The Hotel Guide 2000

AA Lifestyle Guides

33rd edition October 1999

First published by the Automobile Association as the Hotel and Restaurant Guide, 1967

Mapping is produced by the Cartographic Department of the Automobile Association.

Directory compiled by the AA Hotel Services Department and generated from the AA establishment database.

Cover design by Sue Climpson, Whitchurch, England

Typesetting and colour repro by Microset Graphics Ltd, Basingstoke, England

Printed in Italy by Rotolito Lombarda SpA

Advertisement Production: Karen Weeks, telephone 01256 491545

The main cover photograph shows Hintlesham Hall, Ipswich, England

Images courtesy of: AA picture library © 1999 and courtesy of Radisson Edwardian Hotels

A CIP catalogue record for this book is available from the British Library

ISBN: 0 7495 2248 8

Published by AA Publishing, a trading name of Automobile Association Developments Limited, whose registered office is Norfolk House, Priestley Road, Basingstoke, Hampshire RG24 9NY. Registered number 1878835

CONTENTS

Prize Draw

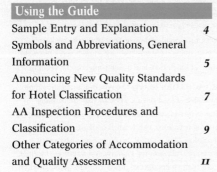

Using the Guide

AA Awards 1999-2000

The Premier Collection

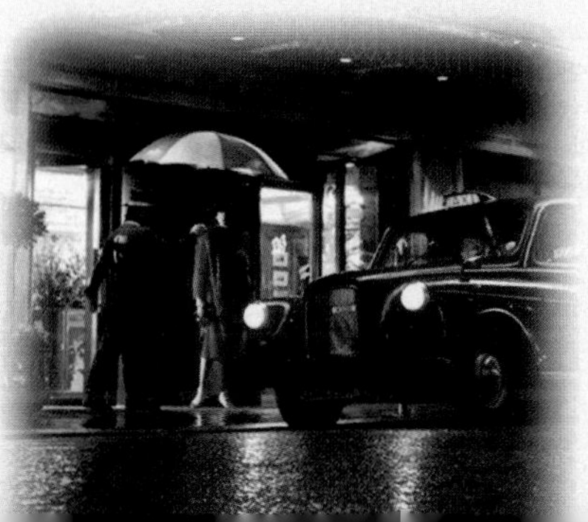

Useful Information

Features

Directory of Hotels

USING THE GUIDE

Sample Entry

Explanation of entries and notes on abbreviations

(see also the key opposite)

1. Town Listed alphabetically within each country section: England, Channel Islands, Isle of Man, Scotland, Wales, Ireland. The administrative county or region follows the town name. Towns on islands are listed under the island (e.g. Wight, Isle of). The map ref gives the map page number, then the National Grid Ref. Read the first figure across and the second figure vertically within the lettered square.

2. Hotel Name Preceded by the star rating and rosette award, followed by address and quality percentage score (see page 11). Listed in star and quality percentage score order within each location. If the hotel name is in *italic type* information that follows has not been confirmed by the hotel management. A company or consortium name or logo may appear (hotel groups are listed on pages 35-38), for those with a central telex or fax service specify the name and location of the hotel when booking.

3. Dir: Directions to the hotel.

4. ROOMS The first figure shows the number of en suite letting bedrooms, or total number of bedrooms, then the number with en suite or family facilities. Bedrooms in an annexe/extension are only noted if they are at least equivalent to those in the main building, but facilities and prices may differ. In some hotels all bedrooms are in an annexe/extension. **Prices** are provided by hoteliers in good faith and are indications not firm quotations. Most hotels only accept cheques if notice is given and a cheque card produced. Not all hotels take travellers cheques.

5. MEALS If there is a fixed-price menu this is the price range quoted. **'&alc'** shows that a carte is also available; its prices may be much higher. **Coffee am/Tea pm** All four and five star hotels serve morning coffee and normally serve afternoon tea, to resident guests. **VAT** does not apply in the Channel Islands, otherwise all prices quoted are inclusive of VAT and of **service** where applicable. **High Tea** In some areas, particularly Scotland, high tea (a savoury dish, followed by bread and butter, cake etc.) is served in early evening instead of dinner. Dinner may be available as an alternative. On Sundays some hotels serve the main meal at lunch time and a cold supper in the evening.

6. FACILITIES Weekly live entertainment should be available at least once a week all year. Some other hotels provide entertainment only in summer or on special occasions, check when booking. **Child Facilities** May include: baby intercom, baby-sitting, playroom, playground, laundry, drying/ironing facilities, cots, high chairs, special meals. In some hotels children can sleep in parents' rooms at no extra cost, check all details when booking. **No children** A minimum age may be given e.g. No children 4 yrs. **No indication** Where neither 'ch fac' or 'no children' appears, hotels accept children, but may not have special facilities (e.g. high chairs). It is essential to check when booking.

7. SERVICES Parking may include covered, charged spaces. **Night Porter** may be there only between certain hours or on certain nights, however four and five star hotels must always have a night porter on duty.

8. NOTES Last d The last time for ordering dinner may vary at weekends. **RS** Some hotels have a restricted service e.g. for the restaurant or leisure facilities, during quieter months, check when booking. **No Dogs** Where hotels allow dogs, some breeds may be forbidden and dogs may be excluded from areas of the hotel, especially the dining room. It is essential to check when booking. **No coaches** This information is supplied by hotels in good faith. Inns have well defined legal obligations towards travellers. In the event of a query the customer should approach the proprietor or the local licensing authority.

9. CARDS Credit cards may be subject to a surcharge, check when booking.

KEY TO SYMBOLS AND ABBREVIATIONS

Symbols

★	New Quality Standards Star Classification (see pages 7-11)
%	Quality Percentage Score (see pages 7-11)
★	Red Stars denote the AA's highest quality awards (see pages 17-24)
❀	Rosette Award for quality of food (see page 15)
🏠	Country House Hotel
○	Hotel likely to open during currency of guide or no classification yet
✚	Star Classification not confirmed under New Quality Standards
*	1999 prices

Different accommodation categories (see page 11 for explanation)

🏘	Townhouse Accommodation
⇧	Travel Accommodation

Rooms

rms	Rooms (and number)
fmly	Family rooms (and number)
bth/shr	En suite bathroom/shower room with own WC
LB	Special leisure breaks available
Off Peak	Lower prices/concessions may be available, check when booking

Bedroom restrictions are stated e.g. no smoking in 15 bedrooms

Meals

V Meals	A choice of vegetarian dishes is normally available, check when booking
cont bkfst	Continental breakfast
Coffee am/Tea pm	morning coffee and/or afternoon tea served to chance callers
alc	A la carte menu

Facilities

TV	Black and White television
CTV	Colour Television
STV	Satellite Television
ch fac	Special facilities for children
Xmas	Special Programme for Christmas/New Year

Leisure facilities are as stated eg indoor swimming pool

Services

P	Parking (preceded by number of spaces e.g. 40P)

Other services as stated eg night porter

Notes

No Dogs	No dogs allowed in bedrooms (Guide dogs for the blind may be excepted)
No children	Indicates that children cannot be accommodated
Last d	Last time dinner may be ordered
RS	Restricted opening e.g. RS Jan-Mar, Closed Xmas/New Year

Other restrictions as stated e.g. no smoking in restaurant area

CONF

Conference facilities available

Thtr	Seats theatre style (and number)
Class	Seats classroom style (and number)
Board	Seats boardroom style (and number)
Del	Typical overnight delegate rate

Cards

Cards accepted where symbols are shown

MasterCard Switch VISA DELTA

General Information

Booking

Book as early as possible, particularly for peak periods (June to September inclusive), public holidays and, in some parts of Scotland, during the ski season. Some hotels ask for a deposit or full payment in advance, especially for one-night bookings from chance callers. Not all hotels will take advance bookings for bed and breakfast, overnight or short stays. Some will not make reservations from mid week. Some hotels charge half-board (bed, breakfast and dinner) whether you eat the meals or not. Some hotels only accept full-board bookings.

Cancellation

Once a booking is confirmed, notify the hotel immediately if you are unable to keep your reservation. If the hotel cannot relet your room you may be liable to pay about two-thirds of the room price (a deposit will count towards this payment). In Britain a legally binding contract is made when an intending guest accepts an offer of accommodation, either in writing or by telephone. Illness is not accepted as a release from this contract. You are advised to effect insurance cover against possible cancellation, for example AA Travelsure **(Telephone 0870 606 1612 for details).**

Complaints

If you have a complaint about hotel food, services or facilities, we strongly advise you to take it up with the management there and then, in order to give the hotelier a chance to put things right straight away. If this personal approach fails, AA members may inform AA Hotel Services, Fanum House, Basing View Basingstoke, Hampshire RG21 4EA; however the AA does not undertake to obtain compensation for complaints.

See page 25 for Useful Information (fire regulations, licensing, prices) and important telephone number changes.

Announcing New Quality Standards for Hotel Classification

Everyone is familiar with the distinctive yellow signs outside hotels showing AA star classification. Stars are the internationally recognised symbol denoting the levels of service, accommodation and facilities a hotel guest can expect.

Until recently, hotels in the UK could approach either the AA or the RAC for their Star Classification, or go to one of the National Tourist Boards of England, Scotland or Wales for a Crown Classification.

Each organisation inspected to its own slightly different standards and requirements, so hotels could end up displaying for example, a 3 Star sign from the AA, a 4 Star sign from the RAC and a 5 Crown sign from one of the Tourist Boards.

Consumer research showed that this was confusing for hotel guests, especially international travellers, and also for hotel proprietors meeting different requirements for each scheme. Discussions began between the AA, RAC and the National Tourist Boards for England, Scotland and Wales, to agree a common symbol and common requirements for hotel accommodation.

Harmonising Standards Across the Board

All aspects of the requirements at the five levels were examined in detail by the Chief Inspectors of the organisations concerned, and agreements were worked out for new quality standards.

A consultation document explaining the agreed quality standards was sent to hoteliers, and their views were taken into account before the final agreement on New Quality Standards was reached. The inspectors working for each organisation went through the same training programme and tested the new standards thoroughly in practice. Stars were adopted as the hotel classification symbol.

Not Quite Unanimous for Scotland and Wales: Unfortunately, at a late stage in the proceedings, the Scottish and Welsh Tourist Boards decided that they wished to act independently and have their own criteria for a classification scheme, although they will still use stars as their symbol.

The AA continues to offer hotels in Scotland and Wales a classification under the new quality standards. A degree of confusion may exist in Scotland and Wales, where hotels display a Tourist Board star classification as well as the New Quality Standards star classification from the AA.

New Quality Standards Consistently Applied in The AA Hotel Guide

Hotels in England now know where they stand and are inspected to the agreed New Quality Standards, with just one Star Classification, whichever organisation carries out the inspection.

All the hotels featured in the Scotland and Wales sections of the AA Hotel Guide, as well as those in England, the Channel Islands and the Isle of Man, have been inspected and classified by the AA Inspectorate according to the same New Quality Standards, and only this classification is shown.

For hotel guests, the New Quality Standards place an even stronger emphasis on quality, as well as a greater range of facilities and services at each of the five star levels.

AA INSPECTION PROCEDURES AND CLASSIFICATION

Hotels applying for AA recognition are visited on a 'mystery guest' basis by one of the AA's team of qualified hotel and restaurant inspectors. The inspector stays overnight to make a thorough test of the accommodation and services, and only after settling the bill the following morning declares his/her identity and asks to be shown round the entire premises. The inspector completes a full report, making a recommendation for the appropriate star classification and quality percentage score. After the first inspection, the hotel receives an annual visit to check that standards are maintained. If hotels change hands, the new owners must re-apply for classification, AA recognition is not transferable.

About the star classification

Star classification is a quality scheme at five levels. The assessment rises from one star, denoting hotels with the simplest range of facilities, to five stars, denoting large, luxury hotels with a range of services and facilities that meet the best international standards. The requirements for the five star levels are outlined as follows:

Minimum Requirements for AA Recognition under the New Quality Standards

AA ★ Hotel

Hotels in this classification are likely to be small and independently owned, with a family atmosphere. Services may be provided by the owner and family on an informal basis. There may be a limited range of facilities and meals may be fairly simple. Lunch, for example, may not be served. Some bedrooms may not have en suite bath/shower rooms. Maintenance, cleanliness and comfort should, however, always be of an acceptable standard.

AA ★★ Hotel

In this classification hotels will typically be small to medium sized and offer more extensive facilities than at the one star level. Some business hotels come into the two star classification and guests can expect comfortable, well equipped, overnight accommodation, usually with an en suite bath/shower room. Reception and other staff will aim for a more professional presentation than at the one star level, and offer a wider range of straightforward services, including food and drink.

AA ★★★ Hotel

At this level, hotels are usually of a size to support higher staffing levels, and a significantly greater quality and range of facilities than at the lower star classifications. Reception and the other public rooms will be more spacious and the restaurant will normally also cater for non-residents. All bedrooms will have fully en suite bath and shower rooms and offer a good standard of comfort and equipment, such as a hair dryer, direct dial telephone, toiletries in the bathroom. Some room service can be expected, and some provision for business travellers.

AA ★★★★ Hotel

Expectations at this level include a degree of luxury as well as quality in the furnishings, decor and equipment, in every area of the hotel. Bedrooms will also usually offer more space than at the lower star levels, and well designed, co-ordinated furnishings and decor. En suite bathrooms will have both bath and fixed shower. There will be a high enough ratio of staff to guests to provide services like porterage, 24-hour room service, laundry and dry-cleaning. The restaurant will demonstrate a serious approach to cuisine.

AA ★★★★★ Hotel

Here you should find spacious and luxurious accommodation throughout the hotel, matching the best international standards. Interior design should impress with its quality and attention to detail, comfort and elegance. Furnishings should be immaculate. Services should be formal, well supervised and flawless in attention to guests' needs, without being intrusive. The restaurant will demonstrate a high level of technical skill, producing dishes to the highest international standards. Staff will be knowledgeable, helpful, well versed in all aspects of customer care, combining efficiency with courtesy.

OTHER CATEGORIES OF ACCOMMODATION

Country House Hotels
Country House Hotels offer a relaxed, informal atmosphere, with an emphasis on personal welcome. They are usually, but not always, in a secluded or rural setting and should offer peace and quiet regardless of location.

Townhouse Accommodation
This classification denotes small, personally run town-centre hotels which afford a high degree of privacy and concentrate on luxuriously furnished bedrooms and suites with high-quality room service, rather than the public rooms or formal dining rooms usually associated with hotels, they are usually in areas well served by restaurants. All fall broadly within the Four or Five Star classification, though no star classification or quality percentage score is shown in the guide.

Travel Accommodation
This classification denotes budget or lodge accommodation suitable for an overnight stay, usually in purpose-built units close to main roads and motorways, often forming part of motorway service areas. They provide consistent levels of accommodation and service, matching today's expectations.

★ ✣

Hotels with a provisional star classification
A small number of hotels in this guide have a provisional classification, denoted by this symbol after the stars, ✣ which means that their classification is still to be confirmed under the new quality standards.

○

Hotels with no star classification
Hotels with this symbol ○ have no star classification as they are due to open during the currency of the guide, or because due to late entry to the scheme it was impossible to make a final overnight visit before our press date.

Further AA quality assessments
In addition to the star classification, the AA makes a further quality assessment to help intending guests in their choice of hotel, the Quality Percentage Score. The highest achievers in this assessment are awarded Red Stars and can be easily identified in the guide, appearing first in their location with a highlighted entry. The quality percentage score and Red Star awards are assessed as follows:

Quality Percentage Score – Making hotel choice easier
AA inspectors supplement their general report with an additional quality assessment of everything the hotel offers, including hospitality, based on what they experience as the 'mystery guest'. This enables them to award an overall quality percentage score.

The quality percentage score offers a comparison of quality within the star classification, so a one star hotel may receive as high a quality percentage score within its classification as a four or five star hotel.

When using the guide, intending guests can see at a glance for example that a two star hotel with a percentage score of 69, offers a higher quality experience within its star classification than a two star hotel with a percentage score of 59.

To gain AA recognition in the first place, a hotel must achieve a minimum quality score of 50 per cent. The quality percentage score for ordinary star classification effectively runs between 50 and 80 per cent.

Red Star Awards - 'Best Hotels in Britain'
At each of the five classification levels, the AA recognises exceptional quality of accommodation and hospitality by awarding Red Stars for excellence. A hotel with Red Stars is judged to be the best in its star classification and recognises that the hotel offers outstanding levels of comfort, hospitality and customer care. Red Star hotels as a general rule achieve a quality percentage score between 81 and 100 per cent, the actual percentage score is not shown in the guide.

★ **Red Star hotels are listed on pages 17-24**

AA Awards 1999-2000

Hotel of the Year Award

Hotel of the Year is the AA's most prestigious award. Winning hotels receive a specially commissioned, framed watercolour of the hotel by artist Duncan Palmar. National awards are made for England, Scotland, Wales and Ireland, a photograph of the hotel appears at the beginning of the relevant country section in the guide. Awards for 1999-2000 are as follows:

Hotel of the Year, England

★★★★★ ❀❀ 75% One Aldwych, London WC2
General Manager: Mr Simon Hirst

Hotel of the Year, Scotland

⌂ ❀ The Bonham, Edinburgh
General Manager: Ms Fiona Vernon

Hotel of the Year, Wales

★★★★★ ❀❀❀ 72% St David's Hotel and Spa, Cardiff
General Manager: Mr Andrew Buchanan

Hotel of the Year, Ireland

★★★★ ❀❀ 75% The Lodge & Spa at Inchydoney Island, Clonakilty, West Cork
Managing Director: Mr Michael Knox-Johnston

Courtesy and Care Awards 1999-2000

This award is made to hotels where staff offer exceptionally high standards of courtesy and care. National awards are made for England, Scotland, Wales and Ireland. Members of staff receive a specially designed lapel badge to wear on duty. In addition, a large framed certificate is commissioned for display by the hotels and they have a highlighted entry with photograph in the guide. Awards for 1999-2000 are as follows:

Courtesy and Care Award, England

★★★ ❀❀ 78% Colwall Park, Malvern
Proprietor: Mr Clive Sturman

Courtesy and Care Award, Scotland

★★★★ ❀❀ 70% The Beardmore, Clydebank
General Manager: Mr David Clarke

Courtesy and Care Award, Wales

★★★ ❀❀ 73% The Conrah, Aberystwyth
Proprietor: Mr F. H. Heading

Courtesy and Care Award, Ireland

★★★ ❀❀❀ 77% The Hibernian Hotel, Ballsbridge, Dublin
General Manager: Ms Siobhan Maher

CARLTON HOTEL
KEEP CLEAR

HOW THE AA ASSESSES RESTAURANTS FOR ROSETTE AWARDS

The AA's rosette award scheme is the only home-grown, nationwide scheme for assessing the quality of food served by restaurants and hotels. The rosette scheme is an award scheme, not a classification scheme and although there is necessarily an element of subjectivity when it comes to assessing taste, we aim for a consistent approach to our awards throughout the UK. It is important to remember however, that many places serve enjoyable food but do not qualify for an AA award.

AA rosette awards are made solely on the basis of a meal visit or visits by one or more of our hotel and restaurant inspectors, who have an unrivalled breadth and depth of experience in assessing quality. Awards are made annually on a rising scale of one to five.

Recommendations from users of the guides are always welcome and will be passed on to the inspectors on merit for their consideration, the AA does not however guarantee a meal visit or an entry in the guide. Rosette awards are made or withdrawn only on the basis of our own inspectors' meal visits.

What makes a restaurant worthy of a rosette award?

The following summaries attempt to explain what inspectors look for, but are intended only as guidelines. The AA is constantly reviewing its award criteria and competition usually results in an all-round improvement in standards, so it becomes increasingly difficult for restaurants to reach award level.

At the simplest level, one rosette, the chef should display a mastery of basic techniques and be able to produce dishes of sound quality and clarity of flavours, using good, fresh ingredients.

To gain two rosettes, the chef must show greater technical skill, more consistency and judgement in combining and balancing ingredients and a clear ambition to achieve high standards. Inspectors will look for evidence of innovation to test the dedication of the kitchen brigade, and the use of seasonal ingredients sourced from quality suppliers.

This award takes a restaurant into the big league, and, in a typical year, fewer than 10 per cent of restaurants in our scheme achieve this distinction. Expectations of the kitchen are high, and inspectors find little room for inconsistencies. Exact technique, flair and imagination will come through in every dish, and balance and depth of flavour are all-important.

This is an exciting award because, at this level, not only should all technical skills be exemplary, but there should also be daring ideas, and they must work. There is no room for disappointment. Flavours should be accurate and vibrant.

This award is the ultimate awarded only when the cooking is at the pinnacle of achievement. Technique should be of such perfection that flavours, combinations and textures show a faultless sense of balance, giving each dish an extra dimension. The sort of cooking that never falters and always strives to give diners a truly memorable taste experience.

Where rosette awards have been made to hotels rosette symbols appear after the star classification. For details of all hotels and restaurants with rosette awards see the AA Restaurant Guide 2000 (page 24).

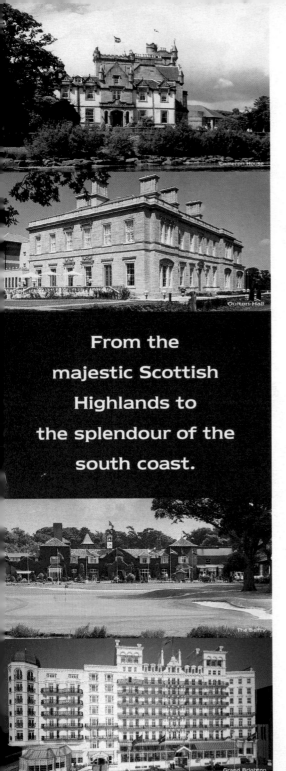

THE PREMIER COLLECTION

★ ★ ★

'Britain's best hotels'

★ ★ ★

Red Star Awards
1999-2000

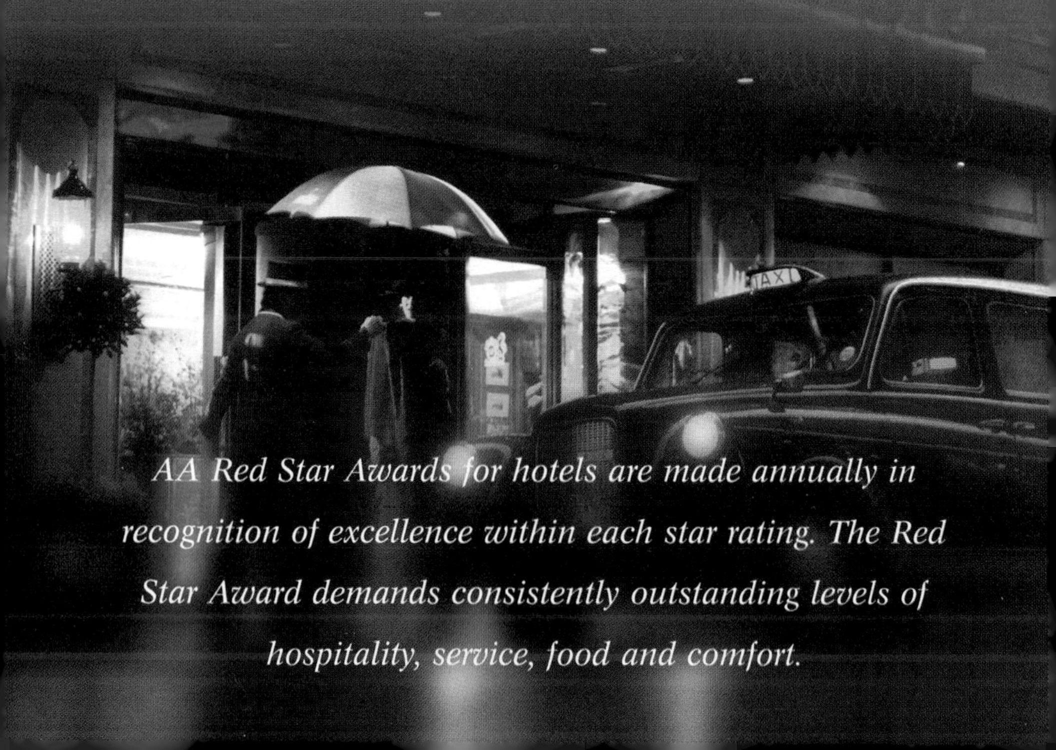

AA Red Star Awards for hotels are made annually in recognition of excellence within each star rating. The Red Star Award demands consistently outstanding levels of hospitality, service, food and comfort.

RED STAR HOTELS MAP

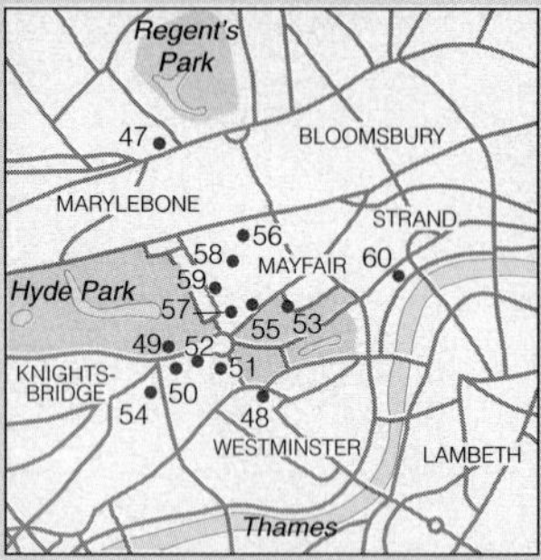

Central London

RED STAR HOTELS REGIONAL INDEX

The number shown against each hotel in the index corresponds with the number given on the Red Star Hotels Map. Hotels are listed in Country and County order, showing their star classification, rosettes and telephone number.

England

BERKSHIRE

1	★★★★	✿✿✿	Fredrick's Hotel	MAIDENHEAD	☎ **01628 581000**
2	★★★	✿✿✿	Hollington Country House	NEWBURY	☎ **01635 255100**
3	★★★★	✿✿✿	The Vineyard at Stockcross	NEWBURY	☎ **01635 528770**

BUCKINGHAMSHIRE

4	★★★★	✿✿✿	Hartwell House	AYLESBURY	☎ **01296 747444**
5	★★★★★	✿✿✿✿	Cliveden Hotel	TAPLOW	☎ **01628 668561**

CHESHIRE

6	★★★	✿✿	Rookery Hall	NANTWICH	☎ **01270 610016**
7	★★★	✿✿✿	Nunsmere Hall Country House Hotel	SANDIWAY	☎ **01606 889100**

CORNWALL & ISLES OF SCILLY

8	★★	✿✿✿	Well House Hotel	LISKEARD	☎ **01579 342001**
9	★★★	✿✿✿	St Martin's on the Isle	ST MARTIN'S	☎ **01720 422092**

CUMBRIA

10	★★★	✿✿	Farlam Hall Hotel	BRAMPTON	☎ **016977 46234**
11	★★★	✿✿✿✿	Michael's Nook Country House Hotel	GRASMERE	☎ **015394 35496**
12	★	✿✿	White Moss House	GRASMERE	☎ **015394 35295**
13	★★★	✿✿✿	Sharrow Bay Country House Hotel	HOWTOWN	☎ **017684 86301**
14	★	✿	Hipping Hall	KIRKBY LONSDALE	☎ **015242 71187**
15	★	✿	Old Church Hotel	WATERMILLOCK	☎ **017684 86204**
16	★★★	✿✿✿	Gilpin Lodge Country House Hotel	WINDERMERE	☎ **015394 88818**
17	★★★	✿✿✿	Holbeck Ghyll Country House Hotel	WINDERMERE	☎ **015394 32375**
18	★★	✿✿	Miller Howe Hotel	WINDERMERE	☎ **015394 42536**
19	★	✿✿	Old Vicarage Country House Hotel	WITHERSLACK	☎ **015395 52381**

DERBYSHIRE

20	★★★	✿✿	Cavendish Hotel	BASLOW	☎ **01246 582311**
21	★★	✿✿✿	Fischer's Baslow Hall	BASLOW	☎ **01246 583259**

DEVON

22	★★	✿✿	Blagdon Manor Country Hotel	ASHWATER	☎ **01409 211224**
23	★★	✿✿	Halmpstone Manor	BARNSTAPLE	☎ **01271 830321**
24	★★★	✿✿✿✿	Gidleigh Park	CHAGFORD	☎ **01647 432367**
25	★★★	✿✿	Lewtrenchard Manor	LEWDOWN	☎ **01566 783256 & 783222**
26	★★	✿✿✿	Whitechapel Manor	SOUTH MOLTON	☎ **01769 573377**

DORSET

27	★★★	✿✿✿	Summer Lodge	EVERSHOT	☎ **01935 83424**
28	★★★	✿✿✿	Stock Hill Country House Hotel	GILLINGHAM	☎ **01747 823626**
29	★★★	✿✿	Priory Hotel	WAREHAM	☎ **01929 551666**
30	★★	✿✿	Beechleas Hotel	WIMBORNE MINSTER	☎ **01202 841684**

ESSEX

31	★★★	✿✿	Maison Talbooth	DEDHAM	☎ **01206 322367**

GLOUCESTERSHIRE

32	★★★	✿✿✿	Buckland Manor	BUCKLAND	☎ **01386 852626**
34	★★★	✿✿	Hotel On the Park	CHELTENHAM	☎ **01242 518898**
35	★★★	✿✿✿	The Greenway	CHELTENHAM	☎ **01242 862352**
36	★★★	✿✿	Cotswold House Hotel & Restaurant	CHIPPING CAMPDEN	☎ **01386 840330**
37	★★★	✿✿✿	Lower Slaughter Manor	LOWER SLAUGHTER	☎ **01451 820456**
38	★★★	✿✿✿	Lords of the Manor	UPPER SLAUGHTER	☎ **01451 820243**
39	★★★	✿✿	Calcot Manor	TETBURY	☎ **01666 890391**
40	★★★	✿✿	Thornbury Castle	THORNBURY	☎ **01454 281182**

HAMPSHIRE

41 ★★ ❀❀ Gordleton Mill Hotel & Restaurant
LYMINGTON ☎ **01590 682219**

42 ★★★★★ ❀❀❀ Chewton Glen Hotel
NEW MILTON ☎ **01425 275341**

43 ★★★★ ❀❀ Tylney Hall Hotel
ROTHERWICK ☎ **01256 764881**

KENT

44 ★★ ❀❀ Kennel Holt Hotel
CRANBROOK ☎ **01580 712032**

LEICESTERSHIRE

45 ★★★★ ❀❀ Stapleford Park
MELTON MOWBRAY ☎ **01572 787522**

LINCOLNSHIRE

46 ★★ ❀❀❀❀ Winteringham Fields
WINTERINGHAM ☎ **01724 733096**

CENTRAL LONDON

47 ★★★★★ ❀❀❀ Landmark Hotel
LONDON NW1 ☎ **020 7631 8000**

48 ★★★★ ❀❀ Goring Hotel
LONDON SW1 ☎ **020 7396 9000**

49 ★★★★★ ❀❀❀❀ Mandarin Oriental Hyde Park
LONDON SW1 ☎ **020 7235 2000**

50 ★★★★★ ❀❀❀❀❀ The Berkeley
LONDON SW1 ☎ **020 7235 6000**

51 ★★★★ ❀❀❀ The Halkin Hotel
LONDON SW1 ☎ **020 7333 1000**

52 ★★★★★ ❀❀❀ The Lanesborough
LONDON SW1 ☎ **020 7259 5599**

53 ★★★★ ❀❀ The Stafford
LONDON SW1 ☎ **020 7493 0111**

54 ★★★★ ❀❀❀ The Capital
LONDON SW3 ☎ **020 7589 5171**

55 ★★★★ ❀ Athenaeum Hotel & Apartments
LONDON W1 ☎ **020 7499 3464**

56 ★★★★★ ❀❀ Claridge's
LONDON W1 ☎ **020 7629 8860**

57 ★★★★★ ❀❀ Four Seasons Hotel
LONDON W1 ☎ **020 7499 0888**

58 ★★★★★ ❀❀ The Connaught
LONDON W1 ☎ **020 7499 7070**

59 ★★★★★ ❀❀❀ The Dorchester
LONDON W1 ☎ **020 7629 8888**

60 ★★★★★ ❀❀❀ The Savoy
LONDON WC2 ☎ **020 7836 4343**

NORFOLK

61 ★★ ❀❀❀ Morston Hall
BLAKENEY ☎ **01263 741041**

62 ★★★ ❀❀ Congham Hall Country House Hotel
GRIMSTON ☎ **01485 600250**

OXFORDSHIRE

63 ★★★★ ❀❀❀❀❀ Le Manoir Aux Quat' Saisons
GREAT MILTON ☎ **01844 278881**

RUTLAND

64 ★★★ ❀❀❀❀ Hambleton Hall
OAKHAM ☎ **01572 756991**

SHROPSHIRE

65 ★★★ ❀❀❀ Old Vicarage Hotel
WORFIELD ☎ **01746 716497**

SOMERSET

66 ★★★ ❀❀ The Queensberry Hotel
BATH ☎ **01225 447928**

67 ★★ ❀ Ashwick House Hotel
DULVERTON ☎ **01398 323868**

68 ★★★ ❀❀❀ Homewood Park Hotel
HINTON CHARTERHOUSE ☎ **01225 723731**

69 ★★★ ❀❀❀ Hunstrete House Hotel
HUNSTRETE ☎ **01761 490490**

70 ★★ ❀❀ The Oaks Hotel
PORLOCK ☎ **01643 862265**

71 ★★★ ❀❀❀ Charlton House Hotel
SHEPTON MALLET ☎ **01749 342008**

72 ★★★★ ❀❀ Ston Easton Park
STON EASTON ☎ **01761 241631**

73 ★★★ ⚜⚜⚜⚜ Castle Hotel
TAUNTON ☎ 01823 272671

74 ★★ ⚜⚜ Langley House Hotel & Restaurant
WIVELISCOMBE ☎ 01984 623318

75 ★ ⚜⚜ Little Barwick House
YEOVIL ☎ 01935 423902

SUFFOLK

76 ★★★★ ⚜⚜⚜ Hintlesham Hall Hotel
HINTLESHAM ☎ 01473 652334

SURREY

77 ★★ ⚜ Langshott Manor
HORLEY ☎ 01293 786680

SUSSEX EAST

78 ★★★ ⚜⚜ Netherfield Place
BATTLE ☎ 01424 774455

79 ★★★★ ⚜⚜ Ashdown Park Hotel
FOREST ROW ☎ 01342 824988

SUSSEX WEST

80 ★★★ ⚜⚜ Amberley Castle
AMBERLEY ☎ 01798 831992

81 ★★★ ⚜⚜⚜ Gravetye Manor Hotel
EAST GRINSTEAD ☎ 01342 810567

82 ★★★★ ⚜⚜⚜ South Lodge Hotel
LOWER BEEDING ☎ 01403 891711

83 ★★★ ⚜⚜ Alexander House
TURNERS HILL ☎ 01342 714914

WARWICKSHIRE

84 ★ ⚜ Lansdowne Hotel
ROYAL LEAMINGTON SPA ☎ 01926 450505

85 ★★★ ⚜⚜⚜ Mallory Court Hotel
ROYAL LEAMINGTON SPA ☎ 01926 330214

WEST MIDLANDS

86 ★★★★ ⚜⚜ New Hall
SUTTON COLDFIELD ☎ 0121 378 2442

WILTSHIRE

87 ★★★★ ⚜⚜⚜ Manor House Hotel
CASTLE COMBE ☎ 01249 782206

88 ★★★★ ⚜⚜⚜ Lucknam Park
COLERNE ☎ 01225 742777

WORCESTERSHIRE

89 ★★★★ ⚜⚜⚜ The Lygon Arms
BROADWAY ☎ 01386 852255

90 ★★★ ⚜⚜⚜ Brockencote Hall Country House
CHADDESLEY CORBETT ☎ 01562 777876

YORKSHIRE NORTH

91 ★★★ ⚜⚜ The Devonshire Arms Country House Hotel
BOLTON ABBEY ☎ 01756 710441

92 ★★★ ⚜⚜⚜ Middlethorpe Hall Hotel
YORK ☎ 01904 641241

93 ★★★ ⚜⚜ The Grange Hotel
YORK ☎ 01904 644744

CHANNEL ISLANDS

JERSEY

94 ★★★ ⚜⚜ Chateau La Chaire
ROZEL BAY ☎ 01534 863354

95 ★★★★ ⚜⚜⚜ Longueville Manor Hotel
ST SAVIOUR ☎ 01534 725501

SCOTLAND

ABERDEENSHIRE

96 ★★ ⚜⚜ Balgonie Country House Hotel
BALLATER ☎ 013397 55482

97 ★★ ⚜⚜ The Old Manse of Marnoch
BRIDGE OF MARNOCH ☎ 01466 780873

98 ★★★ ⚜ Kildrummy Castle Hotel
KILDRUMMY ☎ 019755 71288

ARGYLL & BUTE

99 ★★ ⚜ Killiechronan House
KILLIECHRONAN ☎ 01680 300403

100 ★★★ ⚜⚜⚜ Airds Hotel
PORT APPIN ☎ 01631 730236

CITY OF GLASGOW

101 ★★★ ⚜⚜⚜ One Devonshire Gardens Hotel
GLASGOW ☎ 0141 339 2001

DUMFRIES & GALLOWAY

102 ★ ⚜⚜ Well View Hotel
MOFFAT ☎ 01683 220184

103 ★★★ ⚜⚜⚜ Kirroughtree House
NEWTON STEWART ☎ 01671 402141

104 ★★ ⚜⚜⚜ Knockinaam Lodge Hotel
PORTPATRICK ☎ 01776 810471

EAST LOTHIAN

105 ★★★ ⚜⚜ Greywalls Hotel
GULLANE ☎ 01620 842144

FIFE

106 ★★★★ ⚜⚜ Balbirnie House
MARKINCH ☎ 01592 610066

107 ★★ ⚜⚜⚜ The Peat Inn
PEAT INN ☎ 01334 840206

HIGHLAND

108 ★★★ ❀❀❀ Arisaig House
ARISAIG ☎ **01687 450622**

109 ★★★★ ❀❀❀ Inverlochy Castle Hotel
FORT WILLIAM ☎ **01397 702177**

110 ★ ❀❀ Harlosh House
HARLOSH ☎ **01470 521367**

111 ★★ ❀❀❀ The Cross
KINGUSSIE ☎ **01540 661166**

112 ★ ❀❀ The Dower House
MUIR OF ORD ☎ **01463 870090**

113 ★★ ❀❀ Knockie Lodge Hotel
WHITEBRIDGE ☎ **01456 486276**

NORTH AYRSHIRE

114 ★★ ❀ Kilmichael Country House Hotel
BRODICK ☎ **01770 302219**

PERTH & KINROSS

115 ★★★★★ ❀❀ The Gleneagles Hotel
AUCHTERARDER ☎ **01764 662231**

116 ★★★ ❀❀❀ Kinloch House Hotel
BLAIRGOWRIE ☎ **01250 884237**

117 ★★★ ❀❀❀ Kinnaird
DUNKELD ☎ **01796 482440**

SOUTH AYRSHIRE

118 ★★ ❀ Ladyburn
MAYBOLE ☎ **01655 740585**

119 ★★★ ❀❀❀ Lochgreen House
TROON ☎ **01292 313343**

120 ★★★★★ ❀❀ Turnberry Hotel
TURNBERRY ☎ **01655 331000**

STIRLING

121 ★★★ ❀❀ Cromlix House Hotel
DUNBLANE ☎ **01786 822125**

122 ★ ❀❀ Creagan House
STRATHYRE ☎ **01877 384638**

WALES

CEREDIGION

123 ★★★ ❀❀❀ Ynyshir Hall
EGLWYSFACH ☎ **01654 781209**

CONWY

124 ★★ ❀❀❀ Tan-y-Foel Country House Hotel
BETWS-Y-COED ☎ **01690 710507**

125 ★★ ❀❀❀ The Old Rectory Country House
CONWY ☎ **01492 580611**

126 ★★★ ❀❀❀ Bodysgallen Hall Hotel
LLANDUDNO ☎ **01492 584466**

127 ★★ ❀❀❀ St Tudno Hotel
LLANDUDNO ☎ **01492 874411**

DENBIGHSHIRE

128 ★★ ❀❀❀ Tyddyn Llan Country Hotel & Restaurant
LLANDRILLO ☎ **01490 440264**

GWYNEDD

129 ★★ ❀❀ Hotel Maes y Neuadd
TALSARNAU ☎ **01766 780200**

POWYS

130 ★★★ ❀❀ Lake Country House Hotel
LLANGAMMARCH WELLS ☎ **01591 620202**

131 ★★★★ ❀❀❀ Llangoed Hall
LLYSWEN ☎ **01874 754525**

SWANSEA

132 ★★ ❀❀❀ Fairyhill
REYNOLDSTON ☎ **01792 390139**

IRELAND

CLARE

133 ★★★ ❀❀ Gregans Castle
BALLYVAUGHAN ☎ **065 7077 005**

CORK

134 ★★★ ❀❀❀ Longueville House Hotel
MALLOW ☎ **022 47156**

DUBLIN

135 ★★★★ ❀❀❀ The Clarence
DUBLIN ☎ **01 6709000**

GALWAY

136 ★★★ ❀❀ Cashel House Hotel
CASHEL ☎ **095 31001**

137 ★★★★ ❀❀ Glenlo Abbey Hotel
GALWAY ☎ **091 526666**

KERRY

138 ★★★★ ❀❀❀ Park Hotel Kenmare
KENMARE ☎ **064 41200**

139 ★★★★ ❀❀ Sheen Falls Lodge
KENMARE ☎ **064 41600**

KILDARE

140 ★★★★★ ❀❀❀ The Kildare Hotel & Country Club
STRAFFAN ☎ **01 6017200**

KILKENNY

141 ★★★★ ❀❀ Mount Juliet Hotel
THOMASTOWN ☎ **056 73000**

WEXFORD

142 ★★★ ❀❀ Marlfield House Hotel
GOREY ☎ **055 21124**

WICKLOW

143 ★★★ ❀❀ Tinakilly Country House & Restaurant
RATHNEW ☎ **0404 69274**

THE PREMIER COLLECTION

Red Star Hotels are listed here in star and rosette order.
The number corresponds with the map index and regional listing

5 star
★★★★★

50	The Berkeley	✿✿✿✿✿
5	Cliveden Hotel	✿✿✿✿
49	Mandarin Oriental Hyde Park	✿✿✿✿
42	Chewton Glen Hotel	✿✿✿
47	Landmark Hotel	✿✿✿
59	The Dorchester	✿✿✿
140	The Kildare Hotel & Country Club	✿✿✿
52	The Lanesborough	✿✿✿
60	The Savoy	✿✿✿
56	Claridge's	✿✿
57	Four Seasons Hotel	✿✿
58	The Connaught	✿✿
115	The Gleneagles Hotel	✿✿
120	Turnberry Hotel, Golf Courses & Spa	✿✿

4 star
★★★★

63	Le Manoir Aux Quat' Saisons	✿✿✿✿✿
1	Fredrick's Hotel	✿✿✿
4	Hartwell House	✿✿✿
76	Hintlesham Hall Hotel	✿✿✿
109	Inverlochy Castle Hotel	✿✿✿
131	Llangoed Hall	✿✿✿
95	Longueville Manor Hotel	✿✿✿
88	Lucknam Park	✿✿✿
87	Manor House Hotel	✿✿✿
138	Park Hotel Kenmare	✿✿✿
82	South Lodge Hotel	✿✿✿
54	The Capital	✿✿✿
135	The Clarence	✿✿✿
51	The Halkin Hotel	✿✿✿
89	The Lygon Arms	✿✿✿
3	The Vineyard At Stockcross	✿✿✿
79	Ashdown Park Hotel	✿✿
106	Balbirnie House	✿✿
137	Glenlo Abbey Hotel	✿✿
48	Goring Hotel	✿✿
141	Mount Juliet Hotel	✿✿
86	New Hall	✿✿
139	Sheen Falls Lodge	✿✿
45	Stapleford Park	✿✿
72	Ston Easton Park	✿✿
53	The Stafford	✿✿
43	Tylney Hall Hotel	✿✿
55	Athenaeum Hotel & Apartments	✿

3 star
★★★

24	Gidleigh Park	✿✿✿✿✿
73	Castle Hotel	✿✿✿✿
64	Hambleton Hall	✿✿✿✿
11	Michael's Nook Country House Hotel	✿✿✿✿
100	Airds Hotel	✿✿✿
108	Arisaig House	✿✿✿
126	Bodysgallen Hall Hotel	✿✿✿
90	Brockencote Hall Country House Hotel	✿✿✿
32	Buckland Manor	✿✿✿
71	Charlton House Hotel	✿✿✿
16	Gilpin Lodge Country House Hotel & Restaurant	✿✿✿
81	Gravetye Manor Hotel	✿✿✿
17	Holbeck Ghyll Country House Hotel	✿✿✿
2	Hollington Country House	✿✿✿
68	Homewood Park Hotel	✿✿✿
69	Hunstrete House Hotel	✿✿✿
116	Kinloch House Hotel	✿✿✿
117	Kinnaird	✿✿✿
103	Kirroughtree House	✿✿✿
119	Lochgreen House	✿✿✿
134	Longueville House Hotel	✿✿✿
38	Lords of the Manor	✿✿✿
37	Lower Slaughter Manor	✿✿✿
85	Mallory Court Hotel	✿✿✿
92	Middlethorpe Hall Hotel	✿✿✿
7	Nunsmere Hall Country House Hotel	✿✿✿
65	Old Vicarage Hotel	✿✿✿
101	One Devonshire Gardens Hotel	✿✿✿
13	Sharrow Bay Country House Hotel	✿✿✿
9	St Martin's on the Isle	✿✿✿
28	Stock Hill Country House Hotel	✿✿✿
27	Summer Lodge	✿✿✿
35	The Greenway	✿✿✿
123	Ynyshir Hall	✿✿✿
40	Thornbury Castle	✿✿
83	Alexander House	✿✿
80	Amberley Castle	✿✿
39	Calcot Manor	✿✿
136	Cashel House Hotel	✿✿
20	Cavendish Hotel	✿✿
94	Chateau La Chaire	✿✿
62	Congham Hall Country House Hotel	✿✿
36	Cotswold House Hotel & Restaurant	✿✿
121	Cromlix House Hotel	✿✿
10	Farlam Hall Hotel	✿✿
133	Gregans Castle	✿✿
105	Greywalls Hotel	✿✿
130	Lake Country House Hotel	✿✿
31	Hotel On the Park	✿✿
25	Lewtrenchard Manor	✿✿
31	Maison Talbooth	✿✿
142	Marlfield House Hotel	✿✿
78	Netherfield Place	✿✿
29	Priory Hotel	✿✿
6	Rookery Hall	✿✿
91	The Devonshire Arms Country House Hotel	✿✿
93	The Grange Hotel	✿✿
66	The Queensberry Hotel	✿✿
143	Tinakilly Country House & Restaurant	✿✿
98	Kildrummy Castle Hotel	✿

2 star
★★

46	Winteringham Fields	✿✿✿✿
132	Fairyhill	✿✿✿
21	Fischer's Baslow Hall	✿✿✿
104	Knockinaam Lodge Hotel	✿✿✿
61	Morston Hall	✿✿✿
127	St Tudno Hotel	✿✿✿
124	Tan-y-Foel Country House Hotel	✿✿✿
111	The Cross	✿✿✿
125	The Old Rectory Country House	✿✿✿
107	The Peat Inn	✿✿✿
128	Tyddyn Llan Country Hotel & Restaurant	✿✿✿
8	Well House Hotel	✿✿✿
26	Whitechapel Manor	✿✿✿
96	Balgonie Country House Hotel	✿✿
30	Beechleas Hotel	✿✿
22	Blagdon Manor Country Hotel	✿✿
41	Gordleton Mill Hotel & Restaurant	✿✿
23	Halmpstone Manor	✿✿
129	Hotel Maes y Neuadd	✿✿
44	Kennel Holt Hotel	✿✿
113	Knockie Lodge Hotel	✿✿
74	Langley House Hotel & Restaurant	✿✿
18	Miller Howe Hotel	✿✿
70	The Oaks Hotel	✿✿
97	The Old Manse of Marnoch	✿✿
67	Ashwick House Hotel	✿
99	Killiechronan House	✿
114	Kilmichael Country House Hotel	✿
118	Ladyburn	✿
77	Langshott Manor	✿

1 star
★

122	Cregan House	✿✿
110	Harlosh House	✿✿
75	Little Barwick House	✿✿
19	Old Vicarage Country House Hotel	✿✿
112	The Dower House	✿✿
102	Well View Hotel	✿✿
12	White Moss House	✿✿
14	Hipping Hll	✿
84	Lansdowne Hotel	✿
15	Old Church Hotel	✿

USEFUL INFORMATION

Britain

The Fire Precautions Act does not apply to the Channel Islands, Republic of Ireland, or the Isle of Man, which have their own rules. As far as we are aware, all hotels listed in Great Britain have applied for and not been refused a fire certificate.

Licensing laws differ in England, Wales, Scotland, the Republic of Ireland, the Isle of Man, the Isles of Scilly and the Channel Islands. Public houses are generally open from mid morning to early afternoon, and from about 6 or 7pm until 11pm, closing times may be earlier or later, some are open all afternoon. Unless otherwise stated, establishments listed are licensed. Hotel residents can obtain alcoholic drinks at all times, if the licensee is prepared to serve them. Non-residents eating at the hotel restaurant can have drinks with meals. Children under 14 (or 18 in Scotland) may be excluded from bars where no food is served. Those under 18 may not purchase or consume alcoholic drinks. Club licence means that drinks are served to club members only, 48 hours must elapse between joining and ordering.

Prices The AA encourages the use of the Hotel Industry Voluntary Code of Booking Practice, which aims to ensure that guests know how much they will have to pay and what services and facilities that includes, before entering a financially binding agreement. If the price has not previously been confirmed in writing, guests should be given a card stipulating the total obligatory charge when they register at reception.

The Tourism (Sleeping Accommodation Price Display) **Order of 1977** compels hotels, motels, guest houses, farmhouses, inns and self-catering accommodation with four or more letting bedrooms, to display in entrance halls the minimum and maximum prices charged for each category of room. Tariffs shown are the minimum and maximum for one or two persons but they may vary without warning.

Northern Ireland & Republic of Ireland

Prices for the Republic of Ireland are shown in Irish Punts (IR£), hotels may display prices in Euros, as this guide went to press IR£1 = 1.269 Euros

The Fire Services (NI) Order 1984 covers establishments accommodating more than 6 people, which must have a certificate from the Northern Ireland Fire Authority. Places accommodating fewer than 6 persons need adequate exits. AA officials inspect emergency notices, fire-fighting equipment and fire exits here. Republic of Ireland safety regulations are a matter for local authority regulations. For your own and others' safety, read the emergency notices and be sure you understand them.

Licensing Regulations

Northern Ireland: public houses open Mon-Sat 11.30-23.00 and Sun 12.30-14.30 and 19.00-22.00. Hotels can serve residents without restriction. Non-residents can be served from 12.30-22.00 on Christmas Day. Children under 18 are not allowed in the bar area and may neither buy nor consume liquor in hotels.

Republic of Ireland: General licensing hours are Mon-Sat 10.30-23.00 (23.30 in summer). Sun and St Patrick's Day (17th Mar), 12.30-14.00 and 16.00-23.00. Hotels can serve residents without restriction. There is no service on Christmas Day (except for hotel residents) or Good Friday.

Telephone Numbers Area codes for numbers in the Republic of Ireland apply only within the Republic. If dialling from outside check the telephone directory. Area codes for numbers in Britain and N. Ireland cannot be used directly from the Republic.

IMPORTANT TELEPHONE NUMBER CHANGES

Effective from 22 April 2000 for calls to the following:

London,	dialling code (020) then eight digit local number starting 7 or 8 e.g.(0171) 1234567 becomes (020) 71234567 (0181) 1234567 becomes (020) 81234567
Cardiff,	dialling code (029) then eight-digit local number starting 20 e.g. (01222) 123456 becomes (029) 20123456
Coventry,	dialling code (024) then eight-digit local number starting 76 e.g. (01203) 123456 becomes (024) 76123456
Portsmouth,	dialling code (023) then eight-digit local number starting 92 e.g. (01705) 123456 becomes (023) 92123456
Southampton,	dialling code (023) then eight-digit local number starting 80 e.g. (01703) 123456 becomes (023) 80123456
Northern Ireland,	dialling code (028). There are 38 local conversions to eight-digit numbers, check with directory enquiries.
Belfast,	(01232) 123456 becomes (028) 90123456

'Nowt so Queer as Folk'

by Julia Hynard

In our Millennium Survey we asked hotel-keepers to tell us their funniest stories about the extraordinary things that people do and say while staying in hotels. Once again we have been rewarded with some priceless anecdotes, baffling behaviour, and mind-boggling statistics. While hoteliers have been generous in sharing their extraordinary experiences, names and venues have been withheld to maintain discretion.

We have a tradition in these islands of tolerating eccentric behaviour, and relishing the individualism that might be the mark of creative genius or more likely the bark of the decidedly dotty. This tradition is upheld with pride in our hotel industry, where people of varied disposition are accommodated with remarkable tact and courtesy.

A London hotel reports on a long-staying guest of some panache, who re-decorated her suite with a leopardskin bedcover, leopardskin curtains, 50 helium balloons and a goldfish bowl full of fake goldfish. She also sent herself four bouquets of flowers every day for six weeks. Goldfish seem to be a recurrent theme in London. Chambermaids at another hotel responded to the daily request of one lady guest to 'Hoover away the ghosts in the bathroom and the goldfish in the toilet', after which she was perfectly content.

A stylishly romantic pair booked into a Cornish hotel in March wearing full medieval costume, which they wore throughout the evening. They explained that this was 'their favourite period'. During dinner he proposed to her, on bended knee, and she accepted!

Cloak & dagger

Hotel staff can at times find themselves drawn into a web of intrigue. A couple at a Welsh hotel insisted that their room had been searched by the Secret Service and that they were being watched by two agents in a Ford Sierra in the car park. They complained that they had been followed all day and that the room was bugged. The proprietor was despatched to the car park to check that the 'agents' had gone.

Suspicious behaviour was also observed at a Lincolnshire hotel, where an old man and a young couple stayed for three nights, and only came out of their room at 4am for vodka cocktails - each night.

Sweet complaints

Sometimes, despite the best efforts of management and staff, it's hard to please everyone all of the time. An elderly lady staying at a Cornish hotel at Christmas complained bitterly that all the chocolate triangles had been eaten from the complimentary tin of Quality Street. As any good hotelier would, the proprietor sent on a box of her particular favourites. This confirmed her suspicions and compounded her fury, as she believed that these were those deliberately removed in the first place.

At a Cumbrian hotel a lady swore blind that her expensive diamond brooch had been stolen by the housekeeping staff. When she turned to leave it became clear that her jumper was on the wrong way round and her brooch was displayed for all to see on her back!

Twice a guest came to the reception desk at a hotel in Waterford complaining that her telephone wasn't working. Staff could find nothing wrong with it, and the lady became quite irate. Upon investigation it was discovered that the lady was dialling the TV remote control.

When the customer's not quite right

While the eccentric may be amiable they can also be utterly exasperating. Residents in an Irish hotel were disturbed at five o'clock in the morning by guests performing Irish dancing to loud music. They had simply succumbed to the 'urge to dance'.

From Scotland we hear of a gentleman who spray-painted his shoes in the bath, leaving it black with white footprints (size nine); and another guest who walked around for days with an empty birdcage covered in a cloth talking to a bird that wasn't there.

A German lady staying at a Shropshire hotel for three weeks, insisted on lying down to eat in the restaurant with her bare feet sticking up in the air. She shouted continuously at her calm and long-suffering husband, and had the staff jumping through hoops day and night. On departure she declared that she'd thoroughly enjoyed her stay and made a great play of presenting her hosts with a present, which turned out to be a bar of soap. The husband scuttled back in as they were leaving and, without a word, pressed a £350 tip into the proprietor's hand.

Foreign affairs

Guests from overseas are owed some latitude in getting to grips with our own idiosyncracies. One group of foreigners staying in Cheshire, anxious to observe what they believed to be a local custom, sat down to eat with their napkins on their heads.

An Egyptian child holidaying in Cornwall was deeply disappointed by the lack of rain. He'd come fully equipped for this novel experience. Thus he was found standing under the shower in full spate, in raincoat and wellington boots.

A hotel in the Channel Islands has an attractive display of beans and pastas in jars on the breakfast buffet. One morning a German couple complained that their cereals were 'stale'. They had completely overlooked the cornflakes and tucked into the split peas.

Wild life

Some guests have a less than full appreciation of their natural surroundings, however captivating they may appear to be. One guest in a converted mill requested that 'the noise of the river be turned down', as though it were some Disney special effect. In Scotland, a couple who had passed the local loch on route to their hotel, asked to be moved from the lovely ground floor room allocated to them to a smaller room upstairs. It transpired that the wife had been frightened by the loch and felt that she was in danger of being eaten by a monster during the night.

Passion takes others to the opposite extreme, as a proprietor from South Wales writes: 'They were young, in love and on honeymoon. A birdwatching holiday in Wales to see the famous red kites. I delivered early morning tea and opened the curtains for them. "Great bird morning," I said, "two kites in the air and a pair of goosanders on the lake." They were out of the bed in a flash, grabbing their binoculars and looking out of the window before I'd got out of the door. I wonder how long it was before they realised that neither of them had a stitch on?'

Guests' strange requests... in brief

A bottle of Chateaubriand

A heart made of teddybears on the bed, pierced by an arrow of ducks

A nightingale's heart on toast

Bananas strung around a four-poster bed

Room with a sea view - in Banbury?

Scrambled egg without the yolk

To stop the cathedral bells ringing on Sunday morning

To turn off the light from the lighthouse (on the Scilly Isles)

Turf for the hotel room balcony (in London)

Whale music to be played in the swimming pool

All requests were complied with where possible (a chicken's heart was used as a substitute for the nightingale's, and the waiter tactfully explained that the Chateaubriand was out of stock).

US expectations

There's some evidence of a gulf between fact and expectation for our American visitors. One Scottish hotelier writes, 'American guests were astonished to find that all our bedrooms had en suite facilities, and that we had hot and cold running water.'

A similar experience is related by a proprietor in Somerset who had made quite a feature of the spring-fed stream flowing through his garden. One day he was helping an American guest in with his luggage when he asked, 'Hey son, is that what you'd call an open sewer?'

On the other hand, an American guest at an old world establishment in a sleepy Somerset village was discovered in the middle of the road, outside the hotel at midnight, trying to hail a taxi to take her to Heathrow airport, a three-hour journey away.

Taking the Mickey (and a little more beside)

It is no secret that things 'walk' from hotels. Beautifully decorated and sumptuously furnished establishments are particularly vulnerable to the light-fingered element. Our respondents have reported losing the following:

100 square feet of carpet

A piano from a function suite three floors up

A JCB digger and earth mover

A proprietor's car containing the guests' TV and contents of the cellar

A six-foot yucca plant

CCTV plus surveillance tapes

Twelve place settings (cutlery and crockery)

Thermostatic radiator valves

A 14-stone marble bust of lovers entwined.

Sleeping arrangements

Hotel beds give rise to a number of anecdotes. One hotel was asked to remove the bed from the room as the guest always slept in a chair, and another was asked to remove all the furniture so the guest could sleep on the floor. At a Cumbrian hotel, a couple ignored the bed, leant out and picked all the ivy from around the window and made a nest on the floor in which they slept.

In Shropshire, a man came down to reception and asked for a hacksaw. When asked for what purpose, he explained that the fancy wooden legs on the antique twin beds in his room were getting in his way, so he thought he'd saw them off.

Left Luggage

They say that when you leave something behind in a place it means that, subconsciously, you want to return there. It's a charming thought, but the list of items guests leave in hotels smacks more of reckless abandon: £1,000 in cash under the mattress, artificial limbs, cars, crutches, a diamond ring worth $250,000, fake fur boxer pants, false teeth, glass eyes, inflatable dolls, man's leather leopard print G-string, Mr Blobby nightshirt, suitcases of pornography, innumerable dildos, signed open cheques, goat's carcass, bucket of dates, a hamster and a toupee.

Largesse

The respondents to our Millennium Survey also revealed just how generous appreciative guests can be. The most extravagant tips and gestures of appreciation offered to staff include a £5,000 cash gratuity (at a Knightsbridge hotel), a car (because the registration plate had the same initials as the member of staff), fine wines from a Middle Eastern sheikh, holidays in Barbados, Jamaica, Jeddah, and a private Caribbean island (with private jet flights from the USA thrown in), paintings, antiques, jewellery, porcelain and tickets to a vital Manchester United home game.

Meanness

Of course there are also some spectacular Scrooges, and the meanest behaviour and most ungrateful gestures experienced by hotel staff are as follows:

A guest who had seen a picture of the owners' children in reception left a 3p tip on a £105 bill and whispered in the proprietor's ear, 'Here's a little something for you and your lovely children.'

A guest produced a small bottle containing a faecal sample, claiming he was going to have it analysed because he believed he'd been given mercury food poisoning. The hotel replied by requesting a copy of the test result and, meanwhile, settlement of his account.

An elderly colonel used to come down for breakfast, eat and then doze off. He would then wake up and demand breakfast once again, turning very nasty when told he'd already had it. He had two breakfasts a day for the duration of his stay and never ate lunch.

Instead of providing refreshments, one conference organiser made his delegates go to their rooms and use the complimentary tea and coffee-making facilities

Millennium Entertainment Outrage

Our respondents reveal their most outrageous quotes for Millennium New Year's Eve entertainment:

£20,000 for a band that normally costs £2,000

£10,000 for 15-minute fireworks display

£6,000 for a DJ

£4,000 for a local duo

£3,000 for band that also required 12 free tickets for family

£2,500 for medieval theming of venue

£1,500 for a piper

£1,240 for a marquee that is normally £240

Cocktail Cool

Cocktails are enjoying a revival so we set out to discover what our hotel bars are offering. Some were reluctant to reveal their secret recipes so the *"Elephants Graveyard"* cocktail will remain a mystery! Others were more forthcoming and the three most popular cocktails served in hotel bars are as follows:

Martini Cocktail

007 prefers it shaken not stirred, hotel bars mix it over ice with Martini, Vodka, Gin, Olive and a twist of lemon.

'Bloody Mary'

a combination of vodka, tomato juice, lemon juice, celery salt, pepper, Tabasco, Worcestershire sauce, and an optional splash of dry sherry.

Champagne Cocktail

to create this classic, simply mix champagne, brandy, brown sugar and Angostura Bitters.

Bar of the Millennium

The hotel bar can be a flexible venue for meetings, late-night celebrations, aperitifs or a quiet night-cap. Many offer live entertainment, excellent service and either bar snacks, canapes or a full menu. The hotel bar is an increasingly popular choice for a night out so we asked our inspectors to recommend a 'Bar of the Millennium' for Ireland, Scotland, Wales, England and London.

Ireland

La Marine bistro bar at Kelly's Hotel in Rosslare brings a taste of France to Ireland. The unusual zinc-covered bar counter with carved wooden base was brought back from Burgundy. French and mediterranean influences are found in the eclectic décor, bistro cuisine and the wines, imported directly from France.

Scotland

The Bar at The Gleneagles Hotel captures the atmosphere of a great ocean liner. Guests can enjoy morning coffee and shortbread, light lunch and traditional afternoon tea, an aperitif or relaxing after dinner drink. The Bar has an unrivalled selection of over 120 single malt whiskies, vintage champagne by the glass and excellent wines.

Wales

Tides Bar at The St David's Hotel & Spa looks out over Cardiff Bay. The back of the bar has unusual slow changing coloured lights. Champagne flutes are used for gentlemen and Saucers for ladies. There is also a special glass sloped at a 10-degree angle and heavy steel ashtrays, adding to the nautical feel. The deep bar makes dining easy and comfortable, with an extensive dining list to choose from.

England

The Bar at The French Horn, Sonning-on-Thames, is haunted by an old soldier called Frank! Don't let that deter you from sampling the ducks and other poultry cooked in front of the open fire. The bar is open to diners and residents only so check in to check it out.

London

The Dorchester Coupe aux Fraises is a delightful cocktail of strawberries marinated overnight in brandy and Grand Marnier, topped with Champagne and white wine. Home to the glass and rhinestone baby grand belonging to the late Liberace, the Dorchester Bar offers live Jazz three times a week and live piano every night.

Hotel Groups Information

The following hotel groups have at least 5 hotels and 400 rooms or are part of an internationally significant brand with a central reservations number.

Brand Logo	Company Statement	Central Reservations/ Contact Number
Arcadian Hotels Distinctly Different	A group of three and four star hotels, many are rurally based; all of which have at least one rosette	*0171 340 4800* **(Head Office)**
Best Western	Great Britain's largest group has around 400 independently owned hotels, modern and traditional mainly in the three and four star markets. Many have leisure facilities and over 150 have rosette awards	*0345 73 73 73*
Brend Hotels	A privately owned group of eleven three and four star hotels in Devon and Cornwall	*01271 34 44 96*
Campanile	Campanile offers modern accommodation for the budget market	*0181 569 6969*
Choice Hotels Europe	Choice offers mainly two brands in the UK: Quality Hotels in the three star market, and Comfort Inns at two star	*0800 44 44 44*
corus Corus and Regal hotels	A growing brand of three star hotels, representing the best of Regal Hotel Group	*0345 33 44 00*
Courtyard Marriott	There are ten hotels in the UK, part of the international brand of modern three star hotels	*0800 221 222*
Crowne Plaza	These modern hotels offer four star level accommodation around the country. They often have leisure facilities	*0800 897121*
De Vere Hotels	De Vere comprises around sixteen four and five star hotels, which specialise in leisure, golf and conferences	*01925 639499*
Forestdale Hotels	A privately owned group of about a dozen three star hotels across the south of England	*0500 276440*
Four Pillars Hotels	Half a dozen three and four star hotels based in the Oxfordshire area	*01993 700100*
	A small group of two and three star hotels, located around the southern half of England	*01905 29990*
Greene King	Two and three star hotels, many former coaching inns, mainly in the southern half of England	*01284 768 500* **(Head Office)**
	A small group of three and four star hotels located mainly in the central counties of England	*0345 444 123*
Hastings	A group of four star hotels located in Northern Ireland	*0345 05 10 66*
	A group of provincial hotels across the UK, mainly three star, including many well known former coaching inns	*0800 40 40 40*
Holiday Inn	These modern hotels offer four star level accommodation. They often have leisure facilities	*0800 89 71 21*
Holiday Inn Express	Holiday Inn's most recent development in the UK, which reaches the superior budget marketplace	*0800 89 71 21*
Holiday Inn Garden Court	These modern hotels offer three star level accommodation around the country	*0800 89 71 21*

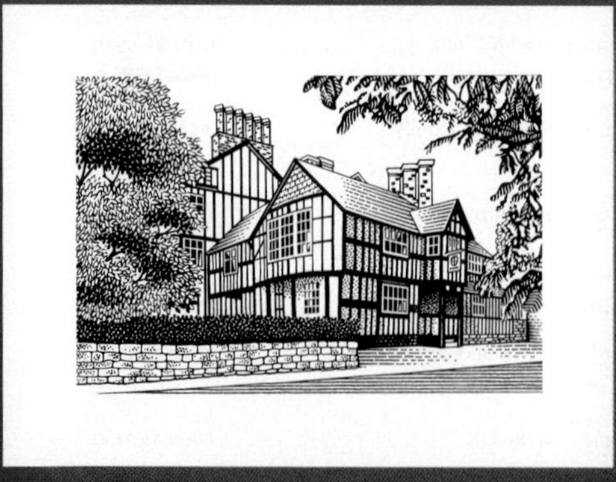

THE GEORGE

ibis hotel	Ibis is a chain of modern two star hotels	*0181 283 4550*
	A consortium of independently owned mainly two and three star hotels across Britain	*0800 88 55 44*
INTER-CONTINENTAL	This internationally known group is primarily represented in the UK with three five star hotels in central London	*0345 581444*
	An association of owner-managed establishments across Ireland	*00 353 (1) 462 3416*
JURYS	This Irish company has a range of three and four star hotels in the UK and the Republic of Ireland	*00 353 (1) 607 5000*
LONDON SIGNATURE HOTELS	A collection of mainly four star hotels in and near London	*0800 40 40 40*
MACDONALD hotels	A large number of hotels in the three and four star markets, traditional and modern	*01506 815215*
Malmaison	A growing brand of three star city centre hotels, all rated over 70%	*0171 340 4800 (Head Office)*
MANOR HOUSE HOTELS	Manor House Hotels of Ireland are country house hotels, they include castles, stately homes and Georgian manors	*0990 300 200* *00 353 (1) 295 8900*
Marriott	This international brand operates four star hotels in primary locations; most are modern and have leisure facilities, some have a focus on golf	*0800 221 222*
MARSTON HOTELS	A small group of three and four star hotels in the southern half of England	*01303 269900*
MENZIES HOTELS	A group of three and four star hotels across Britain	*0870 600 3013*
Le MERIDIEN	An international brand of four and five star hotels, represented mainly in and around London	*0800 40 40 40*
MILLENNIUM	Modern four star hotels in primary provincial locations and Central London	*0845 30 20 001*
MINOTEL Great Britain	A consortium of independently owned mainly two and three star hotels across Britain	*01253 292000*
MOAT HOUSE	Over 40 three and four star hotels, many with leisure facilities	*0645 10 20 30*
Mount Charlotte Hotels	Part of Thistle Hotels Plc, this brand is mainly their three star hotels	*0800 18 17 16*
NOVOTEL	Part of French group Accor, Novotel provides modern three star hotels	*0181 283 4500*
OLD ENGLISH INNS & HOTELS	A large collection of former coaching inns, mainly in the two and three star markets	*0800 917 3085*
PARAMOUNT HOTEL GROUP	A small group of mainly four star hotels	*0500 342 543*
PEEL HOTELS	A group of mainly three star hotels located across the UK	*0845 601 7335*
Posthouse	Over 80 modern three star hotels, often situated on the edge of towns, many have leisure facilities	*0800 40 40 40*
PRIDE OF BRITAIN MEMBER	A consortium of privately owned British hotels, often in the country house style	*01264 324400 (Head Office)*
PRINCIPAL HOTELS	A small group of three and four star hotels in various locations across the country	*0800 454 454*

Radisson Edwardian	There are ten hotels at three, four and five star levels, almost entirely in central London	***0800 37 44 11***
Regal	A large national hotel company with almost a hundred three star hotels in both town centre and country locations	***0345 33 44 00***
Relais & Chateaux	An international consortium of rural privately owned hotels, mainly in the country house style	***0800 960239***
Lodge	Lodge accommodation at motorway services	***0800 834719***
The Savoy Group	Five red star hotels, four in London, one in the Cotswolds	***0171 872 8080 (General Enquiries)***
Scotland's Hotels of Distinction	A consortium of independent Scottish hotels, in the three and four star market	***01333 360 888***
Scottish & Newcastle hotels	Two star hotels across the country generally based round a busy restaurant operation	***0990 39 38 39***
Scottish Highland Hotels	A group of three and four star hotels in Scotland	***0131 472 3102***
The Luxury Collection	Sheraton is represented in the UK by a small number of four and five star hotels in London and Edinburgh	***0800 35 35 35***
Shire Inns	A small group of mostly four star hotels across the country	***01282 416987 (Head Office)***
SLH	Part of an international consortium of mainly privately owned hotels, often in the country house style	***0800 964470***
Swallow Hotels	In most cases modern four star hotels in primary provincial locations and London; most have indoor leisure facilities	***0191 419 4666***
The Circle	A consortium of independently owned mainly two and three star hotels across Britain	***01865 875888***
Thistle Hotels	A large group of mainly four star hotels across the UK, with many in London and some country house properties	***0800 18 17 16***
travel inn	Good quality modern budget accommodation. Every hotel has an adjacent licensed family restaurant, often a Beefeater, Brewers Fayre, or TGI Fridays	***0870 242 8000***
travel inn metro	A new brand of Travel Inn based in city locations	***0870 242 8000***
travel inn capital	A new brand of larger Travel Inn based in London	***0870 242 8000***
Travelodge	Good quality modern budget accommodation across the UK. Almost every lodge has an adjacent family restaurant, often a Little Chef, Harry Ramsden's or Burger King	***0800 850 950***
Virgin Hotel Collection	A group of three and four star hotels, many rurally based	***0800 716 919***
Welcome Break	Lodge accommodation at motorway services	***0800 731 4466***

THE 2000 AA HOTEL GUIDE IN ASSOCIATION WITH ROYAL MAIL

On behalf of Royal Mail, welcome to the 2000 AA Hotel Guide.

Whilst you're away from home, it's good to know that you can stay in touch with the people you've left behind. Whether it's a letter to a colleague, a postcard to a friend or an important international parcel, you can rely on a variety of Royal Mail services.

If you're going away, avoid letting your post build up by leaving it in the safe hands of Royal Mail. With *Keepsafe*, your mail is held for up to 2 months, and then delivered safely upon your return.

Whilst you're away on business we can help you keep in touch with the office or your customers. Use our guaranteed delivery services to ensure that your urgent or important documents reach their destination by 12.30 the next working day. Also the *International Recorded* service provides a signature on delivery to any world-wide destination.

You can even order stamps via the phone, by fax, or by post. We will deliver free anywhere in the UK the next working day - simply call *Royal Mail Direct* on 0345 782677.

If you would like to know more about Royal Mail services, please call 0345 950 950.

Finally, whichever hotel you choose from this guide, Royal Mail would like to wish you a very pleasant stay.

Royal Mail

I saw this and thought of you

WHAT WOULD

YOU SEND?

Royal Mail

Happy Anniversary darling!

WHAT WOULD

IMPROVE
YOUR
MEMORY
by R.E.Member
1ST
Road
YOU SEND?
Royal Mail

Hotel of the Year England

One Aldwych, London

ABBERLEY Worcestershire **Map 07 SO76**
★★★ **The Elms**
Stockton Rd WR6 6AT
Quality Percentage Score: 78%
☎ 01299 896666 Fax 01299 896804
Dir: *on A443 between Worcester and Tenbury Wells 2m beyond Great Witley*

A fine Queen Anne mansion built over 250 years ago. The spacious public rooms and the generously-proportioned bedrooms are full of character and the restaurant overlooks the landscaped gardens. The menu offers imaginative and seasonal dishes.
ROOMS: 16 en suite (bth/shr) s £90; d £140-£175 (incl. bkfst) * LB Off peak **MEALS:** Lunch £15-£19.50 Dinner £30.50-£40 English & Continental Cuisine V meals Coffee am Tea pm **FACILITIES:** CTV in all bedrooms Tennis (hard) Croquet lawn Xmas **CONF:** Thtr 60 Class 30 Board 24 Del from £145 * **SERVICES:** Night porter 61P **NOTES:** No dogs (ex guide dogs) No smoking in restaurant Last d 9.30pm
CARDS:

ABBOT'S SALFORD Warwickshire **Map 04 SP05**
★★★ **Salford Hall**
WR11 5UT
Quality Percentage Score: 75%
☎ 01386 871300 Fax 01386 871301
Dir: *8m W of Stratford-upon-Avon on B439*

Salford Hall is a beautifully restored 15th-century manor house which still retains many of its charming period features including exposed beams, stonework, and large open fireplaces. Staff provide a caring and friendly service under the direction of General Manager Sally Pearce. Public rooms include a cosy bar with leather seating, a conservatory courtyard, and a superb oak panelled restaurant, in which the carte is based around a modern interpretation of regional cooking. Bedrooms are superbly equipped, most featuring mini bars and a wealth of extras. The fabrics and furnishings used throughout are bold and stylish, but still in keeping with the character of the house.
ROOMS: 14 en suite (bth/shr) 19 annexe en suite (bth/shr) s £80-£140; d £115-£150 (incl. bkfst) * LB Off peak **MEALS:** Lunch fr £15.95 Dinner £25-£35 V meals Coffee am Tea pm **FACILITIES:** CTV in all bedrooms Tennis (hard) Snooker Sauna Solarium **CONF:** Thtr 50 Class 35 Board 25 Del from £130 * **SERVICES:** 51P **NOTES:** No dogs (ex guide dogs) No coaches No smoking in restaurant Last d 9.30pm Closed 24-30 Dec
CARDS:

See advert under STRATFORD-UPON-AVON

ABINGDON Oxfordshire **Map 04 SU49**
★★★ **Upper Reaches**
Thames St OX14 3JA
Quality Percentage Score: 68%
☎ 01235 522311 Fax 01235 555182
Dir: *on A415 in Abingdon follow signs for Dorchester and turn left just before the Broad Face public house*
Dating back to the 17th century this hotel was once a water mill and and has an interesting history linking it to the nearby abbey. Set on the banks of the Thames with moorings for boats and within walking distance of the town the hotel appeals to business and leisure guests. The spacious bedrooms have recently been refurbished and now offer a high standard of comfort.
ROOMS: 31 en suite (bth/shr) (4 fmly) No smoking in 15 bedrooms s fr £105; d fr £115 * LB Off peak **MEALS:** Sunday Lunch £9.95 Dinner £3.95-£19.95 & alc British Cuisine V meals Coffee am Tea pm **FACILITIES:** CTV in all bedrooms Boat moorings Xmas **CONF:** Thtr 25 Class 15 Board 20 Del from £135 * **SERVICES:** 80P **NOTES:** No smoking in restaurant Last d 9.30pm
CARDS:

ABINGDON Oxfordshire **Map 04 SU49**
★★★ **Abingdon Four Pillars Hotel**
Marcham Rd OX14 1TZ
Quality Percentage Score: 65%
☎ 01235 553456 Fax 01235 554117
Dir: *turn off A34 at junct with A415, on entry into Abingdon, turn right at rdbt, hotel on right*
This modern hotel particularly appeals to the business user with its fine range of meeting rooms and spacious bedrooms with good desk space. The friendly young team of staff is typical of this small group of hotels.
ROOMS: 63 en suite (bth/shr) (7 fmly) No smoking in 40 bedrooms s £61-£82; d £69-£92 * LB Off peak **MEALS:** Lunch £9-£10 Dinner £14.25-£15.25 English & French Cuisine V meals Coffee am Tea pm **FACILITIES:** CTV in all bedrooms STV Wkly live entertainment Xmas **CONF:** Thtr 140 Class 80 Board 48 Del £125 * **SERVICES:** Night porter 85P **NOTES:** Last d 10pm **CARDS:**

ABINGDON Oxfordshire **Map 04 SU49**
★★ **Crown & Thistle**
Bridge St OX14 3HS
Quality Percentage Score: 62%
☎ 01235 522556 Fax 01235 553281
Dir: *follow A415 towards Dorchester into the centre of Abingdon*
Guests will find a warm welcome at this charming old coaching inn, built in 1605, and whose name signifies the union of England and Scotland under James I. With its quaint cobbled courtyard, this listed building is in a lovely location close to the Abbey grounds and the River Thames. Bedrooms retain much of

contd.

their original character and are attractively decorated with co-ordinated fabrics and pine furniture.
ROOMS: 21 rms (16 bth/shr) (3 fmly) s fr £40; d £62 * Off peak **MEALS:** Lunch £10.75-£17.15alc Dinner £10.75-£17.15alc English & Continental Cuisine V meals Coffee am Tea pm **FACILITIES:** CTV in all bedrooms Snooker Pool table Bar Billards Wkly live entertainment **CONF:** Thtr 30 Class 16 Board 12 Del from £79 * **SERVICES:** Night porter 36P **NOTES:** No dogs (ex guide dogs) No smoking area in restaurant Last d 9.30pm **CARDS:**

ACCRINGTON Lancashire — Map 07 SD72

★★★★ *Dunkenhalgh*

Blackburn Rd, Clayton-le-Moors BB5 5JP
Quality Percentage Score: 62%
☎ 01254 398021 01254 872230
Dir: *adj to M65, junct 7*

This historic country house, considerably extended, is set in attractive grounds. It has a new wing of executive rooms, all providing a high standard of comfort. There are good meeting, banqueting and leisure facilities.
ROOMS: 37 en suite (bth/shr) 42 annexe en suite (bth/shr) (13 fmly) No smoking in 10 bedrooms **MEALS:** International Cuisine V meals Coffee am Tea pm **FACILITIES:** CTV in all bedrooms STV Indoor swimming pool (heated) Snooker Sauna Solarium Gym Steam room Wkly live entertainment **CONF:** Thtr 400 Class 200 Board 100 **SERVICES:** Night porter 400P **CARDS:**

ACCRINGTON Lancashire — Map 07 SD72

★★★ Sparth House Hotel

Whalley Rd, Clayton Le Moors BB5 5RP
Quality Percentage Score: 63%
☎ 01254 872263 01254 872263
Dir: *take A6185 to Clitheroe along Dunkenhalgh Way. right at lights onto A678, left at next lights - A680 to Whalley. Hotel on left after 2 lights*

Situated to the north of the town, this comfortable hotel, an 18th-century listed building, is set in three acres of mature grounds. Bedrooms are individually furnished and nicely spacious in the main house, somewhat more compact in the converted barn, and include one that has the genuine fittings of an ex-ocean liner. A wide range of meals is served in the bar lounge or wood-panelled restaurant.
ROOMS: 16 en suite (bth/shr) (3 fmly) s £53.50-£63.50; d £75-£87 (incl. bkfst) * LB Off peak **MEALS:** Lunch £9.95-£13.95 & alc Dinner fr £19.95 English & French Cuisine V meals Coffee am Tea pm **FACILITIES:** CTV in all bedrooms **CONF:** Thtr 100 Class 75 Board 60 Del from £75 * **SERVICES:** 50P **NOTES:** No smoking in restaurant Last d 9.30pm
CARDS:

ACLE Norfolk — Map 05 TG41

Travelodge

NR13 3BE
☎ 01493 751970 01493 751970
Dir: *junc A47 & Acle Bypass*

This modern building offers accommodation in smart, spacious and well equipped bedrooms, all with en-suite bathrooms. Refreshments may be taken at the nearby family restaurant. For details about current prices, consult the Contents Page under Hotel Groups for the Travelodge phone number.
ROOMS: 40 en suite (bth/shr) d £45.95 *

ACTON TRUSSELL Staffordshire — Map 07 SJ91

★★★ The Moat House

Lower Penkridge Rd ST17 0RJ
Quality Percentage Score: 76%
☎ 01785 712217 01785 715344
Dir: *off M6 junct 13 onto the A449 through the village of Acton Trussell. The hotel is on the right hand side on the way out of the village*

Despite being just a couple of miles from junction 13 of the M6, this 17th century timbered building has a peaceful canalside setting. Newly built bedrooms are spacious, comfortable and have many thoughtful extras. The bar and restaurant are located in the older part of the building and a wide range of bar snacks and meals is offered, carefully prepared and proving popular with both locals and visitors alike.
ROOMS: 21 en suite (bth/shr) (3 fmly) No smoking in 16 bedrooms s fr £95; d fr £105 (incl. bkfst) * LB Off peak **MEALS:** Lunch £10-£14.95 & alc Dinner fr £21.50 & alc V meals Coffee am Tea pm **FACILITIES:** CTV in all bedrooms STV Fishing **CONF:** Thtr 200 Class 60 Board 60 Del from £130 * **SERVICES:** Night porter 200P **NOTES:** No dogs (ex guide dogs) No smoking in restaurant Last d 9.45pm
CARDS:

See advert under STAFFORD

ADLINGTON Lancashire — Map 07 SD61

★★ *Gladmar*

Railway Rd PR6 9RG
Quality Percentage Score: 65%
☎ 01257 480398 01257 482681
Dir: *turn off A6 into Railway Road, cross railway bridge to hotel on left*

Surrounded by mature gardens, this well maintained hotel is peacefully situated, but convenient for the A6 and M61. The comfortable lounge leads into a cosy bar and a wide range of home cooked meals is offered in the restaurant. Bedrooms are attractively furnished and service provided by Christine Maxwell and her team is friendly.
ROOMS: 20 en suite (bth/shr) **MEALS:** **FACILITIES:** CTV in all bedrooms **CONF:** Board 14 **SERVICES:** 35P **NOTES:** No dogs (ex guide dogs) No smoking area in restaurant Last d 9.30pm
CARDS:

> ✚ Indicates that the star classification has not been confirmed under the New Quality Standards, see page 7 for further information.

ALBRIGHTON Shropshire — Map 07 SJ80

★★★ Lea Manor Hotel

Holyhead Rd WV1 3BX

Quality Percentage Score: 64%

☎ 01902 373266 Fax 01902 372853

Dir: *junct 3 of M54, follow A41 towards Wolverhampton then A464 towards Shifnal for approx. 2m hotel on the left*

This much extended hotel offers well equipped bedrooms, half of which are in the original building, and half on the ground floor of a nearby modern building. The restaurant and lounge bar serve a good range of popular dishes and there is also a large function room accommodating up to 200 people.

ROOMS: 6 en suite (bth/shr) 8 annexe en suite (bth/shr) No smoking in 6 bedrooms s fr £55; d fr £65 (incl. bkfst) * LB Off peak
MEALS: Dinner fr £16.50 V meals Coffee am Tea pm **FACILITIES:** CTV in all bedrooms **CONF:** Thtr 200 Class 60 Board 40 Del from £100 *
SERVICES: 200P **NOTES:** No dogs (ex guide dogs) No smoking in restaurant Last d 9.30pm **CARDS:**

ALCESTER Warwickshire — Map 04 SP05

★★★ *Kings Court*

Kings Coughton B49 5QQ

Quality Percentage Score: 65%

☎ 01789 763111 Fax 01789 400242

Dir: *1m N on A435*

This inviting hotel continues to benefit from improvement with modern extensions seamlessly complementing the Tudor origins of the main house. The well equipped bedrooms are spacious and those in the original house boast oak beams, and rustic appeal. Diners are spoilt for choice with several menus served either in the smart restaurant or cosy bar. Dishes reflect a discerning approach and satisfy those in search of a casual snack or more formal treat.

ROOMS: 4 en suite (bth/shr) 38 annexe en suite (bth/shr) (3 fmly)
MEALS: V meals Coffee am Tea pm **FACILITIES:** CTV in all bedrooms
CONF: Thtr 120 Class 40 Board 30 **SERVICES:** 120P **NOTES:** No smoking area in restaurant Closed 24-30 Dec **CARDS:**

ALCESTER Warwickshire — Map 04 SP05

Travelodge

A435 Birmingham Rd, Oversley Mill Roundabout B49 6AA

☎ 0800 850 950

Dir: *at junc A46/A435*

This modern building offers accommodation in smart, spacious and well equipped bedrooms, all with en-suite bathrooms. Refreshments may be taken at the nearby family restaurant. For details about current prices, consult the Contents Page under Hotel Groups for the Travelodge phone number.

ROOMS: 40 en suite (bth/shr) d £39.95 *

ALDEBURGH Suffolk — Map 05 TM45

★★★ Wentworth

Wentworth Rd IP15 5BD

Quality Percentage Score: 73%

☎ 01728 452312 Fax 01728 454343

Dir: *turn off A12 onto A1094, 6m to Aldeburgh, leave church on left and turn left at bottom of hill*

This popular hotel, just a stone's throw from the seafront, has been owned and run by the Pritt family for several decades and has gained a loyal following. The public areas are spacious and comfortably furnished, the homely feel enhanced by an abundance of prints, paintings and fresh flowers. In the winter there are log fires. The comfortable bedrooms are well equipped

contd.

Symbols and Abbreviations are listed and explained on pages 4 and 5

and attractively decorated; some rooms are located in Darfield House across the road, these have a charming Mediterranean feel and are very spacious.
ROOMS: 31 rms (24 bth 4 shr) 7 annexe en suite (bth/shr) No smoking in 7 bedrooms s £69-£79; d £100-£120 (incl. bkfst) * LB Off peak **MEALS:** Lunch £12.95-£14.75 Dinner £12.95-£15.50 English & French Cuisine V meals Coffee am Tea pm **FACILITIES:** CTV in all bedrooms Xmas **CONF:** Thtr 15 Class 8 Board 14 Del from £95 * **SERVICES:** 30P **NOTES:** No coaches No smoking in restaurant Last d 9pm Closed 28 Dec-8 Jan **CARDS:**

See advert on page 51

ALDEBURGH Suffolk — Map 05 TM45

★★★ White Lion

Market Cross Place IP15 5BJ
Quality Percentage Score: 73%
☎ 01728 452720 Fax 01728 452986
***Dir:** from A12 at Saxmundham take A1094 approx 5m, on seafront*

A major upgrading programme is bringing smart results to the bedrooms and public areas of this seaside hotel. Excellent customer care from the general manager and his team continues to charm loyal guests. Fresh shellfish and seafood are the natural speciality of the beamed restaurant in the evenings, there is a modern brasserie for lunch. The comfortable public areas include a smart air-conditioned conference room and two separate lounges with open fires.
ROOMS: 38 en suite (bth/shr) (1 fmly) No smoking in 10 bedrooms s £69.50-£81.50; d £98-£118 (incl. bkfst) * LB Off peak **MEALS:** Sunday Lunch £13.95 High tea fr £6.50 Dinner fr £16.95 English & French Cuisine V meals Coffee am Tea pm **FACILITIES:** CTV in all bedrooms STV Xmas **CONF:** Thtr 120 Class 50 Board 50 Del from £88 * **SERVICES:** 15P **NOTES:** No smoking in restaurant Last d 9pm
CARDS:

See advert on opposite page

ALDEBURGH Suffolk — Map 05 TM45

★★★ The Brudenell

The Parade IP15 5BU
Quality Percentage Score: 64%
☎ 01728 452071 Fax 01728 454082
***Dir:** on seafront, adjoining Fort Green car park*
Aldeburgh's main claim to fame is its music festival. The Brudenell has a loyal clientele, and offers attractively decorated accommodation. Informal meals are served in the bar, and there is also a formal dining room.

ROOMS: 47 en suite (bth/shr) (1 fmly) No smoking in 11 bedrooms **MEALS:** Lunch £2.95-£13.95 Dinner £13.95-£15.95 V meals Coffee am Tea pm **FACILITIES:** CTV in all bedrooms **CONF:** Thtr 50 Class 25 Board 35 Del from £90 * **SERVICES:** Lift Night porter 22P **NOTES:** No smoking in restaurant Last d 9pm
CARDS:

ALDEBURGH Suffolk — Map 05 TM45

★★ Uplands

Victoria Rd IP15 5DX
Quality Percentage Score: 65%
☎ 01728 452420 Fax 01728 454872
***Dir:** turn off A12 onto A1094, Aldeburgh 6m, Parish Church on left, hotel is opposite*
This Regency house was once in the midst of orchards in a country setting; the town may have encroached, but the hotel with its walled garden next to the church has kept much of its tranquillity. There are plenty of spacious public areas, with an airy conservatory, open fires in the two lounges, an elegant dining room and the intimate bar. The bedrooms vary in style and size with period furnishings in the main house and a contemporary approach to the chalet-style garden cottages.

ROOMS: 10 en suite (bth/shr) 7 annexe en suite (bth/shr) (4 fmly) s £49; d £69 (incl. bkfst) * LB Off peak **MEALS:** Dinner £14.50 & alc V meals Coffee am Tea pm **FACILITIES:** CTV in all bedrooms **SERVICES:** 22P **NOTES:** No coaches Last d 8.30pm Closed 23 Dec-3 Jan
CARDS:

ALDERLEY EDGE Cheshire — Map 07 SJ87

★★★ Alderley Edge

Macclesfield Rd SK9 7BJ
Quality Percentage Score: 71%
☎ 01625 583033 Fax 01625 586343
***Dir:** turn off A34 in Alderley Edge onto B5087 towards Macclesfield. Hotel 200yds on right*

contd.

Alderley Edge with its charming grounds was originally a country house built for one of the region's cotton kings. Now a hotel, four suites have been added, offering excellent quality and comfort, whilst the other bedrooms in the house are also attractively furnished, with several executive rooms available. The welcoming bar and adjacent lounge lead into the split-level restaurant, which offers freshly prepared and very satisfying meals.

ROOMS: 46 en suite (bth/shr) s £99.50-£400; d £115-£400 * LB Off peak **MEALS:** Lunch £14.50-£23.95 & alc Dinner £23.95 & alc English & Continental Cuisine V meals Coffee am **FACILITIES:** CTV in all bedrooms STV Wkly live entertainment Xmas **CONF:** Thtr 120 Class 80 Board 40 Del from £100 * **SERVICES:** Lift Night porter 90P **NOTES:** No dogs (ex guide dogs) Last d 10pm **CARDS:**

ALDERMINSTER Warwickshire — Map 04 SP24

★★★★ Ettington Park

CV37 8BU

Quality Percentage Score: 78%

☎ 01789 450123 Fax 01789 450472

Dir: *Off A3400, 5m S of Stratford just outside the village of Alderminster*

Set in 40 acres on the banks of the River Stour, this magnificent Victorian Gothic mansion has kept many of its architectural features. Bedrooms and bathrooms are furnished in keeping, many have views of the gardens and 12th-century chapel. Service is attentive but unobtrusive.

ROOMS: 48 en suite (bth/shr) (5 fmly) s fr £150; d fr £185 (incl. bkfst) * LB Off peak **MEALS:** Lunch £10-£17.50 Dinner £30.50 & alc V meals Coffee am Tea pm **FACILITIES:** CTV in all bedrooms STV Indoor swimming pool (heated) Tennis (hard) Fishing Riding Sauna Solarium Croquet lawn Jacuzzi/spa Clay pigeon shooting Archery Croquet HotAir Ballooning Wkly live entertainment Xmas **CONF:** Thtr 75 Class 40 Board 48 Del £190 * **SERVICES:** Lift Night porter 150P **NOTES:** No dogs (ex guide dogs) No smoking in restaurant Last d 9.30pm

CARDS:

ALDERSHOT Hampshire — Map 04 SU85

★★★ *Potters International*

1 Fleet Rd GU11 2ET

Quality Percentage Score: 69%

☎ 01252 344000 Fax 01252 311611

Dir: *access via A325 and A321 towards Fleet*

This modern hotel and leisure complex stands on the site of a former Army Officers' Mess building. Spacious, well equipped bedrooms have been attractively decorated and furnished. Extensive air conditioned public areas include a coffee shop

Some hotel groups have a central reservations telephone number, see pages 35, 37 and 38 for details.

serving light meals and a more formal restaurant; there are also conference facilities, a business centre and a very good leisure club.

ROOMS: 97 en suite (bth/shr) (6 fmly) No smoking in 10 bedrooms **MEALS:** English & French Cuisine V meals Coffee am Tea pm **FACILITIES:** CTV in all bedrooms STV Indoor swimming pool (heated) Sauna Solarium Gym Pool table Jacuzzi/spa **CONF:** Thtr 200 Class 150 Board 40 **SERVICES:** Lift Night porter 120P **NOTES:** No dogs (ex guide dogs) No smoking in restaurant **CARDS:**

ALDERSHOT Hampshire — Map 04 SU85

⇧ Travel Inn

Wellington Av GU11 1SQ

☎ 01252 344063 Fax 01252 344073

Dir: *from M3 junct 4 follow signs to Aldershot (A331, A3011 and A325). At Wellington rdbt (A323) turn left, Travel Inn on right*

This modern building offers accommodation in smart, spacious and well equipped bedrooms, all with en-suite bathrooms. Refreshments may be taken at the nearby family restaurant. For details about current prices consult the Contents Page under Hotel Groups for the Travel Inn phone number.

ROOMS: 40 en suite (bth/shr) d £39.95 *

ALDWARK North Yorkshire — Map 08 SE46

★★★ Aldwark Manor Hotel, Golf & Country Club

YO61 1UF

Quality Percentage Score: 67%

☎ 01347 838146 & 838251 Fax 01347 838867

Dir: *from A1, A59 towards Green Hammerton, then B6265 towards Little Ouseburn & follow signs Aldwark Bridge/Manor. A19 through Linton on Ouse to Aldwark*

Surrounded by a well designed golf course, this 19th-century

contd.

manor house offers well furnished, spacious bedrooms. Public rooms are furnished in style with the period; service is friendly and the restaurant offers a good range of food. Bunkers Bar is a recent addition.

ROOMS: 25 en suite (bth/shr) 3 annexe rms (2 bth/shr) (2 fmly) s £55; d £80-£100 (incl. bkfst) * LB Off peak **MEALS:** Lunch £11.50-£14 Dinner £25 English & French Cuisine V meals Coffee am Tea pm **FACILITIES:** CTV in all bedrooms STV Golf 18 Fishing Pool table Putting green Coarse fishing Xmas **CONF:** Thtr 80 Class 40 Board 30 Del from £90 * **SERVICES:** Night porter 150P **NOTES:** No smoking in restaurant Last d 9pm **CARDS:**

ALFRETON Derbyshire — Map 08 SK45

Travelodge

Old Swanwick Colliery Rd DE55 1HJ

☎ 01773 520040 🖷 01773 520040

Dir: *3m from junc 28 M1 where the A38 joins the A61*

This modern building offers accommodation in smart, spacious and well equipped bedrooms, all with en-suite bathrooms. Refreshments may be taken at the nearby family restaurant. For details about current prices, consult the Contents Page under Hotel Groups for the Travelodge phone number.

ROOMS: 60 en suite (bth/shr) d £45.95 *

ALFRISTON East Sussex — Map 05 TQ50

★★★ White Lodge Country House

Sloe Ln BN26 5UR

Quality Percentage Score: 69%

☎ 01323 870265 🖷 01323 870284

Dir: *turn off A27 at rdbt take road to Alfriston. After 1.5m note hotel sign and 250yrds on turn sharp right into narrow lane, hotel 60yds on left*

Set in five acres overlooking the River Cuckmere Valley, White Lodge is an extended Edwardian house offering comfort in a tranquil atmosphere. Day rooms have a sumptuous Victorian feel. Bedrooms are individually decorated and well equipped.

ROOMS: 17 en suite (bth/shr) (1 fmly) No smoking in 2 bedrooms s £55-£85; d £110-£135 (incl. bkfst) LB Off peak **MEALS:** Lunch £14-£15 Dinner £21-£22.50 International Cuisine V meals Coffee am Tea pm **FACILITIES:** CTV in all bedrooms STV Snooker Xmas **CONF:** Thtr 25 Class 25 Board 16 Del £105 **SERVICES:** Lift 30P **NOTES:** No coaches No smoking in restaurant Last d 9.30pm **CARDS:**

See advert on opposite page

ALFRISTON East Sussex — Map 05 TQ50

★★★ The Star Inn

BN26 5TA

Quality Percentage Score: 67%

☎ 01323 870495 🖷 01323 870922

Dir: *7m off A27 at Drusillas roundabout*

Originally built in 1345, the Star Inn has been sympathetically modernised over the years whilst still retaining much of its traditional character. Bedrooms, divided between the main building and a modern extension, are comfortably furnished and well equipped. Public areas include a neatly appointed restaurant, flagstoned bar and two lounges which feature exposed beams and open fires.

ROOMS: 37 en suite (bth/shr) (1 fmly) No smoking in 10 bedrooms s £80-£95; d £95-£140 * LB Off peak **MEALS:** Sunday Lunch £9.95-£12.95 Dinner £12.50-£18 V meals Coffee am Tea pm **FACILITIES:** CTV in all bedrooms Xmas **CONF:** Thtr 40 Class 20 Board 30 Del from £99 * **SERVICES:** Night porter 27P **NOTES:** No smoking in restaurant Last d 9pm **CARDS:**

ALFRISTON East Sussex — Map 05 TQ50

★★★ *Deans Place*

Seaford Rd BN26 5TW

Quality Percentage Score: 62%

☎ 01323 870248 🖷 01323 870918

Dir: *Turn off A27 signposted Alfriston & Drusillas Zoo Park. Pass through village towards south side*

This creeper-clad hotel stands in its own grounds on the southern fringes of the village. Bedrooms vary in size and standard, and there is a range of public areas suited to both leisure and conference guests. A wide range of food is offered, and there is an extensive bar menu.

ROOMS: 36 en suite (bth/shr) (2 fmly) No smoking in 4 bedrooms **MEALS:** International Cuisine V meals Coffee am Tea pm **FACILITIES:** CTV in all bedrooms STV Outdoor swimming pool (heated) Croquet lawn Putting green **CONF:** Thtr 170 Class 70 Board 45 **SERVICES:** Night porter 100P **NOTES:** No dogs (ex guide dogs) Last d 9.30pm **CARDS:**

ALNWICK Northumberland — Map 12 NU11

★★★ *White Swan*

Bondgate Within NE66 1TD

Quality Percentage Score: 60%

☎ 01665 602109 🖷 01665 510400

Dir: *from A1 follow signs to town centre. Procede through Bondgate Tower archway to hotel on right*

Situated in the centre of this pretty market town and with ample parking, this long-established hotel provides comfortable bedrooms in a variety of styles. Public areas include the Olympic Suite which features hand-carved panelling from the SS Olympic, sister ship to the ill-fated Titanic.

ROOMS: 58 en suite (bth/shr) (4 fmly) No smoking in 15 bedrooms **MEALS:** English & French Cuisine V meals Coffee am Tea pm **FACILITIES:** CTV in all bedrooms Wkly live entertainment **CONF:** Thtr 200 Class 80 Board 15 Del from £79 * **SERVICES:** Night porter 30P **NOTES:** No smoking in restaurant Last d 9.30pm **CARDS:**

ALRESFORD Hampshire — Map 04 SU53

★★ Swan

11 West St SO24 9AD

Quality Percentage Score: 61%

☎ 01962 732302 & 734427 🖷 01962 735274

Dir: *turn off A31 onto B3047*

The Swan Hotel is conveniently located in the centre of the town and dates back to the 18th century. Bedrooms vary from more traditional standard rooms in the original building to the more spacious ones in the annexe. The lounge bar is open all day and is a popular meeting place for both guests and locals. There is

contd.

also a separate restaurant, and the cellar bar which acts as a function room.
ROOMS: 11 rms (3 bth 7 shr) 12 annexe en suite (bth/shr) (3 fmly)
MEALS: International Cuisine V meals Coffee am Tea pm
FACILITIES: CTV in all bedrooms **CONF:** Thtr 90 Class 60 Board 40
SERVICES: 75P **NOTES:** No dogs (ex guide dogs) No smoking area in restaurant Last d 9.30pm RS 25-26 Dec **CARDS:**

See advert on this page

ALSAGER Cheshire **Map 07 SJ75**
★★★ Manor House
Audley Rd ST7 2QQ
Quality Percentage Score: 73%
☎ 01270 884000 Fax 01270 882483
Dir: *take A500 toward Stoke-on-Trent. In approx 0.5m take 1st slip road, Alsager, turn left at top & continue, hotel on left approaching village*
This modern hotel has been developed around an old farmhouse, the original oak beams of which are still a feature in the restaurant and bars. The bedrooms are well equipped and include ground floor rooms, and family accommodation. Conference and banqueting facilities for up to 200 people are available, and a pleasant patio garden and indoor swimming pool. The staff are helpful and caring, and the cuisine served in the restaurant is imaginative and very satisfying.
ROOMS: 57 en suite (bth/shr) (4 fmly) No smoking in 12 bedrooms s £79-£89; d £89-£109 (incl. bkfst) * LB Off peak **MEALS:** Lunch £12.95-£13.50 & alc Dinner £21 & alc English & French Cuisine V meals Coffee am Tea pm **FACILITIES:** CTV in all bedrooms STV Indoor swimming pool (heated) Jacuzzi/spa Xmas **CONF:** Thtr 200 Class 108 Board 82 Del from £105 * **SERVICES:** Night porter 200P
NOTES: No dogs (ex guide dogs) Last d 9.30pm RS 25-30 Dec
CARDS:

See advert on this page

A

ALSTON Cumbria **Map 12 NY74**
★★ ***Lovelady Shield Country House***
CA9 3LF
Quality Percentage Score: 73%
☎ 01434 381203 & 381305 📠 01434 381515
Dir: *2m E, signposted off A689 where it joins the B6294*

A delightful hotel in two acres of grounds high on the Pennines. Bedrooms vary in size and style, most have moorland views. Staff are friendly and give high levels of service. The stylish restaurant sets the scene for accomplished cooking; the varied menu makes good use of local seasonal produce. An inviting bar, opulent lounge and well stocked library capture the rural charm of the house.
ROOMS: 12 en suite (bth/shr) (1 fmly) **MEALS:** English & French Cuisine Coffee am Tea pm **FACILITIES:** CTV in all bedrooms **CONF:** Class 12 Board 12 **SERVICES:** 20P **NOTES:** No coaches No smoking in restaurant Last d 8.30pm Closed early Jan-early Feb
CARDS:

See advert on opposite page

ALSTON Cumbria **Map 12 NY74**
★★ **Lowbyer Manor Country House**
CA9 3JX
Quality Percentage Score: 68%
☎ 01434 381230 📠 01434 382937
Dir: *on the edge of town on A686 towards Newcastle*
A charming 17th-century manor house. The lounge has plenty of reading material and many homely touches. The attractive restaurant offers hearty home-cooked meals and the dinner menu has tempting vegetarian dishes. A cosy bar with inglenook fireplace, exposed stone walls and oak beams is popular for pre-dinner drinks.
ROOMS: 8 en suite (bth/shr) 4 annexe en suite (bth) s £35.50; d £71 (incl. bkfst) * LB Off peak **MEALS:** Bar Lunch £9.35-£11.50alc Dinner £18-£22.10alc V meals Coffee am Tea pm **FACILITIES:** CTV in all bedrooms Xmas **CONF:** Thtr 40 Class 14 Board 10 Del £75 * **SERVICES:** 14P **NOTES:** Last d 8.30pm **CARDS:**

ALSTON Cumbria **Map 12 NY74**
★★ **Nent Hall Country House Hotel**
CA9 3LQ
Quality Percentage Score: 66%
☎ 01434 381584 📠 01434 382668
Dir: *2m SE of Alston, on the A689*
A smartly presented hotel set in gardens three miles east of Alston. The bedrooms are well equipped, stylish and modern. Public areas have a country house ambience, lounges are filled with displays and antiques. Creative cooking is served in the elegant restaurant.
ROOMS: 8 en suite (bth/shr) 9 annexe en suite (bth/shr) (2 fmly) No smoking in all bedrooms **MEALS:** V meals Coffee am Tea pm **FACILITIES:** CTV in all bedrooms Solarium Croquet lawn **CONF:** Thtr 25 Class 25 **SERVICES:** 37P **NOTES:** No coaches No smoking in restaurant Last d 8.30pm **CARDS:**

ALTARNUN Cornwall & Isles of Scilly **Map 02 SX28**
★★ **Penhallow Manor Country House**
PL15 7SJ
Quality Percentage Score: 77%
☎ 01566 86206 📠 01566 86179
Dir: *8m W of Launceston towards Bodmin village, 1m N of A30. Hotel is next to church*
Built in 1842, Penhallow Manor is a Grade II listed Georgian style house. The individually furnished and decorated bedrooms are well equipped, exceeding expectations at Two Star level. Each evening the well balanced menu offers an interesting choice of dishes, featuring local fish, meat and game in season; complemented by a carefully selected wine list. Breakfast is served in the conservatory overlooking the garden.
ROOMS: 7 en suite (bth/shr) No smoking in all bedrooms s £45-£60; d £90-£120 (incl. bkfst) * LB Off peak **MEALS:** Bar Lunch £1.95-£8 High tea £3.30 Dinner £22.50 English & French Cuisine V meals Coffee am Tea pm **FACILITIES:** CTV in all bedrooms Fishing Croquet lawn Art courses Game Fishing instruction Bird Watching Xmas **CONF:** Thtr 30 Class 16 Board 16 Del from £73.50 * **SERVICES:** 10P **NOTES:** No coaches No children 12yrs No smoking in restaurant Last d 8.45pm Closed 3 Jan-27 Feb **CARDS:**

ALTON Hampshire **Map 04 SU73**
★★★ ***Alton House***
Normandy St GU34 1DW
Quality Percentage Score: 67%
☎ 01420 80033 📠 01420 89222
Dir: *turn off A31, close to railway station*
This pleasant hotel on the edge of the town is popular with both the business and leisure guest for the quality of its spacious and well equipped bedrooms. The restaurant offers a daily set menu and a carte, with dishes served by attentive, friendly staff. There is an attractive rear garden.
ROOMS: 39 en suite (bth/shr) (3 fmly) No smoking in 2 bedrooms **MEALS:** English & Continental Cuisine V meals Coffee am Tea pm **FACILITIES:** CTV in all bedrooms STV Outdoor swimming pool (heated) Tennis (hard) Snooker Sauna Solarium Gym Croquet lawn Jacuzzi/spa **CONF:** Thtr 150 Class 80 Board 50 **SERVICES:** Night porter 94P **NOTES:** No dogs (ex guide dogs) Last d 9.15pm Closed 25-26 Dec RS 27-29 Dec **CARDS:**

See advert on opposite page

ALTON Hampshire **Map 04 SU73**
★★★ **Alton Grange**
London Rd GU34 4EG
Quality Percentage Score: 66%
☎ 01420 86565 📠 01420 541346
Dir: *from A31 take first right at rdbt signed Alton/Holybourne/Bordon B3004, hotel will be found 300yds on left*
Situated on the edge of the town, this friendly, family-run hotel has been sympathetically extended and provides well equipped accommodation. The bedrooms, including some on the ground floor, are spacious and individually decorated. A piano bar overlooks the two-acre Oriental-style garden and the Terrace

contd.

Room is available for private use. Guests may dine in Truffles Restaurant or informally at the bar.
ROOMS: 26 en suite (bth/shr) 4 annexe en suite (bth/shr) (2 fmly) No smoking in 2 bedrooms s £67-£82.50; d £82.50-£95 (incl. bkfst) * LB Off peak **MEALS:** Lunch fr £16.50 & alc Dinner fr £16.50 & alc English & French Cuisine V meals Coffee am Tea pm **FACILITIES:** CTV in all bedrooms STV Hot air ballooning **CONF:** Thtr 80 Class 30 Board 40 Del from £117 * **SERVICES:** 48P **NOTES:** No children 3yrs No smoking in restaurant Last d 10pm Closed 24-30 Dec
CARDS:

ALTRINCHAM Greater Manchester **Map 07 SJ78**
★★★ Woodland Park
Wellington Rd, Timperley WA15 7RG
Quality Percentage Score: 72%
☎ 0161 928 8631 Fax 0161 941 2821
***Dir:** off the A560*
Privately owned, and in a residential area near Manchester and the motorways, this hotel offers good bedrooms, furnished in individual style. Lounges have a welcoming atmosphere and carefully prepared meals are offered in the Terrace Restaurant.
ROOMS: 46 en suite (bth/shr) (2 fmly) No smoking in 20 bedrooms s £77.50-£120; d £120-£145 (incl. bkfst) * LB Off peak **MEALS:** Lunch £11.95-£12.95 & alc Dinner £15.95-£19.90 & alc International Cuisine V meals Coffee am Tea pm **FACILITIES:** CTV in all bedrooms **CONF:** Thtr 150 Class 100 Board 50 Del £120 * **SERVICES:** Night porter 151P **NOTES:** No dogs (ex guide dogs) No smoking in restaurant Last d 9.45pm **CARDS:**

ALTRINCHAM Greater Manchester **Map 07 SJ78**
★★★ Cresta Court
Church St WA14 4DP
Quality Percentage Score: 65%
Best Western
☎ 0161 927 7272 Fax 0161 926 9194
***Dir:** on the A56 town centre Altrincham. Courtesy Transport available from Manchester Airport*
Accommodation at this large town-centre hotel has recently been refurbished, and now includes a number of four-poster suites with spa baths. Meals are available all day in the popular bar, and there is also a restaurant.
ROOMS: 138 en suite (bth/shr) (5 fmly) No smoking in 40 bedrooms s £41.50-£86.50; d £58-£120 * LB Off peak **MEALS:** Lunch £5.95-£15 & alc Dinner £12.50-£16 & alc V meals Coffee am Tea pm **FACILITIES:** CTV in all bedrooms STV Solarium Gym Xmas **CONF:** Thtr 320 Class 140 Board 50 Del from £110 * **SERVICES:** Lift Night porter 200P **NOTES:** No smoking in restaurant Last d 9.30pm
CARDS:

ALTRINCHAM Greater Manchester **Map 07 SJ78**
★★★ Quality Hotel Altrincham
Langham Rd, Bowdon WA14 2HT
Quality Percentage Score: 65%
Comfort Quality Clarion CHOICE HOTELS EUROPE
☎ 0161 928 7121 Fax 0161 927 7560
***Dir:** M6 leave junct 19 to airport continue until 2nd rdbt head for Bowdon/Altrincham hotel is in Langham Road*
A popular hotel within easy reach of the motorways and Manchester airport. The converted, extended Victorian house boasts a smart new leisure complex. The modern Cafe Continental serves drinks and light bites, the main restaurant

contd.

The AA Hotel Booking Service is a free benefit to AA members. See the advertisement on page 47

offers more formal eating. Bedrooms, varying in style and type, are comfortably furnished.
ROOMS: 89 en suite (bth/shr) No smoking in 15 bedrooms s £80-£96; d £96-£120 * LB Off peak **MEALS:** Lunch fr £9.90 & alc Dinner £3.95-£20.50 & alc English & French Cuisine V meals Coffee am Tea pm **FACILITIES:** CTV in all bedrooms Indoor swimming pool (heated) Sauna Solarium Gym Jacuzzi/spa Xmas **CONF:** Thtr 130 Class 60 Board 48 **SERVICES:** Night porter 164P **NOTES:** No smoking area in restaurant Last d 9.45pm **CARDS:**

ALVELEY Shropshire **Map 07 SO78**

★★★★ Mill Hotel & Restaurant

WV15 6HL
Quality Percentage Score: 66%
☎ 01746 780437 01746 780850
Dir: *between Kidderminster/Bridgnorth, turn off A442 signposted Enville/Turley Green*

Built around a 17th-century flour mill, with the original water wheel still on display, this modern hotel is set in eight acres of landscaped grounds with a mill pool, waterfall feature and several woodland walks. Bedrooms are pleasant and include some superior rooms, which have additional sitting areas. Rooms with four-poster beds are also available. The restaurant provides a range of carefully prepared dishes and there are numerous function suites to cater for wedding receptions and conferences.
ROOMS: 21 en suite (bth/shr) (3 fmly) No smoking in 18 bedrooms s £61-£88; d £73-£105 (incl. cont bkfst) * LB Off peak **MEALS:** Lunch £11.50-£15.25 & alc Dinner fr £19.50 & alc English & Continental Cuisine V meals Coffee am Tea pm **FACILITIES:** CTV in all bedrooms STV Pool table **CONF:** Thtr 200 Class 200 Board 100 Del from £100 * **SERVICES:** Lift Night porter 200P **NOTES:** No dogs No smoking in restaurant Last d 10.15pm **CARDS:**

See advert under BRIDGNORTH

ALVESTON Gloucestershire **Map 03 ST68**

★★★ Alveston House

Davids Ln BS35 2LA
Quality Percentage Score: 74%
☎ 01454 415050 01454 415425
Dir: *near A38, between juncts 14 & 16 of M5*

This popular hotel provides well maintained, modern bedrooms. The restaurant and bar areas are open plan and extend into a conservatory. Menus offer a good choice and services are efficient.
ROOMS: 30 en suite (bth/shr) (1 fmly) s £84.50-£94.50; d £94.50-£110.50 (incl. bkfst) * LB Off peak **MEALS:** Lunch £16.75-£22.50 Dinner £18.75-£22.50 & alc English & French Cuisine V meals Coffee am Tea pm **FACILITIES:** CTV in all bedrooms STV **CONF:** Thtr 85 Class 48 Board 50 Del from £115 * **SERVICES:** 75P **NOTES:** No smoking in restaurant Last d 9.30pm **CARDS:**

See advert under BRISTOL

AMBERLEY West Sussex **Map 04 TQ01**

The Premier Collection

★★★ Amberley Castle

BN18 9ND
☎ 01798 831992 01798 831998
Dir: *SW of village, off B2139*

Dating back to the 11th century, this castle is the real thing complete with massive gate-house (with working portcullis) and high curtain walls concealing delightful gardens presided over by white peacocks. Oozing history, there are all sorts of discoveries to be made from an ancient oubliette to garde robes (the last word in 14th-century sanitation). Under Joy and Martin Cummings, the castle has now been transformed into a luxury hotel with individually decorated bedrooms of great charm offering all sorts of comforting extras. Bathrooms, that all have spa bathtubs, are reassuringly 20th-century. Perhaps surprisingly for a castle, the antique-dotted day rooms are positively cosy despite the odd suit of armour and rack of pikes. The Queens Room restaurant boasts a mural commemorating the visit here in 1685 of Catherine of Braganza, and some sophisticated cooking from chef Sam Mahoney. Castle Cuisine, one of several menus, offers dishes based on carefully researched old English recipes.
ROOMS: 15 en suite (bth/shr) d £145-£300 (incl. bkfst) * LB Off peak **MEALS:** Lunch £12.50-£35 Dinner fr £35 English & French Cuisine V meals Coffee am Tea pm **FACILITIES:** CTV in all bedrooms Croquet lawn Jacuzzi/spa Xmas **CONF:** Thtr 60 Class 24 Board 32 Del from £190 * **SERVICES:** 50P **NOTES:** No dogs (ex guide dogs) No coaches No children 12yrs No smoking in restaurant Last d 9pm **CARDS:**

AMBLESIDE Cumbria **Map 07 NY30**
see also **Elterwater**

★★★ Rothay Manor

Rothay Bridge LA22 0EH
Quality Percentage Score: 76%
☎ 015394 33605 015394 33607
Dir: *in Ambleside follow signs for Coniston. Hotel is 0.25m SW on the road to Coniston opposite Rugby pitch*

A Regency-style hotel in landscaped gardens within walking distance of the town centre. Bedrooms are attractive and thoughtfully equipped, some rooms have balconies. Recently

contd.

For Useful Information and Important Telephone Number Changes turn to page 25

refurbished family suites are in contemporary style. The elegant dining room serves a short but well chosen menu.

ROOMS: 15 en suite (bth/shr) 3 annexe en suite (bth/shr) (7 fmly) s £70-£75; d £115-£135 (incl. bkfst) * LB Off peak **MEALS:** Lunch £8.50-£16.50 High tea £4-£8 Dinner £27 English & French Cuisine V meals Coffee am Tea pm **FACILITIES:** CTV in all bedrooms Nearby leisure centre free to guests Xmas **CONF:** Thtr 25 Board 20 Del from £109 * **SERVICES:** 45P **NOTES:** No dogs (ex guide dogs) No smoking in restaurant Last d 9pm Closed 3 Jan-Feb
CARDS:

See advert on this page

AMBLESIDE Cumbria — Map 07 NY30
★★★ Regent
Waterhead Bay LA22 0ES
Quality Percentage Score: 73%
☎ 015394 32254 📠 015394 31474
Dir: *1m S A591*

Situated just across from Waterhead Bay, on the south side of town, the Regent stands out with its abundant hanging baskets. Public areas include inviting lounges, a stylish restaurant and a heated swimming pool. Bedrooms are tastefully decorated and those in the courtyard building are especially comfortable. Staff throughout are delightful and both hospitality and service are excellent.

ROOMS: 30 en suite (bth/shr) (7 fmly) No smoking in 4 bedrooms s £59-£75; d £98-£113 (incl. bkfst) * LB Off peak **MEALS:** Bar Lunch £5-£15alc Dinner £24.50 V meals Coffee am Tea pm **FACILITIES:** CTV in all bedrooms Indoor swimming pool (heated) Jacuzzi/spa Wkly live entertainment **SERVICES:** 38P **NOTES:** No coaches No smoking in restaurant Last d 8.30pm **CARDS:**

AMBLESIDE Cumbria — Map 07 NY30
★★★ Wateredge
Borrans Rd, Waterhead LA22 0EP
Quality Percentage Score: 72%
☎ 015394 32332 📠 015394 31878
Dir: *on A591, at Waterhead Bay, adj Steamer Pier*

Idyllically situated on the shores of Windermere, this delightful hotel has been tastefully converted from two fishermen's cottages and retains oak beams and a great deal of charm. The elegant lounges overlook the gardens and lake. Bedrooms include impressive studio suites, each with their own patio or balcony.

contd.

We endeavour to be as accurate as possible but changes in personnel and data can occur in establishments after the Hotel Guide has gone to press.

A

Freshly prepared dinners, light lunches and home-made afternoon teas are to be recommended.

Wateredge, Ambleside

ROOMS: 17 en suite (bth/shr) 6 annexe en suite (bth/shr) (1 fmly) No smoking in 1 bedroom s fr £84; d £150-£210 (incl. bkfst & dinner) * LB Off peak **MEALS:** Bar Lunch fr £5alc Dinner £29.50 Coffee am Tea pm **FACILITIES:** CTV in all bedrooms Rowing boat Free use of Leisure Club Private jetty, Boat Launching **SERVICES:** 25P **NOTES:** No coaches No children 7yrs No smoking in restaurant Last d 8.30pm Closed mid Dec-mid Jan **CARDS:**

See advert on page 59

AMBLESIDE Cumbria — Map 07 NY30

★★★ The Salutation

Lake Rd LA22 9BX

Quality Percentage Score: 69%

☎ 015394 32244 015394 34157

Dir: *take A591 to Ambleside and follow one way system down Wansfell Road into Compston Road. At traffic lights take right hand lane back into village*

Located in the town centre, this former coaching inn has been transformed into a comfortable modern hotel. Bedrooms vary in size but are well equipped and tastefully decorated, those at the front enjoying open patios with delightful views. There is a spacious new air-conditioned lounge, and a restaurant which serves from an ambitious menu. A wide ranging snack menu is available in the bar.

ROOMS: 38 en suite (bth/shr) 4 annexe en suite (bth/shr) (4 fmly) No smoking in 4 bedrooms s £37-£60; d £74-£100 (incl. bkfst) Off peak **MEALS:** Bar Lunch £4-£11 Dinner £16-£19 English & French Cuisine V meals Coffee am Tea pm **FACILITIES:** CTV in all bedrooms STV Jacuzzi/spa Free membership of nearby leisure club Xmas **CONF:** Thtr 40 Board 16 Del from £73 **SERVICES:** 41P **NOTES:** No smoking in restaurant Last d 9pm **CARDS:**

See advert on opposite page

AMBLESIDE Cumbria — Map 07 NY30

★★★ Skelwith Bridge

Skelwith Bridge LA22 9NJ

Quality Percentage Score: 65%

☎ 015394 32115 015394 34254

Dir: *2.5m W on the A593 at junction of B5343 to Langdale*

A welcoming family-run hotel at the heart of the Lake District National Park. The comfortable, attractive public areas include lounges and bars. The tastefully appointed restaurant offers a tempting range of carefully prepared dishes. Bedrooms are modern in style and offer all the expected amenities.

ROOMS: 23 en suite (bth/shr) 6 annexe en suite (bth/shr) (3 fmly) No smoking in 6 bedrooms s £33.50-£53; d £61-£90 (incl. bkfst) * LB Off peak **MEALS:** Sunday Lunch £10.45 Dinner £19.45 English & French Cuisine V meals Coffee am Tea pm **FACILITIES:** CTV in all bedrooms Fishing Pool table Jacuzzi/spa ch fac **CONF:** Thtr 45 Class 25 Board 25 Del from £52 * **SERVICES:** 60P **NOTES:** No coaches No smoking in restaurant Last d 9pm **CARDS:**

See advert on opposite page

AMBLESIDE Cumbria — Map 07 NY30

★★ Nanny Brow Country House

Clappersgate LA22 9NF

Quality Percentage Score: 77%

☎ 015394 32036 015394 32450

Dir: *on A593, 1.5m from Ambleside*

Set in several acres of grounds and gardens, this country house has beautiful views over the River Brathey towards the Langdale Valley. The bedrooms are well equipped; four-poster rooms and garden suites are available. An elegant drawing room is provided for afternoon tea whilst the comfortable bar is situated in a conservatory. The attractive restaurant is home to accomplished British cuisine.

ROOMS: 17 en suite (bth/shr) (3 fmly) No smoking in all bedrooms s £65-£100; d £110-£180 (incl. bkfst & dinner) LB Off peak **MEALS:** Sunday Lunch £9.95-£15 High tea £3.75-£9.50 Dinner £19.99-£30 V meals Coffee am Tea pm **FACILITIES:** CTV in all bedrooms STV Fishing Solarium Croquet lawn Putting green Jacuzzi/spa Free use of private leisure club Xmas **CONF:** Thtr 30 Class 30 Board 20 Del from £100 * **SERVICES:** 20P **NOTES:** No coaches No smoking in restaurant Last d 8.45pm **CARDS:**

See advert on opposite page

AMBLESIDE Cumbria — Map 07 NY30

★★ *Fisherbeck*

Lake Rd LA22 0DH

Quality Percentage Score: 72%

☎ 015394 33215 015394 33600

Dir: *S of Ambleside on A591*

A welcoming, family-run hotel, offering friendly and attentive service. The delightful bedrooms come in a variety of sizes, those at the front enjoying fine views of the distant fells. Public rooms

contd. on p. 62

Skelwith BRIDGE HOTEL

AA ★★★

AMBLESIDE · CUMBRIA LA22 9NJ
TEL: 015394 32115 · FAX: 015394 34254
Email: skelwithbr@aol.com
Website: www.skelwithbridgehotel.co.uk

This former 17th century farm and inn has over the years been developed into a hotel for today's discerning guests, abundant original features blend beside modern day requirements, with a genuine warm and friendly welcome. Situated in the heart of the National Park it is an ideal base to explore the Lakes, walk the Fells, or simply relax, unwind and recharge your batteries.

Why not take advantage of one of our Seasonal Breaks.

WHERE THE SPIRIT SOARS

LANGDALE

This naturally beautiful Estate is a haven of peace and tranquillity; an ideal touring base to discover the Lake District. Formerly a 19th century gunpowder works, it is dotted with massive millstones and other carefully preserved reminders of its history. The Hotel has two restaurants, a Lakeland pub and leisure facilities. So much to do and so much to remember . . . the scenery, the comfort, the good food and the warm and friendly service.

Langdale Hotel & Country Club,
Great Langdale, Nr. Ambleside, Cumbria LA22 9JD
FREEPHONE 0500 051197
AA ★★★ BTA Award of Distinction
Egon Ronay Recommended Civic Trust Award

Nanny Brow Country House Hotel & Restaurant

An Oasis of Elegance

★★ ❀❀

Elegant country house sits peacefully under Loughrigg Fell with spectacular views of the river Brathay and valley and has direct access onto the Fell. The award winning candle- lit restaurant is cosy and intimate featuring superb cuisine and fine wines. Relax in the charming lounge, library bar or hall - there are log fires on chilly evenings and fresh flowers are attended to daily. All suites and rooms are individually and thoughtfully designed and furnished in traditional style with caring consideration given to the guests' comforts by attentive staff. Private leisure club facilities. Dogs accepted by prior arrangement. Personally managed by the resident owners Michael and Carol Fletcher.

• Two AA Red Rosettes • AA Romantic Hotel of the Year •
• Egon Ronay • Johansens • Best Loved Hotels of the World •
HOTEL OF THE YEAR – *Lancashire and Lake District Life*

CLAPPERSGATE, AMBLESIDE
CUMBRIA LA22 9NF
Tel: (015394) 32036 Fax: (015394) 32450

The Ambleside Salutation Hotel

LAKE ROAD, AMBLESIDE
CUMBRIA LA22 9SS
Tel: 015394 32244 Fax: 015394 34157

Overlooking the market cross at the heart of Ambleside village, this 16th century coaching hotel with its newly refurbished lounge bar, extended lounge and restaurant the Salutation makes the ideal base for a relaxing holiday with good food served by friendly staff. Guests enjoy free membership of nearby luxury leisure club.

Give us a call to book that well-earned break at the heart of The Lakes and remember us first for your Northern meeting venue.

include an attractive restaurant, serving a daily changing menu of creative dishes.

Fisherbeck, Ambleside

ROOMS: 18 en suite (bth/shr) (2 fmly) No smoking in 4 bedrooms **MEALS:** International Cuisine V meals Coffee am Tea pm **FACILITIES:** CTV in all bedrooms Free use of nearby Leisure Complex **SERVICES:** 24P **NOTES:** No dogs No coaches No smoking in restaurant Last d 8.30pm Closed 26 Dec-15 Jan **CARDS:**

AMBLESIDE Cumbria — Map 07 NY30
★★ Elder Grove
Lake Rd LA22 0DB
Quality Percentage Score: 70%
☎ 015394 32504
***Dir:** on A591, half a mile S of village centre*

A friendly family-run hotel offering attractive, well equipped bedrooms and appealing public rooms, including two lounges, a cosy bar and intimate restaurant with genuine Lakeland stone walls. The cooking is very skilful, producing carefully prepared seafood and game.

ROOMS: 10 en suite (bth/shr) (1 fmly) No smoking in all bedrooms **MEALS:** V meals Coffee am **FACILITIES:** CTV in all bedrooms **SERVICES:** 8P **NOTES:** No coaches No smoking in restaurant Closed mid Nov-mid Feb **CARDS:**

AMBLESIDE Cumbria — Map 07 NY30
★★ Kirkstone Foot Country House
Kirkstone Pass Rd LA22 9EH
Quality Percentage Score: 69%
☎ 015394 32232 📠 015394 32805
***Dir:** from the S on A591, in Ambleside village keep in left hand lane past Dodds restaurant, turn right up hill signed Kirkstone 3m, hotel on right 500yds*

A 17th-century manor house, set in secluded gardens with grounds sloping down to a stream. The comfortable lounge has lots of reading material, and pretty bedrooms are decorated in traditional country colours. Staff are attentive and very caring.

ROOMS: 13 en suite (bth/shr) (1 fmly) **MEALS:** High tea £10-£12 & alc Dinner £21.95-£22.50 & alc V meals Coffee am Tea pm **FACILITIES:** CTV in all bedrooms **CONF:** Thtr 40 Class 35 Board 26 **SERVICES:** 36P **NOTES:** No dogs No coaches No smoking in restaurant Last d 8.30pm Closed 3 Jan-10 Feb **CARDS:**

AMBLESIDE Cumbria — Map 07 NY30
★★ Waterhead
Lake Rd LA22 0ER
Quality Percentage Score: 65%
☎ 015394 32566 📠 015394 31255
***Dir:** A591 into Ambleside, hotel is opposite Waterhead Pier*

Best Western

Situated opposite the bay, this tourist hotel offers views of the lakeside, where guests can sit in the gardens. There is an Irish theme bar as well as a modern mediterranean style cafe, and a traditional restaurant. There is a choice of bedroom size and style, all rooms are well equipped.

ROOMS: 28 en suite (bth/shr) (3 fmly) No smoking in 14 bedrooms s £42; d £82-£116 (incl. bkfst) * LB Off peak **MEALS:** Lunch fr £5 High tea £6.95-£10.95 Dinner fr £18.95 English, French, Irish & Italian Cuisine V meals Coffee am Tea pm **FACILITIES:** CTV in all bedrooms STV Use of sister hotel's leisure facilities Wkly live entertainment Xmas **CONF:** Thtr 40 Class 30 Board 25 Del from £87 * **SERVICES:** 50P **NOTES:** No smoking in restaurant Last d 9.30pm **CARDS:**

AMERSHAM Buckinghamshire — Map 04 SU99
★★★ The Crown
High St HP7 0DH
Quality Percentage Score: 66%
☎ 01494 721541 📠 01494 431283
***Dir:** access to car park immediately next to Nags Head pub*

The Georgian façade hides an Elizabethan interior, with inglenooks, beams and wall paintings. Bedrooms vary in shape and size, all are refurbished and attractively furnished. Film-goers may be interested to know that some of the romantic scenes from "Four Weddings and a Funeral" were shot here. Flowers and hanging baskets makes the courtyard an attractive location.

ROOMS: 19 en suite (bth/shr) 4 annexe en suite (bth/shr) No smoking in 7 bedrooms s fr £119; d fr £125 (incl. bkfst) * LB Off peak **MEALS:** Lunch £13.25-£16.95 Dinner £21.95 British & European Cuisine V meals Coffee am Tea pm **FACILITIES:** CTV in all bedrooms Xmas **CONF:** Thtr 30 Class 18 Board 24 **SERVICES:** Night porter 32P **NOTES:** No smoking in restaurant Last d 9.30pm **CARDS:**

AMESBURY Wiltshire — Map 04 SU14
★★ Antrobus Arms
15 Church St SP4 7EU
Quality Percentage Score: 64%
☎ 01980 623163 📠 01980 622112
***Dir:** from rdbt on A303 proceed through town on one way system to T junct, turn left hotel on left*

MINOTEL Great Britain

Advertised as the nearest hotel to Stonehenge, the Antrobus Arms suits local and leisure visitors. Bedrooms, some overlooking the walled Victorian garden, are individually furnished. The wood panelled Fountain Restaurant serves food and there is also a choice of bar meals.

ROOMS: 16 en suite (bth/shr) (2 fmly) s fr £53.50; d fr £75 (incl. bkfst) * LB Off peak **MEALS:** Lunch £5.90-£10 Dinner £12.50-£16.45 English & French Cuisine V meals Coffee am Tea pm **FACILITIES:** CTV in all bedrooms STV Xmas **CONF:** Thtr 40 Class 40 Board 20 **SERVICES:** 15P **NOTES:** No smoking in restaurant Last d 9pm **CARDS:**

AMESBURY Wiltshire **Map 04 SU14**
Travelodge
Countess Services SP4 7AS
01980 624966 01980 624966
Dir: *junc A345 & A303 eastbound*
This modern building offers accommodation in smart, spacious and well equipped bedrooms, all with en-suite bathrooms. Refreshments may be taken at the nearby family restaurant. For details about current prices, consult the Contents Page under Hotel Groups for the Travelodge phone number.
ROOMS: 32 en suite (bth/shr) d £49.95 *

ANDOVER Hampshire **Map 04 SU34**
★★★ **Esseborne Manor**
Hurstbourne Tarrant SP11 0ER
Quality Percentage Score: 68%
01264 736444 01264 736725
Dir: *halfway between Andover and Newbury on A343*

This attractive manor house is set in two acres of well tended gardens surrounded by open countryside. The bedrooms are split between the main house, adjoining courtyard and separate garden cottage. All are individually furnished and offer many thoughtful extras. Recently refurbished public areas are quiet and comfortable.
ROOMS: 6 en suite (bth/shr) 8 annexe en suite (bth/shr) s £88-£95; d £95-£160 (incl. bkfst) * LB Off peak **MEALS:** Lunch £13-£15 High tea fr £8 Dinner fr £18 & alc English & French Cuisine V meals Coffee am Tea pm **FACILITIES:** CTV in all bedrooms STV Tennis (hard) Croquet lawn Putting green Jacuzzi/spa **CONF:** Thtr 35 Class 25 Board 25 Del from £135 * **SERVICES:** 50P **NOTES:** No dogs (ex guide dogs) No coaches No smoking in restaurant Last d 9.30pm
CARDS:

See advert on this page

ANDOVER Hampshire **Map 04 SU34**
★★★ **White Hart**
Bridge St SP10 1BH
Quality Percentage Score: 68%
01264 352266 01264 323767
Dir: *from A303 follow signs to town centre, then signs for London St, Bridge St and High St, hotel is on left hand side halfway along Bridge St*
Dating back to the 17th century, this former coaching inn is now a family-owned property, combining charm with modern facilities. Each of the bedrooms is well equipped and three spacious, superior rooms have recently been created. Simon's Wine Bar offers an informal atmosphere for guests with an additional eating option to the formal restaurant where guests can choose from the fixed-price menu or the carte.
ROOMS: 27 en suite (bth/shr) (2 fmly) No smoking in 6 bedrooms **MEALS:** Lunch £12.95-£13.50 & alc Dinner £14 & alc English & Continental Cuisine V meals Coffee am Tea pm **FACILITIES:** CTV in all bedrooms STV Sauna Solarium Gym **CONF:** Thtr 70 Class 30 Board 30 Del from £105 * **SERVICES:** Night porter 30P **NOTES:** No coaches No smoking in restaurant Last d 9.45pm
CARDS:

★
The Premier Collection, hotels with Red Star Awards are listed on pages 17-23

ANDOVER Hampshire **Map 04 SU34**
★★★ ***Ashley Court***
Micheldever Rd SP11 6LA
Quality Percentage Score: 62%
01264 357344 01264 356755
This peaceful hotel is set in grounds on the outskirts of the town. Bedrooms are comfortable and well equipped, all have trouser presses. The range of conference and meeting rooms make it a popular venue for functions and weddings.
ROOMS: 9 en suite (bth/shr) 26 annexe en suite (bth/shr) No smoking in 7 bedrooms **MEALS:** English & French Cuisine V meals Coffee am **FACILITIES:** CTV in all bedrooms STV Snooker **CONF:** Thtr 180 Class 40 Board 60 **SERVICES:** 100P **NOTES:** No dogs (ex guide dogs) No smoking in restaurant Last d 9.30pm **CARDS:**

Indicates that the star classification has not been confirmed under the New Quality Standards, see page 7 for further information.

A

APPLEBY-IN-WESTMORLAND Cumbria **Map 12 NY62**

★★★ Appleby Manor Country House

Roman Rd CA16 6JB
Quality Percentage Score: 76%
☎ 017683 51571 017683 52888

***Dir:** from M6 junct 40, take A66 towards Brough. Take Appleby turn off, then immediately right and continue for 0.5m*

This friendly, family-run Victorian mansion nestles in colourful grounds and enjoys panoramic views of the valley and Appleby Castle. There are three styles of bedrooms - modern garden rooms, main house rooms and smart coach house rooms across the courtyard. At dinner a full carte offers imaginative dishes in generous portions, and afterwards, guests can sample the impressive range of whiskies.

ROOMS: 23 en suite (bth/shr) 7 annexe en suite (bth/shr) (9 fmly) No smoking in 6 bedrooms s £78-£88; d £116-£136 (incl. bkfst) LB Off peak **MEALS:** Lunch £16.50-£32alc Dinner £16.50-£32alc International Cuisine V meals Coffee am Tea pm **FACILITIES:** CTV in all bedrooms STV Indoor swimming pool (heated) Sauna Solarium Pool table Putting green Jacuzzi/spa Steam room Table tennis **CONF:** Thtr 38 Class 25 Board 28 Del from £109.95 **SERVICES:** 53P **NOTES:** No smoking in restaurant Last d 9pm Closed 24-26 Dec **CARDS:**

See advert on opposite page

APPLEBY-IN-WESTMORLAND Cumbria **Map 12 NY62**

★★★ Tufton Arms

Market Square CA16 6XA
Quality Percentage Score: 70%
☎ 017683 51593 017683 52761

***Dir:** in the centre of Appleby, by-passed by the A66, on B6260*

Conveniently situated in the centre of this popular market town, this family-run hotel is stylishly furbished to reflect its grand Victorian character. The elegant bedrooms include lavish suites and studio rooms, along with two mews rooms; there are also some simpler economy rooms. The smart conservatory restaurant features some ambitious cooking and offers a set-price dinner menu as well as a carte offering less formal dishes.

ROOMS: 21 en suite (bth/shr) (4 fmly) s £49-£90; d £90-£145 (incl. bkfst) * LB Off peak **MEALS:** Lunch £14-£25alc Dinner fr £22 & alc English & French Cuisine V meals Coffee am **FACILITIES:** CTV in all bedrooms STV Fishing Shooting **CONF:** Thtr 100 Class 60 Board 50 Del from £96 * **SERVICES:** 17P **NOTES:** Last d 9pm **CARDS:**

APPLEBY-IN-WESTMORLAND Cumbria **Map 12 NY62**

★★ Royal Oak Inn

Bongate CA16 6UN
Quality Percentage Score: 71%
☎ 017683 51463 017683 52300

***Dir:** from M6 junct 38 follow B6260, hotel is 0.5m from Appleby centre on old A66 in direction of Scotch Corner*

With its rustic atmosphere, wide variety of food and well kept ales, The Royal Oak will appeal to lovers of character inns. Bedrooms are attractive and well equipped while authentic inn style public areas include two lounges, two traditional bars and three smart dining areas.

ROOMS: 9 rms (7 bth/shr) (1 fmly) s £35-£53; d £76-£86 (incl. bkfst) * LB Off peak **MEALS:** Lunch £8-£50alc Dinner £8-£50alc European/International Cuisine V meals Coffee am Tea pm **FACILITIES:** CTV in all bedrooms Xmas **CONF:** Class 20 Board 15 **SERVICES:** 13P **NOTES:** No smoking area in restaurant Last d 9pm **CARDS:**

ARNCLIFFE North Yorkshire **Map 07 SD97**

★★ *Amerdale House*

BD23 5QE
Quality Percentage Score: 75%
☎ 01756 770250 01756 770250

There are fine views of the dale and fells from each bedroom in this delightful former manor house. Nigel and Paula Crapper, the resident proprietors, have furnished the bedrooms in a simple yet elegant manner. There is a choice of welcoming lounges, looking out over the neatly tended gardens, and the dining room is suitably appointed to enjoy the carefully prepared meals, chosen from a short handwritten menu.

ROOMS: 10 en suite (bth/shr) 1 annexe en suite (bth) (3 fmly) **MEALS: FACILITIES:** CTV in all bedrooms **SERVICES:** 30P **NOTES:** No dogs (ex guide dogs) No coaches No smoking in restaurant Last d 8.30pm Closed mid Nov-mid Mar **CARDS:**

ARUNDEL West Sussex **Map 04 TQ00**

★★★ Norfolk Arms

High St BN18 9AD
Quality Percentage Score: 67%
☎ 01903 882101 01903 884275

***Dir:** in centre of High Street*

Originally built as a Georgian coaching inn over 200 years ago, the Norfolk Arms stands in the heart of the town. Bedrooms, including some in a separate courtyard building, are comfortably furnished. The public areas consist of two bars, and a separate, attractively decorated lounge.

ROOMS: 21 en suite (bth) 13 annexe en suite (bth) (4 fmly) No smoking in 3 bedrooms **MEALS:** Lunch fr £7.95 Dinner fr £17.85 International Cuisine V meals Coffee am Tea pm **FACILITIES:** CTV in all bedrooms **CONF:** Thtr 100 Class 40 Board 40 Del from £90 * **SERVICES:** Night porter 34P **NOTES:** No smoking area in restaurant Last d 9.45pm **CARDS:**

ARUNDEL West Sussex **Map 04 TQ00**

★★★ The Arundel Swan Hotel

27-29 High St BN18 9AG
Quality Percentage Score: 65%
☎ 01903 882314 01903 883759

***Dir:** on A27*

Situated in the heart of the town, this well presented Victorian hotel offers smart accommodation in well equipped rooms. Public areas feature a lively tap room bar, a small combined reception and residents' lounge and a tastefully appointed restaurant, where Chef Michael Collis offers guests an interesting range of carefully prepared dishes. Room service and light

contd.

refreshments are also available throughout the day together with bar meals in the evening.

ROOMS: 15 en suite (bth/shr) (5 fmly) No smoking in all bedrooms s £50-£85; d £65-£100 (incl. bkfst) * LB Off peak **MEALS:** Lunch £13.95-£14.95 & alc Dinner £14.95 & alc English & Continental Cuisine V meals Coffee am Tea pm **FACILITIES:** CTV in all bedrooms Xmas **SERVICES:** 15P **NOTES:** No dogs (ex guide dogs) No smoking in restaurant Last d 9.30pm **CARDS:**

ARUNDEL West Sussex — Map 04 TQ00

★★ Burpham Country House

Old Down, Burpham BN18 9RJ
Quality Percentage Score: 76%
☎ 01903 882160 01903 884627

Dir: *3m NE off A27 turning by Arundel Railway Station clearly signed to Hotel Warningcamp & Burpham continue for 2.5m along lane Hotel on right*

This delightful little gem is located in the perfect tranquillity of the countryside just outside Arundel. Bedrooms are comfortable and attractively decorated, all are well equipped and have modern facilities. A daily changing menu is offered in the restaurant which enjoys views of the pretty garden. Mr and Mrs Walker are excellent hosts and with their friendly team a warm welcome is assured.

ROOMS: 10 en suite (bth/shr) No smoking in all bedrooms s £40-£60; d £82-£100 (incl. bkfst) * LB Off peak **MEALS:** Dinner £19-£23.50 English, French & Swiss Cuisine V meals **FACILITIES:** CTV in all bedrooms Croquet lawn Xmas **SERVICES:** 12P **NOTES:** No dogs No coaches No children 10yrs No smoking in restaurant Last d 9pm RS Mon **CARDS:**

See advert on this page

The AA's professional hotel and restaurant inspectors make regular and anonymous visits to all the hotels listed in the guide. They do not accept gifts or favours from hoteliers.

A

ARUNDEL West Sussex **Map 04 TQ00**
★★ Comfort Inn
Junction A27/A284, Crossbush BN17 7QQ
Quality Percentage Score: 68%
☎ 01903 840840 01903 849849
Dir: *from Worthing on the A27 towards Arundel, turn left on the A284 towards Littlehampton and straight right, hotel next to McDonalds restaurant*
Conveniently located just off the A27 and close to the historic town of Arundel, this lodge-type hotel offers good levels of comfort and value for money. The spacious bedrooms are brightly appointed and well equipped. The Arun Restaurant offers guests a good range of dishes with particular emphasis on fish. In addition there are conference rooms and a mini-gym.
ROOMS: 55 en suite (bth/shr) (4 fmly) No smoking in 26 bedrooms d £43.75-£54.50 * LB Off peak **MEALS:** Lunch £2.95-£15.95alc Dinner fr £10.75 & alc English & Continental Cuisine V meals Coffee am Tea pm **FACILITIES:** CTV in all bedrooms STV Gym Mini gym Xmas **CONF:** Thtr 30 Class 12 Board 24 **SERVICES:** Night porter 50P **NOTES:** No smoking in restaurant Last d 10pm
CARDS:

ARUNDEL West Sussex **Map 04 TQ00**
★★ Mill House
16 Chichester Rd BN18 0AD
Quality Percentage Score: 62%
☎ 01903 882677 01903 884154
Dir: *off A27, 0.5m W*
These well-equipped bedrooms are particularly suitable for business travellers. Public areas include an old black-beamed bar and a restaurant serving popular dishes. Bedrooms are in newer wings that blend in well with the original building.
ROOMS: 24 en suite (bth/shr) (3 fmly) No smoking in 16 bedrooms s fr £44.50; d fr £62.99 * LB Off peak **MEALS:** Lunch £3.95-£10.95alc High tea fr 85palc Dinner £3.95-£10.95alc International Cuisine V meals Coffee am Tea pm **FACILITIES:** CTV in all bedrooms STV Xmas **CONF:** Thtr 140 Class 60 Board 60 Del from £65 * **SERVICES:** Night porter 130P **NOTES:** No smoking in restaurant Last d 9.30
CARDS:

ARUNDEL West Sussex **Map 04 TQ00**
Travel Inn
Crossbush Ln BN18 9PQ
☎ 01903 882655 01903 884381
Dir: *1m E of Arundel at intersection of A27/A284*
This modern building offers accommodation in smart, spacious and well equipped bedrooms, all with en-suite bathrooms. Refreshments may be taken at the nearby family restaurant. For details about current prices consult the Contents Page under Hotel Groups for the Travel Inn phone number.
ROOMS: 40 en suite (bth/shr) d £39.95 *

ASCOT Berkshire **Map 04 SU96**
★★★★ The Berystede
Bagshot Rd, Sunninghill SL5 9JH
Quality Percentage Score: 62%
☎ 01344 623311 01344 872301
Dir: *turn off A30 onto B3020 (Windmill Pub). Continue for approx. 1.25m to hotel on left just before junct with A330*
Just 15 miles from Heathrow, and close to Ascot race course, this elegant turreted and timber-framed Victorian residence has been sympathetically extended, and stands in nine acres of wooded grounds. Bedrooms are decorated in period style and the larger rooms are in the main house. The hotel has several comfortable lounges, a bar and restaurant overlooking the gardens.
ROOMS: 91 en suite (bth/shr) (6 fmly) No smoking in 36 bedrooms s £135; d £155 * LB Off peak **MEALS:** Lunch £9-£30alc Dinner £9-£30alc European Cuisine V meals Coffee am Tea pm **FACILITIES:** CTV in all bedrooms STV Outdoor swimming pool (heated) Croquet lawn Putting green Xmas **CONF:** Thtr 120 Class 55 Board 50 Del from £175 * **SERVICES:** Lift Night porter 240P **NOTES:** No smoking in restaurant Last d 9.45pm **CARDS:**

ASCOT Berkshire **Map 04 SU96**
★★ *Highclere*
19 Kings Rd, Sunninghill SL5 9AD
Quality Percentage Score: 74%
☎ 01344 625220 01344 872528
Dir: *opposite Sunninghill Post Office*
The Highclere is situated opposite Sunninghill's post office, in a quiet road off the main street. The location is ideal for visitors to Ascot or the Windsor area. The owners are on hand to ensure guests are cosseted and feel thoroughly at home. Bedrooms are well equipped, and the comfortable lounge and dining areas are spacious, with fresh flowers throughout.
ROOMS: 11 en suite (shr) (1 fmly) No smoking in 3 bedrooms **MEALS:** European Cuisine V meals Coffee am **FACILITIES:** CTV in all bedrooms STV **SERVICES:** 11P **NOTES:** No dogs (ex guide dogs) No coaches No smoking in restaurant Last d 9pm
CARDS:

ASCOT Berkshire **Map 04 SU96**
★★ Brockenhurst
Brockenhurst Rd SL5 9HA
Quality Percentage Score: 66%
☎ 01344 621912 01344 873252
Dir: *on A330*
This attractive Edwardian hotel with large garden is situated just back from the road on the A330 to the south of Ascot. The hotel caters well for both business and leisure guests. Bedrooms are spacious and well equipped, there is an attractive lounge bar and restaurant.
ROOMS: 11 en suite (bth/shr) 4 annexe en suite (bth/shr) (2 fmly) s £79-£100; d £89-£150 (incl. cont bkfst) * Off peak **MEALS:** Lunch fr £12.95 Dinner fr £17.50 English & French Cuisine Coffee am Tea pm **FACILITIES:** CTV in all bedrooms STV Xmas **CONF:** Thtr 50 Class 25 Board 30 **SERVICES:** 32P **NOTES:** No dogs No coaches Last d 9.30pm
CARDS:

ASHBOURNE Derbyshire **Map 07 SK14**
★★★ Callow Hall
Mappleton Rd DE6 2AA
Quality Percentage Score: 75%
☎ 01335 343403 & 342412 01335 343624
Dir: *take A515 through Ashbourne toward Buxton, turn left at Bowling Green pub on left, then first right*
A delightful Victorian house lying in a 44 acre estate, overlooking Bentley Brook and the Dove Valley. The atmosphere is relaxed and welcoming, and service professional and friendly. Bedrooms range in style from cosy to spacious rooms with comfortable sitting areas. The public areas are comfortable and have high ceilings, ornate plasterwork, and antique furniture.
contd.

Symbols and Abbreviations are listed and explained on pages 4 and 5

Food plays an important part here, with a good range of dishes available from daily set-price and carte menus.

ROOMS: 16 en suite (bth/shr) (2 fmly) No smoking in 8 bedrooms s £80-£105; d £120-£150 (incl. bkfst) * LB Off peak **MEALS:** Lunch fr £19.50 Dinner fr £37 & alc English & French Cuisine V meals **FACILITIES:** CTV in all bedrooms Fishing **CONF:** Thtr 30 Board 16 **SERVICES:** 21P **NOTES:** No dogs (ex guide dogs) No coaches No smoking in restaurant Last d 9pm Closed 25-26 Dec
CARDS:

See advert on this page

ASHBOURNE Derbyshire — Map 07 SK14

★★★ Hanover International

Derby Rd DE6 1XH
Quality Percentage Score: 69%
☎ 01335 346666 📠 01335 346549
Dir: *on A52 to Ashbourne at rdbt take right turn to Airfield Ind Est, hotel is 400yds on right*

This modern, purpose built hotel lies just a few minutes' drive from the town and offers well equipped and comfortable accommodation, including some rooms specifically designed for disabled visitors. The Milldale restaurant serves freshly prepared meals whilst the brasserie provides a pleasant alternative for those diners looking for a less formal atmosphere. With a number of function rooms available, as well as the bonus of a leisure centre, the hotel is well equipped to cater for business and leisure guests alike.

ROOMS: 50 en suite (bth/shr) (5 fmly) No smoking in 10 bedrooms s £75; d £90 (incl. bkfst) * LB Off peak **MEALS:** Dinner £17.95 English & French Cuisine V meals Coffee am Tea pm **FACILITIES:** CTV in all bedrooms STV Indoor swimming pool (heated) Sauna Gym Pool table Steam room Wkly live entertainment **CONF:** Thtr 200 Class 100 Board 80 Del £110 * **SERVICES:** Lift Night porter 130P **NOTES:** No dogs (ex guide dogs) No smoking in restaurant Last d 10pm Closed 25 Dec-3 Jan
CARDS:

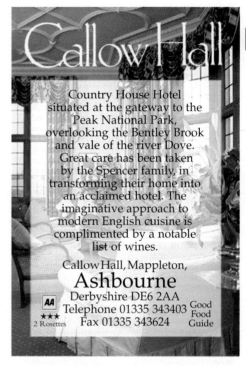

ASHBURTON Devon — Map 03 SX77
★★★ Holne Chase
Two Bridges Rd TQ13 7NS
Quality Percentage Score: 76%
☎ 01364 631471 Fax 01364 631453
Dir: *R3m N on Two Bridges/Tavistock road (unclass)*
Set in idyllic woodland along the Dart Valley, this former hunting lodge continues to thrive. The bedrooms are decorated and furnished to a very high standard and in a variety of styles; some have original fireplaces and four-poster beds. The stables have been converted to provice delightful split-level suites. Public rooms combine the architectural charm of the building with the comfort expected in a country house.
ROOMS: 11 en suite (bth/shr) 6 annexe en suite (bth/shr) (8 fmly) s £85-£100; d £120-£160 (incl. bkfst) * LB Off peak **MEALS:** Lunch fr £20 High tea fr £8.50 Dinner fr £28.50 V meals Coffee am Tea pm **FACILITIES:** CTV in all bedrooms Fishing Croquet lawn Putting green Fly fishing Xmas **CONF:** Thtr 20 Class 20 Board 20 Del from £150 * **SERVICES:** 40P **NOTES:** No coaches No smoking in restaurant Last d 8.45pm **CARDS:**

See advert on page 67

ASHBURTON Devon — Map 03 SX77
★★ *Dartmoor Lodge*
Peartree Cross TQ13 7JW
Quality Percentage Score: 65%
☎ 01364 652232 Fax 01364 653990
Dir: *turn off A38 at Peartree Junction and follow 'Hotel & Services' signs*
This popular hotel, halfway between Plymouth and Exeter, is close to Dartmoor and the South Devon coast. Bedrooms, including two with four-posters, are well equipped; the bar and some of the function rooms display old beams and open fireplaces. There is a choice of menus in the attractive restaurant.
ROOMS: 30 en suite (bth/shr) (5 fmly) No smoking in 5 bedrooms **MEALS:** English & French Cuisine V meals Coffee am Tea pm **FACILITIES:** CTV in all bedrooms STV **CONF:** Thtr 100 Board 32 **SERVICES:** Lift Night porter 80P **NOTES:** No smoking area in restaurant Last d 9.30pm **CARDS:**

ASHFORD Kent — Map 05 TR04
★★★★ Eastwell Manor
Eastwell Park, Boughton Lees TN25 4HR
Quality Percentage Score: 77%
☎ 01233 213000 Fax 01233 635530
Dir: *on A251, 200 yds on left when entering Boughton Aluph*
A fine hotel in 62 acres of gardens and grounds. Its rich history is reflected in stunning architecture and comfortable public rooms with stonework, open fires, antiques, and wood panelling. Bedrooms are spacious with many thoughtful extras. Seasonally-changing menus with a balanced range of dishes make creative use of good local produce.
ROOMS: 23 en suite (bth/shr) 39 annexe en suite (bth/shr) (2 fmly) No smoking in 4 bedrooms s £150-£310; d £180-£340 (incl. bkfst) * Off peak **MEALS:** Lunch £15 & alc High tea fr £9.25 Dinner £30 & alc V meals Coffee am Tea pm **FACILITIES:** CTV in 23 bedrooms STV Outdoor swimming pool (heated) Tennis (hard) Croquet lawn Putting green Jacuzzi/spa Boule Wkly live entertainment Xmas **CONF:** Thtr 100 Class 40 Board 36 Del from £170.50 * **SERVICES:** Lift Night porter 80P **NOTES:** No smoking in restaurant Last d 9.30pm **CARDS:**

> Some hotel groups have a central reservations telephone number, see pages 35, 37 and 38 for details.

ASHFORD Kent — Map 05 TR04
★★★★ Ashford International
Simone Weil Av TN24 8UX
Quality Percentage Score: 62%
☎ 01233 219988 Fax 01233 647743
Dir: *off junct 9, M20*
This modern, purpose-built hotel is within easy reach of the M20. As a central feature it has a long mall containing boutiques and several eating places, including a popular brasserie and a more formal restaurant, the Alhambra. Bedrooms are spacious and provide good facilities.
ROOMS: 200 en suite (bth/shr) (4 fmly) No smoking in 57 bedrooms s £105; d £120 * LB Off peak **MEALS:** Lunch £8.95-£16.90 Dinner £8.95-£16.90 European Cuisine V meals Coffee am Tea pm **FACILITIES:** CTV in all bedrooms Indoor swimming pool (heated) Snooker Sauna Solarium Gym Jacuzzi/spa **CONF:** Thtr 400 Class 160 Board 100 Del £127 * **SERVICES:** Lift Night porter 400P **NOTES:** No smoking area in restaurant Last d 10pm
CARDS:

ASHFORD Kent — Map 05 TR04
★★★ *Master Spearpoint*
Canterbury Rd, Kennington TN24 9QR
Quality Percentage Score: 64%
☎ 01233 636863 Fax 01233 610119
Dir: *on A28 1m N of town centre, and 1m from junct 9/10 on M20*
Set in five acres of mature grounds, this hotel overlooks the South Downs to the rear and a main road to the front. The focal point is the informal bar which leads into the restaurant. Meeting rooms, a small first floor lounge and ample parking are provided.
ROOMS: 34 en suite (bth/shr) (1 fmly) **MEALS:** International Cuisine V meals Coffee am Tea pm **FACILITIES:** CTV in all bedrooms STV **CONF:** Thtr 75 Class 40 Board 40 Del from £95 * **SERVICES:** Night porter 60P **NOTES:** No smoking area in restaurant Last d 9.30pm
CARDS:

ASHFORD Kent — Map 05 TR04
★★★ Posthouse Ashford
Posthouse
Canterbury Rd TN24 8QQ
☎ 01233 625790 Fax 01233 643176
Dir: *off A28*
Suitable for both the business and leisure traveller, this bright hotel provides modern accommodation in well equipped bedrooms with en suite bathrooms.
ROOMS: 103 en suite (bth/shr) (45 fmly) No smoking in 60 bedrooms d £29-£79 * LB Off peak **MEALS:** International Cuisine V meals Coffee am Tea pm **FACILITIES:** CTV in all bedrooms ch fac Xmas **CONF:** Thtr 120 Class 65 Board 40 Del from £79.99 * **SERVICES:** Night porter 130P **NOTES:** No smoking area in restaurant Last d 10.30pm
CARDS:

ASHFORD Kent — Map 05 TR04
Travel Inn
Maidstone Rd, Hothfield Common TN26 1AP
☎ 01233 712571 Fax 01233 713945
Dir: *on A20, between Ashford & Charing*
This modern building offers accommodation in smart, spacious and well equipped bedrooms, all with en-suite bathrooms. Refreshments may be taken at the nearby family restaurant. For details about current prices consult the Contents Page under Hotel Groups for the Travel Inn phone number.
ROOMS: 40 en suite (bth/shr) d £39.95 *

ASHFORD-IN-THE-WATER Derbyshire **Map 07 SK17**

★★★🏵🏵 Riverside House

Fennel St DE45 1QF

Quality Percentage Score: 74%

☎ 01629 814275 📠 01629 812873

Dir: *turn right off A6 Bakewell/Buxton road 2m from Bakewell village, hotel at end of main street*

Part of this delightful hotel dates back to 1630, and stands at the centre of the village surrounded by mature gardens beside the River Wye. The hotel offers comfortably appointed rooms, including a light conservatory, a cosy oak panelled lounge with inglenook fireplace, a drawing room and two separate dining rooms. The kitchen produces quality meals from menus created to provide modern variations of traditional dishes. Service is attentive, and bedrooms are individually designed with attractive fabrics.

ROOMS: 15 en suite (bth/shr) No smoking in all bedrooms s £85-£105; d £115-£150 (incl. bkfst) * Off peak **MEALS:** Lunch £16.95-£21.95alc Dinner £32.45-£39.95alc V meals Coffee am Tea pm **FACILITIES:** CTV in all bedrooms Croquet lawn Xmas **CONF:** Thtr 15 Class 15 Board 15 **SERVICES:** 24P **NOTES:** No dogs (ex guide dogs) No coaches No children 10yrs No smoking in restaurant Last d 9.30pm **CARDS:**

See advert on this page

ASHTON-UNDER-LYNE Greater Manchester **Map 07 SJ99**

★★ York House

York Place, Richmond St OL6 7TT

Quality Percentage Score: 69%

☎ 0161 330 9000 📠 0161 343 1613

Dir: *close to junct A635/A6017*

Developed from a cluster of Victorian houses, set around a courtyard with attractive gardens, this welcoming hotel offers comfortable, well equipped bedrooms. Carefully prepared meals are served in the elegant restaurant, by a professional and friendly staff.

ROOMS: 24 en suite (bth/shr) 10 annexe en suite (bth/shr) (2 fmly) s £52-£65; d £80-£83 (incl. bkfst) * LB Off peak **MEALS:** Lunch fr £9.50 English & French Cuisine V meals Coffee am Tea pm **FACILITIES:** CTV in all bedrooms STV Reduced cost at local gym/pool **CONF:** Thtr 50 Class 20 Board 22 **SERVICES:** Night porter 34P **NOTES:** Closed 26 Dec RS Sun **CARDS:**

ASHWATER Devon **Map 02 SX39**

The Premier Collection

★★🏵🏵 Blagdon Manor Country Hotel

EX21 5DF

☎ 01409 211224 📠 01409 211634

Dir: *leave Launceston on A388 Holsworthy road, pass Chapman's Well & sign to Ashwater, turn right at second sign Ashwater then first right hotel on right*

This delightful retreat, parts of which date back to the 16th century, is situated in rolling Devonshire countryside. The seven bedrooms have luxury touches such as bathrobes and superior quality bed linen. Day rooms include the Georgian lounge, library, and flag-stoned bar with a snooker table. A magnificent table adorns the elegant dining room, where guests sit 'en famille' to enjoy a set dinner, served at 8pm and based on fresh local produce.

ROOMS: 7 en suite (bth/shr) No smoking in all bedrooms s £74; d £115 (incl. bkfst) LB Off peak **MEALS:** Dinner fr £21 British & International Cuisine V meals Coffee am Tea pm **FACILITIES:** CTV in all bedrooms Snooker Croquet lawn 4 hole practice ground **SERVICES:** 14P **NOTES:** No dogs (ex guide dogs) No coaches No children 16yrs No smoking in restaurant Last d 7pm Closed 25-26 Dec **CARDS:**

🏵 AA Rosettes are awarded for quality of food, see page 15 for an explanation of Rosette assessment.

Indicates that the star classification has not been confirmed under the New Quality Standards, see page 7 for further information.

ASKRIGG North Yorkshire **Map 07 SD99**

★★ ***King's Arms Hotel & Clubroom Restaurant***

Market Place DL8 3HQ

Quality Percentage Score: 68%

☎ 01969 650258 01969 650635

Dir: *half a mille off A684 at Worton*

This famous old character inn, which dates back to 1760, was a location for the popular James Herriot TV series. The public rooms and accommodation retain much of their old charm, especially the original bars where real ale is served; there is also a good range of eating options, informally within Silks brasserie and the bars, or a more serious style in the panelled Clubroom Restaurant; here Chef John Barber continues to provide fine cooking through an interesting set priced 5 course carte. Bedrooms are individually furnished with period and antique appointments, in keeping with the style of the house, but equipped to meet the needs of modern day guests.

ROOMS: 11 en suite (bth/shr) (1 fmly) **MEALS:** English French & Oriental Cuisine V meals Coffee am Tea pm **FACILITIES:** CTV in all bedrooms **CONF:** Thtr 40 Class 20 Board 30 Del from £78 * **SERVICES:** 12P **NOTES:** No smoking in restaurant Last d 9pm

CARDS:

ASPLEY GUISE Bedfordshire **Map 04 SP93**

★★★ **Moore Place**

The Square MK17 8DW

Quality Percentage Score: 67%

☎ 01908 282000 01908 281888

Dir: *from junct 13 of M1, take A507 and then follow signs for Aspley Guise and Woburn Sands. Hotel is on left hand side of village square*

This attractive Georgian mansion is set in its own grounds in the centre of the village, and is conveniently located for access to the motorway. Public rooms include a small foyer lounge area, a cosy bar and a Victorian-style conservatory restaurant, where Chef Clive Southgate presents an interesting selection of dishes cooked in the modern British style and also caters for vegetarians and those with special diets. Smartly furnished, well equipped bedrooms are divided between the main house and a courtyard building.

ROOMS: 39 en suite (bth/shr) 15 annexe en suite (bth/shr) s fr £75; d fr £105 (incl. bkfst) * LB Off peak **MEALS:** Lunch £11.50-£14.50 & alc Dinner £18.95-£22.95 & alc English & French Cuisine V meals Coffee am Tea pm **FACILITIES:** CTV in all bedrooms STV Xmas **CONF:** Thtr 50 Class 32 Board 24 Del £150 * **SERVICES:** Night porter 70P **NOTES:** No smoking in restaurant Last d 9.45pm

CARDS:

AA Rosettes are awarded for quality of food, see page 15 for an explanation of Rosette assessment.

ASTON CLINTON Buckinghamshire **Map 04 SP81**

★★★ **Bell Inn**

HP22 5HP

Quality Percentage Score: 72%

☎ 01296 630252 01296 631250

Dir: *on A41 between Aylesbury and Tring*

The Bell Inn has seen recent reinvestment and improvement; staff are attentive and ensure a continuity of tradition. Cooking has been revitalised with delicious combinations of ingredients in well conceived menus, changing seasonally. Bedrooms are spacious and comfortable, many featuring period pieces. The formal gardens are worth a tour.

ROOMS: 5 en suite (bth/shr) 15 annexe en suite (bth/shr) (6 fmly) d £65-£130 * LB Off peak **MEALS:** Lunch £12-£19.50 & alc Dinner £17 & alc English & French Cuisine V meals Coffee am Tea pm **FACILITIES:** CTV in all bedrooms Croquet lawn ch fac **CONF:** Thtr 30 Board 20 Del from £135 * **SERVICES:** Night porter 200P **NOTES:** No dogs (ex guide dogs) No smoking in restaurant Last d 9.45pm

CARDS:

ASTON CLINTON Buckinghamshire **Map 04 SP81**

★★ **West Lodge**

London Rd HP22 5HL

Quality Percentage Score: 67%

☎ 01296 630362 01296 630151

Dir: *on A41*

West Lodge offers a mix of Victorian elegance and modern comforts. Bedrooms, which vary in size, are attractively decorated. There is a pretty water garden to the rear. The Montgolfier Restaurant serves a short menu in the French style.

ROOMS: 6 en suite (bth/shr) s £45-£50; d £70 (incl. bkfst) * Off peak **MEALS:** Lunch £25-£30 Dinner £25-£40 French Cuisine V meals **FACILITIES:** CTV in all bedrooms STV Indoor swimming pool (heated) Sauna Jacuzzi/spa Hot air ballooning Xmas **SERVICES:** 17P **NOTES:** No dogs (ex guide dogs) No coaches No children 8yrs No smoking in restaurant Last d 9pm **CARDS:**

ATHERSTONE Warwickshire **Map 04 SP39**

★★ **Chapel House**

Friar's Gate CV9 1EY

Quality Percentage Score: 75%

☎ 01827 718949 01827 717702

Dir: *next to St Marys Church in Market Square*

Nestling beside the church and partly enclosed by a high red brick wall, this hotel is an oasis of hospitality and good cooking. The house offers nicely appointed dining rooms and a comfortable conservatory lounge overlooking the attractive walled garden. Bedrooms, which are individually appointed, differ in styles and sizes. The kitchen brigade produce an interesting monthly changing carte which is supplemented by a variety of daily dishes. On a recent visit the hotel was hosting one of their special events, a 'Befores and Afters' meal of starters and puddings, leaving out the main course!

ROOMS: 14 en suite (bth/shr) s £49.50-£65; d £65-£75 (incl. bkfst) * LB Off peak **MEALS:** Lunch £12 & alc Dinner £14-£30alc English & French Cuisine V meals **FACILITIES:** CTV in all bedrooms **CONF:** Thtr 15 Board 20 Del from £71.95 * **NOTES:** No dogs (ex guide dogs) No coaches No smoking in restaurant Last d 9.30pm Closed 24-26 Dec RS BH **CARDS:**

See advert on opposite page

AUSTWICK North Yorkshire — Map 07 SD76

★★ The Traddock
LA2 8BY
Quality Percentage Score: 66%
☎ 015242 51224 Fax 015242 51224
Dir: *4m N of Settle, off A65*

Enviably located in the Yorkshire Dales National Park, this smart hotel continues to grow in popularity. The atmosphere is relaxing and informal and the pretty lawns and gardens, together with the function room, are popular for weddings. Bedrooms vary in size and are fitted with period furniture. Family rooms are also available. Two comfortable lounges are provided as well as a cosy bar. Warm hospitality is personally provided by Mr and Mrs Michaelis.

ROOMS: 9 en suite (bth/shr) (3 fmly) No smoking in all bedrooms s £35-£50; d £50-£80 (incl. bkfst) * LB Off peak **MEALS:** Dinner £21.50 International Cuisine V meals Coffee am **FACILITIES:** CTV in all bedrooms Croquet lawn Putting green **CONF:** Thtr 70 Class 30 Board 20 Del from £80 * **SERVICES:** 15P **NOTES:** No dogs (ex guide dogs) No smoking in restaurant Last d 8.30pm Closed Xmas & New Year
CARDS:

AXBRIDGE Somerset — Map 03 ST45

★★ The Oak House
The Square BS26 2AP
Quality Percentage Score: 68%
☎ 01934 732444 Fax 01934 733112
Dir: *2m E of Cheddar, 0.25m off A371*

Situated in the main square of the delightful old town, this small hotel has a popular local following. Hospitality and service are strengths here with the added attraction of award-winning cuisine served in the informal atmosphere of the bistro-style restaurant. Bedrooms vary in style and size, each individually decorated and all offering modern facilities.

ROOMS: 11 en suite (bth/shr) (2 fmly) **MEALS:** English & French Cuisine V meals Coffee am Tea pm **FACILITIES:** CTV in all bedrooms **CONF:** Thtr 40 Class 40 Board 22 Del from £75 * **NOTES:** No smoking area in restaurant Last d 9.15pm **CARDS:**

AXMINSTER Devon — Map 03 SY29

★★★ Fairwater Head
Hawkchurch EX13 5TX
Quality Percentage Score: 74%
☎ 01297 678349 Fax 01297 678459
Dir: *turn off B3165 (Crewkerne to Lyme Regis Road) hotel signposted to Hawkchurch*

A delightful Edwardian house, set in landscaped gardens and rolling countryside. The bedrooms are attractively decorated and furnished, a few rooms are in a modern house in the grounds. Public areas include comfortable sitting rooms and a spacious dining room, where freshly prepared meals using local produce are served.

ROOMS: 14 en suite (bth/shr) 7 annexe en suite (bth/shr) s fr £87; d fr £154 (incl. bkfst & dinner) * LB Off peak **MEALS:** Lunch £12 High tea £2-£10 Dinner £22.50-£32.50 English & French Cuisine V meals Coffee am Tea pm **FACILITIES:** CTV in all bedrooms Croquet lawn Xmas **CONF:** Thtr 20 Class 20 Board 12 **SERVICES:** 30P **NOTES:** No smoking in restaurant Last d 8.30pm Closed 4 Dec-2 Mar
CARDS:

AXMINSTER Devon — Map 03 SY29

★★ Lea Hill
Membury EX13 7AQ
Quality Percentage Score: 77%
☎ 01404 881881 & 881388 Fax 01404 881890
Dir: *in Membury go through village, past the Trout Farm and continue for 0.5m to hotel on right*

Parts of this delightful countryside thatched Devon longhouse date back to the 1300s. Sympathetically restored to provide modern comforts, the bedrooms are mostly situated in thatched cottages and converted barns around the main house. Rooms have been decorated to enhance their cottage style and there is a bar-lounge, a study and a meeting room. The restaurant serves an imaginative fixed-price menu prepared from fresh produce and often featuring local fish.

ROOMS: 2 en suite (bth/shr) 9 annexe en suite (bth/shr) (2 fmly) No smoking in all bedrooms s £59-£69; d £98-£108 (incl. bkfst) LB Off peak **MEALS:** Bar Lunch £3.95-£7.95 Dinner £22.95-£25.95 English & French Cuisine Coffee am Tea pm **FACILITIES:** CTV in all bedrooms Croquet lawn Jacuzzi/spa Par 3 6-hole golf course ch fac Xmas **CONF:** Class 14 Board 12 Del from £95 * **SERVICES:** 25P **NOTES:** No coaches No children 12yrs No smoking in restaurant Last d 8.45pm Closed 3 Jan-28 Feb **CARDS:**

★
The Premier Collection, hotels with Red Star Awards are listed on pages 17-23

AYLESBURY Buckinghamshire — Map 04 SP81

The Premier Collection

★★★★ Hartwell House

Oxford Rd HP17 8NL

☎ 01296 747444 Fax 01296 747450

Dir: signposted 2m SW on A418 towards Oxford

This distinguished country mansion in a 90 acre estate dates from 1600, featuring a grand and well preserved Jacobean staircase. Bedrooms are comfortable and characterful, some are in a converted stable block. The health centre complex houses the Buttery coffee shop and there are separate function rooms. Staff offer polished service, and the cuisine and service on offer in the main dining room is consistently good.

ROOMS: 30 en suite (bth/shr) 16 annexe en suite (bth/shr) No smoking in 12 bedrooms s £130-£165; d £205 * LB Off peak **MEALS:** Lunch £22-£29 Dinner £44 V meals Coffee am Tea pm **FACILITIES:** CTV in all bedrooms Indoor swimming pool (heated) Tennis (hard) Fishing Sauna Solarium Gym Croquet lawn Jacuzzi/spa Treatment room Xmas **CONF:** Thtr 100 Class 40 Board 40 Del from £225 * **SERVICES:** Lift Night porter 91P **NOTES:** No coaches No children 8yrs No smoking in restaurant Last d 9.45pm **CARDS:**

AYLESBURY Buckinghamshire — Map 04 SP81

★★★ Posthouse Aylesbury

Posthouse

Aston Clinton Rd HP22 5AA

Quality Percentage Score: 68%

☎ 01296 393388 Fax 01296 392211

Dir: on A41

Suitable for the business or leisure traveller, this bright hotel provides modern accommodation in well equipped en suite bedrooms. Public areas are spacious and include the Junction dining option and a smart new leisure complex.

ROOMS: 94 en suite (bth/shr) (6 fmly) No smoking in 47 bedrooms s £95-£115; d £95-£125 * LB Off peak **MEALS:** Lunch £15-£30alc Dinner £15-£30alc International Cuisine V meals Coffee am Tea pm **FACILITIES:** CTV in all bedrooms Indoor swimming pool (heated) Sauna Solarium Gym Jacuzzi/spa Xmas **CONF:** Thtr 110 Class 80 Board 40 Del from £120 * **SERVICES:** Night porter 150P **NOTES:** No smoking area in restaurant Last d 10.30pm **CARDS:**

BABBACOMBE See Torquay

We endeavour to be as accurate as possible but changes in personnel and data can occur in establishments after the Hotel Guide has gone to press.

BADMINTON Gloucestershire — Map 03 ST88

★★ Bodkin House

Petty France GL9 1AF

Quality Percentage Score: 70%

☎ 01454 238310 Fax 01454 238422

Dir: on A46, 6m N of junct 18 on M4

This charming 17th-century inn offers a high standard of comfort. Modernisation has not spoiled its historic character, and many original features are displayed in the bar. Restaurant and lounge are attractively decorated and meals can also be taken in the bar.

ROOMS: 9 en suite (bth/shr) (2 fmly) s £49.95-£52; d £70-£75 (incl. bkfst) * LB Off peak **MEALS:** Lunch £5.95-£15.95 & alc Dinner £15.95 & alc English & French Cuisine V meals Coffee am Tea pm **FACILITIES:** CTV in all bedrooms Hot air ballooning Xmas **CONF:** Thtr 20 Class 12 Board 12 **SERVICES:** 35P **NOTES:** No dogs (ex guide dogs) No smoking in restaurant Last d 9pm **CARDS:**

See advert under BATH

BAGINTON Warwickshire — Map 04 SP37

★★ Old Mill

Mill Hill CV8 3AH

Quality Percentage Score: 66%

☎ 024 76302241 Fax 024 76307070

Dir: in village 0.25m from junction A45 & A46

Set in a relatively quiet spot beside the River Sowe, yet having easy access to Coventry and motorway networks, the Old Mill offers comfortable accommodation, with a popular restaurant and traditional bar. These public areas retain many original features - flagstone floors, exposed beams and an iron mill wheel. Bedrooms are well proportioned and equipped, and furnished in rustic pine.

ROOMS: 20 en suite (bth/shr) (6 fmly) d £63 * LB Off peak **MEALS:** International Cuisine V meals Coffee am **FACILITIES:** CTV in all bedrooms **CONF:** Thtr 50 Class 8 Board 25 Del from £90 * **SERVICES:** 200P **NOTES:** No dogs (ex guide dogs) No smoking in restaurant Last d 9.30pm **CARDS:**

BAGSHOT Surrey — Map 04 SU96

★★★★★ Pennyhill Park

London Rd GU19 5ET

Quality Percentage Score: 70%

☎ 01276 471774 Fax 01276 473217

Dir: on A30 between Bagshot and Camberley opposite Texaco garage

Set in 120 acres of grounds, with stables, golf course and formal gardens, the original creeper-clad Victorian building has been much extended and improved to create a fine hotel. Several meeting rooms and a spacious informal restaurant have been added to existing public areas which include the Tudor-style bar, an informal restaurant and a well-appointed restaurant where chef Karl Edmunds' French-influenced menus continue to please.

contd.

Spacious individually decorated bedrooms are particularly impressive with many antique pieces and high levels of comfort.
ROOMS: 28 en suite (bth/shr) 86 annexe en suite (bth/shr) No smoking in 35 bedrooms s £170-£411; d £188-£411 * LB Off peak
MEALS: Lunch £16.95-£26 Dinner £10-£35 & alc English & French Cuisine V meals Coffee am Tea pm **FACILITIES:** CTV in all bedrooms Outdoor swimming pool (heated) Golf 9 Tennis (hard) Fishing Gym Croquet lawn Archery Clay pigeon shooting Volleyball Half size snooker table Xmas
CONF: Thtr 160 Class 80 Board 60 Del from £305.50 **SERVICES:** Lift Night porter 300P **NOTES:** No coaches No children 5yrs No smoking in restaurant Last d 10.30pm **CARDS:**

See advert on this page

BAGSHOT Surrey — Map 04 SU96

Travel Inn
1 London Rd GU19 5HR
☎ 01276 473196 Fax 01276 451357
Dir: *on A30, 0.25m from Bagshot*
This modern building offers accommodation in smart, spacious and well equipped bedrooms, all with en-suite bathrooms. Refreshments may be taken at the nearby family restaurant. For details about current prices consult the Contents Page under Hotel Groups for the Travel Inn phone number.
ROOMS: 40 en suite (bth/shr) d £39.95 *

BAINBRIDGE North Yorkshire — Map 07 SD99

★★ Rose & Crown
Village Green DL8 3EE
Quality Percentage Score: 61%
☎ 01969 650225 Fax 01969 650735
Dir: *on A684 in centre of village*
For almost seven hundred years this appealing coaching inn has welcomed guests who are crossing the Pennines. Its original character is apparent particularly in the bars, yet in contrast, the bedrooms are modern. One can eat in the bars or in the spacious restaurant.
ROOMS: 12 en suite (bth/shr) (1 fmly) s £32-£39; d £52-£66 (incl. bkfst) * LB Off peak **MEALS:** Sunday Lunch £10.95-£13.45alc Dinner £14.95-£23.75alc V meals Coffee am Tea pm **FACILITIES:** CTV in all bedrooms Fishing Pool table **SERVICES:** 65P **NOTES:** No smoking area in restaurant Last d 9.30pm **CARDS:**

BAKEWELL Derbyshire — Map 08 SK26

★★★ Hassop Hall
Hassop DE45 1NS
Quality Percentage Score: 70%
☎ 01629 640488 Fax 01629 640577
Dir: *take B6001 from Bakewell for approx. 2m into Hassop, hotel opposite church*
A magnificent stately home with a rich heritage that still manages to provide all the modern comforts expected by today's visitor. Most bedrooms overlook the fine gardens and grounds. There is a choice of comfortable lounges in which to relax before taking dinner in the bright, pleasantly furnished dining room.
ROOMS: 13 en suite (bth/shr) (2 fmly) d £79-£139 * LB Off peak
MEALS: Lunch £11.45-£19.95 Dinner £19.75-£33.25 V meals
FACILITIES: CTV in all bedrooms Tennis (hard) Wkly live entertainment
SERVICES: Lift 80P **NOTES:** Last d 9pm Closed 24-25 Dec RS 26 Dec
CARDS:

For Useful Information and Important Telephone Number Changes turn to page 25

B

BAKEWELL Derbyshire **Map 08 SK26**

★★★ Rutland Arms

The Square DE45 1BT

Quality Percentage Score: 62%

☎ 01629 812812 01629 812309

Dir: *on main A6 between Matlock/Manchester. In main square opposite War Memorial*

This historic hotel lies at the very centre of Bakewell. There is a wide range of accommodation on offer, which includes a number of bedrooms located in a nearby courtyard annexe. The staff are friendly and welcoming, whether in the adjacent Tavern bar or the main hotel. The Four Seasons restaurant offers an inviting menu and fine dining.

ROOMS: 18 en suite (bth/shr) 17 annexe en suite (bth) (1 fmly) No smoking in 10 bedrooms s £54-£59; d £84-£89 (incl. bkfst) * LB Off peak **MEALS:** Lunch £11.50 Dinner £18.50 V meals Coffee am Tea pm **FACILITIES:** CTV in all bedrooms STV Pool table Xmas **CONF:** Thtr 100 Class 60 Board 40 Del from £90 * **SERVICES:** Night porter 25P **NOTES:** No smoking in restaurant Last d 9pm **CARDS:**

BAKEWELL Derbyshire **Map 08 SK26**

★★ Croft Country House

Great Longstone DE45 1TF

Quality Percentage Score: 73%

☎ 01629 640278

Dir: *from Bakewell follow A6 towards Buxton turn right on to A6020, turn left at sign to Great Longstone, entrance on right 0.25m into village*

Hidden away in mature gardens and grounds, this delightful Victorian house exudes charm from the nature of the hotel and the welcome extended by its dedicated staff. Public rooms lead off the central galleried lounge, including the cosy bar and restaurant, where freshly prepared evening meals are served from an interesting four-course set menu. Bedrooms have modern comforts mixed with some fine period pieces.

ROOMS: 9 en suite (bth/shr) s £45-£60; d £67.50-£97.50 (incl. bkfst) LB Off peak **MEALS:** Dinner £25.50 British & Continental Cuisine V meals **FACILITIES:** CTV in all bedrooms Xmas **SERVICES:** Lift 40P **NOTES:** No dogs (ex guide dogs) No coaches No smoking in restaurant Last d 7.30pm Closed 2 Jan-10 Feb **CARDS:**

See advert on opposite page

BALDOCK Hertfordshire **Map 04 TL23**

Travelodge

Great North Rd, Hinxworth SG7 5EX

Travelodge

☎ 01462 835329 01462 835329

Dir: *on A1, southbound*

This modern building offers accommodation in smart, spacious and well equipped bedrooms, all with en-suite bathrooms. Refreshments may be taken at the nearby family restaurant. For details about current prices, consult the Contents Page under Hotel Groups for the Travelodge phone number.

ROOMS: 40 en suite (bth/shr) d £45.95 *

BALSALL COMMON West Midlands **Map 04 SP27**

★★★★ Nailcote Hall

Nailcote Ln, Berkswell CV7 7DE

Quality Percentage Score: 67%

☎ 024 76466174 024 76470720

Dir: *on B4101*

Steeped in history, this charming Elizabethan manor house remains largely unspoilt and features contemporary wall coverings which enhance the heavy timbers and open fires. A professional staff combine efficient service with courtesy and care. The intimate candlelit restaurant serves an exciting new menu, while more informal dining is offered in a Mediterranean-style bistro. The modern bedroom wing offers a contrast of styles, while the more traditional bedrooms are in the main house.

ROOMS: 21 en suite (bth/shr) 17 annexe en suite (bth/shr) (2 fmly) s fr £135; d £145-£245 (incl. bkfst) * LB Off peak **MEALS:** Lunch £21.50 Dinner fr £29.50 English & Mediterranean Cuisine V meals Coffee am Tea pm **FACILITIES:** CTV in all bedrooms Indoor swimming pool (heated) Golf 9 Tennis (hard) Snooker Solarium Gym Croquet lawn Putting green Jacuzzi/spa Xmas **CONF:** Thtr 120 Class 80 Board 45 Del from £150 * **SERVICES:** Lift Night porter 200P **NOTES:** No smoking in restaurant Last d 9.30pm **CARDS:**

See advert under SOLIHULL

Some hotel groups have a central reservations telephone number, see pages 35, 37 and 38 for details.

BALSALL COMMON West Midlands — Map 04 SP27

★★❀❀ Haigs

Kenilworth Rd CV7 7EL

Quality Percentage Score: 75%

☎ 01676 533004 Fax 01676 535132

Dir: *on A452 4m N of Kenilworth and 6m S of junct 4 of M6. 5m S of M42 junct 6*

Set in a residential area, this charming hotel is owned and run by the Harrises and offers a warm welcome and attentive service. The accommodation is being steadily upgraded, and the new rooms are particularly attractive and comfortable. Public areas

contd.

The AA's professional hotel and restaurant inspectors make regular and anonymous visits to all the hotels listed in the guide. They do not accept gifts or favours from hoteliers.

include a lounge/bar, a meeting room and the Poppies restaurant where an interesting and varied menu is offered.
ROOMS: 23 en suite (bth/shr) No smoking in 8 bedrooms s fr £59.50; d fr £79.50 (incl. bkfst) * Off peak **MEALS:** Sunday Lunch fr £14.95 Dinner fr £22 English & French Cuisine V meals Coffee am Tea pm **FACILITIES:** CTV in all bedrooms **CONF:** Thtr 35 Class 20 Board 20 Del from £80 * **SERVICES:** 22P **NOTES:** No coaches No smoking in restaurant Last d 9.30pm Closed 26 Dec-3 Jan & Etr
CARDS:

See advert under BIRMINGHAM (NATIONAL EXHIBITION CENTRE)

BALSALL COMMON West Midlands **Map 04 SP27**
Travel Inn
Kenilworth Rd CV7 7EX
☎ 01676 533118 📠 01676 535929
Dir: *from junct 6 of M42 take A45 towards Coventry for 0.5m, then A452 towards Leamington, Travel Inn on the right in 3m*
This modern building offers accommodation in smart, spacious and well equipped bedrooms, all with en-suite bathrooms. Refreshments may be taken at the nearby family restaurant. For details about current prices consult the Contents Page under Hotel Groups for the Travel Inn phone number.
ROOMS: 40 en suite (bth/shr) d £39.95 *

BAMBURGH Northumberland **Map 12 NU13**
★★★ Waren House
Waren Mill NE70 7EE
Quality Percentage Score: 68%
☎ 01668 214581 📠 01668 214484
Dir: *3m W off B1342 to Waren Mill, at T-junct turn right, hotel 100yds on right*
A delightful restored country house, Georgian in origin. Themed bedrooms (Victorian or Edwardian, Nursery or Oriental) offer good levels of comfort and plenty of interest. Public rooms are attractively furnished, with an elegant dining room, welcoming drawing room and adjoining library. Many rooms enjoy fine views over gardens and the coastline.
ROOMS: 10 en suite (bth/shr) No smoking in 9 bedrooms s fr £85; d fr £115 (incl. bkfst) * LB Off peak **MEALS:** Dinner £18.45-£25 **FACILITIES:** CTV in all bedrooms STV Croquet lawn Xmas **CONF:** Class 24 Board 24 Del from £98 * **SERVICES:** 20P **NOTES:** No coaches No children 14yrs No smoking in restaurant Last d 8.30pm
CARDS:

BAMBURGH Northumberland **Map 12 NU13**
★★ Lord Crewe Arms
Front St NE69 7BL
Quality Percentage Score: 67%
☎ 01668 214243 📠 01668 214273
Dir: *just below the castle*
Developed from an old country inn, this inviting hotel lies in the centre of the village, where the impressive Bamburgh Castle dominates the skyline.
ROOMS: 20 rms (18 bth/shr) (1 fmly) s £40-£50; d £60-£75 (incl. bkfst) * LB Off peak **MEALS:** Bar Lunch £2.50-£7 & alc Dinner £13-£26alc V meals Coffee am Tea pm **FACILITIES:** CTV in all bedrooms **SERVICES:** 34P **NOTES:** No children 5yrs No smoking in restaurant Last d 8.45pm Closed Nov-Etr **CARDS:**

AA Rosettes are awarded for quality of food, see page 15 for an explanation of Rosette assessment.

BAMBURGH Northumberland **Map 12 NU13**
★★ Victoria
Front St NE69 7BP
Quality Percentage Score: 66%
☎ 01668 214431 📠 01668 214404
Dir: *turn off the A1 North of Alnwick onto the B1342, near Belford & follow signs to Bamburgh. Hotel in centre of Bamburgh opposite the village green.*

This traditional stone built hotel has undergone total refurbishment. The ground floor areas include a modern Brasserie with conservatory roof, a popular bar and an area where all day food is on offer during the season. Bedrooms are well equipped and the effective use of rag roll decor gives them a cheerful appearance. Service is friendly and relaxed; the hotel caters well for families and includes an indoor children's playden.
ROOMS: 29 en suite (bth/shr) (2 fmly) No smoking in 18 bedrooms s £32.50-£48; d £70-£92 (incl. bkfst) * LB Off peak **MEALS:** Lunch £8.50-£21 Dinner £15.85-£22alc English & European Cuisine V meals Coffee am Tea pm **FACILITIES:** CTV in all bedrooms Pool table Games room ch fac Xmas **CONF:** Thtr 50 Class 30 Board 20 Del from £63.50 * **SERVICES:** 12P **NOTES:** No smoking area in restaurant Last d 9.30pm
CARDS:

BAMBURGH Northumberland **Map 12 NU13**
★★ The Mizen Head
Lucker Rd NE69 7BS
Quality Percentage Score: 61%
☎ 01668 214254 📠 01668 214104
Dir: *turn off the A1 onto the B1341 for Bamburgh the hotel is the first building on the left as you enter the village*
Located on the western edge of the village, this family-run hotel offers a relaxed and friendly atmosphere. A wide range of good value meals is served in both the dining room and bar.
ROOMS: 13 rms (11 bth/shr) (2 fmly) s £29-£35.50; d £58-£71 (incl. bkfst) * LB Off peak **MEALS:** Lunch £3.50-£13 Dinner fr £13 V meals Coffee am **FACILITIES:** CTV in all bedrooms Pool table Darts ch fac Xmas **SERVICES:** 30P **NOTES:** No smoking area in restaurant Last d 8.30pm **CARDS:**

BAMFORD Derbyshire **Map 08 SK28**
★★ Yorkshire Bridge Inn
Ashopton Rd, Yorkshire Bridge S33 0AZ
Quality Percentage Score: 67%
☎ 01433 651361 📠 01433 651361
Dir: *A57 Sheffield/Glossop Road, at Ladybower Reservoir take A6013 Bamford Road, Yorkshire Bridge Inn is on the right hand side in 1m*
A well known hostelry, situated close to the Ladybower and Derwent reservoirs. Attractively furnished bedrooms housed in nearby buildings are comfortable and equipped to suit the needs of both business and leisure visitors. A wide range of dishes are

contd.

offered in the bar and dining area, and an excellent range of real ales in the bar.
ROOMS: 10 en suite (bth/shr) (1 fmly) No smoking in 5 bedrooms s £40; d £60-£64 (incl. bkfst) * LB Off peak **MEALS:** English & Continental Cuisine V meals Coffee am **FACILITIES:** CTV in all bedrooms Xmas **SERVICES:** 40P **NOTES:** No coaches **CARDS:**

BAMPTON Devon — Map 03 SS92

★★ Bark House

Oakford Bridge EX16 9HZ
Quality Percentage Score: 76%
☎ 01398 351236
***Dir:** 9m N of Tiverton on the A396*

Quietly situated in a beautiful part of the Exe Valley, this cottage-style hotel offers public areas with great character, including a low ceilinged dining room and a lounge with a log fire. Bedrooms are nicely decorated and have been equipped with some thoughtful touches. Imaginative quality meals are served in the restaurant.
ROOMS: 5 rms (2 bth 2 shr) (1 fmly) s £32.50-£42; d £59-£78 (incl. bkfst) * LB Off peak **MEALS:** Lunch fr £13.75 Dinner fr £19.95 V meals Coffee am Tea pm **FACILITIES:** CTV in all bedrooms Croquet lawn Xmas **SERVICES:** 15P **NOTES:** No coaches No smoking in restaurant Last d 9.15pm RS Nov-Mar

BAMPTON Oxfordshire — Map 04 SP30

★★ The Romany Inn

Bridge St OX18 2HA
Quality Percentage Score: 63%
☎ 01993 850237 Fax 01993 852133
***Dir:** located on the A4095 Witney/Faringdon Road in centre of Bampton*

Situated in the heart of the village, The Romany Inn has been skilfully upgraded. Accommodation is well presented and comfortably furnished. Public areas include a popular village bar and a more formal restaurant. A wide range of food is available in each.
ROOMS: 7 en suite (shr) 3 annexe en suite (shr) (4 fmly) s £26.50-£30; d £42.50-£49.50 (incl. bkfst) * LB Off peak **MEALS:** Lunch £3.95-£10.95alc Dinner £3.95-£10.95alc International Cuisine V meals Coffee am Tea pm **FACILITIES:** CTV in all bedrooms **SERVICES:** 6P **NOTES:** No smoking in restaurant Last d 9.30pm
CARDS:

See advert under BURFORD

BANBURY Oxfordshire — Map 04 SP44

★★★ Banbury House

Oxford Rd OX16 9AH
Quality Percentage Score: 69%
☎ 01295 259361 Fax 01295 270954
***Dir:** approx 200yds from Banbury Cross on the A423 towards Oxford*

This popular family owned hotel offers very good levels of overall comfort and friendly, attentive service. Spacious, well appointed bedrooms suit both leisure and business guests. The smart restaurant offers a good range of dishes and snacks are served in the popular bar.
ROOMS: 63 en suite (bth/shr) (4 fmly) No smoking in 24 bedrooms s £39-£73; d £78-£83 * LB Off peak **MEALS:** Bar Lunch £3-£7 High tea £6-£10 Dinner £19.50 & alc Continental Cuisine V meals Coffee am Tea pm **FACILITIES:** CTV in all bedrooms STV **CONF:** Thtr 70 Class 35 Board 28 Del £125 * **SERVICES:** Night porter 60P **NOTES:** No dogs (ex guide dogs) Last d 9.30pm Closed 24-30 Dec
CARDS:

BANBURY Oxfordshire — Map 04 SP44

★★★ Wroxton House

Wroxton St Mary OX15 6QB
Quality Percentage Score: 69%
☎ 01295 730777 Fax 01295 730800
***Dir:** follow A422 from Banbury, 2.5m to Wroxton, hotel on right on entering village*

Converted from three 17th-century cottages, this charming hotel is situated in the centre of the lovely village of Wroxton and is clearly signposted from Banbury. Guests will find this a pleasant retreat in which to relax. Bedrooms are very well equipped and vary in style from the more traditionally furnished older wing to modern rooms that are well suited to the business guest. Chef Hylton Bradley offers well presented food which combines local produce with sound technical skills.
ROOMS: 29 en suite (bth/shr) 3 annexe en suite (bth/shr) (1 fmly) No smoking in 14 bedrooms s fr £89; d fr £99 * LB Off peak **MEALS:** Lunch £12.50-£15.50 Dinner fr £24.50 English & French Cuisine V meals Coffee am Tea pm **FACILITIES:** CTV in all bedrooms STV Xmas **CONF:** Thtr 40 Class 20 Board 23 Del from £147.50 * **SERVICES:** Night porter 50P **NOTES:** No dogs (ex guide dogs) No smoking in restaurant Last d 9.30pm Closed 28-30 Dec RS 31 Dec & 1 Jan
CARDS:

BANBURY Oxfordshire — Map 04 SP44

★★★ Whately Hall

Banbury Cross OX16 0AN
Quality Percentage Score: 68%
☎ 01295 263451 Fax 01295 271736
***Dir:** from M40 junct 11. Straight over 2 rdbts, turn left at 3rd, carry on to Banbury Cross about 1/4m & Hotel on right*

This former 17th-century coaching inn occupies a central location overlooking Banbury Cross. The well equipped bedrooms, most of which have been refurbished to a high standard, vary in size and style and offer a good range of modern facilities. Spacious, comfortable public areas include several lounges and an informal bar. All are atmospheric with original oak panelling and black beams. The service is generally attentive and friendly.
ROOMS: 72 en suite (bth/shr) (1 fmly) No smoking in 24 bedrooms s £55-£85; d £55-£90 * LB Off peak **MEALS:** Lunch £6.95-£12.95 & alc Dinner £21.95 & alc European Cuisine V meals Coffee am Tea pm **FACILITIES:** CTV in all bedrooms Croquet lawn Xmas **CONF:** Thtr 150 Class 80 Board 40 Del from £100 * **SERVICES:** Lift Night porter 80P **NOTES:** No smoking area in restaurant Last d 9.30pm
CARDS:

BARFORD Warwickshire — Map 04 SP26

★★★ The Glebe at Barford

Church St CV35 8BS
Quality Percentage Score: 69%
☎ 01926 624218 Fax 01926 624625
***Dir:** leave M40 at junct 15 take exit A429 Barford/Wellesboune at mini island turn left, hotel 500mtrs on right*

This former rectory has been considerably modernised and extended to create a friendly hotel. Public rooms have recently been altered and refurbished to provide a new lounge area, upgraded bar and soft furnishings for the inviting conservatory restaurant. The small leisure club is also being improved. Conference facilities continue to be very successful. Bedrooms

contd.

are individually furnished with cheerful soft furnishings and co-ordinated decor, and each room has a range of useful facilities.
ROOMS: 39 en suite (bth/shr) (5 fmly) s fr £90; d fr £110 (incl. bkfst) * Off peak **MEALS:** Lunch £12.50-£12.95 Dinner fr £19.95 European Cuisine V meals Coffee am Tea pm **FACILITIES:** CTV in all bedrooms STV Indoor swimming pool (heated) Sauna Gym Croquet lawn Jacuzzi/spa Beauty salon Xmas **CONF:** Thtr 130 Class 60 Board 60 Del from £145 * **SERVICES:** Lift Night porter 60P **NOTES:** No smoking area in restaurant Last d 9pm **CARDS:**

BAR HILL Cambridgeshire **Map 05 TL36**
★★★ ***Cambridgeshire Moat House***
CB3 8EU
Quality Percentage Score: 66%
☎ 01954 249988 01954 780010
Dir: *turn off A14 Huntingdon to Cambridge road at Bar Hill junction, follow road all way over flyover to roundabout, hotel opposite*
Very accessible for all the main routes in the Cambridge area, this purpose-built hotel offers extensive grounds, including a championship golf course. Bedrooms are furnished to meet modern requirements. The public areas are split-level; the vibrant refurbished bar overlooks the open plan restaurant below. The leisure complex includes a small gym and pool.
ROOMS: 99 en suite (bth/shr) (8 fmly) No smoking in 50 bedrooms **MEALS:** Mediterranean Cuisine V meals Coffee am Tea pm **FACILITIES:** CTV in all bedrooms Indoor swimming pool (heated) Golf 18 Tennis (hard) Gym Pool table Putting green Jacuzzi/spa Beauty treatments **CONF:** Thtr 200 Class 80 Board 40 **SERVICES:** Night porter 200P **NOTES:** No smoking area in restaurant Last d 10pm
CARDS:

BARKING Greater London **Map 05 TQ48**
★★ **Hotel Ibis**
IG11 7BA
Quality Percentage Score: 63%
☎ 020 8477 4100 020 8477 4101
This new hotel is conveniently located off the A406 North Circular road on the outskirts of town. It has ample car parking and the usual range of amenities associated with this popular brand.
MEALS: s fr £47; d £49.50 (incl. bkfst) * Off peak

BARNARD CASTLE Co Durham **Map 12 NZ01**
★★★ **Morritt Arms Hotel & Restaurant**
Greta Bridge DL12 9SE
Quality Percentage Score: 64%
☎ 01833 627232 01833 627392
Dir: *A1 Scotch Corner, turn onto A66 in direction of Penrith and after 9m turn off at Greta Bridge. Hotel just over the bridge on left*
This authentic 17th-century coaching house offers comfortable public rooms, including an open plan lounge and a bar with a delightful Dickensian mural. Bedrooms come in a variety of shapes and sizes, and the wood-panelled dining room is a perfect setting for the appetizing meals. Service is friendly and professional.
ROOMS: 26 en suite (bth/shr) No smoking in 18 bedrooms s £59.50-£65; d £75-£89.50 (incl. bkfst) * LB Off peak **MEALS:** Lunch £12.95-£16.95 Dinner £16.95 English, French & Mediterranean Cuisine V meals Coffee am Tea pm **FACILITIES:** CTV in all bedrooms Pool table Membership of nearby leisure facility Xmas **CONF:** Thtr 200 Class 100 Board 125 Del £85.50 * **SERVICES:** 103P **NOTES:** No smoking in restaurant Last d 9pm **CARDS:**

New AA Guides for the Millennium are featured on page 24

BARNBY MOOR Nottinghamshire **Map 08 SK68**
★★★ **Ye Olde Bell Hotel**
DN22 8QS
Quality Percentage Score: 64%
☎ 01777 705121 01777 860424
Dir: *leave A1 at Blyth rbt onto A634*
This impressive old coaching inn is situated close to Sherwood Forest and is convenient for the A1. It provides comfortable lounges together with a lovely oak panelled restaurant where a good range of dishes are available. Bedrooms offer modern facilities and there are plans to carry out an extensive upgrade. Friendly and polite service is provided by all the staff.
ROOMS: 55 en suite (bth/shr) (5 fmly) No smoking in 20 bedrooms s £52.50-£62.50; d fr £72.50 (incl. bkfst) * LB Off peak **MEALS:** Lunch fr £10.50 Dinner fr £16.75 & alc V meals Coffee am Tea pm **FACILITIES:** CTV in all bedrooms STV Xmas **CONF:** Thtr 250 Class 100 Board 50 Del from £85 * **SERVICES:** Night porter 200P **NOTES:** No smoking in restaurant Last d 9.45pm **CARDS:**

BARNHAM BROOM Norfolk **Map 05 TG00**
★★★ **Barnham Broom**
NR9 4DD
Quality Percentage Score: 70%
☎ 01603 759393 01603 758224
Dir: *signposted from A11 and A47, follow brown tourist signs with Barnham Broom and golf flag*
This renowned golfing and leisure hotel continues to be a popular venue. The extensive public areas offer a wide range of facilities and the modern-style bedrooms are attractively decorated. All-day informal meals are served in the Buttery, while more serious dining is served in the open-plan restaurant. A swimming pool, gym and squash courts are just some of the leisure pursuits to be enjoyed, while there are two 18-hole golf courses on the estate.
ROOMS: 53 en suite (bth/shr) (8 fmly) s £72-£80; d £98-£105 (incl. bkfst) * LB Off peak **MEALS:** Lunch £9.50-£17.45 & alc Dinner £17.45-£18 & alc English & Continental Cuisine V meals Coffee am Tea pm **FACILITIES:** CTV in all bedrooms Indoor swimming pool (heated) Golf 36 Tennis (hard) Squash Sauna Solarium Gym Pool table Putting green Jacuzzi/spa Hairdressing salon Beautician Xmas **CONF:** Thtr 150 Class 90 Board 70 Del from £74 * **SERVICES:** Night porter 200P **NOTES:** No dogs (ex guide dogs) No smoking in restaurant Last d 9.30pm
CARDS:

See advert under NORWICH

BARNSDALE BAR SERVICE AREA North Yorkshire **Map 08 SE51**
Travelodge
Wentbridge WF8 3JB
☎ 01977 620711 01977 620711
Dir: *on A1, southbound*
This modern building offers accommodation in smart, spacious and well equipped bedrooms, all with en-suite bathrooms. Refreshments may be taken at the nearby family restaurant. For details about current prices, consult the Contents Page under Hotel Groups for the Travelodge phone number.
ROOMS: 56 en suite (bth/shr) d £39.95 *

BARNSLEY South Yorkshire **Map 08 SE30**
see also **Tankersley**
★★★ **Ardsley House**
Doncaster Rd, Ardsley S71 5EH
Quality Percentage Score: 69%
☎ 01226 309955 01226 205374
Dir: *on A635, 0.75m from Stainfoot Rdbt*
Quietly situated a couple of miles east of the town, this extended
contd.

Georgian house offers modern bedrooms that are well equipped to meet the needs of todays business traveller. There is a choice of bars, where diners can choose from the carefully prepared dishes on offer. A range of meeting and function rooms is available, and there is a new health club to relax in.

ROOMS: 74 en suite (bth/shr) (12 fmly) No smoking in 35 bedrooms s £70-£72; d £85-£89 (incl. bkfst) LB Off peak **MEALS:** Lunch £10.95 Dinner £18.50 English & French Cuisine V meals Coffee am Tea pm **FACILITIES:** CTV in all bedrooms STV Indoor swimming pool (heated) Sauna Solarium Gym Pool table Jacuzzi/spa Wkly live entertainment Xmas **CONF:** Thtr 350 Class 250 Board 40 **SERVICES:** Night porter 200P **NOTES:** No smoking area in restaurant Last d 10pm
CARDS:

See advert on this page

BARNSLEY South Yorkshire — Map 08 SE30

Travelodge
520 Doncaster Rd S70 3PE
☎ 01226 298799 Fax 01226 298799
Dir: *at Stairfoot roundabout A633/A635*

Travelodge

This modern building offers accommodation in smart, spacious and well equipped bedrooms, all with en-suite bathrooms. Refreshments may be taken at the nearby family restaurant. For details about current prices, consult the Contents Page under Hotel Groups for the Travelodge phone number.
ROOMS: 32 en suite (bth/shr) d £39.95 *

BARNSTAPLE Devon — Map 02 SS53

★★★★ The Imperial
Taw Vale Pde EX32 8NB
Quality Percentage Score: 62%
☎ 01271 345861 Fax 01271 324448
Dir: *from M5, take junct27, A361 Barnstaple. Follow signs for town centre, passing Tescos. Straight ahead at next 2 rdbts. Hotel is on the right*

Brend Hotels

Overlooking the River Taw in the centre of Barnstaple, this traditional Edwardian-style hotel has charming, elegant reception rooms including a sitting room, bar lounge, spacious dining

contd.

B

room and various meeting rooms. Bedrooms are decorated with flair and have rich colour schemes.
ROOMS: 63 en suite (bth/shr) (15 fmly) s £48-£150; d £76-£180 (incl. bkfst) * LB Off peak **MEALS:** Lunch £12-£13.50 Dinner £18 & alc English & French Cuisine V meals Coffee am Tea pm **FACILITIES:** CTV in all bedrooms STV Xmas **SERVICES:** Lift Night porter 80P
NOTES: Last d 9pm **CARDS:**

See advert on opposite page

BARNSTAPLE Devon **Map 02 SS53**
★★★ Royal & Fortescue
Boutport St EX31 1HG
Quality Percentage Score: 71%
☎ 01271 342289 01271 342289
Dir: *follow A361 along Barbican Rd signposted town centre, turn right into Queen St & left (oneway) Boutport St hotel on left*
Originally a coaching inn, this friendly and welcoming hotel is centrally situated in the town. Bedrooms vary in size, but all are neatly decorated and equipped with modern conveniences. A choice of lounges is complemented by a bar that leads into the nicely appointed restaurant. More informal dining is offered at The Bank, a bistro and café bar, open all day and serving both meals and snacks, many with a Mexican influence.
ROOMS: 50 en suite (bth/shr) (5 fmly) s £49-£54; d £60-£70 * LB Off peak **MEALS:** Lunch £9.50-£13.50 & alc Dinner £16.50 & alc English & French Cuisine V meals Coffee am Tea pm **FACILITIES:** CTV in all bedrooms STV Wkly live entertainment Xmas **CONF:** Thtr 50 Class 50 Board 50 **SERVICES:** Lift Night porter 40P **NOTES:** Last d 9pm
CARDS:

BARNSTAPLE Devon **Map 02 SS53**
★★★ Barnstaple Hotel
Braunton Rd EX31 1LE
Quality Percentage Score: 69%
☎ 01271 376221 01271 324101
Dir: *on the outskirts of Barnstaple on A361*
This purpose built hotel offers a range of leisure facilities, including both indoor and outdoor swimming pools, snooker tables and a well equipped gymnasium. Bedrooms are located around the outdoor pool and sun terrace, many having direct access. A range of dishes is available in the restaurant or in the comfortably furnished bar lounge, whilst snacks can be had from the poolside café. There are also meeting rooms and an impressive function suite.
ROOMS: 60 en suite (bth/shr) (6 fmly) s £54-£59; d £74-£84 * LB Off peak **MEALS:** Lunch £9.50 & alc Dinner £16.50 & alc English & French Cuisine V meals Coffee am Tea pm **FACILITIES:** CTV in all bedrooms STV Indoor swimming pool (heated) Outdoor swimming pool (heated) Snooker Sauna Solarium Gym Jacuzzi/spa ch fac Xmas **CONF:** Thtr 250 Class 250 Board 250 **SERVICES:** Night porter 250P
NOTES: Last d 9pm **CARDS:**

BARNSTAPLE Devon **Map 02 SS53**
★★★ Park
Taw Vale EX32 9AE
Quality Percentage Score: 66%
☎ 01271 372166 01271 323157
Dir: *opposite Rock Park, 0.5m from town centre*
This modern hotel is situated opposite the park and within easy walking distance of the town centre. Comfortable bedrooms, varying in size, are split between the main building and Garden Court, located just across the car park. Public areas are laid out in open plan style, the well maintained bar leading straight into the restaurant, with a spacious function suite also being available.
ROOMS: 25 en suite (bth/shr) 17 annexe en suite (bth/shr) (7 fmly) s £49-£54; d £60-£70 * LB Off peak **MEALS:** Lunch £10.50 & alc Dinner £16.50 & alc English & French Cuisine V meals Coffee am Tea pm **FACILITIES:** CTV in all bedrooms STV Wkly live entertainment Xmas **CONF:** Thtr 150 Class 150 Board 150 **SERVICES:** Night porter 80P
NOTES: Last d 9pm **CARDS:**

BARNSTAPLE Devon **Map 02 SS53**

The Premier Collection

★★ Halmpstone Manor
Bishop's Tawton EX32 0EA
☎ 01271 830321 01271 830826
Dir: *5m S off A377, leave A377 at Bishop's Tawton opposite petrol station and follow unclassified road for 2m then turn right at Halmpstone Manor sign*
This historic manor house is surrounded by its rich farmlands. Bedrooms, including two with four-poster beds, have many thoughtful touches. The comfortable lounge has a log fire; dinner is expertly cooked from quality local ingredients and served in the candlelit panelled dining room.
ROOMS: 5 en suite (bth/shr) No smoking in 1 bedroom s £75-£80; d £110-£140 (incl. bkfst) * Off peak **MEALS:** English & French Cuisine V meals Coffee am Tea pm **FACILITIES:** CTV in all bedrooms **SERVICES:** 12P **NOTES:** No coaches No children 12yrs No smoking in restaurant Last d 9pm Closed Xmas & New Year
CARDS:

BARNSTAPLE Devon **Map 02 SS53**
Travel Inn
Eastern Av, Whiddon Valley
☎ 01271 377830
This modern building offers accommodation in smart, spacious and well equipped bedrooms, all with en-suite bathrooms. Refreshments may be taken at the nearby family restaurant. For details about current prices consult the Contents Page under Hotel Groups for the Travel Inn phone number.
ROOMS: 40 en suite (bth/shr) d £39.95 *

BARROW-IN-FURNESS Cumbria **Map 07 SD16**
★★ *Lisdoonie*
307/309 Abbey Rd LA14 5LF
Quality Percentage Score: 64%
☎ 01229 827312 01229 820944
Dir: *on A590, first set of traffic lights in town (Strawberry pub on left), continue for 100yds, hotel on right. Car park right in Furness Park Rd*
This hotel has a friendly and relaxing atmosphere which attracts regular business guests. Two lounges, one with a bar, place

contd.

emphasis on comfort and a convivial atmosphere. Comfortable bedrooms come in a variety of sizes.
ROOMS: 12 en suite (bth/shr) (2 fmly) **MEALS:** English & French Cuisine V meals Coffee am Tea pm **FACILITIES:** CTV in all bedrooms **CONF:** Class 255 **SERVICES:** 30P **NOTES:** Last d 8pm Closed Xmas & New Year **CARDS:**

BARTON Lancashire — Map 07 SD53

★★★ Barton Grange
Garstang Rd PR3 5AA
Quality Percentage Score: 69%
☎ 01772 862551 Fax 01772 861267
Dir: *from M6 junct 32 follow A6, signed Garstang ,for two and half miles, hotel on the right*

Best Western

Set alongside a large garden centre, this friendly hotel has recently undergone a major refurbishment. The upgraded bedrooms, some of them in an adjacent cottage, are comfortable and offer a useful range of extras. There is a gym and swimming *contd.*

IN THE HEART OF NORTH DEVON

The luxurious Imperial Hotel, stands in its own manicured grounds on the banks of the River Taw. Boasting all the elegance and style of a beautiful hotel it provides first class service with the finest of wines and superb cuisine, with ensuite bedrooms, satellite TV and a lift to all floors.

In a central location with free resident parking, The Imperial is the perfect base from which to explore the historic market town of Barnstaple, Englands oldest borough and many time 'Britain in Bloom' winner, or the idyllic surroundings of places like Clovelly, Lynmouth and Saunton.

FOR A FREE COLOUR BROCHURE, PLEASE CONTACT:

THE IMPERIAL HOTEL
AA ★★★★

TAW VALE PARADE, BARNSTAPLE, NORTH DEVON EX32 8NB.
TEL: (01271) 345861 FAX: (01271) 324448
www.brend-imperial.co.uk e-mail: info@brend-imperial.co.uk

Brend Hotels
The Westcountry's Leading Hotel Group

NORTHCOTE MANOR
country house hotel

Stay awhile in timeless tranquillity

Step free from the stresses of life and enjoy the uniquely peaceful and relaxing atmosphere of Northcote Manor Country House Hotel. Twenty acres of mature woodlands, lawns and gardens, including an outstanding view over the Taw River Valley, set the scene for healthy relaxation and gentle leisure.

Each of the 11 bedrooms and suites has been individually designed and luxuriously furnished, providing a wonderful level of comfort and elegance in which to rest.

Dining at Northcote is an experience to savour. The spacious and harmonious Manor House Restaurant makes the ideal setting for a relaxing meal freshly prepared to the highest standards.

AA ★★★

Northcote Manor Country House Hotel, Burrington, Umberleigh, North Devon EX37 9LZ
Telephone: 01769 560501 Fax: 01769 560770 E-mail: rest@northcotemanor.co.uk

B

pool as well as a range of meeting and function rooms. The Walled Garden restaurant offers a wide range of meals and lighter dishes in an informal environment.
ROOMS: 42 en suite (bth/shr) 8 annexe en suite (bth/shr) (4 fmly) s £76-£84; d £86-£99 (incl. bkfst) * LB Off peak **MEALS:** Lunch fr £11.75 & alc High tea £3.95-£6.65alc Dinner fr £19 & alc English, French & Italian Cuisine V meals Coffee am Tea pm **FACILITIES:** CTV in all bedrooms STV Indoor swimming pool (heated) Snooker Sauna Gym Pool table Jacuzzi/spa Garden Centre Beauty salon Xmas **CONF:** Thtr 350 Class 200 Board 60 Del from £99 * **SERVICES:** Lift Night porter 250P **NOTES:** No dogs (ex guide dogs) No smoking area in restaurant Last d 10pm **CARDS:**

BARTON MILLS Suffolk — Map 05 TL77
Travelodge
IP28 6AE
☎ 01638 717675 01638 717675
Dir: *on A11*
This modern building offers accommodation in smart, spacious and well equipped bedrooms, all with en-suite bathrooms. Refreshments may be taken at the nearby family restaurant. For details about current prices, consult the Contents Page under Hotel Groups for the Travelodge phone number.
ROOMS: 40 en suite (bth/shr) d £49.95 *

BARTON-ON-SEA Hampshire — Map 04 SZ29
★★ The Cliff House
Marine Dr West BH25 7QL
Quality Percentage Score: 75%
☎ 01425 619333 01425 612462
Dir: *turn off A337 on to Sea Road at Barton-on-Sea. Hotel at end of road on cliff top*
From a superb clifftop location overlooking the sea, this charming family-run hotel has a warm and welcoming atmosphere. Bedrooms are prettily decorated and many have panoramic sea views. Popular with locals and visitors alike, the restaurant serves a variety of menus.
ROOMS: 9 en suite (bth/shr) No smoking in all bedrooms s £35-£39; d £70-£80 (incl. bkfst) * LB Off peak **MEALS:** Lunch £11.95-£14.75 & alc Dinner fr £18.95 & alc International Cuisine V meals Coffee am Tea pm **FACILITIES:** CTV in all bedrooms STV **SERVICES:** 50P **NOTES:** No dogs (ex guide dogs) No coaches No children 10yrs No smoking in restaurant Last d 8.45pm **CARDS:**

BARTON STACEY Hampshire — Map 04 SU44
Travelodge
SP21 3NP
☎ 01264 720260 01264 720260
Dir: *on A303*
This modern building offers accommodation in smart, spacious and well equipped bedrooms, all with en-suite bathrooms. Refreshments may be taken at the nearby family restaurant. For details about current prices, consult the Contents Page under Hotel Groups for the Travelodge phone number.
ROOMS: 20 en suite (bth/shr) d £49.95 *

BARTON-UNDER-NEEDWOOD Staffordshire — Map 07 SK11
Travelodge (Northbound)
DE13 8EG
☎ 01283 716343 01283 716343
Dir: *on A38,northbound*
This modern building offers accommodation in smart, spacious and well equipped bedrooms, all with en-suite bathrooms. Refreshments may be taken at the nearby family restaurant. For details about current prices, consult the Contents Page under Hotel Groups for the Travelodge phone number.
ROOMS: 20 en suite (bth/shr) d £39.95 *

BARTON-UNDER-NEEDWOOD Staffordshire — Map 07 SK11
Travelodge (Southbound)
Rykneld St DE13 8EH
☎ 01283 716784 01283 716784
Dir: *on A38, southbound*
This modern building offers accommodation in smart, spacious and well equipped bedrooms, all with en-suite bathrooms. Refreshments may be taken at the nearby family restaurant. For details about current prices, consult the Contents Page under Hotel Groups for the Travelodge phone number.
ROOMS: 40 en suite (bth/shr)

BARTON-UPON-HUMBER Lincolnshire — Map 08 TA02
★★★ *Reeds Hotel*
Westfield Lakes, Far-ings Rd DN18 5RG
Quality Percentage Score: 70%
☎ 01652 632313 01652 636361

Nestling beside the Humber, between a couple of freshwater lakes, Reeds enjoys splendid views of the Humber Bridge - the world's largest single span suspension bridge. Public rooms include an attractive restaurant, foyer lounge and 'Clippers Tea Room', with panoramic views. Bedrooms vary in size - all are thoughtfully equipped and nicely presented. Please note that this is a non-smoking establishment.
ROOMS: 6 en suite (bth/shr) (1 fmly) No smoking in all bedrooms **MEALS:** Coffee am Tea pm **FACILITIES:** CTV in all bedrooms Alternative therapy centre Wkly live entertainment **CONF:** Thtr 100 Class 40 Board 35 **SERVICES:** Night porter P **NOTES:** No dogs (ex guide dogs) No smoking in restaurant Last d 10pm
CARDS:

BASILDON Essex — Map 05 TQ78
★★★ Chichester
Old London Rd, Wickford SS11 8UE
Quality Percentage Score: 67%
☎ 01268 560555 01268 560580
Dir: *off A129*
A friendly and relaxed atmosphere prevails at this family-run, commercial hotel, which stands in landscaped grounds surrounded by open farmland. Diners can take an informal bar meal in the character Stable Bar or choose from a set-priced menu in the Gallery Restaurant. The well appointed bedrooms,
contd.

set around an attractive courtyard garden, are comfortably furnished and well maintained.
ROOMS: 2 en suite (bth/shr) 32 annexe en suite (bth/shr) d fr £65 * Off peak **MEALS:** Lunch £9.25-£11.85 Dinner £12.95-£17.25 English & French Cuisine V meals **FACILITIES:** CTV in all bedrooms **SERVICES:** Night porter 150P **NOTES:** No dogs (ex guide dogs) No children 5yrs No smoking in restaurant Last d 9.15pm
CARDS:

BASILDON Essex **Map 05 TQ78**
★★★ Posthouse Basildon
Cranes Farm Rd SS14 3DG
Quality Percentage Score: 64%
☎ 01268 533955 Fax 01268 530119
Dir: *off A1235, via A127*
Suitable for both the business and leisure traveller, this bright hotel provides modern accommodation in well equipped bedrooms.
ROOMS: 149 en suite (bth/shr) (30 fmly) No smoking in 70 bedrooms s £109-£129; d £109-£149 * LB Off peak **MEALS:** Lunch £5.95-£12.50 & alc High tea £6.95 Dinner £10-£18.50 & alc International Cuisine V meals Coffee am Tea pm **FACILITIES:** CTV in all bedrooms Use of nearby Leisure Club (David Lloyd) Xmas **CONF:** Thtr 300 Class 80 Board 80 Del from £135 * **SERVICES:** Lift Night porter 200P **NOTES:** No smoking area in restaurant Last d 10.30pm
CARDS:

BASILDON Essex **Map 05 TQ78**
Campanile
Pipps Hill, Southend Arterial Rd SS14 3AE
☎ 01268 530810 Fax 01268 286710
Dir: *M25 junct29 exit in direction of Basildon take first exit to Basildon, go back under A127 then at roundabout go left*

This modern building offers accommodation in smart well equipped bedrooms, all with en-suite bathrooms. Refreshments may be taken at the informal Bistro. For details about current prices, consult the Contents Page under Hotel Groups for the Campanile phone number.
ROOMS: 98 annexe en suite (bth/shr) **CONF:** Thtr 35 Class 18 Board 20

BASILDON Essex **Map 05 TQ78**
Travel Inn
Felmores, East Mayne SS13 1BW
☎ 01268 522227 Fax 01268 530092
Dir: *take junct 29 off M25 on to the A127 towards Southend, then A132 towards Basildon*
This modern building offers accommodation in smart, spacious and well equipped bedrooms, all with en-suite bathrooms. Refreshments may be taken at the nearby family restaurant. For details about current prices consult the Contents Page under Hotel Groups for the Travel Inn phone number.
ROOMS: 32 en suite (bth/shr) d £39.95 *

BASILDON Essex **Map 05 TQ78**
Travel Inn
High Rd, Fobbing, Stanford le Hope SS17 9NR
☎ 01268 554500 Fax 01268 581752
Dir: *on junc of A13 & A176*
This modern building offers accommodation in smart, spacious and well equipped bedrooms, all with en-suite bathrooms. Refreshments may be taken at the nearby family restaurant. For details about current prices consult the Contents Page under Hotel Groups for the Travel Inn phone number.
ROOMS: 40 en suite (bth/shr) d £39.95 *

BASINGSTOKE Hampshire **Map 04 SU65**
see also **Odiham & Stratfield Turgis**
★★★★ Tylney Hall Hotel
Tylney Hall RG27 9AZ
☎ 01256 764881 Fax 01256 768141
(For full entry see Rotherwick)

BASINGSTOKE Hampshire **Map 04 SU65**
★★★★ Audleys Wood
Alton Rd RG25 2JT
Quality Percentage Score: 76%
☎ 01256 817555 Fax 01256 817500
Dir: *1.5m S of Basingstoke on A339*
Discreetly set back in seven acres of wooded gardens, this Gothic Renaissance style residence offers comfortable and attractively styled accommodation with peaceful views over woodland. Spacious bedrooms are comfortable and well equipped, bathrooms are fitted in marble. The bar and lounges retain much of their original character with fine wood panelling and attractive
contd.

seating. The stylish restaurant, with high vaulted ceiling has our Two rosette award for standards of cuisine.

Audleys Wood, Basingstoke

ROOMS: 71 en suite (bth/shr) (6 fmly) No smoking in 35 bedrooms s £115; d £140 * LB Off peak **MEALS:** Lunch £17.75-£22 & alc Dinner £22-£28 & alc British & French Cuisine V meals Coffee am Tea pm **FACILITIES:** CTV in all bedrooms STV Croquet lawn Putting green Bicycles Archery ch fac Xmas **CONF:** Thtr 50 Class 20 Board 26 Del from £155 * **SERVICES:** Night porter 100P **NOTES:** No smoking area in restaurant Last d 9.45pm **CARDS:**

BASINGSTOKE Hampshire **Map 04 SU65**
★★★ **Romans**
Little London Rd RG7 2PN
Quality Percentage Score: 75%
☎ 0118 970 0421 0118 970 0691
(For full entry see Silchester)

Best Western

BASINGSTOKE Hampshire **Map 04 SU65**
★★★ **Basingstoke Country**
Scures Hill, Nately Scures, Hook RG27 9JS
Quality Percentage Score: 70%
☎ 01256 764161 01256 768341
***Dir:** leave M3 exit 5 take turning on roundabout to Newnham/Basingstoke, proceed 0.5m until reaching T junct, turn left onto A30, hotel is 200yd on right*
This extensive hotel is very popular with the business community who appreciate the well designed rooms and public areas. Bedrooms are spacious and very well equipped. Good conference and meetings facilities can cater for a variety of functions. The Winchester restaurant features contemporary dishes served in comfortable surroundings.
ROOMS: 100 en suite (bth/shr) (8 fmly) No smoking in 35 bedrooms s fr £105; d fr £115 * LB Off peak **MEALS:** V meals Coffee am Tea pm **FACILITIES:** CTV in all bedrooms STV Indoor swimming pool (heated) Sauna Solarium Gym Jacuzzi/spa Beauty salon Dance studio **CONF:** Thtr 200 Class 95 Board 80 **SERVICES:** Lift Night porter 164P **NOTES:** Last d 9.45pm **CARDS:**
See advert on opposite page

BASINGSTOKE Hampshire **Map 04 SU65**
★★★ **The Hampshire Centrecourt Hotel**
Centre Dr, Chineham RG24 8FY
Quality Percentage Score: 69%
☎ 01256 816664 01256 816727

Marston Hotels

***Dir:** off A33 Reading Road behind the Chineham Shopping Centre via Great Binfields Road*
Ideally located in the Chineham area of Basingstoke with easy access to the M3, M4 and business areas. The hotel has extensive leisure facilities centred around a number of indoor and outdoor tennis courts. A fitness suite with full time trainers, a dance and work-out studio and an indoor pool are available for non tennis players. Bedrooms are spacious and well equipped, and some have balconies overlooking the tennis courts. The open plan public areas have a relaxed and friendly atmosphere.
ROOMS: 50 en suite (bth/shr) (6 fmly) No smoking in 25 bedrooms s fr £110; d fr £125 (incl. bkfst) * LB Off peak **MEALS:** Lunch £12.50-£14.95 & alc Dinner £17.95-£19.50 & alc English & Continental Cuisine V meals Coffee am **FACILITIES:** CTV in all bedrooms STV Indoor swimming pool (heated) Tennis (hard) Sauna Solarium Gym Pool table Jacuzzi/spa Steam room **CONF:** Thtr 100 Class 40 Board 40 Del from £149 * **SERVICES:** Lift Night porter 120P **NOTES:** No dogs (ex guide dogs) No smoking area in restaurant Last d 9.30pm Closed 24 Dec-31 Jan **CARDS:**

BASINGSTOKE Hampshire **Map 04 SU65**
★★★ ***Posthouse Basingstoke***
Grove Rd RG21 3EE
Quality Percentage Score: 63%
☎ 01256 468181 01256 840081

Posthouse

***Dir:** on A339 Alton road S of Basingstoke*
Situated on the outskirts of Basingstoke, and ideally place for easy access to the M3, this modern, purpose-built hotel offers a good standard of accommodation in well equipped rooms. In addition to the popular Garfunkel's restaurant, the hotel benefits from function rooms and good parking facilities.
ROOMS: 84 en suite (bth/shr) (3 fmly) No smoking in 42 bedrooms **MEALS:** International Cuisine V meals Coffee am Tea pm **FACILITIES:** CTV in all bedrooms Pool table Childrens indoor/outdoor play areas ch fac **CONF:** Thtr 150 Class 80 Board 80 **SERVICES:** Night porter 150P **NOTES:** No smoking area in restaurant Last d 9.30pm **CARDS:**

BASINGSTOKE Hampshire **Map 04 SU65**
★★★ **Red Lion**
24 London St RG21 7NY
Quality Percentage Score: 61%
☎ 01256 328525 01256 844056
Central to Basingstoke town the Red Lion is an ideal choice for business guests. Bedrooms and bathrooms have recently been refurbished, and most are spacious. The restaurant and bar have an informal feel and there is an attractive residents' lounge and dedicated parking.
ROOMS: 59 en suite (bth/shr) (2 fmly) No smoking in 6 bedrooms s £95-£105; d £112-£130 (incl. bkfst) * Off peak **MEALS:** Sunday Lunch £5.95-£11.95 Dinner £10-£20alc Englidh & American Cuisine V meals Coffee am Tea pm **FACILITIES:** CTV in all bedrooms STV Pool table Wkly live entertainment Xmas **CONF:** Thtr 40 Class 40 Board 20 Del £117 * **SERVICES:** Lift Night porter 62P **NOTES:** No smoking in restaurant Last d 9.30pm **CARDS:**
See advert on opposite page

BASINGSTOKE Hampshire **Map 04 SU65**
★★★ **Ringway**
Popley Way, Aldermaston Roundabout, Ringway North (A339) RG24 9NU
Quality Percentage Score: 61%
☎ 01256 320212 01256 842835
***Dir:** situated off M3 junct 6. Follow ringroad N to exit A340 (Aldermaston), hotel on rdbt take 5th exit for access*
The Ringway is conveniently located for access to major routes
contd. on p. 86

We endeavour to be as accurate as possible but changes in personnel and data can occur in establishments after the Hotel Guide has gone to press.

Red Lion Hotel

London Street
Basingstoke
Hampshire RG21 1NY
Tel: 01256 328525
Fax: 01256 844056

Dating back to the 17th century the Red Lion Hotel is located in the heart of Basingstoke town centre and is the town's most historical hotel. The hotel offers high levels of service and comfort and is ideal for your travelling needs whether for business or leisure. All 58 bedrooms are en-suite with hospitality tray, satellite TV and direct dial telephone.

Once a private country residence now an elegant modern country hotel, set in 4.5 acres adjacent to mature woodland. The Basingstoke Country Hotel offers an almost unique blend of high standards, personal service and excellent facilities including 100 en-suite bedrooms, Winchester Restaurant, Players Sports Bar & Diner, two purpose built conference suites for up to 250 and 'Club Veranda' Leisure Complex.

BASINGSTOKE COUNTRY HOTEL

Scures Hill, Nately Scures
Hook, Hants RG27 9JS
Telephone: 01256 764161
Fax: 01256 768341

Andrew Weir Hotels

ROMANS

Country House Hotel

★ ★ ★

Little London Road, Silchester
Basingstoke RG7 2PN
Tel: 01189 700421 Fax: 01189 700691

ONLY AN HOUR'S DRIVE FROM LONDON.

A PRIVATELY OWNED HOTEL, SET IN THE HISTORIC VILLAGE OF SILCHESTER, THE HOUSE, BUILT IN THE STYLE OF LUTYENS, HAS BEEN SYMPATHETICALLY CONVERTED TO OFFER GUESTS THE BEST IN MODERN FACILITIES, WHILE RETAINING THE ATMOSPHERE AND PERIOD DETAILS OF AN EDWARDIAN COUNTRY RESIDENCE.

DELIGHTFUL RESTAURANT. INNOVATIVE FRENCH CUISINE.

HEALTH AND LEISURE CENTRE WITH GYMNASIUM, SAUNA, TENNIS AND OUTDOOR POOL, HEATED TO A STEAMING 30°c ALL YEAR ROUND.

and remains a popular venue for both corporate and private guests. Now under new ownership the hotel is being upgraded.

Ringway, Basingstoke

ROOMS: 135 en suite (bth/shr) No smoking in 35 bedrooms s £40-£93; d £50-£115 * LB Off peak **MEALS:** Lunch £15 & alc High tea £1.95-£5.75 Dinner £15 & alc V meals Coffee am Tea pm **FACILITIES:** CTV in all bedrooms STV Indoor swimming pool (heated) Sauna Solarium Gym **CONF:** Thtr 140 Class 100 Board 40 Del from £120 * **SERVICES:** Lift Night porter 200P **NOTES:** No dogs (ex guide dogs) No smoking in restaurant Last d 10pm **CARDS:**

See advert on opposite page

BASINGSTOKE Hampshire — Map 04 SU65

Travel Inn

Basingstoke Leisure Park, Worting Rd RG22 6PG

☎ 01256 811477 📠 01256 819329

Dir: *from M3 junct 6 follow signs for Leisure Park*

This modern building offers accommodation in smart, spacious and well equipped bedrooms, all with en-suite bathrooms. Refreshments may be taken at the nearby family restaurant. For details about current prices consult the Contents Page under Hotel Groups for the Travel Inn phone number.

ROOMS: 40 en suite (bth/shr) d £39.95 *

BASINGSTOKE Hampshire — Map 04 SU65

Travelodge

Stag and Hounds, Winchester Rd RG22 5HN

☎ 01256 843566 📠 01256 843566

Dir: *off A30*

This modern building offers accommodation in smart, spacious and well equipped bedrooms, all with en-suite bathrooms. Refreshments may be taken at the nearby family restaurant. For details about current prices, consult the Contents Page under Hotel Groups for the Travelodge phone number.

ROOMS: 32 en suite (bth/shr) d fr £49.95 *

BASLOW Derbyshire — Map 08 SK27

The Premier Collection

★★★ Cavendish

DE45 1SP

☎ 01246 582311 📠 01246 582312

Dir: *on A619*

A country house hotel on the edge of the Chatsworth estate, some of the works of art adorning the walls have been loaned by the Duke and Duchess of Devonshire. Bedrooms are comfortably furnished and thoughtfully equipped with many extras, and the lounge provides a lovely setting in which to relax. Light meals are served all day in the Garden Room conservatory, with more formal dining in the restaurant; the hotel cuisine uses local produce wherever possible.

ROOMS: 24 en suite (bth/shr) No smoking in 2 bedrooms s £95-£115; d £125-£145 * LB Off peak **MEALS:** European Cuisine V meals Coffee am Tea pm **FACILITIES:** CTV in all bedrooms STV Fishing Putting green Xmas **CONF:** Thtr 25 Board 18 Del from £174 * **SERVICES:** Night porter 50P **NOTES:** No dogs (ex guide dogs) No coaches No smoking in restaurant Last d 10pm **CARDS:**

BASLOW Derbyshire — Map 08 SK27

The Premier Collection

★★ Fischer's Baslow Hall

Calver Rd DE45 1RR

☎ 01246 583259 📠 01246 583818

Dir: *on the A623 between Baslow & Calver*

A cosy country house hotel, ideal for business travellers and lovers of good food. This welcoming manor house has sumptuous bedrooms, and a few have kept their period bathroom fittings. Public rooms centre round the restaurant, and the slightly more casual Café-Max with its brasserie-style menu. The hotel cuisine is worth travelling for, and the efficient team of smart staff exude friendly hospitality.

ROOMS: 6 en suite (bth/shr) s £80-£95; d £95-£130 (incl. cont bkfst) * LB Off peak **MEALS:** Lunch £20-£26.75 Dinner £45 European Cuisine V meals Coffee am Tea pm **FACILITIES:** CTV in all bedrooms Xmas **CONF:** Thtr 40 Board 18 Del from £125 * **SERVICES:** 40P **NOTES:** No dogs (ex guide dogs) No coaches No smoking in restaurant Last d 9.30pm Closed 25-26 Dec

CARDS:

BASSENTHWAITE Cumbria **Map 11 NY23**

★★★★ ***Armathwaite Hall***

CA12 4RE

Quality Percentage Score: 70%

☎ 017687 76551 017687 76220

Dir: *M6 junct40, A66 to Keswick roundabout then A591 signposted Carlisle. 8m to Castle Inn junction, turn left hotel 300yds ahead*

Standing in 400 acres of woodland and open meadows, this stately 17th-century mansion is a real slice of the Lake District. Impressive public rooms have superb woodwork and grand fireplaces, while the bedrooms offer a variety of styles and standards. A six-course dinner menu is presented formally in the panelled dining room. Extensive leisure facilities are also available.

ROOMS: 43 en suite (bth/shr) (4 fmly) **MEALS:** English & French Cuisine V meals Coffee am Tea pm **FACILITIES:** CTV in all bedrooms STV Indoor swimming pool (heated) Tennis (hard) Fishing Riding Snooker Sauna Solarium Gym Croquet lawn Putting green Jacuzzi/spa Archery Beauty salon Clay shooting Quad bikes ch fac **CONF:** Thtr 120 Class 50 Board 60 **SERVICES:** Lift Night porter 100P **NOTES:** No smoking in restaurant Last d 9.15pm **CARDS:**

See advert under KESWICK

BASSENTHWAITE Cumbria **Map 11 NY23**

★★★ **Castle Inn**

CA12 4RG

REGAL

Quality Percentage Score: 65%

☎ 017687 76401 017687 76604

Dir: *leave A66 at Keswick and take A591 towards Carlisle, pass Bassenthwaite village on right and hotel is 6m on the left*

The indoor and outdoor leisure facilities are a particular strength of this smartly decorated hotel. All bedrooms are well equipped and there are some top of the range 'superior' rooms. Public areas are spacious and staff offer cheerful service.

ROOMS: 48 en suite (bth/shr) (6 fmly) No smoking in 14 bedrooms s £47-£75; d £94-£115 (incl. bkfst) * LB Off peak **MEALS:** Bar Lunch £4.95-£6.50 Dinner £18.95 & alc English & French Cuisine V meals Coffee am Tea pm **FACILITIES:** CTV in all bedrooms STV Indoor swimming pool (heated) Tennis (grass) Snooker Sauna Solarium Gym Pool table Jacuzzi/spa Badminton Table tennis Golf practice net Health & beauty spa Xmas **CONF:** Thtr 120 Class 35 Board 40 Del from £85 * **SERVICES:** Night porter 100P **NOTES:** No smoking in restaurant Last d 9.45pm **CARDS:**

BASSENTHWAITE Cumbria **Map 11 NY23**

★★ **Overwater Hall**

Ireby CA5 1HH

Quality Percentage Score: 72%

☎ 017687 76566 017687 76566

Dir: *from Keswick on A591, turn right at Castle Inn crossroads, 2m along this road, turn right at sign in wall*

This splendid mansion lies in 18 acres of woodland near the Overwater Tarn. Spacious public rooms include a cosy bar, where the counter, a baby grand piano, is an unusual feature. Bedrooms are comfortable and thoughtfully furnished, while the

contd.

Indicates that the star classification has not been confirmed under the New Quality Standards, see page 7 for further information.

restaurant serves an excellent five-course dinner with imaginative cuisine.

Overwater Hall, Bassenthwaite

ROOMS: 12 en suite (bth/shr) (4 fmly) s £64-£72; d £108-£124 (incl. bkfst & dinner) * LB Off peak **MEALS:** Sunday Lunch £15 Dinner fr £19.50 English & French Cuisine V meals Coffee am Tea pm **FACILITIES:** CTV in all bedrooms Fishing Putting green Xmas **SERVICES:** 25P **NOTES:** No coaches No smoking in restaurant Last d 8.30pm **CARDS:**

BASSENTHWAITE Cumbria — Map 11 NY23

★★ Ravenstone

CA12 4QG
Quality Percentage Score: 66%
☎ 017687 76240 Fax 017687 76733
Dir: *4.5m N of Keswick on Carlisle road A591*

This popular hotel has panoramic views across the valley towards Bassenthwaite Lake. The house retains an original character, with splendid oak panelling, antiques and pictures. There is a comfortable lounge, dining room, bar and games room. The bedrooms are well presented and feature superb hand-carved furniture and there are two four-poster rooms.

ROOMS: 20 en suite (bth/shr) (2 fmly) s £31-£33; d £62-£66 (incl. bkfst) * Off peak **MEALS:** Dinner fr £13.50 V meals Coffee am **FACILITIES:** CTV in all bedrooms Snooker Pool table Table tennis Xmas **SERVICES:** 25P **NOTES:** No coaches No smoking in restaurant Last d 7.30pm Closed Nov-Feb **CARDS:**

BATH Somerset — Map 03 ST76

see also **Chelwood, Colerne & Hinton Charterhouse**

★★★★★ Royal Crescent

16 Royal Crescent BA1 2LS
Quality Percentage Score: 77%
☎ 01225 823333 Fax 01225 339401
Dir: *cont along A4. R at traffic lights. 2nd L onto Bennett St. Cont into the Circus, 2nd exit onto Brock St, proceed ahead to cobbled street & No.16.*

In the centre of John Wood's masterpiece of fine Georgian architecture, the Royal Crescent offers hospitality, service and fine cuisine. There are two restaurants: the Brasserie and Bar offers menus with a Mediterranean slant in a friendly atmosphere; Pimpernels is more intimate and achieves a higher standard of cuisine. Bedrooms are in different period buildings around a spacious garden, so room sizes vary. All include many modern facilities, such as fax, CD and video players. Recent additions include a leisure facility that mixes Roman and Japanese influences, and two superbly equipped meeting rooms.

ROOMS: 45 en suite (bth/shr) (8 fmly) No smoking in 8 bedrooms s fr £190; d fr £190 * Off peak **MEALS:** Lunch £12-£15 & alc High tea fr £16.50 Dinner £28-£36 & alc Modern English & French Cuisine V meals Tea pm **FACILITIES:** CTV in all bedrooms Indoor swimming pool (heated) Sauna Croquet lawn Jacuzzi/spa Outdoor heated Plunge pool, Hot air ballooning, 1920's river launch ch fac Xmas **CONF:** Thtr 100 Class 45 Del from £195 * **SERVICES:** Lift Night porter Air conditioning 27P **NOTES:** No smoking in restaurant Last d 9.30pm **CARDS:**

See advert on opposite page

BATH Somerset — Map 03 ST76

★★★★★ The Bath Spa

Sydney Rd BA2 6JF
Quality Percentage Score: 64%
☎ 01225 444424 Fax 01225 444006

This imposing and sympathetically restored hotel set in immaculately maintained gardens overlooking the city, offers smart, well appointed and thoughtfully equipped bedrooms and suites. The inviting public areas, which include extensive leisure facilities, are no less impressive. Guests have the choice of eating in the Alfresco Restaurant where lighter meals are served in an airy colonnade overlooking the gardens, or in the Vellore Restaurant, a former ballroom, where the quality of the food earns our two rosette award. Nursery, car valeting and chauffeur services are also available.

ROOMS: 98 en suite (bth/shr) (2 fmly) No smoking in 31 bedrooms s £142-£160; d £174-£219 * LB Off peak **MEALS:** Lunch £12.50-£17 & alc Dinner £20-£35alc International Cuisine V meals Coffee am Tea pm **FACILITIES:** CTV in all bedrooms STV Indoor swimming pool (heated) Tennis (hard) Sauna Solarium Gym Croquet lawn Jacuzzi/spa Beauty treatment Hair salon Wkly live entertainment Xmas **CONF:** Thtr 140 Class 72 Board 55 Del from £179 * **SERVICES:** Lift Night porter 156P **NOTES:** No smoking in restaurant Last d 10pm **CARDS:**

BATH Somerset — Map 03 ST76

★★★★ Bath Priory

Weston Rd BA1 2XT
Quality Percentage Score: 77%
☎ 01225 331922 Fax 01225 448276

Carefully extended, this delightful Georgian house offers a recently built wing which includes a smart leisure centre themed on the Roman Baths. The individually styled bedrooms are sumptuously furnished with antiques. The public areas include two elegant sitting rooms and a well appointed dining room overlooking beautiful grounds. Chef Robert Clayton is fast making his mark and uses top quality ingredients to create a very high standard of cooking.

ROOMS: 28 en suite (bth/shr) (6 fmly) s fr £140; d fr £220 (incl. bkfst) * LB Off peak **MEALS:** Lunch £15-£22.50 Dinner £37.50 French Cuisine V meals Coffee am Tea pm **FACILITIES:** CTV in all bedrooms STV Indoor swimming pool (heated) Outdoor swimming pool (heated) Sauna Solarium Gym Croquet lawn Jacuzzi/spa Xmas **CONF:** Thtr 60 Class 30 Board 24 Del £160 * **SERVICES:** Night porter 28P **NOTES:** No dogs (ex guide dogs) No coaches No smoking in restaurant Last d 10pm **CARDS:**

BATH Somerset **Map 03 ST76**

★★★★ Combe Grove Manor Hotel & Country Club

Brassknocker Hill, Monkton Combe BA2 7HS

Quality Percentage Score: 66%

☎ 01225 834644 01225 834961

Dir: *exit at junct 18 of the M4, follow A46 to City Centre. Next follow signs for University and American Museum, hotel is 2m past University on left*

Based around a Georgian manor house this hotel has stunning views. Stylishly furnished, the main house boasts two restaurants. Most bedrooms are in the Garden Lodge, with balconies and garden furniture. There is a superb leisure centre and a popular beauty treatment room.

ROOMS: 9 en suite (bth/shr) 31 annexe en suite (bth/shr) (11 fmly) s £75-£270; d £99-£270 (incl. bkfst) * LB Off peak **MEALS:** Lunch £16.50 Dinner £25 & alc V meals Coffee am Tea pm **FACILITIES:** CTV in all bedrooms STV Indoor swimming pool (heated) Outdoor swimming pool (heated) Golf 5 Tennis (hard) Sauna Solarium Gym Croquet lawn Putting green Jacuzzi/spa Aerobics Beauty salon ch fac Xmas **CONF:** Thtr 100 Class 40 Board 36 **SERVICES:** Night porter 150P **NOTES:** No dogs No smoking in restaurant Last d 9.30pm Closed New Year **CARDS:**

BATH Somerset **Map 03 ST76**

The Premier Collection

★★★ Queensberry

Russel St BA1 2QF

☎ 01225 447928 01225 446065

Dir: *100mtrs from the Assembly Rooms*

A carefully restored Bath-stone town house a few minutes walk from the city centre. Bedrooms are individually decorated and tastefully furnished with sofas, fresh flowers and marble bathrooms with bath robes. A lounge and bar open onto an enclosed courtyard garden. The Olive Tree Restaurant features freshly prepared cuisine. Advance booking is recommended, especially at weekends.

ROOMS: 29 en suite (bth/shr) s £95-£110; d £145-£210 (incl. cont bkfst) * LB Off peak **MEALS:** Lunch £13.50-£15.50 & alc Dinner £24 & alc English, French & Italian Cuisine V meals Coffee am Tea pm **FACILITIES:** CTV in all bedrooms **CONF:** Thtr 35 Board 25 Del £135 * **SERVICES:** Lift Night porter 5P **NOTES:** No dogs (ex guide dogs) No smoking in restaurant Last d 10pm Closed 24 Dec-4 Jan RS Sun **CARDS:**

BATH Somerset **Map 03 ST76**

★★★ Cliffe

Crowe Hill, Limpley Stoke BA3 6HY

Quality Percentage Score: 73%

☎ 01225 723226 01225 723871

Dir: *A36 S from Bath,in approx 3m at traffic lights take B3108 to Lower Limpley Stoke. At sharp left hand bend take minor road to village*

Situated just a short drive from the centre of Bath, this attractive country house property benefits from hill top views and a tranquil setting. Now under the ownership of John Hawken and Carol Nottage, much has been done to improve the property, with the guest lounge now offering a particularly comfortable environment. Bedrooms are all well equipped, with a number

contd.

conveniently situated on the ground floor of the adjacent wing. The restaurant, where guests can sample AA Rosette-worthy cuisine, overlooks the outdoor pool and surrounding garden.
ROOMS: 11 en suite (bth/shr) (4 fmly) s £68-£88; d £88-£110 (incl. bkfst) * LB Off peak **MEALS:** Lunch £9.50-£12.75 Dinner £19-£29alc English & French Cuisine V meals Coffee am Tea pm **FACILITIES:** CTV in all bedrooms STV Outdoor swimming pool (heated) ch fac Xmas **CONF:** Thtr 20 Board 10 Del £110 * **SERVICES:** 40P **NOTES:** No coaches No smoking in restaurant Last d 9.30pm
CARDS:

See advert on opposite page

BATH Somerset **Map 03 ST76**
★★★ ***Lansdown Grove Hotel***
Lansdown Rd BA1 5EH
Quality Percentage Score: 72%
☎ 01225 483888

An established hotel, a steep walk from the city centre. Bedrooms vary in size but are well equipped and tastefully decorated. Public areas include a reception lounge and a comfortable drawing room. Orders for dinner are taken in the bar, the impressive dishes are served in the elegant dining room.
ROOMS: 44 en suite (bth/shr) (3 fmly) No smoking in 9 bedrooms **MEALS:** English & French Cuisine V meals Coffee am Tea pm **FACILITIES:** CTV in all bedrooms **CONF:** Thtr 100 Class 45 Board 40 **SERVICES:** Lift Night porter 44P **NOTES:** Last d 9.30pm
CARDS:

BATH Somerset **Map 03 ST76**
★★★ **The Francis**
Queen Square BA1 2HH
Quality Percentage Score: 69%
☎ 01225 424257 01225 319715
Situated in a prime central location, this well established hotel extends a warm welcome and a feeling of tradition. The lounge is a popular venue for afternoon tea and the restaurant offers more formal dining, while there is an informal bar lounge.
ROOMS: 94 en suite (bth/shr) (1 fmly) No smoking in 38 bedrooms s £94-£99; d £124-£144 * LB Off peak **MEALS:** Lunch fr £12.50 High tea fr £6.75 Dinner fr £23 European Cuisine V meals Coffee am Tea pm **FACILITIES:** CTV in all bedrooms Xmas **CONF:** Thtr 80 Class 40 Board 30 Del from £89 * **SERVICES:** Lift Night porter 42P **NOTES:** No smoking in restaurant Last d 9.30pm **CARDS:**

BATH Somerset **Map 03 ST76**
★★★ ***Duke's***
54 Great Pulteney St BA2 4DN
Quality Percentage Score: 63%
☎ 01225 463512 01225 483733
Located in one of Bath's most sought after addresses, this stylish hotel offers modern facilities combined with the elegance and charm of a fine Georgian building. Bedrooms are comfortable and attractively decorated. In addition to the cosy bar and lounge, the restaurant on the lower ground floor serves an interesting selection of freshly prepared dishes. Unrestricted overnight parking is available on the streets around the hotel, which just a few minutes' walk from some of the most popular attractions.

ROOMS: 24 en suite (bth/shr) (2 fmly) **MEALS:** V meals Coffee am Tea pm **FACILITIES:** CTV in all bedrooms **CONF:** Thtr 20 Class 20 Board 20 **NOTES:** No dogs (ex guide dogs) No coaches No smoking in restaurant Last d 8.30pm **CARDS:**

See advert on opposite page

BATH Somerset **Map 03 ST76**
★★★ **Pratts**
South Pde BA2 4AB
Quality Percentage Score: 63%
☎ 01225 460441 01225 448807
Dir: *take A46 into Bath City Centre*
This old-established hotel forms part of an attractive Georgian terrace in the town centre. Day rooms have kept their traditional atmosphere, and include a quiet writing room as well as lounges. There is also a conservatory bar. Bedrooms, in keeping with the character of the building, vary in style, and those on the third floor have a more cottagey feel.
ROOMS: 46 en suite (bth/shr) (2 fmly) No smoking in 2 bedrooms s fr £75; d fr £95 (incl. bkfst) * LB Off peak **MEALS:** Sunday Lunch fr £12.50 Dinner fr £16.95 English & French Cuisine V meals Tea pm **FACILITIES:** CTV in all bedrooms Xmas **CONF:** Thtr 50 Class 12 Board 30 Del from £105 * **SERVICES:** Lift Night porter **NOTES:** No smoking in restaurant Last d 9.30pm **CARDS:**

BATH Somerset **Map 03 ST76**
★★★ **The Abbey Hotel**
North Pde BA1 1LF
Quality Percentage Score: 62%
☎ 01225 461603 01225 447758
Dir: *close to the Abbey in city centre*

Part of a handsome Georgian terrace, this hotel is close to the heart of the city and its attractions. Bedrooms are equipped with

contd. on p. 92

Bodkin House

HOTEL & RESTAURANT

A46, Petty France, Badminton, S Glos GL9 1AF
Telephone: 01454 238310 Fax: 01454 238422

AA ★★

A warm and friendly welcome awaits you in this 17th century former coaching inn. Being so near the M4, access is easy to Bath, Bristol, the Cotswolds, the Wye Valley and the Forest of Dean. Choose to wine and dine in Bodkin's Restaurant or relax with a drink in front of the log fire in Bodkin's Bar before retiring to one of our nine spacious en-suite rooms.

THE CLIFFE HOTEL

Limpley Stoke, BATH BA3 6HY

Best Western

AA ★★★ 74%

Situated in over 3 acres of wooded grounds, this elegant Country House Hotel offers one of the finest views over the Avon Valley. The hotel is actively run by the resident owners who pride themselves on attention to detail, and good service. All rooms are tastefully and individually decorated to the highest standards. Each room has full en-suite facilities, and most have commanding Valley views. The hotel has an outdoor heated swimming pool and more than adequate parking space.

AA Red Rosette award for à la carte Restaurant.

TELEPHONE 01225 723226 FAX 01225 723871

AA ★★

Les Routiers

WOOLVERTON HOUSE HOTEL

Woolverton, Bath, Somerset BA3 6QS
Telephone: 01373 830415
Fax: 01373 831243

Situated 9 miles south of Bath city centre on A36. The hotel dates back to 1830 with elegant and comfortable rooms throughout the house. Set in lovely gardens with its own stream and pond, guests can enjoy lawn tennis, croquet and pitch and putt. The restaurant is beautifully decorated and specialises in French cuisine and wines offering excellent value.

See gazetteer entry under Woolverton.

★★★ 63%

DUKES HOTEL

Great Pulteney Street
Bath, Avon
BA2 4DN
Tel: (01225) 463512 Fax: (01225) 483733

This Grade II Listed Townhouse is situated on Europe's most elegant Georgian boulevard – just a short stroll from the Roman Baths and Abbey.

Our 24 newly refurbished bedrooms are all equipped with tea and coffee-making facilities, hairdryer, satellite TV and direct-dial telephone.

We offer a peaceful and relaxed atmosphere with emphasis on personal service and excellent food. Dinner is prepared from the finest local produce complemented by our reasonably priced of wines.

modern comforts and the public areas include a smart bar-lounge and a formal restaurant where a fixed price menu is available.
ROOMS: 60 en suite (bth/shr) (4 fmly) No smoking in 23 bedrooms s £75-£85; d £115-£125 (incl. bkfst) LB Off peak **MEALS:** Lunch £6-£11.50 Dinner £9.50-£17.50 British & French Cuisine V meals Coffee am **FACILITIES:** CTV in all bedrooms STV Xmas **CONF:** Thtr 8 Class 14 **SERVICES:** Lift Night porter **NOTES:** No smoking in restaurant
CARDS:

See advert on opposite page

BATH Somerset **Map 03 ST76**

★★ Haringtons

8/10 Queen St BA1 1HE
Quality Percentage Score: 74%
☎ 01225 461728 01225 444804
Dir: *from A4 go to George St and turn into Milsom St. 1st right into Quiet St and 1st left into Queen St*
Located in the centre of the city, Harington's dates back to the 18th century. The cafe-bar is open throughout the day for light meals and refreshment. All bedrooms are of a good standard and offer the expected modern comforts.
ROOMS: 13 en suite (bth/shr) (3 fmly) No smoking in all bedrooms s £65-£78; d £88-£110 (incl. bkfst) LB Off peak **MEALS:** Lunch £12-£17alc High tea £5-£7alc Dinner £12-£17alc V meals Coffee am Tea pm **FACILITIES:** CTV in all bedrooms STV **NOTES:** No dogs (ex guide dogs) No coaches No smoking in restaurant Last d 8.30pm Closed 24-26 Dec
CARDS:

BATH Somerset **Map 03 ST76**

★★ The Bath Tasburgh

Warminster Rd BA2 6SH
Quality Percentage Score: 71%
☎ 01225 425096 01225 463842
Dir: *follow signs for A36. Hotel stands on N side of A36 - Adjacent to Bathampton Ln junct - approx. 0.5m from Bathwick St rdbt and Sydney Gardens*
Set in 7 acres of beautifully tended gardens and meadowland extending down to the Kennet and Avon Canal, this charming Victorian house has glorious views over the Avon Valley. David and Susan Keeling have extended the public areas with the addition of a bright and airy conservatory, opening onto a garden terrace. A short, fixed-price menu is offered in the attractive and intimate surroundings of the dining room, complemented by an interesting choice of wines. Bedrooms vary in size and quality and include a number of four-posters and family rooms, with two rooms being available on the ground floor.
ROOMS: 12 en suite (bth/shr) (3 fmly) No smoking in all bedrooms s £50-£60; d £72-£98 (incl. bkfst) * Off peak **MEALS:** Dinner £21.50-£24 European Cuisine V meals Coffee am Tea pm **FACILITIES:** CTV in all bedrooms Croquet lawn **CONF:** Thtr 15 Class 15 Board 15 **SERVICES:** 16P **NOTES:** No dogs No coaches No smoking in restaurant Last d 7.30pm **CARDS:**

See advert on opposite page

BATH Somerset **Map 03 ST76**

★★ *The Old Mill*

Tollbridge Rd, Batheaston BA1 7DE
Quality Percentage Score: 64%
☎ 01225 858476 01225 852600
Dir: *take A46 for 8 miles, turn left for Bath at large rdbt turn left towards Batheaston in 0.5m turn right after Waggon & Horses to Bathampton Toll Br*
Formerly a flour mill, this attractive creeper-clad hotel is currently being transformed by the new owners, with refurbishment of all public areas and bedrooms. The original waterwheel can be seen from the restaurant, which has a unique revolving floor and overlooks the gardens lying alongside the River Avon. Bedrooms vary in size, but all offer good levels of equipment and comfort.
ROOMS: 16 en suite (bth/shr) 10 annexe en suite (shr) (5 fmly) **MEALS:** English & French Cuisine V meals Coffee am Tea pm **FACILITIES:** CTV in all bedrooms Fishing **CONF:** Thtr 100 Class 80 Board 80 **SERVICES:** 50P **NOTES:** No smoking area in restaurant Last d 10pm **CARDS:**

See advert on opposite page

BATH Somerset **Map 03 ST76**

★★ Old Malt House

Radford, Timsbury BA3 1QF
Quality Percentage Score: 62%
☎ 01761 470106 01761 472726
Dir: *from Bath take A367 south for 1.5m then right onto B3115 towards Timsbury. Continue down hill to Camerton Inn then second left and second left again*
Conveniently located just six miles from Bath, this former brewery malt house provides a tranquil base from which to explore the surrounding area. Bedrooms are well equipped with thoughtful extras such as hairdryers, clock radios and hot water bottles. Guests may enjoy a pre-dinner drink in front of the wood- burning stove in the bar, where home-cooked meals are served, or dine from the a la carte menu in the candle lit restaurant.
ROOMS: 12 en suite (bth/shr) (2 fmly) s £36-£44; d £72 (incl. bkfst) * LB Off peak **MEALS:** Bar Lunch £7.90-£12.45alc Dinner £17 V meals Coffee am Tea pm **FACILITIES:** CTV in all bedrooms **SERVICES:** 40P **NOTES:** No coaches No smoking in restaurant Last d 8.30pm Closed 24-27 Dec **CARDS:**

THE GEORGE at Nunney

★★

Church Street, Nunney
Somerset BA11 4LW

Tel: 01373 836458

Beside the historic and moated Nunney Castle is the equally famous ***George*** which embodies traditional high standards of English hospitality. The extremely well equipped rooms offer every convenience for both the businessman and holidaymaker alike. Off road parking in the pretty conservation area village centre. Close by are many **golf courses - the Georgian splendour of Bath - Longleat Safari Park - The Royal Bath and West Showground** - each within a short drive. Good value Bargain Breaks - including Christmas and New Year - are a feature at the ***George*** as is the cuisine which specialises in the best of local produce.

Telephone or write for a brochure and tariff

The Abbey Hotel

Situated in the very heart of Bath close to the Abbey, Roman Baths and Pump Rooms. The Abbey Hotel is your ideal base for exploring this historic city which has been designated a World Heritage Site because of the importance and magnificence of its Georgian architecture and Roman connections.

Best Western

A member of Best Western Hotels.
The world's largest group of
fine independent hotels.

North Parade, Bath BA1 1LF

Tel: 01225 461603 Fax: 01225 447758

The Old Mill

Under New Ownership

TOLLBRIDGE ROAD
BATHEASTON
BATH BA1 7DE
Tel: 01225 858476
Fax: 01225 852600

★★

In a picturesque position on the banks of the river Avon just 1.4 miles from the centre of Bath.

All bedrooms are en suite and have been totally refurbished in 1999 with the majority having river views, there are some with 4-poster beds. Dine in the Water Wheel Restaurant with views of the historic toll bridge, revolving water wheel, pretty gardens and the river and its wild life.

Free private parking.

Special short breaks available all year.

BATH'S MOST BEAUTIFULLY LOCATED HOTEL

The Bath Tasburgh Hotel

AA ★★

Tel:
01225 425096
Fax:
01225 463842

WARMINSTER ROAD
BATH BA2 6SH

A Victorian mansion standing in seven acres of beautiful gardens and meadowlands stretching down to the Kennet & Avon canal. With spectacular views the hotel provides ideal country comfort in a city setting and is convenient for central Bath. The adjacent canal towpath provides an idyllic walk into Bath. Individually decorated en-suite bedrooms (including 4-posters and family). Elegant Drawing Room and stunning Conservatory. Evening meals. Licensed. Ample parking. Caring and friendly service.

≣ **BATLEY** West Yorkshire   **Map 08 SE22**
★★ *Alder House*
Towngate Rd, Healey Ln WF17 7HR
Quality Percentage Score: 68%
☎ 01924 444777 ▤ 01924 442644
An attractive Georgian house tucked away in a quiet corner, carefully furnished and thoughtfully equipped throughout. There is a cosy dining room, with a good range of very interesting dishes available. The modern bedrooms are well equipped and a delight to occupy. Solid Yorkshire hospitality and service is provided by a dedicated staff.
ROOMS: 20 en suite (bth/shr) (1 fmly) **MEALS:** English & Continental Cuisine V meals Coffee am Tea pm **FACILITIES:** CTV in all bedrooms STV **CONF:** Thtr 80 Class 40 Board 35 **SERVICES:** 52P **NOTES:** No smoking in restaurant Last d 9pm **CARDS:** 💳 ■ ✕ ⚍

See advert on opposite page

≣ **BATTLE** East Sussex   **Map 05 TQ71**

The Premier Collection

★★★✿✿ **Netherfield Place**
Netherfield TN33 9PP
☎ 01424 774455 ▤ 01424 774024
Dir: turn off A21 onto A2100 to Battle. After level crossing take second turning right, hotel approx 1.5m on left
Built in Georgian style, Netherfield Place is surrounded by fine gardens and extensive parkland. A peaceful atmosphere prevails within the lounge and cocktail bar. Bedrooms vary in size but all have extra touches. A well balanced menu is served in the panelled dining room.
ROOMS: 14 en suite (bth/shr) (1 fmly) s fr £68; d £125-£160 (incl. bkfst) * LB Off peak **MEALS:** V meals Coffee am Tea pm **FACILITIES:** CTV in all bedrooms Tennis (hard) Croquet lawn Putting green Clay pigeon & archery by arrangement **CONF:** Thtr 60 Class 40 Board 30 Del from £125 * **SERVICES:** 32P **NOTES:** No dogs (ex guide dogs) No coaches Last d 9.30pm Closed 2 wks Xmas, New Year & 2wks Jan **CARDS:** 💳 ■ ✕ ⚍ 🏧 ✈ ⚍

≣ **BATTLE** East Sussex   **Map 05 TQ71**
★★★⚜ **Powder Mills**
Powdermill Ln TN33 0SP
Quality Percentage Score: 70%
☎ 01424 775511 ▤ 01424 774540
Dir: through town in direction of Hasting, past abbey on A2100, 1st turning on right and hotel on right after a mile
An 18th-century wisteria-clad mansion set in 150 acres of grounds with lakes and woodland. Perhaps the best-furnished rooms are in The Mill, others are in a separate building.

Extensive day rooms are filled with antiques and provide a relaxing setting for drinks and refreshment.
ROOMS: 25 en suite (bth/shr) 10 annexe en suite (bth/shr) s £70-£95; d £85-£150 (incl. bkfst) * LB Off peak **MEALS:** Lunch £14.95 High tea £5.75-£9.50 Dinner £22.50-£25.50alc V meals Coffee am Tea pm **FACILITIES:** CTV in all bedrooms STV Outdoor swimming pool Fishing Xmas **CONF:** Thtr 250 Class 50 Board 16 Del from £115 * **SERVICES:** 101P **NOTES:** No smoking area in restaurant Last d 9pm **CARDS:** 💳 ■ ✕ 🏧 ▦ ✈ ⚍

See advert on opposite page

≣ **BATTLE** East Sussex   **Map 05 TQ71**
★★ *Burnt Wood House*
Powdermill Ln TN33 0SU
Quality Percentage Score: 70%

THE CIRCLE
Selected Individual Hotels

☎ 01424 775151 ▤ 01424 775151
Dir: turn off A2100 onto road signed Catsfield (B2095) hotel 1.5m on left side of road
Surrounded by its own extensive grounds, this substantial Edwardian house is run in a relaxed and informal style. Bedrooms vary in size but all are well equipped and decorated in soft pastel shades. Public areas include a comfortable lounge and separate bar.
ROOMS: 10 en suite (bth/shr) (2 fmly) No smoking in 3 bedrooms **MEALS:** English & French Cuisine V meals Coffee am Tea pm **FACILITIES:** CTV in all bedrooms Outdoor swimming pool (heated) Tennis (hard) Croquet lawn **SERVICES:** 30P **NOTES:** No coaches No smoking in restaurant Last d 9pm **CARDS:** 💳 ■ ✕ 🏧 ▦ ✈ ⚍

≣ **BAWTRY** South Yorkshire   **Map 08 SK69**
★★★ **The Crown**
High St DN10 6JW
Quality Percentage Score: 61%

REGAL

☎ 01302 710341 ▤ 01302 711798
Dir: North/South A1 at S end of A1(M) S of Doncaster take A614 to Bawtry

Situated in the centre of the town, this 17th-century coaching inn retains much of its original character and charm. The public areas consist of an oak panelled bar and cosy restaurant, and there is ample car parking to the rear. Well equipped bedrooms come in variety of styles and sizes, some have recently been refurbished to the new 'Corus' brand standard.
ROOMS: 57 en suite (bth/shr) No smoking in 18 bedrooms s £60; d £75 * LB Off peak **MEALS:** V meals Coffee am Tea pm **FACILITIES:** CTV in all bedrooms **CONF:** Thtr 150 Class 80 Board 60 Del £95 * **SERVICES:** Night porter 50P **NOTES:** No smoking in restaurant **CARDS:** 💳 ■ ✕ 🏧 ▦ ✈ ⚍

BEACONSFIELD Buckinghamshire — Map 04 SU99

★★★★ Bellhouse

Oxford Rd HP9 2XE

DE VERE HOTELS

Quality Percentage Score: 67%

☎ 01753 887211 Fax 01753 888231

Dir: *leave M40 at junct 2, exit signed Gerrards Cross/Beaconsfield. At rdbt take A40 to Gerrards Cross. Hotel is 1m on right hand side*

This smart Mediterranean-style hotel is close to a number of major motorway exits, making it convenient for both central London, the M40 and Heathrow. The compact bedrooms have been refurbished and are well equipped. There is a choice of eating options, either in the casual brasserie, or in the more formal restaurant. Facilities include popular conference and meeting rooms and a leisure club.

ROOMS: 136 en suite (bth/shr) (11 fmly) No smoking in 86 bedrooms s £139-£164; d £159-£184 (incl. bkfst) * LB Off peak **MEALS:** Lunch £15-£17 Dinner £21.50-£27.50 & alc English & Continental Cuisine V meals Coffee am Tea pm **FACILITIES:** CTV in all bedrooms STV Indoor swimming pool (heated) Squash Snooker Sauna Solarium Gym Jacuzzi/spa Beauty therapy room Xmas **CONF:** Thtr 450 Class 220 Board 40 Del from £160 * **SERVICES:** Lift Night porter 405P **NOTES:** No smoking in restaurant Last d 9.45pm **CARDS:**

The AA's professional hotel and restaurant inspectors make regular and anonymous visits to all the hotels listed in the guide. They do not accept gifts or favours from hoteliers.

B

BEAMINSTER Dorset Map 03 ST40

★★★ Bridge House

3 Prout Bridge DT8 3AY

Quality Percentage Score: 71%

☎ 01308 862200 01308 863700

Dir: *off A3066, 100yds from Town Square*

This 13th-century property, with its attractive walled garden, lies in the heart of Beaminster. Bedrooms are tastefully decorated and offer modern comforts. The public rooms feature log fires and beamed ceilings. An imaginative menu is served in the Georgian dining room.

ROOMS: 9 en suite (bth/shr) 4 annexe en suite (bth/shr) s £61-£80; d £88-£112 (incl. bkfst) * LB Off peak **MEALS:** Lunch £8.75-£12 & alc Dinner £21.50-£25.50 International Cuisine V meals Coffee am Tea pm **FACILITIES:** CTV in all bedrooms Tennis (hard) Xmas **CONF:** Thtr 20 Class 16 Board 16 **SERVICES:** 22P **NOTES:** No coaches No smoking in restaurant Last d 9pm Closed 28 Dec-3 Jan

CARDS:

BEAMISH Co Durham Map 12 NZ25

★★★ Beamish Park

Beamish Burn Rd NE16 5EG

Quality Percentage Score: 66%

☎ 01207 230666 01207 281260

Dir: *from A1(M) take A692 towards Consett, then A6076 towards Stanley. Hotel on left behind Causey Arch Inn*

This modern hotel lies within easy reach of the main north-east commercial and heritage centres. Bedrooms come in a variety of styles with comfortable ground floor rooms offering direct access to the car park. Public areas include a spacious lounge bar, and an outside pub. The restaurant is located in a bright conservatory and offers imaginative cuisine with pleasing modern presentation.

ROOMS: 47 en suite (bth/shr) (7 fmly) No smoking in 20 bedrooms s £43-£53; d £57-£65 * LB Off peak **MEALS:** Lunch £12.65-£21.65alc Dinner £18.75-£30.25alc English & French Cuisine V meals Coffee am Tea pm **FACILITIES:** CTV in all bedrooms STV Golf 9 Putting green 20 bay floodlit golf driving range Golf tuition by PGA professional **CONF:** Thtr 30 Class 10 Board 25 Del from £73.50 * **SERVICES:** Night porter 100P **NOTES:** No smoking area in restaurant Last d 9.45pm

CARDS:

BEAULIEU Hampshire Map 04 SU30

★★★ Master Builders House Hotel

Bucklers Hard SO42 7XB

Best Western

Quality Percentage Score: 76%

☎ 01590 616253 01590 616297

Dir: *turn off M27, junct2, follow signs Beaulieu, at T junct left onto B3056 1st left to Bucklers Hard, hotel in 2m on left just before village entrance*

This 18th-century house beside the marina at Bucklers Hard, is now under the same management as the George Hotel at Yarmouth on the Isle of Wight and a boat operates between the two hotels. This was once the home of a master ship builder, as the name suggests, and has kept a nautical theme for its public areas. Many rooms have riverside views and all offer a high standard of comfort. Enjoyable meals are served in the Riverview Restaurant and the Yachtsman's Bar.

ROOMS: 8 en suite (bth/shr) 17 annexe en suite (bth/shr) (2 fmly) No smoking in 12 bedrooms s £90-£145; d £120-£185 (incl. bkfst) * LB Off peak **MEALS:** Lunch £16.95 & alc Dinner £22.50 & alc English & French Cuisine V meals Coffee am Tea pm **FACILITIES:** CTV in all bedrooms STV Fishing Xmas **CONF:** Thtr 50 Class 50 Board 25 Del from £125 * **SERVICES:** Night porter 70P **NOTES:** No coaches Last d 9.45pm

CARDS:

BEAULIEU Hampshire Map 04 SU30

★★★ Montagu Arms

Palace Ln SO42 7ZL

Quality Percentage Score: 70%

☎ 01590 612324 01590 612188

Dir: *leave M27 at junct 2, turn left at rdbt, then follow tourist signs for Beaulieu, continue to Dibden Purlieu, then right at rdbt, hotel is on left*

This attractive, creeper-clad hotel stands in the centre of picturesque Beaulieu. Bedrooms are tastefully decorated and thoughtfully equipped. Public rooms include a cosy bar, elegant lounge and adjoining conservatory which overlooks the pretty walled garden. Guests can choose to dine in either the restaurant or the more informal Monty's.

ROOMS: 24 en suite (bth/shr) s £90-£130; d £125-£205 (incl. bkfst) * LB Off peak **MEALS:** Lunch £14.50-£16.50 High tea £3.50-£6 Dinner £25.90 & alc V meals Coffee am Tea pm **FACILITIES:** CTV in all bedrooms Pool table Use of health club facilities in Brockenhurst Xmas **CONF:** Thtr 50 Class 30 Board 30 Del from £120 * **SERVICES:** Night porter 86P **NOTES:** No smoking in restaurant Last d 9.30pm

CARDS:

See advert on opposite page

BEAULIEU Hampshire Map 04 SU30

★★★ Beaulieu

Beaulieu Rd SO42 7YQ

Quality Percentage Score: 61%

☎ 023 80293344 023 80292729

Dir: *M27 junct 1 follow signs onto A337 towards Lyndhurst. Left at traffic lights in Lyndhurst through village turn right onto B3056 & continue for 3m*

Situated in the heart of the New Forest between Lyndhurst and Beaulieu, this popular small hotel provides an ideal base for exploring the surrounding area. Bedrooms are neatly furnished and equipped with modern amenities throughout. Facilities include an indoor swimming pool and steam room, an outdoor children's play area and an adjoining pub. A daily changing menu is offered in the restaurant which has lovely Forest views.

ROOMS: 15 en suite (bth/shr) 3 annexe en suite (bth/shr) (2 fmly) s fr £70; d fr £125 (incl. bkfst) * LB Off peak **MEALS:** Sunday Lunch fr £10.95 Dinner £21.50 V meals Coffee am Tea pm **FACILITIES:** CTV in all bedrooms Indoor swimming pool (heated) Steam room Xmas **CONF:** Thtr 60 Class 40 Board 30 Del from £90 * **SERVICES:** 60P **NOTES:** Last d 8.45pm **CARDS:**

BEBINGTON Merseyside Map 07 SJ38

Travelodge

New Chester Rd L62 9AQ

Travelodge

☎ 0151 327 2489 0151 327 2489

Dir: *on A41, northbound off, junct 5 on M63*

This modern building offers accommodation in smart, spacious and well equipped bedrooms, all with en-suite bathrooms. Refreshments may be taken at the nearby family restaurant. For details about current

contd.

prices, consult the Contents Page under Hotel Groups for the Travelodge phone number.
ROOMS: 31 en suite (bth/shr) d £39.95-£45.95 *

BECKINGTON Somerset — Map 03 ST85
★★ Woolpack Inn

BA3 6SP
Quality Percentage Score: 73%
☎ 01373 831244 Fax 01373 831223
Dir: *on A36*

This charming coaching inn dates back to the 16th century and retains many original features - flagstone floors, open fireplaces and exposed beams. There is a cosy residents' lounge and a choice of places to eat: the bar for lighter snacks, and for more substantial meals, the Oak Room, or Garden Room which leads onto an inner courtyard.
ROOMS: 12 en suite (bth/shr) No smoking in 1 bedroom
MEALS: English & French Cuisine V meals Coffee am Tea pm
FACILITIES: CTV in all bedrooms STV **CONF:** Thtr 30 Class 20 Board 20
SERVICES: 16P **NOTES:** No coaches No children 5yrs No smoking area in restaurant **CARDS:**

BECKINGTON Somerset — Map 03 ST85
Travelodge

BA3 6SF
☎ 01373 830251 Fax 01373 830251
Dir: *A36*

This modern building offers accommodation in smart, spacious and well equipped bedrooms, all with en-suite bathrooms. Refreshments may be taken at the nearby family restaurant. For details about current prices, consult the Contents Page under Hotel Groups for the Travelodge phone number.
ROOMS: 40 en suite (bth/shr) d £49.95 *

BEDFORD Bedfordshire — Map 04 TL04
★★★ Woodlands Manor

Green Ln, Clapham MK41 6EP
Quality Percentage Score: 74%
☎ 01234 363281 Fax 01234 272390
Dir: *A6 from Bedford, towards Kettering. Clapham is 1st village N of town centre, on entering village first right into Green Lane, Manor 200mtrs on right*

Set in wooded gardens and grounds on the outskirts of the village, the character of the building is echoed in the choice of furnishings and decor. The drawing room, with its rich colour scheme, wood panelled walls and large sofas, is very comfortable, and the elegant restaurant offers imaginative cooking. Bedrooms are pleasantly appointed, with cherry wood furniture and co-ordinated colour schemes.
ROOMS: 30 en suite (bth/shr) 3 annexe en suite (bth/shr) (4 fmly) No smoking in 6 bedrooms s £72.50-£95; d £87.50-£150 (incl. bkfst) * LB Off peak **MEALS:** Lunch £9.95-£14.95 Dinner £19.95-£28.75 English & French Cuisine V meals Coffee am Tea pm **FACILITIES:** CTV in all bedrooms STV Xmas **CONF:** Thtr 80 Class 28 Board 40 Del £135 * **SERVICES:** Night porter 100P **NOTES:** No dogs (ex guide dogs) No smoking in restaurant Last d 9.45pm **CARDS:**

BEDFORD Bedfordshire — Map 04 TL04
★★★ The Barns

Cardington Rd MK44 3SA
Quality Percentage Score: 72%
☎ 01234 270044 Fax 01234 273102
Dir: *take A421 from M1 and turn off at A603 Sandy, turn left to Bedford on A603*

With the Great Ouse flowing behind and a delightful medieval tithe barn, this 17th-century manor house has many original features and a relaxing atmosphere, though it has been sympathetically extended over the centuries. Modern, well equipped bedrooms are found in the more recent extensions and are all of good size and smartly decorated. The riverside public areas include a country pub, a cocktail bar and the Anglers restaurant.

ROOMS: 48 en suite (bth/shr) No smoking in 16 bedrooms s £75-£85; d £85-£95 * LB Off peak **MEALS:** Lunch £4.95-£18alc Dinner £6.95-£18alc International Cuisine V meals Coffee am Tea pm
FACILITIES: CTV in all bedrooms STV Free use of local leisure centre (1mile) Xmas **CONF:** Thtr 120 Class 40 Board 40 Del from £125 *
SERVICES: Night porter 90P **NOTES:** No smoking in restaurant Last d 9.45pm **CARDS:**

For Useful Information and Important Telephone Number Changes turn to page 25

B

BEDFORD Bedfordshire
Map 04 TL04
★★★ *Bedford Moat House*
2 Saint Mary's St MK42 0AR
Quality Percentage Score: 67%
☎ 01234 799988 ▤ 01234 340447

MOAT HOUSE

Dir: from junct 13 on M1 follow signs for town centre hotel is on right just before bridge crossing river Great Ouse
A few minutes' walk from the town centre, this business hotel stands on the south bank of the Great Ouse. The exterior may look plain, but within all is colour and comfort, and public rooms look out on the river. Bedrooms are well equipped and the hotel has very good conference facilities.
ROOMS: 110 en suite (bth/shr) No smoking in 70 bedrooms
MEALS: English & Continental Cuisine V meals Coffee am Tea pm
FACILITIES: CTV in all bedrooms Sauna Solarium Gym **CONF:** Thtr 400 Class 200 Board 50 **SERVICES:** Lift Night porter 120P **NOTES:** No smoking in restaurant Last d 10pm RS Bank hols
CARDS: ● ▬ ▆ ▒ ▧

BEDFORD Bedfordshire
Map 04 TL04
★★❀ Knife & Cleaver
The Grove, Houghton Conquest MK45 3LA
Quality Percentage Score: 67%
☎ 01234 740387 ▤ 01234 740900
Dir: turn off A6 onto unclass road signposted Houghton Conquest, hotel in village on left opposite the church
A few miles south of the town, in a pleasant village setting, this relaxing restaurant-with-rooms consists of an inn-style bar and an elegant conservatory restaurant to the rear. It has a good local following for its freshly produced menu, which specialises in fish dishes, and has won awards for its wine lists. Comfortable bedrooms vary in style, and are located in a separate, purpose-built wing; the three stable rooms are well worth requesting.
ROOMS: 9 annexe en suite (bth/shr) (1 fmly) s £49-£59; d £64-£74 (incl. bkfst) * LB Off peak **MEALS:** Lunch £11.95-£13.95 & alc Dinner fr £20 & alc V meals Coffee am **FACILITIES:** CTV in all bedrooms STV
CONF: Class 30 Board 20 Del from £69 * **SERVICES:** 30P **NOTES:** No coaches No smoking in restaurant Last d 9.30pm Closed 27-30 Dec
CARDS: ● ▬ ▆ ▒ ▨ ▧

BEDFORD Bedfordshire
Map 04 TL04
⌂ Travel Inn
Priory Country Park, Barkers Ln MK41 9DJ
☎ 01234 352883 ▤ 01234 325697
Dir: from junct 13 of M1 follow A421 along bypass to end, turn left onto A428 towards Bedford and follow signs for Priory Country Park
This modern building offers accommodation in smart, spacious and well equipped bedrooms, all with en-suite bathrooms. Refreshments may be taken at the nearby family restaurant. For details about current prices consult the Contents Page under Hotel Groups for the Travel Inn phone number.
ROOMS: 32 en suite (bth/shr) d £39.95 *

BELFORD Northumberland
Map 12 NU13
★★★ Blue Bell
Market Place NE70 7NE
Quality Percentage Score: 68%
☎ 01668 213543 ▤ 01668 213787
Dir: centre of village on left of St Mary's church
This long-established creeper-clad former coaching inn is found in the centre of the village just off the A1. It has a friendly atmosphere and retains much of its original character. Bedrooms are all individual and enhanced by stylish en suite bathrooms. A

variety of menus provide an extensive choice of food in the bar, bistro and main restaurant.
ROOMS: 17 en suite (bth/shr) (1 fmly) No smoking in 4 bedrooms
MEALS: Lunch £10.95-£11.95 High tea £6-£8 Dinner £21-£22 English & French Cuisine V meals Coffee am Tea pm **FACILITIES:** CTV in all bedrooms Pool table **CONF:** Thtr 140 Class 120 Board 30 Del from £68 * **SERVICES:** 17P **NOTES:** No smoking in restaurant Last d 9pm
CARDS: ● ▬ ▆ ▧

BELFORD Northumberland
Map 12 NU13
⌂ Purdy Lodge
Adderstone Services NE70 7JU
☎ 01668 213000 ▤ 01668 213111
Dir: between Alnwick & Berwick turn off A1 to B1341
Part of a roadside complex, this conveniently situated lodge provides practical accommodation with several family rooms. All the bedrooms look out over fields to the rear of the lodge and are insulated from road noise. Public areas include a 24-hour café, lounge bar and restaurant open for dinners.
ROOMS: 20 en suite (bth/shr) d £41.50 *

BELLINGHAM Northumberland
Map 12 NY88
★★❀ Riverdale Hall
NE48 2JT
Quality Percentage Score: 67%
☎ 01434 220254 ▤ 01434 220457
Dir: turn off B6320, after bridge, hotel on left

Standing in grounds overlooking its own cricket pitch and the North Tyne river, this hotel - in the Cocker family for over twenty years - attracts a mixed clientele including families, who appreciate its indoor and outdoor amenities. In the restaurant, menus feature freshly cooked dishes including seafood and vegetarian specialities, all complemented by an interesting wine list. Bedrooms are all well equipped and come in a variety of sizes, the larger ones with their own balconies being particularly favoured.
ROOMS: 20 en suite (bth/shr) (11 fmly) s £40-£48; d £69-£84 (incl. bkfst) * LB Off peak **MEALS:** Lunch £8.95-£9.95 & alc Dinner £19.50 & alc English & Danish Cuisine V meals Coffee am Tea pm **FACILITIES:** CTV in all bedrooms Indoor swimming pool (heated) Fishing Sauna Croquet lawn Putting green Cricket field Petanque ch fac Xmas **CONF:** Thtr 40 Class 40 Board 20 Del from £69 * **SERVICES:** 60P **NOTES:** No smoking area in restaurant Last d 9.30pm **CARDS:** ● ▬ ▆ ▨ ▧

BELPER Derbyshire
Map 08 SK34
★★★❀ Makeney Hall Country House
Makeney, Milford DE56 0RS
Quality Percentage Score: 70%
☎ 01332 842999 ▤ 01332 842777

cOrus
Corus and Regal hotels

Dir: turn off A6 between Belper and Duffield at Milford, signposted Makeney. Hotel is 0.25m further along on left
A beautifully restored Victorian mansion, standing in 6 acres of

contd.

delightful gardens and grounds above the River Derwent. Bedrooms vary in style and size; the main house rooms offer more comfort and quality, whilst the nine ground floor courtyard rooms are more contemporary in style with light oak furniture; two bedrooms have been specifically designed for disabled access. Well appointed public rooms include Lavinia's restaurant, an oak-panelled room with large windows that overlook the garden; here diners are offered a range of unusual and interesting dishes from a choice of menus.

ROOMS: 27 en suite (bth/shr) 18 annexe en suite (bth/shr) No smoking in 6 bedrooms s £85; d £95 * LB Off peak **MEALS:** Lunch £13.50 Dinner £18.50 & alc V meals Coffee am Tea pm **FACILITIES:** CTV in all bedrooms STV Xmas **CONF:** Thtr 180 Class 80 Board 50 Del £130 * **SERVICES:** Lift Night porter 150P **NOTES:** No smoking in restaurant Last d 9.45pm **CARDS:**

BELPER Derbyshire — Map 08 SK34
★★ Lion
Bridge St DE56 1AX

MENZIES HOTELS

Quality Percentage Score: 68%

☎ 0500 636943 (Central Res) 📠 01773 880321

Dir: *on A6*

Situated on the border of the Peak District, yet close to the M1, this 18th century hotel is superbly located for exploring local attractions. Bedrooms are all tastefully decorated and well equipped. In addition to two cosy bars the hotel has a function room.

ROOMS: 20 rms (14 bth/shr) (1 fmly) No smoking in 6 bedrooms s £62.50-£72.50; d fr £72.50 * LB Off peak **MEALS:** Lunch fr £7.95 Dinner fr £16.50 English & Continental Cuisine V meals Coffee am Tea pm **FACILITIES:** CTV in all bedrooms Xmas **CONF:** Thtr 130 Class 60 Board 50 Del from £75 * **SERVICES:** Night porter 25P **NOTES:** No smoking in restaurant Last d 9.30pm

CARDS:

BELTON Lincolnshire — Map 08 SK93
★★★★ Belton Woods
NG32 2LN

DE VERE HOTELS

Quality Percentage Score: 73%

☎ 01476 593200 📠 01476 574547

Dir: *2m N of Grantham on A607*

A destination venue for golf and sports lovers as well as a relaxing executive retreat for seminars, Belton Woods has the benefit of both easy access to major routes such as the A1 and A52, and an idyllic parkland location in 475 acres of rolling countryside, to the north of Grantham.. This stylish and striking hotel complex is a major leisure and golf resort, combined with extensive meeting suites and attractive public areas, including a choice of restaurants and bars. The smartly appointed bedrooms, many of which overlook the golf courses, are both spacious and well equipped. A good range of carefully prepared dishes is available in the Manor restaurant, where staff are welcoming and service is pleasantly attentive.

ROOMS: 136 en suite (bth/shr) No smoking in 48 bedrooms s fr £120; d fr £130 (incl. bkfst) * LB Off peak **MEALS:** Lunch fr £12.50 & alc High tea £6.95 Dinner £18.50-£24.95 & alc English & French Cuisine V meals Coffee am Tea pm **FACILITIES:** CTV in all bedrooms STV Indoor swimming pool (heated) Golf 45 Tennis (hard) Squash Snooker Sauna Solarium Gym Croquet lawn Putting green Jacuzzi/spa Hair & beauty salon Steamroom Xmas **CONF:** Thtr 275 Class 130 Board 80 **SERVICES:** Lift Night porter 500P **NOTES:** No dogs (ex guide dogs) No smoking area in restaurant Last d 9.45pm

CARDS:

BERKELEY Gloucestershire — Map 03 ST69
★★ The Old Schoolhouse
Canonbury St GL13 9BG

Quality Percentage Score: 72%

☎ 01453 811711 📠 01453 511761

Dir: *1.5m off A38 next to Berkeley Castle*

As the name suggests, this fine old building was formerly a school. Bedrooms are all of a generous size, with modern facilities, and the good standard of cooking in the attractive restaurant might surprise former pupils. There is no bar as such, but drinks are served in both lounge and dining room.

ROOMS: 8 en suite (bth/shr) (1 fmly) No smoking in 4 bedrooms s £50-£60; d £60-£70 (incl. bkfst) * LB Off peak **MEALS:** Dinner £17.50-£23.50alc International Cuisine V meals Coffee am Tea pm **FACILITIES:** CTV in all bedrooms **SERVICES:** 20P **NOTES:** No dogs (ex guide dogs) No coaches No smoking in restaurant Last d 9pm

CARDS:

BERKELEY ROAD Gloucestershire — Map 03 ST79
★★★ Prince of Wales
Berkeley Rd GL13 9HD

Quality Percentage Score: 66%

☎ 01453 810474 📠 01453 511370

Dir: *on A38, 6m S of M5 junc 13 and 6m N of junc 14*

A comfortable hotel with modern amenities, attractively furnished, bright modern bedrooms and an informal bar and a restaurant serving food with an Italian influence.

ROOMS: 43 en suite (bth/shr) (2 fmly) No smoking in 10 bedrooms s £50-£55; d £60-£65 * LB Off peak **MEALS:** Lunch £9.40-£25.80alc Dinner £9.40-£25.80alc English & Italian Cuisine V meals Coffee am Tea pm **FACILITIES:** CTV in all bedrooms STV Pool table **CONF:** Thtr 200 Class 60 Board 60 **SERVICES:** Night porter 150P **NOTES:** No smoking area in restaurant Last d 9.30pm **CARDS:**

B

BERWICK-UPON-TWEED Northumberland **Map 12 NT95**

★★★ Marshall Meadows Country House

TD15 1UT

Quality Percentage Score: 71%

☎ 01289 331133 Fax 01289 331438

Dir: *signposted directly off A1, 200 yds from Scottish Border*

This stylish Georgian mansion set in wooded grounds flanked by farmland, is a popular venue for weddings and conferences. Bedrooms are comfortable and well equipped. Public rooms include a cosy bar, inviting lounge and a two-tier restaurant serving imaginative dishes.

ROOMS: 19 en suite (bth/shr) (2 fmly) No smoking in 4 bedrooms s £70-£75; d £85-£100 (incl. bkfst) * LB Off peak **MEALS:** Lunch £7.90-£8.90 High tea £6.95-£7.95 Dinner £18-£22 International Cuisine V meals Coffee am Tea pm **FACILITIES:** CTV in all bedrooms Tennis (hard) Croquet lawn Petanque piste Xmas **CONF:** Thtr 120 Class 180 Board 60 Del from £85 * **SERVICES:** 87P **NOTES:** No smoking in restaurant Last d 9.30pm **CARDS:**

See advert on opposite page

BERWICK-UPON-TWEED Northumberland **Map 12 NT95**

★ Queens Head

Sandgate TD15 1EP

Quality Percentage Score: 60%

☎ 01289 307852 Fax 01289 307852

Dir: *in town centre adjacent to town walls*

Set in the centre, close to the old walls of this garrison town, this commercial hotel provides decent sized bedrooms and good value meals served either in the lounge area or dining room.

ROOMS: 6 en suite (bth/shr) (5 fmly) s £30-£35; d £50-£55 (incl. bkfst) * LB Off peak **MEALS:** Lunch £7.95-£10 & alc High tea £7.25 Dinner £10.50 V meals Coffee am **FACILITIES:** CTV in all bedrooms **NOTES:** No smoking area in restaurant Last d 9pm **CARDS:**

BEVERLEY East Riding of Yorkshire **Map 08 TA03**

★★★ Tickton Grange

Tickton HU17 9SH

Quality Percentage Score: 68%

☎ 01964 543666 Fax 01964 542556

Dir: *3m NE on A1035*

Set in four acres, this is a charming Georgian house that retains much charm and character. The well equipped bedrooms are individually decorated. Public rooms include a comfortable lounge bar, and are smartly presented. Skilfully prepared dinners are served in the refurbished restaurant.

ROOMS: 18 en suite (bth/shr) (2 fmly) s fr £60; d fr £75 * LB Off peak **MEALS:** Lunch £13.95-£15.95alc Dinner £25-£35alc V meals Coffee am Tea pm **FACILITIES:** CTV in all bedrooms STV Croquet lawn Putting green **CONF:** Thtr 80 Class 60 Board 35 Del from £91 * **SERVICES:** 65P **NOTES:** No coaches No smoking in restaurant Last d 9.30pm RS 25-29 Dec **CARDS:**

BEVERLEY East Riding of Yorkshire **Map 08 TA03**

★★★ Beverley Arms

REGAL

North Bar Within HU17 8DD

Quality Percentage Score: 67%

☎ 01482 869241 Fax 01482 870907

Dir: *opposite St Marys Church, just before North Bar*

History relates this hotel with the highwayman Dick Turpin. Today a feature of the hotel is the stone flagged and spacious Shires Lounge in which guests can relax, there are also two bars and an attractively appointed restaurant which looks out on to a patio at the rear. Bedrooms in the older part of the building have more character than those in the newer section, but all have every modern facility. Service is friendly and helpful from a dedicated team.

ROOMS: 56 en suite (bth/shr) (4 fmly) No smoking in 30 bedrooms s fr £46; d fr £92 (incl. bkfst) * LB Off peak **MEALS:** Lunch fr £10.50 Dinner fr £18.95 V meals Coffee am Tea pm **FACILITIES:** CTV in all bedrooms Xmas **CONF:** Thtr 60 Class 40 Board 30 Del £95 * **SERVICES:** Lift Night porter 70P **NOTES:** No smoking in restaurant Last d 9.30pm **CARDS:**

BEVERLEY East Riding of Yorkshire **Map 08 TA03**

★★ *The Manor House*

Northlands, Walkington HU17 8RT

Quality Percentage Score: 71%

☎ 01482 881645 Fax 01482 866501

Dir: *4m SW off B1230. Follow brown 'Walkington' signs from junct 38 on M62*

This delightful country house hotel is set in its own well tended gardens. The spacious bedrooms have been thoughtfully equipped and the public rooms include a conservatory restaurant together with an inviting lounge. A good range of dishes is available from two menus, which emphasise local produce.

ROOMS: 6 en suite (bth/shr) 1 annexe en suite (bth/shr) (1 fmly) **MEALS:** V meals **FACILITIES:** CTV in all bedrooms **CONF:** Thtr 20 **SERVICES:** 40P **NOTES:** No coaches Last d 9.15pm **CARDS:**

BEWDLEY Worcestershire **Map 07 SO77**

★★ The George

Load St DY12 2AW

Quality Percentage Score: 61%

☎ 01299 402117 Fax 01299 401269

Dir: *in town centre opposite town hall*

Conveniently situated in the town centre close to the River Severn this 16th-century inn continues to appeal both to the leisure and business guest. Public rooms have original oak panelling, huge oak beams and magnificent fire places. There is a restaurant and two bars, one of which doubles as a coffee shop during the day. During the evening, the talented chef offers a creative range of classical and modern dishes including steaks and vegetarian options. Bedrooms vary in size but all are comfortable, having benefited from recent refurbishment. Family accommodation and a room with a four-poster bed are also available.

ROOMS: 11 en suite (bth/shr) s £42-£45; d £59-£75 (incl. bkfst) * LB Off peak **MEALS:** Lunch £9.95-£12.50 Dinner £18.40-£28.15alc English & French Cuisine V meals Coffee am Tea pm **FACILITIES:** CTV in all bedrooms **CONF:** Thtr 50 Class 50 Board 40 Del from £61 * **SERVICES:** 50P **NOTES:** No dogs (ex guide dogs) No smoking in restaurant Last d 9.30pm **CARDS:**

BEXLEY Greater London **Map 05 TQ47**

★★★★ **Swallow**

1 Broadway DA6 7JZ

Quality Percentage Score: 69%

☎ 020 8298 1000 📠 020 8298 1234

Dir: *take A2 (London Bound) from junct 2 of M25 exit Black Prince interchange onto A220, follow signs Bexleyheath, 3rd rdbt turn left into*

This very modern, purpose-built hotel is located on the fringes of the town centre, and is linked to a covered municipal car park. The bedrooms are smart, comfortable and well laid out with useful added facilities. There is a choice of two restaurants as

contd.

★

The Premier Collection, hotels with Red Star Awards are listed on pages 17-23

well as full room service. The young team of staff make good efforts at creating a warm and welcoming atmosphere.
ROOMS: 142 en suite (bth/shr) (16 fmly) No smoking in 53 bedrooms s £110-£165; d £135-£165 (incl. bkfst) * LB Off peak **MEALS:** Lunch £14-£18.50 & alc Dinner £10.50-£26 & alc British & European Cuisine V meals Coffee am Tea pm **FACILITIES:** CTV in all bedrooms STV Indoor swimming pool (heated) Solarium Gym Jacuzzi/spa Steam room Xmas **CONF:** Thtr 250 Class 120 Board 40 Del from £114 * **SERVICES:** Lift Night porter Air conditioning 100P
NOTES: Last d 10.30pm **CARDS:**

BEXLEY Greater London — **Map 05 TQ47**
★★★ Posthouse Bexley
Black Prince Interchange, Southwold Rd DA5 1ND
Posthouse
Quality Percentage Score: 65%
☎ 01322 526900 📠 01322 526113
Dir: *follow A2 to exit signposted A220/A223 Black Prince interchange Bexley, Bexleyheath & Crayford*
A purpose built hotel with well equipped bedrooms, all upgraded and smartly appointed in a modern style. Public areas include a choice of bars and the Junction restaurant offering a range of popular dishes. The hotel offers meeting rooms and a business centre.
ROOMS: 105 en suite (bth/shr) (10 fmly) No smoking in 50 bedrooms d £99-£139 * LB Off peak **MEALS:** International Cuisine V meals Coffee am Tea pm **FACILITIES:** CTV in all bedrooms ch fac Xmas **CONF:** Thtr 70 Class 30 Board 30 **SERVICES:** Lift Night porter 200P **NOTES:** No smoking area in restaurant Last d 10.30pm
CARDS:

BIBURY Gloucestershire — **Map 04 SP10**
★★★ *Swan*
GL7 5NW
Quality Percentage Score: 80%
☎ 01285 740695 📠 01285 740473
Dir: *off B4425, by bridge over the River Coln*
Fronted by riverside gardens, this delightful 17th-century inn provides individually styled bedrooms, furnished with quality period pieces. The public rooms include a charming bar, a choice of lounges and two restaurants.
ROOMS: 18 en suite (bth/shr) (1 fmly) **MEALS:** European Cuisine V meals Coffee am Tea pm **FACILITIES:** CTV in all bedrooms Fishing **CONF:** Thtr 85 Class 60 Board 10 Del from £175 * **SERVICES:** Lift 16P **NOTES:** No dogs (ex guide dogs) No coaches No smoking in restaurant Last d 9.45pm **CARDS:**

See advert on opposite page

BIBURY Gloucestershire — **Map 04 SP10**
★★★ Bibury Court
GL7 5NT
Quality Percentage Score: 71%
☎ 01285 740337 & 740324 📠 01285 740660
Dir: *on B4425 beside the River Coln, behind St Marys Church*
Standing in extensive grounds beside the River Colne, this elegant manor house dates back to Tudor times. Spacious public areas have a wealth of charm and character, the bedrooms are furnished in keeping with the style of the building and enjoyable food is served in the restaurant.
ROOMS: 19 en suite (bth/shr) (2 fmly) s £68-£78; d £95-£140 (incl. cont bkfst) * LB Off peak **MEALS:** Sunday Lunch £15.50-£22.15 Dinner £25 English, French & Spanish Cuisine V meals Coffee am Tea pm **FACILITIES:** CTV in all bedrooms Fishing Pool table Croquet lawn **CONF:** Thtr 20 Board 12 Del £150 * **SERVICES:** 100P **NOTES:** No smoking in restaurant Last d 9pm Closed 21 Dec-1 Jan
CARDS:

See advert on opposite page

BICESTER Oxfordshire — **Map 04 SP52**
★★ Bignell Park Hotel & Restaurant
Chesterton OX6 8UE
Quality Percentage Score: 73%
☎ 01869 241444 & 241192 📠 01869 241444
Dir: *on A4095 Witney road*

This thoroughly charming hotel, situated just outside Bicester, is proving popular for small wedding groups. The hotel has many features of real quality including the dramatic galleried restaurant with its artwork, fireplace and exposed beams, where chef Paul Franklin presents imaginative dishes using good local produce. The bedrooms are stylish and comfortably furnished with some unusual pieces of furniture, the newly completed rooms are particularly spacious. Danish proprietor Erling Sorensen acts as host and his friendly dog is always on hand to extend a warm welcome.
ROOMS: 14 en suite (bth/shr) **MEALS:** Lunch £13-£18 & alc Dinner £13-£18 & alc English & French Cuisine V meals Coffee am **FACILITIES:** CTV in all bedrooms **CONF:** Thtr 26 Class 16 Board 16 **SERVICES:** Night porter 40P **NOTES:** No children 6yrs Last d 9.30pm
CARDS:

BICESTER Oxfordshire — **Map 04 SP52**
Travelodge
Northampton Rd, Ardley OX6 9RD
Travelodge
☎ 01869 346060 📠 01869 345030
Dir: *M40 junct 10*
This modern building offers accommodation in smart, spacious and well equipped bedrooms, all with en-suite bathrooms. Refreshments may be taken at the nearby family restaurant. For details about current prices, consult the Contents Page under Hotel Groups for the Travelodge phone number.
ROOMS: 98 en suite (bth/shr) d £49.95 * **CONF:** Thtr 40 Class 20 Board 20

BIDEFORD Devon — **Map 02 SS42**
★★★ Royal
Barnstaple St EX39 4AE
Brend Hotels
Quality Percentage Score: 65%
☎ 01237 472005 📠 01237 478957
Dir: *at eastern end of Bideford Bridge*
Dating back to the late 16th century, this hotel situated near the quay, offers high ceilinged bedrooms that are attractively furnished and well equipped. Freshly prepared meals are a feature of the airy restaurant, bar snacks also being available. Service is both friendly and attentive. The wood panelled

contd.

Kingsley suite, with its feature plaster ceiling, is an ideal room for smaller functions or meetings.
ROOMS: 31 en suite (bth/shr) (3 fmly) s £49-£54; d £60-£70 * LB Off peak **MEALS:** Lunch £9.50 Dinner £16.50 & alc English & French Cuisine V meals Coffee am Tea pm **FACILITIES:** CTV in all bedrooms STV Wkly live entertainment Xmas **CONF:** Thtr 100 Class 100 Board 100 **SERVICES:** Lift Night porter 70P **NOTES:** Last d 9pm
CARDS:

BIDEFORD Devon — Map 02 SS42

★★ Yeoldon Country House
Durrant Ln, Northam EX39 2RL
Quality Percentage Score: 75%
☎ 01237 474400 01237 476618

THE CIRCLE *Selected Individual Hotels* GREAT BRITAIN

***Dir:** from Barnstaple follow A39 over River Torridge Bridge, at rdbt turn right onto A386 towards Northam then 3rd right into Durrant Ln*
An ivy-clad Victorian manor house in a peaceful location. Individually styled bedrooms are brightly decorated and equipped with modern facilities. Public areas include a comfortable bar-lounge and attractive dining room. The interesting menus are based on fresh, and where possible, local produce.
ROOMS: 10 en suite (bth/shr) (2 fmly) s £50-£55; d £80-£90 (incl. bkfst) * LB Off peak **MEALS:** Sunday Lunch £11.25 High tea £3-£5 Dinner £21.50 & alc English, French & Italian Cuisine V meals Coffee am Tea pm **FACILITIES:** CTV in all bedrooms **CONF:** Del from £78 * **SERVICES:** 22P **NOTES:** No coaches No smoking in restaurant Last d 8.30pm Closed 25-27 Dec **CARDS:**

BIDEFORD Devon — Map 02 SS42

★★ *Beaconside*
Landcross EX39 5JL
Quality Percentage Score: 65%
☎ 01237 477205
***Dir:** 1m SW on A388*
Genuine Devonshire hospitality is guaranteed at this friendly and relaxed hotel. Set in farmland, with an outdoor pool and well tended garden, Beaconside House has comfortable bedrooms, and public areas including a function room ideal for weddings. Dishes from the fixed-price menu are freshly prepared from local ingredients.
ROOMS: 8 rms (6 bth/shr) (2 fmly) **MEALS:** Coffee am Tea pm **FACILITIES:** CTV in all bedrooms Outdoor swimming pool Tennis (grass) Putting green Nature trail **SERVICES:** 16P **NOTES:** No dogs (ex guide dogs) No smoking in restaurant Last d 7.45pm

BIGBURY-ON-SEA Devon — Map 03 SX64

★★ Henley
TQ7 4AR
Quality Percentage Score: 67%
☎ 01548 810240 01548 810020
Overlooking Bigbury Bay, this family-run holiday hotel provides comfortable accommodation with modern facilities and friendly service. A sandy beach can be reached by a private cliff path descending through the hotel's pretty gardens. The short table d'hote menu offers dishes cooked with care and imagination.
ROOMS: 7 en suite (bth/shr) (1 fmly) No smoking in all bedrooms s £45-£47; d £70-£74 (incl. bkfst) * LB Off peak **MEALS:** Bar Lunch £5-£10 Dinner £18 European Cuisine Coffee am Tea pm **FACILITIES:** CTV in all bedrooms STV **SERVICES:** 9P **NOTES:** No coaches No smoking in restaurant Last d 8pm Closed Nov-Mar **CARDS:**

B

BIGGLESWADE Bedfordshire
Map 04 TL14

★★ Stratton House Hotel
London Rd SG18 8ED
Quality Percentage Score: 65%
☎ 01767 312442 📠 01767 600416
Dir: *Nthbound; A1 1st turning to Biggleswade, hotel before town centre. Sthbound; A1 leavat Sainsburys rdbt through town on right opposite Red Lion PH*
Ideally situated just a few minutes from the A1 this small hotel offers comfortable accommodation. Rooms are well presented and public areas include a cosy lounge with a fire and a popular bar.
ROOMS: 31 en suite (bth/shr) (1 fmly) No smoking in 6 bedrooms s fr £53; d fr £68 (incl. bkfst) * LB Off peak **MEALS:** Lunch £5.95-£9.25alc Dinner £14.50-£24.50alc V meals Coffee am Tea pm **FACILITIES:** CTV in all bedrooms **CONF:** Thtr 50 Class 30 Board 28 Del from £80 * **SERVICES:** 40P **NOTES:** No dogs (ex guide dogs) No smoking in restaurant Last d 9pm Closed 26 Dec
CARDS:

BILBROUGH North Yorkshire
Map 08 SE54

⇧ Travelodge
Tadcaster LS24 8EG
☎ 01937 531823 📠 01937 531823
Dir: *A64 eastbound*
This modern building offers accommodation in smart, spacious and well equipped bedrooms, all with en-suite bathrooms. Refreshments may be taken at the nearby family restaurant. For details about current prices, consult the Contents Page under Hotel Groups for the Travelodge phone number.
ROOMS: 62 en suite (bth/shr) d £49.95 *

BILLINGHAM See Stockton-on-Tees

BILLINGSHURST West Sussex
Map 04 TQ02

Late entry **○✣ *Newstead Hall***
Adversane RH14 9JH
☎ 01403 783196
This Tudor style hotel is conveniently located just a couple of miles south of the village. Five bedrooms in the older part of the building have an individual character, while the remainder in a modern extension, are more uniform in style. Public rooms include a bar with fire place and a popular restaurant.
ROOMS: 15 rms

BINFIELD Berkshire
Map 04 SU87

⇧ Travelodge
London Rd RG42 4AA
☎ 01344 485940
Dir: *exit junct 10 on M4(Bracknell) take 1st exit towards Binfield*
This modern building offers accommodation in smart, spacious and well equipped bedrooms, all with en-suite bathrooms. Refreshments may be taken at the nearby family restaurant. For details about current prices, consult the Contents Page under Hotel Groups for the Travelodge phone number.
ROOMS: 35 en suite (bth/shr) d £55.95 *

BINGLEY West Yorkshire
Map 07 SE13

★★ *Oakwood Hall*
Lady Ln BD16 4AW
Quality Percentage Score: 67%
☎ 01274 564123 & 563569 📠 01274 561477
Dir: *in town centre turn off A650 signposted Eldnick (Park Road). Continue 1m into Lady Lane then 2nd left and 1st right*
This Grade II listed Victorian building boasts fine wood panelling, ornate plaster work and a William Morris window on the main staircase. It is situated in pleasant, mature gardens. Bedrooms have a homely appearance. A range of dishes is offered in the restaurant.
ROOMS: 20 en suite (bth/shr) **MEALS:** English & French Cuisine V meals Coffee am Tea pm **FACILITIES:** CTV in all bedrooms **CONF:** Thtr 80 Class 50 Board 40 Del from £95 * **SERVICES:** Night porter 100P
NOTES: Last d 10pm Closed 25-31 Dec
CARDS:

See advert on opposite page

BINGLEY West Yorkshire
Map 07 SE13

⇧ Travel Inn
Off Bradford Rd
☎ 0870 242 8000
This modern building offers accommodation in smart, spacious and well equipped bedrooms, all with en-suite bathrooms. Refreshments may be taken at the nearby family restaurant. For details about current prices consult the Contents Page under Hotel Groups for the Travel Inn phone number.
ROOMS: 40 en suite (bth/shr) (incl. bkfst) d £39.95 *

BIRCH MOTORWAY SERVICE AREA (M62) Greater Manchester
Map 07 SD80

⇧ Travelodge
M62 Service Area OL10 2HQ
☎ Central Res 0800 850950 📠 01525 878450
This modern building offers accommodation in smart, spacious and well equipped bedrooms, all with en-suite bathrooms. Refreshments may be taken at the nearby family restaurant. For details about current prices, consult the Contents Page under Hotel Groups for the Travelodge phone number.
ROOMS: 55 en suite (bth/shr) d £49.95 *

BIRKENHEAD Merseyside
Map 07 SJ38

★★★ Bowler Hat
2 Talbot Rd, Prenton CH43 2HH
Quality Percentage Score: 69%
☎ 0151 652 4931 📠 0151 653 8127
Dir: *1m from junct 3 of M53*

This modern business hotel with an enclosed rear car park stands in a quiet area near Oxton village. Extensive function facilities are provided and the hotel is very popular for wedding receptions. The bedrooms are well equipped with modern facilities, those in the older wing tend to be more spacious. The restaurant attracts a good local following and offers a wide choice of dishes.
ROOMS: 32 en suite (bth/shr) No smoking in 18 bedrooms s £60-£75; d £75-£110 (incl. bkfst) * LB Off peak **MEALS:** Lunch £12.50-£24.50alc Dinner £15.50-£24.50alc European Cuisine V meals Coffee am Tea pm **FACILITIES:** CTV in all bedrooms STV Wkly live entertainment Xmas **CONF:** Thtr 150 Class 80 Board 40 Del from £80 * **SERVICES:** Night porter 85P **NOTES:** No smoking in restaurant Last d 9.45pm
CARDS:

BIRKENHEAD Merseyside **Map 07 SJ38**

★★ Riverhill

Talbot Rd, Oxton L43 2HJ

Quality Percentage Score: 65%

☎ 0151 653 3773 📠 0151 653 7162

Dir: *1m from M53 junct 3, along the A552 turn left onto B5151 at traffic lights hotel 0.5m on right*

Pretty lawns and gardens provide the setting for this hotel. Refurbished bedrooms include ground floor, family, and four-poster rooms. Business meetings and functions can be catered for; a wide choice of dishes is available in the restaurant overlooking the garden.

ROOMS: 16 en suite (bth/shr) (1 fmly) d £44.50 * LB Off peak **MEALS:** Lunch £11.95-£13.45 & alc Dinner £14.95-£16.45 & alc English, French & Italian Cuisine V meals **FACILITIES:** CTV in all bedrooms Free use of local leisure facilities **SERVICES:** Night porter 30P **NOTES:** No dogs (ex guide dogs) No coaches Last d 10pm

CARDS:

BIRMINGHAM West Midlands **Map 07 SP08**

see also **Bromsgrove, Lea Marston, Oldbury & Sutton Coldfield**

★★★★★ Swallow

12 Hagley Rd, Five Ways B16 8SJ

Quality Percentage Score: 70%

☎ 0121 452 1144 📠 0121 456 3442

A range of comfortable rooms is on offer at The Swallow, together with welcoming extra touches. A highlight of any visit is a meal in the Sir Edward Elgar Restaurant. For further choice, there is a more traditional restaurant, Langtry's. The hotel also has an enjoyable leisure complex.

ROOMS: 98 en suite (bth/shr) No smoking in 54 bedrooms s £160; d £180 (incl. bkfst) * LB Off peak **MEALS:** English & French Cuisine V meals Coffee am Tea pm **FACILITIES:** CTV in all bedrooms STV Indoor swimming pool (heated) Solarium Gym Jacuzzi/spa Hair & beauty salon Steam room Wkly live entertainment Xmas **CONF:** Thtr 25 Board 20 Del £165 * **SERVICES:** Lift Night porter Air conditioning 70P **NOTES:** No coaches Last d 10.30pm **CARDS:**

BIRMINGHAM West Midlands **Map 07 SP08**

★★★★ The Burlington

Burlington Arcade, 126 New St B2 4JQ

Quality Percentage Score: 69%

☎ 0121 643 9191 📠 0121 628 5005

Dir: *exit M6 junct 6 and follow signs for City Centre, then onto A38*

Having been a hotel for over a hundred years, the former Midland Hotel was closed for two years whilst a major refurbishment took place to re-open recently as the Burlington. Much of the original Victorian design is still in evidence blended with the modern to meet the needs of today's visitor. Bedrooms are furnished and equipped to a good standard, whilst a carefully prepared meal can be had in Berlioz Restaurant, using fresh produce and a few original combinations. There are extensive conference and banqueting facilities. The fifth floor leisure area allows an opportunity to unwind afterwards.

ROOMS: 112 en suite (bth/shr) (6 fmly) No smoking in 49 bedrooms s £135-£150; d £157-£180 LB Off peak **MEALS:** Lunch fr £16 & alc Dinner £19-£25 English & French Cuisine V meals Coffee am Tea pm **FACILITIES:** CTV in all bedrooms STV Sauna Solarium Gym Jacuzzi/spa Xmas **CONF:** Thtr 400 Class 175 Board 60 Del from £99 * **SERVICES:** Lift Night porter **NOTES:** No smoking area in restaurant Last d 10pm **CARDS:**

Indicates that the star classification has not been confirmed under the New Quality Standards, see page 7 for further information.

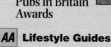

B

BIRMINGHAM West Midlands **Map 07 SP08**
★★★★ Crowne Plaza Birmingham
Central Square B1 1HH
Quality Percentage Score: 68%
☎ 0121 631 2000 🖷 0121 643 9018
Dir: *from A38M over flyover & go through 1st tunnel continue through 2nd tunnel-Queensway- then join left slip road*
Located in the city centre, this smart hotel offers spacious bedrooms with air-conditioning, and all equipped to a high stadard of modern comfort with all the expected facilities. There are numerous conference and meeting rooms, and the polished services include valet parking. There are good leisure facilities.
ROOMS: 284 en suite (bth/shr) (188 fmly) No smoking in 191 bedrooms s £109-£135; d £119-£145 * LB Off peak **MEALS:** Lunch £13.50-£19.50 Dinner £15.95-£18.95 International Cuisine V meals Coffee am Tea pm **FACILITIES:** CTV in all bedrooms STV Indoor swimming pool (heated) Sauna Solarium Gym Jacuzzi/spa Children's pool steam room, Fully equipped Gym Xmas **CONF:** Thtr 150 Class 75 Board 40 Del from £99 * **SERVICES:** Lift Night porter Air conditioning **NOTES:** No smoking area in restaurant Last d 10.30pm **CARDS:**

BIRMINGHAM West Midlands **Map 07 SP08**
★★★★ Copthorne Birmingham
Paradise Circus B3 3HJ
Quality Percentage Score: 66%
☎ 0121 200 2727 🖷 0121 200 1197
Dir: *follow signs to 'International Convention Centre, then bear right for hotel entrance*
This smart, modern hotel is located right in the heart of the city and is ideally placed for the ICC. It has spacious, well laid-out bedrooms. Public areas include useful business and leisure facilities. Guests have the choice of eating less formally in Goldie's Brasserie or Goldsmiths Restaurant where there is more emphasis on higher standards of gastronomy.
ROOMS: 212 en suite (bth/shr) No smoking in 108 bedrooms s £130-£150; d £150-£170 * LB Off peak **MEALS:** Sunday Lunch £5.95-£19.95 High tea £7.75 Dinner £18.95-£26.95alc International Cuisine V meals Coffee am Tea pm **FACILITIES:** CTV in all bedrooms STV Indoor swimming pool (heated) Sauna Gym Jacuzzi/spa **CONF:** Thtr 180 Class 120 Board 30 Del £150 * **SERVICES:** Lift Night porter 88P **NOTES:** No dogs (ex guide dogs) No smoking area in restaurant Last d 11pm **CARDS:**

BIRMINGHAM West Midlands **Map 07 SP08**
★★★ Lombard Room Restaurant & Mill House Hotel
180 Lifford Ln, Kings Norton B30 3NT
Quality Percentage Score: 77%
☎ 0121 459 5800 🖷 0121 459 8553
This elegant hotel and restaurant, set in peaceful landscaped gardens, was once a paper mill and now provides excellent accommodation, together with AA rosette-worthy cuisine. Chef Anthony Morgan offers an interesting menu of both English and continental dishes presented with great care and imagination, in the elegant restaurant. Pre-dinner drinks are served in the spacious conservatory. The bedrooms, all of which are found in a separate building, have been carefully designed and furnished with some luxury, to include such extra facilities as mini bars, bathrobes, fresh fruit, and a selection of videos for guests' use.
ROOMS: 10 annexe en suite (bth/shr) No smoking in 5 bedrooms s £98-£98; d £110-£110 (incl. bkfst) * LB Off peak **MEALS:** Lunch fr £18.50alc Dinner fr £26.50alc English & French Cuisine V meals Coffee am Tea pm **FACILITIES:** CTV in all bedrooms Indoor swimming pool (heated) Jacuzzi/spa ch fac **CONF:** Thtr 60 Class 30 Board 35 **SERVICES:** 40P **NOTES:** No dogs (ex guide dogs) No coaches No smoking in restaurant Last d 9.45pm Closed 27 Dec-16 Jan
CARDS:

BIRMINGHAM West Midlands **Map 07 SP08**
★★★ The Westley
80-90 Westley Rd, Acocks Green B27 7UJ
Quality Percentage Score: 71%
☎ 0121 706 4312 🖷 0121 706 2824
Dir: *take A41 signed Birmingham on Solihull By-Pass and continue to Acocks Green. At roundabout take second exit B4146 Westley Rd, hotel 200 yds on left*
This very pleasant, friendly and popular, privately owned hotel is conveniently located within 15 minutes of the city centre and 10 minutes from Birmingham International Airport and the NEC. It provides good quality, well equipped accommodation, which includes bedrooms on the ground and first floors of an adjacent town house. Facilities here include a choice of bars and both formal and informal eating options. There is also a function suite for up to 200 people.
ROOMS: 27 en suite (bth/shr) 9 annexe en suite (bth/shr) (1 fmly) s £42.50-£82.50; d £42.50-£85 * LB Off peak **MEALS:** Sunday Lunch £12.95 Dinner fr £14.95 English & French Cuisine V meals Coffee am Tea pm **FACILITIES:** CTV in 37 bedrooms STV Wkly live entertainment **CONF:** Thtr 200 Class 80 Board 50 Del from £95 * **SERVICES:** Night porter 150P **NOTES:** No smoking area in restaurant Last d 10pm **CARDS:**

BIRMINGHAM West Midlands **Map 07 SP08**
★★★ Posthouse Birmingham Great Barr
Posthouse
Chapel Ln, Great Barr B43 7BG
Quality Percentage Score: 67%
☎ 0121 357 7444 🖷 0121 357 7503
Dir: *take Jct7 M6. Turn onto A34 signposted Walsall. Hotel located 200yds on the right hand side across the carriage-way in Chapel Lane*
A modern hotel, in pleasant surroundings, with well equipped, comfortable bedrooms. There are good leisure facilities, a popular restaurant, and also an all-day lounge menu, and 24-hour room service. There is a courtyard patio and garden.
ROOMS: 192 en suite (bth/shr) (36 fmly) No smoking in 108 bedrooms d £89-£109 * LB Off peak **MEALS:** International Cuisine V meals Coffee am Tea pm **FACILITIES:** CTV in all bedrooms Indoor swimming pool (heated) Sauna Solarium Gym Pool table Jacuzzi/spa Aerobics studio Beauty treatments **CONF:** Thtr 120 Class 70 Board 50 Del from £105 * **SERVICES:** Night porter 400P **NOTES:** No smoking area in restaurant Last d 10.30pm **CARDS:**

BIRMINGHAM West Midlands **Map 07 SP08**
★★★ *Thistle Birmingham City*
St Chads, Queensway B4 6HY
Quality Percentage Score: 66%
☎ 0121 236 4211 🖷 0121 233 2195
Dir: *In city centre on A38M Aston Expressway. From M6 junct 6 onto A38M, hotel 4th exit*
The majority of the bedrooms have now been refurbished at this modern hotel, conveniently situated adjacent to a large public car park. Public areas include a spacious bar lounge leading into the bright Raffles Restaurant, where a choice of carefully prepared dishes is offered. Conference and banqueting facilities are also available.
ROOMS: 133 en suite (bth/shr) (4 fmly) No smoking in 50 bedrooms **MEALS:** English & French Cuisine V meals Coffee am Tea pm **FACILITIES:** CTV in all bedrooms STV **CONF:** Thtr 150 Class 80 Board 30 **SERVICES:** Lift Night porter **NOTES:** No smoking in restaurant Last d 10pm **CARDS:**

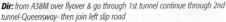

BIRMINGHAM West Midlands **Map 07 SP08**
★★★ Novotel
70 Broad St B1 2HT
Quality Percentage Score: 65%
☎ 0121 643 2000 🖹 0121 643 9796
Dir: *2mins fron the International Conference centre*
A large, modern, purpose built hotel with a secure basement car park. There are six floors of similar, spacious and comfortable bedrooms, half are for non smokers. Bar meals offer an informal option to the Garden Brasserie. Facilities include conference/function suites for up to 250 people and a fitness centre with Jacuzzi, gym and sauna.
ROOMS: 148 en suite (bth/shr) (148 fmly) No smoking in 75 bedrooms s £115; d fr £95 * LB Off peak **MEALS:** Lunch £12-£15 & alc Dinner £14-£16 & alc International Cuisine V meals Coffee am Tea pm **FACILITIES:** CTV in all bedrooms STV Sauna Gym Jacuzzi/spa **CONF:** Thtr 250 Class 100 Board 100 Del from £85 * **SERVICES:** Lift Air conditioning 57P **NOTES:** No smoking area in restaurant Last d m'night **CARDS:**

BIRMINGHAM West Midlands **Map 07 SP08**
★★★ Westmead
Redditch Rd, Hopwood B48 7AL
Quality Percentage Score: 65%
☎ 0121 445 1202 🖹 0121 445 6163
Dir: *M42 junct 2 head towards Birmingham on A441 upto rdbt and turn right, follow A441 for 1m and hotel is on right hand side*

Conveniently situated to the south of Birmingham, and just a few minutes from the M42, this hotel offers spacious, modern bedrooms that are well equipped for both business and leisure travellers. In addition to the main restaurant, a carvery is available at weekends and snacks are served in the Hopwood bar. A range of different meeting rooms is available for conferences and meetings, and the hotel is also a popular local choice for wedding receptions.
ROOMS: 58 en suite (bth/shr) (2 fmly) No smoking in 28 bedrooms s fr £90; d fr £105 * LB Off peak **MEALS:** Lunch fr £5.95 Dinner fr £15.95 & alc International Cuisine V meals Coffee am **FACILITIES:** CTV in all bedrooms STV Sauna Solarium **CONF:** Thtr 300 Class 120 Board 80 Del from £105 * **SERVICES:** Night porter 155P **NOTES:** No dogs (ex guide dogs) No smoking in restaurant Last d 9.30pm
CARDS:

BIRMINGHAM West Midlands **Map 07 SP08**
★★★ Birmingham Grand Moat House
Colmore Row B3 2DA
Quality Percentage Score: 64%
☎ 0121 607 9988 🖹 0121 233 1465
Dir: *opposite cathedral*
This large and rather elegant Victorian property is situated in the city centre, opposite the cathedral. It provides comfortable, well equipped accommodation, which is equally suitable for both business people and tourists. Spacious suites, no smoking bedrooms and family bedded rooms are all available. The spacious public areas include choices of bars and both formal and informal eating options. Facilities here include several rooms for meetings and conferences, plus a large, very impressive and ornately decorated ballroom.
ROOMS: 173 en suite (bth/shr) (4 fmly) No smoking in 130 bedrooms s £11.50-£125; d £135-£145 * LB Off peak **MEALS:** Lunch £5.95-£17.85alc Dinner £5.95-£17.85alc English & French Cuisine V meals Coffee am Tea pm **FACILITIES:** CTV in all bedrooms STV Xmas **CONF:** Thtr 500 Class 250 Board 80 Del £120 * **SERVICES:** Lift Night porter P **NOTES:** No smoking area in restaurant Last d 11pm
CARDS:

BIRMINGHAM West Midlands **Map 07 SP08**
★★★ Plough & Harrow
135 Hagley Rd B16 8LS
Quality Percentage Score: 64%
☎ 0121 454 4111 🖹 0121 454 1868
Dir: *from the city travel along the A456 (Hagley Road), the hotel is on the right hand side after 5 ways roundabout*
A well established hotel, about a mile west of the city centre, has a relaxed, friendly atmosphere. Bedrooms come in a variety of styles and sizes, and the restaurant has a good selection of dishes.
ROOMS: 44 en suite (bth/shr) No smoking in 11 bedrooms s £95; d £115 * LB Off peak **MEALS:** Lunch £7.95-£15.95 & alc Dinner £18.95 & alc V meals Coffee am Tea pm **FACILITIES:** CTV in all bedrooms Xmas **CONF:** Thtr 100 Class 60 Board 50 Del £109 * **SERVICES:** Lift Night porter 80P **NOTES:** No smoking in restaurant Last d 10pm
CARDS:

BIRMINGHAM West Midlands — Map 07 SP08

★★★ Portland

313 Hagley Rd B16 9LQ

Quality Percentage Score: 64%

☎ 0121 455 0535 Fax 0121 456 1841

Dir: *2m from city centre on A456*

A large, purpose built, privately owned hotel just west of the city centre. It provides well equipped modern accommodation including non smoking and ground floor rooms. There is an attractive restaurant and a pleasant lounge bar, a choice of function suites and meeting rooms.

ROOMS: 63 en suite (bth/shr) No smoking in 7 bedrooms s £49.95-£64.95; d £54.50-£79.95 (incl. bkfst) * LB Off peak **MEALS:** Lunch £12.95-£14.95 & alc Dinner £13.95-£15.95 & alc English & French Cuisine V meals Tea pm **FACILITIES:** CTV in all bedrooms STV **CONF:** Thtr 80 Class 40 Board 40 Del from £73.95 * **SERVICES:** Lift Night porter 80P **NOTES:** No dogs (ex guide dogs) No smoking area in restaurant Last d 9.45pm **CARDS:**

BIRMINGHAM West Midlands — Map 07 SP08

★★★ Posthouse Birmingham City

Posthouse

Smallbrook Queensway B5 4EW

Quality Percentage Score: 64%

☎ 0121 643 8171 Fax 0121 631 2528

Dir: *from M6 junct 6 follow signs on A38 for 'City Centre' through two tunnels. Take second slip road off, then 1st left to hotel in 100yds*

A large modern hotel in the city centre. Bedrooms are well designed for their purpose and other hotel amenities include extensive meeting rooms, a business centre and a leisure club. Public areas include a lounge bar with a terrace and an all-day menu; 24-hour room service is also available. Overnight parking vouchers are provided for the adjacent multi-storey car park.

ROOMS: 251 en suite (bth/shr) No smoking in 174 bedrooms **MEALS:** European Cuisine V meals Coffee am Tea pm **FACILITIES:** CTV in all bedrooms STV Indoor swimming pool (heated) Squash Sauna Solarium Gym Pool table Health & fitness club Beauty treatment **CONF:** Thtr 630 Class 380 Board 50 **SERVICES:** Lift Night porter Air conditioning **NOTES:** No smoking area in restaurant Last d 10.30pm **CARDS:**

BIRMINGHAM West Midlands — Map 07 SP08

★★★ Great Barr Hotel & Conference Centre

Pear Tree Dr, Newton Rd, Great Barr B43 6HS

Quality Percentage Score: 61%

☎ 0121 357 1141 Fax 0121 357 7557

Dir: *1m W of junc A34/A4041*

This busy hotel is situated in a residential area just off the A4041. It is popular with conference delegates and business people, for whom the well equipped bedrooms with their modern style of furnishings are ideally suited.

ROOMS: 105 en suite (bth/shr) (1 fmly) s £69-£75; d £85-£115 * LB Off peak **MEALS:** Lunch £9.50-£13.50 & alc High tea £3.50-£5 Dinner £17.50-£18.50 & alc English & Continental Cuisine V meals Coffee am Tea pm **FACILITIES:** CTV in all bedrooms STV Xmas **CONF:** Thtr 120 Class 50 Board 50 Del from £90 * **SERVICES:** Night porter 175P **NOTES:** No dogs (ex guide dogs) No smoking area in restaurant Last d 9pm RS BH (restaurant may be closed) **CARDS:**

See advert on opposite page

> Remember to return your Prize Draw card for a chance to win one of 30 relaxing leisure breaks with Corus and Regal hotels. See inside the front cover for the card and competition details.

BIRMINGHAM West Midlands — Map 07 SP08

★★ Copperfield House

60 Upland Rd, Selly Park B29 7JS

Quality Percentage Score: 71%

☎ 0121 472 8344 Fax 0121 415 5655

Dir: *exit M6 at junct 6, take A38 through city centre, at second set of traffic lights turn left, at next traffic lights turn right (A441), third right*

This large Victorian house, now a privately owned and personally run hotel, is situated in a residential area two miles south-west of the city centre, close to the BBC Pebble Mill Studios. It provides soundly maintained, well equipped accommodation, including bedrooms on ground floor level, which is equally suitable for both business people and tourists.

ROOMS: 17 en suite (bth/shr) (2 fmly) **MEALS:** European Cuisine V meals Coffee am Tea pm **FACILITIES:** CTV in all bedrooms **CONF:** Board 12 **SERVICES:** 11P **NOTES:** No coaches No smoking in restaurant Last d 9pm **CARDS:**

BIRMINGHAM West Midlands — Map 07 SP08

★★ Oxford Hotel

21 Oxford Rd B13 9EH

Quality Percentage Score: 71%

☎ 0121 449 3298 Fax 0121 442 4212

Dir: *3m S of Birmingham A435, on entering Moseley village turn R at traffic lights, then R again at Ford Garage. Hotel is situated 50yds on the L.*

Privately owned and personally run, this large Victorian house has been sympathetically restored to provide a high standard of accommodation. Public rooms are cheerfully decorated and inviting, and the bedrooms are modern and thoughtfully equipped with many useful extras. A high level of customer care is provided by Ann Molloy and her small team of loyal staff.

ROOMS: 15 en suite (bth/shr) 9 annexe en suite (bth/shr) (5 fmly) No smoking in 7 bedrooms s £40-£76; d £60-£80 (incl. bkfst) * LB Off peak **MEALS:** Bar Lunch £3.95-£7.95 Dinner £10.95-£15.95 English Cuisine V meals Coffee am Tea pm **FACILITIES:** CTV in all bedrooms STV Snooker Pool table **CONF:** Thtr 70 Class 70 Board 40 Del from £89.95 * **SERVICES:** Air conditioning 60P **NOTES:** No smoking in restaurant Last d 9pm **CARDS:**

BIRMINGHAM West Midlands — Map 07 SP08

★★ Norwood

87-89 Bunbury Rd, Northfield B31 2ET

Quality Percentage Score: 70%

☎ 0121 411 2202 Fax 0121 411 2202

Dir: *turn left on A38 at Grosvenor shopping centre, 5m S of city centre*

This tastefully appointed and comfortable privately owned hotel provides well equipped modern accommodation which includes a bedroom on ground floor level. The pleasant public rooms have recently been extended by the addition of a conservatory. Well produced home cooking is served in the attractive dining room and the service is both friendly and attentive.

ROOMS: 18 en suite (bth/shr) **MEALS:** English & French Cuisine V meals **FACILITIES:** CTV in all bedrooms STV **CONF:** Thtr 40 Class 24 Board 20 **SERVICES:** 11P **NOTES:** Last d 8.30pm Closed 23-26 Dec RS 27-31 Dec **CARDS:**

BIRMINGHAM West Midlands — Map 07 SP08

★★ Chamberlain Park

Alcester St B12 0PJ

Quality Percentage Score: 68%

☎ 0121 606 9000 Fax 0121 606 9001

This impressive building close to the town centre dates from the turn of the century. Renovated and refurbished to a high standard, it provides well equipped accommodation, with elegant reception rooms and numerous conference and function rooms,

contd.

one of which can accommodate 400 people. Civil weddings can be performed here.

ROOMS: 250 en suite (bth/shr) No smoking in all bedrooms **MEALS:** V meals Coffee am Tea pm **FACILITIES:** CTV in all bedrooms STV **CONF:** Thtr 400 Class 200 Board 112 **SERVICES:** Lift Night porter 200P **NOTES:** No dogs (ex guide dogs) No smoking in restaurant Last d 10pm **CARDS:**

BIRMINGHAM West Midlands **Map 07 SP08**

★★ Heath Lodge

117 Coleshill Rd, Marston Green B37 7HT
Quality Percentage Score: 65%
☎ 0121 779 2218 🖷 0121 779 2218

Dir: *join A446 from M6 J4 travelling nothwards to Coleshill, after 0.5m turn left into Coleshill Heath Rd, signposted to Marston Green. Hotel on right*

This privately owned and personally run hotel is within easy reach of the M6 and M42 motorways and both the NEC and Birmingham Airport are less than two miles away. Its modern bedrooms are well equipped and comfortable, and day rooms consist of a small bar, a lounge and a dining room overlooking the garden.

ROOMS: 17 rms (16 bth/shr) (1 fmly) s £42-£45; d £54-£59 (incl. bkfst) * Off peak **MEALS:** Dinner £7-£12alc English & French Cuisine V meals Coffee am Tea pm **FACILITIES:** CTV in all bedrooms **CONF:** Thtr 36 Class 30 Del from £65 * **SERVICES:** 22P **NOTES:** No coaches No smoking in restaurant Last d 8.30pm **CARDS:**

BIRMINGHAM West Midlands **Map 07 SP08**

★★ Westbourne Lodge

27/29 Fountain Rd, Edgbaston B17 8NJ
Quality Percentage Score: 65%
☎ 0121 429 1003 🖷 0121 429 7436

Dir: *off A456, 3m from junct 3 of the M5, 1.25 m from city*

This friendly family owned and run hotel is conveniently located just off the A456 at Edgbaston, two miles west of the city centre and within easy reach of the motorway. It provides soundly maintained and well equipped bedrooms. Other facilities include a cosy lounge, a small bar and a pleasant dining room, which overlooks the terrace and garden.

ROOMS: 22 en suite (bth/shr) (5 fmly) No smoking in all bedrooms s £39.50-£49.50; d £49.50-£69.50 (incl. bkfst) * LB Off peak **MEALS:** Lunch fr £10.95 High tea fr £5 Dinner fr £14.95 English, French & Italian Cuisine V meals Coffee am Tea pm **FACILITIES:** CTV in all bedrooms Private garden and Patio Area **SERVICES:** 22P **NOTES:** No smoking in restaurant Last d 9pm **CARDS:**

> The AA's professional hotel and restaurant inspectors make regular and anonymous visits to all the hotels listed in the guide. They do not accept gifts or favours from hoteliers.

BIRMINGHAM West Midlands **Map 07 SP08**
★★ ***Astoria***
311 Hagley Rd B16 9LQ
Quality Percentage Score: 64%
☎ 0121 454 0795 ▤ 0121 456 3537
Dir: *on A456 2m from city centre*
This pair of semi-detached mid Victorian houses have been converted into one property. It provides fairly modern, no frills accommodation, including family and ground floor rooms. There is a choice of lounges, a homely bar and a traditionally furnished dining room, where a selection of grill type dishes is available.
ROOMS: 26 en suite (bth/shr) (6 fmly) No smoking in 2 bedrooms **MEALS:** V meals Coffee am Tea pm **FACILITIES:** CTV in all bedrooms STV **SERVICES:** 27P **NOTES:** No dogs (ex guide dogs) No smoking in restaurant Last d 9pm **CARDS:**

BIRMINGHAM West Midlands **Map 07 SP08**
★★ **Fountain Court**
339-343 Fountain Court Hotel B17 8NH
Quality Percentage Score: 64%
☎ 0121 429 1754 ▤ 0121 429 1209
Dir: *on A456, towards Birmingham*
This family owned hotel is on the A456, near the M5 and Birmingham. Bedrooms include a family suite and some rooms on the ground floor. A brightly decorated dining room, a choice of sitting areas and a bar complete the accommodation.
ROOMS: 25 en suite (bth/shr) (4 fmly) s £35-£48.50; d £48.50-£60 (incl. bkfst) * Off peak **MEALS:** Dinner £14.95 V meals **FACILITIES:** CTV in all bedrooms **SERVICES:** 20P **NOTES:** Last d 8.30pm **CARDS:**

BIRMINGHAM West Midlands **Map 07 SP08**
★★ **Hotel Ibis**
Ladywell Walk B5 4ST
Quality Percentage Score: 64%
☎ 0121 622 6010 ▤ 0121 622 6020
Dir: *M6 junct 7 take A34 to city centre & follow signs to Market areas. M5 junct 3 take A456 to centre then Market areas*
This modern red brick building is located in the heart of Chinatown within walking distance of New Street Station. Most bedrooms have been refurbished to a smart, easy, bright specification making them attractive for all users. Breakfast and light evening meals are served on site.
ROOMS: 159 en suite (bth/shr) No smoking in 59 bedrooms d £49.50 * Off peak **MEALS:** High tea 80p-£3 Dinner £2.95-£7.25 International Cuisine V meals Coffee am Tea pm **FACILITIES:** CTV in all bedrooms STV **CONF:** Thtr 100 Class 60 Board 40 Del from £70 * **SERVICES:** Lift **NOTES:** No smoking area in restaurant Last d 11pm
CARDS:

BIRMINGHAM West Midlands **Map 07 SP08**
★★ **Sheriden House**
82 Handsworth Wood Rd, Handsworth Wood B20 2PL
Quality Percentage Score: 63%
☎ 0121 554 2185 & 0121 523 5960 ▤ 0121 551 4761
Dir: *at junct 7 of M6 turn onto A34, through traffic lights at A4041 next right filter onto B4124, straight through to hotel on left*
This privately owned and personally run hotel is situated on the B4124, three and a half miles north-west of the city centre. It provides soundly maintained and well equipped accommodation, which is popular with commercial visitors who appreciate the homely atmosphere. Facilities include a pleasant bar, a cosy lounge and a restaurant which can be partitioned to accommodate private parties.
ROOMS: 11 en suite (bth/shr) No smoking in 3 bedrooms s fr £39; d £54 (incl. bkfst) * LB Off peak **MEALS:** Lunch £9.95-£15 & alc Dinner £15 & alc English & French Cuisine V meals Coffee am Tea pm **FACILITIES:** CTV in all bedrooms **CONF:** Thtr 40 Class 25 Board 20 Del from £55.50 * **SERVICES:** 30P **NOTES:** No dogs (ex guide dogs) No smoking in restaurant Last d 9pm **CARDS:**

See advert on opposite page

BIRMINGHAM West Midlands **Map 07 SP08**
★★ ***Edgbaston Palace***
198 Hagley Rd B16 9PQ
Quality Percentage Score: 62%
☎ 0121 452 1577 ▤ 0121 452 1577
This fine Georgian property has recently been extended and provides a variety of well equipped modern bedrooms, including family rooms and rooms on the ground floor. In addition to the cosy dining room, spacious breakfast room and bar, there is a separate TV lounge, a conference room and a secure car park. A shuttle service to the city centre and the airport is available to guests.
ROOMS: 30 rms (29 bth/shr) (4 fmly) **MEALS:** English & Continental Cuisine V meals Coffee am Tea pm **FACILITIES:** CTV in all bedrooms STV **CONF:** Thtr 150 Class 50 Board 50 Del from £60 *
SERVICES: Night porter 53P **NOTES:** Last d 9pm Closed 24-30 Dec
CARDS:

BIRMINGHAM West Midlands **Map 07 SP08**
⇧ ***Campanile***
Chester St, Aston Rd North B6 4BE
☎ 020 8569 6969 ▤ 020 8814 0887

This modern building offers accommodation in smart well equipped bedrooms, all with en-suite bathrooms. Refreshments may be taken at the informal Bistro. For details about current prices, consult the Contents Page under Hotel Groups for the Campanile phone number.

BIRMINGHAM West Midlands **Map 07 SP08**
⇧ **Travel Inn (Central)**
20 Bridge St B1 2JH
☎ 0121 633 4820 ▤ 0121 633 4779
Dir: *from M6/M5/M42 follow signs for ICC, Bridge St is opposite ICC and Symphony Hall*
This modern building offers accommodation in smart, spacious and well equipped bedrooms, all with en-suite bathrooms. Refreshments may be taken at the nearby family restaurant. For details about current prices consult the Contents Page under Hotel Groups for the Travel Inn phone number.
ROOMS: 54 en suite (bth/shr) d £39.95 *

BIRMINGHAM West Midlands **Map 07 SP08**
Travel Inn (Central East)
Richard St, Aston B7 4AA
0121 333 6484 0121 333 6490
Dir: *off Aston Expresway & inner ring road (A4540 on the Dartmouth Middleway*
This modern building offers accommodation in smart, spacious and well equipped bedrooms, all with en-suite bathrooms. Refreshments may be taken at the nearby family restaurant. For details about current prices consult the Contents Page under Hotel Groups for the Travel Inn phone number.
ROOMS: 60 en suite (bth/shr) d £39.95 *

BIRMINGHAM West Midlands **Map 07 SP08**
Travelodge (Birmingham Central)
230 Broad St B15 1AY
0121 644 5266
This modern building offers accommodation in smart, spacious and well equipped bedrooms, all with en-suite bathrooms. Refreshments may be taken at the nearby family restaurant. For details about current prices, consult the Contents Page under Hotel Groups for the Travelodge phone number.
ROOMS: 136 en suite (bth/shr) d £49.95 *

BIRMINGHAM West Midlands **Map 07 SP08**
Travelodge (Birmingham East)
A45 Coventry Rd, Acocks Green B26 1DS
0800 850950
This modern building offers accommodation in smart, spacious and well equipped bedrooms, all with en-suite bathrooms. Refreshments may be taken at the nearby family restaurant. For details about current prices, consult the Contents Page under Hotel Groups for the Travelodge phone number.
ROOMS: 40 en suite (bth/shr) d fr £45.95 *

BIRMINGHAM West Midlands **Map 07 SP08**
Thistle Birmingham Edgbaston
225 Hagley Rd B16 9RY
0121 455 9777 0121 454 9432
Dir: *from junct 3 on M5 follow signs for Birmingham City Centre A456. Hotel approx 5m on left*
This circular hotel is just outside the city centre on the western side. Smart public areas include a comfortable lobby, a brasserie, two bars (one of which is also an informal restaurant) and extensive conference and banqueting facilities. The unusual shape of the building dictates the design of the well equipped rooms.
ROOMS: 151 en suite (bth/shr) (1 fmly) No smoking in 55 bedrooms **MEALS:** European Cuisine V meals Coffee am Tea pm **FACILITIES:** CTV in all bedrooms STV Pool table Wkly live entertainment **CONF:** Thtr 170 Class 100 Board 50 **SERVICES:** Lift Night porter 200P **NOTES:** No smoking in restaurant Last d 10pm **CARDS:**

BIRMINGHAM West Midlands **Map 07 SP08**
Quality Hotel Birmingham
166 Hagley Rd, Edgbaston B16 9NZ
0121 454 6621 021-454 1910
A large hotel situated on the A456, within easy reach of the city centre, and offering a choice of bedrooms, a popular carvery restaurant and good leisure facilities.
ROOMS: 230 en suite (bth/shr) (8 fmly) No smoking in 40 bedrooms **MEALS:** English & French Cuisine V meals Coffee am Tea pm **FACILITIES:** CTV in all bedrooms Indoor swimming pool (heated) Sauna Solarium Gym jacuzzi **SERVICES:** Lift Night porter 200P **NOTES:** Last d 9.45pm **CARDS:**

BIRMINGHAM West Midlands **Map 07 SP08**
Quality Hotel & Suites
257/267 Hagley Rd, Edgbaston B16 9NA
0121 454 8071 021-454 1910
A large hotel on the A456 close to the city centre, offering modestly decorated and furnished rooms, is particularly popular with commercial travellers.
ROOMS: 175 rms (32 bth 56 shr) No smoking in 15 bedrooms **MEALS:** V meals Coffee am Tea pm **FACILITIES:** CTV in all bedrooms putting green **SERVICES:** Lift Night porter 130P **NOTES:** Last d 9.45pm Closed 24 Dec-2 Jan **CARDS:**

BIRMINGHAM West Midlands **Map 07 SP08**
Hotel Clarine
229 Hagley Rd, Edgbaston B16 9RP
0121 454 6514 0121 456 2722
Dir: *on A456*
ROOMS: 27 en suite (bth/shr) (1 fmly) No smoking in 16 bedrooms s fr £45; d fr £58 (incl. bkfst) * LB Off peak **MEALS:** Bar Lunch fr £3.25 & alc Dinner £9.75-£11.75 & alc English & Continental Cuisine V meals Coffee am Tea pm **FACILITIES:** CTV in all bedrooms STV Xmas **SERVICES:** Night porter 28P **NOTES:** No dogs (ex guide dogs) No coaches No smoking area in restaurant Last d 9.30pm **CARDS:**

BIRMINGHAM West Midlands **Map 07 SP08**
Hotel Ibis
55 Irving St B1 1DH
0121 622 4925 0121 622 4195
Dir: *150yds from Dome Night Club, just off Bristol Street*
This purpose built hotel is conveniently located in the city centre.
contd.

It provides well equipped, modern accommodation. Facilities include a bistro restaurant, a bar and a conference room.
ROOMS: 51 annexe en suite (bth/shr) (5 fmly) No smoking in 23 bedrooms s £39.50; d £39.50 * LB Off peak **MEALS:** French Cuisine V meals Coffee am Tea pm **FACILITIES:** CTV in 50 bedrooms STV Xmas **CONF:** Thtr 35 Class 18 Board 20 **SERVICES:** 60P **NOTES:** No smoking area in restaurant Last d 10pm **CARDS:**

BIRMINGHAM AIRPORT West Midlands **Map 07 SP18**
★★★ Posthouse Birmingham Airport
Coventry Rd B26 3QW
Quality Percentage Score: 65%
☎ 0121 782 8141 Fax 0121 782 2476
Dir: *from junct 6 of M42 take A45 towards Birmingham for 1.5m*
Conveniently located for the airport and NEC this hotel offers recently refurbished bedrooms with every modern facility; further upgrading of public areas and the Junction Restaurant is also scheduled. Conference and meeting facilities are also available.
ROOMS: 141 en suite (bth/shr) (3 fmly) No smoking in 84 bedrooms d £119 * LB Off peak **MEALS:** International Cuisine V meals Coffee am Tea pm **FACILITIES:** CTV in all bedrooms Xmas **CONF:** Thtr 130 Class 100 Board 70 Del from £100 * **SERVICES:** Night porter 250P **NOTES:** No smoking area in restaurant Last d 10.30pm
CARDS:

BIRMINGHAM AIRPORT West Midlands **Map 07 SP18**
★★★ Novotel
B26 3QL
Quality Percentage Score: 64%
☎ 0121 782 7000 Fax 0121 782 0445
Dir: *exit junct 6 of M42 onto A45 direction Birmingham, after 0.25m exit following signs for airport, hotel opposite main terminal*
This modern hotel, opened in 1991, is conveniently located opposite the main passenger terminal and is linked with the monorail allowing direct access to Birmingham International station as well as the N.E.C. Parking is available in the nearby NCP-Two car park. The identically-furnished bedrooms, most with brand new bathrooms, include non-smoking and disabled rooms. Food service is flexible and extensive - meals are available from 5am until midnight.
ROOMS: 195 en suite (bth/shr) (20 fmly) No smoking in 130 bedrooms s £108-£134; d £117.50-£143.50 (incl. bkfst) * Off peak **MEALS:** Lunch £12.50 & alc Dinner £18.50 & alc International Cuisine V meals Coffee am Tea pm **FACILITIES:** CTV in all bedrooms STV Pool table **CONF:** Thtr 35 Class 20 Board 22 Del from £139 * **SERVICES:** Lift Night porter Air conditioning **NOTES:** No smoking area in restaurant Last d mdnt **CARDS:**

BIRMINGHAM (NATIONAL EXHIBITION CENTRE) West Midlands **Map 07 SP18**
see also **Sutton Coldfield**
★★★★ Nailcote Hall
Nailcote Ln, Berkswell CV7 7DE
Quality Percentage Score: 67%
☎ 024 76466174 Fax 024 76470720
(For full entry see Balsall Common)

BIRMINGHAM (NATIONAL EXHIBITION CENTRE) West Midlands **Map 07 SP18**
★★★ Arden Hotel & Leisure Club
Coventry Rd, Bickenhill B92 0EH
Quality Percentage Score: 63%
☎ 01675 443221 Fax 01675 443221
Dir: *from junc 6 of M42 take A45 towards Birmingham, hotel 0.25m on right hand side, just off B'ham Airport Island*
The Arden is a successful family owned and run hotel which is constantly being updated to meet the demands of today's market and particularly business from the adjacent NEC. The bedrooms are all modern and well equipped. Facilities here include a coffee shop, a formal restaurant and terraced water gardens.
ROOMS: 146 en suite (bth/shr) (6 fmly) s £95; d £105 * Off peak **MEALS:** Lunch £10.95-£14.10 & alc Dinner £14.10 & alc French & Italian Cuisine V meals Coffee am Tea pm **FACILITIES:** CTV in all bedrooms STV Indoor swimming pool (heated) Snooker Sauna Solarium Gym Jacuzzi/spa Wkly live entertainment **CONF:** Thtr 220 Class 60 Board 40 Del from £137 * **SERVICES:** Lift Night porter 300P **NOTES:** No smoking area in restaurant Last d 9.45pm
CARDS:

See advert under SOLIHULL

BIRMINGHAM (NATIONAL EXHIBITION CENTRE) West Midlands **Map 07 SP18**
★★★ *Sutton Court*
60-66 Lichfield Rd B74 2NA
Quality Percentage Score: 62%
☎ 0870 6011160 Fax 01543 481551
(For full entry see Sutton Coldfield & advert on p 109)

BIRMINGHAM (NATIONAL EXHIBITION CENTRE) West Midlands **Map 07 SP18**
★★ Haigs
Kenilworth Rd CV7 7EL
Quality Percentage Score: 75%
☎ 01676 533004 Fax 01676 535132
(For full entry see Balsall Common & advert on opposite page)

BISHOP'S STORTFORD Hertfordshire **Map 05 TL42**
★★★★ Down Hall Country House
Hatfield Heath CM22 7AS
Quality Percentage Score: 66%
☎ 01279 731441 Fax 01279 730416
Dir: *follow A1060, at Hatfield Heath keep left, turn right into lane opposite Hunters Meet restaurant & left at the end following signpost*
With its country estate setting, it is hard to believe that this impressive Victorian mansion is so conveniently located. The hotel is set in over 100 acres, and the gardens have undergone major re-landscaping. Bedrooms may vary in size, but all are well furnished with antique-style furniture and a wide range of facilities. The public areas offer an imposing lounge and extensive leisure amenities. The Lambourne restaurant offers a good range of dishes in a traditional atmosphere, while the Downham restaurant offers fine dining in a more formal setting.
ROOMS: 103 en suite (bth/shr) s fr £115; d fr £151 * LB Off peak **MEALS:** Lunch fr £22.50 Dinner fr £29.50 & alc International Cuisine V meals Coffee am Tea pm **FACILITIES:** CTV in all bedrooms STV Indoor swimming pool (heated) Tennis (hard) Snooker Sauna Gym Croquet lawn Putting green Jacuzzi/spa Petanque Giant chess Whirlpool Xmas **CONF:** Thtr 290 Class 154 Board 84 Del £210 * **SERVICES:** Lift Night porter 150P **NOTES:** No smoking in restaurant Last d 9.45pm
CARDS:

BLACKBURN Lancashire **Map 07 SD62**
see also **Langho**
★★★★ Clarion Hotel & Suites Foxfields
Whalley Rd, Billington BB7 9HY
Quality Percentage Score: 64%
☎ 01254 822556 Fax 01254 824613
Dir: *turn off A59 at signpost for Billington/Whalley & hotel after 0.5m on right*
A modern hotel with particularly good bedrooms - including

contd.

many with separate sitting and dressing rooms - situated in a rural location just off the A59 in the direction of Whalley. Expressions Restaurant with cocktail bar, offers mainly English dishes cooked in the modern style. There is also a smart Leisure Club. Further renovation should be underway at time of press.
ROOMS: 44 en suite (bth/shr) (27 fmly) No smoking in 20 bedrooms s £90-£95; d £102-£115 * LB Off peak **MEALS:** Dinner fr £19.50 English & French Cuisine V meals Coffee am Tea pm **FACILITIES:** CTV in all bedrooms STV Indoor swimming pool (heated) Sauna Gym Steam room Wkly live entertainment Xmas **CONF:** Thtr 180 Class 60 Board 60 **SERVICES:** Night porter 170P **NOTES:** No dogs (ex guide dogs) No smoking in restaurant Last d 9.45pm
CARDS:

BLACKBURN Lancashire — Map 07 SD62
★★★ County Hotel Blackburn
REGAL
Preston New Rd BB2 7BE
Quality Percentage Score: 61%
☎ 01254 899988 🖷 01254 682435
Dir: *on A667/A6119 junct W of town*

Situated to the west of the town itself, this hotel offers comfortable and brightly decorated bedrooms, all of them recently refurbished. Public areas are shortly to be upgraded also. Extensive function facilities are available and there is adequate car parking.
ROOMS: 101 en suite (bth/shr) (2 fmly) No smoking in 50 bedrooms s £55-£85; d £65-£95 * LB Off peak **MEALS:** Lunch £3-£15alc Dinner £3-£15alc International Cuisine V meals Coffee am Tea pm **FACILITIES:** CTV in all bedrooms Pool table Xmas **CONF:** Thtr 350 Class 150 Board 100 Del from £75 * **SERVICES:** Lift Night porter 150P **NOTES:** No smoking in restaurant Last d 10pm
CARDS:

BLACKBURN Lancashire — Map 07 SD62
★★ Millstone
SHIRE INNS
Church Ln, Mellor BB2 7JR
Quality Percentage Score: 76%
☎ 01254 813333 🖷 01254 812628
Dir: *3m NW off A59*

Found in the village of Mellor, just off the A59 this inviting stone-built coaching inn offers a very good standard of accommodation. The bedrooms, some of which are located in an adjoining building, have been furnished to a high standard and are very well equipped. The lounge bar is also the village local and in the wood panelled restaurant serves some tempting dishes.
ROOMS: 18 en suite (bth/shr) 6 annexe en suite (bth/shr) (1 fmly) No smoking in 4 bedrooms s fr £84; d fr £104 (incl. bkfst) * LB Off peak **MEALS:** Bar Lunch fr £5 Dinner fr £22 International Cuisine V meals Coffee am Tea pm **FACILITIES:** CTV in all bedrooms STV **CONF:** Thtr 25 Class 15 Board 16 Del from £68 * **SERVICES:** 40P **NOTES:** No coaches No smoking in restaurant Last d 9.30pm Closed 31 Dec
CARDS:

BLACKPOOL Lancashire — Map 07 SD33
★★★★ *De Vere*
DE VERE HOTELS
East Park Dr FY3 8LL
Quality Percentage Score: 67%
☎ 01253 838866 🖷 01253 798800
Dir: *M6 junct32/M55 junct4, A583, at 4th set of traffic lights turn right into South Park Drive & follow signs for zoo. Hotel on right*

This stylish modern hotel is conveniently located on the much quieter edge of the town and offers excellent indoor and outdoor leisure facilities, including a championship golf course. There is a choice of smart bars and dining options, while the leisure area offers lighter meals in addition to the ambitious menus available in the main restaurant. Refurbished bedrooms are comfortable and many have views over the golf course.
ROOMS: 164 en suite (bth/shr) (8 fmly) No smoking in 95 bedrooms **MEALS:** V meals Coffee am Tea pm **FACILITIES:** CTV in all bedrooms STV Indoor swimming pool (heated) Golf 18 Tennis (hard) Squash Snooker Sauna Solarium Gym Pool table Jacuzzi/spa Aerobic studio Beauty room **CONF:** Thtr 600 Class 310 Board 30 **SERVICES:** Lift Night porter 500P **NOTES:** No smoking area in restaurant Last d 10pm
CARDS:

BLACKPOOL Lancashire — Map 07 SD33
★★★ Savoy
Best Western
Queens Promenade, North Shore FY2 9SJ
Quality Percentage Score: 60%
☎ 01253 352561 🖷 01253 595549
Dir: *located along the seafront at Queens Promenade*

This large hotel, on the North Promenade, offers nicely furnished bedrooms, varying in size but generally quite spacious. Many have fine sea views. In addition to the large open plan bar and lounge, there is a separate lounge with a large screen TV and an

contd.

attractive wood panelled restaurant with an interesting stained glass ceiling. A variety of meeting and function suites is also available.
ROOMS: 131 en suite (bth/shr) (14 fmly) No smoking in 58 bedrooms s £57.50-£82.50; d £75-£122.50 (incl. bkfst) * LB Off peak **MEALS:** Sunday Lunch £7.95 Dinner £14.50 & alc International Cuisine V meals Coffee am Tea pm **FACILITIES:** CTV in all bedrooms Xmas **CONF:** Thtr 400 Class 250 Board 50 Del from £75 * **SERVICES:** Lift Night porter 40P **NOTES:** No dogs (ex guide dogs) No smoking in restaurant Last d 9.30pm **CARDS:**

See advert on opposite page

BLACKPOOL Lancashire — Map 07 SD33
★★★ Clifton
Talbot Square, The Promenade FY1 1ND
Quality Percentage Score: 57%
☎ 01253 621481 📠 01253 627345
Dir: *from Blackpool town centre head towards the North Pier, hotel opposite*
With a central location, just opposite the North Pier, this Grade I listed building is ideally situated for all the major attractions within the town. Public areas include a popular bistro restaurant and a choice of three bars, two of which offer entertainment at weekends, whilst many of the bedrooms enjoy fine views.
ROOMS: 77 en suite (bth/shr) (2 fmly) s £25-£75; d £50-£120 (incl. bkfst) * LB Off peak **MEALS:** V meals Coffee am Tea pm **FACILITIES:** CTV in all bedrooms Wkly live entertainment Xmas **SERVICES:** Lift Night porter **NOTES:** No dogs (ex guide dogs) No smoking in restaurant **CARDS:**

See advert on opposite page

BLACKPOOL Lancashire — Map 07 SD33
★★ Brabyns
1-3 Shaftesbury Av, North Shore FY2 9QQ
Quality Percentage Score: 66%
☎ 01253 354263 📠 01253 352915
Situated in a residential area, close to the sea front, this privately owned hotel is being upgraded throughout. Newly decorated bedrooms are comfortable and thoughtfully equipped, with rooms at the back of the house tending to be larger. There is a cosy bar lounge and an attractive, wood panelled dining room. Service is friendly and willingly provided.
ROOMS: 22 en suite (bth/shr) 3 annexe en suite (bth/shr) s £30-£45; d £50-£80 (incl. bkfst) * LB Off peak **MEALS:** Lunch £6.50-£8.50 Dinner £11-£14 V meals Coffee am Tea pm **FACILITIES:** CTV in all bedrooms STV Xmas **SERVICES:** 12P **NOTES:** No children No smoking in restaurant Last d 7.30pm **CARDS:**

BLACKPOOL Lancashire — Map 07 SD33
★★ Hotel Sheraton
54-62 Queens Promenade FY2 9RP
Quality Percentage Score: 65%
☎ 01253 352723 📠 01253 595499
Dir: *1m N from Blackpool Tower on promenade towards Fleetwood*
Ideal for families because of its many facilities, this seafront hotel offers very good value for money accommodation. The bedrooms are modern and well equipped and the spacious lounges include quiet areas. A satisfactory choice of dishes are available in the dining room and the staff are very willing and friendly.
ROOMS: 108 en suite (bth/shr) (44 fmly) s £42.50-£54; d £80-£102 (incl. bkfst) * LB Off peak **MEALS:** Dinner fr £15 V meals Coffee am Tea pm **FACILITIES:** CTV in all bedrooms Indoor swimming pool (heated) Sauna Pool table Table tennis Darts Wkly live entertainment Xmas **CONF:** Thtr 200 Class 100 Board 150 Del from £50 * **SERVICES:** Lift Night porter 20P **NOTES:** No dogs (ex guide dogs) Last d 8pm **CARDS:**

BLACKPOOL Lancashire — Map 07 SD33
★★ *Belgrave*
272 Queens Promenade FY2 9HD
Quality Percentage Score: 61%
☎ 01253 351570 📠 01253 353335
Situated on the quieter north shore, this family run hotel offers bedrooms varying in size, some being suitable for families. There is a cosy TV lounge, in addition to a spacious lounge bar. The bright restaurant and some of the bedrooms have views across the promenade to the sea.
ROOMS: 33 en suite (shr) (7 fmly) **MEALS:** V meals Coffee am **FACILITIES:** CTV in all bedrooms STV Pool table **SERVICES:** Lift 16P **NOTES:** No dogs No smoking in restaurant Last d 7.15pm Closed Jan RS Feb-Mar & Nov-Dec **CARDS:**

BLACKPOOL Lancashire — Map 07 SD33
★★ Revill's
190-194 North Promenade FY1 1RJ
Quality Percentage Score: 61%
☎ 01253 625768 📠 01253 624736
Dir: *just N of Blackpool Tower, almost opposite the North Pier*
This family-run hotel enjoys a seafront location close to the North Pier and yet is in the heart of the town. There is a choice of bars and a good value evening meal is offered in the attractively decorated restaurant that has a sun lounge to relax in afterwards. Bedrooms are comfortable and some of them have fine sea views.
ROOMS: 47 en suite (bth/shr) (10 fmly) s £25-£35; d £40-£50 (incl. bkfst) * LB Off peak **MEALS:** Dinner £8.50-£10.50 V meals Coffee am Tea pm **FACILITIES:** CTV in all bedrooms Snooker Xmas **SERVICES:** Lift Night porter 23P **NOTES:** No dogs Last d 7.30pm **CARDS:**

BLACKPOOL Lancashire — Map 07 SD33
★★ Warwick
603-609 New South Promenade FY4 1NG
Quality Percentage Score: 61%
☎ 01253 342192 📠 01253 405776
Dir: *from M55 junct 4 take A5230 for South Shore then rt on A584, Promenade South*
Standing on the south shore, close to the famous Pleasure Beach, this popular hotel offers comfortable well furnished bedrooms, the largest being on the first floor. Rafferty's Bar has frequent live entertainment, and there is a separate restaurant.
ROOMS: 50 en suite (bth/shr) (11 fmly) s £29-£42; d £58-£84 (incl. bkfst & dinner) * LB Off peak **MEALS:** Bar Lunch £1.75-£7.50 Dinner £12.50-£13.50 International Cuisine V meals Coffee am Tea pm **FACILITIES:** CTV in all bedrooms Indoor swimming pool (heated) Solarium Pool table Table tennis Wkly live entertainment Xmas **CONF:** Thtr 50 Class 24 Board 30 Del from £44 * **SERVICES:** Lift Night porter 30P **NOTES:** No smoking in restaurant Last d 8pm Closed 1 Jan-13 Feb **CARDS:**

BLACKPOOL Lancashire — Map 07 SD33
Travel Inn
Yeadon Way, South Shore FY1 6BF
☎ 01253 341415 📠 01253 343805
Dir: *M55 into Blackpool, keep right at end of dual carriageway, 2nd exit rdbt, follow signs for Main Coach & Car Park, next to Elf Garage*
This modern building offers accommodation in smart, spacious and well equipped bedrooms, all with en-suite bathrooms. Refreshments may be taken at the nearby family restaurant. For details about current prices consult the Contents Page under Hotel Groups for the Travel Inn phone number.
ROOMS: 40 en suite (bth/shr) d £39.95 *

contd.

B

BLACKPOOL Lancashire — **Map 07 SD33**

Travel Inn (Bispham)
Devonshire Rd, Bispham FY2 0AR
☎ 01253 354942 Fax 01253 590498
Dir: *from Fleetwood on A587 for approx 4m*
This modern building offers accommodation in smart, spacious and well equipped bedrooms, all with en-suite bathrooms. Refreshments may be taken at the nearby family restaurant. For details about current prices consult the Contents Page under Hotel Groups for the Travel Inn phone number.
ROOMS: 40 en suite (bth/shr) d £39.95 *

BLAKENEY Norfolk — **Map 09 TG04**

★★★ The Blakeney
The Quay NR25 7NE
Quality Percentage Score: 64%
☎ 01263 740797 Fax 01263 740795
Dir: *off A149*
A charming setting and traditional hospitality are hallmarks of this typically English hotel. The elegant restaurant serves freshly prepared meals, while the refurbished sun lounge has delightful

contd.

Indicates that the star classification has not been confirmed under the New Quality Standards, see page 7 for further information.

views overlooking the marshes. The thoughtfully laid out bedrooms vary in size and style, and all are well furnished.

The Blakeney, Norfolk

ROOMS: 49 en suite (bth/shr) 10 annexe en suite (bth/shr) (11 fmly) s £56-£111; d £112-£222 (incl. bkfst & dinner) * LB Off peak **MEALS:** Lunch fr £13 High tea fr £5 Dinner fr £19 & alc English & Continental Cuisine V meals Coffee am Tea pm **FACILITIES:** CTV in all bedrooms Indoor swimming pool (heated) Snooker Sauna Gym Pool table Jacuzzi/spa Table tennis Xmas **CONF:** Thtr 70 Class 40 Board 32 Del from £96 * **SERVICES:** Lift Night porter 60P **NOTES:** No coaches No smoking in restaurant Last d 9.30pm

CARDS:

See advert on page 115

BLAKENEY Norfolk **Map 09 TG04**

The Premier Collection

★★❀❀❀ Morston Hall

Morston NR25 7AA

☎ 01263 741041 📠 01263 740419

***Dir:** 1m W of Blakeney on A149 Kings Lynn/Cromer Rd*

Morston Hall dates back to the 17th century and stands in delightful, well tended gardens in a small coastal village beside a tidal quay. The bedrooms are spacious and individually decorated, with comfortable furnishings and thoughtful extra touches. Lounges are superbly comfortable and include a sunny conservatory. The elegant dining room is the perfect setting for the excellent set dinners served at Morston Hall along with its extensive wine list.

ROOMS: 6 en suite (bth/shr) **MEALS:** Sunday Lunch £22 Dinner £34 V meals Coffee am Tea pm **FACILITIES:** CTV in all bedrooms **SERVICES:** 40P **NOTES:** No coaches No smoking in restaurant Last d 7.30pm Closed Xmas **CARDS:**

BLAKENEY Norfolk **Map 09 TG04**

★★ The Pheasant

Coast Rd, Kelling NR25 7EG

Quality Percentage Score: 75%

☎ 01263 588382 📠 01263 588101

***Dir:** on A419 coast road, mid-way between Sheringham & Blakeney*

A charming hotel on the coast road, in well landscaped grounds overlooking the sea. There are two styles of bedroom, new wing rooms are modern and spacious, the few main house rooms are traditionally appointed, including a four-poster room. Public rooms include an open plan bar, lounge area, and a large restaurant.

ROOMS: 27 en suite (bth/shr) No smoking in 16 bedrooms s £38-£46; d £64-£76 (incl. bkfst) * LB Off peak **MEALS:** Lunch £7.95-£9.95 Dinner £5-£8.50 & alc V meals Coffee am Tea pm **FACILITIES:** CTV in all bedrooms **CONF:** Thtr 80 Class 50 Board 50 **SERVICES:** 80P **NOTES:** No children 10yrs No smoking in restaurant Last d 9pm

CARDS:

BLAKENEY Norfolk **Map 09 TG04**

★★ Manor

Blakeney NR25 7ND

Quality Percentage Score: 64%

☎ 01263 740376 📠 01263 741116

***Dir:** turn off A149 at St Mary's church*

Up from the quayside, this generously priced hotel has many regular guests returning for the relaxed atmosphere. There is a choice of bedroom sizes and locations, in both the main house and a collection of fully converted flint faced barns and stables; all rooms are tastefully furnished. The spacious public rooms offer guests the choice of dining options, informal bar fare or imaginative restaurant cuisine.

ROOMS: 8 en suite (bth/shr) 30 annexe en suite (bth/shr) s £35-£40; d £70-£90 (incl. bkfst) * LB Off peak **MEALS:** Sunday Lunch fr £11.25 Dinner fr £16 & alc English & French Cuisine V meals Coffee am Tea pm **FACILITIES:** CTV in all bedrooms Xmas **SERVICES:** 40P **NOTES:** No children 14yrs No smoking in restaurant Last d 9pm Closed 31 Dec-21 Jan

CARDS:

BLANCHLAND Northumberland **Map 12 NY95**

★★❀ Lord Crewe Arms

DH8 9SP

Quality Percentage Score: 68%

☎ 01434 675251 📠 01434 675337

***Dir:** 10m S of Hexham via B6306*

Originally a lodging house for monks, this historic hotel dates from medieval times and is the focal point of an attractive conservation village. Public areas feature flagstone floors, vaulted ceilings and original stonework. Restaurant dinners feature an interesting range of dishes, or there is an equally appetising menu in the crypt bar. Bedrooms are split between the main hotel and a former estate building just across the road. All are well equipped, but most retain a period style.

ROOMS: 9 en suite (bth/shr) 10 annexe en suite (bth/shr) (2 fmly) s fr £80; d fr £110 (incl. bkfst) * LB Off peak **MEALS:** Sunday Lunch £14 Dinner £28 V meals Coffee am Tea pm **FACILITIES:** CTV in all bedrooms Xmas **CONF:** Thtr 20 Class 20 Board 16 Del from £68 * **SERVICES:** P **NOTES:** Last d 9.15pm **CARDS:**

BLANDFORD FORUM Dorset **Map 03 ST80**

★★★ Crown

West St DT11 7AJ

Quality Percentage Score: 65%

☎ 01258 456626 📠 01258 451084

***Dir:** 100mtrs from town bridge*

An attractive former coaching house in the centre of Blandford,

contd.

suitable for business and leisure travellers. Bedrooms are well equipped, comfortable and spacious. The wood-panelled bar is popular, there is also a restaurant and small lounge. The separate, self-contained function room overlooking the walled garden is a good venue for wedding receptions and conferences.

ROOMS: 34 en suite (bth/shr) (2 fmly) No smoking in 4 bedrooms s £50-£65; d £70-£85 (incl. bkfst) * LB Off peak **MEALS:** Lunch £12.50-£14 & alc Dinner £14 & alc English & French Cuisine V meals Coffee am Tea pm **FACILITIES:** CTV in all bedrooms STV Fishing Shooting ch fac **CONF:** Thtr 250 Class 200 Board 60 Del £85 * **SERVICES:** 144P **NOTES:** Last d 9.15pm Closed 25-28 Dec **CARDS:**

See advert on this page

BLOCKLEY Gloucestershire — Map 04 SP13

★★★ Crown Inn

High St GL56 9EX

Quality Percentage Score: 67%

☎ 01386 700245 Fax 01386 700247

Built of mellow Cotswold stone, this popular hotel, once a coaching inn, dates back to the 16th century. It has much charm and character, with exposed stone walls and log fires. There is a choice of eating options including one of the best fish and grill menus in the area. The accommodation, in a separate building, includes four-poster rooms and two full suites, all with modern equipment and facilities.

ROOMS: 13 en suite (bth/shr) 8 annexe en suite (bth/shr) (2 fmly) s fr £70; d £99-£135 (incl. bkfst) * LB Off peak **MEALS:** English & Continental Cuisine V meals Coffee am Tea pm **FACILITIES:** CTV in all bedrooms Wkly live entertainment Xmas **CONF:** Board 18 Del from £90 * **SERVICES:** 50P **NOTES:** Last d 10pm **CARDS:**

BLUNDELLSANDS Merseyside — Map 07 SJ39

★★★ Carlton Blundellsands

The Serpentine L23 6YB

Quality Percentage Score: 63%

☎ 0151 924 6515 Fax 0151 931 5364

Dir: *from A565 from Liverpool turn left at College Rd (Merchant Taylors School) to roundabout. Turn left & take third right into Agnes Rd*

An elegant Victorian hotel opposite Crosby Station offering good accommodation. Public areas include the formal Mauretania Restaurant and popular Copper Bar, providing light meals and snacks at lunch time and during the evening. There are conference and banqueting suites and a large car park.

ROOMS: 30 en suite (bth/shr) No smoking in 6 bedrooms s £80-£90; d £90-£100 * LB Off peak **MEALS:** Lunch £9.95-£10.50 Dinner £14.95-£16.95 & alc European Cuisine V meals Coffee am Tea pm **FACILITIES:** CTV in all bedrooms STV Wkly live entertainment **CONF:** Thtr 640 Class 350 Board 320 Del from £95 * **SERVICES:** Lift Night porter 150P **NOTES:** No smoking area in restaurant Last d 9.30pm **CARDS:**

BLYTH Nottinghamshire — Map 08 SK68

★★★ Charnwood

Best Western

Sheffield Rd S81 8HF

Quality Percentage Score: 68%

☎ 01909 591610 Fax 01909 591429

Dir: *A614 into Blyth village, turn right past church onto A634 Sheffield road. Hotel 0.5m on right past humpback bridge*

Conveniently situated for major routes, this hotel enjoys a rural setting and is surrounded by attractive gardens. Bedrooms are comfortably furnished and attractively decorated. A range of carefully prepared meals and snacks is offered in the restaurant, or in the lounge bar overlooking the gardens. Service is friendly and attentive.

ROOMS: 34 en suite (bth/shr) (1 fmly) No smoking in 6 bedrooms s fr £65; d fr £90 (incl. bkfst) * LB Off peak **MEALS:** Lunch £12.45 & alc Dinner £17.95 English & French Cuisine V meals Coffee am Tea pm **FACILITIES:** CTV in all bedrooms STV Mini-gym **CONF:** Thtr 135 Class 60 Board 45 Del £99.95 * **SERVICES:** Night porter 70P **NOTES:** No dogs (ex guide dogs) **CARDS:**

BLYTH Nottinghamshire — Map 08 SK68

Travelodge

Travelodge

Hilltop Roundabout S81 8HG

☎ 01909 591841

Dir: *at junct of A1M/A614*

This modern building offers accommodation in smart, spacious and well equipped bedrooms, all with en-suite bathrooms. Refreshments may be taken at the nearby family restaurant. For details about current prices, consult the Contents Page under Hotel Groups for the Travelodge phone number.

ROOMS: 39 en suite (bth/shr) d £39.95 *

B

BODMIN Cornwall & Isles of Scilly **Map 02 SX06**

★★ *Westberry*

Rhind St PL31 2EL

Quality Percentage Score: 64%

☎ 01208 72772 01208 72212

This family-run hotel is popular with business travellers, being conveniently located for Bodmin town centre and the A30. Bedrooms are comfortably furnished and equipped with a range of facilities for both business and leisure guests. A spacious bar-lounge is provided, plus a billiard room. The restaurant serves both fixed-price and carte menus, and an extensive bar menu is available for lunch.

ROOMS: 14 rms (6 bth 3 shr) 8 annexe en suite (bth/shr) (2 fmly) **MEALS:** V meals Coffee am Tea pm **FACILITIES:** CTV in all bedrooms STV Snooker Gym **CONF:** Thtr 60 Class 20 Board 30 **SERVICES:** 30P **NOTES:** Closed 5 days Xmas/New Year **CARDS:**

BOGNOR REGIS West Sussex **Map 04 SZ99**

★★★ *The Inglenook*

255 Pagham Rd, Nyetimber PO21 3QB

Quality Percentage Score: 61%

☎ 01243 262495 & 265411 01243 262668

This friendly, family-run hotel, formerly a 16th-century inn, retains much of its original charm with exposed beams throughout. Bedrooms, which vary in shape and size, are all individually decorated and well equipped. Public areas include a cosy lounge, and the bar is full of character. The spacious restaurant overlooks the garden, and attentive service is provided by the owners and their team of staff.

ROOMS: 18 en suite (bth/shr) (1 fmly) **MEALS:** English, French & Italian Cuisine V meals Coffee am Tea pm **FACILITIES:** CTV in all bedrooms **CONF:** Thtr 100 Class 50 Board 50 **SERVICES:** 35P **NOTES:** No smoking area in restaurant Last d 9.30pm **CARDS:**

BOGNOR REGIS West Sussex **Map 04 SZ99**

★★ Beachcroft

Clyde Rd, Felpham Village PO22 7AH

Quality Percentage Score: 69%

☎ 01243 827142 01243 827142

Dir: *turn off A259 at Butlins rdbt into Felpham Village, in 800mtrs turn right into Sea Rd then 2nd left into Clyde Rd*

This welcoming family run hotel offers bright, airy accommodation which is well maintained and attractive. Guests enjoy the informal atmosphere and the traditional cuisine. There is a heated indoor swimming pool and a cosy lounge bar.

ROOMS: 38 en suite (bth/shr) (4 fmly) No smoking in 3 bedrooms s £37.50-£41.50; d £56-£65 (incl. bkfst) * LB Off peak **MEALS:** Dinner £14 & alc International Cuisine V meals Coffee am Tea pm **FACILITIES:** CTV in all bedrooms STV Indoor swimming pool (heated) **CONF:** Thtr 50 Class 30 Board 30 Del from £45 * **SERVICES:** 27P **NOTES:** No dogs Last d 9.30pm Closed 24 Dec-10 Jan **CARDS:**

BOGNOR REGIS West Sussex **Map 04 SZ99**

★★ Aldwick Hotel

Aldwick Rd, Aldwick PO21 2QU

Quality Percentage Score: 66%

☎ 01243 821945 01243 821316

Dir: *at rbt junct with A259/A29 take Victoria Drive, signed Aldwick. At traffic lights turn rt into Aldwick Road. Hotel 250yds on left-1km W of Pier*

Under ownership of Tim and Coleen Scargill, this friendly hotel has undergone much refurbishment. Situated close to Marine Park Gardens and the beach, it enjoys a quiet residential location. All bedrooms are neatly decorated and well equipped. Public areas include a spacious dining room, smart bar and cosy lounge.

ROOMS: 19 en suite (bth/shr) No smoking in all bedrooms s £41; d £82 (incl. bkfst) * LB Off peak **MEALS:** Lunch £9-£12 Dinner £13.95-£14.95 English & French Cuisine V meals Coffee am Tea pm **FACILITIES:** CTV in all bedrooms Xmas **CONF:** Thtr 50 Class 20 Board 24 Del from £60 * **SERVICES:** Lift 10P **NOTES:** No smoking in restaurant Last d 8.30pm **CARDS:**

BOLTON Greater Manchester **Map 07 SD70**

★★★★ *Bolton Moat House*

MOAT HOUSE

1 Higher Bridge St BL1 2EW

Quality Percentage Score: 63%

☎ 01204 879988 01204 380777

Dir: *take A666, following signs for town centre north at 2nd set of traffic lights turn right, hotel on left*

This modern hotel is situated in the town centre and features a restaurant in what was once a local church. Although the bedrooms are compact they are well appointed and some have separate sitting rooms. There is a range of conference and banqueting suites, a leisure centre and secure parking facilities.

ROOMS: 128 en suite (bth/shr) (4 fmly) No smoking in 98 bedrooms **MEALS:** V meals Coffee am Tea pm **FACILITIES:** CTV in all bedrooms STV Indoor swimming pool (heated) Sauna Solarium Gym Pool table Jacuzzi/spa **CONF:** Thtr 350 Class 120 Board 80 **SERVICES:** Lift Night porter 83P **NOTES:** No dogs (ex guide dogs) No smoking in restaurant Last d 9.30pm **CARDS:**

BOLTON Greater Manchester **Map 07 SD70**

★★★★ *Last Drop Hotel*

MACDONALD hotels

The Last Drop Village & Hotel, Bromley Cross BL7 9PZ

Quality Percentage Score: 63%

☎ 01204 591131 01204 304122

Dir: *3m N of Bolton off B5472*

Formerly a farm complex, the buildings were transformed into an hotel in the 1960s. There are excellent leisure and conference facilities, and the well appointed bedrooms are either in the main

contd.

building, or in the courtyard and separate cottages. A cobbled way leads from reception to the restaurant and a variety of shops.
ROOMS: 118 en suite (bth/shr) 10 annexe en suite (bth/shr) (72 fmly) No smoking in 60 bedrooms **MEALS:** English & French Cuisine V meals Coffee am Tea pm **FACILITIES:** CTV in all bedrooms STV Indoor swimming pool (heated) Squash Snooker Sauna Solarium Gym Pool table Jacuzzi/spa Craft shops Wkly live entertainment **CONF:** Thtr 700 Class 300 Board 95 **SERVICES:** Lift Night porter 400P **NOTES:** No smoking in restaurant Last d 10pm
CARDS:

BOLTON Greater Manchester — Map 07 SD70

★★★ *The Beaumont*

Beaumont Rd BL3 4TA
Quality Percentage Score: 59%
☎ 01204 651511 Fax 01204 61064
Dir: *on A58 W of town*

A modern hotel conveniently situated close to junction 5 of the M61 motorway. Bedrooms are designed to modern standards and upgrading is planned for the near future. Public areas include 'Seasons' restaurant and bar, a banqueting suite and conference facilities. Staff are friendly and helpful and there is an all day lounge menu and 24 hour room service.
ROOMS: 101 en suite (bth/shr) No smoking in 50 bedrooms **MEALS:** International Cuisine V meals Coffee am Tea pm **FACILITIES:** CTV in all bedrooms Pool table ch fac **CONF:** Thtr 130 Class 100 Board 50 **SERVICES:** Night porter 150P **NOTES:** No smoking area in restaurant Last d 9.30pm **CARDS:**

BOLTON Greater Manchester — Map 07 SD70

Comfort Inn Bolton

Bolton West Service Area, Horwich BL6 5UZ
☎ 01204 468641 Fax 01204 668585
ROOMS: 32 en suite (bth/shr) **CONF:** Thtr 60 Class 60 Board 30

BOLTON ABBEY North Yorkshire — Map 07 SE05

The Premier Collection

★★★ The Devonshire Arms Country House

BD23 6AJ
☎ 01756 710441 Fax 01756 710564
Dir: *on B6160, 250yds N of junct with A59*

Set in the Wharfe valley, this stylish country house hotel is owned by the Duke and Duchess of Devonshire. Bedrooms are well equipped and furnished with some impressive pieces. The smart leisure club includes treatment rooms and is located in a converted stone barn. A diverse range of dishes is offered in a choice of dining areas. The brasserie has a light, eclectic menu, while the restaurant offers more traditional fare.
ROOMS: 41 en suite (bth/shr) No smoking in 12 bedrooms s £110-£325; d £155-£325 (incl. bkfst) * LB Off peak **MEALS:** Lunch fr £17.95 & alc High tea £4.50-£10alc Dinner fr £37 English & French Cuisine V meals Coffee am Tea pm **FACILITIES:** CTV in all bedrooms Indoor swimming pool (heated) Tennis (hard) Fishing Sauna Solarium Gym Croquet lawn Putting green Jacuzzi/spa Laser pigeon shooting Falconry Xmas **CONF:** Thtr 120 Class 80 Board 40 Del from £160 * **SERVICES:** Night porter 150P **NOTES:** No smoking in restaurant Last d 10pm
CARDS:

BONCHURCH See **Wight, Isle of**

BOREHAMWOOD Greater London — Map 04 TQ19

★★★★ *Elstree Moat House*

Barnet Bypass WD6 5PU
Quality Percentage Score: 63%
☎ 020 8214 9988 Fax 020 8207 3194
Dir: *2m from junct 23 of M25*

A modern, primarily corporate hotel. Hemingway's cocktail bar and Hugo's restaurant are popular, there is an alternative, larger bar. Versatile conference suites make this a good business venue. The well equipped gym, small pool and beauty salon appeal to leisure guests. Bedrooms have two styles of décor with the same levels of comfort and amenities.
ROOMS: 130 en suite (bth/shr) (5 fmly) No smoking in 65 bedrooms **MEALS:** International Cuisine V meals Coffee am Tea pm **FACILITIES:** CTV in all bedrooms STV Indoor swimming pool (heated) Sauna Solarium Gym Pool table Jacuzzi/spa Steam room Beautician **CONF:** Thtr 400 Class 100 Board 60 **SERVICES:** Lift Night porter 250P **NOTES:** No dogs (ex guide dogs) No smoking area in restaurant Last d 9.45pm **CARDS:**

BOROUGHBRIDGE North Yorkshire — Map 08 SE36

★★★ *Crown*

Horsefair YO51 9LB
Quality Percentage Score: 69%
☎ 01423 322328 Fax 01423 324512
Dir: *take junct 48 off A1(M). Hotel 1m towards town centre at T-junct*

Situated in this historic market town just off the A1, The Crown boasts a remarkable history. Today it provides well appointed bedrooms and comfortable public areas including the a delightfully refurbished restaurant offering a wide range of well prepared food. A good range of meeting rooms are also available.
ROOMS: 42 en suite (bth/shr) (2 fmly) **MEALS:** International Cuisine V meals Coffee am Tea pm **FACILITIES:** CTV in all bedrooms STV **CONF:** Thtr 200 Class 120 Board 120 Del from £85 * **SERVICES:** Lift Night porter 60P **NOTES:** No smoking in restaurant
CARDS:

BOROUGHBRIDGE North Yorkshire — Map 08 SE36

★★★ Rose Manor

Horsefair YO51 9LL
Quality Percentage Score: 67%
☎ 01423 322245 Fax 01423 324920
Dir: *turn off A1(M) at exit 48 onto B6265, hotel within 1m*

Popular with business people and also attracting both conferences and weddings, Rose Manor is a country mansion lying on the south side of the town with a friendly and relaxing

contd.

atmosphere. It has an inviting lounge and a split level dining room, and bedrooms are well equipped, many being spacious.
ROOMS: 19 en suite (bth/shr) 2 annexe en suite (bth/shr) (1 fmly) No smoking in 11 bedrooms s fr £78.50; d £103-£108 (incl. bkfst) * LB Off peak **MEALS:** Lunch £9.95-£10.75 Dinner fr £17.50 V meals Coffee am Tea pm **FACILITIES:** CTV in all bedrooms STV **CONF:** Thtr 250 Class 250 Board 25 **SERVICES:** 100P **NOTES:** No dogs Last d 10pm
CARDS:

BORROWDALE Cumbria — Map 11 NY21

see also **Keswick & Rosthwaite**

★★★ Borrowdale Gates Country House

CA12 5UQ
Quality Percentage Score: 77%
☎ 017687 77204 017687 77254
Dir: *from Keswick follow Borrowdale signs on B5289, after approx 4m turn right at sign for Grange, hotel is on right approx 0.25m through village*

Enjoying a sedate woodland setting, this family-run hotel commands stunning views of the towering fells that form the Borrowdale valley. Inviting public rooms include lounges complete with an open fire, a cosy bar and an attractive restaurant. The ambitious menu changes daily and makes excellent use of local produce. Many of the bedrooms have been stylishly upgraded and the recently completed superior rooms provide exemplary facilities.
ROOMS: 32 en suite (bth/shr) (2 fmly) s £75-£87.50; d £145-£165 (incl. bkfst & dinner) LB Off peak **MEALS:** Lunch £14.25 & alc Dinner £27.50 & alc English & French Cuisine V meals Coffee am Tea pm
FACILITIES: CTV in all bedrooms ch fac Xmas **SERVICES:** 40P
NOTES: No dogs (ex guide dogs) No coaches No smoking in restaurant Last d 8.45pm Closed Jan **CARDS:**

See advert under KESWICK

BORROWDALE Cumbria — Map 11 NY21

★★★ Borrowdale

CA12 5UY
Quality Percentage Score: 70%
☎ 017687 77224 017687 77338
Dir: *on B5289 at south end of Lake Derwentwater*
A traditional holiday hotel in the beautiful Borrowdale Valley overlooking Derwentwater and 15 minutes drive from Keswick. Extensive public areas include a choice of lounges, a stylish dining room, and a lounge bar and conservatory serving hearty bar meals. There is a wide choice of bedroom size, the larger rooms are best.
ROOMS: 33 en suite (bth/shr) (9 fmly) s £53-£64; d £96-£150 (incl. bkfst & dinner) * LB Off peak **MEALS:** Lunch fr £11.95 High tea £1.50-£4.50alc Dinner fr £19.95 English & Continental Cuisine V meals Coffee am Tea pm **FACILITIES:** CTV in all bedrooms Free use of nearby Health Club Xmas **CONF:** Class 30 **SERVICES:** 100P **NOTES:** No coaches No smoking in restaurant Last d 9.15pm **CARDS:**

BOSCASTLE Cornwall & Isles of Scilly — Map 02 SX09

★★ The Wellington Hotel

The Harbour PL35 0AQ
Quality Percentage Score: 64%
☎ 01840 250202 01840 250621
THE CIRCLE Selected Individual Hotels GREAT BRITAIN
The 'Welly', as it's affectionately known locally, dates back around 400 years and boasts connections with both Thomas Hardy and, more recently, Guy Gibson of 'Dambusters' fame. Stone built, with a crenellated tower on one corner, and comfortable rooms of varying sizes, the hotel offers a choice of comfortable lounges and a cheery beamed bar where local folk singers gather every Monday night. The dining room provides an appetizing menu of home-cooked dishes with a strong French influence.
ROOMS: 16 en suite (bth/shr) (1 fmly) s £32-£44; d £58-£76 (incl. bkfst) * LB Off peak **MEALS:** Bar Lunch fr £3.50alc Dinner £17.50-£22.50 English & French Cuisine V meals Coffee am **FACILITIES:** CTV in all bedrooms Pool table Games room Wkly live entertainment Xmas
CONF: Board 24 **SERVICES:** 20P **NOTES:** No children 7yrs No smoking area in restaurant Last d 9.30pm RS 29 Nov-16 Dec & 10 Jan-10 Feb
CARDS:

BOSHAM West Sussex — Map 04 SU80

★★★ *The Millstream*

Bosham Ln PO18 8HL
Quality Percentage Score: 72%
☎ 01243 573234 01243 573459
Best Western
Dir: *4m W of Chichester on A259, turn left at Bosham roundabout, 1m turn right at T junction follow signs to church & quay hotel 0.5m on right*
Situated in the peaceful village of Bosham, this attractive hotel provides comfortable and attractively decorated bedrooms, each with an individual theme. Public rooms include a cocktail bar, which opens out onto the garden, a lounge and a well appointed restaurant.

ROOMS: 33 en suite (bth/shr) (2 fmly) No smoking in 14 bedrooms
MEALS: English & French Cuisine V meals Coffee am Tea pm
FACILITIES: CTV in all bedrooms Sailing breaks Bridge breaks Wkly live entertainment **CONF:** Thtr 45 Class 20 Board 24 **SERVICES:** Night porter 44P **NOTES:** No coaches No smoking in restaurant Last d 9.30pm
CARDS:

See advert under CHICHESTER

BOSTON Lincolnshire — Map 08 TF34

★★★ New England

49 Wide Bargate PE21 6SH
MENZIES HOTELS
Quality Percentage Score: 59%
☎ 0500 636943 (Central Res) 01773 880321
Dir: *E side of town off John Adams Way*
Situated close to the town centre, this popular hotel continues to be improved. Morning coffee and afternoon tea are served in its

contd.

open-plan public areas, and the restaurant serves a brasserie-style menu.
ROOMS: 25 en suite (bth/shr) (2 fmly) No smoking in 5 bedrooms s £59.50-£75; d fr £75 * LB Off peak **MEALS:** Lunch £8.95-£10.95 Dinner fr £13.50 V meals Coffee am Tea pm **FACILITIES:** CTV in all bedrooms STV Xmas **CONF:** Thtr 40 Class 18 Board 25 Del from £85 * **SERVICES:** Night porter **NOTES:** No smoking in restaurant Last d 9.30pm
CARDS:

BOSTON Lincolnshire **Map 08 TF34**
★★ Comfort Friendly Inn
Donnington Rd, Bicker Bar PE20 3AN
Quality Percentage Score: 67%
☎ 01205 820118 📠 01205 820228
Dir: *at junct of A17/A52*
A purpose-built hotel with well equipped bedrooms offering good levels of comfort and value for money. Facilities include two meeting rooms, a small open plan lounge bar with TV and adjacent restaurant. Reasonably priced meals are available all day. Public areas are air-conditioned.
ROOMS: 55 en suite (bth/shr) (4 fmly) No smoking in 27 bedrooms s £43.75; d £54.50 * LB Off peak **MEALS:** Lunch £2.95-£15.95alc Dinner fr £10.75 & alc English & Continental Cuisine V meals Coffee am Tea pm **FACILITIES:** CTV in all bedrooms STV Gym Xmas **CONF:** Thtr 70 Class 28 Board 35 **SERVICES:** Night porter Air conditioning 50P **NOTES:** No smoking area in restaurant Last d 10pm
CARDS:

BOSTON Lincolnshire **Map 08 TF34**
Travel Inn
Wainfleet Rd PE21 9RW
☎ 01205 362307 📠 01205 366494
Dir: *on A52 Skegness Road, 300yds east of its junction with A16 Boston/Grimsby road*
This modern building offers accommodation in smart, spacious and well equipped bedrooms, all with en-suite bathrooms. Refreshments may be taken at the nearby family restaurant. For details about current prices consult the Contents Page under Hotel Groups for the Travel Inn phone number.
ROOMS: 34 en suite (bth/shr) d £39.95 *

BOTLEY Hampshire **Map 04 SU51**
★★★★ Botley Park Hotel Golf & Country Club
Winchester Rd, Boorley Green SO32 2UA
Quality Percentage Score: 67%
☎ 01489 780888 📠 01489 789242
Dir: *Boorley Green on B3354, approx 2m from village*

Set in 176 acres of landscaped parkland golf course, Botley Park boasts extensive sports and leisure facilities. Bedrooms are spacious, lounges comfortable and guests have a choice of restaurants and bars.
ROOMS: 100 en suite (bth/shr) No smoking in 52 bedrooms
MEALS: International Cuisine V meals Coffee am Tea pm
FACILITIES: CTV in all bedrooms STV Indoor swimming pool (heated) Golf 18 Tennis (hard) Squash Snooker Sauna Solarium Gym Croquet lawn Jacuzzi/spa Aerobics studio Beauty salon Wkly live entertainment
CONF: Thtr 240 Class 100 Board 60 **SERVICES:** Night porter 250P
NOTES: No smoking in restaurant Last d 9.45pm
CARDS:
See advert under SOUTHAMPTON

BOURNE Lincolnshire **Map 08 TF02**
★★ Black Horse Inn
Grimsthorpe PE10 0LY
Quality Percentage Score: 68%
☎ 01778 591247 📠 01778 591373
Dir: *turn off A1 onto A151, hotel 9m on left 0.5m after entrance to Grimsthorpe Castle*
The Black Horse inn sits in a small village, almost on the doorstep of Grimsthorpe Castle. Standards of accommodation and service are good, and the owners offer an extensive range of well prepared dishes in the restaurant and in the bar.
ROOMS: 6 en suite (bth/shr) s £45-£59; d £60-£95 (incl. bkfst) Off peak **MEALS:** Lunch £9.50-£13 & alc Dinner £16.75-£25.20alc V meals **FACILITIES:** CTV in all bedrooms Jacuzzi/spa Xmas **CONF:** Class 40 Board 12 **SERVICES:** 41P **NOTES:** No dogs (ex guide dogs) No children 14yrs No smoking in restaurant Last d 9pm
CARDS:

BOURNEMOUTH Dorset **Map 04 SZ09**
see also **Christchurch**
★★★★★ Royal Bath
Bath Rd BH1 2EW
Quality Percentage Score: 65%
☎ 01202 555555 📠 01202 554158
Dir: *from A338 follow tourist signs for Pier and Beaches. The hotel is on Bath Rd just before Lansdowne rdbt and the Pier*
Surrounded by well tended gardens, this large Victorian hotel enjoys fine sea views. Public areas include a health club in the grounds, spacious lounges and a choice of restaurants, one of which, Oscars, has been completely refurbished to a very high standard. Staff are friendly and courteous.
ROOMS: 140 en suite (bth/shr) s £130; d £155 (incl. bkfst) * LB Off peak **MEALS:** Lunch fr £16.50 & alc High tea fr £4.50 & alc Dinner fr £30 & alc English & French Cuisine V meals Coffee am Tea pm **FACILITIES:** CTV in all bedrooms STV Indoor swimming pool (heated) Sauna Solarium Gym Jacuzzi/spa Beauty salon Hairdressing Wkly live entertainment Xmas **CONF:** Thtr 400 Class 220 Board 100 **SERVICES:** Lift Night porter 70P **NOTES:** No dogs (ex guide dogs) No smoking area in restaurant Last d 10pm
CARDS:

BOURNEMOUTH Dorset **Map 04 SZ09**
★★★★ East Cliff Court
East Overcliff Dr BH1 3AN
Quality Percentage Score: 71%
☎ 0500 636943 (Central Res) 📠 01773 880321
Dir: *from A338 follow signs to East Cliff*
Accommodation here is of high quality, and many rooms have balconies and sea views. Public areas are most attracive and
contd.

Symbols and Abbreviations are listed and explained on pages 4 and 5

south-facing terraces lead down to a heated swimming pool. There is a good restaurant.

East Cliff Court, Bournemouth

ROOMS: 70 en suite (bth/shr) (10 fmly) s £110-£140; d £140-£190 (incl. bkfst) * LB Off peak **MEALS:** Lunch fr £9.95 Dinner fr £18.95 English & French Cuisine V meals Coffee am Tea pm **FACILITIES:** CTV in all bedrooms STV Outdoor swimming pool (heated) Beauty salon Xmas **CONF:** Thtr 200 Class 80 Board 40 Del from £105 * **SERVICES:** Lift Night porter 70P **NOTES:** No smoking in restaurant Last d 9.30pm **CARDS:**

BOURNEMOUTH Dorset — Map 04 SZ09

★★★★ Swallow Highcliff

St Michaels Rd, West Cliff BH2 5DU
Quality Percentage Score: 71%
☎ 01202 557702 Fax 01202 292734

Dir: *take A338 dual carriageway through Bournemouth, then follow signs for Bournemouth International Centre to West Cliff Rd, then 2nd turning right*

From its superb cliff-top location, this splendid hotel enjoys panoramic sea views. Located close to the BIC, yet within easy walking distance of the town centre, it has an excellent range of leisure and meeting and function room facilities which are now supported by a separate business centre. Bedrooms are traditionally furnished and well equipped with extra comforts such as bathrobes, irons and mini fridges. Guests can enjoy traditional dishes with a modern twist in the popular Terrace Restaurant, whilst AA rosette worthy food can be enjoyed in the elegant environment of the Robert Wild Room.

ROOMS: 143 en suite (bth/shr) 14 annexe en suite (bth/shr) (26 fmly) No smoking in 65 bedrooms s £90-£120; d £135-£165 (incl. bkfst) * LB Off peak **MEALS:** Lunch £11.75-£13.95 Dinner fr £24 & alc English & French Cuisine V meals Coffee am Tea pm **FACILITIES:** CTV in all bedrooms STV Indoor swimming pool (heated) Outdoor swimming pool (heated) Tennis (hard) Sauna Solarium Gym Pool table Croquet lawn Putting green Jacuzzi/spa Golf driving net Beautician Volley ball Wkly live entertainment ch fac Xmas **CONF:** Thtr 450 Class 180 Board 90 Del from £125 * **SERVICES:** Lift Night porter 130P **NOTES:** No smoking in restaurant Last d 10.15pm **CARDS:**

BOURNEMOUTH Dorset — Map 04 SZ09

★★★★ Carlton

East Overcliff BH1 3DN
Quality Percentage Score: 70%
☎ 05002 636943 (Central Res) Fax 01773 880321

Dir: *take A338 to the East Cliff*

Set on the East Cliff, with views of the Isle of Wight and Dorset coastline, the Carlton has lovely gardens and good leisure facilities. Most of the spacious bedrooms enjoy sea views.

ROOMS: 74 en suite (bth/shr) s £130-£180; d £180-£230 (incl. bkfst) * LB Off peak **MEALS:** Lunch £12.50-£16.50 Dinner fr £25 English & Continental Cuisine V meals Coffee am Tea pm **FACILITIES:** CTV in all bedrooms STV Indoor swimming pool (heated) Outdoor swimming pool (heated) Sauna Solarium Gym Jacuzzi/spa Xmas **CONF:** Thtr 140 Class 90 Board 45 Del from £145 * **SERVICES:** Lift Night porter 70P **NOTES:** No smoking in restaurant Last d 9.30pm **CARDS:**

BOURNEMOUTH Dorset — Map 04 SZ09

★★★★ Norfolk Royale

Richmond Hill BH2 6EN
Quality Percentage Score: 67%
☎ 01202 551521 Fax 01202 299729

Dir: *from A338 follow signs 'Richmond Hill' and 'Town Square'*

Easily recognisable by its wrought iron balconies, this Edwardian hotel is conveniently located for the centre of the town. Most of the bedrooms are contained in a modern wing at the side of the building, overlooking the pretty landscaped gardens.

ROOMS: 95 en suite (bth/shr) (9 fmly) No smoking in 14 bedrooms s £65-£105; d £85-£155 (incl. bkfst) * LB Off peak **MEALS:** Lunch £12.50-£17.50 Dinner £22.50-£31.50 English & French Cuisine V meals Coffee am Tea pm **FACILITIES:** CTV in all bedrooms STV Indoor swimming pool (heated) Sauna Jacuzzi/spa Steamroom Whirlpool Xmas **CONF:** Thtr 90 Class 45 Board 35 Del from £90 * **SERVICES:** Lift Night porter 95P **NOTES:** No dogs (ex guide dogs) No smoking in restaurant Last d 9.30pm **CARDS:**

See advert on opposite page

BOURNEMOUTH Dorset — Map 04 SZ09

★★★ Chine

Boscombe Spa Rd BH5 1AX
Quality Percentage Score: 75%
☎ 01202 396234 Fax 01202 391737

Set in well tended gardens this hotel benefits from sea views. Public areas are spacious. The attractively decorated bedrooms are well equipped and comfortable, and many front-facing rooms

contd.

have balconies. Head Chef Robert Bird offers a range of skilfully prepared dishes.

ROOMS: 69 en suite (bth/shr) 23 annexe en suite (bth/shr) (13 fmly) No smoking in 14 bedrooms s £57.75-£73.50; d £115.50-£147 (incl. bkfst) LB Off peak **MEALS:** Lunch fr £14.50 Dinner fr £18.50 English & French Cuisine V meals Coffee am Tea pm **FACILITIES:** CTV in all bedrooms STV Indoor swimming pool (heated) Outdoor swimming pool (heated) Sauna Solarium Croquet lawn Putting green Games room Outdoor & indoor childrens play area Xmas **CONF:** Thtr 140 Class 70 Board 30 Del from £80 * **SERVICES:** Lift Night porter 50P **NOTES:** No dogs (ex guide dogs) No smoking in restaurant Last d 8.30pm Closed 30 Dec-4 Jan **CARDS:**

See advert on this page

For Useful Information and Important Telephone Number Changes turn to page 25

B

BOURNEMOUTH Dorset — Map 04 SZ09
★★★ Langtry Manor
26 Derby Rd, East Cliff BH1 3QB
Quality Percentage Score: 72%
☎ 01202 553887 Fax 01202 290115
Dir: *from A31 onto A338 at 1st rdbt by rail station turn left over next rdbt 1st left into Knyveton Rd, hotel on opposite corner of small rdbt*

Built in 1877 by Edward VII as a rendezvous for he and his mistress Lillie Langtry, the house retains a stately atmosphere. The stylish bedrooms are individually furnished and several boast four-poster beds. The high ceilinged dining hall has several large Tudor tapestries.

ROOMS: 14 en suite (bth/shr) 14 annexe en suite (bth/shr) (3 fmly) No smoking in 2 bedrooms s £89.75-£119.75; d fr £119.50 (incl. bkfst & dinner) * LB Off peak **MEALS:** Bar Lunch £7.95-£10.95 Dinner fr £21.75 & alc International Cuisine V meals Coffee am Tea pm **FACILITIES:** CTV in all bedrooms Sports Centre 2min walk Xmas **CONF:** Thtr 100 Class 100 Board 50 Del from £99 * **SERVICES:** 30P **NOTES:** No smoking in restaurant Last d 9pm **CARDS:**

BOURNEMOUTH Dorset — Map 04 SZ09
★★★ Elstead
Knyveton Rd BH1 3QP
Quality Percentage Score: 71%
☎ 01202 293071 Fax 01202 293827

Situated in a quiet residential area, the hotel offers attractively decorated bedrooms that vary in size and style. Public areas include a comfortable lounge and the smart Stagecoach Bar. Conference rooms are exceptionally well equipped.

ROOMS: 50 en suite (bth/shr) (4 fmly) No smoking in 5 bedrooms s £51-£66.50; d £82-£92 (incl. bkfst) * LB Off peak **MEALS:** Lunch £9.95 Dinner £17.50 V meals Coffee am Tea pm **FACILITIES:** CTV in all bedrooms STV Indoor swimming pool (heated) Snooker Sauna Solarium Gym Pool table Jacuzzi/spa **CONF:** Thtr 80 Class 60 Board 40 **SERVICES:** Lift Night porter 40P **NOTES:** No smoking in restaurant Last d 8.30pm **CARDS:**

See advert on opposite page

BOURNEMOUTH Dorset — Map 04 SZ09
★★★ The Connaught
West Hill Rd, West Cliff BH2 5PH
Quality Percentage Score: 70%
☎ 01202 298020 Fax 01202 298028
Dir: *follow signs 'Town Centre West & BIC'*

Best Western

An attractive modern hotel on Bournemouth's West Cliff. Bedrooms are equipped with modern facilities and decorated using bright fabrics. There are extensive meeting facilities and a smart leisure centre for guest use. The professional staff are attentive and friendly.

ROOMS: 60 en suite (bth/shr) (15 fmly) No smoking in 4 bedrooms s £59-£65; d £90-£110 (incl. bkfst) * LB Off peak **MEALS:** Lunch £9.25-£14.50 & alc High tea £2.50-£6 & alc Dinner £15-£19.50 & alc English, French, Italian & Oriental Cuisine V meals Coffee am Tea pm **FACILITIES:** CTV in all bedrooms STV Indoor swimming pool (heated) Snooker Sauna Solarium Gym Pool table Jacuzzi/spa Cardio-vascular suite Table tennis Wkly live entertainment **CONF:** Thtr 200 Class 70 Board 70 Del from £69 * **SERVICES:** Lift Night porter 45P **NOTES:** No smoking in restaurant Last d 9pm **CARDS:**

BOURNEMOUTH Dorset — Map 04 SZ09
★★★ Queens
Meyrick Rd, East Cliff BH1 3DL
Quality Percentage Score: 70%
☎ 01202 554415 Fax 01202 294810

Only yards from the seafront, the hotel enjoys a good location and continues to be popular for conferences and functions. The public areas include a bar lounge and a restaurant. There is also the Queensbury Leisure Club. Bedrooms range in size and style.

ROOMS: 113 en suite (bth/shr) (15 fmly) s £49.50-£56.50; d £80-£113 (incl. bkfst) * LB Off peak **MEALS:** Lunch £8.25-£11.95 High tea £5-£6 Dinner £17.95-£19.95 English & French Cuisine V meals Coffee am Tea pm **FACILITIES:** CTV in all bedrooms Indoor swimming pool (heated) Snooker Sauna Solarium Gym Pool table Jacuzzi/spa Beauty salon Games Room Xmas **CONF:** Thtr 220 Class 120 Board 50 Del from £62 * **SERVICES:** Lift Night porter 80P **NOTES:** No smoking in restaurant Last d 8.30pm **CARDS:**

BOURNEMOUTH Dorset — Map 04 SZ09
★★★ Anglo-Swiss
16 Gervis Rd, East Cliff BH1 3EQ
Quality Percentage Score: 69%
☎ 0500 636943 (Central Res) Fax 01773 880321
Dir: *follow signs to East Cliff from A338*

MENZIES HOTELS

A short walk from East Cliff, but just minutes from the town centre, this attractive hotel is peacefully set amid pine trees. Bedrooms are attractively decorated, and some have balconies. Public areas offer a choice of lounges and bars.

ROOMS: 57 en suite (bth/shr) 8 annexe en suite (bth/shr) (16 fmly) s £70-£110; d £110-£135 (incl. bkfst) * LB Off peak **MEALS:** Lunch fr £9.50 Dinner fr £17.95 English & French Cuisine V meals Coffee am Tea pm **FACILITIES:** CTV in all bedrooms STV Indoor swimming pool (heated) Sauna Solarium Gym Jacuzzi/spa Wkly live entertainment Xmas **CONF:** Thtr 75 Class 30 Board 30 Del from £75 * **SERVICES:** Lift Night porter 70P **NOTES:** Last d 9.30pm
CARDS:

BOURNEMOUTH Dorset

Map 04 SZ09

★★★ East Anglia

6 Poole Rd BH2 5OX
Quality Percentage Score: 69%
☎ 01202 765163 Fax 01202 752949
Dir: *leave A338 at Bournemouth West rdbt, follow signs for B.I.C. and West Cliff, at next rdbt turn right into Poole Rd, hotel on right hand side*

With easy access to the town centre and major road links, this well managed hotel is staffed by a friendly, loyal team. The bedrooms are attractive and public areas are comfortable; they include a pleasant restaurant, ample lounges and a selection of function rooms.

ROOMS: 46 en suite (bth/shr) 24 annexe en suite (bth/shr) (18 fmly) No smoking in 2 bedrooms s £48-£52; d £88-£104 (incl. bkfst) * LB Off peak **MEALS:** Sunday Lunch fr £10.50alc Dinner fr £18alc English & French Cuisine V meals Coffee am Tea pm **FACILITIES:** CTV in all bedrooms STV Outdoor swimming pool (heated) Sauna Pool table Jacuzzi/spa Xmas **CONF:** Thtr 150 Class 75 Board 60 Del from £78 * **SERVICES:** Lift Night porter 70P **NOTES:** No dogs (ex guide dogs) No smoking in restaurant Last d 8.30pm Closed 28 Dec-8 Jan
CARDS:

BOURNEMOUTH Dorset

Map 04 SZ09

★★★ Hotel Miramar

East Overcliff Dr, East Cliff BH1 3AL
Quality Percentage Score: 69%
☎ 01202 556581 Fax 01202 291242

Describing itself as a country house by the sea, the Hotel Miramar sits in landscaped gardens close to the town centre. The bedrooms and public areas are of a high standard and the coffee lounge is spacious. Staff are particularly friendly.

ROOMS: 45 en suite (bth/shr) (6 fmly) No smoking in 10 bedrooms s £73-£78; d £136-£146 (incl. bkfst & dinner) * LB Off peak **MEALS:** Lunch fr £10 Dinner fr £17.95 V meals Coffee am Tea pm **FACILITIES:** CTV in all bedrooms STV Croquet lawn Wkly live entertainment Xmas **CONF:** Thtr 200 Class 50 Board 50 Del from £55 * **SERVICES:** Lift Night porter 80P **NOTES:** No smoking in restaurant Last d 9pm **CARDS:**

BOURNEMOUTH Dorset

Map 04 SZ09

★★★ Piccadilly

Bath Rd BH1 2NN
Quality Percentage Score: 69%
☎ 01202 552559 Fax 01202 298235
Dir: *follow signs for 'Lansdowne'*

This personally run hotel is situated just a few minutes walk from both the promenade and the town centre. Bedrooms are comfortably furnished, attractively decorated and well equipped, and the smart public areas include a large open plan bar and lounge, a modern restaurant and a function room.

ROOMS: 45 en suite (bth/shr) (2 fmly) s £38-£50; d £76-£80 (incl. bkfst) * LB Off peak **MEALS:** Sunday Lunch £9.50 Dinner £16.50 & alc English & French Cuisine V meals Coffee am **FACILITIES:** CTV in all bedrooms STV Ballroom dancing Xmas **CONF:** Thtr 100 Class 50 Board 40 Del from £60 * **SERVICES:** Lift Night porter 30P **NOTES:** No dogs (ex guide dogs) No smoking in restaurant Last d 8.30pm
CARDS:

BOURNEMOUTH Dorset **Map 04 SZ09**

★★★ Cumberland

East Overcliff Dr BH1 3AF

Quality Percentage Score: 68%

☎ 01202 290722 🖷 01202 311394

Dir: *follow signs for East Cliff into East Overcliffe Drive*

Many of the well equipped and attractively decorated bedrooms benefit from sea views and balconies here. The public areas are spacious and comfortable. The restaurant offers a daily changing fixed price menu. Guests have use of the leisure club at the sister hotel, The Queens.

ROOMS: 102 en suite (bth/shr) (12 fmly) s £44-£56; d £88-£112 (incl. bkfst) LB Off peak **MEALS:** Lunch £7.95-£15.95 High tea £9.50-£12.50 Dinner fr £18.95 British & Continental Cuisine V meals Coffee am Tea pm **FACILITIES:** CTV in all bedrooms Outdoor swimming pool (heated) Pool table Free use of pool etc at nearby hotel Wkly live entertainment Xmas **CONF:** Thtr 120 Class 70 Board 45 Del from £59.50 * **SERVICES:** Lift Night porter 51P **NOTES:** No smoking in restaurant Last d 8.30pm **CARDS:**

BOURNEMOUTH Dorset **Map 04 SZ09**

★★★ Durley Hall

Durley Chine Rd, West Cliff BH2 5JS

Quality Percentage Score: 68%

☎ 01202 751000 🖷 01202 757585

Dir: *from A338 follow signs to the West Cliff & Bournemouth International Centre*

Equally suitable for leisure and business guests, this hotel is well situated on the West Cliff. In addition to the Starlight restaurant there is a café overlooking the outdoor pool. The hotel has several executive and honeymoon rooms, some with feature beds and baths.

ROOMS: 70 en suite (bth/shr) 11 annexe en suite (bth/shr) (27 fmly) s £50-£75; d £100-£130 (incl. bkfst) * LB Off peak **MEALS:** Sunday Lunch £9.75 High tea £4.50 Dinner £16.50-£18.50 & alc English & Continental Cuisine V meals Coffee am Tea pm **FACILITIES:** CTV in all bedrooms STV Indoor swimming pool (heated) Outdoor swimming pool (heated) Sauna Solarium Gym Pool table Jacuzzi/spa Beauty therapist Hairdresser Steam room Table tennis Toning table Wkly live entertainment Xmas **CONF:** Thtr 200 Class 80 Board 35 Del from £68 * **SERVICES:** Lift Night porter 150P **NOTES:** No dogs (ex guide dogs) No smoking in restaurant Last d 8.45pm **CARDS:**

BOURNEMOUTH Dorset **Map 04 SZ09**

★★★ *Hermitage*

Exeter Rd BH2 5AH

Quality Percentage Score: 68%

☎ 01202 557363 🖷 01202 559173

Dir: *follow signs for Bournemouth International Centre or pier, hotel opposite both*

This hotel occupies an enviable location on the seafront overlooking the pier and adjacent to the town's Winter Gardens. Bedrooms offer good standards of quality and comfort. There is a spacious restaurant, cosy bar and ample comfortable lounge seating.

ROOMS: 69 en suite (bth/shr) 11 annexe en suite (bth/shr) (10 fmly) No smoking in 18 bedrooms **MEALS:** V meals Coffee am Tea pm **FACILITIES:** CTV in all bedrooms **CONF:** Thtr 100 Class 50 Board 40 Del from £55 * **SERVICES:** Lift Night porter 58P **NOTES:** No dogs No smoking in restaurant Last d 6pm **CARDS:**

See advert on opposite page

BOURNEMOUTH Dorset **Map 04 SZ09**

★★★ Wessex

West Cliff Rd BH2 5EU

Quality Percentage Score: 68%

☎ 01202 551911 🖷 01202 297354

Dir: *via M27/A35 through New Forest. A338 from Dorchester and A347 to the North. Hotel on West Cliff side of the town*

This well presented hotel is centrally located for both the town centre and the beach. Bedrooms which vary in size are smartly appointed with comfortable furnishings and a good range of modern facilities. Spacious public areas include a super leisure club with choice of pools and open plan bar and lounge. The hotel has a relaxing atmosphere with attentive service provided by the friendly young team. Extensive parking available.

ROOMS: 85 en suite (bth/shr) (22 fmly) No smoking in 3 bedrooms s fr £65; d fr £95 (incl. bkfst) * LB Off peak **MEALS:** Bar Lunch fr £1.95 High tea fr £3 Dinner fr £14 & alc International Cuisine V meals Coffee am Tea pm **FACILITIES:** CTV in all bedrooms STV Indoor swimming pool (heated) Outdoor swimming pool (heated) Snooker Sauna Solarium Gym Table tennis Xmas **CONF:** Thtr 400 Class 160 Board 160 Del from £90 * **SERVICES:** Lift Night porter 250P **NOTES:** No smoking area in restaurant Last d 9.30pm **CARDS:**

BOURNEMOUTH Dorset **Map 04 SZ09**

★★★ *Hotel Collingwood*

11 Priory Rd, West Cliff BH2 5DF

Quality Percentage Score: 67%

☎ 01202 557575 🖷 01202 293219

Dir: *from A338 left at Westcliff sign across 1st rdbt left at 2nd rdbt, hotel 500yds on left in Priory Rd*

Privately owned and well managed, this hotel is ideally located for the BIC, the town centre and the seafront, and offers good leisure facilities. Public areas are spacious and each evening in Pinks Restaurant, a fixed-price menu is available.

ROOMS: 53 en suite (bth/shr) (16 fmly) **MEALS:** English & French Cuisine V meals Coffee am Tea pm **FACILITIES:** CTV in all bedrooms STV Indoor swimming pool (heated) Snooker Sauna Solarium Pool table Jacuzzi/spa Mini gym Steam room Games room Pool table Wkly live entertainment **SERVICES:** Lift Night porter 55P **NOTES:** No smoking in restaurant Last d 8.30pm **CARDS:**

See advert on opposite page

BOURNEMOUTH Dorset **Map 04 SZ09**

★★★ Trouville

Priory Rd BH2 5DH

Quality Percentage Score: 67%

☎ 01202 552262 🖷 01202 293324

Dir: *close to International Centre*

Close to Bournemouth's International Centre and the seafront, this large privately-owned hotel is situated on the West Cliff. The bedrooms are attractively decorated and well co-ordinated. In

contd. on p. 128

Sheer indulgence...

- Heated indoor pool.
- Jacuzzi, steam & sauna, solarium.
- 5 course dinner & dancing nightly.
- 53 en-suite rooms, lift to all floors.
- Full size snooker table.
- Minutes from town centre & sea.
- Huge car park.
- Family owned & run for 21 years.

Hotel Collingwood

11 Priory Road
Bournemouth

AA ★★★

(01202) 557575

THE HERMITAGE HOTEL

★★★

Exeter Road, Bournemouth, BH2 5AH

(follow signs for the Bournemouth International Centre)

Tel: 01202 557363 Fax: 01202 559173

Situated in central Bournemouth this recently refurbished hotel offers 77 en suite bedrooms all beautifully furnished in an elegant and classic style. A short walk through the Gardens leads to the local shops, restaurants and extensive entertainment attractions. Parking is available on-site at the Hermitage and complimentary leisure facilities are offered at the BIC directly opposite.

AA ★★★

ARTHUR YOUNG HOTELS

Take a Break and Stay Young!

Arthur Young Hotels comprises four privately owned hotels. The majestic Queens Hotel, renowned for its many awards and indoor leisure complex. The delightful Trouville Hotel, conveniently situated in the town centre with an indoor leisure complex. The beautiful Art Deco Cumberland Hotel has a huge outdoor swimming pool and sun drenched balconies, and the tranquil Cliffeside Hotel provides a haven for relaxation on the terraces and enclosed outdoor swimming pool.

All the bedrooms are en-suite with colour TV, hospitality trays, direct dial telephone, radio alarm and hairdryer. Many of the rooms also enjoy the added luxury of balconies and panoramic views across the bay.

Highly praised and award winning restaurants create imaginative menus using the finest, freshest, local produce. There are fully licensed bars and luxurious lounges complemented by teams of friendly, professional staff that create the perfect atmosphere in which to relax and unwind...

INDOOR AND OUTDOOR LEISURE

Two indoor and outdoor heated swimming pools, Jacuzzi, Spa Bath, Saunas, Steam Room, Table Tennis, Snooker and Pool Tables, Gymnasium, Separate Children's Pools and Play Areas, Trynasium, Beauty Salon featuring "Clarins" treatments.

B

addition to a smart leisure suite, there is a comfortable bar and separate lounge.
ROOMS: 79 en suite (bth/shr) (21 fmly) s £53-£66; d £106-£132 (incl. bkfst & dinner) * LB Off peak **MEALS:** Lunch fr £8.95 Dinner fr £18.45 & alc English & French Cuisine V meals Coffee am Tea pm **FACILITIES:** CTV in all bedrooms Indoor swimming pool (heated) Sauna Solarium Gym Jacuzzi/spa Xmas **CONF:** Thtr 100 Class 45 Board 50 Del from £65 * **SERVICES:** Lift Night porter 60P **NOTES:** No smoking in restaurant Last d 8.30pm **CARDS:**

See advert on page 127

BOURNEMOUTH Dorset — Map 04 SZ09
★★★ Bay View Court
35 East Overcliff Dr BH1 3AH
Quality Percentage Score: 66%
☎ 01202 294449 Fax 01202 292883
Dir: *on A338 left at St Pauls roundabout. Go straight over St Swithuns roundabout. Left down Manor Rd, bear left onto Manor Rd, 1st right, next right*
This friendly family-run hotel enjoys splendid views across the bay. Bedrooms vary in size but are all attractively furnished. The lounges are comfortable and south-facing.
ROOMS: 64 en suite (bth/shr) (11 fmly) s £40-£50; d £80-£100 (incl. bkfst & dinner) * LB Off peak **MEALS:** Sunday Lunch £6.95 Dinner £12.50-£18 International Cuisine V meals Coffee am Tea pm **FACILITIES:** CTV in all bedrooms STV Indoor swimming pool (heated) Snooker Pool table Jacuzzi/spa Wkly live entertainment Xmas **CONF:** Thtr 170 Class 85 Board 50 Del from £50 * **SERVICES:** Lift Night porter 58P **NOTES:** No smoking in restaurant Last d 8.30pm **CARDS:**

BOURNEMOUTH Dorset — Map 04 SZ09
★★★ *Bournemouth Moat House*
Knyveton Rd BH1 3QQ
Quality Percentage Score: 66%
☎ 01202 369988 Fax 01202 292221
Situated in a quiet residential area, the Moat House offers excellent conference rooms and good leisure facilities. Children are catered for with their own play rooms and menu, and there has been significant upgrading of accommodation as well as the introduction of award-winning facilities for disabled guests.
ROOMS: 145 en suite (bth/shr) (20 fmly) No smoking in 40 bedrooms **MEALS:** English & French Cuisine V meals Coffee am Tea pm **FACILITIES:** CTV in all bedrooms Indoor swimming pool (heated) Snooker Gym Pool table Putting green Table tennis Childrens play area outdoor & indoor **CONF:** Thtr 1496 Class 620 Board 224 **SERVICES:** Lift Night porter 100P **NOTES:** No smoking in restaurant Last d 10pm **CARDS:**

BOURNEMOUTH Dorset — Map 04 SZ09
★★★ Cliffeside
East Overcliff Dr BH1 3AQ
Quality Percentage Score: 66%
☎ 01202 555724 Fax 01202 314534
Dir: *from M27 to Ringwood A338. From Ringwood approximately 7m, then first rdbt left into East Cliff*
Many of the public areas and bedrooms benefit from bay views at this popular hotel. The friendly staff create a good rapport with guests and a relaxed atmosphere prevails. The bedrooms are attractively decorated. A set price menu is offered in the restaurant.
ROOMS: 62 en suite (bth/shr) (10 fmly) **MEALS:** Lunch £8.50-£9.50 High tea £6 Dinner £17.95 English & French Cuisine V meals Coffee am Tea pm **FACILITIES:** CTV in all bedrooms Outdoor swimming pool (heated) Pool table Table tennis **CONF:** Thtr 180 Class 140 Board 60 **SERVICES:** Lift Night porter 45P **NOTES:** No smoking in restaurant Last d 8.30pm **CARDS:**

BOURNEMOUTH Dorset — Map 04 SZ09
★★★ Hotel Courtlands
16 Boscombe Spa Rd, East Cliff BH5 1BB
Quality Percentage Score: 66%
☎ 01202 302442 Fax 01202 309880
Dir: *from A338 towards Bournemouth, then East Cliffe, then Boscombe. Turn left over 1st rdbt left at 2nd & next right after Bosocmbe Gdns*
This is a popular hotel close to Boscombe pier and the beach. Bedrooms are neatly decorated and furnished. Public rooms include two comfortable lounges overlooking the south-facing garden. Traditional meals are served in the spacious restaurant.
ROOMS: 58 en suite (bth/shr) (8 fmly) s £39-£45; d £75-£79 * LB Off peak **MEALS:** Sunday Lunch £8.25 Dinner £13.50-£17.50 English & French Cuisine V meals Coffee am Tea pm **FACILITIES:** CTV in all bedrooms STV Outdoor swimming pool (heated) Sauna Solarium Pool table Jacuzzi/spa Free use of nearby Health Club Xmas **CONF:** Thtr 120 Class 85 Board 20 Del from £59 * **SERVICES:** Lift Night porter 50P **NOTES:** No smoking in restaurant Last d 8.30pm **CARDS:**

BOURNEMOUTH Dorset — Map 04 SZ09
★★★ Quality Hotel Bournemouth
8 Poole Rd BH2 5QU
Quality Percentage Score: 66%
☎ 01202 763006 Fax 01202 766168
Dir: *0.5m from A338 road and by-pass. Follow signs B.I.C. from by-pass then right at rbt into Poole Road*
A modern popular hotel on the West Cliff, a good base for visiting the attractions and beach. Bedrooms are attractively decorated and well equipped. Public areas, although not extensive, are bright and comfortable with a relaxed, friendly atmosphere.
ROOMS: 57 en suite (bth/shr) (3 fmly) No smoking in 18 bedrooms s £63.25-£74.25; d £74.25-£85.25 * LB Off peak **MEALS:** Lunch fr £6.75 & alc Dinner fr £14.50 & alc English & European Cuisine V meals Coffee am Tea pm **FACILITIES:** CTV in all bedrooms STV Xmas **CONF:** Thtr 90 Class 50 Board 45 **SERVICES:** Lift Night porter 55P **NOTES:** No smoking in restaurant Last d 9pm **CARDS:**

BOURNEMOUTH Dorset — Map 04 SZ09
★★★ Belvedere
Bath Rd BH1 2EU
Quality Percentage Score: 65%
☎ 01202 297556 Fax 01202 294699
Dir: *from A338 keep railway station & ASDA on left at rdbt take 1st left then 3rd exit at next 2 rdbts. Hotel on Bath Hill just after 4th rdbt*
Spacious public areas and comfortable bedrooms are on offer at this friendly hotel, found close to the town centre and seafront. There is a lively bar, and the attractive restaurant is popular with locals.
ROOMS: 61 en suite (bth/shr) (12 fmly) s £37-£66; d £64-£97 (incl. bkfst) * LB Off peak **MEALS:** English & Continental Cuisine V meals Coffee am Tea pm **FACILITIES:** CTV in all bedrooms STV Wkly live entertainment Xmas **CONF:** Thtr 80 Class 30 Board 30 Del from £59 * **SERVICES:** Lift Night porter 55P **NOTES:** No dogs (ex guide dogs) Last d 9pm **CARDS:**

BOURNEMOUTH Dorset — Map 04 SZ09
★★★ Durlston Court
47 Gervis Rd, East Cliff BH1 3DD
Quality Percentage Score: 65%
☎ 01202 316316 Fax 01202 316999
Dir: *on A338 10m from M27 left at large rdbt, right at next rdbt, 3rd junct at next rdbt (Meyrick Rd) next rdbt right into Gervis Rd then right*
With easy access to the town's attractions and beaches, The

contd.

Durlston Court is located on the East Cliff. The bedrooms offer comfort and quality. Public areas are bright and airy. The bar overlooks the sheltered pool and terrace.
ROOMS: 55 en suite (bth/shr) (16 fmly) No smoking in 10 bedrooms s £34-£38; d £68-£76 (incl. bkfst) * LB Off peak **MEALS:** Lunch fr £9.95alc Dinner fr £16.95alc English & French Cuisine V meals Coffee am Tea pm **FACILITIES:** CTV in all bedrooms STV Outdoor swimming pool (heated) Sauna Solarium Jacuzzi/spa Wkly live entertainment Xmas **CONF:** Thtr 80 Class 80 Board 40 Del from £60 * **SERVICES:** Lift Night porter 50P **NOTES:** No dogs (ex guide dogs) No smoking area in restaurant Last d 9pm **CARDS:**

BOURNEMOUTH Dorset — Map 04 SZ09
★★★ Hinton Firs
Manor Rd, East Cliff BH1 3HB
Quality Percentage Score: 65%
☎ 01202 555409 01202 299607
Dir: *from A338 turn west at St Paul's Rdbt across next 2 rdbts then immediately fork left to side of church, hotel on next corner*

Benefitting from a loyal clientele this friendly hotel is in a quiet residential area of the East Cliff, near the seafront. Public areas include several comfortable lounges, a bar and games room. Bedrooms vary in size and are attractively decorated and furnished.
ROOMS: 46 en suite (bth/shr) 6 annexe en suite (bth) (12 fmly) s £40-£50; d £70-£90 (incl. bkfst & dinner) * LB Off peak **MEALS:** English & French Cuisine V meals Coffee am Tea pm **FACILITIES:** CTV in all bedrooms Indoor swimming pool (heated) Outdoor swimming pool (heated) Sauna Pool table Jacuzzi/spa Games room Wkly live entertainment Xmas **CONF:** Thtr 60 Class 40 Board 30 Del from £55 * **SERVICES:** Lift Night porter 40P **NOTES:** No dogs No coaches No smoking in restaurant **CARDS:**

BOURNEMOUTH Dorset — Map 04 SZ09
★★★ Marsham Court
Russell Cotes Rd BH1 3AB
Quality Percentage Score: 65%
☎ 01202 552111 01202 294744

Conveniently located on the East Cliff and a short walk from the town centre, this hotel enjoys splendid views. Bedrooms vary in size and standard. There is a comfortable bar-lounge and the restaurant serves a daily-changing, fixed-price menu.
ROOMS: 86 en suite (bth/shr) (15 fmly) s £51-£58; d £82-£96 (incl. bkfst) * LB Off peak **MEALS:** Bar Lunch £3-£7 High tea fr £5 Dinner £15-£17 International Cuisine V meals Coffee am Tea pm **FACILITIES:** CTV in all bedrooms STV Outdoor swimming pool (heated) Pool table Free swimming at BIC Xmas **CONF:** Thtr 200 Class 120 Board 80 Del from £70 * **SERVICES:** Lift Night porter 100P **NOTES:** No dogs (ex guide dogs) No smoking in restaurant Last d 9pm
CARDS:

See advert on this page

BOURNEMOUTH Dorset — Map 04 SZ09
★★★ Bournemouth Heathlands
12 Grove Rd, East Cliff BH1 3AY
Quality Percentage Score: 64%
☎ 01202 553336 01202 555937
Dir: *from A338 St Pauls rdbt take Hadenhurst Road, then take 2nd exit off Lansdowne rdbt, into Meyrick Rd. Left into Gervis Rd. Hotel on R*
A large hotel on the East Cliff, Bournemouth Heathlands is popular with groups. Public areas are bright and spacious. The coffee shop is open all day and there is regular live entertainment.
ROOMS: 114 en suite (bth/shr) (13 fmly) No smoking in 15 bedrooms s £57-£72; d £114 (incl. bkfst) * LB Off peak **MEALS:** Lunch £6.50-£9.50 High tea fr £4.50 Dinner £12-£18.50 V meals Coffee am Tea pm **FACILITIES:** CTV in all bedrooms STV Outdoor swimming pool (heated) Sauna Solarium Gym Jacuzzi/spa Health club Wkly live entertainment ch fac Xmas **CONF:** Thtr 270 Class 102 Board 54 Del from £58 * **SERVICES:** Lift Night porter 80P **NOTES:** No smoking in restaurant Last d 8.30pm **CARDS:**

B

BOURNEMOUTH Dorset **Map 04 SZ09**
★★★ Pavilion
22 Bath Rd BH1 2NS
Quality Percentage Score: 64%
☎ 01202 291266 📠 01202 559264
A warm welcome is assured at this hotel, located close to the town centre with easy access to the seafront and attractions. The well equipped bedrooms vary in size and suit the requirements of both the leisure and business guest. There are spacious and comfortable public areas.
ROOMS: 44 en suite (bth/shr) (6 fmly) s £32-£37; d £64-£74 (incl. bkfst) * LB Off peak **MEALS:** Lunch £5.50-£7.50 High tea £6-£12 Dinner £14 & alc English, French & Italian Cuisine V meals Coffee am Tea pm **FACILITIES:** CTV in all bedrooms Special rates for International Centre Wkly live entertainment Xmas **CONF:** Thtr 100 Class 50 Board 50 Del from £50 * **SERVICES:** Lift Night porter 40P **NOTES:** No smoking in restaurant Last d 8.30pm **CARDS:**

BOURNEMOUTH Dorset **Map 04 SZ09**
★★★ Burley Court
Bath Rd BH1 2NP
Quality Percentage Score: 63%
☎ 01202 552824 & 556704 📠 01202 298514
Dir: *leave A338 at St Pauls roundabout, take 3rd exit at next roundabout (Holdenhurst Rd), 3rd exit at next roundabout (Bath Rd), overcrossing, 1st left*
This personally owned and managed hotel attracts many loyal guests. The bedrooms vary in style and standard. Public areas are spacious and comfortable. A daily changing table d'hote menu is served in the dining room.
ROOMS: 38 en suite (bth/shr) (8 fmly) No smoking in 8 bedrooms s £31-£43; d £62-£82 (incl. bkfst) * LB Off peak **MEALS:** Lunch £8-£9 Dinner £16 English & French Cuisine Coffee am Tea pm **FACILITIES:** CTV in all bedrooms Outdoor swimming pool (heated) Solarium Pool table Free use of local indoor leisure pool Xmas **CONF:** Thtr 30 Class 15 Board 15 **SERVICES:** Lift Night porter 35P **NOTES:** No smoking in restaurant Last d 8.30pm Closed 30 Dec-10 Jan **CARDS:**

BOURNEMOUTH Dorset **Map 04 SZ09**
★★★ Chesterwood
East Overcliff Dr BH1 3AR
Quality Percentage Score: 63%
☎ 01202 558057 📠 01202 556285
Enjoying splendid sea views from its elevated position on the East Cliff, this privately owned hotel has been attractively furnished and decorated. A comfortable bar lounge offers an informal seating alternative to the drawing room. There is also a spacious restaurant.
ROOMS: 47 en suite (bth/shr) 4 annexe en suite (bth) (13 fmly) s £46.50-£64.50; d £93-£119 * LB Off peak **MEALS:** Lunch fr £8.95 High tea fr £4.95 Dinner fr £11.95 V meals Coffee am Tea pm **FACILITIES:** CTV in all bedrooms Outdoor swimming pool (heated) Pool table Wkly live entertainment Xmas **CONF:** Thtr 150 Class 100 Board 30 Del from £39.50 * **SERVICES:** Lift Night porter 47P **NOTES:** No smoking in restaurant Last d 8.30pm
CARDS:

BOURNEMOUTH Dorset **Map 04 SZ09**
★★★ Embassy Royale
Meyrick Rd, East Cliff BH1 3DW
Quality Percentage Score: 63%
☎ 01202 290751 📠 01202 557459
Dir: *turn off A338 towards the East Cliff then towards Lansdowne Roundabout. Meyrick Rd is off this roundabout & the Embassy is 200yds along on the right*
Conveniently located within easy reach of the East Cliff and town centre, the Embassy Royale has undergone extensive refurbishment. The bedrooms provide the modern standards of comfort expected by both business and holiday guests.
ROOMS: 37 en suite (bth/shr) 33 annexe en suite (bth/shr) (12 fmly) No smoking in 30 bedrooms s £34.50-£48; d £69-£96 (incl. bkfst) * LB Off peak **MEALS:** Bar Lunch £1.95-£7 Dinner fr £14.95 British & French Cuisine V meals Coffee am Tea pm **FACILITIES:** CTV in all bedrooms STV Outdoor swimming pool (heated) Use of facilities at Queens Park Health Club Xmas **CONF:** Thtr 180 Class 60 Board 50 Del from £55 * **SERVICES:** Lift Night porter 75P **NOTES:** No dogs No smoking in restaurant Last d 8.30pm **CARDS:**

BOURNEMOUTH Dorset **Map 04 SZ09**
★★★ *New Durley Dean*
Westcliff Rd BH2 5HE
Quality Percentage Score: 63%
☎ 01202 557711 📠 01202 292815
Dir: *off A338*
Located on the West Cliff, this large hotel is equally well suited to business and leisure guests. Facilities include a leisure centre with pool and night club where entertainment is provided some evenings.
ROOMS: 121 en suite (bth/shr) (27 fmly) **MEALS:** English & Continental Cuisine V meals Coffee am Tea pm **FACILITIES:** CTV in all bedrooms STV Indoor swimming pool (heated) Sauna Solarium Gym Pool table Jacuzzi/spa Table tennis Steam room Wkly live entertainment **CONF:** Thtr 150 Class 70 Board 40 **SERVICES:** Lift Night porter 45P **NOTES:** No smoking in restaurant Last d 8.30pm **CARDS:**

BOURNEMOUTH Dorset **Map 04 SZ09**
★★★ *Suncliff*
29 East Overcliff Dr BH1 3AG
Quality Percentage Score: 63%
☎ 01202 291711 📠 01202 293788
Dir: *A338 to Bournemouth. 1st left at rdbt into St Pauls Rd, follow signs for East Cliff*
A large privately owned hotel on the East Cliff with glorious views from the public rooms and many bedrooms. Rooms are equipped with modern facilities, and are spacious and comfortably furnished. Public rooms include a pleasant conservatory.
ROOMS: 94 en suite (bth/shr) (29 fmly) **MEALS:** English & French Cuisine V meals Coffee am Tea pm **FACILITIES:** CTV in all bedrooms Indoor swimming pool (heated) Squash Sauna Solarium Gym Pool table Jacuzzi/spa Table tennis Wkly live entertainment **CONF:** Thtr 100 Class 70 Board 60 **SERVICES:** Lift Night porter 60P **NOTES:** No smoking area in restaurant Last d 8.45pm **CARDS:**

BOURNEMOUTH Dorset **Map 04 SZ09**
★★★ Grosvenor
Bath Rd, East Cliff BH1 2EX
Quality Percentage Score: 62%
☎ 01202 558858 📠 01202 298332
Within a short walk of the seafront and conveniently close to the shops, this hotel offers a range of comfortable bedrooms. Guests can relax in the well furnished lounge bar and a separate sitting room is available. A popular indoor leisure suite is provided.
ROOMS: 40 en suite (bth/shr) (12 fmly) s £30-£45; d £60-£90 (incl. bkfst) * LB Off peak **MEALS:** Lunch £7.50-£10 Dinner £14.95-£15.95 English & French Cuisine V meals Coffee am Tea pm **FACILITIES:** CTV in all bedrooms STV Indoor swimming pool (heated) Sauna Solarium Pool table Jacuzzi/spa Wkly live entertainment Xmas **CONF:** Thtr 30 Class 50 Board 20 Del from £55 * **SERVICES:** Lift Night porter 40P **NOTES:** No dogs (ex guide dogs) No coaches No smoking in restaurant Last d 8.45pm **CARDS:**

BOURNEMOUTH Dorset **Map 04 SZ09**

★★★ Roundhouse

REGAL

Lansdowne BH1 2PR

Quality Percentage Score: 61%

☎ 01202 553262 📠 01202 557698

Dir: *from A338 at St Pauls rdbt filter left onto the A35, turn onto B3066 at the next rdbt, hotel is off 2nd exit on next rdbt*

As the name suggests, this unusual building is circular in design with the first two floors forming useful car parking space. Bedrooms are well equipped and many have recently befitted from a comprehensive refurbishment programme. Public areas have also received similar attention with stylish bar and lounge areas augmented by the new dining room, which provides an enjoyable setting from which to sit and watch the world go by!

ROOMS: 99 en suite (bth/shr) (5 fmly) No smoking in 49 bedrooms * LB Off peak **MEALS:** Lunch £1-£6.75alc Dinner £14.75-£24alc English & Mediterranean Cuisine V meals Coffee am Tea pm **FACILITIES:** CTV in all bedrooms Table tennis Darts Skittles Xmas **CONF:** Thtr 90 Class 50 Board 40 **SERVICES:** Lift Night porter 95P **NOTES:** No smoking in restaurant Last d 10pm **CARDS:**

BOURNEMOUTH Dorset **Map 04 SZ09**

★★ Sun Court

West Hill Rd, West Cliff BH2 5PH

Quality Percentage Score: 71%

☎ 01202 551343 📠 01202 316747

This hotel is family-owned and run by friendly long-serving staff. Situated on the West Cliff, it is convenient for the town centre, seafront and theatres. The bedrooms vary in size but are all well equipped, and several have lounge areas. Public areas are comfortable.

ROOMS: 33 en suite (bth/shr) (7 fmly) s £36-£43; d £72-£86 (incl. bkfst) * LB Off peak **MEALS:** Sunday Lunch £7.45 Dinner £16 English, French, Italian & Spanish Cuisine V meals Coffee am Tea pm **FACILITIES:** CTV in all bedrooms Outdoor swimming pool (heated) Solarium Gym Facilities at sister hotel **SERVICES:** Lift Night porter 50P **NOTES:** No smoking in restaurant Last d 8.30pm **CARDS:**

BOURNEMOUTH Dorset **Map 04 SZ09**

★★ Durley Grange

6 Durley Rd, West Cliff BH2 5JL

Quality Percentage Score: 70%

☎ 01202 554473 & 290743 📠 01202 293774

Dir: *turn left off Wessex Way-A338 on St Michaels rdbt, through next rdbt, 1st left into Sommerville Rd, turn right into Durley Rd*

This friendly hotel is located in a quiet area, within easy walking distance of the pier and town centre. Bedrooms are simply decorated, comfortable and well equipped. Home-cooked meals are served in the dining room and there is a lounge bar.

ROOMS: 52 en suite (bth/shr) (4 fmly) No smoking in 2 bedrooms s £32-£38; d £64-£76 (incl. bkfst) * LB Off peak **MEALS:** Bar Lunch £1.50-£4.50 English & Mediterranean Cuisine Coffee am **FACILITIES:** CTV in all bedrooms STV Indoor swimming pool (heated) Sauna Solarium Jacuzzi/spa Wkly live entertainment Xmas **SERVICES:** Lift Night porter 35P **NOTES:** No children 5yrs No smoking in restaurant Closed 2 Jan-1 Feb **CARDS:**

The AA Hotel Booking Service is a free benefit to AA members. See the advertisement on page 47

B

BOURNEMOUTH Dorset **Map 04 SZ09**

★★ Whitehall

Exeter Park Rd BH2 5AX

Quality Percentage Score: 70%

☎ 01202 554682 📠 01202 554682

Dir: *follow signs B.I.C. then turn into Exeter Park Road off Exeter Road*

The warmest of welcomes awaits guests at this comfortable hotel. Bedrooms are bright and attractively decorated in co-ordinating fabrics. There is a small, well stocked bar and two attractive lounges, one of which overlooks the garden.

ROOMS: 47 rms (44 bth/shr) (5 fmly) s £28-£40; d £56-£80 (incl. bkfst) * LB Off peak **MEALS:** Bar Lunch £1.75-£4 Dinner £14 Coffee am Tea pm **FACILITIES:** CTV in all bedrooms **SERVICES:** Lift Night porter 25P **NOTES:** No smoking in restaurant Last d 7.30pm Closed Nov-Feb **CARDS:**

BOURNEMOUTH Dorset **Map 04 SZ09**

★★ Arlington

Exeter Park Rd BH2 5BD

Quality Percentage Score: 69%

☎ 01202 552879 & 553012 📠 01202 298317

Dir: *follow signs to Bournemouth International Centre through Priory Rd, onto rdbt and exit at Royal Exeter Hotel sign. Hotel is along Exeter Park Rd*

Overlooking the Central Gardens, and just a short walk from the seafront and town centre, this relaxed, family-run hotel offers a friendly atmosphere. Bedrooms are comfortably furnished and there are two guests' lounges, a bar with garden views and a patio.

ROOMS: 27 en suite (bth/shr) 1 annexe en suite (shr) (6 fmly) s £38-£43.50; d £76-£87 (incl. bkfst & dinner) * LB Off peak **MEALS:** Bar Lunch £3 Dinner £11 English & French Cuisine V meals Coffee am Tea pm **FACILITIES:** CTV in all bedrooms STV Xmas **SERVICES:** Lift 21P **NOTES:** No dogs No children 2yrs No smoking area in restaurant Last d 8pm Closed 4-15 Jan **CARDS:**

BOURNEMOUTH Dorset **Map 04 SZ09**

★★ Chinehurst

Alum Chine, 18-20 Studland Rd, Westbourne BH4 8JA

Quality Percentage Score: 69%

☎ 01202 764583 📠 01202 762854

Dir: *turn off A338, second junction off Frizzel roundabout, foolow signs for Alum Chine*

Peacefully situated on the west side of the town, this hotel is run by the Griffin family. Well appointed public rooms look out onto woodland, and a path running down to the beach leads past aviaries housing tropical birds. Bedrooms have modern facilities and are well equipped.

ROOMS: 30 en suite (bth/shr) (4 fmly) No smoking in 4 bedrooms s £30-£40; d £60-£80 (incl. bkfst & dinner) * LB Off peak **MEALS:** Lunch £8.50-£9 & alc Dinner fr £15 Continental Cuisine V meals Coffee am Tea pm **FACILITIES:** CTV in all bedrooms Pool table Games room Bird gardens Wkly live entertainment Xmas **CONF:** Thtr 60 Class 40 Board 40 **SERVICES:** Night porter 14P **NOTES:** No children 3yrs No smoking in restaurant Last d 8.30pm **CARDS:**

B

BOURNEMOUTH Dorset — Map 04 SZ09
★★ Winterbourne
Priory Rd, Westcliff BH2 5DJ
Quality Percentage Score: 68%
☎ 01202 296366 📠 01202 780073
Dir: *from A338 follow signs to Bournemouth International Centre. Approach town centre & pier down hill (Priory Road), hotel on right, adjacent B.I.C*
Located near the BIC, this family owned hotel benefits from views over the town and out to sea. Bedrooms have all been upgraded to a good standard and are practically furnished. Public rooms include a spacious lounge overlooking the garden.
ROOMS: 41 en suite (bth/shr) (12 fmly) s £31-£43; d £54-£78 (incl. bkfst) * LB Off peak **MEALS:** Sunday Lunch fr £8.95 High tea £3.50 Dinner £14.50 & alc V meals Coffee am Tea pm **FACILITIES:** CTV in all bedrooms STV Outdoor swimming pool (heated) Pool table Table tennis Xmas **CONF:** Thtr 90 Class 50 Board 36 Del from £45 * **SERVICES:** Lift 33P **NOTES:** No smoking in restaurant Last d 8pm
CARDS:

BOURNEMOUTH Dorset — Map 04 SZ09
★★ Mansfield
West Cliff Gardens BH2 5HL
Quality Percentage Score: 67%
☎ 01202 552659
Dir: *from A338 follow signs for West Cliff, straight on at two rdbts via Cambridge & Durley Chine Rd*
Located in a quiet crescent on the West Cliff, Mansfield Hotel is convenient for access to the seafront and town centre. The bedrooms are comfortably furnished. Staff make every effort to ensure that guests have an enjoyable stay. Two lounges adjoin the cosy bar.
ROOMS: 30 en suite (bth/shr) (7 fmly) s £29-£37; d £58-£74 (incl. bkfst & dinner) LB Off peak **MEALS:** Sunday Lunch fr £8 Dinner fr £10 V meals Coffee am Tea pm **FACILITIES:** CTV in all bedrooms Xmas **SERVICES:** 12P **NOTES:** No dogs No coaches No smoking in restaurant Last d 8.30pm Closed 29 Dec-17 Jan **CARDS:**

BOURNEMOUTH Dorset — Map 04 SZ09
★★ Royal Exeter
Exeter Rd BH2 5AG
Quality Percentage Score: 66%
☎ 01202 290566 📠 01202 297963
Dir: *opposite the Bournemouth International Centre*
Situated opposite the Bournemouth International Centre, parts of the Royal Exeter Hotel date back to 1812 and features castellated towers and gables. The attractively decorated bedrooms are exceptionally well equipped and bar meals are available in addition to an extensive restaurant menu.
ROOMS: 46 en suite (bth/shr) (12 fmly) s fr £39; d fr £62 * LB Off peak **MEALS:** Lunch £8.74-£20.05alc Dinner £8.74-£20.05alc International Cuisine V meals Coffee am Tea pm **FACILITIES:** CTV in all bedrooms Childrens indoor play area Xmas **CONF:** Thtr 40 Class 25 Board 25 Del from £68 * **SERVICES:** Lift Night porter 56P **NOTES:** No dogs (ex guide dogs) No smoking area in restaurant Last d 9.30pm
CARDS:

BOURNEMOUTH Dorset — Map 04 SZ09
★★ Cliff Court
15 Westcliff Rd BH2 5EX
Quality Percentage Score: 65%
☎ 01202 555994 📠 01202 780954
Dir: *A338 (Wessex Way) into Cambridge Road, follow Durley Chine Road into West Cliff Road*
This hotel is on the West Cliff within easy reach of the town centre, local attractions and the beach. A range of comfortable bedrooms is available. Public rooms include a bar and lounge.
ROOMS: 38 en suite (bth/shr) (4 fmly) s £26-£36; d £52-£72 (incl. bkfst) * LB Off peak **MEALS:** Dinner £6-£7.50alc V meals Coffee am Tea pm **FACILITIES:** CTV in all bedrooms STV Wkly live entertainment Xmas **SERVICES:** Lift Night porter 39P **NOTES:** No smoking in restaurant Last d 7.30pm **CARDS:**

BOURNEMOUTH Dorset — Map 04 SZ09
★★ *Croham Hurst*
9 Durley Rd South, West Cliff BH2 5JH
Quality Percentage Score: 65%
☎ 01202 552353 📠 01202 311484
Dir: *off A35 at Cambridge Rd roundabout, follow signs to BIC, hotel on the right just before Durley roundabout*

This popular family run hotel is conveniently situated for access to the beach and town centre. Rooms are a mixture of traditional and modern styles but all are spacious and well equipped. There is a lounge and the spacious restaurant offers traditional home cooked dishes.
ROOMS: 40 en suite (bth/shr) (10 fmly) **MEALS:** English, French & Italian Cuisine V meals Coffee am **FACILITIES:** CTV in all bedrooms STV Wkly live entertainment **SERVICES:** Lift 30P **NOTES:** No dogs (ex guide dogs) No smoking in restaurant Last d 7.30pm Closed 2 Jan-10 Feb
CARDS:

BOURNEMOUTH Dorset — Map 04 SZ09
★★ *Durley Chine Hotel*
29 Chine Crescent, West Cliff BH2 5LB
Quality Percentage Score: 65%
☎ 01202 551926 📠 01202 310671
Dir: *follow signs for Bournemouth International Centre, West Cliff and Town Centre pass Durley Hall Hotel on right, Durley Chine hotel is 50yds on right*
Within minutes of both the town centre and the beach, this family-run hotel is set in its own grounds and beautiful gardens. Bedrooms vary in size and style. Public rooms are comfortable and both the lounge-bar and restaurant overlook the gardens at the rear of the property.
ROOMS: 23 en suite (bth/shr) 17 annexe en suite (bth/shr) (7 fmly) **MEALS:** European Cuisine V meals Coffee am **FACILITIES:** CTV in all bedrooms **SERVICES:** Night porter 40P **NOTES:** No smoking in restaurant Closed 2-16 Jan **CARDS:**

BOURNEMOUTH Dorset — Map 04 SZ09
★★ Fircroft
4 Owls Rd BH5 1AE
Quality Percentage Score: 65%
☎ 01202 309771 📠 01202 395644
Dir: *off A338 signposted Boscombe Pier, hotel is 400yds from pier close to Christchurch Road*
Guests will find a warm welcome at this hotel which is popular with tour groups, and well situated close to Boscombe Pier. Bedrooms are well equipped and comfortable. In addition to a

contd.

separate cocktail bar, there are a number of lounge areas for guests' use.
ROOMS: 51 en suite (bth/shr) (20 fmly) s £22-£28; d £44-£56 (incl. bkfst) * LB Off peak **MEALS:** Bar Lunch £2-£5alc Dinner fr £14.50 English & French Cuisine V meals Coffee am Tea pm **FACILITIES:** CTV in all bedrooms Indoor swimming pool (heated) Squash Sauna Solarium Gym Pool table Jacuzzi/spa Sports at health club owned by hotel Xmas **CONF:** Thtr 200 Class 100 Board 40 Del from £40 * **SERVICES:** Lift Night porter 50P **NOTES:** No smoking in restaurant Last d 8pm **CARDS:**

BOURNEMOUTH Dorset — Map 04 SZ09

★★ Ullswater

West Cliff Gardens BH2 5HW
Quality Percentage Score: 65%
☎ 01202 555181 01202 317896
Dir: *on entering Bournemouth follow signs to Westcliff, hotel just off Westcliff Road*
Situated on the West Cliff, this hotel continues to attract a loyal following. There is a spacious lounge bar and a beautiful dining room where a varied choice of dishes is offered. The bedrooms differ in size but all are well equipped and attractively furnished.
ROOMS: 42 en suite (bth/shr) (7 fmly) s £27-£32; d £54-£64 (incl. bkfst) * LB Off peak **MEALS:** Sunday Lunch fr £7.50 High tea fr £2.50alc Dinner fr £10.50 English & French Cuisine Coffee am Tea pm **FACILITIES:** CTV in all bedrooms Snooker Table tennis Wkly live entertainment Xmas **CONF:** Thtr 40 Class 30 Board 24 Del from £45 * **SERVICES:** Lift 10P **NOTES:** No dogs (ex guide dogs) No smoking in restaurant Last d 8pm **CARDS:**

BOURNEMOUTH Dorset — Map 04 SZ09

★★ *West Cliff Towers*

12 Priory Rd BH2 5DG
Quality Percentage Score: 65%
☎ 01202 553319 01202 553313
Dir: *exit A338 (A35) onto B3066 (Cambridge Road) straight across 1st rdbt, left at 2nd rdbt through traffic lights, hotel 2nd road on right*
This friendly hotel is a stone's throw from sandy beaches and the BIC. A comfortable lounge and well stocked bar are available. Bedrooms are light and airy, and soundly furnished. Fresh local ingredients are used to prepare meals that are served in the lower ground floor dining room.
ROOMS: 28 rms (6 bth 21 shr) (7 fmly) **MEALS:** V meals Coffee am Tea pm **FACILITIES:** CTV in all bedrooms STV **CONF:** Thtr 18 Class 12 Board 12 **SERVICES:** Lift 26P **NOTES:** No dogs (ex guide dogs) No coaches No smoking in restaurant Last d 7.30pm
CARDS:

BOURNEMOUTH Dorset — Map 04 SZ09

★★ *Lynden Court*

8 Durley Rd, West Cliff BH2 5JL
Quality Percentage Score: 63%
☎ 01202 553894 01202 317711
Dir: *A338 from Ringwood, left at Town Centre West rdbt to St Michaels rdbt, straight across and second left, hotel facing*
Conviently located on the West Cliff, this is a friendly, family run hotel. The public areas include a comfortable lounge and bar, and an attractive restaurant. A choice from the English menu is offered at dinner and breakfast.
ROOMS: 32 en suite (bth/shr) (3 fmly) **MEALS:** English & Italian Cuisine V meals Coffee am Tea pm **FACILITIES:** CTV in all bedrooms STV Pool table Wkly live entertainment **SERVICES:** Lift 20P **NOTES:** No smoking in restaurant Last d 7.15pm Closed Jan
CARDS:

BOURNEMOUTH Dorset — Map 04 SZ09

★★ *Taurus Park*

16 Knyveton Rd BH1 3QN
Quality Percentage Score: 61%
☎ 01202 557374 01202 557374
Guests are assured a pleasant stay at Taurus Park. Situated in a quiet residential area, only a short walk from the town centre, it offers comfortable accommodation with modern facilities. There is a large dining room and bar.
ROOMS: 43 rms (38 bth/shr) (7 fmly) **MEALS: FACILITIES:** CTV in all bedrooms Pool table **SERVICES:** Lift 20P **NOTES:** No dogs No children 5yrs No smoking in restaurant Last d 8pm **CARDS:**

BOURNEMOUTH Dorset — Map 04 SZ09

★★ Bourne Hall Hotel

14 Priory Rd, West Cliff BH2 5DN
Quality Percentage Score: 60%
☎ 01202 299715 01202 552669
Dir: *A31 & M27 from Ringwood into Bournemouth on A338 (Wessex Way) - pick up signs to B.I.C. onto West Cliff - Hotel on right*

This spacious hotel is located on the West Cliff, within a short stroll of the town centre, seafront and theatres. Bedrooms are furnished for comfort and well equipped for the needs of both business and leisure guests. The atmosphere throughout is relaxed and welcoming.
ROOMS: 48 en suite (bth/shr) (9 fmly) No smoking in 12 bedrooms s £35-£55; d £55-£75 (incl. bkfst) * LB Off peak **MEALS:** Dinner £10.75-£13.75 V meals **FACILITIES:** CTV in all bedrooms STV Pool table Xmas **CONF:** Thtr 70 Class 70 **SERVICES:** Lift 35P **NOTES:** No smoking in restaurant Last d 7.30pm **CARDS:**

BOURNEMOUTH Dorset — Map 04 SZ09

★★ *St George*

West Cliff Gardens BH2 5HL
Quality Percentage Score: 60%
☎ 01202 556075 01202 557330
Older guests enjoy the friendly atmosphere at this popular hotel on the West Cliff, which is set in its own gardens with direct access to the sea. The bedrooms are uncluttered in style. Public areas include a traditional lounge and a bar; a set menu is offered in the dining room.
ROOMS: 22 rms (20 bth/shr) (5 fmly) **MEALS:** V meals Coffee am Tea pm **FACILITIES:** CTV in all bedrooms STV Use of owner's motor sailor for days sailing **SERVICES:** Lift 4P **NOTES:** No smoking in restaurant Last d 7.30pm Closed mid Nov-mid Dec & 3 Jan-Mar
CARDS:

New AA Guides for the Millennium are featured on page 24

BOURNEMOUTH Dorset **Map 04 SZ09**
★★ ***County***
Westover Rd BH1 2BT
Quality Percentage Score: 56%
☎ 01202 552385 & 0500 141401 Fax 01202 297255
This centrally located hotel offers easy access to the seafront, shops and Bournemouth's nightlife. The bedrooms are mostly spacious and well equipped. Public areas include a quiet lounge bar and a themed Piano Bar for the over 30s.
ROOMS: 48 en suite (bth/shr) (11 fmly) **MEALS:** Coffee am **FACILITIES:** CTV in all bedrooms STV Use of Bournemouth International Pool **CONF:** Thtr 25 Board 25 Del from £30 * **SERVICES:** Lift Night porter 6P **NOTES:** No smoking area in restaurant Last d 8pm
CARDS:

BOURNEMOUTH Dorset **Map 04 SZ09**
★★ ***Russell Court***
Bath Rd BH1 2EP
Quality Percentage Score: 56%
☎ 01202 295819 Fax 01202 293457
This popular coaching hotel offers bright, well-maintained rooms, several benefiting from sea views. Public rooms are spacious and comfortably furnished. There is a lounge bar and live entertainment is provided in the evenings.
ROOMS: 62 rms (54 bth 4 shr) (6 fmly) **MEALS:** V meals Coffee am Tea pm **FACILITIES:** CTV in all bedrooms Wkly live entertainment **CONF:** Thtr 20 **SERVICES:** Lift Night porter 60P **NOTES:** No dogs (ex guide dogs) No smoking in restaurant Last d 8pm
CARDS:

BOURNEMOUTH Dorset **Map 04 SZ09**
Late entry ○ ***Tralee Hotel***
West Hill Rd, West Cliff BH2 5EQ
☎ 01202 556246
The Tralee Hotel is situated within easy reach of the town centre and its many attractions. All rooms are equipped to a very high standard. A choice of bars and lounges is available, including the fourth floor Solarium lounge, with its spectacular views.

BOURTON-ON-THE-WATER **Map 04 SP12**
Gloucestershire
★★★ ***Bourton Lodge***
Whiteshoots Hill GL54 2LE
Quality Percentage Score: 66%
☎ 01451 820387 Fax 01451 821635
Dir: *on A429*
Owned by the Miles family, this hotel has a reputation for its hospitality. Rooms are smartly furnished and equipped with modern amenities; one has a four-poster bed and a spa bath. The restaurant offers a wide choice of dishes.
ROOMS: 11 en suite (bth/shr) (2 fmly) No smoking in all bedrooms **MEALS:** English & Continental Cuisine V meals Coffee am Tea pm **FACILITIES:** CTV in all bedrooms **SERVICES:** 30P **NOTES:** No smoking in restaurant Last d 8.30pm **CARDS:**

BOURTON-ON-THE-WATER **Map 04 SP12**
Gloucestershire
★★ **Dial House**
The Chestnuts, High St GL54 2AN
Quality Percentage Score: 74%
☎ 01451 822244 Fax 01451 810126
Dir: *off A429*
This charming hotel built of mellow Cotswold stone dates back to 1698. Public rooms are tastefully appointed including a cosy bar and adjoining lounge and two small dining rooms. Bedrooms vary in size and style, all are comfortably furnished and well equipped. Guests appreciate the high standard of cooking.

ROOMS: 10 en suite (bth/shr) No smoking in 3 bedrooms s £49.50; d £99-£123 (incl. bkfst) * LB Off peak **MEALS:** Lunch £10.95-£21.95 Dinner £18.45-£25.40alc V meals Coffee am Tea pm **FACILITIES:** CTV in all bedrooms STV Croquet lawn Putting green Xmas **CONF:** Class 16 Board 14 Del from £138.95 * **SERVICES:** 20P **NOTES:** No dogs (ex guide dogs) No coaches No children 10yrs No smoking in restaurant Last d 9pm **CARDS:**
See advert on opposite page

BOURTON-ON-THE-WATER **Map 04 SP12**
Gloucestershire
★★ ***Old New Inn***
High St GL54 2AF
Quality Percentage Score: 67%
☎ 01451 820467 Fax 01451 810236
Dir: *off A429*
Situated near the famous model village, the inn offers a variety of styles of bedroom, some in a nearby cottage. Public areas are full of character.
ROOMS: 16 rms (6 bth 2 shr) 4 annexe rms **MEALS:** English & French Cuisine V meals Coffee am **FACILITIES:** CTV in 19 bedrooms **SERVICES:** 31P **NOTES:** No coaches No smoking in restaurant Last d 8.30pm Closed 25 Dec **CARDS:**

BOURTON-ON-THE-WATER **Map 04 SP12**
Gloucestershire
★★ **Chester House Hotel & Motel**
Victoria St GL54 2BU
Quality Percentage Score: 66%
☎ 01451 820286 Fax 01451 820471
Close to the village green and river, this Cotswold stone hotel has been run by Mr and Mrs Davies for over 30 years. Rooms are comfortable and thoughtfully equipped. Public areas include an attractive restaurant and separate breakfast room. The family and ground floor rooms, and 'pets welcome' philosophy appeal to many visitors. The car park is a bonus.
ROOMS: 13 en suite (bth/shr) 10 annexe en suite (bth/shr) (8 fmly) s fr £54; d £74-£102 (incl. bkfst) * LB Off peak **MEALS:** Sunday Lunch £8.50-£12.50 Dinner £16.25-£17.75 & alc English & French Cuisine V meals Coffee am **FACILITIES:** CTV in 22 bedrooms **CONF:** Board 121 Del from £83 * **SERVICES:** 20P **NOTES:** Last d 9.30pm Closed mid Dec-Jan
CARDS:

BOVEY TRACEY Devon **Map 03 SX87**
★★★ **Edgemoor**
Haytor Rd, Lowerdown Cross TQ13 9LE
Quality Percentage Score: 71%
☎ 01626 832466 Fax 01626 834760
Dir: *from A382 follow signs for Haytor and Widecombe*
This country house hotel was built in 1870 and lies in two acres
contd.

of gardens on the edge of Dartmoor. The individually decorated bedrooms are well equipped and some ground floor rooms are available. Public areas include a spacious lounge and a beamed bar, both featuring welcoming open fires. A tempting selection of cooking is offered in the elegantly furnished dining room.

ROOMS: 12 en suite (bth/shr) 5 annexe en suite (bth/shr) (3 fmly) s £57.50; d £100 (incl. bkfst) * LB Off peak **MEALS:** Lunch £11.95-£18.45 High tea £2.95-£7.95 Dinner £22.50-£26.70 English & French Cuisine V meals Coffee am Tea pm **FACILITIES:** CTV in all bedrooms ch fac **CONF:** Thtr 60 Class 40 Board 30 Del from £70 * **SERVICES:** 45P **NOTES:** No coaches No smoking in restaurant Last d 9pm **CARDS:**

See advert on this page

BOVEY TRACEY Devon — Map 03 SX87

★★ Coombe Cross

Coombe Cross TQ13 9EY

Quality Percentage Score: 66%

THE CIRCLE Selected Individual Hotels GREAT BRITAIN

☎ 01626 832476 01626 835298

***Dir:** from A38 follow signs for Bovey Tracey and town centre, along High St & up the hill 400yds beyond the Parish Church, hotel on the left*

A welcoming hotel set in attractive landscaped gardens within easy walking distance of the local shops. Comfortable public rooms include two lounges, one reserved for non-smokers, a small bar, a heated indoor pool, and a smart dining room. Bedrooms are comfortable and well equipped, and contain many thoughtful extras.

ROOMS: 24 en suite (bth/shr) (2 fmly) s £35-£45; d £60-£70 (incl. bkfst) * LB Off peak **MEALS:** Bar Lunch £3-£10 High tea £5.50-£7.50 Dinner £17.95-£19.95 V meals Coffee am Tea pm **FACILITIES:** CTV in all bedrooms Indoor swimming pool (heated) Sauna Solarium Gym Jacuzzi/spa ch fac **CONF:** Thtr 40 Class 60 Board 30 Del from £65 * **SERVICES:** Night porter 26P **NOTES:** No smoking in restaurant Last d 8.30pm **CARDS:**

BOVEY TRACEY Devon — Map 03 SX87

★★ Riverside Inn

Fore St TQ13 9AF

Quality Percentage Score: 61%

☎ 01626 832293 01626 833880

***Dir:** hotel by bridge in town centre*

Located on the southern edge of Dartmoor, this is an ideal base for touring this beautiful corner of Devon. As an added bonus, the inn enjoys fishing rights on the River Bovey, which flows beside the property. Bedrooms are spacious, comfortably furnished and equipped with a good range of facilities, suitable for both business and leisure guests.

ROOMS: 10 en suite (bth/shr) s £29.50; d £39.50 (incl. bkfst) * LB Off peak **MEALS:** English & French Cuisine V meals Coffee am Tea pm **FACILITIES:** CTV in all bedrooms STV Fishing **CONF:** Thtr 100 Class 80 Board 50 **SERVICES:** Night porter 100P **NOTES:** No smoking area in restaurant Last d 9.30pm **CARDS:**

BOVEY TRACEY Devon **Map 03 SX87**
Late entry *Cromwell Arms*
Fore St TQ13 9AE
☎ 01626 833473

BOWNESS ON WINDERMERE See **Windermere**

BRACKLEY Northamptonshire **Map 04 SP53**
★★ **Crown**
20-22 Market Square NN13 7DP
Quality Percentage Score: 64%
☎ 01280 702210 📠 01280 701840
Dir: *from M40 junc 10 take A43 into town, though Market Place for hotel on left*
This traditional town centre hotel provides bright, comfortable accommodation, well equipped for business and leisure guests. The open plan public areas include a spacious restaurant and bustling bar with log fire. Meeting rooms are available.
ROOMS: 19 en suite (bth/shr) (1 fmly) s fr £65; d fr £75 * LB Off peak **MEALS:** Lunch £8.50 Dinner £12.50-£18.50 & alc International Cuisine V meals Coffee am Tea pm **FACILITIES:** CTV in all bedrooms **CONF:** Thtr 120 Class 60 Board 25 Del from £75 * **SERVICES:** Night porter 25P **NOTES:** Last d 9.30pm
CARDS:

BRACKNELL Berkshire **Map 04 SU86**
see also **Wokingham**
★★★★ **Coppid Beech**
John Nike Way RG12 8TF
Quality Percentage Score: 76%
☎ 01344 303333 📠 01344 301200
Dir: *from junct 10 on M4 take Wokingham/Bracknell option on to A329, in 2 miles at roundabout take B3408 to Binfield, hotel 200yds on the right hand side*
This impressive modern hotel is built in an Alpine style to match the ski slope and ice rink adjacent. Offering an extensive range of amenities, which include indoor leisure centre, a night-club, and Bier keller. Bedrooms are spacious, quiet and well equipped. All beds have feather duvets. Rowans restaurant serves a wide range of classical and modern dishes and carries our award for Two Rosettes.
ROOMS: 205 en suite (bth/shr) (6 fmly) No smoking in 138 bedrooms s £145-£195; d £165-£295 (incl. bkfst) LB Off peak **MEALS:** Lunch £17.95-£22.50 & alc Dinner £22.50 & alc V meals Coffee am Tea pm **FACILITIES:** CTV in all bedrooms STV Indoor swimming pool (heated) Sauna Solarium Gym Jacuzzi/spa Wkly live entertainment Xmas **CONF:** Thtr 400 Class 240 Board 24 Del from £175 * **SERVICES:** Lift Night porter Air conditioning 350P **NOTES:** No smoking area in restaurant Last d 10.30pm **CARDS:**

BRACKNELL Berkshire **Map 04 SU86**
★★★ **Stirrups Country House**
Maidens Green RG42 6LD
Quality Percentage Score: 73%
☎ 01344 882284 📠 01344 882300
Dir: *3m N on B3022 towards Windsor*
Between Maidenhead, Bracknell and Windsor, this friendly hotel is ideal for business or pleasure. Local companies make good use of the spacious meeting rooms, and the friendly attentive staff add an extra touch of warmth. Bedrooms are quiet and well appointed, with recently refurbished bathrooms.
ROOMS: 28 en suite (bth) (4 fmly) s £95-£110; d £99-£120 * LB Off peak **MEALS:** Lunch £12.50-£20 & alc Dinner fr £20 & alc English & Continental Cuisine V meals Coffee am **FACILITIES:** CTV in all bedrooms STV **CONF:** Thtr 100 Class 50 Board 40 Del from £125 * **SERVICES:** Lift Night porter 100P **NOTES:** No dogs (ex guide dogs) No smoking in restaurant Last d 10pm **CARDS:**

BRACKNELL Berkshire **Map 04 SU86**
Travel Inn
Arlington Square, Wokingham Rd RG12 1WA
☎ 01344 486320 📠 01344 486172
Dir: *from M4 junct 10 follow A329(M) sign to Bracknell. Turn left at sign to Arlington Square, Travel Inn at front of Business Park on Wokingham Rd*
This modern building offers accommodation in smart, spacious and well equipped bedrooms, all with en-suite bathrooms. Refreshments may be taken at the nearby family restaurant. For details about current prices consult the Contents Page under Hotel Groups for the Travel Inn phone number.
ROOMS: 40 en suite (bth/shr) d £39.95 *

BRADFORD West Yorkshire **Map 07 SE13**
see also **Shipley**
★★★★ **Cedar Court Hotel Bradford**
Mayo Av, Off Rooley Ln BD5 8HZ
Quality Percentage Score: 64%
☎ 01274 406606 & 406601 📠 01274 406600
Dir: *leave M62 at junct 26, then follow M606. At the end take 3rd exit off rdbt onto A6177 toward Bradford, take 1st sharp right at lghts*
This large modern hotel is well located between the end of the M606 and the city centre. Comfortable bedrooms are nicely furnished, whilst public areas include the elegant Four Seasons restaurant and a spacious central bar lounge. Meeting and function suites are particularly impressive, with a variety of sizes and styles of rooms being available, as well as a manned business centre. Leisure facilities, including a pool and well equipped gym, are also available.
ROOMS: 131 en suite (bth/shr) (7 fmly) No smoking in 75 bedrooms d £55-£95 * LB Off peak **MEALS:** Lunch £7.50-£12.50 & alc Dinner £16-£18.50 & alc International Cuisine V meals Coffee am Tea pm **FACILITIES:** CTV in all bedrooms Indoor swimming pool (heated) Sauna Solarium Gym Pool table Jacuzzi/spa Beauty treatments Xmas **CONF:** Thtr 800 Class 500 Board 100 Del from £75 **SERVICES:** Lift Night porter 350P **NOTES:** No smoking area in restaurant Last d 10pm RS Xmas & New Year **CARDS:**

BRADFORD West Yorkshire **Map 07 SE13**
★★★ **Quality Hotel Bradford**
Bridge St BD1 1JX
Quality Percentage Score: 71%
☎ 01274 728706 📠 01274 736358
Dir: *behind Bradford Interchange Station, next to St Georges Concert Hall*
This Victorian hotel, although totally refurbished to provide modern standards of comfort, has kept its period atmosphere. Bedrooms are very well equipped and include some suites with private sitting rooms. A main attraction of the hotel is Vic and Bert's Brasserie, and there is a lively public bar, the Pie-eyed Parrot.
ROOMS: 60 en suite (bth/shr) (3 fmly) No smoking in 40 bedrooms s £73.25-£81.75; d £88.25-£105.50 * LB Off peak **MEALS:** Lunch £2.95-£15.95alc Dinner fr £14.50 & alc V meals Coffee am Tea pm **FACILITIES:** CTV in all bedrooms STV Sauna Gym Wkly live entertainment Xmas **CONF:** Thtr 150 Class 90 Board 60 **SERVICES:** Lift Night porter 69P **NOTES:** No smoking area in restaurant Last d 10pm **CARDS:**

BRADFORD West Yorkshire **Map 07 SE13**
★★★ **Midland Hotel**
Forster Square BD1 4HU
Quality Percentage Score: 68%
☎ 01274 735735 📠 01274 720003
Centrally located, with the added advantage of secure parking, this hotel has a pleasing mix of historical features. Bedrooms,
contd.

however, are modern in style and in the range of amenities offered. Public areas are spacious and comfortable.
ROOMS: 91 en suite (bth/shr) (10 fmly) No smoking in 9 bedrooms s £70-£80; d £80-£90 (incl. bkfst) * LB Off peak **MEALS:** Lunch £7-£11.95 Dinner fr £11.95 English & Continental Cuisine V meals Coffee am Tea pm **FACILITIES:** CTV in all bedrooms STV Pool table Y Wkly live entertainment **CONF:** Thtr 500 Class 150 Board 100 Del from £95 * **SERVICES:** Lift Night porter 200P **NOTES:** No smoking area in restaurant Last d 11pm **CARDS:**

BRADFORD West Yorkshire **Map 07 SE13**
★★★ Apperley Manor
Apperley Ln, Apperley Bridge BD10 0PQ
Quality Percentage Score: 65%
☎ 0113 250 5626 Fax 0113 250 0075
Dir: *on A658 Bradford to Harrogate road, 2m from Leeds/Bradford Int Airport*
This friendly hotel is conveniently situated between Leeds and Bradford, with easy access to the airport. Generally spacious bedrooms have been nicely furnished, with a full refurbishment programme underway to improve still further. Carefully prepared meals are served in the candlelit restaurant, served by the courteous and welcoming staff.
ROOMS: 13 en suite (bth/shr) (2 fmly) s £59.50-£65; d £69.50-£80 * Off peak **MEALS:** Lunch £12.95-£14.75 & alc Dinner £14.75 & alc International Cuisine V meals Coffee am Tea pm **FACILITIES:** CTV in all bedrooms Jacuzzi in 2 bedrooms **CONF:** Thtr 80 Class 40 Board 30 Del from £82.50 * **SERVICES:** Lift Night porter 100P **NOTES:** No dogs (ex guide dogs) No smoking area in restaurant Last d 9pm
CARDS:

BRADFORD West Yorkshire **Map 07 SE13**
★★★ Courtyard by Marriott Leeds/Bradford
The Pastures, Tong Ln BD4 0RP
Quality Percentage Score: 65%
☎ 0113 285 4646 Fax 0113 285 3661
Dir: *from junct 27 M62, take A650 towards Bradford. 3rd rdbt, take 3rd exit 'Tong Village & Pudsey'. Turn left Tong Lane. Hotel 0.5m on right*
This former eighteenth century vicarage with modern, but sympathetically designed bedroom wings is situated in a rural location (with plenty of parking) just off the A650 only a short distance from Bradford city centre, Leeds and junction 27 of the M62 motorway. The spacious and well equipped bedrooms, are particularly well appointed and several have separate sitting rooms. The hotel also provides a good range of conference and banqueting facilities.
ROOMS: 53 en suite (bth/shr) (5 fmly) No smoking in 28 bedrooms d £72-£75 * LB Off peak **MEALS:** Lunch £10.50-£12.50 & alc Dinner £11-£24alc English, Italian & Indian Cuisine V meals Coffee am Tea pm **FACILITIES:** CTV in all bedrooms STV Gym Pool table **CONF:** Thtr 300 Class 150 Board 100 Del from £109 * **SERVICES:** Lift Night porter 300P **NOTES:** No dogs (ex guide dogs) No smoking area in restaurant Last d 10pm **CARDS:**

BRADFORD West Yorkshire **Map 07 SE13**
★★★ Guide Post Hotel
Common Rd, Low Moor BD12 0ST
Quality Percentage Score: 63%
☎ 01274 607866 Fax 01274 671085
Dir: *follow A638 towards Oakenshaw/Low Moor, pass large factory (CIBA), pass petrol station on left, take 2nd left into Common Road*
Conveniently situated just two miles from the junction of the M606 and M62, this hotel offers a mixture of attractively furnished and spacious bedrooms. An extensive range of dishes, including a daily list of fresh fish according to availability, is offered in the bright restaurant, with lighter meals being served in the bar. The hotel also has two well maintained function suites.

ROOMS: 43 en suite (bth/shr) (3 fmly) No smoking in 7 bedrooms s £57.50-£72.50; d £72.50-£82.50 (incl. bkfst) * LB Off peak **MEALS:** Lunch £9.95 Dinner fr £15.95 & alc English & French Cuisine V meals Coffee am Tea pm **FACILITIES:** CTV in all bedrooms STV **CONF:** Thtr 120 Class 80 Board 60 Del from £84 * **SERVICES:** Night porter 100P **NOTES:** No dogs (ex guide dogs) No smoking area in restaurant Last d 9.45pm **CARDS:**
See advert on this page

BRADFORD West Yorkshire **Map 07 SE13**
★★★ Novotel
Merrydale Rd BD4 6SA
Quality Percentage Score: 62%
☎ 01274 683683 Fax 01274 651342
Dir: *adjacent to M606 junct 2, 3m from city centre*
On the outskirts of the city, close to the motorway, this was one
contd.

of the first Novotels built in this country. An ongoing refurbishment programme is steadily upgrading the spacious bedrooms, and public areas include an open plan bar and lounge leading into the Garden Brasserie. Several function rooms are also available.
ROOMS: 127 en suite (bth/shr) (127 fmly) No smoking in 74 bedrooms d £55-£60 * Off peak **MEALS:** Lunch £4.95-£13.50 High tea £13.50 Dinner £13.50 English & French Cuisine V meals Coffee am Tea pm **FACILITIES:** CTV in all bedrooms STV Outdoor swimming pool (heated) Pool table **CONF:** Thtr 300 Class 150 Board 100 Del from £85 * **SERVICES:** Lift Night porter 180P **NOTES:** No smoking area in restaurant Last d mdnt **CARDS:**

BRADFORD West Yorkshire — Map 07 SE13
★★ Park Drive
12 Park Dr BD9 4DR
Quality Percentage Score: 66%
☎ 01274 480194 📠 01274 484869
Dir: *turn off A650 Keighley road into Emm Lane, at Lister Park, then turn 2nd right*

Pleasantly situated in a quiet residential area, close to Lister Park, the proprietors Mr and Mrs Hilton are always on hand to ensure guest comfort. Spacious bedrooms are currently being refurbished to a very good standard, with attractive soft furnishings and comfortable easy seating. Good home cooking is a feature of the nicely presented dining room and there is also a welcoming lounge.
ROOMS: 11 en suite (bth/shr) (1 fmly) s £47-£52; d £57-£62 (incl. bkfst) LB Off peak **MEALS:** Dinner £13.50 English & Continental Cuisine V meals **FACILITIES:** CTV in all bedrooms **CONF:** Thtr 20 Class 8 Board 12 Del £70 **SERVICES:** 10P **NOTES:** No coaches No smoking in restaurant Last d 8.30pm **CARDS:**

See advert on opposite page

BRADFORD West Yorkshire — Map 07 SE13
★★ Park Grove
28 Park Grove, Frizinghall BD9 4JY
Quality Percentage Score: 65%
☎ 01274 543444 📠 01274 495619
Dir: *off A650 Keighley road, turn right after the Park Pub*
The Singh family converted their large family home, situated in a quiet side road, into a hotel a few years ago and now offer comfortable and generally spacious bedrooms. Friendly service is provided, with a small lounge next to the attractively decorated restaurant, where an interesting mix of Punjabi and English dishes is available.
ROOMS: 15 en suite (bth/shr) (3 fmly) s £40-£47; d £50-£62 (incl. bkfst) * LB Off peak **MEALS:** English & Indian Cuisine V meals **FACILITIES:** CTV in all bedrooms STV **SERVICES:** Night porter 8P **NOTES:** No dogs No coaches No smoking in restaurant Last d 9pm **CARDS:**

BRADFORD West Yorkshire — Map 07 SE13
★★ *Dubrovnik*
3 Oak Av, Mannington BD8 7AQ
Quality Percentage Score: 62%
☎ 01274 543511 📠 01274 480407
Dir: *1.5m from city centre. Take Keighley Road, Queens Road, first left after police station, then second left and hotel on right*
This well established hotel comprises a spacious Victorian house with a modern extension and is quietly located about one mile from the city centre. Bedrooms in the original house, whilst not as large as those in the newer part, have much character and are attractively decorated. A varied range of dishes is offered in generous portions in the traditional dining room.
ROOMS: 46 en suite (bth/shr) (10 fmly) **MEALS:** English & Yugoslavian Cuisine V meals Coffee am Tea pm **FACILITIES:** CTV in all bedrooms ch fac **CONF:** Thtr 250 Class 100 Board 60 **SERVICES:** Night porter 70P **NOTES:** Last d 10pm **CARDS:**

BRADFORD-ON-AVON Wiltshire — Map 03 ST86
★★★ Woolley Grange
Woolley Green BA15 1TX
Quality Percentage Score: 74%
☎ 01225 864705 📠 01225 864059
Dir: *on B3105, 0.5m NE at Woolley Green*
This splendid Cotswold manor house is set in beautiful Wiltshire countryside. Children are made particularly welcome with a trained nanny on duty in the nursery and a special 'den' for the over 8's. Bedrooms and public areas are charmingly furnished and decorated, with lovely fresh flowers and log fires, and lots of luxurious extras. Phil Rimmer's well balanced Rosette worthy menus continue to gain praise.

ROOMS: 14 en suite (bth/shr) 9 annexe en suite (bth/shr) (8 fmly) s fr £90; d £99-£260 (incl. bkfst) * LB Off peak **MEALS:** Lunch £15-£18.50 High tea £5 V meals Coffee am Tea pm **FACILITIES:** CTV in all bedrooms STV Outdoor swimming pool (heated) Tennis (grass) Pool table Croquet lawn Putting green Badminton Games room ch fac Xmas **CONF:** Thtr 40 Class 40 Board 22 Del £140 * **SERVICES:** Night porter 40P **NOTES:** No coaches No smoking in restaurant Last high tea 5pm **CARDS:**

See advert on opposite page

BRADFORD-ON-AVON Wiltshire — Map 03 ST86
★★★ *Leigh Park Hotel*
Leigh Park West BA15 2RA
Quality Percentage Score: 65%
☎ 01225 864885 📠 01225 862315
Dir: *A363 Bath/Frome road, take B3105 signed Holt/Woodley Green) hotel 0.25m on right on crossroads of B3105/B3109, N side of Bradford-on-Avon*
Standing in five-acre grounds, complete with a vineyard, this Georgian hotel combines charm and character with modern

contd.

facilities. The restaurant serves dishes cooked to order, with the majority of fruit and vegetables grown within the grounds.
ROOMS: 21 en suite (bth/shr) (4 fmly) No smoking in 7 bedrooms
MEALS: English & French Cuisine V meals Coffee am Tea pm
FACILITIES: CTV in all bedrooms Tennis (hard) Snooker **CONF:** Thtr 120 Class 60 Board 60 **SERVICES:** 80P **NOTES:** No smoking in restaurant Last d 9.30pm **CARDS:**

BRAINTREE Essex — Map 05 TL72

★★★ *White Hart*
Bocking End CM7 9AB
Quality Percentage Score: 62%
☎ 01376 321401 01376 552628
Dir: *in town centre*

Old English Inns & Hotels

Dating back to the 16th century, this hotel suits both leisure and business guests, as well as being popular with locals. Informal public areas have the feel of a traditional coaching inn and include a bar with a log fire and real ales, and a family restaurant with a broad-appeal menu. The comfortable bedrooms are modern with the exception of a small number of character rooms in the original building.
ROOMS: 31 en suite (bth/shr) (8 fmly) No smoking in 9 bedrooms
MEALS: English & Continental Cuisine V meals Coffee am Tea pm
FACILITIES: CTV in all bedrooms STV Sauna Solarium Gym
CONF: Thtr 40 Class 16 Board 24 **SERVICES:** Night porter 52P
NOTES: No dogs (ex guide dogs) No smoking area in restaurant
CARDS:

The AA Hotel Booking Service is a free benefit to AA members. See the advertisement on page 47

B

BRAINTREE Essex — Map 05 TL72

Travel Inn

Cressing Rd, Galley's Corner CM7 8GG

☎ 01376 340914 Fax 01376 340437

Dir: *on A120 bypass at Galley's Corner*

This modern building offers accommodation in smart, spacious and well equipped bedrooms, all with en-suite bathrooms. Refreshments may be taken at the nearby family restaurant. For details about current prices consult the Contents Page under Hotel Groups for the Travel Inn phone number.

ROOMS: 40 en suite (bth/shr) d £39.95 *

BRAITHWAITE Cumbria — Map 11 NY22

★★ ***Ivy House***

CA12 5SY

Quality Percentage Score: 68%

☎ 017687 78338 Fax 017687 78113

Dir: *in the middle of the village turn left immediately after the Royal Oak pub*

Dating from the 17th century, this fine period house is conveniently situated in the village centre. The cosy lounge features ancient timbers and open fires. The galleried restaurant, candlelit by night, serves a skilfully prepared daily-changing menu.

ROOMS: 12 en suite (bth/shr) **MEALS: FACILITIES:** CTV in all bedrooms **SERVICES:** 17P **NOTES:** No coaches No children No smoking in restaurant Last d 8pm Closed Jan

CARDS:

BRAMHALL Greater Manchester — Map 07 SJ88

★★★ **County Hotel Bramhall**

Bramhall Ln South SK7 2EB

REGAL

Quality Percentage Score: 64%

☎ 0161 455 9988 Fax 0161 440 8071

Dir: *M56 junct6 to Wilmslow A34 bypass towards Manchester, A5102 to Bramhall. From M60 junct3, A34 bypass to Congleton - A5102 to Bramhall*

This modern hotel is in a pleasant suburban area, and offers accommodation in comfortable bedrooms, ranging in size up to spacious family rooms. There is a formal restaurant, and also the Shires Pub for simpler meals.

ROOMS: 65 en suite (bth/shr) (3 fmly) No smoking in 20 bedrooms s £83-£97; d £83-£115 * LB Off peak **MEALS:** Lunch £5.95-£13.50 Dinner £8.99-£13.50 English & French Cuisine V meals Coffee am Tea pm **FACILITIES:** CTV in all bedrooms Xmas **CONF:** Thtr 200 Class 80 Board 60 Del from £110 * **SERVICES:** Night porter 120P **NOTES:** No smoking in restaurant Last d 9.45pm

CARDS:

BRAMHOPE West Yorkshire — Map 08 SE24

★★★ ***Posthouse Bramhope***

Leeds Rd LS16 9JJ

Posthouse

Quality Percentage Score: 69%

☎ 0113 284 2911 Fax 0113 284 3451

Dir: *on A660 6m N of Leeds city centre. Follow signs 'Leeds/Bradford Airport'*

This modern hotel is peacefully situated in 16 acres of grounds. Bedrooms offer a good standard of modern comfort and public areas include a restaurant, conference rooms and a training centre. Refreshments are served all day in the lounge and 24-hour room service is provided.

ROOMS: 124 en suite (bth/shr) No smoking in 40 bedrooms **MEALS:** International Cuisine V meals Coffee am Tea pm **FACILITIES:** CTV in all bedrooms STV Indoor swimming pool (heated) Sauna Solarium Gym Pool table Jacuzzi/spa **CONF:** Thtr 160 Class 80 Board 40 **SERVICES:** Lift Night porter Air conditioning 126P **NOTES:** No smoking in restaurant Last d 10.30pm **CARDS:**

BRAMPTON Cumbria — Map 12 NY56

The Premier Collection

★★★ **Farlam Hall**

Hallbankgate CA8 2NG

RELAIS & CHATEAUX

☎ 016977 46234 Fax 016977 46683

Dir: *from A69 take A689 to Alston, the hotel is approx 2m on the left, not in Farlam village*

A delightful 16th century house in extensive landscaped gardens complete with ornamental lake and tumbling stream. Standards of hospitality and service are excellent. The public rooms are lavishly furnished; in the elegant restaurant guests enjoy ambitious regional cooking which is noteworthy. All bedrooms provide decadent levels of comfort, fine period pieces and thoughtful extras.

ROOMS: 11 en suite (bth/shr) 1 annexe en suite (bth/shr) s £120-£135; d £220-£250 (incl. bkfst & dinner) * LB Off peak **MEALS:** Dinner £30-£31 V meals Coffee am Tea pm **FACILITIES:** CTV in all bedrooms Croquet lawn **CONF:** Thtr 12 Class 12 Board 12 **SERVICES:** 35P **NOTES:** No coaches No children 5yrs Last d 8.30pm Closed 25-30 Dec

CARDS:

BRAMPTON Cumbria — Map 12 NY56

★★ ***Tarn End House***

Talkin Tarn CA8 1LS

Quality Percentage Score: 65%

☎ 016977 2340 Fax 016977 2089

Dir: *from A69 take B6413 for 2m and turn off towards Talkin Village*

There is a warm and relaxed atmosphere at this farmhouse, which enjoys an idyllic location. The hotel provides an ideal

contd.

retreat and is also popular with golfers, the local course being on its doorstep. Dinner is a treat, with an extremely imaginative and daily changing menu.
ROOMS: 7 en suite (bth/shr) (1 fmly) **MEALS:** International Cuisine V meals Coffee am Tea pm **FACILITIES:** CTV in all bedrooms **CONF:** Board 20 Del from £75 * **SERVICES:** 40P **NOTES:** No coaches No smoking in restaurant Last d 9pm **CARDS:**

BRANDESBURTON East Riding of Yorkshire — Map 08 TA14
★★ Burton Lodge
YO25 8RU
Quality Percentage Score: 67%
☎ 01964 542847 Fax 01964 542847
Dir: *7m from Beverley off A165, adjoining Hainsworth Park Golf Club*
Surrounded by landscaped gardens close to a golf course, this modern hotel offers very pleasant accommodation. An open fire is a welcoming feature of the lounge and there is also an attractive dining room with a menu offering a good choice.
ROOMS: 7 en suite (bth/shr) 2 annexe en suite (bth/shr) (2 fmly) s £34-£37; d £46-£52 (incl. bkfst) * LB Off peak **MEALS:** Dinner fr £13.50 V meals Coffee am Tea pm **FACILITIES:** CTV in all bedrooms Golf 18 Tennis (grass) Putting green Pitch and putt **SERVICES:** 14P **NOTES:** No coaches No smoking in restaurant Last d 9.15pm
CARDS:

BRANDON Suffolk — Map 05 TL78
★★ Brandon House
High St IP27 0AX
MINOTEL Great Britain
Quality Percentage Score: 69%
☎ 01842 810171 Fax 01842 814859
Dir:
Strikingly built in red brick, this manor house dates back to the 18th century. The bedrooms vary in size and style, but all are well equipped. The spacious public rooms include the traditional Conifers English Restaurant for serious dining, Smokey Joe's with its informal American-style cooking, and a large comfortable lounge bar to relax in.
ROOMS: 15 en suite (bth/shr) (3 fmly) s £55; d £69.50 (incl. bkfst) * LB Off peak **MEALS:** Lunch £10.95-£16.95 & alc Dinner fr £16.95 & alc English & French Cuisine V meals Coffee am Tea pm **FACILITIES:** CTV in all bedrooms STV **CONF:** Thtr 70 Class 25 Board 20 **SERVICES:** 40P **NOTES:** No coaches Last d 9pm Closed 25-26 Dec & 1 Jan
CARDS:

BRANDON Warwickshire — Map 04 SP47
★★★ The Brandon Hall
Main St CV8 3FW
Quality Percentage Score: 64%
☎ 024 76542571 Fax 024 76544909
Dir: *off A428 to Rugby*
Peacefully located in 17 acres of lawns and woodland, this former shooting lodge is found by following signs for the village centre of Brandon. Many bedrooms have been refurbished to a very good standard, providing a good range of modern facilities and smart bathrooms; the remaining original house rooms and some public rooms are scheduled for similar good work.
ROOMS: 60 en suite (bth/shr) No smoking in 29 bedrooms d fr £94 * LB Off peak **MEALS:** Lunch £13.95 Dinner £21.95 & alc International Cuisine V meals Coffee am Tea pm **FACILITIES:** CTV in all bedrooms Squash Croquet lawn Putting green Xmas **CONF:** Thtr 90 Class 40 Board 40 Del £135 * **SERVICES:** Night porter 250P **NOTES:** No smoking in restaurant Last d 9.30pm
CARDS:

BRANDS HATCH Kent — Map 05 TQ56
★★★★ *Thistle Brands Hatch*
DA3 8PE
THISTLE HOTELS
Quality Percentage Score: 65%
☎ 01474 854900 Fax 01474 853220
Dir: *on A20 N of junct with M20 3m from junct 3 M25, at main entrance to Brands Hatch Racing Circuit*
This conference and leisure hotel is located at the main entrance of the world famous Grand Prix racing circuit. Bedrooms are individually styled and staff are friendly and efficient. In addition to the main restaurant there is an informal brasserie. A recent addition is a range of indoor leisure facilities.
ROOMS: 121 en suite (bth/shr) (4 fmly) No smoking in 41 bedrooms **MEALS:** English & French Cuisine V meals Coffee am Tea pm **FACILITIES:** CTV in all bedrooms STV Indoor swimming pool (heated) Sauna Solarium Gym Jacuzzi/spa **CONF:** Thtr 270 Class 120 Board 50 Del from £118 * **SERVICES:** Night porter 180P **NOTES:** No smoking area in restaurant Last d 10pm **CARDS:**

BRANDS HATCH Kent — Map 05 TQ56
★★★ ❀❀ Brandshatch Place
Fawkham DA3 8NQ
ARCADIAN HOTELS Distinctly Different
Quality Percentage Score: 67%
☎ 01474 872239 Fax 01474 879652
Dir: *from A20 follow signs Fawkham. Tourist sign Brandshatch Place Hotel. After 1 mile follow tourist sign, take third turn left under motorway bridge*

This delightful Georgian country house set in extensive gardens, is peaceful despite being close to the famous racing circuit and M20. The hotel has excellent leisure facilities in the Fredericks Leisure Club, and a range of meeting rooms. Bedrooms are spacious, comfortable and equipped with extra amenities. The kitchen takes pride in its cuisine.
ROOMS: 29 en suite (bth/shr) 12 annexe en suite (bth/shr) (2 fmly) No smoking in 12 bedrooms s £85; d £99 * LB Off peak **MEALS:** Lunch £14.95-£16.95 & alc Dinner £21.95 & alc International Cuisine V meals Coffee am Tea pm **FACILITIES:** CTV in all bedrooms STV Indoor swimming pool (heated) Tennis (hard) Squash Snooker Sauna Solarium Gym Jacuzzi/spa Beauty therapy Steam room ch fac Xmas **CONF:** Thtr 120 Class 50 Board 35 Del £150 * **SERVICES:** Night porter 100P **NOTES:** No smoking in restaurant Last d 9.45pm
CARDS:

BRANKSOME See **Poole**

★
The Premier Collection, hotels with Red Star Awards are listed on pages 17-23

BRANSCOMBE Devon — Map 03 SY18

★★ The Masons Arms
EX12 3DJ
Quality Percentage Score: 64%
☎ 01297 680300 Fax 01297 680500
Dir: *turn off A3052 towards Branscombe, head down hill, hotel in the valley at the bottom of the hill*

This charming 14th-century inn is only half a mile from the sea in the picturesque village of Branscombe. There is a choice of bedroom accommodation with cottage rooms and comfortable berths inside the main house. There is a cosy first floor lounge, whilst the bar, built around a central fireplace, serves many fine ales in addition to an extensive menu. Oak beams are a feature of the restaurant, where a short fixed-price menu offers both innovative and more traditional dishes.

ROOMS: 6 rms (5 bth) 16 annexe en suite (bth/shr) (2 fmly) s £22-£100; d £44-£120 (incl. bkfst) * LB Off peak **MEALS:** Bar Lunch £2.95-£10.95 Dinner £2.95-£10.95 English & French Cuisine V meals Coffee am Tea pm **FACILITIES:** CTV in all bedrooms Xmas **CONF:** Thtr 60 Class 20 Board 20 Del from £90 * **SERVICES:** 43P **NOTES:** No coaches No smoking in restaurant Last d 9pm **CARDS:**

BRANSFORD Worcestershire — Map 03 SO75

★★★ Bank House Hotel Golf & Country Club
Hereford Rd WR6 5JD
Quality Percentage Score: 66%
☎ 01886 833551 Fax 01886 832461
Dir: *M5 junct 7 follow signs to Worcester West, pick up signs for Hereford on A4440 then the A4103 Hereford Rd. Turn left, hotel approx. 2m on left*

Partly dating back to the 17th century, but now considerably extended, Bank House is set in 120 acres overlooking the Malvern Hills, 3 miles west of Worcester just off the A4103. There is a good choice of function and conference suites, and the bedrooms are furnished in the main with Stag furniture. Fixed price and à la carte menus are offered in the attractive first-floor Barclay Restaurant. The hotel has a gymnasium and sauna, and an 18-hole golf course.

ROOMS: 68 en suite (bth/shr) (20 fmly) No smoking in 15 bedrooms **MEALS:** Sunday Lunch £12.50-£14.95 High tea £4.50-£7.50alc Dinner £17.95-£19.95 & alc English, Continental & Oriental Cuisine V meals Coffee am Tea pm **FACILITIES:** CTV in all bedrooms Outdoor swimming pool Golf 18 Tennis Sauna Solarium Gym Pool table Putting green Jacuzzi/spa **CONF:** Thtr 400 Class 150 Board 70 Del from £99 **SERVICES:** Night porter 350P **NOTES:** No dogs (ex guide dogs) No smoking in restaurant Last d 9.30pm
CARDS:

BRANSTON Lincolnshire — Map 08 TF06

★★★ Branston Hall
Branston Park LN4 1PD
Quality Percentage Score: 63%
☎ 01522 793305 Fax 01522 790549
Dir: *3m from Lincoln city centre along B1188 towards Woodhall Spa. On entering Branston village, hotel is located directly opposite the village hall*

Set in 88 acres of woodland within easy reach of Lincoln, this impressive mansion house offers traditionally furnished, well equipped bedrooms. Public rooms include the lounge bar, a lounge with splendid views, and a restaurant serving interesting menus.

ROOMS: 36 en suite (bth/shr) 7 annexe en suite (bth/shr) (3 fmly) s £49-£59.50; d £63-£79.50 (incl. bkfst) * LB Off peak **MEALS:** Lunch £12.95-£16.95 & alc Dinner £16.95 & alc International Cuisine V meals Coffee am Tea pm **FACILITIES:** CTV in all bedrooms Gym Croquet lawn Jogging circuit Xmas **CONF:** Thtr 200 Class 70 Board 60 Del from £90 * **SERVICES:** Lift Night porter 150P **NOTES:** No smoking area in restaurant Last d 9.30pm **CARDS:**

See advert under LINCOLN

BRANSTON Lincolnshire — Map 08 TF06

★★★ *Moor Lodge*
Sleaford Rd LN4 1HU
Quality Percentage Score: 60%
☎ 01522 791366 Fax 01522 794389
Dir: *3m S of Lincoln on B1188*

The restaurant at this old manor house is called 'Arnhem' as wartime paratroopers trained in the area. There is a relaxed atmosphere in the bar and lounge, staff are friendly and welcoming. The restaurant offers a range of well-produced dishes. Most bedrooms are recently redecorated.

ROOMS: 24 en suite (bth/shr) (2 fmly) No smoking in 2 bedrooms **MEALS:** English & French Cuisine V meals Coffee am Tea pm **FACILITIES:** CTV in all bedrooms **CONF:** Thtr 200 Class 80 Board 60 **SERVICES:** Night porter 150P **NOTES:** Last d 9.45pm
CARDS:

BRAY Berkshire — Map 04 SU97

★★★★ *Monkey Island*
SL6 2EE
Quality Percentage Score: 64%
☎ 01628 623400 Fax 01628 784732
Dir: *exit M4 at junct 8/9 and take A308 signposted Windsor, take first left into Bray then first right into Old Mill Lane*

Enjoying an idyllic island location on the River Thames, the access to this peaceful hotel is by footbridge or boat only. There is a feeling of exclusivity and peace and the bedrooms are

contd.

comfortable and smart. The grounds are lovingly maintained and have a population of rabbits and waterfowl.

ROOMS: 26 en suite (bth/shr) (1 fmly) **MEALS:** English & French Cuisine V meals Coffee am Tea pm **FACILITIES:** CTV in all bedrooms STV Fishing Gym Croquet lawn Clay pigeon shooting Boating by request Wkly live entertainment **CONF:** Thtr 150 Class 60 Board 55 **SERVICES:** Night porter 100P **NOTES:** No dogs No smoking area in restaurant Last d 9.30pm Closed 25 Dec-15 Jan RS Sat (no lunch in restaurant)
CARDS:

See advert under MAIDENHEAD

BRAY Berkshire **Map 04 SU97**

★★★ Chauntry House Hotel & Restaurant

SL6 2AB
Quality Percentage Score: 68%
☎ 01628 673991 01628 773089
Dir: *from M4 junct 8/9 take A308(M) towards Windsor then B3028 to Bray village. Hotel on left*

A delightful country house, with charming public rooms. Bedrooms are spacious and individually decorated with attractive appointments. There is a pretty walled garden where guests may relax on warm days. The restaurant is manned by joint proprietor Chris Hope, whose worldwide experiences are reflected in his two rosette awarded menus.

ROOMS: 12 en suite (bth/shr) 4 annexe en suite (bth/shr) s fr £102; d £130-£140 (incl. bkfst) * Off peak **MEALS:** Lunch fr £19.50 & alc V meals Coffee am Tea pm **FACILITIES:** CTV in all bedrooms STV **CONF:** Board 22 Del from £135 * **SERVICES:** 35P **NOTES:** No coaches No smoking in restaurant Closed 24 Dec-2 Jan RS Sun & BH
CARDS:

BREADSALL Derbyshire **Map 08 SK33**

★★★★ Marriott Breadsall Priory Hotel, Country Club

Moor Rd DE7 6DL
Quality Percentage Score: 62%
☎ 01332 832235 01332 833509
Dir: *take A52 to Derby, then 3rd exit signposted Chesterfield. At 4th rdbt take 3rd exit to Village follow road & turn right at church hotel in 1.5m*

This extended mansion house is set in 400 acres of parkland with glorious views over rolling countryside. Guest have full membership of the Country Club which offers a host of facilities including golf, tennis and an impressive indoor leisure complex. Bedrooms are mostly contained within various modern wings and guests are advised to register before unloading. There is a smart and informal Weekend leisure café which serves food all day, a more formal restaurant and an extensive room service.

ROOMS: 12 en suite (bth/shr) 100 annexe en suite (bth/shr) (35 fmly) No smoking in 56 bedrooms d fr £79 * LB Off peak **MEALS:** Lunch fr £11.95 Dinner £25-£30 & alc English & French Cuisine V meals Coffee am Tea pm **FACILITIES:** CTV in all bedrooms STV Indoor swimming pool (heated) Golf 36 Tennis (hard) Sauna Solarium Gym Croquet lawn Putting green Jacuzzi/spa Health/beauty salon Dance studio Xmas **CONF:** Thtr 120 Class 50 Board 36 Del from £135 * **SERVICES:** Lift Night porter 300P **NOTES:** No dogs (ex guide dogs) No smoking in restaurant Last d 9.45pm **CARDS:**

AA Rosettes are awarded for quality of food, see page 15 for an explanation of Rosette assessment.

BRENT KNOLL Somerset **Map 03 ST35**

★★ Woodlands

Hill Ln TA9 4DF
Quality Percentage Score: 68%
☎ 01278 760232 01278 760232
Dir: *from A38 take first left into village, then fifth right and first left*

Bedrooms offer extras like sherry, sweets, sewing kits and bottled waters. They are tastefully decorated and well equipped. The bar-lounge has a log fire on cooler evenings, the elegant dining room serves memorable meals. Breakfast is served in the conservatory, overlooking the outdoor pool and patio.

ROOMS: 8 en suite (bth/shr) No smoking in all bedrooms s £45-£60; d £65-£115 (incl. bkfst) * LB Off peak **MEALS:** English & French Cuisine V meals Coffee am Tea pm **FACILITIES:** CTV in all bedrooms Xmas **CONF:** Thtr 90 Class 45 Board 35 **SERVICES:** 20P **NOTES:** No coaches No children 8yrs No smoking in restaurant **CARDS:**

See advert under WESTON-SUPER-MARE

BRENT KNOLL Somerset **Map 03 ST35**

★★ Battleborough Grange Hotel

Bristol Rd TA9 4HJ
Quality Percentage Score: 60%
☎ 01278 760208 01278 760208
Dir: *on A38 Weston-Super-Mare Rd, opposite the Goat House*

Surrounded by mellow Somerset countryside, the hotel is just
contd.

one mile from the M5, thus making a convenient location for both business and leisure guests. Bedrooms are well equipped and some offer extensive views of the historic Iron Age fort of Brent Knoll. Public rooms include a convivial bar, conservatory restaurant and extensive function facilities.

ROOMS: 14 en suite (bth/shr) s £45-£48; d £59-£68 (incl. bkfst) * LB Off peak **MEALS:** Lunch fr £5 & alc High tea fr £4 Dinner fr £12.50 & alc V meals Coffee am Tea pm **FACILITIES:** CTV in all bedrooms Jacuzzi/spa **SERVICES:** Night porter 50P **NOTES:** No dogs (ex guide dogs) No smoking in restaurant Last d 9pm
CARDS:

BRENTWOOD Essex **Map 05 TQ59**

★★★★ Marygreen Manor

London Rd CM14 4NR
Quality Percentage Score: 71%
☎ 01277 225252 01277 262809
Dir: *on A1023*

This handsome manor house dates back to 1535, and offers easy access to London and the major motorway network. Beamed ceilings and carved panelling are features of the public rooms and the three de luxe bedrooms in the main house. The remaining bedrooms are located around an attractive garden at the rear. Recently gaining its second rosette, the grand baronial restaurant is a popular venue for a wide variety of dishes from good value carte and set price menus.

ROOMS: 3 en suite (bth/shr) 40 annexe en suite (bth/shr) No smoking in 8 bedrooms s £111.50-£129; d £127.50-£134 Off peak **MEALS:** Lunch £14-£17.50 & alc Dinner £25 & alc International Cuisine V meals Coffee am Tea pm **FACILITIES:** CTV in all bedrooms STV **CONF:** Thtr 60 Class 20 Board 25 Del from £155 * **SERVICES:** Night porter 100P **NOTES:** No dogs (ex guide dogs) No coaches No smoking in restaurant Last d 10.15pm **CARDS:**

See advert on opposite page

BRENTWOOD Essex **Map 05 TQ59**

★★★ Posthouse Brentwood

Posthouse

Brook St CM14 5NF
Quality Percentage Score: 69%
☎ 01277 260260 01277 264264
Dir: *close to M25/A12 interchange*

Inside this modern hotel, major refurbishment has taken place: bedrooms are a real strength, smartly decorated, well equipped and supported by extensive room service. In the public areas, guests have a choice of eating options with Café Express and Garfunkels open all day, and Atrio restaurant additional in the evening.

ROOMS: 145 en suite (bth/shr) (30 fmly) No smoking in 80 bedrooms d £109-£129 * LB Off peak **MEALS:** International & Mediterranean Cuisine V meals Coffee am Tea pm **FACILITIES:** CTV in all bedrooms Indoor swimming pool (heated) Sauna Solarium Gym Health & fitness club Xmas **CONF:** Thtr 120 Class 60 Board 50 Del from £155 * **SERVICES:** Lift Night porter 190P **NOTES:** No smoking area in restaurant Last d 10.30pm **CARDS:**

AA Rosettes are awarded for quality of food, see page 15 for an explanation of Rosette assessment.

BRIDGNORTH Shropshire **Map 07 SO79**
see also **Alveley**

★★★ Old Vicarage Hotel

WV15 5JZ
☎ 01746 716497 01746 716552
(For full entry see Worfield)

PRIDE OF BRITAIN MEMBER

BRIDGNORTH Shropshire **Map 07 SO79**

★★ Parlors Hall

Mill St WV15 5AL
Quality Percentage Score: 63%
☎ 01746 761931 01746 767058
Dir: *turn left off A454 then right and right again for 200yds*

Named after the family who lived here between 1419 and 1539, Parlors Hall has been a hotel since 1929 and retains many original features, such as oak panelling and magnificent fireplaces. The bedrooms are well equipped and some have four-poster beds.

ROOMS: 15 en suite (bth/shr) (2 fmly) s £39; d £48 (incl. bkfst) * Off peak **MEALS:** Lunch £7.95-£11.25 & alc Dinner £5-£10.50alc European Cuisine V meals Coffee am Tea pm **FACILITIES:** CTV in all bedrooms Xmas **CONF:** Thtr 50 Class 25 Board 25 **SERVICES:** 24P **NOTES:** No dogs (ex guide dogs) Last d 9.45pm **CARDS:**

See advert on opposite page

BRIDGNORTH Shropshire **Map 07 SO79**

★ Croft

Saint Mary's St WV16 4DW
Quality Percentage Score: 67%
☎ 01746 762416 01746 767431
Dir: *follow signs for town centre and turn right immediately after Town Hall*

This small family run hotel is just off the High Street, and dates back to the 18th century. The traditionally furnished accommodation has modern equipment and facilities, and includes family bedded rooms plus a bedroom on ground floor level. Other facilities here comprise a bar, a lounge and a dining room. There is a public car park just a short walk away.

ROOMS: 22 rms (20 bth/shr) (3 fmly) s £23.50-£41; d £46-£50 (incl. bkfst) * LB Off peak **MEALS:** Dinner £10.20-£16.75alc V meals Coffee am Tea pm **FACILITIES:** CTV in all bedrooms **CONF:** Thtr 30 Class 20 Board 12 **SERVICES:** Night porter **NOTES:** No smoking in restaurant Last d 8.30pm **CARDS:**

BRIDGWATER Somerset **Map 03 ST33**
see also **Holford**

★★★ Walnut Tree Hotel

North Petherton TA6 6QA
Quality Percentage Score: 72%
☎ 01278 662255 01278 663946
Dir: *on A38, 1m S of exit 24 on M5*

Best Western

An 18th-century former coaching inn, modernised and extended with impressive results. Most bedrooms, now of executive standard, are elegantly furnished, decorated and equipped. The formal 'Dukes' restaurant has an interesting carte and the

contd. on p. 146

The Mill Hotel

Alveley, Nr Bridgnorth
Shropshire WV15 6HL
Tel: 01746 780437 Fax: 01746 780850

For full entry see Alveley

AA ★★★★

The beautiful tranquil setting of The Mill provides the perfect venue for a leisure break or business stopover. The luxurious bedrooms are elegantly furnished and most overlook the landscaped gardens and pool and surrounding countryside. The ***Waterside Restaurant*** *is renowned for the high standard of its cuisine and charming ambience. Open daily. Easily accessible from Midland motorway networks, The Mill Hotel is situated just off the A442, midway Kidderminster to Bridgnorth.*

Marygreen Manor Hotel

AA★★★★ ❀❀

In the warm and friendly atmosphere of this genuine Tudor House, you can enjoy the traditional comfort of open log fires in oak panelled lounges. Accommodation consists of 33 garden suites facing onto an olde-worlde garden – three authentic period ensuite rooms with four-posters – and our most recent addition of seven rooms and three Suites in luxurious 'Country House style' incorporating every modern hi-tech facility for the busy executive. The elegant restaurant offers imaginative fresh-produce menus. Twenty-four hour room service, afternoon teas and all day snack menu. You will find us just half a mile from the M25 Junction 28.

London Road, Brentwood, Essex CM14 4NR
Tel: 01277-225252 Fax: 01277-262809
www.marygreenmanor.co.uk

Parlors Hall Hotel ★★

Mill Street, Bridgnorth
Shropshire WV15 5AL
Tel: (01746) 761931 Fax: (01746) 767058

The original Parlors Hall which dates back to the 12th century became an hotel in 1929. Since then it has been carefully refurbished but keeping many of the ancient features, including the fireplaces and oak panelling. Today the hotel offers fifteen luxury en suite bedrooms, each individually decorated in keeping with the character of the building. The attractive restaurant offers an à la carte and carvery menus. Ideally located for business visitors or visiting the many tourist attractions of the area.

The Heybridge Hotel

Roman Road, Ingatestone, Essex CM4 9AB
Tel: 01277 355355 Fax: 01277 353288

This family owned Hotel has been under the direction of Mr Ermis Kyprianou and his family for the past 34 years.

A Traditional welcome awaits you and you are guaranteed a standard of service unrivalled in the area.
You can enjoy the intimate delights of our Restaurant or you can use the extensive facilities in our Banqueting Suites which may hold up to 500 guests for a Banquet or Dinner and Dance.
We look forward to welcoming you to
The Heybridge Hotel

popular 'Cottage Room' serves value for money meals.
ROOMS: 32 en suite (bth) (5 fmly) No smoking in 3 bedrooms s £65-£107; d £86-£115 (incl. bkfst) * LB Off peak **MEALS:** Lunch £9-£14alc Dinner £14 & alc International Cuisine V meals Coffee am Tea pm **FACILITIES:** CTV in all bedrooms STV Solarium ch fac Xmas **CONF:** Thtr 130 Class 76 Board 70 Del from £84.20 * **SERVICES:** Night porter 70P **NOTES:** No dogs (ex guide dogs) No smoking area in restaurant Last d 10pm **CARDS:**

BRIDGWATER Somerset — Map 03 ST33

★★ Friarn Court

37 St Mary St TA6 3LX
Quality Percentage Score: 66%
☎ 01278 452859 01278 452988
Dir: *at junct of A38 & A39 turn into St Mary St*

Service is friendly and relaxed at this popular and homely town centre hotel. Bedrooms, executive and standard, are comfortably furnished and tastefully appointed. There is a popular bar, small lounge and a more spacious restaurant which doubles as a conference venue. During the week a full carte menu is served, on Sundays a range of bar snacks are provided.
ROOMS: 16 en suite (bth/shr) (3 fmly) No smoking in 4 bedrooms s £39.90-£59.90; d £59.90-£69.90 (incl. bkfst) * LB Off peak **MEALS:** Dinner £10-£20alc International Cuisine V meals Coffee am Tea pm **FACILITIES:** CTV in all bedrooms **CONF:** Thtr 60 Class 40 Board 30 **SERVICES:** Night porter 14P **NOTES:** Last d 9pm
CARDS:

BRIDLINGTON East Riding of Yorkshire — Map 08 TA16

★★★ Revelstoke

1-3 Flamborough Rd YO15 2HU
Quality Percentage Score: 67%
☎ 01262 672362 01262 672362
Dir: *take B1255 Flamborough Head rd & in 0.5m turn right at mini rdbt to junct of the Promenade & Flamborough Rd. Hotel across from Holy Trinty*

This family owned and run hotel, near both the town centre and the seafront, is a popular place to stay. Bedrooms offer a good standard of comfort and amenity; public rooms are well furnished and the restaurant serves a wide range of enjoyable dishes.
ROOMS: 25 en suite (bth/shr) (5 fmly) s £35-£50; d £55-£75 * LB Off peak **MEALS:** Lunch £5.95-£11 Dinner £14 English & French Cuisine V meals Coffee am Tea pm **FACILITIES:** CTV in all bedrooms Wkly live entertainment **CONF:** Thtr 250 Class 200 Board 100 **SERVICES:** 14P **NOTES:** No dogs (ex guide dogs) No smoking in restaurant Last d 8.30pm **CARDS:**

See advert on opposite page

BRIDLINGTON East Riding of Yorkshire — Map 08 TA16

★★★ Expanse

North Marine Dr YO15 2LS
Quality Percentage Score: 66%
☎ 01262 675347 01262 604928
Dir: *follow signs North Beach P, pass under railway arch for North Marine Drive. Hotel at bottom of hill*

This traditional seaside hotel overlooks the bay and has been in the same family's ownership for many years. Comfortable public areas include a large bar and inviting lounge. The modern bedrooms are well equipped. Service is relaxed and friendly.
ROOMS: 48 en suite (bth/shr) (4 fmly) s £29.50-£49.50; d £59-£85 (incl. bkfst) * LB Off peak **MEALS:** Lunch £8.95-£9.95 Dinner fr £15.75 & alc English & French Cuisine V meals Coffee am Tea pm **FACILITIES:** CTV in all bedrooms Wkly live entertainment Xmas **CONF:** Thtr 50 Class 30 Board 24 **SERVICES:** Lift Night porter 25P **NOTES:** No dogs (ex guide dogs) No coaches **CARDS:**

BRIDPORT Dorset — Map 03 SY49

★★★ Haddon House

West Bay DT6 4EL
Quality Percentage Score: 58%
☎ 01308 423626 & 425323 01308 427348
Dir: *0.5m off the A35 Crown Inn rdbt signposted to West Bay*

This is an attractive hotel a few minutes from the quay and seafront. Bedrooms offer good standards of accommodation. There is a comfortable lounge and popular bar that serves a wide range of food. The restaurant offers an interesting menu of carefully prepared dishes.
ROOMS: 12 en suite (bth/shr) (2 fmly) d £50-£80 (incl. bkfst) * LB Off peak **MEALS:** Lunch fr £9.95 & alc Dinner fr £21.50 English & French Cuisine V meals Coffee am Tea pm **FACILITIES:** CTV in all bedrooms STV Solarium ch fac Xmas **CONF:** Thtr 50 Class 30 Board 20 **SERVICES:** 74P **NOTES:** No dogs (ex guide dogs) No smoking in restaurant Last d 8.45pm **CARDS:**

BRIDPORT Dorset — Map 03 SY49

★★ Roundham House

Roundham Gardens, West Bay Rd DT6 4BD
Quality Percentage Score: 66%
☎ 01308 422753 & 425779 01308 421500
Dir: *take A35 Bridport road, do not take left turn to Bridport follow A35 to rdbt Crown Inn, follow signs for West Bay along West Bay Rd hotel signed*

This small hotel is located on the edge of the town and benefits from wonderful views across the Dorset countryside. Bedrooms vary in size, but all offer comfort and good levels of equipment. In the restaurant, a choice of fixed-price and à la carte menus is offered.
ROOMS: 8 rms (7 bth/shr) (2 fmly) s £33-£38; d £65-£75 (incl. bkfst) * LB Off peak **MEALS:** Dinner fr £17.50 & alc European Cuisine V meals Coffee am **FACILITIES:** CTV in all bedrooms Xmas **SERVICES:** 13P **NOTES:** No smoking in restaurant Last d 8.30pm Closed Jan-Feb
CARDS:

BRIDPORT Dorset — Map 03 SY49

★ Bridge House

115 East St DT6 3LB

Quality Percentage Score: 64%

☎ 01308 423371 Fax 01308 423371

***Dir:** turn off at rdbt with A35 & A 3066, hotel 150yds on right next to River Asker bridge*

This hotel dates from the 18th century and is equally well suited to business and leisure guests. Bedrooms are well equipped. There is a small bar-lounge, in addition to the main lounge. Good home cooked meals that use top quality produce are offered.

ROOMS: 10 en suite (bth/shr) (3 fmly) s £29-£35; d £42-£50 (incl. bkfst) * LB Off peak **MEALS:** Dinner £16.50 V meals Coffee am **FACILITIES:** CTV in all bedrooms **CONF:** Thtr 20 Board 12 Del £60 * **SERVICES:** 12P **NOTES:** No coaches No smoking in restaurant Last d 9pm **CARDS:**

BRIGG Lincolnshire — Map 08 TA00

★★ *Exchange Coach House Inn*

Bigby St DN20 8EJ

Quality Percentage Score: 62%

☎ 01652 657633 Fax 01652 657636

***Dir:** access via M180 junct 4 onto A18 for 5m*

This grade 11 listed building provides modern and well equipped bedrooms which are located in outbuildings to the rear. There is an extensive range of dishes with a leaning towards the Americas and the Orient. The bars are furnished with many interesting items of bric-a-brac and the service is both friendly and attentive.

ROOMS: 21 en suite (bth/shr) (1 fmly) **MEALS:** American/Mexican/Ethnic Cuisine V meals Coffee am Tea pm **FACILITIES:** CTV in all bedrooms STV Snooker Pool table Wkly live entertainment **CONF:** Thtr 100 Class 50 Board 40 Del from £70 * **SERVICES:** 24P **NOTES:** No smoking area in restaurant Last d 10.30pm

CARDS:

BRIGHOUSE West Yorkshire — Map 07 SE12

★★★ Posthouse Brighouse

Posthouse

Clifton Village HD6 4HW

Quality Percentage Score: 67%

☎ 01484 400400 Fax 01484 400068

***Dir:** on A644 just off junct 25 of M62*

Bedrooms at this modern hotel are spacious and comfortably furnished, and include rooms suitable for disabled guests and family rooms. Public areas are roomy and include an attractively appointed restaurant, several versatile conference and meeting rooms and a leisure club. Service includes the provision of an all-day lounge menu and 24 hour room service.

ROOMS: 94 en suite (bth/shr) (20 fmly) No smoking in 62 bedrooms d £59-£99 * LB Off peak **MEALS:** International Cuisine V meals Coffee am Tea pm **FACILITIES:** CTV in all bedrooms STV Indoor swimming pool (heated) Sauna Solarium Gym Croquet lawn Jacuzzi/spa Xmas **CONF:** Thtr 200 Class 120 Board 60 Del from £99 * **SERVICES:** Night porter 155P **NOTES:** No smoking area in restaurant

CARDS:

B

BRIGHTON & HOVE East Sussex Map 04 TQ30
★★★★★ Grand
Kings Rd BN1 2FW
Quality Percentage Score: 64%
☎ 01273 321188 📠 01273 202694
Dir: *next to Brighton Centre facing Palace Pier & seafront, turn right along Grand Junction Rd into King's Rd.*
This landmark hotel has graced the Brighton seafront since 1864 and continues to be a popular choice for both leisure and corporate guests. Bedrooms, many of which enjoy seaviews, are smartly appointed and well equipped in keeping with the hotel's classification. Public areas include a cosy bar and adjoining conservatory, attractive restaurant and a small leisure club. The hotels also offers extensive conference facilities and a night club open at weekends.
ROOMS: 200 en suite (bth/shr) (70 fmly) s £155; d £195-£285 (incl. bkfst) * LB Off peak **MEALS:** Lunch £19.50-£22 & alc Dinner £26.50-£30 English & French Cuisine V meals Coffee am Tea pm **FACILITIES:** CTV in all bedrooms STV Indoor swimming pool (heated) Sauna Solarium Gym Jacuzzi/spa Hairdresser Masseur Steam room Wkly live entertainment Xmas **CONF:** Thtr 800 Class 420 Del from £190 * **SERVICES:** Lift Night porter 65P **NOTES:** No smoking area in restaurant Last d 10pm **CARDS:**

BRIGHTON & HOVE East Sussex Map 04 TQ30
★★★★ Thistle Brighton
King's Rd BN1 2GS
Quality Percentage Score: 67%
☎ 01273 206700 📠 01273 820692
Dir: *from Palace Pier rbt take Kings Rd for hotel in 0.5m on right*
With a prime position on the seafront between the two piers, this modern hotel also has the advantage of an adjoining underground car park. Smartly appointed bedrooms are well equipped and the open-plan public areas are enclosed in an atrium; the hotel offers a small leisure club and conference facilities.
ROOMS: 204 en suite (bth/shr) No smoking in 40 bedrooms
MEALS: English & French Cuisine V meals Coffee am Tea pm
FACILITIES: CTV in all bedrooms STV Indoor swimming pool (heated) Sauna Solarium Gym Wkly live entertainment **CONF:** Thtr 300 Class 180 Board 120 **SERVICES:** Lift Night porter Air conditioning 70P
NOTES: No smoking area in restaurant Last d 10pm
CARDS:

BRIGHTON & HOVE East Sussex Map 04 TQ30
★★★ Imperial
First Av BN3 2GU
Quality Percentage Score: 66%
☎ 01273 777320 📠 01273 777310

Set in a row of Victorian town houses, close to the seafront, the Imperial offers good quality modern bedrooms that are comfortable and well equipped. Public rooms include a quiet lounge, informal bar and stylish restaurant plus a terrace for summer days.
ROOMS: 76 en suite (bth/shr) (2 fmly) No smoking in 10 bedrooms **MEALS:** V meals Coffee am Tea pm **FACILITIES:** CTV in all bedrooms STV Mountain bike hire **CONF:** Thtr 110 Class 50 Board 32 Del from £75 * **SERVICES:** Lift Night porter 4P **NOTES:** No smoking area in restaurant Last d 9.30pm **CARDS:**
See advert under HOVE & p. 321

BRIGHTON & HOVE East Sussex Map 04 TQ30
★★★ Brighton Hotel
143/145 Kings Rd BN1 2PQ
Quality Percentage Score: 64%
☎ 01273 820555 📠 01273 821555
Dir: *follow signs to Palace Pier, turn right and hotel is 100yds past West Pier*
This friendly family run hotel is located close to the historic West Pier on Brighton's sea front. All rooms are bright and well equipped and the smart public areas are a popular meeting place. Guests benefit from good car parking facilities, a real bonus in Brighton.
ROOMS: 52 en suite (bth/shr) **MEALS:** V meals Coffee am Tea pm **FACILITIES:** CTV in all bedrooms STV Sauna Solarium Gym Jacuzzi/spa **CONF:** Thtr 90 Board 40 Del from £68 * **SERVICES:** Lift Night porter 18P **NOTES:** No smoking area in restaurant Last d 9pm
CARDS:

BRIGHTON & HOVE East Sussex Map 04 TQ30
★★★ Courtlands
21-27 The Drive BN3 3JE
Quality Percentage Score: 64%
☎ 01273 731055 📠 01273 328295
Dir: *A23 junct A27 Worthing-take 1st exit to Hove, 2nd exit at rdbt, then right at 1st junct and turn left at shops. Straight on at junct, hotel on left*
This popular hotel offers spacious and comfortable accommodation. There is a choice of fixed-price and carte menus in the well appointed restaurant, and bar meals are also available in the cosy bar. Friendly staff provide helpful and attentive service.
ROOMS: 56 en suite (bth/shr) 12 annexe en suite (bth/shr) (2 fmly) s £42.50-£55; d £65-£85 (incl. bkfst) * LB Off peak **MEALS:** Lunch £8.95-£15 Dinner fr £13.75 European Cuisine V meals Coffee am Tea pm **FACILITIES:** CTV in all bedrooms STV Indoor swimming pool (heated) Solarium Beach hut on promenade Xmas **CONF:** Thtr 100 Class 70 Board 60 Del from £72.50 * **SERVICES:** Lift Night porter 24P
NOTES: No smoking area in restaurant Last d 9.15pm
CARDS:

BRIGHTON & HOVE East Sussex Map 04 TQ30
★★★ Quality Hotel Brighton
West St BN1 2RQ
Quality Percentage Score: 64%
☎ 01273 220033 📠 01273 778000
Dir: *from A23 take A529 towards city centre. Hotel is just behind Brighton Conference Centre*
This purpose-built hotel is located close to the seafront and town centre. Bedrooms are modern and well equipped, with executive rooms offering more space. The stylish lobby has an ocean liner theme with a feature staircase, sitting area and open-plan bar offering alternative all-day dining, whilst Spinnakers restaurant serves an extensive range of dishes with an international flavour.
ROOMS: 138 en suite (bth/shr) No smoking in 40 bedrooms s £56-£71; d £66-£81 * LB Off peak **MEALS:** Dinner fr £14.50 English & French Cuisine V meals Coffee am Tea pm **FACILITIES:** CTV in all bedrooms STV **CONF:** Thtr 200 Class 80 Board 60 **SERVICES:** Lift Night porter Air conditioning **NOTES:** Last d 10pm **CARDS:**

BRIGHTON & HOVE East Sussex **Map 04 TQ30**

★★ Princes Marine

153 Kingsway BN3 4GR

Quality Percentage Score: 67%

☎ 01273 207660 ▤ 01273 325913

Dir: *turn right at Palace Pier and follow seafront for approx 2m, hotel is approx 200yds from King Alfred sports & leisure centre*

This informal and cheerfully-run hotel is located on the seafront to the west, and has large, comfortable rooms equipped for both commercial and leisure users. The ground floor comprises a cosy restaurant, bar and a useful meeting room.

ROOMS: 47 en suite (bth/shr) (3 fmly) No smoking in 6 bedrooms s £48-£58; d £75-£95 (incl. bkfst) * LB Off peak **MEALS:** Lunch fr £9.95 Dinner fr £14.95 & alc English & Continental Cuisine V meals Coffee am Tea pm **FACILITIES:** CTV in all bedrooms Wkly live entertainment Xmas **CONF:** Thtr 80 Class 40 Board 40 Del from £60 * **SERVICES:** Lift Night porter 30P **NOTES:** Last d 9.30pm **CARDS:**

BRIGHTON & HOVE East Sussex **Map 04 TQ30**

★★ St Catherines Lodge

Seafront, Kingsway BN3 2RZ

Quality Percentage Score: 63%

☎ 01273 778181 ▤ 01273 774949

Dir: *opposite King Alfred Leisure Centre on main A259*

Privately owned and family-run, this hotel is located by the seafront at Hove. Bedrooms are neatly decorated and comfortably appointed. Public areas retain many original features including Adam-style ceilings and antique Delft tiling in the restaurant.

ROOMS: 50 rms (40 bth/shr) (4 fmly) s £36-£55; d £60-£75 (incl. bkfst) * LB Off peak **MEALS:** Lunch £6 Dinner £14.50 & alc European Cuisine V meals Coffee am Tea pm **FACILITIES:** CTV in all bedrooms Games room Xmas **CONF:** Thtr 40 Class 24 Board 24 Del from £50 * **SERVICES:** Lift Night porter 9P **NOTES:** No dogs (ex guide dogs) Last d 9pm **CARDS:**

See advert on this page

The AA Hotel Booking Service is a free benefit to AA members. See the advertisement on page 47

BRISTOL Bristol **Map 03 ST57**

★★★★ ❀❀ Swallow Royal

College Green BS1 5TA

Quality Percentage Score: 75%

☎ 0117 925 5100 ▤ 0117 925 1515

Dir: *in the city centre next to the cathedral*

Adjacent to the cathedral, at the heart of the city, this landmark hotel has been impressively restored in recent years. There are

contd.

plenty of lounges where guests can relax over a drink or traditional afternoon tea, and in addition an impressive leisure club. Dining options include the casual Terrace restaurant, and the splendid Palm Court restaurant with its three-storey-high ceiling. A harpist plays here three nights a week and the restaurant is a showcase for rosette-worthy cuisine. Bedrooms are charmingly decorated with good quality furnishings, comfortable armchairs, luxurious marbled bathrooms and air conditioning.

Swallow Royal, Bristol

ROOMS: 242 en suite (bth/shr) (14 fmly) No smoking in 100 bedrooms s £140-£160; d £160-£200 (incl. bkfst) * LB Off peak **MEALS:** Lunch £16-£18 High tea fr £8 Dinner fr £20 V meals Coffee am Tea pm **FACILITIES:** CTV in all bedrooms STV Indoor swimming pool (heated) Sauna Solarium Gym Jacuzzi/spa Xmas **CONF:** Thtr 300 Class 140 Board 30 Del from £165 * **SERVICES:** Lift Night porter Air conditioning 200P **NOTES:** No smoking area in restaurant Last d 10.30pm **CARDS:**

BRISTOL Bristol **Map 03 ST57**
★★★★ **Aztec**
Aztec West Business Park, Almondsbury BS32 4TS
Quality Percentage Score: 72%
☎ 01454 201090 01454 201593
Dir: *access via M5 (junct 16) & M4*

This impressive modern hotel offers smart well equipped bedrooms and bright public areas that include extensive leisure facilities. Situated close to the M4/M5 junction business guests can make use of a good range of meeting rooms. Staff are enthusiastic and services well marshalled. Quarterjacks restaurant offers a good standard of well executed modern cooking.

ROOMS: 109 en suite (bth/shr) (13 fmly) No smoking in 55 bedrooms **MEALS:** International Cuisine V meals Coffee am Tea pm **FACILITIES:** CTV in all bedrooms STV Indoor swimming pool (heated) Squash Snooker Sauna Solarium Gym Jacuzzi/spa Steam room Childrens splash pool **CONF:** Thtr 250 Class 120 Board 48 Del from £89 * **SERVICES:** Lift Night porter 240P **NOTES:** No smoking in restaurant Last d 9.30pm Closed 31 Dec **CARDS:**

BRISTOL Bristol **Map 03 ST57**
★★★★ **Bristol Marriott**
Lower Castle St BS1 3AD
Quality Percentage Score: 67%
☎ 0117 929 4281 0117 927 6377
Dir: *from M32 follow signs 'City Centre' and 'Temple Meads' - do not take underpass*

A modern hotel with high standards of comfort in a central location. There is a stylish lounge, the Brasserie restaurant is popular for casual dining. The more formal restaurant, Le Chateau, is re-opening as a new concept serving British cuisine. Bedrooms have air conditioning and power showers. The executive floor has its own lounge and extra luxuries. The leisure complex is well-equipped. Parking is adjacent to the hotel with valet parking on request. The team are smartly presented and helpful.

ROOMS: 289 en suite (bth/shr) (136 fmly) No smoking in 221 bedrooms d fr £99 * LB Off peak **MEALS:** Lunch £17-£29alc Dinner £15.95 & alc International Cuisine V meals Coffee am Tea pm **FACILITIES:** CTV in all bedrooms STV Indoor swimming pool (heated) Sauna Solarium Gym Jacuzzi/spa Steam room Whirlpool **CONF:** Thtr 600 Class 280 Board 50 Del from £145 * **SERVICES:** Lift Night porter Air conditioning **NOTES:** No smoking area in restaurant Last d 10.30pm **CARDS:**

BRISTOL Bristol **Map 03 ST57**
★★★★ ***Thistle Bristol***
Broad St BS1 2EL
Quality Percentage Score: 64%
☎ 0117 929 1645 0117 922 7619
Dir: *from M32 end left at lights, 3rd exit at rdbt, immediate right, left at lights, up incline, as road veers left turn right into Broad St*

This stylishly refurbished hotel is situated right in the centre of the city and has attractively decorated bedrooms which offer all the modern facilities expected by the business and leisure guest. Ladies are particularly well catered for with a dedicated floor of rooms offering special security arrangements. Public area space is restricted but there is a choice of bars and eating options. Staff are cheerful and willing.

ROOMS: 182 en suite (bth/shr) (8 fmly) No smoking in 23 bedrooms **MEALS:** English & French Cuisine V meals Coffee am Tea pm **FACILITIES:** CTV in all bedrooms **CONF:** Thtr 600 Class 250 Board 70 **SERVICES:** Lift Night porter 180P **NOTES:** No smoking area in restaurant Last d 10.30pm **CARDS:**

BRISTOL Bristol **Map 03 ST57**
★★★★ ***Crowne Plaza Bristol***
Victoria St BS1 6HY
Quality Percentage Score: 63%
☎ 0117 976 9988 0117 925 5040

Near Temple Meads railway station, this modern hotel offers comfortable bedrooms. Public rooms comprise a bright and airy open-plan lobby, lounge-bar and informal restaurant. The underground car park and small gym are useful amenities.

ROOMS: 128 en suite (bth/shr) (6 fmly) No smoking in 58 bedrooms **MEALS:** International Cuisine V meals Coffee am Tea pm **FACILITIES:** CTV in all bedrooms STV Solarium Gym **CONF:** Thtr 250 Class 80 Board 50 **SERVICES:** Lift Night porter 150P **NOTES:** No smoking area in restaurant Last d 10pm **CARDS:**

BRISTOL Bristol **Map 03 ST57**
★★★ **Redwood Lodge Hotel**
Beggar Bush Ln, Failand BS8 3TG
Quality Percentage Score: 70%
☎ 01275 393901 01275 392104
Dir: *M5 junct 19, take A369 for approx 3m then turn right at lights, hotel is approx 1m on left hand side*

This popular modern hotel offers guests friendly service and well equipped accommodation, as well as an extensive range of conference and leisure facilities. "Steps" cafe bar, which forms part of the leisure club, makes an ideal setting for casual dining, while the attractive split level restaurant provides more formal

contd.

surroundings. Redwood Lodge is situated in a quiet location, yet is convenient for the M5 and the city centre.

ROOMS: 112 en suite (bth/shr) No smoking in 81 bedrooms s £95; d £105 * Off peak **MEALS:** Lunch £7.50-£12.50 Dinner £1-£18 European Cuisine V meals Coffee am Tea pm **FACILITIES:** CTV in all bedrooms STV Indoor swimming pool (heated) Outdoor swimming pool Tennis (hard) Squash Snooker Sauna Solarium Gym Pool table 175 seater Cinema Aerobics/Dance studio Xmas **CONF:** Thtr 175 Class 80 Board 30 Del £135 * **SERVICES:** Night porter 1000P **NOTES:** No dogs (ex guide dogs) No smoking in restaurant Last d 10pm
CARDS:

BRISTOL Bristol **Map 03 ST57**

★★★ Berkeley Square

15 Berkeley Square, Clifton BS8 1HB

Quality Percentage Score: 69%

☎ 0117 925 4000 0117 925 2970

Dir: *from M32 follow signs for Clifton, take first turn left at traffic lights by Willis Memorial Tower (University) into Berkeley Sq*

Set in an elegant and peaceful square close to the university, art gallery and Clifton village, this smart Georgian hotel is thoughtfully furnished with tastefully decorated bedrooms. There is a busy bar, and Nightingales Restaurant features diverse cuisine from a choice of menus. The hotel has its own garage adjacent to the main building offering secure parking.
ROOMS: 42 en suite (bth/shr) No smoking in 12 bedrooms s £86; d £107 (incl. bkfst) * LB Off peak **MEALS:** Lunch £10 European Cuisine V meals Coffee am Tea pm **FACILITIES:** CTV in all bedrooms STV **CONF:** Thtr 15 Class 12 Board 12 Del £120 * **SERVICES:** Lift Night porter 20P **CARDS:**

BRISTOL Bristol **Map 03 ST57**

★★★ Posthouse Bristol

Filton Rd, Hambrook BS16 1QX **Posthouse**

Quality Percentage Score: 69%

☎ 0117 956 4242 0117 956 9735

Dir: *M4 junct 19 onto M32. Take junct 1 off M32 onto A4174 towards Filton, Bristol and Parkway Station. Hotel 800yds on the left*

This popular, modern hotel is right next to the Frenchay Campus of UWE and close to key business locations; the hotel is in an excellent location for both the M4 and M5, and has reasonable access to the city centre. Conferences are attracted by the range of meeting rooms and business and leisure facilities. Bedrooms have been completely refurbished. Meals are served in The

contd.

We endeavour to be as accurate as possible but changes in personnel and data can occur in establishments after the Hotel Guide has gone to press.

B

Junction Brasserie, and snacks are available in the lounge, which is popular for informal business meetings.
ROOMS: 198 en suite (bth/shr) (21 fmly) No smoking in 131 bedrooms d £105-£125 (incl. bkfst) * LB Off peak **MEALS:** International Cuisine V meals Coffee am Tea pm **FACILITIES:** CTV in all bedrooms STV Indoor swimming pool (heated) Sauna Solarium Gym Pool table Outdoor badminton Xmas **CONF:** Thtr 250 Class 130 Board 60 Del from £120 * **SERVICES:** Lift Night porter 400P **NOTES:** No smoking area in restaurant Last d 10.30pm **CARDS:**

BRISTOL Bristol **Map 03 ST57**
★★★ Jurys Bristol Hotel
Prince St BS1 4QF
Quality Percentage Score: 68%
☎ 0117 923 0333 0117 923 0300
Dir: *from city centre, follow brown signs for Yarm Hostel & Arnofini, right at rndbt into Princes St, turn right for hotel beside NC*

This popular hotel, located on the waterside, close to Bristol's Millennium development, offers well-equipped bedrooms. Public rooms are bright, and include a new Quayside pub and a bistro and lounge bar which look over the river. Porterage and room service are a welcome feature. Guests have free parking at the adjacent multi-storey.
ROOMS: 191 en suite (bth/shr) (22 fmly) No smoking in 71 bedrooms d £115 * LB Off peak **MEALS:** Lunch £9.95-£10.95 Dinner fr £15.95 International Cuisine V meals Coffee am Tea pm **FACILITIES:** CTV in all bedrooms STV Boules Discount at local Leisure Club Wkly live entertainment Xmas **CONF:** Thtr 320 Class 140 Board 80 Del £140 * **SERVICES:** Lift Night porter **NOTES:** No dogs (ex guide dogs) No smoking area in restaurant Last d 10.15pm
CARDS:

See advert on opposite page

BRISTOL Bristol **Map 03 ST57**
★★★ *City Inn Bristol*
Temple Way BS1 6HG
Quality Percentage Score: 66%
☎ 0117 925 1001
Freshly opened last year, the City Inn offers spacious, contemporary public areas and a similar style in the bedrooms. The staff are well motivated and friendly. A short carte is offered and the adjacent bar serves tea and coffee all day. The hotel is close to city centre and railway station.

BRISTOL Bristol **Map 03 ST57**
★★★ The Avon Gorge
Sion Hill, Clifton BS8 4LD
Quality Percentage Score: 64%
☎ 0117 973 8955 0117 923 8125
Dir: *from M5 S junct 19/A369 to Clifton via toll bridge then Sion Hill. From M5 N junct 18/A4 to Bristol left at lights under suspension bridge*
Benefiting from a commanding position overlooking Avon Gorge and Brunel's famous suspension bridge, this popular hotel is situated in the heart of fashionable Clifton. Bedrooms, many of which have glorious views, have been refurbished and are extremely well equipped with both business and leisure guests in mind. Two rooms have four poster beds, and guests can expect to find many amenities, including extra telephone points and ceiling fans. The hotel offers a range of function suites, a choice of bars (one with a popular terrace), and an attractive restaurant.
ROOMS: 76 en suite (bth/shr) (6 fmly) No smoking in 30 bedrooms s £99; d £109 (incl. bkfst) * LB Off peak **MEALS:** Lunch £10-£14 Dinner £15-£18 English & French Cuisine V meals Coffee am Tea pm **FACILITIES:** CTV in all bedrooms STV Childrens activity play area Wkly live entertainment Xmas **CONF:** Thtr 100 Class 50 Board 26 Del from £95 * **SERVICES:** Lift Night porter 23P **NOTES:** Last d 10pm
CARDS:

BRISTOL Bristol **Map 03 ST57**
★★★ Henbury Lodge
Station Rd, Henbury BS10 7QQ
Quality Percentage Score: 63%
☎ 0117 950 2615 0117 950 9532
Dir: *4.5m NW of City centre off A4018, 1m from M5 junct 17*
This privately owned hotel dates from 1760 and was once a country house. Conveniently situated in a quiet suburb of Bristol, within half a mile from Junction 17 of the M5, it benefits from ample car parking. Bedrooms are available both within the main house and in the adjoining stable conversion, all being attractively decorated and well equipped. The public areas are very comfortable, and the dining room offers a range of simple, freshly cooked dishes.
ROOMS: 12 en suite (bth/shr) 9 annexe en suite (bth/shr) (4 fmly) No smoking in 6 bedrooms s £89.50; d £99.50 (incl. bkfst) LB Off peak **MEALS:** Lunch £4.50-£18.50 Dinner £18.50 English & Continental Cuisine V meals Coffee am Tea pm **FACILITIES:** CTV in all bedrooms STV Sauna Solarium Gym Xmas **CONF:** Thtr 32 Board 20 Del from £95 **SERVICES:** Night porter 24P **NOTES:** No smoking in restaurant Last d 9.30pm **CARDS:**

BRISTOL Bristol **Map 03 ST57**
★★ Seeley's
17-27 St Paul's Rd, Clifton BS8 1LX
Quality Percentage Score: 70%
☎ 0117 973 8544 0117 973 2406
Dir: *M5 junct17, follow A4018 for 4.5 m to BBC studios, turn right at lights and hotel is on the left*
A privately owned hotel with easy access to Clifton Village, the university and city centre. Comfortable public areas are spacious. A wide selection of dishes are offered in Le Chasseur Restaurant, lighter meals and snacks are served in the bar. The bedrooms, some in adjacent properties, are all pleasing and well equipped.
ROOMS: 37 en suite (bth/shr) 18 annexe en suite (bth/shr) (10 fmly) s £65-£80; d £80-£95 (incl. bkfst) * LB Off peak **MEALS:** Lunch £15 Dinner fr £12.05 & alc International Cuisine V meals Coffee am Tea pm **FACILITIES:** CTV in all bedrooms STV Sauna Solarium Gym Jacuzzi/spa ch fac **CONF:** Thtr 70 Class 30 Board 25 Del from £87.50 * **SERVICES:** Night porter 25P **NOTES:** No dogs (ex guide dogs) No smoking area in restaurant Last d 10.30pm Closed 24 Dec-2 Jan
CARDS:

BRISTOL Bristol **Map 03 ST57**
★★ Rodney Hotel
4 Rodney Place, Clifton BS8 4HY
Quality Percentage Score: 67%
☎ 0117 973 5422 0117 946 7092
Dir: *off Clifton Down Road*
With easy access from the M5, this attractive, listed building in Clifton, is conveniently close to the city centre. The individually

contd.

decorated bedrooms provide a useful range of facilities for the business traveller. Snacks are served in the bar-lounge and the more formal restaurant offers an appealing selection of dishes.
ROOMS: 31 en suite (bth/shr) No smoking in 9 bedrooms s £40-£64; d £60-£78 (incl. bkfst) * Off peak **MEALS:** Lunch £14.95-£17.95 & alc Dinner £14.95-£17.95 & alc English & French Cuisine V meals Coffee am Tea pm **FACILITIES:** CTV in all bedrooms STV **CONF:** Thtr 30 Class 20 Board 15 **SERVICES:** Night porter **NOTES:** No smoking area in restaurant Last d 9.30pm Closed 22 Dec-3 Jan RS Sun
CARDS:

BRISTOL Bristol **Map 03 ST57**
★★ Clifton
St Pauls Rd, Clifton BS8 1LX
Quality Percentage Score: 65%
☎ 0117 973 6882 🖷 0117 974 1082
Dir: *take M32 into Bristol & follow signs for Clifton. Go up Park St (very steep hill) follow road ahead & turn left at traffic lights into St Pauls Rd*
This popular hotel offers well equipped bedrooms. There is a smart lounge at reception, during summer months drinks can be taken on the terrace. Racks Bar and Restaurant offers an interesting selection of modern dishes from an imaginative menu. Street parking is unrestricted, secure parking is available for a small charge.
ROOMS: 60 rms (48 bth/shr) (2 fmly) No smoking in 15 bedrooms s £74; d £84 * Off peak **MEALS:** Bar Lunch £2.50-£8alc Dinner £11.95-£13.95 & alc English & French Cuisine V meals Coffee am Tea pm **FACILITIES:** CTV in all bedrooms STV **SERVICES:** Lift Night porter 20P **NOTES:** Closed 23-29 Dec **CARDS:**

BRISTOL Bristol **Map 03 ST57**
★★ *Glenroy*
Best Western
Victoria Square, Clifton BS8 4EW
Quality Percentage Score: 60%
☎ 0117 973 9058 🖷 0117 973 9058
Dir: *junct 19 of M5, follow signs for Clifton come over suspension bridge and turn left after the bakery, hotel around corner on right*
Convenient for the university and city centre, this hotel is geared to the short stay business guest. Bedrooms, in the main house and an adjacent property, are varied in size, some quite compact, but all well equipped. Facilities include a congenial open-plan bar, carvery restaurant, and the Victoria and Albert conference rooms.
ROOMS: 25 en suite (bth/shr) 19 annexe en suite (bth/shr) (9 fmly) **MEALS:** V meals Coffee am **FACILITIES:** CTV in all bedrooms STV **CONF:** Thtr 45 Class 16 Board 25 **SERVICES:** Night porter 16P **NOTES:** No smoking area in restaurant Last d 9.30pm Closed 24-31 Dec
CARDS:

BRISTOL Bristol **Map 03 ST57**
⌂ Travel Inn
travel inn
200/202 Westerleigh Rd,
Emersons Green BS16 7AN
☎ 0117 956 4755 🖷 0117 956 4644
Dir: *follow A4174 (Avon Ring Rd) E from M32 junct 1*
This modern building offers accommodation in smart, spacious and well equipped bedrooms, all with en-suite bathrooms. Refreshments may be taken at the nearby family restaurant. For details about current prices consult the Contents Page under Hotel Groups for the Travel Inn phone number.
ROOMS: 40 en suite (bth/shr) d £39.95 *

B

BRISTOL Bristol
Map 03 ST57
Travel Inn (Bristol South)
Hengrove Leisure Park, Hengrove Way BS14 0HR
☎ 01275 834340 🖷 01275 834721
Dir: *on A4174*
This modern building offers accommodation in smart, spacious and well equipped bedrooms, all with en-suite bathrooms. Refreshments may be taken at the nearby family restaurant. For details about current prices consult the Contents Page under Hotel Groups for the Travel Inn phone number.
ROOMS: 40 en suite (bth/shr) d £39.95 *

BRISTOL Bristol
Map 03 ST57
Travelodge
Cribbs Causeway BS10 7TL
☎ 0117 950 1530 🖷 0117 950 1530
Dir: *A4018, just off junc17 M5*
This modern building offers accommodation in smart, spacious and well equipped bedrooms, all with en-suite bathrooms. Refreshments may be taken at the nearby family restaurant. For details about current prices, consult the Contents Page under Hotel Groups for the Travelodge phone number.
ROOMS: 56 en suite (bth/shr) d £49.95 *

BRIXHAM Devon
Map 03 SX95
★★★ Berryhead
Berryhead Rd TQ5 9AJ
Quality Percentage Score: 66%
☎ 01803 853225 🖷 01803 882084
Dir: *to Brixham Harbour turn right past statue & then left to Marina; straight on another quarter of a mile past Marina*
Enjoying glorious views from a stunning clifftop position, this imposing property dates back to 1809 and was the former residence of Rev. Henry Lyte who wrote many hymns including 'Abide With Me'. The hotel offers individually designed accommodation, some of which are recent additions. Public areas include popular bars and all-day eating options.
ROOMS: 32 en suite (bth/shr) (7 fmly) s £38-£48; d £76-£148 (incl. bkfst) * LB Off peak **MEALS:** Lunch fr £10 & alc High tea fr £6 Dinner fr £18.50 & alc English & French Cuisine V meals Coffee am Tea pm **FACILITIES:** CTV in 2 bedrooms Indoor swimming pool (heated) Croquet lawn Jacuzzi/spa Petanque Sailing Deep sea fishing Wkly live entertainment Xmas **CONF:** Thtr 350 Class 250 Board 40 Del from £55 * **SERVICES:** Night porter 200P **NOTES:** No coaches No smoking in restaurant Last d 9.30pm **CARDS:**

See advert on opposite page

BRIXHAM Devon
Map 03 SX95
★★★ Quayside
41-49 King St TQ5 9TJ
Quality Percentage Score: 66%
☎ 01803 855751 🖷 01803 882733
Dir: *from Exeter follow signs for Torquay on A380, at the 2nd rdbt at Kinkerswell follow signs for Brixham on A3022, hotel overlooks the harbour*
Created from six cottages and enjoying panoramic views over the harbour and bay, the Quayside Hotel offers friendly and attentive service. The public rooms include a cosy lounge, a snug residents' bar and the busier Ernie Lister's public bar. An extensive range of enjoyable dishes is available in the intimate restaurant, including fresh fish landed directly from the boats. Bedrooms are modern and well equipped.

ROOMS: 29 en suite (bth/shr) (2 fmly) s £60-£81; d £75-£95 (incl. bkfst) * LB Off peak **MEALS:** Bar Lunch £2.95-£10alc Dinner £17.50 & alc English & French Cuisine V meals Coffee am Tea pm
FACILITIES: CTV in all bedrooms Wkly live entertainment Xmas
NOTES: No coaches No smoking in restaurant Last d 9.30pm
CARDS:

BRIXHAM Devon
Map 03 SX95
★★ Maypool Park
Maypool, Galmpton TQ5 0ET
Quality Percentage Score: 71%
☎ 01803 842442 🖷 01803 845782
Dir: *at Churston (A3022) turn SW signed Maypool/Passenger ferry/ Greenway Quay to Manor Vale Rd. Follow signs through village to hotel*

These converted cottages offer stunning views across a wooded valley and the River Dart. Now run as a country hotel, the cottages provide bedrooms equipped with every modern comfort, a choice of comfortable lounges, and an intimate bar. The attractive dining room is where guests can enjoy beautifully presented cuisine. An interesting wine list complements the innovative menus.
ROOMS: 10 en suite (bth/shr) No smoking in all bedrooms s £39-£60; d £58-£94 (incl. bkfst) * LB Off peak **MEALS:** Sunday Lunch £16.50-£19 Dinner £19.50-£22 V meals **FACILITIES:** CTV in all bedrooms
CONF: Thtr 30 Class 20 Board 20 Del from £74 * **SERVICES:** 15P
NOTES: No dogs No coaches No children 12yrs No smoking in restaurant Last d 8.30pm Closed 23 Dec-2 Jan
CARDS:

BRIXHAM Devon
Map 03 SX95
★ Smuggler's Haunt
Church Hill East TQ5 8HH
Quality Percentage Score: 60%
☎ 01803 853050 & 859416 🖷 01803 858738
This 300-year-old hotel in the centre of the historic fishing town, offers clean and pleasing accommodation. The restaurant and

contd.

Indicates that the star classification has not been confirmed under the New Quality Standards, see page 7 for further information.

bar menus provide a wide selection of carefully cooked dishes from around the world.
ROOMS: 14 en suite (bth/shr) (4 fmly) s £22-£28; d £42-£54 (incl. bkfst) * LB Off peak **MEALS:** Lunch £2.25-£8.25 Dinner £2.25-£8.25 & alc English & French Cuisine V meals Coffee am **FACILITIES:** CTV in all bedrooms Xmas **SERVICES:** Night porter **NOTES:** Last d 9.45pm
CARDS:

BROADSTAIRS Kent — Map 05 TR36

★★★ Royal Albion

Albion St CT10 1AN
Quality Percentage Score: 61%
☎ 01843 868071 📠 01843 861509
Dir: *on entering the town follow signs for seafront*

On the sea front with delightful views from some rooms. The bedrooms are attractive and well equipped with modern furnishings. The main hotel houses reception, public bar lounge and breakfast room, the restaurant is two doors down the street in Marchesi's. Staff are friendly, and the atmosphere is very relaxed and informal.
ROOMS: 19 en suite (bth/shr) (3 fmly) No smoking in 3 bedrooms s £55-£90; d £70-£100 * LB Off peak **MEALS:** Lunch £8.95-£11 & alc Dinner £13-£16.50 & alc English & French Cuisine V meals Coffee am Tea pm **FACILITIES:** CTV in all bedrooms STV Xmas **CONF:** Thtr 80 Class 60 Board 20 **SERVICES:** Night porter 22P **NOTES:** No dogs (ex guide dogs) No coaches No smoking area in restaurant Last d 9.30pm RS Sun
CARDS:

BROADWAY Worcestershire — Map 04 SP03

see also **Buckland**

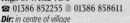

The Premier Collection

★★★★ The Lygon Arms

High St WR12 7DU
☎ 01386 852255 📠 01386 858611
The Savoy Group
Dir: *in centre of village*

Dating back to 1532, this sympathetically extended hotel lists Charles 1 and Oliver Cromwell amongst its guests. Bedrooms vary in style and layout, offering comfort, modern facilities and some fine antique furniture. Public rooms include a variety of lounge areas, some with open fires, and an impressive indoor pool and fitness centre. Guests dine in the main Great Hall restaurant or Oliver's Brasserie.
ROOMS: 65 rms (62 bth/shr) (3 fmly) **MEALS:** Lunch £25.50-£27.50 & alc Dinner £39.50 & alc V meals Coffee am Tea pm
FACILITIES: CTV in all bedrooms STV Indoor swimming pool (heated) Tennis (hard) Snooker Sauna Solarium Gym Pool table Croquet lawn Jacuzzi/spa Beauty treatments Steam Room Bike Hire
CONF: Thtr 80 Class 48 Board 30 **SERVICES:** Night porter 152P
NOTES: No coaches No smoking in restaurant Last d 9.15pm
CARDS:

BROADWAY Worcestershire — Map 04 SP03

★★★ Dormy House

Willersey Hill WR12 7LF
Quality Percentage Score: 74%
☎ 01386 852711 📠 01386 858636
Dir: *2m E off A44, at top of Fish Hill 1.5m from Broadway village, take turn signposted Saintbury/Picnic area. After 0.5m fork left Dormy House on left*

A former 17th-century farmhouse converted into a large complex in extensive grounds. Rooms are traditionally furnished and well equipped, some with four-poster beds. Many are in separate cottage-style buildings, patio doors open onto garden areas with tables and chairs. There are comfortable lounges and a pleasant bar. The attractive restaurant benefits from chef Alan Cuttler's imaginative culinary skills. The 'Barn Owl' pub offers a less formal eating option.
ROOMS: 25 en suite (bth/shr) 23 annexe en suite (bth) (3 fmly) s £73-£97; d £146-£174 (incl. bkfst) LB Off peak **MEALS:** Lunch £19.50 & alc Dinner £30.50 & alc English & French Cuisine V meals Coffee am Tea pm
FACILITIES: CTV in all bedrooms Sauna Gym Pool table Croquet lawn Putting green Games room Nature/jogging trail **CONF:** Thtr 200 Class 100 Board 25 Del from £155 * **SERVICES:** Night porter 80P
NOTES: No coaches No smoking area in restaurant Last d 9.30pm Closed 25 & 26 Dec RS Sat (restaurant closed for lunch)
CARDS:

See advert on page 157

Remember to return your Prize Draw card for a chance to win one of 30 relaxing leisure breaks with Corus and Regal hotels. See inside the front cover for the card and competition details.

B

BROADWAY Worcestershire **Map 04 SP03**

★★★ Broadway

The Green, High St WR12 7AA
Quality Percentage Score: 62%
☎ 01386 852401 🖷 01386 853879
Dir: *set back from the High Street (A44), behind the village green*

Parts of this stone built hostelry date from 1575. It is conveniently located overlooking the village green, and has a very pleasant garden to the rear. The hotel changed hands in 1998 and at the time of our last inspection, the new owners had started to upgrade the bedrooms and public areas. The accommodation is well equipped and includes a room with a four-poster bed and a bedroom on the ground floor of a separate building, with its own direct access onto the garden. Public areas, particularly the cosy bar, have a lot of charm and character.

ROOMS: 20 en suite (bth/shr) (1 fmly) No smoking in 4 bedrooms s £68.50-£75; d £110-£125 (incl. bkfst) * LB Off peak **MEALS:** Bar Lunch £9.95-£10.95 Dinner £14.50-£19.95 V meals Coffee am Tea pm **FACILITIES:** CTV in all bedrooms Xmas **CONF:** Thtr 20 Board 16 Del from £110 * **SERVICES:** 20P **NOTES:** No smoking in restaurant Last d 9pm **CARDS:**

BROADWAY Worcestershire **Map 04 SP03**

★★❀ Collin House

Collin Ln WR12 7PB
Quality Percentage Score: 72%
☎ 01386 858354 🖷 01386 858697
Dir: *1 mile NW of Broadway - the hotel is clearly marked at the roundabout at the junction of the A44 and is 40 metres from the roundabout*

Built in mellow Cotswold stone, this small country house is thought to date back to the 1600s as the home of a wealthy wool merchant. Surrounded by several acres of grounds and gardens, it provides traditionally furnished accommodation, which includes rooms with four-poster beds. The public areas have a wealth of charm and character, enhanced by features such as stone flagged floors, oak beams and an inglenook fireplace in the bar.

ROOMS: 7 rms (6 bth/shr) No smoking in 2 bedrooms s £50-£72; d £95-£105 (incl. bkfst) LB Off peak **MEALS:** Lunch £16.50 Dinner £18-£26alc V meals Coffee am Tea pm **FACILITIES:** CTV in all bedrooms Croquet lawn **SERVICES:** 25P **NOTES:** No dogs (ex guide dogs) No coaches No smoking in restaurant Last d 9pm Closed 24-28 Dec **CARDS:**

BROCKENHURST Hampshire **Map 04 SU30**

★★★❀ Rhinefield House

Rhinefield Rd SO42 7QB
Quality Percentage Score: 75%
☎ 01590 622922 🖷 01590 622800
Dir: *take A35 towards Chistchurch. 3m from Lyndhurst turn left to Rhinefield, 1.5m to hotel*

This splendid 19th-century, mock-Elizabethan mansion is set in beautifully maintained grounds and gardens. Bedrooms are spacious and particularly well equipped. The open plan lounge and bar, elegant restaurant and Alhambra room are impressive. Cuisine under the direction of new chef David Innwood remains a focus of the hotel. 24 hour room service and turndown of beds are available.

ROOMS: 34 en suite (bth/shr) No smoking in 12 bedrooms s £105-£115; d £140-£150 (incl. bkfst) * LB Off peak **MEALS:** Lunch fr £16.95 & alc Dinner fr £25.50 & alc English & French Cuisine V meals Coffee am Tea pm **FACILITIES:** CTV in all bedrooms STV Indoor swimming pool (heated) Outdoor swimming pool (heated) Tennis (hard) Sauna Gym Pool table Croquet lawn Putting green Jacuzzi/spa Xmas **CONF:** Thtr 100 Class 30 Board 40 Del from £140 * **SERVICES:** Night porter 80P **NOTES:** No dogs (ex guide dogs) No coaches No smoking in restaurant Last d 10pm **CARDS:**

BROCKENHURST Hampshire **Map 04 SU30**

★★★❀❀ Whitley Ridge Country House

Beaulieu Rd SO4 7QL
Quality Percentage Score: 74%
☎ 01590 622354 🖷 01590 622856
Dir: *access via B3055 towards Beaulieu*

Originally a royal hunting lodge built in the late 18th century, this charming hotel enjoys a peaceful setting located in 5 secluded acres in the heart of the New Forest. The day rooms include 2 relaxing lounges furnished and decorated by Rennie and Sue Law in true country-house style with fresh flowers and books adding the finishing touch. All the bedrooms, many of which enjoy lovely views over the forest, are individual in style and feature thoughtful extras such as chocolates and mineral water. The elegant dining room offers a high standard cuisine using quality local ingredients.

ROOMS: 13 en suite (bth/shr) 1 annexe en suite (bth/shr) s £60-£70; d £96-£98 (incl. bkfst) * LB Off peak **MEALS:** Sunday Lunch £13.50-£14.50 Dinner £21.50-£23 & alc English & French Cuisine V meals Coffee am Tea pm **FACILITIES:** CTV in all bedrooms Tennis (hard) Xmas **CONF:** Thtr 40 Class 40 Board 20 **SERVICES:** 30P **NOTES:** No coaches No smoking in restaurant Last d 9pm Closed 1-14 Jan **CARDS:**

BROCKENHURST Hampshire **Map 04 SU30**

★★★❀ Careys Manor

SO42 7RH
Quality Percentage Score: 72%
☎ 01590 623551 🖷 01590 622799
Dir: *follow signs for Lyndhurst & Lymington A337, enter Brockenhurst, hotel after 30mph sign*

Originally a hunting lodge, Careys Manor stands in its own grounds on the edge of the village. Bedrooms are comfortably furnished and some have balconies overlooking the garden. Public areas include a large lounge with a log fire, a cocktail bar and a smart restaurant where chef Kevin Dorrington presents a classical menu. The Health Club offers a large pool, beauty

contd.

treatments, sauna and fitness room with qualified instructors. Le Blaireau Cafe provides informal dining in a typically French style.
ROOMS: 15 en suite (bth/shr) 64 annexe en suite (bth/shr) No smoking in 28 bedrooms s £79-£89; d £129-£149 (incl. bkfst) * LB Off peak
MEALS: Lunch £14.75-£15.95 Dinner fr £24.50 & alc English & French Cuisine V meals Coffee am Tea pm **FACILITIES:** CTV in all bedrooms STV Indoor swimming pool (heated) Sauna Gym Croquet lawn Jacuzzi/spa Steam room Beauty therapists Xmas **CONF:** Thtr 120 Class 70 Board 40 Del from £145 * **SERVICES:** Night porter 180P
NOTES: No smoking in restaurant Last d 9.45pm
CARDS:

See advert on this page

BROCKENHURST Hampshire **Map 04 SU30**
★★★ New Park Manor
Lyndhurst Rd SO42 7QH
Quality Percentage Score: 72%
☎ 01590 623467 01590 622268
Dir: *on A337 1.5m from Lyndhurst between Brockenhurst and Lyndhust*
The favourite hunting lodge of Charles II, this well presented hotel enjoys a peaceful setting in acres of parkland with its own equestrian centre. Now under new ownership of Von Essen Hotels, the bedrooms are gradually being refurbished and are comfortably appointed throughout. The smart public areas include an elegant bar with adjoining lounge and a wood

contd.

We endeavour to be as accurate as possible but changes in personnel and data can occur in establishments after the Hotel Guide has gone to press.

panelled restaurant where a good choice of interesting dishes is offered.

New Park Manor, Brockenhurst

ROOMS: 24 en suite (bth/shr) (4 fmly) No smoking in 8 bedrooms s £85; d £110 (incl. bkfst) * Off peak **MEALS:** Lunch £12.95-£14.95 & alc High tea £4.95 Dinner £27.50 & alc English & French Cuisine V meals Coffee am Tea pm **FACILITIES:** CTV in all bedrooms STV Outdoor swimming pool (heated) Tennis (hard) Riding Walking Xmas **CONF:** Thtr 60 Class 45 Board 40 Del from £105 * **SERVICES:** 50P **NOTES:** No smoking in restaurant Last d 9.45pm **CARDS:**

See advert on opposite page

BROCKENHURST Hampshire **Map 04 SU30**

★★★ Forest Park

Forestdale Hotels

Rhinefield Rd SO42 7ZG

Quality Percentage Score: 67%

☎ 01590 622844 📠 01590 623948

Dir: *from A337 to Brockenhurst turn into Meerut Rd, follow winding road through Waters Green, 0.5m to a T junct, turn right into Rhinefield Road*

This friendly hotel in the heart of the New Forest is popular for weekend breaks and quieter midweek stays. There are splendid walks and a riding stables next door. The well equipped, comfortable bedrooms vary in size and style, and there is a choice of lounge areas.

ROOMS: 38 en suite (bth/shr) (2 fmly) No smoking in 2 bedrooms s fr £75; d fr £95 (incl. bkfst) * LB Off peak **MEALS:** Lunch fr £9.95 Dinner fr £19.95 English & French Cuisine V meals Coffee am Tea pm **FACILITIES:** CTV in all bedrooms Outdoor swimming pool (heated) Tennis (hard) Riding Sauna ch fac Xmas **CONF:** Thtr 50 Class 20 Board 24 Del from £105 * **SERVICES:** 80P **NOTES:** No smoking in restaurant Last d 9.45pm **CARDS:**

BROCKENHURST Hampshire **Map 04 SU30**

★★★ Balmer Lawn

Best Western

Lyndhurst Rd SO42 7ZB

Quality Percentage Score: 65%

☎ 01590 623116 📠 01590 623864

Dir: *take A337 towards Lymington, hotel on left hand side behind village cricket green*

One of the best locations in the heart of the New Forest and central to its attractions, this character and historic house provides comfortable public rooms and a good range of bedrooms. Extensive yet discreet, function and leisure facilities skirt the hotel and make this a popular conference venue.

ROOMS: 55 en suite (bth/shr) (4 fmly) No smoking in 45 bedrooms s fr £72; d fr £108 * LB Off peak **MEALS:** Lunch £10-£14.95 High tea £4.50-£10 Dinner £13.30-£23.40alc V meals Coffee am Tea pm **FACILITIES:** CTV in all bedrooms Indoor swimming pool (heated) Outdoor swimming pool (heated) Tennis (hard) Squash Sauna Gym Jacuzzi/spa **CONF:** Thtr 150 Class 50 Board 50 Del from £117.50 * **SERVICES:** Lift Night porter 80P **NOTES:** No smoking in restaurant Last d 9.45pm **CARDS:**

See advert on opposite page

BROCKENHURST Hampshire **Map 04 SU30**

★★ Cloud

Meerut Rd SO42 7TD

Quality Percentage Score: 72%

☎ 01590 622165 📠 01590 622165

Dir: *first turning right off A337 approaching Brockenhurst from Lyndhurst. Follow brown tourist signs*

Personally run by friendly proprietor Avril Owton, this charming hotel enjoys a peaceful location on the edge of the village. The bedrooms are bright and comfortably furnished, with smart en suite facilities. The public rooms include a restaurant specialising in wholesome English food and several cosy lounges with log fires for the winter months.

ROOMS: 18 en suite (bth/shr) (3 fmly) s fr £52; d fr £84 (incl. bkfst) * LB Off peak **MEALS:** Lunch £7.95-£14.25 Dinner fr £18 V meals Coffee am Tea pm **FACILITIES:** CTV in all bedrooms Xmas **SERVICES:** 20P **NOTES:** No coaches No smoking in restaurant Last d 8.45pm **CARDS:**

BROCKENHURST Hampshire **Map 04 SU30**

★★ Watersplash

The Rise SO42 7ZP

Quality Percentage Score: 67%

☎ 01590 622344 📠 01590 624047

This popular Victorian hotel has been in the Foster family for 37 years and is now run by the second generation. Robin and Judy continue to make improvements to all areas, and are at present upgrading the bedrooms, with co-ordinated decor and added facilities. The restaurant overlooks the pretty garden, and there is a comfortable residents' lounge and separate bar. The outdoor pool is particularly popular in the summer months.

ROOMS: 23 en suite (bth/shr) (6 fmly) s £49; d £82-£92 (incl. bkfst) * LB Off peak **MEALS:** English & Continental Cuisine V meals Coffee am Tea pm **FACILITIES:** CTV in all bedrooms Outdoor swimming pool (heated) Motor cruiser Xmas **CONF:** Thtr 80 Class 20 Board 20 **SERVICES:** 29P **NOTES:** Last d 8.30pm **CARDS:**

Indicates that the star classification has not been confirmed under the New Quality Standards, see page 7 for further information.

BROMBOROUGH Merseyside — Map 07 SJ38

Travel Inn
High St, Bromborough Cross L62 7HZ
☎ 0151 334 2917 Fax 0151 334 0443
Dir: *on A41 New Chester Road, 1.5m from junct 5 of the M53*

This modern building offers accommodation in smart, spacious and well equipped bedrooms, all with en-suite bathrooms. Refreshments may be taken at the nearby family restaurant. For details about current prices consult the Contents Page under Hotel Groups for the Travel Inn phone number.
ROOMS: 31 en suite (bth/shr) d £39.95 *

BROME Suffolk — Map 05 TM17

★★★ Cornwallis Arms
IP23 8AJ
Quality Percentage Score: 70%
☎ 01379 870326 Fax 01379 870051
Dir: *off B1077, 50yds from junct with A140 in direction of Eye*

The approach to this striking, 16th-century dower house is by a long tree-lined avenue set in formal grounds with topiary and a duck pond. St Peter's Brewery own the hotel and, naturally, their excellent beers are drawn off the barrels in the Tudor Bar. The elegant open-plan restaurant runs into a relaxing lounge area and a vine-laden conservatory, used for private parties. The bedrooms are furnished in baronial style, in keeping with their period, but facilities are modern.
ROOMS: 10 en suite (bth/shr) 6 annexe en suite (bth/shr) (4 fmly) s £67.50; d £87.50 (incl. bkfst) * LB Off peak **MEALS:** Lunch £16.95-£19.95 Dinner £17.95-£19.95 English & French Cuisine V meals Coffee am Tea pm **FACILITIES:** CTV in all bedrooms STV Archery Xmas **CONF:** Thtr 40 Class 20 Board 20 **SERVICES:** 100P **NOTES:** No smoking area in restaurant Last d 9.30pm **CARDS:**

BROMLEY Greater London

See LONDON SECTION plan 1 *G1*

★★★ Bromley Court
Bromley Hill BR1 4JD
Quality Percentage Score: 70%
☎ 020 8464 5011 Fax 020 8460 0899
Dir: *N, signposted off A21. Opposite Mercedes Benz garage on Bromley Hill*

A grand mansion with modern extensions standing amid three acres of grounds. Accommodation is spread among several buildings, and although rooms vary in character, all are exceptionally well designed. The restaurant features dinner dancing and live entertainment on Friday and Saturday nights. Other facilities include a leisure club and good meeting rooms.
ROOMS: 115 en suite (bth/shr) (3 fmly) No smoking in 14 bedrooms s £85-£90; d £90-£98 (incl. bkfst) * Off peak **MEALS:** Lunch £2.75-£15.95 Dinner £12-£14 & alc Cosmopolitan Cuisine V meals Coffee am Tea pm **FACILITIES:** CTV in all bedrooms STV Sauna Gym Croquet lawn Putting green Jacuzzi/spa Xmas **CONF:** Thtr 150 Class 80 Board 45 Del £130 * **SERVICES:** Lift Night porter 100P **NOTES:** No smoking area in restaurant Last d 10pm **CARDS:**

BROMSGROVE Worcestershire — Map 07 SO97

★★★ Pine Lodge
Kidderminster Rd B61 9AB
Quality Percentage Score: 71%
☎ 01527 576600 Fax 01527 878981
Dir: *on A448 Bromsgrove to Kidderminster road, 1m W of Bromsgrove town centre*

This modern, purpose-built hotel provides a good choice of well equipped accommodation, including full suites, family-bedded rooms, rooms for women, and a room for disabled guests. There

contd.

is a pleasant bar and a choice of formal and informal restaurants, where chef Mark Higgins and his team have a well deserved reputation for their cuisine.
ROOMS: 114 en suite (bth/shr) (18 fmly) No smoking in 18 bedrooms **MEALS:** English & Continental Cuisine V meals Coffee am Tea pm **FACILITIES:** CTV in all bedrooms STV Indoor swimming pool (heated) Snooker Sauna Solarium Gym Jacuzzi/spa Childrens play area **CONF:** Thtr 200 Class 140 Board 30 **SERVICES:** Lift Night porter 250P **NOTES:** No smoking area in restaurant Last d 10pm
CARDS:

See advert on opposite page

BROOK (NEAR CADNAM) Hampshire **Map 04 SU21**
★★★ Bell Inn
SO43 7HE
Quality Percentage Score: 67%
☎ 023 80812214 023 80813958
***Dir:** leave M27 junct 1 onto B3079, hotel a mile and a half on right*
The golf course is the focal point of this popular hotel, although it is also an ideal base from which to visit the New Forest and surrounding sights. Bedrooms are comfortable and attractively furnished, and the public areas offer a cosy, friendly atmosphere. A wide range of fresh local produce is offered in both the oak-beamed bar and the restaurant.
ROOMS: 25 en suite (bth) No smoking in 11 bedrooms **MEALS:** Lunch fr £14.50 Dinner fr £26.50 English & French Cuisine V meals Coffee am Tea pm **FACILITIES:** CTV in all bedrooms Golf 36 Putting green **CONF:** Thtr 40 Class 60 Board 40 Del from £75 * **SERVICES:** 150P **NOTES:** No dogs (ex guide dogs) No smoking in restaurant Last d 9.30pm **CARDS:**

BROXTON Cheshire **Map 07 SJ45**
★★★★ Carden Park Hotel Golf Resort & Spa
Carden Park CH3 9DQ
Quality Percentage Score: 72%
☎ 01829 731000 01829 731032
***Dir:** leave M56 junct 15 for M53 Chester, take A41 for Whitchurch for approx 8m, at Broxton rdbt turn right on to A534 Wrexham continue 1.5m hotel on left*
This fine modern hotel provides a full range of leisure, conference and function facilities. A choice of golf courses is available, including one designed by Jack Nicklaus. A brasserie serves light meals and snacks and the more formal Garden Restaurant offers a fixed price menu and a further carte choice. Bedrooms are spacious and well equipped, many located in nearby buildings with views over the courses.
ROOMS: 115 en suite (bth/shr) 77 annexe en suite (bth/shr) (24 fmly) No smoking in 134 bedrooms s £110-£250; d £125-£250 * LB Off peak **MEALS:** Sunday Lunch fr £14.95 Dinner fr £22.95 & alc V meals Coffee am Tea pm **FACILITIES:** CTV in all bedrooms STV Indoor swimming pool (heated) Golf 45 Tennis (hard) Snooker Sauna Solarium Gym Pool table Croquet lawn Putting green Jacuzzi/spa Archery Quad bikes Jack Nicklaus Golf School Xmas **CONF:** Thtr 400 Class 240 Board 125 Del from £140 * **SERVICES:** Lift Night porter 350P **NOTES:** No dogs (ex guide dogs) No smoking in restaurant Last d 10pm
CARDS:

See advert under CHESTER

BROXTON Cheshire **Map 07 SJ45**
★★★ Broxton Hall Country House
Whitchurch Rd CH3 9JS
Quality Percentage Score: 66%
☎ 01829 782321 01829 782330
***Dir:** on A41 S of Chester at Broxton Rdbt A534, halfway between Whitchurch & Chester*
This impressive half-timbered Tudor Hall is located 10 miles south of Chester, and lies in several acres of well maintained grounds and gardens. Public areas are elegantly equipped with antique and period furnishings in keeping with the Hall's history. A daily fixed-price menu of imaginative dishes is available.
ROOMS: 10 en suite (bth/shr) s £60; d £70 (incl. bkfst) * LB Off peak **MEALS:** Lunch £15.90-£25.50 & alc Dinner £18-£25.50 English & French Cuisine V meals Coffee am Tea pm **FACILITIES:** CTV in all bedrooms Croquet lawn **CONF:** Thtr 23 Board 12 **SERVICES:** 30P **NOTES:** No coaches No children 12yrs Last d 9.30pm Closed 25 Dec & 1 Jan
CARDS:

BRYHER See Scilly, Isles of

BUCKDEN North Yorkshire **Map 07 SD97**
★★ Buck Inn
BD23 5JA
Quality Percentage Score: 67%
☎ 01756 760228 & 760352 01756 760227
***Dir:** on B6160*
This Georgian inn is situated amidst glorious Dales scenery, with fine views from many of the rooms. Bedrooms, varying in size, are attractively furnished and there is a cosy lounge area for visitors. A wide range of snacks and meals is served in the welcoming lounge bar, warmed by a log fire during the cooler months, with a more formal style available in the Courtyard restaurant. Here, fresh ingredients, local wherever possible, are carefully combined to produce satisfying meals.
ROOMS: 14 en suite (bth/shr) (2 fmly) **MEALS:** English & French Cuisine V meals Coffee am Tea pm **FACILITIES:** CTV in all bedrooms **CONF:** Class 30 **SERVICES:** 30P **NOTES:** No children 6yrs No smoking in restaurant **CARDS:**

BUCKHURST HILL Essex **Map 05 TQ49**
See LONDON SECTION plan 5 *F5*
★★★ Roebuck
North End IG9 5QY
Quality Percentage Score: 63%
☎ 020 8505 4636 020 8504 7826

corus
Corus and Regal hotels

The pleasant rural appeal of the climber-clad exterior belies the modern interior which has undergone a major refurbishment. The new restaurant features a bold colour scheme which also extends to the bar.
ROOMS: 28 en suite (bth/shr) No smoking in 10 bedrooms s fr £85; d fr £95 * LB Off peak **MEALS:** Lunch £5-£8 & alc Dinner £10-£13 & alc V meals Coffee am Tea pm **FACILITIES:** CTV in all bedrooms Xmas **CONF:** Thtr 200 Class 60 Board 14 Del £119 * **SERVICES:** Night porter 40P **NOTES:** Last d 9.45pm **CARDS:**

BUCKINGHAM Buckinghamshire — Map 04 SP63

★★★ Villiers

3 Castle St MK18 1BS
Quality Percentage Score: 72%
☎ 01280 822444 Fax 01280 822113

This town centre hotel has much to commend it and is ideal for business travellers, with excellent conference facilities equipped with high-tech audio-visual equipment. The spacious bedrooms have been thoughtfully equipped and carefully planned to ensure guests' comfort. There are two restaurants, Henry's, and Porcini's. The stone-flagged pub is popular with both guests and locals. Staff work with dedication to make guests feel welcome.

ROOMS: 38 en suite (bth/shr) (25 fmly) s £85-£130; d £99-£135 (incl. bkfst) * Off peak **MEALS:** Sunday Lunch £11.75-£15 & alc High tea £8-£12 & alc Dinner £14.25-£17.75 & alc English & Italian Cuisine V meals Coffee am Tea pm **FACILITIES:** CTV in all bedrooms STV Free membership of nearby leisure club Wkly live entertainment Xmas **CONF:** Thtr 250 Class 100 Board 60 Del from £116.73 * **SERVICES:** Lift Night porter 53P **NOTES:** No dogs (ex guide dogs) Last d 10pm
CARDS:

See advert on this page

BUCKINGHAM Buckinghamshire — Map 04 SP63

★★★ Buckingham Four Pillars Hotel

FOUR PILLARS HOTELS

Buckingham Ring Rd South MK18 1RY
Quality Percentage Score: 66%
☎ 01280 822622 Fax 01280 823074
Dir: *on A421 near junct with A413*

A purpose built hotel, designed with the needs of the business traveller in mind, provides extensive conference facilities and large, well appointed bedrooms with plenty of desk space. There is a well equipped leisure suite with pool, spa and fitness room; also a snooker table, which for the less energetic helps with relaxation. The open-plan restaurant and bar offers a good range of dishes including a carvery on selected days.

ROOMS: 70 en suite (bth/shr) (6 fmly) No smoking in 24 bedrooms s £61-£80; d £71-£90 * LB Off peak **MEALS:** Lunch fr £15.95 & alc Dinner fr £15.95 & alc English & French Cuisine V meals Coffee am Tea pm **FACILITIES:** CTV in all bedrooms STV Indoor swimming pool (heated) Snooker Sauna Solarium Gym Jacuzzi/spa Steam room Wkly live entertainment Xmas **CONF:** Thtr 160 Class 90 Board 50 Del £125 * **SERVICES:** Night porter 120P **NOTES:** No smoking area in restaurant Last d 9.45pm Closed 28 Dec-4 Jan
CARDS:

Symbols and Abbreviations are listed and explained on pages 4 and 5

B

BUCKLAND (NEAR BROADWAY) Gloucestershire

Map 04 SP03

The Premier Collection

★★★ Buckland Manor
WR12 7LY
☎ 01386 852626 01386 853557
Dir: off B4632

RELAIS & CHATEAUX

This imposing 13th-century manor house stands in extensive grounds. Bedrooms and public areas are furnished with high quality pieces and decorated in keeping with the style of the manor. Cuisine, based on carefully chosen raw materials, displays skill and confidence.

ROOMS: 13 en suite (bth/shr) (2 fmly) s £195-£335; d £205-£345 (incl. bkfst) * Off peak **MEALS:** Lunch £23.50-£28.50 International Cuisine V meals Coffee am Tea pm **FACILITIES:** CTV in all bedrooms STV Outdoor swimming pool (heated) Tennis (hard) Croquet lawn Putting green Xmas **SERVICES:** 30P **NOTES:** No dogs No coaches No children 12yrs No smoking in restaurant **CARDS:**

BUDE Cornwall & Isles of Scilly

Map 02 SS20

★★★ Falcon
Breakwater Rd EX23 8SD
Quality Percentage Score: 70%
☎ 01288 352005 01288 356359
Dir: turn off A39 into Bude and follow road to Widemouth bay. Hotel is on right as you cross over canal bridge).

Located on the edge of the town, the Falcon Hotel is a popular venue for guests, as well as locals. Public areas include a spacious bar which serves a wide range of bar meals, an intimate cocktail bar, and an elegant restaurant. The extensive menus feature locally caught fish and a variety of vegetarian options. Bedrooms are decorated to a high standard, and are well equipped.

ROOMS: 26 en suite (bth/shr) (5 fmly) s £36-£38; d £72-£76 (incl. bkfst) * LB Off peak **MEALS:** Lunch £8.95 Dinner £16 & alc English & French Cuisine V meals Coffee am **FACILITIES:** CTV in all bedrooms STV Sauna Solarium Gym Croquet lawn Jacuzzi/spa **CONF:** Thtr 60 Class 30 Board 30 **SERVICES:** 40P **NOTES:** No coaches No smoking in restaurant Last d 9.30pm **CARDS:**

See advert on opposite page

BUDE Cornwall & Isles of Scilly

Map 02 SS20

★★★ ***Hartland***
Hartland Ter EX23 8JY
Quality Percentage Score: 69%
☎ 01288 355661 01288 355664

Ideally located close to the centre of the town and yet convenient for the beaches, the Hartland Hotel is continually popular with its guests. Each evening an interesting fixed-price menu is offered in the elegantly furnished restaurant. Entertainment is provided in the ballroom, and the outdoor swimming pool is ideal for a summer's day.

ROOMS: 28 en suite (bth/shr) (2 fmly) No smoking in 5 bedrooms **MEALS:** International Cuisine V meals Coffee am Tea pm **FACILITIES:** CTV in all bedrooms Outdoor swimming pool (heated) Wkly live entertainment **SERVICES:** Lift 30P **NOTES:** No smoking in restaurant Last d 8.30pm Closed mid Nov-Etr (ex Xmas)

BUDE Cornwall & Isles of Scilly

Map 02 SS20

★★ Atlantic House
17-18 Summerleaze Crescent EX23 8HJ
Quality Percentage Score: 66%
☎ 01288 352451 01288 356666
Dir: leave M5 junct 31, follow A30 dual carriageway to bypass Okehampton, follow signs to Bude via Halwill and Holsworthy

Set in a quiet area near the beach and a few minutes walk from the town centre. Each evening in the restaurant, a well balanced, fixed-price menu is offered. Bedrooms are comfortable and well maintained, the front facing rooms are popular with regular guests.

ROOMS: 13 en suite (bth/shr) (3 fmly) No smoking in 1 bedroom s £22.40-£23.90; d £44.80-£47.90 (incl. bkfst) LB Off peak **MEALS:** Bar Lunch £3 Dinner £14.90 V meals Coffee am Tea pm **FACILITIES:** CTV in all bedrooms Pool table Games room Multi-activity sports **SERVICES:** 10P **NOTES:** No dogs (ex guide dogs) No smoking in restaurant Last d 8pm Closed 11 Nov-2 Mar **CARDS:**

BUDE Cornwall & Isles of Scilly

Map 02 SS20

★★ Maer Lodge
Crooklets Beach EX23 8NG
Quality Percentage Score: 65%
☎ 01288 353306 01288 354005
Dir: leave A39 at Stratton to Bude 1m. Go right into The Strand and up Belle Vue past shops. Bear left at Somerfield to Crooklets Beach, hotel to right

THE CIRCLE
Selected Individual Hotels
GREAT BRITAIN

With views over the Downs, this family-run hotel has traditionally furnished public areas that include a cosy bar and spacious lounge. In the dining room a choice from a short fixed-price menu is offered. The bedrooms are tastefully furnished and appointed.

ROOMS: 19 en suite (bth/shr) (4 fmly) No smoking in all bedrooms s £32-£36; d £56-£60 (incl. bkfst) * LB Off peak **MEALS:** Dinner fr £9 English & Continental Cuisine V meals Coffee am **FACILITIES:** CTV in all bedrooms STV Putting green Xmas **CONF:** Class 60 Board 15 **SERVICES:** 15P **NOTES:** No smoking in restaurant Last d 7.30pm **CARDS:**

BUDE Cornwall & Isles of Scilly — Map 02 SS20
★★ Penarvor
Crooklets Beach EX23 8NE
Quality Percentage Score: 64%
☎ 01288 352036 📠 01288 355027
Dir: *on headland 50yds from Crooklets beach*
There is a friendly atmosphere at this family-owned hotel overlooking Crooklets Beach. Particularly popular with golfers, the hotel is adjacent to the golf course and a short walk from the town centre. Bedrooms vary in size but are all equipped to a similar pleasing standard. In the restaurant an interesting selection of dishes is offered using fresh local produce.
ROOMS: 16 en suite (bth/shr) (3 fmly) s £24-£28; d £48-£56 (incl. bkfst) * LB Off peak **MEALS:** Lunch £7.95-£14.95 & alc Dinner £10.95 & alc English, French & Italian Cuisine V meals Coffee am Tea pm **FACILITIES:** CTV in all bedrooms STV Pool table Xmas **SERVICES:** 20P **NOTES:** No coaches No smoking in restaurant Last d 8.30pm
CARDS:

BUDE Cornwall & Isles of Scilly — Map 02 SS20
★★ *Bude Haven*
Flexbury Av EX23 8NS
Quality Percentage Score: 63%
☎ 01288 352305 📠 01288 352305
Within walking distance of the town centre and Crooklets Beach, the hotel has a friendly relaxed atmosphere. In the smartly decorated dining room, an interesting choice of dishes is offered at dinner and breakfast. Bedrooms all have modern facilities and are well equipped.
ROOMS: 12 en suite (bth/shr) (2 fmly) **MEALS:** V meals **FACILITIES:** CTV in all bedrooms **SERVICES:** 8P **NOTES:** No dogs (ex guide dogs) No coaches No smoking in restaurant Last d 7.30pm Closed New Year **CARDS:**

BUDE Cornwall & Isles of Scilly — Map 02 SS20
★★ *Stamford Hill Hotel*
Stratton EX23 9AY
Quality Percentage Score: 62%
☎ 01288 352709 📠 01288 352709
Dir: *on the edge of the village of Stratton, just off A39, brown tourist signs direct to the hotel*
Set in five acres of woodland and gardens, this Georgian Manor was built on the site of the Battle of Stamford Hill. Within half a mile of Bude's sandy beaches, the hotel offers bedrooms that are modestly furnished but well equipped. The comfortable lounge is warmed by crackling log fires and the convivial atmosphere in the bar provides a fitting prelude to the carefully prepared dinners.
ROOMS: 14 en suite (bth/shr) (5 fmly) No smoking in 1 bedroom **MEALS:** V meals Coffee am Tea pm **FACILITIES:** CTV in all bedrooms Outdoor swimming pool (heated) Tennis (grass) Sauna Pool table Badminton court **SERVICES:** 20P **NOTES:** No coaches No smoking in restaurant Last d 8.30pm Closed 18 Dec-18 Jan
CARDS:

BUDE Cornwall & Isles of Scilly — Map 02 SS20
★★ Camelot
Downs View EX23 8RE
Quality Percentage Score: 61%
☎ 01288 352361 📠 01288 355470
Dir: *turn off A39 into Bude, right at rdbt, through one-way system keep left, hotel on left overlooking golf course*
Overlooking Bude and Cornwall Golf Club, this Edwardian property has an enviable reputation among the golfing fraternity. Comfortable public areas include a well furnished lounge and bar, the latter featuring golfing ties from around the world. Bedrooms are light, airy and furnished in a contemporary style.
ROOMS: 21 en suite (bth/shr) (3 fmly) s £24-£29.50; d £48-£59 (incl. bkfst) * LB Off peak **MEALS:** Dinner £15 French & English Cuisine V meals **FACILITIES:** CTV in all bedrooms Pool table Darts Table tennis **SERVICES:** 21P **NOTES:** No dogs (ex guide dogs) No coaches No smoking in restaurant Last d 8.30pm **CARDS:**

BUDE Cornwall & Isles of Scilly — Map 02 SS20
★ Meva Gwin
Upton EX23 0LY
Quality Percentage Score: 66%
☎ 01288 352347 📠 01288 352347
Dir: *take Widemouth Bay road and continue for 1m*
With stunning views over the coastline and surrounding countryside, this well maintained, homely hotel is set in neatly tended gardens. Front facing bedrooms have lovely views, some have balconies. In addition to the comfortable sun lounge, the Surf Rider Bar is a popular meeting place.
ROOMS: 12 rms (4 bth 7 shr) (4 fmly) s £21-£25; d £42-£50 (incl. bkfst) Off peak **MEALS:** Lunch £9.50 Dinner £9.50 Coffee am Tea pm **FACILITIES:** CTV in all bedrooms ch fac **SERVICES:** 44P **NOTES:** No dogs No smoking in restaurant Last d 7.30pm Closed 5 Oct-Mar
CARDS:

BURFORD Oxfordshire — Map 04 SP21
★★★ The Lamb Inn
Sheep St OX18 4LR
Quality Percentage Score: 73%
☎ 01993 823155 📠 01993 822228
Dir: *off Burford High Street*
High levels of hospitality and service are the hallmarks of this

contd.

wonderful old inn set in the pretty Cotswold village of Burford. The en suite bedrooms retain the character of the building and are well equipped with good quality furnishings and fabrics. In the public areas, flagstone floors and log fires set the tone in each of the three comfortable lounges, traditionally furnished with sumptuous sofas and fireside chairs. Meals are taken in the formal rear dining room, where chef Pascal Clavaud presents rosette-worthy cuisine. A pretty cottage garden completes the picture.
ROOMS: 15 en suite (bth/shr) s £60-£75; d £95-£115 (incl. bkfst) * LB Off peak **MEALS:** Sunday Lunch fr £18.50 Dinner £20-£25 English & French Cuisine V meals Coffee am **FACILITIES:** CTV in all bedrooms **SERVICES:** 6P **NOTES:** No coaches No smoking in restaurant Last d 9pm Closed 25-26 Dec **CARDS:**

BURFORD Oxfordshire **Map 04 SP21**
★★★ The Bay Tree
12-14 Sheep St OX18 4LW
Quality Percentage Score: 67%
☎ 01993 822791 Fax 01993 823008
***Dir:** off A40, down hill onto A361 towards Burford, Sheep St 1st left*
Built in the traditional manner from local Cotswold stone, this historic inn is ideally situated in the heart of the pretty village of Burford. The building retains many of its original period features, the main staircase with its heraldic decor being particularly impressive. The bedrooms are all individually decorated with a variety of traditional and modern furnishings, and equipped to a high standard. A number of rooms feature four-poster and half tester beds, whilst the cottage rooms overlook an attractive walled garden.
ROOMS: 9 en suite (bth/shr) 14 annexe en suite (bth/shr) s £90; d £135-£210 (incl. bkfst) * LB Off peak **MEALS:** Lunch £6.25-£9.75alc High tea 95p-£2.20alc Dinner £24.95 English & French Cuisine V meals Coffee am Tea pm **FACILITIES:** CTV in all bedrooms Croquet lawn Xmas **CONF:** Thtr 40 Board 25 Del from £140 * **SERVICES:** 30P **NOTES:** No smoking in restaurant Last d 9.30pm
CARDS:

BURFORD Oxfordshire **Map 04 SP21**
★★★ Cotswold Gateway
Cheltenham Rd OX18 4HX
Quality Percentage Score: 65%
☎ 01993 822695 Fax 01993 823600
***Dir:** situated at the roundabout on the A40 Oxford/Cheltenham at junct with A361*
Situated on the A40 route to Cheltenham, the hotel is a convenient base from which to explore the Cotswolds. The natural friendliness of the staff is one of the hotel's main assets and ensures that guests return. Bedrooms are prettily decorated with pleasant fabrics and attractive furnishings, the two four-poster rooms are particularly good. There is a separate coffee shop and restaurant where traditional and modern dishes are served.
ROOMS: 13 en suite (bth/shr) 8 annexe en suite (bth/shr) (2 fmly) No smoking in all bedrooms s fr £65; d fr £85 (incl. bkfst) * LB Off peak **MEALS:** English & French Cuisine V meals Coffee am Tea pm **FACILITIES:** CTV in all bedrooms Xmas **CONF:** Thtr 40 Class 20 Board 24 **SERVICES:** 60P **NOTES:** No dogs (ex guide dogs) No smoking in restaurant **CARDS:**

BURFORD Oxfordshire **Map 04 SP21**
★★★ The Inn For All Seasons
The Barringtons OX18 4TN
Quality Percentage Score: 60%
☎ 01451 844324 Fax 01451 844375
***Dir:** 3m W on A40*
Guests are assured of a warm and friendly welcome at this 16th-century, family-run coaching inn which provides comfortable and spacious bedrooms. The interior of the hotel, whilst providing modern amenities, has been carefully preserved to retain the original fireplaces, oak beams and period furniture. A good selection of bar meals is available at lunchtime, in addition to a full evening restaurant menu.
ROOMS: 9 en suite (bth) 1 annexe en suite (bth/shr) (2 fmly) s £39.50-£47.50; d £70-£83 (incl. bkfst) * LB Off peak **MEALS:** Bar Lunch £7.50-£12.50alc Dinner fr £18.75 English & Continental Cuisine V meals Coffee am Tea pm **FACILITIES:** CTV in all bedrooms STV Clay pigeon shooting Xmas **CONF:** Thtr 25 Class 30 Board 30 Del from £97.50 * **SERVICES:** 60P **NOTES:** No children 10yrs No smoking in restaurant Last d 9.30pm **CARDS:**

BURFORD Oxfordshire **Map 04 SP21**
★★ Golden Pheasant
91 High St OX18 4QA
Quality Percentage Score: 65%
☎ 01993 823223 Fax 01993 822621
***Dir:** leave M40 at junct 8 and follow signs A40 Cheltenham into Burford*
This attractive old inn on Burford's main street has parts that date back to the 16th century. Bedrooms can be a little compact but all are stylishly furnished; attractive fabrics and period furniture are combined with useful extras. Meals can either be taken in the bar or in the restaurant with its solid-fuel stove.
ROOMS: 12 rms (11 bth/shr) (1 fmly) **MEALS:** English & French Cuisine V meals Coffee am Tea pm **FACILITIES:** CTV in all bedrooms **SERVICES:** 12P **NOTES:** No coaches No smoking area in restaurant Last d 9.30pm **CARDS:**

BURFORD Oxfordshire **Map 04 SP21**
Travelodge
Bury Barn OX7 5TB
☎ 01993 822699 Fax 01993 822699
***Dir:** A40*
This modern building offers accommodation in smart, spacious and well equipped bedrooms, all with en-suite bathrooms. Refreshments may be taken at the nearby family restaurant. For details about current prices, consult the Contents Page under Hotel Groups for the Travelodge phone number.
ROOMS: 40 en suite (bth/shr) d £49.95 *

BURLEY Hampshire **Map 04 SU20**
★★★ Burley Manor
Ringwood Rd BH24 4BS
Quality Percentage Score: 67%
☎ 01425 403522 Fax 01425 403227
***Dir:** leave A31 at Burley signpost, hotel 3m on left*
Set in extensive grounds, this 18th-century hotel overlooks farmland, and is well placed for exploring the New Forest. Half the well equipped bedrooms, including several with four poster beds, are in the main house, while the remainder are in the converted stable block and new wing. Riding can be arranged.
ROOMS: 21 en suite (bth/shr) 17 annexe en suite (bth/shr) (3 fmly) No smoking in 4 bedrooms s fr £85; d fr £110 (incl. bkfst) * LB Off peak **MEALS:** Lunch fr £12.75 High tea fr £5 Dinner fr £18.45 V meals Coffee am Tea pm **FACILITIES:** CTV in all bedrooms Outdoor swimming pool (heated) Fishing Riding Croquet lawn Xmas **CONF:** Thtr 60 Class 40 Board 40 Del from £115 * **SERVICES:** 60P **NOTES:** No smoking in restaurant Last d 9.45pm **CARDS:**

★
The Premier Collection, hotels with Red Star Awards are listed on pages 17-23

BURLEY Hampshire **Map 04 SU20**

★★★ Moorhill House

BH24 4AG

Quality Percentage Score: 63%

☎ 01425 403285 🖷 01425 403715

Dir: *follow A31 for approx 5m pass two shell gardens on either side of the road & sign for Burley, into village. Road opposite Queens Head then 1st left*

Situated in the heart of the New Forest, this hotel continues to be upgraded. The public areas include two lounges overlooking the garden. Service is friendly and relaxed. The bedrooms vary in size.

ROOMS: 24 en suite (bth/shr) (7 fmly) s fr £70; d fr £125 (incl. bkfst) * LB Off peak **MEALS:** Lunch £10.95-£14.95 Dinner £21.50 V meals Coffee am Tea pm **FACILITIES:** CTV in all bedrooms Indoor swimming pool (heated) Sauna Croquet lawn Putting green Jacuzzi/spa ch fac Xmas **CONF:** Thtr 54 Class 48 Board 28 Del from £90 * **SERVICES:** 40P **NOTES:** No coaches No smoking area in restaurant Last d 8.45pm **CARDS:**

BURNHAM Buckinghamshire **Map 04 SU98**

★★★ Burnham Beeches

Grove Rd SL1 8DP

REGAL

Quality Percentage Score: 70%

☎ 01628 429955 🖷 01628 603994

Dir: *follow A355 towards Slough. Straight on at 1st rbt, right at 2nd and right at 3rd then follow signs to hotel*

In its own grounds, this extended Georgian manor house stands on the fringes of woodland convenient for the M4 and M40. Bedrooms are comfortable, quiet and are well equipped. Facilities include a fitness centre inluding pool and a cosy lounge bar where all day snacks are available.

ROOMS: 82 en suite (bth/shr) (19 fmly) No smoking in 18 bedrooms **MEALS:** Lunch £15.50-£20 & alc High tea £4.95-£5 Dinner £22.50-£25 & alc International Cuisine V meals Coffee am Tea pm **FACILITIES:** CTV in all bedrooms STV Indoor swimming pool (heated) Tennis (hard) Snooker Sauna Solarium Gym Croquet lawn Jacuzzi/spa Beauty Treatments by prior arrangement **CONF:** Thtr 180 Class 100 Board 60 Del from £180 * **SERVICES:** Lift Night porter 200P **NOTES:** No dogs (ex guide dogs) No smoking area in restaurant Last d 9.30pm

CARDS:

BURNHAM Buckinghamshire **Map 04 SU98**

★★★ *Grovefield*

Taplow Common Rd SL1 8LP

Quality Percentage Score: 69%

☎ 01628 603131 🖷 01628 668078

Close to Heathrow and Windsor, Grovefield is set in spacious grounds. A popular venue for conferences in the week, its pleasant situation and a nearby golf course also make it ideal for weekend breaks. Bedrooms are spacious and attractively decorated and the restaurant is a comfortable place to eat.

ROOMS: 40 en suite (bth/shr) (5 fmly) No smoking in 24 bedrooms **MEALS:** English & French Cuisine V meals Coffee am Tea pm **FACILITIES:** CTV in all bedrooms STV Fishing Croquet lawn Putting green **CONF:** Thtr 250 Class 80 Board 80 **SERVICES:** Lift Night porter 155P **NOTES:** No smoking in restaurant Last d 10pm

CARDS:

BURNHAM MARKET Norfolk **Map 09 TF84**

★★ Hoste Arms

The Green PE31 8HD

Quality Percentage Score: 71%

☎ 01328 738777 🖷 01328 730103

Dir: *signposted on B1155, 5m W of Wells-Next-the-Sea*

A traditional inn combining a hotel, restaurant and pub in a delightful Georgian village setting. Stylish in appearance, yet down-to-earth in atmosphere, it caters for a real mix of guests ranging from locals enjoying the pub and restaurant to city slickers enjoying a relaxing weekend. Richly decorated accommodation is provided in a variety of charming bedrooms.

ROOMS: (1 fmly) No smoking in 1 bedroom s £60; d £76-£92 (incl. bkfst) * LB Off peak **MEALS:** Sunday Lunch £14-£26alc Dinner £14-£26alc English, French, Mediterranean & Thai Cuisine V meals Coffee am Tea pm **FACILITIES:** CTV in 28 bedrooms Xmas **CONF:** Thtr 30 Class 22 Board 24 **SERVICES:** Night porter 60P **NOTES:** No children 5yrs No smoking area in restaurant Last d 9.15pm **CARDS:**

The AA Hotel Booking Service is a free benefit to AA members. See the advertisement on page 47

B

BURNHAM-ON-SEA Somerset — Map 03 ST34
★★ *Queens Hotel*
1 Pier St TA8 1BT
Quality Percentage Score: 65%
☎ 01278 783045 Fax 01278 793591
Dir: *on seafront & corner of Pier St*
This imposing hotel was built in 1850 and is delightfully situated on the sea front and close to the main shopping area. It is popular with the business and leisure markets and is a good base for touring the area. Bedrooms have recently been refurbished and are well equipped with many having sea views. Some are also suitable for families. There is an attractive restaurant offering dinner and a large comfortable bar where snacks are available. Small parties and functions can also be catered for.
ROOMS: 19 en suite (bth/shr) (5 fmly) No smoking in 2 bedrooms **MEALS:** V meals Coffee am Tea pm **FACILITIES:** CTV in all bedrooms **CONF:** Thtr 30 Class 18 Board 20 **SERVICES:** 12P **NOTES:** No dogs (ex guide dogs) No smoking area in restaurant
CARDS:

BURNLEY Lancashire — Map 07 SD83
★★★ Oaks
Colne Rd, Reedley BB10 2LF
Quality Percentage Score: 72%
☎ 01282 414141 Fax 01282 433401
Dir: *on A56 between Burnley and Nelson*
Conveniently situated for the M65, on the edge of the town, this fine Victorian house stands in 4 acres of mature gardens. The panelled entrance hall leads to a gallery lounge with a splendid stained glass window. Other public areas include a leisure club, the comfortable Quills restaurant and, at lunchtimes, the more informal Archives brasserie. Comfortable bedrooms are well equipped to suit both business and leisure visitors and there is a range of function suites.
ROOMS: 53 en suite (bth/shr) (10 fmly) No smoking in 20 bedrooms s fr £92; d fr £112 (incl. bkfst) * LB Off peak **MEALS:** Bar Lunch fr £5 Dinner fr £22 English & French Cuisine V meals Coffee am Tea pm **FACILITIES:** CTV in all bedrooms STV Indoor swimming pool (heated) Sauna Solarium Gym Jacuzzi/spa Steam room **CONF:** Thtr 120 Class 48 Board 60 Del from £79 * **SERVICES:** Night porter 110P **NOTES:** No smoking in restaurant Last d 9.30pm Closed 31 Dec
CARDS:

BURNLEY Lancashire — Map 07 SD83
★★★ Sparrow Hawk
Church St BB11 2DN
Quality Percentage Score: 69%
☎ 01282 421551 Fax 01282 456506
Dir: *on Inner Ring Road (A682), opposite St Peters Church*
This well maintained Victorian hotel provides comfortable accommodation in modern bedrooms. All are well equipped and female guests are particularly well taken care of, with such items as bathrobes, irons, and quality toiletries provided. There is a choice between the cocktail bar and the popular lounge bar, where a range of real ales is served. A full à la carte menu is available in the first floor restaurant during the week, changing to a grill menu at weekends.
ROOMS: 36 en suite (bth/shr) (2 fmly) No smoking in 18 bedrooms s £48.50-£49.50; d £55-£65 (incl. bkfst) * LB Off peak **MEALS:** Bar Lunch fr £8 Dinner £8-£15 European Cuisine V meals Coffee am **FACILITIES:** CTV in all bedrooms STV Pool table Wkly live entertainment Xmas **CONF:** Thtr 80 Class 40 Board 30 Del from £59 * **SERVICES:** Night porter 24P **NOTES:** No dogs (ex guide dogs) No smoking area in restaurant Last d 9.30pm
CARDS:

BURNLEY Lancashire — Map 07 SD83
★★★ Rosehill House
Rosehill Av BB11 2PW
Quality Percentage Score: 64%
☎ 01282 453931 Fax 01282 455628
Dir: *0.5m S of Burnley town centre, off the A682*
Quietly situated on the edge of the town, in attractive grounds, this Grade II listed building retains many of its original features, including some fine ornate ceilings. Bedrooms continue to be upgraded and are individually furnished and thoughtfully equipped. Public areas include a comfortable bar lounge and a well appointed restaurant, recently enlarged with a conservatory, where a selection of carefully prepared dishes is offered.
ROOMS: 30 en suite (bth/shr) (2 fmly) No smoking in 1 bedroom s £40-£55; d £56-£85 * LB Off peak **MEALS:** Lunch £6-£14.50 & alc Dinner £6-£14.50 & alc English & Continental Cuisine V meals Coffee am Tea pm **FACILITIES:** CTV in all bedrooms STV Snooker Gym **CONF:** Thtr 50 Class 30 Board 30 **SERVICES:** Night porter 52P **NOTES:** No dogs (ex guide dogs) No smoking area in restaurant Last d 9.30pm **CARDS:**

BURNLEY Lancashire — Map 07 SD83
★★ Alexander
2 Tarleton Av, Todmorden Rd BB11 3ET
Quality Percentage Score: 65%
☎ 01282 422684 Fax 01282 424094
Dir: *leave M65 at junct 10 and follow signs for 'Towneley Hall' to Tarleton Avenue*
Quietly situated in a residential area, yet with easy access to the town centre, this family run hotel offers attractively furnished bedrooms, some of which are sited in an adjacent building. An extensive range of dishes is available, served either in the well appointed restaurant or in the more informal café bar.
ROOMS: 11 en suite (bth/shr) 5 annexe en suite (bth/shr) (2 fmly) s £32-£42; d £45-£53 (incl. bkfst) * LB Off peak **MEALS:** Sunday Lunch £7.95 & alc Dinner £7.95 & alc English & Continental Cuisine V meals Coffee am **FACILITIES:** CTV in all bedrooms STV Xmas **CONF:** Thtr 120 Class 40 Board 45 Del from £49 * **SERVICES:** 18P **NOTES:** No dogs (ex guide dogs) Last d 9.15pm **CARDS:**

BURNLEY Lancashire — Map 07 SD83
★★ Comfort Friendly Inn
Keirby Walk BB11 2DH
Quality Percentage Score: 60%
☎ 01282 427611 Fax 01282 436370
Conveniently situated in the centre of the town and with a small underground car park, this hotel offers value for money accommodation in a friendly and informal atmosphere. Bedrooms, although compact, are particularly well equipped and all have full en suite facilities. Cottons Café Bar offers a good range of beers together with carvery style meals and bar snacks. The large Keirby Suite can cater for 200 people and there are also smaller meeting and conference rooms.
ROOMS: 50 en suite (bth/shr) No smoking in 18 bedrooms d £46.75-£54.50 * LB Off peak **MEALS:** Sunday Lunch £2.95-£15.95alc Dinner fr £10.75 & alc English & Continental Cuisine V meals Coffee am Tea pm **FACILITIES:** CTV in all bedrooms STV Mini-gym Xmas **CONF:** Thtr 300 Class 130 Board 35 **SERVICES:** Lift Night porter 75P **NOTES:** No smoking area in restaurant Last d 9.45pm
CARDS:

BURNLEY Lancashire **Map 07 SD83**
Travel Inn
Queen Victoria Rd BB10 3EF
☎ 01282 450250 01282 452811
Dir: *M65 junct 12 right at rdbt past B&Q, follow signs Burnley N, at traffic lights by football ground left, across next rdbt, past Ford garage, in 0.5m*
This modern building offers accommodation in smart, spacious and well equipped bedrooms, all with en-suite bathrooms. Refreshments may be taken at the nearby family restaurant. For details about current prices consult the Contents Page under Hotel Groups for the Travel Inn phone number.
ROOMS: 40 en suite (bth/shr) d £39.95 *

BURNLEY Lancashire **Map 07 SD83**
Travelodge
Cavalry Barracks, Barracks Rd BB11 4AS
☎ 01282 416039 01282 416039
Dir: *junc A671/A679*
This modern building offers a good standard of accommodation for overnight stops. Smart, spacious and well equipped bedrooms, all with en suite bathrooms, are suitable for family use, and meals may be taken at the nearby Happy Eater.
ROOMS: 32 en suite (bth/shr) (32 fmly) No smoking in 15 bedrooms d £39.95 * Off peak **FACILITIES:** CTV in all bedrooms STV **SERVICES:** Night porter 32P **NOTES:** No coaches
CARDS:

BURNSALL North Yorkshire **Map 07 SE06**
★★ ***Red Lion Hotel***
By the Bridge BD23 6BU
Quality Percentage Score: 67%
☎ 01756 720204 01756 720292
Dir: *on B6160 between Grassington and Bolton Abbey*
Dating back to the 16th century this charming Dales inn stands by a bridge that spans the River Wharfe and guests are free to fish the hotel's own stretch of water. Attractively furnished bedrooms offer good levels of comfort, and the homely lounge is complemented by a traditional bar. Chef James Rowley continues to source local produce with care, producing memorable meals in the intimate restaurant - and guests should not miss the breakfasts served here!
ROOMS: 7 en suite (bth/shr) 4 annexe en suite (bth/shr) (2 fmly)
MEALS: V meals Coffee am **FACILITIES:** CTV in all bedrooms Fishing
CONF: Thtr 30 Class 10 Board 20 Del from £100 * **SERVICES:** 80P
NOTES: No dogs No coaches No smoking in restaurant Last d 9.30pm
CARDS:

BURNSALL North Yorkshire **Map 07 SE06**
★★ ***Fell***
BD23 6BT
Quality Percentage Score: 62%
☎ 01756 720209 01756 720605
Dir: *on B6160 beyond Bolton Abbey Hotel*
Set above the village, this friendly hotel offers fine views over the River Wharfe and surrounding hills from the public rooms and many of the modern and comfortably furnished bedrooms. A wide range of dishes is offered either in the bar or in the light and airy restaurant.
ROOMS: 16 en suite (bth/shr) (6 fmly) **MEALS:** V meals Coffee am Tea pm **FACILITIES:** CTV in all bedrooms Pool table **CONF:** Thtr 70 Class 46 Board 30 **SERVICES:** 60P **NOTES:** No smoking area in restaurant Last d 9.30pm **CARDS:**

BURRINGTON (NEAR PORTSMOUTH ARMS STATION) Devon **Map 03 SS61**
★★★ **Northcote Manor**
EX37 9LZ
Quality Percentage Score: 78%
☎ 01769 560501 01769 560770
Dir: *turn off A377 opposite Portsmouth Arms Pub, into hotels own drive marked Northcote Manor. Do not enter Burrington village*
Standing in 20 acres of lawns and woodland, this stone-built gabled manor enjoys views over some beautiful countryside. The accommodation is very comfortable, and all rooms are very well equipped, with a host of extra touches. Award winning cuisine is served in the Manor House Restaurant, which is inventive and satisfying.
ROOMS: 11 en suite (bth/shr) s fr £84; d fr £120 (incl. bkfst & dinner) * LB Off peak **MEALS:** Lunch £18.50-£25.50 Dinner £29.50-£35 English & French Cuisine V meals Coffee am Tea pm **FACILITIES:** CTV in all bedrooms STV Tennis (hard) Croquet lawn Xmas **CONF:** Thtr 12 Class 12 Board 12 **SERVICES:** 20P **NOTES:** No coaches No smoking in restaurant Last d 9.15pm **CARDS:**
See advert on p. 81

BURTON MOTORWAY SERVICE AREA (M6) Cumbria **Map 07 SD57**
Travelodge
Burton in Kendal LA6 1JF
☎ 01524 781234
Dir: *between junct35/36 southbound M6*
This modern building offers accommodation in smart, spacious and well equipped bedrooms, all with en-suite bathrooms. Refreshments may be taken at the nearby family restaurant. For details about current prices, consult the Contents Page under Hotel Groups for the Travelodge phone number. **ROOMS:** 40 en suite (bth/shr) d £39.95 *

BURTON UPON TRENT

BURTONWOOD MOTORWAY SERVICE AREA (M62) Cheshire
Map 07 SJ59

Welcome Lodge

Welcome Break - Burtonwood, M62,
Great Sankey WA5 3AX
☎ 01925 710376 📠 01925 710378
Dir: *between junc 7 & 9 M62 westbound*
This modern building offers accommodation in smart, spacious and well equipped bedrooms, suitable for families and businessmen, and all with en-suite bathrooms. Refreshments may be taken at the nearby family restaurant. For details of current prices, consult the Contents Page under Hotel Groups for the Welcome Break phone number.
ROOMS: 40 en suite (bth/shr) d fr £45 *

BURWARDSLEY Cheshire
Map 07 SJ55

★★ Pheasant Inn

Higher Burwardsley CH3 9PF
Quality Percentage Score: 66%
☎ 01829 770434 📠 01829 771097
Dir: *follow signs 'Cheshire Workshops'*
Set high in the Peckforton Hills, this 17th-century inn commands enriching views over the Cheshire plains. The bar has a warming character with exposed ceiling beams and a roaring open fire. Food is served in the bar, and also in the connecting bistro. The bedrooms are located a stone's throw from the inn, and are comfortable with modern facilities.
ROOMS: 2 en suite (bth/shr) 8 annexe en suite (bth/shr) (1 fmly) No smoking in 4 bedrooms s £49.50; d £70-£80 (incl. bkfst) * LB Off peak **MEALS:** Sunday Lunch fr £12.50 Dinner fr £14.50 English & French Cuisine V meals Coffee am Tea pm **FACILITIES:** CTV in all bedrooms ch fac Xmas **SERVICES:** 60P **NOTES:** No coaches No smoking area in restaurant Last d 9.30pm **CARDS:**

BURY Greater Manchester
Map 07 SD81

★★★ Normandie

Elbut Ln, Birtle BL9 6UT
Quality Percentage Score: 69%
☎ 0161 764 3869 & 764 1170 📠 0161 764 4866
Dir: *leave M66 at junct 2, first right and then first right again into Willow St. At top turn right onto B6222 and after 1m turn left into Elbut Lane*
Enjoying fine views over Greater Manchester to the Pennines beyond, the Normandie Hotel offers warm hospitality and professional service. The restaurant is at the centre of the operation, with good culinary skills apparent. Bedrooms are all spacious and well-equipped.
ROOMS: 20 en suite (bth/shr) 3 annexe en suite (bth/shr) s £59-£69; d £69-£79 (incl. cont bkfst) * LB Off peak **MEALS:** Lunch £12.50 & alc Dinner £15 & alc English & French Cuisine V meals **FACILITIES:** CTV in all bedrooms **CONF:** Thtr 14 Class 14 Board 14 Del from £105 * **SERVICES:** Lift Night porter 60P **NOTES:** No dogs (ex guide dogs) No coaches Last d 9.30pm Closed 26 Dec-5 Jan & 1 wk at Etr RS weekends (restricted meal service) **CARDS:**

BURY Greater Manchester
Map 07 SD81

★★★ *Bolholt Country Park*

Walshaw Rd BL8 1PU
Quality Percentage Score: 65%
☎ 0161 762 4000 📠 0161 762 4100
Dir: *from M66 take turn-off for Bury Town Centre and after 50yds fork right and at 4-lane filter system take right hand lanes and signpost for Walshaw*
Quietly situated but with easy access to the town centre, this former mill owner's house, set in 50 acres of parkland, has been extended to include modern comfortable bedrooms. Spacious public rooms include a choice of lounges and, separate from the hotel, there is a well equipped fitness and leisure centre. Service is friendly and attentive.
ROOMS: 66 en suite (bth/shr) (13 fmly) No smoking in 4 bedrooms **MEALS:** V meals Coffee am Tea pm **FACILITIES:** CTV in all bedrooms STV Indoor swimming pool (heated) Fishing Sauna Solarium Gym Pool table Jacuzzi/spa Fitness & leisure centre Wkly live entertainment **CONF:** Thtr 300 Class 120 Board 40 Del from £90 * **SERVICES:** Night porter 300P **NOTES:** No smoking in restaurant Last d 9.30pm
CARDS:

BURY ST EDMUNDS Suffolk
Map 05 TL86

★★★ *Angel*

Angel Hill IP33 1LT
Quality Percentage Score: 71%
☎ 01284 753926 📠 01284 750092
Dir: *from A134 turn left at rdbt into Northgate St, straight on to T jnct with traffic lights right into Mustow St left onto Angel Hill on right*
Dating back to the 15th century and with such famous past guests as Charles Dickens, the hotel is steeped in history. There is formal dining in the Abbeygate restaurant (where a vivid Eastern colonial feel complements original Georgian features) or lighter meals in the brasserie-styled 12th-century Vaults. Open plan lounge and reception areas and the Pickwick Bar offer comfy seating. Bedrooms vary in size and space, four-poster suites are especially recommended.
ROOMS: 42 en suite (bth/shr) (4 fmly) No smoking in 6 bedrooms **MEALS:** English & French Cuisine V meals Coffee am Tea pm **FACILITIES:** CTV in all bedrooms STV Wkly live entertainment **CONF:** Thtr 160 Class 30 Board 40 **SERVICES:** Night porter 62P **NOTES:** No smoking in restaurant Last d 9.30pm
CARDS:

BURY ST EDMUNDS Suffolk
Map 05 TL86

★★★ Ravenwood Hall

Rougham IP30 9JA
Quality Percentage Score: 69%
☎ 01359 270345 📠 01359 270788
Dir: *3m E off A14*
Personally run, this interesting hotel displays many reminders of its Tudor origins. Combining modern convenience with natural charm, the individually styled bedrooms have been tastefully decorated. Some are in the main house and some in the converted stable mews. The attractive restaurant offers formal dining.
ROOMS: 7 en suite (bth) 7 annexe en suite (bth) No smoking in all bedrooms s £67-£89; d £87-£121 (incl. bkfst) * LB Off peak **MEALS:** Lunch £18.95 & alc High tea £8.95 Dinner £18.95 & alc V meals Coffee am Tea pm **FACILITIES:** CTV in all bedrooms Outdoor swimming pool (heated) Tennis (hard) Riding Croquet lawn Shooting & fishing parties Free membership of local healthclub Xmas **CONF:** Thtr 200 Class 80 Board 40 **SERVICES:** 150P **NOTES:** No smoking in restaurant Last d 9.30pm **CARDS:**

BURY ST EDMUNDS Suffolk
Map 05 TL86

★★★ The Priory

Tollgate IP32 6EH
Quality Percentage Score: 68%
☎ 01284 766181 📠 01284 767604
Dir: *off A1101 towards Mildenhall*
This delightful hotel is popular with business and leisure guests, who appreciate the country house feel. There is a range of spacious public rooms, including two restaurant areas, a conservatory and dining room in the main house and a bustling bar. The attractive mature grounds are well kept. The generally spacious accommodation is split between the main house and the garden wings; some of the bedrooms have been smartly

contd.

refurbished making good use of Laura Ashley fabrics. An ambitious wide-ranging selection of appealing dishes is offered on carte and set price supper menus in the restaurant.

ROOMS: 9 en suite (bth/shr) 18 annexe en suite (bth/shr) (3 fmly) No smoking in 14 bedrooms s £67-£102; d £91-£116 (incl. bkfst) * LB Off peak **MEALS:** Lunch £16 & alc Dinner £22 & alc English & French Cuisine V meals Coffee am Tea pm **FACILITIES:** CTV in all bedrooms Xmas **CONF:** Thtr 40 Class 20 Board 20 Del from £102 * **SERVICES:** 60P **NOTES:** No smoking area in restaurant Last d 10pm Closed 27 Dec-3 Jan RS Sat & Sun **CARDS:**

See advert on this page

BURY ST EDMUNDS Suffolk — Map 05 TL86

★★★ Butterfly

Moreton Hall IP32 7BW

Quality Percentage Score: 65%

☎ 01284 760884 Fax 01284 755476

Dir: *from A14 take Bury East exit and at rndbt take exit for Moreton Hall. Left at next rndbt*

On the town's outskirts the Butterfly offers comfortable bedrooms, especially well laid out for business travellers - ground floor, studio, 'lady' and rooms suitable for the disabled are available. Walt's Restaurant and Bar, offers a comprehensive carte and daily-changing menus, in addition to room and lounge service selections.

ROOMS: 65 en suite (bth/shr) (2 fmly) No smoking in 10 bedrooms d £67.50 * LB Off peak **MEALS:** Lunch fr £7 & alc Dinner fr £18 & alc European & Oriental Cuisine V meals Coffee am Tea pm **FACILITIES:** CTV in all bedrooms **CONF:** Thtr 40 Class 21 Board 22 Del from £95 * **SERVICES:** Night porter 85P **NOTES:** No dogs (ex guide dogs) No smoking area in restaurant Last d 10pm **CARDS:**

BUTTERMERE Cumbria — Map 11 NY11

★★ *Bridge*

CA13 9UZ

Quality Percentage Score: 70%

☎ 017687 70252 Fax 017687 70215

This long-established family-run hotel lies by a stream in the centre of the village in the beautiful Buttermere Valley. Bar meals and real ales can be enjoyed in the traditional beamed bar, and there is also a separate restaurant. Afternoon tea is served to residents in the lounge. There are no televisions in the bedrooms, but all have stunning views and some have balconies.

ROOMS: 22 en suite (bth/shr) No smoking in 10 bedrooms

MEALS: English & French Cuisine V meals Coffee am Tea pm

FACILITIES: **CONF:** Class 30 Board 30 **SERVICES:** 60P **NOTES:** No coaches No smoking in restaurant Last d 8.30pm **CARDS:**

BUXTON Derbyshire — Map 07 SK07

★★★ Best Western Lee Wood

The Park SK17 6TQ

Quality Percentage Score: 74%

☎ 01298 23002 Fax 01298 23228

Dir: *NE on A5004, 300mtrs beyond the Devonshire Royal Hospital*

This elegant Georgian hotel offers high standards of comfort and hospitality. Individually furnished bedrooms are generally spacious, with all the expected modern conveniences. There is a choice of two bars, two comfortable lounges and a conservatory restaurant.

ROOMS: 35 en suite (bth/shr) 2 annexe en suite (bth/shr) (4 fmly) No smoking in 14 bedrooms s £74-£78; d £80-£85 * LB Off peak **MEALS:** Lunch £13.50-£16.50 Dinner £23.50-£25.75 & alc English & French Cuisine V meals Coffee am Tea pm **FACILITIES:** CTV in all bedrooms Xmas **CONF:** Thtr 120 Class 65 Board 40 Del from £95 * **SERVICES:** Lift Night porter 50P **NOTES:** No smoking area in restaurant Last d 9.30pm **CARDS:**

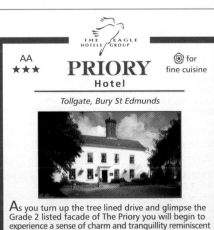

B

BUXTON Derbyshire **Map 07 SK07**

★★★ Buckingham Hotel

1 Burlington Rd SK17 9AS

Quality Percentage Score: 64%

☎ 01298 70481 01298 72186

Dir: *on A53 overlooking the Pavilion Gardens*

One of Buxton's most welcoming hotels, the Buckingham sports pleasantly modern public areas which include Ramsay's Bar, serving bar meals and real ales, and the popular carvery also serving grills and other dishes. Bedrooms are spacious and comfortable, many overlook the Pavilion Gardens.

ROOMS: 30 en suite (bth/shr) (4 fmly) No smoking in 20 bedrooms s £45-£65; d £60-£80 (incl. bkfst) * LB Off peak **MEALS:** Lunch fr £8.95 International Cuisine V meals Coffee am Tea pm **FACILITIES:** CTV in all bedrooms STV Xmas **CONF:** Thtr 40 Class 20 Board 16 **SERVICES:** Lift 20P **NOTES:** No coaches No smoking in restaurant **CARDS:**

BUXTON Derbyshire **Map 07 SK07**

★★ *Hartington*

18 Broad Walk SK17 6JR

Quality Percentage Score: 64%

☎ 01298 22638 01298 22638

This welcoming hotel is in an ideal position opposite the lake and gardens, a short walk from Buxton town centre. Bedrooms are attractively furnished, and the lounge is a comfortable area in which to relax. Good home cooking is provided, service is both friendly and attentive.

ROOMS: 17 rms (3 bth 4 shr) (3 fmly) No smoking in 2 bedrooms **MEALS: FACILITIES:** CTV in all bedrooms **SERVICES:** 15P **NOTES:** No dogs (ex guide dogs) Last d 8pm Closed 17 Dec-4 Jan RS Nov-Mar **CARDS:**

BUXTON Derbyshire **Map 07 SK07**

★★ Portland Hotel & Park Restaurant

32 St John's Rd SK17 6XQ

Quality Percentage Score: 62%

☎ 01298 71493 01298 27464

Dir: *on A53 opposite the Pavilion and Gardens*

This popular hotel is situated near the famous Opera House. Lounge and bar provide comfortable and relaxing areas, and the Park Restaurant, housed in the conservatory, specialises in traditional English dishes.

ROOMS: 22 en suite (bth/shr) (3 fmly) No smoking in 3 bedrooms s £48-£58; d £68-£75 (incl. bkfst) * LB Off peak **MEALS:** V meals Coffee am Tea pm **FACILITIES:** CTV in all bedrooms STV Xmas **CONF:** Thtr 50 Class 30 Board 25 **SERVICES:** 18P **NOTES:** No smoking in restaurant Last d 9.30pm **CARDS:**

CADNAM Hampshire **Map 04 SU21**

★★★❀❀ Bartley Lodge

Lyndhurst Rd SO40 2NR

Quality Percentage Score: 69%

☎ 023 80812248 023 80812075

Dir: *leave M27 junct 1, at 1st rndbt take 1st exit at 2nd rndbt take 3rd exit onto A337. On joining this road hotel sign is on left*

An 18th-century former hunting lodge, with a grand entrance hall, cosy bar, and indoor pool with sauna and fitness suite. Bedrooms vary in size, and all are quiet, comfortable and well equipped. Excellent use is made of local produce in the restaurant, and staff are friendly.

ROOMS: 31 en suite (bth/shr) (14 fmly) s fr £70; d fr £125 (incl. bkfst) * LB Off peak **MEALS:** Sunday Lunch fr £10.95 Dinner £21.50 V meals Coffee am Tea pm **FACILITIES:** CTV in all bedrooms Indoor swimming pool (heated) Tennis (hard) Sauna Gym Croquet lawn ch fac Xmas **CONF:** Thtr 60 Class 40 Board 40 Del from £90 * **SERVICES:** 60P **NOTES:** No smoking in restaurant Last d 8.45pm **CARDS:**

★

The Premier Collection, hotels with Red Star Awards are listed on pages 17-23

CALNE Wiltshire **Map 03 ST97**

★★ Lansdowne Strand

The Strand SN11 0EH

Quality Percentage Score: 68%

☎ 01249 812488 01249 815323

Dir: *on A4*

This 16th century former coaching inn retains much of its original charm. Mr and Mrs Calleya continue to upgrade and improve the property and provide a good standard of accommodation. The recently refurbished lounge area and restaurant are comfortable, and there is a wood panelled 'pub' offering a selection of real ales. Bedrooms, which include a four poster, are individually decorated and well equipped with such additional amenities as clock radio, remote TV, trouser press and hair dryer.

ROOMS: 21 en suite (bth/shr) 5 annexe en suite (bth/shr) (3 fmly) No smoking in 4 bedrooms s £59-£62; d £78-£80 (incl. bkfst) * LB Off peak **MEALS:** Lunch £7.95-£15.50 & alc High tea £5.60-£7.50 Dinner fr £15.50 & alc English & French Cuisine V meals Coffee am Tea pm **FACILITIES:** CTV in all bedrooms Xmas **CONF:** Thtr 90 Class 28 Board 30 Del from £85 * **SERVICES:** 21P **NOTES:** Last d 9.30pm **CARDS:**

CAMBERLEY Surrey **Map 04 SU86**

★★★ Frimley Hall

Portsmouth Rd GU15 2BG

Quality Percentage Score: 69%

☎ 01276 28321 01276 691253

Peacefully situated at the end of a residential road, this handsome Victorian manor lies two acres of grounds. Public rooms comprise the elegant Wellington restaurant and comfortable lounge, together with the smaller, beamed Sandhurst bar. Wood panels and stained glass add to the style of the grand staircase, and wide corridors lead to the original bedrooms which retain fine features. Other more modern rooms are freshly decorated in smart fashionable fabrics and offer good facilities.

ROOMS: 86 en suite (bth/shr) (20 fmly) No smoking in 25 bedrooms d fr £150 LB Off peak **MEALS:** Lunch £13-£25 & alc Dinner £13.95-£28 & alc European Cuisine V meals Coffee am Tea pm **FACILITIES:** CTV in all bedrooms Croquet lawn Putting green Wkly live entertainment **CONF:** Thtr 60 Class 30 Board 40 Del from £154 * **SERVICES:** Night porter 100P **NOTES:** Last d 10pm **CARDS:**

CAMBERLEY Surrey **Map 04 SU86**

★★★ Lakeside International

Wharf Rd, Frimley Green GU16 6JR

Quality Percentage Score: 64%

☎ 01252 838000 & 838808 01252 837857

Dir: *off A321*

The Lakeside International is chiefly geared to conferences and the corporate market, offering well equipped facilities. The overall complex includes a renowned night club and a health and fitness club. Bedrooms are furnished and equipped to a

contd.

similarly good standard, the best with balcony and lakeside views.
ROOMS: 98 en suite (bth/shr) (1 fmly) No smoking in 18 bedrooms s fr £105; d fr £120 (incl. bkfst) * Off peak **MEALS:** Lunch £10.95-£16.50 Dinner fr £16.50 English & French Cuisine V meals Coffee am Tea pm **FACILITIES:** CTV in all bedrooms STV Indoor swimming pool (heated) Squash Snooker Sauna Solarium Gym Pool table Jacuzzi/spa Xmas **CONF:** Thtr 100 Class 100 Board 36 Del £165 * **SERVICES:** Lift Night porter 250P **NOTES:** No dogs (ex guide dogs) No smoking in restaurant Last d 10.30pm **CARDS:**

CAMBERLEY Surrey — Map 04 SU86
Travel Inn
221 Yorktown Rd, College Town GU47 0RT
☎ 01252 878181 📠 01252 890648
***Dir:** at junct of Yorktown Rd & Rackstraw Rd, close to M3 junct 4*
This modern building offers accommodation in smart, spacious and well equipped bedrooms, all with en-suite bathrooms. Refreshments may be taken at the nearby family restaurant. For details about current prices consult the Contents Page under Hotel Groups for the Travel Inn phone number.
ROOMS: 40 en suite (bth/shr) d £39.95 *

CAMBORNE Cornwall & Isles of Scilly — Map 02 SW64
★★★ Tyacks
27 Commercial St TR14 8LD
Quality Percentage Score: 68%
☎ 01209 612424 📠 01209 612435
***Dir:** town centre opposite town clock*
This 18th-century former coaching inn has a large secure car park. The spacious, well furnished public areas include a smart lounge and bar, a popular public bar and a well appointed restaurant serving fixed price and carte menus. The comfortable bedrooms are attractively decorated, with modern facilities.
ROOMS: 15 en suite (bth/shr) (2 fmly) No smoking in 3 bedrooms s fr £45; d fr £75 (incl. bkfst) * LB Off peak **MEALS:** Lunch £8.95-£11.95 & alc Dinner £11.95 & alc English & Continental Cuisine V meals Coffee am **FACILITIES:** CTV in all bedrooms STV Pool table Wkly live entertainment **SERVICES:** 28P **NOTES:** Last d 9.30pm
CARDS:

CAMBRIDGE Cambridgeshire — Map 05 TL45
★★★★ Cambridge Garden House Moat House
Granta Place, Mill Ln CB2 1RT
Quality Percentage Score: 65%
☎ 01223 259988 📠 01223 316605
***Dir:** leave M11 junct 11 onto A1309 follow road into Cambridge. Take left turn into Mill Lane, hotel is at the bottom of Mill Lane*
This purpose-built hotel has a peaceful setting in its own grounds overlooking the river Cam. Bedrooms, some with views over the river, are well equipped with modern amenities, and many have been smartly refurbished. Public areas cater equally well to leisure, corporate and conference users; facilities include a stylish new restaurant and a well-equipped leisure club.
ROOMS: 117 en suite (bth/shr) (4 fmly) No smoking in 82 bedrooms s £130-£210; d £160-£240 * LB Off peak **MEALS:** Lunch £12.95-£18.95 & alc Dinner £8.75-£25alc Modern European Cuisine V meals Coffee am Tea pm **FACILITIES:** CTV in all bedrooms STV Indoor swimming pool (heated) Fishing Sauna Solarium Gym Jacuzzi/spa Punting Beauty salon Steam room Wkly live entertainment Xmas **CONF:** Thtr 250 Class 100 Board 30 Del from £150 * **SERVICES:** Lift Night porter 150P
NOTES: No dogs (ex guide dogs) No smoking in restaurant Last d 10pm
CARDS:

CAMBRIDGE Cambridgeshire — Map 05 TL45
★★★★ University Arms
Regent St CB2 1AD
Quality Percentage Score: 65%
☎ 01223 351241 📠 01223 461319
With a 160-year heritage and imposing position on the edge of Parker's Piece in the heart of the city, this striking Victorian style building embodies much of the traditional elegance of Cambridge. Public areas include the quaintly-domed lounge, ideal for afternoon tea, and a small brasserie at the front of the hotel. Bedrooms, which vary in size and outlook, have recently been totally refurbished, as had the rest of the hotel.
ROOMS: 115 en suite (bth/shr) (5 fmly) No smoking in 38 bedrooms s £118; d £135-£150 (incl. bkfst) * LB Off peak **MEALS:** Lunch fr £10.95 Dinner £21.50-£23.50 English & French Cuisine V meals Coffee am Tea pm **FACILITIES:** CTV in all bedrooms STV Xmas **CONF:** Thtr 350 Class 100 Board 60 Del from £155 * **SERVICES:** Lift Night porter 100P
NOTES: No smoking in restaurant Last d 9.30pm
CARDS:

CAMBRIDGE Cambridgeshire — Map 05 TL45
★★★ Gonville
Gonville Place CB1 1LY
Quality Percentage Score: 70%
☎ 01223 366611 & 221111 📠 01223 315470
***Dir:** leave M11 jct 11 on A1309 follow signs to city centre, at 2nd mini rdbt turn right into Lensfield road, straight over jct with traffic lights*
Situated on the south-eastern edge of the inner ring road, this hotel is only a leisurely walk away across the green to the city centre. Well established, with loyal regular guests and very experienced staff, the Gonville is popular for its relaxing, informal atmosphere. The recently redecorated, air-conditioned public areas are cheerfully furnished, and bedrooms are well appointed and appealing.
ROOMS: 64 en suite (bth/shr) (1 fmly) No smoking in 12 bedrooms s fr £86; d fr £99 * LB Off peak **MEALS:** Lunch fr £13.50 Dinner fr £17.95 English & French Cuisine V meals Coffee am Tea pm
FACILITIES: CTV in all bedrooms Arrangement with nearby gym & swimming pool Xmas **CONF:** Thtr 200 Class 100 Board 50 Del from £115.50 * **SERVICES:** Lift Night porter 80P **NOTES:** No smoking in restaurant Last d 8.45pm **CARDS:**

CAMBRIDGE Cambridgeshire — Map 05 TL45
★★★ Royal Cambridge
Trumpington St CB2 1PY
Quality Percentage Score: 70%
☎ 01223 351631 📠 01223 352972
***Dir:** leave M11 junct 11, follow signs for city centre. At 1st mini rdbt turn left into Fen Causeway, then first right for hotel*

This attractive Georgian townhouse sits on the south western edge of the city centre. Recently smartly upgraded, it offers a wide range of comfortable bedrooms, which are well equipped

contd.

and pleasingly decorated. Relaxing public rooms are intimate, and include an elegant spilt-level restaurant serving modern British cuisine; bar snacks and hot room service meals are also available. Friendly staff are helpful and attentive.
ROOMS: 49 en suite (bth/shr) (8 fmly) No smoking in 28 bedrooms s £88-£104; d £108.50-£114 (incl. bkfst) * LB Off peak **MEALS:** Bar Lunch £3.95-£12 High tea £3.95-£12 Dinner £3.95-£15.95 English & French Cuisine V meals Coffee am Tea pm **FACILITIES:** CTV in all bedrooms STV **CONF:** Thtr 120 Class 40 Board 40 Del from £113.50 * **SERVICES:** Lift Night porter 80P **NOTES:** No smoking in restaurant Last d 10.30pm **CARDS:**

C

CAMBRIDGE Cambridgeshire — Map 05 TL45
★★★ Posthouse Cambridge
Posthouse

Lakeview, Bridge Rd, Impington CB4 9PH
Quality Percentage Score: 68%
☎ 01223 237000 Fax 01223 233426
***Dir:** 2.5m N,on N side of rdbt jct A14/B1049*
Situated in a rural location at the junction of the A14 and B1049, this hotel is ideal for both business and leisure visitors. Bedrooms are spacious and well appointed and include new millennium rooms as well as those with traditional furnishings. There are also facilities for disabled guests. There is a well equipped health club as well as a secluded courtyard garden with a children's play area. The Junction restaurant offers a range of dishes.
ROOMS: 165 en suite (bth/shr) (14 fmly) No smoking in 105 bedrooms d £99-£119 * LB Off peak **MEALS:** International Cuisine V meals Coffee am Tea pm **FACILITIES:** CTV in all bedrooms Indoor swimming pool (heated) Sauna Gym Jacuzzi/spa Xmas **CONF:** Thtr 60 Class 30 Board 30 Del from £140 * **SERVICES:** Night porter 200P **NOTES:** No smoking area in restaurant Last d 11pm RS 24-27 Dec & 31 Dec
CARDS:

CAMBRIDGE Cambridgeshire — Map 05 TL45
★★★ *Cambridgeshire Moat House*
MOAT HOUSE

CB3 8EU
Quality Percentage Score: 66%
☎ 01954 249988 Fax 01954 780010
(For full entry see Bar Hill)

CAMBRIDGE Cambridgeshire — Map 05 TL45
★★ Arundel House
Chesterton Rd CB4 3AN
Quality Percentage Score: 70%
☎ 01223 367701 Fax 01223 367721
***Dir:** on A1303, overlooking the River Cam*
This popular hotel enjoys an enviable position next to the River Cam with views over nearby parkland. The smart public areas on the lower ground floor comprise a conservatory-brasserie for informal snacks, a spacious bar, and an elegant restaurant for serious dining. The bedrooms are attractive, and have a special character as the hotel was originally a row of Victorian terraced townhouses.
ROOMS: 83 rms (80 bth/shr) 22 annexe en suite (bth/shr) (6 fmly) No smoking in 77 bedrooms s £47-£69; d £69-£94 (incl. cont bkfst) * LB Off peak **MEALS:** Lunch £10.75-£12.95 & alc Dinner £13.50-£15.95 & alc International Cuisine V meals Coffee am Tea pm **FACILITIES:** CTV in all bedrooms **CONF:** Thtr 50 Class 34 Board 32 **SERVICES:** Night porter 70P **NOTES:** No dogs No smoking in restaurant Last d 9.30pm Closed 25-26 Dec **CARDS:**

Some hotel groups have a central reservations telephone number, see pages 35, 37 and 38 for details.

CAMBRIDGE Cambridgeshire — Map 05 TL45
★★ Centennial
63-71 Hills Rd CB2 1PG
Quality Percentage Score: 68%
☎ 01223 314652 Fax 01223 315443
***Dir:** from M11 junct 11 take A1309 to Cambridge. Turn right onto Brooklands Av at the end of Av turn left hotel in 100yds on right*
Close to the town centre, but easily accessed by the ring road, this pleasant hotel offers a relaxing bar, welcoming lounge and a friendly restaurant. The bedrooms are well maintained and equipped, including several easy-access rooms on the ground floor.
ROOMS: 39 en suite (bth/shr) (1 fmly) No smoking in 20 bedrooms s fr £69; d fr £85 (incl. bkfst) * LB Off peak **MEALS:** English & French Cuisine V meals Coffee am Tea pm **FACILITIES:** CTV in all bedrooms **CONF:** Thtr 35 Class 26 Board 26 **SERVICES:** Night porter 30P **NOTES:** No dogs Closed 23 Dec-1 Jan
CARDS:

See advert on opposite page

CAMBRIDGE Cambridgeshire — Map 05 TL45
Travelodge
Travelodge

Fourwentways
☎ 01223 839479
***Dir:** adjacent to Little Chef at junct A11/A1307, 5m S of Cambridge*
This modern building offers accommodation in smart, spacious and well equipped bedrooms, all with en-suite bathrooms. Refreshments may be taken at the nearby family restaurant. For details about current prices, consult the Contents Page under Hotel Groups for the Travelodge phone number.
ROOMS: 32 en suite (bth/shr) (incl. bkfst) d £49.95 *

CANNOCK Staffordshire — Map 07 SJ91
★★★ Roman Way
REGAL

Watling St, Hatherton WS11 1SH
Quality Percentage Score: 63%
☎ 01543 572121 Fax 01543 502749
***Dir:** M6 junct 11 towards Cannock (A460), at rdbt take A5 to Telford, hotel 100yds on left. Or M6 junct 12, then A5 towards Cannock, hotel 2m on right*

Named after the Roman road on which it is situated, this modern hotel provides a good standard of accommodation and is in a convenient location close to the M6. Doric columns and marble floors are a feature of the reception area and Nero's Restaurant and Gilpins Lounge provide formal or informal eating options.
ROOMS: 56 en suite (bth/shr) (7 fmly) No smoking in 23 bedrooms **MEALS:** Sunday Lunch £9.25 High tea £5.95 Dinner £17.95 & alc V meals Coffee am Tea pm **FACILITIES:** CTV in all bedrooms STV Wkly live entertainment **CONF:** Thtr 150 Class 100 Board 50 **SERVICES:** Night porter 150P **NOTES:** No smoking in restaurant Last d 9.45pm
CARDS:

CANNOCK Staffordshire — Map 07 SJ91

Travel Inn

Watling St WS11 1SJ

☎ 01543 572721 Fax 01543 466130

Dir: *on the rdbt at junct of A5/A460, 2m from junct 11/junct 12 of the M6*

This modern building offers accommodation in smart, spacious and well equipped bedrooms, all with en-suite bathrooms. Refreshments may be taken at the nearby family restaurant. For details about current prices consult the Contents Page under Hotel Groups for the Travel Inn phone number.

ROOMS: 38 en suite (bth/shr) d £39.95 *

CANTERBURY Kent — Map 05 TR15

★★★ Falstaff

St Dunstans St, Westgate CT2 8AF

Quality Percentage Score: 67%

☎ 01227 462138 Fax 01227 463525

Dir: *turn into St Peters Place off the A2, pass Westgate Towers into St Dunstans St, hotel on right*

Many original features testify to the 16th-century origins of this historic old coaching inn. It stands next to the Westgate Tower, offers easy access to the city centre and motorway network, as

contd.

Remember to return your Prize Draw card for a chance to win one of 30 relaxing leisure breaks with Corus and Regal hotels. See inside the front cover for the card and competition details.

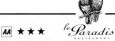

well as the benefit of its own carpark. Bedrooms vary in size and all have very smart bathrooms.

Falstaff, Kent

ROOMS: 32 en suite (bth/shr) (2 fmly) No smoking in 23 bedrooms s £75-£85; d £85-£95 * LB Off peak **MEALS:** Lunch £12.95-£14.95 & alc High tea £5.95 Dinner £14.95 & alc English & French Cuisine V meals Coffee am Tea pm **FACILITIES:** CTV in all bedrooms STV Xmas **SERVICES:** Night porter 41P **NOTES:** No smoking in restaurant Last d 9.45pm **CARDS:**

See advert on page 173

CANTERBURY Kent **Map 05 TR15**

★★★ The Chaucer

Ivy Ln CT1 1TU
Quality Percentage Score: 60%
☎ 01227 464427 📠 01227 450397

Dir: *approaching city on A2, follow signs for Dover. Turn right at first rdbt, then 1st left*

Conveniently located within easy walking distance of the city centre, this former Georgian residence has comfortably furnished bedrooms which vary slightly in style. The lounge and bar area has an old-fashioned charm and the restaurant is smartly furnished.

ROOMS: 42 en suite (bth/shr) (5 fmly) No smoking in 19 bedrooms d £95-£140 * LB Off peak **MEALS:** Lunch £9.95-£12.95 High tea £4 Dinner £14.95-£18 V meals Coffee am Tea pm **FACILITIES:** CTV in all bedrooms Xmas **CONF:** Thtr 120 Class 45 Board 45 Del from £99 * **SERVICES:** Night porter **NOTES:** No smoking in restaurant Last d 9.30pm **CARDS:**

CANTERBURY Kent **Map 05 TR15**

★★ *Ebury*

65/67 New Dover Rd CT1 3DX
Quality Percentage Score: 75%
☎ 01227 768433 📠 01227 459187

Dir: *follow A2, take Canterbury turn off, then ring road around Canterbury follow Dover signs at 5th rdbt signs to Dover in 1m on left is Ebury House*

A delightful family-run hotel in two acres of pretty gardens. Bedrooms are attractively furnished and well equipped. Public areas include a spacious restaurant, with an interesting menu of skilfully prepared dishes. Room service is available, including continental breakfast.

ROOMS: 15 en suite (bth/shr) (2 fmly) **MEALS:** International Cuisine V meals Coffee am Tea pm **FACILITIES:** CTV in all bedrooms Indoor swimming pool (heated) Jacuzzi/spa Exercise equipment **SERVICES:** 30P **NOTES:** No coaches No smoking in restaurant Last d 8.30pm Closed 19 Dec-11 Jan **CARDS:**

CANTERBURY Kent **Map 05 TR15**

★★❀❀ Canterbury

71 New Dover Rd CT1 3DZ
Quality Percentage Score: 68%
☎ 01227 450551 📠 01227 780145

Dir: *on A2, Dover road*

A Georgian style hotel close to the city centre. Bedrooms, standard and superior, are spacious, comfortable and well equipped. Public areas are attractively furnished with a reception/ bar, and a separate TV lounge which can be used for private meetings. The bright attractive restaurant has a continental feel, with French staff and an excellent French menu.

ROOMS: 23 en suite (bth/shr) (1 fmly) s £45-£65; d £65-£80 (incl. bkfst) * LB Off peak **MEALS:** Lunch £15.95-£17.95 & alc Dinner £15.95-£17.95 & alc French Cuisine V meals Coffee am **FACILITIES:** CTV in all bedrooms STV **CONF:** Thtr 25 Board 12 Del from £70 * **SERVICES:** Lift Night porter 50P **NOTES:** No smoking in restaurant Last d 9.45pm **CARDS:**

CANTERBURY Kent **Map 05 TR15**

★★ Victoria

59 London Rd CT2 8JY
Quality Percentage Score: 66%
☎ 01227 459333 📠 01227 781552

Dir: *accessible via main London/Dover M2/A2 onto main A2052, hotel on left off the 1st rdbt*

Situated 15 minutes' walk from the city centre, The Victoria is well suited to the needs of both the business and leisure guest. Attractively decorated bedrooms vary in size and comfort, but all are well maintained and have excellent facilities. The public areas include a bustling bar with satellite TV, and a restaurant where guests can choose to eat from a short menu or the carvery. Staff are friendly and willing.

ROOMS: 34 en suite (bth/shr) (12 fmly) No smoking in 4 bedrooms s £42-£52; d £52-£75 * LB Off peak **MEALS:** Lunch £6.45-£11.45 Dinner £6.45-£11.45 V meals Coffee am Tea pm **FACILITIES:** CTV in all bedrooms **CONF:** Thtr 20 Class 20 Board 20 Del from £68 * **SERVICES:** 70P **NOTES:** No dogs (ex guide dogs) No smoking area in restaurant Last d 9.15pm **CARDS:**

CANTERBURY Kent **Map 05 TR15**

★★ Pointers Hotel

1 London Rd CT2 8LR
Quality Percentage Score: 65%
☎ 01227 456846 📠 01227 452786

Dir: *Canterbury exit off A2, follow signposts for university & Whitstable. Opposite St Dunstans Church*

This small family run hotel is centrally located in historic Canterbury and is an ideal base for visiting the cathedral. Rooms are compact but comfortable and dinners are freshly prepared from quality raw ingredients.

ROOMS: 12 en suite (bth/shr) (3 fmly) s £45-£60; d £55-£70 (incl. bkfst) * LB Off peak **MEALS:** Dinner fr £14.50 Coffee am **FACILITIES:** CTV in all bedrooms **SERVICES:** Night porter 10P **NOTES:** No coaches Last d 8pm Closed 3-20 Jan **CARDS:**

See advert on opposite page

CANTERBURY Kent **Map 05 TR15**

⌂ Travelodge

A2 Gate Services, Dunkirk ME13 9LN
☎ 01227 752781 📠 01227 752781

Dir: *5m W on A2 northbound*

This modern building offers accommodation in smart, spacious and well equipped bedrooms, all with en-suite bathrooms. Refreshments may be taken at the nearby family restaurant. For details about current

contd.

prices, consult the Contents Page under Hotel Groups for the Travelodge phone number.
ROOMS: 40 en suite (bth/shr) d £45.95 *

CARBIS BAY See **St Ives** **Map 02 SW53**

CARCROFT South Yorkshire **Map 08 SE50**
Travelodge
Great North Rd DN6 9LF
☎ 01302 330841 01302 330841
Dir: *on A1 northbound*
This modern building offers accommodation in smart, spacious and well equipped bedrooms, all with en-suite bathrooms. Refreshments may be taken at the nearby family restaurant. For details about current prices, consult the Contents Page under Hotel Groups for the Travelodge phone number.
ROOMS: 40 en suite (bth/shr) d £39.95 *

CARLISLE Cumbria **Map 11 NY45**
see also **Brampton**
★★★ **Crosby Lodge Country House**
High Crosby, Crosby-on-Eden CA6 4QZ
Quality Percentage Score: 76%
☎ 01228 573618 01228 573428
Dir: *leave M6 at junc 44, 3.5m from motorway off A689*
An Aladdin's Cave of antiques and period furnishings, this hotel offers a relaxing atmosphere, with elegant and efficient service. Freshly-made food and delicious home baking are popular features. The opulent bedrooms are all individual, and provide thoughtful little touches; two are in a tastefully converted stable block.
ROOMS: 9 en suite (bth/shr) 2 annexe en suite (bth/shr) (3 fmly) s £80-£85; d £105-£140 (incl. bkfst) * LB Off peak **MEALS:** Lunch £17-£20 & alc Dinner £30-£35 & alc English & French Cuisine V meals Coffee am **FACILITIES:** CTV in all bedrooms **CONF:** Thtr 25 Board 12 **SERVICES:** 40P **NOTES:** No coaches No smoking in restaurant Last d 8.45pm Closed 24 Dec-20 Jan RS Sun evening (restaurant-residents only) **CARDS:**

CARLISLE Cumbria **Map 11 NY45**
★★★ **Crown**
Wetheral CA4 8ES
Quality Percentage Score: 70%
☎ 01228 561888 01228 561637
Situated in the charming village of Wetheral, this attractive 19th-century hotel attracts both business guests and holiday makers. It has two bars, one a cocktail bar, and one a traditional public bar serving bar snacks. Overlooking the gardens is a conservatory restaurant which serves well prepared dishes. There are good leisure and conference facilities.
ROOMS: 49 en suite (bth/shr) 2 annexe en suite (bth/shr) (3 fmly) No smoking in 10 bedrooms s fr £102; d fr £122 (incl. bkfst) * LB Off peak **MEALS:** Bar Lunch fr £5 Dinner fr £20 International Cuisine V meals Coffee am Tea pm **FACILITIES:** CTV in all bedrooms STV Indoor swimming pool (heated) Squash Sauna Solarium Gym Jacuzzi/spa Children's splash pool Steam room **CONF:** Thtr 175 Class 90 Board 50 Del from £88 * **SERVICES:** Night porter 80P **NOTES:** No smoking area in restaurant Last d 9.30pm Closed 31 Dec
CARDS:

★
The Premier Collection, hotels with Red Star Awards are listed on pages 17-23

C

CARLISLE Cumbria
Map 11 NY45

★★★ Posthouse Carlisle

Posthouse

Parkhouse Rd CA3 0HR
Quality Percentage Score: 68%
☎ 01228 531201 Fax 01228 543178

***Dir:** junc 44/M6 take A7 signposted Carlisle, hotel on right at first set of traffic lights*

Refurbishment of the bedrooms has considerably enhanced this modern hotel. There are several eating options including the popular Traders Bar and Grill and an all day lounge menu. The staff are friendly and helpful.

ROOMS: 127 en suite (bth/shr) (34 fmly) No smoking in 85 bedrooms d £59-£79 * LB Off peak **MEALS:** International Cuisine V meals Coffee am Tea pm **FACILITIES:** CTV in all bedrooms Indoor swimming pool (heated) Sauna Gym Pool table Jacuzzi/spa Xmas **CONF:** Thtr 120 Class 64 Board 60 Del from £85 * **SERVICES:** Night porter 150P **NOTES:** No smoking area in restaurant Last d 10pm
CARDS:

CARLISLE Cumbria
Map 11 NY45

★★★ Cumbria Park

Best Western

32 Scotland Rd, Stanwix CA3 9DG
Quality Percentage Score: 67%
☎ 01228 522887 Fax 01228 514796

***Dir:** 1.5m N on A7*

Distinguished by an impressive brick façade, this long established and friendly hotel is attractively furnished and offers relaxing lounge areas. There is a variety of bedroom styles and sizes, with some rooms offering antique four-poster beds.

ROOMS: 47 en suite (bth/shr) (3 fmly) No smoking in 13 bedrooms s fr £71; d £92.50-£122.50 (incl. bkfst) LB Off peak **MEALS:** Lunch fr £12.50 Dinner £12.95-£17.95 English & Italian Cuisine V meals Coffee am Tea pm **FACILITIES:** CTV in all bedrooms STV **CONF:** Thtr 190 Del from £105 * **SERVICES:** Lift Night porter 40P **NOTES:** No dogs (ex guide dogs) No smoking area in restaurant Last d 9.45pm Closed 25-26 Dec
CARDS:

CARLISLE Cumbria
Map 11 NY45

★★★ Swallow Hilltop

SWALLOW HOTELS

London Rd CA1 2PQ
Quality Percentage Score: 64%
☎ 01228 529255 Fax 01228 525238

***Dir:** from M6 junct 42 take A6 to Carlisle. In 1m hotel on left on hill*

Situated on the edge of the town, to the south, this hotel offers a variety of meeting rooms as well as well equipped leisure facilities. Most of the bedrooms have now been refurbished to a good standard, whilst spacious public rooms include a light and airy lounge bar leading into a restaurant that overlooks the surrounding area from the hotel's elevated position.

ROOMS: 92 en suite (bth/shr) (6 fmly) No smoking in 24 bedrooms s £75-£95; d £95-£105 (incl. bkfst) * LB Off peak **MEALS:** Lunch fr £9.50 Dinner fr £18.50 English & French Cuisine V meals Coffee am Tea pm **FACILITIES:** CTV in all bedrooms STV Indoor swimming pool (heated) Sauna Solarium Gym Pool table Jacuzzi/spa Massage Steam room Xmas **CONF:** Thtr 500 Class 250 Board 90 Del £105 * **SERVICES:** Lift Night porter 350P **NOTES:** No smoking area in restaurant Last d 9.30pm **CARDS:**

CARLISLE Cumbria
Map 11 NY45

★★★ Cumbrian

REGAL

Court Square CA1 1QY
Quality Percentage Score: 62%
☎ 01228 531951 Fax 01228 547799

***Dir:** leave M6 at junct43. Follow signs for city centre & railway station. The Hotel is adjacent to the railway station*

This well preserved Victorian hotel, next to the railway station, offers friendly service. The modern bedrooms are well equipped and comfortable, whilst the inviting public rooms include a restaurant as well as an attractive lounge bar. The hotel has good conference and function suites.

ROOMS: 70 en suite (bth/shr) (4 fmly) No smoking in 22 bedrooms s fr £71.50; d fr £98 (incl. bkfst) * LB Off peak **MEALS:** Bar Lunch £3.95-£5.25 High tea £6.50-£7.50 Dinner £9.95-£15.25 English & French Cuisine V meals Coffee am Tea pm **FACILITIES:** CTV in all bedrooms STV Xmas **CONF:** Thtr 300 Class 80 Board 60 Del from £80 * **SERVICES:** Lift Night porter 35P **NOTES:** No smoking in restaurant Last d 9pm **CARDS:**

CARLISLE Cumbria
Map 11 NY45

★★★ Central Plaza

Victoria Viaduct CA3 8AL
Quality Percentage Score: 60%
☎ 01228 520256 Fax 01228 514657

***Dir:** in city centre, just N of main BR station on A6*

Offering accommodation in a variety of styles, this grand example of Victorian architecture lies in the city centre close to the station. Good French and British cuisine is on offer in addition to weekly live entertainment.

ROOMS: 84 en suite (bth/shr) (3 fmly) No smoking in 5 bedrooms s £45-£59; d £55-£69 (incl. bkfst) * LB Off peak **MEALS:** Lunch £8.95-£12.19alc High tea £1-£3.25alc Dinner £9.95-£12.95alc English & French Cuisine V meals Coffee am Tea pm **FACILITIES:** CTV in all bedrooms STV Pool table Xmas **CONF:** Thtr 100 Class 70 Board 50 Del £75 * **SERVICES:** Lift Night porter 15P **NOTES:** No smoking area in restaurant Last d 9.30pm **CARDS:**

See advert on opposite page

Symbols and Abbreviations are listed and explained on pages 4 and 5

CARLISLE Cumbria **Map 11 NY45**

★★★ The Crown & Mitre

4 English St CA3 8HZ
Quality Percentage Score: 60%
☎ 01228 525491 Fax 01228 514553
Dir: *A6 into city centre, pass rly station on left then left past Woolworths. Sharp right into Blackfriars St. Hotel car park and rear entrance at end*
Thoughtful refurbishment is returning this imposing, town-centre Edwardian hotel to its former glory. The bedrooms are decorated to a very high standard and the public rooms, which have many original architectural features, provide a good range of facilities.
ROOMS: 74 en suite (bth/shr) 20 annexe en suite (bth/shr) (4 fmly) No smoking in 10 bedrooms s £84; d £109 (incl. bkfst) * LB Off peak **MEALS:** Bar Lunch £4.50-£5.45 Dinner fr £14.50 V meals Coffee am Tea pm **FACILITIES:** CTV in all bedrooms STV Indoor swimming pool (heated) Pool table Jacuzzi/spa Xmas **CONF:** Thtr 400 Class 250 Board 50 Del from £75 * **SERVICES:** Lift Night porter 42P **NOTES:** Last d 9.30pm **CARDS:**

CARLISLE Cumbria **Map 11 NY45**

★★ County

9 Botchergate CA1 1QP
Quality Percentage Score: 60%
☎ 01228 531316 Fax 01228 401805
Located just across from the railway station, this hotel caters mainly for tourists, but business clients will also appreciate the well equipped bedrooms. A choice of dining venues offer good value meals. There is a secure car park to the rear.
ROOMS: 84 en suite (bth/shr) (14 fmly) No smoking in 6 bedrooms s £49.95-£69.95; d £59.95-£69.95 * LB Off peak **MEALS:** Bar Lunch £4.25 Dinner £15.95 & alc International Cuisine V meals Coffee am Tea pm **FACILITIES:** CTV in all bedrooms Xmas **CONF:** Thtr 150 Class 75 Board 50 Del from £52 * **SERVICES:** Lift Night porter 45P **NOTES:** No smoking in restaurant Last d 10pm
CARDS:

See advert on this page

CARLISLE Cumbria **Map 11 NY45**

★★ *Pinegrove*

MINOTEL Great Britain

262 London Rd CA1 2QS
Quality Percentage Score: 60%
☎ 01228 524828 Fax 01228 810941
Dir: *on A6*
The Pinegrove is an extended late-Victorian mansion which lies on the south side of the city, predominantly serving a commercial and business clientele. Public rooms include a spacious restaurant and an attractive lounge bar; guests also have free access to a local leisure club. While bedroom styles and sizes vary, each is soundly appointed and the majority are en suite.
ROOMS: 27 rms (7 bth 19 shr) 18 annexe rms (8 bth 8 shr) (8 fmly) **MEALS:** English & French Cuisine V meals Coffee am **FACILITIES:** CTV in all bedrooms STV Pool table Darts **CONF:** Thtr 120 Class 100 Board 100 **SERVICES:** 50P **NOTES:** No smoking area in restaurant Last d 9pm Closed 25 Dec **CARDS:**

CARLISLE Cumbria **Map 11 NY45**

⇧ Travel Inn

travel inn

Warwick Rd
☎ 01228 545290 Fax 01228 545354
This modern building offers accommodation in smart, spacious and well equipped bedrooms, all with en-suite bathrooms. Refreshments may be taken at the nearby family restaurant. For details about current prices consult the Contents Page under Hotel Groups for the Travel Inn phone number.
ROOMS: 44 en suite (bth/shr) d £39.95 *

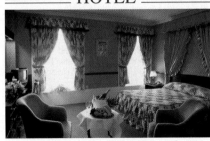

CARNFORTH Lancashire
Map 07 SD47

★ Royal Station
Market St LA5 9BT
Quality Percentage Score: 64%
☎ 01524 732033 & 733636 ▤ 01524 720267
Dir: *leave M6 junct 35 join A6 signed Carnforth & Morecambe, in 1m at x-rds in centre of Carnforth turn rt into Market St. Hotel opposite railway station*

Situated close to the railway station, this grand Victorian hotel provides modern and well equipped bedrooms. There are two atmospheric bars and a good range of food is served either in the bars or the cosy restaurant.

ROOMS: 12 en suite (bth/shr) (1 fmly) s fr £36; d fr £52 (incl. bkfst) * LB Off peak **MEALS:** Sunday Lunch £6.95 High tea £4.95-£6.95 Dinner £13.95-£22.95alc English & French Cuisine V meals Coffee am Tea pm **FACILITIES:** CTV in all bedrooms Pool table Xmas **CONF:** Thtr 150 Class 100 Board 100 Del from £48 * **SERVICES:** 8P **NOTES:** No dogs (ex guide dogs) No smoking in restaurant Last d 9.30pm
CARDS:

CARPERBY North Yorkshire
Map 07 SE08

★ Wheatsheaf
DL8 4DF
Quality Percentage Score: 59%
☎ 01969 663216 ▤ 01969 663019
Dir: *from A1 take west route on A684 to Wensley, turn right signposted Castle Bolton next village is Carperby*

The Wheatsheaf is a typical Dales inn, incidently where author James Herriot spent his honeymoon, that offers cosy and comfortable accommodation. The bedrooms are pleasantly furnished and two have four-poster beds. The lounge features a 17th-century stone fireplace, and guests can eat in either the cosy pub or the dining room.

ROOMS: 8 en suite (bth/shr) (1 fmly) s £26; d £50-£60 (incl. bkfst) * LB Off peak **MEALS:** Sunday Lunch £5.95 Dinner £11.45-£15alc V meals Coffee am Tea pm **FACILITIES:** CTV in all bedrooms Trout fishing can be arranged Xmas **SERVICES:** 42P **NOTES:** No coaches No smoking in restaurant Last d 9pm **CARDS:**

CARTMEL Cumbria
Map 07 SD37

★★ Aynsome Manor
LA11 6HH
Quality Percentage Score: 74%
☎ 015395 36653 ▤ 015395 36016
Dir: *from M6 junc36, follow A590 signed Barrow in Furness. Continue towards Cartmel turn left at end of dual carriageway, hotel just before village*

A lovely old manor house, which stands peacefully in its own well tended gardens on the edge of the village. Many guests return time and time again to enjoy the wonderful hospitality, good food, and relaxing atmosphere. Inviting public areas include a cosy bar, choice of lounges, and an elegant panelled restaurant, where you can enjoy the honest home-cooking which is carefully prepared and very rewarding. There is a choice of bedroom size and style.

ROOMS: 10 en suite (bth/shr) 2 annexe en suite (bth) (2 fmly) s £56-£65; d £98-£115 (incl. bkfst & dinner) * LB Off peak **MEALS:** Sunday Lunch £12-£12.75 Dinner £17-£22 V meals Coffee am **FACILITIES:** CTV in all bedrooms Xmas **SERVICES:** 20P **NOTES:** No coaches No smoking in restaurant Last d 8.30pm Closed 2 Jan-1 Feb
CARDS:

CASTLE ASHBY Northamptonshire
Map 04 SP85

★★ *Falcon*
NN7 1LF
Quality Percentage Score: 75%
☎ 01604 696200 ▤ 01604 696673
Dir: *opposite war memorial*

This hotel has two wings, each with its own character; bedrooms throughout are individually decorated and feature a wealth of extras and stylish bold furnishings and decor. Public rooms include a first-floor lounge area, a choice of bars and a separate restaurant with an interesting menu.

ROOMS: 6 rms (5 bth/shr) 11 annexe en suite (bth/shr) **MEALS:** English & French Cuisine V meals Coffee am Tea pm **FACILITIES:** CTV in all bedrooms STV **CONF:** Thtr 30 Class 30 Board 20 **SERVICES:** 75P **NOTES:** Last d 9.30pm **CARDS:**

CASTLE CARY Somerset
Map 03 ST63

★★ *The George*
Market Place BA7 7AH
Quality Percentage Score: 70%
☎ 01963 350761 ▤ 01963 350035
Dir: *from M5 junct 23 follow A39 to Shepton Mallet then A371 to Castle Cary. From A303 to Wincanton, then A371 to castle Cary*

A 15th-century hotel with a distinctive thatched roof and bay windows. Rooms are generally spacious, offering a good standard of accommodation and comfort. Guests eat in the formal dining room, with its imaginative range of dishes, or one of the two cosy bars. An attractive lounge is also available.

ROOMS: 14 en suite (bth/shr) (1 fmly) No smoking in 4 bedrooms **MEALS:** V meals Coffee am Tea pm **FACILITIES:** CTV in all bedrooms **SERVICES:** 10P **NOTES:** No dogs (ex guide dogs) No coaches No smoking in restaurant Last d 9.30pm **CARDS:**

CASTLE COMBE Wiltshire
Map 03 ST87

The Premier Collection

★★★★ Manor House
SN14 7HR
☎ 01249 782206 ▤ 01249 782159
Dir: *follow Chippenham signs from M4 junc17, onto A420 signed Bristol, then right onto B4039. Go through village, turn rt after crossing river bridge*

Set in 26 acres of grounds with a romantic Italian garden, this 14th-century country house has been sympathetically extended to provide superbly furnished rooms. Public areas include a number of small lounge areas, some with roaring fires during the cooler months. Bedrooms situated in a row of original stone cottages within the grounds are currently being upgraded to the same standard as those in the main house. Service is both professional and friendly, while the

contd.

meals prepared by chef Mark Taylor and his team continue to impress.
ROOMS: 21 en suite (bth/shr) 24 annexe en suite (bth/shr) (8 fmly) s £120-£350; d £120-£350 * LB Off peak **MEALS:** Lunch £16.95-£20 Dinner £35 & alc English & French Cuisine V meals Coffee am Tea pm **FACILITIES:** CTV in all bedrooms STV Outdoor swimming pool (heated) Golf 18 Tennis (hard) Fishing Snooker Sauna Pool table Croquet lawn Jogging track Xmas **CONF:** Thtr 60 Class 36 Board 36 Del from £170 * **SERVICES:** Night porter 100P **NOTES:** No dogs (ex guide dogs) No coaches No smoking in restaurant Last d 9.30pm **CARDS:**

CASTLE COMBE Wiltshire **Map 03 ST87**

★★★ Castle Inn

SN14 7HN
Quality Percentage Score: 67%
☎ 01249 783030 📠 01249 782315
Dir: *Take A420 to Chippenham follow signs for Castle Combe. Hotel is situated in the heart of the village*

Set in the market place of the historic and picturesque village of Castle Combe, this famous hostelry can trace its origins back to the 12th-century and many features of the original construction remain today. Bedrooms, many with old beams, are individually decorated; thoughtful extras include fruit, mineral water and bathrobes. Public areas are cosy and inviting, with the bar being the hub of activity. Interesting and honest fare is available in Oliver's Restaurant and more informal dining is on offer in the bar. Staff help to generate a friendly atmosphere here.
ROOMS: 11 en suite (bth/shr) s £67.50-£75; d £90-£115 (incl. bkfst) * LB Off peak **MEALS:** Bar Lunch £13-£19.50alc Dinner £13-£22.85alc V meals Coffee am Tea pm **FACILITIES:** CTV in all bedrooms STV N Xmas **CONF:** Board 30 **NOTES:** No dogs (ex guide dogs) No smoking in restaurant Last d 9.30pm **CARDS:**

CASTLE DONINGTON Leicestershire **Map 08 SK42**

see also **East Midlands Airport**

★★★ The Priest House on the River

Kings Mills DE74 2RR
Quality Percentage Score: 69%
☎ 01332 810649 📠 01332 811141
Dir: *M1 junct 23A towards airport, pass airport entrance, after 1.5m turn right into Castle Donnington. At 1st traffic lights turn left & follow road*

Peacefully located on a bend in the River Trent, the Priest House is mostly contemporary in style. Bedrooms are in converted cottages as well as the main building. A variety of imaginative modern British dishes are served in the Riverside restaurant.
ROOMS: 25 en suite (bth/shr) 20 annexe en suite (bth/shr) (1 fmly) s £90-£110; d £100-£175 * LB Off peak **MEALS:** Lunch £4-£16.50 Dinner £24.50-£28 & alc V meals Coffee am Tea pm **FACILITIES:** CTV in all bedrooms STV Fishing Archery Clay pigeon shooting Wkly live entertainment **CONF:** Thtr 140 Class 45 Board 36 Del from £150 * **SERVICES:** Night porter 150P **NOTES:** No smoking in restaurant Last d 4.30pm Closed 29 Dec-3 Jan
CARDS:

CASTLE DONINGTON Leicestershire **Map 08 SK42**

★★★ Donington Manor

High St DE74 2PP
Quality Percentage Score: 67%
☎ 01332 810253 📠 01332 850330
Dir: *1m into village on B5430 situated on left at traffic lights*

A graceful Georgian building just off the village centre offers high standards of hospitality and comfort. Many of the original architectural features have been preserved, particularly in the elegant dining room. Bedrooms are individually designed, and among the luxurious bathrooms is one formerly belonging to Elvis Presley.
ROOMS: 25 en suite (bth/shr) 1 annexe en suite (bth/shr) (1 fmly) s £66-£84; d £80-£100 (incl. bkfst) * LB Off peak **MEALS:** English & French Cuisine V meals Coffee am Tea pm **FACILITIES:** CTV in all bedrooms STV **CONF:** Thtr 80 Class 50 Board 20 **SERVICES:** Night porter 40P **NOTES:** No dogs (ex guide dogs) Last d 9.30pm Closed 24-30 Dec RS Sat **CARDS:**

CATTERICK BRIDGE North Yorkshire **Map 08 SE29**

★★ Bridge House

DL10 7PE
Quality Percentage Score: 63%
☎ 01748 818331 📠 01748 818331
Dir: *4m S of Scotch Corner, on bridge opp Catterick Racecourse*

Formerly a coaching inn, this commercial hotel sits by the River Swale close to the racecourse. The bedrooms vary in size, but all are well equipped and have benefited from recent refurbishment. A good range of freshly prepared meals is served in the bar or restaurant.
ROOMS: 15 en suite (bth/shr) (2 fmly) s £40-£45; d £60-£65 (incl. bkfst) * LB Off peak **MEALS:** Lunch £9.50 & alc Dinner £8.95-£15.95alc English & French Cuisine V meals Coffee am **FACILITIES:** CTV in all bedrooms STV Fishing Pool table **CONF:** Thtr 100 Class 50 Board 40 Del from £62.75 * **SERVICES:** 71P **NOTES:** Last d 9.30pm
CARDS:

CHADDERTON Greater Manchester **Map 07 SD90**

Travel Inn

The Broadway OL9 8DW
☎ 0161 681 1373 📠 0161 682 7974
Dir: *from M62 junct 20 join A627(M) follow signs to Manchester. Travel Inn on the left of A663 (Broadway) and A6104 junct*

This modern building offers accommodation in smart, spacious and well equipped bedrooms, all with en-suite bathrooms. Refreshments may be taken at the nearby family restaurant. For details about current prices consult the Contents Page under Hotel Groups for the Travel Inn phone number.
ROOMS: 40 en suite (bth/shr) d £39.95 *

Indicates that the star classification has not been confirmed under the New Quality Standards, see page 7 for further information.

CHADDESLEY CORBETT Worcestershire   Map 07 SO87

The Premier Collection

★★★◉◉◉ 🍴 Brockencote Hall Country House
DY10 4PY
☎ 01562 777876 📠 01562 777872
Dir: 0.50m W, off A448, opposite St Cassians Church
A magnificent Victorian mansion in extensive parkland, with a Tudor dovecote, lake and fine trees. Spacious bedrooms are appointed to a high standard, with many thoughtful extras. Comfortable lounges and an elegant dining room overlook the landscaped grounds. Head Chef Didier Philipot uses top quality ingredients and precise cooking skills.
ROOMS: 17 en suite (bth/shr) (2 fmly) s £97-£112; d £125-£150 (incl. bkfst) * LB Off peak **MEALS:** Lunch £20.50-£24.50 & alc Dinner fr £24.50 & alc French Cuisine V meals Coffee am Tea pm
FACILITIES: CTV in all bedrooms STV Croquet lawn Jacuzzi/spa Xmas **CONF:** Thtr 30 Class 20 Board 20 Del £155 * **SERVICES:** Lift 45P **NOTES:** No dogs (ex guide dogs) No coaches No smoking in restaurant Last d 9.30pm **CARDS:** 🖭 🖭 🖭 🖭 🖭 🖭

CHAGFORD Devon   Map 03 SX78

The Premier Collection

★★★◉◉◉◉ 🍴 Gidleigh Park
TQ13 8HH
☎ 01647 432367 & 432225 📠 01647 432574   RELAIS & CHATEAUX
Dir: approach from Chagford, turn right at Lloyds Bank into Mill St. After 150 yds fork right, follow lane 2 miles to end
Gidleigh Park reflects all that is best in British hotel-keeping. The well kept Tudor-style house, set in 45 acres of Dartmoor National Park, provides a guaranteed warm welcome with its friendly and professional staff. Bedrooms vary in size and style but all rooms provide the comforts expected of a top hotel. The cuisine is superb, with excellent

recipes often using local ingredients in conjunction with a very well chosen wine list. The grounds contain running water, forests, peaceful retreats, a choice of sporting pursuits, and of course the backdrop of wild, wonderful Dartmoor.
ROOMS: 12 en suite (bth/shr) 3 annexe en suite (bth/shr)
MEALS: Lunch £31.50-£67.50 Dinner £62.50-£67.50 French Cuisine Coffee am Tea pm **FACILITIES:** CTV in all bedrooms STV Tennis (hard) Fishing Croquet lawn Putting green Bowls **CONF:** Board 22 **SERVICES:** 25P **NOTES:** No coaches No smoking in restaurant Last d 9pm **CARDS:** 🖭 🖭 🖭 🖭 🖭 🖭

CHAGFORD Devon   Map 03 SX78
★★★◉◉ Mill End
Dartmoor National Park, Sandy Park TQ13 8JN
Quality Percentage Score: 75%
☎ 01647 432282 📠 01647 433106
Dir: from A30 at Whiddon Down follow A382 to Moretonhampstead. After 3.5 miles a hump back bridge at Sandy Park, hotel on right by river

Located in Dartmoor National Park, this charming hotel provides the ideal venue for a tranquil break. Bedrooms vary in size and character, but all benefit from countryside views. A daily changing menu often uses local produce, served in the elegant dining room. The property also benefits from six miles of fishing on the Teign.
ROOMS: 17 rms (15 bth/shr) (2 fmly) s £47-£79; d £64-£100 (incl. bkfst) * LB Off peak **MEALS:** Lunch fr £15 & alc Dinner fr £25 & alc V meals Coffee am Tea pm **FACILITIES:** CTV in all bedrooms Fishing Croquet lawn Xmas **CONF:** Thtr 40 Class 20 Board 30 **SERVICES:** 21P **NOTES:** No smoking in restaurant Last d 8.45pm
CARDS: 🖭 🖭 🖭 🖭

CHAGFORD Devon   Map 03 SX78
★★ Easton Court
Easton Cross TQ13 8JL
Quality Percentage Score: 72%
☎ 01647 433469 📠 01647 433654
Dir: turn off A30 onto A382, hotel 4m on left near turning to Chagford
This lovely Grade II thatched Tudor house offers a wealth of character and charm, with many of its original features preserved, including granite walls, oak beams and an inglenook fireplace complete with bread oven. Bedrooms offer a combination of pretty fabrics, tasteful furnishings and modern facilities. A short fixed price menu is available in the candlelit dining room; look out for home-made terrines, hearty soups and scrumptious puddings.
ROOMS: 8 en suite (bth/shr) **MEALS:** English & Continental Cuisine **FACILITIES:** CTV in all bedrooms **SERVICES:** 20P **NOTES:** No coaches No children 12yrs No smoking in restaurant Last d 8pm Closed Jan
CARDS: 🖭 🖭 🖭 🖭

CHAGFORD Devon **Map 03 SX78**

★★ Three Crowns Hotel

High St TQ13 8AJ

Quality Percentage Score: 64%

☎ 01647 433441 & 433444 Fax 01647 433117

Dir: *turn left off A30 at Whiddon Down, in Chagford town centre opposite church*

Standing in the heart of Chagford, the hotel dates back to the 13th century and many original features have been retained such as mullioned windows and aged-darkened oak beams. Public rooms include a choice of bars, together with an intimate dining room for more formal occasions. Bedrooms retain the character of the building and all have modern facilities. A large function room is also available, with separate bar.

ROOMS: 14 en suite (bth/shr) (1 fmly) **MEALS:** Lunch £10.50-£17.50 & alc High tea £5-£8.50 Dinner £17.50 & alc English & French Cuisine V meals Coffee am Tea pm **FACILITIES:** CTV in all bedrooms STV Pool table **CONF:** Board 90 **SERVICES:** 14P **NOTES:** No smoking in restaurant Last d 9pm **CARDS:**

See advert on this page

CHALE See Wight, Isle of

CHARD Somerset **Map 03 ST30**

★★★ Lordleaze

Henderson Dr, Forton Rd TA20 2HW

Quality Percentage Score: 64%

☎ 01460 61066 Fax 01460 66468

Dir: *from centre of Chard take A358 towards Axminster, pass St Mary's Church on your right then turn left to Forton & Winsham, 3rd left to hotel*

Located on the eastern edge of the town and approached through a modern housing development, the Lordleaze Hotel is owned and professionally managed by the Owen family. A relaxed and friendly atmosphere prevails throughout the hotel, the bar being a focal point for locals and residents alike. In addition to the fixed-price menu served in the restaurant, an interesting selection

contd.

of bar meals are available. Bedrooms are comfortable, with two rooms available on the ground floor.
ROOMS: 16 en suite (bth/shr) (1 fmly) s £49.50-£55; d £69.50-£80 (incl. bkfst) * LB Off peak **MEALS:** Lunch £9.95-£17alc Dinner £15.50-£22.50alc International Cuisine V meals Coffee am Tea pm **FACILITIES:** CTV in all bedrooms Xmas **CONF:** Thtr 180 Class 60 Board 40 Del £69.50 * **SERVICES:** 55P **NOTES:** No smoking in restaurant Last d 9.30pm **CARDS:**

See advert on page 181

CHARINGWORTH Gloucestershire **Map 04 SP13**

★★★ Charingworth Manor
GL55 6NS
Quality Percentage Score: 76%
☎ 01386 593555 01386 593353
Dir: *on B4035 3m E of Chipping Campden*
Standing in its own grounds, this 14th-century manor house makes the most of its beautiful Cotswold setting. The original house has been extended to provide high quality accommodation, with most of the bedrooms in a group of well converted buildings. The main house, while retaining its original character, offers excellent leisure facilities, and the standard of cooking is high.
ROOMS: 26 en suite (bth/shr) **MEALS:** English & French Cuisine V meals Coffee am Tea pm **FACILITIES:** CTV in all bedrooms STV Indoor swimming pool (heated) Tennis (hard) Snooker Sauna Solarium Croquet lawn Jacuzzi/spa Steam room **CONF:** Thtr 36 Class 16 Board 30 Del from £175 * **SERVICES:** Night porter 50P **NOTES:** No dogs (ex guide dogs) No coaches No smoking in restaurant Last d 9.30pm
CARDS:

See advert under CHIPPING CAMPDEN

CHARMOUTH Dorset **Map 03 SY39**
★★ White House
2 Hillside, The Street DT6 6PJ
Quality Percentage Score: 76%
☎ 01297 560411 01297 560702
Dir: *turn off A35-signed Charmouth hotel opposite the church*
This friendly hotel offers comfortable accommodation in a charming Regency property. The beach, famous for its fossils, is nearby. Individually styled bedrooms are equipped with modern facilities. A five course menu is offered at night, based on fresh produce.
ROOMS: 7 en suite (bth/shr) 3 annexe en suite (bth/shr) No smoking in all bedrooms s £38.50-£48.50; d £77-£87 (incl. bkfst) * LB Off peak **MEALS:** Dinner £18.50 V meals **FACILITIES:** CTV in all bedrooms **SERVICES:** 12P **NOTES:** No coaches No children 14yrs No smoking in restaurant Last d 9pm Closed 3 Jan-9 Feb
CARDS:

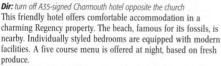

CHATHAM Kent **Map 05 TQ76**
★★★★ Bridgewood Manor Hotel
Bridgewood Roundabout, Walderslade Woods ME5 9AX
Quality Percentage Score: 77%
☎ 01634 201333 01634 201330
Dir: *adjacent to Bridgewood rdbt on A229. Take third exit signed 'Walderslade/Lordswood'. Hotel 50mtrs on left*
Although relatively modern in style, traditional values of service and hospitality are very much to the fore at Bridgewood Manor. On the edge of the historic city of Rochester, the location provides easy access to the motorway network. The hotel offers quality, well equipped accommodation, augmented by a full complement of leisure facilities including heated indoor pool, fitness gym, tennis court and, for lovers of the green baize, a full-size snooker table. Seriously good cuisine is served in the elegant surroundings of Squires Restaurant, where choice includes the 5 Course 'Gourmets' menu. Alternatively, for a lighter bite, try The Terrace.
ROOMS: 100 en suite (bth/shr) (12 fmly) No smoking in 63 bedrooms s £94-£104; d fr £110 * LB Off peak **MEALS:** Lunch £14.50-£18.50 & alc Dinner £26.50 & alc English & French Cuisine V meals Coffee am Tea pm **FACILITIES:** CTV in all bedrooms STV Indoor swimming pool (heated) Tennis (hard) Snooker Sauna Solarium Gym Putting green Jacuzzi/spa Hairdressing Beauty treatments Xmas **CONF:** Thtr 200 Class 110 Board 80 Del from £130 * **SERVICES:** Lift Night porter 178P **NOTES:** No smoking in restaurant Last d 10pm **CARDS:**

CHATTERIS Cambridgeshire **Map 05 TL38**
★ Cross Keys
16 Market Hill PE16 6BA
Quality Percentage Score: 73%
☎ 01354 693036 & 692644 01354 694454
Dir: *at junct A141/142, opposite parish church*
Dating back to Elizabethan times, this small inn with a big character has recently been tastefully extended. The spacious restaurant, cosy bar, dining area and residents lounge are pleasant and relaxing. The older bedrooms offer a wide variety of room sizes and styles, whilst the rooms in the new wing are well equipped and spacious.
ROOMS: 12 rms (10 bth/shr) (1 fmly) No smoking in 5 bedrooms s £21-£35; d £58 (incl. bkfst) * LB Off peak **MEALS:** Lunch £9.45 & alc Dinner £15-£25alc English & French Cuisine V meals Coffee am Tea pm **FACILITIES:** CTV in all bedrooms **CONF:** Class 40 **SERVICES:** 12P **NOTES:** No dogs (ex guide dogs) No smoking in restaurant Closed 26-28 Dec **CARDS:**

CHEADLE Greater Manchester **Map 07 SJ88**
Travel Inn
Royal Crescent SK8 3FE
☎ 0161 491 5884 0161 491 5886
Dir: *off Cheadle Royal rdbt on the A34 behind TGI Friday's*
This modern building offers accommodation in smart, spacious and well equipped bedrooms, all with en-suite bathrooms. Refreshments may be taken at the nearby family restaurant. For details about current prices consult the Contents Page under Hotel Groups for the Travel Inn phone number.
ROOMS: 40 en suite (bth/shr) d £39.95 *

CHEDDAR See **Axbridge**

CHELMSFORD Essex **Map 05 TL70**
★★★★ *Pontlands Park Country*
West Hanningfield Rd, Great Baddow CM2 8HR
Quality Percentage Score: 67%
☎ 01245 476444 01245 478393
Dir: *leave A12 at junct A130. Take A1116 to Chelmsford, then 1st exit 'Great Baddow/Sandon'. Bear left, then left towards 'The Hanningfields*
A country house hotel in the village of Great Baddow. Public rooms include a quiet lounge, a cosy bar and conservatory, and an attractive restaurant. The leisure club has been recently refurbished and bedrooms, which include wedding suites with four-poster beds, are all comfortable.
ROOMS: 17 en suite (bth/shr) (1 fmly) **MEALS:** Euopean Cuisine V meals Coffee am Tea pm **FACILITIES:** CTV in all bedrooms Indoor swimming pool (heated) Outdoor swimming pool (heated) Sauna Solarium Gym Pool table Jacuzzi/spa Beauty salon Dance studio Hairdresser Wkly live entertainment **CONF:** Thtr 40 Class 30 Board 27 **SERVICES:** Night porter 100P **NOTES:** No dogs (ex guide dogs) No coaches Last d 9.45pm Closed 24 Dec-2 Jan (ex 31 Dec) RS Sat/Mon lunch & Sun dinner **CARDS:**

CHELMSFORD Essex **Map 05 TL70**
★★★ County
Rainsford Rd CM1 2QA
Quality Percentage Score: 67%
☎ 01245 491911 01245 492762
Dir: *from town centre continue past railway and bus station to hotel 300yds on left beyond traffic lights*
This town centre hotel continues to improve, and is notable for its willing and attentive staff. Public rooms are comfortable and well presented. Diners choose from carte and fixed-price menus of modern French and British cooking in the restaurant. Several well equipped meeting rooms complement the smartly refurbished ballroom. Bedrooms are attractively decorated and well equipped, they vary in size.
ROOMS: 28 en suite (bth/shr) 8 annexe en suite (bth/shr) s £72; d £82 (incl. bkfst) * LB Off peak **MEALS:** Lunch £11.95-£23 Dinner £16.95-£23 English & French Cuisine V meals Coffee am Tea pm **FACILITIES:** CTV in all bedrooms **CONF:** Thtr 200 Class 60 Board 40 **SERVICES:** Night porter 80P **NOTES:** No smoking area in restaurant Last d 9.30pm Closed 27-30 Dec **CARDS:**

CHELMSFORD Essex **Map 05 TL70**
Travel Inn
Chelmsford Service Area, Colchester Rd, Springfield CM2 5PY
☎ 01245 464008 01245 464010
Dir: *at intersection of A12 Chelmsford by-pass & A130/A138 to Cambridge and services. Follow signs to services*
This modern building offers accommodation in smart, spacious and well equipped bedrooms, all with en-suite bathrooms. Refreshments may be taken at the nearby family restaurant. For details about current prices consult the Contents Page under Hotel Groups for the Travel Inn phone number.
ROOMS: 60 en suite (bth/shr) d £39.95 *

CHELTENHAM Gloucestershire **Map 03 SO92**
see also **Cleeve Hill**
★★★★ Cheltenham/Gloucester Moat House
Shurdington Rd, Brockworth GL3 4PB
Quality Percentage Score: 68%
☎ 01452 519988 01452 519977
Dir: *from M5 junct 11a, follow signs 'Cirencester A417'. Keep left and follow A46 towards Stroud for 0.25m to hotel on left*
Convenient for the M5, this modern hotel is designed in an attractive, contemporary style. Guests can enjoy a varied range of food and drinks in the stylishly furnished open-plan bar/lounge. Coopers restaurant offers a lively menu that includes a carvery, char-grills and local specialities. Bedrooms include some with king size beds and smart, modern bathrooms. An excellent range of function rooms, a business centre and leisure complex are available.
ROOMS: 96 en suite (bth/shr) No smoking in 60 bedrooms s £105; d fr £120 * LB Off peak **MEALS:** Lunch £12.95-£16alc Dinner fr £16alc European Cuisine V meals Coffee am Tea pm **FACILITIES:** CTV in all bedrooms STV Indoor swimming pool (heated) Sauna Solarium Gym Jacuzzi/spa Dance studio Xmas **CONF:** Thtr 344 Class 120 Board 50 Del from £143 * **SERVICES:** Lift Night porter 212P **NOTES:** No smoking in restaurant Last d 9.30pm **CARDS:**

CHELTENHAM Gloucestershire **Map 03 SO92**
★★★★ Cheltenham Park
Cirencester Rd, Charlton Kings GL53 8EA
Quality Percentage Score: 67%
☎ 01242 222021 01242 254880
Dir: *on the A435, 2m SE of Cheltenham near the Lilley Brook Golf Course*

Situated next to a golf course, this smart hotel offers smart public areas and good leisure facilities. There are two bars, a separate restaurant and a choice of lounge areas. Spacious bedrooms offer a good level of modern comfort.
ROOMS: 144 en suite (bth/shr) No smoking in 56 bedrooms s £99-£109; d £128-£148 (incl. bkfst) * LB Off peak **MEALS:** Lunch £10.95-£12.95 Dinner £21.50 International Cuisine V meals Coffee am Tea pm **FACILITIES:** CTV in all bedrooms STV Indoor swimming pool (heated) Sauna Solarium Gym Jacuzzi/spa Steam room Xmas **CONF:** Thtr 320 Class 180 Board 45 Del from £99 * **SERVICES:** Night porter 200P **NOTES:** No smoking in restaurant Last d 9.30pm **CARDS:**

See advert on page 185

CHELTENHAM Gloucestershire **Map 03 SO92**
★★★★ *Thistle Cheltenham*
Gloucester Rd GL51 0TS
Quality Percentage Score: 67%
☎ 01242 232691 01242 221846
Dir: *leave M5 junct 11 onto A40 signed Cheltenham , at 1st rdbt take 2nd exit left into Fiddlers Green Ln, hotel immediately on left*
A smart, modern hotel with a notable range of leisure facilities and a restaurant that offers some punchy, contemporary cooking. Both the public areas and the bedrooms are well kept and the latter have a good level of facilities. Popular as a conference

contd.

★
The Premier Collection, hotels with Red Star Awards are listed on pages 17-23

venue, the hotel is very well located for Cheltenham, Gloucester and the M5.
ROOMS: 122 en suite (bth/shr) (8 fmly) No smoking in 44 bedrooms **MEALS:** International Cuisine V meals Coffee am Tea pm **FACILITIES:** CTV in all bedrooms STV Indoor swimming pool (heated) Tennis (hard) Sauna Solarium Gym Croquet lawn Putting green Jacuzzi/spa Beauty salon **CONF:** Thtr 220 Class 120 Board 60 **SERVICES:** Lift Night porter 250P **NOTES:** No smoking area in restaurant Last d 9.45pm **CARDS:**

CHELTENHAM Gloucestershire **Map 03 SO92**
★★★★ The Queen's
The Promenade GL50 1NN
Quality Percentage Score: 59%
☎ 01242 514724 01242 224145
An elegant, traditional hotel with a fine Regency façade, located in the town centre overlooking the Regency Gardens. Although not large, this hotel does have a spacious feel. In addition to the cocktail bar and the smart restaurant there is now a second eating option - Le Petit Blanc.
ROOMS: 79 en suite (bth/shr) (8 fmly) No smoking in 20 bedrooms s £95-£175; d £100-£175 * LB Off peak **MEALS:** Lunch £12.95-£16.95 Dinner £24.50 V meals Coffee am Tea pm **FACILITIES:** CTV in all bedrooms STV Xmas **CONF:** Thtr 100 Class 60 Board 40 Del £135 * **SERVICES:** Lift Night porter 85P **NOTES:** No smoking in restaurant Last d 9.45pm **CARDS:**

CHELTENHAM Gloucestershire **Map 03 SO92**
The Premier Collection

★★★ The Greenway
Shurdington GL51 5UG
☎ 01242 862352 01242 862780
Dir: *2.5m SW on A46*
The Greenway is a charming Elizabethan manor house dating back to 1587. The spacious, individually decorated bedrooms are divided between the main house and the smartly refurbished Georgian coach house, which overlooks a pretty walled garden. Rooms retain many original features and offer thoughtful extras. Guests can relax in the foyer or drawing room. Meals are served in the conservatory dining room.
ROOMS: 11 en suite (bth/shr) 8 annexe en suite (bth/shr) (1 fmly) No smoking in 8 bedrooms s £95-£120; d £150-£240 (incl. bkfst) * LB Off peak **MEALS:** Lunch £5.50-£21.50 Dinner £29.50-£35 & alc V meals Coffee am Tea pm **FACILITIES:** CTV in all bedrooms STV Croquet lawn Clay pigeon shooting Horse riding Mountain biking Guided walks Xmas **CONF:** Thtr 35 Class 25 Board 22 Del from £135 * **SERVICES:** Night porter 50P **NOTES:** No dogs No coaches No children 7yrs No smoking in restaurant Last d 9.30pm **CARDS:**

CHELTENHAM Gloucestershire **Map 03 SO92**
The Premier Collection

★★★ Hotel On the Park
38 Evesham Rd GL52 2AH
☎ 01242 518898 01242 511526
Dir: *opposite Pittville Park. Join one-way system and turn off A435 towards Evesham*
A country house in style, even though it is in a town, this hotel displays high standards of quality in every department, and polished, professional service. Elegant day rooms comprise a bar, restaurant and drawing room, with period furnishings and fine fabrics adding opulence to comfort. Bedrooms are similarly appointed and many extra little comforts are provided. Cuisine is both distinctive and accomplished.
ROOMS: 12 en suite (bth/shr) No smoking in 4 bedrooms s £76.50; d £94.50-£154.50 * LB Off peak **MEALS:** Lunch fr £14.25 & alc Dinner fr £21.50 & alc V meals Coffee am Tea pm **FACILITIES:** CTV in all bedrooms STV **CONF:** Board 18 **SERVICES:** 9P **NOTES:** No coaches No children 8yrs No smoking in restaurant Last d 9.30pm **CARDS:**

CHELTENHAM Gloucestershire **Map 03 SO92**
★★★ Carlton
Parabola Rd GL50 3AQ
Quality Percentage Score: 67%
☎ 01242 514453 01242 226487
Conveniently close to the town centre, this majestic Regency property provides spacious and comfortable accommodation, including some luxurious bedrooms next door in an extensively renovated house. There is a choice of bars and lounges.
ROOMS: 62 en suite (bth/shr) 13 annexe en suite (bth/shr) (2 fmly) No smoking in 20 bedrooms s £59.50-£65; d £79.50-£85 (incl. bkfst) * LB Off peak **MEALS:** Lunch £12.50-£16.50 & alc Dinner £15.50-£16.50 & alc English & French Cuisine V meals Coffee am **FACILITIES:** CTV in all bedrooms STV Xmas **CONF:** Thtr 225 Class 150 Board 100 Del from £75 * **SERVICES:** Lift Night porter 85P **NOTES:** No smoking area in restaurant Last d 9.30pm **CARDS:**

CHELTENHAM Gloucestershire **Map 03 SO92**
★★★ Charlton Kings
London Rd, Charlton Kings GL52 6UU
Quality Percentage Score: 66%
☎ 01242 231061 01242 241900
Dir: *2.5m SE on A40 1st property on left entering Cheltenham from Oxford on the A40*
A well kept, friendly hotel providing comfortable modern accommodation. Bedrooms are well equipped and attractively furnished and are equally suitable for tourists or business guests.
contd.

The restaurant serves some interesting cooking based on quality ingredients.
ROOMS: 14 en suite (bth/shr) (2 fmly) No smoking in 5 bedrooms s £53-£79.50; d £66-£102 (incl. bkfst) * LB Off peak **MEALS:** Sunday Lunch £13.45-£18.50 High tea fr £6.75 Dinner fr £18.50 & alc English & French Cuisine V meals Coffee am Tea pm **FACILITIES:** CTV in all bedrooms **CONF:** Thtr 30 Class 30 Board 20 Del from £85 * **SERVICES:** 20P **NOTES:** No smoking in restaurant Last d 8.45pm
CARDS:

CHELTENHAM Gloucestershire **Map 03 SO92**
★★★ Hotel Kandinsky (formerly Savoy Hotel)
Bayshill Rd, Montpellier GL50 3AS
Quality Percentage Score: 66%
☎ 01242 527788 Fax 01242 226412

This large, well preserved Regency villa stands in easy reach of the centre. It provides well equipped bedrooms, while the public areas, furnished in a style befitting the character of the house, include a spacious lounge area, a small bar with an adjacent conservatory lounge, and an attractive restaurant offering a set-price menu of interesting dishes.
ROOMS: 41 en suite (bth/shr) No smoking in 10 bedrooms s £70-£85; d £85-£100 * LB Off peak **MEALS:** Dinner fr £21.50 & alc V meals Coffee am Tea pm **FACILITIES:** CTV in all bedrooms STV **CONF:** Thtr 35 Class 20 Board 15 Del from £91 * **SERVICES:** Lift Night porter 45P **NOTES:** No dogs (ex guide dogs) No coaches No smoking in restaurant Last d 9.30pm RS 24-30 Dec **CARDS:**

See advert on this page

CHELTENHAM Gloucestershire **Map 03 SO92**
★★★ White House
Gloucester Rd GL51 0ST
Quality Percentage Score: 66%
☎ 01452 713226 Fax 01452 857590
Dir: *leave M5 junc 11 onto A40 to Cheltenham, then left at roundabout hotel half a mile on left*

Situated between the M5 and Cheltenham, the White House offers comfortable modern accommodation. The lounge bar and

contd.

restaurant are attractively presented and staff offer a warm welcome.
ROOMS: 49 en suite (bth/shr) (4 fmly) No smoking in 13 bedrooms s £60-£75; d £80-£95 (incl. bkfst) * LB Off peak **MEALS:** Lunch £8-£12.50 Dinner £18-£24alc English, French & New World Cuisine V meals Coffee am **FACILITIES:** CTV in all bedrooms STV Pool table **CONF:** Thtr 180 Class 80 Board 45 Del from £90 * **SERVICES:** Night porter 150P **NOTES:** No smoking in restaurant Last d 9.30pm RS 13-16 Mar, 17-28 Jul, 10-12 & 16-28 Nov **CARDS:**

See advert on opposite page

CHELTENHAM Gloucestershire **Map 03 SO92**
★★★ *Royal George*
Birdlip GL4 8JH
Quality Percentage Score: 65%
☎ 01452 862506 01452 862277
Dir: *on the B4070, off the A417*
This Cotswold building has been sympathetically converted and extended into a pleasant hotel. Bedrooms are comfortably furnished with modern facilities. Open-plan public areas are informally designed around the bar and restaurant. A path links the hotel to the Cotswold Way.
ROOMS: 34 en suite (bth/shr) (4 fmly) No smoking in 6 bedrooms **MEALS:** English & Continental Cuisine V meals Coffee am Tea pm **FACILITIES:** CTV in all bedrooms STV Putting green **CONF:** Thtr 100 Class 50 Board 40 **SERVICES:** Night porter 120P **NOTES:** No dogs (ex guide dogs) No smoking area in restaurant Last d 9.30pm
CARDS:

CHELTENHAM Gloucestershire **Map 03 SO92**
★★★ Wyastone
Parabola Rd GL50 3BG
Quality Percentage Score: 64%
☎ 01242 245549 01242 522659
Dir: *from junct 11 M5,travel 3m to end of Lansdown Rd,at Montpellier (rdbt with ornate lampstand) 2nd left around Bank of Scotland into Parabola Rd*

Situated in the elegant Montpelier district, close to the town centre, this charming period hotel is run with great personal care by owners Mr and Mrs Osborne. Public rooms are all furnished in keeping with the style of the building, and the bedrooms offer comfortable accommodation, up to modern standards.
ROOMS: 13 en suite (bth/shr) (2 fmly) No smoking in all bedrooms s £53-£63; d £65-£75 (incl. bkfst) * LB Off peak **MEALS:** Dinner £3.25-£18alc English & French Cuisine V meals **FACILITIES:** CTV in all bedrooms STV Secluded patio garden **CONF:** Thtr 25 Board 15 **SERVICES:** 13P **NOTES:** No dogs No coaches No smoking in restaurant Last d 8.30pm Closed 24 Dec-3 Jan **CARDS:**

CHELTENHAM Gloucestershire **Map 03 SO92**
★★★ The Prestbury House Hotel & Restaurant
The Burgage, Prestbury GL52 3DN
Quality Percentage Score: 63%
☎ 01242 529533 01242 227076
Dir: *2m NE A46 from Cheltenham racecourse follow signs for Prestbury hotel is 2nd on the left half a mile from racecouse*

Ably run by resident proprietors, the hotel has historic charm and easy access to town. The owners also run a management training company, and team-building activities sometimes take place in the hotel grounds. Well equipped accommodation is divided between spacious rooms in the main house and those in a converted coach house.
ROOMS: 8 en suite (bth/shr) 9 annexe en suite (bth/shr) (3 fmly) s £72-£78; d £85-£96 (incl. bkfst) * LB Off peak **MEALS:** Lunch £12.50-£27 & alc High tea £2.50-£10.50 Dinner £24-£27 & alc English, French & Italian Cuisine V meals Coffee am Tea pm **FACILITIES:** CTV in all bedrooms STV Riding Croquet lawn Clay pigeon shooting Archery Mountain bike hire Xmas **CONF:** Thtr 70 Class 30 Board 25 Del from £105 * **SERVICES:** 50P **NOTES:** No dogs (ex guide dogs) No smoking area in restaurant Last d 9pm **CARDS:**

See advert on opposite page

CHELTENHAM Gloucestershire **Map 03 SO92**
★★ Cotswold Grange
Pittville Circus Rd GL52 2QH
Quality Percentage Score: 67%
☎ 01242 515119 01242 241537
Dir: *from town centre follow signs 'Prestbury'. Turn right at first roundabout, hotel 200yds on left*
A popular and friendly family-run hotel situated conveniently for the town centre. The bustling bar is the centre of the operation and there is a spacious restaurant serving a selection of home-made dishes. The bedrooms are well kept and include many in-room extras.
ROOMS: 25 en suite (bth/shr) (4 fmly) s £48-£55; d £70-£80 (incl. bkfst) * LB Off peak **MEALS:** Lunch £3.50-£13.50alc Dinner £8.50-£18.50alc V meals Coffee am Tea pm **FACILITIES:** CTV in all bedrooms **CONF:** Thtr 20 Class 15 Board 15 Del from £80 * **SERVICES:** 20P **NOTES:** No smoking in restaurant Last d 7.30pm Closed 24 Dec-1 Jan RS Sun evening (food by arrangement) **CARDS:**

CHELTENHAM Gloucestershire **Map 03 SO92**
★★ George Hotel
St Georges Rd GL50 3DZ
Quality Percentage Score: 67%
☎ 01242 235751 01242 224359
This popular Regency hotel is close to the town centre and offers

contd.

well eqipped, comfortable bedrooms and relaxing public areas with a convivial atmosphere.
ROOMS: 39 en suite (bth/shr) (1 fmly) No smoking in 2 bedrooms s £55-£60; d fr £75 (incl. bkfst) * LB Off peak **MEALS:** Lunch fr £9.95 & alc Dinner fr £14.95 & alc English & French Cuisine V meals Coffee am **FACILITIES:** CTV in all bedrooms STV **CONF:** Thtr 40 Class 24 Board 20 Del from £80 * **SERVICES:** Night porter 30P **NOTES:** No smoking area in restaurant Last d 9.15pm **CARDS:**

CHELTENHAM Gloucestershire — Map 03 SO92
Travel Inn
Tewkesbury Rd, Uckington GL51 9SL
☎ 01242 233847 Fax 01242 244887
Dir: *2m from junct 10 of M5, on A4019 opposite Sainsbury's*
This modern building offers accommodation in smart, spacious and well equipped bedrooms, all with en-suite bathrooms. Refreshments may be taken at the nearby family restaurant. For details about current prices consult the Contents Page under Hotel Groups for the Travel Inn phone number.
ROOMS: 40 en suite (bth/shr) d £39.95 *

CHELTENHAM Gloucestershire — Map 03 SO92
Travel Inn Cheltenham Central
374 Gloucester Rd GL51 7AP
☎ 0870 242 8000
This modern building offers accommodation in smart, spacious and well equipped bedrooms, all with en-suite bathrooms. Refreshments may be taken at the nearby family restaurant. For details about current prices consult the Contents Page under Hotel Groups for the Travel Inn phone number.
ROOMS: 42 en suite (bth/shr) d £39.95 *

CHELTENHAM Gloucestershire — Map 03 SO92
Late entry ***Hotel De La Bere***
Southam GL52 3NH
☎ 01242 237771 Fax 01242 236016
Dir: *3m NE on B4632, 1m beyond village of Prestbury*
An imposing 15th century building overlooking the racecourse, this hotel retains such original features as oak panelling, ornate plasterwork, beams and fireplaces. Some of the accommodation is located in a converted coach house with the rest in the main house. These rooms tend to vary in size and comfort and in some cases are accessed by winding corridors or old staircases.
ROOMS: 32 en suite (bth/shr) 25 annexe en suite (bth/shr) (2 fmly) No smoking in 14 bedrooms **MEALS:** English & French Cuisine V meals Coffee am Tea pm **FACILITIES:** CTV in all bedrooms Outdoor swimming pool (heated) Tennis (hard) Squash Sauna Solarium Gym Badminton Wkly live entertainment **CONF:** Thtr 80 Class 35 Board 40 **SERVICES:** Night porter 160P **NOTES:** No smoking in restaurant
CARDS:

CHELWOOD Somerset — Map 03 ST66
★★ Chelwood House
BS39 4NH
Quality Percentage Score: 65%
☎ 01761 490730 Fax 01761 490072
Dir: *on A37 200yds S of junct with A368*
This imposing 300-year-old country house is situated near the A37 convenient for Bath or Bristol. Recently acquired by the Cleary family, an ambitious refurbishment plan is now underway. Bedrooms, which include both four-poster and ground floor rooms, are well equipped and comfortable. The smart

contd.

lounges reflect similar high standards and accomplished cuisine is served in the conservatory restaurant.
ROOMS: 12 en suite (bth/shr) (1 fmly) s £49.50-£60; d £82.50-£97.50 (incl. bkfst) * LB Off peak **MEALS:** Dinner £17-£25alc English & French Cuisine V meals Coffee am Tea pm **FACILITIES:** CTV in all bedrooms Croquet lawn **CONF:** Thtr 30 Class 12 Board 12 **SERVICES:** 30P **NOTES:** No coaches No smoking in restaurant Last d 9pm RS Sun **CARDS:**

CHENIES Buckinghamshire — Map 04 TQ09

★★★ Bedford Arms Chenies

WD3 6EQ
Quality Percentage Score: 69%
☎ 01923 283301 ▤ 01923 284825
Dir: *off A404, signposted*
This 19th-century country inn retains a great deal of charm and character. The bedrooms are of varying sizes, and of a superior standard. The traditional bar is popular with guests and non-residents alike and the richly furnished restaurant offers an extensive range of dishes.
ROOMS: 10 en suite (bth/shr) No smoking in 3 bedrooms d £145 * LB Off peak **MEALS:** Lunch fr £15.50 Dinner fr £23 English & French Cuisine V meals Coffee am Tea pm **FACILITIES:** CTV in all bedrooms STV **CONF:** Thtr 25 Class 10 Board 15 Del from £108 * **SERVICES:** Night porter 120P **NOTES:** No coaches Last d 10pm **CARDS:**

CHERTSEY Surrey — Map 04 TQ06

★★★ The Crown

7 London St KT16 8AP
Quality Percentage Score: 67%
☎ 01932 564657 ▤ 01932 570839
Dir: *adjacent to Old Town Hall*
The Crown has been completely refurbished and extended and now offers a range of well proportioned and good quality bedrooms along with public bar, garden bar and conservatory, and an attractive traditional style restaurant. Home-cooked food features some interesting dishes both in the restaurant and the bar. Other facilities include a popular function suite.
ROOMS: 30 annexe en suite (bth/shr) (4 fmly) No smoking in 13 bedrooms s £48-£92; d £58-£104 (incl. bkfst) * LB Off peak **MEALS:** Lunch £2.50-£10.95alc Dinner £2.50-£10.95alc V meals Coffee am Tea pm **FACILITIES:** CTV in all bedrooms STV **CONF:** Thtr 100 Class 40 Board 35 **SERVICES:** Night porter 50P **NOTES:** No smoking area in restaurant Last d 10pm **CARDS:**

CHESHUNT Hertfordshire — Map 05 TL30

★★★★ Cheshunt Marriott

Halfhide Ln, Turnford EN10 6NG
Quality Percentage Score: 65%
☎ 01992 451245 ▤ 01992 440120
Dir: *take Turnford/Wormley exit from A10, turn right at Beefeater, New River Arms rdbt, take 3rd exit from next rdbt. Hotel on 3rd exit*
This modern hotel situated off the A10 offers air-conditioned bedrooms including some de-luxe rooms overlooking a pretty, central garden. Guests may eat in either the busy Washington Bar or the restaurant. Ask for directions when you book.
ROOMS: 143 en suite (bth/shr) (37 fmly) No smoking in 92 bedrooms d £104-£154 * LB Off peak **MEALS:** Sunday Lunch £17.50 Dinner £19.50 & alc English & French Cuisine V meals Coffee am Tea pm **FACILITIES:** CTV in all bedrooms STV Indoor swimming pool (heated) Gym Jacuzzi/spa Wkly live entertainment Xmas **CONF:** Thtr 180 Class 100 Board 90 **SERVICES:** Lift Night porter Air conditioning 200P **NOTES:** No dogs (ex guide dogs) No smoking in restaurant Last d 10pm **CARDS:**

CHESSINGTON Greater London — Map 04 TQ16

Travel Inn

Leatherhead Rd KT9 2NE
☎ 01372 744060 ▤ 01372 720889
Dir: *on A423, 2m from junct 9 of the M25, towards Kingston*
This modern building offers accommodation in smart, spacious and well equipped bedrooms, all with en-suite bathrooms. Refreshments may be taken at the nearby family restaurant. For details about current prices consult the Contents Page under Hotel Groups for the Travel Inn phone number.
ROOMS: 42 en suite (bth/shr) d £39.95 *

CHESTER Cheshire — Map 07 SJ46

see also **Puddington**

★★★★★ The Chester Grosvenor

Eastgate CH1 1LT
Quality Percentage Score: 75%
☎ 01244 324024 ▤ 01244 313246
Dir: *turn off M56 for M53 Chester, then A56 Chester - follow signs for city centre hotels*
Found within the Roman walls of the city, close to the fashionable shops and attractions, this icon of hospitality and excellence continues to be popular with visitors to Chester. The staff are well trained and courteous, while the Brasserie remains a popular meeting point for visitors and locals alike; also appealing is the library which has a discreet club-like feel, and the drawing room is an inviting area in which to relax. In the Arkle restaurant, guests are tantalized by imaginative cuisine using seasonal ingredients in the modern British style. Fully air-conditioned suites and bedrooms are designed for guest comfort and furnished to a high standard.
ROOMS: 85 en suite (bth/shr) s £152.75-£170.38; d £229.13-£264.38 * LB Off peak **MEALS:** Lunch fr £25 British & French Cuisine V meals Coffee am Tea pm **FACILITIES:** CTV in all bedrooms STV Sauna Solarium Gym Membership of Country Club - 2m from hotel with complimentary transport Wkly live entertainment **CONF:** Thtr 250 Class 120 Board 48 Del £211.50 * **SERVICES:** Lift Night porter Air conditioning **NOTES:** No dogs (ex guide dogs) Closed 25-26 Dec **CARDS:**

CHESTER Cheshire — Map 07 SJ46

★★★★ Carden Park Hotel Golf Resort & Spa

Carden Park CH3 9DQ
Quality Percentage Score: 72%
☎ 01829 731000 ▤ 01829 731032
(For full entry see Broxton)

CHESTER Cheshire — Map 07 SJ46

★★★★ *Chester Moat House*

Trinity St CH1 2BD
Quality Percentage Score: 67%
☎ 01244 899988 ▤ 01244 316118
Dir: *from City Inner Ring Road follow signs 'Gateway Theatre'*
A smart city-centre hotel with comfortable and well-equipped bedrooms. The spacious public areas are on the first floor and include a leisure suite, extensive business and meeting facilities. Silks restaurant which offers a wide-ranging menu is bright and strikingly decorated.
ROOMS: 152 en suite (bth/shr) (4 fmly) No smoking in 91 bedrooms **MEALS:** Continental Cuisine V meals Coffee am Tea pm **FACILITIES:** CTV in all bedrooms Sauna Solarium Gym Pool table Jacuzzi/spa Steam bath **CONF:** Thtr 600 Class 250 Board 120 **SERVICES:** Lift Night porter 76P **NOTES:** No smoking area in restaurant Last d 10pm **CARDS:**

CHESTER Cheshire **Map 07 SJ46**

★★★★ **Mollington Banastre**

Parkgate Rd CH1 6NN

Quality Percentage Score: 66%

☎ 01244 851471 📠 01244 851165

Dir: *M56 to junct 16 at next rdbt turn left for Chester A540. Hotel is 2 miles down the A540 on right*

Conveniently situated between the city and the M56, with attractive gardens to the rear. Bedrooms vary in size and include family suites. Meeting and function rooms and a well equipped leisure centre are available. Stylish public areas include a comfortable bar, the Garden Room restaurant and the less formal 'Place Apart'.

ROOMS: 63 en suite (bth) (8 fmly) No smoking in 5 bedrooms s £75-£95; d £95-£115 * LB Off peak **MEALS:** Lunch £9.95-£20alc Dinner £23 & alc V meals Coffee am Tea pm **FACILITIES:** CTV in all bedrooms STV Indoor swimming pool (heated) Squash Sauna Solarium Gym Croquet lawn Jacuzzi/spa Hairdressing Health & beauty salon Wkly live entertainment Xmas **CONF:** Thtr 260 Class 60 Board 50 Del from £130 * **SERVICES:** Lift Night porter 200P **NOTES:** No children No smoking in restaurant Last d 9.45pm **CARDS:**

CHESTER Cheshire **Map 07 SJ46**

★★★★ **Queen**

City Rd CH1 3AH

Quality Percentage Score: 64%

☎ 01244 350100 📠 01244 318483

Dir: *follow signs for railway station, hotel is opposite*

Standing opposite the railway station, this elegant, 19th-century hotel offers bedrooms equipped to modern standards of comfort. The reception area, graced by an impressive central staircase, gives access to the public areas, which include a spacious lounge, separate bar and a restaurant.

ROOMS: 128 en suite (bth/shr) (6 fmly) No smoking in 24 bedrooms s £90-£105; d £120-£130 (incl. bkfst) * LB Off peak **MEALS:** Lunch £9.95-£12.95 Dinner fr £17.95 & alc English & French Cuisine V meals Coffee am Tea pm **FACILITIES:** CTV in all bedrooms STV Croquet lawn Wkly live entertainment Xmas **CONF:** Thtr 280 Class 100 Board 50 Del from £110 * **SERVICES:** Lift Night porter 100P **NOTES:** No smoking in restaurant Last d 9.30pm **CARDS:**

CHESTER Cheshire **Map 07 SJ46**

★★★ **Crabwall Manor**

Parkgate Rd, Mollington CH1 6NE

Quality Percentage Score: 80%

☎ 01244 851666 📠 01244 851400

Dir: *NW off A540*

First mentioned in the Domesday Book, this re-built manor house hotel dates from the 17th century. Spacious bedrooms and suites are attractively decorated and include a number of useful extras and features, including luxuriously large bathtubs. There are a number of small, comfortable lounge areas, in addition to a

contd.

billiard room, and a full leisure centre. An imaginative menu is served in the conservatory restaurant.
ROOMS: 48 en suite (bth/shr) No smoking in 2 bedrooms s fr £116; d fr £160 * LB Off peak **MEALS:** Lunch fr £16.50 High tea fr £9.50 Dinner fr £27.50 & alc English & French Cuisine V meals **FACILITIES:** CTV in all bedrooms STV Indoor swimming pool (heated) Snooker Sauna Solarium Gym Croquet lawn Jacuzzi/spa Heli pad Xmas **CONF:** Thtr 100 Class 60 Board 36 Del from £130 * **SERVICES:** Night porter 120P **NOTES:** No dogs (ex guide dogs) No smoking area in restaurant Last d 9.30pm **CARDS:**

See advert on opposite page

CHESTER Cheshire **Map 07 SJ46**
★★★ *The Gateway To Wales*
Welsh Rd, Sealand, Deeside CH5 2HX
Quality Percentage Score: 70%
☎ 01244 830332 01244 836190
Dir: *4m NW via A548 towards Sealand and Queensferry*
Close to the Welsh border, this pleasant hotel provides an ideal base to explore Chester and North Wales. Public rooms include the Louis XVI lounge bar and the Regency restaurant which serves a very imaginative menu. Bedrooms are tastefully furnished and thoughtfully equipped.
ROOMS: 39 en suite (bth/shr) (4 fmly) No smoking in 10 bedrooms **MEALS:** European Cuisine V meals Coffee am Tea pm **FACILITIES:** CTV in all bedrooms STV Indoor swimming pool (heated) Sauna Solarium Gym Jacuzzi/spa Use of Indoor Bowls & Snooker Club **CONF:** Thtr 110 Class 50 Board 50 Del from £85 * **SERVICES:** Lift Night porter 51P **NOTES:** No dogs (ex guide dogs) No smoking in restaurant Last d 9.30pm **CARDS:**

CHESTER Cheshire **Map 07 SJ46**
★★★ Rowton Hall Country House Hotel
Whitchurch Rd, Rowton CH3 6AD
Quality Percentage Score: 68%
☎ 01244 335262 01244 335464
Dir: *2m SE A41 towards Whitchurch*
This impressive creeper-clad country house dates from the 18th century and lies in several acres of mature grounds. Original features include a superb carved staircase and several fireplaces. Many of the public rooms have wood-panelled walls and the modern extensions include a fully equipped leisure centre and extensive function facilities. Modern rooms are available in the courtyard while the rooms in the manor house are luxuriously spacious.
ROOMS: 42 en suite (bth/shr) (4 fmly) s £85-£138; d £85-£170 (incl. bkfst) * LB Off peak **MEALS:** Lunch £13.50-£14.50 & alc Dinner £22.50 & alc English & French Cuisine V meals Coffee am Tea pm **FACILITIES:** CTV in all bedrooms STV Indoor swimming pool (heated) Tennis (hard) Sauna Solarium Gym Croquet lawn Jacuzzi/spa **CONF:** Thtr 200 Class 48 Board 50 Del from £130 * **SERVICES:** Night porter 120P **NOTES:** No smoking in restaurant Last d 9pm
CARDS:

CHESTER Cheshire **Map 07 SJ46**
★★★ Broxton Hall Country House
Whitchurch Rd CH3 9JS
Quality Percentage Score: 66%
☎ 01829 782321 01829 782330
(For full entry see Broxton)

New AA Guides for the Millennium are featured on page 24

CHESTER Cheshire **Map 07 SJ46**
★★★ *Posthouse Chester*
Posthouse
Wrexham Rd CH4 9DL
Quality Percentage Score: 66%
☎ 01244 680111 01244 674100
Dir: *near Wrexham junct on A483, off A55*
This modern hotel is a short distance from Chester and convenient for major routes into North Wales. Bedrooms are well appointed including several in the new millennium style, rooms specially equipped for disabled guests and family rooms. Other features include a 'Seasons' restaurant, a leisure club and children's play areas. An all day lounge menu and 24-hour room service are available.
ROOMS: 145 en suite (bth/shr) (44 fmly) No smoking in 99 bedrooms **MEALS:** International Cuisine V meals Coffee am Tea pm **FACILITIES:** CTV in all bedrooms Indoor swimming pool (heated) Sauna Solarium Gym Pool table Jacuzzi/spa **CONF:** Thtr 100 Class 50 Board 40 **SERVICES:** Night porter 220P **NOTES:** No smoking area in restaurant Last d 10.30pm **CARDS:**

CHESTER Cheshire **Map 07 SJ46**
★★★ Grosvenor Pulford
Wrexham Rd, Pulford CH4 9DG
Quality Percentage Score: 64%
☎ 01244 570560 01244 570809
Dir: *exit M53/A55 at junct signposted A483 Chester, Wrexham & North Wales. Turn onto B5445, hotel is 2m on right*
Midway between Chester and Wrexham, this imposing hotel offers comfortable and well equipped bedrooms. Ground floor and family rooms are available, as well as suites where the sitting area is separated from the bedroom by a spiral staircase. The restaurant offers an interesting selection of carefully prepared dishes, and breakfast is served in a conservatory overlooking the inner courtyard.
ROOMS: 68 en suite (bth/shr) (4 fmly) No smoking in 3 bedrooms s £60-£67.50; d £80-£85 (incl. bkfst) * LB Off peak **MEALS:** Sunday Lunch fr £7.95 & alc Dinner £9.50-£17alc Continental Cuisine V meals Coffee am Tea pm **FACILITIES:** CTV in all bedrooms STV Indoor swimming pool (heated) Snooker Sauna Solarium Gym Jacuzzi/spa Hairdressing & Beauty salon with latest treatments Xmas **CONF:** Thtr 200 Class 100 Board 50 Del from £90 * **SERVICES:** Night porter 160P **NOTES:** No smoking area in restaurant Last d 10pm
CARDS:

See advert on opposite page

CHESTER Cheshire **Map 07 SJ46**
★★★ Hoole Hall
REGAL
Warrington Rd, Hoole Village CH2 3PD
Quality Percentage Score: 63%
☎ 01244 350011 01244 320251
Dir: *from junct 12 on M53 continue 0.5m on A56 towards city centre*

This hotel, dating from the 18th century, is 2 miles from the city
contd. on p. 192

C

centre and stands in extensive grounds. The hotel is now much extended and modernised, and refurbishment has considerably enhanced the bedroom accommodation. There are a wide range of facilities for meetings, banquets and conferences, and ample car parking to cater for all events.
ROOMS: 97 en suite (bth/shr) (4 fmly) No smoking in 48 bedrooms s fr £80; d fr £95 * LB Off peak **MEALS:** Lunch £10.50-£14.50 High tea fr £6 Dinner fr £17.95 & alc International Cuisine V meals Coffee am Tea pm **FACILITIES:** CTV in all bedrooms STV ch fac Xmas **CONF:** Thtr 150 Class 65 Board 50 Del from £120 * **SERVICES:** Lift Night porter 200P **NOTES:** No smoking in restaurant Last d 9.15pm
CARDS:

C

CHESTER Cheshire — Map 07 SJ46
★★★ Blossoms
St John St CH1 1HL
Quality Percentage Score: 62%
☎ 01244 323186 01244 346433
Dir: *in city centre, around the corner from the Eastgate Clock*
This well established hotel is ideally situated right in the heart of the city and offers smart, refurbished accommodation. The public areas retain some of their Victorian charm and the atmosphere is enhanced at dinner, on occasions, with live piano music in the lobby. Free parking is available nearby in Newgate Street, close to the hotel.
ROOMS: 64 en suite (bth/shr) (2 fmly) No smoking in 43 bedrooms s £85-£90; d £100-£130 * LB Off peak **MEALS:** Lunch £5.95-£13.95alc Dinner £15-£25alc English & Continental Cuisine V meals Coffee am Tea pm **FACILITIES:** CTV in all bedrooms Wkly live entertainment Xmas **CONF:** Thtr 100 Class 60 Board 60 Del £100 * **SERVICES:** Lift Night porter **NOTES:** No smoking in restaurant Last d 9.45pm
CARDS:

CHESTER Cheshire — Map 07 SJ46
★★ Westminster
City Rd CH1 3AF
Quality Percentage Score: 68%
☎ 01244 317341 01244 325369
Dir: *from A56 approx. 3 miles to Chester City Centre, turn left when signposted rail station, hotel directly opposite station*
This long established hotel is near the railway station and all local attractions. Bedrooms are attractively decorated and furnished in a modern style. Public areas include a choice of bars, a comfortable lounge and an attractive restaurant.
ROOMS: 75 en suite (bth/shr) (5 fmly) No smoking in 20 bedrooms s £44.95-£49.95; d £59.95-£65 (incl. bkfst) * LB Off peak **MEALS:** Bar Lunch £2.95-£5.95 Dinner £12.50-£13.95 & alc V meals Coffee am Tea pm **FACILITIES:** CTV in all bedrooms STV Wkly live entertainment Xmas **CONF:** Thtr 30 Class 20 Board 20 **SERVICES:** Lift Night porter **NOTES:** No smoking area in restaurant Last d 9pm
CARDS:

CHESTER Cheshire — Map 07 SJ46
★★ *Brookside*
Brook Ln CH2 2AN
Quality Percentage Score: 66%
☎ 01244 381943 01244 379701
Dir: *0.5m from city, turn off A5116 into Brook Lane, hotel 300yds on left*
The Brookside is a friendly hotel located just north of the city centre. The attractive public areas consist of a foyer lounge, a small bar and a split-level restaurant. Bedrooms are brightly decorated, and well equipped.
ROOMS: 24 en suite (bth/shr) (7 fmly) **MEALS:** V meals Coffee am Tea pm **FACILITIES:** CTV in all bedrooms STV Sauna Solarium Gym Pool table **SERVICES:** 20P **NOTES:** No smoking in restaurant Last d 8.30pm Closed 24-26 Dec **CARDS:**

CHESTER Cheshire — Map 07 SJ46
★★ Cavendish
42-44 Hough Green CH4 8JQ
Quality Percentage Score: 66%
☎ 01244 675100 01244 678844
Dir: *S of Chester, from the A483 take A5104 signposted Saltney. Hotel is approx 350yds on the right, next to Youth hostel*
Less than a mile from the centre of the city, this well maintained Georgian house offers spacious, well-equipped bedrooms, including one on the ground floor, and there is a comfortable lounge. There is also a small bar and lounge beside the restaurant, which overlooks the patio.
ROOMS: 19 en suite (bth/shr) (4 fmly) s £45-£50; d £55-£75 (incl. bkfst) * LB Off peak **MEALS:** Lunch £10-£30 High tea £5-£10 Dinner £10-£30 International Cuisine V meals Coffee am Tea pm **FACILITIES:** CTV in all bedrooms STV Xmas **SERVICES:** 35P **NOTES:** No dogs (ex guide dogs) No coaches No smoking in restaurant Last d 9pm **CARDS:**

CHESTER Cheshire — Map 07 SJ46
★★❀ Curzon
52/54 Hough Green CH4 8JQ
Quality Percentage Score: 66%
☎ 01244 678581 01244 680866
Dir: *on A5104*
Conveniently situated for the racecourse and just one mile from the city centre, this friendly hotel provides pleasing modern accommodation. The bedrooms are well appointed and four-poster and family rooms are both available. The lounge bar is inviting and the cuisine is imaginative; the menu features many authentic Swiss dishes inspired by the owners.
ROOMS: 16 en suite (bth/shr) (7 fmly) No smoking in 7 bedrooms s £45-£55; d £60-£70 (incl. bkfst) * LB Off peak **MEALS:** Dinner £15-£20 Continental & Swiss Cuisine V meals **FACILITIES:** CTV in all bedrooms Pool table Xmas **SERVICES:** 20P **NOTES:** No coaches No smoking in restaurant Last d 9pm Closed 20-29 Dec
CARDS:

CHESTER Cheshire — Map 07 SJ46
★★ Dene
95 Hoole Rd CH2 3ND
Quality Percentage Score: 66%
☎ 01244 321165 01244 350277
Dir: *0.75m E of city centre, from junct 12 of M53 take A56 towards Chester, hotel just after Alexander Park*
Conveniently situated between the city centre and the M53, this hotel offers a variety of comfortably furnished accommodation, ranging up to family suites. The bedrooms are shared between the main house and adjoining buildings. Good food is served in both the restaurant and the bar. There is also a small conference room.
ROOMS: 44 en suite (bth/shr) 8 annexe en suite (bth/shr) (5 fmly) No smoking in 16 bedrooms s £45; d £57 (incl. bkfst) * LB Off peak **MEALS:** Sunday Lunch £8.95 Dinner £6.95-£12.85 & alc French Cuisine V meals Coffee am Tea pm **FACILITIES:** CTV in all bedrooms STV Pool table **CONF:** Thtr 30 Class 12 Board 16 Del from £59 * **SERVICES:** 55P **NOTES:** No smoking in restaurant Last d 10pm
CARDS:

See advert on opposite page

The AA Hotel Booking Service is a free benefit to AA members. See the advertisement on page 47

CHESTER Cheshire
Map 07 SJ46

★★ *Chester Court*

Hoole Rd CH2 3NL

Quality Percentage Score: 62%

☎ 01244 320779 Fax 01244 344795

Dir: *approach city centre on A56 Hoole Road. Hotel on right opposite All Saints Church*

This hotel lies on the leafy outskirts of Chester. Bedrooms are well equipped with modern facilities and many are located at ground level in a peaceful courtyard. Several rooms have four-poster beds, and family accommodation is available. The hotel has a lounge and a bar, and a well appointed restaurant featuring a pleasing conservatory.

ROOMS: 8 en suite (bth/shr) 12 annexe en suite (bth/shr) (2 fmly) **MEALS:** V meals Coffee am Tea pm **FACILITIES:** CTV in all bedrooms STV **CONF:** Thtr 20 Class 9 Board 12 Del from £79 * **SERVICES:** 20P **NOTES:** No smoking in restaurant Last d 8.15pm

CARDS:

CHESTER Cheshire
Map 07 SJ46

★★ Eaton

THE CIRCLE
Selected Individual Hotels
GREAT BRITAIN

29/31 City Rd CH1 3AE

Quality Percentage Score: 62%

☎ 01244 320840 Fax 01244 320850

Dir: *400 metres from the station, towards the city centre, adjacent to the canal*

This privately owned hotel is a short walk from the city centre and conveniently placed for the railway station. There is an attractive cane-furnished bar and a wood-panelled dining room

contd.

with a small daily fixed-price menu. Enclosed car parking is also available.
ROOMS: 16 en suite (bth/shr) s fr £45; d fr £57.50 (incl. bkfst) * LB Off peak **MEALS:** Lunch £8.95 Dinner £8.95-£12.95 English & French Cuisine V meals Coffee am Tea pm **FACILITIES:** CTV in all bedrooms **SERVICES:** 10P **NOTES:** No smoking in restaurant Last d 8pm
CARDS:

C

CHESTER Cheshire **Map 07 SJ46**
Travel Inn
Caldy Valley Rd
☎ 0870 242 8000
This modern building offers accommodation in smart, spacious and well equipped bedrooms, all with en-suite bathrooms. Refreshments may be taken at the nearby family restaurant. For details about current prices consult the Contents Page under Hotel Groups for the Travel Inn phone number.
ROOMS: 70 en suite (bth/shr) d £39.95 *

CHESTERFIELD Derbyshire **Map 08 SK37**
★★★ **Sandpiper**
Sheffield Rd, Sheepbridge S41 9EH
Quality Percentage Score: 62%
☎ 01246 450550 01246 452805
Dir: *leave M1 junct 29 follow A617 to Chesterfield. Follow A61 to Sheffield then at 1st exit take Dronfield Rd. Hotel 0.5m on left*
Conveniently situated for the A61 and M1, just three miles from Chesterfield, this modern hotel offers comfortable and well furnished bedrooms. Public areas are situated in a separate building across the car park and include a cosy bar and open plan restaurant, serving a range of popular dishes.
ROOMS: 28 annexe en suite (bth/shr) (4 fmly) No smoking in 14 bedrooms s £40-£60; d £60-£75 (incl. bkfst) * LB Off peak **MEALS:** Lunch £10 Dinner £15-£20 English & French Cuisine V meals Coffee am Tea pm **FACILITIES:** CTV in all bedrooms STV **CONF:** Thtr 60 Class 30 Board 40 Del from £80 * **SERVICES:** 220P **NOTES:** No dogs (ex guide dogs) No smoking area in restaurant Last d 10pm
CARDS:

CHESTERFIELD Derbyshire **Map 08 SK37**

★★★ ***Chesterfield***
Malkin St S41 7UA
Quality Percentage Score: 59%
☎ 01246 271141 01246 220719
Dir: *from Chesterfield town centre follow signs to railway station hotel is diagonally across from station*
A hotel with a friendly atmosphere, close to both railway station and town centre. Bedrooms offer a good standard of comfort, and the 1920s-style restaurant offers a wide choice of food.
ROOMS: 73 en suite (bth/shr) (5 fmly) No smoking in 19 bedrooms **MEALS:** International Cuisine V meals Coffee am **FACILITIES:** CTV in all bedrooms STV Indoor swimming pool (heated) Snooker Sauna Solarium Gym Jacuzzi/spa **CONF:** Thtr 200 Class 100 Board 80 **SERVICES:** Lift Night porter 100P **NOTES:** No smoking in restaurant Last d 9.45pm **CARDS:**

CHESTERFIELD Derbyshire **Map 08 SK37**
★★ **Abbeydale**
Cross St S40 4TD
Quality Percentage Score: 67%
☎ 01246 277849 01246 558223
Dir: *A617 to Chesterfield, A619 to Buxton & Bakewell, 3rd rdbt (at B62) turn off to Foljambe Rd across lights into West St, rigt at T junctof Cross St*
Situated in a quiet residential area of the town, this friendly hotel offers excellent service and warm hospitality. Bedrooms, two of which are on the ground floor, are bright, fresh and well equipped. A short selection of freshly prepared dishes are served in the dining room, adjacent to the cosy lounge and bar.
ROOMS: 12 rms (11 bth/shr) (1 fmly) No smoking in 3 bedrooms s £43-£49.50; d £60 (incl. bkfst) * Off peak **MEALS:** Dinner £14-£14.50 & alc V meals Coffee am Tea pm **FACILITIES:** CTV in all bedrooms **SERVICES:** 18P **NOTES:** No coaches No smoking in restaurant Last d 8.15pm **CARDS:**

CHESTERFIELD Derbyshire **Map 08 SK37**
★★ **Portland**
West Bars S40 1AY
Quality Percentage Score: 65%
☎ 01246 234502 & 234211 01246 550915
Dir: *in town centre overlooking Market Place*
This popular Victorian town-centre hotel is close to the market place, and offers the benefit of private parking. Public areas include a choice of meeting and function rooms, a popular open-plan bar lounge and pleasant restaurant. Bedrooms are well equipped and nicely furnished.
ROOMS: 24 en suite (bth/shr) (6 fmly) s fr £55; d fr £64 (incl. bkfst) * LB Off peak **MEALS:** Lunch fr £7.99 & alc Dinner £7.50-£25alc V meals Coffee am **FACILITIES:** CTV in all bedrooms **CONF:** Thtr 50 Class 50 Board 20 Del from £87 * **SERVICES:** Night porter 30P **NOTES:** No dogs (ex guide dogs) Last d 9.30pm
CARDS:

CHESTERFIELD Derbyshire **Map 08 SK37**
Travelodge
Brimmington Rd, Inner Ring Rd, Wittington Moor S41 9BE
☎ 01246 455411 01246 455411
Dir: *A61, N of town centre*
This modern building offers accommodation in smart, spacious and well equipped bedrooms, all with en-suite bathrooms. Refreshments may be taken at the nearby family restaurant. For details about current prices, consult the Contents Page under Hotel Groups for the Travelodge phone number.
ROOMS: 20 en suite (bth/shr) d £45.95 *

CHICHESTER West Sussex **Map 04 SU80**
★★★★ **Marriott Goodwood Park**
PO18 0QB
Quality Percentage Score: 69%
☎ 01243 775537 01243 520120
(For full entry see Goodwood)

CHICHESTER West Sussex **Map 04 SU80**
★★★ ❀ ***The Millstream***
Bosham Ln PO18 8HL
Quality Percentage Score: 72%
☎ 01243 573234 Fax 01243 573459
(For full entry see Bosham)

CHICHESTER West Sussex **Map 04 SU80**
★★★ ❀ **Crouchers Bottom Country Hotel**
Birdham Rd PO20 7EH
Quality Percentage Score: 69%
☎ 01243 784995 Fax 01243 539797
Dir: *turn off A27 to the A286, 1.5m from Chichester centre opposite the Black Horse pub*
Conveniently located just a couple of miles from the city centre and close to the harbour, this family run hotel has been greatly extended in keeping with the original character of the property. Guests can enjoy spacious public areas with a comfortable lounge, separate bar and attractive beamed restaurant.
Bedrooms, the majority of which are situated in adjacent, ground floor coach houses offer good levels of space and comfort, feature many thoughtful touches such as tissues and mineral water, and are well equipped.
ROOMS: 15 en suite (bth/shr) (1 fmly) No smoking in 9 bedrooms s £52-£55; d £65-£95 (incl. bkfst) * LB Off peak **MEALS:** Lunch £15 Dinner £19.50-£21.50 & alc French Cuisine V meals Coffee am Tea pm **FACILITIES:** CTV in all bedrooms **SERVICES:** 40P **NOTES:** No coaches No smoking in restaurant Last d 10pm
CARDS:

CHICHESTER West Sussex **Map 04 SU80**
★★★ ❀ **Ship**
North St PO19 1NH
Quality Percentage Score: 67%
☎ 01243 778000 Fax 01243 788000
Dir: *enter Chichester from A27, go round the inner ring road to Northgate, at large Northgate rdbt turn left into North St, hotel is on left*

This well presented Georgian hotel continues to improve. With a major refurbishment programme completed, bedrooms have been upgraded to high standard tastefully decorated and well equipped. An elegant spiral staircase rises from the reception hall. Guests can enjoy a high standard of cooking in the smartly appointed Murrays restaurant.
ROOMS: 34 en suite (bth/shr) (4 fmly) s £65-£73; d £89-£109 (incl. bkfst) * LB Off peak **MEALS:** Lunch £14.95-£15.95 & alc Dinner £18.95 & alc English & French Cuisine V meals Coffee am Tea pm **FACILITIES:** CTV in all bedrooms Xmas **CONF:** Thtr 70 Class 35 Board 30 **SERVICES:** Lift Night porter 38P **NOTES:** No smoking in restaurant Last d 9.30pm **CARDS:**

CHICHESTER West Sussex **Map 04 SU80**
★★ **Bedford**
Southgate PO19 1DP
Quality Percentage Score: 67%
☎ 01243 785766 Fax 01243 533175
Dir: *from A27 (Chichester Bypass) continue N past level crossing at Chichester Station. Hotel 400yds on right*
In a central location convenient for both the city centre and the ring road, this well presented hotel dates back to the 1700s. Bedrooms are attractively decorated, comfortably furnished and well equipped. Public areas include a cosy bar, separate lounge and dining room which overlooks the rear patio. Resident proprietors David and Rita Winship, together with their small team of loyal staff, offer a warm welcome and friendly service.
ROOMS: 19 rms (16 bth/shr) (2 fmly) No smoking in 11 bedrooms s fr £54; d fr £85 (incl. bkfst) * LB Off peak **MEALS:** Dinner £16.50 & alc English & French Cuisine V meals Coffee am **FACILITIES:** CTV in all bedrooms **SERVICES:** 8P **NOTES:** No smoking in restaurant Last d 9pm Closed 24 Dec-4 Jan **CARDS:**

CHICHESTER West Sussex **Map 04 SU80**
★★ **Suffolk House**
3 East Row PO19 1PD
Quality Percentage Score: 67%
☎ 01243 778899 Fax 01243 787282
Dir: *turn right off East St into Little London, follow into East Row, hotel on left*
Friendly proprietors Mr and Mrs Page offer a warm welcome to guests at this intimate Georgian hotel, located just a couple of minutes' walk from the city centre. Bedrooms vary in shape and size but all are comfortably furnished, well equipped and feature

contd.

many thoughtful touches. There is a cosy lounge, small bar, pleasant patio and a restaurant offering an interesting menu. Please telephone beforehand about parking.
ROOMS: 11 en suite (bth/shr) (2 fmly) No smoking in 2 bedrooms s £59-£61; d £86-£112 (incl. bkfst) * LB Off peak **MEALS:** Dinner fr £16.50 & alc English & French Cuisine V meals Coffee am **FACILITIES:** CTV in all bedrooms STV **CONF:** Thtr 25 Class 12 Board 16 **NOTES:** No dogs (ex guide dogs) No coaches No smoking in restaurant Last d 9.15pm **CARDS:**

CHIDEOCK Dorset — Map 03 SY49

★★❀ Chideock House

Main St DT6 6JN
Quality Percentage Score: 69%
☎ 01297 489242 01297 489184
***Dir:** on A35 between Lyme Regis and Bridport*
This delightful, part-thatched house dates back to the 15th century. It is full of character and retains many original beams and fireplaces. Thoughtful touches abound in the bedrooms, and there is a choice of lounges. An interesting menu is offered in the restaurant.
ROOMS: 9 rms (7 bth 1 shr) s £45-£80; d £60-£85 (incl. bkfst) * LB Off peak **MEALS:** Sunday Lunch £9.95-£10.95alc Dinner £17-£25alc English & French Cuisine Coffee am **FACILITIES:** CTV in all bedrooms Xmas **SERVICES:** 20P **NOTES:** No coaches No children 2-12yrs Last d 8.55pm Closed 2 Jan-mid Feb **CARDS:**

CHILDER THORNTON Cheshire — Map 07 SJ37

Travel Inn

New Chester Rd L66 1QW
☎ 0151 339 8101 0151 347 1401
***Dir:** on A41, near junct 5 of M53 heading towards Chester*
This modern building offers accommodation in smart, spacious and well equipped bedrooms, all with en-suite bathrooms. Refreshments may be taken at the nearby family restaurant. For details about current prices consult the Contents Page under Hotel Groups for the Travel Inn phone number.
ROOMS: 31 en suite (bth/shr) d £39.95 *

CHIPPENHAM Wiltshire — Map 03 ST97

★★★ Angel Hotel

Market Place SN15 3HD
Quality Percentage Score: 68%
☎ 01249 652615 01249 443210
***Dir:** follow signs for town centre, hotel next to Borough Pde shopping centre car park*
With good car parking to the rear of the hotel, this centuries-old building is centrally situated. Both the bedrooms in the original building and the new courtyard rooms are comfortable and well equipped. The panelled restaurant serves a carte menu, and there two popular bars.
ROOMS: 15 en suite (bth/shr) 26 annexe en suite (bth/shr) (3 fmly) s fr £82.50; d fr £92.50 * Off peak **MEALS:** Bar Lunch £13.80-£17alc Dinner £16.15-£25alc V meals Coffee am **FACILITIES:** CTV in all bedrooms Indoor swimming pool & Gymnasium from Nov 1999 **CONF:** Thtr 120 Class 50 Board 50 Del from £99 * **SERVICES:** Night porter 50P **NOTES:** No smoking area in restaurant Last d 9.30pm **CARDS:**

CHIPPERFIELD Hertfordshire — Map 04 TL00

★★ The Two Brewers

The Common WD4 9BS
Quality Percentage Score: 70%
☎ 01923 265266 01923 261884
***Dir:** turn left in centre of village, hotel overlooks common*
Formerly a 16th-century inn, with a bar and food operation at its hub, the Two Brewers overlooks the cricket ground and common. Under new ownership, the hotel has undergone an impressive investment and refurbishment programme. Food is available all day and evening in the attractive Chef and Brewer style bar/restaurant. Services here are provided promptly by a willing and friendly team.
ROOMS: 20 en suite (bth/shr) No smoking in 10 bedrooms d fr £85 * LB Off peak **MEALS:** Lunch £7.15-£25alc Dinner £9.50-£25alc International Cuisine V meals Coffee am Tea pm **FACILITIES:** CTV in all bedrooms STV **CONF:** Board 16 Del from £135 * **SERVICES:** Night porter 25P **NOTES:** No dogs (ex guide dogs) No coaches Last d 10pm **CARDS:**

CHIPPING Lancashire — Map 07 SD64

★★★★❀ The Gibbon Bridge

Forest of Bowland PR3 2TQ
Quality Percentage Score: 69%
☎ 01995 61456 01995 61277
***Dir:** at T-junct in Chipping turn right towards Clithroe. Hotel 1m on right*
This fine hotel offers high levels of comfort and service. Bedrooms, including four-poster rooms and split-level suites, are a delight, whilst public areas include a welcoming restaurant and conservatory. Leisure facilites are available and the hotel stands in lovely gardens.
ROOMS: 15 en suite (bth/shr) 14 annexe en suite (bth/shr) s fr £70; d fr £100 (incl. bkfst) * LB Off peak **MEALS:** Lunch £10-£15 Dinner £20 & alc V meals Coffee am Tea pm **FACILITIES:** CTV in all bedrooms STV Tennis (hard) Fishing Sauna Solarium Gym Xmas **CONF:** Thtr 70 Class 30 Board 35 **SERVICES:** Lift Night porter 252P **NOTES:** No dogs (ex guide dogs) No smoking in restaurant Last d 9pm
CARDS:

CHIPPING CAMPDEN Gloucestershire — Map 04 SP13

The Premier Collection

★★★❀❀ Cotswold House

The Square GL55 6AN
☎ 01386 840330 01386 840310
***Dir:** from A44 take B4081 signposted to Chipping Campden village. Turn right into High St at T junct Cotswold House is located at the Square*
This elegant small hotel stands on the town's charming main street. Antiques and works of art decorate the lovely public rooms and bedrooms are individually furnished, with an eye for detail and comfort. Guests can eat either in Forbes

contd.

Brasserie or in the more formal Garden Room Restaurant; food in both is cooked with flair.
ROOMS: 15 en suite (bth/shr) s £55-£75; d £120-£160 (incl. bkfst) * LB Off peak **MEALS:** Sunday Lunch £17 High tea £6-£8alc Dinner £22 & alc V meals Coffee am Tea pm **FACILITIES:** CTV in all bedrooms STV Croquet lawn Access to local Sports Centre Wkly live entertainment **CONF:** Thtr 30 Board 20 Del from £125 * **SERVICES:** 15P **NOTES:** No dogs No coaches No children 7yrs No smoking in restaurant Last d 9.30pm Closed 23-26 Dec
CARDS:

See advert on this page

CHIPPING CAMPDEN Gloucestershire — Map 04 SP13
★★★ Seymour House
High St GL55 6AH
Quality Percentage Score: 71%
☎ 01386 840429 Fax 01386 840369
Dir: *Hotel in middle of High St ooposite Lloyds Bank, Chipping Campden at centre of road links A34/46/44*
Parts of this lovely Cotswold stone property date from the early 18th century, and public rooms, including a drawing room, restaurant and separate bar, have kept their period character. Bedrooms vary in style, and there are some in a cottage in the garden. The hotel has a licence for civil wedding ceremonies.
ROOMS: 11 en suite (bth/shr) 4 annexe en suite (bth/shr) s fr £72.50; d £95-£180 (incl. bkfst) * LB Off peak **MEALS:** Lunch £13-£15.50 Dinner £24.95-£32 English, French & Italian Cuisine V meals Coffee am Tea pm **FACILITIES:** CTV in all bedrooms STV Xmas **CONF:** Thtr 55 Class 20 Board 30 Del from £120 * **SERVICES:** 28P **NOTES:** No dogs (ex guide dogs) No smoking in restaurant Last d 10pm
CARDS:

CHIPPING CAMPDEN Gloucestershire — Map 04 SP13
★★★ Noel Arms
High St GL55 6AT
Quality Percentage Score: 70%
☎ 01386 840317 Fax 01386 841136
Dir: *turn off A44 onto B4081 to Chipping Campden, take 1st right down hill into town. Hotel on right opposite Market Hall.*
Dating from the 14th century, the hotel retains much original character yet has been extensively refurbished. Bedrooms are well co-ordinated and have smart modern en suites. Public areas include a popular bar, conservatory lounge and bright restaurant offering high standards of cuisine.
ROOMS: 26 en suite (bth/shr) (1 fmly) s fr £75; d £105-£125 (incl. bkfst) * LB Off peak **MEALS:** Sunday Lunch £11.95-£13.95 Dinner £19.95 British & French Cuisine V meals Coffee am Tea pm **FACILITIES:** CTV in all bedrooms Membership of leisure club Xmas **CONF:** Thtr 20 Board 12 Del from £110 * **SERVICES:** 30P **NOTES:** No smoking in restaurant Last d 9.30pm
CARDS:

CHIPPING CAMPDEN Gloucestershire — Map 04 SP13
★★★ Three Ways House
Mickleton GL55 6SB
Quality Percentage Score: 70%
THE CIRCLE Selected Individual Hotels GREAT BRITAIN
☎ 01386 438429 Fax 01386 438118
Dir: *situated on B4632 Stratford upon Avon to Broadway Road, Hotel in centre of Mickleton Village*
This delightful old hotel stands in a small village north of Chipping Campden. It is the home of the famous 'Pudding Club' and several of the bedrooms reflect this theme. Meals are served

contd.

in the traditional restaurant, where there is sometimes live piano music, or in Randles Bar/Bistro.

Three Ways House, Chipping Camden

ROOMS: 41 en suite (bth/shr) (5 fmly) s £65-£70; d £92-£115 (incl. bkfst) * LB Off peak **MEALS:** Sunday Lunch £13.50-£16 Dinner fr £21 & alc English & Continental Cuisine V meals Coffee am Tea pm **FACILITIES:** CTV in all bedrooms Wkly live entertainment Xmas **CONF:** Thtr 130 Class 40 Board 35 Del from £105 * **SERVICES:** Night porter 37P **NOTES:** No smoking in restaurant Last d 9.30pm **CARDS:**

See advert on opposite page

CHIPPING NORTON Oxfordshire — Map 04 SP32

★★ *The Crown & Cushion*

23 High St OX7 5AD
Quality Percentage Score: 62%
☎ 01608 642533 📠 01608 642926
Dir: *the Hotel is located on the High Street of Chipping Norton*

Dating back to 1497, this former coaching inn is located on the historic market place and its rather plain frontage belies the extent of the building and the range of facilities offered within or the courtyard to the rear. All the bedrooms, which vary in size, offer modern comforts and several have four-poster beds.

ROOMS: 30 en suite (bth/shr) 10 annexe rms (3 shr) (10 fmly) No smoking in 3 bedrooms **MEALS:** European Cuisine V meals Coffee am Tea pm **FACILITIES:** CTV in all bedrooms Indoor swimming pool (heated) Squash Snooker Solarium Gym Jacuzzi/spa **CONF:** Thtr 200 Class 70 Board 60 **SERVICES:** 34P **NOTES:** No smoking in restaurant Last d 9pm **CARDS:**

CHIPPING NORTON Oxfordshire — Map 04 SP32

★★ The White Hart

16 High St OX7 5AD
Quality Percentage Score: 62%
☎ 01608 642572 📠 01608 644143
Dir: *opposite Market Sq on High St (A44)*

There is an 18th-century façade to this building, parts of which date back to the 13th century. A few of the bedrooms are spacious and have some wonderful older world character but the majority are more contemporary. Centrally located in the town, the lounge is a popular place for morning tea and afternoon refreshments.

ROOMS: 14 en suite (bth/shr) 5 annexe en suite (bth) s £25-£55; d £45-£85 (incl. bkfst) * LB Off peak **MEALS:** Lunch £4.95-£9.95 Dinner £14.95 British & French Cuisine V meals Coffee am Tea pm **FACILITIES:** CTV in all bedrooms Xmas **CONF:** Thtr 60 Class 20 Board 24 Del from £75 * **SERVICES:** 22P **NOTES:** No smoking in restaurant Last d 9pm **CARDS:**

CHITTLEHAMHOLT Devon — Map 03 SS62

★★★ Highbullen

EX37 9HD
Quality Percentage Score: 68%
☎ 01769 540561 📠 01769 540492
Dir: *leave M5 junct 27 onto A361 to South Molton, then B3226 Crediton Rd after 5.2m turn right up hill to Chittlehamholt, hotel 0.5m beyond village*

Set in parkland with its own 18-hole golf course, Highbullen is a Victorian Gothic mansion with glorious countryside views. The extensive cellars feature a daily-changing, fixed-price menu served each evening. The breakfast room has magnificent views of the valley, and light lunches are served in the bar or pleasing courtyard. There is a wide choice of bedrooms in sizes and style, spread between the mansion and fully converted buildings in the grounds.

ROOMS: 12 en suite (bth) 25 annexe en suite (bth/shr) s £70; d £140-£180 (incl. cont bkfst & dinner) * LB Off peak **MEALS:** Lunch £16 & alc High tea £5 & alc Dinner £22 & alc International Cuisine V meals Coffee am Tea pm **FACILITIES:** CTV in all bedrooms Indoor swimming pool (heated) Outdoor swimming pool (heated) Golf 18 Tennis (hard) Fishing Squash Snooker Sauna Solarium Gym Croquet lawn Putting green Hairdressing Beauty treatment Massage Indoor tennis **CONF:** Board 20 Del £90 * **SERVICES:** 60P **NOTES:** No dogs (ex guide dogs) No coaches No children 8yrs No smoking in restaurant Last d 9pm **CARDS:**

CHOLLERFORD Northumberland — Map 12 NY97

★★★ Swallow George Hotel

NE46 4EW
Quality Percentage Score: 73%
☎ 01434 681611 📠 01434 681727
Dir: *0.25m W of Hexham turn off A69 onto A6079, follow road NW for 4m until crossroads, turn left onto B6318, hotel 0.25m on right hand side over bridge*

Situated where the old Roman Road crosses the River Tyne, with terraced gardens running down to the river, this hotel provides stylish, well-equipped accommodation and fine food in an attractive setting. The restaurant and cocktail lounge, plus several bedrooms overlook the gardens and river. Tasteful refurbishment of the lounges has considerably enhanced the remaining public rooms.

ROOMS: 47 en suite (bth/shr) (5 fmly) No smoking in 19 bedrooms s £80-£110; d £110-£150 (incl. bkfst) * LB Off peak **MEALS:** Lunch £9-£16 Dinner fr £24.95 V meals Coffee am Tea pm **FACILITIES:** CTV in all bedrooms STV Indoor swimming pool (heated) Fishing Sauna Solarium Putting green Jacuzzi/spa Jogging track Exercise equipment Xmas **CONF:** Thtr 60 Class 30 Board 32 Del from £120 * **SERVICES:** Night porter 70P **NOTES:** No smoking in restaurant Last d 9.30pm **CARDS:**

CHORLEY Lancashire **Map 07 SD51**

★★★ Park Hall

Park Hall Rd, Charnock Richard PR7 5LP
Quality Percentage Score: 69%
☎ 01257 452090 Fax 01257 451838

Dir: *off A49 W of village. Follow brown tourist signs from M6/M61*

Situated in the Camelot Theme Park and adjoining a village complex complete with a pub and various shops, the hotel provides a choice of bedrooms, some following interesting design themes. There are two restaurant, and a well equipped leisure club.

ROOMS: 54 en suite (bth/shr) 84 annexe en suite (bth/shr) (59 fmly) No smoking in 11 bedrooms d fr £89 * LB Off peak **MEALS:** Lunch £9.50-£9.95 High tea £6.25-£7.75 Dinner fr £16.95 English, American, French & Mexican Cuisine V meals Coffee am Tea pm **FACILITIES:** CTV in all bedrooms STV Indoor swimming pool (heated) Sauna Solarium Gym Pool table Jacuzzi/spa Steam room Weights room Xmas **CONF:** Thtr 700 Class 230 Board 50 Del £119 * **SERVICES:** Lift Night porter 2600P **NOTES:** No dogs (ex guide dogs) No smoking area in restaurant Last d 9.45pm **CARDS:**

See advert under PRESTON

CHORLEY Lancashire **Map 07 SD51**

★★★ Shaw Hill Hotel Golf & Country Club

Preston Rd, Whittle-le-Woods PR6 7PP
Quality Percentage Score: 68%
☎ 01257 269221 Fax 01257 261223

Dir: *from Chorley on A6, then signs for A49, at lghts turn left past golf course, left to Dawson Ln. At T-junct go right. Hotel 50yds on right*

A championship golf course is just one of the attractions at this hotel, which is based on a Georgian mansion. Both standard and 'executive' rooms are available, there is a choice of bars and a well appointed restaurant, overlooking the golf course.

ROOMS: 26 en suite (bth/shr) 4 annexe en suite (bth/shr) (1 fmly) s £70-£100; d £90-£120 (incl. bkfst) * LB Off peak **MEALS:** Bar Lunch £2.70-£5.50 International Cuisine V meals Coffee am Tea pm **FACILITIES:** CTV in all bedrooms STV Indoor swimming pool (heated) Golf 18 Fishing Snooker Sauna Solarium Gym Putting green Jacuzzi/spa Beauty salon Hairdresser Xmas **CONF:** Thtr 350 Class 100 Board 150 **SERVICES:** Night porter 200P **CARDS:**

See advert on this page

CHORLEY Lancashire **Map 07 SD51**

Travelodge

Preston Rd, Clayton-le-Woods PR6 7JB
☎ 01772 311963

Dir: *from M6 junc28 take B5256 for approx 2m, next to Halfway House public house*

This modern building offers accommodation in smart, spacious and well equipped bedrooms, all with en-suite bathrooms. Refreshments may be taken at the nearby family restaurant. For details about current prices, consult the Contents Page under Hotel Groups for the Travelodge phone number.

ROOMS: 40 en suite (bth/shr) d £45.95 *

CHORLEY Lancashire **Map 07 SD51**

Welcome Lodge

Welcome Break, Charnock Richard - M6, Mill Ln PR7 5LR
☎ 01257 791746 Fax 01257 793596

Dir: *on north-bound side of the Welcome Break service area between junct 27 & 28 of the M6. Accessible from south-bound carriageway*

This modern building offers accommodation in smart, spacious and well equipped bedrooms, suitable for families and businessmen, and all with en-suite bathrooms. Refreshments may be taken at the nearby

contd.

family restaurant. For details of current prices, consult the Contents Page under Hotel Groups for the Welcome Break phone number.
ROOMS: 100 en suite (bth/shr) d fr £45 * **CONF:** Thtr 30 Board 20

CHRISTCHURCH Dorset **Map 04 SZ19**
★★★ **Waterford Lodge**
87 Bure Ln, Friars Cliff, Mudeford BH23 4DN
Quality Percentage Score: 73%
☎ 01425 272948 & 278801 📠 01425 279130
Dir: *from A35 Somerford rdbt 2m E of Christichurch take A337 towards Highcliffe, at next rdbt turn towards Mudeford, hotel on left*

Situated in easy reach of Christchurch, the hotel is popular with business guests as well as holiday makers. It offers attractive, spacious bedrooms, a comfortable bar lounge overlooking the gardens and a well appointed restaurant.
ROOMS: 18 en suite (bth) (1 fmly) s £78-£88; d £90-£100 * LB Off peak **MEALS:** Lunch £14.50 Dinner £25.50 English & French Cuisine V meals Coffee am Tea pm **FACILITIES:** CTV in all bedrooms **CONF:** Thtr 100 Class 48 Board 36 Del from £105 * **SERVICES:** 38P **NOTES:** No coaches No smoking in restaurant Last d 9pm
CARDS:

CHRISTCHURCH Dorset **Map 04 SZ19**
★★★ **The Avonmouth**
95 Mudeford BH23 3NT
Quality Percentage Score: 66%
☎ 01202 483434 📠 01202 479004
Dir: *approaching Christchurch on A35 from Lyndhurst, turn left at roundabout and right at next roundabout and continue for 1m*
This friendly hotel appeals to both leisure and business guests, and benefits from a superb location alongside Mudeford Quay and right at the water's edge. Cosy public rooms are traditional in style, but the bedrooms are modern with pretty decor and a good level of comfort; the garden rooms also have small patios.
ROOMS: 26 en suite (bth/shr) 14 annexe en suite (bth/shr) (3 fmly) No smoking in 14 bedrooms s £70; d £110 * LB Off peak **MEALS:** Sunday Lunch £13.50 Dinner £15-£20 V meals Coffee am Tea pm **FACILITIES:** CTV in all bedrooms Outdoor swimming pool (heated) Croquet lawn Putting green Golf practice net Xmas **CONF:** Thtr 60 Class 25 Board 24 Del from £75 * **SERVICES:** Night porter 80P **NOTES:** No coaches Last d 8.45pm **CARDS:**

CHRISTCHURCH Dorset **Map 04 SZ19**
★★ **Fisherman's Haunt**
Sailsbury Rd, Winkton BH23 7AS
Quality Percentage Score: 68%
☎ 01202 477283 & 484071 📠 01202 478883
Dir: *2.5m N on B3347*
The bedrooms, two with four-poster beds, offer exceptional standards of comfort, decor and furnishing. A few rooms are in the main house, but most are in two attractive cottages. The public areas include a lively bar and a restaurant.
ROOMS: 4 en suite (bth/shr) 14 annexe en suite (bth/shr) (3 fmly) No smoking in 6 bedrooms s £48; d £64 (incl. bkfst) * LB Off peak **MEALS:** Sunday Lunch £8-£10 Dinner £11.95-£13.95alc V meals Coffee am Tea pm **FACILITIES:** CTV in all bedrooms STV **SERVICES:** 75P **NOTES:** No smoking in restaurant Last d 9.30pm Closed 25 Dec
CARDS:

CHRISTCHURCH Dorset **Map 04 SZ19**
⌂ **Travel Inn (Christchurch East)**
Somerford Rd BH23 3QG
☎ 01202 485376 📠 01202 474939
Dir: *from M27 take A337 to Lyndhurst, then A35 to Christchurch. Situated on B3059 rdbt towards Somerford*
This modern building offers accommodation in smart, spacious and well equipped bedrooms, all with en-suite bathrooms. Refreshments may be taken at the nearby family restaurant. For details about current prices consult the Contents Page under Hotel Groups for the Travel Inn phone number.
ROOMS: 38 en suite (bth/shr) d £39.95 *

CHRISTCHURCH Dorset **Map 04 SZ19**
⌂ **Travel Inn (Christchurch West)**
Barrack Rd BH23 2BN
☎ 01202 485215 📠 01582 400024
Dir: *from A338 take A3060 towards Christchurch. Turn left onto A35 & Travel Inn is on right*
This modern building offers accommodation in smart, spacious and well equipped bedrooms, all with en-suite bathrooms. Refreshments may be taken at the nearby family restaurant. For details about current prices consult the Contents Page under Hotel Groups for the Travel Inn phone number.
ROOMS: 41 en suite (bth/shr) d £39.95 *

CHURCHILL Somerset **Map 03 ST45**
★★ ***Winston Manor***
Bristol Rd BS25 5NL
Quality Percentage Score: 62%
☎ 01934 852348 📠 01934 852033
Dir: *On A38 100yds N of junction with A368 Bath-Weston-Super-Mare*
This small hotel is conveniently close to Bristol Airport. In addition to standard bedrooms, an attractive honeymoon/VIP room is available. All rooms are well equipped, with thoughtful extras such as mineral water.
ROOMS: 14 en suite (bth/shr) (1 fmly) No smoking in 2 bedrooms **MEALS:** British & Mediterranean Cuisine V meals Coffee am Tea pm **FACILITIES:** CTV in all bedrooms **CONF:** Thtr 40 Class 30 Board 30 **SERVICES:** 25P **NOTES:** No smoking in restaurant Last d 9.15pm 25 & 26 Dec. Restaurant closed Sun eves **CARDS:**

CHURCH STRETTON Shropshire **Map 07 SO49**
★★★ **Stretton Hall Hotel**
All Stretton SY6 6HG
Quality Percentage Score: 63%
☎ 01694 723224 📠 01694 724365
Dir: *from Shrewsbury, travelling along the A49, turn right onto B4370 signed to All Stretton, hotel in 1m on left opposite The Yew Tree PH*
This fine late 18th-century country house stands in its own spacious gardens. Original oak panelling features throughout the lounge bar, lounge and the traditionally furnished restaurant. The bedrooms are traditionally furnished, but have modern facilities and equipment. Family and four-poster rooms are available. New, young and enthusiastic owners Frances and

contd.

Charles Baker-Vilain took over in 1998 and at the time of our last inspection they had already started to make improvements.

ROOMS: 12 en suite (bth/shr) (1 fmly) s fr £40; d fr £55 (incl. bkfst) * LB Off peak **MEALS:** Lunch £10.75 & alc Dinner £18-£25alc English & French Cuisine V meals Coffee am Tea pm **FACILITIES:** CTV in all bedrooms Xmas **CONF:** Thtr 60 Class 24 Board 18 Del from £66 * **SERVICES:** 70P **NOTES:** No smoking in restaurant Last d 9pm
CARDS:

CHURCH STRETTON Shropshire — Map 07 SO49
★★ Mynd House
Ludlow Rd, Little Stretton SY6 6RB
Quality Percentage Score: 69%
☎ 01694 722212 Fax 01694 724180
Dir: *off A49 follow signs for Little Stretton, hotel in main village street, 2m S B4370*
A large Edwardian house reached via a steep driveway. The attractive bedrooms have many thoughtful extras and are well equipped. Two suites are available. Refurbished public areas comprise a comfortable lounge, pleasant bar and attractive, traditional dining room.
ROOMS: 7 en suite (bth/shr) (2 fmly) No smoking in all bedrooms s £45-£55; d £70-£130 (incl. bkfst) * LB Off peak **MEALS:** Lunch £10 Dinner £26 V meals **FACILITIES:** CTV in all bedrooms Jacuzzi/spa Xmas **CONF:** Board 20 **SERVICES:** 12P **NOTES:** No coaches No smoking in restaurant Last d 9pm Closed 6-31 Jan **CARDS:**

CHURT Surrey — Map 04 SU83
★★★ Frensham Pond Hotel
GU10 2QB
Quality Percentage Score: 68%
☎ 01252 795161 Fax 01252 792631
Dir: *from A3 turn right onto A287. After 4m turn left at 'Beware Horses' sign to hotel 0.25m along Pond Lane*
The hotel has a quiet picturesque setting overlooking Frensham Pond with its ducks, swans and geese. Built in the 15th century as a private residence, it offers modern facilities including a leisure club, quality dining and 24-hour room service. All rooms are doubles, garden suites offer family accommodation overlooking the lawns.
ROOMS: 39 en suite (bth/shr) 12 annexe en suite (bth/shr) s £75-£102; d £85-£118 (incl. cont bkfst) * LB Off peak **MEALS:** Lunch £12.50-£14.50 & alc Dinner £19.75-£23 & alc V meals Coffee am Tea pm **FACILITIES:** CTV in all bedrooms Indoor swimming pool (heated) Squash Sauna Solarium Gym Pool table Jacuzzi/spa Steam room **CONF:** Thtr 120 Class 45 Board 40 Del from £115 * **SERVICES:** Night porter 120P **NOTES:** No dogs (ex guide dogs) Last d 9.30pm
CARDS:

CIRENCESTER Gloucestershire — Map 04 SP00
★★★ The Crown of Crucis
Ampney Crucis GL7 5RS
Quality Percentage Score: 69%
☎ 01285 851806 Fax 01285 851735
Dir: *take A417 to Fairford, hotel is approx 2.5m on left hand side of road*
Parts of this hotel date back to the 16th Century and the old coaching inn now forms the bar and restaurant. Recently refurbished, the restaurant serves good food in a bright, bistro environment. The bedrooms, arranged around an open courtyard, are attractively appointed and offer modern facilities.
ROOMS: 25 en suite (bth/shr) (2 fmly) No smoking in 10 bedrooms s fr £58; d fr £86 (incl. bkfst) LB Off peak **MEALS:** Sunday Lunch £10-£18 Dinner £16.50 & alc V meals Coffee am Tea pm **FACILITIES:** CTV in all bedrooms Free membership of local leisure centre **CONF:** Thtr 80 Class 40 Board 25 Del £86.50 * **SERVICES:** 82P **NOTES:** No smoking in restaurant Last d 10pm Closed 24-30 Dec
CARDS:

CIRENCESTER Gloucestershire — Map 04 SP00
★★★ Stratton House
Gloucester Rd GL7 2LE
Quality Percentage Score: 68%
☎ 01285 651761 Fax 01285 640024
Dir: *M4 junct 15, A419 to Cirencester, hotel on left on A417. M5 exit 11 to Cheltenham, follow B4070 to A417, hotel on right*
This attractive 17th-century manor house, just a short walk from the town centre, has a new wing of spacious 'premier' rooms, and well equipped standard rooms in the main house. Day rooms include a split-level drawing room and a traditional

contd.

restaurant overlooking the garden. Food is well prepared and menus offer a wide choice of dishes.
ROOMS: 41 en suite (bth/shr) No smoking in 19 bedrooms s fr £75; d fr £95 (incl. bkfst) * LB Off peak **MEALS:** Lunch fr £12.25 High tea fr £3.75 Dinner fr £18.75 English & French Cuisine V meals Coffee am Tea pm **FACILITIES:** CTV in all bedrooms Xmas **CONF:** Thtr 150 Class 50 Board 40 Del from £110 * **SERVICES:** Night porter 100P **NOTES:** No smoking in restaurant Last d 10pm
CARDS:

CIRENCESTER Gloucestershire — Map 04 SP00
★★ The New Inn at Coln
GL7 5AN
Quality Percentage Score: 78%
☎ 01285 750651 Fax 01285 750657
(For full entry see Coln St Aldwyns)

CLACTON-ON-SEA Essex — Map 05 TM11
★★ Esplanade Hotel
27-29 Marine Pde East CO15 1UU
Quality Percentage Score: 68%
☎ 01255 220450 Fax 01255 221800
Dir: *enter Clacton on Sea on the A133 follow sign to Sea Front (Carnarvon Rd) at sea front turn right, hotel on right in 50yds*

The Simpsons' long established family hotel on the sea front at Clacton offers a warm welcome to guests new and old. Recently refurbished to a very high standard, bedrooms are airy, bright and spacious, and many have sea views. Guests particularly enjoy the convivial atmosphere in the restaurant and lounge and secure parking is available.
ROOMS: 29 en suite (bth/shr) (2 fmly) s £24-£35; d £48-£60 (incl. bkfst) * LB Off peak **MEALS:** Lunch £5.95-£11 & alc Dinner £5.95-£11 & alc International Cuisine V meals Coffee am Tea pm **FACILITIES:** CTV in all bedrooms Xmas **CONF:** Class 50 Del from £40 * **SERVICES:** 13P **NOTES:** No dogs (ex guide dogs) No smoking in restaurant Last d 9pm
CARDS:

CLACTON-ON-SEA Essex — Map 05 TM11
★ Chudleigh
13 Agate Rd, Marine Pde West CO15 1RA
Quality Percentage Score: 73%
☎ 01255 425407 Fax 01255 425407
Dir: *follow signs to Town Centre, Seafront and Pier. Turn right at seafront and then right again into Agate Rd after crossing traffic lights at Pier*
Popular with business and leisure guests, who return for the Oleggini's wonderful hospitality and personal attention, the hotel is a relaxing oasis close to the pier and the bustling seafront. It offers spruced and tidy accommodation in recently refurbished rooms. There is a comfortable lounge where drinks are served, and a spacious restaurant to relax in over dinner.
ROOMS: 10 en suite (bth/shr) (2 fmly) No smoking in 2 bedrooms s £32.50-£35; d £48-£52 (incl. bkfst) Off peak **MEALS:** Dinner £11-£12.50 **FACILITIES:** CTV in all bedrooms **SERVICES:** 7P **NOTES:** No coaches No smoking in restaurant Last d 7.30pm Closed 1st week Oct, 1 week Spring, 4-20 Jan **CARDS:**

CLANFIELD Oxfordshire — Map 04 SP20
★★★ Plough at Clanfield
Bourton Rd OX18 2RB
Quality Percentage Score: 67%
☎ 01367 810222 Fax 01367 810596
Dir: *on edge of village at junct of A4095/B4020*
Full of character, and retaining many original features, the Plough, built in 1560, is the archetypal stone-built Elizabethan manor house with mullioned windows. The cosy bar has two log-burning fires and each of the bedrooms is furnished with individual style. Food here is taken seriously, and the kitchen brigade cooks with flair.
ROOMS: 6 en suite (bth/shr) s £65-£85; d £95-£125 (incl. bkfst) * LB **MEALS:** Lunch £16.75-£23.50 alc Dinner £32.50 alc English & French V meals Coffee am Tea pm **FACILITIES:** CTV in all bedrooms Xmas **SERVICES:** 30P **NOTES:** No dogs (ex guide dogs) No children 12yrs No smoking in restaurant Last d 9pm Closed 25-30 Dec
CARDS:

CLAVERDON Warwickshire — Map 04 SP16
★★★ Ardencote Manor Hotel & Country Club
Lye Green Rd CV35 8LS
Quality Percentage Score: 68%
☎ 01926 843111 Fax 01926 842646
Dir: *follow sign post direction towards Shrewley off A4189 in centre of Claverdon, Hotel 0.5m on right*
The range of public areas and leisure facilities available at Ardencote are unsurpassed in a hotel of this size. Bedrooms are all well equipped, and decorated with pretty fabrics and smart furnishings. There is a varied choice of eating options available; The Oak Room offers a modern imaginative menu with formal service. Informal snacks and meals are served in the members' bar and at the lakeside sports lodge.

ROOMS: 18 en suite (bth/shr) (1 fmly) No smoking in 2 bedrooms **MEALS:** Lunch fr £14.95 High tea fr £1.50 Dinner fr £21.95 English & French Cuisine V meals Coffee am Tea pm **FACILITIES:** CTV in all bedrooms STV Indoor swimming pool (heated) Tennis (hard) Trout fishing 9 hole golf from mid 1999 Wkly live entertainment **CONF:** Thtr 120 Class 60 Board 50 **SERVICES:** Night porter 120P **NOTES:** No dogs (ex guide dogs) No smoking in restaurant Last d 9.30pm
CARDS:

See advert under WARWICK

CLEARWELL Gloucestershire **Map 03 SO50**
★★★ Wyndham Arms
GL16 8JT
Quality Percentage Score: 67%
☎ 01594 833666 📠 01594 836450
Dir: *in centre of village on the B4231*
In the heart of the Forest of Dean, this old village inn traces its history back over 600 years. Exposed stone walls and an impressive inglenook fireplace in the bar, add to its charm and character. Most of the bedrooms are in a modern extension close to the main entrance. There are both bar and restaurant menus.
ROOMS: 5 en suite (bth/shr) 12 annexe en suite (bth/shr) (3 fmly) s £58.50; d £80-£100 (incl. bkfst) * LB Off peak **MEALS:** Lunch £13.75 & alc Dinner £21.25 & alc International Cuisine V meals Coffee am Tea pm **FACILITIES:** CTV in all bedrooms **CONF:** Thtr 56 Class 30 Board 22 Del from £57.50 * **SERVICES:** 54P **NOTES:** No smoking in restaurant Last d 9.30pm **CARDS:**

CLEARWELL Gloucestershire **Map 03 SO50**
★★❀ *Tudor Farmhouse Hotel & Restaurant*
GL16 8JS
Quality Percentage Score: 71%
☎ 01594 833046 📠 01594 837093
Dating back to the 13th-century this charming house has exposed stonework, oak beams, wall panelling and open inglenook fireplace. Friendly service is provided by the owners and staff, the restaurant is the venue for some good cooking. Bedrooms are individually styled and thoughtfully equipped; located in the main house and two converted cottages.
ROOMS: 6 en suite (bth/shr) 7 annexe en suite (bth/shr) (3 fmly) No smoking in 6 bedrooms **MEALS:** V meals **FACILITIES:** CTV in all bedrooms **SERVICES:** 20P **NOTES:** No coaches No smoking in restaurant Last d 9pm Closed 24-30 Dec
CARDS:

CLEATOR Cumbria **Map 11 NY01**
★★★ Ennerdale Country House
CA23 3DT
Quality Percentage Score: 74%
☎ 01946 813907 📠 01946 815260
Dir: *take A5086 towards Egremont after approximately 14m arrive at Cleator Moor. Stay on the A5086 for a further mile until village of Cleator*
This increasingly popular hotel has stylish, well equipped bedrooms that come in a variety of sizes and include superior split-level rooms with four-posters. The old farm buildings in the grounds have recently been converted to provide a high standard of accommodation inclusive of videos, CD players, and games consoles. There is a smart restaurant which offers an appealing variety of both classical and contemporary cuisine. A smart cocktail lounge and a less formal bar provides a choice of venue for pre dinner drinks.
ROOMS: 30 en suite (bth/shr) (4 fmly) No smoking in 4 bedrooms s £65-£95; d £90-£150 (incl. bkfst) * LB Off peak **MEALS:** Lunch £7-£18 & alc Dinner £19-£25 International Cuisine V meals Coffee am Tea pm **FACILITIES:** CTV in all bedrooms STV Xmas **CONF:** Thtr 150 Class 100 Board 40 Del from £45 * **SERVICES:** 65P **NOTES:** No smoking in restaurant Last d 9.30pm **CARDS:**

AA Rosettes are awarded for quality of food, see page 15 for an explanation of Rosette assessment.

CLECKHEATON West Yorkshire **Map 07 SE12**
★★ Prospect Hall Hotel
Prospect Rd BD19 3HD
Quality Percentage Score: 60%
☎ 01274 873022 📠 01274 870376
Dir: *M62 junct 26, follow A638 towards Dewsbury, just before Cleckheaton town ctr take right up Scott St, then 1st left after the Bridge onto Prospect Rd*
ROOMS: 34 en suite (bth/shr) 6 annexe en suite (bth/shr) (1 fmly) No smoking in 17 bedrooms s £40-£43; d £56.50 (incl. bkfst) * Off peak **MEALS:** Lunch £8.50-£14.50 & alc Dinner £11-£14 & alc English & Continental Cuisine V meals **FACILITIES:** CTV in all bedrooms STV ch fac Xmas **CONF:** Thtr 60 Class 90 Board 35 Del from £60 * **SERVICES:** Night porter 150P **NOTES:** No dogs (ex guide dogs) Last d 9.30pm **CARDS:**

CLECKHEATON West Yorkshire **Map 07 SE12**
Travel Inn
Whitehall Rd BD19 6HG
☎ 01274 862828 📠 01274 852973
Dir: *on A58 at intersection with M62 & M606*
This modern building offers accommodation in smart, spacious and well equipped bedrooms, all with en-suite bathrooms. Refreshments may be taken at the nearby family restaurant. For details about current prices consult the Contents Page under Hotel Groups for the Travel Inn phone number.
ROOMS: 40 en suite (bth/shr) d £39.95 *

CLEETHORPES Lincolnshire **Map 08 TA30**
★★★❀ Kingsway
Kingsway DN35 0AE
Quality Percentage Score: 70%
☎ 01472 601122 📠 01472 601381
Dir: *leave A180 at Grimsby, head to Cleethorpes seafront. The hotel is at jct of The Kingsway and Queen Parade (A1098)*
This seafront hotel has been in the same family for four generations and continues to provide traditional comfort and professional friendly service. The lounges are comfortable and good food is served in the pleasant dining room. Most of the bedrooms are of good comfortable proportions, and all are bright and pleasantly furnished.
ROOMS: 50 en suite (bth/shr) s £58-£75; d £84-£90 (incl. bkfst) * LB Off peak **MEALS:** Lunch £12.50-£14.75 & alc Dinner £18.95 & alc English & French Cuisine V meals Coffee am **FACILITIES:** CTV in all bedrooms STV **SERVICES:** Lift Night porter 50P **NOTES:** No dogs (ex guide dogs) No coaches No children 5yrs Last d 9pm Closed 25-28 & 31 Dec
CARDS:

CLEEVE HILL Gloucestershire **Map 03 SO92**
★★★ *Rising Sun*
GL52 3PX
Quality Percentage Score: 65%
☎ 01242 676281 📠 01242 673069
Dir: *on the B4632, 4m N of Cheltenham*
For views, this hotel cannot be bettered. It stands in an elevated position with a commanding panorama across the Severn Vale to the Malvern Hills and beyond. There is a pleasant range of public rooms which include a large bar-bistro and a reception lounge. Bedrooms are not large, but they offer a good range of equipment and many boast glorious views.
ROOMS: 24 en suite (bth/shr) (2 fmly) No smoking in 6 bedrooms **MEALS:** English & French Cuisine V meals Coffee am Tea pm **FACILITIES:** CTV in all bedrooms STV Sauna **CONF:** Thtr 16 Class 12 Board 12 **SERVICES:** Night porter 75P **NOTES:** No dogs (ex guide dogs) No smoking area in restaurant Last d 10pm
CARDS:

CLEOBURY MORTIMER Shropshire — Map 07 SO67

★★★ Redfern

DY14 8AA

Quality Percentage Score: 71%

☎ 01299 270395 Fax 01299 271011

Dir: *on A4117 midway between Kidderminster & Ludlow*

This delightful hotel offers warm hospitality, the culinary skills of young chef Jamie Bailey are praiseworthy. Well equipped accommodation includes six rooms in a purpose-built cottage-style annexe. Other facilities include a restaurant, a pleasant bar and a roof-top conservatory doubling as a coffee shop, where breakfast is served.

ROOMS: 5 en suite (bth/shr) 6 annexe en suite (bth/shr) (4 fmly) s £53-£65; d £80-£95 (incl. bkfst) LB Off peak **MEALS:** Lunch £2.92-£9 & alc Dinner £18.75 & alc English & French Cuisine V meals Coffee am Tea pm **FACILITIES:** CTV in all bedrooms Clay pigeon shooting Pheasant shooting Xmas **CONF:** Thtr 30 Class 30 Board 20 Del from £60 **SERVICES:** 20P **NOTES:** No coaches No smoking in restaurant Last d 9.30pm

CARDS:

CLEOBURY MORTIMER Shropshire — Map 07 SO67

★★ The Crown Inn

Hopton Wafers DY14 0NB

Quality Percentage Score: 65%

☎ 01299 270372 Fax 01299 271127

Dir: *on A4117 8m W of Ludlow, 2m E of Cleobury Mortimer*

A former 16th century coaching inn considerably improved inside and out under new ownership. The bedrooms are tastefully appointed and well equipped. Public areas have exposed beams and log burning fires. Facilities include a pleasant garden with duck pond, and a patio area.

ROOMS: 8 en suite (bth/shr) No smoking in all bedrooms **MEALS:** Lunch £13.95 & alc Dinner £19.95 Coffee am Tea pm **FACILITIES:** CTV in all bedrooms **SERVICES:** 40P **NOTES:** No dogs No smoking in restaurant Last d 9.30pm **CARDS:**

CLEVEDON Somerset — Map 03 ST47

★★★ *Walton Park*

Wellington Ter BS21 7BL

Best Western

Quality Percentage Score: 65%

☎ 01275 874253 Fax 01275 343577

Quietly located, this popular Victorian hotel enjoys glorious views across the Bristol Channel. Bedrooms are well equipped and a high standard of home-cooked food is served in the restaurant. Friendly service is provided by long-serving staff.

ROOMS: 40 en suite (bth/shr) (4 fmly) **MEALS:** English & French Cuisine V meals Coffee am Tea pm **FACILITIES:** CTV in all bedrooms STV **CONF:** Thtr 150 Class 80 Board 80 Del from £75 * **SERVICES:** Lift Night porter 50P **NOTES:** No smoking area in restaurant Last d 9.30pm

CARDS:

CLIMPING West Sussex — Map 04 SU90

★★★ Bailiffscourt

BN17 5RW

Quality Percentage Score: 76%

☎ 01903 723511 Fax 01903 723107

Dir: *turn off A259 Littlehampton to Bognor road marked Climping Beach & Bailiffscourt. The hotel is 0.5 of a mile on right.*

A truly unique 'medieval' hotel created in the 1930s from original 13th-century building materials and other salvaged antique architectural features. The result is quite delightful, with old stone windows, heavy iron-studded doors and ancient arches. A number of inter-connected rooms provide comfortable lounges, and the antique theme is carried through to the beamed restaurant which serves a consistently sound standard of interesting food. Bedrooms, some in adjacent buildings of similar character, come with antique oak furniture and embroidered fabrics that are very much in sympathy with the hotel's style.

ROOMS: 10 en suite (bth/shr) 22 annexe en suite (bth/shr) s £125-£290; d £140-£310 (incl. bkfst) * LB Off peak **MEALS:** Lunch £17.50-£21 & alc Dinner £35 & alc English & French Cuisine V meals Coffee am Tea pm **FACILITIES:** CTV in all bedrooms STV Outdoor swimming pool (heated) Tennis (hard) Pool table Croquet lawn Golf practice area Clay pigeon Xmas **CONF:** Thtr 50 Board 22 Del £145 * **SERVICES:** Night porter 60P **NOTES:** No smoking in restaurant Last d 9.45pm

CARDS:

CLITHEROE Lancashire — Map 07 SD74

★★★ Stirk House

BB7 4LJ

Best Western

Quality Percentage Score: 67%

☎ 01200 445581 Fax 01200 445744

Dir: *W of village, on A59. Hotel 0.5m on left*

With a peaceful location, set well back from the A59, this hotel offers a range of facilities to suit both business and leisure visitors. Modern bedrooms are attractively furnished and the lounges comfortable, whilst service is both friendly and attentive.

ROOMS: 36 en suite (bth/shr) 10 annexe en suite (bth/shr) (2 fmly) No smoking in 25 bedrooms s £50-£70; d £80-£100 (incl. bkfst) * LB Off peak **MEALS:** Lunch £11.50-£11.95 Dinner fr £15 & alc V meals Coffee am Tea pm **FACILITIES:** CTV in all bedrooms STV Indoor swimming pool (heated) Squash Sauna Solarium Gym Xmas **CONF:** Thtr 300 Class 150 Board 50 **SERVICES:** Night porter 130P **NOTES:** No dogs (ex guide dogs) No smoking in restaurant Last d 9.15pm

CARDS:

CLOVELLY Devon — Map 02 SS32

★★ *New Inn*

High St EX39 5TQ

Quality Percentage Score: 71%

☎ 01237 431303 Fax 01237 431636

Dir: *at Clovelly Cross, turn off A39 onto B3237. Follow road down hill for 1.5m. Turn right at sign "All vehicles for Clovelly" and park in main car park*

In a charming fishing village with hilly cobbled streets, vehicles must be left at the visitor centre at the top of the hill, the hotel will collect luggage by landrover, sledge or donkey! The hotel has been carefully renovated, bedrooms and public areas are attractive and comfortable. Meals may be taken in the spacious restaurant upstairs or the cosy downstairs bar.

ROOMS: 8 en suite (bth/shr) (2 fmly) **MEALS:** V meals Coffee am Tea pm **FACILITIES:** CTV in all bedrooms **NOTES:** No dogs (ex guide dogs) No smoking in restaurant Last d 8.30pm **CARDS:**

New AA Guides for the Millennium are featured on page 24

CLOVELLY Devon — Map 02 SS32
★★ Red Lion
The Quay EX39 5TF
Quality Percentage Score: 70%
☎ 01237 431237 Fax 01237 431044
Dir: *turn off A39 at Clovelly Cross on to B3237. Proceed to bottom of hill and take first turning on left by white rails to harbour*

Guests have two options when arriving at this quay-side inn, either walk down the cobbled street or take the Land Rover 'ferry service'. This quaint 18th-century inn, packed with day visitors during the summer, becomes a tranquil haven at night, with only locals for company in the beamed bars. Bedrooms, many of which have glorious views, are well furnished, and now offer a very high level of comfort.

ROOMS: 11 en suite (bth/shr) (2 fmly) s £37.50-£61; d £75-£92 (incl. bkfst) * LB Off peak **MEALS:** Bar Lunch £5.50-£13 Dinner £17.50-£22.50 English & French Cuisine V meals Coffee am Tea pm **FACILITIES:** CTV in all bedrooms Xmas **SERVICES:** 11P **NOTES:** No dogs No smoking in restaurant Last d 8.30pm **CARDS:**

COALVILLE Leicestershire — Map 08 SK41
Charnwood Arms
Beveridge Ln, Bardon Hill LE67 2TB
☎ 01530 813644 Fax 01530 815425
Dir: *1m W of junct 22 of M1, on A50*

The Charnwood Arms offers good value for money accommodation and a popular pub-style restaurant and a large function suite. Public areas have recently been upgraded to create a spacious lounge bar in which home-cooked food and cask conditioned ales are served. Bedrooms are in a pleasing mews development arranged around the main building, providing very well furnished and equipped rooms that are fully en-suite.

ROOMS: 35 en suite (bth/shr) d £28.50-£39.50 * **CONF:** Thtr 200 Class 100 Board 60

See advert on this page

COCKERMOUTH Cumbria — Map 11 NY13
★★★ The Trout
Crown St CA13 0EJ
Quality Percentage Score: 71%
☎ 01900 823591 Fax 01900 827514
Dir: *next to Wordsworth House and Mineral Museum*

This smart hotel lies by the banks of the River Derwent, next to the birthplace of William Wordsworth. Public areas, which include an attractive restaurant, are cosy and inviting, while bedrooms in the original building come in a variety of sizes. In the main house the rooms are comfortable and well equipped. Dinner is highly recommended with an imaginative menu suited to most tastes.

ROOMS: 30 en suite (bth/shr) (4 fmly) No smoking in 12 bedrooms s £59.95-£105; d £84.95-£140 (incl. bkfst) * LB Off peak **MEALS:** Lunch £9.95-£11.95 Dinner £17.95-£21.45 & alc English, French & Italian Cuisine V meals Coffee am **FACILITIES:** CTV in all bedrooms STV Fishing Xmas **CONF:** Thtr 50 Class 30 Board 25 Del from £109.95 * **SERVICES:** Night porter 60P **NOTES:** No smoking in restaurant Last d 9.30pm **CARDS:**

COCKERMOUTH Cumbria — Map 11 NY13
★★★ *Derwent Lodge*
Bassenthwaite Lake, Embleton CA13 9YA
Quality Percentage Score: 66%
☎ 017687 76606 Fax 017687 76766
Dir: *take first turning off A66 (sign posted Embleton), hotel straight in front*

A former farmer's lodge and guest house, Derwent Lodge represents all that is fine in a three-star hotel. The stylish modern bedrooms are well equipped, and offer superb views across the valley. A wide choice is available in the attractive restaurant, and the traditional bars and open plan lounge all contribute to the hotel ambience.

ROOMS: 20 en suite (bth/shr) (5 fmly) **MEALS:** V meals Coffee am Tea pm **FACILITIES:** CTV in all bedrooms Jacuzzi/spa **CONF:** Thtr 40 Class 30 Board 20 **SERVICES:** 40P **NOTES:** No dogs (ex guide dogs) No smoking in restaurant Last d 9pm **CARDS:**

COCKERMOUTH Cumbria — Map 11 NY13
★★★ The Manor House Hotel
Crown St CA13 0EH
Quality Percentage Score: 59%
☎ 01900 828663 Fax 01900 828679
Dir: *turn off A66 at Cockermouth junct, continue 0.75m to T junct to hotel 700yds on left*

Situated near the town centre, this impressive Victorian house has attractive public rooms, an elegant restaurant and a cosy bar. The modern bedrooms are pleasant and well equipped. Both menus offered present an appetising choice of imaginatively cooked and satisfying dishes.

ROOMS: 13 en suite (shr) (1 fmly) s £55-£75; d £69-£85 (incl. bkfst) * LB Off peak **MEALS:** Lunch £8.95 Dinner £16.95 & alc International Cuisine V meals Coffee am Tea pm **FACILITIES:** CTV in all bedrooms Xmas **SERVICES:** Night porter 20P **NOTES:** No smoking in restaurant Last d 9pm **CARDS:**

COCKERMOUTH Cumbria **Map 11 NY13**

★★ **Broughton Craggs**

Great Broughton CA13 0XW

Quality Percentage Score: 64%

☎ 01900 824400 📠 01900 825350

Dir: *leave A66 2m W of town, signposted Great Broughton. Over River Derwent and up Little Brow to T-junction. Turn right.*

Tucked away in its own attractive grounds, this hotel enjoys splendid views across the valley of the River Derwent to distant fells. It has a relaxed and informal atmosphere and its versatile public areas make it a popular venue for weddings and small conferences.

ROOMS: 14 en suite (bth/shr) (1 fmly) s fr £52.50; d fr £70 (incl. bkfst) * LB Off peak **MEALS:** Lunch £8.50-£13 Dinner £19.50 English & French Cuisine V meals Coffee am Tea pm **FACILITIES:** CTV in all bedrooms STV Salmon & trout fishing nearby **CONF:** Thtr 180 Class 100 Board 60 **SERVICES:** 80P **NOTES:** No dogs (ex guide dogs) No smoking area in restaurant Last d 9.30pm **CARDS:**

COGGESHALL Essex **Map 05 TL82**

★★★ *White Hart*

Market End CO6 1NH

Quality Percentage Score: 69%

☎ 01376 561654 📠 01376 561789

Dating from around 1420, this historic inn retains many original features, a good example being the comfortable first-floor Guild Room lounge, encompassing an original bay from what used to be the town's guildhall. Guests can eat either in the bar or the attractive restaurant.

ROOMS: 18 en suite (bth/shr) (1 fmly) **MEALS:** French & Italian Cuisine V meals Coffee am **FACILITIES:** CTV in all bedrooms STV **CONF:** Thtr 30 Class 10 Board 22 Del from £140 * **SERVICES:** 47P **NOTES:** No dogs No coaches Last d 10pm **CARDS:**

See advert on opposite page

COLCHESTER Essex **Map 05 TL92**

★★★ **George**

116 High St CO1 1JD

Quality Percentage Score: 70%

☎ 01206 578494 📠 01206 761732

Dir: *200yds beyond Town Hall on the High Street*

A 15th-century former coaching inn combining a wealth of original features with modern comforts. The property has been transformed under the ownership of Mr Slagle, with warm decor and elegant furnishings. The bedrooms vary in size, as one expects in a listed building, but all are equipped to a high standard. Open-plan public rooms include several lounge areas, where light snacks are served, and the County Suite or Brasserie Restaurant for more serious dining.

ROOMS: 48 en suite (bth/shr) (3 fmly) No smoking in 32 bedrooms s £49.50-£69.50; d £64.50-£74.50 * Off peak **MEALS:** Lunch £10.50-£14.50 High tea fr £6.50alc Dinner £17.50-£19.50alc International Cuisine V meals Coffee am Tea pm **FACILITIES:** CTV in all bedrooms STV **CONF:** Thtr 70 Class 30 Board 30 Del from £120 * **SERVICES:** Night porter 46P **NOTES:** No smoking area in restaurant Last d 10pm **CARDS:**

COLCHESTER Essex **Map 05 TL92**

★★★ **Butterfly**

Old Ipswich Rd CO7 7QY

Quality Percentage Score: 68%

☎ 01206 230900 📠 01206 231095

Dir: *A12/A120 Ardleigh Junction*

On the edge of town, this comfortable hotel overlooks a lake and provides twin and double rooms which are charged by the room - studio singles are particularly comfortable for the business traveller. A wide range of imaginative dishes is served in the restaurant. Conference suites are available.

ROOMS: 50 en suite (bth/shr) (2 fmly) No smoking in 11 bedrooms d fr £67.50 * LB Off peak **MEALS:** Lunch £7-£18 & alc Dinner fr £18 & alc European & Oriental Cuisine V meals Coffee am Tea pm **FACILITIES:** CTV in all bedrooms STV **CONF:** Thtr 80 Class 40 Board 40 Del from £95 * **SERVICES:** Night porter 85P **NOTES:** No dogs (ex guide dogs) No smoking area in restaurant Last d 10pm **CARDS:**

COLCHESTER Essex **Map 05 TL92**

★★★ **Marks Tey**

London Rd, Marks Tey CO6 1DU

Quality Percentage Score: 68%

☎ 01206 210001 📠 01206 212167

Dir: *off A12/A120 junction*

Just off the A12, south of Colchester, this modern hotel is convenient for the ferry terminal at Felixstowe. It offers attractive well furnished rooms and a range of conference suites.

ROOMS: 110 en suite (bth/shr) (12 fmly) No smoking in 16 bedrooms s £68.50; d £76.50 * LB Off peak **MEALS:** Lunch £15.50 & alc Dinner £15.50 & alc English & French Cuisine V meals Coffee am Tea pm **FACILITIES:** CTV in all bedrooms STV Indoor swimming pool (heated) Tennis (hard) Sauna Solarium Gym Pool table Jacuzzi/spa **CONF:** Thtr 200 Class 100 Board 60 Del £105 * **SERVICES:** Night porter 200P **NOTES:** No dogs (ex guide dogs) Last d 9.30pm **CARDS:**

COLCHESTER Essex **Map 05 TL92**

★★★ *Rose & Crown*

East St CO1 2TZ

Quality Percentage Score: 66%

☎ 01206 866677 📠 01206 866616

This historic posting house is located on the edge of Britain's oldest recorded town and retains much of its original character. The bedrooms are smartly decorated and well equipped; public rooms include an Italian themed restaurant and the Tudor bar with its oak beams and flame fireplace. There are also a number of function rooms catering for private dining and conferences.

ROOMS: 29 en suite (bth/shr) (3 fmly) No smoking in 5 bedrooms **MEALS:** English, French, Italian & Portuguese Cuisine V meals Coffee am Tea pm **FACILITIES:** CTV in all bedrooms STV Beauty Salon **CONF:** Thtr 100 Class 40 Board 60 Del from £90 * **SERVICES:** Night porter 50P **NOTES:** No dogs (ex guide dogs) No smoking area in restaurant Last d 10pm **CARDS:**

COLCHESTER Essex **Map 05 TL92**

★★★ **Posthouse Colchester**

Abbotts Ln, Eight Ash Green CO6 3QL

Quality Percentage Score: 65%

☎ 01206 767740 📠 01206 766577

Dir: *junct A1124 of A12 signposted to Halstead*

On the western fringes of the town and suitable for both business and leisure travellers, this relaxing hotel provides modern accommodation in well equipped bedrooms. Pleasant public areas include a bar and restaurant, conference rooms and a leisure club.

ROOMS: 110 en suite (bth/shr) (30 fmly) No smoking in 58 bedrooms d fr £80 * LB Off peak **MEALS:** International Cuisine V meals Coffee am Tea pm **FACILITIES:** CTV in all bedrooms Indoor swimming pool (heated) Sauna Solarium Gym Jacuzzi/spa Steam room Treatment rooms Xmas **CONF:** Thtr 150 Class 70 Board 60 Del from £115 * **SERVICES:** Night porter 150P **NOTES:** No smoking area in restaurant Last d 10pm **CARDS:**

COLCHESTER Essex **Map 05 TL92**

Travel Inn
Ipswich Rd CO4 4NP
☎ 01206 855001 01206 842536
Dir: *take A120 (A1232) junct off A12, follow A1232 towards Colchester, Travel Inn on right*

This modern building offers accommodation in smart, spacious and well equipped bedrooms, all with en-suite bathrooms. Refreshments may be taken at the nearby family restaurant. For details about current prices consult the Contents Page under Hotel Groups for the Travel Inn phone number.

ROOMS: 40 en suite (bth/shr) d £39.95 *

COLEFORD Gloucestershire **Map 03 SO51**

★★★ **The Speech House**
GL16 7EL
Quality Percentage Score: 69%
☎ 01594 822607 01594 823658
Dir: *on B4226 between Cinderford and Coleford*

This 17th-century hunting lodge, tucked away in the the Forest of Dean, offers comfortable bedrooms, several with four-posters, which combine modern facilities with period charm. The beamed restaurant serves good, imaginative food. The hotel has a golf course just over two miles away.

ROOMS: 15 en suite (bth/shr) 16 annexe rms (9 shr) (4 fmly) No smoking in 6 bedrooms s fr £61; d fr £81.50 (incl. bkfst) * LB Off peak **MEALS:** Lunch £1.95-£19.50 High tea £1.50-£3.95 Dinner £19.50-£29.50 & alc European Cuisine V meals Coffee am Tea pm **FACILITIES:** CTV in all bedrooms Golf 18 Sauna Solarium Gym Jacuzzi/spa Cricket Bridge Health Spa Xmas **CONF:** Thtr 70 Class 40 Board 40 Del £105 * **SERVICES:** Night porter 70P **NOTES:** No smoking in restaurant Last d 9.15pm **CARDS:**

COLERNE Wiltshire **Map 03 ST87**

The Premier Collection

★★★★ **Lucknam Park**
SN14 8AZ
☎ 01225 742777 01225 743536
Dir: *leave M4 at junct 17, take A350 to Chippenham, then A420 towards Bristol for 3 miles. At village of Ford, turn south towards Colerne*

The long tree-lined driveway makes a striking first impression at this Palladian mansion, set in 500 acres of parkland. Lucknam Park has elegant day rooms and dates back to 1720. There are many private suites and standards of comfort are high. Leisure facilities include a notable equestrian centre. A choice of menus offers a balanced selection from the kitchen.

ROOMS: 23 en suite (bth/shr) 18 annexe en suite (bth/shr) s £140-£180; d £260-£730 * LB Off peak **MEALS:** Lunch fr £25 Dinner £40 English & French Cuisine V meals Coffee am Tea pm **FACILITIES:** CTV in all bedrooms STV Indoor swimming pool (heated) Tennis (hard) Riding Snooker Sauna Solarium Gym Croquet lawn Jacuzzi/spa Whirlpool Beauty salon Steam room Hair salon Xmas **CONF:** Thtr 80 Class 22 Board 22 Del from £220 * **SERVICES:** Night porter 90P **NOTES:** No dogs (ex guide dogs) No coaches No smoking in restaurant Last d 9.30pm **CARDS:**

C

COLESHILL Warwickshire Map 04 SP28
★★★ Grimstock Country House
Gilson Rd, Gilson B46 1AJ
Quality Percentage Score: 65%
☎ 01675 462121 & 462161 📠 01675 467646
Dir: *turn off A446 onto B4117 to Gilson, hotel 100yds on right*
This privately owned, friendly hotel stands in its own grounds, conveniently close to Birmingham International Airport and the NEC. It is within easy reach of junctions 9 and 6 of the M42 and junction 4 of the M6. It provides modern well equipped bedrooms and the public rooms include a choice of restaurants. Good conference facilities are also available.
ROOMS: 44 en suite (bth/shr) (1 fmly) s fr £75; d fr £85 (incl. bkfst) * LB Off peak **MEALS:** Lunch £5.50-£8.50 & alc Dinner fr £14.50 & alc English & French Cuisine V meals Coffee am Tea pm **FACILITIES:** CTV in all bedrooms STV Solarium Gym Xmas **CONF:** Thtr 100 Class 60 Board 50 Del from £105 * **SERVICES:** Night porter 80P
CARDS:

COLESHILL Warwickshire Map 04 SP28
★★★ *Coleshill*
152 High St B46 3BG
Quality Percentage Score: 64%
☎ 01675 465527 📠 01675 464013
Dir: *from M6 junct 4 take A446. Signposted Coleshill town centre. Situated on main high street*
This popular town-centre hotel is only a short drive from the M6 and M42, and is convenient for both the NEC and Birmingham International Airport. Bedrooms vary in size, but all offer modern facilities. Some, including those at ground level, are in a separate house on the opposite side of the road. The bar and bistro have character and are attractively appointed. Other facilities include two self-contained function suites, one of which is in an adjacent building.
ROOMS: 15 en suite (bth/shr) 8 annexe en suite (bth/shr)
MEALS: English & French Cuisine V meals Coffee am Tea pm
FACILITIES: CTV in all bedrooms STV Wkly live entertainment
CONF: Thtr 150 Class 60 Board 50 **SERVICES:** Night porter 48P
NOTES: No dogs (ex guide dogs) No smoking area in restaurant
Last d 10pm **CARDS:**

COLN ST-ALDWYNS Gloucestershire Map 04 SP10
★★❀❀ The New Inn at Coln
GL7 5AN
Quality Percentage Score: 78%
☎ 01285 750651 📠 01285 750657
Dir: *8m E of Cirencester, between Bibury and Fairford*
Genuine hospitality is one of the hallmarks of this delightful inn, which dates from the reign of Elizabeth I. The well equipped bedrooms are divided between the main building and the Dovecote. The public rooms, with stone floors and roaring fires, include a popular bar and restaurant, both of which serve a high standard of food.
ROOMS: 8 en suite (bth/shr) 6 annexe en suite (bth/shr) (1 fmly) s £68-£99; d £96-£115 (incl. bkfst) * LB Off peak **MEALS:** Lunch £17.50-£22.50 Dinner £22.50-£26.50 & alc English & Mediterranean Cuisine V meals Coffee am Tea pm **FACILITIES:** CTV in all bedrooms
CONF: Thtr 20 Board 12 Del from £119.50 * **SERVICES:** 22P
NOTES: No coaches No children 10 yrs No smoking in restaurant
Last d 9pm **CARDS:**

COLSTERWORTH Lincolnshire Map 08 SK92
⇧ Travelodge
NG33 5JR
☎ 01476 861077 📠 01476 861078
Dir: *on A1/A151 southbound at junct with B151/B676*
This modern building offers accommodation in smart, spacious and well equipped bedrooms, all with en-suite bathrooms. Refreshments may be taken at the nearby family restaurant. For details about current prices, consult the Contents Page under Hotel Groups for the Travelodge phone number.
ROOMS: 31 en suite (bth/shr) d £39.95 *

COLYFORD Devon Map 03 SY29
★★❀ Swallow Eaves
Swan Hill Rd EX24 6QJ
Quality Percentage Score: 77%
☎ 01297 553184 📠 01297 553574
Dir: *on A3052, in centre of village, opposite village store*
This delightful hotel has built up a well deserved reputation for excellent service, food and hospitality. The bedrooms are very comfortable and attractively decorated with many thoughtful extras. The restaurant serves a daily menu of carefully prepared dishes which, often uses fresh local ingredients.
ROOMS: 8 en suite (bth/shr) No smoking in 6 bedrooms s £42-£52; d £64-£84 (incl. bkfst) * LB Off peak **MEALS:** Bar Lunch fr £4.50 Dinner fr £22 Coffee am Tea pm **FACILITIES:** CTV in all bedrooms Free use of nearby Swimming Club Xmas **SERVICES:** 10P **NOTES:** No dogs (ex guide dogs) No coaches No children 14yrs No smoking in restaurant Last d 8pm **CARDS:**

CONGLETON Cheshire Map 07 SJ86
★★★ The Plough Inn & Old Barn Restaurant
Macclesfield Rd, Eaton CW12 2NH
Quality Percentage Score: 66%
☎ 01260 280207 📠 01260 298377
Dir: *turn off A34 onto A536, hotel 1m on left*
This black and white Elizabethan coaching inn has recently been extended by the addition of a timber frame barn, reconstructed on site after being transported from its original home in Wales. Fine dining is offered at the hotel, along with a more informal lounge bar. Comfortable bedrooms are in a fully converted stable block.
ROOMS: 8 annexe en suite (bth/shr) s £50-£60; d £70-£75 (incl. bkfst) * Off peak **MEALS:** Sunday Lunch £13-£18.95alc Dinner £13.60-£28.40alc V meals Coffee am **FACILITIES:** CTV in all bedrooms **SERVICES:** 50P
NOTES: No dogs (ex guide dogs) No smoking in restaurant
Last d 9.30pm **CARDS:**

CONGLETON Cheshire Map 07 SJ86
★★★ *Lion & Swan*
Swan Bank CW12 1JR
Quality Percentage Score: 61%
☎ 01260 273115 📠 01260 299270
Dir: *M6 junct 17, signed Congleton to roundabout, straight over and follow one way system round to right, hotel at top*
A black and white half-timbered coaching inn, dating back to the 16th century. Many original features have been retained, with numerous exposed beams and a fine carved fireplace in the lounge bar. Bedrooms vary in size and are attractively decorated.
ROOMS: 21 en suite (bth/shr) (1 fmly) No smoking in 3 bedrooms
MEALS: English & French Cuisine V meals Coffee am Tea pm
FACILITIES: CTV in all bedrooms **CONF:** Thtr 130 Class 70 Board 40
SERVICES: 49P **NOTES:** No smoking in restaurant Last d 9.30pm Closed Xmas **CARDS:**

CONISTON Cumbria Map 07 SD39
★★ *Sun*
LA21 8HQ
Quality Percentage Score: 62%
☎ 015394 41248
Dir: *signposted from village centre, off A593*
This 16th-century inn, now a family-run hotel, has many

contd.

bedrooms with fine views of the valley and 'Old Man'. The inn's association with Donald Campbell of Bluebird fame is recorded by many photographs and archive items. The Lakeland bar serves an extensive menu and there is a comfortable lounge next to an attractive dining room.

ROOMS: 11 rms (7 bth 3 shr) **MEALS:** English & Continental Cuisine V meals Coffee am Tea pm **FACILITIES:** CTV in all bedrooms **CONF:** Class 20 **SERVICES:** 20P **NOTES:** No smoking in restaurant Last d 9pm **CARDS:** 💳 💳 💳 💳 ⚡

☰ CONSETT Co Durham   **Map 12 NZ15**
○✦ **The Raven Hotel**
Broomhill, Ebchester DH8 6RY
☎ 01207 562562 📠 01207 560262
Dir: on B6309, overlooking village
Spacious and well equipped bedrooms are a feature of this modern and pleasantly furnished hotel, which stands on a hillside overlooking the village. Well prepared dinners are served in the attractive conservatory restaurant and a good range of popular bar meals is available along with a range of hand pulled real ales. Friendly service is provided by a dedicated and smartly turned out staff.

ROOMS: 28 en suite (bth/shr) (7 fmly) s fr £52; d fr £69 (incl. bkfst) * LB Off peak **MEALS:** Sunday Lunch fr £12.95alc V meals Coffee am Tea pm **FACILITIES:** CTV in all bedrooms STV Wkly live entertainment Xmas **CONF:** Thtr 150 Class 80 Board 40 Del £78.95 * **SERVICES:** Night porter Air conditioning 100P **NOTES:** No dogs (ex guide dogs) No smoking area in restaurant **CARDS:** 💳 💳 💳 💳 💳 ⚡

☰ CONSTANTINE Cornwall & Isles of Scilly   **Map 02 SW72**
★★◉◉ **Trengilly Wartha Inn**
Nancenoy TR11 5RP
Quality Percentage Score: 71%
☎ 01326 340332 📠 01326 340332

THE CIRCLE
Selected Individual Hotels
GREAT BRITAIN

Dir: take A39 to Falmouth, at rdbt by Asda store in Penryn follow signs to Constantine then direction Gweek, hotel signposted to the left in 1m
A popular and busy country inn hotel located in a beautiful rural area. Whether you eat in the smart restaurant or the busy bar, the emphasis is on fresh Cornish produce. The lounge, with its easy chairs and ample reading matter, is the place to relax in front of an open log fire.

ROOMS: 6 rms (4 bth 1 shr) 2 annexe en suite (bth/shr) (2 fmly) No smoking in 2 bedrooms s £45; d £68-£83 (incl. bkfst) * LB Off peak **MEALS:** Bar Lunch £2.50-£14 Dinner £25 V meals Coffee am **FACILITIES:** CTV in all bedrooms Pool table ch fac **SERVICES:** 50P **NOTES:** No coaches Last d 9.30pm RS 25 Dec (breakfast only) **CARDS:** 💳 💳 💳 💳 💳 ⚡

☰ CONSTANTINE BAY Cornwall & Isles of Scilly **Map 02 SW87**
★★★◉ **Treglos**
PL28 8JH
Quality Percentage Score: 77%
☎ 01841 520727 📠 01841 521163

Best Western

Dir: turn right at Constantine Bay stores, hotel 50yds on left
This fine hotel has high standards of hospitality and service. A choice of comfortable lounges is available, one specifically for guests wishing to play bridge. Bedrooms vary in size, those with

---

Remember to return your Prize Draw card for a chance to win one of 30 relaxing leisure breaks with Corus and Regal hotels. See inside the front cover for the card and competition details.

---

splendid views are always popular. The restaurant continues to provide imaginative and interesting dishes.

ROOMS: 44 en suite (bth/shr) (12 fmly) s £61-£81; d £122-£162 (incl. bkfst & dinner) * LB Off peak **MEALS:** Lunch £10.50-£16.50 High tea £7-£10 Dinner £23 & alc English & French Cuisine V meals Coffee am Tea pm **FACILITIES:** CTV in all bedrooms Indoor swimming pool (heated) Snooker Pool table Croquet lawn Jacuzzi/spa Converted 'boat house' for table tennis **CONF:** Board 20 **SERVICES:** Lift Night porter 58P **NOTES:** No coaches No smoking in restaurant Last d 9pm Closed 4 Nov-16 Mar **CARDS:** 💳 💳 💳 💳 ⚡

See advert under PADSTOW

☰ COPTHORNE See **Gatwick Airport**

☰ CORBRIDGE Northumberland   **Map 12 NY96**
★★ **Angel Inn**
Main St NE45 5LA
Quality Percentage Score: 68%
☎ 01434 632119 📠 01434 632119
Dir: half a mile off A69, signed Corbridge
The oldest inn in the village, and sympathetic refurbishment has added style to its original character. Relax with the daily papers in the lounge or enjoy a drink in the snug bar. Diners are offered an excellent choice, whether in the restaurant or the more informal lounge bar. Bedrooms vary in size, but all are well equipped and smart. Service is friendly and attentive.

ROOMS: 5 en suite (bth/shr) (2 fmly) **MEALS:** Lunch £12.95-£16.95 High tea £6.95 Dinner £6.95 V meals Coffee am Tea pm **FACILITIES:** CTV in all bedrooms STV **SERVICES:** 20P **NOTES:** No dogs (ex guide dogs) No smoking in restaurant Last d 9pm
CARDS: 💳 💳 💳 💳 💳 ⚡

☰ CORFE CASTLE Dorset   **Map 03 SY98**
★★★◉ **Mortons House**
East St BH20 5EE
Quality Percentage Score: 69%
☎ 01929 480988 📠 01929 480820
Dir: on A351 between Wareham/Swanage
A charming hotel, Mortons House has been sensitively improved over recent years. Traditional features include an oak panelled drawing room and carved timbered friezes. Bedrooms are decorated with style, individuality and taste. Some accomplished cuisine is on offer.

ROOMS: 14 en suite (bth/shr) 3 annexe en suite (bth/shr) (1 fmly) No smoking in 3 bedrooms d £96-£106 (incl. bkfst) * LB Off peak **MEALS:** Sunday Lunch £12.50-£16 Dinner £22.50 & alc English & French Cuisine V meals Coffee am Tea pm **FACILITIES:** CTV in all bedrooms Jacuzzi/spa Xmas **CONF:** Thtr 45 Board 20 Del from £100 * **SERVICES:** 40P **NOTES:** No coaches No smoking in restaurant Last d 8.30pm **CARDS:** 💳 💳 💳 💳 💳 ⚡

CORNHILL-ON-TWEED Northumberland **Map 12 NT83**

★★★ Tillmouth Park

TD12 4UU

Quality Percentage Score: 68%

☎ 01890 882255 📠 01890 882540

Dir: *turn off A1(M) at East Ord roundabout at Berwick-upon-Tweed and follow A698 towards Cornhill and Coldstream. Hotel is 9 miles along A698 on left*

This magnificent country mansion, built in 1882 using stones from nearby Twizel Castle, is set in mature grounds by the banks of the River Till. The house retains all of its period charm, with gracious public rooms, including a galleried lounge which dominates the upper floors. One can dine in the informal bistro or the dining room, with the emphasis on fresh Scottish produce. Bedrooms combine the traditional and the modern with much success.

ROOMS: 12 en suite (bth/shr) 2 annexe en suite (bth/shr) (1 fmly) s £90-£115; d £120-£160 (incl. bkfst) * LB Off peak **MEALS:** Lunch £8.50-£22.65 High tea £12.25-£22 Dinner £25 English & French Cuisine V meals Coffee am Tea pm **FACILITIES:** CTV in all bedrooms Croquet lawn Clay pigeon shooting Snooker table 3/4 size Xmas **CONF:** Thtr 50 Class 20 Board 20 Del £100 * **SERVICES:** 50P **NOTES:** Last d 8.45pm RS 25-26 Dec **CARDS:**

See advert under BERWICK-UPON-TWEED

CORSE LAWN Worcestershire **Map 03 SO83**

★★★ Corse Lawn House

GL19 4LZ

Quality Percentage Score: 75%

☎ 01452 780479 & 780771 📠 01452 780840

Dir: *on B4211 5m SW of Tewkesbury*

A sympathetically extended Queen Anne country house that sits in its own extensive grounds. The public rooms feature a bistro and bar in addition to the main restaurant. A drawing room and other seating areas are also provided. The bedrooms are decorated in a similarly elegant style to the communal areas, and feature many extra touches including fresh fruit, magazines and mineral water. Cooking is of a high standard with good use made of top quality ingredients.

ROOMS: 19 en suite (bth/shr) (2 fmly) s fr £70; d fr £100 (incl. bkfst) * LB Off peak **MEALS:** Lunch £16.95-£17.95 & alc Dinner fr £25 & alc V meals Coffee am Tea pm **FACILITIES:** CTV in all bedrooms STV Outdoor swimming pool (heated) Tennis (hard) Croquet lawn Badminton Xmas **CONF:** Thtr 40 Class 30 Board 25 **SERVICES:** 62P **NOTES:** No smoking in restaurant Last d 9.30pm Closed 24-25 Dec **CARDS:**

COVENTRY West Midlands **Map 04 SP37**

see also **Brandon, Meriden & Nuneaton**

★★★ Brooklands Grange Hotel & Restaurant

Holyhead Rd CV5 8HX

Quality Percentage Score: 74%

☎ 024 76601601 📠 024 76601277

Dir: *leave A45 at roundabout marked city centre onto A4114 go to next roundabout & stay on A4114, hotel 100yds on left*

Behind the Jacobean façade of Brooklands Grange is this modern and comfortable business hotel. The food is worthy of note, with an interesting carte offering carefully presented and tasty dishes. Bedrooms are well equipped and thoughtfully laid-out.

ROOMS: 30 en suite (bth/shr) (1 fmly) No smoking in 15 bedrooms s £105-£110; d £120-£125 (incl. bkfst) * Off peak **MEALS:** Bar Lunch fr £4.65 Dinner £20.65-£26.15alc International Cuisine V meals Coffee am Tea pm **FACILITIES:** CTV in all bedrooms **SERVICES:** Night porter 52P **NOTES:** No dogs (ex guide dogs) No smoking in restaurant Last d 10pm Closed 26-28 Dec & 1-2 Jan **CARDS:**

COVENTRY West Midlands **Map 04 SP37**

★★★ Posthouse Coventry

Posthouse

Hinckley Rd, Walsgrave CV2 2HP

Quality Percentage Score: 70%

☎ 024 76613261 📠 024 76621736

Dir: *on A4600*

This modern hotel offers smartly decorated bedrooms, including some in the new 'Millennium' style. There is a new range of air-conditioned meeting rooms with their own reception and lounge. For meals, there is a choice between the Rotisserie and the coffee lounge.

ROOMS: 160 en suite (bth/shr) (15 fmly) No smoking in 112 bedrooms d fr £95 * LB Off peak **MEALS:** V meals Coffee am Tea pm **FACILITIES:** CTV in all bedrooms Indoor swimming pool (heated) Sauna Gym Jacuzzi/spa Steam room Childrens play areas Wkly live entertainment ch fac Xmas **CONF:** Thtr 250 Class 150 Board 50 Del from £135 * **SERVICES:** Lift Night porter 300P **NOTES:** No smoking in restaurant Last d 10pm **CARDS:**

COVENTRY West Midlands **Map 04 SP37**

★★★ Courtyard by Marriott Coventry

London Rd, Ryton on Dunsmore CV8 3DY

Quality Percentage Score: 69%

☎ 024 76301585 📠 024 76301610

Dir: *junction 10 of M40, take A46 - A45 to Northampton*

This modern hotel is conveniently situated on the outskirts of the city and provides very comfortable and spacious accommodation, particularly suited to the business guest. Public areas are particularly well designed and include a lounge bar, foyer lounge and an informal restaurant. There are versatile meeting and conference facilities.

ROOMS: 49 en suite (bth/shr) (2 fmly) No smoking in 25 bedrooms d £75-£95 * LB Off peak **MEALS:** Lunch £11.50 & alc Dinner £17 & alc English & Continental Cuisine V meals Coffee am Tea pm **FACILITIES:** CTV in all bedrooms STV **CONF:** Thtr 300 Class 100 Board 24 Del from £125 * **SERVICES:** Night porter 120P **NOTES:** No dogs (ex guide dogs) No smoking area in restaurant Last d 10pm **CARDS:**

COVENTRY West Midlands **Map 04 SP37**

★★★ Aston Court

80-90 Holyhead Rd CV1 3AS

Quality Percentage Score: 68%

☎ 024 76258585 📠 024 76225547

Under new management, Aston Court has been completely refurbished and offers smartly decorated bedrooms, well equipped for the business guest. The restaurant offers a choice of menus and there is a range of function rooms.

ROOMS: 82 en suite (bth/shr) s £63.50-£90; d £63.50-£90 * LB Off peak **MEALS:** Lunch £6.50-£9.50 Dinner £12.50-£16.50 & alc International Cuisine V meals Coffee am Tea pm **FACILITIES:** CTV in all bedrooms Xmas **CONF:** Thtr 260 Class 150 Board 80 Del from £80 * **SERVICES:** Lift Night porter 40P **NOTES:** No smoking in restaurant Last d 9.30pm **CARDS:**

COVENTRY West Midlands **Map 04 SP37**

★★★ Hylands

Warwick Rd CV3 6AU

Quality Percentage Score: 68%

☎ 024 76501600 📠 024 76501027

Dir: *on A429, Warwick Rd, approx 500 yds from junct 6 of town centre ring road, opposite Memorial Park*

This hotel is close to the railway station and city centre, yet overlooks an attractive park. Refurbishment programmes have seen the public rooms upgraded and a gradual refreshing and

contd.

refurbishment of the bedroom stock. The restaurant, Restaurant 153, offers good food in very contemporary surroundings.
ROOMS: 54 en suite (bth/shr) (4 fmly) s £86-£96; d £96-£105 * LB Off peak **MEALS:** Lunch £15.75 & alc Dinner £15.75 & alc Modern European Cuisine V meals Coffee am Tea pm **FACILITIES:** CTV in all bedrooms STV **CONF:** Thtr 60 Class 40 Board 30 Del from £105 * **SERVICES:** Night porter 60P **NOTES:** No smoking area in restaurant Last d 10pm **CARDS:**

COVENTRY West Midlands **Map 04 SP37**
★★★ Leofric
Broadgate CV1 1LZ
MENZIES HOTELS
Quality Percentage Score: 66%
0500 636943 (Central Res) 01773 880321
Dir: *opposite West Orchards Car Park*

Reputedly the first hotel to be built in Britain after the Second World War, the Leofric is near the cathedral and the shopping centre. Open plan public areas include a choice of bars and a brasserie. The West Orchards car park gives direct access to the hotel.
ROOMS: 94 en suite (bth/shr) (5 fmly) No smoking in 20 bedrooms s £95-£105; d £105-£125 * LB Off peak **MEALS:** Lunch fr £6.95 Dinner fr £15.50 International Cuisine V meals Coffee am Tea pm **FACILITIES:** CTV in all bedrooms STV Xmas **CONF:** Thtr 600 Class 200 Board 80 Del from £90 * **SERVICES:** Lift Night porter **NOTES:** No dogs (ex guide dogs) No smoking area in restaurant Last d 9.30pm
CARDS:

COVENTRY West Midlands **Map 04 SP37**
★★★ Allesley
Birmingham Rd, Allesley Village CV5 9GP
Quality Percentage Score: 65%
024 76403272 024 76405190
Dir: *from the A45. Turn off slip road A4114 Brownshill Green/City Centre. 4th exit, at next rndbt 1st exit Allesley Village. Hotel is 150yrd on left*
The Allesley hotel is three miles from the city centre and provides well appointed accommodation that is light and inviting, with co-ordinated colour schemes. All rooms are well equipped for today's corporate guest. Public areas are split over two levels, the spacious reception foyer is on the ground floor, while the restaurant and bar are located on a higher level. Bedrooms and public areas are served by a lift. Extensive conference and function facilities are readily available and have dedicated audio-visual and secretarial support.
ROOMS: 75 en suite (bth/shr) 15 annexe en suite (bth/shr) (2 fmly) No smoking in 31 bedrooms s £102; d £130 (incl. bkfst) * LB Off peak **MEALS:** Lunch £11.95-£15.50 & alc Dinner £19.50 & alc European Cuisine V meals Coffee am Tea pm **FACILITIES:** CTV in 91 bedrooms Pool table Wkly live entertainment **CONF:** Thtr 450 Class 150 Board 80 Del from £100 * **SERVICES:** Lift Night porter 500P **NOTES:** No smoking in restaurant Last d 9.30pm **CARDS:**

COVENTRY West Midlands **Map 04 SP37**
★★★ The Chace
London Rd, Toll Bar End CV3 4EQ
corus
Corus and Regal hotels
Quality Percentage Score: 64%
024 76303398 024 76301816
Dir: *from S M40, exit junct 15, A46 to Coventry, right onto A45 & follow to 1st rdbt, turn left onto B4110, straight on at next mini rdbt, Hotel on left*

This much extended hotel displays many of its original Victorian features, such as the stained glass and oak panelling in its open-plan lounge bar and restaurant. Bedrooms are well equipped and mostly decorated in a light, appealing style.
ROOMS: 66 en suite (bth/shr) (23 fmly) No smoking in 34 bedrooms s £85-£90; d £100 * LB Off peak **MEALS:** Lunch £4.95-£12.50 & alc Dinner £5.95-£17.95 & alc International Cuisine V meals Coffee am Tea pm **FACILITIES:** CTV in all bedrooms Pool table Croquet lawn Childrens play area Xmas **CONF:** Thtr 65 Class 40 Board 36 Del from £75 * **SERVICES:** Night porter 120P **NOTES:** No dogs (ex guide dogs) No smoking area in restaurant Last d 9.45pm
CARDS:

COVENTRY West Midlands **Map 04 SP37**

★★★ **Novotel**
Wilsons Ln CV6 6HL
Quality Percentage Score: 62%
☎ 024 76365000 📠 024 76362422
Dir: *exit M6 junct 3, follow signs for B4113 towards Longford, Bedworth. Take 3rd exit on large rndbt*
The first Novotel built in the UK, this modern hotel is conveniently situated close to junction 3 of the M6. The bedrooms are all very similar and include family as well as disabled rooms. They have been upgraded and there is also a useful range of meeting rooms. Guests can dine until midnight in the cheerfully redecorated brasserie, or take meals from the extensive room service menu. The hotel has an outdoor swimming pool and a new children's play area.
ROOMS: 98 en suite (bth/shr) (98 fmly) No smoking in 26 bedrooms d fr £65 * LB Off peak **MEALS:** British & French Cuisine V meals Coffee am Tea pm **FACILITIES:** CTV in all bedrooms STV Outdoor swimming pool (heated) Petanque **CONF:** Thtr 200 Class 100 Board 40 Del from £90 * **SERVICES:** Lift Night porter Air conditioning 120P **NOTES:** No smoking area in restaurant **CARDS:**

COVENTRY West Midlands **Map 04 SP37**

⇧ **Campanile**
4 Wigston Rd, Walsgrave CV2 2SD
☎ 024 76622311 📠 024 76602362
Dir: *exit 2 of M6, at 2nd roundabout turn right*

This modern building offers accommodation in smart well equipped bedrooms, all with en-suite bathrooms. Refreshments may be taken at the informal Bistro. For details about current prices, consult the Contents Page under Hotel Groups for the Campanile phone number.
ROOMS: 50 en suite (bth/shr) **CONF:** Thtr 35 Class 18 Board 20

COVENTRY West Midlands **Map 04 SP37**

⇧ **Travel Inn**
Rugby Rd, Binley Woods CV3 2TA
☎ 024 76636585 📠 024 76431178
Dir: *M6 junct 2 on right hand side of A46 Eastern by-pass at junction with Rugby Rd*
This modern building offers accommodation in smart, spacious and well equipped bedrooms, all with en-suite bathrooms. Refreshments may be taken at the nearby family restaurant. For details about current prices consult the Contents Page under Hotel Groups for the Travel Inn phone number.
ROOMS: 50 en suite (bth/shr) d £39.95 *

COVENTRY West Midlands **Map 04 SP37**

Hotel Ibis
Abbey Rd, Whitley CV3 4BJ
☎ 02476 639922 📠 02476 306898
Dir: *signposted from A46/A423 roundabout, take A423 towards A45 & London stay in left hand lane. Follow signs for the Racquet Centre.*
This modern, purpose built hotel is located to the south of Coventry, via the A423. It is close to the Jaguar Engineering centre and the Racquet club, both of which have directional sign-posting. It provides well equipped accommodation, has a bistro style restaurant and a cosy bar.
ROOMS: 51 en suite (bth/shr) (5 fmly) No smoking in 25 bedrooms s £36.50; d £36.50 * LB Off peak **MEALS:** French Cuisine V meals Coffee am Tea pm **FACILITIES:** CTV in all bedrooms STV Xmas **CONF:** Thtr 35 Class 18 Board 20 **SERVICES:** 50P **NOTES:** Last d 10pm **CARDS:**

See advert under Ibis

COWES See **Wight, Isle of**

CRAMLINGTON Northumberland **Map 12 NZ27**

⇧ **Travel Inn**
Moor Farm Roundabout, off Front St NE23 RGF
☎ 0191 250 2770 📠 0191 250 2216
Dir: *situated on the rdbt junction of the A19/A189 S of Cramlington*
This modern building offers accommodation in smart, spacious and well equipped bedrooms, all with en-suite bathrooms. Refreshments may be taken at the nearby family restaurant. For details about current prices consult the Contents Page under Hotel Groups for the Travel Inn phone number.
ROOMS: 40 en suite (bth/shr) d £39.95 *

CRANBROOK Kent **Map 05 TQ73**

The Premier Collection

★★ **Kennel Holt**
Goudhurst Rd TN17 2PT
☎ 01580 712032 📠 01580 715495
Dir: *between Goudhurst and Cranbrook on A262*
This Elizabethan manor house is a charming retreat with immaculately kept five-acre gardens. The relaxing public rooms are full of original features. Individually-styled
contd.

bedrooms, some including four-poster beds, are comfortable and furnished in keeping with the style of the property.
ROOMS: 10 en suite (bth/shr) s £85-£110; d £135-£165 (incl. bkfst) * LB Off peak **MEALS:** Dinner £27.50-£32.50 European Cuisine V meals **FACILITIES:** CTV in all bedrooms Croquet lawn Putting green **CONF:** Thtr 15 Class 15 Board 10 Del from £195 * **SERVICES:** 20P **NOTES:** No dogs No coaches No smoking in restaurant Last d 8.45pm Closed middle 2 wks Jan
CARDS:

CRANBROOK Kent — Map 05 TQ73

★★ Hartley Mount Country House

Hartley Rd TN17 3QX
Quality Percentage Score: 69%
☎ 01580 712230 📠 01580 715733
Dir: *1m S on A229*

A fine Edwardian manor house with well proportioned bedrooms, attractively decorated, and with thoughtful extra touches. There is a comfortable open-plan lounge with an adjoining conservatory, used as bar, breakfast and smoking room.
ROOMS: 6 en suite (bth/shr) (1 fmly) No smoking in all bedrooms s £65-£90; d £80-£95 (incl. bkfst) * LB Off peak **MEALS:** Lunch fr £17.50 Dinner £17.50-£19.50 European Cuisine V meals Coffee am Tea pm **FACILITIES:** CTV in all bedrooms Croquet lawn Putting green Pitch & putt **SERVICES:** 32P **NOTES:** No dogs (ex guide dogs) No coaches No smoking in restaurant **CARDS:**

CRANTOCK Cornwall & Isles of Scilly — Map 02 SW76

★★ Crantock Bay

West Pentire TR8 5SE
Quality Percentage Score: 67%
☎ 01637 830229 📠 01637 831111
Dir: *off A3075 at West Pentire Headland*

Set in four acres of gardens with direct access to the beach, this family-run hotel offers its many repeat guests a friendly atmosphere with professional service combined with an extensive range of leisure facilities. The bedrooms are comfortably furnished, many with stunning sea views, and all have modern facilities. The dining room serves a traditional menu and enjoys marvellous views over the beach and the open sea which can alos be seen from the various lounges.
ROOMS: 33 en suite (bth/shr) (3 fmly) s £56.50-£69.50; d £100-£139 (incl. bkfst & dinner) * LB Off peak **MEALS:** Sunday Lunch £1.95-£9.70 Dinner £17.95 & alc V meals Coffee am Tea pm **FACILITIES:** CTV in all bedrooms Indoor swimming pool (heated) Tennis (hard) Sauna Gym Pool table Croquet lawn Putting green Jacuzzi/spa Xmas **CONF:** Thtr 80 Board 22 Del £59 * **SERVICES:** 35P **NOTES:** No coaches No smoking in restaurant Last d 8.30pm Closed Dec & Jan RS Nov & Feb-Mar
CARDS:

CRATHORNE North Yorkshire — Map 08 NZ40

★★★★ Crathorne Hall

Virgin Hotel Collection

TS15 0AR
Quality Percentage Score: 73%
☎ 01642 700398 📠 01642 700814
Dir: *off A19, take slip rd marked Teeside Airport and Kirklevington, then a right turn signposted Crathorne leads straight to the hotel*

This fine Edwardian hall offers good comforts in a choice of tastefully appointed lounges. Carefully prepared meals are served in the magnificent restaurant, with a log fire during cooler months. Bedrooms are spacious and well equipped, retaining some original features.
ROOMS: 37 en suite (bth/shr) (4 fmly) No smoking in 15 bedrooms s £120-£130; d £160-£235 (incl. bkfst) * LB Off peak **MEALS:** Lunch £14.95 & alc Dinner £27.50 & alc English & French Cuisine V meals Coffee am Tea pm **FACILITIES:** CTV in all bedrooms STV Fishing Croquet lawn Jogging track Clay pigeon shooting Xmas **CONF:** Thtr 140 Class 80 Board 60 Del from £155 * **SERVICES:** Night porter 120P **NOTES:** No smoking in restaurant Last d 10pm
CARDS:

See advert on this page

CRAWLEY See Gatwick Airport

CREDITON Devon — Map 03 SS80

★★★ Coombe House Country Hotel

Coleford EX17 5BY
Quality Percentage Score: 67%
☎ 01363 84487 📠 01363 84722
Dir: *turn left off A377 Exeter/Barnstaple road 1m NW of Crediton signposted, hotel 1m on left*

A Georgian Manor House nestling in a hidden valley, Coombe House is only 15 minutes drive from Exeter. The bedrooms reflect two styles with bright modern rooms that have recently been furnished and the traditionally appointed rooms with period furniture. The atmosphere is relaxed and friendly.
ROOMS: 15 en suite (bth/shr) (2 fmly) s £50.50-£60.50; d £82-£90 (incl. bkfst) * LB Off peak **MEALS:** Lunch fr £16.50 Dinner fr £5.50 V meals Coffee am Tea pm **FACILITIES:** CTV in all bedrooms Tennis (hard) Croquet lawn Gymnasium equipment Xmas **CONF:** Thtr 80 Board 25 Del from £78.50 * **SERVICES:** 70P **NOTES:** No smoking in restaurant Last d 9pm **CARDS:**

CREWE Cheshire **Map 07 SJ75**
★★★ ***White Lion***
Weston CW2 5NA
Quality Percentage Score: 66%
☎ 01270 587011 & 500303 Fax 01270 500303
Dir: *2m S A5020*
Parts of this this privately owned hotel were once a Tudor farmhouse. Now it provides well equipped modern accommodation and offers a choice of bars and eating options. Facilities here include a conference room and the hotel is also licensed for civil wedding ceremonies.
ROOMS: 16 en suite (bth/shr) (2 fmly) No smoking in 2 bedrooms **MEALS:** English & French Cuisine V meals Coffee am Tea pm **FACILITIES:** CTV in all bedrooms Crown Green bowling **CONF:** Thtr 50 Class 28 Board 20 **SERVICES:** Night porter 100P **NOTES:** No coaches No smoking in restaurant Closed Xmas & New Year
CARDS:

CREWE Cheshire **Map 07 SJ75**
★★★ **Hunters Lodge**
Sydney Rd, Sydney CW1 5LU
Quality Percentage Score: 64%
☎ 01270 583440 Fax 01270 500553
Dir: *1m from Crewe station, off A534*
This hotel has a purpose-built, modern bedroom wing, with several family rooms and a select number of rooms with four poster beds. Imaginative dishes are served in the spacious restaurant, and the popular bar also offers a wide choice of tempting meals.
ROOMS: 47 en suite (bth/shr) (2 fmly) No smoking in 21 bedrooms s £50-£62; d £71-£77 (incl. bkfst) * LB Off peak **MEALS:** Lunch £8.95-£21.50alc Dinner £15.25-£21.50alc International Cuisine V meals Coffee am Tea pm **FACILITIES:** CTV in all bedrooms STV Fishing Sauna Solarium Gym Jacuzzi/spa Xmas **CONF:** Thtr 160 Class 100 Board 80 Del from £79 * **SERVICES:** Night porter 240P **NOTES:** No dogs (ex guide dogs) No smoking in restaurant Last d 9.30pm
CARDS:

CREWE Cheshire **Map 07 SJ75**
⌂ **Travel Inn**
Coppenhall Ln, Woolstanwood CW2 8SD
☎ 01270 251126 Fax 01270 256316
Dir: *at junc A530 & A532, 8m from M6 junct 16*
This modern building offers accommodation in smart, spacious and well equipped bedrooms, all with en-suite bathrooms. Refreshments may be taken at the nearby family restaurant. For details about current prices consult the Contents Page under Hotel Groups for the Travel Inn phone number.
ROOMS: 40 en suite (bth/shr) d £39.95 *

CREWE Cheshire **Map 07 SJ75**
⌂ **Travelodge**
Alsager Rd, Barthomley CW2 5PT
☎ 01270 883157 Fax 01270 883157
Dir: *5m E, at junc 16 M6/A500*
This modern building offers accommodation in smart, spacious and well equipped bedrooms, all with en-suite bathrooms. Refreshments may be taken at the nearby family restaurant. For details about current prices, consult the Contents Page under Hotel Groups for the Travelodge phone number.
ROOMS: 42 en suite (bth/shr) d £45.95 *

New AA Guides for the Millennium are featured on page 24

CRICK Northamptonshire **Map 04 SP57**
★★★ **Posthouse Northampton/Rugby**
NN6 7XR
Quality Percentage Score: 66%
☎ 01788 822101 Fax 01788 823955
Dir: *at junct 18 of M1*
A modern hotel just off the M1, whose spacious grounds include a children's play area. Bedrooms, in various styles, include several family rooms and some have pleasant country views. There is a restaurant, a lounge serving refreshments all day, and 24-hour room service. There are good leisure facilities and ample parking space.
ROOMS: 88 en suite (bth/shr) (17 fmly) No smoking in 51 bedrooms d £95 * LB Off peak **MEALS:** Asian & European Cuisine V meals Coffee am Tea pm **FACILITIES:** CTV in all bedrooms Indoor swimming pool (heated) Sauna Solarium Gym Pool table Jacuzzi/spa ch fac Xmas **CONF:** Thtr 200 Class 100 Board 142 Del from £140 * **SERVICES:** Night porter 200P **NOTES:** No smoking area in restaurant Last d 10.30pm **CARDS:**

CROMER Norfolk **Map 09 TG24**
★★ ***Red Lion***
Brook St NR27 9HD
Quality Percentage Score: 66%
☎ 01263 514964 Fax 01263 512834
Dir: *from town centre take first left after church*
A focal point for the area, the Red Lion dates from Victorian times. Public areas are comfortable, and the snooker room is a popular feature. Locals and residents mingle in the bars, which are Edwardian in style. Bedrooms offer a good standard of comfort and come in a variety of attractive styles and sizes.
ROOMS: 12 en suite (bth/shr) (1 fmly) **MEALS:** English & French Cuisine V meals Coffee am Tea pm **FACILITIES:** CTV in all bedrooms Snooker Sauna Solarium Gym Pool table Discount for local leisure centre **CONF:** Thtr 60 Class 50 Board 40 **SERVICES:** Night porter 12P **NOTES:** No dogs No coaches Last d 10pm **CARDS:**

CROOKLANDS Cumbria **Map 07 SD58**
★★★ **Crooklands**
LA7 7NW
Quality Percentage Score: 67%
☎ 015395 67432 Fax 015395 67525
Dir: *on A65, 1.5m from junct 36 of M6*
Originally a farmhouse, this hotel has been considerably extended, yet much of its character remains. There are several eating options including the Junkers Bar and the upstairs Hayloft Restaurant, which is open five days a week. The bedrooms reside in purpose built wings.
ROOMS: 30 en suite (bth/shr) No smoking in 12 bedrooms d £49.50-£55 * LB Off peak **MEALS:** Lunch fr £9.40alc Dinner fr £13.50alc International Cuisine V meals Coffee am **FACILITIES:** CTV in all bedrooms Pool table **CONF:** Thtr 100 Class 60 Board 50 Del from £85 * **SERVICES:** 150P **NOTES:** No dogs No smoking area in restaurant Last d 9pm Closed 24-26 Dec **CARDS:**
See advert under KENDAL

CROSTHWAITE Cumbria **Map 07 SD49**
★★★ **Damson Dene**
LA8 8JE
Quality Percentage Score: 59%
☎ 015395 68676 Fax 015395 68227
Dir: *on A5074, approx 6m from Bowness on right*
Owned and managed by Methodist Holiday Hotels, the spirit of Christian fellowship is evident throughout this hotel, but attendance of services in the hotel chapel is entirely voluntary. The modern leisure centre is very popular with families. Public
contd.

areas include an traditionally furnished foyer lounge, well-stocked bar, and a spacious restaurant.

ROOMS: 37 en suite (bth/shr) (3 fmly) No smoking in 8 bedrooms s £35-£58; d £70-£116 (incl. bkfst) * LB Off peak **MEALS:** Lunch £9.95-£16.50 Dinner £18.50-£25 English & French Cuisine V meals Coffee am Tea pm **FACILITIES:** CTV in all bedrooms Indoor swimming pool (heated) Squash Snooker Sauna Solarium Gym Pool table Putting green Jacuzzi/spa Steam Room Turkish Bath Xmas **CONF:** Thtr 140 Class 60 Board 40 Del from £40 * **SERVICES:** Night porter 40P **NOTES:** No smoking in restaurant Last d 9pm **CARDS:**

CROWBOROUGH East Sussex — Map 05 TQ53

★★★ Winston Manor Hotel
Beacon Rd TN6 1AD
Quality Percentage Score: 70%
☎ 01892 652772 01892 665537
Dir: *on the A26 Tunbridge Wells to Brighton*
On the main A26 between Tunbridge Wells and Lewes, Winston Manor has recently changed hands and is in private ownership.
ROOMS: 51 en suite (bth/shr) (5 fmly) s £95; d £115 (incl. bkfst) * LB Off peak **MEALS:** Lunch £14.50-£16.50 Dinner £21.50 & alc English & French Cuisine V meals Coffee am Tea pm **FACILITIES:** CTV in all bedrooms STV Indoor swimming pool (heated) Sauna Solarium Gym Jacuzzi/spa **CONF:** Thtr 300 Class 70 Board 50 Del from £90 * **SERVICES:** Lift Night porter 100P **NOTES:** No smoking in restaurant Last d 9.15pm RS 24-30 Dec **CARDS:**
See advert on this page

CROWTHORNE Berkshire — Map 04 SU86

★★★ Waterloo
corus
Corus and Regal hotels
Duke's Ride RG45 6DW
Quality Percentage Score: 68%
☎ 01344 777711 01344 778913
Dir: *M3 junct 3 towards Bracknell follow A322 then follow signs for Crowthorne, once in village follow sign for Hotel & Conference centre*

Conveniently situated for the M3 and M4, this much extended Victorian building offers very smartly decorated accommodation,
contd.

and attractive, well equipped bedrooms. Public areas, including the brasserie and bar, have a real Continental feel.
ROOMS: 58 en suite (bth/shr) No smoking in 26 bedrooms s fr £100; d fr £130 * LB Off peak **MEALS:** Lunch £11-£12.50 & alc Dinner fr £15alc International Cuisine V meals Coffee am Tea pm **FACILITIES:** CTV in all bedrooms Xmas **CONF:** Thtr 75 Class 36 Board 36 Del from £135 * **SERVICES:** Night porter 80P **NOTES:** Last d 10pm
CARDS:

C

CROYDE Devon — Map 02 SS43

★★ Kittiwell House

St Mary's Rd EX33 1PG
Quality Percentage Score: 69%
☎ 01271 890247 Fax 01271 890460
Dir: *0.5m from village centre in direction of Georgeham*
This charming, thatched hotel has a delightful cottage-style atmosphere. The individually decorated and furnished bedrooms offer cosy accommodation, reflecting the character of the property. The relaxing public areas have beamed ceilings and an interesting collection of bric-a-brac, with welcoming log fires. The attractive restaurant is popular for its high standard of cooking, with both carte and fixed price menus on offer.
ROOMS: 12 en suite (bth/shr) (2 fmly) No smoking in 4 bedrooms **MEALS:** English & French Cuisine V meals Coffee am Tea pm **FACILITIES:** CTV in all bedrooms **SERVICES:** 21P **NOTES:** No coaches No smoking in restaurant Closed mid Jan-mid Feb
CARDS:

See advert on page 215

CROYDON Greater London — Map 04 TQ36

★★★★ Coulsdon Manor

MARSTON HOTELS

Coulsdon Court Rd, Coulsdon CR5 2LL
Quality Percentage Score: 77%
☎ 020 8668 0414 Fax 020 8668 3118
Skilfully extended in keeping with its original style, to provide a range of modern and well equipped bedrooms, this fine Victorian manor house is set within 140 acres of parkland. Attentive service and hospitality are provided by a dedicated staff who achieve high standards of customer care. Public rooms include a comfortable lounge bar with separate dining area, a formal restaurant and cocktail bar. Chef Rob Bird provides interesting and innovative a la carte and daily set priced menus that demonstrate a serious and dedicated approach to enjoyable cooking. There is a good range of conference and function facilities. The excellent leisure facilities include a professional 18 hole golf course, access to a resident golf professional, pro shop and fitness assessment.
ROOMS: 35 en suite (bth/shr) No smoking in 2 bedrooms s fr £94; d fr £110 * LB Off peak **MEALS:** Lunch £14-£17.50 & alc High tea fr £12 Dinner £20-£25 & alc V meals Coffee am Tea pm **FACILITIES:** CTV in all bedrooms STV Golf 18 Tennis (hard) Squash Sauna Solarium Gym Putting green ch fac Xmas **CONF:** Thtr 180 Class 90 Board 70 Del from £140 * **SERVICES:** Lift Night porter 200P **NOTES:** No dogs (ex guide dogs) No smoking in restaurant Last d 9.30pm
CARDS:

CROYDON Greater London — Map 04 TQ36

★★★★ Selsdon Park

PRINCIPAL HOTELS

Addington Rd, Sanderstead CR2 8YA
Quality Percentage Score: 69%
☎ 020 8657 8811 Fax 020 8651 6171
Dir: *3m SE off A2022*
The extensive grounds of this imposing Jacobean mansion include a professional, 18-hole golf course. Bedrooms are equipped to a high standard, there is a grand restaurant and good conference facilities.
ROOMS: 204 en suite (bth/shr) (25 fmly) s fr £120; d fr £155 * LB Off peak **MEALS:** Lunch fr £19.95 Dinner £24.95-£40 & alc International Cuisine V meals Coffee am Tea pm **FACILITIES:** CTV in all bedrooms STV Indoor swimming pool (heated) Outdoor swimming pool (heated) Golf 18 Tennis (hard & grass) Squash Sauna Solarium Gym Croquet lawn Putting green Jacuzzi/spa Boules Jogging track Wkly live entertainment Xmas **CONF:** Thtr 200 Class 80 Board 66 Del from £189 * **SERVICES:** Lift Night porter 300P **NOTES:** No dogs (ex guide dogs) No smoking in restaurant Last d 10pm
CARDS:

See advert on opposite page

CROYDON Greater London — Map 04 TQ36

★★★ Posthouse Croydon

Posthouse

Purley Way CR9 4LT
Quality Percentage Score: 65%
☎ 020 8688 5185 Fax 020 8681 6438
Dir: *off A23*
Suitable for both the business and leisure traveller, this bright hotel provides modern accommodation in well equipped bedrooms with en suite bathrooms.
ROOMS: 83 en suite (bth/shr) No smoking in 40 bedrooms **MEALS:** International Cuisine V meals Coffee am Tea pm **FACILITIES:** CTV in all bedrooms **CONF:** Thtr 100 Class 50 Board 40 **SERVICES:** Night porter 70P **NOTES:** No smoking area in restaurant Last d 10.30pm **CARDS:**

CROYDON Greater London — Map 04 TQ36

★★ The South Park Hotel

3-5 South Park Hill Rd, South Croydon CR2 7DY
Quality Percentage Score: 66%
☎ 020 8688 5644 & 020 8688 0840 Fax 020 8760 0861
Dir: *from A235 to Croydon town centre, take A212 towards Addington, continue for 1.5m to rdbt. Take 3rd exit off onto South Park Hill Rd*
Under an owner committed to high standards, the hotel offers recently refurbished bedrooms, with good beds and soft furnishings. The small lounge is furnished with comfortable chesterfields, there is a reception-bar and a terrace overlooking the attractive rear garden.
ROOMS: 20 en suite (bth/shr) (2 fmly) No smoking in 7 bedrooms **MEALS:** V meals Coffee am Tea pm **FACILITIES:** CTV in all bedrooms **SERVICES:** 15P **NOTES:** No dogs (ex guide dogs) No coaches No smoking in restaurant Last d 7.30pm **CARDS:**

CROYDON Greater London — Map 04 TQ36

★★ Markington Hotel & Conference Centre

THE INDEPENDENTS

9 Haling Park Rd CR2 6NG
Quality Percentage Score: 63%
☎ 020 8681 6494 Fax 020 8688 6530
Dir: *travelling N from Purley, Haling Park Rd is 1st on left after bus garage. Hotel on left*
Now under new ownership, this popular hotel is close to Croydon's centre, but in a quiet area. Bedrooms are comfortable and well equipped; public areas comprise a smart bar/lounge and attractive dining room.
ROOMS: 29 rms (28 bth/shr) (3 fmly) No smoking in 5 bedrooms s £50.50-£79; d fr £65 (incl. bkfst) * Off peak **MEALS:** Bar Lunch £5-£7.50 & alc Dinner fr £7.50 & alc Cosmopolitan Cuisine V meals Coffee am Tea pm **FACILITIES:** CTV in all bedrooms STV **CONF:** Thtr 30 Class 20 Board 25 **SERVICES:** Night porter 17P **NOTES:** No dogs (ex guide dogs) No smoking in restaurant Last d 9pm
CARDS:

CROYDON Greater London — Map 04 TQ36

Travel Inn

104 Coombe Rd CR0 5RB

☎ 020 8686 2030 📠 020 8686 6435

Dir: *M25 jnct 7, M23 towards Croydon, at Purley Cross A235 to Croydon. Pass Blue Anchor PH, right at traffic lights, A212 towards Addington for 1m*

This modern building offers accommodation in smart, spacious and well equipped bedrooms, all with en-suite bathrooms. Refreshments may be taken at the nearby family restaurant. For details about current prices consult the Contents Page under Hotel Groups for the Travel Inn phone number.

ROOMS: 39 en suite (bth/shr) d £39.95 *

CROYDON Greater London — Map 04 TQ36

Late entry **Dukes Head**

6 Manor Rd, The Green, Wallington SM6 0AA

☎ 020 8401 7410 📠 020 8401 7420

Located between Croydon and Sutton, this brewery-owned hotel has undergone substantial investment. Spacious bedrooms have been furnished to a high standard, are well equipped and feature smart en-suite facilities. Public areas include a bar and brightly appointed restaurant.

ROOMS: 24 en suite (bth/shr) (4 fmly) No smoking in 15 bedrooms s fr £92; d fr £102 (incl. bkfst) * LB Off peak **MEALS:** Lunch £9.95-£20.50alc Dinner £9.95-£20.50alc V meals Coffee am **FACILITIES:** CTV in all bedrooms STV Xmas **SERVICES:** Night porter 35P **NOTES:** No dogs (ex guide dogs) Last d 9.45pm

CARDS:

CUCKFIELD West Sussex — Map 04 TQ32

★★★ **Ockenden Manor**

Ockenden Ln RH17 5LD

Quality Percentage Score: 77%

☎ 01444 416111 📠 01444 415549

Dir: *turn off A23 in direction of Brighton onto B2115 signed Cuckfield Village. Follow signs into village, take first right into Ockendon Lane, at end*

Set in the village centre, this charming 16th-century hotel enjoys fine views of the South Downs. Public rooms retain much of the original character of the property, such as the stained glass of the restaurant, the cosy panelled bar and elegant sitting room with its open log fire. Bedrooms are divided between the main building and a new wing, and offer a high standard of accommodation all individual in style. The kitchen continues to impress, and attentive staff are a great asset.

ROOMS: 22 en suite (bth/shr) (1 fmly) s £99-£150; d £120-£250 (incl. cont bkfst) * LB Off peak **MEALS:** Lunch £15.50-£20 High tea £10 Dinner £29.50-£32.50 V meals Coffee am Tea pm **FACILITIES:** CTV in all bedrooms STV Croquet lawn Xmas **CONF:** Thtr 50 Class 25 Board 25 Del £188 * **SERVICES:** 45P **NOTES:** No dogs No coaches No smoking in restaurant Last d 9.30pm **CARDS:**

CUCKFIELD West Sussex — Map 04 TQ32

★★ **Hilton Park Hotel**

Tylers Green RH17 5EG

Quality Percentage Score: 70%

☎ 01444 454555 📠 01444 457222

Dir: *halfway between Cuckfield and Haywards Heath on the A272*

Enjoying panoramic views, this delightful, family-run Victorian country house enjoys a peaceful setting in three acres of grounds. The attractive bedrooms are comfortably furnished and public areas include an elegant drawing room, smart dining room and conservatory bar.

ROOMS: 10 en suite (bth/shr) (2 fmly) s £70-£85; d £90-£105 (incl. bkfst) * LB Off peak **MEALS:** Lunch £15-£25alc High tea fr £10 Dinner £15-£25alc English, French & Italian Cuisine V meals Coffee am Tea pm **FACILITIES:** CTV in all bedrooms STV ch fac **CONF:** Thtr 30 Board 12 Del from £105 * **SERVICES:** 50P **NOTES:** No dogs (ex guide dogs) No coaches No smoking in restaurant Last d 8.30pm

CARDS:

DARLINGTON Co Durham — Map 08 NZ21

see also **Tees-Side Airport**

★★★ **Hall Garth Golf & Country Club**

Coatham Mundeville DL1 3LU

Quality Percentage Score: 73%

☎ 01325 300400 📠 01325 310083

Dir: *at junct 59 A1(M) take A167 towards Darlington, after 600yds turn left at top of hill, hotel is on right*

A delightful 16th-century house with well designed extensions, in rural surroundings near the A1. Extensive facilities include a

contd.

Indicates that the star classification has not been confirmed under the New Quality Standards, see page 7 for further information.

golf course, leisure centre, Hugo's Restaurant and Stables Pub. Bedrooms offer a high standard of comfort.

Hall Garth Golf & Country Club, Darlington

ROOMS: 30 en suite (bth/shr) 11 annexe en suite (bth/shr) (4 fmly) No smoking in 10 bedrooms s fr £95; d fr £110 * LB Off peak **MEALS:** Lunch £9.95-£11.95 Dinner £22.95 & alc V meals Coffee am Tea pm **FACILITIES:** CTV in all bedrooms STV Indoor swimming pool (heated) Golf 9 Sauna Gym Putting green Jacuzzi/spa Steam room **CONF:** Thtr 300 Class 120 Board 80 Del from £110 * **SERVICES:** Night porter 150P **NOTES:** No smoking in restaurant Last d 9.45pm **CARDS:**

DARLINGTON Co Durham **Map 08 NZ21**

★★★ Blackwell Grange

Blackwell Grange DL3 8QH

REGAL

Quality Percentage Score: 67%

☎ 01325 509955 01325 380899

Dir: *on A167, 1.5m from central ring road*

This 17th-century mansion is set in attractive parkland, surrounded by an eighteen hole golf course. Many of the bedrooms are in modern extensions, although more spacious rooms are situated in the original building.

ROOMS: 99 en suite (bth/shr) 11 annexe en suite (bth/shr) (3 fmly) No smoking in 14 bedrooms d fr £90 * LB Off peak **MEALS:** Lunch £5-£8.95 Dinner fr £17.95 & alc International Cuisine V meals Coffee am Tea pm **FACILITIES:** CTV in all bedrooms STV Indoor swimming pool (heated) Golf 18 Tennis (hard) Sauna Solarium Gym Pool table Croquet lawn Jacuzzi/spa Boules Xmas **CONF:** Thtr 300 Class 110 Board 50 Del from £95 * **SERVICES:** Lift Night porter 250P **NOTES:** No smoking in restaurant Last d 10pm **CARDS:**

DARLINGTON Co Durham **Map 08 NZ21**

★★★ Headlam Hall

Headlam, Gainford DL2 3HA

Quality Percentage Score: 66%

☎ 01325 730238 01325 730790

Dir: *2m N of A67 between Piercebridge and Gainford*

The former home of two Lords, this Jacobean hall has considerable character throughout; it retains many of its original charms, while moving with the times to provide a wide range of modern amenities. There is a choice of bedroom styles with traditionally styled rooms in the manor house and more contemporary cottage style accommodation in the converted coach house. Guests can relax in the drawing room, hall or in the cosy bar and there is a wide choice of four differently styled dining rooms.

ROOMS: 19 en suite (bth/shr) 17 annexe en suite (bth/shr) (4 fmly) No smoking in 19 bedrooms s £65-£90; d £80-£105 (incl. bkfst) * LB Off peak **MEALS:** Lunch fr £13 & alc Dinner fr £17 & alc English & French Cuisine V meals Coffee am Tea pm **FACILITIES:** CTV in all bedrooms STV Indoor swimming pool (heated) Tennis (hard) Fishing Sauna Croquet lawn Putting green ch fac **CONF:** Thtr 150 Class 40 Board 40 Del from £99 * **SERVICES:** Night porter 60P **NOTES:** No dogs (ex guide dogs) No smoking in restaurant Last d 9.30pm Closed 24-25 Dec **CARDS:**

DARLINGTON Co Durham **Map 08 NZ21**

★★★ Quality Hotel Darlington

Priest Gate DL1 1NW

Comfort Quality Clarion CHOICE HOTELS EUROPE

Quality Percentage Score: 66%

☎ 01325 380222 01325 382006

Dir: *A1 northbound follow signs to Darlington. 3rd exit off next rdbt, 2nd off next, 1st exit off next, 1st right then 1st left. Hotel on right*

Situated next to the Cornmill Shopping Centre, this modern hotel provides a sound standard of accommodation in well equipped bedrooms. Public areas include the Priestgate foyer lounge, open all day for light snacks, and a traditional restaurant on the second floor. The hotel has the advantage of a secure car park, and extensive function facilities.

ROOMS: 85 en suite (bth/shr) (3 fmly) No smoking in 51 bedrooms s fr £75; d £95-£105 * LB Off peak **MEALS:** V meals Coffee am Tea pm **FACILITIES:** CTV in all bedrooms STV Xmas **CONF:** Thtr 250 **SERVICES:** Lift Night porter 24P **NOTES:** No smoking area in restaurant Last d 9.30pm **CARDS:**

DARLINGTON Co Durham **Map 08 NZ21**

★★ *Devonport*

16-18 The Front, Middleton-one-Row DL2 1AS

Best Western

Quality Percentage Score: 68%

☎ 01325 332255 01325 333242

Delightfully situated in a former spa village near Darlington, this popular hotel enjoys fine views across the River Ouse towards open farmland and distant hills. Originally a 300-year old inn, the hotel has been completely upgraded to offer smart public areas which include a pub and restaurant offering a contemporary bistro-style menu. Bedrooms are well equipped and many are particularly spacious. Service is both friendly and efficient and matches the relaxed mood of the house.

ROOMS: 16 en suite (bth/shr) (1 fmly) No smoking in 5 bedrooms **MEALS:** English, French & Oriental Cuisine V meals Coffee am Tea pm **FACILITIES:** CTV in all bedrooms **CONF:** Thtr 50 Class 30 Board 40 Del from £55 * **SERVICES:** 30P **NOTES:** No smoking area in restaurant Last d 9.30pm **CARDS:**

DARRINGTON West Yorkshire **Map 08 SE42**

★★ The Darrington Hotel

Great North Rd WF8 3BL

Scottish Newcastle hotels

Quality Percentage Score: 62%

☎ 01977 791458 01977 602286

Dir: *off A1, 2m S of A1/M62 interchange (junct 33). Signposted*

Conveniently close to the A1 and on the edge of the village of Darrington, this popular hotel offers modern bedrooms which include hair dryers and trouser presses. There are lively bars and

contd.

a Homespreads restaurant. Service throughout is relaxed and friendly.
ROOMS: 27 en suite (bth/shr) (1 fmly) s £29.50-£45; d £38-£45 * LB Off peak **MEALS:** Lunch £6.34-£15.04alc Dinner £6.35-£15.04alc International Cuisine V meals Coffee am Tea pm **FACILITIES:** CTV in all bedrooms STV Wkly live entertainment **CONF:** Thtr 24 Class 12 Board 12 Del from £77.50 * **SERVICES:** 90P **NOTES:** No dogs (ex guide dogs) No smoking area in restaurant Last d 10pm
CARDS:

DARTFORD Kent **Map 05 TQ57**
★★★★ **Rowhill Grange Hotel & Spa**
DA2 7QH
Quality Percentage Score: 71%
☎ 01322 615136 01322 615137
Dir: *on B258 opposite Shell Garage*
This magnificent country house hotel has nine acres of woodland and gardens. Bedrooms are individually decorated to a high standard and have elegant bathrooms. Guests may eat in the Garden Restaurant or in the Topiary Brasserie. All guests have membership of the hotel's new Utopia health and leisure spa.
ROOMS: 30 en suite (bth/shr) (1 fmly) No smoking in 24 bedrooms s £99-£139; d £109-£159 * LB Off peak **MEALS:** Bar Lunch £7-£16 Dinner fr £29.95alc European Cuisine V meals Coffee am Tea pm **FACILITIES:** CTV in all bedrooms STV Indoor swimming pool (heated) Sauna Solarium Gym Croquet lawn Jacuzzi/spa Beauty treatment Hair salon Aerobics studio Therapy pool Xmas **CONF:** Thtr 100 Class 70 Board 30 Del from £159.65 * **SERVICES:** Lift Night porter 100P **NOTES:** No dogs (ex guide dogs) No coaches No smoking in restaurant Last d 9pm **CARDS:**

DARTFORD Kent **Map 05 TQ57**
⌂ **Campanile**
Clipper Boulevard West, Business Park, Crossways DA2 6QN
☎ 01322 278925 01322 278948
Dir: *follow signs for Ferry Terminal from Dartford Bridge*

This modern building offers accommodation in smart well equipped bedrooms, all with en-suite bathrooms. Refreshments may be taken at the informal Bistro. For details about current prices, consult the Contents Page under Hotel Groups for the Campanile phone number.
ROOMS: 125 en suite (bth/shr) **CONF:** Thtr 50 Class 20 Board 25

DARTMOUTH Devon **Map 03 SX85**
★★★ **The Dart Marina**
Sandquay TQ6 9PH
Quality Percentage Score: 72%
☎ 01803 832580 01803 835040
A fine hotel in an unrivalled position by the marina, with direct access to the water. Public rooms are comfortable and inviting with a nautical theme. Bedrooms, each enjoying the view, have extras such as fresh flowers and home made fudge. Locally caught fish are served in the smart restaurant.
ROOMS: 46 en suite (bth/shr) 4 annexe en suite (bth/shr) No smoking in 23 bedrooms s £44-£64; d £88-£128 (incl. bkfst) * LB Off peak **MEALS:** Lunch £2.95-£9.95 Dinner £20.95-£26.95 V meals Coffee am Tea pm **FACILITIES:** CTV in all bedrooms Xmas **SERVICES:** 75P **NOTES:** No smoking in restaurant Last d 9.30pm
CARDS:

DARTMOUTH Devon **Map 03 SX85**
★★★ **Royal Castle**
11 The Quay TQ6 9PS
Quality Percentage Score: 71%
☎ 01803 833033 01803 835445
Dir: *in the centre of the town, overlooking Boatfloat Inner Harbour*

This 17th century coaching inn is stands right on Dartmouth harbour. Its two bars serve traditional ales and a range of locally popular bar meals. Upstairs, there are several quiet lounges and the more formal Adams Restaurant. The attractive, individual bedrooms, several with four-poster beds, offer modern facilities and many personal touches.
ROOMS: 25 en suite (bth/shr) (4 fmly) **MEALS:** Sunday Lunch £6-£9.95 & alc Dinner £18.95-£19.95 & alc V meals Coffee am Tea pm **FACILITIES:** CTV in all bedrooms STV Wkly live entertainment **CONF:** Thtr 70 Class 40 Board 40 Del £60 * **SERVICES:** Night porter 17P **NOTES:** No smoking in restaurant Last d 10pm
CARDS:

DARTMOUTH Devon **Map 03 SX85**
★★★ **Stoke Lodge**
Stoke Fleming TQ6 0RA
Quality Percentage Score: 65%
☎ 01803 770523 01803 770851
Dir: *2m S A379*
Stoke Lodge is a popular hotel with many guests returning year upon year. All bedrooms are comfortably furnished with modern facilities. The spacious restaurant offers an extensive wine list and both carte and fixed-price menus. Hotel sports facilities are extensive.
ROOMS: 25 en suite (bth/shr) (5 fmly) s £47-£53; d £76-£99 (incl. bkfst) * LB Off peak **MEALS:** Lunch £11.95-£15 & alc High tea £5.50-£7.50 Dinner £17.25-£20 & alc English & Continental Cuisine V meals Coffee am Tea pm **FACILITIES:** CTV in all bedrooms Indoor swimming pool (heated) Outdoor swimming pool (heated) Tennis (hard) Snooker Sauna Pool table Putting green Jacuzzi/spa Table tennis Xmas **CONF:** Thtr 80 Class 60 Board 30 Del from £60 * **SERVICES:** 50P **NOTES:** No coaches No smoking in restaurant Last d 9pm
CARDS:

DARTMOUTH Devon **Map 03 SX85**

★★ Townstal Farmhouse

Townstal Rd TQ6 9HY

Quality Percentage Score: 66%

☎ 01803 832300 01803 835428

Dir: *on A3122 opposite Royal Naval College gate*

Elevated above the town centre, the hotel is ideal for visitors to the Royal Naval College opposite. It is a former farmhouse dating from the 16th century, and those rooms in the main building enjoy the benefit of original features. The spacious annexe rooms, one of which is designed for disabled guests, are very popular. Guests will enjoy good home-cooked meals in the beamed dining room, and can relax in front of the log fire in the cosy lounge.

ROOMS: 9 rms (6 bth/shr) 8 annexe en suite (bth/shr) (5 fmly) s fr £39.50; d fr £59 (incl. bkfst) * LB Off peak **MEALS:** Dinner fr £13.50 V meals **FACILITIES:** CTV in all bedrooms Xmas **SERVICES:** 17P **NOTES:** No coaches No smoking in restaurant Last d 8.30pm

CARDS:

See advert on opposite page

DARWEN Lancashire **Map 07 SD62**

★★★ Whitehall

Springbank, Whitehall BB3 2JU

Quality Percentage Score: 66%

☎ 01254 701595 01254 773426

Dir: *off A666 S of town*

Spacious bedrooms are offered at this family-run hotel, situated in its own grounds on the edge of the town. A wide range of dishes is offered in the elegant restaurant, or lighter meals are served in the welcoming bar and adjacent lounge. Leisure facilities include an indoor swimming pool and a snooker room.

ROOMS: 17 en suite (bth/shr) (2 fmly) s fr £55; d fr £90 (incl. bkfst) * LB Off peak **MEALS:** Lunch fr £11.50 Dinner fr £17.50 English & French Cuisine V meals Coffee am Tea pm **FACILITIES:** CTV in all bedrooms STV Indoor swimming pool (heated) Sauna Solarium Pool table 3/4 size snooker table **CONF:** Thtr 50 Class 50 Board 25 **SERVICES:** 60P **NOTES:** No smoking area in restaurant Last d 9.30pm

CARDS:

DARWEN Lancashire **Map 07 SD62**

★★★ *The Old Rosins Inn*

Pickup Bank, Hoddlesden BB3 3QD

Quality Percentage Score: 63%

☎ 01254 771264 01254 873894

Dir: *leave M65 at junct 5, follow signs for Haslingdon then right after 2m signed Egworth, then right after 0.5m and continue 0.5m*

Fine views over the surrounding countryside are to be had from most bedrooms at this hotel, situated in an elevated position just outside the town. Well equipped bedrooms also offer attractive decor and comfort. Public areas, including a popular lounge bar and nicely appointed restaurant, are situated on the first floor to take full advantage of the views.

ROOMS: 15 en suite (bth/shr) (3 fmly) **MEALS:** English & French Cuisine V meals Coffee am Tea pm **FACILITIES:** CTV in all bedrooms STV **CONF:** Thtr 30 Class 24 Board 70 **SERVICES:** 200P **NOTES:** No dogs (ex guide dogs) No smoking area in restaurant

CARDS:

DAVENTRY Northamptonshire **Map 04 SP56**

★★★★ Fawsley Hall

Fawsley NN11 3BA

Quality Percentage Score: 77%

☎ 01327 892000 01327 892001

Dir: *signed 'Fawsley Hall' follow this single track road for 1.5m until you reach wrought iron gates of Fawsley Hall*

This magnificent building, originally a Tudor manor house, is set in beautiful countryside and grounds designed by Capability Brown. A major attraction is the sheer peace and tranquility in the house, along with its history and architecture. Many of the stylish rooms overlook the 14th-century church or the lakes.

ROOMS: 30 en suite (bth/shr) (1 fmly) No smoking in 2 bedrooms **MEALS:** Lunch £14.95-£18.95 & alc Dinner £28-£42alc V meals Coffee am Tea pm **FACILITIES:** CTV in all bedrooms STV Tennis (hard) Squash **CONF:** Thtr 70 Class 36 Board 22 Del from £195 * **SERVICES:** Night porter 100P **NOTES:** No dogs (ex guide dogs) No coaches No smoking area in restaurant Last d 10pm **CARDS:**

DAVENTRY Northamptonshire **Map 04 SP56**

★★★★ *Hanover International Hotel & Club Daventry*

Sedgemoor Way, off Ashby Rd NN11 5SG

Quality Percentage Score: 60%

☎ 01327 301777 01327 706313

This smart, modern hotel set in its own grounds overlooking Drayton Water is within easy reach of both the M1 and the M40. The impressive public areas include a good range of banqueting, meeting and leisure facilities. Also boasting a fully equipped business centre, the hotel represents an excellent venue for conferences. The comfortable bedrooms all offer double beds. The Waterside restaurant provides a pleasant setting for lunch and dinner.

ROOMS: 138 en suite (bth/shr) No smoking in 73 bedrooms **MEALS:** International Cuisine V meals Coffee am Tea pm **FACILITIES:** CTV in all bedrooms STV Indoor swimming pool (heated) Sauna Solarium Gym Jacuzzi/spa Steam room Health & beauty salon **CONF:** Thtr 600 Class 200 Board 30 **SERVICES:** Lift Night porter 350P **NOTES:** Last d 9.45pm **CARDS:**

DAWLISH Devon **Map 03 SX97**

★★★ Langstone Cliff

Dawlish Warren EX7 0NA

Quality Percentage Score: 66%

☎ 01626 868000 01626 868006

Dir: *1.5m NE off A379 Exeter road*

A charming hotel standing in wooded grounds overlooking the sea and the Exe Estuary. Lounges and bars are spacious and comfortable, with a carvery operation in the restaurant.

contd.

Remember to return your Prize Draw card for a chance to win one of 30 relaxing leisure breaks with Corus and Regal hotels. See inside the front cover for the card and competition details.

Bedrooms vary in size and style. During the winter months, special cabaret weekends attract a regular following.

ROOMS: 63 en suite (bth/shr) 4 annexe en suite (bth/shr) (52 fmly) s £53-£60; d £90-£106 (incl. bkfst) * LB Off peak **MEALS:** Lunch £12 Dinner £15.50-£18.50 V meals Coffee am Tea pm **FACILITIES:** CTV in all bedrooms STV Indoor swimming pool (heated) Outdoor swimming pool (heated) Tennis (hard) Snooker Table tennis Golf practice area Wkly live entertainment ch fac Xmas **CONF:** Thtr 400 Class 200 Board 80 Del £78 * **SERVICES:** Lift Night porter 200P **NOTES:** Last d 9pm **CARDS:**

See advert on this page

DEAL Kent — Map 05 TR35

★★★ Dunkerleys Hotel & Restaurant

19 Beach St CT14 7AH
Quality Percentage Score: 66%
01304 375016 01304 380187

***Dir:** from M20 or M2 follow signs for A258 Deal. Hotel is situated on the seafront close to Deal Pier.*

Situated almost opposite the pier, Dunkerley's can be spotted by the bright array of window boxes. Bedrooms are refurbished to high standards with facilities such as trouser presses and hair dryers. The restaurant and bar have views over the channel and are popular with residents and locals, fresh fish always features.

ROOMS: 16 en suite (bth/shr) (2 fmly) s £45-£90; d £70-£150 (incl. bkfst) Off peak **MEALS:** Lunch fr £9.75 Dinner £8-£20 & alc Coffee am Tea pm **FACILITIES:** CTV in all bedrooms STV Jacuzzi/spa Xmas **SERVICES:** Night porter **NOTES:** No dogs (ex guide dogs) No coaches Last d 10.30pm RS Mon **CARDS:**

DEAL Kent — Map 05 TR35

★★ Royal Hotel

Beach St CT14 6JD
Quality Percentage Score: 70%
01304 375555

***Dir:** turn off A2 onto the A258. Follow the road for 5m into Deal. Follow the one-way system onto the seafront. The Royal is 100yrds from the pier*

A spacious imposing hotel on the seafront. The focus is the

contd.

vibrant brasserie, where an appealing selection of dishes can be enjoyed. Comfortable bedrooms feature smart colour schemes, and there is also a conference/function suite.
ROOMS: 22 en suite (bth/shr) (4 fmly) No smoking in 2 bedrooms s £40-£50; d £65-£75 (incl. bkfst) * LB Off peak **MEALS:** Lunch £9.50 & alc Dinner £9.50 & alc French Cuisine V meals Coffee am Tea pm **FACILITIES:** CTV in all bedrooms STV **CONF:** Thtr 50 Class 20 Board 20 Del £65 * **NOTES:** No dogs (ex guide dogs) No coaches Last d 9.30pm **CARDS:**

D

DEDDINGTON Oxfordshire — Map 04 SP43

★★★ Holcombe Hotel & Restaurant

High St OX15 0SL
Quality Percentage Score: 71%
☎ 01869 338274 01869 337167
***Dir:** on the A4260 between Oxford & Banbury*

Best Western

This charming hotel continues to grow in stature due to the efforts of proprietors Carole and Chedley Mahfoudh, who have a gift for hospitality and creating attractive, comfortably furnished rooms. There is a convivial air in the bar, where the informal meals are popular, and there is also a separate, formal restaurant.
ROOMS: 17 en suite (bth/shr) (3 fmly) **MEALS:** English & French Cuisine V meals Coffee am Tea pm **FACILITIES:** CTV in all bedrooms STV **CONF:** Thtr 25 Class 14 Board 18 **SERVICES:** 40P **NOTES:** No smoking area in restaurant Last d 9.30pm Closed 2-10 Jan
CARDS:

See advert on opposite page

DEDDINGTON Oxfordshire — Map 04 SP43

★★★ Deddington Arms

Horsefair OX15 0SH
Quality Percentage Score: 64%
☎ 01869 338364 01869 337010

There has been an inn on this site for over 400 years and the Deddington Arms retains much of its 16th-century character. Accommodation has been upgraded and extended to offer smart modern rooms with modern facilities. In the heart of this historic village the bar has a busy local trade and the restaurant enjoys a good reputation.
ROOMS: 27 en suite (bth/shr) (4 fmly) s £59.50-£80; d £69.50-£100 (incl. bkfst) * LB Off peak **MEALS:** Lunch £8-£20alc Dinner £12-£22alc V meals Coffee am **FACILITIES:** CTV in all bedrooms STV Xmas **CONF:** Thtr 50 Class 40 Board 30 Del from £92 * **SERVICES:** 35P **NOTES:** Last d 9.30pm **CARDS:**

DEDHAM Essex — Map 05 TM03

The Premier Collection

★★★ Maison Talbooth

Stratford Rd CO7 6HN
☎ 01206 322367 01206 322752
***Dir:** A12 towards Ipswich, 1st turning signed Dedham, follow road until nasty left hand bend, take right hand turn, hotel 1m on right*

Pride of Britain Member

Overlooking tranquil Dedham Vale, this pretty Georgian hotel offers a warm welcome. There is a comfortable drawing room where guests may take afternoon tea or snacks. Excellent breakfasts are served in the spacious bedrooms; for dinner, Le Talbooth Restaurant is nearby.
ROOMS: 10 en suite (bth/shr) (1 fmly) s £115-£130; d £150-£175 (incl. cont bkfst) * LB Off peak **MEALS:** Lunch £16.50-£24 & alc Dinner £20.50-£24 & alc English & French Cuisine V meals **FACILITIES:** CTV in all bedrooms STV Croquet lawn Garden chess Xmas **CONF:** Thtr 30 Class 20 Board 16 Del from £140 * **SERVICES:** 20P **NOTES:** No dogs (ex guide dogs) Last d 9.30pm **CARDS:**

DERBY Derbyshire — Map 08 SK33

★★★★ Mickleover Court

Etwall Rd, Mickleover DE3 5XX
Quality Percentage Score: 75%
☎ 01332 521234 01332 521238
***Dir:** take first exit off A516 signposted Mickleover*

Virgin Hotel Collection

Situated on the outskirts of Derby, this impressive modern hotel offers smartly appointed, thoughtfully equipped, air-conditioned bedrooms, each with a balcony. Hallmarks of the impressive public areas are the open-plan circular lounges and an internal glass lift. There is a choice of two restaurants; the Stelline offers an Italian menu while the Avesbury offers a wide choice of brasserie-style dishes to suit every taste.
ROOMS: 80 en suite (bth/shr) (20 fmly) No smoking in 45 bedrooms s £120; d £145 (incl. bkfst) * LB Off peak **MEALS:** Lunch £14.50-£20alc High tea £5-£7.50alc Dinner £15-£20alc English & Italian Cuisine V meals Coffee am Tea pm **FACILITIES:** CTV in all bedrooms STV Indoor swimming pool (heated) Sauna Solarium Gym Jacuzzi/spa Beauty salon Steam room Wkly live entertainment Xmas **CONF:** Thtr 200 Class 80 Board 40 Del from £150 * **SERVICES:** Lift Night porter Air conditioning 270P **NOTES:** No dogs (ex guide dogs) No smoking area in restaurant Last d 11pm **CARDS:**

DERBY Derbyshire — **Map 08 SK33**

★★★★ Marriott Breadsall Priory Hotel, Country Club

Marriott HOTELS · RESORTS · SUITES

Moor Rd DE7 6DL
Quality Percentage Score: 62%
☎ 01332 832235 📠 01332 833509
(For full entry see Breadsall)

DERBY Derbyshire — **Map 08 SK33**

★★★ Midland

Best Western

Midland Rd DE1 2SQ
Quality Percentage Score: 74%
☎ 01332 345894 📠 01332 293522
Dir: *situated opposite Derby central railway station*

This early Victorian hotel situated opposite Derby Midland Station provides good modern accommodation. The executive rooms are ideal for business travellers, equipped with writing desks, fax/computer points and first class bathrooms. Public

contd.

THE HOLCOMBE HOTEL & RESTAURANT

High Street, Deddington, Nr. Woodstock
Oxfordshire OX15 0SL (on A4260, 7m J11 of M40)
Tel: +44-01869 338274 Fax: +44-01869 337167

Be our guest.... ★★★ Best Western

At this delightful 17thC. award winning family run, quality hotel near Woodstock, in a pretty Cotswold village offering exceptional hospitality and personal attention: AA Courtesy and Care Award 1993 – Oak beamed Bar noted for its Ambience and local Ales – Sixteen lovely character rooms, all en-suite, with every amenity – Restaurant renowned for superb food and 150 wines – Elegantly refurbished recently, relaxed old world charm – Free car park – Ideal to visit Stratford, Cotswolds and Bicester Shopping Village (10 miles) 'Bond Street at 50%' – Special Getaway breaks all year, Golf, or just Romance

EN·DIEU·EST·MA·FOY
RISLEY HALL
COUNTRY HOUSE HOTEL

'When thou haply se'est some rare noteworthy object in thy travel, Wish me partaker in thy happiness'

RISLEY HALL HOTEL
DERBY ROAD, RISLEY
DERBYSHIRE DE72 3SS
TEL 0115 939 9000
FAX 01125 939 7766

In the heart of the glorious shires midway between Nottingham and Derby just off Junction 25 M1, in the leafy village of Risley, Risley Hall is set amongst fine historic gardens and offers the traveller fine foods, fine wines, fine beers and a comfortable bed.

The 16 bedroomed manor house built in the early 1700s was added to an earlier building dated 1524 known as the Baronial Hall.

The hotel offers breakfast, lunches, dinners and cream teas to the general public and is open 7 days a week. The Baronial Hall is available for conferences, celebrations and wedding receptions.

THE MIDLAND
DERBY

Situated near the city centre, close to Junction 25 of the M1 motorway, Donington Park and East Midlands Airport. Well placed for visiting Alton Towers, Royal Crown Derby, Chatsworth, Haddon Hall and the outstanding beauty of the Derbyshire Peak District. Extensively refurbished throughout. Conference and Banqueting facilities for up to 150 guests. Wedding licence granted. Excellent restaurant with nightly entertainment on the Grand Piano. Special Weekend rates and discounted tickets for Alton Towers available.

MIDLAND ROAD, DERBY DE1 2SQ
TEL: 01332 345894 FAX: 01332 293522
www.midland-derby.co.uk

rooms have been traditionally decorated and provide a comfortable lounge and a popular restaurant. Service is both professional and friendly. There is also a secluded garden, and a secure car park.
ROOMS: 100 en suite (bth/shr) No smoking in 41 bedrooms s £75-£92; d £81-£98 * LB Off peak **MEALS:** Lunch £8.05-£20.85 Dinner £19.25-£27.65 English & French Cuisine V meals Coffee am Tea pm **FACILITIES:** CTV in all bedrooms **CONF:** Thtr 150 Class 50 Board 40 Del from £90 * **SERVICES:** Lift Night porter 120P **NOTES:** No dogs (ex guide dogs) No smoking in restaurant Last d 9.45pm Closed 24-26 Dec & 31 Dec-1 Jan **CARDS:**

See advert on page 223

DERBY Derbyshire **Map 08 SK33**
★★★ Hotel Ristorante La Gondola
220 Osmaston Rd DE23 8JX
Quality Percentage Score: 65%
☎ 01332 332895 01332 384512
Dir: *on A514 towards Melbourne*
Imaginatively designed and well equipped bedrooms are offered at this elegant Georgian house, situated between the inner and outer ring roads. There are two comfortable lounges and a well established Italian restaurant.
ROOMS: 20 rms (19 bth/shr) (7 fmly) s £51-£58; d £54-£61 * LB Off peak **MEALS:** Lunch £6.90-£9.95 & alc Dinner £11.90-£14.50 & alc Continental Cuisine V meals Coffee am Tea pm **FACILITIES:** CTV in all bedrooms STV Wkly live entertainment Xmas **CONF:** Thtr 80 Class 50 Board 80 Del from £72.50 * **SERVICES:** Night porter 70P **NOTES:** No dogs (ex guide dogs) Last d 10pm **CARDS:**

DERBY Derbyshire **Map 08 SK33**
★★★ Posthouse Derby
Pastures Hill, Littleover DE23 7BA **Posthouse**
Quality Percentage Score: 64%
☎ 01332 514933 01332 518668
Dir: *from M1/A52 head towards Derby. Take A5111 ringroad following signs to Littleover-hotel located through Littleover on rdbt opp Derby High School*
The hotel is situated in grounds and gardens including a children's play area, about 3 miles south west of the city centre and in easy reach of the recently opened southern by-pass. The Junction Restaurant and Bar, reception, meeting and function facilities, are situated in a former manor house. The well equipped bedrooms are in a modern extension at the rear. Both lounge and room service are more extensive than usual, the atmosphere is warm and relaxed with friendly and responsive staff.
ROOMS: 63 en suite (bth/shr) No smoking in 29 bedrooms
MEALS: International Cuisine V meals Coffee am Tea pm
FACILITIES: CTV in all bedrooms Pitch'n'Putt **CONF:** Thtr 85 Class 60 Board 25 Del from £95 * **SERVICES:** Night porter 150P **NOTES:** No smoking area in restaurant Last d 10.30pm
CARDS:

DERBY Derbyshire **Map 08 SK33**
★★★ International
288 Burton Rd DE23 6AD
Quality Percentage Score: 63%
☎ 01332 369321 01332 294430
Dir: *0.5m from city centre on A5250*
Located within easy reach of the city centre, this hotel caters for both leisure and business visitors. Comfortable modern public rooms are provided and an extensive range of dishes is offered in the pleasant restaurant. There is a wide range of bedroom sizes and styles, and each room is very well equipped. The annexe accommodation is generally spacious and modern in style; some suites are also available.
ROOMS: 41 en suite (bth/shr) 21 annexe en suite (bth/shr) (4 fmly) s £52.50-£62.50; d £63.50-£73.50 (incl. bkfst) * LB Off peak **MEALS:** Lunch £7.99-£8.25 Dinner fr £13.95 English & Continental Cuisine V meals Coffee am Tea pm **FACILITIES:** CTV in all bedrooms STV Wkly live entertainment Xmas **CONF:** Thtr 70 Class 40 Board 30 Del from £76 * **SERVICES:** Lift Night porter 100P **NOTES:** Last d 10pm **CARDS:**

DERBY Derbyshire **Map 08 SK33**
★★★ Mackworth
Ashbourne Rd DE22 4LY
Quality Percentage Score: 59%
☎ 01332 824324 01332 824692
Dir: *follow A52 towards Ashbourne to Markeaton island and continue to hotel 1m on right*
This hotel, based around a farmhouse offers comfortable accommodation in attractively decorated bedrooms of varying sizes. There is a choice of bar areas and the carvery restaurant continues to be popular with the locals, there is also a full carte available. Catering can be arranged for wedding receptions and other functions.
ROOMS: 13 en suite (bth/shr) 1 annexe en suite (bth/shr) (3 fmly) s £42-£49; d £65-£80 (incl. bkfst) * Off peak **MEALS:** Lunch £5.95-£8.95 & alc Dinner £7.95-£12.50 & alc English & French Cuisine V meals Coffee am Tea pm **FACILITIES:** CTV in all bedrooms STV Wkly live entertainment Xmas **CONF:** Thtr 180 Class 90 Board 60 Del from £80 * **SERVICES:** Night porter 130P **NOTES:** No dogs (ex guide dogs) No smoking area in restaurant Last d 10pm
CARDS:

See advert on opposite page

DERBY Derbyshire **Map 08 SK33**
★★★ *Royal Stuart Hotel*
119 London Rd DE1 2QR
Quality Percentage Score: 58%
☎ 01332 340633 01332 293502
Dir: *follow signs for Royal Infirmary*

The hotel is close to the town centre and, being opposite the Royal Infirmary, easy to find. Bedrooms are suitably equipped for both the business and the leisure market.
ROOMS: 101 en suite (bth/shr) (9 fmly) No smoking in 65 bedrooms **MEALS:** European Cuisine V meals Coffee am Tea pm **FACILITIES:** CTV in all bedrooms STV Pool table **CONF:** Thtr 175 Class 80 Board 60 **SERVICES:** Night porter 80P **NOTES:** No smoking in restaurant Last d 9.30pm **CARDS:**

DERBY Derbyshire **Map 08 SK33**
★★ Aston Court
Midland Rd DE1 2SL
Quality Percentage Score: 61%
☎ 01332 342716 01332 293503
ROOMS: 58 en suite (shr) (4 fmly) s fr £65; d fr £75 * LB Off peak
MEALS: Lunch fr £11.95 Dinner fr £16.95 V meals Coffee am Tea pm
FACILITIES: CTV in all bedrooms Jacuzzi/spa **CONF:** Thtr 150 Class 80 Board 50 Del from £107.50 * **SERVICES:** Lift Night porter 40P
NOTES: No smoking in restaurant Last d 9.15pm
CARDS:

DERBY Derbyshire **Map 08 SK33**
European Inn
Midland Rd DE1 2SL
☎ 01332 292000 01332 293940
Dir: *200yds from railway station*
Excellent value accommodation is provided at this modern lodge, along with secure car parking and conference facilities. Bedrooms are well appointed and equipped with a range of modern facilities. Shops form part of the complex, including an Italian pizza restaurant. A good choice English breakfast is served buffet-style in the breakfast room, which may also be used for consumption of take-away meals.
ROOMS: 88 en suite (bth/shr) d £44.50-£46.50 * **CONF:** Thtr 80 Class 30 Board 25 Del from £79 *

DERBY Derbyshire **Map 08 SK33**
Travel Inn (Derby East)
The Wyvern Business Park, Chaddesden Sidings DE21 6BF
☎ 01332 667826 01332 667827
Dir: *A52 towards Derby, follow signs for city centre go past Travel Inn on left & take next exit left signed Wyvern Business Park*
This modern building offers accommodation in smart, spacious and well equipped bedrooms, all with en-suite bathrooms. Refreshments may be taken at the nearby family restaurant. For details about current prices consult the Contents Page under Hotel Groups for the Travel Inn phone number.
ROOMS: 80 en suite (bth/shr) d £39.95 *

DERBY Derbyshire **Map 08 SK33**
Travel Inn (Derby West)
Uttoxeter New Rd, Manor Park Way DE22 3HN
☎ 01332 203003 01332 207506
Dir: *from A38 (northbound) go past sign for Mickleover, take next exit for city centre & at rdbt Travel Inn 1st on left*
This modern building offers accommodation in smart, spacious and well equipped bedrooms, all with en-suite bathrooms. Refreshments may be taken at the nearby family restaurant. For details about current prices consult the Contents Page under Hotel Groups for the Travel Inn phone number.
ROOMS: 40 en suite (bth/shr) d £39.95 *

DESBOROUGH Northamptonshire **Map 04 SP88**
Travelodge
Harborough Rd NN14 2UG
☎ 01536 762034 01536 762034
Dir: *on A6, southbound*
This modern building offers accommodation in smart, spacious and well equipped bedrooms, all with en-suite bathrooms. Refreshments may be taken at the nearby family restaurant. For details about current prices, consult the Contents Page under Hotel Groups for the Travelodge phone number.
ROOMS: 32 en suite (bth/shr) d £39.95 *

DEVIZES Wiltshire **Map 04 SU06**
★★★ Bear
Market Place SN10 1HS
Quality Percentage Score: 65%
☎ 01380 722444 🖷 01380 722450
Situated in the market place, this popular coaching inn dates back to 1599. Bedrooms vary in size but all are well equipped and most have refurbished bathrooms. Old beams and log fires feature in the two bars and the comfortable residents' lounge is very relaxing. Morning coffee and afternoon tea with home-made cakes are popular, as are the buffet lunches and the regularly changing restaurant evening menu.
ROOMS: 24 en suite (bth/shr) (5 fmly) s fr £54; d £80-£90 (incl. bkfst) * LB Off peak **MEALS:** Lunch £10-£10.95 & alc Dinner £16.95 & alc English & French Cuisine V meals Coffee am Tea pm **FACILITIES:** CTV in all bedrooms Solarium **CONF:** Thtr 150 Board 50 **SERVICES:** 25P **NOTES:** Last d 9.15pm Closed 25-26 Dec **CARDS:**

DEWSBURY West Yorkshire **Map 08 SE22**
★★ Healds Hall
Leeds Rd, Liversedge WF15 6JA
Quality Percentage Score: 70%
☎ 01924 409112 🖷 01924 401895
Dir: *on A62 between Leeds and Huddersfield*
This 18th-century house in the heart of West Yorkshire offers comfortable and well equipped accommodation. The hotel has earned a good local reputation for the quality of its food, and offers both a fixed-price menu and a full carte. Owners Mr and Mrs Harrington are personally involved in the day-to-day running.
ROOMS: 25 en suite (bth/shr) (3 fmly) s £55-£57; d £75 (incl. bkfst) * LB Off peak **MEALS:** Lunch £2.25-£13 & alc Dinner £18.50 & alc International Cuisine V meals Coffee am Tea pm **FACILITIES:** CTV in all bedrooms STV **CONF:** Thtr 100 Class 60 Board 80 Del from £80 * **SERVICES:** Night porter 80P **NOTES:** No smoking in restaurant Last d 10pm Closed New Years Day
CARDS:

DIDCOT Oxfordshire **Map 04 SU59**
Travel Inn
Milton Heights OX14 4DP
☎ 01235 835168 🖷 01235 835187
Dir: *on main A4130 at Milton Interchange on the A34, which travels between Oxford/Newbury*
This modern building offers accommodation in smart, spacious and well equipped bedrooms, all with en-suite bathrooms. Refreshments may be taken at the nearby family restaurant. For details about current prices consult the Contents Page under Hotel Groups for the Travel Inn phone number.
ROOMS: 40 en suite (bth/shr) d £39.95 *

DONCASTER South Yorkshire **Map 08 SE50**
★★★ Mount Pleasant
Great North Rd DN11 0HW
Quality Percentage Score: 71%
☎ 01302 868696 & 868219 🖷 01302 865130
(For full entry see Rossington)

DONCASTER South Yorkshire **Map 08 SE50**
★★★ *Doncaster Moat House*
Warmsworth DN4 9UX
Quality Percentage Score: 66%
☎ 01302 799988 🖷 01302 310197
Dir: *2.5m SW on A630 at junc with A1(M)*
This hotel is situated in the grounds of the 17th-century Warmsworth Hall, which has been splendidly restored and is now the hotel's conference centre. Many of the bedrooms have been refurbished and are very well appointed. Two rooms have their own separate lounges, and there are also lady guest rooms and rooms designed for disabled guests. The restaurant provides a wide range of dishes and the informal atmosphere is comfortable and relaxing.
ROOMS: 100 en suite (bth/shr) (16 fmly) No smoking in 70 bedrooms **MEALS:** International Cuisine V meals Coffee am Tea pm **FACILITIES:** CTV in all bedrooms Indoor swimming pool (heated) Sauna Solarium Gym Pool table Jacuzzi/spa ch fac **CONF:** Thtr 400 Class 250 Board 40 **SERVICES:** Lift Night porter 200P **NOTES:** No smoking area in restaurant Last d 10pm **CARDS:**

DONCASTER South Yorkshire **Map 08 SE50**
★★★ Quality Hotel Doncaster
High St DN1 1DN
Quality Percentage Score: 64%
☎ 01302 342261 🖷 01302 329034
Dir: *from M18 juct3 A6182 to Doncaster. Cross rdbt, & right at next rdbt. Turn right at Give way sign, left at mini rdbt, & hotel straight ahead*
Situated in the centre of the town, this Edwardian hotel offers spacious public rooms together with well equipped bedrooms. A very pleasant restaurant on the first floor serves adventurous dishes. Car parking is limited and there are good conference facilities available. A new public bar has been added and a business centre is also planned.
ROOMS: 66 en suite (bth/shr) (3 fmly) No smoking in 24 bedrooms s £77-£90; d £90-£120 * LB Off peak **MEALS:** Lunch £9.95-£14.95 Dinner £18.95 French Cuisine V meals Coffee am Tea pm **FACILITIES:** CTV in all bedrooms STV Free entry to local Leisure Centre Wkly live entertainment Xmas **CONF:** Thtr 350 **SERVICES:** Lift Night porter 68P **NOTES:** No dogs No smoking area in restaurant Last d 10pm **CARDS:**

DONCASTER South Yorkshire **Map 08 SE50**
★★★ Grand St Leger
Bennetthorpe DN2 6AX
Quality Percentage Score: 63%
☎ 01302 364111 🖷 01302 329865
Dir: *follow signs for Doncaster Racecourse, at Racecourse rdbt hotel on corner*
This well maintained hotel is situated opposite the racecourse, next to the stables, and offers comfortable accommodation in two styles, - standard and superior - including some rooms with four poster beds. Service is willingly provided in the attractively furnished bar and restaurant, which incorporate a horse racing theme.
ROOMS: 20 en suite (bth/shr) (2 fmly) No smoking in all bedrooms s £75-£80; d £85-£110 (incl. bkfst) * LB Off peak **MEALS:** Lunch £9.95-£13.50 & alc Dinner £15.45-£19.95 & alc English & French Cuisine V meals Coffee am Tea pm **FACILITIES:** CTV in all bedrooms STV Xmas **CONF:** Thtr 65 Class 40 Board 40 Del from £85 * **SERVICES:** Night porter 28P **NOTES:** No smoking in restaurant Last d 9.45pm **CARDS:**

DONCASTER South Yorkshire **Map 08 SE50**
★★ Regent
Regent Square DN1 2DS
Quality Percentage Score: 74%
☎ 01302 364180 🖷 01302 322331
Dir: *on the corner of the A630 & A638, 1m from racecourse*
This hospitable hotel in the centre of town overlooks a small park, and has enthusiastic owners and cheerful staff. The well equipped bedrooms have been furnished along modern lines. The public rooms include a library and O'Gradys Bar. The

contd.

refurbished restaurant offers an interesting range of well prepared food.
ROOMS: 50 en suite (bth/shr) (4 fmly) s £58-£78; d £70-£84 (incl. bkfst) * LB Off peak **MEALS:** Lunch £5-£10 & alc Dinner £15 & alc English & French Cuisine V meals Coffee am Tea pm **FACILITIES:** CTV in all bedrooms STV Sauna Wkly live entertainment **CONF:** Thtr 80 Class 50 Board 40 Del from £85 * **SERVICES:** Lift Night porter 20P **NOTES:** No smoking area in restaurant Last d 10pm Closed New Year's Day Xmas Day RS Bank Hols **CARDS:**

DONCASTER South Yorkshire — Map 08 SE50

Campanile

Doncaster Leisure Park, Bawtry Rd DN4 7PD
☎ 01302 370770 01302 370813
Dir: *follow signs to Dome Leisure Centre and turn left at entrance to Dome complex*

This modern building offers accommodation in smart well equipped bedrooms, all with en-suite bathrooms. Refreshments may be taken at the informal Bistro. For details about current prices, consult the Contents Page under Hotel Groups for the Campanile phone number.
ROOMS: 50 en suite (bth/shr) **CONF:** Thtr 35 Class 18 Board 20

DONCASTER South Yorkshire — Map 08 SE50

Travel Inn

South Entry Dr, White Rose Way, Doncaster Carr DN4 5JH
☎ 01302 361134 01302 364811
Dir: *off A6182 near junct with access road to M18 junct 3*
This modern building offers accommodation in smart, spacious and well equipped bedrooms, all with en-suite bathrooms. Refreshments may be taken at the nearby family restaurant. For details about current prices consult the Contents Page under Hotel Groups for the Travel Inn phone number.
ROOMS: 40 en suite (bth/shr) d £39.95 *

DONNINGTON See **Telford**

DORCHESTER-ON-THAMES Oxfordshire — Map 04 SU59

★★★ *George*

25 High St OX10 7HH
Quality Percentage Score: 66%
☎ 01865 340404 01865 341620
Dir: *Leave M40 junct6 onto B4009 through Watlington & Benson, take A4074 at BP petrol station, follow signposts to Dorchester. Hotel on left.*
The George dates back to the 15th century with historic features throughout such as a vaulted ceiling in the restaurant. Bedrooms, retain the character of the building with beams and furnishings to suit the period. Diners have two options for meals as the hotel has a busy bar meal trade and full menu in the restaurant. The wine list is extensive and a credit to a hotel of this size.
ROOMS: 9 en suite (bth/shr) 9 annexe en suite (bth/shr) (1 fmly) No smoking in 4 bedrooms **MEALS:** V meals Coffee am Tea pm **FACILITIES:** CTV in all bedrooms **CONF:** Thtr 35 Class 25 Board 26 **SERVICES:** 75P **NOTES:** Last d 9.30pm
CARDS:

DORCHESTER-ON-THAMES Oxfordshire — Map 04 SU59

★★ White Hart

High St OX10 7HN
Quality Percentage Score: 67%
☎ 01865 340074 01865 341082
Dir: *just off A415/A4074*
This historic inn, situated on a Thameside village high street, offers good modern cooking in a charming setting. The village is known for its abbey and antique shops. The bar and restaurant are across a courtyard, and the well equipped bedrooms come in all shapes and sizes.
ROOMS: 19 en suite (bth/shr) (3 fmly) s £70-£90; d £80-£100 (incl. bkfst) LB Off peak **MEALS:** Lunch £8.50-£17.95 & alc English & French Cuisine V meals Coffee am Tea pm **FACILITIES:** CTV in all bedrooms Xmas **CONF:** Thtr 50 Class 20 Board 20 Del £115 * **SERVICES:** 25P **NOTES:** No coaches No smoking area in restaurant
CARDS:

DORKING Surrey — Map 04 TQ14

★★★★ The Burford Bridge

Burford Bridge, Box Hill RH5 6BX
Quality Percentage Score: 67%
☎ 01306 884561 01306 880386
Dir: *from M25 junct 9 follow signs for Dorking on A24. Hotel is located on this road on the left hand side*
This hotel nestles at the bottom of Box Hill, a landscape feature that was a source of inspiration for poets Keats and Wordsworth. Some of the bedrooms have balconies overlooking the well-tended gardens. There are extensive conference and banqueting facilities, for which a fine 16th-century tithe barn may be used.
ROOMS: 57 en suite (bth/shr) No smoking in 17 bedrooms d fr £140 LB Off peak **MEALS:** Lunch £13-£28 & alc Dinner fr £20 & alc European Cuisine V meals Coffee am Tea pm **FACILITIES:** CTV in all bedrooms Outdoor swimming pool (heated) Croquet lawn Putting green Xmas **CONF:** Thtr 300 Class 100 Board 60 Del from £154 * **SERVICES:** Night porter 80P **NOTES:** No smoking area in restaurant Last d 10pm
CARDS:

DORKING Surrey — Map 04 TQ14

★★★ The White Horse

High St RH4 1BE
Quality Percentage Score: 67%
☎ 01306 881138 01306 887241
Dir: *from M25 junct 9 take A24 S towards Dorking. Hotel is situated in the centre of the town*
There is plenty of old character to this centrally located hotel which has been an inn/hotel since the 18th century. The focal point is the bar with its adjoining lounges. Bedrooms are distributed between the original main building and a purpose-built annexe.
ROOMS: 36 en suite (bth/shr) 32 annexe en suite (bth/shr) (2 fmly) No smoking in 20 bedrooms d fr £110 LB Off peak **MEALS:** Lunch £10.95-£25 & alc Dinner £12.95-£25 & alc V meals Coffee am Tea pm **FACILITIES:** CTV in all bedrooms Xmas **CONF:** Thtr 50 Class 30 Board 30 Del from £140 **SERVICES:** Night porter 73P **NOTES:** No smoking area in restaurant Last d 10pm **CARDS:**

DORKING Surrey **Map 04 TQ14**
★★★ Gatton Manor Hotel Golf & Country Club
Standon Ln RH5 5PQ
Quality Percentage Score: 63%
☎ 01306 627555 🖷 01306 627713
(For full entry see Ockley)

DORKING Surrey **Map 04 TQ14**
Travelodge
Reigate Rd RH4 1QB
☎ 01306 740361 🖷 01306 740361
Dir: *0.5m E, on A25*
This modern building offers accommodation in smart, spacious and well equipped bedrooms, all with en-suite bathrooms. Refreshments may be taken at the nearby family restaurant. For details about current prices, consult the Contents Page under Hotel Groups for the Travelodge phone number.
ROOMS: 54 en suite (bth/shr) d £55.95 *

DORRIDGE West Midlands **Map 07 SP17**
★★ Forest Hotel
25 Station Approach B93 8JA
Quality Percentage Score: 65%
☎ 01564 772120 🖷 01564 770677
Dir: *take junct 5 off M42, follow A4141 for 2m, after Knowle village turn right (signed Dorridge) in 1.5m left just before rail bridge, hotel 200yds*
This well established, privately run hotel is situated in the heart of Dorridge village. Rooms have been refurbished throughout and are very well equipped with modern facilities. Downstairs there is a choice of bars where meals are available as well as a hotel restaurant.
ROOMS: 12 en suite (bth/shr) (1 fmly) s £50; d £60 (incl. bkfst) * Off peak **MEALS:** Sunday Lunch £9.95-£11.95 Dinner £10.95-£12.50 & alc V meals Coffee am **FACILITIES:** CTV in all bedrooms **SERVICES:** Air conditioning 70P **NOTES:** No dogs (ex guide dogs) No coaches Last d 9pm **CARDS:**

DOVER Kent **Map 05 TR34**
★★★ The Churchill
Dover Waterfront CT17 9BP
Quality Percentage Score: 69%
☎ 01304 203633 🖷 01304 216320
Dir: *from A20 follow signs for Hoverport, turn left onto seafront, hotel 800yds along*

Located on Dover's waterfront overlooking the harbour, this completely refurbished hotel forms part of a listed Regency terrace. Bedrooms are furnished to a comfortable standard; executive rooms have mini bars and there are ten with balconies. Winston's Restaurant serves enjoyable cooking and there is a well appointed bar lounge, sun lounge and front terrace.
ROOMS: 68 rms (67 bth/shr) (5 fmly) No smoking in 6 bedrooms s £59; d £79 * Off peak **MEALS:** Lunch £10.95-£12.95 Dinner £16.50 English & French Cuisine V meals Coffee am Tea pm **FACILITIES:** CTV in all bedrooms STV Xmas **CONF:** Thtr 90 Class 60 Board 60 **SERVICES:** Lift Night porter 32P **NOTES:** No smoking in restaurant Last d 9.10pm **CARDS:**

See advert on opposite page

DOVER Kent **Map 05 TR34**
★★★ County Hotel Dover
Townwall St CT16 1SZ
Quality Percentage Score: 60%
☎ 01304 509955 🖷 01304 213230
Dir: *follow A20 over 3 rdbts, then at 4th stay left signed 'Eastern Docks' and take 2nd slip road on left*

Conveniently located for the ferry terminal, this hotel offers spacious well equipped rooms with air-conditioning. A refurbishment programme is under way and the newly completed rooms are bright and modern. The indoor swimming pool is popular.
ROOMS: 79 en suite (bth/shr) (32 fmly) No smoking in 31 bedrooms s £55-£70; d £65-£80 * LB Off peak **MEALS:** Lunch £7.50-£12 Dinner £12.50 English & French Cuisine V meals Coffee am Tea pm **FACILITIES:** CTV in all bedrooms Indoor swimming pool (heated) Xmas **CONF:** Thtr 80 Class 46 Board 40 Del £85 * **SERVICES:** Lift Night porter 48P **NOTES:** No smoking area in restaurant Last d 10pm **CARDS:**

DOVER Kent **Map 05 TR34**
★★★ Posthouse Dover
Singledge Ln, Whitfield CT16 3LF
☎ 01304 821222 🖷 01304 825576
Dir: *from M2,take A2 towards Dover, turn left immediately before Esso garage OR from M20, at Eastern Docks rdbt turn right, over 2 rdbts then turn right*
Suitable for both the business and leisure traveller, this bright hotel provides accommodation in well equipped bedrooms. It is located to the north of town.
ROOMS: 68 en suite (bth/shr) (19 fmly) No smoking in 37 bedrooms d £59-£69 * LB Off peak **MEALS:** International Cuisine V meals Coffee am Tea pm **FACILITIES:** CTV in all bedrooms ch fac Xmas **CONF:** Thtr 60 Class 20 Board 24 Del from £115 * **SERVICES:** Night porter 80P **NOTES:** No smoking area in restaurant Last d 10pm **CARDS:**

DOVER Kent **Map 05 TR34**

★★ Wallett's Court

West Cliffe, St Margarets-at-Cliffe CT15 6EW

Quality Percentage Score: 76%

☎ 01304 852424 Fax 01304 853430

Dir: *take A258 towards Deal; 1st right to St Margaret's-at-Cliffe & Westcliffe, 1m on right opposite Westcliffe church*

This country house hotel has at its core a lovely Jacobean manor. Bedrooms range from traditionally furnished in the original house to modern rooms in courtyard buildings in the grounds, and all are equipped to a high standard. The restaurant offers well prepared traditional food.

ROOMS: 3 en suite (bth/shr) 12 annexe en suite (bth/shr) (2 fmly) s £70-£110; d £80-£130 (incl. bkfst) * LB Off peak **MEALS:** Sunday Lunch £17.50 & alc Dinner £27.50 & alc V meals Coffee am Tea pm **FACILITIES:** CTV in all bedrooms Indoor swimming pool (heated) Tennis (hard) Sauna Solarium Gym Croquet lawn Putting green Jacuzzi/spa **CONF:** Thtr 25 Class 25 Board 16 Del from £100 * **SERVICES:** 32P **NOTES:** No dogs (ex guide dogs) No coaches No smoking in restaurant Last d 9pm Closed 24 Dec-3 Jan **CARDS:**

See advert on this page

DOVER Kent **Map 05 TR34**

Travel Inn

Folkestone Rd CT15 7AB

☎ 01304 213339 Fax 01304 214504

Dir: *at end of M20 continue through tunnel on A20 to Dover. Take 2nd exit onto B2011 signed "local services"*

This modern building offers accommodation in smart, spacious and well equipped bedrooms, all with en-suite bathrooms. Refreshments may be taken at the nearby family restaurant. For details about current prices consult the Contents Page under Hotel Groups for the Travel Inn phone number.

ROOMS: 62 en suite (bth/shr) d £39.95 *

DOVER Kent **Map 05 TR34**

Travel Inn

Jubilee Way, Guston Wood CT15 5FD

☎ 01304 204660 Fax 01304 215273

Dir: *on the rdbt of the A2 & A258*

This modern building offers accommodation in smart, spacious and well equipped bedrooms, all with en-suite bathrooms. Refreshments may be taken at the nearby family restaurant. For details about current prices consult the Contents Page under Hotel Groups for the Travel Inn phone number.

ROOMS: 40 en suite (bth/shr) d £39.95 *

Symbols and Abbreviations are listed and explained on pages 4 and 5

DOWNHAM MARKET Norfolk **Map 05 TF60**

★★ Castle
High St PE38 9HF
Quality Percentage Score: 68%
☎ 01366 384311 Fax 01366 384311
Dir: *from M11 take A10 for Ely into Downham Market, on reaching town hotel opposite traffic lights, on corner of High St*
For over 300 years, this coaching inn has been welcoming guests and it has recently received a smart and vibrant upgrade. The inviting bedrooms, some with four-poster beds, have colourful furnishings and the cheerful public rooms include a choice of eating options.
ROOMS: 10 en suite (bth/shr) s £52-£59; d £62-£85 (incl. bkfst) LB Off peak **MEALS:** Lunch £9.95-£10.95 High tea £7 Dinner £15.95 & alc English & French Cuisine V meals Coffee am Tea pm **FACILITIES:** CTV in all bedrooms Xmas **CONF:** Thtr 60 Class 30 Board 40 **SERVICES:** Night porter 26P **NOTES:** No smoking area in restaurant Last d 9pm
CARDS:

DRIFFIELD (GREAT) East Riding of Yorkshire **Map 08 TA05**

★★★ Bell
46 Market Place YO25 6AN
Quality Percentage Score: 70%
☎ 01377 256661 Fax 01377 253228
Dir: *enter town from A164, turn right at traffic lights. Car park 50yds on left behind black railings*
This 250-year-old hotel is furnished with many antique and period pieces. The bedrooms vary in shape and size; all have modern facilities and some have their own sitting rooms. There is a good leisure and natural health centre across the courtyard. The hotel has a relaxed, friendly atmosphere.
ROOMS: 16 en suite (bth/shr) No smoking in 4 bedrooms s £75-£85; d £105-£115 (incl. bkfst) LB Off peak **MEALS:** Dinner £15-£25alc V meals Coffee am Tea pm **FACILITIES:** CTV in all bedrooms Indoor swimming pool (heated) Squash Snooker Sauna Solarium Gym Jacuzzi/spa Masseur Wkly live entertainment **CONF:** Thtr 250 Class 200 Board 50 **SERVICES:** Lift Night porter 18P **NOTES:** No children 12yrs No smoking in restaurant Last d 9.30pm
CARDS:

DROITWICH Worcestershire **Map 03 SO86**

★★★★ *Château Impney*
WR9 0BN
Quality Percentage Score: 67%
☎ 01905 774411 Fax 01905 772371
Dir: *on A38, 1m from M5 junct 5*
Built in the style of a French chateau, and a notable landmark, this elegant hotel stands in extensive grounds near junction 5 of the M5. All bedrooms are furnished and equipped to modern standards, but do vary in size. The hotel has excellent conference, function and leisure facilities, and can take up to 1000 delegates. Service is both friendly and professional.
ROOMS: 67 en suite (bth/shr) (1 fmly) **MEALS:** English & French Cuisine V meals Coffee am Tea pm **FACILITIES:** CTV in all bedrooms Tennis (hard) **CONF:** Thtr 1000 Class 550 Board 160 Del from £144.85 * **SERVICES:** Lift Night porter 1000P **NOTES:** No dogs (ex guide dogs) No smoking in restaurant Last d 9pm Closed Xmas
CARDS:

DROITWICH Worcestershire **Map 03 SO86**

★★★★ *Raven*
Victoria Square WR9 8DQ
Quality Percentage Score: 65%
☎ 01905 772224 Fax 01905 797100
Dir: *in town centre on A38, 1.5m from M5 junct 5*
This large black and white, timber framed property dates back to at least the 16th century. Considerably altered and extended over the centuries, it is now an extensive hotel, conference and function complex. It provides modern well equipped accommodation. Public areas include a spacious lounge, pleasant lounge bar with pianist, and charming restaurant with exposed beams and wall timbers.
ROOMS: 72 en suite (bth/shr) (1 fmly) **MEALS:** English & French Cuisine V meals Coffee am Tea pm **FACILITIES:** CTV in all bedrooms **CONF:** Thtr 150 Class 70 Board 40 **SERVICES:** Lift Night porter 250P **NOTES:** No smoking in restaurant Last d 9.30pm Closed Xmas
CARDS:

DROITWICH Worcestershire **Map 03 SO86**

Travelodge
Rashwood Hill WR9 8DA
☎ 01527 861545 Fax 01527 861545
Dir: *2m N, on A38 from junc 5 at M5*
This modern building offers accommodation in smart, spacious and well equipped bedrooms, all with en-suite bathrooms. Refreshments may be taken at the nearby family restaurant. For details about current prices, consult the Contents Page under Hotel Groups for the Travelodge phone number.
ROOMS: 32 en suite (bth/shr) d £49.95 *

DRONFIELD Derbyshire **Map 08 SK37**

★★ *Chantry*
Church St S18 1QB
Quality Percentage Score: 66%
☎ 01246 413014 Fax 01246 413014
Dir: *6m from Sheffield and Chesterfield on A61. Opposite church with spire*
Next to a striking church, this hotel has award-winning gardens and friendly service. Day rooms include a pleasant conservatory coffee shop, and a spacious restaurant and a bar. Bedrooms are thoughtfully designed and seem relatively spacious.
ROOMS: 7 en suite (bth/shr) **MEALS:** Continental Cuisine V meals Coffee am **FACILITIES:** CTV in all bedrooms **SERVICES:** 28P **NOTES:** No coaches Last d 9pm **CARDS:**

DUDLEY West Midlands **Map 07 SO99**

see also **Himley**

★★★★ *The Copthorne Merry Hill-Dudley*
The Waterfront, Level St, Brierley Hill DY5 1UR
Quality Percentage Score: 68%
☎ 01384 482882 Fax 01384 482773
Dir: *follow signs for Merry Hill Centre*
Situated to the west of the city, this new hotel has a scenic position overlooking the Merry Hill development and marina. Polished marbled floors, rich fabrics and striking interior design are features of the stylish public areas which include the informal Faradays bar and restaurant. Bedrooms are spacious and well equipped.
ROOMS: 138 en suite (bth/shr) (14 fmly) No smoking in 60 bedrooms **MEALS:** International Cuisine V meals Coffee am Tea pm **FACILITIES:** CTV in all bedrooms STV Indoor swimming pool (heated) Sauna Solarium Gym Jacuzzi/spa Aerobics studio Beauty Therapist **CONF:** Thtr 250 Class 150 Board 40 Del from £100 * **SERVICES:** Lift Night porter 170P **NOTES:** No dogs (ex guide dogs) No smoking area in restaurant Last d 10.45pm **CARDS:**

DUDLEY West Midlands **Map 07 SO99**

★★★ Ward Arms
Birmingham Rd DY1 4RN
Quality Percentage Score: 60%
☎ 01384 458070 Fax 01384 457502
Dir: *on A461*
This popular, modern hotel is within easy reach of the M5 motorway. Well equipped bedrooms include some on ground-
contd.

floor level and public areas include the traditionally furnished conservatory restaurant and bar. There is also "Morriseys", a very popular Irish theme bar.

ROOMS: 72 en suite (bth/shr) No smoking in 14 bedrooms s fr £65; d fr £75 * LB Off peak **MEALS:** Sunday Lunch £8-£22alc High tea £1.95-£6.50alc Dinner £8-£22alc International Cuisine V meals Coffee am Tea pm **FACILITIES:** CTV in all bedrooms STV Pool table Xmas **CONF:** Thtr 100 Class 50 Board 60 **SERVICES:** Night porter 150P **NOTES:** No smoking area in restaurant Last d 10pm
CARDS:

DUDLEY West Midlands — Map 07 SO99

Travelodge

Dudley Rd, Brierley Hill DY5 1LQ
☎ 01384 481579 Fax 01384 481579
Dir: *3m W, on A461*

Travelodge

This modern building offers accommodation in smart, spacious and well equipped bedrooms, all with en-suite bathrooms. Refreshments may be taken at the nearby family restaurant. For details about current prices, consult the Contents Page under Hotel Groups for the Travelodge phone number.
ROOMS: 32 en suite (bth/shr) d £45.95 *

DULVERTON Somerset — Map 03 SS92

★★★ *Carnarvon Arms*

TA22 9AE
Quality Percentage Score: 71%
☎ 01398 323302 Fax 01398 324022
Dir: *leave A396 at Exbridge onto B3222, hotel 1m on right*

Owned and operated since 1958 by Mrs Toni Jones, the Carnarvon Arms typifies all that is best in the English country house hotel including cosy public rooms with open fires and fresh flowers. It has its own stabling and five miles of fishing on the rivers Exe and Barle, and shooting can be arranged. Two dining options are available: the restaurant which offers a choice of menus and the informal Buttery Bar. Look out for the old railway buildings are a feature of the delightful grounds.
ROOMS: 25 rms (23 bth/shr) (2 fmly) **MEALS:** V meals Coffee am Tea pm **FACILITIES:** CTV in all bedrooms Indoor swimming pool (heated) Outdoor swimming pool (heated) Tennis (hard) Fishing Snooker Sauna Croquet lawn Jacuzzi/spa Clay pigeon shooting Hairdressing salon **CONF:** Thtr 100 Class 25 Board 40 **SERVICES:** 121P **NOTES:** No coaches No smoking in restaurant Last d 9pm
CARDS:

See advert on this page

AA Rosettes are awarded for quality of food,
see page 15 for an explanation of Rosette assessment.

DULVERTON Somerset — Map 03 SS92

The Premier Collection

★★ Ashwick House

TA22 9QD
☎ 01398 323868 Fax 01398 323868
Dir: *turn left at post office, 3m NW on B3223, over two cattlegrids, signposted on left*

Prepare to be pampered at this small Edwardian Hotel set in six acres on the edge of Exmoor. The atmosphere is relaxed and unhurried, guests can take tea or an aperitif on the terrace overlooking the grounds. Public areas are extensive, the main feature being the galleried hall with its welcoming log fire. Bedrooms are spacious and comfortable, with every conceivable facility, plus a few whimsical touches. Each

contd.

evening a set menu is served using the finest of local produce.
ROOMS: 6 en suite (bth) No smoking in 1 bedroom s £68-£84; d £114-£148 (incl. bkfst & dinner) * LB Off peak **MEALS:** Sunday Lunch £14.75 Dinner £19.75 International Cuisine Coffee am Tea pm **FACILITIES:** CTV in all bedrooms Solarium Xmas **SERVICES:** 27P **NOTES:** No dogs No coaches No children 8yrs No smoking in restaurant Last d 8.30pm

D

DULVERTON Somerset **Map 03 SS92**
★★ **Lion**
Bank Square TA22 9BU
Quality Percentage Score: 62%
☎ 01398 323444 01398 323980
The Lion is a charming traditional inn ideally situated for exploring the natural beauty of the Exmoor National Park. The tap bar is popular with locals for the real ales and extensive range of bar meals available at lunchtimes and evenings. Bedrooms are comfortable and well equipped, and a residents' lounge is also available on the first floor.
ROOMS: 13 en suite (bth/shr) (1 fmly) s fr £27.50; d fr £55 (incl. bkfst) * Off peak **MEALS:** Lunch £5-£10alc Dinner £5-£15alc English, French & Italian Cuisine V meals Coffee am **FACILITIES:** CTV in all bedrooms Xmas **SERVICES:** 6P **NOTES:** No coaches No smoking in restaurant Last d 8.30pm **CARDS:**

DUNCHURCH Warwickshire **Map 04 SP47**
Travelodge
London Rd, Thurlaston CV23 9LG
Travelodge
☎ 01788 521538 01788 521538
Dir: *A45, westbound*
This modern building offers accommodation in smart, spacious and well equipped bedrooms, all with en-suite bathrooms. Refreshments may be taken at the nearby family restaurant. For details about current prices, consult the Contents Page under Hotel Groups for the Travelodge phone number.
ROOMS: 40 en suite (bth/shr) d £45.95 *

DUNSTABLE Bedfordshire **Map 04 TL02**
★★★ **Old Palace Lodge**
Church St LU5 4RT
Quality Percentage Score: 68%
☎ 01582 662201 01582 696422
Dir: *exit M1 at junct 11 and take A505. Hotel 2m on right opposite Priory church*

Ideally located close to the town centre and the motorway, this ivy-clad hotel offers comfortable bedrooms. Public areas include an attractive restaurant serving a daily menu and a varied carte. The comfortably furnished lounge/bar is the focal point of the hotel and provides a popular meeting place.
ROOMS: 68 en suite (bth/shr) (7 fmly) No smoking in 21 bedrooms s £95; d £105 * LB Off peak **MEALS:** Lunch £13.50 & alc Dinner £19.95 & alc English & French Cuisine V meals Coffee am Tea pm **FACILITIES:** CTV in all bedrooms STV **CONF:** Thtr 40 Class 18 Board 25 Del £125 * **SERVICES:** Lift Night porter 70P **NOTES:** Last d 9.40pm **CARDS:**

See advert on opposite page

DUNSTABLE Bedfordshire **Map 04 TL02**
Travel Inn
Watling St, Kensworth LU6 3QP
☎ 01582 840509 01582 842811
Dir: *from M1 junct 9 head towards Dunstable on A5, Travel Inn on right just past Packhorse pub*
This modern building offers accommodation in smart, spacious and well equipped bedrooms, all with en-suite bathrooms. Refreshments may be taken at the nearby family restaurant. For details about current prices consult the Contents Page under Hotel Groups for the Travel Inn phone number.
ROOMS: 40 en suite (bth/shr) d £39.95 *

DUNSTABLE Bedfordshire **Map 04 TL02**
Travel Inn
350 Luton Rd LU5 4LL
☎ 01582 609938 01582 664114
Dir: *on A505, from M1 junct 11 follow signs to Dunsatble*
This modern building offers accommodation in smart, spacious and well equipped bedrooms, all with en-suite bathrooms. Refreshments may be taken at the nearby family restaurant. For details about current prices consult the Contents Page under Hotel Groups for the Travel Inn phone number.
ROOMS: 40 en suite (bth/shr) d £39.95 *

DUNSTABLE Bedfordshire **Map 04 TL02**
Travelodge
Watling St LU7 9LZ
Travelodge
☎ 01525 211177 01525 211177
Dir: *3m N, on A5*
This modern building offers accommodation in smart, spacious and well equipped bedrooms, all with en-suite bathrooms. Refreshments may be taken at the nearby family restaurant. For details about current prices, consult the Contents Page under Hotel Groups for the Travelodge phone number.
ROOMS: 28 en suite (bth/shr) d £49.95 *

DUNSTER Somerset **Map 03 SS94**
★★★ **The Luttrell Arms**
High St TA24 6SG
Quality Percentage Score: 66%
☎ 01643 821555 01643 821567
Dir: *20m beyond the Exmoor Visitor Centre on A396, opposite the Yarn Market*
Steeped in history, and dating from the 15th century, The Luttrell Arms welcomes guests through a massive stone porch. Most bedrooms are spacious with interesting features. Those in the Latches are more compact but have been refurbished and are attractively decorated and well equipped. Guests are offered home cooked food in the smart split-level restaurant, and meals are also available in the Old Kitchen Bar. There is a congenial

contd.

bar and comfortable beamed lounge on the first floor and friendly service is carried out by a local team.
ROOMS: 27 en suite (bth/shr) (1 fmly) No smoking in 5 bedrooms s £65-£85; d £75-£95 * LB Off peak **MEALS:** Lunch £7.50-£14.95 Dinner £15-£22.50 V meals Coffee am Tea pm **FACILITIES:** CTV in all bedrooms Xmas **CONF:** Thtr 25 Board 15 **SERVICES:** 3P **NOTES:** No smoking in restaurant Last d 9.30pm **CARDS:**

DURHAM Co Durham **Map 12 NZ24**
★★★★ Swallow Royal County
Old Elvet DH1 3JN
Quality Percentage Score: 72%
☎ 0191 386 6821 📠 0191 386 0704
Dir: *from A1(m) take junct 62 towards Durham, over 1st rdbt, turn left at 2nd rdbt over the bridge. Turn left at traffic lights, hotel on left*

This long established hotel sits by the river in the heart of the city. Bedrooms are split between three different buildings. Public areas include a cocktail bar and foyer and two restaurants, the elegant County earning our Two Rosette award.
ROOMS: 151 en suite (bth/shr) (4 fmly) No smoking in 99 bedrooms s £99-£120; d £135-£165 (incl. bkfst) * LB Off peak **MEALS:** Lunch £16.50-£17.50 & alc High tea fr £10 Dinner fr £25.50 & alc International Cuisine V meals Coffee am Tea pm **FACILITIES:** CTV in all bedrooms STV Indoor swimming pool (heated) Sauna Solarium Gym Jacuzzi/spa Steam room Plunge pool Impulse showers Wkly live entertainment Xmas **CONF:** Thtr 140 Class 50 Board 45 Del from £130 * **SERVICES:** Lift Night porter 72P **NOTES:** No smoking area in restaurant Last d 10.30pm **CARDS:**

DURHAM Co Durham **Map 12 NZ24**
★★★ Ramside Hall
Carrville DH1 1TD
Quality Percentage Score: 71%
☎ 0191 386 5282 📠 0191 386 0399
Dir: *take A690 towards Sunderland from A1M/A690 interchange, 200mtrs after going under railway bridge*

Set in attractive parkland with a golf course, driving range, and an impressive new conference centre, Ramside Hall is ideal for corporate travellers. Facilities include a choice of eating options and a mix of public areas which include an elegant foyer and lounge, plus various bar lounge areas. The majority of bedrooms are extremely spacious, located in an extension of the original building.
ROOMS: 80 en suite (bth/shr) (10 fmly) No smoking in 36 bedrooms s £98-£175; d £118-£210 (incl. bkfst) * LB Off peak **MEALS:** Lunch £12.50-£16 & alc High tea fr £6 Dinner fr £15 & alc Cosmopolitan Cuisine V meals Coffee am Tea pm **FACILITIES:** CTV in all bedrooms STV Golf 27 Snooker Sauna Putting green Wkly live entertainment **CONF:** Thtr 400 Class 160 Board 40 Del from £118 * **SERVICES:** Lift Night porter Air conditioning 500P **NOTES:** No smoking area in restaurant Last d 9.30pm **CARDS:**

DURHAM Co Durham **Map 12 NZ24**
★★★ Swallow Three Tuns
New Elvet DH1 3AQ
Quality Percentage Score: 68%
☎ 0191 386 4326 📠 0191 386 1406
Dir: *from A1 follow A690 for city. At 1st rdbt take 2nd exit at 2nd rdbt take 1st exit. Hotel 100yds on left over bridge and through traffic lights*
With parts dating back to the 16th century, this city centre hotel retains much of its character and individuality. Friendly and committed staff are also influential in its popularity with local customers as well as tourists and business guests. Bedrooms are well equipped, the executive rooms being particularly spacious and comfortable. Although there are no leisure facilities, guests

contd.

can use those at the Swallow County Hotel just a few yards down the road.

Swallow Three Tuns, Durham

ROOMS: 50 en suite (bth/shr) (2 fmly) No smoking in 30 bedrooms s £95-£105; d £105-£130 (incl. bkfst) * LB Off peak **MEALS:** Lunch £9.25-£12.50 Dinner £19.95 English & French Cuisine V meals Coffee am Tea pm **FACILITIES:** CTV in all bedrooms STV Free facilities at Royal County Hotel Wkly live entertainment Xmas **CONF:** Thtr 350 Class 200 Board 160 Del from £80 * **SERVICES:** Night porter 60P **NOTES:** No smoking area in restaurant Last d 9.30pm
CARDS:

DURHAM Co Durham — Map 12 NZ24
★★★ Bowburn Hall
Bowburn DH6 5NH
Quality Percentage Score: 61%
☎ 0191 377 0311 Fax 0191 377 3459
Dir: *head towards Bowburn, go right at Cooperage Pub, then 0.5 miles along country rd toleft junct signposted Durham. Hotel on immediate left*
Standing in five acres of grounds, this former country mansion offers an informal and relaxed style of service. It has a good choice of lounges, as well as a spacious restaurant. Bedrooms come in a variety of sizes, all of which are individual in style.
ROOMS: 19 en suite (bth) s £50-£55; d £55-£65 (incl. bkfst) * LB Off peak **MEALS:** Lunch fr £10.95 Dinner fr £14.95 English & French Cuisine V meals Coffee am Tea pm **FACILITIES:** CTV in all bedrooms STV **CONF:** Thtr 150 Class 80 Board 60 Del from £65 * **SERVICES:** 100P **NOTES:** Last d 9.45pm **CARDS:**

DURHAM Co Durham — Map 12 NZ24
★★ Rainton Lodge
West Rainton DH4 6QY
Quality Percentage Score: 62%
☎ 0191 512 0540 & 512 0534 Fax 0191 584 1221
Dir: *1.5m from junct 62 A1 (M) on A690 towards Sunderland*
Enjoying a fine outlook across the valley, this hotel has an attractive interior. The bar and restaurant feature a good range of dishes, the fixed price dinner is excellent value. Bedrooms vary in style and size, some furnished in a contemporary style, the others with traditional pine.
ROOMS: 27 en suite (bth/shr) (3 fmly) s £34-£38; d £44-£48 (incl. bkfst) * LB Off peak **MEALS:** Lunch £4.75-£9.95 & alc Dinner fr £9.95 & alc V meals Coffee am Tea pm **FACILITIES:** CTV in all bedrooms STV Riding Xmas **CONF:** Thtr 100 Class 70 Board 50 Del from £66 * **SERVICES:** Night porter 80P **NOTES:** No dogs (ex guide dogs) Last d 9.40pm **CARDS:**

DURHAM Co Durham — Map 12 NZ24
Roadchef Lodge
Motorway Service Area, Tursdale Rd, Bowburn DH6 5NP
☎ 0191 377 3666 Fax 0191 377 1448
This modern building offers accommodation in smart, spacious and well equipped bedrooms, all with en-suite bathrooms. Refreshments may be taken at the nearby family restaurant. For details about current prices, consult the Contents Page under Hotel Groups for the Roadchef phone number.
ROOMS: 38 en suite (bth/shr) d fr £47.50 * **CONF:** Thtr 20 Board 10

DURHAM Co Durham — Map 12 NZ24
Travel Inn
Adj Arnison Retail Centre, Pity Me DH1 5GB
☎ 0191 383 9140 Fax 0191 383 9107
Dir: *from A1 take junct 63 south on A167 to Durham. Straight over 3 rdbts and at 4th rdbt turn left, Travel Inn on the right after 200yds*
This modern building offers accommodation in smart, spacious and well equipped bedrooms, all with en-suite bathrooms. Refreshments may be taken at the nearby family restaurant. For details about current prices consult the Contents Page under Hotel Groups for the Travel Inn phone number.
ROOMS: 40 en suite (bth/shr) d £39.95 *

DUXFORD Cambridgeshire — Map 05 TL44
★★★ Duxford Lodge
Ickleton Rd CB2 4RU
Quality Percentage Score: 69%
☎ 01223 836444 Fax 01223 832271
Dir: *junc 10 of M11 and A505. Opposite T junction*

In a quiet residential setting in the middle of Duxford, this delightful village hotel is staffed by a dedicated and welcoming team. Public areas include a convivial bar, separate lounge, and an attractive restaurant where guests can enjoy meals from an excellent and imaginative menu. Accommodation is available in both the main house, and also in ground floor rooms in the pleasing gardens, connected by a covered walkway.
ROOMS: 11 en suite (bth/shr) 4 annexe en suite (bth/shr) s £75-£80; d £95-£100 (incl. bkfst) * LB Off peak **MEALS:** Lunch £16.95-£20.50 & alc Dinner £20.50 & alc English & French Cuisine V meals Coffee am Tea pm **FACILITIES:** CTV in all bedrooms **CONF:** Thtr 30 Class 20 Board 20 Del from £110 * **SERVICES:** 34P **NOTES:** No smoking area in restaurant Last d 9.30pm Closed 25-30 Dec & 1 Jan RS Sat
CARDS:

See advert under CAMBRIDGE

EASINGTON North Yorkshire — Map 08 NZ71
★★★ Grinkle Park
TS13 4UB
Quality Percentage Score: 70%
☎ 01287 640515 Fax 01287 641278
Dir: *9m from Guisborough, signed left off the main A171 Guisborough/Whitby Road*
Standing in extensive grounds, this elegant Victorian house has an attentive and friendly staff and delightfully furnished bedrooms. There are comfortable lounges and a gracious

contd.

restaurant which serves well presented dishes using the best of local produce.
ROOMS: 20 en suite (bth/shr) s £61.95-£77.65; d £76.45-£102 (incl. bkfst) * LB Off peak **MEALS:** Lunch £12-£13.25 Dinner £19.95 & alc English & French Cuisine V meals Coffee am Tea pm **FACILITIES:** CTV in all bedrooms Tennis (hard) Snooker Croquet lawn Xmas **CONF:** Thtr 70 Class 20 Board 25 Del £100.95 * **SERVICES:** 122P **NOTES:** Last d 9pm **CARDS:**

EASINGWOLD North Yorkshire **Map 08 SE56**

★★ George

Market Place Y061 3AD
Quality Percentage Score: 67%
☎ 01347 821698 01347 823448
Dir: *off A19 midway between York & Thirsk, in Market Place*
An old coaching inn overlooking the cobbled market square. Bedrooms to the rear have been upgraded to a very good standard. The dining room is attractive, an extensive well produced range of food is available in the bar or candlelit restaurant. A cosy and comfortable lounge is provided.
ROOMS: 14 en suite (bth/shr) (2 fmly) s fr £50; d fr £66 (incl. bkfst) LB Off peak **MEALS:** Lunch fr £11 & alc Dinner fr £16 & alc European Cuisine V meals Coffee am Tea pm **FACILITIES:** CTV in all bedrooms **SERVICES:** 10P **NOTES:** No dogs (ex guide dogs) No smoking in restaurant Last d 9pm **CARDS:**

EAST AYTON North Yorkshire **Map 08 SE98**

★★★ East Ayton Lodge

Moor Ln, Forge Valley YO13 9EW
Quality Percentage Score: 63%
☎ 01723 864227 01723 862680
Dir: *400 yds off A170*
This family-run hotel stands in three acres of grounds close to the River Derwent, off a quiet lane on the edge of the village. Bedrooms are well equipped and those in the courtyard are particularly spacious. A good range of food is a available.
ROOMS: 11 en suite (bth/shr) 20 annexe en suite (bth/shr) (3 fmly) s £39.50-£49.50; d £65-£99 (incl. bkfst) * LB Off peak **MEALS:** Lunch £5.95-£10.95 Dinner fr £22.50 English & French Cuisine V meals Coffee am Tea pm **FACILITIES:** CTV in all bedrooms Xmas **CONF:** Thtr 46 Class 74 Board 32 Del from £60 * **SERVICES:** 50P **NOTES:** No smoking in restaurant Last d 9pm Closed Jan-12 Feb **CARDS:**

EASTBOURNE East Sussex **Map 05 TV69**

★★★★★ Grand

King Edward's Pde BN21 4EQ
Quality Percentage Score: 64%
☎ 01323 412345 01323 412233
Dir: *on seafront west of Eastbourne 1m from railway station*
This impressive Victorian hotel stands at the western end of the

contd.

seafront before the steep ascent to Beachy Head. Bedrooms provide the expected levels of comfort. The Mirabelle restaurant has been expanded to incorporate a larger bar.
ROOMS: 152 en suite (bth/shr) (20 fmly) No smoking in 4 bedrooms s £115-£285; d £145-£305 (incl. bkfst) * LB Off peak **MEALS:** Lunch £12.50-£21 & alc High tea fr £6 Dinner £31 & alc English & French Cuisine V meals Coffee am Tea pm **FACILITIES:** CTV in all bedrooms STV Indoor swimming pool (heated) Outdoor swimming pool (heated) Snooker Sauna Solarium Gym Putting green Jacuzzi/spa Hairdressing beauty & massage Wkly live entertainment ch fac Xmas **CONF:** Thtr 400 Class 240 Board 60 Del from £195 * **SERVICES:** Lift Night porter 64P **NOTES:** No coaches Last d 9.30pm
CARDS:

See advert on page 235

EASTBOURNE East Sussex — Map 05 TV69

★★★ Lansdowne

King Edward's Pde BN21 4EE
Quality Percentage Score: 73%
☎ 01323 725174 Fax 01323 739721
Dir: *hotel situated at west end of seafront (B2103 facing Western Lawns*

Enjoying one of the best locations on the promenade, this long established hotel has a range of attractively furnished bedrooms, several lounges and a well appointed cocktail bar. The splendid Devonshire Restaurant features enthusiastic traditional cooking.
ROOMS: 121 en suite (bth/shr) (5 fmly) s £53-£61; d £86-£106 (incl. bkfst) LB Off peak **MEALS:** Sunday Lunch £10.25-£13 Dinner £17.95 V meals Coffee am Tea pm **FACILITIES:** CTV in all bedrooms STV Snooker Pool table Darts Table tennis **CONF:** Thtr 120 Class 50 Board 50 Del from £75 * **SERVICES:** Lift Night porter 22P **NOTES:** No smoking in restaurant Last d 8.30pm Closed 29 Dec-13 Jan
CARDS:

See advert on opposite page

EASTBOURNE East Sussex — Map 05 TV69

★★★ Hydro

Mount Rd BN20 7HZ
Quality Percentage Score: 71%
☎ 01323 720643 Fax 01323 641167
Dir: *proceed to pier/seafront, turn right along Grand Parade, at Grand Hotel you will see a road with the sign Hydro Hotel, proceed up South Cliff 200yds*
Well established and popular, this hotel enjoys an elevated position and fine views. Public areas are extensive and have an elegant, traditional feel. Bedrooms are neatly decorated, comfortably furnished and fully equipped. There is a range of lounges and a restaurant.
ROOMS: 83 en suite (bth/shr) (1 fmly) s £33-£55; d £60-£104 (incl. bkfst) * LB Off peak **MEALS:** Lunch £8.50-£10.95 Dinner £15.95 V meals Coffee am Tea pm **FACILITIES:** CTV in all bedrooms Outdoor swimming pool (heated) Sauna Gym Pool table Croquet lawn Putting green Beauty room Hairdressing Xmas **CONF:** Thtr 140 Class 90 Board 40 Del from £65 * **SERVICES:** Lift Night porter 50P **NOTES:** No coaches No smoking in restaurant Last d 8.30pm
CARDS:

> ★
> The Premier Collection, hotels with Red Star Awards are listed on pages 17-23

EASTBOURNE East Sussex — Map 05 TV69

★★★ Chatsworth

Grand Pde BN21 3YR
Quality Percentage Score: 61%
☎ 01323 411016 Fax 01323 643270
Dir: *on seafront between the pier and the bandstand*
This splendid Edwardian hotel enjoys one of the best seafront locations. Bedrooms are comfortably furnished and well equipped. Public rooms include a spacious lounge and foyer, the Devonshire Restaurant and cosy Dukes Bar. Regular live entertainment is provided through the summer.
ROOMS: 47 en suite (bth/shr) (2 fmly) No smoking in 10 bedrooms s £40-£60; d £60-£90 (incl. bkfst) LB Off peak **MEALS:** Lunch £11.75 Dinner fr £16.25 V meals Coffee am Tea pm **FACILITIES:** CTV in all bedrooms STV Wkly live entertainment Xmas **CONF:** Thtr 100 Class 60 Board 30 **SERVICES:** Lift Night porter **NOTES:** No smoking in restaurant Last d 8.30pm **CARDS:**

See advert on opposite page

EASTBOURNE East Sussex — Map 05 TV69

★★★ Quality Hotel Eastbourne

Grand Pde BN21 3YS
Quality Percentage Score: 61%
☎ 01323 727411 Fax 01323 720665
Dir: *take A22 to Eastbourne and follow through to seafront where the hotel is located between the pier and the bandstand*
The hotel is centrally located on the sea front. Bedrooms which vary in shape and size are comfortably appointed and well equipped. Public areas include a comfortable bar, spacious restaurant and sun lounge.
ROOMS: 115 en suite (bth/shr) (6 fmly) No smoking in 47 bedrooms s £63.25-£74.25; d £74.25-£85.25 * LB Off peak **MEALS:** Lunch £2.95-£15.95alc Dinner fr £14.50 & alc English & Continental Cuisine V meals Coffee am Tea pm **FACILITIES:** CTV in all bedrooms STV Gym Xmas **CONF:** Thtr 150 Class 80 Board 20 **SERVICES:** Lift Night porter **NOTES:** No smoking area in restaurant Last d 9pm
CARDS:

EASTBOURNE East Sussex **Map 05 TV69**
★★★ Wish Tower
King Edward's Pde BN21 4EB
Quality Percentage Score: 61%
☎ 01323 722676 📠 01323 721474
Dir: *opposite Wish Tower on seafront, W of the pier*
On the seafront near the Martello Tower, this hotel is also in reach of the Congress Theatre, Winter Gardens and Devonshire Park Theatre. Bedrooms vary in size, but all are well equipped, and more than half enjoy sea views. Public areas include a comfortable bar/lounge and dining room.
ROOMS: 56 en suite (bth/shr) (6 fmly) No smoking in 3 bedrooms s £55-£70; d £84-£110 (incl. bkfst) * LB Off peak **MEALS:** Lunch £9.50-£10.50 Dinner £18-£19 & alc English & French Cuisine V meals Coffee am Tea pm **FACILITIES:** CTV in all bedrooms STV Nearby sports centre free to guests Xmas **CONF:** Thtr 60 Class 30 Board 30 **SERVICES:** Lift Night porter 3P **NOTES:** No smoking area in restaurant Last d 9.15pm
CARDS:

EASTBOURNE East Sussex **Map 05 TV69**
★★ The Downland Hotel & Restaurant
37 Lewes Rd BN21 2BU
Quality Percentage Score: 68%
☎ 01323 732689 📠 01323 720321
Dir: *on A22, take 1st exit at Willingdon rdbt, follow sign to seafront, go past college and hospital straight over rdbt. Hotel in 0.5m*
Owners Thomas and Laurentina Brown maintain high standards at this hotel, which is slightly out of the town centre. Bedrooms are comfortable, and equipped with a range of quality extras. The dining room offers a short menu of dishes, all cooked to order.
ROOMS: 12 en suite (bth/shr) (2 fmly) s £32.50-£37.50; d £55-£75 (incl. bkfst) * LB Off peak **MEALS:** Dinner £17.50 & alc Coffee am **FACILITIES:** CTV in all bedrooms **SERVICES:** 10P **NOTES:** No dogs (ex guide dogs) No coaches No children 10yrs No smoking in restaurant Last d 8.30pm **CARDS:**

EASTBOURNE East Sussex **Map 05 TV69**
★★ West Rocks
Grand Pde BN21 4DL
Quality Percentage Score: 68%
☎ 01323 725217 📠 01323 720421
Dir: *on seafront western end*
This is a popular family-run hotel on the seafront. Bedrooms, varying in shape and size, are neatly appointed and well equipped. Many have bay windows and sea views. There are two traditional lounges and a well stocked bar. The large dining room offers a varied menu of popular dishes.
ROOMS: 45 en suite (bth/shr) (4 fmly) s £35-£50; d £50-£90 (incl. bkfst) * LB Off peak **MEALS:** Bar Lunch £6-£8 Dinner £9-£10.95 English & French Cuisine V meals Coffee am Tea pm **FACILITIES:** CTV in all bedrooms Wkly live entertainment **CONF:** Thtr 50 Class 26 Board 20 **SERVICES:** Lift Night porter **NOTES:** No dogs No children 3yrs Last d 8pm Closed mid Nov-end Feb
CARDS:

EASTBOURNE East Sussex **Map 05 TV69**
★★ New Wilmington
25 Compton St BN21 4DU
Quality Percentage Score: 67%
☎ 01323 721219 📠 01323 728900
Dir: *A22 to Eastbourne along the seafront, turn right along promenade until Wishtower. Turn right off Promenade and Hotel is on the first left*
This family run hotel offers comfortable bedrooms and well presented public areas, including a red plush lounge bar. It is

contd.

conveniently located for the seafront, the Winter Gardens and the theatres.
ROOMS: 40 en suite (bth/shr) (8 fmly) s £45-£51; d £80-£92 (incl. bkfst & dinner) LB Off peak **MEALS:** Lunch £5.95-£7.50 Dinner £10-£12.50 English, French & Italian Cuisine V meals Coffee am Tea pm **FACILITIES:** CTV in all bedrooms Wkly live entertainment Xmas **SERVICES:** Lift Night porter 2P **NOTES:** No smoking in restaurant Last d 7pm Closed Jan & Feb **CARDS:**

EASTBOURNE East Sussex — Map 05 TV69
★★ *Stanley House Hotel*
9/10 Howard Square BN21 4BQ
Quality Percentage Score: 67%
☎ 01323 731393 Fax 01323 738823
Privately owned and run, Stanley House stands close to the bandstand and Pier and overlooks the gardens of Howard Square. The good value accommodation offers all the expected comforts in an attractive setting. A daily changing selection of traditional fare is offered in the dining room.
ROOMS: 25 en suite (bth/shr) (3 fmly) **MEALS:** Coffee am **FACILITIES:** CTV in all bedrooms Wkly live entertainment **SERVICES:** Lift Night porter **NOTES:** No dogs No smoking in restaurant Last d 7.30pm Closed Jan-Feb **CARDS:**

EASTBOURNE East Sussex — Map 05 TV69
★★ *York House*
14/22 Royal Pde BN22 7AP
Quality Percentage Score: 67%
☎ 01323 412918 Fax 01323 646238
Dir: *M25, take M23 outside Brighton take A27 towards Lewes and then Eastbourne. York House is on the sea front .25m east of the pier*

After celebrating a century of being under the same family membership a few years ago, York House continues to provide warm hospitality to guests, while the upgrading of facilities continues. An open verandah makes the best of the seafront location, and the public areas include a spacious reception hall, cosy bar and separate lounge plus a games room and indoor swimming pool.
ROOMS: 97 en suite (bth/shr) (8 fmly) **MEALS:** V meals Coffee am Tea pm **FACILITIES:** CTV in all bedrooms STV Indoor swimming pool (heated) Pool table Games room **CONF:** Thtr 100 Class 30 Board 24 Del from £65 * **SERVICES:** Lift Night porter **NOTES:** No smoking in restaurant Last d 8pm Closed 23-29 Dec
CARDS:

See advert on opposite page

EASTBOURNE East Sussex — Map 05 TV69
★★ Farrar's Hotel
Wilmington Gardens BN21 4JN
Quality Percentage Score: 65%
☎ 01323 723737 Fax 01323 732902
Dir: *turn off seafront by Wish Tower, hotel opposite Congress Theatre*
Conveniently situated opposite Devonshire Park, and just a short walk from the seafront, this privately owned hotel provides comfortable and well equipped bedrooms. Public areas are spacious with a choice of lounges, and the restaurant serves a short menu of traditional fare.
ROOMS: 45 en suite (bth/shr) (3 fmly) **MEALS:** V meals Coffee am Tea pm **FACILITIES:** CTV in all bedrooms **CONF:** Thtr 80 **SERVICES:** Lift Night porter 35P **NOTES:** No smoking in restaurant Closed Jan
CARDS:

EASTBOURNE East Sussex — Map 05 TV69
★★ Langham
Royal Pde BN22 7AH
Quality Percentage Score: 65%
☎ 01323 731451 Fax 01323 646623
Dir: *follow signs for the seafront, hotel half a mile E of the pier, near the Redoubt Fortress*
Privately owned and run for more than 80 years, this friendly hotel is very well maintained. Public areas are comfortable and include sea-facing terraces in addition to the ground floor lounges and bar. Live entertainment provided four nights a week from May to September.
ROOMS: 87 en suite (bth/shr) (5 fmly) s £26-£52; d £52-£96 (incl. bkfst) * LB Off peak **MEALS:** Lunch £5.25-£9.25 Dinner £9.50-£12.50 & alc European Cuisine V meals Coffee am Tea pm **FACILITIES:** CTV in all bedrooms Pool table Temporary membership of Sovereign club Xmas **CONF:** Thtr 80 Class 40 Board 24 **SERVICES:** Lift Night porter 4P **NOTES:** No smoking in restaurant Last d 8.30pm Closed 27 Dec-29 Jan
CARDS:

EASTBOURNE East Sussex — Map 05 TV69
★★ Oban
King Edward's Pde BN21 4DS
Quality Percentage Score: 64%
☎ 01323 731581 Fax 01323 721994
Dir: *opposite Wish Tower seafront area*
This friendly hotel benefits from a seafront location overlooking tidy lawns. Bedrooms, which vary in shape and size, are brightly decorated and well equipped; many have sea views. There is a comfortable bar and sun lounge. Meals are taken in the dining room.
ROOMS: 31 en suite (bth/shr) (2 fmly) **MEALS:** V meals Coffee am Tea pm **FACILITIES:** CTV in all bedrooms Lounge bar activities Wkly live entertainment **SERVICES:** Lift Night porter **NOTES:** No smoking in restaurant Closed Dec-Feb (ex Xmas) **CARDS:**

EASTBOURNE East Sussex — Map 05 TV69
★★ *Lathom*
4-6 Howard Square, Grand Pde BN21 4BG
Quality Percentage Score: 60%
☎ 01323 720985 & 641986 Fax 01323 416405
Privately owned and run, this hotel continues to successfully cater for coach parties. The brightly decorated bedrooms vary in size, and although some are small, good use has been made of available space. Evening entertainment is provided in the lounge and there is a small bar.
ROOMS: 45 en suite (bth/shr) (5 fmly) **MEALS:** V meals Coffee am **FACILITIES:** CTV in all bedrooms Wkly live entertainment **SERVICES:** Lift Night porter 6P **NOTES:** No dogs (ex guide dogs) Last d 8pm Closed Nov-Feb (ex Xmas & New Year) **CARDS:**

The AA Hotel Booking Service is a free benefit to AA members. See the advertisement on page 47

EAST GRINSTEAD West Sussex **Map 05 TQ33**

The Premier Collection

★★★ Gravetye Manor
RH19 4LJ
☎ 01342 810567 Fax 01342 810080
RELAIS & CHÂTEAUX.

Dir: *B2028 towards Haywards Heath. 1 mile after Turners Hill, take left fork towards Sharpthorne, then 1st left into Vowels Lane*

Created by Peter Herbert in 1958, Gravetye was one of the first country house hotels and remains a shining example in its class. The Elizabethan stone manor house is set in 1000 acres that include William Robinson's famous English garden. The flower-filled day rooms are comfortably furnished, bedrooms are decorated in traditional English style, furnished with antiques and include many thoughtful additions such as a good selection of books and tapestry screens concealing the TVs. Bathrooms have quality toiletries and bathrobes. Chef Mark Raffan uses excellent ingredients including produce from the walled kitchen garden, to create an imaginative range of dishes for the restaurant.

ROOMS: 18 en suite (bth/shr) s £135-£145; d £170-£290 * Off peak
MEALS: Lunch £28-£35 & alc Dinner fr £38 & alc V meals
FACILITIES: CTV in all bedrooms Fishing Croquet lawn **CONF:** Thtr 12 Class 12 Board 12 Del from £235 * **SERVICES:** 35P
NOTES: No dogs No coaches No children 7yrs No smoking in restaurant Last d 9.30pm RS 25 Dec **CARDS:**

EAST GRINSTEAD West Sussex **Map 05 TQ33**

★★★ Woodbury House
Lewes Rd RH19 3UD
Quality Percentage Score: 65%
☎ 01342 313657 Fax 01342 314801
Best Western

Dir: *0.5m S of town on A22*

Conveniently located south of the town on the A22, this small, privately owned hotel offers smart accommodation in well

contd.

equipped bedrooms. Guests are provided with a choice of eating options in the hotel restaurant or the more informal bistro. Service is both friendly and attentive from the dedicated team of staff.
ROOMS: 14 en suite (bth/shr) (1 fmly) No smoking in 2 bedrooms s £50-£80; d £70-£100 (incl. bkfst) * LB Off peak **MEALS:** Lunch £12.50-£17.50 Dinner £12.50-£17.50 V meals Coffee am Tea pm **FACILITIES:** CTV in all bedrooms STV Xmas **CONF:** Thtr 40 Class 30 Board 24 Del from £95 * **SERVICES:** 52P **NOTES:** No coaches No smoking in restaurant Last d 9.30pm
CARDS:

See advert on page 239

E

EAST HORNDON Essex — Map 05 TQ68
Travelodge
CM13 3LL
☎ 01277 810819 Fax 01277 810819
Dir: *on A127, eastbound 4m off junc29 M25*
This modern building offers accommodation in smart, spacious and well equipped bedrooms, all with en-suite bathrooms. Refreshments may be taken at the nearby family restaurant. For details about current prices, consult the Contents Page under Hotel Groups for the Travelodge phone number.
ROOMS: 22 en suite (bth/shr) d £49.95 *

EASTLEIGH Hampshire — Map 04 SU41
★★★ Posthouse Eastleigh/Southampton
Leigh Rd SO50 9PG
Quality Percentage Score: 64%
☎ 023 80619700 Fax 023 80643945
Dir: *follow A335 to Eastleigh, hotel on right*
Located close to junction 13 of the M3 motorway, this well sited hotel is suitable for both business and leisure traveller. It is bright and provides modern accommodation in well equipped and well laid-out bedrooms. It has a leisure centre with a decent-sized swimming pool.
ROOMS: 116 en suite (bth/shr) (3 fmly) No smoking in 86 bedrooms d £59-£89 * LB Off peak **MEALS:** International Cuisine V meals Coffee am Tea pm **FACILITIES:** CTV in all bedrooms Indoor swimming pool (heated) Sauna Gym Pool table Jacuzzi/spa Beauty treatment Leisure club Xmas **CONF:** Thtr 250 Class 90 Board 90 Del from £115 * **SERVICES:** Lift Night porter 160P **NOTES:** No smoking area in restaurant Last d 10pm **CARDS:**

EASTLEIGH Hampshire — Map 04 SU41
Travel Inn
Leigh Rd SO50 9YX
☎ 023 80650541 Fax 023 80650531
Dir: *adjacent to junct 13 of the M3, near Eastleigh on A335*
This modern building offers accommodation in smart, spacious and well equipped bedrooms, all with en-suite bathrooms. Refreshments may be taken at the nearby family restaurant. For details about current prices consult the Contents Page under Hotel Groups for the Travel Inn phone number.
ROOMS: 60 en suite (bth/shr) d £39.95 *

EASTLEIGH Hampshire — Map 04 SU41
Travelodge
Twyford Rd SO50 4LF
☎ 023 80616813 Fax 023 80616813
Dir: *off junct 12 on M3 on A335*
This modern building offers accommodation in smart, spacious and well equipped bedrooms, all with en-suite bathrooms. Refreshments may be taken at the nearby family restaurant. For details about current prices, consult the Contents Page under Hotel Groups for the Travelodge phone number.
ROOMS: 32 en suite (bth/shr) d £55.95 *

EAST MIDLANDS AIRPORT Leicestershire — Map 08 SK42
★★★★ Thistle East Midlands Airport
DE74 2SH
Quality Percentage Score: 70%
☎ 01332 850700 Fax 01332 850823
Dir: *on the A453 at entrance to East Midlands Airport, just 1 mile from junction 24 and 23A of the M1 and M1/A42(M) interchange.*
A large, modern hotel in a very peaceful setting. Public areas include a range of leisure facilities, an informal bar, and the Sherwood restaurant, which has a good reputation for fine food. Bedrooms are smartly appointed, well equipped and of comfortable proportions; room service is available.
ROOMS: 110 en suite (bth/shr) (4 fmly) No smoking in 55 bedrooms
MEALS: International Cuisine V meals Coffee am Tea pm
FACILITIES: CTV in all bedrooms STV Indoor swimming pool (heated) Sauna Solarium Gym Jacuzzi/spa Steam room Wkly live entertainment
CONF: Thtr 220 Class 90 Board 30 **SERVICES:** Night porter 250P
NOTES: No smoking in restaurant Last d 10pm
CARDS:

EAST MIDLANDS AIRPORT Leicestershire — Map 08 SK42
★★★ Yew Lodge Hotel & Conference Centre
Packington Hill DE74 2DF
Quality Percentage Score: 72%
☎ 01509 672518 Fax 01509 674730
Dir: *leave M1 at junc 24, then follow signs to Loughborough & Kegworth on the A6. At the bottom of the hill, first right, 400 yards is Yew Lodge on right*
Handy for both the M1 and East Midlands Airport, Yew Lodge has been dramatically improved through refurbishment and extension. The reception rooms are now light, inviting and well appointed, there is a cosy foyer lounge area, a bar and a spacious restaurant, which offers an improved choice through set priced and a la carte menus. Bedrooms look cheerful with co-ordinated decor and matching soft furnishings. The new conference and syndicate rooms are proving very popular.
ROOMS: 64 en suite (bth/shr) (3 fmly) No smoking in 18 bedrooms s £45-£85; d £60-£85 * LB Off peak **MEALS:** Lunch £9-£20 Dinner £15-£25 & alc English & French Cuisine V meals Coffee am Tea pm
FACILITIES: CTV in all bedrooms STV Xmas **CONF:** Thtr 150 Class 60 Board 36 Del from £95 * **SERVICES:** Lift Night porter 120P
NOTES: No smoking area in restaurant Last d 9.30pm
CARDS:

EAST RETFORD Nottinghamshire — Map 08 SK78
★★★ West Retford
24 North Rd DN22 7XG
Quality Percentage Score: 64%
☎ 01777 706333 Fax 01777 709951
Dir: *on A638 on outskirts of East Retford*
Set in attractive grounds close to the town centre this 18th-century manor house offers a good range of well equipped meeting facilities. The spacious, well laid out bedrooms and suites are located in a separate building and extensive upgrading of the hotel is planned.
ROOMS: 62 annexe en suite (bth/shr) (39 fmly) No smoking in 35 bedrooms s £70; d £90 * LB Off peak **MEALS:** Lunch £6.95-£11.95 Dinner £16.95 & alc Italian Cuisine V meals Coffee am Tea pm
FACILITIES: CTV in all bedrooms STV Xmas **CONF:** Thtr 150 Class 40 Board 43 Del from £90 * **SERVICES:** Night porter 110P **NOTES:** No smoking in restaurant Last d 9.30pm
CARDS:

EGHAM Surrey — Map 04 TQ07

★★★★ Runnymede Hotel & Spa

Windsor Rd TW20 0AG
Quality Percentage Score: 72%
☎ 01784 436171 Fax 01784 436340
Dir: *off junc 13 of M25, on A308 towards Windsor*

Located by the Thames and with easy access to Heathrow and west London this successful hotel has steadily improved in recent years. The smart Leftbank restaurant with its nautical theme has views of the river and offers a modern menu. For an alternative there is the lively Charlie Bell's Café/Bar. There are extensive leisure facilities.

ROOMS: 180 en suite (bth/shr) (26 fmly) No smoking in 94 bedrooms s £145-£165; d £180-£205 * LB Off peak **MEALS:** Lunch £17.95-£22 European Cuisine V meals Coffee am Tea pm **FACILITIES:** CTV in all bedrooms STV Indoor swimming pool (heated) Tennis (hard & grass) Snooker Sauna Solarium Gym Croquet lawn Putting green Jacuzzi/spa Steam room Beauty Salon Dance studio Hairdressers **CONF:** Thtr 300 Class 250 Board 76 Del from £220 * **SERVICES:** Lift Night porter Air conditioning 280P **NOTES:** No dogs (ex guide dogs) No smoking area in restaurant RS Restaurant closed Sat lunch/Sun dinner
CARDS:

See advert under WINDSOR

ELLESMERE PORT Cheshire — Map 07 SJ47

★★★ Quality Hotel Chester

Welsh Road/Berwick Rd, Little Sutton L66 4PS
Quality Percentage Score: 64%
☎ 0151 339 5121 Fax 0151 339 3214
Dir: *M53 junct 5 turn left at rdbt at 2nd set of traffic lights, turn right onto A550 over the hump back bridge turn left into Berwick Road*

Set back from the A550 and just a short distance from junction 5 of the M53, this distinctive hotel has attractive modern accommodation, equipped with both business and leisure guests in mind. The recently refurbished public areas are popular for large parties. There is a good range of facilities including a swimming pool and versatile banqueting and conference suites.

ROOMS: 53 en suite (bth/shr) (8 fmly) No smoking in 18 bedrooms s fr £75; d £90-£100 * LB Off peak **MEALS:** Dinner fr £16.50 English & French Cuisine V meals Coffee am Tea pm **FACILITIES:** CTV in all bedrooms Indoor swimming pool (heated) Sauna Steam room Exercise equipment Wkly live entertainment Xmas **CONF:** Thtr 300 Class 150 Board 100 **SERVICES:** Night porter 200P **NOTES:** Last d 9.30pm
CARDS:

> Indicates that the star classification has not been confirmed under the New Quality Standards, see page 7 for further information.

ELLESMERE PORT Cheshire — Map 07 SJ47

★★ Woodcore Hotel & Restaurant

3 Hooton Rd L66 1QU
Quality Percentage Score: 61%
☎ 0151 327 1542 Fax 0151 328 1328
Dir: *M53 junc 5, take A41 towards Chester, first traffic lights turn right towards Willaston. Hotel 300 yards on left*

This popular commercial hotel offers generally spacious, well equipped rooms, many of which are located in a separate building. The bars and restaurant are attractively decorated and there is a separate breakfast room. A range of popular, reasonably priced dishes are on offer.

ROOMS: 7 en suite (bth/shr) 13 annexe en suite (bth/shr) (1 fmly) **MEALS:** Lunch £6.95-£19.60 & alc Dinner £10.45-£19.60 & alc English & Italian Cuisine V meals Coffee am Tea pm **FACILITIES:** CTV in all bedrooms Wkly live entertainment **CONF:** Thtr 90 Class 50 Board 48 **SERVICES:** 35P **NOTES:** No dogs (ex guide dogs) No coaches Last d 9pm **CARDS:**

ELSTREE Hertfordshire — Map 04 TQ19

★★★ Edgwarebury

Barnet Ln WD6 3RE
Quality Percentage Score: 71%
☎ 020 8953 8227 Fax 020 8207 3668
Dir: *M1 junct 5 follow A41 to Harrow, turn left onto A411 into Elstree cont through crossrds into Barnet Ln, hotel entrance is on the right*

Within easy reach of the M1 and M25, this former millionaire's private neo-Tudor residence is set in 10 acres of mature grounds. Comfortable modern bedrooms have been added to the main building, which has retained some original features, such as stone fireplaces and oak panelling. The kitchen team produce an imaginative menu of skilfully prepared dishes and for less adventurous guests there is a selection of 'plain and simple' dishes.

ROOMS: 47 en suite (bth/shr) (1 fmly) No smoking in 19 bedrooms s £115-£120; d £135-£190 * LB Off peak **MEALS:** Lunch £18.95-£29.50 & alc Dinner £29.50 & alc V meals Coffee am Tea pm **FACILITIES:** CTV in all bedrooms STV **CONF:** Thtr 80 Class 50 Board 10 Del £150 * **SERVICES:** Night porter 100P **NOTES:** No smoking in restaurant Last d 9.45pm **CARDS:**

ELTERWATER Cumbria — Map 07 NY30

★★★ Langdale Hotel & Country Club

LA22 9JD
Quality Percentage Score: 70%
☎ 015394 37302 Fax 015394 37694
Dir: *follow road into Langdale, hotel part of private estate on left in the bottom of the valley*

An extensive modern hotel offering a wide range of bedrooms which are comfortable and well equipped. Five rooms are in the main hotel, others in buildings in the grounds. Leisure facilities are extensive and feature a large heated indoor pool, and a well

contd.

equipped gym. An excellent choice of food is served all day in either of the two stylish restaurants.

Langdale Hotel & Country Club, Elterwater

ROOMS: 5 en suite (bth/shr) 60 annexe en suite (bth/shr) (8 fmly) s £105-£125; d £170-£200 (incl. bkfst) * LB Off peak **MEALS:** Sunday Lunch £12-£12.50 Dinner £18.50 & alc International Cuisine V meals Coffee am Tea pm **FACILITIES:** CTV in all bedrooms STV Indoor swimming pool (heated) Tennis (hard) Fishing Squash Sauna Solarium Gym Pool table Jacuzzi/spa Steam room Hair & beauty salon Cycle hire Wkly live entertainment ch fac Xmas **CONF:** Thtr 100 Class 66 Board 50 Del from £95 * **SERVICES:** Night porter 100P **NOTES:** No dogs No smoking in restaurant Last d 9.45pm **CARDS:**

See advert under AMBLESIDE

ELTERWATER Cumbria — Map 07 NY30

★★ Eltermere Country House

LA22 9HY

Quality Percentage Score: 67%

☎ 01539 437207 🖷 01539 437540

***Dir:** on unclass road between A593 & B5343, turn left after cattle grid through village of Elterwater, cross bridge 100 mtrs on left*

An established hotel in colourful landscaped gardens with views over Elterwater Tarn. Well maintained throughout, it offers comfortable, inviting public rooms. Most bedrooms and the public rooms offer fine views.

ROOMS: 19 rms (14 bth/shr) (4 fmly) s £51.50-£55; d £103-£110 (incl. bkfst & dinner) * LB Off peak **MEALS:** Dinner £17.50 Coffee am Tea pm **FACILITIES:** CTV in all bedrooms Fishing Putting green Xmas **SERVICES:** 20P **NOTES:** No coaches No smoking in restaurant Last d 8pm Closed Xmas **CARDS:**

ELY Cambridgeshire — Map 05 TL58

★★★ ❀ *Lamb*

2 Lynn Rd CB7 4EJ

Quality Percentage Score: 68%

☎ 01353 663574 🖷 01353 662023

***Dir:** enter Ely on A10, Hotel in centre of city near Cathedral on the corner of Lynn Rd & the Hogh St*

This pleasant 15th-century coaching inn has been sympathetically developed to provide many creature comforts. Informal snacks are served in the smart bars, modern British cooking features on the appealing menus in the Octagon Restaurant. Bedrooms offer co-ordinated soft furnishings, decor and modern light wood furniture.

ROOMS: 32 en suite (bth/shr) (6 fmly) **MEALS:** English & French Cuisine V meals Coffee am Tea pm **FACILITIES:** CTV in all bedrooms STV **CONF:** Thtr 45 Class 28 Board 30 **SERVICES:** Night porter **NOTES:** No smoking in restaurant Last d 9.15pm

CARDS:

ELY Cambridgeshire — Map 05 TL58

★★ Nyton

7 Barton Rd CB7 4HZ

Quality Percentage Score: 60%

☎ 01353 662459 🖷 01353 666217

***Dir:** from S A10 into Ely. Pass golf course on right, then first right after passing two garages. Hotel 200yds on right*

Set inside two-acre gardens, this family-run hotel offers comfortable bedrooms in a variety of sizes and styles. Informal meals are served in the bar with more serious dining in the wood-panelled restaurant; there is also a relaxing conservatory lounge.

ROOMS: 10 en suite (bth/shr) (3 fmly) s fr £40; d fr £60 (incl. bkfst) * LB Off peak **MEALS:** Sunday Lunch £9.95-£15 Dinner £15 English & French Cuisine V meals Coffee am Tea pm **FACILITIES:** CTV in all bedrooms **SERVICES:** Night porter 25P **NOTES:** No dogs (ex guide dogs) Last d 8.30pm **CARDS:**

ELY Cambridgeshire — Map 05 TL58

Travelodge

Witchford Rd CB6 3NN

☎ 01353 668499 🖷 01353 668499

***Dir:** at roundabout A10/A142*

This modern building offers accommodation in smart, spacious and well equipped bedrooms, all with en-suite bathrooms. Refreshments may be taken at the nearby family restaurant. For details about current prices, consult the Contents Page under Hotel Groups for the Travelodge phone number.

ROOMS: 39 en suite (bth/shr) d £39.95 *

EMPINGHAM Rutland — Map 04 SK90

★★ The White Horse Inn

Main St LE15 8PR

Quality Percentage Score: 65%

☎ 01780 460221 & 460521 🖷 01780 460521

***Dir:** on A606, Oakham-Stamford road*

Situated at the eastern end of Rutland Water, is this attractive stone-built village inn. A wide range of meals is served in the various rooms that make up the bar, whilst a full menu is also available in the comfortable restaurant. Bright and well equipped bedrooms are mainly located in converted outbuildings across the courtyard, whilst some budget bedrooms are available inside the inn.

ROOMS: 4 en suite (bth/shr) 9 annexe en suite (bth/shr) (4 fmly) No smoking in 1 bedroom s £50; d £63-£70 (incl. bkfst) * LB Off peak **MEALS:** Lunch £13.95-£17.95 High tea £8.90 Dinner fr £17.95 & alc English & French Cuisine V meals Coffee am Tea pm **FACILITIES:** CTV in all bedrooms Xmas **CONF:** Thtr 60 Class 60 Board 34 Del from £60 * **SERVICES:** 60P **NOTES:** No smoking in restaurant Last d 10pm

CARDS:

EMSWORTH Hampshire — Map 04 SU70

★★★ Brookfield

Havant Rd PO10 7LF

Quality Percentage Score: 68%

☎ 01243 373363 & 376383 🖷 01243 376342

***Dir:** Emsworth junct off A27, turn onto B529, hotel is 0.5m on the left on the way into Emsworth*

This well established hotel is run by the Gibson family, who provide friendly, attentive service. Bedrooms are in a modern style, and comfortably furnished. The popular Hermitage

contd.

Symbols and Abbreviations are listed and explained on pages 4 and 5

Restaurant offers a seasonally changing menu and an award-winning wine list.
ROOMS: 40 en suite (bth/shr) s £58-£65; d £85-£90 (incl. bkfst) * LB Off peak **MEALS:** Lunch £12.95-£15.95 Dinner fr £15.95 & alc English & French Cuisine V meals Coffee am Tea pm **FACILITIES:** CTV in all bedrooms STV **CONF:** Thtr 100 Class 50 Board 40 Del from £80 * **SERVICES:** Night porter 80P **NOTES:** No dogs (ex guide dogs) No coaches Last d 9.30pm Closed 25 Dec-1 Jan
CARDS:

EMSWORTH Hampshire — Map 04 SU70

Travelodge

PO10 7RB
☎ 01243 370877 Fax 01243 370877
***Dir:** A27*

This modern building offers accommodation in smart, spacious and well equipped bedrooms, all with en-suite bathrooms. Refreshments may be taken at the nearby family restaurant. For details about current prices, consult the Contents Page under Hotel Groups for the Travelodge phone number.
ROOMS: 36 en suite (bth/shr) d £45.95 *

ENFIELD Greater London — Map 04 TQ39

★★★ Royal Chace

The Ridgeway EN2 8AR
Quality Percentage Score: 70%
☎ 020 8366 6500 Fax 020 8367 7191
***Dir:** from junct 24 on M25 take A1005 towards Enfield. Hotel 3m on right*

This bright, modern family-run hotel is well located for the M25. Smart public areas, coupled with attractive bedrooms and excellent housekeeping make the Royal Chace a popular choice. It has two options for **MEALS:** the comfortable bar or the stylish Gallery Restaurant.
ROOMS: 92 en suite (bth/shr) (2 fmly) No smoking in 34 bedrooms s £89.50-£94.50; d £99.50-£150 (incl. bkfst) * Off peak **MEALS:** Lunch £14.40-£16.95 Dinner £19.95-£22.50 V meals Coffee am Tea pm **FACILITIES:** CTV in all bedrooms STV Outdoor swimming pool (heated) Free access to local leisure facilities **CONF:** Thtr 250 Class 100 Board 40 Del from £130 * **SERVICES:** Night porter 300P **NOTES:** No dogs (ex guide dogs) No smoking in restaurant Last d 9.30pm Closed 24-31 Dec RS Restaurant closed lunchtime/Sum eve
CARDS:

See advert under LONDON

ENFIELD Greater London — Map 04 TQ39

★★ Oak Lodge

80 Village Rd, Bush Hill Park EN1 2EU
Quality Percentage Score: 70%
☎ 020 8360 7082

Set in a leafy road, this small country-house hotel has a welcoming atmosphere and attractively furnished bedrooms, some of which look out on the garden, and one is suitable for guests with disabilities. The dining room offers an interesting seasonal menu.
ROOMS: 7 en suite (bth/shr) (1 fmly) No smoking in 6 bedrooms s £69.50-£93.41; d £89.50-£140 (incl. bkfst & dinner) * Off peak **MEALS:** Lunch £12.50-£21.50 & alc High tea £3.50-£5.50 & alc Dinner £20 V meals **FACILITIES:** CTV in all bedrooms Special arrangement with David Lloyd Sports Centre Wkly live entertainment Xmas **CONF:** Board 16 Del from £140 * **SERVICES:** Night porter 4P **NOTES:** No dogs (ex guide dogs) No coaches No smoking in restaurant Last d 9pm
CARDS:

EPPING Essex — Map 05 TL40

★★★ *Posthouse Epping*

High Rd, Bell Common CM16 4DG
Quality Percentage Score: 62%
☎ 01992 573137 Fax 01992 560402
***Dir:** on B1393*

Bedrooms, which are spacious and well equipped, are being upgraded to the new company standard. Public areas include a small popular bar and the Junction restaurant which offers a range of modern dishes. There are good parking facilities, meeting rooms are available.
ROOMS: 79 annexe en suite (bth/shr) (22 fmly) No smoking in 32 bedrooms **MEALS:** International Cuisine V meals Coffee am Tea pm **FACILITIES:** CTV in all bedrooms **CONF:** Thtr 85 Class 50 Board 32 **SERVICES:** Night porter 95P **NOTES:** No smoking area in restaurant Last d 10.30pm **CARDS:**

EPSOM Surrey — Map 04 TQ26

Travel Inn

2-4 St Margarets Dr, Off Dorking Rd
KT18 7LB
☎ 01372 739786 Fax 01372 739761
***Dir:** A24 towards Epsom, hotel on left just before town centre*

This modern building offers accommodation in smart, spacious and well equipped bedrooms, all with en-suite bathrooms. Refreshments may be taken at the nearby family restaurant. For details about current prices consult the Contents Page under Hotel Groups for the Travel Inn phone number.
ROOMS: 40 en suite (bth/shr) d £39.95 *

ESCRICK North Yorkshire — Map 08 SE64

★★★ Parsonage Country House

York Rd YO19 6LF
Quality Percentage Score: 73%
☎ 01904 728111 Fax 01904 728151
***Dir:** next to St Helens Church on A19*

An early 19th-century parsonage with a charming country house atmosphere, standing in well tended grounds. Lounges are comfortable, and bedrooms well equipped and attractive. Staff

contd.

are caring and professional, and a new extension in the grounds includes conference facilities.
ROOMS: 12 en suite (bth/shr) 9 annexe en suite (bth/shr) (3 fmly) No smoking in 13 bedrooms s £75-£95; d fr £110 (incl. bkfst) * LB Off peak **MEALS:** Lunch £12-£13.90 Dinner £24.50 & alc V meals Coffee am Tea pm **FACILITIES:** CTV in all bedrooms STV Putting green Xmas **CONF:** Thtr 160 Class 140 Board 80 Del from £120 * **SERVICES:** Night porter 100P **NOTES:** No dogs (ex guide dogs) No coaches No smoking in restaurant Last d 9.30pm **CARDS:** [card symbols]

See advert under YORK

ESHER Surrey
See LONDON SECTION plan 1 *B1*

★★ Haven
Portsmouth Rd KT10 9AR
Quality Percentage Score: 64%
☎ 020 8398 0023 020 8398 9463
Dir: *1m NE on A307*
With its distinctive black and white timbered facade, the Haven is convenient for visitors to Sandown Racecourse. Bedrooms vary in size and style and are generally well equipped and quiet, four rooms are in a separate Lodge. There is a residential-licensed bar with television.
ROOMS: 16 en suite (bth/shr) 4 annexe en suite (bth/shr) (3 fmly) s £69-£75; d £84-£89 (incl. bkfst) * Off peak **MEALS:** Dinner £17.50 & alc International Cuisine V meals Coffee am Tea pm **FACILITIES:** CTV in all bedrooms STV **CONF:** Thtr 40 Class 24 Board 20 **SERVICES:** 20P **NOTES:** No dogs (ex guide dogs) No coaches No smoking in restaurant Last d 9.30pm **CARDS:** [card symbols]

ESKDALE GREEN Cumbria — Map 06 NY10

★★ Bower House Inn
CA19 1TD
Quality Percentage Score: 66%
☎ 019467 23244 019467 23308
Dir: *4m off A595 1/2 mile west of Eskdale Green*
This former farmhouse combines the character of a country inn with an attractive and popular restaurant. Main meals are the speciality, with an appetizing seasonal menu available in both the bar and restaurant. Some bedrooms are inside the inn, but most are in a smart barn conversion across the courtyard, with some in a secluded Garden House a few footsteps away.
ROOMS: 5 en suite (bth/shr) 19 annexe en suite (bth/shr) (3 fmly) **MEALS:** Bar Lunch fr £13.75 Dinner fr £22.50 & alc English & French Cuisine V meals Coffee am Tea pm **FACILITIES:** CTV in all bedrooms **CONF:** Thtr 50 Class 50 Board 40 **SERVICES:** 60P **NOTES:** No dogs No smoking in restaurant Last d 8.30pm **CARDS:** [card symbols]

EVERSHOT Dorset — Map 03 ST50

The Premier Collection

★★★ Summer Lodge
DT2 0JR
☎ 01935 83424 01935 83005
Dir: *1m W of A37 halfway between Dorchester & Yeovil*
The public rooms at this family-run hotel are comfortably furnished. Floral arrangements, log fires and watercolours add to the elegance. Bedrooms are individually furnished and decorated. There is an imaginative daily set menu, and a seasonal carte is also available.

ROOMS: 11 en suite (bth/shr) 6 annexe en suite (bth/shr) (1 fmly) s fr £125; d £175-£245 (incl. bkfst) * LB Off peak **MEALS:** V meals Coffee am Tea pm **FACILITIES:** CTV in all bedrooms Outdoor swimming pool (heated) Tennis (hard & grass) Croquet lawn Xmas **CONF:** Thtr 20 Board 20 Del from £185 * **SERVICES:** 40P **NOTES:** No coaches No smoking in restaurant Last d 9pm **CARDS:** [card symbols]

EVESHAM Worcestershire — Map 04 SP04
see also **Fladbury**

★★★★ Wood Norton Hall
Wood Norton WR11 4YB
Quality Percentage Score: 73%
☎ 01386 420007 01386 420190
Dir: *2m from Evesham on the A4538, after the village of Chadbury travelling westwards or 4m after Wyre Piddle travelling eastwards*
This impressive Victorian hall stands in a 170-acre estate just north-west of Evesham. For much of the 19th century, it was the home of an exiled family of French aristocrats, then at the start of WWII, after it was purchased by the BBC, it became the largest broadcasting centre in Europe. Since then it has become a training centre for the Corporation and today provides excellent business and conference facilities. The Hall itself retains much of its bygone splendour, including carved oak panelling and ornate fireplaces. Bedrooms are comfortably furnished, well equipped and spacious, and several are located in converted former stables.
ROOMS: 15 en suite (bth/shr) 30 annexe en suite (bth/shr) No smoking in 40 bedrooms s £115-£150; d £155-£225 (incl. bkfst) LB Off peak **MEALS:** Lunch £17.50-£19.50 Dinner £32.50 English & French Cuisine V meals Coffee am Tea pm **FACILITIES:** CTV in all bedrooms STV Outdoor swimming pool Tennis (hard) Fishing Squash Snooker Gym Pool table Croquet lawn **CONF:** Thtr 70 Class 35 Board 32 Del from £164 * **SERVICES:** Night porter 300P **NOTES:** No dogs (ex guide dogs) No smoking in restaurant Last d 9.30pm Closed 26 Dec-4 Jan **CARDS:** [card symbols]

EVESHAM Worcestershire — Map 04 SP04

★★★ The Evesham
Coopers Ln, Off Waterside WR11 6DA
Quality Percentage Score: 71%
☎ 01386 765566 & 0800 716969 (Res) 01386 765443
Dir: *Coopers lane is off the road alongside the River Avon*
This friendly hotel has been privately owned and personally run by the Jenkinson family for almost quarter of a century. Originally built in 1540, the property was considerably altered and extended in 1810, which accounts for the Georgian appearance. The two and a half acres of grounds feature mulberry trees reputed to be 500 years old, as well as a magnificent cedar of Lebanon which was planted in 1809. Well

contd.

equipped accommodation includes no smoking bedrooms and family suites. The hotel has a well deserved reputation for its food, complemented by an extremely extensive wine list. Facilities include a conference room and an indoor pool, and there are lots of things to keep children amused, making the hotel understandably popular with family groups.
ROOMS: 39 en suite (bth/shr) (2 fmly) No smoking in 4 bedrooms s £63.70; d £94.98 (incl. bkfst) * LB Off peak **MEALS:** Lunch £12.25-£28.25alc Dinner £14.75-£28.25alc International Cuisine V meals Coffee am Tea pm **FACILITIES:** CTV in all bedrooms Indoor swimming pool (heated) Croquet lawn Putting green ch fac **CONF:** Thtr 12 Class 12 Board 12 Del from £102 * **SERVICES:** 50P **NOTES:** No coaches No smoking in restaurant Last d 9.30pm Closed 25 & 26 Dec
CARDS:

EVESHAM Worcestershire — Map 04 SP04
★★★ *Waterside*
56 Waterside WR11 6JZ
Quality Percentage Score: 71%
☎ 01386 442420 01386 446272
Dir: *A44/A435 junc 40yds on right alongside river*
Personally run by the same proprietors for over 30 years, this hotel has been constantly developed and upgraded over the years. It stands opposite the River Avon, within walking distance of the town centre, and offers attractively appointed, modern and well equipped bedrooms. Public areas include the popular Strollers restaurant and bar, which has an American theme and provides a wide variety of dishes. Cream teas are served in the riverside gardens when the weather permits.
ROOMS: 14 en suite (bth/shr) 4 annexe en suite (bth/shr) (2 fmly) **MEALS:** English & American Cuisine V meals Coffee am Tea pm **FACILITIES:** CTV in all bedrooms Fishing **SERVICES:** 30P **NOTES:** No smoking area in restaurant **CARDS:**

EVESHAM Worcestershire — Map 04 SP04
★★★ Northwick Hotel
Waterside WR11 6BT
Quality Percentage Score: 67%
☎ 01386 40322 01386 41070
Dir: *turn off A46 onto A44 over traffic lights to next set turn right along B4035 past hospital hotel on right side opposite river*
Once a coaching inn, this hotel stands opposite the River Avon and within walking distance of the town centre. Bedrooms include family rooms, no smoking rooms, a room with a four-poster bed, and a ground floor annexe room which is specially adapted for disabled guests. All public areas were recently renovated and greatly improved. Facilities include a choice of bars, a beautifully appointed restaurant and a choice of meeting rooms.
ROOMS: 31 en suite (bth/shr) (4 fmly) No smoking in 10 bedrooms s £62-£70; d £85-£110 (incl. bkfst) * LB Off peak **MEALS:** Lunch £8-£15 & alc High tea £5-£10 Dinner £14-£17.50alc French Cuisine V meals Coffee am Tea pm **FACILITIES:** CTV in all bedrooms Hot air ballooning Clay pigeon shooting Archery Paint balling Xmas **CONF:** Thtr 240 Class 150 Board 80 Del from £105 * **SERVICES:** Night porter 200P **NOTES:** No smoking in restaurant Last d 9.30pm
CARDS:

EVESHAM Worcestershire — Map 04 SP04
★★ The Mill at Harvington
Anchor Ln, Harvington WR11 5NR
Quality Percentage Score: 80%
☎ 01386 870688 01386 870688
Dir: *Harvington is found 4m NE of Evesham. The hotel is on the banks of the Avon, reached by a bridge over the new A46 and not in village*
A former Georgian house and mill in extensive grounds on the banks of the River Avon. The house was extensively re-furbished in 1998. The comfortable lounge has fine views, there is a conservatory bar and elegant restaurant, cuisine is of a high standard. Bedrooms are mostly well proportioned and thoughtfully equipped. Six spacious, luxury rooms are in a separate building.
ROOMS: 15 en suite (bth/shr) 6 annexe en suite (bth/shr) s £61-£75; d £86-£120 (incl. bkfst) LB Off peak **MEALS:** Lunch £12.95-£14.95 English & French Cuisine V meals Coffee am Tea pm **FACILITIES:** CTV in all bedrooms Outdoor swimming pool (heated) Fishing Croquet lawn **CONF:** Board 12 **SERVICES:** 50P **NOTES:** No dogs (ex guide dogs) No coaches No children 10yrs No smoking in restaurant Closed 24-27 Dec
CARDS:

EVESHAM Worcestershire — Map 04 SP04
★★ Riverside
The Parks, Offenham Rd WR11 5JP
Quality Percentage Score: 73%
☎ 01386 446200 01386 40021
Dir: *off the A46 follow signs for Offenham. Take turning on right B4510 (Offenham) 1/2 mile turn left along private drive called The Parks to end*
Standing in three acres of gardens sloping down to the River Avon, this family-owned and run hotel offers comfortable bedrooms, many of which overlook the river, as do the lounge and restaurant. Cooking remains a strength here, with a menu of imaginative dishes based on really good produce. Service is friendly.
ROOMS: 7 en suite (bth/shr) s fr £60; d fr £80 (incl. bkfst) * LB Off peak **MEALS:** Lunch £17.95-£19.95 Dinner fr £28.95 English & French Cuisine V meals Coffee am **FACILITIES:** CTV in all bedrooms Fishing **SERVICES:** 40P **NOTES:** No dogs (ex guide dogs) No smoking in restaurant Last d 9pm Closed 25 Dec, Sun night & Mon RS 2-20 Jan (wknds only) **CARDS:**

EWEN Gloucestershire — Map 04 SU09

★★ *Wild Duck Inn*

Drakes Island GL7 6BY
Quality Percentage Score: 70%
☎ 01285 770310 📠 01285 770924
Dir: *from Cirencester take A429 on reaching Kemble take left turn to Ewen keep driving to the centre of the village*

A deservedly popular inn that dates back to the early 16th century. Open fires, old beams and rustic pine tables lend character to the bar and restaurant, where honest cooking and cheerful service are further strengths. The bedrooms offer comfortable well equipped accommodation.
ROOMS: 10 en suite (bth) **MEALS:** English & Continental Cuisine V meals Coffee am Tea pm **FACILITIES:** CTV in all bedrooms **SERVICES:** 50P **NOTES:** No dogs (ex guide dogs) No coaches Last d 10pm **CARDS:**

See advert under CIRENCESTER

EXETER Devon — Map 03 SX99

★★★★ The Southgate

Southernhay East EX1 1QF
Quality Percentage Score: 67%
☎ 01392 412812 📠 01392 413549
Dir: *on Southernhay roundabout near cathedral*

This attractive modern hotel, situated close to the town centre, and across from the quay, is popular with business, conference and leisure guests alike. The smart bedrooms offer a good level of comfort and are equipped with such extra facilities as trouser press and mini bar. The elegant public rooms are richly furnished, giving a real country house ambience.
ROOMS: 110 en suite (bth/shr) (6 fmly) No smoking in 55 bedrooms s £79-£105; d £105 * LB Off peak **MEALS:** Lunch fr £12.95 & alc Dinner £22 & alc International Cuisine V meals Coffee am Tea pm **FACILITIES:** CTV in all bedrooms STV Indoor swimming pool (heated) Sauna Solarium Gym Jacuzzi/spa Xmas **CONF:** Thtr 100 Class 70 Board 50 Del from £99 * **SERVICES:** Lift Night porter 115P **NOTES:** No smoking in restaurant Last d 10pm RS Sat (restaurant closed for lunch) **CARDS:**

EXETER Devon — Map 03 SX99

★★★ Barton Cross Hotel & Restaurant

Huxham, Stoke Canon EX5 4EJ
Quality Percentage Score: 73%
☎ 01392 841245 📠 01392 841942
Dir: *0.5m off A396 at Stoke Canon just 3 miles north of Exeter*

'Seventeenth century charm with 20th century luxury' perfectly sums up this lovely countryside hotel. With just seven bedrooms, tastefully decorated and maintained, guests can be sure of a warm welcome and an enjoyable stay. Public areas include the cosy first floor lounge, in addition to the lounge/bar with its warming log fire. The beamed restaurant, with its intimate first floor gallery, serves award-winning cuisine.
ROOMS: 9 en suite (bth/shr) (2 fmly) No smoking in 2 bedrooms s £65.50; d £90 (incl. bkfst) * LB Off peak **MEALS:** English & French Cuisine V meals Coffee am Tea pm **FACILITIES:** CTV in all bedrooms STV Xmas **CONF:** Board 12 **SERVICES:** Night porter 35P **NOTES:** No coaches No smoking in restaurant Last d 9.30pm
CARDS:

See advert on opposite page

EXETER Devon — Map 03 SX99

★★★ *Devon*

Exeter Bypass, Matford EX2 8XU
Quality Percentage Score: 70%
☎ 01392 259268 📠 01392 413142
Dir: *leave M5 at junct 30, follow signpost to Marsh Barton Ind Est A379, hotel is on main A38 rdbt*

Conveniently situated for the city centre and with easy access to the M5, this hotel offers modern accommodation. The recently opened Carriages brasserie is already proving very popular with locals and visitors alike, offering a wide range of dishes from around the world as well as a more traditional carvery. Service is both efficient and friendly. Extensive meeting and function rooms are also available, located, as is Carriages, in a Georgian manor house adjacent to the bedrooms.
ROOMS: 41 annexe en suite (bth/shr) (3 fmly) **MEALS:** English & French Cuisine V meals Coffee am Tea pm **FACILITIES:** CTV in all bedrooms STV Childrens play area Wkly live entertainment ch fac **CONF:** Thtr 150 Class 150 Board 150 **SERVICES:** Night porter 250P **NOTES:** No smoking area in restaurant Last d 10pm
CARDS:

EXETER Devon — Map 03 SX99

★★★ Ebford House

Exmouth Rd EX3 0QH
Quality Percentage Score: 69%
☎ 01392 877658 📠 01392 874424
Dir: *1m E of Topsham on A376*

This charming Georgian house lies between Exeter and Exmouth and has a good repuation for award-winning cuisine. Frisco's Bistro is another eating option for guests and non-residents alike, offering interesting home-cooked dishes and other blackboard specials. Bedrooms are individual in style and size and include many modern facilities.
ROOMS: 16 en suite (bth/shr) No smoking in 6 bedrooms s £60-£68; d £75-£95 (incl. bkfst) * LB Off peak **MEALS:** Lunch £2.75-£20alc High tea £2.50-£5alc Dinner £4-£24alc English, French & Italian Cuisine V meals Coffee am Tea pm **FACILITIES:** CTV in all bedrooms STV Sauna Gym Jacuzzi/spa **CONF:** Thtr 25 Class 10 Board 18 Del from £92 * **SERVICES:** 45P **NOTES:** No dogs (ex guide dogs) No smoking in restaurant Last d 9.45pm Closed 23 Dec-28 Dec
CARDS:

See advert on opposite page

EXETER Devon — Map 03 SX99

★★★ Royal Clarence

Cathedral Yard EX1 1HD
Quality Percentage Score: 69%
☎ 01392 319955 📠 01392 439423
Dir: *facing cathedral*

This historic, 14th Century building is a landmark in Exeter and is situated in the remaining medieval part of the City, opposite the Cathedral. Public areas include an elegant dining room where light lunches, a la carte dinners and afternoon cream teas are served. There is a quiet residents' lounge and a popular bar, in addition to the hotel's Wellhouse Public Bar next door.

contd.

Bedrooms are attractively furnished and decorated and are all equipped with many modern facilities.

ROOMS: 57 en suite (bth/shr) (6 fmly) No smoking in 16 bedrooms s £85-£99; d £125 * LB Off peak **MEALS:** Lunch £5-£11.95 Dinner £11.95-£16.95 English, French & Italian Cuisine V meals Coffee am Tea pm **FACILITIES:** CTV in all bedrooms Wkly live entertainment Xmas **CONF:** Thtr 120 Class 50 Board 50 Del from £110 * **SERVICES:** Lift Night porter 15P **NOTES:** No dogs (ex guide dogs) No smoking in restaurant Last d 10pm **CARDS:**

EXETER Devon **Map 03 SX99**

★★★❀❀ **St Olaves Court**

Mary Arches St EX4 3AZ

Quality Percentage Score: 67%

☎ 01392 217736 Fax 01392 413054

Dir: *drive to City centre, follow signs to Mary Arches Parking. Hotel entrance is directly opposite car park entrance*

St Olaves Court is only a short stroll from the cathedral and

contd.

medieval centre of Exeter and its modern shops. Bedrooms are well appointed, with extra touches including a complimentary decanter of sherry. The intimate Golsworthy's Restaurant offers menus with innovative dishes of a high standard.
ROOMS: 11 en suite (bth) 4 annexe en suite (bth) (4 fmly) s £80-£85; d £90-£100 (incl. cont bkfst) * LB Off peak **MEALS:** Lunch fr £14.50 & alc Dinner fr £14.50 & alc International Cuisine V meals Coffee am Tea pm **FACILITIES:** CTV in all bedrooms Jacuzzi/spa Xmas **CONF:** Thtr 45 Class 35 Board 35 Del from £120 * **SERVICES:** 15P **NOTES:** No coaches No smoking in restaurant Last d 9.30pm
CARDS:

E

EXETER Devon **Map 03 SX99**

★★★ Buckerell Lodge
Topsham Rd EX2 4SQ
Quality Percentage Score: 66%
☎ 01392 221111 01392 491111
***Dir:** M5 junct 30 follow signs for City Centre, hotel is located on the main Topsham Rd approx 0.5m from Exeter*
Very popular for wedding parties, and conveniently situated for the city centre, this hotel offers comfortable accommodation in a relaxed atmosphere. Public areas include a smart cocktail bar and a range of meeting rooms. Fine dining is a feature of Raffles Restaurant where fixed-price and carte menus are offered - call in advance to check dining arrangements at weekends. For snacks and a more informal experience the Lodge Bar makes an ideal alternative.
ROOMS: 53 en suite (bth/shr) (2 fmly) No smoking in 15 bedrooms s £40-£45; d £60-£80 * LB Off peak **MEALS:** Lunch £9.95-£12.50 High tea £4.95-£7.25 Dinner £19.95-£21.95 & alc English & French Cuisine V meals Coffee am Tea pm **FACILITIES:** CTV in all bedrooms STV Jacuzzi/spa Xmas **CONF:** Thtr 50 Class 35 Board 30 Del from £99 * **SERVICES:** Night porter 100P **NOTES:** No smoking in restaurant Last d 9.30pm **CARDS:**

See advert on page 247

EXETER Devon **Map 03 SX99**

★★★ *Gipsy Hill*
Gipsy Hill Ln, Monkerton EX1 3RN
Quality Percentage Score: 66%
☎ 01392 465252 01392 464302
***Dir:** 3m E on B3181, leave M5 at junct 30, follow signs to Sowton Ind Est, turn right on roundabout then first left (Pinn Lane)*
A popular hotel just outside Exeter and close to the M5 and the airport. Set in attractive, well tended gardens with country views, the hotel offers conference and function rooms with comfortable bedroom accommodation and modern facilities. An intimate bar and lounge are next to the elegant restaurant, daily and carte menus are available.
ROOMS: 20 en suite (bth/shr) 17 annexe en suite (bth/shr) (5 fmly) No smoking in 6 bedrooms **MEALS:** English & French Cuisine V meals Coffee am Tea pm **FACILITIES:** CTV in all bedrooms ch fac **CONF:** Thtr 120 Class 55 Board 36 **SERVICES:** Night porter 100P **NOTES:** No smoking in restaurant Last d 9.30pm Closed 25-30 Dec
CARDS:

See advert on opposite page

EXETER Devon **Map 03 SX99**

★★★ Lord Haldon
Dunchideock EX6 7YF
Quality Percentage Score: 65%
☎ 01392 832483 01392 833765
***Dir:** from A30 follow signs to Ide then continue through village for 2.5m. After telephone box turn left. In 0.5m pass under stone bridge turn left*
Situated in some of Devon's most picturesque countryside, the Lord Haldon offers a warm welcome and comfortable accommodation. It is a spacious hotel, proud of its cuisine and its good reputation. Bedrooms are individual in style and well equipped.

ROOMS: 19 en suite (bth/shr) (3 fmly) No smoking in 10 bedrooms s £39.50-£48.50; d £60-£68.50 (incl. bkfst) LB Off peak **MEALS:** Lunch £9.50-£14.50 & alc High tea £9.50-£14alc Dinner £15-£19.50 & alc V meals Coffee am Tea pm **FACILITIES:** CTV in all bedrooms STV ch fac Xmas **CONF:** Thtr 200 Class 140 Board 100 Del from £52.50 * **SERVICES:** 60P **NOTES:** No smoking in restaurant Last d 8.30pm
CARDS:

See advert on opposite page

EXETER Devon **Map 03 SX99**

★★★ *White Hart*
66 South St EX1 1EE
Quality Percentage Score: 65%
☎ 01392 279897 01392 250159
Conveniently situated in the city centre, the White Hart is over 400 years old and an important landmark in Exeter. Bedrooms are comfortable and offer modern facilities. The dining rooms offer both fixed-price and carte menus, while more informal meals are available in the bars.
ROOMS: 57 en suite (bth/shr) (6 fmly) No smoking in 11 bedrooms **MEALS:** European Cuisine V meals Coffee am **FACILITIES:** CTV in all bedrooms STV Reduced entry to neighbouring gym **CONF:** Thtr 60 Class 24 Board 22 **SERVICES:** Lift Night porter 55P **NOTES:** No dogs (ex guide dogs) No coaches No smoking area in restaurant Last d 10pm Closed 24-26 Dec **CARDS:**

See advert on opposite page

The Lord Haldon Hotel

AA ★★★

DUNCHIDEOCK, EXETER, DEVON EX6 7YF
Tel: 01392 832483 Fax: 01392 833765

Described as a Pearl in the Heart of the Devon countryside, this small comfortable family-run hotel attracts many guests back year after year. They come for good food, pleasant company and friendly staff.
As well as the lovely setting in five acres of secluded gardens with breathtaking views over the Exe Valley, the hotel is a short distance from the Cathedral City of Exeter. Horse riding, walking, birds of prey are but some of the attractions of staying at the hotel.

Free colour brochure on request.
Recommended by
Johansens, Ashley Courtenay, and Relais Du Silence.

AA★★★

GIPSY HILL

COUNTRY HOUSE HOTEL

Gipsy Hill Lane, Monkerton, Exeter, Devon EX1 3RN
Tel: 01392 465252 Fax: 01392 464302

The hotel is situated on the eastern edge of the historic city of Exeter, close to the M5, junction 30. Built in the early part of this century it became an hotel just after the Second World War. The hotel still retains its former style and charm, the bedrooms are all individually furnished, decorated and have en suite facilities. The popular restaurant overlooks the gardens and the Devon countryside.

Best Western

The White Hart Hotel

South Street, Exeter, Devon EX1 1EE
Telephone 01392 279897 Fax 01392 250159

A Unique 15th Century Hostelry

This popular city centre hotel is steeped in history, whilst offering

Comfortable and well equipped en-suite bedrooms ★ A superb choice of bars and restaurants, serving excellent cuisine, real ales, fine wines and vintage ports ★ Award winning hotel bar (well worth a visit) ★ Conference facilities ★ Parking for 55 cars (car valeting service available)

EXETER Devon **Map 03 SX99**
★★ St Andrews
28 Alphington Rd EX2 8HN
Quality Percentage Score: 73%
☎ 01392 276784 Fax 01392 250249
Dir: *M5 exit at junct 31 signed Oakhampton.Follow sign for Exeter city centre/Marsh Barton along Alphington Rd.A377 A main route into City, hotel on left*
This welcoming family-run hotel, within walking distance of the city centre, offers brightly decorated, spotless and well equipped bedrooms. There is a comfortable lounge with separate bar, whilst the restaurant menu offers an extensive choice of dishes using the best local meat and vegetables. A room is available for disabled guests.
ROOMS: 17 en suite (bth/shr) (2 fmly) No smoking in 5 bedrooms s £43-£47; d £59-£70 (incl. bkfst) * LB Off peak **MEALS:** Bar Lunch fr £2.80alc Dinner £12-£26alc V meals Coffee am Tea pm **FACILITIES:** CTV in all bedrooms STV **SERVICES:** 21P **NOTES:** No dogs (ex guide dogs) No coaches No smoking in restaurant Last d 8pm Closed 25 Dec-1 Jan **CARDS:**

EXETER Devon **Map 03 SX99**
★★ Fairwinds Hotel
Kennford EX6 7UD
Quality Percentage Score: 68%
☎ 01392 832911 Fax 01392 832911
Dir: *4m S of Exeter, from M5 junct 31, continue along A38, after 2 miles turn left at sign for Kennford. First hotel on the left*
Conveniently situated within easy reach of Exeter, Torbay and Plymouth, Fairwinds is a strictly non-smoking hotel throughout. It has a small bar-lounge adjacent to the restaurant, where enjoyable home-made dishes are served. The comfortable, well maintained bedrooms have many useful facilities.
ROOMS: 6 en suite (bth/shr) (1 fmly) No smoking in all bedrooms s £35-£39; d £50-£54 (incl. bkfst) * LB Off peak **MEALS:** Dinner £11.90-£14.50alc V meals **FACILITIES:** CTV in all bedrooms STV **SERVICES:** 8P **NOTES:** No dogs No coaches No smoking in restaurant Last d 7.30pm Closed Dec **CARDS:**

EXETER Devon **Map 03 SX99**
★★ Red House
2 Whipton Village Rd EX4 8AR
Quality Percentage Score: 60%
☎ 01392 256104 Fax 01392 666145
Dir: *jct 30 off M5,left before services signed Middlemoor,right at rdbt towards Pinhoe & University,in 0.75m left to Whipton/University,hotel 1m on right*

This family-owned hotel, located on the edge of the city, offers an extensive menu including a carvery, served either in the bar or in the adjacent dining room. The bedrooms are modern and well equipped, and suitable for both business or leisure guests.
ROOMS: 12 en suite (bth/shr) (2 fmly) No smoking in 8 bedrooms **MEALS:** Lunch £6.50-£12.95 & alc Dinner £6.50-£12.95 & alc English & French Cuisine V meals Coffee am Tea pm **FACILITIES:** CTV in all bedrooms STV **CONF:** Class 50 Board 20 **SERVICES:** 28P **NOTES:** Last d 9.30pm **CARDS:**

EXETER Devon **Map 03 SX99**
Travel Inn
398 Topsham Rd EX2 6HE
☎ 01392 875441 Fax 01392 876174
Dir: *located 2m from M5 junct 30 and A30 link. Follow signs for Dawlish and Topsham (A379). Situated on the intersection of A379/A377*
This modern building offers accommodation in smart, spacious and well equipped bedrooms, all with en-suite bathrooms. Refreshments may be taken at the nearby family restaurant. For details about current prices consult the Contents Page under Hotel Groups for the Travel Inn phone number.
ROOMS: 44 en suite (bth/shr) d £39.95 *

EXETER Devon **Map 03 SX99**
Travelodge
Moor Ln, Sandygate EX2 4AR
☎ 01392 74044 Fax 01392 410406
Dir: *M5 jnct 30*
This modern building offers accommodation in smart, spacious and well equipped bedrooms, all with en-suite bathrooms. Refreshments may be taken at the nearby family restaurant. For details about current prices, consult the Contents Page under Hotel Groups for the Travelodge phone number.
ROOMS: 74 en suite (bth/shr) d £59.95 * **CONF:** Thtr 80 Class 18 Board 25

EXETER Devon **Map 03 SX99**
Thistle Exeter
Queen St EX4 3SP
☎ 01392 254982 Fax 01392 420928
Dir: *city centre opposite railway station and Royal Albert Museum*
This Victorian hotel, located a short walk from the cathedral, has benefited from substantial investment and refurbishment. The interior has been transformed, especially the reception hall with its splendid staircase. Bedrooms are comfortably furnished, varying in size and style.
ROOMS: 90 en suite (bth/shr) (5 fmly) No smoking in 13 bedrooms **MEALS:** English & French Cuisine V meals Coffee am Tea pm **FACILITIES:** CTV in all bedrooms STV **CONF:** Thtr 300 Class 140 Board 80 Del from £115 * **SERVICES:** Lift Night porter 40P **NOTES:** No smoking area in restaurant Last d 10pm
CARDS:

EXETER Devon **Map 03 SX99**
Queens Court
Bystock Ter EX4 4HY
☎ 01392 272709
ROOMS: 19 rms

EXFORD Somerset **Map 03 SS83**

★★★ Crown

Park St TA24 7PP

Quality Percentage Score: 72%

☎ 01643 831554 Fax 01643 831665

Dir: *leave M5 junct 25 and follow signs for Taunton. Take the A358 out of Taunton, then the B3224 via Wheddon Cross into Exford*

A warm welcome is ensured at the Crown whatever the weather. Hosts Mr and Mrs Bradley have guest comfort at heart offering afternoon teas by the roaring fires in the lounge, and tempting menus in both bar and restaurant. Bedrooms offer space, comfort and modern facilities with quaint traditional village views from most rooms.

ROOMS: 17 en suite (bth) s fr £47.50; d £80-£116 (incl. bkfst) * LB Off peak **MEALS:** Sunday Lunch £15-£18 Dinner £18.50-£21 & alc European Cuisine V meals Coffee am Tea pm **FACILITIES:** CTV in all bedrooms Fishing Riding Shooting Xmas **SERVICES:** 30P **NOTES:** No smoking area in restaurant Last d 9.30pm **CARDS:**

EXMOUTH Devon **Map 03 SY08**

★★★ Royal Beacon

The Beacon EX8 2AF

Quality Percentage Score: 64%

☎ 01395 264886 Fax 01395 268890

Dir: *A376 to Exmouth from Exmouth follow seafront signs to the Beacon Hotel on left*

Originally a Georgian posting house, this elegant hotel overlooks the coastline and town centre. Boasting a magnificent restored ball-room and with friendly, efficient staff, the hotel is ideal for private functions.

ROOMS: 23 en suite (bth/shr) (2 fmly) No smoking in 4 bedrooms s fr £40; d fr £75 (incl. bkfst) * LB Off peak **MEALS:** Lunch £10.25-£12.25 Dinner £14.95-£16.95 V meals Coffee am Tea pm **FACILITIES:** CTV in all bedrooms Xmas **CONF:** Thtr 150 Class 100 Board 40 Del from £70 * **SERVICES:** Lift 10P **NOTES:** No smoking area in restaurant Last d 9pm **CARDS:**

See advert on this page

EXMOUTH Devon **Map 03 SY08**

★★★ The Imperial

REGAL

The Esplanade EX8 2SW

Quality Percentage Score: 62%

☎ 01395 274761 Fax 01395 265161

Dir: *M5 junct30 A376 to Exmouth follow signed for seafront. Over 1st roundabout left at next, hotel at end of T junction*

A traditional hotel set in grounds with an outdoor swimming pool and tennis court, close to the town centre and facing the sea front. A well chosen menu of British dishes can be enjoyed in the spacious restaurant. Bedrooms vary in style and size but are all equipped with modern facilities.

ROOMS: 57 en suite (bth/shr) (3 fmly) No smoking in 18 bedrooms (incl. bkfst) * LB Off peak **MEALS:** Dinner £16.95-£24.45 V meals Coffee am Tea pm **FACILITIES:** CTV in all bedrooms Outdoor swimming pool (heated) Tennis (hard) Wkly live entertainment Xmas **CONF:** Thtr 150 Class 80 Board 30 Del from £75 * **SERVICES:** Lift Night porter 58P **NOTES:** No smoking in restaurant Last d 8.45pm **CARDS:**

EXMOUTH Devon **Map 03 SY08**

★★ Barn

Foxholes Hill, Marine Dr EX8 2DF

Quality Percentage Score: 68%

☎ 01395 224411 Fax 01395 225445

Dir: *M5 junt30 follow signs for Exmouth A376, to seafront in an easterly direction, next rdbt last exit into Foxholes Hill Hotel on right*

This Grade II listed butterfly-shaped property overlooks the sea

contd.

from an elevated position in two acres of attractive gardens. Bedrooms are brightly decorated, and well equipped with modern facilities. The public rooms include a comfortable and quiet lounge and a small bar. In the dining room a short daily-changing table d'hôte menu is based on fresh ingredients.
ROOMS: 11 en suite (bth/shr) (4 fmly) No smoking in all bedrooms s £30-£34; d £60-£68 (incl. bkfst) * LB Off peak **MEALS:** Sunday Lunch £7.50-£8.95 Dinner £14 European Cuisine Coffee am Tea pm **FACILITIES:** CTV in all bedrooms Outdoor swimming pool Putting green **CONF:** Class 40 Board 20 **SERVICES:** 24P **NOTES:** No dogs No coaches No smoking in restaurant Last d 7.30pm Closed 23 Dec-10 Jan
CARDS:

E

EXMOUTH Devon — Map 03 SY08

★★ Manor

The Beacon EX8 2AG
Quality Percentage Score: 61%
☎ 01395 272549 & 274477 Fax 01395 225519
Dir: *M5 junct 30 take A376 to Exmouth take signs for seafront,Hotel located 300 yards from seafront by Tourist Information Office*
Overlooking the town centre and the sea, this family run hotel, now over two hundred years old, provides comfortable accommodation in rooms which vary in style and size. The short table d'hote menu offers traditional dishes.
ROOMS: 38 en suite (bth/shr) (3 fmly) s £27.50-£30; d £50-£60 (incl. bkfst) * LB Off peak **MEALS:** Bar Lunch £4-£12 Dinner £8.50-£15 V meals Coffee am Tea pm **FACILITIES:** CTV in all bedrooms Xmas **CONF:** Thtr 100 **SERVICES:** Lift Night porter 15P **NOTES:** No dogs (ex guide dogs) No smoking in restaurant **CARDS:**

FAIRFORD Gloucestershire — Map 04 SP10

★★ Bull Hotel

The Market Place GL7 4AA
Quality Percentage Score: 64%
☎ 01285 712535 & 712217 Fax 01285 713782
Dir: *on the A417 in the market square adjacent to the post office*
A family-run inn on the picturesque market square offers neatly furnished, well equipped bedrooms. The bar is a popular meeting place, and has kept its original character. There is a good choice of food, either in the bar or in the separate restaurant.
ROOMS: 22 rms (20 bth/shr) (1 fmly) s £32.50-£69.50; d £59.50-£72.50 (incl. bkfst) * LB Off peak **MEALS:** Lunch £5.95-£8.95 Dinner £10.95-£12.95 & alc International Cuisine V meals Coffee am Tea pm **FACILITIES:** CTV in all bedrooms Fishing **CONF:** Thtr 60 Class 40 Board 40 **SERVICES:** 10P **NOTES:** No smoking in restaurant Last d 9.15pm
CARDS:

See advert on opposite page

FAKENHAM Norfolk — Map 09 TF92

★★ *Sculthorpe Mill*

Lynn Rd, Sculthorpe NR21 9QG
Quality Percentage Score: 67%
☎ 01328 856161 Fax 01328 856651
Dir: *turn off A148 from Fakenham to Kings Lynn, just beyond village of Sculthorpe*
Some two miles west of Fakenham, Sculthorpe Mill enjoys close proximity to the town centre as well as an idyllic and tranquil riverside position. With open fires and lots of low beams and nooks and crannies, this 18th-century watermill is popular, both as a watering hole for locals and a fine dining venue. The six bedrooms are rather spacious and well equipped; one has a four-poster bed.
ROOMS: 6 en suite (bth/shr) (1 fmly) No smoking in all bedrooms **MEALS:** International Cuisine V meals Coffee am Tea pm **FACILITIES:** CTV in all bedrooms Fishing ch fac **CONF:** Thtr 25 Class 16 Board 16 **SERVICES:** 60P **NOTES:** No smoking in restaurant Last d 9pm RS Oct-Good Fri Mon-Fri closed 3-6pm
CARDS:

FAKENHAM Norfolk — Map 09 TF92

★★ *Crown*

Market Place NR21 9BP
Quality Percentage Score: 66%
☎ 01328 851418 Fax 01328 862433
Dir: *in town centre*
Originally a coaching inn and focal point of this old market town, parts of The Crown date back to the 16th century. Bedrooms are attractively decorated and well equipped. The bar menu and blackboard offer a range of snacks whilst the restaurant has a carte menu.
ROOMS: 12 en suite (bth/shr) (2 fmly) No smoking in 1 bedroom **MEALS:** V meals Coffee am **FACILITIES:** CTV in all bedrooms Garage lock up for bicycles **SERVICES:** 25P **NOTES:** No dogs (ex guide dogs) No smoking area in restaurant Last d 9.30pm Closed 25 Dec
CARDS:

FALFIELD Gloucestershire — Map 03 ST69

★★★ *Gables Inn*

Bristol Rd GL12 8DL
Quality Percentage Score: 71%
☎ 01454 260502 Fax 01454 261821
Dir: *on A38 just off junct 14 on M5*
Attractive public rooms and good conference and function facilities are one of the strengths of the Gables, which is close to the M5. Bedrooms are decorated and furnished to a good standard with all modern amenities, and the restaurant offers enjoyable dishes.
ROOMS: 32 en suite (bth/shr) (2 fmly) **MEALS:** English & Continental Cuisine V meals Coffee am Tea pm **FACILITIES:** CTV in all bedrooms STV Sauna Solarium Gym **CONF:** Thtr 150 Class 80 Board 60 **SERVICES:** Night porter 100P **NOTES:** No dogs (ex guide dogs) No smoking area in restaurant Last d 10pm
CARDS:

FALMOUTH Cornwall & Isles of Scilly — Map 02 SW83

see also **Mawnan Smith**

★★★★ Royal Duchy

Cliff Rd TR11 4NX
Quality Percentage Score: 69%
☎ 01326 313042 Fax 01326 319420
Dir: *located on Cliff Rd, along Falmouth Sea Front*
A welcoming hotel, situated on the sea front, just a short walk

contd.

For Useful Information and Important Telephone Number Changes turn to page 25

from the centre of the town and the beach. There are also many indoor facilities including a swimming pool, sauna, solarium, and snooker room. Also, lounges have fine views over the bay, and an interesting selection of carefully prepared dishes, using local produce wherever possible, is served in the comfortable restaurant. Bedrooms vary in size and aspect, and family suites are available.

ROOMS: 43 en suite (bth/shr) (6 fmly) s £58-£86; d £108-£192 (incl. bkfst) * LB Off peak **MEALS:** Lunch £9.95-£10.50 & alc Dinner £22 & alc English & French Cuisine V meals Coffee am Tea pm **FACILITIES:** CTV in all bedrooms STV Indoor swimming pool (heated) Sauna Solarium Pool table Jacuzzi/spa Table tennis Wkly live entertainment ch fac Xmas **CONF:** Thtr 50 Class 50 Board 50 **SERVICES:** Lift Night porter 50P **NOTES:** No dogs (ex guide dogs) Last d 9pm
CARDS:

See advert on this page

FALMOUTH Cornwall & Isles of Scilly **Map 02 SW83**
★★★ The Greenbank Hotel & Retreat
Harbourside TR11 2SR
Quality Percentage Score: 74%
☎ 01326 312440 01326 211362
Dir: *200yds past Falmouth Marina*
An established hotel dating back to the 18th century. Florence Nightingale stayed here in 1907, the hotel register with her signature is on display. Bedrooms are mostly spacious, well

contd.

New AA Guides for the Millennium are featured on page 24

equipped and many have balconies overlooking the sea front. The hotel has a hairdressers, beauty salon and gym.
ROOMS: 61 en suite (bth/shr) (3 fmly) No smoking in 3 bedrooms s £45-£150; d £75-£180 (incl. bkfst) * LB Off peak **MEALS:** Lunch fr £15 Dinner £22-£40 English & French Cuisine V meals Coffee am Tea pm **FACILITIES:** CTV in all bedrooms STV Snooker Sauna Solarium Gym Pool table Fishing from hotel quay Hairdressing Beauty salons Xmas **CONF:** Thtr 80 Class 45 Board 20 Del from £79.90 **SERVICES:** Lift Night porter 70P **NOTES:** No smoking in restaurant Last d 9pm **CARDS:** 💳 ■ ⬛ 🖻 🖅 💷

≡ **FALMOUTH** Cornwall & Isles of Scilly   **Map 02 SW83**
★★★❀❀ 🛎 **Penmere Manor**
Mongleath Rd TR11 4PN
Quality Percentage Score: 74%
☎ 01326 211411 📠 01326 317588

Best Western

Dir: *turn right off Hillhead roundabout and follow road for approx 1m then turn left into Mongleath Road*

A wide range of bedrooms are offered at Penmere Manor with the Garden Wing rooms being the largest and most popular. Imaginative dishes using local produce are served in Bolitho's Restaurant, whilst 'Fountains' Bar, part of the fully supervised leisure club, offers light meals and snacks in a more informal setting.
ROOMS: 37 en suite (bth/shr) (14 fmly) No smoking in 29 bedrooms s £53-£59.50; d £60-£93 (incl. bkfst) * LB Off peak **MEALS:** Bar Lunch £9.20-£9.95 Dinner £19.50-£25alc V meals Coffee am Tea pm **FACILITIES:** CTV in all bedrooms STV Indoor swimming pool (heated) Outdoor swimming pool (heated) Sauna Solarium Gym Pool table Croquet lawn Jacuzzi/spa Table tennis Boules Xmas **CONF:** Thtr 40 Class 30 Board 30 Del from £75 * **SERVICES:** 50P **NOTES:** No smoking in restaurant Last d 9pm Closed 24-28 Dec **CARDS:** 💳 ■ ⬛ 🖻 🖅 💷

See advert on opposite page

≡ **FALMOUTH** Cornwall & Isles of Scilly   **Map 02 SW83**
★★★❀ **Falmouth Beach Resort Hotel**
Gyllyngvase Beach, Seafront TR11 4NA
Quality Percentage Score: 71%
☎ 01326 318084 📠 01326 319147

Best Western

Dir: *from A39 to Falmouth follow signs to seafront & Gyllyngvase Beach, hotel opposite Gyllyngvase Beach*
This large, popular hotel has recently seen major investment. Public areas include the new 250 seater Sandpipers Restaurant, Ospreys restaurant with carte menu, the new Features Lounge and extended Feathers bar. Rooms, varying in style and size, are

nicely decorated and have modern amenities. Extensive leisure facilities at 'The Beach Club' are popular with guests and non residents.

ROOMS: 109 en suite (bth/shr) 7 annexe en suite (bth/shr) (20 fmly) No smoking in 94 bedrooms s £45-£56; d £90-£100 (incl. bkfst & dinner) * LB Off peak **MEALS:** Lunch £7.95-£12.95 High tea £3-£8 Dinner £6.95-£13.95 & alc English & French Cuisine V meals Coffee am Tea pm **FACILITIES:** CTV in all bedrooms STV Indoor swimming pool (heated) Tennis (hard) Sauna Solarium Gym Pool table Jacuzzi/spa Wkly live entertainment Xmas **CONF:** Thtr 300 Class 200 Board 150 Del from £45 * **SERVICES:** Lift Night porter 95P **NOTES:** No smoking in restaurant Last d 11pm **CARDS:** 💳 ■ ⬛ 🖻 🖅 💷

See advert on opposite page

≡ **FALMOUTH** Cornwall & Isles of Scilly   **Map 02 SW83**
★★★❀💠 **Falmouth**
Castle Beach TR11 4NZ
Quality Percentage Score: 67%
☎ 01326 312671 & Freephone 0500 602030 📠 01326 319533
Dir: *on the seafront near Pendennis Castle*

This Victorian hotel is set in five acres of gardens overlooking Castle Beach and just a short walk from the town centre. The bedrooms include family, no-smoking and balconied rooms. Public rooms offer a choice of lounges, a restaurant and a leisure club. The hotel also has a large ballroom. Self-catering apartments are available in the hotel grounds.
ROOMS: 69 en suite (bth/shr) 44 annexe rms (4 shr) (6 fmly) No smoking in 12 bedrooms s £50-£102; d £80-£180 (incl. bkfst) * LB Off peak **MEALS:** Lunch £11.20 & alc High tea fr £1.95 & alc Dinner £18-£21 & alc V meals Coffee am Tea pm **FACILITIES:** CTV in all bedrooms STV Indoor swimming pool (heated) Snooker Sauna Solarium Gym Pool table Croquet lawn Putting green Jacuzzi/spa Membership of local tennis & squash club ch fac **CONF:** Thtr 300 Class 150 Board 100 Del from £59 * **SERVICES:** Lift Night porter 175P **NOTES:** No smoking area in restaurant Last d 9.30pm **CARDS:** 💳 ■ ⬛ 🖻 🖅 💷

See advert on opposite page

Symbols and Abbreviations are listed and explained on pages 4 and 5

★★★

Trelawne Hotel

In a beautiful, peaceful and tranquil corner of Cornwall, this fine country house hotel nestles on the coastline between the Helford and the Fal rivers with magnificent views across Falmouth Bay. The Trelawne is ideally situated for endless coastal walks, exploring sandy beaches and coves, visiting many National Trust properties and free entry into some of Cornwall's famous gardens.

Mawnan Smith, Falmouth,
Cornwall TR11 5HS
Tel: (01326) 250226 Fax: (01326) 250909

PENMERE MANOR

One visit to this very special hotel is never enough

Experiencing an oasis of gracious living in 5 acres of sub-tropical gardens and woodland
Savouring very special cuisine including local seafood and over 100 wines . . .
Enjoy our stunning Fountains Leisure Club with indoor and outdoor pool . . .
Feeling pampered and relaxed . . .

That's why our guests return time and time again

AA ★★★ 74%

Mongleath Road, Falmouth
Cornwall TR11 4PN
Telephone: (01326) 211411

INVESTOR IN PEOPLE

Best Western

The Falmouth Hotel

CASTLE BEACH
FALMOUTH
CORNWALL
TR11 4NZ
Tel: 01326 312671
Fax: 01326 319533

AA ★★★ ★★★ **Email: FalHotel@connexions.co.uk**

A beautiful hotel commanding an unrivalled seafront position. 100 luxurious bedrooms, apartments and cottages, some with balconies and jacuzzis, you can choose between B&B, HB or SC.

Delightful restaurants, bars and lounges with stunning views and a wonderfully relaxing ambience. Superb leisure complex with pool, sauna, jacuzzi, solarium and gymnasium. The perfect location for a holiday or short break as well as a delightful venue for weddings, conferences and all functions.

Please call for a brochure and tariff.

What a position to be in!

AA ★★★

Best Western

...sunbathing on the beautiful beach right outside the hotel, or swimming in the pool at 'The Beach Club', or sampling our wonderful food, maybe on the sun terrace overlooking the sea.

Live music, free tennis.
Enjoy Falmouth with all its history, attractions and facilities...shops, golf, sailing, fishing, beautiful gardens.
Just be in the right position to enjoy it.

FALMOUTH BEACH
RESORT HOTEL & Conference Centre

The Falmouth Beach Resort Hotel.
Gyllyngvase Beach, Falmouth, Cornwall.
Tel: 01326 318084 Fax: 319147
Email: falbeach@aol.com
Web site: http://members.aol.com/falbeach

FALMOUTH Cornwall & Isles of Scilly **Map 02 SW83**
★★★ Green Lawns
Western Ter TR11 4QJ
Quality Percentage Score: 67%
☎ 01326 312734 🖷 01326 211427
Dir: *on A39*
A popular hotel with extensive facilities, including a spacious function room and an attractive split-level restaurant where both a table d'hote and a carte menu is available to guests and non-residents alike. Bedrooms vary in size and style, although all offer many modern facilities and comforts.
ROOMS: 39 en suite (bth/shr) (8 fmly) No smoking in 8 bedrooms s £50-£70; d £100-£140 (incl. bkfst) * LB Off peak **MEALS:** Lunch £3.50-£20 & alc High tea £3-£5 Dinner £20-£22 & alc English & French Cuisine V meals Coffee am Tea pm **FACILITIES:** CTV in all bedrooms STV Indoor swimming pool (heated) Tennis (hard & grass) Squash Sauna Solarium Gym Jacuzzi/spa Wkly live entertainment **CONF:** Thtr 200 Class 80 Board 100 Del from £85 * **SERVICES:** Night porter 69P **NOTES:** No smoking area in restaurant Last d 9.45pm Closed 24-30 Dec
CARDS:

FALMOUTH Cornwall & Isles of Scilly **Map 02 SW83**
★★★ Penmorvah Manor
Budock Water TR11 5ED
Quality Percentage Score: 67%
☎ 01326 250277 🖷 01326 250509
Dir: *take A39 to Hillhead roundabout take 2nd exit. At Falmouth Football Club turn right, through Budock, hotel opposite Penjerrick Gardens*
Situated within two miles of central Falmouth, this extended Victorian manor house is peacefully set in six acres of private woodland and gardens. Activity holidays and leisure breaks are available, including a painters' workshop, and garden and golfing holidays. Most of the rooms are located in a modern wing, with half the rooms on the ground floor. In the candlelit restaurant an interesting fixed-price menu is offered.
ROOMS: 27 en suite (bth/shr) (1 fmly) No smoking in all bedrooms s £50-£55; d £75-£100 (incl. bkfst) * LB Off peak **MEALS:** Lunch £10.50 Dinner £19.50 English & French Cuisine V meals Coffee am Tea pm **FACILITIES:** CTV in all bedrooms Pool table Croquet lawn Xmas **CONF:** Thtr 250 Class 100 Board 56 Del from £86.50 * **SERVICES:** 150P **NOTES:** No smoking in restaurant Last d 8.30pm
CARDS:

FALMOUTH Cornwall & Isles of Scilly **Map 02 SW83**
★★★ *Gyllyngdune Manor*
Melvill Rd TR11 4AR
Quality Percentage Score: 65%
☎ 01326 312978 🖷 01326 211881
Dir: *from A39 follow signs for beaches and docks. Hotel 200yds beyond Pavilion and Beer Garden on right*
This fine Georgian manor house, situated above the town in its own mature grounds, has fine views of Falmouth Bay. The hotel has friendly staff and comfortable public areas in addition to an indoor swimming pool, games room and gymnasium. Bedrooms include ground floor, four-poster, and family options.
ROOMS: 30 en suite (bth/shr) (3 fmly) **MEALS:** English & Continental Cuisine V meals Coffee am Tea pm **FACILITIES:** CTV in all bedrooms Indoor swimming pool (heated) Sauna Solarium Gym Pool table Table tennis Wkly live entertainment **SERVICES:** Night porter 27P **NOTES:** No smoking in restaurant Last d 9pm Closed 27 Dec-11 Jan
CARDS:

FALMOUTH Cornwall & Isles of Scilly **Map 02 SW83**
★★★ St Michaels of Falmouth
Gyllyngvase Beach TR11 4NB
Quality Percentage Score: 63%
☎ 01326 312707 🖷 01326 211772
Dir: *follow the A39 into Falmouth, at 2nd rdbt, take Melville Rd, then take the 3rd right turn and right again into Stracey Rd*

Conveniently situated for the beaches and town centre, St Michael's Hotel benefits from spacious public areas and its four acres of gardens. A popular leisure centre, including an indoor pool, sauna, solarium and well equipped gym add to the facilities available to guests. Bedrooms vary in size and style and offer modern facilities.
ROOMS: 57 en suite (bth/shr) 8 annexe en suite (bth/shr) (2 fmly) No smoking in 4 bedrooms **MEALS:** Lunch £9.95 Dinner £17 V meals Coffee am Tea pm **FACILITIES:** CTV in all bedrooms STV Indoor swimming pool (heated) Sauna Solarium Gym Pool table Jacuzzi/spa Concessionary golf rates ch fac **CONF:** Thtr 200 Class 150 Board 120 Del from £56 * **SERVICES:** Night porter 30P **NOTES:** No smoking in restaurant Last d 9pm **CARDS:**

FALMOUTH Cornwall & Isles of Scilly **Map 02 SW83**
★★ *Crill Manor*
Maen Valley, Budock Water TR11 5BL
Quality Percentage Score: 70%
☎ 01326 211880 🖷 01326 211229
Dir: *2.5m W on unclass rd*
This delightful family-run hotel lies in an idyllic spot two miles from Falmouth, set in attractive gardens, with a surrounding area of outstanding natural beauty. Bedrooms are stylishly decorated, well equipped with modern facilities, and two are located in an adjoining building. The open-plan lounge and bar look out over the swimming pool and gardens.
ROOMS: 12 en suite (bth/shr) 2 annexe en suite (bth/shr) (2 fmly) No smoking in all bedrooms **MEALS:** V meals Coffee am Tea pm **FACILITIES:** CTV in all bedrooms Outdoor swimming pool (heated) **SERVICES:** 14P **NOTES:** No dogs No coaches No children 10yrs No smoking in restaurant Last d 8pm **CARDS:**

FALMOUTH Cornwall & Isles of Scilly **Map 02 SW83**
★★ Carthion
Cliff Rd TR11 4AP
Quality Percentage Score: 67%
☎ 01326 313669 🖷 01326 212828
Dir: *from A39 follow signs to sea-front*
The Carthion continues to be popular and is very good at organizing catering for smaller functions and private parties. The lounges, bar and marvellous conservatory, where guests take breakfast, offer stunning views over Falmouth Bay. The bedrooms are generally spacious and comfortably furnished,
contd.

many with sea views. Consistently good traditional cuisine is available on two menus.
ROOMS: 18 en suite (bth/shr) (4 fmly) s £42-£47; d £74-£84 (incl. bkfst & dinner) * LB Off peak **MEALS:** Lunch £8.75 Dinner £8-£14 & alc English & French Cuisine V meals Coffee am Tea pm **FACILITIES:** CTV in all bedrooms STV **SERVICES:** 18P **NOTES:** No dogs (ex guide dogs) No coaches No children 10yrs No smoking in restaurant Last d 8pm RS Nov-Feb **CARDS:**

FALMOUTH Cornwall & Isles of Scilly — Map 02 SW83
★★ Park Grove
Kimberley Park Rd TR11 2DD
Quality Percentage Score: 65%
☎ 01326 313276 Fax 01326 211926
Dir: *turn off A39 at traffic lights by Riders Garage, towards harbour. Hotel is 400yds on left opposite the park*

A long established family-run hotel, conveniently situated opposite Kimberley Gardens within walking distance of Falmouth town centre. Relaxed, friendly service is provided by a small team of loyal staff. Bedrooms are neat and comfortably furnished with many modern facilities. Each evening a four-course meal is served in the dining room, next to the popular bar.
ROOMS: 17 en suite (shr) (6 fmly) s £25-£28; d £50-£56 (incl. bkfst) * LB Off peak **MEALS:** Bar Lunch £4.50-£7.50 Dinner £12.50-£16 Coffee am Tea pm **FACILITIES:** CTV in all bedrooms STV **SERVICES:** 28P **NOTES:** No smoking in restaurant Last d 7.30pm
CARDS:

FALMOUTH Cornwall & Isles of Scilly — Map 02 SW83
★★ Broadmead
THE CIRCLE Selected Individual Hotels GREAT BRITAIN
66-68 Kimberley Park Rd TR11 2DD
Quality Percentage Score: 63%
☎ 01326 315704 & 318036 Fax 01326 311048
Dir: *turn off A39 at traffic lights by Riders Garage, towards town centre, hotel 150yds on left*

This informal family-run hotel overlooks the attractive Kimberley Park and is within easy walking distance of Falmouth town centre. Inside are comfortable lounges for the guests, and a restaurant offering a fixed price menu.
ROOMS: 12 rms (11 bth/shr) (1 fmly) s £28-£38; d £54-£60 (incl. bkfst) * LB Off peak **MEALS:** Dinner £12.75 & alc Coffee am **FACILITIES:** CTV in all bedrooms **SERVICES:** 8P **NOTES:** No dogs No smoking in restaurant Last d 8pm Closed 23 Dec-3 Jan
CARDS:

FALMOUTH Cornwall & Isles of Scilly — Map 02 SW83
★★ Rosslyn
110 Kimberley Park Rd TR11 2JJ
Quality Percentage Score: 62%
☎ 01326 312699 Fax 01326 312699

On the northern edge of Falmouth, this family-run hotel is popular with tour groups. Public areas are spacious and comfortable with a choice of lounges, one specifically for non-smokers. The attractive gardens at the rear of the property are well tended and peaceful. Bedrooms vary in size and are freshly decorated. Live entertainment is provided periodically during the season.
ROOMS: 27 rms (9 bth 12 shr) (2 fmly) No smoking in all bedrooms s fr £27; d fr £53 (incl. bkfst) * LB Off peak **MEALS:** Coffee am Tea pm **FACILITIES:** CTV in all bedrooms Pool table Putting green Table tennis Darts Xmas **CONF:** Class 60 **SERVICES:** 10P **NOTES:** No smoking in restaurant Last d 7pm RS 24 Dec-28 Feb
CARDS:

FALMOUTH Cornwall & Isles of Scilly — Map 02 SW83
★★ *Membly Hall*
Sea Front, Cliff Rd TR11 4NT
Quality Percentage Score: 61%
☎ 01326 312869 & 311115 Fax 01326 211751
Dir: *from A30 turn onto A3076 for Truro then follow A39 to Falmouth. At Falmouth follow signs for seafront and beaches. Hotel located middleof seafront*

This holiday hotel lies on the seafront with superb views over Falmouth Bay. Bedrooms are decorated with pretty wallpapers and are well equipped. Several rooms are located at ground-floor level and many are suitable for families. Public areas are spacious and live entertainment is held regularly.
ROOMS: 37 en suite (bth/shr) (3 fmly) **MEALS:** English & Continental Cuisine V meals Coffee am **FACILITIES:** CTV in all bedrooms STV Pool table Putting green Indoor short bowls Table tennis Darts Wkly live entertainment ch fac **CONF:** Thtr 150 Class 130 Board 60 **SERVICES:** Lift 30P **NOTES:** No smoking in restaurant Last d 7.30pm Closed Xmas week RS Dec to Feb

FALMOUTH Cornwall & Isles of Scilly — Map 02 SW83
★★ Lerryn Hotel
De Pass Rd TR11 4BJ
Quality Percentage Score: 63%
☎ 01326 312489
Dir: *from A389 follow signs for Princess Pavilion and take 2nd turning on right after the Pavilion*

A family-run hotel with a warm welcome that proves consistently popular with its guests. Many bedrooms have been modernised and include various in-room facilities. Traditional home-cooked five-course dinners are served in the spacious dining room, adjacent to the two lounges, with views over Falmouth Bay.
ROOMS: 20 en suite (bth/shr) (2 fmly) No smoking in 10 bedrooms s £25-£27; d £50-£54 (incl. bkfst & dinner) LB Off peak **MEALS:** Lunch £12 & alc High tea £8 Dinner £12 & alc English, French & Italian Cuisine V meals Coffee am Tea pm **FACILITIES:** CTV in all bedrooms **CONF:** Class 50 Board 50 Del from £50 * **SERVICES:** 13P **NOTES:** No smoking in restaurant Last d 12 **CARDS:**

FAREHAM Hampshire — Map 04 SU50
★★★★ Solent
SHIRE INNS
Rookery Av, Whiteley PO15 7AJ
Quality Percentage Score: 76%
☎ 01489 880000 Fax 01489 880007
Dir: *on Solent Business Park just off junct 9 on M27*

Peacefully located midway between Southampton and Portsmouth close to junction 9 of the M27, this smart, purpose built hotel offers well appointed and thoughtfully equipped accommodation. Public areas which offer a good range of meeting and leisure facilities are no less impressive and even include a pub in the grounds which serves real ale and home-

contd.

cooked food. Guests can also dine in Woodlands restaurant where the quality of the food earns our One Rosette award. An undoubted strength of the hotel is the friendly and helpful attitude of the management and staff who make every effort to ensure guests are well looked after.
ROOMS: 117 en suite (bth/shr) (9 fmly) No smoking in 30 bedrooms s fr £112; d fr £132 (incl. bkfst) * LB Off peak **MEALS:** International Cuisine V meals Coffee am Tea pm **FACILITIES:** CTV in all bedrooms STV Indoor swimming pool (heated) Tennis (hard) Squash Snooker Sauna Solarium Gym Jacuzzi/spa Steam room Childrens splash pool **CONF:** Thtr 250 Class 120 Board 80 Del from £95 * **SERVICES:** Lift Night porter 200P **NOTES:** No smoking in restaurant Last d 9.30pm **CARDS:**

F

FAREHAM Hampshire **Map 04 SU50**
★★★ Posthouse Fareham
Posthouse
Cartwright Dr, Titchfield PO15 5RJ
Quality Percentage Score: 68%
☎ 01329 844644 🖷 01329 844666
Dir: *exit M27 at junct 9 and follow signs for A27. Continue across Segensworth roundabout following road for 1.5m, turn left at next roundabout*
This well established Posthouse continues to attract both business and leisure markets. Bedrooms are modern in style, comfortably furnished and well equipped, including a mini-bar. Spacious public areas include several conference rooms, leisure centre and large open-plan restaurant.
ROOMS: 125 en suite (bth/shr) (25 fmly) No smoking in 78 bedrooms d £59-£109 * LB Off peak **MEALS:** International Cuisine V meals Coffee am Tea pm **FACILITIES:** CTV in all bedrooms Indoor swimming pool (heated) Sauna Solarium Gym Pool table Jacuzzi/spa Childrens play area Xmas **CONF:** Thtr 160 Class 80 Board 50 Del from £105 * **SERVICES:** Night porter 130P **NOTES:** No smoking in restaurant Last d 10.30pm **CARDS:**
See advert on opposite page

FAREHAM Hampshire **Map 04 SU50**
★★★ Lysses House
51 High St PO16 7BQ
Quality Percentage Score: 62%
☎ 01329 822622 🖷 01329 822762
Dir: *take M27 junct 11 and stay in left hand lane till rdbt, take third exit in to East St and follow into High St. Hotel is at top on right*
A Georgian hotel in a quiet location on the edge of the town centre. Rooms are well equipped, appealing particularly to the business traveller. There are conference facilities, a lounge and bar, serving a range of snacks. The Richmond Restaurant has an interesting selection of dishes on set and carte menus.
ROOMS: 21 en suite (bth/shr) s £51.50-£65; d £66.50-£80 (incl. bkfst) * Off peak **MEALS:** Lunch £11.95-£13.95 & alc Dinner £16.50-£18.50 & alc English & French Cuisine V meals Coffee am Tea pm **FACILITIES:** CTV in all bedrooms **CONF:** Thtr 95 Class 42 Board 28 Del from £78 * **SERVICES:** Lift Night porter 30P **NOTES:** No dogs (ex guide dogs) No smoking in restaurant Last d 9.45pm Closed 25 Dec-1 Jan
CARDS:

FAREHAM Hampshire **Map 04 SU50**
★★★ *Red Lion*
East St PO16 0BP
Quality Percentage Score: 62%
☎ 01329 822640 🖷 01329 823579
Conveniently located in the heart of town, this Grade II listed coaching inn continues to be popular with business guests. The bedrooms, the majority of which have been refurbished, are generally spacious and well equipped. Public areas include a cosy bar and restaurant offering a range of popular dishes. The hotel benefits from good meeting facilities and ample parking.
ROOMS: 42 en suite (bth/shr) (2 fmly) **MEALS:** English & Continental Cuisine V meals Coffee am **FACILITIES:** CTV in all bedrooms STV Sauna **CONF:** Thtr 80 Class 60 Board 60 **SERVICES:** Night porter 136P **NOTES:** No dogs (ex guide dogs) No smoking area in restaurant Last d 10pm **CARDS:**

FAREHAM Hampshire **Map 04 SU50**
Travel Inn
Southampton Rd, Park Gate SO31 6AF
☎ 01489 579857 🖷 01489 577238
Dir: *on 2nd rdbt off M27 junct 9, signed A27 Fareham*
This modern building offers accommodation in smart, spacious and well equipped bedrooms, all with en-suite bathrooms. Refreshments may be taken at the nearby family restaurant. For details about current prices consult the Contents Page under Hotel Groups for the Travel Inn phone number.
ROOMS: 40 en suite (bth/shr) d £39.95 *

FARINGDON Oxfordshire **Map 04 SU29**
★★★ Sudbury House Hotel & Conference Centre
London St SN7 8AA
Quality Percentage Score: 72%
☎ 01367 241272 🖷 01367 242346
Dir: *off A420, signposted Folly Hill*

Ideally situated on the edge of the Cotswolds, midway between Oxford and Swindon, and set in six acres of well tended grounds, which include a pitch and put course. The hotel is well suited to cater for both business and leisure markets, private rooms are well suited to weddings or conferences. Bedrooms are attractive, spacious and well equipped. Dining options include the restaurant and bar or a comprehensive room service menu is also available.
ROOMS: 49 en suite (bth/shr) (2 fmly) No smoking in 22 bedrooms s £59.50-£82; d £65-£92 (incl. bkfst) * LB Off peak **MEALS:** Lunch £9.95-£14.50 High tea fr £7.95 Dinner fr £18.95 & alc English & Continental Cuisine V meals Coffee am Tea pm **FACILITIES:** CTV in all bedrooms STV Croquet lawn Putting green Pitch & Putt Badminton Xmas **CONF:** Thtr 90 Class 90 Board 40 Del from £132 * **SERVICES:** Lift Night porter 100P **NOTES:** Last d 9.15pm **CARDS:**
See advert on opposite page

★
The Premier Collection, hotels with Red Star Awards are listed on pages 17-23

FARINGDON Oxfordshire — Map 04 SU29
★★ Faringdon
1 Market Place SN7 7HL
Quality Percentage Score: 61%
☎ 01367 240536 Fax 01367 243250
Dir: *M4 junct 15 A419 take A420 signposted to Oxford for 10m follow signs for Faringdon, hotel next to All Saints Church*
Well situated in the market place of this Oxfordshire town, this historic inn sits opposite the 12th-century church. Bedrooms are spacious and equipped with hair dryer, remote TV and clock radio. There is a popular lounge bar and restaurant.
ROOMS: 15 en suite (bth/shr) 5 annexe en suite (bth/shr) (3 fmly) s £50-£60; d £65-£75 (incl. bkfst) * LB Off peak **MEALS:** Bar Lunch £7-£10 & alc Dinner £10-£15 & alc Thai Cuisine V meals Coffee am Tea pm **FACILITIES:** CTV in all bedrooms **CONF:** Thtr 30 Class 15 Board 20 **NOTES:** Last d 10.30pm **CARDS:**

FARNBOROUGH Hampshire — Map 04 SU85
★★★ *Posthouse Farnborough*
Posthouse
Lynchford Rd GU14 6AZ
Quality Percentage Score: 67%
☎ 01252 545051 Fax 01252 377210
Dir: *from M3 junct 4, follow A325 for Farnborough. Take A325 through Farnborough town centre towards Aldershot. Hotel on the left at The Queen's rdbt*
Combining a mix of traditional and modern style, and very conveniently placed for the bi-annual air show, this smart hotel continues to improve, with extensive refurbishment work carried out this year. Well equipped bedrooms are a feature, in addition to a range of meeting rooms, and good leisure facilities.
ROOMS: 143 en suite (bth/shr) (39 fmly) No smoking in 80 bedrooms **MEALS:** V meals Coffee am Tea pm **FACILITIES:** CTV in all bedrooms Indoor swimming pool (heated) Sauna Solarium Gym Jacuzzi/spa Health & fitness centre ch fac **CONF:** Thtr 120 Class 60 Board 60 **SERVICES:** Night porter 175P **NOTES:** No smoking area in restaurant Last d 10pm **CARDS:**

FARNBOROUGH Hampshire — Map 04 SU85
★★★ *Falcon*
68 Farnborough Rd GU14 6TH
Quality Percentage Score: 60%
☎ 01252 545378 Fax 01252 522539
Dir: *on A325 opposite Aerospace Centre airfield*
This hotel is conveniently placed for the town centre and access to major roads. Popular with an international business clientele, the bedrooms are modern and well equipped. There is a pleasant club-like atmosphere in the public areas, which include a small bar and open-plan lounge.
ROOMS: 30 en suite (bth/shr) (1 fmly) **MEALS:** International Cuisine V meals Coffee am Tea pm **FACILITIES:** CTV in all bedrooms STV **CONF:** Thtr 25 Class 10 Board 16 **SERVICES:** Night porter 30P **NOTES:** No dogs (ex guide dogs) Last d 9.30pm RS Xmas & New Year **CARDS:**

FARNBOROUGH Hampshire — Map 04 SU85
Travel Inn
Ively Rd, Southwood GU14 0JP
☎ 01252 546654 Fax 01252 546427
Dir: *2m from M3 junct 4A towards Farnborough, next to Golf Club*
This modern building offers accommodation in smart, spacious and well equipped bedrooms, all with en-suite bathrooms. Refreshments may be taken at the nearby family restaurant. For details about current prices consult the Contents Page under Hotel Groups for the Travel Inn phone number.
ROOMS: 40 en suite (bth/shr) d £39.95 *

FARNHAM Surrey **Map 04 SU84**

★★★ Bishop's Table

27 West St GU9 7DR

Quality Percentage Score: 74%

☎ 01252 710222 01252 733494

Dir: *take the A331 (from M3 J4), or A31 (from A3) and follow signs for town centre, hotel is located next to the library*

The Bishop's Table is a charming Georgian townhouse hotel. A walled garden to the rear houses an extension which takes in the former stable block. Individually-decorated bedrooms come with a good range of facilities and several rooms have fine antique beds. Public areas include a relaxing bar, and a restaurant offering three different menus.

ROOMS: 9 en suite (bth/shr) 8 annexe en suite (bth/shr) s £88-£97; d £102-£105 (incl. bkfst) * LB Off peak **MEALS:** Lunch £15-£23.50 & alc Dinner £21-£23.50 & alc European Cuisine V meals Coffee am Tea pm **FACILITIES:** CTV in all bedrooms **CONF:** Thtr 26 Class 36 Board 15 Del from £146 * **SERVICES:** Night porter **NOTES:** No dogs (ex guide dogs) No coaches No children 16yrs No smoking in restaurant Last d 9.45pm Closed 25 Dec-3 Jan RS Closed for lunch Sat **CARDS:**

See advert on opposite page

FARNHAM Surrey **Map 04 SU84**

★★★ The Bush

The Borough GU9 7NN

Quality Percentage Score: 64%

☎ 01252 715237 01252 733530

Dir: *join A31 Farnham follow signs for town centre. At crossroads left and hotel on the right*

Situated in the centre of town, this ivy-clad 17th-century coaching inn offers a range of different styles of bedroom, some in the original building, some in an extension. Day rooms include a bar, a separate lounge with frescoes depicting historical scenes, and the Georgian-style Thackeray restaurant.

ROOMS: 65 en suite (bth/shr) No smoking in 30 bedrooms d fr £118 LB Off peak **MEALS:** Lunch £10.95-£25 & alc Dinner fr £13.95 & alc V meals Coffee am Tea pm **FACILITIES:** CTV in all bedrooms Xmas **CONF:** Thtr 60 Class 30 Board 30 Del from £140 * **SERVICES:** Night porter 60P **NOTES:** No smoking area in restaurant Last d 10pm **CARDS:**

FARNHAM Surrey **Map 04 SU84**

★★★ Farnham House

Alton Rd GU10 5ER

Quality Percentage Score: 61%

☎ 01252 716908 01252 722583

Dir: *1m from town, off A31 Alton road*

Popular for conferences and weddings, Farnham House is surrounded by its own five acres of grounds. The Victorian architecture is part Tudor, part baronial in style, and features an oak-panelled bar with an inglenook fireplace. Comfortable, well appointed bedrooms are quiet with views over lovely countryside.

ROOMS: 25 en suite (bth/shr) (1 fmly) No smoking in 5 bedrooms s fr £70; d fr £75 * Off peak **MEALS:** Lunch £11.95 & alc Dinner £3-£17.50alc International Cuisine V meals Coffee am Tea pm **FACILITIES:** CTV in all bedrooms STV Outdoor swimming pool (heated) Tennis (hard) Croquet lawn **CONF:** Thtr 65 Class 15 Board 24 Del £130 * **SERVICES:** Night porter 75P **NOTES:** No dogs (ex guide dogs) No coaches Last d 9.15pm **CARDS:**

FAVERSHAM Kent **Map 05 TR06**

Travelodge

Thanet Way ME8 9EL

☎ 01227 770980

Dir: *from junc 7 M2, take A299*

This modern building offers accommodation in smart, spacious and well equipped bedrooms, all with en-suite bathrooms. Refreshments may be taken at the nearby family restaurant. For details about current prices, consult the Contents Page under Hotel Groups for the Travelodge phone number.

ROOMS: 40 en suite (bth/shr) d £45.95 *

FEERING Essex **Map 05 TL82**

Travelodge

A12 London Rd Northbound CO5 9EL

☎ 0800 850950

This modern building offers accommodation in smart, spacious and well equipped bedrooms, all with en-suite bathrooms. Refreshments may be taken at the nearby family restaurant. For details about current prices, consult the Contents Page under Hotel Groups for the Travelodge phone number.

ROOMS: 39 en suite (bth/shr) d £39.95 *

FELIXSTOWE Suffolk **Map 05 TM33**

★★★ Orwell

Hamilton Rd IP11 7DX

Quality Percentage Score: 67%

☎ 01394 285511 01394 670687

Dir: *approaching on A45, straight across Dock Roundabout, straight across next roundabout, 4th exit off third roundabout*

An imposing building, the Orwell's interior decor creates the feel of a grand hotel. Bedrooms are smartly decorated, and it is worth requesting one of the spacious 'Superior' rooms. Guests have a choice of two bars, and for meals, an informal buttery or the spacious restaurant.

ROOMS: 58 en suite (bth/shr) (8 fmly) No smoking in 4 bedrooms **MEALS:** Lunch £12-£13.50 & alc Dinner £16.50 & alc International Cuisine V meals Coffee am Tea pm **FACILITIES:** CTV in all bedrooms STV Wkly live entertainment **CONF:** Thtr 200 Class 100 Board 60 Del £85 * **SERVICES:** Lift Night porter 70P **NOTES:** No dogs (ex guide dogs) No smoking area in restaurant Last d 9.45pm

CARDS:

FELIXSTOWE Suffolk **Map 05 TM33**

★★ Waverley

2 Wolsey Gardens IP11 7DF

Quality Percentage Score: 70%

☎ 01394 282811 01394 670185

Built in the Victorian era and occupying a high position with views over the cliff tops down towards the beach, this traditional resort hotel continues to please many regular business and leisure guests. Well equipped and spacious accommodation comes in a variety of sizes and shapes, and some rooms have balconies and views over the promenade. Public areas include a

contd.

busy bar serving a wide range of hot and cold snacks and the restaurant offering an extensive menu in a more formal setting.
ROOMS: 19 en suite (bth/shr) (4 fmly) s £40-£56.95; d £50-£74.95 * LB Off peak **MEALS:** Lunch £6.95-£16.95 Dinner £12.95-£15.95 & alc English & Continental Cuisine V meals Coffee am Tea pm **FACILITIES:** CTV in all bedrooms Wkly live entertainment Xmas **CONF:** Thtr 85 Class 35 Board 25 Del from £70 * **SERVICES:** 30P **NOTES:** No smoking in restaurant Last d 9.30pm
CARDS:

FELIXSTOWE Suffolk — Map 05 TM33

★★ *Marlborough*

Sea Front IP11 8BJ
Quality Percentage Score: 64%
☎ 01394 285621 Fax 01394 670724
Dir: *follow 'Seafront' signs*

This traditional seaside hotel continues to please its many visitors, especially weekly guests who appreciate the good value tariffs. With the seafront location, south of the pier leisure complex, many of the public areas look out to sea, and guests can enjoy the well appointed Flying Boat bar-lounge, the attractive Rattan Restaurant and L'Aperitif Bar. The recently redecorated accommodation is steadily being upgraded, and all rooms are well equipped and suitably furnished.
ROOMS: 47 en suite (bth/shr) **MEALS:** English, French, Greek & Indian Cuisine V meals Coffee am Tea pm **FACILITIES:** CTV in all bedrooms STV Pool table **CONF:** Thtr 80 Class 80 Board 60 **SERVICES:** Lift Night porter 16P **NOTES:** No smoking in restaurant Last d 9.30pm
CARDS:

FENSTANTON Cambridgeshire — Map 04 TL36

Travelodge

Travelodge

PE18 9JG
☎ 01954 230919 Fax 01954 230919
Dir: *4m SE of Huntingdon, on A14 eastbound*

This modern building offers accommodation in smart, spacious and well equipped bedrooms, all with en-suite bathrooms. Refreshments may be taken at the nearby family restaurant. For details about current prices, consult the Contents Page under Hotel Groups for the Travelodge phone number.
ROOMS: 40 en suite (bth/shr) d £49.95 *

FERNDOWN Dorset — Map 04 SU00

★★★★ Dormy

De Vere Hotels

New Rd BH22 8ES
Quality Percentage Score: 67%
☎ 01202 872121 Fax 01202 895388
Dir: *off A347 from Bournemouth*

Ideal for both conference and leisure guests, this long established hotel is on the outskirts of Ferndown. Public rooms have traditional wood panelling and open fires. Bedrooms are located in the main building and in several nearby cottage wings. There are good leisure facilities, and an informal brasserie as well as a more formal restaurant where dinner dances are held.
ROOMS: 115 en suite (bth/shr) (15 fmly) No smoking in 28 bedrooms s fr £110; d £145-£250 (incl. bkfst) LB Off peak **MEALS:** Lunch £10-£15 High tea £3.50-£8.50 Dinner £19.50-£24.50 French Cuisine V meals Coffee am Tea pm **FACILITIES:** CTV in all bedrooms STV Indoor swimming pool (heated) Tennis (hard) Squash Snooker Sauna Solarium Gym Pool table Putting green Jacuzzi/spa Beauty salon Wkly live entertainment ch fac Xmas **CONF:** Thtr 250 Class 150 Board 60 Del from £115 * **SERVICES:** Lift Night porter 220P **NOTES:** Last d 9.45pm
CARDS:

FERNDOWN Dorset — Map 04 SU00

★★ Coach House Inn

579 Winborne Rd East, Tricketts Cross BH22 9NW
Quality Percentage Score: 59%
☎ 01202 861222 Fax 01202 894130
Dir: *take A31 & follow signs to Ferndwon. Hotel is on the last rdbt before Ferndown. From W A31 Wimborne-by-pass follow Ferndown signs hotel 1m E.*

Equally well suited to business and leisure travellers, The Coach House Inn is convenient for exploring the area. A range of dishes is available in the bar and carte menus are served in the restaurant. The executive bedrooms are the most popular and well equipped.
ROOMS: 44 annexe en suite (bth) (7 fmly) s £33.50-£39; d £45-£50 * LB Off peak **MEALS:** Lunch £6-£10 Dinner £12-£13.50 & alc English & Italian Cuisine V meals Coffee am Tea pm **FACILITIES:** CTV in all bedrooms STV **CONF:** Thtr 150 Class 75 Board 40 Del from £45 * **SERVICES:** 125P **NOTES:** No smoking in restaurant Last d 9.30pm RS Xmas **CARDS:**

FERNDOWN Dorset — Map 04 SU00

Travel Inn

Ringwood Rd, Tricketts Cross BH22 9BB

☎ 01202 874210 Fax 01202 897794

Dir: *off A348 just before Tricketts Cross rdbt*

This modern building offers accommodation in smart, spacious and well equipped bedrooms, all with en-suite bathrooms. Refreshments may be taken at the nearby family restaurant. For details about current prices consult the Contents Page under Hotel Groups for the Travel Inn phone number.

ROOMS: 32 en suite (bth/shr) d £39.95 *

FERRYBRIDGE SERVICE AREA West Yorkshire — Map 08 SE42

Travelodge

WF11 0AF

☎ 01977 672767

Dir: *A1/M62 jnct 33*

This modern building offers accommodation in smart, spacious and well equipped bedrooms, all with en-suite bathrooms. Refreshments may be taken at the nearby family restaurant. For details about current prices, consult the Contents Page under Hotel Groups for the Travelodge phone number.

ROOMS: 36 en suite (bth/shr) d £49.95 *

FILEY North Yorkshire — Map 08 TA18

★★ ***Downcliffe House Hotel***

The Beach YO14 9LA

Quality Percentage Score: 72%

☎ 01723 513310 Fax 01723 516141

Dir: *leave A165 & join A1039 into centre of Filey, continue through centre along Cargate Hill & turn right. Hotel is approx 200yds along sea front*

Standing at the edge of the sea, this delightful hotel has been furnished to a very high standard. There is a pleasant ground floor bar together with a first floor lounge while a good range of dishes is available in the attractive restaurant. Service is provided in a friendly and courteous manner and all bedrooms are well equipped and attractively furnished.

ROOMS: 10 en suite (bth/shr) (2 fmly) **MEALS:** V meals Coffee am Tea pm **FACILITIES:** CTV in all bedrooms STV **SERVICES:** 9P **NOTES:** No dogs (ex guide dogs) No coaches No children 5yrs No smoking in restaurant Closed 2-25 Jan **CARDS:**

FILEY North Yorkshire — Map 08 TA18

★★ **Sea Brink**

3 The Beach YO14 9LA

Quality Percentage Score: 65%

☎ 01723 513257 Fax 01723 514139

Dir: *Leave A165 following A1039 into Filey town centre and to beach. Turn right, hotel is 300yds along seafront*

A friendly sea front hotels with superb views over the bay, offering good value and fine hospitality. The bright, fresh bedrooms are well equipped and the short dining room menu offers an adequate choice of home-cooked food. A newly refurbished, cosy lounge enjoys fine sea views.

ROOMS: 9 en suite (bth/shr) (3 fmly) s £30-£40; d £54-£60 (incl. bkfst) * Off peak **MEALS:** Lunch £1.50-£4.95alc Dinner fr £12 & alc V meals Tea pm **FACILITIES:** CTV in all bedrooms **NOTES:** No coaches No smoking in restaurant Last d 7.30pm Closed Jan & Nov/Dec

CARDS:

For Useful Information and Important Telephone Number Changes turn to page 25

FINDON West Sussex — Map 04 TQ10

★★★ **Findon Manor**

High St BN14 0TA

Quality Percentage Score: 60%

☎ 01903 872733 Fax 01903 877473

Dir: *500yds off A24 at the sign for Findon*

A former rectory once owned by Magdalen College Oxford, surrounded by trees and well kept grounds. A beamed lounge doubles as reception, a cosy bar offers a good range of bar food and is popular with locals. Bedrooms, several with four-posters, are prettily decorated. The restaurant overlooks a garden and offers modern and traditional dishes.

ROOMS: 11 en suite (bth/shr) (2 fmly) s fr £47.50; d fr £75 (incl. bkfst) * LB Off peak **MEALS:** Lunch fr £14.95 Dinner fr £19.50 Anglo French Cuisine V meals Coffee am **FACILITIES:** CTV in all bedrooms Xmas **CONF:** Thtr 45 Class 25 Board 20 Del from £85.95 * **SERVICES:** 28P **NOTES:** No smoking area in restaurant Last d 8.45pm

CARDS:

FIR TREE Co Durham — Map 12 NZ13

★★★ **Helme Park Hall Hotel**

DL13 4NW

Quality Percentage Score: 67%

☎ 01388 730970 Fax 01388 730970

Dir: *1m N of roundabout at A689 intersection*

Dating back to the 13th century, this hospitable family owned hotel commands panoramic views over the Wear Valley. The lounge bar, warmed by roaring fires, is extremely popular for its vast selection of bar meals. The style of furnishings and decoration is modern, and the bedrooms are individually sized and well equipped.

ROOMS: 13 en suite (bth/shr) (1 fmly) s £41; d £67-£91.50 (incl. bkfst) * LB Off peak **MEALS:** Lunch £11.75-£16.50alc Dinner fr £16.50alc English & French Cuisine V meals Coffee am Tea pm **FACILITIES:** CTV in all bedrooms Xmas **CONF:** Thtr 100 Class 50 Board 120 **SERVICES:** 70P **NOTES:** No dogs (ex guide dogs) Last d 9pm

CARDS:

See advert on opposite page

FIVE OAKS West Sussex — Map 04 TQ02

Travelodge

Staines St RH14 9AE

☎ 01403 782711 Fax 01403 782711

Dir: *on A29, northbound, 1m N of Billingshurst*

This modern building offers accommodation in smart, spacious and well equipped bedrooms, all with en-suite bathrooms. Refreshments may be taken at the nearby family restaurant. For details about current prices, consult the Contents Page under Hotel Groups for the Travelodge phone number.

ROOMS: 26 en suite (bth/shr) d £49.95 *

FLADBURY Worcestershire **Map 03 SO94**

★★ **The Chequers Inn**

Chequers Ln WR10 2PZ

Quality Percentage Score: 68%

☎ 01386 860276 & 860527 📠 01386 861286

Dir: *off A4538 between Evesham & Pershore*

This charming old inn, which dates from the 14th century, stands in the centre of a village just west of Evesham. Features include a bar with beamed ceiling and real fires. Meals can be ordered in the bar or in the restaurant, which also offers a carvery buffet. Bedrooms include one suitable for families, and all have modern facilities.

ROOMS: 8 en suite (bth/shr) (1 fmly) s fr £45; d £58-£68 (incl. bkfst) * LB Off peak **MEALS:** Lunch £15-£21.50alc Dinner £15-£21.50alc V meals Coffee am **FACILITIES:** CTV in all bedrooms Fishing Xmas **SERVICES:** 25P **NOTES:** No dogs (ex guide dogs) Last d 9.30pm

CARDS:

See advert under EVESHAM

FLAMBOROUGH East Riding of Yorkshire **Map 08 TA26**

★★ **North Star**

North Marine Dr YO15 1BL

Quality Percentage Score: 70%

☎ 01262 850379

Dir: *in town follow signs for 'North Landing'. Hotel 100yds from the sea*

Standing close to the North Landing of Flamborough Head, this family-run hotel overlooks delightful countryside. The hotel has been tastefully furnished and provides excellent bedrooms together with a busy bar. A good range of well produced food is available in both the bar and the spacious dining room.

ROOMS: 7 en suite (bth/shr) s fr £40; d fr £60 (incl. bkfst) * LB Off peak **MEALS:** Lunch £9.95-£15 & alc Dinner £12.95-£16 & alc English & French Cuisine V meals Coffee am Tea pm **FACILITIES:** CTV in all bedrooms **SERVICES:** 30P **NOTES:** No dogs (ex guide dogs) No smoking in restaurant Last d 9pm Closed Xmas

CARDS:

FLAMBOROUGH East Riding of Yorkshire **Map 08 TA26**

★★ ***Flaneburg***

North Marine Rd YO15 1LF

Quality Percentage Score: 64%

☎ 01262 850284 📠 01262 850284

Dir: *from the centre of Flamborough, follow the signs for "hotel" & "North Landing". The hotel is situated on the very edge of the village on the left*

This friendly hotel, on the North Landing of Flamborough Head, is popular with bird watchers and golfers. Bedrooms are pleasantly furnished in traditional style, and good meals can be taken either in the bar or the dining room.

ROOMS: 14 rms (12 shr) (3 fmly) **MEALS:** International Cuisine V meals **FACILITIES:** CTV in all bedrooms **CONF:** Thtr 30 Class 20 Board 20 **SERVICES:** 50P **NOTES:** No dogs (ex guide dogs) No smoking in restaurant Last d 9.30pm **CARDS:**

FLEET Hampshire **Map 04 SU85**

★★★ ***Lismoyne***

Church Rd GU13 8NA

Quality Percentage Score: 62%

☎ 01252 628555 📠 01252 811761

Dir: *approach town on B3013, cross over railway bridge and continue to town centre. Pass through traffic lights & take fourth right. Hotel 0.25m on left*

The Lismoyne is popular with commercial guests who appreciate the spacious, quiet rooms. Situated in a residential area in its own extensive grounds but close to Fleet centre. The restaurant serves a good range of dishes, room service is also an option. The newly refurbished lounge and bar are comfortable.

ROOMS: 44 en suite (bth/shr) (3 fmly) No smoking in 13 bedrooms **MEALS:** V meals Coffee am Tea pm **FACILITIES:** CTV in all bedrooms ch fac **CONF:** Thtr 150 Class 105 Board 50 **SERVICES:** Night porter 120P **NOTES:** No smoking in restaurant Last d 9.30pm

CARDS:

FLEET MOTORWAY SERVICE AREA (M3) Hampshire **Map 04 SU75**

Welcome Lodge

Welcome Break- Fleet, M3 RG27 8BN

☎ 01252 815587 📠 01252 815587

Dir: *between junct 4a & 5 westbound M3*

This modern building offers accommodation in smart, spacious and well equipped bedrooms, suitable for families and businessmen, and all with en-suite bathrooms. Refreshments may be taken at the nearby family restaurant. For details of current prices, consult the Contents Page under Hotel Groups for the Welcome Break phone number.

ROOMS: 60 en suite (bth/shr) d fr £50 *

FLITWICK Bedfordshire **Map 04 TL03**

★★★ **Flitwick Manor**

Church Rd MK45 1AE

Quality Percentage Score: 79%

☎ 0500 636943 (Central Res) 📠 01773 880321

Dir: *on A5120, 2m from M1 exit 12 towards Ampthill*

A delightful 17th-century mansion, elegant comfortably furnished public rooms are enhanced by paintings and log fires. Bedrooms vary in size, all individually decorated with welcome extra touches. In a choice of dining areas, imaginative dishes are

contd.

based on traditional foundations with occasional confident use of eastern flavours. Staff are cheerful and committed.

Flitwick Manor, Flitwick

ROOMS: 17 en suite (bth/shr) s £120-£145; d £145-£175 * LB Off peak **MEALS:** Lunch fr £24.50 Dinner fr £37.50 English & French Cuisine V meals Coffee am Tea pm **FACILITIES:** CTV in all bedrooms Tennis (hard) Croquet lawn Putting green Xmas **CONF:** Thtr 40 Class 30 Board 24 Del from £150 * **SERVICES:** 50P **NOTES:** No coaches No smoking in restaurant Last d 9.30pm
CARDS:

FLORE Northamptonshire — Map 04 SP66

★★★ Courtyard by Marriott Daventry

The High St NN7 4LP
Quality Percentage Score: 72%
☎ 01327 349022 🖷 01327 349017
Dir: *from junct 16 on M1, follow A45 towards Daventry. Hotel 1m on right between and Upper Heyford and Flore*

Conveniently located for the motorway and set in a rural surrounding, this modern hotel is particularly suited to the business guest. Bedrooms provide smart, soft furnishings, together with good beds and useful workspaces. Public rooms are bright and pleasing to use. The staff go about their duties in a committed and friendly manner.

ROOMS: 53 en suite (bth/shr) (7 fmly) No smoking in 19 bedrooms d £69-£75 * LB Off peak **MEALS:** Lunch £9.95 & alc Dinner £15-£25alc International Cuisine V meals Coffee am Tea pm **FACILITIES:** CTV in all bedrooms STV Gym Xmas **CONF:** Thtr 80 Class 40 Board 48 Del from £120 * **SERVICES:** Night porter 120P **NOTES:** No dogs (ex guide dogs) No smoking area in restaurant Last d 10pm **CARDS:**

FOLKESTONE Kent — Map 05 TR23

★★★ Clifton

The Leas CT20 2EB
Quality Percentage Score: 69%
☎ 01303 851231 🖷 01303 851231
Dir: *from M20 junct 13, quarter mile W of town centre on A259*

This privately owned Victorian-style hotel occupies a prime location with views across the Channel. Proprietor Mr Peter Hail continues to improve all areas and is steadily upgrading the bedrooms, most of which overlook the sea. The public areas include a comfortable, traditionally furnished lounge, a popular bar with a good range of beers and several well appointed conference rooms.

ROOMS: 80 en suite (bth/shr) (5 fmly) No smoking in 6 bedrooms s £58-£76; d £78-£98 (incl. bkfst) * LB Off peak **MEALS:** Lunch £10.25-£10.50 & alc Dinner £16.50-£17.50 & alc English & French Cuisine V meals Coffee am Tea pm **FACILITIES:** CTV in all bedrooms STV Solarium Games room Xmas **CONF:** Thtr 80 Class 72 Board 32 Del from £87.50 * **SERVICES:** Lift Night porter **NOTES:** No smoking area in restaurant Last d 9.15pm **CARDS:**

See advert on opposite page

FOLKESTONE Kent — Map 05 TR23

★★ Sandgate Hotel et Restaurant La Terrasse

The Esplanade, Sandgate CT20 3DY
Quality Percentage Score: 78%
☎ 01303 220444 🖷 01303 220496
Dir: *exit M20 junct12 (Cheriton/Tunnel) and follow directions for Sandgate, go through Sandgate on A249 towards Hythe, hotel on right facing sea*

Under the ownership of Zara and Samuel Gicqueau, this hotel goes from strength to strength. The restaurant is very much the emphasis, and a feeling of style and comfort is evident throughout the hotel. Some of the bedrooms have balconies overlooking the sea.

ROOMS: 15 en suite (bth/shr) s £44-£69; d £56-£74 (incl. bkfst) * Off peak **MEALS:** Lunch £20.50-£29.50 & alc Dinner £20.50-£29.50 & alc French Cuisine V meals Coffee am **FACILITIES:** CTV in all bedrooms Xmas **SERVICES:** Lift 4P **NOTES:** No dogs (ex guide dogs) No coaches No smoking in restaurant Last d 9.30pm Closed 2nd wk Jan-mid Feb, 1st wk Oct, Sun evng **CARDS:**

FOLKESTONE Kent — Map 05 TR23

Travel Inn

Cherry Garden Ln CT19 4AP
☎ 01303 273620 🖷 01303 273641
Dir: *leave M20 junct 13. At 1st large rdbt take 2nd exit signed Folkestone A20, then take 1st right. Travel Inn on right 200yds*

This modern building offers accommodation in smart, spacious and well equipped bedrooms, all with en-suite bathrooms. Refreshments may be taken at the nearby family restaurant. For details about current prices consult the Contents Page under Hotel Groups for the Travel Inn phone number.

ROOMS: 40 en suite (bth/shr) d £39.95 *

FONTWELL West Sussex — Map 04 SU90

Travelodge

BN18 0SB
☎ 01243 543973 🖷 01243 543973
Dir: *on A27/A29 roundabout*

This modern building offers accommodation in smart, spacious and well equipped bedrooms, all with en-suite bathrooms. Refreshments may be taken at the nearby family restaurant. For details about current prices, consult the Contents Page under Hotel Groups for the Travelodge phone number.

ROOMS: 63 en suite (bth/shr) d £45.95 *

FORDINGBRIDGE Hampshire — Map 04 SU11

★★ *Ashburn Hotel & Restaurant*

Station Rd SP6 1JP
Quality Percentage Score: 70%
☎ 01425 652060 🖷 01425 652150
Dir: *from Fordingbridge High St follow road signposted Damerham. Pass police and fire station and hotel is 400yds on left-hand side*

Located on the edge of the charming village, this traditional

contd.

family-run hotel provides a range of comfortable, well equipped bedrooms, many of which look out over the New Forest. In addition to the attractive dining room and residents' lounge, a heated outdoor swimming pool is a bonus.
ROOMS: 20 en suite (bth/shr) (3 fmly) No smoking in 10 bedrooms **MEALS:** English & French Cuisine V meals Coffee am Tea pm **FACILITIES:** CTV in all bedrooms Outdoor swimming pool (heated) **CONF:** Thtr 150 Class 80 Board 50 **SERVICES:** 60P **NOTES:** No smoking in restaurant Last d 9.30pm **CARDS:**

FOREST ROW East Sussex — Map 05 TQ43

The Premier Collection

★★★★ Ashdown Park
Wych Cross RH18 5JR
☎ 01342 824988 Fax 01342 826206
Dir: *take A264 to East Grinstead, then A22 to Eastbourne, 2miles south of Forest Row at Wych Cross, turn left to Hartfield, hotel situated on right*
A splendid country house overlooking a lake and set in fine grounds, Ashdown Park has some some wonderful features such as the chapel with stained glass windows. Bedrooms are spacious and decorated in traditional style. The kitchen provides classically based dishes with light touches.
ROOMS: 95 en suite (bth/shr) s £115-£295; d £145-£305 (incl. bkfst) * LB Off peak **MEALS:** Lunch £15-£23 & alc Dinner £23-£33 International Cuisine V meals Coffee am Tea pm **FACILITIES:** CTV in all bedrooms STV Indoor swimming pool (heated) Golf 18 Tennis (hard) Snooker Sauna Solarium Gym Croquet lawn Putting green Jacuzzi/spa Indoor golf Beauty therapy Hair salon Wkly live entertainment Xmas **CONF:** Thtr 150 Class 60 Board 60 Del from £205 * **SERVICES:** Lift Night porter 149P **NOTES:** No dogs (ex guide dogs) No smoking in restaurant Last d 10pm
CARDS:

See advert under GATWICK AIRPORT (LONDON)

FORMBY Merseyside — Map 07 SD30

★★★ Tree Tops
Southport Old Rd L37 0AB
Quality Percentage Score: 62%
☎ 01704 572430 Fax 01704 572430
Dir: *off A565 Southport to Liverpool road*
The Tree Tops provides chalet-style accommodation adjacent to the main building, an outdoor swimming pool and a permanent marquee used for functions. Bedrooms are well equipped, larger rooms are particularly suitable for families. The lounge bar is comfortably furnished and the restaurant, with attractive conservatory extension, serves carefully prepared meals from an extensive menu.
ROOMS: 11 en suite (bth/shr) (2 fmly) s £53-£68; d £90-£110 (incl. bkfst) * LB Off peak **MEALS:** Lunch £8.50-£12.50 & alc Dinner £8.50 & alc English & French Cuisine V meals Coffee am **FACILITIES:** CTV in all bedrooms Outdoor swimming pool (heated) **CONF:** Thtr 200 Class 80 Board 40 Del £90 * **SERVICES:** 100P **NOTES:** No dogs No smoking area in restaurant Last d 9.30pm **CARDS:**

See advert under SOUTHPORT

FORTON MOTORWAY SERVICE AREA (M6) Lancashire — Map 07 SD55

Travelodge
White Carr Ln, Bay Horse LA2 9DU
☎ 01524 792227 Fax 01524 791703
Dir: *between juncts 32 & 33 M6*
This modern building offers accommodation in smart, spacious and well equipped bedrooms, all with en-suite bathrooms. Refreshments may be taken at the nearby family restaurant. For details about current prices, consult the Contents Page under Hotel Groups for the Travelodge phone number.
ROOMS: 53 en suite (bth/shr) d £49.95 *

FOSSEBRIDGE Gloucestershire — Map 04 SP01

★★ Fossebridge Inn
GL54 3JS
Quality Percentage Score: 67%
☎ 01285 720721 Fax 01285 720793
Dir: *from M4 junct 15 take A419 towards Cirencester, then take A429 towards Stow. Hotel approx 7m on left.*
The Bridge Bar dates from the 15th century, and has kept features such as its old beams, Yorkstone floors and inglenook

contd.

fireplace. There are good bar meals, and the restaurant offers an enjoyable fixed-price menu. Bedrooms are divided between the main inn and a converted stable block.
ROOMS: 11 en suite (bth/shr) (1 fmly) No smoking in all bedrooms s £49.50; d £79.50 (incl. bkfst) * LB Off peak **MEALS:** Sunday Lunch £5.95-£11.95alc Dinner £7.25-£15.95alc V meals Coffee am **FACILITIES:** CTV in all bedrooms Fishing Xmas **CONF:** Thtr 60 Class 30 Board 30 **SERVICES:** 60P **NOTES:** No coaches No smoking in restaurant Last d 9.30pm **CARDS:**

FOUR MARKS Hampshire **Map 04 SU63**
Travelodge
156 Winchester Rd GU34 5HZ
☎ 01420 562659 01420 562659
Travelodge
Dir: *5m S of Alton on the A31, northbound*
This modern building offers accommodation in smart, spacious and well equipped bedrooms, all with en-suite bathrooms. Refreshments may be taken at the nearby family restaurant. For details about current prices, consult the Contents Page under Hotel Groups for the Travelodge phone number.
ROOMS: 31 en suite (bth/shr) d £45.95 *

FOWEY Cornwall & Isles of Scilly **Map 02 SX15**
★★★ Fowey
The Esplanade PL23 1HX
Quality Percentage Score: 71%
☎ 01726 832551 01726 832125
Dir: *turn off A390 onto B3269 for approx 5m, straight across rdbt signposted Fowey and continue along Polvillion Rd for 0.75m. Second right*

This attractive hotel is perched above the estuary, with marvellous views of the river from the public areas and the majority of the bedrooms. High standards of appointment and decor are evident throughout the property. Public areas include a spacious bar, elegant restaurant and smart new drawing room. Imaginative dinners, making use of local ingredients, are enjoyed by regular visitors.
ROOMS: 21 en suite (bth/shr) No smoking in 1 bedroom d £98-£144 (incl. bkfst & dinner) * LB Off peak **MEALS:** Lunch £10.95 Dinner £23.95 English & French Cuisine V meals Coffee am Tea pm **FACILITIES:** CTV in all bedrooms Fishing Jacuzzi/spa ch fac Xmas **CONF:** Thtr 80 Class 20 Board 20 Del from £79.45 * **SERVICES:** Lift 20P **NOTES:** No smoking in restaurant Last d 9.30pm
CARDS:

FOWEY Cornwall & Isles of Scilly **Map 02 SX15**
★★★ Fowey Hall
Hanson Dr PL23 1ET
☎ 01726 833866 01726 834100
Dir: *on arriving in Fowey cross mini rdbt continue until you descend into town centre. Pass school on right after 400mtrs right into Hanson Drive*
Built in 1899, this listed mansion above the estuary looks out into the English Channel. Imaginatively designed bedrooms offer charm and sumptuous comfort. Beautifully appointed public rooms include the wood panelled dining room where accomplished cuisine is served. Families are a priority with a range of facilities to entertain children of all ages. The grounds have a covered pool and sunbathing area.
ROOMS: 17 en suite (bth/shr) 8 annexe en suite (bth/shr) (18 fmly) s £90-£170; d £125-£245 (incl. bkfst) * LB Off peak **MEALS:** Sunday Lunch fr £15.95 High tea fr £5 Dinner fr £29.50 V meals Coffee am Tea pm **FACILITIES:** CTV in all bedrooms STV Indoor swimming pool (heated) Pool table Croquet lawn ch fac Xmas **CONF:** Thtr 35 Class 12 Board 18 Del from £130 * **SERVICES:** Night porter 40P **NOTES:** No smoking in restaurant Last d 9.45pm
CARDS:

FOWEY Cornwall & Isles of Scilly **Map 02 SX15**
★★ Marina
Esplanade PL23 1HY
Quality Percentage Score: 73%
☎ 01726 833315 01726 832779
Dir: *drive into town down Lostwithiel Street, near bottom of hill turn right into Esplanade*

This charming Georgian property has many original features. Along with separate lounges and a bar, the Waterside Restaurant has an extensive carte or daily, fixed-priced menu with local seafood a speciality. Bedrooms have a range of equipment, many benefit from sea views and some have balconies.
ROOMS: 11 en suite (bth/shr) s £52-£60; d £72-£104 (incl. bkfst) * LB Off peak **MEALS:** Dinner £12-£18 & alc English & French Cuisine V meals Coffee am **FACILITIES:** CTV in all bedrooms Fishing Sailing **NOTES:** No dogs (ex guide dogs) No coaches No smoking in restaurant Last d 8.30pm Closed 15 Dec-28 Feb **CARDS:**
See advert on opposite page

FOWNHOPE Herefordshire **Map 03 SO53**
★★ Green Man Inn
HR1 4PE
Quality Percentage Score: 67%
☎ 01432 860243 01432 860207
Dir: *on B4224 midway between Ross-on-Wye and Hereford*
This charming village inn dates back to 1485 and has a wealth of character. Well-equipped accommodation includes bedrooms on ground-floor level, family rooms, and one room with a four-poster bed. Some bedrooms are located in two separate cottage-style buildings. There are two lounges for residents, a choice of bars, and a restaurant with a beamed ceiling. Other facilities include a beer garden and a play area for children. At the time of our last inspection, the construction of a leisure centre with a swimming pool was nearing completion.
ROOMS: 10 en suite (bth/shr) 9 annexe en suite (bth/shr) (3 fmly) s £35.50-£36.50; d £56-£57.50 (incl. bkfst) * LB Off peak **MEALS:** Sunday Lunch £10.95 Dinner £13-£17.50alc V meals Coffee am Tea pm **FACILITIES:** CTV in all bedrooms STV Fishing Xmas **CONF:** Thtr 40 Class 60 Board 30 **SERVICES:** 75P **NOTES:** No smoking in restaurant Last d 9pm **CARDS:**

FRADDON Cornwall & Isles of Scilly **Map 02 SW95**
Travel Inn
Penhale TR9 6NA
01726 861148 01726 861336
Dir: *on A30 2m S of Indian Queens*
This modern building offers accommodation in smart, spacious and well equipped bedrooms, all with en-suite bathrooms. Refreshments may be taken at the nearby family restaurant. For details about current prices consult the Contents Page under Hotel Groups for the Travel Inn phone number.
ROOMS: 40 en suite (bth/shr) d £39.95 *

FRANKLEY MOTORWAY SERVICE AREA (M5) West Midlands **Map 07 SO98**
Travelodge
Illey Ln, Frankley Motorway Service Area, Frankley B32 4AR
0121 550 3131
Dir: *between junc 3 and 4 on southbound carriageway of M5*
This modern building offers accommodation in smart, spacious and well equipped bedrooms, all with en-suite bathrooms. Refreshments may be taken at the nearby family restaurant. For details about current prices, consult the Contents Page under Hotel Groups for the Travelodge phone number.
ROOMS: 62 en suite (bth/shr) d £49.95 *

FRINTON-ON-SEA Essex **Map 05 TM21**
★★ Maplin
Esplanade CO13 9EL
Quality Percentage Score: 71%
01255 673832 01255 673832
Dir: *from A133 towards Clacton, follow local signs to Frinton B1033. Turn at level crossing on to Connaught Av at end turn right onto Esplanade*
An impressive house, built in 1911, at the quiet end of the esplanade. Guests show their appreciation of the hospitality here by returning again and again. Bedrooms are attractively furnished to a high standard, and some have spa baths. Public areas feature beautiful oak panelling and leaded windows.
ROOMS: 11 rms (10 bth/shr) (2 fmly) s £57.50-£85; d £90-£105 (incl. bkfst) * LB Off peak **MEALS:** English & French Cuisine V meals Coffee am **FACILITIES:** CTV in all bedrooms Outdoor swimming pool (heated) Xmas **CONF:** Thtr 35 Class 20 Board 30 Del from £90 * **SERVICES:** 12P **NOTES:** No coaches No smoking in restaurant Last d 9pm Closed Jan **CARDS:**

FRODSHAM Cheshire **Map 07 SJ57**
★★★ Forest Hill Hotel & Leisure Complex
Bellemonte Rd, Overton Hill WA6 6HH
Quality Percentage Score: 67%
01928 735255 01928 735517
Dir: *at Frodsham turn onto B5151 after 1m turn right into Manley Rd after 0.5m turn right into Simons Ln. Hotel 0.5m along road past Frodsham golf course*
This purpose built complex near Frodsham stands at the top of Overton Hill, and many of the well equipped bedrooms enjoy spectacular views of both the Mersey estuary and the Cheshire plains. Family, executive and ground floor rooms are all available, along with a choice of bars, a well equipped leisure centre, and conference facilities.
ROOMS: 57 en suite (bth/shr) (4 fmly) No smoking in 5 bedrooms d £87 * LB Off peak **MEALS:** Lunch £10.25-£15 Dinner £18-£25 International Cuisine V meals Coffee am Tea pm **FACILITIES:** CTV in all bedrooms STV Indoor swimming pool (heated) Squash Snooker Sauna Solarium Gym Jacuzzi/spa Nightclub Wkly live entertainment ch fac Xmas **CONF:** Thtr 200 Class 80 Board 48 Del from £120 * **SERVICES:** Night porter 350P **NOTES:** No smoking in restaurant Last d 10pm **CARDS:**

FROME Somerset — Map 03 ST74
★★ The George at Nunney
11 Church St BA11 4LW
Quality Percentage Score: 68%
☎ 01373 836458 Fax 01373 836565
(For full entry see Nunney)

GARFORTH West Yorkshire — Map 08 SE43
★★★ Milford Lodge
A1 Great North Rd, Peckfield LS25 5LQ
Quality Percentage Score: 69%
☎ 01977 681800 Fax 01977 681245
Dir: *on the southbound carriageway of the A1, E of Leeds where A63 joins A1 from Leeds*
Milford Lodge is well equipped to meet the needs of both business users and passing leisure guests. There is a good range of well furnished bedrooms. Public rooms include an open plan bar and restaurant. Service is helpful and relaxed. Imaginative fare is served in the restaurant.
ROOMS: 47 en suite (bth/shr) (10 fmly) No smoking in 19 bedrooms d £49-£59 * LB Off peak **MEALS:** Lunch £7.95-£16.85alc High tea £10.20-£16.85alc Dinner £15.85-£24.85alc International Cuisine V meals Coffee am Tea pm **FACILITIES:** CTV in all bedrooms STV Xmas **CONF:** Thtr 70 Class 35 Board 30 Del £85 * **SERVICES:** Night porter Air conditioning 80P **NOTES:** No smoking area in restaurant Last d 10pm **CARDS:**

See advert under LEEDS

GARSTANG Lancashire — Map 07 SD44
★★★ Pickering Park Country House
Garstang Rd, Catterall PR3 0HD
Quality Percentage Score: 67%
☎ 01995 600999 Fax 01995 602100
Dir: *from S M6 junct 32 take A6. After Esso garage turn right onto B6430 then right after bus shelter*
New owners are continuing to refurbish this comfortable hotel, a former vicarage dating from the 17th century. Bedrooms are comfortable and generally quite spacious. The lounges are attractively presented and a particular feature of this hotel is the wide range of carefully prepared dishes offered in the restaurant. The gardens to the rear are delightful.
ROOMS: 14 en suite (bth/shr) 2 annexe en suite (bth/shr) (1 fmly) s £60; d £76-£140 (incl. bkfst) * LB Off peak **MEALS:** Lunch £9.95-£16.50 & alc High tea £5-£7.50 Dinner £14.50-£16.50 & alc International Cuisine V meals Coffee am Tea pm **FACILITIES:** CTV in all bedrooms Xmas **CONF:** Thtr 65 Class 50 Board 35 Del £86 * **SERVICES:** 50P **NOTES:** No dogs (ex guide dogs) No smoking in restaurant Last d 9.30pm **CARDS:**

See advert under PRESTON

GARSTANG Lancashire — Map 07 SD44
★★★ Crofters
Cabus PR3 1PH
Quality Percentage Score: 64%
☎ 01995 604128 Fax 01995 601646
Dir: *on A6, midway between junc 32 & 33 of M6*
This family-run hotel offers spacious bedrooms, and a range of executive rooms that have additional comforts. Meals are served either in the Tavern bar, a popular meeting place for locals, or the nicely furnished Crofters Restaurant.
ROOMS: 19 en suite (bth/shr) (3 fmly) s £38-£45; d £44-£65 * Off peak **MEALS:** Sunday Lunch £10.25 Dinner £15.25-£16.25 & alc English & French Cuisine V meals Coffee am **FACILITIES:** CTV in all bedrooms STV Pool table Wkly live entertainment Xmas **CONF:** Thtr 200 Class 120 Board 50 Del from £55 * **SERVICES:** Night porter 200P **NOTES:** No smoking area in restaurant Last d 10pm **CARDS:**

GATESHEAD Tyne & Wear — Map 12 NZ26
see also **Beamish & Whickham**
★★★★ Newcastle Marriott
Metro Centre NE11 9XF
Quality Percentage Score: 68%
☎ 0191 493 2233 Fax 0191 493 2030
Dir: *on A1 follow signs for Metro Centre & then signs for Marriott Hotel*
Conveniently situated just off the Western bypass (A1), this smart modern hotel appeals to business persons, as well as attracting families visiting the nearby MetroCentre at the weekends. Bedrooms are comprehensively equipped and provide either one or two double beds. Public area offer a popular café/bar and a brasserie style restaurant, as well as an impressive range of banqueting and leisure facilities.
ROOMS: 148 en suite (bth/shr) (136 fmly) No smoking in 75 bedrooms d £83 * LB Off peak **MEALS:** Lunch £3.25-£23.45alc High tea £4.75-£7.75alc Dinner £16.50 & alc International Cuisine V meals Coffee am Tea pm **FACILITIES:** CTV in all bedrooms STV Indoor swimming pool (heated) Sauna Solarium Gym Jacuzzi/spa Health & beauty clinic Dance studio Xmas **CONF:** Thtr 450 Class 190 Board 40 Del from £120 * **SERVICES:** Lift Night porter Air conditioning 300P **NOTES:** No dogs (ex guide dogs) No smoking area in restaurant Last d 10.30pm **CARDS:**

GATESHEAD Tyne & Wear — Map 12 NZ26
★★★ Swallow
High West St NE8 1PE
Quality Percentage Score: 68%
☎ 0191 477 1105 Fax 0191 478 7214
Dir: *A1, A148 to Gateshead, follow signs for centre. At mini rdbt turn right, pass bus stn, lights, and two rdbts. Take 3rd left, hotel at bottom of rd*

Situated just across the Tyne from Newcastle city centre, this purpose-built hotel offers a good range of services provided in an efficient manner by friendly and attentive staff. The attractive modern bedrooms come in a variety of sizes, a number of smaller standard single rooms having the benefit of a double bed. There is a secure undercover car park.
ROOMS: 103 en suite (bth/shr) (12 fmly) No smoking in 40 bedrooms s £83-£99; d £99-£108 (incl. bkfst) * LB Off peak **MEALS:** Lunch £10.50-£10.95 Dinner fr £17.50 & alc International Cuisine V meals Coffee am Tea pm **FACILITIES:** CTV in all bedrooms STV Indoor swimming pool (heated) Sauna Solarium Gym Jacuzzi/spa Xmas **CONF:** Thtr 350 Class 150 Board 100 Del £112 * **SERVICES:** Lift Night porter 190P **NOTES:** No smoking in restaurant Last d 10pm **CARDS:**

★

The Premier Collection, hotels with Red Star Awards are listed on pages 17-23

GATESHEAD Tyne & Wear — Map 12 NZ26

★★❀ Eslington Villa

8 Station Rd, Low Fell NE9 6DR
Quality Percentage Score: 74%
☎ 0191 487 6017 & 420 0666 📠 0191 420 0667

Dir: *turn off A1 onto Team Valley Trading Estate, take 2nd rdbt turn right along Eastern Av then turn left just past Belle Vue Motors, hotel on left*

A friendly and relaxed atmosphere has been created by Nick and Melanie Tulip and staff at their stylish hotel which lies secluded in a residential area. Public areas are cosy and comfortable, the restaurant providing an interesting selection of well presented dishes which attracts a good local following.

ROOMS: 12 en suite (bth/shr) (2 fmly) s £45-£64.50; d £55-£74 (incl. bkfst) * Off peak **MEALS:** Lunch £9.95-£16.50 & alc Dinner £18.95-£21.50 & alc English & French Cuisine V meals **FACILITIES:** CTV in all bedrooms **SERVICES:** Night porter 15P **NOTES:** No coaches No smoking in restaurant Last d 9.45pm Closed 25-26 Dec RS Sun/BHs (restricted restaurant service) **CARDS:**

GATESHEAD Tyne & Wear — Map 12 NZ26

⇧ Travel Inn

Derwent Haugh Rd, Swalwell NE16 3BL
☎ 0191 414 6308 📠 0191 414 5032

Dir: *on the Derwent Haugh Road leading from A1/A694 intersection to Metro Centre, near Gateshead*

This modern building offers accommodation in smart, spacious and well equipped bedrooms, all with en-suite bathrooms. Refreshments may be taken at the nearby family restaurant. For details about current prices consult the Contents Page under Hotel Groups for the Travel Inn phone number.

ROOMS: 40 en suite (bth/shr) d £39.95 *

GATWICK AIRPORT (LONDON) — Map 04 TQ24

West Sussex

see also **Dorking, East Grinstead & Reigate**

★★★★❀❀ Copthorne London Gatwick

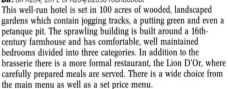

Copthorne Way RH10 3PG
Quality Percentage Score: 70%
☎ 01342 714971 📠 01342 717375

Dir: *on A264, 2m E of A264/B2036 roundabout*

This well-run hotel is set in 100 acres of wooded, landscaped gardens which contain jogging tracks, a putting green and even a petanque pit. The sprawling building is built around a 16th-century farmhouse and has comfortable, well maintained bedrooms divided into three categories. In addition to the brasserie there is a more formal restaurant, the Lion D'Or, where carefully prepared meals are served. There is a wide choice from the main menu as well as a set price menu.

ROOMS: 227 en suite (bth/shr) (10 fmly) No smoking in 98 bedrooms s fr £125; d fr £135 * LB Off peak **MEALS:** Lunch £16.95-£18.95 & alc Dinner £16.95-£25.50 & alc English & Continental Cuisine V meals Coffee am Tea pm **FACILITIES:** CTV in all bedrooms STV Indoor swimming pool (heated) Tennis (hard) Squash Solarium Gym Pool table Croquet lawn Putting green Jacuzzi/spa Petanque pit Wkly live entertainment **CONF:** Thtr 110 Class 65 Board 40 Del £160 * **SERVICES:** Lift Night porter 300P **NOTES:** No smoking area in restaurant Last d 10.30pm RS 24 Dec-4 Jan **CARDS:**

AA Rosettes are awarded for quality of food,
see page 15 for an explanation of Rosette assessment.

GATWICK AIRPORT (LONDON) Map 04 TQ24
West Sussex
★★★★ Le Meridien London Gatwick
North Terminal RH6 0PH
Quality Percentage Score: 69%
☎ 0870 4008494 📠 01293 567739
Dir: *M23 junct9, follow dual carriageway to second rdbt, hotel is large white building straight ahead*
This modern hotel, moments from the terminals, was recently refurbished to become the latest addition to Le Meridien brand. Smart rooms boast a range of facilities and high standards of guest comfort. At the time of going to press, a new executive club floor was due to open, with its own lounge and extra services. Visitors have a range of eating options, including the Brasserie, a French-style café and an Oriental restaurant. There is a useful business centre and both corporate and leisure guests will appreciate the health and fitness facilities. North terminal is accessed via a covered walkway.
ROOMS: 494 en suite (bth/shr) (36 fmly) No smoking in 228 bedrooms s £118-£145; d £128-£155 * Off peak **MEALS:** Lunch £14.50-£15.50 Dinner £18.95 European & Oriental Cuisine V meals Coffee am Tea pm **FACILITIES:** CTV in all bedrooms STV Indoor swimming pool (heated) Sauna Solarium Gym Pool table Xmas **CONF:** Thtr 250 Class 100 Board 40 Del from £130 * **SERVICES:** Lift Night porter Air conditioning **NOTES:** No smoking area in restaurant Last d 11pm
CARDS:

GATWICK AIRPORT (LONDON) Map 04 TQ24
West Sussex
★★★★ Copthorne Effingham Park
West Park Rd RH10 3EU
Quality Percentage Score: 64%
☎ 01342 714994 📠 01342 716039
Dir: *from M23 junct10, take A264 towards East Grinstead. Go straight over rdbt, at 2nd rdbt turn left along B2028. Effingham Park is on right*
There is a very good range of leisure facilities at this peacefully located hotel, set in 40 acres of grounds. It is very popular with conference organisers and for weekend functions, providing an excellent range of meeting rooms. The main restaurant is an open-plan, Mediterranean-themed brasserie, and snacks are also available in the leisure club bar. In line with company policy there are two categories of bedroom : Connoisseur and Classic, both of which are spacious and well cared for.
ROOMS: 122 en suite (bth/shr) (6 fmly) No smoking in 36 bedrooms s fr £125; d fr £135 * LB Off peak **MEALS:** Bar Lunch fr £2.50alc Dinner £13.75-£31.75alc English & Mediterranean Cuisine V meals Coffee am Tea pm **FACILITIES:** CTV in all bedrooms STV Indoor swimming pool (heated) Golf 9 Tennis (hard) Sauna Solarium Gym Croquet lawn Putting green Jacuzzi/spa Dance studio Bowls **CONF:** Thtr 600 Class 250 Board 30 Del £155 * **SERVICES:** Lift Night porter 500P **NOTES:** No dogs (ex guide dogs) No smoking in restaurant Last d 10.15pm
CARDS:

GATWICK AIRPORT (LONDON) Map 04 TQ24
West Sussex
★★★ *Stanhill Court*
Stanhill Rd, Charlwood RH6 0EP
Quality Percentage Score: 66%
☎ 01293 862166 📠 01293 862773
Dir: *N of Charlwood towards Newdigate*
With 35 acres of grounds, this baronial style hotel built in 1881 has original features such as stained glass panels. Many rooms have four-poster beds, all are individually decorated and well equipped. There is a cosy lounge, enclosed conservatory patio bar and wood-panelled restaurant, an extensive range of dishes are offered.
ROOMS: 12 en suite (bth/shr) (3 fmly) No smoking in 2 bedrooms **MEALS:** International Cuisine V meals Coffee am Tea pm **FACILITIES:** CTV in all bedrooms STV Tennis (hard) Fishing Croquet lawn ch fac **CONF:** Thtr 180 Class 60 Board 60 Del from £150 * **SERVICES:** Night porter 100P **NOTES:** No dogs (ex guide dogs) No coaches No smoking in restaurant Last d 9pm
CARDS:

GATWICK AIRPORT (LONDON) Map 04 TQ24
West Sussex
★★★ *Thistle Gatwick*
Brighton Rd RH6 8PH
Quality Percentage Score: 65%
☎ 01293 786992 📠 01293 820625
Dir: *2m N, on A23. At Shell petrol station, turn left into Horley Row, then immediately right*
This could be described as a hotel of two parts : one side comprises the original inn, parts of which date back to the 16th century, and the main part which houses meeting rooms, a restaurant with its own cocktail bar and bedrooms which provide decent levels of comfort. Like most of the hotels in the vicinity, there is a regular shuttle service to and from the airport. It has a sizeable car park.
ROOMS: 78 en suite (bth/shr) (2 fmly) No smoking in 55 bedrooms **MEALS:** International Cuisine V meals Coffee am Tea pm **FACILITIES:** CTV in all bedrooms STV Outdoor swimming pool **CONF:** Thtr 60 Class 24 Board 30 **SERVICES:** Night porter 190P **NOTES:** No smoking in restaurant Last d 9.30pm
CARDS:

GATWICK AIRPORT (LONDON) Map 04 TQ24
West Sussex
★★★ *Posthouse Gatwick Airport*
Povey Cross Rd RH6 0BA
Quality Percentage Score: 63%
☎ 01293 771621 📠 01293 771054
Dir: *from M23 junct 9 follow signs for Gatwick, then Reigate. Hotel on left after 3rd rdbt*
Suitable for both the business and leisure traveller, this bright hotel provides modern accommodation in well equipped bedrooms with en suite bathrooms.
ROOMS: 210 en suite (bth/shr) (19 fmly) No smoking in 105 bedrooms **MEALS:** International Cuisine V meals Coffee am Tea pm **FACILITIES:** CTV in all bedrooms **CONF:** Thtr 160 Class 90 Board 60 Del from £125 * **SERVICES:** Lift Night porter 300P **NOTES:** No smoking area in restaurant Last d 11pm
CARDS:

Remember to return your Prize Draw card for a chance to win one of 30 relaxing leisure breaks with Corus and Regal hotels. See inside the front cover for the card and competition details.

Indicates that the star classification has not been confirmed under the New Quality Standards, see page 7 for further information.

GATWICK AIRPORT (LONDON) West Sussex — Map 04 TQ24

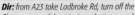

The Premier Collection

★★ Langshott Manor
Langshott Ln RH6 9LN
☎ 01293 786680 🖹 01293 783905
Dir: *from A23 take Ladbroke Rd, turn off the Chequers roundabout to Langshott, proceed for 0.75 miles, entrance to hotel on right*
This small Elizabethan manor house is set in beautiful gardens. The cosy day rooms include a morning room/bar and a gallery sitting room. Bedrooms combine modern comforts with individuality. Rosette worthy dinner is served in the beamed dining room.
ROOMS: 7 en suite (bth/shr) 8 annexe en suite (bth/shr) No smoking in all bedrooms s £125-£210; d £155-£250 (incl. bkfst) * LB Off peak **MEALS:** Lunch fr £24.95 Dinner £37.50 European Cuisine V meals Coffee am Tea pm **FACILITIES:** CTV in all bedrooms Croquet lawn Xmas **CONF:** Thtr 18 Board 12 Del from £188 * **SERVICES:** Night porter 18P **NOTES:** No dogs (ex guide dogs) No coaches No smoking in restaurant Last d 9.30pm
CARDS:

GATWICK AIRPORT (LONDON) West Sussex — Map 04 TQ24

Travel Inn
North Terminal, Longbridge Way RH6 0NX
☎ 01293 568158 🖹 01293 568278
Dir: *from M23 head for North Terminal, at rdbt take 3rd exit, hotel on right*
This modern building offers accommodation in smart, spacious and well equipped bedrooms, all with en-suite bathrooms. Refreshments may be taken at the nearby family restaurant. For details about current prices ring 01582 41 43 41.
ROOMS: 121 en suite (bth/shr) d £44.95 *

GATWICK AIRPORT (LONDON) West Sussex — Map 04 TQ24

Travelodge
Church Rd, Lowfield Heath RH11 0PQ
☎ 01293 533441 🖹 01293 535369
Dir: *1m S, off A23 junc 10 M23*
This modern building offers accommodation in smart, spacious and well equipped bedrooms, all with en-suite bathrooms. Refreshments may be taken at the nearby family restaurant. For details about current prices, consult the Contents Page under Hotel Groups for the Travelodge phone number.
ROOMS: 126 en suite (bth/shr) d £49.95 * **CONF:** Thtr 60 Class 25 Board 25

GERRARDS CROSS Buckinghamshire — Map 04 TQ08

★★★ Bull
Oxford Rd SL9 7PA
Quality Percentage Score: 68%
☎ 01753 885995 🖹 01753 885504
Dir: *from M40 junct 2 follow signs for Beaconsfield (A355). After 0.5m at rdbt take 2nd exit signed A40 Gerrards Cross for 2m to The Bull on right*
Once a favoured haunt of 17th-century highwaymen, the Bull is now firmly in modern times. Overlooking the nearby Common and within close range of the M40 and M25 the hotel has a busy corporate trade. Bedrooms are generally spacious, well equipped and furnished with good quality co-ordinated fabrics. The historic Jack Shrimpton bar is much frequented by locals, while the restaurant provides a comfortable environment in which to dine.
ROOMS: 95 en suite (bth/shr) (2 fmly) No smoking in 58 bedrooms s £120-£140; d £140-£160 * LB Off peak **MEALS:** Lunch £18-£25 High tea £3.50-£6.50 Dinner £20-£25 & alc French & International Cuisine V meals Coffee am Tea pm **FACILITIES:** CTV in all bedrooms STV Leisure facilities available nearby Wkly live entertainment **CONF:** Thtr 200 Class 88 Board 50 Del from £150 * **SERVICES:** Lift Night porter 200P **NOTES:** No dogs (ex guide dogs) No smoking area in restaurant Last d 10pm **CARDS:**

See advert on page 273

GERRARDS CROSS Buckinghamshire — Map 04 TQ08

★★ Ethorpe
Packhorse Rd SL9 8HY
Quality Percentage Score: 66%
☎ 01753 882039 🖹 01753 887012
The Ethorpe stands in its own grounds in the centre of Gerrards Cross, with good access to the motorway network and Heathrow.
contd.

Meals are served in the popular bar and the separate restaurant. Bedrooms are generally a good size, smartly furnished and well equipped.
ROOMS: 34 rms (31 bth/shr) (2 fmly) s £95; d £115-£135 * LB Off peak **MEALS:** Lunch £5.25 & alc Dinner £5-£16alc International Cuisine V meals Coffee am Tea pm **FACILITIES:** CTV in all bedrooms STV Xmas **CONF:** Thtr 30 Board 18 **SERVICES:** Night porter 80P **NOTES:** No dogs (ex guide dogs) No smoking area in restaurant Last d 10pm
CARDS:

GILLAN Cornwall & Isles of Scilly — Map 02 SW72

★★ Tregildry
TR12 6HG
Quality Percentage Score: 80%
☎ 01326 231378 01326 231561
Dir: *from Helston join the A3083 Lizard road and take first turning left for St Keverne and follow signs for Manaccan and Gillan*
Blessed with spectacular sea and pretty river views, Tregildry is a picturesque paradise. Bedrooms and lounges make the most of the wonderful views and are both tasteful and comfortable. The well appointed dining room provides the perfect surroundings to enjoy the daily changing menus. There is direct access from the hotel grounds to the beach and coastal footpath.
ROOMS: 10 en suite (bth/shr) No smoking in all bedrooms s £70; d £120-£150 (incl. bkfst & dinner) * LB Off peak **MEALS:** Dinner £24 English & French Cuisine V meals Coffee am **FACILITIES:** CTV in all bedrooms Boat hire Windsurfing **SERVICES:** 15P **NOTES:** No coaches No children 8yrs No smoking in restaurant Last d 9pm Closed Nov-Feb
CARDS:

G

GILLINGHAM Dorset — Map 03 ST82

The Premier Collection

★★★ Stock Hill Country House
Stock Hill SP8 5NR
☎ 01747 823626 & 822741 01747 825628
Dir: *3m E on B3081 off A303*
Set in 11 acres, this hotel has an impressive beech lined driveway. The bedrooms are luxurious and individually styled. There is a sumptuously furnished lounge where fine teas are served. The cuisine is an interesting blend of traditional Austrian dishes and modern ideas.
ROOMS: 6 en suite (bth/shr) 3 annexe en suite (bth/shr) s £115-£165; d £125-£150 (incl. bkfst & dinner) * LB Off peak
MEALS: Lunch £22-£25 Dinner £32-£35 Austrian Cuisine V meals Coffee am Tea pm **FACILITIES:** CTV in all bedrooms Tennis (hard) Sauna Croquet lawn Putting green Xmas **CONF:** **SERVICES:** 25P **NOTES:** No dogs No coaches No children 7yrs No smoking in restaurant Last d 8.45pm **CARDS:**

GILLINGHAM Kent — Map 05 TQ76

Travelodge
Medway Motorway Service Area, Rainham ME8 8PQ
☎ 01634 233343 01634 360848
Dir: *between juncts 4 & 5 M2*
This modern building offers accommodation in smart, spacious and well equipped bedrooms, all with en-suite bathrooms. Refreshments may be taken at the nearby family restaurant. For details about current prices, consult the Contents Page under Hotel Groups for the Travelodge phone number.
ROOMS: 58 en suite (bth/shr) d £59.95 *

GLASTONBURY Somerset — Map 03 ST53

★★ *George & Pilgrims*
1 High St BA6 9DP
Quality Percentage Score: 63%
☎ 01458 831146 01458 832252
Dir: *hotel situated in Glatonbury High Street (A39) at the bottom of the hill in Town Centre*
Right in the heart of the town, this 15th century inn is steeped in history, and behind its stone facade and mullioned windows lie a tiny lounge, a characterful bar and informal brassiere/grill with flag-stoned floor.
ROOMS: 13 en suite (bth/shr) (1 fmly) **MEALS:** V meals Coffee am Tea pm **FACILITIES:** CTV in all bedrooms **CONF:** Thtr 70 Class 35 Board 40 **NOTES:** Last d 9.30pm **CARDS:**

GLENRIDDING Cumbria — Map 11 NY31

★★★ Glenridding
CA11 0PB
Quality Percentage Score: 70%
☎ 017684 82228 017684 82555
Dir: *on A592 in village*
A friendly village hotel with views of the lake. There is a wide choice of accommodation, with a newly furbished wing offering very good quality. The smart new leisure club has a heated indoor pool, kiddies pool and sauna. Well equipped conference facilities are available. The hotel has a formal carte restaurant, a friendly pub with traditional hearty dishes and a cosy coffee shop for snacks.
ROOMS: 39 en suite (bth/shr) (6 fmly) s £74-£78; d £102-£106 (incl. bkfst) LB Off peak **MEALS:** Bar Lunch £6.50-£14alc Dinner £19-£28.50 European Cuisine V meals Coffee am Tea pm **FACILITIES:** CTV in all bedrooms STV Indoor swimming pool (heated) Sauna Pool table Jacuzzi/spa Billiards 3/4 Snooker table Xmas **CONF:** Thtr 30 Class 30 Board 20 Del from £85 * **SERVICES:** Lift 30P **NOTES:** No smoking in restaurant Last d 8.30pm **CARDS:**

GLOSSOP Derbyshire — Map 07 SK09

★★ Wind in the Willows
Derbyshire Level, Sheffield Rd SK13 7PT
Quality Percentage Score: 77%
☎ 01457 868001 01457 853354
Dir: *1m E on A57 opposite the Royal Oak*
The hospitality is warm and sincere at this charming hotel, situated at the foot of the Snake Pass. Individually designed bedrooms are comfortable and equipped with many thoughtful extras. There are two inviting lounges with warming log fires during the cooler months.
ROOMS: 12 en suite (bth/shr) s £72-£90; d £99-£117 (incl. bkfst) Off peak **MEALS:** Dinner £24 English & French Cuisine V meals Coffee am **FACILITIES:** CTV in all bedrooms **CONF:** Class 12 Board 12 Del from £127 * **SERVICES:** 16P **NOTES:** No coaches No children 10yrs No smoking in restaurant Last d 7.45pm Closed Xmas
CARDS:

GLOUCESTER Gloucestershire **Map 03 SO81**

★★★ Hatton Court

Upton Hill, Upton St Leonards GL4 8DE
Quality Percentage Score: 70%
☎ 01452 617412 Fax 01452 612945
Dir: *3m SE off B4073*

This beautifully preserved and considerably refurbished 17th-century Cotswold Manor House is set in seven acres of well maintained gardens. It stands at the top of Upton Hill, just south of the village of Upton St Leonards, commanding spectacular views of the Severn Valley. The well equipped, modern accommodation includes rooms with four-poster beds, with some bedrooms in a modern purpose-built wing adjacent to the main house. In addition, the elegant Carringtons Restaurant offers a varied choice of menus, there is a traditionally furnished bar, as well as a very comfortable foyer lounge area which is totally in character.

ROOMS: 17 en suite (bth/shr) 28 annexe en suite (bth/shr) No smoking in 2 bedrooms s £95-£105; d £110-£130 (incl. bkfst) * LB Off peak **MEALS:** Lunch fr £14.50 Dinner fr £22.50 English & French Cuisine V meals Coffee am Tea pm **FACILITIES:** CTV in all bedrooms STV Outdoor swimming pool (heated) Sauna Gym Croquet lawn Jacuzzi/spa Mini gym equipment Xmas **CONF:** Thtr 60 Class 30 Board 30 Del from £130 * **SERVICES:** Night porter 80P **NOTES:** No dogs (ex guide dogs) No smoking in restaurant Last d 9.45pm
CARDS:

See advert on this page

Symbols and Abbreviations are listed and explained on pages 4 and 5

GLOUCESTER Gloucestershire **Map 03 SO81**
★★★ Posthouse Gloucester
Crest Way, Barnwood GL4 7RX
Posthouse
Quality Percentage Score: 69%
☎ 01452 613311 01452 371036
Dir: *on A417 ring road to Barnwood, next to Cheltenham & Gloucester building*
This recently refurbished hotel is conveniently located off the Barnwood by-pass, and boasts stylish and well-equipped Millennium rooms and a good leisure complex. The relatively new Seasons restaurant rings the changes in its menus every few months.
ROOMS: 122 en suite (bth/shr) (25 fmly) No smoking in 60 bedrooms d £85-£125 * LB Off peak **MEALS:** International Cuisine V meals Coffee am Tea pm **FACILITIES:** CTV in all bedrooms STV Indoor swimming pool (heated) Sauna Solarium Gym Pool table Jacuzzi/spa Spa pool Sauna Dance Studio Xmas **CONF:** Thtr 100 Class 45 Board 40 Del from £100 * **SERVICES:** Night porter 135P **NOTES:** No smoking in restaurant Last d 10.30pm **CARDS:**

G

GLOUCESTER Gloucestershire **Map 03 SO81**
★★★ New County
44 Southgate St GL1 2DU
Quality Percentage Score: 67%
☎ 01452 307000 01452 500487

This character hotel in the heart of the city has been refurbished to offer modern comforts and bright well furnished bedrooms with good facilities. Public rooms include a small bistro-style restaurant, popular bar and spacious ballroom/function suite. A multi-storey car park is within 2 minutes' walk.
ROOMS: 39 en suite (bth/shr) (3 fmly) s £40-£60; d £50-£65 (incl. bkfst) * LB Off peak **MEALS:** Lunch £13.95 & alc Dinner £13.95 & alc International Cuisine V meals Coffee am **FACILITIES:** CTV in all bedrooms **CONF:** Thtr 130 Class 60 Board 60 Del from £75 * **SERVICES:** Night porter 10P **NOTES:** No smoking in restaurant Last d 9pm **CARDS:**

See advert on opposite page

GLOUCESTER Gloucestershire **Map 03 SO81**
★★★ Hatherley Manor
Down Hatherley Ln GL2 9QA
Quality Percentage Score: 61%
☎ 01452 730217 01452 731032
Dir: *from Gloucester, go through the village of Twigworth on the A38 & take turning for Down Hatherley, hotel 0.25m on left*
This stylish 17th-century manor is near the M5 and a good base for holidaying in the Cotswolds. Bedrooms are well equipped, and the restaurant offers a menu of mostly traditional dishes.
ROOMS: 56 en suite (bth/shr) No smoking in 6 bedrooms s £89.50-£125; d £105-£125 (incl. bkfst) * LB Off peak **MEALS:** Lunch £11.95-£13.50 Dinner fr £18.50 & alc English & French Cuisine V meals Coffee am Tea pm **FACILITIES:** CTV in all bedrooms In-house movies Xmas **CONF:** Thtr 250 Class 90 Board 70 Del £125 * **SERVICES:** Night porter 350P **NOTES:** No smoking in restaurant Last d 9.30pm
CARDS:

We endeavour to be as accurate as possible but changes in personnel and data can occur in establishments after the Hotel Guide has gone to press.

GLOUCESTER Gloucestershire **Map 03 SO81**
★ Rotherfield House
5 Horton Rd GL1 3PX
Quality Percentage Score: 63%
☎ 01452 410500 01452 381922
Dir: *adjacent to Royal Hospital*
Close to the Royal Hospital and only a mile from the city centre, this large Victorian house is privately owned and personally run. It provides well equipped bedrooms and attractive public rooms.
ROOMS: 13 rms (8 shr) (2 fmly) s £25-£36; d £48-£52 (incl. bkfst) * LB Off peak **MEALS:** Dinner £11 & alc English, Continental & Indian Cuisine V meals Coffee am Tea pm **FACILITIES:** CTV in all bedrooms **SERVICES:** 9P **NOTES:** No coaches No smoking in restaurant Last d 7.30pm **CARDS:**

GLOUCESTER Gloucestershire **Map 03 SO81**
⌂ Travel Inn (Gloucester Longford)
Tewkesbury Rd, Longford GL2 9BE
☎ 01452 523519 01452 300924
Dir: *on A38 between Longford and Gloucester*
This modern building offers accommodation in smart, spacious and well equipped bedrooms, all with en-suite bathrooms. Refreshments may be taken at the nearby family restaurant. For details about current prices consult the Contents Page under Hotel Groups for the Travel Inn phone number.
ROOMS: 40 en suite (bth/shr) d £39.95 *

GLOUCESTER Gloucestershire **Map 03 SO81**
⌂ Travel Inn (Gloucester Witcombe)
Witcombe GL3 4SS
☎ 01452 862521 01452 864926
Dir: *from junct 11A of M5 follow A417 (Cirencester) at 1st exit turn right onto A46 towards Stroud/Witcombe. Left at next rdbt by Crosshands PH*
This modern building offers accommodation in smart, spacious and well equipped bedrooms, all with en-suite bathrooms. Refreshments may be taken at the nearby family restaurant. For details about current prices consult the Contents Page under Hotel Groups for the Travel Inn phone number.
ROOMS: 39 en suite (bth/shr) d £39.95 *

GOATHLAND North Yorkshire **Map 08 NZ80**
★★ *Mallyan Spout*
YO22 5AN
Quality Percentage Score: 71%
☎ 01947 896486 01947 896327
Dir: *off A169*
Standing on the edge of a delightful moorland village, this welcoming, personally run hotel offers good service, good food and attractively furnished bedrooms. Guests have a choice of lounges and bars, where snacks and light meals are available,

contd.

and there is also a pleasant, spacious restaurant serving well prepared evening meals.
ROOMS: 20 en suite (bth) 4 annexe en suite (bth) **MEALS:** English & French Cuisine V meals Coffee am Tea pm **FACILITIES:** CTV in all bedrooms **CONF:** Thtr 70 Class 70 Board 40 Del from £100 * **SERVICES:** 50P **NOTES:** Last d 8.45pm Closed 25 Dec
CARDS:

See advert on this page

GOATHLAND North Yorkshire **Map 08 NZ80**
★★ Inn On The Moor
YO22 5LZ
Quality Percentage Score: 70%
☎ 01947 896296 01947 896484
***Dir:** off A169 between Whitby and Pickering*
The kitchen garden of this traditional hotel provides some of the produce served in the restaurant. Bedrooms are generally spacious and well furnished. There is a delightful conservatory and an elegant dining room. The service is both friendly and attentive.
ROOMS: 24 en suite (bth/shr) (2 fmly) s £46-£48 (incl. bkfst) * LB Off peak **MEALS:** Lunch £10.50-£12.50 & alc Dinner £19.50-£38 & alc English, French & Italian Cuisine V meals Coffee am Tea pm **FACILITIES:** CTV in all bedrooms STV Pool table Putting green ch fac **CONF:** Thtr 60 Class 20 Board 30 Del from £54 * **SERVICES:** 40P **NOTES:** Last d 8.30pm Closed 16 Dec-12 Jan
CARDS:

GOLANT Cornwall & Isles of Scilly **Map 02 SX15**
★★ Cormorant
PL23 1LL
Quality Percentage Score: 68%
☎ 01726 833426 01726 833426
***Dir:** in village bear right on approaching the estuary and follow the coastline to hotel via a steep drive on right*

This delightful hotel lies above the fishing village of Golant with unforgettable views over the Fowey Estuary. The bedrooms are equipped with period furnishings and all have full length picture windows that take full advantage of the views. A spacious lounge complete with log fire is available and there is an indoor swimming pool. Local fish features on the menu, and the quality of the cooking has achieved wide recognition.
ROOMS: 11 en suite (bth/shr) s £58.50; d £92 (incl. bkfst) * LB Off peak **MEALS:** Dinner fr £19 & alc English & French Cuisine V meals Coffee am Tea pm **FACILITIES:** CTV in all bedrooms Indoor swimming pool (heated) Boating Xmas **SERVICES:** 20P **NOTES:** Last d 9pm
CARDS:

See advert under FOWEY

GOMERSAL West Yorkshire — Map 08 SE22

★★★ *Gomersal Park*
Moor Ln BD19 4LJ
Quality Percentage Score: 67%
☎ 01274 869386 🖷 01274 861042
Dir: *take A62 towards Huddersfield, at junct with A651 (by Greyhound Pub) turn right, after approx 1m take first right after Oakwell Hall*
Built around a 19th century house, this modern hotel enjoys a peaceful location in its own grounds. A comfortable lounge is provided, and imaginative meals are served in the Harlequin restaurant. Bedrooms are well equipped and there is also a leisure centre and a variety of function rooms.
ROOMS: 52 en suite (bth/shr) (4 fmly) No smoking in 14 bedrooms **MEALS:** English & Continental Cuisine V meals Coffee am Tea pm **FACILITIES:** CTV in all bedrooms STV Indoor swimming pool (heated) Sauna Solarium Gym Jacuzzi/spa 5 a side football pitch **CONF:** Thtr 220 Class 130 Board 60 **SERVICES:** Night porter 220P **NOTES:** Last d 10pm **CARDS:**

G

GOMERSAL West Yorkshire — Map 08 SE22

★★ Gomersal Lodge
Spen Ln BD19 4PJ
Quality Percentage Score: 63%
☎ 01274 861111 🖷 01274 861111
Dir: *M62 junct 26, take A638 to Cleakheaton, 2nd lights turn left along Peg Lane leading to Spen Lane. Hotel on left just after Old Saw Pub on right*
Standing in 5 acres of grounds this 19th century house offers well furnished bedrooms together with a cosy bar and a pleasant restaurant. A good range of dishes are available and service is polite and friendly.
ROOMS: 9 en suite (shr) (1 fmly) No smoking in 4 bedrooms s £39-£43; d fr £55 * Off peak **MEALS:** Lunch £8.50-£13.95 & alc High tea £5-£10 Dinner £9.95-£13.95 & alc V meals Coffee am Tea pm **FACILITIES:** CTV in all bedrooms **CONF:** Thtr 20 Class 12 Board 12 Del from £60 * **SERVICES:** Night porter 70P **NOTES:** No dogs (ex guide dogs) No smoking in restaurant Last d 8.45pm **CARDS:**

GOODRICH Herefordshire — Map 03 SO51

★★ *Ye Hostelrie*
HR9 6HX
Quality Percentage Score: 68%
☎ 01600 890241 🖷 01600 890838
Dir: *1m off the A40, between Ross-on-Wye/Monmouth, within 100yds of Goodrich Castle*
Parts of this unusual building are reputed to date back to 1625. Considerable improvements to both the accommodation and public areas have been made since the Browns took over in 1996, and there is a pleasant garden and patio area.
ROOMS: 6 en suite (bth/shr) (2 fmly) **MEALS:** English & French Cuisine V meals Coffee am Tea pm **FACILITIES:** CTV in all bedrooms ch fac **CONF:** Thtr 60 Class 40 Board 30 **SERVICES:** 32P **NOTES:** No smoking in restaurant Last d 9.30pm **CARDS:**

GOODRINGTON See **Paignton**

GOODWOOD West Sussex — Map 04 SU80

★★★★ Marriott Goodwood Park
PO18 0QB
Quality Percentage Score: 69%
☎ 01243 775537 🖷 01243 520120
Dir: *off the A285, 3m NE of Chichester*
Close to the racecourse and part of the Goodwood Estate, this hotel offers smartly decorated, well equipped accommodation. There are very good leisure facilities, and a choice of eating styles: a sports cafe, and a formal dining room.

ROOMS: 94 en suite (bth/shr) (1 fmly) No smoking in 66 bedrooms s £74-£89; d £88-£118 (incl. bkfst) * LB Off peak **MEALS:** Lunch £15-£19.95 High tea £2.50-£13.90 Dinner fr £25 V meals Tea pm **FACILITIES:** CTV in all bedrooms STV Indoor swimming pool (heated) Golf 18 Tennis (hard) Sauna Solarium Gym Putting green Jacuzzi/spa Beauty salons Xmas **CONF:** Thtr 150 Class 60 Board 60 Del from £120 * **SERVICES:** Night porter 250P **NOTES:** No smoking in restaurant Last d 9.30pm **CARDS:**

GOOLE East Riding of Yorkshire — Map 08 SE72

★★ Clifton
155 Boothferry Rd DN14 6AL
Quality Percentage Score: 70%
☎ 01405 761336 🖷 01405 762350
Dir: *Leave M62 junct 36 & follow town centre signs. At 2nd set of traffic lights turn right into Boothferry Rd. Hotel is on left*
Friendly and attentive service is a feature of this well furnished and comfortable small hotel. Convenient for the town centre, it offers well equipped bedrooms. Public rooms are inviting; a cosy lounge and a small bar complement an attractive restaurant offering a good choice of dishes.
ROOMS: 9 rms (8 bth/shr) (1 fmly) s fr £42; d fr £49 (incl. bkfst) * LB Off peak **MEALS:** Lunch £8.60-£22.75alc Dinner £8.60-£22.75alc English & Continental Cuisine V meals Coffee am **FACILITIES:** CTV in all bedrooms **CONF:** Thtr 40 Class 20 Board 20 **SERVICES:** 8P **NOTES:** No smoking in restaurant **CARDS:**

GORDANO MOTORWAY SERVICE AREA (M5) Somerset — Map 03 ST57

Welcome Lodge
BS20 9XG
☎ 01275 373709 🖷 01275 374104
Dir: *M5 junct 19*
This modern building offers accommodation in smart, spacious and well equipped bedrooms, suitable for families and businessmen, and all with en-suite bathrooms. Refreshments may be taken at the nearby family restaurant. For details of current prices, consult the Contents Page under Hotel Groups for the Welcome Break phone number.
ROOMS: 62 en suite (bth/shr) d fr £45 *

GORLESTON-ON-SEA See **Great Yarmouth**

GOSFORTH Cumbria — Map 11 NY00

★★ Westlakes
CA20 1HP
Quality Percentage Score: 69%
☎ 019467 25221 🖷 019467 25099
Dir: *junc of A595 and B5344*
Warm hospitality is assured at this Georgian country mansion. There is an inviting lounge bar, and an attractive dining room

contd.

comprising three rooms, one of which is ideal for private parties. Bedrooms in the original house are traditional in character, while the three in the extension follow a modern theme. A wide ranging menu is on offer which does not disappoint.
ROOMS: 9 en suite (bth/shr) (1 fmly) s £49.50; d £56.50 (incl. bkfst) * Off peak **MEALS:** Lunch £14-£24.50alc Dinner £14-£24.50alc English & French Cuisine V meals **FACILITIES:** CTV in all bedrooms STV ch fac **SERVICES:** 25P **NOTES:** No dogs (ex guide dogs) No coaches No smoking in restaurant Last d 9pm **CARDS:**

GRANGE-OVER-SANDS Cumbria **Map 07 SD47**
★★★ Netherwood
Lindale Rd LA11 6ET
Quality Percentage Score: 69%
☎ 015395 32552 Fax 015395 34121
Dir: *on B5277 just before the station*
Boasting panoramic views across Morecambe Bay, this Georgian mansion has been tastefully extended to provide a restaurant, swimming pool, fitness centre, and banqueting centre, popular for small conferences and weddings. Features retained from the original house include magnificent oak panelling, roaring log fires and mullioned windows throughout. There is a range of bedroom sizes; all rooms offer stylish Italian furniture and smart modern bathrooms.
ROOMS: 28 en suite (bth/shr) (5 fmly) No smoking in 14 bedrooms s £50-£60; d £100-£120 (incl. bkfst) * LB Off peak **MEALS:** Lunch £15.50-£16.50 High tea £9.75-£11 Dinner £23-£25 English & French Cuisine V meals Coffee am Tea pm **FACILITIES:** CTV in all bedrooms Indoor swimming pool (heated) Solarium Gym Croquet lawn Jacuzzi/spa Beauty salon Steam room ch fac **CONF:** Thtr 150 Class 30 Board 40 Del from £85 * **SERVICES:** Lift Night porter 160P **NOTES:** No smoking in restaurant Last d 8.30pm **CARDS:**

GRANGE-OVER-SANDS Cumbria **Map 07 SD47**
★★★ Graythwaite Manor
Fernhill Rd LA11 7JE
Quality Percentage Score: 64%
☎ 015395 32001 & 33755 Fax 015395 35549
Dir: *follow B5277 through Grange, Fernhill Road opposite fire station behind small traffic island, hotel first left*
Standing in superb landscaped gardens above the town, this welcoming hotel enjoys lovely views. Public areas are comfortable and include a choice of relaxing lounges and an attractive restaurant. The stylishly furnished bedrooms vary in size and style. Cooking remains the highlight of any visit with ambitious dishes served in the elegantly appointed dining room.

ROOMS: 21 en suite (bth/shr) (2 fmly) s £50-£60; d £90-£100 (incl. bkfst) * LB Off peak **MEALS:** Lunch £9.50-£12.50 & alc Dinner £18-£21 & alc English & French Cuisine V meals Coffee am Tea pm **FACILITIES:** CTV in all bedrooms Tennis (hard) Fishing Putting green 3/4 size billiard table Xmas **SERVICES:** 32P **NOTES:** No dogs (ex guide dogs) No coaches No smoking in restaurant Last d 8.30pm Closed 4-24 Jan **CARDS:**

GRANGE-OVER-SANDS Cumbria **Map 07 SD47**
★★ Hampsfell House
Hampsfell Rd LA11 6BG
Quality Percentage Score: 64%
☎ 015395 32567 Fax 015395 35995
Dir: *M6 junct 36, take exit A590 signed Barrow-in-Furness. Continue to junct with B5277 and follow to Grange-over-Sands*
Handy for the town and local amenities, this friendly hotel is situated in its own gardens off a quiet wooded lane. There are two cosy lounges served by one bar, and the well maintained bedrooms are bright and cheerful.
ROOMS: 9 en suite (bth/shr) (1 fmly) No smoking in 3 bedrooms s £30-£35; d £60-£70 (incl. bkfst) LB Off peak **MEALS:** V meals Coffee am Tea pm **FACILITIES:** CTV in all bedrooms Xmas **SERVICES:** 12P **NOTES:** No coaches No children 5yrs No smoking in restaurant Last d 8.15pm **CARDS:**

GRANGE-OVER-SANDS Cumbria **Map 07 SD47**
★ Clare House
Park Rd LA11 7HQ
Quality Percentage Score: 76%
☎ 015395 33026 & 34253
Dir: *turn off A590 onto B5277, through Lindale onto Grange, hotel 0.5m on left past Crown Hill/St Paul's Church*
This family-run hotel stands in beautiful secluded gardens. All the bedrooms are furnished to a high standard of comfort, some have balconies, and most enjoy delightful views across Morecambe Bay. There is a choice of lounges, and very good food is served in the dining room, with breakfast a speciality.
ROOMS: 17 rms (16 bth/shr) (1 fmly) s £48; d £96 (incl. bkfst & dinner) * LB Off peak **MEALS:** Dinner £21 English & French Cuisine Coffee am Tea pm **FACILITIES:** CTV in all bedrooms Croquet lawn Putting green **SERVICES:** 18P **NOTES:** No dogs (ex guide dogs) No coaches No children 5yrs No smoking in restaurant Last d 7.15pm Closed Nov-Mar

GRANTHAM Lincolnshire **Map 08 SK93**

★★★ Swallow
SWALLOW HOTELS
Swingbridge Rd NG31 7XT
Quality Percentage Score: 73%
☎ 01476 593000 Fax 01476 592592
Dir: *junc of A1 southbound with A607*
This modern hotel has extensive public rooms which are particularly comfortable and spacious, in the summer they extend into a pretty courtyard. Bedrooms are attractively presented and well equipped; two rooms have been specially
contd.

For Useful Information and Important Telephone Number Changes turn to page 25

designed for disabled guests and family rooms are available. There is a full range of conference and leisure facilities.
ROOMS: 90 en suite (bth/shr) (6 fmly) No smoking in 55 bedrooms s fr £95; d fr £110 (incl. bkfst) * LB Off peak **MEALS:** Lunch £9.50-£20.50 High tea fr £5.50 Dinner fr £20.50 English & French Cuisine V meals Coffee am Tea pm **FACILITIES:** CTV in all bedrooms STV Indoor swimming pool (heated) Sauna Gym Jacuzzi/spa Steam room Wkly live entertainment **CONF:** Thtr 200 Class 90 Board 50 Del from £125 * **SERVICES:** Night porter 150P **NOTES:** No smoking in restaurant Last d 10pm **CARDS:**

GRANTHAM Lincolnshire **Map 08 SK93**
★★★ Kings
North Pde NG31 8AU
Quality Percentage Score: 67%
☎ 01476 590800 Fax 01476 590800
Dir: *turn off A1 at rdbt northern end of Grantham onto B1174, follow road for 2m. Hotel on left by rail bridge*
This much extended Georgian house offers accommodation of a high standard in attractively decorated bedrooms. The Orangery, which serves as a coffee shop and breakfast room, is popular with residents and locals, as is the more formal Victorian restaurant. There is also a comfortable open-plan foyer lounge and bar.
ROOMS: 21 en suite (bth/shr) (1 fmly) s £43-£48; d £53-£58 (incl. bkfst) * LB Off peak **MEALS:** Lunch £10.75-£13.75 & alc Dinner £13.75 & alc English & French Cuisine V meals Coffee am Tea pm **FACILITIES:** CTV in all bedrooms STV Tennis (hard) Special rates at leisure club ch fac **CONF:** Thtr 100 Class 50 Board 40 Del from £73 * **SERVICES:** Night porter 36P **NOTES:** No smoking in restaurant Last d 10pm **CARDS:**

GRANTHAM Lincolnshire **Map 08 SK93**
Travelodge
Grantham Service Area, Grantham North, Gonerby Moor NG32 2AB
☎ 01476 577500
Dir: *4m N on A1*
This modern building offers accommodation in smart, spacious and well equipped bedrooms, all with en-suite bathrooms. Refreshments may be taken at the nearby family restaurant. For details about current prices, consult the Contents Page under Hotel Groups for the Travelodge phone number.
ROOMS: 40 en suite (bth/shr) d £39.95 *

GRASMERE Cumbria **Map 11 NY30**
★★★★ Wordsworth
LA22 9SW
Quality Percentage Score: 70%
☎ 015394 35592 Fax 015394 35765
Dir: *in centre of village adjacent to St Oswalds church*

This impressive Victorian hotel in the centre of Grasmere continues to be widely popular. The richly furnished public rooms offer peace and serenity, whilst the gardens, swimming pool and terrace allow guests to relax all year round. The Prelude Restaurant provides an imaginative blend of traditional and contemporary dishes cooked in the modern style with fresh fish and seafood featuring strongly. Bedrooms are well appointed, with all the expected facilities.
ROOMS: 37 en suite (bth/shr) (3 fmly) s £65-£75; d £130-£170 (incl. bkfst) * LB Off peak **MEALS:** Lunch £18-£19.50 & alc Dinner £30-£32.50alc English & French Cuisine V meals Coffee am Tea pm **FACILITIES:** CTV in all bedrooms STV Indoor swimming pool (heated) Sauna Solarium Gym Pool table Croquet lawn Jacuzzi/spa Table tennis Wkly live entertainment Xmas **CONF:** Thtr 130 Class 50 Board 40 Del from £98.50 * **SERVICES:** Lift Night porter 60P **NOTES:** No dogs (ex guide dogs) No coaches No smoking in restaurant Last d 9pm **CARDS:**

See advert on opposite page

GRASMERE Cumbria **Map 11 NY30**

The Premier Collection

★★★ Michael's Nook Country House
LA22 9RP
☎ 015394 35496 Fax 015394 35645
Dir: *turn off A591 between The Swan Hotel and its car park just N of village. Hotel 400yds on right*
A fine early Victorian Lakeland hillside house. The delightful bedrooms and day rooms are furnished with fine antique prints, rugs, furniture and porcelain. Open fires burn in the elegant drawing room and cosy bar. Service is extremely friendly, discreet and professional. Excellent cuisine is available which leaves all hotel guests satisfied.
ROOMS: 14 en suite (bth/shr) (2 fmly) **MEALS:** Lunch £36.50 International Cuisine **FACILITIES:** CTV in all bedrooms Croquet lawn Use of leisure facilities at Wordsworth Hotel **CONF:** Thtr 24 Board 20 Del from £155 * **SERVICES:** 20P **NOTES:** No dogs (ex guide dogs) No coaches No smoking in restaurant
CARDS:

GRASMERE Cumbria **Map 11 NY30**
★★★ Gold Rill Country House
Red Bank Rd LA22 9PU
Quality Percentage Score: 72%
☎ 015394 35486 Fax 015394 35486
Dir: *turn off A591 into village centre, turn into road opposite St Oswalds Church. Hotel 300yds on left*
Situated in gardens in a quiet part of the village, enjoying fine open views of the lake and surrounding fells, the hotel has a relaxed and friendly atmosphere. It boasts comfortable lounges and an attractive restaurant, where steamed puddings are an

contd.

irresistible speciality. Most of the attractively decorated bedrooms take advantage of the impressive view.
ROOMS: 25 en suite (bth/shr) 3 annexe en suite (bth/shr) (2 fmly) s £57-£64; d £114-£128 (incl. bkfst & dinner) * LB Off peak
MEALS: Bar Lunch £2-£5 Dinner £19.50 V meals Coffee am
FACILITIES: CTV in all bedrooms STV Outdoor swimming pool (heated) Croquet lawn Putting green Xmas **SERVICES:** 35P **NOTES:** No dogs No coaches No smoking in restaurant Last d 8.30pm Closed mid Dec-mid Jan **CARDS:**

See advert on this page

GRASMERE Cumbria — Map 11 NY30

★★★ *Thistle Grasmere*
Keswick Rd LA22 9PR
THISTLE HOTELS
Quality Percentage Score: 70%
☎ 015394 35666 015394 35565
Dir: *on road from Ambleside just before entering the village on lake shore*
This large hotel stands in its own gardens leading to the lake and many of the bedrooms have fine views over the surrounding fells. Bedrooms are comfortably furnished and include a stylish suite, complete with a four-poster bed. Service is friendly and the choice of meals, from a selection of restaurant and bar menus, should suit most tastes.
ROOMS: 72 en suite (bth/shr) (8 fmly) No smoking in 13 bedrooms
MEALS: International Cuisine V meals Coffee am Tea pm
FACILITIES: CTV in all bedrooms STV Pool table Table tennis Rowing boats **CONF:** Thtr 110 Class 60 Board 40 **SERVICES:** Night porter 100P
NOTES: No smoking in restaurant Last d 8.45pm
CARDS:

GRASMERE Cumbria **Map 11 NY30**

★★★ Red Lion

Red Lion Square LA22 9SS

Quality Percentage Score: 69%

☎ 015394 35456 015394 35579

Dir: *turn off A591, signposted Grasmere Village, hotel is in centre of the village*

This former Grasmere coaching inn provides modern, well equipped bedrooms of varying size. There is a lively pub and buttery as well as the main restaurant, and an attractive conservatory extension to the foyer bar. Leisure facilities are good, and well designed conference facilities include ISDN.

ROOMS: 36 en suite (bth/shr) (4 fmly) s £46-£54; d £92-£108 (incl. bkfst) * Off peak **MEALS:** Bar Lunch £6-£13.25 Dinner £19 V meals Coffee am Tea pm **FACILITIES:** CTV in all bedrooms STV Sauna Solarium Gym Pool table Jacuzzi/spa Hairdressing Xmas **CONF:** Thtr 60 Class 30 Board 30 Del from £79.50 **SERVICES:** Lift 38P **NOTES:** No smoking in restaurant Last d 9pm **CARDS:**

See advert on page 279

GRASMERE Cumbria **Map 11 NY30**

★★★ Rothay Garden

Broadgate LA22 9RJ

Quality Percentage Score: 69%

☎ 015394 35334 015394 35723

Dir: *turn off A591, opposite Swan Hotel, into Grasmere village, 300 yds on left*

Located on the northern edge of the charming village of Grasmere, the Rothay Garden offers a warm welcome. Bedrooms, including some with four-poster beds and whirlpool baths, are comfortable and well equipped. Public areas offer a choice of relaxing lounges and a cosy cocktail bar, as well as a bright conservatory restaurant.

ROOMS: 26 en suite (bth/shr) (2 fmly) s £55-£59; d £110-£138 (incl. bkfst & dinner) LB Off peak **MEALS:** Lunch £10.50-£11 & alc Dinner £22 English & French Cuisine V meals Coffee am Tea pm **FACILITIES:** CTV in all bedrooms STV Fishing Jacuzzi/spa Xmas **CONF:** Thtr 25 Class 16 Board 12 Del from £90 * **SERVICES:** 38P **NOTES:** No coaches No smoking in restaurant Last d 9pm **CARDS:**

GRASMERE Cumbria **Map 11 NY30**

★★★ The Swan

LA22 9RF

Quality Percentage Score: 67%

☎ 015394 35551 015394 35741

Dir: *M6 junct36, take A590 past Windermere, follow signs for Grasmere and Keswick. The Swan Hotel is located on outskirts of village*

A 300 year old inn mentioned by Wordsworth in his poem "The Waggoner". Stylish bedrooms have every modern facility, many enjoy views of the surrounding fells. Fresh flowers decorate the lounges, which include one of Wordsworth's high-backed chairs. The Waggoners Restaurant is renowned for excellent cuisine, less formal meals are taken in the bar or Cygnet lounge.

ROOMS: 36 en suite (bth/shr) No smoking in 20 bedrooms s £70-£90; d £140-£180 (incl. bkfst & dinner) * LB Off peak **MEALS:** Lunch £12-£15 Dinner £19.95-£25 V meals Coffee am Tea pm **FACILITIES:** CTV in all bedrooms Xmas **SERVICES:** Night porter 40P **NOTES:** No smoking in restaurant Last d 9pm **CARDS:**

GRASMERE Cumbria **Map 11 NY30**

★★ *Oak Bank*

Broadgate LA22 9TA

Quality Percentage Score: 73%

☎ 015394 35217 015394 35685

Dir: *in centre of village just off A591*

A very welcoming lake district hotel. The open plan restaurant with conservatory extension serves traditional lakeland four-course dinners. There are stylish lounges with log fires. Bedrooms vary in size, with attractive decor and antique pine furniture.

ROOMS: 15 en suite (bth/shr) (1 fmly) **MEALS:** English & Continental Cuisine V meals Coffee am Tea pm **FACILITIES:** CTV in all bedrooms Jacuzzi/spa ch fac **SERVICES:** 15P **NOTES:** No coaches No smoking in restaurant Last d 8.30pm Closed Jan **CARDS:**

GRASMERE Cumbria **Map 11 NY30**

★★ Grasmere

Broadgate LA22 9TA

Quality Percentage Score: 72%

☎ 015394 35277 015394 35277

Dir: *take A591 from Ambleside, then second turning left into town centre. Follow road over humpbacked bridge, past playing field. Hotel on left*

This family-run hotel has a friendly and relaxing atmosphere. The hotel is sheltered in its own grounds stretching down to the River Rothay. Public rooms are cosy and comfortable, with two lounges (one with a residents bar) and an attractive dining room looking out on to the garden. Careful use of fresh ingredients is evident in the short but thoughtfully chosen dinner menu. Bedrooms are bright and cheerful, most are furnished in pine.

ROOMS: 12 en suite (bth/shr) s £35-£40; d £50-£60 (incl. bkfst) * LB Off peak **MEALS:** Dinner £15-£18.50 English & French Cuisine V meals Coffee am Tea pm **FACILITIES:** CTV in all bedrooms STV Croquet lawn Putting green Xmas **SERVICES:** 16P **NOTES:** No coaches No children 6yrs No smoking in restaurant Last d 8pm Closed Jan-8 Feb

CARDS:

GRASMERE Cumbria — Map 11 NY30

The Premier Collection

★ White Moss House
Rydal Water LA22 9SE
☎ 015394 35295 Fax 015394 35516
Dir: *on A591, 1m S of Grasmere*
This traditional Lakeland house was once owned by William Wordsworth, but is now an intimate country hotel. The creative approach to the classical dishes served here, and the fabulous wine list explains why so many guests regularly return. Bedrooms are all individual, and come in a variety of sizes. A two-room suite is offered in a cottage on the hillside high above the hotel. There is no bar; pre-dinner drinks are served in the lounge.
ROOMS: 7 en suite (bth/shr) 2 annexe en suite (bth/shr) s £65-£90; d £135-£180 (incl. bkfst & dinner) LB Off peak **MEALS:** Dinner £28 **FACILITIES:** CTV in all bedrooms Free use of local leisure club Free fishing at all local waters **SERVICES:** 10P **NOTES:** No dogs No coaches No smoking in restaurant Last d 8pm Closed early Dec-early Mar RS Sun **CARDS:**

GRASSINGTON North Yorkshire — Map 07 SE06

★★ *Grassington House*
5 The Square BD23 5AQ
Quality Percentage Score: 59%
☎ 01756 752406 Fax 01756 752135
Dir: *Take B6265 from Skipton, on right hand side of village square*
In a prime position in the centre of the main square, this hotel enjoys a popular following for both its bar and restaurant meals, which are freshly cooked to provide good quality fare. Bedrooms have a cottagey feel to them, and service is willing and friendly.
ROOMS: 9 en suite (bth/shr) (1 fmly) **MEALS:** English & French Cuisine V meals Coffee am Tea pm **FACILITIES:** CTV in all bedrooms **SERVICES:** 20P **NOTES:** Last d 9pm **CARDS:**

GRAVESEND Kent — Map 05 TQ67

★★★ Manor Hotel
Hever Court Rd, Singlewell DA12 5UQ
Quality Percentage Score: 71%
☎ 01474 353100 Fax 01474 354978
Dir: *A2, eastbound*
This modern privately owned hotel is ideally located for the motorways, channel ports and tunnel. The bedrooms are spacious and well equipped. The bright, attractive public areas include an open plan lounge and smart restaurant offering a small carte. The in-house health club has a swimming pool, sauna and gymnasium.
ROOMS: 52 en suite (bth/shr) No smoking in 39 bedrooms s £75-£85; d £85-£95 (incl. bkfst) * Off peak **MEALS:** International Cuisine V meals Coffee am Tea pm **FACILITIES:** CTV in all bedrooms STV Indoor swimming pool (heated) Sauna Solarium Gym **CONF:** Thtr 210 Class 100 Board 80 Del from £99 * **SERVICES:** Night porter 80P **NOTES:** No dogs (ex guide dogs) Last d 10pm
CARDS:

GRAVESEND Kent — Map 05 TQ67

★★★ Overcliffe
15-16 The Overcliffe DA11 0EF
Quality Percentage Score: 60%
☎ 01474 322131 Fax 01474 536737
Dir: *outside town centre, to the west on the A226*
This family-run hotel, consisting of the main house and a nearby Victorian lodge, is just a short distance from the town centre. It provides comfortable, well equipped accommodation. Live piano entertainment is provided most evenings in the bar/lounge and restaurant.
ROOMS: 19 en suite (shr) 10 annexe en suite (bth/shr) s £59-£65; d £75-£85 (incl. bkfst) * Off peak **MEALS:** English & Continental Cuisine V meals Coffee am Tea pm **FACILITIES:** CTV in all bedrooms STV **SERVICES:** Night porter 35P **NOTES:** Last d 9.30pm
CARDS:

GRAVESEND Kent — Map 05 TQ67

Travel Inn
Wrotham Rd DA11 7LF
☎ 01474 533556 Fax 01474 323776
Dir: *1m from A2 along A227*
This modern building offers accommodation in smart, spacious and well equipped bedrooms, all with en-suite bathrooms. Refreshments may be taken at the nearby family restaurant. For details about current prices consult the Contents Page under Hotel Groups for the Travel Inn phone number.
ROOMS: 36 en suite (bth/shr) d £39.95 *

GRAYS Essex — Map 05 TQ67

★★★ *Lakeside Moat House*
High Rd, North Stifford RM16 5UE
Quality Percentage Score: 69%
☎ 01708 719988 Fax 01375 390426
Dir: *from A13, follow signs Grays/Tilbury/Thurrock Lakeside keep in middle lane, then 2nd turn off A13 signed A1012 to Grays. Take 2nd turning for hotel*
This extended Georgian property provides the ideal location for its main weekday purpose of meetings and conferences. Elegant public areas include a smart restaurant, decorated in sunny colours, and a sports-themed bar. Bedrooms, in the main house and the recently built garden wing, provide an impressive level of comfort.
ROOMS: 97 en suite (bth/shr) (16 fmly) No smoking in 69 bedrooms **MEALS:** International Cuisine V meals Coffee am Tea pm **FACILITIES:** CTV in all bedrooms Tennis (hard) Croquet lawn Petanque Wkly live entertainment **CONF:** Thtr 130 Class 30 Board 36 **SERVICES:** Lift Night porter 150P **NOTES:** No smoking area in restaurant RS Sat & bank holidays (restricted lunch)
CARDS:

GRAYS Essex
Map 05 TQ67

Travel Inn

Fleming Rd, Unicorn Estate, Chafford Hundred RM16 6YJ

☎ 01375 481908 Fax 01375 481876

Dir: *from A13 follow signs for Lakeside Shopping Centre turn right at 1st rdbt straight over next rdbt then 1st slip road turn left at next rdbt*

This modern building offers accommodation in smart, spacious and well equipped bedrooms, all with en-suite bathrooms. Refreshments may be taken at the nearby family restaurant. For details about current prices consult the Contents Page under Hotel Groups for the Travel Inn phone number.

ROOMS: 40 en suite (bth/shr) d £39.95 *

GREAT CHESTERFORD Essex
Map 05 TL54

★★ The Crown House

CB10 1NY

Quality Percentage Score: 67%

☎ 01799 530515 Fax 01799 530683

Dir: *on B1383 1m from junct 9 on M11*

This small, listed hotel dates back to Tudor times. Bedrooms in the main house have most character, those in the courtyard annexe are popular with guests who want peace and quiet. Public rooms are cosy, and include a comfortable lounge, a bar, a cottage style dining room offering appetising meals, and a light conservatory where breakfast is served.

ROOMS: 8 en suite (bth/shr) 10 annexe en suite (bth/shr) (1 fmly) s £58; d £78-£95 (incl. bkfst) * LB Off peak **MEALS:** Lunch £10.95-£12.95 Dinner fr £13.95 & alc English & Continental Cuisine V meals Coffee am Tea pm **FACILITIES:** CTV in all bedrooms **CONF:** Thtr 50 Class 40 Board 30 Del £86 * **SERVICES:** 30P **NOTES:** No smoking area in restaurant Last d 9.30pm **CARDS:**

GREAT DUNMOW Essex
Map 05 TL62

★★ The Saracen's Head

High St CM6 1AG

Quality Percentage Score: 62%

☎ 01371 873901 Fax 01371 875743

Dir: *take A120 towards Colchester turn left at 2nd rndbt, hotel 0.50m downhill*

At the heart of this old Essex market town, this former coaching inn retains much of its original character in the beamed public rooms. Bedrooms are well-equipped and attractively decorated, including three spacious suites with brass beds.

ROOMS: 4 en suite (bth/shr) 20 annexe en suite (bth/shr) (3 fmly) No smoking in 5 bedrooms s fr £70; d fr £85 * LB Off peak **MEALS:** Lunch £5-£16.95 & alc High tea £1.50-£4 Dinner £16.95 & alc V meals Coffee am Tea pm **FACILITIES:** CTV in all bedrooms Xmas **CONF:** Thtr 50 Class 30 Board 34 Del from £90 * **SERVICES:** 50P **NOTES:** No smoking in restaurant Last d 9.15pm

CARDS:

GREAT LANGDALE See Elterwater

GREAT MILTON Oxfordshire
Map 04 SP60

The Premier Collection

★★★★ Le Manoir Aux Quat' Saisons

OX44 7PD

☎ 01844 278881 Fax 01844 278847

Dir: *from A329 take 2nd right turn to Great Milton Manor, hotel 200yds on right*

This delightful mellow stone 15th-century manor house, sympathetically restored and extended by Raymond Blanc, is peacefully positioned in immaculately maintained gardens, complete with interesting sculptures, and a traditional Japanese tea house. Bedrooms and suites, in both the main house and the converted stables, are beautifully appointed and offer a superb level of comfort. Decorated in true country house style, the hallmarks of the public rooms, which include a splendid new lounge/bar, are deep cushioned sofas, wonderful arrangements of flowers and plenty of magazines. The highlight of any stay has to be the outstanding quality of the cuisine which earns our supreme accolade of five rosettes. Head Chef Jonathan Wright now stands alongside Raymond Blanc to ensure the consistently high standards are maintained.

ROOMS: 10 en suite (bth/shr) 22 annexe en suite (bth/shr) d £230-£550 (incl. cont bkfst) * LB Off peak **MEALS:** Lunch fr £32 & alc Dinner £65-£85alc French Cuisine V meals Coffee am Tea pm **FACILITIES:** CTV in all bedrooms STV Croquet lawn Xmas **CONF:** Thtr 24 Board 20 **SERVICES:** Night porter 60P **NOTES:** No dogs (ex guide dogs) No smoking in restaurant Last d 9.45pm **CARDS:**

GREAT YARMOUTH Norfolk
Map 05 TG50

★★★ Cliff

Gorleston NR31 6DH

Quality Percentage Score: 73%

☎ 01493 662179 Fax 01493 653617

Dir: *2m S A12*

This high quality hotel continues to offer excellent accommodation in Great Yarmouth. The relaxing ambience of the public rooms runs through the smart restaurant, a choice of bars and a comfy lounge. Guests have a choice of serious dining in the restaurant, informal fare in the bar, an all-day selection of snacks in the lounge, or from the room service menu. There is a

contd.

wide range of bedroom size and style; all rooms offer well matched furniture and fabrics, enhanced by smart bathrooms.
ROOMS: 39 en suite (bth/shr) (5 fmly) No smoking in 2 bedrooms s £69-£107; d £97-£107 (incl. bkfst) * LB Off peak **MEALS:** Lunch £11.50-£19.75 & alc Dinner £16.50-£19.75 & alc V meals Coffee am Tea pm **FACILITIES:** CTV in all bedrooms STV Xmas **CONF:** Thtr 170 Class 150 Board 80 Del from £84.50 * **SERVICES:** Night porter 70P **NOTES:** No smoking in restaurant Last d 9.30pm
CARDS:

GREAT YARMOUTH Norfolk — Map 05 TG50
★★★ Regency Dolphin
Albert Square NR30 3JH
Quality Percentage Score: 68%
☎ 01493 855070 01493 853798
***Dir:** proceed along seafront and turn right at Wellington Pier, follow road round and turn left. Hotel on left hand side*
Offering smart public areas and attractive accommodation and set back from the beach and its pleasure attractions, this hotel is ideal for business guests visiting Great Yarmouth. A good level of services are readily available, including all-day menus in the lounge and room service. Bedrooms come in varying styles and sizes; each room is well appointed with colour co-ordinated decor and soft furnishings.
ROOMS: 48 en suite (bth/shr) (6 fmly) No smoking in 8 bedrooms s £65; d £75 (incl. bkfst) * LB Off peak **MEALS:** Lunch £16.95 Dinner £16.95 & alc English & French Cuisine V meals Coffee am Tea pm **FACILITIES:** CTV in all bedrooms STV Outdoor swimming pool (heated) Xmas **CONF:** Thtr 140 Class 50 Board 30 Del from £75 * **SERVICES:** Night porter 30P **NOTES:** No smoking in restaurant Last d 9.30pm **CARDS:**

GREAT YARMOUTH Norfolk — Map 05 TG50
★★★ *Star*
Hall Quay NR30 1HG
Quality Percentage Score: 67%
☎ 01493 842294 01493 330215
Overlooking the quayside, the Star is a pleasant hotel, whether it be for a bite to eat or an overnight stay. The bedrooms enjoy modern interior design and are well equipped. The intimate public rooms are richly decorated and welcoming.
ROOMS: 40 en suite (bth/shr) (3 fmly) No smoking in 4 bedrooms **MEALS:** V meals Coffee am Tea pm **FACILITIES:** CTV in all bedrooms STV **CONF:** Class 40 Board 40 Del from £55 * **SERVICES:** Lift Night porter 20P **NOTES:** No smoking area in restaurant Last d 9.30pm
CARDS:

GREAT YARMOUTH Norfolk — Map 05 TG50
★★★ Imperial
North Dr NR30 1EQ
Quality Percentage Score: 66%
☎ 01493 851113 01493 852229
***Dir:** follow signs to seafront and turn left, Hotel opposite tennis courts*
Hospitable proprietors lead a professional staff at this spacious hotel. The extensive public areas include banqueting rooms, the comfortable Savoie Lounge Bar, and the Rambouillet Restaurant and Brasserie. The colour co-ordinated accommodation is attractive and well equipped.
ROOMS: 39 en suite (bth/shr) (4 fmly) No smoking in 12 bedrooms s £66; d £82 (incl. bkfst) * LB Off peak **MEALS:** Lunch £9.95-£12.50 & alc Dinner £19.50 & alc English & French Cuisine V meals Coffee am Tea pm **FACILITIES:** CTV in all bedrooms STV Xmas **CONF:** Thtr 120 Class 30 Board 30 Del from £55 * **SERVICES:** Lift Night porter 50P
NOTES: No smoking area in restaurant
CARDS:

GREAT YARMOUTH Norfolk — Map 05 TG50
★★ *Furzedown*
19-20 North Dr NR30 4EW
Quality Percentage Score: 66%
☎ 01493 844138 01493 844138

This welcoming family-run hotel stands at the north end of the seafront overlooking the Blue Flag beaches and the Venetian Waterways. Most of the pretty rooms have a bright, airy decor. The spacious public areas are comfortable and appealing, the bar decorated with interesting maritime memorabilia. Diners can enjoy a wide selection of appetising dishes from the set price menu.
ROOMS: 23 rms (19 bth/shr) (11 fmly) **MEALS:** English & French Cuisine V meals Coffee am Tea pm **FACILITIES:** CTV in all bedrooms STV **CONF:** Class 60 Board 30 **SERVICES:** 15P **NOTES:** No smoking area in restaurant Last d 8.30pm **CARDS:**

Burlington Hotel
Great Yarmouth

GREAT YARMOUTH Norfolk Map 05 TG50

★★ *Regency*
5 North Dr NR30 1ED
Quality Percentage Score: 65%
☎ 01493 843759 Fax 01493 330411
Dir: *on sea front*
On the wide seafront road at the quieter end of town, this traditional hotel has a friendly ambience and many regular guests. Both tourists and business users appreciate the high standards. There is a variety of bedroom size and style, but all rooms offer good facilities.
ROOMS: 14 en suite (bth/shr) (2 fmly) **MEALS:** V meals **FACILITIES:** CTV in all bedrooms **SERVICES:** 10P **NOTES:** No dogs No children 7yrs No smoking in restaurant Last d 8.15pm
CARDS:

GREAT YARMOUTH Norfolk Map 05 TG50

★★ **Burlington**
11 North Dr NR30 1EG
Quality Percentage Score: 64%
☎ 01493 844568 & 842095 Fax 01493 331848
Dir: *A12 to sea front, turn left at Britannia Pier. Hotel close to tennis courts*
Sitting at the more tranquil end of the seafront, the sister properties, Burlington and Palm Court, provide joint facilities for all residents. Very much a well run traditional resort hotel, the pleasant bedrooms are well equipped, whilst the public areas offer a spacious bar and lounge.
ROOMS: 28 en suite (bth/shr) (9 fmly) No smoking in 5 bedrooms **MEALS:** English & French Cuisine V meals Coffee am Tea pm **FACILITIES:** CTV in all bedrooms STV Indoor swimming pool (heated) Sauna Pool table Jacuzzi/spa Turkish steam room Wkly live entertainment **CONF:** Thtr 120 Class 40 Board 20 **SERVICES:** Lift 40P **NOTES:** No dogs (ex guide dogs) No smoking in restaurant Last d 8pm Closed Jan-Feb RS Dec (group bookings only)
CARDS:

See advert on page 283

GREENFORD Greater London

See LONDON SECTION plan 1 *B4*
★★★ **The Bridge**
Western Av UB6 8ST
Quality Percentage Score: 69%
☎ 020 8566 6246 Fax 020 8566 6140
With easy access via the A40 to London or Oxford, the Bridge is a popular choice. Its spacious bedrooms have very good facilities, there are rooms suitable for guests with disabilities and some with four-poster beds. The bistro serves a good choice of dishes.
ROOMS: 68 en suite (bth/shr) (4 fmly) No smoking in 44 bedrooms s £55-£92; d £65-£102 (incl. bkfst) * Off peak **MEALS:** Sunday Lunch £12.95-£14.95 Dinner £16-£24alc English & French Cuisine V meals Coffee am Tea pm **FACILITIES:** CTV in all bedrooms STV Arrangement with local leisure centre **CONF:** Thtr 130 Class 60 Board 60 **SERVICES:** Lift Night porter 68P **NOTES:** No dogs (ex guide dogs) Last d 9.45pm **CARDS:**

GRIMSBY Lincolnshire Map 08 TA20

★★★ *Posthouse Grimsby*
Posthouse
Littlecoates Rd DN34 4LX
Quality Percentage Score: 63%
☎ 01472 350295 Fax 01472 241354
Dir: *take A1136 signed Greatcoates, left at first rdbt right at second rdbt. Hotel is on right 200 metres down*
The majority of bedrooms at this pleasantly situated hotel have large windows and balconies overlooking the adjoining golf course and are comfortably furnished with every modern convenience. The popular restaurant also overlooks the golf course. Staff are pleasant and helpful and an all day lounge menu and 24 hour room service are available. The hotel also features a large banqueting suite as well as smaller meeting and conference rooms.
ROOMS: 52 en suite (bth/shr) (2 fmly) No smoking in 27 bedrooms **MEALS:** International Cuisine V meals Coffee am Tea pm **FACILITIES:** CTV in all bedrooms Golf 18 Pool table **CONF:** Thtr 300 Class 100 Board 60 **SERVICES:** Lift Night porter 250P **NOTES:** No smoking area in restaurant Last d 10pm
CARDS:

GRIMSBY Lincolnshire Map 08 TA20

Travel Inn
Europa Park, Appian Way, Off Gilbey Rd DN31 2UT
☎ 01472 242630 Fax 01472 250281
Dir: *from junct 5 of M180 take A180 towards Grimsby town centre, Travel Inn is on 2nd exit from 1st rdbt on A180*
This modern building offers accommodation in smart, spacious and well equipped bedrooms, all with en-suite bathrooms. Refreshments may be taken at the nearby family restaurant. For details about current prices consult the Contents Page under Hotel Groups for the Travel Inn phone number.
ROOMS: 40 en suite (bth/shr) d £39.95 *

GRIMSBY Lincolnshire Map 08 TA20

Late entry **Beeches**
42 Waltham Rd, Scartho DN33 2LX
☎ 01472 278830 Fax 01472 278830
ROOMS: 10 en suite (bth/shr) No smoking in all bedrooms s fr £42.50; d fr £59.50 (incl. bkfst) * Off peak **MEALS:** Lunch £18-£18 & alc High tea £4 & alc Dinner fr £18 & alc V meals Coffee am Tea pm **FACILITIES:** CTV in all bedrooms **CONF:** Thtr 30 Class 20 Board 20 **SERVICES:** Lift Night porter 70P **NOTES:** No dogs (ex guide dogs) No coaches No smoking in restaurant Last d 9.30pm
CARDS:

GRIMSTON Norfolk Map 09 TF72

The Premier Collection

★★★ **Congham Hall Country House**
Lynn Rd PE32 1AH
☎ 01485 600250 Fax 01485 601191
Dir: *A149/A148 interchange north east of King's Lynn, follow A148 to Sandringham/Fakenham/Cromer for 100yds. Turn right to Grimston, hotel 2.5m on left*
A Georgian country retreat on the outskirts of Grimston. Inside, elegant public rooms and a winding staircase lead up to a charming variety of individually styled bedrooms. Many overlook the delightful grounds, with open and wooded parkland, lawns, impressive herb and flower gardens and a

contd.

putting green. The Orangery Restaurant overlooks the garden and is an attractive setting in which to enjoy the excellent menu, serving dishes with a combination of Mediterranean and Northern European influences, many using herbs from Congham's gardens.
ROOMS: 14 en suite (bth/shr) No smoking in all bedrooms s £95-£105; d £125-£165 (incl. bkfst) * LB Off peak **MEALS:** Lunch £9.50-£18.50 & alc Dinner £27.50-£34 V meals Coffee am **FACILITIES:** CTV in all bedrooms Outdoor swimming pool (heated) Tennis (hard) Croquet lawn Putting green Jacuzzi/spa Cricket Xmas **CONF:** Thtr 25 Class 12 Board 12 Del from £145 * **SERVICES:** 50P **NOTES:** No dogs No coaches No children 12yrs No smoking in restaurant Last d 9.30pm **CARDS:**

GRINDLEFORD Derbyshire — Map 08 SK27

★★★ Maynard Arms

Main Rd S32 2HE
Quality Percentage Score: 68%
☎ 01433 630321 Fax 01433 630445
Dir: *leave Sheffield on the A625 towards Castleton. Turn left into Grindleford on the B6521 after the Fox House. Hotel is on left*
Enjoying fine views, this fine country mansion provides a good base from which to explore the northern Peak District. Bedrooms are attractively furnished and include some larger, 'superior' rooms and a couple of suites. For dinner, guests can choose either the lounge bar or Padley's Restaurant, which overlooks the garden. There is a comfortable lounge on the first floor.
ROOMS: 10 en suite (bth/shr) s £67-£87; d £77-£97 (incl. bkfst) * LB Off peak **MEALS:** Lunch £13-£20 Dinner £16-£20 British & European Cuisine V meals Coffee am Tea pm **FACILITIES:** CTV in all bedrooms STV Xmas **CONF:** Thtr 140 Class 80 Board 80 Del from £84 * **SERVICES:** 80P **NOTES:** No coaches No smoking in restaurant Last d 9.30pm **CARDS:**

GRIZEDALE Cumbria — Map 07 SD39

★★ Grizedale Lodge

LA22 0QL
Quality Percentage Score: 72%
☎ 015394 36532 Fax 015394 36572
Dir: *at Hawkshead take Newby Bridge Road to right turn for Forest Park Centre.*
Surrounded by rolling meadows and woodland, this former shooting lodge lies in the heart of Grizedale Forest, two miles south of Hawkshead. A friendly hotel, it has attractive and inviting public areas and comfortable, well furnished bedrooms in a variety of styles. The daily-changing dinner menu makes excellent use of fresh ingredients.
ROOMS: 9 en suite (bth/shr) (1 fmly) No smoking in all bedrooms s £61.50-£67.50 (incl. bkfst & dinner) * LB Off peak **MEALS:** Dinner £23.50 English & French Cuisine Coffee am **FACILITIES:** CTV in all bedrooms Xmas **SERVICES:** 20P **NOTES:** No coaches No smoking in restaurant Last d 8pm **CARDS:**

GUILDFORD Surrey — Map 04 SU94

★★★ The Angel Posting House and Livery

91 High St GU1 3DP
Quality Percentage Score: 78%
☎ 01483 564555 Fax 01483 533770
Service standards are high at this historic coaching inn, and the welcome begins with valet parking to the nearest car park. Most of the individually furnished bedrooms are either full or junior suites, some featuring characterful old beams. Extras include complimentary sherry and mineral water, bathrobes and slippers. A Jacobean fireplace and 17th-century parliament clock are among the original features to be found in cosy public areas which include the 13th-century, stone-vaulted Crypt Restaurant where chef Tony O'Hare offers interesting dishes based on the best quality ingredients.

ROOMS: 11 en suite (bth/shr) (4 fmly) d £135-£200 * LB Off peak **MEALS:** Lunch £14.50-£18.50 & alc Dinner £23.50 & alc English & Continental Cuisine V meals Coffee am Tea pm **FACILITIES:** CTV in 21 bedrooms STV **CONF:** Thtr 80 Class 20 Board 40 **SERVICES:** Lift Night porter **NOTES:** No coaches Last d 10.30pm
CARDS:

See advert on this page

GUILDFORD Surrey — Map 04 SU94

★★★ The Manor

Newlands Corner GU4 8SE
Quality Percentage Score: 70%
☎ 01483 222624 Fax 01483 211389
Dir: *3.5m on A25 to Dorking*
Built in the 1890s for the Strachey family, The Manor is a

contd.

popular venue for meetings, conferences, and weddings. There's a frieze painted by Litton Strachey in Squires Restaurant. Recently extended, the hotel has twenty new, well appointed and attractively decorated bedrooms in addition to considerably increased lounge facilities and a new air-conditioned function room. The hotel is set in nine acres of well kept grounds.
ROOMS: 45 en suite (bth/shr) (4 fmly) No smoking in 4 bedrooms s £80-£95; d £90-£125 * LB Off peak **MEALS:** Lunch £12.95-£17.50 & alc Dinner fr £19.50 & alc English & French Cuisine V meals Coffee am Tea pm **FACILITIES:** CTV in all bedrooms Croquet lawn Wkly live entertainment **CONF:** Thtr 200 Class 80 Board 80 Del from £140 * **SERVICES:** Night porter 100P **NOTES:** No coaches Last d 9.30pm
CARDS:

GUILDFORD Surrey — Map 04 SU94
★★★ *Posthouse Guildford*
Egerton Rd GU2 5XZ
Posthouse
Quality Percentage Score: 69%
☎ 01483 574444 01483 506890
Dir: *exit A3 for Hospital and Cathedral, take third exit at rdbt then second exit at next*
Located near the Cathedral, this large, modern hotel has smartly equipped bedrooms, all of which are a good size. The spacious public areas include a comfortable bar lounge and a health club.
ROOMS: 162 en suite (bth/shr) (100 fmly) No smoking in 71 bedrooms **MEALS:** International Cuisine V meals Coffee am Tea pm **FACILITIES:** CTV in all bedrooms STV Indoor swimming pool (heated) Sauna Solarium Gym **CONF:** Thtr 200 Class 100 Board 45 **SERVICES:** Night porter 220P **NOTES:** No smoking area in restaurant Last d 10pm **CARDS:**

GUILDFORD Surrey — Map 04 SU94
Travel Inn
Parkway GU1 1UP
☎ 01483 304932 01483 304935
Dir: *from M25 junct 10 follow signs to Portsmouth A3. Take turn off to Guildford centre/Lesiure Centre A320/A25 turn left hotel on left*
This modern building offers accommodation in smart, spacious and well equipped bedrooms, all with en-suite bathrooms. Refreshments may be taken at the nearby family restaurant. For details about current prices consult the Contents Page under Hotel Groups for the Travel Inn phone number.
ROOMS: 60 en suite (bth/shr) d £39.95 *

GULWORTHY Devon — Map 02 SX47
★★ Horn of Plenty
PL19 8JD
Quality Percentage Score: 79%
☎ 01822 832528 01822 832528
Dir: *from Tavistock take A390 W for 3m and turn right at Gulworthy Cross. After 400yds turn left and continue for a further 400yds to hotel on right*
This beautiful country house is set high above the Tamar valley with stunning views across to Bodmin Moor. Bright and attractively furnished bedrooms overlook the pretty walled garden. The comfortable public rooms are elegantly furnished.
ROOMS: 2 en suite (bth/shr) 6 annexe en suite (bth/shr) (1 fmly) No smoking in 1 bedroom s £105-£240; d £115-£250 (incl. bkfst) * LB Off peak **MEALS:** Lunch £14.50-£21.50 Dinner £35 International Cuisine V meals Coffee am Tea pm **FACILITIES:** CTV in all bedrooms Xmas **CONF:** Thtr 20 Class 20 Board 12 **SERVICES:** 25P **NOTES:** No coaches No smoking in restaurant Last d 9.30pm Closed 25-26 Dec
CARDS:

GUNTHORPE Nottinghamshire — Map 08 SK64
★★ Unicorn
Gunthorpe Bridge NG14 7FB
Quality Percentage Score: 68%
☎ 0115 966 3612 0115 966 4801
Dir: *on A6097, between Lowdham and Bingham*
This popular refurbished riverside inn offers good accommodation and characterful public rooms. The bars and restaurant are spacious, and feature exposed timbers and brickwork. A good range of snacks and meals is offered during the day, and a carte menu during the evening. Bedrooms are well equipped, cheerfully furnished and of good proportions.
ROOMS: 16 en suite (bth/shr) (3 fmly) s £49.50; d £59.50 (incl. bkfst) * LB Off peak **MEALS:** Bar Lunch £3.95-£7.95alc Dinner £12-£18alc English & French Cuisine V meals Coffee am **FACILITIES:** CTV in all bedrooms STV Fishing **SERVICES:** 200P **NOTES:** No dogs (ex guide dogs) No smoking area in restaurant Last d 10pm
CARDS:

See advert under NOTTINGHAM

HACKNESS North Yorkshire — Map 08 SE99
★★★ Hackness Grange Country House
North York National Park YO13 0JW
Quality Percentage Score: 69%
☎ 01723 882345 01723 882391
Dir: *A64 to Scarborough and then A171 to Whitby/Scalby, follow signs to Hackness/Forge Valley National Park, through Hackness village on left hand side*
Close to Scarborough and the North Yorkshire Moors National Park, Hackness Grange is surrounded by its own well tended gardens with tennis courts and a pitch and putt course. Comfortably furnished bedrooms have views of the quiet countryside. Lounges and the restaurant are spacious and relaxing.
ROOMS: 13 en suite (bth/shr) 15 annexe en suite (bth/shr) (5 fmly) **MEALS:** Lunch £12.50-£17.50 Dinner £25-£35 English & French Cuisine V meals Coffee am Tea pm **FACILITIES:** CTV in all bedrooms STV Indoor swimming pool (heated) Tennis (hard) Croquet lawn Jacuzzi/spa 9 hole pitch & putt **CONF:** Thtr 15 Class 8 Board 8 Del from £95 * **SERVICES:** Night porter 60P **NOTES:** No dogs (ex guide dogs) No coaches No smoking in restaurant Last d 9.15pm
CARDS:

HADLEY WOOD Greater London — Map 04 TQ29
★★★★ West Lodge Park
Cockfosters Rd EN4 0PY
Quality Percentage Score: 71%
☎ 020 8216 3900 020 8216 3937
Dir: *on A111, 1m S of exit 24 on M25*
This impressive country house, set in beautiful parkland, has been in the Beale family for more than 50 years. Bedrooms are individually decorated and have many luxurious little touches, particularly in the 'executive' rooms. The Cedar Restaurant has an interesting menu.
ROOMS: 46 en suite (bth/shr) 9 annexe en suite (bth/shr) (1 fmly) No smoking in 19 bedrooms s £92.50-£140; d £130-£188.50 * LB Off peak **MEALS:** Lunch £23.95-£29.95 Dinner £27.50-£34.50 V meals Coffee am Tea pm **FACILITIES:** CTV in all bedrooms STV Croquet lawn Putting green Fitness trail Free membership of David Lloyd Club Wkly live entertainment Xmas **CONF:** Thtr 80 Class 24 Board 30 Del from £155 * **SERVICES:** Lift Night porter 200P **NOTES:** No dogs (ex guide dogs) No coaches No smoking in restaurant Last d 9.30pm
CARDS:

HAGLEY Worcestershire — Map 07 SO98

Travel Inn

Birmingham Rd DY9 9JS
☎ 01562 883120 🖹 01562 884416
Dir: *5m off junct 3 of the M5 on opposite side of the A456 dual carriageway towards Kidderminster*

This modern building offers accommodation in smart, spacious and well equipped bedrooms, all with en-suite bathrooms. Refreshments may be taken at the nearby family restaurant. For details about current prices consult the Contents Page under Hotel Groups for the Travel Inn phone number.

ROOMS: 40 en suite (bth/shr) d £39.95 *

HAILSHAM East Sussex — Map 05 TQ50

★★★ Boship Farm

Lower Dicker BN27 4AT
Quality Percentage Score: 68%
☎ 01323 844826 🖹 01323 843945
Dir: *on A22 at Boship roundabout, junct of A22/A267/A271*

Set in 17 acres of grounds this popular hotel, originally a 17th-century farmhouse, has been extended to offer comfortable accommodation in a relaxed country atmosphere. There are good leisure facilities and public areas include a bar, lounges and numerous function rooms.

ROOMS: 47 annexe en suite (bth/shr) (5 fmly) No smoking in 17 bedrooms s fr £60; d fr £85 (incl. bkfst) * LB Off peak **MEALS:** Lunch fr £12.50 Dinner fr £18 English & French Cuisine V meals Coffee am Tea pm **FACILITIES:** CTV in all bedrooms Outdoor swimming pool (heated) Tennis (hard) Gym Croquet lawn Jacuzzi/spa Xmas **CONF:** Thtr 175 Class 40 Board 46 Del from £90 * **SERVICES:** Night porter 100P **NOTES:** No smoking in restaurant Last d 9.45pm **CARDS:**

HAILSHAM East Sussex — Map 05 TQ50

★★ The Olde Forge Hotel & Restaurant

Magham Down BN27 1PN
Quality Percentage Score: 68%
☎ 01323 842893 🖹 01323 842893
Dir: *off Boship rdbt on A271 to Bexhill. 3m on left*

This small, popular hotel on the edge of town has a small terrace garden. Pine-furnished bedrooms are all well equipped. Public areas consist of a small beamed bar and a candlelit restaurant.

ROOMS: 8 en suite (bth/shr) s £42; d £55 (incl. bkfst) * LB Off peak **MEALS:** Dinner fr £22.50alc English & French Cuisine V meals Coffee am Tea pm **FACILITIES:** CTV in all bedrooms **SERVICES:** 11P **NOTES:** No coaches Last d 9.30pm **CARDS:**

HAILSHAM East Sussex — Map 05 TQ50

Travelodge

Boship Roundabout, Hellingly BN27 4DT
☎ 01323 844556 🖹 01323 844556
Dir: *on A22 at Boship roundabout*

This modern building offers accommodation in smart, spacious and well equipped bedrooms, all with en-suite bathrooms. Refreshments may be taken at the nearby family restaurant. For details about current prices, consult the Contents Page under Hotel Groups for the Travelodge phone number.

ROOMS: 40 en suite (bth/shr) d £45.95 *

HALIFAX West Yorkshire — Map 07 SE02

★★★ Holdsworth House

Holdsworth HX2 9TG
Quality Percentage Score: 72%
☎ 01422 240024 🖹 01422 245174
Dir: *3m NW off A629 Keighley Road*

This beautifully preserved 17th-century Jacobean manor house retaining all of its period features, stands just three miles north of Halifax. The property has been extended in a sympathetic manner over the years and now offers forty bedrooms, all of which are individual in style and well appointed. Guests can relax in the charming lounge and dining room with attentive service and sound cooking using quality ingredients.

ROOMS: 40 en suite (bth/shr) (2 fmly) No smoking in 15 bedrooms s £85-£115; d £101-£130 (incl. cont bkfst) * LB Off peak **MEALS:** Lunch £10-£22.50alc Dinner £22.50-£26alc English & Continental Cuisine V meals Coffee am Tea pm **FACILITIES:** CTV in all bedrooms STV **CONF:** Thtr 150 Class 75 Board 50 Del £122.50 * **SERVICES:** Night porter 60P **NOTES:** No smoking in restaurant Last d 9.30pm **CARDS:**

HALIFAX West Yorkshire — Map 07 SE02

★★★ The Imperial Crown

42/46 Horton St HX1 1QE
Quality Percentage Score: 63%
☎ 01422 342342 🖹 01422 349866
Dir: *opposite Railway Station*

A major refurbishment programme is underway at this imposing building, located in the town centre. Bedrooms are split between the main building and a lodge situated across the road, where there is also a popular American style diner. More traditional dining is to be had in the Wallis Simpson restaurant, adjacent to the characterful lounge bar.

ROOMS: 41 en suite (bth/shr) (3 fmly) No smoking in 10 bedrooms **MEALS:** Bar Lunch fr £3.95 High tea fr £4.95 Dinner £17.50 & alc English & French Cuisine V meals Coffee am Tea pm **FACILITIES:** CTV in all bedrooms STV **CONF:** Thtr 150 Class 120 Board 70 Del from £65 * **SERVICES:** Night porter 63P **NOTES:** Last d 9.45pm **CARDS:**

Some hotel groups have a central reservations telephone number, see pages 35, 37 and 38 for details.

HALIFAX West Yorkshire **Map 07 SE02**
★★ Rock Inn Hotel & Churchills
Holywell Green HX4 9BS
Quality Percentage Score: 70%
☎ 01422 379721 Fax 01422 379110
Dir: *junct 24 off M62, signs for Blackley, left at crossroads approx 1/2m on left*
Quietly situated, yet convenient for the M62, this privately owned hotel offers attractively furnished bedrooms. An extension was being built at the time of our last visit, which will contain additional executive rooms. The bar and brasserie are popular with locals and visitors alike, meals can also be taken in Churchills restaurant.
ROOMS: 30 en suite (bth/shr) (5 fmly) No smoking in 15 bedrooms d £67-£110 * LB Off peak **MEALS:** Lunch £10.50 Dinner £12-£25alc English, French & Thai Cuisine V meals Coffee am Tea pm **FACILITIES:** CTV in all bedrooms STV Games room Xmas **CONF:** Thtr 200 Class 100 Board 100 Del from £75 * **SERVICES:** 122P **NOTES:** No smoking in restaurant Last d 10pm
CARDS:

HALIFAX West Yorkshire **Map 07 SE02**
★★ The Hobbit
Hob Ln, Norland, Sowerby Bridge HX6 3QL
Quality Percentage Score: 69%
☎ 01422 832202 Fax 01422 835381
Located high above Sowerby Bridge, and well signed from the town, this family run hotel has fine views over the area. Modern bedrooms, some in an adjacent building, are brightly decorated and furnished. Meals are available all day in the bistro, and more formal dining is offered in the restaurant. In either case, service is fiendly and prompt.
ROOMS: 17 en suite (bth/shr) 5 annexe en suite (bth/shr) (4 fmly) No smoking in 6 bedrooms s £48-£63; d £69-£79 (incl. bkfst) * LB Off peak **MEALS:** Lunch £8.95 Dinner £8.95-£15.95 & alc English, French, Italian Cuisine V meals Coffee am Tea pm **FACILITIES:** CTV in all bedrooms STV Wkly live entertainment Xmas **CONF:** Thtr 60 Board 16 Del from £69.95 * **SERVICES:** 100P **NOTES:** No dogs (ex guide dogs) No smoking area in restaurant Last d 10.30pm
CARDS:

HALLAND East Sussex **Map 05 TQ41**
★★★ Halland Forge
BN8 6PW
Quality Percentage Score: 64%
☎ 01825 840456 Fax 01825 840773
Dir: *on A22 at junct with B2192, 4m S of Uckfield*

This well established hotel on the A22 offers well maintained accommodation in a two-storey, motel-style block. It has a lounge bar, a popular coffee shop which is open all day, and a restaurant serving reliably good food.
ROOMS: 20 annexe en suite (bth/shr) (2 fmly) s £51-£53.50; d £65-£68 * LB Off peak **MEALS:** Lunch £12.50-£14.50 & alc Dinner fr £17.05 & alc English, French & Italian Cuisine V meals Coffee am Tea pm **FACILITIES:** CTV in all bedrooms **CONF:** Thtr 70 Class 50 Board 50 Del from £60 * **SERVICES:** 70P **NOTES:** No children 5yrs Last d 9.30pm
CARDS:

HAMBLETON North Yorkshire **Map 08 SE53**
★★ *Owl*
Main Rd YO8 9JH
Quality Percentage Score: 64%
☎ 01757 228374 Fax 01757 228125
Dir: *4m W on A63*
Standing in the centre of the village and offering a very extensive range of popular food, this modern and very well equipped hotel offers bedrooms which have been pleasantly decorated and thoughtfully furnished. Some of the bedrooms are located in a nearby annexe.
ROOMS: 7 en suite (bth/shr) 15 annexe en suite (bth/shr) (2 fmly) **MEALS:** International Cuisine V meals Coffee am Tea pm **FACILITIES:** CTV in all bedrooms STV **CONF:** Thtr 80 Class 40 Board 50 **SERVICES:** 101P **NOTES:** No dogs (ex guide dogs) No smoking area in restaurant Last d 10pm **CARDS:**

HAMPSON GREEN Lancashire **Map 07 SD45**
★★ Hampson House
Hampson Ln LA2 0JB
Quality Percentage Score: 61%
☎ 01524 751158 Fax 01524 751779
Dir: *4m S of Lancester adjacent to junct 33 on M6*
This modern hotel is set in over an acre of mature gardens and parts of the building date back to 1666. An imaginative choice of dishes is offered in the open-plan restaurant, and the bedrooms are bright and well equipped.
ROOMS: 12 en suite (bth/shr) 2 annexe en suite (bth/shr) (4 fmly) s £35-£38.50; d £49.50-£55 (incl. bkfst) * LB Off peak **MEALS:** Lunch £8.95-£13 & alc Dinner £9.50-£13 & alc English, French & Italian Cuisine V meals Coffee am Tea pm **FACILITIES:** CTV in all bedrooms Xmas **CONF:** Thtr 90 Class 40 Board 26 Del from £48 * **SERVICES:** 60P **NOTES:** Last d 9.30pm **CARDS:**

HAMPTON COURT Greater London
See LONDON SECTION plan 1 *B1*
★★★★ The Carlton Mitre
Hampton Court Rd KT8 9BN
Quality Percentage Score: 69%
☎ 020 8979 9988 Fax 020 8979 9777
Dir: *from M3 junct1 follow signs to Sunbury & Hampton Court Palace, continue until Hampton Court Palace rdbt, turn right & The Mitre is on the right*
Dating back in parts to the 17th century, this attractive building has a wonderful riverside setting opposite Hampton Court Palace. Bedrooms are all smart, well equipped and spacious, and day rooms include a quiet reading room, a riverside bar and a restaurant.
ROOMS: 36 en suite (bth/shr) (2 fmly) No smoking in 16 bedrooms d fr £150 * Off peak **MEALS:** Sunday Lunch £15-£25 Dinner £20-£30 & alc International Cuisine V meals Coffee am Tea pm **FACILITIES:** CTV in all bedrooms STV Jacuzzi/spa Wkly live entertainment Xmas **CONF:** Thtr 30 Class 15 Board 20 Del from £185 * **SERVICES:** Lift Night porter Air conditioning 13P **NOTES:** No smoking in restaurant
CARDS:

HAMPTON COURT Greater London

★★★ Liongate
Hampton Court Rd KT8 9DD
Quality Percentage Score: 64%
☎ 0500 636943 (Central Res) Fax 01773 880321
Dir: *from London approach via A3 and A308. From SW leave M3 at junct 1 and follow A308*
Opposite the Lion Gate entrance to Hampton Court and by the entrance to Bushy Park (which some of the bedrooms overlook), this hotel has well equipped bedrooms, either in the main house or in a small mews across the road. There is a bar and a separate restaurant.
ROOMS: 29 en suite (bth/shr) s £120-£140; d £140-£160 * LB Off peak **MEALS:** Lunch £4.95-£15 Dinner fr £17alc English & Continental Cuisine V meals Coffee am Tea pm **FACILITIES:** CTV in all bedrooms STV Xmas **CONF:** Thtr 50 Class 20 Board 20 Del from £125 * **SERVICES:** Night porter 30P **NOTES:** No coaches No smoking in restaurant Last d 9.30pm **CARDS:**

HANDFORTH See **Manchester Airport**

HANSLOPE Buckinghamshire **Map 04 SP84**

★★★ Hatton Court
Bullington End MK19 7BQ
Quality Percentage Score: 62%
☎ 01908 510044 Fax 01908 510945
This Victorian house stands at the end of a tree-lined drive, surrounded by six acres of grounds. Its setting makes it a popular venue for all kinds of events. Bedrooms are divided between the main house and nicely converted stables.
ROOMS: 12 en suite (bth/shr) 8 annexe en suite (bth/shr) (4 fmly) No smoking in 6 bedrooms d £87.50-£95 * LB Off peak **MEALS:** Lunch £16.95-£18.95 Dinner £22.50 International Cuisine V meals Coffee am Tea pm **FACILITIES:** CTV in all bedrooms STV Croquet lawn Xmas **CONF:** Thtr 60 Class 36 Board 32 Del from £130 * **SERVICES:** Night porter 120P **NOTES:** No smoking in restaurant Last d 9.45pm **CARDS:**

HAREWOOD West Yorkshire **Map 08 SE34**

★★★ *Harewood Arms*
Harrogate Rd LS17 9LH
Quality Percentage Score: 66%
☎ 0113 288 6566 Fax 0113 288 6064
Dir: *on A61 at junct with A659*
Standing almost opposite Harewood House, this comfortable hotel offers good modern bedrooms together with a busy bar and restaurant, where a good range of well produced food is available. Staff provide some fine Yorkshire hospitality.
ROOMS: 13 en suite (bth/shr) 11 annexe en suite (bth/shr) (2 fmly) **MEALS:** English & French Cuisine V meals Coffee am Tea pm **FACILITIES:** CTV in all bedrooms **CONF:** Thtr 20 Class 12 Board 16 **SERVICES:** Night porter 60P **NOTES:** No smoking in restaurant Last d 9.45pm **CARDS:**

HARLOW Essex **Map 05 TL41**

★★★ Swallow Churchgate Hotel
Churchgate St Village, Old Harlow CM17 0JT
Quality Percentage Score: 73%
☎ 01279 420246 Fax 01279 420246
Dir: *on B183, NE of Old Harlow*
Relaxing surroundings and an emphasis on leisure, conference and banqueting facilities are characteristic of hotels in the Swallow group. The Swallow Churchgate is a Jacobean house, conveniently situated for access to the M11 in a quiet village north-east of Old Harlow. 'Executive' rooms are the best of the high quality bedrooms and there is extensive room service as well as the elegant restaurant.

ROOMS: 85 en suite (bth/shr) (6 fmly) No smoking in 41 bedrooms s £94-£99; d £120-£145 (incl. bkfst) * LB Off peak **MEALS:** Lunch £15.95-£20 & alc Dinner £15.95-£21 English & French Cuisine V meals Coffee am Tea pm **FACILITIES:** CTV in all bedrooms STV Indoor swimming pool (heated) Sauna Solarium Gym Jacuzzi/spa Xmas **CONF:** Thtr 180 Class 70 Board 40 Del from £135 * **SERVICES:** Night porter 120P **NOTES:** No smoking in restaurant Last d 10pm Closed 27-29 Dec **CARDS:**

HARLOW Essex **Map 05 TL41**

★★★ *Harlow Moat House*
Southern Way CM18 7BA
Quality Percentage Score: 66%
☎ 01279 829988 Fax 01279 635094
Dir: *from M11 junct 7 take A414 towards Harlow. Take first exit at first roundabout and then first left*
The relaxing public areas at this purpose-built hotel have recently been refurbished and include a welcoming bar and spacious informal restaurant, with a manned business centre and a small lounge area in the open-plan reception area. Well maintained bedrooms are adequately sized.
ROOMS: 119 en suite (bth/shr) No smoking in 60 bedrooms **MEALS:** English & French Cuisine V meals Coffee am Tea pm **FACILITIES:** CTV in all bedrooms Pool table **CONF:** Thtr 150 Class 150 Board 50 **SERVICES:** Night porter 120P **NOTES:** No dogs (ex guide dogs) No smoking area in restaurant Last d 10pm **CARDS:**

HARLOW Essex **Map 05 TL41**

★★★ Green Man
Mulberry Green, Old Harlow CM17 0ET
Quality Percentage Score: 61%
☎ 01279 442521 Fax 01279 626113
The original inn building houses a popular bar, with a separate restaurant and function rooms, while the bedrooms, in a range of styles, are all in a purpose-built extension in a peaceful setting. The massive refurbishment programme is now complete, creating

contd.

the spacious Olio restaurant, and the upgrade of the accommodation has brought smart co-ordinated results.

Green Man, Harlow

ROOMS: 55 annexe en suite (bth/shr) No smoking in 27 bedrooms s £85; d £95 * LB Off peak **MEALS:** Lunch fr £9.95 & alc Dinner £12.50-£28alc International Cuisine V meals Coffee am Tea pm **FACILITIES:** CTV in all bedrooms Xmas **CONF:** Thtr 60 Class 26 Board 30 Del from £95 * **SERVICES:** Night porter 75P **NOTES:** Last d 10pm **CARDS:**

HARLOW Essex — Map 05 TL41

Travel Inn

Cambridge Rd CM20 2EP
☎ 01279 442545 01279 452169
Dir: *in Old Harlow, just off A414 on the Sawbridgeworth and Bishop's Stortford Road*

This modern building offers accommodation in smart, spacious and well equipped bedrooms, all with en-suite bathrooms. Refreshments may be taken at the nearby family restaurant. For details about current prices consult the Contents Page under Hotel Groups for the Travel Inn phone number.

ROOMS: 38 en suite (bth/shr) d £39.95 *

HARLYN BAY Cornwall & Isles of Scilly — Map 02 SW87

★ Polmark

PL28 8SB
Quality Percentage Score: 66%
☎ 01841 520206 01841 520206
Dir: *A39 to Padstow, then Padstow to Harlyn Bay*

Friendly service is offered at this 1920s Cornish stone property. Bedrooms are well equipped, ranging from rooms in the original property to new bedrooms in a purpose-built wing. On cooler evenings, log fires burn in the bar-lounge. Imaginative menus are offered each evening and Thai specialities are a feature.

ROOMS: 13 en suite (bth/shr) (3 fmly) **MEALS:** Sunday Lunch fr £10.50 English, Continental & Thai Cuisine V meals Coffee am Tea pm **FACILITIES:** CTV in all bedrooms Outdoor swimming pool (heated) **SERVICES:** 20P **NOTES:** No coaches No smoking in restaurant Closed Nov-Mar **CARDS:**

HAROME See **Helmsley**

HARPENDEN Hertfordshire — Map 04 TL11

★★★ Glen Eagle

1 Luton Rd AL5 2PX
Quality Percentage Score: 73%
☎ 01582 760271 01582 460819
Dir: *in town centre just beyond Oggelsby's Garage*

Located on the northern edge of the town, this well established hotel offers smart public areas which, with their bold colour schemes, are particularly striking. Guests have the choice of informal snacks from an all-day lounge menu, or more interesting choices in the restaurant; a room service menu is also available. The newly refurbished bedrooms are modern, attractive and well equipped.

ROOMS: 60 en suite (bth/shr) (12 fmly) No smoking in 25 bedrooms s £95-£125; d £105-£150 * LB Off peak **MEALS:** Lunch fr £12 & alc Dinner fr £14 & alc English & French Cuisine V meals Coffee am Tea pm **FACILITIES:** CTV in all bedrooms STV Free membership of local leisure club **CONF:** Thtr 80 Class 30 Board 35 Del £120 * **SERVICES:** Lift Night porter 100P **NOTES:** Last d 9.45pm **CARDS:**

See advert on opposite page

HARPENDEN Hertfordshire — Map 04 TL11

★★★ Harpenden House

18 Southdown Rd AL5 1PE
Quality Percentage Score: 67%
☎ 01582 449955 01582 769858
Dir: *turn off the A1081 onto Southampton Rd, hotel is 200 yrds on the left set back from the rd*

An elegant Georgian building with easy access to the M1 and Luton airport. The unusual restaurant, with Renaissance painted ceiling, chandelier and alcoves, serves modern international cuisine. The bar may have limited space when busy. Generally spacious and comfortable bedrooms, varying in style, are in the main house and extension. There is a suite and two apartments for long-staying guests.

ROOMS: 17 en suite (bth/shr) 36 annexe en suite (bth/shr) (8 fmly) No smoking in 26 bedrooms s £120-£130; d £155-£220 * LB Off peak **MEALS:** Lunch £12.95-£19.85 & alc Dinner £12.95-£19.85 & alc English & Mediterranean Cuisine V meals Coffee am Tea pm **FACILITIES:** CTV in all bedrooms Croquet lawn **CONF:** Thtr 150 Class 60 Board 70 Del from £110 * **SERVICES:** Night porter 80P **NOTES:** Last d 10pm RS Bank Holidays **CARDS:**

Indicates that the star classification has not been confirmed under the New Quality Standards, see page 7 for further information.

HARROGATE North Yorkshire **Map 08 SE35**
see also **Knaresborough**
★★★★ **Rudding Park House & Hotel**
Rudding Park, Follifoot HG3 1JH
Quality Percentage Score: 76%
☎ 01423 871350 Fax 01423 872286
Dir: *From A61, at rdbt with A658 take exit for York and follow brown signs to Rudding Park*

Part of a 230 acre estate, this imposing hotel has been built in the same elegant style as that of the adjacent Rudding House, which is the venue for conferences, functions and corporate entertainment. The hotel offers quality accommodation, plus a contemporary style bar and brasserie. Lounge facilities are limited, but bedrooms are well proportioned and thoughtfully equipped. The hotel has its own 18 hole golf course.
ROOMS: 50 en suite (bth/shr) No smoking in 31 bedrooms s £112-£132; d £145-£165 (incl. bkfst) * LB Off peak **MEALS:** Lunch fr £9.50 Dinner fr £24.92 Cosmopolitan Cuisine V meals Coffee am Tea pm **FACILITIES:** CTV in all bedrooms STV Golf 18 Croquet lawn Jogging trail Membership of local gym Xmas **CONF:** Thtr 350 Class 170 Board 40 Del from £170 * **SERVICES:** Lift Night porter 150P **NOTES:** No dogs (ex guide dogs) No coaches No smoking area in restaurant Last d 9.30pm **CARDS:**

See advert on this page

HARROGATE North Yorkshire **Map 08 SE35**
★★★★ ***Harrogate Moat House***
Kings Rd HG1 1XX
Quality Percentage Score: 63%
☎ 01423 849988 Fax 01423 524435
Dir: *in Harrogate follow signs to International Conference Centre, hotel adjoins*
Located next to the International Conference Centre, this distinctive glass-fronted building provides smart, well-equipped accommodation. Refurbished spacious public areas include meeting facilities, a business centre and a restaurant offering dishes from around the world.
ROOMS: 214 en suite (bth/shr) No smoking in 69 bedrooms **MEALS:** English & French Cuisine V meals Coffee am Tea pm **FACILITIES:** CTV in all bedrooms Pool table **CONF:** Thtr 360 Class 220 Board 60 **SERVICES:** Lift Night porter 130P **NOTES:** No smoking area in restaurant Last d 11pm **CARDS:**

HARROGATE North Yorkshire **Map 08 SE35**
★★★★ **The Majestic**
Ripon Rd HG1 2HU
Quality Percentage Score: 62%
☎ 01423 700300 Fax 01423 502283
Dir: *leave M1 at Leeds, follow A61 to Harrogate. The hotel is in the town centre, overlooking the Royal Hall*
Very convenient for the town and conference centre, this elegant Edwardian hotel has impressive and comfortable public rooms
contd.

which feature chandeliers, murals, paintings and beautiful wood panelling. The bedrooms have been refurbished and include several spacious suites with separate sitting rooms.
ROOMS: 156 en suite (bth/shr) (10 fmly) No smoking in 46 bedrooms s £95-£110; d £130-£155 * LB Off peak **MEALS:** Bar Lunch £13.25-£17.95alc Dinner £19.95-£21.95 & alc International Cuisine V meals Coffee am Tea pm **FACILITIES:** CTV in all bedrooms STV Indoor swimming pool (heated) Tennis (hard) Squash Snooker Sauna Solarium Gym Jacuzzi/spa Health & beauty salon Wkly live entertainment Xmas **CONF:** Thtr 350 Class 150 Board 60 Del from £128 * **SERVICES:** Lift Night porter 240P **NOTES:** Last d 9.30pm
CARDS:

HARROGATE North Yorkshire **Map 08 SE35**
★★★★ ***Old Swan***
Swan Rd HG1 2SR
Quality Percentage Score: 61%
☎ 01423 500055 01423 501154

One of the best known of the town's hotels, the Old Swan has connections with the 'disappearance' in 1926 of Agatha Christie. Public rooms have been restored and include the ornate Wedgwood Room and the Library Restaurant. Bedrooms vary in style, but are comfortably furnished and include some suites with sitting rooms.
ROOMS: 136 en suite (bth/shr) (10 fmly) No smoking in 40 bedrooms **MEALS:** V meals Coffee am Tea pm **FACILITIES:** CTV in all bedrooms STV Croquet lawn **CONF:** Thtr 450 Class 150 Board 100 **SERVICES:** Lift Night porter 215P **NOTES:** No smoking in restaurant Last d 10pm RS Xmas/New Year **CARDS:**

HARROGATE North Yorkshire **Map 08 SE35**
★★★ **The Boar's Head Hotel**
Ripley Castle Estate HG3 3AY
Quality Percentage Score: 75%
☎ 01423 771888 01423 771509
Dir: *on the A61 Harrogate/Ripon road, the hotel is in the centre of Ripley Village*
In the private village of Ripley Castle estate, Sir Thomas and Lady Ingilby's charming hotel overlooks the cobbled market square. One of the 'Great Inns of England', it is renowned for its warm hospitality, traditional hostelry, and a restaurant which mixes modern dishes with traditional classics. Bedrooms offer many comforts, and the richly decorated public rooms feature family art work from the castle. Guests have free admission to the deer park, the lakeside and the walled gardens.
ROOMS: 13 en suite (bth/shr) 12 annexe en suite (bth/shr) (2 fmly) No smoking in 6 bedrooms s fr £95; d fr £115 (incl. bkfst) * LB Off peak **MEALS:** Lunch £16-£18 Dinner fr £30 V meals Coffee am Tea pm **FACILITIES:** CTV in all bedrooms STV Tennis (hard) Fishing Croquet lawn Clay pigeon shooting Xmas **CONF:** Thtr 60 Class 35 Board 30 Del from £145 * **SERVICES:** Night porter 53P **NOTES:** Last d 9.30pm
CARDS:

HARROGATE North Yorkshire **Map 08 SE35**
★★★ **Grants**
3-13 Swan Rd HG1 2SS
Quality Percentage Score: 71%
☎ 01423 560666 01423 502550
Dir: *off A61*

A welcoming hotel a short walk from the town centre. Individually styled bedrooms are comfortable, attractively furnished and thoughtfully equipped. Freshly prepared meals are served in the smart bistro restaurant where the walls display interesting pictures.
ROOMS: 42 en suite (bth/shr) (2 fmly) **MEALS:** English & French Cuisine V meals Coffee am Tea pm **FACILITIES:** CTV in all bedrooms Use of local Health & Leisure Club **CONF:** Thtr 70 Class 20 Board 30 **SERVICES:** Lift Night porter 26P **NOTES:** Last d 10pm
CARDS:

See advert on opposite page

HARROGATE North Yorkshire **Map 08 SE35**
★★★ **Imperial**
Prospect Place HG1 1LA
Quality Percentage Score: 69%
☎ 01423 565071 01423 500082
Dir: *follow A61 into town centre. Hotel opposite Betty's Tea Rooms*
This town-centre hotel provides attractive, comfortable accommodation, catering well for business and leisure guests. Staff are hospitable, and day rooms include a cocktail bar and the spacious Ambassadors Restaurant, as well as relaxing lounge areas.
ROOMS: 85 en suite (bth/shr) (2 fmly) No smoking in 40 bedrooms s £85; d £99 (incl. bkfst) * LB Off peak **MEALS:** Lunch fr £7.95 Dinner fr £15.50 English & French Cuisine V meals Coffee am Tea pm **FACILITIES:** CTV in all bedrooms STV Wkly live entertainment Xmas **CONF:** Thtr 200 Class 120 Board 40 Del from £110 * **SERVICES:** Lift Night porter 45P **NOTES:** No smoking in restaurant Last d 9.30pm
CARDS:

See advert on opposite page

HARROGATE North Yorkshire **Map 08 SE35**
★★★ ***Studley***
Swan Rd HG1 2SE
Quality Percentage Score: 66%
☎ 01423 560425 01423 530967
This pleasant, hospitable hotel is conveniently located for the Conference centre. Bedrooms are well furnished and thoughtfully equipped, inviting public areas include two bar lounges. The menu in the Le Breton room includes a mix of charcoal-cooked dishes and more classical offerings, excellent cooking.
ROOMS: 36 en suite (bth/shr) **MEALS:** English & French Cuisine Coffee am **FACILITIES:** CTV in all bedrooms STV **SERVICES:** Lift Night porter 14P **NOTES:** Last d 10pm **CARDS:**

THE IMPERIAL HOTEL

HARROGATE

AA ★★★ AA

The Imperial Hotel stands proudly at the heart of this famous spa town. The hotel has recently been refurbished and enjoys a superb central location with spectacular views across award winning gardens and The Stray.

Bygone Breakaways

This spacious hotel exudes a sense of luxury and grandeur normally associated with a bygone era. Our Bygone Break is inclusive of upgraded accommodation, four course evening meal, full English breakfast, complimentary tickets to five of North Yorkshire's finest attractions, a welcome refreshment tray of fresh fruit, chocolate and mineral water. **A minimum of a two night stay from just £49.00 per person per night.**

The Imperial Hotel has extensive conference facilities available and also free car parking at the front of the hotel.

The Imperial
Prospect Place, Harrogate HG1 1LA
Tel: 01423 565071 Fax: 01423 508427

Quality Inns

Hob Green

HOTEL & RESTAURANT

★ ★ ★

Set in 800 acres of glorious rolling countryside Hob Green is a gracious country house which has been carefully altered and restored to provide all the facilities of a first class hotel whilst retaining many original features including antique furniture and paintings. Each of the bedrooms is individually furnished and thoughtfully equpped to provide every comfort. Chef Chris Taylor uses the best local ingredients, including fruit, vegetables and herbs which are grown in the hotel's award winning gardens, to provide a high standard of modern and classical English cooking. Open log fires, a relaxed peaceful atmosphere and friendly helpful staff combine to make Hob Green the perfect retreat whether it be for a leisure break or small business get-together. With Fountains Abbey on the doorstep, the hotel is conveniently situated for Harrogate, Ripon and the Yorkshire Dales.

MARKINGTON, HARROGATE HG3 3PJ
Tel: Harrogate (01423) 770031 Fax: (01423) 771589

Ripon Spa Hotel

Peacefully situated just 5 minutes' walk from the ancient city of Ripon, close to Fountains Abbey and 20 minutes' drive from the spa town of Harrogate, the Ripon Spa Hotel is the ideal base whether on holiday or business.

Set in several acres of landscaped gardens, guests can relax and enjoy the comforts of this privately owned hotel which include 40 individually furnished bedrooms, attractive lounges and choice of dining in either The Restaurant or the informal Turf Tavern.

The hotel has excellent conference and banqueting facilities. Most importantly, the friendly and courteous staff provide the very best of Yorkshire hospitality which is why so many guests return again and again... and again.

For further details please see entry under RIPON.

Best Western   AA ★★★

THE RIPON SPA HOTEL
PARK STREET, RIPON, NORTH YORKS HG4 2BU
Tel. 01765 602172 · Fax. 01765 690770

Grants Hotel

HARROGATE

Are you looking for somewhere special with first class facilities plus a warm welcome and friendly efficient service. 42 well appointed, comfortable rooms. Lovely fresh food served in our Bistro with its casual French atmosphere. Free use of a superb nearby Health and Leisure club plus a host of other leisure activities within a few miles.

Telephone 01423 560666

Swan Road, Harrogate HG1 2SS

≡ HARROGATE North Yorkshire   **Map 08 SE35**
★★★ ⑳⑳✤ White House
10 Park Pde HG1 5AH
Quality Percentage Score: 66%
☎ 01423 501388 📠 01423 527973
Dir: at roundabout junct of A59/A6040, take Skipton direction, first turn left (Church Sq) at bottom turn left and house on right
Proudly owned and run by Jenny Forster, this hotel overlooks the famous Stray. Jenny is also the head chef and her excellent and imaginative dinners are served in the elegant dining room. The thoughtfully equipped bedrooms are stylishly furnished in keeping with the hotel's Victorian character. Two lounges are available for guests.
ROOMS: 10 en suite (bth/shr) (1 fmly) No smoking in all bedrooms s £92; d £125-£138.50 (incl. bkfst) * LB Off peak **MEALS:** Lunch £16.50 & alc Dinner £23-£27alc International Cuisine V meals Coffee am Tea pm **FACILITIES:** CTV in all bedrooms Xmas **CONF:** Thtr 40 Board 20 Del from £110 * **NOTES:** No dogs (ex guide dogs) No coaches No smoking in restaurant Last d 9pm **CARDS:** ➡ ▦ ⬛ ▦ ☒ ▢

≡ HARROGATE North Yorkshire   **Map 08 SE35**
★★★ Swallow St George
1 Ripon Rd HG1 2SY
Quality Percentage Score: 65%
☎ 01423 561431 📠 01423 530037

SWALLOW
HOTELS

Dir: on A61 opposite the Royal Hall, Conference Centre

Situated in the centre of the town and close to the Conference centre, this well furnished hotel offers comfortable accommodation with bedrooms that are particularly well equipped. Public areas include the elegant Swaledale Restaurant, The Brasserie, a leisure centre together with comfortable and well appointed lounges. Facilities are available for meetings and conferences and there is also a small garden, ideal for wedding receptions and private parties.
ROOMS: 90 en suite (bth/shr) (14 fmly) No smoking in 35 bedrooms s fr £100; d fr £110 (incl. bkfst) * LB Off peak **MEALS:** Lunch £11.50 & alc Dinner £13.50-£18.50 English & French Cuisine V meals Coffee am Tea pm **FACILITIES:** CTV in all bedrooms STV Indoor swimming pool (heated) Sauna Solarium Gym Jacuzzi/spa Boutique Beautician Masseuse Steamroom Carsio vascular room Xmas **CONF:** Thtr 200 Class 80 Board 50 Del from £110 * **SERVICES:** Lift Night porter 60P **NOTES:** No smoking in restaurant Last d 9.30pm
CARDS: ➡ ▦ ⬛ ▨ ▢

≡ HARROGATE North Yorkshire   **Map 08 SE35**
★★★ The Harrogate Spa Hotel
Prospect Place, West Park HG1 1LB
Quality Percentage Score: 62%
☎ 01423 564601 📠 01423 507508
Dir: on A61 close to town centre
Overlooking the famous Stray, this converted Georgian terrace property is only a short walk from the main shopping area of the town. A friendly and well managed hotel with slightly dated, but

well equipped and comfortable bedrooms. Drinks can be enjoyed in the warm atmosphere of the David Copperfield bar where lighter meals are also served.
ROOMS: 71 en suite (bth/shr) (5 fmly) No smoking in 9 bedrooms s £85; d £97 (incl. bkfst) * LB Off peak **MEALS:** Sunday Lunch £8.25-£10.50 Dinner fr £15.75 English & French Cuisine V meals Coffee am Tea pm **FACILITIES:** CTV in all bedrooms STV Xmas **CONF:** Thtr 150 Class 75 Board 58 Del from £75 * **SERVICES:** Lift Night porter 40P **NOTES:** No smoking in restaurant Last d 9.30pm
CARDS: ➡ ▦ ⬛ ▨ ☒ ▢

≡ HARROGATE North Yorkshire   **Map 08 SE35**

★★★ The Crown
Crown Place HG1 2RZ
Quality Percentage Score: 59%
☎ 01423 567755 📠 01423 502284

REGAL

Dir: take A61 into Harrogate continue down Parliament St to traffic lights by Royal Hall, left towards Valley Gardens, 1st left to rdbt, hotel on right
Improvements to the lounge and bar areas of this 18th-century coaching inn, situated next to the Royal Pump Room, have enhanced these facilities considerably. When further upgrading of the bedrooms has been completed the accommodation will be of a very good standard. In the meantime, the opulence of the panelled Ripley Restaurant and the elegance of other public rooms is reminiscent of the period, although much modernisation has taken place.
ROOMS: 121 en suite (bth/shr) (8 fmly) No smoking in 61 bedrooms s fr £85; d fr £105 * LB Off peak **MEALS:** Lunch £6.95-£9.95 Dinner £13-£19 English & French Cuisine V meals Coffee am Tea pm **FACILITIES:** CTV in all bedrooms free use of local sports club Xmas **CONF:** Thtr 400 Class 200 Board 80 Del £135 * **SERVICES:** Lift Night porter 70P **NOTES:** No smoking area in restaurant Last d 9.30pm **CARDS:** ➡ ▦ ⬛ ▨ ▦ ☒ ▢

≡ HARROGATE North Yorkshire   **Map 08 SE35**
★★ The Manor
3 Clarence Dr HG1 2QE
Quality Percentage Score: 72%
☎ 01423 503916 📠 01423 568709
Dir: from Ripon Road turn into Swan Road, then onto Clarence Drive
Standing in a quiet residential area close to the Valley Gardens, this attractive Victorian house has been well furnished throughout to provide good standards of comfort. Owners Mr and Mrs Gonzalez provide friendly service and interesting home-cooked food.
ROOMS: 17 en suite (bth/shr) (1 fmly) No smoking in 13 bedrooms s £45-£68; d £65-£90 (incl. bkfst) * LB Off peak **MEALS:** Lunch £18.95 & alc Dinner £18.95 & alc English & French Cuisine V meals Coffee am Tea pm **FACILITIES:** CTV in all bedrooms STV **SERVICES:** Lift 12P **NOTES:** No dogs No coaches No smoking in restaurant Last d 9.45pm Closed 24-27 Dec **CARDS:** ➡ ⬛ ▨ ☒ ▢

HARROGATE North Yorkshire — Map 08 SE35
★★ Ascot House
53 Kings Rd HG1 5HJ
Quality Percentage Score: 71%
☎ 01423 531005 Fax 01423 503523

MINOTEL Great Britain

Dir: *follow signs to town centre/conference and exhibition centre. At Kings Rd, drive past conference centre, Ascot House on left immediately after park*

Attentive service and friendly hospitality are found at this family-owned hotel. Freshly decorated bedrooms are thoughtfully equipped. There is a smartly presented lounge and a spacious lounge bar. A range of freshly prepared meals are served from the daily menu and a short carte in the attractive restaurant.
ROOMS: 19 en suite (bth/shr) (2 fmly) s £49.50-£59.50; d £74-£84 (incl. bkfst) LB Off peak **MEALS:** Dinner £14.95-£15.95 & alc English & Continental Cuisine V meals Coffee am Tea pm **FACILITIES:** CTV in all bedrooms Xmas **CONF:** Thtr 80 Class 36 Board 36 Del from £72 * **SERVICES:** 14P **NOTES:** Last d 8.30pm Closed 29 Dec-4 Jan & 21 Jan-7 Feb **CARDS:**

HARROGATE North Yorkshire — Map 08 SE35
★★ Grafton
1-3 Franklin Mount HG1 5EJ
Quality Percentage Score: 68%
☎ 01423 508491 Fax 01423 523168

Dir: *500yds from Conference Centre*

Convenient for both the town and the Conference Centre this friendly hotel offers good value, pleasant accommodation. The bedrooms have all been recently upgraded, and the public rooms consist of a cosy lounge/bar and a dining room which overlooks the well tended front garden.
ROOMS: 17 en suite (bth/shr) (3 fmly) No smoking in 8 bedrooms s £40-£65; d £59.50-£74 (incl. bkfst) * LB Off peak **MEALS:** Lunch £10-£15 & alc High tea £6-£8 & alc Dinner £17.50 & alc English & Continental Cuisine V meals **FACILITIES:** CTV in all bedrooms **SERVICES:** 3P **NOTES:** No dogs (ex guide dogs) No smoking in restaurant Last d 7pm Closed 16 Dec-5 Jan **CARDS:**

HARROGATE North Yorkshire — Map 08 SE35
★★ Green Park
Valley Dr HG2 0JT
Quality Percentage Score: 68%
☎ 01423 504681 Fax 01423 530811

Best Western

Dir: *S of town centre, turn off A61 on to B6162, right at traffic lights by New Inn pub, left past petrol station*

This friendly hotel is situated opposite Valley Gardens, just a short walk from the Conference and Exhibition Centre and main shopping areas. Bedrooms, including two on the ground floor, are comfortably furnished, while public areas include a bright restaurant offering a varied range of dishes. There is also a choice of light and airy lounges.
ROOMS: 43 en suite (bth/shr) (2 fmly) No smoking in 20 bedrooms **MEALS:** International Cuisine V meals Coffee am Tea pm **FACILITIES:** CTV in all bedrooms **CONF:** Thtr 40 Class 30 Board 24 Del from £69 * **SERVICES:** Lift Night porter 10P **NOTES:** No smoking in restaurant Last d 8.45pm **CARDS:**

HARROGATE North Yorkshire — Map 08 SE35
★★ ❀ Harrogate Brasserie Hotel & Bar
28-30 Cheltenham Pde HG1 1DB
Quality Percentage Score: 68%
☎ 01423 505041 Fax 01423 530920

Dir: *on A61*

Situated in the town centre, this hotel offers a style of operation that is distinctly continental. The Brasserie is very popular and at weekends live jazz is featured. Bedrooms are individual in style and offer a varied standard of appointment. The hotel also provides a comfortable residents' lounge on the first floor.
ROOMS: 13 en suite (bth/shr) (3 fmly) **MEALS:** English & French Cuisine V meals Coffee am Tea pm **FACILITIES:** CTV in all bedrooms STV Wkly live entertainment **SERVICES:** 12P **NOTES:** No coaches Last d 10pm **CARDS:**

See advert on this page

HARROGATE North Yorkshire — Map 08 SE35
★★ The Croft
42-46 Franklin Rd HG1 5EE
Quality Percentage Score: 66%
☎ 01423 563326 Fax 01423 530733

THE CIRCLE Selected Individual Hotels GREAT BRITAIN

Dir: *proceed to Conference Centre, opposite turn into Strawberry Dale Av, first left into Franklin Road*

Mr & Mrs Maas provide friendly and personal service at this hotel, located in a quiet residential road within easy walking distance of both the town and the conference centre. The bright fresh bedrooms are thoughtfully equipped and the lounge and bar are both inviting and comfortable. Quality home-cooked food is available in the cosy rear dining room.
ROOMS: 13 en suite (bth/shr) s £32-£37.50; d £50-£62 (incl. bkfst) * LB Off peak **MEALS:** Lunch £15-£18alc Dinner £15-£18alc English & French Cuisine V meals Coffee am Tea pm **FACILITIES:** CTV in all bedrooms Pool table **CONF:** Class 12 Board 10 **SERVICES:** 10P **NOTES:** No smoking in restaurant Last d 8pm **CARDS:**

H

AA Rosettes are awarded for quality of food,
see page 15 for an explanation of Rosette assessment.

HARROGATE North Yorkshire **Map 08 SE35**
★★ ***Low Hall***
Ripon Rd, Killinghall HG3 2AY
Quality Percentage Score: 66%
☎ 01423 508598 🖷 01423 560848
Dir: *exit Harrogate on A61 northbound in the direction of Ripon in 2m on exiting the village of Killinghall, Low Hall is 300mtrs on the right*
Situated in the village of Killinghall, just to the north of Harrogate, this Grade II listed building, dating back to 1672 in parts, has great charm and character in the public areas. Beams and stone walls are much in evidence and the galleried dining area is an attractive feature. Bedrooms vary in size but are equipped to suit both the business and leisure visitor, and service is friendly.
ROOMS: 7 en suite (bth/shr) No smoking in all bedrooms
MEALS: European Cuisine V meals Coffee am Tea pm **FACILITIES:** CTV in all bedrooms STV **CONF:** Thtr 90 Class 70 Board 70 **SERVICES:** 40P **NOTES:** No dogs (ex guide dogs) No coaches No smoking in restaurant Last d 8.30pm **CARDS:**

HARROGATE North Yorkshire **Map 08 SE35**
★★ **Bay Horse Inn & Motel**
Burnt Yates HG3 3EJ
Quality Percentage Score: 65%
☎ 01423 770230 🖷 01423 771894
Dir: *W on B6165 next to village church*
Located in a quiet village set in rolling open countryside north west of Harrogate this 18th-century inn provides pretty bedrooms which are also well equipped. The hotel offers very good food which is prepared from fresh ingredients and the resident owners are always around either in the bar or the rustic restaurant.
ROOMS: 6 en suite (shr) 10 annexe en suite (shr) (2 fmly) s £40-£45; d £55-£60 (incl. bkfst) * LB Off peak **MEALS:** Lunch £10.95-£15.95 Dinner £15.95 English & French Cuisine V meals Coffee am **FACILITIES:** CTV in all bedrooms **CONF:** Board 35 **SERVICES:** 70P **NOTES:** No dogs (ex guide dogs) No smoking in restaurant Last d 9.30pm **CARDS:**

HARROGATE North Yorkshire **Map 08 SE35**
Late entry ○ **Cedar Court**
Queens Buildings, Park Pde HG1 5AH
☎ 01423 858585 🖷 01423 504950
This grade II listed building has been completely refurbished to 21st century standards. The bedrooms are spacious and well equipped and there are ample meeting rooms and two large banqueting halls.
ROOMS: 100 en suite (bth/shr) s £85-£95; d £90-£110 * Off peak **MEALS:** Lunch £7.50-£12.50 High tea £7.50 Dinner £15-£18.50 & alc International Cuisine V meals Coffee am Tea pm **FACILITIES:** CTV in all bedrooms STV Gym Xmas **CONF:** Thtr 350 Class 180 Board 70 Del from £90 * **SERVICES:** Lift Night porter 150P **NOTES:** No smoking area in restaurant Last d 10pm **CARDS:**

HARROW Greater London
See LONDON SECTION plan 1 *B5*
★★★ ***Cumberland***
1 St Johns Rd HA1 2EF
Quality Percentage Score: 67%
☎ 020 8863 4111 🖷 020 8861 5668
This popular hotel stands in the town centre and caters for both the business and leisure markets. The bedrooms, which are modern and well equipped, are divided between the main house and two other nearby buildings. There is a quiet lounge area, and a restaurant serving a wide choice of food.

ROOMS: 31 en suite (bth/shr) 53 annexe en suite (bth/shr) (6 fmly) No smoking in 51 bedrooms **MEALS:** International Cuisine V meals Coffee am Tea pm **FACILITIES:** CTV in all bedrooms STV Sauna Gym Small Fitness Room **CONF:** Thtr 140 Class 50 Board 40 Del from £90 * **SERVICES:** Night porter 57P **NOTES:** No dogs (ex guide dogs) No smoking area in restaurant Last d 10.30pm
CARDS:

See advert on opposite page

HARROW Greater London
★★★ **Quality Harrow Hotel**
Roxborough Bridge, 12-22 Pinner Rd HA1 4HZ
Quality Percentage Score: 67%
☎ 020 8427 3435 🖷 020 8861 1370
Dir: *at junct of A404/A312*
This privately owned hotel is housed in a number of interlinked houses dating from the early 20th century. Bedrooms are well equipped and smartly furnished, and the five courtyard rooms are particularly peaceful. Public areas include a smart conservatory restaurant.
ROOMS: 53 en suite (bth/shr) 23 annexe en suite (bth/shr) (2 fmly) No smoking in 28 bedrooms s £70-£85; d £95-£110 (incl. bkfst) * Off peak **MEALS:** Lunch £17.95 Dinner £17.95 International Cuisine V meals Coffee am Tea pm **FACILITIES:** CTV in all bedrooms STV **CONF:** Thtr 160 Class 60 Board 60 Del from £117 * **SERVICES:** Night porter 70P **NOTES:** No smoking in restaurant Last d 10.30pm RS Xmas (limited service) **CARDS:**

See advert on opposite page

HARROW Greater London

★★★ **Northwick Park**
2-12 Northwick Park Rd HA1 2NT
Quality Percentage Score: 65%
☎ 0500 636943 (Central Res) 🖷 01773 880321
Dir: *off A4006*
Convenient for access to central London, and sheltered from the
contd.

main road, this long, low building offers a variety of styles of comfortable bedrooms, some being designated as 'superior'. There is a modern bar and restaurant, and a large function room.
ROOMS: 75 en suite (bth/shr) (3 fmly) No smoking in 30 bedrooms s £89; d £99 * Off peak **MEALS:** Lunch £5.95-£20 Dinner fr £18.95alc V meals Coffee am Tea pm **FACILITIES:** CTV in all bedrooms STV Xmas **CONF:** Thtr 200 Class 80 Board 75 Del from £95 * **SERVICES:** Night porter 65P **NOTES:** Last d 9.30pm **CARDS:**

HARROW Greater London
★★ Lindal
2 Hindes Rd HA1 1SJ
Quality Percentage Score: 55%
☎ 020 8863 3164 Fax 020 8427 5435
Dir: *off A409, opposite Tesco Superstore*
This family-run establishment provides easy access to Harrow shopping centre and offers attractively furnished, modern bedrooms. Day rooms consist of a combined bar-lounge, a breakfast room and a dining area.
ROOMS: 19 en suite (bth/shr) (3 fmly) No smoking in 5 bedrooms s £48-£52; d £60-£65 (incl. bkfst) * LB Off peak **MEALS:** V meals Coffee am Tea pm **FACILITIES:** CTV in all bedrooms **SERVICES:** Night porter 17P **NOTES:** No dogs (ex guide dogs) **CARDS:**

HARROW WEALD See LONDON SECTION plan 1 *B6*

HARTLEBURY Worcestershire — Map 07 SO87
Travelodge
Travelodge
Shorthill Nurseries DY13 9SH
☎ 01299 250553 Fax 01299 250553
Dir: *A449 southbound*
This modern building offers accommodation in smart, spacious and well equipped bedrooms, all with en-suite bathrooms. Refreshments may be taken at the nearby family restaurant. For details about current prices, consult the Contents Page under Hotel Groups for the Travelodge phone number.
ROOMS: 32 en suite (bth/shr) d £45.95 *

HARTLEPOOL Co Durham — Map 08 NZ53
★★★ The Grand
Swainson St TS24 8AA
Quality Percentage Score: 64%
☎ 01429 266345 Fax 01429 265217
Dir: *opposite shopping centre, adjacent to Civic Centre*
Standing in the centre of the town, this splendid Victorian building with impressive facade offers many spacious, well equipped bedrooms. Public rooms are extensive and include a pleasant restaurant, a large bar and a magnificent ballroom. A good range of food is available in the bar and the restaurant.
ROOMS: 47 en suite (bth/shr) (4 fmly) s fr £52.50; d fr £65 (incl. bkfst) * LB Off peak **MEALS:** Lunch fr £4.50 Dinner fr £10 & alc English & French Cuisine V meals Coffee am Tea pm **FACILITIES:** CTV in all bedrooms STV Pool table Free use of local leisure centre **CONF:** Thtr 200 Class 150 Board 35 **SERVICES:** Lift Night porter 50P
CARDS:

HARTLEPOOL Co Durham — Map 08 NZ53
★★ Ryedale Moor
3 Beaconsfield St, Headland TS24 0NX
Quality Percentage Score: 67%
☎ 01429 231436 Fax 01429 863787
Dir: *access via A179. Follow signs to Headland*
Looking out to sea in The Headland area of Hartlepool, this hotel offers friendly and attentive service to a mainly commercial
contd.

clientele in a relaxed atmosphere. The interior is attractively decorated and bedrooms are modern in style.
ROOMS: 16 en suite (bth/shr) (2 fmly) No smoking in 5 bedrooms s £38-£43.50; d £48-£54 (incl. bkfst) * LB Off peak **MEALS:** Lunch £4.95-£9.95 & alc High tea £9.95 & alc Dinner £11.50 & alc English, French & Indian Cuisine V meals Coffee am Tea pm **FACILITIES:** CTV in 13 bedrooms STV Xmas **CONF:** Thtr 40 Class 40 Board 30 Del from £49 * **SERVICES:** 8P **NOTES:** No dogs No children 12yrs No smoking in restaurant Last d 9.45pm **CARDS:**

HARTLEPOOL Co Durham — Map 08 NZ53

Travel Inn
Maritme Av, Hartlepool Marina TS24 0XZ
☎ 01429 890115 01429 868674
Dir: *approx 1m from A689/A179 link road on marina*
This modern building offers accommodation in smart, spacious and well equipped bedrooms, all with en-suite bathrooms. Refreshments may be taken at the nearby family restaurant. For details about current prices consult the Contents Page under Hotel Groups for the Travel Inn phone number.
ROOMS: 40 en suite (bth/shr) d £39.95 *

HARTSHEAD MOOR SERVICE AREA West Yorkshire — Map 07 SE12

Welcome Lodge
Hartshead Moor Service Area, Clifton HD6 4JX
☎ 01274 851706 01274 855169
Dir: *M62 eastbound between junct 25 & 26*
This modern building offers accommodation in smart, spacious and well equipped bedrooms, suitable for families and businessmen, and all with en-suite bathrooms. Refreshments may be taken at the nearby family restaurant. For details of current prices, consult the Contents Page under Hotel Groups for the Welcome Break phone number.
ROOMS: 40 en suite (bth/shr) d fr £45 *

HARVINGTON (NEAR EVESHAM) Worcestershire 4 — Map 04 SP0

★★ The Mill at Harvington
Anchor Ln, Harvington WR11 5NR
Quality Percentage Score: 80%
☎ 01386 870688 01386 870688
(For full entry see Evesham)

HARWICH Essex — Map 05 TM23

★★ The Pier at Harwich
The Quay CO12 3HH
Quality Percentage Score: 72%
☎ 01255 241212 01255 551922
Dir: *from A12, take A120 to the Quay, hotel is opposite the Lifeboat Station*
Just across the road from the harbourside, this excellent small hotel is renowned for the quality of its cooking, with seafood a speciality. There is a choice of two restaurants, the family orientated Ha'penny Pier downstairs, and above, for more serious dining, the Pier at Harwich. The six comfortable bedrooms are on the top floor, some with views over the harbour.
ROOMS: 6 en suite (bth) (2 fmly) s £52.50-£67.50; d £75-£85 (incl. cont bkfst) * Off peak **MEALS:** Lunch £16.50-£59.70alc Dinner £4.25-£29.95alc English & French Cuisine V meals Coffee am **FACILITIES:** CTV in all bedrooms **CONF:** Thtr 50 Class 50 Board 24 **SERVICES:** Night porter 10P **NOTES:** No dogs (ex guide dogs) Last d 9.30pm Closed 24-26 Dec RS 25-26 Dec **CARDS:**

HARWICH Essex — Map 05 TM23

★★ Hotel Continental
28/29 Marine Pde, Dovercourt CO12 3RG
Quality Percentage Score: 61%
☎ 01255 551298 01255 551698
Dir: *turn off A120 at Ramsay rdbt onto B1352 continue until reaching a pedestrain crossing & Co-op store on right, turn right here into Fronks Rd*

With its seafront location and easy access to the ferry terminals, this popular hotel is frequented by both overseas travellers and business users. The open plan bar/dining area is a focal point, with its all-day snack selection, wide-screen satellite television and wide ranging dinner menu. There is also a cosy residents' lounge. The bedrooms vary in size and space, but all are suitably furnished and comfortable.
ROOMS: 14 rms (12 shr) (2 fmly) No smoking in 1 bedroom s £25-£40; d £40-£60 (incl. bkfst) LB Off peak **MEALS:** Lunch £9.95-£13.95 & alc Dinner £9.95-£14 & alc Coffee am Tea pm **FACILITIES:** CTV in all bedrooms STV **CONF:** Thtr 30 Board 20 Del from £40 *
SERVICES: 4P **NOTES:** Last d 10pm
CARDS:

HARWICH Essex — Map 05 TM23

Late entry **Cliff**
Marine Pde, Dovercourt CO12 3RE
☎ 01255 503345 & 507373 01255 240358
Dir: *A120 to Parkeston rdbt, take road to Dovercourt, on seafront after Dovercourt town centre*
With views of Felixstowe Harbour and the Stour Estuary, this traditional resort hotel stands in a central position on the cliff between Dovercourt and Harwich. Public rooms are attractive and comfortably furnished; they include a lounge and residents' bar serving a range of light snacks, and a more formal restaurant. Bedroom styles and sizes vary, but the more recently refurbished bedrooms are modern and well appointed.
ROOMS: 26 en suite (bth/shr) (3 fmly) No smoking in 1 bedroom s £48; d £58 (incl. bkfst) * LB Off peak **MEALS:** Lunch £8.95-£14.95 Dinner £11.95-£14.95 V meals Coffee am Tea pm **FACILITIES:** CTV in all bedrooms STV Pool table **CONF:** Thtr 200 Class 150 Board 40 Del from £64.75 * **SERVICES:** Night porter 50P **NOTES:** No smoking area in restaurant Last d 9.30pm RS Xmas & New Year
CARDS:

HASLEMERE Surrey — Map 04 SU93

★★★★ Lythe Hill
Petworth Rd GU27 3BQ
Quality Percentage Score: 71%
☎ 01428 651251 01428 644131
Dir: *turn left from Haslemere High St onto B2131. Lythe Hill 1.25m on right*
Lythe Hill has been created out of a cluster of historic buildings set in 20 acres of fine grounds which include a bluebell wood and several lakes. Most of the individually styled bedrooms are designed around the 15th-century beams and the layout of the

contd.

original dwellings. There are some separate garden suites and five rooms in the original black and white timbered house with its jetted upper storey. It is also here that the oak-panelled Auberge de France restaurant is located (there is another restaurant in the main building), offering sound cooking from long serving chef Roger Clarke.

ROOMS: 41 en suite (bth/shr) (8 fmly) s £98-£148; d £120-£180 * LB Off peak **MEALS:** Lunch £19.50-£24.50 Dinner £19.50-£24.50 & alc English & French Cuisine V meals Coffee am Tea pm **FACILITIES:** CTV in all bedrooms STV Tennis (hard) Fishing Pool table Croquet lawn Boules Games Room Xmas **CONF:** Thtr 60 Class 40 Board 30 Del from £108 * **SERVICES:** Night porter 200P **NOTES:** No smoking in restaurant Last d 9.15pm **CARDS:**

HASTINGS & ST LEONARDS East Sussex **Map 05 TQ80**

★★★ Beauport Park
Battle Rd TN38 8EA
Quality Percentage Score: 69%
☎ 01424 851222 01424 852465
Dir: *3m N off A2100*

An elegant Georgian manor house set in 40 acres just outside Hastings. The bedrooms are tastefully decorated and well equipped. Public rooms convey much of the original character of the building and the Garden restaurant offers an extensive range of dishes.

ROOMS: 23 en suite (bth/shr) (2 fmly) No smoking in 9 bedrooms s fr £85; d fr £110 (incl. bkfst) * LB Off peak **MEALS:** International Cuisine V meals Coffee am Tea pm **FACILITIES:** CTV in all bedrooms STV Outdoor swimming pool (heated) Golf 18 Tennis (hard) Riding Croquet lawn Putting green Wkly live entertainment ch fac Xmas **CONF:** Thtr 70 Class 25 Board 30 Del from £63 * **SERVICES:** 60P **NOTES:** No coaches No smoking in restaurant Last d 9.30pm **CARDS:**

See advert on this page

HASTINGS & ST LEONARDS East Sussex **Map 05 TQ80**

★★★ High Beech
Battle Rd TN37 7BS
Quality Percentage Score: 65%
☎ 01424 851383 01424 854265
Dir: *400yds from A2100 between Hastings and Battle*

Bedrooms at this privately owned hotel are generally of a good size and come with complimentary wine and fresh fruit. The Mountbatten Bar doubles as the lounge area and the attractive

contd.

★

The Premier Collection, hotels with Red Star Awards are listed on pages 17-23

Wedgwood Restaurant is the place to find a good cooked breakfast. Self-catering suites are available.

High Beech, Hastings & St Leonards

ROOMS: 17 en suite (bth/shr) (3 fmly) s £55; d £85-£95 (incl. bkfst) * LB Off peak **MEALS:** Lunch fr £11 Dinner £16-£18 & alc English & Continental Cuisine V meals Coffee am Tea pm **FACILITIES:** CTV in all bedrooms STV Xmas **CONF:** Thtr 250 Class 192 Board 146 Del from £65 * **SERVICES:** 65P **NOTES:** No dogs (ex guide dogs) Last d 9.15pm **CARDS:**

See advert on page 299

HASTINGS & ST LEONARDS East Sussex **Map 05 TQ80**

★★★ Royal Victoria

Marina, St Leonards-on-Sea TN38 0BD
Quality Percentage Score: 64%
☎ 01424 445544 01424 721995
Dir: *on western seafront off A21*

Purpose built as a hotel in 1828, and numbering the eponymous Queen among its famous guests, the Royal Victoria is an imposing presence on the seafront at St Leonards. A fine marble staircase leads up from the lobby to the main public areas on the first floor which are gradually being refurbished. Bedrooms are unusually spacious and include a number of duplex and family suites. Staff are attentive and friendly.

ROOMS: 50 en suite (bth/shr) (15 fmly) s fr £85; d fr £95 (incl. bkfst) * LB Off peak **MEALS:** Lunch fr £12.50 High tea fr £3.50 Dinner fr £17 V meals Coffee am Tea pm **FACILITIES:** CTV in all bedrooms Wkly live entertainment Xmas **CONF:** Thtr 100 Class 50 Board 250 Del from £85 * **SERVICES:** Lift Night porter 6P **NOTES:** No smoking in restaurant Last d 9.30pm **CARDS:**

See advert on opposite page

Indicates that the star classification has not been confirmed under the New Quality Standards, see page 7 for further information.

HASTINGS & ST LEONARDS East Sussex **Map 05 TQ80**

Travel Inn

1 John Macadam Way, St Leonards on Sea TN37 6DB
☎ 01424 754070 01424 753139
Dir: *travelling int Hastings on A21 London Rd, Travel Inn is on right after junct with A2100 Battle road*

This modern building offers accommodation in smart, spacious and well equipped bedrooms, all with en-suite bathrooms. Refreshments may be taken at the nearby family restaurant. For details about current prices consult the Contents Page under Hotel Groups for the Travel Inn phone number.

ROOMS: 44 en suite (bth/shr) d £39.95 *

HATFIELD Hertfordshire **Map 04 TL20**

★★★ Quality Hotel Hatfield

Roehyde Way AL10 9AF
Quality Percentage Score: 66%
☎ 01707 275701 01707 266033
Dir: *M25 junct 23 take A1(M) northbound to junct 2, at rdbt take exit left, hotel in 0.5m on right*

This hotel attracts a thriving conference market. Bedrooms are modern in design and well equipped; executive bedrooms are larger and have extra facilities such as fridges and trouser presses. For meals, there is 24-hour room service or a choice between a bar/brasserie and a more formal dining room.

ROOMS: 76 en suite (bth/shr) (14 fmly) No smoking in 39 bedrooms s £85-£99; d £90-£109 * Off peak **MEALS:** Dinner fr £14.50 V meals Coffee am Tea pm **FACILITIES:** CTV in all bedrooms STV Xmas **CONF:** Thtr 120 Class 60 Board 50 **SERVICES:** Night porter 120P **NOTES:** No smoking area in restaurant Last d 9.45pm **CARDS:**

HATFIELD Hertfordshire **Map 04 TL20**

★★ Hatfield Lodge Hotel

Comet Way AL10 9NG
Quality Percentage Score: 63%
☎ 01707 272661 01707 256282
Dir: *turn off A1 at junct 3 take A1001, Comet Way, towards Hatfield, over rdbt hotel on left (dual carriageway) opposite Galleria shopping centre*

This modern hotel offers extensive conference facilities and is ideally located opposite the Hatfield Galleria with easy access to the A1(M) and M1. Accommodation is divided between the well proportioned and well equipped single rooms which are popular with conference delegates; and the more recent addition of rooms which are more spacious and very smart, there are also three older rooms in the main house. There is a small bar and a bright conservatory restaurant offering a short modern menu.

ROOMS: 37 en suite (bth/shr) No smoking in 9 bedrooms s £52-£68; d fr £68 * Off peak **MEALS:** Dinner £13.75-£15.75 V meals Coffee am Tea pm **FACILITIES:** CTV in all bedrooms STV Swimming pass available for local pool **CONF:** Thtr 300 Class 128 Board 80 Del from £105 * **SERVICES:** Night porter 120P **NOTES:** No dogs (ex guide dogs) No coaches Last d 9.15pm Closed 24-28 Dec **CARDS:**

HATFIELD Hertfordshire **Map 04 TL20**

Travel Inn

Lemsford Rd AL10 0DA
☎ 01707 268990 01707 268293
Dir: *from A1(M) junct 4 follow A1001 towards Hatfield, Travel Inn on top of Hatfield Tunnel*

This modern building offers accommodation in smart, spacious and well equipped bedrooms, all with en-suite bathrooms. Refreshments may be taken at the nearby family restaurant. For details about current prices consult the Contents Page under Hotel Groups for the Travel Inn phone number.

ROOMS: 40 en suite (bth/shr) d £39.95 *

HATHERSAGE Derbyshire **Map 08 SK28**

★★★ George

Main Rd S32 1BB

Quality Percentage Score: 70%

☎ 01433 650436 01433 650099

Dir: *in village centre on A625 from Sheffield*

Recently refurbished, this solid stone built hotel is in the village centre. Spacious bedrooms offer good comfort, as does the inviting bar lounge; carefully prepared dishes are served in the cosy restaurant. Service is professional and friendly.

ROOMS: 19 en suite (bth/shr) (2 fmly) s fr £69.50; d fr £99.50 (incl. bkfst) * LB Off peak **MEALS:** Lunch £14.95-£16.95 & alc Dinner fr £19.95 International Cuisine V meals Coffee am Tea pm **FACILITIES:** CTV in all bedrooms **CONF:** Thtr 30 Class 15 Board 20 Del from £105 * **SERVICES:** 40P **NOTES:** No dogs (ex guide dogs) No smoking in restaurant Last d 10pm

CARDS:

HATHERSAGE Derbyshire **Map 08 SK28**

★★★ Hathersage Inn

Main Rd S32 1BB

Quality Percentage Score: 68%

☎ 01433 650259 01433 651199

Dir: *in village centre on A625*

A charming stone-built inn, situated in the middle of Hathersage. Attractively decorated and comfortable bedrooms, four of which are in an adjacent building, are complemented by the lounge-bar and restaurant, where high quality dishes are always guaranteed. In addition, the Cricketers Bar is a popular with locals and visitors alike.

ROOMS: 11 en suite (bth/shr) 4 annexe en suite (bth/shr) s fr £56; d fr £74 (incl. bkfst) * LB Off peak **MEALS:** Sunday Lunch £7.50-£10 Dinner £13.95-£19.50 English & French Cuisine V meals Coffee am Tea pm **FACILITIES:** CTV in all bedrooms Xmas **CONF:** Thtr 18 Class 12 Board 12 Del from £75 * **SERVICES:** 20P **NOTES:** No coaches Last d 9.30pm **CARDS:**

HAVANT Hampshire **Map 04 SU70**

★★ *The Bear*

East St PO9 1AA

Quality Percentage Score: 63%

☎ 023 92486501 023 92470551

Dir: *£*

This former coaching inn in the heart of the town offers informal public rooms which include a small cocktail bar and the Elizabethan public bar. Bedrooms are gradually being upgraded, though all are fully equipped and well laid out.

ROOMS: 42 en suite (bth/shr) (6 fmly) No smoking in 24 bedrooms **MEALS:** European Cuisine V meals Coffee am Tea pm **FACILITIES:** CTV in all bedrooms STV Wkly live entertainment **CONF:** Thtr 120 Class 60 Board 60 **SERVICES:** Night porter 90P **NOTES:** No dogs (ex guide dogs) No smoking area in restaurant Last d 9.45pn

CARDS:

HAVANT Hampshire **Map 04 SU70**

Travel Inn

65 Bedhampton Hill, Bedhampton PO9 3JN

☎ 023 92472619 023 92453471

This modern building offers accommodation in smart, spacious and well equipped bedrooms, all with en-suite bathrooms. Refreshments may be taken at the nearby family restaurant. For details about current prices consult the Contents Page under Hotel Groups for the Travel Inn phone number.

ROOMS: 36 en suite (bth/shr) d £39.95 *

HAWES North Yorkshire **Map 07 SD88**

★★ *Simonstone Hall*

Simonstone DL8 3LY

Quality Percentage Score: 75%

☎ 01969 667255 01969 667741

Dir: *1.5m N on road signed to Muker and Buttertubs*

Commanding spectacular views across the upper WensleyDale Valley, this former hunting lodge provides an ideal base for exploring the Yorkshire moors. Fully restored and now run as a country house, it offers professional but friendly service in a relaxed atmosphere. The house 'overflows' with collectibles, artefacts and a vast array of gilt framed paintings. There is an inviting drawing room, elegant restaurant and character bar serving pub food. Bedrooms reflect the style of the house and are generally spacious. Dinner is a highlight of any visit and the creative kitchen make excellent use of the local game, fish and delicious cheeses.

ROOMS: 18 en suite (bth/shr) (10 fmly) No smoking in all bedrooms **MEALS:** English & French Cuisine V meals Coffee am Tea pm **FACILITIES:** CTV in all bedrooms **CONF:** Thtr 30 Board 20 **SERVICES:** 40P **CARDS:**

HAWES North Yorkshire **Map 07 SD88**

★★ Stone House

Sedbusk DL8 3PT

Quality Percentage Score: 72%

☎ 01969 667571 01969 667720

Dir: *from Hawes take road signposted 'Muker & The Buttertubs' to T junct then right towards Sedbusk & Askrigg. Hotel 500yds on left*

Overlooking green fields to the north of Hawes, this traditional Edwardian hotel retains the charm of a bygone age. The hotel is well furnished and contemporary fittings blend well with the

contd.

historic architecture. There is a delightful log fire in the lounge and carefully prepared Yorkshire dinners are served each evening in the welcoming restaurant. Bedrooms are well equipped and attractively furnished and the service is friendly and attentive.
ROOMS: 18 rms (17 bth/shr) 4 annexe en suite (bth/shr) (1 fmly) No smoking in all bedrooms s £36-£85; d £62-£85 (incl. bkfst) LB Off peak **MEALS:** Dinner £17.95 British Cuisine V meals Coffee am **FACILITIES:** CTV in all bedrooms Tennis (grass) Pool table Croquet lawn Xmas **CONF:** Thtr 35 Class 35 Board 35 **SERVICES:** 30P **NOTES:** No smoking in restaurant Last d 8pm Closed Jan RS mid Nov-Dec & Feb
CARDS:

HAWKHURST Kent — Map 05 TQ73

★★★ *Tudor Court*

Rye Rd TN18 5DA
Quality Percentage Score: 70%
☎ 01580 752312 Fax 01580 753966
Dir: *from A21 take A268 and continue across traffic lights. Hotel 0.5m on left*

This small hotel offers a particularly warm welcome. The bedrooms are comfortably furnished and well equipped with modern facilities. The public areas include bars, a comfortable lounge and an attractive restaurant overlooking the garden, children's play area, croquet lawn, clock golf and hard tennis courts.
ROOMS: 18 en suite (bth/shr) (2 fmly) No smoking in 2 bedrooms **MEALS:** International Cuisine V meals Coffee am Tea pm **FACILITIES:** CTV in all bedrooms Tennis (hard) Croquet lawn Putting green Clock golf Childrens play area ch fac **CONF:** Thtr 60 Class 40 Board 32 Del from £88.13 * **SERVICES:** 50P **NOTES:** No dogs (ex guide dogs) No smoking in restaurant Last d 9pm
CARDS:

See advert on opposite page

HAWKSHEAD (NEAR AMBLESIDE) Cumbria — Map 07 SD39

★★ *Highfield House Country Hotel*

Hawkshead Hill LA22 0PN
Quality Percentage Score: 75%
☎ 015394 36344 Fax 015394 36793
Dir: *on B5285 towards Coniston three quarters of a mile from Hawkshead village*

From an elevated position above the village of Hawkshead this country house hotel enjoys a stunning panorama. Bedrooms combine the traditional and the contemporary. Public areas include a lounge, cosy bar and dining room serving good food and excellent breakfasts.
ROOMS: 11 en suite (bth/shr) (2 fmly) No smoking in 1 bedroom **MEALS:** English & Continental Cuisine V meals Coffee am Tea pm **FACILITIES:** CTV in all bedrooms ch fac **SERVICES:** 15P **NOTES:** No coaches No smoking in restaurant Last d 8.30pm Closed 20-27 Dec & 3-31 Jan **CARDS:**

HAWKSHEAD (NEAR AMBLESIDE) Cumbria — Map 07 SD39

★★ *Queen's Head*

Main St LA22 0NS
Quality Percentage Score: 66%
☎ 015394 36271 Fax 015394 36722
Dir: *leave M6 at junct 36, then A590 to Newby Bridge. Take 2nd right and continue 8m into Hawkshead*

This black and white 16th-century inn has low oak beamed ceilings in the welcoming bar, which is warmed by an open log fire. Substantial, carefully prepared meals are served in the wood panelled bar. Bedrooms, three of which are in an adjacent cottage, are attractively furnished; four poster and family rooms are available.

ROOMS: 10 rms (1 bth 7 shr) 3 annexe en suite (bth/shr) (2 fmly) No smoking in all bedrooms **MEALS:** English & Continental Cuisine V meals Coffee am Tea pm **FACILITIES:** CTV in all bedrooms **NOTES:** No dogs (ex guide dogs) No smoking in restaurant Last d 9.30pm
CARDS:

See advert on opposite page

HAWORTH West Yorkshire — Map 07 SE03

★★ Old White Lion

6 West Ln BD22 8DU
Quality Percentage Score: 67%
☎ 01535 642313 Fax 01535 646222
Dir: *turn off A629 onto B6142, hotel 0.5m past Haworth Station*

Almost 300 years old, this character hotel is situated at the top of the old cobbled street in the centre of the village. There is a choice of bars, in addition to the oak panelled lounge, where a range of snacks and meals is available. More formal dining is available in the popular restaurant, and function facilities are also offered. Bedrooms, varying in size and style, are comfortably furnished.
ROOMS: 15 en suite (bth/shr) (3 fmly) s £44-£60; d £60-£80 (incl. bkfst) * LB Off peak **MEALS:** Sunday Lunch fr £7.75 Dinner fr £12 & alc English & French Cuisine V meals Coffee am **FACILITIES:** CTV in all bedrooms Xmas **CONF:** Thtr 70 Class 40 Board 30 **SERVICES:** 10P **NOTES:** No dogs (ex guide dogs) Last d 9.30pm
CARDS:

See advert under BRADFORD

HAWORTH West Yorkshire — Map 07 SE03

★★ Three Sisters

Brow Top Rd BD22 9PH
Quality Percentage Score: 64%
☎ 01535 643458 Fax 01535 646842
Dir: *from A629 Keighley/Halifax road take B6144 at Flappit Corner. Hotel 0.75m on right*

Originally a Victorian farmhouse, this popular hotel and inn

contd.

now offers modern spacious bedrooms. An extensive selection of freshly prepared meals and snacks is served, all in generous portions, in either the bar or the spacious restaurant, enjoying fine views over Haworth and the surrounding district.
ROOMS: 9 en suite (bth/shr) (1 fmly) s £33-£38; d £45-£50 (incl. bkfst) * LB Off peak **MEALS:** Lunch £6.95-£9.95 & alc High tea £3.45-£6.95 Dinner £9.95 & alc English & French Cuisine V meals Coffee am Tea pm **FACILITIES:** CTV in all bedrooms STV Pool table Wkly live entertainment Xmas **CONF:** Thtr 250 Class 200 Board 100 Del from £50 * **SERVICES:** Night porter 300P **NOTES:** No dogs (ex guide dogs) No smoking in restaurant Last d 9.30pm **CARDS:**

HAYDOCK Merseyside **Map 07 SJ59**
★★★★ ***Thistle Haydock***
THISTLE HOTELS
Penny Ln WA11 9SG
Quality Percentage Score: 68%
☎ 01942 272000 01942 711092
Dir: *M6 junct23, follow signs for racecourse, around traffic island and onto A49 towards Ashton-in-Makerfield. Take 1st left, under bridge and 1st left*
This smart, purpose built hotel which offers an excellent standard of thoughtfully equipped accommodation, is conveniently situated between Liverpool and Manchester, just off junction 23 of the M6. The public areas, which include a wide range of leisure and meeting facilities, prove popular with both corporate and leisure guests. A friendly team of professional, well supervised staff ensure guests are well looked after.
ROOMS: 139 en suite (bth/shr) (13 fmly) No smoking in 30 bedrooms **MEALS:** English & Continental Cuisine V meals Coffee am Tea pm **FACILITIES:** CTV in all bedrooms STV Indoor swimming pool (heated) Sauna Solarium Gym Jacuzzi/spa Steam room Whirlpool Trim trail ch fac **CONF:** Thtr 300 Class 180 Board 40 **SERVICES:** Night porter 180P **NOTES:** Last d 10pm **CARDS:**

HAYDOCK Merseyside **Map 07 SJ59**
★★★ **Posthouse Haydock**
Posthouse
Lodge Ln WA12 OJG
Quality Percentage Score: 66%
☎ 01942 717878 01942 718419
Dir: *adj to M6 junct 23, on A49*
A modern hotel, conveniently situated for junction 23 of the M6, and Haydock Park racecourse. Bedrooms are comfortable and well appointed and public areas, including the popular Seasons restaurant, are similarly relaxing. A feature of the hotel is the excellent leisure club which incorporates a heated swimming pool, gymnasium and an aerobics studio. An all day menu is available in the lounge and 24 hour room service is also provided. There are also meeting and conference facilities and easy car parking.
ROOMS: 138 en suite (bth/shr) (41 fmly) No smoking in 74 bedrooms d fr £89 * LB Off peak **MEALS:** International Cuisine V meals Coffee am Tea pm **FACILITIES:** CTV in all bedrooms Indoor swimming pool (heated) Sauna Solarium Gym Pool table Jacuzzi/spa ch fac Xmas **CONF:** Thtr 180 Class 100 Board 60 **SERVICES:** Lift Night porter 197P **NOTES:** No smoking area in restaurant
CARDS:

HAYDOCK Merseyside **Map 07 SJ59**
Travelodge
Travelodge
Piele Rd WA11 9TL
☎ 01942 272055 01942 272055
Dir: *2m W of junct 23 on M6, on A580 westbound*
This modern building offers accommodation in smart, spacious and well equipped bedrooms, all with en-suite bathrooms. Refreshments may be taken at the nearby family restaurant. For details about current prices, consult the Contents Page under Hotel Groups for the Travelodge phone number.
ROOMS: 40 en suite (bth/shr) d £39.95 *

HAYES Hotels are listed under **Heathrow Airport**

HAYLING ISLAND Hampshire **Map 04 SU70**

★★★ Posthouse Havant

Posthouse

Northney Rd PO11 0NQ
Quality Percentage Score: 62%
☎ 023 92465011 📠 023 92466468
Dir: *from A27 signposted Havant/Hayling Island follow A3023 across roadbridge onto Hayling Island and take sharp left on leaving bridge*
This purpose built hotel, just south of the A27, overlooks Langstone estuary. Bedrooms are well equipped and benefit from 24 hour room service. Public rooms include a first floor bar and lounge, and an indoor leisure centre.
ROOMS: 92 en suite (bth/shr) (10 fmly) No smoking in 44 bedrooms d £39-£79 (incl. dinner) * LB Off peak **MEALS:** International Cuisine V meals Coffee am Tea pm **FACILITIES:** CTV in all bedrooms Indoor swimming pool (heated) Sauna Gym Pool table Jacuzzi/spa Massage & beauty therapy, Steam Room Xmas **CONF:** Thtr 180 Class 80 Board 50 Del from £70 * **SERVICES:** Night porter 150P **NOTES:** No smoking in restaurant Last d 10pm **CARDS:**

HAYTOR VALE Devon **Map 03 SX77**

★★★ Bel Alp House

TQ13 9XX
Quality Percentage Score: 78%
☎ 01364 661217 📠 01364 661292
Dir: *2.5m W of Bovey Tracey, A38 onto A382*
This delightful Edwardian house offers spacious, well equipped bedrooms and has outstanding views of Dartmoor. Stained glass windows and open fires are features of the public rooms, and the set six-course dinner should not be missed. Picnic lunches can be provided.
ROOMS: 8 en suite (bth/shr) (2 fmly) No smoking in 1 bedroom s £60-£75; d £120-£150 (incl. bkfst) * Off peak **MEALS:** Dinner £22.50 English & French Cuisine **FACILITIES:** CTV in all bedrooms Snooker Croquet lawn **SERVICES:** 20P **NOTES:** No coaches No smoking in restaurant Last d 8.30pm **CARDS:**

HAYTOR VALE Devon **Map 03 SX77**

★★ Rock Inn

TQ13 9XP
Quality Percentage Score: 73%
☎ 01364 661305 & 661465 📠 01364 661242
Dir: *turn off A38 onto A382 to Bovey Tracey, approx 0.5m turn left and join B3387 to Haytor*
This delightful 16th-century inn is set in a village in the Dartmoor National Park. A wide range of dishes is served in a variety of dining areas and the bars are full of character, with flagstone floors and old beams. The bedrooms are all named after Grand National winners, and the 'Lovely Cottage' room, with its four-poster bed, is especially popular.
ROOMS: 9 en suite (bth/shr) (2 fmly) No smoking in 2 bedrooms s £47.95-£57.95; d £65.95-£75.95 (incl. bkfst) * LB Off peak **MEALS:** Bar Lunch £10-£25alc Dinner £12-£25.95alc English, French & Italian Cuisine V meals Coffee am Tea pm **FACILITIES:** CTV in all bedrooms STV Xmas **SERVICES:** 20P **NOTES:** No dogs (ex guide dogs) No coaches No smoking in restaurant Last d 9.15pm
CARDS:

HEATHROW AIRPORT (LONDON) **Map 04 TQ07**
Greater London
see also **Staines**

★★★★ Crowne Plaza London – Heathrow

Stockley Rd UB7 9NA
Quality Percentage Score: 75%
☎ 01895 445555 📠 01895 445122
Dir: *leave M4 junct 4 follow signs to Uxbridge on A408, hotel entrance approx 400yds on left*
Close to Heathrow and the motorways, this modern hotel offers a particularly good range of facilities for the international traveller, as well as service and accommodation of a high quality. There is a choice of bars serving food, and a modern French restaurant. Conference facilities are versatile, and there is a 24-hour leisure complex as well as golfing. Air-conditioning, mini bars and 24-hour room service are standard in all bedrooms, from the 'executive' style through to the 'superiors' and luxurious 'club' rooms.
ROOMS: 458 en suite (bth/shr) (220 fmly) No smoking in 187 bedrooms **MEALS:** European Cuisine V meals Coffee am Tea pm **FACILITIES:** CTV in all bedrooms STV Indoor swimming pool (heated) Golf 9 Sauna Solarium Gym Jacuzzi/spa Beauty therapy room Helipad **CONF:** Thtr 200 Class 120 Board 75 **SERVICES:** Lift Night porter Air conditioning 410P **NOTES:** No smoking area in restaurant Last d 10.30pm
CARDS:

HEATHROW AIRPORT (LONDON) **Map 04 TQ07**
Greater London

★★★★ London Heathrow Marriott Hotel

Bath Rd
Quality Percentage Score: 70%
☎ 020 8990 1100 📠 020 8990 1110
This brand new hotel has all the hallmarks expected of a modern airport hotel. There is a spacious atrium with several eating and drinking options leading from it. Secure car parking, meeting rooms and very good leisure facilities, all in very good condition, make this a well-rounded establishment. Spacious bedrooms are very well sound-proofed and equipped with a useful range of amenities.
ROOMS: 390 en suite (bth/shr) (20 fmly) No smoking in 320 bedrooms d £110-£165 * LB Off peak **MEALS:** Lunch £16-£30alc Dinner £18-£30alc International Cuisine V meals Coffee am Tea pm **FACILITIES:** CTV in all bedrooms STV Indoor swimming pool (heated) Sauna Solarium Gym Jacuzzi/spa **CONF:** Thtr 540 Class 214 Board 50 Del from £195 * **SERVICES:** Lift Night porter Air conditioning 290P **NOTES:** No smoking area in restaurant Last d 11pm **CARDS:**

HEATHROW AIRPORT (LONDON) **Map 04 TQ07**
Greater London

★★★★ Sheraton Skyline

Bath Rd UB3 5BP
Quality Percentage Score: 70%
☎ 020 8759 2535 📠 020 8750 9150
Offering a courtesy bus to all terminals, the Sheraton Skyline sits on the Heathrow 'strip'. At the hotel's heart is a pool within a leafy atrium complex. The ground floor has a range of eating options including snacks in the lobby lounge, the popular sports bar or the more formal Colony Room restaurant. Bedrooms are a

contd.

good size and have the bonus of air-conditioning. Other facilities include a range of conference rooms, and a gym.
ROOMS: 351 en suite (bth/shr) (12 fmly) No smoking in 58 bedrooms d £80-£242 * LB Off peak **MEALS:** Lunch £18.75 & alc Dinner £25-£30 & alc French Cuisine V meals Coffee am Tea pm **FACILITIES:** CTV in all bedrooms STV Indoor swimming pool (heated) Gym Xmas **CONF:** Thtr 600 Class 350 Board 16 Del from £195 * **SERVICES:** Lift Night porter Air conditioning 300P **NOTES:** No smoking area in restaurant Last d 11pm **CARDS:**

HEATHROW AIRPORT (LONDON) Map 04 TQ07
Greater London
★★★★ *Forte Crest Heathrow*
Sipson Rd UB7 0JU
Quality Percentage Score: 67%
☎ 020 8759 2323 📠 020 8897 8659
Dir: *M4 junct4, keep left, take first left into Holloway Lane, left at mini rdbt then immediately left through hotel gates*
This large, modern hotel, well situated for both the airport and M4/M25 motorways, has services and amenities designed for the international traveller. Bedrooms are smart and comfortable, there is a wide choice of restaurant and refreshment facilities and good modern conference and meeting rooms.
ROOMS: 610 en suite (bth/shr) (284 fmly) No smoking in 359 bedrooms **MEALS:** English, Italian & Chinese Cuisine V meals Coffee am Tea pm **FACILITIES:** CTV in all bedrooms STV **CONF:** Thtr 130 Class 60 Board 60 **SERVICES:** Lift Night porter 478P **NOTES:** No dogs (ex guide dogs) Last d mdnt **CARDS:**

HEATHROW AIRPORT (LONDON) Map 04 TQ07
Greater London
★★★★ *The Renaissance London Heathrow Hotel*
Bath Rd TW6 2AQ
Quality Percentage Score: 67%
☎ 020 8897 6363 📠 020 8897 1113
Dir: *leave M4 junct4 follow spur road towards airport, take 2nd turning left & follow road to rdbt take 2nd exit. This road leads to hotel*
This busy hotel, formerly one of the Ramada group, offers views of one of Heathrow's main runways. There are well equipped, up-to-the-minute conference facilities, and the Icarus bar is a popular meeting place.
ROOMS: 650 en suite (bth/shr) No smoking in 140 bedrooms **MEALS:** International Cuisine V meals Coffee am Tea pm **FACILITIES:** CTV in all bedrooms STV Sauna Solarium Gym Wkly live entertainment **CONF:** Thtr 450 Class 280 Board 60 **SERVICES:** Lift Night porter Air conditioning 675P **NOTES:** No dogs (ex guide dogs) No smoking area in restaurant Last d 10.30pm
CARDS:

HEATHROW AIRPORT (LONDON) Map 04 TQ07
Greater London
★★★★ Slough/Windsor Marriott
Ditton Rd, Langley SL3 8PT
Quality Percentage Score: 66%
☎ 01753 544244 📠 01753 540272
Dir: *from junct 5 of M4/A4, follow 'Langley' signs and turn left at traffic lights into Ditton Road*
This large busy hotel, just off the M4, manages successfully to juggle the demands of international travellers without losing the personal touch that makes all guests feel welcome. A wide range of services is offered, plus a choice of eating options and an indoor leisure centre. Bedrooms are comfortable and well equipped.
ROOMS: 380 en suite (bth/shr) (149 fmly) No smoking in 231 bedrooms d £99-£135 * LB Off peak **MEALS:** Lunch £16.95 Dinner fr £19.95 Mediterranean Cuisine V meals Coffee am Tea pm **FACILITIES:** CTV in all bedrooms STV Indoor swimming pool (heated) Tennis (hard) Sauna Solarium Gym Beautician Wkly live entertainment Xmas **CONF:** Thtr 300 Class 150 Board 10 Del from £145 * **SERVICES:** Lift Night porter Air conditioning 600P **NOTES:** No dogs (ex guide dogs) No smoking area in restaurant Last d 10pm **CARDS:**

HEATHROW AIRPORT (LONDON) Map 04 TQ07
Greater London
★★★★ *The Excelsior*
Bath Rd UB7 0DU
Quality Percentage Score: 64%
☎ 020 8759 6611 📠 020 8759 3421
Dir: *adj M4 spur at junc with A4*
Heathrow's largest hotel offers its international clientele a wide range of eating and drinking options, including an Irish-themed pub, a fish restaurant and a carvery, as well as an all-day cafe. There is a choice of room styles, with the Crown Club offering more comfortable rooms.
ROOMS: 830 en suite (bth/shr) (55 fmly) No smoking in 390 bedrooms **MEALS:** V meals Coffee am Tea pm **FACILITIES:** CTV in all bedrooms STV Indoor swimming pool (heated) Sauna Solarium Gym Jacuzzi/spa **CONF:** Thtr 700 Class 310 Board 60 **SERVICES:** Lift Night porter Air conditioning 500P **NOTES:** No smoking area in restaurant Last d 10.30pm **CARDS:**

HEATHROW AIRPORT (LONDON) Map 04 TQ07
Greater London
★★★ Novotel
Junction 4 M4, Cherry Ln UB7 9HB
Quality Percentage Score: 69%
☎ 01895 431431 📠 01895 431221
Dir: *leave M4 junct 4 follow signs for Uxbridge(A408), keep left & take 2nd exit off traffic island into Cherry Ln signed West Drayton. Hotel on left*
With convenient access to the M4 and M25 motorways, the Novotel offers comfortable and well equipped accommodation for business and leisure guests alike. The rooms have been upgraded to the new company standard. Overlooked by bedrooms above, the huge indoor atrium is bright and airy, offering spacious public areas, with a cocktail bar, indoor swimming pool and fitness centre. The keen and enthusiastic team of staff are on hand to assist at all times.
ROOMS: 178 en suite (bth/shr) (29 fmly) No smoking in 112 bedrooms d fr £109 * LB Off peak **MEALS:** International Cuisine V meals Coffee am Tea pm **FACILITIES:** CTV in all bedrooms STV Indoor swimming pool (heated) Gym **CONF:** Thtr 250 Class 100 Board 90 **SERVICES:** Lift Night porter 150P **NOTES:** No smoking area in restaurant Last d mndt **CARDS:**

HEATHROW AIRPORT (LONDON) Map 04 TQ07
Greater London
★★★ Posthouse Heathrow Airport
118 Bath Rd UB3 5AJ
Quality Percentage Score: 66%
☎ 0870 400 9040 📠 020 8564 9265
Dir: *leave M4 junct 4, take spur road to Heathrow Airport, 1st left off towards A4, on to A4 Bath Road, through 3 traffic lights, hotel on left*
Well positioned for both the business and leisure traveller, this bright hotel provides accommodation equipped to up-to-date

contd.

modern standards, especially Posthouse's new Millennium rooms.
ROOMS: 186 en suite (bth/shr) No smoking in 100 bedrooms s £49-£130; d £49-£150 * Off peak **MEALS:** International Cuisine V meals Coffee am Tea pm **FACILITIES:** CTV in all bedrooms Xmas **CONF:** Thtr 50 Class 20 Board 24 **SERVICES:** Lift Night porter Air conditioning 105P **NOTES:** No dogs (ex guide dogs) No smoking area in restaurant Last d 12.30pm **CARDS:**

HEATHROW AIRPORT (LONDON) Greater London — Map 04 TQ07
★★★ Osterley Four Pillars Hotel
764 Great West Rd TW7 5NA
Quality Percentage Score: 65%
☎ 020 8568 9981 020 8569 7819
(For full entry see Osterley)

HEATHROW AIRPORT (LONDON) Greater London — Map 04 TQ07
★★★ Master Robert
Great West Rd TW5 0BD
Quality Percentage Score: 63%
☎ 020 8570 6261 020 8569 4016
Dir: *A4*
Three-and-a-half miles from Heathrow on the A4 towards London, the Master Robert offers well equipped bedrooms in motel-style buildings behind the main hotel premises, which house a pub, a residents bar lounge and a restaurant.
ROOMS: 94 en suite (bth/shr) (8 fmly) No smoking in 33 bedrooms s £92.50-£95; d £104-£107 * LB Off peak **MEALS:** English & Continental Cuisine V meals Coffee am Tea pm **FACILITIES:** CTV in all bedrooms STV **CONF:** Thtr 130 Class 48 Board 40 Del from £115 * **SERVICES:** Night porter 135P **NOTES:** No dogs (ex guide dogs) No smoking area in restaurant **CARDS:**

HEATHROW AIRPORT (LONDON) Greater London — Map 04 TQ07
★★★ *The Heathrow Park*
Bath Rd, Longford UB7 0EQ
Quality Percentage Score: 62%
☎ 020 8759 2400 020 8759 5278
This quiet hotel offers extensive and sizeable meeting facilities, two dining choices, shop and business centre. Three styles of bedroom are available, some of which have more facilities than others. The first-floor restaurant and bar have good views of the airport's western runway. Free use of a nearby health centre is provided.
ROOMS: 310 en suite (bth/shr) (55 fmly) No smoking in 140 bedrooms **MEALS:** Continental Cuisine V meals Coffee am Tea pm **FACILITIES:** CTV in all bedrooms STV Free use of neighbouring Health Club **CONF:** Thtr 700 Class 500 Board 30 **SERVICES:** Night porter Air conditioning 500P **NOTES:** No smoking area in restaurant Last d 11.30pm **CARDS:**

HEATHROW AIRPORT (LONDON) Greater London — Map 04 TQ07
★★ Hotel Ibis
112/114 Bath Rd UB3 5AL
Quality Percentage Score: 62%
☎ 020 8759 4888 020 8564 7894
Dir: *on A4 close to airport*
This busy hotel provides good levels of comfort for the budget conscious business and leisure user. Modern and well maintained facilities are provided in the bedrooms and on the ground floor there is a well run buffet style restaurant as well as a bar where snacks are available throughout most of the day and night. A regular shuttle service is available to and from the airport.
ROOMS: 354 en suite (bth/shr) No smoking in 134 bedrooms d £58 * Off peak **MEALS:** Lunch £4.50-£7.50alc Dinner £7.95-£11.95alc International Cuisine V meals Coffee am Tea pm **FACILITIES:** CTV in all bedrooms STV **SERVICES:** Lift Night porter 120P **NOTES:** No smoking area in restaurant Last d 10.30pm **CARDS:**

HEATHROW AIRPORT (LONDON) Greater London — Map 04 TQ07
Travel Inn
362 Uxbridge Rd UB4 0HF
☎ 020 8573 7479 020 8569 1204
Dir: *from M4 junct 3 follow A312 north, straight across next rdbt onto dual carriageway, at A4020 junc turn left, Travel Inn is 100yds on the right*
This modern building offers accommodation in smart, spacious and well equipped bedrooms, all with en-suite bathrooms. Refreshments may be taken at the nearby family restaurant. For details about current prices consult the Contents Page under Hotel Groups for the Travel Inn phone number.
ROOMS: 40 en suite (bth/shr) d £39.95 *

HEBDEN BRIDGE West Yorkshire — Map 07 SD92
★★★ Carlton
Albert St HX7 8ES
Quality Percentage Score: 66%
☎ 01422 844400 01422 843117
Dir: *turn right at cinema for hotel at top of Hope St*
This town centre Victorian building, originally the town's main store, still has shops at street level, a lift takes guests to the hotel itself. Individually designed bedrooms are attractively furnished, whilst public areas also offer peaceful and comfortable areas for relaxation. Diners can choose between snacks served in the bar or more traditional meals in the airy dining room, where the service is prompt yet friendly.
ROOMS: 16 en suite (bth/shr) s £56-£66; d £75-£85 (incl. bkfst) * LB Off peak **MEALS:** Lunch £6.95-£11.50 Dinner £15.50-£22.85alc International Cuisine V meals Coffee am Tea pm **FACILITIES:** CTV in all bedrooms STV **CONF:** Thtr 120 Class 40 Board 40 Del from £90 * **SERVICES:** Lift **NOTES:** No smoking in restaurant Last d 9.30pm
CARDS:

HECKFIELD Hampshire — Map 04 SU76
★★ New Inn
RG27 0LE
Quality Percentage Score: 68%
☎ 0118 932 6374 0118 932 6550
Dir: *turn off A33 onto B3349, turn right at island and continue on B3349 to hotel 0.5m on left*
A well maintained inn, parts of which date from the 15th century. Low, beamed ceilings and two roaring log fires in the bar create a cosy atmosphere. Guests can eat here or in the restaurant. Bedrooms offer spacious accommodation and are equipped to a high standard of comfort.
ROOMS: 16 en suite (bth/shr) (1 fmly) s £65; d £75 (incl. bkfst) * Off peak **MEALS:** Lunch £6.95-£20.95alc Dinner £11.90-£20.95alc V meals Coffee am Tea pm **FACILITIES:** CTV in all bedrooms STV **CONF:** Thtr 20 Class 14 Board 16 Del £105 * **SERVICES:** 80P **NOTES:** No smoking area in restaurant Last d 10pm Closed 25 Dec
CARDS:

For Useful Information and Important Telephone Number Changes turn to page 25

HEDDON'S MOUTH Devon — Map 03 SS64

★★ Heddon's Gate Hotel

EX31 4PZ

Quality Percentage Score: 76%

☎ 01598 763313 Fax 01598 763363

Dir: *3.5m W of Lynton on A39 turn R, signs Martinhoe & Woody Bay. Follow signs for Hunter's Inn & Heddon's Mouth, hotel on R 0.25m before Hunter's Inn*

Breathtaking countryside surrounds this friendly hotel, which takes great pride in the quality of its food. Do not miss afternoon tea, laid out between four and five o'clock. Bedrooms are individually designed and comfortable day rooms include a bar, a Victorian morning room cum library and an Edwardian sitting room with superb views.

ROOMS: 11 en suite (bth/shr) 3 annexe en suite (bth/shr) s £59-£69; d £112-£160 (incl. bkfst & dinner) LB Off peak **MEALS:** Dinner £20-£25 Tea pm **FACILITIES:** CTV in all bedrooms **SERVICES:** 20P **NOTES:** No coaches No children No smoking in restaurant Last d 8pm Closed Nov-Etr **CARDS:**

See advert on this page

HELLIDON Northamptonshire — Map 04 SP55

★★★★ Hellidon Lakes Hotel & Country Club

NN11 6LN

Quality Percentage Score: 69%

☎ 01327 262550 Fax 01327 262559

Dir: *signposted, off A361 between Daventry and Banbury*

Extensive grounds have twelve lakes, an 18 and a 9 hole golf course. Leisure facilities include a state of the art gym, beauty salon, sauna, pool and a bowling alley. Bedrooms feature striking tulip-wood furniture, all are spacious and well equipped. The restaurant serves modern British cuisine, a spectacular new restaurant was nearing completion at the time of our visit.

ROOMS: 51 en suite (bth/shr) s £89.50-£125; d £125-£145 (incl. bkfst) * LB Off peak **MEALS:** Lunch fr £22.50 Dinner £22.50-£27.50 & alc English & French Cuisine V meals Coffee am Tea pm **FACILITIES:** CTV in all bedrooms STV Indoor swimming pool (heated) Golf 27 Fishing Solarium Gym Putting green Jacuzzi/spa Beautician, Ten Pin Bowling, Golf Simulator. **CONF:** Thtr 150 Class 70 Board 50 Del from £135 * **SERVICES:** Night porter 140P **NOTES:** No dogs (ex guide dogs) No coaches Last d 9.30pm **CARDS:**

HELMSLEY North Yorkshire — Map 08 SE68

★★★ The Black Swan

Market Place YO62 5BJ

Quality Percentage Score: 75%

☎ 01439 770466 Fax 01439 770174

Dir: *follow A170 towards Scarborough into Helmsley and hotel at top of Market Square*

In a prime position overlooking the square, the Black Swan is made up of a Tudor rectory, an Elizabethan coaching inn and a Georgian house. It offers attractively decorated and thoughtfully equipped accommodation which reflects the character and history of the building. There are modern rooms which overlook the gardens at the rear of the building. Deep cushioned sofas, fresh flowers and open fires are the hallmarks of the numerous lounges.

ROOMS: 45 en suite (bth/shr) (4 fmly) No smoking in 13 bedrooms s £120-£145; d £145 * LB Off peak **MEALS:** Lunch £10.75-£16.75alc Dinner £25-£40alc V meals Coffee am Tea pm **FACILITIES:** CTV in all bedrooms Croquet lawn Xmas **CONF:** Thtr 60 Class 16 Board 22 Del £135 * **SERVICES:** Night porter 50P **NOTES:** No smoking in restaurant Last d 9.30pm **CARDS:**

HELMSLEY North Yorkshire — Map 08 SE68

★★★ Feversham Arms

1 High St YO62 5AG

Quality Percentage Score: 70%

☎ 01439 770766 Fax 01439 770346

Dir: *on B1363, 100mtrs from Market Place*

This well-furnished and comfortable hotel has been owned by the same family since 1971. Each summer a colourful display of roses adorns the façade. Both the restaurant and bar menus offer a good selection of dishes, including a wide variety of fish and shellfish. The comfortable bedrooms are well equipped and hospitality is very good.

ROOMS: 18 en suite (bth/shr) (4 fmly) s £55-£65; d £80-£90 (incl. bkfst) * LB Off peak **MEALS:** Lunch fr £15 & alc Dinner £20-£25 & alc English, French & Spanish Cuisine V meals Coffee am **FACILITIES:** CTV in all bedrooms STV Outdoor swimming pool (heated) Tennis (hard) **CONF:** Thtr 30 Class 30 Board 24 Del from £89 * **SERVICES:** 30P **NOTES:** No smoking in restaurant Last d 9pm **CARDS:**

HELMSLEY North Yorkshire — Map 08 SE68
★★★ Pheasant

Harome YO62 5JG

Quality Percentage Score: 70%

☎ 01439 771241 Fax 01439 771744

***Dir:** 2.5m SE, leave A170 after 0.25m, turn right signposted Harome for further 2m*

Enjoying a charming setting next to the village pond, this welcoming hotel has attractive, comfortable bedrooms. The beamed, stone-flagged bar leads into the extended dining room, where honest English food is served, with a nearby and comfortable lounge in which to relax.

ROOMS: 12 en suite (bth) 2 annexe en suite (bth) s £58.50-£64; d £117-£128 (incl. bkfst & dinner) * LB Off peak **MEALS:** Bar Lunch £1.65-£15alc Dinner £20-£22 V meals Coffee am **FACILITIES:** CTV in all bedrooms Indoor swimming pool (heated) **SERVICES:** 20P **NOTES:** No coaches No children 12yrs No smoking in restaurant Last d 8pm Closed Xmas & Jan-Feb **CARDS:**

HELMSLEY North Yorkshire — Map 08 SE68
★★ Carlton Lodge

Bondgate YO62 5EY

Quality Percentage Score: 68%

☎ 01439 770557 Fax 01439 770623

***Dir:** on the A170 Scarborough road, close to Market Sq*

A friendly, welcoming hotel on the edge of the town with comfortable, well furnished bedrooms. Public areas include an inviting lounge with an open fire, and a well appointed dining room where good quality, home-cooked evening meals are served.

ROOMS: 7 rms (6 shr) 4 annexe en suite (bth/shr) (1 fmly) s fr £39.50; d fr £70 (incl. bkfst) * LB Off peak **MEALS:** Lunch £15-£18.50alc Dinner £17.50-£20alc European Cuisine V meals **FACILITIES:** CTV in all bedrooms Xmas **CONF:** Thtr 150 Class 60 Board 50 Del from £49.95 * **SERVICES:** 45P **NOTES:** No smoking in restaurant Last d 9pm **CARDS:**

HELMSLEY North Yorkshire — Map 08 SE68
★★ Crown

Market Square YO62 5BJ

Quality Percentage Score: 68%

☎ 01439 770297 Fax 01439 771595

***Dir:** on A170*

A 16th-century inn, standing in the market square and noted for its colourful flower arrangements. Bedrooms are individual and thoughtfully equipped, and public areas are pleasantly traditional. These include cosy bars, a residents' lounge and a dining room serving wholesome dishes in generous portions.

ROOMS: 12 en suite (bth/shr) (1 fmly) s £32-£35; d £64-£70 (incl. bkfst) * LB Off peak **MEALS:** Lunch fr £10.95 High tea £5.95-£7.95 Dinner fr £15.50 V meals Coffee am Tea pm **FACILITIES:** CTV in all bedrooms Xmas **SERVICES:** 20P **NOTES:** No smoking area in restaurant Last d 8.30pm **CARDS:**

HELMSLEY North Yorkshire — Map 08 SE68
★★ *Feathers*

Market Place YO62 5BH

Quality Percentage Score: 64%

☎ 01439 770275 Fax 01439 771101

***Dir:** in Helmsley market place on A170*

This 15th-century, creeper-clad hotel and inn stands in the Market Place and has been extensively refurbished by the present owners. It offers very pleasantly furnished and well equipped bedrooms while an extensive range of food is available either in the bar or the dining room. The bars are very popular, especially with the friendly locals.

ROOMS: 14 en suite (bth/shr) **MEALS:** English & Continental Cuisine V meals Coffee am **FACILITIES:** CTV in all bedrooms **CONF:** Del from £67 * **SERVICES:** 24P **NOTES:** No dogs (ex guide dogs) No children 12yrs No smoking in restaurant Last d 9.30pm

CARDS:

HELSTON Cornwall & Isles of Scilly — Map 02 SW62
★★ ❀❀ Nansloe Manor

Meneage Rd TR13 0SB

Quality Percentage Score: 78%

☎ 01326 574691 Fax 01326 564680

***Dir:** 300yds on the left from Helston/Lizard roundabout A394/A3083*

Located on the main Helston to Falmouth road and set in five acres of grounds, Nansloe offers its guests a tranquil and civilised atmosphere. There is a choice of bedroom sizes, and all rooms offer modern facilities and many personal touches. The comfortable drawing room looks out over the gardens, where dining orders are taken for the popular cuisine that is served in the elegant restaurant.

ROOMS: 7 rms (6 bth/shr) s £51-£98; d £98-£120 (incl. bkfst) LB Off peak **MEALS:** Sunday Lunch £11.50 Dinner £21.50 & alc English & Mediterranean Cuisine V meals Coffee am Tea pm **FACILITIES:** CTV in all bedrooms Croquet lawn Xmas **SERVICES:** 40P **NOTES:** No dogs No coaches No children 10yrs No smoking in restaurant Last d 8.30pm

CARDS:

HELSTON Cornwall & Isles of Scilly — Map 02 SW62
★★ The Gwealdues

Falmouth Rd TR13 8JX

Quality Percentage Score: 66%

☎ 01326 572808 Fax 01326 561388

***Dir:** Hotel is on approach into Helston on A394, coming from Truro or Falmouth*

Situated on the outskirts of town, this is a friendly hotel for business and tourism and is much in demand for its smart function room. Most bedrooms offer modern accommodation and many useful facilities, in addition to the provision of complimentary newspapers. Guests may choose to eat from the main menu in the homely dining room or sample one of the many bar snacks.

ROOMS: 17 en suite (bth/shr) (5 fmly) s £30-£45; d £40-£60 (incl. bkfst) * LB Off peak **MEALS:** Dinner £12 & alc V meals Coffee am Tea pm **FACILITIES:** CTV in all bedrooms **CONF:** Board 100 **SERVICES:** 60P **NOTES:** No coaches No smoking in restaurant Last d 9pm

CARDS:

HEMEL HEMPSTEAD Hertfordshire — Map 04 TL00
★★★ Posthouse Hemel Hempstead

Posthouse

Breakspear Way HP2 4UA

Quality Percentage Score: 66%

☎ 01442 251122 Fax 01442 211812

***Dir:** exit junct 8 of M1, straight over roundabout and 1st left after BP garage*

Well suited to both the business and leisure traveller, this bright modern hotel provides well equipped in smart bedrooms with en suite bathrooms.

ROOMS: 145 en suite (bth/shr) (33 fmly) No smoking in 76 bedrooms **MEALS:** Lunch £5.95-£15.95 & alc Dinner £4.95-£15.95alc International Cuisine V meals Coffee am Tea pm **FACILITIES:** CTV in all bedrooms Indoor swimming pool (heated) Sauna Solarium Gym Pool table Jacuzzi/spa Children's playroom/play area at weekends ch fac **CONF:** Thtr 60 Class 22 Board 30 **SERVICES:** Lift Night porter 195P **NOTES:** No smoking area in restaurant Last d 10.30pm

CARDS:

HEMEL HEMPSTEAD Hertfordshire — Map 04 TL00

★★★ *Watermill*

London Rd, Bourne End HP1 2RJ
Quality Percentage Score: 64%
☎ 01442 349955 Fax 01442 866130
Dir: *from M1 junct8 or M25 junct 20 follow signs to & join A41 for Aylesbury then A4251 to Bourne End*

The Grand Union Canal lies to the rear of The Watermill, enhancing its peaceful location. The various wings of annexe accommodation are steadily being upgraded to a smart standard, and offer comfortable well equipped rooms, some overlooking the river. A range of snacks is available throughout the day in the bar, or from a wide room service selection, and the Riverside restaurant offers daily changing and carte menus of appetising dishes.

ROOMS: 75 annexe en suite (bth/shr) (4 fmly) No smoking in 26 bedrooms **MEALS:** International Cuisine V meals Coffee am Tea pm **FACILITIES:** CTV in all bedrooms Fishing **CONF:** Thtr 100 Class 70 Board 48 **SERVICES:** Night porter 100P **NOTES:** No dogs (ex guide dogs) No smoking in restaurant Last d 9.30pm
CARDS:

HEMEL HEMPSTEAD Hertfordshire — Map 04 TL00

Travel Inn

Stoney Ln, Bourne End Services HP1 2SB
☎ 01442 879149 Fax 01442 879147
Dir: *from S leave M25 junct 20 (A41) follow service signs. From N at rdbt in Hemel Hempstead 2nd exit (A41 Aylesbury), once on A41 take 3rd exit for svcs*

This modern building offers accommodation in smart, spacious and well equipped bedrooms, all with en-suite bathrooms. Refreshments may be taken at the nearby family restaurant. For details about current prices consult the Contents Page under Hotel Groups for the Travel Inn phone number.

ROOMS: 60 en suite (bth/shr) d £39.95 *

HENFIELD West Sussex — Map 04 TQ21

★★ Tottington Manor Hotel

THE CIRCLE Selected Individual Hotels GREAT BRITAIN

Edburton BN5 9LJ
Quality Percentage Score: 68%
☎ 01903 815757 Fax 01903 879331
Dir: *turn off B2037 between Upper Beeding and Small Dole, hotel is 0.25m on left*

This Sussex Manor house enjoys views of the South Downs and the Sussex Weald and parts of the house can be dated back to the 16th century. The Manor offers comfortable accommodation and a popular restaurant. The six bedrooms are attractively decorated and have lots of thoughtful touches.

ROOMS: 6 en suite (bth/shr) No smoking in 1 bedroom s £50-£60; d £75-£95 (incl. bkfst) * Off peak **MEALS:** Lunch fr £16 & alc Dinner fr £22.50 & alc International Cuisine V meals Coffee am **FACILITIES:** CTV in all bedrooms **CONF:** Thtr 35 Class 15 Board 20 Del from £100 * **SERVICES:** 100P **NOTES:** No dogs (ex guide dogs) No coaches No children 5yrs No smoking area in restaurant Last d 9pm Closed 24 Dec-1 Jan RS Sunday evening **CARDS:**

HENLEY-ON-THAMES Oxfordshire — Map 04 SU78

see also **Stonor**

★★★ Red Lion

Hart St RG9 2AR
Quality Percentage Score: 69%
☎ 01491 572161 Fax 01491 410039
Dir: *adjacent to Henley Bridge*

Situated beside the Thames, the front rooms of this 16th-century ivy-clad coaching inn offer fabulous views of the river and the famous regatta course. The public areas retain many original features such as wood panelling and flagstone floors and the bedrooms have been tastefully decorated and equipped to a high standard. The attractive brasserie features an interesting selection of freshly prepared dishes ranging from light snacks to substantial meals.

ROOMS: 27 en suite (bth/shr) (1 fmly) s £85-£105; d £115-£135 * Off peak **MEALS:** Lunch £12-£19 & alc Dinner £12-£16 & alc V meals Coffee am Tea pm **FACILITIES:** CTV in all bedrooms **CONF:** Thtr 60 Class 20 Board 30 Del from £145 * **SERVICES:** Night porter 25P **NOTES:** No dogs No coaches Last d 9.45pm **CARDS:**

HENLEY-ON-THAMES Oxfordshire — Map 04 SU78

★★ *The White Hart Hotel*

High St, Nettlebed RG9 5DD
Quality Percentage Score: 62%
☎ 01491 641245 Fax 01491 641423
Dir: *on A4130 3.5m from Henley-on-Thames heading towards Oxford*

A recent change in staff here has resulted in an increasing number of regular guests. This 17th-century inn, just five miles from Henley, has the benefit of a strong kitchen led by Manager Andrew Welch.

ROOMS: 6 en suite (bth/shr) No smoking in all bedrooms
MEALS: European Cuisine V meals Coffee am Tea pm **FACILITIES:** CTV in all bedrooms **CONF:** Board 16 **SERVICES:** 50P **NOTES:** No dogs (ex guide dogs) No smoking area in restaurant Last d 10pm
CARDS:

H

HEREFORD Herefordshire **Map 03 SO54**
see also **Much Birch**

★★★ Three Counties Hotel

Belmont Rd HR2 7BP
Quality Percentage Score: 67%
☎ 01432 299955 📠 01432 275114
Dir: *on A465 Abergavveny Rd*

Standing in over three acres, yet just a mile from the city centre, this large, modern complex has well-equipped bedrooms which are all located on the ground floor; some suitable for the less able. The hotel has a large, comfortable lounge, a traditional bar and an attractive restaurant.

ROOMS: 28 en suite (bth/shr) 32 annexe en suite (bth/shr) (4 fmly) No smoking in 23 bedrooms s £37.50-£59.25; d £55-£78 (incl. bkfst) * LB Off peak **MEALS:** Bar Lunch £2.95-£7.95 International Cuisine V meals Coffee am Tea pm **FACILITIES:** CTV in all bedrooms STV Xmas **CONF:** Thtr 300 Class 100 Board 60 Del from £75 * **SERVICES:** Night porter 250P **CARDS:**

HEREFORD Herefordshire **Map 03 SO54**

★★★ Graftonbury Garden Hotel

Grafton Ln HR2 8BN
Quality Percentage Score: 64%
☎ 01432 268826 📠 01432 354633
Dir: *2m S of Hereford, 0.5m off A49 to Ross-on-Wye*

Situated on the A49 south of the Hereford, this hotel occupies a secluded location but is conveniently located for the city. The hotel has been recently refurbished and benefits from bright public areas, incorporating a bar, lounge and bistro as well as extensive function/conference rooms. The bedrooms have also received recent attention and are comfortable and well-equipped.

ROOMS: 25 en suite (bth/shr) 4 annexe en suite (shr) (3 fmly) s fr £45; d fr £55 (incl. bkfst) * LB Off peak **MEALS:** Lunch £6.95-£14.95 Dinner £6.95-£14.95 V meals Coffee am Tea pm **FACILITIES:** CTV in all bedrooms Wkly live entertainment Xmas **CONF:** Thtr 150 Class 100 Board 80 Del £80 * **SERVICES:** Night porter 100P **NOTES:** No smoking in restaurant Last d 9.30pm **CARDS:**

HEREFORD Herefordshire **Map 03 SO54**

★★★ Belmont Lodge & Golf Course

Belmont HR2 9SA
Quality Percentage Score: 62%
☎ 01432 352666 📠 01432 358090
Dir: *from city centre turn off A465 to Abergavenny into Ruckhall Lane, hotel located on right in approx 0.5m*

This hotel and golfing complex occupies a superb location on the slopes above the River Wye. Modern, well equipped bedrooms are located on the ground and first floors of a purpose built lodge, with no smoking bedrooms and family rooms available. The restaurant and bar are located in the clubhouse, which is on the ground floor of the Grade II listed Belmont House.

ROOMS: 30 en suite (bth/shr) (4 fmly) No smoking in 15 bedrooms s £33.50-£49.50; d £50-£65 (incl. bkfst) * LB Off peak **MEALS:** Lunch £13 Dinner £13 English & French Cuisine V meals Coffee am Tea pm **FACILITIES:** CTV in all bedrooms Golf 18 Tennis (hard) Fishing Snooker Putting green Bowls Darts **CONF:** Thtr 60 Class 14 Board 25 Del £64 * **SERVICES:** Night porter 150P **NOTES:** Last d 9.30pm
CARDS:

HEREFORD Herefordshire **Map 03 SO54**

★★★ *The Green Dragon*

Broad St HR4 9BG
Quality Percentage Score: 61%
☎ 01432 272506 📠 01432 352139
Dir: *follow signs for Cathedral and Mappa Mundi to rdbt. First exit, then 2nd left into West St, then 2nd right into Aubrey St and hotel garage*

Located close to the Cathedral, this landmark hotel is on the one-way road system. The public areas have an appealing charm and on most days, visitors throng to the comfortable lounges for leisurely afternoon tea.

ROOMS: 83 en suite (bth/shr) No smoking in 29 bedrooms
MEALS: V meals Coffee am Tea pm **FACILITIES:** CTV in 87 bedrooms N **CONF:** Thtr 200 Class 72 Board 50 **SERVICES:** Lift Night porter 110P **NOTES:** No smoking area in restaurant Last d 9.15pm
CARDS:

HEREFORD Herefordshire **Map 03 SO54**

★★ Ancient Camp Inn

Ruckhall HR2 9QX
Quality Percentage Score: 71%
☎ 01981 250449 📠 01981 251581
Dir: *A465, turn right to Belmont Abbey, 2.5m to hotel*

In an impressive position above the River Wye with stunning views, the inn is named after a nearby Iron Age fort. It has features such as stone flagged floors, exposed beams and real fires in the quaint bar and dining room. Bedrooms currently vary in standard, with improvements planned. In the kitchen, Jason Eland's well crafted, rustic style is proving a genuine success.

ROOMS: 5 en suite (bth/shr) (1 fmly) s £45-£70; d £55-£70 (incl. bkfst) * Off peak **MEALS:** Sunday Lunch £14.95-£18.50alc Dinner £22.50-£25alc International Cuisine V meals Coffee am **FACILITIES:** CTV in all bedrooms Fishing Xmas **SERVICES:** 30P **NOTES:** No dogs (ex guide dogs) No coaches No children 12 No smoking in restaurant Last d 9pm Closed 1-14 Jan RS Mon **CARDS:**

HEREFORD Herefordshire **Map 03 SO54**

★★ Merton Hotel & Governors Restaurant

28 Commercial Rd HR1 2BD
Quality Percentage Score: 63%
☎ 01432 265925 📠 01432 354983
Dir: *on main A4103, close to rail station, opposite the cinema*

A privately owned and run hotel close to the bus station (with its public car park) and in walking distance of the railway station. The modern accommodation is well equipped, two rooms have four-poster beds. The cosy lounge has real fires in cold weather. There is a pleasant restaurant and a lounge bar with adjacent eating area.

ROOMS: 19 en suite (bth/shr) (2 fmly) s £45-£50; d £60-£65 (incl. bkfst) * LB Off peak **MEALS:** Lunch £6-£12 Dinner £14-£20alc V meals Coffee am Tea pm **FACILITIES:** CTV in all bedrooms Fishing Sauna Solarium Gym Shooting fishing (by arrangement) Wkly live entertainment **CONF:** Thtr 30 Class 20 Board 20 Del from £65 * **SERVICES:** 4P
NOTES: Last d 9.30pm **CARDS:**

HEREFORD Herefordshire **Map 03 SO54**

Travel Inn

Holmer Rd, Holmer HR4 9RS

☎ 01432 274853 📠 01432 343003

Dir: *from N leave M5 junct 7, follow A4103 to Worcester. From M50 junct 4 take A49 Leominster road Travel Inn 800yds on left*

This modern building offers accommodation in smart, spacious and well equipped bedrooms, all with en-suite bathrooms. Refreshments may be taken at the nearby family restaurant. For details about current prices consult the Contents Page under Hotel Groups for the Travel Inn phone number.

ROOMS: 40 en suite (bth/shr) d £39.95 *

HERSTMONCEUX East Sussex **Map 05 TQ61**

★★★ **White Friars**

Boreham St BN27 4SE

Quality Percentage Score: 64%

☎ 01323 832355 📠 01323 833882

Dir: *2m E on A271 between Herstmonceux & Ninfield*

This privately owned hotel dates back to the early 1700s and retains much character. Bedrooms vary in size and are traditionally furnished and well equipped. The main bar/lounge has a cosy atmosphere. The elegant Georgian style restaurant serves carefully prepared meals.

ROOMS: 12 en suite (bth/shr) 8 annexe en suite (bth/shr) (2 fmly) **MEALS:** Lunch £10-£20 & alc Dinner £24.50 & alc English & French Cuisine V meals Coffee am Tea pm **FACILITIES:** CTV in all bedrooms Croquet lawn **CONF:** Thtr 40 Class 25 Board 30 Del £84.50 * **SERVICES:** Night porter 60P **NOTES:** No smoking in restaurant Last d 9.30pm **CARDS:**

HERTFORD Hertfordshire **Map 04 TL31**

★★★ **The White Horse**

Hertingfordbury SG14 2LB

Quality Percentage Score: 66%

☎ 01992 586791 📠 01992 550809

Dir: *1m W on A414*

Situated in the quaint village of Hertingfordbury this former coaching inn has a Georgian façade, but a much older interior. Most of the bedrooms are in the modern extension and are of a comfortable size with attractive decor. The restaurant looks onto a lovely garden, where afternoon tea and drinks can be enjoyed on fine days. Light lunches and teas can be taken in the beamed lounge bar.

ROOMS: 42 en suite (bth/shr) No smoking in 14 bedrooms s £95; d £110 * LB Off peak **MEALS:** Lunch £12.95-£15.75alc European Cuisine V meals Coffee am Tea pm **FACILITIES:** CTV in all bedrooms Xmas **CONF:** Thtr 60 Class 30 Board 30 Del from £108 * **SERVICES:** Night porter 60P **CARDS:**

HESLEDEN Co Durham **Map 08 NZ43**

★★ ***Hardwicke Hall Manor***

TS27 4PA

Quality Percentage Score: 69%

☎ 01429 836326 📠 01429 837676

Dir: *NE on B1281, off A19 at the sign for Durham/Blackhall*

This creeper-clad mansion is family owned and offers well furnished and thoughtfully equipped bedrooms. It is very popular for its food and the public rooms are both inviting and relaxing.

ROOMS: 15 en suite (bth/shr) (2 fmly) **MEALS:** English & French Cuisine V meals Coffee am Tea pm **FACILITIES:** CTV in all bedrooms **CONF:** Thtr 60 Board 20 **SERVICES:** 100P **NOTES:** No smoking in restaurant Last d 9.30pm **CARDS:**

HESTON MOTORWAY SERVICE AREA (M4)
Greater London
See LONDON SECTION plan 1 *A3*

Travelodge

Phoenix Way TW5 9NB

☎ Central Res 0800 850950 📠 01384 78578

Dir: *M4 junc 2&3 westbound*

This modern building offers accommodation in smart, spacious and well equipped bedrooms, all with en-suite bathrooms. Refreshments may be taken at the nearby family restaurant. For details about current prices, consult the Contents Page under Hotel Groups for the Travelodge phone number.

ROOMS: 95 en suite (bth/shr) d £69.95 *

HESWALL Merseyside **Map 07 SJ28**

Travel Inn (Wirral North)

Chester Rd, Gayton, Heswall L60 3FD

☎ 0151 342 1982 📠 0151 342 8983

Dir: *from M53 junct 4 follow A5137 signed Heswall for 3m & turn left at next rdbt, hotel on left*

This modern building offers accommodation in smart, spacious and well equipped bedrooms, all with en-suite bathrooms. Refreshments may be taken at the nearby family restaurant. For details about current prices consult the Contents Page under Hotel Groups for the Travel Inn phone number.

ROOMS: 37 en suite (bth/shr) d £39.95 *

HETHERSETT Norfolk **Map 05 TG10**

★★★ **Park Farm**

NR9 3DL

Quality Percentage Score: 69%

☎ 01603 810264 📠 01603 812104

Dir: *5m S of Norwich, off A11 on B1172*

A modern hotel, it has evolved from the existing Georgian farmhouse. Extensively redeveloped public rooms are smart and well maintained. The recently extended modern leisure facilities and conference suites are very popular. Bedrooms are available in the main house and garden annexes rooms, they are thoughtfully equipped and most have rich colour schemes.

ROOMS: 6 en suite (bth/shr) 30 annexe en suite (bth/shr) (8 fmly) s £70-£100; d £90-£130 (incl. bkfst) * LB Off peak **MEALS:** Lunch £13.75 & alc Dinner £19.50 & alc English & French Cuisine V meals Coffee am Tea pm **FACILITIES:** CTV in all bedrooms Indoor swimming pool (heated) Sauna Solarium Gym Croquet lawn Putting green Jacuzzi/spa Beauty salon Xmas **CONF:** Thtr 120 Class 50 Board 50 Del from £102.50 * **SERVICES:** Night porter 151P **NOTES:** No dogs (ex guide dogs) No smoking in restaurant Last d 9.30pm **CARDS:**

See advert under NORWICH

HEVERSHAM Cumbria **Map 07 SD48**
★★★ ***Blue Bell***
Prince's Way LA7 7EE
Quality Percentage Score: 67%
☎ 015395 62018 🖷 015395 62455
Dir: *1m N of Milnthorpe, on A6*
Full of charm and character, this comfortable old Jacobean coaching inn offers well equipped, modern bedrooms, and traditional public areas include a restaurant, cosy lounge and traditional bar. Several skilfully prepared menus offer a good range of food including afternoon tea and an early diners menu served in the restaurant from 4pm to 6pm. Staff throughout are considerate and nothing is too much trouble.
ROOMS: 21 en suite (bth/shr) (4 fmly) **MEALS:** English Cuisine V meals Coffee am Tea pm **FACILITIES:** CTV in all bedrooms Pool table **CONF:** Thtr 85 Class 35 Board 25 Del from £75 * **SERVICES:** Night porter 100P **NOTES:** No smoking in restaurant Last d 9.30pm
CARDS:

H

HEXHAM Northumberland **Map 12 NY96**
★★★★ **De Vere Slaley Hall**
Slaley NE47 0BY
De Vere Hotels
Quality Percentage Score: 71%
☎ 01434 673350 🖷 01434 673050
Superbly situated amidst 1,000 acres of stunning Northumbrian forest and farmland, this smart, stylish hotel provides particularly well equipped bedrooms. Public rooms reflect the Edwardian elegance of the architecture whilst the spacious bars and lounges enjoy panoramic views over the golf course. The brasserie is open for both buffet lunch and dinner although a more ambitious carte is served.
ROOMS: 139 en suite (bth/shr) (23 fmly) No smoking in 17 bedrooms s £120-£140; d £160-£180 (incl. bkfst) * Off peak **MEALS:** Lunch £15.95-£18.50 Dinner £21.50 & alc International Cuisine V meals Coffee am Tea pm **FACILITIES:** CTV in all bedrooms STV Indoor swimming pool (heated) Golf Snooker Sauna Solarium Gym Jacuzzi/spa Quad bikes Monda pilots 4x4 driving Hot air ballooning Archery Clay shooting Wkly live entertainment Xmas **CONF:** Thtr 250 Class 220 Board 150 Del from £125 * **SERVICES:** Lift Night porter Air conditioning 500P **NOTES:** No smoking in restaurant Last d 10pm
CARDS:

HEXHAM Northumberland **Map 12 NY96**
★★★ ***Beaumont***
Beaumont St NE46 3LT
Best Western
Quality Percentage Score: 68%
☎ 01434 602331 🖷 01434 606184
Dir: *on A69 towards Hexham*

Popular with both business guests and tourists, the Beaumont overlooks the park in the town centre. Its bright attractive bedrooms are well equipped; there are two bars, a relaxing foyer lounge and a first-floor restaurant featuring well presented and innovative dishes.
ROOMS: 25 en suite (bth/shr) (3 fmly) No smoking in 18 bedrooms
MEALS: International Cuisine V meals Coffee am Tea pm
FACILITIES: CTV in all bedrooms STV Snooker Solarium **CONF:** Thtr 100 Class 60 Board 40 Del from £65 * **SERVICES:** Lift Night porter 8P
NOTES: No dogs No smoking in restaurant Closed 25-26 Dec & 1 Jan
CARDS:

See advert on opposite page

HEYWOOD Greater Manchester **Map 07 SD81**
★★ **The Albany**
87/89 Rochdale Rd East OL10 1PX
Quality Percentage Score: 61%
☎ 01706 369606 🖷 01706 627914
Dir: *on A58*
Conveniently situated, on the edge of town, by the main road, this hotel offers accommodation in the main house and an adjacent building. Guests may either eat in the bar or in the restaurant.
ROOMS: 7 en suite (shr) 11 annexe en suite (bth/shr) (2 fmly) s £30-£35; d £40-£60 (incl. bkfst) * Off peak **MEALS:** Lunch £7-£10 Dinner £7-£10 English Indian & Italian Cuisine V meals Coffee am Tea pm
FACILITIES: CTV in 20 bedrooms Xmas **CONF:** Thtr 120 Class 100 Board 80 **SERVICES:** 50P **NOTES:** Last d 9.30pm
CARDS:

HICKSTEAD West Sussex **Map 04 TQ22**
★★★ ***The Hickstead Hotel***
Jobs Ln, Bolney RH17 5PA
Quality Percentage Score: 62%
☎ 01444 248023 🖷 01444 245280
Dir: *0.25m E of A23 turn off at Hickstead village towards Burgess Hill*
Set in the heart of West Sussex the hotel enjoys a peaceful location close to the A23. The bedrooms are modern in style and comfortably furnished. Lounge and bar areas are compact but the hotel benefits from an indoor leisure centre, conference rooms and ample car parking.
ROOMS: 50 en suite (bth/shr) (8 fmly) No smoking in 25 bedrooms
MEALS: English & Continental Cuisine V meals Coffee am Tea pm
FACILITIES: CTV in all bedrooms STV Indoor swimming pool (heated) Sauna Solarium Gym Jacuzzi/spa **CONF:** Thtr 120 Class 60 Board 40
SERVICES: Night porter 150P **NOTES:** No smoking in restaurant Last d 10pm **CARDS:**

HICKSTEAD West Sussex **Map 04 TQ22**
Travelodge
Jobs Ln RH17 5NX
Travelodge
☎ 01444 881377 🖷 01444 881377
Dir: *A23 southbound*
This modern building offers accommodation in smart, spacious and well equipped bedrooms, all with en-suite bathrooms. Refreshments may be taken at the nearby family restaurant. For details about current prices, consult the Contents Page under Hotel Groups for the Travelodge phone number.
ROOMS: 40 en suite (bth/shr) d £45.95 *

HIGHBRIDGE Somerset **Map 03 ST34**
★★ ***Sundowner***
74 Main Rd, West Huntspill TA9 3QU
Quality Percentage Score: 62%
☎ 01278 784766 🖷 01278 784766
Dir: *3m south on A38 from M5 junct 22 or 3m N on A35 from M5 junct 23*
An informal atmosphere prevails throughout this cosy hotel, with its open-plan lounge/bar and popular restaurant which offers extensive menus. The bedrooms are well equipped and are

contd.

currently undergoing refurbishment. The friendly owners, Christine and Alan Pepler are enthusiastic and totally involved with the day to day running of the hotel.
ROOMS: 8 en suite (bth/shr) (1 fmly) **MEALS:** English & French Cuisine V meals Coffee am **FACILITIES:** CTV in all bedrooms **CONF:** Thtr 40 Class 24 Board 24 **SERVICES:** 24P **NOTES:** No smoking in restaurant Last d 9.45pm **CARDS:**

HIGHCLERE Hampshire — Map 04 SU45

The Premier Collection

★★★ Hollington Country House

Woolton Hill RG20 9XA
☎ 01635 255100 Fax 01635 255075
Dir: *take A343 from Newbury towards Andover, after 3m turn right & follow signs to hotel & Hollington Herb Garden*
Owners John and Penny Guy never stand still in their search for improvement at this charming country house. Bedrooms are on two floors in the main house, with some in a nearby converted cottage. All are a fine size, and decorated with great comfort, taste and an eye for detail. (To avoid being disturbed just put out the fluffy cat.) Many of the excellent bathrooms feature large spa baths. The public rooms have many architectural highlights and the extensive grounds enjoy wonderful views and woodland walks. The cuisine is of a high standard while the fine wine list must have the best Australian selection in the UK, personally sourced by John Guy. In the end, the real strength of the hotel is the friendly and helpful attitude of the owners and their young team.
ROOMS: 20 en suite (bth/shr) (1 fmly) No smoking in 2 bedrooms d fr £145 (incl. bkfst) * LB Off peak **MEALS:** Lunch £19.50-£22.50 & alc Dinner £22.50-£29.50 & alc English & French Cuisine V meals Coffee am Tea pm **FACILITIES:** CTV in all bedrooms Indoor swimming pool (heated) Outdoor swimming pool (heated) Tennis (hard) Snooker Pool table Croquet lawn Putting green Jacuzzi/spa Free bicycle hire Xmas **CONF:** Thtr 60 Class 25 Board 30 **SERVICES:** Lift Night porter 39P **NOTES:** No dogs (ex guide dogs) No coaches No smoking in restaurant Last d 9.30pm
CARDS:

Remember to return your Prize Draw card for a chance to win one of 30 relaxing leisure breaks with Corus and Regal hotels. See inside the front cover for the card and competition details.

HIGH WYCOMBE Buckinghamshire — Map 04 SU89

★★★ Posthouse High Wycombe

Posthouse

Handy Cross HP11 1TL
Quality Percentage Score: 66%
☎ 01494 442100 Fax 01494 439071
Dir: *intersection of M40 and A4010*
Usefully situated on the junction with the M40, this busy hotel has good modern bedrooms. Spacious public areas have various eating options, including the informal Mongolian Barbecue.
ROOMS: 106 en suite (bth/shr) (4 fmly) No smoking in 55 bedrooms d £99-£129 * LB Off peak **MEALS:** International Cuisine V meals Coffee am Tea pm **FACILITIES:** CTV in all bedrooms Pool table Xmas **CONF:** Thtr 200 Class 100 Board 40 Del from £89 * **SERVICES:** Night porter 173P **NOTES:** No dogs (ex guide dogs) No smoking area in restaurant Last d 10pm **CARDS:**

HIGH WYCOMBE Buckinghamshire — Map 04 SU89

Travel Inn

Thanestead Farm, London Rd, Loudwater HP10 9YL
☎ 01494 537080 Fax 01494 446855
Dir: *on A40 0.5m from junc 3 M40*
This modern building offers accommodation in smart, spacious and well equipped bedrooms, all with en-suite bathrooms. Refreshments may be taken at the nearby family restaurant. For details about current prices consult the Contents Page under Hotel Groups for the Travel Inn phone number.
ROOMS: 60 en suite (bth/shr) d £39.95 *

★
The Premier Collection, hotels with Red Star Awards are listed on pages 17-23

HILLINGTON Norfolk — Map 09 TF72

★★ Ffolkes Arms
Lynn Rd PE31 6BJ
Quality Percentage Score: 68%
☎ 01485 600210 Fax 01485 601196
Dir: *on main A148 turn right towards Cromer at roundabout hotel 6m along A148 at Hillington*
Dating back to the mid 17th century, this is a popular coaching inn sympathetically adapted to create a friendly, family hotel. There is a bar and restaurant plus improved reception and lounge facilities. The spacious bedrooms are in a modern wing, and the courtyard has a popular function suite and social club.
ROOMS: 20 annexe en suite (bth/shr) (2 fmly) No smoking in all bedrooms s £35-£50; d £50-£70 (incl. bkfst) * LB Off peak
MEALS: Lunch £10.50-£17.50 & alc High tea fr £6.75 Dinner £10.50-£15 & alc English, Italian & French Cuisine V meals Coffee am Tea pm
FACILITIES: CTV in all bedrooms Snooker Pool table Xmas **CONF:** Thtr 250 Class 80 Board 50 Del from £60 * **SERVICES:** 200P **NOTES:** No dogs (ex guide dogs) No smoking in restaurant Last d 9.30pm
CARDS:

HILTON PARK MOTORWAY SERVICE AREA (M6) West Midlands — Map 07 SJ90

Travelodge
Hilton Park Services (M6), Essington WV11 2DR
☎ Cen Res 0800 850950 Fax 01922 701967
Dir: *on M6 between juncts 10a & 11*
This modern building offers accommodation in smart, spacious and well equipped bedrooms, all with en-suite bathrooms. Refreshments may be taken at the nearby family restaurant. For details about current prices, consult the Contents Page under Hotel Groups for the Travelodge phone number.
ROOMS: 64 en suite (bth/shr) d £49.95 *

HIMLEY Staffordshire — Map 07 SO89

★★★ Himley Country Hotel
School Rd DY3 4LG
Quality Percentage Score: 63%
☎ 01902 896716 Fax 01902 896668
Dir: *100yds off A449*

This modern hotel has been built around the original Victorian village schoolhouse, which is now part of the restaurant. Other public areas include a pleasant lounge bar, as well as a choice of function rooms, the largest of which can hold up to 150 people. Accommodation includes bedrooms on ground floor level.
ROOMS: 73 en suite (bth/shr) (1 fmly) No smoking in 38 bedrooms s £65-£75; d £75-£85 * LB Off peak **MEALS:** Lunch £11.50-£12.95alc Dinner £10.50-£25alc English & French Cuisine V meals Coffee am Tea pm **FACILITIES:** CTV in all bedrooms STV **CONF:** Thtr 150 Class 80 Board 50 Del from £85 * **SERVICES:** Night porter 100P **NOTES:** No smoking in restaurant Last d 9.30pm
CARDS:

HIMLEY Staffordshire — Map 07 SO89

★★ Himley House Hotel
Stourbridge Rd DY3 4LD
Quality Percentage Score: 65%
☎ 01902 892468 Fax 01902 892604
Dir: *on A449 N of Stourbridge*
A Georgian-style building, dating from the 17th century, once the lodge for nearby Himley Hall, now offers spacious, well equipped and attractive accommodation. Some of the bedrooms are located in separate buildings at the rear of the main house and several are on ground floor level. The restaurant proves popular with families and there are children's play areas both inside and in the garden. Service, from the mainly young staff, is willing and friendly.
ROOMS: 24 en suite (bth/shr) (2 fmly) s £36-£70; d £40-£70 * LB Off peak **MEALS:** Lunch £4.15-£17.50alc Dinner £6.50-£17.50alc International Cuisine V meals Coffee am **FACILITIES:** CTV in all bedrooms Wkly live entertainment **CONF:** Thtr 50 Class 30 Board 22 Del from £90 * **SERVICES:** Night porter 162P **NOTES:** No dogs (ex guide dogs) No smoking area in restaurant Last d 10pm
CARDS:

HINCKLEY Leicestershire — Map 04 SP49

★★★★ Hanover International Hotel & Club Hinckley
Watling St LE10 3JA
Quality Percentage Score: 61%
☎ 01455 631122 Fax 01455 634536
Dir: *on A5, S of junct 1 on M69*
Conveniently situated for the motorway network and airports, this large hotel offers comfortable and well appointed bedrooms, many of which have recently been refurbished. The Club floor is well designed for business visitors, each bedroom having a desk, fax and PC. An extensive range of function suites is complemented by a leisure club and shop. Dinner is served in the Brasserie, lighter meals and snacks also being available in the Snooty Fox pub.
ROOMS: 348 en suite (bth/shr) (47 fmly) No smoking in 197 bedrooms s £80-£85; d £90-£95 * LB Off peak **MEALS:** Lunch £10.50-£16.95 & alc Dinner £10.50-£16.95 & alc V meals Coffee am Tea pm **FACILITIES:** CTV in all bedrooms STV Indoor swimming pool (heated) Fishing Snooker Sauna Solarium Gym Jacuzzi/spa Xmas **CONF:** Thtr 400 Class 190 Board 40 Del from £1300 * **SERVICES:** Lift Night porter Air conditioning 500P **NOTES:** No dogs (ex guide dogs) No smoking in restaurant Last d 9.30pm **CARDS:**

> ✚ Indicates that the star classification has not been confirmed under the New Quality Standards, see page 7 for further information.

HINCKLEY Leicestershire
Map 04 SP49

★★★ Sketchley Grange

Sketchley Ln, Burbage LE10 3HU
Quality Percentage Score: 77%
☎ 01455 251133 Fax 01455 631384

Dir: *SE of town, off A5, take B4109 (Hinckley) turn left at mini rdbt. First right onto Sketchley Lane*

Set among its own landscaped gardens, is this extended country house. Smart public rooms offer a choice of bars and eating options, which include the Willows Restaurant and the lively Terrace Bistro Bar. A further wing of superior bedrooms should soon be nearing completion along with an upgrading programme to existing bedroom stock.

ROOMS: 55 en suite (bth/shr) (9 fmly) No smoking in 15 bedrooms s £82.50-£105; d £95-£225 * LB Off peak **MEALS:** Lunch £13.95 & alc High tea £7.95-£9.95 & alc Dinner £21.95 & alc English & French Cuisine V meals Coffee am Tea pm **FACILITIES:** CTV in all bedrooms STV Indoor swimming pool (heated) Sauna Solarium Gym Jacuzzi/spa Steam room Games room Creche Wkly live entertainment **CONF:** Thtr 300 Class 150 Board 50 Del from £140 * **SERVICES:** Lift Night porter 200P **NOTES:** No smoking in restaurant Last d 9.30pm
CARDS:

See advert under LEICESTER

HINCKLEY Leicestershire
Map 04 SP49

★★ Kings Hotel & Restaurant

13/19 Mount Rd LE10 1AD
Quality Percentage Score: 70%
☎ 01455 637193 Fax 01455 636201

THE CIRCLE Selected Individual Hotels GREAT BRITAIN

Dir: *follow A447 signposted to Hinckley. Under railway bridge and turn right at roundabout. First road left opposite railway station and then third right*

This friendly hotel sits in a quiet part of town, yet is still close to the centre. Public rooms are strikingly decorated, varying from Chinese-style wallpaper in the cosy bar, to Victoriana in the restaurant, where cooking is under the personal supervision of the proprietor. Bedrooms are individually styled and well equipped.

ROOMS: 7 en suite (bth/shr) No smoking in all bedrooms s £69.50-£79.50; d £79.50-£89.50 (incl. bkfst) * LB Off peak **MEALS:** Lunch £12.90-£16.90 & alc Dinner £16.90-£29.90 & alc English, French & Hungarian Cuisine V meals Coffee am **FACILITIES:** CTV in all bedrooms STV **CONF:** Thtr 40 Class 30 Board 24 Del from £80 * **SERVICES:** 12P **NOTES:** No dogs (ex guide dogs) No smoking in restaurant Last d 9.30pm **CARDS:**

HINDON Wiltshire
Map 03 ST93

★★ The Grosvenor Arms

High St SP3 6DJ
Quality Percentage Score: 74%
☎ 01747 820696 Fax 01747 820869

Dir: *village centre 1.5m from A303, through village B3089 to Salisbury*

Originally a 17th-century coaching inn set in the centre of the village, the Grosvenor Arms has undergone major refurbishment to offer a high standard of accommodation. The rooms are smartly appointed with co-ordinating furnishings and fabrics. Public areas include a cosy lounge, spacious bar and attractive dining room where diners can watch the chefs work in the open plan kitchen. Paul Suter's confident cooking offers carefully prepared food using good quality produce. Service throughout is both friendly and attentive.

ROOMS: 7 en suite (bth/shr) (2 fmly) No smoking in all bedrooms s £45-£55; d £65-£75 (incl. bkfst) * Off peak **MEALS:** English & Continental Cuisine V meals Coffee am Tea pm **FACILITIES:** CTV in all bedrooms Fishing Xmas **SERVICES:** 18P **NOTES:** No coaches No children 5yrs No smoking in restaurant **CARDS:**

HINDON Wiltshire
Map 03 ST93

★★ *Lamb at Hindon*

SP3 6DP
Quality Percentage Score: 70%
☎ 01747 820573 Fax 01747 820605

Dir: *1m from A303 & A350, on B3089 in the centre of the village*

This stone-built free house offers a warm welcome with owners John Croft and Cora Scott keen to continue its tradition of genuine hospitality. Bedrooms are comfortably furnished with modern facilities, and are currently undergoing further upgrading. Public areas have beamed ceilings and log fires in winter. Interesting dishes are featured on the fixed price menu, while in the bar a sophisticated choice is available from blackboards. A detailed wine list includes a range of wines by the glass.

ROOMS: 12 en suite (bth/shr) **MEALS:** English & French Cuisine V meals Coffee am Tea pm **FACILITIES:** CTV in all bedrooms Fishing Shooting Mountain bikes **CONF:** Thtr 35 Class 30 Board 20 Del from £68 * **SERVICES:** 26P **NOTES:** No smoking in restaurant Last d 9.30pm **CARDS:**

New AA Guides for the Millennium are featured on page 24

HINTLESHAM Suffolk — Map 05 TM04

The Premier Collection

★★★★ Hintlesham Hall
IP8 3NS
☎ 01473 652334 & 652268 01473 652463
Dir: *4m W of Ipswich on A1071 to Sudbury*
Hintlesham Hall is a fine country house hotel, with polished yet friendly service. The magnificent Georgian façade belies the Tudor origins of the house. The pine-panelled parlour is sometimes used as a second dining room, but the main dining room, The Salon, is a grand, elegant room where classical cuisine is served. Bedrooms vary in style and design, each with individual decor and furniture. Guests may take advantage of the 18-hole golf facilities for a fee, or enjoy the small leisure complex in the Orangery with the hotel's compliments.
ROOMS: 33 en suite (bth/shr) (1 fmly) s £89-£105; d £115-£350 (incl. cont bkfst) * LB Off peak **MEALS:** Lunch £19.99-£23 & alc Dinner fr £26 & alc English & French Cuisine V meals **FACILITIES:** CTV in all bedrooms Outdoor swimming pool (heated) Golf 18 Tennis (hard) Fishing Riding Snooker Sauna Solarium Gym Croquet lawn Putting green Jacuzzi/spa Clay & game shooting Xmas **CONF:** Thtr 80 Class 50 Board 32 Del from £175 * **SERVICES:** Night porter 100P **NOTES:** No coaches No smoking in restaurant Last d 9.30pm RS Sat **CARDS:**

HINTON CHARTERHOUSE Somerset — Map 03 ST75

The Premier Collection

★★★ Homewood Park
BA3 6BB
☎ 01225 723731 01225 723820
Dir: *6m SE of Bath on A36, turn left at 2nd sign for Freshford*
Homewood Park offers relaxed surroundings whilst maintaining high standards. The public areas are welcoming and feature roaring fires on winter days. Bedrooms are individually decorated with great attention to detail. In the kitchen Andrew Hamer produces some masterful cooking.
ROOMS: 19 en suite (bth/shr) s £95; d £139-£174 (incl. bkfst) * LB Off peak **MEALS:** Lunch £19.50-£22.50 Dinner £40-£52alc V meals Coffee am Tea pm **FACILITIES:** CTV in all bedrooms STV Outdoor swimming pool (heated) Tennis (hard) Croquet lawn Xmas **CONF:** Thtr 35 Class 30 Board 25 Del from £159 * **SERVICES:** Night porter 30P **NOTES:** No dogs No smoking in restaurant Last d 9.30pm **CARDS:**

HITCHIN Hertfordshire — Map 04 TL12

★★★ ***Thistle Stevenage/Hitchin***
Blakemore End Rd, Little Wymondley SG4 7JJ
Quality Percentage Score: 61%
☎ 01438 355821 01438 742114
Dir: *from A1 junct 8, 2nd exit for Little Wymondley. Continue through village for approx. 1m then left at mini-rdbt to hotel 150mtrs on left*
A range of smart and versatile function and meeting rooms is provided at this well established hotel, located in six acres of landscaped grounds. Bedrooms are well looked after and offer good guest comfort. An informally arranged bar-lounge adjoins the dining room, which offers an enjoyable dinner menu. The hotel has a mini-bus for local shuttles.
ROOMS: 82 en suite (bth/shr) (6 fmly) No smoking in 23 bedrooms **MEALS:** International Cuisine V meals Coffee am Tea pm **FACILITIES:** CTV in all bedrooms STV Outdoor swimming pool (heated) Croquet lawn Boule Free membership of local David Lloyd health club **CONF:** Thtr 150 Class 80 Board 40 **SERVICES:** Night porter 200P **NOTES:** Last d 9.45pm **CARDS:**

HOCKLEY HEATH West Midlands — Map 07 SP17

★★★ Nuthurst Grange Country House
Nuthurst Grange Ln B94 5NL
Quality Percentage Score: 78%
☎ 01564 783972 01564 783919
Dir: *0.5m S on A3400*
Set at the end of a long, tree-lined avenue is this impressive country house hotel. Bedrooms, each individually furnished, are comfortable and include a wide range of thoughtful extras. Two of the bedrooms are situated on the ground floor. There is a choice of lounges, both overlooking the gardens.
ROOMS: 15 en suite (bth/shr) (2 fmly) s fr £128; d £145-£170 (incl. bkfst) * LB Off peak **MEALS:** Lunch £18-£28alc Dinner £29.50-£45 V meals Coffee am Tea pm **FACILITIES:** CTV in all bedrooms STV Croquet lawn Helipad **CONF:** Thtr 100 Class 50 Board 45 Del from £169 * **SERVICES:** Night porter 86P **NOTES:** No dogs (ex guide dogs) No coaches No smoking in restaurant Last d 9.30pm
CARDS:

HOCKLEY HEATH West Midlands — Map 07 SP17

★★★ Aylesbury House
Aylesbury Rd B94 6PL
Quality Percentage Score: 64%
☎ 01564 779207 01564 770917
Dir: *turn off A3400 left just before Nags Head into Aylesbury Rd, hotel 0.50m along on left after sharp right hand bend*
This manor house stands in 12 acres of grounds, just off the A3400, and in easy reach of the M40 and M42, the NEC and Birmingham Airport. Bedrooms are divided between those in the

contd.

manor house, which are particularly spacious, and some on the ground and first floors of a separate building.
ROOMS: 6 en suite (bth/shr) 28 annexe en suite (bth/shr) (5 fmly) s £89.95; d £105 * LB Off peak **MEALS:** Lunch £9.95 & alc Dinner £12-£16 & alc V meals Coffee am Tea pm **FACILITIES:** CTV in all bedrooms STV Croquet lawn Putting green Xmas **CONF:** Thtr 80 Class 36 Board 32 Del from £85 * **SERVICES:** Night porter 50P **NOTES:** No smoking in restaurant Last d 9.45pm **CARDS:**

HODNET Shropshire **Map 07 SJ62**
★★ Bear
TF9 3NH
Quality Percentage Score: 64%
☎ 01630 685214 01630 685787
Dir: *junct of A53 & A442 on sharp corner in middle of small village*
Now a privately owned and personally run hotel, this 16th-century former coaching inn is in the centre of Hodnet village. It provides modern equipped accommodation, which includes a two bedroom family unit. The public areas have a wealth of charm and character which is enhanced by features such as exposed beams. There is a large baronial style function room and medieval banquets are something of a speciality here.
ROOMS: 6 en suite (bth/shr) 2 annexe en suite (bth/shr) **MEALS:** Lunch £6-£14alc Dinner £10-£20alc International Cuisine V meals Coffee am Tea pm **FACILITIES:** CTV in all bedrooms Ten-pin & Skittles to order Wkly live entertainment **CONF:** Thtr 100 Class 50 Board 40 Del from £72 * **SERVICES:** 70P **NOTES:** No dogs (ex guide dogs) No smoking area in restaurant Last d 9.30pm **CARDS:**

HOLFORD Somerset **Map 03 ST14**
★★ Combe House
TA5 1RZ
Quality Percentage Score: 71%
☎ 01278 741382 01278 741322
Dir: *from A39 in Holford take lane between garage and Plough Inn, bear left at fork and continue for 0.25m to Holford Combe*
Deep in the heart of the Quantocks, this charming 17th-century house was once a tannery and the water wheel still remains. In the dining room, the short menu focuses on fresh produce, simply prepared and served. Bedrooms are tastefully decorated and furnished, all are equipped with modern facilities and like the public areas retain the original character and charm of the property.
ROOMS: 16 en suite (bth/shr) (2 fmly) s £28-£38; d £56-£76 (incl. bkfst) * LB Off peak **MEALS:** Bar Lunch £2.50-£8.25 Dinner fr £18.75 English & Continental Cuisine V meals Coffee am Tea pm **FACILITIES:** CTV in all bedrooms Indoor swimming pool (heated) Tennis (hard) Xmas **SERVICES:** 17P **NOTES:** No coaches No smoking in restaurant Last d 8.30pm **CARDS:**

HOLMES CHAPEL Cheshire **Map 07 SJ76**
★★★ Holly Lodge Hotel & "Truffles" Restaurant
70 London Rd CW4 7AS
Quality Percentage Score: 65%
☎ 01477 537033 01477 535823
Dir: *A50/A54 crossroads, 1m from junc 18 of M6*
Situated near the centre of Holmes Chapel, the Holly Lodge Hotel remains a very popular venue. Inside, a number of the comfortably furnished bedrooms are located around a courtyard overflowing with hanging baskets. A carefully prepared menu is served in Truffles restaurant and several function rooms are also available.
ROOMS: 17 en suite (bth/shr) 25 annexe en suite (bth/shr) (3 fmly) No smoking in 17 bedrooms s fr £73.50; d fr £85 (incl. bkfst) * Off peak **MEALS:** Lunch £11.95 Dinner £15.50 & alc English & French Cuisine V meals Coffee am Tea pm **FACILITIES:** CTV in all bedrooms STV Pool table Xmas **CONF:** Thtr 120 Class 60 Board 60 Del from £99.75 * **SERVICES:** 90P **NOTES:** No smoking in restaurant Last d 9pm
CARDS:

HOLMES CHAPEL Cheshire **Map 07 SJ76**
★★★ Old Vicarage
Knutsford Rd CW4 8EF
Quality Percentage Score: 65%
☎ 01477 532041 01477 535728
Dir: *on the A50, 1m from junct 18 on the M6*
Situated on the edge of the village, parts of this Grade II listed building date back to the 17th century. Most bedrooms are in the newer wing, overlooking the river Dane and open fields beyond. An atmospheric open-beamed bar leads into the restaurant, which offers a wide range of freshly prepared dishes. There is also a light and airy lounge for guests to relax in after dinner.
ROOMS: 29 en suite (bth/shr) s £36.50-£68.50; d £55.50-£80 (incl. bkfst) * LB Off peak **MEALS:** Lunch £11.90-£15.50 & alc Dinner £15.50 & alc English & French Cuisine V meals Coffee am Tea pm **FACILITIES:** CTV in all bedrooms STV **CONF:** Thtr 36 Class 14 Board 22 Del from £108 * **SERVICES:** Night porter 70P **NOTES:** No dogs (ex guide dogs) No smoking in restaurant Last d 9.45pm
CARDS:

HONILEY Warwickshire **Map 04 SP27**
★★★ Honiley Court
CV8 1NP
Corus and Regal hotels
Quality Percentage Score: 64%
☎ 01926 484234 01926 484474
Dir: *from M40 junc 15, take A46 then A4177 to Solihull, at 1st main rdbt turn right to hotel approx 2m on left*

An extension of the Old Boot Inn, this modern hotel gives easy access to the motorways around Birmingham, and to the airport. Bedrooms are spacious and comfortable. Public areas include a restaurant and a lively bar. Conference and meeting room facilities are being extended.
ROOMS: 62 en suite (bth/shr) (4 fmly) No smoking in 31 bedrooms s £85; d £95 * LB Off peak **MEALS:** Lunch £9.95-£11 Dinner £13.95-£17.50 English & French Cuisine V meals Coffee am Tea pm **FACILITIES:** CTV in all bedrooms STV Wkly live entertainment **CONF:** Thtr 170 Class 60 Board 45 Del from £125 * **SERVICES:** Lift Night porter 250P **NOTES:** No smoking in restaurant Last d 9.30pm
CARDS:

HONITON Devon — Map 03 ST10
see also **Yarcombe**

★★★ Combe House Gittisham
EX14 0AD
Quality Percentage Score: 70%
☎ 01404 540400 Fax 01404 46004
Dir: *turn off A30 1m S of Honiton, follow Gittisham signs*

This historic Elizabethan mansion set in extensive parkland offers highly individual, spacious bedrooms, most of which enjoy lovely views, and comfortable, well furnished reception rooms. It is now under new ownership.
ROOMS: 15 en suite (bth/shr) (1 fmly) s £83-£125; d £102-£156 (incl. bkfst) * LB Off peak **MEALS:** Lunch £8-£14 High tea £4.50-£9 Dinner fr £27.50 English, Asian, Mediterranean & Australian Cuisine V meals Coffee am Tea pm **FACILITIES:** CTV in all bedrooms Fishing Croquet lawn ch fac Xmas **CONF:** Thtr 40 Class 40 Board 30 Del from £101 * **SERVICES:** 51P **NOTES:** No coaches No smoking in restaurant Last d 9.30pm **CARDS:**

HONITON Devon — Map 03 ST10
★★★ Deer Park Country Hotel
Weston EX14 0PG
Quality Percentage Score: 63%
☎ 01404 41266 Fax 01404 46598
Dir: *2.5m W off A30*

A Georgian mansion, set amidst 80 acres of parkland, offers elegant public areas, complete with antique furnishings and many interesting pictures. Bedrooms in the main house are traditional in style, but with the expected facilities; those in the Mews are designed along practical, modern lines. Fishing, shooting and other country pursuits are available.
ROOMS: 12 en suite (bth/shr) 10 annexe en suite (bth/shr) (2 fmly) s £50-£100; d £80-£150 (incl. bkfst) * LB Off peak **MEALS:** Lunch £16-£18 & alc High tea £6 Dinner £29 & alc English, French & Italian Cuisine V meals Coffee am Tea pm **FACILITIES:** CTV in all bedrooms Outdoor swimming pool (heated) Tennis (hard) Fishing Squash Snooker Sauna Solarium Pool table Croquet lawn Putting green Walking Ballooning Shooting Archery Sea Fishing Riding ch fac Xmas **CONF:** Thtr 70 Class 40 Board 38 Del from £70 **SERVICES:** Night porter 44P **NOTES:** No coaches No smoking area in restaurant Last d 10.30pm
CARDS:

See advert on opposite page

HONITON Devon — Map 03 ST10
★★ Home Farm
Wilmington EX14 9JR
Quality Percentage Score: 74%
☎ 01404 831278 & 831246 Fax 01404 831411
Dir: *3m E on A35 in village of Wilmington*

A thatched, 16th-century farmhouse is the nucleus of this country house hotel. All rooms, both in the main house and in the 'Stable Block' around the cobbled courtyard, are comfortably furnished and individually decorated. The standard of cooking is good, and guests have a choice of menus.
ROOMS: 6 en suite (bth) 7 annexe en suite (bth/shr) (3 fmly) s £34.50; d £65 (incl. bkfst) * LB Off peak **MEALS:** Lunch £10.70-£14.50 & alc Dinner £14.50 & alc English, French & Italian Cuisine V meals Coffee am **FACILITIES:** CTV in all bedrooms **SERVICES:** 25P **NOTES:** No smoking in restaurant Last d 9.15pm **CARDS:**

HONITON Devon — Map 03 ST10
★★ Monkton Court
Monkton EX14 9QH
Quality Percentage Score: 65%
☎ 01404 42309 Fax 01404 46861
Dir: *2m E of Honiton on A30 towards Illminster, opposite Monkton Church*

Set in a five-acre deer park, this 17th-century manor house retains many original features. The comfortable oak-beamed bar features a central log fire; the traditional bedrooms are well equipped and spacious. An extensive range of home-cooked dishes is available in both the bar and restaurant.
ROOMS: 6 en suite (bth/shr) (2 fmly) s £29.50-£39.50; d £49.50-£59.50 (incl. bkfst) * LB Off peak **MEALS:** Lunch £9.95 Dinner £12.50 & alc English & French Cuisine V meals Coffee am **FACILITIES:** CTV in all bedrooms Xmas **CONF:** Thtr 30 Class 30 Board 20 **SERVICES:** 60P **NOTES:** No dogs (ex guide dogs) No smoking in restaurant Last d 9.15pm **CARDS:**

HONITON Devon — Map 03 ST10
★★ *Honiton Motel*
Turks Head Corner, Exeter Rd EX14 8BL
Quality Percentage Score: 63%
☎ 01404 43440 Fax 01404 47767
Dir: *off A35*

This family-run motel offers comfortable budget accommodation in well maintained rooms with modern facilities. The bar serves snacks and bar food, whilst the Black Swan Restaurant provides an enjoyable menu.
ROOMS: 15 annexe en suite (bth/shr) (3 fmly) **MEALS:** English/French Cuisine V meals Coffee am Tea pm **FACILITIES:** CTV in all bedrooms Pool table **CONF:** Thtr 150 Class 100 Board 50 **SERVICES:** 50P **NOTES:** Last d 9pm **CARDS:**

HOOK Hampshire — Map 04 SU75
★★ *Hook House*
London Rd RG27 9EQ
Quality Percentage Score: 71%
☎ 01256 762630 Fax 01256 760232
Dir: *1m E of Hook on A30*

This charming, family-run hotel in several acres of landscaped grounds has a reputation for warmth and good service.

contd.

Bedrooms are quiet, attractive and well equipped, the more recently refurbished rooms are exceptionally well presented.
ROOMS: 13 en suite (bth/shr) **MEALS:** V meals **FACILITIES:** CTV in all bedrooms Croquet lawn **CONF:** Thtr 20 Class 20 Board 20 **SERVICES:** 20P **NOTES:** No dogs No coaches No children 13yrs No smoking in restaurant Last d 8.39pm Closed Xmas
CARDS:

HOOK Hampshire — Map 04 SU75

★★ ***Raven***
Station Rd RG27 9HS
Quality Percentage Score: 66%
☎ 01256 762541 📠 01256 768677
Dir: *0.75m N of M3 junc 5 on B3349*
Situated in easy reach of the M3 and adjacent to the railway station is this friendly, informal and well run hotel. It is a popular venue which does a brisk bar and restaurant trade. Recently refurbished bedrooms are modern, practical and well equipped for the business traveller.
ROOMS: 38 en suite (bth/shr) (5 fmly) No smoking in 6 bedrooms **MEALS:** European Cuisine V meals Coffee am **FACILITIES:** CTV in all bedrooms STV Wkly live entertainment **CONF:** Thtr 100 Class 80 Board 50 **SERVICES:** Night porter 100P **NOTES:** No dogs (ex guide dogs) No smoking area in restaurant Last d 9.45pm
CARDS:

HOPE COVE Devon — Map 03 SX64

★★ **Cottage**
TQ7 3HJ
Quality Percentage Score: 67%
☎ 01548 561555 📠 01548 561455
Dir: *from Kingsbridge A381 towards Salcombe, it is suggested you take 2nd right at village of Marlborough continue & turn left for Inner Hope*
Owned by the Ireland family for over 20 years, the hotel has a real home-from-home feel. Bedrooms are well equipped and furnished with mostly traditional pieces. Some have balconies and stunning coastal views. Guests have a choice of lounges and a wide range of dishes is served in the restaurant.
ROOMS: 35 rms (25 bth/shr) (5 fmly) s £52.50-£65; d £85-£110 (incl. bkfst & dinner) * LB Off peak **MEALS:** Lunch £9.25 Dinner fr £18.25 & alc V meals Coffee am Tea pm **FACILITIES:** CTV in 29 bedrooms STV Xmas **CONF:** Thtr 50 Class 20 Board 24 Del from £39.50 * **SERVICES:** 50P **NOTES:** No coaches Last d 8.30pm Closed 3-30 Jan

HOPE COVE Devon — Map 03 SX64

★★ **Lantern Lodge**
TQ7 3HE
Quality Percentage Score: 66%
☎ 01548 561280 📠 01548 561736
Dir: *turn right off A381 Kingsbridge-Salcombe road, take first right after passing Hope Cove sign then first left along Grand View Rd*
This attractive small hotel has splendid views and is close to the South Devon coastal path. Bedrooms are all well furnished and the home-cooked meals are a particular strength. Guests have a choice of lounges and there is a pretty, enclosed garden with putting green.
ROOMS: 14 en suite (bth/shr) (1 fmly) s £72-£78; d £120-£130 (incl. bkfst & dinner) * LB Off peak **MEALS:** Bar Lunch £2.50-£6.50 Dinner £17 Coffee am Tea pm **FACILITIES:** CTV in all bedrooms Indoor swimming pool (heated) Sauna Solarium Putting green Multi-gym **SERVICES:** 15P **NOTES:** No dogs (ex guide dogs) No coaches No children 12yrs No smoking in restaurant Last d 8.30pm Closed Dec-Feb
CARDS:

HORLEY Hotels are listed under **Gatwick Airport**

HORNCASTLE Lincolnshire — Map 08 TF26

★★ **Admiral Rodney**
North St LN9 5DX
Quality Percentage Score: 70%
☎ 01507 523131 📠 01507 523104
Dir: *off A153*
This well furnished hotel in the centre of town has good car parking to the rear. Public areas include the Rodney bar, in the style of an old galleon, there is an informal Courtyard restaurant serving a wide range of food and snacks. Modern bedrooms are well appointed, thoughtfully equipped and generally of comfortable proportions.
ROOMS: 31 en suite (bth/shr) (3 fmly) No smoking in 6 bedrooms s £49-£54; d £66-£76 (incl. bkfst) * LB Off peak **MEALS:** Lunch £4.95-£10.30 Dinner £13.95-£17.45 V meals Coffee am Tea pm **FACILITIES:** CTV in all bedrooms STV Xmas **CONF:** Thtr 140 Class 80 Board 80 Del from £64 * **SERVICES:** Lift Night porter 60P **NOTES:** No dogs (ex guide dogs) No smoking area in restaurant Last d 9.30pm
CARDS:

HORNING Norfolk — Map 09 TG31

★★★ **Petersfield House**
Lower St NR12 8PF
Quality Percentage Score: 61%
☎ 01692 630741 📠 01692 630745
Dir: *from Wroxham take A1062 follow for two and a half miles then turn right into Horning Village, hotel in centre of village on left*
Close to the centre of this delightful riverside village, this pleasant hotel sits amid pretty gardens. The friendly environment is enhanced by traditional services. There is a comfortable lounge area and a light airy restaurant. Most of the bedrooms

contd.

have pretty views and are furnished in a modern style, however sizes can vary, ranging from 'cosy' to 'spacious'.
ROOMS: 18 en suite (bth/shr) (1 fmly) s £58-£63; d £75-£85 (incl. bkfst) * LB Off peak **MEALS:** Lunch £10.95-£13.95 & alc High tea fr £4.95 Dinner fr £16.50 & alc English & Continental Cuisine V meals Coffee am Tea pm **FACILITIES:** CTV in all bedrooms Fishing Putting green Boating Wkly live entertainment Xmas **CONF:** Thtr 50 Class 40 Board 30 Del from £75 * **SERVICES:** 70P **NOTES:** No coaches Last d 9.30pm **CARDS:**

HORRABRIDGE Devon — Map 02 SX57

★★ Overcombe

PL20 7RA
Quality Percentage Score: 64%
☎ 01822 853501 01822 85351
Dir: *on A386, 4m S of Tavistock*
With splendid views over Walkham Valley to the high granite tors of Dartmoor, this small hotel has a relaxed atmosphere. The individually decorated bedrooms are comfortable and well equipped. Two rooms are on the ground floor, and one is suitable for disabled guests.
ROOMS: 8 en suite (bth/shr) (3 fmly) No smoking in all bedrooms s £25-£28; d £51 (incl. bkfst) * LB Off peak **MEALS:** V meals **FACILITIES:** CTV in all bedrooms Croquet lawn Walking with professional guide **SERVICES:** 8P **NOTES:** No coaches No smoking in restaurant
CARDS:

See advert on opposite page

HORSHAM West Sussex — Map 04 TQ13

★★★★ South Lodge

Brighton Rd RH13 6PS
☎ 01403 891711 01403 891766
(For full entry see Lower Beeding)

HORSHAM West Sussex — Map 04 TQ13

★★★ Random Hall

Stane St, Slinford RH13 7QX
Quality Percentage Score: 71%
☎ 01403 790558 01403 791046
Dir: *on A29 0.5m from village of Slinfold*
Originally a 16th century farmhouse, public areas have beams and timbers, polished flagstones, open fire places and quiet comfortable corners. The bedrooms are furnished and decorated in keeping with the rest of the hotel. Guests can enjoy modern British cooking in the Tapestry restaurant and professional service from the friendly team of staff.
ROOMS: 15 en suite (bth/shr) (2 fmly) s £77.50; d £87.50 (incl. bkfst) * LB Off peak **MEALS:** Lunch £16.95 Dinner £20.95 European Cuisine V meals Coffee am Tea pm **FACILITIES:** CTV in all bedrooms
CONF: Thtr 16 Class 8 Board 12 Del £90 * **SERVICES:** 50P
NOTES: No dogs No coaches No smoking in restaurant Last d 10pm
CARDS:

HORSHAM West Sussex — Map 04 TQ13

★★ Ye Olde King's Head

Carfax RH12 1EG
Quality Percentage Score: 67%
☎ 01403 253126 01403 242291
Dir: *close to town hall, 0.5m from railway station, at junction of Carfax & East St*
Located in the heart of town, this former coaching inn, dating back to the 14th century, retains many original features. Bedrooms vary in shape and size and are smartly appointed and well equipped. Public areas include an attractive restaurant, cosy bar and wine cellar and a popular coffee shop which ensures a buzz of activity throughout the day.
ROOMS: 42 rms (41 bth/shr) (1 fmly) No smoking in 12 bedrooms **MEALS:** Lunch £7-£18 Dinner £7-£20alc English & French Cuisine V meals Coffee am Tea pm **FACILITIES:** CTV in all bedrooms STV **CONF:** Thtr 45 Class 40 Board 30 **SERVICES:** 40P **NOTES:** No smoking in restaurant Last d 9.30pm **CARDS:**

HORSHAM West Sussex — Map 04 TQ13

Travel Inn

57 North St RH12 1RB
☎ 01403 250141 01403 270797
Dir: *opposite railway station, 5m from junct 11 of M23*
This modern building offers accommodation in smart, spacious and well equipped bedrooms, all with en-suite bathrooms. Refreshments may be taken at the nearby family restaurant. For details about current prices consult the Contents Page under Hotel Groups for the Travel Inn phone number.
ROOMS: 40 en suite (bth/shr) d £39.95 *

HORTON-CUM-STUDLEY Oxfordshire — Map 04 SP51

★★★ Studley Priory

OX33 1AZ
Quality Percentage Score: 78%
☎ 01865 351203 & 351254 01865 351613
Dir: *2.5m off B4027 between Wheatley and Islip*
Set in extensive and pretty grounds, guests cannot fail to be impressed by this very special property. Just six miles from the centre of Oxford, the former Benedictine nunnery was founded in the 12th century, and extended by the Croke family who acquired the property when Henry VIII dissolved the monasteries. A professional yet friendly welcome awaits guests here, and lattice-windowed bedrooms, varying in size, are all tastefully decorated with lots of thoughtful extras. Peter Hewett's imaginative cuisine continues to impress.
ROOMS: 18 en suite (bth/shr) No smoking in 4 bedrooms s £105-£130; d £130-£200 (incl. cont bkfst) * LB Off peak **MEALS:** Lunch £10-£15 & alc Dinner £22.50-£25 & alc English & French Cuisine V meals Coffee am Tea pm **FACILITIES:** CTV in all bedrooms STV Tennis (hard & grass) Croquet lawn Putting green **CONF:** Thtr 40 Class 25 Board 25 Del from £160 * **SERVICES:** Night porter 101P **NOTES:** No dogs No smoking in restaurant Last d 9.30pm Closed 29 Dec-3 Jan
CARDS:

HORTON-CUM-STUDLEY Oxfordshire — Map 04 SP51

★★ Kings Arms Hotel

Horton Hill OX33 1AY
Quality Percentage Score: 67%
☎ 01865 351235 01865 351721
Dir: *from the A40 part of the Oxford ringroad at Headington rdbt follow signs to Horton-cum-Studley*
Although this inn can be dated back to the 14th century most of

contd.

it was rebuilt in 1742 from Cotswold Stone. The hotel has been lovingly restored and extended over the past few years and the accommodation is now comfortable and well presented each with stylish individual decor. Mr Bumbles restaurant has lots of character and offers an 'early birds' menu and an a la carte using good fresh ingredients.
ROOMS: 10 en suite (shr) 8 annexe en suite (bth/shr) (1 fmly) s £39-£49; d £59-£69 (incl. bkfst) * LB Off peak **MEALS:** Lunch £7.95-£9.95 Dinner fr £7.95 & alc English & French Cuisine V meals Coffee am Tea pm **FACILITIES:** CTV in all bedrooms Wkly live entertainment Xmas **SERVICES:** 25P **NOTES:** No dogs (ex guide dogs) No smoking area in restaurant Last d 9pm **CARDS:**

HORWICH Greater Manchester **Map 07 SD61**
★★ ***Swallowfield***
Chorley New Rd BL6 6HN
Quality Percentage Score: 65%
☎ 01204 697914 01204 468900
Dir: *on A673, off junc 6 of M61*
This family run hotel, not far from junction 6 of the M61, offers spacious bedrooms. A friendly atmosphere is generated in the lively bar and good-value meals are served in the restaurant.
ROOMS: 31 en suite (bth/shr) **MEALS:** V meals Coffee am Tea pm **FACILITIES:** CTV in all bedrooms STV Pool table **SERVICES:** 32P **NOTES:** No smoking area in restaurant Last d 8.30pm
CARDS:

AA Rosettes are awarded for quality of food, see page 15 for an explanation of Rosette assessment.

HOUGHTON-LE-SPRING Tyne & Wear **Map 12 NZ34**

★★ **Chilton Lodge**

Black Boy Rd, Chilton Moor, Fencehouses DH4 6LX

Quality Percentage Score: 59%

☎ 0191 385 2694 0191 385 6762

Dir: *leave A1(M) at junct 62, then A690 towards Sunderland. Turn left at Rainton Bridge/Fencehouses sign, cross rdbt and take 1st left*

Set in open countryside near the village of Fencehouses, this hotel has evolved from original farm cottages to a complex providing modern but functional bedrooms, a country pub and a spacious ballroom catering for functions and weddings. Menus offer a wide choice of bar and dining room meals.

ROOMS: 25 en suite (bth/shr) (7 fmly) No smoking in 7 bedrooms s £38-£48; d £48-£58 (incl. bkfst) * LB Off peak **MEALS:** Lunch £7.50-£10.50 Dinner £10.50-£12.95 English, French, Italian & Chinese Cuisine V meals Coffee am **FACILITIES:** CTV in all bedrooms STV Xmas **CONF:** Thtr 60 Class 50 Board 30 Del £60 * **SERVICES:** Night porter 100P **NOTES:** No dogs (ex guide dogs) No smoking area in restaurant Last d 10pm **CARDS:**

HOUNSLOW Hotels are listed under **Heathrow Airport**

HOVE See **Brighton & Hove** and advert on p. 321

HOVINGHAM North Yorkshire **Map 08 SE67**

★★★ **Worsley Arms**

YO62 4LA

Quality Percentage Score: 70%

☎ 01653 628234 01653 628130

Dir: *on B1257*

Forming the focal point of an attractive village, this hotel takes its name from the family who are custodians of the village and the local estate. Lounges are comfortable and relaxing and real fires burn on cooler days. The restaurant offers a modern interpretation of dishes using the best of meats, game and seafood. Although less formal, one can eat equally seriously in the Cricketers Bar and Bistro, and both hold our Two Rosette award. Several bedrooms are contained in cottages across the village green.

ROOMS: 10 en suite (bth/shr) 8 annexe en suite (bth/shr) No smoking in all bedrooms s £60; d £80 (incl. bkfst) * LB Off peak **MEALS:** Lunch £16 Dinner £25 V meals Coffee am Tea pm **FACILITIES:** CTV in all bedrooms Tennis (hard) Squash Shooting Xmas **CONF:** Thtr 40 Class 40 Board 30 Del £100 * **SERVICES:** Night porter 52P **NOTES:** No smoking in restaurant Last d 9.30pm

CARDS:

HOWTOWN (NEAR POOLEY BRIDGE) **Map 12 NY41**

Cumbria

The Premier Collection

★★★ **Sharrow Bay Country House**

Sharrow Bay CA10 2LZ

☎ 017684 86301 & 86483 017684 86349

Dir: *at Pooley Bridge take right hand fork by church towards Howtown. At cross road turn right and follow Lakeside Road for 2m.*

Believed to be the world's first country house hotel, the Sharrow Bay has been warmly welcoming guests since 1948. The Italianate architecture sits in 12-acres of grounds on the shores of Lake Ullswater with inspiring views. Bedrooms are a delight, each room is individually and thoughtfully furnished; accommodation is mainly in cottages and an Elizabethan farmhouse with its own lounge and breakfast room. The comfortable public rooms are beautifully appointed with a myriad of collectibles. Dinner at Sharrow is a celebration, the 6-course meal being served with panache by a smart and attentive team. Breakfasts and afternoon teas are also extremely popular.

ROOMS: 10 rms (8 bth/shr) 16 annexe en suite (bth/shr) s £125-£230; d £210-£390 (incl. bkfst & dinner) * Off peak **MEALS:** Lunch £30-£36.25 Dinner £47.25 English & French Cuisine Coffee am Tea pm **FACILITIES:** CTV in all bedrooms **SERVICES:** 30P **NOTES:** No dogs No coaches No children 13yrs No smoking in restaurant Last d 8.30pm Closed 6 Dec-25 Feb **CARDS:**

HUDDERSFIELD West Yorkshire **Map 07 SE11**

★★★ **Old Golf House Hotel**

New Hey Rd, Outlane HD3 3YP

Quality Percentage Score: 69%

☎ 01422 379311 01422 372694

Dir: *leave M62 at junct 23 (Eastbound only), or junct 24 & follow A640 towards Rochdale. Hotel on A640 (New Hey Rd) at Outlane*

Close to the M62 (Junction 23 - note restricted access), this hotel offers well insulated bedrooms equipped to a good modern standard and is now part of the Corus group. A wide choice of dishes is served in the restaurant, or lighter meals can be had in the comfortable lounge bar. Some leisure facilities and meeting and function suites are available.

ROOMS: 52 en suite (bth/shr) (4 fmly) No smoking in 30 bedrooms s £55-£95; d £55-£105 * LB Off peak **MEALS:** Lunch £9.99-£11.95 High tea fr £5 Dinner £15.95-£17.95 & alc International Cuisine V meals Coffee am Tea pm **FACILITIES:** CTV in all bedrooms STV Sauna Solarium Gym Putting green 5 Hole pitch & putt **CONF:** Thtr 100 Class 50 Board 40 Del from £99 * **SERVICES:** Night porter 100P **NOTES:** No smoking in restaurant Last d 10pm **CARDS:**

HUDDERSFIELD West Yorkshire **Map 07 SE11**

★★★ **Bagden Hall**

Wakefield Rd, Scissett HD8 9LE

Quality Percentage Score: 68%

☎ 01484 865330 01484 861001

Dir: *on A636, between Scissett and Denby Dale*

Set in grounds, with a par three nine hole golf course, this elegant mansion house is close to the village of Scissett. The public rooms include a bright conservatory where light meals are served, and a good conference/function room. Bedrooms vary in size, all are well equipped and pleasingly furnished.

ROOMS: 17 en suite (bth/shr) (3 fmly) No smoking in 2 bedrooms **MEALS:** Lunch £8.95-£12.95 High tea £3.95 Dinner £17.95 & alc English & French Cuisine V meals Coffee am Tea pm **FACILITIES:** CTV in all bedrooms STV Golf 9 Putting green **CONF:** Thtr 80 Class 40 Board 30 Del £99 * **SERVICES:** Night porter 96P **NOTES:** No dogs (ex guide dogs) No smoking area in restaurant Last d 9.15pm RS 24-25 Dec

CARDS:

HUDDERSFIELD West Yorkshire — Map 07 SE11

★★★ George

St George's Square HD1 1JA

Quality Percentage Score: 66%

☎ 01484 515444 Fax 01484 435056

Dir: *M62 Junc 24 follow signs Huddersfield Town Centre, adjacent to railway station*

This Victorian hotel, near the railway station, played its part in the history of Rugby League as the venue for their first meeting, in 1895. Bedrooms, equipped to a good modern standard, are mostly spacious, and public rooms include a pleasant restaurant serving a range of popular dishes, and a comfortable lounge bar. There is some reserved car parking in the railway station car park.

ROOMS: 60 en suite (bth/shr) (1 fmly) No smoking in 15 bedrooms s £80-£90; d £90-£100 * LB Off peak **MEALS:** Lunch £9.95-£11.95 High tea £9-£10.50 Dinner £15.95-£17.95 International Cuisine V meals Coffee am Tea pm **FACILITIES:** CTV in all bedrooms STV Free use of local Sports Centre Xmas **CONF:** Thtr 200 Class 60 Board 60 Del from £85 * **SERVICES:** Lift Night porter 23P **NOTES:** No smoking in restaurant Last d 9.30pm **CARDS:**

HUDDERSFIELD West Yorkshire — Map 07 SE11

★★★ Huddersfield

33-47 Kirkgate HD1 1QT

Quality Percentage Score: 64%

☎ 01484 512111 Fax 01484 435262

Dir: *on A62 ring road, below parish church, opposite sports centre*

This popular hotel, situated in the town centre, close to the ring road, offers comfortable and attractively furnished bedrooms, including family rooms and some with four-posters. A choice of bars and dining areas is available, with an all-day brasserie and evening bistro for meals and snacks. The car park reaches award winning standards for high security.

ROOMS: 50 en suite (bth/shr) (6 fmly) s £39-£52; d £49-£62 (incl. bkfst) * Off peak **MEALS:** Lunch £5-£7 & alc High tea £4-£6 & alc Dinner £12-£15 & alc English & Continental Cuisine V meals Coffee am Tea pm **FACILITIES:** CTV in all bedrooms STV Pool table Wkly live entertainment Xmas **SERVICES:** Lift Night porter 70P **NOTES:** Last d mdnt **CARDS:**

HUDDERSFIELD West Yorkshire — Map 07 SE11

★★★ Briar Court

Halifax Rd, Birchencliffe HD3 3NT

Quality Percentage Score: 60%

☎ 01484 519902 Fax 01484 431812

Dir: *on A629, 300yds S of junc 24 on M62*

Conveniently situated close to junction 24 of the M62, this modern hotel offers well equipped bedrooms. As well as the main restaurant, diners can opt for the popular Da Sandro Restaurant, with its range of Italian dishes, served in a lively atmosphere.

ROOMS: 48 en suite (bth/shr) (3 fmly) No smoking in 20 bedrooms s £65-£75; d £75-£85 (incl. bkfst) Off peak **MEALS:** Lunch £13-£25alc Dinner £13-£30alc English & Italian Cuisine V meals Coffee am Tea pm **FACILITIES:** CTV in all bedrooms STV **CONF:** Thtr 150 Class 50 Board 60 Del from £65 * **SERVICES:** Night porter 140P **NOTES:** No dogs (ex guide dogs) No smoking in restaurant Last d 11pm **CARDS:**

Symbols and Abbreviations are listed and explained on pages 4 and 5

HUDDERSFIELD West Yorkshire — Map 07 SE11

★★ Lodge

48 Birkby Lodge Rd, Birkby HD2 2BG

Quality Percentage Score: 71%

☎ 01484 431001 Fax 01484 421590

Dir: *junct 24 of M62, then exit A629 for Birkby. Turn right at Nuffield Hospital down Birkby Lodge Road, hotel 200yds on left*

This quiet family run hotel offers attractively furnished bedrooms. Public areas include two comfortable lounges and an inviting restaurant, where carefully prepared meals are served. A wood panelled meeting room is available, service is friendly and efficient.

ROOMS: 13 en suite (bth/shr) (2 fmly) No smoking in all bedrooms s £60; d £70-£80 (incl. bkfst) * Off peak **MEALS:** Lunch £13.95-£14.95 Dinner £23.95 English & Continental Cuisine V meals Coffee am **FACILITIES:** CTV in all bedrooms **CONF:** Thtr 40 Class 20 Board 20 Del from £85 * **SERVICES:** 41P **NOTES:** No coaches No smoking in restaurant Last d 9.30pm Closed 25-27 Dec **CARDS:**

HUDDERSFIELD West Yorkshire — Map 07 SE11

★★ The Flying Horse Country Hotel & Restaurant

Nettleton Hill Rd, Scapegoat Hill HD7 4NY

Quality Percentage Score: 64%

☎ 01484 642368 Fax 01484 642866

Dir: *junct 24 M62 follow signs for Rochdale-Outlane Village-left after Tillotsons Arms onto Round Ings Rd-top of Hill turn left onto Nettleton Hill Rd*

This purpose built hotel offers nicely furnished bedrooms. There is a popular bar serving a good selection of snacks and meals,

contd.

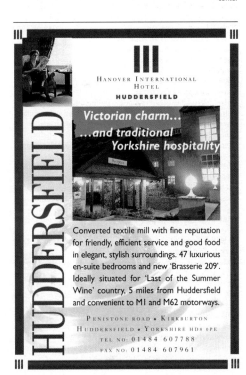

with more formal dining in the well appointed restaurant, overlooking the surrounding countryside.
ROOMS: 31 en suite (bth/shr) (4 fmly) No smoking in 6 bedrooms s £38-£59; d £55-£69 (incl. bkfst) * LB Off peak **MEALS:** Sunday Lunch £9.95 Dinner £15.95 English & French Cuisine V meals Coffee am **FACILITIES:** CTV in all bedrooms STV **CONF:** Thtr 132 Class 56 Board 30 Del from £85 * **SERVICES:** Night porter 115P **NOTES:** No smoking area in restaurant Last d 9.30pm **CARDS:**

HUDDERSFIELD West Yorkshire **Map 07 SE11**
★ Elm Crest
2 Queens Rd, Edgerton HD2 2AG
Quality Percentage Score: 67%
☎ 01484 530990 01484 516227
Dir: *1.5m from M62 (J24), 1m from the town centre on A629*
The attractively furnished bedrooms at this small hotel are generally spacious, and the lounge, on the lower ground floor, is comfortable and cosy. Freshly prepared evening meals and hearty breakfasts are served in the adjacent dining room.
ROOMS: 8 rms (5 shr) (1 fmly) No smoking in all bedrooms s fr £38; d fr £60 (incl. bkfst) * LB Off peak **MEALS:** Lunch £12-£15 & alc High tea £4-£6 Dinner £14-£24 English & French Cuisine V meals Coffee am Tea pm **FACILITIES:** CTV in all bedrooms **CONF:** Thtr 15 Class 15 Board 12 Del from £45 * **SERVICES:** 12P **NOTES:** No dogs No coaches No smoking in restaurant Last d 7pm **CARDS:**

HULL East Riding of Yorkshire **Map 08 TA02**
see also **Little Weighton**
★★★ Willerby Manor
Well Ln HU10 6ER
Quality Percentage Score: 70%
☎ 01482 652616 01482 653901
(For full entry see Willerby)

HULL East Riding of Yorkshire **Map 08 TA02**
★★★ *Posthouse Hull Marina*
The Marina, Castle St HU1 2BX
Posthouse
Quality Percentage Score: 68%
☎ 01482 225221 01482 213299
Dir: *from M62 join A63 to Hull. Follow signs for 'Marina and Ice Arena'. Hotel on left next to Ice Arena*
This modern hotel occupies a prime position overlooking Hull Marina. Bedrooms are particularly well appointed and include several family and executive rooms. The restaurant has a waterside setting and features international and British dishes. Secretarial services can be provided and there is a well equipped Health and Fitness Club.
ROOMS: 99 en suite (bth/shr) (12 fmly) No smoking in 66 bedrooms **MEALS:** International Cuisine V meals Coffee am Tea pm **FACILITIES:** CTV in all bedrooms Indoor swimming pool (heated) Sauna Solarium Gym **CONF:** Thtr 150 Class 60 Board 50 **SERVICES:** Lift Night porter 130P **NOTES:** No smoking in restaurant Last d 10pm **CARDS:**

HULL East Riding of Yorkshire **Map 08 TA02**
★★★ *Portland*
Paragon St HU1 3JP
Quality Percentage Score: 67%
☎ 01482 326462 01482 213460
Dir: *leave M62 onto A63 to 1st main rdbt at 2nd set of lights turn left at x-roads across next junct turn right onto Carr Ln follow 1-way system*
This tall modern hotel is right in the heart of the city and offers well equipped accommodation. Public rooms include a spacious bar-lounge and an elegant restaurant serving a good range of well produced dishes. There is also an all-day coffee shop on the ground floor.
ROOMS: 106 en suite (bth/shr) (4 fmly) No smoking in 9 bedrooms **MEALS:** English & International Cuisine V meals Coffee am Tea pm **FACILITIES:** CTV in all bedrooms STV **CONF:** Thtr 240 Class 70 Board 100 **SERVICES:** Lift Night porter 2P **NOTES:** No smoking area in restaurant Last d 10.30pm **CARDS:**

HULL East Riding of Yorkshire **Map 08 TA02**
★★★ Quality Hotel Hull
170 Ferensway HU1 3UF
Quality Percentage Score: 65%
☎ 01482 325087 01482 323172
Dir: *follow signs for Railway Station*
Although completely renovated a few years ago, this Victorian railway hotel still retains its original façade. Bedrooms are modern and well equipped, while the spacious and practical public areas are well designed and comfortably furnished. The restaurant overlooks the station concourse, and guests have the free use of an adjacent leisure centre.
ROOMS: 155 en suite (bth/shr) No smoking in 85 bedrooms s £73.25-£81.75; d £88.25-£105.50 * LB Off peak **MEALS:** Lunch £2.95-£15.95alc Dinner fr £14.50 & alc English & Continental Cuisine V meals Coffee am Tea pm **FACILITIES:** CTV in all bedrooms STV Indoor swimming pool (heated) Sauna Solarium Gym Pool table Jacuzzi/spa Spa pool Steamroom Xmas **CONF:** Thtr 450 Class 150 Board 105 **SERVICES:** Lift Night porter 130P **NOTES:** No smoking area in restaurant Last d 10pm **CARDS:**

HULL East Riding of Yorkshire **Map 08 TA02**
★★★ Posthouse Hull
Ferriby High Rd HU14 3LG
Posthouse
Quality Percentage Score: 63%
☎ 01482 645212 01482 643332
(For full entry see North Ferriby)

HULL East Riding of Yorkshire **Map 08 TA02**
★★ Rowley Manor
Rowley Rd HU20 3XR
Quality Percentage Score: 64%
☎ 01482 848248 01482 849900
(For full entry see Little Weighton)

HULL East Riding of Yorkshire **Map 08 TA02**
★★ Fox & Coney Inn
Market Place HU15 2AT
Quality Percentage Score: 63%
☎ 01430 422275 01430 421552
(For full entry see South Cave)

HULL East Riding of Yorkshire **Map 08 TA02**
★★ Comfort Inn
11 Anlaby Rd HU1 2PJ
Quality Percentage Score: 58%
☎ 01482 323299 01482 214730
Dir: *turn off A63 onto A1079 - Ferensway*
Centrally located, this city centre hotel offers modern, well equipped accommodation, with open-plan lounge, bar and restaurant on the first floor. Bedrooms are comfortable and provide all expected facilities.
ROOMS: 59 en suite (bth/shr) (5 fmly) No smoking in 29 bedrooms d £46.75-£54.50 * LB Off peak **MEALS:** Lunch £2.95-£15.95alc Dinner fr £10.75 & alc English & Continental Cuisine V meals Coffee am Tea pm **FACILITIES:** CTV in all bedrooms STV Xmas **CONF:** Thtr 140 Class 80 Board 45 **SERVICES:** Lift Night porter 100P **NOTES:** No smoking area in restaurant Last d 10pm **CARDS:**

HULL East Riding of Yorkshire **Map 08 TA02**

Campanile

Beverley Rd, Freetown Way HU2 9AN

01482 325530 01482 587538

Dir: *pass station and first right after crossroads*

This modern building offers accommodation in smart well equipped bedrooms, all with en-suite bathrooms. Refreshments may be taken at the informal Bistro. For details about current prices, consult the Contents Page under Hotel Groups for the Campanile phone number.
ROOMS: 50 annexe en suite (bth/shr) **CONF:** Thtr 35 Class 18 Board 20

HULL East Riding of Yorkshire **Map 08 TA02**

Travel Inn

Ferriby Rd, Hessle HU13 0JA

01482 645285 01482 645299

Dir: *from A63 take exit for A164/A15 to Humber Bridge/Beverley/Hessle Viewpoint, Travel Inn on 1st rdbt*

This modern building offers accommodation in smart, spacious and well equipped bedrooms, all with en-suite bathrooms. Refreshments may be taken at the nearby family restaurant. For details about current prices consult the Contents Page under Hotel Groups for the Travel Inn phone number.
ROOMS: 40 en suite (bth/shr) d £39.95 *

HULL East Riding of Yorkshire **Map 08 TA02**

Travel Inn Hull North

Kingswood Park, Ennerdale HU7 4HS

01482 820225 01482 820300

Dir: *on rdbt junc of A1079 Ennerdale link road & main access road to Kingswood Park*

This modern building offers accommodation in smart, spacious and well equipped bedrooms, all with en-suite bathrooms. Refreshments may be taken at the nearby family restaurant. For details about current prices consult the Contents Page under Hotel Groups for the Travel Inn phone number.
ROOMS: 40 en suite (bth/shr) d £39.95 *

HULL East Riding of Yorkshire **Map 08 TA02**

Travelodge

Beacon Service Area HU15 1RZ

01430 424455 01430 424455

(For full entry see South Cave)

HUNGERFORD Berkshire **Map 04 SU36**

★★ **Three Swans**

117 High St RG17 0LZ

Quality Percentage Score: 67%

01488 682721 01488 681708

Dir: *south of the A4, in the High St opposite the Town Hall*

Located in the centre of town, this popular inn has attractively decorated public areas and well equipped accommodation. Public areas include an oak panelled bar, modern restaurant and a comfortable lounge bar. The atmosphere is informal and the service is both friendly and helpful.
ROOMS: 15 en suite (bth/shr) (1 fmly) No smoking in 2 bedrooms s £50-£65; d £60-£75 * LB Off peak **MEALS:** Lunch £4.95-£9.95 & alc Dinner £8-£14alc English & Continental Cuisine V meals Coffee am Tea pm **FACILITIES:** CTV in all bedrooms STV Xmas **CONF:** Thtr 60 Class 35 Board 30 Del from £70 * **SERVICES:** 50P **NOTES:** No smoking in restaurant Last d 9pm **CARDS:**

HUNMANBY North Yorkshire **Map 08 TA07**

★★ **Wrangham House Hotel**

10 Stonegate YO14 0NS

Quality Percentage Score: 68%

01723 891333 01723 891333

Dir: *from main A64 road, follow the A1039 to Filey, turning right onto Hunmanby road, the hotel is behind All Saints Church in Hunmanby village*

Wrangham House was once the local vicarage, but is now a comfortable hotel offering traditional service and accommodation. The bedrooms are attractively furnished and all have been thoughtfully equipped. Two comfortable lounges are available, while a good menu is served in the elegant dining room. The house is surrounded by delightful gardens.

ROOMS: 8 en suite (bth/shr) 4 annexe en suite (bth/shr) No smoking in all bedrooms s £43.50-£48.50; d £67-£77 (incl. bkfst) * LB Off peak **MEALS:** Lunch fr £9.95 Dinner £14-£17.50 V meals Coffee am Tea pm **FACILITIES:** CTV in all bedrooms Croquet lawn Xmas **CONF:** Thtr 50 Class 20 Board 20 Del from £60 * **SERVICES:** 20P **NOTES:** No dogs (ex guide dogs) No coaches No smoking in restaurant Last d 9.30pm
CARDS:

HUNSTANTON Norfolk **Map 09 TF64**

★★★ ***Le Strange Arms***

Golf Course Rd, Old Hunstanton PE36 6JJ

Quality Percentage Score: 65%

01485 534411 01485 534724

Dir: *turn off A149 1m N of Hunstanton town. Road bends sharply right and access road to hotel is on bend*

With wide lawns sweeping down to the sandy beach, loyal leisure and busines guests return time and again to enjoy the blend of relaxed yet attentive hospitality and the delights of the dining room at this hotel. More informal fare is served in the very popular Ancient Mariners pub, adjacent to the hotel. The attractive bedrooms feature a wide range of styles, from the original bedrooms in the main house with period furnishings, to the more contemporary rooms in a new wing.
ROOMS: 36 en suite (bth/shr) (4 fmly) **MEALS:** English, French & Mediterranean Cuisine V meals Coffee am Tea pm **FACILITIES:** CTV in all bedrooms Tennis Snooker **CONF:** Thtr 180 Class 150 Board 50 **SERVICES:** Night porter 80P **NOTES:** Last d 9pm
CARDS:

See advert on page 327

HUNSTANTON Norfolk **Map 09 TF64**

★★ Caley Hall

Old Hunstanton Rd PE36 6HH
Quality Percentage Score: 72%
☎ 01485 533486 ▯ 01485 533348
Dir: *1m from Hunstanton, on A149*

Based around a 17th-century manor house, this courtyard-style hotel has a variety of pleasantly furnished bedrooms located in tasteful conversions of the manor's authentic buildings. The relaxing public rooms include a cosy bar and an open-plan lounge area, while the spacious restaurant serves a daily-changing menu.

ROOMS: 33 annexe en suite (bth) (5 fmly) s £39-£45; d £48-£64 (incl. bkfst) * LB Off peak **MEALS:** Lunch £14.75-£15.75 & alc Dinner £14.75-£15.75 & alc International Cuisine V meals Coffee am **FACILITIES:** CTV in all bedrooms STV Snooker Xmas **CONF:** Board 40 **SERVICES:** 70P **NOTES:** No smoking in restaurant Last d 9pm Closed Jan-Feb
CARDS:

HUNSTANTON Norfolk **Map 09 TF64**

★★ The Lodge Hotel & Restaurant

Old Hunstanton Rd PE36 6HX
Quality Percentage Score: 70%
☎ 01485 532896 ▯ 01485 535007
Dir: *1m E of Hunstanton on A149*

A friendly hotel within easy reach of the beach and town centre. The attractively decorated rooms are generally spacious, well maintained and all offer good facilities; a four poster room and an executive ground floor suite are available. Spacious public areas include a large garden in which to enjoy cream teas, a popular restaurant, food-serving bar and a comfortable lounge.

ROOMS: 16 en suite (bth/shr) 6 annexe en suite (bth/shr) (3 fmly) No smoking in 6 bedrooms s £44-£52; d £88-£108 (incl. bkfst) * LB Off peak **MEALS:** Lunch £10.95-£30alc Dinner £19-£30alc English, French & Italian Cuisine V meals Coffee am Tea pm **FACILITIES:** CTV in all bedrooms Snooker Pool table Games room Xmas **CONF:** Thtr 30 Class 20 Board 20 **SERVICES:** Night porter 70P **NOTES:** No smoking in restaurant Last d 9.30pm **CARDS:**

See advert on opposite page

HUNSTRETE Somerset **Map 03 ST66**

The Premier Collection

★★★ Hunstrete House

BS39 4NS
☎ 01761 490490 ▯ 01761 490732
Dir: *from Bath A4 to Bristol, take A39 through Marksbury, A368 turn off Hunstrete Village*

Built in the 18th century, Hunstrete House is located in 92 acres of deer park and woodland. Individually furnished and decorated bedrooms have modern facilities and views over the countryside. The elegantly furnished public areas feature antiques and original paintings. Creative cooking uses the finest ingredients.

ROOMS: 23 en suite (bth/shr) (2 fmly) s fr £120; d fr £170 (incl. bkfst) * LB Off peak **MEALS:** Lunch £14.95-£19.95 & alc Dinner £29.95 & alc English & French Cuisine V meals Coffee am Tea pm **FACILITIES:** CTV in all bedrooms Outdoor swimming pool (heated) Tennis (hard) Croquet lawn Xmas **CONF:** Thtr 50 Class 40 Board 30 Del £175 * **SERVICES:** Night porter 75P **NOTES:** No dogs (ex guide dogs) No coaches No smoking in restaurant Last d 9.30pm
CARDS:

HUNTINGDON Cambridgeshire **Map 04 TL27**

★★★★ Swallow

SWALLOW HOTELS

Kingfisher Way, Hinchingbrooke Business Park PE18 8FL
Quality Percentage Score: 71%
☎ 01480 446000 ▯ 01480 451111
Dir: *situated 1m from the centre of Huntington on the A14*

This brand new hotel is located on the fringes of the business park, ideally placed for easy access from the A14 and A1. It has all the trappings of a modern, well planned hotel with excellent meeting and leisure facilities. In addition to the open-plan lounge bar, there is a also a quiet retreat in the form of a cosy drawing room. A good range of services is provided by a smartly uniformed team of staff.

ROOMS: 150 en suite (bth/shr) No smoking in 60 bedrooms s £90-£130; d £100-£140 (incl. bkfst) * LB Off peak **MEALS:** International Cuisine V meals Coffee am Tea pm **FACILITIES:** CTV in all bedrooms STV Indoor swimming pool (heated) Gym Jacuzzi/spa Xmas **CONF:** Thtr 300 Class 150 Board 100 Del from £120 **SERVICES:** Lift Night porter Air conditioning 250P **NOTES:** No smoking in restaurant Last d 9.30pm
CARDS:

HUNTINGDON Cambridgeshire **Map 04 TL27**

★★★ The Old Bridge

1 High St PE18 6TQ
Quality Percentage Score: 75%
☎ 01480 452681 ▯ 01480 411017
Dir: *off A1 signposted from junct with A14*

This delightful hotel sits on the banks of the Ouse, close to Huntingdon town centre. Dating back to the 18th century, it has a delightful combination of the old and the new, with the stylish charm of its architecture complimented by modern interior design. Meals are available in the convivial Terrace and the more formal Restaurant, offering the same appealing menu. All the rooms have been individually designed for full effect, and many are equipped with CD players or air conditioning. There is a

contd.

particularly good modern business centre, with dedicated secretarial services.
ROOMS: 25 en suite (bth/shr) (3 fmly) s £79.50-£89.50; d £89.50-£149.50 (incl. bkfst) * LB Off peak **MEALS:** Lunch £20-£29.50alc Dinner £20-£29.50alc English & Mediterranean Cuisine V meals Coffee am Tea pm **FACILITIES:** CTV in all bedrooms STV Fishing Private mooring for boats Xmas **CONF:** Thtr 50 Class 20 Board 24 Del from £139.50 * **SERVICES:** Night porter 50P **NOTES:** No smoking in restaurant Last d 10.30pm RS 25 Dec night
CARDS:

HUNTINGDON Cambridgeshire — Map 04 TL27

Travel Inn
Brampton Hut PE18 8NQ
01480 810800 01480 811298
Dir: *at junct of A1/A14. From the north do not use junct 14 but take next main exit for Huntingdon and Brampton, access via services*
This modern building offers accommodation in smart, spacious and well equipped bedrooms, all with en-suite bathrooms. Refreshments may be taken at the nearby family restaurant. For details about current prices consult the Contents Page under Hotel Groups for the Travel Inn phone number.
ROOMS: 60 en suite (bth/shr) d £39.95 *

HURST GREEN Lancashire — Map 07 SD63

★★ Shireburn Arms
Whalley Rd BB7 9QJ
Quality Percentage Score: 68%
01254 826518 01254 826208
Dir: *on B6243 at the entrance to Hurst Green village*
This well kept family run inn is peacefully situated in the Ribble

contd.

valley, just a short drive from Clitheroe. Attractively decorated bedrooms are spacious and comfortably furnished. The airy restaurant has fine views over open fields and guests can choose between dining there or in one of the inviting bar lounges.
ROOMS: 18 en suite (bth/shr) (3 fmly) s fr £40; d fr £60 (incl. bkfst) * LB Off peak **MEALS:** Lunch £6.95-£10.95 Dinner £10.95-£20 English & French Cuisine V meals Coffee am Tea pm **FACILITIES:** CTV in all bedrooms Xmas **CONF:** Thtr 100 Class 50 Board 50 Del £70 * **SERVICES:** 71P **NOTES:** No smoking in restaurant Last d 9.30pm
CARDS:

HYTHE Kent — Map 05 TR13

★★★★ The Hythe Imperial

MARSTON HOTELS

Princes Pde CT21 6AE
Quality Percentage Score: 76%
☎ 01303 267441 01303 264610
Dir: *M20, junct 11 take A261*

Set in a 50 acre estate on the Hythe seafront, this magnificent building, evocative of a bygone era, is surrounded by a 9 hole, 18 tee golf course and beautifully maintained gardens. The splendid leisure facilities include an indoor pool with spa, sauna, gymnasium and range of beauty treatment rooms in the most tranquil of settings. Bedrooms are spacious and well equipped with lovely views of either the grounds or sea. The restaurant offers a wide range of carefully prepared dishes served by a professional and friendly staff. For a more informal atmosphere there is the sunny Bistro Bar, where lighter dishes are served throughout the day. The hotel is very popular for functions, boasting extensive conference facilities, and for families there is a creche.
ROOMS: 100 en suite (bth/shr) (5 fmly) No smoking in 38 bedrooms s £95; d £130 (incl. bkfst) * LB Off peak **MEALS:** Lunch £16-£17 & alc Dinner £24 & alc British & French Cuisine V meals Coffee am Tea pm **FACILITIES:** CTV in all bedrooms STV Indoor swimming pool (heated) Golf 9 Tennis (hard & grass) Squash Snooker Sauna Solarium Gym Croquet lawn Putting green Jacuzzi/spa Beauty salon Fitness assessments ch fac Xmas **CONF:** Thtr 250 Class 120 Board 80 Del £140 * **SERVICES:** Lift Night porter 201P **NOTES:** No dogs (ex guide dogs) No smoking in restaurant Last d 9.30pm
CARDS:

HYTHE Kent — Map 05 TR13

★★★ Stade Court

MARSTON HOTELS

West Pde CT21 6DT
Quality Percentage Score: 74%
☎ 01303 268263 01303 261803
Dir: *M20, junc 11 on A261*

Situated just a few steps from the shingle strand and sparkling sea, The Stade Court provides a comfortable and relaxing base from which to explore the local area. Bedrooms are attractively decorated and well equipped and a number also have additional seating overlooking the expanse of the channel. The committed team pride themselves on offering smooth service and genuine hospitality, guests are therefore assured an enjoyable and memorable stay. After indulging in the delightful cuisine on offer, why not take a stroll beside the sea along to the sister hotel the Hythe Imperial, where the extensive leisure facilities may help work off any excesses!
ROOMS: 42 en suite (bth/shr) (5 fmly) No smoking in 7 bedrooms **MEALS:** Lunch fr £12.95 Dinner fr £19.50 English & Continental Cuisine V meals Coffee am Tea pm **FACILITIES:** CTV in all bedrooms STV Indoor swimming pool (heated) Golf 9 Tennis (hard & grass) Squash Snooker Sauna Solarium Gym Croquet lawn Putting green Jacuzzi/spa All leisure facilities at sister hotel **CONF:** Thtr 60 Class 50 Board 30 Del from £75 * **SERVICES:** Lift Night porter 13P **NOTES:** No smoking in restaurant Last d 9pm **CARDS:**

ILFORD Greater London

See LONDON SECTION plan 1 *H5*

Travel Inn

Redbridge Ln East IG4 5BG
☎ 020 8550 7909 020 8550 6214
Dir: *at bottom of M11 (signed London East/A12 Chelmsford) follow A12 Chelmsford signs, Travel Inn on left at bottom of slip road*

This modern building offers accommodation in smart, spacious and well equipped bedrooms, all with en-suite bathrooms. Refreshments may be taken at the nearby family restaurant. For details about current prices consult the Contents Page under Hotel Groups for the Travel Inn phone number.
ROOMS: 43 en suite (bth/shr) d £39.95 *

ILFORD Greater London

Travelodge

Beehive Ln, Gants Hill IG4 5DR
☎ 020 8550 4248 020 8550 4248

This modern building offers accommodation in smart, spacious and well equipped bedrooms, all with en-suite bathrooms. Refreshments may be taken at the nearby family restaurant. For details about current prices, consult the Contents Page under Hotel Groups for the Travelodge phone number.
ROOMS: 32 en suite (bth/shr) d £59.95 *

ILFRACOMBE Devon — Map 02 SS54

★★ Elmfield

Torrs Park EX34 8AZ
Quality Percentage Score: 71%
☎ 01271 863377 01271 866828
Dir: *take A361 to Ilfracombe left at 1st traffic lights, left again at 2nd traffic lights, after 10yds left again hotel near top of hill on left*

Set in pleasant terraced gardens, where a covered swimming pool, sauna and gym are also located, this Victorian house is immaculately maintained. Guests have the choice of deluxe or standard bedrooms, and two of the former have four-poster beds. Good home cooked meals are served in the traditional dining room, and there is also a bar and lounge leading to a small games room.
ROOMS: 11 en suite (bth/shr) 2 annexe en suite (bth/shr) s £39; d £78 (incl. bkfst & dinner) * LB Off peak **MEALS:** Bar Lunch £7-£10 Dinner £16 & alc English & Continental Cuisine V meals **FACILITIES:** CTV in all bedrooms Indoor swimming pool (heated) Sauna Solarium Gym Pool table Jacuzzi/spa Darts Xmas **SERVICES:** 14P **NOTES:** No dogs No coaches No children 8yrs No smoking in restaurant Last d 7.30pm Closed Nov-Mar ex Xmas **CARDS:**

See advert on opposite page

ILFRACOMBE Devon — Map 02 SS54

★★ Ilfracombe Carlton

Runnacleave Rd EX34 8AR
Quality Percentage Score: 66%
☎ 01271 862446 & 863711 01271 865379
Dir: *take A361 to Ilfracombe left at traffic lights, left at next lights follow brown sign 'tunnels, beaches'*

This well maintained hotel in the centre of town has a loyal

AA Rosettes are awarded for quality of food, see page 15 for an explanation of Rosette assessment.

clientele. Bedrooms are attractively decorated, and the dining room is bright and airy.

ROOMS: 48 en suite (bth/shr) (8 fmly) No smoking in all bedrooms **MEALS:** Bar Lunch £1.60-£3.95 Dinner £12.50 V meals Coffee am Tea pm **FACILITIES:** CTV in all bedrooms STV **CONF:** Thtr 50 Class 50 Board 50 Del from £45 * **SERVICES:** Lift Night porter 25P **NOTES:** No dogs (ex guide dogs) No smoking in restaurant Last d 8.30pm Closed Jan-Feb RS Mar **CARDS:**

See advert on this page

ILFRACOMBE Devon — Map 02 SS54

★★ St Helier

Hillsborough Rd EX34 9QQ
Quality Percentage Score: 65%
☎ 01271 864906 📠 01271 864906

Dir: *leave M5 junct 27 onto A361 continue to Ilfracombe, then take Combe Martin road through High St hotel opposite 'Old Thatched Inn'*

This small, family-run hotel is in walking distance of the centre and the harbour. Bedrooms have well chosen colour schemes and from some there are views to the sea. The public areas include a comfortable reception/lounge, a convivial Cellar Bar and separate dining room.

ROOMS: 9 en suite (bth/shr) (3 fmly) s £26-£28; d £48-£52 (incl. bkfst) * LB Off peak **MEALS:** Bar Lunch £3.20-£5.50 Dinner £9.50-£10 English, Austrian, French & Italian Cuisine V meals Coffee am Tea pm **FACILITIES:** CTV in all bedrooms Darts **SERVICES:** 29P **NOTES:** No coaches No smoking in restaurant Last d 8pm Closed Oct-Apr **CARDS:**

ILFRACOMBE Devon — Map 02 SS54

★ Westwell Hall Hotel

Torrs Park EX34 8AZ
Quality Percentage Score: 69%
☎ 01271 862792 📠 01271 862792

Dir: *along Ilfracombe High Street, onto Worthfield road at lights, then L up Torrs Park. Turn R (Upper Torrs). Westwell Hall is 3rd drive on the Left*

Set in large gardens and overlooking the town, this fine Victorian hotel is convenient for both beaches and shops. Well equipped bedrooms are each individually decorated and day rooms include a bar, a lounge and a restaurant looking out on the patio. There is a car park.

ROOMS: 10 en suite (bth/shr) s £20-£23; d £40-£46 (incl. bkfst) * LB Off peak **MEALS:** Dinner £10-£12 V meals **FACILITIES:** CTV in all bedrooms **SERVICES:** 10P **NOTES:** No coaches No smoking in restaurant Last d 6.30pm **CARDS:**

Symbols and Abbreviations are listed and explained on pages 4 and 5

ILFRACOMBE Devon — Map 02 SS54
★ Torrs
Torrs Park EX34 8AY
Quality Percentage Score: 65%
☎ 01271 862334 Fax 01271 862334
Dir: *from Barnstaple (A361), 1st set of lights in Ilfracombe L into Wilder Road. Next set of lights, turn L then L again. Hotel 320yrds on right*
This personally run hotel stands in gardens with views of town and country. Accommodation provides the expected modern amenities and rooms are comfortable, light and airy.
ROOMS: 14 en suite (bth/shr) (5 fmly) s £20-£24; d £40-£48 (incl. bkfst) LB Off peak **MEALS:** Dinner £8-£9 & alc V meals **FACILITIES:** CTV in all bedrooms **SERVICES:** 14P **NOTES:** No children 5yrs No smoking in restaurant Last d 7.30pm Closed Mid Nov - Mid Feb **CARDS:**

ILKLEY West Yorkshire — Map 07 SE14
★★★ Rombalds
11 West View, Wells Rd LS29 9JG
Quality Percentage Score: 71%
☎ 01943 603201 Fax 01943 816586
Dir: *on Leeds/Skipton road A65, left at 2nd lights, follow signs Ilkley Moor. Right at Midland Bank onto Wells Road. Hotel is 600yrds on left*
Standing between the town and the moors, this elegantly furnished hotel provides comfortable lounges, well equipped bedrooms and an attractive restaurant serving well produced meals. Hospitality is good, and the whole atmosphere of the hotel is inviting.
ROOMS: 15 en suite (bth/shr) (2 fmly) No smoking in 4 bedrooms s £55-£105; d £80-£125 (incl. bkfst) * LB Off peak **MEALS:** Lunch £8.95-£12.95 & alc Dinner £9.95-£12.95 & alc English & French Cuisine V meals Coffee am Tea pm **FACILITIES:** CTV in all bedrooms STV Xmas **CONF:** Thtr 70 Class 40 Board 25 Del from £107.50 * **SERVICES:** 28P **NOTES:** No smoking in restaurant Last d 9.30pm **CARDS:**

ILKLEY West Yorkshire — Map 07 SE14
★ Moorview
104 Skipton Rd LS29 9HE
Quality Percentage Score: 64%
☎ 01943 600156 Fax 01943 817313
Dir: *travelling west on A65 through Ilkley hotel on right just on western side of town*

The public rooms of this large Victorian house are furnished to a good standard. There is an inviting, comfortable lounge with a real fire in winter, good home-cooking is provided in the small dining room. Bedroom styles and sizes vary.
ROOMS: 12 en suite (bth/shr) (3 fmly) s £35-£40; d £50 (incl. bkfst) * LB Off peak **MEALS:** V meals **FACILITIES:** CTV in all bedrooms **SERVICES:** 15P **NOTES:** No coaches No smoking in restaurant Last d 7.30pm **CARDS:**

ILMINSTER Somerset — Map 03 ST31
★★★ Pheasant Hotel & Restaurant
Water St, Seavington St Mary TA19 0QH
Quality Percentage Score: 69%
☎ 01460 240502 Fax 01460 242388
Dir: *3m E of Ilminster, off B3168*
This delightful part-thatched former farmhouse, surrounded by well tended gardens, is near the border of Somerset and close to Dorset and Devon. The sympathetic decor and furnishings complement the character of the bar and restaurant, with lovely oak beams and splendid inglenook fireplaces creating a special warmth. Individually styled bedrooms, some in stone-built cottages around the main house, have been equipped with modern comforts and thoughtful extras. The imaginative carte menu offers a wide variety of dishes.
ROOMS: 2 en suite (bth/shr) 6 annexe en suite (bth/shr) s fr £70; d fr £90 (incl. bkfst) * LB Off peak **MEALS:** Sunday Lunch £13.50-£17.50alc Dinner £21-£34alc International Cuisine V meals **FACILITIES:** CTV in all bedrooms STV ch fac **CONF:** Thtr 28 Board 12 **SERVICES:** 30P **NOTES:** No coaches No smoking in restaurant Last d 9.30pm Closed 24 Dec, 26 Dec & 1 Jan RS BH's (bed & breakfast only) **CARDS:**

ILMINSTER Somerset — Map 03 ST31
★★★ Shrubbery
TA19 9AR
Quality Percentage Score: 63%
☎ 01460 52108 Fax 01460 53660
Dir: *half a mile from A303 towards Ilminster town centre*
An established Victorian hotel set in attractive terraced gardens with an outdoor swimming pool. Public areas include extensive function facilities. Well equipped bedrooms vary in size, those in the main house are larger and traditionally furnished, those in the Garden Wing are simpler. A fixed-price restaurant menu supplements the less formal bar selection.
ROOMS: 14 en suite (bth/shr) (3 fmly) s £55-£80; d £70-£100 (incl. bkfst) * LB Off peak **MEALS:** Lunch £10-£15 High tea £7-£12 Dinner £21-£27.50 V meals Coffee am Tea pm **FACILITIES:** CTV in all bedrooms STV Outdoor swimming pool (heated) Tennis (grass) **CONF:** Thtr 250 Class 100 Board 60 **SERVICES:** 100P **NOTES:** No smoking area in restaurant Last d 9.30pm **CARDS:**

ILMINSTER Somerset — Map 03 ST31
Travelodge
Southfields Roundabout, Horton Cross TA19 9PT
☎ 01460 53748 Fax 01460 53748
Dir: *on A303*
This modern building offers accommodation in smart, spacious and well equipped bedrooms, all with en-suite bathrooms. Refreshments may be taken at the nearby family restaurant. For details about current prices, consult the Contents Page under Hotel Groups for the Travelodge phone number.
ROOMS: 32 en suite (bth/shr) d £45.95 *

ILSINGTON Devon — Map 03 SX77
★★★ The Ilsington Country
Ilsington Village TQ13 9RR
Quality Percentage Score: 71%
☎ 01364 661452 Fax 01364 661307
Dir: *take A38 after 12m exit for Newton Abbot/Bovey Tracey take 3rd turn off rdbt towards Ilsington then 1st right, pass P.O, hotel on right*
Standing in extensive grounds on the southern slopes of Dartmoor, the hotel is approached along four miles of winding roads. Bedrooms are individually furnished and include some on

contd.

the ground floor. There are good leisure facilities and the friendly staff help create a relaxing atmosphere.

ROOMS: 25 en suite (bth/shr) (2 fmly) s £69-£86.50; d £110-£140 (incl. bkfst & dinner) * LB Off peak **MEALS:** Lunch £12.50 Dinner £22.50 International Cuisine V meals Coffee am Tea pm **FACILITIES:** CTV in all bedrooms STV Indoor swimming pool (heated) Tennis (hard) Sauna Solarium Gym Croquet lawn Jacuzzi/spa Beautician Table tennis Xmas **CONF:** Thtr 35 Class 30 Board 30 Del from £85 * **SERVICES:** Lift 100P **NOTES:** No smoking in restaurant Last d 9pm **CARDS:**

IMMINGHAM Lincolnshire — Map 08 TA11

★★ Old Chapel Hotel & Restaurant

50 Station Rd, Habrough DN40 3AY
Quality Percentage Score: 65%
☎ 01469 572377 Fax 01469 577883

***Dir:** M180/A180 turn off A180 onto A160 (Killingholme/Immingham) right at 1st rdbt to Harbrough. Straight over mini rdbt, 0.25m on right after flyover*

Dating from 1836, this former Methodist chapel has been extended to provide comfortable and well equipped bedrooms. There is also a traditional bar leading to a bright conservatory lounge and a cosy beamed restaurant where a range of popular dishes are served. Service is friendly and attentive.

ROOMS: 14 en suite (bth/shr) (1 fmly) s £40.50-£50; d £49.50-£55 (incl. bkfst) * Off peak **MEALS:** Lunch £14.50 & alc Dinner £14.50 & alc V meals Coffee am **FACILITIES:** CTV in all bedrooms STV **SERVICES:** 20P **NOTES:** No coaches No smoking area in restaurant Last d 9pm **CARDS:**

INGATESTONE Essex — Map 05 TQ69

★★★ The Heybridge

Roman Rd CM4 9AB
Quality Percentage Score: 66%
☎ 01277 355355 Fax 01277 353288

***Dir:** follow M25 and A12. Take B1002 exit - Ingatestone. Through Mountnessing and take 1st right (A12 London & Heybridge). Hotel 200yrds on left*

This hotel is family run and very popular with both leisure and business guests. Parts of the building date back to the 15th century, including the beamed cocktail bar and the restaurant, which offers a lengthy menu and live music at the weekends. Chalet-style bedrooms are furnished with extra comforts such as king size beds.

ROOMS: 22 en suite (bth/shr) (3 fmly) No smoking in 2 bedrooms s £88-£98; d £98-£108 * Off peak **MEALS:** Lunch £14-£14.50 & alc Dinner £14.50 & alc International Cuisine V meals Coffee am Tea pm **FACILITIES:** CTV in all bedrooms STV Wkly live entertainment Xmas **CONF:** Thtr 600 Class 400 Board 10 Del £132 * **SERVICES:** Night porter 220P **NOTES:** No dogs Last d 10pm **CARDS:**

See advert under BRENTWOOD

INSTOW Devon — Map 02 SS43

★★★ Commodore

Marine Pde EX39 4JN
Quality Percentage Score: 73%
☎ 01271 860347 Fax 01271 861233

***Dir:** leave M5 junct 27 follow N Devon link road to Bideford. Turn right before bridge to Instow hotel 3m from bridge*

Owned for over 30 years by the same family, the hotel is renowned for its award-winning afternoon teas. Bedrooms are well equipped, and some have balconies looking out towards Appledore. Guests have a choice of eating in the bar or in the separate restaurant.

ROOMS: 20 en suite (bth/shr) s £59.50; d £105-£136 (incl. bkfst & dinner) * LB Off peak **MEALS:** Lunch £12-£15 High tea £3.95-£4.20 Dinner £19-£22 & alc English, Continental & Oriental Cuisine V meals Coffee am Tea pm **FACILITIES:** CTV in all bedrooms **CONF:** Thtr 250 Class 250 Board 80 Del from £74 * **SERVICES:** Night porter 200P **NOTES:** No dogs No smoking in restaurant Closed 22-27 Dec **CARDS:**

IPPLEPEN Devon — Map 03 SX86

★★ Old Church House Inn

Torbryan TQ12 5UR
Quality Percentage Score: 67%
☎ 01803 812372 Fax 01803 812180

***Dir:** take A381 from Newton Abbot after 5m turn right into Ipplepen continue a further one & a quarter miles to Torbryan. Hotel opposite the church*

This charming thatched inn can trace its history back to the 13th century and combines an old-world atmosphere with bedrooms furnished and equipped to modern standards. There are a number of rooms in which food can be served, and also a cosy lounge with large open fires.

ROOMS: 12 en suite (bth/shr) (5 fmly) s £45-£55; d £65-£85 (incl. bkfst) * LB Off peak **MEALS:** Lunch £8-£10 & alc Dinner £12.50-£15 & alc English & French Cuisine V meals Coffee am Tea pm **FACILITIES:** CTV in all bedrooms Xmas **CONF:** Thtr 30 Class 30 Board 20 Del from £65 * **SERVICES:** 30P **NOTES:** No dogs No smoking area in restaurant Last d 9.30pm **CARDS:**

IPSWICH Suffolk — Map 05 TM14

★★★★ ❀❀❀ Hintlesham Hall

IP8 3NS
☎ 01473 652334 & 652268 Fax 01473 652463
(For full entry see Hintlesham)

New AA Guides for the Millennium are featured on page 24

IPSWICH Suffolk **Map 05 TM14**
★★★ Marlborough
Henley Rd IP1 3SP
Quality Percentage Score: 73%
☎ 01473 257677 01473 226927
Dir: *take A1156 from A14 or A1214 from A12 turn right at Henley Rd/A1214 x-rds*

The quiet residential surroundings and the red brick exterior belie the country house-style ambience and the polished service of the Gough's delightful hotel. The bedrooms are appointed to a high standard, all well equipped and attractively decorated with lots of personal touches. Drinks are served in the upbeat, contemporary bar, and the smart restaurant overlooks the well tended gardens, illuminated at night for the benefit of diners. Chef Simon Barker offers an adventurous style of cooking supported by a well chosen wine-list.
ROOMS: 22 en suite (bth/shr) (3 fmly) s £69-£85; d £78-£85 * LB Off peak **MEALS:** Lunch £17.80-£17.95 & alc High tea fr £7.50 Dinner £21.85-£31.50 English & French Cuisine V meals Coffee am Tea pm **FACILITIES:** CTV in all bedrooms STV Xmas **CONF:** Thtr 40 Class 20 Board 26 Del from £115 * **SERVICES:** Night porter 60P **NOTES:** No smoking in restaurant Last d 9.30pm
CARDS:

See advert on opposite page

IPSWICH Suffolk **Map 05 TM14**
★★★ Swallow Belstead Brook
Belstead Rd IP2 9HB
Quality Percentage Score: 73%
☎ 01473 684241 01473 681249
Dir: *take A1214 from A12/A14 interchange rdbt & follow signs to hotel*

Standing in grounds of some eight landscaped acres in quiet residential surroundings, this leisure-orientated hotel looks after valued guests well. One of the main assets is the leisure centre. Bedrooms, whilst having the benefit of modern facilities, also give guests good old-fashioned comfort with thoughtful touches. In addition to five suites and a wing of superior garden rooms, there are a number of lady and non-smoking rooms. Public areas include a comfortable lounge area and a smart bar where a pianist plays on some evenings. The historic wood-panelled restaurant is divided up into five intimate areas.
ROOMS: 76 en suite (bth/shr) 12 annexe en suite (bth/shr) (2 fmly) No smoking in 32 bedrooms s fr £95; d £104.75-£144.75 (incl. bkfst) * LB Off peak **MEALS:** Lunch £3.75-£14.95 Dinner £20.50 & alc English & French Cuisine V meals Coffee am Tea pm **FACILITIES:** CTV in all bedrooms STV Indoor swimming pool (heated) Sauna Solarium Gym Croquet lawn Steam Room Wkly live entertainment Xmas **CONF:** Thtr 180 Class 75 Board 50 Del £120 * **SERVICES:** Lift Night porter 120P **NOTES:** No smoking in restaurant Last d 9.45pm
CARDS:

IPSWICH Suffolk **Map 05 TM14**
★★★ Courtyard by Marriott Ipswich
The Havens, Ransomes Europark IP3 9SJ
Quality Percentage Score: 68%
☎ 01473 272244 01473 272484
Dir: *just off A14 Ipswich By Pass at 1st jnct after Orwell Bridge signed Ransomes Europark when travelling towards Felixstowe, hotel faces the slip road*
This modern and well maintained hotel is well suited to the needs of the business or leisure traveller. The interior has been designed with some style, and bedrooms are attractively furnished and spacious. Public rooms include an open plan restaurant and bar, and a suite of popular conference rooms. The small fitness studio is an added bonus.
ROOMS: 60 en suite (bth/shr) (26 fmly) No smoking in 45 bedrooms s £40-£75; d £40-£75 * LB Off peak **MEALS:** Lunch £9.95-£12.95 & alc Dinner £12.95-£22.75alc International Cuisine V meals Coffee am Tea pm **FACILITIES:** CTV in all bedrooms STV Gym Pool table Xmas **CONF:** Thtr 180 Class 80 Board 60 Del from £70 * **SERVICES:** Lift Night porter 150P **NOTES:** No dogs (ex guide dogs) No smoking area in restaurant Last d 10.30pm **CARDS:**

IPSWICH Suffolk **Map 05 TM14**
★★★ County Hotel Ipswich
London Rd, Copdock IP8 3JD
Quality Percentage Score: 66%
☎ 01473 209988 01473 730801
Dir: *close to the A12/A14 interchange S of Ipswich. Exit A12 at junct signposted Washbrook/Copdock. Hotel on old A12 1m on left*
Located close the main Colchester road, this modern hotel is popular with both business and leisure guests. The refurbished bar and restaurant have an informal atmosphere and room service is actively promoted.
ROOMS: 76 en suite (bth/shr) (3 fmly) No smoking in 27 bedrooms d £70-£75 * LB Off peak **MEALS:** Lunch £5-£15.45 & alc Dinner £12.95-£15.45 & alc International Cuisine V meals Coffee am Tea pm **FACILITIES:** CTV in all bedrooms Indoor swimming pool (heated) Sauna Solarium Gym Jacuzzi/spa Xmas **CONF:** Thtr 500 Class 200 Board 35 Del from £80 * **SERVICES:** Lift Night porter 360P **NOTES:** No smoking in restaurant Last d 9.50pm **CARDS:**

IPSWICH Suffolk **Map 05 TM14**
★★★ Novotel
Greyfriars Rd IP1 1UP
Quality Percentage Score: 64%
☎ 01473 232400 01473 232414
Dir: *from A14 towards Felixstowe turn left onto A137 & follow for 2m into centre of town, hotel on double rdbt by Stoke Bridge*
This continental style modern red brick hotel features open plan vibrant public areas, including a Mediterranean style restaurant and a bar with a small games area. It is a popular business and meeting venue. Smartly refurbished bedrooms are simple in

contd.

decor, well designed for most needs and equipped to a modern standard.
ROOMS: 100 en suite (bth/shr) (6 fmly) No smoking in 76 bedrooms d £76 * LB Off peak **MEALS:** Lunch £12-£14 & alc High tea £3.50 & alc Dinner £14-£15 & alc International Cuisine V meals Coffee am Tea pm **FACILITIES:** CTV in all bedrooms STV Pool table **CONF:** Thtr 180 Class 75 Board 45 Del from £99 * **SERVICES:** Lift Night porter Air conditioning 50P **NOTES:** No smoking area in restaurant Last d midnight **CARDS:**

IPSWICH Suffolk **Map 05 TM14**
★★★ Posthouse Ipswich
London Rd IP2 0UA
Posthouse
Quality Percentage Score: 62%
☎ 01473 690313 🖹 01473 680412
Dir: *from A12/A45, go on A1214. At Tesco's go straight over 1st rndbt and hotel is 200yds on left*
This pleasant modern hotel is located to the west of the town centre. Bedrooms and public areas are suited to the needs of both business and leisure guests, and a new leisure club is a useful feature.
ROOMS: 109 en suite (bth/shr) (48 fmly) No smoking in 66 bedrooms d fr £75 * LB Off peak **MEALS:** Lunch £5-£10 High tea £1.95-£6 Dinner £5-£15 International Cuisine V meals Coffee am Tea pm **FACILITIES:** CTV in all bedrooms Indoor swimming pool (heated) ch fac Xmas **CONF:** Thtr 120 Class 50 Board 40 Del from £75 * **SERVICES:** Night porter 200P **NOTES:** No smoking area in restaurant Last d 10.30pm **CARDS:**

IPSWICH Suffolk **Map 05 TM14**
★★ *Claydon Country House*
16-18 Ipswich Rd, Claydon IP6 0AR
Best Western
Quality Percentage Score: 68%
☎ 01473 830382 🖹 01473 832476
Dir: *from A14, north west of Ipswich 4m take Great Blakenham road, B1113 then turn off to Claydon, hotel on left*
West of Ipswich, just of the main A14 bypass, in an easily accessible village location, this welcoming hotel offers a range of modern and well equipped accommodation. All bedrooms have been recently refurbished, and there is a spacious and attractive four poster-room. The smart restaurant, overlooking the lawn to the rear, offers a wide choice of appealing dishes, and on the lower floor there is a relaxing lounge bar.
ROOMS: 14 en suite (bth/shr) (2 fmly) **MEALS:** English & French Cuisine V meals Coffee am Tea pm **FACILITIES:** CTV in all bedrooms STV ch fac **CONF:** Thtr 40 Class 30 Board 20 Del £85 * **SERVICES:** Night porter 60P **NOTES:** No dogs (ex guide dogs) No coaches Last d 9.30pm **CARDS:**

IPSWICH Suffolk **Map 05 TM14**
⌂ Travel Inn
Mockbeggars Hall Farm, Paper Mill Ln, Claydon IP6 0AP
☎ 01473 833125 🖹 01473 833127
Dir: *on A14 W of Ipswich at Gt Blakenham/Claydon/RAF Wattisham junc, a rdbt take exit into Papermill Ln*
This modern building offers accommodation in smart, spacious and well equipped bedrooms, all with en-suite bathrooms. Refreshments may be taken at the nearby family restaurant. For details about current prices consult the Contents Page under Hotel Groups for the Travel Inn phone number.
ROOMS: 61 en suite (bth/shr) d £39.95 *

IPSWICH Suffolk **Map 05 TM14**
⌂ Travel Inn (Wherstead)
Bourne Hill, Wherstead IP2 8ND
☎ 01473 692372 🖹 01473 692283
Dir: *follow signs to Ipswich town centre and docks. Travel Inn on Marina front*
This modern building offers accommodation in smart, spacious and well equipped bedrooms, all with en-suite bathrooms. Refreshments may be taken at the nearby family restaurant. For details about current prices consult the Contents Page under Hotel Groups for the Travel Inn phone number.
ROOMS: 40 en suite (bth/shr) d £39.95 *

IPSWICH Suffolk **Map 05 TM14**
⌂ Travelodge
Capel St Mary IP9 2JP
☎ 01473 312157 🖹 01473 312157
Dir: *5m S on A12*
This modern building offers accommodation in smart, spacious and well equipped bedrooms, all with en-suite bathrooms. Refreshments may be taken at the nearby family restaurant. For details about current prices, consult the Contents Page under Hotel Groups for the Travelodge phone number.
ROOMS: 32 en suite (bth/shr) d £45.95 *

ISLE OF Places incorporating the words 'Isle of' or 'Isle' will be found under the actual name - eg Isle of Wight is listed under Wight, Isle of.

IVYBRIDGE Devon Map 02 SX65
★★ Glazebrook House Hotel & Restaurant
TQ10 9JE
Quality Percentage Score: 72%
☎ 01364 73322 🖷 01364 72350
Dir: *turn off A38 at Avonwick, South Brent jct. proceed 1.5m to South Brent. Pass the London Inn, in 100yds the jct for Glazebrook is on the right*

Glazebrook is a delightful Georgian house set in pretty gardens and grounds. Hospitality and good food are the strengths, and bedrooms are attractively furnished, with many personal touches.
ROOMS: 11 en suite (bth/shr) (3 fmly) s £48; d £68-£125 (incl. bkfst) * LB Off peak **MEALS:** Lunch £16.50 & alc Dinner £19.50-£24 & alc English & French Cuisine V meals Coffee am Tea pm **FACILITIES:** CTV in all bedrooms ch fac Xmas **CONF:** Thtr 100 Class 80 Board 60 Del from £68 * **SERVICES:** 50P **NOTES:** No dogs (ex guide dogs) No smoking in restaurant Last d 8.30pm **CARDS:**

See advert under PLYMOUTH

IVYBRIDGE Devon Map 02 SX65
★★ Sportsmans Inn Hotel & Restaurant
Exeter Rd PL21 0BQ
Quality Percentage Score: 64%
☎ 01752 892280 🖷 01752 690714
Dir: *turn off A38 Devon expressway at Ivybridge exit, follow main road through town, hotel on the main road*

Popular with both locals and visitors, the Sportsmans offers a wide choice of meals and snacks in its open-plan bar and restaurant, and there are well equipped bedrooms, including one on the ground floor.
ROOMS: 10 en suite (bth/shr) s £35-£39.95; d £45-£49.95 (incl. bkfst) * LB Off peak **MEALS:** Lunch £8.95 & alc Dinner £8.95 & alc V meals Coffee am Tea pm **FACILITIES:** CTV in all bedrooms STV Wkly live entertainment **SERVICES:** 40P **NOTES:** No dogs (ex guide dogs) No smoking area in restaurant Last d 9.30pm
CARDS:

See advert under PLYMOUTH

KEGWORTH Leicestershire Map 08 SK42
★★ *Kegworth*
Packington Hill DE74 2DF
Quality Percentage Score: 65%
☎ 01509 672427 🖷 01509 674664
Dir: *0.5m from junct 24 of the M1/A42 on the A6 towards Loughborough*
This modern hotel has been converted from a squash club and there is a leisure centre with a gymnasium and pool, and there are still a few squash courts, too, as well as a good range of modern conference rooms. Public areas include an open plan lounge bar, where informal meals can be taken; the restaurant offers more substantial meals through daily and carte menus and a hot buffet.
ROOMS: 52 en suite (bth/shr) (3 fmly) No smoking in 24 bedrooms
MEALS: International Cuisine V meals Coffee am Tea pm
FACILITIES: CTV in all bedrooms STV Indoor swimming pool (heated) Squash Sauna Solarium Gym Jacuzzi/spa Aromatherapy & massage
CONF: Thtr 300 Class 110 Board 120 Del from £88 * **SERVICES:** Night porter 150P **NOTES:** Last d 9.30pm **CARDS:**

See advert under DERBY

KEIGHLEY West Yorkshire Map 07 SE04
★★ Dalesgate
406 Skipton Rd, Utley BD20 6HP
Quality Percentage Score: 66%
☎ 01535 664930 🖷 01535 611253
Dir: *2m NW A629*

Situated in the village of Utley, just a couple of miles from the town, this hotel, with its cosy bar and comfortable restaurant, was originally the residence of a local chapel minister but has been extended by the addition of a modern wing to provide well furnished bedrooms.
ROOMS: 20 en suite (bth/shr) (2 fmly) s fr £45; d fr £70 (incl. bkfst) * LB Off peak **MEALS:** Dinner £12.95 & alc French & English Cuisine V meals Coffee am Tea pm **FACILITIES:** CTV in all bedrooms ch fac
SERVICES: 25P **NOTES:** No smoking area in restaurant Last d 9pm
CARDS:

KENDAL Cumbria Map 07 SD59
see also **Crooklands**
★★★ The Castle Green Hotel in Kendal
Best Western
LA9 6RG
Quality Percentage Score: 73%
☎ 01539 734000 🖷 01539 735522
Dir: *from M6 junc 36, head for Kendal. Right at 1st traffic lights, left at rdbt to "K" Village then right for 0.75m to hotel at T-junct*
Commanding stunning views of the distant fells, this new hotel has been impressively created from former offices. Public rooms are strikingly decorated, with modern architecture and fine finishes throughout. Bedrooms are stylish and well equipped, those at the front enjoy fine views. The Greenhouse Restaurant

contd.

provides imaginative and skilfully prepared dishes, and an impressive business centre offers extensive conference facilities.
ROOMS: 65 en suite (bth/shr) (3 fmly) s fr £71; d fr £89 (incl. bkfst) * LB Off peak **MEALS:** Lunch £8-£25alc Dinner £8-£25alc European Cuisine V meals Coffee am Tea pm **FACILITIES:** CTV in all bedrooms STV Indoor swimming pool (heated) Tennis (grass) Gym Croquet lawn Steam Room Aerobics Yoga Beauty Salon Hairdressing Wkly live entertainment **CONF:** Thtr 400 Class 200 Board 100 **SERVICES:** Lift Night porter 230P **NOTES:** No dogs (ex guide dogs) No smoking in restaurant Last d 10pm **CARDS:**

KENDAL Cumbria **Map 07 SD59**
★★★ Stonecross Manor Hotel
Milnthorpe Rd LA9 5HP
Quality Percentage Score: 68%
☎ 01539 733559 Fax 01539 736386
Dir: *M6 junct 36 onto A590 and follow signs to Windermere, then take exit for Kendal South. Pass petrol station on right hotel on left*
Originally constructed in 1857, this smart, traditionally styled hotel has been skilfully converted to provide bedrooms equipped with many modern comforts including jacuzzi spa baths. Public rooms include a conservatory restaurant, two comfortable lounges and a discreet bar.
ROOMS: 30 en suite (bth/shr) (4 fmly) No smoking in 15 bedrooms s fr £63.50; d £89-£119 (incl. bkfst) * LB Off peak **MEALS:** Dinner £17.50-£19.50 English & French Cuisine Coffee am **FACILITIES:** CTV in all bedrooms Indoor swimming pool (heated) Sauna Solarium Jacuzzi/spa Xmas **CONF:** Thtr 135 Class 80 Board 40 **SERVICES:** Lift Night porter 55P **NOTES:** No dogs (ex guide dogs) No coaches No smoking in restaurant Last d 9pm **CARDS:**

KENDAL Cumbria **Map 07 SD59**
★★ Garden House
Fowl-ing Ln LA9 6PH
Quality Percentage Score: 63%
☎ 01539 731131 Fax 01539 740064
Dir: *leave M6 junct 36 follow signs for A6 north & turn right at Duke of Cumberland after 200yds turn right into lane near Texaco Garage*
This traditionally furnished house in a quiet residential area is close to the town centre. Bedrooms are well equipped and some have four-poster beds. Day rooms consist of a bar, a separate lounge and a delightful conservatory restaurant that boasts a magnificent mural of the hotel. Service is friendly and informal.
ROOMS: 11 en suite (bth/shr) (2 fmly) No smoking in 4 bedrooms s £49.50-£54.50; d £75-£79 (incl. bkfst) * LB Off peak **MEALS:** Sunday Lunch £9.75 Dinner £16-£18.50 English & French Cuisine V meals Coffee am **FACILITIES:** CTV in all bedrooms Croquet lawn Putting green **CONF:** Thtr 60 Class 40 Board 30 Del £75 * **SERVICES:** 30P **NOTES:** No smoking in restaurant Last d 8.30pm RS 26-30 Dec **CARDS:**

KENILWORTH Warwickshire **Map 04 SP27**
★★★★ Chesford Grange
PRINCIPAL HOTELS
Chesford Bridge CV8 2LD
Quality Percentage Score: 63%
☎ 01926 859331 Fax 01926 859075
Dir: *0.5m SE junct A46/A452 at rdbt take right exit signed Leamington Spa. After approx 250yds at x-rds turn right hotel on left*
With good access to major road links, this successful business
contd.

The AA Hotel Booking Service is a free benefit to AA members. See the advertisement on page 47

Crooklands Hotel, Kendal

and conference hotel offers bedrooms ranging in style from standard to 'executive'. All are well equipped and comfortable.
ROOMS: 145 en suite (bth/shr) 9 annexe en suite (bth/shr) (12 fmly) No smoking in 55 bedrooms s £105-£120; d £115-£140 (incl. bkfst) * LB Off peak **MEALS:** Lunch £11.95-£14.50 & alc Dinner £17.50-£20.95 & alc International Cuisine V meals Coffee am Tea pm **FACILITIES:** CTV in all bedrooms STV Indoor swimming pool (heated) Fishing Sauna Solarium Gym Jacuzzi/spa Wkly live entertainment Xmas **CONF:** Thtr 860 Class 300 Board 50 Del £145 * **SERVICES:** Lift Night porter 550P
NOTES: No smoking in restaurant Last d 9.30pm
CARDS:

KENILWORTH Warwickshire **Map 04 SP27**
★★★★ *De Montfort*
The Square CV8 1ED
Quality Percentage Score: 63%
☎ 01926 855944 01926 855952
Dir: *take A452 into Kenilworth, hotel at top end of main street by rdbt*

Located in the heart of Shakespeare country the De Montfort Hotel offers accommodation of a high standard. Its public areas include a smart café bar and a restaurant.
ROOMS: 104 en suite (bth/shr) (15 fmly) No smoking in 50 bedrooms **MEALS:** French Cuisine V meals Coffee am Tea pm **FACILITIES:** CTV in 103 bedrooms STV Pool table Wkly live entertainment **CONF:** Thtr 250 Class 90 Board 60 Del £145 * **SERVICES:** Lift Night porter 85P
NOTES: No smoking in restaurant Last d 9.45pm
CARDS:

KENILWORTH Warwickshire **Map 04 SP27**
★★ *Clarendon House*
Old High St CV8 1LZ
Quality Percentage Score: 63%
☎ 01926 857668 Cen. Res. 0800 616883 01926 850669
Situated in the conservation area, this building incorporates the original 15th-century timber-framed Castle Tavern, which was supported by an oak tree, into the fabric of the hotel. Bedroom styles and sizes vary considerably, but each is practically designed.
ROOMS: 30 en suite (bth/shr) **MEALS:** V meals Coffee am Tea pm **FACILITIES:** CTV in all bedrooms **CONF:** Thtr 200 Class 50 Board 60 Del from £85 * **SERVICES:** 20P **NOTES:** Last d 9.30pm
CARDS:

KENILWORTH Warwickshire **Map 04 SP27**
Peacock Hotel
149 Warwick Rd CV8 1HY
☎ 01926 851156 01926 864500 01926 864644
Dir: *turn off the A46 into Kenilworth. Hotel located on the Warwick road, opposite the Green Man PH*
ROOMS: 12 en suite (bth/shr) 3 annexe en suite (shr) (3 fmly) No smoking in 9 bedrooms s £50-£55; d £60-£70 (incl. bkfst) * LB Off peak **MEALS:** Lunch £4-£7alc High tea £4-£7alc Dinner £10-£20alc Continental, Indian & Malaysian Cuisine V meals Coffee am Tea pm **FACILITIES:** CTV in all bedrooms STV Xmas **CONF:** Thtr 40 Class 40 Board 30 Del from £90 * **SERVICES:** 18P **NOTES:** No dogs Last d 10.30pm **CARDS:**

KENTON Greater London See LONDON SECTION plan 1 *C5*
Travel Inn
Kenton Rd HA3 8AT
☎ 020 8907 4069 020 8909 1604
Dir: *on A4006 between Harrow and Wembley opposite Kenton Railway Station*
This modern building offers accommodation in smart, spacious and well equipped bedrooms, all with en-suite bathrooms. Refreshments may be taken at the nearby family restaurant. For details about current prices consult the Contents Page under Hotel Groups for the Travel Inn phone number.
ROOMS: 44 en suite (bth/shr) d £39.95 *

KESWICK Cumbria **Map 11 NY22**
★★★★ Keswick Country House
Station Rd CA12 4NQ
Quality Percentage Score: 65%
☎ 017687 72020 017687 71300
Dir: *adjacent to Keswick Leisure Pool*
This elegant Victorian hotel is full of character, and its stylish bedrooms are housed in a well converted former railway station adjoining the main building. Hospitality is a strength, and the hotel is popular for private functions.
ROOMS: 74 en suite (bth/shr) (10 fmly) s £80; d £115 (incl. bkfst) * LB Off peak **MEALS:** Sunday Lunch £12.95 Dinner £16.95 & alc V meals Coffee am Tea pm **FACILITIES:** CTV in all bedrooms STV Snooker Croquet lawn Putting green Pitch & putt Wkly live entertainment Xmas **CONF:** Thtr 80 Class 35 Board 35 Del £110 * **SERVICES:** Lift Night porter 70P **NOTES:** No smoking in restaurant Last d 9.15pm
CARDS:

See advert on opposite page

KESWICK Cumbria **Map 11 NY22**
★★★ Derwentwater
Portinscale CA12 5RE
Quality Percentage Score: 72%
☎ 017687 72538 017687 71002
Dir: *off A66 turn into village of Portinscale, follow signs*
This stately hotel lies in the village of Portinscale, on the peaceful western shores of Derwentwater. The gardens stretch down to the lake and many of the comfortable bedrooms have pleasant views. The conservatory is popular in summer, while out of season the cosy sitting room is a favourite retreat. The

contd. on p. 338

AA Rosettes are awarded for quality of food, see page 15 for an explanation of Rosette assessment.

THE KESWICK COUNTRY HOUSE HOTEL

KESWICK ON DERWENTWATER

AA ★★★★ AA

A splendid fully refurbished Victorian hotel set in four acres of landscaped gardens in the heart of the Lake District, minutes walk from the centre of Keswick.

Bygone Breakaways

Enjoy a luxury break inclusive of dinner, bed, breakfast and free entrance to several of the Lake District's major attractions. **From £55.00 per person per night.**

Free use of adjacent swimming pool.

Conferences and Meetings

A superb range of character function rooms are available for conferences for up to 100 delegates and private dinners.

The hotel has a large car park and the lakeland towns of Windermere and Penrith are only a 20 minute drive away.

The Keswick Country House Hotel
Station Road, Keswick, Cumbria, CA12 4NQ
Tel: (017687) 72020 Fax: (017687) 71300

Quality wins

A PRINCIPAL HOTEL

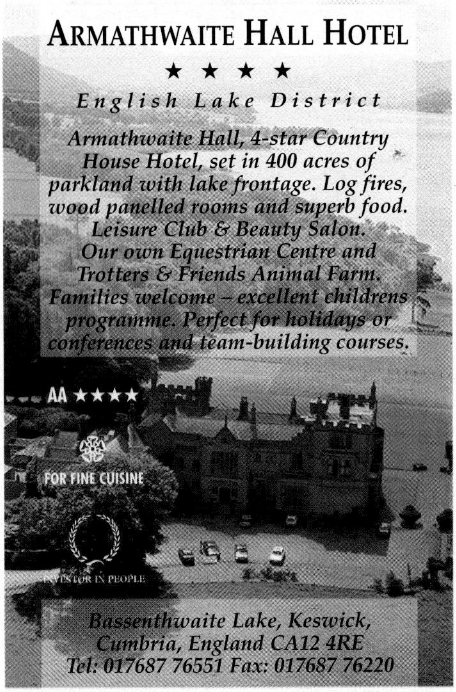

ARMATHWAITE HALL HOTEL

★ ★ ★ ★

English Lake District

Armathwaite Hall, 4-star Country House Hotel, set in 400 acres of parkland with lake frontage. Log fires, wood panelled rooms and superb food. Leisure Club & Beauty Salon. Our own Equestrian Centre and Trotters & Friends Animal Farm. Families welcome – excellent childrens programme. Perfect for holidays or conferences and team-building courses.

AA ★★★★

FOR FINE CUISINE

INVESTOR IN PEOPLE

Bassenthwaite Lake, Keswick, Cumbria, England CA12 4RE
Tel: 017687 76551 Fax: 017687 76220

K

Keswick – Unrivalled Lakeside Location – Lake District

AA ★★★

Best Western

The Derwentwater Hotel

THE EPITOME OF A LAKELAND COUNTRY HOUSE HOTEL

Remaining in private hands. The Derwentwater has a style all of its own. A relaxing haven on the shores of Lake Derwentwater in 16 acres of conservation grounds (designated European area of special Conservation), and refurbished to a high standard. Many of the tastefully decorated and exceptionally well equipped bedrooms and the conservatory enjoy panoramic lake views. Four-poster Beds for that special occasion along with our Deluxe rooms pamper your every need including CD and Video player.

Dine on the very best of local produce in the Deers Leap Restaurant.

Award winning hospitality. Customer Service and Environmental policy.

Something different – why not try our Derwent Manor?

Standing in its own grounds it offers outstanding Self Catering Apartments and Cottages. The freedom of self catering with all the services of a quality 3-star hotel.

THE DERWENTWATER – SUBLIMELY COMFORTABLE YET NOT IN THE LEAST PRETENTIOUS.

Visit our website: http://ds.dial.pipex.com/derwentwater.hotel/

FREEPHONE 0500-432191 TELEPHONE 017687 72538

bedroooms are well equipped, attractively decorated with tasteful fabrics, and have many thoughtful touches.

Derwentwater, Keswick

ROOMS: 46 en suite (bth/shr) (1 fmly) s £75-£79; d £130-£136 (incl. bkfst) LB Off peak **MEALS:** Bar Lunch £2.95-£8.95alc High tea £7.25-£10.95alc Dinner £24.95-£30.50 European Cuisine V meals Coffee am Tea pm **FACILITIES:** CTV in all bedrooms Fishing Pool table Putting green Wkly live entertainment Xmas **SERVICES:** Lift Night porter 120P **NOTES:** No smoking in restaurant Last d 9.30pm
CARDS:

See advert on page 337

K

KESWICK Cumbria **Map 11 NY22**

★★★ Skiddaw

Main St CA12 5BN
Quality Percentage Score: 66%
☎ 017687 72071 017687 74850
Dir: *A66 to Keswick follow signs for town centre. Hotel in the Market Square in heart of the town*

This hotel overlooks the square, upper rooms have views of Skiddaw. There is a high standard of accommodation, particularly in the 'Summit' bedrooms' with smart furnishings and stylish decor. There is a stylish restaurant, the lounge bar is popular for morning coffee, lunch and afternoon tea.
ROOMS: 40 en suite (bth/shr) (7 fmly) No smoking in 10 bedrooms s £38-£42; d £70-£78 (incl. bkfst) * LB Off peak **MEALS:** Lunch £5.50-£10.50 & alc High tea £9.20-£11.80alc Dinner fr £16.95 & alc English & French Cuisine V meals Coffee am Tea pm **FACILITIES:** CTV in all bedrooms STV Sauna Free use of out of town leisure fac Xmas **CONF:** Thtr 70 Class 60 Board 40 **SERVICES:** Lift 22P **NOTES:** No dogs (ex guide dogs) No smoking in restaurant Last d 10pm
CARDS:

See advert on opposite page

KESWICK Cumbria **Map 11 NY22**

★★ Dale Head Hall Lakeside

Lake Thirlmere CA12 4TN
Quality Percentage Score: 77%
☎ 017687 72478 017687 71070
Dir: *mid-way between Keswick & Grasmere, off A591, onto private drive to shores of Lake Thirlmere*
This idyllic country house nestles in extensive woodland and gardens overlooking the inviting waters of Thirlmere. Parts of the house date back to the 16th century. Dinner features good British cooking, along with a recommended wine list and a lavish menu that runs to five courses.
ROOMS: 9 en suite (bth/shr) (1 fmly) No smoking in all bedrooms s £65-£72.50; d £80-£95 (incl. bkfst) LB Off peak **MEALS:** Dinner £27.50 V meals Coffee am Tea pm **FACILITIES:** Tennis (grass) Fishing Croquet lawn Xmas **SERVICES:** 22P **NOTES:** No dogs No coaches No smoking in restaurant Last d 8pm Closed 31 Dec-3 Feb
CARDS:

See advert on opposite page

KESWICK Cumbria **Map 11 NY22**

★★ Highfield

The Heads CA12 5ER
Quality Percentage Score: 71%
☎ 017687 72508
Dir: *approaching from A66 take 2nd exit at rdbt, turn left follow road to t-junc left again & right at mini rdbt, The Heads is 4th turning on right*
Fronted by well tended gardens and overlooking the park with a stunning view of the mountains beyond, this friendly hotel has appealing bedrooms in a variety of sizes, two having their own balcony. There is a choice of homely lounges and a cosy dining room where an imaginative menu is served.
ROOMS: 18 en suite (bth/shr) (2 fmly) No smoking in all bedrooms s £31-£35; d £52-£80 (incl. bkfst) * LB Off peak **MEALS:** Sunday Lunch £10.95-£11.95 Dinner £15.50-£18 English & French Cuisine V meals Coffee am Tea pm **FACILITIES:** CTV in all bedrooms **SERVICES:** 19P **NOTES:** No dogs No coaches No children 8yrs No smoking in restaurant Last d 8.30pm Closed Dec-Jan **CARDS:**

KESWICK Cumbria **Map 11 NY22**

★★ Lairbeck

Vicarage Hill CA12 5QB
Quality Percentage Score: 71%
☎ 017687 73373 017687 73144
Dir: *follow A66 to rdbt with A591 turn left then immediately right onto Vicarage Hill, hotel 150 yds on right*
Close to town and set amidst gardens, this inviting Victorian country house provides attractively furnished bedrooms in a

contd. on p. 340

variety of sizes. There is a welcoming residents' bar and a dining room with views of the garden.
ROOMS: 14 en suite (bth/shr) (1 fmly) No smoking in all bedrooms s £36; d £72-£82 (incl. bkfst) * LB Off peak **MEALS:** Dinner £16 English & Continental Cuisine **FACILITIES:** CTV in all bedrooms **SERVICES:** 16P **NOTES:** No dogs No coaches No children 5yrs No smoking in restaurant Last d 7.30pm Closed Jan & Feb RS Dec
CARDS:

KESWICK Cumbria **Map 11 NY22**
★★ *Lyzzick Hall Country House*
Under Skiddaw CA12 4PY
Quality Percentage Score: 71%
☎ 017687 72277 017687 72278
Dir: *from M6 junct 40, take A66 Keswick do not enter town keep to Keswick by-pass, take 3rd exit off rdbt onto A591 to Carlisle, hotel is 1.5m on right*
A smartly presented country house with views across the valley. There are two spacious lounges, a small bar area and an attractive restaurant. The indoor swimming pool and other facilities are very popular with children. Bedrooms are well equipped and thoughtfully decorated. Lunch and dinner menus offer dishes to suit all tastes.
ROOMS: 28 en suite (bth/shr) 1 annexe en suite (bth/shr) (3 fmly) **MEALS:** International Cuisine V meals Coffee am **FACILITIES:** CTV in all bedrooms Indoor swimming pool (heated) Sauna Jacuzzi/spa ch fac **SERVICES:** 40P **NOTES:** No dogs No coaches No smoking in restaurant Last d 9.30pm Closed 24-26 Dec & Feb
CARDS:

K

KESWICK Cumbria **Map 11 NY22**
★★ *Applethwaite Country House Hotel*
Applethwaite, Underskiddaw CA12 4PL
Quality Percentage Score: 69%
☎ 017687 72413 017687 75706
A former Victorian residence built of local stone and standing in well tended grounds in the shadow of Skiddaw, about 1.5 miles north of Keswick. Traditional public rooms enjoy stunning views over the Borrowdale Valley and include a choice of comfortable non-smoking sitting rooms, and enjoyable home cooking is served in the attractive dining room. Bedrooms are smartly decorated and offer both traditional and modern furnishings.
ROOMS: 12 en suite (bth/shr) (3 fmly) No smoking in all bedrooms **MEALS:** English & French Cuisine V meals **FACILITIES:** CTV in all bedrooms Croquet lawn Putting green Bowling green **SERVICES:** 10P **NOTES:** No dogs (ex guide dogs) No coaches No children 5yrs No smoking in restaurant Last d 6.50pm Closed Dec-10 Feb
CARDS:

KESWICK Cumbria **Map 11 NY22**
★★ Chaucer House
THE CIRCLE Selected Individual Hotels GREAT BRITAIN
Derwentwater Place CA12 4DR
Quality Percentage Score: 69%
☎ 017687 72318 & 73223 017687 75551
Dir: *turn right off A591 into Manor Brow, continue down hill, past Castlerigg Catholic Training Centre and sharp double bend, hotel on right*
In a quiet residential area, enjoying superb views of the surrounding mountains, this traditional hotel is suited to leisure and business guests alike. Attractive public areas and efficient service by smart staff are features of this well maintained hotel. Dinner offers a wide range of imaginative dishes, with a carte augmenting the fixed-price four-course menu.
ROOMS: 34 rms (31 bth/shr) (4 fmly) s £25-£40; d £32-£85.50 (incl. bkfst) * LB Off peak **MEALS:** Dinner £14.50-£18.50 & alc English & French Cuisine V meals Coffee am **FACILITIES:** CTV in 33 bedrooms STV **SERVICES:** Lift 25P **NOTES:** No smoking in restaurant Last d 9pm Closed Dec-Jan **CARDS:**

KESWICK Cumbria **Map 11 NY22**
★★ Thwaite Howe
Thornthwaite CA12 5SA
Quality Percentage Score: 69%
☎ 017687 78281 017687 78529
Dir: *follow signs to Thornthwaite Gallery from A66 approx 3 miles from Keswick. Hotel is signposted from outside Gallery*

A charming Victorian country house hotel set in two acres of gardens with magnificent views across the valley and distant hills, which can also be enjoyed from some of the thoughtfully equipped bedrooms. Public rooms feature a cosy residents' bar, comfortable lounge with a real fire, and an attractive dining room serving delicious five-course dinners.
ROOMS: 8 en suite (bth) No smoking in all bedrooms s £67-£71; d £94-£102 (incl. bkfst & dinner) LB Off peak **MEALS:** Dinner £17.75 **FACILITIES:** CTV in all bedrooms **SERVICES:** 12P **NOTES:** No coaches No children 12yrs No smoking in restaurant Last d 7pm Closed Nov-Feb
CARDS:

KESWICK Cumbria **Map 11 NY22**
★★ Edwardene
26 Southey St CA12 4EF
Quality Percentage Score: 67%
☎ 017687 73586 017687 73824
Dir: *take A591 towards Keswick town centre. At pedestrian traffic lights turn left into Southey St*
Situated in a grand Victorian terrace near the centre of Keswick, this hotel is a blaze of colour in summer with its shrubs, hanging baskets and flower tubs. Attractively decorated throughout, it offers stylish, well equipped bedrooms furnished in pine. There are two cosy lounges, and a delightfully decorated dining room serving three-course dinners and breakfast.
ROOMS: 11 en suite (bth/shr) (1 fmly) No smoking in all bedrooms s fr £25; d fr £50 (incl. bkfst) * Off peak **MEALS:** Dinner fr £13 Coffee am **FACILITIES:** CTV in all bedrooms Xmas **NOTES:** No dogs (ex guide dogs) No coaches No smoking in restaurant Last d 7.30pm
CARDS:

KESWICK Cumbria **Map 11 NY22**
★★ Crow Park
The Heads CA12 5ER
Quality Percentage Score: 65%
☎ 017687 72208 017687 74776
A relaxed welcoming atmosphere prevails at this comfortable family run holiday hotel with views over the lake to the Borrowdale Valley. Attractive public areas include a lounge, a cosy bar, and a dining room decorated with a collection of local
contd.

photographs. Bedrooms are variable in size with practical appointments and a good range of amenities.
ROOMS: 26 en suite (bth/shr) (1 fmly) No smoking in 1 bedroom s £29.50-£30.50; d £59-£61 (incl. bkfst) * LB Off peak **MEALS:** Dinner £10-£14.50 English & Continental Cuisine V meals Coffee am **FACILITIES:** CTV in 27 bedrooms STV Xmas **SERVICES:** 27P **NOTES:** No smoking in restaurant Last d 8pm **CARDS:**

KESWICK Cumbria — Map 11 NY22
★★ *Ladstock Country House*
Thornthwaite CA12 5RZ
Quality Percentage Score: 60%
☎ 017687 78210 & 78249
This traditional country house is set in landscaped gardens overlooking Bassenthwaite and the valley towards Skiddaw. Once the local parsonage, it contains an abundance of oak panelling, mullioned windows and lots of paintings and photographs of the house in earlier days. There are log burning fireplaces in the lounges and the atmosphere throughout is warm and relaxing. Bedrooms are traditionally furnished, but have good modern facilities. One of the main features is a banqueting suite capable of seating up to 150 guests.
ROOMS: 22 rms (11 bth 7 shr) (2 fmly) **MEALS:** V meals Coffee am Tea pm **FACILITIES:** CTV in all bedrooms **SERVICES:** 50P **NOTES:** No dogs (ex guide dogs) Last d 8.30pm Closed Jan **CARDS:**

KESWICK Cumbria — Map 11 NY22
Late entry Horse & Farrier Inn
Threlkeld CA12 4SQ
☎ 017687 79688 017687 79824
Dir: *12m from Penrith M6, just off A66 4m from Keswick*
Both modern inside and retaining many original features, this traditional Lakeland inn, situated under the shadow of Blencathra, offers high levels of comfort throughout. The dining rooms serve an imaginative menu which makes good use of local produce.
ROOMS: 9 en suite (bth/shr) No smoking in all bedrooms s fr £28.50; d fr £57 (incl. bkfst) * LB Off peak **MEALS:** Sunday Lunch fr £10.95alc Dinner £3.75-£13.85alc English & French Cuisine V meals Coffee am Tea pm **FACILITIES:** CTV in all bedrooms **SERVICES:** 60P **NOTES:** No smoking area in restaurant Last d 9.30pm
CARDS:

KETTERING Northamptonshire — Map 04 SP87
★★★★ Kettering Park
Kettering Parkway NN15 6XT
Quality Percentage Score: 70%
☎ 01536 416666 01536 416171
Dir: *just off junct 9 of A14, M1 to A1 link road, on the Kettering Venture Park*
This smart, purpose-built hotel is situated just outside the market town of Kettering and offers spacious, thoughtfully designed bedrooms and suites. Langberrys Restaurant serves a menu showing thought and imagination and is particularly enjoyable to use. Both business and leisure guests will appreciate the excellent leisure facilities and the friendly and helpful nature of the well-supervised staff.
ROOMS: 119 en suite (bth/shr) (28 fmly) No smoking in 60 bedrooms s fr £120; d fr £140 (incl. bkfst) * LB Off peak **MEALS:** Bar Lunch fr £5 Dinner fr £22 International Cuisine V meals Coffee am Tea pm **FACILITIES:** CTV in all bedrooms STV Indoor swimming pool (heated) Squash Snooker Sauna Solarium Gym Jacuzzi/spa Steam rooms Childrens splash pool Xmas **CONF:** Thtr 260 Class 120 Board 40 Del from £105 * **SERVICES:** Lift Night porter 200P **NOTES:** No smoking in restaurant Last d 9.30pm **CARDS:**

KETTERING Northamptonshire — Map 04 SP87
Travel Inn
Rothwell Rd NN16 8XF
☎ 01536 310082 01536 310104
Dir: *on A14 trunk road linking A1 & M1. Off junct7 of the A14 near Telford Way Industrial Estate*
This modern building offers accommodation in smart, spacious and well equipped bedrooms, all with en-suite bathrooms. Refreshments may be taken at the nearby family restaurant. For details about current prices consult the Contents Page under Hotel Groups for the Travel Inn phone number.
ROOMS: 39 en suite (bth/shr) d £39.95 *

KEYNSHAM Somerset — Map 03 ST66
★★ Grange
42 Bath Rd BS31 1SN
Quality Percentage Score: 64%
☎ 0117 986 9181 0117 986 6373
Dir: *from the A4 take B3116 to Keynsham. The Hotel is situated on the E side of town*
Conveniently located mid-way between Bath and Bristol, this popular, commercial hotel was formerly a farm. Smart public areas and well equipped, modern bedrooms are available. Some bedrooms are situated in an adjoining building, all at ground floor level. A good choice of food is offered, with guests having the option of either eating from the bar selection in relaxed atmosphere, or in the more formal restaurant.
ROOMS: 12 rms (11 bth/shr) 18 annexe en suite (bth/shr) (5 fmly) No smoking in 12 bedrooms s £48-£73; d £65-£85 (incl. bkfst) * LB Off peak **MEALS:** Lunch £2.05-£19.95alc High tea £2.25-£5.25alc Dinner £10.25-£19alc English & French Cuisine V meals Coffee am Tea pm **FACILITIES:** CTV in all bedrooms Gym **CONF:** Thtr 20 Class 20 Board 16 Del £85 * **SERVICES:** 25P **NOTES:** No dogs (ex guide dogs) Last d 9pm **CARDS:**

KIDDERMINSTER Worcestershire — Map 07 SO87
★★★★ Stone Manor
Stone DY10 4PJ
Quality Percentage Score: 64%
☎ 01562 777555 01562 777834
Dir: *2m SE on A448*
This converted and much extended former manor house stands in 25 acres of impressive grounds and gardens. The recently refurbished and well equipped accommodation includes no smoking bedrooms, rooms with four-poster beds and bedrooms on ground floor level. The hotel is a popular venue for wedding receptions and there are three self-contained function suites with capacity for up to 250 guests. There are also four conference suites and these, together with its convenient location, make it a popular choice for business seminars.
ROOMS: 52 en suite (bth/shr) No smoking in 6 bedrooms d £70-£120 * LB Off peak **MEALS:** Lunch £14.95 & alc Dinner £19.50 & alc International Cuisine V meals Coffee am Tea pm **FACILITIES:** CTV in all bedrooms STV Outdoor swimming pool Tennis (hard) Pool table Croquet lawn Putting green Xmas **CONF:** Thtr 150 Class 48 Board 60 Del £135 * **SERVICES:** Night porter 400P **NOTES:** No smoking in restaurant Last d 10pm **CARDS:**

KIDDERMINSTER Worcestershire — Map 07 SO87
★★ Cedars
Mason Rd DY11 6AG
Quality Percentage Score: 64%
☎ 01562 515595 01562 751103
Dir: *on ring road follow signs to Bridgnorth (A442) take left turn from last rdbt signed Habberley, 400 metres on left opposite Police Station*
This much extended, large detached house with a delightful

contd.

garden, is situated just off the A442 road to Bridgnorth, close to the Police Station, north of the town centre. Privately owned and personally run, it provides very well equipped accommodation, which includes no smoking bedrooms and bedrooms on ground floor level, some of which have direct access to the garden. Family bedded rooms are also available. Facilities here include a lounge bar and an adjacent conservatory lounge.
ROOMS: 21 en suite (bth/shr) (3 fmly) No smoking in 7 bedrooms s £48-£60; d £62-£75 (incl. bkfst) LB Off peak **MEALS:** Dinner £12-£15 & alc V meals **FACILITIES:** CTV in all bedrooms STV ch fac **CONF:** Thtr 25 Class 15 Board 12 Del from £75 * **SERVICES:** 21P **NOTES:** No dogs (ex guide dogs) No smoking in restaurant Last d 8.30pm Closed 24 Dec-2 Jan **CARDS:**

KILLINGTON LAKE MOTORWAY SERVICE AREA Cumbria — Map 07 SD59
Roadchef Lodge
Killington Lake, Motorway Service Area, Killington LA8 0NW
☎ 01539 621666 01539 621660
Dir: *1m S of junc 37 M6 southbound*
This modern building offers accommodation in smart, spacious and well equipped bedrooms, all with en-suite bathrooms. Refreshments may be taken at the nearby family restaurant. For details about current prices, consult the Contents Page under Hotel Groups for the Roadchef phone number.
ROOMS: 36 en suite (bth/shr) d fr £47.50 *

KINGHAM Oxfordshire — Map 04 SP22
★★★ Mill House Hotel & Restaurant
OX7 6UH
Quality Percentage Score: 72%
☎ 01608 658188 01608 658492
Dir: *turn off A44 at either Chipping Norton or Stow on the Wold onto B4450, hotel is on outskirts of Kingham village*

This delightful Cotswold stone hotel, mentioned in the Domesday book, is set in extensive well kept grounds and bordered by its own trout stream. A warm and relaxing atmosphere prevails and staff are very hospitable. The smart bedrooms are individually decorated and thoughtfully equipped. Guests may relax in the spacious and comfortable lounge or in the bar with its log burning fire. The restaurant is popular with locals and leisure guests alike.
ROOMS: 21 en suite (bth/shr) 2 annexe en suite (bth) (1 fmly) s fr £80; d fr £110 (incl. bkfst & dinner) * LB Off peak **MEALS:** Lunch £13.95 Dinner £22.75 English & French Cuisine V meals Coffee am Tea pm **FACILITIES:** CTV in all bedrooms STV Fishing Croquet lawn Xmas **CONF:** Thtr 70 Class 24 Board 20 Del £125 * **SERVICES:** 62P **NOTES:** No smoking in restaurant Last d 9pm
CARDS:

KINGSBRIDGE Devon — Map 03 SX74
★★★ Buckland-Tout-Saints
Goveton TQ7 2DS
Quality Percentage Score: 75%
☎ 01548 853055 01548 856261
Dir: *turn off A381 Totnes/Kingsbridge Rd towards Goveton, left into Goveton and up hill towards St Peters Church, hotel 2nd right after church*
This beautifully proportioned Queen Anne manor house stands in seven acres of grounds. The bedrooms are individual in style and size and wood-panelled day rooms, furnished in keeping with the style of the building, include a choice of lounges, one with a bar, and an intimate restaurant.
ROOMS: 15 en suite (bth/shr) (1 fmly) No smoking in 1 bedroom s £95-£120; d £190-£280 (incl. bkfst) * Off peak **MEALS:** Lunch £19.50 High tea £2.50-£12 Dinner £20-£30 English & French Cuisine V meals Coffee am Tea pm **FACILITIES:** CTV in all bedrooms Croquet lawn Putting green Xmas **CONF:** Thtr 40 Class 30 Board 30 Del from £150 * **SERVICES:** 42P **NOTES:** No coaches No smoking in restaurant Last d 9pm **CARDS:**

See advert on opposite page

KINGSBRIDGE Devon — Map 03 SX74
★★ *White House*
Chillington TQ7 2JX
Quality Percentage Score: 70%
☎ 01548 580580 01548 581124
Dir: *on the A379 at the eastern end of the village*
This charming hotel, a listed building, has a choice of lounges, two of which are no-smoking areas. The Normandy bar-lounge serves pre-dinner drinks, and an interesting menu is offered in the modern, conservatory-style restaurant.
ROOMS: 8 en suite (bth/shr) (1 fmly) **MEALS:** English, French & Italian Cuisine V meals **FACILITIES:** CTV in all bedrooms Croquet lawn Badminton **CONF:** **SERVICES:** 14P **NOTES:** No dogs (ex guide dogs) No coaches No smoking in restaurant Last d 8.45pm Closed 3 Jan-Feb
CARDS:

KING'S LYNN Norfolk — Map 09 TF62
★★★ Congham Hall Country House
Lynn Rd PE32 1AH
☎ 01485 600250 01485 601191
(For full entry see Grimston)

KING'S LYNN Norfolk — Map 09 TF62
★★★ Knights Hill
Knights Hill Village, South Wootton PE30 3HQ
Quality Percentage Score: 69%
☎ 01553 675566 01553 675568
Dir: *junct A148/A149*
Knights Hill is a hotel village complex, set around a historic site dating back to the 16th century. In the main house and the surrounding 17th century buildings, historical charm has been combined with modern facilities such as conference and banqueting suites and an indoor leisure centre. The accommodation is mainly located in extensions to the original hunting lodge. The various types of bedrooms are pleasantly appointed and attractively furnished. Dining options include

contd.

Indicates that the star classification has not been confirmed under the New Quality Standards, see page 7 for further information.

formal meals in the Garden Restaurant in the main hotel, or informal choices in the Farmers Arms pub.
ROOMS: 40 en suite (bth/shr) 17 annexe en suite (bth/shr) No smoking in 14 bedrooms s £85-£110; d £90-£125 LB Off peak **MEALS:** Sunday Lunch £8.05-£16.80alc Dinner fr £17.95 International Cuisine V meals Coffee am **FACILITIES:** CTV in all bedrooms STV Indoor swimming pool (heated) Tennis (hard) Sauna Solarium Gym Croquet lawn Jacuzzi/spa Heli-pad Xmas **CONF:** Thtr 350 Class 150 Board 30 Del from £99 * **SERVICES:** Night porter 350P **NOTES:** No smoking in restaurant Last d 9.30pm **CARDS:**

KING'S LYNN Norfolk — Map 09 TF62
★★★ Butterfly
Beveridge Way, Hardwick Narrows PE30 4NB
Quality Percentage Score: 65%
☎ 01553 771707 📠 01553 768027
Dir: *situated on A10/A47 roundabout, take exit for Hardwick Narrows Industrial Estate*
Located on the main road interchange to the south of the town centre, this popular modern hotel is ideal for business travellers. A variety of bedroom types are available; ladies', studio and ground floor rooms are all provided. The lounge areas and Walt's Restaurant and Bar are both popular venues, the latter serving a wide selection of appetising dishes.
ROOMS: 50 en suite (bth/shr) (2 fmly) No smoking in 10 bedrooms s fr £67.50; d fr £67.50 * LB Off peak **MEALS:** Lunch fr £18 Dinner fr £18 & alc European & Oriental Cuisine V meals Coffee am Tea pm **FACILITIES:** CTV in all bedrooms STV **CONF:** Thtr 40 Class 21 Board 22 **SERVICES:** Night porter 70P **NOTES:** No dogs (ex guide dogs) No smoking area in restaurant Last d 10pm
CARDS:

KING'S LYNN Norfolk — Map 09 TF62
★★★ The Duke's Head
REGAL
Tuesday Market Place PE30 1JS
Quality Percentage Score: 65%
☎ 01553 774996 📠 01553 763556
Dir: *in town centre one-way system go left when road splits then left at lights, along St Anns St into Chapel St, hotel just past carpark on right*

This spacious, elegant Georgian building has many original features. The hotel has a traditional style, but accommodation offers the expected modern standards. There is a comfortable lounge and bar, public bar and a buttery, in addition to the main restaurant.
ROOMS: 71 en suite (bth/shr) (2 fmly) No smoking in 33 bedrooms s £75; d £90 * LB Off peak **MEALS:** Lunch £11.45 Dinner £13.95-£16.95 & alc English & French Cuisine V meals Coffee am Tea pm **FACILITIES:** CTV in all bedrooms Xmas **CONF:** Thtr 240 Class 120 Board 60 **SERVICES:** Lift Night porter 41P **NOTES:** No smoking in restaurant Last d 9.45pm **CARDS:**

KING'S LYNN Norfolk — Map 09 TF62
★★ Globe Hotel
SCOTTISH NEWCASTLE hotels
Tuesday Market Place PE30 1EZ
Quality Percentage Score: 70%
☎ 01553 772617 📠 01553 761315
Dir: *from A10 or A1/A47 follow signs for King's Lynn centre (Old Town). Hotel overlooks the market place*
Very much a relaxed pub-restaurant with rooms, the focal point of the hotel is the busy popular family style restaurant, offering a wide variety of international dishes, and the informal pub, with weekly karaoke. The Globe is located on a corner of Tuesday Market Square in the 'Old Town' of Kings Lynn. Modern bedrooms are smartly decorated, equipped with a very good range of useful facilities and quality bathrooms.
ROOMS: 38 en suite (bth/shr) (4 fmly) No smoking in 18 bedrooms d £47.50 * LB Off peak **MEALS:** Lunch £5.99-£6.50 & alc International Cuisine V meals Coffee am **FACILITIES:** CTV in all bedrooms STV Pool table Wkly live entertainment Xmas **CONF:** Thtr 60 Class 40 Board 30 Del £75 * **SERVICES:** Night porter 20P **NOTES:** No dogs (ex guide dogs) No smoking area in restaurant
CARDS:

KING'S LYNN Norfolk — Map 09 TF62
★★ *Russet House*
53 Goodwins Rd PE30 5PE
Quality Percentage Score: 67%
☎ 01553 773098 📠 01553 773098
Dir: *follow town centre signs along Hardwick Rd at small rdbt just before Southgates turn right into Vancouver Av after short drive hotel on left*
Russet House dates back to 1890 and is a friendly establishment, a short walk from the River Ouse and the market town of Kings Lynn. The bright and airy bedrooms are spacious

contd.

and attractively decorated. There is a comfortable lounge with a roaring fire in winter, and french doors open onto the garden in summer.
ROOMS: 13 en suite (bth/shr) (2 fmly) No smoking in 1 bedroom **MEALS:** V meals Coffee am **FACILITIES:** CTV in all bedrooms **SERVICES:** 14P **NOTES:** No coaches No smoking in restaurant Last d 9pm Closed 22 Dec-1 Jan RS Sun (restaurant closed) **CARDS:**

See advert on opposite page

KING'S LYNN Norfolk **Map 09 TF62**
★★ Stuart House
35 Goodwins Rd PE30 5QX
Quality Percentage Score: 67%
☎ 01553 772169 📠 01553 774788
Dir: *A47/A10/A149 rdbt follow signs for King Lynn Town Centre. Pass under the Southgate Arch right into Guanock Ter. Right Goodwins Rd*
In quiet residential surroundings, this comfortable hotel has been greatly refurbished over the past few years. The public rooms are informal, and guests may choose between meals in the popular bar, or the carte menu and daily specials on offer in the elegant restaurant. The accommodation is in a variety of sizes and the results of the new owners' upgrade are very smart.
ROOMS: 18 en suite (bth/shr) (2 fmly) No smoking in 4 bedrooms s £45; d £68-£100 (incl. bkfst) * LB Off peak **MEALS:** Lunch £7.95-£15 & alc Dinner £18 & alc International Cuisine V meals Coffee am Tea pm **FACILITIES:** CTV in all bedrooms STV Jacuzzi/spa Wkly live entertainment Xmas **CONF:** Thtr 40 Class 40 Board 30 Del from £50 * **SERVICES:** 30P **NOTES:** No dogs (ex guide dogs) No smoking in restaurant Last d 9.30pm **CARDS:**

KING'S LYNN Norfolk **Map 09 TF62**
★★ The Tudor Rose
St Nicholas St, Tuesday Market Place PE30 1LR
Quality Percentage Score: 65%
☎ 01553 762824 📠 01553 764894
Dir: *Hotel is off Tuesday Market Place in the centre of Kings Lynn*
A Grade II listed building dating back to before the 14th century. There are exposed beams in the charming restaurant, and the entire hotel offers a pleasant and relaxing atmosphere. Public rooms also include a small reception lounge and two bars, where real ales and informal fare are served. Bedroom styles and sizes vary and each room is well equipped.
ROOMS: 13 rms (4 bth 7 shr) s £35-£45.50; d £60 (incl. bkfst) * LB Off peak **MEALS:** English & French Cuisine V meals Coffee am Tea pm **FACILITIES:** CTV in all bedrooms **NOTES:** No smoking in restaurant Last d 9pm **CARDS:**

KING'S LYNN Norfolk **Map 09 TF62**
★★ Grange
Willow Park, South Wootton Ln PE30 3BP
Quality Percentage Score: 64%
☎ 01553 673777 & 671222 📠 01553 673777
Dir: *take A148 towards King's Lynn for 1.5m at traffic lights turn left into Wootton Rd 400yds on right South Wootton Ln hotel 1st on left*
An imposing Edwardian house in a quiet residential area, surrounded by gardens and ample private car parking. Most bedrooms are in the main house, some are in an adjacent courtyard-style garden annexe, all accommodation is well kept. Public rooms are inviting, with a wood-panelled lobby and wide stairwell.
ROOMS: 5 en suite (bth/shr) 4 annexe en suite (bth) s £40-£55; d £50-£65 (incl. bkfst) * LB Off peak **MEALS:** Dinner £7.95-£17alc V meals Coffee am Tea pm **FACILITIES:** CTV in all bedrooms Xmas **CONF:** Thtr 20 Class 15 Board 12 **SERVICES:** 16P **NOTES:** No coaches No smoking in restaurant Last d 7.30pm **CARDS:**

KING'S LYNN Norfolk **Map 09 TF62**
Travel Inn
Freebridge Farm
☎ 01553 772221 📠 01553 775827
This modern building offers accommodation in smart, spacious and well equipped bedrooms, all with en-suite bathrooms. Refreshments may be taken at the nearby family restaurant. For details about current prices consult the Contents Page under Hotel Groups for the Travel Inn phone number.
ROOMS: 40 en suite (bth/shr) d £39.95 *

KINGSTON UPON THAMES Greater London
See LONDON SECTION plan 1 *C1*
★★★ Kingston Lodge
Kingston Hill KT2 7NP
Quality Percentage Score: 69%
☎ 020 8541 4481 📠 020 8547 1013
Dir: *A3 Robin Hood intersection A308 towards Kingston. Hotel 1.5m on left*
The location of this friendly hotel and the quality of many of the bedrooms contribute to its all round popularity. Overlooking the peaceful courtyard there is now a smart, new brasserie, Burnt Orange, which provides a modern style of eating in an informal atmosphere.
ROOMS: 62 en suite (bth/shr) No smoking in 20 bedrooms d £140 * LB Off peak **MEALS:** Lunch £8.95-£10.95 & alc High tea fr £7.50 Dinner fr £12.95 & alc Continental Cuisine V meals Coffee am Tea pm **FACILITIES:** CTV in all bedrooms Wkly live entertainment **CONF:** Thtr 80 Class 50 Board 35 Del from £130 * **SERVICES:** Night porter 74P **NOTES:** Last d 10pm **CARDS:**

KINGSTON UPON THAMES Greater London
★★ *Chase Lodge*
10 Park Rd, Hampton Wick KT1 4AS
Quality Percentage Score: 69%
☎ 020 8943 1862 📠 020 8943 9363
Close to the centre of Kingston in a quiet residential area in Hampton Wick, Chase Lodge offers high standards of comfort and quiet bedrooms, three with four-poster beds and one with fabric-covered walls. Public areas comprise an open plan conservatory restaurant and bar.
ROOMS: 6 en suite (bth/shr) 4 annexe en suite (bth/shr) (1 fmly) **MEALS:** V meals Coffee am Tea pm **FACILITIES:** CTV in all bedrooms STV **SERVICES:** Night porter 20P **NOTES:** No coaches No smoking in restaurant Last d 10pm **CARDS:**

KINGSWINFORD West Midlands **Map 07 SO88**
Travel Inn
Dudley Rd DY6 8WP
☎ 01384 291290 📠 01384 277593
Dir: *on the A4101 leading from Kingswinford to Dudley. Directly opposite the Pensnett Trading Estate in Kingswinford*
This modern building offers accommodation in smart, spacious and well equipped bedrooms, all with en-suite bathrooms. Refreshments may be taken at the nearby family restaurant. For details about current prices consult the Contents Page under Hotel Groups for the Travel Inn phone number.
ROOMS: 43 en suite (bth/shr) d £39.95 *

KINGTON Herefordshire **Map 03 SO25**
★★ Burton
Mill St HR5 3BQ
Quality Percentage Score: 66%
☎ 01544 230323 📠 01544 230323
Dir: *at rdbt of A44/A411 interchange take road signed town centre*
This privately owned and friendly hotel is located in the town centre. It provides spacious bedrooms, which are well equipped

contd.

and suitable for both business people and tourists. Facilities include a lounge bar, a small lounge and a pleasant restaurant. There is also a meeting room and a large ballroom.
ROOMS: 16 en suite (bth/shr) (5 fmly) s £40; d £58 (incl. bkfst) * LB Off peak **MEALS:** Dinner £15 International Cuisine V meals Coffee am Tea pm **FACILITIES:** CTV in all bedrooms Xmas **CONF:** Thtr 150 Class 100 Board 20 **SERVICES:** 50P **NOTES:** Last d 9.30pm
CARDS:

KIRKBURTON West Yorkshire — Map 07 SE11
★★★ Hanover International
Penistone Rd HD8 0PE
Quality Percentage Score: 68%
☎ 01484 607788 01484 607961
Dir: *3m S of Huddersfield town centre, on A629, close to M1 and M62*

This converted former Victorian textile mill lies just a few miles to the south of Huddersfield. Modern bedrooms are generally quite spacious and are nicely furnished. A wide range of dishes is offered in the comfortable restaurant, and a variety of meeting and function suites is also available.
ROOMS: 47 en suite (bth/shr) (2 fmly) No smoking in 20 bedrooms s £45; d £55 * LB Off peak **MEALS:** Sunday Lunch £9.95-£16 & alc Dinner £16 & alc V meals Coffee am Tea pm **FACILITIES:** CTV in all bedrooms STV Pool table Xmas **CONF:** Thtr 150 Class 30 Board 42 Del £80 * **SERVICES:** Night porter 100P **NOTES:** No smoking in restaurant Last d 9.45pm **CARDS:**

See advert under HUDDERSFIELD

KIRKBY LONSDALE Cumbria — Map 07 SD67
★★ Pheasant Inn
LA6 2RX
Quality Percentage Score: 68%
☎ 015242 71230 015242 71230
Dir: *leave M6 junc36 onto A65, turn left at A683 1m onwards in centre of village*
This friendly inn stands in the village of Casterton, near Kirby Lonsdale and has fine views of the surrounding fells. There are cosy bars, a panelled restaurant serving a good range of meals, and bedrooms offer a good standard of comfort.
ROOMS: 11 en suite (bth/shr) s £37.50; d £68 (incl. bkfst) * LB Off peak **MEALS:** International Cuisine V meals Coffee am **FACILITIES:** CTV in all bedrooms Xmas **CONF:** Board 12 **SERVICES:** 40P **NOTES:** No smoking in restaurant Last d 9.30pm Closed 4-6 Jan
CARDS:

KIRKBY LONSDALE Cumbria — Map 07 SD67
★★ Whoop Hall Inn
LA6 2HP
Quality Percentage Score: 66%
☎ 015242 71284 015242 72154
Dir: *6m from M6 junct 36 on A65 1m SE of Kirkby Londsdale*
This popular inn and hotel combines traditional charm with modern facilities. Bedrooms, some with four poster beds, are

spacious and attractively furnished, a number are in converted barns. A fire warms the bar on cooler days and a wide variety of dishes is offered in the galleried restaurant.
ROOMS: 22 en suite (bth/shr) (3 fmly) No smoking in 11 bedrooms **MEALS:** English & Continental Cuisine V meals Coffee am Tea pm **FACILITIES:** CTV in all bedrooms Pool table Jacuzzi/spa **CONF:** Thtr 80 Class 80 Board 60 **SERVICES:** Night porter 120P **NOTES:** Last d 10pm
CARDS:

KIRKBY LONSDALE Cumbria — Map 07 SD67
★★ Plough Hotel
Cow Brow LA6 1PJ
Quality Percentage Score: 58%
☎ 015395 67227 015395 67848
Dir: *turn off junc 36 M6, head for Skipton/Kirkby Lonsdale, 1m from M6*

This coaching inn combines the best of traditional values with many modern amenities. Bedrooms vary in size, but all are soundly furnished and suitably equipped. Guests can enjoy a

contd.

wide range of bar snacks, or more serious fare from the daily-changing fixed-price menu in the dining room. The smart conservatory is used at breakfast.
ROOMS: 12 en suite (bth/shr) (2 fmly) **MEALS:** English & French Cuisine V meals Coffee am Tea pm **FACILITIES:** CTV in all bedrooms STV Fishing ch fac **CONF:** Thtr 100 Class 100 Board 60 **SERVICES:** 72P **NOTES:** No smoking in restaurant Last d 9pm
CARDS:

KIRKBY LONSDALE Cumbria — Map 07 SD67

The Premier Collection

★ Hipping Hall
Cowan Bridge LA6 2JJ
☎ 015242 71187 015242 72452
Dir: on A65, 2.5m E of Kirkby Lonsdale, 8.5m from M6 junct 36
This delightful country house provides comfortable, attractively furnished bedrooms, including two cottage suites with spiral staircases. Excellent home cooking is served at the large table in the baronial hall - complete with minstrels gallery. Breakfast is taken at individual tables in the morning room.
ROOMS: 7 en suite (bth/shr) No smoking in 5 bedrooms s £72; d £88 (incl. bkfst) * LB Off peak **MEALS:** Dinner £24 **FACILITIES:** CTV in all bedrooms Croquet lawn **SERVICES:** 12P **NOTES:** No coaches No children 12yrs No smoking in restaurant Last d 4pm Closed 2 Nov-mid Mar
CARDS:

KIRKBYMOORSIDE North Yorkshire — Map 08 SE68

★★ George & Dragon Hotel
17 Market Place YO62 6AA
Quality Percentage Score: 65%
☎ 01751 433334 01751 432933
Dir: off A170 between Thirsk/Scarborough, in centre of market town

A 17th-century coaching inn in the centre of the town. The pub with its blazing fire and sporting theme has a great atmosphere and a reputation for good food. A range of hearty dishes is offered from the carte and blackboard, served in the bar, small bistro or dining room. Comfortable bedrooms are located in two buildings to the rear.
ROOMS: 12 en suite (bth/shr) 7 annexe en suite (bth/shr) (3 fmly) No smoking in 5 bedrooms s fr £49; d fr £79 (incl. bkfst) * LB Off peak **MEALS:** Sunday Lunch £9.90-£12.90 & alc Dinner £12.95-£17.95 & alc English & Continental Cuisine V meals Coffee am **FACILITIES:** CTV in all bedrooms Gym Xmas **CONF:** Thtr 50 Class 20 Board 20 Del from £75 * **SERVICES:** 20P **NOTES:** No smoking area in restaurant Last d 9.15pm
CARDS:

KIRKBY STEPHEN See advert on opposite page

KNARESBOROUGH North Yorkshire — Map 08 SE35

★★★ Dower House
Bond End HG5 9AL
Quality Percentage Score: 70%
☎ 01423 863302 01423 867665
Dir: A1M to A59 Harrogate through Knaresborough hotel on right after lights at end of High Street
This Grade II listed building is convenient for both the town and the River Nidd. The house is delightfully furnished and offers well equipped bedrooms and inviting public rooms. The Terrace Restaurant is a perfect setting for some quality British cooking, which is prepared with both skill and flair and features much local produce. Conferences and business meetings are well catered for and there is also an excellent leisure and health club.
ROOMS: 28 en suite (bth/shr) 3 annexe en suite (bth/shr) (2 fmly) No smoking in 15 bedrooms d £68-£80 LB Off peak **MEALS:** Sunday Lunch fr £12.50 Dinner fr £21 & alc English & French Cuisine V meals Coffee am Tea pm **FACILITIES:** CTV in all bedrooms Indoor swimming pool (heated) Sauna Gym Jacuzzi/spa Xmas **CONF:** Thtr 65 Class 35 Board 40 Del from £99 * **SERVICES:** Night porter 80P **NOTES:** No smoking in restaurant Last d 9.15pm **CARDS:**

KNARESBOROUGH North Yorkshire — Map 08 SE35

★★★ General Tarleton Inn
Boroughbridge Rd, Ferrensby HG5 0QB
Quality Percentage Score: 64%
☎ 01423 340284 01423 340288
Dir: on A6055, on cross road in Ferrensby
Quality cooking in both the restaurant and the bars is a feature of this hotel and now includes 'early bird' specials. Bedrooms are located in a modern extension and provide all the expected comforts. The reception and foyer area provides comfortable seating, while the delightful covered courtyard makes an additional dining area.
ROOMS: 14 en suite (bth/shr) d fr £65 * LB Off peak **MEALS:** Lunch fr £17.50 Dinner £25 English & French Cuisine V meals Coffee am Tea pm **FACILITIES:** CTV in all bedrooms Xmas **CONF:** Thtr 60 Class 35 Board 28 Del £80 * **SERVICES:** 80P **NOTES:** No coaches No smoking in restaurant Last d 10pm Closed 25 Dec only
CARDS:

See advert on opposite page

KNUTSFORD Cheshire — Map 07 SJ77

★★★★ Cottons
Manchester Rd WA16 0SU
Quality Percentage Score: 68%
☎ 01565 650333 01565 755351
Dir: on A50 1m from junct 19 of M6
Ideally located just a short distance from the M6 and M56 motorways, this successful hotel provides facilities for both business and leisure guests, very well appointed and thoughtfully laid out bedrooms. In addition to the superbly

contd.

equipped leisure facilities, the public areas offer a smart bar and restaurant. The menu has a noticeable Cajun influence and provides an excellent choice of dishes. There is also an informal covered courtyard bar. A friendly and professional level of service is provided throughout.
ROOMS: 99 en suite (bth/shr) (4 fmly) No smoking in 44 bedrooms s £115-£139; d £125-£139 (incl. bkfst) * LB Off peak **MEALS:** Bar Lunch fr £8 Dinner £22-£30 English & French Cuisine V meals Coffee am Tea pm **FACILITIES:** CTV in all bedrooms STV Indoor swimming pool (heated) Tennis (hard) Squash Sauna Solarium Gym Jacuzzi/spa Fitness and beauty rooms Steam room Childrens splash pool Xmas **CONF:** Thtr 200 Class 120 Board 30 Del from £110 * **SERVICES:** Lift Night porter 180P **NOTES:** No smoking in restaurant Last d 9.30pm Closed 31 Dec **CARDS:**

KNUTSFORD Cheshire — Map 07 SJ77

★★★ Cottage Restaurant & Lodge

London Rd, Allostock WA16 9LU
Quality Percentage Score: 67%
☎ 01565 722470 Fax 01565 722749
Dir: *on A50 between Holmes Chapel and Knutsford*

Despite its modern facilities this hotel retains the character and friendliness of the original cottage restaurant. Bedrooms are situated in adjacent buildings and are comfortably furnished. A good choice of freshly prepared dishes is offered, and functions can also be catered for.
ROOMS: 12 en suite (bth/shr) (4 fmly) No smoking in 4 bedrooms s £65-£70; d £75-£80 (incl. bkfst) * Off peak **MEALS:** Lunch fr £10.95 Dinner £10.95 & alc V meals Coffee am Tea pm **FACILITIES:** CTV in all bedrooms STV Xmas **CONF:** Thtr 40 Class 40 Board 40 Del from £90 * **SERVICES:** 60P **NOTES:** No dogs (ex guide dogs) No coaches No smoking in restaurant Last d 9.30pm **CARDS:**

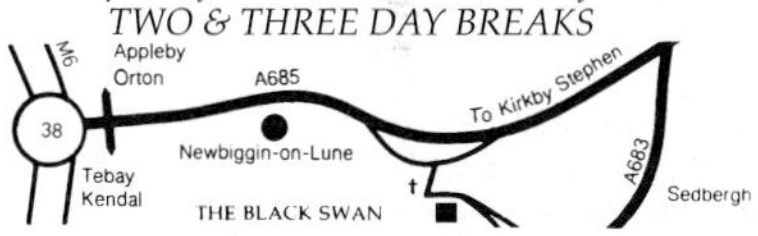

KNUTSFORD Cheshire **Map 07 SJ77**
★★ The Longview Hotel & Restaurant
55 Manchester Rd WA16 0LX
Quality Percentage Score: 71%
☎ 01565 632119 📠 01565 652402
Dir: *from M6 junct 19 take A556 W towards Chester.Left at lights onto A5033 1.5m to rdbt then left. Hotel 200yds on right*

A comfortable Victorian hotel with a long history of satisfied guests. Characterful public areas include a cosy cellar bar and inviting foyer lounge. The attractive restaurant has a Victorian feel and offers an imaginative selection of dishes carefully prepared from fresh local produce. Bedrooms are comfortable with fetching colour schemes, and offer a thoughtful range of amenities.
ROOMS: 13 en suite (bth/shr) 10 annexe en suite (bth/shr) (1 fmly) s £63-£75; d £77.50-£90 (incl. bkfst) * LB Off peak **MEALS:** Bar Lunch £3.50-£5alc Dinner £17.25-£23.20alc English & Continental Cuisine V meals Coffee am **FACILITIES:** CTV in all bedrooms **SERVICES:** Night porter 29P **NOTES:** No coaches No smoking in restaurant Last d 9pm Closed 24 Dec-8 Jan **CARDS:**

See advert on page 347

KNUTSFORD Cheshire **Map 07 SJ77**
★★ The Toft Hotel & Dick Willett's Restaurant
Toft Rd WA16 9EH
Quality Percentage Score: 70%
☎ 01565 633470 & 634443 📠 01565 632603
Dir: *1m S on A50*
Tasteful conversion of old farm buildings created this charming hotel with its friendly and informal atmosphere. Many of the original features remain in the well equipped, beamed bedrooms, and the public areas also display a pleasing character. The restaurant menu is imaginative and offers many speciality vegetarian dishes.
ROOMS: 11 en suite (bth/shr) No smoking in all bedrooms
MEALS: V meals **FACILITIES:** CTV in all bedrooms STV **SERVICES:** 35P
NOTES: No dogs (ex guide dogs) No coaches No children 12yrs No smoking in restaurant Last d 9.30pm Closed Xmas & New Year
CARDS:

KNUTSFORD Cheshire **Map 07 SJ77**
★★ Royal George
King St WA16 6EE
Quality Percentage Score: 64%
☎ 01565 634151 📠 01565 634955
Dir: *exit M6 junct 19 and take A556. Follow signs to town centre. Follow one way system into Princess St and turn left before Midland Bank*
Conveniently situated in the town centre, this former 14th-century coaching inn is reputed to have been visited in the past by such historical figures as Queen Victoria, Winston Churchill and General Patton. Although recently modernised, the rooms retain considerable charm and character. The bedrooms are well equipped, and some have four-poster beds. The Café Bar serves innovative cuisine.
ROOMS: 31 rms (25 bth/shr) (6 fmly) No smoking in 20 bedrooms s £62.45; d £69.40 (incl. bkfst) * LB Off peak **MEALS:** Lunch £4.95-£8.95 & alc High tea £4.75 & alc Dinner £12.95 & alc V meals Coffee am Tea pm **FACILITIES:** CTV in all bedrooms Wkly live entertainment Xmas **CONF:** Thtr 160 Class 120 Board 60 Del £89.95 * **SERVICES:** Lift Night porter 50P **NOTES:** No dogs (ex guide dogs) No smoking in restaurant Last d 10pm **CARDS:**

KNUTSFORD Cheshire **Map 07 SJ77**
Travelodge
Chester Rd, Tabley WA16 0PP
☎ 01565 652187 📠 01565 652187
Dir: *on A556, northbound just E of junct 19 on M6*
This modern building offers accommodation in smart, spacious and well equipped bedrooms, all with en-suite bathrooms. Refreshments may be taken at the nearby family restaurant. For details about current prices, consult the Contents Page under Hotel Groups for the Travelodge phone number.
ROOMS: 32 en suite (bth/shr) d £55.95 *

LANCASTER Lancashire **Map 07 SD46**
★★★★ Lancaster House
Green Ln, Ellel LA1 4GJ
Quality Percentage Score: 64%
☎ 01524 844822 📠 01524 844766
Dir: *M6 junct 33 N towards Lancaster. Through Galgate village, turn right onto Green Lane. Hotel just before University entrance*
This stylish hotel is situated in open countryside next to Lancaster University. The modern bedrooms are spacious and pleasantly furnished. For those wishing to relax a superb leisure complex is on hand. The Gressingham Restaurant provides an extensive à la carte menu of mainly British dishes. As an extra facility for business guests a smart business training centre provides the latest equipment and Internet technology.
ROOMS: 80 en suite (bth/shr) (10 fmly) No smoking in 36 bedrooms d £94-£119 * LB Off peak **MEALS:** Lunch £10.95-£12.95 & alc Dinner £18.50-£21.50 & alc V meals Coffee am Tea pm **FACILITIES:** CTV in all bedrooms STV Indoor swimming pool (heated) Sauna Gym Jacuzzi/spa Activity centre 1 mile Wkly live entertainment Xmas **CONF:** Thtr 180 Class 50 Board 60 Del from £99 * **SERVICES:** Night porter 100P **NOTES:** No smoking in restaurant Last d 9.30pm
CARDS:

LANCASTER Lancashire **Map 07 SD46**
★★★ Posthouse Lancaster
Waterside Park, Caton Rd LA1 3RA
Quality Percentage Score: 67%
☎ 01524 65999 📠 01524 841265
Dir: *take junct 34 off M6, turn towards Lancaster, hotel first on right*
Situated alongside the River Lune, this modern hotel provides spacious bedrooms and refurbished, extended public areas to provide comfortable and convenient lounges. The popular Traders Bar and Grill provides a varied menu and there is an all day eating option.
ROOMS: 157 en suite (bth/shr) (82 fmly) No smoking in 73 bedrooms
MEALS: International Cuisine V meals Coffee am Tea pm
FACILITIES: CTV in all bedrooms Indoor swimming pool (heated) Sauna Gym Jacuzzi/spa Health & fitness centre **CONF:** Thtr 120 Class 60 Board 60 Del from £89 * **SERVICES:** Lift Night porter 300P **NOTES:** No smoking in restaurant Last d 10pm
CARDS:

LANCASTER Lancashire **Map 07 SD46**

★★★ Royal Kings Arms

Market St LA1 1HP

Quality Percentage Score: 65%

☎ 0500 636943 (Central Res) 📠 01773 880321

Dir: *follow 'City Centre' signs from M6, then 'Castle & Railway Station', turn off before traffic lights next to Waterstones bookshop*

This traditional, city-centre hotel, with its own small car park, is also close to the station. It has kept many of its 19th-century features, including a fine galleried restaurant. Bedrooms come in a variety of styles, but all have modern facilities. Staff are friendly and welcoming.

ROOMS: 55 en suite (bth/shr) (2 fmly) No smoking in 15 bedrooms s £69.50-£79.50; d £79.50-£95 * LB Off peak **MEALS:** Lunch £5.95-£7.95 Dinner fr £15.95 European Cuisine V meals Coffee am Tea pm **FACILITIES:** CTV in all bedrooms STV Wkly live entertainment Xmas **CONF:** Thtr 160 Class 50 Board 60 Del from £85 * **SERVICES:** Lift Night porter 20P **NOTES:** No smoking in restaurant Last d 9.30pm **CARDS:**

LANCASTER Lancashire **Map 07 SD46**

★★ Hampson House

Hampson Ln LA2 0JB

Quality Percentage Score: 61%

☎ 01524 751158 📠 01524 751779

(For full entry see Hampson Green)

LANCASTER Lancashire **Map 07 SD46**

★ Scarthwaite Country House

Crook O Lune, Caton LA2 9HR

Quality Percentage Score: 63%

☎ 01524 770267 📠 01524 770711

Dir: *leave M6 at junct 34 onto A683 towards Caton hotel 1.5m on right*

This attractive stone house sits back from the road in a peaceful woodland setting. Recently refurbished bedrooms provide pretty co-ordinated themes. There is a cosy bar, small television lounge and spacious function room. The hotel is a popular wedding reception venue.

ROOMS: 10 en suite (bth/shr) (1 fmly) No smoking in 2 bedrooms s £33-£39.50; d £48-£58 (incl. bkfst) * LB Off peak **MEALS:** Lunch £5.50 V meals Coffee am Tea pm **FACILITIES:** CTV in all bedrooms **CONF:** Thtr 150 Class 90 Board 50 **SERVICES:** Night porter 75P **NOTES:** No smoking area in restaurant **CARDS:**

Remember to return your Prize Draw card for a chance to win one of 30 relaxing leisure breaks with Corus and Regal hotels. See inside the front cover for the card and competition details.

LANCING West Sussex Map 04 TQ10

★★ *Sussex Pad*

Old Shoreham Rd BN15 0RH
Quality Percentage Score: 70%
☎ 01273 454647 Fax 01273 453010
Dir: *situated on the main A27 oposite Shoreham Airport and by Lancing College*

Conveniently situated just off the A27, this popular hotel is personally run by its dedicated owner Mr Wally J Pack. Bedrooms, all named after champagne houses, are comfortably furnished and well equipped. Public areas centre around a spacious conservatory including a well stocked bar. Bar meals and light refreshments are available throughout the day and chef Paul Hornsby offers a fixed-price menu in the Ladywells Restaurant.

ROOMS: 19 en suite (bth/shr) **MEALS:** English & French Cuisine V meals Coffee am Tea pm **FACILITIES:** CTV in all bedrooms STV **CONF:** Thtr 20 Board 20 Del from £80 * **SERVICES:** 60P **NOTES:** No smoking in restaurant Last d 10pm **CARDS:**

LAND'S END Cornwall & Isles of Scilly Map 02 SW32

see also **Sennen**

★★★ The Land's End Hotel

TR19 7AA
Quality Percentage Score: 65%
☎ 01736 871844 Fax 01736 871599
Dir: *from Penzance follow A30 & signs to Land's End. After Sennen continue for 1m to Land's End*

With its famous clifftop location the hotel commands views across the Atlantic and over to the Longships lighthouse. Recently opened is 'Longships' Restaurant and Bar, here fresh local produce is used and fish dishes are a speciality. All bedrooms are comfortably furnished with modern facilities, many with stunning sea views.

ROOMS: 33 en suite (bth/shr) (2 fmly) s £50-£60; d £80-£100 (incl. bkfst) LB Off peak **MEALS:** V meals Coffee am Tea pm **FACILITIES:** CTV in all bedrooms Free entry to Lands End visitor centre & exhibitions Wkly live entertainment Xmas **CONF:** Thtr 200 Class 100 Board 50 **SERVICES:** Night porter 1000P **NOTES:** No smoking in restaurant Last d 9.30pm **CARDS:**

See advert on page 349

LANGAR Nottinghamshire Map 08 SK73

★★ *Langar Hall*

NG13 9HG
Quality Percentage Score: 69%
☎ 01949 860559 Fax 01949 861045
Dir: *accessible via Bingham on the A52 or Cropwell Bishop from the A46, both signposted, the house adjoins the church*

Home of the Skirving family since 1837, Imogen Skirving now presides over this country house hotel with a welcoming and enthusiastic team of staff. The majority of the bedrooms have been upgraded and feature fine antique furniture, lovely paintings and quality soft furnishings. Drinks are served in the elegant white room, dinner in the pillared hall dining room. Public rooms are also being upgraded, there are two private dining rooms leading out on to the herb garden.

ROOMS: 10 en suite (bth/shr) (1 fmly) No smoking in all bedrooms **MEALS:** V meals Coffee am Tea pm **FACILITIES:** CTV in 11 bedrooms Fishing Croquet lawn **CONF:** Thtr 20 Class 20 Board 20 Del from £150 * **SERVICES:** Night porter 20P **NOTES:** No coaches No smoking in restaurant Last d 9.30pm **CARDS:**

New AA Guides for the Millennium are featured on page 24

LANGHO Lancashire Map 07 SD73

★★★ Northcote Manor

Northcote Rd BB6 8BE
Quality Percentage Score: 71%
☎ 01254 240555 Fax 01254 246568
Dir: *M6 junct 31, 8m to Northcote, follow signs to Clitheroe, Hotel is set back on the left just before the rdbt*

Northcote Manor is full of character and provides a very comfortable environment in which to sample the delights of its famous restaurant. Bedrooms have been individually furnished and thoughtfully equipped. Enjoy a drink in one of the comfortable lounges whilst browsing the tempting menus, where the excellent cooking includes much of Lancashire's finest fare.

ROOMS: 14 en suite (bth/shr) s £75-£90; d £90-£110 (incl. bkfst) * LB Off peak **MEALS:** Lunch fr £16 & alc High tea fr £8.50 Dinner fr £37 & alc International Cuisine V meals Coffee am Tea pm **FACILITIES:** CTV in all bedrooms STV Croquet lawn Xmas **CONF:** Thtr 40 Class 20 Board 26 **SERVICES:** 50P **NOTES:** No dogs (ex guide dogs) No coaches No smoking in restaurant Last d 9.30pm Closed 25 Dec & 1-7 Jan **CARDS:**

LANGTOFT East Riding of Yorkshire Map 08 TA06

★★ Old Mill Hotel & Restaurant

Mill Ln YO25 3BQ
Quality Percentage Score: 70%
☎ 01377 267284 Fax 01377 267383
Dir: *6m N of Driffield, on B1249, through village of Langtoft on B1249 approx 1m N, turn left at hotel sign hotel straight ahead*

Set in open countryside, this modern hotel has been very well furnished throughout. It provides thoughtfully equipped, modern bedrooms, and a popular bar-lounge where a good range of well produced food is available. There is a charming restaurant, and a friendly atmosphere throughout.

ROOMS: 8 en suite (bth/shr) No smoking in 2 bedrooms s fr £45.50; d fr £55.50 (incl. bkfst) * LB Off peak **MEALS:** Sunday Lunch fr £10.95alc Dinner fr £20.95alc English & Continental Cuisine V meals Coffee am **FACILITIES:** CTV in all bedrooms **CONF:** Thtr 40 Class 20 Board 20 Del from £90 * **SERVICES:** 30P **NOTES:** No coaches No smoking area in restaurant Last d 9pm Closed 26 Dec-12 Jan **CARDS:**

LASTINGHAM North Yorkshire Map 08 SE79

★★★ *Lastingham Grange*

YO62 6TH
Quality Percentage Score: 72%
☎ 01751 417345 & 417402
Dir: *2m E on A170 towards Scarborough, onto Lastingham, in village turn left uphill towards Moors. Hotel can be found on right*

This charming hotel dating from the 17th-century, has been run by the Wood family for over 40 years. A number of fine antiques are displayed, both in the attractively decorated bedrooms, and in the public areas. Quality home cooking is offered and there is

contd.

a welcoming lounge in which to relax. The colourful grounds feature a sunken rose garden.
ROOMS: 12 en suite (bth) (2 fmly) **MEALS:** V meals Coffee am Tea pm **FACILITIES:** CTV in all bedrooms Large adventure playground ch fac **SERVICES:** 32P **NOTES:** No coaches No smoking in restaurant Last d 8.30pm Closed mid Dec-Feb

LAUNCESTON Cornwall & Isles of Scilly **Map 02 SX38**
see also **Lifton**
★★ Penhallow Manor Country House
PL15 7SJ
Quality Percentage Score: 77%
☎ 01566 86206 Fax 01566 86179
(For full entry see Altarnun)

LAUNCESTON Cornwall & Isles of Scilly **Map 02 SX38**
★★ Eagle House
Castle St PL15 8BA
Quality Percentage Score: 64%
☎ 01566 772036 Fax 01566 772036
Built in 1767, this elegant Georgian house is next to the castle and within walking distance of all local amenities. Bedrooms are well equipped and many have entrancing views of the Cornish countryside. A fixed-price menu is served in the restaurant, with a more modest menu served on Sundays evenings. The hotel benefits from a wide range of function rooms.
ROOMS: 14 en suite (bth/shr) (1 fmly) **MEALS:** V meals Coffee am Tea pm **FACILITIES:** CTV in all bedrooms STV **CONF:** Thtr 190 Class 190 Board 190 **SERVICES:** 100P **NOTES:** No dogs (ex guide dogs) No coaches Last d 9pm **CARDS:**

LAVENHAM Suffolk **Map 05 TL94**
★★★ The Swan
High St CO10 9QA
Quality Percentage Score: 71%
☎ 01787 247477 Fax 01787 248286
Dir: *in centre of village on A134 Bury St Edmunds/Hadleigh*
The Swan is a focal point in the town with its historic architecture and beams. Bedrooms are smart and are gradually being up-dated. Public areas include two bars and a pleasant restaurant with minstrel's gallery. In the evening, there is a choice of two menus using seasonal, fresh ingredients.
ROOMS: 46 en suite (bth/shr) No smoking in 15 bedrooms s £75; d £120 * LB Off peak **MEALS:** Lunch £9.95-£17.95 Dinner £24.95 & alc V meals Coffee am Tea pm **FACILITIES:** CTV in all bedrooms Croquet lawn Wkly live entertainment Xmas **CONF:** Thtr 60 Class 35 Board 25 Del £125 * **SERVICES:** Night porter 60P **NOTES:** No smoking in restaurant Last d 9.30pm **CARDS:**

LAVENHAM Suffolk **Map 05 TL94**
★★ Angel
Market Place CO10 9QZ
Quality Percentage Score: 68%
☎ 01787 247388 Fax 01787 248344
Dir: *from A14 take Bury East/Sudbury turn off A143, after 4m take A1141 to Lavenham, Angel is off the High Street*
Standing in the heart of one of England's finest medieval villages, this popular inn was first licensed in 1420 and is still a popular focal point for locals and visitors. The daily-changing restaurant menu offers appealing dishes that use good raw ingredients; meals can be taken in the garden during warmer weather. The spacious residents' lounge is most relaxing, while the comfortable bedrooms are individually decorated and well furnished.
ROOMS: 8 en suite (bth/shr) (1 fmly) s £42.50-£55; d £69-£80 (incl. bkfst) * LB Off peak **MEALS:** Lunch £11.15-£17.95alc Dinner £13.45-£18.75alc English & French Cuisine V meals Coffee am **FACILITIES:** CTV in all bedrooms Use of Lavenham Tennis Club facilities Wkly live entertainment **SERVICES:** 5P **NOTES:** No coaches No smoking area in restaurant Last d 9.15pm Closed 25-26 Dec
CARDS:

LEA MARSTON Warwickshire **Map 04 SP29**
★★★ Lea Marston Hotel & Leisure Complex
Haunch Ln B76 0BY
Quality Percentage Score: 72%
☎ 01675 470468 Fax 01675 470871
Dir: *leave M42 at junct 9 and take A4097 towards Kingsbury. Hotel signposted 1.5m on right*

This large, modern, hotel complex is close to junction 9 of the M42 motorway, with access via the A4097. The well equipped accommodation includes some suites and some ground-floor rooms. Extensive public areas include a family restaurant with adjacent play areas, and a wide range of indoor and outdoor leisure facilities. The hotel is a popular choice for wedding receptions.
ROOMS: 83 en suite (bth/shr) (6 fmly) No smoking in 34 bedrooms s £110; d £125 (incl. bkfst) * LB Off peak **MEALS:** Lunch £10.95-£13.95 High tea £1.50 Dinner £19.95 English & Continental Cuisine V meals Coffee am Tea pm **FACILITIES:** CTV in all bedrooms STV Indoor swimming pool (heated) Golf 9 Tennis (hard) Sauna Solarium Gym Pool table Croquet lawn Putting green Jacuzzi/spa Golf driving range Wkly live entertainment ch fac Xmas **CONF:** Thtr 110 Class 60 Board 40 Del £145 * **SERVICES:** Night porter 220P **NOTES:** No dogs (ex guide dogs) No smoking in restaurant Last d 10pm
CARDS:

AA Rosettes are awarded for quality of food, see page 15 for an explanation of Rosette assessment.

Indicates that the star classification has not been confirmed under the New Quality Standards, see page 7 for further information.

LEAMINGTON SPA (ROYAL) Warwickshire Map 04 SP36

The Premier Collection

★★★ Mallory Court

Harbury Ln, Bishop's Tachbrook CV33 9QB
☎ 01926 330214 01926 451714
Dir: *2m S off B4087 towards Harbury*

Set in 10 acres of landscaped grounds and formal gardens, this beautifully restored English country house is a fine example of period architecture. Most of the tastefully appointed bedrooms enjoy views over the gardens, and each room is individually styled with attractive decor and quality furnishings. All have a wide array of thoughtful extras and modern facilities and some of the original art deco bathrooms are still in use. Day rooms include two elegant and comfortable lounges and an impressive panelled restaurant, which provides an ideal setting for the innovative cuisine.

ROOMS: 18 en suite (bth/shr) (1 fmly) s £165-£205; d £175-£295 (incl. cont bkfst) * LB Off peak **MEALS:** Lunch £27.50-£29.50 & alc Dinner fr £38 & alc British & French Cuisine V meals Coffee am Tea pm **FACILITIES:** CTV in all bedrooms Outdoor swimming pool Tennis (hard) Croquet lawn Xmas **CONF:** Board 25 Del from £225 * **SERVICES:** 52P **NOTES:** No dogs (ex guide dogs) No coaches No children 9yrs No smoking in restaurant Last d 10pm
CARDS:

LEAMINGTON SPA (ROYAL) Warwickshire Map 04 SP36

★★★ *The Leamington Hotel & Bistro*

64 Upper Holly Walk CV32 4JL
Quality Percentage Score: 68%
☎ 01926 883777 01926 330467

Attractive public rooms include a small welcoming residents' lounge which is a particularly relaxing room with a lovely high ceiling and some ornate plasterwork. The bar and restaurant feature dark wood and an interesting range of paintings and prints. The modern bistro-style menu combines traditional English and French cuisine with a modern twist. Bedrooms are generally spacious, each smartly appointed and with a range of thoughtful extras and modern facilities.

ROOMS: 22 en suite (bth/shr) (6 fmly) No smoking in 4 bedrooms
MEALS: English & French Cuisine V meals Coffee am Tea pm
FACILITIES: CTV in all bedrooms **CONF:** Thtr 45 Class 32 Board 24
SERVICES: 22P **NOTES:** No dogs (ex guide dogs) No coaches
Last d 10pm **CARDS:**

LEAMINGTON SPA (ROYAL) Warwickshire Map 04 SP36

★★★ Courtyard by Marriott Leamington Spa

Olympus Av, Tachbrook Park CV34 6RJ
Quality Percentage Score: 65%
☎ 01926 425522 01926 881322
Dir: *located on the A452, 1m S of the town centre, 3m from the M40*

This modern hotel is situated in Tachbrook Park, a business development on the edge of the town and within easy reach of the M40. Bedrooms are well equipped with good-sized beds, and although the public areas are compact, they are bright and relaxing.

ROOMS: 95 en suite (bth/shr) (15 fmly) No smoking in 48 bedrooms s £75-£95; d £85-£105 (incl. bkfst) * LB Off peak **MEALS:** Lunch £12-£16 & alc Dinner £12.95-£21.20alc European Cuisine V meals Coffee am Tea pm **FACILITIES:** CTV in all bedrooms STV Gym Xmas **CONF:** Thtr 70 Class 35 Board 30 Del from £110 * **SERVICES:** Lift Night porter 120P **NOTES:** No smoking area in restaurant Last d 10pm
CARDS:

LEAMINGTON SPA (ROYAL) Warwickshire Map 04 SP36

★★★ Angel

143 Regent St CV32 4NZ
Quality Percentage Score: 63%
☎ 01926 881296 01926 881296
Dir: *in the town centre at junct of Regent Street and Holly Walk*

A modern extension has been sympathetically added to the existing inn. Public rooms include a comfortable foyer lounge area, a smart restaurant and an informal bar. Bedrooms are thoughtfully equipped, the most recent are contemporary and well laid-out, original rooms are more traditional in style.

ROOMS: 50 en suite (bth/shr) (3 fmly) s £35-£55; d £50-£65 (incl. bkfst) * LB Off peak **MEALS:** Lunch £9.50-£14.50 & alc Dinner £14.50 & alc English & French Cuisine V meals Coffee am Tea pm **FACILITIES:** CTV in all bedrooms STV Xmas **CONF:** Thtr 70 Class 40 Board 40 Del from £70 * **SERVICES:** Lift Night porter 38P **NOTES:** Last d 9.30pm **CARDS:**

LEAMINGTON SPA (ROYAL) Warwickshire Map 04 SP36

★★★ Falstaff

16-20 Warwick New Rd CV32 5JQ
Quality Percentage Score: 61%
☎ 01926 312044 01926 450574
Dir: *from M40 junct 13/14 follow signs for Leamington Spa over 4 rdbts then under bridge. Left into Princes Drive, then right at mini-rdbt*

A friendly young team of staff and an enthusiastic management create a welcoming atmosphere and provide a helpful service. Bedrooms come in a variety of styles and sizes, and are all reasonably well equipped. The restaurant is pleasantly appointed and offers an interesting range of dishes from daily and carte

contd.

menus. There are also extensive conference and banqueting facilities.
ROOMS: 63 en suite (bth/shr) (2 fmly) No smoking in 5 bedrooms s £40-£65; d £50-£75 (incl. bkfst) * LB Off peak **MEALS:** Sunday Lunch £8.50 Dinner £14 & alc English & Continental Cuisine V meals Coffee am Tea pm **FACILITIES:** CTV in all bedrooms STV Xmas **CONF:** Thtr 60 Class 40 Board 32 Del from £80 * **SERVICES:** Night porter 80P **NOTES:** No dogs (ex guide dogs) No smoking in restaurant Last d 9.30pm **CARDS:**

See advert on opposite page

LEAMINGTON SPA (ROYAL) Warwickshire **Map 04 SP36**
★★★ Manor House
Avenue Rd CV31 3NJ
REGAL
Quality Percentage Score: 60%
☎ 01926 423251 Fax 01926 425933
***Dir:** 500yds from railway station*

Near the town centre, this Victorian hotel offers well equipped bedrooms which vary in style and size. The spacious lounge and bar and the atmospheric restaurant all add to the character of the building.
ROOMS: 53 en suite (bth/shr) (2 fmly) No smoking in 19 bedrooms s fr £80; d fr £95 * LB Off peak **MEALS:** Lunch fr £10.95 Dinner £16.50-£22.75 & alc V meals Coffee am Tea pm **FACILITIES:** CTV in all bedrooms Reduced price at nearby leisure club Xmas **CONF:** Thtr 120 Class 46 Board 40 Del from £80 * **SERVICES:** Lift Night porter 70P **NOTES:** No smoking in restaurant Last d 9.30pm
CARDS:

LEAMINGTON SPA (ROYAL) Warwickshire **Map 04 SP36**
★★ Adams
22 Avenue Rd CV31 3PQ
Quality Percentage Score: 71%
☎ 01926 450742 Fax 01926 313110
***Dir:** situated near Library on A452*

This impeccably maintained Georgian house is located just south of the town centre. Public rooms are tastefully furnished and include a comfortable lounge and smart bar - home cooked meals can be enjoyed in the elegant dining room. Bedrooms are individually furnished with quality soft furnishings, all are well equipped.
ROOMS: 14 en suite (bth/shr) s £52.50-£64; d £64 (incl. bkfst) * LB Off peak **MEALS:** V meals Coffee am Tea pm **FACILITIES:** CTV in all bedrooms STV Xmas **CONF:** Class 20 Board 12 **SERVICES:** 14P **NOTES:** No dogs No coaches No smoking in restaurant
CARDS:

LEAMINGTON SPA (ROYAL) Warwickshire **Map 04 SP36**

The Premier Collection

★ Lansdowne
87 Clarendon St CV32 4PF
THE CIRCLE Selected Individual Hotels GREAT BRITAIN
☎ 01926 450505 Fax 01926 421313
***Dir:** town centre at junct of Clarendon St & Warwick St*

David and Gillian Allen and their small team provide consistently charming and caring service within this wonderful small hotel. A Regency property, it is located just a short walk from the town centre. Bedrooms are individually decorated, attractively furnished and equipped with a good range of facilities. The comfortably appointed public rooms include a quiet lounge, a small bar and a pleasant dining room, in which Chef Lucinda Robinson provides a short and interesting set-priced carte, where

quality fresh ingredients are carefully cooked and attractively presented.

ROOMS: 14 en suite (bth/shr) (1 fmly) **MEALS:** Dinner £18.95-£22.85 English, French & Italian Cuisine V meals **FACILITIES:** CTV in all bedrooms **SERVICES:** 11P **NOTES:** No dogs (ex guide dogs) No coaches No children 5yrs No smoking in restaurant Last d 9.30pm RS 26 Dec-2 Jan **CARDS:**

LEATHERHEAD Surrey **Map 04 TQ15**
★★ Bookham Grange
Little Bookham Common, Bookham KT23 3HS
MINOTEL Great Britain
Quality Percentage Score: 60%
☎ 01372 452742 Fax 01372 450080
***Dir:** off A246 first right after Bookham Railway station*

Quietly situated in two-and-a-half acres, this family-run hotel has all the style of an English country house. The accommodation has been upgraded and the new bedrooms are

contd.

well equipped. As well as two popular function and meeting rooms, there is a beamed bar, central sitting area and restaurant. The hotel is convenient for Bookham railway station for access to London.

ROOMS: 21 en suite (bth/shr) (3 fmly) s £64-£70; d £85 (incl. bkfst) * LB Off peak **MEALS:** Lunch fr £13.50 Dinner fr £13.50 International Cuisine V meals Coffee am Tea pm **FACILITIES:** CTV in all bedrooms Xmas **CONF:** Thtr 80 Class 24 Board 24 **SERVICES:** 100P **NOTES:** No smoking area in restaurant Last d 9.30pm **CARDS:**

LEDBURY Herefordshire — Map 03 SO73

★★★ Feathers

High St HR8 1DS

Quality Percentage Score: 72%

☎ 01531 635266 Fax 01531 638955

Dir: *S from Worcester A449, E from HerefordA438, N from Gloucester A417, hotel is situated in the High Street*

Standing in the centre of town, this timber-framed coaching inn has a wealth of charm and character. There is a comfortable lounge and "Fuggles" bar/bistro, where a wide range of soundly prepared dishes is available. Considerable improvements have been made, including the building of a leisure centre and a function suite. New bedrooms have also been added, and these, like the original accomodation, are individually styled and well equipped.

ROOMS: 19 en suite (bth/shr) (2 fmly) No smoking in 2 bedrooms s £69.50-£77.50; d £89.50-£105 (incl. bkfst) * LB Off peak **MEALS:** Lunch £15.70-£29.20alc Dinner £15.70-£29.20alc V meals Coffee am Tea pm **FACILITIES:** CTV in all bedrooms STV Indoor swimming pool (heated) Solarium Gym Jacuzzi/spa Steam room Wkly live entertainment Xmas **CONF:** Thtr 150 Class 80 Board 40 Del £130 * **SERVICES:** Night porter 30P **NOTES:** Last d 9pm **CARDS:**

See advert on opposite page

LEDBURY Herefordshire — Map 03 SO73

★★ The Verzons Country House

Trumpet HR8 2PZ

Quality Percentage Score: 65%

☎ 01531 670381 Fax 01531 670830

Dir: *3m W of Ledbury A438*

This large country house dates back to 1790, and stands in extensive gardens near Ledbury. Bedrooms are well equipped, and many have views of the Malvern Hills. Public areas include a bar, a lounge, an adjacent bistro-style restaurant, and a larger traditionally furnished dining room, which is also available for functions and meetings.

ROOMS: 9 en suite (bth/shr) (2 fmly) s fr £49; d fr £69 (incl. bkfst) * LB Off peak **MEALS:** Sunday Lunch £5.25-£11.95 Dinner £5.95-£25 English & French Cuisine V meals Coffee am **FACILITIES:** CTV in all bedrooms **CONF:** Thtr 50 Class 25 Board 20 Del from £70 * **SERVICES:** 60P **NOTES:** Last d 9.15pm Closed 25 Dec **CARDS:**

LEEDS West Yorkshire — Map 08 SE33

see also **Shipley**

★★★★★ Oulton Hall

Rothwell Ln, Oulton LS26 8HN

DE VERE HOTELS

Quality Percentage Score: 67%

☎ 0113 282 1000 Fax 0113 282 8066

Dir: *2m from M62 junct 30/A639 on the left hand side, or 1m from M1 junct 44 then follow signs to Castleford/Pontefract A639.*

Restored and sympathetically extended, this 19th-century house offers a range of facilities. Public rooms including the galleried Great Hall, have a stately elegance, whilst bedrooms enjoy fine views over the grounds and championship golf course. There is a well-equipped indoor leisure centre and a range of function suites.

ROOMS: 152 en suite (bth/shr) No smoking in 128 bedrooms s fr £140; d fr £160 (incl. bkfst) * LB Off peak **MEALS:** Lunch £15 Dinner £23 & alc English & French Cuisine V meals Coffee am Tea pm **FACILITIES:** CTV in all bedrooms STV Indoor swimming pool (heated) Golf 27 Squash Snooker Sauna Solarium Gym Croquet lawn Jacuzzi/spa Beauty therapy Aerobics ch fac Xmas **CONF:** Thtr 350 Class 150 Board 40 Del £175 * **SERVICES:** Lift Night porter 260P **NOTES:** No smoking in restaurant Last d 9.45pm **CARDS:**

See advert on opposite page

LEEDS West Yorkshire — Map 08 SE33

★★★★ Leeds Marriott

4 Trevelyan Square, Boar Ln LS1 6ET

Marriott HOTELS · RESORTS · SUITES

Quality Percentage Score: 70%

☎ 0113 236 6366 Fax 0113 236 6367

Dir: *from M1 or M62 follow signs to City Centre turn into Sovereign St, left at lights right into NCP car park adjacent to the hotel*

A large, modern hotel in a pedestrianised square in the city centre, offering spacious bedrooms comfortably furnished and equipped. John T's serves light meals from an all day menu, chef Peter McMahon displays his talents in Dysons, named after a jeweller and clock maker, and appropriately themed. A variety of function rooms and leisure centre are available.

ROOMS: 244 en suite (bth/shr) (26 fmly) No smoking in 184 bedrooms s £105-£109; d £105-£109 * LB Off peak **MEALS:** Lunch £5-£18.50alc Dinner £5-£18.50alc International Cuisine V meals Coffee am Tea pm **FACILITIES:** CTV in all bedrooms STV Indoor swimming pool (heated) Sauna Solarium Gym Jacuzzi/spa Subsidised use of NCP car park Xmas **CONF:** Thtr 280 Class 120 Board 80 Del from £135 * **SERVICES:** Lift Night porter Air conditioning **NOTES:** No smoking area in restaurant Last d 10.30pm **CARDS:**

LEEDS West Yorkshire **Map 08 SE33**

★★★★ ***Queen's***

City Square LS1 1PL

Quality Percentage Score: 69%

☎ 0113 243 1323 0113 242 5154

Dir: *follow signs for City Centre, hotel adjacent to the railway station in City Square*

This former railway hotel has been sympathetically restored to ensure that much of its original splendour is retained. Rooms include the comfortable Palm Court Lounge, the elegant Harewood Restaurant, the Carvery Restaurant and the popular Leaders Bar. Bedrooms are spacious and well furnished, while some still contain the sturdy furniture which was made especially for the hotel when it opened. Staff are friendly and helpful and the porters, elegantly dressed in tail coats and top hats, will arrange for cars to be taken to the hotel car park.

ROOMS: 199 en suite (bth/shr) No smoking in 72 bedrooms **MEALS:** International Cuisine V meals Coffee am Tea pm **FACILITIES:** CTV in all bedrooms STV **CONF:** Thtr 600 Class 160 Board 40 **SERVICES:** Lift Night porter 88P **NOTES:** No smoking area in restaurant Last d 10pm **CARDS:**

LEEDS West Yorkshire **Map 08 SE33**

★★★★ **Crowne Plaza Leeds**

Wellington St LS1 4DL

Quality Percentage Score: 68%

☎ 0113 244 2200 0113 244 0460

Dir: *from M1 follow signs to City Centre, at City Square left into Wellington Street*

This large modern hotel provides a number of suites and also rooms dedicated to lady guests. There are two eating options, Hamilton's Restaurant and the more informal Buongiorno's, which specialises in Italian food. There is also a Leisure Centre and numerous conference and function rooms.

ROOMS: 135 en suite (bth/shr) (38 fmly) No smoking in 90 bedrooms d £98-£135 * LB Off peak **MEALS:** Lunch £11.95-£30alc High tea £6.95-£9.95alc Dinner £14-£30alc International Cuisine V meals Coffee am Tea pm **FACILITIES:** CTV in all bedrooms STV Indoor swimming pool (heated) Sauna Solarium Gym Jacuzzi/spa Steam room Childrens playroom Xmas **CONF:** Thtr 200 Class 100 Board 60 Del from £120 * **SERVICES:** Lift Night porter Air conditioning 125P **NOTES:** No dogs (ex guide dogs) No smoking area in restaurant Last d 10.30pm **CARDS:**

LEEDS West Yorkshire **Map 08 SE33**

★★★★ **Metropole**

King St LS1 2HQ

Quality Percentage Score: 65%

☎ 0113 245 0841 0113 242 5156

Dir: *from M1/M62/M621 follow signs for City Centre. Take A65 Airport into Wellington St, at first traffic Island turn right into King St Hotel on right*

This splendid terracotta-fronted hotel stands in the heart of the city. Well equipped bedrooms range in style from standard to 'executive, and public areas include Lloyds Bar and a separate restaurant. Staff are helpful and valet parking is provided.

ROOMS: 118 en suite (bth/shr) No smoking in 98 bedrooms s £99-£119; d £119-£139 * LB Off peak **MEALS:** Lunch fr £12 Dinner fr £16.95 & alc V meals Coffee am Tea pm **FACILITIES:** CTV in all bedrooms STV **CONF:** Thtr 250 Class 100 Board 80 Del from £145 * **SERVICES:** Lift Night porter 40P **NOTES:** No dogs (ex guide dogs) No smoking in restaurant Last d 9.30pm RS 26 Dec-1 Jan **CARDS:**

LEEDS West Yorkshire **Map 08 SE33**

★★ Haley's Hotel & Restaurant

Shire Oak Rd, Headingley LS6 2DE
Quality Percentage Score: 80%
☎ 0113 278 4446 0113 275 3342
Dir: *from city centre follow local signs to University on A660, 1.5m turn right in Headingley between Midland and Yorkshire Banks*
A stone-built Victorian house set in a tree-lined cul-de-sac, convenient for the county cricket ground. Individually styled bedrooms and reception rooms are richly decorated and furnished with fine antiques. The staff are courteous and dedicated, and Jon Vennell's modern British cooking continues to impress.

ROOMS: 22 en suite (bth/shr) 7 annexe en suite (bth/shr) (3 fmly) No smoking in 10 bedrooms s £110-£117; d £130-£150 (incl. bkfst) * LB Off peak **MEALS:** Sunday Lunch £13.95 Dinner £19.99 & alc V meals Coffee am **FACILITIES:** CTV in all bedrooms STV **CONF:** Thtr 30 Class 20 Board 25 Del from £122 * **SERVICES:** Night porter 25P **NOTES:** No dogs (ex guide dogs) No coaches No smoking in restaurant Last d 9.45pm Closed 26-30 Dec RS Sun
CARDS:

See advert on opposite page

LEEDS West Yorkshire **Map 08 SE33**

★★★ The Merrion

Merrion Centre LS2 8NH
Quality Percentage Score: 69%
☎ 0113 243 9191 0113 242 3527
PEEL HOTELS
Dir: *from the M1/M62/A61 join city loop road to junct 7, the Hotel is situated on Wade Lane adjoining the Merrion Centre*
Situated to the north of the city centre, this modern hotel can be entered from the next-door car park. There are comfortable, well equipped bedrooms, and the public rooms include a restaurant and bar with an art deco theme, an open-plan lounge and a conference suite. It is wise to phone for directions.
ROOMS: 109 en suite (bth/shr) No smoking in 76 bedrooms s £109; d £119 * LB Off peak **MEALS:** Lunch fr £14.75 Dinner fr £14.75 English & French Cuisine V meals Coffee am Tea pm **FACILITIES:** CTV in all bedrooms STV Xmas **CONF:** Thtr 80 Class 25 Board 25 Del from £110 * **SERVICES:** Lift Night porter P **NOTES:** No smoking in restaurant Last d 10.15pm **CARDS:**

Remember to return your Prize Draw card for a chance to win one of 30 relaxing leisure breaks with Corus and Regal hotels. See inside the front cover for the card and competition details.

LEEDS West Yorkshire **Map 08 SE33**

★★★ Milford Lodge Hotel

A1 Great North Rd, Peckfield LS25 5LQ
Quality Percentage Score: 69%
☎ 01977 681800 01977 681245
(For full entry see Garforth)
Best Western

LEEDS West Yorkshire **Map 08 SE33**

★★★ Golden Lion

2 Lower Briggate LS1 4AE
Quality Percentage Score: 64%
☎ 0113 243 6454 0113 242 9327
PEEL HOTELS
Dir: *between junct 16 (Bridge End) and 17 (Sovereign Street). Hotel situated on junct of Lower Briggate & Swinegate*
This centrally situated hotel is one of Leeds oldest, but the accommodation provided has every modern facility. Staff are particularly friendly and helpful and the atmosphere is warm and informal. Meeting and conference facilities are available and free parking is provided nearby.
ROOMS: 89 en suite (bth/shr) (5 fmly) No smoking in 29 bedrooms s £99; d £110 (incl. bkfst) * LB Off peak **MEALS:** Lunch £6.50-£8.95 Dinner £13.50-£15.95 V meals Coffee am **FACILITIES:** CTV in all bedrooms STV Xmas **CONF:** Thtr 120 Class 65 Board 45 Del from £110 * **SERVICES:** Lift Night porter 60P **NOTES:** No smoking area in restaurant Last d 9pm **CARDS:**

LEEDS West Yorkshire **Map 08 SE33**

★★★ Posthouse Leeds/Selby

LS25 5LF
Quality Percentage Score: 64%
☎ 01977 682711 01977 685462
(For full entry see Lumby)
Posthouse

LEEDS West Yorkshire **Map 08 SE33**

★ Aragon

250 Stainbeck Ln LS7 2PS
Quality Percentage Score: 65%
☎ 0113 275 9306 0113 275 7166
Dir: *off A61 2.5m N from city centre*
This attractive stone building stands in a leafy part of north Leeds and in its own well tended gardens. It provides bright and modern bedrooms together with comfortable public rooms. The service is both polite and attentive.
ROOMS: 12 en suite (bth/shr) (2 fmly) No smoking in all bedrooms s £42.90; d £52.90 (incl. bkfst) * Off peak **MEALS:** Dinner £9.90-£12.90 Coffee am Tea pm **FACILITIES:** CTV in all bedrooms **CONF:** Thtr 16 Board 16 **SERVICES:** 20P **NOTES:** No coaches No smoking in restaurant Closed 25 Dec-1 Jan **CARDS:**

LEEDS West Yorkshire **Map 08 SE33**

42 The Calls

LS2 7EW

☎ 0113 244 0099 📠 0113 234 4100

Dir: *leave city centre loop road at junct 15 (The Calls). Hotel next to Calls Landing*

This wonderful conversion of a canal side warehouse provides luxury bedrooms complete with many thoughtful extras and comforts. All have CD players as well as large writing desks and mini bars. Breakfast may be taken either in the bedrooms or in the breakfast room which overlooks the canal. There are many good restaurants nearby and one of these is located just next door.

ROOMS: 41 en suite (bth/shr) No smoking in 6 bedrooms s £95-£140; d £125-£145 * LB Off peak **MEALS:** V meals Coffee am Tea pm **FACILITIES:** CTV in all bedrooms STV Fishing **CONF:** Thtr 55 Class 40 Board 42 Del from £160.95 * **SERVICES:** Lift Night porter 28P **NOTES:** No coaches Closed 5 days Xmas **CARDS:**

LEEDS West Yorkshire **Map 08 SE33**

Travel Inn (Leeds Airport)

Victoria Av, Yeadon LS19 7AW

☎ 0113 250 4284 📠 0113 250 5838

Dir: *on A658, less than 2mins drive from Leeds/Bradford Airport*

This modern building offers accommodation in smart, spacious and well equipped bedrooms, all with en-suite bathrooms. Refreshments may be taken at the nearby family restaurant. For details about current prices consult the Contents Page under Hotel Groups for the Travel Inn phone number.

ROOMS: 40 en suite (bth/shr) d £39.95 *

LEEDS West Yorkshire **Map 08 SE33**

Travel Inn (Leeds Centre)

Citygate, Wellington St LS3 1LW

☎ 0113 242 8104 📠 0113 242 8105

Dir: *on junct of A65 with A58 inner ring road*

This modern building offers accommodation in smart, spacious and well equipped bedrooms, all with en-suite bathrooms. Refreshments may be taken at the nearby family restauarant. For details about current prices ring 01582 41 43 41.

ROOMS: 84 en suite (bth/shr) d £44.95 *

LEEDS West Yorkshire **Map 08 SE33**

Travel Inn (Leeds South)

Wakefield Rd, Drighlington BD11 1EA

☎ 0113 287 9132 📠 0113 287 9115

Dir: *on Drighlington bypass, adjacent M62 junct 27*

This modern building offers accommodation in smart, spacious and well equipped bedrooms, all with en-suite bathrooms. Refreshments may be taken at the nearby family restaurant. For details about current prices consult the Contents Page under Hotel Groups for the Travel Inn phone number.

ROOMS: 42 en suite (bth/shr) d £39.95 *

LEEDS West Yorkshire **Map 08 SE33**

Malmaison Hotel Leeds

Kings House, 1 Swinegate LS1 1DQ

☎ 0141 221 1052

ROOMS: 100 en suite (bth/shr) **NOTES:** Due to open Summer 1999

LEEK Staffordshire **Map 07 SJ95**

★★ Three Horseshoes Inn & Restaurant

Buxton Rd, Blackshaw Moor ST13 8TW

Quality Percentage Score: 63%

☎ 01538 300296 📠 01538 300320

Dir: *2m N of Leek on the A53 Leek/Buxton Road*

This family owned and run hostelry stands in its own spacious

contd.

grounds and attractive gardens, which include a beer garden and a play area for young children. There are impressive views from the garden towards the Roches and Tittesworth Reservoir. Bedrooms are tastefully appointed and furnished in a style befitting the character of the hotel. The public areas are traditional in style and include a choice of bars and eating options.
ROOMS: 6 en suite (bth/shr) No smoking in all bedrooms s £45-£55; d £60-£70 (incl. bkfst) * LB Off peak **MEALS:** Lunch £12.95 & alc Dinner £7.50-£21alc International Cuisine V meals Coffee am **FACILITIES:** CTV in all bedrooms Wkly live entertainment **SERVICES:** 80P **NOTES:** No dogs (ex guide dogs) No smoking in restaurant Last d 9pm Closed 24 Dec-1 Jan
CARDS:

LEE-ON-THE-SOLENT Hampshire — Map 04 SU50

★★★ Belle Vue

39 Marine Pde East PO13 9BW
Quality Percentage Score: 61%
☎ 023 92550258 023 92552624
Dir: *M27 junct9/11 to Fareham follow signs to Lee-on-Solent, hotel is on seafront*

Set on the seafront, this popular hotel enjoys views across to the Isle of Wight. The bedrooms are undergoing a refurbishment programme and are comfortably furnished. Public rooms include a spacious bar and an attractive restaurant offering a wide range of popular dishes.
ROOMS: 24 en suite (bth/shr) 3 annexe en suite (bth/shr) (4 fmly) s £47.50-£73.50; d £67.50-£73.50 * LB Off peak **MEALS:** Lunch £17.50 & alc Dinner £17.50 & alc English & Continental Cuisine V meals Coffee am **FACILITIES:** CTV in all bedrooms STV Wkly live entertainment **CONF:** Thtr 150 Class 60 Board 40 Del from £79.50 * **SERVICES:** Night porter 55P **NOTES:** No smoking area in restaurant Last d 9.45pm Closed 25-28 Dec RS 24 Dec **CARDS:**

LEICESTER Leicestershire — Map 04 SK50

★★★ Belmont House

Best Western

De Montfort St LE1 7GR
Quality Percentage Score: 72%
☎ 0116 254 4773 0116 247 0804
Dir: *from A6 in S direction, take first right after BR station, 200yds on right*

Close to the station and town centre, Belmont House is well suited to the needs of the midweek business user or the weekend leisure guest. The extensive public areas have a cosy, welcoming feel to them. There are a choice of dining options, the lower-ground floor Bistro providing informal meals, or the more formal Cherries Restaurant; service is both professional and friendly. The bedrooms are thoughtfully designed and well equipped. A major upgrading programme is underway.
ROOMS: 75 rms (74 bth/shr) (7 fmly) No smoking in 40 bedrooms s £85-£95; d £93-£103 * LB Off peak **MEALS:** Lunch £12.95-£13.95 Dinner £19-£24 English & French Cuisine V meals Coffee am Tea pm **FACILITIES:** CTV in all bedrooms Wkly live entertainment **CONF:** Thtr 120 Class 60 Board 50 Del from £106 * **SERVICES:** Lift Night porter 60P **NOTES:** No smoking area in restaurant Last d 9.45pm Closed 24 Dec-2 Jan **CARDS:**

See advert on opposite page

LEICESTER Leicestershire — Map 04 SK50

★★★ *Posthouse Leicester*

Posthouse

Braunstone Ln East LE3 2FW
Quality Percentage Score: 68%
☎ 0116 263 0500 0116 282 3623
Dir: *from junct 21 of M1 at M69 interchange take A5460 and continue towards city to hotel 1m on right*

A feature of this recently refurbished hotel is the warmth and friendliness reflected by staff throughout. Additional services include 24-hour room service and an all day lounge menu. Meeting and conference facilities are available.
ROOMS: 172 en suite (bth/shr) (35 fmly) No smoking in 110 bedrooms **MEALS:** International Cuisine V meals Coffee am Tea pm **FACILITIES:** CTV in all bedrooms **CONF:** Thtr 85 Class 54 Board 45 **SERVICES:** Lift Night porter 300P **NOTES:** No smoking area in restaurant Last d 10pm **CARDS:**

LEICESTER Leicestershire — Map 04 SK50

★★★ Hermitage

REGAL

Wigston Rd, Oadby LE2 5QE
Quality Percentage Score: 66%
☎ 0116 256 9955 0116 272 0559/272 0686
Dir: *from city centre follow A6 Market Harborough. After 4m pass ASDA on left turn right at lights for Oadby Village and over rdbt to hotel on left*

Located in a residential area, this modern hotel appeals to business guests. Bedrooms are well equipped and there is a good range of meeting and function suites. Service is efficient and friendly.
ROOMS: 57 en suite (bth/shr) (4 fmly) No smoking in 16 bedrooms s fr £75; d fr £85 * LB Off peak **MEALS:** Lunch fr £9.95 Dinner fr £14.95 European Cuisine V meals Coffee am Tea pm **FACILITIES:** CTV in all bedrooms Xmas **CONF:** Thtr 250 Class 100 Board 60 Del from £115 * **SERVICES:** Lift Night porter 160P **NOTES:** No smoking in restaurant Last d 9.45pm **CARDS:**

LEICESTER Leicestershire **Map 04 SK50**

★★★ **Time Out Hotel & Leisure**

Enderby Rd, Blaby LE8 4GD

corus
Corus and Regal hotels

Quality Percentage Score: 66%

☎ 0116 278 7898 Fax 0116 278 1974

Dir: *M1 junct.21, A5460 towards Leicester take 4th exit at 1st rdbt, ahead at 2nd, left at 3rd follow signs to Blaby, over 4th rdbt Hotel on left*

Adjacent to the link road on the outskirts of the city, this small hotel provides bright, comfortable bedrooms with good accommodation and leisure facilities.

ROOMS: 48 en suite (bth/shr) (2 fmly) No smoking in 26 bedrooms s fr £80; d fr £85 * LB Off peak **MEALS:** Sunday Lunch £10.95-£11.95 & alc Dinner £15.45-£18.45 & alc English & Mediterranean Cuisine V meals Coffee am Tea pm **FACILITIES:** CTV in all bedrooms STV Indoor swimming pool (heated) Sauna Solarium Gym Jacuzzi/spa Xmas **CONF:** Thtr 70 Class 30 Board 36 Del from £85 * **SERVICES:** Night porter 110P **NOTES:** Last d 9.45pm

CARDS:

contd.

LEICESTER Leicestershire **Map 04 SK50**

★★★ Leicester Stage Hotel

Leicester Rd, Wigston LE18 1JW

Quality Percentage Score: 65%

☎ 0116 288 6161 Fax 0116 281 1874

Dir: *on A5199*

An imposing glass fronted building to the south of the city centre, the Stage's smart public areas are impressive. In recent years, major investment has dramatically upgraded the conference, leisure and downstairs areas. It is planned that similar positive results will be achieved in the bedrooms in the near future, and they offer all the expected amenities and comfort; executive rooms and four poster bridal suites are worth requesting.

ROOMS: 75 en suite (bth/shr) (10 fmly) No smoking in 9 bedrooms s £85; d £99 (incl. bkfst) * LB Off peak **MEALS:** Lunch £8.95-£12.25 Dinner £17.50 & alc International Cuisine V meals Coffee am Tea pm **FACILITIES:** CTV in all bedrooms STV Indoor swimming pool (heated) Sauna Solarium Gym Jacuzzi/spa Xmas **CONF:** Thtr 450 Class 200 Board 100 Del from £75 * **SERVICES:** Night porter 200P **NOTES:** No dogs (ex guide dogs) No smoking area in restaurant Last d 9.45pm **CARDS:**

LEICESTER Leicestershire **Map 04 SK50**

★★★ Regency

360 London Rd LE2 2PL

Quality Percentage Score: 64%

☎ 0116 270 9634 Fax 0116 2701375

Dir: *on the A6 London Road 1.5m from the city centre, near outer ring road which leads to the M1 & M9 approx 4m away*

Originally a convent, this busy hotel has been completely modernised and now provides bright and well equipped accommodation. The well fitted bedrooms are attractively decorated with rich fabrics and there are several honeymoon suites. The new conservatory brasserie, just off the comfortable lounge bar, is an informal alternative to the restaurant which offers more formal dining and occasional specially themed dinners.

ROOMS: 32 en suite (bth/shr) (4 fmly) s £46-£52; d £62-£67 (incl. bkfst) * Off peak **MEALS:** Lunch £8-£10.95 & alc Dinner fr £11.95 & alc English & French Cuisine V meals Coffee am **FACILITIES:** CTV in all bedrooms Wkly live entertainment Xmas **CONF:** Thtr 70 Class 50 Board 30 Del from £71.50 * **SERVICES:** Night porter 40P **NOTES:** No dogs (ex guide dogs) Last d 9.45pm **CARDS:**

See advert on opposite page

LEICESTER Leicestershire **Map 04 SK50**

★★★ *Saint James*

Abbey St LE1 3TE

Quality Percentage Score: 58%

☎ 0116 251 0666 Fax 0116 251 5183

Dir: *turn right after St Margaret's bus station*

Public areas and accommodation at this hotel are modern in style, guests have the use of a comfortable open plan lounge area, a small bar and a galleried restaurant which has views out over the city skyline; these areas are scheduled for redecoration over the coming year. Bedrooms have benefited from a recent refurbishment, the new richly coloured soft furnishings and decor give the rooms a lift and all have light-wood fitted furniture and a good range of modern facilities.

ROOMS: 73 en suite (bth/shr) (3 fmly) **MEALS:** English & French Cuisine V meals Coffee am Tea pm **FACILITIES:** CTV in all bedrooms **CONF:** Thtr 200 Class 120 Board 35 Del from £60 * **SERVICES:** Lift Night porter **NOTES:** Last d 9.30pm **CARDS:**

LEICESTER Leicestershire **Map 04 SK50**

★★ Red Cow

Hinckley Rd, Leicester Forest East LE3 3PG

Quality Percentage Score: 68%

☎ 0116 238 7878 Fax 0116 238 6539

Dir: *follow A47 out of Leicester towards Hinckley, hotel is on right approx 4m from city centre*

To the west of Leicester this is a modern and popular pub restaurant with an adjacent bedroom block. A good range of food is available in the bar, restaurant and conservatory; the latter overlooks a rear garden and is set aside for families. The accommodation is modern and well equipped.

ROOMS: 31 en suite (bth/shr) (26 fmly) No smoking in 23 bedrooms s £28.50-£39.50; d £28.50-£39.50 * Off peak **MEALS:** Bar Lunch £8.25-£13.95 & alc Dinner £8.25-£13.95 & alc English & French Cuisine V meals Coffee am Tea pm **FACILITIES:** CTV in all bedrooms **SERVICES:** 120P **NOTES:** No dogs (ex guide dogs) No smoking area in restaurant Last d 10pm **CARDS:**

See advert on opposite page

LEICESTER Leicestershire **Map 04 SK50**

★★ Charnwood

48 Leicester Rd, Narborough LE9 5DF

Quality Percentage Score: 65%

☎ 0116 286 2218 Fax 0116 275 0119

Dir: *junct 21 of M1 follow B4114 to Narborough*

Recently refurbished and altered public rooms are smart and cheerful. An attractive restaurant with small dispense bar, separate bar and comfortable seating overlooks gardens. Bar meals supplement a carte offering traditional and international dishes. Bedroom refurbishment is underway, completed rooms are equipped with useful facilities. The hotel is a popular venue for weddings.

ROOMS: 20 en suite (bth/shr) s £45; d £63 (incl. bkfst) * Off peak **MEALS:** Lunch £11.95-£13.50 & alc Dinner £13.50 & alc International Cuisine V meals Coffee am Tea pm **FACILITIES:** CTV in all bedrooms **CONF:** Thtr 50 Class 20 Board 30 Del £77 * **SERVICES:** 30P **NOTES:** No coaches No smoking area in restaurant Last d 9.30pm Closed 26 Dec-3 Jan **CARDS:**

LEICESTER Leicestershire **Map 04 SK50**

★★ *Old Tudor Rectory*

Main St, Glenfield LE3 8DG

Quality Percentage Score: 60%

☎ 0116 2915678 Fax 0116 2911416

Dir: *from M1 exit 21A follow signs for Kirby Muxloe (B5380), then Glenfield. Hotel on right on entering village opposite The Forge Inn*

This popular traditional Grade II listed hotel is situated west of Leicester in the village of Glenfield. The public areas offer a comfortable small lounge bar and an adjoining dining room, with a separate restaurant situated in the grounds. Bedrooms vary considerably in style and size, but all are attractively decorated.

ROOMS: 15 en suite (bth/shr) 1 annexe en suite (bth/shr) (2 fmly) **MEALS:** English & French Cuisine V meals Coffee am Tea pm **FACILITIES:** CTV in all bedrooms Jacuzzi/spa Beauty salon **CONF:** Thtr 20 Class 20 Board 20 **SERVICES:** 37P **NOTES:** Last d 9.30pm Closed 24 Dec-1 Jan **CARDS:**

See advert on opposite page

New AA Guides for the Millennium are featured on page 24

LEICESTER Leicestershire **Map 04 SK50**

★★ ***Gables***

368 London Rd LE2 2PN

Quality Percentage Score: 58%

☎ 0116 270 6969 Fax 0116 270 6969

Dir: *0.5m city side of junction A563 (South East) and A6*

This privately owned commercial hotel is located south of the city centre and conveniently placed for the university. The public rooms include a restaurant and a cosy lounge bar; an adjoining room serves as a popular venue for business meetings and local functions.

ROOMS: 30 en suite (bth/shr) (9 fmly) **MEALS:** English & French Cuisine V meals Coffee am **FACILITIES:** CTV in all bedrooms **CONF:** Thtr 60 Class 12 Board 28 **SERVICES:** 29P **NOTES:** No dogs (ex guide dogs) No coaches No smoking in restaurant Last d 9.30pm

CARDS:

LEICESTER Leicestershire **Map 04 SK50**

Travel Inn

Hinckley Rd, Leicester Forest East LE3 3GD

☎ 0116 239 4677 Fax 0116 239 3429

Dir: *from M1 junct 21 take A5460 over rdbt to 1st traffic lights. Left down Braunstone Lane. At 2nd traffic lights turn left onto A47, Travel Inn 0.25m*

This modern building offers accommodation in smart, spacious and well equipped bedrooms, all with en-suite bathrooms. Refreshments may be taken at the nearby family restaurant. For details about current prices consult the Contents Page under Hotel Groups for the Travel Inn phone number.

ROOMS: 40 en suite (bth/shr) d £39.95 *

LEICESTER Leicestershire **Map 04 SK50**

Travel Inn (Braunstone)
Meridian Business Park, Meridian Way,
Braunstone LE3 2LW
☎ 0116 289 0945 Fax 0116 282 7486
Dir: *from M1 junct 21 follow sign to Leicester ring road, take 1st slip road on left at next rdbt take 3rd exit left onto A563, Travel Inn 0.5m on left*
This modern building offers accommodation in smart, spacious and well equipped bedrooms, all with en-suite bathrooms. Refreshments may be taken at the nearby family restaurant. For details about current prices consult the Contents Page under Hotel Groups for the Travel Inn phone number.
ROOMS: 50 en suite (bth/shr) d £39.95 *

LEIGH DELAMERE MOTORWAY SERVICE AREA (M4) Wiltshire **Map 03 ST87**

Travelodge
SN14 6LB
☎ Central Res 0800 850950 Fax 01666 837112
Dir: *Between junc 17 & 18 on the M4*
This modern building offers accommodation in smart, spacious and well equipped bedrooms, all with en-suite bathrooms. Refreshments may be taken at the nearby family restaurant. For details about current prices, consult the Contents Page under Hotel Groups for the Travelodge phone number.
ROOMS: 70 en suite (bth/shr) d £59.95 *

LENHAM Kent **Map 05 TQ85**

★★★★ **Chilston Park**
Sandway ME17 2BE
Quality Percentage Score: 69%
☎ 01622 859803 Fax 01622 858588
Dir: *turn right at x-roads in Lenham. Then left after 0.5m into Boughton Road. Straight over x-roads, and hotel is on left*

Chilston Park, standing in extensive grounds, is partly an antique-filled country house and partly modern. Many of the well equipped bedrooms have four-poster beds. Public areas include a range of meeting rooms and lounges, and well prepared dishes are served in the dining room.
ROOMS: 30 en suite (bth/shr) 23 annexe en suite (bth/shr) (2 fmly) s £125; d £145 * LB Off peak **MEALS:** Lunch £19.50 & alc High tea £6.50-£10.95 Dinner £29.50 & alc European Cuisine V meals Coffee am Tea pm **FACILITIES:** CTV in all bedrooms STV Tennis (hard) Fishing Croquet lawn 3/4 size Snooker table Xmas **CONF:** Thtr 120 Class 40 Board 44 Del £170 * **SERVICES:** Lift Night porter 100P **NOTES:** No smoking in restaurant Last d 9.30pm
CARDS:

LEOMINSTER Herefordshire **Map 03 SO45**

★★★ **Talbot**
West St HR6 8EP
Quality Percentage Score: 65%
☎ 01568 616347 Fax 01568 614880
Dir: *approach either from A49, A44 or A4112, the Hotel can be found at the centre of the town*
The charm and character of this former coaching inn is enhanced by exposed ceiling beams, antique furniture in the bars and welcoming fires. Bedrooms are well equipped and many have recently been refurbished. Facilities are available for private functions and conferences.
ROOMS: 20 en suite (bth/shr) (3 fmly) s £41-£46; d £56-£62 * LB Off peak **MEALS:** Lunch £11 & alc Dinner £17 & alc English & French Cuisine V meals Coffee am Tea pm **FACILITIES:** CTV in all bedrooms Xmas **CONF:** Thtr 150 Class 35 Board 28 Del £80 * **SERVICES:** 20P **NOTES:** No smoking in restaurant Last d 9pm
CARDS:

LEOMINSTER Herefordshire **Map 03 SO45**

★★ **Royal Oak**
South St HR6 8JA
Quality Percentage Score: 60%
☎ 01568 612610 Fax 01568 612710
Dir: *junct A44/A49*
This privately owned hotel is conveniently located in the town centre. It is personally run in an informal manner and provides warm and friendly hospitality. The recently refurbished public ares have charm and character and they include a bistro style restaurant.
ROOMS: 17 en suite (bth/shr) 1 annexe en suite (bth/shr) (2 fmly) No smoking in 2 bedrooms **MEALS:** Sunday Lunch £7.50 Dinner £10-£25 & alc V meals Coffee am **FACILITIES:** CTV in all bedrooms **CONF:** Thtr 220 Class 100 Board 50 Del from £66 * **SERVICES:** 25P **NOTES:** No smoking in restaurant Last d 9pm **CARDS:**

LEWDOWN Devon **Map 02 SX48**

The Premier Collection

★★★ **Lewtrenchard Manor**
EX20 4PN
☎ 01566 783256 & 783222
Fax 01566 783332
Dir: *A30 from Exeter turn on to Plymouth/Tavistock road. T-junct right and immediately left onto Old A30 Lewdown 6m turn left signposted Lewtrenchard*
Built around 1600, this delightful Jacobean manor house retains the atmosphere of a family home. Spacious, well equipped bedrooms have extensive views; day rooms have ornate ceilings, oak panelling and large fireplaces and are

contd.

richly furnished. The restaurant menus are interesting, and the array of desserts noteworthy.
ROOMS: 9 en suite (bth/shr) s £85-£100; d £110 (incl. bkfst) * LB Off peak **MEALS:** Lunch £19.50 High tea £6 Dinner £32 English & French Cuisine V meals Coffee am Tea pm **FACILITIES:** CTV in all bedrooms Fishing Croquet lawn Clay pigeon shooting Xmas **CONF:** Thtr 50 Class 40 Board 30 Del £140 * **SERVICES:** 50P **NOTES:** No coaches No children 7yrs No smoking in restaurant Last d 9pm **CARDS:**

LEWES East Sussex **Map 05 TQ41**

★★★ Shelleys Hotel

High St BN7 1XS
Quality Percentage Score: 77%
☎ 01273 472361 01273 483152

PEEL HOTELS

Dir: *A27 Lewes across crossroads hotel on left*

Dating back to the 17th century, Shelley's retains much of the ambience of a Georgian manor house. Bedrooms are particularly impressive, individually decorated in country-house style. The traditional feel is supported by modern conveniences, including well-appointed bathrooms. An interesting and sophisticated menu is served in the elegant dining room, which overlooks a peaceful garden.
ROOMS: 19 en suite (bth/shr) (2 fmly) No smoking in 4 bedrooms s £120; d £155 * LB Off peak **MEALS:** Lunch £17.50-£26.50 Dinner £17.50-£26.50 International Cuisine V meals Coffee am Tea pm **FACILITIES:** CTV in all bedrooms STV Wkly live entertainment Xmas **CONF:** Thtr 50 Class 20 Board 28 Del from £160 * **SERVICES:** Night porter 25P **NOTES:** No smoking in restaurant Last d 9.15pm **CARDS:**

LEWES East Sussex **Map 05 TQ41**

★★★ *White Hart*

55 High St BN7 1XE
Quality Percentage Score: 66%
☎ 01273 476694 01273 476695

Best Western

Dir: *from A27 follow signs for town centre. Hotel opposite County Court*

The first draft of the American constitution was written at this town-centre coaching inn. The hotel is a combination of the old and the new. A leisure centre and patio have been added to the original characterful bar and lounge and the panelled restaurant in the Victorian conservatory.
ROOMS: 23 rms (19 bth/shr) 29 annexe en suite (bth/shr) (3 fmly) **MEALS:** English and French Cuisine V meals Coffee am Tea pm **FACILITIES:** CTV in all bedrooms STV Indoor swimming pool (heated) Golf Sauna Solarium Gym Jacuzzi/spa Wkly live entertainment **CONF:** Thtr 250 Class 120 Board 90 Del from £70 * **SERVICES:** Night porter 40P **NOTES:** Last d 10.15pm **CARDS:**

See advert on this page

LEYBURN North Yorkshire **Map 07 SE19**

★ *Golden Lion*

Market Place DL8 5AS
Quality Percentage Score: 61%
☎ 01969 22161 01969 23836
Dir: *set on the A684 in Market Square*

Standing in the market square, this popular Georgian inn offers well equipped bedrooms. There is a good range of value for money food on offer in both the bar and the cosy dining room. The bar serves its own house beer called Oliver John. Staff are friendly and keen to please.
ROOMS: 15 rms (14 bth/shr) (5 fmly) **MEALS:** English & Continental Cuisine V meals Coffee am Tea pm **FACILITIES:** CTV in all bedrooms **SERVICES:** Lift **NOTES:** No coaches Last d 9pm Closed 25 & 26 Dec **CARDS:**

LICHFIELD Staffordshire **Map 07 SK10**

★★★ Little Barrow

Beacon St WS13 7AR
Quality Percentage Score: 66%
☎ 01543 414500 01543 415734
Dir: *200 yds from cathedral on right*

Conveniently situated for the cathedral and the city, this friendly family run hotel offers practical, well equipped accommodation. The cosy lounge bar, popular with locals and visitors alike, has a range of real ales and offers a choice of bar meals, alternatively, more formal meals are available in the bright restaurant.

contd.

A spacious function suite is also available for social functions and meetings.
ROOMS: 24 en suite (bth/shr) (2 fmly) s £55-£65; d £70-£80 (incl. bkfst) * LB Off peak **MEALS:** Lunch £9.50-£12.50 & alc Dinner £13-£15.50 & alc International Cuisine V meals Coffee am Tea pm **FACILITIES:** CTV in all bedrooms **CONF:** Thtr 80 Class 30 Board 30 Del £87 * **SERVICES:** Night porter 70P **NOTES:** No dogs (ex guide dogs) No smoking in restaurant Last d 9.30pm Closed 24-26 Dec
CARDS:

LICHFIELD Staffordshire — Map 07 SK10

★★ The Olde Corner House

Walsall Rd, Muckley Corner WS14 0BG
Quality Percentage Score: 66%
☎ 01543 372182 01543 372211
***Dir:** at junct of A5/A461 5 mins from A38*

This landmark coaching inn, at the junction of the A5 and A461, dates back to the 17th century in parts and much of the character remains, particularly in the public areas. These include two dining rooms, offering a range of well prepared dishes, and a popular bar as well as a separate comfortable lounge. Bedrooms in the newer wing tend to be slightly larger, but all are attractively furnished and well equipped. Service is informal and a warm welcome adds to the welcoming feel of the hotel.
ROOMS: 23 en suite (bth/shr) No smoking in all bedrooms s fr £39.95; d £55.95-£75 (incl. bkfst) * Off peak **MEALS:** Lunch £9.95 International Cuisine V meals Coffee am Tea pm **FACILITIES:** CTV in all bedrooms Pool table Xmas **CONF:** Thtr 24 Class 18 Del from £75 * **SERVICES:** 65P **NOTES:** No dogs No coaches
CARDS:

LICHFIELD Staffordshire — Map 07 SK10

★★ *Angel Croft*

Beacon St WS13 7AA
Quality Percentage Score: 61%
☎ 01543 258737 01543 415605
***Dir:** situated opposite main west gate entrance to Lichfield Cathedral*

Owned and run by the Hilpert family for over a quarter of a century, this traditional, Georgian hotel is close to the cathedral and city centre. Bedrooms are generally spacious, particularly those in the adjacent Westgate House. The comfortable lounge leads into a nicely appointed dining room, and the cosy bar is on lower ground level.
ROOMS: 10 rms (3 bth 5 shr) 8 annexe en suite (bth/shr) (1 fmly) **MEALS:** V meals Coffee am Tea pm **FACILITIES:** CTV in all bedrooms **SERVICES:** Night porter 60P **NOTES:** No dogs (ex guide dogs) No smoking in restaurant Last d 8.45pm Closed 25 & 26 Dec RS Sun evenings **CARDS:**

LIFTON Devon — Map 02 SX38

★★★❀❀❀ Arundell Arms

PL16 0AA
Quality Percentage Score: 75%
☎ 01566 784666 01566 784494
***Dir:** 40m West of Exeter and M5, 1m off A30 in Lifton Village*

Owned by Anne Voss-Bark, this delightful old inn, situated between Dartmoor and Bodmin Moor, is renowned for its excellent cuisine and its 20 miles of salmon and trout fishing. Bedrooms are decorated with restful colour schemes and lounge and bar have a relaxed, inviting atmosphere.

ROOMS: 23 en suite (bth/shr) 5 annexe en suite (bth/shr) s £44-£72; d £88-£110 (incl. bkfst) * LB Off peak **MEALS:** Lunch £19 & alc Dinner £28.50 & alc English & French Cuisine V meals Coffee am Tea pm **FACILITIES:** CTV in all bedrooms STV Fishing Skittle alley Games room Xmas **CONF:** Thtr 100 Class 36 Board 46 Del £107 * **SERVICES:** Night porter 80P **NOTES:** No coaches No smoking in restaurant Last d 9.30pm Closed 3 days Xmas & New Year **CARDS:**

See advert on opposite page

LIFTON Devon — Map 02 SX38

★★ Lifton Hall Country House

PL16 0DR
Quality Percentage Score: 72%
☎ 01566 784863 & 784263 01566 784770
***Dir:** off A30 at Lifton village exit*

This small, luxurious hotel maintains a traditional English style, especially in the bar, where an interesting range of bar meals is served. Bedrooms have individual character and charm, and there is an attractive drawing room for residents.
ROOMS: 11 en suite (bth/shr) (4 fmly) s £42-£48; d £75-£90 * LB Off peak **MEALS:** Bar Lunch £3.50-£12alc Dinner £25 & alc International Cuisine V meals Coffee am Tea pm **FACILITIES:** CTV in all bedrooms Fishing Falconry & hawking Xmas **SERVICES:** 30P **NOTES:** No smoking in restaurant Last d 9.30pm **CARDS:**

LIFTON Devon — Map 02 SX38

★★ *Thatched Cottage*

Sprytown PL16 0AY
Quality Percentage Score: 69%
☎ 01566 784224 01566 784334
***Dir:** leave A30 dual carriageway at Stowford Cross,turn S for 2m until Sprytown Cross is reached, straight across X-roads hotel on right*

This delightful thatched cottage hotel is set in lovely gardens, where there is a separate building housing the bedrooms. The main building contains the beamed lounge and restaurant. Sunday lunches and cream teas are a speciality.
ROOMS: 5 annexe en suite (bth/shr) **MEALS:** International Cuisine V meals Coffee am Tea pm **FACILITIES:** CTV in all bedrooms **CONF:** Thtr 20 Board 16 Del from £60 * **SERVICES:** 12P **NOTES:** No coaches No children 12yrs No smoking area in restaurant
CARDS:

AA Rosettes are awarded for quality of food, see page 15 for an explanation of Rosette assessment.

Indicates that the star classification has not been confirmed under the New Quality Standards, see page 7 for further information.

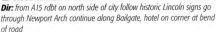

LINCOLN Lincolnshire **Map 08 SK97**
★★★★ The White Hart
Bailgate LN1 3AR
Quality Percentage Score: 59%
☎ 01522 526222 ▤ 01522 531798
Dir: *from A15 rdbt on north side of city follow historic Lincoln signs go through Newport Arch continue along Bailgate, hotel on corner at bend of road*
A centrally located hotel, with convenient car parking, between the castle and imposing cathedral. Bedrooms are attractively decorated and comfortably furnished, many have lovely views over the city. Public areas are traditional in style and furnished with some impressive antique pieces.
ROOMS: 48 en suite (bth/shr) (4 fmly) No smoking in 18 bedrooms d £95-£150 * LB Off peak **MEALS:** Lunch £10.95-£13.95alc Dinner £19.95-£25alc English & Continental Cuisine V meals Coffee am Tea pm **FACILITIES:** CTV in all bedrooms Wkly live entertainment Xmas **CONF:** Thtr 90 Class 40 Board 30 Del from £125 * **SERVICES:** Lift Night porter 57P **NOTES:** No smoking area in restaurant Last d 9.30pm
CARDS:

LINCOLN Lincolnshire **Map 08 SK97**
★★★ Washingborough Hall
Church Hill, Washingborough LN4 1BE
Quality Percentage Score: 69%
☎ 01522 790340 ▤ 01522 792936
Dir: *from B1188 onto B1190 Church Hill, 2m turn right opposite Methodist Church*
This listed Georgian manor stands on the edge of the village, not far from Lincoln. Public rooms are pleasantly furnished and comfortable, and the restaurant offers interesting menus. All the bedrooms are individually designed and most look out on the grounds or surrounding countryside.
ROOMS: 14 en suite (bth/shr) No smoking in 3 bedrooms s £65-£80; d £80-£125 (incl. bkfst) * LB Off peak **MEALS:** Lunch fr £11.25 Dinner fr £19.75 & alc European Cuisine V meals Coffee am Tea pm **FACILITIES:** CTV in all bedrooms Outdoor swimming pool (heated) Pool table Croquet lawn Jacuzzi/spa **CONF:** Thtr 50 Class 18 Board 24 Del from £95 * **SERVICES:** 50P **NOTES:** No coaches No children 15yrs No smoking in restaurant Last d 9.30pm
CARDS:

LINCOLN Lincolnshire **Map 08 SK97**
★★★ Courtyard by Marriott Lincoln
Brayford Wharf North LN1 1YW
Quality Percentage Score: 67%
☎ 01522 544244 ▤ 01522 560805
Dir: *from A46 take A57-Lincoln Central,after Tanvics go straight ahead at the lights hotel on the left*
Overlooking Bayford Pool, this smart modern hotel offers spacious and well equipped bedrooms, many of which look out over the waterfront. The public areas are comfortable and inviting. Staff are smartly uniformed, helpful, and friendly.
ROOMS: 95 en suite (bth/shr) (20 fmly) No smoking in 44 bedrooms s £64-£70; d £77-£80 (incl. bkfst) * LB Off peak **MEALS:** Lunch £12.95-£21.50alc Dinner £12.95-£21.50alc International Cuisine V meals Coffee am Tea pm **FACILITIES:** CTV in all bedrooms STV Gym **CONF:** Thtr 30 Class 20 Board 20 **SERVICES:** Lift Night porter Air conditioning 100P **NOTES:** No dogs (ex guide dogs) Last d 10pm
CARDS:

For Useful Information and Important Telephone Number Changes turn to page 25

LINCOLN Lincolnshire **Map 08 SK97**

★★★ Grand Hotel

Saint Mary's St LN5 7EP

Quality Percentage Score: 67%

☎ 01522 524211 📠 01522 537661

Dir: *from A1 take A46, follow signs for Lincoln Central and then railway station*

This friendly family-owned hotel, in the heart of the city, is ideal for exploring the many attractions on foot. The tastefully decorated bedrooms include a number of smart executive rooms, and several have four-poster beds. Staff are willing and helpful, and the hotel benefits from the option of two restaurants and bars.

ROOMS: 46 en suite (bth/shr) (2 fmly) s £54-£69; d £69-£79 (incl. bkfst) * LB Off peak **MEALS:** Lunch £5.95-£12 & alc High tea £3.50-£7.50 Dinner £13.25 & alc International Cuisine V meals Coffee am Tea pm **FACILITIES:** CTV in all bedrooms STV Xmas **CONF:** Thtr 80 Board 30 Del from £87 * **SERVICES:** Night porter 30P **NOTES:** No dogs (ex guide dogs) No smoking area in restaurant Last d 9.45pm

CARDS:

LINCOLN Lincolnshire **Map 08 SK97**

★★★ Posthouse Lincoln

Eastgate LN2 1PN

Quality Percentage Score: 65%

☎ 01522 520341 📠 01522 510780

Dir: *adjacent to cathedral*

This modern and friendly hotel is situated opposite Lincoln Cathedral and its grounds contain sections of the Roman wall and parts of Roman Eastgate. Bedrooms have every modern facility and some which face the cathedral have balconies. Others on the ground floor have patio doors opening to a secluded garden. Facilities include the 'Seasons' restaurant and bar, an all day lounge sevice, 24-hour room service, a comfortable lounge and ample free parking.

ROOMS: 70 en suite (bth/shr) (7 fmly) No smoking in 46 bedrooms d £65-£85 * LB Off peak **MEALS:** International Cuisine V meals Coffee am Tea pm **FACILITIES:** CTV in all bedrooms Xmas **CONF:** Thtr 90 Class 50 Board 40 Del from £90 * **SERVICES:** Lift Night porter 110P **NOTES:** No smoking area in restaurant Last d 10pm

CARDS:

LINCOLN Lincolnshire **Map 08 SK97**

★★★ *Moor Lodge*

Sleaford Rd LN4 1HU

Quality Percentage Score: 60%

☎ 01522 791366 📠 01522 794389

(For full entry see Branston)

LINCOLN Lincolnshire **Map 08 SK97**

★★ Hillcrest

15 Lindum Ter LN2 5RT

Quality Percentage Score: 71%

☎ 01522 510182 📠 01522 510182

Dir: *from S of town take Wragby Road, pass Adam & Eve public house on right take first right Upper Lindum Street, at end turn left in Lindum Terrace*

The hospitality offered by Jenny Bennett and her small staff is one of the strengths of this very friendly hotel, which sits in a quiet location, within easy walking distance of the town centre. The bedrooms are well equipped and come in a variety of sizes, and there is a cosy dining room and pleasant conservatory which overlooks the adjacent park. A good range of freshly prepared food is also available.

ROOMS: 16 en suite (bth/shr) (4 fmly) No smoking in 6 bedrooms s £52; d £79 (incl. bkfst) * LB Off peak **MEALS:** Bar Lunch £7.50-£9.50 Dinner £15 & alc International Cuisine V meals Coffee am Tea pm **FACILITIES:** CTV in all bedrooms **CONF:** Thtr 16 Class 12 Board 12 Del £72 * **SERVICES:** 8P **NOTES:** No smoking in restaurant Last d 8.30pm Closed 23 Dec-3 Jan **CARDS:**

LINCOLN Lincolnshire **Map 08 SK97**

★★ Castle

Westgate LN1 3AS

Quality Percentage Score: 69%

☎ 01522 538801 📠 01522 575457

Dir: *follow signs for 'Historic Lincoln' Hotel is at North East corner of the Castle*

Standing close to the castle, this family run hotel provides delightful bedrooms which are named after British castles; the Lincoln suite is a recent addition, a flexible bedroom with a lounge area. Public rooms include a small bar, open-plan to an attractive restaurant where Chef Dave Collett offers a wide selection of dishes, featuring quality seafood and local game.

ROOMS: 17 en suite (bth/shr) 3 annexe en suite (shr) (1 fmly) No smoking in 9 bedrooms s £60-£74; d £74-£120 (incl. bkfst) * LB Off peak **MEALS:** English & Continental Cuisine V meals Coffee am Tea pm **FACILITIES:** CTV in all bedrooms Xmas **CONF:** Thtr 50 Class 18 Board 22 **SERVICES:** 20P **NOTES:** No children 10yrs No smoking area in restaurant Last d 9.30pm **CARDS:**

See advert on opposite page

LINCOLN Lincolnshire **Map 08 SK97**

★★ Loudor

37 Newark Rd, North Hykeham LN6 8RB

Quality Percentage Score: 65%

☎ 01522 680333 & 500474 📠 01522 680403

Dir: *Turn off A1 10m on A46 A1434 2m hotel on left opposite shopping forum*

This family run hotel, three miles from the city, provides attentive, friendly service. En suite bedrooms are soundly furnished and suitably equipped with a good level of facilities.

contd.

The relaxing public rooms include a cosy lounge, small bar and welcoming restaurant, traditional freshly prepared English cooking is served.
ROOMS: 9 en suite (bth/shr) 1 annexe en suite (shr) (1 fmly) s £28-£33; d £38-£45 (incl. bkfst) * Off peak **MEALS:** English & French Cuisine Coffee am **FACILITIES:** CTV in all bedrooms STV **SERVICES:** 12P **NOTES:** No dogs No coaches Last d 8.30pm **CARDS:**

LINCOLN Lincolnshire **Map 08 SK97**
Travel Inn
Lincoln Rd, Canwick Hill LN4 2RF
☎ 01522 525216 01522 542521
Dir: *on the junc of B1188 to Branston and B1131 to Bracebridge Heath*
This modern building offers accommodation in smart, spacious and well equipped bedrooms, all with en-suite bathrooms. Refreshments may be taken at the nearby family restaurant. For details about current prices consult the Contents Page under Hotel Groups for the Travel Inn phone number.
ROOMS: 41 en suite (bth/shr) d £39.95 *

LINCOLN Lincolnshire **Map 08 SK97**
Travelodge
Thorpe on the Hill LN6 9AJ
☎ 0800 850950
Dir: *on A46*
This modern building offers accommodation in smart, spacious and well equipped bedrooms, all with en-suite bathrooms. Refreshments may be taken at the nearby family restaurant. For details about current prices, consult the Contents Page under Hotel Groups for the Travelodge phone number.
ROOMS: 32 en suite (bth/shr) d £39.95-£45.95 *

LINCOLN Lincolnshire **Map 08 SK97**
The Bentley Hotel & Leisure Club
Newark Rd, South Hykeham LN6 9NH
☎ 01522 878000
ROOMS: 53 en suite (bth/shr)

LIPHOOK Hampshire **Map 04 SU83**
★★★ **Old Thorns Hotel, Golf & Country Club**
Longmoor Rd, Griggs Green GU30 7PE
Quality Percentage Score: 73%
☎ 01428 724555 01428 725036
Dir: *A3 Guildford to Portsmouth, take Griggs Green exit (first after Liphook). Signposted*
This smartly presented hotel has many attractions: an 18-hole golf course with golf shop, an indoor pool with sauna and solarium, spacious bedrooms, some with balconies, and two restaurants, one of which, the Nippon Kan, is Japanese and specialises in Teppan-Yaki cuisine.
ROOMS: 28 en suite (bth/shr) 4 annexe en suite (shr) s £90-£110; d £120-£135 (incl. bkfst) LB Off peak **MEALS:** Sunday Lunch £10-£16.95 Dinner £20-£25 European & Japanese Cuisine V meals Coffee am Tea pm **FACILITIES:** CTV in all bedrooms STV Indoor swimming pool (heated) Golf 18 Tennis (hard) Sauna Solarium Gym Pool table Putting green Xmas **CONF:** Thtr 100 Class 50 Board 30 Del £145 * **SERVICES:** Night porter 80P **NOTES:** No dogs (ex guide dogs) No coaches Last d 9.30pm **CARDS:**

Symbols and Abbreviations are listed and explained on pages 4 and 5

LIPHOOK Hampshire — Map 04 SU83

Travelodge
GU30 7TT
☎ 0800 850950
Dir: *on northbound carriageway of A3, 1m from Griggs Green exit at Shell services*
This modern building offers accommodation in smart, spacious and well equipped bedrooms, all with en-suite bathrooms. Refreshments may be taken at the nearby family restaurant. For details about current prices, consult the Contents Page under Hotel Groups for the Travelodge phone number.
ROOMS: 40 en suite (bth/shr) d £39.95 *

LISKEARD Cornwall & Isles of Scilly — Map 02 SX26

The Premier Collection

★★ Well House
St Keyne PL14 4RN
☎ 01579 342001 🖷 01579 343891
Dir: *from Liskeard A38 take B3254 to St Keyne, at church take left fork signed St Keynewell, hotel 0.5m from church*
This charming small hotel offers a personal level of hospitality and service. Bedrooms are tastefully furnished and well equipped. Public areas include an elegant sitting room with log fire, and an intimate bar. Guests can relax over afternoon tea with home-made biscuits on the terrace which overlooks the pretty gardens.
ROOMS: 9 en suite (bth/shr) (1 fmly) s £75-£90; d £110-£160 (incl. bkfst) * LB Off peak **MEALS:** Lunch £20.95-£30.50 Dinner £20.95-£30.50 V meals **FACILITIES:** CTV in all bedrooms Outdoor swimming pool (heated) Tennis (hard) Croquet lawn Xmas **SERVICES:** 30P **NOTES:** No coaches No smoking area in restaurant Last d 8.30pm **CARDS:**

LISKEARD Cornwall & Isles of Scilly — Map 02 SX26

★★ Lord Eliot
Castle St PL14 3AU
Quality Percentage Score: 62%
☎ 01579 342717 🖷 01579 347593
Dir: *take A38 into Liskeard, hotel 0.5m on left past St Martins Church*
The Lord Eliot has a friendly team on hand to welcome guests. Bedrooms are undergoing a refurbishment programme and have been decorated smartly. The traditional bar is a popular meeting place for locals, and there is a separate TV lounge across the hall.
ROOMS: 15 rms (14 bth/shr) (1 fmly) No smoking in 2 bedrooms s fr £50; d fr £70 (incl. bkfst) * LB Off peak **MEALS:** Lunch fr £15.95 & alc Dinner fr £15.95 & alc English & French Cuisine V meals Coffee am Tea pm **FACILITIES:** CTV in all bedrooms Xmas **CONF:** Thtr 180 Class 180 Board 180 **SERVICES:** 60P **NOTES:** No smoking in restaurant Last d 9pm RS 25 Dec, closed evening
CARDS:

LITTLEBOURNE Kent — Map 05 TR25

★★ *Bow Window Inn*
50 High St CT3 1ST
Quality Percentage Score: 69%
☎ 01227 721264 🖷 01227 721250
A 300-year-old country cottage offering warm comfortable accommodation. Bedrooms are furnished in keeping with the style of the house and are well equipped. Public areas are limited, the restaurant offers attractive surroundings with exposed oak beams and a large Kentish fireplace.
ROOMS: 8 en suite (bth/shr) (1 fmly) **MEALS:** English & Continental Cuisine V meals Coffee am Tea pm **FACILITIES:** CTV in all bedrooms **SERVICES:** 16P **NOTES:** No dogs (ex guide dogs) No smoking in restaurant Last d 9pm **CARDS:**

LITTLE HALLINGBURY See Bishop's Stortford

LITTLE LANGDALE Cumbria — Map 07 NY30

★★ Three Shires Inn
LA22 9NZ
Quality Percentage Score: 67%
☎ 015394 37215 🖷 015394 37127
Dir: *turn off A593, 2.5m from Ambleside at 2nd junct signposted for the Langdales. 1st left 0.5m, then hotel 1m up lane*
A delightful country hotel and inn amidst dramatic mountain scenery in an area popular with walkers. An extensive menu is served in the dining room or bar and there are tables outside, with a brook running by. Cooking is ambitious and reflects the imagination and skills of the chef. There is a cosy, quiet foyer lounge with log fire as well as a TV lounge.
ROOMS: 10 en suite (bth/shr) (1 fmly) s £33-£37.50; d £66-£80 (incl. bkfst) LB Off peak **MEALS:** Bar Lunch fr £12 & alc Dinner fr £19.95 & alc British & Continental Cuisine V meals Coffee am Tea pm **FACILITIES:** CTV in all bedrooms Xmas **SERVICES:** 22P **NOTES:** No dogs No coaches No smoking in restaurant Last d 8.30pm Closed Jan (ex New Year) RS Dec **CARDS:**

LITTLE WEIGHTON East Riding of Yorkshire — Map 08 SE93

★★ Rowley Manor
Rowley Rd HU20 3XR
Quality Percentage Score: 64%
☎ 01482 848248 🖷 01482 849900
Dir: *9m NW of Hull, W of A164 Beverley to Hessle road*
This hotel is a Georgian country house in over 30 acres of gardens and parkland. Bedrooms are traditionally furnished and decorated, and many have views. Some master rooms are particularly spacious. The magnificent pine panelling in the study is a feature of the public rooms.
ROOMS: 16 en suite (bth/shr) s fr £70; d fr £80 (incl. bkfst) * LB Off peak **MEALS:** Lunch £11.95-£22.50 International Cuisine V meals Coffee am Tea pm **FACILITIES:** CTV in all bedrooms STV Riding Solarium Croquet lawn Xmas **CONF:** Thtr 90 Class 30 Board 50 **SERVICES:** Night porter 80P **CARDS:**

LIVERPOOL Merseyside — Map 07 SJ39

see also **Blundellsands**
★★★★ Swallow
1 Queen Square L1 1RH
Quality Percentage Score: 68%
☎ 0151 476 8000 🖷 0151 474 5000
Dir: *from City Centre follow signs for Queen Square Parking. Hotel adjacent*
This impressive modern hotel is situated in the newly developed Queen Square area, close to St George's Hall. The interior is rich and elegant and the large bedrooms, including three suites, are very tastefully and comfortably furnished, with every modern

contd.

facility. The hotel features a Swallow Leisure Club which includes a large swimming pool and a fitness room. There are also meeting and conference facilities, comprehensively equipped. Olivier's Restaurant on the first floor provides a high standard of cuisine in stylish surrounds and is open for both lunch and dinner. There is free parking for guests in the adjoining multi-storey car park only a few steps from the hotel entrance.

ROOMS: 146 en suite (bth/shr) (29 fmly) No smoking in 90 bedrooms s fr £105; d fr £125 (incl. bkfst) * LB Off peak **MEALS:** Lunch £10.95-£14.95 & alc Dinner fr £22 & alc V meals Coffee am Tea pm **FACILITIES:** CTV in all bedrooms STV Indoor swimming pool (heated) Sauna Solarium Gym Jacuzzi/spa Xmas **CONF:** Thtr 250 Class 90 Board 30 Del from £130 * **SERVICES:** Lift Night porter Air conditioning 158P **NOTES:** No smoking in restaurant Last d 9.45pm Closed 1-2 Jan **CARDS:**

LIVERPOOL Merseyside — Map 07 SJ39
★★★ *The Royal*

Marine Ter, Waterloo L22 5PR
Quality Percentage Score: 63%
☎ 0151 928 2332 0151 949 0320
Dir: *6.50m NW of city centre, turn left off A565 Liverpool/Southport road at monument, hotel at bottom of this road*

This hotel dates from 1815, the Marine Gardens lie at the front and there are fine views towards the Wirral and North Wales. Bedrooms are smart and equipped with modern facilities. Family rooms and one four-poster bed are available. Extensive public areas are provided and provision for meetings and functions.
ROOMS: 25 en suite (bth/shr) (3 fmly) **MEALS:** Continental Cuisine V meals Coffee am Tea pm **FACILITIES:** CTV in all bedrooms STV **CONF:** Thtr 120 Class 70 Board 40 **SERVICES:** Night porter 25P **NOTES:** No dogs (ex guide dogs) No coaches No smoking area in restaurant Last d 9.30pm **CARDS:**

LIVERPOOL Merseyside — Map 07 SJ39
Campanile

Chaloner St, Queens Dock L3 4AJ
☎ 0151 709 8104 0151 709 8725
Dir: *follow brown tourist signs marked "Albert Dock" Hotel is situated south on the waterfront*

This modern building offers accommodation in smart well equipped bedrooms, all with en-suite bathrooms. Refreshments may be taken at the informal Bistro. For details about current prices, consult the Contents Page under Hotel Groups for the Campanile phone number.
ROOMS: 103 en suite (bth/shr) **CONF:** Thtr 35 Class 18 Board 20

LIVERPOOL Merseyside — Map 07 SJ39
Travel Inn (Liverpool North)

Northern Perimiter Rd, Bootle L30 7PT
☎ 0151 531 1497 0151 520 1842
Dir: *on A5207, 0.25m from end of M58/M57*

This modern building offers accommodation in smart, spacious and well equipped bedrooms, all with en-suite bathrooms. Refreshments may be taken at the nearby family restaurant. For details about current prices consult the Contents Page under Hotel Groups for the Travel Inn phone number.
ROOMS: 43 en suite (bth/shr) d £39.95 *

LIVERPOOL Merseyside — Map 07 SJ39
Travel Inn (Liverpool Tarbock)

Wilson Rd, Tarbock L36 6AD
☎ 0151 480 9614 0151 480 9361
Dir: *on intersection of M62/M57, from junct 6 M62 take A5080 towards Huyton then first right into Wilson Rd*

This modern building offers accommodation in smart, spacious and well equipped bedrooms, all with en-suite bathrooms. Refreshments may be taken at the nearby family restaurant. For details about current prices consult the Contents Page under Hotel Groups for the Travel Inn phone number.
ROOMS: 40 en suite (bth/shr) d £39.95 *

LIVERPOOL Merseyside — Map 07 SJ39
Travel Inn (Liverpool West Derby)

Queens Dr, West Derby L13 0DL
☎ 0151 228 4724 0151 220 7610
Dir: *on the Liverpool ring road at end of M62 turn right at 1st traffic lights onto A5058, pass Esso garage and left at next lights*

This modern building offers accommodation in smart, spacious and well equipped bedrooms, all with en-suite bathrooms. Refreshments may be taken at the nearby family restaurant. For details about current prices consult the Contents Page under Hotel Groups for the Travel Inn phone number.
ROOMS: 40 en suite (bth/shr) d £39.95 *

LIVERPOOL Merseyside — Map 07 SJ39

Liverpool Moat House

Paradise St L1 8JD
☎ 0151 471 9988 Fax 0151 709 2706

Refurbishment has enhanced the public areas of this central hotel, the new Conference and Banqueting Centre is particularly impressive. Full meals or simple snacks are enjoyed in the brasserie and bar. Bedrooms are comfortable, staff friendly and helpful. There are special parking arrangements in the adjacent multi-storey car park.

ROOMS: 251 en suite (bth/shr) (202 fmly) No smoking in 130 bedrooms
MEALS: English & French Cuisine V meals Coffee am Tea pm
FACILITIES: CTV in all bedrooms Indoor swimming pool (heated) Sauna Solarium Gym Whirlpool/Steam Room **CONF:** Thtr 600 Class 250 Board 152 **SERVICES:** Lift Night porter Air conditioning **NOTES:** No smoking area in restaurant Last d 10.pm **CARDS:**

LIVERPOOL Merseyside — Map 07 SJ39

Thistle Liverpool

Chapel St L3 9RE
☎ 0151 227 4444 Fax 0151 236 3973

***Dir:** follow signs for the City Centre, Pier Head then Atlantic Tower Hotel. Situated opposite St Nicholas Church on Chapel Street*

A distinctive modern hotel overlooking the River Mersey and similar in shape to a ship's bow. Refurbishment has considerably enhanced the reception lounge and foyer, and work is ongoing on the bedroom floors. Many of the well-equipped bedrooms have splendid views over the river, and there are some interesting themed suites. Public areas include the Stateroom Restaurant, the Club Car Diner and a choice of bars, one resembling the interior of an old sailing ship.

ROOMS: 226 en suite (bth/shr) (4 fmly) No smoking in 120 bedrooms
MEALS: European Cuisine V meals Coffee am Tea pm **FACILITIES:** CTV in all bedrooms STV **CONF:** Thtr 120 Class 60 Board 30 **SERVICES:** Lift Night porter Air conditioning 60P **NOTES:** Last d 10.15pm
CARDS:

LIZARD, THE Cornwall & Isles of Scilly — Map 02 SW71

★★★ Housel Bay

Housel Cove TR12 7PG
Quality Percentage Score: 68%
☎ 01326 290417 & 290917 Fax 01326 290359

***Dir:** follow A39/A394 to Helston, take the A3083 to the Lizard, at Lizard sign bear left, at school turn left and proceed down Lane to Hotel*

This hotel has stunning sea views over to The Lizard, enjoyed from the lounge and many bedrooms. Bedrooms have been extensively upgraded to offer many modern facilities and extras. Home-made cuisine is served in the elegant dining room, in addition to lighter meals served in the bar.

ROOMS: 21 en suite (bth/shr) (1 fmly) No smoking in 2 bedrooms s £27.50-£72.50; d £49-£96.50 (incl. bkfst) * LB Off peak
MEALS: Sunday Lunch £9.50 Dinner £15.50-£19.50 International Cuisine V meals Coffee am Tea pm **FACILITIES:** CTV in all bedrooms STV Xmas
SERVICES: Lift 37P **NOTES:** No dogs (ex guide dogs) No smoking in restaurant Last d 9pm **CARDS:**

LIZARD, THE Cornwall & Isles of Scilly — Map 02 SW71

★★ Tregildry

TR12 6HG
Quality Percentage Score: 80%
☎ 01326 231378 Fax 01326 231561

(For full entry see GILLAN)

LOCKINGTON — Map 08 SK42

Hotels are listed under **East Midlands Airport**

LOLWORTH Cambridgeshire — Map 05 TL36

Travelodge

Huntingdon Rd CB3 8DR
☎ 01954 781335 Fax 01954 781335

***Dir:** on A14 northbound, 3m N of junct 14 on M11*

This modern building offers accommodation in smart, spacious and well equipped bedrooms, all with en-suite bathrooms. Refreshments may be taken at the nearby family restaurant. For details about current prices, consult the Contents Page under Hotel Groups for the Travelodge phone number.

ROOMS: 20 en suite (bth/shr) d £49.95 *

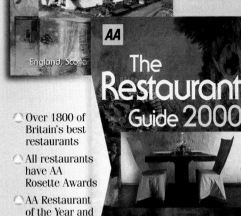

Index of London Hotels

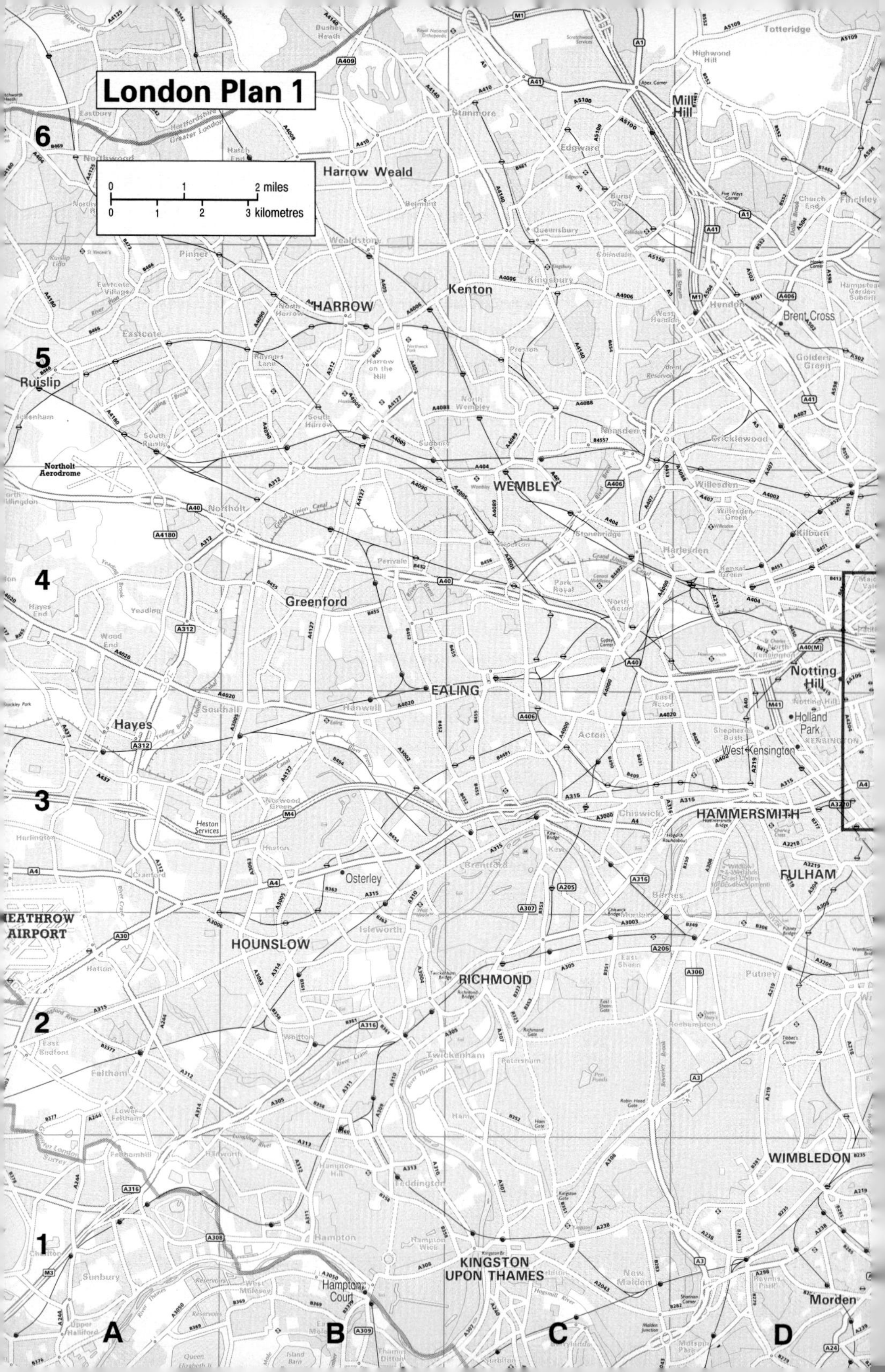
London Plan 1
0 1 2 miles
0 1 2 3 kilometres
6
5
4
3
2
1
A
B
C
D
Mill Hill
Harrow Weald
Stanmore
Edgware
Totteridge
Highwood Hill
Finchley
Church End
Burnt Oak
Queensbury
Colindale
Kingsbury
Kenton
HARROW
Harrow on the Hill
Hendon
Brent Cross
Golders Green
Northwood
Pinner
Eastcote
Ruislip
Ickenham
Northolt Aerodrome
Northolt
South Ruislip
South Harrow
Sudbury
North Wembley
WEMBLEY
Preston
Neasden
Cricklewood
Willesden
Kilburn
Harlesden
Stonebridge
Park Royal
North Acton
Greenford
Perivale
Yeading
Hayes
Southall
EALING
Hanwell
Acton
East Acton
Notting Hill
Holland Park
Shepherd's Bush
West Kensington
HAMMERSMITH
Chiswick
FULHAM
Barnes
Brentford
Osterley
Isleworth
Heston
HOUNSLOW
HEATHROW AIRPORT
Hatton
RICHMOND
East Sheen
Putney
Roehampton
Twickenham
Whitton
Feltham
East Bedfont
Lower Feltham
Hanworth
Hampton
Hampton Hill
Teddington
Hampton Wick
Hampton Court
KINGSTON UPON THAMES
New Malden
WIMBLEDON
Morden
Sunbury
Upper Halliford
M1
M4
A40
A4
A316
A3
A205
A406

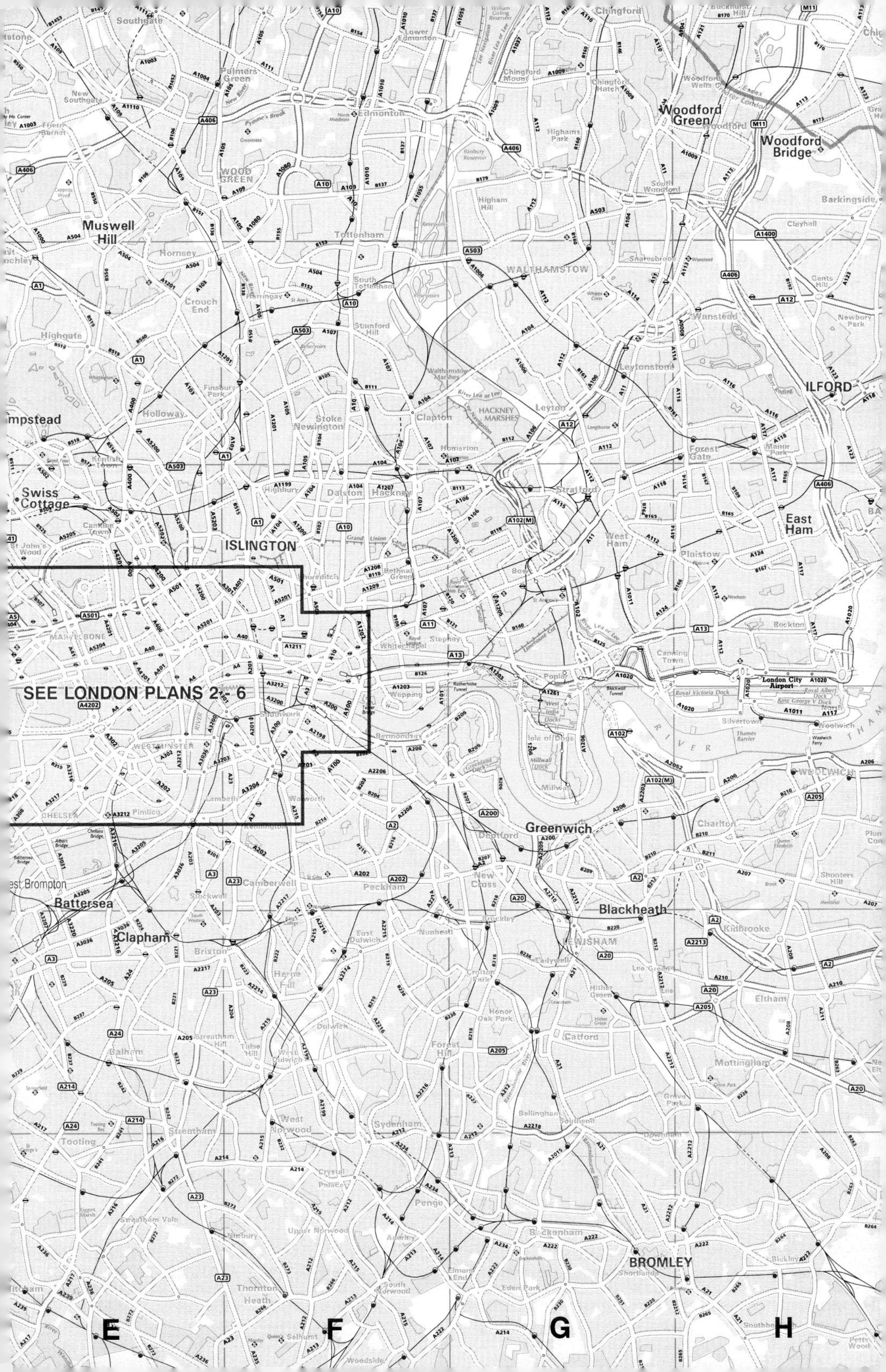

Southgate
Chingford
Palmers Green
Edmonton
Woodford Green
Woodford Bridge
Wood Green
Muswell Hill
Hornsey
Tottenham
Crouch End
Walthamstow
Highgate
Stamford Hill
Barkingside
Holloway
Stoke Newington
Clapton
Hackney Marshes
Leyton
Leytonstone
Ilford
Wanstead
Hampstead
Swiss Cottage
Dalston
Hackney
Homerton
Stratford
Forest Gate
Camden Town
Islington
Shoreditch
Bethnal Green
West Ham
Plaistow
East Ham
Whitechapel
Stepney
Bow
Poplar
Canning Town
London City Airport
SEE LONDON PLANS 2 - 6
Wapping
Southwark
Westminster
Bermondsey
Isle of Dogs
Millwall
Lambeth
Walworth
Chelsea
Pimlico
Greenwich
Deptford
Charlton
Woolwich
Battersea
Camberwell
Peckham
New Cross
Clapham
Brixton
Blackheath
Lewisham
Kidbrooke
East Dulwich
Brockley
Nunhead
Herne Hill
Lee Green
Hither Green
Eltham
Dulwich
Honor Oak Park
Catford
Balham
Streatham Hill
Tulse Hill
West Dulwich
Forest Hill
Mottingham
Tooting
Streatham
West Norwood
Sydenham
Bellingham
Crystal Palace
Penge
Beckenham
Bromley
Norbury
Upper Norwood
Anerley
Thornton Heath
South Norwood
Elmers End
Eden Park
Shortlands
Bickley
Selhurst
Woodside
E
F
G
H

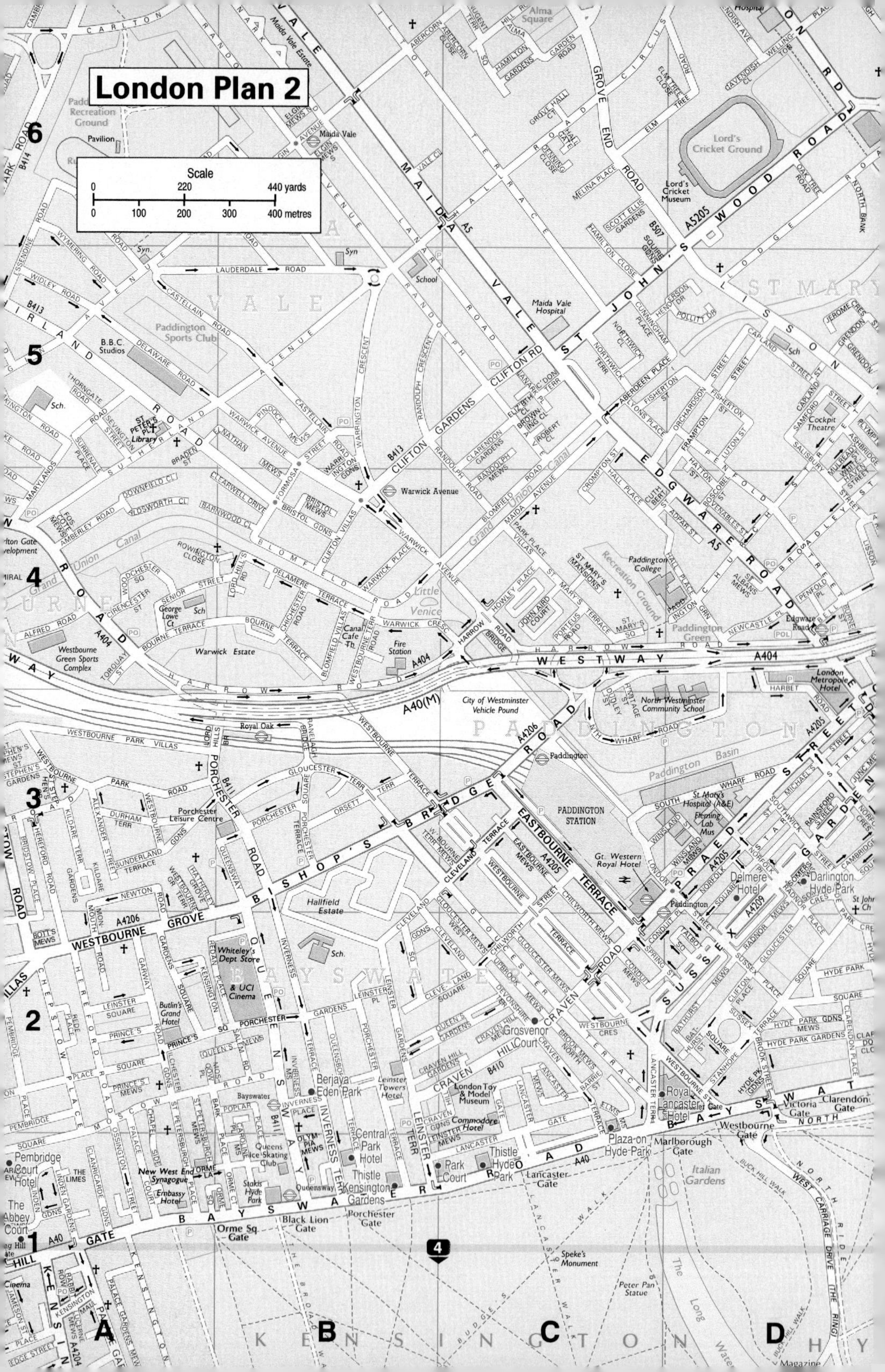
London Plan 2
Scale
0
220
440 yards
0
100
200
300
400 metres
6
5
4
3
2
1
A
B
C
D
Paddington Recreation Ground
Pavilion
Maida Vale
Maida Vale Estate
Alma Square
Lord's Cricket Ground
Lord's Cricket Museum
Maida Vale Hospital
School
Syn
Syn.
Paddington Sports Club
B.B.C. Studios
Sch.
St Peter's Pl
Library
Warwick Avenue
Little Venice
Canal Cafe Th
Fire Station
Warwick Estate
Westbourne Green Sports Complex
George Lowe Ct
Grand Union Canal
Paddington College
Recreation Ground
Paddington Green
Edgware Road
Cockpit Theatre
London Metropole Hotel
City of Westminster Vehicle Pound
North Westminster Community School
Royal Oak
Paddington
Paddington Basin
PADDINGTON STATION
Gt. Western Royal Hotel
St Mary's Hospital (A&E)
Fleming Lab Mus
Delmere Hotel
Darlington Hyde Park
Porchester Leisure Centre
Hallfield Estate
Whiteley's Dept Store & UCI Cinema
Butlin's Grand Hotel
Berjaya Eden Park
Grosvenor Court
London Toy & Model Museum
Commodore Hotel
Leinster Towers Hotel
Bayswater
Queensway
Queens Ice Skating Club
Central Park Hotel
Thistle Kensington Gardens
Park Court
Thistle Hyde Park
Stakis Hyde Park
New West End Synagogue
Embassy Hotel
Pembridge Court Hotel
The Abbey Court
Royal Lancaster Hotel
Plaza-on Hyde-Park
Victoria Gate
Clarendon Gate
Westbourne Gate
Marlborough Gate
Lancaster Gate
Italian Gardens
Black Lion Gate
Porchester Gate
Orme Sq Gate
Speke's Monument
Peter Pan Statue
The Long Water
Cinema
MAIDA VALE
EDGWARE ROAD
ST JOHN'S WOOD ROAD
BISHOP'S BRIDGE ROAD
WESTWAY
HARROW ROAD
BAYSWATER ROAD
WESTBOURNE GROVE
PRAED STREET
SUSSEX GARDENS
EASTBOURNE TERRACE
PORCHESTER ROAD
QUEENSWAY
CLIFTON GARDENS
WARWICK AVENUE
LAUDERDALE ROAD
CARLTON
A5
A40
A40(M)
A404
A4206
A4205
A4209
A205
A4204
B411
B413
B414
B410
B507
4
KENSINGTON GARDENS
HYDE PARK

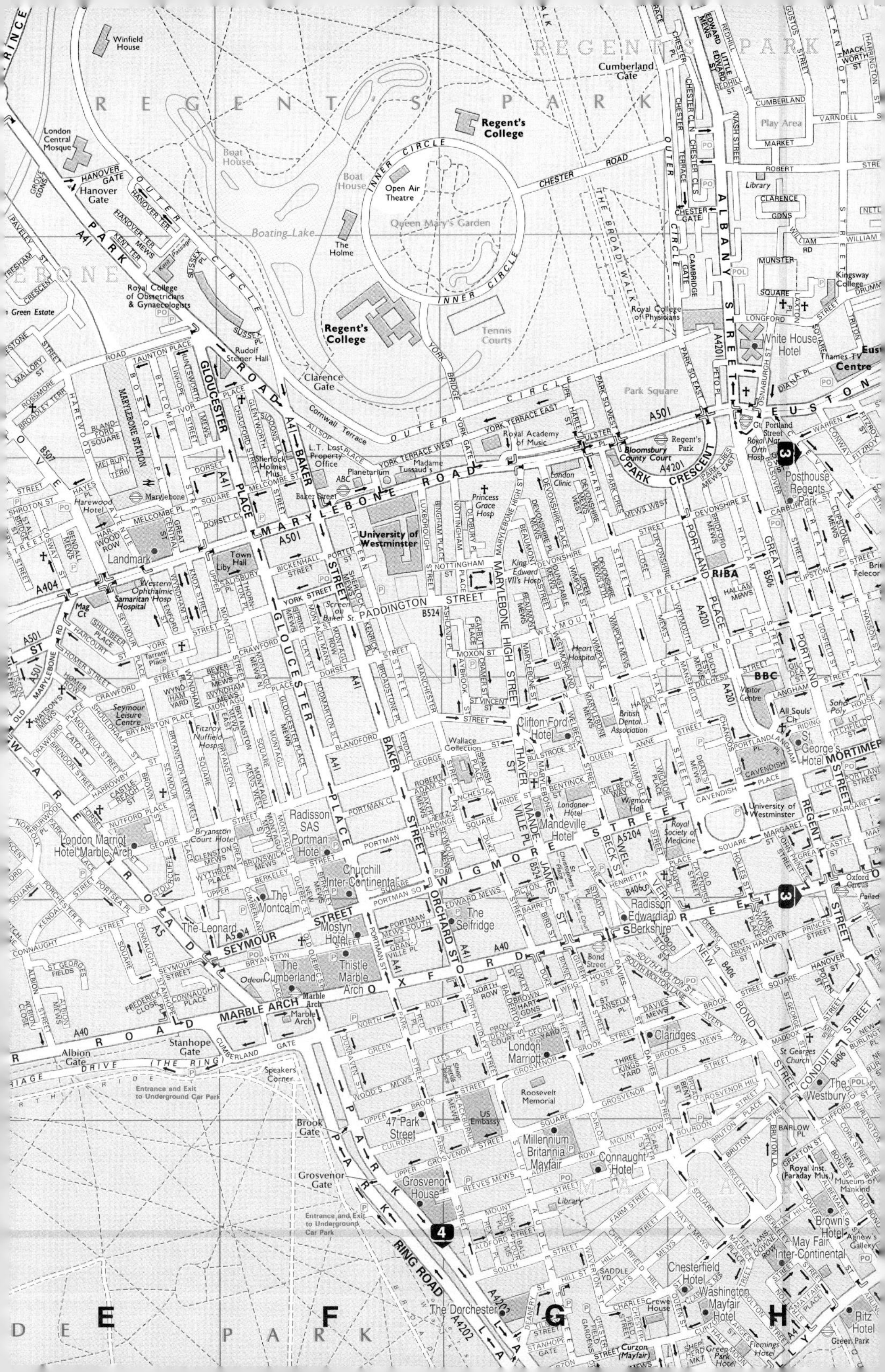

REGENT'S PARK
Winfield House
London Central Mosque
Hanover Gate
Boat House
Boating Lake
Open Air Theatre
Queen Mary's Garden
The Holme
Regent's College
Inner Circle
Chester Road
Cumberland Gate
Outer Circle
The Broad Walk
Royal College of Physicians
Royal College of Obstetricians & Gynaecologists
Tennis Courts
Clarence Gate
York Bridge
Rudolf Steiner Hall
Cornwall Terrace
L.T. Lost Property Office
Planetarium
Madame Tussaud's
Sherlock Holmes Mus.
Marylebone Station
Marylebone
Baker Street
Royal Academy of Music
Park Square
Regent's Park
Bloomsbury County Court
Park Crescent
London Clinic
Portland Street
Royal Nat Orth Hosp
Posthouse Regents Park
White House Hotel
Thames TV Centre
Euston Road
Albany Street
Great Portland Street
Play Area
Library
Kingsway College
Princess Grace Hosp
University of Westminster
Harewood Hotel
Landmark
Town Hall
Liby
Western Ophthalmic
Samaritan Hosp Hospital
Marylebone Road
King Edward VII's Hosp
Marylebone High Street
RIBA
BBC
Visitor Centre
All Souls' Ch
St George's Hotel
Heart Hospital
British Dental Association
Clifton Ford Hotel
Wallace Collection
Screen on Baker St
Paddington Street
Seymour Leisure Centre
Fitzroy Nuffield Hosp
Bryanston Court Hotel
London Marriott Hotel Marble Arch
Radisson SAS Portman Hotel
Churchill Inter-Continental
The Montcalm
The Leonard
Mostyn Hotel
The Cumberland
Thistle Marble Arch
Odeon
Marble Arch
The Selfridge
Londoner Hotel
Wigmore Hall
Mandeville Hotel
Wigmore Street
Royal Society of Medicine
University of Westminster
Radisson Edwardian Berkshire
Oxford Circus
Oxford Street
Bond Street
Regent Street
New Bond Street
Claridges
London Marriott
Roosevelt Memorial
US Embassy
47 Park Street
Millennium Britannia Mayfair
Connaught Hotel
Grosvenor House
Speakers Corner
Stanhope Gate
Albion Gate
Brook Gate
Grosvenor Gate
Entrance and Exit to Underground Car Park
Park Lane
Ring Road
St Georges Church
The Westbury
Royal Inst. (Faraday Mus.)
Museum of Mankind
Brown's Hotel
May Fair Inter-Continental
Agnew's Gallery
Chesterfield Hotel
Washington Mayfair Hotel
Crewe House
The Dorchester
Curzon (Mayfair)
Green Park Hotel
Flemings Hotel
Ritz Hotel
Green Park
MAYFAIR
HYDE PARK
A501
A41
A40
A4202
A5204
B524
3
4
E
F
G
H

London Plan 3
Somers Town
British Library
St Pancras Station
King's Cross St Pancras
King's Cross (Thameslink)
Euston Station
Euston Road
Euston
Euston Square
Kennedy Hotel
National Temperance Hospital
Ibis Euston
Camden Town Hall & St Pancras Liby
St Pancras International Youth Hostel
Elizabeth Garrett Anderson Hosp.
London Euston Travel Inn
New Ambassadors Hotel
County Hotel
Euston Plaza Hotel
Friends House
Wellcome Inst
British Medical Assoc
Kingsway College
Euston Tower
Thames TV Centre
White House Hotel
Play Area
Library
St Pancras
St George's Gardens
Thomas Coram Foundation
Coram's Fields Playground
Brunswick Housing & Shopping Centre
Renoir Cinema
Posthouse Bloomsbury
Tavistock Hotel
Royal National Hotel
University of London
Percival David Foundation of Chinese Art
University College
University College Hosp
Bloomsbury Theatre
Maternity & Childrens Hosp.
Obstetrics Hosp
Warren Street
Great Portland Street
Radisson Edwardian Grafton
Posthouse Regents Park
London Foot Hosp
British Telecom Tower
Middlesex Hospital
Pollock's Toy Museum
Goodge Street
Bloomsbury
Hotel Russell
Russell Square
President Hotel
National Hosp.
Hospital for Sick Children
Royal London Homeopathic Hospital
Imperial Hotel
Waverley House Hotel
Bloomsbury Park
The Bonnington in Bloomsbury
Bedford Hotel
Montague on the Gardens
British Museum and Library
Blooms Hotel
R.A.D.A.
The Academy
Drill Hall
Vanbrugh Th.
Building Centre
Bedford Corner Hotel
Rathbone Hotel
Radisson Edwardian Kenilworth
Thistle Bloomsbury
Radisson Edwardian Mountbatten
Holborn
Holborn Town Hall
Cochrane Theatre
RIBA
BBC
All Souls'
St George's Hotel
University of Westminster
Mag Court
The Berners
YMCA
Dominion
St Giles Circus
New Oxford Street
Oxford Street
Tottenham Court Road
Oxford Circus
Palladium
Centre Pt
Princes Circus
Shaftesbury Eye Hosp
Oasis Sports Centre
Drury Lane Moat House
New London Theatre
Freemason's Hall
House of St Barnabas
Soho
Soho Theatre
Marshall Street Leisure Centre
Phoenix Th & Curzon Cin
Shaftesbury Hosp.
Contemp Applied Arts
Donmar Th
Cambridge Th
Prince Edward Th
Palace Th
Curzon (West End)
Fire Sta
Royal Opera House
Covent Garden
Theatre Royal
The Waldorf Meridien
Theatre Mus.
London Transport Mus.
Africa Centre
Jubilee Mkt
St Paul's
Lyceum Th
Strand Palace
Vaudeville Th
Adelphi Th
Savoy Th
The Savoy
Royal Society of Arts
Charing Cross Hotel
Charing Cross Sta
Embankment
Embankment Pier
Victoria Embankment Gardens
York Water Gate
Players Th
Hungerford Br
Leicester Square
Hippodrome
Wyndhams Th
Albery Th
Garrick Th
Coliseum
St Martin-in-the-Fields
National Portrait Gallery
National Gallery
Trafalgar Square
Nelson's Column
South Africa House
Canada Hse
Admiralty Arch
Mall Galleries
Inst. of Contemporary Arts
Government Offices
Whitehall Th
Min of Agriculture
Northumberland Av
Strand
Radisson Edwardian Hampshire
The Pastoria
Thistle Trafalgar Square
Odeon
Comedy Th
Her Majesty's Th
Haymarket
Prince of Wales Th
Criterion Th
Piccadilly Circus
Piccadilly Pavilion
London Trocadero Centre
MGM (Swiss Centre)
Apollo Th
Lyric Th
Queens Th
Gielgud Th
Piccadilly Th
Empire
Warner
Prince Charles
St John's Hosp
Le Meridien Piccadilly
Royal Academy of Arts
Museum of Mankind
Royal Inst (Faraday Mus.)
22 Jermyn Street
St James's Church
Britain Centre
Cavendish St James
Brown's Hotel
May Fair Inter-Continental
Washington Mayfair Hotel
Ritz Hotel
Green Park
Stafford
Flemings Hotel
The Westbury
St Georges Church
Piccadilly
Regent Street
Bond Street
Conduit Street
Hanover Square
Cavendish Square
Portland Place
Albany Street
Tottenham Court Road
Gower Street
Charing Cross Road
Shaftesbury Avenue
Southampton Row
Kingsway
High Holborn
Long Acre
St Martin's La
St James's
Mayfair
A
B
C
D
1
2
3
4
5
6

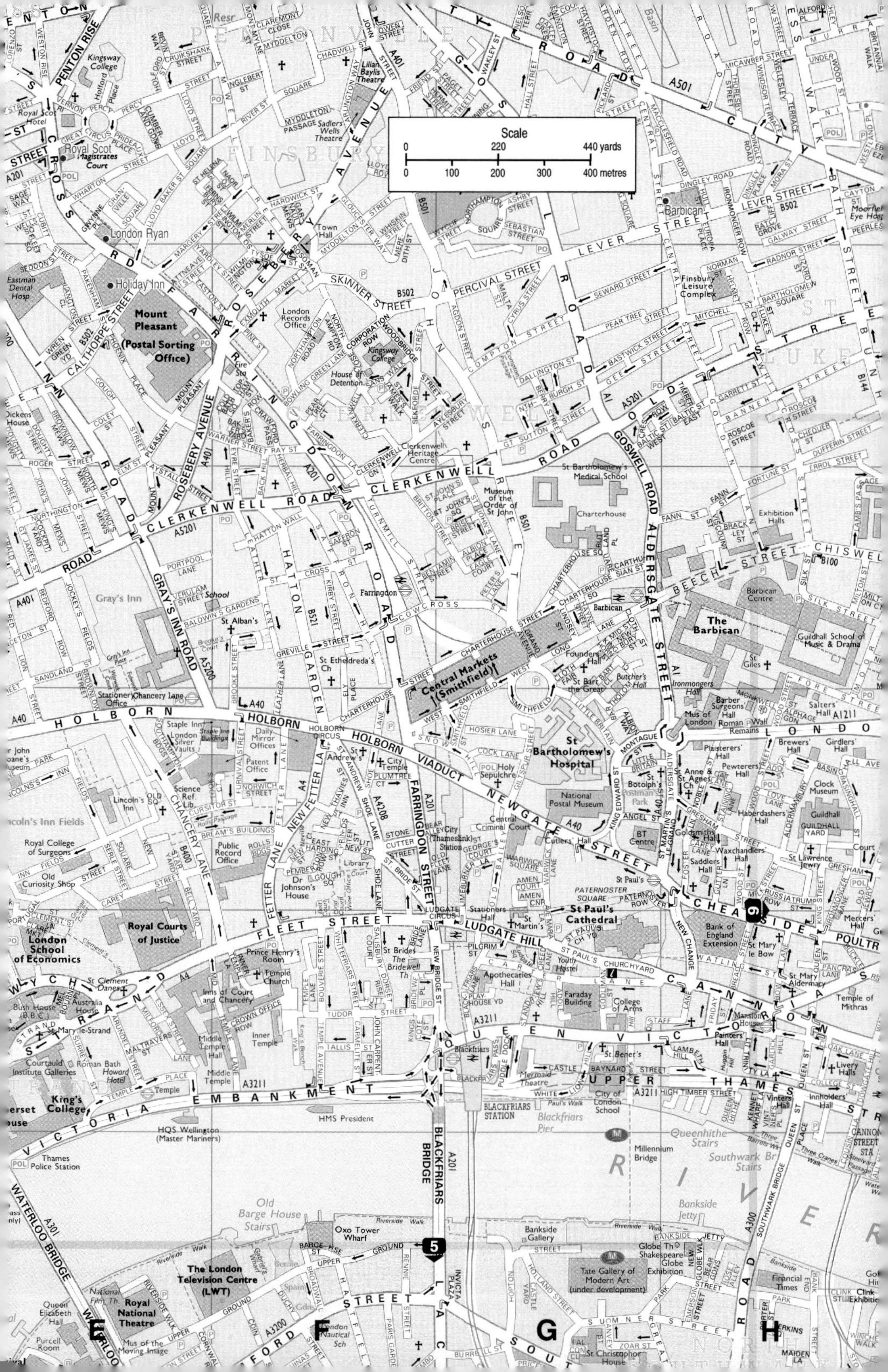
Scale
0
220
440 yards
0
100
200
300
400 metres
PENTONVILLE
FINSBURY
CLERKENWELL
ST LUKE'S
Kingsway College
Royal Scot Hotel
Magistrates Court
London Ryan
Holiday Inn
Mount Pleasant (Postal Sorting Office)
Eastman Dental Hosp.
Lilian Baylis Theatre
Sadlers Wells Theatre
Town Hall
London Records Office
House of Detention
Clerkenwell Heritage Centre
Museum of the Order of St John
St Bartholomew's Medical School
Charterhouse
Barbican
Barbican Centre
The Barbican
Guildhall School of Music & Drama
Finsbury Leisure Complex
Exhibition Halls
Moorfields Eye Hosp
Gray's Inn
Chancery Lane
Staple Inn
London Silver Vaults
Daily Mirror Offices
Patent Office
Science Ref. Lib
Lincoln's Inn
Lincoln's Inn Fields
Royal College of Surgeons
Old Curiosity Shop
Public Record Office
Royal Courts of Justice
London School of Economics
Dickens House
St Alban's
Farringdon
St Etheldreda's Ch
Central Markets (Smithfield)
St Bart the Great
St Bartholomew's Hospital
Holy Sepulchre
City Temple
Dr Johnson's House
Central Criminal Court
National Postal Museum
BT Centre
Goldsmiths' Hall
Saddlers Hall
St Paul's Cathedral
Stationers Hall
St Martin's
Apothecaries Hall
Youth Hostel
Faraday Building
College of Arms
St Brides
The Bridewell Th
Prince Henry's Room
Temple Church
Inns of Court and Chancery
Inner Temple
Middle Temple Hall
Middle Temple
St Clement Danes
Bush House (B.B.C.)
Australia House
St Mary le-Strand
Courtauld Institute Galleries
Roman Bath
Howard Hotel
King's College
Temple
HQS Wellington (Master Mariners)
HMS President
Thames Police Station
Blackfriars
BLACKFRIARS STATION
Blackfriars Pier
City of London School
Mermaid Theatre
St Benet's
Millennium Bridge
Queenhithe Stairs
Southwark Br Stairs
Bankside Jetty
Bankside Gallery
Tate Gallery of Modern Art (under development)
Globe Th Shakespeare Globe Exhibition
Financial Times
Oxo Tower Wharf
Old Barge House Stairs
The London Television Centre (LWT)
National Film Th.
Royal National Theatre
Queen Elizabeth Hall
Purcell Room
Mus of the Moving Image
London Nautical Sch
St Christopher House
Ironmongers Hall
Barber Surgeons Hall
Mus of London
Roman Wall Remains
Salters' Hall
Brewers' Hall
Girdlers' Hall
Plaisterers' Hall
Pewterers' Hall
St Anne & St Agnes Ch
St Botolph's
Postman's Park
Haberdashers' Hall
Clock Museum
Guildhall
Waxchandlers' Hall
St Lawrence Jewry
Mercers' Hall
Bank of England Extension
St Mary le Bow
St Mary Aldermary
Temple of Mithras
Mansion House
Painters' Hall
Vintners Hall
Innholders' Hall
Livery Halls
CANNON STREET STA
Clink Exhibition
HOLBORN
HOLBORN CIRCUS
HOLBORN VIADUCT
FLEET STREET
LUDGATE HILL
LUDGATE CIRCUS
STRAND
VICTORIA EMBANKMENT
QUEEN VICTORIA STREET
UPPER THAMES STREET
CHEAPSIDE
NEWGATE STREET
CLERKENWELL ROAD
FARRINGDON ROAD
FARRINGDON STREET
GRAY'S INN ROAD
ROSEBERY AVENUE
GOSWELL ROAD
ALDERSGATE STREET
CITY ROAD
OLD STREET
BEECH STREET
CHISWELL
LONDON WALL
BLACKFRIARS BRIDGE
WATERLOO BRIDGE
SOUTHWARK BRIDGE
PENTON RISE
PENTONVILLE ROAD
KING'S CROSS ROAD
ST JOHN STREET
CHANCERY LANE
FETTER LANE
NEW BRIDGE ST
CANNON STREET
RIVER
A201
A401
A5201
A40
A4
A3211
A501
B502
A1
A300
A3200
E
F
G
H
5
9

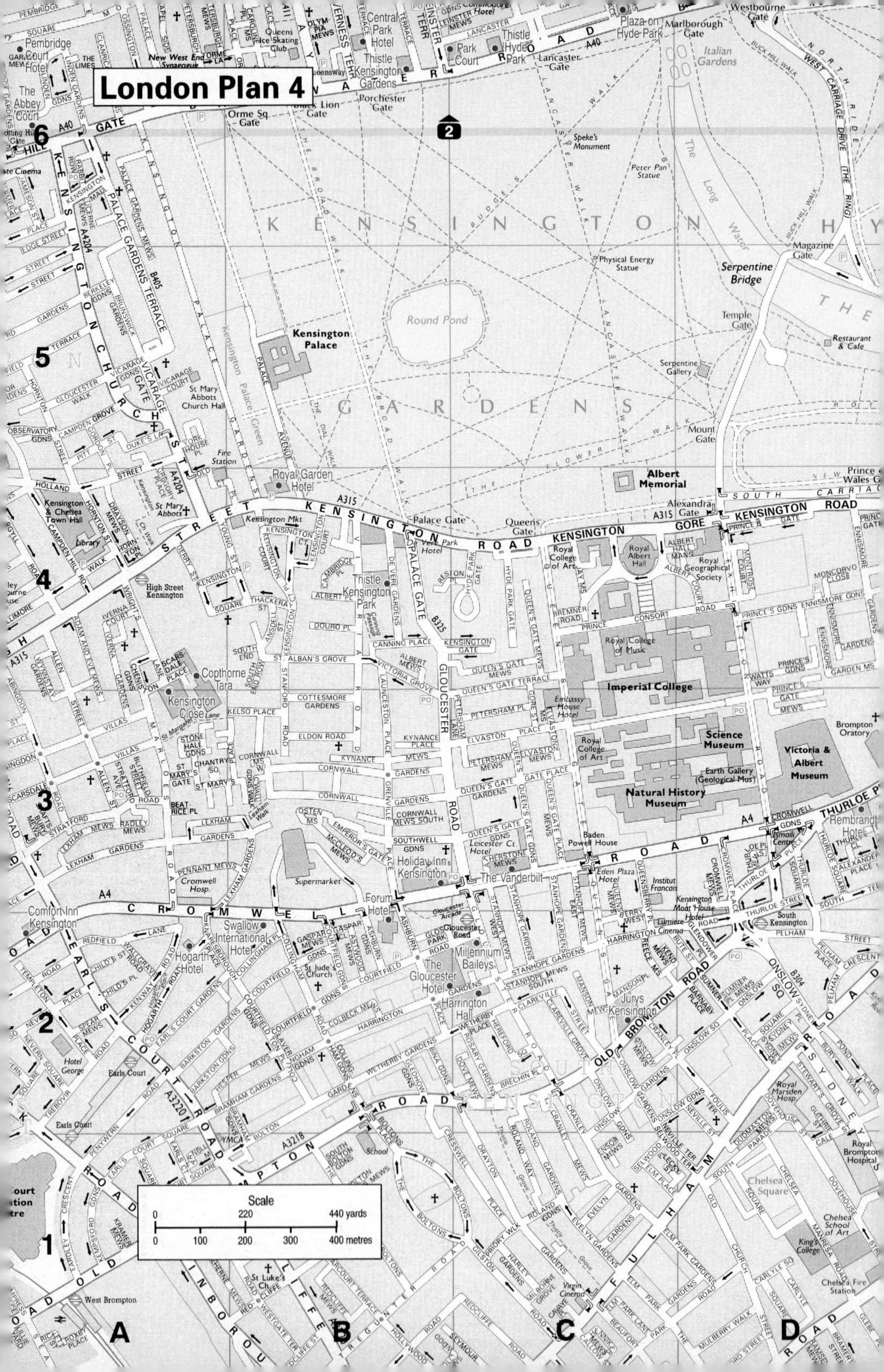

London Plan 4
KENSINGTON GARDENS
Kensington Palace
Round Pond
Albert Memorial
Physical Energy Statue
Speke's Monument
Peter Pan Statue
Serpentine Bridge
Serpentine Gallery
The Long Water
Italian Gardens
Marlborough Gate
Lancaster Gate
Westbourne Gate
Black Lion Gate
Orme Sq Gate
Porchester Gate
Magazine Gate
Temple Gate
Mount Gate
Alexandra Gate
Queens Gate
Palace Gate
Prince of Wales Gate
Restaurant & Cafe
BAYSWATER ROAD
KENSINGTON ROAD
KENSINGTON GORE
KENSINGTON HIGH STREET
KENSINGTON CHURCH STREET
GLOUCESTER ROAD
CROMWELL ROAD
OLD BROMPTON ROAD
FULHAM ROAD
EARL'S COURT ROAD
PALACE GARDENS TERRACE
KENSINGTON PALACE GARDENS
QUEEN'S GATE
EXHIBITION ROAD
PRINCE CONSORT ROAD
Royal Albert Hall
Royal College of Art
Royal College of Music
Royal Geographical Society
Imperial College
Science Museum
Natural History Museum
Victoria & Albert Museum
Earth Gallery (Geological Mus)
Brompton Oratory
Baden Powell House
Institut Français
Kensington Mkt
Royal Garden Hotel
Kensington & Chelsea Town Hall
Library
High Street Kensington
Copthorne Tara
Kensington Close
Thistle Kensington Park
De Vere Park Hotel
Holiday Inn Kensington
The Vanderbilt
Forum Hotel
Swallow International Hotel
Hogarth Hotel
Comfort Inn Kensington
Gloucester Road
Millennium Baileys
The Gloucester Hotel
Harrington Hall
Jurys Kensington
Kensington Moat House Hotel
Eden Plaza Hotel
Rembrandt Hotel
South Kensington
Earls Court
West Brompton
Hotel George
Cromwell Hosp.
Supermarket
Royal Marsden Hosp
Royal Brompton Hospital
Chelsea School of Art
King's College
Chelsea Fire Station
Chelsea Square
Virgin Cinema
St Luke's Ch.
SOUTH KENSINGTON
Scale
0 220 440 yards
0 100 200 300 400 metres
A B C D
1 2 3 4 5 6

Brook Gate
47 Park Street
US Embassy
Millennium Britannia Mayfair
Connaught Hotel
Grosvenor Gate
Grosvenor House
Entrance and Exit to Underground Car Park
2
MAYFAIR
Library
Royal Inst. (Faraday Mus.)
Museum of Mankind
Brown's Hotel
Agnew's Gallery
May Fair Inter-Continental
Chesterfield Hotel
Washington Mayfair Hotel
Crewe House
Ritz Hotel
Green Park
Flemings Hotel
The Dorchester
RING ROAD
A4202
PARK LANE
A4202
HYDE PARK
Curzon (Mayfair)
Green Park Hotel
SHEPHERD MKT
MKT MEWS
Park Lane Hotel
PICCADILLY
A4
Metropolitan Hotel
Four Seasons Hotel
Athenaeum Hotel
The Metropolitan
GREEN PARK
Norwegian/British Monument
Boat House
Pier
SERPENTINE
SERPENTINE ROAD
Queen Mother Gate
Hotel Inter-Continental
Apsley House (Wellington Mus)
Hyde Park Corner
HYDE PARK CORNER
ROTTEN ROW
Albert Gate
SOUTH CARRIAGE DRIVE
Wellington Arch
POL
CONSTITUTION HILL (CLOSED TO TRAFFIC SUNDAYS)
5
Edinburgh Gate
Bowater House
Mandarin Oriental Hyde Park
Knightsbridge Barracks
KNIGHTSBRIDGE
The Berkeley
The Lanesborough
GROSVENOR CRES
B310
Buckingham Palace Gardens
Buckingham Palace
Queen's Gallery
Knightsbridge
A315
Basil Street Hotel
Sheraton Park Tower
The Millennium Chelsea
The Halkin Hotel
GROSVENOR PLACE
A302
RING ROAD
Knightsbridge Fire Sta
Capital Hotel
Lowndes Hyatt Hotel
BELGRAVE SQUARE
Harrods Store
Hyatt Carlton Tower Hotel
SLOANE STREET
A3216
The Royal Mews
LWR GROSVENOR PL
Rubens at the Palace
Westminster Th
The Parkes Hotel
The Beaufort
BROMPTON ROAD
A4
BEAUCHAMP PLACE
B319
PONT STREET
Cadogan Hotel
HOBART PL
A3217
London Tourist Board & Convention Bureau
Goring Hotel
Thistle Westminster
Victoria Palace
BROMPTON
St Columba's Ch
Mag Ct
EATON SQUARE
RING ROAD
ECCLESTON
Edbury Court Hotel
Thistle Victoria
(Victoria)
Victoria TERMINUS PL Bus Sta
Apollo Victoria
VICTORIA STATION
Victoria Place Shopping Centre
Victoria Rail/Air Terminal
Wilbraham Hotel
Royal Ct Hotel
BELGRAVIA
Coach Sta Arrivals
The Colonnades Shopping Centre
B310
Quality London Victoria
Royal Court
Sloane Square
Victoria Coach Sta
School
Guinness Trust Estate
Duke of York's H.Q.
LOWER SLOANE STREET
PIMLICO ROAD
A3214
BUCKINGHAM PALACE ROAD
EBURY BRIDGE
B324
Abbots Manor Estate
KING'S ROAD
A3217
CHELSEA BRIDGE ROAD
Chelsea Barracks
EBURY BRIDGE ROAD
B313
Chelsea Cinema
Burtons Court
Museum
Ranelagh Gardens
Chelsea Old Town Hall
Chelsea Centre
ROYAL HOSPITAL ROAD
B302
Royal Hospital
Lister Hosp
Churchill Gardens
National Army Museum
A3212
GROSVENOR ROAD
EMBANKMENT
E
F
G
H

London Plan 5

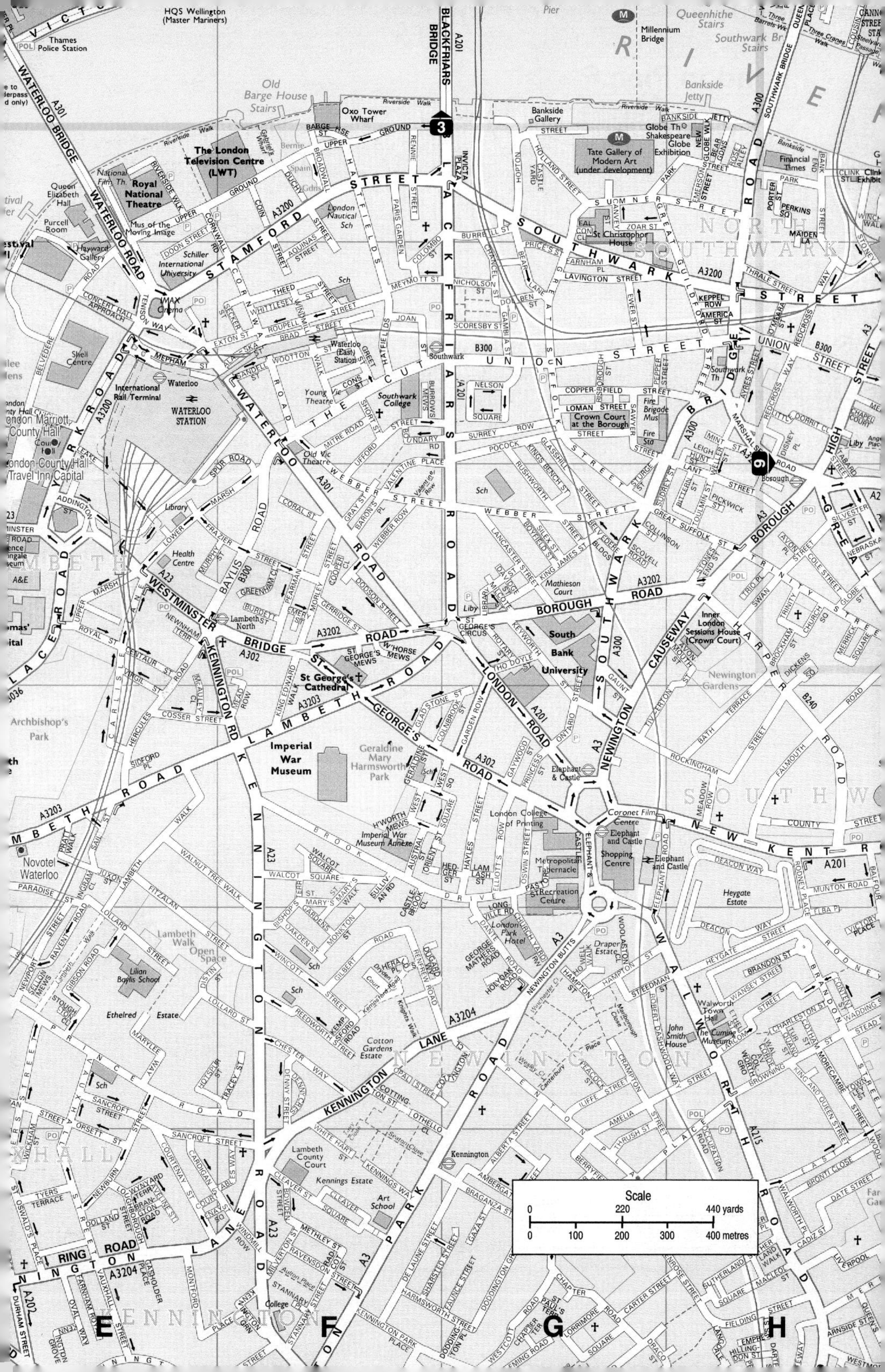

HQS Wellington (Master Mariners)
Thames Police Station
BLACKFRIARS BRIDGE
Millennium Bridge
Queenhithe Stairs
Southwark Br Stairs
RIVER
WATERLOO BRIDGE
Old Barge House Stairs
Oxo Tower Wharf
Riverside Walk
Bankside Gallery
Bankside Jetty
Globe Th Shakespeare Globe Exhibition
Tate Gallery of Modern Art (under development)
The London Television Centre (LWT)
Royal National Theatre
National Film Th.
Queen Elizabeth Hall
Purcell Room
Hayward Gallery
Mus of the Moving Image
Schiller International University
London Nautical Sch
STAMFORD STREET
SOUTHWARK STREET
SOUTHWARK BRIDGE ROAD
Financial Times
St Christopher House
NORTH SOUTHWARK
IMAX Cinema
Shell Centre
International Rail Terminal
WATERLOO STATION
Waterloo
Waterloo (East) Station
Southwark
UNION STREET
THE CUT
Young Vic Theatre
Southwark College
Old Vic Theatre
Crown Court at the Borough
Fire Brigade Mus
Borough
London County Hall
Travel Inn Capital
Library
Health Centre
WESTMINSTER BRIDGE ROAD
Lambeth North
St George's Cathedral
St George's Circus
BOROUGH ROAD
South Bank University
Mathieson Court
Inner London Sessions House (Crown Court)
Newington Gardens
LAMBETH ROAD
KENNINGTON ROAD
LONDON ROAD
ST GEORGE'S ROAD
Imperial War Museum
Geraldine Mary Harmsworth Park
Imperial War Museum Annexe
Elephant & Castle
London College of Printing
Metropolitan Tabernacle
Elephant and Castle Shopping Centre
Coronet Film Centre
NEW KENT ROAD
Heygate Estate
Archbishop's Park
Novotel Waterloo
Lambeth Walk Open Space
Lilian Baylis School
Ethelred Estate
Cotton Gardens Estate
London Park Hotel
Draper Estate
NEWINGTON
Walworth Town Hall
The Cuming Museum
John Smith House
KENNINGTON LANE
KENNINGTON PARK ROAD
Lambeth County Court
Kennings Estate
Art School
Kennington
VAUXHALL
KENNINGTON
WALWORTH ROAD
College
Scale
0 220 440 yards
0 100 200 300 400 metres
E
F
G
H

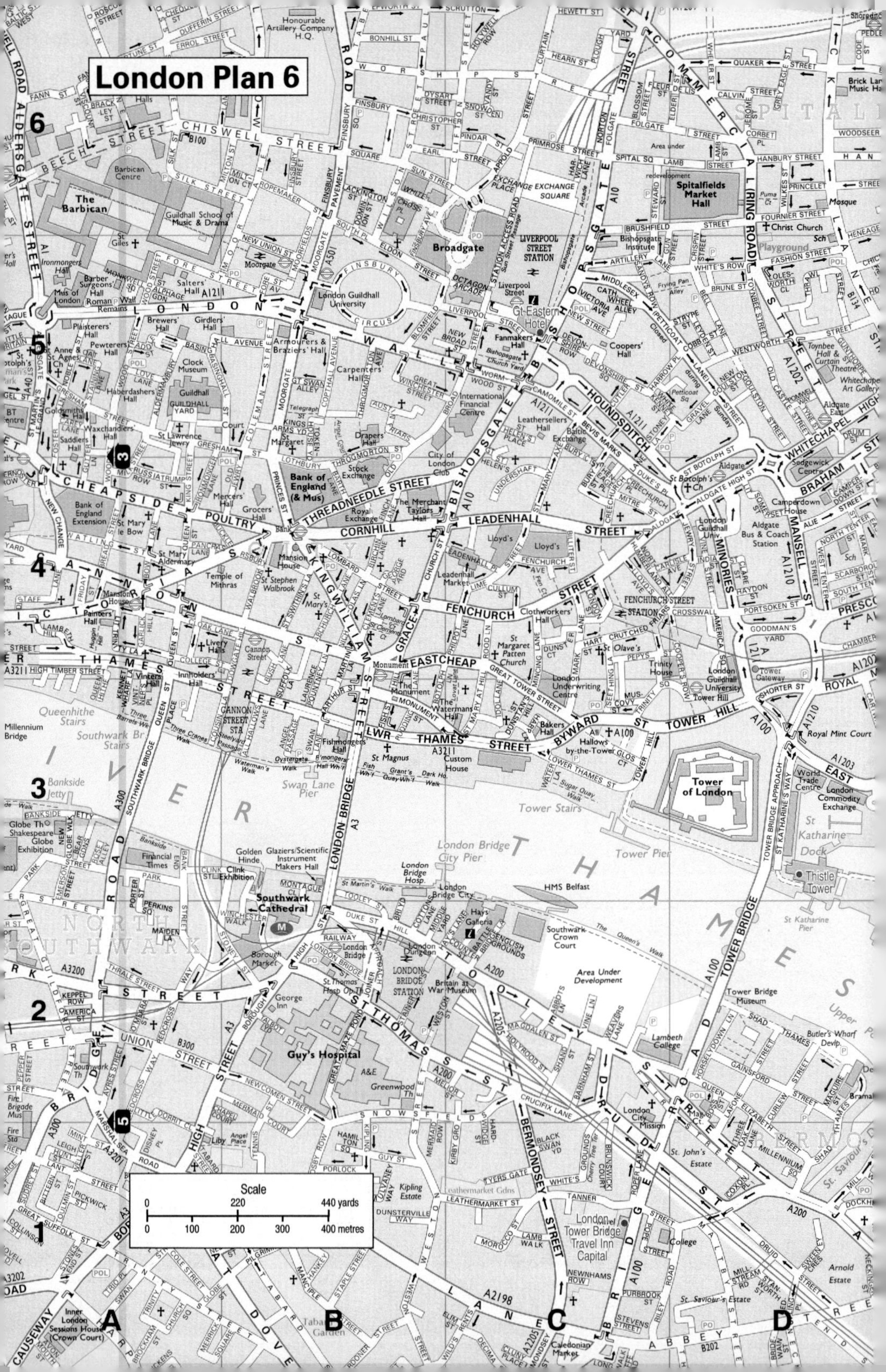
London Plan 6
Scale
0
220
440 yards
0
100
200
300
400 metres
The Barbican
Barbican Centre
Guildhall School of Music & Drama
St Giles
Ironmongers' Hall
Barber Surgeons' Hall
Mus of London
Roman Wall Remains
Salters' Hall
Moorgate
London Guildhall University
Broadgate
Liverpool Street Station
Gt Eastern Hotel
Spitalfields Market Hall
Christ Church
Mosque
Bishopsgate Institute
Playground
Plaisterers' Hall
Pewterers' Hall
Brewers' Hall
Girdlers' Hall
Armourers & Braziers' Hall
Carpenters' Hall
Clock Museum
Guildhall
Haberdashers' Hall
Goldsmiths' Hall
Waxchandlers' Hall
Saddlers' Hall
St Lawrence Jewry
Drapers' Hall
Stock Exchange
Bank of England (& Mus)
Bank of England Extension
St Mary le Bow
Mercers' Hall
Grocers' Hall
Royal Exchange
The Merchant Taylors Hall
City of London Club
International Financial Centre
Leathersellers Hall
Baltic Exchange
Coopers' Hall
Fanmakers Hall
Toynbee Hall & Curtain Theatre
Whitechapel Art Gallery
Aldgate East
Aldgate
Sedgewick Centre
St Botolph's Ch
Camperdown House
Aldgate Bus & Coach Station
London Guildhall Univ
Lloyd's
Leadenhall Market
St Mary Aldermary
Temple of Mithras
St Stephen Walbrook
Mansion House
St Mary's
Painters' Hall
Livery Halls
Cannon Street
Vintners' Hall
Innholders' Hall
Cannon Street Sta
Clothworkers' Hall
St Margaret Pattens Church
London Underwriting Centre
Fenchurch Street Station
St Olave's
Trinity House
London Guildhall University
Tower Hill
Tower Gateway
Monument
The Monument
The Watermans Hall
Bakers Hall
All Hallows by-the-Tower
Fishmongers Hall
St Magnus
Custom House
Swan Lane Pier
Queenhithe Stairs
Millennium Bridge
Southwark Br Stairs
Bankside Jetty
Globe Th Shakespeare Globe Exhibition
Financial Times
Clink Exhibition
Golden Hinde
Glaziers/Scientific Instrument Makers Hall
Southwark Cathedral
Borough Market
London Bridge City Pier
London Bridge Hosp.
London Bridge City
HMS Belfast
Hays Galleria
Southwark Crown Court
Area Under Development
London Dungeon
London Bridge Station
Britain at War Museum
St Thomas Hosp Op Th
George Inn
Guy's Hospital
A&E
Greenwood Th
Tower Stairs
Tower of London
Tower Pier
Royal Mint Court
World Trade Centre
London Commodity Exchange
St Katharine Dock
Thistle Tower
St Katharine Pier
Tower Bridge Museum
Butler's Wharf Devlp.
Lambeth College
London City Mission
St. John's Estate
Kipling Estate
Leathermarket Gdns
London Tower Bridge Travel Inn Capital
College
Arnold Estate
St. Saviour's Estate
Caledonian Market
Inner London Sessions House (Crown Court)
Tabard Garden
Fire Brigade Mus
Fire Sta
RIVER THAMES
NORTH SOUTHWARK
SPITALFIELDS
BERMONDSEY
A
B
C
D
1
2
3
4
5
6

LONDON

Greater London Plans 1-5, pages 372-386. (Small scale maps 4 & 5 at back of book.) Hotels are listed below in postal district order, commencing East, then North, South and West, with a brief indication of the area covered. Detailed plans 2-5 show the locations of AA-appointed hotels within the Central London postal districts. If you do not know the postal district of the hotel you want, please refer to the index preceding the street plans for the entry and map pages.

E1 STEPNEY AND EAST OF THE TOWER OF LONDON

★★★★ ***Thistle Tower***

THISTLE HOTELS

St Katherine's Way E1 9LD
Quality Percentage Score: 67%
☎ 020 7481 2575 📠 020 7488 4106
Dir: *adjacent to Tower Bridge on North side of River Thames*

This busy hotel has wonderful views - even the docks to the rear are attractively landscaped. A large number of the bedrooms are very sumptuous, but few can match the opulence and design of the suites which come with full butler service. The Princes Room provides carefully crafted dishes served by a professional and friendly team of staff. There is a range of very modern state-of-the-art meeting rooms on the top floor.

ROOMS: 800 en suite (bth/shr) No smoking in 478 bedrooms
MEALS: International Cuisine V meals Coffee am Tea pm
FACILITIES: CTV in all bedrooms STV Gym Wkly live entertainment
CONF: Thtr 250 Class 130 Board 40 **SERVICES:** Lift Night porter Air conditioning 102P **NOTES:** No smoking area in restaurant Last d 11pm
CARDS:

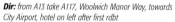

E6 EAST HAM See LONDON plan 1 *H4*

Travel Inn

travel inn

1 Woolwich Manor Way, Beckton E6 4NT
☎ 020 7511 3853 📠 020 7511 4214
Dir: *from A13 take A117, Woolwich Manor Way, towards City Airport, hotel on left after first rdbt*

This modern building offers accommodation in smart, spacious and well equipped bedrooms, all with en-suite bathrooms. Refreshments may be taken at the nearby family restaurant. For details about current prices consult the Contents Page under Hotel Groups for the Travel Inn phone number.

ROOMS: 40 en suite (bth/shr) d £39.95 *

E14 LIMEHOUSE

Travelodge

Travelodge

Coriander Av, East India Dock Rd E14 2AA
☎ 020 7531 9705
Dir: *fronts A13 at East India Dock Road*

This modern building offers accommodation in smart, spacious and well equipped bedrooms, all with en-suite bathrooms. Refreshments may be taken at the nearby family restaurant. For details about current prices, consult the Contents Page under Hotel Groups for the Travelodge phone number.

ROOMS: 132 en suite (bth/shr) (incl. bkfst) d £59.95 *

EC1 CITY OF LONDON

★★★ ***The Barbican***

Mount Charlotte Hotels MH

Central St, Clerkenwell EC1V 8DS
Quality Percentage Score: 63%
☎ 020 7251 1565 📠 020 7253 1005
Dir: *From Kings Cross station follow Pentonville Rd Islington. Over junct at Angel into City Rd. 3rd right into Central St, hotel is 150m on the left*

Very popular with both tourists and corporate guests, this modern hotel is about a ten minute walk from the Barbican, although the hotel does provide a useful shuttle service. The pleasant bedrooms are well decorated including some smart contemporary executive rooms.

ROOMS: 298 en suite (bth/shr) 167 annexe en suite (bth/shr) (57 fmly) No smoking in 30 bedrooms **MEALS:** European Cuisine V meals Coffee am Tea pm **FACILITIES:** CTV in all bedrooms STV **CONF:** Thtr 160 Class 60 Board 50 **SERVICES:** Lift Night porter 12P **NOTES:** No dogs (ex guide dogs) No smoking area in restaurant Last d 10.30pm
CARDS:

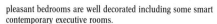

EC2

Great Eastern Hotel

Liverpool St EC2M 7QW
☎ 020 7618 5000
ROOMS: 267 rms **NOTES:**

N1 ISLINGTON See LONDON plan 1 *F4*

★★★ ***Jury's Inn London***

JURYS HOTEL GROUP

60 Pentonville Rd, Islington N1 9LA
Quality Percentage Score: 66%
☎ 020 7282 5500 📠 020 7282 5511

The Jury's Inn concept is based on good value rooms, that can easily be adapted to family use, and single guests will be pleased to have the comfort of a double bed; all rooms are air-conditioned. Other facilities and services are fairly low-key; strengths include hospitality and the fixed room rate. The Angel

contd.

London

For Useful Information and Important Telephone Number Changes turn to page 25

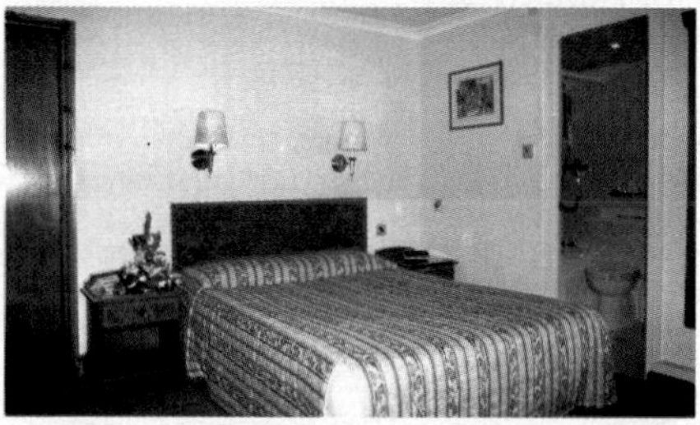

Tube station is nearby and there are several car parks in the neighbourhood.

Jury's Inn, London

ROOMS: 229 en suite (bth/shr) (116 fmly) No smoking in 135 bedrooms **MEALS:** V meals Coffee am **FACILITIES:** CTV in all bedrooms STV **CONF:** Thtr 30 Class 10 Board 15 **SERVICES:** Lift Night porter Air conditioning **NOTES:** No dogs (ex guide dogs) No smoking area in restaurant Last d 10pm Closed 24-27 Dec **CARDS:** 😊 ■ 🔁 💷 🄲

See advert on opposite page

≡ N1 ISLINGTON
★★★ Great Northern
Kings Cross N1 9AN

Best Western

Quality Percentage Score: 64%
☎ 020 7837 5454 📠 020 7278 5270
Dir: *entrance faces side of Kings Cross station*
This hotel is close to Kings Cross and Euston stations. It offers spacious, comfortable accommodation with a good level of facilities. The coffee house is open all day for meals, and there is also a lively bar and a no-smoking lounge. There is 24-hour room service and a laundry service.
ROOMS: 82 en suite (bth/shr) (16 fmly) No smoking in 22 bedrooms s £105-£125; d £125-£135 (incl. bkfst) * LB Off peak **MEALS:** Lunch fr £17 Dinner £13.15-£24.70alc V meals Coffee am Tea pm **FACILITIES:** CTV in all bedrooms STV **CONF:** Thtr 100 Class 60 Board 45 Del from £126 * **SERVICES:** Lift Night porter 12P **NOTES:** No dogs No coaches No smoking area in restaurant Last d 9.30pm
CARDS: 😊 ■ 🔁 💷 🚃 🄲

≡ N10 MUSWELL HILL See LONDON plan 1 *E6*
★★★ Raglan Hall
8-12 Queens Ave, Muswell Hill N10 3NR

Best Western

Quality Percentage Score: 68%
☎ 020 8883 9836 📠 020 8883 5002
Dir: *North Circ B550 for Muswell Hill. At roundabout take last exit to Queens Avenue. Hotel is 75yds on the right.*
Service and hospitality are the hallmarks at Raglan Hall, which has an attractive frontage on the tree-lined Queens Avenue in Muswell Hill. Bedrooms vary in size but all are well equipped. Public areas centre on a relaxing bar and meals are carefully prepared.
ROOMS: 46 en suite (bth/shr) (8 fmly) No smoking in 6 bedrooms s £69-£104; d £69-£109 Off peak **MEALS:** High tea fr £2 Dinner £3.50-£19 & alc Mediterranean Cuisine V meals Coffee am Tea pm **FACILITIES:** CTV in all bedrooms STV **CONF:** Thtr 120 Class 40 Board 50 Del from £120 **SERVICES:** Night porter 12P **NOTES:** No dogs (ex guide dogs) Last d 9.30pm **CARDS:** 😊 ■ 🔁 💷 🚃 🄲

≡ NW1 REGENT'S PARK See LONDON plan 1 *E4*

The Premier Collection

★★★★★ 🏵🏵🏵 *Landmark*
222 Marylebone Rd NW1 6JQ
☎ 020 7631 8000 📠 020 7631 8080
Dir: *located on Marylebone Road in front of Marylebone Railway Station*
At the heart of this magnificent hotel is the spectacular Winter Garden, an eight-storey atrium fringed with high palm trees, where a pianist plays and afternoon teas, drinks and light meals are served. There are two further eating options - the panelled Cellars, and the main dining room where Andrew McLeish and his team produce a modern menu. Bedrooms are generously proportioned and air-conditioned, with marble bathrooms offering deep tubs and separate shower cubicles.

ROOMS: 298 en suite (bth/shr) **MEALS:** Mediterannean & Oriental Cuisine V meals Coffee am Tea pm **FACILITIES:** CTV in all bedrooms STV Indoor swimming pool (heated) Sauna Gym Health club Massage Turkish bath **CONF:** Thtr 350 Class 162 Board 80 **SERVICES:** Lift Night porter Air conditioning 90P **NOTES:** No dogs (ex guide dogs) No smoking area in restaurant Last d 11pm **CARDS:** 😊 ■ 🔁 💷 🚃 🄲

≡ NW1 REGENT'S PARK
★★★★ 🏵🏵 The White House
Albany St NW1 3UP
Quality Percentage Score: 73%
☎ 020 7387 1200 📠 020 7388 0091
Dir: *opposite Gt Portland St Underground and set slightly back from Marylebone & Euston Rd*

This delightful hotel began life as an apartment building in 1936 and offers high standards of comfort and service. Bedrooms on the 'Reserve' floor are the most spacious and have their own dedicated lounge. There are different styles of restaurant, one of

contd.

which, The Wine Press, is often used for private parties. The café bar has a brasserie-style menu, and there is also a formal dining room.
ROOMS: 582 en suite (bth/shr) (1 fmly) No smoking in 166 bedrooms s £163-£210; d £163-£210 * Off peak **MEALS:** Lunch £9.45-£12.95 Dinner £9.45-£11.75 & alc International Cuisine V meals Coffee am Tea pm **FACILITIES:** CTV in all bedrooms STV Sauna Gym Xmas **CONF:** Thtr 120 Class 45 Board 40 **SERVICES:** Lift Night porter 7P **NOTES:** No dogs (ex guide dogs) No smoking area in restaurant Last d 10.30pm **CARDS:**

See advert on this page

NW1 REGENT'S PARK
★★★ *The Kennedy*
Cardington St NW1 2LP
Quality Percentage Score: 61%
☎ 020 7387 4400 020 7387 5122
Dir: *A40 to Euston,then A501 to Euston Stn,turn left before Stn into Melton St, then into Cardington St, hotel is on left 200yds from traffic lights*
The Kennedy is a modern hotel close to Euston Station. Both standard and superior rooms are available, the latter being more spacious and having more amenities. Refurbishment has recently taken place and upgraded rooms look smart and contemporary. Public areas include a lounge bar with satellite TV and all day snacks, Spires restaurant which has a broad appeal, and a range of smart meeting rooms.
ROOMS: 360 en suite (bth/shr) (25 fmly) No smoking in 67 bedrooms **MEALS:** English & French Cuisine V meals Coffee am Tea pm **FACILITIES:** CTV in all bedrooms STV **CONF:** Thtr 100 Class 45 Board 50 **SERVICES:** Lift Night porter Air conditioning 24P **NOTES:** No dogs (ex guide dogs) No smoking area in restaurant Last d 10.30pm
CARDS:

NW1 REGENT'S PARK
★★ Hotel Ibis Euston
3 Cardington St NW1 2LW
Quality Percentage Score: 64%
☎ 020 7388 7777 020 7388 0001
Dir: *from Euston station or Eustaon Rd, turn right to Melton St leading to Cardington St*
This popular, busy hotel is conveniently located for Euston station and has the added advantage of a very secure underground car park. Bedrooms are bright, well maintained and provide good value for this location. The hub of the public areas is the bar/lounge which is open all day and well into the night for drinks and snacks. There is also an informal restaurant.
ROOMS: 300 en suite (bth/shr) No smoking in 150 bedrooms s fr £59.50; d fr £62.50 * Off peak **MEALS:** Lunch £9.50-£12alc Dinner £10-£15alc English & French Cuisine V meals Coffee am Tea pm **FACILITIES:** CTV in all bedrooms STV **CONF:** Thtr 100 Class 50 Board 50 **SERVICES:** Lift Air conditioning 100P **NOTES:** No smoking area in restaurant Last d 10.30pm **CARDS:**

★

The Premier Collection, hotels with Red Star Awards are listed on pages 17-23

Remember to return your Prize Draw card for a chance to win one of 30 relaxing leisure breaks with Corus and Regal hotels. See inside the front cover for the card and competition details.

NW1 REGENT'S PARK

London Euston Travel Inn Capital
141 Euston Rd NW1 2AU
☎ 020 7554 3400 020 7554 3419
Dir: *situated on the corner of Euston Road (south side) and Duke's Road, between Kings Cross/St Pancreas and Euston stations*
This modern building offers accommodation in smart, spacious and well equipped bedrooms, all with en-suite bathrooms. Refreshments may be taken at the nearby family restaurant. For details about current prices ring 01582 41 43 41.
ROOMS: 220 en suite (bth/shr) d £59.95 *

NW3 HAMPSTEAD AND SWISS COTTAGE
See LONDON plan 1 *E5/E4*

★★★★ **London Marriott Hotel Regents Park**
128 King Henry's Rd NW3 3ST
Quality Percentage Score: 68%
☎ 020 7722 7711 020 7586 5822
Dir: *at the junct of Adelaide Rd and King Henry's Rd. Approximately 200yds off Finchley Rd, A41*
Situated at Swiss Cottage, this large, modern hotel boasts a very good standard of accommodation. The spacious bedrooms all have large beds and excellent facilities; executive rooms have the benefit of a dedicated club lounge. Smart public areas comprise an open plan marbled lobby and bar-lounge. Additionally, there is indoor leisure, free parking and a shop.
ROOMS: 303 en suite (bth/shr) (157 fmly) No smoking in 102 bedrooms d £129.25-£159.80 * LB Off peak **MEALS:** Lunch £17.95-£18.95 Dinner £8.50-£16alc International Cuisine V meals Coffee am Tea pm **FACILITIES:** CTV in all bedrooms STV Indoor swimming pool (heated) Sauna Solarium Gym Hair & Beauty salon Wkly live entertainment Xmas **CONF:** Thtr 300 Class 150 Board 90 Del from £180 * **SERVICES:** Lift Night porter Air conditioning 150P **NOTES:** No dogs (ex guide dogs) No smoking area in restaurant Last d 10.30pm
CARDS:

NW3 HAMPSTEAD AND SWISS COTTAGE

★★★ ***Posthouse Hampstead***
215 Haverstock Hill NW3 4RB
Quality Percentage Score: 64%
☎ 020 7794 8121 020 7435 5586
Dir: *take A41 to Swiss Cottage just before this junction take feeder road left into Buckland Cres onto Belsize Av left into Haverstock Hill*
Suitable for business and leisure travellers, this bright hotel provides modern accommodation in well equipped bedrooms. A recent refurbishment has completed two floors of smart 'Millennium' rooms. The Traders bar and restaurant is open for lunch and dinner.
ROOMS: 140 en suite (bth/shr) No smoking in 70 bedrooms
MEALS: V meals Coffee am Tea pm **FACILITIES:** CTV in all bedrooms
CONF: Thtr 35 Board 20 **SERVICES:** Lift Night porter 70P
NOTES: Last d 10pm **CARDS:**

NW7 MILL HILL See LONDON plan 1 *D6*

Welcome Lodge
Welcome Break Service Area, London Gateway, M1, Mill Hill NW7 3HB
☎ 020 8906 0611 020 8906 3654
Dir: *on M1, between junct 2 & 3 - northbound. Accessible from southbound carriageway*
This modern building offers accommodation in smart, spacious and well equipped bedrooms, suitable for families and businessmen, and all with en-suite bathrooms. Refreshments may be taken at the nearby family restaurant. For details of current prices, consult the Contents Page under Hotel Groups for the Welcome Break phone number.
ROOMS: 101 en suite (bth/shr) d fr £55 * **CONF:** Thtr 40 Class 20 Board 25

SE1 SOUTHWARK AND WATERLOO

★★★★★ ***London Marriott County Hall***
County Hall SE1 7PB
Quality Percentage Score: 69%
☎ 020 7928 5200
The redevelopment of London's erstwhile seat of government takes advantage of views over the river towards the Houses of Parliament. Notable features are well laid-out bedrooms and first class leisure facilities. The County Restaurant produces food that shows accuracy of execution and hearty flavours.
ROOMS: 200 en suite (bth/shr)

SE1 SOUTHWARK AND WATERLOO

★★★ **Novotel London Waterloo**
113 Lambeth Rd SE1 7LS
Quality Percentage Score: 69%
☎ 020 7793 1010 020 7793 0202
Dir: *opposite Houses of Parliament on the S bank of the river Thames*
This modern young hotel, close to Waterloo station, benefits from its own secure car park. Bedrooms are spacious and well equipped with modern facilities including air conditioning. The open plan public areas include a garden brasserie, the "Flag and Whistle Pub", a small shop, and leisure facilities.
ROOMS: 187 en suite (bth/shr) (80 fmly) No smoking in 158 bedrooms s fr £119; d fr £139 * LB Off peak **MEALS:** International Cuisine V meals Coffee am Tea pm **FACILITIES:** CTV in all bedrooms STV Sauna Gym Pool table Steam room **CONF:** Thtr 40 Class 25 Board 24 Del from £175 * **SERVICES:** Lift Air conditioning 40P **NOTES:** No coaches No smoking area in restaurant
CARDS:

SE1 SOUTHWARK AND WATERLOO

London County Hall Travel Inn Capital
Belvedere Rd SE1 7PB
☎ 020 7902 1600 020 7902 1619
Dir: *next to the Royal Festival Hall and South Bank Centre*
This modern building offers accommodation in smart, spacious and well equipped bedrooms, all with en-suite bathrooms. Refreshments may be taken at the nearby family restaurant. For details about current prices ring 01582 41 43 41.
ROOMS: 312 en suite (bth/shr) d £59.95 *

SE1 SOUTHWARK AND WATERLOO

London Tower Bridge Travel Inn Capital
Tower Bridge Rd SE1
☎ 020 7940 3700 020 7940 3719
This modern building offers accommodation in smart, spacious and well equipped bedrooms, all with en-suite bathrooms. Refreshments may be taken at the nearby family restaurant. For details about current prices ring 01582 41 43 41.
ROOMS: 195 en suite (bth/shr) d £59.95 *

New AA Guides for the Millennium are featured on page 24

London

SE3 BLACKHEATH See LONDON plan 1 *G3*

★★★ Bardon Lodge

15-17 Stratheden Rd SE3 7TH
Quality Percentage Score: 64%
☎ 020 8853 4051 Fax 020 8858 7387

On the edge of the pretty village of Blackheath, this is a friendly hotel, popular for small conferences during the week and equally in demand by weekend visitors to Greenwich. The Vanbrugh Hotel across the road is under the same ownership and offers budget accommodation.

ROOMS: 32 en suite (bth/shr) (4 fmly) s £75-£80; d £100-£120 (incl. bkfst) * LB Off peak **MEALS:** Bar Lunch £5-£15 Dinner £13.50-£19 & alc English & Continental Cuisine V meals Coffee am Tea pm **FACILITIES:** CTV in all bedrooms STV Xmas **CONF:** Thtr 45 Class 20 Board 20 Del from £80 * **SERVICES:** Night porter 16P **NOTES:** No smoking area in restaurant Last d 9.30pm
CARDS:

SE3 BLACKHEATH

★★ Clarendon

8-16 Montpelier Row, Blackheath SE3 0RW
Quality Percentage Score: 55%
☎ 020 8318 4321 Fax 020 8318 4378

***Dir:** A2, turn off at Blackheath junct, hotel on left just before village overlooking Blackheath & Greenwich Royal Park*

This imposing Georgian building stands on the edge of the Royal Hundred of Blackheath with commanding views over open countryside. Bedrooms are neat and well equipped. Function and meeting rooms are available. The Chart Bar is an attractive feature of the hotel.

ROOMS: 193 en suite (bth/shr) (37 fmly) No smoking in 22 bedrooms s fr £59.50; d fr £79 (incl. bkfst) * LB Off peak **MEALS:** Lunch £5-£12.50 Dinner fr £15 & alc English, French & Italian Cuisine V meals Coffee am Tea pm **FACILITIES:** CTV in all bedrooms Pool table Wkly live entertainment Xmas **CONF:** Thtr 200 Class 50 Board 120 Del from £73.50 * **SERVICES:** Lift Night porter 80P **NOTES:** No smoking area in restaurant Last d 9.45pm **CARDS:**

See advert on this page

SE10 GREENWICH See LONDON plan 1 *G3*

★★ Hotel Ibis

30 Stockwell St SE10 9JN
Quality Percentage Score: 63%
☎ 020 8305 1177 Fax 020 8858 7139

This modern hotel is located in the heart of Greenwich. Public areas are restricted to a bar serving limited snacks and soft

contd.

drinks. The restaurant is operated by a high profile brasserie company which also provides a full choice self-service breakfast.
ROOMS: 82 en suite (bth/shr) No smoking in 22 bedrooms s £55.50; d £58.50 * Off peak **MEALS:** Coffee am **FACILITIES:** CTV in all bedrooms STV **SERVICES:** Lift 30P **NOTES:** No smoking area in restaurant **CARDS:**

SW1 WESTMINSTER

The Premier Collection

★★★★★❀❀❀❀❀ **The Berkeley**
Wilton Place, Knightsbridge SW1X 7RL
☎ 020 7235 6000 020 7235 4330
The Savoy Group
***Dir:** 300mtrs along Knightsbridge from Hyde Park Corner*
Considered to be the bench-mark for the the very best in hotel-keeping and service, the Berkeley has an excellent range of bedrooms, some with sizeable balconies, furnished with care and attention to detail. Reception rooms, including the Lutyens Writing Room, are adorned with magnificent flower arrangements, and there are superb leisure facilities The two restaurants offer a complete contrast of style: modern, influenced by South East Asia at Vong (❀❀) and French cuisine at La Tante Claire (❀❀❀❀❀), where Pierre Koffmann presides.
ROOMS: 168 en suite (bth/shr) No smoking in 28 bedrooms s £317.25-£364.25; d £387.75-£405.38 * LB Off peak **MEALS:** Lunch £16.50-£45 & alc Dinner fr £45 & alc French & Thai Cuisine V meals Coffee am Tea pm **FACILITIES:** CTV in all bedrooms STV Indoor swimming pool (heated) Sauna Solarium Gym Xmas **CONF:** Thtr 220 Class 100 Board 50 **SERVICES:** Lift Night porter Air conditioning 50P **NOTES:** No dogs (ex guide dogs) No coaches No smoking area in restaurant Last d 11.30pm
CARDS:

SW1 WESTMINSTER

The Premier Collection

★★★★★❀❀❀ **Lanesborough**
Hyde Park Corner SW1X 7TA
☎ 020 7259 5599 020 7259 5606
***Dir:** follow signs to central London and Hyde Park Corner*
Occupying an enviable position on Hyde Park Corner, the Lanesborough offers the highest levels of comfort in its range of bedrooms and suites. Twenty-four-hour service from a personal butler ensures that guests are well catered for, and the reception rooms, with their lavish furnishings and magnificent flower arrangements, are a delight to use. The popular cocktail bar has a wonderful supply of vintage cognac, whiskies and ports, and the conservatory restaurant offers an attractive atmosphere for dining.

ROOMS: 95 en suite (bth/shr) No smoking in 24 bedrooms s £276-£323; d £364-£480 * LB Off peak **MEALS:** Lunch £20.50-£25.50 & alc Dinner £30.50-£38 & alc International Cuisine V meals Coffee am Tea pm **FACILITIES:** CTV in all bedrooms STV Gym Jacuzzi/spa Fitness studio Wkly live entertainment Xmas **CONF:** Thtr 90 Class 60 Board 50 Del from £410 * **SERVICES:** Lift Night porter Air conditioning 38P **NOTES:** No coaches Last d mdnt
CARDS:

SW1 WESTMINSTER

The Premier Collection

★★★★★❀❀❀❀ **Mandarin Oriental Hyde Park**
66 Knightsbridge SW1X 7LA
☎ 020 7235 2000 020 7235 4552
***Dir:** after passing Harrods, on the righthand side, the hotel is 0.5m on the left opposite Harvey Nichols department store*
Situated between the fashionable shopping district of Knightsbridge and the peaceful green expanse of Hyde Park, this famous hotel offers a luxurious atmosphere. Marble is used to elegant effect in the reception areas, which include a popular cocktail lounge and the princpal restaurant, The Park, where dishes exemplify subtle flavours and high quality ingredients. The standard of food, accommodation and service are all excellent.
ROOMS: 200 en suite (bth/shr) No smoking in 72 bedrooms s £270-£425; d £295-£425 * LB Off peak **MEALS:** Lunch £19-£23.50 Dinner £32-£37alc English & European Cuisine V meals Coffee am Tea pm **FACILITIES:** CTV in all bedrooms STV Gym Fitness centre Wkly live entertainment Xmas **CONF:** Thtr 250 Class 130 Board 60 **SERVICES:** Lift Night porter Air conditioning P **NOTES:** No dogs (ex guide dogs) No coaches Last d 10.30pm
CARDS:

SW1 WESTMINSTER

★★★★★ Hyatt Carlton Tower
Cadogan Place SW1X 9PY
Quality Percentage Score: 74%
☎ 020 7235 1234 Fax 020 7235 9129
***Dir:** turn down Sloane St, Cadogan Place is the second turning on the left immediately before Pont St*

In the heart of Knightsbridge, the Hyatt Carlton Tower offers stylish bedrooms and bright public areas. Facilities are impressive. The ground floor houses the Chinoiserie lounge and Rib Room restaurant with its clubby bar. Modern Italian cooking is on offer in the Grissini restaurant.

ROOMS: 220 en suite (bth/shr) No smoking in 61 bedrooms s fr £270; d fr £290 * LB Off peak **MEALS:** Lunch £19.50-£28alc Dinner £24.50-£34alc English & Italian Cuisine V meals Coffee am Tea pm **FACILITIES:** CTV in all bedrooms STV Indoor swimming pool (heated) Tennis (hard) Sauna Solarium Gym Jacuzzi/spa Beauty treatment Hair salon Health club Massage & Spa treatments Wkly live entertainment Xmas **CONF:** Thtr 400 Class 250 Board 80 **SERVICES:** Lift Night porter Air conditioning 80P **NOTES:** No dogs (ex guide dogs) No coaches No smoking area in restaurant Last d 22.30pm
CARDS:

SW1 WESTMINSTER

★★★★★ Sheraton Park Tower
101 Knightsbridge SW1X 7RN
Quality Percentage Score: 69%
☎ 020 7235 8050 & 7235 3368 Res Fax 020 7235 3368
***Dir:** close to Knightsbridge Underground Station*

The unique circular, modern hotel has good standard-sized bedrooms, higher tariffs have better views and facilities, up to full butler service. Refurbished public areas have a lively atmosphere; the main bar off the lobby has a 'clubby' feel with tasteful polo prints; afternoon tea can be taken in the Rotunda Lounge. Restaurant One-O-One has undergone a transformation, Chef Pascal Proyart's cuisine de la mer meets a very high standard of cooking.

ROOMS: 289 en suite (bth/shr) (289 fmly) No smoking in 80 bedrooms s fr £285; d fr £305 * Off peak **MEALS:** Lunch fr £25 Dinner fr £42 French Cuisine V meals Coffee am Tea pm **FACILITIES:** CTV in all bedrooms STV Health facilities at affiliated club Wkly live entertainment Xmas **CONF:** Thtr 60 Class 50 Board 30 **SERVICES:** Lift Night porter Air conditioning 90P **NOTES:** No dogs (ex guide dogs) No smoking area in restaurant Last d 10.30pm **CARDS:**

SW1 WESTMINSTER

The Premier Collection

★★★★ Goring
Beeston Place, Grosvenor Gardens
SW1W 0JW

PRIDE OF BRITAIN MEMBER

☎ 020 7396 9000 Fax 020 7834 4393
***Dir:** behind Buckingham Palace, right off Lower Grosvenor Place, just prior to the Royal Mews on the left*

Run by the Goring family since 1910, this hotel is a superb example of the true British tradition of hotel keeping. Bedrooms are traditionally furnished and provide all the modern facilities one would expect from such a highly regarded hotel. Reception rooms include the garden bar and drawing room, both popular for afternoon tea and cocktails. The restaurant menu has a classic repertoire, such as grilled Dover sole and lobster Thermidor, as well as more modern dishes.

ROOMS: 75 en suite (bth/shr) s £202; d £246-£305 * LB Off peak **MEALS:** Lunch £24-£27.50alc English & French Cuisine V meals Coffee am Tea pm **FACILITIES:** CTV in all bedrooms STV Free membership of nearby Health Club Wkly live entertainment Xmas **CONF:** Thtr 60 Class 30 Board 30 **SERVICES:** Lift Night porter Air conditioning 8P **NOTES:** No dogs No coaches
CARDS:

SW1 WESTMINSTER

The Premier Collection

★★★★ The Halkin Hotel
Halkin St, Belgravia SW1X 7DJ
☎ 020 7333 1000 Fax 020 7333 1100

The Halkin is one of the more individual of the capital's top hotels combining the best of modern design with attention to detail. The interior has a cool, relaxed atmosphere and contemporary appeal. Bedrooms have state of the art business communications, lighting and air-conditioning control systems. Service is polished and friendly without being intrusive. Stefano Cavallini's modern Italian cooking continues to set high standards.

ROOMS: 41 en suite (bth/shr) No smoking in 9 bedrooms d £299.63-£381.88 * LB Off peak **MEALS:** Lunch fr £23 & alc Dinner fr £55 Italian Cuisine V meals Coffee am Tea pm **FACILITIES:** CTV in all bedrooms STV Wkly live entertainment **CONF:** Thtr 30 Class 15 Board 26 **SERVICES:** Lift Night porter Air conditioning P **NOTES:** No dogs (ex guide dogs) No coaches Last d 10.30pm
CARDS:

London

SW1 WESTMINSTER

The Premier Collection

★★★★ The Stafford
16-18 St James's Place SW1A 1NJ
☎ 020 7493 0111 020 7493 7121
Dir: *turn off Pall Mall into St James's Street, take second left turn into St James's Place*

Tucked discretely away in exclusive St James, this charming hotel has successfully recaptured the heights of luxury that had been its trademark for decades. Complete refurbishment has left the hotel with elegant, individually designed bedrooms, which include a superb new studio courtyard suite. Public rooms include a comfortable drawing room and the bustling American Bar, famous for its collection of caps and ties. In the restaurant, menus balance traditional grills with more creative dishes. Service throughout the hotel demonstrates a serious commitment to customer care. Ask the sommelier for a tour of the 350-year-old cellars.

ROOMS: 81 en suite (bth/shr) s £234-£305; d £258-£305 * Off peak **MEALS:** Lunch £22.50-£25.50 & alc Dinner £25.50-£29 & alc English & French Cuisine V meals Coffee am Tea pm **FACILITIES:** CTV in all bedrooms STV Membership of Fitness Club available Xmas **CONF:** Thtr 40 Board 24 **SERVICES:** Lift Night porter Air conditioning **NOTES:** No dogs No coaches Last d 10.30pm **CARDS:**

SW1 WESTMINSTER
★★★★ The Rubens at the Palace
Buckingham Palace Rd SW1W 0PS
Quality Percentage Score: 70%
☎ 020 7834 6600 020 7233 6037
Dir: *opposite the Royal Mews*

Overlooking the Royal Mews, behind Buckingham Palace and close to Victoria Station, the Rubens offers bedrooms and public areas that are notably comfortable and well appointed. There is a good choice of eating in the two restaurants and also an extensive lounge menu. Room service provides hot dishes throughout the night.

ROOMS: 174 en suite (bth/shr) No smoking in 64 bedrooms s £116-£145; d £135-£195 * Off peak **MEALS:** Lunch £7.99-£22 High tea £10 Dinner £14.95-£19.95 & alc English & French Cuisine V meals Coffee am Tea pm **FACILITIES:** CTV in all bedrooms STV Wkly live entertainment Xmas **CONF:** Thtr 80 Class 40 Board 40 Del from £170 * **SERVICES:** Lift Night porter Air conditioning **NOTES:** No dogs (ex guide dogs) No smoking in restaurant Last d 10pm **CARDS:**

SW1 WESTMINSTER
★★★★ *The Lowndes Hyatt Hotel*
21 Lowndes St SW1X 9ES
Quality Percentage Score: 69%
☎ 020 7823 1234 020 7235 1154

International standards of accommodation and facilities combine with a welcoming atmosphere and excellent service to make this Hyatt hotel a popular choice for guests to the capital. Many of the smartly decorated bedrooms and suites have balconies, and in-room dining and 24-hour room service are alternatives to the brasserie. Concierge service and car-parking arrangements are available.

ROOMS: 78 en suite (bth/shr) No smoking in 31 bedrooms **MEALS:** International Cuisine V meals Coffee am Tea pm **FACILITIES:** CTV in all bedrooms STV Indoor swimming pool (heated) Tennis (hard) Sauna Gym Jacuzzi/spa **CONF:** Thtr 25 Board 18 **SERVICES:** Lift Night porter Air conditioning **NOTES:** No dogs (ex guide dogs) No coaches Last d 11pm **CARDS:**

SW1 WESTMINSTER
★★★★ The Millennium Chelsea
17 Sloane St, Knightsbridge SW1X 9NU
Quality Percentage Score: 67%
☎ 020 7235 4377 020 7235 3705
Dir: *from A4, Sloane St is located on the left, just past Harrods. Access to the hotel is also available via Pavilion Road*

This Sloane Street hotel is near Harrods, Harvey Nichols and many designer boutiques. All bedrooms have been refurbished to a high standard with an excellent range of modern facilities. The lounge on the ground floor is popular for coffee or snacks. The bright and airy restaurant provides the setting for some seriously enjoyable food.

ROOMS: 222 en suite (bth/shr) No smoking in 70 bedrooms s fr £200; d fr £210 * Off peak **MEALS:** Lunch £16.50 & alc Dinner £19.50 & alc International Cuisine V meals Coffee am Tea pm **FACILITIES:** CTV in all bedrooms STV **CONF:** Thtr 70 Class 40 Board 30 Del from £249 * **SERVICES:** Lift Night porter Air conditioning 10P **NOTES:** No dogs No coaches No smoking area in restaurant Last d 10.30pm **CARDS:**

SW1 WESTMINSTER
★★★★ *Thistle Westminster*
49 Buckingham Palace Rd SW1W 0QT
Quality Percentage Score: 67%
☎ 020 7834 1821 020 7931 7542
Dir: *opposite the Royal Mews*

There is a cosy atmosphere to this discreetly located hotel close to Buckingham Palace and Victoria railway station. One of its strengths is the size of the bedrooms which are spacious by city centre standards. Smartly-dressed staff are friendly and willing to help out. A street-facing brasserie, Le Café, is the setting for informal dining.

ROOMS: 134 en suite (bth/shr) (6 fmly) No smoking in 67 bedrooms **MEALS:** English & French Cuisine V meals Coffee am Tea pm **FACILITIES:** CTV in all bedrooms STV **CONF:** Thtr 180 Class 60 Board 14 **SERVICES:** Lift Night porter Air conditioning **NOTES:** No dogs (ex guide dogs) No smoking area in restaurant Last d 11pm **CARDS:**

The AA Hotel Booking Service is a free benefit to AA members. See the advertisement on page 47

London

SW1 WESTMINSTER
★★★★ The Cavendish St James's

LONDON SIGNATURE HOTELS

81 Jermyn St SW1Y 6JF
Quality Percentage Score: 66%
☎ 020 7930 2111 020 7839 2125
Dir: *follow signs for Marble Arch along Park Lane to Hyde Park Corner left to Piccadilly. Past Ritz hotel right down Dukes St Behind Fortnum and Mason*

Close to both Piccadilly and Green Park this modern hotel is particularly popular with business guests. The Sub Rosa Bar is a cosy, club-like venue off the lobby, and there is a spacious, well maintained lounge on the first floor. '81' Restaurant offers a Mediterranean-style menu with hints of Spanish influence.
ROOMS: 251 en suite (bth/shr) No smoking in 195 bedrooms s fr £193.87; d fr £229.12 (incl. bkfst) * LB Off peak **MEALS:** Lunch fr £14.50 Dinner fr £14.50 Mediterranean Cuisine V meals Coffee am Tea pm **FACILITIES:** CTV in all bedrooms STV Wkly live entertainment Xmas **CONF:** Thtr 100 Class 50 Board 40 Del from £249.50 * **SERVICES:** Lift Night porter 85P **NOTES:** No smoking area in restaurant Last d 10.30pm **CARDS:**

SW1 WESTMINSTER
★★★★ *The Royal Horseguards*

THISTLE HOTELS

Whitehall Court SW1A 2EJ
Quality Percentage Score: 66%
☎ 020 7839 3400 020 7925 2263

Government buildings lie all around this hotel, which is close to the Palace and many major tourist attractions, including the River Thames. A quite remarkable refurbishment has transformed the accommodation which is now spacious and very smart. There is an alliance with the magnificent meeting facilities of the adjacent One Whitehall, owned by the same company.
ROOMS: 280 en suite (bth/shr) No smoking in 189 bedrooms **MEALS:** International Cuisine V meals Coffee am Tea pm **FACILITIES:** CTV in all bedrooms STV Gym **CONF:** Thtr 60 Class 30 Board 24 **SERVICES:** Lift Night porter Air conditioning **NOTES:** No dogs **CARDS:**

SW1 WESTMINSTER
★★★★ *Thistle Victoria*

THISTLE HOTELS

Buckingham Palace Rd, Victoria SW1W 0SJ
Quality Percentage Score: 64%
☎ 020 7834 9494 020 7630 1978
Dir: *adjacent to Victoria railway station*

This Victorian landmark has had a facelift to some of its public areas which has resulted in a clean façade and stunning reception foyer. There is also a quiet Gallery lounge, a ground floor lounge, popular for afternoon tea, the quaint Harvard bar and the Clarence restaurant with its friendly team of staff. Bedrooms, which vary in size and outlook, have some attractive features.
ROOMS: 366 en suite (bth/shr) (35 fmly) No smoking in 129 bedrooms **MEALS:** V meals Coffee am Tea pm **FACILITIES:** CTV in all bedrooms STV **CONF:** Thtr 200 Class 85 Board 85 **SERVICES:** Lift Night porter **NOTES:** No dogs (ex guide dogs) No smoking area in restaurant Last d 10.30pm **CARDS:**

SW1 WESTMINSTER
★★★ Quality Hotel London Victoria

Comfort Quality Clarion CHOICE HOTELS EUROPE

82-83 Eccleston Square SW1V 1PS
Quality Percentage Score: 63%
☎ 020 7834 8042 020 7630 8942

Set close to Victoria station, the hotel has a quiet location and is popular with tourists and business guests. train and bus stations in a quiet location, the hotel is popular with tourist and business guests alike. Bedroom sizes vary, with Premier Plus providing the greatest comfort and additional facilities. Public rooms include the coffee shop a foyer bar, fitness room and various types of meeting room.
ROOMS: 115 en suite (bth/shr) No smoking in 30 bedrooms s £83.50-£95.75; d £95.75-£109 * LB Off peak **MEALS:** Lunch £2.95-£15.95alc Dinner fr £14.50 & alc English & Continental Cuisine V meals Coffee am Tea pm **FACILITIES:** CTV in all bedrooms STV **CONF:** Thtr 150 Class 65 Board 40 **SERVICES:** Lift Night porter **NOTES:** No smoking area in restaurant Last d 9.45pm **CARDS:**

SW1 WESTMINSTER
22 Jermyn Street

SLH

St James's SW1Y 6HL
☎ 020 7734 2353 020 7734 0750

An elegant town house in an equally elegant street just off St James's and behind Piccadilly. Bedrooms offer very high standards of comfort, and are provided with bathrobes, slippers, fruit, flowers and good toiletries. There is also a wide range of office services for the business guest, 24-hour room service and a mini-bar. Restaurants abound in the neighbourhood.
ROOMS: 18 en suite (bth/shr) (13 fmly) d £205-£315 * Off peak **MEALS:** V meals **FACILITIES:** CTV in all bedrooms STV Membership of nearby Health Club (£10 per day) **SERVICES:** Lift Night porter Air conditioning P **NOTES:** No coaches **CARDS:**

SW3 CHELSEA, BROMPTON

The Premier Collection

★★★★ Capital
Basil St, Knightsbridge SW3 1AT
☎ 020 7589 5171 020 7225 0011

Located in the very heart of Knightsbridge, this small and exclusive hotel offers individually designed bedrooms with high quality bedding, soft furnishings and hand-made furniture. Public areas are furnished to the same standard and a highlight of a stay here is dinner in the restaurant, where the chef offers a choice of tasting menus as well as a traditional carte.
ROOMS: 48 en suite (bth/shr) s fr £180; d fr £235 * Off peak **MEALS:** Lunch fr £24.50 & alc Dinner fr £60 & alc French Cuisine V meals Coffee am Tea pm **FACILITIES:** CTV in all bedrooms STV **CONF:** Thtr 30 **SERVICES:** Lift Night porter Air conditioning 15P **NOTES:** No coaches Last d 11.15pm **CARDS:**

SW3 CHELSEA, BROMPTON
★★★ *Basil Street*
Basil St, Knightsbridge SW3 1AH
Quality Percentage Score: 70%
☎ 020 7581 3311 020 7581 3693

Built in Edwardian times, the Basil Street Hotel aims to re-create the restful atmosphere of those days. Day rooms, with their

contd.

London

parquet floors, comfortable armchairs and antiques, suggest more a country-house setting than a city hotel. Bedrooms also follow a traditional style of furnishings, but have up-to-date facilities. Staff are attentive, and an enjoyable range of dishes is served in the dining room.
ROOMS: 93 rms (80 bth/shr) (2 fmly) No smoking in 6 bedrooms
MEALS: English & Continental Cuisine V meals Coffee am Tea pm
FACILITIES: CTV in all bedrooms STV Wkly live entertainment
CONF: Thtr 32 Class 18 Board 20 **SERVICES:** Lift Night porter 2P
NOTES: No coaches Last d 10pm
CARDS:

SW3 CHELSEA, BROMPTON
The Beaufort
33 Beaufort Gardens SW3 1PP
☎ 020 7584 5252 📠 020 7589 2834
Dir: *100yds from Harrods*

Harrods is the local neighbourhood store of the Beaufort, which stands in a quiet, leafy square only 100 yards or so from the world-famous emporium. The hotel offers guests every comfort and luxury in its well equipped bedrooms - chocolates, flowers, bathrobes, books and videos can all be taken for granted. Service is attentive.
ROOMS: 28 en suite (bth/shr) (7 fmly) No smoking in 6 bedrooms s £199.75-£211.50; d £235-£381.88 (incl. bkfst) * Off peak
FACILITIES: CTV in all bedrooms STV ch fac **SERVICES:** Lift Night porter Air conditioning **NOTES:** No dogs (ex guide dogs) No coaches
CARDS:

See advert on opposite page

SW3 CHELSEA, BROMPTON
Cliveden Townhouse
26 Cadogan Gardens SW3 2RP
☎ 020 7730 6466 📠 020 7730 0236
As is expected from the Cliveden group, this townhouse bears all the hallmarks of quality and style and, appropriately, is only yards away from Sloane Square. Bedrooms are beautifully furnished and have luxurious appointments and day rooms consist of two lounges, where refreshments are served; there is also a sheltered garden. A complimentary executive car chauffeurs guests to the City twice each morning.
ROOMS: 35 en suite (bth/shr) (9 fmly) No smoking in 30 bedrooms s £152.75-£229.12; d £276.12-£1034 * LB Off peak **MEALS:** V meals
FACILITIES: CTV in all bedrooms STV Gym Beauty treatment Massage
CONF: Board 12 **SERVICES:** Lift Night porter Air conditioning
NOTES: No coaches **CARDS:**

SW3 CHELSEA, BROMPTON
Parkes
41 Beaufort Gardens, Knightsbridge SW3 1PW
☎ 020 7581 9944 📠 020 7581 1999
Dir: *off Brompton Road, 150yds from Harrods*
Only five minutes from Knightsbridge and the world of fashionable shopping, this charming little hotel is in the oasis of a peaceful square. Its well equipped suites come in a range of sizes, and each has a kitchenette. Breakfast is served in an attractive dining room and there is a small lounge.
ROOMS: 33 en suite (bth/shr) (16 fmly) d £153-£311 * Off peak
FACILITIES: CTV in all bedrooms STV **SERVICES:** Lift Night porter Air conditioning **NOTES:** No dogs (ex guide dogs) No coaches
CARDS:

SW4 CLAPHAM See LONDON plan 1 *E2*
★★★ The Windmill on The Common
Southside, Clapham Common SW4 9DE
Quality Percentage Score: 68%
☎ 020 8673 4578 📠 020 8675 1486
A traditional 18th-century pub forms the nucleus of this comfortable hotel which has been skilfully extended to provide modern bedroom accommodation. There are three large bars, a bistro counter, a small lounge and a separate wood-panelled restaurant.
ROOMS: 29 en suite (bth/shr) No smoking in 15 bedrooms s fr £90; d fr £100 (incl. bkfst) * Off peak **MEALS:** Bar Lunch £7-£15 Dinner £16.95-£20 & alc European Cuisine V meals Coffee am Tea pm
FACILITIES: CTV in all bedrooms STV **CONF:** Thtr 40 Class 25 Board 20
SERVICES: Night porter 16P **NOTES:** Last d 10pm
CARDS:

SW5 EARLS COURT
★★★★ Swallow International
Cromwell Rd SW5 0TH
Quality Percentage Score: 67%
☎ 020 7973 1000 📠 020 7244 8194
Dir: *on the A4, within minutes of the M4*

SWALLOW HOTELS

One of the few London hotels with its own car park. The modern bedrooms, if a little compact, are thoughtfully equipped. In addition to an all-day eating option, there is the more formal Blayneys restaurant where some interesting dishes are offered. The hotel has an indoor leisure facility.
ROOMS: 421 en suite (bth/shr) (36 fmly) No smoking in 76 bedrooms s £145; d £165 * LB Off peak **MEALS:** Lunch £18 High tea £12 Dinner £18 European Cuisine V meals Coffee am Tea pm **FACILITIES:** CTV in all bedrooms STV Indoor swimming pool (heated) Sauna Solarium Gym Jacuzzi/spa Whirlpool spa Turkish Steamroom Wkly live entertainment
CONF: Thtr 200 Class 100 Board 60 Del from £180 * **SERVICES:** Lift Night porter Air conditioning 80P **NOTES:** No smoking area in restaurant Last d 11.30pm Closed 23-26 Dec **CARDS:**

London

SW5 EARLS COURT
★★★ The Hogarth

33 Hogarth Rd, Kensington SW5 0QQ

Quality Percentage Score: 73%

☎ 020 7370 6831 Fax 020 7373 6179

***Dir:** turn into Earls Court Rd from Cromwell Rd (A4), take 3rd turning left into Hogarth Rd. Hotel is at the end of the rd on the left*

Situated off the Earls Court Road, convenient for the Exhibition Centre, and just a few yards from the underground, this purpose built hotel has been completely refurbished to a good standard. Bedrooms do vary in size but are all well equipped, with such extra facilities as safes, trouser press and satellite TV provided. Top floor rooms also benefit from balconies. A good range of room service snacks and light meals are also available for those not wanting to leave the comfort of their rooms. Public areas, although limited in space, are attractive and well designed. There is a popular casual restaurant/bar, The Terrace, where a good range of freshly prepared dishes to suit all tastes and pockets is available throughout the day. There are three smart meeting rooms, and the hotel also benefits from having its own secure car park for about 20 cars. Friendly helpful young staff make a stay at this modern hotel a particular pleasure.

ROOMS: 85 en suite (bth/shr) (12 fmly) No smoking in 18 bedrooms s fr £97; d fr £115 LB Off peak **MEALS:** Lunch £10-£20 High tea £10-£20 Dinner £18-£25 English & French Cuisine V meals Coffee am Tea pm **FACILITIES:** CTV in all bedrooms STV **CONF:** Thtr 50 Class 20 Board 24 Del from £141 * **SERVICES:** Lift Night porter 20P **NOTES:** No smoking in restaurant Last d 10pm **CARDS:**

SW5 EARLS COURT
★★ Comfort Inn Kensington

22-32 West Cromwell Rd, Kensington SW5 9QJ

Quality Percentage Score: 67%

☎ 020 7373 3300 Fax 020 7835 2040

Convenient for Earl's Court, this cheerful, modern hotel is well suited to business and leisure guests. The bedrooms vary in size, but are smartly kept with a range of amenities including air-conditioning. The welcoming public areas are bright and comfortable.

ROOMS: 125 en suite (bth/shr) (6 fmly) No smoking in 48 bedrooms s £83.50-£95.75; d £95.75-£109 * LB Off peak **MEALS:** Lunch £2.95-£15.95alc Dinner fr £14.50 & alc English & Continental Cuisine V meals Coffee am Tea pm **FACILITIES:** CTV in all bedrooms STV **CONF:** Thtr 80 Class 60 Board 40 **SERVICES:** Lift Night porter Air conditioning **NOTES:** No dogs (ex guide dogs) No smoking in restaurant Last d 9.30pm **CARDS:**

SW5 EARLS COURT
Oki Hotel

25 Courtfield Gardens, Kensington SW5 0PG

☎ 020 7565 2222 Fax 020 7565 2223

***Dir:** M4 into London join A4 to Cromwell Rd, turn right at Cromwell Hospital into Knaresborough Pl, hotel is at the end as it becomes Courtfield Gdns*

This townhouse in the heart of fashionable Kensington offers accommodation of a very high standard. Rooms are well equipped and comfortable, there is a bar lounge and a basement dining room where a buffet breakfast is served.

ROOMS: 41 en suite (bth/shr) **FACILITIES:** CTV in all bedrooms STV **SERVICES:** Lift Night porter **NOTES:** No dogs **CARDS:**

SW6 FULHAM See LONDON plan 1 *D3*
★★★★ Chelsea Village

Stamford Bridge, Fulham Rd SW6 1HS

Quality Percentage Score: 71%

☎ 020 7565 1400 Fax 020 7565 1450

This exciting new hotel forms part of the ambititous developments at Chelsea Football Club and is a bold modern structure just next door to the ground. Bedrooms are well equipped and the range of public areas includes four different styles of eating: modern and global at Kings Brasserie, Irish, seafood, and finally, in the sport-themed Shed Bar, pub food.

ROOMS: 160 en suite (bth/shr) (64 fmly) No smoking in 56 bedrooms s fr £135; d fr £145 * Off peak **MEALS:** Lunch £15-£30 & alc Dinner £15-£30 & alc V meals Coffee am Tea pm **FACILITIES:** CTV in all bedrooms STV Xmas **CONF:** Thtr 50 Class 25 Board 30 Del from £160 * **SERVICES:** Lift Night porter Air conditioning 250P **NOTES:** No dogs (ex guide dogs) Last d 10.30pm **CARDS:**

SW6 FULHAM
★★★ Paragon Hotel

47 Lillie Rd SW6 1UD

Quality Percentage Score: 61%

☎ 020 7385 1255 Fax 020 7381 0215

***Dir:** A4 to central London,0.5m after Hammersmith flyover turn right at traffic lights into North End Rd follow for 0.5m to mini rdbt left into Lillie Rd*

This well established hotel is ideally located for the Earls Court Exhibition Centre. There are extensive conference facilities and the bedrooms are modern and well equipped. Two restaurants

contd.

offer the choice of light meals and pizzas or more formal traditional menus. There is an underground car-park.
ROOMS: 501 en suite (bth/shr) No smoking in 96 bedrooms s fr £125; d fr £145 * LB Off peak **MEALS:** Lunch fr £8 Dinner fr £12 International Cuisine V meals Coffee am Tea pm **FACILITIES:** CTV in all bedrooms STV **CONF:** Thtr 1750 Class 900 Board 50 Del from £155 * **SERVICES:** Lift Night porter 130P **NOTES:** No dogs (ex guide dogs) No smoking area in restaurant Last d 10.30pm
CARDS:

SW6 FULHAM
London Putney Bridge Travel Inn Capital

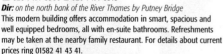

3 Putney Bridge Approach SW6 3JD
☎ 020 7471 8300 020 7471 8315
Dir: *on the north bank of the River Thames by Putney Bridge*
This modern building offers accommodation in smart, spacious and well equipped bedrooms, all with en-suite bathrooms. Refreshments may be taken at the nearby family restaurant. For details about current prices ring 01582 41 43 41.
ROOMS: 154 en suite (bth/shr) d £59.95 *

SW7 SOUTH KENSINGTON
★★★★ The Millennium Gloucester Hotel

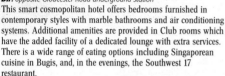

4-18 Harrington Gardens SW7 4LH
Quality Percentage Score: 77%
☎ 020 7373 6030 020 7373 0409
Dir: *opposite Gloucester Road underground station*
This smart cosmopolitan hotel offers bedrooms furnished in contemporary styles with marble bathrooms and air conditioning systems. Additional amenities are provided in Club rooms which have the added facility of a dedicated lounge with extra services. There is a wide range of eating options including Singaporean cuisine in Bugis, and, in the evenings, the Southwest 17 restaurant.
ROOMS: 610 en suite (bth/shr) (4 fmly) No smoking in 232 bedrooms d fr £215 * LB Off peak **MEALS:** Lunch £8-£20alc Dinner £15-£25alc English & Continental Cuisine V meals Coffee am Tea pm **FACILITIES:** CTV in all bedrooms STV Gym Xmas **CONF:** Thtr 800 Class 500 Del from £250 * **SERVICES:** Lift Night porter Air conditioning 100P **NOTES:** No smoking area in restaurant Last d 10.45pm
CARDS:

SW7 SOUTH KENSINGTON

★★★★ Harrington Hall

5-25 Harrington Gardens SW7 4JW
Quality Percentage Score: 71%
☎ 020 7396 9696 020 7396 9090
Dir: *head towards Knightsbridge into Gloucester Rd. Take 2nd right into Harrington Gdns hotel on the left*
A short walk from the South Kensington museums, this modern, air-conditioned hotel offers well equipped bedrooms, furnished to high quality standards, and well designed reception rooms. The restaurant, where there is sometimes live entertainment, offers a choice of a hot buffet or a traditional full menu.
ROOMS: 200 en suite (bth/shr) No smoking in 132 bedrooms d fr £160 * LB Off peak **MEALS:** Lunch fr £19.75 & alc High tea fr £12.50 Dinner fr £19.75 & alc European Cuisine V meals Coffee am Tea pm **FACILITIES:** CTV in all bedrooms STV Sauna Gym Leisure centre Wkly live entertainment Xmas **CONF:** Thtr 260 Class 150 Board 50 Del from £195 * **SERVICES:** Lift Night porter Air conditioning **NOTES:** No dogs (ex guide dogs) No smoking area in restaurant Last d 10.30pm
CARDS:

See advert on opposite page

SW7 SOUTH KENSINGTON
★★★★ The Millennium Baileys Hotel

140 Gloucester Rd SW7 4QH
Quality Percentage Score: 67%
☎ 020 7373 6000 020 7370 3760
Dir: *M4, take A4 which turns into Cromwell Road, turn right onto Gloucester Road, hotel on the right opposite tube station*
Purpose-built in 1876 and given a new lease of life by its current owners, it has modern bedrooms with useful facilities such as air-conditioning and TV guest-link system. Public areas are shared with its large sister hotel. Its own modern restaurant, Olives, produces enjoyable food in contemporary style. Service is provided by a friendly team of staff.
ROOMS: 212 en suite (bth/shr) No smoking in 80 bedrooms s £120-£215; d £225-£265 * Off peak **MEALS:** Bar Lunch £4.50-£6.95alc Dinner £12.50-£15.25 & alc International Cuisine V meals Coffee am **FACILITIES:** CTV in all bedrooms STV Fitness room Xmas **CONF:** Thtr 500 Class 300 Board 16 **SERVICES:** Lift Night porter Air conditioning 70P **NOTES:** No dogs (ex guide dogs) No smoking area in restaurant Last d 10.30pm **CARDS:**

SW7 SOUTH KENSINGTON
★★★★ Rembrandt

11 Thurloe Place SW7 2RS
Quality Percentage Score: 65%
☎ 020 7589 8100 020 7225 3363
Dir: *opp Victoria & Albert Museum*
The ornate architecture of the Rembrandt connects it stylistically to nearby Harrods. A strength of this plush, comfortable hotel is the leisure centre, designed in a style reminiscent of ancient Rome.
ROOMS: 195 en suite (bth/shr) (25 fmly) No smoking in 28 bedrooms s £165; d £185 * LB Off peak **MEALS:** Lunch fr £16.95 & alc Dinner fr £16.95 & alc International Cuisine V meals Coffee am Tea pm **FACILITIES:** CTV in all bedrooms STV Indoor swimming pool (heated) Sauna Solarium Gym Jacuzzi/spa Health, fitness & beauty centre Wkly live entertainment Xmas **CONF:** Thtr 200 Class 90 Board 60 Del from £195 * **SERVICES:** Lift Night porter **NOTES:** No dogs (ex guide dogs) No smoking area in restaurant Last d 10pm
CARDS:

SW7 SOUTH KENSINGTON
★★★★ Forum

97 Cromwell Rd SW7 4DN
Quality Percentage Score: 62%
☎ 020 7370 5757 020 7373 1448
Dir: *from South Circular onto North Circular at Chiswick Flyover, join A4 Cromwell Rd as far as the Gloucseter Rd*
London's tallest hotel has, not surprisingly, panoramic views over London from the majority of its rooms. Bedrooms are

contd.

smartly decorated and well equipped. Public areas include a business centre, a large shop and several eating outlets.
ROOMS: 910 en suite (bth/shr) (36 fmly) No smoking in 176 bedrooms s £150-£170; d £170-£190 LB Off peak **MEALS:** Lunch fr £21 International Cuisine V meals Coffee am Tea pm **FACILITIES:** CTV in all bedrooms STV Fitness room Wkly live entertainment Xmas **CONF:** Thtr 400 Class 200 Board 35 Del from £170 * **SERVICES:** Lift Night porter 75P **NOTES:** No dogs (ex guide dogs) No smoking area in restaurant **CARDS:**

SW7 SOUTH KENSINGTON
★★★★ Jurys Kensington Hotel
109-113 Queensgate, South Kensington SW7 5LR
Quality Percentage Score: 62%
☎ 020 7589 6300 020 7581 1492
Dir: *from A3218 (Old Bromton Rd), hotel is approx 300 yards on left at junction with Queensgate*
This fine hotel offers a traditional Irish welcome. The attractive lobby/bar and library lounge areas are popular. Kavanagh's bar is lively, Copplestones restaurant more sedate. Bedrooms range from stylish fifth-floor cottage rooms with floral fabrics, to smart executive suites. Third-floor bedrooms are non smoking.
ROOMS: 172 en suite (bth/shr) (4 fmly) No smoking in 36 bedrooms s £170; d £170-£190 * LB Off peak **MEALS:** Dinner £18.50 & alc European Cuisine V meals Coffee am Tea pm **FACILITIES:** CTV in all bedrooms STV Wkly live entertainment **CONF:** Thtr 80 Class 42 Board 40 Del £190 * **SERVICES:** Lift Night porter Air conditioning **NOTES:** No dogs (ex guide dogs) No smoking in restaurant Last d 10pm Closed 24-27 Dec **CARDS:**

SW7 SOUTH KENSINGTON
Radisson Edwardian Vanderbilt
68/86 Cromwell Rd SW7 5BT
☎ 020 7589 2424 020 7225 2293
Dir: *A4 into central London*
Situated on Cromwell Road, convenient for several museums, this terraced Victorian property is popular with both business travellers and tourists. Bedrooms vary in size and decor but all have chintzy fabrics and solid, inlaid-wood furniture.
ROOMS: 223 en suite (bth/shr) (17 fmly) s £158.63; d £176.25 * Off peak **MEALS:** Lunch fr £17.50 Dinner fr £24 English & French Cuisine V meals Coffee am Tea pm **FACILITIES:** CTV in all bedrooms Xmas **CONF:** Thtr 120 Class 36 Board 40 **SERVICES:** Lift Night porter **NOTES:** No dogs (ex guide dogs) Last d 10pm **CARDS:**

SW10 WEST BROMPTON See LONDON plan 1 *E3*
★★★★★ Conrad International London
Chelsea Harbour SW10 0XG
Quality Percentage Score: 65%
☎ 020 7823 3000 020 7351 6525
Dir: *A4 Earls Court Rd south towards river. Right into Kings Rd left down Lots Rd Chelsea Harbour is in front of you*
This modern, luxury hotel overlooks a small marina at Chelsea Harbour and accommodation is in the form of superbly equipped private suites, with spacious bathrooms and separate WCs. Most have furnished balconies and are equipped with fax and video. Public rooms look out over the marina.
ROOMS: 160 en suite (bth/shr) (41 fmly) No smoking in 62 bedrooms s £211.50-£317.25; d £246.75-£352.50 * LB Off peak **MEALS:** Lunch £20-£36.50 & alc Dinner £22-£25 & alc International Cuisine V meals Coffee am Tea pm **FACILITIES:** CTV in all bedrooms STV Indoor swimming pool (heated) Sauna Solarium Gym Steam room Massage therapist Wkly live entertainment Xmas **CONF:** Thtr 200 Class 120 Board 50 Del from £319 * **SERVICES:** Lift Night porter Air conditioning 80P **NOTES:** No coaches Last d 10.30pm **CARDS:**

SW11 BATTERSEA
Travelodge
200 York Rd, Battersea SW11 3SA
☎ 020 7228 5508
Dir: *from Wandsworth Bridge southern rdbt, take York Road A3205 towards Battersea. Travelodge 0.5m on left*
This modern building offers accommodation in smart, spacious and well equipped bedrooms, all with en-suite bathrooms. Refreshments may be taken at the nearby family restaurant. For details about current prices, consult the Contents Page under Hotel Groups for the Travelodge phone number.
ROOMS: 80 en suite (bth/shr) d £59.95 *

SW19 WIMBLEDON See LONDON plan 1 *D1*
★★★★ Cannizaro House
West Side, Wimbledon Common SW19 4UE
Quality Percentage Score: 77%
☎ 020 8879 1464 020 8879 7338
Dir: *approaching from A3 follow A219 signed Wimbledon into Parkside and past old fountain sharp right then 2nd on right*
This familiar Wimbledon landmark is a haven of peace and quiet close to London. The bedrooms, furnished and decorated in country-house style, look out on the original park, particularly lovely in spring when daffodils, then bluebells and azaleas are at their best. Reception rooms are richly decorated and endowed with oils, murals and massive fireplaces. The restaurant and private dining rooms serve a high standard of cuisine, and in

contd.

summer, cocktails on the terrace make an elegant prelude to a meal. Staff are professional and attentive.

Cannizaro House, Wimbledon

ROOMS: 45 en suite (bth/shr) No smoking in 6 bedrooms **MEALS:** Lunch fr £17.95 Dinner £23.75-£28.75 English & French Cuisine V meals Coffee am Tea pm **FACILITIES:** CTV in all bedrooms STV **CONF:** Thtr 80 Class 34 Board 40 **SERVICES:** Lift Night porter 60P **NOTES:** No dogs (ex guide dogs) No coaches No children 8yrs No smoking area in restaurant Last d 10.30pm
CARDS:

W1 WEST END

The Premier Collection

★★★★★ *Claridge's*

Brook St W1A 2JQ
☎ 020 7629 8860 Fax 020 7499 2210

The Savoy Group

***Dir:** Between Grosvenor Square and New Bond Street parallel with Oxford Street*

In its centenary year, this classic hotel is set to enter the new millennium much as it began the last - as an example for others to follow. Its latest refurbishment blends state-of-the-art modern design and technology into a traditional setting, and the 7th-floor penthouses are particularly impressive. Reception rooms and public areas are best described as opulent and immaculate, giving an overall impression that is simply majestic. Staff, however, with their professional, cheerful service, ensure that no one need feel intimidated. In addition to the two famous restaurants, refreshments are also served in the Causerie (smorgasbord), the reading room (afternoon tea) and the lounge (aperitifs), to the accompaniment of music from the Hungarian Quartet.

ROOMS: 197 en suite (bth/shr) No smoking in 18 bedrooms **MEALS:** International Cuisine V meals Coffee am Tea pm **FACILITIES:** CTV in all bedrooms STV Sauna Gym Tennis at the Vanderbilt Club Wkly live entertainment **CONF:** Thtr 260 Class 110 Board 50 **SERVICES:** Lift Night porter Air conditioning **NOTES:** No dogs (ex guide dogs) No coaches Last d 10.45pm
CARDS:

W1 WEST END

The Premier Collection

★★★★★ Connaught

Carlos Place W1Y 6AL
☎ 020 7499 7070 Fax 020 7495 3262

The Savoy Group

***Dir:** Situated between Grosvenor Square and Berkeley Square in Mayfair*

The Connaught continues to offer measured service and quiet comfort in one of London's great hotels. The unhurried atmosphere is sustained by bans on both mobile telephones and business meetings. The Restaurant and The Grill Room share the same impeccable service and exhaustive menu, with Chef Michel Bourdin continuing to please the many admirers of his classical cuisine.

ROOMS: 90 en suite (bth/shr) s £280-£325; d £360-£405 * LB Off peak **MEALS:** Lunch £27.50-£32.50 & alc Dinner fr £45 & alc English & French Cuisine Coffee am Tea pm **FACILITIES:** CTV in all bedrooms STV Health & beauty facilities available at sister hotels **CONF:** Class 35 Board 15 **SERVICES:** Lift Night porter Air conditioning **NOTES:** No dogs No coaches Last d 10.45pm
CARDS:

W1 WEST END

The Premier Collection

★★★★★ The Dorchester

Park Ln W1A 2HJ
☎ 020 7629 8888 Fax 020 7409 0114

***Dir:** half way along Park Lane between Hyde Park Corner & Marble Arch, overlooking Hyde Park on corner of Park Lane & Deanery St*

One of London's finest hotels, the Dorchester is sumptuously decorated in every department. Bedrooms have individual design schemes, are beautifully furnished, and their luxurious bathrooms have huge baths which have become a Dorchester hallmark. Leading off from the foyer, the Promenade is the perfect setting for afternoon tea or

contd.

Symbols and Abbreviations are listed and explained on pages 4 and 5

drinks, and in the evenings there is live jazz in the famous bar which specialises in Italian dishes and cocktails. The Grill is a restaurant in the traditional style and there is also an acclaimed Cantonese restaurant, the Oriental.

ROOMS: 248 en suite (bth/shr) No smoking in 24 bedrooms s £311.38-£334.88; d £346.63-£381.88 * LB Off peak **MEALS:** Lunch £25-£29.50 & alc High tea fr £29.50 Dinner £39.50-£42 V meals Coffee am Tea pm **FACILITIES:** CTV in all bedrooms STV Sauna Solarium Gym Jacuzzi/spa The Dorchester Spa Health club Wkly live entertainment ch fac Xmas **CONF:** Thtr 500 Class 300 Board 42 Del from £365 * **SERVICES:** Lift Night porter Air conditioning 21P **NOTES:** No dogs (ex guide dogs) No coaches Last d 11pm **CARDS:**

W1 WEST END

The Premier Collection

★★★★★ Four Seasons

Hamilton Place, Park Ln W1A 1AZ
☎ 020 7499 0888 Fax 020 7493 6629

The grand foyer sets the tone for this elegant but friendly hotel. Accommodation offers excellent standards of comfort, and in addition to the standard rooms, there are suites and impressive 'conservatory' rooms, offering extra touches of luxury. Lanes Restaurant, where service is polished, looks out on one side to Park Lane and serves interesting modern food.

ROOMS: 220 en suite (bth/shr) No smoking in 72 bedrooms s £260-£270; d £305-£315 * LB Off peak **MEALS:** Lunch fr £32 & alc Dinner fr £30.50 & alc International Cuisine V meals Coffee am Tea pm **FACILITIES:** CTV in all bedrooms STV Gym Fitness club Wkly live entertainment Xmas **CONF:** Thtr 500 Class 180 Board 90 **SERVICES:** Lift Night porter Air conditioning 55P **NOTES:** No dogs (ex guide dogs) No coaches No smoking area in restaurant Last d 11pm **CARDS:**

W1 WEST END

★★★★★ The Ritz

150 Piccadilly W1V 9DG
Quality Percentage Score: 80%
☎ 020 7493 8181 Fax 020 7493 2687

Dir: *from Hyde Park Corner travel E on Piccadilly. The Ritz is the first building on the right immediately after Green Park*

One of the world's great metropolitan hotels, the Ritz is a byword for magnificent decor. Bedrooms are furnished in Louis XVI style and have fine marble bathrooms. Elegant reception rooms include the Palm Court, with its famous afternoon-tea ritual, and the sumptuous Ritz Restaurant with its gold chandeliers and extraordinary trompe l'oeil decoration.

ROOMS: 131 en suite (bth/shr) No smoking in 20 bedrooms s £305.50-£352.50; d £340.75-£352.50 * Off peak **MEALS:** Lunch fr £34 & alc Dinner £43-£55 & alc International Cuisine V meals Coffee am Tea pm **FACILITIES:** CTV in all bedrooms STV Gym Wkly live entertainment Xmas **CONF:** Thtr 70 Class 25 Board 30 **SERVICES:** Lift Night porter Air conditioning **NOTES:** No dogs (ex guide dogs) No coaches Last d 11.15pm **CARDS:**

W1 WEST END

★★★★★ Hotel Inter-Continental

1 Hamilton Place, Hyde Park Corner W1V 0QY
Quality Percentage Score: 75%
☎ 020 7409 3131 Fax 020 7493 3476

Dir: *Situated on Hyde Park Corner where junct of Knightsbridge/Park Lane & Piccadilly meet*

Situated in a prominent position on Hyde Park Corner, this fine hotel has a very good reputation. Bedrooms vary from inner courtyard rooms to spacious suites. From the upper floors, views of the surrounding area are excellent. The smart marble foyer houses the Observatory lounge, which provides light meals or afternoon teas, and the Coffee House restaurant provides breakfast and all-day dining, but the jewel in the hotel's crown is Le Soufflé Restaurant, where Peter Kromberg cooks with commendable flair.

ROOMS: 458 en suite (bth/shr) No smoking in 240 bedrooms d £295 * LB Off peak **MEALS:** Lunch £13.50-£26.50 & alc High tea £19.50 Dinner £17.50-£27 & alc French, Oriental & International Cuisine V meals Coffee am Tea pm **FACILITIES:** CTV in all bedrooms STV Sauna Gym Jacuzzi/spa Health centre Wkly live entertainment Xmas **CONF:** Thtr 1000 Class 380 Board 66 **SERVICES:** Lift Night porter Air conditioning 100P **NOTES:** No dogs (ex guide dogs) No coaches No smoking area in restaurant Last d 11pm **CARDS:**

W1 WEST END

★★★★★ Le Meridien Piccadilly

21 Piccadilly W1V 0BH
Quality Percentage Score: 75%
☎ 020 7734 8000 Fax 020 7437 3574

Dir: *100mtrs from Piccadilly Circus*

This well-established hotel has comfortable, well equipped bedrooms. Renowned chef, Marco Pierre White, runs the hotel's opulent Oak Room restaurant as a separate operation while the Terrace restaurant is the London showcase for Parisian chef, Michel Rostang. The hotel has the additional benefit of

contd.

New AA Guides for the Millennium are featured on page 24

London

Champney's health club which has an excellent range of leisure and beauty facilities.
ROOMS: 267 en suite (bth/shr) (19 fmly) No smoking in 91 bedrooms s £311.37-£346.62; d £346.62-£381.87 * LB Off peak **MEALS:** Lunch £23.50 Dinner £23.50 British & French Cuisine V meals Coffee am Tea pm **FACILITIES:** CTV in all bedrooms STV Indoor swimming pool (heated) Squash Sauna Solarium Gym Jacuzzi/spa Beauty treatments Aerobics Massage Xmas **CONF:** Thtr 250 Class 160 Board 80 **SERVICES:** Lift Night porter Air conditioning **NOTES:** No dogs (ex guide dogs) No smoking area in restaurant Last d 10.45pm
CARDS:

W1 WEST END
★★★★★ Churchill Inter-Continental
30 Portman Square W1A 4ZX
Quality Percentage Score: 74%
☎ 020 7486 5800 020 7486 1255
Overlooking Portman Square, this impressive hotel provides luxury accommodation with such modern amenities as dual voltage plugs, modem and fax lines. Club Rooms entitle occupants to a dedicated lounge and reception, breakfast, cocktails and a laundry pressing service. Public areas display a wealth of marble, pillars and chandeliers, and in the relaxed surroundings of The Terrace lounge afternoon tea and other light refreshments are served. By contrast, the Churchill Bar and Cigar Divan has a gentleman's club atmosphere, perfect for a pre-dinner drink before dining in Clementine's Restaurant, an attractive setting for the Mediterranean-inspired cooking. Staff are professional yet friendly and obliging. There is a business centre, theatre desk and nearby car parking facilities.
ROOMS: 440 en suite (bth/shr) No smoking in 135 bedrooms s £276.13-£323.13; d £293.75-£340.75 * LB Off peak **MEALS:** Lunch £18-£25 High tea £16 Dinner £25 V meals Coffee am Tea pm **FACILITIES:** CTV in all bedrooms STV Tennis (hard) Wkly live entertainment Xmas **CONF:** Thtr 250 Class 150 Board 54 **SERVICES:** Lift Night porter Air conditioning P **NOTES:** No dogs (ex guide dogs) No smoking area in restaurant Last d 10.30pm **CARDS:**

W1 WEST END
★★★★★ Grosvenor House
Park Ln W1A 3AA
Quality Percentage Score: 73%
☎ 020 7499 6363 020 7493 3341
***Dir:** Marble Arch, halfway down Park Lane*
Majestically positioned on Park Lane, this internationally recognised hotel, with its noteworthy Lutyens' façade, offers thoughtfully equipped accommodation. There are a number of impressive suites, some enjoying views of Hyde Park, and the latest addition is a floor of Crown Club rooms which have the advantage of a range of extra services and facilities. The public areas include a wide range of banqueting, function and private dining rooms. The leisure centre has been completely overhauled. Guests have the choice of eating at Chez Nico (which boasts the AA's highest award for cuisine), Café Nico (two rosettes) and the hotel's own Italian Restaurant.
ROOMS: 453 en suite (bth/shr) No smoking in 70 bedrooms s fr £225; d fr £245 * LB Off peak **MEALS:** English, French & Italian Cuisine V meals Coffee am Tea pm **FACILITIES:** CTV in all bedrooms STV Indoor swimming pool (heated) Sauna Solarium Gym Jacuzzi/spa Health & Fitness centre Wkly live entertainment Xmas **CONF:** Thtr 110 Class 60 Board 36 **SERVICES:** Lift Night porter Air conditioning 75P **NOTES:** No dogs (ex guide dogs) No smoking area in restaurant Last d 10pm **CARDS:**

W1 WEST END
★★★★★ Park Lane
Piccadilly W1Y 8BX
Quality Percentage Score: 69%
☎ 020 499 6321 020 7499 1965
***Dir:** On Piccadilly opposite Green Park*
Major investment from its new owners has restored the hotel to much of its former glory. Examples of stylish and sophisticated refurbishment of public areas include the art-deco ballroom and period-style Palm Court, the perfect setting for a fine afternoon tea with harp accompaniment. The French-style Brasserie on the Park offers guests an interesting range of modern dishes. Other facilities include hairdressing, a small gym, a business centre and garage.
ROOMS: 305 en suite (bth/shr) (20 fmly) No smoking in 116 bedrooms **MEALS:** Lunch fr £19.50alc High tea fr £16 Dinner fr £19.50alc English Mediterranean & French Cuisine V meals Coffee am Tea pm **FACILITIES:** CTV in all bedrooms STV Gym Wkly live entertainment **CONF:** Thtr 500 Class 250 Board 100 **SERVICES:** Lift Night porter 120P **NOTES:** No dogs (ex guide dogs) No smoking area in restaurant Last d 11pm **CARDS:**

W1 WEST END
★★★★★ May Fair Inter-Continental London
Stratton St W1A 2AN
Quality Percentage Score: 66%
☎ 020 7629 7777 020 7629 1459
***Dir:** from Hyde Park Corner/Piccadilly turn left onto Stratton St & hotel is on left*
A perennial favourite, especially with showbiz celebrities, this friendly, welcoming hotel boasts an intimate atmosphere and congenial surroundings. Public areas offer a varied range, including a choice of restaurants, bars, manned business centre and even a conference auditorium. Air-conditioned bedrooms have been newly refurbished and feature some sumptuous suites. The Opus 70 restaurant proves a fashionable venue for Michael Coaker's fine British cuisine.
ROOMS: 290 en suite (bth/shr) (14 fmly) No smoking in 148 bedrooms s fr £325; d fr £345 * LB Off peak **MEALS:** Lunch £15-£27 & alc High tea £15 Dinner £20-£30alc English, American & French Cuisine V meals Coffee am Tea pm **FACILITIES:** CTV in all bedrooms STV Indoor swimming pool (heated) Sauna Solarium Gym Hair & Beauty salon Wkly live entertainment Xmas **CONF:** Thtr 292 Class 108 Board 90 **SERVICES:** Lift Night porter Air conditioning **NOTES:** No dogs (ex guide dogs) No coaches No smoking area in restaurant Last d 11pm
CARDS:

W1 WEST END

The Premier Collection

★★★★ Athenaeum
116 Piccadilly W1V 0BJ
☎ 020 7499 3464 020 7493 1860
***Dir:** located on Piccadily, overlooking Green Park*
An elegant hotel overlooking Green Park, the Athenaeum is prized for its high standards of service and welcoming atmosphere. Bedrooms are superbly appointed, offering luxurious accommodation, and dining in Bullochs Restaurant from the menu of modern classics is another

contd.

London

highlight. Afternoon tea and other refreshments are served in the Windsor Lounge and there is also a clubby, panelled bar.

ROOMS: 156 en suite (bth/shr) No smoking in 58 bedrooms s £195-£290; d £195-£650 * LB Off peak **MEALS:** Lunch fr £35 Dinner fr £35 International Cuisine V meals Coffee am Tea pm **FACILITIES:** CTV in all bedrooms STV Sauna Gym Jacuzzi/spa Massage & treatment rooms Wkly live entertainment ch fac **CONF:** Thtr 55 Class 35 Board 36 Del from £260 * **SERVICES:** Lift Night porter Air conditioning **NOTES:** No dogs (ex guide dogs) No coaches No smoking area in restaurant Last d 10.30pm
CARDS:

W1 WEST END
★★★★ The Montcalm-Hotel Nikko London

Great Cumberland Place W1A 2LF
Quality Percentage Score: 75%
☎ 020 7402 4288 020 7724 9180
Dir: *By Marble Arch*
Originally named after the 18th-century French General Montcalm, defeated by General Wolfe at Quebec, this Japanese-owned hotel offers extremely comfortable accommodation, ranging from standard to duplex, 'junior' suites and penthouse suites. The Crescent Restaurant has a good reputation for modern cooking.
ROOMS: 120 en suite (bth/shr) No smoking in 28 bedrooms s fr £240.88; d £264.38-£646.25 * LB Off peak **MEALS:** Lunch £19-£24alc Dinner £19-£24alc V meals Coffee am Tea pm **FACILITIES:** CTV in all bedrooms STV **CONF:** Thtr 80 Class 36 Board 36 **SERVICES:** Lift Night porter Air conditioning 10P **NOTES:** No dogs (ex guide dogs) No coaches No smoking area in restaurant Last d 10.30pm
CARDS:

W1 WEST END
★★★★ The Westbury

New Bond St W1A 4UH
Quality Percentage Score: 75%
☎ 020 7629 7755 020 7495 1163
Dir: *from Oxford Circus south down Regent St turn right onto Conduit St, hotel at junct of Conduit St & Bond St*
Set in the heart of London's shopping district, this distinctive property, under new management, is aiming to provide accommodation of the highest standards for an international clientele. Reception rooms include the Polo Lounge, and La Méditerranée Restaurant, serving traditional dishes at lunchtime and a more adventurous evening menu.

ROOMS: 244 en suite (bth/shr) No smoking in 76 bedrooms s £246.75; d £264.38 * LB Off peak **MEALS:** Lunch £17.50-£19.50 & alc Dinner £19.50-£21.50 & alc European Cuisine V meals Coffee am Tea pm **FACILITIES:** CTV in all bedrooms STV Complimentary access to nearby Health Club Xmas **CONF:** Thtr 120 Class 65 Board 36 Del £330 * **SERVICES:** Lift Night porter Air conditioning **NOTES:** No dogs (ex guide dogs) No smoking area in restaurant Last d 10.30pm
CARDS:

See advert on this page

AA Rosettes are awarded for quality of food, see page 15 for an explanation of Rosette assessment.

W1 WEST END
★★★★ London Marriott Grosvenor Square
Grosvenor Square W1A 4AW
Quality Percentage Score: 73%
☎ 020 7493 1232 Fax 020 7491 3201
Dir: *M4 east to Cromwell Rd through Knightsbridge to Hyde Park Corner, Park Lane right at Brook Gate onto upper Brook St to Grosvenor Sq/ Duke St*
Situated in the heart of Mayfair, this popular hotel offers comfortable, well equipped accommodation in a variety of room sizes, all with a good range of facilities. Public areas are smart and inviting, staff are friendly and helpful. Light refreshments are served all day in the Regent Lounge and a full menu is offered in the Diplomat Restaurant, where an impressive breakfast buffet is also laid out.
ROOMS: 221 en suite (bth/shr) (26 fmly) No smoking in 120 bedrooms d £276 * LB Off peak **MEALS:** Lunch £20.50-£27.95 & alc Dinner £12.95 & alc V meals Coffee am Tea pm **FACILITIES:** CTV in all bedrooms STV Gym Exercise & fitness centre Xmas **CONF:** Thtr 1000 Class 550 Board 120 **SERVICES:** Lift Night porter Air conditioning 80P **NOTES:** No dogs (ex guide dogs) No coaches No smoking area in restaurant Last d 10pm **CARDS:**

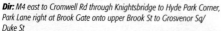

W1 WEST END
★★★★ *Millennium Britannia Mayfair*
Grosvenor Square W1A 3AN
Quality Percentage Score: 73%
☎ 020 7629 9400 Fax 020 7629 7736
The extensive range of facilities includes a cocktail bar and piano bar, plus a choice of two restaurants, one Japanese. The hotel also boasts a fine new ballroom, equipped with state-of-the art communications. Bedrooms vary in size, but all are smartly appointed. The hotel also offers a business centre and fitness room.
ROOMS: 316 en suite (bth/shr) No smoking in 60 bedrooms **MEALS:** English, American, French, Italian & Japanese Cuisine V meals Coffee am Tea pm **FACILITIES:** CTV in all bedrooms STV Gym Wkly live entertainment **CONF:** Thtr 100 Class 54 Board 55 **SERVICES:** Lift Night porter Air conditioning 15P **NOTES:** No dogs (ex guide dogs) Last d 10.30pm **CARDS:**

W1 WEST END
★★★★ Radisson SAS Portman
22 Portman Square W1H 9FL
Quality Percentage Score: 73%
☎ 020 7208 6000 Fax 020 7208 6001
Dir: *100mtrs N of Oxford St and 500mtrs E of Edgware Rd*
Situated off Portman Square, the hotel is just a short stroll from Oxford Street, Marble Arch and Hyde Park. Guests can choose from four distict styles of bedroom: Oriental, Scandinavian, British and Classic. Some rooms, with fax and modem points, are designated 'business class'. The intimate Library Restaurant claims to be the smallest hotel dining room in London, and offers a sophisticated menu. Portman Corner is the more informal restaurant, and afternoon tea is served in the lobby lounge.
ROOMS: 280 en suite (bth/shr) (21 fmly) No smoking in 129 bedrooms s £229.12-£750; d £246.75-£750 * LB Off peak **MEALS:** Lunch £19.95-£23.95 Dinner £19.95-£23.95 International Cuisine V meals Coffee am Tea pm **FACILITIES:** CTV in all bedrooms STV Tennis (hard) Sauna Solarium Gym Wkly live entertainment Xmas **CONF:** Thtr 500 Class 300 Board 65 **SERVICES:** Lift Night porter Air conditioning 400P **NOTES:** No dogs (ex guide dogs) No smoking area in restaurant Last d 11pm **CARDS:**

W1 WEST END
★★★★ Clifton-Ford
47 Welbeck St W1M 8DN
Quality Percentage Score: 71%
☎ 020 7486 6600 Fax 020 7486 7492
This well managed and friendly hotel is popular for business and conference use, as well as keeping its appeal for holidaymakers. Accommodation offers high standards of modern comfort, especially in the private suites. A marbled lobby, where guests may enjoy complimentary sherry and canapés during the cocktail hour, leads into an intimate lounge. There is also a cocktail bar and a brasserie.
ROOMS: 186 en suite (bth/shr) (7 fmly) **MEALS:** Lunch £12-£25 & alc Dinner £12-£25alc European Cuisine V meals Coffee am Tea pm **FACILITIES:** CTV in all bedrooms STV **CONF:** Thtr 150 Class 80 Board 40 **SERVICES:** Lift Night porter Air conditioning 20P **NOTES:** Last d 10pm **CARDS:**

W1 WEST END
★★★★ *The Washington Mayfair Hotel*
5-7 Curzon St, Mayfair W1Y 8DT
Quality Percentage Score: 71%
☎ 020 7499 7000 Fax 020 7495 6172
This smart, air conditioned modern hotel offers a high standard of accommodation. Bedrooms, furnished in burred oak, range from state rooms and suites with spa baths to equally comfortable twins and doubles. Light refreshments are served in the marbled and wood-panelled public areas and there is a wide range of business services, a concierge desk and help with car parking.
ROOMS: 173 en suite (bth/shr) No smoking in 94 bedrooms **MEALS:** International Cuisine V meals Coffee am Tea pm **FACILITIES:** CTV in all bedrooms STV Wkly live entertainment **CONF:** Thtr 80 Class 35 Board 36 **SERVICES:** Lift Night porter Air conditioning **NOTES:** No dogs (ex guide dogs) No smoking area in restaurant Last d 11pm **CARDS:**

W1 WEST END
★★★★ Brown's
Albemarle St, Mayfair W1X 4BP
Quality Percentage Score: 70%
☎ 020 7493 6020 Fax 020 7493 9381
Dir: *from Green Park Underground Station on Piccadilly, take third left into Albemarle Street*
Browns is famous for its English country-house style and traditional emphasis on comfortable furnishings. Accommodation is of good quality and there is a smartly decorated restaurant with an imaginative menu. The hotel is a popular refuge for afternoon tea.
ROOMS: 118 en suite (bth/shr) (15 fmly) **MEALS:** Lunch fr £24 Dinner fr £45alc French Cuisine V meals Coffee am Tea pm **FACILITIES:** CTV in all bedrooms STV Wkly live entertainment **CONF:** Thtr 70 Class 30 Board 35 **SERVICES:** Lift Night porter **NOTES:** No dogs (ex guide dogs) No coaches No smoking area in restaurant Last d 10.30pm **CARDS:**

W1 WEST END
★★★★ *Thistle Marble Arch*
Bryanston St, Marble Arch W1A 4UR
Quality Percentage Score: 69%
☎ 020 7629 8040 Fax 020 7499 7792
Dir: *off Oxford Street*
Just off Oxford Street this very popular hotel offers some of the most spacious, elegant and thoughtfully equipped bedrooms in London with extras such as voice mail, American power outlets and climate control. Public areas including a range of meeting facilities, are impressive in terms of their comfort and quality.

contd.

London

Guests dine in The Charleston restaurant or from the 24-hour room service menu. The hotel offers a business centre and executive lounge facilities.
ROOMS: 689 en suite (bth/shr) (12 fmly) No smoking in 331 bedrooms **MEALS:** International Cuisine V meals Coffee am Tea pm **FACILITIES:** CTV in all bedrooms STV Wkly live entertainment **CONF:** Thtr 300 Class 160 Board 80 **SERVICES:** Lift Night porter P **NOTES:** No dogs (ex guide dogs) No smoking area in restaurant Last d 0.45am **CARDS:**

W1 WEST END
★★★★ The Chesterfield
35 Charles St, Mayfair W1X 8LX
Quality Percentage Score: 68%
☎ 020 7491 2622 020 7491 4793
Dir: *Hyde Park corner along Picadilly, turn right into Half Moon St. At the end turn left and first right into Queens St, then turn right onto Charles St*
Quiet elegance and an atmosphere of exclusivity appropriate to its prestigious Mayfair address characterise this privately owned hotel. The lobby with its marble floor, glittering chandelier and fluted pillars leads into a library lounge and clubby bar. The restaurant, although traditional in decor, provides a modern menu. Bedrooms are stylish and amenities include direct Internet access via the TV.
ROOMS: 110 en suite (bth/shr) (4 fmly) No smoking in 16 bedrooms s fr £182.13; d fr £205.63 * LB Off peak **MEALS:** Lunch £9.50-£12.50 & alc High tea £5.50-£9.50 & alc Dinner £12.50-£15.50 & alc V meals Coffee am Tea pm **FACILITIES:** CTV in all bedrooms STV Wkly live entertainment Xmas **CONF:** Thtr 90 Class 50 Board 45 **SERVICES:** Lift Night porter **NOTES:** No dogs (ex guide dogs) No coaches No smoking area in restaurant Last d 10.45pm **CARDS:**

W1 WEST END
★★★★ London Marriott Hotel Marble Arch
134 George St W1H 6DN
Quality Percentage Score: 68%
☎ 020 7723 1277 020 7402 0666
Dir: *from Marble Arch turn into the Edgware Road then take 4th turning on right into George St. Turn immediate left into Forset Street for main entrance*
This modern hotel, conveniently situated just off the Edgware Road, and close to Oxford Street shops, offers a good standard of accommodation. Bedrooms are well equipped and furnished with quality fittings; executive rooms have their own lounge on the top floor, where breakfast and special check-out facilities are available. Public lounge and bar areas, although not spacious, are comfortable and the hotel also benefits from a leisure centre and car parking.
ROOMS: 240 en suite (bth/shr) (100 fmly) No smoking in 120 bedrooms d £159-£223.25 * LB Off peak **MEALS:** Lunch £20-£25alc Dinner £30-£32alc English & American Cuisine V meals Coffee am Tea pm **FACILITIES:** CTV in all bedrooms STV Indoor swimming pool (heated) Sauna Solarium Gym Jacuzzi/spa Xmas **CONF:** Thtr 150 Class 75 Board 80 Del from £195 * **SERVICES:** Lift Night porter Air conditioning 80P **NOTES:** No dogs (ex guide dogs) No smoking area in restaurant Last d 10.15pm **CARDS:**

W1 WEST END
★★★★ *The Selfridge*
Orchard St W1H 0JS
Quality Percentage Score: 68%
☎ 020 7408 2080 020 7409 2295
Dir: *behind Selfridges Department store*
Situated right in the heart of shopping land, this elegant hotel is very popular. Most of the bedrooms have been refurbished and although on the small side, they are very smartly decorated and equipped. The first floor is a peaceful retreat from the hustle and bustle with a lounge, rustic-themed bar and informal restaurant.
ROOMS: 294 en suite (bth/shr) No smoking in 98 bedrooms **MEALS:** European Cuisine V meals Coffee am Tea pm **FACILITIES:** CTV in all bedrooms STV **CONF:** Thtr 200 Class 120 Board 36 **SERVICES:** Lift Night porter Air conditioning P **NOTES:** No dogs (ex guide dogs) No smoking area in restaurant Last d 10.30pm **CARDS:**

W1 WEST END
★★★★ *The Cumberland*
Marble Arch W1H 8DP
Quality Percentage Score: 66%
☎ 020 7262 1234 020 7724 4621
Dir: *M4 to central London. At Hyde Park Corner take Park Lane to Marble Arch. Hotel is above Marble Arch tube station.*
Convenient for both the capital's shopping area and the greenery of Hyde Park, the Cumberland's position is unrivalled. The vast range of eating and drinking options includes cafés, oriental dining in Sampans, the ever popular Carvery, and Callaghans bar and restaurant for fresh Irish fare and nightly musical entertainment. An excellent, manned business complex with no less than 17 conference rooms is one of the hotel's notable features. Bedrooms are comfortably furnished and up-to-date and guests have the option of upgrading to the Premier Club for extra comfort and amenities.
ROOMS: 917 en suite (bth/shr) (21 fmly) No smoking in 480 bedrooms **MEALS:** English Mediterranean Chinese & Carvery Cuisine V meals Coffee am Tea pm **FACILITIES:** CTV in all bedrooms STV Wkly live entertainment **CONF:** Thtr 750 Class 350 Board 80 **SERVICES:** Lift Night porter **NOTES:** No dogs (ex guide dogs) Last d midnt **CARDS:**

W1 WEST END
★★★★ The Berners Hotel
Berners St W1A 3BE
Quality Percentage Score: 65%
☎ 020 7666 2000 020 7666 2001
Well positioned in the heart of London's West End, just off Oxford Street, this traditional hotel has an elegant, classical marble-columned foyer with a comfortable lounge - popular for afternoon tea - and attractive restaurant. Bedrooms are all equipped with modern comforts.
ROOMS: 217 en suite (bth/shr) No smoking in 100 bedrooms s £160; d £195 * Off peak **MEALS:** Lunch £16.95-£19.20 & alc Dinner fr £10.25 & alc English & French Cuisine V meals Coffee am Tea pm **FACILITIES:** CTV in all bedrooms STV **CONF:** Thtr 180 Class 80 Board 36 Del from £165 * **SERVICES:** Lift Night porter **NOTES:** Last d 10pm **CARDS:**

W1 WEST END
★★★★ Radisson Edwardian Berkshire
Oxford St W1N 0BY
☎ 020 7629 7474 020 7629 8156
Dir: *central London, along Oxford Street*
Situated almost directly opposite Bond Street Tube station in Oxford Street, this is an ideal hotel for shoppers, and also attracts an international business clientele. Bedrooms, though not over-large, are stylishly decorated. Public rooms are intimate

contd.

London

in scale, and include an elegant drawing room, cocktail bar and first-floor restaurant.
ROOMS: 147 en suite (bth/shr) (2 fmly) No smoking in 44 bedrooms s £240.88; d £287.88 * Off peak **MEALS:** Lunch fr £18.50 Dinner fr £22.50 & alc English & French Cuisine V meals Coffee am Tea pm **FACILITIES:** CTV in all bedrooms **CONF:** Thtr 45 Class 20 Board 26 **SERVICES:** Lift Night porter Air conditioning **NOTES:** No dogs (ex guide dogs) Last d 10.30pm **CARDS:**

W1 WEST END
★★★ Posthouse Regents Park
Carburton St, Regents Park W1P 8EE

Posthouse

Quality Percentage Score: 69%
☎ 020 7388 2300 📠 020 7387 2806

This modern hotel with its own car-park is undergoing significant improvements. The smart public areas are modern in design and are air-conditioned. The bedrooms, which have been refurbished, are well designed. There is 24-hour room service and an all day lounge menu.
ROOMS: 326 en suite (bth/shr) No smoking in 184 bedrooms s £139-£149; d £139-£159 * Off peak **MEALS:** International Cuisine V meals Coffee am Tea pm **FACILITIES:** CTV in all bedrooms STV Wkly live entertainment Xmas **CONF:** Thtr 350 Class 180 Board 50 Del from £180 * **SERVICES:** Lift Night porter 85P **NOTES:** No dogs (ex guide dogs) No smoking area in restaurant Last d 10.30pm
CARDS:

London

W1 WEST END
★★★ Mandeville
Mandeville Place W1M 6BE
Quality Percentage Score: 66%
☎ 020 7935 5599 📠 020 7935 9588
Dir: *off Oxford Street & Wigmore St near Bond St underground station*

This quiet hotel is only a short walk from Oxford Street, and the language skills of its reception staff, plus the helpful concierge desk, have made it popular with foreign visitors. There are also good business and conference facilities. Oceana Restaurant offers inventive, up-market cooking, and there is another all-day restaurant and a pub serving bar food.
ROOMS: 165 en suite (bth/shr) No smoking in 30 bedrooms s £125-£135; d fr £165 (incl. cont bkfst) * Off peak **MEALS:** Bar Lunch fr £6alc Dinner fr £13 & alc International Cuisine V meals Coffee am Tea pm **FACILITIES:** CTV in all bedrooms STV **CONF:** Thtr 35 Class 30 Board 24 Del from £160 * **SERVICES:** Lift Night porter **NOTES:** No dogs (ex guide dogs) Last d 10.30pm **CARDS:**

See advert on opposite page

W1 WEST END
★★★ *Mostyn*
4 Bryanston St W1H 8DE
Quality Percentage Score: 65%
☎ 020 7935 2361 📠 020 7487 2759

Close to Oxford Street and Marble Arch, this Georgian hotel has well equipped bedrooms with good quality furnishings and smart marble bathrooms. For meals, guests may choose to dine in the Spanish Tio Taberna or in the Bistro, with its range of provincial French dishes. There are two car-parks within a short walk.
ROOMS: 121 en suite (bth/shr) (15 fmly) No smoking in 54 bedrooms **MEALS:** Spanish Brasserie & French Cuisine V meals Coffee am Tea pm **FACILITIES:** CTV in all bedrooms STV **CONF:** Thtr 140 Class 80 Board 60 **SERVICES:** Lift Night porter **NOTES:** No dogs (ex guide dogs) No coaches No smoking area in restaurant Last d 10.30pm
CARDS:

See advert on opposite page

W1 WEST END
The Leonard
15 Seymour St W1H 5AA
☎ 020 7935 2010 📠 020 7935 6700

Discreetly situated off Portman Square, The Leonard is only two minutes' walk from Oxford Street. Bedrooms are smartly decorated, with all the expected modern comforts, and equipped with fax and modem links. Lounge and bar are furnished with antique pieces and decorated with fresh flowers.
ROOMS: 28 en suite (bth/shr) s fr £199.75; d fr £223.25 * LB Off peak **MEALS:** Bar Lunch £10-£30alc Dinner £15-£30alc English & Italian Cuisine V meals Coffee am Tea pm **FACILITIES:** CTV in all bedrooms STV Gym **CONF:** Thtr 15 Class 15 Board 15 **SERVICES:** Lift Night porter Air conditioning **NOTES:** No dogs (ex guide dogs) No coaches
CARDS:

W1 WEST END
St George's
Langham Place, Regent St W1N 8QS

LONDON SIGNATURE HOTELS

☎ 020 7580 0111 📠 020 7436 7997
Dir: *Located in Langham Place at the intersection of Regent St and Portland Place*

Situated in Henry Wood House, which is shared by the BBC, St George's is quite unique. The reception lobby is on the ground floor, but there are no further public areas until you reach the 15th floor, which has superb views across the city. Here there is a cosy bar area, a few meeting rooms and a restaurant which makes the most of the views.
ROOMS: 86 en suite (bth/shr) (8 fmly) No smoking in 18 bedrooms **MEALS:** V meals Coffee am Tea pm **FACILITIES:** CTV in all bedrooms STV **CONF:** Thtr 30 Class 20 Board 20 **SERVICES:** Lift Night porter 2P **NOTES:** No smoking area in restaurant Last d 9.45pm
CARDS:

W1 WEST END
Radisson Edwardian Grafton
130 Tottenham Court Rd W1P 9HP

Radisson Edwardian

☎ 020 7388 4131 📠 020 7387 7394
Dir: *central London, along Euston Road, turn into Tottenham Court Road. Past Warren Street Tube*

Handily placed next to Warren Street Tube station, and within an easy walk of London's main shopping area and the British Museum, the hotel offers a variety of styles of bedroom, all with modern amenities. Public areas include a smart lounge, a restaurant and a wine bar where food is also available.
ROOMS: 324 en suite (bth/shr) (8 fmly) No smoking in 163 bedrooms s £170.37; d £211.50 * Off peak **MEALS:** Lunch fr £13.50 Dinner fr £19.50 & alc English & French Cuisine V meals **FACILITIES:** CTV in all bedrooms **CONF:** Thtr 100 Class 40 Board 36 **SERVICES:** Lift Night porter **NOTES:** No dogs (ex guide dogs) Last d 10pm
CARDS:

W2 BAYSWATER, PADDINGTON
★★★★ *Thistle Hyde Park*

THISTLE HOTELS

90-92 Lancaster Gate W2 3NR
Quality Percentage Score: 73%
☎ 020 7262 2711 020 7262 2147
Dir: *on Bayswater Rd between Lancaster Gate and Queensway*

Whites has all the atmosphere of a country house hotel but is situated just steps from Hyde Park and the West End. It is a popular place, with a loyal clientele who appreciate the discreet elegance of its interior. Bedrooms are quite spacious and the marble bathrooms are an attractive feature. A cosy club-like bar with a glass-canopied extension leads into a smart restaurant where modern dishes are interpreted with aplomb.

ROOMS: 54 en suite (bth/shr) No smoking in 10 bedrooms
MEALS: International Cuisine V meals Coffee am Tea pm
FACILITIES: CTV in all bedrooms STV **CONF:** Thtr 35 Class 20 Board 25 Del from £190 * **SERVICES:** Lift Night porter Air conditioning 25P
NOTES: No dogs (ex guide dogs) No coaches No smoking area in restaurant Last d 10.30pm **CARDS:**

W2 BAYSWATER, PADDINGTON
★★★★ Royal Lancaster

Lancaster Ter W2 2TY
Quality Percentage Score: 72%
☎ 020 7262 6737 020 7724 3191
Dir: *directly above Lancaster Gate Underground Station*

Overlooking Hyde Park and Kensington Gardens, the Royal Lancaster's upper storeys also offer fine views across London. There is 24-hour room service and efficient porterage. The choice of eating ranges from the lounge, the Pavement Café, the smart Park Restaurant or the exotic and authentic Nipa Thai.

ROOMS: 416 en suite (bth/shr) (9 fmly) No smoking in 51 bedrooms d £215-£290 * LB Off peak **MEALS:** Lunch £19.50-£23.50 Dinner £19.50-£23.50 International Cuisine V meals Coffee am Tea pm
FACILITIES: CTV in all bedrooms STV Wkly live entertainment Xmas
CONF: Thtr 1500 Class 650 Board 40 Del from £210 * **SERVICES:** Lift Night porter Air conditioning 100P **NOTES:** No dogs (ex guide dogs) No smoking area in restaurant Last d 10.30pm
CARDS:

W2 BAYSWATER, PADDINGTON
★★★ Grosvenor Court

27 Devonshire Ter W2 3DP
Quality Percentage Score: 66%
☎ 020 7262 2204 020 7402 9351
Dir: *from A40 take exit signed Paddington Station, at station turn into Craven Road hotel on right*

This centrally located hotel has been recently refurbished to a very high standard and bedrooms are bright, modern and smart. The restaurant offers a short but interesting range of dishes.

contd.

London

Staff are friendly and relaxed and guests enjoy sitting in the smart lounge.
ROOMS: 157 en suite (bth/shr) (34 fmly) s £80-£90; d £90-£120 (incl. cont bkfst) * LB Off peak **MEALS:** Dinner £10-£15alc International Cuisine V meals Coffee am **FACILITIES:** CTV in all bedrooms STV **SERVICES:** Lift Night porter **NOTES:** No dogs (ex guide dogs) No smoking area in restaurant Last d 9.30pm
CARDS:

W2 BAYSWATER, PADDINGTON
★★★ Central Park
Queensborough Ter W2 3SS
Quality Percentage Score: 64%
☎ 020 7229 2424 Fax 020 7229 2904
Central Park is a popular hotel just off the Bayswater Road and close to London's West End. Bedrooms offer all the expected modern comforts, and there are spacious public areas. Garage parking is available.
ROOMS: 252 en suite (bth/shr) **MEALS:** International Cuisine V meals Coffee am Tea pm **FACILITIES:** CTV in all bedrooms **CONF:** Thtr 800 Class 50 Board 50 **SERVICES:** Lift Night porter 30P
NOTES: Last d 10pm **CARDS:**

See advert on opposite page

W2 BAYSWATER, PADDINGTON
★★★ Berjaya Eden Park Hotel
35-39 Inverness Ter, Bayswater W2 3JS
Quality Percentage Score: 63%
☎ 020 7221 2220 Fax 020 7221 2286
Dir: *From Marble Arch, straight across main rdbt onto Bayswater Rd, turn right into Queensway,the first turn left into Inverness Terrace*
This friendly hotel close to Queensway offers attractively furnished and well equipped bedrooms. The restaurant is informal and the stylish bar serves complimentary coffee to hotel residents in the afternoon.
ROOMS: 75 rms (67 bth/shr) 62 annexe en suite (bth/shr) (8 fmly) s £97; d £114 Off peak **MEALS:** Dinner £10.50-£12.50alc European Cuisine V meals Coffee am Tea pm **FACILITIES:** CTV in all bedrooms STV **SERVICES:** Lift Night porter **NOTES:** No dogs (ex guide dogs) Last d 10.30pm **CARDS:**

W2 BAYSWATER, PADDINGTON
★★★ *The Park Court*
75 Lancaster Gate, Hyde Park W2 3NN
Quality Percentage Score: 63%
☎ 020 7402 4272 Fax 020 7706 4156
Dir: *off Bayswater Road*
This busy hotel, fashioned from a terrace of 19th-century houses, has well appointed public rooms, extensive conference facilities, a hotel shop, and a spacious lounge and bar. Ongoing refurbishment has enhanced the comfort and quality of the well equipped bedrooms, which include a spacious suite, interconnecting family rooms, and accommodation on the ground floor suitable for guests with disabilities.
ROOMS: 390 en suite (bth/shr) (25 fmly) No smoking in 194 bedrooms **MEALS:** V meals Coffee am Tea pm **FACILITIES:** CTV in all bedrooms STV **CONF:** Thtr 120 Class 50 Board 40 **SERVICES:** Lift Night porter **NOTES:** No smoking area in restaurant Last d 11pm
CARDS:

W2 BAYSWATER, PADDINGTON
★★★ *Thistle Kensington Gardens*
104 Bayswater Rd W2 3HL
Quality Percentage Score: 63%
☎ 020 7262 4461 Fax 020 7706 4560
Dir: *Corner of Bayswater Rd and Porchester Ter*
There are some wonderful views of the city over Hyde Park from this centrally located hotel. Bedrooms have recently been upgraded and offer smart well equipped accommodation. Public areas, although restricted in size, have been transformed by a complete refurbishment producing an attractive bar and restaurant, and elegant meeting rooms.
ROOMS: 175 en suite (bth/shr) No smoking in 66 bedrooms
MEALS: International Cuisine V meals Coffee am Tea pm
FACILITIES: CTV in all bedrooms STV **CONF:** Thtr 60 Class 22 Board 36 Del from £180 * **SERVICES:** Lift Night porter Air conditioning 60P
NOTES: No smoking area in restaurant Last d 10.30pm
CARDS:

W2 BAYSWATER, PADDINGTON
★★★ Plaza on Hyde Park
1-7 Lancaster Gate W2 3LG
Quality Percentage Score: 58%
☎ 020 7262 5022 Fax 020 7724 8666
Dir: *200yds from Lancaster Gate Underground Station*
Attractively situated opposite Hyde Park and only a few minutes walk from Marble Arch, this busy hotel is popular with overseas visitors. Its interior is bright and modern in style.
ROOMS: 402 en suite (bth/shr) (10 fmly) No smoking in 100 bedrooms s £110-£130; d £130-£150 * LB Off peak **MEALS:** Lunch £10-£15 High tea £3-£10 Dinner £10-£20 Mediterranean Cuisine V meals Coffee am Tea pm **FACILITIES:** CTV in all bedrooms STV **CONF:** Thtr 25 Class 12 Board 20 Del from £140 * **SERVICES:** Lift Night porter **NOTES:** No dogs (ex guide dogs) No smoking area in restaurant Last d 10.30pm
CARDS:

W2 BAYSWATER, PADDINGTON
★★ Delmere
130 Sussex Gardens, Hyde Park W2 1UB
Quality Percentage Score: 68%
☎ 020 7706 3344 Fax 020 7262 1863
Well positioned on historic Sussex Gardens for both Hyde Park and the West End. The welcoming, friendly staff are a big plus at this well-managed hotel. Bedrooms are all well equipped and designed to make the best use of available space. Public rooms include a jazz-themed bar and a particularly comfortable lounge that is provided with books, up-to-date magazines and newspapers.
ROOMS: 38 en suite (bth/shr) (3 fmly) s £70-£92; d £88-£98 (incl. cont bkfst) * LB Off peak **MEALS:** Dinner £8-£15 & alc Italian & Continental Cuisine V meals **FACILITIES:** CTV in all bedrooms **SERVICES:** Lift Night porter 2P **NOTES:** No dogs No coaches Last d 10pm
CARDS:

W2 BAYSWATER, PADDINGTON
The Abbey Court
20 Pembridge Gardens, Kensington W2 4DU
☎ 020 7221 7518 Fax 020 7792 0858
Dir: *2 minute walk from Nottinghill Gate Underground station*
Situated in Notting Hill and close to Kensington, this elegant five-storey townhouse is in a quiet side road. Rooms are individually decorated and furnished to a high standard and there is room-service of light snacks. Breakfast is taken in the conservatory.
ROOMS: 22 en suite (bth/shr) (1 fmly) No smoking in 10 bedrooms **MEALS:** V meals Coffee am Tea pm **FACILITIES:** CTV in all bedrooms STV **SERVICES:** Night porter **NOTES:** No dogs (ex guide dogs) No coaches **CARDS:**

London

W2 BAYSWATER, PADDINGTON

The Darlington Hyde Park

111-117 Sussex Gardens W2 2RU

☎ 020 7460 8800 Fax 020 7460 8828

Dir: *just off Edgware Road*

Although not offering the full range of hotel services, this comfortable townhouse provides smart, well maintained rooms with excellent facilities, including good desk space. Breakfast is served in an airy dining room which also offers drinks and snacks in the early evening.

ROOMS: 40 en suite (bth/shr) (2 fmly) No smoking in 5 bedrooms s £90-£130; d £110-£130 (incl. cont bkfst) * Off peak **FACILITIES:** CTV in all bedrooms STV **SERVICES:** Lift Night porter **NOTES:** No dogs (ex guide dogs) No coaches No smoking in restaurant **CARDS:**

W2 BAYSWATER, PADDINGTON

Pembridge Court

34 Pembridge Gardens W2 4DX

☎ 020 7229 9977 Fax 020 7727 4982

Dir: *off the Bayswater Rd at Nottinghill Gate by underground Station*

Just minutes from Portobello Market and in Notting Hill Gate, this Victorian townhouse provides well appointed bedrooms with 24-hour room service. In the evenings the restaurant and cellar bar are open.

ROOMS: 20 en suite (bth/shr) (4 fmly) s £120-£155; d £150-£190 (incl. bkfst) * Off peak **MEALS:** V meals Coffee am Tea pm **FACILITIES:** CTV in all bedrooms STV Membership of local Health Club **SERVICES:** Lift Night porter Air conditioning 2P **NOTES:** No coaches No smoking area in restaurant **CARDS:**

W6 HAMMERSMITH See LONDON plan 1 *D3*

★★★ Novotel London West

Hammersmith Int. Centre, 1 Shortlands W6 8DR

Quality Percentage Score: 68%

☎ 020 8741 1555 Fax 020 8741 2120

Dir: *turn off A4 onto Hammersmith Broadway, then follow signs for City Centre, take first left and hotel is on the left*

This large purpose-built hotel, situated close to Hammersmith Underground Station, is easily accessible from the M4 and Heathrow Airport, and has the advantage of its own secure car park. Practical, spacious bedrooms are well equipped with a wide range of modern facilities which include air conditioning. The open-plan public areas include a brasserie, a choice of bars including the "Frog and Bulldog Pub", a useful shop and a range of conference and function rooms.

ROOMS: 629 en suite (bth/shr) (184 fmly) No smoking in 415 bedrooms **MEALS:** Lunch £11-£16.95 & alc Dinner £16.95 & alc International Cuisine V meals Coffee am Tea pm **FACILITIES:** CTV in all bedrooms STV Pool table Wkly live entertainment **CONF:** Thtr 900 Class 600 Board 300 Del from £179 * **SERVICES:** Lift Air conditioning 250P **NOTES:** No smoking area in restaurant Last d midnight **CARDS:**

W6 HAMMERSMITH

★★★ Vencourt

255 King St, Hammersmith W6 9LU

Quality Percentage Score: 66%

☎ 020 8563 8855 Fax 020 8563 9988

Dir: *from Central London-A4 to Hammersmith then follow A315 towards Chiswick*

This modern hotel is close to the centre of Hammersmith where there is good public transport. Rooms have the expected modern comforts and most have good views over London, especially on the upper of the 12 storeys. The open-plan public areas include a

contd.

London

lounge bar, where snacks are served all day, and a small restaurant for more substantial meals.
ROOMS: 120 en suite (bth/shr) (25 fmly) No smoking in 18 bedrooms s £86-£99; d £94-£99 * LB Off peak **MEALS:** Lunch £11.55-£16alc High tea £2.10-£4.50alc Dinner £10-£10.65 & alc English & French Cuisine V meals Coffee am Tea pm **FACILITIES:** CTV in all bedrooms STV Xmas **CONF:** Thtr 50 Class 40 Board 26 Del from £99 * **SERVICES:** Lift 27P **NOTES:** No smoking area in restaurant Last d 10.30pm
CARDS:

W8 KENSINGTON See LONDON plan 1 *D3*
★★★★★ Royal Garden Hotel
2-24 Kensington High St W8 4PT
Quality Percentage Score: 71%
☎ 020 7937 8000 020 7361 1991
Dir: *next to Kensington Palace*
Overlooking Kensington Gardens and Hyde Park, the Royal Garden Hotel offers high standards of comfort and service. The spacious lobby leads into extensive reception rooms. Bertie's Bar is housed on a balcony overlooking the foyer and there are two restaurants, one, the Park Terrace, informal, and the other on the 10th floor, famed for its wonderful views. Bedrooms range from Traders rooms to suites and split-level rooms with views of the park.
ROOMS: 401 en suite (bth/shr) (19 fmly) No smoking in 164 bedrooms d £210-£246.75 * Off peak **MEALS:** Lunch £14.95-£28.50 & alc Dinner £24-£37alc International Cuisine V meals Coffee am Tea pm **FACILITIES:** CTV in all bedrooms STV Sauna Solarium Gym Health & fitness centre Wkly live entertainment Xmas **CONF:** Thtr 600 Class 340 Board 80 **SERVICES:** Lift Night porter Air conditioning **NOTES:** No dogs (ex guide dogs) No smoking area in restaurant Last d 11pm
CARDS:

See advert on page 409

W8 KENSINGTON
★★★★ *Thistle Kensington Park*
16-32 De Vere Gardens, Kensington W8 5AG
Quality Percentage Score: 64%
☎ 020 7937 8080 020 7937 7616
Attractive public areas are a feature of this bright modern hotel which has extensive meeting room facilities. Guests enjoy dining in the all day coffee shop and the Eaglescarnie bar is particularly friendly and welcoming. Bedrooms vary in size but all are well presented and some are very quiet. There are now some brand new rooms with excellent facilities including air-conditioning.
ROOMS: 352 en suite (bth/shr) (14 fmly) No smoking in 90 bedrooms **MEALS:** International Cuisine V meals Coffee am Tea pm **FACILITIES:** CTV in all bedrooms STV **CONF:** Thtr 120 Class 75 Board 50 **SERVICES:** Lift Night porter Air conditioning **NOTES:** No dogs (ex guide dogs) No smoking area in restaurant Last d 10.45pm
CARDS:

W8 KENSINGTON
★★★★ Copthorne Tara
Scarsdale Place, Wrights Ln W8 5SR
Quality Percentage Score: 62%
☎ 020 7937 7211 020 7937 7100
This is one of the city's larger hotels catering to both leisure and business guests. It is located in a residential area off Kensington High Street. Public areas have a smart atmosphere about them and include the relaxing setting of Café Mozart or Jerome's Restaurant,. Bedrooms are bright and equipped with a useful range of facilities.
ROOMS: 831 en suite (bth/shr) No smoking in 265 bedrooms s £170-£190; d £185-£205 * LB Off peak **MEALS:** Lunch £16-£19 & alc Dinner £16-£19 & alc International Cuisine V meals Coffee am Tea pm **FACILITIES:** CTV in all bedrooms Xmas **CONF:** Thtr 280 Class 160 Board 92 Del from £185 * **SERVICES:** Lift Night porter Air conditioning 110P **NOTES:** No dogs (ex guide dogs) No smoking area in restaurant Last d 11pm **CARDS:**

W8 KENSINGTON
★★★ Posthouse Kensington
Wright's Ln, Kensington W8 5SP
☎ 020 7937 8170 020 7937 8289
Dir: *off Kensington High Street*
Positioned close to Kensington High Street, this hotel offers well equipped bedrooms and an extensive range of facilities; these include an impressive new leisure club, dedicated conference rooms and several eating outlets, including an all day conservatory coffee shop and two restaurants. A refurbishment programme has enhanced the quality and decor of the public areas. Bedrooms are benefiting from a stylish re-vamp, and although some rooms are quite compact, they all offer good facilities.
ROOMS: 550 en suite (bth/shr) No smoking in 150 bedrooms **MEALS:** Lunch fr £15.95 Dinner £15.95-£16.95 English & Italian Cuisine V meals Coffee am Tea pm **FACILITIES:** CTV in all bedrooms STV Indoor swimming pool (heated) Squash Sauna Solarium Gym Pool table Jacuzzi/spa Health & Fitness centre with Beauty room Steam room **CONF:** Thtr 180 Class 80 Board 60 Del £172 * **SERVICES:** Lift Night porter 70P **NOTES:** No smoking area in restaurant Last d 11pm
CARDS:

W11 HOLLAND PARK, NOTTING HILL
See LONDON plan 1 *D3/D4*
★★★★ *Halcyon*
81 Holland Park W11 3RZ
Quality Percentage Score: 78%
☎ 020 7727 7288 020 7229 8516
Faithfully restored some ten years ago, this elegant hotel is well named. Accommodation is amply proportioned and equipped with every comfort. Staff provide attentive and friendly service, and good modern cooking from a seasonally changing menu is served in The Room restaurant.
ROOMS: 43 en suite (bth/shr) **MEALS:** English & French Cuisine V meals Coffee am Tea pm **FACILITIES:** CTV in all bedrooms STV **CONF:** Class 20 Board 10 **SERVICES:** Lift Night porter Air conditioning **NOTES:** No dogs (ex guide dogs) No coaches Last d 10.30pm
CARDS:

WC1 BLOOMSBURY, HOLBORN
★★★★ The Montague on the Gardens
15 Montague St, Bloomsbury WC1B 5BJ
Quality Percentage Score: 68%
☎ 020 7637 1001 020 7637 2516
Off Russell Square and near the British Museum, this is an elegant hotel with stylish, well designed bedrooms and good IT provision. The clubby bar is the ideal venue for cocktails, meals are taken in the Blue Door Bistro.
ROOMS: 104 en suite (bth/shr) No smoking in 20 bedrooms s fr £110; d fr £145 * LB Off peak **MEALS:** Lunch £15.95 & alc Dinner £15.95 & alc International Cuisine V meals Coffee am Tea pm **FACILITIES:** CTV in all bedrooms STV Sauna Gym Jacuzzi/spa Wkly live entertainment Xmas **CONF:** Thtr 120 Class 50 Board 50 **SERVICES:** Lift Night porter **NOTES:** No dogs (ex guide dogs) No smoking area in restaurant Last d 11pm **CARDS:**

London

WC1 BLOOMSBURY, HOLBORN
★★★★ Radisson Edwardian Marlborough

Bloomsbury St WC1B 3QD
Quality Percentage Score: 67%
☎ 020 7636 5601 020 7636 0532
Dir: *continue past Oxford Street and down New Oxford Street turn into Bloomsbury Street*
This stylish period hotel offers a wide range of services and a choice of eating options for the international traveller. Bedrooms are smart and individually furnished, and are fully equipped with modern facilities.
ROOMS: 173 en suite (bth/shr) (3 fmly) No smoking in 57 bedrooms s £198.58; d £287.88 * LB Off peak **MEALS:** Lunch fr £17.50 High tea fr £8 Dinner fr £20.50 & alc English & French Cuisine V meals Coffee am Tea pm **FACILITIES:** CTV in all bedrooms **CONF:** Thtr 250 Class 90 Board 50 **SERVICES:** Lift Night porter **NOTES:** Last d 10.30pm
CARDS:

WC1 BLOOMSBURY, HOLBORN
★★★★ Holiday Inn Kings Cross/ Bloomsbury

1 Kings Cross Rd WC1X 9HX
Quality Percentage Score: 66%
☎ 020 7833 3900 020 7917 6163
Dir: *0.50m from Kings Cross station on the corner of King Cross Rd and Calthorpe St*
This smart modern hotel is conveniently placed for Kings Cross station and the City. Bedrooms have been fitted to a good standard, each with air conditioning, fridge and power shower. The lobby leads to a range of attractively furnished public rooms including an intimate cocktail bar and two restaurants one of which is Indian.
ROOMS: 405 en suite (bth/shr) (163 fmly) No smoking in 160 bedrooms s fr £180; d fr £180 * LB Off peak **MEALS:** Lunch £6-£17.50alc Dinner £6-£20alc International Cuisine V meals Coffee am Tea pm **FACILITIES:** CTV in all bedrooms STV Indoor swimming pool (heated) Sauna Solarium Gym Jacuzzi/spa Hair & Beauty salon Xmas **CONF:** Thtr 220 Class 120 Board 30 Del £180 * **SERVICES:** Lift Night porter Air conditioning 12P **NOTES:** No dogs (ex guide dogs) No smoking area in restaurant Last d 10pm
CARDS:

WC1 BLOOMSBURY, HOLBORN
★★★★ *Hotel Russell*

Russell Square WC1B 5BE
Quality Percentage Score: 59%
☎ 020 7837 6470 020 7837 2857
This splendid historic Victorian building has bedrooms which are very traditional in design, and are all well equipped. Public areas, which include a choice of restaurants and bars, have real character. Staff are friendly and helpful, and the magnificent ballroom, recently redecorated, is popular for functions and meetings.
ROOMS: 329 en suite (bth/shr) No smoking in 23 bedrooms **MEALS:** V meals Coffee am Tea pm **FACILITIES:** CTV in all bedrooms STV **CONF:** Thtr 450 Class 200 Board 35 **SERVICES:** Lift Night porter **NOTES:** No smoking area in restaurant Last d 10.30pm
CARDS:

New AA Guides for the Millennium are featured on page 24

WC1 BLOOMSBURY, HOLBORN
★★★ The Bonnington in Bloomsbury

92 Southampton Row WC1B 4BH
Quality Percentage Score: 71%
☎ 020 7242 2828 020 7831 9170
Dir: *From M40 Euston Rd opposite Stn turn south into Upper Woburn Place past Russell Sq into Southampton Row Bonnington on left*
Well placed for West End theatres, the hotel offers traditional standards of service and modern comfort. Bedrooms come in a range of sizes and styles, and some are suitable for families. Waterfalls Restaurant offers a good choice of dishes and as an alternative there is a popular bar with a buffet.
ROOMS: 215 en suite (bth/shr) (16 fmly) No smoking in 85 bedrooms s fr £111; d fr £140 (incl. bkfst) * LB Off peak **MEALS:** Lunch £11.50 Dinner £19.75 English & French Cuisine V meals Coffee am Tea pm **FACILITIES:** CTV in all bedrooms STV Business Centre **CONF:** Thtr 250 Class 70 Board 50 Del from £104 * **SERVICES:** Lift Night porter **NOTES:** Last d 10.30pm **CARDS:**

WC1 BLOOMSBURY, HOLBORN
★★★ *Academy*

17-21 Gower St WC1E 6HG
Quality Percentage Score: 69%
☎ 020 7631 4115 020 7636 3442
Dir: *Right turn off Euston Rd onto Gower St*
The Academy provides a welcoming and cosy atmosphere to all who visit. Continuing refurbishment has improved quality and comfort of rooms featuring air conditioning and well designed bathrooms, all in a light modern style. Our award of Two Rosettes is held by the restaurant which specialises in quality eclectic cuisine.
ROOMS: 48 en suite (bth/shr) **MEALS:** English & French Cuisine V meals Coffee am **FACILITIES:** CTV in all bedrooms STV Private Patio Gardens **CONF:** Thtr 24 Class 16 Board 20 **NOTES:** No dogs (ex guide dogs) No coaches Last d 22.45pm **CARDS:**

WC1 BLOOMSBURY, HOLBORN
★★★ *Thistle Bloomsbury*

Bloomsbury Way WC1A 2SD
Quality Percentage Score: 69%
☎ 020 7242 5881 020 7831 0225
Dir: *Euston Rd underpass into Gower St to Bloomsbury St. At junct with New Oxford St left cont into Bloomsbury Way Hotel on Left after St Georges Church*
Well situated for theatregoers, this hotel has recently benefited from significant improvement. Bedrooms have either been refurbished or completely refitted and the ground-floor bar and lounge areas have been impressively remodelled. The well-equipped rooms are generally spacious with good quality fabrics and furnishings, with both family rooms and suites available. There is a public car park nearby.
ROOMS: 138 en suite (bth/shr) (19 fmly) No smoking in 42 bedrooms **MEALS:** International Cuisine V meals Coffee am Tea pm **FACILITIES:** CTV in all bedrooms STV Jacuzzi/spa **CONF:** Thtr 90 Class 40 Board 35 **SERVICES:** Lift Night porter **NOTES:** No smoking area in restaurant Last d 10pm **CARDS:**

WC1 BLOOMSBURY, HOLBORN
★★★ *The London Ryan*

Gwynne Place, Kings Cross Rd WC1X 9QN
Quality Percentage Score: 63%
☎ 020 7278 2480 020 7837 3776
Dir: *M40 Marylebone Rd Euston Rd Kings Cross Rd.M1 West End St Johns Wood Regents Park Baker St Marylebone Rd Euston Kings Cross Rd*
Conveniently situated for King's Cross and Euston stations, the hotel has comfortable, well furnished bedrooms and gives a

contd.

London

choice of standard, executive and family rooms. A ground-floor lounge leads to a small bar area and the Casablanca restaurant serves a good range of meals. Extensive room service is also available.
ROOMS: 211 en suite (bth/shr) (18 fmly) No smoking in 89 bedrooms
MEALS: English & Continental Cuisine V meals Coffee am Tea pm
FACILITIES: CTV in all bedrooms Arrangement with nearby Health Club
CONF: Thtr 50 Class 18 Board 30 **SERVICES:** Lift Night porter 28P
NOTES: No dogs (ex guide dogs) No smoking area in restaurant
Last d 10pm **CARDS:**

WC1 BLOOMSBURY, HOLBORN
★★★ *The Royal Scot*
100 Kings Cross Rd WC1X 9DT
Quality Percentage Score: 61%
☎ 020 7278 2434 020 7833 0798
Well positioned for both Kings Cross and St Pancras stations, this large, modern hotel is well suited to all visitors. A gradual transformation is under way, which is resulting in some excellent standards of comfort and quality. There are two eating options and a shop.
ROOMS: 351 en suite (bth/shr) (22 fmly) No smoking in 4118 bedrooms
MEALS: English & French Cuisine V meals Coffee am Tea pm
FACILITIES: CTV in all bedrooms STV **CONF:** Thtr 170 Class 60 Board 50 Del from £145 * **SERVICES:** Lift Night porter Air conditioning 35P
NOTES: No dogs (ex guide dogs) No smoking area in restaurant
Last d 10pm **CARDS:**

London

WC1 BLOOMSBURY, HOLBORN
★★★ Posthouse Bloomsbury
Coram St WC1N 1HT
Posthouse
Quality Percentage Score: 61%
☎ 020 7837 1200 020 7837 5374
Dir: *off Upper Woburn Place near to Russell Square*
Designed with the business traveller in mind, this large hotel offers a wide range of services and facilities. Newly refurbished rooms are smart, comfortable and well equipped. A new Irish-themed bar has been added, and there is a carpark nearby.
ROOMS: 284 en suite (bth/shr) (29 fmly) No smoking in 211 bedrooms d £90-£140 * LB Off peak **MEALS:** International Cuisine V meals Coffee am Tea pm **FACILITIES:** CTV in all bedrooms STV Xmas **CONF:** Thtr 200 Class 140 Board 22 Del from £180 * **SERVICES:** Lift Night porter 80P **NOTES:** No dogs (ex guide dogs) No smoking area in restaurant
Last d 10.30pm **CARDS:**

WC1 BLOOMSBURY, HOLBORN
★★★ *Bloomsbury Park*
126 Southampton Row WC1B 5AD
Quality Percentage Score: 57%
☎ 020 7430 0434 020 7242 0665
Located midway along Southampton Row, this hotel caters to all markets. Bedrooms vary in size and shape, with some overlooking the road. Public areas are quite compact; there is a small dining area with an open-air extension and a second bar, Peter's, with direct access off the street.
ROOMS: 95 en suite (bth/shr) No smoking in 13 bedrooms
MEALS: International Cuisine V meals Coffee am Tea pm
FACILITIES: CTV in all bedrooms STV **CONF:** Thtr 30 Class 10 Board 20
SERVICES: Lift Night porter **NOTES:** No dogs (ex guide dogs)
Last d 9.30pm **CARDS:**

WC1 BLOOMSBURY, HOLBORN
Blooms
7 Montague St WC1B 5BP
☎ 020 7323 1717 020 7636 6498
Dir: *off Russell Square*
Part of an 18th-century terrace, this elegant townhouse is just around the corner from the British Museum. Bedrooms are furnished in Regency style and day rooms consist of a lobby lounge, a garden terrace, a breakfast room and cocktail bar, all graced with antique pieces, paintings and flowers. The lounge menu is also available as room service, and meals can be delivered from some of the local restaurants.
ROOMS: 27 en suite (bth/shr) **MEALS:** European Cuisine V meals Coffee am Tea pm **FACILITIES:** CTV in all bedrooms STV **CONF:** Thtr 20 Board 18 Del £235 * **SERVICES:** Lift Night porter **NOTES:** No dogs (ex guide dogs) No coaches No smoking area in restaurant
Last d 10.30pm **CARDS:**
See advert on opposite page

WC1 BLOOMSBURY, HOLBORN
Radisson Edwardian Kenilworth
Great Russell St WC1B 3LB
☎ 020 7637 3477 020 7631 3133
Dir: *continue past Oxford Street and down New Oxford Street. Turn into Bloomsbury Street*
This stylish period (Edwardian) hotel offers a wide range of friendly services and a choice of eating options for international and national travellers alike. Bedrooms are smart and individually furnished, and are fully equipped with modern facilities.
ROOMS: 187 en suite (bth/shr) No smoking in 20 bedrooms s £164.50; d £193.88 * LB Off peak **MEALS:** Lunch fr £16 High tea fr £20 Dinner fr £30alc English & French Cuisine V meals Coffee am Tea pm
FACILITIES: CTV in all bedrooms STV **CONF:** Thtr 150 Class 50 Board 50 **SERVICES:** Lift Night porter **NOTES:** Last d 10pm
CARDS:

WC2 SOHO, STRAND

The Premier Collection

★★★★★ The Savoy
Strand WC2R 0EU
The Savoy Group
☎ 020 7836 4343 020 7240 6040
Dir: *situated halfway along The Strand between Trafalgar Square and Aldwych*
This splendid hotel of international renown continues to retain its enviable position as one of the country's best. Bedrooms provide very high standards of comfort and quality, famous Art Deco design features, and a push-button bell system for summoning maid, valet or waiter. The marble bathrooms have celebrated thunderstorm showers, and guests will find all the luxurious extras one has come to expect from a hotel of this calibre. The American bar maintains its popularity as a watering-hole for the discerning, and the Grill has a large business clientele. The River Room is renowned for the flavours and precision of its menu, but whichever dining option is chosen, the excellent quality of the ingredients and care in execution
contd.

demonstrates the skill of executive chef Anton Edelmann. Afternoon tea remains a highlight for both residents and visitors, and Saturday night 'Stomping at the Savoy' is a real treat.
ROOMS: 207 en suite (bth/shr) (6 fmly) No smoking in 48 bedrooms s fr £275; d fr £325 * LB Off peak **MEALS:** International Cuisine V meals Coffee am Tea pm **FACILITIES:** CTV in all bedrooms STV Indoor swimming pool (heated) Sauna Gym Tennis at the Vanderbilt Club Wkly live entertainment Xmas **CONF:** Thtr 500 Class 200 Board 32 **SERVICES:** Lift Night porter 58P **NOTES:** No dogs (ex guide dogs) No coaches Last d 11.30pm **CARDS:**

WC2 SOHO, STRAND

Hotel of the Year

★★★★★ One Aldwych
1 Aldwych WC2B 4BZ
Quality Percentage Score: 75%
☎ 020 7300 1000 020 7300 1001
This magnificent building was chosen as this year's Hotel of the Year for England. From its position on the corner of the Aldwych the hotel enjoys commanding views across Waterloo Bridge and Covent Garden. Once the home of the Morning Post newspaper, the building has been skilfully restored. Accommodation is bright, stylish and fully air-conditioned. All rooms are equipped with satellite TV, CD player and voicemail. The Axis and Indigo restaurants provide quality dining, and the cocktail bar is a popular meeting place. The excellent health club has a gym, sauna, treatment rooms and swimming pool.
ROOMS: 105 en suite (bth/shr) No smoking in 39 bedrooms s £245-£300; d £265-£320 * Off peak **MEALS:** Lunch £14.95-£18.95 & alc Dinner £14.95-£18.95 & alc V meals **FACILITIES:** CTV in all bedrooms STV Indoor swimming pool (heated) Sauna Gym Steam room 2 Treatment rooms **CONF:** Thtr 60 Board 40 **SERVICES:** Lift Night porter Air conditioning **NOTES:** No dogs (ex guide dogs) Last d 11.30pm **CARDS:**

WC2 SOHO, STRAND

★★★★★ Le Meridien Waldorf
Aldwych WC2B 4DD
Quality Percentage Score: 72%
☎ 020 7836 2400 020 7836 7244
***Dir:** from Trafalgar Sq follow road down The Strand signed City. At end of The Strand road becomes Aldwych, Le Meridien Waldorf is situated on left*
This historic hotel continues to go from strength to strength, with continued investment and upgrading, enthusiastic and committed management, and friendly, helpful staff. The Palm Court Lounge stages weekend afternoon tea dances backed up by regular jazz evenings. Bedrooms have been tastefully styled with a degree of

contd.

luxury and all are well equipped and air-conditioned. Imaginative cuisine is served in the romantic setting of the Palm Court, and the French-styled brasserie is open all day.
ROOMS: 292 en suite (bth/shr) No smoking in 154 bedrooms s £246.75-£352.50; d £282-£352.50 * LB Off peak **MEALS:** Lunch £30-£50alc High tea £25-£28 Dinner £13.95-£16.95 & alc European Cuisine V meals Coffee am Tea pm **FACILITIES:** CTV in all bedrooms STV Hairdressing salon Wkly live entertainment Xmas **CONF:** Thtr 250 Class 130 Board 80 Del from £230 * **SERVICES:** Lift Night porter **NOTES:** No dogs (ex guide dogs) No smoking area in restaurant Last d 11pm
CARDS:

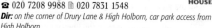

WC2 SOHO, STRAND
★★★★ *Drury Lane Moat House*
10 Drury Ln WC2B 5RE
Quality Percentage Score: 60%
☎ 020 7208 9988 020 7831 1548
Dir: *on the corner of Drury Lane & High Holborn, car park access from High Holborn*
Superbly located for theatre-land and Covent Garden, the Moat House offers public areas which include a comfortable lobby lounge, small bar and informal bistro. Rooms vary in size and all are very well maintained. A fitness room, car park and business centre are also available.
ROOMS: 163 en suite (bth/shr) (95 fmly) No smoking in 86 bedrooms **MEALS:** French Cuisine V meals Coffee am Tea pm **FACILITIES:** CTV in all bedrooms Solarium Gym **CONF:** Thtr 60 Class 40 Board 40 **SERVICES:** Lift Night porter 20P **NOTES:** No smoking in restaurant Last d 10pm **CARDS:**

London

WC2 SOHO, STRAND
★★★★ Radisson Edwardian Mountbatten
Monmouth St, Seven Dials, Covent Garden WC2H 9HD
☎ 020 7836 4300 020 7240 3540
Dir: *just off Shaftesbury Av, on the corner of Seven Dials rdbt*
Situated at Seven Dials, in the heart of theatreland, this hotel is also a popular choice for business guests. Bedrooms are not over-large, but all have an excellent range of facilities, including Internet access. Public areas include a comfortable cocktail bar and restaurant.
ROOMS: 127 en suite (bth/shr) No smoking in 13 bedrooms s £252.63; d £287.88 * Off peak **MEALS:** Lunch fr £18.50 Dinner fr £22 & alc English & French Cuisine V meals Coffee am Tea pm **FACILITIES:** CTV in all bedrooms STV **CONF:** Thtr 90 Class 45 Board 32 **SERVICES:** Lift Night porter **NOTES:** No smoking area in restaurant Last d 11pm
CARDS:

WC2 SOHO, STRAND
★★★ *Strand Palace*
Strand WC2R 0JJ
Quality Percentage Score: 69%
☎ 020 7836 8080 020 7836 2077
This busy hotel offers restaurants and bars ranging from a cosy Italian bistro and lively cafe-bar, to the stylish Mask Bar and contemporary 373 The Strand, with its international menu and buffet. The Academy offers state-of-the-art conference and banqueting suites. Rooms vary in size and style; a supplement buys a room on the smart Club floor, where bedrooms have added luxuries and guests can use an exclusive lounge.
ROOMS: 783 en suite (bth/shr) No smoking in 305 bedrooms **MEALS:** International Cuisine V meals Coffee am Tea pm **FACILITIES:** CTV in all bedrooms STV Discount at nearby Health Club **CONF:** Thtr 160 Class 85 Board 40 Del from £180 * **SERVICES:** Lift Night porter **NOTES:** No dogs (ex guide dogs) Last d mdnt
CARDS:

WC2 SOHO, STRAND
★★★ *Thistle Trafalgar Square*
Whitcomb St WC2H 7HG
Quality Percentage Score: 59%
☎ 020 7930 4477 020 7925 2149
Dir: *Situated 100m from Trafalgar Sq adjacent to the Sainsbury Wing of the National Gallery*
Tucked away in a side street adjacent to the National Gallery and convenient for many of the West End theatres, this popular hotel offers a sound standard of accommodation. Public areas include a pleasant foyer lounge, a busy traditional pub, and a brasserie which opens out onto the pavement in the warmer months.
ROOMS: 108 en suite (bth/shr) No smoking in 36 bedrooms **MEALS:** Modern British Cuisine V meals Coffee am Tea pm **FACILITIES:** CTV in all bedrooms STV **SERVICES:** Lift Night porter **NOTES:** No dogs (ex guide dogs) No smoking area in restaurant Last d 11.30pm **CARDS:**

WC2 SOHO, STRAND
Radisson Edwardian Hampshire
Leicester Square WC2H 7LH
☎ 020 7839 9399 020 7930 8122
Dir: *situated on Leicester Square*
This stylish period hotel enjoys a prime location in Leicester Square. Public areas, although not extensive, have been smartly refurbished and ooze style. The restaurant is particularly enjoyable, complemented by Oscar's wine bar. The smart bedrooms are comfortable and feature access to the Internet.
ROOMS: 124 en suite (bth/shr) No smoking in 20 bedrooms s £329; d £364 * Off peak **MEALS:** Lunch fr £18 Dinner fr £22.50 & alc English & French Cuisine V meals Coffee am Tea pm **FACILITIES:** CTV in all bedrooms STV **CONF:** Thtr 100 Class 40 Board 34 **SERVICES:** Lift Night porter Air conditioning **NOTES:** Last d 10pm
CARDS:

WC2 SOHO, STRAND
Radisson Edwardian Pastoria
3-6 St Martins St WC2H 7HL
☎ 020 7930 8641 020 7925 0551
Dir: *off Leicester Square*
Tucked away in a discreet side street off Leicester Square, this small hotel has smart public areas and an informal restaurant. The bedrooms are tastefully furnished and comfortable, and offer a useful level of room service. Those on the top floor are more spacious and have marble bathrooms.
ROOMS: 58 en suite (bth/shr) No smoking in 16 bedrooms s £205.63; d £235 * Off peak **MEALS:** Lunch fr £13.50 Dinner fr £17 & alc English & American Cuisine V meals Coffee am Tea pm **FACILITIES:** CTV in all bedrooms Xmas **CONF:** Thtr 60 Class 28 Board 26 **SERVICES:** Lift Night porter **NOTES:** No dogs (ex guide dogs) No coaches Last d 10pm
CARDS:

WC2 SOHO, STRAND
○ *Kingsway Hall*
Great Queen St, Covent Garden WC2B 5BZ
☎ 020 7396 1616
ROOMS: 170 en suite (bth/shr) **NOTES:** Please phone for details.

See advert on page 413

LONDON AIRPORTS See under **Gatwick & Heathrow**

LONG EATON Derbyshire — Map 08 SK43
see also **Sandiacre**

★★★ *Novotel*
Bostock Ln NG10 4EP
Quality Percentage Score: 66%
☎ 0115 946 5111 Fax 0115 946 5900
Dir: *M1 junct 25. Take B6002 to Long Eaton, hotel is 400 yds on left*
Conveniently close to junction 25 of the M1 motorway, this purpose-built hotel is ideal for all users - it has a useful range of meeting rooms. Bedrooms are uniform in size and lay-out providing the range of facilities and comfort associated with this international brand. Services are efficiently provided by a young friendly team of staff.
ROOMS: 108 en suite (bth/shr) (31 fmly) No smoking in 58 bedrooms **MEALS:** English & French Cuisine V meals Coffee am Tea pm **FACILITIES:** CTV in all bedrooms STV Outdoor swimming pool (heated) Pool table **CONF:** Thtr 220 Class 100 Board 100 **SERVICES:** Lift 180P **NOTES:** No smoking area in restaurant Last d mdnt
CARDS:

LONG EATON Derbyshire — Map 08 SK43

★★ Europa
20-22 Derby Rd NG10 1LW
Quality Percentage Score: 63%
☎ 0115 972 8481 Fax 0115 946 0229
Dir: *on A6005, in the centre of Long Eaton*
Conveniently located for the town centre and the M1, this commercial hotel offers clean and brightly furnished bedrooms. In addition to the restaurant, light refreshments are available throughout the day in the conservatory. Informal service is provided in a relaxed and cheerful manner by the friendly staff.
ROOMS: 15 en suite (bth/shr) (2 fmly) s £36.95-£42.95; d £42.95-£48.95 (incl. bkfst) * LB Off peak **MEALS:** Lunch £4.25-£10.70 Dinner £9.25-£11.50 International Cuisine V meals Coffee am Tea pm **FACILITIES:** CTV in all bedrooms **CONF:** Thtr 35 Class 35 Board 28 **SERVICES:** 24P **NOTES:** No dogs (ex guide dogs) No smoking in restaurant Last d 8.15pm **CARDS:**

LONGHORSLEY Northumberland — Map 12 NZ19

★★★★ *Linden Hall*
NE65 8XF
Quality Percentage Score: 65%
☎ 01670 516611 Fax 01670 788544
Dir: *1m N on A697*
Set in 400 acres of park and woodlands north of the village, this stately Georgian mansion boasts extensive leisure and conference facilities as well as a golf course. The hotel has evolved into an impressive complex, but modern developments are skilfully blended with the original building. Public areas lead off a grand inner hall and include a drawing room, cocktail lounge and restaurant, named after the architect of the original house. Bedrooms range from cosy to spacious and are divided between the original house and a modern extension.
ROOMS: 50 en suite (bth/shr) (4 fmly) **MEALS:** English & French Cuisine V meals Coffee am Tea pm **FACILITIES:** CTV in all bedrooms STV Indoor swimming pool (heated) Golf 18 Tennis (hard) Snooker Sauna Solarium Gym Pool table Croquet lawn Putting green Jacuzzi/spa Hairdressing Health & beauty spa **CONF:** Thtr 300 Class 100 Board 40 Del from £135 * **SERVICES:** Lift Night porter 260P **NOTES:** No smoking in restaurant Last d 9.45pm
CARDS:

LONG MELFORD Suffolk — Map 05 TL84

★★★ *The Bull*
Hall St CO10 9JG
Quality Percentage Score: 67%
☎ 01787 378494 Fax 01787 880307
Dir: *3m north of Sudbury on the A134*
Close to the green at the end of one of Britain's longest town high streets, the Bull is a fine Elizabethan building. Some original features remain, such as exposed beams and a large fireplace. Bedrooms have modern comforts, and the public areas are spacious, offering a choice of lounges.
ROOMS: 25 en suite (bth/shr) (3 fmly) No smoking in 11 bedrooms **MEALS:** V meals Coffee am Tea pm **FACILITIES:** CTV in all bedrooms **CONF:** Thtr 60 Class 30 Board 35 **SERVICES:** 20P **NOTES:** No smoking in restaurant Last d 9.30pm **CARDS:**

LONG MELFORD Suffolk — Map 05 TL84

★★ The Countrymen
The Green CO10 9DN
Quality Percentage Score: 71%
☎ 01787 312356 Fax 01787 374557
Dir: *at junct of A134/A1092*
On the edge of the green at the end of the high street, this popular and well established hotel continues to delight. The hotel has a loyal following of local diners, and two different eating options; the informal wine bar with its robust cooking, and more serious dining in the main restaurant from several table d'hôte-style menus. The charming bedrooms are comfortable and individually decorated, with modern en suite bathrooms and lots of personal touches.
ROOMS: 9 en suite (bth/shr) (3 fmly) s £60-£75; d £80-£105 (incl. bkfst) * LB Off peak **MEALS:** Lunch £5-£15.75 & alc Dinner £9.95-£20.75 English & Mediterranean Cuisine V meals Coffee am **FACILITIES:** CTV in all bedrooms **SERVICES:** 10P **NOTES:** No coaches No smoking area in restaurant Last d 9.30pm
CARDS:

LONG SUTTON Lincolnshire — Map 09 TF42

Travelodge
Wisbech Rd PE12 9AG
☎ 01406 362230 Fax 01406 362230
Dir: *on junct A17/A1101 roundabout*
This modern building offers accommodation in smart, spacious and well equipped bedrooms, all with en-suite bathrooms. Refreshments may be taken at the nearby family restaurant. For details about current prices, consult the Contents Page under Hotel Groups for the Travelodge phone number.
ROOMS: 40 en suite (bth/shr) d £45.95 *

LOOE Cornwall & Isles of Scilly — Map 02 SX25

★★★ *Hannafore Point*
Marine Dr, West Looe PL13 2DG
Quality Percentage Score: 65%
☎ 01503 263273 Fax 01503 263272
A star feature of the Hannafore Point Hotel is its panoramic coastal views. The hotel appeals to both leisure and business travellers, with several conference and function rooms available. The spacious restaurant enjoys the coastal views, and a short fixed price menu is offered, served by a friendly team of staff. Bedrooms are good quality and of similar style.
ROOMS: 37 en suite (bth/shr) (2 fmly) **MEALS:** V meals Coffee am Tea pm **FACILITIES:** CTV in all bedrooms Indoor swimming pool (heated) Squash Sauna Solarium Gym Jacuzzi/spa **CONF:** Thtr 100 Class 120 Board 40 **SERVICES:** Lift Night porter 37P **NOTES:** No dogs (ex guide dogs) No smoking in restaurant Last d 9pm
CARDS:

See advert on page 417

LOOE Cornwall & Isles of Scilly — Map 02 SX25

★★ Coombe Farm

Widegates PL13 1QN

Quality Percentage Score: 72%

☎ 01503 240223 Fax 01503 240895

***Dir:** just S of Widegates village, on the B3253 3.5m E of looe and 1m W of Hessenford*

Set in 10 acres of grounds with magnificent views down the valley to the sea, Coombe Farm offers attractively decorated and exceptionally well equipped accommodation. Each evening a set four-course dinner is served, and there is a games room in a charmingly converted stone barn.

ROOMS: 7 en suite (shr) 3 annexe en suite (shr) No smoking in all bedrooms s £28-£33; d £56-£66 (incl. bkfst) * LB Off peak **MEALS:** Dinner fr £16 V meals **FACILITIES:** CTV in all bedrooms STV Outdoor swimming pool (heated) Croquet lawn Table tennis 3/4 size snooker table **SERVICES:** 20P **NOTES:** No coaches No children 12yrs No smoking in restaurant Last d 7pm Closed Nov-28 Feb **CARDS:**

LOOE Cornwall & Isles of Scilly — Map 02 SX25

★★ Fieldhead

Portuan Rd, Hannafore PL13 2DR

Quality Percentage Score: 72%

☎ 01503 262689 Fax 01503 264114

***Dir:** from West Looe and follow road alongside estuary left signposted 'Hannafore' around headland, onto promenade then right and right again*

From its elevated position in West Looe, the Fieldhead Hotel enjoys commanding views of the bay and St George's Island. Bedrooms are individually furnished and decorated with modern equipment and facilities. The fixed-price menu changes daily and features fresh ingredients, including local seafood.

ROOMS: 14 en suite (bth/shr) (2 fmly) s £40-£60; d £80-£95 (incl. bkfst) LB Off peak **MEALS:** Lunch £8.50-£11.50 High tea £5.50 Dinner £21 English & French Cuisine V meals Coffee am Tea pm **FACILITIES:** CTV in all bedrooms Outdoor swimming pool (heated) Xmas **SERVICES:** 15P **NOTES:** No coaches No smoking in restaurant Last d 8.45pm **CARDS:**

See advert on opposite page

LOSTWITHIEL Cornwall & Isles of Scilly — Map 02 SX15

★★★ Lostwithiel Hotel Golf & Country Club

Lower Polscoe PL22 0HQ

Quality Percentage Score: 66%

☎ 01208 873550 Fax 01208 873479

***Dir:** turn off A38 at Dobwalls onto the A390, on entering Lostwithiel turn right - signposted from main road*

Leisure facilities at Lostwithiel include a challenging 18-hole golf course and flood-lit driving range, indoor swimming pool, all weather tennis courts and state of the art gym. Salmon and trout fishing are available on the river Fowey bordering the grounds. A range of interesting meals are served in The Sportsman's Bar and the Black Prince restaurant. The bedrooms are well equipped and housed in fully converted stone barns.

ROOMS: 19 en suite (bth/shr) s £42-£46; d £84-£92 (incl. cont bkfst) * LB Off peak **MEALS:** Sunday Lunch £4.95-£7.50alc Dinner £14-£16.95 & alc English, French & Italian Cuisine V meals Coffee am Tea pm **FACILITIES:** CTV in all bedrooms Indoor swimming pool (heated) Golf 18 Tennis (hard) Fishing Snooker Gym Putting green Undercover floodlit driving range Xmas **CONF:** Thtr 200 Class 60 Board 40 Del from £52 * **SERVICES:** 120P **NOTES:** No smoking area in restaurant Last d 9pm **CARDS:**

LOSTWITHIEL Cornwall & Isles of Scilly — Map 02 SX15

★★★ *Restormel Lodge*

Hillside Gardens PL22 0DD

Quality Percentage Score: 64%

☎ 01208 872223 Fax 01208 873568

***Dir:** on A390*

Owned by the same family for over 30 years, a friendly and relaxed atmosphere prevails throughout the hotel. The bar and lounges are located in the original building which is full of character and charm, while the bedrooms are located in purpose-built buildings. The restaurant offers an interesting choice of dishes.

ROOMS: 21 en suite (bth/shr) 12 annexe en suite (bth) (3 fmly) **MEALS:** V meals Coffee am Tea pm **FACILITIES:** CTV in all bedrooms STV Outdoor swimming pool (heated) **CONF:** Thtr 100 Class 80 Board 60 **SERVICES:** 40P **NOTES:** No smoking in restaurant Last d 9.30pm **CARDS:**

LOUGHBOROUGH Leicestershire — Map 08 SK51

★★★ The Quality Hotel

New Ashby Rd LE11 0EX

Quality Percentage Score: 63%

☎ 01509 211800 Fax 01509 211868

***Dir:** leave M1 at junct 23 and take A512 towards Loughborough. Hotel 1m on left*

Conveniently situated within a mile of junction 23 of the M1, this popular modern hotel offers comfortable and well equipped accommodation which meets the needs of both the business traveller and leisure guest. All the bedrooms offer a spacious work area, while some rooms have small lounges and kitchenettes, ideal for the longer stay or families. There is a small leisure centre and the hotel's conference facilities offer versatility.

ROOMS: 94 en suite (bth/shr) (12 fmly) No smoking in 47 bedrooms s £81.50-£107; d £105.50-£107 * LB Off peak **MEALS:** Lunch £2.95-£15.95alc Dinner fr £14.50 & alc English & Continental Cuisine V meals Coffee am Tea pm **FACILITIES:** CTV in all bedrooms STV Indoor swimming pool (heated) Sauna Solarium Gym Jacuzzi/spa Xmas **CONF:** Thtr 225 Class 120 Board 80 **SERVICES:** Night porter 160P **NOTES:** No smoking area in restaurant Last d 9.30pm **CARDS:**

LOUGHBOROUGH Leicestershire — Map 08 SK51

★★ Cedars Hotel

Cedar Rd LE11 2AB

Quality Percentage Score: 67%

☎ 01509 214459 Fax 01509 233573

***Dir:** leaving Loughborough for Leicester on the A6, Cedar Road is last road on the left opposite Crematorium*

This well established and popular hotel, popular with local businessmen and diners, is to the south of the town centre. Modest bedrooms and relaxing open plan public areas with

contd.

partitioned restaurant and banqueting rooms are well suited to the needs of the varied business, leisure and function clientele.

ROOMS: 36 en suite (bth/shr) (4 fmly) s fr £55; d fr £68 (incl. bkfst) * Off peak **MEALS:** Lunch £9.50-£15.95 & alc Dinner £15.95 & alc French Cuisine V meals Coffee am **FACILITIES:** CTV in all bedrooms Outdoor swimming pool (heated) Sauna Solarium **CONF:** Thtr 40 Class 24 Board 25 **SERVICES:** Night porter 50P **NOTES:** No smoking in restaurant Last d 9.15pm **CARDS:**

LOUGHBOROUGH Leicestershire — Map 08 SK51

★★ Great Central

Great Central Rd LE11 1RW

Quality Percentage Score: 58%

☎ 01509 263405 Fax 01509 264130

Dir: *from town centre take A60 towards Nottingham then first right. Hotel on left*

The aptly named hotel is near the Great Central Steam Railway, which runs steam trips from Loughborough to Leicester at weekends. Its high-ceilinged bar follows a Victorian style, and has a convivial atmosphere and a good range of bar meals. Bedrooms are appealing, and most have pine furniture and cheerful colour schemes.

ROOMS: 22 en suite (bth/shr) (5 fmly) s £32; d £48 (incl. bkfst) * LB Off peak **MEALS:** Sunday Lunch £5-£10 & alc Dinner £5-£10 & alc International Cuisine V meals Coffee am **FACILITIES:** CTV in all bedrooms STV Xmas **CONF:** Thtr 100 Class 100 Board 40 Del from £42 * **SERVICES:** 40P **NOTES:** No smoking area in restaurant Last d 9.15pm **CARDS:**

LOUTH Lincolnshire — Map 08 TF38

★★★ Beaumont

66 Victoria Rd LN11 0BX

Quality Percentage Score: 68%

☎ 01507 605005 Fax 01507 607768

Friendly service from a charming young team is one of the key strengths of this personally run hotel, which is located in a peaceful residential street close to the centre of town. The bedrooms are individually decorated and mostly spacious, although there are some small single rooms available. Public areas include a comfortable lounge bar and a smartly appointed restaurant, where chef William McMullan offers set priced and carte menus with a Mediterranean influence, including Italian speciality pasta dishes.

ROOMS: 16 en suite (bth/shr) (2 fmly) s £40-£55; d £60-£75 (incl. bkfst) * LB Off peak **MEALS:** Lunch £13.95 & alc Dinner £13.95 & alc English & Italian Cuisine V meals Coffee am Tea pm **FACILITIES:** CTV in all bedrooms STV Xmas **CONF:** Thtr 112 Class 50 Board 46 **SERVICES:** Lift 70P **NOTES:** No smoking area in restaurant Last d 9pm RS Sun **CARDS:**

LOUTH Lincolnshire Map 08 TF38

★★★ Kenwick Park

Kenwick Park LN11 8NR
Quality Percentage Score: 64%
☎ 01507 608806 Fax 01507 608027
***Dir:** on the A157, take Mablethorpe/Manly signs*

Best Western

An elegant Georgian style house with modern extensions, on the 500 acre Kenwick Park Estate. Bedrooms are of comfortable proportions with every modern facility. The "Fairway" restaurant has an imaginative carte and house menus produced by Chef Paul Harvey. The conservatory style "Keepers" bar overlooks Kenwick Park Golf Course. The excellent leisure centre has a large swimming pool and many other facilities.
ROOMS: 23 rms (19 bth/shr) (3 fmly) s £67-£79.50; d £75-£98 (incl. bkfst) * LB Off peak **MEALS:** Lunch £11.95-£18.50 & alc High tea £6 Dinner £18.50 Modern English/Classical Cuisine V meals Coffee am Tea pm **FACILITIES:** CTV in all bedrooms STV Indoor swimming pool (heated) Golf 18 Tennis (hard) Squash Snooker Sauna Solarium Gym Pool table Putting green Jacuzzi/spa Health & Beauty Centre ch fac Xmas **CONF:** Thtr 100 Class 40 Board 40 Del from £110 * **SERVICES:** Night porter 50P **NOTES:** No smoking in restaurant Last d 9.30pm
CARDS:

See advert on opposite page

LOWER BEEDING West Sussex Map 04 TQ22

The Premier Collection

★★★★ South Lodge

Brighton Rd RH13 6PS
☎ 01403 891711 Fax 01403 891766
***Dir:** off A281*

Enjoying splendid views over the Downs, this Victorian mansion stands in 90 acres of gardens containing over 260 varieties of camellia and rhododendron. Escorted walks can be easily arranged for guests. Bedrooms are individually furnished and have lots of personal touches. Dishes such as John Dory with a foie butter sauce and duck confit with pumpkin risotto display the skills of chef Lewis Hamblet and are served in the elegant restaurant, where traditional Sunday lunch is also much in demand.
ROOMS: 39 en suite (bth) **MEALS:** Lunch £16.50-£21 High tea fr £11.50 Dinner £35 & alc V meals Coffee am Tea pm **FACILITIES:** CTV in all bedrooms STV Tennis (hard) Fishing Snooker Croquet lawn Putting green Golf-driving net Shooting Petanque **CONF:** Thtr 85 Class 40 Board 30 **SERVICES:** Night porter 80P **NOTES:** No dogs (ex guide dogs) No coaches No smoking in restaurant Last d 9.45pm
CARDS:

See advert under HORSHAM

LOWER BEEDING West Sussex Map 04 TQ22

★★ *Brookfield Farm Hotel*

Winterpit Ln, Lower Beeding RH13 6LY
Quality Percentage Score: 64%
☎ 01403 891191

Situated in the heart of the countryside a few mile from Horsham, this property has recently been skilfully extended by the new owners. Rooms are attractively furnished and have smart modern en suites. The bar and dining room overlook a pond and the golf course, guests may enjoy the terrace in the summer months; there is also a comfortable lounge.
ROOMS: 17 rms

LOWER SLAUGHTER Gloucestershire Map 04 SP12

The Premier Collection

★★★ Lower Slaughter Manor

GL54 2HP
☎ 01451 820456 Fax 01451 822150
***Dir:** off A429 signposted "The Slaughters", the manor is 0.5m on right entering village*

This charming Grade II listed Manor dates mainly from the

contd.

17th century and enjoys a tranquil location. Spacious bedrooms are tastefully furnished and thoughtfully equipped. Public areas are appealing, and include an inviting lounge and drawing room with log fires in season.
ROOMS: 11 en suite (bth/shr) 5 annexe en suite (bth/shr) s £135-£325; d £150-£375 (incl. bkfst) * LB Off peak **MEALS:** Lunch £15.95-£24.95 Dinner £25-£75 & alc English & French Cuisine V meals Coffee am Tea pm **FACILITIES:** CTV in all bedrooms Indoor swimming pool (heated) Tennis (hard) Croquet lawn Putting green Xmas **CONF:** Thtr 30 Board 14 Del from £195 *
SERVICES: 35P **NOTES:** No dogs (ex guide dogs) No coaches No children 8yrs No smoking in restaurant Last d 10pm
CARDS:

LOWER SLAUGHTER Gloucestershire **Map 04 SP12**

★★★ Washbourne Court

GL54 2HS
Quality Percentage Score: 79%
☎ 01451 822143 01451 821045
***Dir:** turn off A429 at signpost 'The Slaughters', between Stow-on-the-Wold and Bourton-on-the-Water. Hotel is in the centre of village*
Beamed ceilings, log fires and stone-mullioned windows feature at this 17th-century hotel, set in four acres of grounds by the River Eye. Bedrooms, in the main house and self-contained cottages, are smartly appointed. Public rooms include traditionally furnished sitting areas and an elegant dining room with an interesting menu.
ROOMS: 15 en suite (bth/shr) 13 annexe en suite (bth/shr) s £100-£170; d £110-£180 (incl. bkfst) * LB Off peak **MEALS:** Lunch £13.50-£19 V meals Coffee am Tea pm **FACILITIES:** CTV in all bedrooms Tennis (hard) Xmas **CONF:** Thtr 30 Board 20 Del from £160 *
SERVICES: 40P **NOTES:** No dogs No coaches No children 7yrs No smoking in restaurant **CARDS:**

See advert on this page

LOWESTOFT Suffolk **Map 05 TM59**

★★★ Ivy House Farm

Ivy Ln, Beccles Rd, Oulton Broad NR33 8HY
Quality Percentage Score: 71%
☎ 01502 501353 & 588144 01502 501539
***Dir:** on A146 SW of Oulton Broad turn into Ivy Ln beside Esso petrol station, over small railway bridge & follow private driveway into car park*

The skilfully restored Crooked Barn restaurant is the focal point, chef Richard Pye offers an interesting selection of modern dishes. Attractive bedrooms are spacious and comfortably furnished,

contd.

Symbols and Abbreviations are listed and explained on pages 4 and 5

with bright modern bathrooms. All rooms enjoy views of the garden or neighbouring fields, home to a variety of wildfowl.
ROOMS: 13 annexe en suite (bth/shr) (1 fmly) No smoking in 6 bedrooms s fr £67; d fr £89 (incl. bkfst) * LB Off peak **MEALS:** Lunch £3.50-£12.50alc Dinner £15-£35alc European & Thai Cuisine V meals Coffee am Tea pm **FACILITIES:** CTV in all bedrooms Arrangement with neighbouring leisure club for reduced rates Xmas **CONF:** Thtr 50 Board 24 Del from £105 * **SERVICES:** 50P **NOTES:** No coaches No smoking in restaurant Last d 9.30pm **CARDS:**

LOWESTOFT Suffolk — Map 05 TM59
★★★ Wherry Hotel
Bridge Rd, Oulton Broad NR32 3LN
Quality Percentage Score: 67%
☎ 01502 516845 & 573521 Fax 01502 501350

Aptly named for the sailing barges typical of the Norfolk Broads area, the hotel stands to the south-west of Lowestoft and dates from the turn of the century. Many original features can be seen in the bustling public areas, overlooking the waterfront. Well equipped bedrooms come in a variety of sizes and styles, and there is a carvery-style restaurant, as well as the public and lounge bars.
ROOMS: 29 en suite (bth/shr) (4 fmly) s £41.50-£46; d £59.50-£66 (incl. bkfst) * LB Off peak **MEALS:** V meals Coffee am Tea pm **FACILITIES:** CTV in all bedrooms STV Pool table **CONF:** Thtr 250 Class 150 Board 80 **SERVICES:** Lift Night porter 185P **NOTES:** No smoking area in restaurant Closed 24-26 Dec
CARDS:

LOWESTOFT Suffolk — Map 05 TM59
★★★ *Hotel Hatfield*
The Esplanade NR33 0QP
Quality Percentage Score: 65%
☎ 01502 565337 Fax 01502 511885
Dir: *from town centre follow signs for 'South Beach' (A12 Ipswich). Hotel 200yds on left*
Easily accessible, being directly on the A12 along the esplanade, this traditional resort hotel sits opposite the sea and has many original architectural features. Public areas extend to a lively bar with a choice of real ales and informal snacks, and the sea-facing Chaplins restaurant offering international dishes to suit most tastes; functions are also catered for in a variety of rooms. Bedrooms are generally of good comfortable proportions, although there are a few compact single bedrooms.
ROOMS: 33 en suite (bth/shr) (1 fmly) **MEALS:** English & French Cuisine V meals Coffee am **FACILITIES:** CTV in all bedrooms STV **CONF:** Thtr 100 Class 50 Board 40 **SERVICES:** Lift Night porter 26P **NOTES:** No dogs (ex guide dogs) Last d 10pm
CARDS:

LOWESTOFT Suffolk — Map 05 TM59
Travel Inn
249 Yarmouth Rd NR32 4AA
☎ 01502 572441 Fax 01502 581223
Dir: *on A12, 2m N of Lowestoft*
This modern building offers accommodation in smart, spacious and well equipped bedrooms, all with en-suite bathrooms. Refreshments may be taken at the nearby family restaurant. For details about current prices consult the Contents Page under Hotel Groups for the Travel Inn phone number.
ROOMS: 40 en suite (bth/shr) d £39.95 *

LOWESWATER Cumbria — Map 11 NY12
★ Grange Country House
CA13 0SU
Quality Percentage Score: 69%
☎ 01946 861211 & 861570
Dir: *turn left off A5086 for Mockerkin, through village and after 2m turn left for Loweswater Lake. Hotel at bottom of hill on left*
This delightful country hotel rests in a quiet valley at the north-western end of Loweswater. It has a friendly and relaxed atmosphere, cosy public areas, and very friendly staff. There is a small bar, a residents' lounge, and an attractive dining room. The well equipped, comfortable bedrooms all have en suite bathrooms.
ROOMS: 8 rms (7 bth/shr) 2 annexe en suite (bth) (2 fmly) s £32-£35; d £60-£70 (incl. bkfst) * Off peak **MEALS:** Lunch £8-£14 High tea £8-£12 Dinner £14-£16 V meals Coffee am Tea pm **FACILITIES:** CTV in all bedrooms National Trust boats & fishing Xmas **CONF:** Thtr 25 Class 25 Board 25 Del from £60 * **SERVICES:** 22P **NOTES:** No coaches No smoking in restaurant Last d 8pm RS Jan-Feb

LUDLOW Shropshire — Map 07 SO57
★★★ *Overton Grange*
Hereford Rd SY8 4AD
Quality Percentage Score: 76%
☎ 01584 873500 Fax 01584 873524
Dir: *turn off A49 at B4361 Richards castle, Ludlow and hotel is 200yds on left*
An Edwardian mansion situated above the town with lovely views across the Shropshire countryside. The well manicured gardens and abundant fresh flowers create a pleasing appearance. Public areas include a comfortable lounge and bar, together with a restaurant that offers a high standard of cuisine with a classic French bias.
ROOMS: 14 en suite (bth/shr) (2 fmly) No smoking in 3 bedrooms **MEALS:** British & French Cuisine V meals Coffee am Tea pm **FACILITIES:** CTV in all bedrooms Croquet lawn **CONF:** Thtr 160 Class 80 Board 50 **SERVICES:** Night porter 80P **NOTES:** No dogs (ex guide dogs) No smoking in restaurant Last d 9.45pm
CARDS:

See advert on opposite page

LUDLOW Shropshire — Map 07 SO57
★★★ *Dinham Hall*
By the Castle SY8 1EJ
Quality Percentage Score: 71%
☎ 01584 876464 Fax 01584 876019
Dir: *opposite the castle*
This lovely old house dates back to 1792. Set in an attractive garden, it stands immediately opposite Ludlow Castle. Now a privately owned and professionally run hotel, it has a well deserved reputation for both its warm hospitality and its fine cuisine. The bedrooms, which include two in a converted cottage, are well equipped and include rooms with four poster beds. The

contd.

comfortable public rooms are elegantly appointed. Facilities include a room for private meetings or dinner parties.
ROOMS: 14 en suite (bth/shr) (3 fmly) **MEALS:** International Cuisine V meals Coffee am Tea pm **FACILITIES:** CTV in all bedrooms Sauna Gym **CONF:** Thtr 28 Class 28 Board 24 **SERVICES:** 16P **NOTES:** No coaches No smoking in restaurant Last d 9pm
CARDS:

LUDLOW Shropshire **Map 07 SO57**
★★★ The Feathers at Ludlow
REGAL
Bull Ring SY8 1AA
Quality Percentage Score: 64%
☎ 01584 875261 🖹 01584 876030
Dir: *in the town centre*

Famous for the carved woodwork outside and in, this picturesque hotel dates from the 17th century and is one of the town's best known landmarks. Bedrooms are decorated in traditional style. The lounge and the Prince of Wales function suite are especially noteworthy for their decor.
ROOMS: 40 en suite (bth/shr) (3 fmly) No smoking in 5 bedrooms s £60-£65; d £80-£85 * LB Off peak **MEALS:** Lunch £10.45-£14 Dinner £17.95-£19.95 English & French Cuisine V meals Coffee am Tea pm **FACILITIES:** CTV in all bedrooms Jacuzzi/spa Xmas **CONF:** Thtr 80 Class 40 Board 40 Del from £70 * **SERVICES:** Lift Night porter 39P **NOTES:** No smoking in restaurant Last d 9pm
CARDS:

LUDLOW Shropshire **Map 07 SO57**
★★ Cliffe
Dinham SY8 2JE
Quality Percentage Score: 64%
☎ 01584 872063 🖹 01584 873991
Dir: *through Ludlow town centre to Castle turn left at castle gates to Dinham, follow road beneath castle over bridge, hotel sign 100yds from bridge*
Built in the last century and standing in extensive grounds and gardens, this hotel is quietly located close to the castle and the river. It provides well equipped accommodation, and facilities include a lounge bar, a pleasant restaurant and a patio overlooking the garden.
ROOMS: 9 en suite (bth/shr) (2 fmly) No smoking in all bedrooms s £30-£40; d £50-£60 (incl. bkfst) * LB Off peak **MEALS:** V meals Coffee am **FACILITIES:** CTV in all bedrooms **SERVICES:** 22P **NOTES:** No coaches No smoking in restaurant **CARDS:**

LUDLOW Shropshire **Map 07 SO57**
Travelodge
Travelodge
Woofferton SY8 4AL
☎ 01584 711695 🖹 01584 711695
Dir: *on A49 at junct A456/B4362*
This modern building offers accommodation in smart, spacious and well equipped bedrooms, all with en-suite bathrooms. Refreshments may be taken at the nearby family restaurant. For details about current prices, consult the Contents Page under Hotel Groups for the Travelodge phone number.
ROOMS: 32 en suite (bth/shr) d £45.95 *

LULWORTH COVE See **West Lulworth**

LUMBY North Yorkshire **Map 08 SE43**
★★★ Posthouse Leeds/Selby
Posthouse
LS25 5LF
Quality Percentage Score: 64%
☎ 01977 682711 🖹 01977 685462
Dir: *leave A1 at A63 signposted Selby, hotel on A63 on left*
A modern hotel situated in extensive grounds near the A1/A63 junction. Attractive day rooms include the "Seasons" restaurant and the "Spa" leisure club is a popular feature. Service, provided by friendly staff, includes an all day lounge menu and 24 hour room service.
ROOMS: 97 en suite (bth/shr) (18 fmly) No smoking in 50 bedrooms d fr £80 * LB Off peak **MEALS:** International Cuisine V meals Coffee am Tea pm **FACILITIES:** CTV in all bedrooms Indoor swimming pool (heated) Tennis (hard) Sauna Putting green 9 Hole pitch & putt Xmas **CONF:** Thtr 160 Class 50 Board 40 Del from £89 * **SERVICES:** Night porter 330P **NOTES:** Last d 9.30pm **CARDS:**

LUTON Bedfordshire **Map 04 TL02**
★★★ Thistle Luton
THISTLE HOTELS
Arndale Centre LU1 2TR
Quality Percentage Score: 65%
☎ 01582 734199 🖹 01582 402528
Dir: *from M1 junct 10 take signs to Luton town centre. In St Mary's Rd drive across traffic lights, left at mini rdbt into Guildford St, hotel on left*
Situated next to the Arndale shopping centre, this large, purpose-
contd.

built hotel offers well equipped bedrooms, and for those seeking a higher standard of comfort there are also executive rooms. The spacious lobby leads guests to a cocktail bar and the more formal of two restaurants. There is free parking in an adjacent multi-storey car park.
ROOMS: 150 en suite (bth/shr) No smoking in 88 bedrooms
MEALS: International Cuisine V meals Coffee am Tea pm
FACILITIES: CTV in all bedrooms STV Use of nearby health club
CONF: Thtr 300 Class 150 Board 60 **SERVICES:** Lift Night porter 44P
NOTES: No dogs (ex guide dogs) No smoking area in restaurant
Last d 10pm **CARDS:**

LUTON Bedfordshire — Map 04 TL02

★★★ The Chiltern

Waller Av LU4 9RU
Quality Percentage Score: 56%
☎ 01582 575911 🖷 01582 581859
Dir: *M1 junct 11 take A505 to Luton go past two sets of lights over rdbt left filter lane left at lights hotel on right*

Conveniently positioned close to the M1, the Chiltern Hotel is geared towards the business guest, having a range of conference and meeting rooms. Bedrooms are well equipped, offering good desk space; room service is a bonus. The busy bar is at the hub of the hotel.
ROOMS: 91 en suite (bth/shr) (6 fmly) No smoking in 63 bedrooms s £85-£105; d £85-£105 * LB Off peak **MEALS:** Lunch £4-£7alc Dinner £13.50-£24.50alc English & Italian Cuisine V meals Coffee am Tea pm **FACILITIES:** CTV in all bedrooms STV Xmas **CONF:** Thtr 180 Class 180 Board 30 Del from £110 * **SERVICES:** Lift Night porter 150P **NOTES:** No smoking in restaurant Last d 9.45pm
CARDS:

LUTON AIRPORT Bedfordshire — Map 04 TL12

★★ Hotel Ibis

Spittlesea Rd LU2 9NZ
Quality Percentage Score: 59%
☎ 01582 424488 🖷 01582 455511
Dir: *from junct 10 on M1 follow signs to Airport*

The Ibis is the only hotel within the airport complex. Bedrooms are all equipped to the same standard and furnished on clean, modern lines in a 'no frills' style. All are en suite with a bath as well as shower. The bar and restaurant are open all day.
ROOMS: 98 en suite (bth/shr) No smoking in 30 bedrooms s £46; d £49 * Off peak **MEALS:** Lunch £6.50-£9.50 Dinner £6.50-£12.50 & alc English & French Cuisine V meals Coffee am **FACILITIES:** CTV in all bedrooms STV **CONF:** Thtr 100 Class 55 Board 45 **SERVICES:** Lift Night porter 60P **NOTES:** No smoking area in restaurant Last d 10.30pm
CARDS:

LUTTERWORTH Leicestershire — Map 04 SP58

★★★ Denbigh Arms

High St LE17 4AD
Quality Percentage Score: 55%
☎ 01455 553537 🖷 01455 556627
Dir: *exit M1 junct 20 and turn right at traffic lights, over bridge and past Fox Inn*

Located on the southern edge of the town, this converted Georgian coaching inn has a friendly, informal atmosphere and spacious bedrooms. There is a quiet foyer lounge area and a good-sized bar across the courtyard in addition to a cosy restaurant.
ROOMS: 31 en suite (bth/shr) (3 fmly) No smoking in 2 bedrooms s £45-£65; d £55-£75 (incl. bkfst) * LB Off peak **MEALS:** Lunch £8.95-£12.95 Dinner £13.95-£17.95 V meals Coffee am Tea pm
FACILITIES: CTV in all bedrooms STV Pool table Xmas **CONF:** Thtr 60 Class 29 Board 30 Del from £65 * **SERVICES:** Night porter 30P
NOTES: No smoking in restaurant Last d 9pm
CARDS:

LYDFORD Devon — Map 02 SX58

★★ Lydford House

EX20 4AU
Quality Percentage Score: 74%
☎ 01822 820347 🖷 01822 820442
Dir: *turn off A386 halfway between Okehampton and Tavistock, signpost Lydford, 500yds on right hand side*

Eight acres of grounds on the edge of Dartmoor surround this impressive Victorian country house. Guests can have riding lessons at the stables owned by the same family or go on accompanied rides over the moors. The bedrooms are all attractively decorated, and public areas include a conservatory lounge and a restaurant.
ROOMS: 12 rms (11 bth/shr) (3 fmly) No smoking in 1 bedroom s fr £42.50; d fr £73 (incl. bkfst) * LB Off peak **MEALS:** Sunday Lunch fr £8.50 Dinner fr £15 V meals Coffee am Tea pm **FACILITIES:** CTV in all bedrooms Riding Free use of Tavistock Leisure Centre and Tennis Courts **SERVICES:** 30P **NOTES:** No coaches No children 5yrs No smoking in restaurant Last d 8pm **CARDS:**

LYME REGIS Dorset — Map 03 SY39

★★★ Alexandra

Pound St DT7 3HZ
Quality Percentage Score: 70%
☎ 01297 442010 🖷 01297 443229
Dir: *on the B3052*

Built in 1735 and Grade II listed this hotel features an elegant restaurant with picture windows taking in the magnificent views. Bedrooms have pretty chintz fabrics and attractive furniture.The south facing conservatory opens onto gardens. During winter, log fires burn in the lounge.
ROOMS: 27 rms (26 bth/shr) (8 fmly) s £50-£80; d £85-£122 (incl. bkfst) * LB Off peak **MEALS:** Lunch £12.95 High tea £5.50 Dinner £22.50 International Cuisine V meals Coffee am Tea pm
FACILITIES: CTV in all bedrooms **SERVICES:** Night porter 25P
NOTES: No coaches No smoking in restaurant Last d 8.30pm Closed Xmas & Jan **CARDS:**

See advert on opposite page

LYME REGIS Dorset — Map 03 SY39

★★ Kersbrook

Pound Rd DT7 3HX
Quality Percentage Score: 71%
☎ 01297 442596 🖷 01297 442596
Dir: *Lyme Regis A35 to A3052*

Kersbrook Hotel is a thatched Grade II listed property with well tended gardens. The restaurant offers a varied choice of dishes from a fixed-price menu and lengthy carte. Bedrooms are attractively furnished and well equipped. There is a lounge and separate bar.
ROOMS: 10 en suite (bth/shr) No smoking in all bedrooms s £50-£65; d £75-£85 (incl. bkfst) * LB Off peak **MEALS:** Lunch fr £8.95 Dinner fr £16.50 & alc English, French & Italian Cuisine V meals Coffee am
FACILITIES: CTV in all bedrooms ch fac Xmas **CONF:** Class 16 Board 12 Del from £45 * **SERVICES:** 14P **NOTES:** No smoking area in restaurant Last d 9pm RS 8 Jan-10 Feb **CARDS:**

LYME REGIS Dorset — Map 03 SY39

★★ Orchard Country

Rousdon DT7 3XW
Quality Percentage Score: 68%
☎ 01297 442972 🖷 01297 443670
Dir: *off A3052 in Rousdon, Devon between Lyme Regis & Seaton, brown signposted from the centre of the village*

Within easy reach of many picturesque resorts in Devon and Dorset, this small hotel offers comfortable accommodation and a

contd.

relaxed atmosphere. A short fixed price menu is offered, focusing on fresh local produce.
ROOMS: 12 rms (9 bth/shr) No smoking in all bedrooms s £30-£40; d £60-£74 (incl. bkfst) * LB Off peak **MEALS:** Dinner £16 Coffee am **FACILITIES:** CTV in all bedrooms **SERVICES:** 15P **NOTES:** No dogs No children 8yrs No smoking in restaurant Last d 7.45pm Closed Mid Dec-Feb **CARDS:**

LYME REGIS Dorset — Map 03 SY39

★★ *Buena Vista*

Pound St DT7 3HZ
Quality Percentage Score: 66%
☎ 01297 442494
Dir: *W on A3052 out of town*
Situated in attractive gardens overlooking the harbour and Cobb, this hotel has a private path to the sea. Many bedrooms have balconies to take advantage of the views. There are two comfortable lounges and a south-facing sun terrace.
ROOMS: 18 rms (17 bth/shr) (1 fmly) **MEALS:** V meals Coffee am Tea pm **FACILITIES:** CTV in all bedrooms **SERVICES:** 20P **NOTES:** No coaches No smoking in restaurant Last d 8pm Closed Dec-Jan
CARDS:

LYME REGIS Dorset — Map 03 SY39

★★ Royal Lion

Broad St DT7 3QF
Quality Percentage Score: 64%
☎ 01297 445622 Fax 01297 445859
Built as a coaching inn in 1601, the Royal Lion retains much character. Bedrooms in the newer wing are more spacious, some have balconies, sea views or a private terrace. There are a number of lounge areas. The dining room provides an extensive range of dishes.
ROOMS: 30 en suite (bth/shr) (4 fmly) s £35-£40; d £70-£80 (incl. bkfst) * LB Off peak **MEALS:** V meals Coffee am Tea pm
FACILITIES: CTV in all bedrooms Indoor swimming pool (heated) Snooker Sauna Gym Pool table Jacuzzi/spa Games room Xmas
SERVICES: 36P **NOTES:** Last d 9pm Closed 3 days Xmas
CARDS:

LYME REGIS Dorset — Map 03 SY39

★★ Bay

Marine Pde DT7 3JQ
Quality Percentage Score: 62%
☎ 01297 442059
Dir: *On the seafront in the centre of Lyme Regis*
This family run hotel occupies a prime seafront location. Bedrooms are tastefully decorated, combining style with comfort. Mediterranean colours are found in the dining room, the venue for a daily menu offering an interesting choice of dishes. Additional facilities include a spacious lounge.
ROOMS: 19 en suite (bth/shr) (2 fmly) s £35-£42; d £60-£84 (incl. bkfst) * LB Off peak **MEALS:** Lunch £6.50-£16 Dinner £7-£16.50 English & Continental Cuisine V meals Coffee am Tea pm
FACILITIES: CTV in all bedrooms Snooker Sauna Solarium Gym Pool table Xmas **CONF:** Del from £60 * **SERVICES:** 20P **NOTES:** No coaches No smoking area in restaurant Last d 8.45pm
CARDS:

LYME REGIS Dorset — Map 03 SY39

★ *Tudor House*

Church St DT7 3BU
Quality Percentage Score: 62%
☎ 01297 442472
Dir: *opposite the Tourist Information Bureau*
At this 16th-century town centre hotel bedrooms vary in quality, size and shape, largely due to the age of the building. Public areas include a spacious dining room, two lounges and a flagstoned basement bar which houses the original town well.
ROOMS: 17 en suite (bth/shr) (10 fmly) **MEALS:** Coffee am Tea pm **FACILITIES:** CTV in 8 bedrooms **SERVICES:** 20P **NOTES:** No dogs (ex guide dogs) Last d 7.30pm Closed Oct-end Mar **CARDS:**

LYMINGTON Hampshire — Map 04 SZ39

★★★ Passford House

Mount Pleasant Ln SO41 8LS
Quality Percentage Score: 72%
☎ 01590 682398 Fax 01590 683494
Dir: *from A337 at Lymington straight on at mini rdbt, then first right at Tollhouse public house, then after 1m right into Mount Pleasant Lane*
A peaceful hotel set in attractive grounds on the edge of town. Bedrooms vary in shape and size but all are comfortably furnished, well equipped and attractively decorated. Extensive public areas include lounges, a smartly appointed bar and restaurant and leisure facilities. Attentive service is provided by a friendly and well motivated team.
ROOMS: 53 en suite (bth/shr) 2 annexe en suite (bth/shr) (2 fmly) No smoking in 5 bedrooms s £55-£85; d £90-£130 (incl. bkfst) * LB Off peak **MEALS:** Lunch £15.75-£25.50 & alc Dinner £22.50-£28.50 & alc English & French Cuisine V meals Coffee am Tea pm **FACILITIES:** CTV in all bedrooms Indoor swimming pool (heated) Outdoor swimming pool (heated) Tennis (hard) Sauna Solarium Gym Pool table Croquet lawn Putting green Jacuzzi/spa Petanque Table tennis Xmas **CONF:** Thtr 80 Class 30 Board 30 Del from £120 * **SERVICES:** Night porter 100P
NOTES: No smoking in restaurant Last d 9.30pm
CARDS:

LYMINGTON Hampshire — Map 04 SZ39

★★★ **Stanwell House**
High St SO41 9AA
Quality Percentage Score: 72%
☎ 01590 677123 Fax 01590 677756
Dir: *A337 to town centre, on right hand side of High St before it descends to quay*
A privately owned Georgian hotel in the heart of Lymington, with quality fabrics and furnishings. Bedrooms are attractively decorated, deluxe rooms have four-posters and power showers. Guests can relax in the conservatory lounge and enjoy modern brasserie style cuisine in the main bistro, or a lighter meal in the more informal bar.
ROOMS: 29 en suite (bth/shr) (1 fmly) No smoking in 4 bedrooms
MEALS: English French Cuisine V meals Coffee am Tea pm
FACILITIES: CTV in all bedrooms **CONF:** Thtr 30 Class 20 Board 22
SERVICES: Night porter **NOTES:** No smoking in restaurant Last d 10pm
CARDS:
See advert on opposite page

LYMINGTON Hampshire — Map 04 SZ39

The Premier Collection

★★ **Gordleton Mill**
Silver St, Hordle SO41 6DJ
☎ 01590 682219 Fax 01590 683073
Dir: *on Sway Rd which becomes Silver St*
This delightful 17th-century watermill is set on the banks of the River Avon in picturesque grounds. A Provencal oasis in the midst of Hampshire's greenbelt. The bedrooms are attractively decorated and luxuriously equipped with whirlpool baths, fresh fruit and flowers, bathrobes and Champagne. The public rooms have lots of character and take full advantage of the lovely views, particularly the restaurant, Provence, which has seen the beginning of many illustrious careers. New Chef Alan Dann has already established a reputation for enjoyable food, and his seasonally changing menu fully exploits the high quality local produce.
ROOMS: 9 en suite (bth/shr) (1 fmly) No smoking in 4 bedrooms d £95-£150 (incl. cont bkfst) * Off peak **MEALS:** Lunch £9.50-£14.50 & alc Dinner £14.50 & alc French Cuisine V meals Coffee am Tea pm **FACILITIES:** CTV in all bedrooms Fishing Xmas
SERVICES: 60P **NOTES:** No smoking in restaurant Last d 10.30pm
CARDS:

LYMINGTON Hampshire — Map 04 SZ39

★★ **String of Horses**
Mead End Rd SO41 6EH
Quality Percentage Score: 71%
☎ 01590 682631 Fax 01590 682911
(For full entry see Sway)

LYMPSHAM Somerset — Map 03 ST35

★★ **Batch Country Hotel**
Batch Ln BS24 0EX
Quality Percentage Score: 65%
☎ 01934 750371 Fax 01934 750501
Dir: *off A370. Follow Tourist Board signs for 1.5m through village to hotel*

This attractive property stands peacefully in well tended grounds mid-way between Weston-super-Mare and Burnham-on-Sea. The atmosphere is relaxed and friendly, with a warm welcome from the Brown family. Spacious lounges overlook the gardens and an extensive range of dishes is served in the beamed dining room.
ROOMS: 10 en suite (bth/shr) (6 fmly) No smoking in 2 bedrooms
MEALS: Bar Lunch fr £5.75 High tea fr £7 Dinner £13-£15 & alc English & Continental Cuisine V meals Coffee am Tea pm **FACILITIES:** CTV in 8 bedrooms Fishing **CONF:** Thtr 80 Class 60 Board 100 Del from £70 *
SERVICES: 70P **NOTES:** No dogs No coaches No smoking in restaurant Last d 8.30pm Closed Xmas **CARDS:**

LYNDHURST Hampshire — Map 04 SU30

★★★ **Parkhill Country House Hotel**
Beaulieu Rd SO43 7FZ
Quality Percentage Score: 77%
☎ 023 80282944 Fax 023 80283268
Dir: *off B3056 to Beaulieu*
A delightful, carefully restored Georgian country house in twelve acres of parkland. Elegant public rooms contain open fires and antiques. Comfortable bedrooms, individual in style, are well equipped. Chef Darren Whiffen continues to impress with good use of quality ingredients. Service is professional and friendly.
ROOMS: 15 en suite (bth/shr) 5 annexe en suite (bth/shr) (2 fmly) No smoking in 6 bedrooms s £80-£105; d £100-£115 (incl. bkfst) * LB Off peak **MEALS:** Lunch £13.50-£17 Dinner fr £27 & alc English & French Cuisine V meals Coffee am Tea pm **FACILITIES:** CTV in all bedrooms Outdoor swimming pool (heated) Fishing Croquet lawn Putting green Outdoor chess Xmas **CONF:** Thtr 60 Class 40 Board 35 Del from £110 * **SERVICES:** Night porter 75P **NOTES:** No smoking in restaurant Last d 9.30pm **CARDS:**
See advert on this page

LYNDHURST Hampshire — Map 04 SU30

★★★ **Crown**
High St SO43 7NF
Quality Percentage Score: 69%
☎ 023 80282922 Fax 023 80282751
Dir: *in the centre of the village, opposite the church*
Situated in the heart of the village, this historic hotel has been welcoming visitors to the New Forest for generations. The spacious public rooms retain much of the original character with two comfortable lounges and a popular panelled bar. Bedrooms are all individual in style, attractively furnished and well
contd. on p. 426

WESTOVER HALL

AA ★★★ 76% ✿ ✿

ETC ★★★ Silver Award

PARK LANE, MILFORD ON SEA
LYMINGTON, HAMPSHIRE S041 0PT

Tel: 01590 643044 Fax: 01590 644490

A Grade II Listed Victorian Mansion on the edge of the New Forest, 200 yards from the beach with stunning uninterrupted views across to the Needles and Isle of Wight. Magnificent oak panelled interior with stained glass windows and antique furniture. Family owned and run with a relaxed friendly atmosphere. Excellent cuisine. Individually furnished, luxurious bedrooms, many with sea views, all en-suite.

A fascinating and unusual hotel.

South Lawn Hotel & Restaurant

AA ★★★ 72% ✿

Milford-on-Sea, Lymington, Hampshire SO41 0RF
Tel: Lymington (01590) 643911 Fax: (01590) 644820
Website: www.southlawn.co.uk
Email: enquiries@southlawn.co.uk

Delightful country house hotel in peaceful surroundings where comfort and good food predominate.

Owner/Chef Ernst Barten supervises excellent cuisine.

All rooms en-suite, colour TV and satellite, phone and trouser press. Facilities nearby include windsurfing and sailing from Keyhaven, Golf at Brockenhurst and Barton-on-Sea, the Beach at Milford and walking or riding in the beautiful New Forest.

AN OASIS OF PEACE AND TRANQUILITY IN THE HEART OF THE NEW FOREST

★★★ AA ✿✿ 77%

PARKHILL COUNTRY HOUSE HOTEL

A delightful 20 bedroom Georgian Country House Hotel nestling in 12 acres of glorious pasture and parkland offering the highest standards of hospitality and service together with award winning cuisine in a relaxed and comfortable atmosphere.

Outdoor facilities include Giant Chess, Putting Green, Croquet Lawn and Outdoor Pool, heated in season.

BEAULIEU ROAD, LYNDHURST, HAMPSHIRE
Tel: (01703) 282944 Fax: (01703) 283268

The Stanwell House Hotel is a superb example of Georgian architecture, sympathetically restored to combine luxury, style and informal comfort

The dining facilities are excellent. The Bistro and Bar are a group of rooms, truly Georgian, stunningly simple

The Stanwell House Hotel is ideally located for the New Forest and Lymington Marinas

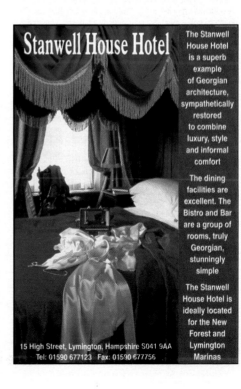

L

equipped. The restaurant offers an interesting range of seasonal dishes, and bar meals provide an informal alternative.

Crown, Lyndhurst

ROOMS: 39 en suite (bth/shr) (8 fmly) s £65-£70; d £97-£110 LB Off peak **MEALS:** Sunday Lunch fr £15.25 High tea £9.50-£14 Dinner fr £19 & alc European Cuisine V meals Coffee am Tea pm **FACILITIES:** CTV in all bedrooms STV Xmas **CONF:** Thtr 70 Class 30 Board 45 Del from £81 * **SERVICES:** Lift Night porter 60P **NOTES:** No smoking in restaurant Last d 9.15pm **CARDS:**

See advert on opposite page

LYNDHURST Hampshire **Map 04 SU30**
★★★ Forest Lodge
Pikes Hill, Romsey Rd SO43 7AS
Quality Percentage Score: 64%
☎ 023 80283677 023 80282940
Dir: *exit M27 at junct 1 and join A337 towards Lyndhurst. On approaching village, police station/courts on right, take first right into Pikes Hill*
Situated on the edge of Lyndhurst, this well maintained hotel has comfortable bedrooms, many ideal for families, and attractively decorated public areas, which include two lounges, a bar and a restaurant. Service is friendly and attentive.
ROOMS: 28 en suite (bth/shr) (7 fmly) s fr £70; d fr £125 (incl. bkfst) * LB Off peak **MEALS:** Sunday Lunch £10.95-£14.95 Dinner £21.50 V meals Coffee am Tea pm **FACILITIES:** CTV in all bedrooms Indoor swimming pool (heated) Sauna Gym ch fac Xmas **CONF:** Thtr 100 Class 70 Board 50 Del from £90 * **SERVICES:** 50P **NOTES:** No smoking in restaurant Last d 8.45pm **CARDS:**

LYNDHURST Hampshire **Map 04 SU30**
★★★ Lyndhurst Park
High St SO43 7NL
Quality Percentage Score: 63%
☎ 023 80283923 023 80283019
Dir: *M27 Junct 1-3 to A35 to Lyndhurst. Hotel is situated at bottom of High Street*
Conveniently situated on the edge of the town and just a short walk away from the high street, this extended Georgian house boasts a fine setting in five acres of mature grounds, good car parking, and outdoor leisure facilities. It is ideally placed for exploring the New Forest. There are two bars and a cosy oak-panelled restaurant with a sunny conservatory addition which is used in warmer weather. Bedrooms vary in size and style but do include several with four poster beds.
ROOMS: 59 en suite (bth/shr) (3 fmly) No smoking in 3 bedrooms s fr £70; d fr £90 (incl. bkfst) * LB Off peak **MEALS:** Lunch fr £11.95 Dinner fr £14.95 English & Continental Cuisine V meals Coffee am Tea pm **FACILITIES:** CTV in all bedrooms Outdoor swimming pool (heated) Tennis (hard) Snooker Sauna Table tennis ch fac Xmas **CONF:** Thtr 300 Class 120 Board 80 Del from £90 * **SERVICES:** Lift Night porter 100P **NOTES:** No smoking in restaurant Last d 9.30pm
CARDS:

LYNDHURST Hampshire **Map 04 SU30**
★★ *Mill House Hotel*
Romsey Rd SO43 7AR
Quality Percentage Score: 68%
☎ 023 80282814 023 80282815
Dir: *leave junct 1 of M27 on to A31, turn right at rdbt onto A337 hotel 4m on left*
Conveniently situated on the edge of the village, the Mill House is ideally placed for both business and leisure guests. Bedrooms are brightly decorated, comfortably furnished and feature modern en suite facilities. Public areas include a very popular bar and restaurant operation which serves food all day. With indoor and outdoor play areas for children, the hotel is ideal for families.
ROOMS: 11 en suite (bth/shr) (3 fmly) **MEALS:** V meals Coffee am Tea pm **FACILITIES:** CTV in all bedrooms **SERVICES:** 56P **NOTES:** No dogs (ex guide dogs) No smoking area in restaurant Last d 9.30pm
CARDS:

LYNDHURST Hampshire **Map 04 SU30**
★ Knightwood Lodge
Southampton Rd SO43 7BU
Quality Percentage Score: 71%
☎ 023 80282502 023 80283730
Dir: *on A35*
This friendly, family-run hotel is situated in the heart of the New Forest and caters well for both the business and tourist guest. The bedrooms are comfortably appointed in modern style and well equipped with many useful extras. The hotel offers an excellent range of facilities which are free to residents. A bright new conservatory dining room has been added and there is a cosy bar in which to relax with a pre-dinner drink.
ROOMS: 14 en suite (bth/shr) 4 annexe en suite (bth/shr) (2 fmly) s £35-£45; d £60-£80 (incl. bkfst) * LB Off peak **MEALS:** Dinner £17.95 V meals **FACILITIES:** CTV in all bedrooms STV Indoor swimming pool (heated) Sauna Solarium Gym Jacuzzi/spa Steam room **SERVICES:** 15P **NOTES:** No coaches No smoking in restaurant Last d 8pm **CARDS:**

LYNMOUTH Devon **Map 03 SS74**
see also **Lynton**
★★★ Tors
EX35 6NA
Quality Percentage Score: 62%
☎ 01598 753236 01598 752544
Dir: *Adjacent to A39 on Countisbuty Hill just before you enter Lynmouth*
A friendly hotel in five acres of woodland. Most of the bedrooms have superb views, as do the public areas, and the restaurant offers a choice of menus.
ROOMS: 33 en suite (bth/shr) (5 fmly) s £40-£85; d £70-£110 (incl. bkfst) * LB Off peak **MEALS:** Bar Lunch £3-£6 Dinner £23-£25 & alc English & French Cuisine V meals Coffee am Tea pm **FACILITIES:** CTV in 35 bedrooms Outdoor swimming pool (heated) Pool table Table tennis ch fac Xmas **CONF:** Thtr 60 Class 40 Board 25 Del from £57 * **SERVICES:** Lift 40P **NOTES:** No coaches No smoking in restaurant Last d 9.15pm Closed 4-31 Jan RS Feb (wknds only)
CARDS:

LYNMOUTH Devon **Map 03 SS74**
★★ Rising Sun
Harbourside EX35 6EQ
Quality Percentage Score: 73%
☎ 01598 753223 01598 753480
Dir: *leave M5 at junct 23 (Minehead), follow A39 to Lynmouth. Hotel is located on Harbourside*
Nestling right on the harbour front, this historic smugglers' inn

contd.

has a good restaurant and a popular bar. Its bedrooms are individually designed and offer good modern facilities. On the first floor there is a comfortable, quiet lounge.
ROOMS: 11 en suite (bth/shr) 5 annexe en suite (bth/shr) No smoking in 11 bedrooms s £55-£60; d £90-£140 (incl. bkfst) * LB Off peak **MEALS:** Lunch fr £14.50 & alc Dinner £27.50 & alc English & French Cuisine V meals Coffee am **FACILITIES:** CTV in all bedrooms Fishing Xmas **NOTES:** No dogs (ex guide dogs) No coaches No children 8yrs No smoking in restaurant Last d 9.30pm
CARDS:

LYNMOUTH Devon — Map 03 SS74
★★ Bath
Sea Front EX35 6EL
Quality Percentage Score: 67%
☎ 01598 752238 Fax 01598 752544
Dir: *M5 junct 25 follow A39 to Minehead then Pollock and Lynmouth*
This well established hotel stands near the harbour, and its sea-facing bedrooms are particularly attractive. Local fish in season features on the restaurant menu and cream teas are served in the sun lounge.
ROOMS: 24 en suite (bth/shr) (9 fmly) s £29-£35; d £58-£80 (incl. bkfst) * LB Off peak **MEALS:** Lunch £4.95-£9.95 Dinner £10.50-£16.50 & alc English & French Cuisine V meals Coffee am Tea pm **FACILITIES:** CTV in all bedrooms Pool table **SERVICES:** 15P **NOTES:** No smoking in restaurant Last d 8.30pm Closed Jan & Dec RS Nov-Mar **CARDS:**

LYNTON Devon — Map 03 SS74
see also **Lynmouth**
★★★ Hewitts
North Walk EX35 6HJ
Quality Percentage Score: 67%
☎ 01598 752293 Fax 01598 752489
Dir: *North Walk runs off the Lee Road, entrance between St Mary's Church and Valley of Rocks hotel*
Perched on the hillside, Hewitt's was built as a gentleman's country house in the late 1800s. Each of the individually designed and decorated bedrooms benefits from panoramic views across the channel to the Welsh coastline. Public areas feature stained glass and carved fireplaces.
ROOMS: 9 en suite (bth/shr) (1 fmly) No smoking in 8 bedrooms s £50-£80; d £99-£120 (incl. bkfst) * Off peak **MEALS:** Lunch £20-£30 & alc High tea £7.50-£9.50 Dinner £20-£30 & alc International Cuisine V meals Coffee am Tea pm **FACILITIES:** CTV in all bedrooms STV Jacuzzi/spa Wkly live entertainment **CONF:** Thtr 20 Class 16 Board 16 Del from £80 * **SERVICES:** Night porter 12P **NOTES:** No coaches No children 10yrs No smoking in restaurant Last d 9pm RS 10 Nov-10 Feb
CARDS:

LYNTON Devon — Map 03 SS74
★★★ Lynton Cottage
North Walk EX35 6ED
Quality Percentage Score: 62%
☎ 01598 752342 Fax 01598 752597
Dir: *turn into North Walk by St Mary's Church, hotel is 100mtrs on right*
Hidden away at the end of a private drive, the 17th-century Lynton Cottage Hotel has stunning views and has kept much of its period character. A spacious lounge, a separate bar and a restaurant make up the public rooms. The menu is well balanced, and puddings are delicious.
ROOMS: 17 en suite (bth/shr) No smoking in 2 bedrooms s £41-£59; d £82-£118 (incl. bkfst) * LB Off peak **MEALS:** Lunch £2.95-£6.75 Dinner £23 & alc International Cuisine V meals Coffee am Tea pm **FACILITIES:** CTV in all bedrooms **SERVICES:** 17P **NOTES:** No dogs No children 15yrs No smoking in restaurant Last d 9pm Closed Jan
CARDS:

LYNTON Devon — Map 03 SS74
★★ *The Crown Hotel*
Sinai Hill EX35 6AG
Quality Percentage Score: 64%
☎ 01598 752253 Fax 01598 753311
Situated in the Old Village area of Lynton, The Crown dates back to 1760 and is popular with locals and tourists alike. A fixed price menu is available in the dining room, and in the Whip and Collar Bar and Restaurant, a wide variety of dishes is offered, including some daily specials. Bedrooms are well equipped, varying in size and style; several rooms have four-poster beds.
ROOMS: 15 en suite (bth/shr) (3 fmly) **MEALS:** V meals Coffee am **FACILITIES:** CTV in all bedrooms Darts **SERVICES:** 25P **NOTES:** No coaches Last d 8.30pm **CARDS:**

LYNTON Devon — Map 03 SS74
★★ Sandrock
Longmead EX35 6DH
Quality Percentage Score: 63%
☎ 01598 753307 Fax 01598 752665
Dir: *follow signs to 'The Valley of the Rocks'*
Situated at the head of the Valley of the Rocks, on the edge of the village, this family-run hotel offers light, airy, modern bedrooms and has a popular public bar, with a comfortable residents lounge on the first floor.
ROOMS: 9 rms (7 bth/shr) (3 fmly) s £22.50-£24; d £47.50-£50 (incl. bkfst) * LB Off peak **MEALS:** V meals Coffee am Tea pm **FACILITIES:** CTV in all bedrooms Pool table **SERVICES:** 9P **NOTES:** No coaches Last d 7.30pm Closed Nov-Jan **CARDS:**

LYNTON Devon — Map 03 SS74
★ Highcliffe House
Sinai Hill EX35 6AR
Quality Percentage Score: 82%
☎ 01598 752235 🖷 01598 752235
Dir: *From the old village take Sinai Hill Hotel 400yrds on left*
This Victorian gentleman's residence high above the bay is a delightful small hotel. Guests lucky enough to secure one of the bedrooms will feel thoroughly pampered. There are two attractive lounges, decorated in keeping with the period of the house. Smoking is not allowed.
ROOMS: 6 en suite (bth/shr) No smoking in all bedrooms s £57; d £70-£84 (incl. bkfst) * LB Off peak **MEALS:** Dinner £25 English & Continental Cuisine V meals **FACILITIES:** CTV in all bedrooms **SERVICES:** 10P **NOTES:** No dogs No coaches No children No smoking in restaurant Last d 7.30pm **CARDS:**

LYNTON Devon — Map 03 SS74
★ Seawood
North Walk EX35 6HJ
Quality Percentage Score: 73%
☎ 01598 752272 🖷 01598 752272
This charming hotel, nestling on wooded cliffs some 400 feet above the sea, provides spectacular views across Lynmouth Bay. Bedrooms are all individually furnished and decorated, and some have four-poster beds. The menu changes daily.
ROOMS: 12 en suite (bth/shr) s £29-£31; d £58-£60 (incl. bkfst) * LB Off peak **MEALS:** Dinner £13.50-£14.50 V meals **FACILITIES:** CTV in all bedrooms **SERVICES:** 10P **NOTES:** No coaches No children 10yrs No smoking in restaurant Last d 6.30pm Closed Nov-Etr

LYNTON Devon — Map 03 SS74
★ Chough's Nest
North Walk EX35 6HJ
Quality Percentage Score: 69%
☎ 01598 753315 🖷 01598 763529
Dir: *turn onto North Walk by Parish Church in the centre of the High St. Chough's Nest last building on the left*
Built as a private residence by a Dutch millionaire, this beautiful stone house has spectacular views over Lynmouth Bay. Bedrooms are individually designed to modern standards, and the restaurant offers a carefully chosen menu with a vegetarian choice always on offer.
ROOMS: 12 en suite (bth/shr) (2 fmly) No smoking in all bedrooms s £29-£44; d £58-£88 (incl. bkfst) * LB Off peak **MEALS:** Dinner £19 International Cuisine V meals Coffee am Tea pm **FACILITIES:** CTV in all bedrooms Beauty Therapist, Reflexology & Aromatherapy **SERVICES:** 10P **NOTES:** No dogs No coaches No smoking in restaurant Last d 8pm Closed Nov-Jan RS Feb & Early March **CARDS:**

LYNTON Devon — Map 03 SS74
★ North Cliff
North Walk EX35 6HJ
Quality Percentage Score: 67%
☎ 01598 752357
Dir: *from Lynton main street Lee Road take North Walk Hill Hotel on left*
With spectacular views over Lynmouth Bay, this small hotel offers guests a genuine welcome. Home-cooked meals are served in the dining room which, like the lounge, enjoys fine views, as do many of the spacious, comfortable bedrooms.
ROOMS: 14 en suite (bth/shr) (3 fmly) No smoking in all bedrooms s fr £31; d fr £62 (incl. bkfst) * LB Off peak **MEALS:** Dinner £17 **FACILITIES:** CTV in all bedrooms Table tennis **SERVICES:** 15P **NOTES:** No coaches No smoking in restaurant Last d 7pm Closed Nov-Feb **CARDS:**

LYTHAM ST ANNES Lancashire — Map 07 SD32
★★★★ Clifton Arms
West Beach, Lytham FY8 5QJ
Quality Percentage Score: 63%
☎ 01253 739898 🖷 01253 730657
Dir: *on the A584 along the seafront*

The restaurant is the latest area to be refurbished, bedrooms are also being upgraded as part of continued improvements. Many are spacious and all are nicely furnished, including a choice of suites and some rooms overlooking the Ribble estuary. A range of dishes is offered and there is a comfortable lounge and separate library. Service is professional and friendly.
ROOMS: 44 en suite (bth/shr) No smoking in 4 bedrooms s £87.50-£97.50; d £108-£118 (incl. bkfst) * LB Off peak **MEALS:** Lunch £16.50 & alc Dinner £25 & alc V meals Coffee am Tea pm **FACILITIES:** CTV in all bedrooms STV Xmas **CONF:** Thtr 300 Class 200 Board 100 Del from £120 * **SERVICES:** Lift Night porter 50P **NOTES:** No dogs (ex guide dogs) No smoking area in restaurant Last d 10pm
CARDS:

See advert on opposite page

LYTHAM ST ANNES Lancashire — Map 07 SD32
★★★ Chadwick
South Promenade FY8 1NP
Quality Percentage Score: 66%
☎ 01253 720061 🖷 01253 714455
Dir: *M6 Junct 32 take M55 Blackpool A5230 South Shore and follow signs for St Annes*

In the same family for over half a century, this traditional hotel caters for different generations of regular visitors. Bedrooms,

contd.

We endeavour to be as accurate as possible but changes in personnel and data can occur in establishments after the Hotel Guide has gone to press.

including some overlooking the sea, are comfortably furnished, whilst the public areas are spacious.

ROOMS: 75 en suite (bth/shr) (28 fmly) s £42-£46; d £60-£68 (incl. bkfst) * LB Off peak **MEALS:** Lunch £7.80-£9.25 Dinner £16 & alc International Cuisine V meals Coffee am Tea pm **FACILITIES:** CTV in all bedrooms STV Indoor swimming pool (heated) Sauna Solarium Gym Pool table Jacuzzi/spa Turkish bath Games room Soft play adventure area Wkly live entertainment ch fac Xmas **CONF:** Thtr 72 Class 24 Board 28 Del from £58 * **SERVICES:** Lift Night porter 40P **NOTES:** No dogs (ex guide dogs) No coaches No smoking in restaurant Last d 8.30pm **CARDS:**

See advert on this page

LYTHAM ST ANNES Lancashire **Map 07 SD32**

★★★ Bedford

307-311 Clifton Dr South FY8 1HN

Quality Percentage Score: 64%

☎ 01253 724636 01253 729244

Dir: *from M55 follow signs for airport to last set of lights. Turn left, through 2 sets of lights hotel is 300yds on left*

This family-run hotel is close to the town centre and the sea front. Bedrooms, those at the front generally being larger, are attractively furnished and well equipped. Diners are offered a wide range of meals in the restaurant, and good bar food in the

contd.

Indicates that the star classification has not been confirmed under the New Quality Standards, see page 7 for further information.

Kitty O'Shea Bar, where there is regular entertainment. The coffee shop serves snacks throughout the day.

Bedford, Lytham St Annes

ROOMS: 36 en suite (bth/shr) (6 fmly) s fr £45; d fr £65 (incl. bkfst) * LB Off peak **MEALS:** Lunch £7.95 & alc High tea £5.50 Dinner £15-£17.50 & alc English & Continental Cuisine V meals Coffee am Tea pm **FACILITIES:** CTV in all bedrooms STV Sauna Solarium Gym Jacuzzi/spa Steam room Wkly live entertainment Xmas **CONF:** Thtr 150 Class 100 Board 40 Del from £60 * **SERVICES:** Lift Night porter 20P **NOTES:** No dogs No smoking in restaurant Last d 8.30pm
CARDS:

See advert on page 429

LYTHAM ST ANNES Lancashire — Map 07 SD32
★★ Lindum
63-67 South Promenade FY8 1LZ
Quality Percentage Score: 68%
☎ 01253 721534 & 722516 01253 721364

THE CIRCLE Selected Individual Hotels GREAT BRITAIN

Dir: *from airport, continue to seafront lights and turn left. Continue onto 2nd set of lights & turn right, then left at jct. Hotel on left*

Popular with the leisure guest, this friendly hotel has been operated by the same family for over 40 years. Bedrooms are generally spacious and comfortable, many were recently refurbished, and some enjoy fine sea views. There are several lounges, one with a large screen TV, also a games room and a health suite. The airy restaurant offers a wide choice of dishes.
ROOMS: 76 en suite (bth/shr) (25 fmly) No smoking in 4 bedrooms s £28-£40; d £55-£65 (incl. bkfst) * LB Off peak **MEALS:** Sunday Lunch fr £9 High tea fr £7.50 Dinner fr £13.50 British & Continental Cuisine V meals Coffee am Tea pm **FACILITIES:** CTV in all bedrooms Sauna Solarium Jacuzzi/spa Beauty salon Xmas **CONF:** Thtr 80 Class 30 Board 25 Del from £45 * **SERVICES:** Lift Night porter Air conditioning 20P **NOTES:** No smoking in restaurant Last d 7pm **CARDS:**

LYTHAM ST ANNES Lancashire — Map 07 SD32
★★ Glendower
North Promenade FY8 2NQ
Quality Percentage Score: 66%
☎ 01253 723241 01253 723241

Best Western

Dir: *M55 follow airport signs turn left at Promenade to St Annes*

This well-established and popular hotel has easy access to the town centre. Some bedrooms have fine sea views, but all are comfortably furnished, with family rooms and four-poster beds available. There is a choice of comfortable lounges and home-style food is served in the restaurant.
ROOMS: 60 en suite (bth/shr) (17 fmly) s £39.95-£44.95; d £72-£82 (incl. bkfst) * LB Off peak **MEALS:** Bar Lunch £2.50-£7.95 Dinner £15.50 V meals Coffee am **FACILITIES:** CTV in all bedrooms Indoor swimming pool (heated) Snooker Sauna Gym Pool table Table tennis Fitness room Childrens playroom Xmas **CONF:** Thtr 150 Class 120 Board 40 Del from £72 * **SERVICES:** Lift Night porter 45P **NOTES:** No smoking in restaurant Last d 8.30pm **CARDS:**

LYTHAM ST ANNES Lancashire — Map 07 SD32
New England
314 Clifton Dr North, St Annes on Sea FY8 2PB
☎ 01253 722355
ROOMS: 10 rms

MACCLESFIELD Cheshire — Map 07 SJ97
★★★★ Shrigley Hall Hotel Golf & Country Club
Shrigley Park, Pott Shrigley SK10 5SB
Quality Percentage Score: 62%
☎ 01625 575757 01625 573323

PARAMOUNT HOTEL · GROUP

Dir: *turn off A523 at Legh Arms, towards Pott Shrigley, hotel is 2m on left just before village*

Set in 262 acres of mature parkland, this lesiure complex offers activities including a championship golf course and fishing by arrangement. There is a wide choice of room size and style with the rooms in the main house being particularly regal, some with four-poster beds. Good food is served in the restaurant, while lighter meals and snacks are available in the airy Courtyard lounge.

ROOMS: 150 en suite (bth/shr) (8 fmly) No smoking in 28 bedrooms s fr £110; d fr £140 (incl. bkfst) * LB Off peak **MEALS:** Lunch £14 Dinner £23-£32 & alc International Cuisine V meals Coffee am Tea pm **FACILITIES:** CTV in all bedrooms STV Indoor swimming pool (heated) Golf 18 Tennis (hard) Fishing Sauna Solarium Gym Putting green Jacuzzi/spa Beauty salon Steam spa Tennis courts Wkly live entertainment Xmas **CONF:** Thtr 280 Class 140 Board 50 Del from £160 * **SERVICES:** Lift Night porter 300P **NOTES:** No coaches No smoking in restaurant Last d 9.30pm **CARDS:**

See advert under MANCHESTER AIRPORT

MACCLESFIELD Cheshire — Map 07 SJ97
★★★ Belgrade Hotel & Restaurant
Jackson Ln, Kerridge, Bollington SK10 5BG
Quality Percentage Score: 67%
☎ 01625 573246 01625 574791

Best Western

Dir: *off A523, 2m along B5090*

Set in the peaceful Cheshire countryside, this hotel is convenient for Manchester Airport, with courtesy transport available. The main building has an impressive carved staircase, public rooms with high ceilings, as well as a restaurant and lounge. Attractively furnished accommodation is situated in a purpose-built annexe nearby.
ROOMS: 54 en suite (bth/shr) (2 fmly) No smoking in 36 bedrooms s £54.50-£70; d £65-£85 * LB Off peak **MEALS:** Lunch £10.50 Dinner fr £18.95 & alc International Cuisine V meals Coffee am Tea pm **FACILITIES:** CTV in all bedrooms STV Pool table Free use of neighbouring Leisure Club **CONF:** Thtr 80 Class 50 Board 50 Del £95 * **SERVICES:** Night porter 200P **NOTES:** No dogs (ex guide dogs) Last d 9.30pm **CARDS:**

MACCLESFIELD Cheshire **Map 07 SJ97**

Travel Inn

Tytherington Business Park, Springwood Way, Tytherington SK10 2XA

☎ 01625 427809 01625 422874

Dir: *on A523 Tytherington rdbt*

This modern building offers accommodation in smart, spacious and well equipped bedrooms, all with en-suite bathrooms. Refreshments may be taken at the nearby family restaurant. For details about current prices consult the Contents Page under Hotel Groups for the Travel Inn phone number.

ROOMS: 40 en suite (bth/shr) d £39.95 *

MADELEY Staffordshire **Map 07 SJ74**

★★ ***Crewe Arms***

Wharf St, Madeley Heath CW3 9LP

Quality Percentage Score: 58%

☎ 01782 750392 01782 750587

Dir: *off A525, near junct with A531*

This small hotel, peacefully located in the charming village of Madeley, is within easy reach of the M6. Spacious bedrooms have been created in a converted barn and a range of popular dishes is offered in the traditional bar, in addition to the main restaurant.

ROOMS: 10 en suite (bth/shr) (2 fmly) **MEALS:** V meals Coffee am **FACILITIES:** CTV in all bedrooms Pool table **SERVICES:** 50P **NOTES:** No dogs (ex guide dogs) Last d 9.30pm **CARDS:**

MAIDENCOMBE See **Torquay**

MAIDENHEAD Berkshire **Map 04 SU88**

see also **Bray** and advert on p. 433

The Premier Collection

★★★★❀❀❀ **Fredrick's**

Shoppenhangers Rd SL6 2PZ

☎ 01628 581000 01628 771054

Dir: *M4, A404 for Henley to Cox Green/White Waltham head to Maindenhead*

Quietly located, this delightful hotel provides individually decorated, well equipped bedrooms. Friendly, efficient service is provided by enthusiastic staff, and a highlight of any visit is a meal in the restaurant, where chef Brian Cutler and his team produce memorable modern dishes.

ROOMS: 37 en suite (bth/shr) s £168-£188; d £210-£230 (incl. bkfst) * LB Off peak **MEALS:** Lunch £25.50-£29.50 & alc Dinner £35.50 & alc English & French Cuisine V meals Coffee am **FACILITIES:** CTV in all bedrooms STV Croquet lawn **CONF:** Thtr 120 Class 80 Board 60 Del from £250 * **SERVICES:** Night porter 90P **NOTES:** No dogs (ex guide dogs) No coaches Last d 9.45pm Closed 24 Dec-3 Jan **CARDS:**

MAIDENHEAD Berkshire **Map 04 SU88**

★★★ **Walton Cottage**

Marlow Rd SL6 7LT

Quality Percentage Score: 68%

☎ 01628 624394 01628 773851

Dir: *A308 towards Marlow, hotel on right after passing town centre*

This family owned and run hotel provides very good accommodation and is close to the centre of town. Some of the bedrooms feature sitting rooms and kitchenettes, while other rooms are smaller, but all are well equipped. The restaurant offers a good choice of dishes through the week but restricted service applies at weekends when meals are only available by prior arrangement.

ROOMS: 25 en suite (bth/shr) 45 annexe en suite (bth/shr) s £94; d £114 * Off peak **MEALS:** Dinner £16.75 International Cuisine V meals Coffee am Tea pm **FACILITIES:** CTV in all bedrooms STV **CONF:** Thtr 70 Class 40 Board 30 **SERVICES:** Lift Night porter 60P **NOTES:** No dogs (ex guide dogs) No coaches No smoking in restaurant Last d 9.30pm Closed 24 Dec-3 Jan

CARDS:

MAIDENHEAD Berkshire **Map 04 SU88**

★★★ **Thames Riviera**

At the Bridge SL6 8DW

Quality Percentage Score: 66%

☎ 01628 674057 01628 776586

Dir: *turn off A4 by Maidenhead Historic Bridge,the hotel is situated by the bridge*

This family owned hotel enjoys an enviable location next to the Thames by the Maidenhead Bridge. There are two bedroom blocks; the main building with its smart restaurant houses around half the rooms and the remainder are in a more modern unit. There are extensive conference and banqueting facilities, a scenic restaurant and small coffee shop.

ROOMS: 34 en suite (bth/shr) 18 annexe en suite (bth/shr) (1 fmly) No smoking in 4 bedrooms s fr £95; d fr £110 * LB Off peak **MEALS:** Dinner fr £19.50 International Cuisine V meals Coffee am Tea pm **FACILITIES:** CTV in all bedrooms STV Wkly live entertainment **CONF:** Thtr 50 Class 30 Board 20 Del from £155 * **SERVICES:** Night porter 60P **NOTES:** No dogs (ex guide dogs) Last d 9.45pm Closed 26-30 Dec **CARDS:**

MAIDENHEAD Berkshire **Map 04 SU88**

★★★❀ **Ye Olde Bell Hotel**

Hurley SL6 5LX

Quality Percentage Score: 66%

☎ 01628 825881 01628 825939

Dir: *take A4130 to Henley look for East Arms public house, High St is on the right just before the pub*

In a charming village, between Henley and Maidenhead, Ye Olde Bell is reputed to be one of the oldest inns in England. In the main building there are a selection of bedrooms, a snug bar and the Garden restaurant with conference rooms housed in the Malt House. On the opposite side of the road, a series of converted barns contain additional accommodation as well as a banqueting suite.

ROOMS: 11 en suite (bth/shr) 31 annexe en suite (bth/shr) (3 fmly) No smoking in 5 bedrooms s £135-£155; d £155-£175 * LB Off peak **MEALS:** Lunch £17.95-£22.90 & alc Dinner £23.50-£26.45 & alc V meals Coffee am Tea pm **FACILITIES:** CTV in all bedrooms STV Tennis (hard) Croquet lawn Badminton Petanque Xmas **CONF:** Thtr 140 Class 60 Board 40 Del from £155 * **SERVICES:** Night porter 85P **NOTES:** No coaches No smoking area in restaurant Last d 9.30pm

CARDS:

≡ **MAIDSTONE** Kent
Map 05 TQ75
★★★★ **Marriott Tudor Park**
Hotel & Country Club
Marriott
HOTELS · RESORTS · SUITES
Ashford Rd, Bearsted ME14 4NQ
Quality Percentage Score: 68%
☎ 01622 734334 📠 01622 735360
Dir: *leave M20 at junct 8 Lenham. At rdbt turn right and head to Bearsted and Maidstone. Hotel is situated 1m on the left hand side*

This fine country hotel provides an excellent venue for both business and leisure users. The superb facilities and good levels of comfort in the bedrooms are part of a successful formula which also includes friendly and helpful staff. The main restaurant, Fairviews, offers uncomplicated dishes which are generally well executed; guests also have the option of the more relaxed environment of the Long Weekend brasserie. Make time to enjoy the excellent range of leisure options, be it golf, a workout, swim or a visit to the beauty salon.
ROOMS: 118 en suite (bth/shr) (47 fmly) No smoking in 65 bedrooms s £74-£81; d £81-£86 * Off peak **MEALS:** Lunch £15.95-£16.95 High tea fr £7.95 Dinner £22.50 & alc Continental Cuisine V meals Coffee am Tea pm **FACILITIES:** CTV in all bedrooms STV Indoor swimming pool (heated) Golf 18 Tennis (hard) Sauna Solarium Gym Putting green Jacuzzi/spa Driving range Beauty salon Steam room Wkly live entertainment ch fac Xmas **CONF:** Thtr 250 Class 120 Board 60 Del from £125 * **SERVICES:** Lift Night porter 250P **NOTES:** No dogs (ex guide dogs) No smoking in restaurant Last d 9.30pm
CARDS: 💳 ■ ■ ■ ■ ■

≡ **MAIDSTONE** Kent
Map 05 TQ75
★★★ *Russell*
136 Boxley Rd ME14 2AE
Best Western
Quality Percentage Score: 65%
☎ 01622 692221 📠 01622 762084

This attractive Victorian house is set in two acres of grounds on the edge of Maidstone, only minutes from the major routes. Bedrooms continually upgraded, have modern en suite facilities including remote control colour TV and hairdryer. The attractive restaurant offers good home-cooked food and has a strong local following. The hotel is a popular venue for wedding receptions

and meetings, Mr Costa is an effusive and attentive host, leading a keen continental team.
ROOMS: 42 en suite (bth/shr) (5 fmly) **MEALS:** French Cuisine V meals Coffee am Tea pm **FACILITIES:** CTV in all bedrooms Jacuzzi/spa ch fac **CONF:** Thtr 300 Class 100 Board 90 **SERVICES:** Night porter 100P **NOTES:** No dogs (ex guide dogs) No smoking area in restaurant Last d 9.30pm **CARDS:** 💳 ■ ■ ■ ■ ■ ■

See advert on opposite page

≡ **MAIDSTONE** Kent
Map 05 TQ75
★★★ **Larkfield Priory**
London Rd, Larkfield ME20 6HJ
REGAL
Quality Percentage Score: 63%
☎ 01732 846858 📠 01732 846786
Dir: *M20 junct 4 take A228 to W Malling at 1st rdbt take 2nd exit signposted to Maidstone (A20), after 1m hotel on left*
Dating from 1890,this hotel has been extended and upgraded to provide levels of comfort demanded by today's business travellers. Accommodation is being steadily refurbished and the new rooms are bright and smart. The restaurant boasts a conservatory annex, and the bar lounge is a pleasant alternative for lighter meals and snacks.

ROOMS: 52 en suite (bth/shr) No smoking in 24 bedrooms s £55-£65; d £55-£75 * LB Off peak **MEALS:** Lunch fr £11.95 Dinner fr £17 International Cuisine V meals Coffee am Tea pm **FACILITIES:** CTV in all bedrooms Xmas **CONF:** Thtr 80 Class 36 Board 30 Del from £99 * **SERVICES:** Night porter 80P **NOTES:** No smoking in restaurant Last d 9.30pm **CARDS:** 💳 ■ ■ ■ ■ ■

≡ **MAIDSTONE** Kent
Map 05 TQ75
★★ **Grange Moor**
St Michael's Rd ME16 8BS
Quality Percentage Score: 66%
☎ 01622 677623 📠 01622 678246
Dir: *off A26, Tonbridge Road. Church on lft, turn left hotel on right*
A friendly, family-run hotel, just off the A26. Bedrooms, some in a nearby building, are well equipped and modern in style, though some have four-poster beds. The popular bar serves a good range of bar meals, there is a small lounge and several dining and function rooms.
ROOMS: 47 en suite (bth/shr) (6 fmly) s £40-£48; d £50-£52 (incl. bkfst) * LB Off peak **MEALS:** Sunday Lunch £10.50 Dinner £13.50-£15 & alc English & French Cuisine V meals Coffee am Tea pm **FACILITIES:** CTV in all bedrooms **CONF:** Thtr 100 Class 50 Board 50 Del from £80 * **SERVICES:** Night porter 60P **NOTES:** Last d 9.30 Closed last week Dec **CARDS:** 💳 ■ ■ ■

Symbols and Abbreviations are listed and explained on pages 4 and 5

MAIDSTONE Kent **Map 05 TQ75**

Roadchef Lodge

ME17 1SS

☎ 01622 631100 📠 01622 739535

Dir: *M20 junct 8*

This modern building offers accommodation in smart, spacious and well equipped bedrooms, all with en-suite bathrooms. Refreshments may be taken at the nearby family restaurant. For details about current prices, consult the Contents Page under Hotel Groups for the Roadchef phone number.

ROOMS: 58 en suite (bth/shr) d fr £49.95 * **CONF:** Thtr 30 Board 18

MAIDSTONE Kent **Map 05 TQ75**

Travel Inn

London Rd ME16 0HG

☎ 01622 752515 📠 01622 672469

Dir: *leave M20 junct 5 take London Rd and head towards Maidstone. Half a mile from junct 5*

This modern building offers accommodation in smart, spacious and well equipped bedrooms, all with en-suite bathrooms. Refreshments may be taken at the nearby family restaurant. For details about current prices consult the Contents Page under Hotel Groups for the Travel Inn phone number.

ROOMS: 40 en suite (bth/shr) d £39.95 *

MAIDSTONE Kent **Map 05 TQ75**

Travel Inn (Leybourne)

Castle Way ME19 5TR

☎ 01732 521630 📠 01732 521609

Dir: *from junct 4 of the M20 take the A228 towards West Malling, hotel on left*

This modern building offers accommodation in smart, spacious and

contd.

well equipped bedrooms, all with en-suite bathrooms. Refreshments may be taken at the nearby family restaurant. For details about current prices consult the Contents Page under Hotel Groups for the Travel Inn phone number.
ROOMS: 40 en suite (bth/shr) d £39.95 *

MAIDSTONE Kent — Map 05 TQ75

Travel Inn (Sandling)

Allington Lock, Sandling ME14 3AS
☎ 01622 717251 Fax 01622 715159
Dir: *off junct 6 M20 follow sign for Museum of Kent Life*
This modern building offers accommodation in smart, spacious and well equipped bedrooms, all with en-suite bathrooms. Refreshments may be taken at the nearby family restaurant. For details about current prices consult the Contents Page under Hotel Groups for the Travel Inn phone number.
ROOMS: 40 en suite (bth/shr) d £39.95 *

MALDON See **Tolleshunt Knights**

MALHAM North Yorkshire — Map 07 SD96

★★ *The Buck Inn*

BD23 4DA
Quality Percentage Score: 61%
☎ 01729 830317 Fax 01729 830670
Dir: *from Skipton, take A65 to Gargrave, signposted in village centre, Malham is 7 miles further along*
At the centre of the village this stone built inn offers attractively furnished and freshly decorated bedrooms. In addition to the menus offered in the comfortable dining room, a wide choice of homemade dishes is available in the two bars.
ROOMS: 10 en suite (bth/shr) (2 fmly) **MEALS:** V meals Coffee am **FACILITIES:** CTV in all bedrooms **SERVICES:** 20P **NOTES:** No dogs (ex guide dogs) Last d 9pm **CARDS:**

MALMESBURY Wiltshire — Map 03 ST98

★★★ Old Bell

Abbey Row SN16 0AG
Quality Percentage Score: 76%
☎ 01666 822344 Fax 01666 825145
Dir: *off A429, in centre of Malmesbury, adjacent to the Abbey*

Reputed to be England's oldest hotel and located next to the abbey in the centre of Malmesbury, this Grade I listed building is ideal for those who crave a little history. Although modern facilities have been provided throughout, many of the property's original features have been retained. There is a choice of comfortable lounges in which to relax. Bedrooms are varied in size and style, ranging from character rooms in the main building, to the stylish Japanese-inspired rooms in the adjoining coach house. Dinner in the elegant Edwardian restaurant provides a perfect end to the day.
ROOMS: 31 en suite (bth/shr) (3 fmly) s £75-£125; d £95-£150 (incl. bkfst) * LB Off peak **MEALS:** Lunch fr £16 Dinner fr £19.75 & alc V meals Coffee am Tea pm **FACILITIES:** CTV in all bedrooms STV Xmas **CONF:** Thtr 40 Class 20 Board 26 Del from £130 * **SERVICES:** Night porter 30P **NOTES:** No coaches No smoking in restaurant Last d 9.30pm **CARDS:**

See advert on opposite page

MALMESBURY Wiltshire — Map 03 ST98

★★★ Whatley Manor

Nr Easton Grey SN16 0RB
Quality Percentage Score: 71%
☎ 01666 822888 Fax 01666 826120
Dir: *3m W of Malmesbury on B4040 between Easton Grey and Malmesbury*

A stone-built manor house in gardens and grounds. The spacious wood-panelled drawing room has a welcoming open fire. Bedrooms in the Manor, Tudor and Terrace wings are spacious and comfortable, Court House rooms are more functional. An interesting fixed price menu is served in the restaurant. Leisure facilities and facilities for guests bringing dogs are available.
ROOMS: 18 en suite (bth) 11 annexe en suite (bth) (3 fmly) s £82-£92; d £96-£132 (incl. bkfst) * LB Off peak **MEALS:** Lunch £16 High tea fr £10 Dinner £29.50 English & Continental Cuisine V meals Coffee am Tea pm **FACILITIES:** CTV in all bedrooms Outdoor swimming pool (heated) Tennis (hard) Fishing Sauna Solarium Croquet lawn Jacuzzi/spa Table tennis Xmas **CONF:** Thtr 50 Class 30 Board 30 Del from £138 * **SERVICES:** Night porter 60P **NOTES:** No coaches Last d 9pm **CARDS:**

See advert on opposite page

MALMESBURY Wiltshire — Map 03 ST98

★★★ Knoll House

Swindon Rd SN16 9LU
Quality Percentage Score: 67%
☎ 01666 823114 Fax 01666 823897
Dir: *from M4 junct 17 follow A429 towards Cirencester, at first rdbt after 5m turn right, 3rd exit. Hotel is on left at top of hill along B4042*
Situated on the outskirts of Malmesbury, this friendly little hotel provides a warm welcome to business and leisure guests alike. Formerly a Victorian family home, the property offers comfortable accommodation and a relaxed yet professional atmosphere. Bedrooms are found in either the main house or a

contd. on p. 436

KNOLL HOUSE HOTEL

AA ★★★

Swindon Road, Malmesbury
Wiltshire SN16 9LU
Telephone Malmesbury (01666) 823114
Fax (01666) 823897

Comfort, quality and service surrounded by beautiful Wiltshire countryside.

The Knoll is ideally situated on the outskirts of this historic town.

England's oldest borough on the southern edge of the Cotswolds.

The Old Bell

Abbey Row ★ Malmesbury
Wiltshire ★ SN16 0AG

Searching for an hotel that understands your requirements whatever your age or occupation?

We will be happy to help you look.

Tel: 01666 822344 ★ Fax: 01666 825145

MAYFIELD HOUSE

HOTEL AND RESTAURANT

"RELAX AND BE WELCOMED"

Delightful, privately owned 2-star country hotel in two acres of walled garden. The village location provides an ideal setting for a few days away. Award winning restaurant. Warm and friendly welcome. Excellent for touring Cotswolds and Bath.

SHORT BREAKS OUR SPECIALITY

TELEPHONE FOR A BROCHURE:
(01666) 577409
MAYFIELD HOUSE HOTEL, CRUDWELL
MALMESBURY, WILTSHIRE SN16 9EW

RELAX IN CIVILISED SURROUNDINGS

WHATLEY MANOR

NR EASTON GREY • MALMESBURY
WILTSHIRE • (01666) 822888

newer wing, but all are well equipped with a good range of modern amenities.

Knoll House, Malmesbury

ROOMS: 12 en suite (bth/shr) 10 annexe en suite (bth/shr) (1 fmly) s fr £60; d fr £82.50 (incl. bkfst) * LB Off peak **MEALS:** English & French Cuisine V meals Coffee am Tea pm **FACILITIES:** CTV in all bedrooms Outdoor swimming pool (heated) Croquet lawn Xmas **CONF:** Thtr 50 Board 30 Del from £110 * **SERVICES:** 40P **NOTES:** No smoking in restaurant Last d 9.30pm **CARDS:**

See advert on page 435

MALMESBURY Wiltshire — Map 03 ST98

★★ Mayfield House

Crudwell SN16 9EW

Quality Percentage Score: 72%

☎ 01666 577409 & 577198 01666 577977

***Dir:** 3m N on A429*

The owners, together with their attentive team offer a warm welcome at this charming hotel on the edge of the Cotswolds. A loyal group of guests return regularly to enjoy the relaxed atmosphere and sample the food. There is a foyer lounge, a bar offering a wide range of dishes and a restaurant with an imaginative menu. Bedrooms, some on the ground floor, are all equipped with modern facilities.

ROOMS: 23 rms (20 bth/shr) (1 fmly) s £48-£50; d £72-£74 (incl. bkfst) * LB Off peak **MEALS:** Sunday Lunch £10.95 Dinner fr £17.95 English & French Cuisine V meals Coffee am Tea pm **FACILITIES:** CTV in all bedrooms Xmas **CONF:** Thtr 40 Class 30 Board 25 Del £72.50 * **SERVICES:** 50P **NOTES:** No smoking in restaurant

CARDS:

See advert on page 435

For Useful Information and Important Telephone Number Changes turn to page 25

MALTON North Yorkshire — Map 08 SE77

★★★ Burythorpe House

Burythorpe YO17 9LB

Quality Percentage Score: 71%

☎ 01653 658200 01653 658204

***Dir:** 4m S of Malton, just outside the village of Burythorpe and 4m from A64 Yprk to Scarborough*

This charming house is set in its own grounds on the edge of a village south of Malton. Bedrooms are mostly well proportioned and individually furnished. There is a comfortable lounge with a bar, and a panelled dining room.

ROOMS: 11 en suite (bth/shr) 5 annexe en suite (bth/shr) (2 fmly) s £45; d £58-£96 (incl. bkfst) * LB Off peak **MEALS:** Lunch fr £11.95 Dinner fr £18 & alc International Cuisine V meals Coffee am **FACILITIES:** CTV in all bedrooms Indoor swimming pool (heated) Tennis (hard) Snooker Sauna Solarium Gym Xmas **SERVICES:** 50P **NOTES:** No coaches No smoking in restaurant Last d 9.30pm **CARDS:**

MALTON North Yorkshire — Map 08 SE77

★★★ Green Man

15 Market St YO17 7LY

Quality Percentage Score: 61%

☎ 01653 600370 01653 696006

***Dir:** from A64 follow signs fo Malton town centre, turn left into Market St, hotel on left*

This charming hotel set in the centre of town includes an inviting reception lounge where a log fire burns in winter. There is also a choice of bars and dining options while the bedrooms are thoughtfully equipped.

ROOMS: 24 en suite (bth/shr) (4 fmly) s £35-£55; d £65-£110 (incl. bkfst) * LB Off peak **MEALS:** Lunch fr £10.50 Dinner fr £17.50 V meals Coffee am Tea pm **FACILITIES:** CTV in all bedrooms Xmas **CONF:** Thtr 40 Class 20 Board 40 Del from £55 * **SERVICES:** Night porter 40P **NOTES:** No smoking in restaurant Last d 9pm **CARDS:**

See advert on opposite page

MALTON North Yorkshire — Map 08 SE77

★★ Talbot

Yorkersgate YO17 7AJ

Quality Percentage Score: 67%

☎ 01653 694031 01653 693355

***Dir:** off A64 towards Malton. The Talbot is on the right*

This well established, ivy-clad hotel overlooks the River Derwent and open countryside and offers friendly and attentive service. The hotel has been refurbished and offers attractive and well equipped bedrooms together with traditional and comfortable public rooms.

ROOMS: 31 en suite (bth/shr) (3 fmly) s £30-£47.50; d £60-£85 (incl. bkfst) * LB Off peak **MEALS:** Lunch £7.50-£12.50 Dinner £15.95-£17.95 V meals Coffee am Tea pm **FACILITIES:** CTV in all bedrooms Xmas **CONF:** Thtr 80 Class 40 Board 40 Del from £60 * **SERVICES:** Night porter 30P **NOTES:** No dogs (ex guide dogs) No smoking in restaurant Last d 8.45pm **CARDS:**

See advert on opposite page

MALTON North Yorkshire — Map 08 SE77

★ Wentworth Arms

Town St, Old Malton YO17 7HD

Quality Percentage Score: 62%

☎ 01653 692618 01653 692618

***Dir:** turn off A64 onto A169 to Malton. Hotel 400yds on right*

This friendly inn in Old Malton, close to the bypass, has a home-like atmosphere and neatly maintained, comfortable

contd.

bedrooms. Meals can be taken either in the dining room, with its exposed stone walls and old beams, or in the bar.
ROOMS: 5 rms (4 shr) s fr £23; d fr £46 (incl. bkfst) * Off peak
MEALS: Lunch £4-£7.50 High tea fr £5 Dinner fr £7.50 Coffee am Tea pm **FACILITIES:** CTV in all bedrooms **SERVICES:** 30P **NOTES:** No dogs No coaches No children 6yrs Last d 9pm Closed 25 Dec
CARDS:

MALVERN Worcestershire **Map 03 SO74**

Courtesy & Care Award

★★★ Colwall Park
Walwyn Rd, Colwall WR13 6QG
Quality Percentage Score: 78%
☎ 01684 540206 01684 540847
Dir: *3m SW on B4218*
Colwall Park, which stands on the western side of the Malvern Hills, was purpose built to serve the local railway station. Head chef Peter Butterill and his team are earning a well deserved high reputation for their talents. The recently refurbished accommodation is well equipped, with family bedded rooms available. The team at Colwall Park hold the Courtesy and Care Award for England 1999-2000.
ROOMS: 23 en suite (bth/shr) (6 fmly) No smoking in 2 bedrooms s £64.50-£92.50; d £105-£135 (incl. bkfst) * LB Off peak
MEALS: Lunch £9.50-£12.50 Dinner fr £25 & alc Modern English Cuisine V meals Coffee am Tea pm **FACILITIES:** CTV in all bedrooms STV Croquet lawn Boule Xmas **CONF:** Thtr 120 Class 80 Board 50 Del from £100 * **SERVICES:** Night porter 40P
NOTES: No coaches No smoking in restaurant Last d 9pm
CARDS:

See advert on page 439

MALVERN Worcestershire **Map 03 SO74**

★★★ Cottage in the Wood
Holywell Rd, Malvern Wells WR14 4LG
Quality Percentage Score: 73%
☎ 01684 575859 01684 560662
Dir: *3m S of Great Malvern off A449 500yds N of B4209 turning on opposite side of road*
This delightful hotel enjoys magnificent views from its superb position on the slopes of the Malvern Hills, once the haunt of Sir Edward Elgar. The cosy bedrooms are divided between the main house, Beech Cottage and the Coach House, all well equipped with lots of thoughtful extras to ensure a pleasant stay. The

contd.

delightful public areas include real fires, deep cushioned sofas and plenty of fresh flowers.
ROOMS: 8 en suite (bth/shr) 12 annexe en suite (bth/shr) s £72-£82; d £89.50-£139 (incl. bkfst) * LB Off peak **MEALS:** Sunday Lunch £9.95-£14.95 & alc Dinner £26-£29alc V meals Coffee am Tea pm **FACILITIES:** CTV in all bedrooms Walking on Malvern hills, direct from hotel ground Xmas **CONF:** Thtr 20 Board 14 Del from £130 * **SERVICES:** 40P **NOTES:** No coaches No smoking in restaurant Last d 9pm **CARDS:**

See advert on opposite page

MALVERN Worcestershire **Map 03 SO74**

★★★ Foley Arms

14 Worcester Rd WR14 4QS
Quality Percentage Score: 68%
☎ 01684 573397 Fax 01684 569665
Dir: *M5 exit 7 north or 8 south, M50 exit 2, proceed to Great Malvern on A449*

This lovely old Georgian property occupies a prominent position in the town centre and commands excellent panoramic views of the Severn Valley. The bedrooms vary in size and style, but all have period furnishings and a good array of modern equipment. Public areas include an attractive restaurant, a popular and busy bar and a choice of comfortable lounges.
ROOMS: 28 en suite (bth/shr) (2 fmly) No smoking in 5 bedrooms s £72-£78; d £88-£98 (incl. bkfst) * LB Off peak **MEALS:** Lunch £9.25-£12.50 Dinner £19.50 English & French Cuisine V meals Coffee am Tea pm **FACILITIES:** CTV in all bedrooms STV Free use of leisure centre pool and sauna Wkly live entertainment Xmas **CONF:** Thtr 150 Class 40 Board 45 Del from £92 * **SERVICES:** 64P **NOTES:** No smoking in restaurant Last d 9.15pm **CARDS:**

See advert on opposite page

MALVERN Worcestershire **Map 03 SO74**

★★★ Abbey

Abbey Rd WR14 3ET
Quality Percentage Score: 64%
☎ 01684 892332 Fax 01684 892662
Dir: *leave M5 junct7, take A449 into Malvern, left hand turn (by Barclays bank) into Church St, turn right at traffic lighs and first right into Abbey Rd*
This large impressive hotel is in the centre of Great Malvern. It provides well equipped modern accommodation. Facilities include a good range of function rooms, the hotel is a popular venue for conferences. It is frequently used by coach tour parties in summer.
ROOMS: 105 en suite (bth/shr) (5 fmly) No smoking in 24 bedrooms s £85-£105; d £95-£115 (incl. bkfst) * LB Off peak **MEALS:** Lunch £9.50-£12.50 Dinner £16.50 V meals Coffee am Tea pm **FACILITIES:** CTV in all bedrooms Free entry to Malvern Leisure Complex toswim Xmas **CONF:** Thtr 300 Class 140 Board 70 Del from £95 * **SERVICES:** Lift Night porter 90P **NOTES:** No smoking in restaurant Last d 9pm **CARDS:**

See advert under WORCESTER

MALVERN Worcestershire **Map 03 SO74**

★★ Holdfast Cottage

Little Malvern WR13 6NA
Quality Percentage Score: 76%
☎ 01684 310288 Fax 01684 311117
Dir: *on A4104 midway between Welland and Little Malvern*
This charming cottage stands in its own extensive grounds, surrounded by farmland, on the A4104, west of Little Malvern, and has impressive views of the Malvern Hills. Accommodation is full of charm and character, with all the expected comforts. A Victorian-style bar, a lounge and dining room furnished in period are pleasant day rooms and the hotel has a well deserved reputation for its cuisine.
ROOMS: 8 en suite (bth/shr) (1 fmly) No smoking in all bedrooms s £45-£48; d £80-£90 (incl. bkfst) * LB Off peak **MEALS:** Dinner £22-£25 Coffee am Tea pm **FACILITIES:** CTV in all bedrooms Croquet lawn **CONF:** Thtr 20 Board 14 Del from £105 * **SERVICES:** 15P **NOTES:** No coaches No smoking in restaurant Last d 8.45pm Closed Xmas & 3 wks in Jan **CARDS:**

See advert on page 441

MALVERN Worcestershire **Map 03 SO74**

★★ Great Malvern

Graham Rd WR14 2HN
Quality Percentage Score: 67%
☎ 01684 563411 Fax 01684 560514
Dir: *from Worcester on A449, turn left just beyond the fire station into Graham Rd. Hotel is at the end of Graham Rd on the right*
This friendly, personally-run hotel is conveniently located in the town centre, and ideal for tourists, business people and theatre goers. The busy bar/brasserie is popular with locals. The recently refurbished and well equipped accommodation includes family rooms. Other facilities include a function/conference room. The first floor restaurant has recently been extensively refurbished to provide an additional, more formal eating option.
ROOMS: 14 rms (13 bth/shr) (3 fmly) s fr £60; d fr £85 (incl. bkfst) * LB Off peak **MEALS:** Bar Lunch £8-£14.50alc Dinner £9.50-£21alc European Cuisine V meals Coffee am Tea pm **FACILITIES:** CTV in all bedrooms **CONF:** Thtr 60 Class 20 Board 30 Del from £75 * **SERVICES:** Lift 9P **NOTES:** No dogs (ex guide dogs) No smoking in restaurant Last d 9pm Closed 24-26 Dec
CARDS:

MALVERN Worcestershire **Map 03 SO74**

★★ Mount Pleasant

Belle Vue Ter WR14 4PZ
Quality Percentage Score: 67%
☎ 01684 561837 Fax 01684 569968
Dir: *on A449, 0.5m from Great Malvern station*
A privately owned and personally run Georgian property situated in an elevated position in the town centre, with impressive views of the Severn Valley. The extensive gardens

contd. on p. 440

Cottage in the Wood, Malvern

lead directly onto the Malvern Hills. It provides well equipped accommodation, a quiet lounge for residents, a lounge bar and the pleasant Café el Sol restaurant which is used as a coffee shop during the day.

Mount Pleasant, Malvern

ROOMS: 15 rms (14 bth/shr) s £49.50-£56; d £74-£85 (incl. bkfst) * LB Off peak **MEALS:** Lunch £11.50-£13 & alc Dinner £16.75-£17.50 English & Spanish Cuisine V meals Coffee am Tea pm **FACILITIES:** CTV in all bedrooms **CONF:** Thtr 80 Class 40 Board 45 Del from £77.50 * **SERVICES:** 20P **NOTES:** No dogs (ex guide dogs) No smoking area in restaurant Last d 9.30pm Closed 25 & 26 Dec
CARDS:

See advert on opposite page

MALVERN Worcestershire **Map 03 SO74**
★★ Cotford
51 Graham Rd WR14 2HU
Quality Percentage Score: 66%
☎ 01684 572427 🖷 01684 572952
Dir: *from Worcester follow signs to Malvern on A449. Left into Graham Rd signed town centre hotel on right*
This large stone-built house, constructed in 1851, stands in spacious gardens, and is within easy reach of the town centre. Many original features such as the lovely stone mullion windows and impressive stone fireplaces remain. Well equipped accommodation includes family rooms and a bedroom on ground floor level. The hotel is popular with business people and tourists. Other facilities include a bar, a comfortable lounge and a pleasant restaurant.
ROOMS: 17 en suite (bth/shr) (4 fmly) s £45-£50; d £65-£75 (incl. bkfst) * LB Off peak **MEALS:** Lunch £10-£15 Dinner £15-£20 V meals Coffee am Tea pm **FACILITIES:** CTV in all bedrooms STV **CONF:** Thtr 26 Class 26 Del from £70 * **SERVICES:** 18P **NOTES:** No smoking in restaurant Last d 9pm **CARDS:**

MALVERN Worcestershire **Map 03 SO74**
★★ The Malvern Hills
Wynds Point WR13 6DW
Quality Percentage Score: 63%
☎ 01684 540690 🖷 01684 540327
Dir: *4m S, at junct of A449 with B4232*
To the west of Malvern and situated opposite the British camp, which was fortified and occupied by the Ancient Britons, this hotel dates back to the 19th century. It is popular with those visiting the area to admire the scenery or walk the hills, yet the well equipped accommodation is equally suitable for commercial visitors.

ROOMS: 15 en suite (bth/shr) (1 fmly) No smoking in 4 bedrooms s £40-£50; d £75-£85 (incl. bkfst) * LB Off peak **MEALS:** Lunch £12.50 & alc V meals Coffee am Tea pm **FACILITIES:** CTV in all bedrooms Pool table Wkly live entertainment Xmas **CONF:** Thtr 40 Class 40 Board 30 Del from £58.50 * **SERVICES:** 35P **NOTES:** No smoking in restaurant
CARDS:

MANCHESTER Greater Manchester **Map 07 SJ89**
see also **Manchester Airport**
★★★★ Le Meridien Victoria & Albert
Le MERIDIEN HOTELS & RESORTS
Water St M60 9EA
Quality Percentage Score: 75%
☎ 0161 832 1188 🖷 0161 834 2484
Dir: *M602 to A57 through lights on Regent Rd pass Sainsbury's then left at lights into Water St go over lights and hotel is on the left*
Created from former warehouses on the banks of the River Irwell, opposite Granada Studios. Bedrooms are named after Granada productions with pictures to match. The interior features exposed brick walls, iron pillars and wooden beams. Guests eat in Cafe Maigret, the all-day brasserie, or the more formal restaurant. Smartly uniformed, dedicated staff provide a range of services.
ROOMS: 156 en suite (bth/shr) (2 fmly) No smoking in 60 bedrooms **MEALS:** V meals Coffee am Tea pm **FACILITIES:** CTV in all bedrooms STV Snooker Sauna Solarium Gym Wkly live entertainment ch fac **CONF:** Thtr 350 Class 200 Board 16 **SERVICES:** Lift Night porter Air conditioning 120P **NOTES:** No dogs (ex guide dogs) No smoking area in restaurant Last d 10.30pm **CARDS:**

See advert on opposite page

MANCHESTER Greater Manchester **Map 07 SJ89**
★★★★ Crowne Plaza Manchester-The Midland
Peter St M60 2DS
Quality Percentage Score: 69%
☎ 0161 236 3333 🖷 0161 932 4100
Dir: *M62 towards Liverpool junct 12 to M602 City Centre. Follow Granada Studios signs and turn left into Water St past studios hotels on right*
An elegant Edwardian building which has kept its original grandeur but introduced modern standards of comfort. Mr Rolls first met Mr Royce here, and the rest is history. Spacious public rooms include the Terrace Lounge, the Trafford Room buffet and

contd. on p. 442

THE PALACE HOTEL MANCHESTER

AA ★★★★ AA

This famous terracotta building is one of the most distinctive and luxurious hotels in Manchester. It provides a haven of quiet calm and tranquility in sharp contrast to the bustling city of Manchester.

Bygone Breakaways

Enjoy a luxury break inclusive of dinner, bed and full English breakfast and complimentary admission to some of Manchester's famous attractions. **From £60.00 per person per night**, minimum 2 night stay.

Conferences and Meetings

The Palace has a new Business and Secretarial Centre with a choice of 12 conference rooms, seven of which are air cooled, plus the magnificent Ballroom which can cater for up to 1,000 delegates.

Oxford Street mainline railway station is opposite the hotel.

The Palace Hotel,
Oxford Street, Manchester. M60 7HA
Tel: 0161 288 1111 Fax: 0161 288 2222

Quality wins

A PRINCIPAL HOTEL

Holdfast Cottage Hotel and Restaurant

Marlbank Road, Little Malvern WR13 6NA
Tel: (01684) 310288 Fax: (01684) 311117
Email: Holdcothot@Aol.com

• A wonderfully warm and relaxing Country House Hotel tucked into the foot of the Malvern Hills • Personal care and service is reflected in everything from the imaginative Dinner Menu which includes home-made Rolls, Ice Creams and Chocolates to the personal touches in the individual pretty en-suite bedrooms • The hotel is family owned and run and offers true hospitality and an ideal centre to discover Elgar's heartland • Away Breaks available all week, all year • Children and Pets welcome •

M

Le MERIDIEN

VICTORIA & ALBERT

The luxurious, four star deluxe, Le Meridien Victoria and Albert Manchester stands on the banks of the River Irwell. This beautiful listed building with its mellowed brickwork and exposed beams creates a country house atmosphere in the city centre.

For the very best in accommodation, food and service visit this wonderful hotel. All 156 bedrooms are lavishly and lovingly appointed with the many features one would expect from Manchester's premier hotel.

The superb Sherlock Holmes Restaurant is a fine dining restaurant with two AA rosettes and the menu is filled with unusual delights to tempt your pallet.

Cafe Maigret is a warm and welcoming French Brasserie with a varied reasonably priced menu to entice you.

So whether it is business or pleasure the only place in Manchester to visit is Le Meridien Victoria and Albert. We look forward to seeing you soon.

Hotel of the Year 1996 – Cheshire Life
Best New Hotel in the World 1995 – Executive Travel Readers

MANCHESTER
Water Street, Manchester M3 4JQ
Tel: 0161 832 1188 Fax: 0161 834 2482

Experience friendly hospitality and relaxation at the

Mount Pleasant Hotel ★★

Great Malvern, Worcs
Tel: 01684 561837 Fax: 01684 569968

Set in attractive gardens this early Georgian hotel is close to the town centre with splendid views overlooking the Priory Church and Severn Valley. It is ideally situated close to the theatre, shops and the Winter Gardens with its leisure pool, and yet has direct access to the Malvern Hills through the 99 steps. The Hotel is owned and run by the proprietors in an efficient and friendly manner for both tourists and travelling business people with an emphasis on personal attention, comfort and good food.

Special Breaks on offer all year
Fully licensed with private car park
Conference and function facilities

carvery, and a good French restaurant with formal service. Bedrooms vary in style but are all well equipped.
ROOMS: 303 en suite (bth/shr) (62 fmly) No smoking in 180 bedrooms d £145-£155 * LB Off peak **MEALS:** Lunch £14.95-£16.95 & alc High tea £19.95-£22.95alc Dinner £19.95-£22.95 & alc English & French Cuisine V meals Coffee am Tea pm **FACILITIES:** CTV in all bedrooms STV Indoor swimming pool (heated) Squash Sauna Solarium Gym Jacuzzi/spa Hairdressing Beauty salon Wkly live entertainment Xmas **CONF:** Thtr 500 Class 360 Board 40 Del from £120 * **SERVICES:** Lift Night porter Air conditioning **NOTES:** No smoking area in restaurant Last d 10.30pm **CARDS:**

MANCHESTER Greater Manchester — Map 07 SJ89
★★★★ Palace
Oxford St M60 7HA
Quality Percentage Score: 69%
☎ 0161 288 1111 Fax 0161 288 2222
A striking and unique Victorian building, once the headquarters of the Refuge Assurance Company. The brass and marble staircase, ornately tiled pillars and the overall spaciousness of the public areas reflect the grandeur of the age. Some bedrooms and suites follow the Victorian theme, and all are comfortable and nicely furnished.
ROOMS: 252 en suite (bth/shr) (59 fmly) No smoking in 30 bedrooms s £139-£279; d £155-£279 * LB Off peak **MEALS:** Lunch £12.50-£14.95 High tea £5.50 Dinner £17.95 English & Continental Cuisine V meals Coffee am Tea pm **FACILITIES:** CTV in all bedrooms STV Wkly live entertainment **CONF:** Thtr 1000 Class 450 Board 100 Del £170 * **SERVICES:** Lift Night porter **NOTES:** No dogs (ex guide dogs) No smoking in restaurant Last d 10pm
CARDS:

See advert on page 441

MANCHESTER Greater Manchester — Map 07 SJ89
★★★★ Marriott Manchester Hotel & Country Club
Worsley Park, Worsley M28 2QT
Quality Percentage Score: 67%
☎ 0161 975 2000 Fax 0161 799 6341
Dir: *leave junct 13 M60, go straight on at 1st rdbt take A575 hotel 400yds on left*

This newly opened hotel was developed from an old farm and offers modern, attractively furnished accommodation while preserving some interesting original features. There are extensive indoor leisure facilities.
ROOMS: 159 en suite (bth/shr) (5 fmly) No smoking in 116 bedrooms d £85-£125 * LB Off peak **MEALS:** Lunch £12 & alc Dinner £18-£23 & alc International Cuisine V meals Coffee am Tea pm **FACILITIES:** CTV in all bedrooms STV Indoor swimming pool (heated) Golf 18 Sauna Solarium Gym Putting green Jacuzzi/spa Steam room Health & Beauty salon Tennis court for summer 1999 Xmas **CONF:** Thtr 200 Class 150 Board 100 Del from £130 * **SERVICES:** Lift Night porter 400P **NOTES:** No dogs (ex guide dogs) No smoking area in restaurant Last d 10pm **CARDS:**

MANCHESTER Greater Manchester — Map 07 SJ89
★★★★ Copthorne Manchester
Clippers Quay, Salford Quays M5 2XP
Quality Percentage Score: 65%
☎ 0161 873 7321 Fax 0161 873 7318
Dir: *from M602 follow signs for Salford Quays/Trafford Park (A5063)-Trafford Road, hotel is 3/4 mile along road on right*
Situated within the re-developed Salford Quays, this hotel offers a high standard of accommodation, including the more luxurious Connoisseur rooms overlooking the quay. Fine dining can be had in the more formal Chandlers restaurant, whilst a range of freshly prepared dishes is offered in Clippers. Breakfast is also served in Clippers and includes a fine selection of fruits and cold meats. Extensive conference and banqueting suites, as well as a small leisure club, completes the package.
ROOMS: 166 en suite (bth/shr) (6 fmly) No smoking in 63 bedrooms s £145-£170; d £165-£190 * LB Off peak **MEALS:** Lunch £13-£21 & alc Dinner £13-£21 & alc International Cuisine V meals Coffee am Tea pm **FACILITIES:** CTV in all bedrooms STV Indoor swimming pool (heated) Sauna Gym Jacuzzi/spa Steam room **CONF:** Thtr 150 Class 70 Board 70 Del from £95 * **SERVICES:** Lift Night porter 120P **NOTES:** No dogs (ex guide dogs) No smoking area in restaurant Last d 10.15pm
CARDS:

MANCHESTER Greater Manchester — Map 07 SJ89
★★★ Malmaison
Gore St, Piccadilly M1 3AQ
Quality Percentage Score: 74%
☎ 0161 278 1000 Fax 0161 278 1002
Dir: *follow signs for city centre then for railway station, hotel opposite station*
Epitomising the chic and refreshing style of the Malmaison brand, the Manchester hotel is now in its second year. The smart bedrooms are a strength of this brand, and all have such desirable extras as CD players and air-conditioning. The bar, bright lounge, and French-style brasserie are all well worth a visit.
ROOMS: 112 en suite (bth/shr) d £99 * Off peak **MEALS:** Lunch £12.50-£18.50 & alc Dinner £18.50-£21.50 & alc V meals Coffee am Tea pm **FACILITIES:** CTV in all bedrooms STV Sauna Solarium Gym Jacuzzi/spa **CONF:** Thtr 40 Class 32 Board 25 Del from £150 * **SERVICES:** Lift Night porter Air conditioning **NOTES:** No coaches Last d 11pm **CARDS:**

MANCHESTER Greater Manchester — Map 07 SJ89
★★★ Old Rectory Hotel
Meadow Ln, Haughton Green, Denton M34 7GD
Quality Percentage Score: 67%
☎ 0161 336 7516 Fax 0161 320 3212
This former Victorian rectory enjoys the twin advantages of a peaceful location and easy access to the centre of town and to Manchester Airport. Bedrooms offer a high standard of modern comfort, and staff provide helpful service. The attractively

contd.

appointed restaurant has a good local reputation and the hotel has good meeting facilities and a small garden.
ROOMS: 30 en suite (bth/shr) 6 annexe en suite (bth/shr) (1 fmly) No smoking in 3 bedrooms s £69-£79; d £79-£89 (incl. bkfst) * LB Off peak **MEALS:** Lunch £8.95-£11.95 & alc Dinner £16.95 & alc English & Mediterranean Cuisine V meals Coffee am Tea pm **FACILITIES:** CTV in all bedrooms STV Pool table Games room Xmas **CONF:** Thtr 100 Class 45 Board 50 Del from £100 * **SERVICES:** Night porter 50P **NOTES:** No smoking in restaurant Last d 9.30pm
CARDS:

MANCHESTER Greater Manchester **Map 07 SJ89**
★★★ Novotel
Worsley Brow M28 4YA
Quality Percentage Score: 66%
☎ 0161 799 3535 0161 703 8207
(For full entry see Worsley)

MANCHESTER Greater Manchester **Map 07 SJ89**
★★★ Posthouse Manchester
Palatine Rd, Northenden M22 4FH
Quality Percentage Score: 64%
☎ 0161 998 7090 0161 946 0139
Dir: *at end of M56 follow B5166 Northenden right at lights Posthouse on left*
A modern hotel conveniently situated for both the city and the International Airport, offering a range of services including an all day lounge menu and 24 hour room service. 'Seasons' restaurant provides traditional British and international dishes, and is open for lunch and dinner. Bedrooms have every modern facility and many enjoy panoramic views over the city and the hills beyond. There is a secure car park with many spaces under cover and transport to the airport can also be arranged.
ROOMS: 190 en suite (bth/shr) (5 fmly) No smoking in 67 bedrooms **MEALS:** Lunch £5.95-£12.95alc Dinner £10 & alc International Cuisine V meals Coffee am Tea pm **FACILITIES:** CTV in all bedrooms Free admittance to local Leisure Centre **CONF:** Thtr 120 Class 60 Board 80 Del from £99 * **SERVICES:** Lift Night porter 370P **NOTES:** Last d 10pm Closed 22 Dec-5 Jan **CARDS:**

MANCHESTER Greater Manchester **Map 07 SJ89**
★★★ Waterside
Wilmslow Rd, Didsbury M20 5WZ
Quality Percentage Score: 64%
☎ 0161 445 0225 0161 446 2090
Dir: *M60 junct 3, A34 Disbury, at 3rd set of lights turn left, then left again on B5095 towards Cheadle. Hotel 2nd turning on right*
Conveniently situated for both the motorway network and the city centre, this modern hotel has a really well equipped leisure centre. The brasserie and adjacent café bar, overlooking the river, offer a wide choice of meals and snacks.
ROOMS: 46 en suite (bth/shr) (1 fmly) No smoking in 18 bedrooms s £75-£80; d £94-£104 * Off peak **MEALS:** Sunday Lunch £10.95-£12.50 Dinner fr £18 & alc V meals Coffee am Tea pm **FACILITIES:** CTV in all bedrooms STV Indoor swimming pool (heated) Tennis (hard) Sauna Solarium Gym Jacuzzi/spa Beauty salon Wkly live entertainment Xmas **CONF:** Thtr 160 Class 90 Board 56 Del from £125 * **SERVICES:** Night porter 250P **NOTES:** No dogs (ex guide dogs) No smoking area in restaurant Last d 9.45pm **CARDS:**

MANCHESTER Greater Manchester **Map 07 SJ89**
★★★ Trafford Hall
23 Talbot Rd, Old Trafford M16 0PE
Quality Percentage Score: 60%
☎ 0161 848 7791 0161 848 0219
Dir: *600yds from Old Trafford Cricket Ground towards City Centre*
A Victorian building which retains some original features, including a splendid central staircase. It is conveniently located for the city and Old Trafford. Spacious bedrooms are well equipped, with a number of them being suitable for families.
ROOMS: 31 en suite (bth/shr) 3 annexe en suite (bth/shr) (7 fmly) s £39.50-£48.50; d £49.50-£66.50 (incl. bkfst) * LB Off peak **MEALS:** English and Continental Cuisine V meals Coffee am Tea pm **FACILITIES:** CTV in all bedrooms STV Pool table **CONF:** Thtr 30 Class 10 Board 20 **SERVICES:** Night porter 60P **NOTES:** No dogs (ex guide dogs) Last d 9.45pm **CARDS:**

MANCHESTER Greater Manchester **Map 07 SJ89**
★★ *Crescent Gate*
Park Crescent, Victoria Park, Rusholme M14 5RE
Quality Percentage Score: 67%
☎ 0161 224 0672 0161 257 2822
Dir: *off B5117*

Situated in a quiet residential area, this friendly hotel gives easy access to the centre and the airport. Bedrooms are attractively
contd.

furnished and offer a good standard of comfort. There is a cosy bar and a comfortable lounge.
ROOMS: 14 rms (9 bth/shr) 11 annexe en suite (bth/shr) (1 fmly) **MEALS:** V meals Coffee am Tea pm **FACILITIES:** CTV in all bedrooms STV **SERVICES:** 18P **NOTES:** No coaches Last d 8pm Closed Xmas **CARDS:**

See advert on page 443

MANCHESTER Greater Manchester **Map 07 SJ89**
★★ Albany
21 Albany Rd, Chorlton-c-Hardy M21 0AY
Quality Percentage Score: 65%
☎ 0161 881 6774 🖹 0161 862 9405
Dir: *turn off A5103 onto A5143 follow for approx 1m turn right at Safeways store into Albany Road, hotel 100mtrs on left*

This suburban hotel has a good reputation for its friendly welcome. Bedrooms are very well equipped, including those in a nearby building. Day rooms consist of a cosy lounge, with a small bar and an attractive dining room.
ROOMS: 2 en suite (bth/shr) 13 annexe en suite (bth/shr) (4 fmly) s £49.50-£79.50; d £59.50-£89.50 (incl. bkfst) * Off peak **MEALS:** Lunch £13.95 High tea £6.95-£8.95 Dinner £15.95 V meals Coffee am Tea pm **FACILITIES:** CTV in all bedrooms Pool table **CONF:** Thtr 40 Class 20 Board 25 Del from £46.50 * **SERVICES:** 5P **NOTES:** No coaches No smoking area in restaurant Last d 9.30pm RS 25 Dec-2 Jan **CARDS:**

MANCHESTER Greater Manchester **Map 07 SJ89**
★★ *Elm Grange*
Wilmslow Rd, Withington M20 4GJ
Quality Percentage Score: 65%
☎ 0161 445 3336 🖹 0161 445 3336
Dir: *4m from city centre on B5093, 0.5m from Didsbury opposite Christie Hospital*
This family owned and run hotel is situated in a pleasant residential area and has been attractively furnished throughout. Bedrooms are modern and public areas inviting.
ROOMS: 31 rms (16 bth/shr) (1 fmly) No smoking in 12 bedrooms **MEALS:** English & French Cuisine V meals Coffee am **FACILITIES:** CTV in all bedrooms **SERVICES:** 42P **NOTES:** No dogs No smoking in restaurant Last d 9pm Closed 23 Dec-4 Jan **CARDS:**

MANCHESTER Greater Manchester **Map 07 SJ89**
★★ Comfort Friendly Inn
Hyde Rd, Birch St, West Gorton M12 5NT
Quality Percentage Score: 64%
☎ 0161 220 8700 🖹 0161 220 8848
Dir: *3m SE on A57*
A feature of this hotel, 3 miles from the city centre, is the attentive attitude of staff and the friendly atmosphere. Bedrooms are functional and unfussy, with every modern facility. Public areas, although not extensive, include a lounge bar and attractive restaurant serving good value meals.
ROOMS: 90 en suite (bth/shr) (5 fmly) No smoking in 45 bedrooms d fr £46.75 * LB Off peak **MEALS:** Lunch £2.95-£15.95alc Dinner fr £10.75 & alc English & Continental Cuisine V meals Coffee am Tea pm **FACILITIES:** CTV in all bedrooms STV Gym Xmas **CONF:** Thtr 100 Class 50 Board 50 **SERVICES:** Night porter 70P **NOTES:** No smoking in restaurant Last d 9.30pm **CARDS:**

MANCHESTER Greater Manchester **Map 07 SJ89**
★★ *Royals*
Altrincham Rd M22 4BJ
Quality Percentage Score: 63%
☎ 0161 998 9011 🖹 0161 998 4641
Dir: *on A560 towards Wythenshawe*
Conveniently situated for both the city and motorway network, this hotel also offers parking for guests using Manchester International airport. Refurbished bedrooms are attractive, and the conservatory restaurant offers informal dining, attracting local residents and families as well as visitors. A children's play area has been created on the lower ground floor, and function facilities are also available.
ROOMS: 32 en suite (bth/shr) (6 fmly) No smoking in 6 bedrooms **MEALS:** International Cuisine V meals Coffee am Tea pm **FACILITIES:** CTV in all bedrooms Childrens dungeons and dragons play centre Wkly live entertainment **CONF:** Thtr 100 Class 50 Board 40 Del from £75 * **SERVICES:** Night porter 150P **NOTES:** No dogs (ex guide dogs) No coaches No smoking area in restaurant Last d 9.30pm **CARDS:**

MANCHESTER Greater Manchester **Map 07 SJ89**
★★ Willow Bank
340-342 Wilmslow Rd, Fallowfield M14 6AF
Quality Percentage Score: 63%
☎ 0161 224 0461 🖹 0161 257 2561
Dir: *on B5093*
This privately owned hotel is situated just three miles from the city centre and has plenty of car parking space. Traditionally furnished bedrooms vary in size and style - those in the original part of the building tend to be larger. The popular restaurant offers a range of carefully prepared dishes.
ROOMS: 116 en suite (bth/shr) (4 fmly) s £40-£52; d £62-£66 * LB Off peak **MEALS:** Lunch £7 & alc Dinner £6.50-£12 & alc English & Continental Cuisine V meals Coffee am Tea pm **FACILITIES:** CTV in all bedrooms Wkly live entertainment Xmas **CONF:** Thtr 50 Class 28 Board 28 Del from £45 * **SERVICES:** Night porter 100P **NOTES:** No dogs (ex guide dogs) No smoking area in restaurant Last d 10pm **CARDS:**

MANCHESTER Greater Manchester **Map 07 SJ89**
★★ Montana
59 Palatine Rd, Withington M20 3LJ
Quality Percentage Score: 58%
☎ 0161 445 6427 🖹 0161 448 9458
Dir: *near Christies Hospital*
There is a welcoming atmosphere at this family run hotel, just 10 minutes drive from the city centre. Bedrooms offer good value accommodation, and enjoyable freshly prepared meals are served.
ROOMS: 21 rms (17 bth/shr) 3 annexe en suite (bth) (2 fmly) No smoking in 10 bedrooms s £28-£30; d £48-£50 (incl. bkfst) * LB Off peak **MEALS:** Dinner £7.50-£10 Continental Cuisine Coffee am **FACILITIES:** CTV in 21 bedrooms STV Wkly live entertainment **CONF:** Class 50 Board 30 **SERVICES:** 40P **NOTES:** No smoking in restaurant Last d 8pm **CARDS:**

MANCHESTER Greater Manchester **Map 07 SJ89**
Campanile
55 Ordsall Ln, Salford M5 4RS
0161 833 1845 0161 833 1847
Dir: *take M602 towards Manchester, then A57, after large rdbt Sainsbury's on left turn left at next traffic lights, hotel on right*

This modern building offers accommodation in smart well equipped bedrooms, all with en-suite bathrooms. Refreshments may be taken at the informal Bistro. For details about current prices, consult the Contents Page under Hotel Groups for the Campanile phone number.
ROOMS: 105 en suite (bth/shr) **CONF:** Thtr 50 Class 40 Board 30

MANCHESTER Greater Manchester **Map 07 SJ89**
Travel Inn
Wilderspool Wood, Trafford Centre,
Urmston M17 8WW
0161 747 8850 0161 747 4763
Dir: *at junct 10 of the M60 on W side of Manchester*
This modern building offers accommodation in smart, spacious and well equipped bedrooms, all with en-suite bathrooms. Refreshments may be taken at the nearby family restaurant. For details about current prices consult the Contents Page under Hotel Groups for the Travel Inn phone number.
ROOMS: 60 en suite (bth/shr) d £39.95 *

MANCHESTER Greater Manchester **Map 07 SJ89**
Travel Inn (Heaton Park)
Middleton Rd, Crumpsall M8 6NB
0870 242 8000
This modern building offers accommodation in smart, spacious and well equipped bedrooms, all with en-suite bathrooms. Refreshments may be taken at the nearby family restaurant. For details about current prices consult the Contents Page under Hotel Groups for the Travel Inn phone number.
ROOMS: 45 en suite (bth/shr) d £39.95 *

MANCHESTER Greater Manchester **Map 07 SJ89**
Travel Inn Manchester (Denton)
Manchester Rd, Denton M34 3SH
0161 320 1116 0161 320 1098
Dir: *at junc M67/M60 in Denton*
This modern building offers accommodation in smart, spacious and well equipped bedrooms, all with en-suite bathrooms. Refreshments may be taken at the nearby family restaurant. For details about current prices consult the Contents Page under Hotel Groups for the Travel Inn phone number.
ROOMS: 40 en suite (bth/shr) d £39.95 *

MANCHESTER Greater Manchester **Map 07 SJ89**
Travelodge
Townbury House, Blackfriars St
0800 850950 A3
This modern building offers accommodation in smart, spacious and well equipped bedrooms, all with en-suite bathrooms. Refreshments may be taken at the nearby family restaurant. For details about current prices, consult the Contents Page under Hotel Groups for the Travelodge phone number.
d £49.95 *

MANCHESTER Greater Manchester **Map 07 SJ89**
Thistle Manchester
3/5 Portland St, Piccadilly Gardens M1 6DP
0161 228 3400 0161 228 6347
Dir: *in city centre, overlooking Piccadilly Gardens*
Situated in the city centre, overlooking Piccadilly Gardens, this hotel offers comfortable public areas, including Winston's restaurant, where diners can choose from the brasserie menu or the full carte. Mr Manchester's Bar opens during the day to serve light meals to shoppers and office workers. Bedroom refurbishment continues and, although compact in some cases, they are nicely decorated and furnished.
ROOMS: 205 en suite (bth/shr) (6 fmly) No smoking in 108 bedrooms **MEALS:** International/Modern English Cuisine V meals Coffee am Tea pm **FACILITIES:** CTV in all bedrooms STV Indoor swimming pool (heated) Sauna Solarium Gym Jacuzzi/spa **CONF:** Thtr 300 Class 120 Board 40 **SERVICES:** Lift Night porter Air conditioning 80P **NOTES:** No smoking area in restaurant Last d 9.45pm **CARDS:**

MANCHESTER AIRPORT Greater Manchester **Map 07 SJ88**
see also **Altrincham**
★★★★ **Belfry**
Stanley Rd SK9 3LD
Quality Percentage Score: 63%
0161 437 0511 0161 499 0597
Dir: *off A34, approx 4m S of junct 3 M60*
Situated in Handforth, the Belfry House Hotel is convenient for the Cheshire countryside and Manchester Airport. Inside, the cocktail bar and restaurant both have a welcoming ambience. Accommodation is provided in traditionally furnished bedrooms with several suites and executive rooms available. Other features include a number of function rooms and a nearby health and fitness centre.
ROOMS: 80 en suite (bth/shr) (2 fmly) No smoking in 40 bedrooms s £79-£89; d £90-£99 LB Off peak **MEALS:** Lunch £17.50-£20.50 High tea £5-£7.50 Dinner £19.50-£20.50 International Cuisine V meals Coffee am Tea pm **FACILITIES:** CTV in all bedrooms STV Wkly live entertainment Xmas **CONF:** Thtr 120 Class 70 Board 50 Del from £120 * **SERVICES:** Lift Night porter 150P **NOTES:** No dogs (ex guide dogs) Last d 10pm **CARDS:**

MANCHESTER AIRPORT Greater Manchester **Map 07 SJ88**
★★★ **Etrop Grange**
Thorley Ln M90 4EG
Quality Percentage Score: 70%
0161 499 0500 0161 499 0790
Dir: *M56 junct 5 follow signs for terminal 2, go up slip rd to rdbt take 1st exit, take immediate left, hotel is 400yds ahead*
This Georgian mansion has recently been extended, but retains the aura of a stylish country house and although it is near the

contd.

airport, noise is minimal. Bedrooms are particularly well appointed and have every modern facility. Some rooms have four-poster beds, and two have separate sitting rooms. Public rooms are also comfortably furnished and the Coach House Restaurant provides a high standard of cuisine. A chauffeured limousine is available for airport passengers.

Etrop Grange, Manchester Airport

ROOMS: 64 en suite (bth/shr) No smoking in 10 bedrooms s £70-£115; d £90-£135 * LB Off peak **MEALS:** Lunch £12.95-£16.50 Dinner £23.50-£32.50 English & French Cuisine V meals Coffee am Tea pm **FACILITIES:** CTV in all bedrooms STV Wkly live entertainment **CONF:** Thtr 80 Class 30 Board 36 Del from £105 * **SERVICES:** Night porter 80P **NOTES:** No coaches No smoking in restaurant Last d 10pm **CARDS:**

See advert on opposite page

M

MANCHESTER AIRPORT Greater Manchester **Map 07 SJ88**
★★★ *Manchester Airport Moat House*
Altrincham Rd SK9 4LR
Quality Percentage Score: 67%
☎ 01625 889988 🖷 01625 531876

MOAT HOUSE

Dir: *take A538, follow road for approximtely 1m, the hotel is on the left*

This hotel is conveniently situated for Manchester Airport and the M6 motorway. Bedrooms are modern and well equipped and public areas are spacious and comfortable. Other useful amenities are the leisure centre and long-term parking.

ROOMS: 126 en suite (bth/shr) (23 fmly) No smoking in 44 bedrooms **MEALS:** International Cuisine V meals Coffee am Tea pm **FACILITIES:** CTV in all bedrooms Indoor swimming pool (heated) Squash Sauna Solarium Gym Jacuzzi/spa Steam room Beauty therapy **CONF:** Thtr 300 Class 150 Board 100 **SERVICES:** Lift Night porter 400P **NOTES:** Last d 9.45pm **CARDS:**

MANCHESTER AIRPORT Greater Manchester **Map 07 SJ88**
★★★ Posthouse Manchester Airport
Ringway Rd, Wythenshawe M90 3NS
Quality Percentage Score: 66%
☎ 0161 437 5811 🖷 0161 436 2340

Posthouse

A large modern hotel set within the airport complex with facilities including a leisure club and numerous conference and meeting rooms. Bedrooms have every modern facility and include several in a new millennium design and others in traditional Posthouse style. Services include an all day lounge menu and 24 hour room service. Transport is also provided to the various airport terminals. Gazingi's Brasserie offers a varied menu ranging from simple snacks to traditional British and international dishes and there is also an Expresso Lounge open during the day. Ample car parking facilities are avaiable.

ROOMS: 290 en suite (bth/shr) (6 fmly) No smoking in 80 bedrooms d £79-£109 * LB Off peak **MEALS:** International Cuisine V meals Coffee am Tea pm **FACILITIES:** CTV in all bedrooms STV Indoor swimming pool (heated) Sauna Solarium Gym Health & fitness centre **CONF:** Thtr 80 Class 26 Board 30 Del from £120 * **SERVICES:** Lift Night porter Air conditioning 290P **NOTES:** No smoking area in restaurant Last d 10pm **CARDS:**

MANCHESTER AIRPORT Greater Manchester **Map 07 SJ88**
★★★ Swallow Four Seasons
Hale Rd, Hale Barns WA15 8XW
Quality Percentage Score: 66%
☎ 0161 904 0301 🖷 0161 980 1787

SWALLOW HOTELS

A modern hotel at junction 6 of the M56, the Swallow Four Seasons is five minutes from Manchester Airport and operates a courtesy coach service on a 24-hour basis. Many of the bedrooms, which include executive rooms and luxury suites, are situated around courtyard gardens and are reached by covered verandas. Other features include an elegant restaurant, a bar, business and meeting facilities, and extensive car parking.

ROOMS: 147 en suite (bth/shr) (16 fmly) No smoking in 21 bedrooms s £50-£119.50; d £50-£129.50 * LB Off peak **MEALS:** Lunch £15.95-£20.95 & alc Dinner £20.95 & alc French Cuisine V meals Coffee am **FACILITIES:** CTV in all bedrooms Sauna Solarium Gym Jacuzzi/spa Indoor swimming pool ready for Dec 1999 **CONF:** Thtr 120 Class 80 Board 45 Del from £125 * **SERVICES:** Lift Night porter 401P **NOTES:** No dogs (ex guide dogs) No smoking area in restaurant Last d 10.30pm **CARDS:**

MANCHESTER AIRPORT Greater Manchester **Map 07 SJ88**
⌂ Travel Inn
Finney Ln, Heald Green SK8 2QH
☎ 0161 499 1944 🖷 0161 437 4910

travel inn

Dir: *from M56 junct 5 follow signs to Terminal 1, At rdbt take 2nd exit. At traffic lights turn left, then right at next lights*

This modern building offers accommodation in smart, spacious and well equipped bedrooms, all with en-suite bathrooms. Refreshments may be taken at the nearby family restaurant. For details about current prices consult the Contents Page under Hotel Groups for the Travel Inn phone number.

ROOMS: 60 en suite (bth/shr) d £39.95 *

MANCHESTER AIRPORT Greater Manchester **Map 07 SJ88**
Thistle Manchester Airport
180 Wilmslow Rd, Handforth SK9 3LG
☎ 01625 529211 🖷 01625 536812

THISTLE HOTELS

Dir: *3m from junct 5 of M56 turn off A34 onto B5358 towards Wilmslow. Hotel on left before Handforth Station*

This modern hotel is conveniently situated for Manchester and

contd.

The AA Hotel Booking Service is a free benefit to AA members. See the advertisement on page 47

the airport. Bedrooms are most attractively furnished. Service is friendly, particularly in the restaurant, which opens onto the gardens. There is a wide range of meeting and function suites.
ROOMS: 58 en suite (bth/shr) (3 fmly) No smoking in 20 bedrooms **MEALS:** International Cuisine V meals Coffee am Tea pm **FACILITIES:** CTV in all bedrooms STV **CONF:** Thtr 200 Class 100 Board 60 **SERVICES:** Lift Night porter 100P **NOTES:** No dogs (ex guide dogs) Last d 9.45pm **CARDS:**

MANSFIELD Nottinghamshire — Map 08 SK56

★★ Pine Lodge

281-283 Nottingham Rd NG18 4SE
Quality Percentage Score: 66%
☎ 01623 622308 🖹 01623 656819
Dir: *on A60 Nottingham to Mansfield road*

Located on the edge of town, this owner-managed small hotel offers a welcoming and personal service to its many repeat guests. Ground floor public rooms include a comfortable lounge bar, a small restaurant and a choice of meeting and function rooms. Bedrooms are attractively furnished and well equipped. There is also a sauna available for guest use.
ROOMS: 20 en suite (bth/shr) (2 fmly) s £35-£55; d £50-£65 (incl. bkfst) * LB Off peak **MEALS:** Dinner £12.95 & alc English & Italian Cuisine V meals Coffee am Tea pm **FACILITIES:** CTV in all bedrooms STV Sauna **CONF:** Thtr 50 Class 30 Board 35 Del from £55 * **SERVICES:** Night porter 40P **NOTES:** No dogs No coaches No smoking in restaurant Last d 9pm Closed 25-26 Dec
CARDS:

MANSFIELD Nottinghamshire — Map 08 SK56

★★ Portland Hall

Carr Bank Park, Windmill Ln NG18 2AL
Quality Percentage Score: 63%
☎ 01623 452525 Fax 01623 452550

Dir: *from town centre take A60 towards Worksop for 100yds then right at Pelican Crossing into Nursery Street - Carr Bank Park 50yds on right*

Portland Hall, a former Georgian mansion, sits in 15 acres of parkland. The house retains some fine examples of its past, with original plasterwork and friezes in the cosy lounge bar, and around the magnificent domed skylight over the spiral stairs. There is an attractive restaurant in which carvery and carte menus offer a flexible choice to diners.

ROOMS: 11 en suite (bth/shr) (1 fmly) No smoking in 7 bedrooms s £40-£50; d £50-£60 (incl. bkfst) * LB Off peak **MEALS:** Lunch £3.50-£8.50 High tea £5 Dinner £8.50-£9.95 V meals Coffee am Tea pm **FACILITIES:** CTV in all bedrooms Wkly live entertainment Xmas **CONF:** Thtr 60 Class 60 Board 30 Del from £46 * **SERVICES:** 150P **NOTES:** No smoking in restaurant Last d 8.30pm
CARDS:

MARAZION Cornwall & Isles of Scilly — Map 02 SW53

★★ Mount Haven

Turnpike Rd TR17 0DQ
Quality Percentage Score: 72%
☎ 01736 710249 Fax 01736 711658

Dir: *from A30 follow signs for 'Marazion' and 'St Michael's Mount'. Continue through village to hotel on right*

A former coaching inn set on the outskirts of Marazion. Bedrooms are bright and cheerful with modern facilities, those at the front enjoying the views over Mount's Bay to St. Michael's Mount. The split-level restaurant offers guests both a fixed-price menu and a short carte, using fresh local produce.

ROOMS: 17 en suite (bth/shr) (5 fmly) s £39-£59; d £75-£85 (incl. bkfst) * LB Off peak **MEALS:** Sunday Lunch fr £9.50 Dinner fr £19.75 & alc V meals Coffee am Tea pm **FACILITIES:** CTV in all bedrooms **SERVICES:** 30P **NOTES:** No coaches No smoking in restaurant Last d 9pm Closed 20 Dec-Jan RS Oct-May
CARDS:

See advert under PENZANCE

MARCH Cambridgeshire — Map 05 TL49

★★ Olde Griffin

High St PE15 9JS
Quality Percentage Score: 64%
☎ 01354 652517 Fax 01354 650086

Dir: *March is on A141/142 north of Ely Cambs and off A47 east of Peterborough towards Norwich*

On the town square, this former coaching inn dates back to the 16th century, and is popular for its good value food and accommodation. The pleasing bedrooms vary in style and size but are all fully equipped with creature comforts. The public rooms offer a choice of eating and drinking areas; meals are available in the lounge or bar areas, and there is a restaurant for more formal dining.

ROOMS: 20 rms (19 bth/shr) (1 fmly) s fr £38.50; d fr £55 (incl. bkfst) * LB Off peak **MEALS:** Sunday Lunch fr £10.95 High tea fr £1.20 Dinner fr £10alc International Cuisine V meals Coffee am Tea pm **FACILITIES:** CTV in all bedrooms **CONF:** Thtr 100 Class 50 Board 36 Del from £62.45 * **SERVICES:** 50P **NOTES:** No dogs (ex guide dogs) No smoking area in restaurant Last d 9.30pm
CARDS:

MARGATE Kent — Map 05 TR37

Travel Inn

Station Green, Marine Ter
☎ 01843 299280 Fax 01843 221453

This modern building offers accommodation in smart, spacious and well equipped bedrooms, all with en-suite bathrooms. Refreshments may be taken at the nearby family restaurant. For details about current prices consult the Contents Page under Hotel Groups for the Travel Inn phone number.

ROOMS: 44 en suite (bth/shr) d £39.95 *

MARKET DRAYTON Shropshire — Map 07 SJ63

★★★ Goldstone Hall

Goldstone TF9 2NA
Quality Percentage Score: 72%
☎ 01630 661202 & 661487 Fax 01630 661585

Dir: *4m S of Market Drayton off A529 signposted Goldstone Hall Gardens. 4m N of Newport signed off A41*

Situated in extensive grounds, this charming old house is now a family run hotel. It provides traditionally furnished, but well equipped accommodation. Public rooms provide a choice of lounges, a snooker room and a conservatory. The hotel has a well deserved reputation for its food.

ROOMS: 8 en suite (bth/shr) s fr £65; d £87.50-£100 (incl. bkfst) * LB Off peak **MEALS:** Lunch £5-£15 & alc Dinner fr £25alc V meals Coffee am Tea pm **FACILITIES:** CTV in all bedrooms Fishing Snooker **CONF:** Thtr 50 Board 30 **SERVICES:** 60P **NOTES:** No dogs (ex guide dogs) No coaches Last d 10.30pm
CARDS:

MARKET DRAYTON Shropshire — Map 07 SJ63

★★ Rosehill Manor

Rosehill TF9 2JF
Quality Percentage Score: 67%
☎ 01630 637000 Fax 01630 637008

Dir: *from the rdbt at Turnhill A53/41 head towards Newport or M54 hotel 2m on right*

Parts of this charming house, set in an acre and a half of mature gardens, date back to the 16th century. Friendly and enthusiastic proprietors Jane and Phil Eardley have made many improvements in recent years. The well equipped accommodation includes family rooms, and public areas comprise a pleasant restaurant, a new bar and a comfortable lounge, where a welcoming solid fuel stove is lit in cold weather.

ROOMS: 9 en suite (bth/shr) s fr £45; d fr £60 (incl. bkfst) * LB Off peak **MEALS:** Dinner £18.50-£20.50 & alc English & French Cuisine V meals Coffee am Tea pm **FACILITIES:** CTV in all bedrooms **SERVICES:** 80P **NOTES:** No coaches No smoking in restaurant Last d 9pm **CARDS:**

Symbols and Abbreviations are listed and explained on pages 4 and 5

MARKET HARBOROUGH Leicestershire Map 04 SP78
★★★ Three Swans
21 High St LE16 7NJ
Quality Percentage Score: 68%
☎ 01858 466644 Fax 01858 433101
Dir: *at junct 20 take A4304 to Market Harborough. Passing through town centre on A6, the Hotel is on right*
This former coaching inn in the centre of an attractive and popular market town, has been much extended and completely renovated to make a welcoming hotel with a convivial public bar, much used as a meeting place. It also boasts a select cocktail bar and a formal restaurant serving good food. The bedrooms, like the public areas, are furnished in character and offer a high standard of comfort and a wide range of facilities.
ROOMS: 18 en suite (bth/shr) 31 annexe en suite (bth/shr) (7 fmly) No smoking in 20 bedrooms s £75-£85; d £85-£95 (incl. bkfst) * LB Off peak **MEALS:** Lunch £13.95-£15.50 & alc Dinner fr £19.95 & alc International Cuisine V meals Coffee am Tea pm **FACILITIES:** CTV in all bedrooms STV **CONF:** Thtr 100 Class 60 Board 50 Del from £95 * **SERVICES:** Night porter 100P **NOTES:** No dogs (ex guide dogs) Last d 10pm **CARDS:**

MARKET HARBOROUGH Leicestershire Map 04 SP78
★★★ Angel
37 High St LE16 7NL
Quality Percentage Score: 67%
☎ 0500 636943 (Central Res) Fax 01773 880321
Dir: *on A6*

A former coaching inn, The Angel stands on the town's main street. Public rooms are cheerfully decorated and nicely furnished. Bedrooms come in a variety of styles and are all well appointed.
ROOMS: 37 en suite (bth/shr) s £75-£85; d £85-£99 * LB Off peak **MEALS:** Lunch £5.95-£9.95 Dinner fr £17.50alc English & Continental Cuisine V meals Coffee am Tea pm **FACILITIES:** CTV in all bedrooms Jacuzzi/spa Xmas **CONF:** Thtr 110 Class 45 Board 50 Del from £95 * **SERVICES:** 30P **NOTES:** No smoking in restaurant Last d 9.30pm **CARDS:**

MARKET WEIGHTON East Riding of Yorkshire Map 08 SE84
★★★ *Londesborough Arms Hotel*
High St YO43 3AH
Quality Percentage Score: 70%
☎ 01430 872214 Fax 01430 872219
Dir: *Follow signs into Market Weighton from Shiptonthorpe rdbt at intersection of A1079 & A614, hotel on north side of High St, next to All Saints Church*
Carefully restored, this Georgian hotel in the town centre features high standards of interior design. The thoughtfully equipped bedrooms are spacious by design and include several regal four-posters. Head chef Andrew Dixon prepares some imaginative cooking.
ROOMS: 19 en suite (bth/shr) **MEALS:** V meals Coffee am Tea pm **FACILITIES:** CTV in all bedrooms **CONF:** Thtr 100 Class 100 Board 50 **SERVICES:** Night porter 25P **NOTES:** No coaches Last d 9.30pm **CARDS:**

MARKFIELD Leicestershire Map 08 SK41
★★★ Field Head
Markfield Ln LE6 9PS
Quality Percentage Score: 65%
☎ 01530 245454 Fax 01530 243740
Dir: *access via B5327, off rdbt junct with the A50, 1m from junct 22 of the M1*
This conveniently situated hotel appears very popular with both business and leisure guests. Dating back to the 17th century, it was once a farmhouse and has been considerably extended over recent years. Within the public areas, the bar and lounge are the focal point for residents and non-residents alike, whilst formal meals are taken in a series of four separate dining rooms, each with its own fireplace. Bedrooms are modern and comfortable, each equipped with a good range of useful facilities. The staff are friendly and the atmosphere is relaxed.
ROOMS: 28 en suite (bth/shr) (2 fmly) No smoking in 6 bedrooms s £45-£74; d £56-£84 (incl. bkfst) * LB Off peak **MEALS:** Lunch £8.50-£18.50alc Dinner £8.50-£18.50alc European Cuisine V meals Coffee am Tea pm **FACILITIES:** CTV in all bedrooms STV **CONF:** Thtr 50 Class 30 Board 30 Del from £80 * **SERVICES:** Night porter 85P **NOTES:** No dogs (ex guide dogs) No smoking in restaurant Last d 9.30pm **CARDS:**

MARKFIELD Leicestershire Map 08 SK41
Travelodge
Littleshaw Ln LE67 0PP
☎ Central Res 0800 850950
Dir: *on A50 fom junct22 with M1*
This modern building offers accommodation in smart, spacious and well equipped bedrooms, all with en-suite bathrooms. Refreshments may be taken at the nearby family restaurant. For details about current prices, consult the Contents Page under Hotel Groups for the Travelodge phone number.
ROOMS: 40 en suite (bth/shr) d £49.95 *

MARKHAM MOOR Nottinghamshire Map 08 SK77
Travelodge
DN22 0QU
☎ 01777 838091 Fax 01777 838091
Dir: *on A1 northbound*
This modern building offers accommodation in smart, spacious and well equipped bedrooms, all with en-suite bathrooms. Refreshments may be taken at the nearby family restaurant. For details about current prices, consult the Contents Page under Hotel Groups for the Travelodge phone number.
ROOMS: 40 en suite (bth/shr) d £39.95 *

MARKINGTON North Yorkshire Map 08 SE26
★★★ Hob Green
HG3 3PJ
Quality Percentage Score: 76%
☎ 01423 770031 Fax 01423 771589
Dir: *exit A61 4m after Harrogate and turn left at Wormald Green and follow brown hotel signs*
Set in 800 acres of beautiful countryside and yet very convenient for Harrogate, this charming country house offers tranquillity and comfort. The public rooms include delightful lounges with open fires, together with a charming restaurant which places an

contd.

emphasis on quality local produce and is backed by a well balanced wine list. The staff here are very caring and are naturally friendly and helpful.

Hob Green, Markington

ROOMS: 12 en suite (bth/shr) s £85; d £95-£105 (incl. bkfst) LB Off peak **MEALS:** Sunday Lunch £9.95-£14.95 & alc Dinner fr £23.50 & alc English & French Cuisine V meals Coffee am Tea pm **FACILITIES:** CTV in all bedrooms Croquet lawn **SERVICES:** 40P **NOTES:** No coaches Last d 9.30pm **CARDS:**

See advert under HARROGATE

MARLBOROUGH Wiltshire **Map 04 SU16**

★★★ Ivy House Hotel

High St SN8 1HJ
Quality Percentage Score: 74%
☎ 01672 515333 01672 515338
***Dir:** M4 junct 15 take A346 to Marlborough hotel is situatd on main High St*

This Grade II listed Georgian property was built originally for the Earl of Aylesbury in 1707. Well equipped bedrooms are individually decorated. Public areas include the Beeches conference suite, lounges and the elegant Garden restaurant, where fixed proce and carte menus offer a good mix of traditional dishes and modern imaginative cooking.

ROOMS: 28 en suite (bth/shr) (2 fmly) No smoking in 8 bedrooms s £65-£79; d £79-£105 (incl. bkfst) * LB Off peak **MEALS:** Lunch fr £12.50 & alc Dinner £15-£30alc International Cuisine V meals Coffee am Tea pm **FACILITIES:** CTV in all bedrooms STV Xmas **CONF:** Thtr 100 Class 40 Board 30 **SERVICES:** 36P **NOTES:** No smoking area in restaurant Last d 9.30pm **CARDS:**

See advert on opposite page

MARLBOROUGH Wiltshire **Map 04 SU16**

★★★ The Castle & Ball

High St SN8 1LZ
Quality Percentage Score: 61%
☎ 01672 515201 01672 515895
***Dir:** both the A338 and A4 lead into Marlborough and eventually into the High St*

This traditional town-centre coaching inn is right in the centre of Marlborough market square. An open-plan lounge and bar is a popular meeting place for locals, and guests. Meeting rooms have recently been upgraded. Bedrooms are spacious.

ROOMS: 34 en suite (bth/shr) (1 fmly) No smoking in 13 bedrooms d £49 * LB Off peak **MEALS:** Lunch £6.95-£12.95 Dinner £14-£22 V meals Coffee am Tea pm **FACILITIES:** CTV in all bedrooms Xmas **CONF:** Thtr 45 Class 20 Board 30 Del from £60 * **SERVICES:** 48P **NOTES:** No smoking in restaurant Last d 9pm
CARDS:

MARLOW Buckinghamshire **Map 04 SU88**

★★★★ Danesfield House

Henley Rd SL7 2EY
Quality Percentage Score: 74%
☎ 01628 891010 01628 890408
***Dir:** 2m from Marlow on A4155 towards Henley*

The Renaissance-style building and formal gardens overlooking the Thames create a pleasing impression of Danesfield. The interior is no less impressive, the Great Hall almost cathedral-like with its minstrel's gallery, containing a snooker table, and the panelled Oak Room restaurant. Bedrooms are well proportioned and some have patios with river views. The restaurant is the choice for more formal dining, while the Orangery has a contemporary brasserie-style menu.

ROOMS: 87 en suite (bth/shr) (3 fmly) No smoking in 5 bedrooms s £145; d £175-£205 (incl. bkfst) * LB Off peak **MEALS:** Lunch £19.50-£26.50 Dinner £35.50 & alc English & French Cuisine V meals Coffee am Tea pm **FACILITIES:** CTV in all bedrooms STV Outdoor swimming pool (heated) Tennis (hard) Snooker Croquet lawn Putting green Jacuzzi/spa Jogging trail Wkly live entertainment Xmas **CONF:** Thtr 80 Class 60 Board 65 Del from £240 * **SERVICES:** Lift Night porter 100P **NOTES:** No dogs (ex guide dogs) No smoking in restaurant Last d 9.45pm **CARDS:**

See advert on opposite page

MARLOW Buckinghamshire **Map 04 SU88**

★★★★ The Compleat Angler

Marlow Bridge SL7 1RG
Quality Percentage Score: 72%
☎ 01628 484444 01628 486388
***Dir:** from M40 junct 4 follow A404 to Bisham rdbt, right through Bisham Village. Hotel is on right before Marlow Bridge*

Enjoying an enviable position right beside the River Thames, this internationally famous hotel has kept a traditional atmosphere. Bedrooms are furnished in country-house style. Some, in a newer wing, have balconies overlooking a rushing weir. Reception rooms consist of a lounge and a panelled bar, with a choice for meals of the bistro or the smart Riverside Restaurant.

ROOMS: 65 en suite (bth/shr) (20 fmly) No smoking in 24 bedrooms s fr £175; d fr £195 * LB Off peak **MEALS:** Lunch £17.50-£33.50 Dinner £33.50 & alc English & French Cuisine V meals Coffee am Tea pm **FACILITIES:** CTV in all bedrooms STV Tennis (hard) Fishing Croquet lawn Boating Wkly live entertainment Xmas **CONF:** Thtr 120 Class 60 Board 45 Del from £195 * **SERVICES:** Lift Night porter 100P **NOTES:** No smoking area in restaurant Last d 10pm
CARDS:

See advert on opposite page

MARPLE Greater Manchester **Map 07 SJ98**

★★ ***Springfield***

Station Rd SK6 6PA

Quality Percentage Score: 70%

☎ 0161 449 0721 Fax 0161 4490766

Dir: *beside A626*

Situated on the edge of the Peak District, and convenient for both Stockport and Manchester, this charming hotel offers comfortable and well equipped bedrooms. There are two lounges and a Victorian-style dining room serving home-cooked dinners.

ROOMS: 7 en suite (bth/shr) No smoking in all bedrooms

MEALS: French & Italian Cuisine V meals **FACILITIES:** CTV in all bedrooms STV **SERVICES:** 10P **NOTES:** No dogs (ex guide dogs) No coaches No children 6yrs No smoking in restaurant Last d 8pm

CARDS:

MARSTON MORETAINE Bedfordshire **Map 04 SP94**

Travelodge

Beancroft Rd Junction MK43 0PZ

☎ 01234 766755 Fax 01234 766755

Dir: *on A421, northbound*

This modern building offers accommodation in smart, spacious and well equipped bedrooms, all with en-suite bathrooms. Refreshments may be taken at the nearby family restaurant. For details about current prices, consult the Contents Page under Hotel Groups for the Travelodge phone number.

ROOMS: 32 en suite (bth/shr) d £45.95 *

New AA Guides for the Millennium are featured on page 24

MARSTON TRUSSELL Northamptonshire **Map 04 SP68**

★★ *The Sun Inn*

Main St LE16 9TY

Quality Percentage Score: 66%

☎ 01858 465531 01858 433155

***Dir:** off A4304, between villages of Lubenham and Theddingworth*

This pleasant inn has been extended over the years, public areas are in the old part, predominantly devoted to the busy restaurant trade, with two separate dining areas. Complete refurbishment is planned following a change in ownership, to include the modern wing of bedrooms, bringing smart decor and high levels of comfort.

ROOMS: 19 en suite (bth/shr) (3 fmly) **MEALS:** English & French Cuisine V meals Coffee am Tea pm **FACILITIES:** CTV in all bedrooms Fishing **CONF:** Thtr 60 Class 40 Board 28 **SERVICES:** 60P **NOTES:** No smoking area in restaurant Last d 9.30pm **CARDS:**

MARTINHOE Devon **Map 03 SS64**

★★ **Old Rectory**

EX31 4QT

Quality Percentage Score: 75%

☎ 01598 763368 01598 763567

***Dir:** exit M5 jct27 onto A361, right onto A399 Blackmore Gate, right onto A39 Parracombe. At Martinhoe Cross, 3rd road on left to Woody Bay/ Martinhoe*

Within 500 yards of the Coastal Footpath, the Old Rectory provides an ideal base for exploring Exmoor. Two comfortably furnished sitting rooms open onto a light and airy vinery. In the spacious dining room, the chef produces interesting menus. Each bedroom is tastefully decorated, two are on the ground floor and there are also two self-catering cottages.

ROOMS: 9 en suite (bth/shr) No smoking in all bedrooms s £71; d £63-£73 (incl. bkfst & dinner) * Off peak **MEALS:** Dinner £28.50 English & French Cuisine **FACILITIES:** CTV in all bedrooms **SERVICES:** 10P **NOTES:** No dogs No coaches No children 14yrs No smoking in restaurant Last d 6pm Closed Nov-Easter

MARTOCK Somerset **Map 03 ST41**

★★★ **The Hollies**

Bower Hinton TA12 6LG

Quality Percentage Score: 70%

☎ 01935 822232 01935 822249

***Dir:** on B3165 S of town centre just off A303*

The bar and restaurant of this popular venue are located in an attractive former farmhouse which dates back some 300 years. Bar meals are available in addition to an interesting carte menu. Spacious, well equipped bedrooms, most of which lead onto a grassy courtyard, form part of a modern purpose-built annexe, and both suites and half-suites are available. A range of conference and function rooms are also available.

ROOMS: 32 annexe en suite (bth/shr) (2 fmly) No smoking in 4 bedrooms s £60-£90; d £70-£100 (incl. bkfst) LB Off peak **MEALS:** Lunch £15-£25alc Dinner £15-£25alc English & French Cuisine V meals **FACILITIES:** CTV in all bedrooms STV **CONF:** Thtr 150 Class 80 Board 60 Del from £75 * **SERVICES:** 80P **NOTES:** No dogs (ex guide dogs) No smoking in restaurant Last d 9pm RS Xmas & New Year **CARDS:**

MASHAM North Yorkshire **Map 08 SE28**

★★ **The Kings Head**

Market Place HG4 4EF

Quality Percentage Score: 60%

☎ 01765 689295 01765 689070

***Dir:** off the A6108 Ripon to Leyburn Rd in centre of village*

This historic stone-built hotel, with its uneven floors, beamed bars, and attractive window boxes, looks out over the large market square. Bedrooms are well decorated and comfortable, the bar is full of character and there is good food in the separate restaurant.

ROOMS: 10 en suite (bth/shr) s £45-£70; d £60-£70 * LB Off peak **MEALS:** Lunch £13-£30alc Dinner £13-£30alc V meals Coffee am **FACILITIES:** CTV in all bedrooms **CONF:** Thtr 40 Class 20 Board 20 Del from £90 * **NOTES:** No dogs (ex guide dogs) No coaches Last d 9pm **CARDS:**

MATLOCK Derbyshire **Map 08 SK36**

★★★ **Riber Hall**

DE4 5JU

Quality Percentage Score: 73%

☎ 01629 582795 01629 580475

***Dir:** 1m off A615 at Tansley*

This charming Elizabethan manor house has a walled garden containing a number of rare plants and a peaceful conservatory. Highly individual, beautifully furnished bedrooms have carved oak four poster beds and comfortable sitting areas. The lounge, with glowing log fire, is the perfect place to relax before heading into the restaurant to enjoy a carefully prepared dinner and sample the excellent wine list.

ROOMS: 3 en suite (bth/shr) 11 annexe en suite (bth/shr) No smoking in 4 bedrooms s £92.50-£107; d £118.50-£162 (incl. cont bkfst) * LB Off peak **MEALS:** Lunch £13-£16 Dinner £27-£32 English & French Cuisine V meals Coffee am Tea pm **FACILITIES:** CTV in all bedrooms STV Tennis (hard) Croquet lawn **CONF:** Thtr 20 Class 20 Board 20 **SERVICES:** 50P **NOTES:** No coaches No children 10yrs No smoking area in restaurant Last d 9.30pm **CARDS:**

MATLOCK Derbyshire **Map 08 SK36**

★★★ **New Bath**

New Bath Rd DE4 3PX

Quality Percentage Score: 65%

☎ 01629 583275 01629 580268

***Dir:** M1 junct 28 to Alfreton follow signs for Matlock and then Matlock Bath. Hotel is on the A6 just after Matlock Bath on the right*

Built in 1802, this comfortable and traditional hotel is set in five acres of grounds at one of Derbyshire's finest locations. Two of the bedrooms have four-poster beds and others have half-testers; balconied rooms are also available.

ROOMS: 55 en suite (bth/shr) (5 fmly) No smoking in 11 bedrooms s fr £80; d fr £100 * LB Off peak **MEALS:** Lunch £5.95-£10.95 Dinner £19.95 French Cuisine V meals Coffee am Tea pm **FACILITIES:** CTV in all bedrooms Indoor swimming pool (heated) Outdoor swimming pool Tennis (hard) Sauna Solarium Xmas **CONF:** Thtr 180 Class 60 Board 50 Del from £90 * **SERVICES:** Night porter 200P **NOTES:** No smoking in restaurant Last d 9.30pm **CARDS:**

MATLOCK Derbyshire **Map 08 SK36**

★★ **Red House**

Old Rd, Darley Dale DE4 2ER

Quality Percentage Score: 72%

☎ 01629 734854 01629 734885

***Dir:** just off A6 onto Old Road signposted Carriage Museum, 2.5m N of Matlock*

This peaceful country retreat, set lovely gardens, is only a short drive from the A6 just outside Matlock. Rich colour schemes are used to excellent effect throughout all the public rooms and accommodation. Bedrooms are well equipped and include three ground floor rooms situated in the adjacent coach house. A comfortably appointed lounge, with delightful views of the surrounding countryside, serves refreshments and pre-dinner

contd.

drinks, and carefully presented meals are served in separate breakfast and dining rooms.
ROOMS: 7 en suite (bth/shr) 3 annexe en suite (bth/shr) No smoking in 1 bedroom s £50-£55; d £80 (incl. bkfst) * LB Off peak **MEALS:** Lunch £13.25 Dinner £19.50-£22.50 V meals Coffee am **FACILITIES:** CTV in all bedrooms Xmas **CONF:** Class 70 Board 12 Del from £70 * **SERVICES:** 15P **NOTES:** No dogs (ex guide dogs) No coaches No smoking in restaurant Last d 8.30pm **CARDS:**

MAWGAN PORTH Cornwall & Isles of Scilly **Map 02 SW86**

★★ Tredragon

TR8 4DQ
Quality Percentage Score: 67%
☎ 01637 860213 🖷 01637 860269

Situated above the bay of Mawgan Porth, The Tredragon has panoramic views over the sea to the hills beyond. The bedrooms are all comfortably furnished and equipped. In the dining room guests can enjoy home-made cooking, served by efficient and friendly staff. The hotel offers special residential courses, including lace-making, cooking and painting.
ROOMS: 26 en suite (bth/shr) (15 fmly) s £27.50-£40; d £55-£80 (incl. bkfst) * LB Off peak **MEALS:** Lunch £7-£9 High tea £1.75-£2.25 Dinner £17.50-£18.50 English & French Cuisine V meals Coffee am Tea pm **FACILITIES:** CTV in all bedrooms Indoor swimming pool (heated) Sauna Solarium Pool table Wkly live entertainment ch fac Xmas **CONF:** Thtr 50 Class 40 Board 30 Del from £47.25 * **SERVICES:** 30P **NOTES:** No smoking in restaurant Last d 8pm **CARDS:**

MAWGAN PORTH Cornwall & Isles of Scilly **Map 02 SW86**

★★ *Thorncliff*

Trenance TR8 4DA
Quality Percentage Score: 63%
☎ 01637 860898 🖷 01637 860893
Dir: *from Mawgan Porth take B3276 towards Padston for 1m then left Trenance telephone box then first left again*
This comfortable hotel, situated above the bay of Mawgan Porth, has commanding views over the beach and countryside. There is, in addition to the lounge, a pool room and wide-screen T.V room. Food is freshly prepared and home cooked while the bedrooms all have modern facilities and equipment.
ROOMS: 17 en suite (bth/shr) (5 fmly) No smoking in 2 bedrooms **MEALS:** English & Continental Cuisine V meals Coffee am **FACILITIES:** CTV in all bedrooms Pool table **CONF:** Class 40 **SERVICES:** 18P **NOTES:** No smoking in restaurant Last d 8pm Closed Nov RS Dec, Jan & Feb **CARDS:**

Symbols and Abbreviations are listed and explained on pages 4 and 5

MAWNAN SMITH Cornwall & Isles of Scilly **Map 02 SW72**

★★★★ Budock Vean Golf & Country House

TR11 5LG
Quality Percentage Score: 73%
☎ 01326 252100 & Freephone 0800 833927 🖷 01326 250892
Dir: *from A39 Truro/Falmouth road follow the brown tourist info signs to Trebah Gdns, then continue for 0.5m to the hotel*
With 65 acres of mature grounds beside the Helford River, this impressive hotel has the advantage of a new health spa centre in addition to extensive leisure facilities. Most bedrooms benefit from views over the valley and golf course.
ROOMS: 58 en suite (bth/shr) (4 fmly) No smoking in 6 bedrooms s £49-£95; d £98-£190 (incl. bkfst & dinner) * LB Off peak **MEALS:** Lunch £11.50-£12.50 & alc High tea £3-£7.50alc Dinner £24.50 & alc English & French Cuisine V meals Coffee am Tea pm **FACILITIES:** CTV in all bedrooms STV Indoor swimming pool (heated) Golf 18 Tennis (hard) Fishing Snooker Putting green Natual health spa Wkly live entertainment Xmas **CONF:** Thtr 100 Class 100 Board 80 Del from £60 * **SERVICES:** Lift Night porter 100P **NOTES:** No coaches No smoking in restaurant Last d 9pm **CARDS:**

MAWNAN SMITH Cornwall & Isles of Scilly **Map 02 SW72**

★★★ Meudon

TR11 5HT
Quality Percentage Score: 78%
☎ 01326 250541 🖷 01326 250543
Dir: *leave A39 at hillhead rdbt and follow signs to Maenporth beach, Meudon on left one mile after beach*

Set in nine acres of sub-tropical gardens leading down to Bream Cove and its own beach and surrounded by National Trust land, this late Victorian mansion has a very elegant drawing room and bar. In addition, two modern wings provide beautifully furbished, well-equipped bedrooms. An attractive conservatory

contd.

M

restaurant offers guests a fixed-price dinner, with local seafood a speciality.
ROOMS: 29 en suite (bth/shr) (1 fmly) s £90-£105; d £160-£190 (incl. bkfst & dinner) * LB Off peak **MEALS:** Lunch £12.50-£15 & alc High tea £4-£6 Dinner fr £25 & alc International Cuisine V meals Coffee am Tea pm **FACILITIES:** CTV in all bedrooms Fishing Riding Pool table Private beach Hair salon Subtropical gardens Xmas **CONF:** Thtr 30 Class 30 Board 30 Del from £65 * **SERVICES:** Lift Night porter 52P **NOTES:** No coaches Last d 9pm Closed 3 Jan-13 Feb
CARDS:

See advert under FALMOUTH

MAWNAN SMITH Cornwall & Isles of Scilly **Map 02 SW72**

★★★ *Trelawne*

TR11 5HS
Quality Percentage Score: 67%
☎ 01326 250226 01326 250909
Dir: *A39 towards Falmouth, turn right at Hillhead rdbt take exit signed Maenporth past beach and up the hill, hotel on left overlooking Falmouth Bay*

The Trelawne is surrounded by attractive lawns and gardens and command superb views over the coastline from St Mawes to the Lizard. Inside, the hotel provides neat and well equipped bedrooms and comfortable public areas. At dinner, award winning cuisine is available which brings many guests back year after year.
ROOMS: 14 en suite (bth/shr) (2 fmly) **MEALS:** English & French Cuisine Coffee am Tea pm **FACILITIES:** CTV in all bedrooms Indoor swimming pool (heated) **SERVICES:** 20P **NOTES:** No coaches No smoking in restaurant Last d 9pm Closed 23 Dec-12 Feb
CARDS:

See advert under FALMOUTH

MELKSHAM Wiltshire **Map 03 ST96**

★★★ *Kings Arms*

Market Place SN12 6EX
Quality Percentage Score: 62%
☎ 01225 707272 01225 702085
Dir: *in town centre opposite Lloyds Bank*
Built of Bath stone with cobbled courtyard, the Kings Arms is situated in the heart of this Wiltshire market town. Much of the character and charm of the building has been retained, and bedrooms are equipped with a number of extra facilities to ensure guest comfort. A good range of bar meals is available in addition to full restaurant service in the dining room. There is also a cosy guest lounge.
ROOMS: 13 rms (10 bth/shr) **MEALS:** V meals Coffee am Tea pm **FACILITIES:** CTV in all bedrooms **SERVICES:** 30P **NOTES:** No coaches Last d 9pm **CARDS:**

MELKSHAM Wiltshire **Map 03 ST96**

★★ Shaw Country

Bath Rd, Shaw SN12 8EF
Quality Percentage Score: 68%
☎ 01225 702836 & 790321 01225 790275
Dir: *2m NW A365*

This friendly hotel, on the outskirts of Melksham is run by the Lewis family. The creeper-clad house is said to date from the late 16th century. Accommodation provides comfortable bedrooms with modern facilities. Downstairs there is a cosy bar, and a separate lounge where guests can relax. Fresh ingredients are used in the production of the interesting dishes offered from a choice of menus in the Mulberry Restaurant.
ROOMS: 13 en suite (bth/shr) (2 fmly) s fr £44; d fr £65 (incl. bkfst) * LB Off peak **MEALS:** Lunch £11-£12.50 Dinner fr £17.95 English & French Cuisine V meals Coffee am Tea pm **FACILITIES:** CTV in all bedrooms Jacuzzi/spa **CONF:** Thtr 30 Class 20 Board 30 **SERVICES:** 30P **NOTES:** No coaches No smoking in restaurant Last d 9pm Closed 26-27 Dec **CARDS:**

See advert under BATH

MELTON MOWBRAY Leicestershire **Map 08 SK71**

The Premier Collection

★★★★ Stapleford Park

Stapleford LE14 2EF
☎ 01572 787522 01572 787651
Dir: *1m SW of B676 4m E of Melton Mowbray and 9m W of Colsterworth*
Set in a 500-acre estate, this delightful stately home is surrounded by woods and parkland, originally laid out by Capability Brown. The main reception rooms are sumptuously decorated and furnished in grand country-house style. The dining room features carvings by Grinling Gibbons, and makes a fine setting for the daily-changing menu. Each of the bedrooms has been designed by a

contd.

sponsor, such as Turnbull & Asser and David Hicks, and those in a cottage in the grounds by companies such as IBM and Coca-Cola.
ROOMS: 44 en suite (bth/shr) 7 annexe en suite (bth/shr) No smoking in 44 bedrooms d £193.88-£581.63 (incl. bkfst) * Off peak **MEALS:** Lunch £25 High tea £3-£6 Dinner £39.50 European Cuisine V meals **FACILITIES:** CTV in all bedrooms STV Indoor swimming pool (heated) Golf 3 Tennis (hard) Fishing Riding Sauna Solarium Gym Pool table Croquet lawn Putting green Jacuzzi/spa Shooting Falconry Off road driving Archery Petanque Wkly live entertainment Xmas **CONF:** Thtr 200 Class 140 Board 80 Del from £245 * **SERVICES:** Lift Night porter 120P **NOTES:** No coaches No children 9yrs No smoking in restaurant Last d 10pm
CARDS:

MELTON MOWBRAY Leicestershire **Map 08 SK71**

★★★ Sysonby Knoll

Asfordby Rd LE13 0HP
Quality Percentage Score: 64%
☎ 01664 563563 Fax 01664 410364
Dir: *0.5m from town centre beside A6006*
This Edwardian country house, sympathetically extended over the years, has attractive grounds leading to the River Eye. Bedrooms vary in size and style, major upgrading is creating attractive results. The spacious four poster room is worth requesting. An appealing menu is offered in the restaurant.
ROOMS: 23 en suite (bth/shr) 1 annexe en suite (bth/shr) (2 fmly) s £42.50-£59; d £59-£75 (incl. bkfst) * LB Off peak **MEALS:** Lunch £7-£10 Dinner £13.25-£14.50 & alc English & French Cuisine V meals Coffee am Tea pm **FACILITIES:** CTV in all bedrooms STV Outdoor swimming pool Fishing Croquet lawn **CONF:** Thtr 30 Class 16 Board 24 Del from £75 * **SERVICES:** 40P **NOTES:** No smoking in restaurant Last d 9pm Closed 25 Dec-1 Jan **CARDS:**

See advert on this page

AA Rosettes are awarded for quality of food, see page 15 for an explanation of Rosette assessment.

MELTON MOWBRAY Leicestershire **Map 08 SK71**

★★ Quorn Lodge

46 Asfordby Rd LE13 0HR
Quality Percentage Score: 70%
☎ 01664 566660 & 562590 Fax 01664 480660
Dir: *from town centre take A6006, hotel 300 yds from junct of A606/A607 on right*
Originally a hunting lodge, this hotel is popular for its friendly and welcoming atmosphere. Good standards are maintained throughout. Bedroom styles differ, with Deluxe and Standard options; each room is individually decorated and thoughtfully designed. An elegant restaurant, cosy lounge bar, ample rear car parking and a modern function suite are available.
ROOMS: 19 en suite (bth/shr) (2 fmly) No smoking in 11 bedrooms s £39.50-£49.50; d £55-£75 (incl. bkfst) * LB Off peak **MEALS:** Lunch £7.50-£9.50 & alc Dinner £15.75 & alc V meals Coffee am Tea pm **FACILITIES:** CTV in all bedrooms STV **CONF:** Thtr 90 Class 60 Board 85 Del £75 * **SERVICES:** 33P **NOTES:** No dogs No smoking in restaurant Last d 10pm **CARDS:**

MEMBURY MOTORWAY SERVICE AREA (M4) Berkshire — Map 04 SU37

Welcome Lodge

Membury Service Area RG17 7TZ

☎ 01488 72336

***Dir:** M4 between junct 14 & 15 westbound*

This modern building offers accommodation in smart, spacious and well equipped bedrooms, suitable for families and businessmen, and all with en-suite bathrooms. Refreshments may be taken at the nearby family restaurant. For details of current prices, consult the Contents Page under Hotel Groups for the Welcome Break phone number.

ROOMS: 40 en suite (bth/shr) d fr £45 *

MERIDEN West Midlands — Map 04 SP28

★★★★ Marriott Forest of Arden

Maxstoke Ln CV7 7HR

Quality Percentage Score: 71%

☎ 01676 522335 Fax 01676 523711

***Dir:** M42 junct 6 onto A45 towards Coventry straight on at Stonebridge flyover, after 0.75m turn left into Shepherds Lane, hotel 1.5m on left*

Within easy reach of both the M6 and M42, this impressive modern hotel is convenient for the NEC, Birmingham and Coventry. Moreover, it also happens to enjoy a rural location surrounded by lakes, gardens, two golf courses and a driving range. Popular with conference and leisure guests alike, it offers an extensive range of sporting and leisure activities including an attractive pool area, three gyms and a beauty salon. In this club, one can also enjoy a drink, snack or meal in an informal, family setting. Alternatively, the hotel offers a comfortable cocktail lounge and a split-level restaurant serving noteworthy cuisine. The spacious bedrooms, many of which overlook the golf course, boast an extensive range of facilities.

ROOMS: 215 en suite (bth/shr) (4 fmly) No smoking in 135 bedrooms s fr £70; d £80-£140 * LB Off peak **MEALS:** Lunch £12.95-£16.50 Dinner £10.95-£23alc English & French Cuisine V meals Coffee am Tea pm **FACILITIES:** CTV in all bedrooms STV Indoor swimming pool (heated) Golf 18 Tennis (hard) Fishing Sauna Solarium Gym Croquet lawn Putting green Jacuzzi/spa Health & Beauty salon Xmas **CONF:** Thtr 300 Class 200 Board 40 Del from £135 * **SERVICES:** Lift Night porter Air conditioning 300P **NOTES:** No smoking in restaurant Last d 10pm **CARDS:**

MERIDEN West Midlands — Map 04 SP28

★★★ Manor

Main Rd CV7 7NH

Quality Percentage Score: 72%

☎ 01676 522735 Fax 01676 522186

***Dir:** from M42 junct 6, take A45 towards Coventry, after approx 2m cross dual carriageway onto B4104 for Meriden. Straight ahead at mini-rdbt*

An extended Georgian manor in a quiet village, within easy reach of the NEC and motorway network. Bedrooms are spacious and well equipped. Public areas include the Regency Restaurant and Triumph Buttery, which offers guests a lighter alternative and is open all day. The young, friendly staff offer attentive service.

ROOMS: 114 en suite (bth/shr) No smoking in 54 bedrooms s £75-£135; d £85-£155 (incl. bkfst) * LB Off peak **MEALS:** Lunch £19.75-£20.75 & alc Dinner £19.75-£20.75 & alc English & French Cuisine V meals Coffee am Tea pm **FACILITIES:** CTV in all bedrooms STV **CONF:** Thtr 250 Class 150 Board 60 **SERVICES:** Lift Night porter 200P **NOTES:** No smoking in restaurant Last d 9.45pm **CARDS:**

MEVAGISSEY Cornwall & Isles of Scilly — Map 02 SX04

★★ Spa Hotel

Polkirt Hill PL26 6UY

Quality Percentage Score: 68%

☎ 01726 842244 Fax 01726 842244

***Dir:** from Mevagissey take Portmellion Rd. At the top of Polkirt Hill, turning on right, Hotel sign at this turning*

In an elevated position, the Spa enjoys wonderful coastal views. There is a wide choice of bedroom size, all are light, airy and colourful, and some have patio areas leading onto well tended gardens. A comfortable, cane-furnished lounge and a cosy bar are provided. A short fixed price menu is offered, using fresh local produce.

ROOMS: 11 en suite (bth/shr) (4 fmly) No smoking in all bedrooms s £30-£35; d £60 (incl. bkfst) LB Off peak **MEALS:** Dinner £13.50 V meals Coffee am Tea pm **FACILITIES:** CTV in all bedrooms Putting green Xmas **SERVICES:** 12P **NOTES:** No coaches No smoking in restaurant Last d 7pm **CARDS:**

MEVAGISSEY Cornwall & Isles of Scilly — Map 02 SX04

★★ Tremarne

Polkirt PL26 6UY

Quality Percentage Score: 68%

☎ 01726 842213 Fax 01726 843420

***Dir:** from A390 at St Austell take B3273 to Mevagissey, follow Portmellon signs through Mevagissey, at top of Polkirt Hill turn right*

Secluded on a private road, a relaxed and friendly atmosphere ensures an unhurried holiday in this peaceful location. Many of the bedrooms benefit from coastal views, and all are attractively co-ordinated and well equipped. Public areas are spacious and include a recently refurbished lounge, a cosy bar and the dining room where home-cooked dinners are served.

ROOMS: 14 en suite (bth/shr) (2 fmly) No smoking in all bedrooms s £32; d £64 (incl. bkfst) * LB Off peak **MEALS:** Dinner £16 European Cuisine V meals **FACILITIES:** CTV in all bedrooms Outdoor swimming pool (heated) **SERVICES:** 14P **NOTES:** No coaches No smoking in restaurant Last d 7.30pm Closed 1 Nov-1 Apr

CARDS:

MICHAEL WOOD MOTORWAY SERVICE AREA (M5) Gloucestershire — Map 03 ST79
Welcome Lodge
Lower Wick GL11 6DD
☎ 01454 261513 Fax 01454 261513
Dir: *M5 northbound between junct 13 & 14*
This modern building offers accommodation in smart, spacious and well equipped bedrooms, suitable for families and businessmen, and all with en-suite bathrooms. Refreshments may be taken at the nearby family restaurant. For details of current prices, consult the Contents Page under Hotel Groups for the Welcome Break phone number.
ROOMS: 40 en suite (bth/shr) d fr £45 *

MIDDLEHAM North Yorkshire — Map 07 SE18
★★ Millers House
DL8 4NR
Quality Percentage Score: 75%
☎ 01969 622630 Fax 01969 623570
Dir: *from A1 onto A684 to Leyburn. Turn left to Middleham, hotel set back from market square*
This Georgian house sits secluded just off the market square. Judith and Crossley Sunderland offer excellent hospitality and create a relaxing atmosphere. There are a cosy lounge and bar for residents and diners, and a stylish dining room which extends to a small conservatory at the rear. Bedrooms are very attractive, all individual and thoughtfully equipped.
ROOMS: 7 rms (6 bth/shr) s £39.50-£94; d £79-£94 (incl. bkfst) * LB Off peak **MEALS:** Dinner £20 Modern English Cuisine V meals **FACILITIES:** CTV in all bedrooms Xmas **CONF:** Class 12 Board 12 Del from £70.80 * **SERVICES:** 8P **NOTES:** No dogs (ex guide dogs) No coaches No children 10yrs No smoking in restaurant Last d 8.30pm Closed Jan **CARDS:**

MIDDLEHAM North Yorkshire — Map 07 SE18
★ Waterford House
Kirkgate DL8 4PG
Quality Percentage Score: 73%
☎ 01969 622090 Fax 01969 624020
Dir: *A1 to B6267 via Masham to Middleham. Hotel in right corner of Market Sq*
Brian and Everyl Madell have created a very special restaurant with rooms in this fine period house. A mix of antiques and treasures create a veritable Aladdin's Cave. Add super food, wine and delightful bedrooms and one has a package of enviable quality. Brian is a something of a wine buff and his list runs to some 800 wines. Everyl's cooking is equally serious and her skilful touch is brought to seafood, meats and game.
ROOMS: 5 en suite (bth/shr) s £50-£60; d £70-£90 (incl. bkfst) LB Off peak **MEALS:** Lunch £19.50-£29.50 & alc Dinner £22.50-£29.50 & alc English & Continental Cuisine Coffee am Tea pm **FACILITIES:** CTV in all bedrooms **CONF:** Thtr 12 Board 12 **SERVICES:** 8P **NOTES:** No coaches No smoking in restaurant Last d 10pm **CARDS:**

MIDDLEHAM North Yorkshire — Map 07 SE18
The White Swan
Market Place DL8 4PE
☎ 01969 622093 Fax 01969 624551
Dir: *exit A1 at Leeming Bar, take A684 to Leyburn, before Leyburn Centre take A6108 to Ripon, Middleham is 1.5m from this junct, in the Market Place*
ROOMS: 11 en suite (bth/shr) (3 fmly) **MEALS:** V meals Coffee am Tea pm **FACILITIES:** CTV in all bedrooms **SERVICES:** 5P **NOTES:** No smoking area in restaurant Last d 9pm RS first 2 weeks in Jan ex 1st
CARDS:

MIDDLESBROUGH North Yorkshire — Map 08 NZ42
★★ Highfield
358 Marton Rd TS4 2PA
Quality Percentage Score: 65%
☎ 01642 817638 Fax 01642 821219
Dir: *off A172. From A1 (M) Darlington exit follow A1085 towards town centre*
This popular hotel has been refurbished throughout and provides friendly and attentive service. The pleasant restaurant is popular with families, as a play area is provided. The modern bedrooms are well equipped and pleasantly decorated.
ROOMS: 23 en suite (bth/shr) (1 fmly) d £45-£73.50 * Off peak **MEALS:** Lunch £10.45-£20.35alc Dinner £12.45-£20.35alc International Cuisine V meals Coffee am Tea pm **FACILITIES:** CTV in all bedrooms STV Indoor childrens play area **CONF:** Thtr 200 Class 100 Board 50 Del £108.50 * **SERVICES:** Night porter 100P **NOTES:** No dogs (ex guide dogs) Last d 9.30pm **CARDS:**

MIDDLESBROUGH North Yorkshire — Map 08 NZ42
Travel Inn
Middlesbrough Dock
☎ 0870 242 8000
This modern building offers accommodation in smart, spacious and well equipped bedrooms, all with en-suite bathrooms. Refreshments may be taken at the nearby family restaurant. For details about current prices consult the Contents Page under Hotel Groups for the Travel Inn phone number.
ROOMS: 40 en suite (bth/shr) d £39.95 *

MIDDLETON STONEY Oxfordshire — Map 04 SP52
★★ Jersey Arms
OX6 8SE
Quality Percentage Score: 68%
☎ 01869 343234 & 343505 Fax 01869 343565
Dir: *on the B430 10m N of Oxford, between junct 9 & 10 of M40*
A charming small hotel located close to the M40 and to Bicester, The Jersey Arms has a long tradition of welcoming guests which continues to the present day. A coaching inn in times past the original courtyard houses the more spacious bedrooms which can be a little quieter than those in the main house. The cosy bar is full of village atmosphere and meals may be taken here or in the more formal setting of the restaurant.
ROOMS: 6 en suite (bth) 10 annexe en suite (bth) (3 fmly) s fr £75; d fr £89 (incl. bkfst) * LB Off peak **MEALS:** Lunch £20-£22alc Dinner £20-£22alc English & French Cuisine V meals Coffee am Tea pm **FACILITIES:** CTV in all bedrooms Xmas **SERVICES:** 55P **NOTES:** No dogs (ex guide dogs) No coaches No smoking in restaurant Last d 9.30pm **CARDS:**

MIDDLE WALLOP Hampshire — Map 04 SU23
★★★ *Fifehead Manor*
SO20 8EG
Quality Percentage Score: 71%
☎ 01264 781565 Fax 01264 781400
Dir: *from M3 exit at junct 8 onto A303 to Andover, then take A343 S for 6m to Middle Wallop*
Dating back to the 11th Century, Fifehead Manor retains many original features such as old beams and exterior. Bedrooms are extremely well equipped and feature many thoughtful touches such as mineral water and bathrobes. Public areas have also had

contd.

a makeover which includes the addition of a new bar and front entrance. Service from the friendly team of staff is attentive.
ROOMS: 10 en suite (bth/shr) 6 annexe en suite (bth/shr)
MEALS: V meals Coffee am Tea pm **FACILITIES:** CTV in all bedrooms STV Croquet lawn **CONF:** Thtr 30 Class 18 Board 12 **SERVICES:** 40P **NOTES:** No dogs (ex guide dogs) No coaches No smoking in restaurant Last d 9.30pm **CARDS:**

See advert on opposite page

MIDDLEWICH Cheshire — Map 07 SJ76

Travelodge

M6 Junction 18, A54
☎ 0800 850 950

Travelodge

This modern building offers accommodation in smart, spacious and well equipped bedrooms, all with en-suite bathrooms. Refreshments may be taken at the nearby family restaurant. For details about current prices, consult the Contents Page under Hotel Groups for the Travelodge phone number.
ROOMS: 32 en suite (bth/shr) d £49.95 *

MIDHURST West Sussex — Map 04 SU82

★★★ *Angel*

North St GU29 9DN
Quality Percentage Score: 77%
☎ 01730 812421 📠 01730 815928
Dir: *on South side of A272 in centre of Midhurst*

An English market town hotel which has consistently been at the fore with high standards of hospitality and cuisine. The lounge offers country house comfort and style while the bar and brasserie have a more rustic feel. Further contrast is provided by the elegant, well-appointed Cowdray Room restaurant. Individually decorated bedrooms combine style with comfort.
ROOMS: 24 en suite (bth/shr) 4 annexe en suite (bth/shr) (2 fmly) No smoking in 6 bedrooms **MEALS:** English, French, Italian & Caribbean Cuisine V meals Coffee am Tea pm **FACILITIES:** CTV in all bedrooms Wkly live entertainment **CONF:** Thtr 60 Class 40 Board 40 **SERVICES:** Night porter 28P **NOTES:** No dogs (ex guide dogs) Last d 10pm **CARDS:**

MIDHURST West Sussex — Map 04 SU82

★★★ *Spread Eagle*

South St GU29 9NH
Quality Percentage Score: 77%
☎ 01730 816911 📠 01730 815668
Dir: *on A286*

Full of character with sloping floors, ancient beams and inglenook fireplaces. Individually-decorated bedrooms, furnished with antique and reproduction pieces, provide modern comforts. The leisure centre with pool, gym and beauty treatments is popular. Chef Stephen Crane has a modern unfussy style of cuisine.
ROOMS: 35 en suite (bth/shr) 4 annexe en suite (shr) No smoking in 6 bedrooms **MEALS:** English & French Cuisine V meals Coffee am Tea pm **FACILITIES:** CTV in all bedrooms STV Indoor swimming pool (heated) Sauna Gym Jacuzzi/spa Health & beauty treatment rooms Steam room Fitness trainer **CONF:** Thtr 70 Class 40 Board 35 **SERVICES:** Night porter 70P **NOTES:** No coaches No smoking in restaurant Last d 9.30pm **CARDS:**

MIDHURST West Sussex — Map 04 SU82

★★★ Southdowns Country

Dumpford Ln, Trotton GU31 5JN
Quality Percentage Score: 72%
☎ 01730 821521 📠 01730 821790
Dir: *on A272, after town turn left at Keepers Arms*

Best Western

Hidden down a country lane, this attractive hotel offers peaceful surroundings and good facilities for conferences and wedding receptions or a break from city life. Bedrooms, most with views of surrounding countryside, are attractively furnished and well equipped. The beamed Tudor bar has a roaring log fire in winter and is an informal location for drinks or light meals. The spacious Country restaurant offers more substantial fare and menus change regularly, focusing on seasonal, quality produce.

ROOMS: 20 en suite (bth/shr) (3 fmly) No smoking in 4 bedrooms s fr £69; d fr £89 (incl. bkfst) * LB Off peak **MEALS:** Lunch £7.50-£15 High tea fr £6.95 Dinner £20-£30 & alc European Cuisine V meals Coffee am Tea pm **FACILITIES:** CTV in all bedrooms Indoor swimming pool (heated) Tennis (hard) Sauna Solarium Croquet lawn Exercise equipment Xmas **CONF:** Thtr 120 Class 30 Board 30 Del from £85 * **SERVICES:** 70P **NOTES:** No children 10yrs No smoking in restaurant Last d 9.30pm **CARDS:**

See advert under PETERSFIELD

MIDSOMER NORTON Somerset — Map 03 ST65

★★★ Centurion

Charlton Ln BA3 4BD
Quality Percentage Score: 70%
☎ 01761 417711 📠 01761 418357
Dir: *off A367, 10m S of Bath*

This modern family-run hotel, situated between the cities of Bath and Wells, incorporates the adjacent Fosseway Country Club with its 9 hole golf course and other leisure amenities. Comfortable bedrooms are ideally suited for both leisure and business guests, being well equipped and furnished to a high standard with co-ordinating fabrics. The public areas include a choice of bars, an attractive lounge and a range of meeting and function rooms. The short menu provides an interesting selection of freshly prepared dishes, served in the smart restaurant, overlooking the garden.
ROOMS: 44 en suite (bth/shr) (4 fmly) s fr £62; d fr £72 (incl. bkfst & dinner) * LB Off peak **MEALS:** Lunch £8.30-£12.50 High tea fr £3.30 Dinner £16.50-£19.25 English & Continental Cuisine V meals Coffee am Tea pm **FACILITIES:** CTV in all bedrooms STV Indoor swimming pool (heated) Golf 9 Squash Pool table Bowling green Sports field **CONF:** Thtr 180 Class 70 Board 50 Del from £90 * **SERVICES:** Night porter 100P **NOTES:** No dogs (ex guide dogs) No smoking in restaurant Last d 9.30pm Closed 24-26 Dec **CARDS:**

MIDSOMER NORTON Somerset — Map 03 ST65

★★ *Country Ways*

Marsh Ln BS39 6TT
Quality Percentage Score: 71%
☎ 01761 452449 📠 01761 452706
Dir: *off A37 next to Farrington Gurney Golf Club*

A warm welcome is provided by owner Janet Richards at this cosy little hotel. Situated in a quiet location, convenient for both Bath and Bristol, the property benefits from lovely country views, and the proximity of a local golf course. Janet is also responsible for the freshly prepared and enjoyable food served in the

contd.

intimate dining room. Bedrooms are individually styled, well furnished with stripped pine furniture, and decorated with Laura Ashley fabrics. Comfortable public areas include a small bar-lounge, and a conservatory sitting room.
ROOMS: 6 en suite (bth/shr) **MEALS:** V meals Coffee am Tea pm **FACILITIES:** CTV in all bedrooms Fishing **SERVICES:** 12P **NOTES:** No dogs No coaches No smoking in restaurant Last d 8.45pm Closed 24-31 Dec RS Sun **CARDS:**

MILDENHALL Suffolk — Map 05 TL77
★★★ Riverside
Mill St IP28 7DP
Quality Percentage Score: 66%
☎ 01638 717274 📠 01638 715997
Dir: *taking A1101 into town, left at mini-rdbt along High St, hotel is last building on left before bridge*
An imposing 18th-century, red-brick property, the Riverside Hotel sits on the banks of the River Lark, on the outskirts of this busy market town. The recently refurbished public rooms include the river-facing restaurant to the rear. Bedroom styles and sizes are quite variable, and the more recently refurbished rooms are light and cheerful. There are three separate cottage bedrooms on the ground floor close to the car park.
ROOMS: 20 en suite (bth/shr) (4 fmly) s fr £56; d fr £85 (incl. bkfst) * LB Off peak **MEALS:** Lunch fr £16 High tea fr £5 Dinner fr £20 International Cuisine V meals Coffee am Tea pm **FACILITIES:** CTV in all bedrooms Fishing Croquet lawn Xmas **CONF:** Thtr 50 Class 40 Board 30 Del from £95 * **SERVICES:** Lift 50P **NOTES:** No smoking area in restaurant Last d 9pm **CARDS:**

MILDENHALL Suffolk — Map 05 TL77
★★★ The Smoke House
Beck Row IP28 8DH
Quality Percentage Score: 64%
☎ 01638 713223 📠 01638 712202
Dir: *A1101 into Mildenhall, follow Beck Row signs. Hotel located immediately after mini-rdbt through Beck Row on right-hand side*

This busy complex is popular with visitors to the nearby airbases as well as tour parties, it has a shopping mall and conference centre. Public areas owe their character to 16th-century origins, with open log fires, beams and exposed brickwork. There are two bars and a choice of dining options. The refurbished accommodation is mainly based around modern wings of well proportioned, comfortably appointed bedrooms.
ROOMS: 94 en suite (bth/shr) s fr £80; d fr £100 (incl. bkfst) * LB Off peak **MEALS:** Dinner £14.95-£22.50 English Cuisine V meals Coffee am Tea pm **FACILITIES:** CTV in all bedrooms Tennis Pool table Wkly live entertainment Xmas **CONF:** Thtr 120 Class 80 Board 50 Del £95 * **SERVICES:** 200P **NOTES:** No dogs (ex guide dogs) No smoking in restaurant Last d 9.45pm **CARDS:**

See advert on this page

MILFORD ON SEA Hampshire
Map 04 SZ29

★★★ **Westover Hall**
Park Ln SO41 0PT
Quality Percentage Score: 76%
☎ 01590 643044 01590 644490
Dir: *M3/M27 W and the A337 to Lymington. Follow signs from Lymington fro Milford-on-Sea B3058 hotel is situated just outside village centre towards cliff*

Built for the Siemens family, this splendid mansion commands truly spectacular views. There is a superb galleried entrance hall with original wood panelling. The restaurant, with views of the Needles on the Isle of Wight, offers guests an interesting menu of freshly prepared dishes. A friendly and relaxed atmosphere prevails throughout. Accommodation is spacious and well equipped, with such thoughtful extras as fresh flowers and bathrobes. The hotel also has a wedding licence.
ROOMS: 13 en suite (bth/shr) (1 fmly) s £80; d £110-£140 (incl. bkfst) LB Off peak **MEALS:** Lunch £21.50-£23 High tea £10 Dinner £25 European Cuisine V meals Coffee am Tea pm **FACILITIES:** CTV in all bedrooms Xmas **CONF:** Thtr 50 Class 30 Board 25 **SERVICES:** 50P **NOTES:** No coaches No smoking in restaurant Last d 9pm
CARDS:

See advert under LYMINGTON

MILFORD ON SEA Hampshire
Map 04 SZ29

★★★ **South Lawn**
Lymington Rd SO41 0RF
Quality Percentage Score: 72%
☎ 01590 643911 01590 644820
Dir: *turn left off A337 at Everton onto B3058. Hotel approx 1m on right*

This former dower house, in four acres on the edge of the New Forest, is close to the sea. The bedrooms are spacious and attractively decorated, and the large lounge is a comfortable area to relax in. The bright dining room serves a good range of local produce prepared with care by Ernst Barten and his team.
ROOMS: 24 en suite (bth/shr) No smoking in all bedrooms s fr £52.50; d fr £97 (incl. bkfst) * LB Off peak **MEALS:** Lunch £6-£15 & alc Dinner fr £19.75 English, French & German Cuisine V meals Coffee am Tea pm **FACILITIES:** CTV in all bedrooms STV **SERVICES:** 60P **NOTES:** No dogs No children 7yrs No smoking in restaurant Last d 8.30pm Closed 20 Dec-18 Jan **CARDS:**

See advert under LYMINGTON

MILTON COMMON Oxfordshire
Map 04 SP60

★★★ **The Oxford Belfry**
OX9 2JW
Quality Percentage Score: 68%
☎ 01844 279381 01844 279624
Dir: *M40 junct 7 - A329 to Thame. Turn left onto A40 by 3 Pigeons Pub. Hotel 300yds on right*

MARSTON HOTELS

This smart modern hotel, with mock-Tudor creeper-clad façade, is well situated for the M40. Ambitious plans are further improving the physical standards. Bedrooms vary in size and style but are mostly spacious and well equipped with an excellent range of facilities including satellite TV. The newly refurbished rooms are particularly impressive, attractively furnished and decorated in co-ordinated colours. Fresh, tasty food is served in the restaurant by a team of young, attentive staff. Dinner dances are a popular weekend feature.
ROOMS: 130 en suite (bth/shr) (10 fmly) No smoking in 68 bedrooms s fr £97; d fr £115 LB Off peak **MEALS:** Lunch £13.95-£17 & alc High tea £9.50-£15.50 Dinner £20-£25 & alc English & Continental Cuisine V meals Coffee am Tea pm **FACILITIES:** CTV in all bedrooms STV Indoor swimming pool (heated) Tennis (hard) Sauna Solarium Gym Xmas **CONF:** Thtr 370 Class 220 Board 120 Del from £140 * **SERVICES:** Lift Night porter 200P **NOTES:** No smoking area in restaurant Last d 9.45pm
CARDS:

MILTON KEYNES Buckinghamshire
Map 04 SP83

see also **Flitwick, Hanslope & Woburn**

★★★ **Courtyard by Marriott Milton Keynes**
London Rd, Newport Pagnell MK16 0JA
Quality Percentage Score: 68%
☎ 01908 613688 01908 617335
Dir: *0.5m from junct 14 of M1 on the A509*

COURTYARD. Marriott

Very conveniently positioned for the M1 motorway, yet in a quiet spot, this popular hotel is designed around a handsome three-story Georgian House and a pretty courtyard. The Coach House offers bright, inviting public rooms, including a range of conference rooms; a small gym is an added bonus. Bedrooms are smartly decorated and offer good facilities, particularly to the business guest.
ROOMS: 49 en suite (bth/shr) (1 fmly) No smoking in 26 bedrooms d £89 * LB Off peak **MEALS:** Lunch £14.95-£18.95 Dinner £15.95-£25.95 & alc International Cuisine V meals Coffee am Tea pm **FACILITIES:** CTV in all bedrooms STV Gym **CONF:** Thtr 200 Class 90 Board 50 Del from £124 * **SERVICES:** Night porter 160P **NOTES:** No dogs (ex guide dogs) No smoking in restaurant Last d 9.45pm
CARDS:

MILTON KEYNES Buckinghamshire
Map 04 SP83

★★★ **Posthouse Milton Keynes**
500 Saxon Gate West MK9 2HQ
Quality Percentage Score: 66%
☎ 01908 667722 01908 674714
Dir: *M1 junct 14 over 7 roundabouts right at 8th hotel on left*

Posthouse

This large modern hotel is situated in the city centre, and offers opulent public areas, with glass-sided lifts overlooking the

contd.

lounges and restaurants. Bedrooms are comfortably appointed and include several designed for women.
ROOMS: 150 en suite (bth/shr) No smoking in 79 bedrooms d fr £119 * LB Off peak **MEALS:** International Cuisine V meals Coffee am Tea pm **FACILITIES:** CTV in all bedrooms STV Indoor swimming pool (heated) Sauna Solarium Gym Health & fitness centre Wkly live entertainment Xmas **CONF:** Thtr 150 Class 85 Board 35 Del from £60 * **SERVICES:** Lift Night porter 80P **NOTES:** No smoking area in restaurant Last d 10.30pm **CARDS:**

MILTON KEYNES Buckinghamshire — Map 04 SP83
★★★ Quality Hotel & Suites Milton Keynes
]Monks Way, Two Mile Ash MK8 8LY
Quality Percentage Score: 64%
☎ 01908 561666 📠 01908 568303
Dir: *junct A5/A422*
Bedrooms at this purpose built hotel are particularly well equipped, having extra phones and mini bars; there are also a number of suites with fax machines. All day room and lounge service are additional eating options. A small leisure complex adds to guest comfort.
ROOMS: 88 en suite (bth/shr) (15 fmly) No smoking in 44 bedrooms s fr £81.50; d fr £105.50 * LB Off peak **MEALS:** Lunch £2.95-£15.95alc Dinner fr £14.50 & alc English & Continental Cuisine V meals Coffee am Tea pm **FACILITIES:** CTV in all bedrooms STV Indoor swimming pool (heated) Sauna Solarium Gym Jacuzzi/spa Steam room Whirlpool spa Xmas **CONF:** Thtr 150 Class 70 Board 60 **SERVICES:** Night porter Air conditioning 200P **NOTES:** No dogs (ex guide dogs) No smoking in restaurant Last d 9.30pm **CARDS:**

MILTON KEYNES Buckinghamshire — Map 04 SP83
★★ *Different Drummer*
94 High St, Stony Stratford MK11 1AH
Quality Percentage Score: 67%
☎ 01908 564733 📠 01908 260646
This attractive townhouse hotel on historic Stony Stratford's High Street offers a warm welcome to its guests. The smart Italian restaurant, Al Tamborista, is a popular dining spot and enjoys a good local reputation. Bedrooms are generally spacious, whilst the hotel lounge incorporates a bar and is particularly comfortable.
ROOMS: 8 en suite (bth/shr) 4 annexe en suite (shr) (2 fmly) **MEALS:** English & Italian Cuisine V meals **FACILITIES:** CTV in all bedrooms **NOTES:** No dogs (ex guide dogs) No coaches Last d 10.30pm **CARDS:**

MILTON KEYNES Buckinghamshire — Map 04 SP83
★★ Swan Revived
High St, Newport Pagnell MK16 8AR
Quality Percentage Score: 65%
☎ 01908 610565 📠 01908 210995
Dir: *on B526*
This charming coaching inn has stood in the heart of Newport Pagnell for centuries. Service is friendly, and bedrooms well equipped and spacious. The restaurant serves a wide variety of enjoyable dishes, and there is a cosy hotel bar, as well as a pub to the rear of the building, popular with locals.
ROOMS: 42 en suite (bth/shr) (2 fmly) s £75; d £79.50 (incl. bkfst) * LB Off peak **MEALS:** Lunch £9.95-£11.95 & alc Dinner £15.50-£22.50alc English & Continental Cuisine V meals Coffee am Tea pm **FACILITIES:** CTV in all bedrooms STV **CONF:** Thtr 70 Class 30 Board 28 Del from £109 * **SERVICES:** Lift Night porter 18P **NOTES:** Last d 10pm RS 25 Dec-1 Jan **CARDS:**

MILTON KEYNES Buckinghamshire — Map 04 SP83
⌂ *Campanile*
40 Penn Rd, Fenny Stratford, Bletchley MK2 2AU
☎ 01908 649819 📠 01908 649818

This modern building offers accommodation in smart well equipped bedrooms, all with en-suite bathrooms. Refreshments may be taken at the informal Bistro. For details about current prices, consult the Contents Page under Hotel Groups for the Campanile phone number.

MILTON KEYNES Buckinghamshire — Map 04 SP83
⌂ Travel Inn
Secklow Gate West MK9 3BZ
☎ 01908 663388 📠 01908 607481
Dir: *from M1 junct 14 follow H6 route over 6 rdbts at the 7th (called Sth Secklow) turn right, Travel Inn on left*
This modern building offers accommodation in smart, spacious and well equipped bedrooms, all with en-suite bathrooms. Refreshments may be taken at the nearby family restaurant. For details about current prices consult the Contents Page under Hotel Groups for the Travel Inn phone number.
ROOMS: 38 en suite (bth/shr) d £39.95 *

MILTON KEYNES Buckinghamshire — Map 04 SP83
⌂ Travelodge
109 Grafton Gate MK9 1AL
☎ 0800 850950
This modern building offers accommodation in smart, spacious and well equipped bedrooms, all with en-suite bathrooms. Refreshments may be taken at the nearby family restaurant. For details about current prices, consult the Contents Page under Hotel Groups for the Travelodge phone number.
ROOMS: 80 en suite (bth/shr) d £55.95 *

MILTON KEYNES Buckinghamshire — Map 04 SP83
⌂ Welcome Lodge
Newport Pagnell Service Area MK16 8DS
☎ 01908 610878 📠 01908 216539
Dir: *M1 northbound between junct 14 & 15, access available from southbound carriageway*
This modern building offers accommodation in smart, spacious and well equipped bedrooms, suitable for families and businessmen, and all with en-suite bathrooms. Refreshments may be taken at the nearby family restaurant. For details of current prices, consult the Contents Page under Hotel Groups for the Welcome Break phone number.
ROOMS: 92 en suite (bth/shr) d fr £45 * **CONF:** Thtr 20 Class 10 Board 15

M

MINEHEAD Somerset — Map 03 SS94

★★★ Benares

Northfield Rd TA24 5PT
Quality Percentage Score: 71%
☎ 01643 704911 Fax 01643 706373
Dir: *along sea front 75yds before harbour turn left into Blenheim Rd then right into Northfield Rd*

From an elevated position on North Hill this extended Edwardian house is set in over an acre of beautifully maintained gardens and has views over the Bristol Channel, and on a clear day the Welsh coast is visible. Italian fireplaces and stained glass windows are two of the original features in the spacious and comfortable public areas. Each evening a short fixed-price, five-course dinner is served, including delicious home-made puddings. Peter Maskrey and his small team of loyal and smiling staff, provide friendly service.

ROOMS: 19 en suite (bth/shr) (3 fmly) s £52; d £94 (incl. bkfst) * LB Off peak **MEALS:** Bar Lunch £3-£15alc Dinner £22 English, French & Italian Cuisine V meals Coffee am Tea pm **FACILITIES:** CTV in all bedrooms Xmas **SERVICES:** 22P **NOTES:** No coaches No smoking in restaurant Last d 8.30pm Closed 9 Nov-25 Mar (ex Xmas)
CARDS:

See advert on opposite page

MINEHEAD Somerset — Map 03 SS94

★★★ Northfield

Northfield Rd TA24 5PU
Quality Percentage Score: 67%
☎ 01643 705155 Fax 01643 707715

Set in well maintained gardens, not far from the town centre and sea front. Front rooms have views across the bay, there are comfortable sitting rooms and leisure facilities. An evening fixed price menu is served in the oak-panelled dining room, extra dishes are on a short carte. Attractively co-ordinated bedrooms vary in size and are equipped to a good standard.

ROOMS: 25 en suite (bth/shr) (7 fmly) s £52-£58; d £84-£96 (incl. bkfst) * LB Off peak **MEALS:** Lunch £6.75-£12.75 Dinner £18.95-£19.95 V meals Coffee am Tea pm **FACILITIES:** CTV in 24 bedrooms Indoor swimming pool (heated) Solarium Gym Putting green Jacuzzi/spa Steam room Xmas **CONF:** Thtr 70 Class 45 Board 30 **SERVICES:** Lift 44P **NOTES:** No coaches No smoking in restaurant Last d 8.30pm
CARDS:

MINEHEAD Somerset — Map 03 SS94

★★ Periton Park

Middlecombe TA24 8SN
Quality Percentage Score: 75%
☎ 01643 706885 Fax 01643 706885
Dir: *Hotel located on south side of A39 from Minehead*

Nestling in its own wooded grounds on the northern edge of Exmoor, this delightful country house offers magnificent views and tranquillity. Modern facilities such as a meeting room and helicopter pad have not affected its special atmosphere. Spacious bedrooms with rich fabrics and lounges with deep arm chairs and sofas, are a just a few of the comforts offered. A seasonal menu tempts with a selection of interesting dishes based on fresh local produce; look out for the Somerset House Wines - a real find!

ROOMS: 8 en suite (bth/shr) No smoking in 3 bedrooms s £54-£59.50; d £88-£99 (incl. bkfst) * LB Off peak **MEALS:** Dinner £23.50 V meals **FACILITIES:** CTV in all bedrooms Riding Croquet lawn Xmas **CONF:** Thtr 24 Board 16 Del from £95 * **SERVICES:** 12P **NOTES:** No coaches No children 12yrs No smoking in restaurant Last d 9pm Closed Jan **CARDS:**

MINEHEAD Somerset — Map 03 SS94

★★ Channel House Hotel

Church Path TA24 5QG
Quality Percentage Score: 74%
☎ 01643 703229 Fax 01643 708925
Dir: *from A39, at rdbt turn right to seafront, then left onto promenade, 1st right, then 1st left to Blenheim Gardens 1st right Northfield Road*

Set in two acres of superb gardens, this charming and well-run hotel offers relaxing and tranquil surroundings. Decorated in pastel shades, many bedrooms have wonderful views, while the dining room serves an imaginative menu using the best local produce. The South West coastal path starts from the hotel garden.

ROOMS: 8 en suite (bth/shr) (1 fmly) s £67-£79; d £104-£128 (incl. bkfst & dinner) LB Off peak **MEALS:** Bar Lunch £5-£10 Dinner fr £20 & alc International Cuisine V meals Coffee am Tea pm **FACILITIES:** CTV in all bedrooms Xmas **SERVICES:** Air conditioning 10P **NOTES:** No dogs No coaches No children 10yrs No smoking in restaurant Last d 8.30pm Closed Dec-Feb ex open Xmas **CARDS:**

MONK FRYSTON North Yorkshire — Map 08 SE52

★★★ Monk Fryston Hall

LS25 5DU
Quality Percentage Score: 68%
☎ 01977 682369 Fax 01977 683544
Dir: *A1/A63 junct towards Selby. Left-hand side in centre of Monk Fryston*

This historic mansion stands in attractive and mature grounds in the centre of the village. Inviting fires, oak panelling and large paintings are features, whilst service is attentive and the cooking is traditional in style. The bedrooms have been equipped to meet the needs of today's traveller, which makes the hotel popular with business persons.

ROOMS: 30 en suite (bth/shr) (2 fmly) No smoking in 10 bedrooms s £79-£99; d £99-£150 (incl. bkfst) * LB Off peak **MEALS:** Lunch £15.20-£18.95 Dinner £22.50-£27.50 V meals Coffee am Tea pm **FACILITIES:** CTV in all bedrooms STV Riding Croquet lawn Putting green Xmas **CONF:** Thtr 100 Class 40 Board 30 Del from £115 * **SERVICES:** Night porter 100P **NOTES:** No smoking in restaurant Last d 9.45pm **CARDS:**

See advert on opposite page

MORCOTT Rutland — Map 04 SK90

Travelodge

Uppingham LE15 9DL
☎ 01572 747719 Fax 01572 747719
Dir: *on A47, eastbound*

This modern building offers accommodation in smart, spacious and well equipped bedrooms, all with en-suite bathrooms. Refreshments may be taken at the nearby family restaurant. For details about current prices, consult the Contents Page under Hotel Groups for the Travelodge phone number.

ROOMS: 40 en suite (bth/shr) d £39.95 *

MORDEN Greater London
See LONDON SECTION plan 1 *D1*
Travelodge
Epsom Rd SM4 5PH
☎ 020 8640 8227 🖷 020 8640 8227
Dir: *on A24*
This modern building offers accommodation in smart, spacious and well equipped bedrooms, all with en-suite bathrooms. Refreshments may be taken at the nearby family restaurant. For details about current prices, consult the Contents Page under Hotel Groups for the Travelodge phone number.
ROOMS: 32 en suite (bth/shr) d £59.95 *

MORECAMBE Lancashire **Map 07 SD46**
★★★ **Strathmore**
Marine Rd East LA4 5AP
Quality Percentage Score: 67%
☎ 01524 421234 🖷 01524 414242
Dir: *from Lancaster A589 to Morecambe 3rd rdbt follow signs for the Promenade on reaching coast road turn left and hotel on the left*
Commanding a fine position on the promenade and boasting panoramic views out to sea and over the bay towards the Lake District, this friendly hotel provides modern and well furnished bedrooms together with spacious and comfortable public rooms.
contd.

A skilfully prepared range of well prepared food is available. The hotel gains its name from a once famous ocean liner.

Strathmore, Morecambe

ROOMS: 50 en suite (bth/shr) (5 fmly) No smoking in 15 bedrooms s £45-£65; d £75-£95 (incl. bkfst) * LB Off peak **MEALS:** Lunch £9.50-£12.50 Dinner £17.50 English & French Cuisine V meals Coffee am **FACILITIES:** CTV in all bedrooms STV Wkly live entertainment Xmas **CONF:** Thtr 180 Class 100 Board 50 Del from £70 * **SERVICES:** Lift Night porter 19P **NOTES:** No dogs (ex guide dogs) No smoking in restaurant Last d 9.30pm **CARDS:** ● ▬ ▬ ▣ ▬ ▬ ▢

See advert on page 463

≡ **MORECAMBE** Lancashire   **Map 07 SD46**
★★★✦ **Headway**
Marine Rd East LA4 5AW
Quality Percentage Score: 62%
☎ 01524 412525 ▤ 01524 832630
Dir: *from the seafront, the Headway hotel is 200 yards along the promenade on the left hand side*
Offering fine views over the bay and with the Lakeland hills beyond, this hotel - directed by the Knights of St Columba - caters mainly for the coach tour trade. Many of the bedrooms have benefited from refurbishment and now offer all the expected amenities. There are spacious public rooms where entertainment is provided during the season.
ROOMS: 54 en suite (bth/shr) (4 fmly) s fr £35; d fr £70 (incl. bkfst) * LB Off peak **MEALS:** Sunday Lunch £8.95 High tea £3.50 Dinner £10.95 & alc V meals Coffee am Tea pm **FACILITIES:** CTV in all bedrooms Wkly live entertainment Xmas **CONF:** Thtr 200 Class 50 Board 100 Del from £49.95 * **SERVICES:** Lift Night porter 30P **NOTES:** Last d 8.30pm RS 3-10 Jan **CARDS:** ● ▬ ▬ ▣

≡ **MORECAMBE** Lancashire   **Map 07 SD46**
★★★ **Elms**
Bare Village LA4 6DD
Quality Percentage Score: 61%
☎ 01524 411501 ▤ 01524 831979
This well-established hotel stands in pleasant gardens, just off the North Promenade at Bare. The well equipped bedrooms have pretty soft furnishings and include a number of spacious rooms with four-poster beds. Public rooms include a cheery lounge bar and an elegant Victorian-style restaurant. The hotel also owns The Owl's Nest pub, close to the main building, where bar meals are served at lunch time and guests can enjoy a quiet drink in the evening.
ROOMS: 40 en suite (bth/shr) (3 fmly) s £53-£61; d £73-£90 (incl. bkfst) * LB Off peak **MEALS:** Lunch £10.25 Dinner £16.95 English & French Cuisine V meals Coffee am Tea pm **FACILITIES:** CTV in all bedrooms Xmas **CONF:** Thtr 200 Class 72 Board 60 Del from £64 * **SERVICES:** Lift Night porter 80P **NOTES:** No smoking in restaurant Last d 9.30pm **CARDS:** ● ▬ ▬ ▣ ▬ ▢

≡ **MORECAMBE** Lancashire   **Map 07 SD46**
★★✦ *Clarendon*
Marine Rd West, West End Promenade LA4 4EP
Quality Percentage Score: 62%
☎ 01524 410180 ▤ 01524 421616
Commanding superb views over the bay, this popular resort hotel is just a short walk from the local attractions. The public rooms include a spacious dining room with front aspects and a popular lounge bar where a good range of attractively priced food is served. Residents have a spacious first floor lounge with splendid views and the bedrooms provide a range of sizes and styles with good facilities. Staff are friendly and keen to please.
ROOMS: 31 rms (28 bth/shr) (2 fmly) **MEALS:** V meals Coffee am Tea pm **FACILITIES:** CTV in all bedrooms Pool table **CONF:** Thtr 60 Class 50 Board 50 **SERVICES:** Lift Night porter **NOTES:** Last d 9pm **CARDS:** ● ▬ ▬ ▣ ▬ ▬ ▢

≡ **MORETON** Merseyside   **Map 07 SJ28**
★★★ *Leasowe Castle*
Leasowe Rd L46 3RF
Quality Percentage Score: 65%
☎ 0151 606 9191 ▤ 0151 678 5551
Dir: *leave M53 junct 1 take 1st exit from rdbt at 1st slip road join A551 hotel three quarters of a mile on right*

Dating back in parts to 1592, many impressive features of this hotel design remain, including ornately carved wall panels and a ceiling brought from the Palace of Westminster. Bedrooms, most with sea views, are well equipped and comfortable. The beamed bar offers a range of snacks and bar meals and there is also a more formal restaurant.
ROOMS: 47 en suite (bth/shr) (3 fmly) No smoking in 3 bedrooms **MEALS:** English & Continental Cuisine V meals Coffee am Tea pm **FACILITIES:** CTV in all bedrooms STV Sauna Gym Water sports ch fac **CONF:** Thtr 220 Board 40 **SERVICES:** Lift Night porter 200P **NOTES:** No dogs (ex guide dogs) No smoking area in restaurant Last d 10pm **CARDS:** ● ▬ ▬ ▣ ▬ ▬ ▢

≡ **MORETONHAMPSTEAD** Devon   **Map 03 SX78**
★★★★ ⊛ **Manor House**
TQ13 8RE
Quality Percentage Score: 66%
☎ 01647 440355 ▤ 01647 440961
Dir: *2m from Moretonhampstead towards Princetown on B3212*
A substantial Victorian manor house set in quiet grounds which include a championship golf course and a lake. Bedrooms are

contd.

⬚ PRINCIPAL HOTELS

We endeavour to be as accurate as possible but changes in personnel and data can occur in establishments after the Hotel Guide has gone to press.

---

brightly decorated and have an inviting atmosphere. The Hambleden Restaurant serves interesting menus.
ROOMS: 90 en suite (bth/shr) (5 fmly) s £69-£75; d £118-£150 (incl. bkfst & dinner) * LB Off peak **MEALS:** Lunch fr £11.95 High tea £5-£12 Dinner fr £17.95 & alc English & French Cuisine V meals Coffee am Tea pm **FACILITIES:** CTV in all bedrooms STV Golf 18 Tennis (hard) Fishing Snooker Croquet lawn Putting green Xmas **CONF:** Thtr 100 Class 50 Board 40 Del £145 * **SERVICES:** Lift Night porter 100P **NOTES:** No smoking in restaurant Last d 9.30pm **CARDS:**

MORETON-IN-MARSH Gloucestershire — Map 04 SP23

★★★ Manor House Hotel
High St GL56 0LJ
Quality Percentage Score: 73%
☎ 01608 650501 01608 651481
Dir: *off A429 at south end of the town*
Built from honey-coloured Cotswold stone, this charming 16th-century property makes an elegant hotel, retaining much of its original character and providing comfortable accommodation and professional service. Bedrooms vary in size but all are well equipped and some are particularly opulent.
ROOMS: 38 en suite (bth/shr) (2 fmly) s £65-£75; d £90-£135 (incl. bkfst) * LB Off peak **MEALS:** Lunch £14.50-£16.95 Dinner £24.50 & alc English & French Cuisine V meals Coffee am Tea pm **FACILITIES:** CTV in all bedrooms Indoor swimming pool (heated) Sauna Jacuzzi/spa Xmas **CONF:** Thtr 100 Class 55 Board 50 Del from £125 * **SERVICES:** Lift Night porter 30P **NOTES:** No dogs (ex guide dogs) No smoking in restaurant Last d 9.30pm **CARDS:**

MORLEY West Yorkshire — Map 08 SE22

★★ The Old Vicarage
Bruntcliffe Rd LS27 0JZ
Quality Percentage Score: 65%
☎ 0113 2532174 0113 2533549
Dir: *follow signs for A650, go through traffic lights and pass two gargaes on the left. Hotel is located just before St Andrew's Church*

This elegant stone building provides modern well equipped bedrooms. The interesting public rooms have a delightful Victorian theme. A good range of well produced food is available and service is both friendly and attentive.
ROOMS: 21 en suite (bth/shr) (1 fmly) No smoking in 14 bedrooms s £34-£48; d £55-£62 (incl. bkfst) * LB Off peak **MEALS:** Dinner £10.95 V meals Coffee am **FACILITIES:** CTV in all bedrooms **SERVICES:** 21P **NOTES:** No dogs (ex guide dogs) No coaches No smoking in restaurant Last d 8pm **CARDS:**

MORPETH Northumberland — Map 12 NZ28

★★★★ *Linden Hall*
NE65 8XF
Quality Percentage Score: 65%
☎ 01670 516611 01670 788544
(For full entry see Longhorsley)

MORTEHOE See Woolacombe

MOULSFORD Oxfordshire — Map 04 SU58

★★ Beetle & Wedge
Ferry Ln OX10 9JF
Quality Percentage Score: 73%
☎ 01491 651381 01491 651376
Once the home of Jerome K Jerome, bedrooms at this fine Thames-side hotel are individually decorated. Bathrooms all feature huge enamelled tubs. Guests can choose from two dining options; the popular brasserie-style Boathouse, or the dining room which offers a more formal environment.
ROOMS: 6 en suite (bth/shr) 4 annexe en suite (bth/shr) No smoking in all bedrooms s £90-£110; d £120-£150 (incl. bkfst) * LB Off peak **MEALS:** Lunch fr £27.50 Dinner fr £35 & alc V meals Coffee am **FACILITIES:** CTV in all bedrooms Fishing Wkly live entertainment **CONF:** Thtr 50 Class 30 Board 25 Del £145 * **SERVICES:** 44P **NOTES:** No smoking area in restaurant Last d 10pm RS 25 Dec (restaurant closed) **CARDS:**

MOUNT HAWKE Cornwall & Isles of Scilly — Map 02 SW74

★ *Tregarthen Country Cottage*
Banns Rd TR4 8BW
Quality Percentage Score: 75%
☎ 01209 890399 01209 891041
Dir: *from the A30 turn off at Three Burrows roundabout onto the B3277 St Agnes road, take first left and follow signs to Mount Hawke approx 2m*
Situated in pleasant rural surroundings on the edge of the village, this delightful cottage-style hotel provides a warm welcome to guests, many of whom return on a regular basis. Guests enjoy the comfort of the lounge, with its deep armchairs and roaring log fire. In the well appointed dining room guests can choose from a set menu of traditional home-cooking.
ROOMS: 6 en suite (bth/shr) No smoking in all bedrooms **SERVICES:** 12P **NOTES:** No dogs (ex guide dogs) No coaches No smoking in restaurant

M

MOUSEHOLE Cornwall & Isles of Scilly — Map 02 SW42

★★ Old Coastguard Inn
The Parade TR19 6PR
Quality Percentage Score: 66%
☎ 01736 731222 01736 731720
Dir: *take A30 to Penzance, keep to waterfront & drive to Newlyn, turn left at bridge & follow coastal road 2m to village, hotel 1st building on left*
Situated on the edge of Mousehole, this charming hotel offers comfortable accommodation and modern facilities, and many rooms have sea views. An imaginative menu is offered, many dishes based on fresh fish from nearby Newlyn. The stylish bar, restaurant and sun lounge have wonderful views of the sea.
ROOMS: 14 rms (12 bth/shr) 9 annexe rms (7 bth/shr) (2 fmly) No smoking in all bedrooms s £32-£51; d £64-£80 (incl. bkfst) * LB Off peak **MEALS:** Lunch £3.95-£12.95alc Dinner £22.50 & alc V meals Coffee am Tea pm **FACILITIES:** CTV in all bedrooms **SERVICES:** 12P **NOTES:** No coaches No smoking in restaurant Last d 9.30pm RS Nov-Apr1 **CARDS:**

MOUSEHOLE Cornwall & Isles of Scilly — Map 02 SW42

★★ Carn Du
Raginnis Hill TR19 6SS
Quality Percentage Score: 61%
☎ 01736 731233 01736 731233
Dir: *through village, up hill towards bird hospital, house on right overlooking harbour*
Situated on the edge of the village, Carn Du has commanding views over the sea and Mounts Bay. This hotel combines an
contd.

informal atmosphere with enjoyable home cooked food and comfortably furbished bedrooms.
ROOMS: 7 en suite (bth/shr) s £30-£32; d £60-£64 (incl. bkfst) * LB Off peak **MEALS:** Bar Lunch £3-£10 Dinner fr £15.95 English & German Cuisine V meals Coffee am **FACILITIES:** CTV in all bedrooms **SERVICES:** 12P **NOTES:** No dogs No coaches No smoking in restaurant Last d 8.30pm **CARDS:**

MUCH BIRCH Herefordshire — Map 03 SO53
★★★ Pilgrim
Ross Rd HR2 8HJ
Quality Percentage Score: 62%
☎ 01981 540742 🖷 01981 540620
Dir: *midway between Hereford and Ross-on-Wye off A49*
This much extended former rectory stands in extensive grounds between Ross-on-Wye and Hereford. Accommodation offers good modern comfort and there are some ground-floor rooms and some large enough for families. Reception rooms consist of bar, restaurant and lounge, and also a small meeting room.
ROOMS: 20 en suite (bth/shr) (3 fmly) No smoking in 5 bedrooms s £49.50-£59.50; d £46.50-£90 (incl. bkfst) * LB Off peak **MEALS:** Lunch £9.75 High tea £3.95 Dinner £21.50 & alc English & French Cuisine V meals Coffee am Tea pm **FACILITIES:** CTV in all bedrooms Croquet lawn Putting green Pitch & putt Badminton Xmas **CONF:** Thtr 45 Class 45 Board 25 **SERVICES:** 40P **NOTES:** No coaches **CARDS:**

MUCH WENLOCK Shropshire — Map 07 SO69
★★★ *Raven*
Barrow St TF13 6EN
Quality Percentage Score: 73%
☎ 01952 727251 🖷 01952 728416
Dir: *M54 junct 4 or 5, take the A442 S, then A4169 to Much Wenlock*
This personally run, town-centre hotel has as its core a 17th-century coaching inn, but has also extended into other historic old buildings adjacent to it. Accommodation is all well furnished and equipped to offer modern comfort, and rooms include some, reached by an inner courtyard, on the ground and first floors of a converted stable and coach house, one of which is a delightful suite with a galleried bedrooom. Public areas feature an interesting collection of prints and other memorabilia connected with the Olympic Games.
ROOMS: 8 en suite (bth/shr) 7 annexe en suite (bth/shr) **MEALS:** International Cuisine V meals Coffee am **FACILITIES:** CTV in all bedrooms STV **CONF:** Thtr 16 Board 14 **SERVICES:** 30P **NOTES:** No dogs (ex guide dogs) No coaches No smoking in restaurant **CARDS:**

MUCH WENLOCK Shropshire — Map 07 SO69
★★ Wheatland Fox
TF13 6AD
Quality Percentage Score: 68%
☎ 01952 727292 🖷 01952 727301
Dir: *just off A458 Shrewsbury/Bridgnorth road turn into Much Wenlock*
In common with a number of other buildings in this historic town, the half-timbered structure was built in the 17th century, with a Georgian frontage added later. It is now a small and friendly hotel, offering well equipped and comfortable bedrooms. Snacks are available in the cosy beamed bar and a full menu of popular dishes is served in the adjacent dining room.
ROOMS: 7 en suite (bth/shr) s fr £45; d fr £55 (incl. bkfst) * LB Off peak **MEALS:** Sunday Lunch £2-£8.50alc Dinner fr £8.50alc English & French Cuisine V meals Coffee am Tea pm **FACILITIES:** CTV in all bedrooms **SERVICES:** 12P **NOTES:** No coaches Last d 9.30pm **CARDS:**

MUDEFORD See Christchurch

MULLION Cornwall & Isles of Scilly — Map 02 SW61
★★★ Polurrian
TR12 7EN
Quality Percentage Score: 71%
☎ 01326 240421 🖷 01326 240083
Situated with marvellous views over Mullion Cove and the sea, this impressive Edwardian hotel has spacious and comfortable public areas and a well equipped leisure centre. Bedrooms, all individual in style and decor, are pleasing and comfortable, many have sea views.
ROOMS: 39 en suite (bth/shr) (22 fmly) s £55-£100; d £110-£200 (incl. bkfst & dinner) * LB Off peak **MEALS:** Lunch £7.50-£16.50 High tea £12.50 Dinner £22.50 English & French Cuisine V meals Coffee am Tea pm **FACILITIES:** CTV in all bedrooms STV Indoor swimming pool (heated) Outdoor swimming pool (heated) Tennis (hard) Squash Snooker Sauna Solarium Gym Croquet lawn Putting green Jacuzzi/spa Cricket net Whirlpool Mountain bikes & Wet suit hire ch fac Xmas **CONF:** Thtr 100 Class 60 Board 20 Del from £55 * **SERVICES:** Night porter 80P **NOTES:** No smoking area in restaurant Last d 9pm **CARDS:**

See advert on opposite page

MULLION Cornwall & Isles of Scilly — Map 02 SW61
★★ Mullion Cove Hotel
TR12 7EP
Quality Percentage Score: 71%
☎ 01326 240328 🖷 01326 240998
Dir: *in Helston follow signs to The Lizard, turn right at Mullion Holiday Park. Through village & turn left for Cove & Hotel*

This large hotel features spacious public areas which include an elegant restaurant serving freshly prepared dishes; bar meals are available in the popular 'Cove Bar'. Bedrooms are furnished to a high standard and include many modern facilities.
ROOMS: 28 en suite (bth/shr) (9 fmly) s fr £38; d £76-£158 (incl. bkfst & dinner) * LB Off peak **MEALS:** Bar Lunch £1.50-£15alc High tea £1.50-£10alc Dinner £17.50 V meals Coffee am Tea pm **FACILITIES:** CTV in all bedrooms Outdoor swimming pool (heated) Sauna Solarium Xmas **SERVICES:** 60P **NOTES:** No coaches No smoking in restaurant Last d 8.45pm **CARDS:**

MUNGRISDALE Cumbria — Map 11 NY33
★ The Mill
CA11 0XR
Quality Percentage Score: 78%
☎ 01768 779659 🖷 01768 779155
Dir: *exit M6 at junct 40, 2m N of A66*
Formerly a mill cottage dating from 1651, this charming hotel and restaurant lies beside a tranquil stream. Inside there are cosy lounges, low ceilings and a wealth of antiques, paintings and period pieces. Dinner is something of a special occasion.
contd.

The menu is short, but extends to five courses and will satisfy the heartiest of Lakeland appetites.
ROOMS: 7 rms (5 bth/shr) s £65-£75; d £125-£145 (incl. bkfst & dinner) * Off peak **MEALS:** Dinner £27 English & French Cuisine V meals Coffee am Tea pm **FACILITIES:** CTV in all bedrooms Fishing Games room **SERVICES:** 15P **NOTES:** No coaches No smoking in restaurant Last d 8pm Closed Nov-Feb

NAILSWORTH Gloucestershire **Map 03 ST89**

★★ Egypt Mill

GL6 0AE
Quality Percentage Score: 70%
☎ 01453 833449 01453 836098
Dir: *on A46*

A 17th-century flour mill has been converted to create this interesting hotel. It offers a restaurant with adjoining bar, and a cellar bar with a popular bistro. The millstones and lifting equipment are still in evidence, as well as working waterwheels. There are a riverside patio and gardens. Bedrooms are well equipped and delightfully furnished.
ROOMS: 8 en suite (bth/shr) 10 annexe en suite (bth/shr) (2 fmly) s £45.50-£50; d £75-£95 (incl. bkfst) * LB Off peak **MEALS:** Lunch £9-£12.80 Dinner £8-£25alc V meals Coffee am Tea pm **FACILITIES:** CTV in all bedrooms STV Wkly live entertainment ch fac Xmas **CONF:** Thtr 100 Class 80 Del from £70 * **SERVICES:** 120P **NOTES:** No dogs (ex guide dogs) Last d 9.45pm **CARDS:**

NANTWICH Cheshire **Map 07 SJ65**

The Premier Collection

★★★ Rookery Hall

Worleston CW5 6DQ
☎ 01270 610016 01270 626027
Dir: *take B5074 off the 4th rdbt on the Nantwich by-pass. Rookery Hall is 1.5m on the right*

An imposing Regency mansion in extensive gardens and grounds. Although modernised, it retains much period charm and elegance. Bedrooms, some in the adjacent coach house, are very spacious, with sumptuous bathrooms. Public rooms include an impressive hall and attractive drawing room. Well-prepared dishes are offered in the mahogany-panelled dining room.
ROOMS: 30 en suite (bth/shr) 15 annexe en suite (bth/shr) (3 fmly) No smoking in 12 bedrooms s £130-£230; d £175-£275 (incl. bkfst) * LB Off peak **MEALS:** Lunch £18.50 & alc High tea £3.75-£22.50alc Dinner £39.50 European Cuisine V meals Coffee am Tea pm **FACILITIES:** CTV in all bedrooms STV Tennis (hard) Fishing Croquet lawn Clay pigeon shooting Archery Falconry Xmas **CONF:** Thtr 90 Class 40 Board 40 Del from £140 * **SERVICES:** Lift Night porter 150P **NOTES:** No smoking in restaurant Last d 9.45pm **CARDS:**

NANTWICH Cheshire **Map 07 SJ65**

★★ Crown

High St CW5 5AS
Quality Percentage Score: 69%
☎ 01270 625283 01270 628047
Dir: *take A52 to Nantwich hotel in centre of town*

A Grade I listed building and former 16th century coaching inn, this hotel is ideally situated within the pedestrianised main street of Nantwich. The building retains much of its original character; there are exposed timbers in abundance, uneven floors and narrow corridors adding to its historic appeal. Bedrooms vary in size but all are neatly furnished and equipped to meet the needs of today's traveller. The restaurant serves a varied Italian menu, with a short list of traditional English dishes also available for residents. Ask about parking arrangements when booking.
ROOMS: 18 en suite (bth/shr) (2 fmly) No smoking in 2 bedrooms s fr £59; d fr £69 * LB Off peak **MEALS:** English & Italian Cuisine V meals Coffee am Tea pm **FACILITIES:** CTV in all bedrooms STV **CONF:** Thtr 200 Class 150 Board 70 **SERVICES:** Night porter 18P **NOTES:** Last d 10pm Closed 25 Dec **CARDS:**

NEEDHAM MARKET Suffolk **Map 05 TM05**

Travelodge

Beacon Hill IP6 8NY
☎ 01449 721640 01449 721640
Dir: *A14/A140*

This modern building offers accommodation in smart, spacious and well equipped bedrooms, all with en-suite bathrooms. Refreshments may be taken at the nearby family restaurant. For details about current prices, consult the Contents Page under Hotel Groups for the Travelodge phone number.
ROOMS: 40 en suite (bth/shr) d £39.95 *

NESSCLIFFE Shropshire **Map 07 SJ31**

★★ Nesscliffe

Nesscliffe SY4 1DB
Quality Percentage Score: 70%
☎ 01743 741430 Fax 01743 741104
Dir: *on A5 between Shrewsbury/Oswestry*

This privately owned Grade II listed property, which dates back to the early 19th century, stands in the historic village of Nesscliffe, between Shrewsbury and Oswestry. It provides good quality, tastefully appointed and well equipped accommodation, including two rooms with four-poster beds. The open plan public areas comprise an attractive lounge bar and a very pleasant restaurant area, where a wide range of dishes is available.

ROOMS: 8 en suite (bth/shr) (1 fmly) s fr £45; d fr £55 (incl. bkfst) * LB Off peak **MEALS:** Lunch fr £6.50 & alc Dinner fr £9.95 & alc English & Continental Cuisine V meals Coffee am Tea pm **FACILITIES:** CTV in all bedrooms STV ch fac **SERVICES:** 50P **NOTES:** No dogs (ex guide dogs) No smoking in restaurant Last d 9.15pm
CARDS:

NETHER STOWEY Somerset **Map 03 ST13**

★★ Apple Tree

Keenthorne TA5 1HZ
Quality Percentage Score: 64%
☎ 01278 733238 Fax 01278 732693
Dir: *on A39 approx. 7m W of Bridgwater and 2m E of Nether Stowey*

Conveniently located between Bridgwater and Minehead, this attractive roadside inn is now under enthusiastic new ownership and provides comfortable accommodation for both the leisure and commercial user. The bedrooms, several in a garden annexe, are well equipped and smartly presented. The bar, attractive conservatory and lounge offer areas in which to enjoy a quiet drink and meal.

ROOMS: 15 en suite (bth/shr) (1 fmly) No smoking in 3 bedrooms s fr £37.50; d £47.50-£57.50 (incl. bkfst) * LB Off peak **MEALS:** Lunch £5.95-£12.95alc Dinner £12.95-£17.95alc European & Middle Eastern Cuisine V meals Coffee am Tea pm **FACILITIES:** CTV in all bedrooms **SERVICES:** 60P **NOTES:** No dogs (ex guide dogs) No smoking in restaurant Last d 9.30pm **CARDS:**

NETHER WASDALE Cumbria **Map 06 NY10**

★★ Low Wood Hall Hotel & Restaurant

CA20 1ET
Quality Percentage Score: 70%
☎ 019467 26100 Fax 019467 26111
Dir: *turn off A595 at Gosforth and bear left for Wasdale, after 3m turn right for Nether Wasdale*

This delightful country house hotel is set in the village of Nether Wasdale. Bedrooms are contained in both the main house and a modernised barn adjoining, offering modern, practical accommodation. A cosy bar leads off the main hall, as do the lounge and the Mediterranean-styled dining room. The hotel is also the base of an integral training company that attracts both national and international delegates.

ROOMS: 8 en suite (bth/shr) 6 annexe en suite (bth/shr) (3 fmly) No smoking in all bedrooms s £50; d £100 (incl. bkfst) * LB Off peak **MEALS:** Dinner £24.95 & alc English & French Cuisine V meals Coffee am Tea pm **FACILITIES:** CTV in all bedrooms Xmas **CONF:** Thtr 30 Class 30 Board 16 **SERVICES:** 20P **NOTES:** No dogs No smoking in restaurant Last d 8.45pm Closed Jan (unless booked) RS Sun
CARDS:

NEWARK-ON-TRENT Nottinghamshire **Map 08 SK75**

★★ South Parade

117-119 Baldertongate NG24 1RY
Quality Percentage Score: 73%
☎ 01636 703008 & 703030 Fax 01636 605593
Dir: *from B6326 follow Newark signs drive into Newark turn right at lights on x-rds then right again hotel on left opposite Fountain Gardens*

Situated just a few minutes walk from the town centre, this Grade II Listed Georgian building houses a most welcoming hotel, ably and professionally run by the hardworking Lock family. Bedrooms have all been recently refurbished, offering attractively decorated and comfortably appointed accommodation, that has a good range of useful facilities. In addition to the homely lounge, there is a bar and restaurant on the lower ground floor, where good home cooking and friendly service is the order of the day.

ROOMS: 13 en suite (bth/shr) (3 fmly) No smoking in 11 bedrooms s £39.50-£54; d £54-£74.50 (incl. bkfst) LB Off peak **MEALS:** Sunday Lunch £9.75 & alc Dinner £10.50-£18alc V meals Coffee am Tea pm **FACILITIES:** CTV in all bedrooms **CONF:** Thtr 20 Class 20 Board 20 **SERVICES:** Night porter 14P **NOTES:** No coaches No smoking in restaurant Last d 8.45pm **CARDS:**

NEWARK-ON-TRENT Nottinghamshire **Map 08 SK75**

★★ Grange

73 London Rd NG24 1RZ
Quality Percentage Score: 71%
☎ 01636 703399 Fax 01636 702328
Dir: *outskirts of town off southern approach road to A1*

Quietly situated in a residential area, this family run hotel offers high standards of hospitality and a professional approach to service. Public rooms include a smart lounge bar, a quiet comfortable lounge, and a restaurant, in which daily and carte menus are offered. Bedrooms, some of which are located in an adjacent house, are comfortably furnished, well equipped and nicely decorated.

ROOMS: 10 en suite (bth/shr) 5 annexe en suite (bth/shr) (2 fmly) No smoking in 2 bedrooms s £44.95-£52.50; d £62.50-£72.50 (incl. bkfst) * LB Off peak **MEALS:** Dinner £12.95 & alc V meals **FACILITIES:** CTV in all bedrooms **CONF:** Thtr 20 Class 20 Board 20 **SERVICES:** 19P **NOTES:** No dogs No smoking in restaurant Last d 9pm Closed 24 Dec-2 Jan **CARDS:**

NEWARK-ON-TRENT Nottinghamshire **Map 08 SK75**

Travel Inn

Lincoln Rd NG24 2DB
☎ 01636 640690 Fax 01636 605135
Dir: *at intersection of A1/A46/A17*

This modern building offers accommodation in smart, spacious and well equipped bedrooms, all with en-suite bathrooms. Refreshments may be taken at the nearby family restaurant. For details about current prices consult the Contents Page under Hotel Groups for the Travel Inn phone number.

ROOMS: 40 en suite (bth/shr) d £39.95 *

NEWBURY Berkshire **Map 04 SU46**

The Premier Collection

★★★★ The Vineyard at Stockcross
Stockcross RG20 8JU
☎ 01635 528770 📠 01635 528398
Dir: *2.5m W of Newbury on B4000 north of the A4 Newbury to Hungerford road*
To stay at this recently transformed hotel just outside Newbury is to be surrounded by beautiful artwork, sumptuous furnishings, excellent food and superb wine. You will first be greeted by sculptor William Pye's impressive Fire & Water sculpture, then one of the team will seamlessly whisk you to your room. Staff provide a discreet, friendly and highly professional service. If the restaurant is the focal point of the hotel, then artist blacksmith Alan Dawson's stunning steel balustrade is the focal point of the restaurant. Chef David Sharland has come from the Savoy Grill and offers an impressive menu including a gourmet fusion menu which includes wine with each course. The wine is also a great feature with two lists, one devoted entirely to wines of California, home of proprietor Sir Peter Michael's 'other' vineyard.
ROOMS: 33 en suite (bth/shr) No smoking in 10 bedrooms s fr £158.62; d £188-£511.12 (incl. bkfst) * LB Off peak **MEALS:** Lunch fr £20 & alc Dinner fr £39 & alc English & French Cuisine V meals Coffee am Tea pm **FACILITIES:** CTV in all bedrooms STV Indoor swimming pool (heated) Sauna Gym Jacuzzi/spa Treatment rooms Wkly live entertainment **CONF:** Thtr 50 Class 32 Board 20 Del from £235 * **SERVICES:** Lift Night porter Air conditioning 60P **NOTES:** No dogs (ex guide dogs) No coaches No smoking area in restaurant Last d 9.45pm
CARDS:

NEWBURY Berkshire **Map 04 SU46**
★★★★ **Donnington Valley**
Old Oxford Rd, Donnington RG14 3AG
Quality Percentage Score: 79%
☎ 01635 551199 📠 01635 551123
Dir: *exit M4 junct 13, take A34 southbound and exit at Donnington Castle. Turn right over bridge then left hotel is 1m on right*
Guests cannot fail to be impressed by this exceptional hotel, which has justifiably gained an enviable reputation for the outstanding levels of hospitality displayed by its team of dedicated staff. The public areas offer a high standard of comfort throughout and include a sumptuously furnished lounge and bar with a choice of seating areas. The well equipped meeting rooms, much in demand for conferences, have been cleverly decorated and furnished to give character to the striking modern structure of the building. Food remains a strength throughout, whether at breakfast, afternoon tea, or dinner in the impressive galleried restaurant. The hotel also benefits from golfing facilities, which include a popular bar, where guests may enjoy a range of quality snacks.

ROOMS: 58 en suite (bth/shr) (11 fmly) No smoking in 30 bedrooms d £120-£200 * LB Off peak **MEALS:** Lunch £13.50-£15 Dinner £23.50 & alc English & French Cuisine V meals Coffee am Tea pm **FACILITIES:** CTV in all bedrooms STV Golf 18 Putting green Xmas **CONF:** Thtr 140 Class 60 Board 50 **SERVICES:** Lift Night porter 160P **NOTES:** No dogs (ex guide dogs) No coaches No smoking in restaurant Last d 10pm **CARDS:**

NEWBURY Berkshire **Map 04 SU46**
★★★★ **Regency Park Hotel**
Bowling Green Rd, Thatcham RG18 3RP
Quality Percentage Score: 74%
☎ 01635 871555 📠 01635 871571
Dir: *from Newbury take A4 signed Thatcham/Reading. At 2nd rdbt follow signs to Cold Ash. Hotel 1 mile on the left*
Regency Park stands in five acres of grounds and gardens, offering excellent facilities for conferences and weddings. The spacious bedrooms are tastefully decorated, and there is a good restaurant.
ROOMS: 46 en suite (bth/shr) (7 fmly) No smoking in 15 bedrooms s £95-£125; d £110-£145 * LB Off peak **MEALS:** Lunch £12.95-£16.50 & alc Dinner £16.50-£22 & alc English & French Cuisine V meals Coffee am Tea pm **FACILITIES:** CTV in all bedrooms STV Tennis (hard) Wkly live entertainment Xmas **CONF:** Thtr 150 Class 70 Board 45 Del from £138 * **SERVICES:** Lift Night porter 100P **NOTES:** No smoking in restaurant Last d 9.30pm **CARDS:**

NEWBURY Berkshire **Map 04 SU46**
★★★ **Hollington Country House**
Woolton Hill RG20 9XA
☎ 01635 255100 📠 01635 255075
(For full entry see Highclere)

NEWBURY Berkshire **Map 04 SU46**
★★★ **The Chequers**
REGAL
Oxford St RG14 1JB
Quality Percentage Score: 63%
☎ 01635 38000 📠 01635 37170
Dir: *M4 junct 13 follow signs Newbury town centre. At rdbt with A4 take 4th exit. Over mini rdbt & right at Clocktower rdbt. Hotel on right*
The Chequers is an extended 18th-century coaching inn, conveniently located at the northern end of the town centre. The bedrooms vary in size and outlook; most are in the original buildings and some are in modern wings accessed from the car park. A programme of bedroom refurbishment is underway with upgraded rooms looking smart and inviting. Guests enjoy a
contd.

N

choice of public areas and dinner is served in the attractive Secret Garden restaurant.
ROOMS: 45 en suite (bth/shr) 11 annexe en suite (bth/shr) (3 fmly) No smoking in 40 bedrooms s £105; d £115 * LB Off peak **MEALS:** Lunch £8-£20 High tea £2-£8 Dinner £9-£20 European Cuisine V meals Coffee am Tea pm **FACILITIES:** CTV in all bedrooms STV **CONF:** Thtr 200 Class 100 Board 50 Del from £140 * **SERVICES:** 60P **NOTES:** No dogs (ex guide dogs) No coaches No smoking in restaurant Last d 9pm Closed 24 Dec-4 Jan **CARDS:**

NEWBURY Berkshire — Map 04 SU46
★★★ Millwaters
London Rd RG14 2BY
Quality Percentage Score: 50%
☎ 01635 528838 01635 523406
Dir: take A34 S to Newbury. At end of dual carriageway take A4 at rdbt towards Reading. Hotel 1m on right nearly opposite Swan public house
Millwaters is set away from the road by an attractive pond and waterfall. The house is Georgian in origin but the interior design is modern, with many interesting features. Bedrooms are generally spacious and well equipped, the Oasis Restaurant offers brasserie-style menus.
ROOMS: 30 en suite (bth/shr) **MEALS:** Lunch £9.95-£11.95 Dinner £16.50 & alc English & French Cuisine V meals Coffee am Tea pm **FACILITIES:** CTV in all bedrooms Fishing Jacuzzi/spa **CONF:** Thtr 50 Class 20 Board 28 **SERVICES:** Night porter 50P **NOTES:** Last d 10pm **CARDS:**

NEWBURY Berkshire — Map 04 SU46
Travelodge
Chieveley, Oxford Rd RG18 9XX
☎ 01635 248024
Dir: on A34/off junc 13 M4
This modern building offers accommodation in smart, spacious and well equipped bedrooms, all with en-suite bathrooms. Refreshments may be taken at the nearby family restaurant. For details about current prices, consult the Contents Page under Hotel Groups for the Travelodge phone number.
ROOMS: 64 en suite (bth/shr) d £59.95 *

NEWBY BRIDGE Cumbria — Map 07 SD38
★★★★ Lakeside
Lakeside LA12 8AT
Quality Percentage Score: 71%
☎ 015395 31207 015395 31699
Dir: from M6 junct 36 join A590 to Barrow and follow signs to Newby Bridge. Turn right over the bridge, the hotel is 1 mile along on the right
Peacefully situated by the southern shore of Lake Windermere and next to the steam railway terminus, this spacious and well furnished hotel provides all-round comfort. There is a delightful conservatory lounge, and the elegant restaurant is the place to sample some good British and European cooking. Ruskin's Brasserie provides more informal dining. Bedrooms are generally spacious and thoughtfully equipped.
ROOMS: 80 en suite (bth/shr) (7 fmly) No smoking in 34 bedrooms s fr £95; d fr £135 (incl. bkfst) * LB Off peak **MEALS:** Sunday Lunch £14.95 & alc High tea £11.95-£15.50alc Dinner £32.50-£38.50 & alc English & French Cuisine V meals Coffee am Tea pm **FACILITIES:** CTV in all bedrooms STV Indoor swimming pool (heated) Fishing Pool table Croquet lawn Jacuzzi/spa Private jetty Use of Health club Wkly live entertainment Xmas **CONF:** Thtr 100 Class 50 Board 40 Del from £120 * **SERVICES:** Lift Night porter 200P **NOTES:** No smoking in restaurant Last d 9.30pm **CARDS:**

NEWBY BRIDGE Cumbria — Map 07 SD38
★★★ The Swan
LA12 8NB
Quality Percentage Score: 69%
☎ 015395 31681 015395 31917
Dir: leave M6 junct 36 follow A590 sigposted Barrow for 16m, hotel on right of the old 5 arch bridge, in Newby Bridge

This long-established hotel is set on the banks of the River Leven at the southern end of Lake Windermere, with riverside walks past all the moorings. The main restaurant, occupying an old barn with lofted ceiling and stone walls, is adjoined by a cocktail lounge. There is also a lounge bar and less formal restaurant. Bedrooms are traditionally furnished, well equipped and include some excellent family units.
ROOMS: 56 en suite (bth/shr) (4 fmly) No smoking in 10 bedrooms s fr £75; d fr £140 (incl. bkfst) * LB Off peak **MEALS:** Sunday Lunch fr £10.95 & alc Dinner fr £21.50 & alc English & French Cuisine V meals Coffee am Tea pm **FACILITIES:** CTV in all bedrooms STV Indoor swimming pool (heated) Fishing Sauna Solarium Gym Pool table Croquet lawn Jacuzzi/spa Boules Golf swing practice net Table tennis Wkly live entertainment Xmas **CONF:** Thtr 65 Class 20 Board 28 Del from £80 * **SERVICES:** Lift Night porter 100P **NOTES:** No dogs (ex guide dogs) No coaches No smoking in restaurant Last d 9.30pm **CARDS:**

NEWBY BRIDGE Cumbria — Map 07 SD38
★★★ Whitewater
The Lakeland Village LA12 8PX
Quality Percentage Score: 65%
☎ 015395 31133 015395 31881
Dir: leave M6 junct 36 follow signs for A590 Barrow 1m through Newby Bridge, turn right at signpost for Lakeland Village, hotel on left
On the banks of the spectacular River Leven, this smart hotel has been created by a stylish conversion of an old mill, linked to a superbly equipped leisure centre where children are well catered for. Public areas include a choice of bars and a restaurant offering meals prepared from fresh local produce. Bedrooms, with exposed natural stone, are especially spacious, modern, and comfortable.
ROOMS: 35 en suite (bth/shr) (10 fmly) s £75-£80; d £110-£135 (incl. bkfst) * LB Off peak **MEALS:** Sunday Lunch £9.95-£12.95 Dinner £19 & alc European Cuisine V meals Coffee am Tea pm **FACILITIES:** CTV in all bedrooms STV Indoor swimming pool (heated) Tennis (hard) Squash Sauna Solarium Gym Putting green Jacuzzi/spa Beauty treatment spa steam room table tennis golf driving net Wkly live entertainment Xmas **CONF:** Thtr 80 Class 32 Board 40 Del from £80 * **SERVICES:** Lift Night porter 50P **NOTES:** No dogs (ex guide dogs) No smoking in restaurant Last d 9pm **CARDS:**

NEWCASTLE-UNDER-LYME Staffordshire **Map 07 SJ84**
★★★ **Posthouse Stoke-on-Trent**
Clayton Rd ST5 4DL
☎ 01782 717171 📠 01782 717138
Dir: *on A519 at junct 15 of M6*
This modern hotel is situated in spacious grounds. Facilities include a "Spa" leisure centre and a popular "Traders" restaurant as well as versatile meeting and function rooms. Bedrooms are comfortably furnished and include interactive TV, hairdryers and trouser presses. Extended room service and all day lounge service are also features. Staff are professional, friendly and willing. There are good parking facilities.
ROOMS: 119 en suite (bth/shr) (41 fmly) No smoking in 54 bedrooms d fr £69 * LB Off peak **MEALS:** International Cuisine V meals Coffee am Tea pm **FACILITIES:** CTV in all bedrooms Indoor swimming pool (heated) Sauna Solarium Gym Pool table Jacuzzi/spa Childrens play areas Beauty & therapy room Xmas **CONF:** Thtr 70 Class 40 Board 34 Del from £89 * **SERVICES:** Night porter 128P **NOTES:** No smoking area in restaurant Last d 10pm **CARDS:**

NEWCASTLE-UNDER-LYME Staffordshire **Map 07 SJ84**
★★ **Comfort Inn**
Liverpool Rd ST5 9DX
Quality Percentage Score: 63%
☎ 01782 717000 📠 01782 713669
Dir: *M6 junct 16 onto A500 towards Stoke-on-Trent. Take A34 to Newcastle-under-Lyme, hotel on right after 1.5m*
Some of the well equipped bedrooms at this purpose built hotel are in a separate block at the rear. There is a large lounge bar, an attractively appointed restaurant and a small gymnasium.
ROOMS: 48 en suite (bth/shr) 24 annexe en suite (bth/shr) (5 fmly) No smoking in 25 bedrooms d £46.75-£54.50 * LB Off peak
MEALS: Sunday Lunch £2.95-£15.95alc Dinner fr £10.75 & alc English & Continental Cuisine V meals Coffee am Tea pm **FACILITIES:** CTV in all bedrooms STV Xmas **CONF:** Thtr 130 Class 80 Board 50
SERVICES: Night porter 160P **NOTES:** No smoking area in restaurant Last d 9.30pm **CARDS:**

NEWCASTLE UPON TYNE Tyne & Wear **Map 12 NZ26**
see also **Seaton Burn & Whickham**
★★★★ **Vermont**
Castle Garth NE1 1RQ
Quality Percentage Score: 78%
☎ 0191 233 1010 📠 0191 233 1234
Dir: *city centre by the high level bridge & Castle Keep*
Previously the County Hall, and opened as an hotel in 1994, the Vermont is an imposing building in the city centre next to the castle. There is a choice of bars and restaurants, two with live music in the evening. The Brasserie provides meals throughout the day and evening, but the Blue Room is the place for fine dining in a classical setting.
ROOMS: 101 en suite (bth/shr) (12 fmly) No smoking in 20 bedrooms s fr £145; d fr £165 * LB Off peak **MEALS:** Lunch £12-£15.50 Dinner £18.50 International Cuisine V meals Coffee am Tea pm
FACILITIES: CTV in all bedrooms STV Solarium Gym Wkly live entertainment Xmas **CONF:** Thtr 210 Class 60 Board 36 Del £155 *
SERVICES: Lift Night porter 100P **NOTES:** No coaches No smoking area in restaurant Last d 10.45pm **CARDS:**

NEWCASTLE UPON TYNE Tyne & Wear **Map 12 NZ26**
★★★★ **Swallow Gosforth Park**
High Gosforth Park, Gosforth NE3 5HN
Quality Percentage Score: 74%
☎ 0191 236 4111 📠 0191 236 8192
Dir: *off A1 Western Bypass at A1056 junct signed Killingworth and Wideopen 2nd exit off rdbt to Gosforth Park hotel ahead*
Providing high levels of hospitality and customer care, this purpose built hotel is set in attractively landscaped grounds, just off the A1. It is close to the racecourse and conveniently located for the airport. Bedrooms are smart and well equipped, whilst the extensive public areas provide a wide range of leisure, banqueting and conference facilities. The food served in the elegant Brandling Restaurant, where the service is polished and a pianist plays, earns our Two Rosette award. The Conservatory Restaurant provides a less formal eating option.

ROOMS: 178 en suite (bth/shr) (7 fmly) No smoking in 99 bedrooms s fr £130; d fr £140 (incl. bkfst) * LB Off peak **MEALS:** Lunch £16-£20 & alc High tea fr £8.50 Dinner £25-£32.50 International Cuisine V meals Coffee am Tea pm **FACILITIES:** CTV in all bedrooms STV Indoor swimming pool (heated) Tennis (hard) Squash Sauna Solarium Gym Pool table Jacuzzi/spa Steam room Beauty salon Hairdressing salon Trim-Trail Wkly live entertainment Xmas **CONF:** Thtr 550 Class 300 Board 50 Del from £147 * **SERVICES:** Lift Night porter 300P **NOTES:** No smoking area in restaurant Last d 10pm
CARDS:

NEWCASTLE UPON TYNE Tyne & Wear **Map 12 NZ26**
★★★★ ***Copthorne Newcastle***
The Close, Quayside NE1 3RT
Quality Percentage Score: 71%
☎ 0191 222 0333 📠 0191 230 1111
Dir: *east of A189 off B1600*
This modern hotel overlooking the River Tyne, is close to the heart of the city, and guests have direct access from the hotel concourse to a quayside walk. First-floor bedrooms have balconies overlooking the river and there are some 'Connoisseur' rooms with a dedicated lounge on the same floor. There are two restaurants, Harry's and Le Rivage, the latter being a stylish setting for evening meals. The hotel has internal access to its own multi-storey carpark.
ROOMS: 156 en suite (bth/shr) (16 fmly) No smoking in 53 bedrooms
MEALS: International Cuisine V meals Coffee am Tea pm
FACILITIES: CTV in all bedrooms STV Indoor swimming pool (heated) Sauna Solarium Gym Jacuzzi/spa Steam room **CONF:** Thtr 200 Class 85 Board 60 Del from £145 * **SERVICES:** Lift Night porter Air conditioning 180P **NOTES:** No smoking area in restaurant Last d 10.30pm
CARDS:

NEWCASTLE UPON TYNE Tyne & Wear **Map 12 NZ26**
★★★★ **Newcastle Marriott**
Metro Centre NE11 9XF
Quality Percentage Score: 68%
☎ 0191 493 2233 📠 0191 493 2030
(For full entry see Gateshead)

NEWCASTLE UPON TYNE Tyne & Wear **Map 12 NZ26**
★★★★ *Holiday Inn*
Great North Rd NE13 6BF
Quality Percentage Score: 63%
☎ 0191 201 9988 Fax 0191 236 8091
(For full entry see Seaton Burn)

NEWCASTLE UPON TYNE Tyne & Wear **Map 12 NZ26**
★★★ Malmaison
Quayside NE1 3DX
Quality Percentage Score: 74%
☎ 0191 245 5000 Fax 0191 245 4545
Dir: *follow signs for Newcastle city centre. Take road for Quayside/Law Courts. Hotel is approx 100yds past the Law Courts overlooking the river*
Overlooking the river in the heart of the redeveloped quayside, this stylishly transformed old building is popular with visiting stars, as well as business and leisure guests seeking something different. The spacious, modern style of the boldly designed bedrooms, with their large beds, good desk space, communications and music systems, marks a refreshing change from tradition. Meals are served in the bustling riverside brasserie.
ROOMS: 116 en suite (bth/shr) (10 fmly) d £99-£165 * Off peak **MEALS:** Lunch £9.50-£15.95 Dinner £11.50-£14.50 French Cuisine V meals Coffee am Tea pm **FACILITIES:** CTV in all bedrooms STV Sauna Solarium Gym **CONF:** Thtr 60 Class 10 Board 22 Del from £140 * **SERVICES:** Lift Night porter 50P **NOTES:** No dogs (ex guide dogs) No coaches Last d 11pm **CARDS:**

NEWCASTLE UPON TYNE Tyne & Wear **Map 12 NZ26**
★★★ Swallow
High West St NE8 1PE
Quality Percentage Score: 68%
☎ 0191 477 1105 Fax 0191 478 7214
(For full entry see Gateshead)

NEWCASTLE UPON TYNE Tyne & Wear **Map 12 NZ26**
★★★ Posthouse Newcastle upon Tyne
New Bridge St NE1 8BS
Quality Percentage Score: 67%
☎ 0191 232 6191 Fax 0191 261 8529
Dir: *follow signs for Gateshead/Newcastle A167M over Tyne Bridge take A193 Wallsend and City Centre left to Carliol Sq hotel on corner infront of junct*
This hotel is situated in the city centre, but is well signed after leaving the A 167(M)and its adjoining multi-storey car park provides secure parking facilities. Many bedrooms have been designed in the new millennium style whilst others have been retained in the more conventional Posthouse style. All are very well equipped and most have panoramic views over the city. The Junction Restaurant is situated on the second floor together with the lounge and residents bars. These facilities can be reached by lift and there is also a special lift for disabled guests. Other facilities include an excellent leisure club, a business centre and numerous conference and meeting rooms. 24 hour room and lounge service is available, provided by friendly and helpful staff.
ROOMS: 166 en suite (bth/shr) (2 fmly) No smoking in 108 bedrooms d £55-£89 * LB Off peak **MEALS:** International Cuisine V meals Coffee am Tea pm **FACILITIES:** CTV in all bedrooms Indoor swimming pool (heated) Sauna Solarium Gym Jacuzzi/spa adjoning leisure club Xmas **CONF:** Thtr 600 Class 350 Board 50 Del from £90 * **SERVICES:** Lift Night porter 132P **NOTES:** No smoking area in restaurant Last d 10pm **CARDS:**

NEWCASTLE UPON TYNE Tyne & Wear **Map 12 NZ26**
★★★ Novotel
Ponteland Rd, Kenton NE3 3HZ
Quality Percentage Score: 66%
☎ 0191 214 0303 Fax 0191 214 0633
Dir: *off A1(M) Airport junct - A696, take Kingston Park exit*
Convenient for the airport, this bright, modern hotel offers stylish public areas and spacious, well equipped accommodation. As well as room service, the Garden Brasserie is open for meals until late. A residents-only leisure club, a range of well equipped meeting rooms and security patrolled car parking are other features.
ROOMS: 126 en suite (bth/shr) (126 fmly) No smoking in 82 bedrooms d £72 * LB Off peak **MEALS:** Lunch £10.95-£12.95 & alc Dinner £10.95 & alc English & French Cuisine V meals Coffee am Tea pm **FACILITIES:** CTV in all bedrooms STV Indoor swimming pool (heated) Sauna Exercise equipment **CONF:** Thtr 220 Class 100 Board 25 Del from £99 * **SERVICES:** Lift 260P **NOTES:** No smoking area in restaurant Last d mdnt **CARDS:**

NEWCASTLE UPON TYNE Tyne & Wear **Map 12 NZ26**
★★★ Posthouse Washington
Emerson District 5 NE37 1LB
Quality Percentage Score: 66%
☎ 0191 416 2264 Fax 0191 415 3371
(For full entry see Washington)

NEWCASTLE UPON TYNE Tyne & Wear **Map 12 NZ26**
★★★ Quality Hotel Newcastle
Newgate St NE1 5SX
Quality Percentage Score: 66%
☎ 0191 232 5025 Fax 0191 232 8428
Dir: *from A6082 cross Redhuegh Bridge. Turn rightt 1st set of lights, then left, continue to Bingo hall & straight on, right*
Situated right in the heart of the city, this high-rise hotel is reached directly from its secure car park. The sixth-floor restaurant and cocktail bar provide a comfortable and relaxing retreat, as well as offering fine rooftop views across the city, as do the well equipped bedrooms.
ROOMS: 93 en suite (bth/shr) No smoking in 41 bedrooms s fr £95; d £105-£112 * LB Off peak **MEALS:** Dinner fr £14.50 V meals Coffee am Tea pm **FACILITIES:** CTV in all bedrooms STV Wkly live entertainment Xmas **CONF:** Thtr 154 **SERVICES:** Lift Night porter 120P **NOTES:** No smoking area in restaurant Last d 9.30pm **CARDS:**

NEWCASTLE UPON TYNE Tyne & Wear **Map 12 NZ26**
★★★ Swallow Imperial
Jesmond Rd NE2 1PR
Quality Percentage Score: 66%
☎ 0191 281 5511 Fax 0191 281 8472
Dir: *turn off A167(M) onto A1058 (Tynemouth/East Coast). Hotel 0.25m on left just after second mini rdbt*
Lying east of the city centre, this business hotel is popular for conferences and seminars, both residential and non-residential and has the added benefits of an undercover car park with the

contd.

Indicates that the star classification has not been confirmed under the New Quality Standards, see page 7 for further information.

Metro only a few minutes walk away. Public areas include a comfortable club style lounge.

ROOMS: 122 en suite (bth/shr) (6 fmly) No smoking in 90 bedrooms s £90-£105; d £99-£110 (incl. bkfst) * LB Off peak **MEALS:** Lunch fr £12.50 High tea £4.95-£8.95alc Dinner fr £19.50 & alc V meals Coffee am Tea pm **FACILITIES:** CTV in all bedrooms STV Indoor swimming pool (heated) Sauna Solarium Gym Jacuzzi/spa Steam room Xmas **CONF:** Thtr 150 Class 60 Board 50 Del from £85 * **SERVICES:** Lift Night porter 100P **NOTES:** No smoking area in restaurant Last d 9.45pm
CARDS:

NEWCASTLE UPON TYNE Tyne & Wear **Map 12 NZ26**
★★★ George Washington County Hotel
Stone Cellar Rd, District 12,
High Usworth NE37 1PH
Quality Percentage Score: 65%
☎ 0191 402 9988 📠 0191 415 1166
(For full entry see Washington)

REGAL

NEWCASTLE UPON TYNE Tyne & Wear **Map 12 NZ26**
★★★ The Caledonian Hotel, Newcastle
64 Osborne Rd, Jesmond NE2 2AT
Quality Percentage Score: 64%
☎ 0191 281 7881 📠 0191 281 6241

PEEL HOTELS

***Dir:** take B1318 through Gosforth to large rdbt turn left onto A189 to 2nd set of lights B1600/A1058 turn right hotel beyond St George's Church*
Situated on the east side of the city, this business and conference hotel provides comfortable well equipped bedrooms along with a relaxed informal atmosphere.
ROOMS: 89 en suite (bth/shr) (6 fmly) No smoking in 17 bedrooms s £115; d £135 * LB Off peak **MEALS:** Lunch £9.50-£11.50 Dinner £14.95-£17.95 European Cuisine V meals Coffee am Tea pm **FACILITIES:** CTV in all bedrooms STV Xmas **CONF:** Thtr 100 Class 60 Board 46 Del from £85 * **SERVICES:** Lift Night porter 52P **NOTES:** No smoking area in restaurant Last d 10pm
CARDS:

NEWCASTLE UPON TYNE Tyne & Wear **Map 12 NZ26**
★★★ New Kent Hotel
127 Osborne Rd NE2 2TB
Quality Percentage Score: 64%
☎ 0191 281 7711 📠 0191 281 3369

Best Western

***Dir:** beside B1600, opposite St Georges Church*
This business hotel is situated in Jesmond and provides generously portioned meals in its attractive restaurant. The well equipped bedrooms come in a variety of sizes.
ROOMS: 32 en suite (bth/shr) (4 fmly) s £59.50-£69.50; d £69.50-£79.50 (incl. bkfst) * LB Off peak **MEALS:** Lunch £5.95-£8.95 & alc High tea fr £4.95 & alc Dinner fr £12.95 & alc International Cuisine V meals Coffee am Tea pm **FACILITIES:** CTV in all bedrooms STV Xmas **CONF:** Thtr 90 Class 50 Board 24 Del from £80 * **SERVICES:** Night porter 22P **NOTES:** No smoking in restaurant Last d 9.30pm
CARDS:

NEWCASTLE UPON TYNE Tyne & Wear **Map 12 NZ26**
★★ Eslington Villa
8 Station Rd, Low Fell NE9 6DR
Quality Percentage Score: 74%
☎ 0191 487 6017 & 420 0666 📠 0191 420 0667
(For full entry see Gateshead)

NEWCASTLE UPON TYNE Tyne & Wear **Map 12 NZ26**
★★ Whites
38-42 Osborne Rd, Jesmond NE2 2AL
Quality Percentage Score: 65%
☎ 0191 281 5126 📠 0191 281 9953
***Dir:** 1m N, traveling from N or S follow A1058 signs for coast and turn left into Osborne Road at first rdbt*
This commercial hotel in Jesmond has the benefit of a secure car park and a bus stop right outside. Service is cheery, the bedrooms well equipped with cable TV, iron/board and trouser press. Good value meals are offered in the restaurant.
ROOMS: 39 rms (38 bth/shr) (3 fmly) No smoking in 3 bedrooms s £39-£49; d £55-£69 (incl. bkfst) * LB Off peak **MEALS:** Lunch £7-£10.95 & alc Dinner £12.95-£14.95 & alc French Cuisine V meals Coffee am Tea pm **FACILITIES:** CTV in all bedrooms STV Xmas **CONF:** Thtr 75 Class 50 Board 40 Del from £59 * **SERVICES:** Night porter 40P **NOTES:** No smoking area in restaurant Last d 9.30pm
CARDS:

NEWCASTLE UPON TYNE Tyne & Wear **Map 12 NZ26**
★★ Hadrian Lodge Hotel
Hadrian Rd, Wallsend NE28 6HH
Quality Percentage Score: 63%
☎ 0191 262 7733 📠 0191 263 0714
***Dir:** from Tyne tunnel (A19) take A187 to Wallsend follow this route for 1.5m, hotel on left opposite Hadrian Road Metro Station*

Situated just a few miles from Newcastle, this modern, stylish hotel provides a convenient base for the business guest. Bedrooms are comfortable, well equipped and are insulated from the main road by triple glazing. The Italian restaurant is an appealing venue for dinner with a wide-ranging menu offering dishes to suit all tastes and budgets. Staff throughout are friendly and keen to please.
ROOMS: 25 en suite (bth/shr) (1 fmly) s £45; d £59.50 (incl. bkfst) * LB Off peak **MEALS:** Lunch £3.95-£8.95 & alc Dinner £5.50-£8.95 & alc Italian Cuisine V meals Coffee am Tea pm **FACILITIES:** CTV in all bedrooms STV Xmas **SERVICES:** Night porter 60P **NOTES:** No dogs (ex guide dogs) No coaches No smoking area in restaurant Last d 9.30pm **CARDS:**

N

NEWCASTLE UPON TYNE Tyne & Wear **Map 12 NZ26**

★★ *Cairn*

97/103 Osborne Rd, Jesmond NE2 2TJ
Quality Percentage Score: 60%
☎ 0191 281 1358 📠 0191 281 9031

Situated in the suburb of Jesmond, east of the city centre, this commercial hotel offers friendly informal service, bright, well - equipped bedrooms and straightforward dinners from a short menu, served in the split-level bar/restaurant.

ROOMS: 50 en suite (bth/shr) (2 fmly) **MEALS:** V meals Coffee am Tea pm **FACILITIES:** CTV in all bedrooms STV none **CONF:** Thtr 150 Class 110 Board 100 **SERVICES:** Night porter 22P **NOTES:** No smoking area in restaurant Last d 9.15pm **CARDS:**

See advert on opposite page

NEWCASTLE UPON TYNE Tyne & Wear **Map 12 NZ26**

Travel Inn

City Rd, Quayside NE1 2AN
☎ 0191 232 6533 📠 0191 232 6557

Dir: *at corner of City Rd (A186) & Crawhall Rd*

This modern building offers accommodation in smart, spacious and well equipped bedrooms, all with en-suite bathrooms. Refreshments may be taken at the nearby family restaurant. For details about current prices consult the Contents Page under Hotel Groups for the Travel Inn phone number.

ROOMS: 80 en suite (bth/shr) d £44.95 *

NEWCASTLE UPON TYNE Tyne & Wear **Map 12 NZ26**

Travel Inn (Holystone)

Holystone Roundabout
☎ 0191 2702704 📠 0191 2599509

This modern building offers accommodation in smart, spacious and well equipped bedrooms, all with en-suite bathrooms. Refreshments may be taken at the nearby family restaurant. For details about current prices consult the Contents Page under Hotel Groups for the Travel Inn phone number.

ROOMS: 40 en suite (bth/shr) d £39.95 *

NEWCASTLE UPON TYNE AIRPORT Tyne & Wear **Map 12 NZ17**

★★★ *Newcastle Airport Moat House*

Woolsington NE13 8DJ
Quality Percentage Score: 64%
☎ 0191 401 9988 📠 01661 860157

Dir: *from the A1 onto the A696 following signs for Newcastle International Airport*

This modern hotel is situated in the airport complex and many areas have recently been upgraded. The Old Rangoon Restaurant, which provides a wide range of dishes from around the world, contains lots of old photographs, colonial headgear and other paraphernalia from various corners of the globe. The hotel is pleasantly situated in semi-rural surroundings and its location is very convenient for Newcastle, which is only six miles away.

ROOMS: 100 en suite (bth/shr) (6 fmly) No smoking in 35 bedrooms **MEALS:** International Cuisine V meals Coffee am Tea pm **FACILITIES:** CTV in all bedrooms STV Gym Pool table **CONF:** Thtr 400 Class 200 Board 50 **SERVICES:** Lift Night porter 200P **NOTES:** No smoking in restaurant Last d 10.30pm **CARDS:**

NEWCASTLE UPON TYNE AIRPORT Tyne & Wear **Map 12 NZ17**

Travel Inn (Newcastle Airport)

Newcastle Int. Airport, Ponteland Rd, Prestwick NE20 9DB
☎ 01661 825040 📠 01661 824940

Dir: *situated immediately adjacent to the main entrance to airport*

This modern building offers accommodation in smart, spacious and well equipped bedrooms, all with en-suite bathrooms. Refreshments may be taken at the nearby family restaurant. For details about current prices consult the Contents Page under Hotel Groups for the Travel Inn phone number.

ROOMS: 86 en suite (bth/shr) d £39.95 *

NEWHAVEN East Sussex **Map 05 TQ40**

Travel Inn

The Drove, Avis Rd BN9 0AG
☎ 01273 612356 📠 01273 612359

Dir: *from A26 (New Rd) take left turn into Avis Rd towards Bishoptone & Seaford (A259) hotel on right by rdbt*

This modern building offers accommodation in smart, spacious and well equipped bedrooms, all with en-suite bathrooms. Refreshments may be taken at the nearby family restaurant. For details about current prices consult the Contents Page under Hotel Groups for the Travel Inn phone number.

ROOMS: 40 en suite (bth/shr) d £39.95 *

NEWICK East Sussex **Map 05 TQ42**

★★★ Newick Park Country Estate

BN8 4SB
Quality Percentage Score: 80%
☎ 01825 723633 📠 01825 723969

Dir: *turn S off A272 in Newick between Haywards Heath and Uckfield, pass the church and turn left at junct, entrance to Newick Park is 0.25m on right*

Part of this grade II listed Georgian house dates back to the 16th century and was once owned by an Ironmaster. The house has recently been restored and bedrooms are beautifully decorated. The restaurant offers innovative cooking using fresh local produce.

ROOMS: 13 en suite (bth/shr) 3 annexe en suite (bth/shr) (5 fmly) No smoking in 12 bedrooms s fr £95; d £170-£230 (incl. cont bkfst) * LB Off peak **MEALS:** Lunch fr £15.50 Dinner £32 & alc V meals **FACILITIES:** CTV in all bedrooms STV Outdoor swimming pool (heated) Tennis (hard) Fishing Croquet lawn Badminton Golf on East Sussex National Horseriding Glyndebourne Opera close by. Xmas **CONF:** Thtr 80 Class 80 Board 25 Del from £140 * **SERVICES:** 52P **NOTES:** No smoking in restaurant Last d 10pm **CARDS:**

See advert on opposite page

NEWMARKET Suffolk **Map 05 TL66**

★★★ Bedford Lodge

Bury Rd CB8 7BX
Quality Percentage Score: 72%
☎ 01638 663175 📠 01638 667391

Dir: *take Bury St Edmunds road from town centre, hotel half a mile on the left*

This 18th-century Georgian hunting lodge is dedicated to the town's heritage in 'the sport of kings', with its Roxana bar and the tastefully decorated bedrooms all named after one of the country's racecourses. The wide variety of well prepared dishes

contd.

N

in the Godolphin Restaurant satisfies most tastes. There is a superb modern leisure centre.
ROOMS: 56 en suite (bth/shr) (3 fmly) s £84-£175; d £109-£200 (incl. bkfst) * LB Off peak **MEALS:** Lunch £11.50-£16.95 & alc Dinner fr £16.95 & alc International Cuisine V meals Coffee am Tea pm
FACILITIES: CTV in all bedrooms Indoor swimming pool (heated) Sauna Solarium Gym Jacuzzi/spa Steam room & beauty salon Xmas
CONF: Thtr 200 Class 80 Board 60 Del from £120 * **SERVICES:** Lift Night porter 90P **NOTES:** Last d 9.30pm
CARDS:

NEWMARKET Suffolk — Map 05 TL66

★★★ Heath Court

Moulton Rd CB8 8DY
Quality Percentage Score: 69%
☎ 01638 667171 Fax 01638 666533
Dir: *from A14 leave at Newmarket/Ely exit (A142) follow town centre signs through mini-rdbt at clocktower turn immediately left into Moulton Rd*
Close to the famed Newmarket Heath, this modern red-brick hotel is popular for its pleasant facilities. The bedrooms are spacious and smartly presented. Meals are served in the carvery which offers an a la carte menu in addition to the roasts.
ROOMS: 41 en suite (bth/shr) (2 fmly) No smoking in 10 bedrooms s £75-£95; d £90-£100 (incl. bkfst) * LB Off peak **MEALS:** Lunch £7.95-£15.45 & alc Dinner £11-£20alc V meals Coffee am Tea pm
FACILITIES: CTV in all bedrooms STV **CONF:** Thtr 150 Class 40 Board 40 Del from £110 **SERVICES:** Lift Night porter 60P **NOTES:** No smoking area in restaurant Last d 9.45pm
CARDS:

NEWMARKET Suffolk **Map 05 TL66**
★★★ **Swynford Paddocks Hotel**
CB8 0UE
Quality Percentage Score: 66%
☎ 01638 570234 🖷 01638 570283
(For full entry see Six Mile Bottom)

NEW MILTON Hampshire **Map 04 SZ29**

The Premier Collection

★★★★★ **Chewton Glen**
Christchurch Rd BH25 6QS
☎ 01425 275341 🖷 01425 272310
Dir: *on A35 from Lyndhurst, drive 10 miles and turn left at staggered junct. Following brown tourist sign for hotel through Walkford, take second left*
Chewton Glen goes from strength to strength and since its inception over 30 years ago owners Martin and Brigitte Skan have transformed their hotel into a luxurious and hospitable retreat. The conscientious management of Peter Crome, together with the infectious hospitality of stalwart Joe Simonini, inspires the dedicated and professional team. Sumptuous bathrooms and an abundance of comfort and quality are the result of continued investment and upgrading, particularly of the junior suites. High standards are complemented by many thoughtful touches and excellent housekeeping. The cooking of Pierre Chevillard continues to please. Good use is made of excellent raw ingredients in imaginative and innovative dishes. A comprehensive three course table d' hote menu is offered at both lunch and dinner, as well as a lighter alternative at lunch. An impressive wine list complements.
ROOMS: 52 en suite (bth/shr) 2 annexe en suite (bth/shr) d £245-£465 * LB Off peak **MEALS:** Lunch £13.50-£23 Dinner fr £45 French Cuisine V meals Coffee am Tea pm **FACILITIES:** CTV in all bedrooms STV Indoor swimming pool (heated) Outdoor swimming pool Golf 9 Tennis (hard) Sauna Gym Croquet lawn Putting green Jacuzzi/spa Steam room Treatment rooms Hairdresser Indoor tennis courts Xmas **CONF:** Thtr 150 Class 70 Board 40 Del from £180 * **SERVICES:** Night porter 100P **NOTES:** No dogs (ex guide dogs) No coaches No children 7yrs No smoking in restaurant Last d 9.30pm **CARDS:**

NEWPORT Shropshire **Map 07 SJ71**
★★ **Royal Victoria**
St Mary's St TF10 7AB
Quality Percentage Score: 63%
☎ 01952 820331 🖷 01952 820209
Dir: *Turn off A41 at 2nd Newport by-pass rdbt towards town centre turn right at 1st traffic lights. Hotel car park 150 metres on left*
This privately owned town centre hotel is tucked away behind St Nicholas church. It dates back to Georgian times and its name derives from a visit by the then Princess Victoria, in 1832. The property has been much extended in more recent times. It provides well equipped, modern accommodation which is equally suitable for business people and tourists. Facilities here include an attractively appointed restaurant, a choice of bars and a large function/conference suite.
ROOMS: 24 en suite (bth/shr) (2 fmly) **MEALS:** Lunch £2.95-£10.95 Dinner £3.95-£15.95 V meals Coffee am Tea pm **FACILITIES:** CTV in all bedrooms **CONF:** Thtr 140 Class 80 Del £90 * **SERVICES:** 57P **NOTES:** Last d 9.30pm **CARDS:**

See advert on opposite page

NEWQUAY Cornwall & Isles of Scilly **Map 02 SW86**
★★★ **Barrowfield**
Hilgrove Rd TR7 2QY
Quality Percentage Score: 69%
☎ 01637 878878 🖷 01637 879490
Dir: *take A3058 to Newquay towards Quintrell Downs, turn right at rdbt continue into town and turn left at Shell garage*
A popular, large hotel close to the town centre and beaches. Inside, there is an elegant new restaurant, and intimate 'Piano Bar'. Bedrooms, some with sea views, offer comfortable accommodation with modern facilities. Extensive leisure and fitness facilities are available.
ROOMS: 81 en suite (bth/shr) 2 annexe en suite (bth/shr) (18 fmly) s £30-£60; d £60-£120 (incl. bkfst & dinner) * LB Off peak **MEALS:** Dinner £16 & alc English & French Cuisine V meals Coffee am Tea pm **FACILITIES:** CTV in 81 bedrooms STV Indoor swimming pool (heated) Outdoor swimming pool (heated) Snooker Sauna Solarium Gym Pool table Jacuzzi/spa Table tennis Wkly live entertainment Xmas **CONF:** Thtr 150 Class 60 Board 40 **SERVICES:** Lift Night porter 70P **NOTES:** No smoking in restaurant Last d 8.30pm
CARDS:

See advert on opposite page

NEWQUAY Cornwall & Isles of Scilly **Map 02 SW86**
★★★ **Hotel Bristol**
Narrowcliff TR7 2PQ
Quality Percentage Score: 68%
☎ 01637 875181 🖷 01637 879347
Dir: *turn off A30 onto A392, then onto A3058. Hotel is located 2.5m on left*

The Hotel Bristol is conveniently situated opposite the Barrowfields and with fine views over the sea. Appealing to both leisure and conference markets, the hotel offers comfortable bedrooms, many with sea views. Spacious public areas include a
contd.

selection of lounges, a cocktail bar and an elegant restaurant where traditional, classical dishes are offered.
ROOMS: 74 en suite (bth/shr) (23 fmly) **MEALS:** Lunch fr £12 & alc Dinner fr £19 & alc English & French Cuisine V meals Coffee am Tea pm **FACILITIES:** CTV in all bedrooms Indoor swimming pool (heated) Snooker Sauna Solarium Pool table Table tennis ch fac **CONF:** Thtr 200 Class 80 Board 20 Del from £65 * **SERVICES:** Lift Night porter 105P **NOTES:** No smoking in restaurant Last d 8.45pm
CARDS:

See advert on this page

NEWQUAY Cornwall & Isles of Scilly **Map 02 SW86**

★★★ Headland
Fistral Beach TR7 1EW
Quality Percentage Score: 68%
☎ 01637 872211 01637 872212
Dir: *turn off A30 onto A392 at Indian Queens, on approaching Newquay follow signs for Fistral Beach*
Built in one of the most marvellous settings in Cornwall, this unique Victorian hotel is a grand place to stay and yet is still excellent value for money. Many bedrooms have been upgraded, and all offer modern facilities. Set against the backdrop of Fistral Beach, guests can enjoy the swimming pool and putting course.

contd.

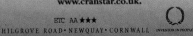

The 'Garden Room' offers lighter meals than the more formal dining room.
ROOMS: 107 en suite (bth/shr) (56 fmly) s £55-£69; d £110-£138 (incl. bkfst) LB Off peak **MEALS:** Bar Lunch £4-£14 High tea £4.95-£7.95 Dinner £18 & alc English & French Cuisine V meals Coffee am Tea pm **FACILITIES:** CTV in all bedrooms STV Indoor swimming pool (heated) Outdoor swimming pool (heated) Golf 9 Tennis (hard) Snooker Sauna Pool table Croquet lawn Putting green Surfing Play areas Wkly live entertainment ch fac **CONF:** Thtr 250 Class 120 Board 50 Del from £82 * **SERVICES:** Lift Night porter 400P **NOTES:** No smoking in restaurant Last d 9pm Closed 23-27 Dec **CARDS:**

NEWQUAY Cornwall & Isles of Scilly **Map 02 SW86**
★★★ Trebarwith
Trebarwith Crescent TR7 1BZ
Quality Percentage Score: 67%
☎ 01637 872288 01637 875431
Dir: *From A3058 forward until Mount Wise Rd then 3rd right down Marcus Hill and across East St into Trebarwith Crescent. Hotel at end*

Set in its own grounds, with a path leading to the beach, this hotel is close to the town centre. Public rooms are spacious, including a lounge, a ballroom, and The Wedgwood Restaurant. The comfortable bedrooms include both four-poster and family rooms.
ROOMS: 41 en suite (bth/shr) (8 fmly) s £35-£57; d £62-£110 (incl. bkfst & dinner) * LB Off peak **MEALS:** Bar Lunch fr £1.50 & alc Dinner £14.50 & alc International Cuisine V meals Coffee am Tea pm **FACILITIES:** CTV in all bedrooms Indoor swimming pool (heated) Fishing Snooker Sauna Solarium Pool table Jacuzzi/spa Video theatre Games room **CONF:** Thtr 45 **SERVICES:** Night porter 41P **NOTES:** No dogs (ex guide dogs) No smoking in restaurant Last d 8.30pm Closed Nov-8 Apr **CARDS:**

See advert on opposite page

NEWQUAY Cornwall & Isles of Scilly **Map 02 SW86**
★★★ Esplanade Hotel
Esplanade Rd, Pentire TR7 1PS
Quality Percentage Score: 65%
☎ 01637 873333 01637 851413
Dir: *from A30 take A392 at Indian Queens towards Newquay, follow holiday route until rdbt, take left to Pentire, then right hand fork towards beach*
This modern hotel overlooks the spectacular expanse of Fistral Beach. Hospitality is warm and the friendly team of staff make every effort to ensure that guests enjoy their stay. There is a wide choice of bedroom sizes, with all the rooms having modern facilities, and many enjoying the stunning sea views. The hotel boasts a number of bars, a continental style coffee shop and the more formal surroundings of the Ocean View restaurant. A range of leisure facilities are available.
ROOMS: 83 en suite (bth/shr) (44 fmly) s £25-£50; d £50-£100 (incl. bkfst & dinner) * LB Off peak **MEALS:** Dinner £11-£20 & alc International Cuisine V meals Coffee am Tea pm **FACILITIES:** CTV in all bedrooms STV Indoor swimming pool (heated) Outdoor swimming pool (heated) Sauna Solarium Pool table Jacuzzi/spa Table tennis Wkly live entertainment Xmas **CONF:** Thtr 300 Class 180 Board 150 Del from £30 * **SERVICES:** Lift Night porter 40P **NOTES:** No smoking in restaurant Last d 8.30pm **CARDS:**

See advert on opposite page

NEWQUAY Cornwall & Isles of Scilly **Map 02 SW86**
★★★ *Glendorgal*
Lusty Glaze Rd, Porth TR7 3AB
Quality Percentage Score: 62%
☎ 01637 874937 01637 851341
Dir: *from A392 at Quintrell Downs rdbt turn right towards the sea do not turn towards Porth. Straight ahead of road & turn right at Hotel Riviera*
The Glendorgal enjoys dramatic views out to sea and enjoys direct access to the beach. Bedrooms are mainly spacious, and comfortably furnished. Freshly prepared meals are served in the restaurant, and entertainment is periodically provided in the bar.
ROOMS: 38 en suite (bth/shr) (16 fmly) **MEALS:** English & French Cuisine V meals Coffee am Tea pm **FACILITIES:** CTV in all bedrooms STV Outdoor swimming pool (heated) Tennis (hard) Fishing Snooker Sauna Solarium Gym Jacuzzi/spa Wkly live entertainment **CONF:** Class 48 Board 25 **SERVICES:** Night porter 60P **NOTES:** No smoking in restaurant Last d 8.30pm **CARDS:**

See advert on opposite page

NEWQUAY Cornwall & Isles of Scilly **Map 02 SW86**
★★★ Kilbirnie
Narrowcliff TR7 2RS
Quality Percentage Score: 61%
☎ 01637 875155 01637 850769
Dir: *on A392*
Overlooking the Barrowfields and the Atlantic Ocean, this family owned hotel has spacious reception rooms, including a ballroom, cocktail bar and a comfortable foyer lounge. Bedrooms vary in size and style and the hotel offers a good range of indoor facilities. The restaurant offers a fixed-price menu.
ROOMS: 66 en suite (bth/shr) (3 fmly) s fr £30; d fr £60 (incl. bkfst & dinner) * LB Off peak **MEALS:** Dinner fr £12.50 V meals Coffee am Tea pm **FACILITIES:** CTV in all bedrooms Indoor swimming pool (heated) Outdoor swimming pool (heated) Snooker Sauna Solarium Pool table Jacuzzi/spa Table tennis Xmas **CONF:** Thtr 80 Class 40 Board 20 **SERVICES:** Lift Night porter Air conditioning 68P **NOTES:** No smoking in restaurant Last d 8.30pm **CARDS:**

See advert on page 481

NEWQUAY Cornwall & Isles of Scilly **Map 02 SW86**
★★❁ Corisande Manor
Riverside Av, Pentire TR7 1PL
Quality Percentage Score: 75%
☎ 01637 872042 874557
Dir: *from A392 Newquay road follow signs for Pentire*
Peacefully situated in three acres of grounds, yet still close to the town centre, this Victorian hotel has direct access to the Gannel Sands. It has a friendly, informal atmosphere with the bedrooms offering modern facilities and decorated and furnished with great

contd.

care and imagination. In the restaurant, the short menu offers an innovative choice of dishes supported by an extensive wine list.
ROOMS: 12 en suite (bth/shr) s £64-£74; d £95-£125 (incl. bkfst) * LB Off peak **MEALS:** Dinner £20.50-£22.50 English, French Cuisine V meals **FACILITIES:** CTV in all bedrooms Croquet lawn Putting green Xmas **SERVICES:** 19P **NOTES:** No coaches No smoking in restaurant Last d 8pm **CARDS:**

NEWQUAY Cornwall & Isles of Scilly **Map 02 SW86**

★★ Whipsiderry

Trevelgue Rd, Porth TR7 3LY
Quality Percentage Score: 71%
☎ 01637 874777 ▤ 01637 874777
Dir: *turn right onto Padstow road B3276 out of Newquay, in half a mile turn right at Trevelgue Rd*

A friendly family-run hotel with superb views over Newquay's Porth Beach. Inside, there is a wide choice of bedrooms in size and style, many of which enjoy the superb scenery. The dining room offers a well balanced fixed-price menu, and badger watching has become a special pastime for guests after sunset.
ROOMS: 24 rms (5 bth 14 shr) (5 fmly) s £36-£47; d £72-£94 (incl. bkfst & dinner) * LB Off peak **MEALS:** Bar Lunch £1.95-£5 Dinner £14.50-£18 English & Continental Cuisine V meals Coffee am Tea pm **FACILITIES:** CTV in all bedrooms Outdoor swimming pool (heated) Sauna Pool table Wkly live entertainment ch fac Xmas **SERVICES:** 30P **NOTES:** No smoking in restaurant Last d 8.30pm Closed Nov-Etr (ex Xmas) **CARDS:**

New AA Guides for the Millennium are featured on page 24

NEWQUAY Cornwall & Isles of Scilly **Map 02 SW86**
★★ Porth Veor Manor
Porth Way TR7 3LW
Quality Percentage Score: 68%
☎ 01637 873274 01637 851690
Dir: *on B3276 quarter of a mile from junct with A3058*
Standing in two acres of gardens and grounds, this 19th-century stone house overlooks Porth Beach. It is a family-run hotel, with a friendly relaxed atmosphere. There is a variety of rooms available in both size and style. The dining room, which benefits from splendid coastal views, serves a fixed-price menu with an emphasis on fresh local produce.
ROOMS: 22 en suite (bth/shr) (7 fmly) No smoking in 6 bedrooms s £42.50-£50; d £85-£100 (incl. bkfst & dinner) * LB Off peak **MEALS:** Sunday Lunch £7.95-£8.95 Dinner fr £12.45 & alc International Cuisine V meals **FACILITIES:** CTV in all bedrooms Croquet lawn Putting green Xmas **CONF:** Class 24 Board 24 Del from £50 **SERVICES:** 40P **NOTES:** No smoking in restaurant Last d 8.30pm
CARDS:

NEWQUAY Cornwall & Isles of Scilly **Map 02 SW86**
★★ *Beachcroft*
Cliff Rd TR7 1SW
Quality Percentage Score: 65%
☎ 01637 873022 01637 873022
Dir: *turn off A30 towards St Mawgan RAF camp then onto Newquay opposite railway station*
The Beachcroft is a competitively priced hotel in the centre of Newquay. Public rooms include several lounge areas, a bar serving real ales, and a small coffee shop. A varied range of both indoor and outdoor leisure facilities is available, whilst popular entertainment is provided nightly in the spacious ballroom.
ROOMS: 69 en suite (bth/shr) (13 fmly) **MEALS:** V meals Coffee am Tea pm **FACILITIES:** CTV in all bedrooms Indoor swimming pool (heated) Outdoor swimming pool (heated) Tennis (hard) Sauna Solarium Pool table Putting green Games room Table tennis Wkly live entertainment ch fac **SERVICES:** Lift Night porter 80P **NOTES:** Last d 8pm Closed early Oct-early Apr
CARDS:

N

NEWQUAY Cornwall & Isles of Scilly **Map 02 SW86**
★★ Philema
1 Esplanade Rd, Pentire TR7 1PY
Quality Percentage Score: 65%
☎ 01637 872571 01637 873188
Dir: *from A30 follow A392 signs then signs for Fistral Beach & Pentire, turn left at rdbt for Pentire. Hotel at bottom of Pentire Rd*
This family-run hotel prides itself on its hospitality and is situated facing Fistral Bay and is close to the town centre and shops. All bedrooms are comfortably furnished, some face the beach and all have modern amenities. There are spacious public areas and leisure facilities. Home-cooked food is served in the pleasant dining room.
ROOMS: 29 en suite (bth/shr) (16 fmly) s £20-£40; d £40-£80 (incl. bkfst) * LB Off peak **MEALS:** Bar Lunch £2-£4 High tea £4-£7 Dinner £7.50-£9.50 & alc English & Continental Cuisine V meals Coffee am Tea pm **FACILITIES:** CTV in all bedrooms STV Indoor swimming pool (heated) Snooker Sauna Solarium Pool table Jacuzzi/spa Table tennis ch fac **SERVICES:** 37P **NOTES:** No smoking in restaurant Last d 7.30pm Closed Nov-Feb **CARDS:**

Symbols and Abbreviations are listed and explained on pages 4 and 5

NEWQUAY Cornwall & Isles of Scilly **Map 02 SW86**
★★ Tremont
Pentire Av TR7 1PB
Quality Percentage Score: 63%
☎ 01637 872984 01637 851984
Dir: *from A30 onto B3902 into Newquay and follow Pentire signs*
This popular hotel is within walking distance of Fistral Beach and the town centre. The hotel has spacious lounges where entertainment is regularly held, a cosy bar, and excellent leisure facilities. Bedrooms are sensibly furnished, all with modern facilities.
ROOMS: 54 en suite (bth/shr) (26 fmly) s £24-£35; d £48-£70 (incl. bkfst & dinner) * LB Off peak **MEALS:** Bar Lunch £1.70-£5 Dinner £6-£11.50 Coffee am Tea pm **FACILITIES:** CTV in all bedrooms Indoor swimming pool (heated) Tennis (hard) Squash Sauna Solarium Gym Pool table Putting green Table tennis Wkly live entertainment Xmas **CONF:** Thtr 160 Del from £21 * **SERVICES:** Lift 60P **NOTES:** No smoking in restaurant Last d 7.30pm **CARDS:**

NEWQUAY Cornwall & Isles of Scilly **Map 02 SW86**
★★ *Cedars*
Mount Wise TR7 2BA
Quality Percentage Score: 61%
☎ 01637 874225 01637 87225
Dir: *enter Newquay via Narrowcliff follow one way system into Berry Rd & Mountwise approx 500yds on right from Mountwise public car park*
This family-run hotel attracts holidaymakers, including private guests and coach parties. Most bedrooms have sea views and a selection of very high quality rooms is available. The comfortable public areas are spacious with a lounge/bar and entertainment on certain evenings during the season. Filling dinners are served in the dining room by friendly and efficient staff.
ROOMS: 42 rms (15 bth 16 shr) (8 fmly) No smoking in 9 bedrooms **MEALS:** Coffee am Tea pm **FACILITIES:** CTV in all bedrooms Outdoor swimming pool (heated) Sauna Solarium Gym Pool table Jacuzzi/spa Wkly live entertainment **SERVICES:** 42P **NOTES:** No smoking in restaurant Last d 7.30pm Closed Nov-Mar (ex New Year)
CARDS:

NEWTON ABBOT Devon **Map 03 SX87**
see also **Ilsington**
★★★ Passage House
Hackney Ln, Kingsteignton TQ12 3QH
Quality Percentage Score: 71%
☎ 01626 355515 01626 363336
Dir: *leave the A380 for the A381 and follow racecourse signs*
Enjoying a lovely location on the Teign estury, this hotel caters well for business meetings and offers a modern health and leisure centre. The restaurant provides a choice of menus both at lunch and dinner, and a well known historic inn, also called the Passage House stands next door to the hotel.
ROOMS: 38 en suite (bth/shr) (32 fmly) No smoking in 3 bedrooms s £65-£75; d £75-£85 (incl. bkfst) LB Off peak **MEALS:** Lunch £9.95 Dinner £18.95 & alc V meals Coffee am Tea pm **FACILITIES:** CTV in all bedrooms STV Indoor swimming pool (heated) Sauna Solarium Gym Pool table Jacuzzi/spa Xmas **CONF:** Thtr 120 Class 30 Board 40 Del from £80 * **SERVICES:** Lift Night porter 300P **NOTES:** No smoking area in restaurant Last d 9.30pm **CARDS:**

NEWTON ABBOT Devon **Map 03 SX87**
★★ Queens
Queen St TQ12 2EZ
Quality Percentage Score: 65%
☎ 01626 363133 & 354106 01626 364922
Dir: *Opposite the railway station, beside Courtenay Park*
A busy hotel near the railway station, Azarats (the hotel's wine

contd.

bar) attracts business guests and younger guests at weekends, serving designer beers and wines. Guest dine in the Regency Restaurant or from the extensive bar or room service menus. Bedrooms are being upgraded and offer comfortable accommodation with modern facilities.
ROOMS: 22 rms (20 bth/shr) (3 fmly) No smoking in 4 bedrooms **MEALS:** Bar Lunch £2.20-£6.75 Dinner £14.95-£19.75 English & French Cuisine V meals Coffee am Tea pm **FACILITIES:** CTV in all bedrooms Pool table **CONF:** Thtr 80 Class 40 Board 40 **SERVICES:** 8P **NOTES:** No coaches No smoking area in restaurant Last d 8.45pm
CARDS:

NEWTON ABBOT Devon — Map 03 SX87
★ Hazelwood Hotel
33a Torquay Rd TQ12 2LW
Quality Percentage Score: 63%
☎ 01626 366130 01626 365021
Within easy walking distance of the town centre, The Hazelwood is an ideal base from which to explore South Devon and Torbay. The modern bedrooms are well equipped, and a short menu is available at dinner.
ROOMS: 8 en suite (bth/shr) s £34-£39; d £48-£54 (incl. bkfst) * LB Off peak **MEALS:** Dinner £11.50-£13.95 V meals Coffee am **FACILITIES:** CTV in all bedrooms **SERVICES:** 10P **NOTES:** No coaches No smoking in restaurant Last d 6.30pm **CARDS:**

NEWTON-LE-WILLOWS Merseyside — Map 07 SJ59
★★ Kirkfield Hotel
2/4 Church St WA12 9SU
Quality Percentage Score: 62%
☎ 01925 228196 01925 291540
Dir: *on A49 Newton-le-Willows opposite St Peter's Church*
Situated directly opposite the church, where parking is available, this hotel offers accomodation with straightforward furnishings. A good range of meals is available in the bar or adjacent dining room, and the mainly young staff help to create a relaxing and informal atmosphere.
ROOMS: 15 en suite (bth/shr) (3 fmly) No smoking in 5 bedrooms s £30-£43.50; d £50 (incl. bkfst) * LB Off peak **MEALS:** Lunch £6.95-£10.95 Dinner £6.95-£10.95 International Cuisine V meals Coffee am Tea pm **FACILITIES:** CTV in all bedrooms Pool table **CONF:** Thtr 70 Class 60 Board 20 Del from £75 * **SERVICES:** 50P **NOTES:** No dogs (ex guide dogs) Last d 9pm Closed 25 Dec **CARDS:**

NORMAN CROSS Cambridgeshire — Map 04 TL19
★★★ Posthouse Peterborough
Great North Rd PE7 3TB
Posthouse
Quality Percentage Score: 64%
☎ 01733 240209 01733 244455
Dir: *on southbound A1(M) take A15 junct to Yaxley. On northbound A1(M take A15 junct to Yaxley*
Situated at the junction of the A1(M) and A15, about 6 miles from the town centre, this hotel offers traditionally furnished and well-equipped rooms, and refurbishment is planned. A health club is a feature of the hotel together with Seasons restaurant which serves British and international dishes.
ROOMS: 93 en suite (bth/shr) No smoking in 47 bedrooms d fr £79 * LB Off peak **MEALS:** International Cuisine V meals Coffee am Tea pm **FACILITIES:** CTV in all bedrooms Indoor swimming pool (heated) Sauna Gym Pool table Jacuzzi/spa Steam room Xmas **CONF:** Thtr 50 Class 16 Board 24 Del from £90 * **SERVICES:** Night porter 150P **NOTES:** No smoking area in restaurant Last d 10.30pm
CARDS:

N

NORTHALLERTON North Yorkshire **Map 08 SE39**

★★★ Solberge Hall

Newby Wiske DL7 9ER

Quality Percentage Score: 68%

☎ 01609 779191 01609 780472

Dir: *3.25kms S of Northallerton on the A167. Hotel is located on the right as you pass through North Otterington*

Standing proudly in its own extensive grounds, with fine views over surrounding countryside, this attractive Victorian hotel provides well equipped bedrooms. Public rooms are stylishly comfortable and a good choice of food is available in the elegant Garden Room Restaurant. Staff are professional, friendly and pleasantly enthusiastic.

ROOMS: 24 en suite (bth/shr) (2 fmly) s £75-£85; d £100-£110 (incl. bkfst) * LB Off peak **MEALS:** Lunch £8.95-£12.50 Dinner £22.50 & alc International Cuisine V meals Coffee am Tea pm **FACILITIES:** CTV in all bedrooms STV Croquet lawn Xmas **CONF:** Thtr 100 Class 50 Board 40 **SERVICES:** 100P **NOTES:** No smoking in restaurant Last d 9.30pm **CARDS:**

NORTHALLERTON North Yorkshire **Map 08 SE39**

★★ The Golden Lion

High St DL7 8PP

Quality Percentage Score: 63%

☎ 01609 777411 01609 773250

Dir: *take A684 travel approx 5m onto A167 through built-up area 3rd exit at next rdbt to town centre at 3rd rdbt turn left into High St*

Situated in the town centre, this popular coaching inn has comfortable lounges with blazing open fires during winter. The attractively appointed restaurant gives the hotel much character and charm, and the traditional, comfortably furnished bedrooms offer every modern facility. Staff are friendly and helpful.

ROOMS: 25 en suite (bth/shr) No smoking in 18 bedrooms s £45-£65; d £70-£90 (incl. bkfst) * LB Off peak **MEALS:** Sunday Lunch £11.95 & alc Dinner £10.95-£36alc V meals Coffee am Tea pm **FACILITIES:** CTV in all bedrooms Xmas **CONF:** Thtr 150 Class 80 Board 40 **SERVICES:** 100P **NOTES:** No smoking in restaurant Last d 9.30pm **CARDS:**

NORTHAMPTON Northamptonshire **Map 04 SP76**

see also **Flore**

★★★★ Swallow

Eagle Dr NN4 7HW

Quality Percentage Score: 67%

☎ 01604 768700 01604 769011

Dir: *off A45, between A428 & A508*

Conveniently positioned, this hotel is custom-made for conferences and even has its own self-contained management centre. The public areas are bright and inviting with bedrooms equally appealing and equipped with a comprehensive range of modern facilities. The dining options include Spires, an elegant room overlooking the lake, and La Fontana, an Italian restaurant with a less formal atmosphere; alternatively lounge and room service options are available.

ROOMS: 120 en suite (bth/shr) (12 fmly) No smoking in 82 bedrooms s £110-£120; d £120-£140 (incl. bkfst) * LB Off peak **MEALS:** Lunch £14-£14.75 & alc Dinner £21.75 & alc English, French & Italian Cuisine V meals Coffee am Tea pm **FACILITIES:** CTV in all bedrooms STV Indoor swimming pool (heated) Sauna Solarium Gym Jacuzzi/spa Steam room Wkly live entertainment Xmas **CONF:** Thtr 220 Class 100 Board 36 Del £143 * **SERVICES:** Night porter 187P **NOTES:** No smoking area in restaurant Last d 10.30pm **CARDS:**

NORTHAMPTON Northamptonshire **Map 04 SP76**

★★★ Lime Trees

8 Langham Place, Barrack Rd NN2 6AA

Quality Percentage Score: 70%

☎ 01604 632188 01604 233012

Dir: *from city centre 0.5m N on A508 Leicester near racecourse park & cathedral*

This charming hotel goes from strength to strength under the careful management of proprietor Bob Elkin and his partner Val. Bedrooms are well equipped and very comfortable. Popular with business guests through the week who appreciate the efficient, friendly attitude of staff, the weekends see more leisure and special occasion business. The smart restaurant offers a range of popular dishes which are carefully prepared.

ROOMS: 27 en suite (bth/shr) (2 fmly) s £59-£69; d £77-£90 (incl. bkfst) * LB Off peak **MEALS:** Bar Lunch £6-£9 High tea £5-£7 Dinner £14.50-£19alc English & Continental Cuisine V meals Coffee am Tea pm **FACILITIES:** CTV in all bedrooms **CONF:** Thtr 50 Class 30 Board 30 **SERVICES:** Night porter 24P **NOTES:** No dogs (ex guide dogs) No coaches No smoking area in restaurant Last d 9.30pm RS 27 Dec-New Year **CARDS:**

NORTHAMPTON Northamptonshire **Map 04 SP76**

★★★ Courtyard by Marriott Northampton

Bedford Rd NN4 7YF

Quality Percentage Score: 68%

☎ 01604 622777 01604 635454

Dir: *from M1 junct 15 follow A508 towards Northampton. Follow A45 towards Wellingborough for 2m then A428 towards Bedford, hotel on left*

On the eastern edge of the town centre and easily accessible for the business traveller, this modern, purpose-built hotel offers a good standard of facilities and refurbished and spacious accommodation. The open-plan public areas offer a congenial, informal atmosphere and have been extended to give more space. Friendly staff provide a good range of services, including comprehensive in-room food provision.

ROOMS: 104 en suite (bth/shr) (55 fmly) No smoking in 50 bedrooms d £75-£95 * LB Off peak **MEALS:** Lunch £1.95-£20.75 High tea £1.50-£4.95 Dinner £13-£20.75alc European Cuisine V meals Coffee am Tea pm **FACILITIES:** CTV in all bedrooms STV Gym Xmas **CONF:** Thtr 40 Board 26 Del from £110 * **SERVICES:** Lift Night porter Air conditioning 150P **NOTES:** No dogs (ex guide dogs) No smoking in restaurant Last d 10.30pm **CARDS:**

NORTHAMPTON Northamptonshire **Map 04 SP76**

★★★ Northampton Moat House

Silver St NN1 2TA

Quality Percentage Score: 67%

☎ 01604 739988 01604 230614

A busy city-centre hotel, popular for conferences and nearby sporting events. Smart new public areas include a contemporary restaurant and Club Moativation Leisure Centre, with indoor pool, gym, sauna and steam-room. Bedrooms are comfortable

contd.

and have an extra telephone and inter-active TVs. The manned 'Work Base' facility is useful.
ROOMS: 145 en suite (bth/shr) No smoking in 123 bedrooms s fr £95; d fr £110 * LB Off peak **MEALS:** Lunch £8.50-£16.50 Dinner fr £15.50 & alc International Cuisine V meals Coffee am Tea pm **FACILITIES:** CTV in all bedrooms STV Indoor swimming pool (heated) Sauna Gym Pool table Steam room **CONF:** Thtr 600 Class 300 Board 160 Del from £90 * **SERVICES:** Lift Night porter 150P **NOTES:** No smoking area in restaurant Last d 10pm **CARDS:**

NORTHAMPTON Northamptonshire **Map 04 SP76**
★★★ Quality Hotel Northampton
Ashley Way, Weston Favell NN3 3EA
Quality Percentage Score: 64%
☎ 01604 739955 📠 01604 415023
Dir: *leave A45 at junct with A43, towards Weston Favell. After 0.5m bear left to town centre. Turn left at top of slip road, hotel signposted off A4500*
Quietly situated, this established hotel offers smartly presented, well equipped accommodation. Attractive public rooms include comfortable lounge areas and an elegant restaurant, where interesting, well prepared dishes are available. The hotel has a number of excellent meeting rooms.
ROOMS: 31 en suite (bth/shr) 35 annexe en suite (bth/shr) (4 fmly) No smoking in 21 bedrooms s £84-£99; d £97-£114 * LB Off peak **MEALS:** Dinner fr £16.95 V meals Coffee am Tea pm **FACILITIES:** CTV in all bedrooms STV Pool table Croquet lawn Putting green Wkly live entertainment Xmas **CONF:** Thtr 120 Class 65 Board 50 **SERVICES:** Lift Night porter 100P **NOTES:** No smoking in restaurant Last d 9.45pm **CARDS:**

NORTHAMPTON Northamptonshire **Map 04 SP76**
★★★ Grand
15 Gold St NN1 1RE
Quality Percentage Score: 63%
☎ 01604 250511 📠 01604 234534
Dir: *follow A508 to town centre, over traffic lights at the Carlsberg Brewery, take the road to left, hotel car park is 300m on left*
This impressive town centre hotel offers bright attractive accommodation. The bedrooms vary in size, but all are comfortably furnished and well equipped. Public areas include the Kasbah bar which offers a range of hot and cold snacks, and the lower ground floor dining room offering a daily set menu and small grill menu.
ROOMS: 56 en suite (bth/shr) (2 fmly) No smoking in 21 bedrooms s fr £65; d fr £89.50 (incl. bkfst) * LB Off peak **MEALS:** Dinner £15 V meals Coffee am **FACILITIES:** CTV in all bedrooms STV Pool table **CONF:** Thtr 120 Class 50 Board 40 Del from £99 * **SERVICES:** Lift Night porter 82P **NOTES:** No smoking in restaurant Last d 9.30pm **CARDS:**

NORTHAMPTON Northamptonshire **Map 04 SP76**
⇧ Travel Inn
Harpole Turn, Weedon Rd, Harpole NN7 4DD
☎ 01604 832340 📠 01604 831807
Dir: *1m from junct 16 of the M1 on A45 towards Northampton*
This modern building offers accommodation in smart, spacious and well equipped bedrooms, all with en-suite bathrooms. Refreshments may be taken at the nearby family restaurant. For details about current prices consult the Contents Page under Hotel Groups for the Travel Inn phone number.
ROOMS: 51 en suite (bth/shr) d £39.95 *

NORTHAMPTON Northamptonshire **Map 04 SP76**
⇧ Travelodge
Upton Way NN5 6EG
☎ 01604 758395 📠 01604 758395
Dir: *A45, towards M1 junct 16*
This modern building offers accommodation in smart, spacious and well equipped bedrooms, all with en-suite bathrooms. Refreshments may be taken at the nearby family restaurant. For details about current prices, consult the Contents Page under Hotel Groups for the Travelodge phone number.
ROOMS: 62 en suite (bth/shr) d £44.95 *

NORTH FERRIBY East Riding of Yorkshire **Map 08 SE92**
★★★ Posthouse Hull
Ferriby High Rd HU14 3LG
Quality Percentage Score: 63%
☎ 01482 645212 📠 01482 643332
Dir: *from M62 join A63 to Hull. Take exit for Humber Bridge. At rdbt follow signs for North Ferriby. Hotel is 0.5m on left*
This hotel commands fine views of the Humber Bridge and and offers well maintained bedrooms with every modern facility. Public areas are functional and include the popular restaurant which looks over the river. Staff are friendly and helpful and as well as an all day lounge menu, 24 hour room service is also provided. A children's play area has been created at the rear and there is ample car parking space.
ROOMS: 95 en suite (bth/shr) No smoking in 66 bedrooms d £59-£75 * LB Off peak **MEALS:** International Cuisine V meals Coffee am Tea pm **FACILITIES:** CTV in all bedrooms Pool table ch fac Xmas **CONF:** Thtr 100 Class 40 Board 40 Del from £75 * **SERVICES:** Night porter 140P **NOTES:** No smoking area in restaurant Last d 10pm **CARDS:**

NORTHLEACH Gloucestershire **Map 04 SP11**
★★ Wheatsheaf
West End GL54 3EZ
Quality Percentage Score: 66%
☎ 01451 860244 📠 01451 861037
Dir: *junct A40/A429, take A429 for Cirencester. After 0.5m turn left at traffic lights, hotel 300yds on left*
This former coaching inn, built of Cotswold stone, provides well equipped and soundly maintained accommodation. Public areas include a pleasant restaurant with period furniture, and two adjoining bars where welcoming real fires burn when the weather is cold.
ROOMS: 9 en suite (bth/shr) (1 fmly) s £45; d £59-£65 (incl. bkfst) * LB Off peak **MEALS:** Bar Lunch £10.20-£16.45alc Dinner £13.40-£22.15alc English & Mediterranean Cuisine V meals Coffee am Tea pm **FACILITIES:** CTV in all bedrooms **SERVICES:** 15P **NOTES:** No smoking in restaurant Last d 9pm Closed 25 Dec **CARDS:**

NORTH MUSKHAM Nottinghamshire **Map 08 SK75**
⇧ Travelodge
NG23 6HT
☎ 01636 703635 📠 01636 703635
Dir: *3m N, on A1 southbound*
This modern building offers accommodation in smart, spacious and well equipped bedrooms, all with en-suite bathrooms. Refreshments may be taken at the nearby family restaurant. For details about current prices, consult the Contents Page under Hotel Groups for the Travelodge phone number.
ROOMS: 30 en suite (bth/shr) d £39.95 *

contd.

NORTH WALSHAM Norfolk **Map 09 TG23**
★★ Beechwood
Cromer Rd NR28 0HD
Quality Percentage Score: 79%
☎ 01692 403231 Fax 01692 407284
Dir: *take B1150 from Norwich, at North Walsham turn left at first set of traffic lights then right at the next*

Close to the North Norfolk coast, this delightful hotel is excellent value for money and its country house seclusion ensures the regular return of many guests. The comfortable and elegant public areas and accommodation are tastefully designed, and the restaurant is a pleasant venue to enjoy the culinary delights on offer. Bedrooms, which vary in size, are individually decorated and offer good facilities.
ROOMS: 9 en suite (bth/shr) No smoking in 7 bedrooms s £48-£58; d £68-£88 (incl. bkfst) * LB Off peak **MEALS:** Lunch £11-£12 Dinner fr £21 New World Cuisine V meals Coffee am Tea pm **FACILITIES:** CTV in all bedrooms **SERVICES:** 17P **NOTES:** No coaches No children 10yrs No smoking in restaurant Last d 9pm **CARDS:**

See advert on opposite page

NORTHWICH Cheshire **Map 07 SJ67**
★★ Hartford Hall
School Ln, Hartford CW8 1PW
Quality Percentage Score: 66%
☎ 01606 75711 Fax 01606 782285
Dir: *in village of Hartford, between Northwich and Chester on the A556*
This 17th-century former manor house is situated in four acres of gardens and grounds. The bedrooms are very well equipped. Public areas are characteristic of the period and feature the heavily beamed Nunn's Room in which civil weddings and other functions are held.
ROOMS: 20 en suite (bth/shr) (2 fmly) d £64 * LB Off peak **MEALS:** Lunch £6.95-£23.45alc Dinner £13.35-£23.45alc International Cuisine V meals Coffee am Tea pm **FACILITIES:** CTV in all bedrooms STV Croquet lawn Xmas **CONF:** Thtr 40 Class 12 Board 25 Del £110 * **SERVICES:** Night porter 50P **NOTES:** No dogs (ex guide dogs) No smoking area in restaurant Last d 9.30pm
CARDS:

NORTHWICH Cheshire **Map 07 SJ67**
★★ Wincham Hall
Hall Ln, Wincham CW9 6DG
Quality Percentage Score: 65%
☎ 01606 43453 Fax 01606 40128
Dir: *leave M6 junct 19 take A556 to Chester. Turn right onto A559 to Northwich. At lights turn right. Hotel 0.5m on left*
This family run hotel offers well presented pine furnished bedrooms. Many of the rooms overlook the five acres of grounds, which include a walled garden and lily pond. Guests can relax in the lounge bar before enjoying a meal.
ROOMS: 10 rms (9 bth/shr) (1 fmly) s £58-£68 (incl. bkfst) * Off peak **MEALS:** Lunch fr £12.95 Dinner fr £17.50 English & Continental Cuisine V meals Coffee am Tea pm **FACILITIES:** CTV in 9 bedrooms Croquet lawn **CONF:** Thtr 100 Class 50 Board 20 **SERVICES:** 200P **NOTES:** Last d 9.30pm **CARDS:**

NORTHWICH Cheshire **Map 07 SJ67**
Quality Hotel Northwich
London Rd CW9 5HD
☎ 01606 44443 Fax (0606) 42596
A first in the UK! This floating hotel has been built over the river and a very successful concept it is. The bedrooms are modern and well equipped and there is a carvery restaurant which, not surprisingly, overlooks the river.
ROOMS: 60 en suite (bth) No smoking in 10 bedrooms **MEALS:** English & French Cuisine V meals Coffee am Tea pm **FACILITIES:** CTV in all bedrooms **SERVICES:** Night porter 40P **NOTES:** Last d 9.30pm
CARDS:

NORTHWOLD Norfolk **Map 05 TL79**
★★ Comfort Inn Thetford
Thetford Rd IP26 5LQ
Quality Percentage Score: 67%
☎ 01366 728888 Fax 01366 727121
Dir: *W of Mundford on A134*
Set in a delightful rural location, this hotel is based around an attractive cluster of buildings. The large bedrooms are set around a courtyard and are ideal for families. The beamed Woodland Inn combines the role of a country public house and the hotel restaurant.
ROOMS: 34 en suite (bth/shr) (5 fmly) No smoking in 17 bedrooms d £46.75-£54.50 * LB Off peak **MEALS:** Lunch £2.95-£15.95alc Dinner fr £10.75 & alc English & Continental Cuisine V meals Coffee am Tea pm **FACILITIES:** CTV in all bedrooms STV Gym Xmas **CONF:** Thtr 150 Class 55 Board 60 **SERVICES:** Night porter Air conditioning 250P **NOTES:** No smoking area in restaurant Last d 9.30pm
CARDS:

NORWICH Norfolk **Map 05 TG20**
see also **South Walsham**
★★★★ Swallow Sprowston Manor
Sprowston Park, Wroxham Rd,
Sprowston NR7 8RP
Quality Percentage Score: 73%
☎ 01603 410871 Fax 01603 423911
Dir: *2m NE A1151-from A11 take the Wroxham road (A1151 and follow signs to Sprowston Park*

Set on the fringes of the city, in attractive parkland and adjacent to the local golf course, Sprowston Manor provides some of the best conference, banqueting and leisure facilities in East Anglia.
contd.

The elegant restaurant serves interesting daily and carte menus featuring modern European cooking. Accommodation comes in a range of styles and sizes, from four-poster beds to full suites.
ROOMS: 94 en suite (bth/shr) (3 fmly) No smoking in 68 bedrooms s £102-£112; d £115-£150 (incl. bkfst) LB Off peak **MEALS:** Lunch £12.50-£16 & alc High tea fr £6.95 Dinner fr £22 V meals Coffee am Tea pm **FACILITIES:** CTV in all bedrooms STV Indoor swimming pool (heated) Golf 18 Sauna Solarium Gym Croquet lawn Jacuzzi/spa Beauty salon Health spa Steam room Wkly live entertainment Xmas **CONF:** Thtr 160 Class 80 Board 50 Del from £134 * **SERVICES:** Lift Night porter 150P **NOTES:** No smoking in restaurant Last d 10pm
CARDS:

NORWICH Norfolk — Map 05 TG20

★★★★ De Vere Dunston Hall

Ipswich Rd, Dunston NR14 8PQ

DE VERE HOTELS

Quality Percentage Score: 65%

☎ 01508 470444 Fax 01508 471499

Dir: *from A47, take A140 Ipswich Road, hotel directly off this road on left after approx 0.25m*

Set in landscaped grounds, this fine listed building stands 2 miles south of the city. It offers spacious, well equipped bedrooms and a wide range of leisure facilities.
ROOMS: 72 en suite (bth/shr) s £89-£139; d £140-£180 (incl. bkfst) * LB Off peak **MEALS:** Lunch £17 High tea £5.25-£7.50 Dinner £19.95-£23 & alc English & French Cuisine V meals Coffee am Tea pm **FACILITIES:** CTV in all bedrooms STV Indoor swimming pool (heated) Golf 18 Snooker Sauna Solarium Gym Pool table Putting green Jacuzzi/spa Bowling green Xmas **CONF:** Thtr 299 Class 140 Board 90 Del from £125 * **SERVICES:** Lift Night porter 500P **NOTES:** No coaches No smoking in restaurant Last d 9.30pm
CARDS:

NORWICH Norfolk **Map 05 TG20**

★★★ **Swallow Nelson Hotel**

Prince of Wales Rd NR1 1DX

Quality Percentage Score: 67%

☎ 01603 760260 📠 01603 620008

Dir: *follow signs for city centre & football ground & railway station. Hotel is on riverside opposite station*

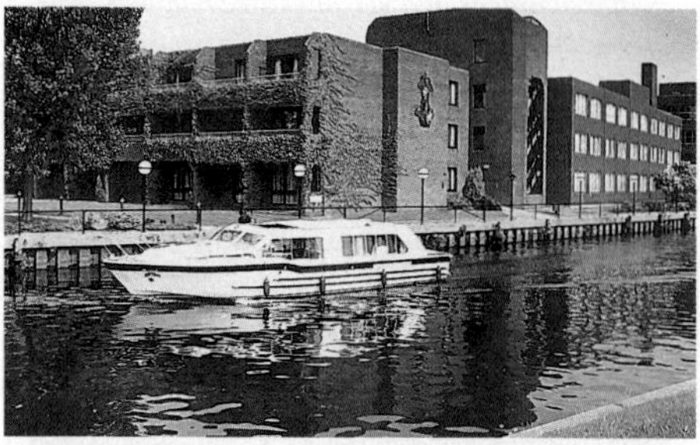

Overlooking the River Wensum and close by the station, this pleasant hotel has a nautical theme, featuring many references to its namesake. Public areas are well designed in a variety of styles, and the well appointed bedrooms have refrigerators; 24-hour room service is on offer. The choice of eating options, the leisure complex and conference suites make this a popular hotel.
ROOMS: 132 en suite (bth/shr) s fr £88; d fr £99 (incl. bkfst) * LB Off peak **MEALS:** Sunday Lunch £10.50-£12.50 & alc Dinner £16.50-£18.50 & alc European Cuisine V meals Coffee am Tea pm **FACILITIES:** CTV in all bedrooms Indoor swimming pool (heated) Sauna Solarium Gym Steam room Beauty & hair salon Xmas **CONF:** Thtr 90 Board 44 **SERVICES:** Lift Night porter 210P **NOTES:** No dogs (ex guide dogs) Last d 9.45pm **CARDS:**

NORWICH Norfolk **Map 05 TG20**

★★★ ***Posthouse Norwich***

Ipswich Rd NR4 6EP

Quality Percentage Score: 66%

☎ 01603 456431 📠 01603 506400

Dir: *take A47, southern bypass, until sign for A140, then turn N into Norwich. Hotel 0.5m on right*

A modern hotel just out of the city. Public areas, including 'Seasons' restaurant, are comfortably appointed, the well equipped "Spa" leisure club is a prominent feature. Bedrooms have every modern facility including mini bars and in-house movies. Staff are friendly and helpful, there is an all day lounge menu and 24 hour room service
ROOMS: 116 en suite (bth/shr) (54 fmly) No smoking in 44 bedrooms **MEALS:** International Cuisine V meals Coffee am Tea pm **FACILITIES:** CTV in all bedrooms Indoor swimming pool (heated) Sauna Gym Jacuzzi/spa Health & fitness centre ch fac **CONF:** Thtr 100 Class 48 Board 40 **SERVICES:** Night porter 200P **NOTES:** No smoking area in restaurant Last d 10.30pm **CARDS:**

NORWICH Norfolk **Map 05 TG20**

★★★ **Quality Hotel**

2 Barnard Rd, Bowthorpe NR5 9JB

Quality Percentage Score: 66%

☎ 01603 741161 📠 01603 741500

Dir: *on Barnard Rd just off the A1074 Dereham rd, 5m from Norwich city centre*

Close to the western side of the city centre and near the bypass, this modern hotel gives easy access to routes around Norwhich. The atmosphere is friendly, and bedrooms are well equipped. There is a good leisure centre and a wide choice of meeting rooms.
ROOMS: 80 en suite (bth/shr) (10 fmly) No smoking in 40 bedrooms s fr £81.75; d fr £105.50 (incl. bkfst) * LB Off peak **MEALS:** Lunch £2.95-£15.95alc Dinner fr £14.50 & alc English & Continental Cuisine V meals Coffee am Tea pm **FACILITIES:** CTV in all bedrooms STV Indoor swimming pool (heated) Sauna Solarium Gym Jacuzzi/spa Xmas **CONF:** Thtr 200 Class 80 Board 60 **SERVICES:** Night porter 140P **NOTES:** No smoking area in restaurant Last d 9.30pm **CARDS:**

NORWICH Norfolk **Map 05 TG20**

★★★ **Maids Head**

Tombland NR3 1LB

Quality Percentage Score: 65%

☎ 01603 209955 📠 01603 613688

Dir: *follow city centre signs, continue past Norwich Castle, 3rd turning after castle into Upper King St, hotel opposite Norman cathedral*

In a dominant position in the heart of the city, close to the impressive Norman cathedral, this historic hotel dates in part back to the 13th century. The Courtyard Restaurant, where coach and horses once drove through, the panelled Jacobean bar and many of the oak beamed bedrooms - particularly in the Cathedral Wing - bear witness to the hotel's earlier days. The bedrooms are well equipped and there is a private car park to the rear of the building.
ROOMS: 84 en suite (bth/shr) (3 fmly) No smoking in 30 bedrooms s £69-£79; d £89-£99 * LB Off peak **MEALS:** Lunch £10-£15 & alc High tea £3.95-£7 Dinner £13.50-£17.50 & alc International Cuisine V meals Coffee am Tea pm **FACILITIES:** CTV in all bedrooms Xmas **CONF:** Thtr 300 Class 120 Board 40 Del from £100 * **SERVICES:** Lift Night porter 60P **NOTES:** No smoking in restaurant Last d 9.45pm **CARDS:**

NORWICH Norfolk **Map 05 TG20**

★★★ **The George Hotel**

10 Arlington Ln, Newmarket Rd NR2 2DA

Quality Percentage Score: 64%

☎ 01603 617841 📠 01603 663708

Dir: *approach on A11, follow City Ctr signs across outer ring rd, large rdbt and inner ring rd smaller rdbt. 3rd turning on left, Hotel on right*

In a residential area within easy walking distance of the city centre, guests will find a warm welcome from the friendly team at the George Hotel. This well maintained hotel offers a good standard of accommodation in well decorated bedrooms. Public

contd.

For Useful Information and Important Telephone Number Changes turn to page 25

areas include an attractive and comfortable lounge bar and small grill restaurant serving home cooked meals.
ROOMS: 36 en suite (bth/shr) 4 annexe en suite (bth/shr) (3 fmly) No smoking in 9 bedrooms s £61.50-£72.50; d £83.50-£100 (incl. bkfst) * LB Off peak **MEALS:** Bar Lunch £10.50-£16.50alc Dinner £16.50-£20 & alc English & French Cuisine V meals Coffee am Tea pm **FACILITIES:** CTV in all bedrooms STV Xmas **CONF:** Thtr 60 Class 25 Board 32 Del from £60 * **SERVICES:** 40P **NOTES:** No smoking in restaurant Last d 10pm **CARDS:**

See advert on this page

NORWICH Norfolk **Map 05 TG20**
★★★ Norwich Sport Village Hotel
Drayton High Rd, Hellesdon NR6 5DU
Quality Percentage Score: 64%
☎ 01603 788898 01603 406845
Dir: *at junct of A140 Ring Road and A1067 to Fakenham follow brown tourist signs*

This modern hotel forms part of an impressive sports and leisure complex. Public areas tend to mingle with sports facilities, and there are numerous informal eating outlets from which to choose. The accommodation is modern and quite spacious, each room equipped with many useful amenities. There is a comprehensive range of sporting facilities, which include an ultra modern gym and an aqua-park; there are also several meeting rooms ideal for business use.
ROOMS: 55 en suite (bth/shr) (2 fmly) No smoking in 10 bedrooms s fr £52; d fr £74 (incl. bkfst) * LB Off peak **MEALS:** Sunday Lunch fr £10 High tea fr £2.50 Dinner fr £15.95 V meals Coffee am Tea pm **FACILITIES:** CTV in all bedrooms STV Indoor swimming pool (heated) Tennis (hard) Squash Snooker Sauna Solarium Gym Jacuzzi/spa Badminton Table tennis Beauty salon Toning salon **CONF:** Thtr 5000 Class 46 Board 80 Del from £85 * **SERVICES:** Lift Night porter 800P **NOTES:** No dogs (ex guide dogs) No smoking in restaurant Last d 9.15pm **CARDS:**

NORWICH Norfolk **Map 05 TG20**
★★ The Old Rectory
103 Yarmouth Rd, Thorpe St Andrew NR7 0HF
Quality Percentage Score: 76%
☎ 01603 700772 01603 300772
Dir: *from A47 Norwich Southern Bypass, take A1042 towards Norwich N & E. At mini-rdbt bear left (A1242), straight over at lights, hotel 100mtrs on right*

This hotel is a delightful haven of classical style and elegance combined with a modern touch. In quiet residential surroundings, the well tended gardens give a secluded air, along with the relaxing conservatory. The elegant dining room is a

contd.

N

good backdrop for the enjoyable food offered on the daily changing menu.
ROOMS: 5 en suite (bth/shr) 3 annexe en suite (bth/shr) No smoking in all bedrooms s £60-£70; d £77-£87 (incl. bkfst) * LB Off peak **MEALS:** High tea £3.50 Dinner £15.95-£17.50 English & French Cuisine V meals Coffee am Tea pm **FACILITIES:** CTV in all bedrooms STV Outdoor swimming pool (heated) **CONF:** Thtr 25 Class 18 Board 18 Del from £92 * **SERVICES:** 17P **NOTES:** No dogs (ex guide dogs) No coaches No smoking in restaurant Last d 8.30pm Closed 23 Dec-11 Jan
CARDS:

See advert on page 487

NORWICH Norfolk **Map 05 TG20**
★★ Annesley House
6 Newmarket Rd NR2 2LA
Quality Percentage Score: 74%
☎ 01603 624553 01603 621577
Dir: *on A11 half a mile before city centre*
The recent addition of a conservatory restaurant and a water feature to the three acres of landscaped gardens has added even more to the appeal of this city-centre hotel. It is an attractive Georgian property, consisting of three houses, two of which are joined. Bedrooms are all comfortable and well equipped.
ROOMS: 18 en suite (bth/shr) 8 annexe en suite (bth/shr) (3 fmly) s £66-£77.50; d £77.50-£90 (incl. bkfst) * LB Off peak **MEALS:** Lunch £8.95-£9.95 High tea fr £6.50 Dinner fr £17.50 & alc English, French & Mediterranean Cuisine V meals Coffee am Tea pm **FACILITIES:** CTV in all bedrooms STV **SERVICES:** 25P **NOTES:** No dogs (ex guide dogs) No smoking in restaurant Last d 9pm Closed 24-27 & 30-31 Dec
CARDS:

NORWICH Norfolk **Map 05 TG20**
★★ Beeches Hotel & Victorian Gardens
4-6 Earlham Rd NR2 3DB
Quality Percentage Score: 69%
☎ 01603 621167 01603 620151
Dir: *on B1108, behind St Johns RC Cathedral just off inner ring road*
A delightful Grade II listed building convenient for the heritage-packed city of Norwich. Consisting of two neighbouring houses, the hotel offers charming and well maintained bedrooms with a good level of facilities. Guests can enjoy the smart bar with its all day snack menu, and the bistro style restaurant that tempts diners with appealing, freshly prepared dishes. The hotel is renowned for its sunken Victorian garden in the spacious landscaped grounds.
ROOMS: 16 en suite (bth/shr) 19 annexe en suite (bth/shr) No smoking in all bedrooms s £59-£64; d £76-£88 (incl. bkfst) * LB Off peak **MEALS:** Dinner fr £14 English & Continental Cuisine V meals Coffee am Tea pm **FACILITIES:** CTV in all bedrooms STV English Heritage Grade 1 listed garden of 3 acres **CONF:** Class 20 **SERVICES:** Night porter 34P **NOTES:** No dogs (ex guide dogs) No children 12yrs No smoking in restaurant Last d 9pm Closed 22-31 Dec RS 31 Dec
CARDS:

See advert on opposite page

NORWICH Norfolk **Map 05 TG20**
★★ Cumberland
212-216 Thorpe Rd NR1 1TJ
Quality Percentage Score: 68%
☎ 01603 434550 & 434560 01603 433355
Dir: *on A1242, 1m from railway station*
The exterior of this small hotel belies the hospitality and jovial warmth offered within by the friendly team. An interesting menu is offered in the vibrant restaurant, whilst the welcoming public rooms are generally spacious. Bedroom sizes vary, but all are individually furnished.
ROOMS: 23 en suite (bth/shr) 4 annexe en suite (bth/shr) (2 fmly) No smoking in 6 bedrooms s £45-£65; d £59.95-£75 (incl. bkfst) * LB Off peak **MEALS:** Dinner £17.95-£24.95 & alc English & French Cuisine V meals Coffee am Tea pm **FACILITIES:** CTV in all bedrooms **CONF:** Thtr 120 Class 80 Board 60 Del from £64.95 * **SERVICES:** Night porter 63P **NOTES:** No dogs (ex guide dogs) No children 12yrs No smoking in restaurant Last d 9.15pm Closed 26 Dec-2 Jan
CARDS:

NORWICH Norfolk **Map 05 TG20**
★★ *The Georgian House*
32-34 Unthank Rd NR2 2RB
Quality Percentage Score: 67%
☎ 01603 615655 01603 765689
Dir: *follow signs for Roman Catholic Cathedral from city centre*

Close to the Catholic cathedral and within walking distance of the city centre, this welcoming hotel was originally two Victorian houses. Bedrooms come in a variety of styles with attractive decor. The smart public areas include a cosy bar and a television lounge; the elegant restaurant offers a table d'hôte menu and a full carte.
ROOMS: 27 en suite (bth/shr) (4 fmly) No smoking in 6 bedrooms **MEALS:** English & French Cuisine V meals Coffee am Tea pm **FACILITIES:** CTV in all bedrooms **CONF:** Class 20 **SERVICES:** 40P **NOTES:** No dogs No coaches No smoking in restaurant Last d 8.30pm
CARDS:

See advert on opposite page

NORWICH Norfolk **Map 05 TG20**
Travel Inn
Longwater Interchange, Dereham Rd, New Costessey NR5 0TL
☎ 01603 749140 01603 741219
Dir: *adjacent to Longwater Interchange at rdbt junct of A47 Norwich southern by-pass & Dereham Rd*
This modern building offers accommodation in smart, spacious and well equipped bedrooms, all with en-suite bathrooms. Refreshments may be taken at the nearby family restaurant. For details about current prices consult the Contents Page under Hotel Groups for the Travel Inn phone number.
ROOMS: 40 en suite (bth/shr) d £39.95 *

NORWICH Norfolk **Map 05 TG20**
Travelodge
Thickthorn Service Area, Norwich Southern Bypass NR9 3AU
☎ 01603 457549 01603 457549
Dir: *A11/A47 interchange*
This modern building offers accommodation in smart, spacious and well equipped bedrooms, all with en-suite bathrooms. Refreshments

contd. on p. 490

may be taken at the nearby family restaurant. For details about current prices, consult the Contents Page under Hotel Groups for the Travelodge phone number.
ROOMS: 40 en suite (bth/shr) d £49.95 *

NOTTINGHAM Nottinghamshire **Map 08 SK54**
see also **Langar**
★★★ *Posthouse Nottingham City*
St James's St NG1 6BN
Posthouse
Quality Percentage Score: 65%
☎ 0115 947 0131 Fax 0115 948 4366
Dir: *from M1 junct 24,25,26 follow signs to city centre, then brown tourist signs to Nottingham Castle & Tales of Robin Hood, hotel is located next door*
This modern city centre hotel is close to all the main attractions of the city. There is a business centre, and good conference and function facilities. Behan's Irish Bar is a popular feature and there is also a separate restaurant.
ROOMS: 130 en suite (bth/shr) (17 fmly) No smoking in 88 bedrooms **MEALS:** International Cuisine V meals Coffee am Tea pm **FACILITIES:** CTV in all bedrooms Wkly live entertainment **CONF:** Thtr 600 Class 350 Board 120 **SERVICES:** Lift Night porter Air conditioning **NOTES:** No smoking area in restaurant Last d 10.30pm
CARDS:

NOTTINGHAM Nottinghamshire **Map 08 SK54**
★★★ Holiday Inn Garden Court
Castle Marina Park NG7 1GX
Holiday Inn Garden Court
Quality Percentage Score: 64%
☎ 0115 993 5000 Fax 0115 993 4000
Dir: *between A6005 Castle Boulevard & A453 Queens Drive at Castle Marina*
Conveniently situated within the Castle Marina Business and Retail Park, and close to the TV studios, this attractive modern hotel offers smart, well equipped and spacious bedrooms. Public areas and services are restricted, but staff are friendly and welcoming.
ROOMS: 130 en suite (bth/shr) (49 fmly) No smoking in 80 bedrooms d £82-£97 * LB Off peak **MEALS:** Bar Lunch fr £3.50 Dinner fr £12.95 V meals Coffee am Tea pm **FACILITIES:** CTV in all bedrooms STV **CONF:** Thtr 40 Class 12 Board 25 **SERVICES:** Lift Night porter 100P **NOTES:** No smoking area in restaurant Last d 10pm
CARDS:

NOTTINGHAM Nottinghamshire **Map 08 SK54**
★★★ Nottingham Gateway
Nuthall Rd, Cinderhill NG8 6AZ
Quality Percentage Score: 64%
☎ 0115 979 4949 Fax 0115 979 4744
Dir: *take A610 from junct 26 of M1*

A modern hotel, convenient for the city and the motorway network. Well-equipped bedrooms are comfortable and there is a choice of restaurants, with a carvery and the Tum-Nuk Thai restaurant. With a number of meeting rooms leading off the glass atrium, this hotel offers a flexible range of facilities.
ROOMS: 107 en suite (bth/shr) (18 fmly) No smoking in 54 bedrooms s £68; d £75 * LB Off peak **MEALS:** Lunch £6.95-£9.95 High tea fr £3.95 Dinner £12.95-£15.50 & alc English, French & Thai Cuisine V meals Coffee am Tea pm **FACILITIES:** CTV in all bedrooms STV Xmas **CONF:** Thtr 300 Class 100 Board 50 Del £105 * **SERVICES:** Lift Night porter Air conditioning 250P **NOTES:** No dogs (ex guide dogs) No smoking area in restaurant Last d 10.30pm **CARDS:**
See advert on opposite page

NOTTINGHAM Nottinghamshire **Map 08 SK54**
★★★ *Nottingham Moat House*
Mansfield Rd NG5 2BT
MOAT HOUSE
Quality Percentage Score: 64%
☎ 0115 935 9988 Fax 0115 969 1506
Dir: *hotel approx 1m from city centre on A60 Mansfield Rd*
This business hotel has smartly appointed public areas and a welcoming brasserie-style restaurant and bar. Modern accommodation is provided in differing styles and sizes of bedrooms. Recent additions include smartly appointed, well equipped meeting rooms and improved car parking.
ROOMS: 172 en suite (bth/shr) No smoking in 89 bedrooms **MEALS:** V meals Coffee am Tea pm **FACILITIES:** CTV in all bedrooms Pool table **CONF:** Thtr 180 Class 80 Board 60 Del £121 * **SERVICES:** Lift Night porter 350P **NOTES:** No smoking area in restaurant Last d 10.30pm **CARDS:**

NOTTINGHAM Nottinghamshire **Map 08 SK54**

★★★ Westminster Hotel
312 Mansfield Rd, Carrington NG5 2EF
Best Western
Quality Percentage Score: 64%
☎ 0115 955 5000 Fax 0115 955 5005
Dir: *on A60 1m N of town centre*
This family run hotel offers well presented accommodation, including spacious superior rooms. Other bedrooms vary in size, reflecting the Victorian origins of the building, though all are equipped to the same good standard. There is a lounge bar and a beamed restaurant.
ROOMS: 72 en suite (bth/shr) No smoking in 40 bedrooms s £72-£75; d £87-£90 LB Off peak **MEALS:** Bar Lunch £4-£15alc Dinner £16-£21alc English & Continental Cuisine V meals Coffee am Tea pm **FACILITIES:** CTV in all bedrooms STV **CONF:** Thtr 60 Class 30 Board 30 Del from £95 * **SERVICES:** Lift Night porter 66P **NOTES:** No dogs (ex guide dogs) No smoking in restaurant Last d 9.15pm Closed 25 Dec-2 Jan
CARDS:
See advert on opposite page

AA ★★★ THE

BESTWOOD LODGE HOTEL

Bestwood Country Park
Arnold, Nottingham NG5 8NE
Tel: 0115 920 3011 Fax: 0115 967 0409

Once the former home of Charles II and Nell Gwynn this historic royal hunting lodge is set in 700 acres of beautiful parkland nestling on the edge of Sherwood Forest.
All 40 bedrooms are en-suite including 4-poster and executive suites.
Dine in the elegant Parkside Restaurant offering a superb A La Carte and Table D'hôte menu or the Brasserie menu, to suit all, served in the oak panelled bar.
Professional tailor-made conference service available.
Ideally located for business or pleasure four miles north of Nottingham City centre. Close to junc 26 of the M1.

★★★ The Nottingham

GATEWAY HOTEL

NUTHALL ROAD
NOTTINGHAM
NG8 6AZ
TEL: 0115 979 4949
FAX: 0115 979 4744

We are located in the heart of Robin Hood Country making it easy to explore Nottingham Castle, Tales of Robin Hood, The Lace Market and Nottingham's popular shopping centres – plus many more attractions.
During your stay we are delighted to offer you a menu choice ranging from the daily Brasserie, to an evening meal in our Carvery, A la Carte or Thai restaurants.

★★★

WESTMINSTER HOTEL

312 Mansfield Road, Nottingham NG5 2EF
Telephone: 0115 955 5000 Fax: 0115 955 5005
Website: www.westminster-hotel.co.uk Email: mail@westminster-hotel.co.uk

Best Western

Conveniently located for Nottingham's tourist attractions, its celebrated shopping centres and wealth of sporting venues our family-owned and run hotel is decorated and equipped to the highest standards. Included in our 72 rooms are 2 four-poster bedded rooms and also our 19 superior rooms which are air-conditioned and offer the additional attraction of king-size beds, dedicated PC/Fax connection points and in the bathroom, the luxury of a shower unit which also provides a relaxing steam shower. Dinner in the informal atmosphere of our highly acclaimed restaurant where excellent food and good wines are sensibly priced will simply add to the enjoyment of your stay. The hotel also has 5 meeting rooms including 2 function suites for up to 60 all of which are fully air conditioned.

N

NOTTINGHAM Nottinghamshire **Map 08 SK54**

★★★ Bestwood Lodge

Bestwood Country Park, Arnold NG5 8NE
Quality Percentage Score: 63%
☎ 0115 920 3011 🖷 0115 967 0409
Dir: *3m N off A60 at lights turn left into Oxclose Lane, at next lights, turn right onto Queens Bower Rd then 1st right, where road forks keep right*
A Victorian hunting lodge in 700 acres of parkland. Contemporary bedrooms vary in size and style. Internal architecture includes Gothic features and high vaulted ceilings in the lounge bar and the gallery. The restaurant serves a good range of dishes and a choice of menus. A popular venue for weddings and conferences.
ROOMS: 40 en suite (bth/shr) (5 fmly) s £75-£125; d £85-£125 (incl. bkfst) LB Off peak **MEALS:** Lunch £10.95-£12.50 Dinner £18.95-£19.95 & alc English & Continental Cuisine V meals Coffee am Tea pm **FACILITIES:** CTV in all bedrooms Riding Guided walking, Horse-riding Xmas **CONF:** Thtr 200 Class 65 Board 50 Del from £85 * **SERVICES:** Night porter 120P **NOTES:** No smoking in restaurant Last d 9.45pm RS Acc. unavailable Xmas Day/New Year's Day
CARDS:

See advert on page 491

NOTTINGHAM Nottinghamshire **Map 08 SK54**

★★★ Rutland Square Hotel by the Castle

St James St NG1 6FJ
Quality Percentage Score: 63%
☎ 0115 941 1114 🖷 0115 941 0014
Dir: *on entering the city follow brown signs to the castle, hotel on right 50yds on from the castle*
As the name suggests, this hotel is situated adjacent to the castle, and is close to the heart of the city centre. Behind its Regency facade the hotel is modern and comfortable with particularly good business facilities; the conference centre, which sits on the opposite side of the square, has recently been refurbished, and on the lower floors the creation of a smart new Terrace Café Bar has proved to be a great success. Bedrooms vary considerably in size, each room is decorated in appealing warm colour schemes and offers a good range of facilities.
ROOMS: 105 en suite (bth/shr) (3 fmly) No smoking in 38 bedrooms s fr £85; d £95-£200 * LB Off peak **MEALS:** English & French Cuisine V meals Coffee am Tea pm **FACILITIES:** CTV in all bedrooms STV Xmas **CONF:** Thtr 200 Class 70 Board 45 Del from £85 * **SERVICES:** Lift Night porter 38P **NOTES:** Last d 9.30pm
CARDS:

See advert on opposite page

NOTTINGHAM Nottinghamshire **Map 08 SK54**

★★★ The Strathdon

Derby Rd NG1 5FT
Quality Percentage Score: 61%
☎ 0115 941 8501 🖷 0115 948 3725
PEEL HOTELS
Dir: *from M1 junct 25, follow A52 into city centre. Hotel is situated on the right on Wollaton Street*
Situated close to the city centre, opposite the Albert Hall Conference and Exhibition Centre, this popular hotel provides modern accommodation for a predominantly business clientele. Public areas include a conservatory lounge, the Boston Bean bar, a comfortable cocktail bar and the attractive Bobbins restaurant. A variety of conference rooms, including a modern boardroom, are available.
ROOMS: 68 en suite (bth/shr) (4 fmly) No smoking in 22 bedrooms s £95; d £125 * LB Off peak **MEALS:** Lunch £11-£14.20 Dinner fr £16.50 International Cuisine V meals Coffee am Tea pm **FACILITIES:** CTV in all bedrooms STV **CONF:** Thtr 150 Class 65 Board 40 Del from £108 * **SERVICES:** Lift Night porter 14P **NOTES:** No smoking area in restaurant Last d 10pm
CARDS:

NOTTINGHAM Nottinghamshire **Map 08 SK54**

★★★ *Windsor Lodge*

116 Radcliffe Rd, West Bridgford NG2 5HG
Quality Percentage Score: 60%
☎ 0115 952 8528 🖷 0115 952 0020
Dir: *A6011 & A52 Grantham, 0.5m Trent Bridge Cricket Ground*
Situated close to Trent Bridge cricket ground, and owned and run by the same family for over 25 years, Windsor Lodge offers well maintained bedrooms, some on the ground floor. Executive rooms offer extra comfort, and public areas include a comfortable bar lounge and a separate billiards room.
ROOMS: 47 en suite (bth/shr) (8 fmly) **MEALS:** Coffee am Tea pm **FACILITIES:** CTV in 41 bedrooms STV Snooker **CONF:** Thtr 40 Class 25 Board 24 **SERVICES:** 50P **NOTES:** No dogs (ex guide dogs) No coaches Last d 8.30pm Closed 25-26 Dec **CARDS:**

See advert on opposite page

NOTTINGHAM Nottinghamshire **Map 08 SK54**

★★★ Swans Hotel & Restaurant

84-90 Radcliffe Rd, West Bridgford NG2 5HH
Quality Percentage Score: 57%
☎ 0115 981 4042 🖷 0115 945 5745
Dir: *on A6011, approached from either A60 or A52 close to Trent Bridge*
This privately owned hotel offers comfortable accommodation. While varying in size, each bedroom is well equipped and decorated in a different style. A welcoming atmosphere is generated in the cosy lounge bar while an interesting and varied choice of freshly prepared dishes is served in Maximes restaurant.
ROOMS: 30 en suite (bth/shr) (4 fmly) s £50-£55; d £60-£65 (incl. bkfst) * LB Off peak **MEALS:** Sunday Lunch £9.95-£13.95 & alc Dinner £13.95 & alc English & French Cuisine V meals Coffee am Tea pm **FACILITIES:** CTV in all bedrooms STV **CONF:** Thtr 50 Class 10 Board 15 Del from £45 * **SERVICES:** Lift Night porter 31P **NOTES:** No dogs (ex guide dogs) No coaches No smoking in restaurant Last d 9pm Closed 24-28 Dec **CARDS:**

See advert on opposite page

NOTTINGHAM Nottinghamshire **Map 08 SK54**

★★ Rufford

53 Melton Rd, West Bridgford NG2 7NE
Quality Percentage Score: 65%
☎ 0115 981 4202 🖷 0115 945 5801
Dir: *on A606, near junct A60 Loughborough Road*
Conveniently situated for all the major sporting arenas, this family run hotel offers a bright conservatory bar and wood panelled restaurant; service is friendly and informal, supervised by the hardworking resident proprietors. Bedrooms, which vary

contd. on p. 494

The AA Hotel Booking Service is a free benefit to AA members. See the advertisement on page 47

★

The Premier Collection, hotels with Red Star Awards are listed on pages 17-23

in size and layout, are comfortably furnished and thoughtfully designed to make full use of the space available.

Rufford, Nottingham

ROOMS: 34 en suite (bth/shr) No smoking in 3 bedrooms s fr £42.50; d £48-£55 (incl. bkfst) * Off peak **MEALS:** V meals Coffee am Tea pm **FACILITIES:** CTV in all bedrooms STV Pool table **SERVICES:** 35P **NOTES:** No dogs (ex guide dogs) No smoking area in restaurant Closed Xmas **CARDS:**

See advert on opposite page

NOTTINGHAM Nottinghamshire **Map 08 SK54**

★★ ***The Stage***

Stephen Pritchard NG7 6LB

Quality Percentage Score: 60%

☎ 0115 960 3261 📠 0115 969 1040

Dir: *on A6130, opposite Forest Park*

Situated opposite Forest Park, where the famous Goose Fair is held, this commercial hotel is just a mile from the centre of the city. Public rooms include a spacious lounge bar, restaurant and various function rooms; a simple menu of popular dishes is offered within the restaurant. Bedroom sizes and styles vary, ranging from executive to standard rooms, but all are well equipped and generally of comfortable proportions, and fully en suite.

ROOMS: 52 en suite (bth/shr) (5 fmly) No smoking in 4 bedrooms **MEALS:** International Cuisine V meals Coffee am Tea pm **FACILITIES:** CTV in all bedrooms **CONF:** Thtr 100 Class 50 Board 35 **SERVICES:** Night porter 80P **NOTES:** No dogs (ex guide dogs) Last d 9pm **CARDS:**

NOTTINGHAM Nottinghamshire **Map 08 SK54**

★★ ***Balmoral***

55-57 Loughborough Rd, West Bridgford NG2 7LA

Quality Percentage Score: 53%

☎ 0115 945 5020 & 955 2992 📠 0115 955 2991

Dir: *beside A60 Loughborough Road*

With a convenient location for the major sporting venues of the city, this popular hotel offers comfortable accommodation throughout, including bedrooms on the ground floor for visitors with difficulty climbing stairs. Public rooms include a bar and an open-plan dining area.

ROOMS: 31 en suite (bth/shr) **MEALS:** V meals **FACILITIES:** CTV in all bedrooms Pool table **SERVICES:** 30P **NOTES:** No dogs (ex guide dogs) No coaches **CARDS:**

NOTTINGHAM Nottinghamshire **Map 08 SK54**

Travel Inn

The Pheonix Centre, Millennium Way West NG8 6AS

☎ 0115 951 9971 📠 0115 977 0113

Dir: *under 1m from junct 26 of the M1 on A610 towards Nottingham*

This modern building offers accommodation in smart, spacious and well equipped bedrooms, all with en-suite bathrooms. Refreshments may be taken at the nearby family restaurant. For details about current prices consult the Contents Page under Hotel Groups for the Travel Inn phone number.

ROOMS: 60 en suite (bth/shr) d £39.95 *

NOTTINGHAM Nottinghamshire **Map 08 SK54**

Travel Inn (Nottingham Central)

Castle Marina Park, Castle Bridge Rd NG8 2DG

☎ 0115 947 3419 📠 0115 958 2362

Dir: *0.5m from Nottingham city centre, follow directions for Castle Marina*

This modern building offers accommodation in smart, spacious and well equipped bedrooms, all with en-suite bathrooms. Refreshments may be taken at the nearby family restaurant. For details about current prices consult the Contents Page under Hotel Groups for the Travel Inn phone number.

ROOMS: 38 en suite (bth/shr) d £39.95 *

NOTTINGHAM Nottinghamshire **Map 08 SK54**

Travelodge (Nottingham Riverside)

Riverside Retail Park NG2 1RT

☎ 0115 985 0934

Dir: *on Riverside Retail Park*

This modern building offers accommodation in smart, spacious and well equipped bedrooms, all with en-suite bathrooms. Refreshments may be taken at the nearby family restaurant. For details about current prices, consult the Contents Page under Hotel Groups for the Travelodge phone number.

ROOMS: 61 en suite (bth/shr) d £49.95 *

NOTTINGHAM Nottinghamshire **Map 08 SK54**

Nottingham Royal Moat House

Wollaton St NG1 5RH

☎ 0115 936 9988 📠 0115 947 5888

Dir: *take A52 towards Nottingham follow signs for Royal Centre & into Wollaton St, hotel is on the left & car park is just before hotel*

This city-centre hotel features a verdant covered arcade, several bars and a choice of three restaurants. The new Penthouse bedrooms on the top floor have panoramic views and good levels of comfort. Some of the single rooms are compact, but all are comprehensively equipped.

ROOMS: 210 en suite (bth/shr) (30 fmly) No smoking in 130 bedrooms **MEALS:** International Cuisine V meals Coffee am Tea pm **FACILITIES:** CTV in all bedrooms Gym Wkly live entertainment **CONF:** Thtr 600 Class 300 Board 100 **SERVICES:** Lift Night porter Air conditioning 605P **NOTES:** No smoking area in restaurant Last d 10pm **CARDS:**

NUNEATON Warwickshire **Map 04 SP39**

★★★ **Weston Hall**

Weston Ln, Weston in Arden, Bulkington CV12 9RU

Quality Percentage Score: 60%

☎ 024 76312989 📠 024 76640846

Dir: *leave M6 junct 2 follow B4065 through Ansty turn left in Shilton, follow Nuneaton signs out of Bulkington, turn into Weston Ln at 30mph sign*

This impressive manor house, with period-style decor in many of its public areas, is set in seven acres of peaceful grounds. Bedrooms vary in size, are decorated in contemporary style and

contd.

New AA Guides for the Millennium are featured on page 24

well equipped. There are also extensive conference facilities and staff are friendly and helpful.

ROOMS: 40 en suite (bth/shr) (7 fmly) No smoking in 6 bedrooms s £69.50-£95; d £85-£105 (incl. bkfst) * LB Off peak **MEALS:** Sunday Lunch £12.95 Dinner £12.50-£17.50 International Cuisine V meals Coffee am Tea pm **FACILITIES:** CTV in all bedrooms Fishing Sauna Gym Croquet lawn Jacuzzi/spa Steam room Wkly live entertainment ch fac Xmas **CONF:** Thtr 200 Class 100 Board 80 Del from £105 * **SERVICES:** 300P **NOTES:** No smoking in restaurant Last d 9.30pm **CARDS:**

See advert under COVENTRY

NUNEATON Warwickshire **Map 04 SP39**

Travel Inn

Coventry Rd CV10 7PJ

☎ 024 76343584 024 76327156

Dir: *from M6 junct 3 follow A444 towards Nuneaton. Travel Inn on the right just off Griff rdbt towards Bedworth on the B4113*

This modern building offers accommodation in smart, spacious and well equipped bedrooms, all with en-suite bathrooms. Refreshments may be taken at the nearby family restaurant. For details about current prices consult the Contents Page under Hotel Groups for the Travel Inn phone number.

ROOMS: 48 en suite (bth/shr) d £39.95 *

NUNEATON Warwickshire **Map 04 SP39**

Travelodge

Bedworth CV10 7TF

☎ 024 76382541 024 76382541

Dir: *2m S, on A444*

This modern building offers accommodation in smart, spacious and well equipped bedrooms, all with en-suite bathrooms. Refreshments may be taken at the nearby family restaurant. For details about current prices, consult the Contents Page under Hotel Groups for the Travelodge phone number.

ROOMS: 40 en suite (bth/shr) d £39.95 *

NUNEATON Warwickshire **Map 04 SP39**

Travelodge

St Nicholas Park Dr CV11 6EN

☎ 024 76353885 024 76353885

Dir: *on A47*

This modern building offers accommodation in smart, spacious and well equipped bedrooms, all with en-suite bathrooms. Refreshments may be taken at the nearby family restaurant. For details about current prices, consult the Contents Page under Hotel Groups for the Travelodge phone number.

ROOMS: 30 en suite (bth/shr) d £39.95 *

NUNNEY Somerset — Map 03 ST74

★★ The George at Nunney
11 Church St BA11 4LW
Quality Percentage Score: 68%
☎ 01373 836458 Fax 01373 836565
Dir: *0.5m N off A361 Frome/Shepton Mallet*

Situated in the centre of the village, opposite the castle, The George dates back to the 17th century. An extensive range of bar meals is served that are complemented by a commendable selection of whiskies. In the restaurant, Darren Boddy provides an imaginative combination of flavours and textures. The cosy bedrooms are neatly furnished and well equipped.
ROOMS: 9 rms (8 bth/shr) (2 fmly) No smoking in 2 bedrooms s £35-£48; d £62-£72 (incl. bkfst) * LB Off peak **MEALS:** Lunch £6.95-£12 Dinner £12 & alc English & French Cuisine V meals Coffee am **FACILITIES:** CTV in all bedrooms STV Pool table Xmas **SERVICES:** 30P **NOTES:** No dogs (ex guide dogs) No coaches No smoking area in restaurant Last d 9pm **CARDS:**

See advert under BATH

N

OAKHAM Rutland — Map 04 SK80

The Premier Collection

★★★ *Hambleton Hall*
Hambleton LE15 8TH
☎ 01572 756991 Fax 01572 724721
Dir: *3m E off A606*

RELAIS & CHATEAUX

Hambleton Hall in its landscaped grounds is the epitome of the English country hotel. Individually decorated bedrooms owe much to the initial input of designer Nina Campbell. Public rooms including the red lacquered bar and elegant drawing room, share views over the lake. The restaurant with its silk wall coverings showcases the inspired cooking of chef Aaron Patterson, with a superb seasonal menu.
ROOMS: 15 en suite (bth/shr) **MEALS:** V meals Coffee am Tea pm **FACILITIES:** CTV in all bedrooms Outdoor swimming pool (heated) Tennis (hard) **CONF:** Thtr 40 Board 20 Del from £200 * **SERVICES:** Lift 40P **NOTES:** No coaches No smoking in restaurant Last d 9.30pm **CARDS:**

OAKHAM Rutland — Map 04 SK80

★★★ Barnsdale Lodge
The Avenue, Rutland Water, North Shore LE15 8AH
Quality Percentage Score: 72%
☎ 01572 724678 Fax 01572 724961
Dir: *turn off A1 onto A606. Hotel is located 5m on right hand side, 2m E of Oakham*

A very popular roadside farmhouse built in mellowed local stone and overlooking Rutland Water, bedrooms and public areas surround a large, colourfully planted courtyard. The restaurant, which is a series of three intimate dining rooms, offers a good range of internationally appealing freshly cooked dishes; the recent addition of a bakery ensures a fresh supply of delicious breads, brioche, croissants and pastries. Morning coffee and afternoon teas are readily available within the lounge bar area and the adjacent conservatory buttery. Bedrooms are comfortable with really good beds on iron bedsteads and contemporary, stylish soft furnishings, each room is well equipped with thoughtful extras.
ROOMS: 45 en suite (bth/shr) (4 fmly) No smoking in 12 bedrooms s fr £65; d £85-£109.50 (incl. bkfst) * LB Off peak **MEALS:** Lunch £16.95 & alc Dinner £15-£35alc English & French Cuisine V meals Coffee am Tea pm **FACILITIES:** CTV in all bedrooms STV Fishing Shooting Archery Golf arranged Pitch'n'Putt ch fac Xmas **CONF:** Thtr 330 Class 120 Board 76 **SERVICES:** Night porter 200P **NOTES:** Last d 9.45pm
CARDS:

OAKHAM Rutland — Map 04 SK80

★★★ Barnsdale Hall Hotel & Country Club
Barnsdale LE15 8AB
Quality Percentage Score: 66%
☎ 01572 757901 Fax 01572 756235
Dir: *from A1 take A606 towards Oakham, travel through the villages of Empingham then Whitwell, after approx 1m hotel on left overlooking Rutland Water*

Best Western

Overlooking Rutland Water, this complex offers extensive leisure facilities and is set in attractive gardens. Spacious modern bedrooms, sited in separate buildings in the grounds, are comfortable and well equipped, and many have the added benefit of a balcony and views. Public rooms offer a choice of modern dining options and new reception facilities, with a lounge area, have just been added.
ROOMS: 61 annexe rms (55 bth/shr) (11 fmly) No smoking in 9 bedrooms s fr £70; d fr £90 (incl. bkfst) * LB Off peak **MEALS:** Lunch £5-£15 Dinner £8-£20 & alc V meals Coffee am Tea pm **FACILITIES:** CTV in all bedrooms Indoor swimming pool (heated) Tennis (hard) Squash Snooker Sauna Solarium Gym Pool table Croquet lawn Putting green Jacuzzi/spa Xmas **CONF:** Thtr 200 Class 80 Board 50 Del from £115 * **SERVICES:** Lift Night porter 100P **NOTES:** No dogs (ex guide dogs) No smoking area in restaurant Last d 9.45pm
CARDS:

OAKHAM Rutland **Map 04 SK80**

★★★ ❀ ***The Boultons Country House***

4 Catmose St LE15 6HW

Quality Percentage Score: 64%

☎ 01572 722844 📠 01572 724473

Dir: *town centre location opposite Rutland County Council*

Standing next to the Rutland museum in quiet residential surroundings, this pleasant hotel has a welcoming atmosphere, and its original building has been extended to provide attractive bedrooms.

ROOMS: 25 en suite (bth/shr) (2 fmly) **MEALS:** V meals Coffee am Tea pm **FACILITIES:** CTV in all bedrooms **CONF:** Thtr 60 Class 40 Board 30 **SERVICES:** 15P **NOTES:** No smoking in restaurant

CARDS:

OAKHAM Rutland **Map 04 SK80**

★★★ ❀ ***Whipper-in Hotel***

Market Place LE15 6DT

Quality Percentage Score: 60%

☎ 01572 756971 📠 01572 757759

Dir: *from A1 take B668 for Oakham and head for the Market Square*

A fashionable market town coaching inn furnished in English country house style, with antiques, old prints and pictures. An open fire warms the recently refurbished lounge bar, a popular meeting place for locals, whilst in the candlelit restaurant an interesting carte of modern British dishes is presented. Each bedroom is individually designed, four-poster and executive rooms are available.

ROOMS: 24 en suite (bth/shr) No smoking in 4 bedrooms **MEALS:** European Cuisine V meals Coffee am Tea pm **FACILITIES:** CTV in all bedrooms **CONF:** Thtr 80 Class 25 Board 30 Del from £95 * **SERVICES:** Night porter 40P **NOTES:** No smoking in restaurant Last d 9.30pm **CARDS:**

See advert on this page

OCKLEY Surrey **Map 04 TQ14**

★★★ **Gatton Manor Hotel Golf & Country Club**

Standon Ln RH5 5PQ

Quality Percentage Score: 63%

☎ 01306 627555 📠 01306 627713

Dir: *off A29 at Ockley turn into Cat Hill Lane, signposted for 2m hotel entrance on the right*

Enjoying a peaceful setting, this popular golf and country club offers a range of comfortable, modern bedrooms. Public areas feature the main club bar, small restaurant and attractive drawing room. Other facilities include a health club and the 18 hole professional golf course.

ROOMS: 16 en suite (bth/shr) (2 fmly) No smoking in 2 bedrooms s fr £67.50; d fr £105 (incl. bkfst) * LB Off peak **MEALS:** Lunch £10.95-£13.95 & alc High tea £5-£10alc Dinner £15-£25alc English & Continental Cuisine V meals Coffee am Tea pm **FACILITIES:** CTV in all bedrooms STV Golf 18 Fishing Sauna Solarium Gym Putting green Jacuzzi/spa Bowling green Wkly live entertainment Xmas **CONF:** Thtr 66 Class 60 Board 30 Del from £120 * **SERVICES:** Night porter 250P **NOTES:** No dogs (ex guide dogs) No coaches Last d 9pm

CARDS:

The AA Hotel Booking Service is a free benefit to AA members. See the advertisement on page 47

ODIHAM Hampshire — Map 04 SU75
★★ George
High St RG29 1LP
Quality Percentage Score: 70%
☎ 01256 702081 Fax 01256 704213
Dir: *from M3 junct 5 follow signs to Alton/Odiham. In Odiham left at mini-rdbt, hotel is on left*
Popular with both locals and travellers, the George offers a warm welcome to all. Bedrooms are characterful in the main house and spacious, smart and modern in the two wings. All rooms are well equipped and feature lots of extra touches. The restaurant serves an extensive menu, and two cosy bars and a small meeting room complete the picture.
ROOMS: 19 en suite (bth/shr) 9 annexe en suite (bth/shr) (1 fmly) No smoking in 14 bedrooms s fr £75; d fr £85 (incl. bkfst) * LB Off peak **MEALS:** Lunch £14.50-£17.95 & alc Dinner fr £17.95 & alc English & French Cuisine V meals Coffee am Tea pm **FACILITIES:** CTV in all bedrooms STV **CONF:** Thtr 30 Class 20 Board 26 Del from £95 * **SERVICES:** Night porter 20P **NOTES:** No coaches Last d 10pm
CARDS:

OKEHAMPTON Devon — Map 02 SX59
★★ White Hart
Fore St EX20 1HD
Quality Percentage Score: 63%
☎ 01837 52730 & 54514 Fax 01837 53979
Dir: *located in town centre, adjacent to the only town traffic lights, car park at rear of hotel*
This 17th-century, town-centre hotel caters well for local functions. Bedrooms, all well equipped, are furnished in similar style and vary in size. Bars display old beams and have preserved some period character. There is a separate restaurant serving a small menu of dishes.
ROOMS: 19 en suite (bth/shr) (2 fmly) No smoking in 4 bedrooms s £35-£40; d £55 (incl. bkfst) * Off peak **MEALS:** Sunday Lunch £12-£15alc Dinner fr £16.50 & alc European Cuisine V meals Coffee am Tea pm **FACILITIES:** CTV in all bedrooms Games room Skittle alley Xmas **CONF:** Thtr 100 Class 80 Board 40 **SERVICES:** 22P **NOTES:** No dogs (ex guide dogs) No smoking area in restaurant Last d 9.30pm
CARDS:

See advert on opposite page

OKEHAMPTON Devon — Map 02 SX59
⇧ Travelodge
Whiddon Down EX20 2QT
☎ 01647 231626 Fax 01647 231626
Dir: *at Merrymeet rdbt on A30/A382*
This modern building offers accommodation in smart, spacious and well equipped bedrooms, all with en-suite bathrooms. Refreshments may be taken at the nearby family restaurant. For details about current prices, consult the Contents Page under Hotel Groups for the Travelodge phone number.
ROOMS: 40 en suite (bth/shr) d £45.95 *

OLDBURY West Midlands — Map 07 SO98
⇧ Travel Inn
Wolverhampton Rd B69 2BH
☎ 0121 552 3031 Fax 0121 552 1012
Dir: *from M5 junct 2 take A4123 towards Wolverhampton, hotel 0.75m on left*
This modern building offers accommodation in smart, spacious and well equipped bedrooms, all with en-suite bathrooms. Refreshments may be taken at the nearby family restaurant. For details about current prices consult the Contents Page under Hotel Groups for the Travel Inn phone number.
ROOMS: 40 en suite (bth/shr) d £39.95 *

OLDBURY West Midlands — Map 07 SO98
⇧ Travelodge
Wolverhampton Rd B69 2BH
☎ 0121 552 2967 Fax 0121 552 2967
Dir: *on A4123, northbound off junct 2 of M5*
This modern building offers accommodation in smart, spacious and well equipped bedrooms, all with en-suite bathrooms. Refreshments may be taken at the nearby family restaurant. For details about current prices, consult the Contents Page under Hotel Groups for the Travelodge phone number.
ROOMS: 33 en suite (bth/shr) d £45.95 *

OLDHAM Greater Manchester — Map 07 SD90
★★★ *Hotel Smokies Park*
Ashton Rd, Bardsley OL8 3HX
Quality Percentage Score: 70%
☎ 0161 624 3405 Fax 0161 627 5262
Dir: *on A627 between Oldham and Ashton-under-Lyne*
This modern hotel offers comfortable bedrooms and a small but well equipped fitness centre. An extensive range of Italian and English dishes is offered in the refurbished restaurant and there is a welcoming lounge bar where live entertainment is offered at weekends. Residents gain free admission to the nightclub, opening on Monday, Friday and Saturday evenings.
ROOMS: 47 en suite (bth/shr) (2 fmly) No smoking in 10 bedrooms **MEALS:** English, French & Italian Cuisine V meals Coffee am Tea pm **FACILITIES:** CTV in all bedrooms STV Sauna Solarium Gym Night club Cabaret lounge Wkly live entertainment **CONF:** Thtr 300 Class 125 Board 50 **SERVICES:** Night porter 120P **NOTES:** No dogs (ex guide dogs) Last d 11pm **CARDS:**

OLDHAM Greater Manchester — Map 07 SD90
★★★ Avant
Windsor Rd, Manchester St OL8 4AS
Quality Percentage Score: 67%
☎ 0500 636943 (Central Res) Fax 01773 880321
Dir: *from junct 20 of M62 (East or West) follow Oldham town centre signs A627(M) then A62 Manchester St, hotel is on left*

Enjoying wide views over the town, this purpose-built hotel has smartly decorated accommodation. A covered walkway leads to public areas including a bright and comfortable restaurant and a large bar.
ROOMS: 103 en suite (bth/shr) (2 fmly) No smoking in 16 bedrooms s £79.50-£89.50; d £89.50-£99.50 * LB Off peak **MEALS:** Sunday Lunch fr £12 Dinner fr £16.75 V meals Coffee am Tea pm **FACILITIES:** CTV in all bedrooms STV Xmas **CONF:** Thtr 200 Class 100 Board 60 Del from £95 * **SERVICES:** Lift Night porter 120P **NOTES:** No smoking area in restaurant Last d 9.30pm **CARDS:**

OLDHAM Greater Manchester **Map 07 SD90**

★★★ *Pennine Way Hotel*

Manchester St OL8 1UZ

Quality Percentage Score: 62%

☎ 0161 624 0555 Fax 0161 627 2031

Dir: *exit M62 junct 20 and foloow signs for town centre*

A modern hotel close to the town centre. Bedrooms are well equipped and staff are friendly and helpful. The fixed price dinner menu is good value and there is a special children's menu. The ballroom, accommodating up to 350, is popular for functions.

ROOMS: 130 en suite (bth/shr) (50 fmly) No smoking in 70 bedrooms **MEALS:** European Cuisine V meals Coffee am Tea pm **FACILITIES:** CTV in all bedrooms STV Gym Pool table **CONF:** Thtr 320 Class 70 Board 70 **SERVICES:** Lift Night porter 250P **NOTES:** No smoking in restaurant Last d 9.30pm **CARDS:**

OLDHAM Greater Manchester **Map 07 SD90**

★★ High Point

64 Napier St East OL8 1TR

Quality Percentage Score: 68%

☎ 0161 624 4130 Fax 0161 627 2757

Dir: *take M62 junct 20 onto M627 Oldham onto A627(Manchester) under "Glass Bridge". Turn left onto Lee Street right at T-junct onto Napier St East*

A friendly welcome awaits at this privately owned town centre hotel, just a short drive from junction 20 of the M62. Bedrooms are attractively furnished and the conservatory restaurant, which enjoys fine views, serves an extensive range of dishes.

ROOMS: 19 en suite (bth/shr) (3 fmly) s £38.50-£45; d £49.50-£55 (incl. bkfst) * LB Off peak **MEALS:** Lunch £10.95 & alc Dinner £11.95-£18.95 & alc English & Continential Cuisine V meals Coffee am Tea pm **FACILITIES:** CTV in all bedrooms STV **CONF:** Thtr 40 Class 25 Board 25 Del £65 * **SERVICES:** 42P **NOTES:** No dogs (ex guide dogs) No coaches Last d 9.30pm **CARDS:**

OLLERTON Nottinghamshire **Map 08 SK66**

★★ Hop Pole

Main St NG22 9AD

Quality Percentage Score: 67%

☎ 01623 822573

Dir: *from Ollerton rdbt take A616 Newark road, turn 1st right signed Ollerton village only, hotel 400yds on left*

This 200-year-old inn is situated in the picturesque village of Ollerton, close to Sherwood Forest. Bedrooms are generally of comfortable proportions, however there are a few very cosy singles. Each room is soundly appointed, well equipped and very well maintained. Public rooms offer a choice of bars and a popular carvery food operation; service is friendly and informal.

ROOMS: 11 rms (10 bth/shr) (1 fmly) **MEALS:** English Carvery Cuisine V meals Coffee am Tea pm **FACILITIES:** CTV in all bedrooms Pool table Darts **SERVICES:** 30P **NOTES:** No dogs (ex guide dogs) No smoking in restaurant **CARDS:**

O

ONNELEY Staffordshire **Map 07 SJ74**

★★ Wheatsheaf Inn at Onneley

Barhill Rd CW3 9QF

Quality Percentage Score: 69%

☎ 01782 751581 🖷 01782 751499

Dir: *on A525 between Madeley/Woore, 6.5m W of Newcastle-under-Lyme*

This 18th century inn is situated next to Onneley golf club. There was a change of ownership in the first half of 1999, and at the time of our last visit, extensive alterations and restructuring work was being carried out. The hotel was scheduled to re-open in August 1999, following completion of this work.

ROOMS: 6 en suite (shr) d £60-£75 (incl. bkfst) * LB Off peak **MEALS:** Sunday Lunch £10-£15 High tea £5-£10 Dinner £10-£20 & alc V meals Coffee am Tea pm **FACILITIES:** CTV in all bedrooms STV ch fac **CONF:** Thtr 60 Class 30 Board 30 **SERVICES:** Night porter 150P **NOTES:** No dogs (ex guide dogs) No smoking in restaurant Last d 9.30pm **CARDS:**

ORMSKIRK Lancashire **Map 07 SD40**

★★★ Beaufort

High Ln, Burscough L40 7SN

Quality Percentage Score: 62%

☎ 01704 892655 🖷 01704 895135

Dir: *from M58 junct 3 follow signs for Ormskirk which is 7m. Hotel is situated between Ormskirk and Burscough*

A smart, modern, privately owned hotel with good open-plan lounge, bar and restaurant areas. A wide choice of food is available all day. Bedrooms are well equipped and comfortable.

ROOMS: 20 en suite (bth/shr) s fr £65; d fr £90 (incl. dinner) * LB Off peak **MEALS:** Lunch £7.50-£12.95 & alc High tea fr £1.50 Dinner £15.95 & alc International Cuisine V meals Coffee am Tea pm **FACILITIES:** CTV in all bedrooms STV Free use of sister Hotel's (Stutelea Hotel, Southport - 8m) facilities Xmas **CONF:** Thtr 50 Class 30 Board 30 Del from £75 * **SERVICES:** Night porter 126P **NOTES:** No dogs (ex guide dogs) No smoking in restaurant Last d 9.30pm

CARDS:

O

OSTERLEY Greater London

See LONDON SECTION plan 1 *B3*

★★★ Osterley Four Pillars Hotel

764 Great West Rd TW7 5NA

Quality Percentage Score: 65%

☎ 020 8568 9981 🖷 020 8569 7819

Dir: *hotel at junct of A4 and Wood Lane. 1m past Osterley Tube Station, Eastbound on A4. 0.5m past Gillette, Westbound on A4*

On the A4, with easy access to the airport and central London, the Four Pillars has long been a local favourite. Friendly staff, the Tudor-style pub, and Greshams Restaurant are the attractions. Bedrooms are mainly in a modern extension.

ROOMS: 61 en suite (bth/shr) (9 fmly) No smoking in 21 bedrooms s £47-£85; d £47-£95 * LB Off peak **MEALS:** Lunch £9.25-£12.95 Dinner £10.95-£12.95 V meals Coffee am Tea pm **FACILITIES:** CTV in all bedrooms STV Pool table Wkly live entertainment **CONF:** Thtr 250 Class 126 Board 80 Del £130 * **SERVICES:** Night porter 98P **NOTES:** No smoking area in restaurant Last d 10pm Closed 26-27 Dec

CARDS:

OSWESTRY Shropshire **Map 07 SJ22**

★★★ Pen-y-Dyffryn Hall Country Hotel

Rhydycroesau SY10 7JD

Quality Percentage Score: 74%

☎ 01691 653700 🖷 01691 650066

Dir: *from A5 into Oswestry town centre, follow signs to Llansilin on B4580, hotel is 3m W of Oswestry just before Rhydycroesau village*

A charming old house built as a rectory in 1840 and set in five acres of grounds. Head chef Paul Thomasson has earned a well deserved reputation for the quality of his food. The accommodation is well equipped, public rooms are comfortably and tastefully appointed and welcoming real fires burn in the lounge and bar during cold weather.

ROOMS: 8 en suite (bth/shr) 2 annexe en suite (bth/shr) (1 fmly) s £59; d £80-£92 (incl. bkfst) * LB Off peak **MEALS:** Bar Lunch £3-£7 High tea £4-£6 Dinner £19.50-£24.50 V meals **FACILITIES:** CTV in all bedrooms Fishing Guided walks **SERVICES:** 30P **NOTES:** No coaches No smoking in restaurant Last d 8.30pm Closed 24 Dec-19 Jan

CARDS:

OSWESTRY Shropshire **Map 07 SJ22**

★★★ *Wynnstay*

Church St SY11 2SZ

Quality Percentage Score: 68%

☎ 01691 655261 🖷 01691 670606

Dir: *centre of town, opposite parish church*

This Georgian property, a former posting house, surrounds a unique 200 year old Crown Bowling Green. A good health, leisure and beauty centre plus extensive function facilities have been added. Well equipped bedrooms are individually styled and decorated, there are several suites and four-poster beds. The restaurant has an Italian theme and there is also a full range of bar food.

ROOMS: 27 en suite (bth/shr) (4 fmly) No smoking in 12 bedrooms **MEALS:** Italian Cuisine V meals Coffee am Tea pm **FACILITIES:** CTV in all bedrooms Indoor swimming pool (heated) Sauna Solarium Gym Jacuzzi/spa Crown green bowling Beauty suite **CONF:** Thtr 290 Class 150 Board 50 **SERVICES:** Night porter 70P **CARDS:**

See advert on opposite page

OSWESTRY Shropshire **Map 07 SJ22**

Travelodge

Mile End Service Area SY11 4JA

☎ 01691 658178 🖷 01691 658178

Dir: *junct A5/A483*

This modern building offers accommodation in smart, spacious and well equipped bedrooms, all with en-suite bathrooms. Refreshments may be taken at the nearby family restaurant. For details about current prices, consult the Contents Page under Hotel Groups for the Travelodge phone number.

ROOMS: 40 en suite (bth/shr) d £45.95 *

OTTERBURN Northumberland **Map 12 NY89**

★★ *Percy Arms*

NE19 1NR

Quality Percentage Score: 64%

☎ 01830 520261 🖷 01830 520567

Dir: *centre of Otterburn village on A696*

This 17th-century coaching inn stands in the centre of the village and is surrounded by beautiful Northumberland moors. Bedrooms are attractively decorated and furnished mostly in

pine. One can eat well in either the restaurant or the brasserie area of the cosy bar.
ROOMS: 28 en suite (bth/shr) (2 fmly) No smoking in 2 bedrooms **MEALS:** V meals Coffee am Tea pm **FACILITIES:** CTV in all bedrooms Fishing Pool table **CONF:** Thtr 100 Class 60 Board 40 **SERVICES:** 74P **NOTES:** Last d 9pm **CARDS:**

OTTERSHAW Surrey — Map 04 TQ06

Foxhills
Stonehill Rd KT16 0EL
☎ 01932 872050 Fax 01932 874762
Dir: *A320 to Woking from M25. At 2nd rdbt take last exit Chobham Road, turn right into Foxhills Rd, follow until T junct, turn right into Stonehill Rd*
ROOMS: 38 en suite (bth/shr) (1 fmly) s £120-£250; d £120-£250 * LB Off peak **MEALS:** Lunch £15.50-£18.50 Dinner £18.50-£26 & alc European Cuisine V meals Coffee am Tea pm **FACILITIES:** CTV in all bedrooms STV Indoor swimming pool (heated) Outdoor swimming pool (heated) Golf 45 Tennis (hard) Squash Snooker Sauna Solarium Gym Croquet lawn Putting green Boules Adventure playground ch fac Xmas **CONF:** Thtr 60 Class 52 Board 56 Del £195 * **SERVICES:** Night porter 450P **NOTES:** No dogs (ex guide dogs) No coaches Last d 10.30pm **CARDS:**

OTTERY ST MARY Devon — Map 03 SY19

★★ **Tumbling Weir Hotel & Restaurant**
EX11 1AQ
Quality Percentage Score: 71%
☎ 01404 812752 Fax 01404 812752
Dir: *turn off A30, take B3177 into Ottery St Mary, hotel adjoining 'Land of Canaan/long stay carpark'*
Situated between the River Otter and its millstream, this 17th-century cottage has old-world charm and attractive bedrooms. Old beams and candles help create an intimate atmosphere in the dining room. Parking is available.
ROOMS: 11 en suite (bth/shr) s fr £44.65; d fr £67.20 (incl. bkfst) LB Off peak **MEALS:** Lunch £3.50-£10.50 Dinner £16.95-£19.95 English & French Cuisine V meals Coffee am Tea pm **FACILITIES:** CTV in all bedrooms STV Fishing Xmas **CONF:** Thtr 95 Class 95 Board 95 **SERVICES:** 10P **NOTES:** No smoking in restaurant Last d 8.30pm **CARDS:**

OUNDLE Northamptonshire — Map 04 TL08

★★★ ***The Talbot***
New St PE8 4EA
Quality Percentage Score: 67%
☎ 01832 273621 Fax 01832 274545
In the heart of this historic town, the Talbot dates from the 1600s. It has kept many of its original features and an atmosphere of old-world charm. Bedrooms are attractively furnished and public rooms display ancient beams. Ruined Fotheringhay Castle, where Mary, Queen of Scots spent her final, tragic days, provided some of the original building materials.
ROOMS: 39 en suite (bth/shr) No smoking in 10 bedrooms **MEALS:** V meals Coffee am Tea pm **FACILITIES:** CTV in all bedrooms **CONF:** Thtr 100 Class 40 Board 40 **SERVICES:** Night porter 50P **NOTES:** No smoking in restaurant Last d 9.30pm **CARDS:**

OXFORD Oxfordshire — Map 04 SP50

see also **Milton Common**

★★★★ **Le Manoir Aux Quat' Saisons**
OX44 7PD
☎ 01844 278881 Fax 01844 278847
(For full entry see Great Milton)

OXFORD Oxfordshire — Map 04 SP50

★★★★ **The Randolph**
Beaumont St OX1 2LN
Quality Percentage Score: 70%
☎ 01865 247481 Fax 01865 791678
Dir: *from M40 head for A40 Northern Bypass and at Pear Tree rdbt take exit S towards city centre into St Giles. Hotel on corner of Beaumont St*
This fine landmark hotel has an excellent location across from the Ashmolean Museum and is fortunate to have an adjoining garage. Built in 1864 in a Neo-Gothic style, the Randolph's public areas boast superb architectural features together with tasteful interior design. The drawing room is known for its traditional afternoon teas. Spires restaurant is the place to watch the world go by from the huge picture windows. Bedrooms are elegantly furnished with restful colour schemes and beautiful fabrics.
ROOMS: 119 en suite (bth/shr) No smoking in 60 bedrooms s fr £125; d £155-£325 * LB Off peak **MEALS:** Lunch £12-£18.50alc High tea £4.95-£12.50alc Dinner £14.50-£32alc European Cuisine V meals Coffee am Tea pm **FACILITIES:** CTV in all bedrooms STV Xmas **CONF:** Thtr 300 Class 120 Board 35 Del from £145 * **SERVICES:** Lift Night porter 64P **NOTES:** No smoking in restaurant Last d 10pm **CARDS:**

OXFORD Oxfordshire — Map 04 SP50

★★★★ **Oxford Thames Four Pillars Hotel**
Henley Rd, Sandford-on-Thames OX4 4GX
Quality Percentage Score: 67%
☎ 01865 334444 Fax 334400
Dir: *turn off Eastern Bypass A4142 at rdbt onto A4074. Take first exit and follow signs to Sandford (1m)*
An impressive Victorian mansion in extensive grounds, extended
contd.

to become a hotel in 1987. The main house retains its galleried staircase leading to manor house bedrooms, individually decorated and with views of the river and gardens. Many rooms in the new wing have small balconies, all are well equipped. Public areas include a comfortable lounge and open plan bar. The leisure suite includes a pool, sauna, steam room and gym.
ROOMS: 60 en suite (bth/shr) (4 fmly) No smoking in 34 bedrooms s £94-£119; d £125-£150 * LB Off peak **MEALS:** Lunch £12.50-£17.50 & alc Dinner £22.50-£26.50 & alc International Cuisine V meals Coffee am Tea pm **FACILITIES:** CTV in all bedrooms STV Indoor swimming pool (heated) Tennis (hard) Fishing Snooker Sauna Gym Croquet lawn Jacuzzi/spa Private launch for hire Wkly live entertainment Xmas **CONF:** Thtr 160 Class 80 Board 60 **SERVICES:** Night porter 120P **NOTES:** No dogs (ex guide dogs) No smoking area in restaurant Last d 10pm **CARDS:**

OXFORD Oxfordshire — Map 04 SP50
★★★ Studley Priory
OX33 1AZ
Quality Percentage Score: 78%
☎ 01865 351203 & 351254 01865 351613
(For full entry see Horton-cum-Studley)

OXFORD Oxfordshire — Map 04 SP50
★★★ Hawkwell House
Church Way, Iffley Village OX4 4DZ
Quality Percentage Score: 70%
☎ 01865 749988 01865 748525

Enjoying a quiet residential location, Hawkwell is only minutes from the Oxford ring road. One of the strengths of this extended hotel is its really smart and well designed new accommodation, and plans are afoot to enhance the older bedrooms. A lively menu is offered in the bright and attractive Orangery restaurant.
ROOMS: 49 en suite (bth/shr) (2 fmly) No smoking in 13 bedrooms s fr £90; d £100-£150 (incl. bkfst) * LB Off peak **MEALS:** Lunch £12.95 Dinner £17.95 & alc European Cuisine V meals Coffee am Tea pm **FACILITIES:** CTV in all bedrooms Xmas **CONF:** Thtr 200 Class 100 Board 200 Del from £120 * **SERVICES:** Lift Night porter 60P **NOTES:** No smoking in restaurant Last d 9.45pm
CARDS:

OXFORD Oxfordshire — Map 04 SP50
★★★ *Cotswold Lodge*
66a Banbury Rd OX2 6JP
Quality Percentage Score: 66%
☎ 01865 512121 01865 512490
Dir: *turn off the A40 Oxford ring road onto the A4165, Banbury Road - signposted City centre/Summertown. Hotel 1.5m on left*
A family run hotel close to the centre of Oxford. The Victorian building, extended round a pretty patio area, is undergoing refurbishment. Bedrooms are completed and very smartly presented. A smart new restaurant/bar and lounge were planned at the time of our visit. The hotel is popular with business guests and caters for conferences and banquets.
ROOMS: 50 en suite (bth/shr) (2 fmly) **MEALS:** English & French Cuisine V meals Coffee am Tea pm **FACILITIES:** CTV in all bedrooms **CONF:** Thtr 100 Class 32 Board 32 Del from £105 * **SERVICES:** Night porter 60P **NOTES:** No smoking in restaurant Last d 10pm Closed 26 Dec-2 Jan **CARDS:**

OXFORD Oxfordshire — Map 04 SP50
★★★ Eastgate
The High, Merton St OX1 4BE
Quality Percentage Score: 66%
☎ 01865 248244 01865 791681
Dir: *follow signs to Headington and Oxford City centre. Hotel is on corner of High St and Merton St after Magdalen Bridge and a set of traffic lights*
The hotel is in the city centre amongst many buildings of historic and architectural interest, and close to Magdalen Bridge. Bedrooms are comfortably appointed and well equipped. Smart public areas, recently refurbished, include a popular bar, small lounge area and Cafe Boheme which offers modern, French bistro style cuisine.
ROOMS: 64 en suite (bth/shr) (3 fmly) No smoking in 25 bedrooms s £110; d £150 * LB Off peak **MEALS:** French Cuisine V meals Coffee am Tea pm **FACILITIES:** CTV in all bedrooms Xmas **SERVICES:** Lift Night porter 27P **CARDS:**

OXFORD Oxfordshire — Map 04 SP50
★★★ Linton Lodge
Linton Rd OX2 6UJ
Quality Percentage Score: 65%
☎ 01865 553461 01865 310365
Dir: *take Banbury Rd leading out of Oxford City centre. Turn right into Linton Rd after approx 0.5m. Hotel is located opposite St Andrews Church*
Located in a residential area, Linton Lodge is within walking distance of the town centre. Bedrooms are spacious and comfortable. There are some quaint period features such as the wood-panelled restaurant and a bar overlooking the croquet lawn.
ROOMS: 71 en suite (bth/shr) (2 fmly) No smoking in 20 bedrooms s £105; d £125 (incl. bkfst) * LB Off peak **MEALS:** Lunch £9.95-£12.50alc Dinner £17.50 English & French Cuisine V meals Coffee am **FACILITIES:** CTV in all bedrooms Croquet lawn Putting green Bowls Area **CONF:** Thtr 120 Class 50 Board 35 Del from £110 * **SERVICES:** Lift Night porter 40P **NOTES:** No smoking area in restaurant Last d 9.30pm
CARDS:
See advert on opposite page

OXFORD Oxfordshire — Map 04 SP50
★★★ *Oxford Moat House*
Godstow Rd, Wolvercote Roundabout OX2 8AL
Quality Percentage Score: 65%
☎ 01865 489988 01865 310259
Dir: *adjacent to A34/A40, 2m from city centre*
This modern, purpose-built hotel is located to the north of the city centre and has a range of indoor and outdoor leisure facilities. Bedrooms are well maintained and designed to suit business, conference and leisure guests. Guests can eat in the restaurant or try the more relaxed bar menu.
ROOMS: 155 en suite (bth/shr) (17 fmly) No smoking in 31 bedrooms **MEALS:** English & French Cuisine V meals Coffee am Tea pm **FACILITIES:** CTV in all bedrooms STV Indoor swimming pool (heated) Squash Snooker Sauna Solarium Gym Whirlpool 9 Hole mini golf **CONF:** Thtr 150 Class 60 Board 40 **SERVICES:** Night porter 250P **NOTES:** No smoking area in restaurant Last d 9.45pm
CARDS:

OXFORD Oxfordshire **Map 04 SP50**

★★★ **Weston Manor Hotel**
OX6 8QL
Quality Percentage Score: 64%
☎ 01869 350621 📠 01869 350901
(For full entry see Weston-on-the-Green)

OXFORD Oxfordshire **Map 04 SP50**

★★ **The Balkan Lodge Hotel**
315 Iffley Rd OX4 4AG
Quality Percentage Score: 67%
☎ 01865 244524 📠 01865 251090
This small family owned hotel is ideally located for the city centre and major routes. The comfortable accommodation is impeccably presented and well equipped. Public areas include a small bar, restaurant and lounge; there is private parking at the rear.
ROOMS: 13 en suite (bth/shr) No smoking in all bedrooms s £55.50-£57.50; d £62.50-£68.50 (incl. bkfst) * LB Off peak **FACILITIES:** CTV in all bedrooms STV **SERVICES:** P

OXFORD Oxfordshire **Map 04 SP50**

★★ **Kings Arms Hotel**
Horton Hill OX33 1AY
Quality Percentage Score: 67%
☎ 01865 351235 📠 01865 351721
(For full entry see Horton-cum-Studley)

OXFORD Oxfordshire **Map 04 SP50**

★★ **Palace**
250 Iffley Rd OX4 1SE
Quality Percentage Score: 63%
☎ 01865 727627 📠 01865 200478
Dir: *on A4158*
A small family hotel close to the city centre and all routes. The attractive bedrooms are bright and thoughtfully equipped. There is a comfortable lounge and bar/dining facilities are available. Mrs Parojcic will prepare traditional Yugoslavian dishes with prior notice.
ROOMS: 8 en suite (bth/shr) (2 fmly) No smoking in all bedrooms **MEALS:** V meals Coffee am Tea pm **FACILITIES:** CTV in all bedrooms **SERVICES:** 6P **NOTES:** No dogs No coaches No smoking area in restaurant Last d 9pm **CARDS:**

OXFORD Oxfordshire **Map 04 SP50**

★★ **Victoria**
180 Abingdon Rd OX1 4RA
Quality Percentage Score: 60%
☎ 01865 724536 📠 01865 794909
Dir: *from M40/A40 take South bypass and head into the city*
The Victoria is a friendly hotel run by its hospitable owners, Mr and Mrs Parojcic. It is within about fifteen minutes of the city centre and is a convenient base for touring the area. Accommodation offers sound standards of comfort and quality.
ROOMS: 15 en suite (bth/shr) 5 annexe en suite (bth/shr) (1 fmly) s £55.50-£59.50; d £72.50-£79.50 (incl. bkfst) * LB Off peak **MEALS:** Italian & Yugoslav Cuisine V meals Coffee am Tea pm **FACILITIES:** CTV in all bedrooms **CONF:** Board 20 Del from £125 * **SERVICES:** 20P **NOTES:** No smoking in restaurant Last d 9.30pm **CARDS:**

OXFORD Oxfordshire **Map 04 SP50**

Travel Inn
Oxford Businees Park, Garsington Rd OX4 2JZ
☎ 01865 779230 📠 01865 775887
Dir: *just off A4142 on junc with B480 opposite Rover works*
This modern building offers accommodation in smart, spacious and well equipped bedrooms, all with en-suite bathrooms. Refreshments may be taken at the nearby family restaurant. For details about current prices consult the Contents Page under Hotel Groups for the Travel Inn phone number.
ROOMS: 60 en suite (bth/shr) d £39.95 *

OXFORD Oxfordshire **Map 04 SP50**

Travelodge
Peartree Roundabout, Woodstock Rd OX2 8JZ
☎ 01865 554301 📠 01865 513474
Dir: *junc A34/A43*
This modern building offers accommodation in smart, spacious and well equipped bedrooms, all with en-suite bathrooms. Refreshments may be taken at the nearby family restaurant. For details about current prices, consult the Contents Page under Hotel Groups for the Travelodge phone number.
ROOMS: 98 en suite (bth/shr) d £49.95 *

OXFORD Oxfordshire **Map 04 SP50**

Travelodge
London Rd, Wheatley OX33 1JH
☎ 01865 875705 📠 01865 875905
Dir: *off A40 next to The Harvester on the outskirts of Wheatley*
This modern building offers accommodation in smart, spacious and well equipped bedrooms, all with en-suite bathrooms. Refreshments may be taken at the nearby family restaurant. For details about current prices, consult the Contents Page under Hotel Groups for the Travelodge phone number.
ROOMS: 36 en suite (bth/shr) d £55.95 *

OXFORD Oxfordshire **Map 04 SP50**
Welcome Lodge
OX33 1JN
☎ 01865 877000 01865 877016
Dir: *situated at the Welcome Break service area of M40 junct 8A. Access available from both Southbound & northbound carriageways*
This modern building offers accommodation in smart, spacious and well equipped bedrooms, suitable for families and businessmen, and all with en-suite bathrooms. Refreshments may be taken at the nearby family restaurant. For details of current prices, consult the Contents Page under Hotel Groups for the Welcome Break phone number.
ROOMS: 59 en suite (bth/shr) d fr £45 *

OXFORD Oxfordshire **Map 04 SP50**
Oxford Spires Four Pillars Hotel
Abingdon Rd OX1 4PS
☎ 01865 324324
NOTES: Due to open Nov 1999

PADSTOW Cornwall & Isles of Scilly **Map 02 SW97**
see also **Constantine Bay**

★★★ The Metropole
Station Rd PL28 8DB
Quality Percentage Score: 70%
☎ 01841 532486 01841 532867
Dir: *leave M5 junct 31. Take A3 until it joins the A39 then the A389 following signs for Padstow*
With glorious views across the Camel Estuary, The Metropole provides friendly, efficient service, and comfortable public areas in which to relax. The smart lounge, bar and veranda are popular for afternoon teas, and bedrooms, which have now all been upgraded, vary in size and aspect but are well equipped. The smart new Garden rooms are particularly spacious and attractively decorated. The hotel also has its own outdoor swimming pool.
ROOMS: 50 en suite (bth/shr) (5 fmly) No smoking in 19 bedrooms s £85-£90; d £110-£160 * LB Off peak **MEALS:** Sunday Lunch £10.39-£16.50 Dinner £17.85-£23.90 V meals Coffee am Tea pm **FACILITIES:** CTV in all bedrooms Outdoor swimming pool (heated) Xmas **SERVICES:** Lift 38P **NOTES:** No smoking in restaurant Last d 9pm
CARDS:

PADSTOW Cornwall & Isles of Scilly **Map 02 SW97**
★★★ *Old Custom House Inn*
South Quay PL28 8ED
Quality Percentage Score: 66%
☎ 01841 532359 01841 533372
Dir: *A359 from Wadebridge take 2nd right, once in Padstow follow road round hairpin bend at bottom of hill & cont, hotel is 2nd building*
Situated by the harbour, this charming little inn offers many bedrooms with sea views. The restaurant menus feature locally caught fish and other captivating dishes. The popular bar serves real ales and good bar meals at lunch-time and in the evening.
ROOMS: 27 en suite (bth/shr) (8 fmly) **MEALS:** English & French Cuisine V meals Coffee am Tea pm **FACILITIES:** CTV in all bedrooms STV Pool table **CONF:** Board 85 **SERVICES:** 9P **NOTES:** Last d 9pm
CARDS:

PADSTOW Cornwall & Isles of Scilly **Map 02 SW97**
★★ Seafood Restaurant
Riverside PL28 8BY
Quality Percentage Score: 76%
☎ 01841 532485 532700 01841 532942
Rick Stein's television fame has brought people from afar to visit his celebrated seafood restaurant, which has put the fishing village of Padstow on the map. Bedrooms were added a decade ago to enable diners to stay overnight and wake to the wonderful harbour views. Rooms are individually priced and modern in style. Residents and diners can enjoy drinks in a sunny conservatory and the restaurant itself has a bright and summery feel. Menus change twice daily, and there is always a stunning array of fresh fish and seafood.
ROOMS: 13 en suite (bth/shr) 16 annexe en suite (bth/shr) (3 fmly) s £40-£105; d £60-£140 (incl. bkfst) * LB Off peak **MEALS:** Lunch fr £28 & alc Dinner fr £34 & alc **FACILITIES:** CTV in all bedrooms **SERVICES:** 24P **NOTES:** No coaches Last d 10pm Closed 1 May, 19-26 Dec **CARDS:**

PADSTOW Cornwall & Isles of Scilly **Map 02 SW97**
★★ Green Waves
West View Rd, Trevone Bay PL28 8RD
Quality Percentage Score: 66%
☎ 01841 520114 01841 520568
The Green Waves is a friendly, family-run, and neatly kept hotel. Many of the tastefully furnished bedrooms are located on the ground floor, and all are comfortable and well equipped. Public areas include a spacious lounge, a separate bar and small snooker room. In the dining room a choice of home-cooked dishes is available.
ROOMS: 19 en suite (bth/shr) s £27-£29; d £54-£58 (incl. bkfst) * LB Off peak **MEALS:** Coffee am **FACILITIES:** CTV in all bedrooms Half size snooker table **SERVICES:** 16P **NOTES:** No coaches No children 4yrs No smoking in restaurant Apr-mid Oct **CARDS:**

See advert on opposite page

PAIGNTON Devon **Map 03 SX86**
★★★ Redcliffe
Marine Dr TQ3 2NL
Quality Percentage Score: 70%
☎ 01803 526397 01803 528030
Dir: *follow signs for Paignton & sea front, hotel on sea front at Torquay end of Paignton Green*

Standing in three acres of grounds, this well-established hotel enjoys uninterrupted views across Tor Bay. Service is friendly and attentive and all bedrooms are comfortably furnished, with modern facilities. Spacious public rooms include the 'Dick Francis' suite and a leisure centre.
ROOMS: 65 en suite (bth/shr) (8 fmly) s £48-£60; d £96-£120 (incl. bkfst) LB Off peak **MEALS:** Sunday Lunch £9.95-£10.95 Dinner £15.75-£16.75 & alc English & French Cuisine V meals Coffee am Tea pm **FACILITIES:** CTV in all bedrooms STV Indoor swimming pool (heated) Outdoor swimming pool (heated) Fishing Sauna Solarium Gym Pool table Putting green Jacuzzi/spa Table tennis Carpet Bowls Wkly live entertainment ch fac Xmas **CONF:** Thtr 150 Class 50 Board 50 Del from £58 * **SERVICES:** Lift Night porter 80P **NOTES:** No dogs (ex guide dogs) No smoking in restaurant Last d 8.30pm
CARDS:

contd.

PAIGNTON Devon **Map 03 SX86**

★★ Preston Sands

10/12 Marine Pde TQ3 2NU

Quality Percentage Score: 69%

☎ 01803 558718 Fax 01803 522875

Dir: *approx 1.5 miles from Paignton rail station, situated on Preston Beach*

Many of the bedrooms in this small, family-run hotel, situated right on the seafront, benefit from fine sea views. Owners Mr and Mrs Mitchell take pains to ensure that guests enjoy their stay and the good, home-cooked meals.

ROOMS: 31 en suite (bth/shr) (3 fmly) s £22-£28; d £44-£56 (incl. bkfst) * LB Off peak **MEALS:** Dinner £13-£16 & alc V meals Coffee am Tea pm **FACILITIES:** CTV in all bedrooms STV Xmas **SERVICES:** 24P **NOTES:** No children 8yrs No smoking in restaurant Last d 7.30pm

CARDS:

PAIGNTON Devon **Map 03 SX86**

★★ Sunhill

Alta Vista Rd TQ4 6DA

Quality Percentage Score: 68%

☎ 01803 557532 Fax 01803 663850

Dir: *directly overlooking Goodrington Sands. Near Paignton Harbour in Alta Vista rd*

Enjoying fine sea views, the hotel has friendly staff and high standards of comfort. Entertainment is a regular feature in the bar-lounge and some of the bright, airy bedrooms have balconies.

ROOMS: 30 en suite (bth/shr) (3 fmly) s £25-£30; d £50-£60 (incl. bkfst) * LB Off peak **MEALS:** Lunch £4-£6 Dinner £6.50-£7.50 English & French Cuisine V meals Coffee am Tea pm **FACILITIES:** CTV in all bedrooms Wkly live entertainment Xmas **SERVICES:** Lift Night porter 31P **NOTES:** No smoking in restaurant Last d 8pm

CARDS:

PAIGNTON Devon **Map 03 SX86**

★★ Clennon Valley Hotel

Clennon Rise, Goodrington TQ4 5HG

Quality Percentage Score: 67%

☎ 01803 550304 Fax 01803 550304

Dir: *400yds N of Quay West Water Park*

Pleasantly revovated, this Victorian house stands between the town centre and beaches. Accommodation is well equipped and facilities include an attractive lounge, small bar and traditionally furnished dining room.

ROOMS: 9 en suite (bth/shr) No smoking in all bedrooms s £25-£28; d £50-£56 (incl. bkfst) * Off peak **MEALS:** V meals Coffee am Tea pm **FACILITIES:** CTV in all bedrooms STV **SERVICES:** 8P **NOTES:** No dogs No coaches No children 12yrs No smoking in restaurant Last d 7.30pm Closed Nov-Feb **CARDS:**

PAIGNTON Devon **Map 03 SX86**

★★ Tor Sands

8 Sands Rd TQ4 6EH

Quality Percentage Score: 66%

☎ 01803 559695 Fax 01803 526786

Continuing the family tradition, brother and sister Sally and Andrew Linskey run a comfortable and friendly hotel, providing regular entertainment and themed events for their guests. Attractive bedrooms all have modern facilities and enjoyable food is served in the dining room.

ROOMS: 29 rms (15 bth 11 shr) 5 annexe en suite (bth/shr) No smoking in all bedrooms s £30-£35; d £52-£60 (incl. bkfst & dinner) * LB Off peak **MEALS:** V meals Coffee am Tea pm **FACILITIES:** CTV in all bedrooms Wkly live entertainment Xmas **SERVICES:** Night porter 15P **NOTES:** No smoking in restaurant Last d 7pm Closed Jan-Feb

PAIGNTON Devon **Map 03 SX86**

★★ Dainton

95 Dartmouth Rd, Three Beaches, Goodrington TQ4 6NA

Quality Percentage Score: 64%

☎ 01803 550067 📠 01803 666339

Dir: *located on the A379 at Goodrington*

Situated at Goodrington, this attractive Tudor-style property is in easy walking distance of the beach and leisure park. Bedrooms have been well designed and guests can either eat in the bar, or choose between a fixed-price menu served at 6.30pm, or the full carte, available later in the evening.

ROOMS: 11 en suite (bth/shr) (2 fmly) No smoking in all bedrooms s fr £30; d fr £60 (incl. bkfst) * LB Off peak **MEALS:** Lunch £7.50-£8.75 Dinner fr £10 & alc English & Continental Cuisine V meals Coffee am Tea pm **FACILITIES:** CTV in all bedrooms Wkly live entertainment Xmas **SERVICES:** Night porter 20P **NOTES:** No coaches No smoking in restaurant Last d 9.30pm **CARDS:**

PAIGNTON Devon **Map 03 SX86**

★★ Torbay Holiday Motel

Totnes Rd TQ4 7PP

Quality Percentage Score: 63%

☎ 01803 558226 📠 01803 663375

Dir: *on A385 Totnes/Paignton road, 2.5m from Paignton*

Situated outside Paignton, this purpose-built complex houses a motel, self-catering apartments and leisure facilities. The comfortable bedrooms are spacious; the dining room serves traditional food, whilst a less formal menu is available in the bar-lounge.

ROOMS: 16 en suite (bth/shr) s £32-£35; d £50-£56 (incl. bkfst) Off peak **MEALS:** Dinner £11.50 & alc English & French Cuisine V meals Coffee am **FACILITIES:** CTV in all bedrooms STV Indoor swimming pool (heated) Outdoor swimming pool (heated) Sauna Solarium Gym Pool table Putting green Crazy golf Adventure playground **SERVICES:** 150P **NOTES:** Last d 9pm Closed 24-31 Dec

CARDS:

See advert on opposite page

P

PAIGNTON Devon **Map 03 SX86**

★ *Sattva*

Esplanade TQ4 6BL

Quality Percentage Score: 63%

☎ 01803 557820 📠 01803 557820

Dir: *hotel located on the seafront by the pier*

The Sattva is close to all the resort's beaches, shops and theatres and to Paignton Green. Strengths are its lively bar, with regular entertainment, its traditional English food and its comfortable bedrooms, accessible by lift.

ROOMS: 20 en suite (bth/shr) (2 fmly) No smoking in 3 bedrooms **MEALS:** V meals Coffee am Tea pm **FACILITIES:** CTV in all bedrooms **SERVICES:** Lift 10P **NOTES:** No smoking in restaurant Last d 6.30pm Closed Jan-Feb **CARDS:**

PAINSWICK Gloucestershire **Map 03 SO80**

★★★❀❀ Painswick

Kemps Ln GL6 6YB

Quality Percentage Score: 78%

☎ 01452 812160 📠 01452 814059

Dir: *turn off A46 in centre of village by the church. Hotel is located off 2nd road behind church off Tibbiwell Lane*

A delightful 18th-century house in the heart of the village, overlooking the valley. Some bedrooms are in the main house, some in an adjacent building, and all are well equipped. Elegant day rooms have much character with antiques and high quality furnishings. The restaurant menu provides an interesting choice of dishes. Service is friendly.

ROOMS: 19 en suite (bth/shr) (4 fmly) s £75-£125; d £110-£175 (incl. bkfst) * LB Off peak **MEALS:** Lunch £13-£17.50 High tea £5-£10 Dinner £23-£26 & alc French Cuisine V meals Coffee am Tea pm **FACILITIES:** CTV in all bedrooms Croquet lawn Xmas **CONF:** Thtr 40 Class 20 Board 20 **SERVICES:** 25P **NOTES:** No coaches Last d 9.30pm **CARDS:**

See advert on opposite page

PANGBOURNE Berkshire **Map 04 SU67**

★★★❀❀ The Copper Inn

Church Rd RG8 7AR

Best Western

Quality Percentage Score: 77%

☎ 0118 984 2244 📠 0118 984 5542

Dir: *from M4 junct 12 take A4 west then A340 to Pangbourne. Hotel located next to Pangbourne parish church at the junction of A329/A340*

Well known locally for its high standards of hospitality and service, the Copper Inn provides individually decorated, spacious and well equipped bedrooms. Bathrooms in particular are stylish, and all have both bath and shower. The lovely restaurant has a Mediterranean feel, and chef Stuart Shepherd's cuisine has gained two AA Rosettes.

ROOMS: 14 en suite (bth/shr) 8 annexe en suite (bth/shr) (1 fmly) s £80-£100; d £115-£135 * LB Off peak **MEALS:** Lunch £13.95-£17.95 & alc Dinner £21.95 & alc French & English Cuisine V meals Coffee am Tea pm **FACILITIES:** CTV in all bedrooms STV Xmas **CONF:** Thtr 60 Class 24 Board 30 Del £135 * **SERVICES:** 20P **NOTES:** No smoking area in restaurant Last d 9.30pm **CARDS:**

PANGBOURNE Berkshire **Map 04 SU67**

★★★ George Hotel

The Square RG8 7AJ

Best Western

Quality Percentage Score: 69%

☎ 0118 9842237 📠 0118 9844354

Dir: *leave M4/junct12 take A4 towards Newbury at 2nd rdbt take 3rd exit onto A340, in village turn right at mini-rdbt, hotel 100yds on left*

Parts of this historic building date back to 1295, and a resident ghost is part of the colourful history. Well thought out spacious bedrooms are equipped with modern facilities and furnishings. The very popular restaurant, although part of the original building, has an Italian feel to it and booking at weekends is recommended.

ROOMS: 24 en suite (bth/shr) (3 fmly) s £75-£85; d £90-£115 (incl. bkfst) * LB Off peak **MEALS:** Italian Cuisine V meals Coffee am Tea pm **FACILITIES:** CTV in all bedrooms STV **CONF:** Thtr 80 Class 60 Board 50 Del from £130 * **SERVICES:** 30P **NOTES:** Last d 10pm RS Bank Holidays **CARDS:**

PARBOLD Lancashire **Map 07 SD41**

★★ Lindley

Lancaster Ln WN8 7AB

Quality Percentage Score: 67%

☎ 01257 462804 01257 464628

Dir: *exit M6 at junct 27 and take A5209 signposted Burscough. Turn right onto B5246, signposted Rufford, 500yds right hand side*

This hotel offers attractively furnished bedrooms with a range of facilities. The restaurant, popular with locals and visitors alike, has a wide selection of dishes, available from the menu or blackboard. Service is both willingly provided and friendly.

ROOMS: 8 en suite (bth/shr) (1 fmly) s £45-£55; d £55-£75 (incl. bkfst) * Off peak **MEALS:** Lunch fr £9.95 & alc Dinner £12.50-£13.75 & alc English & Continental Cuisine V meals Coffee am Tea pm **FACILITIES:** CTV in all bedrooms **SERVICES:** 46P **NOTES:** No dogs (ex guide dogs) No smoking in restaurant Last d 9.30pm **CARDS:**

PARKHAM Devon **Map 02 SS32**

★★★ *Penhaven Country House*

EX39 5PL

Quality Percentage Score: 73%

☎ 01237 451388 & 451711 01237 451878

Dir: *turn off A39 at Horns Cross and follow signs to Parkham, turn left after church*

Set in 11 acres of grounds, with distant views of Exmoor, this 17th-century hotel offers well equipped bedrooms in the main building, and some cottage suites in buildings in the grounds. Local produce features on the interesting restaurant menu. The grounds are a haven for wildlife.

ROOMS: 12 en suite (bth/shr) **MEALS:** English & French Cuisine V meals Coffee am Tea pm **FACILITIES:** CTV in all bedrooms **SERVICES:** 50P **NOTES:** No coaches No children 10yrs No smoking in restaurant Last d 9pm **CARDS:**

PATELEY BRIDGE North Yorkshire **Map 07 SE16**

★★ Grassfields Country House

Low Wath Rd HG3 5HL

Quality Percentage Score: 68%

☎ 01423 711412 01423 712844

Dir: *turn off A59 onto B6451 and turn left at Summerbridge onto B6165. Cross bridge and take first right at petrol pumps*

This elegant Georgian house which stands in its own well tended gardens provides a delightfully comfortable drawing room together with a bar which has recently been extended. A conservatory has been added and the hotel can now cater for functions. A very friendly atmosphere prevails around the hotel and bedrooms are mainly spacious and have been furnished in

contd.

P

the style of a country house. Good home cooking is served in the elegant dining room.
ROOMS: 9 en suite (bth/shr) (3 fmly) s £28.50-£31.50; d £53-£59 (incl. bkfst) * LB Off peak **MEALS:** Bar Lunch £8.75-£14.95alc Dinner £14.95 & alc English & French Cuisine V meals Coffee am Tea pm **FACILITIES:** CTV in all bedrooms Xmas **CONF:** Thtr 100 Class 70 Board 50 Del from £55.95 * **NOTES:** No smoking in restaurant Last d 9pm **CARDS:**

PATTERDALE Cumbria — Map 11 NY31

★★ Patterdale

CA11 0NN
Quality Percentage Score: 58%
☎ 017684 82231 📠 017684 82440
Dir: *M6 junct 40, take A592 towards Ullsware, then 10m up Lakeside Rd to Patterdale*
Enjoying fine views of the valley and fells, this roadside hotel lies at the southern end of Ullswater. The hotel's core business is touring and accordingly it offers practical and functional accommodation.
ROOMS: 63 en suite (bth/shr) (4 fmly) s fr £30; d fr £60 (incl. bkfst) * LB Off peak **MEALS:** Lunch £8.50 Dinner £16 V meals Coffee am **FACILITIES:** CTV in all bedrooms Tennis (hard) Fishing Pool table **CONF:** Class 20 Del from £50 * **SERVICES:** Lift 31P **NOTES:** No smoking in restaurant Last d 8pm Closed Jan-Feb **CARDS:**

PATTINGHAM Staffordshire — Map 07 SO89

★★★ Patshull Park Hotel Golf & Country Club

Patshull Park WV6 7HR
Quality Percentage Score: 66%
☎ 01902 700100 📠 01902 700874
Dir: *1.5m W of Pattingham at Pattingham Church take the Patshull Rd hotel 1.5m on right*

There has been a manor house here since before the Norman Conquest. The present house, dating back to the 1730s, and its 280 acres of parkland have been developed into a hotel with golf, fishing, leisure and conference complex. Facilities include a coffee shop, golf shop, leisure club and swimming pool. There are extensive conference and banqueting suites. Bedrooms are well equipped.
ROOMS: 49 en suite (bth/shr) (2 fmly) s £75-£90; d £80-£95 (incl. bkfst) * LB Off peak **MEALS:** Lunch fr £11.95 High tea £3.50-£6 Dinner fr £17.95 & alc English & French Cuisine V meals Coffee am Tea pm **FACILITIES:** CTV in all bedrooms STV Indoor swimming pool (heated) Golf 18 Fishing Sauna Solarium Gym Pool table Putting green Jacuzzi/spa Beauty therapist Bar billiards Wkly live entertainment Xmas **CONF:** Thtr 250 Class 75 Board 44 Del from £95 * **SERVICES:** Night porter 200P **NOTES:** No smoking in restaurant Last d 9.30pm **CARDS:**

See advert under WOLVERHAMPTON

PEASMARSH East Sussex — Map 05 TQ82

★★★ Flackley Ash

MARSTON HOTELS

TN31 6YH
Quality Percentage Score: 74%
☎ 01797 230651 📠 01797 230510
Dir: *3m from Rye, beside A268*
Set in attractive and well kept grounds just a short distance to the north of Rye, this Georgian country house has been sympathetically restored to provide a range of individually furnished bedrooms, including some splendid new garden rooms added this year. All are well equipped and extra personal touches include the provision of good quality toiletries and hot water bottles. There are also a number of spacious executive rooms, ideal for business guests. Amenities include conference and banqueting facilities for up to 100 people and there is a fully equipped indoor leisure suite. The restaurant now boasts an airy conservatory where guests can sample the traditional cuisine of chef Dale Skinner, whose specialities include local seafood and seasonal fresh vegetables. Efficient service is provided by a friendly team of young staff.
ROOMS: 42 en suite (bth/shr) (3 fmly) s £75-£90; d £115-£165 (incl. bkfst) * LB Off peak **MEALS:** Lunch £10.95-£12.95 & alc High tea £3.95-£7.20 Dinner £22.50-£32.20 English & French Cuisine V meals Coffee am Tea pm **FACILITIES:** CTV in all bedrooms Indoor swimming pool (heated) Sauna Solarium Gym Croquet lawn Putting green Jacuzzi/spa Float tank Beautician Xmas **CONF:** Thtr 100 Class 50 Board 40 Del from £100 * **SERVICES:** 70P **NOTES:** No smoking in restaurant Last d 9.30pm **CARDS:**

PELYNT Cornwall & Isles of Scilly — Map 02 SX25

★★ Jubilee Inn

PL13 2JZ
Quality Percentage Score: 64%
☎ 01503 220312 📠 01503 220920
Dir: *take A390 signposted St Austell at village of East Taphouse turn left onto B3359 signposted Looe & Polperro. Jubilee Inn on left on leaving Pelynt.*
A popular 16th-Century inn with flagstone floors and charming old-fashioned rooms. There is a choice of bars, while the menus have an emphasis on fresh local produce served in the bar or dining room. Bedrooms are individual in size and decor and provide comfortable accommodation with modern facilities.
ROOMS: 12 en suite (bth/shr) (3 fmly) s fr £38.50; d fr £65 (incl. bkfst) * Off peak **MEALS:** Lunch £7.90 & alc Dinner £14.50-£23.90alc English & Continental Cuisine V meals Coffee am Tea pm **FACILITIES:** CTV in all bedrooms Pool table Xmas **SERVICES:** 80P **NOTES:** Last d 9pm **CARDS:**

PENKRIDGE Staffordshire — Map 07 SJ91

★★★ Quality Hotel Stafford

Comfort Quality Clarion CHOICE HOTELS EUROPE

Pinfold Ln ST19 5QP
Quality Percentage Score: 63%
☎ 01785 712459 📠 01785 715532
Dir: *from M6 junct 12 A5 towards Telford at 1st rdbt turn right onto A440, 2m into Penkridge turn left just beyond Ford garage, opposite White Hart*
Nestling in a quiet backwater of Staffordshire and surrounded by countryside, this hotel is located just a few minutes drive from the M6. Bedrooms are spacious and well presented with good facilities. There is an attractive lounge and a smart restaurant offering an interesting menu. Guests have full use of the Leisure Centre.
ROOMS: 47 en suite (bth/shr) (1 fmly) No smoking in 10 bedrooms s £75-£85; d £95-£115 * LB Off peak **MEALS:** Dinner fr £16.50 International Cuisine V meals Coffee am Tea pm **FACILITIES:** CTV in all bedrooms Indoor swimming pool (heated) Squash Sauna Solarium Gym Wkly live entertainment Xmas **CONF:** Thtr 300 Class 120 Board 90 **SERVICES:** Night porter 160P **NOTES:** No smoking in restaurant Last d 9.30pm **CARDS:**

PENRITH Cumbria **Map 12 NY53**
see also **Shap & Temple Sowerby**
★★★★ North Lakes
Ullswater Rd CA11 8QT
Quality Percentage Score: 70%
☎ 01768 868111 01768 868291
Dir: *M6 junct 40 at intersection with A66*

Conveniently located just off junction 40 of the M6, this smartly appointed modern hotel is very well positioned for both the business and leisure guests and offers an excellent standard of accommodation. There are two types of bedroom, both providing modern comforts with the higher category offering extra personal touches. The comfortable public areas include a good range of meeting and leisure facilities.

ROOMS: 84 en suite (bth/shr) (6 fmly) No smoking in 25 bedrooms s £102-£137; d £122-£157 (incl. bkfst) * LB Off peak **MEALS:** Bar Lunch fr £8 Dinner fr £22 English & French Cuisine V meals Coffee am Tea pm **FACILITIES:** CTV in all bedrooms STV Indoor swimming pool (heated) Squash Sauna Solarium Gym Jacuzzi/spa Spa pool Childrens pool Childrens Club room Health & Beauty treatment rooms **CONF:** Thtr 200 Class 140 Board 24 Del from £88 * **SERVICES:** Lift Night porter 150P **NOTES:** No smoking in restaurant Last d 9.30pm Closed 31 Dec **CARDS:**

PENRITH Cumbria **Map 12 NY53**
★★★ Westmorland Hotel
Orton CA10 3SB
Quality Percentage Score: 69%
☎ 015396 24351 015396 24354
(For full entry see Tebay)

PENRITH Cumbria **Map 12 NY53**
★★ *Brantwood Country Hotel*
Stainton CA11 0EP
Quality Percentage Score: 66%
☎ 01768 862748 01768 890164
Dir: *From M6 junct 40 join A66 Keswick road and in 0.5 mile turn left then right signposted Stainton*

Just two minutes drive from the M6, this family run hotel enjoys an open outlook to the rear. The bedroom decor is individual and cheerful in colour; five rooms are in a converted courtyard building. Good meals are served both in the bar and the restaurant.

ROOMS: 6 en suite (shr) 5 annexe en suite (bth/shr) (3 fmly) No smoking in 5 bedrooms **MEALS:** English & Continental Cuisine V meals Coffee am Tea pm **FACILITIES:** CTV in all bedrooms Croquet lawn Putting green **CONF:** Thtr 60 Class 30 Board 30 **SERVICES:** 35P **NOTES:** No dogs No coaches No smoking in restaurant Last d 8.45pm **CARDS:**

See advert on this page

PENRITH Cumbria **Map 12 NY53**
Travelodge
Redhills CA11 0DT
☎ 01768 866958 01768 866958
Dir: *on A66*

This modern building offers accommodation in smart, spacious and well equipped bedrooms, all with en-suite bathrooms. Refreshments may be taken at the nearby family restaurant. For details about current prices, consult the Contents Page under Hotel Groups for the Travelodge phone number.

ROOMS: 40 en suite (bth/shr) d £49.95 *

PENZANCE Cornwall & Isles of Scilly **Map 02 SW43**
★★★ *Higher Faugan*
Newlyn TR18 5NS
Quality Percentage Score: 65%
☎ 01736 362076 01736 351648
Dir: *off B3115, 0.75m from Newlyn crossroads*

This gracious turn-of-the-century hotel is surrounded by acres of well kept gardens. Personal touches, including needlepoint cushions in the comfortable lounges, make it a real home from home. Bedrooms are generally spacious and some have luxurious corner-baths.

ROOMS: 11 en suite (bth/shr) (2 fmly) **MEALS:** English, French & Italian Cuisine Coffee am Tea pm **FACILITIES:** CTV in all bedrooms Outdoor swimming pool (heated) Tennis (hard) Snooker Solarium Pool table Croquet lawn Putting green Exercise equipment available **SERVICES:** 20P **NOTES:** No smoking in restaurant Last d 8.30pm RS Nov-Mar **CARDS:**

PENZANCE Cornwall & Isles of Scilly **Map 02 SW43**

★★★ Mount Prospect

Britons Hill TR18 3AE

Quality Percentage Score: 65%

☎ 01736 363117 📠 01736 350970

THE CIRCLE
Selected Individual Hotels
GREAT BRITAIN

Dir: *from A30 pass heliport on right straight onto next rdbt, bear left for town centre take 3rd right by Pirates Hotel, hotel is on right*

Situated in sub-tropical gardens with panoramic views across Mounts Bay, The Mount Prospect is a well established hotel. There is a choice of lounges and an inviting bar, with a separate restaurant serving well prepared food. Bedrooms are attractive and modern in style.

ROOMS: 21 en suite (bth/shr) (1 fmly) No smoking in 14 bedrooms s £34-£49; d £58-£80 (incl. bkfst) * LB Off peak **MEALS:** Dinner £17.50 English & French Cuisine V meals Coffee am Tea pm **FACILITIES:** CTV in all bedrooms STV Outdoor swimming pool (heated) Pool table **CONF:** Thtr 80 Class 50 Board 12 **SERVICES:** Night porter 14P **NOTES:** No smoking in restaurant Last d 8.30pm Closed 23 Dec-3 Jan **CARDS:**

PENZANCE Cornwall & Isles of Scilly **Map 02 SW43**

★★★ Queen's

The Promenade TR18 4HG

Quality Percentage Score: 64%

☎ 01736 362371 📠 01736 350033

Dir: *A30 to Penzance, follow signs for seafront pass harbour & into promenade, hotel half a mile on right*

Overlooking the picturesque Mounts Bay, this large Victorian hotel has a fine and distinguished history. Inside, the bedrooms provide all modern comforts. The dining room has fine views over the bay and offers both a daily and carte menu.

ROOMS: 70 en suite (bth/shr) (9 fmly) s £47-£53; d £80-£114 (incl. bkfst) * LB Off peak **MEALS:** Sunday Lunch £9.50-£15 Dinner £15.95-£18.95 & alc English & French Cuisine V meals Coffee am Tea pm **FACILITIES:** CTV in all bedrooms STV Sauna Solarium Gym Xmas **CONF:** Thtr 200 Class 100 Board 80 Del from £60 * **SERVICES:** Lift Night porter 50P **NOTES:** No smoking in restaurant Last d 8.45pm **CARDS:**

See advert on opposite page

PENZANCE Cornwall & Isles of Scilly **Map 02 SW43**

★★ Tarbert

11-12 Clarence St TR18 2NU

Quality Percentage Score: 69%

☎ 01736 363758 & 364317 📠 01736 331336

Dir: *take Land's End turning at town approach. At 2nd roundabout turn left, continue past next mini rdbt - 100yds turn right into Clarence St*

Dating back to the 1830s, this former sea captain's house is now a small friendly hotel. There is a spacious reception and an attractive bar-lounge, while the candlelit restaurant serves a bistro-style menu. The comfortable bedrooms are decorated with style.

ROOMS: 12 en suite (bth/shr) s £31.50-£35; d £53-£76 (incl. bkfst) LB Off peak **MEALS:** Dinner fr £18.50 International Cuisine V meals Coffee am **FACILITIES:** CTV in all bedrooms **SERVICES:** 5P **NOTES:** No dogs No coaches No smoking in restaurant Last d 8.30pm Closed Jan-10 Feb & 20 Nov-Dec **CARDS:**

PENZANCE Cornwall & Isles of Scilly **Map 02 SW43**

★★ Union Hotel

Chapel St TR18 4AE

Quality Percentage Score: 65%

☎ 01736 362319 📠 01726 362319

Located in the centre of the town amidst many interesting shops, parts of this charming hotel date back to Tudor times. The Nelson bar is popular with locals and visitors alike, and offers a range of traditional bar meals. The Hamilton Restaurant offers a more formal dining option, with both fixed price and a la carte menus available. There is a variety of sizes and styles of accommodation, with all bedrooms having modern facilities.

ROOMS: 28 rms (22 bth/shr) (4 fmly) s fr £37; d fr £65 (incl. bkfst) * LB Off peak **MEALS:** V meals Coffee am Tea pm **FACILITIES:** CTV in all bedrooms **SERVICES:** 15P **NOTES:** No dogs Last d 9pm **CARDS:**

PENZANCE Cornwall & Isles of Scilly **Map 02 SW43**

★★ The Sea & Horses

Seafront, 6 Alexandra Ter TR18 4NX

Quality Percentage Score: 61%

☎ 01736 361961 📠 01736 330499

Dir: *enter town on A30, stay on seafront follow signs Newlyn/Mousehole for approx 1m, hotel set back off main road, on seafront just past filling station*

Forming part of a Victorian terrace, this friendly hotel is just off the main street of Penzance and looks out over Mounts Bay. Inside, there is a comfortable lounge and bright dining room where good home-made food is served. The bedrooms are individual in style and size.

ROOMS: 11 en suite (bth/shr) (4 fmly) No smoking in 2 bedrooms s £29.50-£35; d £59-£70 (incl. bkfst) * LB Off peak **MEALS:** Lunch fr £12.50 High tea fr £3 Dinner fr £12.50 V meals Coffee am Tea pm **FACILITIES:** CTV in all bedrooms Sunbed available Wkly live entertainment Xmas **SERVICES:** 12P **NOTES:** No smoking in restaurant Last d 5.30pm **CARDS:**

AA Rosettes are awarded for quality of food,
see page 15 for an explanation of Rosette assessment.

PENZANCE Cornwall & Isles of Scilly — Map 02 SW43

★ Estoril

46 Morrab Rd TR18 4EX
Quality Percentage Score: 71%
☎ 01736 362468 & 367471 Fax 01736 367471
Dir: *from bus/train station keep left along promenade towards Newlyn, take 1st turning past "The Lugger", Estoril is 300yds along on left*

Great attention is given to the comfort and well being of guests at this small private hotel, ideally situated in a quiet location midway between the town centre and seafront. All bedrooms are comfortably equipped with a number thoughtful extras. Fresh produce is frequently used for meals, which are served in the well-appointed dining room.

ROOMS: 10 en suite (bth/shr) (2 fmly) No smoking in all bedrooms s £26-£29; d £52-£58 (incl. bkfst) * LB Off peak **MEALS:** Dinner £13-£16 V meals **FACILITIES:** CTV in all bedrooms **SERVICES:** 4P **NOTES:** No dogs No coaches No smoking in restaurant Last d 6.45pm Closed Jan **CARDS:**

PERRANPORTH Cornwall & Isles of Scilly — Map 02 SW75

★★ Beach Dunes

Ramoth Way, Reen Sands TR6 0BY
Quality Percentage Score: 63%
☎ 01872 572263 Fax 01872 573824
Dir: *turn off A30 onto B3075 at Goonhavern continue onto B3285 at 30mph sign private road on right Ramoth Way, Beach Dunes at end of road*

Situated at the end of a private road adjoining the local 18-hole Golf Course, this small hotel enjoys views over Perran Bay, the village and surrounding countryside. In the dining room

contd.

enjoyable home cooking is offered from a short menu. Bedrooms are well equipped, neatly furnished and well decorated.
ROOMS: 6 rms (5 bth/shr) 3 annexe en suite (bth/shr) (2 fmly) No smoking in all bedrooms s £26.50-£29.50; d £53-£59 (incl. bkfst) * LB Off peak **MEALS:** Bar Lunch £5-£10 Dinner £10-£12.50 V meals Coffee am Tea pm **FACILITIES:** CTV in all bedrooms Indoor swimming pool (heated) Squash Bar billiards **SERVICES:** 15P **NOTES:** No coaches No children 3yrs No smoking in restaurant Last d 8pm Closed Nov & Dec
CARDS:

PETERBOROUGH Cambridgeshire **Map 04 TL19**
★★★★ Swallow
Peterborough Business Park, Lynchwood PE2 6GB
Quality Percentage Score: 65%
☎ 01733 371111 01733 236725
Dir: *opposite East of England Showground at Alwalton*

Opposite the East of England showground, this modern hotel is popular with business guests. Bedrooms are well equipped and comfortable. The fully air-conditioned public rooms include lounge and cocktail bars. The brasserie offers a variety of dishes to suit all tastes, and the formal restaurant is ideal for serious dining. There is also a wide range of conference and banqueting facilities. The leisure club includes a children's pool.
ROOMS: 163 en suite (bth/shr) (8 fmly) No smoking in 108 bedrooms s £120; d £140 (incl. bkfst) * LB Off peak **MEALS:** Lunch £13.50-£15 Dinner £17.50-£25 English & French Cuisine V meals Coffee am Tea pm **FACILITIES:** CTV in all bedrooms STV Indoor swimming pool (heated) Sauna Solarium Gym Putting green Jacuzzi/spa Beauty therapist Hairdressing Wkly live entertainment Xmas **CONF:** Thtr 300 Class 160 Board 45 Del £135 * **SERVICES:** Night porter 200P **NOTES:** No smoking in restaurant Last d 9.30pm
CARDS:

PETERBOROUGH Cambridgeshire **Map 04 TL19**
★★★ Orton Hall
Orton Longueville PE2 7DN
Quality Percentage Score: 67%
☎ 01733 391111 01733 231912
Dir: *off A605 (East) opposite Orton Mere*
Set in 20 acres of woodland grounds, this impressive country house has been skilfully converted to a commendable hotel. Public areas are spacious and relaxing, with the hotel facilities dotted throughout the grounds. There are lots of original features, including oak panelling in the Huntly Restaurant, the Grand Hall which is a popular banqueting venue, and even some 16th-century terracotta floors. Across the courtyard is an English pub, the Ramblewood Inn.
ROOMS: 65 en suite (bth/shr) (2 fmly) No smoking in 42 bedrooms s £72-£100; d £97.50-£125 * LB Off peak **MEALS:** Lunch £14.95-£19.50 & alc Dinner fr £19.50 & alc International Cuisine V meals Coffee am Tea pm **FACILITIES:** CTV in all bedrooms Three quarter size snooker table **CONF:** Thtr 120 Class 48 Board 42 Del from £105 * **SERVICES:** Night porter 200P **NOTES:** No smoking in restaurant Last d 9pm Closed 27 Dec-4 Jan **CARDS:**

PETERBOROUGH Cambridgeshire **Map 04 TL19**
★★★ *Peterborough Moat House*
Thorpe Wood PE3 6SG
Quality Percentage Score: 67%
☎ 01733 289988 01733 262737
Dir: *exit A1 S at Peterborough sign onto A1139. Follow city centre signs at junct 3 & 33. Take route marked Thorpe Wood, hotel on right.*
Well suited to the needs of the midweek business traveller and the weekend leisure guest, this modern hotel on the outskirts of Peterborough overlooks a 500 acre Country Park and a golf course. Facilities include extensive conference rooms, a business centre and a brand new leisure centre. Bedrooms are spacious and well equipped; four have their own sitting rooms.
ROOMS: 125 en suite (bth/shr) No smoking in 87 bedrooms
MEALS: International Cuisine V meals Coffee am Tea pm
FACILITIES: CTV in all bedrooms Indoor swimming pool (heated) Sauna Solarium Gym Jacuzzi/spa Beauty Treatment, Aerobics Wkly live entertainment **CONF:** Thtr 400 Class 150 Board 50 **SERVICES:** Lift Night porter 230P **NOTES:** No smoking in restaurant Last d 10pm
CARDS:

PETERBOROUGH Cambridgeshire **Map 04 TL19**
★★★ Bell Inn
Great North Rd PE7 3RA
Quality Percentage Score: 66%
☎ 01733 241066 01733 245173
(For full entry see Stilton)

PETERBOROUGH Cambridgeshire **Map 04 TL19**
★★★ Bull
Westgate PE1 1RB
Quality Percentage Score: 66%
☎ 01733 61364 01733 557304
Dir: *turn off A1 follow signs to city centre, hotel in heart of city opposite Queensgate shopping centre*
The committed new owner and his enthusiastic manager are planning great results for this very pleasant city centre hotel, offering well equipped and prettily furnished modern accommodation. The recently refurbished public rooms are extensive and include a good range of meeting rooms and conference facilities. An interesting range of dishes are served in the elegant restaurant.
ROOMS: 103 en suite (bth) (3 fmly) s £74.50; d £85 * LB Off peak **MEALS:** Lunch fr £17.50 Dinner fr £17.50 English & French Cuisine V meals Coffee am Tea pm **FACILITIES:** CTV in all bedrooms **CONF:** Thtr 200 Class 80 Board 60 Del from £98 * **SERVICES:** Night porter 100P **NOTES:** Last d 10.30pm **CARDS:**

PETERBOROUGH Cambridgeshire **Map 04 TL19**
★★★ Posthouse Peterborough
Great North Rd PE7 3TB
Quality Percentage Score: 64%
☎ 01733 240209 01733 244455
(For full entry see Norman Cross)

Symbols and Abbreviations are listed and explained on pages 4 and 5

PETERBOROUGH Cambridgeshire **Map 04 TL19**
★★★ Butterfly
Thorpe Meadows, Longthorpe Parkway PE3 6GA
Quality Percentage Score: 63%
☎ 01733 64240 01733 65538
Dir: *from A1179 take exit for Thorpe Meadows and city centre, turn right at next two roundabouts*
A popular hotel chain with four properties in East Anglia, the Butterfly name stands for a friendly atmosphere, with pleasant modern accommodation, and a popular vibrant restaurant and bar. Sitting in a pretty location beside the international rowing course in Thorpe Meadows, this hotel offers easy access to parkland, lake and river walks, and the local steam railway. The accommodation is thoughtfully designed, with consideration to the needs of corporate guests; ground floor, studio and ladies' rooms are available.
ROOMS: 70 en suite (bth/shr) (2 fmly) No smoking in 10 bedrooms d £69.50 * LB Off peak **MEALS:** Lunch £7-£15 Dinner fr £18 & alc European Cuisine V meals Coffee am Tea pm **FACILITIES:** CTV in all bedrooms STV **CONF:** Thtr 80 Class 50 Board 50 Del from £95 * **SERVICES:** Night porter 85P **NOTES:** No dogs (ex guide dogs) No smoking area in restaurant Last d 10pm
CARDS:

PETERBOROUGH Cambridgeshire **Map 04 TL19**
Holiday Inn Express
East of England Way, Alwalton PE2 6HE
☎ 01733 284450 01733 284451
Dir: *1m E of the A1 and 4m from city centre on the A605 Oundle Road, adjacent to East of England Showground*
This modern building offers accommodation in smart, spacious and well equipped bedrooms, all with en-suite bathrooms. Refreshments may be taken at the informal restaurant. For details about current prices, consult the Contents Page under Hotel Groups for the Holiday Inn Express phone number.
ROOMS: 80 en suite (shr) (incl. cont bkfst) s £45-£49.50; d £45-£49.50 * **CONF:** Thtr 25 Class 20 Board 16

PETERBOROUGH Cambridgeshire **Map 04 TL19**
Travel Inn
Ham Ln, Orton Meadows, Nene Park PE2 5UU
☎ 01733 235794 01733 391055
Dir: *from A1 take A605 Peterborough exit & follow signs to Nene Park*
This modern building offers accommodation in smart, spacious and well equipped bedrooms, all with en-suite bathrooms. Refreshments may be taken at the nearby family restaurant. For details about current prices consult the Contents Page under Hotel Groups for the Travel Inn phone number.
ROOMS: 40 en suite (bth/shr) d £39.95 *

PETERBOROUGH Cambridgeshire **Map 04 TL19**
Travelodge
Great North Rd, Alwalton PE7 3UR
☎ 01733 231109 01733 231109
Dir: *on A1, southbound*
This modern building offers accommodation in smart, spacious and well equipped bedrooms, all with en-suite bathrooms. Refreshments may be taken at the nearby family restaurant. For details about current prices, consult the Contents Page under Hotel Groups for the Travelodge phone number.
ROOMS: 32 en suite (bth/shr) d £45.95 *

PETERSFIELD See advertisement on this page

PETTY FRANCE Gloucestershire **Map 03 ST78**
★★★ Petty France
GL9 1AF
Quality Percentage Score: 68%
☎ 01454 238361 01454 238768
Dir: *on A46 S of junct with A433, 6m N of M4 junction 18, A46*
There was a coaching inn here from the early 18th Century. The elegant dower house has pretty walled gardens, a courtyard stable block is converted into comfortable, modern bedrooms. Rooms in the main hotel reflect country house style. The attractive bar, lounge and restaurant have open fires. The menus feature herbs and vegetables from the hotel gardens.
ROOMS: 8 en suite (bth/shr) 12 annexe en suite (bth/shr) (1 fmly) No smoking in 2 bedrooms s £69-£99; d £79-£125 (incl. cont bkfst) * LB Off peak **MEALS:** Lunch £13-£21 Dinner £13-£21 International Cuisine V meals Coffee am Tea pm **FACILITIES:** CTV in all bedrooms Croquet lawn Bicycle hire Xmas **CONF:** Thtr 55 Class 20 Board 24 Del from £90 * **SERVICES:** 70P **NOTES:** No smoking in restaurant Last d 9.30pm
CARDS:

PEVENSEY East Sussex **Map 05 TQ60**
★★ Priory Court
Castle Rd BN24 5LG
Quality Percentage Score: 64%
☎ 01323 763150 01323 769030
Dir: *turn left from A22 look for Historic Pevensey Castle*
Standing directly opposite Pevensey Castle, this charming hotel is owned by friendly proprietor Mr Finlay. Public areas have undergone much refurbishment and include a smartly appointed
contd.

lounge, beamed dining room and character bar. Bedrooms are traditionally furnished and well equipped.

Priory Court, Pevensey

ROOMS: 9 rms (7 bth/shr) (1 fmly) s £32-£40; d £44-£57 (incl. bkfst) * LB Off peak **MEALS:** Lunch £9.95 & alc Dinner £13.50-£24.75alc English & French Cuisine V meals Coffee am Tea pm **FACILITIES:** CTV in all bedrooms Xmas **CONF:** Class 25 Board 15 Del from £70 * **SERVICES:** 50P **NOTES:** No coaches Last d 9.30pm **CARDS:**

PICKERING North Yorkshire — Map 08 SE78

★★ Fox & Hounds Country Inn

Main St, Sinnington YO62 6SQ
Quality Percentage Score: 72%
☎ 01751 431577 01751 432791
Dir: *3m W of Pickering, off A170*

This inviting country inn lies in the quiet village of Sinnington just off the main road. It offers attractive well equipped bedrooms together with a cosy residents lounge with lots of reading matter. The restaurant provides a good selection of British dishes cooked in the modern style and there is also a good range of bar meals. Service throughout is friendly and attentive by a dedicated team.

ROOMS: 10 en suite (bth/shr) (1 fmly) No smoking in all bedrooms s £40-£44; d £58-£64 (incl. bkfst) * LB Off peak **MEALS:** Sunday Lunch £5.95-£20alc Dinner £13-£22alc V meals Coffee am Tea pm **FACILITIES:** CTV in all bedrooms Xmas **SERVICES:** 40P **NOTES:** No coaches No smoking in restaurant Last d 9pm **CARDS:**

PICKERING North Yorkshire — Map 08 SE78

★★ Forest & Vale

Best Western

Malton Rd YO18 7DL
Quality Percentage Score: 72%
☎ 01751 472722 01751 472972
Dir: *Hotel is at junction of A169 & A170 in town of Pickering, just off the roundabout*

This pleasantly furnished hotel is well managed by the owners, together with their friendly and efficient staff. The bedrooms are comfortable and include some spacious superior rooms, one with a four-poster bed. A good range of food is available and is served either in the bar or the restaurant, while room service is also provided.

ROOMS: 14 en suite (bth/shr) 5 annexe en suite (bth/shr) (5 fmly) No smoking in 6 bedrooms s £52.50-£58; d £68-£90 (incl. bkfst) * LB Off peak **MEALS:** Lunch £11.95 Dinner £16.50-£21 English & French Cuisine V meals Coffee am **FACILITIES:** CTV in all bedrooms STV Xmas **CONF:** Thtr 120 Class 50 Board 50 Del from £90 * **SERVICES:** 70P **NOTES:** No smoking in restaurant Last d 9pm **CARDS:**

See advert under YORK

PICKERING North Yorkshire — Map 08 SE78

★★ White Swan

Market Place YO18 7AA
Quality Percentage Score: 68%
☎ 01751 472288 01751 472288
Dir: *in the market place between the Church and the Steam Railway Station*

A historic old inn in the centre of this attractive Yorkshire market town, the White Swan combines traditional character with the best of modern hotel-keeping. Bedrooms are particularly appealing and comfortable, and the restaurant provides an interesting carte, with a range of enjoyable dishes to choose from, well complemented by a wine list with an excellent selection of Bordeaux from St Emilion. The bar also serves good food.

ROOMS: 12 en suite (bth/shr) (3 fmly) No smoking in all bedrooms s £50-£55; d £80-£90 (incl. bkfst) * LB Off peak **MEALS:** Lunch £8.95-£10.95alc Dinner £14.20-£26.90alc Modern European Cuisine V meals Coffee am **FACILITIES:** CTV in all bedrooms Jacuzzi/spa Motorised Treasure hunt Mountain bike hire Horseriding Golf Micro-Lyte Xmas **CONF:** Thtr 15 Class 12 Board 20 **SERVICES:** 35P **NOTES:** No coaches No smoking in restaurant Last d 9.30pm **CARDS:**

PICKHILL North Yorkshire — Map 08 SE38

★★ Nags Head Country Inn

YO7 4JG
Quality Percentage Score: 66%
☎ 01845 567391 & 567570 01845 567212
Dir: *6m SE of Leeming Bar, 1.25m E of A1*

Convenient for the A1, this country inn offers an extensive range of food either in the bar or the restaurant. It is owned and run by brothers Raymond and Edward Boynton, and service is friendly and attentive. The bars are full of character and include an extensive collection of ties. Bedrooms are well equipped and modern.

ROOMS: 8 en suite (bth/shr) 7 annexe en suite (bth/shr) s £40; d £60 (incl. bkfst) * LB Off peak **MEALS:** Lunch £10-£20alc Dinner £10-£25alc International Cuisine V meals Coffee am Tea pm **FACILITIES:** CTV in all bedrooms Horse-racing Putting Green ch fac **CONF:** Thtr 36 Class 18 Board 24 Del from £60 * **SERVICES:** 50P **NOTES:** No smoking in restaurant Last d 10pm **CARDS:**

PLYMOUTH Devon — Map 02 SX45

see also **St Mellion**

★★★★ Copthorne Plymouth

MILLENNIUM HOTELS AND RESORTS

Armada Way PL1 1AR
Quality Percentage Score: 64%
☎ 01752 224161 01752 670688
Dir: *from M5, follow A38 to Plymouth city centre. Follow continental ferryport signs over 3 rdbts. Hotel visible on first exit left before 4th rdbt*

This modern, centrally-located hotel provides well equipped bedrooms. Public areas, which are divided over two floors, include a choice of restaurants, a modern leisure complex and a *contd.*

wide range of function rooms. The hotel has an arrangement with an adjacent multi-storey car park.
ROOMS: 135 en suite (bth/shr) (29 fmly) No smoking in 38 bedrooms s £75-£115; d £90-£130 * LB Off peak **MEALS:** Lunch £15 Dinner £18.50 & alc International Cuisine V meals Coffee am Tea pm **FACILITIES:** CTV in all bedrooms STV Indoor swimming pool (heated) Gym Steam room **CONF:** Thtr 140 Class 60 Board 60 Del £130 * **SERVICES:** Lift Night porter 50P **NOTES:** No smoking area in restaurant Last d 10pm **CARDS:**

PLYMOUTH Devon **Map 02 SX45**
★★★★ *Plymouth Hoe Moat House*
Armada Way PL1 2HJ
Quality Percentage Score: 61%
☎ 01752 639988 01752 673816
Dir: *A374 city centre then follow signs for Barbican & Hoe B3240*

MOAT HOUSE

Overlooking The Hoe and out to Plymouth Sound, this modern, high-rise hotel offers extensive facilities, including a leisure club and conference and function rooms. Most bedrooms are very spacious, sea-facing rooms are the most popular. Panoramic views of the city can be enjoyed from the restaurant and bar on the 11th floor.
ROOMS: 206 en suite (bth/shr) (99 fmly) **MEALS:** International Cuisine V meals Coffee am Tea pm **FACILITIES:** CTV in all bedrooms STV Indoor swimming pool (heated) Sauna Solarium Gym Pool table Steam room **CONF:** Thtr 500 Class 240 Board 80 Del from £136 * **SERVICES:** Lift Night porter Air conditioning 180P **NOTES:** No dogs (ex guide dogs) No smoking in restaurant Last d 10.15pm
CARDS:

PLYMOUTH Devon **Map 02 SX45**
★★★ Kitley House Hotel
Yealmpton PL8 2NW
Quality Percentage Score: 73%
☎ 01752 881555 01752 881667

A mile long tree-lined drive leads to this fine Grade I Tudor-revival house built of Devonshire granite, set in 300 acres of peaceful wooded parkland along the Yealm estuary. Large bedrooms and suites are traditionally furnished to a high standard. The impressive entrance boasts a grand piano. Other public rooms include a striking book-lined dining room and a cosy bar.
ROOMS: 20 en suite (bth/shr) (8 fmly) s £65-£95; d £80-£110 (incl. bkfst) * LB Off peak **MEALS:** Lunch £9.50-£12.50 High tea £6.95 Dinner £19.50 & alc V meals Coffee am Tea pm **FACILITIES:** CTV in all bedrooms Fishing Gym Croquet lawn Xmas **CONF:** Thtr 100 Class 80 Board 40 Del from £95 * **SERVICES:** Night porter 100P **NOTES:** No smoking in restaurant Last d 9.30pm
CARDS:

See advert on this page

PLYMOUTH Devon **Map 02 SX45**

★★★ New Continental

Millbay Rd PL1 3LD
Quality Percentage Score: 70%
☎ 01752 220782 🖷 01752 227013
Dir: *from the city centre follow signs for the Pavilions which are adjacent to hotel*
Within easy reach of the town centre and the Hoe, this privately owned hotel offers high standards of service and hospitality. There is a leisure centre and a choice of restaurants, and bedrooms vary in size and style.
ROOMS: 99 en suite (bth/shr) (20 fmly) No smoking in 28 bedrooms s £58-£80; d £73-£160 (incl. bkfst) * LB Off peak **MEALS:** English, French & Greek Cuisine V meals Coffee am Tea pm **FACILITIES:** CTV in all bedrooms STV Indoor swimming pool (heated) Sauna Solarium Gym Steam Room Beautician **CONF:** Thtr 400 Class 100 Board 70 Del from £65 * **SERVICES:** Lift Night porter 100P **NOTES:** Closed 24 Dec-2 Jan
CARDS:

See advert on opposite page

PLYMOUTH Devon **Map 02 SX45**

★★★❀❀ Duke of Cornwall

Millbay Rd PL1 3LG
Quality Percentage Score: 69%
☎ 01752 266256 🖷 01752 600062
Dir: *follow signs to city centre then to Plymouth Pavilions Conference & Leisure Centre which leads you past hotel*

The distinctive façade of this Grande Dame of Victorian hotels graces the Plymouth skyline. Guests will be charmed by such original features as the GWR carriage lamps that adorn many of the bedrooms, all of which are individual in style. Reception rooms include a number of small meeting rooms and an elegant restaurant.
ROOMS: 72 en suite (bth/shr) (6 fmly) No smoking in 20 bedrooms s £79.50-£84.50; d £94.50-£150 (incl. bkfst) * LB Off peak **MEALS:** Lunch £12.95-£16.50alc English & French Cuisine V meals Coffee am Tea pm **FACILITIES:** CTV in all bedrooms Games room Xmas **CONF:** Thtr 300 Class 125 Board 84 Del from £55 * **SERVICES:** Lift Night porter 50P **NOTES:** No smoking in restaurant
CARDS:

PLYMOUTH Devon **Map 02 SX45**

★★★❀ *Boringdon Hall*

Colebrook, Plympton PL7 4DP
Quality Percentage Score: 68%
☎ 01752 344455 🖷 01752 346578
Dir: *A38 at Marsh Mills rdbt follow signs for Plympton along dual carriageway to small island turn left over bridge and follow brown tourist signs*
Set in 10 acres of grounds, this historic, listed property is only 6 miles from the city centre. Most of the comfortable bedrooms are set round a central courtyard, and some have four-poster beds. Meals are served in the Gallery Restaurant, overlooking the Great Hall.

ROOMS: 41 en suite (bth/shr) (5 fmly) No smoking in 16 bedrooms **MEALS:** English & French Cuisine V meals Coffee am Tea pm **FACILITIES:** CTV in all bedrooms STV Indoor swimming pool (heated) Tennis (hard) Sauna Gym pitch & putt 9 hole **CONF:** Thtr 120 Class 40 Board 50 **SERVICES:** Night porter 200P **NOTES:** No smoking in restaurant Last d 9.30pm **CARDS:**

PLYMOUTH Devon **Map 02 SX45**

★★★ *Grand*

Elliot St, The Hoe PL1 2PT
Quality Percentage Score: 66%
☎ 01752 661195 🖷 01752 600653
Dir: *A38 to city centre, turn left at "Barbican" sign, follow road until 3rd set traffic lights, turn left, over crossroads, hotel is at top on right*
Spectacular views over the Hoe and Plymouth Sound are an attractive feature of the Grand. Spacious public areas include a restaurant, bar and small lounge. Front-facing bedrooms are always in high demand, and some have balconies.

ROOMS: 77 en suite (bth/shr) (6 fmly) No smoking in 45 bedrooms **MEALS:** International Cuisine V meals Coffee am Tea pm **FACILITIES:** CTV in all bedrooms STV Wkly live entertainment **CONF:** Thtr 70 Class 35 Board 30 Del from £75 * **SERVICES:** Lift Night porter 70P **NOTES:** No smoking in restaurant Last d 9.45pm
CARDS:

See advert on opposite page

PLYMOUTH Devon **Map 02 SX45**

★★★ *Posthouse Plymouth*

Cliff Rd, The Hoe PL1 3DL
Quality Percentage Score: 66%
☎ 01752 662828 🖷 01752 660974
Dir: *turn off A38 at Plymouth follow signs for City Centre, then follow signs for Hoe, the Hotel is situated on Cliff Road West Hoe*
This purpose built hotel, which commands superb views over Plymouth Sound, is equally suited to business and leisure travellers. The bedrooms are comfortable and well equipped.

contd. on p. 518

New Continental HOTEL

★★★ AA

Plymouth's largest independent hotel

The New Continental, Plymouth's largest independent hotel, is situated in the City Centre adjacent to the Plymouth Pavilion Conference Centre and close to the Theatre Royal, Barbican and historic Plymouth Hoe.

99 beautifully appointed bedrooms, all with private bathroom, offer some of the finest accommodation available within Plymouth today. Take advantage of our superb indoor Leisure Club with its heated swimming pool, sauna, solarium, steam room and fully equipped gymnasium. Then relax and enjoy service and cuisine of the highest standards in the new refurbished Executive Restaurant, alternatively a light healthy snack in the Cafe Continental may be the order of the day or unwind in the Regency bar, in a word it's choice that we provide.

- **Conference facilities for 4-400** • **Free coach and car parking on site**
- **Children under 12 free (B&B basis when sharing with 2 adults)**
- **Short breaks available on request**

MILLBAY ROAD · PLYMOUTH · DEVON · PL1 3LD
Telephone: (01752) 220782 · Fax: (01752) 227013
Email: newconti@aol.com

MANAGED BY MACDONALD HOTELS

GIVE YOURSELF A BREAK

Relax in this elegant Victorian hotel, situated in an unrivalled location on Plymouth Hoe with magnificent seaviews over the Sound.

◆ 77 bedrooms from executive rooms to balcony suites ◆ Saturday night supper dances ◆ Weekend breaks available on DB&B or B&B ◆ Children stay FREE when sharing a room with two adults

A comfortable base to explore Dartmoor, South Devon's Scenic Coastline and Cornwall

The Grand Hotel

Elliot Street, The Hoe, Plymouth PL1 2PT
info@plymouthgrand.macdonald-hotels.co.uk
www.macdonaldhotels.co.uk/grand-hotel/

Tel: 01752 661195 Fax: 01752 600653

★★★

A Grade I Listed Elizabethan Manor House tastefully restored to its former glory set on the edge of Dartmoor close to the A38.

All year round leisure breaks in a place of tranquil calm away from the world of hustle and bustle. Unwind in our Leisure Club including indoor heated swimming pool, sauna, tennis court and 9 hole pitch and putt course. 40 luxury bedrooms standing around a courtyard including four traditional 4-poster rooms and family rooms. Gallery Restaurant serving the finest quality fresh food overlooking the magnificent Great Hall Bar. Conference and banqueting rooms with natural daylight for up to 120 delegates. Car parking for over 200 cars.

BORINGDON HALL HOTEL

Colebrook, Plympton, Devon PL7 4DP
Tel: 01752 344455 Fax: 01752 346578

★★★

Lounge service is available throughout the day, and dinner is served in the Mayflower Restaurant.
ROOMS: 106 en suite (bth/shr) No smoking in 65 bedrooms
MEALS: International Cuisine V meals Coffee am Tea pm
FACILITIES: CTV in all bedrooms Outdoor swimming pool (heated) Pool table Childrens play area **CONF:** Thtr 90 Class 60 Board 40
SERVICES: Lift Night porter 149P **NOTES:** No smoking area in restaurant Last d 9.45pm **CARDS:**

PLYMOUTH Devon **Map 02 SX45**
★★★ Novotel
Marsh Mills PL6 8NH
Quality Percentage Score: 64%
☎ 01752 221422 01752 223922
Dir: *take 1st exit off A38 Plymouth/Kingsbridge, onto Marsh Mills rdbt, follow signs for Plympton the Hotel is straight ahead*
Conveniently located on the outskirts of the city, this modern hotel offers good value accommodation suited to business and leisure guests. All rooms are spacious and adapted for family use. Public areas are open-plan and meals are available throughout the day in either the Garden Brasserie, the bar, or from room service. There is a heated outdoor swimming pool.
ROOMS: 100 en suite (bth/shr) (15 fmly) No smoking in 50 bedrooms d £59-£65 * LB Off peak **MEALS:** Lunch £15 & alc High tea £3.75 Dinner £15.50 & alc French Cuisine V meals Coffee am Tea pm
FACILITIES: CTV in all bedrooms STV Outdoor swimming pool (heated) ch fac Xmas **CONF:** Thtr 300 Class 120 Board 100 Del from £65 *
SERVICES: Lift Night porter 140P **NOTES:** No smoking area in restaurant Last d Midnight **CARDS:**

PLYMOUTH Devon **Map 02 SX45**
★★ *Invicta*
11-12 Osborne Place, Lockyer St, The Hoe PL1 2PU
Quality Percentage Score: 69%
☎ 01752 664997 01752 664994
Dir: *approaching Plymouth, follow signs for City Centre, then look for the HOE park, the hotel is situated opposite the park entrance*
An elegant Victorian building, opposite the famous bowling green, and just a short stroll from the city centre and Barbican. The atmosphere is relaxed and friendly; bedrooms are attractively decorated, and the dining room offers a full menu, with grills a popular feature.
ROOMS: 23 rms (21 bth/shr) (6 fmly) **MEALS:** Mainly grills V meals
FACILITIES: CTV in all bedrooms **CONF:** Thtr 35 Class 40 Board 60
SERVICES: Night porter 10P **NOTES:** No dogs (ex guide dogs) No smoking in restaurant Last d 9pm Closed 24 Dec-3 Jan
CARDS:

PLYMOUTH Devon **Map 02 SX45**
★★ Camelot
5 Elliot St, The Hoe PL1 2PP
Quality Percentage Score: 68%
☎ 01752 221255 & 669667 01752 603660
Dir: *from the A38 follow signs fot the city centre, The Hoe, Citadel Rd and then onto Elliot St*
Standing in easy walking distance of the centre, the Hoe and the Barbican, Camelot offers bedrooms equipped to modern standards. Day rooms include a bar, a separate residents' lounge and a restaurant.
ROOMS: 17 en suite (bth/shr) (4 fmly) s fr £40; d fr £52 (incl. bkfst) * LB Off peak **MEALS:** Lunch fr £13 Dinner fr £13 English & French Cuisine V meals Coffee am Tea pm **FACILITIES:** CTV in all bedrooms
CONF: Thtr 60 Class 40 Board 20 Del from £65 * **NOTES:** No dogs (ex guide dogs) No coaches No smoking in restaurant Last d 8.30pm
CARDS:

PLYMOUTH Devon **Map 02 SX45**
★★ Langdon Court
Down Thomas PL9 0DY
Quality Percentage Score: 68%
☎ 01752 862358 01752 863428
Dir: *follow HMS Cambridge signs from Elburton and brown tourist signs on A379*
Langden Court is set in six acres of woodlands and features an attractive walled garden. It is a Tudor manor where Edward VII is said to have entertained Lillie Langtry. In the restaurant a fixed-price menu is offered, featuring fish straight from the Barbican fish market. The well equipped bedrooms vary from spacious rooms on the first floor to smaller rooms on the second floor.
ROOMS: 18 en suite (bth/shr) (4 fmly) s £39.50-£56 (incl. bkfst) * LB Off peak **MEALS:** Sunday Lunch £10.95-£21 & alc Dinner £16.50-£21 & alc International Cuisine V meals Coffee am Tea pm **FACILITIES:** CTV in all bedrooms **CONF:** Thtr 30 Class 15 Board 15 Del from £64 *
SERVICES: 100P **NOTES:** No smoking in restaurant Last d 9.30pm
CARDS:

PLYMOUTH Devon **Map 02 SX45**
★★ *Grosvenor*
9 Elliot St, The Hoe PL1 2PP
Quality Percentage Score: 63%
☎ 01752 260411 01752 668878
Dir: *when approaching city centre turn left marked "Barbican", follow this road until the Walrus Pub, turn left, go over crossroads, hotel is on the left*
Converted from two adjoining Victorian buildings, the Grosvenor offers easy access to the city centre, the Hoe and the Barbican. Staff provide friendly service and meals are served in a smart modern bistro.
ROOMS: 28 en suite (bth/shr) (2 fmly) **MEALS:** V meals
FACILITIES: CTV in all bedrooms STV **SERVICES:** 3P **NOTES:** No coaches Last d 8.30pm Closed 24 Dec-1 Jan
CARDS:

PLYMOUTH Devon **Map 02 SX45**
★★★ Strathmore
Elliot St, The Hoe PL1 2PR
Quality Percentage Score: 58%
☎ 01752 662101 01752 223690
Dir: *off A38 at Marsh Mills and head for city centre, when you come to Exeter St, follow signs to the 'HOE', hotel is at end opposite the 'Grand Hotel'*
The city centre and The Hoe are in easy walking distance of this hotel. Bedrooms come in a variety of shapes and sizes, but all are equipped to a similar standard. The smartly decorated restaurant offers a sensible menu, often featuring locally caught fish.
ROOMS: 54 en suite (bth/shr) (6 fmly) s £35-£40; d £47-£52 (incl. bkfst) * Off peak **MEALS:** Dinner fr £12.50 English & Continental Cuisine V meals Coffee am **FACILITIES:** CTV in all bedrooms STV **CONF:** Thtr 60 Class 40 Board 20 Del from £56 * **SERVICES:** Lift Night porter
NOTES: Last d 9pm **CARDS:**

PLYMOUTH Devon **Map 02 SX45**
★ Victoria Court
62/64 North Rd East PL4 6AL
Quality Percentage Score: 70%
☎ 01752 668133 01752 668133
Dir: *from A38 follow signs for city centre, past railway station follow North Road East for approx 200yds hotel on left*
Situated in walking distance of the centre, this family-run hotel offers comfortable accommodation. The public areas retain much of the Victorian character of the building, and include an

contd.

attractive lounge, bar and dining area. The attractively decorated bedrooms are well maintained with modern facilities.
ROOMS: 13 en suite (shr) (4 fmly) s £37-£42; d £49-£52 (incl. bkfst) * LB Off peak **MEALS:** Dinner £14.50 European Cuisine V meals Coffee am Tea pm **FACILITIES:** CTV in all bedrooms **SERVICES:** 6P **NOTES:** No dogs No coaches Last d 7pm Closed 22 Dec-1 Jan
CARDS:

PLYMOUTH Devon **Map 02 SX45**
★ Imperial
Lockyer St, The Hoe PL1 2QD
Quality Percentage Score: 68%
☎ 01752 227311 Fax 01752 674986
Dir: *in city centre*
Close to the city centre, this Grade II listed hotel is suitable for both commercial and leisure travellers. The Jones family offer old fashioned hospitality in a friendly and convivial atmosphere. Guests can relax in either the cosy bar or TV lounge, both before and after sampling a menu offering a varied selection of dishes.
ROOMS: 23 rms (17 bth/shr) (4 fmly) s £35-£46; d £48-£59 (incl. bkfst) * LB Off peak **MEALS:** Dinner £12 & alc V meals Coffee am Tea pm **FACILITIES:** CTV in all bedrooms **CONF:** Thtr 25 Class 25 Board 16 **SERVICES:** 14P **NOTES:** No dogs (ex guide dogs) No smoking area in restaurant Last d 8.15pm Closed 25-31 Dec
CARDS:

PLYMOUTH Devon **Map 02 SX45**
★ Grosvenor Park
114-116 North Rd East PL4 6AH
Quality Percentage Score: 67%
☎ 01752 229312 Fax 01752 252777
Dir: *first hotel on exiting Plymouth Station, approx 150yds from the main entrance*
In a quiet area of Plymouth, Grosvenor Park Hotel is convenient for both the city centre and the railway station. Public areas comprise a comfortable lounge, separate bar and dining room where a range of popular dishes is on offer.
ROOMS: 14 rms (11 shr) (1 fmly) No smoking in 3 bedrooms s £22-£33; d £44 (incl. bkfst) * Off peak **MEALS:** Lunch fr £5alc High tea fr £5alc Dinner fr £5alc International Cuisine V meals Coffee am Tea pm **FACILITIES:** CTV in all bedrooms STV **SERVICES:** 6P **NOTES:** No dogs (ex guide dogs) No smoking in restaurant Last d 8pm
CARDS:

PLYMOUTH Devon **Map 02 SX45**
★ Drake
1 & 2 Windsor Villas, Lockyer St, The Hoe PL1 2QD
Quality Percentage Score: 64%
☎ 01752 229730 Fax 01752 255092
Dir: *follow City Centre signs, left at Theatre Royal, last left, first right*
Two adjoining Victorian houses have been linked to form this family run hotel. Bedrooms are well equipped, and public areas offer a lounge, bar and spacious dining room, where there is a choice of times for evening meals which should be pre-arranged when booking.
ROOMS: 35 rms (30 bth/shr) (3 fmly) s £34-£42; d £46-£52 (incl. bkfst) * LB Off peak **MEALS:** Lunch £12-£15 Dinner £12-£15 European Cuisine V meals Coffee am **FACILITIES:** CTV in all bedrooms **SERVICES:** Night porter 25P **NOTES:** No dogs (ex guide dogs) No smoking area in restaurant Last d 9pm Closed 24 Dec-3 Jan
CARDS:

PLYMOUTH Devon   Map 02 SX45
⌂ **Travel Inn**
300 Plymouth Rd, Crabtree, Marsh Mills PL3 6RW
☎ 01752 600660 📠 01752 600112
Dir: A38 to Marsh Mills rdbt, hotel access off rdbt just before exit signed Cornwall
This modern building offers accommodation in smart, spacious and well equipped bedrooms, all with en-suite bathrooms. Refreshments may be taken at the nearby family restaurant. For details about current prices consult the Contents Page under Hotel Groups for the Travel Inn phone number.
ROOMS: 40 en suite (bth/shr)   d £39.95 *

PLYMOUTH Devon   Map 02 SX45
⌂ **Travel Inn (Plymouth Barbican)**
Lockyers Quay, Coxside PL4 0DX
☎ 01752 254180 📠 01752 663872
Dir: follow A374 into Plymouth from A38 Marsh Mills rdbt. Continue along Gdynia Way and follow signs for Coxside, adjacent t new Barbican car park
This modern building offers accommodation in smart, spacious and well equipped bedrooms, all with en-suite bathrooms. Refreshments may be taken at the nearby family restaurant. For details about current prices consult the Contents Page under Hotel Groups for the Travel Inn phone number.
ROOMS: 40 en suite (bth/shr)   d £39.95 *

PLYMOUTH Devon   Map 02 SX45
○✲ **Hotel Ibis**
Marsh Mills, Longbridge Rd PL6 8LD
☎ 01752 601087 📠 01752 223213
Dir: from Exeter take the A38 towards Plymouth, continue over the fly over take the slip road to the roundabout, the Hotel is on the 4th exit
A nearby bar and bistro restaurant provides refreshments for travellers staying at this modern accommodation building. Bedrooms are well equipped and have en suite bathrooms.
ROOMS: 51 en suite (bth/shr) (5 fmly) No smoking in 25 bedrooms d £39.50 * LB Off peak **MEALS:** French Cuisine V meals Coffee am Tea pm **FACILITIES:** CTV in all bedrooms STV Xmas **CONF:** Thtr 35 Class 18 Board 20 **SERVICES:** 56P **NOTES:** No smoking area in restaurant Last d 10pm **CARDS:** ●● ■■ ⚊ 🖭 🖼 ✈ ▢

POCKLINGTON East Riding of Yorkshire   Map 08 SE84
★★ **Yorkway Motel**
Hull-York Rd YO42 2NX
Quality Percentage Score: 65%
☎ 01759 303071 📠 01759 305215
Dir: between Beverley & York on the A1079 with the junc of B1247
This family owned and run motel and diner is close to the village of Pocklington and offers value-for-money accommodation. Bedrooms are thoughtfully equipped and public rooms include a bar and cosy dining room, where a good range of food is served all day.
ROOMS: 15 annexe en suite (bth/shr) (6 fmly) d £36-£40 * LB Off peak **MEALS:** Lunch £2.40-£11.25alc High tea fr £1.85alc Dinner £4.85-£17alc V meals Coffee am Tea pm **FACILITIES:** CTV in all bedrooms Pool table **CONF:** Thtr 30 Class 12 Board 16 **SERVICES:** 40P
NOTES: No dogs (ex guide dogs) No smoking in restaurant Last d 9pm
CARDS: ●● ■■ ⚊ 🖭 🖼 ✈ ▢

POCKLINGTON East Riding of Yorkshire   Map 08 SE84
★★ **Feathers**
Market Place YO42 2AH
Quality Percentage Score: 64%
☎ 01759 303155 📠 01759 304382
Dir: from York, take B1246 signposted Pocklington. Hotel just off A1079
A popular inn which has been fully modernised to provide comfortable accommodation, with some bedrooms in a separate nearby building. Public areas are busy and enjoyable meals are served in the bar or in the conservatory restaurant.
ROOMS: 6 en suite (bth/shr) 6 annexe en suite (bth/shr) (1 fmly) d £44.50-£65 * Off peak **MEALS:** Sunday Lunch £9.99 & alc V meals Coffee am Tea pm **FACILITIES:** CTV in all bedrooms **CONF:** Thtr 20 Class 8 Board 12 **SERVICES:** 56P **NOTES:** No dogs (ex guide dogs) No smoking area in restaurant **CARDS:** ●● ■■ ⚊ 🖭 🖼 ✈ ▢

PODIMORE Somerset   Map 03 ST52
⌂ **Travelodge**
BA22 8JG
☎ 01935 840074 📠 01935 840074
Dir: on A303, near junct with A37
This modern building offers accommodation in smart, spacious and well equipped bedrooms, all with en-suite bathrooms. Refreshments may be taken at the nearby family restaurant. For details about current prices, consult the Contents Page under Hotel Groups for the Travelodge phone number.
ROOMS: 31 en suite (bth/shr)   d £45.95 *

POLPERRO Cornwall & Isles of Scilly   Map 02 SX25
★★★⚜ ᪲ **Talland Bay**
PL13 2JB
Quality Percentage Score: 75%
☎ 01503 272667 📠 01503 272940
Dir: Signposted from crossroads on A387 Looe/Polperro road
Dating back to the 16th century, this Cornish stone manor house has a tropical influence, with delightful views over the gardens to the sea beyond. Public areas have been upgraded, while the menu incorporates the finest regional produce, with seafood featuring strongly. Bedrooms are charmingly furnished and decorated, each having its own character; several are located in cottages in the garden.
ROOMS: 16 en suite (bth/shr) 3 annexe en suite (bth) (2 fmly) s £67-£96; d £134-£192 (incl. bkfst & dinner) * LB Off peak **MEALS:** Bar Lunch £10-£16.50alc High tea £1.75-£8.50alc Dinner £22-£27 & alc English & French Cuisine V meals Coffee am Tea pm **FACILITIES:** CTV in all bedrooms Outdoor swimming pool (heated) Sauna Pool table Croquet lawn Putting green Games room Xmas **CONF:** Thtr 30 Board 30 Del from £70 * **SERVICES:** 20P **NOTES:** No coaches No smoking in restaurant Last d 9pm Closed 2 Jan-late Feb
CARDS: ●● ■■ ⚊ 🖭 🖼 ▢

POLPERRO Cornwall & Isles of Scilly   Map 02 SX25
★ **Claremont**
The Coombes PL13 2RG
Quality Percentage Score: 69%
☎ 01503 272241 📠 01503 272241
Dir: on Polperro's main street
This small, intimate hotel lies in the picturesque village of Polperro. There is an à la carte menu with various interesting, home made dishes served in the bistro style restaurant and a small comfortable lounge and bar. The bedrooms vary in size and style and offer modern amenities and facilities.
ROOMS: 12 en suite (bth/shr) (2 fmly) **MEALS:** V meals Coffee am Tea pm **FACILITIES:** CTV in all bedrooms STV **SERVICES:** 16P **NOTES:** No coaches No smoking in restaurant RS Oct-Mar
CARDS: ●● ■■ ⚊ ✈ ▢

New AA Guides for the Millennium are featured on page 24

contd.

POLZEATH Cornwall & Isles of Scilly **Map 02 SW97**

★★❀❀ ***The Cornish Cottage Hotel & Restaurant***

New Polzeath PL27 6UF

Quality Percentage Score: 73%

☎ 01208 862213 🖷 01208 862259

Dir: *off B3314*

A warm welcome is assured at this cosy hotel. The kitchen is at the heart of this establishment, using the very best of local ingredients. The bedrooms are all well equipped and range from cottage-style rooms in the original building to more recent purpose-built accommodation. There are spacious lounge areas, a conservatory, and a cosy bar.

ROOMS: 13 en suite (bth/shr) **MEALS:** English & French Cuisine V meals Coffee am Tea pm **FACILITIES:** CTV in 14 bedrooms Outdoor swimming pool (heated) **SERVICES:** 20P **NOTES:** No dogs No coaches No children 16yrs No smoking in restaurant Last d 9pm

CARDS:

PONTEFRACT West Yorkshire **Map 08 SE42**

★★★ **Rogerthorpe Manor Hotel**

Thorpe Ln, Badsworth WF9 1AB

Quality Percentage Score: 65%

☎ 01977 643839 🖷 01977 641571

Dir: *take A639 S from Pontefract, in approx 3m turn right at Fox & Hounds PH, Rogerthorpe Manor 1m on left*

Today a comfortable, friendly hotel, Rogerthorpe Manor has a long, interesting history. It provides well equipped bedrooms, ample lounges, and a popular Jacobean bar serving real ale and good bar food. The hotel caters well for weddings and other functions.

ROOMS: 14 en suite (bth/shr) (2 fmly) s £75-£95; d £90-£110 (incl. bkfst) * LB Off peak **MEALS:** Lunch £14.95-£20.95alc High tea £5.25-£9.95 Dinner £14.95-£20.95alc English & French Cuisine V meals Coffee am Tea pm **FACILITIES:** CTV in all bedrooms STV Croquet lawn Xmas **CONF:** Thtr 150 Class 60 Board 50 Del from £95 * **SERVICES:** 90P **NOTES:** No dogs (ex guide dogs) No smoking in restaurant Last d 9pm

CARDS:

PONTEFRACT West Yorkshire **Map 08 SE42**

Travel Inn

Knottingley, Knottingley Rd WF11 0BU

☎ 01977 607946 🖷 01977 607954

Dir: *on A645, close to A1/M62 intersection & adjacent to A1 Business Park*

This modern building offers accommodation in smart, spacious and well equipped bedrooms, all with en-suite bathrooms. Refreshments may be taken at the nearby family restaurant. For details about current prices consult the Contents Page under Hotel Groups for the Travel Inn phone number.

ROOMS: 40 en suite (bth/shr) d £39.95 *

POOLE Dorset **Map 04 SZ09**

★★★★❀❀ **Haven**

Banks Rd, Sandbanks BH13 7QL

Quality Percentage Score: 76%

☎ 01202 707333 🖷 01202 708796

Dir: *take the B3965 towards Poole Bay and turn left onto the Peninsula. Hotel 1.5m on left next to the Swanage Toll Ferry point*

Overlooking Poole Bay, this attractive hotel has enviable views. There are ample lounges, a waterside restaurant and a brasserie. The bedrooms vary in style and size, and some have sea views. The main restaurant serves skilfullly prepared dishes and lighter meals are available in the conservatory.

ROOMS: 94 en suite (bth/shr) (4 fmly) s £78-£130; d £156-£260 (incl. bkfst) LB Off peak **MEALS:** Lunch fr £15 Dinner fr £24.50 & alc English & French Cuisine V meals Coffee am Tea pm **FACILITIES:** CTV in all bedrooms STV Indoor swimming pool (heated) Outdoor swimming pool (heated) Tennis (hard) Squash Sauna Solarium Gym Jacuzzi/spa Steam room Spa pool Hair and Beauty salon Xmas **CONF:** Thtr 150 Class 40 Board 25 Del from £125 * **SERVICES:** Lift Night porter 150P **NOTES:** No dogs (ex guide dogs) No coaches No smoking in restaurant Last d 9.15pm Closed 30 Dec-4 Jan

CARDS:

See advert under BOURNEMOUTH

POOLE Dorset **Map 04 SZ09**

★★★★ ***Thistle Poole***

The Quay BH15 1HD

Quality Percentage Score: 64%

☎ 01202 666800 🖷 01202 684470

Dir: *take A350 into Poole town centre, hotel signposted from here approx 0.50m*

This modern hotel enjoys uninterrupted views across the large natural harbour to the Purbeck Hills. The smart accommodation has been refurbished to a high standard with thoughtfully laid out bedrooms. Some of the public areas are located on the first floor and include a pleasant cocktail bar and a restaurant with a panoramic view.

ROOMS: 68 en suite (bth/shr) No smoking in 22 bedrooms **MEALS:** French Cuisine V meals Coffee am Tea pm **FACILITIES:** CTV in all bedrooms STV Wkly live entertainment **CONF:** Thtr 60 Class 20 Board 30 **SERVICES:** Lift Night porter 150P **NOTES:** No smoking area in restaurant Last d 10pm **CARDS:**

POOLE Dorset **Map 04 SZ09**

★★★❀❀ **Salterns**

38 Salterns Way, Lilliput BH14 8JR

Quality Percentage Score: 80%

☎ 01202 707321 🖷 01202 707488

Dir: *in Poole follow B3369 Sandbanks road. In 1m at Lilliput shops turn into Salterns Way by Barclays Bank*

Situated beside its own marina and enjoying views across to Brownsea Island, this hotel has an enviable repuation. The

contd.

bedrooms are mostly spacious and comfortably furnished. In the restaurant an interesting menu makes good use of local game and fish, there is also a bistro.
ROOMS: 20 en suite (bth/shr) (4 fmly) No smoking in 3 bedrooms s £73-£86; d £92-£120 * LB Off peak **MEALS:** Lunch £14.50-£20 & alc Dinner £19-£25 & alc English & French Cuisine V meals Coffee am **FACILITIES:** CTV in all bedrooms STV Fishing Leisure facilities available at sister hotel Xmas **CONF:** Thtr 100 Class 50 Board 50 Del from £110 * **SERVICES:** Night porter 300P **NOTES:** No coaches No smoking area in restaurant Last d 9.30pm **CARDS:**

See advert on opposite page

POOLE Dorset — Map 04 SZ09
★★★ Mansion House
Thames St BH15 1JN
Quality Percentage Score: 78%
☎ 01202 685666 📠 01202 665709
Dir: *A31 to Poole, follow signs to channel ferry, turn onto Poole quay, take first left (St James St), hotel is opposite church*

Tucked away off the Old Quay, this sophisticated hotel provides individually designed bedrooms and pleasant public areas that include a flagstoned entrance and a quiet drawing room. The comfortable restaurant and the bistro serve enjoyably honest British food.
ROOMS: 32 en suite (bth/shr) (2 fmly) No smoking in 4 bedrooms s £80-£85; d £115-£125 (incl. bkfst) * LB Off peak **MEALS:** Lunch £14.25-£16.50 Dinner £23.50-£27 English & French Cuisine V meals Coffee am Tea pm **FACILITIES:** CTV in all bedrooms STV All facilities available locally Watersports Xmas **CONF:** Thtr 40 Class 18 Board 20 Del from £115 * **SERVICES:** Night porter 46P **NOTES:** No dogs No coaches No smoking area in restaurant Last d 9.30pm
CARDS:

POOLE Dorset — Map 04 SZ09
★★★ Sandbanks
15 Banks Rd, Sandbanks BH13 7PS
Quality Percentage Score: 74%
☎ 01202 707377 📠 01202 708885
Dir: *follow A338 from Bournemouth onto Wessex Way to Liverpool Victoria rdbt. Keep left & take 2nd exit - B3965 to Sandbanks Bay. Hotel on left*
Popular with both leisure and business guests, this large hotel has beach access and superb views across Poole Harbour. In addition to the main restaurant, a brasserie serves an imaginative selection of dishes. Many of the well equipped bedrooms have balconies.

ROOMS: 113 en suite (bth/shr) (30 fmly) No smoking in 22 bedrooms s £66-£103; d £132-£206 (incl. bkfst & dinner) * LB Off peak **MEALS:** Lunch £9.50-£14.50 High tea £2.50-£5 Dinner £12.50-£18.50 & alc International Cuisine V meals Coffee am Tea pm **FACILITIES:** CTV in all bedrooms STV Indoor swimming pool (heated) Sauna Solarium Gym Pool table Putting green Jacuzzi/spa Hobie Cat Sailing Mountain bike hire Indoor children's play area Wkly live entertainment ch fac Xmas **CONF:** Thtr 150 Class 40 Board 25 Del from £85.80 * **SERVICES:** Lift Night porter 200P **NOTES:** No dogs (ex guide dogs) No smoking in restaurant Last d 9pm Closed 30 Dec-4 Jan
CARDS:

See advert under BOURNEMOUTH

POOLE Dorset — Map 04 SZ09
★★★ Harbour Heights
73 Haven Rd, Sandbanks BH13 7LW
Quality Percentage Score: 65%
☎ 01202 707272 📠 01202 708594
Dir: *from M27 to Ringwood, follow signs to Poole and then to Sandbanks*
This pleasant hotel, with magnificent views of Brownsea Island and Studland Bay, caters admirably for its mix of business and leisure guests. The bedrooms are smartly furnished and comfortable and most have sea views. There is a choice of menus in the two popular restaurants.
ROOMS: 48 en suite (bth/shr) (5 fmly) s fr £48; d fr £80 (incl. bkfst) * LB Off peak **MEALS:** Lunch fr £11.50 Dinner fr £16.50 & alc English, French, Italian & Oriental Cuisine V meals Coffee am Tea pm **FACILITIES:** CTV in all bedrooms STV ch fac **SERVICES:** Lift Night porter 84P **NOTES:** No smoking area in restaurant Last d 9.30pm Closed 24 Dec-8 Jan **CARDS:**

POOLE Dorset — Map 04 SZ09
★★★ Arndale Court
62/66 Wimborne Rd BH15 2BY
Quality Percentage Score: 64%
☎ 01202 683746 📠 01202 668838
Dir: *on th A349 close to Town Centre, opposite Poole Stadium entrance*
Popular with business guests during the week but equally well suited to ferry travellers and leisure guests, this hotel is located

contd.

Indicates that the star classification has not been confirmed under the New Quality Standards, see page 7 for further information.

Remember to return your Prize Draw card for a chance to win one of 30 relaxing leisure breaks with Corus and Regal hotels. See inside the front cover for the card and competition details.

close to the town centre. All the bedrooms are very well equipped. The bright public areas include the restaurant, and the bar.

ROOMS: 39 en suite (bth/shr) (7 fmly) s £61; d £70 (incl. bkfst) * Off peak **MEALS:** Lunch £9.50-£13 Dinner £14 & alc English & French Cuisine V meals Coffee am **FACILITIES:** CTV in all bedrooms STV **CONF:** Thtr 50 Class 35 Board 35 Del from £63 * **SERVICES:** Night porter 32P **NOTES:** No smoking in restaurant Last d 9pm
CARDS:

POOLE Dorset — Map 04 SZ09

★★ *Norfolk Lodge*

1 Flaghead Rd, Canford Cliffs BH13 7JL
Quality Percentage Score: 62%
☎ 01202 708614 & 708661 🖷 01202 708614
Dir: *between Poole & Bournemouth hotel on corner of Haven & Flaghead Rd*

Located in a quiet residential area, the Norfolk Lodge is just a few minutes' walk from the beach. The bedrooms are pleasantly decorated. A short, fixed price menu is offered each evening in the restaurant, overlooking the garden and its aviaries full of exotic birds.

ROOMS: 19 rms (17 bth/shr) (4 fmly) **MEALS:** **FACILITIES:** CTV in all bedrooms ch fac **SERVICES:** 16P **NOTES:** No coaches No smoking in restaurant Last d 8pm **CARDS:**

POOLE Dorset — Map 04 SZ09

Travel Inn

Holes Bay Rd BH15 2BD
☎ 01202 669944 🖷 01202 669954
Dir: *follow Poole Channel Ferry signs, hotel S A35/A349 on A350 dual carriageway*

This modern building offers accommodation in smart, spacious and well equipped bedrooms, all with en-suite bathrooms. Refreshments may be taken at the nearby family restaurant. For details about current prices consult the Contents Page under Hotel Groups for the Travel Inn phone number.

ROOMS: 40 en suite (bth/shr) d £39.95 *

PORLOCK Somerset — Map 03 SS84

★★★ Anchor Hotel & Ship Inn

Porlock Harbour TA24 8PB
Quality Percentage Score: 66%
☎ 01643 862753 🖷 01643 862843
Dir: *From A39 take the B3225 Porlock Weir road. Hotel is located after 1.5 miles in a cul-de-sac*

Situated just yards from the water's edge, this long established family hotel overlooks the harbour. Bedrooms fall into two categories; spacious rooms in the main hotel, and more compact rooms of great character in the adjacent 16th-century Ship Inn. The comfortable public areas, are enhanced by log fires during

contd.

cooler months. Both fixed price and a la carte menus are offered in the Harbour Restaurant, while the Ship Inn provides an extensive range of bar meals.
ROOMS: 14 en suite (bth/shr) 6 annexe en suite (bth/shr) (2 fmly) s £70.75-£82.75; d £117.50-£165.50 (incl. bkfst & dinner) * LB Off peak **MEALS:** Lunch £13.75 Dinner £22.75 & alc English & Continental Cuisine V meals Coffee am Tea pm **FACILITIES:** CTV in all bedrooms Xmas **CONF:** Thtr 20 Board 12 Del from £59.75 * **NOTES:** No smoking in restaurant Last d 9pm RS Jan & Feb **CARDS:**

See advert on opposite page

PORLOCK Somerset **Map 03 SS84**

The Premier Collection

★★ The Oaks
TA24 8ES
☎ 01643 862265 01643 863131
This Edwardian country house offers distant views of Porlock Bay and Exmoor. Bedrooms vary in size and have many thoughtful extras. Public rooms are furnished with period pieces. During the summer, the garden is the perfect place to enjoy a drink before sampling the mouth-watering cooking.
ROOMS: 9 en suite (bth/shr) No smoking in all bedrooms s fr £55; d fr £90 (incl. bkfst) * LB Off peak **MEALS:** Dinner £25 **FACILITIES:** CTV in all bedrooms Xmas **SERVICES:** 12P **NOTES:** No coaches No children 8yrs No smoking in restaurant Last d 8.30pm Closed Nov-Mar (excl. Xmas)
CARDS:

PORT GAVERNE Cornwall & Isles of Scilly **Map 02 SX08**

★★ Port Gaverne
PL29 3SQ
Quality Percentage Score: 70%
☎ 01208 880244 01208 880151
Dir: *signposted from B3314*

Half a mile from the old fishing village of Port Isaac, this hotel is set back from a small cove. It retains the flagged floors, beamed ceilings and steep stairways typical of an old fishing inn, while containing modern facilities in all the rooms. Local produce is used whenever possible to provide interesting menus, including bar meals.
ROOMS: 17 en suite (bth/shr) s fr £51; d fr £102 (incl. bkfst) * LB Off peak **MEALS:** Lunch fr £10.75alc Dinner fr £22.50alc International Cuisine V meals Coffee am **FACILITIES:** CTV in all bedrooms **SERVICES:** 30P **NOTES:** No coaches No smoking in restaurant Last d 9.30pm Closed 5 Jan-11 Feb **CARDS:**

PORT GAVERNE Cornwall & Isles of Scilly **Map 02 SX08**

★★ *Headlands*
PL29 3SH
Quality Percentage Score: 67%
☎ 01208 880260 01208 880885
Dir: *on cliff top, 0.50m E of Port Isaac*

THE CIRCLE
Selected Individual Hotels
GREAT BRITAIN

From its unrivalled position overlooking the tiny cove of Port Gaverne, the Headlands Hotel has spectacular views of the North Cornish coastline, which are enjoyed from the majority of the bedrooms and public areas. In the relaxed restaurant a choice of menus is available, often using fresh local produce. Out of season the hotel is the venue for creative arts courses.
ROOMS: 11 en suite (bth/shr) (1 fmly) **MEALS:** International Cuisine V meals Coffee am Tea pm **FACILITIES:** CTV in all bedrooms Sauna **CONF:** Class 20 Board 12 Del from £65 * **SERVICES:** 40P **NOTES:** No coaches No smoking in restaurant Last d 9.30pm
CARDS:

PORTHLEVEN Cornwall & Isles of Scilly **Map 02 SW62**

Late entry **Tye Rock Country House Hotel**
Loe Bar Rd TR13 9EW
☎ 01326 572695 01326 572695
Built in 1883, this charming cliff-top hideaway is surrounded by National Trust land. The setting is quite magnificent and the spectacular views across Mounts Bay remain long in the memory. Each bedroom is styled according to a specific theme, including African, Spanish and 1920s. Traditional home-cooked cuisine is offered in the dining room, accompanied by occasional sightings of Dolphins in the Bay!
ROOMS: 7 en suite (bth/shr) d £80-£98 (incl. bkfst) * LB Off peak **FACILITIES:** CTV in all bedrooms 3acre cliff top garden **SERVICES:** 16P **NOTES:** No dogs (ex guide dogs) No coaches Closed 2wks in Nov
CARDS:

PORT ISAAC Cornwall & Isles of Scilly **Map 02 SW98**

see also **Port Gaverne**

★★ *Castle Rock*
4 New Rd PL29 3SB
Quality Percentage Score: 68%
☎ 01208 880300 01208 880219
Dir: *from A30 turn off after Launceston onto A395. Turn left at junction with A39 then take first right signposted Port Isaac, follow signs to village*
This friendly hotel is an ideal base for holidaymakers to explore this rugged part of Cornwall. The hotel has comfortable and spacious accommodation with public rooms offering guests marvellous views over the cliffs and sea. There is an extensive choice of skilfully cooked dishes from the carte and daily menus.
ROOMS: 13 en suite (bth/shr) 3 annexe en suite (bth/shr) (1 fmly) **MEALS:** International Cuisine V meals Coffee am Tea pm **FACILITIES:** CTV in all bedrooms ch fac **CONF: SERVICES:** 20P **NOTES:** No dogs (ex guide dogs) No children 5yrs No smoking in restaurant Last d 9.30pm **CARDS:**

See advert on opposite page

PORTLAND Dorset — Map 03 SY67

★★★ Portland Heights

Yeates Corner DT5 2EN

Quality Percentage Score: 69%

☎ 01305 821361 Fax 01305 860081

Dir: *from A354 follow signs for Portland Bill, the hotel is on the summit of the island*

Well known for its fabulous outlook across Chesil Beach and Portland Bay, this popular hotel offers a wide range of leisure facilities, well equipped bedrooms, a restaurant and an all-day coffee shop.

ROOMS: 65 en suite (bth/shr) (8 fmly) No smoking in 2 bedrooms s £64; d £74 (incl. bkfst) * LB Off peak **MEALS:** Lunch £9-£14 High tea fr £2.50 Dinner fr £17.50 International Cuisine V meals Coffee am Tea pm **FACILITIES:** CTV in all bedrooms Outdoor swimming pool (heated) Squash Sauna Solarium Gym Pool table Steam room Games room Xmas **CONF:** Thtr 200 Class 120 Board 80 Del from £75 * **SERVICES:** Night porter 160P **NOTES:** No smoking area in restaurant Last d 9pm **CARDS:**

PORTSCATHO Cornwall & Isles of Scilly — Map 02 SW83

★★★ Rosevine

Porthcurnick Beach TR2 5EW

Quality Percentage Score: 79%

☎ 01872 580206 Fax 01872 580230

Dir: *from St Austell take A390 for Truro and turn left onto B3287 to Tregony. Leave Tregony by A3078 through Ruan High Lanes. Hotel third turning left*

A Georgian country house situated on the Roseland peninsula. Bedrooms are tastefully furnished and well equipped, many enjoying lovely sea views. Extensive public rooms include a choice of lounges and spacious dining room. A heated indoor pool is available with an adjacent paddling pool for children.

ROOMS: 11 en suite (shr) 6 annexe en suite (bth/shr) (7 fmly) s £65-£109; d £130-£180 (incl. bkfst) * LB Off peak **MEALS:** Lunch £10-£25 & alc Dinner £27-£36 V meals Coffee am Tea pm **FACILITIES:** CTV in all bedrooms Indoor swimming pool (heated) Table tennis Childrens playroom ch fac **SERVICES:** 20P **NOTES:** No coaches No smoking in restaurant Last d 8.30pm Closed Nov-11 Feb

CARDS:

See advert under ST MAWES

PORTSCATHO Cornwall & Isles of Scilly — Map 02 SW83

★★★ Roseland House

Rosevine TR2 5EW

Quality Percentage Score: 66%

☎ 01872 580644 Fax 01872 580801

Dir: *A3078 for St Mawes. Pass through Ruan-High-Lanes and signposted after 2m*

Roseland House is successful in attracting many of its guests back each year, due to its natural friendliness and high level of informal yet professional service. The spacious, comfortable

contd.

bedrooms have modern facilities, many personal touches and luxurious bathrooms. Award winning cuisine is served in the elegant restaurant with stunning views over the Roseland Peninsula.

ROOMS: 10 en suite (bth/shr) (2 fmly) No smoking in all bedrooms d fr £92 (incl. bkfst & dinner) * LB Off peak **MEALS:** Lunch fr £12 & alc High tea fr £5 Dinner fr £18.50 English & French Cuisine V meals Coffee am Tea pm **FACILITIES:** CTV in all bedrooms Fishing Private beach with safe bathing ch fac **SERVICES:** 25P **NOTES:** No dogs (ex guide dogs) No coaches No smoking in restaurant Last d 9pm Closed Xmas & New Year **CARDS:**

PORTSCATHO Cornwall & Isles of Scilly **Map 02 SW83**

★★ Gerrans Bay

Gerrans TR2 5ED

Quality Percentage Score: 71%

☎ 01872 580338 📠 01872 580250

Dir: *turn off A3078 at Trewithian follow signs for Gerrans Hotel past church on road to St Anthony Head*

Situated in the beautiful heart of the Roseland Peninsula, the Gerrans Bay Hotel offers comfortable accommodation with modern facilities and carefully cooked dishes using local produce. Guests can relax in the spacious, comfortable lounges and bar, which overlook the well kept gardens.

ROOMS: 13 rms (11 bth/shr) (2 fmly) s £53; d £106 (incl. bkfst & dinner) * LB Off peak **MEALS:** Sunday Lunch £11.95 Dinner £18.50-£25 European Cuisine V meals Coffee am Tea pm **FACILITIES:** CTV in all bedrooms Xmas **SERVICES:** 14P **NOTES:** No coaches No smoking in restaurant Last d 8.15pm Closed Nov-Feb **CARDS:**

PORTSMOUTH & SOUTHSEA Hampshire **Map 04 SZ69**

★★★★ Portsmouth Marriott

North Harbour PO6 4SH

Quality Percentage Score: 65%

☎ 023 92383151 📠 023 92388701

Dir: *from M27 junct 12-keep left, hotel on lef*

This large, busy hotel is on the north side of the city. Well equipped bedrooms offer a high standard of comfort. Open plan public areas include a modern bar and restaurant, shop and extensive leisure facilities.

ROOMS: 172 en suite (bth/shr) (76 fmly) No smoking in 122 bedrooms s £79-£119; d £79-£139 * LB Off peak **MEALS:** Lunch fr £19.95 & alc Dinner fr £19.95 & alc English & French Cuisine V meals Coffee am Tea pm **FACILITIES:** CTV in all bedrooms STV Indoor swimming pool (heated) Sauna Solarium Gym Jacuzzi/spa New Health Club available Xmas **CONF:** Thtr 350 Class 180 Board 36 Del from £125 * **SERVICES:** Lift Night porter Air conditioning 300P **NOTES:** No smoking area in restaurant Last d 10.30pm **CARDS:**

PORTSMOUTH & SOUTHSEA Hampshire **Map 04 SZ69**

★★★ Queen's Hotel

Clarence Pde PO5 3LJ

Quality Percentage Score: 66%

☎ 023 92822466 📠 023 9282190

Dir: *from M27 take junct 12 onto M275 and follow signs for Southsea seafront. Hotel is located opp. Hovercraft terminal*

This elegant Edwardian hotel has dominated the Southsea seafront for over 100 years, and enjoys magnificent views over the Solent and Isle of Wight. The bedrooms are smartly decorated and well equipped; there are family rooms available and many have sea views. The restaurant offers a selection of menus, and overlooks the garden and pool. There are two comfortable bars and a members nightclub.

ROOMS: 73 en suite (bth/shr) (3 fmly) No smoking in 51 bedrooms s £50-£85; d £65-£95 (incl. bkfst) * LB Off peak **MEALS:** Lunch £12.75-£14.75 & alc Dinner fr £17.75 & alc English & French Cuisine V meals Coffee am Tea pm **FACILITIES:** CTV in all bedrooms STV Outdoor swimming pool (heated) Private garden Xmas **CONF:** Thtr 150 Class 120 Del from £79.50 * **SERVICES:** Lift Night porter 70P **NOTES:** No dogs (ex guide dogs) No smoking area in restaurant Last d 9.30pm

CARDS:

See advert on opposite page

PORTSMOUTH & SOUTHSEA Hampshire **Map 04 SZ69**

★★★ Innlodge Hotel

Burrfields Rd PO3 5HH

Quality Percentage Score: 65%

☎ 023 92650510 📠 023 92693458

Dir: *from A3(M) & M27 follow A27, take Southsea exit and follow A2030. At 3rd set of traffic lights. Turn right into Burrfields Rd-hotel 2nd car-park on*

Situated on the eastern fringe of the city, the hotel is ideally placed for all major routes. The spacious bedrooms are modern in style, comfortable and well appointed. Guests are offered a choice of two eating options: the Farmhouse Inn or the American-style Beiderbecks restaurant and bar.

ROOMS: 73 en suite (bth/shr) (10 fmly) No smoking in 9 bedrooms d £49.95-£59.95 * LB Off peak **MEALS:** Sunday Lunch £9.95-£18 Dinner £13-£18 English, American & Mexican Cuisine V meals Coffee am Tea pm **FACILITIES:** CTV in all bedrooms STV Golf 18 Pool table Indoor & outdoor children's play area Wkly live entertainment Xmas **CONF:** Thtr 150 Class 72 Board 40 Del from £80 * **SERVICES:** Night porter 200P **NOTES:** No dogs (ex guide dogs) No smoking area in restaurant Last d 10.30pm **CARDS:**

PORTSMOUTH & SOUTHSEA Hampshire **Map 04 SZ69**

★★★ Royal Beach

South Pde PO4 0RN

Quality Percentage Score: 63%

☎ 023 92731281 📠 023 92817572

Dir: *follow M27 to M275, then follow signs to seafront, hotel is situated on seafront*

This well established hotel occupies a prime seafront location directly opposite Southsea Pier. Bedrooms are well equipped, most are spacious, and many have views across the Solent. Public areas include a spacious reception foyer, a bar/lounge and

contd.

the Ark Royal Restaurant. Service is well supervised and friendly.

ROOMS: 115 en suite (bth/shr) (3 fmly) No smoking in 30 bedrooms s £81; d £91 (incl. bkfst) * LB Off peak **MEALS:** Lunch fr £12.50 Dinner fr £15 English & French Cuisine V meals Coffee am **FACILITIES:** CTV in all bedrooms STV Xmas **CONF:** Thtr 250 Class 160 Board 30 Del from £60 * **SERVICES:** Lift Night porter 62P **NOTES:** No smoking in restaurant Last d 9.45pm **CARDS:**

PORTSMOUTH & SOUTHSEA Hampshire Map 04 SZ69

★★★ Posthouse Portsmouth

Posthouse

Pembroke Rd PO1 2TA
Quality Percentage Score: 61%
☎ 023 92827651 023 92756715

Dir: *from M275, follow signs for Southsea and I.O.W Hovercroft for 1 mile, at Southsea Common the Hotel can be found on the right*

Conveniently located for the seafront, local shops and city centre, the hotel is a popular venue for functions at weekends. Bedrooms are gradually being refurbished, and are all well equipped. Guests can take advantage of the hotel's leisure facilities, including an indoor swimming pool and gym. The hotel also has a range of meeting rooms and a business centre.

ROOMS: 167 en suite (bth/shr) (12 fmly) No smoking in 82 bedrooms s £59-£89; d £69-£99 * LB Off peak **MEALS:** International Cuisine V meals Coffee am Tea pm **FACILITIES:** CTV in all bedrooms Indoor swimming pool (heated) Sauna Solarium Gym Pool table Jacuzzi/spa Turkish steam room,Beauty Room, Pool room, Play room Xmas **CONF:** Thtr 220 Class 120 Board 80 Del from £99 * **SERVICES:** Lift Night porter 80P **NOTES:** No smoking in restaurant Last d 10pm **CARDS:**

PORTSMOUTH & SOUTHSEA Hampshire Map 04 SZ69

★★ *The Beaufort*

71 Festing Rd PO4 0NQ
Quality Percentage Score: 73%
☎ 023 92823707 023 92870270

Dir: *follow signs for seafront at South Parade Pier take left fork, Festing Rd is fourth turning on left*

This well established, personally run hotel is ideally situated for both the seafront and town centre. The bedrooms are thoughtfully equipped, attractively furnished and all feature en suite facilities. Well presented public areas include the basement restaurant and bar, and the elegant lounge.

ROOMS: 19 en suite (bth/shr) (1 fmly) No smoking in 10 bedrooms **MEALS:** English & French Cuisine V meals **FACILITIES:** CTV in all bedrooms STV **CONF:** Class 20 **SERVICES:** 10P **NOTES:** No dogs No smoking in restaurant Last d 8.15pm **CARDS:**

PORTSMOUTH & SOUTHSEA Hampshire Map 04 SZ69

★★ Seacrest

MINOTEL Great Britain

11/12 South Pde PO5 2JB
Quality Percentage Score: 71%
☎ 023 92733192 023 92832523

Dir: *from M27 follow signs for Southsea seafront or the Pyramids. Hotel opposite Rock Gardens and the Pyramids*

In a premier seafront location, this friendly hotel provides the ideal base for exploring the historic maritime resort. Bedrooms, many benefiting from sea views, are all en suite and decorated to a high standard. All rooms are well equipped with the usual modern amenities. Guests can relax in either the front-facing lounge furnished with comfortable leather chesterfields or the

contd.

adjacent cosy bar, before enjoying a home-cooked meal in the downstairs dining room.
ROOMS: 28 en suite (bth/shr) (3 fmly) No smoking in 10 bedrooms s £45-£55; d £48-£75 (incl. bkfst) * LB Off peak **MEALS:** Dinner £16.50 English & French Cuisine V meals Coffee am Tea pm **FACILITIES:** CTV in all bedrooms STV Xmas **SERVICES:** Lift Night porter 12P **NOTES:** No smoking in restaurant Last d 7.45pm **CARDS:**

PORTSMOUTH & SOUTHSEA Hampshire **Map 04 SZ69**
★★ Westfield Hall
65 Festing Rd PO4 0NQ
Quality Percentage Score: 70%
☎ 023 92826971 023 92870200
Dir: *follow signs Seafront, bear left at South Parade Pier then 3rd turning left*
Close to the seafront and town, this popular, family-run hotel provides a warm welcome to guests. Split between two houses, all the rooms offer en suite facilities and comfortable furnishings. Evening meals and breakfasts are served in the downstairs dining room.
ROOMS: 16 en suite (bth/shr) 11 annexe en suite (bth/shr) (5 fmly) No smoking in 14 bedrooms s £42-£50; d £50-£70 (incl. bkfst) * LB Off peak **MEALS:** Bar Lunch £4-£6 Dinner £16.95-£18.95 & alc V meals **FACILITIES:** CTV in all bedrooms STV Xmas **SERVICES:** 18P **NOTES:** No dogs No smoking in restaurant Last d 8.30pm
CARDS:

PORTSMOUTH & SOUTHSEA Hampshire **Map 04 SZ69**
★★ St Margarets
3 Craneswater Gate PO4 0NZ
Quality Percentage Score: 69%
☎ 023 92820097 023 92820097
Dir: *follow signs for D Day Museum/Sea Life Centre through city to sea front, head for South Parade Pier, at pier take left fork then 2nd left*
Enjoying a quiet residential location close to both the seafront and the town centre, St Margarets is personally run by friendly proprietors Gwen and Danny Spellar. The bedrooms are well presented with comfortable, co-ordinated furnishings. Guests can relax in the quiet lounge, enjoy a drink in the bar, and sample good home cooking in the spacious dining room.
ROOMS: 13 en suite (bth/shr) (1 fmly) No smoking in 2 bedrooms s £30-£35; d £40-£55 (incl. bkfst) * LB Off peak **MEALS:** Dinner fr £11 Coffee am **FACILITIES:** CTV in all bedrooms **SERVICES:** 5P **NOTES:** No dogs No coaches No smoking in restaurant Last d 7.30pm Closed 21 Dec-2 Jan **CARDS:**

P

PORTSMOUTH & SOUTHSEA Hampshire **Map 04 SZ69**
★★ Hotel Ibis
Winston Churchill Av PO1 2LX
Quality Percentage Score: 61%
☎ 023 92640000 023 92641000
Dir: *M27 junct 2 onto M275 and follow signs first for city centre, then sealife centre, then Guildhall. Turn right at rdbt into Winston Churchill Ave*
This modern hotel is centrally located and has the added advantage of secure parking. The bedrooms are furnished to the company standard with bright, modern amenities. On the ground floor there are meeting rooms, an open-plan bar/lounge area and an informal restaurant.
ROOMS: 144 en suite (shr) No smoking in 72 bedrooms s fr £39.50; d fr £42 * Off peak **MEALS:** Bar Lunch £1.95-£3.25alc Dinner £6.50-£12alc English & French Cuisine V meals Coffee am **FACILITIES:** CTV in all bedrooms STV **CONF:** Thtr 70 Class 24 Board 24 **SERVICES:** Lift Night porter 50P **NOTES:** No smoking area in restaurant Last d 10.30pm
CARDS:

PORTSMOUTH & SOUTHSEA Hampshire **Map 04 SZ69**
★★ Sandringham
7 Osborne Rd, Clarence Pde PO5 3LR
Quality Percentage Score: 60%
☎ 023 92826969 & 92822914 023 92822330
Dir: *turn off M275 at Portsmouth junct, follow signs to historic ships, then to Southsea, along seafront, hotel on left, opposite council car park*
Now under new ownership, this well established hotel continues to be a popular venue for tourists. The hotel is ideally located for the seafront, Southsea Common and the town centre. Bedrooms are comfortably furnished and all offer en suite facilities. Well presented lounges offer large screen TVs and the beamed dining room serves hearty meals.
ROOMS: 44 en suite (bth/shr) (7 fmly) s £29-£45; d £40-£80 (incl. bkfst) * LB Off peak **MEALS:** Dinner £6-£11.50 V meals Coffee am Tea pm **FACILITIES:** CTV in all bedrooms Xmas **CONF:** Thtr 150 Class 100 Board 40 Del from £60 * **SERVICES:** Lift Night porter **NOTES:** No dogs (ex guide dogs) No smoking in restaurant Last d 8.30pm
CARDS:

PORTSMOUTH & SOUTHSEA Hampshire **Map 04 SZ69**
Travel Inn
Southampton Rd, North Harbour, Cosham PO6 4SA
☎ 023 92321122 023 92324895
Dir: *on A27, close to junct 12 of the M27, 1m from Port Solent Marina*
This modern building offers accommodation in smart, spacious and well equipped bedrooms, all with en-suite bathrooms. Refreshments may be taken at the nearby family restaurant. For details about current prices consult the Contents Page under Hotel Groups for the Travel Inn phone number.
ROOMS: 40 en suite (bth/shr) d £39.95 *

PORTSMOUTH & SOUTHSEA Hampshire **Map 04 SZ69**
Travel Inn (Southsea)
Long Curtain Rd, Clarence Pier PO4 3AA
☎ 023 92734622 023 92733048
Dir: *overlooking Portsmouth Harbour entrance*
This modern building offers accommodation in smart, spacious and well equipped bedrooms, all with en-suite bathrooms. Refreshments may be taken at the nearby family restaurant. For details about current prices consult the Contents Page under Hotel Groups for the Travel Inn phone number.
ROOMS: 40 en suite (bth/shr) d £39.95 *

PRESTBURY Cheshire **Map 07 SJ97**
★★★ Bridge
The Village SK10 4DQ
Quality Percentage Score: 69%
☎ 01625 829326 01625 827557
Dir: *off A538 through village, hotel next to church*

Dating in parts from the 17th century, this delightful hotel stands *contd.*

sideways to the village street, between the River Bollin and the ancient church. The cocktail bar provides the ideal place to relax before a satisfying meal in the restaurant while a wide range of bedrooms are available in the original building and a purpose-built extension.

ROOMS: 23 en suite (bth/shr) (1 fmly) s £85-£90; d £90-£100 * LB Off peak **MEALS:** Lunch £5-£11.95 V meals Coffee am Tea pm **FACILITIES:** CTV in all bedrooms Wkly live entertainment **CONF:** Thtr 100 Class 56 Board 48 Del £107.50 * **SERVICES:** Night porter 52P **NOTES:** No dogs (ex guide dogs) **CARDS:**

PRESTBURY Cheshire **Map 07 SJ97**

White House Manor

New Rd SK10 4HP

☎ 01625 829376 ⎙ 01625 828627

Dir: *on the A538 Macclesfield Road*

This elegant Georgian house, situated in attractive gardens on the edge of the village, offers charming individually styled bedrooms, with four-poster beds frequently making guest appearances. Meals can be ordered from the room service menu and breakfast is served in the conservatory. The White House restaurant, under the same ownership, is just a short walk away.

ROOMS: 11 en suite (bth/shr) No smoking in all bedrooms s £70-£95; d £100-£120 * Off peak **MEALS:** Lunch £13.50-£16.75 & alc Dinner £14.95-£20.45 & alc V meals **FACILITIES:** CTV in all bedrooms STV Jacuzzi/spa **CONF:** Thtr 60 Class 40 Board 26 Del from £100 * **SERVICES:** 11P **NOTES:** No dogs (ex guide dogs) No coaches No children 10yrs Last d 10pm **CARDS:**

PRESTON Lancashire **Map 07 SD52**

see also **Barton**

★★★★ Preston Marriott

Garstang Rd, Broughton PR3 5JB

Quality Percentage Score: 67%

☎ 01772 864087 ⎙ 01772 861728

Dir: *M6 junct 32 onto M55 junct 1, follow A6 towards Garstang, the Hotel is .05m on the right*

Originally a farmhouse, this building has been greatly extended with much sympathy, retaining a good deal of character. It is quietly situated in its own grounds and within easy reach of the motorway network. The larger bedrooms are located in the original house, with all rooms being comfortably furnished and equipped to suit both the business and leisure visitor. A good standard of cooking is offered in the Broughton Park restaurant, with snacks and lighter meals also available in the Poolside Grill, adjacent to an impressive up-to-the-minute leisure complex.

ROOMS: 150 en suite (bth/shr) (40 fmly) No smoking in 75 bedrooms s £82-£89; d £90-£97 (incl. bkfst) * LB Off peak **MEALS:** Lunch £11.50-£14 High tea £6-£12 Dinner £12-£18.95 & alc English & French Cuisine V meals Coffee am Tea pm **FACILITIES:** CTV in all bedrooms STV Indoor swimming pool (heated) Sauna Solarium Gym Croquet lawn Jacuzzi/spa Steam room Beauty salon Wkly live entertainment ch fac Xmas **CONF:** Thtr 200 Class 120 Board 40 Del from £99 * **SERVICES:** Lift Night porter 220P **NOTES:** No dogs (ex guide dogs) No smoking in restaurant Last d 10pm **CARDS:**

PRESTON Lancashire **Map 07 SD52**

★★★★ *Tickled Trout*

Preston New Rd, Samlesbury PR5 0UJ

Quality Percentage Score: 63%

☎ 01772 877671 ⎙ 01772 877463

Dir: *close to M6 junct 31*

Popular with business guests, bedrooms are well equipped with good standards of quality and comfort. In addition to an open plan lounge, there are facilities for meetings and conferences, and a small leisure club.

ROOMS: 72 en suite (bth/shr) (56 fmly) No smoking in 40 bedrooms **MEALS:** International Cuisine V meals Coffee am Tea pm **FACILITIES:** CTV in all bedrooms STV Fishing Sauna Solarium Wave pool Steam room **CONF:** Thtr 100 Class 40 Board 4 **SERVICES:** Night porter 150P **NOTES:** No smoking in restaurant Last d 9.45pm **CARDS:**

PRESTON Lancashire **Map 07 SD52**

★★★ Swallow

Preston New Rd, Samlesbury PR5 0UL

Quality Percentage Score: 68%

☎ 01772 877351 ⎙ 01772 877424

Dir: *1m from M6, on A59/A677 junct*

Well suited to the business, conference and leisure guest alike, this hotel is located alongside the A59 just a couple of miles from junction 31 of the M6. Bedrooms are nicely furnished and public

contd.

areas are spacious, with a range of leisure facilities also being available. Services are provided readily by the friendly team of staff.

Swallow, Preston

ROOMS: 78 en suite (bth/shr) No smoking in 24 bedrooms s £78-£87; d £115 (incl. bkfst) LB Off peak **MEALS:** Lunch £11.50-£12.95 Dinner £19.25 International Cuisine V meals Coffee am Tea pm **FACILITIES:** CTV in all bedrooms STV Indoor swimming pool (heated) Sauna Solarium Gym Jacuzzi/spa Steam room Xmas **CONF:** Thtr 250 Class 100 Board 60 Del from £110 * **SERVICES:** Lift Night porter 300P **NOTES:** No smoking in restaurant Last d 9.30pm
CARDS:

PRESTON Lancashire **Map 07 SD52**
★★★ Mill Hotel
Moor Rd, Croston PR5 7HP
Quality Percentage Score: 66%
☎ 01772 600110 📠 01772 601623
Dir: *M6 S j27 onto B5209, left off slip road and right at garage towards Eccleston. Turn left after bridge 5m on onto A581, left at T-junct. Hotel 0.75m*

A well furnished and modern hotel that retains a rustic charm around the spacious public rooms which include two bars and a pleasant restaurant. A good range of family-style cooking is offered and the mainly spacious bedrooms have been well equipped. A playhouse is provided for the younger guests.
ROOMS: 46 en suite (bth/shr) (3 fmly) No smoking in 4 bedrooms s fr £49.50; d fr £65 (incl. bkfst) * Off peak **MEALS:** Lunch £9.95 & alc Dinner £12.50-£22.50alc V meals Coffee am Tea pm **FACILITIES:** CTV in all bedrooms Pool table Xmas **CONF:** Thtr 150 Class 50 Board 30 Del from £70 * **SERVICES:** 130P **NOTES:** No smoking area in restaurant Last d 9.45pm **CARDS:**

PRESTON Lancashire **Map 07 SD52**
★★★ Pines
Clayton le Woods PR6 7ED
Quality Percentage Score: 66%
☎ 01772 338551 📠 01772 629002
Dir: *on A6, 1m S of M6 junc 29*

Enjoying easy access to the motorway network, this privately owned hotel is set in four acres of mature gardens. Thoughtfully equipped bedrooms, some with their own sitting area, are comfortable, whilst public areas include a nicely furnished lounge. Haworths restaurant and bistro, a light and airy room, offers an interesting choice of dishes, from a full traditional meal to pasta or a light snack. Meeting and function suites are available and service throughout is friendly and attentive.
ROOMS: 37 en suite (bth/shr) (12 fmly) No smoking in 11 bedrooms s £70-£95; d £80-£110 (incl. bkfst) * LB Off peak **MEALS:** V meals Coffee am Tea pm **FACILITIES:** CTV in all bedrooms STV Jacuzzi/spa Wkly live entertainment Xmas **CONF:** Thtr 200 Class 100 Board 50 Del from £105 * **SERVICES:** Night porter 120P **NOTES:** No dogs (ex guide dogs) No smoking area in restaurant Closed 26 Dec
CARDS:

PRESTON Lancashire **Map 07 SD52**
★★★ Novotel
Reedfield Place, Walton Summit PR6 8AA
Quality Percentage Score: 64%
☎ 01772 313331 📠 01772 627868
Dir: *M6 junct 29 M61 junct 9,then A6 Chorley Road Hotel is next to Bamber Bridge roundabout*

A modern hotel containing all the usual features associated with the group and although decor is unfussy, bedrooms are spacious, have modern facilities, and are particularly attractive to guests with families. Business guests will also find the facilities useful and the convenience of extended restaurant opening times and the provision of lounge and room service allow for a lot of flexibility. There is also a good range of meeting and conference rooms.
ROOMS: 98 en suite (bth/shr) (98 fmly) No smoking in 49 bedrooms d £55-£59 * LB Off peak **MEALS:** Lunch £6.95-£13.50 & alc Dinner £13.50 & alc English & Continental Cuisine V meals Coffee am **FACILITIES:** CTV in all bedrooms STV Outdoor swimming pool (heated) Pool table **CONF:** Thtr 180 Class 80 Board 52 Del from £85 * **SERVICES:** Lift Night porter 140P **NOTES:** No smoking area in restaurant Last d midnight **CARDS:**

PRESTON Lancashire **Map 07 SD52**
★★★ Posthouse Preston
Ringway PR1 3AU
Quality Percentage Score: 59%
☎ 01772 259411 📠 01772 201923
Dir: *M6 junct 31 follow A59 signs for the Town Centre right at T junct, Forte Posthouse is on the left*

A modern, town-centre hotel, many of whose well equipped bedrooms have panoramic views over the town. Public rooms, including the restaurant and bar are located on the first floor. There is an all-day lounge menu and 24 hour room service.
ROOMS: 119 en suite (bth/shr) (11 fmly) No smoking in 73 bedrooms d fr £79 * LB Off peak **MEALS:** International Cuisine V meals Coffee am Tea pm **FACILITIES:** CTV in all bedrooms Pool table Xmas **CONF:** Thtr 120 Class 50 Board 40 Del from £90 * **SERVICES:** Lift Night porter 30P **NOTES:** No smoking in restaurant Last d 10.15pm
CARDS:

PRESTON Lancashire **Map 07 SD52**
★★ Brook House Hotel
662 Preston Rd, Clayton-le-Woods PR6 7EH
Quality Percentage Score: 67%
☎ 01772 336403 📠 01772 336403
Dir: *on A6 towards Chorley, 0.5m from junct 29 of M6*

Spacious and comfortable bedrooms are offered at this former farmhouse, sympathetically modernised and extended by the present owners. There is a conservatory lounge, also available for

contd.

meetings, and home-cooked food is served in the adjacent restaurant or in the bar.
ROOMS: 20 en suite (bth/shr) (2 fmly) s £40-£45; d £50-£55 (incl. bkfst) * Off peak **MEALS:** V meals **FACILITIES:** CTV in all bedrooms STV **CONF:** Thtr 32 Class 20 Board 20 Del from £49 * **SERVICES:** 28P **NOTES:** No dogs (ex guide dogs) No coaches No smoking in restaurant Closed Xmas & New Year **CARDS:**

PRESTON Lancashire — Map 07 SD52

★★ Claremont

516 Blackpool Rd, Ashton-on-Ribble PR2 1HY
Quality Percentage Score: 66%
☎ 01772 729738 Fax 01772 726274
Dir: *from M6 junct 31 take A59 towards Preston. At hilltop rdbt turn right onto A583. Hotel can be seen on the right just past pub and over bridge*
This friendly hotel, personally run by the proprietor and family, is conveniently situated for both the town centre and the motorways. Freshly decorated bedrooms are bright and thoughtfully equipped, and the public areas include a cosy lounge, as well as a comfortable bar and adjacent dining room. The self-contained function room is nicely presented and the garden, to the rear of the hotel, is most attractive.
ROOMS: 14 en suite (bth/shr) s fr £38.50; d fr £55 (incl. bkfst) * Off peak **MEALS:** Dinner £11.95 European Cuisine V meals Coffee am Tea pm **FACILITIES:** CTV in all bedrooms **CONF:** Thtr 85 Class 45 Board 50 **SERVICES:** 27P **NOTES:** No dogs (ex guide dogs) No coaches No smoking in restaurant Last d 8.30pm
CARDS:

PRESTON Lancashire — Map 07 SD52

★★ Vineyard

Cinnamon Hill, Chorley Rd, Walton-Le-Dale PR5 4JN
Quality Percentage Score: 62%
☎ 01772 254646 Fax 01772 258967
Dir: *from M6 junct 29 take A6 to Preston. Then B6230 to Walton-le-Dale. Right at rdbt. Hotel up hill on left*
The exterior of this hotel has an Alpine look and provides an extensive range of food including many of the more popular dishes. Bedrooms are well equipped and comfortable while the service is both friendly and attentive. The public rooms include an extensive split level restaurant together with a cosy bar in the same style. A conference/function room is also available.
ROOMS: 16 en suite (bth/shr) (1 fmly) d £49 * LB Off peak **MEALS:** Lunch £9.99-£13.99 Dinner £13.99 & alc International Cuisine V meals Coffee am **FACILITIES:** CTV in all bedrooms **CONF:** Thtr 100 Class 40 Board 50 Del £85 * **SERVICES:** Night porter 150P **NOTES:** No dogs (ex guide dogs) No smoking area in restaurant Last d 9.30pm **CARDS:**

PRESTON Lancashire — Map 07 SD52

Travel Inn

Blackpool Rd, Lea PR4 0XB
☎ 01772 720476 Fax 01772 729971
Dir: *from junct 31 turn towards Preston. At the mini rdbt turn right onto A5085 which leads onto the A583*
This modern building offers accommodation in smart, spacious and well equipped bedrooms, all with en-suite bathrooms. Refreshments may be taken at the nearby family restaurant. For details about current prices consult the Contents Page under Hotel Groups for the Travel Inn phone number.
ROOMS: 38 en suite (bth/shr) d £39.95 *

PRESTWICH Greater Manchester — Map 07 SD80

Travel Inn

Bury New Rd M25 3AJ
☎ 0161 798 0827 Fax 0161 773 8099
Dir: *on A56 just off junct 17 of the M60 (formerley M62)*
This modern building offers accommodation in smart, spacious and well equipped bedrooms, all with en-suite bathrooms. Refreshments may be taken at the nearby family restaurant. For details about current prices consult the Contents Page under Hotel Groups for the Travel Inn phone number.
ROOMS: 60 en suite (bth/shr) d £39.95 *

PUCKERIDGE Hertfordshire — Map 05 TL32

★★★ Vintage Court

Vintage Corner SG11 1SA
Quality Percentage Score: 61%
☎ 01920 822722 Fax 01920 822877
Dir: *turn off A10 onto A120-turn left 100 yards off roundabout, the hotel is 200 yards on the right*
Convenient for Stansted airport, this hotel caters well for conferences, with separate meeting rooms, and a dedicated conference help desk. Bedrooms are modern in style, thoughtfully equipped and generally of good comfortable proportions.
ROOMS: 25 en suite (bth/shr) No smoking in 13 bedrooms s £68.55-£85.50; d £77.50-£94.45 (incl. bkfst) * LB Off peak **MEALS:** Lunch £11.85-£13.35 Dinner fr £18.85 & alc English & French Cuisine V meals Coffee am Tea pm **FACILITIES:** CTV in all bedrooms Snooker **CONF:** Thtr 90 Class 40 Board 36 Del £135 * **SERVICES:** 80P **NOTES:** No smoking area in restaurant Last d 9.15pm Closed 26 Dec-2 Jan **CARDS:**

PUDDINGTON Cheshire — Map 07 SJ37

Craxton Wood

Parkgate Rd L66 9PB

☎ 0151 339 4717 Fax 0151 339 1740

Dir: *leave M6 take M56 direction North Wales, take A5117, A540 direction Hoylake, hotel is 200 yards past the traffic lights*

This large house is set in its own attractive wooded grounds. Bedrooms are spacious, comfortably furnished and well equipped. Restaurant menus are changed seasonally, and the list of wines is notable.

ROOMS: 14 en suite (bth/shr) **MEALS:** French Cuisine V meals Coffee am Tea pm **FACILITIES:** CTV in all bedrooms STV **CONF:** Thtr 30 Board 20 **SERVICES:** 41P **NOTES:** No dogs (ex guide dogs) No coaches Last d 9.45pm **CARDS:**

PULBOROUGH West Sussex — Map 04 TQ01

★★ Chequers

Church Place RH20 1AD

Quality Percentage Score: 73%

☎ 01798 872486 Fax 01798 872715

Dir: *off A29, opposite the church on N side of village*

This small, charming hotel is located just north of the centre of the village overlooking the South Downs and dates back to the time of Queen Anne. All rooms are individual in style, comfortably furnished and well equipped. There is no separate bar but drinks are served in a cosy lounge or the conservatory Coffee Shop. The restaurant serves an interesting range of carefully prepared dishes using quality fresh produce.

ROOMS: 11 en suite (bth/shr) (3 fmly) No smoking in 2 bedrooms s £49.50; d £85-£95 (incl. bkfst) * LB Off peak **MEALS:** Lunch £12.50-£15 Dinner £22.95 V meals Coffee am Tea pm **FACILITIES:** CTV in all bedrooms Xmas **CONF:** Thtr 19 Class 19 Board 19 Del from £75 * **SERVICES:** 16P **NOTES:** No smoking in restaurant Last d 8.45pm **CARDS:**

PURFLEET Essex — Map 05 TQ57

Travel Inn

High St RM16 1QA

☎ 01708 865432 Fax 01708 860852

Dir: *from Dartford Tunnel follow signs Dagenham(A13), at rdbt take 1st exit to Purfleet(A1090)*

This modern building offers accommodation in smart, spacious and well equipped bedrooms, all with en-suite bathrooms. Refreshments may be taken at the nearby family restaurant. For details about current prices consult the Contents Page under Hotel Groups for the Travel Inn phone number.

ROOMS: 30 en suite (bth/shr) d £39.95 *

PURTON Wiltshire — Map 04 SU08

★★★ The Pear Tree at Purton

Church End SN5 9ED

Quality Percentage Score: 79%

☎ 01793 772100 Fax 01793 772369

Dir: *from junct 16 of M4 follow signs to Purton, at Spar grocers turn right hotel is 0.25m on left*

Transformed into an elegant country retreat by Francis and Anne Young, this Cotswold stone house was originally a vicarage. Overlooking the attractive gardens, the prettily decorated conservatory restaurant continues to gain praise and a loyal following. The well balanced, creative menu features local produce where possible. Most of the superbly equipped bedrooms are to be extended.

ROOMS: 18 en suite (bth/shr) (2 fmly) d £90-£95 (incl. bkfst) * Off peak **MEALS:** Lunch £12.50-£17.50 Dinner £29.50 V meals Coffee am Tea pm **FACILITIES:** CTV in all bedrooms STV Croquet lawn **CONF:** Thtr 70 Class 30 Board 30 Del from £145 * **SERVICES:** 60P **NOTES:** No coaches Last d 9.30pm **CARDS:**

QUORN Leicestershire — Map 08 SK51

★★★★ Quorn Country

Charnwood House, Leicester Rd LE12 8BB

Quality Percentage Score: 70%

☎ 01509 415050 Fax 01509 415557

Dir: *M1 junct 23-A512 into Loughborough and follow A6 signs. At 1st rdbt after town follow signs for Quorn, through lights-hotel 500yds from 2nd rdbt*

This pleasant hotel is set in four acres of landscaped grounds, leading down to the River Soar. The open plan public areas are intimate and relaxing, and there are two restaurants, the Shires and the conservatory style Orangery. The friendly team of staff offer a warm welcome.

ROOMS: 23 en suite (bth/shr) (1 fmly) No smoking in 3 bedrooms s £78-£98; d £90-£110 * LB Off peak **MEALS:** Lunch fr £17.50 Dinner fr £22 English & Continental Cuisine V meals Coffee am Tea pm **FACILITIES:** CTV in all bedrooms STV Fishing **CONF:** Thtr 100 Class 32 Board 26 Del from £150 * **SERVICES:** Night porter Air conditioning 100P **NOTES:** No dogs RS 26 Dec & New Year **CARDS:**

See advert under LEICESTER

RADLETT Hertfordshire — Map 04 TL10

Travel Inn

Smug Oak Ln

☎ 01727 875557 Fax 01727 873289

This modern building offers accommodation in smart, spacious and well equipped bedrooms, all with en-suite bathrooms. Refreshments may be taken at the nearby family restaurant. For details about current prices consult the Contents Page under Hotel Groups for the Travel Inn phone number.

ROOMS: 56 en suite (bth/shr) d £39.95 *

RAINHILL Merseyside **Map 07 SJ49**

★ Rockland

View Rd L35 0LG

Quality Percentage Score: 61%

☎ 0151 426 4603 Fax 0151 426 0107

Dir: *leave M62 junc 7, take A57 towards Rainhill,after 1m turn left into View Rd, hotel 0.25m on left*

A family-run hotel in a quiet residential area, set in pretty gardens which offer an attractive backdrop for weddings. The hotel is used by local groups for regular meetings, and small conferences can be accommodated. Bedrooms are well equipped and generally spacious; good-value food is provided.

ROOMS: 11 rms (9 bth 1 shr) (2 fmly) s £32.50-£34.50; d £42-£45 (incl. bkfst) * LB Off peak **MEALS:** Sunday Lunch £6-£7.50 Dinner £10.75-£11.75 V meals Coffee am Tea pm **FACILITIES:** CTV in all bedrooms **SERVICES:** 30P **NOTES:** Last d 8.15pm **CARDS:**

RAMSGATE Kent **Map 05 TR36**

★★★ San Clu

Victoria Pde, East Cliff CT11 8DT

Quality Percentage Score: 66%

☎ 01843 592345 Fax 01843 580157

Dir: *opposite Granville Theatre*

This Victorian hotel stands on the seafront, close to the ferry and the town. Bedrooms, some with balconies, are generously sized and well equipped. Meals are served both in the bar lounge and in the restaurant.

ROOMS: 44 en suite (bth/shr) (14 fmly) **MEALS:** International Cuisine V meals Coffee am Tea pm **FACILITIES:** CTV in all bedrooms **CONF:** Thtr 180 Class 100 Board 100 **SERVICES:** Lift Night porter 16P **NOTES:** Last d 9.15pm **CARDS:**

See advert on this page

RAMSGILL North Yorkshire **Map 07 SE17**

★★ Yorke Arms

HG3 5RL

Quality Percentage Score: 73%

☎ 01423 755243 Fax 01423 755330

Dir: *turn off B6265 at Pateley Bridge at the Nidderdale filling station onto Low Wath rd. signed to Ramsgill, continue for 3.5m*

This creeper-clad hotel stands in the heart of Upper Nidderdale close to Gouthwaite reservoir and provides very comfortable and well furnished bedrooms. The highlight of any stay here is the well produced dinner based on the best of local produce where available, very friendly and attentive service is provided by Mr and Mrs Atkins and their dedicated staff.

ROOMS: 13 en suite (bth/shr) (1 fmly) s £70-£85; d £130-£250 (incl. bkfst & dinner) * LB Off peak **MEALS:** Sunday Lunch £3.50-£25alc Dinner £3.50-£25alc V meals Coffee am Tea pm **FACILITIES:** CTV in all bedrooms Xmas **CONF:** Thtr 20 **SERVICES:** 20P **NOTES:** No dogs (ex guide dogs) No coaches No smoking in restaurant Last d 8.45pm RS Sun **CARDS:**

See advert on this page

R

RANGEWORTHY Gloucestershire **Map 03 ST68**

★★ **Rangeworthy Court**

Church Ln, Wotton Rd BS37 7ND

Quality Percentage Score: 72%

☎ 01454 228347 01454 228945

Dir: *signposted off B4058*

This welcoming manor house hotel is within easy reach of the motorway network. It offers a choice of comfortable lounges, and bedrooms equipped to modern standards. Its restaurant provides a varied and interesting menu.

ROOMS: 13 en suite (bth/shr) (4 fmly) s £62-£75; d £70-£85 (incl. bkfst) * LB Off peak **MEALS:** Lunch £11.95-£14 & alc Dinner £19-£23alc V meals Coffee am **FACILITIES:** CTV in all bedrooms STV Outdoor swimming pool (heated) Xmas **CONF:** Thtr 22 Class 14 Board 16 Del from £90 * **SERVICES:** 40P **NOTES:** No coaches No smoking in restaurant Last d 9pm **CARDS:**

See advert under BRISTOL

RAVENSCAR North Yorkshire **Map 08 NZ90**

★★★ **Raven Hall Country House**

YO13 0ET

Quality Percentage Score: 64%

☎ 01723 870353 01723 870072

Dir: *from Scarborough take A171 to Whitby Rd, go through Cloughton Village turn right to Ravenscar*

Raven Hall Hotel occupies a dramatic location in 100 acres of grounds and gardens some 600 feet above sea level, with views towards Robin Hood's Bay. The bedrooms are traditional in style as is the dining room where a satisfactory range of food is available. Public areas are in keeping with a country mansion while good leisure facilities are provided. A new function suite has been added.

ROOMS: 53 en suite (bth/shr) (22 fmly) No smoking in 1 bedroom s £65-£75; d £90-£100 (incl. bkfst) * LB Off peak **MEALS:** Lunch £4.95-£11.95 Dinner £19.95 English & French Cuisine V meals Coffee am Tea pm **FACILITIES:** CTV in all bedrooms Indoor swimming pool (heated) Outdoor swimming pool Golf 9 Tennis (hard) Snooker Sauna Pool table Croquet lawn Putting green Crown green bowls Giant chess Wkly live entertainment Xmas **CONF:** Thtr 160 Class 100 Board 60 Del from £105 * **SERVICES:** Night porter 200P **NOTES:** No dogs (ex guide dogs) No smoking in restaurant Last d 8.45pm **CARDS:**

See advert under SCARBOROUGH

RAVENSTONEDALE Cumbria **Map 07 NY70**

★★ **Black Swan**

CA17 4NG

Quality Percentage Score: 70%

☎ 015396 23204 015396 23604

Dir: *Ravenstondale is less than ten minutes from junct 38 on M6*

This friendly hotel is the focal point of a picturesque village only ten minutes drive from the M6. Popular for its imaginative menus and real ales, dinner is served in the dining room with its antique furniture, or in the cosy bar where a log fire burns on cooler nights. Bedrooms are well equipped and include ground floor chalet-style rooms.

ROOMS: 13 en suite (bth/shr) 4 annexe en suite (bth/shr) (1 fmly) s £45-£50; d £70-£80 (incl. bkfst) * LB Off peak **MEALS:** Lunch fr £9.75 & alc Dinner £23 & alc V meals Coffee am Tea pm **FACILITIES:** CTV in all bedrooms Tennis (hard) Fishing Xmas **SERVICES:** 30P **NOTES:** No coaches No smoking in restaurant Last d 9pm **CARDS:**

See advert under KIRKBY STEPHEN

RAVENSTONEDALE Cumbria **Map 07 NY70**

★★ ***The Fat Lamb***

Crossbank CA17 4LL

Quality Percentage Score: 63%

☎ 01539 623242 01539 623285

Dir: *on A683, between Kirkby Stephen/Sedbergh*

Formerly a 17th-century farmhouse, the Fat Lamb is now a roadside country inn. The bar features an old range, and paintings and prints of the area adorn the walls. Bedrooms are in the house and a ground-floor extension which includes facilities for the disabled. An extensive bar menu, plus blackboard specials, complement the fixed-price dinner menu.

ROOMS: 12 en suite (bth/shr) (4 fmly) No smoking in all bedrooms **MEALS:** British & French Cuisine V meals Coffee am Tea pm **FACILITIES:** CTV in all bedrooms Fishing Private 5 acre nature reserve **SERVICES:** 60P **NOTES:** No smoking in restaurant Last d 9pm **CARDS:**

READING Berkshire **Map 04 SU77**

see also **Swallowfield & Wokingham**

★★★★ ***Holiday Inn***

Caversham Bridge, Richfield Av RG1 8BD

Quality Percentage Score: 59%

☎ 0118 925 9988 0118 939 1665

Dir: *M4 junct 10/A329M to Reading. Join A4 follow signs to Caversham*

Next to Caversham Bridge, this purpose-built hotel offers a range of facilities and well equipped, smartly decorated bedrooms. The open-plan bar and restaurant is topped with an eye-catching atrium roof and there is also a riverside bar.

ROOMS: 111 en suite (bth/shr) No smoking in 15 bedrooms **MEALS:** International Cuisine V meals Coffee am Tea pm **FACILITIES:** CTV in all bedrooms STV Indoor swimming pool (heated) Sauna Solarium Gym Aromatherapy Beauty treatment by appoitment **CONF:** Thtr 200 Class 160 Board 76 **SERVICES:** Lift Night porter 200P **NOTES:** No smoking area in restaurant Last d 10pm **CARDS:**

READING Berkshire **Map 04 SU77**

★★★ ***Posthouse Reading***

Basingstoke Rd RG2 0SL

Quality Percentage Score: 69%

☎ 01189 875485 01189 311958

Dir: *from junct 11 on M4 follow A33 towards Reading. Hotel 0.5m on left*

Suitable for both the business and leisure traveller, this bright hotel provides very modern accommodation in well equipped bedrooms. Meals are served in the Rotisserie restaurant, or snacks are on offer in the lounge, which is also popular for informal one-to-one business meetings. The leisure centre is a bonus. The hotel offers easy access to both Reading and the M4.

ROOMS: 202 en suite (bth/shr) (56 fmly) No smoking in 94 bedrooms **MEALS:** International Cuisine V meals Coffee am Tea pm **FACILITIES:** CTV in all bedrooms Indoor swimming pool (heated) Sauna Solarium Gym Jacuzzi/spa Health & fitness centre ch fac **CONF:** Thtr 100 Class 50 Board 45 **SERVICES:** Night porter 450P **NOTES:** No smoking area in restaurant Last d 10.30pm **CARDS:**

READING Berkshire — Map 04 SU77

★★★ Courtyard by Marriott Reading

Bath Rd, Padworth RG7 5HT
Quality Percentage Score: 68%
☎ 0118 9714411 📠 0118 9714442

Dir: *leave the M4 at junct 12 and follow A4 towards Newbury, hotel is 3.5m on left*

A modern purpose-built hotel, air-conditioned bedrooms are comfortably furnished, well equipped and suitable for business guests. The reception area features an attractive gallery lounge and there is a small gym. In the conservatory-style dining room dishes from the branded menu are supplemented by a small choice of daily specials.

ROOMS: 50 en suite (bth/shr) No smoking in 30 bedrooms d fr £80 * LB Off peak **MEALS:** Lunch £10.95-£11.95 & alc Dinner fr £12.95alc International Cuisine V meals Coffee am **FACILITIES:** CTV in all bedrooms STV Gym Fitness room Xmas **CONF:** Thtr 200 Class 100 Board 80 Del from £130 * **SERVICES:** Night porter Air conditioning 200P **NOTES:** No dogs (ex guide dogs) No smoking in restaurant Last d 9.45pm **CARDS:**

READING Berkshire — Map 04 SU77

★★★ *Hanover International*

Pingewood RG30 3UN
Quality Percentage Score: 67%
☎ 0118 9500885 📠 0118 9391996

Dir: *from M4 junct 11-A33 S. At 1st rdbt turn right then 2nd right. Follow road across M'way, through lights and over bridge, hotel 750meters on left*

Located a short distance south of Reading, with convenient access to the major routes, this modern hotel has the attractive feature of being built around a man-made lake, occasionally used for water sports. All rooms are spacious and have balconies overlooking the lake. Guests have the choice of dinner from the Lakeside restaurant or from the less formal 'Wokery' where oriental dishes are cooked to order.

ROOMS: 81 en suite (bth/shr) (4 fmly) No smoking in 18 bedrooms **MEALS:** International Cuisine V meals Coffee am **FACILITIES:** CTV in all bedrooms STV Indoor swimming pool (heated) Tennis (hard) Fishing Squash Snooker Sauna Solarium Gym Pool table Jacuzzi/spa Jetskiing Waterskiing can be pre-booked **CONF:** Thtr 110 Class 50 Board 45 **SERVICES:** Lift Night porter 225P **NOTES:** No dogs (ex guide dogs) No smoking in restaurant Last d 9.30pmm
CARDS:

READING Berkshire — Map 04 SU77

★★★ Ship

4-8 Duke St RG1 4RY
Quality Percentage Score: 63%
☎ 0118 958 3455 📠 0118 950 4450

Dir: *M4 junct 10-A329(M) take junct for A4 Reading towards town centre. Follow through 1st lights, turn left at 2nd. Left at next lights,hotel on right*

Situated in the city centre and handy for Reading's business district and railway station, the Ship Hotel remains a firm favourite. Its public rooms are being moved into a new purpose-built courtyard, while its bedrooms are well equipped with designated no-smoking and 'ladies only' rooms both available.

ROOMS: 52 en suite (bth/shr) (2 fmly) No smoking in 13 bedrooms s fr £95; d fr £105 * LB Off peak **MEALS:** English & Continental Cuisine V meals Coffee am Tea pm **FACILITIES:** CTV in all bedrooms STV **CONF:** Thtr 80 Class 40 Board 35 **SERVICES:** Night porter 25P **NOTES:** No dogs (ex guide dogs) No smoking area in restaurant Last d 10.30pm **CARDS:**

READING Berkshire — Map 04 SU77

★★ The Mill House

Old Basingstoke Rd RG7 1PY
Quality Percentage Score: 69%
☎ 0118 988 3124 📠 0118 988 5550
(For full entry see Swallowfield)

READING Berkshire — Map 04 SU77

★★ Rainbow Corner

132-138 Caversham Rd RG1 8AY
Quality Percentage Score: 66%
☎ 0118 9588140 📠 0118 9586500

Dir: *from junct 11 of M4 take A327 to town centre then follow signs to Caversham*

North of the city centre, the hotel has private parking, appreciated by business clients using the hotel during the week. Staff are friendly and welcoming, creating a home from home atmosphere. The cosy bar is a focus of activity in the evenings.

contd.

Spacious, comfortable, well equipped bedrooms all have extra facilities.
ROOMS: 24 en suite (bth/shr) (1 fmly) **MEALS:** Dinner £13.95 & alc International Cuisine V meals Coffee am Tea pm **FACILITIES:** CTV in all bedrooms STV **CONF:** Thtr 30 Class 30 Board 20 **SERVICES:** Night porter 15P **NOTES:** No coaches No smoking in restaurant Last d 9.30pm **CARDS:**

READING Berkshire **Map 04 SU77**
★★ George Hotel
10-12 King St RG1 2HE
Quality Percentage Score: 65%
☎ 0118 9573445 📠 0118 9508614
Dir: *leave M4 junct 11/12 (Newbury & West) or junct 10/11 (London & East). The hotel is located at the junct of Broad St & King St*
This old coaching inn with modern comforts is located right in the centre of the city - ask for directions if arriving for the first time. Great progress has been made with a new Café Bar and an attractive brasserie-style restaurant. Alternatively, Albert's serves a traditional fish and chips option. The bar is very relaxing, and the bedrooms are comfortable.
ROOMS: 64 en suite (bth/shr) (2 fmly) s £64; d £70 * LB Off peak **MEALS:** Lunch fr £5.95 & alc Dinner fr £12.95 & alc International Cuisine V meals Coffee am Tea pm **FACILITIES:** CTV in all bedrooms Wkly live entertainment Xmas **CONF:** Thtr 50 Class 36 Board 24 **SERVICES:** Night porter **NOTES:** No dogs (ex guide dogs) Last d 10.30pm **CARDS:**

READING Berkshire **Map 04 SU77**
⇧ Travelodge
387 Basingstoke Rd RG2 0JE
☎ 01734 750618 📠 01734 750618
Dir: *on A33, southbound*
This modern building offers accommodation in smart, spacious and well equipped bedrooms, all with en-suite bathrooms. Refreshments may be taken at the nearby family restaurant. For details about current prices, consult the Contents Page under Hotel Groups for the Travelodge phone number.
ROOMS: 36 en suite (bth/shr) d £55.95 *

READING Berkshire **Map 04 SU77**
⇧ Travelodge (Eastbound)
Burghfield RG30 3UQ
☎ 0118 9566966 📠 01734 595444
Dir: *M4 between junc 11&12*
This modern building offers accommodation in smart, spacious and well equipped bedrooms, all with en-suite bathrooms. Refreshments may be taken at the nearby family restaurant. For details about current prices, consult the Contents Page under Hotel Groups for the Travelodge phone number.
ROOMS: 45 en suite (bth/shr) d £59.95 * **CONF:** Thtr 20 Class 20 Board 20

READING Berkshire **Map 04 SU77**
Late entry **Abbey House**
118 Connaught Rd RG30 2UF
☎ 0118 9590549 📠 0118 9569299
Dir: *from town centre take A329 towards Pangborne after Reading West Railway bridge take 3rd left*
Close to Reading centre but in a quiet location, the Abbey House, with its spacious, well appointed bedrooms (including four in a separate building) is a popular choice for visitors. Public areas include dining room, bar and comfortable lounge.
ROOMS: 14 en suite (bth/shr) 4 annexe en suite (shr) (1 fmly) No smoking in 6 bedrooms s fr £54.50; d fr £74 (incl. bkfst) * LB Off peak **MEALS:** V meals **FACILITIES:** CTV in all bedrooms STV **SERVICES:** 14P **NOTES:** No dogs (ex guide dogs) No coaches No smoking in restaurant Closed Xmas-New Year **CARDS:**

New AA Guides for the Millennium are featured on page 24

REDDITCH Worcestershire **Map 07 SP06**
★★★ The Abbey Hotel Golf & Country Club
Hither Green Ln, Dagnel End Rd, Bordesley B98 7BD
Quality Percentage Score: 68%
☎ 01527 63918 📠 01527 584112
Dir: *from M42 junct 2 take A441 to Redditch, at end dual carriage way turn left still on A441, Dagnell End Rd is on the left*

Situated just to the north of the town this modern hotel is set in 175 acres of grounds. Bedrooms are comfortable, designed to meet the needs of business and leisure visitors alike. There is a choice of bars and leisure facilities.
ROOMS: 38 en suite (bth/shr) s fr £90; d fr £110 (incl. bkfst) * LB Off peak **MEALS:** Lunch £12.95 Dinner £17.95 English, French & Italian Cuisine V meals Coffee am Tea pm **FACILITIES:** CTV in all bedrooms Indoor swimming pool (heated) Golf 18 Fishing Sauna Solarium Gym Putting green Jacuzzi/spa Steam room & Health Club Xmas **CONF:** Thtr 40 Class 24 Board 24 Del £125 * **SERVICES:** Night porter 150P **NOTES:** No dogs (ex guide dogs) No smoking in restaurant Last d 9.30pm **CARDS:**

REDDITCH Worcestershire **Map 07 SP06**
★★★ Quality Hotel
Pool Bank, Southcrest B97 4JS
Quality Percentage Score: 63%
☎ 01527 541511 📠 01527 402600
Dir: *follow signs to hotel, 2nd on right after B & Q DIY store*
Originally a country house dating back in parts to the beginning of the century, this hotel has been considerably extended over the last 25 years. Set back within extensive wooded grounds, which include a Japanese garden, it enjoys commanding views. Bedrooms in the main house are spacious; the majority of rooms however are in the more modern wings, and all are well equipped. As well as a restaurant and recently expanded bar there are function suites and meeting rooms.
ROOMS: 58 en suite (bth/shr) (2 fmly) No smoking in 6 bedrooms s £73.25-£81.75; d £88.25-£105.50 * LB Off peak **MEALS:** Lunch £2.95-£15.95alc Dinner fr £14.50 & alc French Cuisine V meals Coffee am Tea pm **FACILITIES:** CTV in all bedrooms STV **CONF:** Thtr 100 Class 25 Board 50 **SERVICES:** Night porter 100P **NOTES:** No smoking in restaurant Last d 9.30pm **CARDS:**

REDDITCH Worcestershire **Map 07 SP06**

Campanile

Far Moor Ln, Winyates Green B98 0SD

☎ 01527 510710 01527 517269

Dir: *A435 towards Redditch, then A4023 Redditch/Bromsgrove*

This modern building offers accommodation in smart well equipped bedrooms, all with en-suite bathrooms. Refreshments may be taken at the informal Bistro. For details about current prices, consult the Contents Page under Hotel Groups for the Campanile phone number.
ROOMS: 50 annexe en suite (bth/shr) **CONF:** Thtr 35 Class 18 Board 20

REDHILL Surrey **Map 04 TQ25**

★★★★ **Nutfield Priory**

Nutfield RH1 4EL

Quality Percentage Score: 69%

☎ 01737 824400 01737 823321

Dir: *1 m E of Redhill on A25*

An extravagant gothic style folly built in 1872, high on Nutfield Ridge. Individually styled bedrooms, some with dramatic themes, are generally spacious and well equipped. Public areas include a foyer lounge with pipe organ, an oak-panelled library and a small bar. Cloisters Restaurant offers enjoyable cuisine. The Priory leisure complex adjacent to the hotel has a popular beauty salon.

ROOMS: 60 en suite (bth/shr) (4 fmly) No smoking in 12 bedrooms s fr £120; d £150-£300 * LB Off peak **MEALS:** Lunch £15-£18 & alc Dinner £25 & alc V meals Coffee am Tea pm **FACILITIES:** CTV in all bedrooms STV Indoor swimming pool (heated) Squash Sauna Solarium Gym Jacuzzi/spa Steam room Creche Beauty therapy Hairdressing **CONF:** Thtr 80 Class 45 Board 40 Del £215 * **SERVICES:** Lift Night porter 130P **NOTES:** No coaches No smoking in restaurant Last d 10pm Closed 26-30 Dec **CARDS:**

REDHILL Surrey **Map 04 TQ25**

Travel Inn

Brighton Rd, Salfords RH1 5BT

☎ 01737 767277 01737 778099

Dir: *on A23, betwen Horley and Redhill on Salfords Stream*

This modern building offers accommodation in smart, spacious and well equipped bedrooms, all with en-suite bathrooms. Refreshments may be taken at the nearby family restaurant. For details about current prices consult the Contents Page under Hotel Groups for the Travel Inn phone number.
ROOMS: 49 en suite (bth/shr) d £39.95 *

REDRUTH Cornwall & Isles of Scilly **Map 02 SW64**

★★★ **Penventon**

TR15 1TE

Quality Percentage Score: 66%

☎ 01209 203000 01209 203001

Dir: *turn off A30 at Redruth, hotel is 1m S*

This Georgian mansion is conveniently located for the A30 and a short walk from Redruth town centre. Public areas are luxurious, and additional facilities include a health spa and the lively Spice of Life bar. There is a wide choice of bedrooms, with the largest incorporating separate sitting areas. The restaurant,

contd.

R

featuring a pianist, offers extensive menus of Italian, French, British and Cornish dishes.
ROOMS: 50 en suite (bth/shr) (3 fmly) s £28-£50; d £54-£100 (incl. bkfst) LB Off peak **MEALS:** Lunch £10-£13 & alc Dinner £14-£16 & alc English French & Italian Cuisine V meals Coffee am Tea pm **FACILITIES:** CTV in all bedrooms Indoor swimming pool (heated) Sauna Solarium Gym Pool table Jacuzzi/spa Leisure spa Masseuse Steam bath Wkly live entertainment Xmas **CONF:** Thtr 200 Class 100 Board 60 Del from £50 * **SERVICES:** Night porter 100P **NOTES:** Last d 9.30pm
CARDS:

REDRUTH Cornwall & Isles of Scilly — Map 02 SW64
★★ Aviary Court
Mary's Well, Illogan TR16 4QZ
Quality Percentage Score: 69%
☎ 01209 842256 01209 843744
Dir: *turn off A30 at sign A3047 Camborne, Pool & Portreath. Follow Portreath & Illogan signs for approx 2 miles to Alexandra Rd*
This charming property is set in well tended gardens, on the edge of Illogan Woods. The bedrooms are individually furnished and decorated and provide many thoughtful extras. The meals served are generous in size and make full use of Cornish produce; Sunday lunches are a speciality and booking is essential.
ROOMS: 6 en suite (bth/shr) (1 fmly) s £42.50; d £60 (incl. bkfst) * Off peak **MEALS:** Sunday Lunch £10 Dinner £13.50 & alc English & French Cuisine **FACILITIES:** CTV in all bedrooms **CONF:** Thtr 20 Class 20 Board 20 **SERVICES:** 25P **NOTES:** No dogs No coaches No children 3yrs No smoking in restaurant Last d 8.30pm **CARDS:**

REDRUTH Cornwall & Isles of Scilly — Map 02 SW64
★★ Crossroads
Scorrier TR16 5BP
Quality Percentage Score: 68%
☎ 01209 820551 01209 820392
Dir: *off A30, Scorrier/Helston exit*
A purpose-built hotel, bedrooms differ in style and decor, nine executive rooms offer extra space and facilities. Twenty-four hour room service is available. The intimate restaurant serves a choice of menus, there is a separate breakfast room, a convivial red-plush bar and a comfortable lounge area.
ROOMS: 36 en suite (bth/shr) (4 fmly) No smoking in 4 bedrooms s £40-£48; d £50-£58 (incl. bkfst) * LB Off peak **MEALS:** Dinner fr £11.45 & alc English & French Cuisine V meals Coffee am Tea pm **FACILITIES:** CTV in 35 bedrooms Pool table **CONF:** Thtr 100 Class 30 Board 30 **SERVICES:** Lift 140P **NOTES:** Last d 9.30pm
CARDS:

REDWORTH Co Durham — Map 08 NZ22
★★★★ Redworth Hall Hotel & Country Club
DL5 6NL
Quality Percentage Score: 71%
☎ 01388 772442 01388 775112
SCOTTISH HIGHLAND HOTELS
Dir: *from A1(M) take A68 Corbridge road, at first rdbt turn right onto A6072 Shildon road, straight over next rdbt, hotel entrance 0.5m on left*
Housed in an extended Elizabethan mansion, this hotel and health club makes a fine impression. There are spacious, comfortable lounges, and two restaurants, of which the Blue Room is the best showcase for the chef's talents. Bedrooms are comfortable, stylish and well equipped. Leisure, conference and banqueting facilities are all of good quality.
ROOMS: 100 en suite (bth/shr) (10 fmly) No smoking in 30 bedrooms s £112-£122; d £132-£162 * LB Off peak **MEALS:** Lunch £13.50-£14.50 High tea fr £5.50 Dinner fr £21.75 English & Continental Cuisine V meals Coffee am Tea pm **FACILITIES:** CTV in all bedrooms STV Indoor swimming pool (heated) Tennis (hard) Squash Sauna Solarium Gym Croquet lawn Jacuzzi/spa Spa pool Health club Childrens indoor & outdoor play area Beauty treatments Xmas **CONF:** Thtr 300 Class 150 Board 100 Del from £150 * **SERVICES:** Lift Night porter 200P **NOTES:** No smoking area in restaurant Last d 9.45pm
CARDS:

We endeavour to be as accurate as possible but changes in personnel and data can occur in establishments after the Hotel Guide has gone to press.

REIGATE Surrey — Map 04 TQ25
★★★ Bridge House
Reigate Hill RH2 9RP
Quality Percentage Score: 65%
☎ 01737 246801 & 244821 01737 223756
Dir: *on A217 between M25 and Reigate*
High on Reigate Hill, this established hotel has panoramic views over surrounding countryside. Bedrooms, many with a balcony, have been refurbished and are thoughtfully equipped. Lanni's restaurant offers a high standard of cooking with a strong Mediterranean influence, and features live music and dancing most nights.
ROOMS: 39 en suite (bth/shr) (3 fmly) s £55-£85; d £98-£125 * Off peak **MEALS:** Lunch £18.50 & alc Dinner £22.50-£28.50 & alc English, French & Italian Cuisine V meals Coffee am **FACILITIES:** CTV in all bedrooms STV Wkly live entertainment Xmas **CONF:** Thtr 100 Class 70 Board 60 Del £125.50 * **SERVICES:** Night porter 110P **NOTES:** No dogs (ex guide dogs) Last d 10pm RS BH
CARDS:

See advert on opposite page

REIGATE Surrey — Map 04 TQ25
★★★ Reigate Manor Hotel
Reigate Hill RH2 9PF
Quality Percentage Score: 65%
☎ 01737 240125 01737 223883
Dir: *on A217, 1m S of junct 8 on M25*
Conveniently located close to the town on Reigate Hill, this Georgian mansion has benefited from the caring long-term ownership of Graeme Attridge, and a policy of continuous refurbishment. Good-sized bedrooms are well appointed and equipped and public areas appealing and comfortable. The hotel is a popular venue for both business meetings and social functions.
ROOMS: 50 en suite (bth/shr) (1 fmly) No smoking in 30 bedrooms s £90-£110; d £110-£130 * LB Off peak **MEALS:** Lunch £12.75-£17.50 Dinner £20.50-£21.50 English & French Cuisine V meals Coffee am **FACILITIES:** CTV in all bedrooms STV Sauna Solarium Gym **CONF:** Thtr 200 Class 80 Board 50 Del from £125 * **SERVICES:** Night porter 130P **NOTES:** No dogs (ex guide dogs) No smoking in restaurant Last d 10pm **CARDS:**

RENISHAW Derbyshire — Map 08 SK47
★★★ Sitwell Arms
Station Rd S21 3WF
Quality Percentage Score: 59%
☎ 01246 435226 01246 433915
Dir: *on A6135 to Sheffield, W of junct 30 of M1*
Dating back to the 18th century, this stone-built hotel offers a range of bedrooms, most of which are of good comfortable proportions. The public rooms are a focal point for the local

contd.

community and offer a choice of bars and a restaurant serving a range of popular dishes.

ROOMS: 30 en suite (bth/shr) (6 fmly) No smoking in 10 bedrooms s £49.95-£57.95; d £59.95-£67.95 (incl. bkfst) * LB Off peak **MEALS:** Lunch £6.95-£20alc Dinner £16-£20alc V meals Coffee am Tea pm **FACILITIES:** CTV in all bedrooms Xmas **CONF:** Thtr 160 Class 60 Board 60 Del from £56.45 * **SERVICES:** Night porter 150P **NOTES:** No dogs (ex guide dogs) No smoking area in restaurant Last d 9.45pm **CARDS:** *See advert under SHEFFIELD*

RICHMOND North Yorkshire — Map 07 NZ10

★★ King's Head

Market Place DL10 4HS
Quality Percentage Score: 68%
☎ 01748 850220 🖷 01748 850635

Dir: *in Richmond Market Place, 5m from A1/A66 at Scotch Corner on the A6108*

Conveniently located in the historic market square, The Kings Head offers well equipped, modern bedrooms, and its lounges, furnished with deep sofas, display an interesting collection of antique clocks. Afternoon tea is worth sampling, whilst the restaurant offers a good choice for dinner.

ROOMS: 26 en suite (bth/shr) 4 annexe en suite (bth/shr) (1 fmly) No smoking in 11 bedrooms s £55-£63; d £86-£109 (incl. bkfst) * LB Off peak **MEALS:** Sunday Lunch £8.95-£11.50 Dinner £18.95 & alc International Cuisine V meals Coffee am Tea pm **FACILITIES:** CTV in all bedrooms STV Xmas **CONF:** Thtr 180 Class 80 Board 50 Del from £70 * **SERVICES:** Night porter 25P **NOTES:** No smoking in restaurant Last d 9.15pm **CARDS:**

RICHMOND North Yorkshire — Map 07 NZ10

★ *Frenchgate*

59-61 Frenchgate DL10 7AE
Quality Percentage Score: 60%
☎ 01748 822087 🖷 01748 823596

Dir: *turn off at Scotch Corner on the A6108 Richmond. Through Richmond to New Queens Road rdbt, turn left into Dundas St and left again into Frenchgate*

This small, personally run hotel offers a warm welcome to both leisure and business guests. The public rooms include a lounge, bar and a small dining room. The bedrooms have recently been refurbished and provide all the expected facilities.

ROOMS: 12 rms (2 bth 4 shr) 1 annexe en suite (bth) (1 fmly) No smoking in all bedrooms **MEALS:** English, Chinese & Thai Cuisine V meals Coffee am Tea pm **FACILITIES:** CTV in all bedrooms **SERVICES:** 9P **NOTES:** No smoking in restaurant **CARDS:**

RICHMOND UPON THAMES Greater London

See LONDON SECTION plan 1 *C2*

★★★★ Richmond Gate

Richmond Hill TW10 6RP
Quality Percentage Score: 75%
☎ 020 8940 0061 🖷 020 8332 0354

Dir: *from Richmond head to the top of Richmond hill and the hotel on left opposite the Star & Garter home at Richmond gate exit*

A Georgian country house offering high standards of hospitality and service. Stylish bedrooms equipped to a very high standard *contd.*

include luxury doubles and suites, smaller garden wing rooms and several four-posters; best rooms are in the main house. Dining options are the informal Victorian conservatory bistro and candlelit Gates on the Park Restaurant. Cedars health and leisure club has a fitness room, swimming pool, jacuzzi, sauna, steam room and snack bar.
ROOMS: 66 en suite (bth/shr) (2 fmly) No smoking in 11 bedrooms s £110-£195; d £135-£195 (incl. bkfst) * LB Off peak **MEALS:** Lunch £19.25-£19.75 Dinner fr £29.75 International Cuisine V meals Coffee am Tea pm **FACILITIES:** CTV in all bedrooms STV Indoor swimming pool (heated) Sauna Solarium Gym Jacuzzi/spa Health & beauty suite Steam room Wkly live entertainment Xmas **CONF:** Thtr 50 Class 25 Board 30 Del from £185 * **SERVICES:** Night porter 50P **NOTES:** No dogs (ex guide dogs) No smoking in restaurant Last d 9.30pm
CARDS:

RICHMOND UPON THAMES Greater London
★★★ Richmond Hill
Richmond Hill TW10 6RW
Quality Percentage Score: 69%
☎ 020 8940 2247 & 940 5466
020 8940 5424
***Dir:** located at the top of Richmond Hill on B321*

An imposing Georgian Manor house built in 1726 on Richmond Hill, nearby are views of the Thames and open parkland. Rooms come in a variety of sizes and styles. The restaurant offers a fixed price menu and an impressive array of dishes on its carte. The stylish, well designed health club with large pool is shared with sister hotel the Richmond Gate.
ROOMS: 138 en suite (bth/shr) (9 fmly) No smoking in 48 bedrooms s £120-£130; d £130-£175 * LB Off peak **MEALS:** Lunch £15-£16 Dinner £21.50 & alc English & French Cuisine V meals Coffee am Tea pm **FACILITIES:** CTV in all bedrooms STV Indoor swimming pool (heated) Sauna Solarium Gym Jacuzzi/spa Steam room Health & beauty suite Wkly live entertainment Xmas **CONF:** Thtr 180 Class 150 Board 50 Del from £180 * **SERVICES:** Lift Night porter 150P **NOTES:** No smoking area in restaurant Last d 9.30pm **CARDS:**

RINGWOOD Hampshire — Map 04 SU10
★★★ Tyrrells Ford Country House
Avon BH23 7BH
Quality Percentage Score: 69%
☎ 01425 672646 01425 672262
***Dir:** turn off A31 to Ringwood. Follow B3347, Hotel 3m S on left at Avon*
This friendly hotel is peacefully situated in 10 acres of grounds and woodland. There is a wide choice of menus available, whether guests wish to eat in the bar or the restaurant. Bedrooms are comfortably furnished and well equipped.
ROOMS: 16 en suite (bth/shr) s £55-£90; d £80-£100 (incl. bkfst) * LB Off peak **MEALS:** Lunch £13.95-£14.95 Dinner fr £21 & alc English & French Cuisine V meals Coffee am **FACILITIES:** CTV in all bedrooms Xmas **CONF:** Thtr 40 Class 20 Board 20 Del from £100 * **SERVICES:** 100P **NOTES:** No dogs (ex guide dogs) No smoking in restaurant Last d 9.30pm **CARDS:**

> Symbols and Abbreviations are listed and explained on pages 4 and 5

RINGWOOD Hampshire — Map 04 SU10
★★ Moortown Lodge Hotel
244 Christchurch Rd BH24 3AS
Quality Percentage Score: 74%
☎ 01425 471404 01425 476052
***Dir:** off A31 onto B3347. Hotel 1.5m S on right*
This delightful little hotel is personally run by Jilly and Bob Burrows-Jones, who provide a warm welcome to their guests. The attractively decorated bedrooms are cosy, well maintained and have several thoughtful, extra features. Each evening Jilly cooks from an excellent fixed price menu, using local produce wherever possible.
ROOMS: 6 rms (2 bth 3 shr) (1 fmly) No smoking in 3 bedrooms s £45-£50; d £60-£85 (incl. bkfst) * LB Off peak **MEALS:** Dinner £18.95-£21.95 British & French Cuisine V meals **FACILITIES:** CTV in all bedrooms **SERVICES:** 8P **NOTES:** No dogs No coaches No smoking in restaurant Last d 8.30pm Closed 24 Dec-mid Jan
CARDS:

RINGWOOD Hampshire — Map 04 SU10
★★ The Struan Country Inn
Horton Rd, Ashley Heath BH24 2EG
Quality Percentage Score: 66%
☎ 01425 473553 01425 480529
***Dir:** from A31, exit onto the A338. Right at island, follow signs for Ashley Heath, after 0.5m take 2nd on right at hotel sign*
With its close proximity to Bournemouth and the New Forest, the Struan Country Inn is ideally located for both leisure and business travellers. The neatly presented bedrooms are well equipped and comfortable. In the spacious bar, a relaxed and friendly atmosphere prevails and in addition to the imaginative carte an extensive range of bar meals is available.
ROOMS: 10 en suite (bth/shr) (1 fmly) s fr £45; d fr £65 (incl. bkfst) * LB Off peak **MEALS:** Lunch £14.95-£23alc Dinner £14.95-£23alc English & Continental Cuisine V meals Coffee am **FACILITIES:** CTV in all bedrooms STV Xmas **SERVICES:** 75P **NOTES:** No smoking area in restaurant Last d 9.15pm **CARDS:**

RINGWOOD Hampshire — Map 04 SU10
★★ Candlesticks Inn
136 Christchurch Rd BH24 3AP
Quality Percentage Score: 64%
☎ 01425 472587 01425 471600
***Dir:** from M27/A31, take B3347 towards Christchurch, hotel on right hand side approx 1m from intersection/flyover*
This pretty 15th-century thatched inn, a consistent 'Ringwood in Bloom' winner, is on the edge of the town. The well equipped bedrooms are located in a modern lodge to the rear. One room is equipped for disabled guests. There is a bright conservatory bar-lounge where snacks can be taken, and a cosy beamed restaurant that serves a more extensive menu.
ROOMS: 8 en suite (shr) (4 fmly) s £37; d £54 (incl. bkfst) * LB Off peak **MEALS:** Lunch £7.95 & alc Dinner fr £9.95 & alc English & French Cuisine V meals Coffee am **FACILITIES:** CTV in all bedrooms Jacuzzi/spa **SERVICES:** 45P **NOTES:** No dogs No coaches No children 2yrs No smoking area in restaurant Last d 9pm Closed Xmas
CARDS:

contd.

RIPON North Yorkshire **Map 08 SE37**

★★★ Ripon Spa

Park St HG4 2BU

Quality Percentage Score: 68%

☎ 01765 602172 📠 01765 690770

Dir: *follow signs to the B6265, at T junct to join this road, turn right back towards Ripon, hotel on this section of B6265*

Standing in superb grounds, this Edwardian hotel provides traditional service. There are two bars which serve less formal meals, while the impressive restaurant serves a daily menu. The bedrooms are mostly spacious and are well equipped.

ROOMS: 40 en suite (bth/shr) (5 fmly) s £73-£85; d £89-£102 (incl. bkfst) * LB Off peak **MEALS:** Lunch £13.75 High tea £9.95 Dinner £18.25 & alc V meals Coffee am Tea pm **FACILITIES:** CTV in all bedrooms STV Croquet lawn Xmas **CONF:** Thtr 150 Class 35 Board 40 Del from £95 * **SERVICES:** Lift Night porter 80P **NOTES:** No smoking area in restaurant Last d 8.45pm **CARDS:**

See advert under HARROGATE

RIPON North Yorkshire **Map 08 SE37**

★★ Unicorn

Market Place HG4 1BP

Quality Percentage Score: 63%

☎ 01765 602202 📠 01765 690734

Dir: *on south east corner of Market Place, 4m from A1 on A61*

There is plenty of history surrounding this pleasant hotel which overlooks the market square. It offers quite spacious, well furnished bedrooms which continue to improve, and public rooms include a popular bar with excellent murals depicting Ripon. There is a cosy rear dining room where a good range of dishes is available.

ROOMS: 33 en suite (bth/shr) (4 fmly) s £47; d £67 (incl. bkfst) * LB Off peak **MEALS:** Lunch £8.95-£9.95 Dinner £14.95 & alc English & French Cuisine V meals Coffee am **FACILITIES:** CTV in all bedrooms **CONF:** Thtr 60 Class 10 Board 26 Del £72 * **SERVICES:** Night porter 20P **NOTES:** Last d 9pm Closed 24-25 Dec

CARDS:

RISLEY Derbyshire **Map 08 SK43**

★★★ *Risley Hall*

Derby Rd DE72 3SS

Quality Percentage Score: 73%

☎ 0115 9399000 📠 0115 9397766

Dir: *off junct 25 on M1, Sandiacre exit, left at T junct, 0.5m on left*

Dating from the 11th century, this impressive manor house is set in beautiful listed gardens. Public rooms include a comfortable morning room, choice of bars, private dining rooms and a grand baronial hall for larger functions. Bedrooms are individually styled, many with antique furnishings, exposed beams and wall timbers. Food is of a high standard, a carte menu is offered which is supplemented by daily dishes; service is both professional and friendly.

ROOMS: 16 en suite (bth/shr) (8 fmly) **MEALS:** British & European Cuisine V meals Coffee am Tea pm **FACILITIES:** CTV in all bedrooms STV Indoor swimming pool (heated) Snooker Gym Pool table Croquet lawn Jacuzzi/spa Archery **CONF:** Thtr 150 Class 80 Board 60 Del £145 * **SERVICES:** Lift Night porter 100P **NOTES:** No dogs (ex guide dogs) No smoking in restaurant Last d 9.30pm

CARDS:

See advert under DERBY

ROCHDALE Greater Manchester **Map 07 SD81**

★★★★ *Norton Grange*

Manchester Rd, Castleton OL11 2XZ

Quality Percentage Score: 64%

☎ 01706 630788 📠 01706 649313

Dir: *junct 20 of M62 follow signs for A627 (M) Oldham then A664 Middleton/Manchester then follow signs for Castleton on A664 on left*

This extended Victorian house stands in nine acres of grounds. Facilities include an attractive restaurant, bistro and bar. Bedrooms are modern and well equipped, and staff friendly and helpful.

ROOMS: 51 en suite (bth/shr) (28 fmly) No smoking in 25 bedrooms **MEALS:** International Cuisine V meals Coffee am Tea pm **FACILITIES:** CTV in all bedrooms STV **CONF:** Thtr 250 Class 80 Board 60 Del from £118 * **SERVICES:** Lift Night porter 150P **NOTES:** No smoking in restaurant Last high tea 6pm

CARDS:

ROCHDALE Greater Manchester **Map 07 SD81**

★★ *Midway Park*

Manchester Rd, Castleton OL11 2XX

Quality Percentage Score: 62%

☎ 01706 32881 📠 01706 53522

Dir: *off M62 junct 20, A627, then A664, 0.5m on right*

Situated just outside the town, near the A664, this hotel offers comfortable accommodation. There is a carvery and short menu in the restaurant, and also a popular wine bar. Regular entertainment is provided in the large ballroom.

ROOMS: 24 en suite (bth/shr) (1 fmly) **MEALS:** V meals Coffee am Tea pm **FACILITIES:** CTV in all bedrooms STV **CONF:** Thtr 200 Class 100 Board 150 **SERVICES:** Night porter 200P **NOTES:** Last d 9.30pm

CARDS:

ROCHDALE Greater Manchester **Map 07 SD81**

Travel Inn

Newhey Rd, Milnrow OL16 4JF

☎ 01706 299999 📠 01706 299074

Dir: *leave M62 junct 21 at rdbt turn right towards Shaw, go back under motorway bridge & take 1st left*

This modern building offers accommodation in smart, spacious and well equipped bedrooms, all with en-suite bathrooms. Refreshments

contd.

R

may be taken at the nearby family restaurant. For details about current prices consult the Contents Page under Hotel Groups for the Travel Inn phone number.
ROOMS: 40 en suite (bth/shr) d £39.95 *

ROCHESTER Kent **Map 05 TQ76**
★★★ Posthouse Rochester
Maidstone Rd ME5 9SF
Posthouse
Quality Percentage Score: 65%
☎ 01634 687111 🖷 01634 684512
Dir: *on A229 1m N of M2 jnct 3-from A229 head stright on over rdbt. Hotel and airport are signposted 100yds on the left*
Suitable for both the business and leisure traveller, this bright hotel provides modern accommodation in well equipped bedrooms with en suite bathrooms.
ROOMS: 145 en suite (bth/shr) (45 fmly) No smoking in 93 bedrooms d £99 * LB Off peak **MEALS:** International Cuisine V meals Coffee am Tea pm **FACILITIES:** CTV in all bedrooms Indoor swimming pool (heated) Sauna Solarium Gym Pool table Jacuzzi/spa Steam room Beautician available at charge Xmas **CONF:** Thtr 110 Class 48 Board 40 Del £119 * **SERVICES:** Lift Night porter 250P **NOTES:** Last d 10pm
CARDS:

ROCHESTER Kent **Map 05 TQ76**
★ Royal Victoria & Bull Hotel
16-18 High St ME1 1PX
Quality Percentage Score: 68%
☎ 01634 846266 🖷 01634 832312
Dir: *from M25 or London follow A2 into Rochester. Take second right after large bridge (over Medway River) then first right. Hotel located on the left*
A historic coaching inn, at the top end of the High Street, the Royal Victoria was visited by the Queen, its namesake, and features in some of Charles Dickens' novels. Its restaurant serves Italian food, and there is a popular bar. Bedrooms are smartly furnished.
ROOMS: 25 rms (22 bth/shr) (2 fmly) s £45-£57.50; d £57.50-£72.50 (incl. bkfst) * Off peak **MEALS:** Lunch £4.95-£15 & alc Dinner £7.50-£15 & alc Italian/International Cuisine V meals Coffee am Tea pm **FACILITIES:** CTV in all bedrooms STV Jacuzzi/spa **CONF:** Thtr 100 Class 60 Board 40 Del from £90 * **SERVICES:** Night porter 25P **NOTES:** No smoking area in restaurant Last d 11pm
CARDS:

R

ROCHFORD Essex **Map 05 TQ89**
★★★ Hotel Renouf
Bradley Way SS4 1BU
Quality Percentage Score: 68%
☎ 01702 541334 🖷 01702 549563
Dir: *turn off A127 onto B1013 to Rochford, at 3rd mini roundabout turn right & keep right*
A smart, red-brick establishment in the centre of Rochford, owned and run by the Renouf family. There is a small foyer seating area and a comfortable bar filled with cricket and sporting memorabilia. The attractive French restaurant overlooks the garden and Derek Renouf and his son Melvin offer imaginative set-price and carte menus. The bedrooms are spacious and modern in style, with limed oak furniture and co-ordinated decor.
ROOMS: 24 en suite (bth/shr) (2 fmly) **MEALS:** Lunch £12.50-£25 & alc Dinner £15.50-£25 & alc French Cuisine V meals **FACILITIES:** CTV in all bedrooms STV **CONF:** Thtr 30 Class 30 Board 20 Del from £91 * **SERVICES:** Night porter 25P **NOTES:** No coaches No smoking in restaurant Last d 9.45pm Closed 26-31 Dec
CARDS:

ROMALDKIRK Co Durham **Map 12 NY92**
★★ Rose & Crown
DL12 9EB
Quality Percentage Score: 76%
☎ 01833 650213 🖷 01833 650828
Dir: *6m NW from Barnard Castle on B6277*

This splendid Jacobean inn manages to retain much of its original charm, which is especially noticable in the bar and in the comfortable lounge. Accommodation includes several tastefully styled bedrooms and separate from the main house there is a stone-built row of spacious chalet-style rooms, well suited to business travellers, dog owners and shooters. For meals, there is a choice between the bar's blackboard menu or a seasonally changing four-course menu in the restaurant.
ROOMS: 7 en suite (bth/shr) 5 annexe en suite (bth/shr) (1 fmly) s £62; d £84 (incl. bkfst) * LB Off peak **MEALS:** Sunday Lunch £13.50-£15.50 Dinner £24-£26.50 English & French Cuisine V meals Coffee am Tea pm **FACILITIES:** CTV in all bedrooms **SERVICES:** 40P **NOTES:** No children 6yrs No smoking in restaurant Last d 9pm Closed 24-26 Dec
CARDS:

ROMFORD Greater London **Map 05 TQ58**
Travel Inn
Mercury Gardens RM1 3EN
☎ 01708 760548 🖷 01708 760456
travel inn
Dir: *on Mercury Gardens on the Romford Inner Ring Rd*
This modern building offers accommodation in smart, spacious and well equipped bedrooms, all with en-suite bathrooms. Refreshments may be taken at the nearby family restaurant. For details about current prices consult the Contents Page under Hotel Groups for the Travel Inn phone number.
ROOMS: 47 en suite (bth/shr) d £39.95 *

ROMSEY Hampshire **Map 04 SU32**
★★★ Potters Heron
Winchester Rd, Ampfield SO51 9ZF
corus
Corus and Regal hotels
Quality Percentage Score: 67%
☎ 023 80266611 🖷 023 80251359
Dir: *M3 junct 12 follow signs for Chandlers Ford at rdbt take 2nd exit, follow signs for Ampfield, go over crossrds, hotel is on left hand side after 1m*
This distinctive thatched hotel retains many original features. Extensive refurbishment has taken place to offer a good standard of accommodation and public areas, all are comfortably and

contd.

attractively furnished. The re-styled pub and restaurant operation offers an interesting range of dishes at dinner.

ROOMS: 54 en suite (bth/shr) (4 fmly) No smoking in 32 bedrooms d fr £85 * LB Off peak **MEALS:** Lunch £6.95-£13.95 Dinner £15.95 V meals Coffee am Tea pm **FACILITIES:** CTV in all bedrooms STV Sauna Wkly live entertainment Xmas **CONF:** Thtr 150 Class 70 Board 45 Del from £119 * **SERVICES:** Lift Night porter 150P **NOTES:** No smoking in restaurant Last d 9.30pm **CARDS:**

ROMSEY Hampshire Map 04 SU32

★★★ The White Horse

Market Place SO51 8ZJ

Quality Percentage Score: 59%

☎ 01794 512431 01794 517485

Dir: *from M27 junct 3, follow A3057 to Romsey, then signs to town centre. Hotel can be seen on left, car park found on next turn on in Latimer St*

Set in the heart of this historic town, the White Horse dates back to Elizabethan times despite its Georgian facade and more recent additions. Bedrooms, which are gradually being refurbished are attractively furnished and equipped with modern amenities. Public areas include a large restaurant, separate bar and cosy lounge which is a popular venue for coffee and afternoon teas. Rear parking is a real plus.

ROOMS: 33 en suite (bth/shr) (7 fmly) No smoking in 11 bedrooms s fr £65; d £85-£105 * LB Off peak **MEALS:** Sunday Lunch £5.95-£12.95 Dinner £8.50-£18 V meals Coffee am Tea pm **FACILITIES:** CTV in all bedrooms Free use of nearby leisure facilities Xmas **CONF:** Thtr 40 Class 20 Board 20 Del from £75 * **SERVICES:** Night porter 60P **NOTES:** No smoking area in restaurant Last d 9pm **CARDS:**

ROSEDALE ABBEY North Yorkshire Map 08 SE79

★★★ Blacksmith's Country House

Hartoft End YO18 8EN

Quality Percentage Score: 64%

☎ 01751 417331 01751 417167

Dir: *A64 from York turn off for Pickering A169. In Pickering turn left for Thirsk A170. Turn left at Wrelton sign post to Hartoft 5 miles*

The Blacksmiths Arms is a former farm house which has been extended and restored into a comfortable and friendly hotel. It offers a choice of bars and lounges, but the main feature is the dining room designed in the style of stables and furnished in attractive solid pine. Bedrooms are comfortable and staff friendly.

ROOMS: 14 en suite (bth/shr) (1 fmly) s £35-£40; d £70-£80 (incl. bkfst) * LB Off peak **MEALS:** Sunday Lunch £13-£15 & alc Dinner £15.50 & alc International Cuisine V meals Coffee am Tea pm **FACILITIES:** CTV in all bedrooms Pool table **SERVICES:** 60P **NOTES:** No coaches No smoking in restaurant Last d 9pm **CARDS:**

See advert on this page

ROSEDALE ABBEY North Yorkshire Map 08 SE79

★★ Milburn Arms

YO18 8RA

Quality Percentage Score: 72%

☎ 01751 417312 01751 417312

Dir: *7m N off A170 from Wrelton village*

Set in the centre of a village in a fold of the North Yorkshire Moors, this welcoming hotel dates in part from the 16th century. The well equipped bedrooms vary in style between traditional and modern, there is a delightful bar, a comfortable lounge, and the Priory Restaurant for good food.

ROOMS: 3 en suite (bth/shr) 8 annexe en suite (bth/shr) (2 fmly) s £41.50-£49.50; d £68-£76 (incl. bkfst) * LB Off peak **MEALS:** Sunday Lunch fr £11.50 Dinner £22-£28alc English & French Cuisine V meals Coffee am **FACILITIES:** CTV in all bedrooms **SERVICES:** 35P **NOTES:** No children 8yrs No smoking in restaurant Last d 9.30pm Closed 23-27 Dec & 12-29 Jan **CARDS:**

ROSEDALE ABBEY North Yorkshire **Map 08 SE79**

★★ White Horse Farm

YO18 8SE
Quality Percentage Score: 65%
☎ 01751 417239 📠 01751 417781
Dir: *turn off A170, follow signs to Rosedale for approx 7m, hotel sign points up steep hill out of village, hotel 300yds on left*

From its position above the village, this hotel enjoys lovely views over the moors. Bedrooms, whether in the main house or an adjoining building in the gardens, are individually and attractively decorated. Meals are served either in the bar or in the restaurant, and there is also a residents' lounge.

ROOMS: 11 en suite (bth/shr) 4 annexe en suite (bth/shr) (3 fmly) s £47.50-£59.50; d £75-£87 (incl. bkfst) * LB Off peak **MEALS:** Lunch £8.95-£12 Dinner £17-£25 English & French Cuisine V meals Coffee am Tea pm **FACILITIES:** CTV in all bedrooms Pool table Xmas **CONF:** Board 30 **SERVICES:** 100P **NOTES:** No coaches No smoking in restaurant Last d 8.45pm Closed 31 Dec
CARDS:

ROSSINGTON South Yorkshire **Map 08 SK69**

★★★ Mount Pleasant

Great North Rd DN11 0HW
Quality Percentage Score: 71%
☎ 01302 868696 & 868219 📠 01302 865130
Dir: *on A638 Great North Rd between Bawtry and Doncaster*

This charming house dates back to the 18th century and stands in 100 acres of wooded parkland. Bedrooms have been thoughtfully equipped and pleasingly furnished, the new Premier bedrooms being particularly spacious. There are comfortable lounges, a small bar and a traditionally styled restaurant.

ROOMS: 42 en suite (bth/shr) (15 fmly) No smoking in all bedrooms s £57-£81; d £86-£98 (incl. bkfst) * LB Off peak **MEALS:** Lunch £11-£16 Dinner £19.95-£25 English & French Cuisine V meals Coffee am Tea pm **FACILITIES:** CTV in all bedrooms STV **CONF:** Thtr 100 Class 50 Board 50 Del from £105 * **SERVICES:** Night porter 100P **NOTES:** No dogs (ex guide dogs) No coaches No smoking in restaurant Last d 9.30pm
CARDS:

ROSS-ON-WYE Herefordshire **Map 03 SO62**

see also **Goodrich and Symonds Yat**

★★★❀❀ Pengethley Manor

Pengethley Park HR9 6LL
Quality Percentage Score: 77%
☎ 01989 730211 📠 01989 730238
Dir: *4m N on A49 Hereford road*

This fine Georgian mansion, north of Ross-on-Wye, is set in extensive grounds which contain two commercial vineyards. The hotel provides a high level of professional and friendly service and has a well deserved reputation for its cuisine. The accommodation is tastefully appointed and there is a wide variety of bedroom styles, all similarly well equipped. Half are in separate buildings across a courtyard. The elegant public rooms are furnished in a style sympathetic to the character of the house.

ROOMS: 11 en suite (bth/shr) 14 annexe en suite (bth/shr) (3 fmly) s £75-£115; d £120-£160 (incl. bkfst) * LB Off peak **MEALS:** Lunch fr £13.95 & alc High tea fr £8 Dinner £25-£40alc English & French Cuisine V meals Coffee am Tea pm **FACILITIES:** CTV in all bedrooms Outdoor swimming pool (heated) Golf 9 Fishing Snooker Croquet lawn Golf improvement course ch fac Xmas **CONF:** Thtr 50 Class 25 Board 28 **SERVICES:** 70P **NOTES:** No smoking in restaurant Last d 9.30pm
CARDS:

See advert on opposite page

ROSS-ON-WYE Herefordshire **Map 03 SO62**

★★★❀ Hunsdon Manor

Gloucester Rd, Weston under Penyard HR9 7PE
Quality Percentage Score: 70%
☎ 01989 562748 & 563376 & 768348 📠 01989 768348
Dir: *two miles east of M50 on the A40 road to Gloucester*

Hunsdon Manor is built of mellow local sandstone and dates back to Elizabethan times. Set in extensive grounds and gardens, it stands on the A40 in the village of Weston-under-Penyard, two miles south-east of Ross-on-Wye. It is now a privately owned and personally run hotel, with a reputation for friendly hospitality and good food. The accommodation, which includes family bedded rooms and rooms with four-poster beds, has modern facilities and equipment. Some bedrooms are located on the ground and first floors of cleverly converted outbuildings. Public rooms include a pleasant bar and a very attractive restaurant. The hotel can offer a choice of function and conference rooms.

ROOMS: 12 en suite (bth/shr) 13 annexe en suite (bth/shr) (3 fmly) s £48-£56; d £60-£76 (incl. bkfst) * LB Off peak **MEALS:** Lunch £14-£16 Dinner £18 & alc English & Continental Cuisine V meals Coffee am Tea pm **FACILITIES:** CTV in all bedrooms **CONF:** Thtr 60 Class 46 Board 36 Del from £84 * **SERVICES:** 55P **NOTES:** No coaches No smoking area in restaurant Last d 9.30pm
CARDS:

See advert on opposite page

ROSS-ON-WYE Herefordshire **Map 03 SO62**

★★★❀❀ *Chase*

Gloucester Rd HR9 5LH
Quality Percentage Score: 69%
☎ 01989 763161 📠 01989 768330
Dir: *leave M5 junct 8 for M50, leave M50 at junct 4, continue towards town centre, turn right onto B4260, the hotel is situated on the left hand side*

This Regency mansion is set in extensive grounds and gardens within easy reach of the town centre. Bedrooms vary in size, all have modern furnishings and are well equipped. Four-poster rooms are available. Public rooms include an attractive restaurant, where diners can enjoy the culinary skills of chef Ian

contd. on p. 546

Pencraig Court Hotel

Pencraig, Nr. Ross-On-Wye
Herefordshire HR9 6HR
Tel: 01989 770306   Fax: 01989 770040
Email: mike@pencraig-court.co.uk

Georgian Country House Hotel with lovely gardens and views over the River Wye. Situated midway between Ross and Monmouth in the heart of Wye Valley country, it also offers easy access to the Forest of Dean and Rural Herefordshire. The hotel provides a quiet, comfortable relaxing atmosphere with good home-made food all of which is cooked fresh daily to your requirements. There is a well stocked Wine Cellar to suit all tastes.

Open All Year Round.

Price guide for Dinner (Table d'Hote), Bed & Breakfast around £56.50.

Pengethley Manor

GEORGIAN COUNTRY HOTEL & RESTAURANT

Nr. Ross-on-Wye, Herefordshire HR9 6LL
Tel: (01989) 730211 Fax: (01989) 730238

This delightful hotel and restaurant is quietly situated in 15 acres of gardens and grounds, has its own vineyard, with lovely views of the Herefordshire countryside. The attractive, elegant restaurant features fresh local produce and fresh herbs. A la Carte and Table d'hôte menus are available.

A separate Conference Centre provides everything you need for meetings 'away from it all'.

To help you relax, we have a heated outdoor swimming pool, 9 hole golf improvement course, designer walks, trout pond, croquet and snooker.

AA★★★ 76% ◎◎   Egon Ronay
BTA Commended Country House Hotel
Derek Johansen Recommended Hotels

Hunsdon Manor Hotel ★★★

& CONFERENCE CENTRE

A 16th century Manor House given to Baron Hunsdon by Queen Elizabeth I.

Weston Under Penyard · Ross-on-Wye · Hereford & Worcester
Tel: (01989) 562748 and 563376 · Fax: (01989) 768348

Fully licensed hotel and restaurant standing in 2 acres of gardens on the A40, 2 miles from Ross-on-Wye, 14 miles Gloucester. Ideally situated for exploring the beautiful Wye Valley, Royal Forest of Dean and the Welsh Borders. Colour TV, tea and coffee making facilities and direct dial telephone in all rooms. Ground floor rooms available overlooking garden. The Restaurant offers a wide choice of dishes.

PERSONAL ATTENTION FROM RESIDENT OWNER AND MANAGER.

Beale. There is also a pleasant bar and lounge. Other facilities include conference rooms and a large function suite. The hotel is a popular venue for wedding receptions.

Chase, Ross-on-Wye

ROOMS: 38 en suite (bth/shr) (1 fmly) No smoking in 10 bedrooms **MEALS:** International Cuisine V meals Coffee am Tea pm **FACILITIES:** CTV in all bedrooms STV **CONF:** Thtr 300 Class 150 Board 50 **SERVICES:** Night porter 200P **NOTES:** No dogs (ex guide dogs) No children 12yrs Last d 9.45pm Closed 26 & 27 Dec **CARDS:**

ROSS-ON-WYE Herefordshire **Map 03 SO62**

★★★ Pencraig Court

Pencraig HR9 6HR
Quality Percentage Score: 68%
☎ 01989 770306 01989 770040
Dir: *off A40, 4m S of Ross-on-Wye*

A large Georgian house, standing in extensive grounds and gardens, with impressive views of the River Wye. Personally run, it provides well equipped, traditionally furnished accommodation, including family rooms and a room with a four-poster. There is no bar, but drinks are dispensed in both lounges and the restaurant.

ROOMS: 11 en suite (bth) (1 fmly) s £50-£55; d £67.50-£75 (incl. bkfst) * LB Off peak **MEALS:** Lunch £10-£12.50 High tea fr £7.50 Dinner £25 English, American, French & Italian Cuisine V meals Coffee am Tea pm **FACILITIES:** CTV in all bedrooms Fishing Riding Croquet lawn ch fac **CONF:** Board 20 Del from £46 * **SERVICES:** 20P **NOTES:** No smoking in restaurant Last d 9.30pm **CARDS:**

See advert on page 545

ROSS-ON-WYE Herefordshire **Map 03 SO62**

★★★ *The Royal*

Palace Pound HR9 5HZ
Quality Percentage Score: 66%
☎ 01989 565105 01989 768058
Dir: *from M5 junct 8- Take M50 until end of M'way. At 2nd rdbt turn right. Hotel located on the left hand side after 0.5m close to St Marys Church*

Located next to St Mary's church, this character hotel has commanding views out over the river and the countryside beyond. Public rooms include a cosy lounge, small bar and a spacious restaurant. Bedrooms are generally comfortable and well presented.

ROOMS: 40 en suite (bth/shr) (4 fmly) No smoking in 11 bedrooms **MEALS:** English & French Cuisine V meals Coffee am Tea pm **FACILITIES:** CTV in all bedrooms Fishing Pool table **CONF:** Thtr 80 Class 50 Board 30 **SERVICES:** Night porter 70P **NOTES:** No smoking in restaurant Last d 9.30pm **CARDS:**

ROSS-ON-WYE Herefordshire **Map 03 SO62**

★★ Glewstone Court

Glewstone HR9 6AW
Quality Percentage Score: 74%
☎ 01989 770367 01989 770282
Dir: *from Ross Market Place take A40/A49 Monmouth/Hereford, over Wilton Bridge to rdbt, turn left onto A40 to Monmouth, after 1m turn right for Glewstone*

Surrounded by three acres of mature grounds, this country house hotel offers a friendly and relaxed environment for both leisure and business guests. Informal service is delivered with great enthusiasm with owner Bill Reeve-Tucker leading from the front. The kitchen is the domain of Christine Reeve-Tucker who offers an extensive menu of well executed dishes. Throughout, the hotel is decorated and furnished with great flair.

ROOMS: 7 en suite (bth/shr) (2 fmly) s £50-£75; d £90-£105 (incl. bkfst) LB Off peak **MEALS:** Bar Lunch £5-£12alc English & French Cuisine V meals Coffee am **FACILITIES:** CTV in all bedrooms Croquet lawn **CONF:** Thtr 35 Board 16 **SERVICES:** 25P **NOTES:** No coaches Closed 25-27 Dec **CARDS:**

ROSS-ON-WYE Herefordshire **Map 03 SO62**

★★ King's Head

8 High St HR9 5HL
Quality Percentage Score: 68%
☎ 01989 763174 01989 769578
Dir: *near Ancient Town Centre on the High St*

Located in the town centre, this 14th-century coaching inn provides well-equipped accommodation, including some in a converted stable block. The traditionally-furnished dining room serves a good choice of popular dishes, while the bar has much charm and character and there is a comfortable coffee lounge.

ROOMS: 14 en suite (bth) 9 annexe en suite (bth) (6 fmly) s £30-£41; d £70 (incl. bkfst) * LB Off peak **MEALS:** Sunday Lunch £9-£12alc V meals Coffee am Tea pm **FACILITIES:** CTV in all bedrooms Xmas **SERVICES:** 26P **NOTES:** No coaches No smoking in restaurant Closed 24-26 Dec **CARDS:**

ROSS-ON-WYE Herefordshire **Map 03 SO62**

★★ Bridge House

Wilton HR9 6AA
Quality Percentage Score: 65%
☎ 01989 562655 01989 567652
Dir: *0.5m N of Ross-on-Wye, at joining of A40/A49 is a rdbt at Wilton, hotel 200yds from rdbt, towards Ross, at end of Wilton Bridge*

This Georgian house has a large garden extending to the bank of the River Wye. The hotel has a well deserved reputation for

contd.

friendliness. Modern equipped accommodation includes several spacious rooms, and one with a four-poster bed.
ROOMS: 8 en suite (bth/shr) (1 fmly) s fr £35; d fr £52 (incl. bkfst) * LB Off peak **MEALS:** Dinner fr £15.50 & alc English & French Cuisine V meals **FACILITIES:** CTV in all bedrooms Xmas **SERVICES:** 14P
NOTES: No coaches No smoking in restaurant Last d 8pm
CARDS:

ROSS-ON-WYE Herefordshire **Map 03 SO62**
★★ Castle Lodge Hotel
Wilton HR9 6AD
Quality Percentage Score: 65%
☎ 01989 562234 01989 768322
Dir: *on roundabout at junct of A40/A49, 0.5m from centre of Ross-on-Wye*
Dating back to the 16th century, with exposed timbers, this friendly hotel provides pleasant bedrooms, most of them pine-furnished. A good range of bar meals is offered, together with a varied restaurant menu, served in the cane-furnished restaurant. A large function room is available.
ROOMS: 10 en suite (bth/shr) (3 fmly) **MEALS:** Bar Lunch fr £3.50 & alc V meals Coffee am Tea pm **FACILITIES:** CTV in all bedrooms
CONF: Thtr 100 Class 80 Board 60 **SERVICES:** 40P
CARDS:

ROSS-ON-WYE Herefordshire **Map 03 SO62**
★★ Chasedale
Walford Rd HR9 5PQ
Quality Percentage Score: 65%
☎ 01989 562423 01989 567900
Dir: *from Ross-on-Wye town centre head south on B4234, hotel 0.5m on left*
A large, mid-Victorian country house in extensive gardens, the Chasedale provides well equipped accommodation, including ground-floor and family rooms. There is a spacious lounge and a restaurant with a good selection of wholesome food.
ROOMS: 10 en suite (bth/shr) (2 fmly) No smoking in 1 bedroom s £29.50-£32.50; d £59-£65 (incl. bkfst) * LB Off peak **MEALS:** Lunch £9.75-£10.75 Dinner fr £13.75 & alc English & French Cuisine V meals Coffee am Tea pm **FACILITIES:** CTV in all bedrooms Xmas **CONF:** Thtr 40 Class 30 Board 25 **SERVICES:** 14P **NOTES:** No coaches No smoking in restaurant Last d 9pm **CARDS:**

ROSS-ON-WYE Herefordshire **Map 03 SO62**
★★ *Orles Barn*
Wilton HR9 6AE
Quality Percentage Score: 65%
☎ 01989 562155 01989 768470
Dir: *off junct A40/A49*
This privately owned and personally run hotel stands in extensive gardens, which contain an outdoor heated swimming pool. Bedrooms are well maintained and equipped, and some are on the ground floor of an adjoining building.
ROOMS: 9 en suite (bth/shr) (1 fmly) **MEALS:** English & Continental Cuisine V meals **FACILITIES:** CTV in all bedrooms Outdoor swimming pool (heated) Fishing **CONF:** Board 15 **SERVICES:** Night porter 16P
NOTES: No smoking area in restaurant Last d 9.15pm Closed Nov
CARDS:

ROSS-ON-WYE Herefordshire **Map 03 SO62**
Travel Inn
Ledbury Rd HR9 7QJ
☎ 01989 563861 01989 566124
Dir: *1m from town centre on the M50 rdbt*
This modern building offers accommodation in smart, spacious and well equipped bedrooms, all with en-suite bathrooms. Refreshments may be taken at the nearby family restaurant. For details about current prices consult the Contents Page under Hotel Groups for the Travel Inn phone number.
ROOMS: 40 en suite (bth/shr) d £39.95 *

ROSTHWAITE Cumbria **Map 11 NY21**
see also **Borrowdale**
★★ *Scafell*
CA12 5XB
Quality Percentage Score: 63%
☎ 017687 77208 017687 77280
Dir: *6m S of Keswick on B5289*

An established hotel run by an experienced and friendly team. A wide ranging menu of imaginative dishes is presented in the spacious dining room, or you can enjoy supper in the cocktail bar and the less formal 'Walkers Inn' pub. There is a wide choice

contd.

of accommodation with the most sylish rooms in the main house.

ROOMS: 24 en suite (bth/shr) (3 fmly) **MEALS:** International Cuisine V meals Coffee am Tea pm **FACILITIES:** CTV in all bedrooms
SERVICES: 50P **NOTES:** No coaches No smoking in restaurant Last d 8.15pm **CARDS:** 💳 🎫 ✈ 💷

See advert on page 547

ROTHERHAM South Yorkshire — Map 08 SK49
★★★★ Hellaby Hall
Old Hellaby Ln, Hellaby S66 8SN
Quality Percentage Score: 66%
☎ 01709 702701 📠 01709 700979

SCOTTISH HIGHLAND HOTELS

Dir: 1m off junct 1 of the M18 on the A631 towards Bawtry from Rotherham, in village of Hellaby

Just off the M1, this 17th-century hotel was built according to a Flemish design. Reception rooms, with their high, beamed ceilings, are of grand proportions and staircases lead off to the private meeting rooms and a series of oak-panelled lounges. Bedrooms are all decorated in the same pleasantly spacious manner. Good, freshly cooked food is served in the smart restaurant.

ROOMS: 52 en suite (bth/shr) (4 fmly) No smoking in 15 bedrooms s £45-£90; d £79-£105 * LB Off peak **MEALS:** Lunch £10.50-£12.50 & alc Dinner £20-£21.50 & alc English, French & Italian Cuisine V meals Coffee am Tea pm **FACILITIES:** CTV in all bedrooms STV Indoor swimming pool (heated) Sauna Solarium Gym Croquet lawn Putting green Jacuzzi/spa Petanque Outdoor skittles Health Club Wkly live entertainment Xmas **CONF:** Thtr 140 Class 75 Board 40 Del from £95 * **SERVICES:** Lift Night porter 235P **NOTES:** No smoking area in restaurant Last d 10pm **CARDS:** 💳 ■ 🎫 💷 📧

ROTHERHAM South Yorkshire — Map 08 SK49
★★★ Consort
Brampton Rd, Thurcroft S66 9JA
Quality Percentage Score: 69%
☎ 01709 530022 📠 01709 531529

Best Western

Dir: exit 1 M18 right towards Bawtry on A631 in 50yds turn right, 1.5m to crossroads hotel opposite

Bedrooms at this friendly modern hotel are comfortable and attractively decorated, with the added benefit of air conditioning. A wide range of dishes is offered in the open plan bar and restaurant area, a comfortable foyer lounge also being offered. Excellent conference and function facilities include one suite catering for up to 300 people.

ROOMS: 18 en suite (bth/shr) (1 fmly) No smoking in 8 bedrooms
MEALS: V meals Coffee am Tea pm **FACILITIES:** CTV in all bedrooms STV **CONF:** Thtr 300 Class 120 Board 50 **SERVICES:** Night porter 90P
NOTES: No dogs (ex guide dogs) Last d 9.30pm
CARDS: 💳 ■ 🎫 💷 💷

ROTHERHAM South Yorkshire — Map 08 SK49
★★★❀ Swallow
West Bawtry Rd S60 4NA
Quality Percentage Score: 68%
☎ 01709 830630 📠 01709 830549

SWALLOW HOTELS

Dir: from junct 33 of the M1 take A630 towards Rotherham, hotel is approx 0.5m on right hand side

This large modern hotel is well situated for the motorway and the town centre. The bedrooms are spacious and well equipped. A good standard of cooking is provided in the restaurant and an interesting range of snacks is also offered.

ROOMS: 100 en suite (bth/shr) (5 fmly) No smoking in 47 bedrooms s £65-£90; d £80-£115 (incl. bkfst) * LB Off peak **MEALS:** Lunch £7.95-£10.25 High tea £4.50-£9 Dinner £19 English & Continental Cuisine V meals Coffee am Tea pm **FACILITIES:** CTV in all bedrooms STV Indoor swimming pool (heated) Solarium Gym Jacuzzi/spa Steam room Sunbeds Childrens pool Xmas **CONF:** Thtr 300 Class 120 Board 40 Del £130 * **SERVICES:** Lift Night porter 222P **NOTES:** No smoking area in restaurant Last d 9.30pm **CARDS:** 💳 ■ 🎫 💷 📧 ✈ 💷

ROTHERHAM South Yorkshire — Map 08 SK49
★★★ Elton
Main St, Bramley S66 2SF
Quality Percentage Score: 67%
☎ 01709 545681 📠 01709 549100

Best Western

Dir: 3m E A631, from M18 junct 1 follow A631 Rotheram, turn right to Ravenfield, hotel at end Bramley village

Enjoying easy access to the M18, this welcoming, stone-built hotel offers nicely furnished bedrooms, the larger ones being in an adjacent building, reached via a covered walkway. Carefully prepared meals are served in the traditional restaurant and conference rooms are available.

ROOMS: 13 en suite (bth/shr) 16 annexe en suite (bth/shr) (4 fmly) No smoking in 5 bedrooms s £56-£72; d £80 LB Off peak **MEALS:** Lunch £13.50 & alc Dinner £21 & alc English & French Cuisine V meals Coffee am Tea pm **FACILITIES:** CTV in all bedrooms STV **CONF:** Thtr 44 Class 24 Board 26 Del from £85 * **SERVICES:** Night porter 48P **NOTES:** No smoking area in restaurant Last d 9.30pm
CARDS: 💳 ■ 🎫 💷 📧 ✈ 💷

ROTHERHAM South Yorkshire — Map 08 SK49
★★★ Carlton Park
102/104 Moorgate Rd S60 2BG
Quality Percentage Score: 63%
☎ 01709 849955 📠 01709 368960

REGAL

Dir: M1 junct 33, turn right onto A631 (Bawtry) and left onto A618. Hotel 800yds past Rotherham General Hospital

This modern hotel is situated in a pleasant residential area of the town. Bedrooms are furnished and decorated to a good standard and three have separate sitting rooms. A feature of the hotel is
contd.

the recently opened "Nelsons" Restaurant and Bar which offers hot and cold meals and incorporates a Pizza and Pasta section.

ROOMS: 76 en suite (bth/shr) (6 fmly) No smoking in 33 bedrooms s £69-£80; d £95 (incl. bkfst) * LB Off peak **MEALS:** Lunch £2.50-£12.50alc Dinner £2.50-£12.50alc International Cuisine V meals Coffee am Tea pm **FACILITIES:** CTV in all bedrooms STV Sauna Solarium Gym Jacuzzi/spa Wkly live entertainment Xmas **CONF:** Thtr 250 Class 160 Board 60 Del from £85 * **SERVICES:** Lift Night porter 95P **NOTES:** No smoking area in restaurant Last d 11pm
CARDS:

ROTHERHAM South Yorkshire — Map 08 SK49

Campanile

Hellaby Industrial Estate, Lowton Way, Denby Way S66 8RY
☎ 01709 700255 📠 01709 545169
Dir: *junct 1 of M18. Follow directions to Maltby off rdbt. At traffic lights turn left and take 2nd road on left*

This modern building offers accommodation in smart well equipped bedrooms, all with en-suite bathrooms. Refreshments may be taken at the informal Bistro. For details about current prices, consult the Contents Page under Hotel Groups for the Campanile phone number.
ROOMS: 50 en suite (bth/shr) **CONF:** Thtr 35 Class 18 Board 20

ROTHERHAM South Yorkshire — Map 08 SK49

Travel Inn

Bawtry Rd S65 3JB
☎ 01709 543216 📠 01709 531546
Dir: *on A631 towards Wickersley, between junct 1 of M18 and junct 33 of M1*
This modern building offers accommodation in smart, spacious and well equipped bedrooms, all with en-suite bathrooms. Refreshments may be taken at the nearby family restaurant. For details about current prices consult the Contents Page under Hotel Groups for the Travel Inn phone number.
ROOMS: 37 en suite (bth/shr) d £39.95 *

ROTHERWICK Hampshire — Map 04 SU75

The Premier Collection

★★★★ Tylney Hall

Tylney Hall RG27 9AZ
☎ 01256 764881 📠 01256 768141
Dir: *M3 junct 5-A287 to Basingstoke, straight on at junct with A30, over railway bridge, towards Newnham. At Newnham Green turn right. Hotel 1m on left*
Set in 66 acres of beautiful parkland, this Victorian country house offers spacious and comfortable accommodation. The gardens, originally laid out by Gertrude Jekyll, are stunning, having been lovingly restored to their former glory with lakes and ornamental fountains. Public rooms feature log fires, fragrant fresh flowers and fine ceilings, guests can enjoy afternoon tea on beautifully embroided cloths. Traditionally furnished bedrooms range from the spacious to the huge, and offer handsome extras such as fine quality toiletries and linen, towelling robes and mineral water. The splendid Oak Room is the setting for Stephen Hine's cooking which is modern in style and features good quality ingredients. The table d'hote menu changes daily, whilst the other menu evolves seasonally, retaining some favourite dishes; the highlight of a recent inspection was a delicate starter of warm sole souffle.
ROOMS: 35 en suite (bth/shr) 75 annexe en suite (bth/shr) (1 fmly) s £115-£285; d £145-£305 (incl. bkfst) * LB Off peak
MEALS: Lunch £15-£21 Dinner £33 English & French Cuisine V meals Coffee am Tea pm **FACILITIES:** CTV in all bedrooms STV Indoor swimming pool (heated) Outdoor swimming pool (heated) Tennis (hard) Snooker Sauna Gym Croquet lawn Jacuzzi/spa Clay pigeon shooting Archery Falconry Xmas **CONF:** Thtr 110 Class 70 Board 40 Del from £205 * **SERVICES:** Night porter 120P
NOTES: No dogs (ex guide dogs) No coaches No smoking in restaurant Last d 9.30pm **CARDS:**

See advert under BASINGSTOKE

ROTHLEY Leicestershire — Map 08 SK51

★★★ *Rothley Court*

Westfield Ln LE7 7LG
Quality Percentage Score: 61%
☎ 0116 237 4141 📠 0116 237 4483
Dir: *on B5328*
In places dating back to the 11th century, Rothley Court stands in six acres of gardens edged by the river and rolling hills. The public areas are impressive, dominated by a chapel of the Knights Templar, and full of original features and historical charm, even a suit of armour. Accommodation is offered either in

contd.

R

the traditionally furnished rooms of the main house, or modern garden annexe bedrooms.
ROOMS: 13 en suite (bth/shr) 21 annexe en suite (bth/shr) No smoking in 14 bedrooms **MEALS:** V meals Coffee am Tea pm **FACILITIES:** CTV in all bedrooms **CONF:** Thtr 100 Class 35 Board 35 Del from £120 * **SERVICES:** Night porter 100P **NOTES:** No smoking in restaurant Last d 9.30pm **CARDS:**

ROTHLEY Leicestershire — Map 08 SK51

★★ The Limes

35 Mountsorrel Ln LE7 7PS
Quality Percentage Score: 72%
☎ 0116 230 2531
Dir: *turn of old A6, Hotel off village green*

The Limes, just beyond the village green, is owned and run by Mr and Mrs Soper. Public areas offer a comfortable lounge bar and a smart restaurant. The well maintained accommodation is equipped for the needs of the predominantly business clientele, with excellent facilities and comfortable executive swivel chairs.
ROOMS: 11 en suite (bth/shr) s £42.50; d £55 (incl. bkfst) * Off peak **MEALS:** Dinner £11.50-£20 V meals **FACILITIES:** CTV in all bedrooms STV **SERVICES:** Air conditioning 15P **NOTES:** No dogs (ex guide dogs) No coaches No children 14yrs No smoking in restaurant Last d 8.30pm Closed 23 Dec-2 Jan **CARDS:**

ROWNHAMS MOTORWAY SERVICE AREA Hampshire — Map 04 SU31

⇧ Roadchef Lodge

Rownhams Service Area, M27 Westbound
SO16 8AP
☎ 023 80741144 ▤ 023 80740204
Dir: *M27 1m E of junct 3*

This modern building offers accommodation in smart, spacious and well equipped bedrooms, all with en-suite bathrooms. Refreshments may be taken at the nearby family restaurant. For details about current prices, consult the Contents Page under Hotel Groups for the Roadchef phone number.
ROOMS: 39 en suite (bth/shr) d fr £47.50 *

ROWSLEY Derbyshire — Map 08 SK26

★★★❀ East Lodge Country House

DE4 2EF
Quality Percentage Score: 73%
☎ 01629 734474 ▤ 01629 733949
Dir: *A6, Rowsley Village, 3m from Bakewell, 5m from Matlock*

This Victorian lodge stands in 10 acres of attractive grounds. The public rooms consist of an elegant lounge with a roaring log fire and a pleasantly appointed restaurant, where a range of interesting dishes are offered from a weekly changing, set price menu. Individually furnished bedrooms come in a variety of sizes and styles; each room is comfortably appointed, attractively decorated and thoughtfully equipped.
ROOMS: 15 en suite (bth/shr) (2 fmly) s £75-£90; d £95-£125 (incl. bkfst) * LB Off peak **MEALS:** Lunch £10-£25alc High tea fr £6alc Dinner £23-£26alc International Cuisine V meals Coffee am Tea pm **FACILITIES:** CTV in all bedrooms Croquet lawn Xmas **CONF:** Thtr 75 Class 20 Board 22 Del from £105 * **SERVICES:** Night porter 25P **NOTES:** No dogs No coaches No smoking in restaurant Last d 9pm **CARDS:**

See advert under BAKEWELL

RUAN HIGH LANES Cornwall & Isles of Scilly — Map 02 SW93

★★❀ Hundred House

TR2 5JR
Quality Percentage Score: 75%
☎ 01872 501336 ▤ 01872 501151
Dir: *from A390, 4m W of St Austell turn left onto B3287 to Tregony/St Mawes, turn left onto A3078 to St Mawes, hotel 4m along on right*

This Edwardian house on the Roseland Peninsular lies in one of the prettiest parts of Cornwall. The grounds and gardens are beautifully kept and include a croquet lawn. The house is tastefully furnished with fine antiques and pictures, and the bedrooms offer modern comforts and facilities. Guests meet in the bar before enjoying the award-winning cuisine in the restaurant.
ROOMS: 10 en suite (bth/shr) (2 fmly) s £60-£70; d £120-£140 (incl. bkfst & dinner) LB Off peak **MEALS:** Dinner fr £25 Coffee am Tea pm **FACILITIES:** CTV in all bedrooms Croquet lawn **SERVICES:** 15P **NOTES:** No coaches No children 8yrs No smoking in restaurant Last d 8.30pm Closed Nov-Feb **CARDS:**

RUGBY Warwickshire — Map 04 SP57

★★★ Brownsover Hall

Brownsover Ln, Old Brownsover CV21 1HU
Quality Percentage Score: 67%
☎ 01788 546100 ▤ 01788 579241
Dir: *come off M6 junct 1 and follow signs to Rugby A426, follow dual carriageway for 0.5m until slip road to right, follow for 400m, hotel on right*

A mock-Gothic hall in seven acres of wooded parkland. Bedrooms are spacious and well equipped, sixteen new rooms are being created in the converted stable block. The former chapel makes a stylish restaurant with mullion windows and stately chandeliers. For a less formal meal or a relaxing drink, the rugby themed bar is popular.
ROOMS: 27 en suite (bth/shr) 4 annexe en suite (bth/shr) (3 fmly) No smoking in 15 bedrooms s fr £90; d fr £105 * LB Off peak **MEALS:** Lunch £11.95-£13.85 Dinner fr £19.95 & alc V meals Coffee am Tea pm **FACILITIES:** CTV in all bedrooms STV Tennis Xmas **CONF:** Thtr 80 Class 36 Board 36 Del from £119 * **SERVICES:** Night porter 60P **NOTES:** No smoking in restaurant Last d 9.30pm
CARDS:

RUGBY Warwickshire **Map 04 SP57**
★★★ Posthouse Northampton/Rugby
Posthouse
NN6 7XR
Quality Percentage Score: 66%
☎ 01788 822101 Fax 01788 823955
(For full entry see Crick)

RUGBY Warwickshire **Map 04 SP57**
★★★ The Rugby Grosvenor
Clifton Rd CV21 3QQ
Quality Percentage Score: 58%
☎ 01788 535686 Fax 01788 541297
Dir: *M6 junct 1, turn right on to A426 towards Rugby centre, at first rdbt turn left continue to T junct and turn right onto B5414 hotel in 2m on right*
Standing close to the town centre, this family owned hotel has grown over the years into a large corner sited property. While the accomodation may vary in size, it is well equipped, and five new bedrooms were added this year. The public rooms are inviting and pleasantly furnished and service is both friendly and attentive.
ROOMS: 26 en suite (bth/shr) (1 fmly) s £60-£74.50; d £70-£84.50 * LB Off peak **MEALS:** Lunch £21.50 Dinner £21.50 V meals Coffee am Tea pm **FACILITIES:** CTV in all bedrooms Indoor swimming pool (heated) Sauna Solarium Jacuzzi/spa Aromatherapy by appointment **CONF:** Thtr 45 Class 25 Board 50 Del £97 * **SERVICES:** Night porter 33P **NOTES:** No coaches Last d 10pm
CARDS:

RUGBY Warwickshire **Map 04 SP57**
★★ Hillmorton Manor
78 High St, Hillmorton CV21 4EE
Quality Percentage Score: 65%
☎ 01788 565533 & 572403 Fax 01788 540027
Dir: *leave M1 junct 18 & onto A428 to Rugby*
A Victorian manor house on the outskirts of Rugby. Public rooms are very inviting, and include a pleasant lounge bar and attractive restaurant, a good range of well prepared food is served. The bedroom styles and sizes vary, but all are well equipped.
ROOMS: 11 en suite (bth/shr) (1 fmly) s £35-£49; d £45-£62 (incl. bkfst) * Off peak **MEALS:** Lunch £10.95-£11.75 & alc Dinner £18.95 & alc English & French Cuisine V meals Coffee am Tea pm **FACILITIES:** CTV in all bedrooms Xmas **CONF:** Class 30 Board 65 **SERVICES:** 40P **NOTES:** No smoking in restaurant Last d 9.30pm
CARDS:

RUGBY Warwickshire **Map 04 SP57**
★★ Whitefields Hotel Golf & Country Club
Coventry Rd, Thurlaston CV23 9JR
Quality Percentage Score: 61%
☎ 01788 521800 & 522393 Fax 01788 521695
Dir: *4m SW close to junc 1 M45*
A purpose built hotel centred on an 18-hole golf course, which provides straightforward and modern accommodation; bedrooms come in varying styles and sizes, with ground floor rooms generally more spacious. An open plan bar and lounge offers comfortable seating, and there are several well equipped conference suites available; public areas are shared with golf club members.
ROOMS: 34 en suite (bth/shr) (2 fmly) No smoking in all bedrooms s fr £52.50; d fr £72.50 (incl. bkfst) * LB Off peak **MEALS:** Sunday Lunch £2.95-£9.95 Dinner £3.25-£11.50 & alc International Cuisine V meals Coffee am Tea pm **FACILITIES:** CTV in all bedrooms STV Golf 18 Fishing Putting green Driving range Xmas **CONF:** Thtr 80 Class 50 Board 45 Del from £78.95 * **SERVICES:** Night porter 150P **NOTES:** No dogs (ex guide dogs) Last d 9.30pm
CARDS:

RUGELEY Staffordshire **Map 07 SK01**
Travelodge
Travelodge
Western Springs Rd WS15 2AS
☎ 01889 570096 Fax 01889 570096
Dir: *on A51/B5013*
This modern building offers accommodation in smart, spacious and well equipped bedrooms, all with en-suite bathrooms. Refreshments may be taken at the nearby family restaurant. For details about current prices, consult the Contents Page under Hotel Groups for the Travelodge phone number.
ROOMS: 32 en suite (bth/shr) d £45.95 *

RUISLIP Greater London
See LONDON SECTION plan 1 *A5*
★★★ Barn Hotel
West End Rd HA4 6JB
Quality Percentage Score: 64%
☎ 01895 636057 Fax 01895 638379
Dir: *take A4180 (Polish War Memorial) exit off the A40 to Ruislip, 2m to hotel entrance off a mini rdbt before Ruislip Underground Station*
A skilfully extended hotel, parts of which date from 1628. Rooms in the oldest part have four-poster beds and have kept their old beams and uneven floors, while those in the extension
contd.

We endeavour to be as accurate as possible but changes in personnel and data can occur in establishments after the Hotel Guide has gone to press.

are modern in character. There is a pleasant restaurant and a timber-clad bar.

Barn Hotel, Ruislip

ROOMS: 57 en suite (bth/shr) (3 fmly) No smoking in 3 bedrooms s £60-£89; d £70-£95 (incl. bkfst) * LB Off peak **MEALS:** Lunch £10.95 Dinner £18.75 & alc International Cuisine V meals Coffee am Tea pm **FACILITIES:** CTV in all bedrooms STV Xmas **CONF:** Thtr 100 Class 50 Board 40 Del from £108.50 * **SERVICES:** Night porter 60P **NOTES:** No smoking in restaurant Last d 9.30pm

CARDS:

See advert on page 551

RUNCORN Cheshire — Map 07 SJ58

★★★ Posthouse Warrington/Runcorn

Posthouse

Wood Ln, Beechwood WA7 3HA

Quality Percentage Score: 66%

☎ 01928 714000 📠 01928 714611

Dir: *off M56 junc 2, turn left at roundabout then 100 yards on left turn into Halton Station Road under a railway bridge and continue into Wood Lane*

A modern hotel, conveniently situated just off junction 12 of the M56. Ample parking and spacious, comfortable, public areas make it an ideal venue for impromptu meetings as well as more formal gatherings. Bedrooms have every modern facilities and are shortly to be upgraded. The spacious Seasons restaurant is open for lunch and dinner and an all day menu is provided in the lounge and bar. 24 hour room service is also available. There are excellent conference and meeting facilities and a very well equipped leisure club which includes an indoor heated swimming pool.

ROOMS: 135 en suite (bth/shr) No smoking in 86 bedrooms d £99 * LB Off peak **MEALS:** International Cuisine V meals Coffee am Tea pm **FACILITIES:** CTV in all bedrooms Indoor swimming pool (heated) Sauna Solarium Gym Pool table Jacuzzi/spa Beauty therapy Steam room Xmas **CONF:** Thtr 500 Class 60 Board 36 Del from £110 * **SERVICES:** Lift Night porter 210P **NOTES:** Last d 10pm

CARDS:

RUNCORN Cheshire — Map 07 SJ58

Campanile

Lowlands Rd WA7 5TP

☎ 01928 581771 📠 01928 581730

Dir: *leave M56 at junct 12, take A557, then follow signs for Runcorn railway station*

This modern building offers accommodation in smart well equipped bedrooms, all with en-suite bathrooms. Refreshments may be taken at the informal Bistro. For details about current prices, consult the Contents Page under Hotel Groups for the Campanile phone number.

ROOMS: 53 en suite (bth/shr) **CONF:** Thtr 35 Class 28 Board 20

★ The Premier Collection, hotels with Red Star Awards are listed on pages 17-23

RUNCORN Cheshire — Map 07 SJ58

Travel Inn

Chester Rd, Preston Brook WA7 3BB

☎ 01928 716829 📠 01928 719852

Dir: *1m from M56 junct 11, at Preston Brook*

This modern building offers accommodation in smart, spacious and well equipped bedrooms, all with en-suite bathrooms. Refreshments may be taken at the nearby family restaurant. For details about current prices consult the Contents Page under Hotel Groups for the Travel Inn phone number.

ROOMS: 40 en suite (bth/shr) d £39.95 *

RUSHDEN Northamptonshire — Map 04 SP96

Travelodge

Travelodge

Saunders Lodge NN10 9AP

☎ 01933 57008 📠 01933 57008

Dir: *on A45, eastbound*

This modern building offers accommodation in smart, spacious and well equipped bedrooms, all with en-suite bathrooms. Refreshments may be taken at the nearby family restaurant. For details about current prices, consult the Contents Page under Hotel Groups for the Travelodge phone number.

ROOMS: 40 en suite (bth/shr) d £39.95 *

RUSHYFORD Co Durham — Map 08 NZ22

★★★ Swallow Eden Arms

SWALLOW HOTELS

DL17 0LL

Quality Percentage Score: 69%

☎ 01388 720541 📠 01388 721871

Dir: *follow A689 to Rushyford rbt. Hotel on opposite side of rbt*

Built around the original 17th-century foundations, this modern-styled hotel offers comfortable and attractively furnished bedrooms. A choice of dining is available, with lighter snacks in

contd.

the conservatory overlooking the leisure centre, or more formal dining in the spacious main restaurant.
ROOMS: 45 en suite (bth/shr) (4 fmly) No smoking in 20 bedrooms s fr £92; d fr £110 (incl. bkfst) * LB Off peak **MEALS:** Lunch fr £10.50 Dinner £22 English & French Cuisine V meals Coffee am Tea pm **FACILITIES:** CTV in all bedrooms STV Indoor swimming pool (heated) Sauna Solarium Gym Pool table Jacuzzi/spa Steam room Plunge Pool Xmas **CONF:** Thtr 100 Class 40 Board 50 Del from £92 * **SERVICES:** Night porter 200P **NOTES:** No smoking area in restaurant Last d 9.30pm **CARDS:**

RUSTINGTON West Sussex — Map 04 TQ00

Travelodge

Worthing Rd BN17 6JN
☎ 01903 733150 Fax 01903 733150
Dir: on A259, 1m E of Littlehampton

This modern building offers accommodation in smart, spacious and well equipped bedrooms, all with en-suite bathrooms. Refreshments may be taken at the nearby family restaurant. For details about current prices, consult the Contents Page under Hotel Groups for the Travelodge phone number.
ROOMS: 36 en suite (bth/shr) d £45.95 *

RYDE See Wight, Isle of

RYE East Sussex — Map 05 TQ92

★★★ Mermaid Inn

Mermaid St TN31 7EY
Quality Percentage Score: 69%
☎ 01797 223065 & 223788 Fax 01797 225069
Dir: A259, follow signposts to town centre then up Mermaid St

In business for over 150 years by the time Elizabeth I came to the throne, this famous smugglers' inn is steeped in history. The interior has ancient beamed ceilings and huge fireplaces. The public rooms include several lounge areas and the restaurant. Bedrooms vary considerably in size and shape.
ROOMS: 31 en suite (bth/shr) (5 fmly) s £68-£72; d £136-£154 (incl. bkfst) * LB Off peak **MEALS:** Lunch £13.50-£16 & alc Dinner £29-£32 & alc French & Continental Cuisine V meals Coffee am Tea pm **FACILITIES:** CTV in all bedrooms Xmas **CONF:** Thtr 80 Class 50 Board 40 Del from £110 * **SERVICES:** Night porter 25P **NOTES:** No dogs No smoking area in restaurant Last d 9.30pm
CARDS:

RYE East Sussex — Map 05 TQ92

★★★ *The George*

High St TN31 7JP
Quality Percentage Score: 61%
☎ 01797 222114 Fax 01797 224065

Right in the heart of this historic town, near the myriad of small specialist shops, The George is full of character with cosy public rooms reflecting the period of the building. The majority of bedrooms have been sympathetically modernised and are well equipped. Although the restaurant is small, it blends in well with the architecture and style of the building.
ROOMS: 22 en suite (bth/shr) No smoking in 5 bedrooms **MEALS:** V meals Coffee am Tea pm **FACILITIES:** CTV in all bedrooms **CONF:** Thtr 100 Class 40 Board 40 **SERVICES:** 7P **NOTES:** No smoking in restaurant Last d 9pm **CARDS:**

RYE East Sussex — Map 05 TQ92

★★ Broomhill Lodge

Rye Foreign TN31 7UN
Quality Percentage Score: 71%
☎ 01797 280421 Fax 01797 280402
Dir: 1.5m N on A268

Built in the 1820s and set in three acres of grounds, this establishment has individually decorated bedrooms that are comfortably furnished and well equipped. There are two elegant lounges, and a brightly decorated restaurant where a choice of menus is offered at dinner.
ROOMS: 12 en suite (bth/shr) s fr £48; d fr £84 (incl. bkfst) * LB Off peak **MEALS:** Lunch fr £15.50 Dinner fr £26.50 English & French Cuisine V meals Coffee am Tea pm **FACILITIES:** CTV in all bedrooms Sauna Mini gym Xmas **CONF:** Thtr 60 Class 60 Board 30 Del from £80 * **SERVICES:** 20P **NOTES:** No dogs No smoking in restaurant Last d 9pm
CARDS:

RYE East Sussex — Map 05 TQ92

★★ *Hope Anchor*

Watchbell St TN31 7HA
Quality Percentage Score: 66%
☎ 01797 222216 Fax 01797 223796

Featured in Malcolm Saville's childrens' books, this historic inn is on one of Rye's oldest cobbled streets. The spacious bedrooms are attractively furnished and some have lovely views over the harbour and Romney Marsh.
ROOMS: 13 rms (12 bth/shr) (2 fmly) No smoking in 2 bedrooms **MEALS:** V meals Coffee am Tea pm **FACILITIES:** CTV in all bedrooms **NOTES:** Last d 9pm **CARDS:**

ST AGNES Cornwall & Isles of Scilly — Map 02 SW75

★★★ Rose in Vale Country House

Rose in Vale, Mithian TR5 OQD
Quality Percentage Score: 68%
☎ 01872 552202 Fax 01872 552700
Dir: B3284 to Perranporth approx 0.75miles along turn left, signposted "Rose-in-Vale"

A Georgian Manor House, spacious gardens include a pond with waterfowl and an area to play croquet. There is a variety of accommodation in size and style, with many rooms looking onto the attractive gardens. An imaginative fixed price menu and a carte are offered in the spacious dining room each evening.
ROOMS: 18 en suite (bth/shr) (4 fmly) s £48; d £86-£126 (incl. bkfst) * LB Off peak **MEALS:** Lunch £10.50 Dinner £21.95 English & Continental Cuisine V meals Coffee am Tea pm **FACILITIES:** CTV in all bedrooms Outdoor swimming pool (heated) Solarium Croquet lawn Jacuzzi/spa Badminton Table tennis Billiards Scenic flights in hotel's own aeroplane Xmas **CONF:** Thtr 50 Class 50 Board 50 Del £75 * **SERVICES:** 40P **NOTES:** No coaches No smoking in restaurant Last d 8.30pm Closed Jan-Feb **CARDS:**

ST AGNES Cornwall & Isles of Scilly — Map 02 SW75

★★ Sunholme

Goonvrea Rd TR5 0NW
Quality Percentage Score: 69%
☎ 01872 552318
Dir: on B3277, museum on left at mini rdbt, follow brown & white signs

Set in attractive grounds on the southern slopes of St Agnes Beacon, the hotel enjoys spectacular views over the surrounding countryside to the sea. Guests are assured a friendly welcome, and many return on a regular basis. The bedrooms are well equipped and furnished, most having been upgraded to an excellent standard. The inter-connecting lounges and intimate bar are an ideal venue for guests to meet before dinner.
ROOMS: 10 en suite (shr) (2 fmly) s £28-£33; d £56-£66 (incl. bkfst) * LB Off peak **MEALS:** Bar Lunch £2.50-£5 High tea £2-£5 Dinner £14 International Cuisine V meals Coffee am Tea pm **FACILITIES:** CTV in all bedrooms **SERVICES:** 12P **NOTES:** No coaches No children 7yrs No smoking in restaurant Last d 7pm Closed Nov-Mar
CARDS:

S

ST AGNES Cornwall & Isles of Scilly **Map 02 SW75**

★★ Rosemundy House

Rosemundy TR5 0UF

Quality Percentage Score: 68%

☎ 01872 552101 🖷 01872 552101

Dir: *turn off A30 to St Agnes continue for approx 3m on entering village take 1st turning on the right signposted Rosemundy, hotel is at foot of the hill*

Set in extensive gardens, this elegant Queen Anne house has been sympathetically extended to provide comfortable accommodation. The hotel has a secluded position, but the main street is only 100 metres away. The hotel offers bedrooms that are tastefully decorated and consistently well maintained.

ROOMS: 44 en suite (bth/shr) (12 fmly) **MEALS:** Coffee am **FACILITIES:** CTV in all bedrooms Outdoor swimming pool (heated) Pool table Croquet lawn Putting green Badminton/Games room **SERVICES:** 40P **NOTES:** No smoking in restaurant Last d 8pm Closed Nov-Mar **CARDS:**

ST ALBANS Hertfordshire **Map 04 TL10**

★★★★ Sopwell House Hotel & Country Club

Cottonmill Ln, Sopwell AL1 2HQ

Quality Percentage Score: 74%

☎ 01727 864477 🖷 01727 844741/845636

Dir: *follow St Albans sign to M10 rbt then take A414, first left and follow Sopwell signs*

Sopwell House and the surrounding land was once owned by the Mountbatten family. Public areas include a conservatory lounge bar, the Library Lounge, and the Magnolia Conservatory Restaurant. Guests also have the option of informal dining in the Brasserie. Bedrooms are attractively decorated, and many rooms offer four-poster beds. For the football enthusiast, the superb range of leisure facilities attract many top flight domestic and international teams, and a 'hall of fame' is dedicated to those clubs that have won trophies whilst staying at Sopwell.

ROOMS: 122 en suite (bth/shr) 16 annexe en suite (bth/shr) (6 fmly) s fr £79.75; d £109.75-£184.75 * LB Off peak **MEALS:** Lunch £14.95-£18.95 & alc Dinner fr £24.50 & alc English & International Cuisine V meals Coffee am Tea pm **FACILITIES:** CTV in all bedrooms STV Indoor swimming pool (heated) Snooker Sauna Solarium Gym Jacuzzi/spa Health & beauty spa Hairdressing salon Xmas **CONF:** Thtr 400 Class 220 Board 90 Del from £180 * **SERVICES:** Lift Night porter 360P **NOTES:** No smoking in restaurant Last d 9.30pm Closed 31 Dec-1 Jan **CARDS:**

See advert on opposite page

S

ST ALBANS Hertfordshire **Map 04 TL10**

★★★★ *Thistle St Albans*

Watford Rd AL2 3DS

Quality Percentage Score: 69%

☎ 01727 854252 🖷 01727 841906

Dir: *2.75m S at junct A405/B4630*

Committed management and a loyal team of staff ensure that service at the Noke remains as attentive, friendly and professional as ever. Executive rooms are more spacious and comfortable than the Club rooms but all have attractive fabrics and co-ordinated decor. Public rooms are elegant but slightly compact and Bertie's Restaurant has a good local reputation for the seriousness and quality of its food. The Baltimore Bean Company provides more informal dining in an American style in the main bar.

ROOMS: 111 en suite (bth/shr) (4 fmly) No smoking in 60 bedrooms **MEALS:** English & French Cuisine V meals Coffee am Tea pm **FACILITIES:** CTV in all bedrooms STV Gym Membership of local Health Club **CONF:** Thtr 50 Class 26 Board 26 Del from £155 * **SERVICES:** Night porter 150P **NOTES:** Last d 9.45pm RS 26-31 Dec **CARDS:**

ST ALBANS Hertfordshire **Map 04 TL10**

★★★ St Michael's Manor

Fishpool St AL3 4RY

Quality Percentage Score: 76%

☎ 01727 864444 🖷 01727 848909

Dir: *from St Albans Abbey follow Fishpool Street toward St Michael's village. Hotel located 0.5m on left hand side*

Set in five acres of gardens complete with lake and river, this fine hotel is one of the most stunning properties in this part of the country. The hotel provides a welcoming atmosphere and a choice of comfortable lounges in which to relax. Bedrooms boast a wealth of extra touches. The restaurant serves an imaginative menu with enough diversity to satisfy the most jaded of palates, and the bar is a malt whisky drinker's paradise.

ROOMS: 23 en suite (bth/shr) No smoking in 3 bedrooms s £110-£225; d £145-£295 (incl. bkfst) LB Off peak **MEALS:** Lunch £15.75-£22.50alc V meals Coffee am Tea pm **FACILITIES:** CTV in all bedrooms STV Croquet lawn Xmas **CONF:** Thtr 30 Class 18 Board 20 Del from £185 **SERVICES:** Night porter 70P **NOTES:** No dogs (ex guide dogs) No coaches **CARDS:**

See advert on opposite page

ST ALBANS Hertfordshire **Map 04 TL10**

★★ Apples Hotel

133 London Rd AL1 1TA

Quality Percentage Score: 68%

☎ 01727 844111 🖷 01727 861100

Dir: *sited on the main A1081, 0.5m from city centre*

This friendly, small family run hotel is centrally located in historic St Albans. The hotel is very smartly decorated throughout, with excellently equipped comfortable bedrooms. There is an outdoor swimming pool and a cosy lounge. Dinners and breakfasts are served in a bright airy dining room and the proprietors are committed to serving only fresh food, often discussing guests' needs by telephone before arrival.

ROOMS: 9 en suite (bth/shr) (1 fmly) No smoking in 2 bedrooms s £43-£50; d £60-£70.50 (incl. bkfst) * LB Off peak **MEALS:** Lunch £16.50 High tea fr £8.90 Dinner fr £17.50 V meals Coffee am Tea pm **FACILITIES:** CTV in all bedrooms Outdoor swimming pool (heated) **SERVICES:** 9P **NOTES:** No coaches No smoking in restaurant Last d 8.45pm **CARDS:**

ST ALBANS Hertfordshire **Map 04 TL10**

★★ ***Lake***

234 London Rd AL1 1JQ

Quality Percentage Score: 66%

☎ 01727 840904 📠 01727 862750

Dir: *junct 22 off M25 follow A1081 to St Albans, after Colney rdbt hotel is 1m on left*

The Lake offers easy access to the motorways and the railway station. The bedrooms vary in size but all are smartly decorated. The bar and restaurant are attractively presented and there is a comfortable guest lounge with large screen TV. The large function room is a popular venue for wedding receptions.

ROOMS: 43 en suite (bth/shr) (2 fmly) No smoking in 18 bedrooms **MEALS:** International Cuisine V meals Coffee am **FACILITIES:** CTV in all bedrooms STV **CONF:** Thtr 150 Class 60 Board 50 **SERVICES:** 70P **NOTES:** No dogs (ex guide dogs) Last d 9.30pm **CARDS:**

ST ANNES See **Lytham St Annes**

ST AUSTELL Cornwall & Isles of Scilly **Map 02 SX05**

★★★★ ❀ **Carlyon Bay**

Sea Rd, Carlyon Bay PL25 3RD

Quality Percentage Score: 73%

☎ 01726 812304 📠 01726 814938

Dir: *from St Austell, follow signs for Charlestown Carlyon Bay is signposted on left, hotel lies at end of Sea Road*

This hotel is well suited to the leisure visitor yet can also cater for small conferences and business guests. Set in 250 acres of grounds, leisure facilities include a championship golf course, indoor and outdoor swimming pools, tennis courts and snooker tables. Children's activities are arranged in the supervised

contd.

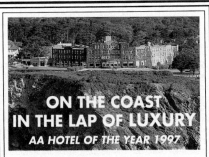

nursery. Bedrooms vary in size, the best being supplied with such extras as fresh fruit and flowers. The spacious lounges provide a relaxing area and a choice of bars is also available.

Carlyon Bay, St Austell

ROOMS: 73 en suite (bth/shr) (14 fmly) s £76-£93; d £146-£220 (incl. bkfst) * LB Off peak **MEALS:** Lunch £12.50-£13.95 & alc Dinner £24 & alc English & French Cuisine V meals Coffee am Tea pm **FACILITIES:** CTV in all bedrooms STV Indoor swimming pool (heated) Outdoor swimming pool (heated) Golf 18 Tennis (hard) Snooker Sauna Solarium Putting green Jacuzzi/spa Table tennis 9-hole approach course Wkly live entertainment ch fac Xmas **CONF:** Thtr 100 **SERVICES:** Lift Night porter 101P **NOTES:** No dogs (ex guide dogs) No coaches Last d 9pm **CARDS:**

See advert on page 555

ST AUSTELL Cornwall & Isles of Scilly — Map 02 SX05

★★★ *Porth Avallen*

Sea Rd, Carlyon Bay PL25 3SG
Quality Percentage Score: 66%
☎ 01726 812802 01726 817097
Dir: *leave A30 onto A391. Follow signs to St Austell and then Charlestown and then Carlyon Bay. Turn right into Sea Rd*

A traditional hotel with panoramic views over the rugged Cornish coastline and Carlyon Bay; owing to the stunning scenery, front facing bedrooms are always popular. A function room is available for private parties, and a comfortable oak-panelled lounge with a conservatory for guests, plus a spacious bar. Both fixed price and carte menus are offered each evening in the dining room.

ROOMS: 24 en suite (bth/shr) (4 fmly) **MEALS:** English & French Cuisine V meals Coffee am Tea pm **FACILITIES:** CTV in all bedrooms STV N **CONF:** Thtr 80 Class 40 Board 35 **SERVICES:** Night porter 50P **NOTES:** No dogs (ex guide dogs) No smoking in restaurant Last d 9pm Closed 26 Dec-4 Jan **CARDS:**

ST AUSTELL Cornwall & Isles of Scilly — Map 02 SX05

★★★ Cliff Head

Sea Rd, Carlyon Bay PL25 3RB
Quality Percentage Score: 65%
☎ 01726 812345 01726 815511
Dir: *2m E off A390*

Set in extensive grounds, the hotel faces south and enjoys views over Carlyon Bay. Attractively decorated day rooms offer guests a choice of lounges and high standards of comfort. Entertainment is provided in the summer season and a covered outdoor swimming pool is popular. The friendly staff provide relaxed, yet efficient service.

ROOMS: 54 en suite (bth/shr) (2 fmly) s £42-£52; d £72-£82 (incl. bkfst) * LB Off peak **MEALS:** Lunch £7.95-£8.95 Dinner £18.95 & alc V meals Coffee am Tea pm **FACILITIES:** CTV in all bedrooms Outdoor swimming pool (heated) Sauna Solarium Gym Pool table Xmas **CONF:** Thtr 150 Class 130 Board 170 Del from £65 * **SERVICES:** Night porter 60P **NOTES:** No dogs (ex guide dogs) No smoking in restaurant Last d 9.30pm **CARDS:**

See advert on opposite page

ST AUSTELL Cornwall & Isles of Scilly — Map 02 SX05

★★ Boscundle Manor

Tregrehan PL25 3RL
Quality Percentage Score: 78%
☎ 01726 813557 01726 814997
Dir: *2m E on A390 signposted 'Tregrehan'*

This handsome 18th century stone-built mansion house offers very comfortable, well equipped bedrooms. The beautiful grounds extend to over ten acres and include lots of secluded corners, ponds and woodland. There is also a games room. The daily menu uses fresh produce to create traditional dishes to satisfy the appetite.

ROOMS: 9 en suite (bth/shr) 3 annexe en suite (bth/shr) (1 fmly) s £65-£75; d £110-£160 (incl. bkfst) Off peak **MEALS:** Dinner £20 International Cuisine **FACILITIES:** CTV in all bedrooms Indoor swimming pool (heated) Outdoor swimming pool (heated) Snooker Gym Croquet lawn Golf practice area Table Tennis Badminton **SERVICES:** 15P **NOTES:** No coaches No smoking in restaurant Last d 8.30pm Closed end Oct-mid Mar RS Sun **CARDS:**

ST AUSTELL Cornwall & Isles of Scilly — Map 02 SX05

★★ Pier House

Harbour Front, Charlestown PL25 3NJ
Quality Percentage Score: 66%
☎ 01726 67955 01726 69246
Dir: *follow A390 to St Austell, Mt Charles rdbt turn left down Charlestown Road*

Overlooking St. Austell, this friendly hotel was formerly a pair of late 18th century cottages. Inside there are comfortable bedrooms, many of which have sea views. The public bar is popular with locals and tourists alike, and guests have their own lounge in addition to the restaurant where locally caught fish regularly features on the menu.

ROOMS: 26 en suite (bth/shr) (4 fmly) No smoking in 5 bedrooms s £37-£46; d £60-£70 (incl. bkfst) * LB Off peak **MEALS:** Lunch £2.50-£5.95alc High tea £3.30-£5.10alc Dinner £10.45-£14.95alc V meals Coffee am Tea pm **FACILITIES:** CTV in all bedrooms **SERVICES:** Night porter 56P **NOTES:** No dogs (ex guide dogs) No smoking in restaurant Last d 9.30pm **CARDS:**

ST AUSTELL Cornwall & Isles of Scilly — Map 02 SX05

★★ *White Hart*

Church St PL25 4AT
Quality Percentage Score: 62%
☎ 01726 72100 01726 74705

This 16th-century, stone-built inn is popular with visitors and locals alike. The two bars are in demand, one has a collection of movie memorabilia. Alternative seating is available in the foyer lounge, where cream teas may be taken. Meals are available at the bar or from a fixed price menu in the restaurant.

ROOMS: 18 en suite (bth/shr) **MEALS:** V meals Coffee am Tea pm **FACILITIES:** CTV in all bedrooms STV **CONF:** Thtr 50 Board 20 Del from £70 * **NOTES:** No dogs (ex guide dogs) Last d 9pm Closed 25 & 26 Dec **CARDS:**

ST HELENS Merseyside — Map 07 SJ59

see also **Rainhill**

★★★ Posthouse Haydock

Posthouse

Lodge Ln WA12 OJG
Quality Percentage Score: 66%
☎ 01942 717878 01942 718419
(For full entry see Haydock)

S

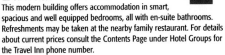

ST HELENS Merseyside — Map 07 SJ59
Travel Inn
Mickle Head Green, Eurolink, Lea Green WA9 4TT
☎ 01744 818971 Fax 01744 813724
This modern building offers accommodation in smart, spacious and well equipped bedrooms, all with en-suite bathrooms. Refreshments may be taken at the nearby family restaurant. For details about current prices consult the Contents Page under Hotel Groups for the Travel Inn phone number.
ROOMS: 40 en suite (bth/shr) d £39.95 *

ST IVES Cambridgeshire — Map 04 TL37
★★★ Olivers Lodge
Needingworth Rd PE17 4JP
Quality Percentage Score: 69%
☎ 01480 463252 Fax 01480 461150
Dir: *follow A14 towards Huntingdon, take B1040 to St Ives, cross 1st rdbt, left at 2nd then 1st right. Hotel 500m on right*
Olivers Lodge is a popular and well run hotel, set in quiet residential surroundings on the edge of St. Ives. The welcoming public rooms include an attractive conservatory dining area and breakfast room, a lounge bar and an air-conditioned restaurant. There are bedrooms in both the main house and an adjoining annexe, housing modern appointments and a good range of useful facilities.
ROOMS: 12 en suite (bth/shr) 5 annexe en suite (bth/shr) (3 fmly) No smoking in 1 bedroom s £55-£68; d £65-£75 (incl. bkfst) * LB Off peak **MEALS:** Lunch £12-£18alc Dinner £12-£18alc International Cuisine V meals Coffee am Tea pm **FACILITIES:** CTV in all bedrooms STV Croquet lawn Motor cruiser for hire Free use of local health club inc swimming, sauna, gym Wkly live entertainment **CONF:** Thtr 65 Class 45 Board 40 Del from £80 * **SERVICES:** 30P **NOTES:** Last d 9.30pm
CARDS:

ST IVES Cambridgeshire — Map 04 TL37
★★★ Slepe Hall
Ramsey Rd PE17 4RB
Quality Percentage Score: 67%
☎ 01480 463122 Fax 01480 300706
Dir: *leave A14 on A1096 & follow by-pass signed Huntingdon towards St Ives, turn into Ramsey Rd at set of traffic lights by Toyota and Ford garages*
Close to the town centre, this convivial hotel is popular with business guests, leisure guests and local diners. The friendly staff create a relaxed atmosphere, and the spacious public rooms are welcoming in nature. A wide range of food is offered, from lighter meals in the bar to a choice of menus in the more formal restaurant. There is also a choice in bedroom style with traditional rooms in the original house and a selection of modern rooms in the new wing.
ROOMS: 16 en suite (bth/shr) (1 fmly) s £55-£75; d £80-£95 (incl. bkfst) * LB Off peak **MEALS:** Lunch £12.95-£14.95 & alc Dinner £14.95-£16.95 & alc English and Continental Cuisine V meals Coffee am Tea pm **FACILITIES:** CTV in all bedrooms STV **CONF:** Thtr 200 Class 80 Board 60 Del from £90 * **SERVICES:** 70P **NOTES:** No coaches No smoking in restaurant Last d 9.30pm Closed 26 Dec-3 Jan
CARDS:

ST IVES Cambridgeshire — Map 04 TL37
★★★ Dolphin
London Rd PE17 4EP
Quality Percentage Score: 65%
☎ 01480 466966 & 497497 Fax 01480 495597
Dir: *on B1040*
A modern hotel with views of the River Ouse, a pedestrian bridge leads to the market town centre. Open-plan public rooms include a choice of bars and a pleasant restaurant offering

contd.

pleasing cuisine. Bedrooms are divided between the hotel and adjacent annexe. There are modern conference and function suites, and secure parking is available.

Dolphin, St Ives

ROOMS: 31 en suite (bth/shr) 36 annexe en suite (bth/shr) (4 fmly) No smoking in 20 bedrooms s fr £70; d fr £90 (incl. bkfst) * LB Off peak **MEALS:** Lunch £5-£15 Dinner £16.50-£17.50 English & Continental Cuisine V meals Coffee am Tea pm **FACILITIES:** CTV in all bedrooms STV Fishing **CONF:** Thtr 150 Class 50 Board 50 Del from £98 * **SERVICES:** Night porter 400P **NOTES:** No dogs (ex guide dogs) Last d 9.30pm RS 25-31 Dec **CARDS:**

See advert on page 557

ST IVES Cornwall & Isles of Scilly **Map 02 SW54**

★★★ *Carbis Bay*

Carbis Bay TR26 2NP
Quality Percentage Score: 73%
☎ 01736 795311 01736 797677

This established, professionally run hotel overlooks its own sandy beach. The hotel has spacious, newly furbished public rooms. Upgraded bedrooms provide comfort, quality and modern facilities; the attentive, natural hospitality is an attraction.

ROOMS: 30 en suite (bth/shr) (9 fmly) No smoking in 5 bedrooms **MEALS:** English & Continental Cuisine V meals Coffee am Tea pm **FACILITIES:** CTV in all bedrooms Outdoor swimming pool (heated) Fishing Snooker Pool table Private beach Wkly live entertainment **CONF:** Thtr 150 Class 100 Board 100 Del from £30 * **SERVICES:** 206P **NOTES:** No smoking in restaurant Last d 8.30pm Closed Jan-Mar **CARDS:**

See advert under CARBIS BAY

ST IVES Cornwall & Isles of Scilly **Map 02 SW54**

★★★ Porthminster

The Terrace TR26 2BN
Quality Percentage Score: 72%
☎ 01736 795221 01736 797043
Dir: *on A3074*

With its enviable position overlooking the sandy beach, the Porthminster Hotel continues to provide excellent hospitality together with very good facilities which includes both an indoor and outdoor pool. Trevor Richards and his loyal team, many of whom have worked at the hotel for over 20 years, welcome guests, some of whom holiday at the hotel on a regular basis. Bedrooms are both comfortable and well equipped and all have been upgraded to meet modern demands. The public rooms are spacious and benefit from the spectacular views over the bay.

ROOMS: 43 en suite (bth/shr) (14 fmly) s £54-£65; d £108-£130 (incl. bkfst) LB Off peak **MEALS:** Lunch £9-£31alc Dinner £19.50 & alc English & French Cuisine V meals Coffee am **FACILITIES:** CTV in all bedrooms Indoor swimming pool (heated) Outdoor swimming pool (heated) Sauna Solarium Gym Pool table Jacuzzi/spa Xmas **CONF:** Thtr 90 Board 24 **SERVICES:** Lift Night porter 43P **NOTES:** Last d 8.30pm Closed 28 Dec-14 Jan **CARDS:**

See advert on opposite page

ST IVES Cornwall & Isles of Scilly **Map 02 SW54**

★★★ Tregenna Castle Hotel

TR26 2DE
Quality Percentage Score: 69%
☎ 01736 795254 01736 796066
Dir: *main A30 from Exeter to Penzance, at Lelant just west of Hayle take A3074 to St Ives, through Carbis Bay, signposted main entrance on left*

The Treganna Castle commands spectacular views over St. Ives and its beaches. Leisure facilities are extensive and include an 18-hole golf course. The bedrooms are generally modern and have excellent facilities. Guests have a choice of eating in the magnificent restaurant or in the informal bistro. Afternoon teas are also served inside or in the garden.

ROOMS: 84 en suite (bth/shr) (12 fmly) No smoking in 49 bedrooms s £70-£99; d £140-£198 (incl. bkfst & dinner) * LB Off peak **MEALS:** V meals Coffee am Tea pm **FACILITIES:** CTV in all bedrooms STV Indoor swimming pool (heated) Outdoor swimming pool (heated) Golf 18 Tennis (hard) Squash Snooker Sauna Solarium Gym Pool table Jacuzzi/spa Health spa Steam room ch fac Xmas **CONF:** Thtr 400 Class 200 Board 50 **SERVICES:** Lift Night porter 200P **NOTES:** No dogs (ex guide dogs) No smoking in restaurant **CARDS:**

See advert on opposite page

ST IVES Cornwall & Isles of Scilly **Map 02 SW54**

★★★ Garrack

Burthallan Ln, Higher Ayr TR26 3AA
Quality Percentage Score: 68%
☎ 01736 796199 01736 798955
Dir: *turn off A30 for St Ives. Follow yellow holiday route signs on B3311. In St Ives, hotel is signposted from first mini rdbt*

The Garrack provides superb views over Porthmeor beach and stands in extensive grounds. Bedrooms are available in both the modern wing and in the original building; all are well equipped and comfortably furnished, including a room designed for disabled guests. A small leisure complex includes an all day

contd.

coffee shop, while in the restaurant both fixed price and carte menus are offered to guests and non-residents. The dishes are skilfully prepared, making good use of home grown produce and local seafood.

ROOMS: 16 rms (14 bth/shr) (2 fmly) s £58-£62; d £116-£146 (incl. bkfst) * LB Off peak **MEALS:** Dinner £22.50 & alc V meals Coffee am Tea pm **FACILITIES:** CTV in 18 bedrooms Indoor swimming pool (heated) Sauna Solarium Gym Jacuzzi/spa Xmas **CONF:** Thtr 30 Board 16 **SERVICES:** 30P **NOTES:** No coaches No smoking in restaurant Last d 9pm **CARDS:**

See advert on this page

ST IVES Cornwall & Isles of Scilly **Map 02 SW54**

★★★ **Boskerris**

Boskerris Rd, Carbis Bay TR26 2NQ

Quality Percentage Score: 63%

☎ 01736 795295 01736 798632

Dir: *upon entering Carbis Bay take 3rd turning right after garage*

With magnificent views over Carbis Bay, Boskerris Hotel is set in an acre and a half of gardens, in a quiet residential area. This family-run hotel continues to attract a regular clientele. Comfortable lounge areas and an attractive dining room are

contd.

Indicates that the star classification has not been confirmed under the New Quality Standards, see page 7 for further information.

provided. Bedrooms vary in size and shape, each being well decorated and equipped.

Boskerris, St Ives

ROOMS: 13 en suite (bth/shr) 5 annexe en suite (bth/shr) (4 fmly) **MEALS:** English & French Cuisine V meals Coffee am Tea pm **FACILITIES:** CTV in all bedrooms STV Outdoor swimming pool (heated) Solarium Putting green Games room **SERVICES:** 20P **NOTES:** No smoking in restaurant Last d 8.30pm Closed Nov-Xmas & 29 Dec-Etr RS Xmas **CARDS:**

ST IVES Cornwall & Isles of Scilly **Map 02 SW54**

★★ Chy-an-Dour

Trelyon Av TR26 2AD

Quality Percentage Score: 70%

☎ 01736 796436 01736 795772

Dir: *turn off A30 onto A3074, follow signs to St Ives for approx 3 miles, hotel on the right just past garage*

Built in 1890, this delightful family-owned hotel has inspiring views over St Ives, the harbour and Porthminster Beach. Good home cooking is provided in the restaurant at both dinner and breakfast. The four-course dinner menu changes daily, often using fresh local produce. Most of the bedrooms enjoy the splendid views, and all the rooms are well equipped.

ROOMS: 23 en suite (bth/shr) (2 fmly) No smoking in 9 bedrooms s £37-£49; d £64-£84 (incl. bkfst) * LB Off peak **MEALS:** Dinner fr £17 English & Continental Cuisine V meals Coffee am **FACILITIES:** CTV in all bedrooms **SERVICES:** Lift 23P **NOTES:** No dogs (ex guide dogs) No children 5yrs No smoking in restaurant Last d 8pm **CARDS:**

ST IVES Cornwall & Isles of Scilly **Map 02 SW54**

★★ *Pedn-Olva*

The Warren TR26 2EA

Quality Percentage Score: 68%

☎ 01736 796222 01736 797710

On a quiet street, this privately-owned hotel stands right at the water's edge. The majority of the comfortably furnished bedrooms have glorious views across the bay, while the public rooms have vast picture windows to take advantage of its unique location. In the restaurant, both a fixed-price and carte menu are offered; there is also a smaller dining room.

ROOMS: 28 en suite (bth/shr) 7 annexe rms (4 bth/shr) (5 fmly) **MEALS:** English & French Cuisine V meals Coffee am Tea pm **FACILITIES:** CTV in all bedrooms Outdoor swimming pool (heated) **SERVICES:** Night porter 21P **NOTES:** Last d 9.15pm **CARDS:**

For Useful Information and Important Telephone Number Changes turn to page 25

ST IVES Cornwall & Isles of Scilly **Map 02 SW54**

★★ *Skidden House*

Skidden Hill TR26 2DU

Quality Percentage Score: 68%

THE CIRCLE Selected Individual Hotels GREAT BRITAIN

☎ 01736 796899 01736 798619

Dir: *turn off A30 at St Erth rdbt, follow road sign A3074 to St Ives & railway station 1st right after rail/bus station*

Situated in the town centre, Skidden House is said to be the oldest hotel in St Ives. Its cosy bedrooms are well equipped with modern facilities. In the bistro-style dining room both fixed-price and à la carte menus are offered, often using fresh local produce. There is also a cosy bar and lounge.

ROOMS: 7 en suite (shr) No smoking in 2 bedrooms **MEALS:** English & French Cuisine V meals Coffee am **FACILITIES:** CTV in all bedrooms **SERVICES:** 7P **NOTES:** No coaches Last d 9.15pm **CARDS:**

ST IVES Cornwall & Isles of Scilly **Map 02 SW54**

★★ *Chy-an-Albany*

Albany Ter TR26 2BS

Quality Percentage Score: 64%

☎ 01736 796759 01736 795584

Dir: *turn of A30 onto A3074 signposted St Ives, hotel on left just before junction*

An ideally located hotel with the town and beaches within easy walking distance. All bedrooms, many with sea views, are well furbished with modern facilities. A fixed-price menu is offered in the attractive dining room, adjacent to the comfortable lounges and intimate bar.

ROOMS: 37 en suite (bth/shr) (15 fmly) No smoking in all bedrooms **MEALS:** V meals **FACILITIES:** CTV in all bedrooms Wkly live entertainment **CONF:** Class 30 Board 20 **SERVICES:** Lift 37P **NOTES:** No dogs (ex guide dogs) No smoking in restaurant Last d 7.30pm **CARDS:**

ST IVES Cornwall & Isles of Scilly **Map 02 SW54**

★★ Hotel St Eia

Trelyon Av TR26 2AA

Quality Percentage Score: 60%

☎ 01736 795531 01736 793591

Dir: *turn off A30 onto A3074, follow signs to St Ives, when approaching St Ives, the hotel is prominently on the right hand side*

Under new ownership, this conveniently located hotel offers a friendly welcome and spectacular views over St Ives, the harbour and Porthminster Beach. Guests can relax with a drink from the well stocked bar before dining in the attractive restaurant.

ROOMS: 19 en suite (bth/shr) (3 fmly) s £23.50-£31.50; d £47-£63 (incl. bkfst) * Off peak **MEALS:** Dinner £12.50-£14.50 Traditional Cuisine V meals **FACILITIES:** CTV in all bedrooms **SERVICES:** 16P **NOTES:** No dogs (ex guide dogs) No coaches No children 5yrs No smoking in restaurant Last d 7.30pm Closed Nov-Jan **CARDS:**

ST IVES Cornwall & Isles of Scilly **Map 02 SW54**

★ Dunmar

Pednolver Ter TR26 2EL

Quality Percentage Score: 59%

☎ 01736 796117 Freephone 0500 131218 01736 796117

Dir: *take A3074 and fork left at the Porthminster Hotel into Albert Road. Hotel is 200yds along at junction of Pednolver and Porthminster Terrace*

Close to the town centre and enjoying an elevated position above the town, the Dunmar is very good value. The comfortable, mostly en suite accommodation has excellent facilities. Traditional English food is served in the spacious dining room,

contd.

adjacent to the attractive split-level lounge bar which enjoys fine views over St. Ives and the ocean.
ROOMS: 13 en suite (bth/shr) (5 fmly) **MEALS:** English Cuisine V meals Coffee am Tea pm **FACILITIES:** CTV in all bedrooms **SERVICES:** 20P **NOTES:** No smoking in restaurant **CARDS:**

ST KEYNE Cornwall & Isles of Scilly **Map 02 SX26**

★★ Old Rectory House
PL14 4RL
Quality Percentage Score: 70%
☎ 01579 342617 📠 01579 342293
Dir: *turn off A38 at Liskeard, take B3254 following signs to St Keyne, pass church on left, hotel is 200 yds on left*
This delightful old house was built in 1820; surrounded by three acres of grounds and gardens, it is quietly situated in a secluded location near St Keyne. Bedrooms provide soundly maintained accommodation which includes rooms with four-poster beds. There is a comfortable lounge and an attractively appointed dining room, where creative and imaginative cuisine makes for a satisfying meal.
ROOMS: 8 rms (4 bth 3 shr) s £40-£45; d £58-£70 (incl. bkfst) * LB Off peak **MEALS:** English & French Cuisine V meals **FACILITIES:** CTV in all bedrooms **CONF:** Board 30 **SERVICES:** 30P **NOTES:** No coaches No smoking in restaurant Last d 8.30pm Closed Xmas **CARDS:**

See advert under LISKEARD

ST LAWRENCE See Wight, Isle of

ST LEONARDS Dorset **Map 04 SU10**

★★★ St Leonards Hotel
Ringwood Rd (A31) BH24 2NP
Quality Percentage Score: 64%
☎ 01425 471220 📠 01425 480274
Dir: *1.5m from Ringwood on the A31 between Ferndown and Ashley Heath*
Close to Ringwood and Bournemouth, this hotel has an attractive bar and restaurant offering an ambitious carte, extensive menu of popular dishes and children's menu. The spacious bedrooms are furnished to a high standard with modern facilities.
ROOMS: 34 en suite (bth/shr) (4 fmly) No smoking in 17 bedrooms **MEALS:** European Cuisine V meals Coffee am Tea pm **FACILITIES:** CTV in all bedrooms STV ch fac **CONF:** Thtr 100 Class 50 Board 40 **SERVICES:** Night porter 250P **NOTES:** No dogs No smoking area in restaurant Last d 9.45pm **CARDS:**

ST LEONARDS-ON-SEA See **Hastings & St Leonards**

ST MARTIN'S See Scilly, Isles of

ST MARY CHURCH See **Torquay**

ST MARY'S See Scilly, Isles of

ST MAWES Cornwall & Isles of Scilly **Map 02 SW83**

★★★ Idle Rocks
Harbour Side TR2 5AN
Quality Percentage Score: 77%
☎ 01326 270771 📠 01326 270062
Dir: *A30, A39, A3078*
With commanding views over the quayside, this smart friendly hotel offers wonderful views from many of its well furbished bedrooms which are all tastefully decorated and co-ordinated. The bedrooms in nearby Bohella House are very spacious, some with four-poster beds. A delightful view is assured on the waterfront terrace; a popular place to relax and enjoy a light

contd.

lunch on sunny days. The hotel cuisine has been awarded two AA Rosettes for the last seven years running. Two contrasting fixed price menus are offered with many innovative dishes using the finest local produce.

ROOMS: 17 en suite (bth/shr) 11 annexe en suite (bth/shr) (6 fmly) s £56-£99; d £112-£198 (incl. bkfst & dinner) * LB Off peak **MEALS:** Bar Lunch £3.50-£7.50alc High tea £3.95-£6.50alc Dinner £24.95 English & French Cuisine Coffee am Tea pm **FACILITIES:** CTV in all bedrooms Xmas **CONF:** Thtr 30 Class 20 Board 20 Del from £65 * **SERVICES:** 5P **NOTES:** No smoking in restaurant Last d 9.15pm **CARDS:**

See advert on page 561

ST MAWES Cornwall & Isles of Scilly — Map 02 SW83

★★ Rising Sun

TR2 5DJ

Quality Percentage Score: 71%

☎ 01326 270233 01326 270198

Dir: *from A39 take A3078 signposted St Mawes, hotel is in centre of village*

The haunt of artists for decades and popular with the yachting enthusiasts, the pretty harbour of St Mawes is the setting for The Rising Sun Hotel. The bar is a focal point and the new brasserie and lounge bar offer imaginative cooking featuring local seafood. Pleasant rooms are individually decorated.

ROOMS: 9 en suite (bth/shr) (1 fmly) s £35-£45; d £70-£99 (incl. bkfst) * LB Off peak **MEALS:** Sunday Lunch fr £11.75alc Dinner fr £21.75alc V meals Coffee am Tea pm **FACILITIES:** CTV in all bedrooms **SERVICES:** 6P **NOTES:** No coaches No smoking in restaurant Last d 9pm **CARDS:**

ST MELLION Cornwall & Isles of Scilly — Map 02 SX36

★★★ St Mellion International

PL12 6SD

Quality Percentage Score: 72%

☎ 01579 351351 01579 350537

Dir: *from A388 to Callington/Launceston, take St Mellion exit, hotel on left in village*

This purpose built hotel, golfing and leisure complex is surrounded by 450 acres of land with two 18 hole golf courses. The bedrooms generally have views over the courses, but with the vast array of leisure facilities on offer, most guests spend little time in their rooms! Public areas include a choice of bars and eating options. Other facilities include function suites for up to 180 people.

ROOMS: 39 annexe en suite (bth/shr) (15 fmly) s £101-£124; d £152-£198 (incl. bkfst & dinner) * LB Off peak **MEALS:** International Cuisine V meals Coffee am Tea pm **FACILITIES:** CTV in all bedrooms Indoor swimming pool (heated) Golf 36 Tennis (hard) Squash Snooker Sauna Solarium Gym Putting green Jacuzzi/spa Steam room,Skincare & Spa centre Xmas **CONF:** Thtr 150 Class 80 Board 26 Del from £89 * **SERVICES:** Lift Night porter 400P **NOTES:** No dogs (ex guide dogs) No smoking in restaurant Last d 9.30pm **CARDS:**

ST NEOTS Cambridgeshire — Map 04 TL16

★★ Abbotsley Golf

Potton Rd, Eynesbury Hardwicke PE19 4XN

Quality Percentage Score: 64%

☎ 01480 474000 01480 471018

Dir: *leave A1 at junct with A428 to Cambridge. take 1st left at 2nd rdbt and then last exit at next rdbt. Left after 300 yds and 1st right*

Popular with touring golf parties, this purpose-built hotel caters well for its many avid golfing guests with a 250-acre estate, 36-hole golf complex and the Vivien Saunders Golf School. The public rooms overlook the adjacent greens. Bedrooms are generally spacious, some converted from old farm buildings which surround a pleasing courtyard garden and putting green.

ROOMS: 17 en suite (bth/shr) (2 fmly) s £45-£55; d fr £80 (incl. bkfst) * LB Off peak **MEALS:** Dinner fr £16.95 International Cuisine V meals Coffee am Tea pm **FACILITIES:** CTV in all bedrooms Golf 36 Squash Gym Putting green Xmas **CONF:** Thtr 80 Class 46 Board 32 Del from £78 * **SERVICES:** 120P **NOTES:** No smoking in restaurant Last d 9pm **CARDS:**

SALCOMBE Devon — Map 03 SX73

see also **Hope Cove, Kingsbridge & Thurlestone**

★★★★ The Marine Hotel

Cliff Rd TQ8 8JH

MENZIES HOTELS

Quality Percentage Score: 72%

☎ 0500 636943 (Central Res) 01773 880321

Dir: *from A38 Exeter take A384 to Totnes then follow A381 direct to Kingsbridge and Salcombe*

This splendid hotel overlooks the estuary from all its public areas. It appeals particularly to guests wanting peace and quiet and has an excellent leisure complex. All the bedrooms are well equipped and stylishly furnished, and the restaurant serves appetising food.

ROOMS: 51 en suite (bth/shr) (10 fmly) s £90-£150; d £150-£170 (incl. bkfst) * LB Off peak **MEALS:** Lunch £9.50-£13.50 Dinner fr £27alc English & Continental Cuisine V meals Coffee am Tea pm **FACILITIES:** CTV in all bedrooms STV Indoor swimming pool (heated) Sauna Solarium Gym Jacuzzi/spa Xmas **CONF:** Del from £125 * **SERVICES:** Lift Night porter 50P **NOTES:** No coaches No smoking in restaurant Last d 9.30pm **CARDS:**

SALCOMBE Devon — Map 03 SX73

★★★★ Thurlestone Hotel

TQ7 3NN

Quality Percentage Score: 72%

☎ 01548 560382 01548 561069

(For full entry see Thurlestone)

SALCOMBE Devon — Map 03 SX73

★★★ Tides Reach

South Sands TQ8 8LJ

Quality Percentage Score: 80%

☎ 01548 843466 01548 843954

Dir: *turn off the A38 at Buckfastleigh towards Tothes. At Tothes join A381 then into Salcombe follow signs to South Sands*

This personally run hotel has a delightful waterside location and staff are both professional and friendly. Many of the spacious

contd. on p. 564

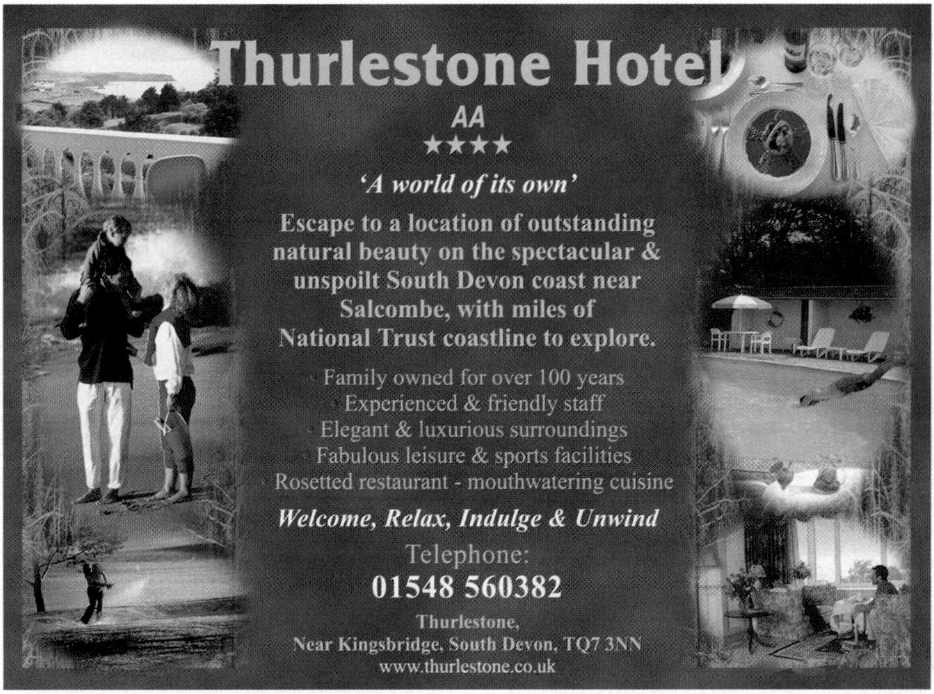
Thurlestone Hotel
AA
★★★★
'A world of its own'
Escape to a location of outstanding natural beauty on the spectacular & unspoilt South Devon coast near Salcombe, with miles of National Trust coastline to explore.
• Family owned for over 100 years
• Experienced & friendly staff
• Elegant & luxurious surroundings
• Fabulous leisure & sports facilities
• Rosetted restaurant - mouthwatering cuisine
Welcome, Relax, Indulge & Unwind
Telephone:
01548 560382
Thurlestone,
Near Kingsbridge, South Devon, TQ7 3NN
www.thurlestone.co.uk

Imagine Waking Up In This Bay...
Come & be spoilt at this superbly positioned hotel overlooking the Salcombe Estuary. Relax in style & enjoy our superb Indoor Pool, Health, Beauty & Leisure facilities, lovely walks along the South Devon coastal path, Fine Food & Friendly Service. (Children 8 & Over)
AA ★★★ 80% AA 2 Rosettes
Salcombe, South Devon Tel: 01548 843466
www.tidesreach.com enquire@tidesreach.com
The Tides Reach

S

bedrooms have balconies and the Garden Room restaurant has a good reputation.

ROOMS: 38 en suite (bth/shr) (5 fmly) s £83-£111; d £146-£222 (incl. bkfst & dinner) * LB Off peak **MEALS:** Bar Lunch £5-£12.50alc Dinner £28 & alc English & Continental Cuisine V meals Coffee am Tea pm **FACILITIES:** CTV in all bedrooms Indoor swimming pool (heated) Squash Snooker Sauna Solarium Gym Jacuzzi/spa Windsurfing Dingy sailing Water skiing **SERVICES:** Lift Night porter 100P **NOTES:** No coaches No children 8yrs No smoking in restaurant Last d 9pm Closed 1 Dec-12 Feb **CARDS:**

See advert on page 563

SALCOMBE Devon — Map 03 SX73

★★★ Soar Mill Cove

Soar Mill Cove, Malborough TQ7 3DS

Quality Percentage Score: 79%

☎ 01548 561566 Fax 01548 561223

***Dir:** 3m W of town off A381 at Malborough. Follow signs 'Soar'*

The hotel is set in extensive grounds, overlooking the bay, and has been in the ownership of the same family for more than 20 years. All the spacious bedrooms are well equipped, with either sea or garden views, and have private balconies or patios. The dining room has a very good reputation for its cuisine.

ROOMS: 21 en suite (bth/shr) (5 fmly) No smoking in all bedrooms s £98-£168; d £196-£224 (incl. bkfst & dinner) * LB Off peak **MEALS:** Lunch £15-£30 & alc High tea £5-£10 & alc Dinner £34-£43 & alc V meals Coffee am Tea pm **FACILITIES:** CTV in all bedrooms Indoor swimming pool (heated) Outdoor swimming pool (heated) Tennis (grass) Putting green Table tennis Large childrens games room & outdoor play area Wkly live entertainment ch fac **SERVICES:** 30P **NOTES:** No coaches No smoking in restaurant Last d 9pm Closed Nov-5 Feb **CARDS:**

See advert on opposite page

SALCOMBE Devon — Map 03 SX73

★★★ Bolt Head

TQ8 8LL

Quality Percentage Score: 77%

☎ 01548 843751 Fax 01548 843061

***Dir:** follow signs to South Sands*

Built in 1901, the hotel is at the entrance to the National Trust-owned Sharpitor and enjoys magnificent views of Salcombe estuary. Public rooms are comfortable and the restaurant has a local reputation for seafood and fish. Pine furniture and well chosen colour schemes make the bedrooms attractive.

ROOMS: 28 en suite (bth/shr) (6 fmly) s £56-£82; d £112-£184 (incl. bkfst) * LB Off peak **MEALS:** Lunch £5.50-£16 Dinner £25-£39 English & French Cuisine V meals Coffee am Tea pm **FACILITIES:** CTV in all bedrooms Outdoor swimming pool (heated) Pool table **SERVICES:** 30P **NOTES:** No coaches No smoking in restaurant Last d 9pm Closed mid Nov-mid Mar **CARDS:**

See advert on opposite page

SALCOMBE Devon — Map 03 SX73

★★★ South Sands

South Sands TQ8 8LL

Quality Percentage Score: 69%

☎ 01548 843741 Fax 01548 842112

***Dir:** off A38 at Buckfastleigh, travel to Totnes and follow A381 to Salcombe, then follow signs to South Sands*

A popular family hotel on the Salcombe estuary, the atmosphere is relaxed and informal, facilities include an indoor swimming pool and children's playroom. Bedrooms are comfortably furnished and equipped, many with superb views. The waterside dining room offers a range of interesting dishes, the beachside Terrace bar is a more informal setting.

ROOMS: 30 en suite (bth/shr) (10 fmly) s £59.50-£90; d £119-£170 (incl. bkfst & dinner) * LB Off peak **MEALS:** Bar Lunch £5.50-£12.50 High tea £3.50-£6.50 Dinner fr £20 & alc English & Continental Cuisine V meals Coffee am Tea pm **FACILITIES:** CTV in all bedrooms Indoor swimming pool (heated) Jacuzzi/spa ch fac **SERVICES:** 50P **NOTES:** No coaches No smoking in restaurant Last d 9pm Closed Nov-Mar **CARDS:**

See advert on opposite page

SALCOMBE Devon — Map 03 SX73

★★ Grafton Towers

Moult Rd, South Sands TQ8 8LG

Quality Percentage Score: 71%

☎ 01548 842882 Fax 01548 842857

***Dir:** approach Salcombe from Kingsbridge,follow signs for South Sands,look for Hotel sign*

Enjoying superb views over the estuary, and standing in gardens, this family owned hotel offers bright, cheerful accommodation and comfortable public rooms, including a lounge and separate bar as well as a dining room.

ROOMS: 13 en suite (bth/shr) s £31.50-£34; d £63-£88 (incl. bkfst) * LB Off peak **MEALS:** Dinner £17.50 Coffee am Tea pm **FACILITIES:** CTV in all bedrooms Croquet lawn **SERVICES:** 13P **NOTES:** No coaches No children 14yrs No smoking in restaurant Last d 8pm Closed Nov-Feb **CARDS:**

Indicates that the star classification has not been confirmed under the New Quality Standards, see page 7 for further information.

AA ★★★ 79%

SOAR MILL COVE HOTEL

Imagine waking to only the sound of birds and the waves breaking upon the golden sand. A late breakfast on your private terrace whilst watching the lobster pots being brought in.
Then stroll amongst the sea pinks to a dramatically beautiful beach surrounded by 2,000 acres of National Trust coastline indented with sandy bays and bubbling streams.
Later, dinner in the elegant restaurant prepared by the award-winning brigade of Keith Stephen, Maitre Association Culinaire Francaise.

SALCOMBE, DEVON TQ7 3DS
Tel: 01548 561566

Heron House Hotel

A small comfortable hotel (17 bedrooms) in an area of outstanding beauty

- ★ *At the edge of the sea, 50 yards from large safe sandy beach in National Trust area*
- ★ *Overlooking Bird Reserve*
- ★ *All rooms en-suite and furnished to a high standard*
- ★ *Gourmet cuisine*
- ★ *Coastal walks and Golf*
- ★ *Heated outdoor pool (May to September)*
- ★ *Ample Parking*

AA ★★ 72% FOR FOOD

80% of our guests return
Non-residents welcome
Thurlestone Sands,
Nr. SALCOMBE, South Devon

(01548) 561308/561600

AA ★★★ 77%

BOLT HEAD HOTEL

Sharpitor, Salcombe, Devon TQ8 8LL
Telephone: 01548 843751
Fax: 01548 843061

Magnificently situated with panoramic views over Salcombe Estuary, the sea and surrounding coastline. The hotel adjoins National Trust Property incorporating Overbecks Gardens & Museum and miles of unspoilt coastal paths for breathtaking walks. Our warm, friendly hotel is only two minutes from a lovely sheltered sandy beach, or you can have a swim in our heated pool. There are lots of interesting places to visit, or you can simply relax and enjoy the views.

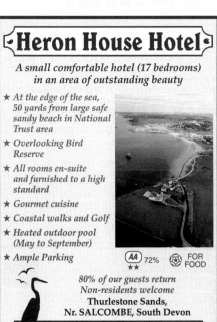

SALCOMBE Devon **Map 03 SX73**
★★ *Lyndhurst*
Bonaventure Rd TQ8 8BG
Quality Percentage Score: 64%
☎ 01548 842481 01548 842481
Dir: *Follow signs to Salcombe, in Salcombe take 1st left (Onslow Rd) then 1st right (St Dunstan's Rd) & 1st left (Raleigh Rd) leads into Bonaventure Rd*
Wonderful views of the countryside and estuary are a feature of many of the bedrooms and the dining room of this comfortable, peaceful hotel which stands high above the town. Enjoyable cuisine is a strength here.
ROOMS: 8 rms (4 fmly) No smoking in all bedrooms **MEALS:** French Cuisine V meals Coffee am **FACILITIES:** CTV in all bedrooms Arrangements with Marine Hotel for use of leisure facilities **SERVICES:** 4P **NOTES:** No smoking in restaurant **CARDS:**

SALCOMBE Devon **Map 03 SX73**
★ **Sunny Cliff**
Cliff Rd TQ8 8JX
Quality Percentage Score: 67%
☎ 01548 842207 01548 843388
Dir: *A381 into Salcombe follow rd down hill, sharp left to South Sands, hotel 150m on left*
This small, friendly hotel enjoys an enviable elevated position above the water's edge. The bar-lounge has been moved to the ground floor and has marvellous views, shared by the dining room and all the bedrooms. The gardens lead down to the outdoor heated pool and the hotel's six private moorings. Bedrooms are mostly spacious with light decor and modern facilities.
ROOMS: 10 rms (5 bth/shr) 4 annexe en suite (bth/shr) (4 fmly) s £38-£42; d £81-£99 (incl. bkfst) * LB Off peak **MEALS:** Dinner £12-£13.50 English & Continental Cuisine **FACILITIES:** CTV in all bedrooms Outdoor swimming pool (heated) Fishing Moorings and Landing stage Xmas **SERVICES:** 17P **NOTES:** No smoking in restaurant Last d 8pm Closed Jan RS Nov-Mar **CARDS:**

SALE Greater Manchester **Map 07 SJ79**
Travel Inn
Carrington Ln, Ashton-Upon-Mersey M33 5NL
☎ 0161 962 8113 0161 905 1742
Dir: *from junct 6 of the M60 take A6144(M) towards Partington and Lymm. Turn left at 1st set of traffic lights, Travel Inn on left*
This modern building offers accommodation in smart, spacious and well equipped bedrooms, all with en-suite bathrooms. Refreshments may be taken at the nearby family restaurant. For details about current prices consult the Contents Page under Hotel Groups for the Travel Inn phone number.
ROOMS: 40 en suite (bth/shr) d £39.95 *

SALFORD Greater Manchester **Map 07 SJ89**
see also **Manchester**
Travel Inn
Basin 8 The Quays, Salford Quays M5 4SQ
☎ 0161 872 4026 0161 876 0094
Dir: *just off A5063 on Salford Quays, 1m from Manchester United Stadium*
This modern building offers accommodation in smart, spacious and well equipped bedrooms, all with en-suite bathrooms. Refreshments may be taken at the nearby family restaurant. For details about current prices consult the Contents Page under Hotel Groups for the Travel Inn phone number.
ROOMS: 52 en suite (bth/shr) d £39.95 *

SALISBURY Wiltshire **Map 04 SU12**
★★★ **Milford Hall**
206 Castle St SP1 3TE
Quality Percentage Score: 74%
☎ 01722 417411 01722 419444
Dir: *hotel is a few hundred yds from the conjunction of Castle St, the A30 ring road and the A345 Amesbury Rd. It is 0.5m from Market Sq*

The hotel is quietly situated, within easy walking distance of the city centre and with a reputation for good hospitality. Bedrooms fall into two categories, traditional rooms in the original Georgian house and spacious, modern rooms recently refurbished, all are well equipped. The smartly appointed restaurant is popular with guests and locals alike.
ROOMS: 35 en suite (bth/shr) (1 fmly) No smoking in 6 bedrooms s £75-£100; d £85-£110 (incl. bkfst) LB Off peak **MEALS:** Lunch £9.95-£12.95 Dinner fr £15.50 & alc English & French Cuisine V meals Coffee am Tea pm **FACILITIES:** CTV in all bedrooms STV Free facilities at local leisure centre **CONF:** Thtr 90 Class 70 Board 40 Del from £95 * **SERVICES:** Night porter 60P **NOTES:** No smoking in restaurant Last d 9.45pm **CARDS:**
See advert on opposite page

SALISBURY Wiltshire **Map 04 SU12**
★★★ **The White Hart**
St John St SP1 2SD
Quality Percentage Score: 70%
☎ 01722 327476 01722 412761
Dir: *from M3 junct 7 take A3, A338 for Salisbury and follow signs for city centre. Hotel on Exeter St, parking at rear*
Dating in parts from the 16th century, this character hotel is directly opposite the cathedral precinct. Bedrooms vary in size, but all are tastefully decorated, bright and inviting. The traditional bar and lounge are popular for morning coffee and afternoon tea.
ROOMS: 68 en suite (bth/shr) (3 fmly) No smoking in 28 bedrooms s £80-£85; d £110-£115 LB Off peak **MEALS:** Lunch £7.95-£15.95 & alc High tea £5-£8.50alc Dinner £18.50-£30alc V meals Coffee am Tea pm **FACILITIES:** CTV in all bedrooms Wkly live entertainment Xmas **CONF:** Thtr 80 Class 40 Board 40 Del from £99 **SERVICES:** Night porter 90P **NOTES:** No smoking in restaurant Last d 9.30pm **CARDS:**

SALISBURY Wiltshire **Map 04 SU12**
★★★ **Red Lion**
Milford St SP1 2AN
Quality Percentage Score: 68%
☎ 01722 323334 01722 325756
Dir: *in city centre off Market Sq*
This 13th-century coaching inn is older than the Cathedral and offers traditional standards of hospitality. Bedrooms are individually furnished and decorated, with attractive co-ordinated fabrics; several have four-poster beds. There is a
contd.

creeper clad courtyard, dinner is taken in the refurbished restaurant.

ROOMS: 54 en suite (bth/shr) (3 fmly) No smoking in 36 bedrooms s £81.50-£91.50; d £96.50-£115 * LB Off peak **MEALS:** Lunch £13.95 & alc Dinner £16.50-£18.50 English & French Cuisine V meals Coffee am Tea pm **FACILITIES:** CTV in all bedrooms **CONF:** Thtr 100 Class 50 Board 40 Del from £98 * **SERVICES:** Lift Night porter 10P **NOTES:** No dogs (ex guide dogs) No smoking in restaurant Last d 9pm
CARDS:

See advert on opposite page

SALISBURY Wiltshire — Map 04 SU12

★★★ Rose & Crown
Harnham Rd, Harnham SP2 8JQ
REGAL
Quality Percentage Score: 68%
☎ 01722 399955 Fax 01722 339816
Dir: *M3 junct 8 to A303 then A30 to centre of Salisbury*

A charming hotel on the banks of the river Avon, with views of the Cathedral. Bedrooms, in the main house or new wing, are well designed and smartly furnished. The Pavilions restaurant is virtually on the water's edge, an evening fixed price menu is offered. Public areas are cosy and attractively furnished, the two bars have log fires.

ROOMS: 28 en suite (bth/shr) s £105; d £130 * LB Off peak **MEALS:** Lunch £9.95-£11.95 & alc High tea fr £3.95 Dinner fr £19.50 & alc V meals Coffee am Tea pm **FACILITIES:** CTV in all bedrooms STV Fishing Xmas **CONF:** Thtr 80 Class 40 Board 40 Del from £110 * **SERVICES:** Night porter 42P **NOTES:** No smoking in restaurant Last d 9.30pm **CARDS:**

SALISBURY Wiltshire — Map 04 SU12

★★★ Grasmere House
Harnhan Rd SP2 8JN
MINOTEL Great Britain
Quality Percentage Score: 66%
☎ 01722 338388 Fax 01722 333710
Dir: *on A3094 on S side of Salisbury next to All Saints Church in Harnham*

This Victorian house has gardens which run down to the River Nadder, and views towards the cathedral. Public areas include a

contd.

spacious conservatory, traditionally furnished lounge, and cosy bar. In the restaurant, the daily changing menu offers an interesting range of dishes. Bedrooms are tastefully furnished and decorated.
ROOMS: 4 en suite (bth/shr) 16 annexe en suite (bth/shr) (2 fmly) No smoking in 4 bedrooms s £65-£70; d £105-£155 (incl. bkfst) * LB Off peak **MEALS:** Lunch £10.50-£15.50 High tea £5-£7.50 Dinner £17.50-£22.50 International Cuisine V meals Coffee am Tea pm
FACILITIES: CTV in all bedrooms Fishing Croquet lawn Xmas
CONF: Thtr 85 Class 65 Board 45 Del from £105 * **SERVICES:** 36P
NOTES: No smoking area in restaurant Last d 9.30pm
CARDS:

See advert on opposite page

SALISBURY Wiltshire — Map 04 SU12
★★ Howard's House
Teffont Evias SP3 5RJ
Quality Percentage Score: 78%
☎ 01722 716392 Fax 01722 716820
Dir: *turn off B3089 at Teffont Magna follow signs to Howards House Hotel*
Set in two acres of colourful gardens, this welcoming hotel is located in a most picturesque village. Spacious bedrooms are comfortably furnished and the welcoming lounge is complemented by an unusual restaurant and a well presented menu.
ROOMS: 9 en suite (bth/shr) (1 fmly) s £70-£75; d £105-£145 (incl. bkfst) * LB Off peak **MEALS:** Sunday Lunch £18.50 Dinner £22-£25 British & Continental Cuisine V meals Coffee am Tea pm
FACILITIES: CTV in all bedrooms Croquet lawn Xmas **CONF:** Class 20 Board 12 **SERVICES:** 23P **NOTES:** No coaches No smoking in restaurant Last d 9.30pm Closed 30 Dec-2 Jan
CARDS:

SALISBURY Wiltshire — Map 04 SU12
Travel Inn
Bishopdown Retail Park, Pearce Way SP1 3GU
☎ 01722 339836 Fax 01722 337889
Dir: *on rdbt adjoining Bishopdown Retail Park*
This modern building offers accommodation in smart, spacious and well equipped bedrooms, all with en-suite bathrooms. Refreshments may be taken at the nearby family restaurant. For details about current prices consult the Contents Page under Hotel Groups for the Travel Inn phone number.
d £39.95 *

SALTASH Cornwall & Isles of Scilly — Map 02 SX45
Travelodge
Callington Rd, Carkeel PL12 6LF
☎ Central Res 0800 850950 Fax 01752 849028
Dir: *on A38 Saltash By-Pass - 1m from Tamar Bridge*
This modern building offers accommodation in smart, spacious and well equipped bedrooms, all with en-suite bathrooms. Refreshments may be taken at the nearby family restaurant. For details about current prices, consult the Contents Page under Hotel Groups for the Travelodge phone number.
ROOMS: 31 en suite (bth/shr) d £49.95 * **CONF:** Thtr 25 Class 15 Board 12

SAMPFORD PEVERELL Devon — Map 03 ST01
Travelodge
Sampford Peverell Service Area EX16 7HD
☎ 01884 821087
Dir: *junc 27, M5*
This modern building offers accommodation in smart, spacious and well equipped bedrooms, all with en-suite bathrooms. Refreshments may be taken at the nearby family restaurant. For details about current prices, consult the Contents Page under Hotel Groups for the Travelodge phone number.
ROOMS: 40 en suite (bth/shr) d £45.95 *

SANDBACH Cheshire — Map 07 SJ76
★★★ Chimney House
Congleton Rd CW11 4ST
Quality Percentage Score: 66%
☎ 01270 764141 Fax 01270 768916
Dir: *on A534, 1m from M6 junct 17 heading for Congleton*

Corus and Regal hotels

Set in eight acres of attractive grounds, this half-timbered Tudor style building offers a variety of bedrooms. Those in the older wing tend to be more spacious. Dinner is served in the attractive Patio restaurant. Meeting and function suites are available, together with a sauna and spa bath.
ROOMS: 49 en suite (bth/shr) (6 fmly) No smoking in 33 bedrooms s £90-£105; d £105-£115 * LB Off peak **MEALS:** Lunch £12 & alc Dinner £18 & alc English & French Cuisine V meals Coffee am Tea pm
FACILITIES: CTV in all bedrooms STV Sauna Putting green Jacuzzi/spa
CONF: Thtr 100 Class 60 Board 50 **SERVICES:** Night porter 110P
NOTES: No dogs (ex guide dogs) No smoking in restaurant Last d 10pm
CARDS:

SANDBACH Cheshire — Map 07 SJ76
★★ Saxon Cross
Holmes Chapel Rd CW11 1SE
Quality Percentage Score: 64%
☎ 01270 763281 Fax 01270 768723
Dir: *heading towards Congleton, first turning on left after motorway bridge on A5022 towards Holmes Chapel*
This purpose built hotel is close to junction 17 of the M6. Bedrooms are spacious and well equipped, and there is the added advantage that visitors can park their car right outside their rooms. There is a choice of meeting rooms which are available for functions.
ROOMS: 52 en suite (bth/shr) (2 fmly) No smoking in 3 bedrooms s £45-£69.50; d £57-£72 (incl. bkfst) * LB Off peak **MEALS:** Lunch £9-£10 Dinner £16 English & French Cuisine V meals Coffee am Tea pm
FACILITIES: CTV in all bedrooms STV **CONF:** Thtr 150 Class 200 Board 80 Del from £80 * **SERVICES:** Night porter 150P **NOTES:** No smoking area in restaurant Last d 9.30pm **CARDS:**

SANDBANKS See **Poole**

SANDIACRE Derbyshire — Map 08 SK43
★★★ Posthouse Nottingham/Derby
Bostocks Ln NG10 5NJ
Quality Percentage Score: 65%
☎ 0115 9397800 Fax 0115 9490469
Dir: *M1 J25 follow exit to Sandiacre, hotel on right*
This modern hotel is conveniently situated just off junction 25 of the M1 motorway. Bedrooms offer a good standard of

contd.

contemporary furnishings and are well equipped, and public areas, including the popular restaurant, are well maintained and comfortable. Staff are friendly and helpful, and an all day lounge menu and 24 hour room service are available. There are numerous conference rooms and plenty of parking.

ROOMS: 93 en suite (bth/shr) (6 fmly) No smoking in 50 bedrooms s £94-£105; d £94-£125 (incl. bkfst) * LB Off peak
MEALS: International Cuisine V meals Coffee am Tea pm
FACILITIES: CTV in all bedrooms Pool table Day membership to David Lloyd Leisure Xmas **CONF:** Thtr 60 Class 26 Board 28 Del from £90 *
SERVICES: Night porter 180P **NOTES:** No smoking area in restaurant Last d 10.30pm **CARDS:**

SANDIWAY Cheshire — Map 07 SJ67

The Premier Collection

★★★ Nunsmere Hall Country House
Tarporley Rd CW8 2ES
☎ 01606 889100 Fax 01606 889055

***Dir:** from Chester follow A51, A556-Manchester, reach intersection at A49 turn right to Whitchurch, Nunsmere Hall is 1m on left hand side*

This hotel lies on a mini peninsula surrounded by a lake. The bedrooms are stylishly decorated and thoughtfully equipped. Guests can relax in the opulent lounge, the library or the oak-panelled bar. In the restaurant, the cosmopolitan menu delivers dishes to suit all tastes.

ROOMS: 37 en suite (bth/shr) No smoking in 10 bedrooms s £110-£130; d £150-£325 * LB Off peak **MEALS:** Lunch £22.50 Dinner fr £32 French Cuisine V meals Coffee am Tea pm **FACILITIES:** CTV in all bedrooms Snooker Croquet lawn Putting green Archery Air Rifle Shooting Falconry Clay pigeon shooting Xmas **CONF:** Thtr 50 Class 24 Board 32 Del £180 * **SERVICES:** Lift Night porter 80P **NOTES:** No dogs (ex guide dogs) No coaches No smoking in restaurant Last d 9.45pm RS Sun
CARDS:

SANDOWN See Wight, Isle of

SANDWICH Kent — Map 05 TR35

★★★ *The Blazing Donkey Country Hotel & Inn*
Hay Hill, Ham CT13 0HU
Quality Percentage Score: 67%
☎ 01304 617362 Fax 01304 615264

***Dir:** turn off A256 at Eastry into the village, turn at the "five bells" public house, hotel is 0.75 mile along the lane situated on the left*

The Blazing Donkey is a hotel with lots of charm. Proprietor John Martin and his friendly staff are real characters, in love with the game of golf - handy as the hotel is so close to Royal St George's. Rooms are all chalet style, with wood panelling and

contd.

polished wooden floors. Bar and restaurant have been designed to look venerable.

The Blazing Donkey, Sandwich

ROOMS: 19 en suite (bth/shr) (2 fmly) No smoking in 5 bedrooms **MEALS:** International Cuisine V meals Coffee am Tea pm **FACILITIES:** CTV in all bedrooms STV Tennis (hard) Croquet lawn Putting green Childrens playground Wkly live entertainment **SERVICES:** Air conditioning 108P **NOTES:** No dogs (ex guide dogs) No smoking area in restaurant Last d 10.30pm **CARDS:**

SAUNDERTON Buckinghamshire — Map 04 SP70

★★ Rose & Crown

Wycombe Rd HP27 9NP
Quality Percentage Score: 62%
☎ 01844 345299 01844 343140
Dir: *on A4010, 6m from Exit4 M40*

This long established family run hotel is located conveniently between High Wycombe and Aylesbury. Accommodation is comfortable and well appointed. The popular bar boasts a log fire; guests may select from an extensive blackboard menu of freshly prepared dishes and eat in the relaxed ambience of the bar or the more secluded restaurant.

ROOMS: 15 en suite (bth/shr) s £49.50-£78.45; d £69.95-£88 (incl. bkfst) LB Off peak **MEALS:** Lunch fr £13.50 & alc Dinner £10.95-£23.75alc English & French Cuisine V meals Coffee am Tea pm **FACILITIES:** CTV in all bedrooms **CONF:** Thtr 30 Board 15 **SERVICES:** 50P **NOTES:** No dogs (ex guide dogs) No coaches No smoking in restaurant Last d 9.30pm Closed 25 Dec-1 Jan **CARDS:**

SAUNTON Devon — Map 02 SS43

★★★★ Saunton Sands

EX33 1LQ
Quality Percentage Score: 69%
☎ 01271 890212 01271 890145
Dir: *turn off A361 at Braunton, signposted Croyde B3231 hotel 2m on left*

This popular hotel enjoys fine sea views, as well as direct access to five miles of sandy beach. A range of leisure facilities is available, including both indoor and outdoor swimming pools, regular entertainment, and a supervised nursery. There is a choice of comfortable lounges which are designed, as is the case with the air conditioned restaurant, to make the best use of the views. Many of the bedrooms, varying in size, have private balconies and include a number of family suites.

ROOMS: 92 en suite (bth/shr) (39 fmly) s £68-£98; d £132-£210 (incl. bkfst) * LB Off peak **MEALS:** Lunch £10.50-£13.50 & alc Dinner £22.50 & alc English & French Cuisine V meals Coffee am Tea pm **FACILITIES:** CTV in all bedrooms STV Indoor swimming pool (heated) Outdoor swimming pool (heated) Tennis (hard) Squash Snooker Sauna Solarium Gym Pool table Putting green Jacuzzi/spa Table tennis Wkly live entertainment ch fac Xmas **CONF:** Thtr 150 **SERVICES:** Lift Night porter 142P **NOTES:** No dogs (ex guide dogs) No coaches Last d 9pm **CARDS:**

See advert on page 569

SCARBOROUGH North Yorkshire — Map 08 TA08

★★★ Ox Pasture Hall Country Hotel

Lady Ediths Dr, Raincliffe Woods YO12 5TD
Quality Percentage Score: 71%
☎ 01723 365295 01723 355156
Dir: *A171 out of Scarborough, after passing hospital, follow tourist sign for "Forge Valley & Raincliffe Woods" turn left, hotel 1.5m on right*

This delightful small country hotel is a sympathetic conversion of a farmhouse in the North Riding Forest Park. Three bedrooms are in the main house and the others around an attractive garden courtyard to which a covered walk gives access. Public areas include a split-level bar, a quiet lounge, and attractive restaurant offering both a carte and a fixed-price menu.

ROOMS: 17 en suite (bth/shr) (2 fmly) No smoking in 4 bedrooms s £34.50-£47.50; d £59-£85 (incl. bkfst) * Off peak **MEALS:** Lunch £9.80-£13.20 & alc Dinner £16.50 & alc International Cuisine V meals Coffee am Tea pm **FACILITIES:** CTV in all bedrooms Fishing Croquet lawn Putting green Xmas **SERVICES:** 30P **NOTES:** No coaches No smoking in restaurant Last d 9.30pm **CARDS:**

See advert on page 573

SCARBOROUGH North Yorkshire — Map 08 TA08

★★★ Wrea Head Country Hotel

Scalby YO13 0PB
Quality Percentage Score: 70%
☎ 01723 378211 01723 371780
Dir: *from Scarborough follow A171 until hotel signpost on left, turn into Barmoor Lane, hotel drive is on left*

Wrea Head Country Hotel is an elegant Victorian country house, standing in 14 acres of well tended grounds and gardens close to the National Park. The house has been delightfully furnished throughout and includes a cosy library and a comfortable bar. Bedrooms vary in size and all are thoughtfully equipped to a

contd. on p. 572

ENGLISH ROSE HOTELS

WREA HEAD

COUNTRY HOUSE HOTEL

Sample the delights of this beautifully restored Victorian Country House set in acres of glorious gardens and park lands at the edge of the North York Moors National Park. Twenty individually styled bedrooms. Award winning Four Seasons restaurant offers superb cuisine using fresh local produce. Ample free car parking. Situated three miles north of Scarborough – a perfect base for touring the heritage coast. Meeting facilities for up to 20 persons in privacy and seclusion.

For details ring 01723 378211
Barmoor Lane, Scalby
Scarborough YO13 0PB
Fax: 01723 355936

AA ★★★

HACKNESS GRANGE COUNTRY HOTEL

AA ★★★

North Yorkshire Moors National Park
nr Scarborough YO13 0JW

Situated on the outskirts of Scarborough, this gracious Country House is set in acres of beautiful gardens and grounds beside the River Derwent, within the North York Moors National Park. Excellent leisure choices - indoor heated swimming pool with jacuzzi, tennis court, trout fishing (in season), croquet and nine hole pitch 'n putt. Delightful en-suite bedrooms, many with scenic country views, and award winning restaurant renowned for good food. Some ground floor rooms available. Perfect location for Board Meetings and available for exclusive use for corporated events and activities.

See entry under Hackness

Tel: 01723 882345 Fax: 01723 882391

S

THE CLIFTON HOTEL

QUEENS PARADE, NORTH SHORE
SCARBOROUGH YO12 7HX
Tel: 01723 375691 Fax: 01723 364203

AA ★★★

The finest location on Scarborough's North Shore with many of the 71 en-suite bedrooms having panoramic sea views over the Bay and Scarborough Castle headland.
Excellent food with good old fashioned Yorkshire portions! Free private car parking.
Adjacent to Alexander Bowls Centre and Scarborough Cricket Ground.

ENGLISH ROSE HOTELS

high standard. Service is professional and friendly from smartly presented staff.

ROOMS: 20 en suite (bth/shr) (2 fmly) s £50-£77.50; d £115-£185 (incl. bkfst) * LB Off peak **MEALS:** Lunch £12.50-£17.50 Dinner £25-£35 English & Continental Cuisine V meals Coffee am Tea pm **FACILITIES:** CTV in all bedrooms STV Croquet lawn Putting green Xmas **CONF:** Thtr 30 Class 16 Board 20 Del from £95 * **SERVICES:** Night porter 50P **NOTES:** No dogs (ex guide dogs) No coaches No smoking in restaurant Last d 9.15pm **CARDS:**

See advert on page 571

SCARBOROUGH North Yorkshire — Map 08 TA08

★★★ Esplanade

Belmont Rd YO11 2AA

Quality Percentage Score: 65%

☎ 01723 360382 ⎙ 01723 376137

Dir: *from Scarborough town centre cross Valley Bridge, left after bridge then immediate right onto Belmont Rd, hotel 100mtrs on right*

This hotel enjoys a spectacular position overlooking the South Bay and harbour. Both the terrace leading off the lounge bar, and the restaurant with its striking oriel window, take advantage of these views. Most bedrooms have been refurbished to a stylish modern standard to match the public areas and the hotel is popular with coach tours and the conference trade.

ROOMS: 73 en suite (bth/shr) (9 fmly) s £45; d £82-£92 (incl. bkfst) * LB Off peak **MEALS:** Bar Lunch £1.95-£5.50 Dinner £16.25-£24.25 English & French Cuisine V meals Coffee am **FACILITIES:** CTV in all bedrooms Pool table Darts Table tennis Xmas **CONF:** Thtr 140 Class 100 Board 40 Del from £45 * **SERVICES:** Lift Night porter 24P **NOTES:** No smoking in restaurant Last d 8.30pm

CARDS:

SCARBOROUGH North Yorkshire — Map 08 TA08

★★★ *Ambassador*

Centre of the Esplanade YO11 2AY

Quality Percentage Score: 64%

☎ 01723 362841 ⎙ 362841

Dir: *A64, right at 1st small rdbt opposite, then right at next small rdbt, take immediate left down Avenue Vicoria to the Cliff Top*

Standing in a prime position on the South Cliff and having excellent views over the bay, this friendly hotel offers well equipped bedrooms together with pleasantly refurbished public rooms. A 40' indoor pool is available together with a sauna and solarium and entertainment is provided during the season.

ROOMS: 59 en suite (bth/shr) (10 fmly) **MEALS:** International Cuisine V meals Coffee am Tea pm **FACILITIES:** CTV in all bedrooms STV Indoor swimming pool (heated) Sauna Solarium Jacuzzi/spa Wkly live entertainment **CONF:** Thtr 140 Class 90 Board 60 **SERVICES:** Lift Night porter **NOTES:** No smoking in restaurant Last d 8.30pm

CARDS:

See advert on opposite page

SCARBOROUGH North Yorkshire — Map 08 TA08

★★★ Crown

Esplanade YO11 2AG

Quality Percentage Score: 64%

☎ 01723 373491 ⎙ 01723 362271

REGAL

Occupying a prime position on the South Cliff, this elegant hotel overlooks the sea and is only a short walk from the town centre. The majority of the bedrooms have been refurbished to a good modern standard, with several enjoying spectacular views over Scarborough Bay. There is a comfortable lounge and good conference and meeting facilities.

ROOMS: 78 en suite (bth/shr) (7 fmly) No smoking in 9 bedrooms s £65; d £85 * LB Off peak **MEALS:** V meals Coffee am Tea pm **FACILITIES:** CTV in all bedrooms Snooker Pool table Xmas **CONF:** Thtr 180 Class 60 Board 70 **SERVICES:** Lift Night porter **NOTES:** No smoking in restaurant Last d 9.00pm **CARDS:**

SCARBOROUGH North Yorkshire — Map 08 TA08

★★★ Palm Court

St Nicholas Cliff YO11 2ES

Quality Percentage Score: 64%

☎ 01723 368161 ⎙ 01723 371547

Dir: *follow signs for Town Centre and Town Hall, hotel is on route to Town Hall situated on right hand side*

The public rooms are spacious and comfortable at this modern hotel and the bedrooms are well equipped. Traditional cooking is provided in the attractive restaurant.

ROOMS: 46 en suite (bth/shr) (7 fmly) s £40-£45; d £37-£82 (incl. bkfst) * LB Off peak **MEALS:** Lunch £9.25 Dinner £13.50 & alc English & French Cuisine V meals Coffee am Tea pm **FACILITIES:** CTV in all bedrooms Indoor swimming pool (heated) Table tennis Xmas **CONF:** Thtr 200 Class 100 Board 60 Del from £48 * **SERVICES:** Lift Night porter 80P **NOTES:** No dogs (ex guide dogs) No smoking area in restaurant Last d 9pm **CARDS:**

See advert on opposite page

PALM COURT HOTEL

St. Nicholas Cliff
Scarborough
YO11 2ES
telephone
01723 368161
facsimile
01723 371547

Superb central location with guaranteed free covered car parking and indoor heated swimming pool, minutes to the beach, town centre, theatres and spa. All 46 bedrooms en-suite with colour television. Ideal for the discerning conference delegate offering in-house conference facilities.

Weekend, midweek and weekly breaks all year.

Open Christmas and New Year.

AA ★★★

Ox Pasture Hall Country Hotel

AA ★★★

Set in 20 acres of glorious National Parkland and nestling on the edge of Forge Valley, with panoramic views from every aspect. A Grade II Listed building of great character newly opened in 1996 after careful renovation combining the best of traditional and modern comforts. Only 3 miles from Scarborough. An ideal base for exploring, moors and coast. Spacious and well equipped accommodation with excellent table d'hôte or à la carte menus, and wine list.

Lady Edith's Drive, Throxenby, Scarborough
North Yorkshire YO12 5TD
Telephone 01723 365295

★★★ *Raven Hall*

COUNTRY HOUSE HOTEL & GOLF COURSE

Half way between Scarborough and Whitby, this historic country house hotel is situated in 100 acres of award winning gardens and battlements.

★ 53 en-suite bedrooms ★ Private cliff top golf course ★ Tennis ★ Croquet ★ Putting ★ Crown Bowls ★ Swimming Pools - outdoor and indoor ★ Snooker ★ Hair & Beauty Salon ★ Sauna ★ Conference facilities ★ Medieval Banqueting Hall ★ Children welcome ★ Parking for 200 cars . . . and an enviable reputation for good food & warm hospitality

Tel: (01723) 870353 Fax: (01723) 870072
Ravenscar, North Yorkshire YO13 0ET

Prime clifftop gracious and individual award winning AA 3-star Victorian hotel, above spa entertainment/conference centre, offering friendly professional service and fine cuisine. 59 en-suite bedrooms with full facilities, lift, satellite TV, panoramic bay views. Conference facilities for the discerning delegate. 40ft indoor heated swimming pool, spa and sauna. Tasteful entertainment. Opposite famous Italian rose gardens, cliff lift to beach and town, free unrestricted street parking and much more!

AMBASSADOR HOTEL

Centre of the Esplanade
Scarborough, North Yorkshire YO11 2AY
Tel/Fax: 01723 362841
www.ambassador-hotel.co.uk
Les Routiers

S

SCARBOROUGH North Yorkshire **Map 08 TA08**
★★★ Hotel St Nicholas
St Nicholas Cliff YO11 2EU
Quality Percentage Score: 64%
☎ 01723 364101 📠 01723 500538
Dir: *in town centre, railway station on right, turn right at traffic lights, left at next set, follow road along, across rdbt, take next left*
A splendid Victorian hotel with fine views over the sea and with access to the town. Bedrooms are well equipped and vary in size. There are good lounge and bar facilities as well as a leisure club. Traditional food is served in the restaurant and there is also a theme pub.
ROOMS: 144 en suite (bth/shr) (17 fmly) No smoking in 8 bedrooms s £35-£71; d £65-£95 (incl. bkfst) * LB Off peak **MEALS:** Sunday Lunch £8-£10 High tea £2-£10 Dinner £14.50 V meals Coffee am Tea pm **FACILITIES:** CTV in all bedrooms STV Indoor swimming pool (heated) Sauna Solarium Gym Pool table Hair & Beauty salon Wkly live entertainment ch fac Xmas **CONF:** Thtr 400 Class 150 Board 50 **SERVICES:** Lift Night porter 20P **NOTES:** No smoking in restaurant Last d 9.15pm **CARDS:**

SCARBOROUGH North Yorkshire **Map 08 TA08**
★★★ Clifton
Queens Pde, North Cliff YO12 7HX
Quality Percentage Score: 60%
☎ 01723 375691 📠 01723 364203
Dir: *on entering the town centre, follow signs for North Bay*
Standing in an impressive position overlooking the bay, this large holiday hotel provides pleasing, well equipped bedrooms together with spacious public rooms where entertainment is provided during the season. It is convenient for Peasholm Park and other leisure attractions.
ROOMS: 71 en suite (bth/shr) (11 fmly) **MEALS:** Lunch £10.50-£15 Dinner £17.50 V meals Coffee am Tea pm **FACILITIES:** CTV in all bedrooms Sauna Solarium Pool table **CONF:** Thtr 120 Class 50 Board 50 Del from £55 * **SERVICES:** Lift Night porter 45P **NOTES:** No smoking in restaurant Last d 9pm Closed 29 Dec-3 Jan
CARDS:

SCARBOROUGH North Yorkshire **Map 08 TA08**
★★ Gridley's Crescent
The Crescent YO11 2PP
Quality Percentage Score: 74%
☎ 01723 360929 & 507507 📠 01723 354126
Dir: *on entering Scarborough travel towards railway station then follow signs to Brunswick Pavilion, at traffic lights turn into Crescent*
This listed building overlooks a small park, and is near the town centre. The bedrooms have been thoughtfully equipped and there are two dining styles - an elegant restaurant serving a set price menu and carte, and a less formal option offering carvery style dishes.
ROOMS: 20 en suite (bth/shr) No smoking in 7 bedrooms s fr £43; d fr £75 (incl. bkfst) * LB Off peak **MEALS:** Lunch fr £10.25 Dinner fr £16.50 & alc V meals Coffee am **FACILITIES:** CTV in all bedrooms **CONF:** Thtr 40 Board 15 Del from £75 * **SERVICES:** Lift Night porter **NOTES:** No dogs (ex guide dogs) No coaches No children 6yrs No smoking in restaurant Last d 9pm **CARDS:**

SCARBOROUGH North Yorkshire **Map 08 TA08**
★★ *The Mount*
Cliff Bridge Ter, Saint Nicholas Cliff YO11 2HA
Quality Percentage Score: 69%
☎ 01723 360961 📠 01723 360961
Standing in a fine elevated position overlooking the sea and enjoying superb views of the bay, this elegant Regency hotel is personally owned and run to a high standard. The richly furnished and comfortable public rooms are inviting, and the well equipped bedrooms have been attractively decorated.The suites are especially good while very attentive and friendly service is provided.
ROOMS: 50 en suite (bth/shr) (5 fmly) No smoking in 2 bedrooms **MEALS:** V meals Coffee am Tea pm **FACILITIES:** CTV in all bedrooms **SERVICES:** Lift Night porter **NOTES:** Closed Jan-mid Mar
CARDS:

See advert on opposite page

SCARBOROUGH North Yorkshire **Map 08 TA08**
★★ *Bradley Court Hotel*
Filey Rd, South Cliff YO11 2SE
Quality Percentage Score: 65%
☎ 01723 360476 📠 01723 376661
Dir: *from A64 enter Scarborough Town limits, at 1st rdbt turn right signposted Filey & South Cliff, at next rdbt turn left, hotel 50yds on left*
Situated on the Filey road, just a short walk from South Cliff and the town centre, this is a predominantly modern hotel offering well equipped accommodation and all the usual amenities.
ROOMS: 40 en suite (bth/shr) (4 fmly) No smoking in 6 bedrooms **MEALS:** European Cuisine V meals Coffee am Tea pm **FACILITIES:** CTV in all bedrooms Pool table **CONF:** Thtr 160 Class 100 Board 60 Del from £48 * **SERVICES:** Lift Night porter 40P **NOTES:** No dogs No smoking in restaurant Last d 8.30pm **CARDS:**

SCARBOROUGH North Yorkshire **Map 08 TA08**
★★ Red Lea
Prince of Wales Ter YO11 2AJ
Quality Percentage Score: 65%
☎ 01723 362431 📠 01723 371230
Dir: *follow signs for South Cliff, Prince of Wales Terrace leads off the esplanade opp the cliff lift*
This family-owned and run hotel on the South cliff provides very good value for money. It offers well equipped bedrooms and adequate public areas, with an indoor pool. A good value five-course dinner is served in the spacious dining room, staff are friendly and attentive.
ROOMS: 67 en suite (bth/shr) (7 fmly) s £34-£35; d £68-£70 (incl. bkfst) * LB Off peak **MEALS:** Lunch fr £8.50 Dinner fr £12 International Cuisine V meals Coffee am Tea pm **FACILITIES:** CTV in all bedrooms Indoor swimming pool (heated) Sauna Solarium Gym Pool table Xmas **CONF:** Thtr 40 Class 25 Board 25 Del from £60 * **SERVICES:** Lift Night porter **NOTES:** No dogs (ex guide dogs) No smoking in restaurant Last d 8.30pm **CARDS:**

SCARBOROUGH North Yorkshire **Map 08 TA08**
★★ La Baia Hotel
24 Blenheim Ter YO12 7HD
Quality Percentage Score: 64%
☎ 01723 370780
Dir: *A64 to centre of town, left at railway station, 1st right Victoria Rd/Castle Rd, left St Peters Church onto Blenheim St and left into Blenheim Terrace*
This family owned and run hotel offers fine hospitality and enjoys superb views over the bay. Bedrooms are pleasantly furnished and have been thoughtfully equipped whilst a friendly

contd.

bar and cosy dining room are also provided. A good range of home cooking is served each evening.

ROOMS: 12 en suite (bth/shr) (2 fmly) s £26; d £44-£52 (incl. bkfst) * Off peak **MEALS:** Dinner £9-£15.95 V meals **FACILITIES:** CTV in all bedrooms **NOTES:** No dogs No coaches No smoking in restaurant Last d 7.30pm Closed 27 Oct-28 Feb **CARDS:**

SCARBOROUGH North Yorkshire **Map 08 TA08**

★★ Southlands

15 West St, South Cliff YO11 2QW

Quality Percentage Score: 63%

☎ 01723 361461 📠 01723 376035

***Dir:** in Scarborough, follow town centre signs, turn right at railway station, at 2nd set of traffic lights turn left, car park is 200yds on left*

Situated in a quiet area close to the South Cliff, this hotel is popular with tour groups and offers spacious bedrooms and well proportioned public areas. Friendly and attentive service is provided by a pleasant and well managed team.

ROOMS: 58 en suite (bth/shr) (9 fmly) No smoking in 2 bedrooms s £30-£34; d £60-£68 (incl. bkfst) * Off peak **MEALS:** Lunch £5.25-£7.45 Dinner £11-£15 V meals Coffee am Tea pm **FACILITIES:** CTV in all bedrooms Wkly live entertainment Xmas **CONF:** Thtr 150 Class 100 Board 20 Del from £43 * **SERVICES:** Lift Night porter 35P **NOTES:** No smoking in restaurant Last d 8.30pm **CARDS:**

SCARBOROUGH North Yorkshire **Map 08 TA08**

★★ Manor Heath Hotel

67 Northstead Manor Dr YO12 6AF

Quality Percentage Score: 61%

☎ 01723 365720 📠 01723 365720

***Dir:** follow signs for North Bay and Peasholme Park*

Brian Smith offers a warm welcome to his pleasant traditional private hotel, situated on the North Bay beside Peasholm Park. Public areas include bar, lounge, and dining room. Bedrooms are modern and bright, offering all expected comforts.

ROOMS: 11 en suite (bth/shr) (6 fmly) s £20-£23; d £40-£46 (incl. bkfst) * LB Off peak **FACILITIES:** CTV in all bedrooms **SERVICES:** 16P **NOTES:** No smoking in restaurant Closed Dec-1 Jan **CARDS:**

SCARBOROUGH North Yorkshire **Map 08 TA08**

★★✤ Brooklands

Esplanade Gardens, South Cliff YO11 2AW

Quality Percentage Score: 60%

☎ 01723 376576 📠 01723 376576

***Dir:** from A64 York turn left at B&Q rdbt, right at next mini rdbt then 1st left onto Victoria Av, at the end turn left then 2nd left*

The Brooklands is a traditional family owned and run seaside hotel offering good value for money. It stands on the South Cliff overlooking a small park and is close to the sea. There are ample lounges and adequate dinners are served.

ROOMS: 63 rms (57 bth 5 shr) (11 fmly) s £40-£42; d £80-£84 (incl. bkfst & dinner) * Off peak **MEALS:** Lunch £5-£8 High tea £2-£3 Dinner £7-£10 V meals Coffee am Tea pm **FACILITIES:** CTV in all bedrooms Riding Pool table Wkly live entertainment Xmas **CONF:** Thtr 120 Class 80 Board 30 Del from £30 * **SERVICES:** Lift 1P **NOTES:** No dogs (ex guide dogs) No smoking in restaurant Last d 7.30pm Closed Jan-Feb **CARDS:**

✤ Indicates that the star classification has not been confirmed under the New Quality Standards, see page 7 for further information.

SCILLY, ISLES OF — Map 02

BRYHER — Map 02

★★★ Hell Bay Hotel

TR23 0PR

Quality Percentage Score: 68%

☎ 01720 422947 🖷 01720 423004

Dir: *only accessiible by helicopter from Penzance, ship from Penzance or plane from Bristol, Exeter, Plymouth or Land's End*

This friendly hotel is located on the smallest of the inhabited Scilly islands and offers a warm welcome to all visitors, including families with children. The comfortable bedrooms all have sitting rooms and garden access and many have marvellous sea views. The public rooms include a choice of comfortable lounges, where guests may enjoy the sea views. The popular bar serves snacks, whilst the restaurant offers a menu featuring many fresh local dishes.

ROOMS: 14 en suite (bth/shr) (3 fmly) d £138-£172 (incl. bkfst & dinner) * LB Off peak **MEALS:** Bar Lunch £7-£12alc Dinner £22 V meals Coffee am Tea pm **FACILITIES:** CTV in all bedrooms Croquet lawn Putting green Boules ch fac **NOTES:** No dogs (ex guide dogs) No coaches No smoking in restaurant Last d 8.45pm Closed Nov-30 Mar

CARDS:

ST MARTIN'S — Map 02

The Premier Collection

★★★ St Martin's on the Isle

Pride of Britain Member

Lower Town TR25 0QW

☎ 01720 422092 🖷 01720 422298

Dir: *20 minute helicopter flight to St Marys, then 20 minute launch to St Martins*

This island hideaway is ideal for those looking for peace and tranquility. The hotel has its own beach, jetty, and yacht, and enjoys an unrivalled panorama of sea and surrounding islands. Individually decorated and furnished bedrooms have been named after local legends, places, and events; most have sea views. Public rooms are cleverly designed with stone floors, split levels, and refreshingly bold decor. Snacks and refreshments can be enjoyed on the lawn or in the lounge. In the restaurant, guests can choose from the daily menu or the a la carte.

ROOMS: 30 en suite (bth/shr) (10 fmly) s £95-£125; d £190-£250 (incl. bkfst & dinner) * LB Off peak **MEALS:** Bar Lunch £3.50-£10 High tea fr £7 Dinner fr £25 French Cuisine Tea pm **FACILITIES:** CTV in all bedrooms STV Indoor swimming pool (heated) Tennis (hard) Fishing Snooker Sailing on own yacht Clay pigeon shooting **CONF:** Thtr 50 Class 50 Board 50 **NOTES:** No coaches No smoking in restaurant Last d 10pm Closed Nov-Feb

CARDS:

ST MARY'S — Map 02

★★★ Star Castle

The Garrison TR21 0JA

Quality Percentage Score: 71%

☎ 01720 422317 & 423342 🖷 01720 422343

Dir: *overlooking the Harbour.*

Built in 1593 as a fortress, this historic landmark now houses a comfortable hotel complete with modern facilities and panoramic views over St. Mary's and the surrounding islands. Bedrooms vary in style and size, and most have sea views. The garden apartments are the most spacious whilst the castle rooms include four-poster beds and oak beamed ceilings. The cuisine is a strong feature of the hotel, and guests can choose between a bar meal on the ramparts, a seafood extravaganza in the garden conservatory or a traditional dinner from the carte menu in the castle restaurant.

ROOMS: 10 en suite (bth/shr) 23 annexe en suite (bth/shr) (17 fmly) s £82; d £72-£105 (incl. bkfst & dinner) * LB Off peak **MEALS:** Bar Lunch £3-£7.50 Dinner £26 V meals Coffee am Tea pm

FACILITIES: CTV in all bedrooms Indoor swimming pool (heated) Pool table Games room **SERVICES:** 6P **NOTES:** No coaches No smoking in restaurant Last d 8.30pm Closed end Oct-Feb **CARDS:**

ST MARY'S — Map 02

★★ Tregarthens

Hugh Town TR21 0PP

Quality Percentage Score: 75%

☎ 01720 422540 🖷 01720 422089

Dir: *100yds from the quay*

This well-established, privately owned hotel was first opened in 1848 by Captain Tregarthen, a steam packet owner. The present chairman being the grandson of Mr W H Lane, the original chairman in 1911. Tregarthens Hotel overlooks St Mary's harbour and some of the many islands, including Tresco and Bryher. The professional staff offer a warm and natural welcome to guests either staying for the first time, or to their many repeat visitors. The majority of bedrooms benefit from marvellous views out to sea; all are well equipped and neatly furnished. Traditional cuisine, with some wonderful home made desserts, is served in the restaurant, many tables here also enjoying the unique views.

ROOMS: 32 en suite (bth/shr) 1 annexe en suite (bth/shr) (5 fmly) s £59-£67; d £102-£152 (incl. bkfst) * LB Off peak **MEALS:** Bar Lunch £2.10-£12.50 High tea £5.50 Dinner £22.50 English & French Cuisine V meals Coffee am Tea pm **FACILITIES:** CTV in all bedrooms

NOTES: No dogs No smoking in restaurant Last d 8.30pm Closed late Oct-mid Mar **CARDS:**

TRESCO — Map 02

★★★ *The Island*

TR24 0PU

Quality Percentage Score: 80%

☎ 01720 422883 🖷 01720 423008

Dir: *helicopter service Penzance to Tresco, hotel on north east side of island*

The magnificent island setting and stunning gardens are only the first impressions of this splendid hotel. Guests are met at the heliport or pier and always receive a warm welcome. Sunny public rooms include a popular lounge and bar, together with a quiet library for residents. Bedroom accommodation has been designed to make the best of the sea views. Local fish and shellfish are staples on the enticing daily-changing menus.

ROOMS: 48 en suite (bth/shr) (27 fmly) **MEALS:** British Cuisine V meals Coffee am Tea pm **FACILITIES:** CTV in all bedrooms Outdoor swimming pool (heated) Tennis (hard) Fishing Pool table Croquet lawn Boating Table tennis Bowls **NOTES:** No dogs (ex guide dogs) No coaches Last d 9.30pm Closed Nov-Feb **CARDS:**

TRESCO — Map 02

★★ New Inn
TR24 0QQ
Quality Percentage Score: 73%
☎ 01720 422844 Fax 01720 423200
Dir: *by New Grimsby Quay*

The New Inn is a byword of hospitality between the residents of Tresco and the many visitors who come to this delightful island. The original part of the inn, made mostly with driftwood, is where the main bar and lounge form a social focal point. The bedrooms are decorated with vibrant colours and offer many modern facilities, and the AA rosette-winning cuisine does not disappoint.

ROOMS: 14 en suite (bth/shr) s £74-£97; d £114-£178 (incl. bkfst & dinner) * LB Off peak **MEALS:** Bar Lunch £11.50-£18.50alc Dinner £21.50 English French & Italian Cuisine V meals Coffee am **FACILITIES:** CTV in all bedrooms Outdoor swimming pool (heated) Tennis (hard) Pool table Sea fishing Xmas **NOTES:** No dogs No coaches No smoking in restaurant **CARDS:**

SCOTCH CORNER (NEAR RICHMOND) North Yorkshire — Map 08 NZ20

★★★ Quality Hotel, Scotch Corner
DL10 6NR
Quality Percentage Score: 65%
☎ 01748 850900 Fax 01748 825417
Dir: *at A1/A66 junct turn off towards Penrith*

Attractive decor characterises the spacious lounges, conference facilities and a smart leisure club while bedrooms fall into two well equipped and comfortable categories: Standard and Premier Plus. Food is served all day in the lounges and the restaurant, where there is a choice of evening menus.

ROOMS: 90 en suite (bth/shr) (5 fmly) No smoking in 45 bedrooms s £70-£81.50; d £81.50-£93.75 * LB Off peak **MEALS:** Lunch £2.95-£15.95alc Dinner fr £14.50 & alc English & Continental Cuisine V meals Coffee am Tea pm **FACILITIES:** CTV in all bedrooms STV Indoor swimming pool (heated) Sauna Solarium Gym Jacuzzi/spa Beauty therapist Hairdressers Golf simulator Xmas **CONF:** Thtr 280 Class 110 Board 40 **SERVICES:** Lift Night porter 200P **NOTES:** No smoking area in restaurant Last d 9.45pm **CARDS:**

SCOTCH CORNER (NEAR RICHMOND) North Yorkshire — Map 08 NZ20

Travelodge
Skeeby DL10 5EQ
☎ 01748 823768 Fax 01748 823768
Dir: *0.5m S on A1*

This modern building offers accommodation in smart, spacious and well equipped bedrooms, all with en-suite bathrooms. Refreshments may be taken at the nearby family restaurant. For details about current prices, consult the Contents Page under Hotel Groups for the Travelodge phone number.

ROOMS: 40 en suite (bth/shr) d £39.95 *

SCOTCH CORNER (NEAR RICHMOND) North Yorkshire — Map 08 NZ20

Travelodge
Middleton Tyas Ln DL10 6PQ
☎ 01325 377177 Fax 01325 377890
Dir: *A1/A66*

This modern building offers accommodation in smart, spacious and well equipped bedrooms, all with en-suite bathrooms. Refreshments may be taken at the nearby family restaurant. For details about current prices, consult the Contents Page under Hotel Groups for the Travelodge phone number.

ROOMS: 50 en suite (bth) d £49.95 *

SCUNTHORPE Lincolnshire — Map 08 SE81

see also **Althorpe**

★★★ Briggate Lodge Inn
Ermine St, Broughton DN20 0AQ
Quality Percentage Score: 74%
☎ 01652 650770 Fax 01652 650495
Dir: *200yds from junct 4 on the M180, on the Brigg-Scunthorpe rdbt*

This modern hotel boasts a championship golf course, and a new leisure complex. The buttery, open all day, offers a range of snacks and meals in addition to the more formal restaurant. The bars often feature live entertainment, and executive bedrooms offer extra space and comfort.

ROOMS: 86 en suite (bth/shr) (40 fmly) No smoking in 50 bedrooms s £79-£86; d £88-£94 (incl. bkfst) LB Off peak **MEALS:** Lunch £11.50-£17.25 & alc High tea fr £4.95 Dinner £19.50-£22 & alc International Cuisine V meals Coffee am Tea pm **FACILITIES:** CTV in all bedrooms STV Indoor swimming pool (heated) Golf 27 Sauna Gym Putting green Jacuzzi/spa Golf practice nets Driving range Mountain bikes Jogging track Wkly live entertainment ch fac Xmas **CONF:** Thtr 250 Class 120 Board 60 Del from £116 * **SERVICES:** Lift Night porter 300P **NOTES:** No dogs (ex guide dogs) No smoking in restaurant Last d 10pm **CARDS:**

Remember to return your Prize Draw card for a chance to win one of 30 relaxing leisure breaks with Corus and Regal hotels. See inside the front cover for the card and competition details.

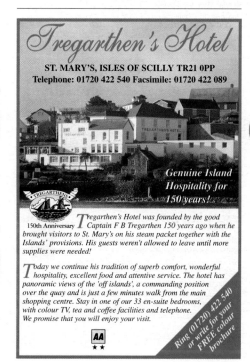

SCUNTHORPE Lincolnshire — Map 08 SE81
★★★ Royal
Doncaster Rd DN15 7DE
Quality Percentage Score: 67%
☎ 0500 636943 (Central Res) 🖹 01773 880321
Dir: *from M181, follow A18 to Scunthorpe centre, hotel is on left at a crossroads*

Standing on the A18 approach to the town, this hotel provides modern, freshly decorated bedrooms and attentive service. There is an extensive range of conference and banqueting facilities.
ROOMS: 33 en suite (bth/shr) (1 fmly) No smoking in 10 bedrooms s £69.50-£79.50; d £79.50-£95 * LB Off peak **MEALS:** Lunch £6.95-£8.95 Dinner fr £14.95 European Cuisine V meals Coffee am Tea pm **FACILITIES:** CTV in all bedrooms Gym Xmas **CONF:** Thtr 240 Class 200 Board 100 Del from £85 * **SERVICES:** Night porter 33P **NOTES:** No smoking in restaurant Last d 9.30pm
CARDS:

SCUNTHORPE Lincolnshire — Map 08 SE81
★★★ Wortley House
Rowland Rd DN16 1SU
Quality Percentage Score: 66%
☎ 01724 842223 🖹 01724 280646
Dir: *leave M181 at J3 and take A18. At 1st rdbt turn R, at 2nd take 3rd exit, take 2nd L over rdbt, hotel 200m on R*
Catering mainly for the commercial trade, this friendly hotel is near the railway station on the southern edge of town. It has cheerfully decorated public rooms, informal bar meals are very popular, alternatively the bistro-style dining room offers daily and carte menu choices. Bedrooms are pleasantly furnished and well equipped.
ROOMS: 38 en suite (bth/shr) (3 fmly) No smoking in 18 bedrooms s £70.50-£80; d £77-£90 (incl. bkfst) * LB Off peak **MEALS:** Lunch £8.50-£10 Dinner £8.50-£15.50 & alc English & French Cuisine V meals Coffee am Tea pm **FACILITIES:** CTV in all bedrooms STV Xmas **CONF:** Thtr 300 Class 120 Board 80 Del from £80 * **SERVICES:** Night porter 100P **NOTES:** No smoking area in restaurant Last d 9.30pm
CARDS:

SCUNTHORPE Lincolnshire — Map 08 SE81
Travel Inn
Lakeside Retail Park, Lakeside Parkway DN16 3NA
☎ 01724 870030 🖹 01724 851809
Dir: *A18 towards Scunthorpe, at Morrisons rdbt turn left, hotel behind Morrisons filling station*
This modern building offers accommodation in smart, spacious and well equipped bedrooms, all with en-suite bathrooms. Refreshments may be taken at the nearby family restaurant. For details about current prices consult the Contents Page under Hotel Groups for the Travel Inn phone number.
ROOMS: 40 en suite (bth/shr) d £39.95 *

SEAHOUSES Northumberland — Map 12 NU23
★★ Olde Ship
NE68 7RD
Quality Percentage Score: 73%
☎ 01665 720200 🖹 01665 721383
Dir: *lower end of main street above harbour*
Just a stone's throw from the harbour, this friendly family-run hotel has tremendous character with its cosy public areas and corridors adorned with nautical and period memorabilia. Residents have their own lounge and there is cabin bar well as the popular saloon bar. Apart from two rooms with four-posters, bedrooms are compact, but they are well equipped and have been stylishly upgraded to a high standard.
ROOMS: 12 en suite (bth/shr) 7 annexe en suite (bth/shr) s £32-£38.50; d £64-£77 (incl. bkfst) * LB Off peak **MEALS:** Lunch £8.75 Dinner £13.50-£15.50 V meals Coffee am Tea pm **FACILITIES:** CTV in all bedrooms STV Putting green **SERVICES:** 19P **NOTES:** No dogs No coaches No children 10yrs No smoking in restaurant Last d 8.30pm Closed Dec-Jan **CARDS:**

SEAHOUSES Northumberland — Map 12 NU23
★★ Bamburgh Castle
NE68 7SQ
Quality Percentage Score: 68%
☎ 01665 720283 🖹 01665 720848
Dir: *from A1 follow signs for Seahouses*
This holiday hotel overlooks the harbour, with views of Bamburgh Castle, the Farne Islands and Lindisfarne. You can watch the fishing boats from the restaurant or relax in one of the lounges. Bedrooms vary in size, all are well equipped and have comfortable seating.
ROOMS: 20 en suite (bth/shr) (2 fmly) No smoking in 5 bedrooms s £37.95-£41.95; d £70.95-£81.90 (incl. bkfst) * LB Off peak **MEALS:** Sunday Lunch £3-£9 High tea £4.95-£6.95 Dinner fr £19.95 V meals Coffee am Tea pm **FACILITIES:** CTV in all bedrooms Putting green Small exercise room Outdoor table tennis **CONF:** Thtr 40 Class 20 Board 25 Del from £70 * **SERVICES:** 30P **NOTES:** No smoking area in restaurant Last d 8.30pm Closed 24-26 Dec & 2wks mid Jan

SEAHOUSES Northumberland — Map 12 NU23
★★ *Beach House*
Sea Front NE68 7SR
Quality Percentage Score: 68%
☎ 01665 720337 🖹 01665 720921
Dir: *Seahouses signposted from A1*
This tourist hotel lies well back from the road and enjoys fine views out to sea towards the Farne Islands. Hazel and Malcolm Brown offer informal service in a friendly, relaxed and at times humorous atmosphere. There is now a residents bar to complement the comfortable lounge. Both dinner and breakfast place emphasis on freshly cooked dishes using local produce. This is a non smoking establishment.
ROOMS: 14 en suite (bth/shr) (1 fmly) No smoking in all bedrooms **MEALS:** V meals Coffee am Tea pm **FACILITIES:** CTV in all bedrooms Jacuzzi/spa **SERVICES:** 16P **NOTES:** No dogs No coaches No smoking in restaurant Last d 6pm Closed Jan **CARDS:**

SEATON BURN Tyne & Wear — Map 12 NZ27
★★★★ *Holiday Inn*
Great North Rd NE13 6BF
Quality Percentage Score: 63%
☎ 0191 201 9988 🖹 0191 236 8091
Dir: *3m W of Tyne Tunnel towards Morpeth*
This purpose-built hotel with its smart foyer lounge is popular with business guests. Many bedrooms have been refurbished; executive rooms are more modern with useful extras. Public

contd.

areas have been smartly upgraded, the hotel offers a good range of conference and banqueting facilities.
ROOMS: 150 en suite (bth/shr) (77 fmly) No smoking in 74 bedrooms **MEALS:** International Cuisine V meals Coffee am Tea pm **FACILITIES:** CTV in all bedrooms Indoor swimming pool (heated) Sauna Solarium Gym Pool table Putting green Jacuzzi/spa Games room Wkly live entertainment **CONF:** Thtr 400 Class 200 Board 100 Del from £85 * **SERVICES:** Night porter Air conditioning 300P **NOTES:** No smoking area in restaurant Last d 10pm **CARDS:**

SEATON BURN Tyne & Wear — Map 12 NZ27

Travelodge (Newcastle North)

Front St NE13 6ED
☎ 0191 217 0107

Travelodge

This modern building offers accommodation in smart, spacious and well equipped bedrooms, all with en-suite bathrooms. Refreshments may be taken at the nearby family restaurant. For details about current prices, consult the Contents Page under Hotel Groups for the Travelodge phone number.
ROOMS: 40 en suite (bth/shr) d £45.95 *

SEAVIEW See Wight, Isle of

SEDGEFIELD Co Durham — Map 08 NZ32

★★★ Hardwick Hall

TS21 2EH
Quality Percentage Score: 64%
☎ 01740 620253 Fax 01740 622771
Dir: *off A1M junct 60 towards Sedgefield, left at 1st rdbt hotel 400m on left*
Set in extensive parkland with a country park nearby, this classic mansion makes an ideal venue for weddings and functions. Bedrooms are all individually decorated and thoughtfully equipped. Guests can dine in either the elegant gilded restaurant or in the comfortable bar.
ROOMS: 17 en suite (bth/shr) (2 fmly) s fr £68; d fr £78 (incl. bkfst) * LB Off peak **MEALS:** Lunch £11.25-£18 & alc Dinner fr £18 & alc English & French Cuisine V meals Coffee am Tea pm **FACILITIES:** CTV in all bedrooms STV **CONF:** Thtr 80 Class 30 Board 40 **SERVICES:** 200P **NOTES:** No dogs (ex guide dogs) Last d 9.45pm
CARDS:

SEDGEFIELD Co Durham — Map 08 NZ32

★★ *Crosshill*

1 The Square TS21 2AB
Quality Percentage Score: 64%
☎ 01740 620153 Fax 01740 621206
Dir: *access via A689, overlooking church*
A friendly atmosphere is found at this comfortable family-run hotel and pub beside the village square. Bedrooms are pleasantly decorated with homely furnishings and a good range of amenities. There is no lounge but an extensive selection of food is available in the comfortable bar and cosy restaurant.
ROOMS: 8 en suite (bth/shr) (2 fmly) **MEALS:** English & Continental Cuisine V meals Coffee am Tea pm **FACILITIES:** CTV in all bedrooms **CONF:** Thtr 20 Class 30 Board 40 **SERVICES:** Night porter 9P **NOTES:** No smoking area in restaurant Last d 9.45pm
CARDS:

SEDGEFIELD Co Durham — Map 08 NZ32

Travelodge

TS21 2JX
☎ 01740 623399 Fax 01740 623399

Travelodge

Dir: *on A689, 3m E of junct A1M*
This modern building offers accommodation in smart, spacious and well equipped bedrooms, all with en-suite bathrooms. Refreshments may be taken at the nearby family restaurant. For details about current prices, consult the Contents Page under Hotel Groups for the Travelodge phone number.
ROOMS: 40 en suite (bth/shr) d £45.95 *

SEDGEMOOR MOTORWAY SERVICE AREA (M5) Somerset — Map 03 ST35

Welcome Lodge

Welcome Break Service Area BS24 0JL
☎ 01934 750831 Fax 01934 750808

Welcome Break

Dir: *between junct 22 & 23 M5 northbound*
This modern building offers accommodation in smart, spacious and well equipped bedrooms, suitable for families and businessmen, and all with en-suite bathrooms. Refreshments may be taken at the nearby family restaurant. For details of current prices, consult the Contents Page under Hotel Groups for the Welcome Break phone number.
ROOMS: 40 en suite (bth/shr) d fr £45 *

SEDLESCOMBE East Sussex — Map 05 TQ71

★★★ Brickwall

The Green TN33 0QA
Quality Percentage Score: 67%
☎ 01424 870253 Fax 01424 870785
Dir: *off A21 on B2244 at top of Sedlescombe Green*
Dating in part from 1597, the original house here retains its Tudor character and a sympathetic extension houses modern bedrooms. The attractive wood-panelled and oak-beamed restaurant and lounge bar offer a fixed-price four-course menu of traditionally cooked food.
ROOMS: 26 en suite (bth/shr) (2 fmly) s £50-£55; d £76-£80 (incl. bkfst) * LB Off peak **MEALS:** Lunch £12.50-£16.50 High tea £5-£10 Dinner £18.50-£21.50 English, French & Italian Cuisine V meals Coffee am **FACILITIES:** CTV in all bedrooms STV Outdoor swimming pool (heated) Xmas **CONF:** Thtr 30 Class 40 Board 30 Del from £85 * **SERVICES:** 40P **NOTES:** No smoking in restaurant Last d 9pm
CARDS:

SELBY North Yorkshire — Map 08 SE63

★★ *Owl*

Main Rd YO8 9JH
Quality Percentage Score: 64%
☎ 01757 228374 Fax 01757 228125
(For full entry see Hambleton (4m W A63))

SELBY North Yorkshire — Map 08 SE63

★★ *Park View*

20 Main St, Riccall YO4 6PX
Quality Percentage Score: 63%
☎ 01757 248458 Fax 01757 249211
Dir: *turn left off A19 northbound 3m from Selby signed Riccall, hotel on right 300yds from junct*
Located just off the A19 in the village of Riccall, this family-owned hotel offers well equipped bedrooms, a bar and a pleasant dining room providing a good range of dishes. Service is personal and friendly.
ROOMS: 7 en suite (bth/shr) **MEALS:** V meals **FACILITIES:** CTV in all bedrooms **CONF:** Board 24 **SERVICES:** 26P **NOTES:** No smoking in restaurant Last d 10pm **CARDS:**

SENNEN Cornwall & Isles of Scilly — Map 02 SW32

★★ *Old Success Inn*

Sennen Cove TR19 7DG
Quality Percentage Score: 65%
☎ 01736 871232 Fax 01736 871457
Dir: *turn right off the A30 approx 1mile before Land's End, signposted Sennen Cove. The Hotel is situated on the left at the bottom of the hill*
Situated on a well known cove, popular with surfers and

contd.

S

walkers, this 17th-century inn offers a number of rooms with marvellous sea views. There is a comfortable lounge and a bar around which village and hotel life revolves and where bar meals are served. The restaurant offers traditional dishes and fish specialities.
ROOMS: 12 rms (1 fmly) **MEALS:** V meals Coffee am Tea pm **FACILITIES:** CTV in all bedrooms STV Wkly live entertainment **SERVICES:** 12P **NOTES:** No smoking in restaurant **CARDS:**

SETTLE North Yorkshire **Map 07 SD86**
★★★ Falcon Manor
Skipton Rd BD24 9BD
Quality Percentage Score: 67%
☎ 01729 823814 01729 822087
Dir: *turn off A65 on roundabout at southern end of Settle by-pass, continue for 0.50m*
This Grade II listed building, originally the home of a local clergyman, was built in 1841 and many of the original features remain, combined now with the modern conveniences expected by today's visitor. A number of the rooms have four poster beds and family rooms are also available, whilst all are freshly decorated and comfortably furnished. Freshly made dishes are offered in the restaurant, overlooking the colourful gardens, and the bar, popular with locals, has a welcoming character.
ROOMS: 15 en suite (bth/shr) 5 annexe en suite (bth/shr) (3 fmly) s £50-£62.50; d £70-£95 * LB Off peak **MEALS:** Lunch £11.95 Dinner £24.50-£45alc English & Continental Cuisine V meals Coffee am Tea pm **FACILITIES:** CTV in all bedrooms Croquet lawn Bowling green Xmas **CONF:** Thtr 45 Class 20 Board 20 Del from £75 * **SERVICES:** 85P **NOTES:** No smoking in restaurant Last d 9.30pm
CARDS:

SEVENOAKS Kent **Map 05 TQ55**
★★★ *Donnington Manor*
London Rd, Dunton Green TN13 2TD
Quality Percentage Score: 67%
☎ 01732 462681 01732 458116
Set in the Weald, near Sevenoaks, the hotel centres on a 15th-century manor with modern extensions. The attractive oak-beamed restaurant keeps its historic character, and the smart well equipped bedrooms are housed in the extension. The small leisure complex has squash courts.
ROOMS: 62 en suite (bth/shr) No smoking in 20 bedrooms **MEALS:** English & French Cuisine V meals Coffee am Tea pm **FACILITIES:** Indoor swimming pool (heated) Squash Sauna Gym Jacuzzi/spa **CONF:** Thtr 180 Class 60 Board 60 Del from £100 * **SERVICES:** Night porter 120P **NOTES:** No dogs (ex guide dogs) No smoking area in restaurant Last d 9pm

SEVENOAKS Kent **Map 05 TQ55**
★★★ *Royal Oak*
Upper High St TN13 1HY
Quality Percentage Score: 63%
☎ 01732 451109 01732 740187
Dir: *on A225, opp Sevenoaks School*
Situated in the centre of Sevenoaks this flint-fronted hotel dates from the 17th century. Bedrooms are divided between the main building and an adjacent one and all are well equipped. Public areas include a bar and brasserie.

ROOMS: 21 en suite (bth/shr) 16 annexe en suite (bth/shr) (2 fmly) **MEALS:** V meals Coffee am Tea pm **FACILITIES:** CTV in all bedrooms Tennis (hard) **CONF:** Thtr 35 Class 14 Board 20 **SERVICES:** Night porter 50P **NOTES:** Last d 10pm **CARDS:**
See advert on opposite page

SEVERN STOKE Worcestershire **Map 03 SO84**
★★★ *Old School House Hotel & Restaurant*
WR8 9JA
Quality Percentage Score: 66%
☎ 01905 371368 & 371464 01905 371591
Dir: *midway beween Worcester and Tewkesbury - just off the A38*
This timber-framed property was originally a farm, then, until the sixties, the village school. Bedrooms have their own character and are equipped to modern standards, some are on the ground floor. There is an attractively decorated restaurant.
ROOMS: 13 en suite (bth/shr) (1 fmly) No smoking in 3 bedrooms **MEALS:** V meals Coffee am **FACILITIES:** CTV in all bedrooms Outdoor swimming pool (heated) Fishing Boat for charter Clay pigeon shooting **CONF:** Thtr 100 Class 40 Board 40 Del from £79.50 * **SERVICES:** 80P **NOTES:** No smoking in restaurant Last d 9.30pm
CARDS:

SEVERN VIEW MOTORWAY SERVICE AREA (M4) Gloucestershire **Map 03 ST58**
Travelodge
M48 Motorway, Severn Bridge BS12 3BH
☎ 0800 850950 01454 632482
Dir: *junct 21 M48*
This modern building offers accommodation in smart, spacious and well equipped bedrooms, all with en-suite bathrooms. Refreshments may be taken at the nearby family restaurant. For details about current prices, consult the Contents Page under Hotel Groups for the Travelodge phone number.
ROOMS: 51 en suite (bth/shr) d £59.95 *

SHAFTESBURY Dorset **Map 03 ST82**
see also **Ludwell**
★★★ Royal Chase
Royal Chase Roundabout SP7 8DB
Quality Percentage Score: 72%
☎ 01747 853355 01747 851969
Dir: *take A303 to within 7m of town and then A350 signposted Blandford Forum. Avoid town centre and follow road to second roundabout*
A well known local landmark, this personally managed hotel is a popular place to stay for both leisure and business guests.
contd.

Indicates that the star classification has not been confirmed under the New Quality Standards, see page 7 for further information.

S

There are two categories of bedroom - standard and 'crown'. There are also good conference and leisure facilities.
ROOMS: 35 en suite (bth/shr) (13 fmly) No smoking in 10 bedrooms s £50-£85; d £85-£105 * LB Off peak **MEALS:** Lunch £12.50-£21 & alc Dinner £21 & alc English & Continental Cuisine V meals Coffee am Tea pm **FACILITIES:** CTV in all bedrooms STV Indoor swimming pool (heated) Turkish steam bath Xmas **CONF:** Thtr 140 Class 90 Board 50 Del from £85 * **SERVICES:** Night porter 100P **NOTES:** No smoking in restaurant Last d 9pm **CARDS:**

SHALDON See Teignmouth

SHANKLIN See Wight, Isle of

SHAP Cumbria — Map 12 NY51

★★★ Shap Wells

CA10 3QU
Quality Percentage Score: 65%
☎ 01931 716628 Fax 01931 716377
Dir: *from M6 junct 39, follow signs for Kendal, turn left at A6, after approx 1m turn left into hotel drive, hotel is situated about 1m down*

Minutes from the M6 in a secluded valley, this hotel was built in 1833 as a therapeutic spa, and the hotel has been popular with vistors ever since. There are a variety of sizes and styles in the bedrooms which are traditionally furnished. There is a choice of comfortable lounges. Extensive conference and banqueting facilities are available.
ROOMS: 90 en suite (bth/shr) 6 annexe en suite (bth/shr) (10 fmly) **MEALS:** Lunch £7.50-£8.50 & alc Dinner £15-£17 & alc English & French Cuisine V meals Coffee am **FACILITIES:** CTV in all bedrooms STV Tennis (hard) Snooker Pool table Games room **CONF:** Thtr 200 Class 100 Board 50 Del from £75 * **SERVICES:** Lift 200P
NOTES: Last d 8.30pm Closed 2 Jan-20 Feb RS 22 Dec-1 Jan
CARDS:

See advert under KENDAL

SHEDFIELD Hampshire — Map 04 SU51

★★★★ Marriott Meon Valley Hotel & Country Club

Sandy Ln SO32 2HQ
Quality Percentage Score: 69%
☎ 01329 833455 Fax 01329 834411
Dir: *from W, M27 junct7 take A334 then towards Wickham and Botley. Sandy Lane is on left 2m from Botley*
This very smartly appointed hotel and country club with golf course provides good, modern bedrooms, extensive leisure facilities and a choice of restaurants and bars.

ROOMS: 113 en suite (bth/shr) No smoking in 80 bedrooms s £82-£97; d £92-£105 (incl. bkfst) * LB Off peak **MEALS:** Lunch £13.50-£15 High tea fr £6 Dinner £22 & alc English & French Cuisine V meals Coffee am Tea pm **FACILITIES:** CTV in all bedrooms STV Indoor swimming pool (heated) Golf 27 Tennis (hard) Sauna Solarium Gym Putting green Jacuzzi/spa Cardio-Vascular suite Aerobics studio Health & Beauty salon ch fac Xmas **CONF:** Thtr 110 Class 60 Board 40 Del from £130 * **SERVICES:** Lift Night porter 320P **NOTES:** No dogs (ex guide dogs) No smoking in restaurant Last d 10pm
CARDS:

The AA's professional hotel and restaurant inspectors make regular and anonymous visits to all the hotels listed in the guide. They do not accept gifts or favours from hoteliers.

SHEFFIELD South Yorkshire **Map 08 SK38**

★★★★ Swallow

Kenwood Rd S7 1NQ

Quality Percentage Score: 65%

☎ 0114 258 3811 Fax 0114 2500138 /0114 2554744

Dir: *2m from Sheffield city centre*

Set in a quiet residential area, just a short drive from the city centre, this extended former private residence is surrounded by 11 acres of landscaped gardens. The majority of bedrooms have been refurbished and range from spacious rooms with private balconies overlooking the ornamental lake, to rooms with much character in the original section. A wide range of dishes is offered in the restaurant and lighter meals are also available.

ROOMS: 116 en suite (bth/shr) (33 fmly) No smoking in 65 bedrooms s fr £105; d fr £120 (incl. bkfst) * LB Off peak **MEALS:** English & French Cuisine V meals Coffee am Tea pm **FACILITIES:** CTV in all bedrooms STV Indoor swimming pool (heated) Fishing Sauna Solarium Gym Jacuzzi/spa Steam room Xmas **CONF:** Thtr 200 Class 100 Board 60 Del from £140 * **SERVICES:** Lift Night porter 200P **NOTES:** No smoking in restaurant Last d 9.45pm **CARDS:**

SHEFFIELD South Yorkshire **Map 08 SK38**

★★★ *Charnwood*

10 Sharrow Ln S11 8AA

Quality Percentage Score: 70%

☎ 0114 258 9411 Fax 0114 255 5107

Dir: *Sharrow Lane is near London Rd/Abbeydale Rd junction, on A621, 1.5 miles SW of city centre*

The Charnwood is within walking distance of the city centre, just off the London Road. It was once a Georgian mansion house owned by a Master Cutler. The bedrooms are well equipped; lounges and bars are ample and comfortable. Leo's Brasserie is an informal restaurant serving a freshly cooked interesting menu. The Hotel has seven individually decorated meeting rooms which are popular with local businesses.

ROOMS: 22 en suite (bth/shr) (1 fmly) No smoking in 10 bedrooms **MEALS:** V meals Coffee am Tea pm **FACILITIES:** CTV in all bedrooms **CONF:** Thtr 90 Class 40 Board 35 Del from £90 * **SERVICES:** Night porter 22P **NOTES:** No dogs (ex guide dogs) No coaches Last d 10.30pm Closed 24-31 Dec **CARDS:**

SHEFFIELD South Yorkshire **Map 08 SK38**

★★★ *Harley*

334 Glossop Rd S10 2HW

Quality Percentage Score: 70%

☎ 0114 275 2288 Fax 0114 272 2383

Dir: *situated west of the city centre on the inner ring road close to its junction with the A57*

Ideally situated in close proximity to both city centre and university campus, this town house-style hotel caters well to the business market. Modern appointed bedrooms offer quality accommodation and all feature en suite showers. Compact public rooms provide both comfort and quality with an elegant dining room producing a good choice of freshly cooked dishes.

ROOMS: 23 en suite (bth/shr) No smoking in 11 bedrooms **MEALS:** International Cuisine V meals Coffee am Tea pm **FACILITIES:** CTV in all bedrooms STV **CONF:** Thtr 20 Class 14 Board 16 **SERVICES:** Night porter **NOTES:** No dogs (ex guide dogs) No coaches No children 12yrs Last d 9.30pm Closed 25 Dec-1 Jan RS Sun **CARDS:**

SHEFFIELD South Yorkshire **Map 08 SK38**

★★★ Beauchief

161 Abbeydale Rd South S7 2QW

Quality Percentage Score: 69%

☎ 0114 262 0500 Fax 0114 235 0197

Dir: *on A621, at junct with B6068*

This comfortable and relaxing hotel is situated in well-tended grounds and gardens, with a stream running though the middle, three miles from the city centre. The bedrooms are very well appointed and include two with four-poster beds. The more formal Beauchief Restaurant and Michels Bar, in which lighter meals are served, are situated on one side of the stream and the bedrooms and reception on the other, linked by a covered corridor. Staff throughout are helpful and friendly.

ROOMS: 50 en suite (bth/shr) No smoking in 30 bedrooms s fr £75; d fr £85 * LB Off peak **MEALS:** Lunch fr £12.25 Dinner fr £19.95 English & Continental Cuisine V meals Coffee am Tea pm **FACILITIES:** CTV in all bedrooms STV Pool table Xmas **CONF:** Thtr 100 Class 50 Board 50 **SERVICES:** Night porter 200P **NOTES:** No dogs (ex guide dogs) No smoking area in restaurant Last d 9.45pm **CARDS:**

SHEFFIELD South Yorkshire **Map 08 SK38**

★★★ Whitley Hall

Elliott Ln, Grenoside S35 8NR

Quality Percentage Score: 68%

☎ 0114 245 4444 Fax 0114 245 5414

Dir: *A61 past football ground and 2m further, turn right just before Norfolk Arms, turn left at bottom of hill. Hotel is on left*

This 16th-century house, owned and managed by the same family for over 30 years, is set in 30 acres of landscaped grounds a short drive from the city centre. Individually furnished bedrooms are comfortable, and public areas include an impressive gallery, plenty of oak panelling and mullioned windows.

ROOMS: 19 en suite (bth/shr) (1 fmly) s £68-£78; d £86-£99 (incl. bkfst) * LB Off peak **MEALS:** Lunch £10-£14 & alc Dinner £21 & alc V meals Coffee am Tea pm **FACILITIES:** CTV in all bedrooms Croquet lawn Putting green Wkly live entertainment **CONF:** Thtr 70 Class 50 Board 40 Del from £120 * **SERVICES:** Night porter 100P **NOTES:** No coaches No smoking in restaurant Last d 9.30pm RS Sat - No lunch **CARDS:**

SHEFFIELD South Yorkshire — Map 08 SK38
★★★ *Mosborough Hall*
High St, Mosborough S20 5EA
Quality Percentage Score: 65%
☎ 0114 248 4353 Fax 0114 247 7042
Dir: *after leaving M1 at junct 30, travel 7m SE on A616*

This 16th-century manor house, a Grade II listed building, is set in its own gardens not far from the M1 and convenient for the centre of the city. Bedrooms vary from modern to characterful and some of them are very spacious. Apart from the galleried bar, there is a conservatory lounge, and freshly prepared dishes are served in the brightly furnished dining room.

ROOMS: 23 en suite (bth/shr) (1 fmly) **MEALS:** English & French Cuisine V meals Coffee am Tea pm **FACILITIES:** CTV in all bedrooms Pool table **CONF:** Thtr 50 Class 40 Board 40 **SERVICES:** Night porter 100P **NOTES:** Last d 9.30pm **CARDS:**

SHEFFIELD South Yorkshire — Map 08 SK38
★★★ Novotel
50 Arundel Gate S1 2PR
Quality Percentage Score: 65%
☎ 0114 278 1781 Fax 0114 278 7744
Dir: *between Registry Office and Crucible/Lyceum Theatres, follow signs to Town Hall/Theatres & Hallam University*

A modern hotel situated in the centre of the city close to the Lyceum and Crucible theatres. Bedrooms are well proportioned and suitable for families as well as being appropriately equipped for business guests. Public areas are spaciously designed and include an attractive restaurant, banqueting and meeting rooms and an indoor heated swimming pool.

ROOMS: 144 en suite (bth/shr) (40 fmly) No smoking in 108 bedrooms d £76 * Off peak **MEALS:** Lunch £2.95-£6.95 & alc Dinner £15 International Cuisine V meals Coffee am Tea pm **FACILITIES:** CTV in all bedrooms STV Indoor swimming pool (heated) Gym Pool table Gym is not owned by hotel, but is free for residents use **CONF:** Thtr 200 Class 30 Board 100 Del from £99 * **SERVICES:** Lift 30P **NOTES:** No smoking area in restaurant Last d midnight RS 24 Dec-2 Jan
CARDS:

SHEFFIELD South Yorkshire — Map 08 SK38
★★★ Staindrop Hotel & Restaurant
Ln End, Chapeltown S35 3UH
Quality Percentage Score: 65%
☎ 0114 284 6727 Fax 0114 284 6783
Dir: *M1 junct 35, take A629 for 1m straight over 1st rdbt, right at 2nd rdbt, hotel is situated about 0.5m on right*

Just a mile from the M1, this pleasant hotel has a friendly and relaxed atmosphere and has earned a good reputation for the quality of its cooking. The spacious bedrooms have been thoughtfully furnished and co-ordinated.

ROOMS: 13 en suite (bth/shr) (1 fmly) s fr £55; d fr £65 (incl. bkfst) * LB Off peak **MEALS:** Lunch fr £8 & alc High tea fr £8 Dinner fr £20 & alc V meals Coffee am Tea pm **FACILITIES:** CTV in all bedrooms Xmas **CONF:** Thtr 90 Class 60 Board 40 **SERVICES:** Night porter 70P **NOTES:** No dogs (ex guide dogs) No smoking in restaurant Last d 10pm **CARDS:**

SHEFFIELD South Yorkshire — Map 08 SK38
★★★ *Posthouse Sheffield*
Mancheater Rd, Broomhill S10 5DX
Quality Percentage Score: 63%
☎ 0114 267 0067 Fax 0114 268 2620
Dir: *M1 J23, follow signs to city centre, then A57 Glossop. Hotel on L after 2.5 miles*

A high rise hotel that dominates the skyline west of the city centre where the majority of the bedrooms have fine views. It is situated in a residential area that is within easy reach of central Sheffield. The hotel features a Spa Leisure Club, the Hallam Banqueting Suite and a range of meeting and conference rooms. The Junction Restaurant is open for lunch and dinner, and there is an all day lounge menu plus, for residents, 24-hour room service.

ROOMS: 136 en suite (bth/shr) No smoking in 70 bedrooms **MEALS:** International Cuisine V meals Coffee am Tea pm **FACILITIES:** CTV in all bedrooms Indoor swimming pool (heated) Sauna Solarium Gym Jacuzzi/spa Health & fitness centre **CONF:** Thtr 300 Class 130 Board 80 **SERVICES:** Lift Night porter 120P **NOTES:** No smoking area in restaurant Last d 10.30pm **CARDS:**

SHEFFIELD South Yorkshire — Map 08 SK38
★★★ The Regency
High St, Ecclesfield S35 9XB
Quality Percentage Score: 62%
☎ 0114 246 7703 Fax 0114 240 0081
Dir: *A629 to Chapeltown, turn left onto Nether Ln, straight across traffic lights, left into Church St, turn left opp church, left again, hotel on right*

A sympathetically extended mansion house in the centre of the village. The restaurant, serving a range of popular dishes, is a favourite amongst locals. Bedrooms offer good comfort levels and are well equipped. Conference and banqueting facilities are available.

ROOMS: 19 en suite (bth/shr) (1 fmly) s fr £66; d fr £80 (incl. bkfst) * LB Off peak **MEALS:** Lunch £4.95-£11.95 & alc High tea fr £1.20 Dinner £11.95 English & Continental Cuisine V meals Coffee am Tea pm **FACILITIES:** CTV in all bedrooms STV **CONF:** Thtr 250 Class 120 Board 40 Del from £85 * **SERVICES:** Night porter 80P **NOTES:** No dogs (ex guide dogs) No smoking area in restaurant Last d 9.45pm Closed 25-26 Dec, 1 Jan **CARDS:**

SHEFFIELD South Yorkshire — Map 08 SK38
★★★ Rutland
452 Glossop Rd, Broomhill S10 2PY
Quality Percentage Score: 62%
☎ 0500 636943 (Central Res) Fax 01773 880321
Dir: *on A57, located next to the Royal Hallamshire Hospital*

This friendly hotel, close to the university, has been created from a cluster of seven Victorian houses, all but one interconnected. Bedrooms vary in size and shape, but all are comfortable. There is a choice of lounges and a restaurant with a conservatory overlooking the garden.

ROOMS: 70 en suite (bth/shr) 13 annexe en suite (bth/shr) (5 fmly) No smoking in 10 bedrooms s £69.50-£79.50; d £79.50-£95 * LB Off peak **MEALS:** Lunch £9.95-£10.25 Dinner fr £14.95 International Cuisine V meals Coffee am Tea pm **FACILITIES:** CTV in all bedrooms STV Xmas **CONF:** Thtr 100 Class 40 Board 40 Del from £95 * **SERVICES:** Lift Night porter 80P **NOTES:** No smoking area in restaurant Last d 9.30pm **CARDS:**

S

SHEFFIELD South Yorkshire Map 08 SK38

Cutlers Hotel

George St S1 2PF

☎ 0114 273 9939 Fax 0114 276 8332

Dir: *city centre adjacent to Crucible Theatre*

Situated close to the Crucible Theatre in the city centre, this hotel offers budget accommodation in well equipped bedrooms. A new dining area featuring pasta and grills has opened, and free overnight parking is provided in the nearby public car park.

ROOMS: 50 en suite (bth/shr) (incl. bkfst) s £43.50-£48.50; d £54.50-£59.50 *

SHEFFIELD South Yorkshire Map 08 SK38

Travel Inn

Attercliffe Common Rd S9 2LU

☎ 0114 242 2802 Fax 0114 242 3703

Dir: *from M1 junct34, follow signs to Sheffield city centre. Travel Inn is opposite the Arena*

This modern building offers accommodation in smart, spacious and well equipped bedrooms, all with en-suite bathrooms. Refreshments may be taken at the nearby family restaurant. For details about current prices consult the Contents Page under Hotel Groups for the Travel Inn phone number.

ROOMS: 61 en suite (bth/shr) d £39.95 *

SHEFFIELD South Yorkshire Map 08 SK38

Travelodge

340 Prince of Wales Rd S2 1FF

☎ 0114 253 0935 Fax 0114 253 0935

Dir: *follow A630, take turn off for ring road & services*

This modern building offers accommodation in smart, spacious and well equipped bedrooms, all with en-suite bathrooms. Refreshments may be taken at the nearby family restaurant. For details about current prices, consult the Contents Page under Hotel Groups for the Travelodge phone number.

ROOMS: 60 en suite (bth/shr) d £49.95 * **CONF:** Thtr 30 Board 20

SHEFFIELD South Yorkshire Map 08 SK38

Sheffield Moat House

Chesterfield Rd South S8 8BW

☎ 0114 282 9988 Fax 0114 237 8140

Dir: *from Sheffield city centre follow signs A61, turn left at rdbt, to Meadowhwead. Hotel 200m on right*

Situated to the south of the city centre, this modern hotel offers facilities to suit both the business and leisure visitor. Recently refurbished bedrooms, including suites, are well appointed, and conference and banqueting facilities are impressive. A varied range of dishes is offered in the restaurant, snacks are also served in the lively Huntsman bar. The leisure club includes a swimming pool and well equipped gym.

ROOMS: 95 en suite (bth/shr) (9 fmly) No smoking in 40 bedrooms **MEALS:** English & French Cuisine V meals Coffee am Tea pm **FACILITIES:** CTV in all bedrooms Indoor swimming pool (heated) Sauna Solarium Gym Pool table Jacuzzi/spa Health & beauty treatment room **CONF:** Thtr 500 Class 300 Board 95 **SERVICES:** Lift Night porter 260P **NOTES:** No smoking in restaurant Last d 9.45pm **CARDS:**

SHEFFORD Bedfordshire Map 04 TL13

★★ *Beadlow Manor*

Beadlow SG17 5PH

Quality Percentage Score: 61%

☎ 01525 860800 Fax 01525 861345

Situated in its own grounds, yet providing good access to major routes and towns, this privately owned hotel offers above average facilities. Rooms vary in size and style, those on the ground floor are more spacious and retain their original character, first floor rooms are compact. There is a golf course and pro-shop, a leisure and beauty suite, an Italian restaurant and conference facilities.

ROOMS: 33 en suite (bth/shr) (7 fmly) **MEALS:** Italian Cuisine V meals Coffee am Tea pm **FACILITIES:** CTV in all bedrooms Golf 36 Sauna Solarium Gym Pool table Jacuzzi/spa Health & Leisure Club Beauty treatments **CONF:** Thtr 450 Class 70 Board 70 **SERVICES:** Night porter 850P **NOTES:** Last d 9.45pm **CARDS:**

SHEPPERTON Surrey

See LONDON SECTION plan 1 *A1*

★★★ *Shepperton Moat House*

Felix Ln TW17 8NP

Quality Percentage Score: 63%

☎ 01932 241404 Fax 01932 245231

The well equipped modern bedrooms help to make this a popular conference and meeting venue. Executive rooms each have a personal hi-fi system, and full room service is an extra benefit in addition to the carvery-style restaurant.

ROOMS: 156 en suite (bth/shr) (5 fmly) No smoking in 17 bedrooms **MEALS:** English & French Cuisine V meals Coffee am **FACILITIES:** CTV in all bedrooms Snooker Sauna Solarium Gym Putting green **CONF:** Thtr 500 Class 160 Board 50 **SERVICES:** Lift Night porter 225P **NOTES:** Last d 10pm Closed 27-30 Dec **CARDS:**

SHEPTON MALLET Somerset Map 03 ST64

The Premier Collection

★★★ Charlton House

Charlton Rd BA4 4PR

☎ 01749 342008 Fax 01749 346362

Dir: *on A371, 1m beyond Shepton town centre, travelling towards Frome*

Situated just outside the town in its own landscaped grounds, this delightful country house dates in part back to the 16th century. Professional service is enhanced by the friendliness of the young staff. In the restaurant, Adam Fellows produces some very distinctive cooking, with a focus on local ingredients.

ROOMS: 12 en suite (bth/shr) 5 annexe en suite (bth/shr) (1 fmly) s £90-£120; d £135-£300 (incl. cont bkfst) * LB Off peak **MEALS:** Lunch £16.50 & alc Dinner £35-£46alc V meals Coffee am Tea pm **FACILITIES:** CTV in all bedrooms STV Indoor swimming pool (heated) Tennis (hard) Fishing Sauna Croquet lawn Archery Clay pigeon shooting Hot air ballooning Xmas **CONF:** Thtr 50 Class 18 Board 20 Del £150 * **SERVICES:** Night porter 41P **NOTES:** No dogs (ex guide dogs) No smoking in restaurant Last d 9.30pm **CARDS:**

SHEPTON MALLET Somerset — Map 03 ST64

★★ Shrubbery

Commercial Rd BA4 5BU

Quality Percentage Score: 71%

☎ 01749 346671 Fax 01749 346581

Dir: *turn off A37 at Shepton Mallet onto A371 Wells Rd, hotel 50mtrs past traffic lights in town centre).*

Under the ownership of Christopher West, this attractive town centre hotel has been transformed into an elegant and thoroughly charming place of relaxation and fine food. The many improvements have included complete refurbishment of the bedrooms, where rich fabrics and co-ordinating colour schemes have been used to good effect. The intimate restaurant overlooks a delightful garden and offers a varied choice of dishes in the modern style, often with Mediterranean influences.

ROOMS: 8 en suite (bth/shr) (1 fmly) s £49.50; d £69-£75 (incl. bkfst) * LB Off peak **MEALS:** Sunday Lunch £10.95-£15.95 & alc Dinner £15.95-£16.95 & alc English, French, Italian & Spanish Cuisine V meals Coffee am Tea pm **FACILITIES:** CTV in all bedrooms ch fac Xmas **CONF:** Thtr 36 Class 30 Board 24 Del from £61.50 * **SERVICES:** 20P **NOTES:** No coaches No smoking in restaurant Last d 9pm RS Sundays **CARDS:**

SHEPTON MALLET Somerset — Map 03 ST64

★★ Pecking Mill Inn & Hotel

Evercreech BA4 6PG

Quality Percentage Score: 64%

☎ 01749 830336 & 830006 Fax 01749 831316

Dir: *on A371 1m W of village*

This popular roadside inn is conveniently located near the Bath & West Show-ground, and retains many of its original features. The best possible use has been made of the available space in the well equipped bedrooms. A wide selection of bar and restaurant food is available; booking is essential for the value for money Sunday lunches.

ROOMS: 6 en suite (shr) s £35; d £50 (incl. bkfst) * LB Off peak **MEALS:** Lunch £7.95 & alc Dinner £10.90-£21.05alc V meals Coffee am **FACILITIES:** CTV in all bedrooms **SERVICES:** 26P **NOTES:** No children 8yrs No smoking in restaurant Last d 9.15pm **CARDS:**

SHERBORNE Dorset — Map 03 ST61

★★★ ❀ *Eastbury*

Long St DT9 3BY

Quality Percentage Score: 67%

☎ 01935 813131 Fax 01935 817296

Dir: *turn left off A30, westbound, into Sherborne high street, at the bottom turn left 800yds along on the right is the Eastbury hotel*

Located on a quiet road in the centre of the town, the hotel has its own walled garden, and a private dining room. Bedrooms are well equipped, with extras such as bathrobes and fresh flowers. The conservatory restaurant offers an interesting menu of quality dishes.

ROOMS: 15 en suite (bth/shr) (1 fmly) No smoking in 3 bedrooms **MEALS:** English & French Cuisine V meals Coffee am Tea pm **FACILITIES:** CTV in all bedrooms STV Croquet lawn **CONF:** Thtr 60 Class 40 Board 28 **SERVICES:** 50P **NOTES:** No dogs (ex guide dogs) No coaches Last d 9.30pm **CARDS:**

AA Rosettes are awarded for quality of food, see page 15 for an explanation of Rosette assessment.

▤ SHERBORNE Dorset ★★★ The Sherborne
Map 03 ST61

Horsecastles Ln DT9 6BB
Quality Percentage Score: 63%
☎ 01935 813191 🖻 01935 816493
Dir: close to A30 on W outskirts of Sherborne

Set in grounds, the hotel is within walking distance of the town centre. The public rooms have picturesque views. Bedrooms are well equipped but a little functional, all are recently refurbished. Staff are friendly with prompt services delivered by a willing team.

ROOMS: 59 en suite (bth/shr) (11 fmly) No smoking in 30 bedrooms s £69-£79; d £79-£89 * LB Off peak **MEALS:** Sunday Lunch £6.50-£12.50 Dinner £10-£22 & alc V meals Coffee am Tea pm **FACILITIES:** CTV in all bedrooms Croquet lawn Putting green Mini driving range Xmas **CONF:** Thtr 80 Class 30 Board 30 **SERVICES:** Night porter Air conditioning 100P **NOTES:** No smoking in restaurant Last d 9pm **CARDS:** ⬤ 🔲 💳 🖺 📇 ✈ 💲

▤ SHERBORNE Dorset ★★★ Antelope
Map 03 ST61

Greenhill DT9 4EP
Quality Percentage Score: 62%
☎ 01935 812077 🖻 01935 816473

THE CIRCLE
Selected Individual Hotels
GREAT BRITAIN

Dir: stay on the A30 into Sherborne, hotel is located at the top of town with parking at rear

Centrally located in Sherbourne, this 18th century coaching inn is an ideal base for those exploring Hardy country. Many bedrooms have retained their original beams and fireplaces. The bar is popular with residents and locals alike. A more formal setting is offered in the restaurant.

ROOMS: 19 en suite (bth/shr) (1 fmly) No smoking in 1 bedroom s £44-£60; d £49.95-£70 (incl. bkfst) * LB Off peak **MEALS:** Lunch £4.50-£10 & alc Dinner £5-£15 & alc English & Continental Cuisine V meals Coffee am Tea pm **FACILITIES:** CTV in all bedrooms Xmas **CONF:** Thtr 80 Class 60 Board 40 **SERVICES:** Night porter 22P **NOTES:** No smoking in restaurant Last d 9.30pm **CARDS:** ⬤ 🔲 💳 🖺

▤ SHERBORNE Dorset
Map 03 ST61

Late entry ◯✦ The Grange Hotel & Restaurant
Oborne DT9 4LA
☎ 01935 813463 🖻 01935 817464
Dir: turn of the A30. 1m out of Sherborne (heading East). At Oborne hotel is clearly marked by road sign

This hotel is a delightful and peaceful 200 year old country house. Bedrooms are spacious and many overlook the beautiful gardens. The owners' overseas travels are reflected in an eclectic menu with Pacific rim influences.

ROOMS: 10 en suite (bth/shr) (2 fmly) No smoking in 2 bedrooms s £52-£55; d £75-£85 (incl. bkfst) * LB Off peak **MEALS:** Sunday Lunch fr £14.90 Dinner £18.50-£27.50alc English, French & Italian Cuisine V meals **FACILITIES:** CTV in all bedrooms STV **SERVICES:** 30P **NOTES:** No dogs (ex guide dogs) No coaches No smoking area in restaurant Last d 9pm Closed 26 Dec-12 Jan RS Sun evening (no dinner) **CARDS:** ⬤ 🔲 💳 🖺 💲

▤ SHERINGHAM Norfolk ★★ Beaumaris
Map 09 TG14

South St NR26 8LL
Quality Percentage Score: 70%
☎ 01263 822370 🖻 01263 821421
Dir: turn off A148, turn left at rdbt, 1st right over railway bridge, 1st left by church, 1st left into South Street

This very pleasant hotel is well established and its many loyal guests regularly return to enjoy the friendly hospitality. In quiet residential surroundings with well kept gardens, it is just five minutes' walk from the seafront, town centre and the golf course.

Public rooms include two quiet lounges, an inviting bar, and a spacious dining room.

ROOMS: 21 en suite (bth/shr) (5 fmly) s £38-£45; d £76-£90 (incl. bkfst) * LB Off peak **MEALS:** Sunday Lunch £1.50-£15 High tea £6.50 Dinner £14.95 & alc V meals Coffee am Tea pm **FACILITIES:** CTV in all bedrooms **SERVICES:** 25P **NOTES:** No smoking in restaurant Last d 8.30pm Closed mid Dec-1 Mar
CARDS: ⬤ 🔲 💳 🖺 📇 ✈ 💲

▤ SHERINGHAM Norfolk ★★ Southlands
Map 09 TG14

South St NR26 8LL
Quality Percentage Score: 68%
☎ 01263 822679 🖻 01263 822679

This pleasant hotel is a home from home where guests are treated more like friends. A short walk from the town centre, it offers well maintained and attractively decorated accommodation and facilities. Day rooms include open plan lounges and several dining areas, an appetising menu of hearty home cooking is offered.

ROOMS: 17 en suite (bth) (3 fmly) s fr £32.50; d fr £65 (incl. bkfst) * Off peak **MEALS:** Coffee am Tea pm **FACILITIES:** CTV in all bedrooms **SERVICES:** 20P **NOTES:** Closed Oct-Etr **CARDS:** ⬤ 💳 ✈

▤ SHIFNAL Shropshire ★★★★ ❀❀ *Park House*
Map 07 SJ70

Park St TF11 9BA
Quality Percentage Score: 63%
☎ 01952 460128 🖻 01952 461658

MACDONALD 🏨 *hotels*

Dir: leave M54 at junct 4 follow A464 Wolverhampton Rd for approx 2m, under railway bridge and hotel is 100yds on left

Service is friendly at this sympathetically extended hotel. Originally two separate 17th-century houses, situated on the edge of this historic market town, within easy reach of junction 4 of the M54. Accommodation is spacious and well appointed, with extra personal touches provided. Elegant public areas include a good choice of meeting facilities, as well as a health club.

ROOMS: 38 en suite (bth/shr) 16 annexe en suite (bth/shr) (4 fmly) No smoking in 10 bedrooms **MEALS:** English & French Cuisine V meals Coffee am Tea pm **FACILITIES:** CTV in all bedrooms STV Indoor swimming pool (heated) Sauna Solarium Jacuzzi/spa **CONF:** Thtr 180 Class 100 Board 40 Del from £115 * **SERVICES:** Lift Night porter 200P **NOTES:** No smoking in restaurant Last d 9.30pm
CARDS: ⬤ 🔲 💳 🖺 📇 ✈ 💲

▤ SHIPHAM Somerset ★★★ ❀❀ ⚑ Daneswood House
Map 03 ST45

Cuck Hill BS25 1RD
Quality Percentage Score: 71%
☎ 01934 843145 & 843945 🖻 01934 843824
Dir: turn off A38 towards Cheddar, travel through village, hotel on left

Built in Edwardian times as a homeopathic health hydro, this
contd.

charming hotel offers breathtaking views across the Bristol Channel towards Wales. Bedrooms are continually being improved and are individually decorated and well equipped. There are also several cottage suites with private lounges. The popular restaurant offers a daily fixed-price menu featuring quality local ingredients.
ROOMS: 9 en suite (bth/shr) 3 annexe en suite (bth/shr) (3 fmly) s £75-£89.50; d £79.50-£125 (incl. bkfst) * LB Off peak **MEALS:** Lunch £12.95-£17.95 Dinner £23.95-£29.95 V meals Coffee am Tea pm **FACILITIES:** CTV in all bedrooms **CONF:** Thtr 40 Board 25 Del from £125 * **SERVICES:** Night porter 27P **NOTES:** No dogs (ex guide dogs) No coaches No smoking in restaurant Last d 9.30pm RS 24 Dec-6 Jan **CARDS:**

SHIPLEY West Yorkshire — Map 07 SE13

★★★★ Marriott Hollins Hall Hotel

Hollins Hill, Baildon BD17 7QW
Quality Percentage Score: 70%
☎ 01274 530053 🖷 01274 530187
Dir: *from A650 follow signs to Salt Mill. At lights in Shipley take A6038. Hotel is 3m on left*

Smartly appointed new bedrooms have recently been added to this attractive hotel overlooking the Esholt Valley. There are extensive leisure facilities and function suites and a formal restaurant, Heathcliff's.
ROOMS: 122 en suite (bth/shr) (6 fmly) No smoking in 75 bedrooms d £74-£85 * LB Off peak **MEALS:** Lunch £12-£20 & alc Dinner £12-£20 & alc English & French Cuisine V meals Coffee am Tea pm **FACILITIES:** CTV in all bedrooms STV Indoor swimming pool (heated) Golf 18 Sauna Solarium Gym Croquet lawn Putting green Jacuzzi/spa Creche, Health Spa **CONF:** Thtr 200 Class 90 Board 60 Del from £99 * **SERVICES:** Lift Night porter 260P **NOTES:** No dogs (ex guide dogs) No smoking area in restaurant Last d 10pm **CARDS:**

SHIPSTON ON STOUR Warwickshire — Map 04 SP24

★★ The Red Lion

Main St, Long Compton CV36 5JS
Quality Percentage Score: 60%
☎ 01608 684221 🖷 01608 684221
Dir: *on B3400 between Shipston on Stour/Chipping Norton*
This friendly inn is run by Jenny Parkin who takes care to ensure that her guests have an enjoyable visit. The public rooms are charming, the focal point being the taproom with its friendly atmosphere and selection of real ales. Bedrooms, decorated in pretty pastel colours, vary in size and layout, and each has a useful range of facilities.
ROOMS: 5 en suite (bth/shr) (1 fmly) s £30; d £50 (incl. bkfst) * LB Off peak **MEALS:** Lunch £9.55-£16.50alc Dinner £10-£20alc English & French Cuisine V meals Coffee am **FACILITIES:** CTV in all bedrooms Pool table ch fac **SERVICES:** 60P **NOTES:** No smoking in restaurant Last d 9pm **CARDS:**

SHIPTON-UNDER-WYCHWOOD Oxfordshire — Map 04 SP21

★★ Shaven Crown

OX7 6BA
Quality Percentage Score: 66%
☎ 01993 830330 🖷 01993 832136
Dir: *on A361, halfway between Burford and Chipping Norton opposite village green and church*
Dating back to the 14th century this charming hotel, formerly a hospice attached to Bruern Abbey, retains all its historic atmosphere. The dramatic reception lounge has an unusual collection of period weapons, and the Monk's Bar is a popular haunt for locals. The spacious bedrooms are furnished and decorated in keeping with the age of the building. Guests may dine in the restaurant or less formally from the extensive bar menu.
ROOMS: 9 rms (8 bth/shr) (3 fmly) s £55; d £85-£120 (incl. bkfst) * LB Off peak **MEALS:** Continental Cuisine V meals Coffee am Tea pm **FACILITIES:** CTV in all bedrooms Tennis (hard) Bowling green Xmas **CONF:** Board 25 **SERVICES:** 15P **NOTES:** No smoking in restaurant Last d 9pm **CARDS:**

SHREWSBURY Shropshire — Map 07 SJ41

see also **Nesscliffe**

★★★★ *Albrighton Hall*

Albrighton SY4 3AG
Quality Percentage Score: 63%
☎ 01939 291000 🖷 01939 291123
Dir: *2.5m N on A528*
Set in 14 acres of grounds, this 17th-century country house has elegant public rooms with beautiful oak panelling. Bedrooms in the main house are mostly spacious and have been refurbished; several have four-poster beds and the attic rooms are popular for their sloping beams.

ROOMS: 29 en suite (bth/shr) 41 annexe en suite (bth/shr) (2 fmly) No smoking in 30 bedrooms **MEALS:** International Cuisine V meals Coffee am Tea pm **FACILITIES:** CTV in all bedrooms STV Indoor swimming pool (heated) Squash Snooker Sauna Solarium Gym Pool table Croquet lawn Jacuzzi/spa Beauty treatment Wkly live entertainment **CONF:** Thtr 400 Class 120 Board 60 **SERVICES:** Night porter 120P **NOTES:** No smoking in restaurant Last d 9.45pm **CARDS:**

SHREWSBURY Shropshire — Map 07 SJ41

★★★ Albright Hussey

Ellesmere Rd SY4 3AF
Quality Percentage Score: 75%
☎ 01939 290571 & 290523 🖷 01939 291143
Dir: *2m N, on A528*
Converted from a farmhouse some twenty years ago, this timber-framed Tudor house offers a choice of accommodation, with spacious and lavishly furnished bedrooms in the older part of
contd.

the building and well equipped modern rooms in a new wing; many look out on to the four acres of mature landscaped gardens. Dinner is taken in the fine, beamed restaurant. A comfortable cocktail bar and lounge are separated from the new function suite, furnished to create a marquee effect.
ROOMS: 14 en suite (bth) (4 fmly) No smoking in 3 bedrooms s £73-£85; d £95-£135 (incl. bkfst) * LB Off peak **MEALS:** Lunch £6.50-£13.50 & alc Dinner £24.50 & alc English, French & Italian Cuisine V meals Tea pm **FACILITIES:** CTV in all bedrooms Croquet lawn Jacuzzi/spa Xmas **CONF:** Thtr 250 Class 180 Board 80 Del from £110 * **SERVICES:** Night porter 85P **NOTES:** No children 3yrs No smoking in restaurant Last d 10pm **CARDS:**

SHREWSBURY Shropshire **Map 07 SJ41**
★★★ The Lion
Wyle Cop SY1 1UY
REGAL
Quality Percentage Score: 66%
☎ 01743 353107 Fax 01743 352744
Dir: *from S: cross English Bridge, take right fork, hotel at top of hill on left. From N: to town centre, follow Castle St into Dogpole, hotel is ahead*

This 14th-century coaching inn where Dickens and other famous people once stayed, is situated in the centre of town. Public areas are elegant and comfortable, particularly the Tapestry Lounge in which log fires blaze during colder months. Bedrooms have every modern facility and are decorated and furnished to a good standard. The beamed Dickens Suite is particularly characteristic of the age of the building.
ROOMS: 59 en suite (bth/shr) (3 fmly) No smoking in 30 bedrooms s fr £65; d fr £85 * LB Off peak **MEALS:** Lunch £4.95-£11.95 High tea fr £5.50 Dinner £14.95-£17.95 & alc V meals Coffee am Tea pm **FACILITIES:** CTV in all bedrooms Xmas **CONF:** Thtr 200 Class 80 Board 60 Del from £87.50 * **SERVICES:** Lift Night porter 70P **NOTES:** No smoking in restaurant Last d 9.30pm
CARDS:

SHREWSBURY Shropshire **Map 07 SJ41**
★★★ Lord Hill
Abbey Foregate SY2 6AX
Quality Percentage Score: 66%
☎ 01743 232601 Fax 01743 369734
Dir: *from M54 take A5, at 1st rdbt left then right into London Rd. At next rdbt (Lord Hill Column) take 3rd exit for hotel on left*
A pleasant and attractively appointed hotel that has been extensively refurbished over the past few years. Most of the bedrooms are located in a purpose-built, separate building but those in the main building include one with a four-poster and a newly created suite. There is also a conservatory restaurant and large function suite.
ROOMS: 12 en suite (bth/shr) 24 annexe en suite (bth/shr) s fr £58.50; d fr £74.50 (incl. bkfst) * LB Off peak **MEALS:** Lunch £12.50-£15.75 Dinner fr £17.95 & alc Continental Cuisine V meals Coffee am Tea pm **FACILITIES:** CTV in all bedrooms Xmas **CONF:** Thtr 300 Class 120 Board 150 Del from £85.50 * **SERVICES:** Night porter 120P **NOTES:** Last d 10pm **CARDS:**

SHREWSBURY Shropshire **Map 07 SJ41**

★★★ Prince Rupert
Butcher Row SY1 1UQ
Quality Percentage Score: 68%
☎ 01743 499955 Fax 01743 357306
Dir: *follow signs to Town Centre, drive over English Bridge and Wyle Cop Hill. Turn right into Fish St and continue for 200 yds till hotel is in view*
This town centre hotel dates back, in parts, to medieval times and many bedrooms have exposed beams and attractive wood panelling. Many local people use the hotel as a meeting point for lunch or morning coffee, adding to the general 'buzz'. In addition to the main 'Cavalier' restaurant, diners can eat at the nearby Italian restaurant, or in 'Chambers' bar-bistro. At the time of our last inspection, four luxury suites were being created as well as a fitness and beauty centre. Improvements for the existing bedrooms and public areas were also being planned. The hotel car park is not the easiest place to find, and guests are recommended to take advantage of the hotel's car parking service.
ROOMS: 69 en suite (bth/shr) (4 fmly) s £75; d £85-£160 (incl. bkfst) * LB Off peak **MEALS:** Lunch £9.50-£11.50 & alc Dinner fr £18.50 & alc English, French & Italian Cuisine V meals Coffee am Tea pm **FACILITIES:** CTV in all bedrooms Snooker Sauna Gym Jacuzzi/spa Weight training room Beauty Salon Xmas **CONF:** Thtr 120 Class 80 Board 20 Del from £95 * **SERVICES:** Lift Night porter 70P **NOTES:** Last d 9.45pm **CARDS:**
See advert on opposite page

SHREWSBURY Shropshire **Map 07 SJ41**
★★ Radbrook Hall
Radbrook Rd SY3 9BQ
SCOTTISH NEWCASTLE hotels
Quality Percentage Score: 69%
☎ 01743 236676 Fax 01743 359194
Dir: *exit M54, join new A5 at Telford. Follow signs Welshpool/Owestry, turn right at 4th rdbt onto A488. Continue towards Shrewsbury, hotel on left*
Parts of this hotel date back to the 15th century, but most of it was built more recently. It is surrounded by spacious grounds. The well equipped accommodation is suitable for both leisure
contd.

and business guests. Public areas feature a pleasant lounge bar and an attractive and popular family restaurant.
ROOMS: 22 en suite (bth/shr) (10 fmly) d £49-£69 * LB Off peak
MEALS: Lunch £10.35-£20.05alc Dinner £10.35-£20.05alc International Cuisine V meals Coffee am Tea pm **FACILITIES:** CTV in all bedrooms Squash Sauna Solarium Gym Jacuzzi/spa 3x Sunbeds ch fac Xmas
CONF: Thtr 360 Class 160 Board 80 Del from £48.90 *
SERVICES: Night porter 200P **NOTES:** No dogs (ex guide dogs) No smoking in restaurant Last d 9.15pm
CARDS:

SHREWSBURY Shropshire **Map 07 SJ41**
★★ ***Lion & Pheasant***
49-50 Wyle Cop SY1 1XJ
Quality Percentage Score: 66%
☎ 01743 236288 ▤ 01743 244475
Dir: *town centre, by English Bridge, 2m from M54 motorway link*
Now a personally-run hotel, this 16th-century former coaching inn stands close to the town centre, near the English Bridge crossing of the River Severn. The accommodation is well equipped for both business and leisure guests. The public areas are full of character, with original features such as exposed

contd.

Remember to return your Prize Draw card for a chance to win one of 30 relaxing leisure breaks with Corus and Regal hotels. See inside the front cover for the card and competition details.

beams and wall timbers. The narrow entrance to the car park should be negotiated with care.

Lion & Pheasant, Shrewsbury

ROOMS: 19 rms (17 bth/shr) (1 fmly) **MEALS:** English & Continental Cuisine V meals Coffee am **FACILITIES:** CTV in all bedrooms **CONF:** Thtr 25 Class 20 Board 16 **SERVICES:** 20P **NOTES:** No smoking in restaurant Last d 9.30pm Closed 24-30 Dec
CARDS:

See advert on page 589

SHREWSBURY Shropshire — Map 07 SJ41

★★ *Shelton Hall*

Shelton SY3 8BH
Quality Percentage Score: 64%
☎ 01743 343982 Fax 01743 241515
***Dir:** M54-A5 heading towards Oswestry, right off A5 at Welshpool, left Shelton, right at rdbt, hotel 1m further on B4380*

A large country house, thought to date back to around 1650 and established as a hotel in 1977, is surrounded by extensive and mature gardens. The bedrooms vary in size and style but all are equipped to suit both business guests and tourists. Family bedded rooms are available.

ROOMS: 9 en suite (bth/shr) (2 fmly) **MEALS:** English & Continental Cuisine V meals Coffee am **FACILITIES:** CTV in 10 bedrooms **CONF:** Thtr 50 Class 24 Board 24 **SERVICES:** 50P **NOTES:** No dogs No coaches Last d 8.30pm **CARDS:**

See advert on opposite page

SHREWSBURY Shropshire — Map 07 SJ41

★★ Abbots Mead

9 St Julian's Friars SY1 1XL
Quality Percentage Score: 63%
☎ 01743 235281 Fax 01743 369133
***Dir:** first left after English Bridge coming into Shrewsbury from S*

This neatly maintained Georgian town house is tucked away in a quiet cul-de-sac near the English Bridge, close to both the river and town centre. Bedrooms are compact but neatly decorated and well equipped. The hotel also has a bright dining room, overlooking the garden, and a bar with walls adorned by horse racing pictures. The hotel is privately owned and personally run.

ROOMS: 14 en suite (shr) s £37-£39; d £54-£56 (incl. bkfst) * LB Off peak **MEALS:** Dinner £11-£15 & alc English & Continental Cuisine V meals Coffee am **FACILITIES:** CTV in all bedrooms **SERVICES:** 10P **NOTES:** No smoking in restaurant Last d 9pm
CARDS:

SHREWSBURY Shropshire — Map 07 SJ41

Travelodge

Bayston Hill Services SY3 0DA
☎ 01743 874256 Fax 01743 874256
***Dir:** A5/A49 junct*

This modern building offers accommodation in smart, spacious and well equipped bedrooms, all with en-suite bathrooms. Refreshments may be taken at the nearby family restaurant. For details about current prices, consult the Contents Page under Hotel Groups for the Travelodge phone number.

ROOMS: 40 en suite (bth/shr) d £45.95 *

SIDMOUTH Devon — Map 03 SY18

★★★★ Riviera

The Esplanade EX10 8AY
Quality Percentage Score: 72%
☎ 01395 515201 Fax 01395 577775
***Dir:** leave M5 junc 30 & follow A3052*

Situated in a prime location, overlooking the sea, the Riviera is a fine Regency building, offering a high standard of service and stylishly furnished bedrooms with modern facilities. There is a good restaurant menu, supported by very good room service.

ROOMS: 27 en suite (bth/shr) (6 fmly) s £84-£109; d £148-£198 (incl. bkfst & dinner) * LB Off peak **MEALS:** Lunch £16 & alc Dinner £26 & alc English & French Cuisine V meals Coffee am Tea pm **FACILITIES:** CTV in all bedrooms STV Wkly live entertainment Xmas **CONF:** Thtr 85 Class 60 Board 30 **SERVICES:** Lift Night porter 26P **NOTES:** No coaches Last d 9pm **CARDS:**

See advert on opposite page

SIDMOUTH Devon — Map 03 SY18

★★★★ Victoria

Esplanade EX10 8RY
Quality Percentage Score: 72%
☎ 01395 512651 Fax 01395 579154
***Dir:** on Sidmouth seafront*

Set within its own carefully tended gardens, this imposing building, completed just after the turn of the century, occupies a prime position on the esplanade. Regular evening entertainment is provided and leisure facilities include both indoor and outdoor swimming pools, as well as tennis courts and a snooker room. Bedrooms, many enjoying fine sea views, are comfortable and nicely furnished, with further improvements continually being made. Extensive public areas include the wood panelled foyer lounge and a sun lounge. Carefully prepared meals are served, in

contd.

a professional yet friendly way, in the recently refurbished restaurant.
ROOMS: 61 en suite (bth/shr) (18 fmly) s £68-£104; d £124-£226 (incl. bkfst) * LB Off peak **MEALS:** Lunch £15-£16 & alc Dinner £25-£27.50 & alc English & French Cuisine V meals Coffee am Tea pm
FACILITIES: CTV in all bedrooms STV Indoor swimming pool (heated) Outdoor swimming pool (heated) Tennis (hard) Snooker Sauna Solarium Pool table Putting green Jacuzzi/spa Wkly live entertainment ch fac Xmas **CONF:** Thtr 60 **SERVICES:** Lift Night porter 104P **NOTES:** No dogs (ex guide dogs) No coaches Last d 9pm
CARDS:

See advert on page 593

SIDMOUTH Devon **Map 03 SY18**
★★★★ Belmont
The Esplanade EX10 8RX
Brend Hotels
Quality Percentage Score: 68%
☎ 01395 512555 Fax 01395 579101
Dir: *on Sidmouth seafront*
Situated in a prime position on the sea front, a short level walk from the town centre, this Georgian hotel offers all the traditional comforts of a resort hotel. There is a choice of lounges, one being non smoking, allowing visitors to relax over afternoon tea. A pianist often plays in the high ceilinged restaurant, air conditioned for extra comfort during the warmer months, whilst service is both efficient and friendly. Bedrooms are currently being upgraded, but all are attractively furnished
contd.

New AA Guides for the Millennium are featured on page 24

S

and many enjoy fine views over the esplanade. Leisure facilities are available to residents at the adjacent Victoria Hotel.

Belmont, Sidmouth

ROOMS: 54 en suite (bth/shr) (10 fmly) s £57-£102; d £104-£204 (incl. bkfst & dinner) * LB Off peak **MEALS:** Lunch £14-£15 & alc Dinner £24-£25.50 & alc English & French Cuisine V meals Coffee am Tea pm **FACILITIES:** CTV in all bedrooms STV Putting green Wkly live entertainment ch fac Xmas **CONF:** Thtr 50 **SERVICES:** Lift Night porter 45P **NOTES:** No dogs (ex guide dogs) No coaches Last d 9pm
CARDS:

SIDMOUTH Devon **Map 03 SY18**
★★★ Westcliff
Manor Rd EX10 8RU
Quality Percentage Score: 79%
☎ 01395 513252 🖷 01395 578203
Dir: *turn off A3052 to Sidmouth and proceed to the seafront and esplanade, turn right, hotel is directly ahead*

This charming hotel is in walking distance of the Promenade and has been run by the same family for more than 30 years. Elegant lounges and the cocktail bar open onto a terrace leading to the pool and croquet lawn. Bedrooms are spacious, some with balconies, and the restaurant offers a good choice of dishes.
ROOMS: 40 en suite (bth/shr) (4 fmly) No smoking in 4 bedrooms s £68-£73; d £126-£174 (incl. bkfst & dinner) * LB Off peak **MEALS:** Sunday Lunch £12.50 Dinner £22 & alc English & Continental Cuisine V meals Coffee am Tea pm **FACILITIES:** CTV in all bedrooms STV Outdoor swimming pool (heated) Gym Pool table Croquet lawn Putting green Jacuzzi/spa Mini tennis Wkly live entertainment **SERVICES:** Lift 40P **NOTES:** No dogs No coaches No children 5yrs No smoking in restaurant Last d 8.45pm Closed Nov-Mar
CARDS:

See advert on opposite page

SIDMOUTH Devon **Map 03 SY18**
★★★ Fortfield
Station Rd EX10 8NU
Quality Percentage Score: 64%
see entry on page 595

SIDMOUTH Devon **Map 03 SY18**
★★★ Abbeydale
Manor Rd EX10 8RP
Quality Percentage Score: 71%
☎ 01395 512060 🖷 515566
Dir: *enter town on A3052 towards seafront, 200 yds before Esplanade turn right into Manor Road*
This friendly hotel, owned and run by the Shardlow family for nearly 40 years, is a short walk from the sea-front and shops, with a private path to the cricket ground. The lounge enjoys fine views of the sea. Bar lunches and a daily dinner menu are offered to residents.
ROOMS: 18 en suite (bth/shr) (2 fmly) s £44-£60; d £88-£120 (incl. bkfst & dinner) * LB Off peak **MEALS:** Bar Lunch fr £8alc Dinner fr £14.50 English & French Cuisine Coffee am Tea pm **FACILITIES:** CTV in all bedrooms **SERVICES:** Lift 24P **NOTES:** No dogs No coaches No children 4yrs No smoking in restaurant Last d 7.45pm Closed Nov-Feb RS 1st wk Aug **CARDS:**

SIDMOUTH Devon **Map 03 SY18**
★★★ Salcombe Hill House
Beatlands Rd EX10 8JQ
Quality Percentage Score: 69%
☎ 01395 514697 & 514398 🖷 01395 578310
Just a short walk from the seafront, this family run hotel stands in large gardens and has lovely views. It is south-facing, so the lounge and patio get the best of the sun; bedrooms are bright and spacious, and served by a lift.
ROOMS: 28 en suite (bth/shr) (7 fmly) s £57.75; d £115.50 (incl. bkfst & dinner) * Off peak **MEALS:** Sunday Lunch £9.95 Dinner £15.50 & alc V meals Coffee am Tea pm **FACILITIES:** CTV in all bedrooms Outdoor swimming pool (heated) Tennis (grass) Putting green Games room **SERVICES:** Lift Night porter 39P **NOTES:** No coaches No smoking in restaurant Last d 8.15pm Closed Nov-Feb
CARDS:

SIDMOUTH Devon **Map 03 SY18**
★★★ Royal Glen
Glen Rd EX10 8RW
Quality Percentage Score: 64%
☎ 01395 513221 & 513456 🖷 01395 514922
Dir: *take A303 to Honiton, turn onto A375 to Sidford, then onto the B175 to Sidmouth, follow seafront signs, turn right onto esplanade, turn right at end*
This historic 19th-century hotel has associations with the then Duke of Kent and Queen Victoria. The connection is emphasised in the names of the comfortable bedrooms which are furnished in period. Day rooms included a 'smoking room' with open fire, and a dining room serving well prepared food.
ROOMS: 32 en suite (bth/shr) (4 fmly) s £43; d £86 (incl. bkfst) * LB Off peak **MEALS:** Lunch £4.95-£9.50 Dinner fr £14 English & French Cuisine V meals Coffee am Tea pm **FACILITIES:** CTV in all bedrooms Indoor swimming pool (heated) **SERVICES:** 24P **NOTES:** No coaches No smoking in restaurant Last d 8.30pm RS 2-31 Jan
CARDS:

SIDMOUTH Devon **Map 03 SY18**
★★ Brownlands
Sid Rd EX10 9AG
Quality Percentage Score: 77%
☎ 01395 513053 🖷 01395 513053
Dir: *turn off A3052 at Sidford, at Fortescue/Sidford sign, hotel 1m on left*
This fine Victorian country hotel has superb views to the town and sea from its peaceful setting on the wooded slopes of Salcombe Hill. The smartly decorated bedrooms are well equipped, and guests have a choice of comfortable lounges, and

contd. on p. 594

S

a separate bar and dining room where a five-course dinner is served.
ROOMS: 14 en suite (bth/shr) s £61.90-£65; d £108-£130 (incl. bkfst & dinner) LB Off peak **MEALS:** Sunday Lunch £12.50 Dinner £19.95 International Cuisine V meals Coffee am Tea pm **FACILITIES:** CTV in all bedrooms Tennis (hard) Putting green Xmas **SERVICES:** 25P **NOTES:** No coaches No children 8yrs No smoking in restaurant Last d 8pm Closed Nov-mid Mar RS Dec

See advert on page 593

SIDMOUTH Devon **Map 03 SY18**
★★ Kingswood
Esplanade EX10 8AX
Quality Percentage Score: 75%
☎ 01395 516367 Fax 01395 513185
Dir: *in the centre of the Esplanade*
Owned by the same family for over 40 years, the hotel has many regular guests. Bedrooms are furnished to a high standard of quality, many with marvellous sea views. There are two lounges and a dining room serving good, traditional English cooking.
ROOMS: 26 rms (25 bth/shr) (7 fmly) No smoking in all bedrooms s £47-£53; d £94-£106 (incl. bkfst & dinner) * LB Off peak **MEALS:** Bar Lunch £2.75-£7.50alc Dinner £16.50 V meals Coffee am **FACILITIES:** CTV in all bedrooms **SERVICES:** Lift 17P **NOTES:** No smoking in restaurant Last d 7.30pm Closed Dec-25 Feb
CARDS:

SIDMOUTH Devon **Map 03 SY18**
★★ *Littlecourt*
Seafield Rd EX10 8HF
Quality Percentage Score: 73%
☎ 01395 515279 Fax 01395 578373
Dir: *turn off A3052 to Sidmouth at the Bown Inn about 1.5 miles. Take directions to Sea Front after mini rdbt first right off Station Rd to Seafield Rd*
Set in beautiful gardens, this listed Regency hotel stands in a quiet road near the town centre and sea front. Bedrooms are bright, attractively furnished and comfortable. Guests have a choice of pleasant sitting areas, including a conservatory. Traditional home-cooking is a strength.
ROOMS: 20 rms (19 bth/shr) (3 fmly) No smoking in all bedrooms **MEALS:** English & French Cuisine V meals Coffee am Tea pm **FACILITIES:** CTV in all bedrooms Outdoor swimming pool (heated) **CONF:** Thtr 45 Class 22 **SERVICES:** 17P **NOTES:** No smoking in restaurant Last d 7.30pm Closed 1 Jan-28 Feb
CARDS:

S

SIDMOUTH Devon **Map 03 SY18**
★★ Royal York & Faulkner
The Esplanade EX10 8AZ
Quality Percentage Score: 73%
☎ 01395 513043 & 0800 220714 (Freephone) Fax 01395 577472
Dir: *from M5 take A3052, travel 10m to Sidmouth, the hotel is on the esplanade in the centre*
A fine Regency building facing the sea, The Royal York & Faulkner is a family run operation. Bedrooms are modern in style and many have balconies and sea views. Light lunches are served in Tappers Bistro, next to the well equipped leisure centre, and dinner in the elegant restaurant.
ROOMS: 68 en suite (bth/shr) (8 fmly) s £34.50-£56.50; d £69-£113 (incl. bkfst & dinner) * LB Off peak **MEALS:** Bar Lunch £3.95-£9.50alc Dinner £13 English & French Cuisine V meals Coffee am Tea pm **FACILITIES:** CTV in all bedrooms Snooker Sauna Solarium Gym Jacuzzi/spa Indoor short mat bowls Free swimming at local indoor pool(200yds away) Wkly live entertainment Xmas **SERVICES:** Lift 18P **NOTES:** No smoking in restaurant Last d 8.30pm Closed Jan
CARDS:

SIDMOUTH Devon **Map 03 SY18**
★★ Mount Pleasant
Salcombe Rd EX10 8JA
Quality Percentage Score: 72%
☎ 01395 514694
Dir: *turn off A3052 at Sidford x-rds after one & quarter miles turn left into Salcombe Rd, hotel opposite Radway Cinema*
A sympathetically modernised Georgian hotel, a short walk from the town centre and sea front, offering comfortable accommodation and a relaxed atmosphere. The dining room features a short fixed-price menu of home-cooked dishes, special requests are willingly catered for.
ROOMS: 16 en suite (bth/shr) (2 fmly) No smoking in 12 bedrooms s £38-£46; d £76-£92 (incl. bkfst & dinner) * LB Off peak **MEALS:** Dinner £14-£16 Coffee am **FACILITIES:** CTV in all bedrooms Putting green **SERVICES:** 20P **NOTES:** No coaches No children 8yrs Last d 7.30pm Closed Dec-Feb

SIDMOUTH Devon **Map 03 SY18**
★★ Devoran
Esplanade EX10 8AU
Quality Percentage Score: 71%
☎ 01395 513151 & 0800 317171 Fax 01395 579929
Dir: *turn off B3052 at Bowd Inn follow Sidmouth sign for approx 2m turn left onto sea front, hotel is 50yds along at the centre of Esplanade*

Directly facing the seafront, The Devoran has spacious and comfortable bedrooms, some with their own balconies. Well maintained public rooms include a large dining room where guests can enjoy a five-course dinner cooked from fresh local produce, and then relax in the comfortable lounge. The hotel is a short stroll to the shops and centre of Sidmouth.
ROOMS: 23 en suite (bth/shr) (4 fmly) No smoking in all bedrooms s £29-£38; d £58-£76 (incl. bkfst) * LB Off peak **MEALS:** Dinner £12.25-£13.25 Coffee am **FACILITIES:** CTV in all bedrooms **SERVICES:** Lift 4P **NOTES:** No smoking in restaurant Last d 7.15pm Closed mid Nov-mid Mar RS Dec-Mar **CARDS:**

SIDMOUTH Devon **Map 03 SY18**
★★ Hunters Moon
Sid Rd EX10 9AA
Quality Percentage Score: 67%
☎ 01395 513380 Fax 01395 514270
Dir: *From A3052 to Sidford, pass Blue Ball Pub, then next turn on right at Fortescue, hotel 1 mile from turning*
This personally owned and run Georgian manor house is set in three acres of grounds, close to the town centre. Accommodation

contd.

is comfortable, facilities are modern, and the restaurant serves enjoyable meals.

ROOMS: 18 en suite (bth/shr) (6 fmly) s £47-£49; d £90-£100 (incl. bkfst & dinner) * Off peak **MEALS:** Bar Lunch £2.50-£3.10 Dinner fr £15.95 French Cuisine Coffee am Tea pm **FACILITIES:** CTV in all bedrooms Putting green Xmas **SERVICES:** 20P **NOTES:** No smoking in restaurant Last d 7.30pm Closed 2nd Nov-Feb ex open Xmas
CARDS:

See advert on this page

SIDMOUTH Devon **Map 03 SY18**
★★ ***Westbourne***
Manor Rd EX10 8RR
Quality Percentage Score: 65%
☎ 01395 513774 01395 512231
Dir: *200yds from Connaught Gardens*

Quietly situated, this family owned and run hotel is convenient for the town centre and the seafront. Set in well tended gardens, this hotel offers an elegant drawing room and a spacious dining room, where a daily menu is available. Bedrooms vary in size and style, and most have views over the town and surrounding countryside.

ROOMS: 12 rms (8 bth/shr) (1 fmly) **MEALS:** V meals Coffee am Tea pm **FACILITIES:** CTV in all bedrooms Croquet lawn Garden with sun terrace **SERVICES:** 16P **NOTES:** No coaches No children 5yrs No smoking in restaurant Last d 7.15pm Closed Nov-Feb

SIDMOUTH Devon **Map 03 SY18**
★★★ **Fortfield**
Station Rd EX10 8NU
Quality Percentage Score: 64%
☎ 01395 512403 01395 512403

Just a short walk from the town centre, the hotel offers good standards of service, hospitality and cuisine. There are spacious lounges and a bar with a maritime theme. Some of the comfortable bedrooms have sea views.

ROOMS: 52 en suite (bth/shr) 3 annexe en suite (bth/shr) (7 fmly) s £37-£42; d £74-£84 (incl. cont bkfst) * LB Off peak **MEALS:** Sunday Lunch £6.50-£8.50 Dinner £18.75 & alc English & Scandinavian Cuisine V meals Coffee am Tea pm **FACILITIES:** CTV in all bedrooms Indoor swimming pool (heated) Sauna Solarium Health & beauty salon Wkly live entertainment Xmas **CONF:** Thtr 70 Class 40 Board 20 Del from £40 * **SERVICES:** Lift Night porter 60P **NOTES:** No smoking in restaurant Last d 8.30pm **CARDS:**

SIDMOUTH Devon **Map 03 SY18**
★★ ***Sidmount***
Station Rd EX10 8XJ
Quality Percentage Score: 62%
☎ 01395 513432
Dir: *on B3176, 0.50m from esplanade*

This fine Georgian house is set in gardens with fine views over the town to the sea. The comfortably furnished bedrooms vary in size and style, with some on the ground floor. The restaurant offers buffet service and looks out on the gardens.

ROOMS: 16 en suite (bth/shr) (1 fmly) No smoking in 14 bedrooms **MEALS:** Coffee am Tea pm **FACILITIES:** CTV in all bedrooms **SERVICES:** 17P **NOTES:** No dogs No coaches No children 9yrs No smoking in restaurant Last d 7pm Closed Nov-Feb

See advert on this page

SILCHESTER Hampshire **Map 04 SU66**

★★★ Romans

Little London Rd RG7 2PN
Quality Percentage Score: 75%
☎ 0118 970 0421 📠 0118 970 0691
***Dir:** A340 Basingstoke to Reading, hotel is signposted*

This privately owned Elizabethan house is set in its own grounds in the village of Silchester, between Basingstoke and Reading. Gardens, heated outdoor pool and fitness room are some of the attractions. The bedrooms, which have benefited from near complete refurbishment, are divided between the main house, where they are spacious and individually styled, and those in a separate wing, which are a little more compact. The public rooms include a comfortable lounge and a pleasant restaurant. Friendly and efficient staff are a strength here.
ROOMS: 11 en suite (bth/shr) 14 annexe en suite (bth/shr) (1 fmly) No smoking in 2 bedrooms s fr £85; d fr £105 (incl. bkfst) * Off peak **MEALS:** Lunch £12.50-£16.50 & alc Dinner fr £16.50 & alc English & French Cuisine V meals Coffee am Tea pm **FACILITIES:** CTV in all bedrooms STV Outdoor swimming pool (heated) Sauna Gym **CONF:** Thtr 60 Class 15 Board 24 Del from £130 * **SERVICES:** Night porter 60P **NOTES:** No smoking in restaurant Last d 9.30pm Closed 24 Dec-2 Jan **CARDS:**

See advert under BASINGSTOKE

SILLOTH Cumbria **Map 11 NY15**

★★★ *The Skinburness*

CA5 4QY
Quality Percentage Score: 61%
☎ 016973 32332 📠 016973 32549
***Dir:** M6 junct 41, take B5305 to Wigton, then B5302 to Silloth. M6 junct 44, take A595 to Carlisle then on to Wigton, then the B5302 to Silloth*

Standing on the peaceful Solway Estuary, close to sandy beaches and coastal walks, this hotel provides traditionally furnished bedrooms, with a host of modern facilities. There is also a leisure complex with pool and spa. Good meals are available in the Mediterranean styled bar, and the pleasing hotel restaurant.
ROOMS: 33 en suite (bth/shr) (2 fmly) **MEALS:** English & French Cuisine V meals Coffee am Tea pm **FACILITIES:** CTV in 32 bedrooms STV Indoor swimming pool (heated) Fishing Sauna Solarium Gym Pool table Croquet lawn Jacuzzi/spa **CONF:** Thtr 120 Class 100 Board 60 Del from £47.50 * **SERVICES:** 120P **NOTES:** Last d 9.30pm
CARDS:

SILLOTH Cumbria **Map 11 NY15**

★ *Golf Hotel*

Criffel St CA5 4AB
Quality Percentage Score: 62%
☎ 016973 31438 📠 016973 32582
***Dir:** off B5302, in Silloth at T-junct turn left hotel overlooks the corner of the green*

This Victorian-styled hotel lies in the centre of Silloth. Bedrooms are mainly well proportioned, all being bright and fresh. Guests can eat in the cosy restaurant with its wide range of dishes, or dine equally well in the spacious lounge bar. The games room is popular with holiday-makers and golfers in poor weather. Staff throughout are good-natured and keen to please.
ROOMS: 22 en suite (bth/shr) (4 fmly) **MEALS:** English & Continental Cuisine V meals Coffee am Tea pm **FACILITIES:** CTV in all bedrooms Snooker Pool table ch fac **CONF:** Thtr 100 Class 40 Board 40 Del £65 * **NOTES:** No smoking area in restaurant Last d 9pm Closed 25 Dec
CARDS:

SIMONSBATH Somerset **Map 03 SS73**

★★ Simonsbath House

TA24 7SH
Quality Percentage Score: 76%
☎ 01643 831259 📠 01643 831557
***Dir:** situated in the village of Simonsbath on the B3223*

This delightful 17th-century house is said to be the first to be built in the forest of Exmoor. Bedrooms are equipped with modern facilities and there is a choice of delightful lounges with original features like wood panelling and ornate fireplaces.
ROOMS: 7 en suite (bth/shr) s £56-£66; d £96 (incl. bkfst) * LB Off peak **MEALS:** Dinner £20 **FACILITIES:** CTV in all bedrooms **SERVICES:** 40P **NOTES:** No dogs No coaches No children 10yrs No smoking in restaurant Last d 8.30pm Closed Dec-Jan
CARDS:

SIX MILE BOTTOM Cambridgeshire **Map 05 TL55**

★★★ Swynford Paddocks

CB8 0UE
Quality Percentage Score: 66%
☎ 01638 570234 📠 01638 570283
***Dir:** M11 junct 9, take A11 towards Newmarket, turn onto the A1304 to Newmarket, hotel is on left 0.75m along*

A very popular venue for marquee weddings and other functions, this pleasant country house sits in rural grounds, between Newmarket and Cambridge. The relaxing accommodation comes in a variety of shapes and styles, ranging from comfortably appointed quarters to regal bedrooms, with several offering four poster beds. The hotel restaurant provides an excellent choice of modern dishes in elegant surroundings.
ROOMS: 15 en suite (bth/shr) s £90-£110; d £127-£188 (incl. bkfst) LB Off peak **MEALS:** Lunch £18.50 & alc High tea £3-£6.50 Dinner £26.50 & alc English & Continental Cuisine V meals Coffee am Tea pm **FACILITIES:** CTV in all bedrooms STV Tennis (hard) Croquet lawn Putting green Outdoor chess ch fac **CONF:** Thtr 200 Class 120 Board 60 Del £125 * **SERVICES:** Night porter 180P **NOTES:** No coaches No smoking in restaurant Last d 9.30pm
CARDS:

See advert under NEWMARKET

SKEGNESS Lincolnshire **Map 09 TF56**

★★★ Crown

Drummond Rd, Seacroft PE25 3AB
Quality Percentage Score: 62%
☎ 01754 610760 📠 01754 610847
***Dir:** take A52 to town centre, hotel 1m from clock tower*

An imposing spacious building close to the seafront and the dunes, this pleasant resort hotel is popular with holidaymakers and business travellers. Peter McGonagle and his team provide a friendly welcome, and a wide selection of enjoyable dishes is

contd.

For Useful Information and Important Telephone Number Changes turn to page 25

available either in the attractive modern bar or in the more formal restaurant.
ROOMS: 27 en suite (bth/shr) (7 fmly) s £45-£50; d £65-£70 (incl. bkfst) * LB Off peak **MEALS:** Lunch £10.75-£14.95 Dinner £14.95 English & French Cuisine V meals Coffee am **FACILITIES:** CTV in all bedrooms STV Indoor swimming pool (heated) Xmas **CONF:** Thtr 120 Class 130 Board 120 **SERVICES:** Lift Night porter 90P **NOTES:** No dogs (ex guide dogs) Last d 9pm **CARDS:**

See advert on this page

SKEGNESS Lincolnshire **Map 09 TF56**

★★★ Vine Hotel

Vine Rd, Seacroft PE25 3DB
Quality Percentage Score: 61%
☎ 01754 763018 & 610611 📠 01754 769845
Dir: *A52 to Skegness, head South towards Gibraltar Point, hotel is approxmately 1m from the clocktower*
Owned by the local brewery, it is reputedly the second oldest

contd.

building in Skegness. Recently refurbished to modern standards, it has spacious, comfortable bedrooms. There are two bars, the Tennyson Lounge, (the poet wrote some of his works in the garden), and the Oak Room with open fire and excellent beers. Freshly prepared dishes are served in the bar and restaurant.
ROOMS: 20 en suite (bth/shr) (6 fmly) s £50-£60; d £70-£80 (incl. bkfst) * LB Off peak **MEALS:** Lunch £9.50-£12.50 & alc Dinner fr £16.50 & alc V meals Coffee am Tea pm **FACILITIES:** CTV in all bedrooms Croquet lawn Bowling green Xmas **CONF:** Thtr 100 Class 80 Board 50 **SERVICES:** 50P **NOTES:** No coaches Last d 9pm
CARDS:

See advert on page 597

SKEGNESS Lincolnshire **Map 09 TF56**
★★ North Shore
North Shore Rd PE25 1DN
Quality Percentage Score: 63%
☎ 01754 763298 01754 761902
Dir: *1m N of town centre on the right hand side of the A52 heading towards Mablethorpe*
Part of a championship course complex, the hotel is popular with golfers and has a clubhouse ambience, as well as satisfying the needs of the business or leisure traveller. There are ample public rooms including a busy bar where simple informal fare is offered; alternatively more formal dining is available in the restaurant. The bedrooms vary in size and comfort but all are suitably equipped and furnished.
ROOMS: 30 en suite (bth/shr) 3 annexe en suite (bth/shr) (4 fmly) s fr £32; d fr £64 (incl. bkfst) * LB Off peak **MEALS:** Lunch £8.95 Dinner £14 English & Continental Cuisine V meals Coffee am Tea pm **FACILITIES:** CTV in all bedrooms Golf 18 Snooker Putting green Xmas **CONF:** Thtr 140 Class 80 Board 36 Del from £75 * **SERVICES:** Night porter 200P **NOTES:** No dogs (ex guide dogs) No coaches No smoking in restaurant Last d 9pm **CARDS:**

SKIPTON North Yorkshire **Map 07 SD95**
★★★ Hanover International
Keighley Rd BD23 2TA
Quality Percentage Score: 66%
☎ 01756 700100 01756 700107
Dir: *on A629, 1m from town*

This large, modern hotel is situated on the edge of the town, beside a canal and overlooking hills. The spacious bedrooms are well equipped and there is a restaurant and comfortable lounges on both the ground and first floors. There are comprehensive leisure and business facilities and a children's nursery is also available to residents.
ROOMS: 75 en suite (bth/shr) (10 fmly) No smoking in 14 bedrooms s fr £76; d fr £86 * LB Off peak **MEALS:** Bar Lunch £1.95-£6.95 Dinner £16.95-£18.95 European Cuisine V meals Coffee am Tea pm **FACILITIES:** CTV in all bedrooms STV Indoor swimming pool (heated) Squash Sauna Solarium Gym Pool table Jacuzzi/spa Whirlpool spa Steam room ch fac Xmas **CONF:** Thtr 400 Class 180 Board 120 Del from £90 * **SERVICES:** Lift Night porter 150P **NOTES:** No smoking in restaurant Last d 9.45pm **CARDS:**

SKIPTON North Yorkshire **Map 07 SD95**
★★ *Herriots*
Broughton Rd BD23 1RT
Quality Percentage Score: 68%
☎ 01756 792781 01756 792781
Dir: *off A59, opposite railway station*
Situated close to the centre of the town and on the doorstep of the Yorkshire Dales National Park, this hotel offers brightly decorated and generally spacious bedrooms. The brasserie is a relaxing area in which to dine from the varied menu, meals and snacks also being available in the bar. Entertainment is normally provided on Sunday evenings and service is willingly provided.
ROOMS: 13 en suite (bth/shr) (2 fmly) No smoking in 8 bedrooms **MEALS:** International Cuisine V meals Coffee am **FACILITIES:** CTV in all bedrooms Bar Billiards Wkly live entertainment **CONF:** Thtr 20 Class 15 Board 14 Del from £76 * **SERVICES:** 26P **NOTES:** No smoking in restaurant Last d 9.15pm **CARDS:**

SKIPTON North Yorkshire **Map 07 SD95**
Travelodge
Gargrave Rd BD23 1UD
☎ 01756 798091 01756 798091
Dir: *A65/A59 roundabout*
This modern building offers accommodation in smart, spacious and well equipped bedrooms, all with en-suite bathrooms. Refreshments may be taken at the nearby family restaurant. For details about current prices, consult the Contents Page under Hotel Groups for the Travelodge phone number.
ROOMS: 32 en suite (bth/shr) d £45.95 *

SKIPTON North Yorkshire **Map 07 SD95**
○ Coniston Hall Lodge
Coniston Cold BD23 4EB
☎ 01756 748080 01756 749487
Dir: *situated on the A65 5m NW of Skipton*
ROOMS: 40 en suite (bth/shr) (4 fmly) s £48-£59.50; d £48-£59.50 * LB Off peak **MEALS:** Lunch £3.50-£15alc High tea £4-£15alc Dinner £12.95-£16 & alc English & Continental Cuisine V meals Coffee am Tea pm **FACILITIES:** CTV in all bedrooms STV Fishing Xmas **CONF:** Thtr 100 Class 50 Board 20 Del from £90 * **SERVICES:** Night porter 120P **NOTES:** No smoking area in restaurant Last d 9.30pm
CARDS:

See advert on opposite page

SLEAFORD Lincolnshire **Map 08 TF04**
★★ Carre Arms
1 Mareham Ln NG34 7JP
Quality Percentage Score: 68%
☎ 01529 303156 01529 303139
Dir: *take A153 to Sleaford, hotel on right at level crossing*
Standing close to the railway station, this friendly hotel offers well equipped bedrooms. The hotel is family owned and run, and a good range of well produced food is offered in either the smartly restyled Brasserie or the more formal restaurant; a good range of bar food is also available. Whilst there is no lounge, the

contd.

The AA Hotel Booking Service is a free benefit to AA members. See the advertisement on page 47

bars are comfortable and the spacious conservatory is a riot of colour during the summertime.
ROOMS: 13 en suite (bth/shr) (1 fmly) s £50; d £70 (incl. bkfst) * Off peak **MEALS:** Lunch £11.50-£15 & alc Dinner fr £11.50alc English & Continental Cuisine V meals Coffee am **FACILITIES:** CTV in all bedrooms **CONF:** Thtr 50 Class 20 Board 30 **SERVICES:** 100P **NOTES:** No dogs (ex guide dogs) Last d 10pm **CARDS:**

SLEAFORD Lincolnshire — Map 08 TF04
Travelodge
Holdingham NG34 8NP
☎ 01529 414752 Fax 01529 414752
Dir: *1m N, at roundabout A17/A15*
This modern building offers accommodation in smart, spacious and well equipped bedrooms, all with en-suite bathrooms. Refreshments may be taken at the nearby family restaurant. For details about current prices, consult the Contents Page under Hotel Groups for the Travelodge phone number.
ROOMS: 40 en suite (bth/shr) d £45.95 *

SLOUGH Berkshire — Map 04 SU97
see also **Heathrow Airport**
★★★★ Copthorne Slough/Windsor
400 Cippenham Ln SL1 2YE
Quality Percentage Score: 68%
☎ 01753 516222 Fax 01753 516237
Dir: *leave M4 junct 6 towards Slough at next rdbt turn left & left again for hotel entrance*
This modern, purpose-built hotel is conveniently located between Slough and junction 6 of the M4. Bedrooms are well thought out, providing excellent facilities for business guests. Leisure facilities include a good sized pool and workout room. There is a choice of two restaurants, one more formal than the other.
ROOMS: 219 en suite (bth/shr) (19 fmly) No smoking in 111 bedrooms s fr £150; d fr £175 LB Off peak **MEALS:** Lunch fr £16.50 Dinner fr £19.50 International Cuisine V meals Coffee am Tea pm
FACILITIES: CTV in all bedrooms STV Indoor swimming pool (heated) Sauna Gym Jacuzzi/spa Steam room Beauty Salon Wkly live entertainment **CONF:** Thtr 250 Class 160 Board 60 Del £180 *
SERVICES: Lift Night porter Air conditioning 300P **NOTES:** No dogs (ex guide dogs) No smoking area in restaurant Last d 10pm
CARDS:

SLOUGH Berkshire — Map 04 SU97
★★★ *Courtyard by Marriott Slough/Windsor*
Church St SL1 2NH
Quality Percentage Score: 68%
☎ 01753 551551 Fax 01753 553333
Dir: *from junct 6 of M4 follow A355 to rdbt, turn right hotel approx 50 yds on right*
This tall, purpose-built hotel is conveniently located for junction 6 of the M4. The very comfortable bedrooms offer good facilities and are particularly well designed for the business traveller. Public areas are more restricted, but have a lively, modern and informal atmosphere.
ROOMS: 148 en suite (bth/shr) (73 fmly) No smoking in 72 bedrooms
MEALS: International Cuisine V meals Coffee am Tea pm
FACILITIES: CTV in all bedrooms STV Gym **CONF:** Thtr 45 Class 24 Board 24 **SERVICES:** Lift Night porter Air conditioning 162P
NOTES: No dogs (ex guide dogs) No smoking in restaurant Last d 10pm
CARDS:

SOLIHULL West Midlands
See advert for Nailcote Hall on this page

SOLIHULL West Midlands **Map 07 SP17**
see also **Dorridge**

★★★★ *Solihull Moat House*

61 Homer Rd B91 3QD
Quality Percentage Score: 68%
☎ 0121 623 9988 Fax 0121 711 2696

MOAT HOUSE

Dir: *leave M42 junc5 follow signs to town centre, turn left at St Alphege Church into Church Hill Rd continue to rdbt hotel on right*

This modern hotel is ideally positioned for guests visiting the NEC, Cadbury World, or the shopping centre just two minutes' walk away. Bedrooms are spacious and well equipped and there are a number of Executive rooms and suites available. Public areas include an attractive foyer lounge, modern meeting facilities and a leisure club. Dining options include an extensive room service menu, the informal bar, or the stylish Brookes restaurant.

ROOMS: 115 en suite (bth/shr) (6 fmly) No smoking in 42 bedrooms **MEALS:** International Cuisine V meals Coffee am Tea pm **FACILITIES:** CTV in all bedrooms Indoor swimming pool (heated) Sauna Solarium Gym Jacuzzi/spa Beauty salon **CONF:** Thtr 200 Class 116 Board 102 **SERVICES:** Lift Night porter 164P **NOTES:** No smoking area in restaurant Last d 10pm **CARDS:**

SOLIHULL West Midlands **Map 07 SP17**

★★★★ Swallow St John's

651 Warwick Rd B91 1AT
Quality Percentage Score: 64%
☎ 0121 711 3000 Fax 0121 705 6629

SWALLOW HOTELS

Dir: *leave M42 junct 5 & follow signs for Solihull centre. At rdbt 2nd left - Warwick Rd. At Barley Mow Pub on left, 2nd left at rdbt, hotel on right*

Conveniently situated for the M42, NEC and Birmingham airport, this attractive modern hotel, with its bright, spacious reception rooms and well equipped bedrooms, is popular with business guests. There are good leisure and conference facilities.

ROOMS: 178 en suite (bth/shr) (6 fmly) No smoking in 78 bedrooms s £55-£135; d £75-£140 (incl. bkfst) * LB Off peak **MEALS:** Lunch £14.50 & alc Dinner £22.50 & alc English & French Cuisine V meals Coffee am Tea pm **FACILITIES:** CTV in all bedrooms STV Indoor swimming pool (heated) Sauna Solarium Gym Jacuzzi/spa Beauty therapist Wkly live entertainment Xmas **CONF:** Thtr 700 Class 350 Board 60 Del from £145 * **SERVICES:** Lift Night porter 380P **NOTES:** No smoking area in restaurant Last d 11pm **CARDS:**

SOLIHULL West Midlands **Map 07 SP17**

★★★ Regency

Stratford Rd, Shirley B90 4EB
Quality Percentage Score: 66%
☎ 0121 745 6119 Fax 0121 733 3801

REGAL

Dir: *beside A34, 0.5m from junct 4 of M42*

Convenient for the motorways, NEC and city centre, this popular hotel provides bedrooms in a range of styles, some of which are very smart indeed. Public areas include a restaurant and choice of bars; Morrissey's Irish Bar provides a lively venue with music.

ROOMS: 112 en suite (bth/shr) (10 fmly) No smoking in 17 bedrooms s £75-£130; d £85-£140 * LB Off peak **MEALS:** Lunch £7.50-£18.95 High tea 95p-£5.25alc Dinner £18.95 & alc International Cuisine V meals Coffee am Tea pm **FACILITIES:** CTV in all bedrooms STV Indoor swimming pool (heated) Sauna Solarium Gym Jacuzzi/spa Beauty health salon Wkly live entertainment **CONF:** Thtr 180 Class 80 Board 60 Del from £75 * **SERVICES:** Lift Night porter 275P **NOTES:** No smoking area in restaurant Last d 10pm **CARDS:**

SOLIHULL West Midlands **Map 07 SP17**

★★ Flemings

141 Warwick Rd, Olton B92 7HW
Quality Percentage Score: 63%
☎ 0121 706 0371 Fax 0121 706 4494

Dir: *on A41, near Olton Station*

This privately owned hotel close to Olton railway station offers convenient access to the M42, the NEC and Birmingham International Airport. The accommodation is sensibly and unfussily equipped with business travellers particularly in mind. There are some ground-floor rooms, and some suitable for family use. Facilities include a small bistro adjacent to the bar, as an alternative to the main restaurant, and there is also a snooker room.

ROOMS: 77 en suite (bth/shr) (6 fmly) No smoking in 4 bedrooms s £32-£50; d £45-£56 (incl. bkfst) * LB Off peak **MEALS:** Lunch £4-£4.75 Dinner £5.75-£10 & alc International Cuisine V meals Coffee am Tea pm **FACILITIES:** CTV in all bedrooms Snooker **CONF:** Thtr 40 Class 40 Board 22 **SERVICES:** Night porter 80P **NOTES:** No smoking in restaurant Last d 9.30pm Closed 24-28 Dec **CARDS:**

SOLIHULL West Midlands **Map 07 SP17**

★★ Richmond House Hotel

47 Richmond Rd, Olton B92 7RP
Quality Percentage Score: 63%
☎ 0121 707 9746 Fax 0121 707 9746

Set in a residential suburb and convenient for the NEC, this family-run hotel offers a cosy residents bar and a restaurant offering a good choice of British and European dishes.

ROOMS: 17 en suite (bth/shr) No smoking in all bedrooms s £45-£63; d £55-£73 (incl. bkfst) * Off peak **MEALS:** Lunch fr £12.95 High tea fr £2 Dinner fr £15.95 English & Portuguese Cuisine V meals Coffee am Tea pm **FACILITIES:** CTV in all bedrooms Tennis (grass) Pool table **CONF:** Thtr 60 Class 60 Board 30 **SERVICES:** Night porter 40P **NOTES:** No smoking in restaurant **CARDS:**

S

SOLIHULL West Midlands — Map 07 SP17

Travel Inn

Stratford Rd, Shirley B90 4EP
☎ 0121 744 2942 Fax 0121 733 7075
Dir: *on A34 N of junct 4 of the M42*

This modern building offers accommodation in smart, spacious and well equipped bedrooms, all with en-suite bathrooms. Refreshments may be taken at the nearby family restaurant. For details about current prices consult the Contents Page under Hotel Groups for the Travel Inn phone number.

ROOMS: 51 en suite (bth/shr) d £39.95 *

SOLIHULL West Midlands — Map 07 SP17

Travel Inn

Stratford Rd, Hockley Heath B94 6NX
☎ 01564 782144 Fax 01564 783197
Dir: *on A3400 Birmingham to Stratford-upon-Avon road 2m S of junct 4 of the M42*

This modern building offers accommodation in smart, spacious and well equipped bedrooms, all with en-suite bathrooms. Refreshments may be taken at the nearby family restaurant. For details about current prices consult the Contents Page under Hotel Groups for the Travel Inn phone number.

ROOMS: 40 en suite (bth/shr) d £39.95 *

SONNING Berkshire — Map 04 SU77

★★★ French Horn

RG4 6TN
Quality Percentage Score: 76%
☎ 0118 969 2204 Fax 0118 944 2210
Dir: *turn left off A4 into Sonning follow road through village over bridge, hotel on right, car park on left*

This long established Thames-side restaurant with rooms has a lovely village setting and retains the traditions of classical hotel-keeping. The restaurant is a particular attraction where the signature dish is duck, spit-roasted in front of the fire in the bar, and carved at the table. (The bar appears in our bar of the millennium feature on page 33.) Bedrooms are spacious and comfortable, many offering stunning views over the river. There are also four cottage suites. A private board room and dining facilities are attractive to corporate guests.

ROOMS: 12 en suite (bth/shr) 8 annexe en suite (bth/shr) s £95-£135; d £100-£155 (incl. bkfst) * Off peak **MEALS:** Lunch £19.50-£35 & alc Dinner £32 & alc English & French Cuisine V meals **FACILITIES:** CTV in all bedrooms Fishing **CONF:** Board 20 Del from £200 * **SERVICES:** 40P **NOTES:** No dogs (ex guide dogs) No coaches Last d 9.30pm Closed 26 Dec-2 Jan & Good Fri **CARDS:**

See advert under READING

SOURTON Devon — Map 02 SX59

★★ Collaven Manor

EX20 4HH
Quality Percentage Score: 67%
☎ 01837 861522 Fax 01837 861614
Dir: *turn off A30 onto A386 to Tavistock hotel 2m on right*

This small 15th-century manor house stands in five acres of gardens on the edge of Dartmoor. The comfortable bedrooms are individually designed and overlook the grounds. Stone walls, old beams and an inglenook fireplace are features of the lounge and there is a separate bar and dining room.

ROOMS: 9 en suite (bth/shr) (1 fmly) s £58-£69; d £116-£138 (incl. bkfst & dinner) * LB Off peak **MEALS:** Sunday Lunch fr £10.50 Dinner fr £19.50 V meals Coffee am Tea pm **FACILITIES:** CTV in all bedrooms Croquet lawn Bowls Badminton **CONF:** Thtr 30 Class 20 Board 16 Del from £63.95 * **SERVICES:** 50P **NOTES:** No coaches No smoking in restaurant Last d 9pm **CARDS:**

See advert under OKEHAMPTON

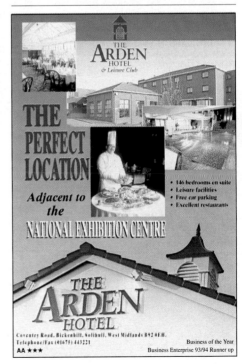

SOURTON CROSS Devon — Map 02 SX59

Travelodge

☎ 01837 52124 Fax 01837 52124

Dir: *4m W, at junct of A30/A386*

This modern building offers accommodation in smart, spacious and well equipped bedrooms, all with en-suite bathrooms. Refreshments may be taken at the nearby family restaurant. For details about current prices, consult the Contents Page under Hotel Groups for the Travelodge phone number.

ROOMS: 42 en suite (bth/shr) d £45.95 *

SOUTHAMPTON Hampshire — Map 04 SU41

see also **Shedfield**

★★★★★ De Vere Grand Harbour

West Quay Rd SO15 1AG

Quality Percentage Score: 63%

☎ 023 80633033 Fax 023 80633066

Dir: *leave M27 junc3 or M3 junc 13 follow Waterfront signs to West Quay Rd*

Ideally located close to the quays, this striking modern building offers a split-level leisure centre, with a modern gym and good sized swimming pool. Other public areas include a variety of lounge areas and two restaurants, offering a choice of dining styles. Bedrooms are comfortably furnished (executive rooms are particularly spacious) and all rooms offer a variety of extra facilities, such as mini bars, safes and faxes.

ROOMS: 172 en suite (bth/shr) No smoking in 139 bedrooms s fr £140; d fr £160 (incl. bkfst) * LB Off peak **MEALS:** Lunch £12.75-£18.50 & alc High tea fr £8.50alc Dinner £26-£28.50 & alc International Cuisine V meals Coffee am Tea pm **FACILITIES:** CTV in all bedrooms STV Indoor swimming pool (heated) Snooker Sauna Solarium Gym Jacuzzi/spa Steam room Beauty treatments Wkly live entertainment Xmas **CONF:** Thtr 500 Class 270 Board 48 Del from £145 * **SERVICES:** Lift Night porter Air conditioning 200P **NOTES:** No dogs (ex guide dogs) No smoking area in restaurant Last d 10pm

CARDS:

SOUTHAMPTON Hampshire — Map 04 SU41

★★★ Botleigh Grange

Hedge End SO30 2GA

Quality Percentage Score: 71%

☎ 01489 787700 Fax 01489 788535

Dir: *follow A334 to Botley & hotel is on the left just before Botley*

A much extended mansion set in grounds, a popular venue for weddings. Spacious bedrooms are comfortably furnished and well equipped. Public areas include a large bar, elegant lounge and attractive dining room, offering interesting, carefully prepared dishes. The hotel has a choice of function and conference rooms.

ROOMS: 59 en suite (bth/shr) (4 fmly) No smoking in 3 bedrooms s £72.50-£75; d £89-£99 (incl. bkfst) * LB Off peak **MEALS:** Lunch £10.95-£15.95 & alc Dinner £12.95-£17.95 & alc English & French Cuisine V meals Coffee am **FACILITIES:** CTV in all bedrooms STV Fishing Xmas **CONF:** Thtr 400 Class 175 Board 60 Del £125 **SERVICES:** Lift Night porter 200P **NOTES:** No dogs (ex guide dogs) No smoking in restaurant Last d 9.30pm **CARDS:**

See advert on opposite page

SOUTHAMPTON Hampshire — Map 04 SU41

★★★ The Woodlands Lodge

Bartley Rd, Woodlands SO40 7GN

Quality Percentage Score: 70%

☎ 023 80292257 Fax 023 80293090

Dir: *take A326 towards Fawley. 2nd rdbt turn right, after 0.25m turn left by White Horse PH. In 1.5m cross cattle grid, hotel is 70mtrs on left*

This beautifully restored 18th-century hunting lodge is set in four acres of attractive grounds on the edge of the New Forest. Bedrooms are furnished and decorated to a high standard, and there are a pleasant lounge and bar, both opening onto the gardens.

ROOMS: 16 en suite (bth/shr) (1 fmly) No smoking in 2 bedrooms s fr £63; d £118-£178 (incl. bkfst) * LB Off peak **MEALS:** Lunch fr £11.95 Dinner fr £25 V meals Coffee am Tea pm **FACILITIES:** CTV in all bedrooms Jacuzzi/spa Xmas **CONF:** Thtr 55 Class 16 Board 20 Del from £98 * **SERVICES:** 31P **NOTES:** No coaches No smoking in restaurant Last d 9pm **CARDS:**

SOUTHAMPTON Hampshire — Map 04 SU41

★★★ Southampton Park

Cumberland Place SO15 2WY

Quality Percentage Score: 66%

☎ 023 80343343 Fax 023 80332538

Dir: *hotel at northern end of the Inner Ring Rd opposite Watts Park & Civic Centre*

Located in the heart of the city opposite Watts Park, this modern hotel provides well equipped, smartly appointed bedrooms with comfortable furnishings. The public areas include a good leisure centre, spacious bar and lounge, and a choice of eating options. Parking is available in the multi-storey car park behind the hotel.

ROOMS: 72 en suite (bth/shr) (10 fmly) No smoking in 20 bedrooms s fr £73.75; d fr £95 (incl. bkfst) * LB Off peak **MEALS:** Bar Lunch fr £2.25 Dinner fr £16.95 English & French Cuisine V meals Coffee am Tea pm **FACILITIES:** CTV in all bedrooms STV Indoor swimming pool (heated) Sauna Solarium Gym Jacuzzi/spa Massage Jet Steam room **CONF:** Thtr 200 Class 60 Board 70 Del from £90 * **SERVICES:** Lift Night porter 8P **NOTES:** Last d 10pm Closed 25 & 26 Dec nights

CARDS:

SOUTHAMPTON Hampshire — Map 04 SU41

★★★ Novotel

1 West Quay Rd SO15 1RA

Quality Percentage Score: 64%

☎ 023 80330550 Fax 023 80222158

Dir: *turn right onto Southern Rd, Dock Gate 10, from the A3057. Turn left into West Quay Rd, all signposted West Quay Shopping*

This modern, purpose built hotel is conveniently located in the heart of the city centre yet close to both the railway station and motorway access. The spacious bedrooms are brightly appointed and ideal for both families and business guests. Public areas include the garden brasserie and bar which is open throughout

contd.

the day, a small leisure complex as well as extensive conference and banqueting facilities.
ROOMS: 121 en suite (bth/shr) (50 fmly) No smoking in 71 bedrooms d £72.50-£75 * LB Off peak **MEALS:** Lunch £11.45-£21.95alc Dinner fr £11.95 & alc International Cuisine V meals Coffee am Tea pm **FACILITIES:** CTV in all bedrooms STV Indoor swimming pool (heated) Sauna Gym **CONF:** Thtr 500 Class 300 Board 150 Del £110 * **SERVICES:** Lift Night porter Air conditioning 300P **NOTES:** No smoking area in restaurant Last d midnight **CARDS:**

SOUTHAMPTON Hampshire — Map 04 SU41

★★★ *Posthouse Southampton*

Posthouse

Herbert Walker Av SO15 1HJ
Quality Percentage Score: 64%
☎ 023 80330777 Fax 023 80332510
Dir: *from M27 follow signs for 'Western Docks 1-10'. Posthouse situated next to Dock Gate 8*

Conveniently located for both the port and the town centre, this modern Posthouse remains a popular choice with business guests, with a range of meeting rooms available. The well equipped bedrooms are comfortably furnished and modern in style. Public areas include an informal lounge bar and the Traders Restaurant which offers an extensive range of popular dishes.
ROOMS: 128 en suite (bth/shr) (14 fmly) No smoking in 75 bedrooms **MEALS:** International Cuisine V meals Coffee am Tea pm **FACILITIES:** CTV in all bedrooms Indoor swimming pool (heated) Sauna Solarium Gym Jacuzzi/spa Beauty therapy room **CONF:** Thtr 250 Class 80 Board 50 **SERVICES:** Lift Night porter 250P **NOTES:** No smoking area in restaurant Last d 10.30pm **CARDS:**

SOUTHAMPTON Hampshire — Map 04 SU41

★★★ Dolphin

REGAL

34-35 High St SO14 2HN
Quality Percentage Score: 59%
☎ 023 80339955 Fax 023 80333650
Dir: *A33 follow signs for Docks & Old Town/I.O.W ferry, at ferry terminal turn right into High Street, hotel 400yds up on the left hand side*

Originally an old coaching inn, The Dolphin enjoys a very central location set almost in the heart of the town centre, yet close to the ferry terminals. Bedrooms are gradually being refurbished as part of an on-going investment program. Spacious public areas include a traditional bar and lounge, upstairs dining room and a selection of function rooms.
ROOMS: 73 en suite (bth/shr) (3 fmly) s fr £65; d fr £80 * LB Off peak **MEALS:** Sunday Lunch fr £6.95 Dinner fr £16 & alc English & Continental Cuisine V meals Coffee am Tea pm **FACILITIES:** CTV in all bedrooms Xmas **CONF:** Thtr 90 Class 30 Board 45 Del from £80 * **SERVICES:** Lift Night porter 90P **NOTES:** No smoking in restaurant Last d 9.00pm **CARDS:**

SOUTHAMPTON Hampshire — Map 04 SU41

★★★ *County Hotel Southampton*

Highfield Ln, Portswood SO17 1AQ
Quality Percentage Score: 58%
☎ 023 80359955 Fax 023 80583910
Dir: *take A335 follow signs for Portswood & university*

Close to the university and within easy reach of the motorway, this hotel remains popular with conference and business guests. Now under new ownership a major refurbishment programme is currently under way to upgrade bedrooms and public areas.
ROOMS: 66 en suite (bth/shr) (6 fmly) No smoking in 20 bedrooms **MEALS:** International Cuisine V meals Coffee am Tea pm **FACILITIES:** CTV in all bedrooms Sauna Gym **CONF:** Thtr 200 Class 100 Board 60 **SERVICES:** Night porter 80P **NOTES:** No smoking area in restaurant Last d 10pm **CARDS:**

SOUTHAMPTON Hampshire **Map 04 SU41**
★★ *Busketts Lawn*
174 Woodlands Rd, Woodlands SO40 7GL
Quality Percentage Score: 68%
☎ 023 80292272 & 80292077 🖹 023 80292487
Dir: *A35 W of city through Ashurst, over railway bridge, sharp right into Woodlands Road*
In a tranquil location on the edge of the New Forest, yet close to Southampton, this charming hotel is personally run by the Hayes family. Bedrooms vary in size but are attractively furnished, with many thoughtful extras. There is a cosy lounge, a small separate bar and a dining room, where home cooked meals are served. The hotel is a popular venue for weddings and also has an outdoor swimming pool.
ROOMS: 14 en suite (bth/shr) (3 fmly) **MEALS:** English & Continental Cuisine V meals Coffee am Tea pm **FACILITIES:** CTV in all bedrooms Outdoor swimming pool (heated) Croquet lawn Putting green Football **CONF:** Thtr 150 Class 75 Board 40 Del £75 * **SERVICES:** 50P **NOTES:** No smoking in restaurant Last d 8.30pm
CARDS:

SOUTHAMPTON Hampshire **Map 04 SU41**
★★ Elizabeth House
43-44 The Avenue SO17 1XP
Quality Percentage Score: 64%
☎ 023 80224327 🖹 023 80224327
Dir: *on the A33, left hand side travelling towards city centre, after Southampton Common, before main traffic lights*
Bedrooms, gradually being refurbished under the ownership of Mr and Mrs Hockin, are comfortably appointed and thoughtfully equipped. Guests can take dinner in the dining room or the popular, informal Cellar Bar. The hotel is equipped with a smart meeting room.
ROOMS: 22 rms (20 bth/shr) (3 fmly) s fr £45; d fr £55 (incl. bkfst) * Off peak **MEALS:** Bar Lunch £2.75-£6.25alc Dinner £8-£15alc V meals Coffee am Tea pm **FACILITIES:** CTV in all bedrooms **CONF:** Thtr 40 Class 24 Board 24 Del from £72.50 * **SERVICES:** 23P **NOTES:** No coaches No smoking in restaurant Last d 9pm
CARDS:

SOUTHAMPTON Hampshire **Map 04 SU41**
★★ Hotel Ibis
West Quay Rd, Western Esplanade SO15 1RA
Quality Percentage Score: 63%
☎ 023 80634463 🖹 023 80223273
Dir: *leave M27 junct 3 joining M271. Turn left to Southampton City. At 2nd set of traffic lights turn right*
Located close to the western docks and the M27, this modern, budget hotel offers bright, well equipped bedrooms. The bar and restaurant provide a short choice of hot meals in the evening, an all-day snack menu and a self-service breakfast buffet.
ROOMS: 93 en suite (bth/shr) (8 fmly) No smoking in 27 bedrooms s £46; d £49.50 * Off peak **MEALS:** Lunch £1.95-£3.25alc Dinner £10.40-£19.15alc English & French Cuisine V meals Coffee am Tea pm **FACILITIES:** CTV in all bedrooms STV **CONF:** Thtr 70 Class 40 Board 28 **SERVICES:** Lift Night porter Air conditioning 280P **NOTES:** No smoking area in restaurant Last d 10.30pm **CARDS:**

SOUTHAMPTON Hampshire **Map 04 SU41**
★★ Rosida Garden
25-27 Hill Ln SO15 5AB
Quality Percentage Score: 63%
☎ 023 80228501 🖹 023 80635501
Dir: *M3, A33 exit, rdbt 2nd exit, next rdbt 2nd exit, 1st exit next rdbt, straight across mini rdbt, 1.5m ahead, hotel on left*
Situated close to the city centre, this hotel is conveniently located for both the docks and ferry ports. The bedrooms are comfortably furnished, and guests can enjoy hearty home-cooked food in the well presented dining room. There is also a TV lounge and a licensed bar.
ROOMS: 27 en suite (bth/shr) (6 fmly) s £46-£58; d £58-£64 (incl. bkfst) * LB Off peak **MEALS:** Dinner £10-£17.50alc Coffee am Tea pm **FACILITIES:** CTV in all bedrooms Outdoor swimming pool (heated) **CONF:** Thtr 35 Class 20 Board 20 **SERVICES:** Night porter 50P **NOTES:** Last d 8.25pm **CARDS:**

SOUTHAMPTON Hampshire **Map 04 SU41**
★★ *The Star Hotel & Restaurant*
26 High St SO14 2NA
Quality Percentage Score: 63%
☎ 023 80339939 🖹 023 80335291
Dir: *enter city from A33 follow signs for city centre at Isle of Wight ferry terminal turn into High St, hotel on right just beyond zebra crossing*
This friendly city centre hotel continues to improve. The bedrooms are bright and comfortably furnished. Public areas include a popular bar, smart reception area and dining room. There are several function rooms including a self-contained conference suite, secure parking is available.
ROOMS: 43 rms (37 bth/shr) (7 fmly) No smoking in 7 bedrooms **MEALS:** Coffee am Tea pm **FACILITIES:** CTV in all bedrooms **CONF:** Thtr 75 Class 25 Board 35 **SERVICES:** Lift Night porter 30P **NOTES:** No coaches Closed 24 Dec-1 Jan **CARDS:**

SOUTHAMPTON Hampshire **Map 04 SU41**
⌂ Travel Inn
Romsey Rd, Nursling SO16 0XJ
☎ 023 80732262 🖹 023 80740947
Dir: *from M27 junct 3 take M271 towards Romsey. At next rdbt take 3rd exit towards Southampton (A3057) Travel Inn 1.5m on right*
This modern building offers accommodation in smart, spacious and well equipped bedrooms, all with en-suite bathrooms. Refreshments may be taken at the nearby family restaurant. For details about current prices consult the Contents Page under Hotel Groups for the Travel Inn phone number.
ROOMS: 32 en suite (bth/shr) d £39.95 *

SOUTHAMPTON Hampshire **Map 04 SU41**
⌂ Travelodge
Lodge Rd SO17 1XS
☎ 023 80229023
This modern building offers accommodation in smart, spacious and well equipped bedrooms, all with en-suite bathrooms. Refreshments may be taken at the nearby family restaurant. For details about current prices, consult the Contents Page under Hotel Groups for the Travelodge phone number.
ROOMS: 48 en suite (bth/shr) d £49.95 *

SOUTH CAVE East Riding of Yorkshire **Map 08 SE93**
★★ Fox & Coney Inn
Market Place HU15 2AT
Quality Percentage Score: 63%
☎ 01430 422275 🖹 01430 421552
Dir: *from A63, main Market Weighton to York road, then A1034 into village, close to Midland Bank*
Standing in the centre of the village, this friendly inn provides modern, well equipped bedrooms which vary in size. An extensive range of food is available, either in the bar or the

contd.

stylish Italian restaurant. The staff are very friendly and the atmosphere is relaxed and informal.
ROOMS: 12 en suite (bth/shr) (2 fmly) s £32.50-£35.50; d £39-£42.50 * LB Off peak **MEALS:** Lunch £6.95-£8.95 & alc Italian and Continental Cuisine V meals Coffee am Tea pm **FACILITIES:** CTV in all bedrooms Xmas **SERVICES:** 28P **NOTES:** No coaches No smoking area in restaurant **CARDS:**

SOUTH CAVE East Riding of Yorkshire **Map 08 SE93**

Travelodge

Beacon Service Area HU15 1RZ
01430 424455 01430 424455
Dir: *A63 eastbound*
This modern building offers accommodation in smart, spacious and well equipped bedrooms, all with en-suite bathrooms. Refreshments may be taken at the nearby family restaurant. For details about current prices, consult the Contents Page under Hotel Groups for the Travelodge phone number.
ROOMS: 40 en suite (bth/shr) d £39.95 *

SOUTHEND-ON-SEA Essex **Map 05 TQ88**

★★★ Westcliff

Westcliff Pde, Westcliff-on-Sea SS0 7QW
Quality Percentage Score: 66%
01702 345247 01702 431814
Dir: *M25 J29, A127 towards Southend, follow signs for Cliffs Pavillion when approaching town centre*

This gleaming white Victorian building overlooks the esplanade and estuary from its cliff-top position. Large public areas include meeting rooms as well as a smart bar and airy restaurant. Well equipped bedrooms have been thoroughly refurbished to a high standard. Friendly staff take a pride in their work.
ROOMS: 55 en suite (bth/shr) (3 fmly) No smoking in 7 bedrooms s £70; d £85 (incl. bkfst) * LB Off peak **MEALS:** Lunch £9.95-£12.95 & alc Dinner £13.95-£15.95 & alc English & Continental Cuisine V meals Coffee am Tea pm **FACILITIES:** CTV in all bedrooms STV Wkly live entertainment Xmas **CONF:** Thtr 225 Class 90 Board 64 Del £80 * **SERVICES:** Lift Night porter **NOTES:** No dogs (ex guide dogs) No smoking in restaurant **CARDS:**

See advert on this page

SOUTHEND-ON-SEA Essex **Map 05 TQ88**

★★★ Roslin Hotel

Thorpe Esplanade SS1 3BG
Quality Percentage Score: 64%
01702 586375 01702 586663
This long established family run hotel on the sea front at Thorpe Bay offers comfortable traditional accommodation. Bedrooms are smart, attractive and well equipped. The restaurant serves a wide choice of classic favourites and the extensive public areas are inviting and cosy.

ROOMS: 39 rms (35 bth/shr) (4 fmly) s fr £43; d £60-£80 (incl. bkfst) * LB Off peak **MEALS:** Lunch £10-£15 & alc Dinner £14-£15 & alc International Cuisine V meals Coffee am Tea pm **FACILITIES:** CTV in all bedrooms STV Temporary membership of local sports centre **CONF:** Thtr 30 Class 30 Board 28 **SERVICES:** Night porter 34P **NOTES:** No smoking area in restaurant Last d 9.30pm
CARDS:

SOUTHEND-ON-SEA Essex **Map 05 TQ88**

★★★ County Hotel Southend

Aviation Way SS2 6UN
Quality Percentage Score: 62%
01702 279955 01702 541961
Dir: *turn off A127 at Tesco rdbt follow signs for Aviation Way, turn right at next rdbt straight over rdbt & then left at mini-rdbt, hotel on right*
This purpose-built hotel offers bedrooms which are divided

contd.

between the main house and several separate buildings. All are spacious and equipped with both single and double beds. Public areas are combined in a bar with an informal brasserie.
ROOMS: 18 en suite (bth/shr) 47 annexe en suite (bth/shr) (65 fmly) No smoking in 22 bedrooms s £67; d £77 * LB Off peak **MEALS:** Sunday Lunch £9.95 Dinner £9.50-£12.50 & alc International Cuisine V meals Coffee am Tea pm **FACILITIES:** CTV in all bedrooms Xmas **CONF:** Thtr 200 Class 120 Board 60 Del from £90 * **SERVICES:** Night porter 200P **NOTES:** No smoking in restaurant Last d 9.45pm
CARDS:

SOUTHEND-ON-SEA Essex **Map 05 TQ88**
★★★ **Erlsmere**
24/32 Pembury Rd, Westcliff-on-Sea SS0 8DS
Quality Percentage Score: 61%
☎ 01702 349025 01702 337724
Quietly located in a mainly residential area just off the seafront, this hotel offers well equipped bedrooms. The Restaurant serves a short fixed-price menu, and guests can relax in the Wellington Bar at the rear of the building. Friendly service is provided by a young, uniformed staff.
ROOMS: 30 en suite (bth/shr) 2 annexe en suite (bth/shr) (2 fmly) s £42-£45; d £60-£100 (incl. bkfst) * LB Off peak **MEALS:** Bar Lunch £1.85-£5 Dinner £12.95 & alc French Cuisine V meals Coffee am Tea pm **FACILITIES:** CTV in all bedrooms Outdoor swimming pool (heated) Xmas **CONF:** Thtr 100 Class 40 Board 45 Del from £65 **SERVICES:** Night porter 12P **NOTES:** No dogs (ex guide dogs) No smoking area in restaurant Last d 10pm **CARDS:**
See advert on opposite page

SOUTHEND-ON-SEA Essex **Map 05 TQ88**
★★ **Balmoral**
34 Valkyrie Rd, Westcliffe-on-Sea SS0 8BU
Quality Percentage Score: 70%
☎ 01702 342947 01702 337828
Dir: *off A13*
Conveniently situated close to Westcliff Station and a short distance from the town centre, the Balmoral was built around the turn of the century. The bedrooms are modern, smart and particularly well equipped. Room service is readily available. Day rooms comprise a restaurant, small cocktail bar, and reception sitting area.
ROOMS: 29 en suite (bth/shr) (4 fmly) s £41-£80; d £65-£100 (incl. bkfst) LB Off peak **MEALS:** Sunday Lunch £5-£11.95 Dinner £12.95 English & French Cuisine V meals Coffee am Tea pm **FACILITIES:** CTV in all bedrooms STV Arrangement with nearby health club **SERVICES:** Night porter 23P **NOTES:** No coaches Last d 9.30pm
CARDS:

SOUTHEND-ON-SEA Essex **Map 05 TQ88**
★★ **Camelia**
178 Eastern Esplanade, Thorpe Bay SS1 3AA
Quality Percentage Score: 70%
☎ 01702 587917 01702 585704
Dir: *from A13 or A127 follow signs to Southend seafront, on seafront turn left, hotel 1m east of the pier*
On the seafront at Thorpe Bay, this small hotel provides modern en suite accommodation, with each bedroom decorated in light, fresh colours. Staff provide informal and friendly service in the spacious air-conditioned restaurant, and there are also a bar and a small lounge area.
ROOMS: 21 en suite (bth/shr) (1 fmly) No smoking in 19 bedrooms s £46-£65; d £60-£90 (incl. bkfst) * LB Off peak **MEALS:** Sunday Lunch fr £10.95 Dinner £10.95-£12.95 & alc English & French Cuisine V meals **FACILITIES:** CTV in all bedrooms STV Jacuzzi/spa Wkly live entertainment **SERVICES:** 102P **NOTES:** No dogs (ex guide dogs) No smoking area in restaurant Last d 10pm
CARDS:

SOUTHEND-ON-SEA Essex **Map 05 TQ88**
★★ ***Schulers Hotel & Restaurant***
161 Eastern Esplanade SS1 2YB
Quality Percentage Score: 65%
☎ 01702 610172 01702 466835
Dir: *from A127 change to A1159 continue to roundabout, turn right into Hamstel Rd and drive straight on into Lifstan Way, at seafront turn right*
This small family-run, seafront restaurant with rooms has a loyal local following It is here that Manfred Schuler presents fixed-price and carte menus of continental dishes; home-made breads, fish and seafood dishes are strengths of the kitchen. Bedrooms are bright and modern.
ROOMS: 9 rms (7 bth/shr) (1 fmly) **MEALS:** International Cuisine V meals Coffee am Tea pm **FACILITIES:** CTV in all bedrooms **SERVICES:** 10P **NOTES:** No dogs (ex guide dogs) No coaches Closed 25-30 Dec RS Sunday eves and Monday morns
CARDS:

SOUTHEND-ON-SEA Essex **Map 05 TQ88**
★★ **Tower Hotel & Restaurant**
146 Alexandra Rd SS1 1HE
Quality Percentage Score: 57%
☎ 01702 348635 01702 433044
Dir: *off A13 Cricketers Inn into Milton road, then left into Cambridge road and take 3rd turn right into Wilson Rd.*
ROOMS: 15 rms (14 bth/shr) 17 annexe en suite (bth/shr) (4 fmly) s £39-£49; d £45-£65 (incl. bkfst) * Off peak **MEALS:** Lunch £5.50-£10 Dinner £5.50-£9.50 & alc **FACILITIES:** CTV in all bedrooms Residents Memebership of local sports club. **SERVICES:** 4P
CARDS:

SOUTHEND-ON-SEA Essex **Map 05 TQ88**
Travel Inn
Thanet Grange SS2 6GB
☎ 01702 338787 01702 337436
Dir: *on A127 at intersection with B1013 adjacent to Tesco*
This modern building offers accommodation in smart, spacious and well equipped bedrooms, all with en-suite bathrooms. Refreshments may be taken at the nearby family restaurant. For details about current prices consult the Contents Page under Hotel Groups for the Travel Inn phone number.
ROOMS: 60 en suite (bth/shr) d £39.95 *

SOUTH MIMMS Hertfordshire **Map 04 TL20**
★★★ ***Posthouse South Mimms***
EN6 3NH
Posthouse
Quality Percentage Score: 61%
☎ 01707 643311 01707 646728
Dir: *junc 23 on M25 & A1 take services exit off main rdbt then 1st left & follow hotel signs*
Located at the junction of the A1 and M25 motorways, this busy meeting and conference venue has facilities well geared to its target market. Of the two styles of bedroom on offer, the Millennium layout is very smart and up-to-the-minute.
ROOMS: 143 en suite (bth/shr) (25 fmly) No smoking in 70 bedrooms **MEALS:** European Cuisine V meals Coffee am Tea pm **FACILITIES:** CTV in all bedrooms Indoor swimming pool (heated) Sauna Solarium Gym Pool table Jacuzzi/spa Outdoor childrens play area **CONF:** Thtr 170 Class 85 Board 40 **SERVICES:** Night porter 200P **NOTES:** No smoking area in restaurant Last d 10.30pm **CARDS:**

SOUTH MIMMS Hertfordshire **Map 04 TL20**

Welcome Lodge

South Mimms Service Area, Bignells Corner
EN6 3QQ
☎ 01707 665440 01707 665440
Dir: *junct 23 on M25*
This modern building offers accommodation in smart, spacious and well equipped bedrooms, suitable for families and businessmen, and all with en-suite bathrooms. Refreshments may be taken at the nearby family restaurant. For details of current prices, consult the Contents Page under Hotel Groups for the Welcome Break phone number.
ROOMS: 75 en suite (bth/shr) d fr £55 *

SOUTH MOLTON Devon **Map 03 SS72**

The Premier Collection

★★ ***Whitechapel Manor***
EX36 3EG
☎ 01769 573377 01769 573797
Dir: *leave M5 junc27 towards Barnstaple on A361, after 30 minutes turn right at rdbt, after 1m turn right at hotel signpost*
A listed manor house set in attractive grounds, the hotel is renowned for its cuisine. Bedrooms each have their own style and there is a small meeting room and private dining room as well as the usual, elegant reception rooms.
ROOMS: 11 en suite (bth/shr) (1 fmly) **MEALS:** English & Mediterranean Cuisine Coffee am Tea pm **FACILITIES:** CTV in all bedrooms Croquet lawn **CONF:** Thtr 20 Class 20 Board 20 **SERVICES:** 40P **NOTES:** No dogs (ex guide dogs) No coaches No smoking in restaurant Last d 8.45pm
CARDS:

SOUTH MOLTON Devon **Map 03 SS72**

★★ **Marsh Hall Country House**
EX36 3HQ
Quality Percentage Score: 76%
☎ 01769 572666 01769 574230
Dir: *1.25m N towards North Molton off A361*
This personally owned hotel stands in large grounds in easy reach of Exmoor and the coast. Dating from the 17th century, its romantic story says it was built by the local squire for his mistress. Bedrooms are furnished in keeping with the house, and there are two lounges, one with a bar.
ROOMS: 7 en suite (bth/shr) s £52.50-£77; d £85-£110 (incl. bkfst) LB Off peak **MEALS:** Bar Lunch £10 Dinner £22 English & Continental Cuisine **FACILITIES:** CTV in all bedrooms Xmas **SERVICES:** 20P **NOTES:** No dogs (ex guide dogs) No coaches No children 12yrs No smoking in restaurant Last d 8pm **CARDS:**

SOUTH MOLTON Devon **Map 03 SS72**

Late entry **George Hotel**
1 Broad St EX36 3AB
☎ 01769 572514 01769 572514
Dir: *turn off A361 at road island signposted 'South Molton 1.5m' to town centre, hotel is in square*
This charming hotel has a long tradition of hospitality and offers accommodation equally suited to business and leisure guests. There is a separate bar and dining room.
ROOMS: 8 en suite (bth/shr) (2 fmly) s fr £35; d fr £55 (incl. bkfst) * LB Off peak **MEALS:** Lunch £10.75-£13.25alc Dinner £11.25-£18.95alc V meals Coffee am Tea pm **FACILITIES:** CTV in all bedrooms **CONF:** Thtr 100 Class 16 Board 20 **SERVICES:** 12P **NOTES:** No dogs (ex guide dogs) No smoking area in restaurant Last d 9pm
CARDS:

SOUTH NORMANTON Derbyshire **Map 08 SK45**

★★★★ **Swallow**
Carter Ln East DE55 2EH
Quality Percentage Score: 67%
☎ 01773 812000 01773 580032
Dir: *situated on the E side of M1 junct 28 on A38 to Mansfield*
This modern hotel is conveniently located just off junction 28 of the M1. All the spacious bedrooms have modern facilities and comfortable furnishings. There are two eating options: Lacemaker, which is a more informal restaurant and Pavilion which has a commitment to serving imaginatively prepared dishes. There is a well-equipped conference and banqueting

contd.

S

centre and a secure car park. Service is provided by a friendly team of staff.

Swallow, South Normanton

ROOMS: 160 en suite (bth/shr) (7 fmly) No smoking in 100 bedrooms s fr £110; d fr £120 (incl. bkfst) * LB Off peak **MEALS:** Lunch £13.95-£18.95 Dinner £14.95-£18.95 & alc International Cuisine V meals Coffee am Tea pm **FACILITIES:** CTV in all bedrooms STV Indoor swimming pool (heated) Sauna Solarium Gym Jacuzzi/spa Whirlpool Steam room Xmas **CONF:** Thtr 220 Class 100 Board 60 Del £130 * **SERVICES:** Night porter 220P **NOTES:** No smoking area in restaurant Last d 9.45pm **CARDS:**

See advert under SOUTH NORMANTON

SOUTH NORMANTON Derbyshire **Map 08 SK45**

Travel Inn

Carter Ln East DE55 2EH
☎ 01773 862899 01773 861155
Dir: *just off junct 28 of the M1*

This modern building offers accommodation in smart, spacious and well equipped bedrooms, all with en-suite bathrooms. Refreshments may be taken at the nearby family restaurant. For details about current prices consult the Contents Page under Hotel Groups for the Travel Inn phone number.

ROOMS: 80 en suite (bth/shr) d £39.95 *

SOUTHPORT Merseyside **Map 07 SD31**

see also **Formby**

★★★ Royal Clifton

Promenade PR8 1RB
Quality Percentage Score: 69%
☎ 01704 533771 01704 500657
Dir: *hotel on Promenade adjacent to Marine Lake*

In a prime position on the promenade, this large hotel offers extensive banqueting facilities, as well as a leisure and fitness club. Spacious bedrooms, including mini suites and family rooms, are comfortable and modern. There is a welcoming lounge in the entrance area. A range of popular meals and snacks is available in the lively conservatory bar, while more formal dining is available in the Pavilion Restaurant.

ROOMS: 106 en suite (bth/shr) (22 fmly) No smoking in 10 bedrooms s fr £72; d fr £99 * LB Off peak **MEALS:** Sunday Lunch £7.95-£8.95 High tea fr £7.50 Dinner fr £17.50 English & French Cuisine V meals Coffee am Tea pm **FACILITIES:** CTV in all bedrooms STV Indoor swimming pool (heated) Sauna Solarium Gym Jacuzzi/spa Hair & beauty salon Steam room Wkly live entertainment Xmas **CONF:** Thtr 300 Class 170 Board 80 Del from £65.80 * **SERVICES:** Lift Night porter 60P **NOTES:** No dogs (ex guide dogs) No smoking area in restaurant Last d 9.30pm **CARDS:**

SOUTHPORT Merseyside **Map 07 SD31**

★★★ Stutelea Hotel & Leisure Club

Alexandra Rd PR9 0NB
Quality Percentage Score: 68%
☎ 01704 544220 01704 500232
Dir: *off the promenade near town & Hesketh Park*

A fully equipped leisure centre is one of the attractions at this popular family run hotel, situated not far from the Marine Lake. Nicely furnished bedrooms include family suites and rooms on the ground floor, as well as some having balconies overlooking the award winning garden. Carefully prepared evening meals are served in generous portions and snacks can also be had in the Garden bar.

ROOMS: 20 en suite (bth/shr) (4 fmly) **MEALS:** Dinner £18 & alc English & French Cuisine V meals Coffee am Tea pm **FACILITIES:** CTV in all bedrooms STV Indoor swimming pool (heated) Sauna Solarium Gym Pool table Jacuzzi/spa Games room Keep fit classes Steam room **CONF:** Thtr 30 Board 20 **SERVICES:** Lift Night porter 18P **NOTES:** No dogs (ex guide dogs) No smoking area in restaurant Last d 9pm **CARDS:**

See advert on opposite page

SOUTHPORT Merseyside **Map 07 SD31**

★★★ Scarisbrick

Lord St PR8 1NZ
Quality Percentage Score: 67%
☎ 01704 543000 01704 533335
Dir: *from South:M6 junct 26, M55 to Ormskirk then onto Southport. from North:A59 from Preston, well signposted. Also junct 26 M6, then M58 junct A570*

Sitting in the centre of Lord Street, this privately owned hotel offers attractively furnished bedrooms. A wide range of eating options is available, from the bistro style of Maloneys Kitchen to the more formal Knightsbridge restaurant.

ROOMS: 90 en suite (bth/shr) (5 fmly) s £55-£115; d £85-£160 (incl. bkfst) * LB Off peak **MEALS:** Lunch £8.90-£12 & alc High tea £4.25-£6.50 Dinner £12-£15.95 English & French Cuisine V meals Coffee am Tea pm **FACILITIES:** CTV in 77 bedrooms STV Pool table Use of private leisure centre (New Leisure centre due to open Aug 199) Wkly live entertainment Xmas **CONF:** Thtr 200 Class 100 Board 80 Del from £80 * **SERVICES:** Lift Night porter 73P **NOTES:** No smoking in restaurant Last d 9.30pm **CARDS:**

SOUTHPORT Merseyside **Map 07 SD31**

★★ Balmoral Lodge

41 Queens Rd PR9 9EX
Quality Percentage Score: 68%
☎ 01704 544298 & 530751 01704 501224
Dir: *edge of town on A565 Preston road*

This family run hotel, located in a residential area close to Lord Street, offers attractively furnished bedrooms, some of which have a private patio overlooking the gardens. Meals are served in

contd.

the dining room, and there is a comfortable lounge in addition to the cosy bar.
ROOMS: 15 en suite (bth/shr) (1 fmly) s £30-£52; d £56-£62 (incl. bkfst) * LB Off peak **MEALS:** English & French Cuisine V meals **FACILITIES:** CTV in all bedrooms STV Sauna **SERVICES:** 12P **NOTES:** No dogs No coaches No smoking in restaurant **CARDS:**

See advert on this page

SOUTHPORT Merseyside **Map 07 SD31**

★★ ***Bold***
585 Lord St PR9 0BE
Quality Percentage Score: 67%
☎ 01704 532578 01704 532528
Dir: *near M57 & M58, at the top end of Lord Street near the Casino*
Occupying a prime position on Lord Street, this hotel offers easy access to the seafront and all the main attractions. Bedrooms, a number of which are suitable for families, are generally spacious. Downstairs, there is a nightclub (open at weekends only) and a popular bar and bistro, where the menu ranges from snacks to full meals and is available all day.
ROOMS: 23 rms (9 bth 11 shr) (4 fmly) **MEALS:** International Cuisine V meals Coffee am Tea pm **FACILITIES:** CTV in all bedrooms Special rates for local squash club Wkly live entertainment **CONF:** Thtr 40 Class 40 Board 11 **SERVICES:** Night porter Air conditioning 15P **NOTES:** No dogs (ex guide dogs) Last d 10pm **CARDS:**

See advert on this page

New AA Guides for the Millennium are featured on page 24

SOUTHPORT Merseyside **Map 07 SD31**

★★ Metropole

Portland St PR8 1LL

Quality Percentage Score: 65%

☎ 01704 536836 📠 01704 549041

Dir: *turn left off Lord St after Prince of Wales Hotel & Metropole is directly behind Prince of Wales*

This family-run hotel is located just 100 yards from the famous Lord Street and offers bright and modern bedrooms, with family rooms available. There is a choice of lounges, in addition to the bar-lounge, and a selection of freshly prepared dishes is offered in the restaurant.

ROOMS: 23 en suite (bth/shr) (4 fmly) s £30-£35; d £52-£60 (incl. bkfst) * LB Off peak **MEALS:** Lunch £3.75-£10 Dinner £12-£15 English & French Cuisine V meals Coffee am **FACILITIES:** CTV in all bedrooms Snooker Xmas **SERVICES:** 12P **NOTES:** Last d 8.30pm **CARDS:**

SOUTHPORT Merseyside **Map 07 SD31**

★★ *Shelbourne*

1 Lord St West PR8 2BH

Quality Percentage Score: 65%

☎ 01704 541252 & 530278 📠 01704 501293

Dir: *on A565, Lord St signposted from motorway*

A family-run hotel, situated at the head of Lord Street. New bedrooms are spacious and brightly furnished, whilst the enlarged bar-lounge and sun terrace are a popular choice for visitors and locals alike. Service is both friendly and willingly provided.

ROOMS: 20 en suite (bth/shr) (1 fmly) No smoking in 4 bedrooms **MEALS:** V meals Coffee am Tea pm **FACILITIES:** CTV in all bedrooms **CONF:** Thtr 150 Class 75 Board 50 **SERVICES:** 20P **NOTES:** No smoking area in restaurant Last d 9pm **CARDS:**

SOUTHPORT Merseyside **Map 07 SD31**

⌂ Travel Inn

Marine Pde

☎ 0870 242 8000

This modern building offers accommodation in smart, spacious and well equipped bedrooms, all with en-suite bathrooms. Refreshments may be taken at the nearby family restaurant. For details about current prices consult the Contents Page under Hotel Groups for the Travel Inn phone number.

ROOMS: 44 en suite (bth/shr) d £39.95 *

S

SOUTHSEA See **Portsmouth & Southsea**

SOUTH SHIELDS Tyne & Wear **Map 12 NZ36**

★★★ Sea

Sea Rd NE33 2LD

Quality Percentage Score: 64%

☎ 0191 427 0999 📠 0191 454 0500

Dir: *on A183*

Situated on the promenade overlooking the River Tyne, this long-established hotel was originally built in the 1930s. Now a popular business hotel, the atmosphere is relaxed and the staff friendly. The restaurant and bar serve a good range of generously portioned dishes.

ROOMS: 33 en suite (bth/shr) (2 fmly) **MEALS:** English, French & Italian Cuisine V meals Coffee am Tea pm **FACILITIES:** CTV in all bedrooms STV **CONF:** Thtr 200 Class 100 Board 50 Del from £55 * **SERVICES:** Night porter 70P **CARDS:**

SOUTHWAITE MOTORWAY SERVICE AREA (M6) Cumbria **Map 12 NY44**

⌂ Travelodge

Broadfield Site CA4 0NT

☎ Central Res 0800 850950 📠 01525 878450

Dir: *on M6 junc 41/42*

This modern building offers accommodation in smart, spacious and well equipped bedrooms, all with en-suite bathrooms. Refreshments may be taken at the nearby family restaurant. For details about current prices, consult the Contents Page under Hotel Groups for the Travelodge phone number.

ROOMS: 39 en suite (bth/shr) d £49.95 *

SOUTH WALSHAM Norfolk **Map 09 TG31**

★★★ *South Walsham Hall*

The Street NR13 6DQ

Quality Percentage Score: 64%

☎ 01603 270378 & 270591 📠 01603 270519

Dir: *E of Norwich on B1140 towards Acle*

This imposing hall dates back to Elizabethan times (with Victorian extensions) and is surrounded by the Fairhaven Trust gardens. There is a wide choice of bedrooms in style and size, all of which are well appointed with some excellent furnishings and a fresh colour scheme. There is a spacious bar-lounge and an intimate dining room.

ROOMS: 10 en suite (bth/shr) 6 annexe en suite (bth) (1 fmly) **MEALS:** English & Continental Cuisine V meals Coffee am Tea pm **FACILITIES:** CTV in all bedrooms Outdoor swimming pool (heated) Tennis (hard) Fishing 50 acres of woodland-water gardens ch fac **CONF:** Thtr 25 Class 15 Board 15 **SERVICES:** 100P **NOTES:** No coaches Last d 9.45pm **CARDS:**

SOUTH WITHAM Lincolnshire **Map 08 SK91**

⌂ Travelodge

New Fox NG33 5LN

☎ 01572 767586 📠 01572 767586

Dir: *on A1, northbound*

This modern building offers accommodation in smart, spacious and well equipped bedrooms, all with en-suite bathrooms. Refreshments may be taken at the nearby family restaurant. For details about current prices, consult the Contents Page under Hotel Groups for the Travelodge phone number.

ROOMS: 32 en suite (bth/shr) d £39.95 *

SOUTHWOLD Suffolk **Map 05 TM57**

★★★ Swan

Market Place IP18 6EG

Quality Percentage Score: 69%

☎ 01502 722186 📠 01502 724800

Dir: *take A1095 to Southwold, hotel is located in the centre of town, parking is via an archway to the left of the building*

The Adnams brewery's flagship property, The Swan is situated on the marketplace and backs onto the brewery itself. A stylish upgrading programme is improving all the comfortable accommodation; some newly enlarged and well appointed bedrooms are clustered around the landscaped gardens. The public rooms include the drawing room and the intimate bar. In the dining room, chef David Smith's daily menus offer guests a selection of appetising, well flavoured and imaginative dishes. An excellent, innovative selection of reasonably priced wines is offered.

ROOMS: 26 rms (25 bth/shr) 17 annexe en suite (bth/shr) (2 fmly) s £59-£80; d £99-£165 (incl. bkfst) * LB Off peak **MEALS:** Lunch £16-£18 High tea £5-£8 Dinner £24-£34 English & French Cuisine V meals Coffee am Tea pm **FACILITIES:** CTV in all bedrooms Croquet lawn Xmas **CONF:** Thtr 50 Class 32 Board 12 Del from £125 * **SERVICES:** Lift Night porter 35P **NOTES:** No coaches No smoking in restaurant Last d 9.30pm RS Nov-Mar **CARDS:** *contd.*

SOUTHWOLD Suffolk
Map 05 TM57

★★ *The Crown*
90 High St IP18 6DP
Quality Percentage Score: 69%
☎ 01502 722275 Fax 01502 727263
Dir: *off A12 take A1094 to Southwold, stay on main road into town centre, hotel on left in High St*

The vibrant bars and restaurant at this Adnam's hotel are very much the emphasis; the wine bar is always very popular, and offers light meals featuring cosmopolitan cooking; tables are offered on a first come, first served basis. In contrast, bookings are taken for the adjacent intimate restaurant, where more serious yet similarly modern cuisine is served. At the back a locals' snug bar is a focal point for gossip and, naturally, Adnams beers. The comfortable and suitably furnished accommodation comes in a variety of sizes and styles; residents can also relax in the parlour.

ROOMS: 12 rms (8 bth 1 shr) (1 fmly) **MEALS:** Eclectic Cuisine V meals Coffee am **FACILITIES:** CTV in all bedrooms **CONF:** Thtr 40 Class 20 Board 20 **SERVICES:** 23P **NOTES:** No dogs (ex guide dogs) No coaches No smoking in restaurant Last d 9.30pm Closed 1st or 2nd wk Jan **CARDS:**

SOUTH ZEAL Devon
Map 03 SX69

★★ Oxenham Arms
EX20 2JT
Quality Percentage Score: 66%
☎ 01837 840244 & 840577 Fax 01837 840791
Dir: *just off A30 4m E of Okehampton in centre of village*

The creeper-clad Oxenham Arms traces its long history back to the 12th century, and features an even more ancient standing stone, around which the inn was built, in the family/TV lounge. The bar and other lounge are also full of character, as are the individually decorated bedrooms.

ROOMS: 8 rms (7 bth/shr) s £40-£50; d £60-£70 (incl. bkfst) * Off peak **MEALS:** Lunch £9.50-£12alc Dinner £15-£18 International Cuisine V meals Coffee am Tea pm **FACILITIES:** CTV in all bedrooms Xmas **SERVICES:** 8P **NOTES:** No coaches No smoking in restaurant Last d 9pm **CARDS:**

SPALDING Lincolnshire
Map 08 TF22

★★ Cley Hall
22 High St PE11 1TX
Quality Percentage Score: 64%
☎ 01775 725157 Fax 01775 710785
Dir: *remain on A16 to B1165, take 1st turning on rdbt across mini-rdbt to river turn left*

This Georgian house near the River Welland once belonged to the Cley family from Cockley Cley in Norfolk - hence the name. It enjoys a high reputation for hospitality, and its comfortable bedrooms are divided between the main house and an adjacent building. The restaurant serves appetising meals.

ROOMS: 4 en suite (bth/shr) 8 annexe en suite (bth/shr) (4 fmly) s £46-£55; d £60-£70 (incl. bkfst) * Off peak **MEALS:** Lunch £11.95 & alc Dinner £11.95 & alc International Cuisine V meals Coffee am Tea pm **FACILITIES:** CTV in all bedrooms ch fac **CONF:** Thtr 40 Class 23 Board 20 **SERVICES:** 20P **NOTES:** No smoking area in restaurant Last d 9.30pm **CARDS:**

STAFFORD Staffordshire
Map 07 SJ92

★★★ *Tillington Hall*
Eccleshall Rd ST16 1JJ
Quality Percentage Score: 65%
☎ 01785 253531 Fax 01785 259223
Dir: *exit M6 junc 14 take A5013*

This large, privately owned hotel is situated on the A5013, north-

contd.

west of the town centre and conveniently close to junction 14 of the M6 motorway. The well equipped accommodation includes bedrooms on ground floor level, no smoking bedrooms, family bedded rooms and rooms which interconnect. It offers a selection of rooms for functions and conferences and is understandably a popular venue for business people. Its well equipped leisure centre and convenience to the Potteries ensure its popularity with tourists, including families visiting Alton Towers theme park.
ROOMS: 90 en suite (bth/shr) (7 fmly) No smoking in 42 bedrooms **MEALS:** English, French & German Cuisine V meals Coffee am Tea pm **FACILITIES:** CTV in all bedrooms STV Indoor swimming pool (heated) Tennis Sauna Solarium Gym Pool table Jacuzzi/spa **CONF:** Thtr 200 Class 80 Board 40 **SERVICES:** Lift Night porter 200P **NOTES:** No smoking in restaurant Last d 9.45pm **CARDS:**

STAFFORD Staffordshire **Map 07 SJ92**
★★★ Garth
Wolverhampton Rd, Moss Pit ST17 9JR
Quality Percentage Score: 64%
☎ 01785 256124 01785 255152
Dir: *exit M6 at Junc 13 take A449*

Conveniently located between the town and junction 13 of the M6, this hotel, originally the home of an Edwardian industrialist, is situated in pleasant gardens. Recently refurbished bedrooms are comfortable and attractively furnished. Light meals and snacks are served in the popular bar, a range of real ales also being available, whilst more substantial fare can be had in the light and airy restaurant.
ROOMS: 60 en suite (bth/shr) (4 fmly) No smoking in 28 bedrooms s £75; d £85 (incl. bkfst) * LB Off peak **MEALS:** Lunch £9.50-£18.75alc International Cuisine V meals Coffee am Tea pm **FACILITIES:** CTV in all bedrooms STV ch fac Xmas **CONF:** Thtr 120 Class 30 Board 48 Del £99 * **SERVICES:** Night porter 175P **NOTES:** No smoking in restaurant RS 25-26 Dec **CARDS:**

STAFFORD Staffordshire **Map 07 SJ92**
★★ Swan Hotel
Greengate St ST16 2JA
Quality Percentage Score: 64%
☎ 01785 258142 01785 223372
Dir: *south along A449 from north follow A34 access via Mill Street in town centre*
This former coaching inn is over 400 years old and was built on the site of monastic college buildings. Situated in the centre of the town, it has an enclosed car park at the rear. Oak beams and oak panelling in the restaurant are just some of its many features. The Romany Bar is open all day and is popular with younger customers. The well-equipped modern bedrooms have been tastefully decorated and include some rooms with four-poster beds and some family-bedded rooms.
ROOMS: 32 en suite (bth/shr) (4 fmly) No smoking in 5 bedrooms s £42.50; d £52 * LB Off peak **MEALS:** Lunch £5.75-£12.95 & alc Dinner £5.95-£12.95 & alc International Cuisine V meals Coffee am Tea pm **FACILITIES:** CTV in all bedrooms STV Xmas **CONF:** Thtr 30 Class 20 Board 20 Del from £75 * **SERVICES:** Night porter 80P **NOTES:** No dogs (ex guide dogs) No smoking area in restaurant Last d 9.30pmm **CARDS:**

STAFFORD Staffordshire **Map 07 SJ92**
★★ Abbey
65-68 Lichfield Rd ST17 4LW
Quality Percentage Score: 63%
☎ 01785 258531 01785 246875
Dir: *A449 to Stafford until Esso garage on right, turn right before garage, cont until mini rdbt, take 1st exit, next rdbt 2nd exit, hotel on right*
This small privately-owned, personally-run hotel is situated alongside the Lichfield road, south of the town centre but within easy reach of the motorway. Bedrooms vary in size but all are neatly decorated, with some available on the ground floor. There is a choice of dining options, with a range of bar snacks and meals in the cosy bar or a more extensive menu in the restaurant, which is also used by guests from the adjacent guest house.
ROOMS: 17 en suite (bth/shr) (3 fmly) s £32-£35; d £46-£50 (incl. bkfst) * LB Off peak **MEALS:** Bar Lunch £3.50-£8alc Dinner £9-£9.80 & alc English & French Cuisine V meals Coffee am **FACILITIES:** CTV in all bedrooms **SERVICES:** 26P **NOTES:** No dogs (ex guide dogs) No coaches No smoking in restaurant Last d 8.30pm Closed 22 Dec-7 Jan **CARDS:**

STAFFORD MOTORWAY SERVICE AREA (M6) Staffordshire **Map 07 SJ83**
Roadchef Lodge Stafford South
Stafford Motorway Service Area, M6 Motorway Southbound ST15 0EU
☎ 01785 826300 01785 826303
This modern building offers accommodation in smart, spacious and well equipped bedrooms, all with en-suite bathrooms. Refreshments may be taken at the nearby family restaurant. For details about current prices, consult the Contents Page under Hotel Groups for the Roadchef phone number.

STAINES Surrey **Map 04 TQ07**
★★★ The Thames Lodge
Thames St TW18 4SF
Quality Percentage Score: 70%
☎ 01784 464433 01784 454858
Dir: *follow signs A30 Staines town centre, join one way system in right hand lane, bus station on right, hotel straight ahead*
This extended Victorian hotel is situated close to the railway bridge and opposite the local rowing club. It has a riverside setting with its own mooring jetty. There is a broad range of modern bedrooms, some of which have balconies and river views. Services are willingly provided by a friendly team of staff.
ROOMS: 79 en suite (bth/shr) (16 fmly) No smoking in 49 bedrooms s £125; d £135 * LB Off peak **MEALS:** Lunch £8.95-£10.95 & alc High tea fr £7.50 Dinner fr £12.95 & alc International Cuisine V meals Coffee am Tea pm **FACILITIES:** CTV in all bedrooms Xmas **CONF:** Thtr 40 Class 20 Board 20 Del from £130 * **SERVICES:** Night porter 33P **NOTES:** Last d 10pm **CARDS:**

STALHAM Norfolk — Map 09 TG32

★★ Kingfisher

High St NR12 9AN
Quality Percentage Score: 69%
☎ 01692 581974 Fax 01692 582544
Dir: *Stalham is by-passed by A149 between Gt Yarmouth & North Walsham, hotel is located just off High St at west end*
In the heart of the Norfolk Broadlands, the hotel is a focal point for this bustling market town. Bedrooms are spacious and bright. The large bar is popular with locals and residents alike for the wide menu. In the more intimate restaurant, fixed price and carte menus offer an interesting choice of dishes.
ROOMS: 18 en suite (bth/shr) (2 fmly) s £45; d £55-£75 (incl. bkfst) * LB Off peak **MEALS:** Dinner £11.95 International Cuisine V meals Coffee am Tea pm **FACILITIES:** CTV in all bedrooms Xmas **CONF:** Thtr 100 Class 40 Board 30 **SERVICES:** 40P **NOTES:** No smoking in restaurant Last d 9pm **CARDS:**

STALLINGBOROUGH Lincolnshire — Map 08 TA11

★★★ Stallingborough Grange Hotel

Riby Rd DN41 8BU
Quality Percentage Score: 64%
☎ 01469 561302 Fax 01469 561338
Dir: *from A180 take signs for Stallingborough Ind Est and then through the village, from rdbt take A1173 Caistor, hotel 1m on left just past windmill*
Originally an 18th-century country house, Stallingborough Grange is just outside the village. It has now developed into a popular business hotel, family-run and offering two different styles of food. The Tavern provides a good range of bar meals while the restaurant is the place to eat for a more serious dinner. Bedrooms provide good facilities and service is both attentive and friendly.
ROOMS: 32 en suite (bth/shr) (2 fmly) s fr £68; d fr £80 (incl. bkfst) * LB Off peak **MEALS:** Sunday Lunch £10.50 Dinner £8-£15alc English & French Cuisine V meals Coffee am **FACILITIES:** CTV in all bedrooms STV **CONF:** Thtr 60 Class 40 Board 28 Del from £98 * **SERVICES:** 100P **NOTES:** No dogs (ex guide dogs) No smoking in restaurant Last d 9.30PM **CARDS:**

STAMFORD Lincolnshire — Map 08 TF00

★★★ The George of Stamford

71 St Martins PE9 2LB
Quality Percentage Score: 75%
☎ 01780 750750 & 750700 (Res) Fax 01780 750701
Dir: *turn off A1 onto B1081, 1m on left*
A charming coaching inn dating back hundreds of years, The George exudes quality and comfort. Staff are friendly the atmosphere relaxed, bedrooms are decorated to a very high standard with lots of extras. Guests have a choice of dining options; and the cobbled courtyard is the ideal place to dine in the summer months.
ROOMS: 47 en suite (bth/shr) (2 fmly) No smoking in 3 bedrooms s £78-£105; d £103-£220 (incl. bkfst) * LB Off peak **MEALS:** Lunch £14.50-£16.50 & alc High tea £2.25-£9.95alc Dinner £27.60-£40.15alc English, French & Italian Cuisine V meals Coffee am Tea pm **FACILITIES:** CTV in all bedrooms STV Croquet lawn Xmas **CONF:** Thtr 50 Class 25 Board 25 Del £130 * **SERVICES:** Night porter 120P **NOTES:** Last d 11pm **CARDS:**

STAMFORD Lincolnshire — Map 08 TF00

★★★ Garden House

St Martin's PE9 2LP
Quality Percentage Score: 65%
☎ 01780 763359 Fax 01780 763339
Dir: *A1 to South Stamford, B1081, signposted Stamford and Burghley House, Hotel on left on entering the town*
Run by Chris and Irene Quinn and their friendly, eager staff, this sympathetically transformed 18th-century house has been steadily refurbished and now provides very pleasant accommodation. It stands only a short walk from the town centre and boasts many modern facilities. The bedrooms are well equipped and comfortable, whilst the public rooms include a charming bar and conservatory, where light meals are available. More serious dining is offered from an appetising menu in the prettily furnished restaurant.
ROOMS: 20 en suite (bth/shr) (1 fmly) No smoking in 4 bedrooms s £58-£65; d £85-£95 (incl. bkfst) * LB Off peak **MEALS:** Lunch £7.75-£15 & alc Dinner £15 & alc V meals Coffee am Tea pm **FACILITIES:** CTV in all bedrooms STV Xmas **CONF:** Thtr 40 Class 20 Board 20 Del from £65 * **SERVICES:** 30P **NOTES:** No smoking area in restaurant Last d 9.30pm **CARDS:**

STAMFORD Lincolnshire — Map 08 TF00

★★ *Crown*

All Saints Place PE9 2AG
Quality Percentage Score: 66%
☎ 01780 763136 Fax 01780 756111
Dir: *off A1 onto A43, straight through town until Red Lion Sq, hotel is behind All Saints church in the square*
Tucked behind the church in the main square, this 15th-century hotel offers comfortable and well equipped bedrooms. Service is friendly and attentive, and the inviting public rooms include two dining rooms and a spacious bar. A good range of freshly cooked meals is available and can be taken either in the bar or cosy restaurant.
ROOMS: 17 en suite (bth/shr) (2 fmly) **MEALS:** European Cuisine V meals Coffee am Tea pm **FACILITIES:** CTV in all bedrooms **CONF:** Thtr 50 Class 40 Board 35 **SERVICES:** 40P **NOTES:** No smoking area in restaurant Last d 9.15pm Closed 25 Dec
CARDS:

STANSTEAD ABBOTS Hertfordshire — Map 05 TL31

★★★★ Briggens House

Stanstead Rd SG12 8LD
Quality Percentage Score: 60%
☎ 01279 829955 Fax 01279 793685
Dir: *A414 to Hertford, after 8th rdbt look for left hand turn signposted Briggens Park, this is the hotel*

Enjoying views of the 80-acre estate in which it is set, Briggens House dates back to the 17th century and was formerly the home of Lord Aldenham. Conferences are a major part of the operation here and there is a good range of meeting rooms; however, this does mean there is limited lounge space. The bedroom refurbishment continues and the completed rooms are

contd.

very smart. Outdoor attractions include an arboretum, swimming pool and golf.
ROOMS: 54 en suite (bth/shr) (3 fmly) s £70-£110; d £85-£128 * LB Off peak **MEALS:** Lunch £6.95-£14.95 Dinner £11.75-£18.95 & alc International Cuisine V meals Coffee am Tea pm **FACILITIES:** CTV in all bedrooms Outdoor swimming pool (heated) Golf 9 Tennis (hard) Croquet lawn Putting green Wkly live entertainment Xmas **CONF:** Thtr 120 Class 50 Board 50 Del from £120 * **SERVICES:** Lift Night porter 100P **NOTES:** No smoking in restaurant Last d 9.30pm
CARDS:

STANSTED AIRPORT Essex **Map 05 TL52**

★★★ *Whitehall*

Church End CM6 2BZ
Quality Percentage Score: 74%
☎ 01279 850603 01279 850385
Dir: *leave M11 J8, follow signs to Stansted Airport, then hotel signs to Broxted village*
This friendly hotel dates back to the Tudor period and boasts good-sized, well equipped bedrooms all of which are stylishly decorated in fresh, bright colours. The character of the original building is reflected in the log-burning fires and the timber-vaulted restaurant, with its feature murals, where guests can enjoy soundly prepared dishes in a modern country style. The walled garden shelters the landscaped lawns and yew trees.
ROOMS: 25 en suite (bth/shr) (3 fmly) **MEALS:** V meals Coffee am Tea pm **FACILITIES:** CTV in all bedrooms Outdoor swimming pool **CONF:** Thtr 120 Class 80 Board 48 **SERVICES:** Night porter 37P **NOTES:** No dogs (ex guide dogs) No coaches Last d 9.30pm Closed 26-30 Dec **CARDS:**

STANSTED AIRPORT Essex **Map 05 TL52**

Welcome Lodge

Birchanger Green, Old Dunmow Rd CM23 5QZ
☎ 01279 656477 01279 656590
Dir: *M11 junct 8*
This modern building offers accommodation in smart, spacious and well equipped bedrooms, suitable for families and businessmen, and all with en-suite bathrooms. Refreshments may be taken at the nearby family restaurant. For details of current prices, consult the Contents Page under Hotel Groups for the Welcome Break phone number.
ROOMS: 60 en suite (bth/shr) d fr £55 *

STAVERTON Devon **Map 03 SX76**

★★ *Sea Trout Inn*

TQ9 6PA
Quality Percentage Score: 66%
☎ 01803 762274 01803 762506
Dir: *turn off A38 onto A384 at Buckfastleigh, follow signs to Staverton*
The Sea Trout Inn is a charming 15th-century building with a popular conservatory restaurant and a separate bar, also serving food. All the bedrooms are furnished to a high standard of comfort.
ROOMS: 10 en suite (bth/shr) (1 fmly) **MEALS:** V meals Coffee am **FACILITIES:** CTV in all bedrooms STV Pool table **SERVICES:** 48P **NOTES:** No coaches No smoking area in restaurant Last d 9.30pm RS 24-26 Dec **CARDS:**

STEEPLE ASTON Oxfordshire **Map 04 SP42**

★★★ The Holt Hotel

OX6 3QQ
Quality Percentage Score: 66%
☎ 01869 340259 01869 340865
Dir: *junct of B4030/A4260*
This attractive stone-built hotel is located on the Woodstock to Banbury road. Popular with corporate guests, the hotel offers well presented conference facilities and smart, spacious public areas. Bedrooms, which are being steadily upgraded, are comfortably furnished and well equipped for the business guest.
ROOMS: 84 en suite (bth/shr) (19 fmly) No smoking in 10 bedrooms s fr £92.83; d fr £116.33 (incl. bkfst) * LB Off peak **MEALS:** Lunch £5.95-£12.95 Dinner £18-£22 & alc English & French Cuisine V meals Coffee am Tea pm **FACILITIES:** CTV in all bedrooms STV Pool table Xmas **CONF:** Thtr 150 Class 70 Board 40 Del from £100 * **SERVICES:** Night porter 200P **NOTES:** No smoking in restaurant Last d 9.45pm **CARDS:**

STEVENAGE Hertfordshire **Map 04 TL22**

★★★ Novotel

Knebworth Park SG1 2AX
Quality Percentage Score: 64%
☎ 01438 742299 01438 723872
Dir: *off junct 7 of A1(M), at entrance to Knebworth park*
Pleasantly located in a Green Belt site, this modern red-brick buidling is only moments from the A1(M), which makes it a popular meeting and conference venue. The informal bar and restaurant are set up to deal with this kind of business. All the large bedrooms are well appointed for both business guests and families.
ROOMS: 100 en suite (bth/shr) (20 fmly) No smoking in 75 bedrooms d £82-£85 * Off peak **MEALS:** Dinner fr £16 International Cuisine V meals Coffee am Tea pm **FACILITIES:** CTV in all bedrooms STV Outdoor swimming pool (heated) Pool table **CONF:** Thtr 150 Class 80 Board 70 Del from £110 * **SERVICES:** Lift 100P **NOTES:** No smoking area in restaurant Last d mdnt **CARDS:**

STEVENAGE Hertfordshire **Map 04 TL22**

★★★ Cromwell

High St, Old Town SG1 3AZ
Quality Percentage Score: 62%
☎ 01438 779954 01438 742169
Dir: *leave A1(M1) junct8. Follow signs for town centre, over 2 rdbts. Join one-way system. Turn off into Old Town. Hotel is on the left after mini rdbt*

Easily accessible from the nearby A1(M), this High Street hotel has retained much of its historic charm, and offers many useful facilities for business and leisure guests alike. The attractive bedrooms are well equipped, and some are more modern in style than others. Amongst the range of public areas, there are two bars and large meeting rooms.
ROOMS: 57 en suite (bth/shr) (4 fmly) No smoking in 14 bedrooms s fr £95; d fr £110 * LB Off peak **MEALS:** Lunch £5-£10.95 Dinner fr £9.95 & alc V meals Coffee am Tea pm **FACILITIES:** CTV in all bedrooms STV Pool table Xmas **CONF:** Thtr 200 Class 60 Board 60 Del from £138 * **SERVICES:** Night porter 50P **NOTES:** No smoking area in restaurant Last d 9.45pm RS 25-31 Dec
CARDS:

STEVENAGE Hertfordshire **Map 04 TL22**
★★★ ***Posthouse Stevenage***
Old London Rd, Broadwater SG2 8DS
Quality Percentage Score: 61%
☎ 01438 365444 Fax 01438 741308
Dir: *off B1970*
Suitable for both the business and leisure traveller, this hotel provides spacious accommodation in well equipped bedrooms. There is some character to the older part of the building which contains the bar and restaurant.
ROOMS: 54 en suite (bth/shr) No smoking in 27 bedrooms
MEALS: International Cuisine V meals Coffee am Tea pm
FACILITIES: CTV in all bedrooms **CONF:** Thtr 60 Class 20 Board 30
SERVICES: Night porter 80P **NOTES:** No smoking area in restaurant Last d 10.30pm **CARDS:**

STEVENAGE Hertfordshire **Map 04 TL22**
★★★ ***Thistle Stevenage/Hitchin***
Blakemore End Rd, Little Wymondley SG4 7JJ
Quality Percentage Score: 61%
☎ 01438 355821 Fax 01438 742114
(For full entry see Hitchin)

STEVENAGE Hertfordshire **Map 04 TL22**
★★★ **Hertfordpark**
Danestrete SG1 1EJ
Quality Percentage Score: 59%
☎ 01438 779955 Fax 01438 741880
Dir: *in town centre adjacent to BHS & Westgate Multi-Store*

Situated in the heart of the new town, surrounded on all sides by shops, this purpose-built hotel is well used by business guests and is a popular local venue. Spacious well equipped bedrooms offer peace and quiet. The coffee shop is an ideal meeting place. The bar and restaurant are located on the first floor. Conference and meeting facilities are available. Free car parking is available at the nearby multi storey.
ROOMS: 98 en suite (bth/shr) No smoking in 42 bedrooms s £60-£80; d £70-£90 * LB Off peak **MEALS:** Lunch £8.50-£14.50 & alc High tea fr £4.50 Dinner fr £14.50 & alc International Cuisine V meals Coffee am Tea pm **FACILITIES:** CTV in all bedrooms Pool table Xmas **CONF:** Thtr 200 Class 80 Board 60 Del from £115 * **SERVICES:** Lift Night porter **NOTES:** No smoking in restaurant Last d 10pm
CARDS:

STEVENAGE Hertfordshire **Map 04 TL22**
Travel Inn
Corey's Mill Ln SG1 4AA
☎ 01438 351318 Fax 01438 721609
Dir: *close to A1(M) at intersection of the A602 Hitchin Rd & Corey's Mill Lane*
This modern building offers accommodation in smart, spacious and well equipped bedrooms, all with en-suite bathrooms. Refreshments may be taken at the nearby family restaurant. For details about current prices consult the Contents Page under Hotel Groups for the Travel Inn phone number.
ROOMS: 40 en suite (bth/shr) d £39.95 *

STEYNING West Sussex **Map 04 TQ11**
★★★ ***The Old Tollgate***
The Street BN44 3WE
Quality Percentage Score: 69%
☎ 01903 879494 Fax 01903 813399
Dir: *on A283 at Steyning rdbt, turn off to Bramber, the hotel is situated approx 200yds along on the right*
A well presented hotel on the site of the old Toll-House. Bedrooms are spacious, smartly designed and furnished to a high standard, some with 4-poster bed, jacuzzi and sitting room. An extensive choice of dishes are offered in the popular carvery style restaurant. The hotel has adaptable function rooms for weddings and conferences.
ROOMS: 11 en suite (bth/shr) 20 annexe en suite (bth/shr) (5 fmly)
MEALS: International Cuisine V meals **FACILITIES:** CTV in all bedrooms STV **CONF:** Thtr 60 Class 32 Board 26 **SERVICES:** Lift Night porter 60P **NOTES:** No dogs (ex guide dogs) No coaches No smoking area in restaurant Last d 9.30pm **CARDS:**

STILTON Cambridgeshire **Map 04 TL18**
★★★ **Bell Inn**
Great North Rd PE7 3RA
Quality Percentage Score: 66%
☎ 01733 241066 Fax 01733 245173
Dir: *turn off A1(M) at junct 16 then follow signs for Stilton, hotel is situated on the main road in centre of village*
A wealth of original rural features makes the Bell a charming place to stay. Now even easier to get to, despite its lovely village setting, with the A1(M) motorway just minutes away. With its beamed ceilings and open log fires, the village bar is full of character, as is the galleried restaurant above which offers an exciting menu, mixing modern and traditional influences to good effect. The pleasant bedrooms vary in size and style, offering a wide choice of accommodation.
ROOMS: 19 en suite (bth/shr) (1 fmly) No smoking in 7 bedrooms s £69.50-£89.50; d £89.50-£109.50 (incl. bkfst) * LB Off peak
MEALS: Lunch £11.95-£19.95 Dinner £19.95 English & French Cuisine V meals Coffee am Tea pm **FACILITIES:** CTV in all bedrooms STV
CONF: Thtr 100 Class 46 Board 46 Del £89.50 * **SERVICES:** Night porter 30P **NOTES:** No dogs (ex guide dogs) No smoking area in restaurant Last d 9.30pm Closed 25 Dec
CARDS:

STOCKBRIDGE Hampshire **Map 04 SU33**
★★★ ***Grosvenor***
High St SO20 6EU
Quality Percentage Score: 63%
☎ 01264 810606 Fax 01264 810747
Dir: *on main A30 in centre of Stockbridge*
Originally a Georgian coaching inn, situated at the heart of this pretty village, the Grosvenor provides a relaxed and informal atmosphere. There is a traditional bar with an angling theme, a cosy panelled dining room and a choice of bedrooms, either in the main house or a rear extension with smaller, quieter rooms.
ROOMS: 25 en suite (bth/shr) No smoking in 3 bedrooms
MEALS: Continental Cuisine V meals Coffee am Tea pm
FACILITIES: CTV in all bedrooms STV Sauna **CONF:** Thtr 80 Class 20 Board 30 **SERVICES:** Night porter 60P **NOTES:** No smoking in restaurant Last d 9.45pm **CARDS:**

STOCKPORT Greater Manchester **Map 07 SJ88**
see also **Manchester Airport & Marple**
★★★ *Bredbury Hall Hotel & Country Club*
Goyt Valley SK6 2DH
Quality Percentage Score: 67%
☎ 0161 430 7421 🖷 0161 430 5079
Dir: *M60 J25 signposted Bredbury, left at traffic ligts, left onto Osbourne St, hotel 500m on right*
With views over open countryside, this large modern hotel is near the M60. Bedrooms offer space and comfort and the restaurant serves a range of freshly prepared dishes. There is a popular nightclub next door to the hotel.
ROOMS: 120 en suite (bth/shr) (2 fmly) **MEALS:** European Cuisine V meals Coffee am Tea pm **FACILITIES:** CTV in all bedrooms STV Fishing Snooker Pool table Night club Wkly live entertainment **CONF:** Thtr 140 Class 90 Board 70 Del from £95 * **SERVICES:** Night porter 400P **NOTES:** No dogs (ex guide dogs) Last d 11.00pm
CARDS:

STOCKPORT Greater Manchester **Map 07 SJ88**
★★★ County Hotel Bramhall
Bramhall Ln South SK7 2EB
Quality Percentage Score: 64%
☎ 0161 455 9988 🖷 0161 440 8071
(For full entry see Bramhall)

STOCKPORT Greater Manchester **Map 07 SJ88**
★★ Red Lion Inn
112 Buxton Rd, High Ln SK6 8ED
Quality Percentage Score: 67%
☎ 01663 765227 🖷 01663 762170
Dir: *beside A6, 1m N from Lyme Country Park*
Just a mile from Lyme Park in High Lane, this well known hotel and inn offers comfortably furnished bedrooms. Restaurant and bar serve a good range of meals, and fish features regularly on the menu.
ROOMS: 6 en suite (bth/shr) (1 fmly) s £30-£49.50; d £49.50-£60 * Off peak **MEALS:** Lunch fr £6.25alc Dinner £10.45-£23.20alc V meals Coffee am Tea pm **FACILITIES:** CTV in all bedrooms **SERVICES:** 100P **NOTES:** No dogs (ex guide dogs) No coaches Last d 10.00pm
CARDS:

STOCKPORT Greater Manchester **Map 07 SJ88**
★★ Saxon Holme
230 Wellington Rd SK4 2QN
Quality Percentage Score: 66%
☎ 0161 432 2335 🖷 0161 431 8076
Dir: *N, beside A6*
This well run hotel is situated outside the town, on the Manchester side, and gives easy access to the airport. Bedrooms, including a number on the ground floor, have modern facilities, and reception rooms are elegant, with ornately decorated plaster ceilings.
ROOMS: 33 en suite (bth/shr) (3 fmly) No smoking in 11 bedrooms s £39.50-£49.50; d £49.50-£59.50 (incl. bkfst) * Off peak **MEALS:** Dinner £12.95-£18.95 & alc English & French Cuisine V meals Coffee am **FACILITIES:** CTV in all bedrooms STV Pool table **CONF:** Thtr 70 Class 10 Board 20 Del from £80 * **SERVICES:** Lift Night porter 40P **NOTES:** No dogs (ex guide dogs) No smoking in restaurant Last d 9pm
CARDS:

STOCKPORT Greater Manchester **Map 07 SJ88**
★★ Wycliffe
74 Edgeley Rd, Edgeley SK3 9NQ
Quality Percentage Score: 66%
☎ 0161 477 5395 🖷 0161 476 3219
Dir: *from M60 junct 2 follow A560 for Stockport, at 1st lights turn right, hotel half a mile on left*
This family run, welcoming hotel has immaculately maintained bedrooms, some in houses just across the road. The main building houses the restaurant and well stocked bar. The menu has an Italian bias.
ROOMS: 20 en suite (bth/shr) s £44; d £56 (incl. bkfst) * Off peak **MEALS:** Lunch £8-£12 & alc Dinner fr £16 & alc French & Italian Cuisine V meals Tea pm **FACILITIES:** CTV in all bedrooms STV Xmas **CONF:** Thtr 20 Class 20 Board 20 **SERVICES:** Night porter 46P **NOTES:** No dogs (ex guide dogs) No coaches Last d 9.30pm
CARDS:

STOCKPORT Greater Manchester **Map 07 SJ88**
Travel Inn
Buxton Rd SK2 6NB
☎ 0161 480 2968 🖷 0161 477 8320
Dir: *on A6 1.5m from town centre*
This modern building offers accommodation in smart, spacious and well equipped bedrooms, all with en-suite bathrooms. Refreshments may be taken at the nearby family restaurant. For details about current prices consult the Contents Page under Hotel Groups for the Travel Inn phone number.
ROOMS: 40 en suite (bth/shr) d £39.95 *

STOCKPORT Greater Manchester **Map 07 SJ88**
Travelodge
London Rd South SK12 4NA
☎ 01625 875292 🖷 01625 875292
Dir: *on A523*
This modern building offers accommodation in smart, spacious and well equipped bedrooms, all with en-suite bathrooms. Refreshments may be taken at the nearby family restaurant. For details about current prices, consult the Contents Page under Hotel Groups for the Travelodge phone number.
ROOMS: 32 en suite (bth/shr) d £45.95 *

STOCKTON-ON-TEES Co Durham **Map 08 NZ41**
★★★★ Swallow
John Walker Square TS18 1AQ
Quality Percentage Score: 63%
☎ 01642 679721 0800 7317549 🖷 01642 601714
Dir: *head for Stockton centre, follow A1130 Stockton. At MFI rdbt take 3rd exit, then 1st left into multi-storey car park. Deck 6 is hotel car park*

Easily recognisable as the tallest building in town, this hotel forms part of a shopping development and has direct access to a multi-storey car park. A steady refurbishment programme now

contd.

offers smart, well equipped bedrooms and the public areas provide two restaurants. Attentive service is offered by friendly staff.
ROOMS: 125 en suite (bth/shr) (12 fmly) No smoking in 77 bedrooms s £90-£110; d £99-£120 (incl. bkfst) * LB Off peak **MEALS:** English & French Cuisine V meals Coffee am Tea pm **FACILITIES:** CTV in all bedrooms STV Indoor swimming pool (heated) Sauna Solarium Gym Jacuzzi/spa Sunbeach tanning area Xmas **CONF:** Thtr 300 Class 150 Board 40 Del from £110 * **SERVICES:** Lift Night porter 400P **NOTES:** No smoking area in restaurant Last d 9.45pm **CARDS:**

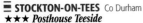

STOCKTON-ON-TEES Co Durham — Map 08 NZ41
★★★ Parkmore
636 Yarm Rd, Eaglescliffe TS16 0DH
Quality Percentage Score: 70%
☎ 01642 786815 01642 790485
Dir: *3m S A19*
In this Victorian house hotel, bedrooms are well equipped and have modern fittings, public rooms are comfortable and inviting. Extensive menus are available in Reeds restaurant with inventive combinations of flavours used in the cuisine. There is a well equipped leisure centre and good conference facilities.
ROOMS: 55 en suite (bth/shr) (3 fmly) No smoking in 20 bedrooms s £58-£64; d £74-£80 * LB Off peak **MEALS:** Lunch £11.25 & alc Dinner £15-£22alc V meals Coffee am Tea pm **FACILITIES:** CTV in all bedrooms STV Indoor swimming pool (heated) Sauna Solarium Gym Jacuzzi/spa Beauty salon **CONF:** Thtr 140 Class 40 Board 40 Del from £94 * **SERVICES:** Night porter 120P **NOTES:** No smoking in restaurant Last d 9.30pm **CARDS:**

STOCKTON-ON-TEES Co Durham — Map 08 NZ41
★★★ *Posthouse Teeside*
low Ln, Stainton Village, Thornaby TS17 9LW
Quality Percentage Score: 66%
☎ 01642 591213 01642 594989
Dir: *off A19 onto A174, then B1380 towards Stainton Village, 2nd exit at rdbt towards Stainton Village again, hotel is on right*
A large modern hotel situated in spacious open grounds on the A1044 close to its junction with the A19, south east of the town. Bedrooms are of a particularly good standard and include several of "Millennium" style as well as executive and family rooms. The menu in "Seasons" restaurant provides a good choice of dishes, consistent with the brand, but additionally supplements the choice with a daily special.
ROOMS: 136 en suite (bth/shr) (10 fmly) No smoking in 87 bedrooms **MEALS:** International Cuisine V meals Coffee am Tea pm **FACILITIES:** CTV in all bedrooms **CONF:** Thtr 120 Class 60 Board 70 **SERVICES:** Night porter 250P **NOTES:** No smoking area in restaurant Last d 10.00pm **CARDS:**

STOCKTON-ON-TEES Co Durham — Map 08 NZ41
★★ Claireville
519 Yarm Rd, Eaglescliffe TS16 9BG
Quality Percentage Score: 67%
☎ 01642 780378 01642 784109
Dir: *on A135 adjacent to Eaglescliffe Golf Course, between Stockton-On-Tees and Yarm*
A family-run hotel with comfortable, pleasantly furnished bedrooms. There is a cosy bar-lounge and attractive dining room which offers a reasonably priced carte. A delightful conservatory has been added to the rear, providing extra function and lounge facilities.
ROOMS: 18 en suite (bth/shr) (2 fmly) No smoking in 4 bedrooms s £36-£46; d £46-£56 (incl. bkfst) * Off peak **MEALS:** Lunch fr £10.65 Dinner fr £11.65 & alc English & French Cuisine V meals Coffee am Tea pm **FACILITIES:** CTV in all bedrooms STV **CONF:** Thtr 40 Class 20 Board 25 **SERVICES:** 30P **NOTES:** Last d 8.30pm RS Xmas & New Year **CARDS:**

STOCKTON-ON-TEES Co Durham — Map 08 NZ41
Travel Inn
Yarm Rd TS18 3RT
☎ 01642 633354 01642 633339
Dir: *junc A66/A135*
This modern building offers accommodation in smart, spacious and well equipped bedrooms, all with en-suite bathrooms. Refreshments may be taken at the nearby family restaurant. For details about current prices consult the Contents Page under Hotel Groups for the Travel Inn phone number.
ROOMS: 40 en suite (bth/shr) d £39.95 *

STOCKTON-ON-TEES Co Durham — Map 08 NZ41
Travel Inn (Thornaby)
Whitewater Way, Thornaby TS17 6QB
☎ 01642 671573 01642 671464
Dir: *off A66, adjacent to Canoe Slalom Centre*
This modern building offers accommodation in smart, spacious and well equipped bedrooms, all with en-suite bathrooms. Refreshments may be taken at the nearby family restaurant. For details about current prices consult the Contents Page under Hotel Groups for the Travel Inn phone number.
ROOMS: 40 en suite (bth/shr) d £39.95 *

STOKE D'ABERNON Surrey — Map 04 TQ15
★★★★ Woodlands Park
Woodlands Ln KT11 3QB
Quality Percentage Score: 66%
☎ 01372 843933 01372 842704
Dir: *from A3 towards London, exit at Cobham. Through town centre & Stoke D'Abernon, left at garden centre into Woodlands Ln, hotel 0.5m on right*

A Victorian mansion with impressive Grand Hall. Versatile conference rooms make this a popular venue. Eating options are Langtry's Bar & Brasserie, and fine dining in the Oak Room Restaurant. Most bedrooms are refurbished and thoughtful extras, such as a turndown service, are welcome.
ROOMS: 59 en suite (bth/shr) (4 fmly) No smoking in 9 bedrooms s £125-£255; d £155-£255 * LB Off peak **MEALS:** Lunch fr £18.95 & alc Dinner £25.50 & alc European Cuisine V meals Coffee am Tea pm **FACILITIES:** CTV in all bedrooms STV Tennis (hard) Croquet lawn Xmas **CONF:** Thtr 280 Class 100 Board 50 Del from £185 * **SERVICES:** Lift Night porter 150P **NOTES:** No dogs (ex guide dogs) No smoking area in restaurant Last d 10pm **CARDS:**

contd.

STOKE GABRIEL Devon **Map 03 SX85**

★★★ Gabriel Court
TQ9 6SF
Quality Percentage Score: 71%
☎ 01803 782206 📠 01803 782333
Dir: *off A38 down the A384 onto the A385 towards Paignton, turn right by the Parkers Arms, follow road down until reaching Stoke Gabriel*
A charming old house, mainly Victorian in character and set in lovely gardens, is a comfortable, civilised hotel, with elegant reception rooms and individually designed bedrooms which retain a sense of period.
ROOMS: 19 en suite (bth/shr) s fr £55; d fr £79 (incl. bkfst) * Off peak **MEALS:** Sunday Lunch fr £13 Dinner fr £26 Coffee am Tea pm **FACILITIES:** CTV in all bedrooms Outdoor swimming pool (heated) Tennis (grass) Croquet lawn ch fac Xmas **CONF:** Thtr 20 Board 20 Del from £110 * **SERVICES:** 20P **NOTES:** No coaches No smoking in restaurant Last d 8.30pm **CARDS:**

STOKENCHURCH Buckinghamshire **Map 04 SU79**

★★★ *The Kings Arms*
Oxford Rd HP12 3TA
Quality Percentage Score: 67%
☎ 01494 609090 📠 01494 484582
Dir: *junct 5 of M40 turn right over motorway bridge, hotel 600yds on the left*
Conveniently located just a few minutes from J5 of the M40. Rooms are smartly decorated and well equipped for the business guest. Public areas include a busy bar offering an extensive range of hot and cold dishes, and a more formal restaurant and several conference rooms.
ROOMS: 43 en suite (bth/shr) (3 fmly) No smoking in 22 bedrooms **MEALS:** V meals Coffee am Tea pm **FACILITIES:** CTV in all bedrooms STV **CONF:** Thtr 150 Class 80 Board 50 **SERVICES:** Lift Night porter Air conditioning 95P **NOTES:** No dogs (ex guide dogs) No smoking in restaurant **CARDS:**

STOKE-ON-TRENT Staffordshire **Map 07 SJ84**

see also **Newcastle-under-Lyme**

★★★★ *Stoke-on-Trent Moat House*
Etruria Hall, Festival Way, Etruria ST1 5BQ
Quality Percentage Score: 64%
☎ 01782 609988 📠 01782 284500
Dir: *from M6 take A500, leave A500 at Brown tourist info signs for Festival Park, hotel is situated on the Festival Park*
A large modern hotel located in Stoke's Festival Park, that adjoins Etruria Hall, the former home of Josiah Wedgwood. The bedrooms are spacious and well equipped and include family rooms, no-smoking rooms, suites and executive rooms. Other facilities include a business centre and a leisure club.
ROOMS: 143 en suite (bth/shr) (42 fmly) No smoking in 100 bedrooms **MEALS:** International Cuisine V meals Coffee am Tea pm **FACILITIES:** CTV in all bedrooms STV Indoor swimming pool (heated) Snooker Sauna Solarium Gym Pool table Jacuzzi/spa Leisure club Dance studio Residential beautician **CONF:** Thtr 600 Class 250 Board 30 **SERVICES:** Lift Night porter 350P **NOTES:** No dogs (ex guide dogs) Last d 10pm **CARDS:**

STOKE-ON-TRENT Staffordshire **Map 07 SJ84**

★★★ George
Swan Square, Burslem ST6 2AE
Quality Percentage Score: 69%
☎ 01782 577544 📠 01782 837496
Dir: *take A53 towards Leek, turn left at 1st set of traffic lights onto A50, follow road to Burslem centre, George hotel is on right*
This soundly maintained and friendly hotel is situated in the centre of Burslem, close to the Royal Doulton factory. It provides well equipped modern accommodation, which is equally suitable for business people and tourists. A good choice of dishes is available in the elegant restaurant. In addition to the spacious lounge bar, there is a comfortable lounge for residents, a choice of function rooms, plus a large ballroom.
ROOMS: 39 en suite (bth/shr) (5 fmly) **MEALS:** Lunch £9.95-£10.95 Dinner £12.95-£15.95 & alc English & Continental Cuisine V meals Coffee am Tea pm **FACILITIES:** CTV in all bedrooms STV Wkly live entertainment **CONF:** Thtr 180 Class 150 Board 60 Del from £80 * **SERVICES:** Lift Night porter 28P **NOTES:** No dogs (ex guide dogs) Last d 9.30pm **CARDS:**

STOKE-ON-TRENT Staffordshire **Map 07 SJ84**

★★★ North Stafford
Station Rd, Winton Square ST4 2AE
Quality Percentage Score: 68%
☎ 01782 744477 📠 01782 744580
Dir: *follow signs for Railway Station and hotel is directly opposite*
This modernised Victorian hotel stands opposite the railway station. Bedrooms retain much of their historic character. The Clayhanger Bar, named after one of Arnold Bennett's famous novels, displays memorabilia of the pottery industry, and there is also a pleasant restaurant.
ROOMS: 80 en suite (bth/shr) (8 fmly) s £95-£105; d £105-£115 * LB Off peak **MEALS:** Lunch £6.50-£9.50 Dinner £12.95-£17.95 & alc English/French Cuisine V meals Coffee am Tea pm **FACILITIES:** CTV in all bedrooms STV Pool table Xmas **CONF:** Thtr 450 Class 150 Board 85 Del from £85 * **SERVICES:** Lift Night porter 120P **NOTES:** No smoking area in restaurant Last d 9.30pm **CARDS:**

STOKE-ON-TRENT Staffordshire **Map 07 SJ84**

★★★ Haydon House
Haydon St, Basford ST4 6JD
Quality Percentage Score: 66%
☎ 01782 711311 📠 01782 717470
Dir: *from M6 junct 15 A500 to Stoke-on-Trent, turn onto A53 Hanley/Newcastle, at rdbt take 1st exit, go up hill, take 2nd left at top of hill,*
This Victorian property is within easy reach of Newcastle-under-Lyme town centre. Now a family run hotel, it has public rooms which have been furnished in a style befitting the age and character of the house. Facilities here include a choice of function rooms, including a new conference room. The hotel is also licensed for marriage ceremonies. The bedrooms all have modern furnishings, and several are located in a separate house across the road.
ROOMS: 17 en suite (bth/shr) 6 annexe en suite (bth/shr) (4 fmly) s £62-£77; d £79-£94 (incl. bkfst) * Off peak **MEALS:** Lunch fr £11.50 & alc Dinner fr £15.90 & alc English & French Cuisine V meals Coffee am Tea pm **FACILITIES:** CTV in all bedrooms **CONF:** Thtr 80 Class 25 Board 30 Del from £79 * **SERVICES:** 52P **NOTES:** Last d 9.30pm **CARDS:**

STONE Staffordshire **Map 07 SJ93**

★★★ Stone House
Stafford Rd ST15 0BQ
Quality Percentage Score: 63%
☎ 01785 815531 📠 01785 814764
Dir: *beside A34, 0.5m S of town centre*
Set in carefully landscaped grounds, this former country house has been extended by two modern wings, one for bedrooms, one

contd.

for leisure and banqueting facilities. The hotel offers convenient access to the M6.

ROOMS: 50 en suite (bth/shr) (1 fmly) No smoking in 33 bedrooms s £25-£85; d £95 * LB Off peak **MEALS:** Lunch £11.95 & alc European Cuisine V meals Coffee am Tea pm **FACILITIES:** CTV in all bedrooms STV Indoor swimming pool (heated) Tennis (hard) Sauna Solarium Gym Putting green Xmas **CONF:** Thtr 190 Class 60 Board 50 Del from £93.75 * **SERVICES:** Lift Night porter 120P **NOTES:** No dogs No smoking area in restaurant RS Sat **CARDS:**

See advert under GLOUCESTER

STONE Staffordshire — Map 07 SJ93

Travelodge

Eccleshall Rd ST15 0EU

01785 811188

Travelodge

***Dir:** between junc 14&15 M6 northbound only*

This modern building offers accommodation in smart, spacious and well equipped bedrooms, all with en-suite bathrooms. Refreshments may be taken at the nearby family restaurant. For details about current prices, consult the Contents Page under Hotel Groups for the Travelodge phone number.

ROOMS: 49 en suite (bth/shr) d £49.95 *

STON EASTON Somerset — Map 03 ST65

The Premier Collection

★★★★ Ston Easton Park

BA3 4DF

01761 241631 01761 241377

RELAIS & CHATEAUX

***Dir:** turn off A37 onto A39, hotel is one mile from junction in village of Ston Easton*

This Palladian mansion is set in extensive parkland and grounds with a river and man-made lake. The interior, painstakingly restored and refurbished, includes a saloon and a cosy library. Food is taken seriously, from breakfast croissants to excellent afternoon teas. Dinner offers a balanced menu of mainly traditional British cuisine.

ROOMS: 18 en suite (bth/shr) 2 annexe en suite (bth/shr) s £155-£195; d £185-£195 * LB Off peak **MEALS:** Lunch £11-£26 & alc Dinner fr £39.50 & alc English & French Cuisine V meals Coffee am Tea pm **FACILITIES:** CTV in all bedrooms Tennis (hard) Snooker Croquet lawn Hot air ballooning Archery Clay Shooting Horse riding Xmas **CONF:** Thtr 50 Class 25 Board 26 Del from £210 * **SERVICES:** 52P **NOTES:** No dogs (ex guide dogs) No children 7yrs No smoking in restaurant Last d 10pm **CARDS:**

STONEHOUSE Gloucestershire — Map 03 SO80

★★★ Stonehouse Court

GL10 3RA

Quality Percentage Score: 72%

01453 825155 01453 824611

***Dir:** off M5 at J13, follow signs for Stonehouse, hotel is on right hand side approx 0.25m after 2nd rdbt*

This Grade II listed manor house has been considerably extended, but has kept some period character in its day rooms. Bedrooms offer all modern comforts and include two with four-poster beds.

ROOMS: 9 en suite (bth/shr) 27 annexe en suite (bth/shr) (1 fmly) No smoking in 4 bedrooms s £84-£94; d £115-£125 (incl. bkfst) * LB Off peak **MEALS:** Lunch £12-£18 & alc High tea £7-£15alc Dinner £25-£30 & alc English & French Cuisine V meals Coffee am Tea pm **FACILITIES:** CTV in all bedrooms STV Fishing Pool table Croquet lawn Bowls Xmas **CONF:** Thtr 150 Class 75 Board 50 Del from £115 * **SERVICES:** Night porter 150P **NOTES:** No smoking in restaurant Last d 9.45pm **CARDS:**

See advert under GLOUCESTER

STONELEIGH Warwickshire — Map 04 SP37

Stoneleigh Park Lodge

The NAC Stoneleigh Park CV8 2LZ

024 7669 0123 024 7669 0789

MARSTON HOTELS

ROOMS: 58 en suite (bth/shr) (incl. cont bkfst) d fr £45 *

STONOR Oxfordshire — Map 04 SU78

★★★ Stonor Arms Hotel

RG9 6HE

Quality Percentage Score: 73%

01491 638866 01491 638863

***Dir:** off A4130 onto B480, hotel 3m on R in Stonor village*

Picturesque scenery and a pretty village set the scene for this small hotel which has bags of historic charm. The spacious bedrooms are well furnished and comfortable; there is a lounge where tea and pre-dinner drinks can be served, and also a bar

contd.

with a boating theme. Dinner can be enjoyed either in the conservatory or a more formal dining room.
ROOMS: 10 en suite (bth/shr) No smoking in 4 bedrooms s £95-£115; d £115-£140 (incl. bkfst) * LB Off peak **MEALS:** Lunch £18.50-£21 & alc Dinner £23.15-£37.70alc English & French Cuisine V meals Coffee am Tea pm **FACILITIES:** CTV in all bedrooms Xmas **CONF:** Thtr 20 Board 12 Del £150 * **SERVICES:** 27P **NOTES:** No coaches No smoking in restaurant Last d 9.30pm **CARDS:**

See advert on opposite page

STOURPORT-ON-SEVERN Worcestershire **Map 07 SO87**
★★★★ Stourport Manor
Hartlebury Rd DY13 9LT
Quality Percentage Score: 69%
☎ 0500 636943 (Central Res) 01773 880321
Dir: *E, off B4193*

Once the home of a former Prime Minister, Sir Stanley Baldwin, this hotel stands in extensive grounds on the eastern edge of town. Bedrooms all have the expected modern facilities and reception rooms are spacious and comfortable. Service is friendly and helpful.
ROOMS: 68 en suite (bth/shr) (4 fmly) No smoking in 25 bedrooms s £85-£95; d £95-£125 * LB Off peak **MEALS:** Lunch £8.95-£13 Dinner fr £19.95alc International Cuisine V meals Coffee am Tea pm **FACILITIES:** CTV in all bedrooms STV Indoor swimming pool (heated) Outdoor swimming pool (heated) Tennis (hard) Squash Sauna Solarium Gym Pool table Putting green Xmas **CONF:** Thtr 420 Class 120 Board 80 Del from £110 * **SERVICES:** Night porter 200P **NOTES:** No dogs (ex guide dogs) No smoking area in restaurant Last d 9.30pm
CARDS:

STOW CUM QUY Cambridgeshire **Map 05 TL56**
★★★ Cambridge Quy Mill Hotel
Newmarket Rd CB5 9AG
Quality Percentage Score: 69%
☎ 01223 293383 01223 293770
Dir: *turn off A14 at junct east of Cambridge onto B1102 for 50yds, hotel entrance opposite church*
Convenient for Cambridge city centre, this 19th-century former watermill is set in water meadows. Well designed public areas include several spacious bar and lounge areas and there are informal and formal eating areas. Bedrooms are smartly appointed and brightly decorated.
ROOMS: 22 en suite (bth/shr) (4 fmly) s £75-£100; d £90-£140 LB Off peak **MEALS:** Lunch £16.95 Dinner £15-£25alc International Cuisine V meals Coffee am Tea pm **FACILITIES:** CTV in all bedrooms STV Fishing Clay pigeon shooting **CONF:** Thtr 80 Class 25 Board 30 Del from £105 * **SERVICES:** Night porter 100P **NOTES:** No dogs (ex guide dogs) Last d 9.45pm Closed 26 Dec
CARDS:

STOWMARKET Suffolk **Map 05 TM05**
★★ Cedars
Needham Rd IP14 2AJ
Quality Percentage Score: 64%
☎ 01449 612668 01449 674704
Dir: *A1308 1m outside Stowmarket on road to Needham Market, close to junction with A1120*
Easily accessible on a main route, about a mile from the town centre, this convivial hotel combines historic charm, oak beams and open fireplaces in the public areas with modern facilities in its comfortable accommodation, located mainly in sympathetic extensions. The spacious restaurant and bar both offer a wide choice of appetising dishes, served by a friendly team.
ROOMS: 25 en suite (bth/shr) (4 fmly) s fr £42.50; d fr £48 (incl. bkfst) * LB Off peak **MEALS:** Lunch £5-£15alc Dinner £5-£15alc English & French Cuisine V meals Coffee am Tea pm **FACILITIES:** CTV in all bedrooms STV **CONF:** Thtr 160 Class 60 Board 60 Del from £65 * **SERVICES:** 75P **NOTES:** No smoking in restaurant Last d 10pm Closed 25 Dec-1 Jan **CARDS:**

STOWMARKET Suffolk **Map 05 TM05**
Travelodge
IP14 3PY
☎ 01449 615347 01449 615347
Dir: *on A14 westbound*
This modern building offers accommodation in smart, spacious and well equipped bedrooms, all with en-suite bathrooms. Refreshments may be taken at the nearby family restaurant. For details about current prices, consult the Contents Page under Hotel Groups for the Travelodge phone number.
ROOMS: 40 en suite (bth/shr) d £39.95 *

STOW-ON-THE-WOLD Gloucestershire **Map 04 SP12**
★★★★ Wyck Hill House
Burford Rd GL54 1HY
Quality Percentage Score: 71%
☎ 01451 831936 01451 832243
Dir: *1.5m SE on A424*
Set in 100 acres of woodlands and gardens, this delightful 18th-century house enjoys superb views across the Windrush Valley. The spacious and thoughtfully equipped bedrooms are divided between the main house and the original coach house. An open fire burns in the magnificent front hall and there is a cosy bar in the restaurant.

ROOMS: 16 en suite (bth/shr) 16 annexe en suite (bth/shr) s fr £105; d fr £150 (incl. bkfst) * LB Off peak **MEALS:** Lunch £13.50-£19.95 High tea £32-£35.50alc British & French Cuisine V meals Coffee am Tea pm **FACILITIES:** CTV in all bedrooms STV Croquet lawn Archery Clay pigeon shooting Ballooning Xmas **CONF:** Thtr 40 Class 20 Board 20 Del from £150 * **SERVICES:** Lift Night porter 100P **NOTES:** No smoking in restaurant **CARDS:**

STOW-ON-THE-WOLD Gloucestershire **Map 04 SP12**

★★★ Fosse Manor

GL54 1JX
Quality Percentage Score: 74%
☎ 01451 830354 Fax 01451 832486
Dir: *1m S on A429, 300yds past junction with A424*

This welcoming Cotswold Stone house sits in six acres of grounds, the friendly staff are attentive and efficient. Bedrooms are individually styled, some suitable for families and one with a four-poster bed. Guests enjoy an appealing lounge, cheerful bar serving a wide range of meals, and a restaurant offering imaginative cooking. Croquet, giant chess, a golf driving range, function room and beauty salon are also available.

ROOMS: 13 en suite (bth/shr) 3 annexe en suite (bth/shr) (3 fmly) s £49-£80; d fr £118 (incl. bkfst) * LB Off peak **MEALS:** Lunch £12.50-£15.50 High tea fr £6.50 Dinner fr £25 & alc English & Continental Cuisine V meals Coffee am Tea pm **FACILITIES:** CTV in 17 bedrooms Croquet lawn Beautician Golf practice net ch fac **CONF:** Thtr 40 Class 20 Board 20 Del from £125 * **SERVICES:** 40P **NOTES:** No smoking in restaurant Last d 9.30pm Closed 23 Dec-4 Jan
CARDS:

STOW-ON-THE-WOLD Gloucestershire **Map 04 SP12**

★★★ Grapevine

Sheep St GL54 1AU
Quality Percentage Score: 74%
☎ 01451 830344 Fax 01451 832278
Dir: *on A436 towards Chipping Norton. 150 yds on right, facing green*

Named after the gnarled old Hamburg vine growing in the Conservatory Restaurant, this 17th-century hotel draws its many loyal guests to stay again and again. Its bedrooms vary in style, but all are charming and comfortable, with some displaying historic features, such as beamed ceilings. Accomplished cooking is offered in the restaurant, with a more informal, brasserie-style menu in the bar.

ROOMS: 12 en suite (bth/shr) 10 annexe en suite (bth/shr) (2 fmly) No smoking in all bedrooms s £73.50-£94.50; d £110-£130 * LB Off peak **MEALS:** Lunch £14.95-£20.40 Dinner £26-£32 V meals Coffee am Tea pm **FACILITIES:** CTV in all bedrooms Xmas **CONF:** Thtr 30 Class 18 Board 20 Del from £115 * **SERVICES:** 23P **NOTES:** No dogs (ex guide dogs) No smoking in restaurant Last d 9.15pm
CARDS:

STOW-ON-THE-WOLD Gloucestershire **Map 04 SP12**

★★★ Stow Lodge

The Square GL54 1AB
Quality Percentage Score: 66%
☎ 01451 830485 Fax 831671
Dir: *in town centre*

Set in large grounds, this family-run hotel has direct access to the market square. It offers comfortable accommodation in traditionally styled bedrooms, some in a converted coach house, and good home cooking.

ROOMS: 11 en suite (bth/shr) 10 annexe en suite (bth/shr) (2 fmly) No smoking in all bedrooms s £50-£100; d £70-£120 (incl. bkfst) LB Off peak **MEALS:** Sunday Lunch £13.50-£21.50alc Dinner £16.75-£18.50 & alc V meals **FACILITIES:** CTV in all bedrooms **SERVICES:** Night porter 30P **NOTES:** No dogs No coaches No children 5yrs No smoking in restaurant Last d 9pm Closed Xmas & Jan **CARDS:**

STOW-ON-THE-WOLD Gloucestershire **Map 04 SP12**

★★★ The Unicorn

Sheep St GL54 1HQ
Quality Percentage Score: 65%
☎ 01451 830257 Fax 01451 831090
Dir: *situated at the junct of A429 & A436*

This busy hotel has kept much of its original, 17th-century character, while offering accommodation equipped to modern standards of comfort. Bedrooms are individual in style, and brightly decorated.

ROOMS: 20 en suite (bth/shr) No smoking in 6 bedrooms s £60-£70; d £105-£120 (incl. bkfst) * LB Off peak **MEALS:** Bar Lunch £5.95-£6.25alc V meals Coffee am Tea pm **FACILITIES:** CTV in all bedrooms Xmas **CONF:** Thtr 50 Board 24 Del from £110 * **SERVICES:** 60P **NOTES:** No smoking in restaurant
CARDS:

> Indicates that the star classification has not been confirmed under the New Quality Standards, see page 7 for further information.

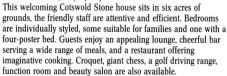

STOW-ON-THE-WOLD Gloucestershire **Map 04 SP12**
★★❀ Old Farmhouse
Lower Swell GL54 1LF
Quality Percentage Score: 70%
☎ 01451 830232 0800 0561150 Fax 01451 870962
Dir: *1m W on B4068*

Pleasantly off the beaten track, this 16th-century farmhouse and its buildings have been converted to provide delightful accommodation, full of character. The food is good and the bar keeps an extensive range of malt whisky.
ROOMS: 6 rms (4 bth/shr) 7 annexe en suite (bth/shr) (3 fmly) No smoking in 6 bedrooms s £31-£74; d £47-£113 (incl. bkfst) * LB Off peak **MEALS:** Sunday Lunch £9.99-£15 High tea £5 Dinner £10.75 V meals Coffee am Tea pm **FACILITIES:** CTV in all bedrooms STV Air pistol hire available Xmas **CONF:** Thtr 30 Board 8 Del from £50 * **SERVICES:** 25P **NOTES:** No smoking in restaurant Last d 9pm
CARDS:

See advert on opposite page

STOW-ON-THE-WOLD Gloucestershire **Map 04 SP12**
★★ Old Stocks
The Square GL54 1AF
Quality Percentage Score: 70%
☎ 01451 830666 Fax 01451 870014
At the heart of the old market square, this historic building has plenty of original charm with its stone walls and beamed ceilings. The lounge, restaurant and bar are tastefully furnished, offering attractive, comfortable areas in which to relax, and the bedrooms are well maintained.
ROOMS: 15 en suite (bth/shr) 3 annexe en suite (bth/shr) (1 fmly) No smoking in 10 bedrooms s £40-£70; d fr £80 (incl. bkfst) * LB Off peak **MEALS:** Sunday Lunch £12 Dinner £17.25 English, Italian and French Cuisine V meals Coffee am Tea pm **FACILITIES:** CTV in all bedrooms ch fac Xmas **SERVICES:** 14P **NOTES:** No smoking in restaurant Last d 9.30pm Closed 18-27 Dec **CARDS:**

STOW-ON-THE-WOLD Gloucestershire **Map 04 SP12**
★★ Royalist
Digbeth St GL54 1BN
Quality Percentage Score: 67%
☎ 01451 830670 Fax 01451 870048
Dir: *turn off A429 onto A436*
The oldest building in Stow, this friendly family-run hotel has a wealth of history and character. Public areas and the charming bedrooms are freshly decorated and look bright and cheerful. Guests have a choice of eating either in the restaurant or the bar.
ROOMS: 8 en suite (bth/shr) 4 annexe en suite (shr) (2 fmly) No smoking in 6 bedrooms s fr £40; d fr £60 (incl. bkfst) * LB Off peak **MEALS:** Lunch fr £10.50alc Dinner fr £15alc French & Spanish Cuisine V meals Coffee am Tea pm **FACILITIES:** CTV in all bedrooms **CONF:** Board 10 Del from £55 * **SERVICES:** 12P **NOTES:** No smoking in restaurant Last d 9.30pm **CARDS:**

STRATFIELD TURGIS Hampshire **Map 04 SU65**
★★★ Wellington Arms
RG27 0AS
Quality Percentage Score: 65%
☎ 01256 882214 Fax 01256 882934
Dir: *A33 between Basingstoke & Reading*
Situated at one of the entrances to the ancestral home of the Duke of Wellington, the white Georgian facade is a familiar landmark. The bar-lounge offers seating around a log fire and an extensive selection of bar meals while the restaurant offers both fixed-price and carte menus. The majority of bedrooms are located in the purpose-built Garden Wing and offer every modern convenience, rooms in the original building are equipped to the same standard but tend to be smaller.
ROOMS: 35 en suite (bth/shr) (2 fmly) No smoking in 3 bedrooms s £55-£100; d £65-£110 (incl. bkfst) * LB Off peak **MEALS:** Lunch £18-£25alc V meals Coffee am Tea pm **FACILITIES:** CTV in all bedrooms **CONF:** Thtr 100 Class 50 Board 40 Del from £130 * **SERVICES:** 150P
CARDS:

STRATFORD-UPON-AVON Warwickshire **Map 04 SP25**
★★★★❀❀ *Welcombe Hotel and Golf Course*
Warwick Rd CV37 0NR
Quality Percentage Score: 72%
☎ 01789 295252 Fax 01789 414666
Dir: *1.5m NE of Stratford on A439*
This Jacobean manor house is set in 800 acres of attractively landscaped parkland, part of which was once owned by Shakespeare. A friendly team of staff offer traditional standards of service in a professional and caring manner. The public rooms are attractive, the lounge looking particularly magnificent with its wood panelling and ornate black marble fireplace. In the light airy dining room chef Mark Naylor offers accomplished cooking from an interesting menu. Bedrooms are divided between the modern garden wing and the original house; each room is thoughtfully equipped and most of the bedrooms have delightful views out over the formal gardens.
ROOMS: 67 en suite (bth/shr) (2 fmly) **MEALS:** French & English Cuisine V meals Coffee am Tea pm **FACILITIES:** CTV in all bedrooms STV Golf 18 Tennis (hard) Snooker Solarium Gym Putting green Table tennis **CONF:** Thtr 120 Class 55 Board 26 **SERVICES:** Night porter 210P **NOTES:** No dogs (ex guide dogs) No smoking in restaurant Last d 9.30pm **CARDS:**

See advert on opposite page

STRATFORD-UPON-AVON Warwickshire **Map 04 SP25**
★★★★ Stratford Manor
Marston Hotels
Warwick Rd CV37 0PY
Quality Percentage Score: 68%
☎ 01789 731173 Fax 01789 731131
Dir: *3m N of Stratford town centre on A439, or leave M40 junct 15, take Stratford-upon-Avon road, hotel is 2m on left*
This purpose built hotel with attractive murals, is set in extensive well-manicured grounds just outside Stratford. Bedrooms are spacious, and cater well for the business traveller with generous desk space and a wealth of extras, including in-house movies. There are excellent conference and meetings facilities and dedicated staff help ensure that events run smoothly. The attractive split-level restaurant offers meals prepared from fresh ingredients and the lounge bar serves as a

contd.

focal point. Energetic guests will enjoy the smart leisure centre with a hi-tech gym, and the tennis courts.
ROOMS: 103 en suite (bth/shr) (8 fmly) No smoking in 52 bedrooms s £94-£114; d £110-£130 * LB Off peak **MEALS:** Lunch fr £15.50 Dinner fr £25 & alc English & Continental Cuisine V meals Coffee am Tea pm **FACILITIES:** CTV in all bedrooms STV Indoor swimming pool (heated) Tennis (hard) Sauna Solarium Gym Pool table Jacuzzi/spa ch fac Xmas **CONF:** Thtr 360 Class 200 Board 100 **SERVICES:** Lift Night porter 220P **NOTES:** No smoking in restaurant Last d 10pm
CARDS:

STRATFORD-UPON-AVON Warwickshire **Map 04 SP25**
★★★★ Stratford Victoria
Arden St CV37 6QQ
Quality Percentage Score: 68%
☎ 01789 271000 01789 271001
Dir: *A439 into Stratford, in town follow A3400 Birmingham, at traffic light junct turn left into Arden St, the hotel is 150yds on right hand side*

This new hotel has enthusiastic and friendly young staff. Open plan public areas include a lounge and a restaurant which also operates a popular weekend carvery. There is a fitness room, jacuzzi and use of Stratford's leisure centre. Bedrooms are spacious and comfortably equipped. Conference facilities and extensive parking are an asset.
ROOMS: 100 en suite (bth/shr) (35 fmly) No smoking in 40 bedrooms s £87.50-£92.50; d £107.50-£125 (incl. bkfst) LB Off peak **MEALS:** Lunch £14.50-£16.50 & alc Dinner £19.50-£22.50 & alc English & Continental Cuisine V meals Coffee am Tea pm **FACILITIES:** CTV in all bedrooms STV Gym Jacuzzi/spa Beauty Salon **CONF:** Thtr 110 Class 66 Board 54 Del from £120 **SERVICES:** Lift Night porter 96P **NOTES:** No smoking in restaurant Last d 9.45pm **CARDS:**

STRATFORD-UPON-AVON Warwickshire **Map 04 SP25**
★★★★ *Billesley Manor*
MOAT HOUSE
Billesley, Alcester B49 6NF
Quality Percentage Score: 67%
☎ 01789 279955 01789 764145
This 16th-century manor is set in peaceful grounds and parkland with a delightful topiary garden. The spacious bedrooms and suites, most in traditional country house style, are thoughtfully designed and well equipped. The public areas have undergone refurbishment and many original features, such as oak panelling and magnificent fireplaces, have been retained. The kitchen brigade continue to produce a range of interesting rosette worthy dishes.
ROOMS: 41 en suite (bth/shr) (6 fmly) No smoking in 5 bedrooms **MEALS:** English & French Cuisine V meals Coffee am Tea pm **FACILITIES:** CTV in all bedrooms Indoor swimming pool (heated) Tennis (hard) Croquet lawn Putting green Croquet Pitch & putt **CONF:** Thtr 100 Class 60 Board 40 Del from £174 * **SERVICES:** Night porter 100P **NOTES:** No dogs (ex guide dogs) No smoking in restaurant Last d 9.30pm RS Sat **CARDS:**
See advert on page 625

S

STRATFORD-UPON-AVON Warwickshire   **Map 04 SP25**
★★★★⧉ **The Shakespeare**
Chapel St CV37 6ER
Quality Percentage Score: 66%
☎ 01789 294771 📠 01789 415411
Dir: adjoining town hall

Right in the heart of the town, this 18th-century hotel is a landmark site with its gabled timber façade. Public rooms are full of charm with a profusion of exposed beams, creaking staircases and open fires. Bedrooms vary in size but provide modern comforts; an annexe wing of bedrooms is new this year. The quality cooking of Chef Gordon Inglis combines traditional and modern trends through an interesting carte; informal dining is also available in the bistro which adjoins the hotel.

ROOMS: 74 en suite (bth/shr) No smoking in 20 bedrooms s £110; d £150-£180 * LB Off peak **MEALS:** Lunch £9.50-£15.50 Dinner £18-£21 International Cuisine V meals Coffee am Tea pm **FACILITIES:** CTV in all bedrooms Xmas **CONF:** Thtr 120 Class 50 Board 40 **SERVICES:** Lift Night porter 34P **NOTES:** No smoking in restaurant Last d 9.30pm
CARDS: 🔵 ■ ⌦ 🖭 🅲

STRATFORD-UPON-AVON Warwickshire   **Map 04 SP25**
★★★★⧉ **The Alveston Manor**
Clopton Bridge CV37 7HP
Quality Percentage Score: 65%
☎ 01789 204581 📠 01789 414095
Dir: South of Clopton Bridge

A striking red brick and wooden facade, well tended grounds, and a giant cedar tree all contribute to the charm of this well established hotel. Bedrooms vary in size and character, but all provide modern comforts - the recent conversion of a coach house offers an impressive mix of comfortable full and junior suites. The Manor Grill menu, based on popular traditional choices, operates mid-week whilst a set price menu is offered at the weekend. Service is friendly and willing.

ROOMS: 114 en suite (bth/shr) No smoking in 30 bedrooms s £110; d £140-£180 * LB Off peak **MEALS:** Lunch £7.50-£14.50 Dinner £18-£26.50 V meals Coffee am Tea pm **FACILITIES:** CTV in all bedrooms STV Xmas **CONF:** Thtr 140 Class 80 Board 40 **SERVICES:** Night porter 200P **NOTES:** No smoking in restaurant Last d 9.30pm
CARDS: 🔵 ■ ⌦ 🖭 🅲

STRATFORD-UPON-AVON Warwickshire   **Map 04 SP25**
★★★★ *Stratford Moat House*
Bridgefoot CV37 6YR
Quality Percentage Score: 65%
☎ 01789 279988 📠 01789 298589
Dir: adjoining Stratford Leisure Centre

Located next to the River Avon, yet a stone's throw from the town centre, this large, modern hotel is popular with both business guests and overseas groups. There is a choice of restaurants and bars, an attractive garden, and a riverside terrace and the manned business centre is a bonus. Guests can take advantage of the well-equipped gym which overlooks the river.

ROOMS: 247 en suite (bth/shr) (8 fmly) No smoking in 91 bedrooms **MEALS:** European Cuisine V meals Coffee am Tea pm **FACILITIES:** CTV in all bedrooms Indoor swimming pool (heated) Fishing Snooker Sauna Solarium Gym Pool table Jacuzzi/spa Beautician Hair stylist Video games room ch fac **CONF:** Thtr 450 Class 260 Board 100 **SERVICES:** Lift Night porter Air conditioning 350P **NOTES:** No smoking area in restaurant Last d 11pm **CARDS:** 🔵 ■ ⌦ 🖭 🅲

STRATFORD-UPON-AVON Warwickshire   **Map 04 SP25**
★★★⧉⧉ **Salford Hall**
WR11 5UT
Quality Percentage Score: 75%
☎ 01386 871300 📠 01386 871301
(For full entry see Abbot's Salford)

STRATFORD-UPON-AVON Warwickshire   **Map 04 SP25**
★★★⧉ **Grosvenor House**
Warwick Rd CV37 6YT
Quality Percentage Score: 70%
☎ 01789 269213 📠 01789 266087
Dir: turn off jct 15 on M40 follow Stratford signs to A439 Warwick Rd, hotel is 7m from jct on town centre one way system

Grosvenor House is located on the Warwick road, a short distance from the town centre and many of the historic attractions. Staff are both friendly and efficient, and useful services, such as an all-day menu of refreshments in the lounge, and room service, are readily available. The Garden Room restaurant, with its hand-painted murals, offers a choice of interesting modern dishes from set priced and carte menus. Bedroom styles and sizes vary; the most recent wing of new rooms are spacious and cheerfully appointed, with smart modern bathrooms.

ROOMS: 67 en suite (bth/shr) (1 fmly) No smoking in 5 bedrooms s £75; d £85 * LB Off peak **MEALS:** Lunch £15.50 & alc Dinner £15.50 & alc English & Continental Cuisine V meals Coffee am Tea pm **FACILITIES:** CTV in all bedrooms Xmas **CONF:** Thtr 100 Class 50 Board 40 Del from £105 * **SERVICES:** Night porter 53P **NOTES:** No dogs (ex guide dogs) Last d 9.30pm **CARDS:** 🔵 ■ ⌦ 🖭 🖭 🕦 🅲

STRATFORD-UPON-AVON Warwickshire   **Map 04 SP25**
★★★ **The Falcon**
Chapel St CV37 6HA
Quality Percentage Score: 66%
☎ 01789 279953 📠 01789 414260
Dir: town centre-opposite Guild Chapel and Nash House

Situated in the heart of the town this traditional inn provides a choice of bars, a sun lounge, pretty gardens and a modern brasserie style restaurant. Well equipped bedrooms vary in style; the older, beamed rooms in the original section are smaller but have their own charm.

ROOMS: 73 en suite (bth/shr) 11 annexe en suite (bth/shr) (13 fmly) No smoking in 38 bedrooms s £80-£105; d £105-£135 LB Off peak **MEALS:** Lunch £9.95-£15.50 & alc High tea £4.95-£7 Dinner £9.95-£15.50 & alc European Cuisine V meals Coffee am Tea pm **FACILITIES:** CTV in all bedrooms Xmas **CONF:** Thtr 200 Class 110 Board 40 Del from £100 * **SERVICES:** Lift Night porter 124P **NOTES:** No smoking area in restaurant Last d 9pm **CARDS:** 🔵 ■ ⌦ 🖭 🖭 🕦 🅲

STRATFORD-UPON-AVON Warwickshire **Map 04 SP25**

★★★ The Swan's Nest

Bridgefoot CV37 7LT
Quality Percentage Score: 65%
☎ 0870 400 8182 📠 01789 414547

Dir: *from M40 junct 15,A46 to Stratford,leave at 1st rdbt A439 to town centre,entering town follow one way system left over river bridge hotel by river*

The original part of this hotel, which has its own river frontage, dates back to the 17th century and is only a short walk from The Royal Shakespeare Theatre and the town centre. Most bedrooms are in a more modern wing and include several in the new millennium design, executive rooms and those in traditional Posthouse style. Extended lounge and room service is a feature of the hotel supplementing the wide ranging menu in "Seasons Restaurant". There is also a courtyard garden, ideal for weddings and outdoor activities, a number of meeting and conference rooms and a large car park.

ROOMS: 68 en suite (bth/shr) (3 fmly) No smoking in 30 bedrooms s £85-£115; d £85-£135 * LB Off peak **MEALS:** Lunch £5.95-£12.50 Dinner £18-£25 International Cuisine V meals Coffee am Tea pm **FACILITIES:** CTV in all bedrooms STV Xmas **CONF:** Thtr 150 Class 80 Board 50 **SERVICES:** Night porter 72P **NOTES:** No smoking area in restaurant Last d 9.30pm **CARDS:**

STRATFORD-UPON-AVON Warwickshire **Map 04 SP25**

★★★ Charlecote Pheasant

Charlecote CV35 9EW
Quality Percentage Score: 63%
☎ 01789 279954 📠 01789 470222

Dir: *leave M40 junc15, take A429 towards Cirencester through Barford village after 2m turn right into Charlecote, hotel opp Charlecote Manor Park*

Located just outside Stratford, this large complex is set in extensive grounds. There is a distinctly rustic feel to the public rooms, restaurant and bars. Bedrooms are well equipped and range from functional to quite luxurious.

ROOMS: 70 en suite (bth/shr) (2 fmly) No smoking in 26 bedrooms s £90-£120; d £105-£135 * LB Off peak **MEALS:** Lunch £6.95-£13.95 Dinner £16.95-£17.95 & alc International Cuisine V meals Coffee am Tea pm **FACILITIES:** CTV in all bedrooms Outdoor swimming pool (heated) Tennis (hard) Pool table Childrens Play area ch fac Xmas **CONF:** Thtr 160 Class 90 Board 50 Del from £110 * **SERVICES:** Night porter 100P **NOTES:** No dogs (ex guide dogs) No smoking in restaurant Last d 9.45pm **CARDS:**

AA Rosettes are awarded for quality of food, see page 15 for an explanation of Rosette assessment.

STRATFORD-UPON-AVON Warwickshire Map 04 SP25

★★★ The White Swan

Rother St CV37 6NH

Quality Percentage Score: 61%

☎ 01789 297022 Fax 01789 268773

Dir: *leave M40 junct15 signposted Stratford on Avon. Hotel is in the Market Square*

Right in the heart of the town, this half-timbered building has retained many of its original features and offers cosy, traditionally styled public areas. Bedrooms come in a variety of shapes and sizes; all are well equipped, and a few boast beamed ceilings.

ROOMS: 41 en suite (bth/shr) (3 fmly) No smoking in 16 bedrooms s £75; d £85 * LB Off peak **MEALS:** Sunday Lunch fr £11.95 & alc Dinner fr £14.95 European Cuisine V meals Coffee am Tea pm **FACILITIES:** CTV in all bedrooms Wkly live entertainment Xmas **CONF:** Thtr 30 Class 25 Board 25 Del from £99 * **SERVICES:** Night porter 9P **NOTES:** No smoking in restaurant Last d 9pm **CARDS:**

STRATFORD-UPON-AVON Warwickshire Map 04 SP25

★★ Stratford Court

Avenue Rd CV37 6UX

Quality Percentage Score: 73%

☎ 01789 297799 Fax 01789 262449

Dir: *Stratford town centre: follow one way system taking A439, 1st left after one way system into Welcombe Rd, continue to top. Stratford Court on right*

Stratford Court is a delightful Edwardian property in a quiet residential area of Stratford, close to the theatres and town centre. The atmosphere is very much one of informal friendliness in charming surroundings. Bedrooms have all been furnished and equipped to a very high standard with the use of some dramatic fabrics and furnishings; period pieces of furniture live in harmony with modern techniques such as rag rolling. The comfortable and tastefully furnished lounge and cosy bar are conducive to socialising, and the hands-on approach of the proprietors means guests quickly feel at home. Dining takes a back seat but is a useful standby for guests wishing to stay in rather than explore the town.

ROOMS: 13 en suite (bth/shr) (2 fmly) s £55-£65; d £95-£150 (incl. bkfst) Off peak **MEALS:** Dinner £16.50 English, French & German Cuisine V meals Coffee am Tea pm **FACILITIES:** CTV in all bedrooms **SERVICES:** 20P **NOTES:** No coaches No children 14yrs No smoking in restaurant Last d 8pm **CARDS:**

Symbols and Abbreviations are listed and explained on pages 4 and 5

STRATFORD-UPON-AVON Warwickshire Map 04 SP25

★★ The Coach House Hotel

16-17 Warwick Rd CV37 6YW

Quality Percentage Score: 65%

☎ 01789 204109 Fax 01789 415916

Dir: *leave M40 junct 15. Follow A46 - Stratford. Exit next rdbt onto A439 - Town Centre. Hotel on the right, just after St Gregory's church*

Conveniently positioned for the town centre, this popular hotel provides well equipped bedrooms that are either in the main house or an adjacent annexe. There is a small lounge, a cellar bar and a restaurant. Residents have free use of the leisure centre just a few minutes' walk away.

ROOMS: 10 en suite (bth/shr) 11 annexe rms (10 bth/shr) (3 fmly) No smoking in 14 bedrooms s £50-£60; d £68-£79 (incl. bkfst) * LB Off peak **MEALS:** Sunday Lunch £10.95 & alc Dinner £12.50 & alc English, Continental & Irish Cuisine V meals **FACILITIES:** CTV in all bedrooms Whirlpool bath (2 rms) Local Leisure centre free to guests Wkly live entertainment Xmas **CONF:** Board 10 Del from £82.50 * **SERVICES:** 30P **NOTES:** No dogs (ex guide dogs) No smoking in restaurant Last d 9.30pm **CARDS:**

See advert on opposite page

STRATFORD-UPON-AVON Warwickshire Map 04 SP25

Thistle Stratford-upon-Avon

Waterside CV37 6BA

☎ 01789 294949 Fax 01789 415874

Dir: *follow town centre signs turn left into High Street from Bridge Street then 2nd left into Chapel Lane*

This hotel is at the water's edge opposite the Royal Shakespeare and Swan theatres. Architectural restraints limit the size of the public rooms but they are cosy and pleasing to use, especially the Theatre bar and elegant restaurant, serving interesting menus. Bedrooms have period-style furnishings but are not overly spacious, executive rooms offer more comfort.

ROOMS: 63 en suite (bth/shr) (2 fmly) No smoking in 25 bedrooms **MEALS:** English & Continental Cuisine V meals Coffee am Tea pm **FACILITIES:** CTV in all bedrooms STV **CONF:** Thtr 60 Class 22 Board 30 **SERVICES:** Night porter 70P **NOTES:** No dogs (ex guide dogs) No smoking in restaurant Last d 9.30pm **CARDS:**

STREATLEY Berkshire Map 04 SU58

★★★★ Swan Diplomat

High St RG8 9HR

Quality Percentage Score: 69%

☎ 01491 878800 Fax 01491 872554

Dir: *M4 junct12 towards Theale, at 2nd rdbt A340 to Pangbourne, A329 to Streatley. Right at 1st traffic lights, hotel 200yds on left, before bridge*

The Swan Diplomat has the perfect riverside location for the quintessential English summer's day. Lounges and restaurant all look onto the superb gardens and river. Bedrooms are spacious and thoughtfully equipped, most enjoying the lovely views. The hotel is well suited to both leisure and business guests with several conference rooms and a modern leisure suite.

ROOMS: 46 en suite (bth/shr) No smoking in 2 bedrooms s £99-£125; d £135-£150 * LB Off peak **MEALS:** Lunch £18.50-£25 Dinner £32 & alc European Cuisine V meals Coffee am Tea pm **FACILITIES:** CTV in all bedrooms STV Sauna Solarium Gym Croquet lawn Jacuzzi/spa Exercise pool Boat hire Bicycle hire Steam room Xmas **CONF:** Thtr 80 Class 50 Board 40 Del from £159 * **SERVICES:** Night porter 135P **NOTES:** Last d 10pm **CARDS:**

See advert on opposite page

STREET Somerset **Map 03 ST43**

★★★ ***Wessex***

High St BA16 0EF

Quality Percentage Score: 62%

☎ 01458 443383 🖷 01458 446589

Dir: *from A303 follow road B3151 to Somerton and Street*

A purpose built hotel in the centre of town with ample parking, a short walk from Clarks village. Spacious bedrooms are equipped with modern facilities. Public areas include function rooms, a cosy bar, and a comfortable restaurant offering a fixed price menu and popular carvery.

ROOMS: 50 en suite (bth/shr) (2 fmly) No smoking in 24 bedrooms **MEALS:** V meals Coffee am Tea pm **FACILITIES:** CTV in all bedrooms STV **CONF:** Thtr 250 Class 150 Board 50 Del £65 * **SERVICES:** Lift Night porter 90P **NOTES:** No smoking in restaurant Last d 9.30pm

CARDS:

STRENSHAM MOTORWAY SERVICE AREA (M5) Worcestershire **Map 03 SO94**

Roadchef Lodge Strensham

WR8 0BZ

☎ 01684 293004 🖷 01684 295960

Dir: *0.5m N of junct 8 on M5*

This modern building offers accommodation in smart, spacious and well equipped bedrooms, all with en-suite bathrooms. Refreshments may be taken at the nearby family restaurant. For details about current prices, consult the Contents Page under Hotel Groups for the Roadchef phone number.

ROOMS: 48 en suite (bth/shr) s fr £47.50; d fr £47.50 * **CONF:** Class 18 Board 24

STRETTON Rutland **Map 08 SK91**

★★❀ **Ram Jam Inn**

Great North Rd LE15 7QX

Quality Percentage Score: 71%

☎ 01780 410776 🖷 01780 410361

Dir: *on 'N'bound carriageway of A1 past the B1668 turn off, thru service station into hotel carpark. 'S'bound take A668 - Oakham & follow signs under A1*

Bedrooms have cheerful soft furnishings and modern en suite bathrooms, and all but one overlook the rear garden and orchard of this informal roadside inn. Continental and English country house influences blend well together, with polished pine, terracotta floors and marble tops interspersed with deep sofas, elegant wall coverings and open fires.

ROOMS: 7 en suite (bth/shr) (1 fmly) s £45; d £55 * Off peak **MEALS:** English & Continental Cuisine V meals Coffee am Tea pm **FACILITIES:** CTV in all bedrooms **CONF:** Thtr 60 Class 40 Board 40 Del from £72.50 * **SERVICES:** 64P **NOTES:** Closed 25 Dec

CARDS:

STROUD Gloucestershire **Map 03 SO80**

see also **Amberley (Gloucestershire)**

★★★❀ **The Bear of Rodborough**

Rodborough Common GL5 5DE

Quality Percentage Score: 69%

☎ 01453 878522 🖷 01453 872523

Dir: *1m S on A46, turn left to Rodborough Common*

Situated at Rodborough Common, high above Stroud, this is a bear of character, with lounges, cocktail bar and elegant restaurant epitomising the inherent charm of the building. There is also a traditional and popular public bar. Food is good, and

contd.

based where possible on local produce, with the long list of local cheeses an interesting feature.
ROOMS: 46 en suite (bth/shr) (2 fmly) No smoking in 23 bedrooms s £65-£75; d £110-£120 (incl. bkfst) * LB Off peak **MEALS:** Bar Lunch £5.95-£6.25alc Dinner £19.95 V meals Coffee am Tea pm **FACILITIES:** CTV in all bedrooms Croquet lawn Xmas **CONF:** Thtr 60 Class 30 Board 30 Del from £115 * **SERVICES:** Night porter 122P **NOTES:** No smoking in restaurant Last d 9.30pm **CARDS:**

STROUD Gloucestershire **Map 03 SO80**

★★★ Burleigh Court

Minchinhampton GL5 2PF
Quality Percentage Score: 69%
☎ 01453 883804 01453 886870
Dir: *0.75m off A419 E of Stroud*

A charming manor house set in attractive grounds. Spacious public areas include a panelled bar, pleasant lounge and attractive restaurant serving well prepared, interesting food. Bedrooms are individually decorated, well equipped and split between the main house and adjoining coach house.
ROOMS: 11 en suite (bth/shr) 7 annexe en suite (bth/shr) (2 fmly) No smoking in 4 bedrooms s £87-£97; d £130-£150 (incl. bkfst & dinner) * LB Off peak **MEALS:** Lunch £13.95-£19.50 High tea £5-£10 Dinner £22.50-£36 British & Continental Cuisine V meals Coffee am Tea pm **FACILITIES:** CTV in all bedrooms Outdoor swimming pool (heated) Putting green Xmas **CONF:** Thtr 60 Board 16 Del from £115 * **SERVICES:** 41P **NOTES:** No coaches No smoking in restaurant Last d 9pm **CARDS:**

STROUD Gloucestershire **Map 03 SO80**

★★ The Bell

Wallbridge GL5 3JA
Quality Percentage Score: 64%
☎ 01453 763556 01453 758611
Dir: *at junct of A419/A46*

Close to the town centre, this friendly small hotel offers well equipped modern accommodation and caters well for business guests and tourists. There is good home-cooking and a small meeting room.
ROOMS: 12 en suite (bth/shr) (1 fmly) s £32-£45; d £45-£60 (incl. bkfst) * LB Off peak **MEALS:** Lunch fr £15alc Dinner fr £15alc Continental Cuisine V meals Coffee am **FACILITIES:** CTV in all bedrooms STV Pool table Xmas **CONF:** Thtr 35 Class 20 Board 16 **SERVICES:** 30P **NOTES:** No smoking in restaurant Last d 8.45pm **CARDS:**

S

STROUD Gloucestershire **Map 03 SO80**

Travelodge

A 419 Easington, Stonehouse GL10 3SQ
☎ 01962 760779

This modern building offers accommodation in smart, spacious and well equipped bedrooms, all with en-suite bathrooms. Refreshments may be taken at the nearby family restaurant. For details about current prices, consult the Contents Page under Hotel Groups for the Travelodge phone number.
ROOMS: 40 en suite (bth/shr) d £45.95 *

STUDLAND Dorset **Map 04 SZ08**

★★ Manor House

BH19 3AU
Quality Percentage Score: 67%
☎ 01929 450288 01929 450288
Dir: *via Bournemouth: in Bournemouth, follow signs to Sandbanks/Sandbanks ferry, over ferry, then 3m to Studland*

Surrounded by 20 acres of secluded gardens, this hotel has charm in abundance. Some bedrooms have four-poster beds. There is a lounge and an oak-panelled dining room. Afternoon tea al fresco is on offer in the pretty gardens, which command views across Studland Bay.
ROOMS: 20 en suite (bth/shr) (9 fmly) s £79.50-£89.50; d £124-£144 (incl. bkfst & dinner) * LB Off peak **MEALS:** English, French & German Cuisine V meals Coffee am Tea pm **FACILITIES:** CTV in all bedrooms Tennis (hard) Croquet lawn **CONF:** Class 25 **SERVICES:** 80P **NOTES:** No children 5yrs No smoking in restaurant Last d 8.30pm Closed 20 Dec-13 Jan **CARDS:**

STURMINSTER NEWTON Dorset **Map 03 ST71**

★★★ Plumber Manor

Hazelbury Bryan Rd DT10 2AF
Quality Percentage Score: 71%
☎ 01258 472507 01258 473370
Dir: *1.5m SW of Sturminster Newton, off A357 towards Hazelbury Bryan*

Set in extensive grounds, this striking Jacobean Manor has been owned by the Prideaux-Brune family for over 300 years. Bedrooms in the main house are traditionally furnished but rooms in the converted barns are more spacious. The hub of the house, though, is the restaurant.
ROOMS: 6 en suite (bth/shr) 10 annexe en suite (bth/shr) s £75-£90; d £95-£140 (incl. bkfst) * LB Off peak **MEALS:** Sunday Lunch fr £17.50alc Dinner £21.50-£30alc English & French Cuisine V meals **FACILITIES:** CTV in all bedrooms Tennis (hard) Croquet lawn **CONF:** Thtr 25 Board 12 Del from £135 * **SERVICES:** 30P **NOTES:** No coaches Last d 9pm Closed Feb **CARDS:**

SUDBURY Derbyshire **Map 07 SK13**

★★★ The Boars Head

Lichfield Rd DE6 5GX
Quality Percentage Score: 68%
☎ 01283 820344 01283 820075
Dir: *Turn off A50 onto A515 towards Lichfield, hotel 1m on right close to railway crossing*

This roadside inn offers comfortable accommodation in well equipped bedrooms, some of which are on the ground floor. The public rooms offer a choice of bars and dining options, the

contd.

refurbished beamed lounge bar offers informal dining from a popular carvery operation, while the restaurant and cocktail bar offer a more formal environment.
ROOMS: 22 en suite (bth/shr) 1 annexe en suite (shr) (1 fmly) s £42.50-£52.50; d £52.50-£64.50 (incl. bkfst) * LB Off peak **MEALS:** Lunch fr £5.95 Dinner £12.95-£13.95 International Cuisine V meals Coffee am Tea pm **FACILITIES:** CTV in all bedrooms STV Xmas **CONF:** Thtr 35 Class 45 Board 25 Del from £95 * **SERVICES:** Night porter 85P
NOTES: Last d 9.30pm **CARDS:**

See advert under BURTON UPON TRENT

SUDBURY Suffolk **Map 05 TL84**
★★★ Mill
Walnut Tree Ln CO10 1BD
Quality Percentage Score: 69%
☎ 01787 375544 📠 01787 373027
Dir: *from Colchester take A134 to Sudbury, follow signs for Chelmsford after town square take 2nd right*
Complete with a millpond and flocks of ducks, this character hotel is on the fringe of the pleasant market town, backing onto open pastures and the banks of the River Stour. The range of comfortable public rooms retain many charming original features from the building's 300 year history, open fires, exposed oak beams, and the working waterwheel, which divides the restaurant and lounge bar areas. Bedrooms may vary in style and size, ranging from the spacious to the cosy, but all are attractively furnished, well appointed and many enjoy river or millpond views.
ROOMS: 52 en suite (bth/shr) (2 fmly) s £59; d £69-£99 * LB Off peak **MEALS:** Lunch £14.50 Dinner £19.85-£31.50alc English & French Cuisine V meals Coffee am Tea pm **FACILITIES:** CTV in all bedrooms STV Fishing Xmas **CONF:** Thtr 90 Class 50 Board 40 Del £75 * **SERVICES:** Night porter 60P **NOTES:** No smoking in restaurant Last d 9.15pm **CARDS:**

SUNDERLAND Tyne & Wear **Map 12 NZ35**
★★★★ Swallow
Queen's Pde, Seaburn SR6 8DB
Quality Percentage Score: 67%
☎ 0191 529 2041 📠 0191 529 3843
Dir: *off A19 to Sunderland N on A1231, at traffic lights follow A183 for approx 3m to seafront, where hotel is situated*

Occupying a sea-front position overlooking the promenade, this hotel now boasts a fine extension providing thirty three impressive bedrooms and a secure covered car park. Stylish public areas include a comfortable foyer lounge and lounge bar. The Promenade Restaurant features a unique Victorian 'bandstand' where a pianist plays at dinner.
ROOMS: 98 en suite (bth/shr) (3 fmly) No smoking in 37 bedrooms s fr £99; d £130-£165 (incl. bkfst) * LB Off peak **MEALS:** Lunch £10-£15 High tea fr £6.95 Dinner fr £22 English & French Cuisine V meals Coffee am Tea pm **FACILITIES:** CTV in all bedrooms STV Indoor swimming pool (heated) Sauna Solarium Gym Jacuzzi/spa Steam room Wkly live entertainment Xmas **CONF:** Thtr 300 Class 120 Board 90 Del from £95 * **SERVICES:** Lift Night porter 130P **NOTES:** No smoking in restaurant Last d 9.45pm **CARDS:**

SUNDERLAND Tyne & Wear **Map 12 NZ35**
★★★ Quality Friendly Hotel
Witney Way, Boldon NE35 9PE
Quality Percentage Score: 68%
☎ 0191 519 1999 📠 0191 519 0655
Dir: *junct A19/A184*
Situated in the business park (turn into Witney Way), this modern purpose-built hotel focuses well on the needs of the business person. It offers spacious, very well equipped bedrooms, whilst public areas include a leisure centre and a variety of meeting rooms. Dinner offers a good choice of menu options.
ROOMS: 82 en suite (bth/shr) (10 fmly) No smoking in 42 bedrooms s fr £81.50; d fr £105.50 * LB Off peak **MEALS:** Lunch £2.95-£15.95alc Dinner fr £14.50 & alc English & Continental Cuisine V meals Coffee am Tea pm **FACILITIES:** CTV in all bedrooms STV Indoor swimming pool (heated) Sauna Solarium Gym Jacuzzi/spa ch fac Xmas **CONF:** Thtr 200 Class 100 Board 75 **SERVICES:** Night porter 150P **NOTES:** No smoking area in restaurant Last d 9.45pm
CARDS:

SUNDERLAND Tyne & Wear **Map 12 NZ35**
★★ Roker
Roker Ter SR6 0PH
Quality Percentage Score: 68%
☎ 0191 567 1786 📠 0191 510 0289
Dir: *1m N of Sunderland town centre on the sea front, follow signs to Roker A183*
This sea-front business hotel provides well equipped bedrooms, a stylish bar and smart new themed restaurant with a good selection of popular dishes. There is secure undercover parking with direct assess to and from the hotel.
ROOMS: 45 en suite (bth/shr) (8 fmly) d £47.50-£57.50 * Off peak **MEALS:** Lunch £1.95-£12.95 & alc Dinner £1.95-£12.95 & alc International Cuisine V meals Coffee am **FACILITIES:** CTV in all bedrooms STV Pool table Xmas **CONF:** Thtr 350 Class 100 Board 50 Del £80 * **SERVICES:** Night porter 140P **NOTES:** No dogs (ex guide dogs) No smoking area in restaurant Last d 10pm
CARDS:

SUNDERLAND Tyne & Wear **Map 12 NZ35**
Travel Inn
Wessington Way, Castletown SR5 3HR
☎ 0191 548 9384 📠 0191 548 4148
Dir: *from A19 take A1231 towards Sunderland, Travel Inn 100yds from junction*
This modern building offers accommodation in smart, spacious and well equipped bedrooms, all with en-suite bathrooms. Refreshments may be taken at the nearby family restaurant. For details about current prices consult the Contents Page under Hotel Groups for the Travel Inn phone number.
ROOMS: 41 en suite (bth/shr) d £39.95 *

S

The AA Hotel Booking Service is a free benefit to AA members. See the advertisement on page 47

SUTTON Greater London — Map 04 TQ26

★★ Thatched House
135 Cheam Rd SM1 2BN
Quality Percentage Score: 63%
☎ 020 8642 3131 📠 020 8770 0684
Dir: *junct 8 of M25, follow A217 to London until reaching A232, turn right onto A232, hotel is half a minute's drive on the right*

As its name suggests, this is a thatched, cottage-style hotel on the Epsom/Croydon road. Bedrooms, either in the main building or a separate extension, are neatly decorated and well equipped. Public rooms include a lounge, a bar and a dining room overlooking the garden.

ROOMS: 27 rms (24 bth/shr) 5 annexe en suite (bth/shr) s £62.50-£75; d £75-£95 (incl. bkfst) * LB Off peak **MEALS:** Lunch £8.95-£12.50 Dinner £13.50-£15.50 V meals Coffee am Tea pm **FACILITIES:** CTV in all bedrooms **CONF:** Thtr 50 Class 30 Board 26 **SERVICES:** 26P **NOTES:** No smoking area in restaurant Last d 9.15pm **CARDS:**

SUTTON COLDFIELD West Midlands — Map 07 SP19

The Premier Collection

★★★★ New Hall
Walmley Rd B76 1QX
THISTLE HOTELS
☎ 0121 378 2442 📠 0121 378 4637
Dir: *take the A38 until you reach the B4148, follow this road until you reach the forked road, take the left fork and New Hall is up on the left*

Set in immaculate grounds and gardens, this beautifully restored hotel is reputedly the oldest moated manor house in England and is personally run by committed managers and a dedicated team of staff. The lovely grounds include a walled rose garden, a yew tree walk and an ornamental pool, as well as several leisure facilities. Hallmarks of the delightful day rooms, which retain many original features are deep cushioned sofas, fresh flowers and plenty of magazines and newspapers. The thoughtfully-equipped bedrooms vary in size and are divided between the main house and a purpose-built wing. The delightful dining room is the showcase for the kitchen brigade to show off their care and dedication in creating fresh-tasting dishes.

ROOMS: 60 en suite (bth/shr) No smoking in 54 bedrooms s £125-£140; d £148-£170 * LB Off peak **MEALS:** Lunch fr £20.50 Dinner £36.50-£42.50 International Cuisine V meals Coffee am Tea pm **FACILITIES:** CTV in all bedrooms STV Golf 9 Fishing Croquet lawn Putting green Golf driving net Xmas **CONF:** Thtr 50 Class 30 Board 30 Del from £175 * **SERVICES:** Night porter 70P **NOTES:** No dogs (ex guide dogs) No smoking in restaurant Last d 10pm RS Sat **CARDS:**

SUTTON COLDFIELD West Midlands — Map 07 SP19

★★★ Moor Hall
Moor Hall Dr, Four Oaks B75 6LN
Best Western
Quality Percentage Score: 71%
☎ 0121 308 3751 📠 0121 308 8974
Dir: *at jct of A38/A453 take A453 towards Sutton Coldfield, at traffic lights turn right into Weeford Rd, Moor Hall drive is 150 yds on left*

Although only a short distance from the city centre and just over 15 minutes drive from the NEC and the motorway network, this much-extended hotel enjoys a peaceful setting, overlooking extensive grounds and an adjacent golf course. Bedrooms are well equipped and the executive rooms particularly spacious. In the evenings, there are two choices for dinner: a formal restaurant, the Oak Room, and the informal Country Kitchen, offering a carvery and blackboard specials.

ROOMS: 75 en suite (bth/shr) (5 fmly) No smoking in 34 bedrooms s £99-£110; d £112-£122 (incl. bkfst) LB Off peak **MEALS:** Lunch £8.95-£12.75 Dinner £21 & alc International Cuisine V meals Coffee am Tea pm **FACILITIES:** CTV in all bedrooms STV Indoor swimming pool (heated) Sauna Solarium Gym Jacuzzi/spa Steam room **CONF:** Thtr 250 Class 120 Board 45 Del £130 * **SERVICES:** Lift Night porter 164P **NOTES:** Last d 10.20pm **CARDS:**

SUTTON COLDFIELD West Midlands — Map 07 SP19

★★★ Marston Farm
Bodymoor Heath B76 9JD
Quality Percentage Score: 65%
☎ 01827 872133 📠 01827 875043
Dir: *take A4091 in direction of Tamworth and turn right for Bodymoor Heath. Turn right after humpback bridge*

This 17th-century farmhouse was previously owned by Robert Peel and Lord Norton. Birmingham city centre, the NEC and the airport are all in easy reach. The hotel provides attractively appointed public rooms and well equipped modern bedrooms,

contd.

which include rooms on ground floor level, and a room for disabled guests.
ROOMS: 37 en suite (bth/shr) No smoking in 5 bedrooms s £85-£100; d £100-£110 (incl. bkfst) * LB Off peak **MEALS:** Lunch £12.95-£13.95 & alc Dinner fr £14.95 & alc English & French Cuisine V meals Coffee am Tea pm **FACILITIES:** CTV in all bedrooms STV Tennis (hard) Fishing Croquet lawn Boules Golf practice net Mountain bikes Xmas **CONF:** Thtr 150 Class 80 Board 50 Del from £110 * **SERVICES:** Night porter 150P **NOTES:** No smoking in restaurant Last d 9.30pm
CARDS:

See advert under BIRMINGHAM

SUTTON COLDFIELD West Midlands — Map 07 SP19
★★★ *Sutton Court*
60-66 Lichfield Rd B74 2NA
Quality Percentage Score: 62%
☎ 0870 6011160 Fax 01543 481551
Dir: *on junct of A5127/A453*
This well run hotel, close to the town centre, provides modern, well equipped bedrooms with special arrangements for female guests. Public rooms are comfortable and a good range of conference and function rooms are available. There is secure parking, and leisure facilities are offered at a nearby centre.
ROOMS: 56 en suite (bth/shr) 8 annexe en suite (bth/shr) (9 fmly) No smoking in 40 bedrooms **MEALS:** V meals Coffee am Tea pm **FACILITIES:** CTV in all bedrooms STV Free use of local leisure centre Wkly live entertainment **CONF:** Thtr 90 Class 70 Board 50 **SERVICES:** Night porter 90P **NOTES:** No smoking area in restaurant Last d 9.30pm **CARDS:**

See advert under BIRMINGHAM

SUTTON COLDFIELD West Midlands — Map 07 SP19
★★ Royal
High St B72 1UD
Quality Percentage Score: 66%
☎ 0121 355 8222 Fax 0121 355 1837
Dir: *from A38/A453 to Sutton Coldfield turn left at 2nd set of traffic lights, hotel 400metres on right hand side*
This town-centre hotel, dating from the Georgian era, offers attractively furnished bedrooms, some with four-posters, and serves a wide range of bar and restaurant meals. It is conveniently placed for Birmingham, the NEC and the International Airport.
ROOMS: 22 en suite (bth/shr) (3 fmly) s fr £49.50; d £56-£62 * LB Off peak **MEALS:** Lunch £9.95-£20alc Dinner £11-£20alc V meals Coffee am **FACILITIES:** CTV in all bedrooms STV **CONF:** Thtr 60 Class 40 Board 30 Del from £79 * **SERVICES:** Night porter 80P **NOTES:** No dogs (ex guide dogs) No smoking area in restaurant Last d 10pm
CARDS:

SUTTON COLDFIELD West Midlands — Map 07 SP19
Travelodge
Boldmere Rd B73 5UP
☎ 0121 355 0017 Fax 0121 355 0017
Dir: *2m S, on B4142*
This modern building offers accommodation in smart, spacious and well equipped bedrooms, all with en-suite bathrooms. Refreshments may be taken at the nearby family restaurant. For details about current prices, consult the Contents Page under Hotel Groups for the Travelodge phone number.
ROOMS: 32 en suite (bth/shr) d £45.95 *

SUTTON IN THE ELMS Leicestershire — Map 04 SP59
Mill On The Soar
Coventry Rd LE9 6QD
☎ 01455 282419 Fax 01455 285937
Dir: *SE of Leicester, on B4114*
The Mill On The Soar is a busy roadside inn which caters well for family dining. The accommodation is housed in a separate wing and offers pleasing colour co-ordinated bedrooms that are very well equipped and fully en-suite. The public areas centre around the open-plan bar where there is an extensive range of bar meals, informally served. The gardens to the rear lead to a falconry centre, play area, river and small well stocked lake.
ROOMS: 20 en suite (bth/shr) d £28.50-£39.50 * **CONF:** Thtr 50 Class 20 Board 15

See advert on this page

SUTTON ON SEA Lincolnshire — Map 09 TF58
★★★ Grange & Links
Sea Ln, Sandilands LN12 2RA
Quality Percentage Score: 62%
☎ 01507 441334 Fax 01507 443033
Dir: *A1111 to Sutton-on-Sea, follow signs to Sandilands*
This friendly seaside hotel is very popular with golfers and also caters well for families with children. Delightful public rooms include an attractive bar together with ample lounge areas. Good home cooking is served in the traditional style dining room and most of the bedrooms have been well equipped and pleasantly furnished. Service is friendly and attentive.
ROOMS: 23 en suite (bth/shr) (10 fmly) s fr £59.50; d fr £71.50 (incl. bkfst) * LB Off peak **MEALS:** Sunday Lunch fr £14 High tea fr £6 Dinner fr £20 & alc French Cuisine V meals Coffee am Tea pm **FACILITIES:** CTV in all bedrooms Golf 18 Tennis (hard) Snooker Gym Croquet lawn Putting green Bowls Xmas **CONF:** Thtr 200 Board 100 Del from £75 * **SERVICES:** Night porter 60P **NOTES:** No dogs (ex guide dogs) Last d 9pm **CARDS:**

SUTTON SCOTNEY Hampshire **Map 04 SU43**

Travelodge (North)

SO21 3JY

☎ 01962 761016

Dir: *on A34 northbound*

This modern building offers accommodation in smart, spacious and well equipped bedrooms, all with en-suite bathrooms. Refreshments may be taken at the nearby family restaurant. For details about current prices, consult the Contents Page under Hotel Groups for the Travelodge phone number.

ROOMS: 30 en suite (bth/shr) d £49.95 *

SUTTON SCOTNEY Hampshire **Map 04 SU43**

Travelodge (South)

SO21 3JY

☎ 01962 760779

Dir: *on A34 southbound*

This modern building offers accommodation in smart, spacious and well equipped bedrooms, all with en-suite bathrooms. Refreshments may be taken at the nearby family restaurant. For details about current prices, consult the Contents Page under Hotel Groups for the Travelodge phone number.

ROOMS: 40 en suite (bth/shr) d £49.95 *

SUTTON UPON DERWENT **Map 08 SE74**

East Riding of Yorkshire

★★ Old Rectory

Sandhill Ln YO41 4BX

Quality Percentage Score: 64%

☎ 01904 608548

Dir: *off A1079 at Grimston Bar rdbt onto B1228 for Howden, through Elvington to Sutton-upon-Derwent, the hotel is situated on left opposite tennis courts*

This former rectory stands close to the village centre and overlooks the Derwent valley. The house provides spacious bedrooms together with a separate bar and lounge. Home cooking is served in the traditional-style dining room, and service is friendly and polite.

ROOMS: 6 rms (5 bth/shr) (2 fmly) s £28-£32; d £50-£52 (incl. bkfst) LB Off peak **MEALS:** Coffee am **FACILITIES:** CTV in all bedrooms **SERVICES:** 30P **NOTES:** No coaches Closed 2 wks Xmas

CARDS:

SWAFFHAM Norfolk **Map 05 TF80**

★★★ George

Station Rd PE37 7LJ

Quality Percentage Score: 64%

☎ 01760 721238 📠 01760 725333

Dir: *turn off A47 signposted Swaffham, hotel opposite the church of St Peter & St Paul*

In the market square of this bustling Norfolk town, this family run coaching inn continues to be popular. The well equipped bedrooms are in the main house and a modern wing. There is a popular bar serving a range of snacks, a more formal restaurant and several function and conference rooms. A gradual refurbishment programme is underway.

ROOMS: 27 en suite (bth/shr) (1 fmly) s £50-£60; d £60-£75 (incl. bkfst) * LB Off peak **MEALS:** Lunch £9.95 & alc Dinner £15.95 & alc English & French Cuisine V meals Coffee am Tea pm **FACILITIES:** CTV in all bedrooms STV Xmas **CONF:** Thtr 150 Class 70 Board 70 Del from £70 * **SERVICES:** Night porter 100P **NOTES:** No smoking in restaurant Last d 9.30pm **CARDS:**

SWALLOWFIELD Berkshire **Map 04 SU76**

★★ The Mill House

Old Basingstoke Rd RG7 1PY

Quality Percentage Score: 69%

☎ 0118 988 3124 📠 0118 988 5550

Dir: *M4 junct11, S on A33, left at 1st rdbt onto B3349. Approx 1m after signpost for Three Mile Cross and Spencer's Wood, hotel is on right*

The Mill House is a comfortable hotel which is conveniently located in a rural setting between the M3 and M4, with easy access to both Reading and Basingstoke. A real strength is the welcoming atmosphere proprietors and staff create. Bedrooms are spacious and very well equipped, with attractive decor. The restaurant offers a well prepared, popular menu, and pleasing rural views through its large picture windows.

ROOMS: 10 en suite (bth/shr) (2 fmly) No smoking in 2 bedrooms s £70-£90; d £80-£100 (incl. bkfst) * LB Off peak **MEALS:** Lunch £15-£20 & alc Dinner £20 & alc English & French Cuisine V meals Coffee am Tea pm **FACILITIES:** CTV in all bedrooms STV Croquet lawn **CONF:** Thtr 90 Class 30 Board 30 Del from £95 * **SERVICES:** 125P **NOTES:** No smoking area in restaurant Last d 10pm RS Sun

CARDS:

SWANAGE Dorset **Map 04 SZ07**

★★★ The Pines

Burlington Rd BH19 1LT

Quality Percentage Score: 68%

☎ 01929 425211 📠 01929 422075

Dir: *follow A351 to seafront, turn left then take second right and continue to end of road*

This popular family run hotel enjoys a superb location with spectacular views over the sea and Ballard Down. The cheerful bedrooms have attractive decor. Public areas include two comfortably furnished lounges. The restaurant offers good value food from a daily menu and an additional carte.

ROOMS: 49 en suite (bth/shr) (26 fmly) s £42.50-£53; d £85-£106 (incl. bkfst) * LB Off peak **MEALS:** Lunch fr £12.50 Dinner fr £19 English & Continental Cuisine V meals Coffee am Tea pm **FACILITIES:** CTV in all bedrooms Xmas **CONF:** Thtr 60 Class 60 Board 30 Del from £55 * **SERVICES:** Lift Night porter 60P **NOTES:** No coaches No smoking in restaurant Last d 8.30pm **CARDS:**

See advert on page 635

SWANAGE Dorset **Map 04 SZ07**

★★★ Purbeck House

91 High St BH19 2LZ

Quality Percentage Score: 66%

☎ 01929 422872 📠 01929 421194

Dir: *A351 to Swanage via Wareham, turn right into Shore road and on into Institute road, right into High Street*

Located close to the town centre, this former convent is set in well tended grounds. The bedrooms are tastefully decorated and appointed with old pine furnishings. Smartly presented public

contd.

areas have some stunning features, such as painted ceilings, wood panelling and fine tiled floors.
ROOMS: 18 en suite (bth/shr) (5 fmly) No smoking in 3 bedrooms s £40-£52; d £80-£104 (incl. bkfst) * LB Off peak **MEALS:** Lunch £9.95-£11.95 Dinner £16.50-£18.50 International Cuisine V meals Coffee am Tea pm **FACILITIES:** CTV in all bedrooms STV Pool table Croquet lawn Xmas **CONF:** Thtr 100 Class 70 Board 70 Del £75 * **SERVICES:** 39P
NOTES: No smoking in restaurant Last d 9pm
CARDS:

See advert on this page

SWANAGE Dorset **Map 04 SZ07**
★★★ Grand
Burlington Rd BH19 1LU
Quality Percentage Score: 64%
☎ 01929 423353 Fax 01929 427068
Dir: *via Sandbanks Toll Ferry from Bournemouth, follow signs to Swanage, at 2nd town centre sign take 4th left into Burlington Rd*
Spectacular views across Swanage Bay can be enjoyed from this hotel, which has access to a private beach. A sunny conservatory, a bar and well tended gardens are available for guests' use.

contd.

Bedrooms vary in size, but all are smartly decorated. An imaginative menu is offered in the restaurant.

Grand, Swanage

ROOMS: 30 en suite (bth/shr) (2 fmly) s £55-£58; d £110-£116 (incl. bkfst & dinner) * LB Off peak **MEALS:** Sunday Lunch £12.50 Dinner £17.95-£21.95 English & French Cuisine V meals Coffee am Tea pm **FACILITIES:** CTV in all bedrooms STV Indoor swimming pool (heated) Fishing Sauna Solarium Gym Jacuzzi/spa Table tennis Xmas **SERVICES:** Lift Night porter 15P **NOTES:** No smoking in restaurant Last d 9.30pm **CARDS:**

See advert on page 633

SWANAGE Dorset **Map 04 SZ07**

★★ Havenhurst

Cranborne Rd BH19 1EA

Quality Percentage Score: 66%

☎ 01929 424224 📠 01929 422173

This personally run small hotel offers a friendly welcome to guests. A comfortable lounge is provided in addition to the popular bar. Each evening, home cooked meals are served, featuring an enormous range of home made desserts. Bedrooms are bright and sunny.

ROOMS: 17 en suite (bth/shr) (4 fmly) s £20-£30; d £40-£60 (incl. bkfst) * LB Off peak **MEALS:** Lunch £8 & alc Dinner £14 & alc V meals Coffee am Tea pm **FACILITIES:** CTV in all bedrooms **SERVICES:** 20P **NOTES:** No dogs No smoking in restaurant Last d 8pm

CARDS:

SWANWICK See **Alfreton**

SWAVESEY Cambridgeshire **Map 05 TL36**

Travelodge

Cambridge Rd CB4 5QA

☎ 01954 789113 📠 01954 789113

Dir: *on eastbound carriageway of the A14*

This modern building offers accommodation in smart, spacious and well equipped bedrooms, all with en-suite bathrooms. Refreshments may be taken at the nearby family restaurant. For details about current prices, consult the Contents Page under Hotel Groups for the Travelodge phone number.

ROOMS: 36 en suite (bth/shr) d £49.95 *

SWAY Hampshire **Map 04 SZ29**

★★ String of Horses

Mead End Rd SO41 6EH

Quality Percentage Score: 71%

☎ 01590 682631 📠 01590 682911

Dir: *A337 Lyndhurst/Brockenhurst, right opposite Carey's Manor Hotel onto B3055 to Sway, right onto Stn Rd, 2nd left,after railway station 350m on left*

The hotel enjoys a peaceful location in mature grounds adjoining the New Forest. The bedrooms are well presented and the majority are equipped with large spa baths and feature many thoughtful extras such as dressing gowns. The spacious public areas include a cosy bar, separate breakfast room and comfortable lounge, which overlooks the pool and garden. The beamed restaurant offers freshly prepared meals from both table d'hôte and carte menus.

ROOMS: 8 en suite (bth/shr) s £65; d £96-£114 (incl. bkfst) LB Off peak **MEALS:** Sunday Lunch £13.95-£14.50 Dinner £23 & alc English & French Cuisine V meals Coffee am Tea pm **FACILITIES:** CTV in all bedrooms STV Outdoor swimming pool (heated) Jacuzzi/spa Xmas **CONF:** Board 30 Del from £88 * **SERVICES:** 32P **NOTES:** No dogs No coaches No children 16yrs No smoking in restaurant Last d 9.30pm

CARDS:

SWAY Hampshire **Map 04 SZ29**

★★ White Rose

Station Rd SO41 6BA

Quality Percentage Score: 65%

☎ 01590 682754 📠 01590 682955

Dir: *turn off B3055 Brockenhurst/New Milton rd into Sway village centre*

Situated in the heart of the village, this spacious Victorian house is set in well tended gardens. The bedrooms, some of which are being upgraded, provide comfortable accommodation, with modern pine furniture throughout. Public areas are smartly presented and friendly staff provide attentive service.

ROOMS: 14 en suite (bth/shr) (3 fmly) s £45-£55; d £79-£85 (incl. bkfst) * LB Off peak **MEALS:** Lunch £11.50-£15 Dinner £11-£15 & alc V meals Coffee am Tea pm **FACILITIES:** CTV in all bedrooms Outdoor swimming pool Xmas **SERVICES:** Lift 50P **NOTES:** No coaches No smoking in restaurant Last d 9pm **CARDS:**

SWINDON Wiltshire **Map 04 SU18**

see also **Wootton Bassett**

★★★★ Blunsdon House Hotel & Leisure Club

Blunsdon SN2 4AD

Quality Percentage Score: 72%

☎ 01793 721701 📠 01793 721056

Dir: *3m N off A419*

Blunsdon House is a family-run hotel set in 30 acres of well tended grounds, offering a plethora of leisure options. The public rooms include three bars and a choice of eating operations. Carrie's Carverie is the more informal choice, while The Ridge

contd.

Indicates that the star classification has not been confirmed under the New Quality Standards, see page 7 for further information.

Restaurant offers an extensive selection of freshly prepared dishes. Bedrooms are spacious and comfortable.
ROOMS: 135 en suite (bth/shr) (16 fmly) No smoking in 77 bedrooms s £94-£124; d £122-£152 (incl. bkfst) * LB Off peak **MEALS:** Lunch £13.75-£14.75 & alc Dinner £15-£21.50 & alc International Cuisine V meals Coffee am Tea pm **FACILITIES:** CTV in all bedrooms STV Indoor swimming pool (heated) Golf 9 Tennis (hard) Squash Sauna Solarium Gym Pool table Putting green Jacuzzi/spa Beauty therapy Woodland walk ch fac Xmas **CONF:** Thtr 300 Class 200 Board 40 Del from £140 * **SERVICES:** Lift Night porter 300P **NOTES:** No dogs (ex guide dogs) No smoking area in restaurant Last d 10.15pm
CARDS:

See advert on this page

SWINDON Wiltshire **Map 04 SU18**
★★★★ De Vere
Shaw Ridge Leisure Park, Whitehill Way SN5 7DW
DE VERE HOTELS
Quality Percentage Score: 71%
☎ 01793 878785 🖹 01793 877822
Dir: *M4 junct 16, signs for Swindon off 1st rdbt, 2nd rdbt follow signs for Link Centre over next 2 rdbts, 2nd left at 3rd rdbt, left onto slip road*
A purpose built hotel offering a wide range of facilities to suit business and leisure guests. Located adjacent to an entertainment park (offering ten-pin bowling and a multiplex cinema) the hotel has a fitness centre, indoor swimming pool and conference rooms. Eating options include the bar, a restaurant and snacks in the leisure club. The bedrooms are bright with a range of useful amenities.
ROOMS: 154 en suite (bth/shr) (10 fmly) No smoking in 77 bedrooms s £80-£205; d £95-£205 (incl. bkfst) * LB Off peak **MEALS:** Lunch £8.95-£18.50 & alc High tea £7-£11.70 & alc Dinner £18.50 & alc English & Continental Cuisine V meals Coffee am Tea pm **FACILITIES:** CTV in all bedrooms STV Indoor swimming pool (heated) Sauna Solarium Gym Jacuzzi/spa Beauty therapist Turkish bath Xmas **CONF:** Thtr 400 Class 168 Board 80 Del from £135 * **SERVICES:** Lift Night porter 170P **NOTES:** No smoking in restaurant Last d 10pm
CARDS:

SWINDON Wiltshire **Map 04 SU18**
★★★★ Swindon Marriott
Pipers Way SN3 1SH
Marriott HOTELS · RESORTS · SUITES
Quality Percentage Score: 64%
☎ 01793 512121 🖹 01793 513114
Dir: *from junct 15 of M4 follow A419, then A4259 to Coate roundabout and B4006 signed 'Old Town'*
A busy, modern hotel, suitable for business and leisure travellers. Good conference and leisure facilities are offered. The air-conditioned rooms are well equipped and comfortable. Staff on our last visit showed high levels of customer care.
ROOMS: 153 en suite (bth/shr) (42 fmly) No smoking in 86 bedrooms d £89-£104 * LB Off peak **MEALS:** Lunch £12.95-£18.95 Dinner £15-£19 & alc English & Continental Cuisine V meals Coffee am Tea pm **FACILITIES:** CTV in all bedrooms STV Indoor swimming pool (heated) Tennis (hard) Sauna Solarium Gym Jacuzzi/spa Hair Salon Steam Room Health & Beauty from Nov99 Xmas **CONF:** Thtr 250 Class 100 Board 40 Del from £148 * **SERVICES:** Lift Night porter Air conditioning 185P **NOTES:** No smoking area in restaurant Last d 10.30pm
CARDS:

SWINDON Wiltshire **Map 04 SU18**
★★★ The Pear Tree at Purton
Church End SN5 9ED
Quality Percentage Score: 79%
☎ 01793 772100 🖹 01793 772369
(For full entry see Purton)

S

SWINDON Wiltshire

Map 04 SU18

★★★ Chiseldon House

New Rd, Chiseldon SN4 0NE

Quality Percentage Score: 70%

☎ 01793 741010 Fax 01793 741059

Dir: *M4 junct 15, onto A346 signposted Marlborough, at brow of hill turn right by Esso garage onto B4005 into New Rd, hotel is 200yds along on right*

This traditional country house hotel, situated in a village just outside Swindon, is a popular venue for weddings and small conferences. Quiet bedrooms, most of which are very spacious, include two four-poster rooms. All are decorated with individual style using quality fabrics and furnishings, and have extras such as trouser presses and luxury bathrooms. The Orangerie restaurant is the showcase for the cuisine of chef Kai Taylor.

ROOMS: 21 en suite (bth/shr) (4 fmly) No smoking in 6 bedrooms s fr £75; d fr £95 (incl. bkfst) * Off peak **MEALS:** Lunch £10-£15 Dinner fr £24.95 V meals Coffee am Tea pm **FACILITIES:** CTV in all bedrooms STV Outdoor swimming pool (heated) **CONF:** Thtr 40 Class 40 Board 35 Del from £125 * **SERVICES:** Night porter 50P **NOTES:** No smoking area in restaurant Last d 9.30pm Closed 26 Dec **CARDS:**

SWINDON Wiltshire

Map 04 SU18

★★★ *Thistle Wiltshire*

THISTLE HOTELS

Fleming Way SN1 1TN

Quality Percentage Score: 67%

☎ 01793 528282 Fax 01793 541283

Dir: *from M4 follow signs for Swindon town centreonto Fleming Way. Hotel is on corner of Islington St and Fleming Way*

The Wiltshire offers well equipped and furnished bedrooms suitable for both leisure and business guests. All rooms have work areas with sockets for computers. The Havana Bar and Café and Shelleys restaurant provide a choice of dining options. There is also the alternative of room-service dishes. Free car parking is available in the adjacent multi-storey car park.

ROOMS: 93 en suite (bth/shr) No smoking in 28 bedrooms **MEALS:** English & French Cuisine V meals Coffee am Tea pm **FACILITIES:** CTV in all bedrooms STV **CONF:** Thtr 230 Class 60 Board 60 **SERVICES:** Lift Night porter **NOTES:** No dogs (ex guide dogs) No smoking in restaurant Last d 9.45pm RS Sat lunchtimes **CARDS:**

SWINDON Wiltshire

Map 04 SU18

★★★ Goddard Arms

High St, Old Town SN1 3EG

Quality Percentage Score: 65%

☎ 01793 692313 Fax 01793 512984

Dir: *M4 junct 15, go along A419 towards Cirencester, at 1st rdbt take a left, go straight across 2nd and 3rd rdbts, hotel is on the right hand side*

Backing onto acres of natural park-land, this historic hotel is in the heart of Old Town. Bedrooms are in the original building and two wings, all are recently refurbished. Public areas include the vaults cellar bar, a charming restaurant with food to suit all palates, and extensive conference facilities.

ROOMS: 18 en suite (bth/shr) 47 annexe en suite (bth/shr) (3 fmly) No smoking in 31 bedrooms s £35-£85; d £49-£90 (incl. bkfst) * LB Off peak **MEALS:** Lunch £12.50-£15.95 Dinner fr £15.95 English, French & Italian Cuisine V meals Coffee am Tea pm **FACILITIES:** CTV in all bedrooms **CONF:** Thtr 180 Class 100 Board 40 **SERVICES:** Night porter 90P **NOTES:** No smoking in restaurant Last d 9.30pm **CARDS:**

See advert on opposite page

SWINDON Wiltshire

Map 04 SU18

★★★ Posthouse Swindon

Posthouse

Marlborough Rd SN3 6AQ

Quality Percentage Score: 65%

☎ 01793 524601 Fax 01793 512887

Dir: *off A419 for Swindon at rdbt, onto A4259. Continue for 1m, hotel is on right opposite Coate Water Country Park*

This modern hotel is convenient for the town centre and for the road network. All accommodation is well equipped, and the new Millennium Rooms are particularly comfortable. Traders Restaurant serves a good variety of dishes, and snacks can be ordered in the lounge. There is a small leisure complex.

ROOMS: 98 en suite (bth/shr) (30 fmly) No smoking in 65 bedrooms s £109; d £89-£129 * LB Off peak **MEALS:** International Cuisine V meals Coffee am Tea pm **FACILITIES:** CTV in all bedrooms Indoor swimming pool (heated) Sauna Solarium Gym Pool table Jacuzzi/spa Xmas **CONF:** Thtr 70 Class 30 Board 30 Del from £90 * **SERVICES:** Night porter 200P **NOTES:** No smoking area in restaurant Last d 10.30pm **CARDS:**

SWINDON Wiltshire

Map 04 SU18

★★★ *Stanton House*

The Avenue, Stanton Fitzwarren SN6 7SD

Quality Percentage Score: 65%

☎ 01793 861777 Fax 01793 861857

Dir: *off A419 onto A361 towards Highworth, pass Honda factory and turn left towards Stanton Fitzwarren about 600yds past business park, hotel is on left*

Situated close to Swindon and the M4, this beautiful Cotswold stone manor house is set in extensive grounds and is owned and operated by Honda. Every effort is made to ensure European guests feel welcome. The spacious bedrooms are simply but tastefully decorated in muted colours and are well equipped. A number of private rooms are popular venues for meetings and weddings. Bilingual staff provide a number of business services. Traditional Japanese dishes are prepared by the kitchen, try the Beneto boxes for a selection of classics such as sashami, sushi and tempura.

ROOMS: 86 en suite (bth/shr) No smoking in 3 bedrooms **MEALS:** English & Japanese Cuisine V meals Coffee am **FACILITIES:** CTV in all bedrooms STV Tennis (hard) Table tennis Darts Mah Jong **CONF:** Thtr 110 Class 70 Board 40 **SERVICES:** Lift Night porter Air conditioning 110P **NOTES:** No dogs (ex guide dogs) No coaches Last d 10pm **CARDS:**

See advert on opposite page

SWINDON Wiltshire

Map 04 SU18

★★★ Villiers Inn

Moormead Rd, Wroughton SN4 9BY

Quality Percentage Score: 62%

☎ 01793 814744 Fax 01793 814119

Dir: *1m S of Swindon, on A4361*

This attractive period property has a modern extension which houses most of the bedrooms. Public areas include a comfortable library lounge, spacious conservatory and the Pig on the Wall

contd.

AA Rosettes are awarded for quality of food,
see page 15 for an explanation of Rosette assessment.

bar and bistro which serves a range of dishes. Conference and function facilities are available.

ROOMS: 33 en suite (bth/shr) No smoking in 10 bedrooms s £69-£79; d £79-£89 (incl. bkfst) * LB Off peak **MEALS:** Lunch £12-£14 & alc High tea £7.50-£12 & alc Dinner £18-£28 & alc International Cuisine V meals Coffee am Tea pm **FACILITIES:** CTV in all bedrooms STV Xmas **CONF:** Thtr 80 Class 30 Board 32 Del from £115 * **SERVICES:** Night porter 60P **NOTES:** No smoking area in restaurant Last d 9.30pm **CARDS:**

See advert on this page

Indicates that the star classification has not been confirmed under the New Quality Standards, see page 7 for further information.

SWINDON Wiltshire
Map 04 SU18

★★ Hotel Ibis Swindon

Delta Business Park, Great Western Way SN5 7XG
Quality Percentage Score: 65%
☎ 01793 514777 📠 01793 514777
Dir: *2m from M4 junct 16 & 1m W of town centre*

This modern hotel offers bedrooms that are bright and practical in style. Open plan facilities include a congenial bistro serving dinner and a self-service breakfast. There is also a bar-lounge open all day to residents. Prompt service is carried out by a friendly team.

ROOMS: 120 en suite (bth/shr) (6 fmly) No smoking in 42 bedrooms d £39.50 * Off peak **MEALS:** Bar Lunch £3.25-£10alc Dinner £6.50-£28alc English & Continental Cuisine V meals Coffee am Tea pm **FACILITIES:** CTV in all bedrooms STV **CONF:** Thtr 90 Class 40 Board 40 **SERVICES:** Lift Night porter 120P **NOTES:** No smoking area in restaurant Last d 10.30pm **CARDS:**

SWINDON Wiltshire
Map 04 SU18

Travel Inn

Great Western Way SN5 8UY
☎ 01793 881490 📠 01793 886890
Dir: *3m SW of Swindon town centre on junct 16 of the M4*

This modern building offers accommodation in smart, spacious and well equipped bedrooms, all with en-suite bathrooms. Refreshments may be taken at the nearby family restaurant. For details about current prices consult the Contents Page under Hotel Groups for the Travel Inn phone number.

ROOMS: 60 en suite (bth/shr) d £39.95 *

SYMONDS YAT (EAST) Herefordshire
Map 03 SO51

★★ Royal

HR9 6JL
Quality Percentage Score: 65%
☎ 01600 890238 📠 01600 890238
Dir: *off A40 onto B4229, after 0.5m turn right on B4432*

The Royal Hotel enjoys a picturesque location at the foot of a wooded cliff, overlooking the River Wye. The mainly spacious accommodation, which includes four-poster rooms, has modern equipment, but no TV, as reception is too poor. Most rooms have either river or garden views, as does the attractive restaurant. Welcoming fires burn in chilly weather in both the bar and the comfortable lounge.

ROOMS: 20 en suite (bth/shr) s £30-£45; d £60-£90 (incl. bkfst) * LB Off peak **MEALS:** Lunch £12.50 Dinner £18.50 & alc British & French Cuisine V meals Coffee am Tea pm **FACILITIES:** Fishing Abseiling Canoeing Clay pigeon shooting Walking Mountain bikes **CONF:** Thtr 70 Class 25 Board 30 Del from £80 * **SERVICES:** 80P **NOTES:** No coaches No children 12yrs Last d 8.30pm Closed 2-16 Jan
CARDS:

SYMONDS YAT (EAST) Herefordshire
Map 03 SO51

★★ Saracens Head

HR9 6JL
Quality Percentage Score: 65%
☎ 01600 890435 📠 01600 890034
Dir: *A40 Monmouth-Ross-on-Wye, turn off at Little Chef, signpost Goodrich & Symonds. 0.5m turn right, 1m fork right alongside river Wye to hotel*

This family owned hostelry stands alongside the River Wye, at the heart of a renowned beauty spot. It provides traditionally furnished but well equipped accommodation, the majority of the bedrooms having river views. In addition to the cosy residents' lounge, there is a very attractive dining room and a popular bar full of character.

ROOMS: 9 en suite (bth/shr) (1 fmly) s £30-£35; d £49-£54 (incl. bkfst) * LB Off peak **MEALS:** Lunch £12-£15 & alc Dinner £16-£20 & alc V meals Coffee am Tea pm **FACILITIES:** CTV in 1 bedroom Fishing Pool table Canoeing Mountain bike hire Walking Climbing Horse riding **SERVICES:** 15P **NOTES:** No dogs (ex guide dogs) No coaches No smoking in restaurant Last d 9.15pm **CARDS:**

See advert on opposite page

TALKE Staffordshire
Map 07 SJ85

Travelodge

Newcastle Rd ST7 1UP
☎ 01782 777000 📠 01782 777000
Dir: *at junct of A34/A500*

This modern building offers accommodation in smart, spacious and well equipped bedrooms, all with en-suite bathrooms. Refreshments may be taken at the nearby family restaurant. For details about current prices, consult the Contents Page under Hotel Groups for the Travelodge phone number.

ROOMS: 62 en suite (bth/shr) d £45.95 * **CONF:** Thtr 50 Class 25 Board 32

TAMWORTH Staffordshire
Map 07 SK20

★★ Globe Inn

Lower Gungate B79 7AW
Quality Percentage Score: 65%
☎ 01827 60455 📠 01827 63575
Dir: *follow signs Lower Gungate car park and shops, Hotel is adjacent to car park*

This popular town centre hostelry provides well equipped modern accommodation, including a family bedroom. Attractive open plan public areas feature a spacious lounge bar and adjacent dining area. There is a function room for up to 100 people and public parking adjacent to the hotel.

ROOMS: 18 en suite (bth/shr) (2 fmly) No smoking in 2 bedrooms **MEALS:** V meals Coffee am **FACILITIES:** CTV in all bedrooms STV **CONF:** Class 90 Board 90 **NOTES:** No dogs (ex guide dogs) No smoking in restaurant **CARDS:**

TAMWORTH Staffordshire
Map 07 SK20

★★ Drayton Court Hotel

65 Coleshill St, Fazeley B78 3RG
Quality Percentage Score: 64%
☎ 01827 285805 📠 01827 284842
Dir: *from M42 junct 9 then A446 to Litchfield at next rdbt turn right onto A4091 after 2m Drayton Manor Park on left hotel further along on right*

Built in the 18th century, this friendly small hotel has undergone major refurbishment and is conveniently situated for local business parks and nearby recreational facilities. The accommodation varies in style, although most of the bedrooms feature carved wooden furniture and colourful soft furnishings; there is one four-poster bedroom available. Service throughout is friendly and helpful.

ROOMS: 19 en suite (bth/shr) (3 fmly) s £55; d £65 (incl. bkfst) * LB Off peak **MEALS:** Dinner £15-£20alc International Cuisine V meals **FACILITIES:** CTV in all bedrooms **SERVICES:** 22P **NOTES:** No coaches No smoking area in restaurant Last d 8pm Closed 24-27 Dec
CARDS:

New AA Guides for the Millennium are featured on page 24

S

TAMWORTH Staffordshire **Map 07 SK20**

Travel Inn

Bonehill Rd, Bitterscote B78 3HQ

☎ 01827 54414 🖹 01827 310420

Dir: *M42 junct 10 follow A5 towards Tamworth. After 3m turn left onto A51. Straight over 1st rdbt, 3rd exit off next rdbt*

This modern building offers accommodation in smart, spacious and well equipped bedrooms, all with en-suite bathrooms. Refreshments may be taken at the nearby family restaurant. For details about current prices consult the Contents Page under Hotel Groups for the Travel Inn phone number.

ROOMS: 40 en suite (bth/shr) d £39.95 *

TAMWORTH Staffordshire **Map 07 SK20**

Travelodge

Green Ln B77 5PS

☎ Central Res 0800 850950 🖹 01525 878450

Dir: *A5/M42 junct 10*

This modern building offers accommodation in smart, spacious and well equipped bedrooms, all with en-suite bathrooms. Refreshments may be taken at the nearby family restaurant. For details about current prices, consult the Contents Page under Hotel Groups for the Travelodge phone number.

ROOMS: 62 en suite (bth/shr) d £49.95 *

TANKERSLEY South Yorkshire **Map 08 SK39**

★★★ Tankersley Manor

Church Ln S75 3DQ

Quality Percentage Score: 69%

☎ 01226 744700 🖹 01226 745405

Dir: *from M1 junct 36 take A61 Sheffield road. Hotel 0.5m on left*

Conveniently situated, this stone-built hotel, originally a farmhouse, offers modern, attractive bedrooms. Recently an adjoining building has been converted, providing additional bedrooms and meeting rooms. Public areas include a spacious restaurant and a popular pub; a good range of meals are available in both.

ROOMS: 70 en suite (bth/shr) (2 fmly) No smoking in all bedrooms **MEALS:** Lunch £12-£15 & alc Dinner £17.95-£19 & alc English & French Cuisine V meals Coffee am Tea pm **FACILITIES:** CTV in all bedrooms STV Golf 18 **CONF:** Thtr 500 Class 160 Board 50 **SERVICES:** Night porter Air conditioning 300P **NOTES:** No dogs (ex guide dogs) No coaches No smoking in restaurant Last d 9.45pm

CARDS:

See advert under BARNSLEY

TANKERSLEY South Yorkshire **Map 08 SK39**

Travel Inn

Maple Rd S75 3DL

☎ 01226 350035 🖹 01226 741524

Dir: *from junct 35A of M1(northbound exit only) follow A616 for 2m. From junct 36 take A61 towards Sheffield, Travel Inn 1m*

This modern building offers accommodation in smart, spacious and well equipped bedrooms, all with en-suite bathrooms. Refreshments may be taken at the nearby family restaurant. For details about current prices consult the Contents Page under Hotel Groups for the Travel Inn phone number.

ROOMS: 40 en suite (bth/shr) d £39.95 *

★

The Premier Collection, hotels with Red Star Awards are listed on pages 17-23

TAPLOW Buckinghamshire **Map 04 SU98**

The Premier Collection

★★★★★ Cliveden

SL6 0JF

☎ 01628 668561 🖹 01628 661837

Approached through a 375-acre National Trust managed estate, the impact of Cliveden Hotel is awesome, standing at the top of a wide, gravelled boulevard. The house has a colourful past from its links with the influential Astor family. Visitors are treated as house guests and staff recapture the country house tradition of service. Bedrooms are steeped in quality and individual style. There is a range of reception rooms, for private dining and business purposes, with state-of-the-art facilities. The view across the parterre from the main dining room, the Terrace Restaurant,

contd.

is one of the many delights. As an alternative, try the excellent menu at Waldo's, a place for serious dining in discreet, well upholstered luxury. Exceptional leisure facilites include cruises in the Astor electric canoe or Thames Slipper Launch along Cliveden Reach.
ROOMS: 32 en suite (bth/shr) 7 annexe en suite (bth/shr) No smoking in 13 bedrooms d £290-£360 * LB Off peak **MEALS:** Lunch £26-£42.50 & alc Dinner fr £50alc British & French Cuisine V meals **FACILITIES:** CTV in all bedrooms STV Indoor swimming pool (heated) Outdoor swimming pool (heated) Tennis (hard) Fishing Squash Riding Snooker Sauna Solarium Gym Jacuzzi/spa Indoor tennis/Turkish bath/massage Wkly live entertainment Xmas **CONF:** Thtr 42 Class 70 Board 28 **SERVICES:** Lift Night porter 63P **NOTES:** No coaches No smoking in restaurant Last d 9.30pm **CARDS:**

TAPLOW Buckinghamshire **Map 04 SU98**
Late entry **Taplow House Hotel**
Berry Hill SL6 0DA
☎ 01628 670056 01628 773625
A hotel set in a Georgian mansion, built in six acres of parkland, with a pleasant sun terrace. Bedrooms are designed with luxury and comfort in mind, mostly air conditioned: facilities are numerous. Hotel transport is available for transfers to nearby Heathrow Airport, ideal for business and leisure.
ROOMS: 32 en suite (bth/shr) (4 fmly) No smoking in all bedrooms s £130-£140; d £160-£425 * LB Off peak **MEALS:** Lunch £20 & alc Dinner £25 & alc European Cuisine V meals Coffee am Tea pm **FACILITIES:** CTV in all bedrooms STV Croquet lawn Xmas **CONF:** Thtr 100 Class 50 Board 40 Del from £150 * **SERVICES:** Night porter Air conditioning 100P **NOTES:** No dogs (ex guide dogs) No coaches No smoking area in restaurant Last d 10pm
CARDS:

TARPORLEY Cheshire **Map 07 SJ56**
★★★ **The Wild Boar**
Whitchurch Rd, Beeston CW6 9NW
Quality Percentage Score: 64%
☎ 01829 260309 01829 261081
Dir: *turn off A51 Nantwich/Chester rd onto A49 to Whitchurch at Red Fox pub traffic lights, hotel on left at brow of hill after about 1.5m*
This classical black and white half-timbered building was built in the 17th century as a hunting lodge. Later extensions, built in a style complimenting the original, have resulted in spacious and comfortably furnished bedrooms. Extensive lounge areas allow guests to relax, and a good standard of cooking is offered in the warm and intimate restaurant.
ROOMS: 37 en suite (bth/shr) (10 fmly) No smoking in 10 bedrooms s £60-£75; d £70-£90 (incl. bkfst) * LB Off peak **MEALS:** Lunch £14.95 & alc Dinner £24.50 & alc International Cuisine V meals Coffee am Tea pm **FACILITIES:** CTV in all bedrooms STV Xmas **CONF:** Thtr 150 Class 33 Board 36 Del from £85 * **SERVICES:** Night porter 80P **NOTES:** Last d 9pm **CARDS:**

TAUNTON Somerset **Map 03 ST22**

The Premier Collection

★★★ **Castle**
Castle Green TA1 1NF
☎ 01823 272671 01823 336066
Dir: *from M5 junct 25 follow signs 'Town Centre' then 'Castle & Museum'*
Ideally situated just a stone's throw from the town centre and adjacent to the castle museum, this impressive wisteria-clad hotel is set in a Norman garden. The tastefully furnished bedrooms vary in size, with the garden rooms and the stunning Penthouse Suite being especially popular. The imaginatively decorated and comfortable public rooms feature many nooks and crannies and a new brasserie. Afternoon tea is a speciality. Local produce features strongly in Chef Phil Vickery's imaginative and constantly changing British menus and includes both the adventurous and classical dishes.

ROOMS: 44 en suite (bth/shr) s £88-£115; d £139-£230 (incl. bkfst) * LB Off peak **MEALS:** Lunch £17-£28 & alc Dinner £25-£27.50 & alc V meals Coffee am Tea pm **FACILITIES:** CTV in all bedrooms STV Xmas **CONF:** Thtr 100 Class 45 Board 40 Del from £125 * **SERVICES:** Lift Night porter 40P **NOTES:** No smoking in restaurant Last d 9pm **CARDS:**

TAUNTON Somerset **Map 03 ST22**
★★★ ***The Mount Somerset***
Henlade TA3 5NB
Quality Percentage Score: 75%
☎ 01823 442500 01823 442900
Dir: *turn off M5 at junct 25, take A358 towards Chard/Ilminster, at Henlade right into Stoke Rd, left at T junct at end Stoke Rd then right into drive*
This splendid Georgian house, stands high on the Blackdown Hills with wonderful views of the Somerset countryside. Public rooms are a blend of elegance, style and intimacy with sumptuous sofas beside a crackling log fire. Bedrooms are well appointed with rich fabrics and some wonderful beds. Many bathrooms have spa baths and marble handbasins. A daily changing menu is served in the dining room.
ROOMS: 11 en suite (bth/shr) No smoking in 6 bedrooms **MEALS:** International Cuisine V meals Coffee am Tea pm **FACILITIES:** CTV in all bedrooms Arrangement with health club adjacent Wkly live entertainment **CONF:** Thtr 50 Class 30 Board 20 **SERVICES:** Lift 100P **NOTES:** No dogs Last d 9.30pm **CARDS:**

See advert on opposite page

TAUNTON Somerset **Map 03 ST22**
★★★ **Rumwell Manor**
Rumwell TA4 1EL
Quality Percentage Score: 71%
☎ 01823 461902 01823 254861
Dir: *leave M5 junct 26 follow signs to Wellington, turn onto A38 to Taunton, hotel is 2.5m on right*
Situated in five acres of grounds and surrounded by mellow Somerset countryside, Rumwell Manor was built in 1805, and has a wonderful relaxed atmosphere. Bedrooms vary, with those in the main house offering greater space and character, whilst those around the small courtyard have recently been upgraded. In the candlelit restaurant both fixed-price and carte menus offer

contd.

T

dishes based on fresh produce. A cosy bar and adjacent lounge are also available.
ROOMS: 10 en suite (bth/shr) 10 annexe en suite (bth/shr) (3 fmly) No smoking in 2 bedrooms s £59-£68; d £85-£105 (incl. bkfst) * LB Off peak **MEALS:** Lunch £7.50-£14 & alc Dinner £13-£18.50 & alc English & French Cuisine V meals Coffee am Tea pm **FACILITIES:** CTV in all bedrooms Xmas **CONF:** Thtr 40 Class 24 Board 26 Del from £89 * **SERVICES:** 40P **NOTES:** No coaches No smoking in restaurant Last d 9pm **CARDS:**

TAUNTON Somerset **Map 03 ST22**
★★★ ***Posthouse Taunton***
Deane Gate Av TA1 2UA **Posthouse**
Quality Percentage Score: 63%
☎ 01823 332222 01823 332266
Dir: *adjacent to junct 25 on M5*
Situated at Junction 25 of the M5, this newly refurbished hotel is suitable for both business and leisure travellers. In addition to a range of meeting rooms and good leisure facilities, this bright establishment provides smart modern accommodation in well equipped bedrooms with en suite bathrooms.
ROOMS: 99 en suite (bth/shr) (68 fmly) No smoking in 55 bedrooms **MEALS:** International Cuisine V meals Coffee am Tea pm **FACILITIES:** CTV in all bedrooms Gym Pool table ch fac **CONF:** Thtr 300 Class 110 Board 105 Del from £105 * **SERVICES:** Lift Night porter 300P **NOTES:** Last d 10.30pm **CARDS:**

TAUNTON Somerset **Map 03 ST22**
★★ ***Farthings Hotel & Restaurant***
Hatch Beauchamp TA3 6SG
Quality Percentage Score: 73%
☎ 01823 480664 01823 481118
Dir: *from A358, between Taunton and Ilminster turn into Hatch Beauchamp for hotel in village centre*

Situated in the village of Hatch Beauchamp, this family run Georgian hotel offers tastefully furnished and decorated bedrooms which include many thoughtful extras. One room has an internal spiral staircase leading to the en suite bathroom. Public areas include a comfortable sitting room and a separate bar-lounge. There is a choice of dining rooms where a frequently changing menu focuses upon innovative use of local produce.
ROOMS: 9 en suite (bth/shr) (2 fmly) No smoking in all bedrooms **MEALS:** V meals Coffee am Tea pm **FACILITIES:** CTV in all bedrooms Croquet lawn **CONF:** Thtr 24 Class 18 Board 16 **SERVICES:** 22P **NOTES:** No dogs (ex guide dogs) No coaches No smoking in restaurant Last d 8.30pm **CARDS:**

Symbols and Abbreviations are listed and explained on pages 4 and 5

TAUNTON Somerset **Map 03 ST22**
★★ ***Corner House Hotel***
Park St TA1 4DQ
Quality Percentage Score: 66%
☎ 0823 284683 & 272665 (0823) 323464
Just a short walk from the town centre, this Victorian house with modern extensions still retains much of its original character. A choice of freshly prepared dishes is offered in either the cosy bar or the more formal surroundings of the restaurant.
ROOMS: 33 rms (23 bth 4 shr) (4 fmly) **MEALS:** English & French Cuisine V meals Coffee am Tea pm **FACILITIES:** CTV in all bedrooms **SERVICES:** 42P **NOTES:** No dogs (ex guide dogs) No coaches Last d 9.15pm **CARDS:**

TAUNTON Somerset **Map 03 ST22**
★★ **Falcon**
Henlade TA3 5DH
Quality Percentage Score: 61%
☎ 01823 442502 01823 442670
Dir: *M5 junct 25 1m E of A358 Taunton to Yeovil Road*
This brick-built Victorian house is conveniently located, and provides bedrooms of varying sizes, equipped with modern comforts. Recent developments include the completion of two cottage style annexe rooms. Fixed-price and carte menus are available in the dining room and the convivial bar is a popular meeting place.
ROOMS: 11 en suite (bth/shr) (2 fmly) No smoking in 3 bedrooms s fr £49.50; d fr £65 (incl. bkfst) * LB Off peak **MEALS:** Dinner fr £16.50 & alc International Cuisine V meals Coffee am **FACILITIES:** CTV in all bedrooms STV **CONF:** Thtr 65 Class 40 Board 40 Del from £75 * **SERVICES:** 25P **NOTES:** No coaches No smoking in restaurant Last d 8.30pm Closed 25 Dec **CARDS:**

TAUNTON Somerset **Map 03 ST22**

Travel Inn

81 Bridgwater Rd TA1 2DU

01823 321112 01823 322054

Dir: *leave M5 junct 25 follow signs to Taunton keep left at rdbt and flow left at Creech Castle traffic lights, following signs for Corfe 200yds on right*

This modern building offers accommodation in smart, spacious and well equipped bedrooms, all with en-suite bathrooms. Refreshments may be taken at the nearby family restaurant. For details about current prices consult the Contents Page under Hotel Groups for the Travel Inn phone number.

ROOMS: 40 en suite (bth/shr) d £39.95 *

TAUNTON Somerset **Map 03 ST22**

Travelodge

Riverside Retail Park, Hankridge Farm TA1 2LR

01823 444702

Dir: *M5 junc25*

This modern building offers accommodation in smart, spacious and well equipped bedrooms, all with en-suite bathrooms. Refreshments may be taken at the nearby family restaurant. For details about current prices, consult the Contents Page under Hotel Groups for the Travelodge phone number.

ROOMS: 48 en suite (bth/shr) d £45.95 *

TAUNTON DEANE MOTORWAY SERVICE AREA (M5) Somerset **Map 03 ST12**

Roadchef Lodge

M5 Southbound, Trull TA3 7PF

01823 332228 01823 338131

Dir: *between junct 25 & 26 of M5*

This modern building offers accommodation in smart, spacious and well equipped bedrooms, all with en-suite bathrooms. Refreshments may be taken at the nearby family restaurant. For details about current prices, consult the Contents Page under Hotel Groups for the Roadchef phone number.

ROOMS: 39 en suite (bth/shr) d fr £47.50 *

TAVISTOCK Devon **Map 02 SX47**

★★★ **Bedford**

REGAL

Plymouth Rd PL19 8BB

Quality Percentage Score: 65%

01822 613221 01822 618034

Dir: *leave M5 Jct31 - Launceston/Okehampton A30. Take A386 - Tavistock. On entering Tavistock follow signs for town centre. Hotel opposite church*

Situated in the town centre, the Bedford is an impressive, castellated building, built in 1820 on the site of a Benedictine Abbey. Recent refurbishment has greatly improved bedrooms, which are ideally equipped for both business and leisure guests, and public areas combine comfort with the hotel's abundant character. A fixed-price menu is served in the Woburn Restaurant.

ROOMS: 30 en suite (bth/shr) (1 fmly) No smoking in 11 bedrooms s fr £55; d fr £43 (incl. bkfst) * LB Off peak **MEALS:** Sunday Lunch £5.50-£13.30 Dinner fr £16.95 & alc V meals Coffee am Tea pm **FACILITIES:** CTV in all bedrooms Xmas **CONF:** Thtr 70 Class 45 Board 25 Del from £85 * **SERVICES:** 50P **NOTES:** No smoking in restaurant Last d 9pm **CARDS:**

For Useful Information and Important Telephone Number Changes turn to page 25

TEBAY Cumbria **Map 12 NY60**

★★★ **Westmorland Hotel & Bretherdale Restaurant**

Orton CA10 3SB

Quality Percentage Score: 69%

015396 24351 015396 24354

Dir: *next to Westmorland's Tebay Services on the M6, easily reached from the southbound carriageway using the road linking the two service areas between*

This family-owned hotel enjoys stunning views of the moors. The stylish bedroom wing and refurbished public rooms reflect a cosmopolitan approach. Staff are keen to please and a pleasant menu is offered in the open-plan restaurant.

ROOMS: 53 en suite (bth/shr) (30 fmly) No smoking in 20 bedrooms s £55-£80.50; d £70.50-£96 (incl. bkfst) * LB Off peak **MEALS:** Bar Lunch fr £2.95 Dinner fr £21 & alc V meals Coffee am Tea pm **FACILITIES:** CTV in all bedrooms STV Xmas **CONF:** Thtr 100 Class 36 Board 24 Del from £95 * **SERVICES:** Lift Night porter 100P **NOTES:** No smoking in restaurant Last d 9pm **CARDS:**

See advert on opposite page

TEES-SIDE AIRPORT Co Durham **Map 08 NZ31**

★★★ **The St George**

Middleton St George DL2 1RH

Quality Percentage Score: 62%

01325 332631 01325 333851

Dir: *turn off A67 by pass directly into Airport grounds*

This former wartime officers' mess is conveniently situated within walking distance of the airport terminal building. Bedrooms are modern and well equipped and public areas, including Carriages Restaurant which enjoys a good reputation for its Continental and English cuisine, are practical and comfortable. Staff throughout are friendly and professional and there are also versatile banqueting and conference facilities.

ROOMS: 59 en suite (bth/shr) (2 fmly) No smoking in 8 bedrooms s £85; d £95 (incl. bkfst) * LB Off peak **MEALS:** Lunch £8.50-£10.95 Dinner £12.50-£15.50 English & French Cuisine V meals Coffee am **FACILITIES:** CTV in all bedrooms Sauna Solarium Xmas **CONF:** Thtr 160 Class 60 Board 50 Del from £75 * **SERVICES:** Night porter 220P **NOTES:** Last d 9.45pm **CARDS:**

TEIGNMOUTH Devon **Map 03 SX97**

★★ **Ness House**

Marine Dr, Shaldon TQ14 0HP

Quality Percentage Score: 70%

01626 873480 01626 873486

Dir: *from M5 take A380 turn onto A381 to Teignmouth, cross bridge to Shaldon, hotel 0.5m on left on Torquay Rd*

Overlooking the Teign Estuary, this Georgian house has kept its original character as a nobelman's summer residence. As an alternative to formal dining in the elegant restaurant, meals are

contd.

also served in the bar and conservatory. Bedrooms are spacious and comfortable.
ROOMS: 7 en suite (bth/shr) 5 annexe en suite (bth/shr) (2 fmly) No smoking in 4 bedrooms s £45-£69; d £79-£99 (incl. bkfst) * LB Off peak **MEALS:** Lunch £7.50-£17.50 & alc Dinner £17.50 & alc English & French Cuisine V meals Coffee am Tea pm **FACILITIES:** CTV in all bedrooms STV ch fac Xmas **SERVICES:** 20P **NOTES:** No dogs (ex guide dogs) No coaches No smoking in restaurant Last d 10.15pm Closed 24 & 25 Dec **CARDS:**

TELFORD Shropshire **Map 07 SJ60**
see also **Worfield**
★★★★ *Buckatree Hall*
The Wrekin, Wellington TF6 5AL
Quality Percentage Score: 64%
☎ 01952 641821 📠 01952 247540
Dir: *exit 7 of M54, turn left and left again for 1m*

Dating from 1820, this former hunting lodge is located in an extensive wooded estate on the slopes of The Wrekin. Bedrooms are well equipped and have been refurbished to a high standard. A suite is available, some rooms are inter-connecting, and some have balconies. Public rooms include function and conference facilities.
ROOMS: 60 en suite (bth/shr) (3 fmly) No smoking in 4 bedrooms **MEALS:** V meals Coffee am Tea pm **FACILITIES:** CTV in 59 bedrooms STV Pool table Wkly live entertainment **CONF:** Thtr 200 Class 100 Board 60 **SERVICES:** Lift Night porter 100P **NOTES:** No smoking in restaurant Last d 9.30pm **CARDS:**

TELFORD Shropshire **Map 07 SJ60**
★★★ Clarion Hotel Madely Court
Castlefields Way, Madeley TF7 5DW
Quality Percentage Score: 68%
☎ 01952 680068 📠 01952 684275
Dir: *M54 junct 4, A4169 Telford, A442 at 2nd rdbt signs for Kidderminster, continue along (ignore sign to Madeley & Kidderminster) 1st left off rdbt*
A delightful 16th-century manor house with a lakeside setting in the grounds of Madeley Court Mill. Panelled walls, large fireplaces and a solid oak spiral staircase give character to the original house, where the bedrooms have fine antique furnishings, whilst the modern wing has, appropriately, modern bedrooms. Meals can be taken either in the Priory Restaurant, also used for functions, or the brasserie.
ROOMS: 29 en suite (bth/shr) 19 annexe en suite (bth/shr) (1 fmly) No smoking in 6 bedrooms s fr £98; d £115-£150 * LB Off peak **MEALS:** Dinner fr £19.50 French & Mediterranean Cuisine V meals Coffee am Tea pm **FACILITIES:** CTV in all bedrooms Fishing Archery Horse riding arranged Xmas **CONF:** Thtr 220 Class 150 Board 50 **SERVICES:** Night porter 180P **NOTES:** No smoking in restaurant Last d 9.45pm **CARDS:**

TELFORD Shropshire **Map 07 SJ60**
★★★ Telford Golf & Country Club
Great Hay Dr, Sutton Hill TF7 4DT
Quality Percentage Score: 66%
☎ 01952 429977 📠 01952 586602
Dir: *M54 junct 4, A442 - Kiderminster, follow signs for Telford Golf Club*
A modern and much extended former farmhouse situated in an elevated position overlooking Ironbridge Gorge. The well equipped bedrooms are located in several different wings some with fine views over the gorge and others looking out over the golf course. The Ironbridge Restaurant offers carvery and a la carte menus, and Darby's Pantry provides light meals in a more informal setting. The many facilities include an 18-hole golf course and driving range, a large indoor swimming pool, squash courts, a gymnasium and a billiards room.
ROOMS: 96 en suite (bth/shr) (16 fmly) No smoking in 36 bedrooms s £105; d £125 * LB Off peak **MEALS:** Lunch £9.95-£12.25 Dinner £15.95 International Cuisine V meals Coffee am Tea pm **FACILITIES:** CTV in all bedrooms Indoor swimming pool (heated) Golf 18 Squash Snooker Sauna Solarium Gym Pool table Putting green Jacuzzi/spa Xmas **CONF:** Thtr 200 Class 140 Board 60 Del from £85 * **SERVICES:** Night porter 200P **NOTES:** No smoking in restaurant Last d 9.45pm **CARDS:**

TELFORD Shropshire **Map 07 SJ60**
★★★ *Telford Moat House*
Forgegate, Telford Centre TF3 4NA
Quality Percentage Score: 66%
☎ 01952 429988 📠 01952 292012
Dir: *junct 5 M54*
A large modern hotel just off the M54. Bedrooms are spacious and comfortably furnished, public areas are designed to cater for

contd.

a wide variety of needs. The Casa Med Bar and Brasserie is popular, there is a well equipped leisure centre and excellent facilities for conferences.
ROOMS: 147 en suite (bth/shr) (7 fmly) No smoking in 44 bedrooms **MEALS:** English & French Cuisine V meals Coffee am **FACILITIES:** CTV in all bedrooms Indoor swimming pool (heated) Sauna Solarium Gym Pool table Jacuzzi/spa Childrens play area **CONF:** Thtr 400 Class 200 Board 40 **SERVICES:** Lift Night porter 300P **NOTES:** Last d 9.45pm **CARDS:**

TELFORD Shropshire **Map 07 SJ60**
★★★ **Valley**
TF8 7DW
Quality Percentage Score: 66%
☎ 01952 432247 01952 432308
Dir: *M6, M54 junct 6 onto A5223 to Ironbridge*
Situated in attractive gardens and close to the famous iron bridge, this house was once the home of Arthur Maw, the distinguished tile manufacturer. Bedrooms vary in size and are split between the main house and an attractive mews development, accessed via covered walkways. A wide range of dishes is offered in the restaurant, including a selection of healthier options and vegetarian meals. The hotel also benefits from good conference facilities.
ROOMS: 35 en suite (bth/shr) s £83; d £92 * LB Off peak **MEALS:** Lunch £14.50-£19.50 & alc High tea £5.50 Dinner £19.50 & alc International Cuisine V meals Coffee am Tea pm **FACILITIES:** CTV in all bedrooms STV ch fac **CONF:** Thtr 250 Class 100 Board 50 Del £120 * **SERVICES:** Night porter 100P **NOTES:** No dogs (ex guide dogs) No smoking in restaurant Last d 9.30pm **CARDS:**

TELFORD Shropshire **Map 07 SJ60**
★★ **White House**
Wellington Rd, Muxton TF2 8NG
Quality Percentage Score: 68%
☎ 01952 604276 & 603603 01952 670336
Dir: *off A518 Telford-Stafford road*
The Swindley family have owned and run this hotel for over 30 years. It provides well equipped modern accommodation. The attractive public areas offer a choice of bars and a very pleasant restaurant, where a wide range of dishes is available. There is also a small lounge for resident guests and a beer garden.
ROOMS: 32 en suite (bth/shr) (3 fmly) s fr £62.50; d fr £75 (incl. bkfst) * LB Off peak **MEALS:** Lunch £9.50-£9.95 & alc Dinner fr £13.50 & alc Continental Cuisine V meals Coffee am Tea pm **FACILITIES:** CTV in all bedrooms **CONF:** Thtr 12 Class 6 Board 10 **SERVICES:** Night porter 100P **NOTES:** No dogs (ex guide dogs) No coaches No smoking area in restaurant Last d 9.30pm **CARDS:**

T

TELFORD Shropshire **Map 07 SJ60**
★★ ***Oaks Hotel & Restaurant***
Redhill, St Georges TF2 9NZ
Quality Percentage Score: 63%
☎ 01952 620126 01952 620257
Dir: *M54 junct 4, A5 Cannock 1.5 miles*
The Oaks is a small, family-run hotel, that is popular with both commercial visitors and tourists. It provides well equipped accommodation, including family rooms. There is an attractively appointed restaurant, where a good choice of popular dishes is available, a pleasant bar, a function room and a beer garden.
ROOMS: 12 en suite (bth/shr) (4 fmly) **MEALS:** English & French Cuisine V meals Coffee am **FACILITIES:** CTV in all bedrooms **CONF:** Thtr 40 Class 40 Board 25 **SERVICES:** 36P **NOTES:** No dogs (ex guide dogs) Last d 9.30pm **CARDS:**

TELFORD Shropshire **Map 07 SJ60**
★★ ***Arleston Inn***
Arleston Ln, Wellington TF1 2LA
Quality Percentage Score: 62%
☎ 01952 501881 01952 506429
Dir: *from M54 junct 6 take A523 Ironbridge road and right at next roundabout past Lawley School then right into Arleston Lane*
This small hotel has a lot of charm and character and was once a coaching inn. The well maintained accommodation has modern furnishings and equipment. Apart from the bar, there is a conservatory lounge which overlooks the lovely garden, and a popular restaurant where a good choice of dishes is available.
ROOMS: 7 en suite (shr) **MEALS:** V meals **FACILITIES:** CTV in all bedrooms **SERVICES:** Night porter 40P **NOTES:** No dogs (ex guide dogs) No smoking in restaurant **CARDS:**

TELFORD Shropshire **Map 07 SJ60**
Travel Inn
Euston Way TF3 4LY
☎ 01952 201075 01952 290742
Dir: *M54 junct 5 follow signs for Cenrtral Railway Station (A442) Travel Inn at next rdbt 2nd exit*
This modern building offers accommodation in smart, spacious and well equipped bedrooms, all with en-suite bathrooms. Refreshments may be taken at the nearby family restaurant. For details about current prices consult the Contents Page under Hotel Groups for the Travel Inn phone number.
ROOMS: 40 en suite (bth/shr) d £39.95 *

TELFORD Shropshire **Map 07 SJ60**
Travelodge
Whitchurch Dr, Shawbirch TF1 3QA
☎ 01952 251244 01952 251244
Dir: *1m NW, on A5223*
This modern building offers accommodation in smart, spacious and well equipped bedrooms, all with en-suite bathrooms. Refreshments may be taken at the nearby family restaurant. For details about current prices, consult the Contents Page under Hotel Groups for the Travelodge phone number.
ROOMS: 40 en suite (bth/shr) d £45.95 *

TEMPLE SOWERBY Cumbria **Map 12 NY62**
★★★ ***Temple Sowerby House***
CA10 1RZ
Quality Percentage Score: 71%
☎ 017683 61578 (Freephone 0800 146157) 017683 61958
Dir: *midway between Penrith and Appleby, 7 miles from M6 junct 40*
This delightful former Cumbrian farmhouse is a very hospitable hotel with a country house atmosphere. Attractive public rooms include a choice of comfortable lounges, a dispense bar and two elegant dining areas featuring traditional English fare. The bedrooms are individual with a mixture of traditional and modern furnishings.
ROOMS: 9 en suite (bth/shr) 4 annexe en suite (bth/shr) (1 fmly) **MEALS:** International Cuisine V meals Coffee am Tea pm **FACILITIES:** CTV in all bedrooms Fishing Croquet lawn Badminton Boules **CONF:** Thtr 30 Class 20 Board 20 **SERVICES:** 30P **NOTES:** No coaches No smoking in restaurant Last d 8.45pm **CARDS:**

The AA Hotel Booking Service is a free benefit to AA members. See the advertisement on page 47

TENBURY WELLS Worcestershire — Map 07 SO56

★★ *Cadmore Lodge*

Berrington Green, St Michaels WR15 8TQ

Quality Percentage Score: 66%

☎ 01584 810044 Fax 01584 810044

Dir: *on A4112 from Tenbury Wells to Leominster, turn right at St Michaels Church, signposted to Cadmore Lodge, hotel 0.75m on left*

Built some 10 years ago, this small privately-owned and personally run hotel enjoys a secluded location on a 70-acre private estate containing many outdoor leisure facilities. The bedrooms, which include family accommodation, are traditionally furnished with modern facilities. Six new bedrooms and impressive indoor leisure facilities are recent additions, while a large room with lake views is a popular venue for functions.

ROOMS: 14 en suite (bth/shr) (1 fmly) No smoking in all bedrooms **MEALS:** French Cuisine V meals Coffee am Tea pm **FACILITIES:** CTV in all bedrooms Indoor swimming pool (heated) Golf 9 Tennis (hard) Fishing Gym Pool table Jacuzzi/spa Bowling green Steam room **CONF:** Thtr 100 Class 40 Board 30 **SERVICES:** 60P **NOTES:** No dogs No smoking in restaurant Last d 9pm

CARDS:

See advert on this page

TENTERDEN Kent — Map 05 TQ83

★★ *Collina House Hotel*

5 East Hill TN30 6RL

Quality Percentage Score: 66%

☎ 01580 764852 & 764004 Fax 01580 762224

Dir: *from Tenterden High Street, A28, turn into Oaks Road B20. Collina House is opposite an orchard before Appledore Road junction*

This friendly family run hotel in the Wealden market town of Tenterden offers comfortable, spacious accommodation. The hotel is a good base for touring the Weald with its many National Trust properties.

ROOMS: 11 en suite (bth/shr) 3 annexe en suite (bth/shr) (7 fmly) No smoking in 4 bedrooms **MEALS:** English, French & Italian Cuisine V meals Coffee am **FACILITIES:** CTV in all bedrooms **SERVICES:** 16P **NOTES:** No dogs (ex guide dogs) No smoking in restaurant Last d 9pm RS 24 Dec-5 Jan **CARDS:**

TETBURY Gloucestershire — Map 03 ST89

The Premier Collection

★★★ Calcot Manor

Calcot GL8 8YJ

☎ 01666 890391 Fax 01666 890394

Dir: *4m West of Tetbuty W at junct A4135/A46*

Originally belonging to Cistercian monks, this charming manor still has a 14th-century barn among its outbuildings. It offers high standards of accommodation, with some well designed family rooms, and its public areas include a choice of lounges, a smart restaurant opening into a conservatory, and a really well equipped children's playroom. The complex also includes the Gumstool, a bar with a country-pub atmosphere.

ROOMS: 9 en suite (bth/shr) 19 annexe en suite (bth/shr) (10 fmly) s fr £110; d £120-£175 (incl. bkfst) * LB Off peak **MEALS:** Lunch £13.50-£18 & alc Dinner £18-£30alc English & French Cuisine V meals Coffee am Tea pm **FACILITIES:** CTV in all bedrooms Outdoor swimming pool (heated) Croquet lawn Clay pigeon shooting ch fac Xmas **CONF:** Thtr 60 Class 40 Board 30 Del from £150 * **SERVICES:** 82P **NOTES:** No dogs (ex guide dogs) No coaches No smoking in restaurant Last d 9pm

CARDS:

TETBURY Gloucestershire
Map 03 ST89

★★★ *Close*

8 Long St GL8 8AQ

Quality Percentage Score: 82%

☎ 01666 502272 01666 504401

***Dir:** in the centre of Tetbury, from M4 junct 17 onto A429 to Malmesbury, Tetbury signposted from here. M5 junct 14 onto B4509 follow signs to Tetbury*

Set at the heart of this pretty Cotswold town, this special hotel has a genuine country house feel to it. Bedrooms are decorated and furnished with an air of luxury and include many extra touches such as robes, Madeira and fresh flowers. The public rooms include a number of relaxing areas to sit and take refreshment including a terrace in the walled garden. The restaurant is the venue for some impressive, modern country house style cooking.

ROOMS: 15 en suite (bth/shr) **MEALS:** V meals Coffee am Tea pm **FACILITIES:** CTV in all bedrooms STV Croquet lawn **CONF:** Thtr 35 Board 22 **SERVICES:** Night porter 22P **NOTES:** No coaches No smoking in restaurant Last d 10pm **CARDS:**

TETBURY Gloucestershire
Map 03 ST89

★★★ **Snooty Fox**

Market Place GL8 8DD

Quality Percentage Score: 74%

☎ 01666 502436 01666 503479

***Dir:** in the centre of the town, by market place*

Smart bedrooms and relaxed service sum up this former stone coaching inn in the heart of Tetbury. The Snooty Fox has many commendable attributes, not least the warm and friendly hospitality of the very attentive staff. Accommodation has recently been refurbished, offering bedrooms which are stylishly designed with many thoughtful extras. The charming public areas include a popular bar and an attractive restaurant, which offers well-priced, enjoyable fare suited to just about every taste.

ROOMS: 12 en suite (bth/shr) s fr £67.50; d fr £90 (incl. bkfst) * LB Off peak **MEALS:** V meals Coffee am Tea pm **FACILITIES:** CTV in all bedrooms STV Xmas **CONF:** Thtr 30 Board 15 **NOTES:** No dogs (ex guide dogs) Last d 9.45pm **CARDS:**

TETBURY Gloucestershire
Map 03 ST89

★★★ **Hare & Hounds**

Westonbirt GL8 8QL

Quality Percentage Score: 70%

☎ 01666 880233 01666 880241

***Dir:** 2.5m SW of Tetbury on A433*

This impressive country house is close to Westonbirt Arboretum, just south of Tetbury. The sizeable bedrooms, some of which are in the coach house, are furnished in keeping with the building's character, and the comfortable day rooms have a welcoming feel.

ROOMS: 24 en suite (bth/shr) 7 annexe en suite (bth/shr) (3 fmly) No smoking in 12 bedrooms s £65-£110; d £75-£120 * LB Off peak **MEALS:** Lunch £12.75-£23.50 & alc Dinner £19.50-£23.50 & alc English & French Cuisine V meals Coffee am Tea pm **FACILITIES:** CTV in all bedrooms Tennis (hard) Squash Pool table Croquet lawn Table tennis Xmas **CONF:** Thtr 120 Class 80 Board 30 **SERVICES:** 85P **NOTES:** No smoking in restaurant Last d 9pm **CARDS:**

TETBURY Gloucestershire
Map 03 ST89

★★★ *Priory Inn*

London Rd GL8 8JJ

Quality Percentage Score: 67%

☎ 01666 502251 01666 503534

***Dir:** on A433, Cirencester/Tetbury road 200yds from High St*

This modern hotel offers a good all-round standard of comfort, and parts of the house have an interesting theatrical theme. Bedrooms are attractive, with well chosen fabrics and decor, and the lounge has an airy 'colonial' style.

ROOMS: 14 en suite (bth/shr) (1 fmly) No smoking in 3 bedrooms **MEALS:** International Cuisine V meals Coffee am Tea pm **FACILITIES:** CTV in all bedrooms STV Wkly live entertainment **CONF:** Thtr 70 Class 25 Board 35 Del from £75 * **SERVICES:** 40P **NOTES:** No smoking area in restaurant Last d 9pm **CARDS:**

TEWKESBURY Gloucestershire
Map 03 SO83

★★★ **Tewkesbury Park Hotel**

Lincoln Green Ln GL20 7DN

Quality Percentage Score: 68%

☎ 01684 295405 01684 292386

***Dir:** M5 junct 9 take A438 through Tewkesbury onto A38 passing Abbey on left, turn right into Lincoln Green Lane before Esso Station*

An extended 18th-century mansion with fine views over the Vale of Evesham and River Severn. There is a fully equipped leisure centre and an 18-hole golf course in the grounds. A choice of dining areas and a number of function rooms are available.

ROOMS: 78 en suite (bth/shr) (16 fmly) No smoking in 57 bedrooms d £75-£85 * LB Off peak **MEALS:** Lunch £9.95-£12 Dinner £19.50 & alc English & French Cuisine V meals Coffee am Tea pm **FACILITIES:** CTV in all bedrooms STV Indoor swimming pool (heated) Golf 18 Tennis (hard) Squash Sauna Solarium Gym Putting green Jacuzzi/spa Health & beauty salon Xmas **CONF:** Thtr 150 Class 100 Board 50 Del £135 * **SERVICES:** Night porter 200P **NOTES:** No smoking in restaurant Last d 10pm **CARDS:**

TEWKESBURY Gloucestershire
Map 03 SO83

★★★ **Bell**

57 Church St GL20 5SA

Quality Percentage Score: 65%

☎ 01684 293293 01684 295938

***Dir:** on A38 in town centre opposite Abbey*

This former 14th century coaching house is on the edge of town, opposite the Norman Abbey. Bedrooms are comfortably furnished and feature thoughtful extras such as sherry. Open plan public areas are bright and inviting and include a popular restaurant where cuisine continues to show much promise.

ROOMS: 25 en suite (bth/shr) (1 fmly) No smoking in 5 bedrooms s £55.50-£65; d £65-£95 (incl. bkfst) * LB Off peak **MEALS:** V meals Coffee am Tea pm **FACILITIES:** CTV in all bedrooms Xmas **CONF:** Thtr 40 Class 15 Board 20 **SERVICES:** Night porter 35P **NOTES:** No smoking in restaurant Last d 9.15pm RS 25 Dec & 1 Jan **CARDS:**

Symbols and Abbreviations are listed and explained on pages 4 and 5

TEWKESBURY Gloucestershire — Map 03 SO83

★★★ Royal Hop Pole

Church St GL20 5RT

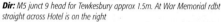

Quality Percentage Score: 58%

☎ 01684 293236 📠 01684 296680

Dir: *M5 junct 9 head for Tewkesbury approx 1.5m. At War Memorial rdbt straight across Hotel is on the right*

This former coaching inn at the heart of the town dates back to the 14th century. Though largely rebuilt in Georgian times, it retains much of its original charm in sloping floors, exposed beams and character interior work. The bedroom renovation programme is still in hand although all rooms are well equipped. The hotel is a popular venue, offering a comfortable lounge, cosy bar and restaurant.

ROOMS: 24 en suite (bth/shr) 5 annexe en suite (bth/shr) (1 fmly) No smoking in 14 bedrooms s £70-£90; d £80-£100 * LB Off peak **MEALS:** Sunday Lunch £9.95-£11.95 Dinner £14.95-£27.90 & alc V meals Coffee am Tea pm **FACILITIES:** CTV in all bedrooms Xmas **CONF:** Thtr 50 Class 25 Board 20 Del from £85 * **SERVICES:** Night porter 30P **NOTES:** No smoking in restaurant Last d 9.30pm

CARDS:

TEWKESBURY Gloucestershire — Map 03 SO83

★★ Tudor House

High St GL20 5BH

Quality Percentage Score: 65%

☎ 01684 297755 📠 01684 290306

Dir: *M5 junct 9 towards Tewkesbury 1.5m to the Town Centre*

A historic, town centre hotel that retains much of its Tudor character, including many beams and sloping floors. The bedrooms are are all well equipped. There is a good range of eating options from restaurant and bar menus. Friendly service is carried out by a local team.

ROOMS: 16 rms (12 bth/shr) 5 annexe rms (3 bth/shr) (1 fmly) s £45-£55; d £65-£75 (incl. bkfst) * LB Off peak **MEALS:** Lunch £8.95-£12.95 Dinner £14.95-£18.95 V meals Coffee am Tea pm **FACILITIES:** CTV in all bedrooms Wkly live entertainment Xmas **CONF:** Thtr 36 Class 18 Board 20 Del from £70 * **SERVICES:** 25P **NOTES:** No smoking in restaurant Last d 9pm **CARDS:**

THAME Oxfordshire — Map 04 SP70

★★★ Spread Eagle

Cornmarket OX9 2BW

Quality Percentage Score: 76%

☎ 01844 213661 📠 01844 261380

Dir: *town centre on A418 Oxford to Aylesbury Road, exit 6 M40 south exit 8 north*

The tradition of hospitality is upheld by proprietors Mr and Mrs Barrington who have assembled a friendly yet professional staff. Bedrooms vary in character depending on which part of the much extended property they are in, with the modern wings offering more space but the older areas having more period charm. There are extensive banqueting facilities and the traditional restaurant offers a wide selection of menus, including some traditional favourites from Fothergill's day like the incredibly rich Chocolate Mud.

ROOMS: 33 en suite (bth/shr) (1 fmly) s £93-£108; d £108-£127 (incl. cont bkfst) * LB Off peak **MEALS:** Lunch £8.50-£25 & alc Dinner £22.95-£28 & alc English & French Cuisine V meals Coffee am Tea pm **FACILITIES:** CTV in all bedrooms Xmas **CONF:** Thtr 250 Class 100 Board 50 Del from £144.95 * **SERVICES:** Night porter 80P **NOTES:** No dogs (ex guide dogs) Last d 10pm Closed 28-30 Dec

CARDS:

THAME Oxfordshire — Map 04 SP70

Travelodge

OX9 3XD

☎ 01844 218740 📠 01844 218740

Dir: *A418/B4011*

This modern building offers accommodation in smart, spacious and well equipped bedrooms, all with en-suite bathrooms. Refreshments may be taken at the nearby family restaurant. For details about current prices, consult the Contents Page under Hotel Groups for the Travelodge phone number.

ROOMS: 31 en suite (bth/shr) d £49.95 *

THAXTED Essex — Map 05 TL63

★★ Four Seasons

Walden Rd CM6 2RE

Quality Percentage Score: 70%

☎ 01371 830129 📠 01371 830835

Dir: *0.5m N on the B184 at the junction with the B1051 Gt Sampford/Haverhill road*

This delightful country hotel, set in two acres of gardens, is distinguished for its courteous personal service. Other notable features are the lovely plaster-work moulding and weatherboarding. Public areas include a new grill room, an intimate, partitioned restaurant, situated within the relaxing lounge bar, and a quiet first-floor residents lounge. A dress code operates in the bar and restaurant.

ROOMS: 9 rms (8 bth/shr) No smoking in all bedrooms s £55; d £65 * LB Off peak **MEALS:** Lunch £14-£22alc Dinner £14-£25alc **FACILITIES:** CTV in all bedrooms **CONF:** Thtr 70 Class 60 Board 40 **SERVICES:** 100P **NOTES:** No dogs No coaches No children 12yrs No smoking in restaurant Last d 8.45pm **CARDS:**

THEALE Berkshire — Map 04 SU67

Travelodge (Westbound)

Burghfield RG30 3UQ

☎ 0118 9566966

Dir: *M4 between junc 11&12*

This modern building offers accommodation in smart, spacious and well equipped bedrooms, all with en-suite bathrooms. Refreshments may be taken at the nearby family restaurant. For details about current prices, consult the Contents Page under Hotel Groups for the Travelodge phone number.

ROOMS: 40 en suite (bth/shr) d £59.95 *

THETFORD Norfolk — Map 05 TL88

see also **Brandon (Suffolk)**

★★★ *The Bell*

King St IP24 2AZ

Quality Percentage Score: 62%

☎ 01842 754455 📠 01842 755552

Dir: *off A134*

In the heart of the old part of town near King Street South, this historic 15th century coaching inn has been sympathetically extended over the years, and enjoys a striking position in a crossroads location. Historic charm permeates through much of

contd.

the building and the oak beamed bar is most pleasant. More modern areas house the restaurant, conference facilities and the newer extension of bedrooms which overlook the river.
ROOMS: 47 en suite (bth/shr) (1 fmly) No smoking in 20 bedrooms **MEALS:** European Cuisine V meals Coffee am Tea pm **FACILITIES:** CTV in all bedrooms **CONF:** Thtr 80 Class 45 Board 40 Del from £115 * **SERVICES:** Night porter 82P **NOTES:** No smoking in restaurant Last d 9.30pm **CARDS:**

THETFORD Norfolk **Map 05 TL88**

★★ The Thomas Paine Hotel

White Hart St IP24 1AA
Quality Percentage Score: 65%
☎ 01842 755631 📠 01842 766505
Dir: *heading N on the A11, at rdbt immediately before Thetford take A1075, the hotel is on the right hand side as you approach the town*
Close to the town centre, this popular hotel extends a friendly welcome and offers spacious public rooms and a choice of eating options in the open-plan bar and more formal restaurant. The bedrooms vary in size but all offer character and comfort.
ROOMS: 13 en suite (bth/shr) (1 fmly) s £50-£55; d £60-£70 (incl. bkfst) * LB Off peak **MEALS:** Lunch £12.50-£16.50 High tea fr £5.20 Dinner fr £16.50 V meals Coffee am Tea pm **FACILITIES:** CTV in all bedrooms Xmas **CONF:** Thtr 70 Class 35 Board 30 Del from £62 * **SERVICES:** 30P **NOTES:** No smoking in restaurant Last d 9pm
CARDS:

THIRSK North Yorkshire **Map 08 SE48**

★★ Sheppard's

Church Farm, Front St, Sowerby YO7 1JF
Quality Percentage Score: 71%
☎ 01845 523655 📠 01845 524720
Dir: *take A61 Ripon road from Market Sq, at mini rdbt turn left towards Sowerby. Hotel on right 0.25m along Sowerby road*
Set in the village suburb of Sowerby, this former farm has evolved from the original granary and stables, grouped around the yard. Attractive bedrooms are decorated in cottage style with stripped pine, and are thoughtfully equipped. Public areas include a cheery bistro with a glass domed conservatory, and a more intimate restaurant.
ROOMS: 8 en suite (bth/shr) No smoking in all bedrooms s £62; d £84 (incl. bkfst) * LB Off peak **MEALS:** Lunch fr £12.95 & alc Dinner £12-£25alc International Cuisine V meals **FACILITIES:** CTV in all bedrooms **CONF:** Thtr 80 Class 40 Board 30 **SERVICES:** 30P **NOTES:** No dogs No children 10yrs Last d 9.30pm Closed 1st wk Jan
CARDS:

T

THIRSK North Yorkshire **Map 08 SE48**

★★ Golden Fleece

42 Market Place YO7 1LL
Quality Percentage Score: 68%
☎ 01845 523108 📠 01845 523996
Dir: *off A19 at the Thirsk turn off, proceed to the town centre, Hotel is situated on the southern edge of Market Place*
This delightful old coaching inn, once the haunt of Dick Turpin, lies behind a Queen Anne facade in the market square. Gradually upgraded over the last few years, it offers modern well equipped bedrooms, a cosy bar and a restaurant which provides a good choice of dishes.
ROOMS: 18 en suite (bth/shr) (3 fmly) s £60; d £80 (incl. bkfst) * LB Off peak **MEALS:** Lunch £8.50 Dinner £17.50 & alc English & French Cuisine V meals Coffee am Tea pm **FACILITIES:** CTV in all bedrooms ch fac Xmas **CONF:** Thtr 100 Class 40 Board 40 Del from £70 * **SERVICES:** 50P **NOTES:** No smoking in restaurant Last d 9pm
CARDS:

THIRSK North Yorkshire **Map 08 SE48**

★★ Three Tuns Hotel

Market Place YO7 1LH
Quality Percentage Score: 62%
☎ 01845 523124 📠 01845 526126
Dir: *directly on A19, A61, 6m from A1 on A168 & A61*
This Georgian hotel stands in the corner of the Market Square and offers bedrooms that have been mostly upgraded. There is also a wide range of well produced food available.
ROOMS: 11 en suite (bth/shr) (3 fmly) No smoking in all bedrooms s £40-£45; d £60-£65 (incl. bkfst) * LB Off peak **MEALS:** V meals Coffee am Tea pm **FACILITIES:** CTV in 10 bedrooms **CONF:** Thtr 50 Board 35 **SERVICES:** 52P **NOTES:** No smoking in restaurant
CARDS:

THORNBURY Gloucestershire **Map 03 ST69**

The Premier Collection

★★★ Thornbury Castle

Castle St BS35 1HH
☎ 01454 281182 📠 01454 416188
Dir: *on A38 travelling N from Bristol take the first turning to Thornbury. At end of the High St left into Castle St, entrance to Castle on left*
Honoured guests at this historic castle in its Tudor period include Henry VIII, Anne Boleyn and Mary Tudor. Now a fine country-house hotel, its lovely handmade furnishings combine with modern standards of comfort and attentive service to create a luxurious atmosphere. The excellent cuisine shows the Scandinavian influence of its chef's home country, and there is a vineyard in the grounds.
ROOMS: 20 en suite (bth/shr) s £85-£105; d £105-£350 (incl. cont bkfst) * LB Off peak **MEALS:** Lunch £16.50-£39.50 Dinner £39.50 English & French Cuisine V meals Tea pm **FACILITIES:** CTV in all bedrooms STV Croquet lawn Hot air ballooning Archery Xmas **CONF:** Thtr 36 Class 12 Board 24 **SERVICES:** Night porter 40P **NOTES:** No dogs (ex guide dogs) No coaches No smoking in restaurant Last d 10pm Closed 4 days Jan
CARDS:

See advert under BRISTOL

THORNE South Yorkshire **Map 08 SE61**

★★ Belmont

Horsefair Green DN8 5EE
Quality Percentage Score: 68%
☎ 01405 812320 📠 01405 740508
Dir: *M18 exit 6 A614 signed Thorne. Hotel is on the right of the Market place*
Standing is the centre of the town, this very friendly and well managed hotel features a delightful bar and well furnished restaurant offering a wide choice of dishes. There is also a small

contd.

bistro. The bedrooms are modern, well equipped and have been delightfully furnished with pine furniture.
ROOMS: 23 en suite (bth/shr) (3 fmly) s £58.95-£63.95; d £73.95-£96.95 (incl. bkfst) * LB Off peak **MEALS:** Lunch £8-£12.95 & alc Dinner £11-£12.95 & alc English & French Cuisine V meals Coffee am Tea pm **FACILITIES:** CTV in all bedrooms STV Xmas **CONF:** Thtr 60 Class 20 Board 25 Del from £69.95 * **SERVICES:** Night porter 30P **NOTES:** Last d 10pm **CARDS:**

THORNHAM Norfolk — Map 09 TF74

★★ *Lifeboat Inn*

Ship Ln PE36 6LT
Quality Percentage Score: 66%
☎ 01485 512236 Fax 01485 512323
Dir: *follow coast road from Hunstanton A149 for approx 6m and take first left after Thornham sign*

A welcome sight for many a traveller over the centuries, this 16th-century ale house now combines historic charm with 20th century comforts. The relaxing views over the open meadows lead to the distant horizon of Thornham Harbour and the sea beyond. The attractive bedrooms may vary in size and space but all are well equipped and suitably furnished with free-standing pine furniture. The popular bar and restaurant provide a wide choice of appealing food.
ROOMS: 13 en suite (bth/shr) (3 fmly) No smoking in all bedrooms **MEALS:** English & French Cuisine V meals Coffee am Tea pm **FACILITIES:** CTV in all bedrooms **CONF:** Thtr 50 Class 30 Board 30 **SERVICES:** 120P **NOTES:** Last d 9.30pm **CARDS:**

THORNTON HOUGH Merseyside — Map 07 SJ38

★★★ Thornton Hall

Neston Rd CH63 1JF
Quality Percentage Score: 68%
☎ 0151 336 3938 Fax 0151 336 7864
Dir: *M53 junct 4 take B5151 Neston onto B5136 to Thornton Hough*

Lying in several acres of mature grounds in the village of Thornton Hough, this country house was built in the 18th-century by a shipping magnate. The hall still features original stained glass windows and impressive oak panelling. The restaurant also has its original leather and mother-of-pearl ceiling and carved fireplace. Most of the rooms are located in a purpose-built wing and these are well equipped with modern amenities.
ROOMS: 5 en suite (bth/shr) 58 annexe en suite (bth/shr) (1 fmly) s fr £76; d fr £86 * LB Off peak **MEALS:** Lunch £11.50-£15.50 Dinner fr £22 European Cuisine V meals Coffee am Tea pm **FACILITIES:** CTV in all bedrooms STV Indoor swimming pool (heated) Tennis (grass) Sauna Solarium Gym Croquet lawn Jacuzzi/spa Hot tub **CONF:** Thtr 200 Class 80 Board 40 Del from £115 * **SERVICES:** Night porter 250P **NOTES:** Last d 9.30pm **CARDS:**

THORNTON WATLASS North Yorkshire — Map 08 SE28

★ Buck Inn

HG4 4AH
Quality Percentage Score: 69%
☎ 01677 422461 Fax 01677 422447
Dir: *A684 towards Bedale, B6268 towards Masham, after 2m turn right at crossroads to Thornton Watlass, the Hotel is situated by the Cricket Green*

A charming inn overlooking the village green and the cricket pitch. Traditional bedrooms are comfortably and attractively decorated and there is also a cosy residents' lounge. The bar is full of character and charm with a good range of food available. The dining room is decorated with cricketing memorabillia.
ROOMS: 7 rms (5 bth/shr) (1 fmly) s fr £38; d fr £55 (incl. bkfst) * LB Off peak **MEALS:** Lunch £5-£9.95 Dinner fr £11 V meals Coffee am Tea pm **FACILITIES:** Fishing Pool table Quoits Childrens play area Wkly live entertainment **CONF:** Thtr 70 Class 40 Board 30 Del from £35 * **SERVICES:** 10P **NOTES:** No smoking in restaurant Last d 9.30pm **CARDS:**

THORPE (DOVEDALE) Derbyshire — Map 07 SK15

★★★ Izaak Walton

DE6 2AY
Quality Percentage Score: 70%
☎ 01335 350555 Fax 01335 350539
Dir: *leave A515 on B5054, follow road to Thorpe village, continue straight through over cattle grids & 2 small bridges, take 1st right & sharp left*

This hotel, named after the renowned fisherman and author, enjoys a fine location overlooking Thorpe Cloud. Many of the

contd.

bedrooms have lovely views, and 'executive' rooms are particularly spacious. Meals are served in the bar area, with more formal dining in the Haddon restaurant, which also has splendid views. Fishing on the River Dove can be arranged.
ROOMS: 30 en suite (bth/shr) (4 fmly) No smoking in 21 bedrooms s fr £81; d £105-£135 (incl. bkfst) * LB Off peak **MEALS:** Sunday Lunch fr £14.75 Dinner £23.50-£34.40 English & French Cuisine V meals Coffee am Tea pm **FACILITIES:** CTV in all bedrooms Fishing Fly fishing Xmas **CONF:** Thtr 50 Class 40 Board 30 Del from £110 * **SERVICES:** Night porter 80P **NOTES:** No smoking in restaurant Last d 9.15pm
CARDS:

See advert on page 649

THORPE (DOVEDALE) Derbyshire — Map 07 SK15
★★★ The Peveril of the Peak
DE6 2AW
Quality Percentage Score: 64%
☎ 01335 350333 Fax 01335 350507
Dir: *from M1 junct25, A52 towards Ashbourne then A515 towards Buxton for 1m to Thorpe. From M6 junct15/16, A50 to Stoke then A515 to Ashbourne and Thorpe*
This comfortable hotel, situated in the beautiful scenery of Dovedale, is named after one of Sir Walter Scott's heroic novels and provides modern accommodation in a relaxed and peaceful atmosphere. Most of the bedrooms have doors opening on to the gardens whilst others have individual patios. Some rooms have been adapted for disabled guests. There is a cosy cocktail bar a traditional and comfortable lounge and an attractively appointed restaurant which overlooks over the gardens. Conference and meeting rooms are also available and there is ample car parking space.
ROOMS: 46 en suite (bth/shr) (2 fmly) No smoking in 20 bedrooms s fr £80; d fr £95 (incl. bkfst) * LB Off peak **MEALS:** Lunch £9.95-£11.95 Dinner £21.95 & alc V meals Coffee am Tea pm **FACILITIES:** CTV in all bedrooms Tennis (hard) Xmas **CONF:** Thtr 70 Class 30 Board 36 Del £97.50 * **SERVICES:** Night porter 65P **NOTES:** Last d 9.30pm **CARDS:**

THORPE MARKET Norfolk — Map 09 TG23
★★ Elderton Lodge
Gunton Park NR11 8TZ
Quality Percentage Score: 69%
☎ 01263 833547 Fax 01263 834673
Dir: *at N Walsham take A149 towards Cromer, the hotel is on the left hand side just prior to entering Thorpe Market village*
The original shooting lodge to Gunton Hall and its 1000-acre deer park, the favoured retreat of Lillie Langtry and King Edward VII, Elderton Lodge maintains its sporting heritage with lots of field-sport paintings and prints, its resident gundog, and frequent shooting parties. This means, of course, a wealth of local seasonal game on the menu. The very attractive, comfortable bedrooms offer different styles and space, but all have good facilities.
ROOMS: 11 en suite (bth/shr) (2 fmly) No smoking in 2 bedrooms s £50-£60; d £80-£100 (incl. bkfst) * LB Off peak **MEALS:** Sunday Lunch £12.95-£14.95 & alc Dinner £15-£28alc European Cuisine V meals Coffee am Tea pm **FACILITIES:** CTV in all bedrooms Fishing Croquet lawn Shooting by arrangement Xmas **CONF:** Thtr 30 Class 30 Board 16 **SERVICES:** 30P **NOTES:** No coaches No children 10yrs No smoking in restaurant Last d 9.30pm **CARDS:**

THRAPSTON Northamptonshire — Map 04 SP97
Travelodge
Thrapston Bypass NN14 4UR
☎ 01832 735199 Fax 01832 735199
Dir: *on A14 link road A1/M1*
This modern building offers accommodation in smart, spacious and well equipped bedrooms, all with en-suite bathrooms. Refreshments may be taken at the nearby family restaurant. For details about current prices, consult the Contents Page under Hotel Groups for the Travelodge phone number.
ROOMS: 40 en suite (bth/shr) d £45.95 *

THRUSSINGTON Leicestershire — Map 08 SK61
Travelodge
LE7 8TF
☎ 01664 424525 Fax 01664 424525
Dir: *on A46, southbound*
This modern building offers accommodation in smart, spacious and well equipped bedrooms, all with en-suite bathrooms. Refreshments may be taken at the nearby family restaurant. For details about current prices, consult the Contents Page under Hotel Groups for the Travelodge phone number.
ROOMS: 32 en suite (bth/shr) d £45.95 *

THURLESTONE Devon — Map 03 SX64
★★★★ Thurlestone
TQ7 3NN
Quality Percentage Score: 72%
☎ 01548 560382 Fax 01548 561069
Dir: *A38 take A384 into Totnes, A381 towards Kingsbridge, onto A379 towards Churchstow, onto B3197 turn into lane signposted to Thurlestone*
Fabulous views and superb leisure facilities are two of the major attractions of this family owned hotel which stands in beautiful grounds. Many of the bedrooms have sea views, and some also have balconies. There is a stylish restaurant serving enjoyable meals, and entertainment is provided in the summer season.
ROOMS: 64 en suite (bth/shr) (17 fmly) s £52-£102; d £104-£204 (incl. bkfst & dinner) * LB Off peak **MEALS:** Lunch fr £13 Dinner fr £28 & alc International Cuisine V meals Coffee am Tea pm **FACILITIES:** CTV in all bedrooms Indoor swimming pool (heated) Outdoor swimming pool (heated) Golf 9 Tennis (hard) Squash Snooker Sauna Solarium Gym Croquet lawn Putting green Jacuzzi/spa Games room Badminton ch fac Xmas **CONF:** Thtr 140 Class 100 Board 40 Del from £85 * **SERVICES:** Lift Night porter 119P **NOTES:** No coaches No smoking in restaurant Last d 9pm **CARDS:**

See advert under SALCOMBE

THURLESTONE Devon — Map 03 SX64
★★ Heron House
Thurlestone Sands TQ7 3JY
Quality Percentage Score: 71%
☎ 01548 561308 & 561600 Fax 01548 560180
Dir: *off A381 3m S of Kingsbridge, turn right signed Hope Cove, continue over x-rds, then fork right 50 yds after Galmpton Village sign*

Standing on the coast near Thurlestone Stands, this hotel offers comfortable modern accommodation, and superb sea views from many of its rooms. The smart open-plan lounge bar overlooks

contd.

the swimming pool and a small games room. The restaurant is popular for its freshly prepared dishes.
ROOMS: 16 en suite (bth/shr) (3 fmly) No smoking in 6 bedrooms s £50-£85; d £80-£130 (incl. bkfst) LB Off peak **MEALS:** Lunch £5-£12 High tea fr £10 Dinner fr £25 English & French Cuisine V meals Coffee am Tea pm **FACILITIES:** CTV in all bedrooms Outdoor swimming pool (heated) Pool table Golf breaks Xmas **SERVICES:** 50P **NOTES:** No smoking in restaurant Last d 8.30pm **CARDS:**

See advert under SALCOMBE

TIBSHELF MOTORWAY SERVICE AREA (M1) Derbyshire — Map 08 SK46

Roadchef Lodge

Tibshelf Motorway Service Area, Junction 28/29 M1 DE55 5TZ
☎ 01773 876600 01773 876609
This modern building offers accommodation in smart, spacious and well equipped bedrooms, all with en-suite bathrooms. Refreshments may be taken at the nearby family restaurant. For details about current prices, consult the Contents Page under Hotel Groups for the Roadchef phone number.

TICEHURST East Sussex — Map 05 TQ63

★★★★ *Dale Hill Hotel & Golf Club*

TN5 7DQ
Quality Percentage Score: 67%
☎ 01580 200112 01580 201249
Dir: *situated on B2087 1.25m off A21*
This impressive modern hotel offers spacious bedrooms, good leisure facilities, and elegantly furnished public areas. The brasserie serves light meals all day, and the formal restaurant overlooks the 18th green. Hotel guests can enjoy the the clubby atmosphere of Spikes Bar.
ROOMS: 26 en suite (bth/shr) (6 fmly) **MEALS:** V meals Coffee am Tea pm **FACILITIES:** CTV in all bedrooms STV Indoor swimming pool (heated) Golf 36 Sauna Solarium Gym Pool table Putting green **CONF:** Thtr 44 Class 30 Board 24 **SERVICES:** Lift Night porter 220P **NOTES:** No coaches Last d 9.30pm **CARDS:**

TINTAGEL Cornwall & Isles of Scilly — Map 02 SX08

★★ Trebrea Lodge

Trenale PL34 0HR
Quality Percentage Score: 78%
☎ 01840 770410 01840 770092
Dir: *from A39 take Tintagel sign about 1m before Tintagel turn into Trenale*

In an elevated position, with four acres of grounds, the hotel has stunning views over Tintagel and the Cornish coastline. Bedrooms are individually decorated with thoughtful extras. There is an elegant drawing room on the first floor, and a popular snug with a log fire and honesty bar. Set dinners in the panelled dining room continue to earn praise.
ROOMS: 6 en suite (bth/shr) 1 annexe en suite (bth/shr) No smoking in all bedrooms s £60-£65; d £84-£94 (incl. bkfst) LB Off peak **MEALS:** Dinner £23 English & French Cuisine **FACILITIES:** CTV in all bedrooms **SERVICES:** 12P **NOTES:** No coaches No children 12yrs No smoking in restaurant Last d 8pm Closed Jan-mid Feb
CARDS:

TINTAGEL Cornwall & Isles of Scilly — Map 02 SX08

★★ Bossiney House

Bossiney PL34 0AX
Quality Percentage Score: 65%
☎ 01840 770240 01840 770501
Dir: *from A39 take B3263 into Tintagel, then Boscastle road for 0.5m to hotel on left*
Located on the outskirts of the village, Bossiney House is family run, with a relaxed and friendly atmosphere. The well stocked lounge bar overlooks the putting green and a cosy lounge is also available. An attractive, Scandinavian style log cabin in the grounds houses the majority of the leisure facilities.
ROOMS: 17 en suite (bth/shr) 2 annexe en suite (bth) (1 fmly) s fr £28; d fr £56 (incl. bkfst) * LB Off peak **MEALS:** Dinner £14 & alc V meals Coffee am **FACILITIES:** CTV in 20 bedrooms Indoor swimming pool (heated) Sauna Solarium Putting green **SERVICES:** 30P **NOTES:** No smoking in restaurant Last d 7.00pm Closed Dec-Jan
CARDS:

TINTAGEL Cornwall & Isles of Scilly — Map 02 SX08

★★ The Wootons Country Hotel

Fore St PL34 0DD
Quality Percentage Score: 65%
☎ 01840 770170 01840 770978
Dir: *Follow A30 until sign for N Cornwall, then right onto A395. continue & then turn right onto B3314 go straight over x-rds onto B3263 to Tintagel*
Located in the main street of Tintagel, this hotel offers exceptionally well equipped bedrooms, equally suitable for both business and leisure guests. An extensive range of meals is available from restaurant and bar menus. The hotel's rear terrace commands glorious views over a wooded valley.
ROOMS: 11 en suite (bth/shr) s £25-£35; d £50-£60 (incl. bkfst) * LB Off peak **MEALS:** Lunch fr £4.95 High tea fr £1.75 Dinner fr £9 & alc V meals Coffee am Tea pm **FACILITIES:** CTV in all bedrooms Snooker Pool table ch fac Xmas **SERVICES:** 35P **NOTES:** No dogs (ex guide dogs) Last d 9.30pm **CARDS:**

TINTAGEL Cornwall & Isles of Scilly — Map 02 SX08

★★ Atlantic View

Treknow PL34 0EJ
Quality Percentage Score: 61%
☎ 01840 770221 01840 770995
Dir: *B3263 to Tregatta turn left into Treknow, Hotel in situated on road to Trebarwith Strand Beach*
Peacefully located in the hamlet of Treknow, with coastal views, and convenient for all the attractions of Tintagel, this hotel is family run and has a relaxed atmosphere. Public areas include a cosy bar, comfortable lounge and a separate TV/games room. The sea is visible from a number of the spacious bedrooms.
ROOMS: 9 en suite (bth/shr) (1 fmly) No smoking in 3 bedrooms s £38-£46; d £76-£92 (incl. bkfst & dinner) * LB Off peak **MEALS:** Dinner fr £14 European Cuisine V meals Coffee am Tea pm **FACILITIES:** CTV in all bedrooms STV Indoor swimming pool (heated) Pool table ch fac **SERVICES:** 10P **NOTES:** No coaches No smoking in restaurant Last d 8.15pm Closed Nov-Jan **CARDS:**

T

TITCHWELL Norfolk — Map 09 TF74
★★ Titchwell Manor
PE31 8BB
Quality Percentage Score: 72%
☎ 01485 210221 📠 01485 210104
Dir: *on A149 between Brancaster and Thornham on A149 coast road*
A charming hotel in an unspoilt coastal location, Titchwell Manor makes the best use of the wealth of local produce, specialising in fish and shellfish, either in the seafood bar or the Garden Restaurant. The hotel is attractively decorated, with bold colour schemes throughout the comfortable public areas and a lighter floral style through the well appointed bedrooms.
ROOMS: 11 rms (7 bth/shr) 4 annexe en suite (bth/shr) (2 fmly) s £35-£65; d £70-£110 (incl. bkfst) * LB Off peak **MEALS:** Lunch £15 High tea £5-£15 Dinner £15-£26 European Cuisine V meals Coffee am Tea pm **FACILITIES:** CTV in all bedrooms ch fac Xmas **CONF:** Thtr 20 Class 35 Board 25 **SERVICES:** 50P **NOTES:** Last d 9.30pm Closed 18-31 Jan
CARDS:

See advert on opposite page

TITCHWELL Norfolk — Map 09 TF74
★★ Briarfields
Main St PE31 8BB
Quality Percentage Score: 70%
☎ 01485 210742 📠 01485 210933
Dir: *A149 coastal road towards Wells-next-Sea, Titchwell is the 3rd village & 7m from Hunstanton, hotel is situated on left of main road into village*
This relaxing country hotel is very popular with birdwatchers and nature lovers. The comfortable public areas feature two eating areas, a restaurant, and a bar serving meals. All the accommodation is attractively decorated, and many bedrooms are spacious with comfy seating; some are separate from the main building, set out courtyard-style with private terrace doors.
ROOMS: 18 en suite (bth/shr) (2 fmly) No smoking in 15 bedrooms s fr £45; d fr £70 (incl. bkfst) * LB Off peak **MEALS:** Lunch £11.95 High tea £2.25-£4.95 Dinner £16.95 English & French Cuisine V meals Coffee am Tea pm **FACILITIES:** CTV in all bedrooms Xmas **CONF:** Thtr 25 Class 12 Board 16 **SERVICES:** 50P **NOTES:** No smoking in restaurant Last d 9pm **CARDS:**

See advert under HUNSTANTON

TIVERTON Devon — Map 03 SS91
★★★ Tiverton
Blundells Rd EX16 4DB
Quality Percentage Score: 67%
☎ 01884 256120 📠 01884 258101
Dir: *M5 junct 27, go onto dual carraigeway A361 N Devon link road, Tiverton exit 7m W. Hotel on Blundells Rd next to business park*
A modern hotel located on the outskirts of Tiverton, offering a comfortable relaxed atmosphere. Many bedrooms and bathrooms have been either redecorated or totally refurbished. There are several menus from which to choose; both table d'hote and a la carte in the restaurant, or a more informal bar menu. Bedrooms are spacious and well equipped, with such extra facilities as trouser presses, irons, and a 24 hour room service menu.
ROOMS: 74 en suite (bth/shr) (10 fmly) No smoking in 54 bedrooms **MEALS:** V meals Coffee am Tea pm **FACILITIES:** CTV in all bedrooms STV **CONF:** Thtr 300 Class 140 Board 70 **SERVICES:** Night porter 130P **NOTES:** No smoking in restaurant Last d 9.45pm
CARDS:

TODDINGTON MOTORWAY SERVICE AREA (M1) Bedfordshire — Map 04 TL02
Travelodge
LU5 6HR
☎ Central Res 0800 850950 📠 01525 878452
Dir: *between junct 11 & 12 M1*
This modern building offers accommodation in smart, spacious and well equipped bedrooms, all with en-suite bathrooms. Refreshments may be taken at the nearby family restaurant. For details about current prices, consult the Contents Page under Hotel Groups for the Travelodge phone number.
ROOMS: 66 en suite (bth/shr) d £59.95 *

TOLLESHUNT KNIGHTS Essex — Map 05 TL91
★★★★ Five Lakes Country House, Golf & Country Club
Colchester Rd CM9 8HX
Quality Percentage Score: 71%
☎ 01621 868888 📠 01621 869696
Dir: *exit A12 follow signs to Tiptree, over staggered x-rds past Wilkin's Jam Factory, fork left to Salcott, at x-rds turn right, 500 metres on right*
Five Lakes is a striking contemporary hotel, standing in 320 acres of countryside, offering an excellent range of sporting and leisure amenities. Richly appointed bedrooms include suites and four-poster rooms. Bathrooms are particularly nice, many with separate shower cubicles. The spacious public areas include a variety of bars, the all-day Berjerano's Brasserie, and the Camelot Restaurant. Two 18-hole golf courses are available - the par 71 links course and the par 72 Lakes Championship course.
ROOMS: 114 en suite (bth/shr) (7 fmly) No smoking in 11 bedrooms s fr £100; d fr £142 * LB Off peak **MEALS:** Lunch £12.95-£17.85 Dinner £18.50 English & Continental Cuisine V meals Coffee am Tea pm **FACILITIES:** CTV in all bedrooms STV Indoor swimming pool (heated) Golf 36 Tennis (hard) Squash Snooker Sauna Solarium Gym Pool table Putting green Jacuzzi/spa Steam room Health & Beauty Spa Aerobics **CONF:** Thtr 3000 Class 1000 Board 50 Del from £119.50 * **SERVICES:** Lift Night porter 700P **NOTES:** No smoking in restaurant Last d 10pm RS 30 Dec-3 Jan **CARDS:**

TONBRIDGE Kent — Map 05 TQ54
★★★ The Langley
18-20 London Rd TN10 3DA
Quality Percentage Score: 65%
☎ 01732 353311 📠 01732 771471
Dir: *turn off A21 signposted Tonbridge N on B245, hotel 500 metres on left beyond Oast Theatre*
Set in the heart of Kent, the Langley Hotel offers good access to county's historical attractions. The atmosphere is relaxed and friendly. Bedrooms are spacious and attractive, with high levels of comfort. The restaurant offers a varied menu of carefully prepared fresh produce and there is a popular bar.
ROOMS: 34 en suite (bth/shr) (3 fmly) No smoking in 12 bedrooms s £60-£65; d £60-£85 (incl. bkfst) * Off peak **MEALS:** Lunch fr £10.95 Dinner fr £10.95 & alc English & French Cuisine V meals Coffee am Tea pm **FACILITIES:** CTV in all bedrooms STV **CONF:** Thtr 25 Class 15 Board 18 Del from £100 * **SERVICES:** Lift 50P **NOTES:** No dogs (ex guide dogs) No smoking in restaurant Last d 9.30pm
CARDS:

TONBRIDGE Kent — Map 05 TQ54
★★★ Rose & Crown
125 High St TN9 1DD
Quality Percentage Score: 62%
☎ 01732 357966 📠 01732 357194
Dir: *on High St opposite castle ruins*
This old coaching inn, close to the Norman castle, can trace its

contd.

history back to the 15th century. Bedrooms are divided between a new extension to the rear, and the main building. The bar with its cricket memorabilia and the beamed restaurant are located in the older part of the building.

ROOMS: 48 en suite (bth/shr) (3 fmly) No smoking in 20 bedrooms **MEALS:** Sunday Lunch fr £12.95 Dinner fr £15.95 & alc V meals Coffee am Tea pm **FACILITIES:** CTV in all bedrooms **CONF:** Thtr 100 Class 40 Board 50 Del £85 * **SERVICES:** Night porter 40P **NOTES:** No smoking area in restaurant Last d 9.30pm **CARDS:**

TOPCLIFFE North Yorkshire **Map 08 SE47**

★★ The Angel Inn

Long St YO7 3RW

Quality Percentage Score: 69%

☎ 01845 577237 01845 578000

Dir: *turn off the A168 link road (between A1(M) & A19) & the Angel Inn is situated in the centre of Topcliffe*

At the heart of the village, this attractive inn is very popular for its country-style cooking using the best available produce. Pleasant bars lead to a fine pub water garden, the bedrooms are well equipped and very comfortable. Staff are friendly and weddings can now be carried out at the hotel.

ROOMS: 15 en suite (bth/shr) (1 fmly) s fr £42.50; d fr £59 (incl. bkfst) * LB Off peak **MEALS:** Lunch £11.95-£19.95 & alc High tea £4.95-£7.95 & alc Dinner £14.95-£22.95 & alc English & Continental Cuisine V meals Coffee am Tea pm **FACILITIES:** CTV in all bedrooms STV Fishing Pool table **CONF:** Thtr 150 Class 60 Board 50 Del from £77 * **SERVICES:** 150P **NOTES:** No dogs (ex guide dogs) Last d 9.30pm **CARDS:**

TORBAY See under **Brixham, Paignton & Torquay**

TORCROSS Devon **Map 03 SX84**

★ *Grey Homes*

TQ7 2TH

Quality Percentage Score: 70%

☎ 01548 580220 01548 580220

Dir: *take A379 to village square, then take right fork and second turning on left*

Built in the 1920s by the grandfather of the present owner, this delightful hotel enjoys spectacular views over Start Bay and Slapton Ley Nature Reserve. Public rooms retain much of the elegant character of the original period, and bedrooms have modern facilities.

ROOMS: 6 en suite (bth/shr) (1 fmly) **MEALS:** English & French Cuisine V meals Coffee am Tea pm **FACILITIES:** CTV in all bedrooms Tennis (hard) **SERVICES:** 15P **NOTES:** No coaches No children 4yrs No smoking in restaurant Last d 7.30pm Closed Nov-Mar **CARDS:**

TORMARTON Gloucestershire **Map 03 ST77**

★★ *Compass Inn*

GL9 1JB

Best Western

Quality Percentage Score: 69%

☎ 01454 218242 & 218577 01454 218741

Dir: *0.5m from junct 18, M4*

This welcoming hotel caters for the full spectrum of guests, with good facilities for business, leisure and conferences. Many of the bedrooms are in a modern extension, with the bars and public rooms concentrated in the main building.

ROOMS: 26 en suite (bth/shr) (7 fmly) **MEALS:** V meals Coffee am Tea pm **FACILITIES:** CTV in all bedrooms STV **CONF:** Thtr 100 Class 30 Board 34 **SERVICES:** 160P **NOTES:** Last d 9.30pm Closed 24-26 Dec **CARDS:**

TORPOINT Cornwall & Isles of Scilly **Map 02 SX45**

★★ Whitsand Bay Hotel Golf & Country Club

Portwrinkle PL11 3BU

Quality Percentage Score: 68%

☎ 01503 230276 01503 230329

Dir: *5m W, off B3247. Turn off A30 at Trevlefoot rdbt on A374 to Crafthole, then take turn for Portwrinkle*

A Victorian stone building with oak panelling, stained glass windows and a sweeping staircase. Bedrooms range from family rooms and a suite with balcony to children's rooms named after pirates. Facilities include an 18-hole cliff-top golf course. The

contd.

T

fixed price menu offers an interesting selection of dishes; light meals and snacks are served in the bar.
ROOMS: 39 rms (37 bth/shr) (15 fmly) s £23-£57.50; d £46-£92 (incl. bkfst) * LB Off peak **MEALS:** Sunday Lunch £9.50 Dinner £18.50 English & Continental Cuisine V meals Coffee am Tea pm **FACILITIES:** CTV in 51 bedrooms Indoor swimming pool (heated) Golf 18 Sauna Solarium Gym Pool table Putting green Beauty salon Steam room Hairdressers Games room ch fac Xmas **CONF:** Thtr 100 Class 100 Board 40 **SERVICES:** Night porter 60P **NOTES:** No smoking area in restaurant Last d 8.30pm **CARDS:**

TORQUAY Devon — Map 03 SX96
★★★★ The Imperial
Park Hill Rd TQ1 2DG
Quality Percentage Score: 67%
☎ 01803 294301 Fax 01803 298293

PARAMOUNT HOTEL GROUP

***Dir:** from A380, when in town, head towards the seafront. Turn left and follow the road to the harbour, at clocktower turn right. Hotel 300yrds on right*

An established hotel with views over the harbour towards the opposite coastline. It has grand public areas which include the Sundeck brasserie, a large lounge, meeting rooms and the Haldon Restaurant. Bedrooms vary in size and opulence.
ROOMS: 154 en suite (bth/shr) (7 fmly) No smoking in 26 bedrooms s £90-£135; d £150-£250 * LB Off peak **MEALS:** Lunch £18.50 & alc Dinner £21 & alc European Cuisine V meals Coffee am Tea pm **FACILITIES:** CTV in all bedrooms STV Indoor swimming pool (heated) Outdoor swimming pool (heated) Tennis (hard) Squash Snooker Sauna Solarium Gym Pool table Croquet lawn Jacuzzi/spa Beauty salon Hairdresser Wkly live entertainment Xmas **CONF:** Thtr 350 Class 200 Board 30 Del from £100 * **SERVICES:** Lift Night porter 140P **NOTES:** No smoking in restaurant Last d 9.30pm **CARDS:**

TORQUAY Devon — Map 03 SX96
★★★★ Grand
Sea Front TQ2 6NT
Quality Percentage Score: 68%
☎ 01803 296677 Fax 01803 213462

***Dir:** from M5, A380 to Torquay. At sea front turn right, then first right. Hotel is on corner, entrance is in the first turning on left*

This Edwardian hotel offers modern facilities. Bedrooms are very well equipped with extras such as irons and trouser presses. Many rooms and various suites have sea views and balconies. Boaters Bar is popular for buffet lunches and afternoon tea. In the evening guests enjoy the more formal atmosphere of the Gainsborough Restaurant.

ROOMS: 112 en suite (bth/shr) (30 fmly) No smoking in 30 bedrooms s £80-£120; d £140-£250 (incl. bkfst) * LB Off peak **MEALS:** Lunch fr £15.50 High tea fr £6.50 Dinner fr £23.50 & alc English & French Cuisine V meals Coffee am Tea pm **FACILITIES:** CTV in all bedrooms STV Indoor swimming pool (heated) Outdoor swimming pool (heated) Tennis (hard) Snooker Sauna Solarium Gym Pool table Jacuzzi/spa Hairdressers Beauty clinic Wkly live entertainment ch fac Xmas **CONF:** Thtr 350 Class 100 Board 60 Del from £110 * **SERVICES:** Lift Night porter 55P **NOTES:** No smoking in restaurant Last d 9.30pm **CARDS:**

See advert on opposite page

★ The Premier Collection, hotels with Red Star Awards are listed on pages 17-23

TORQUAY Devon — Map 03 SX96
★★★★ Palace
Babbacombe Rd TQ1 3TG
Quality Percentage Score: 68%
☎ 01803 200200 Fax 01803 299899

***Dir:** on entering Torquay, head for the harbour, turn left by the clocktower into Babbacombe Rd, hotel on right after about 1m*

The hotel was formerly the summer residence of the Bishop of Exeter. Bedrooms are attractively decorated and offer many modern amenities. Public areas include a choice of lounges, a cocktail bar, and leisure facilities. The restaurant offers traditional cuisine in a formal atmosphere.
ROOMS: 141 en suite (bth/shr) (20 fmly) No smoking in 18 bedrooms s £69-£79; d £138-£158 (incl. bkfst) * LB Off peak **MEALS:** Lunch £14.50 & alc High tea £4 Dinner £22.50 & alc English & French Cuisine V meals Coffee am Tea pm **FACILITIES:** CTV in all bedrooms Indoor swimming pool (heated) Outdoor swimming pool (heated) Golf 9 Tennis (hard) Squash Snooker Sauna Gym Pool table Croquet lawn Putting green Fitness suite Table tennis Wkly live entertainment ch fac Xmas **CONF:** Thtr 1000 Class 150 Board 40 Del from £110 * **SERVICES:** Lift Night porter 180P **NOTES:** No dogs (ex guide dogs) No smoking in restaurant Last d 9.15pm **CARDS:**

See advert on opposite page

T

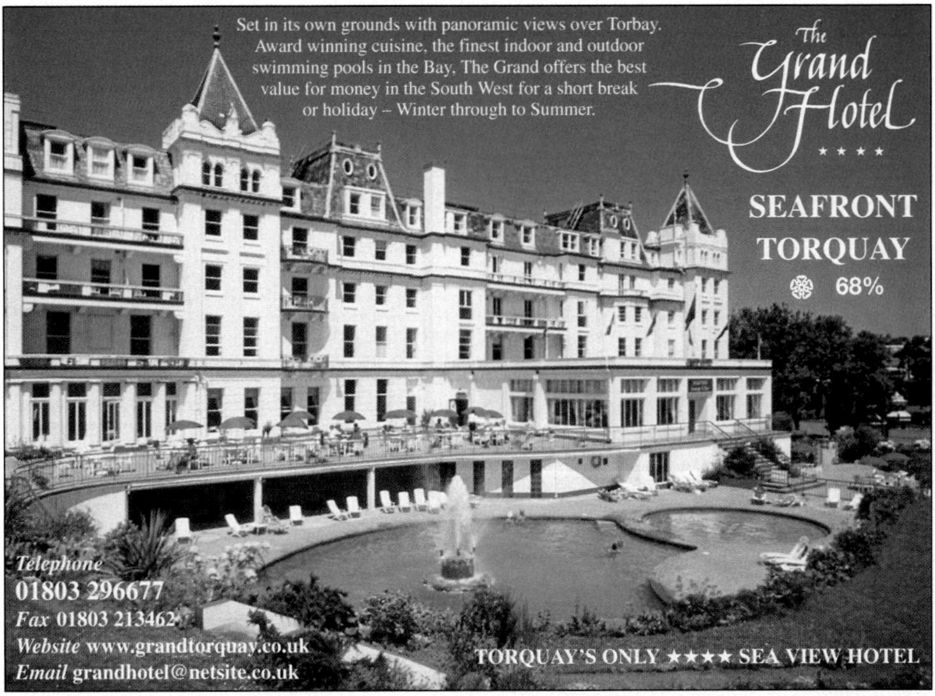

Set in its own grounds with panoramic views over Torbay. Award winning cuisine, the finest indoor and outdoor swimming pools in the Bay, The Grand offers the best value for money in the South West for a short break or holiday – Winter through to Summer.
The Grand Hotel
★★★★
SEAFRONT
TORQUAY
68%
Telephone
01803 296677
Fax 01803 213462
Website www.grandtorquay.co.uk
Email grandhotel@netsite.co.uk
TORQUAY'S ONLY ★★★★ SEA VIEW HOTEL

the A
to Z of
The Palace Hotel
TORQUAY
Set in 25 acres of magnificent landscaped grounds
9 hole par 3 championship short golf course
Indoor and outdoor swimming pools and tennis courts
Croquet lawn
Putting green
2 squash courts
Saunas
Snooker room
Fitness suite
An unrivalled standard of service and excellent cuisine awaits
★★★★
facilities
ring 01803 200200
to make a reservation
www.palacetorquay.co.uk

T

TORQUAY Devon **Map 03 SX96**

★★★ The Osborne

Hesketh Crescent, Meadfoot TQ1 2LL
Quality Percentage Score: 78%
☎ 01803 213311 01803 296788
Dir: *A380 via Newton Abbot, follow signs to seafront, follow road, A3022, down and turn left, turn onto B3199 and follow road up to hotel*

Forming the centrepiece of an elegant Regency terrace, The Osborne looks over the beach and Torbay from five acres of gardens, leading down to the sea. Bedrooms are smartly appointed and some have sea views. The refurbished public areas include an informal brasserie offering all-day service, the restaurant provides a more formal eating option.

ROOMS: 29 en suite (bth/shr) (2 fmly) s £50-£80; d £110-£136 (incl. bkfst) * LB Off peak **MEALS:** Bar Lunch £12.50-£24alc Dinner £18.50 & alc V meals Coffee am Tea pm **FACILITIES:** CTV in all bedrooms STV Indoor swimming pool (heated) Outdoor swimming pool (heated) Tennis (hard) Snooker Sauna Solarium Gym Pool table Putting green Plunge pool Xmas **CONF:** Thtr 30 Class 28 Board 30 Del from £75 * **SERVICES:** Lift Night porter 90P **NOTES:** No dogs (ex guide dogs) No smoking in restaurant **CARDS:**

See advert on opposite page

TORQUAY Devon **Map 03 SX96**

★★★ Orestone Manor

Rockhouse Ln, Maidencombe TQ1 4SX
Quality Percentage Score: 75%
☎ 01803 328098 01803 328336
Dir: *off A379 coast road, Torquay-Teignmouth. Road was formerly B3199*

An attractive Georgian country house hotel with views across Lyme Bay and surrounding countryside. Bedrooms are mainly spacious and vary in style, attractively furnished with modern facilities. The restaurant offers innovative cuisine from master chef Wayne Pearson.

ROOMS: 18 en suite (bth/shr) (6 fmly) s £55-£70; d £110-£160 (incl. bkfst) * LB Off peak **MEALS:** Sunday Lunch £12.95-£21 Dinner £24.50-£37 English & Mediterranean Cuisine V meals Coffee am Tea pm **FACILITIES:** CTV in all bedrooms Outdoor swimming pool (heated) Snooker Xmas **CONF:** Class 20 Board 16 Del from £85 * **SERVICES:** 40P **NOTES:** No coaches No smoking in restaurant Last d 9pm Closed 1st 2 wks Jan **CARDS:**

See advert on opposite page

TORQUAY Devon **Map 03 SX96**

★★★ Corbyn Head

Torquay Rd, Sea Front, Livermead TQ2 6RH
Quality Percentage Score: 74%
☎ 01803 213611 01803 296152
Dir: *follow signs to Torquay seafront, turn right on seafront. Hotel situated on right hand side of seafront with green canopies*

Overlooking Tor Bay, and within easy walking distance of the town and harbour, Corbyn Head offers traditional hospitality and a relaxed atmosphere. The accommodation is carefully designed, and all furnishings are well co-ordinated. Many bedrooms benefit from wonderful sea views. Facilities include an outdoor pool and a choice of restaurants.

ROOMS: 51 en suite (bth/shr) (1 fmly) No smoking in 3 bedrooms s £40-£70; d £80-£140 (incl. bkfst & dinner) * LB Off peak **MEALS:** Lunch fr £10.95 Dinner £19.75 V meals Coffee am Tea pm **FACILITIES:** CTV in all bedrooms Outdoor swimming pool (heated) Wkly live entertainment Xmas **CONF:** Thtr 30 Class 20 Board 20 Del from £40 * **SERVICES:** Night porter 50P **NOTES:** No dogs (ex guide dogs) No smoking in restaurant Last d 9pm **CARDS:**

TORQUAY Devon **Map 03 SX96**

★★★ Livermead Cliff

Torbay Rd TQ2 6RQ
Quality Percentage Score: 73%
☎ 01803 299666 & 292881 01803 294496
Dir: *take A380 towards Newton Abbot, at Penn Inn rdbt, take A380/3022 to Torquay seafront, turn right, Livermead Cliff is 600yds on left*

Situated on the edge of the bay, the hotel provides well appointed upgraded bedrooms, many with superb sea views. The comfortable lounges and bar are spacious and tastefully decorated. The elegant restaurant offers carefully prepared cuisine.

ROOMS: 64 en suite (bth/shr) (21 fmly) s £41.50-£65; d £78-£128 (incl. bkfst) * LB Off peak **MEALS:** Lunch £9-£10 & alc High tea fr £8 & alc Dinner £17.75-£18 & alc English & Continental Cuisine V meals Coffee am Tea pm **FACILITIES:** CTV in all bedrooms Outdoor swimming pool (heated) Fishing Solarium Sun terrace ch fac Xmas **CONF:** Thtr 100 Class 40 Board 30 Del from £53 * **SERVICES:** Lift Night porter 72P **NOTES:** Last d 8.30pm **CARDS:**

TORQUAY Devon **Map 03 SX96**

★★★ *Lincombe Hall*

Meadfoot Rd TQ1 2JX
Quality Percentage Score: 71%
☎ 01803 213361 01803 211485

Lincombe Hall is a short walk from the town centre, with views over Torquay and five acres of grounds. The spacious bedrooms are tastefully furnished and equipped. An interesting and comprehensive selection of menus and wines are available in

contd. on p. 658

The
GROSVENOR
Torquay

AA ★★★ ❀

"Traditional hospitality, excellent facilities, friendly personal attention, perfect for every occasion"

Belgrave Road, Torquay, Devon TQ2 5HG
Tel 01803 294373 Fax 01803 291032
Email: @grosvenor-torquay.co.uk
Internet: http://www.grosvenor-torquay.co.uk/

★★★ 78% ❀ ❀

THE OSBORNE HOTEL AND LANGTRY'S

A 29 bedroomed hotel, which is the centrepiece of an elegant Regency crescent, overlooks Meadfoot Beach and is 'probably' Torquay's most romantic hotel. Having recently achieved the Courtesy & Care Award, this 3-star AA rated hotel offers a friendly ambience complemented by superior standards of comfort and service. Facilities include five acres of lovely gardens, indoor and outdoor pools, tennis court, putting green, Hesketh's Health Club, The Brasserie and Langtry's guide-acclaimed restaurant, one of the foremost restaurants on the English Riviera.

Hesketh Crescent, Meadfoot, nr Torquay TQ1 2LL
Tel: 01803 213311 Fax: 01803 296788

The ORESTONE MANOR HOTEL *& Restaurant*

AA ★★★ 75% RATING

A.A. ROSETTES FOR FINE CUISINE

BEST LOVED

- Fine Gabled Manor House built in 1809
- Nestling in 2 acres of beautifully landscaped grounds
- 18 individually appointed ensuite bedrooms with colour television, direct dial telephone and beverage facilities
- Comfortable lounges & bar
- Snooker room
- Heated outdoor pool
- Ideally situated for exploring the surrounding area
- Superb coastal walking, National Trust properties, Dartmoor National Park, Golf, horseriding, sailing & tennis nearby

- The highest rated A.A. Country House Hotel in Torbay
- One of the finest restaurants in the South West
- Superb, award winning cuisine prepared by Head Chef Wayne Pearson one of only 80 "Master Chefs of Great Britain"

In the countryside, yet by the sea, offering seclusion and that "away from it all feeling". The idyllic place to unwind.

Write or telephone for a brochure and tariff:

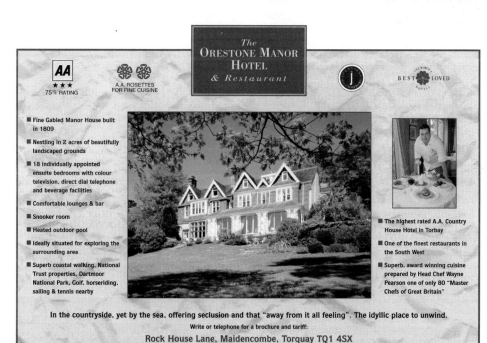

Rock House Lane, Maidencombe, Torquay TQ1 4SX
Telephone 01803 328098 Fax 01803 328336 Email manor@orestone.co.uk

'Harleys' restaurant. Guests can relax in the spacious lounges adjoining the bar.
ROOMS: 42 en suite (bth/shr) (8 fmly) **MEALS:** V meals Coffee am Tea pm **FACILITIES:** CTV in all bedrooms STV Outdoor swimming pool (heated) Tennis (hard) Sauna Solarium Gym Pool table Putting green Jacuzzi/spa Play area Crazy golf **CONF:** Thtr 50 Class 30 Board 20 **SERVICES:** Night porter 40P **NOTES:** No smoking in restaurant
CARDS:

TORQUAY Devon **Map 03 SX96**
★★★ The Grosvenor
Belgrave Rd TQ2 5HG
Quality Percentage Score: 69%
☎ 01803 294373 01803 291032
Dir: *hotel on first left, just off main beach/seafront road*
Close to the seafront and the main attractions of the bay, The Grosvenor has upgraded its spacious, attractively furnished bedrooms. Guests can dine in the restaurant, coffee shop or Mima's Bistro. There is a nightclub in addition to the refurbished ballroom, where dinner dances and functions are held.
ROOMS: 46 en suite (bth/shr) (8 fmly) s fr £48; d fr £96 (incl. bkfst) * LB Off peak **MEALS:** Bar Lunch fr £3 Dinner fr £14.95 English & French Cuisine V meals Coffee am Tea pm **FACILITIES:** CTV in all bedrooms STV Indoor swimming pool (heated) Outdoor swimming pool (heated) Tennis Sauna Solarium Gym Pool table Jacuzzi/spa coffee shop/conservatory Wkly live entertainment Xmas **CONF:** Thtr 150 Class 100 Board 40 Del from £72 * **SERVICES:** Night porter 40P **NOTES:** No dogs (ex guide dogs) No smoking in restaurant Last d 8.30pm **CARDS:**

See advert on page 657

TORQUAY Devon **Map 03 SX96**
★★★ Livermead House
Torbay Rd TQ2 6QJ
Quality Percentage Score: 69%
☎ 01803 294361 01803 200758
Dir: *from seafront turn right, follow A379 towards Paignton and Livermead, the hotel is opposite Institute beach*

Situated on the waterfront, Livermead House was built in the 1820s and is where Charles Kingsley wrote 'The Water Babies'. Bedrooms have been refurbished to a high standard, and the excellent public rooms are popular for private parties, functions and meetings. The attractive restaurant offers a wide choice of classic dishes with friendly, efficient service.
ROOMS: 66 en suite (bth/shr) (6 fmly) No smoking in 12 bedrooms s £43-£68; d £86-£156 (incl. bkfst & dinner) * LB Off peak
MEALS: Lunch £9.75 High tea £5-£15alc Dinner £19.75-£22.75 English & French Cuisine V meals Coffee am Tea pm **FACILITIES:** CTV in all bedrooms Outdoor swimming pool (heated) Squash Snooker Sauna Solarium Gym Wkly live entertainment Xmas **CONF:** Thtr 320 Class 175 Board 80 Del from £42 * **SERVICES:** Lift Night porter 131P **NOTES:** No smoking in restaurant Last d 8.30pm **CARDS:**

See advert on opposite page

TORQUAY Devon **Map 03 SX96**
★★★ Toorak
Chestnut Av TQ2 5JS
Quality Percentage Score: 69%
☎ 01803 291444 01803 291666
Dir: *opposite Riviera Conference Centre*
Facilities are found here and in 'sister' hotels. Conference rooms are popular and there are a number of lounges. Bedrooms have modern facilities, superior 'Terrace' bedrooms are very spacious and well decorated. A fixed price menu and international buffet are available in the restaurant.
ROOMS: 92 en suite (bth/shr) (29 fmly) s £47-£66; d £94-£132 (incl. bkfst & dinner) * LB Off peak **MEALS:** Bar Lunch £2.75-£7.50alc Dinner fr £16.75 English & French Cuisine V meals Coffee am Tea pm **FACILITIES:** CTV in all bedrooms Indoor swimming pool (heated) Outdoor swimming pool (heated) Tennis (hard) Snooker Sauna Solarium Pool table Croquet lawn Jacuzzi/spa Childrens play area Indoor Games Arena Xmas **CONF:** Thtr 200 Class 150 Board 80 Del from £68 * **SERVICES:** Lift Night porter 90P **NOTES:** No dogs (ex guide dogs) No smoking area in restaurant Last d 9pm
CARDS:

See advert on page 661

TORQUAY Devon **Map 03 SX96**
★★★ *Belgrave*
Seafront TQ2 5HE
Quality Percentage Score: 66%
☎ 01803 296666 01803 211308
Dir: *Turn off A38 onto the A380 then onto A3022 for 4 miles head for seafront*
Situated in a prime position on the seafront, the Belgrave offers spacious lounges and a choice of two bars. There is an impressive ballroom, and a restaurant serving a daily table d'hôte menu, in addition to lunchtime snacks. The bedrooms all offer modern facilities.
ROOMS: 68 en suite (bth/shr) (16 fmly) No smoking in 20 bedrooms
MEALS: English & French Cuisine V meals Coffee am Tea pm
FACILITIES: CTV in all bedrooms Outdoor swimming pool (heated) Pool table **CONF:** Thtr 150 Class 70 Board 50 **SERVICES:** Lift Night porter 86P **NOTES:** No coaches No smoking in restaurant Last d 8.30pm
CARDS:

TORQUAY Devon **Map 03 SX96**
★★★ *Kistor Hotel*
Belgrave Rd TQ2 5HF
Quality Percentage Score: 61%
☎ 01803 212632 01803 293219
Dir: *A380 to Torquay, hotel is next to Belgrave hotel at junct of Belgrave Rd and the promenade at the seafront*
The hotel is near the promenade. Bedrooms vary in size and are equipped with modern facilities. In the restaurant, a fixed price menu is offered, with straightforward cooking.
ROOMS: 50 en suite (bth/shr) (14 fmly) **MEALS:** English & French Cuisine V meals Coffee am Tea pm **FACILITIES:** CTV in all bedrooms STV Indoor swimming pool (heated) Sauna Gym Pool table Putting green Jacuzzi/spa Childrens play area Wkly live entertainment
CONF: Thtr 60 Class 50 Board 30 **SERVICES:** Lift Night porter 40P
NOTES: No smoking area in restaurant Last d 8.30pm
CARDS:

For Useful Information and Important Telephone Number Changes turn to page 25

T

TORQUAY Devon **Map 03 SX96**
★★ ***Oscar's Hotel & Restaurant***
56 Belgrave Rd TQ2 5HY
Quality Percentage Score: 73%
☎ 01803 293563 Fax 01803 296685
Dir: *from A3022 into Torquay turn left, then right at next set of lights, head down hill towards seafront, hotel is at the junction with Falkland Rd*
This attractive hotel is close to the shops and seafront. It offers comfortable, smartly decorated and furnished bedrooms.The bistro-style restaurant offers an extensive range of enjoyable dishes.
ROOMS: 13 en suite (bth/shr) (3 fmly) **MEALS:** International Cuisine V meals **FACILITIES:** CTV in all bedrooms **SERVICES:** 4P **NOTES:** No coaches No smoking area in restaurant Last d 7.30pm
CARDS:

TORQUAY Devon **Map 03 SX96**
★★ **Albaston House**
27 St Marychurch Rd TQ1 3JF
Quality Percentage Score: 72%
☎ 01803 296758 Fax 01803 211509
Albaston House is situated between the town centre, historic St Marychurch and the beaches of Babbacombe. Standards of housekeeping, hospitality and service are high and accommodation is smartly decorated, offering modern standards of comfort.
ROOMS: 13 en suite (bth/shr) (4 fmly) s £30-£32; d £60-£64 (incl. bkfst) * LB Off peak **MEALS:** Bar Lunch £5-£8 Dinner £10-£12 English & French Cuisine V meals Coffee am Tea pm **FACILITIES:** CTV in all bedrooms **SERVICES:** 12P **NOTES:** No coaches Last d 8pm Closed Jan
CARDS:

TORQUAY Devon **Map 03 SX96**
★★ **Bute Court**
Belgrave Rd TQ2 5HQ
Quality Percentage Score: 71%
☎ 01803 293771 Fax 01803 213429
Dir: *take A380 to Torquay, continue until traffic lights, bear right past police station, straight across at traffic lights, hotel 200yds on right*
A short walk from the seafront, this popular, hotel (once home to Lord Bute) has been owned by the Jenkins family since 1940. The newly refurbished bedrooms are comfortably furnished with modern facilities. Spacious public rooms, night-time entertainment and leisure facilities are added attractions.
ROOMS: 45 en suite (bth/shr) (10 fmly) s £28-£40; d £56-£80 (incl. bkfst & dinner) * LB Off peak **MEALS:** Bar Lunch £1.65-£3.55 Dinner £8.50 English & Continental Cuisine Coffee am Tea pm **FACILITIES:** CTV in all bedrooms Outdoor swimming pool (heated) Snooker Table tennis Darts Xmas **CONF:** Class 40 **SERVICES:** Lift Night porter 37P **NOTES:** Last d 8.00pm **CARDS:**

T

See advert on opposite page

TORQUAY Devon **Map 03 SX96**
★★ **Hotel Sydore**
Meadfoot Rd TQ1 2JP
Quality Percentage Score: 70%
☎ 01803 294758 Fax 01803 294489
Dir: *A380 to Harbour, left at clock tower 40 metres to traffic lights, right into Meadfoot Rd hotel 100 metres on left*
A charming Georgian villa set in smart, well tended gardens. It offers traditional cuisine in the attractive restaurant, adjacent to the cosy bar and lounge, both decorated and furnished with interesting and unusual objects. Bedrooms are individual in style and decor.
ROOMS: 13 en suite (bth/shr) (5 fmly) No smoking in 11 bedrooms s £19.95-£35; d £42-£70 (incl. bkfst) * LB Off peak **MEALS:** Lunch fr £8.95 Dinner fr £8.95 V meals Coffee am Tea pm **FACILITIES:** CTV in all bedrooms Croquet lawn Bar billiards Table tennis Xmas
SERVICES: 16P **NOTES:** No coaches No smoking in restaurant Last d 8pm **CARDS:**

TORQUAY Devon **Map 03 SX96**
★★ **Hotel Balmoral**
Meadfoot Sea Rd TQ1 2LQ
Quality Percentage Score: 68%
☎ 01803 293381 & 299224 Fax 01803 299224
Dir: *at Torquay harbour go left at Clock Tower towards Babbacombe, after 100yds right at lghts. Follow the rd to Meadfoot beach. Hotel on right*
Situated near Meadfoot Beach with views to the sea, the Balmoral is a friendly, well run hotel with modern bedrooms and bathrooms. The spacious lounges and bar offer guests every comfort. The daily menu offers traditional home cooking in the bright, attractive dining room, with views over the gardens.
ROOMS: 24 en suite (bth/shr) (7 fmly) s £25-£32; d £50-£64 (incl. bkfst) * LB Off peak **MEALS:** Lunch fr £7.50 Dinner fr £12.50 English & French Cuisine Coffee am Tea pm **FACILITIES:** CTV in all bedrooms Wkly live entertainment ch fac Xmas **SERVICES:** 18P **NOTES:** No smoking in restaurant Last d 8.30pm **CARDS:**

TORQUAY Devon **Map 03 SX96**
★★ **Frognel Hall**
Higher Woodfield Rd TQ1 2LD
Quality Percentage Score: 68%
☎ 01803 298339 Fax 01803 215115
Dir: *follow signs to seafront, then follow esplanade to harbour, left to Babbacombe, right at lights towards Meadfoot beach, 3rd left, Hotel on left*
In an elevated position with fine views over Torquay, the hotel has comfortable bedrooms with modern facilities and a newly installed lift. The Croppers and their friendly staff ensure a pleasant stay. The traditional English food includes many vegetarian items.
ROOMS: 28 rms (27 bth/shr) (4 fmly) s £26-£30; d £52-£60 (incl. bkfst) LB Off peak **MEALS:** Lunch £8-£10 & alc Dinner £10 & alc English & French Cuisine V meals Coffee am Tea pm **FACILITIES:** CTV in all bedrooms Sauna Pool table Croquet lawn Putting green Games room Exercise equipment Wkly live entertainment Xmas **CONF:** Thtr 50 Class 30 Board 15 Del from £32 * **SERVICES:** Lift 25P **NOTES:** No smoking in restaurant Last d 8pm **CARDS:**

TORQUAY Devon **Map 03 SX96**
★★ ***Torcroft***
Croft Rd TQ2 5UE
Quality Percentage Score: 68%
☎ 01803 298292
Dir: *follow signs to seafront & town centre, at traffic lights junct turn left, take 1st right into Croft Rd, hotel is 200yds along on left*
A Grade II listed Victorian property overlooking Torbay, convenient for the town centre, shops and sea front. A comfortable, well maintained hotel offering high standards of hospitality, service and cuisine.
ROOMS: 16 en suite (bth/shr) (2 fmly) **MEALS:** English & Italian Cuisine V meals **FACILITIES:** CTV in all bedrooms **SERVICES:** 18P **NOTES:** No dogs No coaches No smoking in restaurant
CARDS:

TORQUAY Devon — Map 03 SX96

★★ Ansteys Lea

Babbacombe Rd, Wellswood TQ1 2QJ
Quality Percentage Score: 67%
☎ 01803 294843 Fax 01803 214333
Dir: *from Torquay Harbour take the Babbacombe road, hotel approx 0.75m towards Babbacombe*

This friendly hotel is a short walk from Ansteys Cove. Bedrooms offer comfortable, well furnished accommodation with a good range of facilities. There is an attractive lounge/TV room overlooking the garden and a heated outdoor pool. The set five-course dinner menu offers a choice of home-cooked dishes.

ROOMS: 24 en suite (bth/shr) (4 fmly) s fr £33; d fr £66 (incl. bkfst) * LB Off peak **MEALS:** V meals Coffee am Tea pm **FACILITIES:** CTV in all bedrooms Outdoor swimming pool (heated) Sauna Gym Pool table Putting green Table tennis Xmas **SERVICES:** Night porter Air conditioning 18P **NOTES:** No smoking in restaurant Last d 7.30pm Closed 3 Jan-13 Feb **CARDS:**

TORQUAY Devon — Map 03 SX96

★★ *Bancourt*

Avenue Rd TQ2 5LG
Quality Percentage Score: 66%
☎ 01803 295077 Fax 01803 201114
Dir: *off M5 onto A38 straight into Torquay, when you reach Torre Station and Halford superstore, stay in R-hand lane through the lights, hotel is on left*

A lively hotel, popular with business guests and coach parties, offers comfortable bedrooms and spacious public rooms, where

contd.

entertainment is regularly provided. There is also an indoor pool and pretty gardens.
ROOMS: 46 en suite (bth/shr) (11 fmly) **MEALS:** English, French & Italian Cuisine Coffee am Tea pm **FACILITIES:** CTV in all bedrooms Indoor swimming pool (heated) Snooker Games room Wkly live entertainment **CONF:** Thtr 60 **SERVICES:** Night porter 50P **NOTES:** No smoking in restaurant Last d 7.30pm **CARDS:**

See advert on page 661

TORQUAY Devon — Map 03 SX96
★★ Carlton
Falkland Rd TQ2 5JJ
Quality Percentage Score: 66%
☎ 01803 400300 Fax 01803 400130
***Dir:** take A380 into Torquay, follow signs to seafront, at traffic light junction on Belgrave Rd turn right into Falkland Rd hotel is 100yds on left*
This popular holiday hotel stands in the town centre, close to beaches and other amenities. Guests can use the leisure facilities here and at other hotels in the same group. Regular entertainment is staged in the spacious ballroom and bar, and the bedrooms are individual in style, all equipped to a good modern standard.
ROOMS: 47 en suite (bth/shr) (26 fmly) s £42-£58; d £84-£116 (incl. bkfst & dinner) * Off peak **MEALS:** Bar Lunch £2.50-£10alc Dinner fr £12alc V meals Coffee am Tea pm **FACILITIES:** CTV in all bedrooms Indoor swimming pool (heated) Outdoor swimming pool (heated) Tennis (hard) Snooker Sauna Solarium Gym Childrens playden & Adventure playground Ten-Pin Bowling Wkly live entertainment Xmas **CONF:** Thtr 120 Class 60 Board 25 Del from £55 * **SERVICES:** Lift Night porter 28P **NOTES:** No dogs (ex guide dogs) No smoking in restaurant Last d 8.15pm **CARDS:**

TORQUAY Devon — Map 03 SX96
★★ Gresham Court
Babbacombe Rd TQ1 1HG
Quality Percentage Score: 66%
☎ 01803 293007 & 293658 Fax 01803 215951
***Dir:** 0.25m from harbourside, also close to Torquay museum*
Close to the harbour and shops, this well run family hotel enjoys high levels of hospitality and service. The fresh, home-cooked food offers a choice. The bedrooms are comfortable and vary in style and size. Entertainment is provided in one of the well-maintained public rooms.
ROOMS: 30 en suite (bth/shr) (6 fmly) s £30-£37; d £60-£74 (incl. bkfst & dinner) * LB Off peak **MEALS:** Bar Lunch £1.50-£3.50 Dinner £9 V meals **FACILITIES:** CTV in all bedrooms Pool table **SERVICES:** Lift 14P **NOTES:** No smoking in restaurant Last d 7.30pm Closed Dec-Feb **CARDS:**

TORQUAY Devon — Map 03 SX96
★★ Red House
Rousdown Rd, Chelston TQ2 6PB
Quality Percentage Score: 66%
☎ 01803 607811 Fax 01803 200592
***Dir:** Make for seafront/Chelston, turn into Avenue Rd, 1st set of traffic lights turn R follow road past shops and church, take next L hotel is on R*
The health and leisure centre managed by trained staff, is a feature of the hotel. The restaurant and all-day informal 'coffee shop' operation offer extensive menus for residents and non-residents. Bedrooms are comfortable, varying in size and style, offering modern facilities and amenities.

ROOMS: 10 en suite (bth/shr) (5 fmly) s £22-£31; d £44-£62 (incl. bkfst) * LB Off peak **MEALS:** Bar Lunch £3.45-£8.25alc Dinner fr £11.75 & alc English & French Cuisine V meals Coffee am Tea pm **FACILITIES:** CTV in all bedrooms Indoor swimming pool (heated) Outdoor swimming pool (heated) Sauna Solarium Gym Pool table Jacuzzi/spa Games room Table tennis Beauty salon Xmas **CONF:** Thtr 20 Class 20 Board 16 **SERVICES:** 10P **NOTES:** No coaches No smoking in restaurant Last d 8pm **CARDS:**

See advert on opposite page

TORQUAY Devon — Map 03 SX96
★★ *Shelley Court*
Croft Rd TQ2 5UD
Quality Percentage Score: 66%
☎ 01803 295642 Fax 01803 215793
***Dir:** A380 from Newton Abbot, then onto A3022 to seafront, hotel is 250yds turning off Shedden Hill into Croft Rd*
This popular hotel is close to the town and beach. Entertainment is provided three nights a week. All rooms are bright and well appointed with many modern facilities. The attractive dining room offers home-cooked, traditional cuisine with a sweet buffet.
ROOMS: 27 en suite (bth/shr) (3 fmly) **MEALS:** Coffee am **FACILITIES:** CTV in all bedrooms Wkly live entertainment **SERVICES:** 20P **NOTES:** No dogs No smoking in restaurant Last d 7.30pm Closed 21 Dec-Jan **CARDS:**

TORQUAY Devon — Map 03 SX96
★★ *Coppice*
Babbacombe Rd TQ1 2QJ
Quality Percentage Score: 65%
☎ 01803 297786 Fax 01803 211085
Conveniently situated just off the Babbacombe Road and within walking distance of the beaches and shops, the Coppice is a friendly and comfortable hotel which appeals to both business visitors and tourists. Rooms are bright and airy with modern amenities and the hotel also offers a variety of leisure and sports facilities. Evening entertainment is often available in the spacious and attractive bar.
ROOMS: 39 en suite (bth/shr) (16 fmly) **MEALS:** Coffee am Tea pm **FACILITIES:** CTV in all bedrooms Indoor swimming pool (heated) Outdoor swimming pool (heated) Sauna Solarium Gym Pool table Putting green Jacuzzi/spa **SERVICES:** Night porter 36P **NOTES:** No coaches Last d 7.30pm Closed 1 Dec-31 Jan

AA Rosettes are awarded for quality of food, see page 15 for an explanation of Rosette assessment.

Symbols and Abbreviations are listed and explained on pages 4 and 5

TORQUAY Devon **Map 03 SX96**
★★ ***The Court Hotel***
Lower Warberry Rd TQ1 1QS
Quality Percentage Score: 65%
☎ 01803 212011 📠 01803 292648
Dir: *From the harbour turn left at the clock tower for Babbacombe, hotel 5th turning on left after traffic lights. Hotel on left at corner with Daphne Cl*
The hotel is in a quiet residential area in easy walking distance of the harbour. Bedrooms are spacious and comfortable with modern facilities. Guests can sample tasty Italian dishes in the attractive dining room, overlooking the gardens and sun terrace.
ROOMS: 16 en suite (bth/shr) (6 fmly) No smoking in all bedrooms **MEALS:** Italian Cuisine V meals **FACILITIES:** CTV in all bedrooms Outdoor swimming pool (heated) **SERVICES:** 16P **NOTES:** No dogs (ex guide dogs) No coaches No smoking in restaurant Last d 7pm Closed Dec-Mar except Xmas RS Nov **CARDS:**
See advert on this page

TORQUAY Devon **Map 03 SX96**
★★ **Burlington**
462-466 Babbacombe Rd TQ1 1HN
Quality Percentage Score: 64%
☎ 01803 294374 📠 01803 200189
Dir: *A380 to Torquay, follow signs to seafront, left at harbour, left at clock tower, the hotel is 0.5m on right hand side*
The Burlington is a short walk from the harbour and shops of Torquay offering a convenient base from which to enjoy the attractions of Torbay. The comfortable bedrooms vary in size and public areas include a pool room and popular bar, whilst in the spacious dining room, traditional dishes are served by friendly staff.
ROOMS: 55 en suite (bth/shr) (7 fmly) s fr £35; d fr £60 (incl. bkfst & dinner) * LB Off peak **MEALS:** Lunch £10 Dinner £10 English, French & Italian Cuisine V meals Coffee am Tea pm **FACILITIES:** CTV in all bedrooms Indoor swimming pool (heated) Sauna Solarium Pool table Jacuzzi/spa Games room Games machines Table tennis Pinball Wkly live entertainment Xmas **SERVICES:** Night porter 20P **NOTES:** No smoking in restaurant Last d 7.50pm **CARDS:**

TORQUAY Devon **Map 03 SX96**
★★ **Dunstone Hall**
Lower Warberry Rd TQ1 1QS
Quality Percentage Score: 64%
☎ 01803 293185
An imposing mansion overlooking Torbay, restored to its former glory. It has comfortable bedrooms equipped with modern facilities. Public areas include a choice of lounges, an atrium with wooden staircase and gallery. The Victorian conservatory houses the bar and dining room.
ROOMS: 13 en suite (bth/shr) (3 fmly) s £35; d £50-£70 (incl. bkfst) * Off peak **MEALS:** Dinner £8.95-£10.50 English & French Cuisine V meals Coffee am Tea pm **FACILITIES:** CTV in all bedrooms Outdoor swimming pool (heated) Pool table **SERVICES:** 18P **NOTES:** No dogs (ex guide dogs) No coaches No smoking in restaurant Last d 7.30pm Closed Nov-Mar **CARDS:**

TORQUAY Devon **Map 03 SX96**
★★ ***Maycliffe***
St Lukes Rd North TQ2 5DP
Quality Percentage Score: 64%
☎ 01803 294964 📠 01803 201167
Dir: *left from Kings Dr, along sea front keep left lane, next lights (Belgrave Rd) proceed up Shedden Hill, 2nd right into St Lukes Rd then 1st left*
In a quiet locatation with views over Torbay from some bedrooms. Rooms are individual in design and decor and have modern facilities. There is a comfortable lounge and attractive
contd.

bar with cabaret three nights a week. Good home cooked food is served in the pretty dining room.
ROOMS: 28 en suite (bth/shr) (1 fmly) No smoking in 9 bedrooms **MEALS:** English & Continental Cuisine V meals Coffee am Tea pm **FACILITIES:** CTV in all bedrooms Wkly live entertainment **SERVICES:** Lift Night porter 10P **NOTES:** No dogs No children 10yrs No smoking in restaurant Last d 7.30pm Closed 2 Jan-12 Feb
CARDS:

TORQUAY Devon **Map 03 SX96**
★★ Ansteys Cove
327 Babbacombe Rd TQ1 3TB
Quality Percentage Score: 63%
☎ 01803 211150 01803 211150
Dir: *turn off A380 Torquay to A3022 turn left onto the B3199. At Babbacombe turn right onto Babbacombe Rd hotel 1m on right opposite Place Hotel*
The hotel is close to the beaches and the Coastal Footpath and its owners extend a warm welcome, and are a mine of local information. Bedrooms are comfortable and attractive, and there is a spacious bar lounge available to residents.
ROOMS: 11 en suite (bth/shr) (2 fmly) No smoking in 9 bedrooms s £25-£31; d £40-£56 (incl. bkfst) * LB Off peak **MEALS:** Dinner fr £12.95 Coffee am Tea pm **FACILITIES:** CTV in all bedrooms STV Xmas **SERVICES:** 12P **NOTES:** No dogs (ex guide dogs) No coaches No smoking in restaurant Last d 8.30pm
CARDS:

TORQUAY Devon **Map 03 SX96**
★★ Anchorage Hotel
MINOTEL Great Britain
Cary Park, Aveland Rd TQ1 3NQ
Quality Percentage Score: 61%
☎ 01803 326175 01803 316439

The Anchorage is situated in a residential part of town and offers a friendly welcome. A lift serves most of the bedrooms, and there are also some on the ground floor. The fixed-price menu at dinner offers a wide choice.
ROOMS: 53 en suite (bth/shr) (5 fmly) No smoking in all bedrooms s £16.50-£24; d £33-£48 (incl. bkfst) * LB Off peak **MEALS:** Sunday Lunch fr £4.75 Dinner fr £9.85 V meals Coffee am Tea pm **FACILITIES:** CTV in all bedrooms Outdoor swimming pool (heated) Wkly live entertainment Xmas **CONF:** Thtr 50 Class 20 Board 24 **SERVICES:** Lift Night porter 26P **NOTES:** No smoking in restaurant Last d 7.30pm **CARDS:**

TORQUAY Devon **Map 03 SX96**
★★ Elmington Hotel
St Agnes Ln, Chelston TQ2 6QE
Quality Percentage Score: 60%
☎ 01803 605192
Dir: *to thr rear of Torquay station*
Lovingly restored, this splendid Victorian villa has Art Deco additions and is set in sub-tropical gardens in a quiet residential area, close to the centre and harbour. Comfortable bedrooms are attractively decorated. There is a spacious lounge, bar and dining room with views over the bay.
ROOMS: 22 rms (19 bth/shr) (5 fmly) No smoking in all bedrooms s £25-£32; d £40-£54 (incl. bkfst) * Off peak **MEALS:** V meals Tea pm **FACILITIES:** CTV in 20 bedrooms Outdoor swimming pool (heated) Pool table Croquet lawn Xmas **SERVICES:** 18P **NOTES:** No dogs (ex guide dogs) No smoking in restaurant Closed Nov
CARDS:

TORQUAY Devon **Map 03 SX96**
★★ *Norcliffe*
7 Babbacombe Downs Rd, Babbacombe TQ1 3LF
Quality Percentage Score: 60%
☎ 01803 328456 01803 328023
Dir: *from M5,take A380, after Sainsburys turn left at lights, across rdbt, left next at lights into Manor road, from Babbacombe Rd turn left*
Situated on the Babbacombe Downs, with marvellous views across Lyme Bay, the Norcliffe is convenient for visitors to St Marychurch or nearby Oddicombe Beach. All bedrooms are comfortable, varying in style and size.
ROOMS: 27 en suite (bth/shr) (3 fmly) **MEALS:** V meals Coffee am Tea pm **FACILITIES:** CTV in all bedrooms Indoor swimming pool (heated) Sauna 3/4 size snooker table ch fac **SERVICES:** Lift 20P **NOTES:** No smoking in restaurant Last d 7.45pm **CARDS:**

TORQUAY Devon **Map 03 SX96**
★★ Roseland
Warren Rd TQ2 5TT
Quality Percentage Score: 58%
☎ 01803 213829 01803 291266
Dir: *at sea front turn left, up Sheddon Hill and turn right at Warren Road*
The former home of Lord Lytton, Viceroy of India, this hotel enjoys views over Torbay. Bedrooms are simply furnished with modern facilities, some with patios and sea views. There is entertainment in the bar-lounge throughout the season, and a small leisure complex.
ROOMS: 39 en suite (bth/shr) 1 annexe en suite (shr) (8 fmly) s £36; d £60 (incl. bkfst) * LB Off peak **MEALS:** Bar Lunch £1.50-£4 Dinner £10 V meals Coffee am Tea pm **FACILITIES:** CTV in all bedrooms Indoor swimming pool (heated) Sauna Solarium Pool table Jacuzzi/spa Games room Wkly live entertainment ch fac Xmas **SERVICES:** Lift Night porter **NOTES:** No smoking in restaurant Last d 8.15pm
CARDS:

TORQUAY Devon **Map 03 SX96**
★★ Seascape
8-10 Tor Church Rd TQ2 5UT
Quality Percentage Score: 58%
☎ 01803 292617 01803 292617
Dir: *take A380 Torquay, at Torre station turn R, at 2nd traffic lights turn L, go through 1 set of lights, hotel is 100yds on right after lights*
It offers panoramic views and is a short stroll from the town centre. A number of public rooms are available and entertainment is provided several times a week. Traditional English cooking is served in the bright dining room, the hotel also has leisure facilities.
ROOMS: 60 en suite (bth/shr) (14 fmly) s £30-£36; d £54-£66 (incl. bkfst & dinner) * LB Off peak **MEALS:** Dinner £15-£20 V meals Tea pm **FACILITIES:** CTV in all bedrooms STV Sauna Solarium Gym Pool table Table tennis Darts Wkly live entertainment Xmas **SERVICES:** Lift 27P **NOTES:** No dogs No smoking in restaurant Last d 7.30pm Closed Jan-Feb
CARDS:

TORQUAY Devon **Map 03 SX96**

★ ***Rawlyn House***

Rawlyn Rd, Chelston TQ2 6PL

Quality Percentage Score: 73%

☎ 01803 605208

A delightful hotel in the quiet residential area of Chelston, within easy reach of the centre of Torquay. Surrounded by an acre of well kept gardens, the hotel has individually styled bedrooms with modern facilities. Dinners are prepared from fresh ingredients, lunchtime bar meals are available.

ROOMS: 14 rms (4 bth 8 shr) 2 annexe en suite (shr) (2 fmly) No smoking in all bedrooms **MEALS:** V meals **FACILITIES:** CTV in all bedrooms Outdoor swimming pool (heated) Pool table Badminton Table tennis **SERVICES:** 16P **NOTES:** No dogs No coaches No smoking in restaurant Last d 7pm Closed Nov-Apr **CARDS:**

TORQUAY Devon **Map 03 SX96**

★ ***Ashley Rise***

18 Babbacombe Rd, Babbacombe TQ1 3SJ

Quality Percentage Score: 68%

☎ 01803 327282

Ashley Rise is situated in historic Babbacombe, close to both shops and beaches, and provides spacious accommodation. The large lounge-bar is the venue for nightly entertainment, traditional meals are served in the attractive dining room.

ROOMS: 25 en suite (bth/shr) (8 fmly) **MEALS:** Coffee am **FACILITIES:** CTV in all bedrooms Solarium Wkly live entertainment **SERVICES:** 14P **NOTES:** No smoking in restaurant Last d 7pm Closed Dec-Mar (ex Xmas & New Year)

TORQUAY Devon **Map 03 SX96**

★ **Westwood**

111 Abbey Rd TQ2 5NP

Quality Percentage Score: 67%

☎ 01803 293818 🖷 01803 293818

Dir: *near town centre*

A small family-run hotel within walking distance of the town centre. Regular guests enjoy the informal atmosphere, particularly in the comfortable bar. Bedrooms are tastefully decorated, offering many modern facilities.

ROOMS: 26 en suite (bth/shr) (4 fmly) s £18-£24; d £36-£48 (incl. bkfst) * LB Off peak **MEALS:** Dinner £10 V meals Tea pm **FACILITIES:** CTV in all bedrooms Xmas **SERVICES:** 12P **NOTES:** No dogs (ex guide dogs) No smoking in restaurant Last d 7pm RS Oct-Jan Jan-Mar **CARDS:**

TORQUAY Devon **Map 03 SX96**

★ **Sunleigh**

Livermead Hill TQ2 6QY

Quality Percentage Score: 62%

☎ 01803 607137

Dir: *from A380 follow signs to Livermead/sea front. Turn right along promenade, right at Cockington sign, take left hand fork Livermead Hill*

With views over Torbay this Victorian villa hotel offers traditional home-made food in an attractive dining room. The simply furnished bedrooms all have modern facilities. The hotel is near the sea front.

ROOMS: 20 en suite (shr) (4 fmly) **MEALS:** Dinner £7-£9.95 **FACILITIES:** CTV in all bedrooms **SERVICES:** 14P **NOTES:** No smoking in restaurant Last d 7pm Closed 2 Jan-Mar & Nov-23 Dec **CARDS:**

TORQUAY Devon **Map 03 SX96**

Late entry **Ashley Court**

107 Abbey Rd TQ2 5NP

☎ 01803 292417 & 292541 🖷 01803 215035

Dir: *A380 onto seafront, left to Sheddon Hill to traffic lights, hotel opposite*

Close to the sea-front, local amenities and attractions, this hotel has been in the same family for over three decades. Staff are committed to ensuring a relaxed, comfortable stay for guests. Bedrooms are well maintained, an outdoor pool and patio are provided as well as live entertainment in the attractive lounge.

ROOMS: 53 en suite (bth/shr) (5 fmly) s £20-£30; d £40-£60 (incl. bkfst) * LB Off peak **MEALS:** Sunday Lunch £5-£7.50 Dinner £5-£7.50 V meals Coffee am Tea pm **FACILITIES:** CTV in all bedrooms Outdoor swimming pool (heated) Wkly live entertainment Xmas **SERVICES:** Lift 28P **NOTES:** No smoking in restaurant Last d 7pm Closed 2 Jan-13 Feb **CARDS:**

TORQUAY Devon **Map 03 SX96**

Late entry ***Villa Marina***

Cockington Ln, Livermead TQ2 6QU

☎ 01803 605440

A family owned hotel a short walk from the sea front, with sea views from public rooms and a number of bedrooms. Live entertainment is provided during the high season and a heated outdoor pool is available.

TOTLAND BAY See Wight, Isle of

TOTNES Devon **Map 03 SX86**

see also **Staverton**

★★ **Royal Seven Stars**

The Plains TQ9 5DD

Quality Percentage Score: 65%

☎ 01803 862125 & 863241 🖷 01803 867925

Dir: *A38 Devon expressway, exit Buckfastleigh turn off onto A384, follow the signs to Totnes town centre*

This 17th-century town centre hotel exudes charm and atmosphere, successfully combined with comfortable accommodation and also providing traditional cuisine. It is a popular local meeting spot with a large bar open to non-residents.

ROOMS: 16 rms (14 bth/shr) (2 fmly) s £49-£59; d £62-£69 (incl. bkfst) LB Off peak **MEALS:** Lunch £11.50-£12.50 & alc Dinner £15-£18 & alc English & Continental Cuisine V meals Coffee am **FACILITIES:** CTV in all bedrooms Xmas **CONF:** Thtr 70 Class 20 Board 20 **SERVICES:** 20P **NOTES:** No smoking area in restaurant Last d 9.15pm **CARDS:**

TOWCESTER Northamptonshire **Map 04 SP64**

⇧ **Travelodge**

NN12 6TQ

☎ 01327 359105 🖷 01327 359105

Dir: *A43 East Towcester by-pass*

This modern building offers accommodation in smart, spacious and well equipped bedrooms, all with en-suite bathrooms. Refreshments may be taken at the nearby family restaurant. For details about current prices, consult the Contents Page under Hotel Groups for the Travelodge phone number.

ROOMS: 33 en suite (bth/shr) d £45.95 *

TRESCO See Scilly, Isles of

TREYARNON BAY Cornwall & Isles of Scilly **Map 02 SW87**

★★ Waterbeach

PL28 8JW

Quality Percentage Score: 67%

☎ 01841 520292 📠 01841 521102

Dir: *from A389 take B3276 signed Newquay, after 2.5m straight across St Merryn X-rds, 3rd turning on right signed Treyarnon then 1st right and 1st left*

Set in grounds three miles south of Padstow, the Waterbeach is a popular coastal hotel. Bedrooms of varying size are all equipped to a high standard. Cottage rooms are especially suited for families. Public areas are comfortable and well proportioned. Each evening, guests enjoy home-cooked six-course dinners.

ROOMS: 13 rms (12 bth/shr) 5 annexe en suite (bth/shr) (7 fmly) s £38-£50; d £76-£100 (incl. bkfst & dinner) Off peak **MEALS:** Dinner £15 V meals Coffee am Tea pm **FACILITIES:** CTV in all bedrooms Tennis (hard) Pool table Putting green **SERVICES:** 20P **NOTES:** No coaches No smoking in restaurant Last d 8.15pm Closed Nov-Etr

CARDS:

TRING Hertfordshire **Map 04 SP91**

★★★★ Pendley Manor

Cow Ln HP23 5QY

Quality Percentage Score: 65%

☎ 01442 891891 📠 01442 890687

Dir: *M25 junct20. Take A41 leaving at Tring exit. At rdbt take exit for Berkhamsted & London. Take 1st left signposted Tring Station & Pendley Manor*

An impressive Victorian mansion, set in extensive grounds. A galleried staircase leads to individually decorated manor house bedrooms with beautiful views. New wing rooms, many with four-poster beds, are well equipped and more spacious. Public areas include a comfortable drawing room and conservatory bar. The conference facilities and business centre are self-contained and extensive, cuisine is deserving of a One Rosette award.

ROOMS: 71 en suite (bth/shr) (4 fmly) s fr £100; d fr £120 (incl. bkfst) * LB Off peak **MEALS:** Lunch £17-£23 & alc Dinner fr £23 & alc English & French Cuisine V meals Coffee am Tea pm **FACILITIES:** CTV in all bedrooms STV Tennis (hard) Snooker Gym Pool table Croquet lawn Games room Archery Laser shooting Hot Air balloon rides Xmas **CONF:** Thtr 180 Class 80 Board 40 Del from £185 * **SERVICES:** Lift Night porter 250P **NOTES:** No smoking in restaurant Last d 10pm

CARDS:

See advert on opposite page

TRING Hertfordshire **Map 04 SP91**

★★★ Rose & Crown

High St HP23 5AH

Quality Percentage Score: 63%

☎ 01442 824071 📠 01442 890735

Dir: *just off the A41 between Aylesbury/Hemel Hempstead, hotel in town centre*

Located in the town centre, this imposing Tudor-style hotel is opposite the church of St Peter and St Paul. The bedrooms vary in size and are comfortably furnished. Bar meals are served in the lounge bar with a more formal menu in the adjacent restaurant.

ROOMS: 27 en suite (bth/shr) (2 fmly) No smoking in 5 bedrooms s £50-£85; d £80-£95 * LB Off peak **MEALS:** English & Continental Cuisine V meals Coffee am Tea pm **FACILITIES:** CTV in all bedrooms STV Xmas **CONF:** Thtr 60 Board 30 Del from £125 * **SERVICES:** Night porter 70P **NOTES:** No dogs (ex guide dogs) No smoking in restaurant Last d 9.30pm **CARDS:**

TRING Hertfordshire **Map 04 SP91**

Travel Inn

Tring Hill HP23 4LD

☎ 01442 824819 📠 01442 890787

Dir: *from M25 junct 20 take A41 towards Aylesbury, at end of Hemel Hempstead/Tring bypass go straight over rdbt, Travel Inn on the right in approx 100yds*

This modern building offers accommodation in smart, spacious and well equipped bedrooms, all with en-suite bathrooms. Refreshments may be taken at the nearby family restaurant. For details about current prices consult the Contents Page under Hotel Groups for the Travel Inn phone number.

ROOMS: 30 en suite (bth/shr) d £39.95 *

TROUTBECK (NEAR WINDERMERE) Cumbria **Map 07 NY40**

★★ Mortal Man

LA23 1PL

Quality Percentage Score: 71%

☎ 015394 33193 📠 015394 31261

Dir: *2.5m N from junct of A591/A592, turn left before church into village, right at T junction, hotel 800m on right*

Situated in a pretty hamlet, this delightful hotel combines the character of a village inn with the charm of a country house hotel. A cosy lounge adjoins the bar with its beams and open fire, whilst the dining room affords stunning views of the valley. The tastefully decorated and exceptionally well eqipped bedrooms also enjoy the scenery. There is an emphasis placed on enjoyable fresh food both in the dining room and the bar.

ROOMS: 12 en suite (bth/shr) s fr £70; d fr £90 (incl. bkfst) * LB Off peak **MEALS:** Sunday Lunch £11-£16alc Dinner £15.65-£25alc International Cuisine V meals Coffee am Tea pm **FACILITIES:** CTV in all bedrooms Wkly live entertainment Xmas **SERVICES:** 20P **NOTES:** No coaches No smoking in restaurant Last d 9.30pm

CARDS:

TROWBRIDGE Wiltshire **Map 03 ST85**

★★ *Polebarn*

Polebarn Rd BA14 7EW

Quality Percentage Score: 67%

☎ 01225 777006 📠 01225 754164

Dir: *off A361 in town centre, follow signs 'Police Station'*

Expect a warm and friendly welcome at this late Georgian Grade II listed building in the heart of Trowbridge. Close to Bath, it is also ideally placed for visiting a number of other tourist attractions such as Stonehenge, Longleat, and Stourhead. Bedrooms are simply decorated, well equipped and suited to the demands of both business and leisure guests. There is a cosy lounge/bar and attractive restaurant.

ROOMS: 12 en suite (bth/shr) (2 fmly) **MEALS:** French Cuisine **FACILITIES:** CTV in all bedrooms **SERVICES:** 12P **NOTES:** Last d 8.15pm

CARDS:

TROWELL MOTORWAY SERVICE AREA (M1) Nottinghamshire
Map 08 SK44

Travelodge

Travelodge

NG9 3PL

☎ 01159 320291

Dir: *M1 junc 25/26 northbound*

This modern building offers accommodation in smart, spacious and well equipped bedrooms, all with en-suite bathrooms. Refreshments may be taken at the nearby family restaurant. For details about current prices, consult the Contents Page under Hotel Groups for the Travelodge phone number.

ROOMS: 35 en suite (bth/shr) d £59.95 *

TRURO Cornwall & Isles of Scilly
Map 02 SW84

see also **Mount Hawke**

★★★ Royal

Lemon St TR1 2QB

Quality Percentage Score: 74%

☎ 01872 270345 📠 01872 242453

Dir: *follow A30 to Carland Cross then Truro. Follow brown tourists signs to hotel in city centre. Drive up to barrier to obtain a pass from reception*

Perfectly situated in the centre of Truro, The Royal Hotel boast some extremely impressive bedrooms. These comfortable rooms, with their modern bathrooms, are complemented by some 'executive' rooms complete with fax machines, CD players and work stations. Mannings Brasserie, open all day and highly

contd.

For Useful Information and Important Telephone Number Changes turn to page 25

popular, offers interesting modern, ethnic and classical dishes in an informal atmosphere, served by friendly and helpful staff.
ROOMS: 35 en suite (bth/shr) (4 fmly) No smoking in 22 bedrooms s £69; d £85 (incl. bkfst) * LB Off peak **MEALS:** Lunch £3-£12alc Dinner £7-£15alc International Cuisine V meals Coffee am Tea pm **FACILITIES:** CTV in all bedrooms STV Snooker Fitness area **SERVICES:** Night porter 40P **NOTES:** No dogs (ex guide dogs) No smoking area in restaurant Last d 10pm Closed 25 & 26 Dec
CARDS:

See advert on page 667

TRURO Cornwall & Isles of Scilly **Map 02 SW84**
★★★ Alverton Manor
Tregolls Rd TR1 1ZQ
Quality Percentage Score: 72%
☎ 01872 276633 01872 222989
Dir: *from M5 Exeter take A30 through Cornwall, at Froddon take the A39 to Truro*

Formerly a convent, this impressive sandstone property stands in six acres of grounds, within walking distance of the city centre. Alverton Manor provides a wide range of smart bedrooms. Stylish public areas include the library and the former chapel, now a striking function room, licensed for wedding ceremonies. Both a carte and fixed price menu are offered in the candlelit restaurant, and dishes are innovative and highly enjoyable.
ROOMS: 34 en suite (bth/shr) s fr £67; d fr £99 (incl. bkfst) * LB Off peak **MEALS:** Lunch £3.25-£17 Dinner fr £21.50 & alc English & French Cuisine V meals Coffee am Tea pm **FACILITIES:** CTV in all bedrooms Golf Snooker Xmas **CONF:** Thtr 370 Class 178 Board 136 Del from £85 * **SERVICES:** Lift Night porter 120P **NOTES:** No smoking in restaurant Last d 9.30pm **CARDS:**

See advert on opposite page

TRURO Cornwall & Isles of Scilly **Map 02 SW84**
★★ Carlton
Falmouth Rd TR1 2HL
Quality Percentage Score: 63%
☎ 01872 272450 01872 223938
Dir: *just off A390 towards city centre*

This family-run hotel is within walking distance of Truro city centre. Bedrooms, some recently refurbished, vary in size and style, but all are well equipped and suited to the hotel's mainly business clientele. Guests can enjoy drinks in the attractive lounge bar. The restaurant, useful for functions, serves a wide selection of home cooked food.
ROOMS: 28 en suite (bth/shr) (4 fmly) No smoking in 12 bedrooms s £33.95-£38.95; d £46.95 (incl. bkfst) * LB Off peak **MEALS:** Dinner £8.95 & alc V meals **FACILITIES:** CTV in all bedrooms Sauna Jacuzzi/spa **CONF:** Thtr 80 Class 40 Board 40 **SERVICES:** 31P **NOTES:** No smoking area in restaurant Last d 8pm Closed 20 Dec-3 Jan
CARDS:

See advert on opposite page

TRURO Cornwall & Isles of Scilly **Map 02 SW84**
★ *Tregarthen Country Cottage*
Banns Rd TR4 8BW
Quality Percentage Score: 75%
☎ 01209 890399 01209 891041
(For full entry see Mount Hawke)

TRURO Cornwall & Isles of Scilly **Map 02 SW84**
Travel Inn
Old Carnon Hill, Carnon Downs TR3 6JT
☎ 01872 863370 01872 865620
Dir: *on A39 3m SW of Truro*

This modern building offers accommodation in smart, spacious and well equipped bedrooms, all with en-suite bathrooms. Refreshments may be taken at the nearby family restaurant. For details about current prices consult the Contents Page under Hotel Groups for the Travel Inn phone number.
ROOMS: 40 en suite (bth/shr) d £39.95 *

TUNBRIDGE WELLS (ROYAL) Kent **Map 05 TQ53**
★★★ *The Spa*
Mount Ephraim TN4 8XJ
Quality Percentage Score: 76%
☎ 01892 520331 01892 510575
Dir: *follow signposts to A264 East Grinstead, hotel is on right hand side*

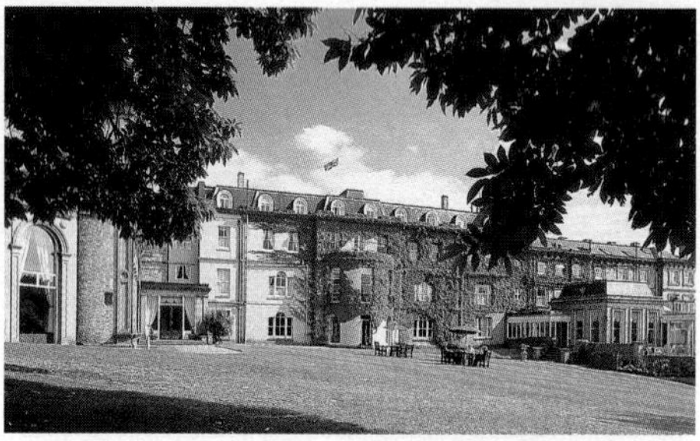

Set in 15 acres of parkland, with ponds and floodlit tennis courts, this 18th-century country house retains much of its original character. Bedrooms, many of which overlook the attractive gardens, are smartly furnished. Wood-panelled public rooms include a comfortable lobby lounge, a bar and a grand restaurant which serves a fixed-price menu and an interesting carte.
ROOMS: 74 en suite (bth) (10 fmly) No smoking in 13 bedrooms **MEALS:** English, French & Italian Cuisine V meals Coffee am Tea pm **FACILITIES:** CTV in all bedrooms STV Indoor swimming pool (heated) Tennis (hard) Sauna Gym Croquet lawn Dance studio Steam room Beauty Salon **CONF:** Thtr 300 Class 93 Board 90 **SERVICES:** Lift Night porter 120P **NOTES:** No smoking area in restaurant Last d 9.30pm
CARDS:

TUNBRIDGE WELLS (ROYAL) Kent **Map 05 TQ53**
★★★ Royal Wells Inn
Mount Ephraim TN4 8BE
Quality Percentage Score: 71%
☎ 01892 511188 01892 511908
Dir: *turn off A21 onto A26 follow it into Tunbridge Wells avoiding town centre, at junct of A264 takr right fork, Inn is 150mtrs on right*

This delightful family-run hotel is situated high above the town with stunning views. The accommodation is being continually upgraded, and all rooms are comfortably furnished. There are two eating options, The Brasserie with its extensive blackboard menu, and the newly refurbished Conservatory with a full carte

contd.

and daily menu. The dishes are interesting and carefully prepared by chef Robert Sloan who makes good use of fresh local produce. The wine list is well chosen and offers a range of reasonably priced selections to complement the menu. The staff provide relaxed and cheerful service.

ROOMS: 19 en suite (bth/shr) (2 fmly) s £65-£85; d £85-£115 (incl. bkfst) LB Off peak **MEALS:** Lunch £12.75-£14.50 & alc Dinner £19.50-£26.50alc International Cuisine V meals Coffee am **FACILITIES:** CTV in all bedrooms STV Wkly live entertainment **CONF:** Thtr 100 Class 40 Board 40 Del from £97.50 **SERVICES:** Lift Night porter 31P **NOTES:** Last d 10pm Closed 25-26 Dec **CARDS:**

See advert on this page

TUNBRIDGE WELLS (ROYAL) Kent **Map 05 TQ53**

★★ **Swan**

The Pantiles TN2 5TD

Quality Percentage Score: 69%

☎ 01892 541450 & 543319 📠 01892 541465

Dir: *from M25 take A26 towards Tunbridge Wells, 0.5m from town centre follow signs for hotel*

This informal, town-centre hotel stands in The Pantiles, at the heart of Tunbridge Wells. Its stylish restaurant offers a brasserie-style menu in a light and airy environment. Bedrooms range from spacious twins and doubles to luxury suites.

ROOMS: 20 en suite (bth/shr) (2 fmly) s £55-£61; d £77-£87 (incl. bkfst) * LB Off peak **MEALS:** Lunch £10-£15 High tea £8 Dinner £15-£25 International Cuisine V meals Coffee am Tea pm **FACILITIES:** CTV in all bedrooms STV Pool table Wkly live entertainment Xmas **CONF:** Thtr 60 Class 30 Board 30 Del from £85 * **SERVICES:** Night porter 18P **NOTES:** No dogs Last d 9.30pm **CARDS:**

TUNBRIDGE WELLS (ROYAL) Kent **Map 05 TQ53**

★★ Russell

80 London Rd TN1 1DZ

Quality Percentage Score: 64%

☎ 01892 544833 Fax 01892 515846

Dir: *at junct A26/A264 uphill onto A26, hotel on right*

A bustling, friendly Victorian hotel, The Russell is very close to the town centre. Bedrooms are spacious and well equipped, and there is 24-hour room service. A separate building houses self-contained luxury suites. Enjoyable meals are served in the restaurant and there is a popular bar.

ROOMS: 19 en suite (bth/shr) 5 annexe en suite (bth/shr) (2 fmly) No smoking in 10 bedrooms s £48-£68; d £58-£82 (incl. bkfst) * LB Off peak **MEALS:** Lunch £11.50-£14.95 Dinner £11.50-£14.95 V meals Coffee am Tea pm **FACILITIES:** CTV in all bedrooms STV **CONF:** Thtr 50 Class 20 Board 32 Del from £79.50 * **SERVICES:** Night porter 15P **NOTES:** No smoking area in restaurant Last d 9.30pm

CARDS:

TUNBRIDGE WELLS (ROYAL) Kent **Map 05 TQ53**

Hotel Du Vin & Bistro

Crescent Rd TN1 2LY

☎ 01892 526455 Fax 01892 512044

Dir: *Follow town centre to main intersection of Mount Pleasant Rd & Crescent Rd/Church Rd. Hotel 150yds along Crescent Rd on R just past Phillips House*

An old-fashioned hotel offering simple but spacious accommodation, many of the rooms having pleasant views over the rear gardens, is conveniently located for the centre of the town.

ROOMS: 25 en suite (bth/shr) **MEALS:** V meals Coffee am Tea pm **FACILITIES:** CTV in all bedrooms STV Snooker Pool table **CONF:** Thtr 40 Board 25 **SERVICES:** Lift 40P **NOTES:** No dogs (ex guide dogs) No coaches No smoking in restaurant Last d 9.30pm

CARDS:

TURNERS HILL West Sussex **Map 04 TQ33**

The Premier Collection

★★★ *Alexander House*

East St RH10 4QD

☎ 01342 714914 Fax 01342 717328

Dir: *on B2110 between Turners Hill and East Grinstead, 6m from junct 10 on M23*

Dating in part from the 17th century, this fine house is set in 135 acres of grounds. Reception rooms include the sunny south drawing room, and oak-panelled library. Individually decorated bedrooms include some full suites, one with a four-poster bed believed to have been made for Napoleon. All rooms are equipped with little extra touches like fruit and mineral water, with good quality toiletries in the bathrooms. In the restaurant tail-coated waiters impress with highly polished service which complements confident modern British cooking.

ROOMS: 15 en suite (bth/shr) **MEALS:** English & French Cuisine V meals Coffee am Tea pm **FACILITIES:** CTV in all bedrooms STV Tennis (hard) Snooker Croquet lawn Putting green Clay pigeon shooting Archery by arrangement Wkly live entertainment **CONF:** Thtr 70 Class 24 Board 24 Del from £195 * **SERVICES:** Lift Night porter 50P **NOTES:** No dogs (ex guide dogs) No coaches No smoking in restaurant Last d 9.30pm

CARDS:

See advert under GATWICK AIRPORT

TURVEY Bedfordshire **Map 04 SP95**

★★ *Laws*

High St MK43 8DB

Quality Percentage Score: 65%

☎ 01234 881213 & 881655 Fax 01234 888864

Dir: *A428 Bedford-Northampton*

The most notable feature of this relaxing hotel is the informality and friendliness of the enthusiastic owners, Jerome and Francesca Mack. An attractive stone property set in well tended gardens, facilities are very good, with comfortable public rooms (including a leisure centre) and spacious and well equipped bedrooms. Guests can choose from a wide choice of dishes in the dining room or opt for a snack in the bar.

ROOMS: 23 rms (20 bth/shr) (2 fmly) No smoking in 21 bedrooms **MEALS:** Continental Cuisine V meals Coffee am Tea pm **FACILITIES:** CTV in 19 bedrooms STV Indoor swimming pool (heated) Gym Jacuzzi/spa **CONF:** Thtr 50 Class 20 Board 18 **SERVICES:** 35P **NOTES:** No dogs (ex guide dogs) No coaches No smoking in restaurant

CARDS:

TUTBURY Staffordshire **Map 08 SK22**

★★★ Ye Olde Dog & Partridge

High St DE13 9LS

Quality Percentage Score: 64%

☎ 01283 813030 Fax 01283 813178

Dir: *exit A50 between Burton-on-Trent and Uttoxeter, signposted off A50 as A511*

Dating in parts from the 15th century, this half-timbered hotel enjoys a pleasant village setting, yet is within easy access of major routes. Bedrooms, which vary in sizes and styles, are available in the main hotel or an adjacent Georgian building; each room is thoughtfully equipped and comfortably furnished. A new brasserie-style restaurant and bar were being created as we went to press and should offer an alternative to the very popular carvery, where locals and visitors alike enjoy informal dining.

ROOMS: 6 en suite (bth/shr) 14 annexe en suite (bth/shr) (1 fmly) No smoking in 6 bedrooms s £55-£75; d £80-£99 (incl. bkfst) * LB Off peak **MEALS:** Lunch £10-£18 & alc High tea fr £3 Dinner £15-£22alc V meals Coffee am Tea pm **FACILITIES:** CTV in all bedrooms STV Full Leisure pass to Branston Golf & Country Club Wkly live entertainment **SERVICES:** Night porter 150P **NOTES:** Last d 10.30pm RS evenings 25 & 26 Dec & 1 Jan **CARDS:**

See advert on opposite page

TWO BRIDGES Devon **Map 02 SX67**

★★ Prince Hall

PL20 6SA

Quality Percentage Score: 78%

☎ 01822 890403 Fax 01822 890676

Dir: *on B3357 1m East of Two Bridges road junct*

Set in the heart of Dartmoor National Park, Prince Hall offers

contd.

spectacular views. Each of the spacious bedrooms is named after one of the tors. Public areas include a bar-lounge and a sitting room. The impressive, but short, fixed-price menu changes daily. Breakfast is equally memorable.
ROOMS: 8 en suite (bth/shr) (1 fmly) s £67-£75; d £123-£145 (incl. bkfst & dinner) * LB Off peak **MEALS:** Dinner £25 English & French Cuisine Coffee am Tea pm **FACILITIES:** CTV in all bedrooms Fishing Croquet lawn Horse riding,Guided Walks,Fly-Fishing Tuition,Spooks and Local Ledgends wknd **SERVICES:** 13P **NOTES:** No coaches No children 10yrs No smoking in restaurant Last d 8.30pm Closed Jan
CARDS:

TWO BRIDGES Devon **Map 02 SX67**
★★ Two Bridges Hotel
PL20 6SW
Quality Percentage Score: 72%
☎ 01822 890581 01822 890575
Dir: *junc of B3212 & B3357*

The hotel is surrounded by Dartmoor National Park. Log fires, easy chairs and a collection of ephemera and artwork contribute to the ambience. Traditional bar food is found in the Saracen's Bar, serving locally brewed 'Jail Ale'. The restaurant provides more formal dining with a choice of menus featuring locally sourced produce, cooked with style and flair. Three standards of bedrooms are available.
ROOMS: 29 en suite (bth/shr) (2 fmly) No smoking in 21 bedrooms s £35-£45; d fr £70 (incl. bkfst) * LB Off peak **MEALS:** Sunday Lunch £9.95-£15.50 Dinner £19.95-£21.95 & alc V meals Coffee am Tea pm **FACILITIES:** CTV in all bedrooms STV Fishing Xmas **CONF:** Thtr 150 Class 58 Board 40 Del from £75 * **SERVICES:** 100P **NOTES:** No smoking in restaurant Last d 9pm **CARDS:**

See advert on this page

TYNEMOUTH Tyne & Wear **Map 12 NZ36**
★★★ Grand
Grand Pde NE30 4ER
Quality Percentage Score: 66%
☎ 0191 293 6666 0191 293 6665
Dir: *A1058 for Tynemouth, when reach coastline rdbt turn right. The Grand Hotel is on right approx 0.5 mile along road*
Situated on the seafront, with many of the rooms taking advantage of the view, this family-owned hotel has been completely refurbished, returning the fine Victorian building to its former glory. A smart reception lobby and grand staircase set

contd.

AA Rosettes are awarded for quality of food,
see page 15 for an explanation of Rosette assessment.

the scene, whilst there are many impressive bedrooms with smart fully tiled bathrooms.

Grand, Tynemouth

ROOMS: 40 en suite (bth/shr) 5 annexe en suite (bth/shr) (12 fmly) s £40-£80; d £45-£140 (incl. bkfst) * Off peak **MEALS:** Lunch £12.75-£13.75 & alc Dinner £14.75-£15.75 & alc English Cuisine V meals Coffee am Tea pm **FACILITIES:** CTV in all bedrooms Public Bar, Restaurant. Xmas **CONF:** Thtr 130 Class 40 Board 40 Del from £60 * **SERVICES:** Lift Night porter 18P **NOTES:** No dogs (ex guide dogs) Last d 9.45 **CARDS:**

See advert on opposite page

UCKFIELD East Sussex **Map 05 TQ42**

★★★★ *Buxted Park Country House Hotel*

Buxted TN22 4AY
Quality Percentage Score: 71%
☎ 01825 732711 01825 732770
Dir: *on A272. Turn off the A22, A26, or A267 on to the A27 towards Heathfield then Buxted*

A Georgian mansion set in 300 acres of beautiful Sussex countryside, Buxted Park retains a grand country house atmosphere in its extensive day rooms. A gilt coat-of-arms above the fireplace in the elegant chandeliered drawing room is one of many original features. Bedrooms, mostly in the Garden Wing, (a 20th-century addition) are stylishly decorated and well appointed. The original Victorian orangery is the stylish setting for some good cooking from an interesting menu.

ROOMS: 44 en suite (bth/shr) (10 fmly) **MEALS:** V meals Coffee am Tea pm **FACILITIES:** CTV in all bedrooms STV Outdoor swimming pool (heated) Snooker Sauna Solarium Gym Croquet lawn Putting green Jacuzzi/spa Beauty salon **CONF:** Thtr 150 Class 60 Board 40 **SERVICES:** Night porter 150P **NOTES:** No dogs (ex guide dogs) No smoking in restaurant Last d 9.30pm
CARDS:

UCKFIELD East Sussex **Map 05 TQ42**

★★★ Horsted Place Sporting Estate & Hotel

Little Horsted TN22 5TS
Quality Percentage Score: 75%
☎ 01825 750581 01825 750459
Dir: *2m S on A26 towards Lewes*

One of Britain's finest examples of Gothic revivalist architecture, Horsted Place is surrounded by its own estate which includes a golf club. Inside there are many fine architectural features, including a splendid Pugin staircase. Bedrooms are notably spacious and well appointed, many are suites.

ROOMS: 17 en suite (bth/shr) (5 fmly) d £105-£290 (incl. bkfst) * LB Off peak **MEALS:** Lunch £10-£18.95 Dinner £32 English & French Cuisine V meals Coffee am Tea pm **FACILITIES:** CTV in all bedrooms STV Indoor swimming pool (heated) Golf 36 Tennis (hard) Croquet lawn Tennis Wkly live entertainment Xmas **CONF:** Thtr 100 Class 50 Board 40 **SERVICES:** Lift Night porter 36P **NOTES:** No dogs (ex guide dogs) No smoking in restaurant Last d 9.30pm
CARDS:

The AA Hotel Booking Service is a free benefit to AA members. See the advertisement on page 47

ULLESTHORPE Leicestershire **Map 04 SP58**

★★★ Ullesthorpe Court Hotel & Golf Club

Frolesworth Rd LE17 5BZ
Quality Percentage Score: 70%
☎ 01455 209023 01455 202537
Dir: *from junct 20 of M1 head towards Lutterworth then follow brown tourist signs*

This impressive hotel, golf and country club complex has extensive gournds and is near the motorway network, the NEC and Birmingham Airport. Bedrooms are spacious and well equipped, there is a choice of restaurants, and there are leisure facilities and rooms for private functions.

ROOMS: 38 en suite (bth/shr) (1 fmly) s fr £76.50; d fr £99.50 (incl. bkfst) * LB Off peak **MEALS:** Dinner £15.50 & alc V meals Coffee am Tea pm **FACILITIES:** CTV in all bedrooms STV Indoor swimming pool (heated) Golf 18 Tennis (hard) Snooker Sauna Solarium Gym Pool table Putting green Jacuzzi/spa Beauty room **CONF:** Thtr 70 Class 40 Board 30 Del from £87.50 * **SERVICES:** Night porter 500P **NOTES:** Last d 10pm **CARDS:**

ULLINGSWICK Herefordshire **Map 03 SO54**

★★ The Steppes Country House

HR1 3JG
Quality Percentage Score: 75%
☎ 01432 820424 01432 820042
Dir: *off A417, 1.5m NW of junct with A465, signposted 'Ullingswick'*

Parts of this delightful country house date back to 1380, though much of it is 17th century. It has a wealth of charm and character, with beamed ceilings, stone flagged and tiled floors, as well as antique furnishings. Surrounded by pleasant gardens, the comfortable and well equipped bedrooms are located in converted outbuildings, including a beautifully restored timber framed barn. Tricia Howland is an award winning cook, who produces some imaginative dishes.

ROOMS: 6 annexe en suite (bth/shr) No smoking in all bedrooms s £90; d £142 (incl. bkfst & dinner) * LB Off peak **MEALS:** Dinner fr £26 French Cuisine V meals **FACILITIES:** CTV in all bedrooms **SERVICES:** 8P **NOTES:** No coaches No children 12yrs No smoking in restaurant Last d 7pm Closed early Dec-late Jan **CARDS:**

ULLSWATER See **Glenridding, Patterdale, & Watermillock**

ULVERSTON Cumbria **Map 07 SD27**

★★ Bay Horse Hotel & Restaurant

Canal Foot LA12 9EL

Quality Percentage Score: 74%

☎ 01229 583972 Fax 01229 580502

Dir: *from A590 on entering Ulverston follow signs for Canal Foot on left side of road*

Standing at the end of the Ulverston canal, this well-established inn enjoys stunning views over the picturesque Leven estuary. The comfortable bedrooms are stylishly furnished, well equipped and boast patio doors and balconies. Excellent meals are served in the conservatory restaurant, and food is also available at lunchtime in the bar.

ROOMS: 7 en suite (bth/shr) s £93.50; d £176 (incl. bkfst & dinner) * LB Off peak **MEALS:** Lunch fr £16.75 & alc Dinner £24.70-£30alc V meals Coffee am Tea pm **FACILITIES:** CTV in all bedrooms **SERVICES:** 6P **NOTES:** No coaches No children 12yrs No smoking in restaurant Last d 8pm **CARDS:**

UMBERLEIGH Devon **Map 02 SS62**

★★ *Rising Sun Inn*

EX37 9DU

Quality Percentage Score: 70%

☎ 01769 560447 Fax 01769 560764

Dir: *situated at Umberleigh Bridge on the A377, Exeter/Barnstaple road, at the junct of the B3227*

This period inn has been extensively renovated. Most of the comfortable, well equipped bedrooms are in the main building, three are across the courtyard. The Angler's Arms bar features an inglenook fireplace and interesting memorabilia. There is a restaurant and a range of bar meals is served.

ROOMS: 6 en suite (bth/shr) 3 annexe en suite (bth/shr) (1 fmly) No smoking in all bedrooms **MEALS:** V meals Coffee am Tea pm **FACILITIES:** CTV in all bedrooms Fishing **CONF:** Thtr 50 Class 30 Board 18 Del from £75 * **SERVICES:** 30P **NOTES:** No dogs (ex guide dogs) No coaches Last d 9.30pm **CARDS:**

UPHOLLAND Lancashire **Map 07 SD50**

★★★ *Holland Hall*

6 Lafford Ln WN8 0QZ

Quality Percentage Score: 65%

☎ 01695 624426 Fax 01695 622433

Dir: *off A577 on right after Upholland Church*

A delightfully positioned hotel with lovely views, Holland Hall is furnished and decorated to a high standard. Interesting food is served in the oak-panelled restaurant and there is also a pizzeria.

ROOMS: 36 en suite (bth/shr) (1 fmly) **MEALS:** International Cuisine V meals Coffee am Tea pm **FACILITIES:** CTV in all bedrooms **CONF:** Thtr 150 Class 100 Board 50 **SERVICES:** Night porter 200P **NOTES:** No dogs (ex guide dogs) No smoking area in restaurant Last d 10pm **CARDS:**

UPHOLLAND Lancashire **Map 07 SD50**

★★★ Quality Hotel Skelmersdale

Comfort Quality Clarion CHOICE HOTELS EUROPE

Prescott Rd WN8 9PU

Quality Percentage Score: 63%

☎ 01695 720401 Fax 01695 50953

Dir: *leave M58 at junct 5 follow road round to hotel on one way system*

One of the main features of this hotel is the magnificent Great Hall, now used for banquets and weddings, which was built in 1580 and has been sympathetically restored. The modern bedrooms are attractively decorated and well equipped, and include facilities for disabled persons. One room also has a four-poster bed. Bare stone walls in the bar and restaurant give character to the public areas and there are also numerous meeting and conference rooms in addition to the Great Hall. Staff throughout are particularly friendly and helpful.

ROOMS: 55 en suite (bth/shr) (2 fmly) No smoking in 9 bedrooms s fr £70; d fr £81.50 * LB Off peak **MEALS:** Lunch £2.95-£15.95alc Dinner fr £14.50 & alc English & French Cuisine V meals Coffee am Tea pm **FACILITIES:** CTV in all bedrooms STV **CONF:** Thtr 200 Class 125 Board 70 **SERVICES:** Night porter 200P **NOTES:** No smoking area in restaurant **CARDS:**

Indicates that the star classification has not been confirmed under the New Quality Standards, see page 7 for further information.

Remember to return your Prize Draw card for a chance to win one of 30 relaxing leisure breaks with Corus and Regal hotels. See inside the front cover for the card and competition details.

U

UPPER SLAUGHTER Gloucestershire **Map 04 SP12**

The Premier Collection

★★★ Lords of the Manor

GL54 2JD

☎ 01451 820243 01451 820696

Dir: *2m W of A429. Turn off A40 onto A429, take 'The Slaughters' turning. Continue through Lower Slaughter for 1m until Upper Slaughter-hotel on right*

The eight acres of gardens and parkland form an idyllic setting for this lovely old manor house, and it is a delight to take an aperitif on the lawn, overlooking the lake, or on the terrace by the formal garden. Bedrooms, including some at ground-floor level, are furnished to a high standard, and the restaurant offers a cuisine that successfully combines modern and classical styles.

ROOMS: 27 en suite (bth/shr) s £98; d £138-£295 (incl. bkfst) * LB Off peak **MEALS:** Lunch £21 Dinner £59 & alc V meals Coffee am Tea pm **FACILITIES:** CTV in all bedrooms STV Fishing Croquet lawn Xmas **CONF:** Thtr 30 Class 20 Board 20 Del £150 * **SERVICES:** Night porter 40P **NOTES:** No dogs (ex guide dogs) No smoking in restaurant Last d 9.30pm **CARDS:**

UPPINGHAM Rutland **Map 04 SP89**

★★ Lake Isle

High St East LE15 9PZ

Quality Percentage Score: 73%

☎ 01572 822951 01572 822951

Dir: *in the centre of Uppingham via Queen street*

Developed from the original restaurant, this town house hotel has bedrooms both in the main building and in the adjacent converted cottages; all are cheerfully decorated, tastefully appointed and well equipped with numerous thoughtful extras. The ground floor public rooms are dominated by the rustic restaurant, however drinks can be taken around an open log fire in the adjacent small bar, and residents also have use of a comfortable first floor lounge.

ROOMS: 10 en suite (bth/shr) 2 annexe en suite (bth/shr) s £52-£62; d £69-£79 (incl. bkfst) * LB Off peak **MEALS:** Lunch £7.50-£13.50 Dinner £23.50-£27.50 English & French Cuisine V meals **FACILITIES:** CTV in all bedrooms Xmas **CONF:** Board 8 Del from £92 * **SERVICES:** 7P **NOTES:** No coaches Last d 9.30pm **CARDS:**

U

UPTON UPON SEVERN Worcestershire **Map 03 SO84**

★★ Fownes Star

High St WR8 0HQ

Quality Percentage Score: 64%

☎ 01684 592300 01684 592929

Dir: *close to junct 1 off M50 on A38 towards Worcester for approx 3m, turn left on A104, over River Bridge, left then 1st left*

This 17th century inn is situated close to both the town centre and the River Severn. The traditionally furnished public rooms are not without charm and character and include a choice of bars. The accommodation, which includes family bedded rooms, is well equipped and equally suitable for both tourists and commercial visitors. The hotel also has a function room for up to 100 people.

ROOMS: 16 en suite (bth/shr) (4 fmly) s £39-£45; d £59-£65 (incl. bkfst) * LB Off peak **MEALS:** Lunch £4.50-£8.95 Dinner £12.95 V meals Coffee am Tea pm **FACILITIES:** CTV in all bedrooms Xmas **CONF:** Thtr 80 Class 50 Board 30 **SERVICES:** 8P **NOTES:** No smoking in restaurant Last d 9.30pm **CARDS:**

UTTOXETER Staffordshire **Map 07 SK03**

★★ *Bank House*

Church St ST14 8AG

Quality Percentage Score: 66%

☎ 01889 566922 01889 567565

Dir: *next to main Parish Church, nearest main road A50 Stoke - Derby*

The Bank House Hotel was built in 1777 and, as the name would suggest, was the first bank in Uttoxeter. The original vault still remains as a feature in the restaurant. The recently refurbished accommodation is well equipped and suitable for both business people and tourists.

ROOMS: 14 en suite (bth/shr) (3 fmly) No smoking in 2 bedrooms **MEALS:** European Cuisine V meals Coffee am Tea pm **FACILITIES:** CTV in all bedrooms **CONF:** Thtr 30 Class 30 Board 35 **SERVICES:** 16P **NOTES:** No smoking in restaurant Last d 9.30pm **CARDS:**

UTTOXETER Staffordshire **Map 07 SK03**

Travelodge

Ashbourne Rd ST14 5AA

☎ 01889 562043 01889 562043

Dir: *on A50/A5030*

This modern building offers accommodation in smart, spacious and well equipped bedrooms, all with en-suite bathrooms. Refreshments may be taken at the nearby family restaurant. For details about current prices, consult the Contents Page under Hotel Groups for the Travelodge phone number.

ROOMS: 32 en suite (bth/shr) d £49.95 *

VENTNOR See Wight, Isle of

VERYAN Cornwall & Isles of Scilly **Map 02 SW93**

★★★★ Nare

Carne Beach TR2 5PF

Quality Percentage Score: 77%

☎ 01872 501279 01872 501856

Dir: *from Tregony follow A3078 for approx 1.5m turn left at signpost Veryan, drive straight through village towards sea and hotel*

This delightful property offers country house care and courtesy in a seaside setting. Many of the bedrooms have balconies. Fresh flowers and antiques add to the warm atmosphere, and a choice

contd.

of restaurants offers a wide range of food from light snacks to superb local seafood.

ROOMS: 38 en suite (bth/shr) (4 fmly) s £107-£160; d £235-£290 (incl. bkfst & dinner) LB Off peak **MEALS:** Lunch £15 Dinner £31 & alc English & French Cuisine V meals Coffee am Tea pm **FACILITIES:** CTV in all bedrooms STV Indoor swimming pool (heated) Outdoor swimming pool (heated) Tennis (hard) Snooker Sauna Gym Croquet lawn Jacuzzi/spa Windsurfing Health & Beauty clinic Hotel Boat Xmas **SERVICES:** Lift Night porter 80P **NOTES:** No coaches No smoking in restaurant Last d 9.30pm Closed 4 Jan-1 Feb **CARDS:**

WADEBRIDGE Cornwall & Isles of Scilly — Map 02 SW97

★★ Molesworth Arms

Molesworth St PL27 7DP
Quality Percentage Score: 64%
☎ 01208 812055 Fax 01208 814254

Dir: *A30 to Bodmin town centre and follow directions to Wadebridge. Over old bridge turn right and then 1st left*

This 16th-century former coaching inn stands on the town centre pedestrian area. Recently upgraded, bedrooms offer comfort and modern facilities while maintaining their charm. In addition to the menu in the Courtyard Restaurant, meals and snacks are served in the charming bar. Short golfing breaks are popular with guests.

ROOMS: 16 rms (14 bth/shr) (2 fmly) s £35-£39.50; d £55-£59.50 (incl. bkfst) * LB Off peak **MEALS:** English Cuisine V meals Coffee am Tea pm **FACILITIES:** CTV in all bedrooms STV **CONF:** Thtr 60 Class 50 Board 40 Del from £45 * **SERVICES:** 16P **CARDS:**

WAKEFIELD West Yorkshire — Map 08 SE32

★★★ St Pierre

Barnsley Rd, Newmillerdam WF2 6QG
Quality Percentage Score: 73%
☎ 01924 255596 Fax 01924 252746

Dir: *A636 to Wakefield, 3rd exit at rdbt, across 2 mini rdbts, right lane at lights follow signs Barnsley(A61). Pass Newmillerdam hotel 500yds on left*

This well furnished hotel is found three miles to the south of Wakefield. The bedrooms are very thoughtfully equipped and also offer good comforts. A small gym has now been added. A good range of food is available in the elegantly furnished and intimate restaurant and staff are exceptionally friendly and very helpful.

ROOMS: 54 en suite (bth/shr) (3 fmly) No smoking in 33 bedrooms d £69-£99 * LB Off peak **MEALS:** Lunch £8.95-£9.95 High tea £6 Dinner £14.95-£20.95 & alc English & Continental Cuisine V meals Coffee am Tea pm **FACILITIES:** CTV in all bedrooms STV Gym Xmas **CONF:** Thtr 130 Class 70 Board 50 Del from £65 * **SERVICES:** Lift Night porter 70P **NOTES:** No smoking area in restaurant Last d 10pm **CARDS:**

WAKEFIELD West Yorkshire — Map 08 SE32

★★★ Waterton Park

Walton Hall, The Balk, Walton WF2 6PW
Quality Percentage Score: 72%
☎ 01924 257911 & 249800 Fax 01924 240082

Dir: *3m SE off B6378 - off M1 at junct 39 towards Wakefield. At rdbt take right for Crofton. At the second set of traffic lights turn right follow signs*

Surrounded by a moat and with its own large lake and extensive grounds, this impressive stone built hotel now has a golf course and a well equipped leisure club. There are attractive, modern bedrooms and the public rooms include two bars and a delightful beamed restaurant serving a good range of well produced dishes. Staff are friendly and provide an attentive style of service.

ROOMS: 30 en suite (bth/shr) 35 annexe en suite (bth/shr) s £65-£95; d £100-£130 (incl. bkfst) LB Off peak **MEALS:** Lunch £15 High tea £5.50 Dinner £20 English & French Cuisine V meals Coffee am Tea pm **FACILITIES:** CTV in all bedrooms STV Indoor swimming pool (heated) Golf 18 Fishing Snooker Sauna Solarium Gym Putting green Jacuzzi/spa Steam room Xmas **CONF:** Thtr 150 Class 80 Board 60 Del from £105 * **SERVICES:** Night porter 180P **NOTES:** No dogs No smoking in restaurant Last d 9.30pm **CARDS:**

WAKEFIELD West Yorkshire — Map 08 SE32

★★★ Posthouse Wakefield

Posthouse

Queen's Dr, Ossett WF5 9BE
Quality Percentage Score: 68%
☎ 01924 276388 Fax 01924 276437

Dir: *exit M1 at junct 40 following signs for Wakefield. Hotel is on the right after 200yrds*

This modern hotel provides a good standard of accommodation in smartly decorated bedrooms, many in the new 'Millennium'style. Traders' Restaurant offers a full menu, and refreshments are served all day in the lounge, or there is 24-hour room service. Parking facilities are ample.

ROOMS: 99 en suite (bth/shr) (27 fmly) No smoking in 71 bedrooms s fr £29; d £49-£99 * LB Off peak **MEALS:** International Cuisine V meals Coffee am Tea pm **FACILITIES:** CTV in all bedrooms Xmas **CONF:** Thtr 160 Class 70 Board 100 Del from £99 * **SERVICES:** Lift Night porter 130P **NOTES:** No smoking area in restaurant Last d 10pm **CARDS:**

WAKEFIELD West Yorkshire — Map 08 SE32

★★★ Quality Hotel Wakefield

Queen St WF1 1JU
Quality Percentage Score: 66%
☎ 01924 372111 Fax 01924 383648

Dir: *leave M1 junct 39 & follow signs for town centre. Queen St is on the Left*

Situated in the centre of the city and close to the cathedral, this modern multi-storey hotel offers well equipped and pleasantly furnished bedrooms. There is a comfortable bar lounge next to

contd.

W

the spacious restaurant where a set price menu with a good choice is offered. The smartly turned out staff are attentive and friendly. Conference facilities are also available.
ROOMS: 64 en suite (bth/shr) (4 fmly) No smoking in 16 bedrooms s £75-£90; d fr £90 * Off peak **MEALS:** V meals Coffee am Tea pm **FACILITIES:** CTV in all bedrooms STV Xmas **CONF:** Thtr 250 Class 90 Board 54 **SERVICES:** Lift Night porter 30P **NOTES:** No smoking area in restaurant Last d 10.45pm **CARDS:**

WAKEFIELD West Yorkshire **Map 08 SE32**
★★★ Cedar Court
Denby Dale Rd, Calder Grove WF4 3QZ
Quality Percentage Score: 65%
☎ 01924 276310 01924 280221
Dir: *adjacent to junct 39 on M1*
Conveniently situated next to junction 39 of the M1, this large commercial hotel provides well equipped modern bedrooms together with comfortable public rooms. There is an extensive range of conference facilities available and a good choice of well-produced dishes is served in the elegant split-level restaurant.
ROOMS: 151 en suite (bth/shr) (11 fmly) No smoking in 85 bedrooms s £105; d £95-£120 * LB Off peak **MEALS:** Lunch £10.95-£12.50 Dinner fr £18.95 English & French Cuisine V meals Coffee am Tea pm **FACILITIES:** CTV in all bedrooms STV Gym Xmas **CONF:** Thtr 400 Class 200 Board 80 Del from £99 * **SERVICES:** Lift Night porter 350P **NOTES:** No smoking area in restaurant Last d 10pm **CARDS:**

WAKEFIELD West Yorkshire **Map 08 SE32**
★★★ Stoneleigh
Doncaster Rd WF1 5HA
Quality Percentage Score: 64%
☎ 01924 369461 01924 201041
Dir: *1.5m S from Wakefield on A638*
Converted from a row of terraced houses, a short distance from the city centre, The Stoneleigh is a popular hotel. The modern bedrooms are situated on two floors.
ROOMS: 32 en suite (bth/shr) s £50-£55; d £60-£65 (incl. bkfst) * Off peak **MEALS:** Lunch £7.95-£10.95 International Cuisine V meals Coffee am Tea pm **FACILITIES:** CTV in all bedrooms STV Free use of adjacent Private Health Club for all residents **CONF:** Thtr 200 Class 100 Board 100 **SERVICES:** Lift Night porter 80P **NOTES:** No dogs (ex guide dogs) Closed New Years day **CARDS:**

WAKEFIELD West Yorkshire **Map 08 SE32**
Campanile
Monckton Rd WF2 7AL
☎ 01924 201054 01924 201055
Dir: *M1 junct 39, 1m towards Wakefield, left onto Monckton Road, hotel on left*

This modern building offers accommodation in smart well equipped bedrooms, all with en-suite bathrooms. Refreshments may be taken at the informal Bistro. For details about current prices, consult the Contents Page under Hotel Groups for the Campanile phone number.
ROOMS: 77 annexe en suite (bth/shr) **CONF:** Thtr 35 Class 18 Board 20

WAKEFIELD West Yorkshire **Map 08 SE32**
Travel Inn
Thornes Park, Denby Dale Rd WF2 8DY
☎ 01924 367901 01924 373620
Dir: *from M1 junct 39 take A636 towards town centre hotel on left at 2nd rdbt*
This modern building offers accommodation in smart, spacious and well equipped bedrooms, all with en-suite bathrooms. Refreshments may be taken at the nearby family restaurant. For details about current prices consult the Contents Page under Hotel Groups for the Travel Inn phone number.
ROOMS: 42 en suite (bth/shr) d £39.95 *

WAKEFIELD West Yorkshire **Map 08 SE32**
Travelodge
M1 Service Area, West Bretton WF4 4LQ
☎ Central Res 0800 850950
(For full entry see Woolley Edge)

WALLASEY Merseyside **Map 07 SJ29**
★★ *Grove House*
Grove Rd L45 3HF
Quality Percentage Score: 72%
☎ 0151 639 3947 & 0151 630 4558 0151 639 0028
Dir: *M53 junct 1, follow A544*
An immaculately maintained family owned hotel. Many bedrooms enjoy a view over attractive gardens to the rear, all are comfortably furnished and particularly well equipped. The bar lounge provides a venue for drinks, before dinner in the oak panelled restaurant.
ROOMS: 14 en suite (bth/shr) (3 fmly) **MEALS:** English & French Cuisine V meals **FACILITIES:** CTV in all bedrooms STV **CONF:** Thtr 60 Class 40 Board 50 Del £74.50 * **SERVICES:** Night porter 28P **NOTES:** No dogs (ex guide dogs) Last d 9.30pm **CARDS:**

WALLINGFORD Oxfordshire **Map 04 SU68**

★★★ Springs
Wallingfrod Rd, North Stoke OX10 6BE
Quality Percentage Score: 75%
☎ 01491 836687 01491 836877
Dir: *turn off the A4074 Oxford-Reading Rd onto the B4009 - Goring. The Springs and Golf club is approx. 1m on the right hand side*
The Springs Hotel is set in 30 acres of gardens edged by woods in the heart of the Thames Valley. The house dates back to 1874 and offers 30 spacious and well equipped bedrooms, many with balconies. The attractive restaurant enjoys beautiful views over the lake, and the seasonally changing menu produced by chef Paul Wilkins offers an interesting range of imaginative dishes.
contd.

Public rooms include a cosy lounge with a log fire and several private dining rooms.
ROOMS: 31 en suite (bth/shr) s fr £86; d fr £112 * LB Off peak **MEALS:** Sunday Lunch £15.50-£18.50 High tea fr £9.25 Dinner fr £27.50 & alc International Cuisine V meals Coffee am Tea pm **FACILITIES:** CTV in all bedrooms STV Outdoor swimming pool (heated) Golf 18 Fishing Sauna Croquet lawn Putting green Xmas **CONF:** Thtr 50 Class 16 Board 26 **SERVICES:** Night porter 120P **NOTES:** No dogs (ex guide dogs) No smoking in restaurant Last d 9.45pm
CARDS:

See advert on this page

WALLINGFORD Oxfordshire — Map 04 SU68

★★★ The George

High St OX10 0BS
Quality Percentage Score: 67%
☎ 01491 836665 Fax 01491 825359
PEEL HOTELS
Dir: *E side of A329 on N entry to town*
It is said that this hotel opened originally as a coaching inn in the 16th century, a claim supported by the abundance of beams, uneven floors, and preserved examples of early building techniques. There are some bedrooms in the old house, but most are in a newer building; all are similarly equipped. In addition to two bars and Wealh's Restaurant, there are popular conference and banqueting rooms.
ROOMS: 39 en suite (bth/shr) (1 fmly) No smoking in 9 bedrooms s £85; d £99 * LB Off peak **MEALS:** Lunch £12.50-£14.50 Dinner £14.50-£19.50 English & French Cuisine V meals Coffee am Tea pm **FACILITIES:** CTV in all bedrooms STV Xmas **CONF:** Thtr 120 Class 60 Board 40 Del from £89 * **SERVICES:** Night porter 60P **NOTES:** Last d 9.45pm **CARDS:**

WALLINGFORD Oxfordshire — Map 04 SU68

★★★ Shillingford Bridge

Shillingford OX10 8LZ
Quality Percentage Score: 64%
☎ 01865 858567 Fax 01865 858636
Forestdale Hotels
Dir: *from M4 junct 10 follow A329 through Wallingford towards Thame. From M40 junct 6 join B4009. Take A4074 then turn left on to A329 to Wallingford*
This popular hotel, situated on the banks of the Thames, has its own moorings and a waterside open-air swimming pool. The public areas make good use of the view from the large picture windows, where guests can relax or enjoy a meal in the restaurant. Bedrooms are well equipped and furnished with comfort in mind.
ROOMS: 34 en suite (bth/shr) 8 annexe en suite (bth/shr) (6 fmly) No smoking in 5 bedrooms s fr £70; d fr £95 (incl. bkfst) * LB Off peak **MEALS:** Lunch £13.95-£17.95 High tea fr £5 Dinner fr £17.95 International Cuisine V meals Coffee am Tea pm **FACILITIES:** CTV in all bedrooms Outdoor swimming pool (heated) Fishing Squash Xmas **CONF:** Thtr 80 Class 36 Board 26 Del from £115 * **SERVICES:** 100P
NOTES: Last d 9.45pm **CARDS:**

WALSALL West Midlands — Map 07 SP09

★★★ The Fairlawns at Aldridge

178 Little Aston Rd, Aldridge WS9 0NU
Quality Percentage Score: 75%
☎ 01922 455122 Fax 01922 743210
Best Western
Dir: *off A452 towards Aldridge at crossroads with A454, Hotel 600 yards on right*
An attractive red brick hotel that has been greatly extended over recent years, yet retains the charm of a smaller hotel. New developments include a smart leisure club with hydrotherapy suite, and a further eleven bedrooms, which complement the existing comfortable and well equipped accommodation. The kitchen brigade, under head chef Todd Hubble, continue to provide quality food through imaginative modern British menus. Service is professional, attentive and friendly.
ROOMS: 46 en suite (bth/shr) (7 fmly) No smoking in 20 bedrooms s £49.50-£89.50; d £65-£112.50 (incl. bkfst) LB Off peak **MEALS:** Lunch £16.95-£17.50 & alc Dinner £14.99-£24.50 & alc English & French Cuisine V meals Coffee am Tea pm **FACILITIES:** CTV in all bedrooms STV Indoor swimming pool (heated) Tennis (hard) Sauna Solarium Gym Croquet lawn Putting green Jacuzzi/spa Dance studio Hair and Beauty Salon Petanque **CONF:** Thtr 80 Class 40 Board 30 Del from £89.50 **SERVICES:** Night porter 140P **NOTES:** No smoking in restaurant Last d 10pm RS 24 Dec-3 Jan **CARDS:**

WALSALL West Midlands — Map 07 SP09

★★★ Beverley

58 Lichfield Rd WS4 2DJ
Quality Percentage Score: 66%
☎ 01922 614967 622999 Fax 01922 724187
Dir: *1m N of Walsall town centre on A461 to Lichfield*
The friendly proprietor and his enthusiastic staff ensure that guests receive a warm welcome at this privately owned hotel. Bedrooms, though varying in size, are thoughtfully equipped, tastefully appointed and pleasantly decorated. The public rooms include a lounge bar with a conservatory extension, which opens onto an attractive patio terrace, and a pleasantly appointed restaurant where daily and carte menus offer a varied choice to diners; there is also a good range of meeting rooms available.
ROOMS: 40 en suite (bth/shr) (2 fmly) No smoking in 2 bedrooms s £58-£85; d £70-£95 * LB Off peak **MEALS:** Lunch £9.50-£14.50 High tea fr £4 Dinner fr £16.50 & alc V meals Coffee am Tea pm **FACILITIES:** CTV in all bedrooms Pool table Games room **CONF:** Thtr 60 Class 30 Board 30 Del from £85 * **SERVICES:** Night porter 68P **NOTES:** No dogs (ex guide dogs) No smoking in restaurant Last d 9.30pm **CARDS:**

W

WALSALL West Midlands **Map 07 SP09**

★★★ Quality Hotel & Suites Walsall

20 Wolverhampton Rd West, Bentley WS2 0BS
Quality Percentage Score: 65%
☎ 01922 724444 01922 723148
Dir: *situated back on the rdbt at junct 10, M6*

Clearly signed from the M6at junction 10, the hotel offers easy access to the city. All the accommodation is well equipped, including air conditioned suites with a personal fax and a kitchen with microwave and fridge. There is an extensive all day menu, room service and carvery restaurant.

ROOMS: 155 en suite (bth/shr) (20 fmly) No smoking in 64 bedrooms s fr £81.50; d fr £105.50 * LB Off peak **MEALS:** Lunch £2.95-£15.95alc Dinner fr £14.50 & alc English & Continental Cuisine V meals Coffee am Tea pm **FACILITIES:** CTV in all bedrooms STV Indoor swimming pool (heated) Sauna Gym Jacuzzi/spa Xmas **CONF:** Thtr 180 Class 70 Board 80 **SERVICES:** Night porter 160P **NOTES:** No smoking area in restaurant Last d 10pm **CARDS:**

WALSALL West Midlands **Map 07 SP09**

★★★ Baron's Court

Walsall Rd, Walsall Wood WS9 9AH
Quality Percentage Score: 63%
☎ 0500 636943 (Central Res) 01773 880321
Dir: *3m NE A461*

This informal hotel has a striking mock Tudor façade, with the same theme carried throughout the public areas.The well equipped bedrooms vary in style and there are good leisure, conference and banqueting facilities. A popular carvery-style menu operates in the evenings.

ROOMS: 95 en suite (bth/shr) (2 fmly) No smoking in 19 bedrooms s £75-£85; d £85-£105 * LB Off peak **MEALS:** Lunch £5-£10 Dinner £13.95-£14.50 V meals Coffee am Tea pm **FACILITIES:** CTV in all bedrooms STV Indoor swimming pool (heated) Sauna Solarium Gym Pool table Jacuzzi/spa Wkly live entertainment Xmas **CONF:** Thtr 200 Class 100 Board 100 Del from £85 * **SERVICES:** Lift Night porter 200P **NOTES:** No smoking in restaurant Last d 9.30pm **CARDS:**

W

WALSALL West Midlands **Map 07 SP09**

★★★ *The Boundary*

Birmingham Rd WS5 3AB
Quality Percentage Score: 60%
☎ 01922 633555 01922 612034
Dir: *off M6 at junc 7, A34 to Walsall. Hotel 2m on left*

This modern, purpose-built hotel, which is easily reached from both junctions 7 and 9 of the M6, offers a sound standard of well equipped accommodation. Guests have the choice of eating from the bar, lounge or room service menus, as well as in the carvery restaurant.

ROOMS: 94 en suite (bth/shr) (3 fmly) No smoking in 53 bedrooms **MEALS:** International Cuisine V meals Coffee am Tea pm **FACILITIES:** CTV in all bedrooms Tennis (hard) Pool table Wkly live entertainment **CONF:** Thtr 65 Class 35 Board 30 **SERVICES:** Lift Night porter 250P **NOTES:** Last d 10pm RS 25-30 Dec **CARDS:**

WALSALL West Midlands **Map 07 SP09**

★★ Abberley

Bescot Rd WS2 9AD
Quality Percentage Score: 65%
☎ 01922 627413 01922 720933
Dir: *junct 9 of M6, take A461 towards Walsall town. Bear to the left at the first set of traffic lights and hotel is visible on the right*

This family-owned and run hotel is conveniently situated between the M6 and the town centre. It combines the charm of a bygone era with modern facilities. The house dates from 1887 and provides modern, thoughtfully equipped bedrooms. The restaurant offers both table d'hôte and carte menus, and the service is friendly and welcoming.

ROOMS: 28 en suite (bth/shr) (4 fmly) No smoking in 4 bedrooms s £41.95-£45.95; d £54.95-£62.95 (incl. bkfst) LB Off peak **MEALS:** Lunch £9-£15 Dinner £12-£14 & alc V meals Coffee am Tea pm **FACILITIES:** CTV in all bedrooms STV Practice Golf Nets Xmas **CONF:** Thtr 80 Class 60 Board 50 Del from £58 * **SERVICES:** Night porter 29P **NOTES:** No smoking in restaurant Last d 9pm **CARDS:**

WALSALL West Midlands **Map 07 SP09**

★★ Bescot

87 Bescot Rd WS2 9DG
Quality Percentage Score: 60%
☎ 01922 622447 01922 630256
Dir: *200yrds off junct 9 M6 on A461*

The Bescot is a privately owned and business oriented hotel. The Public rooms have recently been refurbished and there are plans to refresh the bedroom stock over the coming year; rooms have a good range of facilities and seven annexe bedrooms are particularly spacious and nicely appointed. There are several ground floor bedrooms available.

ROOMS: 18 en suite (bth/shr) 15 annexe en suite (bth/shr) (2 fmly) s fr £40; d £55-£60 (incl. bkfst) * LB Off peak **MEALS:** Lunch £7.95-£13.95 Dinner £13.95 International Cuisine V meals Coffee am Tea pm **FACILITIES:** CTV in all bedrooms STV Xmas **CONF:** Thtr 100 Class 50 Board 30 Del £75 * **SERVICES:** Night porter 150P **NOTES:** No dogs (ex guide dogs) No smoking area in restaurant Last d 9.30pm **CARDS:**

WALSALL West Midlands **Map 07 SP09**

Travel Inn

Bentley Green, Bentley Rd North WS2 0WB
☎ 01922 724485 01922 724098
Dir: *from M6 junct 10 head west on A454 take 2nd slip road signed Bentley South*

This modern building offers accommodation in smart, spacious and well equipped bedrooms, all with en-suite bathrooms. Refreshments may be taken at the nearby family restaurant. For details about current prices consult the Contents Page under Hotel Groups for the Travel Inn phone number.

ROOMS: 40 en suite (bth/shr) d £39.95 *

WALTERSTONE Herefordshire — Map 03 SO32

★★★ Allt-yr-Ynys Country House Hotel

HR2 0DU
Quality Percentage Score: 65%
☎ 01873 890307 📠 01873 890539
Dir: *take A465 N of Abergavenny. After 5m turn left at Old Pandy Inn in Pandy. After 300 yrds turn right and hotel is 300yds on the right*

This lovely house dates back to around 1550; Queen Elizabeth I is reputed to have been a guest here. It stands on the Welsh border in 16 acres of woods and grounds, which include a walled garden. Most of the modern equipped bedrooms are located in single storey stone buildings. Public rooms, which include a comfortable lounge with an ornate ceiling, are contained within the main house. Facilities include a leisure centre and a function room and the hotel holds a license to perform civil wedding ceremonies.

ROOMS: 1 en suite (bth/shr) 18 annexe en suite (bth/shr) (2 fmly) No smoking in 6 bedrooms s £60-£70; d £80-£90 (incl. bkfst) * LB Off peak **MEALS:** Lunch £15-£20alc Dinner £17.50-£25alc English, Welsh, French & Italian Cuisine V meals Coffee am Tea pm **FACILITIES:** CTV in all bedrooms Indoor swimming pool (heated) Fishing Sauna Jacuzzi/spa Clay pigeon range Xmas **CONF:** Thtr 100 Class 30 Board 40 Del from £90 * **SERVICES:** Night porter 100P **NOTES:** No smoking in restaurant Last d 9.30pm **CARDS:**

See advert under ABERGAVENNY

WALTHAM ABBEY Essex — Map 05 TL30

★★★★ Swallow

Old Shire Ln EN9 3LX
Quality Percentage Score: 64%
☎ 01992 717170 📠 01992 711841
Dir: *off junct 26 of M25*

Close to the M25, this Swallow hotel gives easy access to London. Useful facilities include extensive meeting rooms, a leisure club and a bus shuttle to nearby public transport. Bedrooms are comfortable and modern, and there are two restaurants, as well as a cocktail bar cum coffee lounge.

ROOMS: 163 en suite (bth/shr) (14 fmly) No smoking in 60 bedrooms s fr £110; d £135-£150 (incl. bkfst) * LB Off peak **MEALS:** Lunch £14.50-£16.50 Dinner £19.50-£23.50 & alc English & Continental Cuisine V meals Coffee am Tea pm **FACILITIES:** CTV in all bedrooms STV Indoor swimming pool (heated) Sauna Solarium Gym Jacuzzi/spa Steam room, Beauty Salon Wkly live entertainment Xmas **CONF:** Thtr 250 Class 120 Board 50 Del from £150 * **SERVICES:** Night porter 240P **NOTES:** No smoking in restaurant Last d 10pm **CARDS:**

WALTON UPON THAMES See Shepperton & Weybridge

WANSFORD Cambridgeshire — Map 04 TL09

★★★ The Haycock Hotel

PE8 6JA
Quality Percentage Score: 74%
☎ 01780 782223 📠 01780 783031
Dir: *at junct of A47/A1*

In its prominent position north-west of Peterborough, this 17th-century hotel is housed in attractively restored stone buildings. Accommodation is well equipped and service is provided in a traditional, formal style. Meals can be taken either in the restaurant or in Orchards Brasserie. Bar and lounges have an inviting atmosphere and form the hub of the hotel. Conference suites are housed together on one side of the courtyard and there are extensive grounds.

ROOMS: 50 en suite (bth/shr) (3 fmly) No smoking in 6 bedrooms s £110; d £50-£150 (incl. bkfst) * LB Off peak **MEALS:** Lunch £8.95-£13.50 & alc High tea £4.95 Dinner £9.75-£15 & alc V meals Coffee am Tea pm **FACILITIES:** CTV in all bedrooms STV Fishing Petanque Xmas **CONF:** Thtr 150 Class 100 Board 30 Del from £140 * **SERVICES:** Night porter 300P **NOTES:** No smoking in restaurant Last d 9.45pm **CARDS:**

WARDLEY Tyne & Wear — Map 12 NZ36

Travelodge

Leam Ln, Whitemare Pool NE10 8YB
☎ 0191 438 3333 📠 0191 438 3333
Dir: *at junc of A194M/A184*

This modern building offers accommodation in smart, spacious and well equipped bedrooms, all with en-suite bathrooms. Refreshments may be taken at the nearby family restaurant. For details about current prices, consult the Contents Page under Hotel Groups for the Travelodge phone number.

ROOMS: 71 en suite (bth/shr) d £45.95 *

WARE Hertfordshire — Map 05 TL31

★★★★★ Marriott Hanbury Manor

SG12 0SD
Quality Percentage Score: 78%
☎ 01920 487722 📠 01920 487692
Dir: *on A10 12m N of junc 25 of M25*

The range of leisure facilities at this impressive Jacobean-style mansion is outstanding. Set in 200 acres of grounds and wonderful gardens, this hotel offers a golf course of growing international reputation, together with excellent indoor leisure facilities. Bedrooms, both in the main building and in the separate stable wing, are comfortably furnished in the country house-style and have smart marbled bathrooms. The extensive public areas feature fine wood panelling, crystal chandeliers, antique furniture and open fires. There are a number of options

contd.

for food and refreshment, of which the most renowned is the Zodiac Restaurant which maintains high standards of cooking.

Marriott Hanbury Manor, Ware

ROOMS: 69 en suite (bth/shr) 27 annexe en suite (bth/shr) No smoking in 10 bedrooms s £125-£140; d £178-£240 (incl. bkfst) * LB Off peak **MEALS:** Lunch fr £25 & alc Dinner fr £33 & alc English & French Cuisine V meals Coffee am Tea pm **FACILITIES:** CTV in all bedrooms STV Indoor swimming pool (heated) Golf 18 Tennis (hard) Snooker Sauna Solarium Gym Croquet lawn Putting green Jacuzzi/spa Health & beauty treatments Aerobics ch fac Xmas **CONF:** Thtr 150 Class 72 Board 42 Del from £180 * **SERVICES:** Lift Night porter 200P **NOTES:** No smoking in restaurant Last d 9.30pmm
CARDS:

WARE Hertfordshire — Map 05 TL31

★★★ County Hotel Ware

Baldock St SG12 9DR
Quality Percentage Score: 62%
☎ 01920 409955 01920 468016
Dir: *turn off A10 onto B1001 turn left at rdbt first left behind Fire Station*

This modern hotel is ideally suited to conference and business users, and is near the town centre. Bedrooms are spacious, and among the amenities of the public rooms is a bar with a pool table and satellite wide-screen TV.

ROOMS: 50 en suite (bth/shr) (1 fmly) No smoking in 16 bedrooms s £91.50; d £111 (incl. bkfst) * Off peak **MEALS:** Lunch £12.95-£14.50 Dinner £12.95-£14.50 International Cuisine V meals Coffee am Tea pm **FACILITIES:** CTV in all bedrooms Pool table **CONF:** Thtr 175 Class 75 Board 60 Del from £105 * **SERVICES:** Lift Night porter 64P **NOTES:** No dogs (ex guide dogs) No smoking in restaurant Last d 9.30pm **CARDS:**

WAREHAM Dorset — Map 03 SY98

The Premier Collection

★★★ Priory

Church Green BH20 4ND
☎ 01929 551666 01929 554519
Dir: *A351 at Station roundabout take North Causeway/North St, left into East St at lights, 1st right into Church St, hotel between church and river*

This historic former priory is set in four acres on the banks of the River Frome. Bedrooms are luxurious and characterful. Those in the adjacent boathouse are especially spacious. Public areas have log fires and comfortable furnishings. The restaurant, in the vaulted stone cellars, offers both carte and set menus.

ROOMS: 15 en suite (bth/shr) 4 annexe en suite (bth/shr) s £80-£125; d £100-£240 (incl. bkfst) * LB Off peak **MEALS:** Lunch £26.95-£49.50alc High tea £8.50-£8.50 Dinner £26.50-£31.50 & alc English & French Cuisine V meals Coffee am Tea pm **FACILITIES:** CTV in all bedrooms Fishing Croquet lawn Sailing Moorings for guests Wkly live entertainment Xmas **CONF:** Board 20 **SERVICES:** Night porter 25P **NOTES:** No dogs (ex guide dogs) No coaches No children 8yrs No smoking in restaurant Last d 10pm
CARDS:

WAREHAM Dorset — Map 03 SY98

★★★ *Springfield Country Hotel & Leisure Club*

Grange Rd BH20 5AL
Quality Percentage Score: 71%
☎ 01929 552177 01929 551862
Dir: *from Wareham take Stoborough road then first right in village to join by-pass. Turn left and the take first turn immediately on right for hotel*

Situated in attractive countryside, this smart hotel is notable for its extensive leisure and conference facilities.

ROOMS: 48 en suite (bth/shr) (7 fmly) **MEALS:** English & Continental Cuisine V meals Coffee am Tea pm **FACILITIES:** CTV in all bedrooms Indoor swimming pool (heated) Outdoor swimming pool (heated) Tennis (hard) Squash Snooker Sauna Solarium Gym Pool table Jacuzzi/spa Steam room Table tennis Beauty treatment **CONF:** Thtr 200 Class 50 Board 60 **SERVICES:** Lift Night porter 150P **NOTES:** No coaches No smoking in restaurant Last d 9pm **CARDS:**

WAREHAM Dorset — Map 03 SY98

★★ Kemps Country House

East Stoke BH20 6AL
Quality Percentage Score: 69%
☎ 01929 462563 01929 405287
Dir: *mid-way between Wareham/Wool on A352*

A relaxed atmosphere prevails at this family owned hotel with views of the Purbeck Hills. Bedrooms are spacious, those in the coach house being more modern in style. There are two comfortable lounges and an adjoining bar. An extensive choice is available from the set menu and carte.

ROOMS: 5 rms (4 bth/shr) 10 annexe en suite (bth/shr) (4 fmly) s fr £62; d fr £94 (incl. bkfst) * LB Off peak **MEALS:** Lunch £9.95-£11.95 & alc Dinner £20.95 & alc V meals Coffee am **FACILITIES:** CTV in all bedrooms Xmas **CONF:** Thtr 50 Class 20 Board 20 **SERVICES:** 50P **NOTES:** No dogs (ex guide dogs) No coaches No smoking in restaurant Last d 9.50pm **CARDS:**

W

WAREHAM Dorset **Map 03 SY98**

★★ ***Worgret Manor***

Worgret Rd BH20 6AB

Quality Percentage Score: 65%

☎ 01929 552957 🖷 01929 554804

Dir: *on A352 from Wareham to Wool-0.5m from Wareham rdbt*

On the edge of Wareham, with easy access to major routes, this privately owned hotel has a friendly, cheerful atmosphere. The bedrooms come in a variety of sizes. Day rooms comprise a popular bar, a quiet lounge and a restaurant where good, home cooked meals are served.

ROOMS: 13 rms (11 bth/shr) (1 fmly) No smoking in 4 bedrooms **MEALS:** International Cuisine V meals Coffee am Tea pm **FACILITIES:** CTV in all bedrooms Free use of local sports centre **CONF:** Thtr 90 **SERVICES:** Night porter 25P **NOTES:** No smoking in restaurant Last d 9.30pm **CARDS:**

WARMINSTER Wiltshire **Map 03 ST84**

★★★★ **Bishopstrow House**

BA12 9HH

Quality Percentage Score: 73%

☎ 01985 212312 🖷 01985 216769

Dir: *A303, A36, B3414, premises 2m on right*

This classical Georgian house is set in 27 acres of lovely Wiltshire countryside, and ideally placed for a number of tourist attractions. Comfortably furnished with English antiques, 19th-century paintings and log fires, all intended to provide guests with a luxurious yet relaxing atmosphere. All bedrooms are en-suite and equipped with thoughtful extras such as home made biscuits. The choice includes a four-poster room and several suites with whirlpool baths. The Mulberry Restaurant and the Wilton Room offer traditional English fare with a flair, whilst afternoon tea is served in one of several lounges.

ROOMS: 31 en suite (bth/shr) (3 fmly) No smoking in 1 bedroom s £90-£99; d £170-£185 (incl. cont bkfst) * LB Off peak **MEALS:** Lunch £14.50-£35alc High tea £1.50-£9.50 English & French Cuisine V meals Coffee am Tea pm **FACILITIES:** CTV in all bedrooms STV Indoor swimming pool (heated) Outdoor swimming pool (heated) Tennis (hard) Fishing Sauna Gym Croquet lawn Clay pigeon shooting Archery Cycling Wkly live entertainment ch fac Xmas **CONF:** Thtr 65 Class 32 Board 36 Del from £155 * **SERVICES:** Night porter 60P **NOTES:** No smoking in restaurant Last high tea 7.30pm **CARDS:**

WARMINSTER Wiltshire **Map 03 ST84**

Travelodge

A36 Bath Rd BA12 7RU

☎ Central Res 0800 850950 🖷 01525 878450

Dir: *junc A350/A36*

This modern building offers accommodation in smart, spacious and well equipped bedrooms, all with en-suite bathrooms. Refreshments may be taken at the nearby family restaurant. For details about current prices, consult the Contents Page under Hotel Groups for the Travelodge phone number.

ROOMS: 31 en suite (bth/shr) d £49.95 *

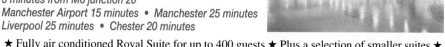

Indicates that the star classification has not been confirmed under the New Quality Standards, see page 7 for further information.

WARRINGTON Cheshire — Map 07 SJ68
★★★★ Park Royal International Hotel
Stretton Rd, Stretton WA4 4NS
Quality Percentage Score: 69%
☎ 01925 730706 Fax 01925 730740
Dir: *off M56 junc 10, A49 to Warrington, at traffic lights turn right to Appleton Thorn, hotel 200 yards on right*
Situated between Warrington and the M56, this large modern hotel still enjoys a peaceful location. Spacious bedrooms are comfortable and attractive. Meals in the Harlequin Restaurant are carefully prepared and enjoyable. The hotel has good function suites and leisure facilities, including outdoor tennis courts.

ROOMS: 140 en suite (bth/shr) (15 fmly) No smoking in 39 bedrooms s £77.50-£101.50; d £87-£111.50 * LB Off peak **MEALS:** Lunch £12.50-£12.95 & alc Dinner £17.95 & alc English & French Cuisine V meals Coffee am Tea pm **FACILITIES:** CTV in all bedrooms STV Indoor swimming pool (heated) Tennis (hard) Sauna Solarium Gym Jacuzzi/spa Retreat Beauty centre with beauty rooms,including Hydrotherapy bath & Solarium Xmas **CONF:** Thtr 400 Class 250 Board 90 Del £142 * **SERVICES:** Lift Night porter 400P **NOTES:** No smoking area in restaurant Last d 10pm
CARDS:

See advert on page 681

WARRINGTON Cheshire — Map 07 SJ68
★★★★ Daresbury Park
Chester Rd, Daresbury WA4 4BB
Quality Percentage Score: 65%
☎ 01925 267331 Fax 01925 601496
Dir: *100yds from junc 11 of M56, on A56*
Bedrooms are currently being refurbished and upgraded at this large, modern hotel. An extensive choice of meeting and function suites and leisure facilities are available. Friendly and attentive staff serve a range of carefully prepared dishes in the Terrace Restaurant.
ROOMS: 181 en suite (bth/shr) (14 fmly) No smoking in 114 bedrooms s £115-£195; d £130-£205 (incl. bkfst) * LB Off peak **MEALS:** Lunch £10-£18.50 & alc Dinner £18.50-£22.50 & alc English & French Cuisine V meals Coffee am Tea pm **FACILITIES:** CTV in all bedrooms STV Indoor swimming pool (heated) Squash Snooker Sauna Solarium Gym Jacuzzi/spa Steam room Beautician Hairdresser Xmas **CONF:** Thtr 500 Class 240 Board 100 Del from £115 * **SERVICES:** Lift Night porter 400P **NOTES:** No smoking area in restaurant Last d 10pm
CARDS:

AA Rosettes are awarded for quality of food, see page 15 for an explanation of Rosette assessment.

WARRINGTON Cheshire — Map 07 SJ68
★★★ *Fir Grove*
Knutsford Old Rd WA4 2LD
Quality Percentage Score: 66%
☎ 01925 267471 Fax 01925 601092
Dir: *turn off M6 at junc 20, follow signs for A50, at Warrington stop before the swing bridge over canal, turn right, and right again*
Situated in a quiet residential area, this privately owned hotel provides modern bedrooms, attractively decorated, whilst public areas include a choice of bars. A variety of function suites is also available.
ROOMS: 40 en suite (bth/shr) No smoking in 4 bedrooms
MEALS: English & French Cuisine V meals Coffee am Tea pm
FACILITIES: CTV in all bedrooms STV **CONF:** Thtr 200 Class 80 Board 40 **SERVICES:** Night porter 100P **NOTES:** Last d 9.45pm
CARDS:

WARRINGTON Cheshire — Map 07 SJ68
★★ Rockfield
Alexandra Rd, Grappenhall WA4 2EL
Quality Percentage Score: 74%
☎ 01925 262898 Fax 01925 263343
Dir: *turn off M6 at junct 20, A50 to Warrington, at junct A50/A56 take side road into Victoria Road. Hotel 60 yds on right*
This privately owned hotel offers a very warm welcome to guests and is locally revered for its authentic Swiss cuisine in the hotel's attractively furnished restaurant. Bedrooms are available in the main hotel and an adjacent house, all of which are comfortable and well equipped, while the lounge and bar are also very welcoming.
ROOMS: 6 en suite (bth/shr) 6 annexe en suite (bth/shr) s £51-£56; d £61-£65 (incl. bkfst) * LB Off peak **MEALS:** Lunch £11.50-£14 & alc High tea £5.50-£11 Dinner £15-£16.50 & alc Swiss & British Cuisine V meals Coffee am Tea pm **FACILITIES:** CTV in all bedrooms STV ch fac Xmas **CONF:** Thtr 60 Class 40 Board 28 **SERVICES:** 25P
NOTES: No dogs (ex guide dogs) No smoking area in restaurant Last d 9pm **CARDS:**

WARRINGTON Cheshire — Map 07 SJ68
★★ Paddington House
514 Old Manchester Rd WA1 3TZ
Quality Percentage Score: 63%
☎ 01925 816767 Fax 01925 816651
Dir: *located 1m from junct 21 M6 off the A57, 2 miles from Warrington town centre*
Just over a mile from junction 21 of the M6, Paddington Hotel is a vibrant commercial venue. The bedrooms are attractively furnished, with rooms available with four-poster beds and some on the ground floor. Diners can eat in the wood-panelled Padgate restaurant, in addition to a wide choice of meals served in the cosy bar.
ROOMS: 37 en suite (bth/shr) (9 fmly) No smoking in 16 bedrooms s £55-£60; d £67.50-£72.50 (incl. bkfst) * LB Off peak **MEALS:** Lunch £9.50-£12.50 & alc High tea £4.50-£6.50 Dinner £9.50-£12.50 & alc English & French Cuisine V meals Coffee am Tea pm **FACILITIES:** CTV in all bedrooms **CONF:** Thtr 200 Class 100 Board 40 Del from £90 * **SERVICES:** Lift Night porter Air conditioning 50P **NOTES:** No smoking area in restaurant Last d 9.30pm **CARDS:**

WARRINGTON Cheshire — Map 07 SJ68
Travel Inn
Woburn Rd WA2 8RN
☎ 01925 414417 Fax 01925 414544
Dir: *just off junct 9 of M62 towards Warrington*
This modern building offers accommodation in smart, spacious and well equipped bedrooms, all with en-suite bathrooms. Refreshments *contd.*

may be taken at the nearby family restaurant. For details about current prices consult the Contents Page under Hotel Groups for the Travel Inn phone number.
ROOMS: 40 en suite (bth/shr) d £39.95 *

WARRINGTON Cheshire **Map 07 SJ68**
Travel Inn (Warrington East)
1430 Centre Park, Park Boulevard WA1 1QR
☎ 01925 242692 🖹 01925 244259
Dir: *at Bridgefoot junct in centre of Warrington, where A49/A50/A56 meet*
This modern building offers accommodation in smart, spacious and well equipped bedrooms, all with en-suite bathrooms. Refreshments may be taken at the nearby family restaurant. For details about current prices consult the Contents Page under Hotel Groups for the Travel Inn phone number.
ROOMS: 42 en suite (bth/shr) d £39.95 *

WARWICK Warwickshire **Map 04 SP26**
see also **Claverdon, Honiley & Leamington Spa (Royal)**
★★★ Ardencote Manor Hotel & Country Club
Lye Green Rd CV35 8LS
Quality Percentage Score: 68%
☎ 01926 843111 🖹 01926 842646
(For full entry see Claverdon)

See advert on this page

WARWICK Warwickshire **Map 04 SP26**
★★ Haseley House Hotel
Haseley, Hatton CV35 7LS
Quality Percentage Score: 67%
☎ 01926 484222 🖹 01926 484227
Dir: *heading W on the A4177 take a right turn at Hatton village hall crossroads. The hotel is 500m down the lane on the right hand side*
A former Georgian rectory in four acres of grounds with easy access to major routes. Proprietors Jane and Stephen Richards are continually upgrading the hotel. A wide range of snacks and light lunches are served in the bar and lounge; an eclectic range of dishes is offered in the brasserie in the evening.
ROOMS: 6 en suite (bth/shr) 8 annexe en suite (shr) (4 fmly) s £65-£95; d £75-£110 (incl. bkfst) * LB Off peak **MEALS:** Lunch £16.95 Dinner £14.50-£17.50 English & French Cuisine V meals Coffee am Tea pm **FACILITIES:** CTV in all bedrooms STV Croquet lawn Xmas **CONF:** Thtr 100 Class 40 Board 40 Del from £110 * **SERVICES:** 70P **NOTES:** No dogs (ex guide dogs) No smoking in restaurant Last d 10pm
CARDS:

WARWICK Warwickshire **Map 04 SP26**
★★ *Warwick Arms*
17 High St CV34 4AT
Quality Percentage Score: 63%
☎ 01926 492759 🖹 01926 410587
Dir: *off M40 junc 15, main road into Warwick, premises 100 yards past Lord Leycester Hospital*
There is a relaxed and friendly atmosphere within the Warwick Arms, which sits right in the heart of the town and near to the castle walls. Public rooms offer a cosy bar and comfortable foyer lounge area, and a good choice of meals is served in the restaurant from a daily set priced menu and a carte; light snacks and informal meals are available in the bar. Bedrooms vary in styles and sizes, each is fully en-suite and has a good range of facilities.
ROOMS: 35 en suite (bth/shr) (4 fmly) **MEALS:** English & French Cuisine V meals Coffee am Tea pm **FACILITIES:** CTV in all bedrooms **CONF:** Thtr 110 Class 50 Board 50 **SERVICES:** Night porter 21P **NOTES:** Last d 9.30pm **CARDS:**

WARWICK MOTORWAY SERVICE AREA Warwickshire **Map 04 SP35**
Welcome Lodge
Welcome Break - Warwick, Northbound M40, Banbury CV35 0AA
☎ 01926 651681 🖹 01926 651634
Dir: *M40 northbound between junct 12 & 13*
This modern building offers accommodation in smart, spacious and well equipped bedrooms, suitable for families and businessmen, and all with en-suite bathrooms. Refreshments may be taken at the nearby family restaurant. For details of current prices, consult the Contents Page under Hotel Groups for the Welcome Break phone number.
ROOMS: 56 en suite (bth/shr) d fr £45 *

WARWICK MOTORWAY SERVICE AREA Warwickshire **Map 04 SP35**
Welcome Lodge
Welcome Break-Warwick, M40 Southbound, Banbury Rd CV35 0AA
☎ 01926 651681 🖹 01926 651601
Dir: *M40 southbound between junct 13 & 12*
This modern building offers accommodation in smart, spacious and well equipped bedrooms, suitable for families and businessmen, and all with en-suite bathrooms. Refreshments may be taken at the nearby family restaurant. For details of current prices, consult the Contents Page under Hotel Groups for the Welcome Break phone number.
ROOMS: 40 en suite (bth/shr) d fr £45 *

W

WASHINGTON Tyne & Wear **Map 12 NZ35**
★★★ **Posthouse Washington**
Emerson District 5 NE37 1LB
Quality Percentage Score: 66%
☎ 0191 416 2264 📠 0191 415 3371
Dir: *off A1 (M) exit A195-take left hand sliproad signposted district 5. Turn left at rdbt and hotel is on the left*
This modern hotel is close to the A1(M) south of Newcastle. Well equipped bedrooms include a number of rooms in the new Millennium design. The Junction Restaurant offers a full menu and there is also a wide-ranging lounge menu and 24-hour room service.
ROOMS: 138 en suite (bth/shr) (7 fmly) No smoking in 89 bedrooms d fr £75 * LB Off peak **MEALS:** International Cuisine V meals Coffee am Tea pm **FACILITIES:** CTV in all bedrooms Pitch & putt Xmas **CONF:** Thtr 100 Class 40 Board 50 Del from £99 * **SERVICES:** Lift Night porter 198P **NOTES:** Last d 10pm
CARDS:

WASHINGTON Tyne & Wear **Map 12 NZ35**
★★★ **George Washington Golf & Country Club**
Stone Cellar Rd, District 12, High Usworth NE37 1PH
Quality Percentage Score: 65%
☎ 0191 402 9988 📠 0191 415 1166
Dir: *off A1 (M), follow signs for District 12 and Golf Course*
Surrounded by its own 18-hole golf course, this popular, purpose-built hotel offers smart well equipped accommodation, including some suites and family rooms. A leisure club and business centre form part of the hotel's many facilities.
ROOMS: 103 en suite (bth/shr) (9 fmly) No smoking in 44 bedrooms s fr £90; d fr £105 * LB Off peak **MEALS:** Lunch £5-£16.50 & alc Dinner £16.50 & alc International Cuisine V meals Coffee am Tea pm **FACILITIES:** CTV in all bedrooms Indoor swimming pool (heated) Golf 18 Squash Sauna Solarium Gym Pool table Putting green Jacuzzi/spa Golf driving range Pitch and putt **CONF:** Thtr 200 Class 100 Board 80 Del £115 * **SERVICES:** Night porter 200P **NOTES:** No smoking in restaurant Last d 9.45pm **CARDS:**
See advert on opposite page

WASHINGTON Tyne & Wear **Map 12 NZ35**
Campanile
Emerson Rd NE37 1LE
☎ 0191 416 5010 📠 0191 416 5023
Dir: *turn off A1 at junct 64, A195 to Washington, first left at rdbt into Emerson Road, Hotel 800yds on left*

This modern building offers accommodation in smart well equipped bedrooms, all with en-suite bathrooms. Refreshments may be taken at the informal Bistro. For details about current prices, consult the Contents Page under Hotel Groups for the Campanile phone number.
ROOMS: 77 annexe en suite (bth/shr) **CONF:** Thtr 35 Class 18 Board 20

WASHINGTON SERVICE AREA Tyne & Wear **Map 12 NZ25**
Travelodge (North)
Motorway Service Area, Portobello DH3 2SJ
☎ 01914 103436
Dir: *northbound carriageway of A1(M)*
This modern building offers accommodation in smart, spacious and well equipped bedrooms, all with en-suite bathrooms. Refreshments may be taken at the nearby family restaurant. For details about current prices, consult the Contents Page under Hotel Groups for the Travelodge phone number.
ROOMS: 31 en suite (bth/shr) d £39.95 *

WASHINGTON SERVICE AREA Tyne & Wear **Map 12 NZ25**
Travelodge (South)
Portobello DH3 2SJ
☎ 01914 103436
Dir: *A1M*
This modern building offers accommodation in smart, spacious and well equipped bedrooms, all with en-suite bathrooms. Refreshments may be taken at the nearby family restaurant. For details about current prices, consult the Contents Page under Hotel Groups for the Travelodge phone number.
ROOMS: 36 en suite (bth/shr) d £39.95 *

WATCHET Somerset **Map 03 ST04**
★★ **Downfield Hotel**
16 St Decuman's Rd TA23 0HR
Quality Percentage Score: 68%
☎ 01984 631267
Dir: *from A39 1.5m out of Williton onto B3190, ignore signs to town ctr 200m past Railway St turn right at jct into St Decuman's Rd, hotel 200m on right*
Built in the 1890's of generous Victorian proportions, Downfield stands in its own large gardens, in an elevated position. Bedrooms in the main house are more spacious than those in the Coach House. A limited choice of freshly prepared dinners is offered and served in the chandeliered dining room. For those wishing to explore the surrounding area the Quantock Hills and Exmoor are not far away.
ROOMS: 5 en suite (bth/shr) 2 annexe en suite (bth/shr) (1 fmly) No smoking in all bedrooms s £39-£43; d £54-£62 (incl. bkfst) Off peak **MEALS:** Dinner £20 V meals **FACILITIES:** CTV in all bedrooms **SERVICES:** 14P **NOTES:** No coaches No smoking in restaurant Last d 8pm **CARDS:**

WATERGATE BAY Cornwall & Isles of Scilly **Map 02 SW86**
★★ ***Tregurrian***
TR8 4AB
Quality Percentage Score: 59%
☎ 01637 860540 📠 01637 860280
Dir: *on B3276, 3m from Newquay*
Conveniently located for walkers, or families wishing to make use of the famous beach, this seaside hotel offers value-for-money accommodation and has well maintained bedrooms. In the dining room, a short fixed-price dinner menu offers filling dishes.
ROOMS: 27 rms (2 bth 20 shr) (8 fmly) **MEALS:** English & Continental Cuisine Coffee am Tea pm **FACILITIES:** CTV in all bedrooms Outdoor swimming pool (heated) Sauna Solarium Pool table Jacuzzi/spa Games room **SERVICES:** 26P **NOTES:** No dogs (ex guide dogs) Last d 7.45pm Closed Nov-Feb **CARDS:**

WATERMILLOCK Cumbria **Map 12 NY42**

★★★ Rampsbeck Country House

CA11 0LP

Quality Percentage Score: 78%

☎ 017684 86442 & 86688 017684 86688

Dir: *leave M6 at junct 40, follow signs for A592 to Ullswater, at T-junct with lake in front, turn right, hotel is 1.5m along lake's edge*

A grand Edwardian residence, with a lakeside setting in 18 acres of grounds. Public rooms include a traditional bar, opulent lounges and an elegant drawing room. Bedrooms are comfortably furnished, most have lake views, the finest have lovely antique pieces. Three menus are offered in the hotel and include extras like canapes, a sorbet and petit fours with coffee. Home-made bread and pastry are excellent.

ROOMS: 20 en suite (bth/shr) No smoking in 2 bedrooms s £60-£110; d £98-£180 (incl. bkfst) * LB Off peak **MEALS:** Lunch £25 Dinner £26 & alc English & French Cuisine V meals Coffee am Tea pm **FACILITIES:** CTV in all bedrooms Fishing Croquet lawn Xmas **SERVICES:** 30P **NOTES:** No coaches No smoking in restaurant Last d 8.15pm Closed End of Jan - early Feb

CARDS:

WATERMILLOCK Cumbria **Map 12 NY42**

★★★ Leeming House

CA11 0JJ

Quality Percentage Score: 73%

☎ 017684 86622 017684 86443

Dir: *exit junct 40 M6 and take A66 to Keswick. Turn left after 1m (to Ullswater). Continue for 5m until T-junct and turn right. Hotel on left (3m)*

Enjoying superb views over Lake Ullswater and the breathtaking backdrop of the mountain fells behind, this delightful hotel is peacefully situated in extensive grounds and gardens. The stylish and comfortable bedrooms are thoughtfully equipped and many have their own balcony or patio. The variety of lounges, warmed in winter by real fires, provide plenty of corners in which to relax and enjoy afternoon tea, or perhaps a quiet drink.

ROOMS: 40 en suite (bth/shr) No smoking in 11 bedrooms s £90-£120; d £180-£240 (incl. bkfst & dinner) * LB Off peak **MEALS:** Lunch £13.95-£15 & alc Dinner £23.50-£25 & alc V meals Coffee am Tea pm **FACILITIES:** CTV in all bedrooms STV Fishing Croquet lawn Xmas **CONF:** Thtr 45 Board 20 Del from £100 * **SERVICES:** Night porter 50P **NOTES:** No smoking in restaurant Last d 9pm

CARDS:

WATERMILLOCK Cumbria **Map 12 NY42**

The Premier Collection

★ Old Church

Old Church Bay CA11 0JN

☎ 017684 86204 017684 86368

Dir: *7m from junc 40 M6, 2.50m S of Pooley Bridgeon A592*

An 18th-century country house with views of the lake and fells. Bedrooms come in three styles, all excel in comfort, quality and equipment. The lounge has board games and reading material, and the cosy bar is inviting. Ambitious dishes are produced at mealtimes from an imaginative menu. A soft furnishings course is often run at the hotel.

ROOMS: 10 en suite (bth) s £59-£99; d £85-£135 (incl. bkfst) * LB Off peak **MEALS:** Dinner £10-£25 & alc English & French Cuisine Coffee am **FACILITIES:** CTV in all bedrooms Fishing Boat hire Moorings/fishing **SERVICES:** 30P **NOTES:** No dogs (ex guide dogs) No coaches No smoking in restaurant Last d 8.30pm Closed Nov-Mar **CARDS:**

Remember to return your Prize Draw card for a chance to win one of 30 relaxing leisure breaks with Corus and Regal hotels. See inside the front cover for the card and competition details.

WATFORD Hertfordshire **Map 04 TQ19**

★★★ The White House

Upton Rd WD1 7EL

Quality Percentage Score: 64%

☎ 01923 237316 01923 233109

Dir: *main Watford centre ring road goes into Exchange Rd, Upton Rd left turn off, hotel can be seen on left*

This popular commercial hotel is centrally located and offers

contd.

smart well equipped bedrooms. The open plan public areas offer a lounge/bar and attractive conservatory restaurant. There are several function rooms and off-street parking.

The White House, Watford

ROOMS: 60 en suite (bth/shr) 26 annexe en suite (bth/shr) (1 fmly) No smoking in 9 bedrooms s £69-£89; d £79-£129 * LB Off peak **MEALS:** Lunch £16.95-£18.95 & alc Dinner £16.95-£18.95 & alc English & French Cuisine V meals Coffee am Tea pm **FACILITIES:** CTV in all bedrooms **CONF:** Thtr 200 Class 80 Board 50 Del from £100 * **SERVICES:** Lift Night porter 40P **NOTES:** No smoking in restaurant Last d 9.45pm **CARDS:**

See advert on opposite page

WATFORD Hertfordshire — Map 04 TQ19

★★★ Watford Moat House

30-40 St Albans Rd WD1 1RN
Quality Percentage Score: 63%
☎ 01923 429988 📠 01923 254638

MOAT HOUSE

***Dir:** from S leave M1 junct 5 and from N junct 6 towards Watford and join A412. Continue to Watford and entrance to hotel is on Wellington Road*

This conference hotel is ideally located for the railway station and the town centre. The modern bar and restaurant have an informal atmosphere and a style of menu to match. Bedrooms are modern and practically laid out.

ROOMS: 90 en suite (bth/shr) (2 fmly) No smoking in 60 bedrooms s fr £105; d fr £120 * LB Off peak **MEALS:** Lunch £8-£20alc Dinner £10-£25alc V meals Coffee am Tea pm **FACILITIES:** CTV in all bedrooms STV Gym **CONF:** Thtr 300 Class 132 Board 80 Del from £125 * **SERVICES:** Lift Night porter 116P **NOTES:** No dogs (ex guide dogs) No smoking in restaurant Last d 11pm
CARDS:

WATFORD GAP MOTORWAY SERVICE AREA (M1) Northamptonshire — Map 04 SP66

Roadchef Lodge Watford Gap

NN6 7UZ
☎ 01327 879001 📠 01327 311658

RoadChef Lodge

***Dir:** on M1 between junct 16 & 17*

This modern building offers accommodation in smart, spacious and well equipped bedrooms, all with en-suite bathrooms. Refreshments may be taken at the nearby family restaurant. For details about current prices, consult the Contents Page under Hotel Groups for the Roadchef phone number.

ROOMS: 36 en suite (bth/shr) d fr £47.50 *

WATTON Norfolk — Map 05 TF90

★★ Broom Hall Country Hotel

Richmond Rd, Saham Toney IP25 7EX
Quality Percentage Score: 68%
☎ 01953 882125 📠 01953 882125

***Dir:** leave A11 at Thetford on A1075 to Watton (12m) B1108 to Swaffham, in 0.5m at rdbt take B1077 to Saham Toney, hotel 0.5m on the left*

A family run Victorian country house hotel set in 15 acres of garden and parkland. Guests can enjoy facilities such as an indoor swimming pool, a full size snooker table or during the winter just sit and relax by the open fire in the large lounge. The hotel makes an excellent base for guests wishing to take advantage of local tourist attractions, such as Sandringham.

ROOMS: 9 en suite (bth/shr) (3 fmly) No smoking in all bedrooms s £32-£39; d £60-£90 (incl. bkfst) * LB Off peak **MEALS:** Lunch £10.75-£12.50 Dinner £11.75-£13.50 V meals Coffee am Tea pm **FACILITIES:** CTV in all bedrooms Indoor swimming pool (heated) Snooker **SERVICES:** 60P **NOTES:** No dogs (ex guide dogs) No smoking in restaurant Last d 8pm Closed 24 Dec-4 Jan

WEEDON Northamptonshire — Map 04 SP65

★★ Globe

High St NN7 4QD
Quality Percentage Score: 65%
☎ 01327 340336 📠 01327 349058

***Dir:** at crossroads of A5/A45*

This friendly coaching inn on the junction of two major roads and a just three miles from the M1 is very popular with both locals and business guests. There is a charming family atmosphere and new proprietors Lucy and David Talbot are making lots of improvements. Bedrooms are all tastefully decorated and well equipped, and those guests staying on a special occasion may enjoy sleeping in one of the four-poster rooms.

ROOMS: 15 en suite (bth/shr) 3 annexe en suite (bth/shr) (3 fmly) No smoking in 2 bedrooms s £45-£50; d £55-£60 (incl. bkfst) * LB Off peak **MEALS:** Lunch £7.95-£19.50alc Dinner £12.50-£19.50alc V meals Coffee am **FACILITIES:** CTV in all bedrooms STV Wkly live entertainment **CONF:** Thtr 30 Board 16 Del from £70 * **SERVICES:** 22P **NOTES:** No smoking in restaurant Last d 10pm **CARDS:**

WELLINGBOROUGH Northamptonshire — Map 04 SP86

★★★ Hind

Sheep St NN8 1BY
Quality Percentage Score: 65%
☎ 0500 636943 (Central Res) 📠 01773 880321

MENZIES HOTELS

***Dir:** on A509 in town centre*

Dating back to Jacobean times, this central hotel provides a good base for visiting the town. The all-day coffee shop is a smart meeting place for locals. There are extensive function and

contd.

Indicates that the star classification has not been confirmed under the New Quality Standards, see page 7 for further information.

meeting rooms, bedrooms are mainly spacious and well designed. A wide range of food is available in the restaurant.

ROOMS: 34 en suite (bth/shr) (2 fmly) No smoking in 5 bedrooms s £75-£85; d £85-£105 * LB Off peak **MEALS:** Lunch £6.95-£8.95 Dinner fr £14.95 International Cuisine V meals Coffee am Tea pm **FACILITIES:** CTV in all bedrooms Xmas **CONF:** Thtr 130 Class 60 Board 50 Del from £85 * **SERVICES:** Night porter 15P **NOTES:** No smoking in restaurant Last d 9.30pm **CARDS:**

WELLINGBOROUGH Northamptonshire — Map 04 SP86

★★ High View

156 Midland Rd NN8 1NG
Quality Percentage Score: 64%
☎ 01933 278733 01933 225948
Dir: *turn off A45 onto B573, follow sign post to rail station, at Midland road T-junct turn left towards town centre, hotel approx 100yds on left*

This small hotel is close to the centre of town and is personally run by Mr and Mrs Lam. Bedrooms are spacious and functional but all have the expected facilities.

ROOMS: 14 en suite (bth/shr) (2 fmly) s £34-£45; d £45-£56 (incl. bkfst) * Off peak **MEALS:** Dinner £6.95-£9.95alc V meals **FACILITIES:** CTV in all bedrooms **SERVICES:** 8P **NOTES:** No dogs No children 3yrs No smoking in restaurant Last d 8.15pm Closed 25 Dec-1 Jan **CARDS:**

WELLINGBOROUGH Northamptonshire — Map 04 SP86

★★ *Columbia*

19-31 Northampton Rd NN8 3HG
Quality Percentage Score: 63%
☎ 01933 229333 01933 440418
Dir: *access from town centre via Oxford Street*

A friendly hotel in the centre of town, the Columbia offers good value accommodation for both business and leisure guests. Bedrooms are well presented and offer good modern facilities. A conference room is available for both meetings and private dining and the bright restaurant serves an extensive menu of popular items.

ROOMS: 29 en suite (bth/shr) (5 fmly) **MEALS:** English, French & Italian Cuisine V meals Coffee am Tea pm **FACILITIES:** CTV in all bedrooms STV **CONF:** Thtr 30 Class 30 Board 20 **SERVICES:** 20P **NOTES:** No smoking in restaurant Last d 8.45pm
CARDS:

WELLINGBOROUGH Northamptonshire — Map 04 SP86

Travel Inn

London Rd NN8 2DP
☎ 01933 278606 01933 275947
Dir: *0.5m from Wellingborough town centre on A5193 near Dennington Ind Est.*

This modern building offers accommodation in smart, spacious and well equipped bedrooms, all with en-suite bathrooms. Refreshments may be taken at the nearby family restaurant. For details about current prices consult the Contents Page under Hotel Groups for the Travel Inn phone number.

ROOMS: 40 en suite (bth/shr) d £39.95 *

WELLINGTON See **Telford (Shropshire)**

WELLINGTON Somerset — Map 03 ST12

★★★ Bindon Country House Hotel & Restaurant

Pride of Britain Member

Langford Budville TA21 0RU
Quality Percentage Score: 76%
☎ 01823 400070 01823 400071
Dir: *from Wellington B3187 to Langford Budville, through village, right towards Wiveliscombe, right at junct, pass Bindon Farm, right after 450yds*

Mentioned in the Domesday Book, this delightful country retreat is set in seven acres of formal and woodland gardens. Each bedroom is named after a battle fought by the Duke of Wellington, and is decorated with sumptuous fabrics and

contd.

W

equipped with every modern facility. The public rooms are equally stunning, with original features such as a wonderful staircase, tiled floors and fireplaces. Dinner is a memorable affair prepared from the best of fresh ingredients.
ROOMS: 12 en suite (bth/shr) (2 fmly) No smoking in all bedrooms s fr £85; d £95-£155 (incl. bkfst) * LB Off peak **MEALS:** Lunch £12.95-£18.95 High tea £12.95 Dinner £29.50 English & French Cuisine V meals Coffee am Tea pm **FACILITIES:** CTV in all bedrooms Outdoor swimming pool (heated) Tennis (hard) Croquet lawn Wkly live entertainment Xmas **CONF:** Thtr 50 Class 30 Board 20 Del from £130 * **SERVICES:** 30P **NOTES:** No coaches No smoking in restaurant Last d 9pm
CARDS:

WELLINGTON Somerset — Map 03 ST12
★★★ The Cleve Country House Hotel
Mantle St TA21 8SN
Quality Percentage Score: 59%
☎ 01823 662033 🖷 01823 660874
Dir: *from M5 junct 26 follow signs to Wellington, then left before Elf Petrol Station in town*

Located in an elevated position above the town of Wellington, The Cleve Hotel and Country Club enjoys glorious views of the Blackdown Hills. Most bedrooms and public areas have now been sympathetically refurbished, offering comfortable accommodation with modern facilities. The atmosphere is relaxed and guests can enjoy dining in the open plan restaurant or make use of the varied leisure facilities available.
ROOMS: 15 en suite (bth/shr) (5 fmly) No smoking in 12 bedrooms s £47.50-£57.50; d £59.50-£69.50 (incl. bkfst) * LB Off peak **MEALS:** Lunch £6-£15 High tea £3-£5 Dinner £13.95-£15.95 English & French Cuisine V meals Coffee am Tea pm **FACILITIES:** CTV in all bedrooms Snooker Sauna Solarium **CONF:** Thtr 150 Class 70 Board 50 **SERVICES:** 120P **NOTES:** No smoking in restaurant Last d 9.30pm
CARDS:

WELLINGTON Somerset — Map 03 ST12
★★ Beambridge
Sampford Arundel TA21 0HB
Quality Percentage Score: 63%
☎ 01823 672223 🖷 01823 673100
Dir: *1.5m W on A38 between junct 26 & 27 of M5*

The Beambridge, a relaxed and friendly hotel, is conveniently located for a stopover for weary travellers en route to the West Country. The dedicated team provide a smooth service, thus ensuring your stay will be stress free! A wide range of bar food is served, plus more formal restaurant dining. The comfortable bedrooms are well equipped and equally suitable for both leisure and business guests.
ROOMS: 9 en suite (bth/shr) (1 fmly) s £39; d £47 (incl. bkfst) * Off peak **MEALS:** Lunch £9.45-£15.50alc Dinner £9.45-£16alc International Cuisine V meals Coffee am **FACILITIES:** CTV in all bedrooms **CONF:** Thtr 100 Class 100 Board 50 **SERVICES:** 100P **NOTES:** No dogs (ex guide dogs) No smoking in restaurant Last d 9pm
CARDS:

W

WELLS Somerset — Map 03 ST54
★★★❀❀ The Market Place
One Market Place BA5 2RW
Quality Percentage Score: 70%
☎ 01749 672616 🖷 01749 679670
Dir: *A39, A371 - in City Centre (Market Place) along one way system*

This friendly hotel, situated in the lee of Wells Cathedral, was built over 500 years ago, and is now a fascinating blend of unique original features, cleverly interwoven with clean and uncluttered contemporary styling. Many rooms overlook an inner courtyard, ideal for al fresco dining and others form part of The Courthouse, a more recent conversion in an adjacent building. There is a comfortable residents' lounge, whilst the busy bar and restaurant downstairs have a lively atmosphere and a choice of innovative dishes.

ROOMS: 24 en suite (bth/shr) 10 annexe en suite (bth/shr) (4 fmly) s £74-£79; d £92.50-£100.50 (incl. bkfst) * LB Off peak **MEALS:** Lunch £10.50-£17alc Dinner £19.50-£24alc English & French Cuisine Coffee am Tea pm **FACILITIES:** CTV in all bedrooms Xmas **CONF:** Thtr 150 Class 75 Board 75 Del from £95 * **SERVICES:** Night porter 30P **NOTES:** No smoking in restaurant Last d 10pm Closed 28 Dec-31 Dec
CARDS:

WELLS Somerset — Map 03 ST54
★★★ Swan
Sadler St BA5 2RX
Quality Percentage Score: 67%
☎ 01749 678877 🖷 01749 677647
Dir: *A39, A371, opp cathedral*

The Swan is a former coaching inn, which can justifiably claim to have one of the best views of the West front of the cathedral. The individually decorated bedrooms vary in size and style, and the majority have recently been refurbished. A third of the rooms have four-poster beds, which seems entirely appropriate within a building dating from the 15th century. Open fires feature in the panelled public rooms. A fixed-price menu is served in the dining room, with the added bonus of a roast trolley, rarely seen in smaller hotels today.
ROOMS: 38 en suite (bth/shr) (2 fmly) s £75-£79.50; d £95-£105 (incl. bkfst) * LB Off peak **MEALS:** Lunch fr £13.95 Dinner fr £18.50 V meals Coffee am Tea pm **FACILITIES:** CTV in all bedrooms Xmas **CONF:** Thtr 100 Class 30 Board 30 Del from £99 * **SERVICES:** Night porter 30P **NOTES:** No smoking in restaurant Last d 9.30pm
CARDS:

WELLS Somerset — Map 03 ST54

★★ White Hart

Sadler St BA5 2RR

Quality Percentage Score: 69%

☎ 01749 672056 Fax 01749 672056

Dir: *Sadler St is the start of the one-way system. Hotel opposite the cathedral*

A short stroll from the cathedral, this former coaching inn dates back to the 15th century. Completely refurbished several years ago, the bedrooms offer comfortable, modern accommodation. Many rooms are located in a converted stable block at the rear of the property. Public areas include a spacious bar-lounge, a cosy landing lounge for residents and a beamed restaurant. Guests can choose between the formal fixed-price menu or the brasserie-style menu in the bar-lounge.

ROOMS: 13 en suite (bth/shr) (1 fmly) No smoking in 5 bedrooms s £50-£55; d £70-£80 (incl. bkfst) * LB Off peak **MEALS:** Sunday Lunch £7.50-£12.50 & alc Dinner £15-£17.50 & alc French Cuisine V meals Coffee am Tea pm **FACILITIES:** CTV in all bedrooms STV Xmas **CONF:** Thtr 80 Class 40 Board 35 **SERVICES:** 17P **NOTES:** No smoking area in restaurant Last d 9.30pm **CARDS:**

WELLS Somerset — Map 03 ST54

★★ The Star

18 High St BA5 2SQ

Quality Percentage Score: 63%

☎ 01749 670500 & 673055 Fax 01749 672654

Dir: *on A36-from M5 junct 23 take the A39 to Wells. Hotel is situated in the town centre High Street*

Right in the heart of this small cathedral city, this quaint, traditional coaching inn has a congenial atmosphere and a cosy, popular bar. Bedrooms vary in size, but all are well equipped, designed to make the best use of space. There are local car parks nearby and on-street parking is available overnight.

ROOMS: 12 en suite (bth/shr) (2 fmly) s £50-£57; d £60-£67 (incl. bkfst) * LB Off peak **MEALS:** Lunch £4.95-£9.95 Dinner £11.95-£14.95 English & Mid-European Cuisine V meals Coffee am Tea pm **FACILITIES:** CTV in all bedrooms Xmas **CONF:** Thtr 130 Class 60 Board 40 Del from £70 * **NOTES:** No smoking area in restaurant Last d 9.30pm **CARDS:**

WELLS Somerset — Map 03 ST54

★ Ancient Gate House

20 Sadler St BA5 2RR

Quality Percentage Score: 69%

☎ 01749 672029 Fax 01749 670319

Dir: *first hotel on left situated on the Cathedral Green, overlooking the West Front of the Cathedral*

One cannot fail to be enchanted by the character of this charming family-run hotel, where guests are treated to good old fashioned hospitality in a friendly informal atmosphere. A designated Ancient Monument, Browne's Gate is so old it needed rebuilding as long ago as 1473. Bedrooms, many of which boast unrivalled cathedral views and four poster beds, are furnished entirely in keeping with the age of the building, but have the advantage of modern facilities. The hotel's Rugantino Restaurant offers a typically Italian menu.

ROOMS: 9 rms (2 bth 5 shr) (1 fmly) s £40-£50; d £60-£70 (incl. bkfst) * LB Off peak **MEALS:** Lunch £5.90-£7.90 Dinner £11.50-£13.50 English & Italian Cuisine V meals Coffee am **FACILITIES:** CTV in all bedrooms **NOTES:** No smoking in restaurant Last d 10pm Closed 25-26 Dec **CARDS:**

WELWYN Hertfordshire — Map 04 TL21

★★★ Quality Hotel Welwyn

The Link AL6 9XA

Quality Percentage Score: 64%

☎ 01438 716911 Fax 01438 714065

A popular venue for business guests due to its conference facilities and convenient location. Bedrooms offer a good level of comfort, quality and range of facilities, enhanced by a refurbishment programme.

ROOMS: 96 en suite (bth/shr) (6 fmly) No smoking in 47 bedrooms s £73.25-£81.75; d £88.25-£105.50 * LB Off peak **MEALS:** Lunch £2.95-£15.95alc Dinner fr £14.50 & alc English & Continental Cuisine V meals Coffee am Tea pm **FACILITIES:** CTV in 95 bedrooms STV Gym Xmas **CONF:** Thtr 200 Class 60 Board 50 **SERVICES:** Night porter 150P **NOTES:** No smoking area in restaurant Last d 9.15pm **CARDS:**

WELWYN GARDEN CITY Hertfordshire — Map 04 TL21

★★★ *The Homestead Court Hotel*

Homestead Ln AL7 4LX

Quality Percentage Score: 62%

☎ 01707 324336 Fax 01707 326447

Dir: *turn off A1000 into Woodhall Lane and left at Pear Tree public house into Cole Green Lane. After 2 mini-rdbts turn right into Homestead Lane*

Located in a residential area, this hotel has been completely refurbished. Bedrooms are comfortable and well equipped with good lighting and attractive decor. Public areas are bright and modern, meeting the needs of the business guest.

ROOMS: 58 en suite (bth/shr) No smoking in 25 bedrooms **MEALS:** International Cuisine V meals Coffee am Tea pm **FACILITIES:** CTV in all bedrooms **CONF:** Thtr 80 Class 45 Board 40 **SERVICES:** Lift Night porter 80P **NOTES:** No smoking area in restaurant Last d 9.45pm **CARDS:**

WELWYN GARDEN CITY Hertfordshire **Map 04 TL21**

Travel Inn
Gosling Park
☎ 01707 391345 Fax 01707 393789
This modern building offers accommodation in smart, spacious and well equipped bedrooms, all with en-suite bathrooms. Refreshments may be taken at the nearby family restaurant. For details about current prices consult the Contents Page under Hotel Groups for the Travel Inn phone number.
ROOMS: 60 en suite (bth/shr) d £39.95 *

WENTBRIDGE (NEAR PONTEFRACT) West Yorkshire **Map 08 SE41**

★★★ **Wentbridge House**
WF8 3JJ
Quality Percentage Score: 70%
☎ 01977 620444 Fax 01977 620148
Dir: *Wentbridge is 0.5m off A1 and 4m S of the M62/A1 interchange*

An established hotel in 15 acres of landscaped gardens offers spacious, well equipped bedrooms. Service in the Fleur de Lys restaurant is polished and there is a varied menu of traditional dishes.
ROOMS: 16 en suite (bth/shr) 4 annexe en suite (bth/shr) s £75-£95; d £85-£105 (incl. bkfst) * LB Off peak **MEALS:** Lunch £12.50-£15.25 & alc Dinner fr £21 & alc English & French Cuisine V meals Coffee am Tea pm **FACILITIES:** CTV in all bedrooms **CONF:** Thtr 120 Class 60 Board 50 Del from £76.50 * **SERVICES:** Night porter 100P **NOTES:** No dogs (ex guide dogs) No coaches Last d 9.30pm Closed 25 Dec-evening only **CARDS:**

WEOBLEY Herefordshire **Map 03 SO45**

★★ ***Ye Olde Salutation Inn***
Market Pitch HR4 8SJ
Quality Percentage Score: 73%
☎ 01544 318443 Fax 01544 318216
Dir: *Weobley is 12m NW of Hereford, on the A4112, Ye Old Salutation Inn is in the village centre, facing Broad Street*
A delightful timber-framed property in the centre of the medieval village, dating back over 500 years. Owned and personally run by Chris and Frances Anthony, it has a good reputation for hospitality and food. The well equipped, traditionally furnished accommodation includes a family room, and a room with a four-poster bed.
ROOMS: 4 en suite (bth/shr) No smoking in all bedrooms
MEALS: English & French Cuisine V meals Coffee am Tea pm
FACILITIES: CTV in all bedrooms STV Gym **SERVICES:** 14P
NOTES: No coaches No children 14yrs No smoking in restaurant Last d 9.30pm **CARDS:**

WEST BAY See **Bridport**

WEST BEXINGTON Dorset **Map 03 SY58**

★★ **Manor**
Beach Rd DT2 9DF
Quality Percentage Score: 69%
☎ 01308 897616 Fax 01308 897035
Amidst dramatic scenery on the South Dorset coast, this ancient manor house features flagstoned floors, panelled walls and beamed ceilings. Bedrooms feature many thoughtful extras. The Cellar Bar provides a range of meals, and an imaginative selection of dishes is offered in the restaurant.
ROOMS: 13 rms (8 bth 4 shr) (1 fmly) s fr £55.50; d fr £95 (incl. bkfst) * LB Off peak **MEALS:** Lunch £14.95-£16.95alc V meals Coffee am Tea pm **FACILITIES:** CTV in all bedrooms **CONF:** Thtr 50 Class 60 Board 30 **SERVICES:** 28P **NOTES:** No dogs **CARDS:**

WEST BROMWICH West Midlands **Map 07 SP09**

★★★ ***Birmingham/West Bromwich Moat House***
Birmingham Rd B70 6RS
Quality Percentage Score: 68%
☎ 0121 609 9988 Fax 0121 525 7403
Dir: *take Birmingham Rd to West Bromich town centre, turn 1st right, take 2nd right, the hotel is situated at the bottom of rd on right hand side*
Located close to the M5, this large, purpose-built complex provides versatile, well-equipped accommodation including a good selection of conference rooms. Following refurbishemnt there is the new Club Moativation leisure complex. A key strength here is a friendly, willing team.
ROOMS: 168 en suite (bth/shr) (3 fmly) No smoking in 55 bedrooms
MEALS: English & French Cuisine V meals Coffee am Tea pm
FACILITIES: CTV in all bedrooms Solarium Gym Pool table Games room ch fac **CONF:** Thtr 180 Class 80 Board 60 **SERVICES:** Lift Night porter 250P **NOTES:** Last d 9.45pm **CARDS:**

WESTBURY Wiltshire **Map 03 ST85**

★★ **The Cedar**
Warminster Rd BA13 3PR
Quality Percentage Score: 68%
☎ 01373 822753 Fax 01373 858423
Dir: *on A350, 0.5m from Westbury towards Warminster*
Built towards the end of the 18th century, and converted into a hotel after the last war, this family run property offers attractive accommodation in well equipped bedrooms. There are some ground floor rooms in an adjacent cottage, and all are individually decorated, with such extras as bathrobes and trouser presses, which make for a most comfortable stay. Situated on the edge of town, the hotel provides a convenient base for exploring Bath and the surrounding area. A variety of meals is available in both the bar lounge and conservatory, whilst the Regency restaurant is popular for more formal dining.
ROOMS: 8 en suite (bth/shr) 8 annexe en suite (bth/shr) (4 fmly) s £49-£52; d £55-£65 (incl. bkfst) * LB Off peak **MEALS:** Lunch £9.25 English & Continental Cuisine V meals Coffee am **FACILITIES:** CTV in all bedrooms STV **CONF:** Thtr 40 Class 30 Board 20 Del £85 * **SERVICES:** 35P **NOTES:** No coaches No smoking in restaurant Closed 27-29 Dec **CARDS:**

WEST CHILTINGTON West Sussex **Map 04 TQ01**

★★★ ***Roundabout***
Monkmead Ln RH20 2PF
Quality Percentage Score: 65%
☎ 01798 813838 Fax 01798 812962
Dir: *A24 onto A283 turn right at mini rdbt in Storrington, left at hill top. After 1m bear left*
This well established hotel, under the ownership of Richard Begley for nearly 30 years, enjoys a most peaceful setting,

contd.

surrounded by gardens deep in the Sussex countryside. Mock Tudor in style, the hotel has lots of character. Bedrooms are comfortably furnished and well equipped. Public areas include a spacious lounge and bar and neatly appointed restaurant where guests are offered an extensive range of dishes.

ROOMS: 23 en suite (bth/shr) (4 fmly) No smoking in 2 bedrooms **MEALS:** English & French Cuisine V meals Coffee am Tea pm **FACILITIES:** CTV in all bedrooms STV **CONF:** Thtr 60 Class 20 Board 26 Del from £102.40 * **SERVICES:** 46P **NOTES:** No children 3yrs No smoking in restaurant Last d 9pm **CARDS:**

See advert on this page

WEST DRAYTON Hotels are listed under **Heathrow Airport**

WESTERHAM Kent **Map 05 TQ45**

★★★ ***Kings Arms***

Market Square TN16 1AN

Quality Percentage Score: 68%

☎ 01959 562990 01959 561240

Dir: *from junct 6 of M25 follow signs to Westerham on A25, enter Westerham and hotel is on right hand side in middle of town*

This attractive Georgian hotel is located in the centre of the town and is steadily improving. The bedrooms, all named after past Kings of England, are well proportioned and individually decorated to retain their character. The public areas include the Conservatory Restaurant with its imaginative menu, a comfortable lounge and the popular downstairs Jail House Sports Cafe and bar. The hotel also has its own secure car park.

ROOMS: 17 en suite (bth/shr) No smoking in 3 bedrooms **MEALS:** English & French Cuisine V meals Coffee am Tea pm **FACILITIES:** CTV in all bedrooms **CONF:** Thtr 35 Class 14 Board 20 **SERVICES:** 70P **NOTES:** No smoking area in restaurant Last d 10pm **CARDS:**

WESTERHAM Kent **Map 05 TQ45**

Roadchef Lodge Clacket Lane

TN16 2ER

☎ 01959 565789 01959 561311

Dir: *between junct 5 & 6 on M25 westbound*

This modern building offers accommodation in smart, spacious and well equipped bedrooms, all with en-suite bathrooms. Refreshments may be taken at the nearby family restaurant. For details about current prices, consult the Contents Page under Hotel Groups for the Roadchef phone number.

ROOMS: 58 en suite (bth/shr) d fr £49.95 * **CONF:** Thtr 50 Board 30

We endeavour to be as accurate as possible but changes in personnel and data can occur in establishments after the Hotel Guide has gone to press.

WESTLETON Suffolk **Map 05 TM46**

★★ ***The Crown at Westleton***

IP17 3AD

Quality Percentage Score: 74%

☎ 01728 648777 01728 648239

Dir: *turn off A12 just beyond Yoxford, northbound, and follow AA signs for 2m*

With its quiet village location, well signed off the main road, this delightful inn continues to charm its many valued guests. A main attraction is the excellent hospitality and attentive service from the Prices and their small team. Guests have a range of eating options, the main restaurant with its appealing menus, including vegetarian and seafood specialities, and simpler more informal cooking offered in the bar, with its real ales, blazing fire and vast array of malt whiskies. Bedrooms of varying sizes are spread through the main house and three converted outbuildings.

ROOMS: 10 en suite (bth/shr) 9 annexe en suite (bth/shr) (2 fmly) No smoking in all bedrooms **MEALS:** International Cuisine V meals Coffee am **FACILITIES:** CTV in all bedrooms **CONF:** Thtr 60 Class 40 Board 30 **SERVICES:** Night porter 40P **NOTES:** No smoking area in restaurant Last d 9.30pm RS 24-26 Dec (Meals only) **CARDS:**

WEST LULWORTH Dorset **Map 03 SY88**

★★ **Shirley**

Main Rd BH20 5RL

Quality Percentage Score: 70%

☎ 01929 400358 01929 400167

Dir: *on B3070 in centre of village*

Hospitality is high on the agenda at this attractive family-run hotel, with a loyal following of guests. The bedrooms are

contd.

attractively decorated, and have modern facilities. Public areas include two comfortable lounges. Proprietor Mr Williams offers good home-cooked evening meals.
ROOMS: 15 en suite (bth/shr) (2 fmly) s £33.50-£44; d £67-£88 (incl. bkfst) * LB Off peak **MEALS:** Dinner £14.50-£16 V meals Coffee am **FACILITIES:** CTV in all bedrooms Indoor swimming pool (heated) Jacuzzi/spa Giant chess **SERVICES:** 20P **NOTES:** No coaches No smoking in restaurant Last d 8pm Closed mid Nov-mid Feb
CARDS:

WEST LULWORTH Dorset — Map 03 SY88

★★ *Cromwell House*
Lulworth Cove BH20 5RJ
Quality Percentage Score: 65%
☎ 01929 400253 & 400332 📠 01929 400566
***Dir:** 200 yds beyond end of West Lulworth village, turn left at Lulworth Lodge, Cromwell House 100yds on left*
With spectacular views across the sea and countryside, this family-run hotel is an ideal base from which to explore the area. Bedrooms are bright and attractive. There is a traditionally furnished dining room that serves home cooked meals. Cream teas are also popular.
ROOMS: 14 en suite (bth/shr) (2 fmly) **MEALS:** International Cuisine V meals Coffee am Tea pm **FACILITIES:** CTV in all bedrooms Outdoor swimming pool (heated) **CONF:** **SERVICES:** 15P **NOTES:** No smoking in restaurant Closed 22 Dec-3 Jan **CARDS:**

WESTON-ON-THE-GREEN Oxfordshire — Map 04 SP51

★★★ Weston Manor
OX6 8QL
Quality Percentage Score: 64%
☎ 01869 350621 📠 01869 350901
***Dir:** M40 junct 9 towards Oxford (A34), leave A34 at 1st exit, turn right at rdbt (B4030), hotel is 100yds on the left*
Convenient for Blenheim Palace and the Cotswolds, and only eight miles from Oxford, this splendid manor house, with a wealth of history, is popular with the business community and has impressive conference and banqueting facilities. Rooms are split between the main house and a converted coach house and though they vary in size all are particularly well equipped. The public areas include an imposing foyer lounge and a magnificent vaulted restaurant with minstrels' gallery and original panelling, where chef Michael Keenleyside offers rosette worthy cuisine.
ROOMS: 16 en suite (bth/shr) 20 annexe en suite (bth/shr) (5 fmly) No smoking in 6 bedrooms s £90-£115; d £115-£135 (incl. bkfst) * LB Off peak **MEALS:** Lunch £30-£39.60alc Dinner £30-£39.60alc English & French Cuisine V meals Coffee am Tea pm **FACILITIES:** CTV in all bedrooms Outdoor swimming pool (heated) Squash Croquet lawn Xmas **CONF:** Thtr 40 Class 20 Board 25 **SERVICES:** 100P **NOTES:** No dogs (ex guide dogs) No smoking in restaurant Last d 9.30pm
CARDS:

WESTON-SUPER-MARE Somerset — Map 03 ST36

★★★ *Commodore*
Beach Rd, Sand Bay, Kewstoke BS22 9UZ
Quality Percentage Score: 68%
☎ 01934 415778 📠 01934 636483
***Dir:** M5 junct 21 onto A371 take the A370 from the 1st rdbt and head towards the town centre, hotel is situated 1.5m NW of town centre*
At the foot of Kewstoke woods by unspoilt Sand Bay, there is direct access to the beach. Comfortable bedrooms, tastefully decorated and furnished, are equipped with modern facilities and thoughtful touches. There is an attractive beamed bar with popular carvery, and a more formal restaurant serving a range of dishes.
ROOMS: 12 en suite (bth/shr) 6 annexe en suite (bth/shr) (4 fmly) **MEALS:** English & French Cuisine V meals Coffee am Tea pm **FACILITIES:** CTV in all bedrooms Putting green Adventure play park Wkly live entertainment **CONF:** Thtr 120 Class 80 Board 32 Del from £65 * **SERVICES:** 85P **NOTES:** No smoking area in restaurant Last d 9pm **CARDS:**

WESTON-SUPER-MARE Somerset — Map 03 ST36

★★★ The Grand Atlantic
Beach Rd BS23 1BA
Quality Percentage Score: 62%
☎ 01934 626543 📠 01934 415048
***Dir:** M5 junct 21, follow signs for town centre, drive through town to the Grand Pier, turn left onto seafront, hotel is 500yds along on the left*

An imposing building on the famous promenade, this hotel retains much of its historic charm with high ceilings, sweeping stairwells and some delightful plasterwork. The refurbished banqueting and conference suites are popular locally, and friendly staff provide traditional service.
ROOMS: 74 en suite (bth/shr) (5 fmly) No smoking in 22 bedrooms s £60-£70; d £75-£85 * LB Off peak **MEALS:** Sunday Lunch £11.95 Dinner £16.95 & alc English & French Cuisine V meals Coffee am Tea pm **FACILITIES:** CTV in all bedrooms Tennis (hard) Xmas **CONF:** Thtr 180 Class 80 Board 35 Del from £70 * **SERVICES:** Lift Night porter 100P **NOTES:** No smoking in restaurant Last d 9.30pm
CARDS:

WESTON-SUPER-MARE Somerset — Map 03 ST36

★★ Beachlands
17 Uphill Rd North BS23 4NG
Quality Percentage Score: 66%
☎ 01934 621401 📠 01934 621966
***Dir:** follow tourist signs for Tropicana from M5 junct 21, hotel overlooks golf course, it is situated 6.5m away from motorway, before reaching Tropicana*
This delightful hotel has a 10 metre indoor pool and sauna. It is very close to the 18-hole links course and a short walk from the sea front. Elegantly decorated public areas include a bar, a choice of lounges and a bright dining room, offering a fixed price daily changing menu. Bedrooms vary in size and comfort but are well equipped.
ROOMS: 24 en suite (bth/shr) (4 fmly) s fr £39.50; d fr £79 (incl. bkfst) * LB Off peak **MEALS:** Lunch £11.95 High tea £6.50 Dinner £15.50-£21.25 English & French Cuisine V meals Coffee am Tea pm **FACILITIES:** CTV in all bedrooms Indoor swimming pool (heated) Sauna **CONF:** Thtr 80 Class 30 Board 36 Del from £70 * **SERVICES:** 28P **NOTES:** No smoking in restaurant Last d 8.30pm Closed 23 Dec-2 Jan
CARDS:

WESTON-SUPER-MARE Somerset — Map 03 ST36

★★ Royal

South Pde BS23 1JN

Quality Percentage Score: 65%

☎ 01934 623601 Fax 01934 415135

Dir: *on the seafront, adjacent to the Winter Gardens*

Overlooking the promenade and Weston Bay, this hotel has benefited from substantial refurbishment and its close proximity to the town's centre. Bedrooms are bright and well equipped. Public rooms include a ballroom, family restaurant and choice of bars, including the adjacent O'Malley's Bar which has a lively, local following.

ROOMS: 37 en suite (bth/shr) (8 fmly) No smoking in 16 bedrooms s fr £39; d fr £58 * LB Off peak **MEALS:** Lunch £6.50-£15 High tea £2.50-£5 Dinner £8-£15 & alc V meals Coffee am Tea pm **FACILITIES:** CTV in all bedrooms Wkly live entertainment Xmas **CONF:** Thtr 250 Class 60 Board 40 Del from £79 * **SERVICES:** Lift Night porter 150P **NOTES:** No dogs (ex guide dogs) No smoking area in restaurant Last d 9.30pm **CARDS:**

WESTON-SUPER-MARE Somerset — Map 03 ST36

★★ Rozel

Madeira Cove BS23 2BU

Quality Percentage Score: 62%

☎ 01934 415268 Fax 01934 644364

Dir: *A370, follow rd until 'Seafront' sign at Poacher's Pocket Inn rdbt right towards seafront, right at Grand Pier, hotel 0.5m along promenade*

The Rozel Hotel, owned by the same family for over 70 years, enjoys an enviable position overlooking the North Shore, with the town centre and all the resort's amenities but a short level walk away. Bedrooms offer a good range of facilities geared towards the leisure market but equally suitable for the needs of business guests. In the restaurant, a short, straightforward menu is available, but for more informal dining, the stylish brasserie in the basement is ideal.

ROOMS: 46 en suite (bth/shr) (15 fmly) s fr £43; d fr £68 (incl. bkfst) * LB Off peak **MEALS:** Sunday Lunch £6.95-£8.95 Dinner fr £13.50 English & French Cuisine V meals Coffee am Tea pm **FACILITIES:** CTV in all bedrooms Outdoor swimming pool (heated) Xmas **CONF:** Thtr 160 Class 80 Board 50 Del from £65 * **SERVICES:** Lift Night porter 80P **NOTES:** No smoking in restaurant Last d 8pm **CARDS:**

WESTON-SUPER-MARE Somerset — Map 03 ST36

Travel Inn

Hutton Moor Rd BS22 8LY

☎ 01934 622625 Fax 01934 627401

Dir: *from M5 junct 21 follow A370 turn right at traffic lights into the Hutton Moor Leisure Centre*

This modern building offers accommodation in smart, spacious and well equipped bedrooms, all with en-suite bathrooms. Refreshments may be taken at the nearby family restaurant. For details about current prices consult the Contents Page under Hotel Groups for the Travel Inn phone number.

ROOMS: 40 en suite (bth/shr) d £39.95 *

WEST THURROCK Essex — Map 05 TQ57

Travelodge

Arterial Rd RM16 3BG

☎ 01708 891111 Central Res 0800 850950 Fax 01525 878450

Dir: *off A1306 Arterial Rd*

This modern building offers accommodation in smart, spacious and well equipped bedrooms, all with en-suite bathrooms. Refreshments may be taken at the nearby family restaurant. For details about current

contd.

W

prices, consult the Contents Page under Hotel Groups for the Travelodge phone number.
ROOMS: 44 en suite (bth/shr) d £59.95 *

WEST WITTON North Yorkshire **Map 07 SE08**
★★ Wensleydale Heifer Inn
DL8 4LS
Quality Percentage Score: 70%
☎ 01969 622322 01969 624183
Dir: *A684, at west end of village*
This historic inn has been a landmark since the 17th century, its original character remains in the traditional lounge and bar. It has a high reputation for comfortable accommodation, friendly service and excellent cuisine, prepared by a professional team. Bedrooms are in the inn or a house across the road.
ROOMS: 9 en suite (bth/shr) 6 annexe en suite (bth/shr) (1 fmly) s £60; d £76 (incl. bkfst) * LB Off peak **MEALS:** Sunday Lunch fr £14.50 Dinner fr £24.50 V meals Coffee am Tea pm **FACILITIES:** CTV in all bedrooms Xmas **CONF:** Thtr 20 Class 20 Board 20 Del £85 * **SERVICES:** 40P **NOTES:** No smoking area in restaurant Last d 9pm **CARDS:**

WETHERBY West Yorkshire **Map 08 SE44**
★★★ Wood Hall
Trip Ln, Linton LS22 4JA
Quality Percentage Score: 75%
☎ 01937 587271 01937 584353
Dir: *from Wetherby town centre take Harrogate road N from market place and turn left to Linton, hotel is then signposted*
A striking Georgian hall in 100 acres of parkland. Conference and banqueting facilities are stylish, the leisure club has a beauty room, pool and gym. Day rooms include a smart drawing room with open fire, and an oak-panelled bar. Food is imaginative and well prepared.

ROOMS: 36 en suite (bth/shr) 6 annexe en suite (bth/shr) d £105-£155 * LB Off peak **MEALS:** Lunch £13.50-£15.95 High tea £3.75-£7.95 Dinner £24.95 & alc British & French Cuisine V meals Coffee am Tea pm **FACILITIES:** CTV in all bedrooms STV Indoor swimming pool (heated) Fishing Snooker Solarium Gym Jacuzzi/spa Treatment room for massage and facials Steam room Xmas **CONF:** Thtr 150 Class 70 Board 30 Del from £135 * **SERVICES:** Lift Night porter 120P **NOTES:** No smoking in restaurant Last d 10pm RS Sat **CARDS:**

WEYBRIDGE Surrey
See LONDON SECTION plan 1 *A1*
★★★★ Oatlands Park
146 Oatlands Dr KT13 9HB
Quality Percentage Score: 73%
☎ 01932 847242 01932 842252
Dir: *through Weybridge High Street to top of Monument Hill. Hotel third of a mile on left*
An impressive 19th-century building, Oatlands Park Hotel is set in 10 acres of grounds overlooking Broadwater Lake. Once inside the glass covered atrium, the marble-pillared lounge leads onto a comfortable bar. The Broadwater Restaurant is spacious and well appointed, with candlelit tables popular for celebrations. Bedrooms include a number of suites, and several comfortable single rooms. All rooms are well equipped with a number of extras. There is a range of air conditioned meeting and function rooms, together with a fitness centre for the more active guest.
ROOMS: 134 en suite (bth/shr) (5 fmly) No smoking in 20 bedrooms s £99.50-£105; d £152-£167 (incl. bkfst) * LB Off peak **MEALS:** Lunch £18.50-£19 & alc Dinner fr £24 & alc International Cuisine V meals Coffee am Tea pm **FACILITIES:** CTV in all bedrooms STV Golf 9 Tennis (hard) Gym Croquet lawn Jogging course Fitness suite Wkly live entertainment **CONF:** Thtr 300 Class 200 Board 70 Del from £165 * **SERVICES:** Lift Night porter 140P **NOTES:** No smoking area in restaurant Last d 9.30pm **CARDS:**

WEYBRIDGE Surrey
★★★ The Ship
Monument Green KT13 8BQ
Quality Percentage Score: 65%
☎ 01932 848364 01932 857153
Dir: *turn off M25 junc 11, A317, at third rdbt turn left into the High Street, hotel on left*
This town-centre hotel has bright, spacious, well maintained bedrooms, a popular, bustling bar and a large restaurant.
ROOMS: 39 en suite (bth/shr) No smoking in 10 bedrooms s £115; d £135 * Off peak **MEALS:** Lunch £13.75-£14.75 Dinner fr £19.75 International Cuisine V meals Coffee am Tea pm **FACILITIES:** CTV in all bedrooms STV **CONF:** Thtr 140 Class 70 Board 60 Del from £129 * **SERVICES:** Night porter 75P **NOTES:** No dogs (ex guide dogs) No smoking in restaurant Last d 9.45pm **CARDS:**

WEYMOUTH Dorset **Map 03 SY67**
★★★ Moonfleet Manor
Fleet DT3 4ED
Quality Percentage Score: 75%
☎ 01305 786948 01305 774395
Dir: *A354 to Weymouth; turn right on B3157 to Bridport. At Chickerell turn left at mini rdbt to Fleet*
Tucked away at the end of a winding country lane, Moonfleet Manor is an enchanting hideaway. Near to Chesil Beach, the hotel is furnished with style and panache. Bedrooms are well equipped, spacious and comfortable. Accomplished cuisine is served in the beautiful restaurant.

ROOMS: 34 en suite (bth/shr) 6 annexe en suite (bth/shr) (22 fmly) s fr £75; d £95-£200 (incl. bkfst) * LB Off peak **MEALS:** Lunch fr £15 High tea fr £5 Dinner fr £19.50 & alc V meals Coffee am Tea pm **FACILITIES:** CTV in all bedrooms STV Indoor swimming pool (heated) Tennis (hard) Squash Snooker Sauna Solarium Pool table Croquet lawn Childrens nursery ch fac Xmas **CONF:** Thtr 50 Class 18 Board 26 Del from £95 * **SERVICES:** Lift Night porter 50P **NOTES:** No smoking in restaurant Last d 9.30pm **CARDS:**
See advert on opposite page

WEYMOUTH Dorset **Map 03 SY67**

★★★ Hotel Rex

29 The Esplanade DT4 8DN
Quality Percentage Score: 61%
☎ 01305 760400 Fax 01305 760500
Dir: *on seafront opposite Alexandra Gardens*

Situated on the esplanade this period hotel has superb views accross Weymouth Bay. Bedrooms are well equipped, and the sea-facing rooms are especially popular. A wide range of dishes is available in the restaurant, which was formerly a wine cellar. A comfortable lounge and a bar are also provided.

ROOMS: 31 en suite (bth/shr) (5 fmly) s £47-£54; d £69-£95 (incl. bkfst) * LB Off peak **MEALS:** Bar Lunch £2.50-£7.50 Dinner fr £11.25 & alc International Cuisine V meals Coffee am Tea pm **FACILITIES:** CTV in all bedrooms STV Wkly live entertainment **CONF:** Thtr 40 Class 30 Board 25 Del from £64 * **SERVICES:** Lift Night porter 6P **NOTES:** No smoking area in restaurant Last d 10pm Closed Xmas
CARDS:

WEYMOUTH Dorset **Map 03 SY67**

★★ Glenburn

42 Preston Rd DT3 6PZ
Quality Percentage Score: 68%
☎ 01305 832353 Fax 01305 835610
Dir: *on A353 1.5m E of town centre*

A warm welcome is assured at this small hotel, which is just a short, level walk from the seafront. Bedrooms and public areas now offer good standards of comfort. The restaurant offers an interesting selection of dishes from both fixed-price and carte menus.

ROOMS: 12 en suite (bth/shr) (2 fmly) No smoking in 10 bedrooms s £35-£38; d £60-£70 (incl. bkfst) * Off peak **MEALS:** Dinner fr £11.95 & alc European Cuisine V meals Tea pm **FACILITIES:** CTV in all bedrooms **SERVICES:** 15P **NOTES:** No dogs (ex guide dogs) No coaches No smoking in restaurant Last d 9.30pm **CARDS:**

WEYMOUTH Dorset **Map 03 SY67**

★★ Hotel Prince Regent

139 The Esplanade DT4 7NR
Quality Percentage Score: 66%
☎ 01305 771313 Fax 01305 778100
Dir: *from A354 follow signs for Seafront. At Jubilee Clock turn left along Seafront,for 0.25m*

Overlooking Weymouth Bay, this resort hotel was built in 1855. On the Esplanade and a level walk to the town centre, beaches and the harbour, the hotel's staff provide a warm welcome to all guests. Bedrooms are simply furnished and decorated, and sea-facing rooms are generally spacious. The Restaurant is popular, serving both fixed price and a la carte menus. In addition there is a comfortable lounge, bar and ballroom where entertainment is provided on certain days during the season.

ROOMS: 50 en suite (bth/shr) (23 fmly) s £55-£75; d £65-£85 (incl. bkfst) * LB Off peak **MEALS:** Lunch £9.95 Dinner £12.50 & alc English & French Cuisine V meals Coffee am Tea pm **FACILITIES:** CTV in all bedrooms STV Pool table Table tennis Xmas **CONF:** Thtr 225 Class 120 Board 70 Del from £90 * **SERVICES:** Lift Night porter 20P **NOTES:** No dogs No smoking in restaurant Last d 8.30pm
CARDS:

WEYMOUTH Dorset **Map 03 SY67**

★★ Crown

51-53 St Thomas St DT4 8EQ
Quality Percentage Score: 63%
☎ 01305 760800 Fax 01305 760300
Dir: *turn off A35 at Dorchester, take A354 to Weymouth, pass over second bridge, premises on left*

Situated close to the harbour, beach and town amenities, this popular tourist hotel provides comfortable accommodation. The public areas include a spacious ballroom, a first-floor lounge and a brightly decorated bar. Guests can eat either in the restaurant or the bar.

ROOMS: 86 en suite (bth/shr) (11 fmly) s fr £35; d fr £64 (incl. bkfst) * LB Off peak **MEALS:** Lunch £5.50-£8 & alc Dinner £9.50-£11 V meals Coffee am **FACILITIES:** CTV in all bedrooms STV **CONF:** Class 140 Board 80 **SERVICES:** Lift Night porter 12P **NOTES:** No dogs (ex guide dogs) No smoking area in restaurant Last d 7.30pm Closed 25-26 Dec
CARDS:

W

WEYMOUTH Dorset — Map 03 SY67

Travel Inn

Green Hill DT4 7SX

☎ 0870 242 8000

This modern building offers accommodation in smart, spacious and well equipped bedrooms, all with en-suite bathrooms. Refreshments may be taken at the nearby family restaurant. For details about current prices consult the Contents Page under Hotel Groups for the Travel Inn phone number.

ROOMS: 40 en suite (bth/shr) d £39.95 *

WHATTON Nottinghamshire — Map 08 SK73

★★ The Haven

Grantham Rd NG13 9EU

Quality Percentage Score: 61%

☎ 01949 850800 01949 851454

Dir: *off A52, take turning to Redmile/Belvoir Castle*

Having started as a family home in 1969, Les and Betty Hydes have extended this hostelry considerably over the years, to include a large public bar and dining room in which a good range of popular dishes are available. A continual programme of upgrading and refurbishment to the modern accommodation is having a positive effect, with the most recently refurbished rooms offering colourful and pleasantly appointed bedrooms.

ROOMS: 33 en suite (bth/shr) (5 fmly) s fr £37.50; d fr £49.50 (incl. bkfst) * LB Off peak **MEALS:** Lunch fr £4.95 International Cuisine V meals Coffee am Tea pm **FACILITIES:** CTV in all bedrooms STV Pool table Leisure centre at Bingham, 3 miles away **CONF:** Thtr 100 Class 20 Board 60 Del from £85 * **SERVICES:** 70P **NOTES:** No smoking area in restaurant **CARDS:**

WHEDDON CROSS Somerset — Map 03 SS93

★★ Raleigh Manor

TA24 7BB

Quality Percentage Score: 70%

☎ 01643 841484 01643 841484

Dir: *at Wheddon Cross, turn right on A396 for Dunster. Private drive to Raleigh Manor on left. Raleigh Manor on right if coming from A39*

A charming Victorian country house, set in an elevated position and surrounded by the beautiful scenery of Exmoor National Park. Bedrooms are comfortably furnished and equipped, and some feature original fireplaces. The public rooms make the most of the lovely views, and include a relaxing lounge, a snug library with a lots of books, and a conservatory. The daily-changing menu offers a limited choice of carefully prepared dishes, making the most of local produce.

ROOMS: 7 en suite (bth/shr) No smoking in all bedrooms s £27-£31; d £54-£62 (incl. bkfst) * LB Off peak **MEALS: FACILITIES:** CTV in all bedrooms **SERVICES:** 10P **NOTES:** No dogs No coaches No children 5yrs No smoking in restaurant Last d 7.30pm Closed Dec-Feb

CARDS:

W

WHICKHAM Tyne & Wear — Map 12 NZ26

see also **Newcastle upon Tyne**

★★★ Gibside Arms

Front St NE16 4JG

Quality Percentage Score: 68%

☎ 0191 488 9292 0191 488 8000

Dir: *turn off A1M towards Whickham on the B6317, B6317 leads onto Whickham Front Street, 2m on right*

This modern hotel is situated in the old village centre and enjoys spectacular views over the Tyne Valley towards Newcastle. It offers modern well equipped bedrooms, some in trendy minimalist style. The public rooms include a cocktail lounge and restaurant, and on the floor above there is a bar offering food throughout the day.

ROOMS: 45 en suite (bth/shr) (2 fmly) No smoking in 10 bedrooms s fr £56.50; d fr £69 * LB Off peak **MEALS:** Lunch fr £12.50 Dinner fr £15.95 & alc English & French Cuisine V meals Coffee am Tea pm **FACILITIES:** CTV in all bedrooms STV Wkly live entertainment **CONF:** Thtr 100 Class 50 Board 50 Del from £74 * **SERVICES:** Lift Night porter 28P **NOTES:** No smoking area in restaurant Last d 9.45pm RS 23-29 Dec **CARDS:**

WHITBY North Yorkshire — Map 08 NZ81

★★★ *Dunsley Hall*

Dunsley YO21 3TL

Quality Percentage Score: 67%

☎ 01947 893437 01947 893505

Dir: *3 miles North of Whitby, signposted off the A171*

Fine hospitality is a strong feature at this country house, situated a few miles out of the town in a peaceful location with fine sea views. Owners Bill and Carol Ward are continuing to upgrade the accommodation and have now added a comfortable bar/bistro to the facilities. The house features oak panelling, carved fireplaces and mullion windows. Spacious bedrooms are complemented by two nicely appointed dining rooms and the house stands in 4 acres of well tended gardens.

ROOMS: 18 en suite (bth/shr) (2 fmly) No smoking in 4 bedrooms **MEALS:** English & French Cuisine V meals Coffee am Tea pm **FACILITIES:** CTV in all bedrooms Indoor swimming pool (heated) Tennis (hard) Sauna Solarium Gym Croquet lawn Putting green **CONF:** Thtr 60 Class 30 Board 30 Del from £85 * **SERVICES:** 20P **NOTES:** No dogs (ex guide dogs) No smoking in restaurant Last d 9.30pm

CARDS:

WHITBY North Yorkshire — Map 08 NZ81

★★ Saxonville

Ladysmith Av, Argyle Rd YO21 3HX

Quality Percentage Score: 71%

☎ 01947 602631 01947 820523

Dir: *A174 on to North Promenade. Turn inland at large four towered building visable on West Cliff into Argyle Road, then first turning on right*

For over 50 years the Newton family have been welcoming guests to their comfortable holiday hotel which provides bedrooms that are nicely presented in modern style and offer all the expected amenities. Public areas include a choice of lounges, a small bar, and spacious restaurant with an extensive range of carefully prepared English fare.

ROOMS: 22 en suite (bth/shr) (6 fmly) s £35-£40; d £70-£80 (incl. bkfst) * LB Off peak **MEALS:** Bar Lunch £2.50-£6alc Dinner fr £18.50 & alc V meals Coffee am **FACILITIES:** CTV in all bedrooms **CONF:** Thtr 100 Class 64 Board 56 Del from £56 * **SERVICES:** 20P **NOTES:** No dogs (ex guide dogs) No smoking in restaurant Last d 8.30pm Closed mid Oct-Etr **CARDS:**

WHITBY North Yorkshire **Map 08 NZ81**
★★ Stakesby Manor
Manor Close, High Stakesby YO21 1HL
Quality Percentage Score: 68%
☎ 01947 602773 01947 602140
Dir: *at roundabout junct of A171/B1416 take road for West Cliff. Third turning on right*
Situated in a residential area, this Georgian mansion has been under the same family ownership for over a decade. Modern bedrooms vary in size and style while all are well maintained and neatly presented. Quality cooking is served in the oak panelled dining room, and there is a cosy lounge upstairs in addition to the lounge bar.
ROOMS: 13 en suite (bth/shr) (2 fmly) No smoking in 6 bedrooms s £51; d £71-£76 (incl. bkfst) LB Off peak **MEALS:** Dinner £18 & alc International Cuisine V meals **FACILITIES:** CTV in all bedrooms **CONF:** Thtr 100 Class 46 Board 40 **SERVICES:** 40P **NOTES:** No dogs (ex guide dogs) No coaches No smoking in restaurant Last d 9.30pm Closed 25-30 Dec **CARDS:**

WHITBY North Yorkshire **Map 08 NZ81**
★★ White House
Upgang Ln, West Cliff YO21 3JJ
Quality Percentage Score: 67%
☎ 01947 600469 01947 821600
Dir: *on A174 beside the golf course*
This family-run hotel is on the north side of town and overlooks the golf course at Sandsend Bay. Attractively appointed bedrooms vary in size, and there is a choice of two bars where locals and visitors mingle. The bars and dining room offer a varied selection of dishes including fresh local fish.
ROOMS: 10 en suite (bth/shr) (3 fmly) s £28.50-£32.50; d £57-£65 (incl. bkfst) * LB Off peak **MEALS:** English & French Cuisine V meals Coffee am **FACILITIES:** CTV in all bedrooms Xmas **SERVICES:** 50P **NOTES:** Last d 9pm **CARDS:**

WHITBY North Yorkshire **Map 08 NZ81**
★★ Cliffemount Hotel
Runswick Bay TS13 5HU
Quality Percentage Score: 66%
☎ 01947 840103 01947 841025
Dir: *turn off A174 N of Whitby, follow road 1m to dead end where hotel is situated on clifftop*
Standing in a delightful elevated position, overlooking the pretty village and with splendid views over the bay, this family run hotel offers good hospitality together with a wide range of quality home cooking. The bedrooms, some of which have balconies, are well equipped and comfortable.
ROOMS: 12 en suite (bth/shr) s £38-£43; d £53.50-£72.50 (incl. bkfst) * LB Off peak **MEALS:** Lunch £10.25 Dinner fr £16.95 & alc V meals Coffee am Tea pm **FACILITIES:** CTV in all bedrooms **SERVICES:** 30P **NOTES:** No coaches Last d 9pm Closed 25-26 Dec
CARDS:

WHITBY North Yorkshire **Map 08 NZ81**
★★ Old West Cliff Hotel
42 Crescent Av YO21 3EQ
Quality Percentage Score: 62%
☎ 01947 603292 01947 821716
Dir: *Leave A171, follow signs for West Cliff, approach spa complex. Hotel 100yds fron centre off Crescent Gardens*
This family owned and run hotel is close to the sea and convenient for the town centre. It provides well equipped bedrooms which are in the process of being upgraded, a cosy lounge and separate bar. A good range of food is served in the cosy basement restaurant.
ROOMS: 12 en suite (bth/shr) (6 fmly) s fr £30; d fr £49 (incl. bkfst) * Off peak **MEALS:** Dinner £11 **FACILITIES:** CTV in all bedrooms **NOTES:** No dogs (ex guide dogs) No smoking in restaurant Last d 4pm Closed 6 Nov-31 Jan **CARDS:**

WHITEHAVEN Cumbria **Map 11 NX91**
★★★ *Howgate*
Howgate CA28 6PL
Quality Percentage Score: 66%
☎ 01946 66286 01946 66286
Dir: *on A595 just outside Whitehaven*
Friendly staff help to create a relaxed atmosphere at this hotel midway between Whitehaven and Workington. The Howgate offers attractive well equipped bedrooms, a split-level restaurant and a choice of bars. A function suite is also available and proves a popular venue for weddings and social events.
ROOMS: 20 en suite (bth/shr) (1 fmly) No smoking in 8 bedrooms **MEALS:** V meals Coffee am Tea pm **FACILITIES:** CTV in all bedrooms STV **SERVICES:** 100P **NOTES:** No smoking area in restaurant Last d 9.15pm **CARDS:**

WHITEHAVEN Cumbria **Map 11 NX91**
Travel Inn
CA28 6PL
☎ 01946 66286 01946 63497
This modern building offers accommodation in smart, spacious and well equipped bedrooms, all with en-suite bathrooms. Refreshments may be taken at the nearby family restaurant. For details about current prices consult the Contents Page under Hotel Groups for the Travel Inn phone number.
ROOMS: 38 en suite (bth/shr) d £39.95 *

WHITLEY BAY Tyne & Wear **Map 12 NZ37**
★★★ Windsor
South Pde NE26 2RF
Quality Percentage Score: 63%
☎ 0191 251 8888 0191 297 0272
Dir: *A191 to Whitley Bay, at third rdbt take first exit, turn right at lights, turn left at Woolworths, then right*

Modern, well equipped bedrooms, some quite spacious, along with comfortable public rooms, are features of this business hotel, set between the town centre and the seafront.
ROOMS: 63 en suite (bth/shr) (24 fmly) s £59; d £60 (incl. bkfst) * LB Off peak **MEALS:** European Cuisine V meals Coffee am Tea pm **FACILITIES:** CTV in 62 bedrooms STV **CONF:** Thtr 100 Class 60 Board 40 **SERVICES:** Lift Night porter 35P **NOTES:** RS 25 Dec
CARDS:

See advert on page 699

WHITLEY BAY Tyne & Wear **Map 12 NZ37**

★★ High Point

The Promenade NE26 2NJ

Quality Percentage Score: 65%

☎ 0191 251 7782 ⎙ 0191 251 6318

Dir: *from A1058 follow signs for Tynemouth, then seafront, turn left at Sealife Centre, follow rd for 1.5m, hotel on left going into Whitley Bay*

This friendly, well managed hotel, offers a sound standard of comfort, and some of its rooms are not only spacious but also have sea views. Meals are served in the attractive little restaurant or the lounge bar. On Sunday nights, catering arrangements are restricted.

ROOMS: 14 en suite (bth/shr) (3 fmly) s fr £49.50; d fr £58 (incl. bkfst) * LB Off peak **MEALS:** Sunday Lunch £7.95 Dinner £8.95 & alc V meals Coffee am **FACILITIES:** CTV in 15 bedrooms STV Pool table Wkly live entertainment **SERVICES:** Night porter 20P **NOTES:** No dogs (ex guide dogs) Last d 8.50pm **CARDS:**

WHITLEY BAY Tyne & Wear **Map 12 NZ37**

★★ Seacrest

North Pde NE26 1PA

Quality Percentage Score: 63%

☎ 0191 253 0140 ⎙ 0191 253 0140

Dir: *from A1058 head towards seafront. With the lighthouse in front, turn left at 42nd St bar, on North Parade, hotel is half way up rd*

A relaxed and friendly atmosphere prevails at this family run hotel, situated between the town and the seafront. Bedrooms vary in size and are brightly decorated, as is the bar. A range of dishes, including a good vegetarian selection, is offered in the bar and the restaurant.

ROOMS: 22 en suite (bth/shr) (4 fmly) s £30-£46; d £50-£60 (incl. bkfst) * LB Off peak **MEALS:** V meals Coffee am Tea pm **FACILITIES:** CTV in all bedrooms Pool table **CONF:** Thtr 50 Class 30 Board 30 Del from £39 * **SERVICES:** Night porter 6P **NOTES:** No dogs (ex guide dogs) No smoking in restaurant

CARDS:

WHITSTABLE Kent **Map 05 TR16**

Travel Inn

Thanet Way CT5 3DB

☎ 01227 272459 ⎙ 01227 263151

Dir: *2m W of town centre on B2205*

This modern building offers accommodation in smart, spacious and well equipped bedrooms, all with en-suite bathrooms. Refreshments may be taken at the nearby family restaurant. For details about current prices consult the Contents Page under Hotel Groups for the Travel Inn phone number.

ROOMS: 40 en suite (bth/shr) d £39.95 *

WICKHAM Hampshire **Map 04 SU51**

★★ Old House

The Square PO17 5JG

Quality Percentage Score: 73%

☎ 01329 833049 ⎙ 01329 833672

Dir: *2m N of Fareham off A32*

A charming Georgian house now under the ownership of Mr and Mrs Ruthven-Stuart. Characterful bedrooms have much character, they are tastefully appointed and well equipped. Spacious public rooms include a choice of lounges, a small bar and an attractive restaurant where cooking reaches a high standard.

ROOMS: 9 en suite (bth/shr) (1 fmly) s £75; d £90 * LB Off peak **MEALS:** Lunch £13.50-£17.50 Dinner £26-£30alc British & French Cuisine V meals Coffee am **FACILITIES:** CTV in all bedrooms **SERVICES:** 12P **NOTES:** No dogs (ex guide dogs) No coaches No smoking in restaurant Last d 9.30pm Closed 10 days Xmas RS Mon-Sat

CARDS:

WIDNES Cheshire **Map 07 SJ58**

★★★ Everglades Park

Derby Rd WA8 3UJ

Quality Percentage Score: 64%

☎ 0151 495 2040 ⎙ 0151 424 6536

Dir: *from M62 junct follow A557 for Widnes, take first exit signed Widnes N A5080, right at rdbt, left at 2nd rdbt onto A5080 hotel 200mts on right*

Bedrooms are clean and spacious at this modern hotel and include executive suites and family rooms. A wide choice of snacks and bar meals are served in Glades bar, as well as a full menu in the restaurant which overlooks the swimming pool.

ROOMS: 65 en suite (bth/shr) (4 fmly) No smoking in 20 bedrooms s £55-£78.50; d £70-£97 (incl. bkfst) * LB Off peak **MEALS:** Lunch £7.95-£9.50 & alc Dinner £15.95 & alc International Cuisine V meals Coffee am **FACILITIES:** CTV in all bedrooms Indoor swimming pool (heated) Pool table Croquet lawn Xmas **CONF:** Thtr 200 Class 90 Board 50 Del from £96 * **SERVICES:** Night porter Air conditioning 200P **NOTES:** No dogs (ex guide dogs) Last d 9.30pm

CARDS:

WIDNES Cheshire **Map 07 SJ58**

★★★ Hill Crest

75 Cronton Ln WA8 9AR

Quality Percentage Score: 63%

☎ 0151 424 1616 ⎙ 0151 495 1348

Dir: *take A5080 Cronton to traffic lights turn right and drive for 0.75m, right at T-junct, follow A5080 for 500yds. Hotel on right*

This modern hotel is situated on the A5080 north west of the town and can be reached from junctions 6 and 7 of the M62 motorway. The majority of bedrooms are comfortable and well equipped especially those designated as executive rooms. Palms Restaurant is a colourful venue in which to enjoy a wide variety

contd.

of popular dishes and Nelson's Bar, depicting a nautical theme, provides a wide range of drinks and regular entertainment.
ROOMS: 50 en suite (bth/shr) (5 fmly) No smoking in 20 bedrooms s £42-£75; d £57-£75 (incl. bkfst) * LB Off peak **MEALS:** Lunch £6.45-£14.95 & alc Dinner £14.95-£16.20 & alc English and Continental Cuisine V meals Coffee am Tea pm **FACILITIES:** CTV in all bedrooms STV Wkly live entertainment Xmas **CONF:** Thtr 140 Class 80 Board 40 Del from £63.75 * **SERVICES:** Lift Night porter Air conditioning 150P
NOTES: Last d 10pm **CARDS:**

WIDNES Cheshire — Map 07 SJ58

Travelodge
Fiddlers Ferry Rd WA8 2NR
☎ 0800 850950
Dir: *on A562*
This modern building offers accommodation in smart, spacious and well equipped bedrooms, all with en-suite bathrooms. Refreshments may be taken at the nearby family restaurant. For details about current prices, consult the Contents Page under Hotel Groups for the Travelodge phone number.
ROOMS: 32 en suite (bth/shr) d £39.95 *

WIGAN Greater Manchester — Map 07 SD50

★★★★ ***Kilhey Court***
Chorley Rd, Standish WN1 2XN
Quality Percentage Score: 64%
☎ 01257 472100 01257 422401
Dir: *on A5106 1.5m N of A49/A5106 junct*

This much extended Victorian mansion, set in ten acres of grounds overlooking the Worthington lakes, offers well appointed accommodation, including a number of magnificent suites. There are two restaurants, one featuring a Victorian conservatory, and a health and leisure club.
ROOMS: 62 en suite (bth/shr) (3 fmly) No smoking in 38 bedrooms **MEALS:** V meals Coffee am Tea pm **FACILITIES:** CTV in all bedrooms STV Indoor swimming pool (heated) Fishing Sauna Solarium Gym Jacuzzi/spa **CONF:** Thtr 180 Class 60 Board 60 **SERVICES:** Lift Night porter 400P **NOTES:** No smoking in restaurant Last d 10pm
CARDS:

WIGAN Greater Manchester — Map 07 SD50

★★★ ***Wrightington Hotel & Restaurant***
Moss Ln, Wrightington WN6 9PB
Quality Percentage Score: 71%
☎ 01257 425803 01257 425830
Dir: *M6 junct 27, 0.25m W, hotel situated on right after church*
This privately owned, modern hotel is situated in open countryside. It provides well equipped accommodation and has
contd.

an excellent leisure centre and a high reputation for service and cuisine.

Wrightington Hotel & Restaurant, Wigan

ROOMS: 47 en suite (bth/shr) (4 fmly) No smoking in 12 bedrooms **MEALS:** V meals Coffee am Tea pm **FACILITIES:** CTV in all bedrooms STV Indoor swimming pool (heated) Squash Sauna Solarium Gym Jacuzzi/spa Sports Injuries Clinic Health & Beauty clinic Hairdresser **CONF:** Thtr 200 Class 120 Board 40 **SERVICES:** Night porter 170P **NOTES:** No smoking area in restaurant Last d 9.30pm **CARDS:**

See advert on page 699

WIGAN Greater Manchester **Map 07 SD50**

★★★ **Quality Hotel Wigan**

Riverway WN1 3SS

Quality Percentage Score: 64%

☎ 01942 826888 Fax 01942 825800

***Dir:** from A49 take B5238 from rdbt, continue for 1.5m through trafic lights, through 3 more sets of lights, at 4th set turn right and take first left*

Close to the centre of the town, opposite Wigan Rugby League ground, this modern hotel offers spacious bedrooms. The open plan public areas include a comfortable lounge bar, adjacent to the popular restaurant which serves a good range of dishes.

ROOMS: 88 en suite (bth/shr) No smoking in 35 bedrooms s £75-£95; d fr £85 * LB Off peak **MEALS:** Dinner fr £14.50 International Cuisine V meals Coffee am Tea pm **FACILITIES:** CTV in all bedrooms STV **CONF:** Thtr 200 Class 90 Board 60 **SERVICES:** Lift Night porter 100P **NOTES:** Last d 9.45pm **CARDS:**

WIGAN Greater Manchester **Map 07 SD50**

★★★ ***Wigan/Standish Moat House***

Almond Brook Rd, Standish WN6 0SR

Quality Percentage Score: 63%

☎ 01257 499988 Fax 01257 427327

***Dir:** 200yds from junct 27 of M6, on A5209*

Conveniently situated just off junction 27 of the M6, this modern hotel has well-equipped bedrooms, including executive rooms and some for the less able. The refurbished public areas are comfortable and spacious and there is a leisure centre and versatile banqueting and conference facilities.

ROOMS: 124 en suite (bth/shr) (13 fmly) No smoking in 64 bedrooms **MEALS:** V meals Coffee am Tea pm **FACILITIES:** CTV in all bedrooms Indoor swimming pool (heated) Sauna Solarium Gym Pool table Jacuzzi/spa **CONF:** Thtr 170 Class 50 Board 50 Del £114 * **SERVICES:** Lift Night porter Air conditioning 400P **NOTES:** Last d 10pm **CARDS:**

WIGAN Greater Manchester **Map 07 SD50**

★★★ ***Bellingham***

141-149 Wigan Ln WN1 2NB

Quality Percentage Score: 61%

☎ 01942 243893 Fax 01942 821027

***Dir:** hotel is situated on the A49 Wigan Lane approximately 0.5m out of Wigan town centre heading North, directly opposite Wigan Infirmary*

The Bellingham provides well equipped, modern accommodation. The pleasant public areas offer a choice of bars and a selection of function rooms, the largest of which can accommodate up to 180 people.

ROOMS: 32 en suite (bth/shr) (4 fmly) No smoking in 2 bedrooms **MEALS:** V meals Coffee am **FACILITIES:** CTV in all bedrooms STV Pool table **CONF:** Thtr 150 Class 50 Board 40 **SERVICES:** Lift Night porter 40P **NOTES:** No smoking in restaurant Last d 9.30pm **CARDS:**

WIGAN Greater Manchester **Map 07 SD50**

★★ **Bel-Air**

236 Wigan Ln WN1 2NU

Quality Percentage Score: 63%

☎ 01942 241410 Fax 01942 243967

***Dir:** M6 junct 27, follow signs for Standish. In Standish turn right at traffic lights towards A49. Hotel is on right, 1.5m from Standish towards Wigan*

This family-run hotel is just to the north of the town. Bedrooms are well equipped and maintained, there is a pleasant bar and the Gaslight Restaurant offers a range of carefully prepared meals.

ROOMS: 11 en suite (bth/shr) (1 fmly) s fr £39.50; d fr £49.50 * Off peak **MEALS:** Lunch fr £6.95 & alc High tea fr £6.95 & alc Dinner fr £6.95 & alc English & French Cuisine V meals Coffee am Tea pm **FACILITIES:** CTV in all bedrooms **CONF:** Thtr 30 Board 8 **SERVICES:** 10P **NOTES:** No dogs (ex guide dogs) Last d 9.30pm **CARDS:**

WIGAN Greater Manchester **Map 07 SD50**

⌂ **Travel Inn (Wigan South)**

Warrington Rd, Marus Bridge WN3 6XB

☎ 01942 493469 Fax 01942 498679

***Dir:** M6 junct 25 slip road to rdbt turn left towards Wigan, hotel on left, off A49. If travelling S on M6 exit junct 24 and return N to junct 25*

This modern building offers accommodation in smart, spacious and well equipped bedrooms, all with en-suite bathrooms. Refreshments may be taken at the nearby family restaurant. For details about current prices consult the Contents Page under Hotel Groups for the Travel Inn phone number.

ROOMS: 40 en suite (bth/shr) d £39.95 *

WIGAN Greater Manchester — Map 07 SD50

Travel Inn (Wigan West)
Orrell Rd, Orrell WN5 8HQ
☎ 01942 211516 Fax 01942 215002
Dir: *M6 junct 26 follow signs Upholland & Orrell, at 1st traffic lights turn left, hotel on right*
This modern building offers accommodation in smart, spacious and well equipped bedrooms, all with en-suite bathrooms. Refreshments may be taken at the nearby family restaurant. For details about current prices consult the Contents Page under Hotel Groups for the Travel Inn phone number.
ROOMS: 40 en suite (bth/shr) d £39.95 *

WIGHT, ISLE OF

BONCHURCH See **Ventnor**

CHALE — Map 04 SZ47

★★ **Clarendon Hotel & Wight Mouse Inn**
PO38 2HA
Quality Percentage Score: 69%
☎ 01983 730431 Fax 01983 730431
Dir: *on B3099 main coast road junct of B3055*
A charming 17th-century former coaching inn with comfortable accommodation at the Clarendon Hotel. The bedrooms, including three suites, feature modern en suite facilities. Guests enjoy freshly prepared food in the smart Clarendon Restaurant or informally at the inn.
ROOMS: 13 en suite (bth/shr) (9 fmly) s £28-£39; d £58-£78 (incl. bkfst) * LB Off peak **MEALS:** Lunch £5-£10 & alc High tea £5-£10 & alc Dinner £12-£17 & alc International Cuisine V meals Coffee am Tea pm **FACILITIES:** CTV in 14 bedrooms Riding Pool table Wkly live entertainment ch fac Xmas **SERVICES:** 200P **NOTES:** No smoking area in restaurant Last d 10pm **CARDS:**

Indicates that the star classification has not been confirmed under the New Quality Standards, see page 7 for further information.

COWES — Map 04 SZ49

★★★ ***New Holmwood***
Queens Rd, Egypt Point PO31 8BW
Quality Percentage Score: 66%
☎ 01983 292508 Fax 01983 295020
Dir: *from Cowes Parade turn right by Royal Yacht Squadron*

A well presented hotel on the Cowes Esplanade with superb views of the Solent. Public rooms include a cosy bar, sea facing restaurant with adjoining sun terrace and comfortable lounge.

contd.

Isle Wight

The bedrooms are well equipped with extras such as mineral water and sweets. Service is friendly and attentive.
ROOMS: 25 en suite (bth/shr) **MEALS:** French Cuisine V meals Coffee am Tea pm **FACILITIES:** CTV in all bedrooms Outdoor swimming pool (heated) **CONF:** Thtr 120 Class 50 Board 32 **SERVICES:** 17P
NOTES: Last d 9.30pm **CARDS:**

See advert on page 701

COWES — Map 04 SZ49

Late entry ○ Duke of York
Mill Hill Rd PO31 7BT
☎ 01983 295171 Fax 01983 295047
This family-run inn is close to the town centre. Bedrooms are split between the main building and a nearby annexe, and are neatly appointed. There is a well stocked bar and a pleasant restaurant, offering a range of popular dishes.
ROOMS: 8 rms (7 bth) (2 fmly) No smoking in 4 bedrooms s fr £35; d fr £45 (incl. bkfst) * Off peak **MEALS:** Lunch fr £4.95 Dinner fr £9.95 English & French Cuisine V meals Coffee am Tea pm **FACILITIES:** CTV in all bedrooms **SERVICES:** Night porter P **NOTES:** No coaches Last d 10pm **CARDS:**

RYDE — Map 04 SZ59

★★ ***Biskra Beach Hotel & Restaurant***
17 Saint Thomas's St PO33 2DL
Quality Percentage Score: 70%
☎ 01983 567913 Fax 01983 616976

Biskra House has undergone complete refurbishment. Public areas convey a stylish, light colonial feel with a spacious bar, cosy lounge and popular basement restaurant. The large rear terrace enjoys stunning views across the Solent and direct access to the shore. There is a childrens' games room and outdoor hot tub.
ROOMS: 14 en suite (bth/shr) (2 fmly) **MEALS:** V meals Coffee am Tea pm **FACILITIES:** CTV in all bedrooms **CONF:** Thtr 30 Class 30 Board 25 Del from £75 * **SERVICES:** 12P **NOTES:** No coaches Last d 10pm Closed 23 Dec-27 Dec **CARDS:**

RYDE — Map 04 SZ59

★★ **Appley Manor**
Appley Rd PO33 1PH
Quality Percentage Score: 65%
☎ 01983 564777 Fax 01983 564704
Dir: *on B3330*
Originally a Victorian Manor House, Appley is set in peaceful grounds five minutes from the town centre. Bedrooms are spacious and well furnished with useful modern facilities. There is a lovely lounge and breakfast room overlooking the gardens. The adjoining Manor Inn offers well-cooked evening meals.
ROOMS: 12 en suite (bth/shr) (2 fmly) No smoking in 3 bedrooms s fr £33; d fr £43 * Off peak **MEALS:** Lunch £7.50-£7.95 Dinner fr £9.70 English, French & Italian Cuisine V meals Coffee am Tea pm **FACILITIES:** CTV in all bedrooms **SERVICES:** Night porter 60P **NOTES:** No dogs (ex guide dogs) No coaches No smoking area in restaurant Last d 9.30pm **CARDS:**

RYDE — Map 04 SZ59

★★ ***Yelf's***
Union St PO33 2LG
Quality Percentage Score: 61%
☎ 01983 564062 Fax 01983 563937
This former coaching inn is undergoing refurbishment, under new ownership. Public areas are smartly appointed and include a busy bar, separate lounge and attractive dining room. Bedrooms, being upgraded, are comfortably furnished and well equipped.
ROOMS: 21 en suite (bth/shr) (2 fmly) **MEALS:** English Cuisine V meals Coffee am Tea pm **FACILITIES:** CTV in all bedrooms **CONF:** Thtr 70 Class 10 Board 20 **NOTES:** No smoking area in restaurant
CARDS:

ST LAWRENCE — Map 04 SZ57

★★ ***Rocklands***
PO38 1XH
Quality Percentage Score: 69%
☎ 01983 852964 Fax 01983 852964
Dir: *A3055 from Ventnor to Niton, pass botanical gardens, Rare Breeds, & St Lawrence Church, hotel is 200m on R*
A charming Victorian house set in peaceful grounds. Public rooms convey much of the original character of the building with a cosy bar, elegant dining room and comfortable lounge. Bedrooms are neatly decorated and thoughtfully equipped. The interesting range of evening meals make use of local fresh produce.

ROOMS: 15 en suite (bth/shr) 4 annexe en suite (bth/shr) (6 fmly) **MEALS:** English & Continental Cuisine V meals Coffee am Tea pm **FACILITIES:** CTV in all bedrooms Outdoor swimming pool (heated) Snooker Sauna Solarium Croquet lawn Table tennis Games room Wkly live entertainment ch fac **CONF:** Class 50 Board 40 **SERVICES:** 20P **NOTES:** No dogs (ex guide dogs) No smoking in restaurant May-Oct

SANDOWN — Map 04 SZ58

★★ ***Cygnet Hotel***
58 Carter St PO36 8DQ
Quality Percentage Score: 67%
☎ 01983 402930 Fax 01983 405112
Popular with tour groups, this family run hotel offers bedrooms that are mostly spacious, comfortably furnished and well equipped. Public areas include two lounge areas and a large bar which regularly stages live entertainment.

SEAVIEW Map 04 SZ69

★★★ Seaview Hotel & Restaurant

High St PO34 5EX
Quality Percentage Score: 77%
☎ 01983 612711 Fax 01983 613729
Dir: *B3330 Ryde-Seaview rd, turn left via Puckpool along seafront Duver Rd, hotel is situated on left hand side adjecent to sea*
A little gem of a hotel, the Seaview is run by a friendly, well motivated team. Bedrooms vary in size and style, but all are decorated with flair. The residents lounge is on the first floor, and there are two bars and a separate, two-roomed restaurant serving good food on the ground floor.
ROOMS: 16 en suite (bth/shr) (1 fmly) No smoking in 4 bedrooms s £65-£90; d £90-£120 (incl. bkfst) * LB Off peak **MEALS:** Lunch £13.95 & alc Dinner £20.45-£25.15alc V meals Coffee am Tea pm **FACILITIES:** CTV in all bedrooms Sailing lessons Painting breaks Special arrangement with local sports club **CONF:** Thtr 30 Class 15 Board 16 Del from £105 * **SERVICES:** 16P **NOTES:** No coaches No smoking area in restaurant Last d 9.30pm Closed 24-28 Dec
CARDS:

SEAVIEW Map 04 SZ69

★★★ *Priory Bay*

Priory Dr PO34 5BU
Quality Percentage Score: 75%
☎ 01983 613146 Fax 01983 616539

This hotel with its own stretch of beach has re-opened following extensive refurbishment. Public areas are comfortable as are the upgraded bedrooms. Chef Pascal Payrere creates interesting and imaginative dishes, using local produce as much as possible.
ROOMS: 19 en suite (bth/shr) 15 annexe en suite (bth) (17 fmly) **MEALS:** European Cuisine V meals Coffee am Tea pm **FACILITIES:** CTV in all bedrooms Outdoor swimming pool Golf 9 Tennis (hard) Pool table Croquet lawn Private beach ch fac **CONF:** Class 60 Board 30 **SERVICES:** Night porter 65P **NOTES:** No coaches No smoking area in restaurant Last d 9.30pm **CARDS:**

SEAVIEW Map 04 SZ69

★★ Springvale Hotel

Springvale PO34 5AN
Quality Percentage Score: 64%
☎ 01983 612533
A friendly hotel in a quiet beach front location with views across the Solent. Bedrooms, varying in shape and size, are attractive and well equipped. Public areas are traditionally furnished and include a cosy bar, dining room and small separate lounge.
ROOMS: 13 en suite (bth/shr) (2 fmly) s £60; d £110 (incl. bkfst) * LB Off peak **MEALS:** Lunch £10 High tea £4-£6 Dinner £14-£18 V meals Coffee am Tea pm **FACILITIES:** CTV in all bedrooms Tennis (grass) Jacuzzi/spa Sailing dinghy hire & tuition Xmas **CONF:** Class 30 Board 20 Del £120 **SERVICES:** 1P **NOTES:** No dogs (ex guide dogs) No coaches No smoking in restaurant Last d 9.30pm **CARDS:**

SHANKLIN Map 04 SZ58

★★★ Keats Green

3 Queens Rd PO37 6AN
Quality Percentage Score: 65%
☎ 01983 862742 Fax 01983 868572
Dir: *on A3055 follow signs Old Village/Ventnor, avoiding town centre, hotel on left past St Saviors church*
This well established hotel enjoys a super location overlooking Keats Green and Sandown Bay. Bedrooms are attractively decorated and pine furnished. Public rooms include a comfortable bar/lounge and a smartly appointed dining room.
ROOMS: 33 en suite (bth/shr) (7 fmly) s £25-£30; d £50-£60 (incl. bkfst) * LB Off peak **MEALS:** Dinner £10-£12.50 V meals Coffee am **FACILITIES:** CTV in all bedrooms Outdoor swimming pool (heated) **SERVICES:** 34P **NOTES:** No smoking in restaurant Last d 8pm Closed Nov-Mar **CARDS:**

SHANKLIN Map 04 SZ58

★★★ Brunswick

Queens Rd PO37 6AN
Quality Percentage Score: 62%
☎ 01983 863245 Fax 01983 868398
This established hotel, on the cliff-top path known as Keat's Green, has lovely sea views. Bedrooms are comfortably furnished, with well chosen colour schemes. Public rooms include a spacious lounge/bar, attractive restaurant and choice of swimming pools.
ROOMS: 27 en suite (bth/shr) 5 annexe en suite (bth/shr) (9 fmly) **MEALS:** International Cuisine V meals **FACILITIES:** CTV in all bedrooms Indoor swimming pool (heated) Outdoor swimming pool (heated) Sauna Pool table Jacuzzi/spa **SERVICES:** Night porter 30P **NOTES:** No smoking in restaurant Closed Dec & Jan **CARDS:**

SHANKLIN Map 04 SZ58

★★★ Holliers Hotel

5 Church Rd, Old Village PO37 6NU
Quality Percentage Score: 60%
☎ 01983 862764 Fax 01983 867134
A popular 18th-century hotel in the heart of the old village. Bedrooms are comfortably appointed and equipped with modern amenities. Public areas include a quiet first floor lounge, a smart bar with live entertainment and a spacious, brightly decorated restaurant with a comprehensive dinner menu.
ROOMS: 30 en suite (bth/shr) (6 fmly) s £45-£50; d £70-£80 (incl. bkfst) * LB Off peak **MEALS:** Bar Lunch fr £2.95 Dinner fr £16.95 European Cuisine V meals Coffee am Tea pm **FACILITIES:** CTV in all bedrooms STV Indoor swimming pool (heated) Outdoor swimming pool (heated) Sauna Pool table Jacuzzi/spa Xmas **SERVICES:** 50P **NOTES:** No dogs (ex guide dogs) Last d 8.30pm
CARDS:

SHANKLIN Map 04 SZ58

★★ *Fernbank*

Highfield Rd PO37 6PP
Quality Percentage Score: 67%
☎ 01983 862790 Fax 01983 864412
Dir: *at Shanklin's old village traffic lights turn onto Victoria Ave, take 3rd left into Highfield Rd*
An established hotel in a peaceful location minutes from the old village. Bedrooms are comfortably appointed and equipped with modern facilities. Guests enjoy the sheltered lawns and leisure
contd.

Isle Wight

facilities. The smartly presented dining room overlooks gardens and countryside.
ROOMS: 19 en suite (bth/shr) 5 annexe en suite (bth/shr) (8 fmly) **MEALS:** English, French & Italian Cuisine V meals Coffee am Tea pm **FACILITIES:** CTV in all bedrooms Indoor swimming pool (heated) Sauna Pool table Jacuzzi/spa Petanque **SERVICES:** 22P **NOTES:** No coaches No children 7yrs No smoking in restaurant Last d 8.30pm Closed Xmas **CARDS:**

SHANKLIN — Map 04 SZ58
★★ *Luccombe Hall*
Luccombe Rd PO37 6RL
Quality Percentage Score: 67%
☎ 01983 862719 Fax 01983 863082
Dir: *take A3055 to Shanklin, through old village then 1st L into Priory Rd, L into Popham Rd, 1st R into Luccombe Rd. Hotel on R*
This hotel was originally built as a summer home for the Bishop of Portsmouth in 1870. Enjoying a peaceful clifftop location the property benefits from sea views and direct access to the beach. Bedrooms are comfortably furnished and well equipped.
ROOMS: 30 en suite (bth/shr) (19 fmly) **MEALS:** English & Continental Cuisine V meals Coffee am Tea pm **FACILITIES:** CTV in all bedrooms Indoor swimming pool (heated) Outdoor swimming pool (heated) Tennis (grass) Squash Sauna Solarium Gym Pool table Jacuzzi/spa Games room Wkly live entertainment ch fac **CONF: SERVICES:** 20P **NOTES:** Last d 8.30pm **CARDS:**

SHANKLIN — Map 04 SZ58
★★ Hambledon
Queens Rd PO37 6AW
Quality Percentage Score: 64%
☎ 01983 862403 & 863651 Fax 01983 867894
Dir: *off A3055*
A small, well maintained hotel. Bedrooms are comfortably furnished, well equipped and feature modern shower facilities. There is a cosy bar, adjacent lounge and a smartly appointed dining room. The hotel specialises in walking holidays which it arranges.
ROOMS: 11 en suite (shr) (4 fmly) s £19-£25; d £38-£50 (incl. bkfst) * LB Off peak **MEALS:** V meals **FACILITIES:** CTV in all bedrooms Free use of nearby indoor leisure facilities Xmas **SERVICES:** 8P **NOTES:** No smoking in restaurant **CARDS:**

SHANKLIN — Map 04 SZ58
★★ *Malton House*
8 Park Rd PO37 6AY
Quality Percentage Score: 64%
☎ 01983 865007 Fax 01983 865576
A well kept Victorian hotel. Recently refurbished bedrooms are brightly appointed. Public rooms include a small comfortable lounge, bar and dining room. The hotel is conveniently located for cliff top walks and the public lift down to the promenade.
ROOMS: 15 en suite (bth/shr) (3 fmly) **MEALS:** English & Continental Cuisine V meals **FACILITIES:** CTV in all bedrooms **SERVICES:** 12P **NOTES:** No dogs No coaches No smoking in restaurant
CARDS:

SHANKLIN — Map 04 SZ58
★★ Melbourne Ardenlea
Queen's Rd PO37 6AP
Quality Percentage Score: 63%
☎ 01983 862283 Fax 01983 862865
Dir: *turn left at Fiveways Crossroads, off A3055, hotel on right 150yds past the tall spired church*
Conveniently located for both the town centre and the lift down to the promenade, this friendly hotel continues to successfully cater for coach parties. Spacious public areas are smartly presented, bedrooms are traditionally furnished.
ROOMS: 57 en suite (bth/shr) (9 fmly) s £30-£45; d £60-£90 (incl. bkfst & dinner) LB Off peak **MEALS:** Bar Lunch £2-£6alc Dinner £11-£14 & alc English & French Cuisine V meals **FACILITIES:** CTV in all bedrooms Indoor swimming pool (heated) Solarium Pool table Jacuzzi/spa Pool Table tennis **SERVICES:** Lift 28P **NOTES:** Closed mid Dec-mid Feb RS Nov-mid Dec & mid Feb-Mar **CARDS:**

TOTLAND BAY — Map 04 SZ38
★★★ Sentry Mead
Madeira Rd PO39 0BJ
Quality Percentage Score: 66%
☎ 01983 753212 Fax 01983 753212
Dir: *turn off A3054 at Totland war memorial rdbt, 300yds on right just before going to beach*
Just two minutes from the sea at Totland Bay, this well kept Victorian villa includes a comfortable lounge and separate bar as well as a conservatory overlooking the garden. Bedrooms feature co-ordinated soft furnishings and extras like mineral water, biscuits and pot-pourri.
ROOMS: 14 en suite (bth/shr) (4 fmly) s fr £30; d fr £60 (incl. bkfst) * LB Off peak **MEALS:** Bar Lunch fr £7.50 Dinner fr £16.50 European Cuisine V meals Coffee am Tea pm **FACILITIES:** CTV in all bedrooms Putting green **SERVICES:** 10P **NOTES:** No coaches No smoking in restaurant Last d 8pm Closed 22 Dec-2 Jan **CARDS:**

VENTNOR — Map 04 SZ57
★★★★ The Royal Hotel
Belgrave Rd PO38 1JJ
Quality Percentage Score: 70%
☎ 01983 852186 Fax 01983 855395
Dir: *A3055 main coastal road, into Ventnor follow one way system around Town, after traffic lights turn left into Belgrave road, Hotel is on right*
Part Georgian and part Edwardian, this honey-coloured stone hotel has been totally transformed over the last few years. Public areas include a sunny conservatory and restful lounge. The restaurant provides an appropriate setting for good cooking from modern, eclectic menus.
ROOMS: 55 en suite (bth/shr) (7 fmly) No smoking in 2 bedrooms s £50-£115; d £100-£160 (incl. bkfst) * LB Off peak **MEALS:** Bar Lunch £15.50-£22 Dinner £22 & alc French Cuisine V meals Coffee am Tea pm **FACILITIES:** CTV in all bedrooms STV Outdoor swimming pool (heated) Croquet lawn Xmas **CONF:** Thtr 100 Class 80 Board 50 Del from £75 * **SERVICES:** Lift Night porter 56P **NOTES:** No dogs (ex guide dogs) No coaches No smoking in restaurant Last d 9.15pm
CARDS:

See advert on opposite page

VENTNOR — Map 04 SZ57
★★★ *Burlington*
Bellevue Rd PO38 1DB
Quality Percentage Score: 65%
☎ 01983 852113 Fax 01983 853862
Eight of the attractively decorated bedrooms have balconies, three ground floor rooms have french doors into the garden. There is a cosy bar, comfortable lounge and a dining room where home-made bread rolls accompany the five-course dinners. Service is both friendly and attentive.
ROOMS: 24 en suite (bth/shr) (8 fmly) **MEALS:** Various Cuisine V meals Coffee am Tea pm **FACILITIES:** CTV in all bedrooms Outdoor swimming pool (heated) Pool table **SERVICES:** 20P **NOTES:** No dogs No coaches No children 3yrs No smoking in restaurant Last d 8.30pm Closed Nov-Etr **CARDS:**

Isle Wight

VENTNOR
Map 04 SZ57

★★★ ***Ventnor Towers***

Madeira Rd PO38 1QT

Quality Percentage Score: 63%

☎ 01983 852277 📠 01983 855536

Dir: *first left after Trinity church, follow road for 0.25m*

This mid-Victorian hotel set in spacious grounds (from which a path leads down to the shore) is high above the bay and enjoys some splendid sea views. Lots of potted plants and fresh flowers grace day rooms which include two lounges and a roomy bar. Bedrooms include two four-posters and some with their own balconies.

ROOMS: 27 en suite (bth/shr) (4 fmly) **MEALS:** English & Continental Cuisine V meals Coffee am Tea pm **FACILITIES:** CTV in all bedrooms Outdoor swimming pool (heated) Tennis (hard) Pool table Croquet lawn Putting green Games room Wkly live entertainment ch fac **CONF:** Thtr 80 Class 50 Board 35 **SERVICES:** 26P **NOTES:** Last d 8.30pm **CARDS:**

VENTNOR
Map 04 SZ57

★★ **Eversley**

Park Av PO38 1LB

Quality Percentage Score: 67%

☎ 1983 852244 📠 01983 853948

Dir: *on A3055 west of Ventnor*

Conveniently located to the west of town by Ventnor Park, this friendly hotel offers bedrooms which are comfortably appointed and well equipped. Public areas include a choice of lounges, bright dining room and a separate bar with a terrace overlooking a sunny lawn.

ROOMS: 32 en suite (bth/shr) (8 fmly) s £28-£30; d £56-£60 (incl. bkfst) * LB Off peak **MEALS:** Bar Lunch £3.50-£7 Dinner £12-£15 English & Continental Cuisine V meals Coffee am Tea pm **FACILITIES:** CTV in all bedrooms Outdoor swimming pool (heated) Tennis (hard) Pool table Xmas **CONF:** Class 40 Board 20 Del from £50 * **SERVICES:** 23P **NOTES:** No smoking in restaurant Last d 8.30pm Closed 16 Nov-22 Dec & 2 Jan-15 Feb **CARDS:**

VENTNOR
Map 04 SZ57

★★ **St Maur Hotel**

Castle Rd PO38 1LG

Quality Percentage Score: 67%

☎ 01983 852570 & 853645 📠 01983 852306

Dir: *W of Ventnor off main A3055 (Park Avenue)*

Guests will find a warm welcome awaits them at this hotel, where six course home cooked dinners are on offer. The well equipped bedrooms are traditionally decorated. In addition to a spacious lounge the hotel benefits from a cosy residents' bar.

ROOMS: 14 en suite (bth/shr) (2 fmly) s £25-£37; d £50-£74 (incl. bkfst & dinner) * LB Off peak **MEALS:** Dinner £6-£12 V meals **FACILITIES:** CTV in all bedrooms STV **SERVICES:** 12P **NOTES:** No dogs No coaches No children 5yrs No smoking in restaurant Last d 7pm Closed Dec **CARDS:**

VENTNOR
Map 04 SZ57

Late entry ***Hillside Hotel***

Mitchell Av PO38 1DR

☎ 01983 852271

Built in 1801 and enjoying an elevated position above the town, this small hotel offers bedrooms which vary in shape and size, are smartly appointed, and equipped with modern facilities. Public rooms include a lounge, conservatory and dining room where guests can enjoy home cooking featuring good vegetarian options.

YARMOUTH
Map 04 SZ38

★★★ ❀❀❀ ***George Hotel***

Quay St PO41 0PE

Quality Percentage Score: 80%

☎ 01983 760331 📠 01983 760425

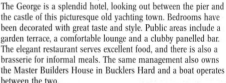

Dir: *between the castle and the pier*

The George is a splendid hotel, looking out between the pier and the castle of this picturesque old yachting town. Bedrooms have been decorated with great taste and style. Public areas include a garden terrace, a comfortable lounge and a clubby panelled bar. The elegant restaurant serves excellent food, and there is also a brasserie for informal meals. The same management also owns the Master Builders House in Bucklers Hard and a boat operates between the two.

ROOMS: 16 en suite (bth/shr) No smoking in 4 bedrooms **MEALS:** British with International influences Cuisine V meals Coffee am Tea pm **FACILITIES:** CTV in all bedrooms STV **CONF:** Thtr 40 Class 20 Board 20 **SERVICES:** Night porter **NOTES:** No coaches No children 8 No smoking area in restaurant Last d 10pm **CARDS:**

WILLERBY East Riding of Yorkshire
Map 08 TA03

★★★ ❀ **Willerby Manor**

Well Ln HU10 6ER

Quality Percentage Score: 70%

☎ 01482 652616 📠 01482 653901

Dir: *turn off A63, signposted Humber Bridge- Follow road, take right at rdbt by Safeway. At next rdbt hotel is signposted*

Standing in its own well tended gardens, this elegant Victorian house has been thoughtfully extended. The hotel provides well equipped and pleasant bedrooms, many of which are very

contd.

spacious. Comfortable public rooms are available and the cooking is to be commended.
ROOMS: 51 en suite (bth/shr) No smoking in 18 bedrooms s £71; d £82-£87 * LB Off peak **MEALS:** Lunch £12.50-£14.50 & alc Dinner fr £17.25 & alc V meals Coffee am Tea pm **FACILITIES:** CTV in all bedrooms STV Indoor swimming pool (heated) Sauna Solarium Gym Croquet lawn Jacuzzi/spa Steam room Beauty therapist Aerobic classes Wkly live entertainment **CONF:** Thtr 500 Class 200 Board 100 Del from £90 * **SERVICES:** Night porter 300P **NOTES:** No dogs (ex guide dogs) No coaches Last d 9.30pm RS 24-26 Dec & New Year
CARDS:

WILLINGTON Co Durham — Map 12 NZ13
★★ Kensington Hall
Kensington Ter DL15 0PJ
Quality Percentage Score: 66%
☎ 01388 745071 Fax 01388 745800
Dir: *off A690*
This friendly family-run business and tourist hotel is also a popular venue for local weddings. The comfortable, well equipped bedrooms are attractively furnished in the modern style, and public areas include a choice of smart bars and a cosy restaurant.
ROOMS: 10 en suite (bth/shr) (3 fmly) No smoking in 2 bedrooms s £38; d £48 (incl. bkfst) * LB Off peak **MEALS:** Lunch £5-£10 & alc Dinner £11-£12 & alc V meals Coffee am Tea pm **FACILITIES:** CTV in all bedrooms **CONF:** Class 80 Board 50 Del from £60 * **SERVICES:** Night porter 40P **NOTES:** No dogs (ex guide dogs) Last d 9.30pm
CARDS:

WILLITON Somerset — Map 03 ST04
★★ Curdon Mill
Vellow TA4 4LS
Quality Percentage Score: 73%
☎ 01984 656522 Fax 01984 656197
Dir: *1m SE off A358*
Outstanding hospitality and good food are the strengths of this charming small hotel. Bedrooms are compact and designed to make the best use of space. The restaurant incorporates original machinery from the water mill, providing an atmospheric environment in which to enjoy a menu dominated by high quality local produce and home-grown vegetables. Weather permitting, an outdoor pool is available.
ROOMS: 8 rms (1 bth 5 shr) No smoking in all bedrooms s fr £45; d fr £70 (incl. bkfst) * LB Off peak **MEALS:** Sunday Lunch £12-£14.50alc Dinner fr £24alc European Cuisine V meals Coffee am Tea pm **FACILITIES:** CTV in all bedrooms Outdoor swimming pool (heated) Tennis Fishing Riding Croquet lawn Xmas **CONF:** Thtr 50 Class 50 Board 20 **SERVICES:** 100P **NOTES:** No dogs (ex guide dogs) No children 8yrs No smoking in restaurant Last d 9.00pm
CARDS:

W

WILLITON Somerset — Map 03 ST04
★★ White House
Long St TA4 4QW
Quality Percentage Score: 72%
☎ 01984 632306 & 632777
Dir: *on A39*
A wonderfully relaxed and easy going atmosphere is the hallmark of this lovely little Georgian hotel, where Dick and Kay Smith make every effort to make guests feel welcome. Many visitors to the north coast of Devon stop here on their travels and when they sample the lovely dinners on offer, they find themselves staying overnight. Fresh fish from Brixham, and local game, is hard to beat and the delicious puddings are irresistible. The White House has something of the feel of a French artist's retreat about it, with the public rooms being decorated and furnished with stylish simplicity. Bedrooms vary in size, those in the main building being rather more spacious and up to date, but all are well equipped with those extra touches that make this charming place more of a home than a hotel.
ROOMS: 6 rms (5 bth/shr) 4 annexe en suite (bth) (1 fmly)
MEALS: Dinner £31.50 English & French Cuisine **FACILITIES:** CTV in all bedrooms **SERVICES:** 12P **NOTES:** No coaches No smoking in restaurant Last d 8.15pm Closed Nov-mid May

WILMSLOW Cheshire — Map 07 SJ88
see also **Manchester Airport**
★★★★ Mottram Hall
Wilmslow Rd, Mottram St Andrew, Prestbury SK10 4QT
De Vere Hotels
Quality Percentage Score: 67%
☎ 01625 828135 Fax 01625 828950
Conveniently located for Manchester airport and the motorway network, this extended Georgian house lies in attractive grounds. Many of the bedrooms have fine views over the golf course and there is a smart cocktail bar and an elegant restaurant.
ROOMS: 132 en suite (bth/shr) (6 fmly) No smoking in 26 bedrooms s fr £140; d fr £165 (incl. bkfst) * LB Off peak **MEALS:** Lunch £12-£19 & alc Dinner £26-£35 & alc English & French Cuisine V meals Coffee am Tea pm **FACILITIES:** CTV in all bedrooms STV Indoor swimming pool (heated) Golf 18 Tennis (hard & grass) Squash Snooker Sauna Solarium Gym Croquet lawn Putting green Jacuzzi/spa Beautitian & Nail Salon Wkly live entertainment ch fac Xmas **CONF:** Thtr 275 Class 140 Board 110 Del £165 * **SERVICES:** Lift Night porter 400P **NOTES:** No smoking in restaurant Last d 9.45pm **CARDS:**

WILMSLOW Cheshire — Map 07 SJ88
★★★ Stanneylands
Stanneylands Rd SK9 4EY
Quality Percentage Score: 73%
☎ 01625 525225 Fax 01625 537282
Dir: *leave M56 at Airport turn off, follow signs to Wilmslow, turn left into Station Rd, onto Stanneylands Rd, hotel is on the right*
Public rooms feature fine wood panelling and real fires at this privately owned hotel, which stands in delightful grounds and provides well equipped bedrooms. The cuisine on offer in the restaurant is from a well chosen carte and gourmet selection.
ROOMS: 31 en suite (bth/shr) (2 fmly) No smoking in 10 bedrooms s fr £94; d £104.58-£128.08 * LB Off peak **MEALS:** Lunch £10.50-£30 & alc High tea £8-£12 Dinner fr £25 & alc English & Continental Cuisine V meals Coffee am Tea pm **FACILITIES:** CTV in all bedrooms STV **CONF:** Thtr 100 Class 50 Board 40 Del from £135 * **SERVICES:** Night porter 80P **NOTES:** No dogs (ex guide dogs) Last d 9.45pm
CARDS:
See advert under MANCHESTER AIRPORT

WIMBORNE MINSTER Dorset — Map 04 SZ09
★★★ *King's Head*
The Square BH21 1GA
Old English Inns & Hotels
Quality Percentage Score: 60%
☎ 01202 880101 Fax 01202 881667
Dir: *off A31 follow Wimborne town centre signs, car park at rear of hotel on one way system*
Prominently positioned, in the square of this historic town, the King's Head retains much of its original character and charm, offering comfortable accommodation with modern facilities. A regularly changing, fixed price menu is available for residents and guests in the formal restaurant, while in the bar an extensive
contd.

choice is offered. The comfortable, spacious lounge is popular with both residents and non-residents alike.
ROOMS: 27 en suite (bth/shr) (1 fmly) No smoking in 8 bedrooms **MEALS:** V meals Coffee am Tea pm **FACILITIES:** CTV in all bedrooms **CONF:** Thtr 40 Class 30 Board 30 **SERVICES:** Lift 25P **NOTES:** No smoking in restaurant Last d 9pm **CARDS:**

WIMBORNE MINSTER Dorset — Map 04 SZ09

The Premier Collection

★★ Beechleas
17 Poole Rd BH21 1QA
☎ 01202 841684 01202 849344
Dir: *on A349*
Furnished to a high standard, the spacious bedrooms at this elegant Georgian townhouse are well equipped. The lounge is very comfortable and the conservatory restaurant is bright and airy. Dinner menus provide honest food, many ingredients sourced from a local organic farm.
ROOMS: 5 en suite (bth/shr) 4 annexe en suite (bth/shr) No smoking in all bedrooms **MEALS:** **FACILITIES:** CTV in all bedrooms **SERVICES:** 9P **NOTES:** No dogs (ex guide dogs) No coaches No smoking in restaurant Last d 9.30pm Closed 25 Dec-11 Jan
CARDS:

WIMBORNE MINSTER Dorset — Map 04 SZ09

★★ Coach House Inn
579 Winborne Rd East, Tricketts Cross BH22 9NW
Quality Percentage Score: 59%
☎ 01202 861222 01202 894130
(For full entry see Ferndown)

WINCANTON Somerset — Map 03 ST72

★★★ *Holbrook House*
Holbrook BA9 8BS
Quality Percentage Score: 68%
☎ 01963 32377 01963 32681
Dir: *from A303 at Wincanton, turn left on A371 towards Castle Cary and Shepton Mallet*
This charming country house is set in pretty grounds with mature trees and clipped box hedges. The comfortable lounges have log fires and deep armchairs, and imaginative dishes are offered in the elegant dining room. There are also a recently completed function room and health spa, and the hotel holds a licence for civil weddings.
ROOMS: 19 rms (4 fmly) **MEALS:** European Cuisine V meals Coffee am Tea pm **FACILITIES:** CTV in all bedrooms Outdoor swimming pool (heated) Tennis (hard & grass) Squash Croquet lawn Table tennis **CONF:** Thtr 50 Board 40 **SERVICES:** Night porter 70P **NOTES:** Last d 9.15pm **CARDS:**

See advert on this page

WINCHESTER Hampshire — Map 04 SU42

★★★★ *Lainston House*
Sparsholt SO21 2LT
Quality Percentage Score: 76%
☎ 01962 863588 01962 776672
Dir: *2m NW off B3049 towards Stockbridge*
This endearing hotel embodies the fine traditions of a quality British country house and stands as a shining example within the region. Set in well manicured grounds the house dates back to the Norman conquest, although the Lainston estate didn't take shape until the 17th century. Rooms vary from spacious and well equipped rooms in Chudleigh Court to spectacular suites in the main house. Chef Friedrich Litty has been presiding over the stove for many years and his distinctive style combines fresh clear flavours with imaginative presentation.
ROOMS: 38 en suite (bth/shr) (1 fmly) **MEALS:** English & French Cuisine V meals Coffee am Tea pm **FACILITIES:** CTV in all bedrooms STV Tennis (hard) Fishing Croquet lawn Archery Clay pigeon shooting Wkly live entertainment **CONF:** Thtr 80 Class 50 Board 40 **SERVICES:** Night porter 150P **NOTES:** No coaches Last d 10.00pm
CARDS:

See advert on page 709

WINCHESTER Hampshire — Map 04 SU42

★★★★ The Wessex
Paternoster Row SO23 9LQ
Quality Percentage Score: 62%
☎ 01962 861611 01962 841503
Dir: *from M3 follow signs for town centre, at rdbt by King Alfred's statue proceed past the Guild Hall and take the next left, hotel on right*
This large modern hotel is ideally positioned, tucked away in the heart of the city, and boasting unrestricted views of the cathedral

contd.

from the public rooms and many bedrooms. Designed with the business and leisure guest in mind the bedrooms are smart, comfortable and well equipped.
ROOMS: 94 en suite (bth/shr) No smoking in 61 bedrooms s £94-£99; d £99-£124 LB Off peak **MEALS:** Lunch £7.50-£17.95 & alc High tea £7.95-£8.50alc Dinner £22-£32alc International Cuisine V meals Coffee am Tea pm **FACILITIES:** CTV in all bedrooms STV Wkly live entertainment Xmas **CONF:** Thtr 100 Class 60 Board 60 Del from £135 **SERVICES:** Lift Night porter 60P **NOTES:** No smoking in restaurant Last d 10pm **CARDS:**

WINCHESTER Hampshire — Map 04 SU42

★★★ Royal
Saint Peter St SO23 8BS
Quality Percentage Score: 68%
☎ 01962 840840 01962 841582
Located in the city centre, this hotel continues to be popular with both leisure and business markets. The bedrooms are split between the main house and a modern wing. Guests have use of the smartly appointed lounge and bar, and the air-conditioned dining room. Professional and friendly service is provided by the dedicated team of staff.
ROOMS: 75 en suite (bth/shr) No smoking in 25 bedrooms s £79-£86.50; d £86.50-£98.50 * LB Off peak **MEALS:** Lunch £12-£18alc Dinner £30 British, French & Italian Cuisine V meals Coffee am Tea pm **FACILITIES:** CTV in all bedrooms STV Xmas **CONF:** Thtr 150 Class 50 Board 40 Del £111.50 * **SERVICES:** Night porter 80P **NOTES:** No smoking in restaurant Last d 9.30pm
CARDS:

See advert on opposite page

WINCHESTER Hampshire — Map 04 SU42

★★★ *Winchester Moat House*
Worthy Ln SO23 7AB
Quality Percentage Score: 67%
☎ 01962 709988 01962 840862
Staff are friendly and helpful at this modern hotel, which is situated on the outskirts of the town, within easy walking distance of the centre. Bedrooms are well equipped and generally spacious. In addition to good meeting facilities, the hotel has a smart leisure centre.
ROOMS: 72 en suite (bth/shr) (4 fmly) No smoking in 27 bedrooms **MEALS:** English & French Cuisine V meals Coffee am Tea pm **FACILITIES:** CTV in all bedrooms Indoor swimming pool (heated) Sauna Solarium Gym Jacuzzi/spa Steam room **CONF:** Thtr 200 Class 100 Board 70 **SERVICES:** Night porter 72P **NOTES:** No smoking in restaurant Last d 9.15pm **CARDS:**

WINCHESTER Hampshire — Map 04 SU42

★★★ *Marwell*
Thompson Ln, Colden Common, Marwell SO21 1JY
Quality Percentage Score: 62%
☎ 01962 777681 01962 777625
Dir: *on B2177 opposite Marwell Zoological Park*
This modern hotel, built on stilts and set in the grounds of Marwell Zoological Park, and offers spacious well equipped bedrooms. Breakfast and dinner are served in the colonial style La Bambouserie Restaurant and a good snack menu is available either in the lounge or bedrooms.
ROOMS: 68 en suite (bth/shr) (35 fmly) No smoking in 47 bedrooms **MEALS:** English & Continental Cuisine V meals Coffee am Tea pm **FACILITIES:** CTV in all bedrooms STV Indoor swimming pool (heated) Sauna Solarium Gym Pool table Jacuzzi/spa **CONF:** Thtr 160 Class 60 Board 60 **SERVICES:** Night porter 85P **NOTES:** No smoking in restaurant Last d 9.30pm RS Sat **CARDS:**

WINCHESTER Hampshire — Map 04 SU42

Hotel du Vin & Bistro
14 Southgate St SO23 9EF
☎ 01962 841414 01962 842458
Dir: *M3 junct 11 towards Winchester, follow all signs. Hotel du Vin is situated approx 2m from junct 11 on left hand side just past cinema*
Robin Hutson's and Gérard Basset's centrally located town house maintains a relaxed yet lively atmosphere in elegant, informal surroundings - also to be found at their new venture in Tunbridge Wells. The comfortable bedrooms, each sponsored by a different wine house, offer considerable originality of style. The bistro serves imaginative and enjoyable food, and there is plenty of choice to be found on the daily changing carte. The wine list has been selected by a master hand and offers a great choice.
ROOMS: 23 en suite (bth/shr) (1 fmly) d £90-£130 Off peak **MEALS:** Lunch £25 & alc Dinner £25-£35alc British & Mediterranean Cuisine V meals **FACILITIES:** CTV in all bedrooms STV Xmas **CONF:** Thtr 40 Class 30 Board 25 Del from £145 * **SERVICES:** Night porter 45P **NOTES:** No dogs (ex guide dogs) No coaches Last d 9.45pm
CARDS:

WINDERMERE Cumbria — Map 07 SD49

The Premier Collection

★★★ Gilpin Lodge Country House Hotel & Restaurant
Crook Rd LA23 3NE
☎ 015394 88818 015394 88058
Dir: *M6 junct 36, take A590/A591 to rdbt North of Kendal, take B5284, hotel is 5m on the right*
A splendid Victorian residence nestling in 20 acres of woodlands, moors and gardens. The dedicated team of staff instantly create a really welcoming and relaxing atmosphere. Furnished with antiques and fresh flowers, and warmed by real fires, the public rooms offer the perfect place to unwind and take afternoon tea. The stylish bedrooms are very comfortably furnished and some have four-poster beds and private sun terraces. Exceptional food, served in one of the three dining rooms, is another highlight of any stay.
ROOMS: 14 en suite (bth/shr) s £110; d £100-£180 (incl. bkfst) LB Off peak **MEALS:** Lunch £16.50 & alc Dinner £29.50 V meals Coffee am Tea pm **FACILITIES:** CTV in all bedrooms Croquet lawn Free membership of local private Leisure Club Xmas **CONF:** Thtr 30 Class 16 Board 12 **SERVICES:** 30P **NOTES:** No dogs No coaches No children 7yrs No smoking in restaurant Last d 9pm
CARDS:

W

WINDERMERE Cumbria **Map 07 SD49**

The Premier Collection

★★★ Holbeck Ghyll Country House

Holbeck Ln LA23 1LU

☎ 015394 32375 015394 34743

Dir: *3m North of Windermere on A591, turn right into Holbeck Lane (sign Troutbeck), hotel is 0.5m along on left*

A delightful Victorian house with delightful views; panoramic vistas stretch across Windermere Lake to the Langdale Fells beyond. Staff are friendly and efficient, and nothing is too much trouble. Bedrooms are thoughtfully equipped and some have private balconies.

ROOMS: 14 en suite (bth/shr) 6 annexe en suite (bth/shr) (1 fmly) No smoking in 6 bedrooms s £95-£175; d £160-£300 (incl. bkfst & dinner) LB Off peak **MEALS:** Lunch fr £18.50 Dinner fr £39.50 English & French Cuisine V meals Coffee am Tea pm **FACILITIES:** CTV in all bedrooms STV Tennis (hard) Sauna Gym Croquet lawn Putting green Jacuzzi/spa Beautician Steam room Xmas **CONF:** Thtr 45 Class 25 Board 25 Del from £125 * **SERVICES:** 30P **NOTES:** No smoking in restaurant Last d 9.30pm **CARDS:**

WINDERMERE Cumbria **Map 07 SD49**

★★★ Linthwaite House Hotel

Crook Rd LA23 3JA

Quality Percentage Score: 78%

☎ 015394 88600 015394 88601

Dir: *A591 towards the lakes for 8m to large rdbt, take 1st exit (B5284), continue for 6m, hotel is on left hand side 1m past Windermere golf club*

Linthwaite House lies in delightful gardens and enjoys spectacular views of the lake and distant fells. Formerly an Edwardian residence, this luxury hotel has friendly staff who provide superb service. Public areas include two lounges, a conservatory and an attractive restaurant. A sun terrace is relaxing in summer, and the hotel has its own tarn, providing opportunities for fishing and swimming. Bedrooms are well equipped and mainly modern in style. Food is imaginative and well presented.

ROOMS: 25 en suite (bth/shr) (1 fmly) No smoking in 19 bedrooms s £110-£120; d £95-£250 (incl. bkfst) * LB Off peak **MEALS:** Sunday Lunch £14.95-£15.95 Dinner £35-£36.50 V meals Coffee am Tea pm **FACILITIES:** CTV in all bedrooms STV Fishing Croquet lawn Putting green Free use of nearby leisure spa Xmas **CONF:** Thtr 47 Class 19 Board 22 Del from £100 * **SERVICES:** 40P **NOTES:** No dogs (ex guide dogs) No coaches No smoking in restaurant Last d 9.30pm **CARDS:**

See advert on opposite page

WINDERMERE Cumbria **Map 07 SD49**

★★★ Storrs Hall

Storrs Park LA23 3LG

Quality Percentage Score: 76%

☎ 015394 47111 015394 47555

Dir: *on the A592 2m S of Bowness on the Newby Bridge road*

This fine Georgian mansion is set on a peninsula of Lake Windermere, enjoying half a mile of lakeside frontage and magnificent views. Bedrooms and the spacious public areas are furnished comfortably with antiques and fine works of art. The atmosphere is relaxed, the hospitality warm, and the food satisfying.

ROOMS: 26 en suite (bth/shr) s £95-£150; d £245-£345 (incl. bkfst & dinner) * LB Off peak **MEALS:** Lunch £18-£22 Dinner fr £38 V meals Coffee am Tea pm **FACILITIES:** CTV in all bedrooms STV Fishing Croquet lawn Sailing Water skiing Xmas **CONF:** Board 15 **SERVICES:** 50P **NOTES:** No dogs (ex guide dogs) No coaches No smoking in restaurant Last d 9pm **CARDS:**

WINDERMERE Cumbria **Map 07 SD49**

★★★ Beech Hill

Newby Bridge Rd LA23 3LR

Quality Percentage Score: 74%

☎ 015394 42137 015394 43745

Dir: *A591 towards Windermere, turn onto A590 to Newby Bridge, then take A592 toward Bowness, hotel is on left hand side 4m S from Bowness*

This delightful hotel stands on the lakeside to the south of Bowness and is constructed from a series of attractive terraced extensions leading eventually down to a jetty on Lake Windermere. Public rooms are very comfortable and bedrooms, which are being continually upgraded, are well equipped and generally very spacious. There is an indoor heated swimming pool and lake activities can be arranged. Dinner is the highlight of any visit to the Beech Hill and the daily-changing menu together with the newly added carte presents innovative and carefully cooked dishes.

ROOMS: 57 en suite (bth/shr) (4 fmly) s £62-£82; d £52-£72 (incl. bkfst) * LB Off peak **MEALS:** Lunch £11.95-£12.95 Dinner £27 English & French Cuisine V meals Coffee am Tea pm **FACILITIES:** CTV in all bedrooms Indoor swimming pool (heated) Fishing Sauna Solarium Wkly live entertainment Xmas **CONF:** Thtr 80 Class 50 Board 40 Del from £105 * **SERVICES:** 70P **NOTES:** No smoking in restaurant Last d 9.30pm **CARDS:**

WINDERMERE Cumbria **Map 07 SD49**

★★★ Burn How Garden House Hotel

Back Belsfield Rd, Bowness LA23 3HH

Quality Percentage Score: 72%

☎ 015394 46226 015394 47000

Dir: *200mtrs S of Bowness Bay*

A short walk from the lakeside and town centre this hotel nestles in leafy woodland. Accommodation is spacious, well furnished and soundly equipped. Rooms are available in a nearby Victorian house and chalet-style rooms along the main drive. The attractive

contd.

lounges, bar, and elegant restaurant offer panoramic views of the surrounding area. Daily-changing menus employ fresh local produce and the cooking has both flair and imagination.

ROOMS: 26 annexe en suite (bth/shr) (10 fmly) s £38-£75; d £70-£92 (incl. bkfst) * LB Off peak **MEALS:** Lunch £5-£10alc Dinner £13.50-£21.50 English & French Cuisine V meals Coffee am **FACILITIES:** CTV in all bedrooms Water sports Xmas **SERVICES:** 30P **NOTES:** No dogs (ex guide dogs) No coaches No smoking in restaurant Last d 8.30pm
CARDS:

See advert on this page

WINDERMERE Cumbria **Map 07 SD49**
★★★ *Wild Boar*
Crook LA23 3NF
Quality Percentage Score: 68%
☎ 015394 45225 015394 42498
Dir: *2.5m S of Windermere on B5284 Crook road. From rdbt where A591, A5284 & B5284 intersect take B5284 to Crook. Continue for 3.5m, hotel is on right*

This former coaching inn lies in the peaceful Winster Valley mid-way between Kendal and Windermere. The hotel has been extended over the years and the comfortable bedrooms provide a wide range of modern facilities. An extensive choice is available on the dinner menu.

ROOMS: 36 en suite (bth/shr) (3 fmly) No smoking in 6 bedrooms **MEALS:** English & French Cuisine V meals Coffee am Tea pm **FACILITIES:** CTV in all bedrooms STV Use of leisure facilities at sister hotel whilst in residence. **CONF:** Thtr 40 Class 20 Board 26 **SERVICES:** 60P **NOTES:** No smoking in restaurant Last d 9.15pm
CARDS:

WINDERMERE Cumbria **Map 07 SD49**
★★★ Burnside
Kendal Rd, Bowness LA23 3EP
Quality Percentage Score: 67%
☎ 015394 42211 015394 43824
Dir: *from M6 junct 36 follow A590 signs to Lakeside Steamers or follow A591 for Bowness and Ambleside. Hotel is 300 yds past steamer pier on the left*

A contemporary complex with well-tended gardens and views to the lake. At its heart is a Victorian house, extended to include comfortably furnished lounges, restaurants and spacious modern bedrooms. There is a wide range of conference and leisure facilities.

ROOMS: 57 en suite (bth/shr) (15 fmly) No smoking in 18 bedrooms s £90; d £106-£235 (incl. bkfst) * LB Off peak **MEALS:** Sunday Lunch £9.50 High tea £6.50-£8 Dinner £18-£24 & alc V meals Coffee am Tea pm **FACILITIES:** CTV in all bedrooms Indoor swimming pool (heated) Squash Snooker Sauna Solarium Gym Jacuzzi/spa Steam room Badminton Beauty salon Wkly live entertainment Xmas **CONF:** Thtr 100 Class 70 Board 38 Del from £75 * **SERVICES:** Lift Night porter 100P **NOTES:** No smoking in restaurant Last d 9.45pm
CARDS:

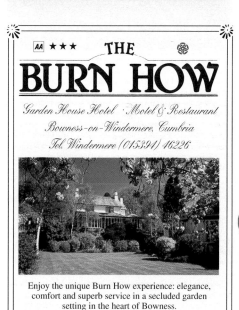

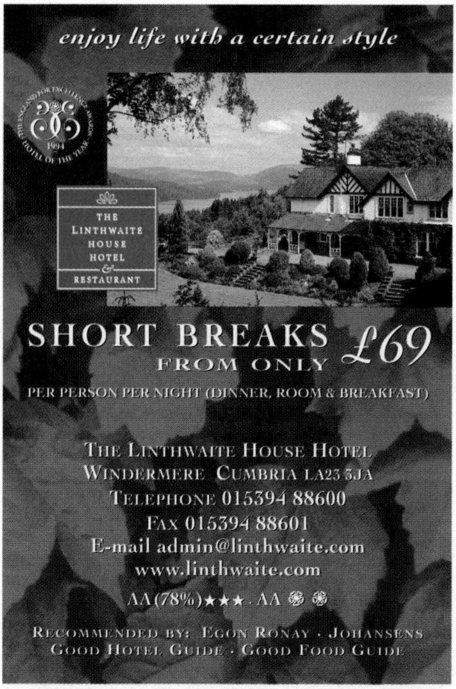

WINDERMERE Cumbria — Map 07 SD49

★★★ *Craig Manor*

Lake Rd LA23 3AR

Quality Percentage Score: 66%

☎ 015394 88877 Fax 015394 88878

Dir: *A590 to Windermere, then A591 into Windermere, turn left at Windermere hotel go through village, pass Magistrates court, hotel is on left*

Just north of Bowness town centre, and five minutes walk from the lake, the hotel is a converted Victorian house with smartly furnished bedrooms and stylish day rooms, consisting of a restaurant, lounge bar and a choice of sitting rooms with splendid Lakeland views.

ROOMS: 16 en suite (bth/shr) **MEALS:** French & English Cuisine V meals Coffee am Tea pm **FACILITIES:** CTV in all bedrooms Pool table Table tennis **SERVICES:** 70P **NOTES:** No coaches No smoking in restaurant Last d 9.30pm **CARDS:**

WINDERMERE Cumbria — Map 07 SD49

★★★ *Langdale Chase*

Langdale Chase Hotel LA23 1LW

Quality Percentage Score: 66%

☎ 015394 32201 Fax 015394 32604

Dir: *2m S of Ambleside and 3m N of Windermere*

A country mansion in a picturesque setting amid colourful terraced gardens running down to the lake. Inside, the public areas have carved fireplaces, oak panelling, and a galleried staircase. The lounges offer lovely views of Lake Windermere, along with the restaurant, and most of the spacious bedrooms.

ROOMS: 29 en suite (bth/shr) (1 fmly) **MEALS:** English & French Cuisine V meals Coffee am Tea pm **FACILITIES:** CTV in 30 bedrooms Tennis (grass) Fishing Croquet lawn Putting green Sailing boats **CONF:** Thtr 25 Class 16 Board 20 Del from £90 * **SERVICES:** Night porter 50P **NOTES:** No coaches No smoking in restaurant Last d 9.30pm **CARDS:**

See advert on opposite page

WINDERMERE Cumbria — Map 07 SD49

★★★ The Old England

Church St, Bowness LA23 3DF

Quality Percentage Score: 66%

☎ 015394 42444 Fax 015394 43432

Dir: *M6 junct 36- follow signs for Windermere. Continue through Windermere town centre to Bowness. Hotel is behind St Martins Church near pier*

An elegant former Georgian country house with lake-front views and access to Bowness. Stylish, comfortable bedrooms have modern facilities. Several rooms in a more modern wing are well equipped and comfortable. The Vinand Restaurant is noted for imaginative cuisine, with a pianist some evenings. There is an outdoor heated swimming pool, banqueting and function suites.

ROOMS: 76 en suite (bth/shr) (8 fmly) No smoking in 26 bedrooms s £70-£100; d £140-£200 (incl. bkfst & dinner) * LB Off peak **MEALS:** Lunch £13-£15 Dinner £20-£25 V meals Coffee am Tea pm **FACILITIES:** CTV in all bedrooms Outdoor swimming pool (heated) Snooker Wkly live entertainment Xmas **CONF:** Thtr 140 Class 50 Board 42 Del from £75 * **SERVICES:** Lift Night porter 82P **NOTES:** No smoking in restaurant Last d 9.15pm **CARDS:**

WINDERMERE Cumbria — Map 07 SD49

★★★ Low Wood

LA23 1LP

Quality Percentage Score: 65%

☎ 015394 33338 Fax 015394 34072

Dir: *M6 junct 36, follow A590 then A591 to Windermere, continue along A591 for 3m towards Ambleside, hotel is situated on the right hand side*

This popular hotel has excellent leisure and conference facilities, and enjoys stunning views of Lake Windermere and the fells beyond. The modern bedrooms are well equipped and come in a variety of sizes. Guests can make use of the hotels water sports centre, learn how to water ski or simply just enjoy a high speed jaunt around the lake in a speed boat. Cooking in the Windemere restaurant is skilled and accomplished.

ROOMS: 117 en suite (bth/shr) (13 fmly) No smoking in 18 bedrooms s £60; d £120-£140 (incl. bkfst) * LB Off peak **MEALS:** Sunday Lunch £9.50-£12.50 Dinner £23 & alc English & French Cuisine V meals Coffee am Tea pm **FACILITIES:** CTV in all bedrooms STV Indoor swimming pool (heated) Fishing Squash Snooker Sauna Solarium Gym Pool table Croquet lawn Putting green Jacuzzi/spa Water skiing Sub aqua diving Windsurfing Canoeing Laser clay pigeon shooting Wkly live entertainment Xmas **CONF:** Thtr 340 Class 180 Board 150 Del from £98 * **SERVICES:** Lift Night porter 200P **NOTES:** No smoking in restaurant Last d 9.30pm **CARDS:**

WINDERMERE Cumbria — Map 07 SD49

★★★ Belsfield

Kendal Rd, Bowness LA23 3EL

Quality Percentage Score: 64%

☎ 015394 42448 Fax 015394 46397

Dir: *from M6 junct 36 follow Windermere signs take 1st left into Windermere follow Bowness signs & the lake. In Bowness take 1st left after Royal Hotel*

The hotel stands in six acres of gardens, many of its rooms look over a lake. Bedrooms are comfortable and guests have a choice

contd.

of lounges. Meals are served in the Chandelier Restaurant and there are good leisure facilities.
ROOMS: 64 en suite (bth/shr) (6 fmly) No smoking in 17 bedrooms s £65-£85; d £130-£160 (incl. bkfst & dinner) * LB Off peak **MEALS:** Bar Lunch £2.50-£6.95 Dinner £15.95 V meals Coffee am Tea pm **FACILITIES:** CTV in all bedrooms Indoor swimming pool (heated) Snooker Sauna Solarium Putting green Mini golf - Pitch & Putt 9 holes Wkly live entertainment Xmas **CONF:** Thtr 130 Class 60 Board 50 Del from £90 * **SERVICES:** Lift Night porter 64P **NOTES:** No smoking in restaurant Last d 9.30pm **CARDS:**

WINDERMERE Cumbria **Map 07 SD49**

The Premier Collection

★★ Miller Howe
Rayrigg Rd LA23 1EY
☎ 015394 42536 015394 45664
Dir: *on A592 between Bowness & Windermere*
A popular hotel with a real flavour of the Lake District. The delightfully furnished bedrooms are generally spacious and share the wonderful views from the inviting lounges and the dining room, where many guests find themselves concentrating instead on the carefully prepared meals.
ROOMS: 12 en suite (bth/shr) d £80-£125 (incl. bkfst & dinner) * LB Off peak **MEALS:** Lunch £15-£18.50 Dinner fr £35 V meals Coffee am Tea pm **FACILITIES:** CTV in all bedrooms Wkly live entertainment Xmas **SERVICES:** 40P **NOTES:** No coaches No children 8yrs No smoking in restaurant Last d 8pm Closed 3 Jan-10 Feb **CARDS:**

WINDERMERE Cumbria **Map 07 SD49**
★★ Lindeth Fell
Lyth Valley Rd, Bowness LA23 3JP
Quality Percentage Score: 77%
☎ 015394 43286 & 44287 015394 47455
Dir: *1m South of Bowness on A5074*
Enjoying delightful views over the lake and fells, this smart Edwardian residence stands in glorious gardens just a short walk

contd.

Indicates that the star classification has not been confirmed under the New Quality Standards, see page 7 for further information.

from the town. The comfortable bedrooms vary in style and size, while skilfully prepared dinners are served in the dining room.

Lindeth Fell, Windermere

ROOMS: 15 en suite (bth/shr) (2 fmly) s £65-£80; d £130-£160 (incl. bkfst & dinner) * LB Off peak **MEALS:** Sunday Lunch £9.50-£15 Dinner £14-£19 English & French Cuisine V meals Coffee am Tea pm **FACILITIES:** CTV in all bedrooms Tennis Fishing Croquet lawn Putting green Bowling Green Xmas **CONF:** Board 12 Del from £87.50 * **SERVICES:** 20P **NOTES:** No dogs No coaches No smoking in restaurant Last d 8.30pm 3 Jan-14 Feb **CARDS:**

See advert on page 713

WINDERMERE Cumbria **Map 07 SD49**

★★ Cedar Manor Hotel & Restaurant

Ambleside Rd LA23 1AX
Quality Percentage Score: 76%
☎ 015394 43192 015394 45970
Dir: *0.25m N on A591 by St Marys Church*

Cedar Manor was built in 1860, and a number of original architectural features still remain in the public rooms. Bedrooms, some of which are contained in a new wing, or a pretty little cottage to the back, are bright and well equipped. The imaginative menu offered here contains an appetizing choice from a table d'hôte menu.

ROOMS: 10 en suite (bth/shr) 2 annexe en suite (bth/shr) (4 fmly) s £30-£51; d £60-£82 (incl. bkfst) * LB Off peak **MEALS:** Dinner £13-£18.50 & alc English, French & Italian Cuisine V meals Coffee am Tea pm **FACILITIES:** CTV in all bedrooms Private arrangements nearby free of charge to guests eg pool, sauna, solarium Xmas **SERVICES:** 15P **NOTES:** No coaches No smoking in restaurant Last d 8.30pm
CARDS:

WINDERMERE Cumbria **Map 07 SD49**

★★ Fayrer Garden House

Lyth Valley Rd, Bowness on Windermere LA23 3JP
Quality Percentage Score: 75%
☎ 015394 88195 015394 45986
Dir: *on A5074 1m from Bowness Bay*

THE CIRCLE
Selected Individual Hotels
GREAT BRITAIN

Located high above the lake and away from the hubbub of Bowness, this turn-of-the-century residence continues to be a popular destination for tourists and business guests alike. Elegant public rooms include a welcoming panelled hall which leads into a cosy sitting room and a richly furnished conservatory restaurant. The appealing bedrooms are stylishly furnished. A friendly atmosphere prevails and the cuisine shows ambitious flair and imagination.

ROOMS: 18 en suite (bth/shr) (3 fmly) s £59-£95; d £118.50-£195 (incl. bkfst & dinner) * LB Off peak **MEALS:** Dinner £24-£29.50 & alc V meals Coffee am Tea pm **FACILITIES:** CTV in all bedrooms STV Fishing Free membership of leisure club Xmas **SERVICES:** 25P **NOTES:** No dogs No coaches No smoking in restaurant Last d 8.30pm
CARDS:

See advert on opposite page

WINDERMERE Cumbria **Map 07 SD49**

★★ *Quarry Garth Country House Hotel & Restaurant*

Troutbeck Bridge LA23 1LF
Quality Percentage Score: 72%
☎ 015394 88282 015394 46584
Dir: *on A591*

THE CIRCLE
Selected Individual Hotels
GREAT BRITAIN

A smart country house hotel in a lovely woodland setting. Public areas are very comfortable and the restaurant is the perfect setting for many ambitious dishes. Bedrooms are richly furnished and come in two sizes; spacious master rooms and the smaller cottage-style rooms. A further three rooms are situated in a picturesque lodge in the grounds.

ROOMS: 11 en suite (bth/shr) (2 fmly) No smoking in all bedrooms **MEALS:** English & Continental Cuisine V meals Coffee am Tea pm **FACILITIES:** CTV in all bedrooms Croquet lawn Putting green Woodland walks **CONF:** Thtr 20 Class 20 Board 20 **SERVICES:** 35P **NOTES:** No coaches No smoking in restaurant Last d 9.15pm
CARDS:

See advert on opposite page

WINDERMERE Cumbria **Map 07 SD49**

★★ Glenburn

New Rd LA23 2EE
Quality Percentage Score: 68%
☎ 015394 42649 015394 88998
Dir: *M6 junct 36, 16m to Windermere A591, through Windermere village, go past shops and the hotel is 500yds along on the left hand side*

Located between Windermere and Bowness, this family-run hotel is set in attractive surroundings. The stylish bedrooms come in a variety of sizes and are well equipped. A smart new reception has enhanced the interior. Dinner in the attractive dining room is available from 6.30pm.

ROOMS: 16 en suite (bth/shr) (4 fmly) No smoking in all bedrooms d £56-£75 (incl. bkfst) LB Off peak **MEALS:** V meals Coffee am Tea pm **FACILITIES:** CTV in all bedrooms **SERVICES:** 17P **NOTES:** No dogs (ex guide dogs) No coaches No children 5yrs No smoking in restaurant
CARDS:

WINDERMERE Cumbria **Map 07 SD49**

★★ Hideaway

Phoenix Way LA23 1DB
Quality Percentage Score: 67%
☎ 015394 43070 015394 48664
Dir: *turn left off A591 at the Ravenswood Hotel into Phoenix Way. Hideaway Hotel is situated 100yds down the hill on the right hand side*

This welcoming family run hotel has a secluded location a short walk from the town centre. Bedrooms, some in a separate building across the courtyard, are individually furnished, with four poster and family rooms available. Good home cooked

contd.

W

meals are served in the dining room, there is a cosy bar and inviting lounge.

ROOMS: 10 en suite (bth/shr) 5 annexe en suite (bth/shr) (3 fmly) s £51-£58; d £88-£140 (incl. bkfst & dinner) * LB Off peak **MEALS:** Bar Lunch £2.50-£9alc Dinner fr £17.50 & alc English & Continental Cuisine V meals Coffee am Tea pm **FACILITIES:** CTV in all bedrooms Free use of nearby leisure facilities Xmas **SERVICES:** 16P **NOTES:** No coaches No smoking in restaurant Last d 8.30pm Closed 3-31 Jan
CARDS:

See advert on this page

Remember to return your Prize Draw card for a chance to win one of 30 relaxing leisure breaks with Corus and Regal hotels. See inside the front cover for the card and competition details.

WINDERMERE Cumbria **Map 07 SD49**
★★ Lindeth Howe Country House
Longtail Hill LA23 3JF
Quality Percentage Score: 67%
☎ 015394 45759 015394 46368
Dir: *turn off A592 onto B5284 (Longtail Hill), hotel is the last driveway on the right hand side*
Once the home of Beatrix Potter, this delightful country house lies in six acres of secluded woodland and gardens, with wonderful views of Lake Windermere and the distant fells beyond. There is a choice of bedroom size; all rooms are comfortable and thoughtfully equipped. Dinner, which earns our one Rosette award, is a pleasing highlight.
ROOMS: 37 en suite (bth/shr) (3 fmly) No smoking in 25 bedrooms s £52.50-£67.50; d £85-£135 (incl. bkfst) * LB Off peak **MEALS:** Sunday Lunch £10.95-£12.50 Dinner £19.50-£24.50 & alc V meals Coffee am Tea pm **FACILITIES:** CTV in all bedrooms Indoor swimming pool (heated) Sauna Solarium Use of adjacent leisure club Xmas **CONF:** Thtr 30 Class 20 Board 18 **SERVICES:** 50P **NOTES:** No dogs (ex guide dogs) No coaches No smoking in restaurant Last d 8.30pm
CARDS:

WINDERMERE Cumbria **Map 07 SD49**
★★ Ravensworth
Ambleside Rd LA23 1BA
Quality Percentage Score: 67%
☎ 015394 43747 015394 43903
Dir: *M6 junct 36, take A590/A591 and travel for 16m into Windermere, hotel is on the left hand side of road*
A very welcoming Victorian hotel situated on the A591. Guests have use of a lounge and a small bar, and evening meals are served in the attractive conservatory restaurant. Bedrooms (including family and four-poster rooms) are modern in style and vary in size, but all are well equipped and comfortable. Two ground floor rooms have their own patios.
ROOMS: 12 en suite (bth/shr) 2 annexe en suite (bth/shr) (1 fmly) s £24.50-£36.50; d £49-£73 (incl. bkfst) * LB Off peak **MEALS:** Dinner £13.95-£20alc English & French Cuisine V meals Coffee am **FACILITIES:** CTV in all bedrooms STV Membership of local Leisure Club Xmas **SERVICES:** 17P **NOTES:** No coaches No smoking in restaurant Last d 8pm **CARDS:**

WINDERMERE Cumbria **Map 07 SD49**
★★ Cranleigh
Kendal Rd, Bowness on Windermere LA23 3EW
Quality Percentage Score: 64%
☎ 015394 43293 015394 47283
Dir: *turn off Lake Road, opposite St Martin's church and continue along Kendal Road for 150mts*
Within walking distance of the town centre, this welcoming, traditional hotel offers a choice of lounges and an attractive dining room which serves a tempting dinner menu. The bedrooms are very pleasant with a few rooms located in a nearby building.
ROOMS: 9 en suite (bth/shr) 6 annexe en suite (bth/shr) (3 fmly) s £35-£57; d £52-£90 (incl. bkfst) * LB Off peak **MEALS:** Bar Lunch £8-£10alc High tea £10.95-£15 & alc Dinner £10.95-£15 & alc European Cuisine V meals Coffee am Tea pm **FACILITIES:** CTV in all bedrooms Free membership of leisure club **SERVICES:** 17P **NOTES:** No dogs (ex guide dogs) No smoking in restaurant Last d 8.30pm **CARDS:**

W

WINDERMERE Cumbria **Map 07 SD49**
★ Willowsmere
Ambleside Rd LA23 1ES
Quality Percentage Score: 65%
☎ 015394 43575 & 44962 015394 44962
Dir: *stay on A591, just past St Marys Church*
Good all-round standards of comfort are provided at this friendly, family-run hotel. Bedrooms vary in size, but all have their own bathrooms. The lounges are particularly comfortable and guests can enjoy good home cooking in the attractive dining room.
ROOMS: 13 en suite (bth/shr) (7 fmly) s £25-£32; d £50-£64 (incl. bkfst) * LB Off peak **MEALS:** Dinner £12.50-£14.50 English & Austrian Cuisine V meals Coffee am Tea pm **FACILITIES:** CTV in all bedrooms **CONF:** **SERVICES:** 20P **NOTES:** No coaches No smoking in restaurant Last d 8pm Closed Nov-Feb RS Dec-Jan
CARDS:

WINDSOR Berkshire **Map 04 SU97**
★★★★ Oakley Court
Windsor Rd, Water Oakley SL4 5UR
Quality Percentage Score: 75%
☎ 01753 609988 01628 637011
Dir: *leave M4 junct 6, head for Windsor, then right onto A308 Maidenhead. Pass racecourse & hotel is 2.5m on right*

This stately, extended Gothic Victorian mansion is enviably situated in extensive grounds leading down to the Thames, where boating trips can be arranged. Stylish public rooms are comfortable and there are a number of useful conference suites. In this main building all the spacious, beautifully furnished rooms enjoy river views, as do a number of rooms in an annexed wing. A further wing was recently completed, boasting deluxe rooms with air-conditioning, and a leisure complex. There are two restaurants under the control of chef Murdo MacSween; Le Boulestin specialises in modern English and French cuisine, and Boaters Brasserie offers lighter meals.
ROOMS: 63 en suite (bth/shr) 52 annexe en suite (bth/shr) No smoking in 45 bedrooms s fr £175; d fr £200 * LB Off peak **MEALS:** Lunch £23.50-£24.50 High tea fr £13.50 Dinner fr £29.50 English & French Cuisine V meals Coffee am Tea pm **FACILITIES:** CTV in all bedrooms STV Indoor swimming pool (heated) Golf 9 Fishing Snooker Sauna Solarium Gym Croquet lawn Jacuzzi/spa Boating Wkly live entertainment Xmas **CONF:** Thtr 160 Class 100 Board 48 **SERVICES:** Night porter 120P **NOTES:** No dogs (ex guide dogs) No smoking in restaurant Last d 9.45pm **CARDS:**

We endeavour to be as accurate as possible but changes in personnel and data can occur in establishments after the Hotel Guide has gone to press.

WINDSOR Berkshire — Map 04 SU97

★★★ The Castle

High St SL4 1LJ
Quality Percentage Score: 68%
☎ 01753 851011 Fax 01753 830244

***Dir:** M4 junct 6/M25 junct 15-follow signs to Windsor town centre and castle. Hotel located at the top of hill by the castle opposite the Guildhall*

Situated in the shadow of Windsor Castle, this hotel is popular with tourists, but also offers strong conference and banqueting services. Bedrooms in the older main building have been tastefully modernised and are traditionally furnished in keeping with the style of the property, whilst the mews boasts splendid executive rooms, all very well equipped. The elegant restaurant serves innovative British cooking, and there is also a less formal café offering a bistro and snack service. The lounge is an attractive venue for afternoon tea and there is a small open-plan bar.

ROOMS: 111 en suite (bth/shr) (26 fmly) No smoking in 32 bedrooms s £135; d £155 * LB Off peak **MEALS:** Lunch £9-£30alc Dinner £9-£30alc English & Continental Cuisine V meals Coffee am Tea pm **FACILITIES:** CTV in all bedrooms STV Xmas **CONF:** Thtr 370 Class 155 Board 80 Del from £175 * **SERVICES:** Lift Night porter 156P **NOTES:** No smoking in restaurant Last d 10pm **CARDS:**

WINDSOR Berkshire — Map 04 SU97

★★★ *Christopher Hotel*

110 High St, Eton SL4 6AN
Quality Percentage Score: 68%
☎ 01753 852359 & 811677 Fax 01753 830914

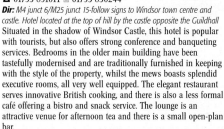

This 16th-century hotel, with modern extension to the rear, is located in the heart of the famous town of Eton. The front of the building is divided equally between a traditional pub and an informal French-style bistro. Bedrooms are comfortable and quiet with good facilities.

ROOMS: 11 en suite (bth/shr) 22 annexe en suite (bth/shr) No smoking in 21 bedrooms **MEALS:** International Cuisine V meals Coffee am Tea pm **FACILITIES:** CTV in all bedrooms **CONF:** Thtr 40 Class 40 Board 28 **SERVICES:** 23P **NOTES:** No smoking area in restaurant Last d 9.30pm **CARDS:**

WINDSOR Berkshire — Map 04 SU97

★★★ Ye Harte & Garter

High St SL4 1PH
Quality Percentage Score: 65%
☎ 01753 863426 Fax 01753 830527

***Dir:** in town centre opposite front entrance to Windsor Castle*

Located in the heart of Windsor, close to the Castle, which can be seen from many of the bedrooms, this inn is an extended and modernised Victorian building. There is a choice of bars serving a range of informal meals, and there is also a separate restaurant with a full menu.

ROOMS: 42 en suite (bth/shr) (4 fmly) s £90-£125; d £100-£180 * LB Off peak **MEALS:** Lunch £4.95-£9.95 & alc High tea fr £4.95 Dinner £4.95-£9.95 & alc International Cuisine V meals Coffee am Tea pm **FACILITIES:** CTV in all bedrooms STV Pool table Wkly live entertainment **CONF:** Thtr 300 Class 150 Board 80 Del from £145 * **SERVICES:** Lift Night porter **NOTES:** No dogs (ex guide dogs) No smoking area in restaurant Last d 9.30pm **CARDS:**

Symbols and Abbreviations are listed and explained on pages 4 and 5

W

WINDSOR Berkshire **Map 04 SU97**

★★ **Aurora Garden**

Bolton Av SL4 3JF

Quality Percentage Score: 75%

☎ 01753 868686 01753 831394

Dir: *take junct 6 M4 onto the A332 for Windsor. At first rdbt, second exit towards Staines. At third rdbt third exit for 500yds. Hotel is on right*

A naturally welcoming and friendly atmosphere characterizes this privately run hotel. Located in a quiet residential neighbourhood, close to Windsor park and half a mile or so from town. The landscaped water gardens and patio are enjoyed by guests throughout the year. The restaurant, which overlooks the garden, provides a wide choice of cuisine at dinner. Breakfast is a hearty affair, the cold buffet is particularly good. Bedrooms offer many extras including cable TV.

ROOMS: 19 en suite (bth/shr) (7 fmly) s fr £80; d fr £100 (incl. bkfst) * LB Off peak **MEALS:** Lunch £5-£11.95 High tea fr £6.95 Dinner £13.95-£15.95 & alc English & French Cuisine V meals Coffee am Tea pm **FACILITIES:** CTV in all bedrooms STV **CONF:** Thtr 90 Class 30 Board 25 Del from £120 * **SERVICES:** 25P **NOTES:** No smoking in restaurant Last d 9.30pm **CARDS:**

See advert on page 717

WINDSOR Berkshire **Map 04 SU97**

Late entry **Sir Christopher Wren's House Hotel**

Thames St SL4 1PX

☎ 01753 861354 01753 860172

An authentic hotel with views over the River Thames. Public areas are comfortable, lounge space is plentiful and the restaurant and terrace enjoy river views. Bedrooms are very well equipped, and offer a wide choice of room sizes, some of which have private courtyards overlooking the Thames.

ROOMS: 70 en suite (bth/shr) (11 fmly) No smoking in 40 bedrooms s £99-£125; d £135-£165 * LB Off peak **MEALS:** Lunch £14.50-£21 & alc High tea £12.50 Dinner £18.50-£23 V meals Coffee am Tea pm **FACILITIES:** CTV in all bedrooms STV Xmas **CONF:** Thtr 120 Class 70 Board 50 Del from £170 * **SERVICES:** Night porter 30P **NOTES:** No dogs (ex guide dogs) Last d 9.30pm

CARDS:

WINDSOR Berkshire **Map 04 SU97**

Late entry ***Royal Adelaide***

46 Kings Rd SL4 2AG

☎ 01753 863916 01753 830682

An elegant Georgian property sporting a fully refurbished interior which overlooks the Long Walk running from Windsor Castle to Virginia Water. Public areas include a bar/reception lounge and an informal restaurant serving à la carte and table d'hôte menus. Bedrooms are tastefully decorated and furnished.

ROOMS: 39 en suite (bth/shr) (1 fmly) **MEALS:** English & French Cuisine V meals Coffee am **FACILITIES:** CTV in all bedrooms **SERVICES:** Night porter 30P **NOTES:** Last d 9.30pm **CARDS:**

W

WINSFORD Somerset **Map 03 SS93**

★★★ **Royal Oak Inn**

Exmoor National Park TA24 7JE

Quality Percentage Score: 70%

☎ 01643 851455 01643 851009

Dir: *N from Tiverton on A396 for 15m then left to Winsford. First turning left on entering village*

Tucked away in the heart of Exmoor, this impressive 12th-century thatched inn offers lively bars. A selection of bar meals are available, complemented by an a la carte menu of traditional old English cuisine. Bedrooms have been restored to retain the charm of the building, while the courtyard rooms are of a simpler, 'cottage' style. A choice of lounges is provided.

ROOMS: 8 en suite (bth/shr) 6 annexe en suite (bth) (1 fmly) d £95-£135 * LB Off peak **MEALS:** V meals Coffee am Tea pm **FACILITIES:** CTV in all bedrooms Fishing Hunting Shooting Xmas **SERVICES:** 23P **NOTES:** Last d 9.15pm **CARDS:**

WINTERINGHAM Lincolnshire **Map 08 SE92**

The Premier Collection

★★ **Winteringham Fields**

DN15 9PF

☎ 01724 733096 01724 733898

Dir: *in the centre of the village at the X-roads*

This delightful hotel is somewhat off the beaten track, but well worth the detour for the excellent quality of the cooking. This is a restaurant-with-rooms and food is very much the focus, with the imaginative menu drawing gourmets from all over the country. The bedrooms are very comfortable, and some are in a building in the village.

ROOMS: 4 en suite (bth/shr) 6 annexe en suite (bth/shr) No smoking in all bedrooms s £70-£89; d £88-£150 (incl. cont bkfst) * Off peak **MEALS:** Lunch £18.50-£22.50 & alc Dinner £29-£54 & alc French & Swiss Cuisine V meals **FACILITIES:** CTV in all bedrooms **SERVICES:** 17P **NOTES:** No coaches No children 8yrs No smoking in restaurant Last d 9.30pm Closed Sun & BH/2wks Xmas/early Aug/late Mar **CARDS:**

WISBECH Cambridgeshire **Map 05 TF40**

★★ **Crown Lodge**

Downham Rd, Outwell PE14 8SE

Quality Percentage Score: 69%

☎ 01945 773391 & 772206 01945 772668

Dir: *on A1122/A1101 approx 5m from Wisbech and 7m from Downham Market*

On the banks of Well Creek in the village of Outwell, this convivial

contd.

hotel is popular with its loyal guests. The well equipped modern accommodation offers good levels of space and comfort, especially suited to the business traveller; the hotel has a convenient conference room as well as numerous leisure facilities. Guests have a wide selection of food, and the restaurant is highly regarded for its cuisine.
ROOMS: 10 en suite (bth/shr) s £45.95-£48.25; d £60.95-£64 (incl. bkfst) * LB Off peak **MEALS:** Lunch £9.95-£13.95 & alc Dinner £13.95-£16.95 & alc International Cuisine V meals Coffee am Tea pm **FACILITIES:** CTV in all bedrooms Squash Snooker Solarium **CONF:** Thtr 50 Class 30 Board 20 **SERVICES:** 57P **NOTES:** No smoking area in restaurant Last d 10.00pm **CARDS:**

WISBECH Cambridgeshire **Map 05 TF40**

★★ *Rose & Crown Hotel*

Market Place PE13 1DG
Quality Percentage Score: 63%
☎ 01945 589800 📠 01945 474610
Dir: *in centre of Wisbech, access from A47 & A1101*
For over 500 years this former hostelry has provided hospitality for adventurers and travellers. The wide range of spacious public rooms includes the Tidnams Tipple Inn, the coffee shop/delicatessen, the traditional Rose Restaurant and several function rooms. Accommodation is modern and comfortable.
ROOMS: 20 en suite (bth/shr) (1 fmly) **MEALS:** International Cuisine V meals Coffee am Tea pm **FACILITIES:** CTV in all bedrooms **CONF:** Thtr 100 Class 60 Board 60 **SERVICES:** 20P **NOTES:** Last d 9.30pm Closed 25-26 Dec **CARDS:**

WISHAW Warwickshire **Map 07 SP19**

★★★★ The Belfry

B76 9PR
DE VERE HOTELS
Quality Percentage Score: 74%
☎ 01675 470301 📠 01675 470256
Dir: *take junct 9 off M42 and follow A446 towards Lichfield, the Belfry is 1m on right*
Well known as a venue for the Ryder Cup, The Belfry, quietly situated close to junction 9 of the M42, offers three golf course amongst the many leisure facilities. The well equipped leisure club includes squash courts and snooker tables, whilst there is also a jogging trail to burn off some of the calories from any of the five restaurants. The dedicated team of staff are friendly and welcoming. Bedrooms vary in size, the best having fine views over the golf course, and a wide range of conference suites and a nightclub complete the package at this busy resort hotel.
ROOMS: 324 en suite (bth/shr) No smoking in 124 bedrooms s £150; d £175 (incl. bkfst) * LB Off peak **MEALS:** Lunch £13.50-£15.95 & alc High tea fr £9.95 Dinner fr £21.95 & alc English & French Cuisine V meals Coffee am Tea pm **FACILITIES:** CTV in all bedrooms STV Indoor swimming pool (heated) Golf 36 Tennis (hard) Squash Snooker Sauna Solarium Gym Putting green Jacuzzi/spa Bel Air night club in grounds Wkly live entertainment Xmas **CONF:** Thtr 400 Class 220 Board 60 Del from £130 * **SERVICES:** Lift Night porter 870P **NOTES:** No smoking area in restaurant Last d 10pm **CARDS:**

WITHERSLACK Cumbria **Map 07 SD48**

The Premier Collection

★ Old Vicarage Country House

Church Rd LA11 6RS
☎ 015395 52381 📠 015395 52373
Dir: *from A590 turn into Witherslack, take left after phone box signposted to the church, continue straight on for 0.75m*
Dating back to 1803, this delightful house retains many of its original features and is surrounded by lush gardens. Bedrooms in the main house are attractively decorated and furnished, with a number of fine antique pieces, while the garden rooms are in modern buildings and are very spacious. There is a choice of two lounges, one with an open log fire, and an intimate restaurant serving satisfying cuisine.

ROOMS: 9 en suite (bth/shr) 5 annexe en suite (bth/shr) (1 fmly) s £65-£85; d £98-£158 (incl. bkfst) * LB Off peak **MEALS:** Sunday Lunch £15.50 Dinner £32.50 V meals Coffee am Tea pm **FACILITIES:** CTV in all bedrooms Tennis (hard) Arrangement with local leisure club Xmas **CONF:** Thtr 12 Class 12 Board 12 Del from £110 * **SERVICES:** 25P **NOTES:** No coaches No smoking in restaurant Last d 9pm **CARDS:**

See advert on this page

W

WITHYPOOL Somerset **Map 03 SS83**

★★ ***Royal Oak Inn***

TA24 7QP

Quality Percentage Score: 72%

☎ 01643 831506 & 831236 📠 01643 831659

Dir: *7m N of Dulverton, off B3223*

Combining the character and charm of a typical village inn with high standards of service and comfort, the Royal Oak Inn will meet most guests' expectations. In addition to the range of bar meals, guests have the choice of either a fixed-price menu or a short carte. Meals are carefully prepared, using as much local produce as possible. Bedrooms are well equipped and all have modern facilities. The bars are popular meeting places for both locals and visitors alike.

ROOMS: 8 rms (7 bth) **MEALS:** V meals Coffee am Tea pm **FACILITIES:** CTV in all bedrooms Riding Shooting **SERVICES:** 20P **NOTES:** No coaches RS 25 & 26 Dec **CARDS:**

WITNEY Oxfordshire **Map 04 SP30**

★★★ **Witney Four Pillars Hotel**

Ducklington Ln OX8 7TJ

Quality Percentage Score: 70%

☎ 01993 779777 📠 01993 703467

FOUR PILLARS HOTELS

Dir: *M40 off junc 9, A34 to A40, exit A415 Witney/Abingdon, Hotel on left, second exit for Witney*

This smart modern hotel offers well equipped rooms. There is a popular restaurant which operates a carvery on certain evenings. Facilities include a swimming pool, gym and sauna.

ROOMS: 74 en suite (bth/shr) (10 fmly) No smoking in 16 bedrooms s £66-£80; d £77-£90 * LB Off peak **MEALS:** Lunch £7.95-£12.95 Dinner £14.25-£15.95 & alc V meals Coffee am Tea pm **FACILITIES:** CTV in all bedrooms STV Indoor swimming pool (heated) Snooker Sauna Solarium Gym Jacuzzi/spa Whirlpool spa Wkly live entertainment Xmas **CONF:** Thtr 160 Class 80 Board 46 Del £130 * **SERVICES:** Night porter Air conditioning 170P **NOTES:** No smoking area in restaurant Last d 10pm **CARDS:**

WIVELISCOMBE Somerset **Map 03 ST02**

The Premier Collection

★★ **Langley House**

Langley Marsh TA4 2UF

☎ 01984 623318 📠 01984 624573

Dir: *follow signs to Wiveliscombe town centre, turn right at town centre. Hotel 0.5m on right*

Parts of Langley House date back to the 16th century, while later additions add Georgian elegance. Over the last twelve years Peter and Annie Wilson have lovingly restored and refurbished the property, including the four acre garden. There are deep armchairs in the boldly decorated sitting room where a log fire burns on colder evenings. Bedrooms vary in size and design, but all have thoughtful touches including fresh flowers, books, mineral water and hot water bottles in winter. Mr Wilson's set menu continues to please guests and makes use of the best of fresh and, whenever possible, local ingredients.

ROOMS: 8 en suite (bth/shr) (1 fmly) No smoking in 2 bedrooms s £75-£82.50; d £95-£127.50 (incl. bkfst) * LB Off peak **MEALS:** Dinner £26.50-£32.50 Coffee am Tea pm **FACILITIES:** CTV in all bedrooms Croquet lawn ch fac Xmas **SERVICES:** 20P **NOTES:** No coaches No smoking in restaurant Last d 8.30pm **CARDS:**

WOBURN Bedfordshire **Map 04 SP93**

★★★ ***Thistle Bedford Arms Woburn***

George St MK17 9PX

Quality Percentage Score: 70%

☎ 01525 290441 📠 290432

Dir: *off M1 junc 13, left to Woburn, at Woburn left at T-junc, hotel in village*

This former inn has been nicely refurbished and now provides high standard accommodation. Bedrooms are divided between the original house and a modern extension. A good choice of imaginatively described dishes is available in the restaurant, and guests may enjoy a drink either in the cocktail bar or the beamed Tavistock bar.

ROOMS: 53 en suite (bth/shr) (4 fmly) No smoking in 10 bedrooms **MEALS:** International Cuisine V meals Coffee am Tea pm **FACILITIES:** CTV in all bedrooms STV **CONF:** Thtr 60 Class 40 Board 40 **SERVICES:** Night porter 80P **NOTES:** No dogs (ex guide dogs) Last d 10pm **CARDS:**

WOKING Surrey **Map 04 TQ05**

⌂ **Travel Inn**

Bridge Barn Ln, Horsell GU21 1NL

☎ 01483 763642 📠 01483 771735

This modern building offers accommodation in smart, spacious and well equipped bedrooms, all with en-suite bathrooms. Refreshments may be taken at the nearby family restaurant. For details about current prices consult the Contents Page under Hotel Groups for the Travel Inn phone number.

ROOMS: 34 en suite (bth/shr) d £39.95 *

WOKINGHAM Berkshire **Map 04 SU86**

★★★★ **Reading Moat House**

Mill Ln, Sindlesham RG41 5DF

Quality Percentage Score: 64%

☎ 0118 949 9988 📠 0118 966 6530

Dir: *head towards Reading on the A329(m) to Winnersh, Woodley & Garley. Follow signs to Lower Garley. Hotel is located on the L hand side.*

In a pleasing out-of-town setting between Reading and Wokingham, this smart, modern hotel has been sympathetically built around an 18th-century mill house, which now houses the hotel pub. Additional facilities include good conference rooms, a business centre and a small leisure complex. The well-maintained bedrooms, many overlooking the small river, all offer good facilities.

ROOMS: 100 en suite (bth/shr) (10 fmly) No smoking in 53 bedrooms s £135; d £150 * LB Off peak **MEALS:** Lunch £18.95-£25 Dinner £18.95-£25 International Cuisine V meals Coffee am Tea pm **FACILITIES:** CTV in all bedrooms Fishing Sauna Gym Steam room, Nightclub Xmas **CONF:** Thtr 80 Class 50 Board 40 **SERVICES:** Lift Night porter 350P **NOTES:** No smoking in restaurant Last d 10.30pm **CARDS:**

W

WOLVERHAMPTON West Midlands — Map 07 SO99
see also **Himley & Worfield**

★★★ Quality Hotel Wolverhampton
Penn Rd WV3 0ER
Quality Percentage Score: 64%
☎ 01902 429216 Fax 01902 710419
Dir: *on A449, Wolverhampton to Kidderminster, 0.25m from ring road on right, opposite Safeway super market*
The original Victorian house has been considerably extended to create a large, busy and popular hotel. Some of the impressive features in the original part remain, and include ornately carved woodwork and ceilings. The well equipped accommodation features rooms with four-poster beds and bedrooms for non smokers. The pleasant public areas have a lot of character and offer a choice of bars. Other facilities include a leisure club with an indoor swimming pool, a business centre, and conference rooms for up to 140 people.
ROOMS: 66 en suite (bth/shr) 26 annexe en suite (bth/shr) (1 fmly) No smoking in 46 bedrooms s £79-£89; d fr £105 * LB Off peak **MEALS:** Dinner fr £16.95 English & French Cuisine V meals Coffee am Tea pm **FACILITIES:** CTV in all bedrooms STV Indoor swimming pool (heated) Sauna Gym Steam room Xmas **CONF:** Thtr 140 Class 70 Board 40 **SERVICES:** Night porter 120P **NOTES:** No dogs (ex guide dogs) No smoking in restaurant Last d 9.30pm
CARDS:

WOLVERHAMPTON West Midlands — Map 07 SO99

★★★ Novotel
Union St WV1 3JN
Quality Percentage Score: 62%
☎ 01902 871100 Fax 01902 870054
Dir: *6m from jct10 of M6. Following Black Country route. Take A454 to Wolverhampton. Hotel is situated on the main ring road*
This large, modern, purpose built hotel stands in the town centre, close to the ring road. It provides well equipped, spacious accommodation and all the bedrooms contain convertible bed settees for family occupancy. In addition to the open plan lounge and bar area, there is a pleasant brasserie style restaurant, which overlooks the small outdoor swimming pool.
ROOMS: 132 en suite (bth/shr) (10 fmly) No smoking in 88 bedrooms d £70-£80 * LB Off peak **MEALS:** Lunch £12-£15 & alc Dinner £15-£17 & alc International Cuisine V meals Coffee am **FACILITIES:** CTV in all bedrooms STV Outdoor swimming pool (heated) Pool table **CONF:** Thtr 200 Class 100 Board 80 Del from £100 * **SERVICES:** Lift Night porter 120P **NOTES:** No smoking area in restaurant Last d midnght
CARDS:

WOLVERHAMPTON West Midlands — Map 07 SO99

★★★ Park Hall Hotel
Park Dr, Goldthorn Park WV4 5AJ
Quality Percentage Score: 62%
☎ 01902 331121 Fax 01902 344760
Dir: *turn off A4039 towards Penn and Womborne, take 2nd road on left (Ednam Road) hotel is at end of road*
Situated in a residential area, this imposing 18th-century house offers bedrooms which vary in size and standard with those in the original wing offering sound all-round standards. The carvery restaurant is popular with locals and the staff are friendly and efficient. When booking, it advisable to ask for directions.
ROOMS: 57 en suite (bth/shr) No smoking in 4 bedrooms s £64.50-£74.50; d £74.50 (incl. bkfst) * LB Off peak **MEALS:** Lunch £9.95 Dinner £13.95 & alc European & Asian Cuisine V meals Coffee am Tea pm **FACILITIES:** CTV in all bedrooms STV Pool table Table Tennis **CONF:** Thtr 450 Class 300 Board 100 Del from £75 * **SERVICES:** Night porter 300P **NOTES:** No dogs (ex guide dogs) No smoking in restaurant Last d 9.30pm **CARDS:**

WOLVERHAMPTON West Midlands **Map 07 SO99**

★★ Ely House

53 Tettenhall Rd WV3 9NB
Quality Percentage Score: 68%
☎ 01902 311311 🖹 01902 421098
Dir: *take A41 towards Whitchurch from town centre-ring road. 200yds on left hand side after traffic lights*

This large Victorian property was for many years a girls' school, but has been well converted to offer spacious, comfortably furnished bedrooms, some of which, on the ground floor, can be reached from the secure car park. There is a pleasant dining room and large lounge bar.
ROOMS: 18 en suite (bth/shr) s £48-£56; d £58-£78 (incl. bkfst) Off peak **MEALS:** Sunday Lunch £12.95 & alc Dinner £14.25 & alc English & Continental Cuisine V meals Coffee am **FACILITIES:** CTV in all bedrooms **SERVICES:** 20P **NOTES:** No dogs (ex guide dogs) No coaches No children 7yrs Last d 8.45pm Closed 24-26 Dec
CARDS:

See advert on page 721

WOLVERHAMPTON West Midlands **Map 07 SO99**

★★ Fox Hotel International

118 School St WV3 0NR
Quality Percentage Score: 59%
☎ 01902 21680 🖹 01902 711654

This privately owned, purpose-built hotel is situated on the inner ring road, close to the town centre. Its modern, well equipped bedrooms are popular with business guests. There is a choice of bars and good meeting and function rooms.
ROOMS: 33 en suite (bth/shr) (1 fmly) No smoking in 5 bedrooms s £33-£36; d £49-£55 (incl. bkfst) * LB Off peak **MEALS:** Lunch £3-£8 & alc International Cuisine V meals Coffee am Tea pm **FACILITIES:** CTV in all bedrooms STV Wkly live entertainment Xmas **CONF:** Thtr 60 Class 60 Board 40 **SERVICES:** Night porter 20P **NOTES:** No dogs (ex guide dogs) No smoking area in restaurant
CARDS:

WOLVERHAMPTON West Midlands **Map 07 SO99**

⌂ Travel Inn

Wolverhampton Business Park, Stafford Rd
☎ 01902 311564 🖹 01902 785280
Dir: *M54 junc2, hotel on rdbt*
This modern building offers accommodation in smart, spacious and well equipped bedrooms, all with en-suite bathrooms. Refreshments may be taken at the nearby family restaurant. For details about current prices consult the Contents Page under Hotel Groups for the Travel Inn phone number.
ROOMS: 54 en suite (bth/shr) d £39.95 *

WOOBURN COMMON Buckinghamshire **Map 04 SU98**

★★ Chequers Inn

Kiln Ln, Wooburn HP10 0JQ
Quality Percentage Score: 65%
☎ 01628 529575 🖹 01628 850124
Dir: *from M40 junct 2 take A40 through Beaconsfield Old Town towards High Wycombe. 2m outside town turn left into Broad Lane. Hotel is 2.5m along road*

In a tranquil, rural setting, this lovely 17th-century inn is intimate and inviting, yet convenient for the M25 which is seemingly a world away. The comfortable bedrooms, with stripped pine furniture and co-ordinated fabrics, offer many convenient extras. The choice of food is varied and temtping, with bar snacks, two restaurant menus, and hot dishes provided by room service.
ROOMS: 17 en suite (bth/shr) s fr £92.50; d fr £97.50 (incl. bkfst) * LB Off peak **MEALS:** Lunch £17.95-£21.95 & alc English & French Cuisine V meals Coffee am **FACILITIES:** CTV in all bedrooms STV **CONF:** Thtr 50 Class 30 Board 20 **SERVICES:** 60P **NOTES:** No dogs (ex guide dogs) No coaches **CARDS:**

See advert under BEACONSFIELD

WOODALL South Yorkshire **Map 08 SK48**

⌂ Welcome Lodge

Welcome Break - Woodall, M1 Motorway, Woodall S31 8XR
☎ 0114 248 7992 🖹 0114 248 5634
Dir: *situated on the southbound side of the M1 at Woodall services between jct31/jct31*
This modern building offers accommodation in smart, spacious and well equipped bedrooms, suitable for families and businessmen, and all with en-suite bathrooms. Refreshments may be taken at the nearby family restaurant. For details of current prices, consult the Contents Page under Hotel Groups for the Welcome Break phone number.
ROOMS: 40 en suite (bth/shr) d fr £45 *

W

WOODBRIDGE Suffolk **Map 05 TM24**

★★★ Seckford Hall

IP13 6NU
Quality Percentage Score: 74%
☎ 01394 385678 🖷 01394 380610
Dir: *signposted on A12 (Woodbridge bypass). Do not follow signs for town centre*
An attractive Elizabethan manor house, reputedly the court of Queen Elizabeth I, Seckfield Hall sits in 34 acres of grounds. The delightful public areas include a panelled lounge with relaxing sofas and an open fire, and the elegant restaurant offering serious cooking from an imaginative menu. For a lighter selection and less formal atmosphere, there is the courtyard brasserie, adjacent to the extensive leisure facilities. The bedrooms in the main house retain much of the original character of the building while those in the courtyard are more spacious.
ROOMS: 22 en suite (bth/shr) 10 annexe en suite (bth/shr) (4 fmly) s £79-£125; d £110-£165 (incl. bkfst) * LB Off peak **MEALS:** Lunch £13.50 & alc High tea £4-£7.50 Dinner £26-£35alc International Cuisine V meals Coffee am Tea pm **FACILITIES:** CTV in all bedrooms STV Indoor swimming pool (heated) Golf 18 Fishing Solarium Gym Putting green Jacuzzi/spa Xmas **CONF:** Thtr 100 Class 46 Board 40 Del £140 * **SERVICES:** Night porter 200P **NOTES:** No smoking in restaurant Last d 10pm Closed 31 Dec **CARDS:**

WOODBRIDGE Suffolk **Map 05 TM24**

★★★ Ufford Park Hotel Golf & Leisure

Best Western

Yarmouth Rd, Ufford IP12 1QW
Quality Percentage Score: 69%
☎ 01394 383555 🖷 01394 383582
Dir: *A12 N to A1152, in Melton turn left at traffic lights, premises 1m on right*
This golf and leisure orientated hotel complex is set in rolling Suffolk countryside with a challenging 18-hole course. Public areas include a bar and lounge area, as well as popular meeting and banqueting suites. The restaurant offers carvery meals and à la carte menus. Accommodation is modern and well appointed, and many of the rooms overlook the golf course.
ROOMS: 42 en suite (bth/shr) 2 annexe en suite (bth/shr) (20 fmly) No smoking in 20 bedrooms * LB Off peak **MEALS:** Sunday Lunch £3.50-£12 Dinner £14-£16 & alc mixed Cuisine V meals Coffee am Tea pm **FACILITIES:** CTV in all bedrooms Indoor swimming pool (heated) Golf 18 Sauna Solarium Gym Pool table Putting green Jacuzzi/spa Beautician Dance studio Games room Xmas **CONF:** Thtr 200 Class 80 Board 80 **SERVICES:** Night porter 160P **NOTES:** No dogs (ex guide dogs) No smoking in restaurant Last d 10pm
CARDS:

WOODFORD BRIDGE Greater London
See LONDON SECTION plan 1 *H6*

★★★★ Prince Regent

MENZIES HOTELS

Manor Rd IG8 8AE
Quality Percentage Score: 64%
☎ 0500 636943 (Central Res) 🖷 01773 880321
This impressive hotel on the edge of Woodford Bridge and Chingford, offers easy access to London and the M25. There are comfortable, well equipped bedrooms and good conference and banqueting rooms.

ROOMS: 61 en suite (bth/shr) No smoking in 10 bedrooms s £105-£130; d £130-£170 * LB Off peak **MEALS:** Lunch £6.50-£16.95 Dinner fr £16.95alc English & Continental Cuisine V meals Coffee am Tea pm **FACILITIES:** CTV in all bedrooms STV Xmas **CONF:** Thtr 350 Class 150 Board 120 Del from £110 * **SERVICES:** Lift Night porter 60P **NOTES:** Last d 9.30pm **CARDS:**

WOODFORD GREEN Greater London
See LONDON SECTION plan 1 *G6*

★★★ County Hotel Epping Forest

REGAL

Oak Hill IG8 9NY
Quality Percentage Score: 66%
☎ 020 8787 9988 🖷 020 8506 0941
Dir: *M25 junct 27 onto M11 S. At junct 4 take first exit left onto A104 towards Epping. At rdbt keep right then take first left turn into Oakhill*

In a residential area on the edge of Epping Forest, this modern hotel is convenient for both the North Circular and M11. Bedrooms are fresh and practical - business guests will appreciate the business centre. Public areas also include an informal brasserie.
ROOMS: 99 en suite (bth/shr) No smoking in 60 bedrooms s £75-£89; d £95-£105 * LB Off peak **MEALS:** Lunch £5.95-£9.95 & alc Dinner £15.95 & alc English & French Cuisine V meals Coffee am Tea pm **FACILITIES:** CTV in all bedrooms Pool table Xmas **CONF:** Thtr 150 Class 80 Board 40 Del from £86 * **SERVICES:** Lift Night porter 90P **NOTES:** No smoking in restaurant Last d 10pm
CARDS:

WOODHALL SPA Lincolnshire **Map 08 TF16**

★★★ Petwood

Stixwould Rd LN10 6QF
Quality Percentage Score: 66%
☎ 01526 352411 🖷 01526 353473
Dir: *from Sleaford take A153 (signposted Skegness). At Tattershall turn left on B1192. Hotel is signposted from the village*
This lovely Edwardian house has historic and interesting
contd.

Indicates that the star classification has not been confirmed under the New Quality Standards, see page 7 for further information.

W

connections. It was built for Lady Weignall on a site chosen by her in the area of her favourite 'pet wood' and was used by royal visitors to the 'Dambusters' squadron. It stands in thirty acres of mature woodland and gardens filled with colourful Rhododendron, flowers and lawns. The hotel is furnished in the character of the period, with original features retained in the elegantly proportioned public rooms and bedrooms.
ROOMS: 47 en suite (bth/shr) No smoking in 6 bedrooms s £75-£85; d £100-£110 (incl. bkfst) * LB Off peak **MEALS:** Sunday Lunch fr £11.75 Dinner fr £17.95 & alc English & French Cuisine V meals Coffee am Tea pm **FACILITIES:** CTV in all bedrooms Snooker Croquet lawn Putting green Complimentary pass to leisure centre Xmas **CONF:** Thtr 160 Class 60 Board 50 Del from £90 * **SERVICES:** Lift Night porter 80P **NOTES:** No smoking in restaurant Last d 9pm
CARDS:

WOODHALL SPA Lincolnshire — Map 08 TF16
★★★ Golf Hotel
The Broadway LN10 6SG
Quality Percentage Score: 60%
☎ 01526 353535 01526 353096
***Dir:** from A158 Lincoln-Horncastle turn onto B1191 towards Woodhall Spa. Hotel is located in the village centre just past Woodhall Spa Golf Club*
Situated in the heart of the village, famous for its golf course, this traditional hotel offers a range of well appointed bedrooms, of which the 'Club' style are particularly well adapted for business guests. Meals are available either in the Wentworth Restaurant or the Sunningdale Bar.
ROOMS: 50 en suite (bth/shr) (4 fmly) s fr £65; d fr £85 (incl. bkfst) * LB Off peak **MEALS:** Lunch fr £8.95 High tea fr £5.95 Dinner fr £15.95 & alc V meals Coffee am Tea pm **FACILITIES:** CTV in all bedrooms STV Tennis (hard) Pool table Croquet lawn Xmas **CONF:** Thtr 150 Class 45 Board 50 Del from £70 * **SERVICES:** Night porter 100P **NOTES:** No smoking in restaurant Last d 9.30pm
CARDS:

See advert on opposite page

WOODHALL SPA Lincolnshire — Map 08 TF16
★★ Eagle Lodge
The Broadway LN10 6ST
Quality Percentage Score: 60%
☎ 01526 353231 01526 352797
***Dir:** in the centre of Woodhall Spa*
Family owned and run, this hotel is located in the town centre, providing soundly appointed accommodation together with comfortable public rooms. A good choice of food is available, including daily blackboard specials, which are served in the bar or the dining room.
ROOMS: 23 en suite (bth/shr) (2 fmly) s £35-£45; d £52-£65 (incl. bkfst) * LB Off peak **MEALS:** Lunch £9-£11 & alc Dinner £13.50 & alc English & Continental Cuisine V meals Coffee am Tea pm
FACILITIES: CTV in all bedrooms STV Wkly live entertainment Xmas **CONF:** Thtr 100 Class 50 Board 50 **SERVICES:** 70P
NOTES: Last d 9.30pm **CARDS:**

W

WOODSTOCK Oxfordshire — Map 04 SP41
★★★ Feathers
Market St OX20 1SX
Quality Percentage Score: 79%
☎ 01993 812291 01993 813158
***Dir:** from Oxford take A44 to Woodstock, after traffic lights take first left, the hotel is on the left*
This historic hotel has been welcoming guests for many years. New manager Martin Godward continues to move forward with his young team. In the kitchen Mark Treasure introduces an impressive menu which won him great acclaim in the Lake District. Accommodation combines tradition with modern facilities. Several of the rooms are reached by rather steep narrow stairways, but all are well equipped and comfortable. The elegant public areas include a smart first floor lounge and the Whinchat bar which adjoins a courtyard garden.
ROOMS: 21 en suite (bth/shr) (4 fmly) s £99-£165; d £105-£275 (incl. cont bkfst) * LB Off peak **MEALS:** Lunch £17.50-£21 Dinner £14 & alc European Cuisine V meals Coffee am Tea pm **FACILITIES:** CTV in all bedrooms STV Mountain bikes Xmas **CONF:** Thtr 20 Board 25 Del £160 * **NOTES:** No coaches No smoking in restaurant Last d 9.15pm
CARDS:

WOODSTOCK Oxfordshire — Map 04 SP41
★★★ The Bear
Park St OX20 1SZ
Quality Percentage Score: 67%
☎ 01993 811511 01993 813380
***Dir:** M 40 junct 8 onto A40 to Oxford/M40 junct 9 onto A34 S to Oxf'd. Take A44 into Woodstock. Turn left to town centre hotel on left opp town hall*
This former 13th-century coaching inn has exposed stone walls, heavily beamed ceilings and log fires. Bedrooms have been refurbished and provide a good standard of accommodation. The attractive restaurant offers imaginative rosette worthy cuisine, with a menu of traditional and contemporary dishes that is changed seasonally.
ROOMS: 32 en suite (bth/shr) 12 annexe en suite (bth/shr) (2 fmly) No smoking in 15 bedrooms s £70-£115; d £100-£135 * LB Off peak **MEALS:** Lunch £11.50-£22.50alc Dinner £20-£35alc V meals Coffee am Tea pm **FACILITIES:** CTV in all bedrooms Xmas **CONF:** Thtr 40 Class 12 Board 24 Del from £145 * **SERVICES:** Night porter 30P **NOTES:** No smoking in restaurant Last d 9.45pm **CARDS:**

WOODSTOCK Oxfordshire — Map 04 SP41
★★ Kings Arms
19 Market St OX20 1SU
Quality Percentage Score: 66%
☎ 01993 813636 01993 813737
***Dir:** located on the corner of Market St and the A44 Oxford Road in the centre of Woodstock*
Located in the heart of Woodstock, the Kings Arms is a short walk from Blenheim Palace. Having recently undergone a total refurbishment under the new ownership of David and Sara Sykes the accommodation is very smart and comfortable. Rooms have bright modern en suite facilities and stylish decor.
ROOMS: 9 en suite (bth/shr) No smoking in all bedrooms s £45-£60; d £70-£90 (incl. bkfst) * Off peak **MEALS:** Lunch £3.75-£11.25 Dinner £12-£20alc English & French Cuisine V meals Coffee am Tea pm **FACILITIES:** CTV in all bedrooms **CONF:** Class 40 Board 20 **NOTES:** No dogs (ex guide dogs) No smoking in restaurant Last d 9.30pm
CARDS:

WOODY BAY Devon — Map 03 SS64
★★ *Woody Bay Hotel*
EX31 4QX
Quality Percentage Score: 63%
☎ 01598 763264 01598 763563
Commanding sweeping views over Woody Bay to the sea beyond, this hotel is popular with walkers. Bedrooms vary in style and size, and some have stunning views. Guests have a choice of dining options, including a simple bar menu which is available in the public bar.
ROOMS: 10 en suite (bth/shr) (1 fmly) **MEALS:** V meals Coffee am Tea pm **FACILITIES:** CTV in all bedrooms **SERVICES:** 10P **NOTES:** No coaches Last d 8.30pm Closed Jan RS Nov, Dec & Feb
CARDS:

WOOKEY HOLE Somerset — Map 03 ST54

★★❀ Glencot House

Glencot Ln BA5 1BH

Quality Percentage Score: 70%

☎ 01749 677160 Fax 01749 670210

Dir: *from Wells follow signs to Wookey Hole. On entering village look for a pink cottage on the left and turn sharp left into Glencot Lane after 100yds*

This late Victorian mansion, built in grand Jacobean style, stands in 18 peaceful acres of grounds and gardens, adjacent to the River Axe. Furnished with an impressive selection of European and Middle Eastern antiques and objets d'art, the house has been lovingly restored to its former glory. Bedrooms are individually styled and furnished, combining the unique character of the building with contemporary comforts. Dinner is served in the elegant surroundings of the oak panelled dining room. Additional facilities include a sauna, plunge pool and snooker room.

ROOMS: 13 en suite (bth/shr) (2 fmly) No smoking in all bedrooms s £65-£75; d £85-£105 (incl. bkfst) * LB Off peak **MEALS:** Dinner £25.50-£28.50 V meals Tea pm **FACILITIES:** CTV in all bedrooms Indoor swimming pool (heated) Fishing Snooker Sauna Pool table Croquet lawn Table tennis Xmas **CONF:** Thtr 40 Class 22 Board 20 Del from £115 * **SERVICES:** 26P **NOTES:** No smoking in restaurant Last d 8.30pm **CARDS:**

See advert under WELLS

WOOLACOMBE Devon — Map 02 SS44

★★★❀ Watersmeet

Mortehoe EX34 7EB

Quality Percentage Score: 74%

☎ 01271 870333 Fax 01271 870890

Dir: *follow B3343 into Woolacombe, turn right onto the esplanade, hotel is situated 0.75m on left*

This is a popular hotel overlooking the bay. The attractive restaurant forms the centrepiece with magnificent sea views and carefully prepared dishes. The bedrooms range in size. Professional and attentive service is provided.

ROOMS: 23 en suite (bth/shr) (3 fmly) s £73-£125; d £116-£220 (incl. bkfst & dinner) * LB Off peak **MEALS:** Bar Lunch £2.40-£9 Dinner £17.50-£26.50 English & French Cuisine V meals Coffee am Tea pm **FACILITIES:** CTV in all bedrooms Indoor swimming pool (heated) Outdoor swimming pool (heated) Tennis (grass) Pool table Croquet lawn Jacuzzi/spa **CONF:** Thtr 40 Class 25 Board 25 **SERVICES:** 38P **NOTES:** No dogs No coaches No children 8yrs No smoking in restaurant Last d 8.30pm Closed Dec-mid Feb **CARDS:**

See advert on this page

WOOLACOMBE Devon — Map 02 SS44
★★★ Woolacombe Bay
South St EX34 7BN
Quality Percentage Score: 73%
☎ 01271 870388 Fax 01271 870613
Dir: *from M5 junct 27 follow A361 to Mullacot Cross. Take first left onto B3343 to Woolacombe. Hotel in centre of village on the left*

Adjacent to the beach, this is a family-oriented hotel in six acres of grounds. Bedrooms are well equipped and some have balconies with views across the bay. The public areas are spacious. Maxwell's bistro is an informal alternative to the fixed-price menu served in the restaurant.
ROOMS: 65 en suite (bth/shr) (27 fmly) s £93-£104; d £186-£208 (incl. bkfst & dinner) * LB Off peak **MEALS:** Sunday Lunch £9.50 High tea £7 Dinner £20 English & French Cuisine V meals Coffee am Tea pm **FACILITIES:** CTV in all bedrooms STV Indoor swimming pool (heated) Outdoor swimming pool (heated) Golf 9 Tennis (hard) Squash Snooker Sauna Solarium Gym Pool table Croquet lawn Jacuzzi/spa Table tennis Beautician Children's Club Aerobics Classes Wkly live entertainment ch fac Xmas **CONF:** Thtr 200 Class 150 Board 150 Del from £92 * **SERVICES:** Lift Night porter 150P **NOTES:** No dogs No smoking in restaurant Last d 9pm Closed 3rd week Jan-mid Feb
CARDS:

WOOLACOMBE Devon — Map 02 SS44
★★ Little Beach
The Esplanade EX34 7DJ
Quality Percentage Score: 75%
☎ 01271 870398
Dir: *A361 at Barnstaple turn onto B3343 to Woolacombe*
Built in the Edwardian era, Little Beach Hotel has splendid views over Morte Bay. The individually furnished and decorated bedrooms are light and airy, some have their own balconies. Public areas include a sun lounge and a drawing room. Wholesome home cooking is served in the dining room.
ROOMS: 9 en suite (bth/shr) s £32-£48; d £44-£76 (incl. bkfst) * LB Off peak **MEALS:** V meals Coffee am **FACILITIES:** CTV in all bedrooms **SERVICES:** 8P **NOTES:** No coaches No children 10yrs No smoking in restaurant Last d 8pm Closed Nov-Jan **CARDS:**

W

WOOLACOMBE Devon — Map 02 SS44
★★ The Royal Hotel
Beach Rd EX34 7AB
Quality Percentage Score: 62%
☎ 01271 870001 Fax 01271 870701
Dir: *turn off A361 at Mullacott Cross rdbt on to B3343. Follow the main road into Woolacombe, hotel on the right*
In an elevated position high above Woolacombe Bay, this family hotel offers comfortable bedrooms, some providing wonderful views. A games area is available and evening entertainment is regular and varied in season.
ROOMS: 95 en suite (bth/shr) (40 fmly) s £30-£45; d £60-£90 (incl. bkfst & dinner) * Off peak **MEALS:** Dinner £9.95 V meals Coffee am Tea pm **FACILITIES:** CTV in all bedrooms Indoor swimming pool (heated) Squash Snooker Sauna Solarium Pool table Wkly live entertainment Xmas **SERVICES:** Lift Night porter 80P **NOTES:** No dogs (ex guide dogs) No smoking in restaurant Last d 8.30pm Closed 15-23 Dec & 2-15 Jan **CARDS:**

WOOLACOMBE Devon — Map 02 SS44
★ Crossways
The Esplanade EX34 7DJ
Quality Percentage Score: 70%
☎ 01271 870395 Fax 01271 870395
Dir: *M5 junct 27 onto A361 to Barnstaple, follow signs for Ilfracombe, then Woolacombe. On reaching sea-front turn right onto esplanade, hotel 0.5m on*
Away from the bustle of the high season crowds, Crossways Hotel overlooks Combesgate Beach and has access to National Trust moorland at the rear. Bedrooms are attractively decorated, many enjoying the dramatic sea views. Public areas include a lounge, bar and spacious dining room
ROOMS: 9 rms (7 shr) (3 fmly) s £27-£34; d £54-£68 (incl. bkfst & dinner) * LB Off peak **MEALS:** Bar Lunch 80p-£4 Dinner £5 English Cuisine V meals **FACILITIES:** CTV in all bedrooms **SERVICES:** 9P **NOTES:** No coaches No smoking in restaurant Last d 6.30pm Closed last Sat in Oct-1st Sat in Mar

WOOLER Northumberland — Map 12 NT92
★★ Tankerville Arms
Cottage Rd NE71 6AD
Quality Percentage Score: 62%
☎ 01668 281581 Fax 01668 281387
Dir: *on A697*
Originally a 17th-century coaching inn, this long-established roadside hotel offers cosy and characterful public rooms and well equipped bedrooms which come in a variety of styles and sizes. In the evening one can eat well in either the bar or restaurant, whilst bar lunches are equally popular.
ROOMS: 15 en suite (bth/shr) (2 fmly) s fr £45; d fr £80 (incl. bkfst) * LB Off peak **MEALS:** V meals Coffee am **FACILITIES:** CTV in 16 bedrooms **CONF:** Thtr 60 Class 60 Board 30 **SERVICES:** 100P **NOTES:** No smoking in restaurant Closed 22-28 Dec
CARDS:

WOOLLEY EDGE MOTORWAY SERVICE AREA (M1) West Yorkshire — Map 08 SE31
Travelodge
M1 Service Area, West Bretton WF4 4LQ
☎ Central Res 0800 850950
Dir: *between junct 38/39, adj to service area*
This modern building offers accommodation in smart, spacious and well equipped bedrooms, all with en-suite bathrooms. Refreshments may be taken at the nearby family restaurant. For details about current prices, consult the Contents Page under Hotel Groups for the Travelodge phone number.
ROOMS: 32 en suite (bth/shr) d £59.95 *

WOOLVERTON Somerset — Map 03 ST75
★★ *Woolverton House*
BA3 6QS
Quality Percentage Score: 70%
☎ 01373 830415 Fax 01373 831243
Dir: *On A36 halfway between Bath and Warminster*
Built in the early 19th century as a rectory, this solid stone house
contd.

has been sympathetically converted to provide a delightful family-run hotel. It is set in two and a half acres of grounds, adjacent to the A36 Bath to Warminster road, and provides a convenient base for touring the area. A good value, fixed-price menu is offered in the restaurant, where rustic French-style cuisine is served, complemented by a carefully selected list of French wines.

ROOMS: 12 en suite (bth/shr) (2 fmly) No smoking in all bedrooms **MEALS:** French Cuisine V meals Coffee am Tea pm **FACILITIES:** CTV in all bedrooms STV Tennis (hard) Fishing Croquet lawn Putting green **CONF:** Board 14 Del from £57.50 * **SERVICES:** 50P **NOTES:** No dogs (ex guide dogs) No coaches No smoking in restaurant Last d 9pm **CARDS:**

See advert under BATH

WOOTTON BASSETT Wiltshire — Map 04 SU08

★★★ Marsh Farm

Coped Hall SN4 8ER

Quality Percentage Score: 71%

☎ 01793 848044 Fax 01793 851528

Dir: *take A3102 from M4, go straight on at first rdbt, at next rdbt (with garage on the left) turn right. Hotel is 200 yds on the left*

In three acres of gardens and grounds, this attractive Victorian farmhouse has been carefully restored and extended. The well equipped bedrooms include executive rooms and some on the ground floor. Fixed price and carte menus are available in the Rawlings Restaurant, with light snacks in the lounge.

ROOMS: 11 en suite (bth/shr) 27 annexe en suite (bth/shr) (1 fmly) No smoking in 11 bedrooms s £85-£95; d £99-£109 (incl. bkfst) * LB Off peak **MEALS:** Lunch £12-£17 Dinner £21 & alc French Cuisine V meals Coffee am Tea pm **FACILITIES:** CTV in all bedrooms STV **CONF:** Thtr 120 Class 50 Board 35 Del from £105 * **SERVICES:** Night porter 150P **NOTES:** No dogs (ex guide dogs) No coaches No smoking in restaurant Last d 9pm RS 26-30 Dec **CARDS:**

See advert on this page

WORCESTER Worcestershire — Map 03 SO85

★★★ Pear Tree Inn & Country Hotel

Smite WR3 8SY

Quality Percentage Score: 75%

☎ 01905 756565 Fax 01905 756777

Dir: *From M5 junct 6 take Droitwich road after 300yds turn 1st right into small country lane over canal bridge, up a hill, hotel on left*

A much expanded country inn, this attractive hotel is well located for Worcester, Droitwich and the M5 motorway. The bedrooms are well kept and particularly spacious with a good range of modern facilities. The public areas are centred around the bar of the original pub and a large open plan restaurant which serves good food based on quality ingredients. Conference and function rooms are available and include a particularly impressive main hall. There is a warm atmosphere, promoted by friendly staff.

ROOMS: 24 en suite (bth/shr) (2 fmly) No smoking in 6 bedrooms s £52-£75; d £70-£95 (incl. bkfst) * LB Off peak **MEALS:** Lunch fr £13.50 High tea fr £7.50 Dinner £15-£18 & alc English & French Cuisine V meals Coffee am Tea pm **FACILITIES:** CTV in all bedrooms STV **CONF:** Thtr 280 Board 30 Del from £120.50 * **SERVICES:** 200P **NOTES:** No dogs (ex guide dogs) No smoking area in restaurant Last d 10pm **CARDS:**

New AA Guides for the Millennium are featured on page 24

WORCESTER Worcestershire
Map 03 SO85

★★★ The Gifford

High St WR1 2QR
Quality Percentage Score: 63%
☎ 01905 726262 Fax 01905 723458
Dir: *leave M5 at junct 7 and follow signs for city centre. Hotel opp Worcester Cathedral*

Conveniently situated in the centre of the city opposite the cathedral and close to the racecourse and County Cricket Ground. Public areas are situated on two floors which include the Royal Worcester Restaurant and lounge bar. The more informal coffee shop is situated on the ground floor. Some bedrooms are compact although with modern facilities whilst other larger rooms are especially suitable for families. There is also 24 hour room service. Banqueting and conference facilities are available together with car parking in the adjacent multi-storey.

ROOMS: 103 en suite (bth/shr) (3 fmly) No smoking in 50 bedrooms s £47-£54; d £94-£108 (incl. bkfst & dinner) * LB Off peak **MEALS:** Sunday Lunch £6.50-£7 High tea £3.50-£5 Dinner £15.95-£21.95 & alc V meals Coffee am Tea pm **FACILITIES:** CTV in all bedrooms Xmas **CONF:** Thtr 150 Class 140 Board 40 Del from £75 * **SERVICES:** Lift Night porter **NOTES:** No smoking in restaurant Last d 9.30pm **CARDS:**

WORCESTER Worcestershire
Map 03 SO85

★★★ Star

Foregate St WR1 1EA
REGAL
Quality Percentage Score: 63%
☎ 01905 24308 Fax 01905 23440
Dir: *take A44 to city centre, right at lights into City Walls Road. Straight on at rdbt, left at lights then right at lights, follow signs for A38*

This city-centre hotel has a popular lounge bar and coffee shop, attracting much local trade. Bedrooms, including some suitable for family use, are comfortably furnished, and other amenities include a restaurant and a cosy residents bar.

ROOMS: 45 en suite (bth/shr) (2 fmly) No smoking in 9 bedrooms s £60; d £70 * LB Off peak **MEALS:** Lunch £7.95 Dinner £15.50 International Cuisine V meals Coffee am Tea pm **FACILITIES:** CTV in all bedrooms STV Xmas **CONF:** Thtr 125 Class 50 Board 50 Del from £85 * **SERVICES:** Lift Night porter 55P **NOTES:** No smoking area in restaurant Last d 9.30pm **CARDS:**

WORCESTER Worcestershire
Map 03 SO85

★★★ Fownes

City Walls Rd WR1 2AP
THE FOWNES HOTEL GROUP
Quality Percentage Score: 62%
☎ 01905 613151 Fax 01905 23742
Dir: *beside A38 Inner Ring Road, 100yds from Cathedral*

This former Victorian glove factory has been converted into an interesting-looking, modern hotel with well proportioned bedrooms.

ROOMS: 61 en suite (bth/shr) (4 fmly) No smoking in 32 bedrooms s fr £85; d fr £95 * LB Off peak **MEALS:** Lunch £7.50-£10 Dinner £12-£17.50 English & European Cuisine V meals Coffee am Tea pm **FACILITIES:** CTV in all bedrooms STV Xmas **CONF:** Thtr 120 Class 50 Board 50 **SERVICES:** Lift Night porter 94P **NOTES:** No smoking in restaurant Last d 10pm **CARDS:**

WORCESTER Worcestershire
Map 03 SO85

★★ *Ye Olde Talbot*

Friar St WR1 2NA
GREENE KING INNS & HOTELS
Quality Percentage Score: 63%
☎ 01905 23573 Fax 01905 612760
Dir: *in city centre opposite Cathedral*

Situated in the city centre close to the cathedral, this former coaching inn offers a congenial bar, popular family restaurant and a welcoming, informal atmosphere. The bedrooms are well equipped and have been improved by redecoration. Limited covered car parking is available.

ROOMS: 26 en suite (bth/shr) (6 fmly) No smoking in 2 bedrooms **MEALS:** English & Continental Cuisine V meals Coffee am Tea pm **FACILITIES:** CTV in all bedrooms STV **CONF:** Thtr 15 Class 10 Board 10 Del £78 * **SERVICES:** Night porter 8P **NOTES:** No dogs (ex guide dogs) No smoking area in restaurant Last d 9.45pm
CARDS:

WORCESTER Worcestershire
Map 03 SO85

Travel Inn

Wainwright Way, Warndon WR4 9FA
ti travel inn
☎ 01905 451240 Fax 01905 756601
Dir: *M5 junc6*

This modern building offers accommodation in smart, spacious and well equipped bedrooms, all with en-suite bathrooms. Refreshments may be taken at the nearby family restaurant. For details about current prices consult the Contents Page under Hotel Groups for the Travel Inn phone number.

ROOMS: 60 en suite (bth/shr) d £39.95 *

WORFIELD Shropshire
Map 07 SO79

The Premier Collection

★★★ Old Vicarage

WV15 5JZ
PRIDE OF BRITAIN MEMBER
☎ 01746 716497 Fax 01746 716552
Dir: *off A454 between Bridgnorth & Wolverhampton*

Nestling in the unspoilt Shropshire countryside this hotel is based around an early Edwardian Vicarage. Bedrooms have been thoughtfully furnished and equipped. There is a

contd.

welcoming conservatory lounge and a beautiful restaurant where meals are prepared to a high standard.
ROOMS: 10 en suite (bth/shr) 4 annexe en suite (bth/shr) (1 fmly) No smoking in all bedrooms s £70-£105; d £107.50-£170 (incl. bkfst) * LB Off peak **MEALS:** Sunday Lunch fr £17.50 Dinner £25-£35 V meals Coffee am Tea pm **FACILITIES:** CTV in all bedrooms Croquet lawn Xmas **CONF:** Thtr 30 Class 30 Board 20 Del from £140 * **SERVICES:** 30P **NOTES:** No coaches No smoking in restaurant Last d 9pm **CARDS:**

WORKINGTON Cumbria — Map 11 NY02

★★★ Washington Central

Washington St CA14 3AY
Quality Percentage Score: 74%
☎ 01900 65772 📠 01900 68770
Dir: *M6 junct 40 onto A66 towards Keswick, follow to Workington. At the bottom of Ramsey Brow, turn left and hotel is immediatly on the right*
Continued investment and helpful staff ensure the popularity of this modern business hotel. There is a choice of eating options and the bedrooms have been furbished to a high standard of comfort with good facilities.
ROOMS: 46 en suite (bth/shr) (4 fmly) No smoking in 10 bedrooms s £64.95-£79.95; d £94.95-£109.95 (incl. bkfst) * LB Off peak **MEALS:** Lunch £12.50-£14.50 & alc High tea £4.50-£7.95 Dinner £3.95-£18.95 & alc English, French & Italian Cuisine V meals Coffee am Tea pm **FACILITIES:** CTV in all bedrooms STV Indoor swimming pool (heated) Sauna Solarium Gym Jacuzzi/spa Mountain biking Nightclub Wkly live entertainment ch fac **CONF:** Thtr 300 Class 250 Board 150 Del from £99.95 * **SERVICES:** Lift Night porter 20P **NOTES:** No dogs (ex guide dogs) No coaches No smoking in restaurant Last d 9.30pm
CARDS:

WORKINGTON Cumbria — Map 11 NY02

★★★ Hunday Manor

Hunday CA14 4JF
Quality Percentage Score: 64%
☎ 01900 61798 📠 01900 601202
Dir: *turn off A66 onto A595, hotel is 3m along on right hand side, signposted 'Hunday'*
Delightfully situated in its own grounds, enjoying distant views of the Solway Firth, this charming hotel offers attractive and thoughtfully equipped bedrooms. The open plan bar and foyer lounge boast welcoming open fires and the spacious, attractive restaurant overlooks the gardens. A choice of menus offer an interesting range of dishes.
ROOMS: 13 en suite (bth/shr) s £50-£60; d £60-£75 (incl. bkfst) * LB Off peak **MEALS:** Lunch £9.95-£15.95 & alc Dinner £13.45-£17.95 & alc English & Continental Cuisine V meals Coffee am **FACILITIES:** CTV in all bedrooms STV Tennis (grass) **CONF:** Thtr 30 Class 10 Board 16 Del from £75 * **SERVICES:** 40P **NOTES:** No coaches No smoking area in restaurant Last d 9.30pm **CARDS:**

WORKSOP Nottinghamshire — Map 08 SK57

★★★ Clumber Park

Clumber Park S80 3PA
Quality Percentage Score: 68%
☎ 01623 835333 📠 01623 835525
Dir: *M1 junct 30/31 follow signs for Worksop. A1 fiveways rdbt onto A614 5m NE*
With easy access to the A1, this hotel is situated in open countryside, edging on to Sherwood Forest and Clumber Park. Bedrooms are comfortably furnished and well equipped to meet travellers needs, while public areas include a choice of two restaurants. Dukes Tavern is lively and informal, while the Limetree offers a more traditional style of service.

ROOMS: 48 en suite (bth/shr) (6 fmly) No smoking in 31 bedrooms s £55-£65; d £70-£80 * LB Off peak **MEALS:** Lunch £11.95 High tea £6.50 Dinner £16 English & Continental Cuisine V meals Coffee am Tea pm **FACILITIES:** CTV in all bedrooms STV Xmas **CONF:** Thtr 270 Class 150 Board 90 Del from £90 * **SERVICES:** Night porter 200P **NOTES:** No smoking in restaurant Last d 10pm
CARDS:

WORKSOP Nottinghamshire — Map 08 SK57

★★ Lion

112 Bridge St S80 1HT
Quality Percentage Score: 71%
☎ 01909 477925 📠 01909 479038
Dir: *A57 to town centre, turn at Walkers Garage on right and follow road to Norfolk Arms and turn left*
This former coaching inn, dating from the 16th century, has been extended to offer spacious and comfortable accommodation, including a number of suites. It is conveniently situated on the edge of the main shopping and business area of the town, encouraging many locals to join visitors in enjoying the wide range of dishes offered in the bar and nicely furnished restaurant.
ROOMS: 32 en suite (bth/shr) (3 fmly) s £55-£67.50; d £65-£80 (incl. bkfst) * LB Off peak **MEALS:** Lunch fr £12.75 Dinner fr £12.75 & alc French Cuisine V meals Coffee am Tea pm **FACILITIES:** CTV in all bedrooms STV Sauna Solarium Gym Xmas **CONF:** Thtr 60 Class 60 Board 60 Del from £70 * **SERVICES:** Night porter 50P
NOTES: Last d 9.30pm **CARDS:**

WORKSOP Nottinghamshire — Map 08 SK57

⌂ Travelodge

St Anne's Dr, Dukeries Dr S80 3QD
☎ 01909 501528 📠 01909 501528
Dir: *on rdbt junct of A60/A57*
This modern building offers accommodation in smart, spacious and well equipped bedrooms, all with en-suite bathrooms. Refreshments may be taken at the nearby family restaurant. For details about current prices, consult the Contents Page under Hotel Groups for the Travelodge phone number.
ROOMS: 40 en suite (bth/shr) d £45.95 *

WORSLEY Greater Manchester — Map 07 SD70

★★★ Novotel

Worsley Brow M28 4YA
Quality Percentage Score: 66%
☎ 0161 799 3535 📠 0161 703 8207
Dir: *adjacent to M60 junc 13*
This modern hotel stands in its own mature grounds. It provides well equipped, spacious and comfortable accommodation. The

contd.

open plan public areas include a pleasant restaurant, a bar and lounge area.
ROOMS: 119 en suite (bth/shr) (5 fmly) No smoking in 72 bedrooms d £75 * LB Off peak **MEALS:** European Cuisine V meals Coffee am Tea pm **FACILITIES:** CTV in all bedrooms STV Outdoor swimming pool (heated) Pool table **CONF:** Thtr 220 Class 140 Board 50 Del £119 * **SERVICES:** Lift 133P **NOTES:** No smoking area in restaurant
CARDS:

WORTHING West Sussex **Map 04 TQ10**
★★★ Ardington
Steyne Gardens BN11 3DZ
Quality Percentage Score: 71%
☎ 01903 230451 01903 526526
Dir: *A27 - turn off at Lancing Leisure centre rdbt to seafront. Follow coast rd to right. Turn left at 1st Church into Steyne Gardens*
Run with professionalism and commitment by Richard and Simon Margaroli, the fourth generation of the family which has owned the Ardington since 1928, the policy of constant investment and improvement continues. Bedrooms are modern in style, very well equipped and feature smartly appointed bathrooms. Public rooms include a comfortable bar-lounge and an attractive restaurant where an interesting range of dishes is served. Service is excellent and includes a 24-hour room service menu.
ROOMS: 45 en suite (bth/shr) (4 fmly) No smoking in 10 bedrooms s £57-£80; d £80-£95 (incl. bkfst) LB Off peak **MEALS:** Bar Lunch fr £2.75 Dinner fr £20.75 & alc International Cuisine V meals Coffee am Tea pm **FACILITIES:** CTV in 47 bedrooms STV ch fac **CONF:** Thtr 140 Class 60 Board 35 Del from £65 * **SERVICES:** Night porter 25P **NOTES:** Last d 8.45pm Closed 25 Dec-4 Jan
CARDS:

WORTHING West Sussex **Map 04 TQ10**
★★★ Beach
Marine Pde BN11 3QJ
Quality Percentage Score: 68%
☎ 01903 234001 01903 234567
Dir: *W of town centre, about 1 third of a mile from pier*

This well established, popular hotel, with its impressive 1930's frontage, has been in the Farnes' family ownership for more than 50 years. Bedrooms, some which have sea views and balconies, are traditionally furnished and fully equipped with modern amenities. Public areas are spacious and comfortable, with the restaurant offering a wide choice of popular dishes. Service is both professional and friendly. Secure parking at the rear is a real plus.
ROOMS: 80 en suite (bth/shr) (8 fmly) s £55.75-£65; d £83.50-£94 (incl. bkfst) * LB Off peak **MEALS:** Lunch £14.50 & alc Dinner £18.95 & alc English & Continental Cuisine V meals Coffee am Tea pm **FACILITIES:** CTV in all bedrooms STV Pool table Xmas **CONF:** Thtr 200 Class 40 Board 12 **SERVICES:** Lift Night porter 55P **NOTES:** No dogs (ex guide dogs) Last d 8.40pm Closed 30 Dec-3 Jan
CARDS:

See advert on opposite page

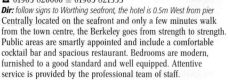

WORTHING West Sussex **Map 04 TQ10**
★★★ Berkeley
86-95 Marine Pde BN11 3QD
Quality Percentage Score: 68%
☎ 01903 820000 01903 821333
Dir: *follow signs to Worthing seafront, the hotel is 0.5m West from pier*
Centrally located on the seafront and only a few minutes walk from the town centre, the Berkeley goes from strength to strength. Public areas are smartly appointed and include a comfortable cocktail bar and spacious restaurant. Bedrooms are modern, furnished to a good standard and well equipped. Attentive service is provided by the professional team of staff.
ROOMS: 84 en suite (bth/shr) (3 fmly) No smoking in 29 bedrooms s £66.50-£70.50; d £91-£96 (incl. bkfst) * LB Off peak **MEALS:** Lunch fr £11.95 Dinner fr £14.95 Carvery Cuisine V meals Coffee am Tea pm **FACILITIES:** CTV in all bedrooms STV Xmas **CONF:** Thtr 150 Class 50 Board 50 Del from £65 * **SERVICES:** Lift Night porter 25P **NOTES:** No dogs (ex guide dogs) No smoking in restaurant Last d 9.15pm
CARDS:

WORTHING West Sussex **Map 04 TQ10**
★★★ *Kingsway*
Marine Pde BN11 3QQ
Quality Percentage Score: 67%
☎ 01903 237542 01903 204173
Dir: *A24 to seafront, turn West past pier and lido*
This seafront hotel comes with all modern comforts including multi-channel satellite TV. For the business traveller, the dressing tables provide good work space, and some also have work-height tables. Rooms at the front of the hotel benefit from recently added bathrooms. Day rooms include two comfortable lounge areas, a bar offering a good range of meals and a well appointed restaurant.
ROOMS: 28 en suite (bth/shr) (2 fmly) **MEALS:** English & French Cuisine V meals Coffee am Tea pm **FACILITIES:** CTV in all bedrooms STV **CONF:** Thtr 50 Class 20 Board 30 **SERVICES:** Lift Night porter 12P **NOTES:** No coaches No smoking in restaurant Last d 8.30pm
CARDS:

WORTHING West Sussex **Map 04 TQ10**
★★★ *Windsor House*
14/20 Windsor Rd BN11 2LX
Quality Percentage Score: 67%
☎ 01903 239655 01903 210763
Dir: *A259 from Brighton, 2nd right past Half Brick Pub*
Popular with business guests, this well maintatined hotel stands in a quiet road near the seafront. The Armstrong family and their staff create a relaxed atmosphere. Rooms are attractively decorated and equipped to a good standard. Public areas include a smart bar, well appointed restaurant and appealing conservatory/reception area.
ROOMS: 30 en suite (bth/shr) (4 fmly) No smoking in 5 bedrooms **MEALS:** English & French Cuisine V meals Coffee am Tea pm **FACILITIES:** CTV in all bedrooms STV Pool table **CONF:** Thtr 120 Class 48 Board 40 **SERVICES:** 18P **NOTES:** No dogs (ex guide dogs) No smoking in restaurant Last d 9.30pm Closed 24-25 Dec
CARDS:

WORTHING West Sussex **Map 04 TQ10**
★★★ Chatsworth
Steyne BN11 3DU
Quality Percentage Score: 62%
☎ 01903 236103 01903 823726
Dir: *A24 to Worthing town centre, left at rdbt by Blockbuster Video, follow signs to seafront. Hotel 200yds E of pier, adjacent to Promenade*
Distinguished by an imposing creeper-clad frontage, the

contd.

W

privately-owned Chatsworth has a prime position overlooking a garden square close to the pier and the town centre. Public areas include a lounge bar and a games room with two full-size snooker tables, table tennis, bar billiards and darts. Bedrooms, reached via a maze of corridors, are equipped with the usual modern facilities. There are parking meters in the street and hotel guests have a preferential rate at a car park across the square.
ROOMS: 107 en suite (bth/shr) (5 fmly) s £55-£59; d £82-£92 (incl. bkfst) * LB Off peak **MEALS:** Lunch £6.95-£13.95 Dinner £9.95-£15.95 English & Continental Cuisine V meals Coffee am Tea pm **FACILITIES:** CTV in all bedrooms STV Snooker Pool table Games room Xmas **CONF:** Thtr 150 Class 60 Board 40 Del from £69 * **SERVICES:** Lift Night porter **NOTES:** No smoking in restaurant Last d 8.45pm **CARDS:**

WORTHING West Sussex **Map 04 TQ10**
★★ Cavendish
115 Marine Pde BN11 3QG
Quality Percentage Score: 64%
☎ 01903 236767 01903 823840
Dir: *on Worthing seafront*
This small popular hotel enjoys a sea front location. Bedrooms are neatly decorated, comfortably furnished and well equipped. Dining options are extensive bar snacks in the traditional bar-lounge or a carte menu in the attractive restaurant. Limited parking is available at the rear.
ROOMS: 17 en suite (bth/shr) (4 fmly) No smoking in 3 bedrooms s £45; d £65-£75 (incl. bkfst) * LB Off peak **MEALS:** Lunch £6.95-£9.95 & alc Dinner £5-£10 & alc English & French Cuisine V meals Coffee am **FACILITIES:** CTV in all bedrooms STV **CONF:** Thtr 30 Class 20 Board 16 Del from £65 * **SERVICES:** Air conditioning 5P **NOTES:** No coaches Last d 8.45pm **CARDS:**

WROTHAM Kent **Map 05 TQ65**
★★★ Posthouse Maidstone/Sevenoaks
London Rd, Wrotham Heath TN15 7RS
Quality Percentage Score: 66%
☎ 01732 883311 01732 885850
Conveniently situated just off the M26 at Wrotham Heath, this is a busy, popular hotel. Bedrooms are comfortably appointed and well equipped. Public areas include an open plan lounge/bar, attractive restaurant and a health and fitness club.
ROOMS: 106 en suite (bth/shr) (15 fmly) No smoking in 42 bedrooms d £49-£95 * LB Off peak **MEALS:** International Cuisine V meals Coffee am Tea pm **FACILITIES:** CTV in all bedrooms Indoor swimming pool (heated) Sauna Solarium Gym Jacuzzi/spa Health & fitness centre ch fac Xmas **CONF:** Thtr 60 Class 30 Board 30 Del from £99 * **SERVICES:** Night porter 110P **NOTES:** No smoking area in restaurant Last d 10.30pm **CARDS:**

WROTHAM Kent **Map 05 TQ65**
Travel Inn
London Rd, Wrotham Heath TN15 7RX
☎ 01732 884214 01732 780368
Dir: *follow A20 Wrotham & West Malling road*
This modern building offers accommodation in smart, spacious and well equipped bedrooms, all with en-suite bathrooms. Refreshments may be taken at the nearby family restaurant. For details about current prices consult the Contents Page under Hotel Groups for the Travel Inn phone number.
ROOMS: 40 en suite (bth/shr) d £39.95 *

WROXHAM Norfolk **Map 09 TG21**
★★ *Broads*
Station Rd NR12 8UR
Quality Percentage Score: 67%
☎ 01603 782869 & 784157 01603 784066
Dir: *turn off A1151 onto Station Rd, Hotel 200yds on right*
Well established under the ownership by the friendly Bales family, this pleasant hotel takes its name from the nearby waterways. The accommodation is modern and well cared for and there are some more spacious 'superior' bedrooms. Entertainment is often laid on in the bar, and diners have the choice of carvery or a full menu in the Rose Restaurant.
ROOMS: 21 en suite (bth/shr) 7 annexe en suite (bth/shr) (1 fmly) **MEALS:** International Cuisine V meals Coffee am **FACILITIES:** CTV in all bedrooms Wkly live entertainment **SERVICES:** 40P **NOTES:** Last d 9.30pm **CARDS:**

WROXHAM Norfolk **Map 09 TG21**
★★ Kings Head
Station Rd NR12 8UR
Quality Percentage Score: 60%
☎ 01603 782429 01603 784622
Dir: *in centre of village*
This popular hotel has a strong local clientele, and being in the heart of Wroxham makes it popular with tourists holidaying on the Norfolk Broads. Day rooms open out onto the hotel's river frontage and gardens; the carvery restaurant specialises in traditional food. Bedrooms are attractive and comfortable.
ROOMS: 8 en suite (bth/shr) (2 fmly) No smoking in all bedrooms d £41 * LB Off peak **MEALS:** Lunch £6.45-£11.45 Dinner £6.45-£11.45 V meals Coffee am **FACILITIES:** CTV in all bedrooms Fishing Pool table **SERVICES:** 45P **NOTES:** No dogs (ex guide dogs) No smoking in restaurant Last d 9pm **CARDS:**

WYMONDHAM Norfolk

Map 05 TG10

★★ Abbey

10 Church St NR18 0PH
Quality Percentage Score: 70%
☎ 01953 602148 01953 606247

Dir: *from A11 follow Wymondham sign. At traffic lights left and first left into one-way system. Continue and left into Church St*

Hospitality is the keyword at this delightful hotel, close to the historic abbey. Its origins go back to the 16th century, and it has kept much of its character, although the bedrooms have modern comforts. There is a pleasant ambience in the public areas, with a convivial lounge and a cosy bar in which pre-dinner drinks can be enjoyed.

ROOMS: 22 en suite (bth/shr) 1 annexe en suite (bth/shr) (3 fmly) s £58-£65; d £65-£79 (incl. bkfst) * LB Off peak **MEALS:** Dinner £17.50-£18.50 English & Continental Cuisine V meals Coffee am Tea pm **FACILITIES:** CTV in all bedrooms Xmas **SERVICES:** Lift 4P **NOTES:** No smoking in restaurant Last d 9pm **CARDS:**

See advert under NORWICH

WYMONDHAM Norfolk

Map 05 TG10

★★ Wymondham Consort Hotel

28 Market St NR18 0BB
Quality Percentage Score: 70%
☎ 01953 606721 01953 601361

Dir: *Hotel situated off A11 (M11) Thetford to Norwich road, turn left at traffic lights and left again*

The Fiddaman family's very pleasant hotel is to be found in the centre of this bustling market town, and they and their enthusiastic team offer a warm welcome to all. The well maintained and comfortable bedrooms may vary in size and character, but all are bright and well appointed with modern en suite facilities; they also have thoughtful extras such as mineral water and fresh fruit. A wide range of spacious public areas include a cosy lounge bar, buzzing coffee shop and an intimate restaurant serving good freshly prepared meals from appealing wide-ranging menus.

ROOMS: 20 en suite (bth/shr) (1 fmly) No smoking in 10 bedrooms s £55-£60; d £68-£75 (incl. bkfst) * LB Off peak **MEALS:** Lunch £8.95-£10.95 Dinner fr £16.50 & alc English & Continental Cuisine V meals Coffee am Tea pm **FACILITIES:** CTV in all bedrooms STV ch fac **CONF:** Thtr 40 Class 30 Board 20 **SERVICES:** 18P **NOTES:** No smoking in restaurant Last d 9.30pm **CARDS:**

See advert under NORWICH

YARCOMBE Devon

Map 03 ST20

★★ The Belfry Country Hotel

EX14 9BD
Quality Percentage Score: 76%
☎ 01404 861234 01404 861579

Dir: *on A30, 7m E of Honiton, 5m W of Chard, 10m S of M5 junct 25 at Taunton*

This hotel is based on a converted Victorian school house, with spacious, attractively decorated bedrooms. An extensive menu is offered in the panelled bar/restaurant. Please note that this is a no smoking establishment.

ROOMS: 6 en suite (bth/shr) (1 fmly) No smoking in all bedrooms s fr £44; d fr £68 * LB Off peak **MEALS:** Dinner £18.95 & alc English & French Cuisine V meals Coffee am Tea pm **FACILITIES:** CTV in all bedrooms Xmas **SERVICES:** 10P **NOTES:** No coaches No children 12yrs No smoking in restaurant Last d 8pm **CARDS:**

YARM North Yorkshire

Map 08 NZ41

★★★ Judges Hotel

Kirklevington TS15 9LW
Quality Percentage Score: 74%
☎ 01642 789000 01642 782878

Dir: *located 1.5m from A19. At A67 junct, follow the Yarm road and hotel is clearly visible on the left hand side*

Set in beautiful gardens and parkland, this imposing country mansion has been restored to its former glory. Once a judge's lodgings, it now offers elegant public areas which include an attractive restaurant with a conservatory extension overlooking the gardens. Bedrooms are all individual and impressively furnished, with smart bathrooms - some having airflow baths - and are very well equipped to include trouser presses and mini bars.

ROOMS: 21 en suite (bth/shr) (3 fmly) s £120; d £152 (incl. bkfst) * LB Off peak **MEALS:** Lunch £9.95-£14.95 & alc Dinner £25 & alc English & French Cuisine V meals Coffee am Tea pm **FACILITIES:** CTV in all bedrooms STV Croquet lawn Xmas **CONF:** Thtr 70 Class 16 Board 24 Del £150 * **SERVICES:** Night porter 102P **NOTES:** No dogs (ex guide dogs) No coaches No smoking in restaurant Last d 10pm **CARDS:**

W

YARMOUTH See Wight, Isle of

YATTENDON Berkshire **Map 04 SU57**

★★❀❀❀ Royal Oak

The Square RG18 0UG

REGAL

Quality Percentage Score: 77%

☎ 01635 201325 📠 01635 201926

Dir: *M4 junct 12 follow A4-Newbury & at 2nd rdbt 3rd exit to Pangbourne, then left to Yattendon*

Welcoming guests for 300 years, this quintessential English country inn is a veritable little haven with wisteria-clad walls and an attractive garden. Public rooms are cosy and congenial, while the stylishly furnished bedrooms have smart bathrooms. Guests can eat informally in the bar from a great choice of modern and traditional dishes. Alternatively, the full range of the team's confident abilities can be sampled in the pretty country restaurant.

ROOMS: 5 en suite (bth) s fr £95; d £115-£125 * LB Off peak **MEALS:** Lunch £20-£25alc Dinner £32.50 & alc English & French Cuisine V meals Coffee am **FACILITIES:** CTV in all bedrooms STV Croquet lawn Xmas **CONF:** Thtr 30 Class 18 Board 22 Del from £150 * **SERVICES:** 20P **NOTES:** No coaches No smoking in restaurant Last d 9.30pm Closed 31 Dec **CARDS:**

YELVERTON Devon **Map 02 SX56**

★★★❀ Moorland Links

PL20 6DA

Forestdale Hotels

Quality Percentage Score: 72%

☎ 01822 852245 📠 01822 855004

Dir: *from A38 dual carriageway from Exeter to Plymouth, take the A386 towards Tavistock. Continue for 5m onto open moorland, hotel is 1m on the left*

Standing in nine acres of grounds in the Dartmoor National Park, this hotel has a regular clientele. Rooms range from well equipped standard to stylish executive rooms, many of which have balconies. The restaurant looks out over lovely gardens and the hotel also has a number of meeting rooms.

ROOMS: 45 en suite (bth/shr) (4 fmly) No smoking in 21 bedrooms s fr £75; d fr £95 (incl. bkfst) * LB Off peak **MEALS:** Lunch £12.45-£18alc Dinner fr £18.20alc English & French Cuisine V meals Coffee am Tea pm **FACILITIES:** CTV in all bedrooms Tennis (hard) Xmas **CONF:** Thtr 120 Class 60 Board 60 Del from £110 * **SERVICES:** Night porter 120P **NOTES:** No smoking in restaurant Last d 9.45pm **CARDS:**

See advert under PLYMOUTH

YEOVIL Somerset **Map 03 ST51**

see also **Martock**

★★★❀ Yeovil Court

West Coker Rd BA20 2NE

Quality Percentage Score: 72%

☎ 01935 863746 📠 01935 863990

Dir: *2.5m W of town centre on the A30 (Exeter)*

This comfortable, family-run hotel has a relaxed atmosphere. All bedrooms are well equipped, some of them are located in an adjacent new building. Public areas consist of a smart lounge, a popular bar and an attractive restaurant. An extensive selection of dishes is available to suit all tastes and pockets.

ROOMS: 15 en suite (bth/shr) 11 annexe en suite (bth/shr) (4 fmly) s fr £65; d £75-£90 (incl. bkfst) * LB Off peak **MEALS:** Lunch £5-£8.95 & alc English & French Cuisine V meals Coffee am Tea pm **FACILITIES:** CTV in all bedrooms Xmas **CONF:** Thtr 44 Class 20 Board 28 **SERVICES:** 65P **NOTES:** No smoking in restaurant **CARDS:**

See advert on this page

Y

Symbols and Abbreviations are listed and explained on pages 4 and 5

YEOVIL Somerset **Map 03 ST51**

The Premier Collection

★ Little Barwick House
Barwick Village BA22 9TD
☎ 01935 423902 01935 420908
Dir: *turn left off A37, Yeovil/Dorchester road, at first rdbt. Hotel 0.25m on left*
Bedrooms at this charming property are attractively decorated and feature many personal touches. Christopher Colley plays host, while his wife Veronica cooks with great care and skill. Guests can enjoy afternoon tea in front of the fire in the cosy lounge or in the secluded garden.
ROOMS: 6 en suite (bth/shr) s £56.50; d £84-£93 (incl. bkfst) * LB Off peak **MEALS:** Dinner £20.90-£27.90 V meals **FACILITIES:** CTV in all bedrooms **SERVICES:** P **NOTES:** No coaches No smoking in restaurant Last d 9.00pm Closed Xmas & New Year
CARDS:

YEOVIL Somerset **Map 03 ST51**
★ ***Preston***
64 Preston Rd BA20 2DL
Quality Percentage Score: 62%
☎ 01935 474400 01935 410142
Dir: *from A30 (hospital rdbt) head north on A37 Bristol road for 0.25m. At rdbt take first exit for Preston Road*
Popular with business guests during the week, a friendly welcome is extended at this family run hotel on the outskirts of Yeovil. Bedrooms and public areas are smartly presented and a good choice of freshly prepared food is offered in the dining room.
ROOMS: 5 en suite (bth/shr) 8 annexe en suite (bth/shr) (7 fmly) **MEALS:** English & French Cuisine V meals Coffee am Tea pm **FACILITIES:** CTV in all bedrooms **SERVICES:** 19P **NOTES:** No smoking in restaurant Last d 9pm **CARDS:**

YORK North Yorkshire **Map 08 SE65**
see also **Aldwark, Escrick & Pocklington**
★★★★ **Swallow**
Tadcaster Rd YO24 1QQ
Quality Percentage Score: 63%
☎ 01904 701000 01904 702308
Dir: *heading E turn off A64 at York 'West' onto A1036, hotel is on right after church and traffic lights*
Situated less than a mile from the city walls and overlooking the Knavesmire and the racecourse, The Swallow offers modern, thoughtfully equipped bedrooms. Some rooms have balconies and enjoy fine views. The smartly refurbished public areas offer good levels of comfort and provide a wide range of leisure and meeting facilities. The hotel also has its own purpose built training centre.

ROOMS: 113 en suite (bth/shr) (14 fmly) No smoking in 40 bedrooms **MEALS:** Lunch £10.95-£14.10 High tea fr £7.25 Dinner fr £20.45 & alc English & French Cuisine V meals Coffee am Tea pm **FACILITIES:** CTV in all bedrooms STV Indoor swimming pool (heated) Tennis (hard) Sauna Solarium Gym Pool table Croquet lawn Putting green Jacuzzi/spa Beauty treatment Golf practice **CONF:** Thtr 170 Class 90 Board 40 **SERVICES:** Lift Night porter 200P **NOTES:** No smoking in restaurant Last d 10pm **CARDS:**

YORK North Yorkshire **Map 08 SE65**
★★★★ **Royal York**
Station Rd YO24 2AA
Quality Percentage Score: 62%
☎ 01904 653681 01904 653271
Dir: *adjacent to railway station*
This magnificent Victorian hotel, with its own private gardens, is close to the city walls, the railway station, and five minutes walk from the Minster. Its attractive, well equipped bedrooms are divided between the main building and the garden mews. Guests have a choice of eating options: Tiles Bar, room service, or the main Rose Room restaurant.
ROOMS: 131 en suite (bth/shr) 27 annexe en suite (bth/shr) (4 fmly) s £115-£125; d £135-£145 * LB Off peak **MEALS:** Lunch £11.95-£18.50 & alc V meals Coffee am Tea pm **FACILITIES:** CTV in all bedrooms STV Sauna Solarium Gym Pool table Croquet lawn Mini pitch & putt Steam room Wkly live entertainment Xmas **CONF:** Thtr 280 Class 120 Board 80 Del from £150 * **SERVICES:** Lift Night porter 100P **NOTES:** No smoking in restaurant **CARDS:**

See advert on opposite page

YORK North Yorkshire **Map 08 SE65**

The Premier Collection

★★★ **The Grange**
1 Clifton YO30 6AA
☎ 01904 644744 01904 612453
Dir: *on A19 York/Thirsk road, approx 500 yds from city centre*
This bustling Regency town house is just a few minutes' walk from York's centre, and is furnished in country house style. The individually designed bedrooms have been thoughtfully equipped for both business and leisure guests. There is a sunny morning room, a first-floor drawing room and a library, which are both licensed for wedding

contd.

ceremonies and receptions. There is a seafood bar, a popular and informal Brasserie and the Ivy Restaurant that serves seasonal, rosette-worthy cuisine.

ROOMS: 30 en suite (bth/shr) s £99-£160; d £120-£210 (incl. bkfst) * LB Off peak **MEALS:** Lunch £11.50 Dinner fr £25 & alc V meals Coffee am Tea pm **FACILITIES:** CTV in all bedrooms STV Xmas **CONF:** Thtr 50 Class 20 Board 24 Del £138 * **SERVICES:** Night porter 26P **NOTES:** Last d 10pm
CARDS:

YORK North Yorkshire **Map 08 SE65**

The Premier Collection

★★★ Middlethorpe Hall

Bishopthorpe Rd, Middlethorpe YO23 2GB
☎ 01904 641241 01904 620176

RELAIS & CHATEAUX

Dir: *from A1036 signed York (west), follow signs to Bishopthorpe and racecourse. Hotel is on right just before racecourse*

This splendid country house overlooks the racecourse. Lovingly restored, there is much to admire in the elegant drawing room before a carefully prepared dinner is taken in the wood panelled dining room, looking over the extensive grounds. Individually furnished bedrooms are split between the main house and a sympathetically renovated courtyard, and the new Spa includes a pool, solarium and beauty treatment rooms.

ROOMS: 30 en suite (bth/shr) s £99-£125; d £140-£250 * LB Off peak **MEALS:** Lunch £17.50-£18.50 Dinner fr £32 V meals Coffee am Tea pm **FACILITIES:** CTV in all bedrooms Indoor swimming pool (heated) Sauna Solarium Croquet lawn Jacuzzi/spa Leisure Spa Xmas **CONF:** Thtr 56 Class 30 Board 25 Del from £150 * **SERVICES:** Lift Night porter 70P **NOTES:** No dogs No children 8yrs No smoking in restaurant Last d 9.30pm RS 25 & 31 Dec
CARDS:

Y

YORK North Yorkshire **Map 08 SE65**
★★★✿ ***Dean Court***
Duncombe Place YO10 7EF
Quality Percentage Score: 74%
☎ 01904 625082 🖷 01904 620305
Dir: *city centre opposite York Minster*

Once housing the clergy of York Minster, this centrally located hotel provides quiet, well equipped and comfortable bedrooms. Inviting public rooms provide a restful respite from the city. The restaurant has a good reputation and there is also a popular tea room and coffee shop.
ROOMS: 39 en suite (bth/shr) (2 fmly) No smoking in 12 bedrooms **MEALS:** English & French Cuisine V meals Coffee am Tea pm **FACILITIES:** CTV in all bedrooms **CONF:** Thtr 60 Class 24 Board 32 Del from £111.50 * **SERVICES:** Lift Night porter 30P **NOTES:** No dogs (ex guide dogs) No coaches No smoking area in restaurant Last d 9.30pm RS 25 Dec evening **CARDS:**

See advert on page 735

YORK North Yorkshire **Map 08 SE65**
★★★✿ **Mount Royale**
The Mount YO24 1GU
Quality Percentage Score: 73%
☎ 01904 628856 🖷 01904 611171
Dir: *W on A1036, towards racecourse*
The charming Oxtoby family have owned and run this hotel for many years and continue to offer friendly professional service. Public rooms include a relaxing lounge, a cosy bar, and separate cocktail lounge attached to the restaurant which overlooks the garden. Freshly prepared food is presented from a daily-changing menu in the very capable hands of chef Karen Brotherton. Bedrooms are comfortable and come in a wide variety of styles.
ROOMS: 23 en suite (bth/shr) (2 fmly) s £80; d £90 (incl. bkfst) * LB Off peak **MEALS:** Dinner £5.75-£30alc International Cuisine V meals Coffee am **FACILITIES:** CTV in all bedrooms STV Outdoor swimming pool (heated) Snooker Sauna Solarium Beauty treatment centre **CONF:** Thtr 25 Board 16 **SERVICES:** Night porter 18P **NOTES:** No coaches No smoking in restaurant Last d 9.30pm RS Rest closed & hotel B&B only on 31/12/99 **CARDS:**

YORK North Yorkshire **Map 08 SE65**
★★★✿✿ **Parsonage Country House**
York Rd YO19 6LF
Quality Percentage Score: 73%
☎ 01904 728111 🖷 01904 728151
(For full entry see Escrick)

YORK North Yorkshire **Map 08 SE65**
★★★✿✿ **York Pavilion**
45 Main St, Fulford YO10 4PJ
Quality Percentage Score: 72%
☎ 01904 622099 🖷 01904 626939
Dir: *on A19, opposite garage on Fulford Main St*
An attractive Georgian hotel situated in its own gardens and grounds. The individually designed and well equipped bedrooms are situated in the main house and in the converted stables. There is a comfortable lounge, a newly created conference centre and an inviting Brasserie-style restaurant, where the regulary changing menu has daily specials always on offer.

ROOMS: 44 en suite (bth/shr) (2 fmly) No smoking in 3 bedrooms s £76-£92; d £94-£115 (incl. bkfst) * LB Off peak **MEALS:** Lunch £14-£25 & alc Dinner £20-£35 & alc European Cuisine V meals Coffee am **FACILITIES:** CTV in all bedrooms STV Xmas **CONF:** Thtr 150 Class 75 Board 50 Del from £110 * **SERVICES:** Night porter 72P **NOTES:** No dogs (ex guide dogs) No smoking in restaurant Last d 9.30pm **CARDS:**

See advert on opposite page

YORK North Yorkshire **Map 08 SE65**
★★★✿ **Ambassador**
123 The Mount YO24 1DU
Quality Percentage Score: 67%
☎ 01904 641316 🖷 01904 640259
Dir: *from A1036 York/Bishopthorpe, follow city centre signs along Tadcaster Road. Hotel is located on the right 300yds after the racecourse*
An elegant Georgian house which offers a quiet and relaxing atmosphere. The well-equipped bedrooms are mostly spacious with the larger ones generally overlooking the attractive and secluded gardens to the rear. The spacious and richly furnished Grays Restaurant is a delightful setting in which to enjoy well produced British dishes. Service is friendly and very attentive.
ROOMS: 25 en suite (bth/shr) (2 fmly) s £98; d £118 (incl. bkfst) * LB Off peak **MEALS:** Lunch £10.50-£12.50 Dinner fr £19.50 & alc English & French Cuisine V meals Coffee am Tea pm **FACILITIES:** CTV in all bedrooms STV Wkly live entertainment Xmas **CONF:** Thtr 60 Class 24 Board 30 Del from £95 * **SERVICES:** Lift 35P **NOTES:** No dogs (ex guide dogs) No coaches No smoking in restaurant Last d 9.30pm **CARDS:**

YORK North Yorkshire **Map 08 SE65**
★★★ ***The Judges Lodging***
9 Lendal YO1 8AQ
Quality Percentage Score: 67%
☎ 01904 638733 🖷 01904 679947
Dir: *from West Door York Minster, 250yds towards Lendal bridge. Turn left into Lendal*
This 18th-century listed building with many Georgian features has been thoughtfully renovated and is situated right in the heart of the city. There is a lively basement bar, or one can enjoy a

contd.

Y

drink outside under the trees. Bedrooms complement the character of the house and include two suites.

ROOMS: 14 en suite (bth/shr) No smoking in 4 bedrooms **MEALS:** International Cuisine V meals Coffee am **FACILITIES:** CTV in all bedrooms STV **SERVICES:** Night porter 16P **NOTES:** No dogs (ex guide dogs) No coaches No children 10yrs No smoking area in restaurant Last d 9.30pm **CARDS:**

YORK North Yorkshire **Map 08 SE65**

★★★ Monkbar

St Maurices Rd YO31 7JA

Quality Percentage Score: 67%

☎ 01904 638086 📠 01904 629195

Dir: *situated overlooking City Walls and Monkbar, 300yds from York Minster fronting onto York inner ring rd*

Standing in a prominent position by the city walls, this large hotel provides well equipped modern bedrooms, some in an

The Parsonage AA ★★★ ETC **ESCRICK YORK YO19 6LF**

Country House, Hotel, Restaurant and Conference Centre

Tel: 01904 728111 Fax: 01904 728151

A charming country house hotel situated in six acres of beautiful gardens and woodlands. The hotel provides an oasis of comfort and tranquillity with the opportunity to be transported back to the days of elegance, tradition and lavish hospitality. All rooms attractively and elegantly designed with comfort in mind with four-poster and ground floor rooms available. Our Head Chef Kenny Noble creates exquisite mouth watering dishes from the finest quality local ingredients which is complimented by fine wines from our extensive wine cellar.

Four conference and banqueting suites available to cater for up to 150 people with superb choice of menus.

Ample parking available.

MONKBAR HOTEL

AA ★★★

The 3-star 99 Bedroomed Monkbar Hotel is situated next to the City Walls and 300 metres from the Minster.
All our bedrooms have been carefully designed to meet the comfort of our guests.
Dine in the Cloisters Restaurant - choice of A La Carte or Table D'Hote Menu.

St. Maurice's Road, York YO31 7JA
Tel: (01904) 638086 Fax: (01904) 629195

YORK PAVILION HOTEL

Country House Hotel & Brasserie in the City of York

This privately owned Grade II Listed hotel offers a relaxed and unpretentious atmosphere which compliments the charming interior.

We provide the finest quality food and the highest standard of service with many exciting wines all at sensible prices.

With 44 bedrooms individually designed and decorated to create a feeling of stylish comfort.

The Sandys'-Richardson Suite provides the most unique setting for a conference, a formal banquet to a Wedding Reception.

MAIN STREET
FULFORD
YORK
YO10 4PJ
Telephone
01904 622099
Facsimile
01904 626939

Y

adjoining courtyard building. There is a choice of styles of restaurant; hospitality is a strength of the operation.
ROOMS: 99 en suite (bth/shr) (3 fmly) s £82-£92; d £124-£148 (incl. bkfst) * Off peak **MEALS:** Lunch £9.50-£9.95 & alc High tea £2.95-£9.75 & alc Dinner £16.95 & alc English & French Cuisine V meals Coffee am Tea pm **FACILITIES:** CTV in all bedrooms Xmas **CONF:** Thtr 200 Class 80 Board 50 Del from £95 * **SERVICES:** Lift Night porter 80P
NOTES: No smoking in restaurant Last d 11pm
CARDS:

See advert on page 737

YORK North Yorkshire **Map 08 SE65**
★★★ *Posthouse York*
Tadcaster Rd YO24 1QF
Quality Percentage Score: 66%
☎ 01904 707921 🖹 01904 702804
Dir: *from A1(M) take A64 towards York. Continue for 7m, then take A106 to York Straight over at rdbt to York city centre. Hotel 0.5m on right*

Posthouse

A modern hotel situated on the main western approach to the city centre and close to the famous racecourse. Many of the spacious, comfortable bedrooms look oout either on the racecourse or the countryside. Public rooms include the popular 'Seasons' Bar and Grill, and flexible meeting rooms. There is a large carpark.
ROOMS: 143 en suite (bth/shr) (37 fmly) No smoking in 83 bedrooms
MEALS: International Cuisine V meals Coffee am Tea pm
FACILITIES: CTV in all bedrooms Childrens mini-golf **CONF:** Thtr 100 Class 40 Board 40 **SERVICES:** Lift Night porter 137P **NOTES:** No smoking area in restaurant Last d 10pm
CARDS:

YORK North Yorkshire **Map 08 SE65**
★★★ *Kexby Bridge*
Hull Rd, Kexby YO41 5LD
Quality Percentage Score: 63%
☎ 01759 388223 & 388154 🖹 01759 388822
Dir: *Turn off A64 onto A1079, travel 3 miles away from York A1079-Hull hotel on left hand side of main road*

THE CIRCLE
Selected Individual Hotels
GREAT BRITAIN

This family-run hotel backs onto extensive gardens. Its spacious bedrooms meet modern standards of comfort, its restaurant serves enjoyable food and it has a pleasant bar lounge.
ROOMS: 32 en suite (bth/shr) No smoking in 8 bedrooms
MEALS: English & French Cuisine V meals Coffee am Tea pm
FACILITIES: CTV in all bedrooms Fishing **CONF:** Thtr 30 Class 30 Board 30 **SERVICES:** 60P **NOTES:** No dogs (ex guide dogs) No smoking area in restaurant **CARDS:**

YORK North Yorkshire **Map 08 SE65**
★★★ Novotel
Fishergate YO10 4FD
Quality Percentage Score: 63%
☎ 01904 611660 🖹 01904 610925
Dir: *S off A19*

NOVOTEL
YOU'RE WELCOME

This smart modern hotel is just outside the city walls, and offers well equipped accommodation in identical, spacious bedrooms. Guests can dine from the extensive room-service menu, or in the garden brasserie until midnight.
ROOMS: 124 en suite (bth/shr) (124 fmly) No smoking in 93 bedrooms d £50-£99 (incl. bkfst) * LB Off peak **MEALS:** Lunch £9.95-£12.95 & alc Dinner £12.85-£16.85 & alc English, French & Italian Cuisine V meals Coffee am Tea pm **FACILITIES:** CTV in all bedrooms STV Indoor swimming pool (heated) Playstations Juke Box Games machines Internet use Childrens play area ch fac **CONF:** Thtr 210 Class 80 Board 60 **SERVICES:** Lift Night porter 150P **NOTES:** No smoking area in restaurant Last d midnight **CARDS:**

YORK North Yorkshire **Map 08 SE65**
★★ Clifton Bridge
Water End, Clifton YO30 6LL
Quality Percentage Score: 71%
☎ 01904 610510 🖹 01904 640208
Dir: *NW side of city between A19 & A59*

Standing between Clifton Green and the River Ouse and within walking distance of the city this family owned and run hotel offers good hospitality and service. The house is well furnished and features oak panelled walls in the public rooms whilst the modern bedrooms are well equipped and attractively decorated. Good home cooked dinners are served in the cosy dining room with the menu offering a pleasing choice of dishes.
ROOMS: 14 en suite (bth/shr) (1 fmly) s £35-£44; d £56-£72 (incl. bkfst) * LB Off peak **MEALS:** Dinner £10 & alc English & French Cuisine V meals Coffee am Tea pm **FACILITIES:** CTV in all bedrooms
CONF: Thtr 20 Board 16 Del from £50 * **SERVICES:** 14P **NOTES:** No smoking in restaurant Last d 8pm Closed 24-25 Dec
CARDS:

YORK North Yorkshire **Map 08 SE65**
★★ Ashcroft
294 Bishopthorpe Rd YO23 1LH
Quality Percentage Score: 70%
☎ 01904 659286 🖹 01904 640107
Dir: *turn off A64 on to A1036 and follow signs to Bishopthorpe, turn left in village and take road to York, hotel is 1.5m on right*

MINOTEL
Great Britain

Standing on the banks of the River Ouse, this Victorian mansion has been carefully furbished by the resident owners. Service is friendly and the pleasantly decorated bedrooms have been thoughtfully equipped. A very inviting lounge is provided and good home cooking is served in the stylish restaurant.
ROOMS: 11 en suite (bth/shr) 4 annexe en suite (bth/shr) (3 fmly) s £43-£48; d £50-£85 (incl. bkfst) * LB Off peak **MEALS:** Bar Lunch £6-£9 Dinner £14.50 & alc V meals Coffee am Tea pm **FACILITIES:** CTV in all bedrooms River moorings **SERVICES:** 40P **NOTES:** No children 5yrs No smoking in restaurant Last d 8.30pm Closed 24-30 Dec
CARDS:

YORK North Yorkshire **Map 08 SE65**
★★ Heworth Court
76 Heworth Green YO31 7TQ
Quality Percentage Score: 70%
☎ 01904 425156 🖹 01904 415290
Dir: *drive around th outer ring rd towards Scarborough rdbt on NE side of York, exit onto A1036 Malton Rd, hotel is on left*
Friendly and attentive service is provided at this family owned hotel, situated within walking distance of the city. Public rooms are comfortable, and the well furnished bedrooms are

contd. on p. 740

Y

thoughtfully equipped. An extensive range of freshly prepared food is served in the Lamp Light restaurant.

Heworth Court Hotel, York

ROOMS: 15 en suite (bth/shr) 10 annexe en suite (bth/shr) (7 fmly) No smoking in 2 bedrooms s £45-£57.50; d £52-£85 (incl. bkfst) * LB Off peak **MEALS:** Lunch £10.95 & alc High tea £1.25 & alc Dinner £10.95 & alc English & European Cuisine V meals Coffee am Tea pm **FACILITIES:** CTV in all bedrooms STV Whisky bar Xmas **CONF:** Thtr 22 Class 12 Board 16 Del from £67 * **SERVICES:** 27P **NOTES:** No dogs No coaches No smoking in restaurant Last d 9pm **CARDS:**

See advert on page 739

YORK North Yorkshire **Map 08 SE65**

★★ Beechwood Close

19 Shipton Rd, Clifton YO30 5RE
Quality Percentage Score: 69%
☎ 01904 658378 01904 647124

Dir: *the hotel is situated on the A19 (Thirsk Rd, between ring rd and city centre) on the right hand side when entering the 30mph zone*

Just a mile north of the city centre, this family owned hotel is very well run and offers spacious, well equipped bedrooms. Public areas are maintained to a high standard and enjoyable food is served by friendly staff in the traditionally furnished dining room. room and is served by an attentive and friendly staff. The hotel is located a mile to the north of the city centre.

ROOMS: 14 en suite (bth/shr) (2 fmly) s £46-£48; d £75-£80 (incl. bkfst) * LB Off peak **MEALS:** Lunch £7.75 High tea £7.25-£9.95 Dinner fr £13.75 V meals Coffee am Tea pm **FACILITIES:** CTV in all bedrooms STV **CONF:** Thtr 60 Class 35 Board 42 Del from £63.50 * **SERVICES:** 36P **NOTES:** No dogs No coaches Last d 9pm Closed 25 Dec **CARDS:**

YORK North Yorkshire **Map 08 SE65**

★★ Kilima Hotel

129 Holgate Rd YO24 4AZ
Quality Percentage Score: 69%
☎ 01904 658844 & 625787 01904 612083

Dir: *on A59, on W outskirts*

On the western edge of the city and within easy walking distance, this Victorian parsonage is now a well furnished and comfortable hotel, offering well equipped bedrooms and helpful service. There is a cosy lounge and an intimate restaurant.

ROOMS: 15 en suite (bth/shr) (1 fmly) s £55; d £82-£94 (incl. bkfst) * LB Off peak **MEALS:** Lunch £13.50-£18.95 & alc Dinner £13.50-£18.95 & alc English & French Cuisine V meals Coffee am Tea pm **FACILITIES:** CTV in all bedrooms Xmas **CONF:** Thtr 25 Board 14 Del £84.50 * **SERVICES:** 20P **NOTES:** No coaches No smoking in restaurant Last d 9.30pm **CARDS:**

YORK North Yorkshire **Map 08 SE65**

★★ Knavesmire Manor

302 Tadcaster Rd YO2 2HE
Quality Percentage Score: 69%
☎ 01904 702941 01904 709274

Dir: *follow signs for York (West) A1036*

This well furnished hotel has many antiques and period furniture in the public rooms. It overlooks the famous racecourse and is convenient for the city. The Brasserie provides a modern menu while the bedrooms include several styles including the Queen's Suite with a four poster.

ROOMS: 12 en suite (bth/shr) 9 annexe en suite (shr) (2 fmly) s £45-£65; d £59-£89 (incl. bkfst) * LB Off peak **MEALS:** Lunch £7.95-£10.95 Dinner £13.50-£15.50 & alc English & Continental Cuisine V meals Coffee am Tea pm **FACILITIES:** CTV in all bedrooms STV Indoor swimming pool (heated) Sauna Xmas **CONF:** Thtr 36 Class 30 Board 28 Del from £59 * **SERVICES:** Lift 27P **NOTES:** No smoking in restaurant Last d 9.15pm **CARDS:**

See advert on opposite page

YORK North Yorkshire **Map 08 SE65**

★★ *Hudsons*

60 Bootham YO30 7BZ
Quality Percentage Score: 68%
☎ 01904 621267 01904 654719

Dir: *situated on the A19 which runs from the north of the city into city centre, just after Bootham Park and before city walls*

Converted from two Victorian houses in 1981 and is within easy walking distance of the city centre. An archway leads to a secured car park and a modern mews development of purpose-built bedrooms. Many of the bedrooms in the original building retain a period style as does the elegant dining room. Downstairs there is a refurbished cosy bar as well as a bistro featuring flagstone floors and an old original cooking range.

ROOMS: 31 en suite (bth/shr) **MEALS:** English & French Cuisine V meals Coffee am **FACILITIES:** CTV in all bedrooms STV **CONF:** Thtr 80 Class 30 Board 25 **SERVICES:** Lift 34P **NOTES:** No dogs (ex guide dogs) Last d 9.30pm **CARDS:**

See advert on opposite page

YORK North Yorkshire **Map 08 SE65**

★★ Alhambra Court

31 St Mary's, Bootham YO30 7DD
Quality Percentage Score: 67%
☎ 01904 628474 01904 610690

Dir: *off Bootham A19*

In a quiet side road within easy walking distance of the city, this attractive Georgian building is pleasantly furnished and offers

contd. on p. 742

Y

Knavesmire Manor HOTEL & RESTAURANT

AA ★★

Proprietors Ian and Margaret Senior

302 TADCASTER ROAD, YORK, YO2 2HE

Telephone: 01904 702941

Fax: 709274

Logis of Great Britain

This late Regency villa (c.1833) was once a Rowntree family home and overlooks York Racecourse whilst close to the city centre. The house became affectionately known as 'a place of friendliness refreshment and peace' and it is in this same tradition of hospitality that guests are welcomed today. The Manor retains many original features, the Oak Room Bar providing added relaxation together with a private indoor swimming pool and spa with sauna, housed in a Victorian style conservatory • Hotel & Motel accommodation • Arnold's Brasserie Restaurant (Red Rosette award) • Conferences & meetings (2-40 delegates) • Walled gardens & car park • Private tropical pool & spa • *All major credit cards accepted*

Forest & Vale

Built in 1786 this former Georgian manor house located on the edge of the breathtaking North Yorkshire Moors, offering a personal and attentive service is the perfect place to relax and unwind. Superb traditional food can be enjoyed in both the restaurant and the Forest Bar. Ideally placed for exploring the moors, Whitby, Scarborough, Castle Howard, shopping in York or a scenic trip on the steam railway.

FOREST & VALE HOTEL
Malton Road, Pickering
North Yorkshire YO18 7DL
Tel: (01751) 472722 Fax: (01751) 472972

Consort HOTELS GROUP

Jacobean Lodge Hotel

WIGGINTON, YORK YO3 3RG

Tel: 01904 762749 Fax: 01904 768403

AA ★★

Converted 17th century detached farmhouse situated in rural surroundings four miles north of York.

Fourteen tastefully decorated and well equipped bedrooms including four-posters.

In winter, relax by open fires in the oak beamed bars – while in summer enjoy 'al fresco' on the patio in our 1½ acre gardens.

★★

Hudson's HOTEL

60 BOOTHAM YORK YO30 7BZ

Tel: 01904 621267

Fax: 01904 654719

Only two minutes from York Minster.
Victorian styled Restaurant and Bar.
Secure Car Park.
Conference facilities.

well equipped accommodation. Service is cheerful and attentive, good home cooking is a feature, the hotel has a car park.

Alhambra Court Hotel, York

ROOMS: 24 en suite (bth/shr) (5 fmly) No smoking in 12 bedrooms s £35-£47.50; d £47-£75 (incl. bkfst) * LB Off peak **MEALS:** Dinner fr £13.50 English & French Cuisine **FACILITIES:** CTV in all bedrooms **SERVICES:** Lift 25P **NOTES:** No dogs (ex guide dogs) No smoking in restaurant Last d 8.30pm Closed 24-31 Dec & 1-7 Jan
CARDS:

YORK North Yorkshire **Map 08 SE65**

★★ Cottage

3 Clifton Green YO30 6LH

Quality Percentage Score: 67%

☎ 01904 643711 🖷 01904 611230

Overlooking Clifton Green, this well furnished and comfortable hotel is within easy walking distance of the city. Bedrooms, some of which are located in the rear courtyard, are all well equipped. The public rooms are cosy and pleasantly appointed, and there is a good range of food available.

ROOMS: 16 en suite (bth/shr) 3 annexe en suite (bth/shr) (3 fmly) d £45-£75 (incl. bkfst) * LB Off peak **MEALS:** Dinner £11.50-£18.95 & alc V meals Coffee am Tea pm **FACILITIES:** CTV in all bedrooms STV **SERVICES:** 10P **NOTES:** Last d 8.30pm Closed 24-26 Dec
CARDS:

YORK North Yorkshire **Map 08 SE65**

★★ *Jacobean Lodge*

Plainville Ln, Wigginton YO32 2RG

Quality Percentage Score: 66%

☎ 01904 762749 🖷 01904 768403

Dir: *Northern ring road A1237 towards Helmsley sign B1363. Left to Shipton, follow hotel sign*

This comfortable hotel stands in open countryside and is within easy driving distance of the city. Bedrooms are modern and well equipped, and a good range of home cooked meals is available in the pleasant bars or the cosy restaurant. The hotel is family owned and run, and is set in extensive gardens.

ROOMS: 8 en suite (bth/shr) 6 annexe en suite (bth/shr) (2 fmly)
MEALS: English & Continental Cuisine V meals Coffee am
FACILITIES: CTV in all bedrooms Giant chess Childrens play area Wkly live entertainment ch fac **CONF:** Thtr 40 Class 30 Board 30
SERVICES: 52P **NOTES:** No smoking in restaurant Last d 10pm RS all yr
CARDS:

See advert on page 741

YORK North Yorkshire **Map 08 SE65**

★★ Elmbank

The Mount YO24 1GE

Quality Percentage Score: 65%

☎ 01904 610653 🖷 01904 627139

Dir: *on A1036 Tadcaster road following signs for racecourse*

Designed in the style of Charles Rennie Mackintosh and with some interesting architectural features, including a fine staircase and gallery, this hotel is very convenient for the racecourse. It caters mainly for conferences and business people, and has a good range of services carried out by friendly staff. Bedrooms are thoughtfully equipped and are gradually being upgraded.

ROOMS: 48 rms (46 bth/shr) 15 annexe en suite (bth/shr) (7 fmly) s £49.50-£69; d £70-£95 (incl. bkfst) * LB Off peak **MEALS:** Sunday Lunch £9 Dinner £15-£17 & alc V meals Coffee am Tea pm **FACILITIES:** CTV in all bedrooms Xmas **CONF:** Thtr 100 Class 35 Board 40 Del from £75 * **SERVICES:** Night porter 20P **NOTES:** No smoking in restaurant Last d 9pm **CARDS:**

See advert on opposite page

YORK North Yorkshire **Map 08 SE65**

★★ *Savages*

St Peters Grove, Clifton YO30 6AQ

Quality Percentage Score: 65%

☎ 01904 610818 🖷 01904 627729

Dir: *off A19 at Clifton*

Standing in a quiet side road and within easy walking distance of the city and the Minster this family-owned and run hotel offers a good standard of both accommodation and service. Good honest home cooking is served in the dining room and the bedrooms are well equipped. A lounge is a pleasant area in which to relax both before and after dinner.

ROOMS: 20 en suite (bth/shr) (3 fmly) **MEALS:** V meals Coffee am Tea pm **FACILITIES:** CTV in all bedrooms **CONF:** **SERVICES:** 14P **NOTES:** No dogs (ex guide dogs) No smoking in restaurant Last d 9pm Closed 25 & 26 Dec **CARDS:**

See advert on opposite page

YORK North Yorkshire **Map 08 SE65**

★★ Lady Anne Middletons Hotel

Skeldergate YO1 6DS

Quality Percentage Score: 64%

☎ 01904 632257 & 630456 01904 613043

Dir: *from A1036 towards City Centre. Right at City Walls lights, keep left, 1st left before bridge, then 1st left into Cromwell Rd. Hotel on right*

This nicely furnished city-centre hotel has been created from several buildings. Among its amenities are a bar lounge and a dining room where a satisfying range of dishes is served.

ROOMS: 40 rms (37 bth/shr) 15 annexe en suite (bth/shr) (3 fmly) No smoking in 15 bedrooms s £70-£80; d £90-£120 (incl. bkfst) * LB Off peak **MEALS:** Lunch £8.50 Dinner £16.95 V meals Coffee am Tea pm **FACILITIES:** CTV in 52 bedrooms Indoor swimming pool (heated) Sauna Solarium Gym No leisure facilities for under 16yrs Xmas **CONF:** Thtr 50 Class 50 Board 20 Del from £95 * **SERVICES:** Night porter 56P **NOTES:** No smoking in restaurant Last d 9.30pm Closed 24-27 Dec **CARDS:**

YORK North Yorkshire **Map 08 SE65**

★★ Newington

147 Mount Vale YO24 1DJ

Quality Percentage Score: 64%

☎ 01904 625173 01904 679937

Dir: *A1036 W from bypass to city centre, hotel is on the right*

Next to York racecourse, this value-for-money hotel provides modern well equipped bedrooms, some in a rear coach house. Lounges are comfortable and a good range of home-cooked food is available in the attractive dining room.

ROOMS: 28 en suite (bth/shr) 14 annexe en suite (bth/shr) (3 fmly) No smoking in 6 bedrooms s £42-£44; d £60-£68 (incl. bkfst) * LB Off peak **MEALS:** Bar Lunch £3.95-£5.95 Dinner £13.95-£16.45 Coffee am **FACILITIES:** CTV in all bedrooms Indoor swimming pool (heated) Sauna Xmas **SERVICES:** Lift 40P **NOTES:** No dogs No smoking in restaurant Last d 8.30pm **CARDS:**

YORK North Yorkshire **Map 08 SE65**

★★ Abbots' Mews

6 Marygate Ln, Bootham YO30 7DE

Quality Percentage Score: 63%

☎ 01904 634866 01904 612848

Dir: *overlooking Marygate car park*

This Victorian cottage and other nearby buildings have been converted into a comfortable hotel. It provides modern bedrooms together with cosy public rooms overlooking a floodlit garden. A good range of food is available in the spacious restaurant.

ROOMS: 12 en suite (shr) 39 annexe en suite (bth/shr) (9 fmly) s fr £40; d fr £70 (incl. bkfst) * LB Off peak **MEALS:** Lunch £10-£15 Dinner £15-£20 International Cuisine V meals Coffee am Tea pm **FACILITIES:** CTV in all bedrooms Xmas **CONF:** Thtr 30 Class 30 Board 20 **SERVICES:** Night porter 30P **NOTES:** No dogs (ex guide dogs) Last d 9.30pm Closed New Year **CARDS:**

See advert on page 743

YORK North Yorkshire **Map 08 SE65**

★★ Elliotts

Sycamore Place, Bootham YO30 7DW

Quality Percentage Score: 62%

☎ 01904 623333 01904 654908

Dir: *A19 Thirsk follow road to York centre under footbridge, 2nd turning on right alongside railway lines, hotel at the bottom*

This delightful Victorian house has a friendly and relaxing atmosphere and offers good accommodation together with freshly prepared meals in both bar and restaurant.

ROOMS: 18 en suite (bth/shr) (2 fmly) No smoking in 1 bedroom s £35-£45; d £52-£66 (incl. bkfst) * Off peak **MEALS:** Lunch fr £8.95 Dinner £8.95-£11.95 V meals Coffee am **FACILITIES:** CTV in all bedrooms **SERVICES:** Night porter 14P **NOTES:** No dogs (ex guide dogs) Last d 9.30pm Closed 24 Dec-3 Jan **CARDS:**

YORK North Yorkshire **Map 08 SE65**

Travel Inn

Bilborough Top, Colton YO24 1LR

☎ 01937 835067 01937 835934

Dir: *on A64 between Tadcaster & York*

This modern building offers accommodation in smart, spacious and well equipped bedrooms, all with en-suite bathrooms. Refreshments may be taken at the nearby family restaurant. For details about current prices consult the Contents Page under Hotel Groups for the Travel Inn phone number. **ROOMS:** 60 en suite (bth/shr) d £39.95 *

YORK North Yorkshire **Map 08 SE65**

Travel Inn

White Rose Close, York Business Park, Nether Poppleton YO26 6RA

☎ 01904 787630 01904 787663

Dir: *on A1237 York Ring Rd between A19 Thirsk rd & A59 Harrogate rd*

This modern building offers accommodation in smart, spacious and well equipped bedrooms, all with en-suite bathrooms. Refreshments may be taken at the nearby family restaurant. For details about current prices consult the Contents Page under Hotel Groups for the Travel Inn phone number. **ROOMS:** 44 en suite (bth/shr) d £39.95 *

YORK North Yorkshire **Map 08 SE65**

York Viking Moat House

North St YO1 6JF

☎ 01904 459988 01904 641793

Dir: *turn off A1 onto A64, then onto A1036 into York centre, between Ouse bridge and Lendal bridge*

Many of the well equipped bedrooms in this modern hotel overlook the River Ouse. The hotel provides extensive banqueting and conference facilities, a Work Base business centre and a Health and Fitness club.

ROOMS: 200 en suite (bth/shr) (7 fmly) No smoking in 144 bedrooms s £60-£115; d £90-£135 * LB Off peak **MEALS:** Bar Lunch £3.50-£10 Dinner fr £16.95 & alc International Cuisine V meals Coffee am Tea pm **FACILITIES:** CTV in all bedrooms Sauna Solarium Gym Jacuzzi/spa Beauty therapy room Xmas **CONF:** Thtr 300 Class 150 Board 50 Del from £100 * **SERVICES:** Lift Night porter 85P **NOTES:** No dogs (ex guide dogs) No smoking in restaurant Last d 9.30pm **CARDS:**

YOXFORD Suffolk **Map 05 TM36**

★★ Satis House

IP17 3EX

Quality Percentage Score: 71%

☎ 01728 668418 01728 668640

Dir: *set back from A12 midway between Ipswich & Lowerstoft*

Charles Dickens visited this 18th-century house and in Great Expectations gave the meaning of 'Satis' as 'enough'. East really does meet West here; Mrs Blackmore is Malaysian and the elegant public rooms combine English charm with Oriental exoticism. The individually decorated bedrooms vary in size and space but all have lovely period furniture. The Malaysian cuisine is a real treat, the Kenduri banquet is well worth a try.

ROOMS: 8 en suite (bth/shr) s £55-£59.50; d £75-£95 (incl. bkfst) * LB Off peak **MEALS:** Lunch £13.95-£19.95alc Dinner £19.95-£23.95alc English, French & Malaysian Cuisine V meals **FACILITIES:** CTV in all bedrooms Tennis (hard) Sauna Jacuzzi/spa **CONF:** Thtr 26 Class 20 Board 14 **SERVICES:** 30P **NOTES:** No dogs No coaches No children 7yrs No smoking in restaurant Last d 9pm **CARDS:**

Y

Channel Islands

Directory of establishments in alphabetical order of location.

CHANNEL ISLANDS — Map 16

GUERNSEY

CATEL

★★★ Cobo Bay

Cobo GY5 7HB

Quality Percentage Score: 75%

☎ 01481 257102 Fax 01481 254542

Dir: *on main coast road*

A popular family-run hotel, overlooking Cobo Bay, provides a range of tastefully decorated modern bedrooms, those at the front having balconies. Public rooms include the Chesterfield Bar, furnished with leather sofas and armchairs, the large Cobo Suite, available for private functions and a candle-lit restaurant.

ROOMS: 36 en suite (bth/shr) (4 fmly) **MEALS:** International Cuisine V meals **FACILITIES:** CTV in all bedrooms STV Snooker Sauna Solarium Pool table Jacuzzi/spa Wkly live entertainment **CONF:** Thtr 50 Class 30 Board 30 **SERVICES:** Lift Night porter 60P **NOTES:** No dogs (ex guide dogs) No coaches Last d 9.45pm Closed 5 Jan-6 Mar

CARDS:

CATEL

★★ Hotel Hougue du Pommier

Hougue Du Pommier Rd GY5 7FQ

Quality Percentage Score: 75%

☎ 01481 56531 Fax 01481 56260

In a quiet location, close to the beach and shopping, the hotel provides high standards of accommodation. Bedrooms are well equipped, especially the 'deluxe' rooms. Public arcas have kept the character of the building's 18th-century origins.

ROOMS: 44 en suite (bth/shr) (5 fmly) **MEALS:** English & Continental Cuisine V meals Coffee am Tea pm **FACILITIES:** CTV in all bedrooms STV Outdoor swimming pool (heated) Golf 10 Sauna Solarium Pool table Putting green Games room Table tennis ch fac **SERVICES:** 87P **NOTES:** No smoking in restaurant Last d 9pm

CARDS:

FERMAIN BAY

★★★ La Favorita

GY4 6SD

Quality Percentage Score: 75%

☎ 01481 235666 Fax 01481 235413

Dir: *at the junct of Fort Road, Sausmarez Road and Fermain Lane take the road (Fermain Lane) signposted to La Favorita Hotel and Fermain Bay*

This charming hotel is on the side of a wooded valley in walking distance of Fermain Bay. Bedrooms are smartly decorated, comfortably furnished and well equipped. Spacious public areas include a choice of lounges, bar, restaurant and a café/brasserie, open all day.

ROOMS: 37 en suite (bth/shr) (6 fmly) No smoking in all bedrooms **MEALS:** English & French Cuisine V meals Coffee am Tea pm **FACILITIES:** CTV in all bedrooms Indoor swimming pool (heated) Sauna Jacuzzi/spa ch fac **CONF:** Thtr 70 Class 30 Board 30 **SERVICES:** Lift 40P **NOTES:** No dogs No coaches No smoking in restaurant Last d 9pm Closed 4 Jan-12 Feb **CARDS:**

See advert on this page

F

FERMAIN BAY

★★★ Le Chalet

GY4 6SD

Quality Percentage Score: 68%

☎ 01481 235716 01481 235718

Dir: *from airport turn left, heading towards St Martins village. At filter turn right to Sausmarez Rd then follow sign for Fermain bay & Le Chalet hotel*

On one side of a wooded valley leading down to Fermain Bay, Le Chalet enjoys a peaceful setting. Bedrooms are generally spacious, comfortably furnished and well equipped. Public areas include the bright dining room, popular bar and wood panelled lounge.

ROOMS: 41 en suite (bth/shr) (5 fmly) s £50-£75; d £64-£100 (incl. bkfst) * LB Off peak **MEALS:** Sunday Lunch £11 Dinner £16 & alc English, Austrian & French Cuisine V meals Coffee am Tea pm **FACILITIES:** CTV in all bedrooms Indoor swimming pool (heated) Sauna Solarium Jacuzzi/spa **SERVICES:** 35P **NOTES:** No coaches Last d 9.30pm Closed mid Oct-mid Apr **CARDS:**

FOREST

★★ Le Chene

Forest Rd GY8 0AH

Quality Percentage Score: 65%

☎ 01481 235566 01481 239456

This Victorian manor, set on the hillside, has been skilfully extended to house a range of well equipped modern bedrooms, some on the lower floor. Public rooms are on the same level, and include a dining room sun lounge and cellar bar. Service is particularly friendly.

ROOMS: 26 en suite (bth/shr) (2 fmly) s £37-£47; d £54-£74 (incl. bkfst) * Off peak **MEALS:** Dinner £12 English & Continental Cuisine V meals Coffee am Tea pm **FACILITIES:** CTV in all bedrooms Outdoor swimming pool (heated) **SERVICES:** 21P **NOTES:** No dogs No coaches No children 12yrs No smoking in restaurant Last d 7.45pm Closed 13 Oct-29 Apr **CARDS:**

PERELLE

★★★ L'Atlantique

Perelle Bay GY7 9NA

Quality Percentage Score: 73%

☎ 01481 264056 01481 263800

Dir: *exit Guernsey airport, turn right and continue on this route until you reach the sea. Turn right and follow the coast road for 1.5m*

Situated on the west coast, flanked by safe sandy beaches, this modern hotel offers comfortable accommodation and a friendly atmosphere. Some bedrooms look out over Perelle Bay, some have balconies; all are equipped with modern facilities. Public areas include the Victoriana Bar, serving a range of popular dishes, a cocktail bar, with sun terrace and lounge, and the Restaurant l'Atlantique whose imaginative menus feature local seafood.

ROOMS: 23 rms (21 bth/shr) (4 fmly) No smoking in 12 bedrooms s £43-£51.50; d £73-£90 (incl. bkfst) * LB Off peak **MEALS:** Sunday Lunch £11.95 Dinner £17 & alc International Cuisine V meals Coffee am **FACILITIES:** CTV in all bedrooms Outdoor swimming pool (heated) Tariff prices include car hire **SERVICES:** 80P **NOTES:** No dogs (ex guide dogs) No coaches No smoking area in restaurant Last d 9.30pm Closed Nov-Feb **CARDS:**

ST MARTIN

★★★ *Idlerocks*

Jerbourg Point GY4 6BJ

Quality Percentage Score: 71%

☎ 01481 237711 01481 235592

This family run cliff top hotel enjoys sea views towards the Channel islands and French coast. Bedrooms, varying in shape and size, are individually decorated and well equipped. Guests relax in the small cosy lounge and dine in Admirals Restaurant or the more informal Lounge and Terrace.

ROOMS: 28 en suite (bth/shr) (4 fmly) No smoking in 11 bedrooms **MEALS:** English & French Cuisine V meals Coffee am Tea pm **FACILITIES:** CTV in all bedrooms STV Outdoor swimming pool (heated) **CONF:** Board 30 **SERVICES:** Night porter 100P **NOTES:** Last d 9pm **CARDS:**

ST MARTIN

★★★ La Barbarie

Saints Rd, Saints Bay GY4 6ES

Quality Percentage Score: 70%

☎ 01481 235217 01481 235208

Dating from the 17th century, this former priory enjoys a peaceful setting. The character and charm of the original building has been retained and carefully combined with modern facilities. The bedrooms are tastefully decorated and the beamed restaurant offers a wide range of interesting dishes, while the bar menu features fresh fish.

ROOMS: 23 en suite (bth/shr) (4 fmly) s £36-£52; d £50-£80 (incl. bkfst) * LB Off peak **MEALS:** Sunday Lunch £11.25 Dinner £14.95 & alc English & French Cuisine V meals Coffee am Tea pm **FACILITIES:** CTV in all bedrooms Outdoor swimming pool (heated) Xmas **SERVICES:** 50P **NOTES:** No dogs No smoking area in restaurant Last d 9.30pm **CARDS:**

ST MARTIN

★★★ Bella Luce Hotel & Restaurant

La Fosse GY4 6EB

Quality Percentage Score: 70%

☎ 01481 238764 01481 239561

Dir: *from airport, turn left to St Peter Port. At second set of traffic lights contiue 40yds and turn right to hotel*

A 12th-century manor house, extended to offer attractive, comfortable accommodation. Bar, lounge and dining room have kept much of their character, and bar lunches are popular. The restaurant offers more formal dining.

ROOMS: 32 en suite (bth/shr) (6 fmly) s £27-£51; d £54-£100 (incl. bkfst) * LB Off peak **MEALS:** Sunday Lunch fr £9.50 High tea fr £2.50 Dinner £16 English & Continental Cuisine V meals Coffee am Tea pm **FACILITIES:** CTV in all bedrooms STV Outdoor swimming pool (heated) Sauna Solarium ch fac Xmas **CONF:** Thtr 40 Class 40 Board 30 Del from £56 **SERVICES:** Night porter 50P **NOTES:** No coaches No smoking in restaurant Last d 9.45pm **CARDS:**

See advert on opposite page

ST MARTIN

★★★ Hotel Bon Port

Moulin Huet Bay GY4 6EW

Quality Percentage Score: 70%

☎ 01481 239249 01481 239596

Dir: *exit airport turn left into St Martins village, at final traffic lights turn right, follow signs from here*

This well presented hotel enjoys beautiful coastal scenery from its peaceful, cliff top location. The bedrooms, some of which offer sea-facing balconies, are neatly decorated, comfortably furnished and well equipped with items such as mini bars. Public areas include a spacious lounge, a large sun terrace overlooking the outdoor pool and a smartly appointed restaurant where guests can enjoy Phil Ashman's high quality cooking.

ROOMS: 18 en suite (bth/shr) (2 fmly) **MEALS:** Lunch fr £12.50 Dinner fr £18.50 English & French Cuisine V meals Coffee am Tea pm **FACILITIES:** CTV in all bedrooms STV Outdoor swimming pool (heated) Sauna Gym Croquet lawn Putting green **SERVICES:** 30P **NOTES:** No dogs (ex guide dogs) No smoking in restaurant Last d 9.30pm **CARDS:**

See advert on opposite page

ST MARTIN

★★★ *St Margaret's Lodge*
Forest Rd GY4 6UE
Quality Percentage Score: 69%
☎ 01481 235757 Fax 01481 237594
Dir: *1m W*

Conveniently located for the airport, this well presented hotel caters well for the business and leisure markets. Bedrooms offer modern standards of comfort, and public areas include a large bar with adjoining conservatory and a smartly refurbished restaurant.

ROOMS: 47 en suite (bth) (2 fmly) **MEALS:** English & French Cuisine V meals Coffee am Tea pm **FACILITIES:** CTV in all bedrooms STV Outdoor swimming pool (heated) Sauna Solarium Croquet lawn Putting green Table tennis Wkly live entertainment **CONF:** Thtr 120 Class 80 Board 20 **SERVICES:** Lift Night porter 100P **NOTES:** No dogs No smoking in restaurant Last d 9.30pm
CARDS:

ST MARTIN

★★★ Green Acres
Les Hubits GY4 6LS
Quality Percentage Score: 68%
☎ 01481 235711 Fax 01481 235978
Dir: *behind parish church, 2m from airport*

Peacefully situated in its own grounds, this well managed hotel is within walking distance of Fermain Bay and only a mile from St Peter Port. Comfortable bedrooms are decorated in modern styles and the public areas include a lounge, a bar-lounge and a restaurant. Bar meals are popular at lunchtime, and the menu regularly features local seafood.

ROOMS: 48 en suite (bth/shr) (3 fmly) s £30-£53; d £60-£86 (incl. bkfst) * Off peak **MEALS:** Bar Lunch £3-£10alc Dinner £14 & alc English & French Cuisine V meals Coffee am Tea pm **FACILITIES:** CTV in all bedrooms Outdoor swimming pool (heated) **CONF:** Thtr 30 Class 20 Board 20 **SERVICES:** 75P **NOTES:** No dogs (ex guide dogs) No smoking in restaurant Last d 8.30pm Closed mid-end Mar **CARDS:**

ST MARTIN

★★★ Hotel Jerbourg
Jerbourg Point GY4 6BJ
Quality Percentage Score: 68%
☎ 01481 238826 Fax 01481 238238
Dir: *from airport turn left and follow rd to St Martins village, the right onto filter rd thenstraight on at lghts, hotel is at end of the rd on right*

A cliff top hotel at the end of a quiet lane, with fine sea views. Smartly appointed public areas include an extensive bar and lounge and bright conservatory-style restaurant. Bedrooms have

contd.

a variety of aspects, all are well fitted out, newer luxury Bay rooms are more spacious.
ROOMS: 32 en suite (bth/shr) (4 fmly) No smoking in all bedrooms s £40-£75; d £80-£130 (incl. bkfst) * LB Off peak **MEALS:** Lunch £11.50 High tea £5.25 Dinner fr £15.95 & alc English & French Cuisine V meals Coffee am Tea pm **FACILITIES:** CTV in all bedrooms STV Outdoor swimming pool (heated) Y Xmas **CONF:** Thtr 50 Class 50 Board 50 Del from £65 * **SERVICES:** 50P **NOTES:** No dogs (ex guide dogs) No smoking area in restaurant Last d 9.30pm **CARDS:**

ST MARTIN
★★★ *La Trelade*
Forest Rd GY4 6UB
Quality Percentage Score: 64%
☎ 01481 235454 📠 01481 237855
The hotel is close to the rugged cliffs and sandy bays of Guernsey's south coast. Tastefully decorated bedrooms are equipped with modern comforts. Public areas include lounges, a bar and attractive gardens with a pool.
ROOMS: 45 en suite (bth/shr) (3 fmly) **MEALS:** English & French Cuisine V meals Coffee am Tea pm **FACILITIES:** CTV in all bedrooms STV Outdoor swimming pool (heated) Pool table Putting green Wkly live entertainment ch fac **CONF:** Thtr 120 Class 48 Board 40 **SERVICES:** Lift Night porter 120P **NOTES:** No smoking in restaurant Last d 9pm
CARDS:

See advert on opposite page

ST MARTIN
★★ La Michele
Les Hubits GY4 6NB
Quality Percentage Score: 73%
☎ 01481 238065 📠 01481 239492
Dir: *located in a quiet country lane, about 10 minutes walk from Fermain Bay, about 1.5m from St Peter Port*
This delightful family-run hotel enjoys a peaceful location not far from Fermain Bay. Bedrooms are neatly presented, comfortably furnished and very well equipped. Public areas include a new conservatory and extended restaurant which overlook the attractive garden and outdoor pool.
ROOMS: 16 en suite (bth/shr) (3 fmly) s £30-£43; d £60-£86 (incl. bkfst & dinner) * LB Off peak **MEALS:** V meals **FACILITIES:** CTV in all bedrooms Outdoor swimming pool (heated) **SERVICES:** 16P **NOTES:** No dogs (ex guide dogs) No coaches No children 8yrs No smoking in restaurant Last d 7.30pm Closed Nov-Mar
CARDS:

S

ST MARTIN
★★ La Villette
GY4 6QG
Quality Percentage Score: 67%
☎ 01481 235292 📠 01481 237699
A family-run Georgian house standing in peaceful grounds. Bedrooms are decorated in a modern style, and day rooms consist of a large bar offering a range of snacks, and regular live music, a separate restaurant and a lounge.
ROOMS: 41 en suite (bth/shr) s £29-£39; d £58-£78 (incl. bkfst) * LB Off peak **MEALS:** English & French Cuisine V meals Coffee am Tea pm **FACILITIES:** CTV in all bedrooms Indoor swimming pool (heated) Outdoor swimming pool (heated) Gym Jacuzzi/spa Steam room Xmas **SERVICES:** 50P **NOTES:** No smoking in restaurant Last d 8.30pm
CARDS:

ST MARTIN
★★ *Carlton*
Les Caches, Forest Rd GY4 6PR
Quality Percentage Score: 66%
☎ 01481 235678 📠 01481 236590
Dir: *on road from airport to main twon of St Peter Port*
Extensive refurbishment has created smart public areas with an inviting atmosphere, especially the dining room. There is also a public bar, serving meals, and residents have a separate lounge. Bedrooms offer good modern standards of comfort.
ROOMS: 45 en suite (bth/shr) 2 annexe en suite (bth/shr) (4 fmly) **MEALS:** V meals Coffee am Tea pm **FACILITIES:** CTV in all bedrooms STV Pool table Wkly live entertainment ch fac **NOTES:** No dogs (ex guide dogs) No smoking in restaurant Last d 8pm
CARDS:

See advert on opposite page

ST PETER PORT
★★★★ Old Government House Hotel
PO BOX 47 ANN'S PLACE GY1 4AZ
Quality Percentage Score: 70%
☎ 01481 724921 📠 01481 724429
Dir: *from airport hotel is located in centre of island, overlooking harbour*
With fine views over the harbour, the 'OGH' has been here for a long time, with buildings added along the way. This explains the variety of the bedrooms, some of which are particularly small. The entrance hall is most attractive, but some of the public areas are looking a little tired. The food can disappoint at times, but there are three bars (one a night club in summer) and staff are friendly.
ROOMS: 68 en suite (bth/shr) s £75-£85.50; d £115-£155 (incl. bkfst) * LB Off peak **MEALS:** Lunch fr £14 High tea £6.50-£7.50 Dinner £19.75 & alc International Cuisine V meals Coffee am Tea pm **FACILITIES:** CTV in all bedrooms STV Outdoor swimming pool (heated) Xmas **CONF:** Thtr 180 Class 150 Board 90 **SERVICES:** Lift Night porter 24P **NOTES:** No dogs (ex guide dogs) No coaches No smoking in restaurant Last d 9.30pm **CARDS:**

ST PETER PORT
★★★★ St Pierre Park
Rohais GY1 1FD
Quality Percentage Score: 68%
☎ 01481 728282 📠 01481 712041
Dir: *10 minutes from airport*
Close to St Peter Port and set in 45 acres of parkland, this purpose-built hotel caters for all markets. Bedrooms feature either a balcony or terrace and guests can either eat in the elegant Victor Hugo Restaurant or the smart but casual Café Renoir.
ROOMS: 132 en suite (bth/shr) (4 fmly) No smoking in 17 bedrooms s fr £125; d fr £165 (incl. bkfst) * LB Off peak **MEALS:** Lunch £10.50-£14.50 & alc Dinner £16-£21.50 & alc English, Italian & French Cuisine V meals Coffee am Tea pm **FACILITIES:** CTV in all bedrooms STV Indoor swimming pool (heated) Golf 9 Tennis (hard) Snooker Sauna Solarium Gym Pool table Croquet lawn Putting green Jacuzzi/spa Bird watching Trim trail Child playground Crazy golf ch fac Xmas **CONF:** Thtr 200 Class 100 Board 30 Del from £99 * **SERVICES:** Lift Night porter 150P **NOTES:** No dogs (ex guide dogs) No smoking area in restaurant Last d 10pm **CARDS:**

The CARLTON Hotel

Les Caches, St Martin's, Guernsey
Channel Islands
Tel: 01481 35678 · Fax: 01481 36590

Situated in the lovely parish of St Martin's, this charming country hotel is ideally placed, close to town with many cliff walks and beaches just a short drive away. The hotel is an ideal choice for holidays or short breaks. First child stays free, second child at 50% rate, when sharing with an adult. Car hire can be arranged with preferential rates. Holidays and short breaks can be booked through the hotel, travelling by air or sea, please ask for package prices and availability. The **Fox & Hound** traditional pub is part of the hotel complex and is a popular meeting place for visitors and locals alike.

Grand opening 1st July 1999
of the Island's newest Health Suite and Swimming Pool complex situated within the hotel – ideal for Family Days of Fun.

★★★

La Trelade Hotel

Forest Road, St Martin's, Guernsey,
Channel Islands GY4 6UB
Telephone: 01481 35454 Fax: 01481 37855

Standing in its own beautiful grounds in the most picturesque part of Guernsey. Originally a traditional Guernsey country house. All the tastefully decorated bedrooms are en suite and have full amenities there are also 4 poster bedroom suites. The majority of the rooms have pleasant views over the gardens or swimming pool area. The use of fresh local produce including seafood and traditional English and French cuisine has given the hotel a reputation for good food and fine wines. Smaller in-house conferences for up to 80 persons and parking for over 100 cars can be catered for.

La Frégate Hotel & Restaurant

3 STARS

St Peter Port, Guernsey, Channel Islands
Telephone: (01481) 724624 Fax: (01481) 720443

La Frégate is a Country House Hotel tucked away in scented gardens in a quiet corner of St Peter Port with views over the harbour and islands of Herm and Sark. The French Restaurant is superb. Open all year round, 13 bedrooms, en suite, central heating, trouser press, hair dryer, TV.

ST PETER PORT
★★★ Hotel de Havelet
Havelet GY1 1BA
Quality Percentage Score: 73%
☎ 01481 722199 🖷 01481 714057
Dir: *from Guernsey airport follow signs for St Peter Port through St. Martins. At bottom of 'Val de Terres' hill turn left into Havelet*
This extended Georgian hotel looks over the harbour to Castle Cornet. Many of the well equipped bedrooms are set around a pretty colonial-style courtyard. Day rooms in the original building have period elegance, the restaurant and bar are on the other side of the car park in a converted stables.
ROOMS: 34 en suite (bth/shr) (4 fmly) s £50-£85; d £80-£120 (incl. bkfst) * LB Off peak **MEALS:** Lunch £9.50-£10.75 Dinner £14.50 & alc English, Austrian & French Cuisine V meals Coffee am Tea pm **FACILITIES:** CTV in all bedrooms STV Indoor swimming pool (heated) Sauna Jacuzzi/spa Xmas **CONF:** Thtr 40 Class 24 Board 26 Del from £90 * **SERVICES:** 40P **NOTES:** No dogs (ex guide dogs) No coaches No smoking area in restaurant Last d 9.30pm
CARDS:

ST PETER PORT
★★★ La Fregate
Les Cotils GY1 1UT
Quality Percentage Score: 72%
☎ 01481 724624 🖷 01481 720443

This secluded hotel is not too easy to find, so guests should ask for directions. Bedrooms are comfortable, attractive and well equipped, many with balconies. There is a popular cocktail bar and restaurant, with menus featuring local seafood and fresh local vegetables.
ROOMS: 13 en suite (bth/shr) s £60; d £75-£100 (incl. bkfst) * Off peak **MEALS:** Lunch £13.50 & alc Dinner £20 & alc Continental Cuisine V meals **FACILITIES:** CTV in all bedrooms **SERVICES:** 25P **NOTES:** No dogs No coaches No children 14yrs Last d 9.30pm
CARDS:

See advert on page 749

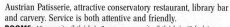

ST PETER PORT
★★★ Moore's
Pollet GY
Quality Percentage Score: 68%
☎ 01481 724452 🖷 01481 714037
Enjoying a central location set in the heart of St Peter Port just back from the harbour, Moore's is ideal for both business and leisure markets. With some parts dating back to the 18th century the hotel combines much of the original character together with more modern facilities such as the Sanctuary health suite. Bedrooms, which include three full suites are comfortably furnished and well equipped. Extensive public areas include an Austrian Patisserie, attractive conservatory restaurant, library bar and carvery. Service is both attentive and friendly.
ROOMS: 46 en suite (bth/shr) 3 annexe en suite (bth/shr) (8 fmly) s £50-£75; d £75-£100 (incl. bkfst) LB Off peak **MEALS:** Lunch £10 & alc Dinner £16 & alc English & French Cuisine V meals Coffee am Tea pm **FACILITIES:** CTV in all bedrooms STV Sauna Solarium Gym Jacuzzi/spa Xmas **CONF:** Thtr 35 Class 20 Board 15 Del from £80 * **SERVICES:** Lift Night porter **NOTES:** No dogs (ex guide dogs) No coaches Last d 9pm
CARDS:

ST PETER PORT

★★ Sunnycroft
5 Constitution Steps GY1 2PN
Quality Percentage Score: 69%
☎ 01481 723008 🖷 01481 712225
Glorious views across the harbour to neighbouring islands are a feature of this small, comfortable hotel. An old stepped and cobbled street gives access, and car parking can be arranged nearby. Many of the nicely decorated bedrooms have balconies and public rooms include a bar-lounge, a sitting room, a small reading room and a dining room.
ROOMS: 12 en suite (bth/shr) s £27-£37; d £54-£54 (incl. bkfst) * Off peak **MEALS:** Bar Lunch £2.75-£5.75 Dinner £9.50-£12.50 International Cuisine V meals Coffee am Tea pm **FACILITIES:** CTV in all bedrooms STV **SERVICES:** 3P **NOTES:** No dogs (ex guide dogs) No coaches No children 12yrs No smoking in restaurant Last d 8pm Closed mid Nov-mid Mar **CARDS:**

See advert on opposite page

VALE
★★★ *Pembroke Bay*
Pembroke Bay GY3 5BY
Quality Percentage Score: 64%
☎ 01481 247573 🖷 01481 248838
Situated near an excellent bathing beach, this popular hotel offers comfortable accommodation with a continental flair. Bedrooms are smartly equipped to modern standards, and public areas include a lounge and a restaurant with an interesting menu making fresh local fish a speciality.
ROOMS: 12 en suite (bth/shr) (2 fmly) No smoking in 6 bedrooms **MEALS:** Italian Cuisine V meals Coffee am **FACILITIES:** CTV in all bedrooms STV Outdoor swimming pool (heated) Tennis (hard) Sailing Surfing Bicycle hire **NOTES:** No smoking area in restaurant Last d 9.30pm Closed Oct-early Apr **CARDS:**

VALE
★★★ Peninsula
Les Dicqs GY6 8JP
Quality Percentage Score: 62%
☎ 01481 248400 🖷 01481 248706
Set in five acres of grounds next to a sandy beach, this modern hotel continues to improve. Bedrooms have all recently been

contd.

refurbished with new carpeting and co-ordinating fabrics. All have additional sofa beds to suit families and good work space for the business traveller. The open-plan public areas have a feeling of spaciousness.
ROOMS: 99 en suite (bth/shr) (99 fmly) No smoking in 18 bedrooms s £30.50-£52; d £45-£88 (incl. bkfst) * LB Off peak **MEALS:** Sunday Lunch fr £10.50 Dinner fr £14.50 & alc English & Continental Cuisine V meals Coffee am Tea pm **FACILITIES:** CTV in all bedrooms STV Outdoor swimming pool (heated) Croquet lawn Putting green Petanque Playground Wkly live entertainment **CONF:** Thtr 250 Class 140 Board 105 Del from £73 * **SERVICES:** Lift Night porter 120P **NOTES:** No smoking in restaurant Last d 9.30pm Closed for the Millennium
CARDS:

HERM

★★ White House

GY1 3HR
Quality Percentage Score: 73%
☎ 01481 722159 🖷 01481 710066
This attractive island hotel enjoys a unique setting on the harbour offering superb sea views. Set in well tended gardens, the main house and adjacent cottages contain neatly decorated bedrooms, all of which feature modern en suite bathrooms. Guests can relax in one of several comfortable lounges, enjoy a drink in one of two bars and choose from the interesting range of dishes in the popular restaurant.
ROOMS: 16 en suite (bth/shr) 22 annexe en suite (bth/shr) (12 fmly) s £62.50-£89; d £125-£152 (incl. bkfst & dinner) * LB Off peak **MEALS:** Lunch £11-£18 Dinner £18.25-£19.25 English & French Cuisine V meals Coffee am Tea pm **FACILITIES:** Outdoor swimming pool (heated) Tennis (hard) Croquet lawn **NOTES:** No dogs (ex guide dogs) No coaches No smoking in restaurant Last d 9pm Closed 9 Oct-5 Apr
CARDS:

JERSEY

ARCHIRONDEL

★★★ Les Arches

Archirondel Bay JE3 6DY
Quality Percentage Score: 62%
☎ 01534 853839 🖷 01534 856660
Dir: *Situated on the East coast of the island, 200yds from beach overlooking the French Coast*
Rooms facing the sea have private balconies, guests may enjoy sea views from the dining room or pool with sun terrace. Other public areas include two bars, one for residents and another with a more lively atmosphere, and a comfortable lounge. Staff are friendly and helpful.
ROOMS: 54 en suite (bth/shr) s £30-£43; d £59-£85 (incl. bkfst) * LB Off peak **MEALS:** English & Continental Cuisine V meals Coffee am **FACILITIES:** CTV in all bedrooms STV Outdoor swimming pool (heated) Tennis (hard) Sauna Gym Pool table Wkly live entertainment ch fac Xmas **CONF:** Thtr 180 Class 120 Board 120 **SERVICES:** Night porter 120P **NOTES:** No coaches **CARDS:**

BEAUMONT

★★ Hotel L'Hermitage

JE3 7BR
Quality Percentage Score: 65%
☎ 01534 733314 & 758272 🖷 01534 721207
Dir: *on N12*
L'Hermitage is based on a fine period house, many bedrooms open directly onto a lawned 'Piazza' to the rear. Rooms are generally spacious with bright fresh decor. Public rooms include a comfortable bar, non-smoking lounge and large dining room which features regular after dinner entertainment. Sandy beaches are two minutes away.
ROOMS: 43 en suite (bth/shr) 65 annexe rms (64 bth/shr) s £27-£42; d £50-£80 (incl. bkfst & dinner) * Off peak **MEALS:** Dinner £8.50 English & French Cuisine Coffee am Tea pm **FACILITIES:** CTV in all bedrooms Indoor swimming pool (heated) Outdoor swimming pool (heated) Sauna Solarium Jacuzzi/spa Wkly live entertainment **SERVICES:** Night porter 100P **NOTES:** No dogs No coaches No children 14yrs No smoking in restaurant Last d 8pm Closed mid Oct-mid Apr

GOREY

★★★ The Moorings

Gorey Pier JE3 6EW
Quality Percentage Score: 66%
☎ 01534 853633 🖷 01534 857618
Dir: *Situated beneath Mont Orgueil Castle, Gorey Pier overlooking the sandy beach of Grouville*
The Moorings enjoys an enviable position by the harbour. A well-appointed restaurant, featuring local seafood, is at the heart of public areas. There is a cosy bar and comfortable first-floor residents' lounge. Rooms at the front have a fine view of the harbour, three have access to a balcony.
ROOMS: 16 en suite (bth/shr) s £38-£47; d £74-£92 (incl. bkfst) * LB Off peak **MEALS:** English & Continental Cuisine V meals Coffee am **FACILITIES:** CTV in all bedrooms Xmas **CONF:** Thtr 20 Class 20 Board 20 **SERVICES:** Night porter **NOTES:** No coaches No smoking area in restaurant **CARDS:**

Symbols and Abbreviations are listed and explained on pages 4 and 5

GOREY

★★★ Old Court House

JE3 9FS
Quality Percentage Score: 66%
☎ 01534 854444 📠 01534 853587

Situated on the fringe of the village of Gorey, a short walk from the beaches of the island's east coast. The most popular bedrooms have balconies overlooking the gardens and heated pool. Five ground floor rooms have a private terrace. Spacious public areas include a beamed restaurant, large bar with dance floor and a comfortable separate lounge.

ROOMS: 58 en suite (bth/shr) (4 fmly) s £32-£49.50; d £64-£107 (incl. bkfst) * LB Off peak **MEALS:** Dinner £15 & alc English, French & Italian Cuisine V meals Coffee am Tea pm **FACILITIES:** CTV in all bedrooms STV Outdoor swimming pool (heated) Sauna Solarium Wkly live entertainment **SERVICES:** Lift Night porter 40P **NOTES:** No smoking area in restaurant Last d 9pm Closed Nov-Mar
CARDS:

G

L'ETACQ

★★★ Lobster Pot Hotel & Restaurant

JE3 2FB
Quality Percentage Score: 72%
☎ 01534 482888 📠 01534 455584
Dir: *turn off A12 at St Ouens parish hall onto B64. Hotel signposted at fork junct for B35*

A 17th-century former farmhouse overlooking St Ouens Bay. Public rooms are stylishly refurbished with a smart bar, air conditioned restaurant and cosy lounge. Spacious bedrooms have thoughtful touches such as robes, quality toiletries, CD music centres and video players. A good standard of cooking is offered in the restaurant, featuring much local seafood.

ROOMS: 12 en suite (bth/shr) (1 fmly) **MEALS:** Lunch £12.95-£15.95 & alc Dinner £18-£50alc English & Continental Cuisine V meals Tea pm **FACILITIES:** CTV in all bedrooms STV Wkly live entertainment **SERVICES:** Night porter Air conditioning 56P **NOTES:** No dogs (ex guide dogs) No smoking in restaurant Last d 9pm **CARDS:**

ROZEL BAY

The Premier Collection

★★★ Château la Chaire

Rozel Bay JE3 6AJ
☎ 01534 863354 📠 01534 865137
Dir: *from direction of St Helier on B38 turn left in village by the Rozel Bay Inn, hotel 100yds on right*

Chateau La Chaire is positioned on the side of a wooded valley and surrounded by five acres of terraced gardens. Built in 1843, the Chateau retains much of the atmosphere of a private country house, including some exquisite decorative plaster work in the drawing room. The oak-panelled dining room, with an conservatory extension, is a fine setting for some skilful and consistent cooking which features the best of local produce.

ROOMS: 14 en suite (bth/shr) (1 fmly) s £82-£108; d £132-£200 (incl. bkfst) * LB Off peak **MEALS:** Lunch £14.75 Dinner fr £26.50alc English & French Cuisine V meals Coffee am Tea pm **FACILITIES:** CTV in all bedrooms STV Xmas **CONF:** Board 20 **SERVICES:** Night porter 30P **NOTES:** No dogs (ex guide dogs) No children 7yrs No smoking area in restaurant Last d 9.30pm
CARDS:

ST AUBIN

★★★ Somerville

Mont du Boulevard JE3 8AD
Quality Percentage Score: 72%
☎ 01534 741226 📠 01534 746621
Dir: *from village, follow harbour then take Mont du Boulevard and second right hand bend*

This handsome 100-year old building overlooks St Aubin Bay, and has superb views from the restaurant, lounge areas and from some of the bedrooms. Rooms are well furnished, and there are some 'superior' rooms offering extra luxury.

ROOMS: 59 rms (58 bth/shr) (7 fmly) s £48-£54; d £96-£122 (incl. bkfst) * Off peak **MEALS:** Lunch £2-£12 High tea £1.60-£4 Dinner £15 English & French Cuisine V meals Coffee am Tea pm **FACILITIES:** CTV in all bedrooms STV Outdoor swimming pool (heated) Wkly live entertainment Xmas **SERVICES:** Lift Night porter 40P **NOTES:** No dogs No coaches No children 4yrs No smoking area in restaurant Last d 9pm
CARDS:

See advert on opposite page

ST BRELADE

★★★★ Hotel L'Horizon

St Brelade's Bay JE3 8EF
Quality Percentage Score: 78%
☎ 01534 743101 📠 01534 746269

L'Horizon's is on the golden sands of St Brelade's bay. Bedrooms

contd.

have been refurbished, many stylishly decorated in sunny colours, with a seashore theme. All are well equipped, the best enjoy views over the bay. Public areas include three eating options, the most serious being the art deco style Grill.
ROOMS: 107 en suite (bth/shr) (7 fmly) s £115-£170; d £165-£240 (incl. bkfst) * LB Off peak **MEALS:** Lunch £15-£17.50 & alc Dinner £25 & alc English, French & Mediterranean Cuisine V meals Coffee am Tea pm **FACILITIES:** CTV in all bedrooms STV Indoor swimming pool (heated) Sauna Gym Jacuzzi/spa Windsurfing Water skiing Wkly live entertainment Xmas **CONF:** Thtr 250 Class 58 Board 40 Del from £140 * **SERVICES:** Lift Night porter 125P **NOTES:** No dogs (ex guide dogs) No coaches No smoking area in restaurant Last d 10pm **CARDS:**

ST BRELADE

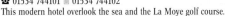

★★★★ The Atlantic
Le Mont de la Pulente JE3 8HE
Quality Percentage Score: 73%
☎ 01534 744101 📠 01534 744102
This modern hotel overlook the sea and the La Moye golf course. Bedrooms, although compact, are tastefully furnished and have balconies. Ground floor rooms are more spacious and have their own patios. Public rooms are elegant, there is a range of leisure facilities. Cuisine remains a focus here with an interesting range of dishes.
ROOMS: 50 en suite (bth/shr) s £100-£150; d £125-£225 (incl. bkfst) * LB Off peak **MEALS:** Lunch fr £16.50 Dinner fr £25 & alc British Cuisine V meals Coffee am Tea pm **FACILITIES:** CTV in all bedrooms STV Indoor swimming pool (heated) Outdoor swimming pool (heated) Tennis (hard) Sauna Solarium Gym Jacuzzi/spa Xmas **CONF:** Thtr 60 Class 40 Board 20 Del from £148 * **SERVICES:** Lift Night porter 60P **NOTES:** No dogs (ex guide dogs) No coaches Last d 9.30pm Closed Jan-Feb **CARDS:**

ST BRELADE

★★★★ Hotel La Place
Route Du Coin, La Haule JE3 8BT
Quality Percentage Score: 68%
☎ 01534 744261 📠 01534 745164
Dir: *turn off the main St Helier/St Aubin coast road at La Haule Manor (B25). Up the hill, take 2nd Left (to Redhouses), then 1st R. Hotel is 100m on R*
Created around a 17th-century farmhouse, the hotel offers a range of bedrooms, some are designed for the business traveller, others have access to the pool-side terrace and a couple have four-poster beds. Day rooms include a beamed lounge, a

contd.

The AA Hotel Booking Service is a free benefit to AA members. See the advertisement on page 47

refurbished cocktail bar and Knights Restaurant, with medieval style decor.

Hotel La Place, St Brelade

ROOMS: 43 en suite (bth/shr) (1 fmly) No smoking in 25 bedrooms s £84-£100; d £128-£184 (incl. bkfst) LB Off peak **MEALS:** Lunch £13.50 High tea £6-£10 Dinner £24 & alc V meals Coffee am Tea pm **FACILITIES:** CTV in all bedrooms STV Outdoor swimming pool (heated) Sauna ch fac Xmas **CONF:** Thtr 120 Class 40 Board 40 Del from £100 * **SERVICES:** Night porter 100P **NOTES:** Last d 9.30pm
CARDS:

See advert on opposite page

ST BRELADE
★★★★ St Brelade's Bay
JE3 8EF
Quality Percentage Score: 67%
☎ 01534 746141 📠 01534 747278

Attractions include extensive terraced gardens and a forsythia-covered terrace, where a buffet and bar operate at lunch-time. Public areas are furnished to a high standard, the well appointed bedrooms are comfortable. A great beach is just across the road.
ROOMS: 72 en suite (bth/shr) (50 fmly) s £53-£93; d £106-£186 (incl. bkfst) * Off peak **MEALS:** Lunch £15 & alc High tea £10 & alc Dinner £25 & alc English & French Cuisine V meals Coffee am **FACILITIES:** CTV in all bedrooms STV Outdoor swimming pool (heated) Tennis (hard & grass) Snooker Sauna Solarium Pool table Croquet lawn Putting green Petanque Mini-gym Wkly live entertainment ch fac **SERVICES:** Lift Night porter 60P **NOTES:** No dogs (ex guide dogs) No coaches No smoking in restaurant Last d 9pm Closed 11 Oct-22 Apr
CARDS:

ST BRELADE
★★★ *Château Valeuse*
Rue de Valeuse, St Brelade's Bay JE3 8EE
Quality Percentage Score: 69%
☎ 01534 746281 📠 01534 747110

With fine views of the bay, this well presented hotel offers comfortable accommodation and a warm and friendly atmosphere. The public areas include a spacious lounge, separate bar and a sun terrace which overlooks the pretty gardens. Guests can enjoy freshly prepared food in the Gallery Restaurant.
ROOMS: 34 en suite (bth/shr) (1 fmly) **MEALS:** English & French Cuisine V meals Coffee am Tea pm **FACILITIES:** CTV in all bedrooms Outdoor swimming pool (heated) Putting green **SERVICES:** Night porter 50P **NOTES:** No dogs No coaches No children 5yrs Last d 9pm Closed Nov-Mar **CARDS:**

ST BRELADE
★★★ Golden Sands
St Brelade's Bay JE3 8EF
Quality Percentage Score: 69%
☎ 01534 741241 📠 01534 499366

Centrally located in St Brelade's Bay, this hotel enjoys direct access to the beach. Different styles of bedroom are offered with the majority sea-facing and with balconies. Public areas include a smart reception foyer, separate lounge and spacious bar and restaurant which overlook the bay.

ROOMS: 62 en suite (bth/shr) (5 fmly) s £41-£78.75; d £52-£90 (incl. bkfst) * Off peak **MEALS:** Bar Lunch £2.50-£7 English & French Cuisine V meals Coffee am Tea pm **FACILITIES:** CTV in all bedrooms STV Childrens play room Wkly live entertainment **SERVICES:** Lift Night porter **NOTES:** No dogs No smoking in restaurant Closed mid Oct-mid Apr
CARDS:

See advert on page 753

ST BRELADE
★★★ Silver Springs
La Route des Genets JE3 8DB
Quality Percentage Score: 69%
☎ 01534 746401 📠 01534 746823

Dir: *turn R from leaving Airport onto B36 till you reach traffic lights. Turn L onto A13 & Hotel is 0.5m along this road.*

Silver Springs is set in seven acres of gardens and woodland, and is very popular with families. Public areas are spacious with separate lounges, a smart bar, and a restaurant that overlooks a wooded valley. Bedrooms are neatly decorated and comfortably furnished, some with balconies.
ROOMS: 88 en suite (bth/shr) (14 fmly) s £41.75-£68.75; d £33.75-£53.75 (incl. bkfst) * Off peak **MEALS:** Bar Lunch £2.10-£6 Dinner fr £14 English & French Cuisine V meals **FACILITIES:** CTV in all bedrooms STV Outdoor swimming pool (heated) Tennis (hard) Pool table Croquet lawn Putting green Boules Children's pool & playground Table tennis Wkly live entertainment ch fac **SERVICES:** Night porter 50P **NOTES:** No dogs (ex guide dogs) No coaches No smoking in restaurant Last d 8.45pm Closed 25 Oct-23 Apr **CARDS:**

See advert on opposite page

ST BRELADE
★★ Beau Rivage
St Brelade's Bay JE3 8EF
Quality Percentage Score: 71%
☎ 01534 745983 📠 01534 747127

A well kept sea front hotel. Most bedrooms are sea facing and nine have large, furnished balconies. Public areas include a sun deck and a patio outside the popular conservatory bar, with games machines and a juke box (turned off at 11pm). There is live music most nights during the season.
ROOMS: 27 en suite (bth/shr) (9 fmly) No smoking in 1 bedroom d £29.50-£70.50 (incl. bkfst & dinner) * LB Off peak **MEALS:** Lunch £5-£12 High tea £3-£6 Dinner £12.50 English, French & Italian Cuisine V meals Coffee am Tea pm **FACILITIES:** CTV in all bedrooms STV Sunbathing terrace Video games Wkly live entertainment **SERVICES:** Lift Night porter 14P **NOTES:** No dogs No smoking in restaurant Last d 7.45pm Closed 1 Nov-18 Apr
CARDS:

ST HELIER

★★★★ The Grand

The Esplanade JE4 8WD

De Vere Hotels

Quality Percentage Score: 67%

☎ 01534 722301 📠 01534 737815

Right on the sea front, overlooking St Aubin's Bay and Elizabeth Castle, this busy hotel offers a smart new leisure complex. Bedrooms vary in size and outlook and all are thoughtfully equipped. Staff are friendly, dedicated and smartly turned out. Victoria's, one of two restaurants, is an elegant setting where guests can enjoy a high standard of cooking.

ROOMS: 115 en suite (bth/shr) s £85-£105; d £135-£150 (incl. bkfst) * LB Off peak **MEALS:** Dinner £21-£23.50 English, French & Italian Cuisine V meals Coffee am Tea pm **FACILITIES:** CTV in all bedrooms STV Indoor swimming pool (heated) Snooker Sauna Solarium Gym Jacuzzi/spa Beauty therapy Massage parlour Wkly live entertainment Xmas **CONF:** Thtr 180 Class 100 Board 40 **SERVICES:** Lift Night porter 27P **NOTES:** No smoking area in restaurant **CARDS:**

ST HELIER

★★★ Pomme d'Or

Liberation Square JE1 3UF

Quality Percentage Score: 70%

☎ 01534 880110 📠 01534 737781

Dir: *opposite the harbour*

Overlooking Liberation Square and the marina, this established hotel offers comfortably furnished and well equipped bedrooms with modern amenities. Public areas include extensive conference facilities and a choice of restaurants, where Steve Le Corre's cooking continues to impress.

ROOMS: 141 en suite (bth/shr) (3 fmly) No smoking in 72 bedrooms s £57.50-£130; d £85-£180 (incl. bkfst) * LB Off peak **MEALS:** Lunch £8.50-£14.25 & alc Dinner £10-£16.50 & alc International Cuisine V meals Coffee am Tea pm **FACILITIES:** CTV in all bedrooms STV Use of Aquadome at Merton Hotel Xmas **CONF:** Thtr 220 Class 100 Board 50 Del from £72.50 * **SERVICES:** Lift Night porter **NOTES:** No dogs (ex guide dogs) No smoking area in restaurant Last d 10pm **CARDS:**

ST HELIER

★★★ Apollo

St Saviours Rd JE2 4GJ

Quality Percentage Score: 68%

☎ 01534 725441 📠 01534 722120

Located in the centre of the town, this popular hotel has recently been refurbished. Bedrooms are attractively furnished. Service is professional and attentive and the restaurant serves from a

contd.

varied and imaginative menu. Indoor and outdoor pools are major attractions.
ROOMS: 85 en suite (bth/shr) (5 fmly) s £41.50-£68.50; d £83-£105 (incl. bkfst) * LB Off peak **MEALS:** Sunday Lunch fr £11 High tea fr £5 Dinner fr £13.50 English & French Cuisine V meals Coffee am Tea pm **FACILITIES:** CTV in all bedrooms STV Indoor swimming pool (heated) Outdoor swimming pool (heated) Sauna Solarium Gym Jacuzzi/spa Xmas **CONF:** Thtr 150 Class 100 Board 80 **SERVICES:** Lift Night porter **NOTES:** No dogs (ex guide dogs) No smoking area in restaurant Last d 8.45pm **CARDS:**

See advert on opposite page

ST HELIER
★★★ Royal
David Place JE2 4TD
Quality Percentage Score: 68%
☎ 01534 726521 📠 01534 724035

Bedrooms at the Royal are well equipped and are being steadily upgraded. The elegant public areas consist of a very comfortable lounge, No 27 bar and Brasserie, a well presented lounge bar, and a stylish restaurant. The hotel also boasts one of the largest conference rooms on the island.
ROOMS: 91 en suite (bth/shr) (39 fmly) s £64.50-£72; d £104-£119 (incl. bkfst) * LB Off peak **MEALS:** Lunch £11.50-£13.50 Dinner £13.50-£15.50 English & French Cuisine V meals Coffee am Tea pm **FACILITIES:** CTV in all bedrooms **CONF:** Thtr 400 Class 150 Board 30 Del from £110 * **SERVICES:** Lift Night porter 20P **NOTES:** No coaches No smoking area in restaurant Last d 9pm
CARDS:

See advert on opposite page

ST HELIER
★★★ Beaufort
Green St JE2 4UH
Quality Percentage Score: 66%
☎ 01534 732471 📠 01534 720371

Just a few minutes walk from the town centre, this modern hotel offers spacious, well equipped bedrooms. Public areas include a bright dining room, smart bar and comfortable lounge with adjoining sun terrace. A heated outdoor pool is a relatively new addition.
ROOMS: 54 en suite (bth/shr) (4 fmly) s £55.50-£76; d £87-£116 (incl. bkfst) * LB Off peak **MEALS:** Bar Lunch £3.30-£4.75 Dinner fr £14.80 English, French & Italian Cuisine V meals Coffee am Tea pm **FACILITIES:** CTV in all bedrooms STV Indoor swimming pool (heated) Outdoor swimming pool (heated) Jacuzzi/spa Xmas **CONF:** Thtr 160 Class 140 **SERVICES:** Lift Night porter 30P **NOTES:** No dogs No smoking area in restaurant Last d 8.40pm **CARDS:**

See advert on page 759

ST HELIER
★★★ Royal Yacht
The Weighbridge JE2 3NF
Quality Percentage Score: 66%
☎ 01534 720511 📠 01534 767729
Dir: *Situated in town centre, opposite the Marina and harbour, 0.5 mile from beach*
Enjoying a central location overlooking the harbour and marina, the Royal Yacht is thought be the oldest established hotel on the island. Bedrooms, being refurbished, are comfortably furnished and well equipped. Public areas have benefitted from redecoration with several bars and a grill room in addition to the main first-floor restaurant.
ROOMS: 45 en suite (bth/shr) s £45-£51; d £88-£102 (incl. bkfst) * LB Off peak **MEALS:** Lunch £12.50-£27.50 & alc Dinner £18.50-£39 & alc English, French & Italian Cuisine V meals Coffee am Tea pm **FACILITIES:** CTV in all bedrooms STV Sauna ch fac Xmas **CONF:** Thtr 20 Class 20 Board 20 **SERVICES:** Lift Night porter
NOTES: Last d 9.30pm **CARDS:**

ST HELIER
★★★ Rex
St Saviours Rd JE2 4GJ
Quality Percentage Score: 61%
☎ 01534 731668 📠 01534 766922
Leisure-oriented, with live entertainment and heated pool to laze around in summer, guests have plenty to choose from at this centrally located hotel. Public areas include a spacious lounge, comfortable bar and restaurant.
ROOMS: 53 en suite (bth/shr) (5 fmly) s £32-£51; d £54-£92 (incl. bkfst & dinner) * Off peak **MEALS:** Lunch £11-£13 Dinner £12-£14 & alc British & Continental Cuisine V meals **FACILITIES:** CTV in all bedrooms Outdoor swimming pool (heated) Wkly live entertainment **SERVICES:** Lift Night porter 20P **NOTES:** No coaches No smoking in restaurant Last d 8.30pm Closed 1 Nov-15 Mar **CARDS:**

ST HELIER
★★ Hotel Revere
Kensington Place JE2 3PA
Quality Percentage Score: 70%
☎ 01534 611111 📠 01534 611116
This former 17th Century coach house retains many original features. Bedrooms are tastefully decorated and well equipped. Public areas include several cosy lounges, and the characterful Candlelight Restaurant where guests can enjoy freshly prepared French cuisine. Parking is available in the adjoining public car park.
ROOMS: 58 en suite (bth/shr) (4 fmly) No smoking in 14 bedrooms s fr £79; d fr £98 (incl. bkfst) * LB Off peak **MEALS:** Lunch £11.95 & alc High tea £6.95 Dinner £12.95-£28alc English & French Cuisine V meals Coffee am Tea pm **FACILITIES:** CTV in all bedrooms STV Outdoor swimming pool (heated) Jacuzzi/spa Wkly live entertainment ch fac Xmas **SERVICES:** Night porter **NOTES:** No smoking area in restaurant Last d 9.30pm **CARDS:**

S

S

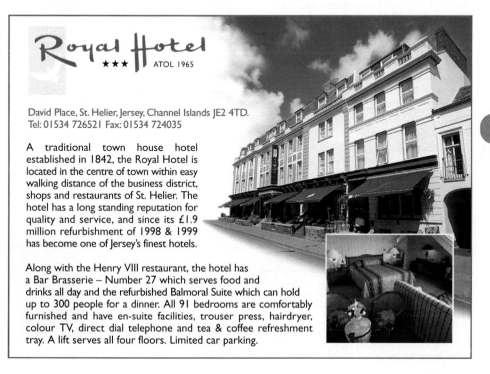

ST HELIER
★★ *Sarum Hotel*
19-21 New St Johns Rd JE2 3LD
Quality Percentage Score: 69%
☎ 01534 758163 Fax 01534 731340
Situated in a residential area, this well presented hotel is five minutes walk from the town centre. All bedrooms are neatly decorated and comfortably furnished. Public areas include a well stocked bar, spacious restaurant and outdoor swimming pool with adjacent garden.
ROOMS: 49 en suite (bth/shr) (9 fmly) **MEALS:** English & Continental Cuisine V meals Coffee am Tea pm **FACILITIES:** CTV in all bedrooms STV Outdoor swimming pool (heated) Pool table Games room Children's play area Wkly live entertainment ch fac **SERVICES:** Lift Night porter 6P **NOTES:** No dogs No smoking in restaurant Last d 7.45pm Closed 1 Nov-25 Mar **CARDS:**

ST HELIER
★★ Uplands
St John's Rd JE2 3LE
Quality Percentage Score: 68%
☎ 01534 730151 Fax 01534 639899
Dir: *turn off main esplanade (A1) onto Pierson Rd by Grand Hotel, follow ring road for 200mtrs, third on left into St Johns Rd, hotel in 0.5m).*
Based around the granite buildings of a 17th-century dairy farm, Uplands Hotel is set in 12 acres of farmland, a mile from St Helier. Bedrooms are modern, spacious and comfortable, some overlooking the swimming pool, some with country views. 12 self-catering cottages are available.
ROOMS: 43 en suite (bth/shr) (3 fmly) s £25-£38; d £50-£76 (incl. bkfst) * Off peak **MEALS:** Lunch £6.75 Dinner £9.25 English & French Cuisine V meals Coffee am Tea pm **FACILITIES:** CTV in all bedrooms STV Outdoor swimming pool (heated) Wkly live entertainment Xmas **SERVICES:** Night porter 44P **NOTES:** No dogs (ex guide dogs) No coaches No children 3yrs No smoking in restaurant Last d 7.45pm
CARDS:

ST LAWRENCE
★★★ Hotel Cristina
Mont Feland JE3 1JA
Quality Percentage Score: 68%
☎ 01534 758024 Fax 01534 758028
Dir: *turn off the A10 on to Mont Felard, hotel on the left*

In a prime position above St Aubin's Bay, the Christina has unrivalled views of the bay. Most bedrooms have good views and balconies. Two bars, a dining room with panoramic views and a heated pool are other attractions.
ROOMS: 62 en suite (bth/shr) s £38-£82.25; d £74-£88 (incl. bkfst) * Off peak **MEALS:** Lunch £12-£16 Dinner £12-£16 English & French Cuisine V meals Coffee am Tea pm **FACILITIES:** CTV in all bedrooms STV Outdoor swimming pool (heated) Swimming pool May-Sep Wkly live entertainment **SERVICES:** Night porter 80P **NOTES:** No dogs No children 4yrs No smoking in restaurant Last d 8.30pm Closed Nov-Mar
CARDS:

ST LAWRENCE
★★ Hotel White Heather
Rue de Haut, Millbrook JE3 1JZ
Quality Percentage Score: 67%
☎ 01534 720978 Fax 01534 720968
A friendly hotel in a smart residential area within easy reach of the beach and a short bus ride from St Helier. Most bedrooms have their own balconies, the day rooms are equally relaxing and well furnished. A spacious sun terrace and an indoor swimming pool are popular amenities.
ROOMS: 33 en suite (bth/shr) (3 fmly) s £25-£39; d £42-£64 (incl. bkfst) * LB Off peak **MEALS:** Dinner fr £9 **FACILITIES:** CTV in all bedrooms Indoor swimming pool (heated) **SERVICES:** 11P **NOTES:** No dogs No smoking in restaurant Last d 7.30pm Closed Nov-Mar
CARDS:

ST PETER
★★★ Mermaid
JE3 7BN
Quality Percentage Score: 69%
☎ 01534 741255 Fax 01534 745826

A wide range of leisure facilities are available at this impressive hotel. Most of the well equipped bedroom have their own furnished balcony overlooking the lake in the grounds.
ROOMS: 68 en suite (bth/shr) s fr £45.50; d £77-£100.50 (incl. bkfst) * LB Off peak **MEALS:** Lunch fr £11 Dinner fr £13.50 English & French Cuisine V meals Coffee am Tea pm **FACILITIES:** CTV in all bedrooms STV Indoor swimming pool (heated) Outdoor swimming pool (heated) Tennis (hard) Sauna Solarium Gym Croquet lawn Putting green Jacuzzi/spa Wkly live entertainment Xmas **CONF:** Thtr 100 Class 60 Board 50 **SERVICES:** Night porter 250P **NOTES:** No dogs (ex guide dogs) Last d 9pm **CARDS:**

See advert on opposite page

Beaufort Hotel

St. Helier, Jersey, JE2 4UH, Channel Islands
Telephone: (01534) 732471 Fax: (01534) 720371

INDOOR SWIMMING POOL AND SPA

Modern 3 Star Hotel well situated for shopping, business or beach in St. Helier's centre. The Beaufort has been designed to offer every amenity for today's traveller. Brummels Bar for aperitifs. The Rib Room for fine cuisine. Ample car parking. New outdoor pool with waterfall.

All Bedrooms are equipped with:

- ★ FULL BATHROOM AND SHOWER
- ★ HAIRDRYER AND TROUSER PRESS
- ★ TEA AND COFFEE MAKING FACILITIES
- ★ 2 DIRECT DIAL TELEPHONES
- ★ COLOUR TELEVISION WITH SATELLITE CHANNELS
- ★ FULL LOUNGE ARMCHAIRS
- ★ WRITING DESK
- ★ MINI BAR

AA ★★★ A Huggler Hotel

Mermaid Hotel

St. Peter, Jersey, JE3 7BN, Channel Islands
Telephone: (01534) 741255 Fax: (01534) 745826

Incorporating an original ancient Tavern and beautiful old Granite Grill Room dating back to 1710 The Mermaid is a modern hotel built around a natural lake.

The Mermaid has a superb indoor Leisure Centre including a 44ft. swimming pool, jacuzzi, solarium, sun beds, saunas and gymnasium and also a 45ft. outdoor heated pool, 2 tennis courts, putting green and croquet lawn.

All bedrooms have bathrooms en suite and balconies. Deluxe rooms also available with mini bars etc.

AMPLE CAR PARKING OPEN ALL YEAR

AA ★★★ A Huggler Hotel

S

ST SAVIOUR

The Premier Collection

★★★★ **Longueville Manor**
JE2 7WF
☎ 01534 725501 🖷 01534 731613
RELAIS & CHATEAUX.
Dir: *off St Helier/Grouville Rd A3*
Dating back in part to the 13th century, Longueville Manor is set in 17 acres of grounds. Antique-furnished bedrooms are individually decorated with ornaments and fresh flowers providing a personal touch. The twin dining rooms offer fine cooking with some home-grown produce.
ROOMS: 32 en suite (bth/shr) s £165-£192.50; d £200-£255 (incl. bkfst) * LB Off peak **MEALS:** Lunch £20-£22.50 Dinner £37.75-£45.50alc English & French Cuisine V meals Coffee am Tea pm **FACILITIES:** CTV in all bedrooms STV Outdoor swimming pool (heated) Tennis (hard) Croquet lawn Xmas **CONF:** Thtr 40 Class 30 Board 30 Del from £190 * **SERVICES:** Lift Night porter 40P **NOTES:** No coaches No smoking area in restaurant Last d 9.30pm
CARDS:

TRINITY

★★★ **Highfield Country**
Route d'Ebenezer JE3 5DT
Quality Percentage Score: 68%
☎ 01534 862194 🖷 01534 865342
A well presented hotel set amidst unspoilt countryside. It offers well equipped bedrooms furnished in modern style. In addition to the cosy bar and large conservatory there is a quiet lounge. In the restaurant, the fixed price menu offers good value for money. Self catering apartments are available.
ROOMS: 38 en suite (bth/shr) (32 fmly) s £33-£48; d £72-£102 (incl. bkfst) * Off peak **MEALS:** Dinner fr £13 & alc International Cuisine V meals Coffee am Tea pm **FACILITIES:** CTV in all bedrooms Indoor swimming pool (heated) Outdoor swimming pool Sauna Solarium Gym Pool table Petanque **SERVICES:** Lift 41P **NOTES:** No dogs No coaches No smoking in restaurant Last d 8pm Closed Nov-Mar
CARDS:

SARK

★★ ***Dixcart***
Dixcart Valley GY9 0SD
Quality Percentage Score: 69%
☎ 01481 832015 🖷 01481 832164
Dir: *ten minutes S of village, following signed footpath*

The 16th-century farm longhouse of La Jaspellerie Tenement, Dixcart is now the oldest established hotel on this feudal isle. It enjoys a peaceful setting surrounded by 50 acres, and the hotel's public areas include a choice of lounges and a small bar, which retain much of the original character of the property. The bedrooms are comfortably furnished with modern facilities. Guests can dine in either the candlelit restaurant or the more informal public bar.
ROOMS: 15 en suite (bth/shr) (5 fmly) **MEALS:** English & French Cuisine V meals Coffee am Tea pm **FACILITIES:** Horse-drawn carriage tours available ch fac **CONF:** Thtr 60 Class 20 Board 10 **NOTES:** Last d 9pm
CARDS:

S

Isle of Man

Directory of establishments in alphabetical order of location.

MAN, ISLE OF — Map 06

CASTLETOWN — Map 06 SC26

★★★ *Castletown Golf Links*
Fort Island IM9 1UA
Quality Percentage Score: 67%
☎ 01624 822201 Fax 01624 824633

Enjoying a unique setting with sea on three sides and adjoining a championship golf course. The accommodation is modern and well equipped. Bedrooms on ground floor level and full suites are available. Function facilities and conference rooms, with the hotel's proximity to the airport, make it a popular venue with business people.

ROOMS: 58 en suite (bth/shr) (3 fmly) **MEALS:** European Cuisine V meals Coffee am Tea pm **FACILITIES:** CTV in all bedrooms STV Indoor swimming pool (heated) Golf 18 Snooker Sauna Solarium Putting green **CONF:** Thtr 200 Class 50 Board 20 Del from £95 * **SERVICES:** Night porter 200P **NOTES:** Last d 9.30pm
CARDS:

DOUGLAS — Map 06 SC37

★★★★ Mount Murray
Santon IM4 2HT
Quality Percentage Score: 67%
☎ 01624 661111 Fax 01624 611116
Dir: *from Douglas turn off main Douglas/Castletown road at Santon. Hotel is signposted on the road*

This purpose built hotel and country club offers leisure facilities and a health and beauty salon. The extensive public areas give a choice of bars and eating options. The spacious bedrooms are well equipped, many enjoy fine views over the 200 acre grounds. There is a large function suite.

ROOMS: 90 en suite (bth/shr) (4 fmly) No smoking in 12 bedrooms s £49.50-£79; d £69.50-£149 (incl. bkfst) * LB Off peak **MEALS:** Lunch £12.50 Dinner £14.95 V meals Coffee am Tea pm **FACILITIES:** CTV in all bedrooms Indoor swimming pool (heated) Golf 18 Tennis (hard) Squash Snooker Sauna Solarium Gym Putting green Bowling green Driving range Sports hall ch fac Xmas **CONF:** Thtr 300 Class 260 Board 70 Del £99 * **SERVICES:** Lift Night porter 400P **NOTES:** No dogs (ex guide dogs) No coaches No smoking area in restaurant Last d 9.45pm
CARDS:

DOUGLAS — Map 06 SC37

★★★★ Sefton
Harris Promenade IM1 2RW
Quality Percentage Score: 67%
☎ 01624 645500 Fax 01624 676004
Dir: *500yrds from the Ferry Dock*

This imposing Victorian hotel has comfortable, well equipped bedrooms. There is a choice of dining options: bistro, carvery or restaurant. A range of ales is offered in the Tramshunter's Arms. Transformation of the hotel was well underway at the time of our last inspection.

ROOMS: 107 en suite (bth/shr) (3 fmly) No smoking in 22 bedrooms s £62-£74; d £78-£95 (incl. bkfst) * LB Off peak **MEALS:** Lunch £12.75-£13.75alc Dinner £10.50-£15 & alc V meals Coffee am Tea pm **FACILITIES:** CTV in all bedrooms STV Indoor swimming pool (heated) Sauna Solarium Gym Jacuzzi/spa Massage Beauty therapy service Aerobics Xmas **CONF:** Thtr 180 Class 40 Board 20 Del from £95 * **SERVICES:** Lift Night porter 42P **NOTES:** No dogs (ex guide dogs) No coaches No smoking area in restaurant Last d 9.50pm
CARDS:

D

DOUGLAS
Map 06 SC37

★★★ *Ascot Hotel*
7/8 Empire Ter IM2 4LE
Quality Percentage Score: 68%
☎ 01624 675081 📠 01624 661512
A friendly, family run hotel, close to the sea front, shops, theatre, and attractions. It provides soundly maintained, well equipped accommodation. Refurbishment has greatly enhanced the public areas.
ROOMS: 40 en suite (bth/shr) (4 fmly) **MEALS:** V meals
FACILITIES: CTV in all bedrooms STV **SERVICES:** Lift Night porter
NOTES: No dogs Last d 9.15pm **CARDS:**

DOUGLAS
Map 06 SC37

★★★ Empress
Central Promenade IM2 4RA
Quality Percentage Score: 68%
☎ 01624 661155 📠 01624 673554

BROOK HOTELS

A large Victorian hotel on the central promenade, overlooking Douglas Bay. Well equipped, modern bedrooms include suites and rooms with sea views. A pianist entertains in the lounge bar most evenings, and there is a lounge, a sun lounge and a brasserie-style restaurant.
ROOMS: 102 en suite (bth/shr) No smoking in 6 bedrooms s fr £65; d fr £70 * LB Off peak **MEALS:** Lunch £10-£14.95 Dinner £14.95 & alc International Cuisine V meals Coffee am Tea pm **FACILITIES:** CTV in all bedrooms STV Indoor swimming pool (heated) Sauna Solarium Gym Jacuzzi/spa Wkly live entertainment Xmas **CONF:** Thtr 200 Class 150 Board 50 Del £95 * **SERVICES:** Lift Night porter **NOTES:** No dogs (ex guide dogs) No smoking area in restaurant Last d 10.45pm
CARDS:

See advert on page 761

DOUGLAS
Map 06 SC37

★★★ Welbeck Hotel
13/15 Mona Dr IM2 4LF
Quality Percentage Score: 68%
☎ 01624 675663 📠 01624 661545
Dir: *at the crossroads of Mona & Empress Drive off Central Promenade*
This family owned and run hotel provides well equipped, attractively appointed accommodation. It is conveniently located for the sea front as well as other attractions. Facilities include a function room for up to 60 people.
ROOMS: 27 en suite (bth/shr) (7 fmly) s £43-£53; d £67-£82 (incl. bkfst) * Off peak **MEALS:** Bar Lunch £2-£11alc Dinner £14-£21 & alc International Cuisine V meals Coffee am Tea pm **FACILITIES:** CTV in all bedrooms STV **CONF:** Thtr 60 Class 36 Board 30 Del from £65 * **SERVICES:** Lift **NOTES:** No dogs (ex guide dogs) No smoking area in restaurant Last d 8.30pm **CARDS:**

PORT ERIN
Map 06 SC16

★★★ Cherry Orchard
Bridson St IM9 6AN
Quality Percentage Score: 67%
☎ 01624 833811 📠 01624 833583
Dir: *from Seaport/Airport take main road south past Castletown to Port Erin*
The comfortable bedrooms at this modern hotel are well equipped and attractively furnished. There are self-catering apartments in the same complex, guests here can use the public areas, including a well appointed restaurant, cosy lounge bar and leisure centre. There is a choice of function rooms.
ROOMS: 31 en suite (bth/shr) (12 fmly) s £48.50-£55.50; d £67-£81 (incl. bkfst) * LB Off peak **MEALS:** Lunch £15-£16 Dinner £16.50 & alc English & French Cuisine V meals Coffee am Tea pm **FACILITIES:** CTV in all bedrooms STV Indoor swimming pool (heated) Sauna Solarium Gym Pool table Croquet lawn Jacuzzi/spa Games room Xmas **CONF:** Thtr 200 Class 120 Board 70 Del from £65 * **SERVICES:** Lift Night porter 80P **NOTES:** No dogs (ex guide dogs) No smoking in restaurant Last d 9.45pm **CARDS:**

Hotel of the Year Scotland

The Bonham, Edinburgh

A

ABERDEEN Aberdeen City **Map 15 NJ90**
see also **Aberdeen Airport**
★★★★ ❀❀ ***Ardoe House***
South Deeside Rd, Blairs AB12 5YP
Quality Percentage Score: 71%
☎ 01224 867355 📠 01224 861283
Dir: *4m W of city off B9077*

Situated to the west of Aberdeen, this impressive mansion house stands in extensive grounds. Its charming public rooms give a choice of contrasting bars and eating options. The Garden Room restaurant displays the talents of the kitchen brigade to best advantage. Bedrooms in the main house are traditional in style, and there are more modern rooms in a new wing.
ROOMS: 71 en suite (bth/shr) (3 fmly) No smoking in 40 bedrooms **MEALS:** International Cuisine V meals Coffee am Tea pm **FACILITIES:** CTV in all bedrooms STV Croquet lawn Putting green Petanque **CONF:** Thtr 200 Class 100 Board 60 **SERVICES:** Lift Night porter 200P **NOTES:** No smoking in restaurant Last d 9.45pm
CARDS:

ABERDEEN Aberdeen City **Map 15 NJ90**
★★★★ **The Marcliffe at Pitfodels**
North Deeside Rd AB15 9YA
Quality Percentage Score: 71%
☎ 01224 861000 📠 01224 868860
Dir: *turn off A90 onto A93 signposted Braemar. 1m on right after turn off at traffic lights*

Situated in the west end and beautifully set in attractive grounds, this distinguished hotel combines traditional values with modern amenities. Elegant reception rooms include an impressive foyer and a drawing room where refreshments are served. The conservatory restaurant offers interesting Scottish food in an informal atmosphere which contrasts with the more sophisticated ambience of the formal Invery Room. Bedrooms range from master rooms with period furnishings, to well equipped standard rooms.
ROOMS: 42 en suite (bth/shr) (4 fmly) No smoking in 10 bedrooms s £135-£145; d £155-£185 (incl. bkfst) LB Off peak **MEALS:** Lunch £19.50-£25.50 & alc Dinner £29.50-£35.50 & alc Scottish & French Cuisine V meals Coffee am Tea pm **FACILITIES:** CTV in all bedrooms STV Snooker Croquet lawn Putting green Xmas **CONF:** Thtr 500 Class 300 Board 24 Del from £160 * **SERVICES:** Lift Night porter 160P **NOTES:** No coaches No smoking area in restaurant Last d 10pm
CARDS:

See advert on opposite page

ABERDEEN Aberdeen City **Map 15 NJ90**
★★★★ ❀ **Patio**
Beach Boulevard AB24 5EF
Quality Percentage Score: 67%
☎ 01224 633339 📠 01224 638833
Dir: *from the A90 follow signs for city centre, then for sea beach. On Beach Boulevard, turn left at traffic lights and hotel is on right*
A good range of banqueting and leisure facilities is offered at this purpose-built hotel, near the seafront. The Premier Club rooms in the new wing are of a particularly good standard, and those in the original building are modern, bright and airy. Public areas radiate from a central atrium and include a continental-style café/bar, small lounge area, and a choice of eating options - informal in the conservatory and more serious food in Footdee's Restaurant.
ROOMS: 124 en suite (bth/shr) (8 fmly) No smoking in 58 bedrooms d £60-£117 * LB Off peak **MEALS:** Lunch fr £9.95 & alc High tea fr £6.75 Dinner fr £15.50 French & Continental Cuisine V meals Coffee am Tea pm **FACILITIES:** CTV in all bedrooms STV Indoor swimming pool (heated) Sauna Solarium Gym Jacuzzi/spa Steam room, Treatment Room **CONF:** Thtr 150 Class 80 Board 50 Del £135 * **SERVICES:** Lift Night porter 196P **NOTES:** No smoking area in restaurant Last d 10.45pm
CARDS:

See advert on opposite page

ABERDEEN Aberdeen City **Map 15 NJ90**
★★★★ ❀ **Copthorne Aberdeen**
122 Huntly St AB10 1SU
Quality Percentage Score: 62%
☎ 01224 630404 📠 01224 640573
Dir: *W of city centre, off Union Street, up Rose Street, hotel quarter of a mile on right on corner with Huntly Street*
Conveniently positioned just off Union Street, close to the shops and within easy reach of the theatre, this smart business hotel offers spacious, thoughtfully equipped accommodation. For the more discerning guest, the attractive Connoisseur rooms will appeal, and the Classic rooms are in the process of being refurbished. Guests have the choice of eating less formally in the comfort of Mac's bar, or in the tastefully appointed Poachers restaurant, where the menus have a Scottish theme.
ROOMS: 89 en suite (bth/shr) (15 fmly) No smoking in 30 bedrooms s £50-£157; d £70-£172 * LB Off peak **MEALS:** Lunch £9.95-£18.50 & alc Dinner £9.95-£18.50 & alc International Cuisine V meals Coffee am Tea pm **FACILITIES:** CTV in all bedrooms STV Wkly live entertainment **CONF:** Thtr 220 Class 100 Board 80 Del from £140 * **SERVICES:** Lift Night porter 20P **NOTES:** No smoking area in restaurant Last d 10pm
CARDS:

AA Rosettes are awarded for quality of food,
see page 15 for an explanation of Rosette assessment.

ABERDEEN Aberdeen City **Map 15 NJ90**

★★★★ *Thistle Aberdeen Altens*

THISTLE HOTELS

Souter Head Rd, Altens AB12 3LF

Quality Percentage Score: 58%

☎ 01224 877000 Fax 01224 896964

Dir: *3m S of Aberdeen, off A90*

This modern purpose-built hotel has a bright foyer area with marbled floor, a spacious split-level bar, and choice of eating options. The best rooms on the upper levels are all smartly refurbished, standards are varied on other levels, although improvements continue.

ROOMS: 221 en suite (bth/shr) (70 fmly) No smoking in 105 bedrooms **MEALS:** International Cuisine V meals Coffee am Tea pm **FACILITIES:** CTV in all bedrooms STV Outdoor swimming pool (heated) Gym **CONF:** Thtr 400 Class 250 Board 100 **SERVICES:** Lift Night porter 300P **NOTES:** No smoking area in restaurant Last d 9.30pm RS Xmas wk **CARDS:**

ABERDEEN Aberdeen City **Map 15 NJ90**

★★★ Atholl

54 Kings Gate AB15 4YN

Quality Percentage Score: 72%

☎ 01224 323505 Fax 01224 321555

Dir: *in West End 400yds from Anderson Drive, the main ring road*

An immaculately maintained business hotel in a desirable west end residential area, within easy reach of the ring road and central amenities. Comfortably modern bedrooms have attractive decor and pretty fabrics. There is a well stocked bar, foyer

contd.

lounge, and popular restaurant offering competitively priced dishes from a carte.
ROOMS: 35 en suite (bth/shr) (1 fmly) No smoking in all bedrooms s £71-£81; d £89 (incl. bkfst) * LB Off peak **MEALS:** Lunch £10-£25alc Dinner £10-£25alc V meals Coffee am Tea pm **FACILITIES:** CTV in all bedrooms STV **CONF:** Thtr 60 Class 25 Board 25 Del from £115 * **SERVICES:** Night porter 60P **NOTES:** No dogs (ex guide dogs) No coaches Last d 9.30pm **CARDS:**

See advert on page 765

ABERDEEN Aberdeen City **Map 15 NJ90**
★★★ Simpsons
59 Queens Rd AB15 4YP
Quality Percentage Score: 72%
☎ 01224 327777 01224 327700
Opened in 1998, this exciting new hotel, created from two granite town houses, has quickly become popular. One building contains modern, boldly decorated and well-equipped bedrooms, the other a large split-level bar and brasserie with Moroccan columns supporting a colonnade of arches. The menus offer a range of modern brasserie dishes.
ROOMS: 37 en suite (bth/shr) (8 fmly) No smoking in all bedrooms s £110-£120; d £120-£130 (incl. bkfst) * Off peak **MEALS:** Lunch £8.95-£23.45alc Dinner £15.40-£23.95alc V meals Coffee am Tea pm **FACILITIES:** CTV in all bedrooms STV Complimentary use of Health Club **CONF:** Thtr 25 Class 12 Board 20 Del from £130 * **SERVICES:** Lift Night porter Air conditioning 102P **NOTES:** No coaches No smoking area in restaurant Last d 9.45pm Closed 1 Jan
CARDS:

ABERDEEN Aberdeen City **Map 15 NJ90**
★★★ *Thistle Aberdeen Caledonian*
10 Union Ter AB10 1WE
Quality Percentage Score: 69%
☎ 01224 640233 01224 641627
Dir: *follow directions to city centre, Union Terrace is half way along Union St, Aberdeen's main thoroughfare and is opposite Union Terrace Gardens*
Good progress is being made with refurbishment at this established hotel. The cocktail bar and restaurant offer a formal environment while Elrond's busy cafe bar and restaurant, provides an informal alternative. Bedrooms remain variable in size and style, the enhancement programme is gradually bringing about more consistent standards.
ROOMS: 80 en suite (bth/shr) (4 fmly) No smoking in 25 bedrooms **MEALS:** International Cuisine V meals Coffee am Tea pm **FACILITIES:** CTV in all bedrooms STV Wkly live entertainment **CONF:** Thtr 40 Class 10 Board 20 **SERVICES:** Lift Night porter 25P **NOTES:** No smoking area in restaurant Last d 10pm
CARDS:

ABERDEEN Aberdeen City **Map 15 NJ90**
★★★ Norwood Hall
Garthdee Rd, Cults AB15 9FX
Quality Percentage Score: 66%
☎ 01224 868951 01224 869868
Dir: *off the A92, at 1st rdbt cross Bridge of Dee and turn left at the rdbt onto Garthdee Rd (B&Q and Sainsbury on the left) continue until hotel sign*
This extended Victorian mansion, standing in wooded grounds, has been carefully refurbished and many of its original features, such as stained glass windows, panelling, ornate fireplaces, gold leaf and leather wall coverings, have been retained. The elegant Ogston Restaurant is the setting for enjoyable meals. The larger bedrooms are in the main house, and those in the newer wing are smartly decorated.
ROOMS: 21 en suite (bth/shr) (3 fmly) No smoking in 8 bedrooms s £75-£105; d £95-£125 (incl. bkfst) LB Off peak **MEALS:** Lunch £12.95-£25.50 Dinner £23.50-£25.50 Scottish & French Cuisine V meals Coffee am Tea pm **FACILITIES:** CTV in all bedrooms Xmas **CONF:** Thtr 200 Class 80 Board 40 Del from £138 * **SERVICES:** Night porter 80P **NOTES:** No dogs (ex guide dogs) No smoking in restaurant Last d 9.30pm **CARDS:**

ABERDEEN Aberdeen City **Map 15 NJ90**
★★★ Palm Court
81 Seafield Rd AB15 7YU
Quality Percentage Score: 66%
☎ 01224 310351 01224 312707
Dir: *take A92 to the Seafield rdbt, drive up Seafield Rd and Hotel is on left hand side*
A smart modern hotel with a welcoming atmosphere stands on the west side of town, convenient for the ring road. There are both standard and executive bedrooms, and reception areas focus on the open-plan conservatory bar and the brasserie restaurant.
ROOMS: 24 en suite (bth/shr) (1 fmly) s £79-£89; d £89-£99 (incl. bkfst) * LB Off peak **MEALS:** Lunch £9.20-£15.20alc Dinner £12.95-£21.50alc International Cuisine V meals Coffee am Tea pm **FACILITIES:** CTV in all bedrooms STV **CONF:** Thtr 110 Class 80 Board 80 Del £110 * **SERVICES:** Night porter 65P **NOTES:** Last d 9.30pm Closed 26 Dec & 1-2 Jan **CARDS:**

ABERDEEN Aberdeen City **Map 15 NJ90**
★★★ Westhill
Westhill AB32 6TT
Quality Percentage Score: 66%
☎ 01224 740388 01224 744354
Dir: *follow A944 West of the city towards Alford, Westhill is 6m out of centre on the right*
Popular with business guests, the Westhill is in 15 minutes drive of the airport. Bedrooms offer the expected standard of modern comfort, there are popular bars, a split-level restaurant and good leisure and function facilities.
ROOMS: 37 en suite (bth/shr) 13 annexe en suite (bth/shr) (2 fmly) No smoking in 8 bedrooms s £54-£70; d £72-£88 (incl. bkfst) LB Off peak **MEALS:** Bar Lunch £4.50-£14.95alc High tea £7.50-£8.50 Dinner £5.95-£18.95alc International Cuisine V meals Coffee am **FACILITIES:** CTV in all bedrooms STV Sauna Solarium Gym Pool table Wkly live entertainment Xmas **CONF:** Thtr 300 Class 200 Board 200 Del from £65 **SERVICES:** Lift Night porter 250P **NOTES:** Last d 9.30pm
CARDS:

ABERDEEN Aberdeen City **Map 15 NJ90**
★★★ The Craighaar
Waterton Rd, Bankhead AB21 9HS
Quality Percentage Score: 65%
☎ 01224 712275 01224 716362
Dir: *NW near the airport off A947*
Situated in a residential area close to the airport this smart modern hotel offers bedrooms ranging from delightful 'gallery suites' and executive rooms to the smaller standard rooms. Inviting public areas include a restaurant, a popular bar, and various sitting areas.
ROOMS: 55 en suite (bth/shr) (2 fmly) s £79; d £89 (incl. bkfst) * LB Off peak **MEALS:** Lunch fr £5.95 & alc Dinner fr £17.95 & alc Scottish, French & Italian Cuisine V meals Coffee am Tea pm **FACILITIES:** CTV in all bedrooms STV **CONF:** Thtr 90 Class 35 Board 30 Del £110 * **SERVICES:** Night porter 80P **NOTES:** Last d 9.30pm Closed 26 Dec & 1-2 Jan **CARDS:**

ABERDEEN Aberdeen City **Map 15 NJ90**
★★★ ***Grampian***
Stirling St AB11 6JU
Quality Percentage Score: 65%
☎ 01224 589101 ▤ 01224 574288
Close to the station and city centre shops, this attractively decorated Victorian building claims to be the oldest hotel in Aberdeen. The modern bedrooms offer the usual amenities; the focal point of the public rooms is the popular McDuffy's bar and brasserie.
ROOMS: 108 en suite (bth/shr) (3 fmly) **MEALS:** Scottish & French Cuisine V meals Coffee am **FACILITIES:** CTV in all bedrooms **SERVICES:** Lift Night porter **NOTES:** Last d 9.30pm
CARDS:

ABERDEEN Aberdeen City **Map 15 NJ90**
★★★ ***Maryculter House Hotel***
South Deeside Rd AB12 5GB
Quality Percentage Score: 65%
☎ 01224 732124 ▤ 01224 733510
Dir: *8 miles along B9077 off the A90 on south side of Aberdeen*

Situated off the South Deeside Road, this hotel on the Banks of the Dee was built on the site of an ancient preceptory of the Knights Templar. The cocktail bar has an impressive vaulted ceiling, and Poachers Bar provides light meals. There is also a formal restaurant. Bedrooms have good quality furniture.
ROOMS: 23 en suite (bth/shr) (1 fmly) No smoking in 12 bedrooms **MEALS:** European Cuisine V meals Coffee am Tea pm **FACILITIES:** CTV in 24 bedrooms STV Fishing Clay pigeon shooting **CONF:** Thtr 250 Class 120 Board 40 **SERVICES:** Night porter 100P **NOTES:** No smoking in restaurant Last d 9.30pm **CARDS:**

ABERDEEN Aberdeen City **Map 15 NJ90**
★★★ **Queens Hotel**
51-53 Queens Rd AB15 4YP
Quality Percentage Score: 64%
☎ 01224 209999 ▤ 01224 209009
This personally run hotel in the west end has particular appeal to the visiting businessman and is a popular venue for local functions. The well equipped modern bedrooms are currently undergoing a programme of enhancement. Public areas include a foyer lounge, a well stocked bar, and a small restaurant.
ROOMS: 27 en suite (bth/shr) (3 fmly) No smoking in 4 bedrooms s £60-£90; d £70-£110 (incl. bkfst) * Off peak **MEALS:** Lunch £12-£18 & alc Dinner £12-£22 & alc European Cuisine V meals Coffee am Tea pm **FACILITIES:** CTV in all bedrooms STV **CONF:** Thtr 400 Class 150 Board 60 Del from £97.50 * **SERVICES:** Night porter 80P **NOTES:** No dogs (ex guide dogs) No smoking in restaurant Last d 9.45pm Closed 25-26 Dec & 1-2 Jan **CARDS:**

ABERDEEN Aberdeen City **Map 15 NJ90**
★★★ **Posthouse Aberdeen**
Claymore Dr, Bridge of Don AB23 8BL **Posthouse**
☎ 01224 706707 ▤ 01224 823923
Dir: *follow signs for Peterhead and Aberdeen Exhibition Conference Centre hotel is adjacent to AECC*
Popular with both business and leisure visitors, this modern purpose-built hotel is situated on the north side of the city adjacent to the Exhibition and Conference Centre. The comfortable, modern bedrooms are attractively decorated, with a good range of amenities. Day rooms are of the open-plan style, and contained within the bright foyer area.
ROOMS: 123 en suite (bth/shr) (23 fmly) No smoking in 49 bedrooms s £39-£85; d £50-£85 * LB Off peak **MEALS:** Chinese, French & Italian Cuisine V meals Coffee am Tea pm **FACILITIES:** CTV in all bedrooms ch fac Xmas **SERVICES:** Lift Night porter 200P **NOTES:** No smoking area in restaurant Last d 10pm **CARDS:**

ABERDEEN Aberdeen City **Map 15 NJ90**
★★ **Mariner**
349 Great Western Rd AB10 6NW
Quality Percentage Score: 66%
☎ 01224 588901 ▤ 01224 571621
This smart, popular business hotel is within easy reach of central amenities and the ring road. There is a nautical theme to public areas; the Atlantis Restaurant specialises in seafood and steaks. Less formal meals are available in the bar. Bedrooms, some

contd.

accessed externally, offer modern appointments and a good range of amenities.
ROOMS: 14 en suite (bth/shr) 8 annexe en suite (bth/shr) s fr £65; d fr £75 (incl. bkfst) * Off peak **MEALS:** Lunch £11.50-£20alc High tea £7.50-£10.50alc Dinner £11.50-£20alc International Cuisine V meals Coffee am Tea pm **FACILITIES:** CTV in all bedrooms STV Xmas **SERVICES:** Night porter 48P **NOTES:** No dogs (ex guide dogs) No coaches Last d 9.30pm **CARDS:**

ABERDEEN Aberdeen City **Map 15 NJ90**
★ Travel Inn (Aberdeen South)
Mains of Balquharn, Portlethen AB12 4QS
☎ 01224 783856 01224 783836
Dir: *on A90 exit signed Portlethen Shopping Centre & Badentoy Industrial Estate*
ROOMS: 40 en suite (bth/shr) d £39.95 * Off peak **FACILITIES:** CTV in all bedrooms **SERVICES:** P **NOTES:** No dogs (ex guide dogs)
CARDS:

ABERDEEN Aberdeen City **Map 15 NJ90**
⇧ Travel Inn
Murcar, Bridge of Don AB23 8BP
☎ 01224 821217 01224 706869
Dir: *on A90 Ellon Road N of city centre, 1m past Aberdeen Exhibition Centre*
This modern building offers accommodation in smart, spacious and well equipped bedrooms, all with en-suite bathrooms. Refreshments may be taken at the nearby family restaurant. For details about current prices consult the Contents Page under Hotel Groups for the Travel Inn phone number.
ROOMS: 40 en suite (bth/shr) d £39.95 *

ABERDEEN Aberdeen City **Map 15 NJ90**
⇧ Travelodge
9 Bridge St AB11 6JL
☎ 01224 584555 01224 584587
This modern building offers accommodation in smart, spacious and well equipped bedrooms, all with en-suite bathrooms. Refreshments may be taken at the nearby family restaurant. For details about current prices, consult the Contents Page under Hotel Groups for the Travelodge phone number.
ROOMS: 95 en suite (bth/shr) d £49.95 *

ABERDEEN Aberdeen City **Map 15 NJ90**
Aberdeen Moat House
Malcolm Rd, Bucksburn AB21 9LN
☎ 01224 409988 01224 714020
Dir: *turn off A96 onto A947, then first left into Malcolm road*
A smart modern business hotel, with easy access to the airport and central amenities. Bedrooms are nicely decorated and comfortable, public areas well presented and enjoyable to use, including a foyer lounge, choice of bars, and a brasserie restaurant. A range of banqueting and leisure facilities are available.
ROOMS: 144 en suite (bth/shr) (35 fmly) No smoking in 81 bedrooms s £38-£105; d £76-£120 (incl. bkfst) * LB Off peak **MEALS:** Lunch £6-£25alc Dinner £6-£25alc International Cuisine V meals Coffee am Tea pm **FACILITIES:** CTV in all bedrooms STV Indoor swimming pool (heated) Sauna Solarium Gym Pool table Steam room Xmas **CONF:** Thtr 450 Class 200 Board 300 Del from £120 * **SERVICES:** Lift Night porter 195P **NOTES:** No smoking area in restaurant Last d 10pm
CARDS:

ABERDEEN AIRPORT Aberdeen City **Map 15 NJ81**
★★★★ Aberdeen Marriott
Overton Circle, Dyce AB21 7AZ
Quality Percentage Score: 69%
☎ 01224 770011 01224 722347
Dir: *follow A96 to Bucksburn village, turn right at the rdbt onto the A947. After 2m you will see the hotel at the second rdbt*
Business and leisure guests continue to appreciate the standards offered at this smart modern hotel. Public areas include the Café/Bar which overlooks the pool, a foyer lounge, and a spacious split level restaurant. Bedrooms are comfortably modern in style, and range in size with the standard rooms being smaller.
ROOMS: 155 en suite (bth/shr) (68 fmly) No smoking in 88 bedrooms d £93-£99 * LB Off peak **MEALS:** Lunch £12.95-£16.95 Dinner £18-£22 & alc International Cuisine V meals Coffee am Tea pm **FACILITIES:** CTV in all bedrooms STV Indoor swimming pool (heated) Sauna Solarium Gym Jacuzzi/spa Xmas **CONF:** Thtr 400 Class 200 Board 60 Del from £130 * **SERVICES:** Night porter Air conditioning 180P **NOTES:** No dogs (ex guide dogs) No smoking area in restaurant Last d 10pm
CARDS:

ABERDEEN AIRPORT Aberdeen City **Map 15 NJ81**
★★★★ *Thistle Aberdeen Airport*
Argyll Rd AB21 7DU
Quality Percentage Score: 66%
☎ 01224 725252 01224 723745
Dir: *adjacent to main airport entrance 1m N of A96*
The attractive, smartly decorated interior of this hotel may come as a surprise after the rather austere outside. Facilities include a foyer lounge, bar and formal restaurant. Bedrooms offer a sound standard of comfort.
ROOMS: 147 en suite (bth/shr) (44 fmly) No smoking in 60 bedrooms **MEALS:** Scottish & French Cuisine V meals Coffee am Tea pm **FACILITIES:** CTV in all bedrooms STV Outdoor swimming pool (heated) **CONF:** Thtr 600 Class 350 Board 25 **SERVICES:** Night porter 250P **NOTES:** No coaches No smoking area in restaurant Last d 9.45pm
CARDS:

ABERDEEN AIRPORT Aberdeen City **Map 15 NJ81**
★★ *The Skean Dhu*
Farburn Ter, Dyce AB21 7DW
Quality Percentage Score: 66%
☎ 01224 723101 01224 722965
Dir: *follow A947 out of Aberdeeen, hotel 2m on left along Farburn terrace*
A purpose built hotel, with motel style accommodation blocks, situated close to the airport, and offering good banqueting and leisure facilities, as well as a choice of bars, and the restaurant provides a varied menu selection. Bedrooms are mixed in size and in style.
ROOMS: 220 en suite (bth/shr) No smoking in 44 bedrooms **MEALS:** International Cuisine V meals Coffee am Tea pm **FACILITIES:** CTV in all bedrooms Squash Sauna Solarium Gym Pool table **CONF:** Thtr 400 Class 160 Board 60 **SERVICES:** Night porter 300P **NOTES:** Last d 10pm **CARDS:**

ABERDEEN AIRPORT Aberdeen City **Map 15 NJ81**
⇧ Travel Inn
Burnside Dr, off Riverside Dr, Dyce AB21 0HW
☎ 01224 772787 01224 772968
Dir: *from Aberdeen A96 towards Inverness, turn right at rdbt onto A947, at 2nd rdbt turn right then 2nd turning on right*
This modern building offers accommodation in smart, spacious and well equipped bedrooms, all with en-suite bathrooms. Refreshments may be taken at the nearby family restaurant. For details about current

contd.

prices consult the Contents Page under Hotel Groups for the Travel Inn phone number.
ROOMS: 40 en suite (bth/shr) d £39.95 *

ABERDOUR Fife **Map 11 NT18**
★★ *Woodside*
High St KY3 0SW
Quality Percentage Score: 67%
☎ 01383 860328 01383 860920
Dir: *E of Forth Road Bridge, across rbt into town, hotel on left after garage*

In recent years this welcoming business and tourist hotel has benefited from substantial refurbishment. Attractive public areas include a bright foyer lounge, a tastefully appointed restaurant offering both Chinese and Scottish dishes, and a delightful nautical themed bar where the smoking lounge of the liner Orontes has been carefully preserved and reinstalled. Bedrooms, all of which are well equipped, range from deluxe rooms to the smaller and more practical standard rooms.
ROOMS: 20 en suite (bth/shr) (1 fmly) **MEALS:** Scottish, French & Chinese Cuisine V meals Coffee am Tea pm **FACILITIES:** CTV in all bedrooms **CONF:** Thtr 25 Class 40 Board 25 **SERVICES:** Night porter 30P **NOTES:** No smoking area in restaurant Last d 9.30pm
CARDS:

See advert on this page

ABERDOUR Fife **Map 11 NT18**
★★ The Aberdour Hotel
38 High St KY3 0SW
Quality Percentage Score: 62%
☎ 01383 860325 01383 860808
Dir: *from Admiralty Interchange travel E on A291 for 5m. Hotel is located in the centre of the village opposite the post office*
A small, friendly commercial hotel in the village centre. Public areas are limited in extent, however the cosy bar features real ales, and good value home cooked fare is served in the beamed dining room. Main house bedrooms have modern and traditional furnishings, more spacious bedrooms are in the stable block annexe, all offer a good range of amenities.
ROOMS: 16 en suite (bth/shr) (4 fmly) s £41.50-£45; d £52-£58 (incl. bkfst) * LB Off peak **FACILITIES:** CTV in all bedrooms STV **SERVICES:** 8P **NOTES:** No coaches

ABERFELDY Perth & Kinross **Map 14 NN84**
★★ *Guinach House*
"By The Birks", Urlar Rd PH15 2ET
Quality Percentage Score: 71%
☎ 01887 820251 01887 829607
Dir: *access off A826 Crieff road*
For ten years Bert and Marion MacKay have been welcoming guests to their delightful small hotel. Marion looks after the front of house, whilst Bert's domain is the kitchen. His innovative style of cooking has deservedly earned high praise. The elegant

contd.

dining room is the focal point of the house but there is also a charming sitting room. Bedrooms, which vary in size and in style, offer both modern and traditional appointments.
ROOMS: 7 en suite (bth/shr) **MEALS:** British, French & Italian Cuisine V meals **FACILITIES:** CTV in all bedrooms **SERVICES:** 12P **NOTES:** No coaches No smoking in restaurant Last d 9.30pm Closed 4 days Xmas
CARDS:

ABERFELDY Perth & Kinross — Map 14 NN84

★★ The Weem

Weem PH15 2LD
Quality Percentage Score: 68%
☎ 01887 820381 Fax 01887 829720
Dir: *1m NW B846*

The wonderfully relaxed and informal atmosphere is a major part of the appeal of this historic roadside inn, and the many guests who return regularly proudly regard themselves as 'Weemies'. Many of the bedrooms have benefited from recent redecoration, and improvements are ongoing. Some rooms can be adapted for self catering use. Public areas are full of character with panelled and natural stone walls and include the Trencherman bar and restaurant, where the carte offers both fun and serious dishes.
ROOMS: 12 en suite (bth/shr) (4 fmly) No smoking in 4 bedrooms s £25-£45; d £50-£80 (incl. bkfst) * LB Off peak **MEALS:** European Cuisine V meals Coffee am Tea pm **FACILITIES:** CTV in all bedrooms Shooting Fishing Golf (can be arranged) Xmas **CONF:** Thtr 60 Class 30 Board 30 **SERVICES:** 20P **NOTES:** No coaches No smoking in restaurant
CARDS:

ABERFOYLE Stirling — Map 11 NN50

★★★★ *Forest Hills*

Kinlochard FK8 3TL
Quality Percentage Score: 65%
☎ 01877 387277 Fax 01877 387307
Dir: *3m W on B829*

Part of a resort complex with a variety of indoor and outdoor leisure activities. Bedrooms, split between the original house and a recent extension, are comfortably furnished, newer rooms are most attractive. Dining takes place in the Garden restaurant or more informal Bonspiel above the leisure complex, with comfortable and welcoming lounges to relax in after dinner.
ROOMS: 56 en suite (bth/shr) (16 fmly) No smoking in 26 bedrooms **MEALS:** British, French & Italian Cuisine V meals Coffee am Tea pm **FACILITIES:** CTV in all bedrooms Indoor swimming pool (heated) Tennis (hard) Fishing Squash Riding Snooker Sauna Solarium Gym Pool table Putting green Jacuzzi/spa Bowls Curling Wkly live entertainment ch fac **CONF:** Thtr 150 Class 60 Board 45 Del from £125 * **SERVICES:** Night porter 80P **NOTES:** Last d 9.30pm **CARDS:**

ABERLADY East Lothian — Map 12 NT47

★★ Kilspindie House

Main St EH32 0RE
Quality Percentage Score: 66%
☎ 01875 870682 Fax 01875 870504
Dir: *on A198 - centre of village on main street, from Edinburgh take A1 South then A198 signed to North Berwick, from South A1 then A6137 to Aberlady*

Just 20 minutes from Edinburgh and a short drive from some excellent golf courses, this is an ideal location for tourists, golfers and business travellers alike. Bedrooms are well equipped and attractively decorated.
ROOMS: 26 en suite (bth/shr) d £60-£74 (incl. bkfst) LB Off peak **MEALS:** Sunday Lunch £10-£16alc High tea £7.95-£10.75 Dinner £12-£18alc V meals Coffee am Tea pm **FACILITIES:** CTV in all bedrooms Xmas **CONF:** Thtr 60 Class 40 Board 8 Del from £50 * **SERVICES:** 30P **NOTES:** No smoking in restaurant Last d 9pm
CARDS:

ABERLOUR See Archiestown

ABINGTON South Lanarkshire — Map 11 NS92

Welcome Lodge

Welcome Break Service Area ML12 6RE
☎ 01864 502782 Fax 01864 502759
Dir: *off junct 13 of M74, accesible from northbound and southbound carriageways*

This modern building offers accommodation in smart, spacious and well equipped bedrooms, suitable for families and businessmen, and all with en-suite bathrooms. Refreshments may be taken at the nearby family restaurant. For details of current prices, consult the Contents Page under Hotel Groups for the Welcome Break phone number.
ROOMS: 56 en suite (bth/shr) d fr £45 *

ABOYNE Aberdeenshire — Map 15 NO59

★★ Birse Lodge

20 Charleston Rd AB34 5EL
Quality Percentage Score: 60%
☎ 013398 86253 Fax 013398 87796
Dir: *in centre of Aboyne turn off A93 and follow road round the side of the green towards River Dee, hotel is at edge of village green*

New owners John and Sue Brotchie look forward to welcoming guests old and new, to their small hotel which stands in its own grounds close to the River Dee. Public areas include a choice of comfortable lounges, a snug bar and attractive conservatory restaurant offering carefully prepared dishes. The bedrooms, of various sizes, are comfortable with both modern and traditional furnishings.
ROOMS: 12 en suite (bth/shr) (3 fmly) s £39-£42; d £58-£74 (incl. bkfst) * LB Off peak **MEALS:** Lunch £3-£15alc Dinner £7-£20alc V meals Coffee am **FACILITIES:** CTV in all bedrooms Wkly live entertainment Xmas **CONF:** Thtr 35 Board 25 Del from £60 * **SERVICES:** 25P **NOTES:** No coaches No children No smoking in restaurant Last d 9pm **CARDS:**

ACHNASHEEN Highland — Map 14 NH15

★★★ Ledgowan Lodge

IV22 2EJ
Quality Percentage Score: 65%
☎ 01445 720252 Fax 01445 720240
Dir: *0.25m on A890 to Kyle of Lochalsh - from Achnasheen*

For over 30 years the Millard family have been welcoming guests to their popular Highland holiday hotel which is ideally situated for exploring Wester Ross. Relaxing public areas, which feature an interesting aquarium and collection of whisky artefacts in the hall, also offer a lounge, a cosy bar and coffee shop serving meals and snacks all day and an attractive dining room with an extensive carte. Bedrooms are comfortable and solidly traditional and the staff are friendly and willing to please.
ROOMS: 12 en suite (bth/shr) (2 fmly) s £27.50-£29.50; d £55-£59 * Off peak **MEALS:** Lunch £10-£20alc Dinner £15-£30alc International Cuisine V meals Coffee am Tea pm **FACILITIES:** CTV in all bedrooms STV **SERVICES:** 25P **NOTES:** No dogs No coaches No smoking in restaurant Last d 9pm Closed Jan-Mar & Nov-Dec RS Apr & Oct
CARDS:

ANNAN Dumfries & Galloway — Map 11 NY16

★★ Queensberry Arms

DG12 6AD
Quality Percentage Score: 63%
☎ 01461 202024 Fax 01461 205998
Dir: *in town square, 1.5m from A75*

This former coaching inn, with its distinctive black and white facade, sits right in the centre of the town. Public areas offer a variety of lounges where morning coffees and afternoon teas are

contd.

popular. Upstairs there is an attractive restaurant that has a nautical theme.

ROOMS: 24 en suite (bth/shr) (3 fmly) s £42.50-£54.50; d £54.50-£65.50 (incl. bkfst) * LB Off peak **MEALS:** Lunch £8.50-£9.25 & alc High tea fr £7.50 Dinner £10-£15 & alc International Cuisine V meals Coffee am Tea pm **FACILITIES:** CTV in all bedrooms STV Darts Wkly live entertainment Xmas **CONF:** Thtr 70 Class 30 Board 30 Del from £48 * **SERVICES:** Night porter 50P **NOTES:** No smoking area in restaurant Last d 9pm **CARDS:**

See advert under GRETNA (WITH GRETNA GREEN)

ANNANDALE WATER MOTORWAY SERVICE AREA Dumfries & Galloway — Map 11 NY19

Roadchef Lodge Annandale Water

Johnstonbridge DG11 1HD
☎ 01576 470870 01576 470395
Dir: *A74(M) junct 16*

This modern building offers accommodation in smart, spacious and well equipped bedrooms, all with en-suite bathrooms. Refreshments may be taken at the nearby family restaurant. For details about current prices, consult the Contents Page under Hotel Groups for the Roadchef phone number.

ROOMS: 42 en suite (bth/shr) d fr £47.50 *

ANSTRUTHER Fife — Map 12 NO50

★★ Smugglers Inn

High St East KY10 3DQ
Quality Percentage Score: 62%
☎ 01333 310506 01333 312706
Dir: *on High Street East A719 after bridge*

This welcoming inn, steeped in Jacobite history, is in the centre of the village with views over the harbour. Much original character is retained in the public areas, there is a small practical lounge, a bar with natural stone walls, cosy fire, and nautical artefacts and a beamed dining room.

ROOMS: 9 en suite (bth/shr) (1 fmly) s £29.50-£35; d £59-£70 (incl. bkfst) * Off peak **MEALS:** Lunch £4.15-£8.50 Dinner £6.15-£12.50 European Cuisine V meals Coffee am **FACILITIES:** CTV in all bedrooms Pool table **SERVICES:** 14P **NOTES:** No dogs (ex guide dogs) No smoking in restaurant Last d 9pm **CARDS:**

ARBROATH Angus — Map 12 NO64

★★★★ The Letham Grange Mansion House Hotel

Colliston DD11 4RL
Quality Percentage Score: 64%
☎ 01241 890373 01241 890725
Dir: *leave A92 onto A933 to Brechin, Letham Grange signposted at village of Colliston*

An impressive Victorian mansion dating back to 1884. Two golf courses and a curling rink are among the attractions. Elegant public areas have panelling, ornate ceilings, and period paintings. The drawing room invites relaxation, the conservatory is ideal for light lunches and coffee. A formal dining experience is found in the Rosehaugh Restaurant. Many main house bedrooms are spacious and traditional in style, modern annexe accommodation is popular with visiting golfers.

ROOMS: 19 en suite (bth/shr) 22 annexe en suite (bth/shr) (1 fmly) No smoking in 2 bedrooms s £65-£100; d £85-£145 (incl. bkfst) * LB Off peak **MEALS:** Lunch £10.50-£12.50 High tea £6.50-£12.50alc Dinner £22.50-£27.50 & alc Scottish & International Cuisine V meals Coffee am Tea pm **FACILITIES:** CTV in all bedrooms STV Golf 36 Snooker Croquet lawn Putting green Curling rink Xmas **CONF:** Thtr 700 Class 300 Board 20 Del from £85 * **SERVICES:** Night porter 150P **NOTES:** No smoking in restaurant Last d 9.30pm **CARDS:**

See advert on this page

The AA Hotel Booking Service is a free benefit to AA members. See the advertisement on page 47

A

ARBROATH Angus — Map 12 NO64

★★ *Hotel Seaforth*
Dundee Rd DD11 1QF
Quality Percentage Score: 64%
☎ 01241 872232 ▯ 01241 877473
Dir: *on southern outskirts, on A92*
Enthusiastic new owners Bill & Sandra Rennie have major improvement plans for this long established commercial hotel at the west end of town. Good progress is being made with a rolling programme of bedroom refurbishment and additional amenities are being provided. Indeed a start has been made with refurbishment of the restaurant and leisure centre, and also the creation of a new fitness room.
ROOMS: 21 rms (19 bth/shr) (4 fmly) **MEALS:** V meals Coffee am **FACILITIES:** CTV in all bedrooms Indoor swimming pool (heated) Snooker Solarium Jacuzzi/spa **CONF:** Thtr 120 Class 60 Board 40 **SERVICES:** 60P **NOTES:** Last d 8.45pm
CARDS:

ARCHIESTOWN Moray — Map 15 NJ24

★★❀❀ Archiestown
AB38 7QL
Quality Percentage Score: 75%
☎ 01340 810218 ▯ 01340 810239
Dir: *on B9102, 5m SW of Craigellachie*
As ever, anglers have a particular 'soft spot' for this welcoming hotel, but the touring holidaymaker is equally at home. The well presented public areas include a choice of inviting and relaxing lounges, and two dining rooms. The pleasantly decorated bedrooms are comfortably furnished.
ROOMS: 9 rms (7 bth) s £37.50-£45; d £90 (incl. bkfst) * Off peak **MEALS:** Sunday Lunch fr £10alc Dinner fr £15alc International Cuisine V meals Coffee am Tea pm **FACILITIES:** CTV in all bedrooms **SERVICES:** 20P **NOTES:** No coaches No smoking area in restaurant Last d 8.45pm Closed Oct-9 Feb **CARDS:**

ARDBEG See Bute, Isle of

ARDELVE Highland — Map 14 NG82

★ Loch Duich
IV40 8DY
Quality Percentage Score: 68%
☎ 01599 555213 ▯ 01599 555214
Dir: *from Inverness A82 towards Fort William, turn right at Invermoriston on to A887 then A87 towards Kyle of Lochalsh and Ardelve*
Improvements continue at this welcoming tourist hotel, a former drovers inn beside the Road to the Isles. Many bedrooms have been individually refurbished. Relaxing public areas include a choice of lounges and a cosy dining room, serving the same good food available in the popular Duich Pub.
ROOMS: 11 rms (9 shr) (1 fmly) s £26.50-£31.50; d £53-£62 (incl. bkfst) * LB Off peak **MEALS:** Bar Lunch £7.50-£19.50alc Dinner £9.50-£20alc Scottish & French Cuisine V meals Coffee am Tea pm **FACILITIES:** CTV in all bedrooms Fishing Shooting Sailing Wkly live entertainment **CONF:** Board 40 Del from £55 * **SERVICES:** 41P **NOTES:** No coaches No smoking in restaurant Last d 8.45pm Closed 4 Jan-1 Mar & 19-28 Dec RS Nov-18 Dec **CARDS:**

ARDUAINE Argyll & Bute — Map 10 NM71

★★★❀❀ Loch Melfort
PA34 4XG
Quality Percentage Score: 76%
☎ 01852 200233 ▯ 01852 200214
Dir: *on A816, midway between Oban and Lochgilphead*
Genuine hospitality, good food and a superb setting with glorious views over Loch Asknish Bay are all part of the appeal of this hotel. The public areas include a library, a modern cocktail bar, the Chartroom Bar where lighter meals are served and a formal restaurant. Both specialise in seafood. Some bedrooms are located in the main house, though most are in a purpose built wing where each room has splendid sea views from either a patio or balcony.

ROOMS: 7 en suite (bth/shr) 20 annexe en suite (bth/shr) (2 fmly) s £45-£75; d £60-£110 (incl. bkfst) LB Off peak **MEALS:** Bar Lunch £7.50-£20 High tea £2.50-£5 Dinner fr £31 Scottish & French Cuisine V meals Coffee am Tea pm **FACILITIES:** CTV in all bedrooms Xmas **CONF:** Thtr 50 Board 24 Del from £70 * **SERVICES:** 65P **NOTES:** No smoking in restaurant Last d 9pm Closed 4 Jan-15 Feb
CARDS:

ARISAIG Highland — Map 13 NM68

The Premier Collection

★★★❀❀❀ Arisaig House
Beasdale PH39 4NR
☎ 01687 450622 ▯ 01687 450626
Dir: *3m E A830*
This splendid Scottish mansion stands peacefully amid extensive woodland and carefully tended gardens with beautiful azaleas and rhododendrons providing breathtaking colour displays. The Smither family, together with daughter Alison and husband David Wilkinson have been busy over the past winter enhancing the bedrooms. Two rooms have been sacrificed to allow enlargement of more Prime Rooms, and regulars will be delighted to see the change in their favourite bedrooms. Bathrooms have also benefited from upgrade and many are now quite luxurious. Inviting day rooms include a choice of wonderfully relaxing sitting rooms, the atmosphere of which are enhanced by fine furnishings, fresh floral displays, and, on the cooler evenings, welcoming open fires. The elegant panelled dining room provides an appropriately civilised setting for the creative cooking of the kitchen team headed up by David

contd.

Gibson. Using the finest ingredients prepared with loving care and great skill, David and his team resist the temptation to over complicate dishes, thus allowing natural flavours to shine through.
ROOMS: 12 en suite (bth/shr) s £80-£260; d £160-£275 (incl. bkfst) * LB Off peak **MEALS:** Lunch £5-£25alc Scotish & French Cuisine V meals Coffee am Tea pm **FACILITIES:** CTV in all bedrooms Snooker Croquet lawn **SERVICES:** 16P **NOTES:** No dogs (ex guide dogs) No coaches No children 10yrs No smoking in restaurant Closed Nov-Mar **CARDS:**

ARISAIG Highland — Map 13 NM68

★★ Arisaig Hotel

PH39 4NH
Quality Percentage Score: 68%
☎ 01687 450210 Fax 01687 450310
Dir: *on A830 opposite the harbour*
This roadside hotel sits on the shores of Loch Nan Ceal with fine sea views towards the islands of Rhum, Eigg, Muck and Skye. Bedrooms are smartly appointed and thoughtfully equipped. The comfortable public areas include a choice of lounges and bars, and a children's playroom. The atmosphere is very friendly and relaxed.
ROOMS: 13 en suite (bth/shr) (2 fmly) s £30-£34; d £60-£68 (incl. bkfst) * LB Off peak **MEALS:** Bar Lunch £8.25-£17.30 Dinner £12.20-£21.85alc V meals Coffee am Tea pm **FACILITIES:** CTV in all bedrooms Pool table ch fac **SERVICES:** 30P **NOTES:** No coaches No smoking in restaurant Last d 8.30pm **CARDS:**

See advert on this page

ARRAN, ISLE OF North Ayrshire — Map 10

BRODICK — Map 10 NS03

The Premier Collection

★★ Kilmichael Country House

Glen Cloy KA27 8BY
☎ 01770 302219 Fax 01770 302068
Dir: *from Brodwick Ferry Terminal follow northbound (Lochranza) road for 1m. At golf course turn inland past sports field & church, follow signs*
Believed to be the oldest house on the island, today Kilmichael is a charming hotel, set in attractive grounds tucked away in a peaceful glen. Bedrooms are thoughtfully equipped and furnished in traditional country house style, those in the converted barns being particularly elegant. The restaurant occupies a cheery new extension on the ground floor and the dinner menu has been simplified to five courses, offering a single choice for each.
ROOMS: 6 en suite (bth/shr) 3 annexe en suite (bth/shr) No smoking in all bedrooms s £65; d £88-£136 (incl. bkfst) * LB Off peak **MEALS:** Dinner £24.50-£29.50 International Cuisine V meals **FACILITIES:** CTV in all bedrooms Jacuzzi/spa **SERVICES:** 12P **NOTES:** No coaches No children 12yrs No smoking in restaurant Last d 8.30pm Closed Xmas **CARDS:**

BRODICK — Map 10 NS03

★★★ Auchrannie Country House

KA27 8BZ
Quality Percentage Score: 75%
☎ 01770 302234 Fax 01770 302812
Dir: *turn right from Brodick Ferry terminal, through Brodick village, turn second left after Brodick Golf Course clubhouse, 300yds to Hotel*
Genuine hospitality and extensive leisure facilities are all part of the appeal at this Victorian mansion, which stands in six acres of landscaped grounds just to the north of Wymodham. Bedrooms are well equipped, those in the new wing being particularly spacious. Public areas include a choice of relaxing lounges, a bistro and the Garden Restaurant with its conservatory extension, where the daily changing fixed-price menu has earned a two Rosette award for quality cooking.
ROOMS: 28 en suite (bth/shr) (3 fmly) s £58-£88.50; d £96-£157 (incl. bkfst & dinner) * LB Off peak **MEALS:** Lunch £1.95-£11.95alc Dinner £17.50-£24 & alc Scottish & French Cuisine V meals Coffee am Tea pm **FACILITIES:** CTV in all bedrooms STV Indoor swimming pool (heated) Snooker Sauna Solarium Gym Jacuzzi/spa Hair salon Aromatherapy Shiatsu Xmas **CONF:** Thtr 120 Board 30 **SERVICES:** Night porter 50P **NOTES:** No dogs (ex guide dogs) No smoking in restaurant Last d 9.30pm **CARDS:**

A

AUCHENCAIRN Dumfries & Galloway Map 11 NX75

★★★ Balcary Bay
DG7 1QZ
Quality Percentage Score: 70%
☎ 01556 640217 & 640311 Fax 01556 640272
Dir: on coast 2m from village

This hotel is pleasantly located on Balcary Bay. The main part of the building dates from 1625 and has associations with smuggling. Bedrooms are bright, attractive and thoughtfully equipped. Public areas include a choice of lounges and a conservatory adjoining the bar.

ROOMS: 17 en suite (bth/shr) (1 fmly) s £59; d £104-£118 (incl. bkfst) * LB Off peak **MEALS:** Lunch £10.75 Dinner £25 V meals Coffee am Tea pm **FACILITIES:** CTV in all bedrooms **SERVICES:** 50P **NOTES:** No coaches Last d 8.30pm Closed Dec-Feb
CARDS:

AUCHTERARDER Perth & Kinross Map 11 NN91

The Premier Collection

★★★★★ *The Gleneagles Hotel*
PH3 1NF
☎ 01764 662231 Fax 01764 662134
Dir: on A823

Renowned world-wide as a Mecca for sports enthusiasts, and as a top class international resort hotel, Gleneagles is set in beautiful countryside, surrounded by its famous golf courses and extensive grounds. It offers an outstanding range of activities, as well as a country club and health spa. The drawing room still serves its famous afternoon teas, and has a smart cocktail bar as a centrepiece. The elegant Strathearn Restaurant is the place for dinner, and bedrooms range from luxurious suites to standard rooms.

ROOMS: 229 en suite (bth/shr) No smoking in 118 bedrooms **MEALS:** International Cuisine V meals Coffee am Tea pm **FACILITIES:** CTV in all bedrooms STV Indoor swimming pool (heated) Golf 36 Tennis (hard & grass) Fishing Squash Riding Snooker Sauna Solarium Gym Pool table Croquet lawn Putting green Jacuzzi/spa Bowls Shooting Falconry Esquestrian Off-Road Driving ch fac **CONF:** Thtr 360 Class 240 Board 70 **SERVICES:** Lift Night porter 200P **NOTES:** No coaches No smoking area in restaurant **CARDS:**

AUCHTERARDER Perth & Kinross Map 11 NN91

★★★ Auchterarder House
PH3 1DZ
Quality Percentage Score: 77%
☎ 01764 663646 Fax 01764 662939
Dir: NW off B8062 1.2m from village

Set in 17 acres of wooded and landscaped grounds, this handsome mansion house is undergoing fine restoration. The interior is enhanced by oak panelling, ornate ceilings, and lovely fireplaces, with a choice of sitting rooms and a winter garden conservatory. The restaurant has been relocated to the former drawing room, where excellent Scottish produce cooked with flair and imagination can be sampled. Bedrooms range from opulent, well proportioned superior rooms with fine antique furnishings and luxurious bathrooms, to smaller standard rooms in the Turret wing which are more modern.

ROOMS: 15 en suite (bth/shr) (3 fmly) s £120; d £160 (incl. bkfst) * LB Off peak **MEALS:** Lunch £12.50-£18 Dinner fr £39.50 Scottish & French Cuisine V meals Coffee am Tea pm **FACILITIES:** CTV in all bedrooms STV Croquet lawn Putting green Xmas **CONF:** Thtr 50 Class 20 Board 25 Del from £150 * **SERVICES:** 30P **NOTES:** No children 12yrs No smoking in restaurant Last d 9pm
CARDS:

AUCHTERARDER Perth & Kinross Map 11 NN91

★★ *Cairn Lodge*
Orchil Rd PH3 1LX
Quality Percentage Score: 77%
☎ 01764 662634 & 662431 Fax 01764 664866
Dir: from the A9 take A824 into Auchterarder then A823 signposted Crieff & Gleneagles in approx 200yds hotel on the Y junct

A warm Scottish welcome awaits at this turreted house on the edge of the village. Bedrooms, recently fitted with double glazed windows, are decorated to a high standard. There is a comfortable lounge and a spacious bar offering a tempting range of malt whiskies, a comfortable setting for the informal supper menu. The elegant Capercaille Restaurant has an innovative carte based on quality ingredients.

ROOMS: 7 en suite (bth/shr) (2 fmly) **MEALS:** V meals **FACILITIES:** CTV in all bedrooms Putting green **SERVICES:** 40P **NOTES:** No dogs (ex guide dogs) No smoking in restaurant Last d 9.30pm **CARDS:**

Indicates that the star classification has not been confirmed under the New Quality Standards, see page 7 for further information.

AUCHTERHOUSE Angus — Map 11 NO33
★★★ Old Mansion House
DD3 0QN
Quality Percentage Score: 75%
☎ 01382 320366 🖷 01382 320400
Dir: *take A923 off Kingsway ringroad, Dundee to Muirhead then B954 for 2m, hotel is on left*

This fine baronial mansion has all sorts of legends associated with it. William Wallace is reported to have stayed here, and a grey lady ghost appears on occasion. There are cosy lounge areas with an abundance of seating and reading material, and large fires burn on cooler evenings. The restaurant has some distinctive architectural features, and for less formal dining there is the Courtyard Bar. Bedrooms are mostly spacious and furnished in traditional style.
ROOMS: 5 en suite (bth/shr) 2 annexe en suite (bth/shr) (1 fmly) s £80; d £105 (incl. bkfst) * LB Off peak **MEALS:** Lunch £15-£17.50 & alc Dinner £26-£33 Scottish & European Cuisine V meals Coffee am Tea pm **FACILITIES:** CTV in all bedrooms Outdoor swimming pool (heated) Tennis (grass) Squash Croquet lawn Xmas **CONF:** Thtr 30 Class 30 Board 20 **SERVICES:** 50P **NOTES:** No dogs (ex guide dogs) No coaches No smoking in restaurant Last d 9.30pm
CARDS:

AULTBEA Highland — Map 14 NG88
★★ Aultbea
IV22 2HX
Quality Percentage Score: 70%
☎ 01445 731201 🖷 01445 731214
Dir: *turn off A832 at Aultbea signs, hotel will be seen at lochside after 400yds*
This holiday hotel on the shore of Loch Ewe offers traditional comfort, pleasant bedrooms of various sizes and attractive public rooms, including a lounge, separate bar and two dining rooms, one formal, and one, the Waterside, offering a bistro-style menu.
ROOMS: 8 en suite (bth/shr) 3 annexe en suite (bth/shr) (1 fmly) s £42-£59.50; d £84-£94 (incl. bkfst) LB Off peak **MEALS:** Lunch fr £22 Dinner fr £22 Scottish & International Cuisine V meals Coffee am Tea pm **FACILITIES:** CTV in all bedrooms Pool table Wkly live entertainment Xmas **SERVICES:** 40P **NOTES:** No coaches Last d 8.30pm
CARDS:

Remember to return your Prize Draw card for a chance to win one of 30 relaxing leisure breaks with Corus and Regal hotels. See inside the front cover for the card and competition details.

AVIEMORE Highland — Map 14 NH81
★★★ Aviemore Highlands
Aviemore Mountain Resort PH22 1PJ
Quality Percentage Score: 67%
☎ 01479 810771 🖷 01479 811473
Dir: *off A9 signed Aviemore B9152, turn left opposite railway station around Ring road Hotel is 2nd on left*
Lovely views of the Cairngorms can be enjoyed from this smart modern hotel in the Aviemore Centre. Bedrooms offer comfortable modern appointments and there is a good range of rooms available for family use. Spacious public areas include a choice of bars, foyer lounge, and a spacious restaurant.
ROOMS: 103 en suite (bth/shr) (37 fmly) s fr £80; d fr £95 LB Off peak **MEALS:** Bar Lunch £1.75-£8.50 Dinner fr £17.50 Scottish, English & French Cuisine V meals Coffee am Tea pm **FACILITIES:** CTV in all bedrooms Pool table ch fac Xmas **CONF:** Thtr 140 Class 80 Board 60 Del from £65 * **SERVICES:** Lift Night porter 140P **NOTES:** No smoking in restaurant Last d 9pm **CARDS:**

AVIEMORE Highland — Map 14 NH81
★★★ Freedom Inn
Aviemore Centre PH22 1PF
Quality Percentage Score: 58%
☎ 01479 810781 🖷 01479 811167
Dir: *from A9 follow directions to Aviemore, hotel is in the Leisure Centre*
This purpose built hotel in the Aviemore Centre is a popular base for visiting tour groups. Most of the bedrooms are spacious and offer the expected amenities, plus small kitchenette areas. The bar has a lively atmosphere and the restaurant offers a short fixed priced menu.
ROOMS: 94 en suite (bth/shr) (85 fmly) No smoking in 6 bedrooms s £67; d £87 (incl. bkfst) * LB Off peak **MEALS:** Dinner fr £13.75 European Cuisine V meals Coffee am **FACILITIES:** CTV in all bedrooms Wkly live entertainment Xmas **CONF:** Thtr 100 Class 60 Board 50 Del from £65 * **SERVICES:** Lift Night porter 94P **NOTES:** Last d 8.30pm
CARDS:

AYR South Ayrshire — Map 10 NS32
★★★★ Fairfield House
12 Fairfield Rd KA7 2AR
Quality Percentage Score: 65%
☎ 01292 267461 🖷 01292 261456
Dir: *from A77 head for Ayr South (A30). Follow signs for the town centre, down Miller Road and turn left then right into Fairfield Road*
This fine Victorian mansion is quietly located with unrestricted views across the promenade towards the Firth of Clyde, yet is still within easy walking distance of the town centre. Whilst not spacious, the public areas are stylish and elegant and provide a smart wine and dine restaurant for dinner, as well as club style lounges. Alternatively one can drink and dine more informally in the conservatory Brasserie/bar. Bedrooms offer a choice of styles, from splendid spacious rooms furnished in period style to the standard modern rooms.
ROOMS: 39 rms (25 bth/shr) 4 annexe en suite (bth/shr) (3 fmly) No smoking in 7 bedrooms **MEALS:** French Cuisine V meals Coffee am Tea pm **FACILITIES:** CTV in all bedrooms STV Indoor swimming pool (heated) Sauna Solarium Gym Jacuzzi/spa **CONF:** Thtr 150 Class 60 Board 60 Del from £115 * **SERVICES:** Night porter 52P
NOTES: Last d 9.30pm **CARDS:**

AYR South Ayrshire **Map 10 NS32**

★★★ Savoy Park

16 Racecourse Rd KA7 2UT
Quality Percentage Score: 62%
☎ 01292 266112 📠 01292 611488
Dir: *from A77 follow Holmston Road(A70)for 2 miles, go through Parkhouse Street and turn left into Beresford Terrace, take first right onto Bellevue Road*

Under the same family ownership for over thirty years, this long-established hotel is unashamedly traditional, whilst offering the services and amenities expected by the modern traveller. Public rooms feature impressive panelled walls and ornate ceilings, whilst the restaurant is reminiscent of the dining room of a Highland shooting lodge. Both it and the relaxing bar lounge have open fires in season. It's worth asking for one of the superior bedrooms, which are spacious and furnished in keeping with the character of the building; others are smaller and more functionally appointed. Staff are friendly and hospitable, and families are made very welcome.
ROOMS: 15 en suite (bth/shr) (3 fmly) s £55-£65; d £75-£95 (incl. bkfst) * LB Off peak **MEALS:** Lunch £8-£10alc High tea fr £7.25alc Dinner £16-£19 Scottish & French Cuisine V meals Coffee am Tea pm **FACILITIES:** CTV in all bedrooms ch fac Xmas **CONF:** Thtr 50 Class 40 Board 30 Del from £80 * **SERVICES:** Night porter 60P **NOTES:** No smoking in restaurant Last d 9.30pm **CARDS:**

See advert on opposite page

AYR South Ayrshire **Map 10 NS32**

★★★ Quality Hotel Ayr

Burns Statue Square KA7 3AT
Quality Percentage Score: 56%
☎ 01292 263268 📠 01292 262293
Dir: *A70 from South/A77 from North*
This Victorian railway hotel sits right by the station in the centre of town. Bedrooms are spacious, with high ceilings and large windows; all have modern amenities and the Premier Rooms are particularly well equipped. Public areas include a small leisure club with a jacuzzi and gymnasium, as well as a number of meeting rooms.
ROOMS: 75 en suite (bth/shr) (3 fmly) No smoking in 26 bedrooms s £70-£81.50; d £81.50-£93.75 * LB Off peak **MEALS:** Lunch £2.95-£15.95alc Dinner fr £14.50 & alc European Cuisine V meals Coffee am Tea pm **FACILITIES:** CTV in all bedrooms STV Sauna Solarium Gym Jacuzzi/spa Xmas **CONF:** Thtr 250 Class 120 Board 100 **SERVICES:** Lift Night porter 50P **NOTES:** Last d 9pm **CARDS:**

AYR South Ayrshire **Map 10 NS32**

★★ Ladyburn

KA19 7SG
☎ 01655 740585 📠 01655 740580
(For full entry see MAYBOLE)

AYR South Ayrshire **Map 10 NS32**

★★ *Grange*

37 Carrick Rd KA7 2RD
Quality Percentage Score: 71%
☎ 01292 265679 📠 01292 285061
Dir: *0.5m from rail station & city centre, turn off A77 at A713 into Ayr, straight through rdbt 0.25m to Chalmers Rd, at the end turn right hotel 100yds*
Located in a residential area, within walking distance of both the town centre and the seafront, this small hotel is run by owners Leo and Jennifer Martin, who along with their charming staff provide friendly personal service. Bedrooms are individually styled, and public areas include an open plan lounge/bar and dining room. Well presented meals regularly feature local seafood.
ROOMS: 8 en suite (bth/shr) (2 fmly) **MEALS:** Scottish Cuisine V meals Coffee am Tea pm **FACILITIES:** CTV in all bedrooms **CONF:** Thtr 100 Class 50 Board 24 **SERVICES:** 25P **NOTES:** Last d 9.30pm
CARDS:

AYR South Ayrshire **Map 10 NS32**

★★ Carrick Lodge

46 Carrick Rd KA7 2RE
Quality Percentage Score: 66%
☎ 01292 262846 📠 01292 611101
Dir: *from A77, take A79 until T-junct, then right, hotel on left*
This family run hotel is located on the south side of town and offers friendly attentive service in a relaxed atmosphere. The popular bar is divided into two areas, one attractively wood-panelled, and both are ideal for enjoying the bar meals that offer good fresh produce and value for money. The more formal dining room has a carte menu and there is a separate suite for private functions. The bright, cheerful bedrooms include several that are suitable for families.
ROOMS: 8 en suite (bth/shr) (3 fmly) s £35-£45; d £50-£70 (incl. bkfst) * LB Off peak **MEALS:** Lunch £8-£12 & alc High tea £6-£8 & alc Dinner £10-£20 & alc Scottish & French Cuisine V meals Coffee am Tea pm **FACILITIES:** CTV in all bedrooms Xmas **CONF:** Thtr 50 Class 50 Board 50 Del from £50 * **SERVICES:** Night porter 25P **NOTES:** No dogs No smoking in restaurant Last d 9.45pm **CARDS:**

AYR South Ayrshire **Map 10 NS32**

Travel Inn

Kilmarnock Rd, Monkton KA9 2RJ
☎ 01292 678262 📠 01292 678248
Dir: *on A77/A78 rdbt by Prestwick Airport*
This modern building offers accommodation in smart, spacious and well equipped bedrooms, all with en-suite bathrooms. Refreshments may be taken at the nearby family restaurant. For details about current prices consult the Contents Page under Hotel Groups for the Travel Inn phone number.
ROOMS: 40 en suite (bth/shr) d £39.95 *

BALLANTRAE South Ayrshire **Map 10 NX08**

Glenapp Castle

KA26 0NZ
☎ 01465 831212
ROOMS: 17 rms

BALLATER Aberdeenshire **Map 15 NO39**

★★★ Darroch Learg

Braemar Rd AB35 5UX
Quality Percentage Score: 71%
☎ 013397 55443 📠 013397 55252
Dir: *hotel situated on the A93, at western edge of Ballater*
A delightful, family-operated country house overlooking the golf

contd.

course and facing the River Dee towards Lochnagar. The public rooms are really comfortable, with a delightful no-smoking lounge and a spacious restaurant looking out on the gardens. Bedrooms, both in the hotel and adjacent mansion are well equipped, comfortable and individually styled.
ROOMS: 13 en suite (bth/shr) 5 annexe en suite (bth/shr) No smoking in 4 bedrooms s £83-£98; d £136-£196 (incl. bkfst & dinner) * LB Off peak **MEALS:** Sunday Lunch £12-£24 Dinner £31.50-£36.50 Coffee am Tea pm **FACILITIES:** CTV in all bedrooms Xmas **CONF:** Thtr 25 Board 12 Del from £87 * **SERVICES:** 25P **NOTES:** No coaches No smoking in restaurant Last d 9pm Closed Xmas & Jan (ex New Year)
CARDS:

BALLATER Aberdeenshire **Map 15 NO39**

The Premier Collection

★★ Balgonie Country House

Scotland's Hotels of Distinction

Braemar Place AB35 5NQ
☎ 013397 55482 Fax 013397 55482
Dir: *turn off A93 [Aberdeen - Perth] on western outskirts of village of Ballater, hotel is sign-posted*
A charming small country house in the Edwardian style, is set in four acres of gardens with superb views towards the hills. Well maintained bedrooms are named after fishing pools on the River Dee and offer a choice of modern (top floor) or traditional (first-floor). Day rooms include a choice of inviting lounges, one with a bar. The elegant dining room is a perfect setting for the well produced food.
ROOMS: 9 en suite (bth/shr) s £65-£75; d £110-£115 (incl. bkfst) * LB Off peak **MEALS:** Lunch £17.50-£18.50 Dinner £28.50-£33.50 French Cuisine Coffee am Tea pm **FACILITIES:** CTV in all bedrooms Croquet lawn Xmas **SERVICES:** 12P **NOTES:** No dogs (ex guide dogs) No coaches No smoking in restaurant Last d 9pm Closed 6 Jan-Feb **CARDS:**

BALLATER Aberdeenshire **Map 15 NO39**

★★ The Deeside Hotel

Braemar Rd AB35 5RQ
Quality Percentage Score: 67%
☎ 013397 55420 Fax 013397 55357
Dir: *set back from A93 Ballater/Braemar road near edge of village*
A welcoming atmosphere prevails at this family run tourist hotel, where the well maintained bedrooms offer the expected level of comfort and are furnished in traditional style. There is a residents lounge and a combined bar/dining room where menus feature Taste of Scotland specialities.
ROOMS: 9 en suite (bth/shr) (1 fmly) s £30; d £50 (incl. bkfst) LB Off peak **MEALS:** Dinner £14-£17alc V meals **FACILITIES:** CTV in all bedrooms **SERVICES:** 15P **NOTES:** No coaches No smoking in restaurant Last d 9pm Closed 4 Jan-6 Feb & Xmas **CARDS:**

BALLATER Aberdeenshire **Map 15 NO39**

★★ *Alexandra*

THE CIRCLE Selected Individual Hotels GREAT BRITAIN

12 Bridge Square AB35 5QJ
Quality Percentage Score: 66%
☎ 013397 55376 Fax 013397 55466
This welcoming family-run business and tourist hotel, situated close to the River Dee, provides good value for money. Although compact, the attractive bedrooms are comfortably modern in style and offer all the expected amenities. Public areas include a well stocked bar and a tastefully appointed restaurant where the menus offer a varied selection of tempting dishes.
ROOMS: 7 en suite (bth/shr) (1 fmly) **MEALS:** Scottish & French Cuisine V meals Coffee am Tea pm **FACILITIES:** CTV in all bedrooms **SERVICES:** 9P **NOTES:** Last d 9pm **CARDS:**

BALLOCH West Dunbartonshire **Map 10 NS38**

★★★★★ Cameron House Hotel

DE VERE HOTELS

G83 8QZ
Quality Percentage Score: 72%
☎ 01389 755565 Fax 01389 759522
Dir: *from M8 (W) junct 30 for Erskine Bridge. Then A82 for Crainlarich. After 14m, at rdbt signed Luss straight on towards Luss, hotel on right*
Set on the shores of Loch Lomond, there are fine views to be had from many of this hotel's bedrooms and public areas. Accomodation is split between the old mansion building and the
contd.

Symbols and Abbreviations are listed and explained on pages 4 and 5

B

sympathetic extension. Public areas include a lounge, library and drawing room and a choice of dining rooms.
ROOMS: 96 en suite (bth/shr) (9 fmly) No smoking in all bedrooms s £140-£160; d £185-£225 (incl. bkfst) * LB Off peak **MEALS:** Lunch £17.50-£21.50 & alc Dinner £19.50-£41.50 & alc International Cuisine V meals Coffee am Tea pm **FACILITIES:** CTV in all bedrooms STV Indoor swimming pool (heated) Golf 9 Tennis (hard) Fishing Squash Snooker Sauna Solarium Gym Pool table Croquet lawn Jacuzzi/spa Quad Bikes Jet Ski Wkly live entertainment ch fac Xmas **CONF:** Thtr 300 Class 80 Board 80 Del from £150 * **SERVICES:** Lift Night porter 250P **NOTES:** No dogs (ex guide dogs) No smoking area in restaurant Last d 9.45pm **CARDS:**

See advert on opposite page

BALQUHIDDER Stirling — Map 11 NN52
★★ Monachyle Mhor
FK19 8PQ
Quality Percentage Score: 69%
☎ 01877 384622 01877 384305
Dir: *11m N of Callander on A84, turn right at Kingshouse Hotel this road takes you under the A84 towards Balquhidder, the hotel is 6m on the right*
The Lewis family preside over this peaceful converted farmhouse which forms part of a 2000-acre estate in the heart of the beautiful Braes of Balquhidder. Bedrooms, including those in the rear courtyard annexe, combine modern amenities with traditional comforts. Public areas include a cosy snug bar, a comfortable lounge and an attractive small dining room in the front extension overlooking the lochs Voile and Donie.
ROOMS: 5 en suite (bth/shr) 5 annexe en suite (bth/shr) No smoking in all bedrooms d £70-£90 (incl. bkfst) * Off peak **MEALS:** Lunch £7.50-£19.50alc Dinner £26.50-£29.50 & alc Scottish & French Cuisine V meals Coffee am Tea pm **FACILITIES:** CTV in all bedrooms Fishing Xmas **SERVICES:** Air conditioning 20P **NOTES:** No dogs (ex guide dogs) No coaches No children 12yrs No smoking in restaurant Last d 8.45pm **CARDS:**

See advert on opposite page

BANCHORY Aberdeenshire — Map 15 NO69
★★★ Tor-na-Coille
AB31 4AB
Quality Percentage Score: 74%
☎ 01330 822242 01330 824012
Dir: *on the main A93 Aberdeen/Braemar road, 0.5m west of Banchory town centre, opposite golf course*
Standing in its own grounds, this ivy-clad Victorian mansion has a growing reputation. Bedroom decor is remarkably attractive, and public areas include a smart lounge, a bar, and an elegant restaurant serving Taste of Scotland specialities.
ROOMS: 23 en suite (bth/shr) (4 fmly) s £55-£73; d £95-£120 (incl. bkfst) * LB Off peak **MEALS:** Sunday Lunch £13.50-£15.75 Dinner £26.50 Scottish & French Cuisine V meals Coffee am Tea pm **FACILITIES:** CTV in all bedrooms Croquet lawn Xmas **CONF:** Thtr 90 Class 60 Board 30 Del from £95 * **SERVICES:** Lift 130P **NOTES:** No smoking area in restaurant Last d 9.30pm Closed 25-28 Dec
CARDS:

BANCHORY Aberdeenshire — Map 15 NO69
★★★ Banchory Lodge
AB31 5HS
Quality Percentage Score: 73%
☎ 01330 822625 01330 825019
Dir: *off A93 13m west of Aberdeen*
This Georgian mansion, popular for small conferences and functions, stands in wooded grounds beside the River Dee. Bedrooms offer a choice of traditional or modern styles, and the inviting sitting rooms have river views. Fresh local produce features strongly on the dinner menu.
ROOMS: 22 en suite (bth/shr) (11 fmly) s £65-£85; d £95-£130 (incl. bkfst) * LB Off peak **MEALS:** Sunday Lunch fr £17.50 High tea fr £6.50 Dinner fr £21 English & French Cuisine V meals Coffee am Tea pm **FACILITIES:** CTV in all bedrooms Fishing Sauna Pool table Xmas **CONF:** Thtr 30 Class 30 Board 28 Del from £105 * **SERVICES:** 50P **NOTES:** No coaches Last d 9.30pm **CARDS:**

BANCHORY Aberdeenshire — Map 15 NO69
★★★ Raemoir House
Raemoir AB31 4ED
Quality Percentage Score: 73%
☎ 01330 824884 01330 822171
Dir: *take the A93 to Banchory turn right onto the A980, to Torphins, main drive is 2m ahead at T-junct*

This country house forms part of a 3,500 acre estate and has a unique atmosphere. Public rooms, including a choice of sitting rooms, a bar and a Georgian dining room, have tapestry-covered walls, open fires, and fine antiques. Bedrooms are individual in style, the 'master' rooms being furnished in period.
ROOMS: 17 en suite (bth/shr) 6 annexe en suite (bth/shr) (1 fmly) s £60-£70; d £80-£130 (incl. bkfst) * LB Off peak **MEALS:** Sunday Lunch £16.50 Dinner £26.50 V meals Coffee am Tea pm **FACILITIES:** CTV in all bedrooms Golf 9 Tennis (hard) Croquet lawn Putting green Shooting Stalking **CONF:** Thtr 40 Class 50 Board 30 Del from £96 * **SERVICES:** 100P **NOTES:** No smoking in restaurant Last d 9pm **CARDS:**

BANCHORY Aberdeenshire — Map 15 NO69
★★ *Burnett Arms*
25 High St AB31 5TD
Quality Percentage Score: 66%
☎ 01330 824944 01330 825553
Dir: *town centre on north side of A93, 18m from centre of Aberdeen*

Conveniently central in the town, this former coaching inn has been completely modernised to provide the comforts and facilities expected by the present day visitor. The tastefully

contd.

decorated bedrooms are comfortably furnished in the modern style and offer a good range of amenities. Public areas include a popular foyer coffee lounge and a choice of contrasting, well stocked bars. The dining room offers good value high teas and dinner.
ROOMS: 16 en suite (bth/shr) **MEALS:** European Cuisine V meals Coffee am Tea pm **FACILITIES:** CTV in all bedrooms STV Pool table **CONF:** Thtr 100 Class 50 Board 50 Del from £68 * **SERVICES:** 40P **NOTES:** No smoking in restaurant Last d 9pm
CARDS:

See advert under ABERDEEN

BANFF Aberdeenshire **Map 15 NJ66**
★★★ *Banff Springs*
Golden Knowes Rd AB45 2JE
Quality Percentage Score: 66%
☎ 01261 812881 01261 815546
Dir: *western outskirts of the town overlooking the beach on the A98 Banff to Inverness road*
This popular hotel offers a good standard of comfort in attractively decorated, modern bedrooms. Owners and staff have created a friendly atmosphere.
ROOMS: 31 en suite (bth/shr) **MEALS:** V meals Coffee am **FACILITIES:** CTV in all bedrooms STV Gym **CONF:** Thtr 400 Class 100 Board 40 **SERVICES:** Night porter 200P **NOTES:** No smoking in restaurant Last d 9pm Closed 25 Dec **CARDS:**

For Useful Information and Important Telephone Number Changes turn to page 25

B

BARRA, ISLE OF Western Isles Map 13

TANGASDALE Map 13 NF60

★★ Isle of Barra
Tangasdale Beach HS9 5XW
Quality Percentage Score: 68%
☎ 01871 810383 🖷 01871 810385
Dir: *turn left after leaving ferry terminal on to the A888, hotel is 2m on the left*
This purpose built hotel occupies a stunning position overlooking the white sands of the crescent shaped Halaman Bay and of the Atlantic Ocean beyond. The public areas are comfortable and optimise the views, as do most of the pleasant bedrooms. Peter and Diane Worthington run the hotel with commitment and dedication, assisted by many very friendly local staff. An attractive table d'hôte dinner is served and it is worth the supplement to savour the local scallops.
ROOMS: 30 en suite (bth/shr) (2 fmly) s £39-£47; d £68-£84 (incl. bkfst) LB Off peak **MEALS:** Bar Lunch £10-£16 Dinner £20.95-£24.95 V meals Coffee am Tea pm **FACILITIES:** CTV in all bedrooms STV Pool table Wkly live entertainment Xmas **CONF:** Class 70 Board 60 Del from £48 * **SERVICES:** 50P **NOTES:** No smoking in restaurant Last d 8.30pm Closed Oct-Apr exc Xmas & New Year **CARDS:**

BARRHEAD East Renfrewshire Map 11 NS45

★★★ Dalmeny Park Country House
Lochlibo Rd G78 1LG
Quality Percentage Score: 69%
☎ 0141 881 9211 🖷 0141 881 9214
Dir: *on A736 towards Glasgow*
Dalmeny Park is located on the outskirts of town, set in seven acres. Bedrooms offer good levels of comfort and quality with many extras such as mineral water and fruit. The hotel is well equipped for both business and leisure markets and is also popular as a wedding venue.
ROOMS: 20 en suite (bth/shr) (2 fmly) No smoking in 2 bedrooms s £70-£95; d £95-£120 (incl. bkfst) * Off peak **MEALS:** Bar Lunch £6.50-£9.99 & alc Dinner £19.50 & alc V meals Coffee am Tea pm **FACILITIES:** CTV in all bedrooms Jacuzzi/spa Xmas **CONF:** Thtr 200 Class 100 Board 60 **SERVICES:** Night porter 150P **NOTES:** No smoking area in restaurant Last d 9.30pm **CARDS:**

BATHGATE West Lothian Map 11 NS96

★★★ *Cairn Hotel*
Blackburn Rd EH48 2EL
Quality Percentage Score: 67%
☎ 01506 633366 🖷 01506 633444
Dir: *M8 exit 3A, at rdbt 1st left, next rdbt 1st left, small rdbt straight on then 1st slip rd signed Blackburn, at T junct turn right, hotel next right*
Originally the Golden Circle, this purpose-built landmark of the late sixties has been transformed into a smart modern hotel. Plush public areas provide ample comfortable seating and an attractive restaurant. There are also several meeting rooms. Bedrooms are not large, but stylishly furnished and well equipped.
ROOMS: 61 en suite (bth/shr) (2 fmly) No smoking in 49 bedrooms **MEALS:** Scottish & French Cuisine V meals Coffee am Tea pm **FACILITIES:** CTV in all bedrooms STV **CONF:** Thtr 250 Class 100 Board 50 Del from £75 * **SERVICES:** Lift Night porter 150P **NOTES:** No dogs (ex guide dogs) No smoking in restaurant Last d 9.45pm
CARDS:

BEATTOCK Dumfries & Galloway Map 11 NT00
see also **Moffat**

★ *Beattock House*
DG10 9QB
Quality Percentage Score: 62%
☎ 01683 300403 🖷 01683 300403
Dir: *turn off A74 at junct for 701 Moffat. Hotel 400yds on left*
A fine Victorian house in grounds which incorporate a small caravan park. Quaintly old fashioned, it is comfortable and homely. Bedrooms are generally well proportioned, with two magnificent Victorian bathrooms serving rooms without en suite facilities. Public areas include a quiet lounge, spacious dining room and cosy bar.
ROOMS: 7 rms (3 shr) (2 fmly) **MEALS:** V meals Coffee am Tea pm **FACILITIES:** CTV in all bedrooms Fishing **SERVICES:** 30P **NOTES:** Last d 9pm **CARDS:**

BEAULY Highland Map 14 NH54

★★★ Priory
The Square IV4 7BX
Quality Percentage Score: 70%
☎ 01463 782309 🖷 01463 782531
Dir: *signposted from A832*
Located in the village square, this friendly business and tourist hotel continues to improve, with more spacious and non-smoking bedrooms complementing the existing rooms, all of which offer a wide range of amenities. The attractive open plan public areas include a comfortable foyer lounge and a split-level restaurant.
ROOMS: 36 en suite (bth/shr) (3 fmly) No smoking in 6 bedrooms s £39.50-£47.50; d £59-£79 (incl. bkfst) * LB Off peak **MEALS:** Lunch £7-£13alc High tea £6-£10alc Dinner £17.50-£19.50 V meals Coffee am Tea pm **FACILITIES:** CTV in all bedrooms STV Snooker Pool table Wkly live entertainment ch fac Xmas **CONF:** Thtr 40 Class 40 Board 30 Del from £67.50 * **SERVICES:** Lift Night porter **NOTES:** No smoking in restaurant Last d 11pm **CARDS:**

BELLSHILL North Lanarkshire Map 11 NS76

Travel Inn
Belziehill Farm ML4 3HH
☎ 01698 740180 🖷 01698 845969
Dir: *from M74 junct 5 follow signs towards Bellshill on the A725. At the 2nd exit off the A725 Travel Inn on left of rdbt*
This modern building offers accommodation in smart, spacious and well equipped bedrooms, all with en-suite bathrooms. Refreshments may be taken at the nearby family restaurant. For details about current prices consult the Contents Page under Hotel Groups for the Travel Inn phone number.
d £39.95 *

BIGGAR South Lanarkshire Map 11 NT03

★★★ Shieldhill
Quothquan ML12 6NA
Quality Percentage Score: 66%
☎ 01899 220035 🖷 01899 221092
Dir: *turn off A702 onto B7016 Biggar to Carnwath rd in the middle of Biggar, after 2m turn left into Shieldhill rd, Hotel 1.5m on right*
Surrounded by lawns and woodland, this fortified mansion has parts dating from 1199. The oak-panelled lounge is a comfortable focal point, while the Chancellor restaurant with its baronial furnishings offers a daily-changing dinner menu.
contd.

Bedrooms vary in size, but some - such as the honeymoon suite with its raised spa bath dominating the room - are enormous.
ROOMS: 16 en suite (bth/shr) No smoking in all bedrooms s £75-£195; d £114-£390 (incl. bkfst) * LB Off peak **MEALS:** Lunch £15-£30alc High tea £12.95-£20 Dinner £20-£45alc Scottish & French Cuisine V meals Coffee am Tea pm **FACILITIES:** CTV in all bedrooms Croquet lawn Cycling Clay shoot Hot air ballooning Xmas **CONF:** Thtr 500 Class 200 Board 250 **SERVICES:** 25P **NOTES:** No smoking in restaurant Last d 8.30pm **CARDS:**

BIGGAR South Lanarkshire — Map 11 NT03

★★★ Tinto
Symington ML12 6FT
Quality Percentage Score: 63%
☎ 01899 308454 Fax 01899 308520
Dir: *SW on A72*
This hotel has a friendly atmosphere and provides comfortable well equipped bedrooms. It is also popular for weddings, while its Tapestry restaurant offers a wide ranging menu in an informal setting.
ROOMS: 29 en suite (bth/shr) (2 fmly) s £53; d £70 (incl. bkfst) * LB Off peak **MEALS:** International Cuisine V meals Coffee am Tea pm **FACILITIES:** CTV in all bedrooms ch fac Xmas **CONF:** Thtr 200 Class 180 Board 30 **SERVICES:** Night porter 100P **NOTES:** No smoking in restaurant Last d 10.00pm **CARDS:**

BIRNAM Perth & Kinross — Map 11 NO04

★★ Birnam House
PH8 0BQ
Quality Percentage Score: 65%
☎ 01350 727462 Fax 01350 728979
Dir: *off A9*
Offering a relaxed and welcoming atmosphere, this substantial baronial style hotel provides public areas include a well stocked bar with welcoming open fire, a foyer lounge, and an attractive restaurant where the short fixed-price menu offers interesting dishes based on fresh ingredients. All the expected amenities are provided in the bedrooms which vary in size and style.
ROOMS: 28 en suite (bth/shr) (6 fmly) s £39-£50; d £66-£80 (incl. bkfst) * LB Off peak **MEALS:** Bar Lunch £7.50-£15alc Dinner fr £17.50 V meals Coffee am Tea pm **FACILITIES:** CTV in all bedrooms STV Pool table Wkly live entertainment Xmas **CONF:** Thtr 150 Class 60 Board 60 Del from £65 * **SERVICES:** Lift Night porter 50P **NOTES:** No smoking in restaurant Last d 10pm **CARDS:**

See advert under DUNKELD

BLAIR ATHOLL Perth & Kinross — Map 14 NN86

★★ Atholl Arms
PH18 5SG
Quality Percentage Score: 68%
☎ 01796 481205 Fax 01796 481550
Dir: *off main A9 to B8079, 1m into Blair Atholl, hotel is situated in the village near entrance to Blair Castle*
A long established Highland hotel, situated close to the castle and railway station. Public areas include a choice of relaxing lounges and contrasting bars, but the most striking feature is the impressive Baronial dining room with its minstrels' gallery, where the fixed price menu offers a tempting range of Scottish fare. Bedrooms vary in size and offer mixed practical appointments.
ROOMS: 30 en suite (bth/shr) (3 fmly) **MEALS:** International Cuisine V meals Coffee am Tea pm **FACILITIES:** CTV in all bedrooms Fishing Pool table Rough shooting, fishing **SERVICES:** 103P **NOTES:** No smoking in restaurant Last d 9pm **CARDS:**

BLAIR ATHOLL Perth & Kinross — Map 14 NN86

★★ Bridge of Tilt
Bridge of Tilt PH18 5SU
Quality Percentage Score: 59%
☎ 01796 481333 Fax 01796 481335
Dir: *turn off A9 onto B8079, hotel is three quarters of a mile on left, with wishing well in front*
Situated close to Blair Castle, this long established Highland hotel in the centre of the village is a popular base for visiting tour groups. Though variable in size, the bedrooms are modern in style and offer all the expected amenities. Public areas include a spacious and well stocked bar, a lounge, and the dining room.
ROOMS: 20 en suite (bth/shr) 7 annexe en suite (bth/shr) (7 fmly) **MEALS:** V meals Coffee am Tea pm **FACILITIES:** CTV in all bedrooms Fishing Pool table Jacuzzi/spa **SERVICES:** 40P **NOTES:** No smoking in restaurant Last d 8.30pm Closed Jan **CARDS:**

BLAIRGOWRIE Perth & Kinross — Map 15 NO14

see also **Coupar Angus**

The Premier Collection

★★★ Kinloch House
PH10 6SG
☎ 01250 884237 Fax 01250 884333
Dir: *3m W on A923*
Set in 25 acres of woods and parkland with its own loch. Wood panelling and open fires characterise the reception rooms. The focal point is the cocktail bar its extensive range of malt whiskies, and adjoining conservatory. Bedrooms in the main house have character and individuality, wing rooms are spacious with luxury bathrooms. Chef Bill McNicoll conjures up mouth-watering dinners, breakfasts feature original dishes like salmon fish cakes with leek and homemade butteries, a type of croissant.
ROOMS: 21 en suite (bth/shr) s £83.55-£160; d £174.75-£235 (incl. bkfst & dinner) * LB Off peak **MEALS:** Lunch £15.95 Dinner £29.90 V meals Coffee am Tea pm **FACILITIES:** CTV in all bedrooms Indoor swimming pool (heated) Fishing Sauna Gym Croquet lawn Jacuzzi/spa Sailing Cycling Xmas **CONF:** Thtr 12 Class 12 Board 12 Del from £130 * **SERVICES:** 40P **NOTES:** No coaches No smoking in restaurant Last d 9.15pm Closed 18-29 Dec **CARDS:**

We endeavour to be as accurate as possible but changes in personnel and data can occur in establishments after the Hotel Guide has gone to press.

BLAIRGOWRIE Perth & Kinross **Map 15 NO14**
★★ **Altamount House Hotel**
Coupar Angus Rd PH10 6JN
Quality Percentage Score: 66%
☎ 01250 873512 01250 876200
Dir: *on entering Blairgowrie on A93 turn right onto Golf Course Rd, after one and a half miles at t-junct turn left, hotel 1m on left*
The Glashan family look forward to welcoming guests to this delightful small hotel, a converted Georgian House set in six acres of well tended gardens. The lounges are comfortable places to relax, while the elegant dining room provides an appropriate setting for the innovative Scottish cuisine prepared by Chef Robert Ramsay.
ROOMS: 7 en suite (bth/shr) (2 fmly) s £30-£70; d £80-£100 (incl. bkfst) * LB Off peak **MEALS:** Sunday Lunch £7.95-£20.75 High tea £8.50-£11.95 Dinner £22.50-£33.50 Modern Scottish Cuisine Coffee am Tea pm **FACILITIES:** CTV in all bedrooms Xmas **CONF:** Thtr 150 Class 40 Board 60 Del from £85 * **SERVICES:** 60P **NOTES:** No dogs (ex guide dogs) No smoking in restaurant Last d 9pm Closed 2-14 Jan
CARDS:

BLAIRGOWRIE Perth & Kinross **Map 15 NO14**
★★ **Angus**
46 Wellmeadow PH10 6NQ
Quality Percentage Score: 63%
☎ 01250 872455 01250 875615
Dir: *on the main A93 Perth/Blairgowrie Rd overlooking the Wellmeadow in the town centre*
Situated in the centre of town overlooking the square and gardens, this long established hotel is a popular base for visiting tour groups. The comfortable bedrooms have been smartly upgraded and offer a good range of amenities. The spacious bar has a no-smoking area while the attractive restaurant offers a good value fixed-price menu.
ROOMS: 81 en suite (bth/shr) s £39-£60; d £78-£120 (incl. bkfst & dinner) * LB Off peak **MEALS:** European Cuisine V meals Coffee am Tea pm **FACILITIES:** CTV in all bedrooms Indoor swimming pool (heated) Sauna Solarium Jacuzzi/spa Xmas **CONF:** Thtr 200 Class 60 Board 40 **SERVICES:** Lift Night porter 62P **NOTES:** No smoking in restaurant Last d 9pm **CARDS:**

BOAT OF GARTEN Highland **Map 14 NH91**
★★★ ***Boat***
PH24 3BH
Quality Percentage Score: 65%
☎ 01479 831258 01479 831414
Dir: *turn off A9 N of Aviemore onto A95 & follow signposts to Boat of Garten*
Holidaymakers and golfers use this comfortable Highland hotel by the Strathspey steam railway. A comfortable and inviting lounge, well stocked bar and smart restaurant are available. Several bedrooms have benefited from refurbishment, others are gradually being enhanced. Chef Peter Woods produces innovative fare on the regularly changing fixed price menu.
ROOMS: 32 en suite (bth/shr) (1 fmly) **MEALS:** Scottish, English & French Cuisine V meals Coffee am Tea pm **FACILITIES:** CTV in all bedrooms STV Pool table ch fac **CONF:** Thtr 35 Class 20 Board 16 Del from £49 * **SERVICES:** 36P **NOTES:** No smoking in restaurant Last d 9pm **CARDS:**

AA Rosettes are awarded for quality of food, see page 15 for an explanation of Rosette assessment.

BOTHWELL South Lanarkshire **Map 11 NS75**
★★★ **Bothwell Bridge**
89 Main St G71 8EU
Quality Percentage Score: 66%
☎ 01698 852246 01698 854686
Dir: *turn off M74 at junct 5 & follow signs to Uddingston, turn right at mini-rndabt. Hotel located just past shops on left*
This red sandstone mansion house has been considerably extended to become a popular business, function and conference centre. The bedrooms are mostly spacious and all are well equipped. The conservatory drawing room provides comfortable seating and a versatile, informal bar/meal operation in addition to the more formal restaurant which has a strong Italian influence.
ROOMS: 90 en suite (bth/shr) (14 fmly) No smoking in 14 bedrooms s fr £58; d fr £68 (incl. bkfst) * LB Off peak **MEALS:** Lunch £9-£12 & alc Dinner £13-£18.50 & alc Continental Cuisine V meals Coffee am Tea pm **FACILITIES:** CTV in all bedrooms STV Wkly live entertainment Xmas **CONF:** Thtr 200 Class 80 Board 350 Del from £85 * **SERVICES:** Lift Night porter 125P **NOTES:** No dogs (ex guide dogs) Last d 10.30pm
CARDS:

See advert on opposite page

BOWMORE See Islay, Isle of

BRAE See Shetland

BRAEMAR Aberdeenshire **Map 15 NO19**
★★★ **The Invercauld Arms**
AB35 5YR
Quality Percentage Score: 67%
☎ 013397 41605 013397 41428
PEEL HOTELS
Dir: *on the A93 equidistant between Perth and Aberdeen*
This impressive Victorian Hotel stands proudly beside the main road at the eastern edge of the village and is popular both with tour groups and private visitors alike. The spacious public areas are comfortably traditional in style and include a choice of inviting lounges, a well stocked tartan themed bar, and a smart dining room. Bedrooms are variable in size with solid furnishings and offer all the expected amenities. Staff are friendly and willing to please.
ROOMS: 68 en suite (bth/shr) (11 fmly) No smoking in 18 bedrooms s £83; d £109 (incl. bkfst) * LB Off peak **MEALS:** Sunday Lunch £15-£18 Dinner £15-£18 International Cuisine V meals Coffee am Tea pm **FACILITIES:** CTV in all bedrooms STV Wkly live entertainment Xmas **CONF:** Thtr 60 Class 20 Board 24 Del from £84 * **SERVICES:** Lift Night porter 80P **NOTES:** No smoking in restaurant Last d 9.45pm
CARDS:

BRAEMAR Aberdeenshire **Map 15 NO19**
★★ **Braemar Lodge**
Glenshee Rd AB35 5YQ
Quality Percentage Score: 70%
☎ 013397 41627 013397 41627
Dir: *on the A93 south approach to Braemar*
Situated on the edge of the village, this friendly hotel has recently added self-catering accommodation in attractive log cabins in the grounds. Bedrooms are comfortably furnished, and downstairs there are a lounge and bar. Substantial meals are served in the light and airy restaurant.
ROOMS: 7 rms (6 shr) (2 fmly) No smoking in all bedrooms s £25-£40; d £50-£80 (incl. bkfst) * LB Off peak **MEALS:** Coffee am **FACILITIES:** CTV in all bedrooms Xmas **SERVICES:** 16P **NOTES:** No smoking in restaurant **CARDS:**

BRECHIN Angus — Map 15 NO66

★★ *Northern*

2/4 Clerk St DD9 6AE

Quality Percentage Score: 62%

☎ 01356 625505 Fax 01356 622714

Jan and Donald MacIntyre are making good progress with improvements at this established town centre hotel. Good value meals are offered in the cocktail bar and restaurant, plans are progressing for a new bar. Bedroom standards remain mixed, smart pine furnishings are being introduced as rooms are refurbished.

ROOMS: 20 rms (5 bth 12 shr) (1 fmly) No smoking in 5 bedrooms **MEALS:** V meals Coffee am Tea pm **FACILITIES:** CTV in all bedrooms Pool table **CONF:** Thtr 120 Class 80 Board 40 **SERVICES:** 20P **NOTES:** No smoking in restaurant Last d 9pm **CARDS:**

BRIDGEND See Islay, Isle of

BRIDGE OF ALLAN Stirling — Map 11 NS79

★★★ Royal

Henderson St FK9 4HG

Quality Percentage Score: 64%

☎ 01786 832284 Fax 01786 834377

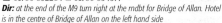

Dir: *at the end of the M9 turn right at the rndbt for Bridge of Allan. Hotel is in the centre of Bridge of Allan on the left hand side*

A popular business hotel with well equipped bedrooms in a variety of sizes, many particularly spacious. The stylish, attractive restaurant offers a contemporary slant on uncomplicated dishes.

ROOMS: 32 en suite (bth/shr) (2 fmly) s £68-£83; d £90-£115 (incl. bkfst) * LB Off peak **MEALS:** Lunch £15 Dinner £20.50-£23.50 & alc Taste of Scotland Cuisine V meals Coffee am Tea pm **FACILITIES:** CTV in all bedrooms STV Xmas **CONF:** Thtr 150 Class 60 Board 50 Del from £120 * **SERVICES:** Lift Night porter 40P **NOTES:** No dogs (ex guide dogs) Last d 9.30pm **CARDS:**

See advert under STIRLING

★

The Premier Collection, hotels with Red Star Awards are listed on pages 17-23

Remember to return your Prize Draw card for a chance to win one of 30 relaxing leisure breaks with Corus and Regal hotels. See inside the front cover for the card and competition details.

BRIDGE OF MARNOCH Aberdeenshire **Map 15 NJ55**

The Premier Collection

★★ Old Manse of Marnoch
AB54 7RS
☎ 01466 780873 Fax 01466 780873
Dir: *on B9117 less than 1m off A97 route midway between Huntly and Banff*

Standing peacefully by the Deveron in four acres of gardens, this Georgian manse is run by owners Patrick and Keren Carter. The well proportioned bedrooms are individual and feature fine antiques as well as modern hand-crafted pieces. The inviting lounge is full of mementoes of the owners' extensive travels, while the dining room has a nautical theme and makes a fine setting for innovative cooking.
ROOMS: 8 en suite (bth/shr) No smoking in 2 bedrooms s £54-£60; d £84.60-£94 (incl. bkfst) * LB Off peak **MEALS:** Dinner fr £27 **FACILITIES:** CTV in all bedrooms Fishing **SERVICES:** 14P **NOTES:** No coaches No children 12yrs No smoking in restaurant Last d 8.30pm Closed 2 wks Nov Xmas & New Year
CARDS:

BRIDGE OF ORCHY Argyll & Bute **Map 10 NN23**
★★ Bridge of Orchy Hotel
PA36 4AD
Quality Percentage Score: 75%
☎ 01838 400208 Fax 01838 400313
Dir: *located on main A82 6m N of Tydrum*

This well established hotel has recently been completely refurbished by new owners. Bedrooms are comfortable and have all expected facilities, as well as a few thoughtful extras. Guests can relax in the comfortable lounge with its roaring fire or enjoy the busy bar. Meals are available in the bar and dining room.
ROOMS: 10 en suite (bth/shr) (2 fmly) No smoking in all bedrooms s £45-£79.50; d £60-£79.50 (incl. bkfst) * LB Off peak **MEALS:** Bar Lunch £10.50-£17.50alc Dinner £16.50-£21alc V meals Coffee am Tea pm **FACILITIES:** CTV in all bedrooms STV Fishing **CONF:** Thtr 40 Class 30 Board 20 Del £89.50 * **SERVICES:** 50P **NOTES:** No dogs (ex guide dogs) No coaches No smoking in restaurant Last d 8.30pm Closed 1 Dec-1 Jan **CARDS:**

BRODICK See Arran, Isle of

BRORA Highland **Map 14 NC90**
★★★ Royal Marine
Golf Rd KW9 6QS
Quality Percentage Score: 72%
☎ 01408 621252 Fax 01408 621181
Dir: *turn off A9 in village toward beach and golf course*

This distinctive house was built in 1913 by Scottish architect, Sir Robert Latimer. An attractive bedroom wing has been added and the swimming pool renewed. The leisure centre has full curling facilities. Both the restaurant and the bar enjoy busy trade, and the Garden Room provides bistro style meals.
ROOMS: 22 en suite (bth/shr) (1 fmly) s £60-£80; d £90-£150 (incl. bkfst) * LB Off peak **MEALS:** Lunch £13-£15alc Dinner £15-£25alc Scottish & French Cuisine V meals Coffee am Tea pm **FACILITIES:** CTV in all bedrooms STV Indoor swimming pool (heated) Golf 18 Tennis (hard) Fishing Snooker Sauna Solarium Gym Pool table Croquet lawn Putting green Jacuzzi/spa Ice curling rink in season Table Tennis Xmas **CONF:** Thtr 70 Class 40 Board 40 Del from £85 * **SERVICES:** Night porter 40P **NOTES:** No coaches No smoking in restaurant Last d 9pm
CARDS:

BRORA Highland **Map 14 NC90**
★★★ The Links
Golf Rd KW9 6QS
Quality Percentage Score: 66%
☎ 01408 621225 Fax 01408 621383
Dir: *turn off A9 in village of Brora towards beach and golf course, hotel overlooks golf course*

Owned and run by The Powell family, this hotel overlooks the golf course towards the North Sea. The attractive bedrooms include a number of family rooms and suites. Guests can enjoy marvellous views from the lounges and restaurant, where a choice of interesting dishes are available from the carte and table d'hote menus.
ROOMS: 23 en suite (bth/shr) (2 fmly) s £60-£80; d £90-£150 (incl. bkfst) LB Off peak **MEALS:** Lunch £13-£15 Dinner £15-£25alc International Cuisine V meals Coffee am Tea pm **FACILITIES:** CTV in all bedrooms Indoor swimming pool (heated) Fishing Snooker Sauna Solarium Gym Croquet lawn Putting green Jacuzzi/spa Xmas **CONF:** Thtr 100 Class 40 Board 20 Del from £85 * **SERVICES:** 55P **NOTES:** No smoking in restaurant Last d 9pm Closed 31 Oct-Mar RS Apr/Oct (dinner may be in sister hotel)
CARDS:

BUCKIE Moray **Map 15 NJ46**
★★ *Mill House*
Tynet AB56 5HJ
Quality Percentage Score: 66%
☎ 01542 850233 Fax 01542 850331
Dir: *on A98 between Buckie and Fochabers*

A former mill has been converted into this popular business and tourist hotel, which stands between Buckie and Fochabers. The original water-driven wheel machinery is still in place in the
contd.

entrance lobby. Other public areas include a well stocked bar and an attractive restaurant.
ROOMS: 15 en suite (bth/shr) (2 fmly) **MEALS:** V meals Coffee am Tea pm **FACILITIES:** CTV in all bedrooms **CONF:** Thtr 100 Class 60 Board 30 Del from £55 * **SERVICES:** Night porter 101P **NOTES:** No smoking in restaurant Last d 9.00pm **CARDS:**

BUNESSAN See Mull, Isle of

BURNTISLAND Fife — Map 11 NT28

★★ *Inchview Hotel*

THE CIRCLE
Selected Individual Hotels
GREAT BRITAIN

69 Kinghorn Rd KY3 9EB
Quality Percentage Score: 62%
☎ 01592 872239 Fax 01592 874866
Dir: *on A921 on entering Burntisland head towards town centre, hotel overlooks The Links on Kinghorn Road*
A friendly family run hotel, part of a listed Georgian terrace, overlooking the Links to the Firth of Forth. Bedrooms are well equipped and come in a range of styles, including a four-poster room. A good choice of popular meals is available in the bar, while in the restaurant more adventurous fare is offered.
ROOMS: 12 en suite (bth/shr) (1 fmly) **MEALS:** International Cuisine V meals Coffee am Tea pm **FACILITIES:** CTV in all bedrooms **CONF:** Thtr 80 Class 40 Board 30 **SERVICES:** 15P **NOTES:** Last d 9.45pm **CARDS:**

BUTE, ISLE OF Argyll & Bute

ARDBEG — Map 10 NS06

★★ Ardmory House Hotel & Restaurant

Ardmory Rd PA20 0PG
Quality Percentage Score: 77%
☎ 01700 502346 Fax 01700 505596
Dir: *N from Rothesay on A844, 1m turn left up Ardmory Road, hotel 300mtrs on left*
Dedicated owners Donald Cameron and Bill Jeffery and their staff provide high levels of attention and care at this most welcoming of small hotels. Set in its own grounds on a hillside overlooking the bay, it offers a wonderfully relaxed atmosphere. The smart bar and lounge now has a conservatory extension. The attractive restaurant is where chef Eddie McGarvey presents a competitively priced four-course table d'hôte menu as well as a carte. The no-smoking bedrooms, though not large, offer a wide range of amenities as well as thoughtful extras.
ROOMS: 5 en suite (bth/shr) No smoking in all bedrooms s £47.50; d £75 (incl. bkfst) * Off peak **MEALS:** Lunch £12.50-£18.50 & alc Dinner £18.50 & alc V meals Coffee am Tea pm **FACILITIES:** CTV in all bedrooms **CONF:** Thtr 60 Class 30 Board 30 **SERVICES:** 12P **NOTES:** No smoking in restaurant Last d 9pm
CARDS:

CALLANDER Stirling — Map 11 NN60

★★★ *Roman Camp Country House*

FK17 8BG
Quality Percentage Score: 72%
☎ 01877 330003 Fax 01877 331533
Dir: *heading north on the A84 turn left at the east end of Callander High street, down a 300 yard driveway into the hotel grounds*
A charming country house hotel on the banks of the River Teith. Bedrooms vary in size and individual style, extras include sherry, mineral water and fruit. Day rooms comprise an inviting drawing room, comfortable library, and informal sun lounge. The new restaurant is the setting for accomplished modern cooking from chef Ian McNaught.
ROOMS: 14 en suite (bth/shr) (3 fmly) **MEALS:** Scottish & French Cuisine V meals Coffee am Tea pm **FACILITIES:** CTV in all bedrooms Fishing **CONF:** Thtr 100 Class 40 Board 20 **SERVICES:** 80P **NOTES:** No children 4 No smoking in restaurant Last d 9pm
CARDS:

See advert on this page

CALLANDER Stirling — Map 11 NN60

★★ Lubnaig

Leny Feus FK17 8AS
Quality Percentage Score: 71%
☎ 01877 330376 Fax 01877 330376
Dir: *travelling W on the A84 through main street of Callander to the W outskirts, turn right into Leny Feus, just after Poppies sign*
Crawford and Sue Low provide plenty of local information and each bedroom has a tourist newsletter compiled by Crawford. Usually wearing the kilt in the evening, Crawford dispenses drinks and answers questions while Sue produces home-cooked dinners and hearty breakfasts. There are three lounges, one of which gives direct access to the garden patio.
ROOMS: 6 en suite (shr) 4 annexe en suite (shr) d £60-£78 (incl. bkfst) LB Off peak **MEALS:** Dinner £13.50-£23alc International Cuisine V meals **FACILITIES:** CTV in all bedrooms **SERVICES:** 10P **NOTES:** No dogs No coaches No children 7yrs No smoking in restaurant Last d 8pm Closed Nov-Etr RS Apr (B&B only) **CARDS:**

CALLANDER Stirling — Map 11 NN60
★★ ***Bridgend House***
Bridgend FK17 8AH
Quality Percentage Score: 63%
☎ 01877 330130 📠 01877 331512
Dir: *proceed down Callander main st, turn onto A81 (Aberfoyle rd) pass over red sandstone bridge, hotel on right*
Easily recognised by its black and white façade, this is a welcoming, personally-run hotel beside the River Teith. Public areas include a popular bar, comfortable lounge, and a dining room that overlooks the garden. The bedrooms, two with four posters, have good quality furnishings and all the expected amenities.
ROOMS: 6 rms (5 bth/shr) **MEALS:** V meals Coffee am Tea pm **FACILITIES:** CTV in all bedrooms STV Pool table Wkly live entertainment **SERVICES:** 30P **NOTES:** Last d 9pm **CARDS:**

CALLANDER Stirling — Map 11 NN60
★★ **Dalgair House**
113-115 Main St FK17 8BQ
Quality Percentage Score: 63%
☎ 01877 330283 📠 01877 331114
Dir: *300 metres beyond access road to golf course on main street*

THE CIRCLE
Selected Individual Hotels
GREAT BRITAIN

New owners the Nietos have begun a rolling improvement programme at this long established hotel on the main street. Public areas include an open-plan lounge and restaurant and there is also a cosy and welcoming bar. Bedrooms, all with a wide range of amenities, are benefiting from enhancement.
ROOMS: 8 en suite (bth/shr) (1 fmly) s £35-£47; d £60-£70 (incl. bkfst) * LB Off peak **MEALS:** Lunch £12-£15 High tea fr £7.50 Dinner £15-£20 & alc International Cuisine V meals Coffee am Tea pm **FACILITIES:** CTV in all bedrooms STV Xmas **CONF:** Del from £25 * **SERVICES:** 12P **NOTES:** Last d 9pm **CARDS:**

CAMPBELTOWN Argyll & Bute — Map 10 NR72
★★ **Seafield**
Kilkerran Rd PA28 6JL
Quality Percentage Score: 67%
☎ 01586 554385 📠 01586 552741
Situated close to the Ferry Terminal and enjoying views over the bay, this family run hotel combines a welcoming atmosphere with good value for money. Bedrooms, several of which are in the garden annexe, vary in size and offer mixed modern furnishings together with a good range of amenities. Public areas include an open-plan foyer with bar and lounge while enjoyable home cooked fare is served in the attractive restaurant.
ROOMS: 3 en suite (bth/shr) 6 annexe en suite (shr) s £45-£55; d £65-£80 (incl. bkfst) * LB Off peak **MEALS:** Lunch £12.50 High tea £8.75 Dinner £20 V meals Coffee am **FACILITIES:** CTV in all bedrooms **SERVICES:** 11P **NOTES:** No children 14yrs No smoking in restaurant Last d 8.30pm **CARDS:**

CANNICH Highland — Map 14 NH33
★★★ ***Mullardoch House***
Glen Cannich IV4 7LX
Quality Percentage Score: 70%
☎ 01456 415460 📠 01456 415460
Dir: *8m W on unclass Glen Cannich road*
The dramatic location of this former hunting lodge well up Glen Cannich, almost at the base of the Mullardoch dam, will take your breath away at any time of the year. Andy Johnston runs the hotel in a very homely manner and offers high standards of comfort. A set four course menu is served at 8pm each evening in the elegant dining room. There is a cosy bar area where a choice of attractive dishes is available.
ROOMS: 6 en suite (bth/shr) (1 fmly) **MEALS:** V meals Coffee am Tea pm **FACILITIES:** CTV in all bedrooms Fishing Deer stalking **SERVICES:** 12P **NOTES:** No coaches No smoking in restaurant **CARDS:**

CARNOUSTIE Angus — Map 12 NO53
★★ **Carlogie House**
Carlogie Rd DD7 6LD
Quality Percentage Score: 68%
☎ 01241 853185 📠 01241 856528
Dir: *take A92 turn off at cross road on to A930, hotel 1km on right side*
The MacKenzie family look forward to welcoming you to their popular business and tourist hotel which stands in lovely gardens just north of the town. Main house bedrooms, though variable in size, are modern in appointment and offer a good range of amenities. Opposite, a former stable block has been converted to provide accommodation for the disabled traveller. Public areas are nicely presented, comfortable, and enjoyable to use. The adventure playground in the garden is a big hit with the children.
ROOMS: 13 en suite (bth/shr) 4 annexe en suite (shr) (2 fmly) s fr £55; d fr £85 (incl. bkfst) * LB Off peak **MEALS:** Lunch £15 & alc High tea £7 & alc Dinner £15 & alc Scottish & French Cuisine V meals Coffee am Tea pm **FACILITIES:** CTV in all bedrooms STV **SERVICES:** 100P **NOTES:** No dogs (ex guide dogs) No smoking area in restaurant Last d 9.00pm Closed 1-3 Jan **CARDS:**

CARNOUSTIE Angus — Map 12 NO53
★★ **Hogan House**
Links Pde DD7 7JF
Quality Percentage Score: 68%
☎ 01241 853273 📠 01241 853319
Dir: *off A92, adjoining Golf Course*
From its position overlooking the 18th green of the championship course, it is not surprising that this family-run hotel has particular appeal for visiting golfers. Public areas include a well stocked themed bar, a comfortable lounge and small restaurant, as well as a popular golf shop. Bedrooms have attractive colour schemes and are comfortably modern in style.
ROOMS: 7 en suite (bth/shr) (4 fmly) s fr £40; d fr £65 (incl. bkfst) * LB Off peak **MEALS:** Scottish & French Cuisine V meals Coffee am Tea pm **FACILITIES:** CTV in all bedrooms **SERVICES:** 10P **NOTES:** No smoking in restaurant **CARDS:**

CARNOUSTIE Angus — Map 12 NO53
○ ***Carnoustie Golf Course Hotel***
The Links DD7 7JE
☎ 01241 411999
Opened in the Spring of 1999 this smart hotel enjoys a spectacular setting beside the Championship Course, and is expected to attract visitors from around the world, many of whom will appreciate the facility to book guaranteed tee times on the town's three links courses. World class designers were

contd.

commissioned to create the hotel interiors. Bedrooms range from opulent suites to superior and regular rooms, all of which are appointed to a high standard. Public areas radiate from the attractive foyer and include a well stocked bar, and an attractive restaurant overlooking the course. Other facilities include a golf shop as well as banqueting and leisure facilities.

CARRBRIDGE Highland — Map 14 NH92
★★★ Dalrachney Lodge
PH23 3AT
Quality Percentage Score: 68%
☎ 01479 841252 01479 841383
Dir: *off A938*
This comfortable Highland hotel is a converted hunting lodge. Public areas, which are nicely presented, include an inviting sitting room, a well stocked bar, and tastefully appointed dining room. Bedrooms are well proportioned and offer comfortable period furnishings.
ROOMS: 11 en suite (bth/shr) (3 fmly) No smoking in 4 bedrooms s £35-£65; d £55-£110 (incl. bkfst) * LB Off peak **MEALS:** Lunch £12.95 & alc Dinner £25 & alc Scottish & French Cuisine V meals Coffee am **FACILITIES:** CTV in all bedrooms STV Fishing Xmas **SERVICES:** 40P **NOTES:** No coaches No smoking in restaurant Last d 8.30pm **CARDS:**

CARRBRIDGE Highland — Map 14 NH92
★★ Fairwinds
PH23 3AA
Quality Percentage Score: 68%
☎ 01479 841240 01479 841240
Dir: *turn off A9 1m N of Aviemore. Follow A95 signposted Carrbridge for 3m then onto B9153, hotel on left side of main road*
A very personal level of attention is offered by Roger and Liz Reed at their comfortable small hotel, where there are a number of self-catering chalets standing in the seven-acre grounds. The comfortable hotel bedrooms are bright and airy and the public areas include a smart conservatory which joins the attractive dining area and the lounge. Smoking is permitted in an adjacent lounge with an honesty bar.
ROOMS: 5 en suite (bth/shr) s £27-£28; d £52-£58 (incl. bkfst) * LB Off peak **MEALS:** Dinner £17 & alc Scottish & Continental Cuisine V meals **FACILITIES:** CTV in all bedrooms **SERVICES:** 6P **NOTES:** No dogs (ex guide dogs) No coaches No children 12yrs No smoking in restaurant Last d 8.00pm Closed 2 Nov-20 Dec **CARDS:**

CARRUTHERSTOWN Dumfries & Galloway — Map 11 NY17
★★★ *Hetland Hall*
DG1 4JX
Quality Percentage Score: 70%
☎ 01387 840201 01387 840211
Dir: *midway between Annan & Dumfries on A75*

An extended Georgian mansion, this hotel is set in 45 acres of parkland. Bedrooms come in a variety of sizes but all are well equipped and attractively decorated. Lounges with log fires are a feature of the public areas. A honeymoon suite with a four-poster bed is available.
ROOMS: 27 en suite (bth/shr) (3 fmly) No smoking in 3 bedrooms **MEALS:** International Cuisine V meals Coffee am Tea pm **FACILITIES:** CTV in all bedrooms STV Indoor swimming pool (heated) Fishing Snooker Sauna Solarium Gym Putting green Indoor badminton ch fac **CONF:** Thtr 200 Class 100 Board 70 Del from £78 * **SERVICES:** Night porter 60P **NOTES:** No smoking in restaurant Last d 9.30pm **CARDS:**
See advert under DUMFRIES

CASTLE DOUGLAS Dumfries & Galloway — Map 11 NX76
★★ Douglas Arms
King St DG7 1DB
Quality Percentage Score: 70%
☎ 01556 502231 01556 504000
Dir: *in centre of town, adjacent to Clock Tower*
Friendly service is a feature of this former coaching inn situated in the centre of the town. There is a choice of lounges, plus a cosy bar adjoining an informal restaurant, both offering good value meals. Bedrooms are well equipped.
ROOMS: 24 en suite (bth/shr) (1 fmly) No smoking in 8 bedrooms s fr £37.50; d fr £68.50 (incl. bkfst) * LB Off peak **MEALS:** Sunday Lunch £6.95-£9.95 Dinner £13.50 & alc International Cuisine V meals Coffee am Tea pm **FACILITIES:** CTV in all bedrooms STV Pool table Xmas **CONF:** Thtr 150 Class 40 Board 40 Del from £62.50 * **SERVICES:** 16P **NOTES:** No smoking in restaurant Last d 10pm **CARDS:**

CASTLE DOUGLAS Dumfries & Galloway — Map 11 NX76
★★ Urr Valley Country House
Ernespie Rd DG7 3JG
Quality Percentage Score: 68%
☎ 01556 502188 01556 504055
Dir: *off A75 towards Castle Douglas, approx 1m on left*
Reached by a long drive, this country house is set in 14 acres of woodland a mile from town. The wood-panelled lounge and bar are filled with shooting and fishing memorabilia. Guests can eat well in both the bar and restaurant. Bedrooms are well equipped and comfortable.
ROOMS: 18 rms (17 bth/shr) (5 fmly) No smoking in 2 bedrooms s £37.50-£47.50; d £50-£85 (incl. bkfst) * LB Off peak **MEALS:** Lunch £9.95 Dinner £17.50 Scottish & French Cuisine V meals Coffee am Tea pm **FACILITIES:** CTV in all bedrooms STV Xmas **CONF:** Thtr 300 Class 100 Board 100 **SERVICES:** 200P **NOTES:** No smoking in restaurant Last d 9pm **CARDS:**

CASTLE DOUGLAS Dumfries & Galloway — Map 11 NX76
★★ Imperial
35 King St DG7 1AA
Quality Percentage Score: 65%
☎ 01556 502086 01556 503009
Dir: *turn off A75 at sign for Castle Douglas go down main street hotel opposite the town library*
Situated in the main street, this former coaching inn, popular with golfers, offers well equipped and cheerfully decorated bedrooms. There is a choice of bars, and good meals are served either in the foyer bar or the upstairs dining room.
ROOMS: 12 en suite (bth/shr) (1 fmly) No smoking in 6 bedrooms s £37-£45; d £56-£60 (incl. bkfst) * LB Off peak **MEALS:** Lunch £8.75-£11.25 High tea £6.50 Dinner £12.50-£15 & alc V meals Coffee am Tea pm **FACILITIES:** CTV in all bedrooms Pool table ch fac **CONF:** Thtr 40 Class 20 Board 20 Del from £55 * **SERVICES:** 29P **NOTES:** No smoking in restaurant Last d 8.30pm **CARDS:**

CASTLE DOUGLAS Dumfries & Galloway **Map 11 NX76**

★★ King's Arms

St Andrew's St DG7 1EL
Quality Percentage Score: 64%
☎ 01556 502626 📠 01556 502097
Dir: *through main street, left at town clock, hotel situated on corner site*
On a corner site just off the main street, this former coaching inn's plain façade contrasts with its characterful interior. This includes a choice of cosy bar areas and a restaurant, overlooking an ivy clad courtyard. Both the bar and the restaurant offer a good choice of menus.
ROOMS: 10 rms (9 bth/shr) (2 fmly) No smoking in 2 bedrooms s £35-£45; d £54-£62 (incl. bkfst) * LB Off peak **MEALS:** Lunch £7.50-£14.50 High tea £6.25-£8 Dinner £12.50-£15 & alc Scottish & French Cuisine V meals Coffee am Tea pm **FACILITIES:** CTV in all bedrooms Pool table ch fac **CONF:** Thtr 35 Class 20 Board 25 Del from £60 * **SERVICES:** 15P **NOTES:** No smoking in restaurant Last d 8.45pm Closed 25-26 Dec & 1-2 Jan **CARDS:**

CLACHAN-SEIL Argyll & Bute **Map 10 NM71**

★★❀❀ Willowburn

PA34 4TJ
Quality Percentage Score: 72%
☎ 01852 300276 📠 300597
Dir: *0.5m from Atlantic Bridge, on left*
This pretty cottage hotel occupies an idyllic position by the water's edge on the Island of Seil, just south of Oban. Peace and quiet along with fine food cooked with passion and sourced from reliable local suppliers along with caring service are the keys to the hotel's success. There is a small bar, a formal dining room and a comfortable homely lounge all of which enjoy lovely views. Bedrooms are all pretty and thoughtfully equipped.
ROOMS: 7 en suite (bth/shr) No smoking in all bedrooms s £51-£58; d £102-£116 (incl. bkfst & dinner) LB Off peak **MEALS:** Bar Lunch £5-£10alc Dinner £26 Scottish & French Cuisine V meals Coffee am Tea pm **FACILITIES:** CTV in all bedrooms Xmas **SERVICES:** 36P **NOTES:** No coaches No smoking in restaurant Last d 8.30pm Closed Jan-Feb **CARDS:**

CLYDEBANK West Dunbartonshire **Map 11 NS56**

Courtesy & Care Award

★★★★❀❀ Beardmore

Beardmore St G81 4SA
Quality Percentage Score: 70%
☎ 0141 951 6000 📠 0141 951 6018
Dir: *M8 J19 follow the A814 towards Dumbarton then follow tourist signs. Turn left onto Beardsmore St and follow signs*
Situated beside the banks of the River Clyde, near the Erskine Bridge, this impressive modern hotel is well placed for business guests and holidaymakers. Bedrooms are attractive and some are of 'executive' standard. Business and conference facilities are extensive and the restaurant, now re-styled and called Citrus, serves interesting modern food. The friendly service and standards of customer care have earned it the AA Courtesy and Care Award for Scotland 1999-2000.
ROOMS: 168 en suite (bth/shr) No smoking in 112 bedrooms d £90-£110 * Off peak **MEALS:** Lunch £13.50-£16.50 Dinner £18-£25alc European Cuisine V meals Coffee am Tea pm **FACILITIES:** CTV in all bedrooms STV Indoor swimming pool (heated) Sauna Solarium Gym Jacuzzi/spa full range of beauty treatments available **CONF:** Thtr 170 Class 40 Board 30 Del from £110 * **SERVICES:** Lift Night porter Air conditioning 150P **NOTES:** Last d 10pm **CARDS:**

CLYDEBANK West Dunbartonshire **Map 11 NS56**

★★★ Patio

1 South Av, Clydebank Business Park G81 2RW
Quality Percentage Score: 63%
☎ 0141 951 1133 📠 0141 952 3713
Situated in the local business park, this modern hotel is a popular conference and function venue. Public areas are in the modern, mainly open-plan style and the restaurant offers a range of menus at lunch and dinner. Bedrooms have interesting lacquer and marble furniture.
ROOMS: 80 en suite (bth/shr) No smoking in 16 bedrooms s £39-£69; d £49-£79 (incl. bkfst) * LB Off peak **MEALS:** Lunch £12.95-£12.95 Dinner £12.95-£15.50 French & Scottish Cuisine V meals Coffee am Tea pm **FACILITIES:** CTV in all bedrooms **CONF:** Thtr 150 Class 30 Board 30 Del from £75 * **SERVICES:** Lift Night porter 120P **NOTES:** Last d 10pm **CARDS:**

COLONSAY, ISLE OF Argyll & Bute **Map 10**

SCALASAIG **Map 10 NR39**

★★❀ Colonsay

PA61 7YP
Quality Percentage Score: 70%
☎ 01951 200316 📠 01951 200353
Dir: *400mtrs W of Ferry Pier*
Enthusiastic new owners Claude and Christine Reysenn look forward to welcoming guests old and new to their delightful small island hotel. Colonsay, a Hebridean island with a ferry service from the mainland every other day, is well worth a visit to sample the wonderfully relaxed atmosphere and good food which is personally prepared by Claude. Relaxing public areas include a choice of inviting lounges, a popular bar, and a timber-clad dining room. Bedrooms, which are variable in size and style are currently in the process of being upgraded.
ROOMS: 11 rms (9 bth/shr) (2 fmly) s £70-£85; d £140-£170 (incl. bkfst & dinner) * LB Off peak **MEALS:** Bar Lunch £1.95-£5 Dinner £25 English, Belgian & French Cuisine V meals Coffee am Tea pm **FACILITIES:** CTV in all bedrooms Bicycles Sailing equipment available Xmas **SERVICES:** 8P **NOTES:** No coaches No smoking in restaurant Last d 7.30pm **CARDS:**

COLVEND Dumfries & Galloway **Map 11 NX85**

★★ Clonyard House

DG5 4QW
Quality Percentage Score: 64%
☎ 01556 630372 📠 01556 630422
Dir: *through Dalbeattie and turn left onto A710 for aprrox. 4m*
This family run hotel is set in seven acres of grounds, which include a childrens' play area and an 'enchanted tree'. Most of the spacious, comfortable bedrooms are housed in a purpose-

contd.

built extension. Meals are served in the bar lounge or in the restaurant proper.

ROOMS: 15 en suite (bth/shr) (2 fmly) s £30-£40; d £60-£70 (incl. bkfst) * LB Off peak **MEALS:** Sunday Lunch £10.50 & alc Dinner £15 & alc British & French Cuisine V meals Coffee am **FACILITIES:** CTV in all bedrooms ch fac **CONF:** Class 35 Board 20 **SERVICES:** 40P **NOTES:** No coaches Last d 8.55pm **CARDS:**

COMRIE Perth & Kinross — Map 11 NN72

★★★ Royal

Melville Square PH6 2DW
Quality Percentage Score: 70%
☎ 01764 679200 01764 679219

Dir: *situated on the main square in Comrie, which the A85 runs through*

Under the care of Edward Gibbons and his friendly, helpful staff, many improvements have taken place at this long-established, town-centre hotel. Public rooms include an inviting library/lounge, a choice of bars, a brasserie and a formal dining room where the emphasis is on Taste of Scotland specialities. Stylish fabrics lend a touch of elegance to the well equipped bedrooms.

ROOMS: 11 en suite (bth/shr) s £45-£95; d £90-£190 (incl. bkfst) * LB Off peak **MEALS:** Lunch £7.95-£21 Dinner £15-£21 V meals Coffee am Tea pm **FACILITIES:** CTV in all bedrooms STV Fishing Pool table Croquet lawn Xmas **SERVICES:** 8P **NOTES:** No dogs (ex guide dogs) No coaches No children 5yrs Last d 9.45pm
CARDS:

See advert on this page

CONNEL Argyll & Bute — Map 10 NM93

★★ Falls of Lora

PA37 1PB
Quality Percentage Score: 70%
☎ 01631 710483 01631 710694

Dir: *off A85, overlooking Loch Etive, 5m from Oban*

This friendly, personally run hotel enjoys views of Loch Etive. The inviting public areas include a comfortable lounge, a well stocked bar, a bistro offering an informal, yet good food service all day, and a formal dining room, which may be closed when the demand is insufficient. Bedrooms range from spacious, luxury rooms to standard cabin rooms.

ROOMS: 30 en suite (bth/shr) (4 fmly) s £35.50-£53.50; d £43-£111 (incl. bkfst) * LB Off peak **MEALS:** Bar Lunch £7.50-£12alc High tea £6.50-£8.50alc Dinner £15-£25alc Scottish & French Cuisine V meals Coffee am Tea pm **FACILITIES:** CTV in all bedrooms **CONF:** Thtr 45 Class 20 Board 15 **SERVICES:** 40P **NOTES:** No coaches No smoking area in restaurant Last d 9.30pm Closed mid Dec & Jan
CARDS:

See advert under OBAN

CONTIN Highland — Map 14 NH45

★★★ Coul House

IV14 9EY
Quality Percentage Score: 74%
☎ 01997 421487 01997 421945

Dir: *from South by passing Inverness continue on A9 over Moray Firth bridge, after 5m take 2nd exit at rdbt on to A835 follow to Contin*

Martyn and Ann Hill and staff provide hospitable attention at this lovely Victorian country house. Individually decorated bedrooms have good amenities. A log fire invites relaxation in the foyer lounge in contrast with the more refined atmosphere of the octagonal drawing room. In the elegant dining room, chef Chris Bentley offers an enjoyable range of Taste of Scotland specialities, with more informal meals available in the new Bistro or the Kitchen Bar.

ROOMS: 20 en suite (bth/shr) (3 fmly) s £66; d £108-£156 (incl. bkfst) LB Off peak **MEALS:** Lunch £20.15-£32alc Dinner £24-£29.50 & alc Scottish & International Cuisine V meals Coffee am Tea pm **FACILITIES:** CTV in all bedrooms STV Pool table Putting green Pitch & putt Xmas **CONF:** Thtr 50 Class 30 Board 30 Del from £62.25 **SERVICES:** 40P **NOTES:** No coaches No smoking in restaurant Last d 9pm **CARDS:**

C

CONTIN Highland
Map 14 NH45

★★ Achilty

IV14 9EG
Quality Percentage Score: 69%
☎ 01997 421355 🖷 01997 421923
Dir: *on A835, at the northern edge of Contin*

Neil and Alison Vaughan set high standards at this renovated 18th-century former coaching inn just west of the village. There is a choice of two comfortable lounges one of which is no-smoking. An extensive carte is available in the restaurant, as well as in the lounge bar, where rough-cut stone walls and a beamed ceiling add character. Bedrooms, four of which have external access, have all been charmingly refurbished in a bright and modern style, with good facilities.

ROOMS: 12 en suite (bth/shr) (3 fmly) No smoking in 6 bedrooms s £26.50-£54.50; d £53-£73 (incl. bkfst) LB Off peak **MEALS:** Sunday Lunch £9.75 & alc High tea £7.95 Dinner £17 & alc Scottish & International Cuisine V meals Coffee am Tea pm **FACILITIES:** CTV in all bedrooms Xmas **CONF:** Thtr 50 Class 50 Board 30 Del £52 * **SERVICES:** 150P **NOTES:** No smoking in restaurant Last d 9.30pm
CARDS:

COUPAR ANGUS Perth & Kinross
Map 11 NO23

★★★ Moorfield House

Myreriggs Rd PH13 9HS
Quality Percentage Score: 71%
☎ 01828 627303 🖷 01828 627339
Dir: *from Perth follow the A94 to Coupar Angus then the A923 to Blairgowrie, in 2.5m hotel on the right*

Efficiently run by the Bjormark family, this delightful country hotel is set amid lovely landscaped gardens. All the comfortable bedrooms are decorated to a high standard and furnishings exude an air of quality. Public areas include an inviting library lounge and a spacious bar where the bar food operation enjoys a popular local following. The elegant restaurant offers a fine dining experience with a short daily fixed-price menu.

ROOMS: 12 en suite (bth/shr) No smoking in 5 bedrooms s £45-£60; d £86-£94 (incl. bkfst) * LB Off peak **MEALS:** Lunch £14.50 Dinner fr £25.50 V meals Coffee am Tea pm **FACILITIES:** CTV in all bedrooms **CONF:** Thtr 140 Class 80 Board 40 Del from £80 * **SERVICES:** 100P **NOTES:** Last d 10.00pm Closed 23 Dec-7 Jan **CARDS:**

See advert under BLAIRGOWRIE

CRAIGELLACHIE Moray
Map 15 NJ24

★★★ Craigellachie

AB38 9SR
Quality Percentage Score: 75%
☎ 01340 881204 🖷 01340 881253
Dir: *on the A95 in Craigellachie, 300yds from the A95/A941 crossing*

The atmosphere throughout this hotel, ever popular with the fishing fraternity, is warmly welcoming. Public areas include a choice of lounges and three dining areas. The majority of bedrooms have been tastefully upgraded and there is a wide range of bedroom sizes, rising up to very well proportioned Master rooms.

ROOMS: 26 en suite (bth/shr) (1 fmly) s £94.50-£124.50; d £114.50-£144.50 (incl. bkfst) * LB Off peak **MEALS:** Lunch fr £13.95 Dinner fr £27.50 European Cuisine V meals Coffee am Tea pm **FACILITIES:** CTV in all bedrooms Gym Pool table Xmas **CONF:** Thtr 60 Class 36 Board 24 Del from £135 * **SERVICES:** 50P **NOTES:** No smoking in restaurant Last d 9.30pm **CARDS:**

See advert on opposite page

CRAIL Fife
Map 12 NO60

★★ *Balcomie Links*

Balcomie Rd KY10 3TN
Quality Percentage Score: 68%
☎ 01333 450237 🖷 01333 450540
Dir: *take A917, on approaching Crail follow road for golf course, hotel last large building on left*

Under the welcoming ownership of the McGachy family, this hotel on the eastern edge of the village is particularly popular with golfers. Comfortable bedrooms come in a range of styles and sizes; public areas include a choice of bars and an attractive restaurant.

ROOMS: 11 en suite (bth/shr) (1 fmly) **MEALS:** V meals Coffee am Tea pm **FACILITIES:** CTV in all bedrooms Snooker Games room **SERVICES:** 40P **NOTES:** Last d 8.45pm **CARDS:**

CRAIL Fife
Map 12 NO60

★ *Croma*

Nethergate KY10 3TU
Quality Percentage Score: 65%
☎ 01333 450239
Dir: *take A917 to Crail*

Situated in a quiet residential area within a few minutes walk of the seafront the Croma Hotel, which is especially popular with families and golfers, offers a welcoming atmosphere together with a very personal level of attention from the resident owners. Bedrooms, some of which are well proportioned, offer comfortable modern appointments and two new family rooms have been created. Public areas include a cosy bar and traditional dining room.

ROOMS: 8 rms (4 bth 2 shr) (6 fmly) **MEALS:** V meals Coffee am **FACILITIES:** CTV in 6 bedrooms **SERVICES:** 6P **NOTES:** No coaches No smoking in restaurant Closed Dec-Mar

CRIEFF Perth & Kinross
Map 11 NN82

★★★ *Crieff Hydro*

Ferntower Rd PH7 3LQ
Quality Percentage Score: 72%
☎ 01764 655555 🖷 01764 653087
Dir: *from Perth first right up Connaught Terrace, first right again*

The hallmark of this multi-faceted hotel on the northern edge of town, is the successful way in which it combines traditional

contd.

values and standards with every modern comfort and amenity. The range and extent of the leisure and sporting amenities on offer are beyond compare, which enables the hotel to cater for the family visitor just as comfortably as it can for large conference groups. A welcome development has been the recent opening of the Brasserie, which provides an informal alternative to the large dining room. Bedrooms range from opulent suites and executive rooms, to the smaller standard rooms. Excellent facilities and services for children are available.

ROOMS: 203 en suite (bth/shr) 6 annexe en suite (bth/shr) (67 fmly) **MEALS:** International Cuisine V meals Coffee am Tea pm **FACILITIES:** CTV in all bedrooms Indoor swimming pool (heated) Golf 9 Tennis (hard) Fishing Squash Riding Snooker Sauna Solarium Gym Pool table Croquet lawn Putting green Jacuzzi/spa Bowling Off-road Football pitch Adventure playground Water ski-ing Cinema Wkly live entertainment ch fac **CONF:** Thtr 335 Class 125 Board 68 Del from £105 * **SERVICES:** Lift Night porter 205P **NOTES:** No dogs (ex guide dogs) Last d 8.30pm **CARDS:**

See advert on this page

CRIEFF Perth & Kinross **Map 11 NN82**

★★ ***Murraypark***

MINOTEL Great Britain

Connaught Ter PH7 3DJ

Quality Percentage Score: 70%

☎ 01764 653731 01764 655311

Dir: *off A85 to Perth, near Crieff Golf Club*

Murraypark Hotel stands in in a quiet residential area at the east end of the town. The well equipped bedrooms are variable in size and style, with the most spacious rooms being located in the new wing. Inviting public areas include a choice of relaxing lounges, a cosy well stocked bar, and an attractive restaurant.

ROOMS: 20 en suite (bth/shr) (1 fmly) **MEALS:** Scottish & French Cuisine V meals Coffee am **FACILITIES:** CTV in all bedrooms Shooting Stalking **CONF:** Thtr 25 Board 20 **SERVICES:** 50P **NOTES:** No smoking in restaurant Last d 9.30pm **CARDS:**

CRIEFF Perth & Kinross **Map 11 NN82**

★★ **Lockes Acre**

7 Comrie Rd PH7 4BP

Quality Percentage Score: 64%

☎ 01764 652526 01764 652526

Dir: *take A9/M9 for Perth, turn off at A822 Crieff, once in Crieff take A85 Comrie/Lochearnhead Rd, hotel on right hand side of A85 just outside Crieff*

A high level of personal attention is assured at this friendly hotel which is situated at the west end of town and enjoys views over the surrounding hills. Though variable in size, the bright airy bedrooms are comfortably modern in appointment. Public areas

contd.

include a relaxing conservatory lounge, and enjoyable home cooked fare is served in either the bar or dining room.
ROOMS: 7 rms (4 shr) (1 fmly) s £25-£29; d £48-£54 (incl. bkfst) * Off peak **MEALS:** Lunch £6.90-£15.30alc Dinner £14 & alc V meals Coffee am **FACILITIES:** CTV in all bedrooms **SERVICES:** 35P **NOTES:** No dogs (ex guide dogs) No coaches No smoking in restaurant **CARDS:**

CRIEFF Perth & Kinross — Map 11 NN82
★★ *Crieff*
49 East High St PH7 3HY
Quality Percentage Score: 60%
☎ 01764 652632 & 653854 📠 01764 655019
Dir: *M80 to Stirling then A9 to Dunblane, leave A9 at Braco and follow A82 to A822 into Crieff, go through town centre to East High St hotel on right*
This is a long established business and tourist hotel in the centre of town. Under new ownership, a programme of alterations and improvements is planned. Public areas include a restaurant and lounge bar. Bedrooms are variable in size and in style.
ROOMS: 10 rms (9 bth/shr) (1 fmly) **MEALS:** V meals Coffee am **FACILITIES:** CTV in all bedrooms Solarium Pool table Hair & beauty salon Beauty therapist **SERVICES:** 9P **NOTES:** No smoking area in restaurant Last d 9pm **CARDS:**

CRIEFF Perth & Kinross — Map 11 NN82
★★ The Drummond Arms
James Square PH7 3HX
Quality Percentage Score: 60%
☎ 01764 652151 📠 01764 655222
In 1745 Bonnie Prince Charlie and his generals held a Council of War at the Drummond Arms. Today, this family run town center hotel attracts tour groups. The variable sized bedrooms offer modern and traditional furnishings and a range of amenities. Public areas include a well stocked cocktail bar and attractive restaurant, both named The '45'.
ROOMS: 37 rms (18 bth 18 shr) 7 annexe en suite (bth/shr) (3 fmly) s fr £25; d fr £50 (incl. bkfst) * LB Off peak **MEALS:** Lunch £4.95-£9.95 High tea £7.50-£11.50 Dinner £7.95-£14 English, Scottish & French Cuisine V meals Coffee am **FACILITIES:** CTV in 36 bedrooms Pool table Wkly live entertainment ch fac Xmas **CONF:** Thtr 120 Class 60 Board 30 Del from £50 * **SERVICES:** Lift 30P **NOTES:** No smoking area in restaurant Last d 8.30pm **CARDS:**

CROCKETFORD Dumfries & Galloway — Map 11 NX87
★ *Lochview Motel*
Crocketford Rd DG2 8RF
Quality Percentage Score: 59%
☎ 01556 690281 📠 01556 690277
Dir: *on the A75, 10 m W of Dumfries on route to Stranraer*
Set by the roadside right on the shores of Auchenreoch Loch, Lochview is well named and makes a convenient stop-off for food and accommodation. A modern chalet houses the bedrooms, four of which have their own veranda right over the loch. The main block offers two large dining areas, one with a bar, serving food all day.
ROOMS: 7 en suite (shr) **MEALS:** V meals Coffee am Tea pm **FACILITIES:** CTV in all bedrooms Fishing **SERVICES:** 80P **NOTES:** Closed 26 Dec & 5 Jan **CARDS:**

CRUDEN BAY Aberdeenshire — Map 15 NK03
★★ Red House
Aulton Rd AB42 0NJ
Quality Percentage Score: 65%
☎ 01779 812215 📠 01779 812320
Dir: *turn off A952 Aberdeen/Peterhead road at Little Chef onto the A975 towards Cruden Bay, hotel opposite golf course*
This personally run small hotel is situated opposite the golf course. The smartly decorated bedrooms are modern in style and offer a good range of amenities. Inviting public areas include a choice of bars, a foyer lounge and attractive dining room. Varied menus offer a wide range of reasonably priced dishes.
ROOMS: 6 rms (5 bth/shr) (1 fmly) s £25-£49.50; d £50-£99 (incl. bkfst) * LB Off peak **MEALS:** V meals Coffee am Tea pm **FACILITIES:** CTV in all bedrooms STV Pool table ch fac **CONF:** Board 180 **SERVICES:** 40P **CARDS:**

CUMBERNAULD North Lanarkshire — Map 11 NS77
★★★★ Westerwood Hotel Golf & Country Club
1 St Andrews Dr, Westerwood G68 0EW
Quality Percentage Score: 61%
☎ 01236 457171 📠 01236 738478
Dir: *A80 exit after passing Oki factory signposted Wardpark/Castlecary second left at Old Inns rdbt then right at mini rdbt*
The 18-hole golf course, designed by Seve Ballesteros, together with the range of leisure, conference and function facilities, are major attractions at this modern purpose built business hotel. There is a wide choice of accommodation, ranging up to well proportioned suites and executive rooms. All have attractive pastel colour schemes and are smartly furnished. The Tipsy Laird restaurant on the first floor provides a modern style of cooking with good results achieved from commendable use of the best local fresh ingredients.
ROOMS: 49 en suite (bth/shr) (20 fmly) No smoking in 19 bedrooms s £90-£94; d £104-£108 (incl. bkfst) * LB Off peak **MEALS:** Lunch £9.50-£9.95 & alc Dinner £17 & alc International Cuisine V meals Coffee am Tea pm **FACILITIES:** CTV in all bedrooms STV Indoor swimming pool (heated) Golf 18 Tennis (hard) Snooker Solarium Gym Pool table Putting green Jacuzzi/spa Steam room Bowling green Driving range Xmas **CONF:** Thtr 300 Class 160 Board 40 Del from £99 * **SERVICES:** Lift Night porter Air conditioning 204P **NOTES:** No dogs (ex guide dogs) No smoking in restaurant Last d 9.45pm **CARDS:**

CUMBERNAULD North Lanarkshire — Map 11 NS77
Travel Inn
4 South Muirhead Rd G67 1AX
☎ 01236 725339 📠 01236 736380
Dir: *from A80 take A8011 following signs to Cumbernauld & then town centre, Travel Inn opposite supermarket*
This modern building offers accommodation in smart, spacious and well equipped bedrooms, all with en-suite bathrooms. Refreshments may be taken at the nearby family restaurant. For details about current prices consult the Contents Page under Hotel Groups for the Travel Inn phone number.
ROOMS: 37 en suite (bth/shr) d £39.95 *

CUPAR Fife — Map 11 NO31
★★ Eden House
2 Pitscottie Rd KY15 4HF
Quality Percentage Score: 67%
☎ 01334 652510 📠 01334 652277
Dir: *overlooking Haugh Park, Cupar on A91, 8m W of St.Andrews*
The Vizan family look forward to welcoming you to their comfortable small hotel on the edge of town. Bedrooms vary in size and are attractively decorated, with individual furnishings. Public areas include a cosy bar, small TV lounge, and an attractive conservatory which continues to earn much local praise for the freshness and honesty of its carefully prepared cuisine.
ROOMS: 9 en suite (bth/shr) 2 annexe en suite (bth/shr) (3 fmly) s £50-£55; d £82-£88 (incl. bkfst) * LB Off peak **MEALS:** Lunch £19-£23 & alc Dinner £19-£23 & alc French & Scottish Cuisine V meals Coffee am Tea pm **FACILITIES:** CTV in all bedrooms STV **CONF:** Thtr 40 Class 40 Board 40 **SERVICES:** 18P **NOTES:** No dogs (ex guide dogs) No coaches Last d 9pm **CARDS:**

contd.

DALKEITH Midlothian **Map 11 NT36**

★ ***Eskbank***
29 Dalhousie Rd EH22 3AT
Quality Percentage Score: 61%
☎ 0131 663 3234 📠 0131 660 4347
Dir: *on B6392*
Bright well equipped bedrooms are contained in a motel/chalet block to the rear of this hotel. Extensive alterations to transform its public areas into a food pub are underway.
ROOMS: 16 en suite (bth/shr) (3 fmly) **MEALS:** International Cuisine V meals Coffee am Tea pm **FACILITIES:** CTV in all bedrooms STV Golf parties catered for/Le Boulle rink Wkly live entertainment **CONF:** Class 20 Board 20 **SERVICES:** Night porter 46P **NOTES:** Last d 9.30pm
CARDS:

See advert under EDINBURGH

DERVAIG See Mull, Isle of

DINGWALL Highland **Map 14 NH55**

★★ **Kinkell House**
Easter Kinkell, Conon Bridge IV7 8HY
Quality Percentage Score: 76%
☎ 01349 861270 📠 01349 865902
Dir: *10m N of Inverness turn off A9 onto B9169 for 1m*
Owners Steve and Marsha Fraser have restored and extended this 19th-century farmhouse to create a comfortable small hotel with splendid views over the Cromarty Firth. Bedrooms in the original house are well proportioned and have period furnishings, and those in the new extension offer highly polished furnishings on traditional lines. There are three comfortable lounges, one of which is a conservatory. Marsha provides a tempting fixed-price menu featuring the best local produce available.
ROOMS: 9 en suite (bth/shr) (1 fmly) No smoking in all bedrooms s £45-£55; d £70-£90 (incl. bkfst) * LB Off peak **MEALS:** Lunch £13-£20alc Dinner £18-£27alc V meals Coffee am Tea pm **FACILITIES:** CTV in all bedrooms Croquet lawn **SERVICES:** 20P **NOTES:** No coaches No smoking in restaurant Last d 8.30pm **CARDS:**

DIRLETON East Lothian **Map 12 NT58**

★★★ **The Open Arms**
EH39 5EG
Quality Percentage Score: 65%
☎ 01620 850241 📠 850570
Dir: *from A1 take signs for North Berwick, pass through Gullane, 2m on left*
The Open Arms has the ambience of a country house and looks across to Dirleton Castle. The public areas include a choice of relaxing lounges and a cosy bar. For informal meals there is a smart brasserie, with a separate restaurant for fine dining. Bedrooms come in a variety of sizes.
ROOMS: 10 en suite (bth/shr) s £65-£90; d £100-£180 (incl. bkfst) * LB Off peak **MEALS:** V meals Coffee am Tea pm **FACILITIES:** CTV in all bedrooms Xmas **CONF:** Thtr 200 Class 150 Board 100 **SERVICES:** 30P **NOTES:** No smoking in restaurant Last d 9.15pm
CARDS:

DORNIE Highland **Map 14 NG82**

★★ ***Dornie***
Francis St IV40 8DT
Quality Percentage Score: 64%
☎ 01599 555205 📠 01599 555429
Dir: *follow A87 turn into village of Dornie, hotel on right*
Enthusiastic owners Ian and Olive Robin extend a warm welcome at their small comfortable hotel beside the shore of Loch Duich. Bedrooms have comfortable modern appointments. Public areas include a cosy lounge, a choice of bars, and an attractive restaurant. Ian's pride in the quality of his food has earned him a reputation for the meals served in both restaurant and bar.
ROOMS: 12 rms (1 bth 5 shr) (2 fmly) **MEALS:** Scottish & French Cuisine V meals Coffee am Tea pm **FACILITIES:** CTV in all bedrooms Pool table Wkly live entertainment ch fac **SERVICES:** 20P **NOTES:** No coaches Closed 25 Dec RS Jan (ex New Year) (bar suppers only)
CARDS:

DORNOCH Highland **Map 14 NH78**

★★★ **Royal Golf Hotel**
The First Tee, Grange Rd IV25 3LG
Quality Percentage Score: 64%
☎ 01862 810283 📠 01862 810923
Dir: *from A9, turn right to Dornoth and continue through main street. Straight ahead at cross roads then hotel is 200yds on the right*
Situated beside the Royal Dornoch Golf Club and overlooking the first tee and the Dornoch Firth, this well established hotel attracts golfers from all around the world. Non-golfers and business visitors are well catered for too. There are two fine bedroom suites on the top floor and the sun lounge is a popular venue for watching the course.
ROOMS: 25 en suite (bth/shr) 8 annexe rms (2 fmly) s £50-£75; d £87-£122 (incl. bkfst) * LB Off peak **MEALS:** Bar Lunch £10-£12alc High tea £5-£7alc Dinner £20-£24alc European Cuisine V meals Coffee am Tea pm **FACILITIES:** CTV in 25 bedrooms Tennis (hard) Fishing Xmas **CONF:** Thtr 120 Class 50 Board 50 Del from £85 * **SERVICES:** Night porter 20P **NOTES:** No smoking in restaurant Last d 9pm Closed Jan-Feb RS Nov, Dec & Mar **CARDS:**

DORNOCH Highland **Map 14 NH78**

★★ ***Dornoch Castle***
Castle St IV25 3SD
Quality Percentage Score: 70%
☎ 01862 810216 📠 01862 810981
Dir: *2m North of Dornoch Firth Bridge on A9, turn right onto A949*
Once the Palace of the Bishops of Caithness, dating back to the 16th century, this family run hotel is popular with tourists and golfers. The lounge overlooks the gardens, and the cocktail bar retains much of the character of the house. Main house bedrooms tend to be more spacious and traditional than those in the wing. The Green Room offers an more informal alternative to the dining room.
ROOMS: 4 en suite (bth/shr) 13 annexe en suite (bth/shr) (4 fmly) **MEALS:** Scottish & Continental Cuisine V meals Coffee am Tea pm **FACILITIES:** CTV in all bedrooms **SERVICES:** Lift 16P **NOTES:** No coaches No smoking area in restaurant Last d 9pm Closed Nov-Mar
CARDS:

DORNOCH Highland **Map 14 NH78**

★★ **Burghfield House**
IV25 3HN
Quality Percentage Score: 65%
☎ 01862 810212 📠 01862 810404
Dir: *turn off A9 at Evelix junct. travel 1m into Dornoch, just before War Memorial turn left and follow road up hill to tower in the trees*
This extended Victorian mansion stands in well kept gardens and is under new ownership for the first time in over 50 years. Bedrooms are located either in the main house or in the Garden Wing annexe, with various styles of decor. Public areas, including a large comfortable lounge, are enhanced with antiques, fresh flowers and real fires, while the bright dining room features an interesting table d'hôte menu
ROOMS: 13 en suite (bth/shr) 15 annexe en suite (bth/shr) **MEALS:** V meals Coffee am Tea pm **FACILITIES:** CTV in all bedrooms Sauna Putting green **CONF:** Thtr 100 Board 80 Del from £40 * **SERVICES:** Night porter 62P **NOTES:** No smoking area in restaurant Last d 9pm **CARDS:**

D

DOUNE Stirling — Map 11 NN70

★★ Doune Arms
Stirling Rd FK16 6DJ
Quality Percentage Score: 67%
☎ 01786 841237 & 841210 Fax 01786 841464
Dir: *on A84 between Stirling & Calendar*
This well established hotel has been completely refurbished and provides pleasant bedrooms with stained pine furniture. Service is friendly, there is a comfortable lounge bar as well as a popular public bar, and the restaurant is a bistro-style operation.
ROOMS: 12 rms (11 bth/shr) (3 fmly) s £35-£40; d £70 (incl. bkfst) * LB Off peak **MEALS:** Lunch £5.95-£18alc High tea fr £8.50alc Dinner £8-£18alc V meals Coffee am Tea pm **FACILITIES:** CTV in all bedrooms Pool table **SERVICES:** 30P **NOTES:** No smoking in restaurant Last d 8.30pm **CARDS:**

DRUMNADROCHIT Highland — Map 14 NH53

★★★ Polmaily House
IV3 6XT
Quality Percentage Score: 67%
☎ 01456 450343 Fax 01456 450813
Dir: *in Drumnadrocht turn onto A831 signposted to Cannich, hotel is 2m on right. 1.5m from Loch Ness*
An unpretentious atmosphere is part of the appeal of this country house which is run by the owners. Standing in 18 acres of lawns and woods, a welcome environment is created for children with facilities such as a popular pets' corner; there are plenty of leisure facilities for all to enjoy. The informal conservatory bar is accessed through the inviting drawing room, while the quiet upstairs library can be a welcome retreat. The elegant dining room provides a pleasant setting for the four-course dinner.
ROOMS: 10 en suite (bth/shr) (6 fmly) s £50-£75; d £100-£150 (incl. bkfst & dinner) * LB Off peak **MEALS:** Bar Lunch £2.95-£10.95 & alc Dinner £16.90-£21.90 & alc European Cuisine V meals Coffee am Tea pm **FACILITIES:** CTV in all bedrooms Indoor swimming pool (heated) Tennis (hard) Fishing Riding Croquet lawn Indoor/outdoor childs play area Boating Pony rides Beauty/massage Pets corner ch fac Xmas **CONF:** Thtr 16 Class 8 Board 14 Del from £50 * **SERVICES:** 20P **NOTES:** No smoking in restaurant Last d 9pm Closed 14 Nov-27 Dec & 12 Jan-1 Feb
CARDS:

DRYMEN Stirling — Map 11 NS48

★★★ Buchanan Arms
G63 0BQ
Quality Percentage Score: 67%
☎ 01360 660588 Fax 01360 660943
SCOTTISH HIGHLAND HOTELS
Dir: *travelling N from Glasgow on the A81 take the turn off onto the A811, the hotel is situated at the S end of Main Street*
This former coaching inn has been extended and modernised to offer a wide range of leisure and conference facilities. Bedrooms are attractively decorated and well equipped. Public areas include a bar with wooden flooring and oak beams, a spacious lounge and conservatory, and a very popular restaurant.
ROOMS: 52 en suite (bth/shr) (3 fmly) No smoking in 6 bedrooms s £83; d £122 * LB Off peak **MEALS:** Lunch £8.50-£10.50 & alc Dinner £20.50 & alc Scottish & French Cuisine V meals Coffee am Tea pm **FACILITIES:** CTV in all bedrooms STV Indoor swimming pool (heated) Squash Sauna Solarium Gym Jacuzzi/spa Xmas **CONF:** Thtr 150 Class 60 Board 60 Del £108 * **SERVICES:** Night porter 100P **NOTES:** No smoking in restaurant Last d 9.30pm **CARDS:**

DRYMEN Stirling — Map 11 NS48

★★★ Winnock
The Square G63 0BL
Quality Percentage Score: 64%
☎ 01360 660245 Fax 660267
Best Western
Dir: *from S follow M74 onto M8 through Glasgow. Exit junct 16B, follow A809 to Aberfoyle*
Prominently situated by the village green, this welcoming 17th-century inn has been extensively modernised. The popular bar with stucco walls and beamed ceiling is a popular rendezvous, whilst the restaurant offers Scottish fare. The bedrooms, which vary in size, are part of on ongoing refurbishment programme.
ROOMS: 48 en suite (bth/shr) (12 fmly) No smoking in 17 bedrooms s £49-£59; d £69-£80 (incl. bkfst) * LB Off peak **MEALS:** Lunch £7.50-£9.75 High tea £6.50 Dinner £17 & alc V meals Coffee am Tea pm **FACILITIES:** CTV in all bedrooms Petanque Wkly live entertainment ch fac Xmas **CONF:** Thtr 140 Class 60 Board 70 Del from £49 * **SERVICES:** 60P **NOTES:** No dogs (ex guide dogs) No smoking in restaurant Last d 9.30pm **CARDS:**

DULNAIN BRIDGE Highland — Map 14 NH92

★★★ Muckrach Lodge
PH26 3LY
Quality Percentage Score: 68%
☎ 01479 851257 Fax 01479 851325
Scotland's Hotels of Distinction
Dir: *from A95 Dulain Bridge exit follow A938 towards Carrbridge. Hotel 500mtrs on right*

James and Dawn MacFarlane have transformed this long-established former Victorian shooting lodge into a welcoming and friendly hotel. The conservatory restaurant is an attractive setting for the short 4-course dinner menu. Bedrooms are smart and well appointed, some being contained in the stable block, and include two suites.
ROOMS: 9 en suite (bth/shr) 4 annexe en suite (bth/shr) (2 fmly) s £49.50-£79; d £99-£119 (incl. bkfst) * LB Off peak **MEALS:** Lunch £12.95 High tea £8.45-£19.45 Dinner fr £26.50 Scottish & French Cuisine V meals Coffee am Tea pm **FACILITIES:** CTV in all bedrooms Beauty & aroma therapy ch fac Xmas **CONF:** Thtr 80 Class 20 Board 24 Del from £100 * **SERVICES:** 53P **NOTES:** No dogs (ex guide dogs) No coaches No smoking in restaurant Last d 9pm **CARDS:**

DUMBARTON West Dunbartonshire — Map 10 NS37

★★ Dumbuck House
Glasgow Rd G82 1EG
Quality Percentage Score: 66%
☎ 01389 734336 Fax 01389 742270
Dir: *from S follow M8 for Glasgow and exit junct 30, follow A82 for 4m, at traffic lights follow A814 and hotel is 0.5m on right*
As well as catering for visiting business people, this family-owned hotel is a popular venue for local functions. Bedrooms are modern in style and offer all the expected amenities, though rooms in the newer wing are perhaps more practical than those

contd.

in the original house. Recently refurbished public areas include a comfortable foyer lounge, a spacious bar and an attractive restaurant serving a wide range of dishes.
ROOMS: 22 en suite (bth/shr) (2 fmly) s £50; d £74 (incl. bkfst) * LB Off peak **MEALS:** Lunch £10.95 Dinner £16.95 International Cuisine V meals Coffee am Tea pm **FACILITIES:** CTV in all bedrooms STV Pool table **CONF:** Thtr 200 Class 140 Board 60 Del from £59 * **SERVICES:** Night porter 140P **NOTES:** Last d 9.30pm
CARDS:

DUMBARTON West Dunbartonshire Map 10 NS37

Travelodge

Milton G82 2TY
☎ 01389 765202 📠 01389 765202
Dir: *1m E, on A82 westbound*
This modern building offers accommodation in smart, spacious and well equipped bedrooms, all with en-suite bathrooms. Refreshments may be taken at the nearby family restaurant. For details about current prices, consult the Contents Page under Hotel Groups for the Travelodge phone number.
ROOMS: 32 en suite (bth/shr) d £45.95 *

DUMFRIES Dumfries & Galloway Map 11 NX97

see also **Carrutherstown**

★★★ Cairndale Hotel & Leisure Club

English St DG1 2DF
Quality Percentage Score: 68%
☎ 01387 254111 📠 01387 250555
Dir: *from S turn off M6 onto A75 to Dumfries, left at first rdbt, cross railway bridge, continue to traffic lights, hotel is 1st building on left*
Within walking distance of the town centre, this hotel provides a wide range of amenities and extensive leisure facilities. The modern bedrooms range from spacious studio rooms to cosy singles. Restaurants and a coffee shop offer everything from a full dinner to a quick snack.
ROOMS: 76 en suite (bth/shr) (19 fmly) No smoking in 16 bedrooms s fr £85; d fr £105 (incl. bkfst) * LB Off peak **MEALS:** Lunch £10 Dinner £15-£17.50 British, French & Italian Cuisine V meals Coffee am Tea pm **FACILITIES:** CTV in all bedrooms STV Indoor swimming pool (heated) Sauna Solarium Gym Jacuzzi/spa Steam room Toning tables Wkly live entertainment Xmas **CONF:** Thtr 120 Class 60 Board 30 Del from £65 * **SERVICES:** Lift Night porter 70P **NOTES:** No smoking area in restaurant Last d 9.30pm **CARDS:**

See advert on this page

DUMFRIES Dumfries & Galloway Map 11 NX97

★★★ Station

49 Lovers Walk DG1 1LT
Quality Percentage Score: 67%
☎ 01387 254316 📠 01387 250388
Dir: *from A75 follow signs to Dumfries town centre, hotel is opposite the railway station*
Sympathetically modernised to blend with its fine Victorian characteristics, this hotel has well equipped bedrooms and a choice of eating options; the Courtyard Bistro has an informal atmosphere and extensive menu, whilst the Pullman dining

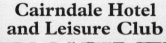

contd.

Remember to return your Prize Draw card for a chance to win one of 30 relaxing leisure breaks with Corus and Regal hotels. See inside the front cover for the card and competition details.

room offers a short but carefully chosen dinner menu which changes weekly.

Station Hotel, Dumfries

ROOMS: 32 en suite (bth/shr) (2 fmly) s £60-£75; d £85-£110 (incl. bkfst) * LB Off peak **MEALS:** Bar Lunch £5.95-£6.95 & alc Dinner £9.95-£16.50 & alc British & International Cuisine V meals Coffee am Tea pm **FACILITIES:** CTV in all bedrooms STV Jacuzzi/spa Xmas **CONF:** Thtr 60 Class 20 Board 30 **SERVICES:** Lift Night porter 40P **NOTES:** No smoking area in restaurant Last d 10pm
CARDS:

See advert on opposite page

DUMFRIES Dumfries & Galloway — Map 11 NX97

Travel Inn
Annan Rd, Collin DG1 3JX
☎ 01387 249785 01387 249287
Dir: *on the main central rdbt junct of the Euroroute bypass (A75)*
This modern building offers accommodation in smart, spacious and well equipped bedrooms, all with en-suite bathrooms. Refreshments may be taken at the nearby family restaurant. For details about current prices consult the Contents Page under Hotel Groups for the Travel Inn phone number.
ROOMS: 40 en suite (bth/shr) d £39.95 *

DUMFRIES Dumfries & Galloway — Map 11 NX97

Travelodge
Annan Rd, Collin DG1 3SE
☎ 01387 750658 01387 750658
Dir: *on A75*
This modern building offers accommodation in smart, spacious and well equipped bedrooms, all with en-suite bathrooms. Refreshments may be taken at the nearby family restaurant. For details about current prices, consult the Contents Page under Hotel Groups for the Travelodge phone number.
ROOMS: 40 en suite (bth/shr) d £45.95 *

DUNBAR East Lothian — Map 12 NT67

★★ Bayswell
Bayswell Park EH42 1AE
Quality Percentage Score: 65%
☎ 01368 862225 01368 862225
Dir: *off A1 into Dunbar High st, turn left and follow road, take first left into Bayswell Park*
There is a friendly and informal atmosphere at this family-run hotel, which enjoys panoramic views over the Firth of Forth from its striking clifftop position. Bedrooms offer mixed modern appointments. As well as the cosy ground floor bar, there is a residents' bar adjacent to the restaurant.
ROOMS: 13 en suite (bth/shr) (4 fmly) s £39.50-£49.50; d £69-£79 (incl. bkfst) * LB Off peak **MEALS:** V meals Coffee am Tea pm **FACILITIES:** CTV in all bedrooms STV Petanque Wkly live entertainment Xmas **SERVICES:** 20P **NOTES:** Last d 9pm
CARDS:

DUNBLANE Stirling — Map 11 NN70

The Premier Collection

★★★ Cromlix House
Kinbuck FK15 9JT
☎ 01786 822125 01786 825450
Dir: *off the A9 N of Dunblane. Exit B8033 to Kinbuck Village cross narrow bridge drive 200yds on left*
A charming Edwardian mansion house in a 3000 acre estate. Day rooms have log fires and pretty floral displays, deep cushioned sofas and easy chairs. Breakfast, and occasionally lunch, is served in the conservatory overlooking the gardens. Evening dining is offered in two elegant dining rooms. Bedrooms are individual in style, and most have private sitting rooms.
ROOMS: 14 en suite (bth/shr) s £135-£215; d £195-£295 (incl. bkfst) * LB Off peak **MEALS:** Lunch £19-£26 Dinner fr £39 V meals Coffee am Tea pm **FACILITIES:** CTV in all bedrooms Tennis (hard) Fishing Croquet lawn Clay pigeon shooting Falconry Xmas **CONF:** Thtr 40 Class 30 Board 22 **SERVICES:** 51P **NOTES:** No coaches No smoking in restaurant Last d 8.30pm Closed 2-29 Jan RS Oct-Apr **CARDS:**

DUNDEE Dundee City — Map 11 NO43

see also **Auchterhouse**

★★★ Swallow
Kingsway West, Invergowrie DD2 5JT
Quality Percentage Score: 70%
☎ 01382 641122 01382 568340
Dir: *turn off from A90/A929 rdbt following sign for Denhead of Gray, hotel on left*
Situated in a peaceful spot off the Dundee bypass, this extended Victorian mansion is surrounded by gardens and close to the city's business parks. Accommodation is equipped to a good standard, and bedrooms range from standard size to attractive

contd.

'executive' rooms and spacious suites. There is a leisure centre and a smart, airy restaurant.

ROOMS: 107 en suite (bth/shr) (11 fmly) No smoking in 60 bedrooms s £105-£125; d £145-£160 (incl. bkfst) * LB Off peak **MEALS:** Lunch £10.95-£14.20 Dinner £17.35-£36.20alc Scottish & European Cuisine V meals Coffee am Tea pm **FACILITIES:** CTV in all bedrooms STV Indoor swimming pool (heated) Sauna Solarium Gym Putting green Jacuzzi/spa Trim trail Mountain bike hire Wkly live entertainment Xmas **CONF:** Thtr 80 Class 20 Board 50 Del from £95 * **SERVICES:** Night porter 140P **NOTES:** No smoking in restaurant Last d 9.30pm
CARDS:

DUNDEE Dundee City — **Map 11 NO43**
★★★ The Woodlands Hotel
13 Panmure Ter, Broughty Ferry DD5 2QL
Quality Percentage Score: 68%
☎ 01382 480033 🖷 01382 480126
Dir: *from Perth A85 to Dundee, from Dundee A930 to Broughty Ferry; from Tay Bridge A930 East to Broughty Ferry*
Set in its own mature wooded grounds, this popular business and tourist hotel offers a good range of leisure and function facilities. The attractively presented public areas include a well stocked bar, a choice of elegant lounges, and a smart restaurant offering both carte and fixed price menus as well as flambe specialities.
ROOMS: 38 en suite (bth/shr) (1 fmly) s £68-£80; d £90-£120 (incl. bkfst) * Off peak **MEALS:** Sunday Lunch £9.95-£12.75 High tea £6-£13.95alc Dinner fr £14 & alc International Cuisine V meals Coffee am Tea pm **FACILITIES:** CTV in all bedrooms STV Indoor swimming pool (heated) Sauna Solarium Gym Jacuzzi/spa Steam room **CONF:** Thtr 200 Class 60 Board 40 Del from £67 * **SERVICES:** Night porter 70P **NOTES:** No smoking in restaurant Last d 9pm Closed 26 Dec & 1-2 Jan
CARDS:

DUNDEE Dundee City — **Map 11 NO43**
★★★ Invercarse
371 Perth Rd DD2 1PG
Quality Percentage Score: 65%
☎ 01382 669231 🖷 01382 644112
Dir: *from the A90 Perth to Aberdeen Road take the A85 (Taybridge) then follow signs*
This popular business hotel, an extended period house, offers convenient access to central amenities. Public areas, where much of the original character has been sympathetically retained, include a choice of bars and a restaurant. Bedrooms, though variable in size, are comfortably modern.
ROOMS: 42 en suite (bth/shr) No smoking in 29 bedrooms s £68; d £90 (incl. bkfst) * Off peak **MEALS:** Lunch £4-£14alc High tea £5-£14alc Dinner fr £17.95 Cosmopolitan Cuisine V meals Coffee am Tea pm **FACILITIES:** CTV in all bedrooms STV **CONF:** Thtr 300 Class 100 Board 50 Del from £69 * **SERVICES:** Night porter 119P **NOTES:** No smoking in restaurant Last d 9.30pm Closed 24-26 Dec & 31 Dec-2 Jan
CARDS:

DUNDEE Dundee City — **Map 11 NO43**
★★★ *Sandford Hotel*
Newport Hill, Wormit DD6 8RG
Quality Percentage Score: 62%
☎ 01382 541802 🖷 01382 542136
Dir: *Hotel located 4m S of the Tay Bridge at the junction with A914/B946*
Sandford Hotel is a listed country house built around 1900. Bedrooms are individually styled and many offer wonderful views. Pre-dinner drinks can be taken in the gracious surroundings of the Minstrel's Gallery. Dinner is served in the Garden Room, and incorporates fresh produce.
ROOMS: 16 en suite (bth/shr) (1 fmly) **MEALS:** Scottish & European Cuisine V meals Coffee am Tea pm **FACILITIES:** CTV in all bedrooms STV **CONF:** Thtr 45 Class 24 Board 28 **SERVICES:** 30P
NOTES: Last d 9.30pm **CARDS:**

DUNDEE Dundee City — **Map 11 NO43**
★★ The Shaftesbury
1 Hyndford St DD2 1HQ
Quality Percentage Score: 70%
☎ 01382 669216 🖷 01382 641598
Dir: *from Perth follow signs to Airport, take first left at circle then turn right, follow Perth Road and turn right*
The Smiths welcome guests to this comfortable hotel which is in the west end, convenient for the University. Bedrooms, though variable in size, are comfortably modern in style and offer a

contd.

good range of amenities. The public areas include a lounge, bar and restaurant.
ROOMS: 12 en suite (bth/shr) (2 fmly) s £46-£53; d £56-£86 (incl. bkfst) * LB Off peak **MEALS:** Lunch £7.50-£12alc Dinner £4-£18alc Scottish & French Cuisine V meals Coffee am **FACILITIES:** CTV in all bedrooms **NOTES:** No coaches No smoking in restaurant Last d 8.30pm **CARDS:**

See advert on opposite page

DUNDEE Dundee City **Map 11 NO43**
Travel Inn
Discovery Quay, Riverside Dr DD1 4XA
☎ 01382 203240 01382 203237
Dir: *follow signs for Discovery Quay, situated on waterfront*
This modern building offers accommodation in smart, spacious and well equipped bedrooms, all with en-suite bathrooms. Refreshments may be taken at the nearby family restaurant. For details about current prices consult the Contents Page under Hotel Groups for the Travel Inn phone number.
ROOMS: 40 en suite (bth/shr) d £39.95 *

DUNDEE Dundee City **Map 11 NO43**
Travel Inn (Dundee East)
Arbroath Rd, Monifieth
☎ 01382 530565 01382 530468
Dir: *on A92 Carnoustie/Arbroath road to the N of Monifieth and Broughty Ferry*
This modern building offers accommodation in smart, spacious and well equipped bedrooms, all with en-suite bathrooms. Refreshments may be taken at the nearby family restaurant. For details about current prices consult the Contents Page under Hotel Groups for the Travel Inn phone number.
ROOMS: 40 en suite (bth/shr) d £39.95 *

DUNDEE Dundee City **Map 11 NO43**
Travel Inn (Dundee West)
Kingsway West, Invergowrie DD2 5JU
☎ 01382 561115 01382 568431
Dir: *approaching Technology Park rdbt take A90 towards Aberdeen, Travel Inn on left after 25yds*
This modern building offers accommodation in smart, spacious and well equipped bedrooms, all with en-suite bathrooms. Refreshments may be taken at the nearby family restaurant. For details about current prices consult the Contents Page under Hotel Groups for the Travel Inn phone number.
ROOMS: 40 en suite (bth/shr) d £39.95 *

DUNDEE Dundee City **Map 11 NO43**
Travelodge
A90 Kingsway DD2 4TD
☎ 0800 850950
Dir: *on A90*
This modern building offers accommodation in smart, spacious and well equipped bedrooms, all with en-suite bathrooms. Refreshments may be taken at the nearby family restaurant. For details about current prices, consult the Contents Page under Hotel Groups for the Travelodge phone number.
ROOMS: 30 en suite (bth/shr) (incl. bkfst) d fr £39.95 *

DUNDONNELL Highland **Map 14 NH08**
★★★ **Dundonnell**
Little Loch Broom IV23 2QR
Quality Percentage Score: 74%
☎ 01854 633204 01854 633366
Dir: *turn off A835 at Braemore junct on to A832*
Situated by the roadside at the head of Little Loch Broom, this hospitable hotel has been extensively developed over 25 years by the Florence family as a haven of relaxation and good food. The bedrooms are well equipped and most enjoy fine views.

ROOMS: 28 en suite (bth/shr) (2 fmly) s £57.50-£70; d £105-£115 (incl. bkfst) * LB Off peak **MEALS:** Bar Lunch £8.50-£17.50alc Dinner £25-£27.50 V meals Coffee am Tea pm **FACILITIES:** CTV in all bedrooms Pool table Xmas **CONF:** Thtr 70 Class 50 Board 40 Del from £75 * **SERVICES:** 60P **NOTES:** No smoking in restaurant Last d 8.30pm Closed 22 Nov-Feb (ex Xmas/New Year) **CARDS:**

See advert under ULLAPOOL

DUNFERMLINE Fife **Map 11 NT08**
★★★ **Keavil House**
Crossford KY12 8QW
Quality Percentage Score: 72%
☎ 01383 736258 01383 621600
Dir: *2m W of Dunfermline on A994*

A warm welcome is assured at this smart business and leisure hotel. Relaxing public areas include a choice of bars, a range of leisure and banqueting facilities, and an attractive conservatory restaurant, serving award winning fare. Bedrooms are comfortably modern in appointment.
ROOMS: 47 en suite (bth/shr) (4 fmly) No smoking in 24 bedrooms s £50-£85; d £85-£115 * LB Off peak **MEALS:** Lunch fr £8.99 Dinner fr £19.95 & alc Scottish & French Cuisine V meals Coffee am **FACILITIES:** CTV in all bedrooms STV Indoor swimming pool (heated) Sauna Solarium Gym Jacuzzi/spa Aerobics studio Steam room ch fac Xmas **CONF:** Thtr 200 Class 60 Board 50 Del from £88 * **SERVICES:** Night porter 150P **NOTES:** No dogs (ex guide dogs) No smoking in restaurant Last d 8.45pm **CARDS:**

See advert on opposite page

DUNFERMLINE Fife **Map 11 NT08**

★★★ Garvock House Hotel

St John's Dr, Transy KY12 7TU

Quality Percentage Score: 71%

☎ 01383 621067 🖷 01383 621168

Dir: *from M90 junct 3 take A907 into Dunfermline . After football stadium turn left into Garvock Hill, then 1st right St John's Drive, hotel on right*

A restored, extended Georgian building in grounds east of the town centre and near the football stadium. Spacious non-smoking bedrooms have many thoughtful touches. The elegant dining room has a 3 course dinner menu offering a short selection of interesting dishes. A small bar services two pleasant ground floor lounges, there is a further lounge on the first floor.

ROOMS: 11 en suite (bth/shr) (1 fmly) No smoking in all bedrooms s fr £65; d fr £95 * LB Off peak **MEALS:** Lunch £12-£20alc High tea £8-£12.50alc Dinner £17-£27alc V meals Coffee am **FACILITIES:** CTV in all bedrooms Xmas **CONF:** Thtr 25 Class 25 Board 25 **SERVICES:** 38P **NOTES:** No coaches No smoking in restaurant Last d 9pm

CARDS:

DUNFERMLINE Fife **Map 11 NT08**

★★★ *Pitbauchlie House*

Aberdour Rd KY11 4PB

Quality Percentage Score: 66%

☎ 01383 722282 🖷 01383 620738

Dir: *1m S of town centre on B916*

A comfortable business and tourist hotel in wooded grounds. Public areas are bright and modern with contrasting bars, foyer lounge, and a restaurant which overlooks the garden. Bedrooms include smart deluxe, executive and practical standard rooms which vary in size.

ROOMS: 40 en suite (bth/shr) (2 fmly) **MEALS:** International Cuisine V meals Coffee am Tea pm **FACILITIES:** CTV in all bedrooms STV Gym **CONF:** Thtr 150 Class 80 Board 60 **SERVICES:** Night porter 70P **NOTES:** No smoking in restaurant Last d 9pm

CARDS:

DUNFERMLINE Fife **Map 11 NT08**

★★★ Elgin

Charlestown KY11 3EE

Quality Percentage Score: 63%

☎ 01383 872257 🖷 01383 873044

Dir: *3m W of M90, junct 1, on loop road off A985, signposted Limekilns & Charlestown*

This welcoming family run business and tourist hotel enjoys an outlook over the Firth of Forth to the Pentland Hills beyond. The smart new conference and function room has added another dimension to the business. Other public areas include a well

contd.

stocked bar and attractive restaurant. Bedrooms, which vary in size, are now benefiting from enhancement.
ROOMS: 12 en suite (bth/shr) (3 fmly) No smoking in 6 bedrooms s £49-£63.50; d £68-£100 (incl. bkfst) * LB Off peak **MEALS:** Lunch £6.45-£13.95alc High tea £6.95-£11.75alc Dinner £6.45-£13.95alc V meals Coffee am **FACILITIES:** CTV in all bedrooms STV Xmas **CONF:** Thtr 150 Class 80 **SERVICES:** 70P **NOTES:** No dogs (ex guide dogs) No smoking in restaurant Last d 9pm **CARDS:**

DUNFERMLINE Fife **Map 11 NT08**
★★★ King Malcolm
Queensferry Rd KY11 5DS
Quality Percentage Score: 61%
☎ 01383 722611 01383 730865
PEEL HOTELS
Dir: *on A823, S of town*
Situated on the south side of town, this modern purpose built hotel has particular appeal for the visiting businessman and is also a popular venue for local functions. Bedrooms tend to be compact, but best use has been made of available space and a good range of amenities is provided. Good value meals are offered in Richmonds Restaurant while the adjacent bar, with its conservatory extension, provides a comfortable corner to relax in comfort.
ROOMS: 48 en suite (bth/shr) (2 fmly) No smoking in 12 bedrooms s £80; d £110 * Off peak **MEALS:** Lunch £9.50-£12.50 Dinner £16.50-£18.50 Scottish & French Cuisine V meals Coffee am Tea pm **FACILITIES:** CTV in all bedrooms Xmas **CONF:** Thtr 150 Class 60 Board 50 Del from £90 * **SERVICES:** Night porter 60P **NOTES:** Last d 10pm **CARDS:**

DUNFERMLINE Fife **Map 11 NT08**
★★★ Pitfirrane Arms
Main St, Crossford KY12 8NJ
Quality Percentage Score: 58%
☎ 01383 736132 01383 621760
Dir: *from Kincardine-follow the A985 at large rdbt take the A994 to Dunfermline, Crossford is the second village from the rdbt, hotel on right*
Good value accommodation and meals are the hallmarks of this popular hotel which is located in the village of Crossford to the west of town. The bedrooms, which are compact and practical in appointment, are benefiting from a programme of enhancement. Public areas include a choice of contrasting bars, a smart restaurant and a range of conference and function rooms.
ROOMS: 40 en suite (bth/shr) (1 fmly) s £39-£58; d £70 (incl. bkfst) * LB Off peak **MEALS:** Dinner £16.50-£18.50 Scottish & International Cuisine V meals Coffee am Tea pm **FACILITIES:** CTV in all bedrooms STV Xmas **CONF:** Thtr 90 Class 60 Board 40 Del from £49.50 * **SERVICES:** Night porter 72P **NOTES:** No smoking in restaurant Last d 9pm **CARDS:**

DUNKELD Perth & Kinross **Map 11 NO04**

The Premier Collection

★★★ Kinnaird
Kinnaird Estate PH8 0LB
☎ 01796 482440 01796 482289
RELAIS & CHATEAUX.
Dir: *from Perth, A9 towards Inverness until Dunkeld but do not enter, continue N for 2m then B898 on left*
Part of a 9000 acre estate in the heart of the Perthshire countryside this Edwardian mansion provides a warm welcome. There are several inviting sitting rooms warmed by open fires. Innovative cooking is offered in one of the two dining rooms. Bedrooms are generously proportioned and luxurious in appointment.

ROOMS: 9 en suite (bth/shr) d £255-£350 (incl. bkfst) * LB Off peak **MEALS: FACILITIES:** CTV in all bedrooms STV Tennis (hard) Fishing Snooker Croquet lawn Shooting **CONF:** Thtr 25 Class 10 Board 15 Del from £185 * **SERVICES:** Lift 22P **NOTES:** No dogs No coaches No children 12yrs No smoking in restaurant RS Jan-Mar (closed Mon-Wed) **CARDS:**

DUNKELD Perth & Kinross **Map 11 NO04**
★★ *Atholl Arms*
Bridgehead PH8 0AQ
Quality Percentage Score: 64%
☎ 01350 727219 & 727759 01350 727219
Dir: *12m N of Perth, turn off A9 into Dunkeld, the hotel will be found on the right overlooking the bridge and the River Tay*
This former coaching inn is at the centre of the village by the bridge. Bedrooms are comfortably furnished in traditional style, a number have views over the River Tay. There are two bars, one frequented by locals. Dinner, featuring local produce where possible, is served in the dining room or homely lounge area.
ROOMS: 14 rms (11 bth/shr) (1 fmly) No smoking in all bedrooms **MEALS:** V meals Coffee am Tea pm **FACILITIES:** CTV in all bedrooms Pool table **CONF:** Thtr 40 Board 30 **SERVICES:** 21P **NOTES:** No coaches No children 8 No smoking area in restaurant Last d 8.45pm **CARDS:**

DUNOON Argyll & Bute **Map 10 NS17**
★★ Enmore
Marine Pde, Kirn PA23 8HH
Quality Percentage Score: 76%
☎ 01369 702230 01369 702148
SCOTLAND'S HOTELS OF DISTINCTION
Dir: *on coastal route between two ferries, 1m N of Dunoon*
Wonderful views over the Firth of Clyde can be enjoyed from this comfortable hotel which stands in its own well tended garden on the seafront between the two Ferry Terminals. Fresh flower displays enhance the inviting public areas, which include a spacious and relaxing lounge and an elegant dining room where David Wilson's varied menus offer a range of carefully prepared Taste of Scotland specialities. Bedrooms, with individual colour schemes, are furnished in various styles and range from a new suite and four-poster rooms, to the smaller standard rooms. A warm welcome is assured.
ROOMS: 10 en suite (bth/shr) (2 fmly) **MEALS:** Lunch £10-£15 High tea £5.95-£10.95 Dinner £23-£25 Scottish & French Cuisine V meals Coffee am Tea pm **FACILITIES:** CTV in all bedrooms Squash **CONF:** Thtr 14 Class 16 Board 12 Del from £65 * **SERVICES:** 20P **NOTES:** No coaches No smoking in restaurant Last d 9pm Closed 2-12 Jan RS Nov-Feb **CARDS:**

DUNOON Argyll & Bute **Map 10 NS17**

★★ Royal Marine

Hunters Quay PA23 8HJ
Quality Percentage Score: 68%
☎ 01369 705810 🖷 01369 702329
Dir: *on A815 opposite Western Ferries terminal*

This welcoming family-run hotel overlooks the Hunters Quay Ferry Terminal. Views over the Firth of Clyde are enjoyed from the front facing modern bedrooms, undergoing a programme of refurbishment. Additional rooms are in an adjacent lodge. The smart new Ghillies cafe/bar offers a varied and extensive range of dishes, the dining room has a more formal atmosphere. Views of the Clyde are enjoyed from the spacious first floor lounge.

ROOMS: 28 en suite (bth/shr) 10 annexe en suite (bth/shr) (3 fmly) s £36.50-£43; d £59-£66 (incl. bkfst) * LB Off peak **MEALS:** Bar Lunch £6.95-£9.95 & alc High tea £3.95-£7 Dinner £14.50-£16 International Cuisine V meals Coffee am Tea pm **FACILITIES:** CTV in all bedrooms Wkly live entertainment Xmas **CONF:** Thtr 80 Class 30 Board 30 Del from £50 * **SERVICES:** 30P **NOTES:** No dogs (ex guide dogs) No smoking in restaurant Last d 8.30pm **CARDS:**

DUNOON Argyll & Bute **Map 10 NS17**

★ Lyall Cliff

141 Alexandra Pde, East Bay PA23 8AW
Quality Percentage Score: 69%
☎ 01369 702041 🖷 01369 702041
Dir: *on A815 between Kirn and Dunoon on sea front, between the ferry terminals at Dunoon amd Hunters Quay*

Owners Philip and Lynda Norris offer a warm welcome to their comfortable seafront hotel. Bedrooms, many with views over the Firth of Clyde, are brightly decorated and modern in style. Public areas include a lounge and small library where refreshments are served on request. Enjoyable meals are served in the dining room.

ROOMS: 10 en suite (shr) (3 fmly) No smoking in 8 bedrooms s £26-£35; d £46-£60 (incl. bkfst) LB Off peak **MEALS:** Lunch £7-£10 Dinner £8-£10 V meals Coffee am **FACILITIES:** CTV in all bedrooms **CONF:** Board 22 Del from £37 * **SERVICES:** 9P **NOTES:** No coaches No smoking in restaurant Last d 6.30pm Closed Nov-Dec RS Jan-Mar **CARDS:**

DUNVEGAN See Skye, Isle of

EAST KILBRIDE South Lanarkshire **Map 11 NS65**

★★★★❀ Crutherland Country House Hotel

MACDONALD hotels

Strathaven Rd G75 0QZ
Quality Percentage Score: 70%
☎ 01355 577000 🖷 01355 220855
Dir: *off A725, in East Kilbride follow signs for Strathaven A726, approx 1.5m on A726 through Torrance rdbt and Crutherland House is on left in 150 yds*

This renovated mansion is set in 37 acres of landscaped grounds, two miles from the town centre. Behind the Georgian façade is a very spacious and comfortable hotel with extensive banqueting and leisure facilities. The bedrooms are all spacious and comfortable.

ROOMS: 76 en suite (bth/shr) (26 fmly) No smoking in 62 bedrooms s £75-£110; d £100-£160 * LB Off peak **MEALS:** Lunch £12-£25alc Dinner £20-£50alc European Cuisine V meals Coffee am Tea pm **FACILITIES:** CTV in all bedrooms STV Indoor swimming pool (heated) Sauna Solarium Gym Steam room Technogym Xmas **CONF:** Thtr 500 Class 100 Board 100 Del from £100 * **SERVICES:** Lift Night porter 150P **NOTES:** No dogs (ex guide dogs) No smoking in restaurant Last d 9.45pm **CARDS:**

EAST KILBRIDE South Lanarkshire **Map 11 NS65**

★★★ Stuart

2 Cornwall Way, Town Centre G74 1JR
Quality Percentage Score: 63%
☎ 013552 21161 🖷 013552 64410
Dir: *6m from junct 5 off M74, head for town centre as sign posted, hotel on rdbt*

This business, conference and function hotel is convenient for the central shopping area. The spacious lounge bar has recently been upgraded and is complemented by a split-level cocktail bar which is adjacent to Jellowickis, an informal and popular American Western themed diner offering a varied good value menu. Executive rooms provide the best accommodation.

ROOMS: 38 en suite (bth/shr) (1 fmly) No smoking in 4 bedrooms s £62-£72; d £80-£90 (incl. bkfst) * Off peak **MEALS:** Lunch £6-£7 & alc Dinner £14 & alc European & Mexican Cuisine V meals Coffee am Tea pm **FACILITIES:** CTV in all bedrooms STV Wkly live entertainment **CONF:** Thtr 200 Class 80 Board 60 Del from £91 * **SERVICES:** Lift Night porter **NOTES:** No dogs (ex guide dogs) No smoking area in restaurant Last d 10pm RS Christmas & New Year's Day **CARDS:**

E

EAST KILBRIDE South Lanarkshire **Map 11 NS65**
★★★ **Bruce Hotel**
Cornwall St G74 1AF
Quality Percentage Score: 62%
☎ 01355 229771 Fax 01355 242216
Dir: *leave M74 at junct 5 on to A725 and follow to East Kilbride, follow town centre signs and turn right into Cornwall St, hotel 200yds on left*
Situated in the centre of East Kilbride and forming part of the main shopping centre, this purpose-built hotel offers various sizes, styles and grades of rooms, all pleasantly appointed and well equipped. Public areas consist of a comfortable lounge bar and a formal restaurant where an interesting Scottish-themed table d'hôte menu forms an alternative to the full carte in the evenings. Some secure car parking is available underneath the hotel.
ROOMS: 65 en suite (bth/shr) No smoking in 23 bedrooms s £75-£90; d £95-£140 (incl. bkfst) * Off peak **MEALS:** Lunch £9.50 & alc Dinner £16.50 & alc V meals Coffee am **FACILITIES:** CTV in all bedrooms STV Xmas **CONF:** Thtr 400 Class 120 Board 300 Del from £85 * **SERVICES:** Lift Night porter 30P **NOTES:** No smoking area in restaurant Last d 9.30pm **CARDS:**

EAST KILBRIDE South Lanarkshire **Map 11 NS65**
Travel Inn
Brunel Way, The Murray G75 0JY
☎ 01355 222809 Fax 01355 230517
Dir: *take junct 5 off M74, follow signs for East Kilbride A725 then signs Paisley A726, turn left at Murray rdbt and left into Brunel Way*
This modern building offers accommodation in smart, spacious and well equipped bedrooms, all with en-suite bathrooms. Refreshments may be taken at the nearby family restaurant. For details about current prices consult the Contents Page under Hotel Groups for the Travel Inn phone number.
ROOMS: 40 en suite (bth/shr) d £39.95 *

EDINBURGH City of Edinburgh **Map 11 NT27**
★★★★★ **Balmoral**
1 Princes St EH2 2EQ
Quality Percentage Score: 67%
☎ 0131 556 2414 Fax 0131 557 8740
Dir: *the East end of Princes Street. Corner of North Bridge*
This classic Edwardian building dominates the east end of Princes Street, and is the flagship of Sir Rocco Forte. The bedrooms are regal and tastefully decorated while the public areas provide a welcome retreat for the hotel guests. The Palm Court is a popular meeting place, particularly for afternoon tea, while there is a real clubland feel to the Lobby Bar. The brasserie has been transformed into a stylish restaurant, but for absolute gourmet cuisine, head for No.1 The Restaurant.
ROOMS: 186 en suite (bth/shr) No smoking in 82 bedrooms s fr £160; d £185-£750 LB Off peak **MEALS:** Lunch £14.50-£18.50 & alc Dinner fr £35 & alc Scottish & International Cuisine V meals Coffee am Tea pm **FACILITIES:** CTV in all bedrooms STV Indoor swimming pool (heated) Sauna Solarium Gym Beauty salon Aromatheraphy massage Hairdressers Wkly live entertainment Xmas **CONF:** Thtr 380 Class 180 Board 40 Del from £220 * **SERVICES:** Lift Night porter Air conditioning 100P **NOTES:** No smoking area in restaurant Last d 10.30pm **CARDS:**

EDINBURGH City of Edinburgh **Map 11 NT27**
★★★★★ **Sheraton Grand**
1 Festival Square EH3 9SR
Quality Percentage Score: 66%
☎ 0131 229 9131 Fax 0131 228 4510
Dir: *follow signs for city centre (A8) Haymarket Station. Turn right at 2nd lights, keep left, left at lights - Morrison St, hotel on right*
This striking modern building forms part of an evolving development to be known as Exchange Square. Public rooms include a marble entrance hall with grand central staircase leading up to the popular Lobby Bar. The Terrace restaurant enjoys floodlit views of the Usher Hall and the historic castle beyond, The Grill Room is a discreet fine-dining restaurant suited to executive lunches. Bedrooms are mostly well proportioned; a smart refurbishment programme was progressing at a good pace at the time of our inspection, completion was expected by the time of Guide publication.
ROOMS: 261 en suite (bth/shr) (27 fmly) No smoking in 124 bedrooms s £165-£230; d £205-£270 * LB Off peak **MEALS:** Lunch £16.50-£19.50 Dinner £24.50-£35.50 & alc Scottish, French & Continental Cuisine V meals Coffee am Tea pm **FACILITIES:** CTV in all bedrooms STV Indoor swimming pool (heated) Sauna Solarium Gym Jacuzzi/spa Wkly live entertainment Xmas **CONF:** Thtr 485 Class 350 Board 120 Del from £185 * **SERVICES:** Lift Night porter Air conditioning 80P **NOTES:** No dogs (ex guide dogs) Last d 11pm
CARDS:

EDINBURGH City of Edinburgh **Map 11 NT27**
★★★★ **Marriott Dalmahoy**
Kirknewton EH27 8EB
Quality Percentage Score: 72%
☎ 0131 333 1845 Fax 0131 333 1433
Dir: *7m W of Edinburgh on the A71*

Set in extensive parkland with glorious views and conveniently located for the airport and city centre. A converted and extended Adam House attracting many returning guests, there are two golf courses, a tennis court and well equipped leisure centre with its own bar and restaurant. Bedrooms in the main house are comfortably traditional in style. Accommodation in the wing is bright, modern and well suited to the needs of business guests. Recently refurbished public areas include a choice of bars, informal and formal eating options. Serious eating takes place in the elegant Pentland Restaurant, which well deserves its two rosettes.
ROOMS: 43 en suite (bth/shr) 108 annexe en suite (bth/shr) (3 fmly) No smoking in 67 bedrooms d £69-£139 * LB Off peak
MEALS: Scottish & French Cuisine V meals Coffee am Tea pm
FACILITIES: CTV in all bedrooms STV Indoor swimming pool (heated) Golf 18 Tennis (hard) Sauna Solarium Gym Putting green Jacuzzi/spa Health & beauty treatments Steam room Dance Studio Driving range Xmas
CONF: Thtr 500 Class 200 Board 110 **SERVICES:** Lift Night porter 350P
NOTES: No dogs (ex guide dogs) No smoking in restaurant Last d 10pm
CARDS: *contd.*

EDINBURGH City of Edinburgh **Map 11 NT27**

★★★★ **George Inter-Continental**

19-21 George St EH2 2PB

Quality Percentage Score: 69%

☎ 0131 225 1251 ▤ 0131 226 5644

Dir: *city centre, East side parallel to Princes Street*

A short walk from Princes Street, this stylish hotel, as its name suggests, attracts an international clientele. Original architectural features include an impressive marble-floored foyer, a welcoming bar, and a choice of restaurants, of which Le Chambertin offers fine dining. Bedrooms come in a variety of sizes, but all are comfortable and well equipped.

ROOMS: 195 en suite (bth/shr) No smoking in 73 bedrooms **MEALS:** Lunch £18.50 & alc Dinner £18.50 & alc International Cuisine V meals Coffee am Tea pm **FACILITIES:** CTV in all bedrooms STV Complimentary Fitness club nearby **CONF:** Thtr 200 Class 80 Board 80 Del from £160 * **SERVICES:** Lift Night porter 24P **NOTES:** No dogs (ex guide dogs) No smoking area in restaurant Last d 10pm

CARDS:

EDINBURGH City of Edinburgh **Map 11 NT27**

★★★★ **Carlton Highland**

North Bridge EH1 1SD

Quality Percentage Score: 66%

☎ 0131 472 3000 ▤ 0131 556 2691

Dir: *on North Bridge which links Princes St to the Royal Mile, opposite 'The Scotsman' offices*

This hotel occupies a prime position in the heart of the city close to the Royal Mile and railway Station. Its facilities include two restaurants, a coffee shop and leisure centre. Public rooms are comfortably furnished and the bedrooms although traditional in style, have every modern facility. Quills Restaurant offers fine dining in an intimate setting, while the Eureka restaurant is less formal.

ROOMS: 197 en suite (bth/shr) (20 fmly) No smoking in 56 bedrooms s £100-£125; d £190-£250 * LB Off peak **MEALS:** Lunch £10-£20 Dinner £18.95-£26 Scottish & Continental Cuisine V meals Coffee am Tea pm **FACILITIES:** CTV in all bedrooms STV Indoor swimming pool (heated) Squash Sauna Solarium Gym Jacuzzi/spa Table tennis Dance studio Creche Night club Fri & Sat Wkly live entertainment Xmas **CONF:** Thtr 300 Class 160 Board 60 Del from £130 * **SERVICES:** Lift Night porter **NOTES:** No smoking area in restaurant Last d 10pm

CARDS:

EDINBURGH City of Edinburgh **Map 11 NT27**

★★★★ **Royal Terrace**

18 Royal Ter EH7 5AQ

Quality Percentage Score: 64%

☎ 0131 557 3222 ▤ 0131 557 5334

Dir: *from A1 - follow sign into city centre, turn left at the end of London Road into Bleinheim Place continuing onto Royal Terrace*

Close to Princess Street, and forming part of quiet Georgian terrace, this attractive hotel offers a variety of styles of bedroom, some lofty and spacious, with four-poster beds, and all looking out, either over the Forth, or over the gardens at the back of the hotel. Service is attentive.

ROOMS: 108 en suite (bth/shr) (19 fmly) s £95-£125; d £115-£160 * LB Off peak **MEALS:** Lunch £12.50-£16.95 Dinner £15-£17.85 Scottish & French Cuisine V meals Coffee am Tea pm **FACILITIES:** CTV in all bedrooms STV Indoor swimming pool (heated) Sauna Solarium Gym Jacuzzi/spa Beauty salon Giant Chess Xmas **CONF:** Thtr 100 Class 36 Board 40 Del from £145 * **SERVICES:** Lift Night porter **NOTES:** No dogs (ex guide dogs) No smoking area in restaurant Last d 9.15pm

CARDS:

EDINBURGH City of Edinburgh **Map 11 NT27**

★★★★ **Swallow Royal Scot**

111 Glasgow Rd EH12 8NF

Quality Percentage Score: 61%

☎ 0131 334 9191 ▤ 0131 316 4507

Dir: *on A8 on western outskirts of city*

From its position in the city's western fringes, close to the bypass and convenient to the airport and also the showground and business park, this purpose-built hotel attracts an international clientele. The bedrooms are contained in two wings, one offering executive rooms, the other housing the smaller standard rooms. Public areas radiate from the attractive marbled foyer and include an informal Club bar, spacious restaurant offering both carvery and carte meals, and a leisure centre. One of the strengths of the hotel is its conference facilities and its ability to accommodate large corporate groups.

ROOMS: 259 en suite (bth/shr) (17 fmly) No smoking in 160 bedrooms s £115; d £145 (incl. bkfst) * LB Off peak **MEALS:** Lunch fr £14.50 Dinner £22.50 & alc International Cuisine V meals Coffee am Tea pm **FACILITIES:** CTV in all bedrooms STV Indoor swimming pool (heated) Sauna Solarium Gym Jacuzzi/spa Steam room Xmas **CONF:** Thtr 300 Class 120 Board 45 Del from £115 * **SERVICES:** Lift Night porter 300P **NOTES:** No smoking in restaurant Last d 10pm

CARDS:

EDINBURGH City of Edinburgh **Map 11 NT27**

★★★ **Norton House**

Ingliston EH28 8LX

Quality Percentage Score: 78%

☎ 0131 333 1275 ▤ 0131 333 5305

Dir: *off A8, 5m W of city centre*

An extended Victorian mansion in 55 acres of parkland. Bedrooms are comfortably furnished, offering many useful extras, rooms in the original house are very spacious and attractive. The Gathering, in the grounds, is a popular meeting place for an informal meal. Fine dining is found in the Conservatory Restaurant, recognised by our two rosette award. Service is attentive and friendly. Guests can relax in welcoming lounges, meeting rooms are available.

ROOMS: 47 en suite (bth/shr) (2 fmly) No smoking in 27 bedrooms s £120-£160; d £140-£180 (incl. bkfst) * LB Off peak **MEALS:** Lunch fr £15.50 & alc Dinner fr £23.50 & alc International Cuisine V meals Coffee am Tea pm **FACILITIES:** CTV in all bedrooms STV Archery Laser clay pigeon shooting Xmas **CONF:** Thtr 300 Class 100 Board 60 Del from £135 * **SERVICES:** Night porter 200P **NOTES:** No smoking area in restaurant Last d 10pm **CARDS:**

EDINBURGH City of Edinburgh **Map 11 NT27**

★★★ **Channings**

South Learmonth Gardens EH4 1EZ

Quality Percentage Score: 75%

☎ 0131 315 2225 🖷 0131 332 9631

Dir: *approach Edinburgh on the A90 from Forth Road Bridge, follow signs for city centre*

This Edwardian town house hotel was originally five terraced houses, and the many different public rooms and bold colour schemes give a distinct feeling of clubland. Many of the comfortable bedrooms have been recently refurbished to a high standard, with smart, individual interior design. All the bedrooms are well equipped and attractively decorated. Downstairs, guests can enjoy dishes from a vibrant modern menu in the brasserie.

ROOMS: 48 en suite (bth/shr) (1 fmly) No smoking in 16 bedrooms s fr £110; d fr £135 (incl. bkfst) LB Off peak **MEALS:** Lunch £14 Dinner £23.50 & alc Contemporary Scottish & French Cuisine V meals Coffee am Tea pm **FACILITIES:** CTV in all bedrooms STV Xmas **CONF:** Thtr 35 Board 20 Del from £115 * **SERVICES:** Lift Night porter **NOTES:** No dogs (ex guide dogs) No smoking in restaurant Last d 9.30pm Closed 24-28 Dec **CARDS:**

EDINBURGH City of Edinburgh **Map 11 NT27**

★★★ **Prestonfield House**

Priestfield Rd EH16 5UT

Quality Percentage Score: 74%

☎ 0131 668 3346 🖷 668 3976

Dir: *A720 City Bypass exit Sherrifhall rdbt A7 into Edinburgh, right after 3m onto Priestfield Rd, 400 metres on left*

Built in 1687, Prestonfield House is set in thirteen acres of gardens and parkland, with a golf course on its doorstep and Arthur's Seat (a glacial hill) as a backdrop. Smartly appointed and thoughtfully equipped bedrooms are housed in an extension. The public rooms still hold much of their charm from the days when this was a private house as the Tapestry, Leather and Italian rooms all contain their original late 17th and 18th-century decorative schemes.

ROOMS: 31 rms (30 bth/shr) No smoking in 16 bedrooms d £125-£245 (incl. bkfst) * LB Off peak **MEALS:** Lunch £19 Dinner £26-£28 & alc Scottish & French Cuisine V meals Coffee am Tea pm **FACILITIES:** CTV in all bedrooms STV Golf 18 Xmas **CONF:** Thtr 800 Class 350 Board 30 Del from £155 * **SERVICES:** Lift Night porter 200P **NOTES:** No coaches No smoking area in restaurant Last d 9.30pm

CARDS:

EDINBURGH City of Edinburgh **Map 11 NT27**

★★★ **Bruntsfield**

69/74 Bruntsfield Place EH10 4HH

Quality Percentage Score: 73%

☎ 0131 229 1393 🖷 0131 229 5634

Dir: *on A702, S of city centre*

Colourful flowering baskets adorn the front of this long established hotel which overlooks the Bruntsfield Links. Available in a variety of sizes, the bedrooms have been tastefully furbished to provide comfortable modern accommodation. Public areas include lounges, a choice of contrasting bars, and meeting rooms. The Potting Shed restaurant offers an excellent choice of Bistro meals, which include several speciality dishes native to Scotland.

ROOMS: 75 en suite (bth/shr) (5 fmly) No smoking in 49 bedrooms s £69-£102; d £90-£140 * LB Off peak **MEALS:** Lunch £6.50-£11.50 & alc Dinner £18.50 & alc International Cuisine V meals Coffee am Tea pm **FACILITIES:** CTV in all bedrooms STV Xmas **CONF:** Thtr 75 Class 30 Board 30 Del from £103 * **SERVICES:** Lift Night porter 25P **NOTES:** No smoking in restaurant Last d 9.30pm

CARDS:

See advert on opposite page

EDINBURGH City of Edinburgh **Map 11 NT27**

★★★ **Posthouse Edinburgh**

Corstorphine Rd EH12 6UA

Quality Percentage Score: 73%

☎ 0131 334 0390 🖷 0131 334 9237

Dir: *adjacent to Edinburgh Zoo*

This modern hotel next to Edinburgh zoo, has undergone extensive refurbishment and provides smart accommodation of a high standard in well equipped 'millennium' bedrooms. The hotel has a new business meeting room complex 'The Academy', and in addition to the main restaurant and popular bar, there is the exciting 'Sampans' where a range of Oriental dishes can be sampled. A new leisure centre is planned.

ROOMS: 303 en suite (bth/shr) (35 fmly) No smoking in 176 bedrooms d fr £109 * LB Off peak **MEALS:** International Cuisine V meals Coffee am Tea pm **FACILITIES:** CTV in all bedrooms **CONF:** Thtr 110 Class 70 Board 50 Del from £110 * **SERVICES:** Lift Night porter 100P **NOTES:** No smoking in restaurant Last d 10pm

CARDS:

EDINBURGH City of Edinburgh **Map 11 NT27**

★★★ **Malmaison Hotel et Brasserie**

1 Tower Place EH6 7DB

Quality Percentage Score: 71%

☎ 0131 468 5000 🖷 0131 468 5002

Dir: *A900 from city centre towards Leith, at end of Leith Walk continue over lights through 2 more sets of lights, left into Tower St-hotel on right*

Renowned for their fashionable modern style, this Malmaison (now one of five in the group) brings this treatment to a fine period building, formerly a Seaman's Mission, right next to Leith port. Bedroom decor here is less minimal than was originally the Malmaison style, but have the same up-to-the-minute facilities. The café bar and brasserie are the "in places" to be, the latter offering a short and snappy Mediterranean menu.

ROOMS: 60 en suite (bth/shr) (6 fmly) d fr £99 * Off peak **MEALS:** Lunch £12.50-£15.95 & alc Dinner £14.50 & alc French Cuisine V meals Coffee am **FACILITIES:** CTV in all bedrooms STV Gym **CONF:** Thtr 50 Class 16 Board 26 Del £146 * **SERVICES:** Lift Night porter 50P **NOTES:** No coaches Last d 10.30pm Closed 1-2 Jan

CARDS:

EDINBURGH City of Edinburgh **Map 11 NT27**

★★★ ***Thistle Edinburgh***

107 Leith St EH1 3SW

Quality Percentage Score: 71%

☎ 0131 556 0111 🖷 0131 557 5333

Dir: *situated on the corner of Leith St and Prince's St*

This purpose-built hotel adjoins a large shopping mall at the east end of Princes Street in the heart of the city. A good range of services is backed by smart well equipped bedrooms. Public

contd.

areas include a restaurant and cocktail bar as well as an American-style diner.
ROOMS: 143 en suite (bth/shr) (4 fmly) No smoking in 48 bedrooms **MEALS:** International Cuisine V meals Coffee am Tea pm **FACILITIES:** CTV in all bedrooms Wkly live entertainment **CONF:** Thtr 250 Class 150 Board 40 **SERVICES:** Lift Night porter 20P **NOTES:** No dogs (ex guide dogs) Last d 9.45pm **CARDS:**

EDINBURGH City of Edinburgh **Map 11 NT27**
★★★ Braid Hills
134 Braid Rd EH10 6JD
Quality Percentage Score: 70%
☎ 0131 447 8888 Fax 0131 452 8477
Dir: *2.5m S A702, opposite Braid Burn Park*
From its elevated postion, this hotel enjoys panoramic views. Bedrooms are smart and well equipped, though varied in size; some rooms even have their own turret. The public areas are inviting, and good food is available in the restaurant or bistro.
ROOMS: 68 en suite (bth/shr) (6 fmly) No smoking in 8 bedrooms s fr £75; d fr £125 (incl. bkfst) * LB Off peak **MEALS:** Lunch £8-£9.50 Dinner £16.95-£18.95 Scottish & French Cuisine V meals Coffee am Tea pm **FACILITIES:** CTV in all bedrooms STV Xmas **CONF:** Thtr 100 Class 50 Board 30 Del from £90 * **SERVICES:** Night porter 38P **NOTES:** No dogs (ex guide dogs) No smoking in restaurant Last d 9.30pm
CARDS:

See advert on this page

EDINBURGH City of Edinburgh **Map 11 NT27**
★★★ Dalhousie Castle Hotel
Bonnyrigg EH19 3JB
Quality Percentage Score: 70%
☎ 01875 820153 Fax 01875 821936
Dir: *take A7 S from Edinburgh through Lasswade & Newtongrange, turn right at Shell Garage onto B704, hotel 0.5m from junction*
This imposing 13th-century castle sits by the River South Esk, with a delightful outlook across meadowland. Just twenty minutes drive from Edinburgh it offers a peaceful retreat and is also popular for weddings, having its own chapel. The vaulted dungeon restaurant is a plus point, and while there is no bar, drinks are served in the two lounges. Accommodation ranges from grand period rooms, including one baronial suite, to cottage-style rooms in a quiet house in the grounds.
ROOMS: 34 en suite (bth/shr) (5 fmly) No smoking in 2 bedrooms **MEALS:** Scottish & French Cuisine V meals Coffee am Tea pm **FACILITIES:** CTV in 29 bedrooms STV Fishing Clay pigeon shooting, Archery, Falconry ch fac **CONF:** Thtr 120 Class 60 Board 40 **SERVICES:** Night porter 110P **NOTES:** No smoking in restaurant Last d 8.45pm Closed 10-26 Jan **CARDS:**

EDINBURGH City of Edinburgh **Map 11 NT27**
★★★ Greens Hotel
24 Eglinton Crescent EH12 5BY
Quality Percentage Score: 66%
☎ 0131 337 1565 Fax 0131 346 2990
Four Georgian houses have been converted to create this comfortable hotel in the west end. Bedrooms are smartly furnished and well equipped, superior rooms are particularly spacious. Public rooms include a cosy panelled bar adjacent to the Club Room Bistro offering an appealing alternative to the main restaurant.
ROOMS: 57 en suite (bth/shr) (3 fmly) No smoking in 20 bedrooms s £50-£70; d £80-£120 (incl. bkfst) * LB Off peak **MEALS:** Lunch £6.50-£10.50 High tea £4.95-£7.95 Dinner fr £17.95 European Cuisine V meals Coffee am Tea pm **FACILITIES:** CTV in all bedrooms STV Xmas **CONF:** Thtr 50 Board 24 Del from £80 * **SERVICES:** Lift Night porter **NOTES:** No smoking area in restaurant Last d 9.15pm
CARDS:

EDINBURGH City of Edinburgh **Map 11 NT27**

★★★ *Edinburgh Capital Moat House*

187 Clermiston Rd EH12 6UG

Quality Percentage Score: 65%

☎ 0131 535 9988 Fax 0131 334 9712

Dir: *take A90 over the Forth Road Bridge, along Queensbury Rd, hotel at top on the right*

A modern hotel three miles from the airport and the city centre, close to Corstorphine Park. Bedrooms are bright and well equipped. Meals are available in rooms, or in Monty's Restaurant which enjoys views over the city. The hotel has a manned business centre and well-equipped meeting rooms. The smart leisure club is a further attraction.

ROOMS: 111 en suite (bth/shr) (10 fmly) No smoking in 20 bedrooms **MEALS:** Scottish & French Cuisine V meals Coffee am Tea pm **FACILITIES:** CTV in all bedrooms Indoor swimming pool (heated) Sauna Solarium Gym Pool table Jacuzzi/spa Leisure Club Steam room Wkly live entertainment **CONF:** Thtr 300 Class 170 Board 120 Del from £114 * **SERVICES:** Lift Night porter 150P **NOTES:** No smoking in restaurant Last d 9.30pm **CARDS:**

EDINBURGH City of Edinburgh **Map 11 NT27**

★★★ Apex European

90 Haymarket Ter EH12 5LQ

Quality Percentage Score: 64%

☎ 0131 474 3456 Fax 0131 474 3400

Within easy reach of Haymarket Station and the Conference Centre, this smart modern hotel is ideal for business guests. Bedrooms are bright, with a contemporary feel and a wide range of amenities. Public areas centre around the brasserie-style restaurant. There is also a small business centre.

ROOMS: 67 en suite (bth/shr) No smoking in 51 bedrooms d £90-£120 * Off peak **MEALS:** Lunch £6.99 Dinner £13.95 & alc European Cuisine V meals Coffee am Tea pm **FACILITIES:** CTV in all bedrooms STV **CONF:** Thtr 100 Class 60 Board 40 Del from £110 * **SERVICES:** Lift Night porter 17P **NOTES:** No dogs (ex guide dogs) No smoking area in restaurant **CARDS:**

EDINBURGH City of Edinburgh **Map 11 NT27**

★★★ Apex International

31/35 Grassmarket EH1 2HS

Quality Percentage Score: 64%

☎ 0131 300 3456 Fax 0131 220 5345

Dir: *turn into Lothian Rd at the West End of Princes Street, then turn 1st left along King Stables Rd. This leads onto the Grassmarket Square*

Situated in the city's Old Town, this modern hotel shares historic Grassmarket Square with several fashionable pubs and cafes. It has an impressive business and conference centre, designed to attract that growing market. Bedrooms are spacious and well equipped, whilst the restaurant enjoys a dramatic view, looking across to Edinburgh Castle, which is floodlit in the evening.

ROOMS: 175 en suite (bth/shr) (99 fmly) No smoking in 100 bedrooms d £90-£160 * LB Off peak **MEALS:** Lunch £6.99 Dinner £13.95 & alc European Cuisine V meals Coffee am Tea pm **FACILITIES:** CTV in all bedrooms STV Xmas **CONF:** Thtr 225 Class 120 Board 50 Del from £110 * **SERVICES:** Lift Night porter 60P **NOTES:** No dogs (ex guide dogs) Last d 10pm **CARDS:**

EDINBURGH City of Edinburgh **Map 11 NT27**

★★★ Grange Hotel

8 Whitehouse Ter EH9 2EU

Quality Percentage Score: 64%

☎ 0131 667 5681 Fax 0131 668 3300

Dir: *turn off A702 (Morningside Road) onto Newbattle Terrace which lead into Whitehouse Terrace*

This delightful little hotel has inviting public areas that include a small library lounge, a well stocked bar, and a conservatory restaurant offering modern cooking from a short seasonal menu. Bedrooms are all individual with their own unique sizes and styles, completing the country house feel.

ROOMS: 15 rms (13 bth/shr) (3 fmly) s £80-£90; d £120-£160 (incl. bkfst) * LB Off peak **MEALS:** Sunday Lunch £10-£15alc Dinner £15.50-£30alc Scottish & French Cuisine V meals Coffee am **FACILITIES:** CTV in all bedrooms Putting green **CONF:** Thtr 40 Class 16 Board 22 Del from £65 * **SERVICES:** Night porter 25P **NOTES:** No dogs No coaches No smoking in restaurant Last d 9.15pm

CARDS:

EDINBURGH City of Edinburgh **Map 11 NT27**

★★★ The Barnton

Queensferry Rd, Barnton EH4 6AS

Quality Percentage Score: 62%

☎ 0131 339 1144 Fax 0131 339 5521

Dir: *cross Forth Road Bridge towards Edinburgh, follow A90, 4m on left by rdbt*

This long-established business hotel is ideally positioned on the A90, four miles from the city centre, the Forth Road Bridge and the airport. It offers well equipped bedrooms - some larger than others - a choice of bars and a classical restaurant.

ROOMS: 50 en suite (bth/shr) (9 fmly) s £99; d £109 * LB Off peak **MEALS:** Lunch £8.50-£10.50 Dinner £15.50-£17.75 International Cuisine V meals Coffee am Tea pm **FACILITIES:** CTV in all bedrooms STV Sauna Xmas **CONF:** Thtr 150 Class 60 Board 50 Del from £95 * **SERVICES:** Lift Night porter 100P **NOTES:** Last d 9.45pm

CARDS:

EDINBURGH City of Edinburgh **Map 11 NT27**

★★★ Kings Manor

100 Milton Rd East EH15 2NP

Quality Percentage Score: 62%

☎ 0131 669 0444 Fax 0131 669 6650

Dir: *follow A720 E until Old Craighall Junction then left into city until turning right at the A1/A199 intersection, hotel 200mtrs on right*

A former Laird's home on the eastern side of Edinburgh, this friendly hotel is popular with business travellers, conferences and tour groups. There is a wide choice of bedroom styles on offer, while the public rooms comprise a cheerful foyer, a pleasing restaurant, and a choice of bars, one of which was formerly a chapel.

ROOMS: 69 en suite (bth/shr) (8 fmly) No smoking in 22 bedrooms s £67-£88; d £90-£125 (incl. cont bkfst) LB Off peak **MEALS:** Lunch £10-£25alc Dinner £12-£30alc Scottish & French Cuisine V meals Coffee am Tea pm **FACILITIES:** CTV in all bedrooms STV Indoor swimming pool (heated) Sauna Solarium Gym Xmas **CONF:** Thtr 140 Class 70 Board 70 Del from £85 * **SERVICES:** Lift Night porter 100P **NOTES:** Last d 9.30pm **CARDS:**

See advert on opposite page

EDINBURGH City of Edinburgh **Map 11 NT27**
★★★ **Old Waverley**
43 Princes St EH2 2BY
Quality Percentage Score: 61%
☎ 0131 556 4648 📠 0131 557 6316
SCOTTISH HIGHLAND HOTELS
Dir: *in the centre of city, opposite the Scott Monument*
Positioned on Princes Street right in the heart of the city, this long-established hotel (dating back to 1883) enjoys views of the Edinburgh skyline, including the Scott Monument and the Castle behind. Sharing these, are the front-facing bedrooms, as well as public rooms, all of which are at first floor level and include the restaurant, lounge and cosy bar.
ROOMS: 66 en suite (bth/shr) (6 fmly) No smoking in 8 bedrooms s £79-£99; d £129-£158 * LB Off peak **MEALS:** Bar Lunch £9-£19alc Dinner £18.50-£22.50 & alc International Cuisine V meals Coffee am Tea pm **FACILITIES:** CTV in all bedrooms STV Xmas **CONF:** Thtr 70 Class 30 Board 26 Del from £107.50 * **SERVICES:** Lift Night porter **NOTES:** No smoking in restaurant Last d 9.30pm
CARDS:

EDINBURGH City of Edinburgh **Map 11 NT27**
★★★ ***Quality Hotel***
Edinburgh Airport, Ingliston EH28 8NF
Quality Percentage Score: 58%
☎ 0131 333 4331 📠 0131 333 4124
Situated right next to the Royal Showground at Ingliston this hotel is also convenient for the airport. The spacious executive bedrooms are the pick of the accommodation, and there is a café restaurant offering a good choice of contemporary dishes.
ROOMS: 95 en suite (bth/shr) No smoking in 64 bedrooms **MEALS:** Scottish & French Cuisine V meals Coffee am Tea pm **FACILITIES:** CTV in all bedrooms STV **CONF:** Thtr 70 Class 24 Board 24 **SERVICES:** Lift Night porter 100P **NOTES:** No smoking in restaurant Last d 9.30pm **CARDS:**

EDINBURGH City of Edinburgh **Map 11 NT27**
★★★ ***Roxburghe***
38 Charlotte Square EH2 4HG
☎ 0131 225 3921 📠 0131 220 2518
MACDONALD hotels
Dir: *located in central Edinburgh, on corner of Charlotte st & George st*
The Roxburghe is a well-established hotel in the heart of Edinburgh's New Town, overlooking the fashionable Charlotte Square Gardens. The informal bistro is popular for lunches, and there is also a formal restaurant.
ROOMS: 75 en suite (bth/shr) (1 fmly) **MEALS:** Scottish & French Cuisine V meals Coffee am Tea pm **FACILITIES:** CTV in all bedrooms **CONF:** Thtr 200 Class 80 Board 60 **SERVICES:** Lift Night porter 2P **NOTES:** No smoking in restaurant Last d 9.45pm
CARDS:

EDINBURGH City of Edinburgh **Map 11 NT27**
★★ ***Allison House***
15/17 Mayfield Gardens EH9 2AX
Quality Percentage Score: 67%
☎ 0131 667 8049 📠 0131 667 5001
Dir: *1m S of city centre on A701*
This welcoming hotel has a wide choice of bedroom sizes; the rooms are smart, and particularly complimented by a tasteful selection of fabrics. Public areas include an attractive restaurant and an inviting lounge, with a small residents dispense bar.
ROOMS: 23 rms (21 shr) (5 fmly) **MEALS:** Scottish Cuisine V meals Coffee am Tea pm **FACILITIES:** CTV in all bedrooms ch fac **CONF:** Thtr 25 Class 12 Board 16 Del from £65 * **SERVICES:** 12P **NOTES:** No smoking in restaurant Last d 9pm **CARDS:**

EDINBURGH City of Edinburgh **Map 11 NT27**
★★ ***Murrayfield***
18 Corstophine Rd EH12 6HN
Quality Percentage Score: 67%
☎ 0131 337 1844 📠 0131 346 8159
Friendly and attentive service is a feature of this popular hotel, close to the national rugby stadium. A smart restaurant serves good food, which is accompanied by a spacious bar. There is a wide choice of well appointed bedrooms of varying sizes and styles, both in the main building, and in a converted mansion fifty yards away.
ROOMS: 23 en suite (bth/shr) 10 annexe en suite (shr) (1 fmly) **MEALS:** Scottish & European Cuisine Coffee am **FACILITIES:** CTV in all bedrooms **CONF:** Thtr 30 Class 12 Board 20 **SERVICES:** Night porter 30P **NOTES:** Last d 9pm Closed 2 days Xmas & 2 days New Year
CARDS:

EDINBURGH City of Edinburgh **Map 11 NT27**
★★ **Salisbury View Hotel**
64 Dalkeith Rd EH16 5AE
Quality Percentage Score: 67%
☎ 0131 667 1133 📠 0131 667 1133
Dir: *on the A7/A68, approx 1.5m to the south of the city centre Holyrood Park*
A small Georgian hotel with a relaxed atmosphere, a cosy bar lounge (residents and diners only) and an attractive restaurant.
contd.

Dishes are well presented and modern in style. Bedrooms are smart and well equipped.

Salisbury View Hotel, Edinburgh

ROOMS: 8 en suite (shr) (1 fmly) s £28-£45; d £54-£74 (incl. bkfst) * LB Off peak **MEALS:** Dinner £21.95 Scottish & French Cuisine V meals Coffee am **FACILITIES:** CTV in all bedrooms STV **SERVICES:** 8P **NOTES:** No coaches No smoking in restaurant Last d 9.30pm Closed 24-26 Dec **CARDS:**

EDINBURGH City of Edinburgh **Map 11 NT27**

★★ Iona

Strathearn Place EH9 2AL

Quality Percentage Score: 64%

☎ 0131 447 6264 & 0131 447 5050 📠 0131 452 8574

Dir: *from Morningside Rd (main access into Edinburgh) turn left at lights into Chamberlain Rd, turn right at the end of the road, at junction turn left*

This hotel lies in a leafy suburb on the south side of Edinburgh. It offers comfortable accommodation, and a bar which is very popular amongst the local residents. There is a selection of good value meals served in both in the bar, and in the hotel restaurant.

ROOMS: 17 en suite (bth/shr) (3 fmly) s £25-£60; d £60-£90 (incl. bkfst) * LB Off peak **MEALS:** Lunch fr £7 High tea fr £7 Dinner fr £13.50alc V meals Coffee am **FACILITIES:** CTV in all bedrooms **CONF:** Thtr 40 Board 22 **SERVICES:** 20P **NOTES:** No coaches Last d 9pm **CARDS:**

EDINBURGH City of Edinburgh **Map 11 NT27**

★★ *Orwell Lodge*

29 Polwarth Ter EH11 1NH

Quality Percentage Score: 64%

☎ 0131 229 1044 📠 0131 228 9492

Dir: *From A702 turn into Gilmore Place (opposite King's theatre) hotel 1m on the left*

Friendly staff offer attentive service at this hotel, a sympathetic conversion and extension of an elegant Victorian mansion. Bedrooms are comfortable, smartly furnished and well equipped. The spacious bar is a focal point which offers food, along with a restaurant upstairs.

ROOMS: 10 en suite (bth/shr) No smoking in all bedrooms **MEALS:** International Cuisine V meals Coffee am Tea pm **FACILITIES:** CTV in all bedrooms Wkly live entertainment **CONF:** Thtr 250 Class 120 Board 80 **SERVICES:** 40P **NOTES:** No dogs (ex guide dogs) No smoking in restaurant Last d 8.30pm Closed 25 Dec **CARDS:**

EDINBURGH City of Edinburgh **Map 11 NT27**

★★ Thrums Private Hotel

14 Minto St EH9 1RQ

Quality Percentage Score: 61%

☎ 0131 667 5545 & 0131 667 8545 📠 0131 667 8707

Dir: *off A701 follow city bypass - Edinburgh South - Newington/A7 - A701*

Two Georgian houses have been converted to create this family-run hotel. Informal public areas include a lounge where drinks are available, and a smart restaurant. Bedrooms, which are well equipped, are available in a variety of sizes leading up to several spacious rooms with period furnishings.

ROOMS: 6 en suite (bth/shr) 8 annexe rms (7 bth/shr) (5 fmly) s £30-£50; d £60-£80 (incl. bkfst) * LB Off peak **MEALS:** Lunch £7-£10alc High tea £4.25-£6.50 Dinner £10.50 & alc V meals Coffee am Tea pm **FACILITIES:** CTV in all bedrooms **SERVICES:** 10P **NOTES:** Last d 8.30pm Closed Xmas **CARDS:**

EDINBURGH City of Edinburgh **Map 11 NT27**

★★ Hotel Ibis

Hunter Square EH1 1QW

Quality Percentage Score: 60%

☎ 0131 240 7000 📠 0131 240 7007

Dir: *from Queen St (M8/M9) or Waterloo Pl (A1) crossover North Bridge (A7) & High St, take 1st right off South Bridge, this is Hunter Sq*

Set right in the heart of the city, close to the famous Royal Mile, this hotel has been converted from old warehouses. It offers practical modern accommodation, self-service breakfast and a simple menu for those wishing to dine in. Public areas include an open plan foyer lounge, reception and bar.

ROOMS: 99 en suite (bth/shr) No smoking in 38 bedrooms d £55-£60 * Off peak **MEALS:** V meals Coffee am Tea pm **FACILITIES:** CTV in all bedrooms STV **SERVICES:** Lift **NOTES:** No smoking area in restaurant **CARDS:**

EDINBURGH City of Edinburgh **Map 11 NT27**

★★ *Royal Ettrick*

13 Ettrick Rd EH10 5BJ

Quality Percentage Score: 60%

☎ 0131 228 6413 📠 0131 229 7330

Dir: *from W end of Princes Street follow Lothian Road, turn right onto Gilmour Place for 0.75m, hotel on right behind Bowling Green*

Set in a leafy suburb just west of the city centre, this family-run hotel offers well equipped bedrooms, a popular lounge bar and a split-level conservatory overlooking the garden. Tasty home-cooked meals are served in an attractive and informal setting from a competitively priced and wide ranging menu.

ROOMS: 12 rms (9 bth/shr) (2 fmly) **MEALS:** Scottish & French Cuisine V meals Coffee am Tea pm **FACILITIES:** CTV in all bedrooms STV **CONF:** Thtr 80 Class 40 Board 30 Del from £60 * **SERVICES:** 20P **NOTES:** No coaches No smoking area in restaurant Last d 8.15pm **CARDS:**

See advert on opposite page

EDINBURGH City of Edinburgh **Map 11 NT27**

Hotel of the Year

The Bonham

35 Drumsheugh Gardens EH3 7RN

☎ 0131 226 6050 & 603 6060

📠 0131 226 6080

Dir: *located close to West End & Princes St*

Chosen as Hotel of the Year for Scotland, this imaginative conversion of a former university residence looks set to be very popular. Imaginatively designed bedrooms are extremely comfortable and spacious, with hi-tech communications systems, and splendid bathrooms. A striking modern restaurant, in the brasserie style, features

contd.

interesting light cuisine. Staff throughout the hotel are very capable.

ROOMS: 48 en suite (bth/shr) No smoking in 24 bedrooms s fr £125; d fr £158 (incl. cont bkfst) LB Off peak **MEALS:** Lunch fr £12.50 & alc Dinner £18-£22alc Californian Cuisine V meals Coffee am Tea pm **FACILITIES:** CTV in all bedrooms STV Xmas **CONF:** Thtr 50 Board 26 **SERVICES:** Lift Night porter **NOTES:** No dogs (ex guide dogs) Last d 9.30pm Closed 24-28 Dec **CARDS:**

EDINBURGH City of Edinburgh **Map 11 NT27**

The Howard

34 Great King St EH3 6QH

☎ 0131 557 3500 0131 557 6515

Dir: *travelling E on Queen St, take 2nd left, Hanover St. Continue through 3 sets of lights, turn right & hotel on left*

A splendid town house hotel, made of three linked Georgian

contd.

houses, providing beautiful accommodation with luxurious bathrooms. Public rooms retain their period charm, with sumptuous furnishings and ornate chandeliers, while the bar-restaurant has a contemporary look and offers a stylish menu of innovative cooking.
ROOMS: 15 en suite (bth/shr) s £130-£135; d £245 (incl. bkfst) * LB Off peak **MEALS:** Lunch £10.50-£14 Dinner £20-£31.50alc International Cuisine V meals Coffee am Tea pm **FACILITIES:** CTV in all bedrooms STV **CONF:** Thtr 45 Class 25 Board 25 **SERVICES:** Lift Night porter 10P **NOTES:** No dogs (ex guide dogs) No smoking in restaurant Last d 10pm Closed 22-28 Dec **CARDS:**

EDINBURGH City of Edinburgh **Map 11 NT27**
Travel Inn
288 Willowbrae Rd EH8 7NG
☎ 0131 661 3396 Fax 0131 652 2789
Dir: *2m from city (east), just before Esso garage*
This modern building offers accommodation in smart, spacious and well equipped bedrooms, all with en-suite bathrooms. Refreshments may be taken at the nearby family restaurant. For details about current prices consult the Contents Page under Hotel Groups for the Travel Inn phone number.
ROOMS: 39 en suite (bth/shr) d £39.95 *

EDINBURGH City of Edinburgh **Map 11 NT27**
Travel Inn
Carberry Rd, Inveresk, Musselburgh EH21 8PT
☎ 0131 665 3005 Fax 0131 653 2270
Dir: *from Wallyford A6094, follow signs for Dalkeith until mini-rdbt & turn right, Travel Inn is 300yds on right*
This modern building offers accommodation in smart, spacious and well equipped bedrooms, all with en-suite bathrooms. Refreshments may be taken at the nearby family restaurant. For details about current prices consult the Contents Page under Hotel Groups for the Travel Inn phone number.
ROOMS: 40 en suite (bth/shr) d £39.95 *

EDINBURGH City of Edinburgh **Map 11 NT27**
Travel Inn (City Centre)
1 Morrison Link EH3 8DN
☎ 0131 228 9819 Fax 0131 228 9836
Dir: *next to Edinburgh International Conference Centre*
This modern building offers accommodation in smart, spacious and well equipped bedrooms, all with en-suite bathrooms. Refreshments may be taken at the nearby family restauarant. For details about current prices consult the Contents Page under Hotel Groups for the Travel Inn phone number.
ROOMS: 128 en suite (bth/shr) d £44.95 *

EDINBURGH City of Edinburgh **Map 11 NT27**
Travel Inn (Leith)
Pier Place, Newhaven Dicks EH6 4LP
☎ 0131 555 1570 Fax 0131 554 5994
This modern building offers accommodation in smart, spacious and well equipped bedrooms, all with en-suite bathrooms. Refreshments may be taken at the nearby family restaurant. For details about current prices consult the Contents Page under Hotel Groups for the Travel Inn phone number.
ROOMS: 60 en suite (bth/shr) d £39.95 *

EDINBURGH City of Edinburgh **Map 11 NT27**
Travelodge
Old Craighall EH21 8RE
☎ 0131 653 6070
Dir: *off A1, 2m from eastern outskirts Edinburgh*
This modern building offers accommodation in smart, spacious and well equipped bedrooms, all with en-suite bathrooms. Refreshments may be taken at the nearby family restaurant. For details about current prices, consult the Contents Page under Hotel Groups for the Travelodge phone number.
ROOMS: 45 en suite (bth/shr) d £49.95 *

EDINBURGH City of Edinburgh **Map 11 NT27**
Travelodge
46 Dreghorn Link EH13 9QR
☎ 0131 441 4296 Fax 0131 441 4296
Dir: *6m S, A720 Ring Rd South*
This modern building offers accommodation in smart, spacious and well equipped bedrooms, all with en-suite bathrooms. Refreshments may be taken at the nearby family restaurant. For details about current prices, consult the Contents Page under Hotel Groups for the Travelodge phone number.
ROOMS: 40 en suite (bth/shr) d £49.95 *

EDINBURGH City of Edinburgh **Map 11 NT27**
Jurys Inn Edinburgh
43 Jeffrey St EH1 1DG
☎ 0131 200 3300
Dir: *A8/M8 onto Princes Street - 1m turn right at the Waverley Station, next left*
Located next to Waverley Station and close to key attractions, this inexpensive hotel is ideal for anyone that wants to explore the delights of Edinburgh. Eating options include the Inn Pub and the Arches Restaurant, while the rooms are brand new and contain the majority of the essentials.
ROOMS: 186 en suite (bth/shr) (68 fmly) No smoking in 121 bedrooms d £61-£82 * Off peak **MEALS:** Bar Lunch £4.95-£8.95 Dinner fr £15 & alc V meals Coffee am Tea pm **FACILITIES:** CTV in all bedrooms STV Wkly live entertainment **CONF:** Thtr 60 Class 35 Board 30 Del £110 * **SERVICES:** Lift Night porter **NOTES:** No smoking area in restaurant Last d 9.30pm **CARDS:**

EDINBURGH City of Edinburgh **Map 11 NT27**
Caledonian
Princes St EH1 2AB
☎ 0131 459 9988 Fax 0131 225 6632
Affectionately known as "The Caley", this bastion of Victorian splendour boasts fine views of the Castle. Public areas now have a smart, elegant feel, and bedrooms vary in style and size, so discuss before booking. In the Pompadour restaurant, a pianist plays, and service provided is discreet and attentive; the newly refurbished Chisholms is more informal. The hotel has its own car park and valet parking is provided.
ROOMS: 249 en suite (bth/shr) (9 fmly) No smoking in 58 bedrooms s £155-£175; d £225-£315 LB Off peak **MEALS:** Lunch £18 & alc Dinner £24 & alc Scottish, French & American Cuisine V meals Coffee am Tea pm **FACILITIES:** CTV in all bedrooms STV Indoor swimming pool (heated) Sauna Solarium Gym Jacuzzi/spa Beauty salon, steam room Wkly live entertainment Xmas **CONF:** Thtr 300 Class 150 Board 60 Del from £164 * **SERVICES:** Lift Night porter 65P **NOTES:** No dogs (ex guide dogs) No smoking area in restaurant Last d 10.45pm
CARDS:

EDINBURGH City of Edinburgh **Map 11 NT27**
Quality Hotel Edinburgh
Marine Dr, Cramond Foreshore EH4 5EP
☎ 0131 336 1700 Fax 0131 336 4934
Dir: *A90 to Davidsons Mains Quality Street over mini rbut Craymond Rd Sth 2nd right Lauriston Farm Rd left at rbut to seafront turn right hotel on left*
This much extended hotel enjoys marvellous views over the Firth of Forth. Bedrooms vary in size and style, although all are well equipped. Guests have the use of a small leisure centre and

contd.

although the public areas are somewhat limited, they are comfortably furnished. The best views are from the first-floor restaurant.
ROOMS: 86 en suite (bth/shr) (6 fmly) No smoking in 30 bedrooms
MEALS: English & Continental Cuisine V meals Coffee am
FACILITIES: CTV in all bedrooms STV Sauna Solarium Gym Jacuzzi/spa
CONF: Thtr 200 Class 80 Board 40 **SERVICES:** Lift Night porter 86P
NOTES: No smoking in restaurant Last d 9.15pm
CARDS:

EDINBURGH City of Edinburgh **Map 11 NT27**
Holyrood Hotel
Holyrood Rd EH8 6AE
☎ 0131 225 3921

EDZELL Angus **Map 15 NO66**
★★★ **Glenesk**
High St DD9 7TF
Quality Percentage Score: 62%
☎ 01356 648319 📠 01356 647333
Dir: *off A90 just after Brechin Bypass*
This family-run hotel is situated by the main road at the south end of the village beside the golf course. As well as a fully equipped leisure centre, public areas offer a choice of inviting lounges and contrasting bars, as well as a dining room that looks onto the garden.
ROOMS: 24 en suite (bth/shr) (5 fmly) s £40-£52; d £60-£85 (incl. bkfst) * LB Off peak **MEALS:** V meals Coffee am **FACILITIES:** CTV in all bedrooms Indoor swimming pool (heated) Snooker Sauna Solarium Gym Pool table Croquet lawn Jacuzzi/spa Xmas **CONF:** Board 30 **SERVICES:** 81P **NOTES:** No coaches Last d 8.45pm
CARDS:

ELGIN Moray **Map 15 NJ26**
see also **Rothes**
★★★ **Mansion House**
The Haugh IV30 1AW
Quality Percentage Score: 76%
☎ 01343 548811 📠 01343 547916
Dir: *in Elgin turn off the A96 into Haugh Rd, hotel at the end of the road by the river*
A baronial-style mansion close to the River Lossie. Bedrooms are individual in size and style with four poster beds, and a wide range of amenities. Attractive public areas include a lounge, a bar with adjacent lounge, a billiard room, and a Leisure Club. The popular Bistro is an informal alternative to the elegant restaurant where the emphasis is on gourmet cooking.
ROOMS: 23 en suite (bth/shr) (3 fmly) s £70-£95; d £120-£150 (incl. bkfst) * LB Off peak **MEALS:** Lunch fr £15.50 & alc High tea fr £10.50 Dinner fr £25 & alc V meals Coffee am Tea pm **FACILITIES:** CTV in all bedrooms STV Indoor swimming pool (heated) Snooker Sauna Solarium Gym Jacuzzi/spa Hairdresser Beauty therapist Steam room Xmas **CONF:** Thtr 200 Class 150 Board 50 Del from £120 * **SERVICES:** Night porter 150P **NOTES:** No dogs (ex guide dogs) No smoking in restaurant Last d 9pm **CARDS:**

See advert on this page

ELGIN Moray **Map 15 NJ26**
★★★ **Laichmoray**
Maisondieu Rd IV30 1QR
Quality Percentage Score: 67%
☎ 01343 540045 📠 01343 540055
Dir: *opposite the railway station*
Close to the railway station on the south side of town, this hotel offers well equipped bedrooms with a variety of styles. Service is friendly throughout and a full range of meals is available in both the bar, the new conservatory and, during the evening, in the more formal restaurant.
ROOMS: 35 rms (34 bth/shr) (5 fmly) No smoking in 4 bedrooms s fr £52; d £60-£78 (incl. bkfst) * LB Off peak **MEALS:** V meals Coffee am Tea pm **FACILITIES:** CTV in all bedrooms Pool table Darts Xmas **CONF:** Thtr 200 Class 160 Board 40 **SERVICES:** 60P
NOTES: Last d 9pm **CARDS:**

ELGIN Moray **Map 15 NJ26**
Travel Inn
1 Linkwood Way IV30 1HY
☎ 01343 550747 📠 01343 540635
Dir: *on A96, 1.5m E of city centre*
This modern building offers accommodation in smart, spacious and well equipped bedrooms, all with en-suite bathrooms. Refreshments may be taken at the nearby family restaurant. For details about current prices consult the Contents Page under Hotel Groups for the Travel Inn phone number.
ROOMS: 40 en suite (bth/shr) d £39.95 *

ELIE Fife **Map 12 NO40**
★★★ **Golf Hotel**
Bank St KY9 1EF
Quality Percentage Score: 62%
☎ 01333 330209 📠 01333 330381
Dir: *on entering Elie turn right off A917 at T-junct, hotel 100mtrs on right*
As it's name suggests, this well run and friendly hotel enjoys a quiet location on the edge of Elie's splendid links course. Bedrooms are currently varied in size and in style but plans are

contd.

in hand to upgrade them. Public areas include an extensive lounge bar and a useful banqueting room.

The Golf Hotel, Elie

ROOMS: 22 en suite (bth/shr) (2 fmly) s £50-£70; d £90-£120 (incl. bkfst) * LB Off peak **MEALS:** Lunch £15 Dinner £22 V meals Coffee am Tea pm **FACILITIES:** CTV in all bedrooms Golf 27 **CONF:** Thtr 120 Class 60 Board 40 Del from £85 * **SERVICES:** 50P **NOTES:** No dogs (ex guide dogs) No smoking in restaurant Last d 9.30pm
CARDS:

ERISKA Argyll & Bute **Map 10 NM94**
★★★★ Isle of Eriska
Eriska, Ledaig PA37 1SD
Quality Percentage Score: 78%
☎ 01631 720371 01631 720531
Dir: *leave A85 at Conneland join A828 and follow for 4m, then follow signs*

On an island which is reached via a private bridge, the grounds of this hotel are perhaps unrivalled. Guests have unrestricted access to beaches, woodlands and moor and are free to wander and explore. The hotel itself is an imposing Victorian granite house furnished with style. Bedrooms are sympathetically furnished, spacious and very well equipped.
ROOMS: 17 en suite (bth/shr) s fr £170; d fr £210 (incl. bkfst) * LB Off peak **MEALS: FACILITIES:** CTV in all bedrooms Indoor swimming pool (heated) Golf 6 Tennis (hard) Fishing Sauna Gym Croquet lawn Putting green Jacuzzi/spa Xmas **CONF:** Thtr 30 Class 30 Board 30 **SERVICES:** Night porter 76P **NOTES:** No smoking in restaurant Last d 9pm Closed Jan **CARDS:**

ERSKINE Renfrewshire **Map 11 NS47**
★★★ Posthouse Glasgow/Erskine
North Barr PA8 6AN
Quality Percentage Score: 65%
☎ 0141 812 0123 0141 812 7642
Dir: *M8 junct 30 and take A726 to Erskine. At 1st rndbt turn right 2nd straight through 3rd turn left*

Located on the banks of the River Clyde within sight of Erskine Bridge, this is a bright, modern hotel with well equipped bedrooms and a good leisure centre.
ROOMS: 177 en suite (bth/shr) (3 fmly) No smoking in 77 bedrooms d £65 * LB Off peak **MEALS:** International Cuisine V meals Coffee am Tea pm **FACILITIES:** CTV in all bedrooms Indoor swimming pool (heated) Sauna Gym Pool table Jacuzzi/spa Xmas **CONF:** Thtr 600 Class 400 Board 40 Del from £89 * **SERVICES:** Lift Night porter 200P **NOTES:** Last d 10.30pm **CARDS:**

FALKIRK Falkirk **Map 11 NS88**
★★★ Park Lodge Hotel
Camelon Rd FK1 5RY
Quality Percentage Score: 64%
☎ 01324 628331 01324 611593
Dir: *from M8 take A803 into Falkirk, hotel 1m beyond Mariner Leisure Ctr, opposite Dollar Park. From M9, A803 through Falkirk follow signs Dollar Park*

This purpose built business hotel on the western side of the town is now under new ownership and many improvements are planned. Bedrooms are bright and well equipped and the foyer lounge and bar is open-plan; the spacious restaurant offers a popular selection of international dishes and the friendly staff provide good standards of willing service.
ROOMS: 55 en suite (bth/shr) (3 fmly) No smoking in 32 bedrooms d £55 (incl. bkfst) * LB Off peak **MEALS:** Lunch £9.50-£12.50 High tea £8.95 Dinner £18.50 & alc French Mediterreanean Cuisine V meals Coffee am Tea pm **FACILITIES:** CTV in all bedrooms STV **CONF:** Thtr 300 Class 180 Board 80 Del from £85 * **SERVICES:** Lift Night porter 160P **NOTES:** No dogs (ex guide dogs) No smoking in restaurant Last d 9.30pm **CARDS:**
See advert on opposite page

FALKIRK Falkirk **Map 11 NS88**
★★ Comfort Inn
Manor St FK1 1NT
Quality Percentage Score: 59%
☎ 01324 624066 01324 611785
Dir: *Hotel adjacent to Callendor Square Shopping Mall*

This tourist and commercial hotel is situated in the centre of town beside a new shopping mall and offers competitively priced accommodation in either premier or standard rooms. Public areas are split on two levels and include a well stocked bar and restaurant on the first floor. Staff are friendly and willing to please.
ROOMS: 33 en suite (bth/shr) (5 fmly) No smoking in 16 bedrooms d £46.75-£54.50 * LB Off peak **MEALS:** Lunch £2.95-£15.95alc Dinner fr £10.75 & alc V meals Coffee am Tea pm **FACILITIES:** CTV in all bedrooms STV Gym Xmas **CONF:** Thtr 170 Class 80 Board 50 **SERVICES:** Lift Night porter Air conditioning 17P **NOTES:** No smoking in restaurant Last d 9.30pm **CARDS:**

FENWICK East Ayrshire **Map 11 NS44**
★★★ *Fenwick*
KA3 6AU
Quality Percentage Score: 67%
☎ 01560 600478 01560 600334
Dir: *2nd Fenwick junct on A77*

Situated by the A77 and convenient for both Glasgow and the Ayrshire coast, this hotel has been expanded and upgraded to provide a new reception foyer, restaurant, comfortable lounge bar and a wing of smart modern bedrooms. It is the hospitality and
contd.

the refreshingly good cooking that makes this a hotel worth seeking out. Seafood and game feature regularly on a menu.
ROOMS: 31 en suite (bth/shr) (2 fmly) No smoking in 4 bedrooms **MEALS:** V meals Coffee am Tea pm **FACILITIES:** CTV in all bedrooms Clay pigeon Quad bike ch fac **CONF:** Thtr 160 Class 60 Board 18 Del from £108 * **SERVICES:** Night porter 80P **NOTES:** No smoking area in restaurant Last d 9.45pm **CARDS:**

FORFAR Angus — Map 15 NO45

★★★ Idvies House
Letham DD8 2QJ
Quality Percentage Score: 67%
☎ 01307 818787 01307 818933
Dir: *from Forfar B9128 signed Carnoustie, 2m left at fork Letham & Arbroath ignoring Letham signs, 1m to T-Jct, turn left Arbroath, Hotel on left*
Set among wooded ground, this Victorian country house hotel offers comfortable bedrooms with period furnishings and a range of modern amenities. The bar has comfortable Chesterfield seating and an adjacent small study. Local produce features strongly on the extensive menu.
ROOMS: 11 en suite (bth/shr) (1 fmly) s £47.50-£50; d £65-£75 (incl. bkfst) * LB Off peak **MEALS:** Lunch £6-£20alc Dinner £18.50-£28.50 Scottish & French Cuisine V meals **FACILITIES:** CTV in all bedrooms STV Squash Snooker Croquet lawn **CONF:** Thtr 50 Class 30 Board 30 Del from £70 * **SERVICES:** 60P **NOTES:** No coaches No smoking in restaurant Last d 9pm Closed 25 Dec-2 Jan
CARDS:

FORRES Moray — Map 14 NJ05

★★★ Knockomie
Grantown Rd IV36 2SG
Quality Percentage Score: 72%
☎ 01309 673146 01309 673290
Dir: *S on A940 towards Grantown*

Scotland's Hotels of Distinction

Genuine hospitality and good food are part of the appeal of this charming country house, which stands in four acres of grounds to the south of town. Bedrooms range from well proportioned Grand Master and Master rooms, with individual colour schemes and period furnishings, to the pleasing standard rooms. Inviting public rooms include a choice of relaxing lounges a cosy cocktail bar with a wide range of malt whiskies. An informal bistro provides an alternative to the elegant main restaurant.
ROOMS: 15 en suite (bth/shr) (1 fmly) No smoking in 3 bedrooms s £74-£115; d £115-£150 (incl. bkfst) * LB Off peak **MEALS:** Lunch £14.50-£18.50 Dinner £28.50 & alc European Cuisine V meals Coffee am Tea pm **FACILITIES:** CTV in all bedrooms STV Putting green Xmas **CONF:** Thtr 40 Class 20 Board 20 Del from £125 * **SERVICES:** 45P **NOTES:** No smoking in restaurant Last d 9.30pm Closed 24 Dec-27 Dec & 29 Dec-2 Jan **CARDS:**

FORRES Moray — Map 14 NJ05

★★★ *Ramnee*

Victoria Rd IV36 0BN

Quality Percentage Score: 66%

☎ 01309 672410 Fax 01309 673392

Dir: *turn off A96 at roundabout on eastern side of Forres, hotel 200yds on right*

Situated in two acres of gardens, the Ramnee Hotel was built in 1907 as a private residence, and has been transformed into a country house-style hotel. Public areas are inviting and the lounge bar is very popular for meals and can get very busy. Bedrooms have all the expected modern facilities.

ROOMS: 20 en suite (bth/shr) (4 fmly) **MEALS:** Modern Scottish & French Cuisine V meals Coffee am Tea pm **FACILITIES:** CTV in all bedrooms STV **CONF:** Thtr 100 Class 30 Board 45 Del from £97.50 * **SERVICES:** 50P **NOTES:** No smoking in restaurant Last d 9pm RS Xmas day 1-3 Jan **CARDS:**

See advert on page 813

FORT AUGUSTUS Highland — Map 14 NH30

★★ *Lovat Arms*

PH32 4DU

Quality Percentage Score: 63%

☎ 01320 366206 & 366204 Fax 01320 366677

Dir: *on A82 near the centre of the village*

This well established hotel is close to both the Abbey and the canal. Public areas are spacious and comfortable and include the lounge bar, where meals are served. A more formal dinner is offered in the dining room. Bedrooms are mostly spacious and some have fine furnishings.

ROOMS: 23 en suite (bth/shr) (4 fmly) **MEALS:** V meals Coffee am Tea pm **FACILITIES:** CTV in all bedrooms Pool table **CONF:** Thtr 50 Class 30 Board 50 **SERVICES:** 50P **NOTES:** No smoking in restaurant Last d 9.30pm **CARDS:**

FORTINGALL Perth & Kinross — Map 14 NN74

★★ **Fortingall**

PH15 2NQ

Quality Percentage Score: 65%

☎ 01887 830367 & 830368 Fax 01887 830367

Dir: *take B846 out of Aberfeldy for 6m, then turn left (Fortingall) for 3m, hotel is in centre of village*

Offering traditional services and comforts, this family run hotel is the focal point of the picturesque conservation village of Fortingall. Public areas have a comfortable feel while many of the well equipped bedrooms are smartly furnished with period pieces.

ROOMS: 10 en suite (bth/shr) (3 fmly) s £30-£35; d £48-£60 (incl. bkfst) * LB Off peak **MEALS:** Lunch £10-£18alc Dinner £12-£20alc V meals Coffee am Tea pm **FACILITIES:** CTV in all bedrooms Fishing Sailing Pony trekking ch fac **SERVICES:** 20P **NOTES:** Last d 9pm Closed Nov-Feb **CARDS:**

FORT WILLIAM Highland — Map 14 NN17

The Premier Collection

★★★★ **Inverlochy Castle**

RELAIS & CHATEAUX.

Torlundy PH33 6SN

☎ 01397 702177 Fax 01397 702953

Dir: *accessible from either A82 Glasgow-Fort William or A9 Edinburgh-Dalwhinnie. Hotel 3m N of Fort William on A82, in Torlundy*

Set amidst glorious scenery this impressive Victorian building has 500 acres of grounds. Bedrooms are lavishly appointed and spacious. Private dining rooms are available, but the main dining room, adjacent to the elegant drawing room, has fine views. Top quality ingredients are carefully cooked.

ROOMS: 17 en suite (bth/shr) s £180-£225; d £250-£450 (incl. bkfst) * Off peak **MEALS:** Lunch £23-£28.50 Dinner £45 International Cuisine V meals Tea pm **FACILITIES:** CTV in all bedrooms STV Tennis (hard) Fishing Snooker Wkly live entertainment Xmas **SERVICES:** Night porter 18P **NOTES:** No dogs No coaches No smoking in restaurant Last d 9.15pm Closed 5 Jan-12 Feb **CARDS:**

FORT WILLIAM Highland — Map 14 NN17

★★★ **Moorings**

Banavie PH33 7LY

Quality Percentage Score: 71%

☎ 01397 772797 Fax 01397 772441

Dir: *3m N of Fort William off A830. Take A830 for approx 1m, cross the Caledonian canal and take first right*

This modern hotel west of Fort William is beside 'Neptune's Staircase' of the Caledonian Canal with views of Ben Nevis on clear days. Interesting meals are available as a two or four course fixed price menu in the Jacobean-style dining room, or as

contd. on p. 816

AA ★★★

Allt-nan-Ros Hotel

FOR BEN NEVIS AND GLENCOE
Onich, by Fort William
Inverness-shire PH33 6RY
Tel: 01855 821210/250 Fax: 01855 821462

Set in four acres with truly panoramic views from all bedrooms, restaurant and lounge across the garden and over Loch Linnhe to the hills of Appin and Morvern, it is no wonder that the MacLeod family's celebrated hotel is endorsed by so many leading authorities. Superb "Taste of Scotland" cuisine, log fire and malt whiskies — indeed, everything a Scottish West Highland Hotel should be!

For Special Offers check
Email: allt-nan-ros@zetnet.co.uk
Web: www.allt-nan-ros.co.uk

Onich Hotel — Onich

NEAR FORT WILLIAM
INVERNESS-SHIRE PH33 6RY
Tel: Onich (01855) 821214 Fax: (01855) 821484
★ ★ ★

Superbly situated on Route A82 midway between Ben Nevis and Glencoe with uninterrupted access to the shores of Loch Linnhe through well tended gardens. The hotel has recently been tastefully refurbished throughout creating a high level of comfort. The Restaurant enjoys an excellent reputation and features the best of fresh Scottish produce – seafood, beef, venison and game in season. The Deerstalkers Bar and Garden Lounge remain open all day for meals and refreshments. This is the ideal base for touring, walking or just relaxing in the Western Highlands. Open throughout the year. *Consort Scottish Hotel of the Year 1998.*

Discover seclusion and serenity

THE LODGE ON THE LOCH

In the heart of the Highlands, where mountains and Gulf Stream meet in tranquillity. Panoramic views from memorable bedrooms, specially furnished in a contemporary Highland style. Renowned Restaurant serving local seafood, salmon, trout and venison with home baking as well as health foods. This is one of three hotels in the Freedom of the Glen group of family hotels, each with a distinctive style of its own and all located around the Loch.

ONICH nr Fort William
The Scottish Highlands
PH33 6RY
Tel: 01855 821582 Fax: 01855 821463

AA ★★★

See gazetteer entry under ONICH

GLENSPEAN LODGE HOTEL

An extremely attractive Country House Hotel in 5 acres of landscaped gardens with truly spectacular views of the Nevis Range, providing an oasis of peace and tranquility. Superior comfort, excellent service and imaginative cuisine all delivered with care and attention to detail. Luxuriously designed bedrooms, Four Posters and Honeymoon Suite. Ben Nevis, Loch Ness, Urquhart Castle and Ski Centre nearby.

ROY BRIDGE, NR. FORT WILLIAM, INVERNESS-SHIRE
Tel: 01397-712223 Fax: 01397-712660

AA ★★★

bar food in the Upper Deck lounge bar or popular Mariners Bar. Bedrooms have fresh decor and good facilities.
ROOMS: 21 en suite (bth/shr) (1 fmly) No smoking in 4 bedrooms s £50-£80; d £72-£104 (incl. bkfst) LB Off peak **MEALS:** Bar Lunch £10-£17alc Dinner £21-£26 V meals Coffee am Tea pm **FACILITIES:** CTV in all bedrooms STV Xmas **CONF:** Thtr 120 Class 40 Board 30 Del from £75 * **SERVICES:** 60P **NOTES:** No smoking in restaurant Last d 9.30pm Closed 22-26 Dec **CARDS:**

See advert on opposite page

FORT WILLIAM Highland — Map 14 NN17
★★ Imperial
Fraser's Square PH33 6DW
Quality Percentage Score: 69%
☎ 01397 702040 & 703921 📠 01397 706277
Dir: *from town centre travel along Middle St approx 400mtrs from junction with A82*
This well established friendly family-run hotel in the town centre provides comfortable standards throughout, including an attractive cocktail bar as well as a busier lounge bar. There is a quiet first floor lounge and an adjacent conference room. Bedrooms feature a good range of facilities.
ROOMS: 32 en suite (bth/shr) (3 fmly) **MEALS:** Bar Lunch £2.50-£12.50 & alc High tea £7.50-£12.50 Dinner £18.50-£21.50 Scottish & French Cuisine V meals Coffee am Tea pm **FACILITIES:** CTV in all bedrooms Pool table **CONF:** Thtr 60 Class 30 Board 30 **SERVICES:** 15P **NOTES:** No smoking in restaurant Last d 8.45pm
CARDS:

FORT WILLIAM Highland — Map 14 NN17
★★ Grand
Gordon Square PH33 6DX
Quality Percentage Score: 68%
☎ 01397 702928 📠 01397 702928
Dir: *on A82 at W end of High St*
Considerable improvements have taken place at this friendly family run hotel at the south end of the pedestrianised High Street. Most bedrooms are refurbished and bathrooms continue to be enhanced. Public areas include comfortable non smoking lounges, a spacious bar and an attractive dining room.
ROOMS: 33 en suite (bth/shr) (4 fmly) s £25-£45; d £44-£70 (incl. bkfst) * LB Off peak **MEALS:** Dinner fr £16.95 V meals Coffee am Tea pm **FACILITIES:** CTV in all bedrooms **CONF:** Thtr 110 Class 60 Board 20 **SERVICES:** Night porter 20P **NOTES:** No smoking in restaurant Last d 8.30pm Closed Jan **CARDS:**

See advert on opposite page

FORT WILLIAM Highland — Map 14 NN17
★★ Alexandra
The Parade PH33 6AZ
Quality Percentage Score: 65%
☎ 01397 702241 📠 01397 705554
Dir: *North end of town centre*
Situated at the north end of the High Street, this long established and welcoming Victorian hotel remains a popular base for visiting tour groups. The best bedrooms are the executive rooms on the top floor which contrast with the smaller and more practical standard rooms on the other levels. Meals are available all day in the coffee shop. Leisure facilities are available to guests at the nearby sister hotel.
ROOMS: 97 en suite (bth/shr) (14 fmly) s £69-£89; d £79-£119 (incl. bkfst) * LB Off peak **MEALS:** Bar Lunch £3-£15alc Dinner £12.50-£17.50 & alc European Cuisine V meals Coffee am Tea pm **FACILITIES:** CTV in all bedrooms Free use of nearby leisure club Wkly live entertainment Xmas **CONF:** Thtr 140 Class 40 Board 26 **SERVICES:** Lift Night porter 65P **NOTES:** No smoking in restaurant Last d 10.45pm
CARDS:

FORT WILLIAM Highland — Map 14 NN17
★★ Milton Hotel & Leisure Club
North Rd PH33 6TG
Quality Percentage Score: 65%
☎ 01397 702331 📠 01397 700132
Dir: *N of town, on A82*
A popular base for visiting tour groups, and families, attracted by the smart new leisure centre. Refurbishment has enhanced the comfortable foyer lounge and large dining room, the covered walkway is appreciated by guests staying in the wing bedrooms. Bedrooms range from spacious executive rooms to smaller, more practical standard rooms.
ROOMS: 52 en suite (bth/shr) 67 annexe en suite (bth/shr) (14 fmly) s £59-£89; d £79-£119 (incl. bkfst) * LB Off peak **MEALS:** Bar Lunch £4-£9 High tea £5.95-£9 Dinner £12.50-£18 European Cuisine V meals Coffee am Tea pm **FACILITIES:** CTV in all bedrooms Indoor swimming pool (heated) Sauna Solarium Gym Pool table Jacuzzi/spa Beauty salon Wkly live entertainment Xmas **CONF:** Thtr 220 Class 70 Board 60 **SERVICES:** Night porter 140P **NOTES:** No smoking in restaurant Last d 9.30pm **CARDS:**

FORT WILLIAM Highland — Map 14 NN17
★★ The Caledonian
Achintore Rd PH33 6RW
Quality Percentage Score: 63%
☎ 01397 703117 📠 01397 700550
Dir: *on A 82, just south of Fort William centre*
Popular with tour groups, this modern hotel enjoys views over Loch Linnhe from its position south of town. The loch can also be seen from the open plan public areas.
ROOMS: 86 en suite (bth/shr) (12 fmly) s £75; d £95 (incl. bkfst) * LB Off peak **MEALS:** Lunch fr £15 Dinner fr £15 V meals Coffee am Tea pm **FACILITIES:** CTV in all bedrooms Sauna Pool table Wkly live entertainment Xmas **CONF:** Thtr 60 Class 40 Board 30 Del from £65 * **SERVICES:** Lift Night porter 60P **NOTES:** No smoking in restaurant Last d 9pm **CARDS:**

FORT WILLIAM Highland — Map 14 NN17
Travel Inn
Loch Iall, An Aird PH33 6AN
☎ 01397 703707 📠 01397 703618
Dir: *N end of Fort William Shopping Centre, just off A82 ring road, close to railway and bus station*
This modern building offers accommodation in smart, spacious and well equipped bedrooms, all with en-suite bathrooms. Refreshments may be taken at the nearby family restaurant. For details about current prices consult the Contents Page under Hotel Groups for the Travel Inn phone number.
ROOMS: 40 en suite (bth/shr) d £39.95 *

FREUCHIE Fife — Map 11 NO20
★★ Lomond Hills
Parliament Square KY15 7EY
Quality Percentage Score: 61%
☎ 01337 857329 & 857498 📠 01337 858180
Dir: *in centre of village off A914 2m north of Glenrothes*
A welcoming, privately owned hotel in the village centre, a former coaching inn which has been considerably extended. Though variable in size, bedrooms offer mixed modern styles

contd. on p. 818

Symbols and Abbreviations are listed and explained on pages 4 and 5

AA ★★ 76%

The Prince's House

Glenfinnan, By Fort William
Inverness-shire PH37 4LT
Tel: 01397 722246 Fax: 01397 722307
Email: princeshouse@glenfinnan.co.uk
web: www.glenfinnan.co.uk

Scottish Tourist Board COMMENDED · The Taste of Scotland

The Prince's House provides that special atmosphere, personal service and memorable food traditionally found in a small family run hotel. Mountain grandeur on the romantic Road to the Isles makes Glenfinnan a special holiday base with walking, fishing, beaches, ferries and steam trains nearby. This charming hotel, originally an Inn dating back to 1658, has recently been refurbished throughout. Our restaurant *'Flora's'* offers gourmet Scottish cuisine based on quality local produce, especially seafood.

THE MOORINGS HOTEL

Moorings Hotel AA ★★★
Banavie, Fort William
Inverness-shire, Scotland PH33 7LY
Tel: (01397) 772797 Fax: (01397) 772441

Set in a peaceful countryside location beside the Caledonian Canal with panoramic views of Ben Nevis, yet just a five minute drive to the town of Fort William. The Moorings offers a warm friendly welcome with a relaxing ambience and superb cuisine. Dine in the award winning restaurant or enjoy a freshly prepared bar meal in the Mariner's Bar.

AA★★

CREAG MHOR HOTEL

ONICH, BY GLENCOE, FORT WILLIAM
INVERNESS-SHIRE PH33 6RY
TEL: 01855 821379 FAX: 01855 821579

A picturesque Victorian house, built in 1890 as a private residence centrally situated for visiting the West of Scotland. Although the building has been upgraded in quality and comfort it still retains many of its interesting features. All bedrooms are fully en suite with full facilities and many enjoy superb views over Loch Linnhe and the surrounding countryside. Children and pets welcome. The elegant restaurant with open log fire in season, is the ideal place to relax and enjoy the best of local produce from the table d'hôte menu. Bar lunches and suppers are served daily in the comfortable lounge bar with its panoramic views.

AA ★★

The GRAND HOTEL

Fort William · Highland PH33 6DX
Telephone/Fax: 01397 702928

INVESTOR IN PEOPLE

Conveniently located in the town centre of Fort William, this family run hotel is an ideal base from which you can explore the surrounding area of Lochaber.
All bedrooms and public areas have recently been redecorated to a comfortable standard.
The *Salmon Leap* Restaurant enjoys an enviable reputation for food whilst *Rab's Bar* has a fine selection of Malt Whiskies and spirits.

and a good range of amenities. Public areas include a choice of inviting lounges as well as the popular leisure centre.
ROOMS: 25 en suite (bth/shr) (3 fmly) No smoking in 3 bedrooms s £50-£54; d £76-£80 (incl. bkfst) * LB Off peak **MEALS:** Lunch fr £17.50 & alc High tea fr £6 & alc Dinner fr £17.50 & alc Scottish & French Cuisine V meals Coffee am Tea pm **FACILITIES:** CTV in all bedrooms STV Indoor swimming pool (heated) Sauna Solarium Gym Jacuzzi/spa Xmas **CONF:** Thtr 200 Class 100 Board 80 Del from £62 *
SERVICES: 21P **NOTES:** No smoking area in restaurant Last d 9.15pm
CARDS:

GAIRLOCH Highland — Map 14 NG87
★★★ Creag Mor
Charleston IV21 2AH
Quality Percentage Score: 67%
☎ 01445 712068 01445 712044
Dir: *A9 to Inverness, then A832 following signs to Ullapool, pass through village of Garve and follow signs for Gairloch, hotel 1st on right*
Bedrooms at this comfortable hotel are pleasantly decorated and offer every modern convenience. Tranquil public areas include an inviting split level gallery bar/lounge from which views of the harbour can be enjoyed. Local produce features strongly in the dining room and there is also an all-day menu.
ROOMS: 17 en suite (bth/shr) (1 fmly) s £38-£57; d £76-£90 (incl. bkfst) * LB Off peak **MEALS:** Dinner £28 Scottish & French Cuisine V meals Coffee am Tea pm **FACILITIES:** CTV in all bedrooms Fishing Pool table **CONF:** Class 40 **SERVICES:** Night porter 29P **NOTES:** No smoking in restaurant Last d 9pm Closed 16 Nov-Feb
CARDS:

See advert on opposite page

GAIRLOCH Highland — Map 14 NG87
★★ Myrtle Bank
Low Rd IV21 2BS
Quality Percentage Score: 70%
☎ 01445 712004 01445 712214
Dir: *off B8012 Melvaig road*
The MacLean family provide a warm welcome at their hotel by the shore of Loch Gairloch. The bedrooms are comfortably furnished and several enjoy views over the loch to the Skye hills. Day rooms consist of a lounge, conservatory, and a bar and dining room, both serving enjoyable food.
ROOMS: 12 en suite (bth/shr) (2 fmly) s £35-£45; d £70-£90 (incl. bkfst) * Off peak **MEALS:** Dinner £20-£23 V meals Coffee am Tea pm **FACILITIES:** CTV in all bedrooms Pool table **SERVICES:** 20P
NOTES: No coaches No smoking in restaurant Last d 8.30pm
CARDS:

GAIRLOCH Highland — Map 14 NG87
★★ *The Old Inn*
Flowerdale IV21 2BD
Quality Percentage Score: 66%
☎ 01445 712006 01445 712445
Dir: *on A832 - at south end of village near the harbour*
Standing by a small river, and close to the harbour, this former coaching inn stocks a good range of cask-conditioned ales and serves food all day, in the two popular bars and the no-smoking bistro. There is also a restaurant serving a table d'hote dinner. Bedrooms are mostly spacious, and all are well equipped.
ROOMS: 14 en suite (bth/shr) (4 fmly) **MEALS:** Coffee am Tea pm **FACILITIES:** CTV in all bedrooms Pool table **CONF:** Class 60 Board 40 **SERVICES:** 30P **NOTES:** No smoking area in restaurant Last d 8.55pm
CARDS:

GALASHIELS Scottish Borders — Map 12 NT43
★★★ Woodlands House Hotel & Restaurants
Windyknowe Rd TD1 1RG
Quality Percentage Score: 66%
☎ 01896 754722 01896 754892
Dir: *A7 into Galashiels, take A72 towards Peebles, take the 1st left into Hall St, then 2nd road on right to hotel*

This Victorian Gothic mansion lies in two acres of grounds in a quiet area above the town. It combines the relaxed atmosphere of a country house with amenities that make it popular with business guests as well as tourists. It is worth asking for one of the larger bedrooms. Guests can eat in the restaurant or the bar and there are plans for a bistro.
ROOMS: 10 en suite (bth/shr) (1 fmly) s £48-£52; d £68-£90 (incl. bkfst) * LB Off peak **MEALS:** Sunday Lunch fr £8.95alc Dinner £11.15-£29alc V meals Coffee am Tea pm **FACILITIES:** CTV in all bedrooms **CONF:** Thtr 50 Class 30 Board 24 **SERVICES:** 35P **NOTES:** No smoking in restaurant Last d 9pm **CARDS:**

GALASHIELS Scottish Borders — Map 12 NT43
★★★ Kingsknowes
Selkirk Rd TD1 3HY
Quality Percentage Score: 63%
☎ 01896 758375 01896 750377
Dir: *off A7 at Galashiels/ Selkirk rdbt*
A friendly and informal atmosphere can be enjoyed at this family-run hotel, which stands in its own grounds south of the town, close to the river Tweed. A Victorian turreted mansion, its public areas feature a marble entrance and imposing staircase, whilst there is a choice of bars, one offering a good range of bar meals to complement the restaurant. Bedrooms are tastefully furnished and several on the first floor are massive.
ROOMS: 11 en suite (bth/shr) (3 fmly) s £42-£49; d £68-£74 (incl. bkfst) * LB Off peak **MEALS:** Lunch £9.50-£15 & alc High tea £6-£8 & alc Dinner £19.25-£22 & alc English & Continental Cuisine V meals Coffee am Tea pm **FACILITIES:** CTV in all bedrooms Tennis (hard) Wkly live entertainment Xmas **CONF:** Thtr 65 Class 45 Board 30 Del from £52 *
SERVICES: 72P **NOTES:** No smoking area in restaurant Last d 9.30pm
CARDS:

GALASHIELS Scottish Borders — Map 12 NT43
★★ King's
56 Market St TD1 3AN
Quality Percentage Score: 65%
☎ 01896 755497 01896 755497
Dir: *adjacent to southbound A7 in town centre*
This family-run hotel lies just off the town centre and has a friendly and relaxing atmosphere. It offers good value, freshly prepared meals. Home baking accompanies the morning coffees

contd.

and afternoon teas. Although not spacious, bedrooms are well equipped.
ROOMS: 7 en suite (bth/shr) (2 fmly) s £35-£45; d £50-£70 (incl. bkfst) * LB Off peak **MEALS:** Lunch £8.50-£11.25alc High tea £6.50-£7.50alc Dinner £12-£18.50 & alc Scottish & French Cuisine V meals Coffee am Tea pm **FACILITIES:** CTV in all bedrooms ch fac **CONF:** Thtr 80 Class 30 Board 40 Del from £60 * **NOTES:** No dogs (ex guide dogs) Last d 9.30pm Closed 1-3 Jan **CARDS:**

GALASHIELS Scottish Borders — Map 12 NT43

★★ Abbotsford Arms

63 Stirling St TD1 1BY
Quality Percentage Score: 62%
☎ 01896 752517 Fax 01896 750744
***Dir:** turn off A7 down Ladhope Vale, turn left opposite bus station*

A friendly and informal hotel, the Abbotsford Arms lies just off the inner ring road within walking distance of the town centre. It serves food throughout the day, and is very popular for its good range of dishes and generous portions, both in the bar and restaurant.
ROOMS: 14 en suite (bth/shr) (2 fmly) s £38; d £58 (incl. bkfst) * LB Off peak **MEALS:** V meals Coffee am **FACILITIES:** CTV in all bedrooms STV **CONF:** Thtr 150 Class 100 Board 100 Del from £45 * **SERVICES:** Night porter 10P **NOTES:** No dogs (ex guide dogs) No coaches Last d 9pm Closed 24-25 & 31 Dec & 1 Jan
CARDS:

GARVE Highland — Map 14 NH36

★★ *Inchbae Lodge*

THE CIRCLE
Selected Individual Hotels
GREAT BRITAIN

Inchbae IV23 2PH
Quality Percentage Score: 64%
☎ 01997 455269 Fax 01997 455207
***Dir:** on the A835, 6m W of Garve*

Situated six miles west of the village, this relaxing holiday hotel has a choice of lounges and a bar featuring a beamed ceiling and natural stone walls. The bedrooms have no televisions or telephones to detract from the peace and quiet; those in the main house are somewhat larger than those in the cedar chalet annexe. Enjoyable dinners are served in the dining room, or lighter meals are available in the bar.
ROOMS: 6 en suite (bth/shr) 6 annexe en suite (shr) (3 fmly) No smoking in all bedrooms **MEALS:** Scottish Cuisine V meals Coffee am Tea pm **FACILITIES:** Fishing Walking-routes are available Clay pigeon shooting Bird watching **CONF:** Board 20 Del from £70 * **SERVICES:** 30P **NOTES:** No coaches No smoking in restaurant Last d 8pm Closed 25-29 Dec **CARDS:**

GATEHOUSE OF FLEET Dumfries & Galloway — Map 11 NX55

★★★★ Cally Palace

DG7 2DL
Quality Percentage Score: 67%
☎ 01557 814341 Fax 01557 814522
***Dir:** 1m from Gatehouse. From M6 & A74, follow signs for Dumfries and then A75 Stranraer*

Set in 500 acres, this grand 17th century building is now a hotel boasting extensive leisure facilities. The public rooms include a
contd.

AA Rosettes are awarded for quality of food,
see page 15 for an explanation of Rosette assessment.

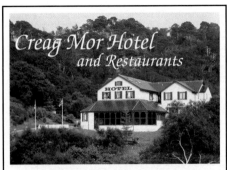

conservatory bar. All bedrooms are spacious, and offer extra touches. There is a short dinner menu of freshly prepared dishes.
ROOMS: 56 en suite (bth) (7 fmly) s £96-£108; d £152-£176 (incl. bkfst & dinner) * LB Off peak **MEALS:** Lunch £8-£15alc Dinner £24 & alc Scottish & French Cuisine V meals Coffee am Tea pm **FACILITIES:** CTV in all bedrooms STV Indoor swimming pool (heated) Golf 18 Tennis (hard) Fishing Snooker Sauna Solarium Pool table Croquet lawn Putting green Jacuzzi/spa Table tennis Practice fairway Xmas **CONF:** Thtr 80 Class 40 Board 35 **SERVICES:** Lift Night porter 100P **NOTES:** No dogs (ex guide dogs) No coaches No smoking in restaurant Last d 9.15pm Closed 3 Jan-3 Feb RS Feb
CARDS:

See advert on page 819

GATEHOUSE OF FLEET Dumfries & Galloway — Map 11 NX55

★★★ Murray Arms

DG7 2HY
Quality Percentage Score: 62%
☎ 01557 814207 🖷 01557 814370
Dir: *off A75, hotel at edge of town, near clock tower*

This former coaching inn retains much of its character, and offers an informal atmosphere. Bedrooms have individuality, enhanced by attractive fabrics. The Lunky Hole Restaurant is open all day for good value meals as well as dinners, and the bar and lounges are cosy.
ROOMS: 12 en suite (bth/shr) 1 annexe en suite (bth/shr) (3 fmly) s £45-£50; d £85-£100 (incl. bkfst) * LB Off peak **MEALS:** Bar Lunch £5-£15alc High tea £5-£10alc Dinner £9-£20alc V meals Coffee am Tea pm **FACILITIES:** CTV in all bedrooms Tennis (hard) Croquet lawn Xmas **CONF:** Thtr 120 Class 50 Board 30 Del from £50 * **SERVICES:** Night porter 50P **NOTES:** No smoking area in restaurant Last d 9.30pm
CARDS:

GIFFNOCK East Renfrewshire — Map 11 NS55

★★★ The Macdonald

Eastwood Toll G46 6RA
Quality Percentage Score: 66%
☎ 0141 638 2225 🖷 0141 638 6231
Dir: *on A77 Kilmarnock/Ayr Rd at Eastwood Toll, Giffnock - take 1st exit onto A726 East Kilbride, then 1st right to hotel*

The MacDonald, a well established friendly and comfortable, mainly business hotel, is conveniently situated for both the city centre and the Ayrshire coast. The bedrooms are neat and well equipped, with four comfortable suites with their own sitting rooms. The public rooms include a choice of bars and modern Scottish cuisine is served in generous portions in the elegant Oscar's Restaurant. There are also meeting and function facilities and ample car parking.
ROOMS: 56 en suite (bth/shr) (4 fmly) No smoking in 12 bedrooms s £85; d £95 * LB Off peak **MEALS:** Lunch fr £18.95 Dinner fr £18.95 International Cuisine V meals Coffee am Tea pm **FACILITIES:** CTV in all bedrooms STV Sauna Solarium Pool table Xmas **CONF:** Thtr 160 Class 60 Board 35 Del from £88 * **SERVICES:** Night porter 130P **NOTES:** No smoking area in restaurant Last d 10.00pm
CARDS:

GIFFNOCK East Renfrewshire — Map 11 NS55

★★ The Redhurst

Eastwoodmains Rd G46 6QE
Quality Percentage Score: 65%
☎ 0141 638 6465 🖷 0141 620 0419
Dir: *on A726 main Paisley route, from city centre take M74/M8 follow signs for A77/A726 to East Kilbride*

Situated in a suburb south of the city, this popular hotel attracts local custom, though it also suits the business market, with access to the city via the M77 being close at hand. Tourists will find this to be a useful base. Bedrooms are well decorated and equipped and the attractively refurbished bar and restaurant offers a popular menu that should suit all tastes and pockets.
ROOMS: 19 en suite (bth/shr) (2 fmly) d £49.50 * LB Off peak **MEALS:** Lunch £6.50-£19alc Dinner £9.50-£19alc V meals Coffee am Tea pm **FACILITIES:** CTV in all bedrooms Wkly live entertainment **CONF:** Thtr 200 Class 150 Board 40 Del from £79 * **SERVICES:** Night porter 50P **NOTES:** No dogs (ex guide dogs) No smoking area in restaurant Last d 9.30pm **CARDS:**

GLAMIS Angus — Map 15 NO34

★★★ *Castleton House*

Castleton of Eassie DD8 1SJ
Quality Percentage Score: 70%
☎ 01307 840340 🖷 01307 840506
Dir: *on A94 midway between Forfar/Cupar Angus, 2m W of Glamis*

A delightful Victorian house in its own grounds, set back from the main road, Castleton House offers bedrooms which vary in size and are furnished in keeping with the character of the house. Public areas include an inviting lounge, a comfortable well stocked bar, with the adjacent conservatory providing an informal alternative to the elegant dining room where a tempting range of Scottish fare is available.
ROOMS: 6 en suite (bth/shr) **MEALS:** French Cuisine Coffee am Tea pm **FACILITIES:** CTV in all bedrooms Riding Croquet lawn Jogging track Wkly live entertainment **CONF:** Thtr 25 Class 25 Board 20 **SERVICES:** 100P **NOTES:** No dogs (ex guide dogs) Last d 9.30pm
CARDS:

GLASGOW City of Glasgow — Map 11 NS56

see also **Clydebank**

★★★★ Beardmore

Beardmore St G81 4SA
Quality Percentage Score: 70%
☎ 0141 951 6000 🖷 0141 951 6018
(For full entry see Clydebank)

GLASGOW City of Glasgow — Map 11 NS56

★★★★ Glasgow Marriott

500 Argyle St, Anderston G3 8RR
Quality Percentage Score: 69%
☎ 0141 226 5577 🖷 0141 221 7676
Dir: *off junct 19 of M8*

The Glasgow Marriott is a well-established and conveniently located operation that has recently undergone major refurbishment. The net result is a smart ground floor with a bar/lounge, informal café, and attractive restaurant. The hotel boasts its own leisure club, which includes a gym and pool. High quality, well-equipped bedrooms benefit from air conditioning and generous beds; the suites are particularly comfortable.
ROOMS: 300 en suite (bth/shr) (89 fmly) No smoking in 212 bedrooms s £89-£119; d £99-£129 (incl. bkfst) * LB Off peak **MEALS:** European Cuisine V meals Coffee am Tea pm **FACILITIES:** CTV in all bedrooms STV Indoor swimming pool (heated) Squash Sauna Solarium Gym Jacuzzi/spa Heated whirlpool Hairdresser Beautician Xmas **CONF:** Thtr 700 Class 400 Board 30 Del from £145 * **SERVICES:** Lift Night porter Air conditioning 250P **NOTES:** No smoking area in restaurant Last d 10.00pm **CARDS:**

GLASGOW City of Glasgow **Map 11 NS56**
★★★★ ❀ ***Glasgow Moat House***
Congress Rd G3 8QT
Quality Percentage Score: 67%
☎ 0141 306 9988 📠 0141 221 2022

MOAT HOUSE

Dir: *junct 19 M8, follow signs for SEC (Scottish Exhibition Centre)` hotel adjacent to centre*
This ultra modern building, instantly recognisable from its mirrored glass exterior, is one of the tallest in Scotland and its convenient location alongside the River Clyde and next to the Scottish Exhibition Centre is ideal for both business and leisure purposes. A feature of its lofty public rooms is a huge wall mural, depicting much of the city's history, which looks down over the informal Pointhouse Restaurant and the stylish Mariners Restaurant, which offers a range of Rosette-worthy dishes. Bedrooms are comfortable and well appointed and most enjoy splendid panoramic views over the river and city. There is a well equipped leisure centre as well as a wide range of meeting and conference rooms.
ROOMS: 283 en suite (bth/shr) (45 fmly) No smoking in 120 bedrooms
MEALS: International Cuisine V meals Coffee am Tea pm
FACILITIES: CTV in all bedrooms STV Indoor swimming pool (heated) Sauna Solarium Gym Wkly live entertainment **CONF:** Thtr 800 Class 350 Board 66 **SERVICES:** Lift Night porter Air conditioning 300P
NOTES: No smoking area in restaurant Last d 10.30pm
CARDS:

GLASGOW City of Glasgow **Map 11 NS56**
★★★★ **Copthorne Glasgow**
George Square G2 1DS
Quality Percentage Score: 64%
☎ 0141 332 6711 📠 0141 332 4264

MILLENNIUM HOTELS AND RESORTS
MILLENNIUM HOTELS COPTHORNE HOTELS

Dir: *take junct 15 from M8 follow signs City Centre/George Sq, travel along Cathedral St past Strathclyde University, turn left into Hanover St*
This Victorian building overlooks George Square in the heart of the city. An elegant reception hall with cosy cocktail bar retains much original character, in contrast a smart restaurant and cafe bar meet the needs of the modern customer. Bedrooms are well equipped, the original building has some very spacious rooms, a wing contains smaller purpose built rooms.
ROOMS: 141 en suite (bth/shr) (4 fmly) No smoking in 45 bedrooms s £75-£130; d £94-£140 (incl. bkfst) * LB Off peak **MEALS:** Lunch £10-£17.95 & alc Dinner £11.95-£17.95 & alc International & Scottish Cuisine V meals Coffee am Tea pm **FACILITIES:** CTV in all bedrooms STV Gym Xmas **CONF:** Thtr 100 Class 40 Board 40 Del £135 * **SERVICES:** Lift Night porter **NOTES:** No dogs (ex guide dogs) No smoking area in restaurant Last d 9.45pm **CARDS:**

GLASGOW City of Glasgow **Map 11 NS56**
★★★★ ***Thistle Glasgow***
36 Cambridge St G2 3HN
Quality Percentage Score: 64%
☎ 0141 332 3311 📠 0141 332 4050

THISTLE HOTELS

Dir: *behind Sauchiehall St, opposite back entrance to Marks & Spencer and Boots*
With the benefit of its own underground car park, this busy hotel is near Sauchiehall Street, the Concert Hall and the Theatre Royal. Bedrooms are attractively decorated and smartly appointed. There is a choice of two dining rooms, a business centre, and impressive conference and banqueting facilities.
ROOMS: 300 en suite (bth/shr) (69 fmly) No smoking in 160 bedrooms
MEALS: International Cuisine V meals Coffee am Tea pm
FACILITIES: CTV in all bedrooms STV **CONF:** Thtr 1500 Class 800 Del from £125 * **SERVICES:** Lift Night porter 250P **NOTES:** Last d 11.30pm
CARDS:

GLASGOW City of Glasgow **Map 11 NS56**

The Premier Collection

★★★❀❀❀ **One Devonshire Gardens**
1 Devonshire Gardens G12 0UX
☎ 0141 339 2001 📠 0141 337 1663
Dir: *M8 junct 17, follow signs for A82, after 1.5m turn left into Hyndland Rd, 1st right, right at mini rdbt, right at end then continue to end*
Three town houses form this highly individual hotel, which stands in a quiet terrace on the west side of the city. Bedrooms each follow an individual and distinctive decorative theme, and offer luxurious comfort, with an impressive array of extras. One house has a stylish drawing room, while there is a cocktail bar and restaurant in another, where diners can enjoy the tempting selection of classic dishes with a modern touch.
ROOMS: 27 en suite (bth/shr) (3 fmly) s £130-£205; d £130-£230 * Off peak **MEALS:** Lunch £19.75-£25 Dinner £33.50-£44.75alc Scottish & French Cuisine V meals Coffee am Tea pm **FACILITIES:** CTV in all bedrooms STV **CONF:** Thtr 40 Class 20 Board 26 **SERVICES:** Night porter 12P **NOTES:** No coaches No smoking in restaurant Last d 10pm **CARDS:**

GLASGOW City of Glasgow **Map 11 NS56**
★★★❀ **The Devonshire Hotel of Glasgow**
5 Devonshire Gardens G12 0UX
Quality Percentage Score: 77%
☎ 0141 339 7878 📠 0141 339 3980

SCOTLAND'S HOTELS OF DISTINCTION

Standing on the corner of an imposing tree-lined Victorian terrace, the Devonshire remains one of the most stylish hotels in the city. The drawing room is the focal point of the day rooms, with all the charm, elegance and comfort expected in such a grand house. An imaginatively prepared Scottish menu is served in the small dining room and there is extensive 24-hour room service. Bedrooms offer designer decor and fabrics to complement the antique pine furnishings.
ROOMS: 14 en suite (bth/shr) (3 fmly) s £115-£145; d £135-£195 * LB Off peak **MEALS:** Lunch £16.50-£25.50 & alc Dinner £16.50-£25.50 & alc Scottish & French Cuisine V meals Coffee am Tea pm **FACILITIES:** CTV in all bedrooms STV Xmas **CONF:** Thtr 50 Class 30 Board 30
SERVICES: Night porter **NOTES:** Last d 9.45pm
CARDS:

New AA Guides for the Millennium are featured on page 24

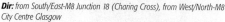

GLASGOW City of Glasgow **Map 11 NS56**
★★★ **Malmaison**
278 West George St G2 4LL
Quality Percentage Score: 72%
☎ 0141 572 1000 Fax 0141 572 1002
Dir: *from South/East-M8 Junction 18 (Charing Cross), from West/North-M8 City Centre Glasgow*
Relax in style in one of Glasgow's most upbeat hotels; the brand may have been replicated in England, but its origins are firmly rooted in Scotland. The highlight of any stay will be the strikingly decorated bedrooms, all equipped with CD players, mini-bars and ISDN telephone lines. Guests who manage to drag themselves away from the rooms can enjoy the all-day Café Mal, which has a Mediterranean feel, or the brasserie.
ROOMS: 72 en suite (bth/shr) (4 fmly) No smoking in 20 bedrooms d £99-£165 * Off peak **MEALS:** Lunch £9.50-£15.95 Dinner £11.50-£14.50 French & Meditteranean Cuisine V meals Coffee am **FACILITIES:** CTV in all bedrooms STV Gym **CONF:** Thtr 35 Class 20 Board 20 Del £145 * **SERVICES:** Lift Night porter **NOTES:** No dogs (ex guide dogs) No coaches Last d 11pm **CARDS:**

G

GLASGOW City of Glasgow **Map 11 NS56**
★★★ **Swallow**
517 Paisley Rd West G51 1RW
Quality Percentage Score: 68%
☎ 0141 427 3146 Fax 0141 427 4059
Dir: *off junc 23 of M8, from S M6/M8 off junct 24 of M8, from W M8*

Just five minutes from the Burrell Collection and ten minutes from the city centre and The Airport, this purpose-built hotel is conveniently situated close to Bellahouston Park and Ibrox and is close to Junction 23 of the M8. The bedrooms offer good levels of comfort and the majority have been refurbished to an attractive standard. The open-plan public areas are comfortable and there are good leisure facilities.
ROOMS: 117 en suite (bth/shr) (11 fmly) No smoking in 63 bedrooms s £90-£99 (incl. bkfst) * LB Off peak **MEALS:** Lunch £10-£12.50 Dinner fr £18.75 & alc Scottish & French Cuisine V meals Coffee am Tea pm **FACILITIES:** CTV in all bedrooms STV Indoor swimming pool (heated) Sauna Solarium Gym Jacuzzi/spa Steam room Xmas **CONF:** Thtr 300 Class 150 Board 30 Del from £100 * **SERVICES:** Lift Night porter 150P **NOTES:** No smoking in restaurant Last d 9.30pm
CARDS:

GLASGOW City of Glasgow **Map 11 NS56**
★★★ ***Holiday Inn***
161 West Nile St G1 2RL
Quality Percentage Score: 66%
☎ 0141 352 8300 Fax 0141 332 7447
Dir: *M8 jnct 16, follow signs for Royal Concert Hall, hotel is opposite*
Purpose built on a corner site close to the Theatre Royal and the Concert Hall, this contemporary hotel features a trendy cafe style French restaurant, a bar area and conservatory. Bedrooms vary in size and include suites. Staff are friendly and attentive. There is a multi-storey park almost opposite.
ROOMS: 113 en suite (bth/shr) (24 fmly) No smoking in 78 bedrooms **MEALS:** French/Mediterranean Cuisine V meals Coffee am Tea pm **FACILITIES:** CTV in all bedrooms STV **CONF:** Thtr 130 Class 80 Board 80 **SERVICES:** Lift **NOTES:** No dogs (ex guide dogs) No smoking area in restaurant Last d 10.15pm **CARDS:**

GLASGOW City of Glasgow **Map 11 NS56**
★★★ ***Jurys Glasgow***
Great Western Rd G12 0XP
Quality Percentage Score: 66%
☎ 0141 334 8161 Fax 0141 334 3846
Dir: *W of city, off A82*
Improvements continue at this popular business and leisure hotel which is situated in the west end beside the A82. Most bedrooms have benefited from refurbishment and plans are in hand to upgrade the remainder to the same standard. Inviting public areas include a choice of contrasting bars, a well equipped leisure centre, conference and banqueting facilities, and an attractive split-level restaurant offering both carte and fixed-price menus as well as the good value carvery. Staff are friendly and willing to please.
ROOMS: 136 en suite (bth/shr) (12 fmly) No smoking in 100 bedrooms **MEALS:** Scottish & European Cuisine V meals Coffee am Tea pm **FACILITIES:** CTV in all bedrooms STV Indoor swimming pool (heated) Sauna Solarium Gym Jacuzzi/spa Whirlpool Wkly live entertainment **CONF:** Thtr 140 Class 80 Board 40 **SERVICES:** Lift Night porter 300P **NOTES:** No dogs (ex guide dogs) No smoking area in restaurant Last d 9.30pm **CARDS:**

GLASGOW City of Glasgow **Map 11 NS56**
★★★ ***Posthouse Glasgow City***
Bothwell St G2 7EN
Quality Percentage Score: 66%
☎ 0141 248 2656 Fax 0141 221 8986
This large, modern city centre hotel, popular for its conferencing facilities, offers two eating outlets in the form of a Traditional Carvery and Jules restaurant, with its range of international dishes. Bedroom styles vary; the smart Millennium rooms offer the highest standards, but all accommodation is very well equipped. Extra services include a concierge and all-day room service. There is limited parking, but extra free parking is offered, courtesy of the hotel, in the nearby NCP.
ROOMS: 247 en suite (bth/shr) (28 fmly) No smoking in 102 bedrooms **MEALS:** International Cuisine V meals Coffee am Tea pm **FACILITIES:** CTV in all bedrooms **CONF:** Thtr 850 Class 450 Board 100 Del from £100 * **SERVICES:** Lift Night porter Air conditioning 40P **NOTES:** No smoking area in restaurant Last d 10.30pm
CARDS:

GLASGOW City of Glasgow **Map 11 NS56**
★★★ **Quality Hotel Glasgow**
99 Gordon St G1 3SF
Quality Percentage Score: 65%
☎ 0141 221 9680 Fax 0141 226 3948
Dir: *exit 19 of M8, left into Argyle St and left into Hope St*
A splendid Victorian railway hotel, forming part of Central Station. It retains much original charm yet has modern facilities. Public rooms are impressive and continue to be upgraded and improved. Bedrooms are well equipped and mostly spacious.

contd.

Guests can eat informally in the Coffee Shop or in the main restaurant.
ROOMS: 222 en suite (bth/shr) (8 fmly) No smoking in 70 bedrooms s £73.25-£81.75; d £88.25-£105.50 * LB Off peak **MEALS:** Lunch £2.95-£15.95alc Dinner fr £14.50 & alc English & Continental Cuisine V meals Coffee am Tea pm **FACILITIES:** CTV in all bedrooms STV Indoor swimming pool (heated) Sauna Solarium Gym Jacuzzi/spa Hair & beauty salon Steamroom Xmas **CONF:** Thtr 600 Class 170 Board 40 **SERVICES:** Lift Night porter **NOTES:** No smoking area in restaurant Last d 9.30pm **CARDS:**

GLASGOW City of Glasgow **Map 11 NS56**
★★★ The Tinto Firs
470 Kilmarnock Rd G43 2BB
Quality Percentage Score: 64%
☎ 0141 637 2353 ▯ 0141 633 1340
Dir: *4m S of Glasgow City Centre on the A77*
This modern, purpose-built hotel is four miles south of the city centre and convenient for the airport and the Burrell Collection. Comfortably furnished public areas include a choice of bars, an attractive restaurant and a smart boardroom. Bedrooms are mostly cosy studio singles which are very well equipped.
ROOMS: 27 en suite (bth/shr) (4 fmly) No smoking in 10 bedrooms s £85; d £94 * LB Off peak **MEALS:** Lunch £9.95-£12.95 Dinner £14.50-£17.95 International Cuisine V meals Coffee am Tea pm **FACILITIES:** CTV in all bedrooms STV Xmas **CONF:** Thtr 150 Class 50 Board 50 Del from £88 * **SERVICES:** Night porter 46P **NOTES:** No smoking area in restaurant Last d 9.30pm
CARDS:

GLASGOW City of Glasgow **Map 11 NS56**
★★★ Kelvin Park Lorne
923 Sauchiehall St G3 7TE
Quality Percentage Score: 63%
☎ 0141 314 9955 ▯ 0141 337 1659

This popular city centre hotel is five minutes walk from the S E C and art galleries, it offers a mixed style of accommodation. Investment is well underway and recently refurbished rooms, although still quite small, are smart and attractive. Larger bedrooms are located in the Apsley Wing, which also houses some useful conference facilities. Guests can either eat informally in the bar, from the room service menu or in the restaurant. There is a small, private car park beneath the hotel.
ROOMS: 100 en suite (bth/shr) (7 fmly) No smoking in 20 bedrooms s £67.50-£85; d £75-£105 * LB Off peak **MEALS:** Bar Lunch £1.95-£8.95alc Dinner £11.95-£14.95 Scottish & Continental Cuisine V meals Coffee am Tea pm **FACILITIES:** CTV in all bedrooms Xmas **CONF:** Thtr 300 Class 100 Board 80 Del from £85 * **SERVICES:** Lift Night porter 40P **NOTES:** No dogs (ex guide dogs) Last d 9.30pm
CARDS:

GLASGOW City of Glasgow **Map 11 NS56**
★★★ Kings Park
Mill St G73 2LX
Quality Percentage Score: 63%
☎ 0141 647 5491 ▯ 0141 613 3022
Dir: *on A730 East Kilbride road*
This hotel is conveniently located in Rutherglen with close proximity to both Glasgow city centre and East Kilbride. The interior has a modern outlook; the bedrooms are suitably equipped and feature comfortable furnishings and fittings. The conference and banqueting suites are particularly impressive.
ROOMS: 26 en suite (bth/shr) s £60-£95; d £70-£100 (incl. bkfst) * Off peak **MEALS:** Bar Lunch £6.75-£8.25 & alc Dinner £17.25 & alc V meals Coffee am Tea pm **FACILITIES:** CTV in all bedrooms Pool table Jacuzzi/spa Xmas **CONF:** Thtr 250 Class 80 Board 50 **SERVICES:** Night porter 150P **NOTES:** No coaches No smoking area in restaurant Last d 9.30pm **CARDS:**

GLASGOW City of Glasgow **Map 11 NS56**
★★★ *Ewington*
Balmoral Ter, 132 Queens Dr, Queens Park G42 8QW
Quality Percentage Score: 62%
☎ 0141 423 1152 ▯ 0141 422 2030
Dir: *M8 junct 20 onto A77, go trough 8 sets of traffic lights, at crossroads the hotel is on 2nd left after crossroads*
Part of a Victorian terrace on the south side opposite Queens Park, this is a stylish town house hotel. Dedicated staff provide excellent service in the public areas which include an inviting foyer lounge and a smart restaurant which is opposite the comfortable cocktail lounge. Bedrooms are available in a rich

contd.

mixture of sizes and styles ranging up to spacious executive rooms.

Ewington, Glasgow

ROOMS: 44 en suite (bth/shr) (1 fmly) No smoking in 6 bedrooms **MEALS:** International Cuisine V meals Coffee am Tea pm **FACILITIES:** CTV in all bedrooms Internet terminal **CONF:** Thtr 70 Class 20 Board 22 **SERVICES:** Lift Night porter 16P **NOTES:** No smoking area in restaurant Last d 9pm **CARDS:**

See advert on page 823

GLASGOW City of Glasgow **Map 11 NS56**
★★★ Carrick
377 Argyle St G2 8LL
Quality Percentage Score: 60%
☎ 0141 248 2355 🖹 0141 221 1014
Dir: *junct 19 M8 bear left onto Argyle St, hotel opposite Cadogan Square*

REGAL

A modern hotel at the west end of one of the city's well known streets. The compact but well equipped bedrooms have all the essential facilities. The restaurant, lounge bar and a number of meeting rooms are on the first floor. Free overnight car parking is available nearby.
ROOMS: 121 en suite (bth/shr) No smoking in 79 bedrooms s £70; d £85 * LB Off peak **MEALS:** Continental Cuisine V meals Coffee am Tea pm **FACILITIES:** CTV in all bedrooms Xmas **CONF:** Thtr 80 Class 40 Board 24 Del from £69 * **SERVICES:** Lift Night porter **NOTES:** No smoking area in restaurant **CARDS:**

GLASGOW City of Glasgow **Map 11 NS56**
⇧ Travel Inn (Glasgow City Centre)
Montrose House, 187 George St G1 1YU
☎ 0870 80000
This modern building offers accommodation in smart, spacious and well equipped bedrooms, all with en-suite bathrooms. Refreshments may be taken at the nearby family restauarant. For details about current prices ring 01582 41 43 41.
ROOMS: 254 en suite (bth/shr) d £44.95 *

GLASGOW City of Glasgow **Map 11 NS56**
⇧ Travel Inn (Glasgow Cambuslang)
Cambuslang
☎ 0141 764 2655 🖹 0141 778 1703
Dir: *on the rdbt at end of the M74, by Cambuslang exit off the A74*
This modern building offers accommodation in smart, spacious and well equipped bedrooms, all with en-suite bathrooms. Refreshments may be taken at the nearby family restaurant. For details about current prices consult the Contents Page under Hotel Groups for the Travel Inn phone number.
ROOMS: 40 en suite (bth/shr) d £39.95 *

GLASGOW City of Glasgow **Map 11 NS56**
⇧ Travel Inn (Glasgow East)
Glasgow Zoo, Hamilton Rd G71 7SA
☎ 0141 773 1133 🖹 0141 771 8354
Dir: *at entrance to Glasgow Zoo alongside junc M73 & M74*
This modern building offers accommodation in smart, spacious and well equipped bedrooms, all with en-suite bathrooms. Refreshments may be taken at the nearby family restaurant. For details about current prices consult the Contents Page under Hotel Groups for the Travel Inn phone number.
ROOMS: 40 en suite (bth/shr) d £39.95 *

GLASGOW City of Glasgow **Map 11 NS56**
⇧ Travelodge
251 Paisley Rd G5 8RA
☎ 0141 420 3882
Dir: *0.5m from city centre just off junc 20 M8 from south/junc 21 M8 from north. Behind Harry Ramsden's*
This modern building offers accommodation in smart, spacious and well equipped bedrooms, all with en-suite bathrooms. Refreshments may be taken at the nearby family restaurant. For details about current prices, consult the Contents Page under Hotel Groups for the Travelodge phone number.
ROOMS: 100 en suite (bth/shr) d £49.95 *

GLASGOW City of Glasgow **Map 11 NS56**
⇧ Travelodge
9 Hill St G3 6PR
☎ 0141 333 1515
This modern building offers accommodation in smart, spacious and well equipped bedrooms, all with en-suite bathrooms. Refreshments may be taken at the nearby family restaurant. For details about current prices, consult the Contents Page under Hotel Groups for the Travelodge phone number.
ROOMS: 93 en suite (bth/shr) d £49.95 *

GLASGOW AIRPORT Renfrewshire **Map 11 NS46**
see also **Howwood**
★★★ Posthouse Glasgow Airport
Abbotsinch PA3 2TR
Quality Percentage Score: 70%
☎ 0141 887 1212 🖹 0141 887 3738
Dir: *from E M8 off at junc 28 follow signs for Hotel; from W M8 off at junc 29 follow airport slip road to Hotel*

Posthouse

This Posthouse is situated opposite the departure hall of the airport, and offers modern accommodation, including smartly

contd.

decorated 'Millennium' bedrooms, as well as good public areas and a comfortable restaurant and bar.
ROOMS: 298 en suite (bth/shr) (9 fmly) No smoking in 158 bedrooms d £89-£109 * LB Off peak **MEALS:** International Cuisine V meals Coffee am Tea pm **FACILITIES:** CTV in all bedrooms Solarium Xmas **CONF:** Thtr 250 Class 120 Board 20 Del from £85 * **SERVICES:** Lift Night porter Air conditioning 60P **NOTES:** No smoking area in restaurant Last d 10.00pm **CARDS:**

GLASGOW AIRPORT Renfrewshire **Map 11 NS46**
★★★ Dalmeny Park Country House
Lochlibo Rd G78 1LG
Quality Percentage Score: 69%
☎ 0141 881 9211 📠 0141 881 9214
(For full entry see Barrhead)

GLASGOW AIRPORT Renfrewshire **Map 11 NS46**
★★★ Glynhill Hotel & Leisure Club
Paisley Rd PA4 8XB
Quality Percentage Score: 68%
☎ 0141 886 5555 & 885 1111 📠 0141 885 2838
Dir: *on M8 towards Glasgow airport,turn off at junct 27,take A741 towards Renfrew cross small rdbt approx 300yds from motorway exit Hotel on right*
The Nicholas family look forward to welcoming guests to their smart hotel. Bedrooms range from spacious executive rooms to smaller standard rooms, and are tastefully appointed with a good range of amenities. The hotel boasts a luxurious leisure complex and extensive conference facilities; and the choice of contrasting bars and restaurants will suit most tastes and pockets.
ROOMS: 125 en suite (bth/shr) (25 fmly) No smoking in 51 bedrooms s £76-£94; d £86-£104 (incl. bkfst) * LB Off peak **MEALS:** Lunch fr £9.95 Dinner fr £15.50 International Cuisine V meals Coffee am Tea pm **FACILITIES:** CTV in all bedrooms STV Indoor swimming pool (heated) Snooker Sauna Solarium Gym Jacuzzi/spa Wkly live entertainment Xmas **CONF:** Thtr 450 Class 240 Board 60 Del from £106 * **SERVICES:** Night porter 230P **NOTES:** No dogs (ex guide dogs) No smoking area in restaurant Last d 10.30pm
CARDS:

GLASGOW AIRPORT Renfrewshire **Map 11 NS46**
★★★ Lynnhurst
Park Rd PA5 8LS
Quality Percentage Score: 67%
☎ 01505 324331 📠 01505 324219
Created from two detached Victorian houses, handy for Glasgow Airport and a popular venue for functions. Bright bedrooms are modern in style with a range of amenities. Public areas include a spacious bar, conservatory lounge, and an attractive panelled dining room with ornate ceiling. Competitively priced dishes are offered on a varied menu.
ROOMS: 21 en suite (bth/shr) (2 fmly) s £53-£57; d £83 (incl. bkfst) * Off peak **MEALS:** Lunch £7.75-£9 Dinner £10.95-£15.50 European Cuisine V meals Coffee am **FACILITIES:** CTV in all bedrooms STV Arrangement with local leisure centre **CONF:** Thtr 160 Class 160 Board 20 Del from £62 * **SERVICES:** 100P **NOTES:** No dogs (ex guide dogs) No smoking area in restaurant Last d 9pm Closed 1-3 Jan
CARDS:

See advert on this page

GLASGOW AIRPORT Renfrewshire **Map 11 NS46**
★★★ Posthouse Glasgow/Erskine
Posthouse
North Barr PA8 6AN
Quality Percentage Score: 65%
☎ 0141 812 0123 📠 0141 812 7642
(For full entry see Erskine)

GLASGOW AIRPORT Renfrewshire **Map 11 NS46**
★★★ Dean Park
91 Glasgow Rd PA4 8YB
Quality Percentage Score: 64%
☎ 0141 304 9955 📠 0141 885 0681
Dir: *3m NE A8 - turn off M8 at junct 26 onto A8 for Renfrew, follow road for 600yds, hotel is on the left*
Most of the bedrooms at this versatile hotel are compact but well equipped; recent re-decoration has enhanced many of them. Public rooms are particularly well appointed, and include the elegant Fountains Restaurant and the comfortable Quills Bar. There is a wide range of conference and banqueting facilities.
ROOMS: 118 en suite (bth/shr) (6 fmly) **MEALS:** International Cuisine V meals Coffee am Tea pm **FACILITIES:** CTV in all bedrooms Snooker Beautician & arrangement with leisure club **CONF:** Thtr 350 Class 150 Board 100 **SERVICES:** Night porter 200P **NOTES:** No smoking area in restaurant Last d 9.45pm **CARDS:**

GLASGOW AIRPORT Renfrewshire **Map 11 NS46**
★★ The Watermill Hotel
Lonend PA1 1SR
Quality Percentage Score: 66%
☎ 0141 889 3201 📠 0141 889 5938
A popular business and tour group hotel, refurbishment and the addition of bedrooms are planned during the currency of this guide. The foyer has been refurbished, new banqueting facilities and an improved bar facility are planned. The spacious

contd.

restaurant with beamed ceiling and stone walls offers an extensive range of dishes from a carte.
ROOMS: 45 en suite (bth/shr) (2 fmly) No smoking in 15 bedrooms s £49.50-£69.50; d £69.50-£89.50 (incl. bkfst) * Off peak
MEALS: Lunch £4.95-£6.95alc Dinner £12-£15alc International Cuisine V meals Coffee am Tea pm **FACILITIES:** CTV in all bedrooms STV Xmas
CONF: Thtr 100 Class 50 Board 30 Del from £69.50 * **SERVICES:** Lift Night porter Air conditioning 50P **NOTES:** No smoking area in restaurant Last d 9.30pm **CARDS:**

GLASGOW AIRPORT Renfrewshire — Map 11 NS46
Travel Inn
Phoenix Retail Park PA1 2BH
☎ 0141 887 4865 📠 0141 887 2799
***Dir:** M8 junct 28A St James Interchange follow A737 signed Irvine, take 1st exit signed Linwood & turn left at 1st rdbt to Phoenix Park*
This modern building offers accommodation in smart, spacious and well equipped bedrooms, all with en-suite bathrooms. Refreshments may be taken at the nearby family restaurant. For details about current prices consult the Contents Page under Hotel Groups for the Travel Inn phone number.
ROOMS: 40 en suite (bth/shr) d £39.95 *

GLASGOW AIRPORT Renfrewshire — Map 11 NS46
Travel Inn (Glasgow Airport)
Whitecart Rd PA3 2TH
☎ 0141 842 1563 📠 0141 842 1570
***Dir:** close to airport terminal follow signs*
This modern building offers accommodation in smart, spacious and well equipped bedrooms, all with en-suite bathrooms. Refreshments may be taken at the nearby family restauarant. For details about current prices consult the Contents Page under Hotel Groups for the Travel Inn phone number.
ROOMS: 81 en suite (bth/shr) d £44.95 *

GLENCOE Highland — Map 14 NN15
★★ *Glencoe*
PA39 4HW
Quality Percentage Score: 66%
☎ 01855 811245 📠 01855 811687
***Dir:** on A82 in Glencoe village, 15m S of Fort William*
A welcoming atmosphere prevails at this long established family-run Highland holiday hotel. Bedrooms are pleasantly decorated with good appointments and functional furniture. The tastefully appointed restaurant overlooks the loch, and at peak times the bar and lounge can get very busy due to the popularity of the bar food.
ROOMS: 15 en suite (bth/shr) (4 fmly) **MEALS:** International Cuisine V meals Coffee am Tea pm **FACILITIES:** CTV in all bedrooms STV Games room **CONF:** Thtr 100 **SERVICES:** 30P **NOTES:** No smoking in restaurant Last d 9.30pm **CARDS:**

GLENEAGLES See **Auchterarder**

GLENFARG Perth & Kinross — Map 11 NO11
★★ Glenfarg
Main St PH2 9NU
Quality Percentage Score: 64%
☎ 01577 830241 📠 01577 830665
***Dir:** travelling S on M90, off at junc 9, turn left, Hotel 5m; travelling N on M90, off at junc 8, second left, Hotel 2m*
Situated in the centre of the village, this hotel has a relaxed, informal atmosphere which particularly appeals to visiting golfers. Bedrooms come in a variety of sizes and for families, the outside adventure playground proves a big hit with the children. The restaurant offerd enjoyable food, but the popular bar is well worth considering as an alternative.
ROOMS: 16 rms (15 bth/shr) (4 fmly) No smoking in 8 bedrooms s £38.50; d £64 (incl. bkfst) * LB Off peak **MEALS:** Lunch £6-£19alc Dinner £12-£25alc French, Scottish, & Italian Cuisine V meals Coffee am Tea pm **FACILITIES:** CTV in all bedrooms STV Pool table Wkly live entertainment Xmas **CONF:** Thtr 60 Board 30 **SERVICES:** 20P
NOTES: No smoking in restaurant Last d 9pm
CARDS:

GLENFINNAN Highland — Map 14 NM98
★★ The Princes House
PH37 4LT
Quality Percentage Score: 76%
☎ 01397 722246 📠 01397 722307
***Dir:** 15m W of Fort William on A830, 0.5m on right past monument*

Genuine hospitality and fine food are part of the appeal of this charming hotel, which stands beside the 'Road To The Isles' and close to the historic site where Bonnie Prince Charlie raised the Jacobite standard in 1745. With its light natural wood, the Pretender's Bar is a cosy place to unwind and enjoy a casual meal whilst Flora's Restaurant offers an interesting two or four course menu within a more formal environment. Attractive fabrics have been used to good effect in the well equipped bedrooms which range from spacious Chieftain rooms to smaller Clansman rooms.
ROOMS: 9 en suite (bth/shr) (1 fmly) No smoking in all bedrooms s £60-£70; d £116-£154 (incl. bkfst & dinner) * LB Off peak
MEALS: Bar Lunch £11-£20alc Dinner £21-£29 V meals Coffee am Tea pm **FACILITIES:** CTV in all bedrooms Fishing Mountain bike hire
CONF: Thtr 40 Class 20 **SERVICES:** 20P **NOTES:** No coaches No children 5yrs No smoking in restaurant Last d 9pm Closed Dec-Feb RS Feb, Mar, Nov & Dec **CARDS:**
See advert under FORT WILLIAM

GLENLUCE Dumfries & Galloway — Map 10 NX15
★★ Kelvin House Hotel
53 Main St DG8 0PP
Quality Percentage Score: 66%
☎ 01581 300303 📠 01581 300303
***Dir:** midway between Newton Stewart & Stranraer, just off the A75.*
This small privately run hotel is in the centre of a village in unspoilt countryside. The bedrooms are bright and spacious and there is a comfortable residents' lounge. Meals are served either in the popular bar or the separate restaurant overlooking the garden.
ROOMS: 6 rms (5 bth/shr) (3 fmly) No smoking in 3 bedrooms s £25-£30; d £22.50-£26.50 (incl. bkfst) * LB Off peak **MEALS:** Lunch £15-£15 & alc High tea £6.95-£10 Dinner £15-£15 & alc Coffee am Tea pm
FACILITIES: CTV in all bedrooms ch fac Xmas **CONF:** Thtr 50 Class 20 Board 20 Del from £51 * **NOTES:** No smoking area in restaurant Last d 9.30pm **CARDS:**

contd.

GLENROTHES Fife — Map 11 NO20

★★★ *Balgeddie House*

Balgeddie Way KY6 3ET
Quality Percentage Score: 62%
☎ 01592 742511 Fax 01592 621702
Dir: *from A911 E of Leslie follow the signs to the hotel*

Situated to the north west of the town and surrounded by a modern housing development, yet set in its own landscaped grounds, this comfortable, family-run hotel offers a relaxed style of service and is especially popular with business visitors. Bedrooms come in a variety of styles and sizes, some are really spacious. Public areas include a lounge, cocktail bar and restaurant.

ROOMS: 19 en suite (bth/shr) (1 fmly) No smoking in 3 bedrooms **MEALS:** Scottish, French & Italian Cuisine V meals Coffee am Tea pm **FACILITIES:** CTV in all bedrooms STV Pool table Croquet lawn Putting green Wkly live entertainment **CONF:** Thtr 40 Class 25 Board 30 Del from £90 * **SERVICES:** Night porter 100P **NOTES:** No dogs (ex guide dogs) Last d 9pm **CARDS:**

GLENROTHES Fife — Map 11 NO20

Travel Inn

Beaufort Dr, Bankhead Roundabout KY7 4UJ
☎ 01592 773473 Fax 01592 773453
Dir: *from M90 junct 3 take A92 to Glenrothes. First rdbt is Bankhead*

This modern building offers accommodation in smart, spacious and well equipped bedrooms, all with en-suite bathrooms. Refreshments may be taken at the nearby family restaurant. For details about current prices consult the Contents Page under Hotel Groups for the Travel Inn phone number.

ROOMS: 40 en suite (bth/shr) d £39.95 *

GLENSHEE (SPITTAL OF) Perth & Kinross — Map 15 NO16

★★ *Dalmunzie House*

PH10 7QG
Quality Percentage Score: 68%
☎ 01250 885224 Fax 01250 885225
Dir: *turn left off A93 to Spittal of Glenshee, hotel entrance 400yds on left*

Walkers, skiers, sports enthusiasts and visitors enjoy staying at this turreted house in a 6,500 acre mountain estate. Bedrooms, some larger than others, are individually furnished and enjoy fine views, there are comfortable lounges. Carefully prepared meals offer local produce whenever possible.

ROOMS: 18 rms (16 bth/shr) s £52-£59; d £82-£100 (incl. bkfst) * LB Off peak **MEALS:** Bar Lunch fr £3alc Dinner £20-£24 & alc V meals Coffee am Tea pm **FACILITIES:** CTV in 16 bedrooms Golf 9 Tennis (hard) Fishing Croquet lawn Clay pigeon shooting Deer stalking Mountain bikes Pony trekking Xmas **CONF:** Thtr 20 Class 20 Board 20 Del from £75 * **SERVICES:** Lift 32P **NOTES:** No coaches No smoking in restaurant Last d 8.30pm Closed end Nov-28 Dec
CARDS:

GRANGEMOUTH Falkirk — Map 11 NS98

★★★ Grange Manor

Glensburgh FK3 8XJ
Quality Percentage Score: 63%
☎ 01324 474836 Fax 01324 665861
Dir: *travelling E; off M9 at junc 6, Hotel 200m to right. Travelling W; off M9 at junc 5, A905 for 2m*

This family-run hotel with convenient access to the M9, will benefit from a new extension providing further bedrooms and a function room. The restaurant continues to produce rosette food at both lunch and dinner, whilst Wallace's, an informal bar/brasserie housed in a separate building, provides an alternative.

ROOMS: 7 en suite (bth/shr) 30 annexe en suite (bth/shr) (6 fmly) No smoking in 16 bedrooms s £65-£85; d £98-£118 (incl. bkfst) * LB Off peak **MEALS:** Lunch £13.20-£16.70 Dinner £22.85-£27.85 & alc Scottish & French Cuisine V meals Coffee am Tea pm **FACILITIES:** CTV in all bedrooms STV Xmas **CONF:** Thtr 150 Class 68 Board 40 Del from £90.85 * **SERVICES:** 154P **NOTES:** No dogs (ex guide dogs) No smoking area in restaurant Last d 9pm **CARDS:**

G

GRANTOWN-ON-SPEY Highland — Map 14 NJ02

★★ Culdearn House

Woodlands Ter PH26 3JU
Quality Percentage Score: 77%
☎ 01479 872106 Fax 01479 873641
Dir: *enter Grantown on the A95 from SW and turn at 30mph sign*

THE CIRCLE
Selected Individual Hotels
GREAT BRITAIN

Genuine hospitality and good food are part of the appeal at this small hotel. Bedrooms, with pretty colour schemes, offer mixed modern furnishings and a good range of amenities. There is no bar, but guests can relax in the charming lounge and enjoy some of the ever increasing range of malt whiskies.

ROOMS: 9 en suite (bth/shr) No smoking in 3 bedrooms s £45-£65; d £90-£130 (incl. bkfst & dinner) * LB Off peak **FACILITIES:** CTV in all bedrooms **SERVICES:** 12P **NOTES:** No dogs (ex guide dogs) No coaches No children 10yrs No smoking in restaurant Closed 30 Oct-28 Feb **CARDS:**

GREENOCK Inverclyde — Map 10 NS27

Travel Inn

James Watt Dock PA15 2AJ
☎ 01475 730911 Fax 01475 730890
Dir: *from A8 at Langbank, turn right off A8 at 3rd rdbt, next to McDonalds*

This modern building offers accommodation in smart, spacious and well equipped bedrooms, all with en-suite bathrooms. Refreshments may be taken at the nearby family restaurant. For details about current prices consult the Contents Page under Hotel Groups for the Travel Inn phone number.

ROOMS: 40 en suite (bth/shr) d £39.95 *

GRETNA (WITH GRETNA GREEN) — Map 11 NY36

Dumfries & Galloway

★★★ *Garden House*

Sarkfoot Rd DG16 5EP
Quality Percentage Score: 66%
☎ 01461 337621 Fax 01461 337692
Dir: *just off junct 45 on the M6 at Gretna*

Situated close to the border, this modern hotel is only a couple of miles from the famous blacksmith's shop. The lounge and dining room are open plan, and there is a cosy bar off the lounge

contd.

area. Bedrooms are spacious and there are several honeymoon suites available.

Garden House, Gretna Green

ROOMS: 21 en suite (bth/shr) (2 fmly) **MEALS:** Continental Cuisine V meals Coffee am Tea pm **FACILITIES:** CTV in all bedrooms STV Indoor swimming pool (heated) Jacuzzi/spa **CONF:** Thtr 100 Class 80 Board 40 **SERVICES:** 105P **NOTES:** No dogs (ex guide dogs) Last d 9pm **CARDS:**

See advert on opposite page

GRETNA (WITH GRETNA GREEN) Map 11 NY36
Dumfries & Galloway

★★ Gretna Chase
DG16 5JB
Quality Percentage Score: 70%
☎ 01461 337517 Fax 01461 337766
Dir: *off A74 onto B7076, left at top of slip road, hotel 400 yards on right*
Seemingly situated in 'no man's land', between the signs for Scotland and England, this hotel is a popular venue for wedding parties. Bedrooms are well equipped and full of character. The spacious dining room can accommodate dinner parties and wedding breakfasts, the lounge bar is also popular.
ROOMS: 9 en suite (bth/shr) (4 fmly) No smoking in 3 bedrooms s £55-£70; d £75-£120 (incl. bkfst) * Off peak **MEALS:** Lunch £9.50-£22alc Dinner £9.50-£22alc English & French Cuisine V meals Coffee am **FACILITIES:** CTV in all bedrooms Jacuzzi/spa **CONF:** Thtr 50 Class 30 Board 20 **SERVICES:** 40P **NOTES:** No dogs (ex guide dogs) Last d 10.30pm **CARDS:**

GRETNA (WITH GRETNA GREEN) Map 11 NY36
Dumfries & Galloway

★★ Solway Lodge
Annan Rd DG16 5DN
Quality Percentage Score: 68%
☎ 01461 338266 Fax 01461 337791
Dir: *A74(M), take Gretna/Longtown exit, turn left at top of road past Welcome to Scotland sign, BP petrol stn turn left for town centre 250 yds on right*
Close to the blacksmith's shop, this friendly family run hotel offers a choice of accommodation. There are two honeymoon suites in the main house, and the chalet block rooms are ideal for overnight stops. A range of home-made meals is offered in the restaurant and lounge bar.
ROOMS: 3 en suite (bth/shr) 7 annexe en suite (bth/shr) s £39.50-£50; d £55-£80 (incl. bkfst) * Off peak **MEALS:** Bar Lunch £2.50-£14 Dinner £12-£19alc V meals Coffee am Tea pm **FACILITIES:** CTV in all bedrooms **SERVICES:** 25P **NOTES:** No coaches No smoking in restaurant Last d 8.45pm Closed 25 & 26 Dec RS 10 Oct-Mar
CARDS:

GRETNA (WITH GRETNA GREEN) Map 11 NY36
Dumfries & Galloway

Welcome Lodge
Welcome Break - Gretna Green, A74M Trunk Rd
DG16 5HQ
☎ 01461 337566 Fax 01461 337823
Dir: *situated at the Welcome Break service area Gretna Green on A74 - Accessible from both Northbound & Southbound carriageway*
This modern building offers accommodation in smart, spacious and well equipped bedrooms, suitable for families and businessmen, and all with en-suite bathrooms. Refreshments may be taken at the nearby family restaurant. For details of current prices, consult the Contents Page under Hotel Groups for the Welcome Break phone number.
ROOMS: 64 en suite (bth/shr) d fr £45 *

GULLANE East Lothian Map 12 NT48

The Premier Collection

★★★ Greywalls
Muirfield EH31 2EG
☎ 01620 842144 Fax 01620 842241
Dir: *A198, hotel is signposted at E end of village*
Designed by Lutyens, and with gardens created by Gertrude Jekyll, Greywalls overlooks the famous Muirfield Golf Course. Public areas include a library with a log fire and grand piano. At dinner a simple cooking style allows top quality ingredients to shine through. Bedrooms are furnished in period style.
ROOMS: 17 en suite (bth/shr) 5 annexe en suite (bth/shr) s £100-£188; d £170-£200 (incl. bkfst) LB Off peak **MEALS:** Lunch £15-£20 Dinner fr £35 Coffee am **FACILITIES:** CTV in all bedrooms STV Tennis (hard & grass) Croquet lawn Putting green **CONF:** Thtr 30 Class 20 Board 20 Del from £140 * **SERVICES:** Night porter 40P **NOTES:** No coaches No smoking in restaurant Last d 9.15pm Closed Nov-Mar **CARDS:**

HALKIRK Highland Map 15 ND15

★★ Ulbster Arms
Bridge St KW12 6XY
Quality Percentage Score: 63%
☎ 01847 831206 & 831641 Fax 01847 831206
Dir: *A9 to Thurso from Perth, 3m after village of Spittal turn Left*
Next to the River Thurso, this long-established hotel is particularly popular with its sporting clientele. Public areas include an attractive dining room, a quiet lounge and a lively lounge bar, which is popular for meals. Bedrooms vary in size

contd.

and style and all have the expected facilities. The chalet rooms at the rear have their own entrances.
ROOMS: 10 en suite (bth/shr) 16 annexe en suite (bth) s £37-£43; d £61-£76 (incl. bkfst) * Off peak **MEALS:** Bar Lunch £2.50-£9.95 Dinner fr £21.50 V meals Coffee am Tea pm **FACILITIES:** CTV in all bedrooms Fishing Wkly live entertainment **SERVICES:** 36P **NOTES:** Last d 8.45pm **CARDS:**

HAMILTON South Lanarkshire **Map 11 NS75**
see also **Bothwell**

Holiday Inn Express
Strathclyde Country Park ML1 3RB
☎ 01698 858585 📠 01698 852375
Dir: *junct 5 off M74 follow signs for Strathclyde Country park*
This modern building offers accommodation in smart, spacious and well equipped bedrooms, all with en-suite bathrooms. Refreshments may be taken at the informal restaurant. For details about current prices, consult the Contents Page under Hotel Groups for the Holiday Inn Express phone number.
ROOMS: 120 en suite (shr) **CONF:** Thtr 30 Class 10 Board 15

HAMILTON MOTORWAY SERVICE AREA (M74) South Lanarkshire **Map 11 NS75**

Roadchef Lodge
Hamilton Motorway Service Area, M74 Northbound ML3 6JW
☎ 01698 891904 📠 01698 891682
Dir: *M74, 1m N of junc 6*
This modern building offers accommodation in smart, spacious and well equipped bedrooms, all with en-suite bathrooms. Refreshments may be taken at the nearby family restaurant. For details about current prices, consult the Contents Page under Hotel Groups for the Roadchef phone number.
ROOMS: 36 en suite (bth/shr) d fr £47.50 * **CONF:** Thtr 30 Board 16

HARLOSH See Skye, Isle of

HAWICK Scottish Borders **Map 12 NT51**

★★ ***Kirklands***
West Stewart Place TD9 8BH
Quality Percentage Score: 69%
☎ 01450 372263 📠 01450 370404
Dir: *0.5m N from Hawick High St, 200yds W of A7*
This fine Victorian house and long-established hotel lies in gardens in a quiet residential area of the town. Bedrooms are comfortable and extremely well equipped, with even more spacious ones in an adjoining mansion, which also houses a snooker room and two lounges. The hotel has a cosy lounge bar featuring a collection of toby jugs, and a popular restaurant, both offering a good choice of freshly cooked dishes.
ROOMS: 5 en suite (bth/shr) 4 annexe en suite (bth/shr) **MEALS:** International Cuisine V meals Coffee am **FACILITIES:** CTV in all bedrooms Snooker Pool table ch fac **CONF:** Thtr 20 Board 12 **SERVICES:** 20P **NOTES:** No smoking area in restaurant Last d 9pm **CARDS:**

HAWICK Scottish Borders **Map 12 NT51**

★★ **Elm House**
17 North Bridge St TD9 9BD
Quality Percentage Score: 62%
☎ 01450 372866 📠 01450 374715
Dir: *on A7 in centre of Hawick. N 200yds, on the right past the Horse Monument*
Situated on the main road through the town, this family-run hotel offers good value accommodation and food in a relaxed

contd.

and informal atmosphere. Bedrooms are a good size - those in the main house are particularly large - and some are contained in a chalet extension in the rear courtyard. Meals are served in either the bar or restaurant.
ROOMS: 7 en suite (bth/shr) 8 annexe en suite (shr) (3 fmly) s £30; d £40-£44 (incl. bkfst) * LB Off peak **MEALS:** Bar Lunch £6.90-£8 Dinner £11 & alc European Cuisine V meals Coffee am Tea pm **FACILITIES:** CTV in all bedrooms **CONF:** Board 20 **SERVICES:** 13P **NOTES:** No smoking in restaurant Last d 9.30pm
CARDS:

HELENSBURGH Argyll & Bute — Map 10 NS28
★★★ Rosslea Hall Country House
Ferry Rd G84 8NF
Quality Percentage Score: 57%
☎ 01436 439955 01436 820897
Dir: *on A814, opposite church*
This early Victorian mansion stands in its own grounds by the shore of Gareloch and gives some fine views of the River Clyde. The comfortable bar provides an informal eating alternative to the main restaurant where there is a choice of menus. Versatile meeting and function rooms are available.
ROOMS: 29 en suite (bth/shr) 5 annexe en suite (bth/shr) (2 fmly) No smoking in 5 bedrooms s £65-£70; d £80-£90 (incl. bkfst) * LB Off peak **MEALS:** Bar Lunch £9-£13.50alc High tea £5-£9 Dinner £13.50-£28.85alc Scottish, Italian, Chinese & German Cuisine V meals Coffee am Tea pm **FACILITIES:** CTV in all bedrooms STV Pool table Xmas **CONF:** Thtr 100 Class 40 Board 50 Del £114 * **SERVICES:** Night porter 60P **NOTES:** No smoking in restaurant Last d 9.15pm
CARDS:

HOWWOOD Renfrewshire — Map 10 NS36
★★★ *Bowfield Hotel & Country Club*
PA9 1DB
Quality Percentage Score: 66%
☎ 01505 705225 01505 705230
Dir: *M8, A737 for 6m, left onto B787, right after 2m, follow road for 1m to hotel*
A former textile mill, carefully converted and extended to create this popular hotel, a convenient stop-over for travellers using Glasgow Airport. Extensive leisure facilities are a major attraction, public areas have beamed ceilings, brick and white painted walls, and welcoming open fires. Bedrooms are in their own wing and offer good modern comforts and facilities.
ROOMS: 23 en suite (bth/shr) (3 fmly) **MEALS:** Scottish & French Cuisine V meals Coffee am Tea pm **FACILITIES:** CTV in all bedrooms Indoor swimming pool (heated) Squash Snooker Sauna Solarium Gym Pool table Jacuzzi/spa Health & beauty studio Wkly live entertainment **CONF:** Thtr 80 Class 60 Board 20 **SERVICES:** 100P **NOTES:** No dogs (ex guide dogs) No coaches No smoking in restaurant Last d 10pm
CARDS:

See advert on opposite page

HUMBIE East Lothian — Map 12 NT46
★★★ The Johnstounburn House
EH36 5PL
Quality Percentage Score: 63%
☎ 01875 833696 01875 833626
PEEL HOTELS
Dir: *A68, B6368, 1.5m S of Humbie village is the hotel*
Surrounded by acres of gardens and the rolling farmland of the Lammermuir Hills, this 17th-century country house provides friendly and relaxed service in a peaceful atmosphere. Bedrooms, some of which are in a converted coach house five minutes walk through the gardens, are furnished in keeping with the style of the house. Public areas have open fires, fine wood panelling and stone stairs.
ROOMS: 11 rms (10 bth/shr) 9 annexe en suite (bth/shr) (5 fmly) s £115; d £150 (incl. bkfst) * LB Off peak **MEALS:** Lunch £14-£18 Dinner fr £30 V meals Coffee am Tea pm **FACILITIES:** CTV in all bedrooms STV Fishing Croquet lawn Clay pigeon shooting All terrain vehicleOff rd driving Xmas **CONF:** Thtr 50 Class 24 Board 30 Del from £101 * **SERVICES:** 100P **NOTES:** No smoking in restaurant Last d 9pm
CARDS:

HUNTLY Aberdeenshire — Map 15 NJ53
★★★ Castle
AB54 4SH
Best Western
Quality Percentage Score: 62%
☎ 01466 792696 01466 792641
Dir: *from Aberdeen turn into Huntly from A96 at the rdbt & follow signs for Huntly Castle. From Inverness take B9022 Portsoy Rd & follow signs for hotel*

This impressive 18th-century stone-built house stands in extensive grounds close to the ruins of the original castle, and remains a popular base for sporting enthusiasts and holidaymakers alike. Public areas, where the atmosphere is relaxed and welcoming, include a comfortably traditional lounge, a well stocked bar, and elegant dining room. Bedrooms come in mixed sizes and styles but all are well equipped.
ROOMS: 19 en suite (bth/shr) (4 fmly) s £50-£58; d £71-£85 (incl. bkfst) * LB Off peak **MEALS:** Lunch £12.50-£25alc Dinner £12.50-£25alc Scottish & French Cuisine V meals Coffee am Tea pm **FACILITIES:** CTV in all bedrooms STV Fishing Xmas **CONF:** Thtr 60 Class 40 Board 36 Del £80 * **SERVICES:** 50P **NOTES:** No smoking in restaurant Last d 9pm **CARDS:**

See advert on opposite page

INVERGARRY Highland — Map 14 NH30
★★★ Glengarry Castle
PH35 4HW
SCOTLAND'S HOTELS OF DISTINCTION
Quality Percentage Score: 68%
☎ 01809 501254 01809 501207
Dir: *on A82 beside Loch Oich, 0.5m from A82/A87 junction*
Situated beside Loch Oich, this impressive Victorian baronial mansion is surrounded by 50 acres of park and woodland. Run by the MacCallum family for over 40 years, the hotel has been refurbished and there is a choice of smart standard rooms or more spacious superior ones, some of which have four-poster or half-tester beds. Public areas include a panelled reception

contd.

Symbols and Abbreviations are listed and explained on pages 4 and 5

hall and two comfortable lounges. The dining room offers a traditional menu.

ROOMS: 26 en suite (bth/shr) (2 fmly) No smoking in 6 bedrooms s fr £54; d £88-£136 (incl. bkfst) Off peak **MEALS:** Sunday Lunch £9.95 Dinner £25-£28 Scottish, English & Continental Cuisine V meals Coffee am Tea pm **FACILITIES:** CTV in all bedrooms Tennis (hard) Fishing **SERVICES:** 32P **NOTES:** No coaches No smoking in restaurant Last d 8.30pm Closed early Nov-late Mar **CARDS:**

See advert on this page

INVERKEITHING Fife — Map 11 NT18

★★★ Queensferry Lodge

St Margaret's Head, North Queensferry
KY11 1HP
Quality Percentage Score: 63%
☎ 01383 410000 Fax 01383 419708
Dir: *from M90 junct 1 left onto A921, right thru Inverkeithing, at rdbt head under m'way - hotel on left*

Fine views of both the Forth bridges are a feature of the public areas and some of the bedrooms. The hotel is on the north side of the Firth and offers good facilities for business users, expecially in the newly built bedroom wing. The restaurant offers a good range of dishes and at weekends is supplemented by a coffee shop.

ROOMS: 77 en suite (bth/shr) (4 fmly) No smoking in 51 bedrooms s £85; d £95 * LB Off peak **MEALS:** Lunch £4.85-£12.95 High tea fr £7.95 Dinner £4.85-£12.95 International Cuisine V meals Coffee am Tea pm **FACILITIES:** CTV in all bedrooms STV Xmas **CONF:** Thtr 200 Class 70 Board 40 Del £101 * **SERVICES:** Lift Night porter 180P **NOTES:** No smoking area in restaurant Last d 9.45pm
CARDS:

INVERMORISTON Highland — Map 14 NH41

★★ Glenmoriston Arms Hotel & Restaurant

IV3 6YA
Quality Percentage Score: 74%
☎ 01320 351206 Fax 01320 351308
Dir: *at the junct of A82/A877*

A warm welcome awaits at this friendly family-run hotel close to Loch Ness. Comfortable, well equipped bedrooms include a four-poster room with a spa bath. There is an attractive bar, and the refurbished restaurant offers a range of Taste of Scotland dishes.

ROOMS: 8 en suite (bth/shr) s £55-£70; d £70-£90 (incl. bkfst) * LB Off peak **MEALS:** Lunch fr £5alc Dinner £24-£30 International Cuisine V meals Coffee am Tea pm **FACILITIES:** CTV in all bedrooms Fishing Stalking Shooting Xmas **SERVICES:** 24P **NOTES:** No coaches No smoking in restaurant Last d 9pm Closed early Jan-mid Feb
CARDS:

INVERNESS Highland — Map 14 NH64

see also **Kirkhill**

★★★★ Culloden House

Culloden IV2 7BZ
Quality Percentage Score: 71%
☎ 01463 790461 Fax 01463 792181
Dir: *take A96 from town and turn right for Culloden. After 1m, turn left at White Church after second traffic lights*

A fine Adam-style Georgian mansion in 40 acres of grounds. Bonnie Prince Charlie left from here for the battle of Culloden. Now under American ownership, considerably altered and upgraded. Day rooms with chandeliers, marble fireplaces and ornate plasterwork include an inviting drawing room, clubby bar and the refined Adam dining room. Chef Michael Simpson prepares a fine daily changing 5 course menu. Bedrooms range from opulent period suites and master rooms, to contemporary refurbished rooms. No-smoking suites are in a separate mansion house in the grounds, suitable for small seminars.

ROOMS: 23 en suite (bth/shr) 5 annexe en suite (bth/shr) (1 fmly) No smoking in 8 bedrooms s £135-£145; d £190-£270 (incl. bkfst) * LB Off peak **MEALS:** Lunch £11.50-£18.50 & alc High tea £7.50-£9.50 & alc Dinner £35 Scottish & French Cuisine V meals Coffee am Tea pm **FACILITIES:** CTV in all bedrooms STV Tennis (hard) Sauna Croquet lawn Boules Badminton Wkly live entertainment Xmas **CONF:** Thtr 70 Class 40 Board 30 Del from £110 * **SERVICES:** Night porter 50P **NOTES:** No coaches No smoking in restaurant Last d 9pm
CARDS:

See advert on opposite page

INVERNESS Highland — Map 14 NH64

★★★★ Swallow Kingsmills

Culcabock Rd IV2 3LP
Quality Percentage Score: 69%
☎ 01463 237166 Fax 01463 225208
Dir: *from A9 S, exit Culduthell/Kingsmills 5th exit at rdbt, follow rd 0.5m, over mini-rdbt pass golf club, hotel on left after traffic lights*

Set in four acres of gardens on the south side of town, this long established business and tourist hotel provides a warm welcome to the Highland capital. Public areas include a choice of relaxing lounges, a well stocked bar, and a bright and spacious conservatory. The refurbished Inglis restaurant specialises in dishes using fine Scottish ingredients. The spacious bedrooms are well equipped, and range from impressive executive rooms to standard rooms, several of which overlook the gardens.

ROOMS: 76 en suite (bth/shr) 6 annexe en suite (bth/shr) (11 fmly) No smoking in 29 bedrooms s fr £110; d fr £155 (incl. bkfst) * LB Off peak **MEALS:** Lunch fr £14 Dinner fr £24 & alc International Cuisine V meals Coffee am Tea pm **FACILITIES:** CTV in all bedrooms STV Indoor swimming pool (heated) Sauna Solarium Gym Putting green Jacuzzi/spa Hair & beauty salon Steam room Xmas **CONF:** Thtr 100 Class 28 Board 40 Del from £105 * **SERVICES:** Lift Night porter 120P **NOTES:** No smoking in restaurant Last d 9.30pm
CARDS:

contd.

INVERNESS Highland — Map 14 NH64

★★★ Craigmonie

9 Annfield Rd IV2 3HX
Quality Percentage Score: 75%
☎ 01463 231649 Fax 01463 233720
Dir: *off A9/A96 follow signs Hilton, Culcabock pass golf course second road on right*

Bedrooms at this welcoming hotel range from the attractive poolside suites with spa bath and balcony, to the variable-sized standard rooms which provide a high level of comfort and a wide range of amenities. Public areas include a lounge and club-styled panelled bar with conservatory extension. Guests can dine in Chardonnay which offers a wide range of seafood specialities, or in the informal Poolside Brasserie. There is also a leisure club.

ROOMS: 35 en suite (bth/shr) (3 fmly) No smoking in 10 bedrooms s £72-£85.50; d £90-£110 (incl. bkfst) * LB Off peak **MEALS:** Lunch £10.50-£12.50 Dinner £22-£24 & alc Scottish & French Cuisine V meals Coffee am Tea pm **FACILITIES:** CTV in all bedrooms STV Indoor swimming pool (heated) Sauna Solarium Gym Jacuzzi/spa **CONF:** Thtr 180 Class 70 Board 50 Del from £110 * **SERVICES:** Lift Night porter 60P **NOTES:** No smoking in restaurant Last d 9.30pm
CARDS:

INVERNESS Highland — Map 14 NH64

★★★ Glenmoriston Town House Hotel

20 Ness Bank IV2 4SF
Quality Percentage Score: 71%
☎ 01463 223777 Fax 01463 712378
Dir: *located on riverside opposite theatre, 5 minutes from town centre*

Situated on the north bank of the River Ness overlooking the cathedral and Eden Court Theatre, this popular hotel has benefited from substantial refurbishment. Bedrooms, with pretty colour schemes and smart modern furnishings have particular appeal for the business guest, as they include modem points. Public areas are nicely presented with the stylish restaurant being the focal point. Here the kitchen team offer a tempting range of mostly Italian specialities from the carte and fixed price menus.

ROOMS: 15 en suite (bth/shr) (1 fmly) s £65-£85; d £85-£135 (incl. bkfst) * LB Off peak **MEALS:** Lunch £12.95-£20 & alc Dinner £24.95 & alc Italian Cuisine V meals Coffee am Tea pm **FACILITIES:** CTV in all bedrooms STV Xmas **CONF:** Thtr 50 Class 50 Board 30 Del from £100 * **SERVICES:** Night porter 40P **NOTES:** No dogs (ex guide dogs) No coaches Last d 9pm **CARDS:**

For Useful Information and Important Telephone Number Changes turn to page 25

INVERNESS Highland **Map 14 NH64**

★★★ Bunchrew House

Bunchrew IV3 8TA

Quality Percentage Score: 70%

☎ 01463 234917 🖷 01463 710620

Dir: *leave Inverness heading W on the A862 along the shore of the Beauly Firth. Hotel on right of road 2m after crossing canal*

A lovely 17th-century mansion set in 20 acres of wooded grounds on the shore of the Beauly Firth. Public areas have many original features, a relaxing atmosphere, natural fires and lots of reading material. The fixed priced dinner menu provides a good choice of enjoyable dishes featuring local produce, carefully cooked by chef Walter Walker.

ROOMS: 11 en suite (bth/shr) (2 fmly) s £70-£105; d £90-£140 (incl. bkfst) * LB Off peak **MEALS:** Lunch £18-£23 & alc Dinner £14-£28alc Scottish & French Cuisine V meals Coffee am Tea pm **FACILITIES:** CTV in all bedrooms Fishing Xmas **CONF:** Thtr 80 Class 30 Board 30 Del from £110 * **SERVICES:** 40P **NOTES:** No smoking in restaurant Last d 8.45pm **CARDS:**

See advert on page 833

INVERNESS Highland **Map 14 NH64**

★★★ Lochardil House

Stratherrick Rd IV2 4LF

Quality Percentage Score: 67%

☎ 01463 235995 🖷 01463 713394

Dir: *follow Island Bank Road for 1m, fork left into Drummond Crescent, into Stratherrick Road, 0.5m hotel on left*

A castellated Victorian house with attractive gardens and a friendly atmosphere, found in a residential area of the town. Bedrooms are comfortable and modern. Adjacent to the cocktail bar is the popular conservatory restaurant which offers a wide range of both light and substantial dishes at lunch and dinner. The new function suite is a well utilised feature.

ROOMS: 12 en suite (bth/shr) s £68-£75; d £98-£108 (incl. bkfst) * LB Off peak **MEALS:** Scottish & French Cuisine V meals Coffee am Tea pm **FACILITIES:** CTV in all bedrooms STV **CONF:** Thtr 120 Class 100 Board 60 Del from £105 **SERVICES:** Night porter 123P **NOTES:** No dogs (ex guide dogs) No coaches Last d 9pm

CARDS:

INVERNESS Highland **Map 14 NH64**

★★★ Loch Ness House

Glenurquhart Rd IV3 6JL

Quality Percentage Score: 65%

☎ 01463 231248 🖷 01463 239327

Dir: *1.5m from town centre, overlooking Tomnahurich Bridge on canal. From A9 turn L at Longman rdbt, follow signs for A82 for 2.5miles*

Close to the Caledonian Canal, this popular, family-run hotel provides welcoming public areas and modern bedrooms which vary in size. The restaurant features Scottish fare and fresh seafood, while lighter meals are served in the bars.

ROOMS: 22 en suite (bth/shr) (3 fmly) No smoking in 6 bedrooms s £60-£85; d £98-£110 (incl. bkfst) * LB Off peak **MEALS:** Bar Lunch £5-£15 Scottish & French Cuisine V meals Coffee am Tea pm **FACILITIES:** CTV in all bedrooms STV Wkly live entertainment Xmas **CONF:** Thtr 150 Class 60 Board 40 Del from £75 * **SERVICES:** 60P **NOTES:** No smoking in restaurant

CARDS:

INVERNESS Highland **Map 14 NH64**

★★★ Palace Milton

8 Ness Walk IV3 5NE

Quality Percentage Score: 64%

☎ 01463 223243 🖷 01463 236865

Dir: *town centre on banks of River Ness*

Beside the river with views of the castle, this well run hotel remains a popular base for visiting tour groups. Public areas enjoy views of the river and include a foyer lounge, well stocked bar and large dining room. Most bedrooms have been upgraded and the new leisure centre is popular.

ROOMS: 88 en suite (bth/shr) (12 fmly) No smoking in 6 bedrooms s £75; d £95 (incl. bkfst) * LB Off peak **MEALS:** Bar Lunch fr £5 High tea fr £6.95 Dinner fr £12.50 European Cuisine V meals Coffee am Tea pm **FACILITIES:** CTV in all bedrooms STV Indoor swimming pool (heated) Sauna Solarium Gym Jacuzzi/spa Beauty salon Wkly live entertainment Xmas **CONF:** Thtr 100 Class 40 Board 40 Del from £69 * **SERVICES:** Lift Night porter 20P **NOTES:** No smoking in restaurant Last d 9.30pm **CARDS:**

INVERNESS Highland **Map 14 NH64**

★★★ Thistle Inverness

Millburn Rd IV2 3TR

Quality Percentage Score: 64%

☎ 01463 239666 🖷 01463 711145

Dir: *from A9 head N, turn off at A96 and follow signs to town centre (B865) Millburn Rd*

Ongoing improvements continue at this modern business and tourist hotel situated at the east end of town. Bright modern public areas include an impressive foyer containing a semi open-plan bar and lounge area. The popular Laird's Restaurant offers a tempting range of Scottish and International fare.

ROOMS: 118 en suite (bth/shr) (11 fmly) No smoking in 24 bedrooms **MEALS:** International Cuisine V meals Coffee am Tea pm **FACILITIES:** CTV in all bedrooms STV **CONF:** Thtr 230 Class 72 Board 70 **SERVICES:** Lift Night porter 150P **NOTES:** Last d 9.30pm RS 1 Jan **CARDS:**

INVERNESS Highland **Map 14 NH64**

★★ Windsor Town House

22 Ness Bank IV2 4SF

Quality Percentage Score: 62%

☎ 01463 715535 🖷 01463 713262

Dir: *follow signs Dores/Holm Mills-rd B862, hotel below castle along riverside*

Situated close to the castle, this friendly "off centre" Town House hotel has a beautiful location beside the River Ness and opposite the Eden Court Theatre. It is only a few minutes' walk from the town centre. All the bedrooms are non-smoking and have been furnished with pine and pretty fabrics and all the expected amenities. The conservatory dining room offers a short and simple menu and a good breakfast buffet, while the cosy lounge is a quiet place to relax.

ROOMS: 18 en suite (bth/shr) (5 fmly) No smoking in 16 bedrooms s £55-£95; d £75-£120 (incl. bkfst) * LB Off peak **MEALS:** Dinner £15-£20 & alc V meals **FACILITIES:** CTV in all bedrooms STV **CONF:** Class 30 **SERVICES:** 14P **NOTES:** No dogs (ex guide dogs) No coaches No smoking in restaurant Last d 7.30pm Closed 23 Dec-4 Jan RS 1 Nov-15 May **CARDS:**

INVERNESS Highland **Map 14 NH64**

★★ Smithton

Smithton IV1 2NL

Quality Percentage Score: 59%

☎ 01463 791999 🖷 01463 794559

Dir: *A96, 2m turn first right, 2m to Smithton Hotel*

This purpose-built hotel is in the centre of the small village of Smithton, about three miles east of Inverness. Bedrooms are

contd.

attractively furnished in pine and offer good amenities, while both the lounge and public bars are popular with the locals.
ROOMS: 16 en suite (bth/shr) (2 fmly) s £35-£38.50; d £57-£59 (incl. bkfst) * Off peak **MEALS:** Lunch £1.35-£9.95 & alc High tea £1.35-£9.95 & alc Dinner £9.95 & alc Coffee am Tea pm **FACILITIES:** CTV in all bedrooms STV Snooker Pool table Wkly live entertainment
SERVICES: 60P **NOTES:** No dogs (ex guide dogs) Last d 8pm
CARDS:

INVERNESS Highland — Map 14 NH64
Travel Inn
Millburn Rd IV2 3QX
☎ 01463 712010 01463 717826
Dir: *on A9 junc with A96, follow B865 towards town centre, hotel 100yds past next rdbt*
This modern building offers accommodation in smart, spacious and well equipped bedrooms, all with en-suite bathrooms. Refreshments may be taken at the nearby family restaurant. For details about current prices consult the Contents Page under Hotel Groups for the Travel Inn phone number.
ROOMS: 40 en suite (bth/shr) d £39.95 *

INVERNESS Highland — Map 14 NH64
Travel Inn (Inverness East)
Beechwood Business Park IV2 3BW
☎ 01463 232727 01463 231553
Dir: *on A9, 2m E of Inverness, opposite Raigmore Hospital*
This modern building offers accommodation in smart, spacious and well equipped bedrooms, all with en-suite bathrooms. Refreshments may be taken at the nearby family restaurant. For details about current prices consult the Contents Page under Hotel Groups for the Travel Inn phone number.
ROOMS: 40 en suite (bth/shr) d £39.95 *

INVERURIE Aberdeenshire — Map 15 NJ72
★★★★ *Thainstone House Hotel and Country Club*
AB51 5NT
Quality Percentage Score: 69%
☎ 01467 621643 01467 625084
Dir: *A96 from Aberdeen, through Kintore, entrance to hotel at first rdbt*

Situated close to the airport and set in lovely grounds, Thainstone House is a palatial Scottish mansion which combines modern amenities with classical elegance. As well as the leisure centre, the elegant public rooms include inviting lounges, bars and a Georgian-style restaurant. Bedrooms vary in size and style, have bold colour schemes and period furniture.
ROOMS: 48 en suite (bth/shr) (3 fmly) No smoking in 32 bedrooms
MEALS: V meals Coffee am Tea pm **FACILITIES:** CTV in all bedrooms STV Indoor swimming pool (heated) Snooker Gym Jacuzzi/spa Archery Shooting Grass Karts Quad Bikes **CONF:** Thtr 300 Class 100 Board 40
SERVICES: Lift Night porter 100P **NOTES:** No dogs (ex guide dogs) No smoking in restaurant Last d 9.30pm **CARDS:**

INVERURIE Aberdeenshire — Map 15 NJ72
★★★★ *Pittodrie House*
Chapel of Garioch, Pitcaple AB51 5HS
Quality Percentage Score: 66%
☎ 01467 681444 01467 681648
Dir: *A96, Chapel of Garioch turn off*
This impressive turreted baronial mansion is set in a 2000 acre estate in the shadow of Bennachie. Reception rooms, decorated with family paintings and antiques, are unashamedly opulent and consist of a bar, two dining rooms and a drawing room. Well proportioned bedrooms are furnished in period style.
ROOMS: 27 en suite (bth/shr) (7 fmly) **MEALS:** V meals Coffee am Tea pm **FACILITIES:** CTV in all bedrooms STV Squash Snooker Croquet lawn Off road driving Clay pigeon shooting Archery Quads Grass karting
CONF: Thtr 130 Class 60 Board 50 **SERVICES:** Night porter 150P
NOTES: No coaches No smoking in restaurant Last d 8.45pm
CARDS:

INVERURIE Aberdeenshire — Map 15 NJ72
★★★ Strathburn
Burghmuir Dr AB51 4GY
Quality Percentage Score: 69%
☎ 01467 624422 01467 625133
Dir: *at Blackhall rbt into Blackhall Rd for 100yds then into Burghmuir Drive*
A comfortable modern hotel on the west side of town. Bedrooms of varying sizes are well maintained and offer comfortable modern appointments with a good range of amenities. Attractive public areas include a bright foyer lounge, a popular bar and a tastefully appointed restaurant.
ROOMS: 25 en suite (bth/shr) (2 fmly) No smoking in 18 bedrooms s £65-£80; d £80-£95 (incl. bkfst) * LB Off peak **MEALS:** Sunday Lunch £11.25-£18.25alc Dinner £19.75-£27.75 & alc V meals Coffee am Tea pm
FACILITIES: CTV in all bedrooms STV **CONF:** Thtr 30 Class 24 Board 16 Del from £92.75 * **SERVICES:** 40P **NOTES:** No dogs (ex guide dogs) No coaches No smoking in restaurant Last d 9pm
CARDS:

IRVINE North Ayrshire — Map 10 NS33
★★★ *Hospitality Inn Irvine*
46 Annick Rd KA11 4LD
Quality Percentage Score: 67%
☎ 01294 274272 01294 277287
Dir: *follow signs to Irvine/Irvine central, at end dual carriageway take 2nd exit down to rdbt, 2nd exit follow rd to rdbt turn right hotel on left*
This spacious, purpose-built, business hotel offers smart executive bedrooms, or larger deluxe rooms, some leading out onto the leisure pool. Public areas include two eating options, the main restaurant, plus a summer-like bistro set around the pool, which has a South Sea theme.
ROOMS: 127 en suite (bth/shr) (44 fmly) No smoking in 16 bedrooms
MEALS: Scottish, French & International Cuisine V meals Coffee am Tea pm **FACILITIES:** CTV in all bedrooms STV Indoor swimming pool (heated) Golf 9 Pool table Putting green Jacuzzi/spa Wkly live entertainment **CONF:** Thtr 200 Class 120 Board 120 **SERVICES:** Night porter 250P **NOTES:** No smoking area in restaurant Last d 10.00pm
CARDS:

ISLAY, ISLE OF Argyll & Bute **Map 10**

BOWMORE **Map 10 NR35**

★★ *Lochside*
19 Shore St PA43 7LB
Quality Percentage Score: 59%
☎ 01496 810244 📠 01496 810390
Dir: *on A846, 100yds from main village square on shore side of road*
The unassuming main street frontage gives no clue to the stunning outlook over Loch Indaal that guests can enjoy from the rear of this family-run business and tourist hotel. Bedrooms, already well equipped, are being steadily upgraded. Seafood is a speciality of the popular and varied menu, served in the small dining room and the bar, where a very extensive selection of malt whisky is on display.
ROOMS: 8 en suite (bth/shr) (1 fmly) **MEALS:** International Cuisine V meals Coffee am Tea pm **FACILITIES:** CTV in all bedrooms Pool table **NOTES:** Last d 9pm **CARDS:**

BRIDGEND **Map 10 NR36**

★★ Bridgend
PA44 7PQ
Quality Percentage Score: 69%
☎ 01496 810212 📠 01496 810960
A warm welcome is assured at this Victorian hotel, positioned in the heart of the island. Bedrooms vary in size and are comfortably furnished in mixed styles, with a wide range of amenities. There is a quiet first floor lounge and a choice of bars, the attractive dining room features island produce on the dinner menu.
ROOMS: 10 rms (5 bth 4 shr) (3 fmly) s £42-£45.50; d £82-£90 (incl. bkfst) * LB Off peak **MEALS:** Lunch £12.50-£20 Dinner £18.50-£22 V meals Coffee am Tea pm **FACILITIES:** CTV in all bedrooms Fishing Bowls **SERVICES:** 30P **NOTES:** No smoking in restaurant Last d 9pm **CARDS:**

PORT ASKAIG **Map 10 NR46**

★★ Port Askaig
PA46 7RD
Quality Percentage Score: 63%
☎ 01496 840245 📠 01496 840295
Dir: *at Ferry Terminal*
Situated right beside the ferry terminal, overlooking the Sound of Islay towards Jura, this welcoming hotel combines traditional hospitality with modern amenities. Relaxing public areas include a snug bar, a dining room and a quiet first-floor lounge. Bedrooms are modern in design and come in a variety of sizes. A range of home-cooked food is served in the bar or the cosy dining room.
ROOMS: 8 rms (5 bth/shr) (1 fmly) s £35-£40; d £72 (incl. bkfst) * LB Off peak **MEALS:** Sunday Lunch £9-£15 High tea £9-£15 Dinner £15.75-£17.85 & alc V meals Coffee am Tea pm **FACILITIES:** CTV in all bedrooms **SERVICES:** 21P **NOTES:** No coaches No children 5yrs No smoking in restaurant Last d 8.30pm

ISLE OF

Placenames incorporating the words 'Isle' or 'Isle of' will be found under the actual name, eg Isle of Arran is under Arran, Isle of.

ISLE ORNSAY See Skye, Isle of

JEDBURGH Scottish Borders **Map 12 NT62**

★★★ Jedforest Hotel
Camptown TD8 6PJ
Quality Percentage Score: 72%
☎ 01835 840222 📠 01835 840226
Dir: *3m S of Jedburgh off A68*

A fully restored country house hotel in 35 acres of grounds. Bardoulets Restaurant is the focal point, with well prepared, cooked and presented meals served at lunch and dinner in the formal dining room. The bedrooms are all pleasantly furnished and equipped.
ROOMS: 8 en suite (bth/shr) (1 fmly) No smoking in all bedrooms s £47.50-£70; d £65-£105 (incl. bkfst) * LB Off peak **MEALS:** Lunch £9.50-£12.50 Dinner £14.50-£18.50 & alc French Cuisine V meals **FACILITIES:** CTV in all bedrooms Fishing Xmas **CONF:** Class 40 Board 25 **SERVICES:** 20P **NOTES:** No dogs No coaches No smoking in restaurant Last d 9pm **CARDS:**

JOHN O'GROATS See **Halkirk** and **Lybster**

KELSO Scottish Borders **Map 12 NT73**

★★★ The Roxburghe Hotel & Golf Course
Heiton TD5 8JZ
Quality Percentage Score: 73%
☎ 01573 450331 📠 01573 450611
Dir: *from A68 Jedburgh join A698 to Heiton, 3m SW of Kelso*
Formerly called Sunlaws House, the name change reflects ownership by the Duke of Roxburghe. Jacobean in style, this impressive mansion close to the River Teviot is surrounded by park and woodland. The area is popular for fishing and shooting, and of course, for golf. Bedrooms are in the grand style, several have four-posters and two have open fires. Reception rooms include a lobby, drawing room, conservatory and restaurant.
ROOMS: 16 en suite (bth/shr) 6 annexe en suite (bth/shr) (3 fmly) No smoking in 1 bedroom s £105-£110; d £145-£165 (incl. bkfst) * LB Off peak **MEALS:** Lunch £13-£17alc Dinner £21-£38.50alc V meals Coffee am Tea pm **FACILITIES:** CTV in all bedrooms STV Golf 18 Tennis (hard) Fishing Croquet lawn Putting green Shooting Health & Beauty Salon Xmas **CONF:** Thtr 40 Class 20 Board 20 Del from £105 * **SERVICES:** Night porter 50P **NOTES:** No smoking in restaurant Last d 9.30pm Closed 23-29 Dec **CARDS:**

KELSO Scottish Borders **Map 12 NT73**

★★★ Ednam House
Bridge St TD5 7HT
Quality Percentage Score: 67%
☎ 01573 224168 📠 01573 226319
This fine Georgian mansion overlooks the River Tweed, so proves popular with salmon fishermen - rods, and sometimes the days' catch, can be found in the lobby! The hotel has been in the Brooks family since 1928 and the present generation and their

contd.

loyal staff provide traditional standards of service to their guests. Bedrooms range from standard to grand, and there are several lounges, two bars and a dining room offering honest British cooking.
ROOMS: 32 en suite (bth/shr) (2 fmly) No smoking in 3 bedrooms s £74-£76; d £108-£143 (incl. bkfst & dinner) * LB Off peak **MEALS:** Sunday Lunch £12 & alc High tea £8-£11alc Dinner £11.50-£22 V meals Coffee am Tea pm **FACILITIES:** CTV in all bedrooms Croquet lawn Free access to Abbey Fitness Centre **CONF:** Thtr 250 Board 200 Del from £62.50 * **SERVICES:** Night porter 100P **NOTES:** Last d 9pm Closed 25 Dec-10 Jan **CARDS:**

KELSO Scottish Borders **Map 12 NT73**

★★★ Cross Keys

36-37 The Square TD5 7HL
Quality Percentage Score: 63%
☎ 01573 223303 01573 225792
Dir: *on approaching Kelso, follow signs for Town centre. The hotel is located in main square*
Originally a coaching inn rebuilt in the Georgian era, this family-run hotel overlooks Kelso's fine cobbled square and its window boxes provide a mass of colour in summer. Bedrooms offer a choice of superior or standard, whilst the spacious lounge bar and restaurant, are supplemented by the Oak Room bar/bistro.
ROOMS: 28 en suite (bth/shr) (5 fmly) No smoking in 8 bedrooms s £46.90-£60.50; d £63.80-£95.80 (incl. bkfst) LB Off peak **MEALS:** Dinner £18.90 & alc Scottish & Continental Cuisine V meals Coffee am Tea pm **FACILITIES:** CTV in all bedrooms STV Xmas **CONF:** Thtr 280 Class 220 Board 70 **SERVICES:** Lift Night porter Air conditioning **NOTES:** Last d 9pm **CARDS:**

KENTALLEN Highland **Map 14 NN05**

★★ *Holly Tree*

Kentallen Pier PA38 4BY
Quality Percentage Score: 73%
☎ 01631 740292 01631 740345
Dir: *3m S of Ballachulish on A828*
Glorious views over Loch Linnhe to the hills of Morvern beyond are enjoyed from this welcoming family run hotel which has been created by sympathetic extension and conversion of the former village railway station. All of the attractive modern bedrooms overlook the loch, and two ground floor rooms are suitable for disabled guests. Both the lounge and restaurant enjoy loch views and the extensive carte offers a tempting range of delicious seafood and game specialities. There is also a small cosy bar which was once the station tea-room.
ROOMS: 10 en suite (bth/shr) **MEALS:** International Cuisine V meals Coffee am Tea pm **FACILITIES:** CTV in all bedrooms Fishing **CONF:** Class 20 **SERVICES:** 30P **NOTES:** No smoking in restaurant Last d 9.30pm Closed 1 Nov-31 Jan **CARDS:**

KILCHRENAN Argyll & Bute **Map 10 NN02**

★★★ Taychreggan

PA35 1HQ
Quality Percentage Score: 77%
☎ 01866 833211 & 833366 01866 833244
Dir: *W from Glasgow A82 to Crianlarich, W from Crianlarich on A85 to Taynuilt, S for 7m on B845 to Kilchrenan and Taychreggan*
A former drovers inn by the shores of loch Awe enjoying superb views. Set around a cobbled courtyard, the house is reminiscent of a villa. Bedrooms and public rooms come in traditional and modern styles. Food is taken seriously here, but above all, Taychreggan is noted for its friendly service and relaxing atmosphere.
ROOMS: 19 en suite (bth/shr) No smoking in 3 bedrooms s £97.50-£97.50; d £160-£250 (incl. bkfst & dinner) * LB Off peak **MEALS:** Bar Lunch £7.50-£17 Dinner £30-£30 International Cuisine V meals Coffee am Tea pm **FACILITIES:** Fishing Snooker Xmas **CONF:** Class 15 Board 20 Del from £155 * **SERVICES:** 40P **NOTES:** No coaches No children 14yrs No smoking in restaurant Last d 8.45pm **CARDS:**

KILDRUMMY Aberdeenshire **Map 15 NJ41**

The Premier Collection

★★★ Kildrummy Castle

AB33 8RA
☎ 019755 71288 019755 71345
Dir: *off A97, Huntly/Ballater road, 35 miles W of Aberdeen*
In the heart of the Grampian countryside, this splendid Victorian mansion overlooks the ruins of a 13th-century castle. There are some splendid reception rooms. Bedrooms are individually decorated, some furnished with antiques. Cooking is traditional in style.
ROOMS: 16 en suite (bth/shr) (4 fmly) s £80-£85; d £130-£160 (incl. bkfst) * LB Off peak **MEALS:** Lunch £16.50-£20 & alc Dinner £30-£31 & alc Scottish & French Cuisine V meals Coffee am Tea pm **FACILITIES:** CTV in all bedrooms Fishing Snooker Xmas **SERVICES:** 30P **NOTES:** No coaches No smoking in restaurant Last d 9pm Closed 4-31 Jan **CARDS:**

KILFINAN Argyll & Bute **Map 10 NR97**

★★ Kilfinan

PA21 2EP
Quality Percentage Score: 78%
☎ 01700 821201 01700 821205
Dir: *on B8000 east coast of Loch Fyne, between Otter Ferry and Tignabruaich*
Guests return time and again to this delightful small hotel which has been skilfully renovated to preserve its character. Bedrooms are comfortably furnished and offer a good range of amenities, while reception rooms, with open fires in season, have an inviting atmosphere. The focal point of a stay is the excellent cooking of Swiss-trained chef/patron Rolf Mueller. Dinner is served in an attractive candle-lit restaurant, and there is also an informal bistro/bar.
ROOMS: 11 en suite (bth/shr) (1 fmly) s fr £49; d £78-£98 (incl. bkfst) * Off peak **MEALS:** Bar Lunch £10-£20alc Dinner £28 Coffee am Tea pm **FACILITIES:** CTV in all bedrooms Fishing Private beach Xmas **SERVICES:** 40P **NOTES:** No dogs (ex guide dogs) No coaches No children 12yrs No smoking in restaurant Last d 8.45pm Closed Feb **CARDS:**

K

KILLIECHRONAN See Mull, Isle of

KILLIECRANKIE Perth & Kinross — Map 14 NN96

★★ Killiecrankie

PH16 5LG
Quality Percentage Score: 74%
☎ 01796 473220 📠 01796 472451
Dir: *turn off A9 at Killiecrankie, hotel is 3m along B8079 on right*
Many guests return time and time again to the Anderson family's delightful holiday hotel, set in extensive grounds close to the historic Pass of Killiecrankie. The bright airy bedrooms are equipped with a wide range of amenities and most are comfortably furnished in pine. Inviting public areas include a cosy, well stocked bar which has a lovely sun lounge adjacent which caters for the bar food operation. A more serious approach to food is taken in the elegant dining room where new chef Mark Easton relies on quality ingredients to produce his innovative Scottish fare.
ROOMS: 10 en suite (bth/shr) (1 fmly) No smoking in 1 bedroom s £78.50-£84; d £157-£168 (incl. bkfst & dinner) * LB Off peak
MEALS: Bar Lunch £2.50-£20alc Dinner £31 V meals Coffee am
FACILITIES: CTV in all bedrooms Croquet lawn Putting green Xmas
SERVICES: 30P **NOTES:** No coaches No children 5yrs No smoking in restaurant Last d 8.30pm Closed 3 Jan-4 Feb & 10 days early Dec
CARDS:

KILLIN Stirling — Map 11 NN53

★★★ Dall Lodge Country House

Main St FK21 8TN
Quality Percentage Score: 64%
☎ 01567 820217 📠 01567 820726
Dir: *from M9 at Stirling turn left A84-Crianlarich, 3m after Lochearnhead turn right onto A827-Killin*

A warm welcome is provided to all at this family-run hotel, situated beside the main road at the north end of the village. Bedrooms, including one suitable for a disabled guest, are smartly decorated and offer mixed modern furnishings. There is a dining room and attractive conservatory lounge which contains a dispense bar.
ROOMS: 10 en suite (bth/shr) (2 fmly) s £42.50-£49.50; d £65-£79 (incl. bkfst) * LB Off peak **MEALS:** Lunch £5.50-£15.50alc Dinner £23.50 Scottish, French & Oriental Cuisine V meals Coffee am **FACILITIES:** CTV in all bedrooms Tennis (grass) ch fac **CONF:** Thtr 20 Class 16 Board 10
SERVICES: 20P **NOTES:** No coaches No smoking in restaurant Last d 8.30pm Closed Nov-Feb **CARDS:**

See advert on opposite page

KILMARNOCK East Ayrshire — Map 10 NS43

Travel Inn

The Moorfield, Moorfield Roundabout, Annadale KA2 0BE
☎ 01563 570534 📠 01563 570536
Dir: *W of Kilmarnock, on A71 at Moorfield rdbt*
This modern building offers accommodation in smart, spacious and well equipped bedrooms, all with en-suite bathrooms. Refreshments may be taken at the nearby family restaurant. For details about current prices consult the Contents Page under Hotel Groups for the Travel Inn phone number.
ROOMS: 40 en suite (bth/shr) d £39.95 *

KILMARNOCK East Ayrshire — Map 10 NS43

Travelodge

Kilmarnock By Pass KA1 5LQ
☎ 01563 573810 📠 01563 573810
Dir: *at Bellfield Interchange just off A77*
This modern building offers accommodation in smart, spacious and well equipped bedrooms, all with en-suite bathrooms. Refreshments may be taken at the nearby family restaurant. For details about current prices, consult the Contents Page under Hotel Groups for the Travelodge phone number.
ROOMS: 40 en suite (bth/shr) d £45.95 *

KILWINNING North Ayrshire — Map 10 NS34

★★★ Montgreenan Mansion House

Montgreenan Estate KA13 7QZ
Quality Percentage Score: 74%
☎ 01294 557733 📠 01294 850397
Dir: *4m N of Irvine on A736*
Set in 48 acres of parkland and woods, this 19th-century mansion offers a peaceful atmosphere. Gracious day rooms retain many original features such as ornate ceilings and marble fireplaces and include a splendid drawing room, library and a club-style bar. The restaurant offers a five-course, fixed-price menu, and a small carte. Bedrooms are well equipped and come in a variety of sizes.
ROOMS: 21 en suite (bth/shr) s £60-£80; d £80-£165 (incl. bkfst) * LB Off peak **MEALS:** Lunch £9.95-£13.75 & alc High tea fr £6.50 & alc Dinner fr £25.80 & alc V meals Coffee am Tea pm **FACILITIES:** CTV in all bedrooms STV Golf 5 Tennis (hard) Snooker Croquet lawn Jacuzzi/spa Clay pigeon shooting Xmas **CONF:** Thtr 110 Class 60 Board 60 Del from £95 * **SERVICES:** Lift Night porter 50P **NOTES:** No coaches No smoking in restaurant Last d 9.30pm
CARDS:

KINCARDINE Fife — Map 11 NS98

Travel Inn

Bowtrees Farm FK2 8PJ
This modern building offers accommodation in smart, spacious and well equipped bedrooms, all with en-suite bathrooms. Refreshments may be taken at the nearby family restaurant. For details about current prices consult the Contents Page under Hotel Groups for the Travel Inn phone number.
d £39.95 *

KINCLAVEN Perth & Kinross — Map 11 NO13

★★★ Ballathie House

PH1 4QN
Quality Percentage Score: 80%
☎ 01250 883268 📠 01250 883396
Dir: *from A9 2m north of Perth, B9099 through Stanley & signposted or off A93 at Beech Hedge follow signs for Ballathie 2.5m*
Forming part of a 1,500 acre estate by the banks of the River Tay, Ballathie is an impressive Scottish mansion. Much of the

contd.

original charm has been retained in the day rooms. There is a bar and an elegant restaurant. Bedrooms range in standard, though all feature fine antique furnishings.
ROOMS: 27 en suite (bth/shr) (2 fmly) s £70-£85; d £140-£210 (incl. bkfst) LB Off peak **MEALS:** Lunch £18.50 & alc Dinner £29.90-£33 V meals Coffee am Tea pm **FACILITIES:** CTV in all bedrooms STV Tennis (hard) Fishing Croquet lawn Putting green Xmas **CONF:** Thtr 50 Class 20 Board 26 **SERVICES:** 50P **NOTES:** No coaches No smoking in restaurant Last d 9pm **CARDS:**

KINGUSSIE Highland — Map 14 NH70

The Premier Collection

★★❀❀❀ The Cross

Tweed Mill Brae, Ardbroilach Rd PH21 1TC
☎ 01540 661166 Fax 01540 661080
Dir: *from traffic lights in centre of Kingussie, travel uphill along Ardbroilach Rd for 300mtrs, turn left into Tweed Mill Brae*
A former tweed mill, this charming hotel provides high standards of comfort. Bedrooms combine contemporary fittings with traditional furnishings. There is an attractive lounge with ample reading material. A five-course dinner menu and impressive wine list are offered in the stone walled dining room.
ROOMS: 9 en suite (bth/shr) No smoking in all bedrooms s £115; d £190 (incl. bkfst & dinner) * LB Off peak **MEALS:** Dinner £35 **FACILITIES:** CTV in all bedrooms Xmas **SERVICES:** 12P **NOTES:** No dogs (ex guide dogs) No coaches No children 12yrs No smoking in restaurant Last d 9pm Closed 1-26 Dec & 8 Jan-28 Feb RS Tuesdays **CARDS:**

KINGUSSIE Highland — Map 14 NH70

★★❀ The Scot House

Newtonmore Rd PH21 1HE
Quality Percentage Score: 74%
☎ 01540 661351 Fax 01540 661111
Dir: *from A9 trunk road, take Kingussie exit, hotel is approx 0.50m at S end of village main street*
An immaculately maintained Highland hotel. Bedrooms are smartly presented with comfortable modern furnishings and amenities. Inviting public areas are decorated to a high standard, facilities include a well stocked bar and inviting lounge. The restaurant provides wholesome Scottish fare on carte and fixed price menus.
ROOMS: 9 en suite (bth/shr) (1 fmly) s fr £39; d fr £65 (incl. bkfst) * LB Off peak **MEALS:** Lunch fr £12.50 Dinner fr £19.50 & alc V meals Coffee am **FACILITIES:** CTV in all bedrooms Xmas **SERVICES:** 30P **NOTES:** No coaches No smoking in restaurant Last d 8.45pm Closed 6-31 Jan **CARDS:**

See advert on this page

KINGUSSIE Highland — Map 14 NH70

★★ Osprey

Ruthven Rd PH21 1EN

Quality Percentage Score: 73%

☎ 01540 661510 01540 661510

Dir: *S end of Kingussie High St*

A charming small hotel overlooking Memorial Gardens. The short fixed price menu offers a tempting range of Taste of Scotland dishes, carefully prepared from quality ingredients. Bedrooms, with pretty decor and attractive co-ordinated fabrics, are comfortably furnished in traditional style. A tastefully appointed dining room and delightful small lounges are available.

ROOMS: 8 en suite (bth/shr) No smoking in 6 bedrooms s £50-£55; d £90-£102 (incl. bkfst & dinner) LB Off peak **MEALS:** Dinner £22 English & Scottish Cuisine Coffee am Tea pm **FACILITIES:** CTV in all bedrooms **NOTES:** No coaches No smoking in restaurant Last d 7.30pm **CARDS:**

KINLOCHBERVIE Highland — Map 14 NC25

★★★ Kinlochbervie

IV27 4RP

Quality Percentage Score: 61%

☎ 01971 521275 01971 521438

Dir: *turn off A838 onto B801, through village, turn right at junct above harbour, hotel is 250mtrs on left*

This modern holiday and sporting hotel enjoys a lovely outlook over the fishing harbour. Bedrooms range from well-proportioned premier rooms to standard rooms with practical fitted furnishings. Public areas include a small lounge and timber-lined lounge bar, as well as the popular public bar.

ROOMS: 14 en suite (bth/shr) (5 fmly) s £45-£65; d £70-£110 * LB Off peak **MEALS:** Bar Lunch £1.75-£4.95alc Dinner £20 European Cuisine V meals Coffee am Tea pm **FACILITIES:** CTV in all bedrooms Fishing Pool table **SERVICES:** 28P **NOTES:** No smoking in restaurant Last d 8.30pm Closed 23 Dec-4 Jan RS Nov-Mar **CARDS:**

See advert on opposite page

KINNESSWOOD Perth & Kinross — Map 11 NO10

★★ Lomond Country Inn

THE CIRCLE Selected Individual Hotels GREAT BRITAIN

KY13 9HN

Quality Percentage Score: 66%

☎ 01592 840253 01592 840693

Dir: *M90 junct 5, follow signs for Glenrothes then Scotlandwell, Kinnesswood next village*

A welcoming small country hotel which looks out over Loch Leven. Though variable in size, bedrooms in both the main building and adjacent annexe are modern in style and offer a good range of amenities. Public areas include a cosy well stocked bar, a small sitting room, and an attractive dining room with an emphasis on freshly prepared Scottish fare.

ROOMS: 4 en suite (bth/shr) 8 annexe en suite (bth/shr) (2 fmly) s £40-£48; d £60-£65 (incl. bkfst) * LB Off peak **MEALS:** Lunch £5-£10 & alc High tea £6.50-£8.50alc Dinner £10-£15 & alc Scottish & International Cuisine V meals Coffee am Tea pm **FACILITIES:** CTV in all bedrooms Xmas **SERVICES:** 50P **NOTES:** No smoking in restaurant Last d 9pm **CARDS:**

KINROSS Perth & Kinross — Map 11 NO10

★★★ Green

2 The Muirs KY13 8AS

Quality Percentage Score: 72%

☎ 01577 863467 01577 863180

Dir: *(M90 junct 6 follow signs for Kinross, turn onto A922, the hotel is situated on this road*

With two golf courses, a curling rink, tennis and squash courts, and a well equipped leisure centre, this former coaching inn has been substantially upgraded to appeal to the tastes of the 21st century. Built around a garden courtyard, the spacious, comfortable bedrooms are decorated in pleasing colours. Bars, lounge, restaurant and shop all have an inviting atmosphere.

ROOMS: 47 en suite (bth/shr) (4 fmly) s £75-£100; d £130-£155 (incl. bkfst) * LB Off peak **MEALS:** Bar Lunch £8.25-£15alc High tea £8.95-£14alc Dinner £25-£30 Scottish & French Cuisine V meals Coffee am Tea pm **FACILITIES:** CTV in all bedrooms STV Indoor swimming pool (heated) Golf 36 Fishing Squash Sauna Solarium Gym Pool table Croquet lawn Putting green Curling in season Xmas **CONF:** Thtr 140 Class 100 Board 60 Del from £100 * **SERVICES:** Night porter 60P **NOTES:** Last d 9.30pm **CARDS:**

See advert on opposite page

KINROSS Perth & Kinross — Map 11 NO10

★★★ Windlestrae Hotel Business & Leisure Centre

REGAL

Windlestrae Hotel, The Muirs KY13 8AS

Quality Percentage Score: 71%

☎ 01577 863217 01577 864733

Dir: *leave M90 junct 6 turn E into Kinross, stop at mini rdbt turn left in approx 350yds Windlestrae on right*

The swimming pool, leisure centre, and conference facilities are among the attractions at this friendly hotel. Situated off the main road on the north side of town, Windlestrae is close to a number of Scotland's main tourist attractions. Bedrooms are nicely

contd.

Symbols and Abbreviations are listed and explained on pages 4 and 5

presented and offer good amenities while public areas include a split-level bar, spacious foyer lounge and an attractive restaurant.

ROOMS: 45 en suite (bth/shr) (5 fmly) No smoking in 15 bedrooms s £80-£100; d £100-£120 * LB Off peak **MEALS:** Lunch £11.95-£13.95 High tea £6.50-£8.50 Dinner fr £21.50 International Cuisine V meals Coffee am Tea pm **FACILITIES:** CTV in all bedrooms STV Indoor swimming pool (heated) Snooker Sauna Solarium Gym Jacuzzi/spa Beautician Steam room Toning tables Xmas **CONF:** Thtr 250 Class 100 Board 80 Del from £85 * **SERVICES:** Night porter Air conditioning 80P **NOTES:** No smoking in restaurant Last d 9.30pm **CARDS:**

KINROSS Perth & Kinross — Map 11 NO10

★★ *Kirklands*
20 High St KY13 7AN
Quality Percentage Score: 66%
☎ 01577 863313 Fax 01577 863313

A completely renovated former coaching inn in the town centre. Bedrooms, though variable in size, are smartly decorated and offer modern furnishings and a good range of amenities. The nicely presented public areas include a choice of popular bars, a coffee lounge and a tastefully appointed restaurant.
ROOMS: 9 en suite (bth/shr) **MEALS:** V meals Coffee am Tea pm **FACILITIES:** CTV in all bedrooms STV **SERVICES:** 30P **NOTES:** No dogs (ex guide dogs) Last d 9pm **CARDS:**

KINROSS Perth & Kinross — Map 11 NO10

Travelodge
Kincardine Rd KY13 7NQ
☎ Central Res 0800 850950 Fax 01577 864108
Dir: *on A977, off junct 6 of M90 Turthills Tourist Centre*

This modern building offers accommodation in smart, spacious and well equipped bedrooms, all with en-suite bathrooms. Refreshments may be taken at the nearby family restaurant. For details about current prices, consult the Contents Page under Hotel Groups for the Travelodge phone number.
ROOMS: 35 en suite (bth/shr) d £49.95 *

KINTORE Aberdeenshire — Map 15 NJ71

★★ *Torryburn*
School Rd AB51 0XP
Quality Percentage Score: 64%
☎ 01467 632269 Fax 01467 632271
Dir: *travelling north from Aberdeen leave off dual carriage way for the village of Kintore. Hotel on the corner of Dunecht Rd*

This family run hotel has a walled garden, children's play area and tennis court. Public areas include a conservatory restaurant with adjacent lounge area, and bar with adjoining supper room, offering a range of competitively priced dishes. Bedrooms,

contd.

although compact, have attractive colour schemes and comfortable modern furnishings.
ROOMS: 9 rms (8 shr) (1 fmly) No smoking in all bedrooms **MEALS:** International Cuisine V meals Coffee am Tea pm **FACILITIES:** CTV in all bedrooms STV Tennis (hard) Fishing Snooker Shooting **CONF:** Class 50 Board 50 **SERVICES:** 30P **NOTES:** No smoking area in restaurant Last d 9.30pm Closed 1 Jan
CARDS:

KIRKCALDY Fife **Map 11 NT29**
★★★ **Dean Park**
Chapel Level KY2 6QW
Quality Percentage Score: 64%
☎ 01592 261635 01592 261371
Dir: *signposted from A92, Kirkcaldy West junc*
Major improvements have taken place at this smart business hotel on the northern edge of town, a popular venue for conferences and functions. Bedrooms in the main house have been smartly upgraded while those in the annexe have been completely refurbished. Public areas include a choice of bars which are nicely presented, work continues with the extension and refurbishment of the restaurant.
ROOMS: 29 en suite (bth/shr) 12 annexe en suite (bth/shr) (2 fmly) s £49.50-£69; d £65-£89 (incl. bkfst) * Off peak **MEALS:** Lunch fr £10.25 High tea fr £6.50 Dinner fr £18.50 Scottish, French & Italian Cuisine V meals Coffee am **FACILITIES:** CTV in all bedrooms STV **CONF:** Thtr 250 Class 125 Board 54 **SERVICES:** Lift Night porter 150P **NOTES:** No dogs (ex guide dogs) Last d 9.30pm
CARDS:

K

KIRKCALDY Fife **Map 11 NT29**
★★ **The Belvedere**
Coxstool, West Wemyss KY1 4SL
Quality Percentage Score: 65%
☎ 01592 654167 01592 655279
THE CIRCLE
Selected Individual Hotels
GREAT BRITAIN
Dir: *A92 from M90 junct 3, at Kirkaldy East take A915, 1m NE turn right to Coaltown, at T-junct turn right then left, hotel 1st building in village*
This small hotel enjoys a beautiful outlook over the Firth of Forth. Bedrooms, mostly in a cluster of houses within the grounds, have pleasing colour schemes, modern furnishings and a range of amenities. The rather limited public areas include a cosy well stocked bar and an attractive restaurant, where seafood features strongly on the fixed price menu.
ROOMS: 5 en suite (bth/shr) 15 annexe en suite (bth/shr) (2 fmly) s £40-£57.50; d £50-£70 (incl. bkfst) * LB Off peak **MEALS:** Lunch fr £14.50 High tea fr £10 Dinner fr £18.50 Scottish & Continental Cuisine V meals Coffee am Tea pm **FACILITIES:** CTV in all bedrooms STV Xmas **CONF:** Thtr 18 Class 18 Board 12 Del from £75 * **SERVICES:** Night porter 50P **NOTES:** No smoking area in restaurant Last d 9.15pm
CARDS:

KIRKCALDY Fife **Map 11 NT29**
Late entry ○ ***Dunnikier House Hotel***
Dunnikier Park KY1 3LP
☎ 01592 268393
ROOMS: 14 rms

KIRKCUDBRIGHT Dumfries & Galloway **Map 11 NX65**
★★★ ***Selkirk Arms***
Old High St DG6 4JG
Quality Percentage Score: 67%
☎ 01557 330402 01557 331639
Best Western
Dir: *turn off A75 5m W of Castle Douglas onto A711, 5m to Kirkcudbright in centre of town*
Once frequented by Robert Burns this delightful hotel has been refurbished to a standard which will appeal to the present day tourist and business person. Inviting public areas feature a smart restaurant and lounge bar as well as cosy lounge, whilst the well equipped bedrooms are furnished in contemporary style and enhanced by tasteful fabrics. The staff are very friendly and attentive and the owners, Mr & Mrs Morris are fully involved.
ROOMS: 14 en suite (bth/shr) 3 annexe en suite (bth/shr) (2 fmly) No smoking in 5 bedrooms **MEALS:** Scottish & Continental Cuisine V meals Coffee am **FACILITIES:** CTV in all bedrooms STV **CONF:** Thtr 70 Class 60 Board 40 **SERVICES:** Night porter 11P **NOTES:** No smoking in restaurant Last d 9.30pm **CARDS:**

KIRKCUDBRIGHT Dumfries & Galloway **Map 11 NX65**
★★ **Royal**
St Cuthbert St DG6 4DY
Quality Percentage Score: 60%
☎ 01557 331213 01557 331513
Dir: *turn off A75 onto A711 hotel is in the centre of Kirkcudbright, on the corner at crossroads*
Situated in the town centre, this tourist and commercial hotel offers reasonably priced accommodation and good value meals in the grill room.
ROOMS: 17 en suite (bth/shr) (7 fmly) s fr £25; d fr £45 (incl. bkfst) * Off peak **MEALS:** Lunch £3.95-£8.95 High tea £6.25 Dinner £9.50 Mainly grills V meals Coffee am Tea pm **FACILITIES:** CTV in all bedrooms Wkly live entertainment **CONF:** Class 60 Board 60 **NOTES:** Last d 9pm **CARDS:**

KIRKHILL Highland **Map 14 NH54**
★★ **Bogroy Inn**
IV5 7PX
Quality Percentage Score: 65%
☎ 01463 831296 01463 831296
Dir: *at junct A862/B9164*
In the 16th century the inn was closely associated with whisky smuggling, it is now a small, friendly hotel. The neat bedrooms are nicely presented in modern style. Public areas include a choice of bars and a pleasant dining room offering wholesome fare.
ROOMS: 7 en suite (bth/shr) (3 fmly) s £27.50-£30; d £50-£55 (incl. bkfst) * LB Off peak **MEALS:** V meals Coffee am Tea pm **FACILITIES:** CTV in all bedrooms Pool table **SERVICES:** 40P **NOTES:** No dogs (ex guide dogs) No smoking in restaurant
CARDS:

KIRKWALL See Orkney

KYLE OF LOCHALSH Highland **Map 13 NG72**
★★★ ***Lochalsh***
Ferry Rd IV40 8AF
Quality Percentage Score: 63%
☎ 01599 534202 01599 534881
Dir: *turn off A82 onto A87*
Almost next to the new Skye Bridge, this established hotel has a prominent position by the former ferry slip. The modern bedrooms vary in size and are brightly decorated. Fine views are enjoyed from public areas, including an open plan foyer lounge and bar. The formal restaurant serves interesting modern food from a short carte.
ROOMS: 38 en suite (bth/shr) (8 fmly) **MEALS:** Scottish & French Cuisine V meals Coffee am Tea pm **FACILITIES:** CTV in all bedrooms STV **CONF:** Thtr 20 Class 20 Board 20 **SERVICES:** Lift Night porter 50P **NOTES:** No smoking in restaurant Last d 9.30pm
CARDS:

See advert on opposite page

KYLE OF LOCHALSH Highland **Map 13 NG72**

★★ Kyle

Main St IV40 8AB
Quality Percentage Score: 68%
☎ 01599 534204 📠 01599 534932
Dir: *A87 just before new bridge to Skye, turn right into main street in village*
This personally-run holiday hotel has an upgraded dining room and new lounge. Although the bedrooms are compact, all are cheerfully decorated and offer a good range of facilities. Staff are most friendly, interesting meals are served.
ROOMS: 31 en suite (bth/shr) No smoking in 2 bedrooms s £38-£47; d £64-£78 (incl. bkfst) LB Off peak **MEALS:** Lunch £8.50-£8.95 & alc Dinner £15 & alc Scottish, French & German Cuisine V meals Coffee am Tea pm **FACILITIES:** CTV in all bedrooms STV **CONF:** Class 50 **SERVICES:** 80P **NOTES:** No smoking in restaurant Last d 9.30pm **CARDS:**

LADYBANK Fife **Map 11 NO30**

★★★ Fernie Castle

Letham KY15 7RU
Quality Percentage Score: 61%
☎ 01337 810381 📠 01337 810422
Dir: *from M90 junct 6 take A91 east (Tay Bridge/St Andrews) to Melville Lodges rdbt. Left onto A92 signed Tay Bridge. Hotel 1.2m on right*

This historic castle, dating from the 12th century, has been ambitiously refurbished under the ownership of Neil Blackburn. The attractive foyer lounge leads into the splendid, vaulted Keep Bar. The Auld Alliance Restaurant boasts a massive Georgian chandelier, setting the scene for enjoyable, formal dining. Bedrooms vary in style and size.
ROOMS: 15 en suite (bth/shr) (2 fmly) No smoking in 3 bedrooms s £45-£85; d £90-£170 (incl. bkfst & dinner) * LB Off peak **MEALS:** Lunch £15.95-£17.95 & alc High tea £4.95-£5.95 Dinner £22.95 Scottish & French Cuisine V meals Coffee am Tea pm **FACILITIES:** CTV in all bedrooms Croquet lawn Putting green 17 acres woodland with loch Wkly live entertainment Xmas **CONF:** Thtr 120 Class 120 Board 25 Del from £50 * **SERVICES:** 60P **NOTES:** No smoking in restaurant Last d 9.30pm **CARDS:**

LAIRG Highland **Map 14 NC50**

★★ *Overscaig*

Loch Shin IV27 4NY
Quality Percentage Score: 67%
☎ 01549 431203
Dir: *on A838*
An idyllic Highland holiday and fishing hotel beside Loch Shin. Bedrooms are cheerfully decorated and have comfortable modern furnishings. Public rooms include a bar with pool room, coffee lounge for snacks, quiet lounge and a smart dining room with panoramic views of the loch. Fishing rights and boats are provided for the loch.
ROOMS: 9 en suite (bth/shr) (2 fmly) **MEALS:** Coffee am Tea pm **FACILITIES:** CTV in all bedrooms Fishing **SERVICES:** 30P **NOTES:** No dogs (ex guide dogs) No coaches No smoking in restaurant Last d 8.30pm

LANARK South Lanarkshire **Map 11 NS84**

see also **Biggar**

★★★ New Lanark Mill Hotel

Mill One, New Lanark Mills ML11 9DB
Quality Percentage Score: 70%
☎ 01555 667200 📠 667222
Dir: *signposted from all major roads, M74 junct 7 also signed from M8*
A unique development, this hotel occupies an impressively restored 18-century cotton mill building which towers over the Falls of Clyde and is part of a heritage village nestling in the river valley. Views from the upper floors are breath-taking and guests have the bonus of being able to enjoy the village. Inside, a bright modern style is balanced with original mill features; an iron staircase leads from the lounge up to the galleried restaurant.
ROOMS: 38 en suite (bth/shr) (2 fmly) No smoking in 28 bedrooms s £57.50-£65; d £75-£85 (incl. bkfst) * LB Off peak **MEALS:** Lunch £8-£15alc Dinner £16.50-£20.50 V meals Coffee am Tea pm **FACILITIES:** CTV in all bedrooms Fishing Access to Wildlife Reserve Xmas **CONF:** Thtr 200 Class 50 Board 50 Del from £70 * **SERVICES:** Lift Night porter 75P **NOTES:** No smoking in restaurant Last d 10pm **CARDS:**

See advert on page 845

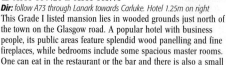

LANARK South Lanarkshire — Map 11 NS84
★★★ *Cartland Bridge*
Glasgow Rd ML11 9UF
Quality Percentage Score: 62%
☎ 01555 664426 Fax 01555 663773
Dir: *follow A73 through Lanark towards Carluke. Hotel 1.25m on right*
This Grade I listed mansion lies in wooded grounds just north of the town on the Glasgow road. A popular hotel with business people, its public areas feature splendid wood panelling and fine fireplaces, while bedrooms include some spacious master rooms. One can eat in the restaurant or the bar and there is also a small cocktail lounge.
ROOMS: 18 en suite (bth/shr) (2 fmly) No smoking in 9 bedrooms **MEALS:** International Cuisine V meals Coffee am Tea pm **FACILITIES:** CTV in all bedrooms STV **CONF:** Thtr 350 Class 100 Board 80 **SERVICES:** Night porter 120P **NOTES:** No smoking in restaurant Last d 9.15pm **CARDS:**

LANGBANK Renfrewshire — Map 10 NS37
★★★★ Gleddoch House
PA14 6YE
Quality Percentage Score: 67%
☎ 01475 540711 Fax 01475 540201
Dir: *signposted from B789 at Langbank rdbt*
Formerly owned by shipping baron Sir James Lithgow, this impressive mansion has been extended and sympathetically converted. Set in 360 acres above the village, it enjoys spectacular views over the River Clyde to the hills of Loch Lomond beyond. The cocktail bar with adjoining conservatory provides a formal environment, while those seeking a more relaxed atmosphere will enjoy the clubhouse. The elegant restaurant is the setting for innovative fare, offered from both the carte and fixed price menus. Bedrooms come in a range of styles, those in the main part of the house retain much of the original character, whilst the two wings are more modern in style.
ROOMS: 39 en suite (bth/shr) (4 fmly) No smoking in 6 bedrooms s £45-£95; d £90-£175 (incl. bkfst) * LB Off peak **MEALS:** Lunch £16.50-£19.50 Dinner £33.95 Scottish & French Cuisine V meals Coffee am Tea pm **FACILITIES:** CTV in all bedrooms STV Golf 18 Fishing Squash Riding Snooker Putting green Clay pigeon shooting Xmas **CONF:** Thtr 100 Class 60 Board 40 Del from £125 * **SERVICES:** Night porter 200P **NOTES:** Last d 9.30pm **CARDS:**

LARGS North Ayrshire — Map 10 NS25
★★★ Brisbane House
14 Greenock Rd, Esplanade KA30 8NF
Quality Percentage Score: 72%
☎ 01475 687200 Fax 01475 676295
Dir: *on A78 midway between Greenock and Irvine, on seafront*
Friendly staff offer a high level of hospitality, and attentive service at this modernised Georgian house, looking out over the promenade to the Isle of Cumbrae. There is a choice of bars and eating options. The conservatory adjoining the lounge bar offers informal dining, whilst the restaurant has its own conservatory cocktail bar adjacent. Bedrooms come in a variety of sizes, and are all well equipped.
ROOMS: 23 en suite (bth/shr) (2 fmly) No smoking in 5 bedrooms s £75-£100; d £95-£120 (incl. bkfst) * LB Off peak **MEALS:** Bar Lunch £7-£20alc High tea £6.95-£11 Dinner £19.75 & alc V meals Coffee am Tea pm **FACILITIES:** CTV in all bedrooms Jacuzzi/spa Wkly live entertainment Xmas **CONF:** Thtr 120 Class 60 Board 50 Del from £90 * **SERVICES:** Night porter 60P **NOTES:** No dogs (ex guide dogs) No coaches No smoking area in restaurant Last d 9.30pm
CARDS:

LARGS North Ayrshire — Map 10 NS25
★★★ Priory House
Broomfields KA30 8DR
Quality Percentage Score: 72%
☎ 01475 686460 Fax 01475 689070
Dir: *on A78 midway between Greenock and Irvine, hotel on seafront*
Standing on the seafront looking out across the Firth of Clyde, this hotel boasts a fine new conservatory in which to relax and take in the views. Food is available in the restaurant, or in the bar with its own dining conservatory and extensive menu. The friendly staff provide attentive service throughout. Bedrooms vary in size, but all are thoughtfully equipped.
ROOMS: 21 en suite (bth/shr) (2 fmly) No smoking in 5 bedrooms s £65-£85; d £80-£110 (incl. bkfst) * LB Off peak **MEALS:** Bar Lunch £5-£15alc High tea £6.95-£13.95alc Dinner £21.95 & alc V meals Coffee am Tea pm **FACILITIES:** CTV in all bedrooms STV Jacuzzi/spa Xmas **CONF:** Thtr 100 Class 50 Board 50 **SERVICES:** Night porter 50P **NOTES:** No smoking area in restaurant Last d 9.15pm
CARDS:

LARGS North Ayrshire — Map 10 NS25
★★★ *Manor Park*
PA17 5HE
Quality Percentage Score: 58%
☎ 01475 520832 Fax 01475 520832
Dir: *2m N of Largs, 200 yds off A78*
An impressive Victorian mansion, standing in 15 acres of gardens and enjoying glorious views over the Firth of Clyde. Original features such as ornate cornices and ceilings have been retained in the public areas - the circular cupola in the hall is particularly fine. Main house bedrooms are traditional in style, while more contemporary styled bedrooms are housed in a converted stable block.
ROOMS: 10 en suite (bth/shr) 13 annexe en suite (bth/shr) **MEALS:** British & Continental Cuisine V meals Coffee am Tea pm **FACILITIES:** CTV in all bedrooms Putting green ch fac **CONF:** Thtr 80 Class 50 Board 40 **SERVICES:** 150P **NOTES:** Last d 9.15pm
CARDS:

LARGS North Ayrshire — Map 10 NS25
★★ Willowbank
96 Greenock Rd KA30 8PG
Quality Percentage Score: 68%
☎ 01475 672311 Fax 01475 672311
Dir: *on A77*
A relaxed, friendly atmosphere prevails at this well maintained hotel. The well decorated bedrooms tend to be spacious and offer comfortable modern appointments, while public areas include a large, well stocked bar, a lounge and dining room. Attractive floral baskets hanging outside are a feature during summer.
ROOMS: 30 en suite (bth/shr) (4 fmly) s £48-£60; d £76-£100 (incl. bkfst) LB Off peak **MEALS:** Lunch £13.95-£16.95 High tea £6-£10.50 Dinner £17.50-£25.50 & alc Scottish, French & Italian Cuisine V meals Coffee am Tea pm **FACILITIES:** CTV in all bedrooms Wkly live entertainment Xmas **CONF:** Board 40 **SERVICES:** 40P **NOTES:** Last d 9pm **CARDS:**

LAUDER Scottish Borders — Map 12 NT54
★★ Lauderdale
1 Edinburgh Rd TD2 6TW
Quality Percentage Score: 66%
☎ 01578 722231 Fax 01578 718642
Dir: *on A68 from S, drive through centre of Lauder, hotel is on right. From Edinburgh, hotel is on left at first bend after passing sign for Lauder*
Friendly attentive service and enjoyable good value meals, served in either the bar or cosy dining room, are features of this hotel
contd.

which lies on the main road on the northern side of the village.
ROOMS: 9 en suite (bth/shr) s £30-£37; d £50-£56 (incl. bkfst) * LB Off peak **MEALS:** Lunch £7.75-£12.20alc High tea £6.15-£8.75alc Dinner £9.80-£26alc V meals Coffee am Tea pm **FACILITIES:** CTV in all bedrooms STV Pool table **SERVICES:** 50P **NOTES:** No dogs (ex guide dogs) Last d 9.30pm **CARDS:**

LERWICK See Shetland

LETTERFINLAY Highland — Map 14 NN29

★★ Letterfinlay Lodge

PH34 4DZ
Quality Percentage Score: 67%
☎ 01397 712622
Dir: *7m N of Spean Bridge, on A82 beside Loch Lochy*

The hotel is set in grounds and enjoys a spectacular outlook over Loch Lochy. Relaxing public areas include a choice of lounges, one of which is popular for bar meals, a snug bar with a pool table, and an attractive dining room. Bedrooms vary in size and offer modern and traditional appointments.
ROOMS: 13 rms (11 bth/shr) (5 fmly) s £27.50-£38; d £55-£76 (incl. bkfst) * LB Off peak **MEALS:** Sunday Lunch £15 Dinner £19.50 & alc V meals Coffee am Tea pm **FACILITIES:** CTV in all bedrooms Fishing **SERVICES:** 100P **NOTES:** No coaches No smoking in restaurant Last d 8.30pm Closed Nov-Feb (ex New Year)
CARDS:

LEUCHARS Fife — Map 11 NO42

★★★ Drumoig Golf Hotel

Drumoig KY16 OBE
Quality Percentage Score: 69%
☎ 01382 541800 🖷 01382 542211
Dir: *M90 to Tay Bridge turn off, then A92 Taybridge/Dundee at the Forgan rdbt turn right to Leuchars/St Andrews, hotel at bottom of the hill on the left*

This smart purpose-built hotel is the focal point for the golf course and is adjacent to the Scottish National Golf Centre. The comfortable modern bedrooms are located in three Lodges close to the main building, and five executive rooms are shortly to be developed in the main house. Public areas have a contemporary

contd.

For Useful Information and Important Telephone Number Changes turn to page 25

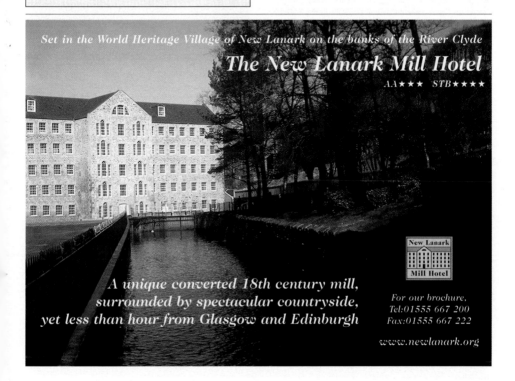

feel. Future development plans include a banqueting centre and a new clubhouse.
ROOMS: 24 annexe en suite (bth/shr) No smoking in 12 bedrooms s £40-£60.50; d £60-£86 (incl. bkfst) * LB Off peak **MEALS:** Bar Lunch £1.60-£17 Dinner £15 & alc V meals Coffee am Tea pm **FACILITIES:** CTV in all bedrooms STV Golf 18 Putting green Home of Scottish National golf centre **CONF:** Thtr 50 Class 15 Board 24 Del from £74.99 * **SERVICES:** 120P **NOTES:** No dogs (ex guide dogs) No smoking in restaurant Last d 10-11.30 **CARDS:**

LEVEN Fife — Map 11 NO30

★★★ Caledonian

81 High St KY8 4NG
Quality Percentage Score: 58%
☎ 01333 424101 🖹 01333 421241
Dir: *follow A912 until Letham Glen rdbt then turn right, 0.5m on turn right into Mitchell St*

Built in 1986 on the site of a former coaching inn, this modern hotel is popular with business guests and visiting tour groups. There is no lounge and the restaurant is small, however there are spacious contrasting bars, one with a lively atmosphere. Newer bedrooms offer good standards and older rooms are being refurbished.
ROOMS: 24 en suite (bth/shr) (1 fmly) s £35-£39.50; d £55 (incl. bkfst) * LB Off peak **MEALS:** Bar Lunch £5-£10 High tea £5-£8 Dinner £10-£12.50 & alc V meals Coffee am Tea pm **FACILITIES:** CTV in all bedrooms STV Wkly live entertainment Xmas **CONF:** Thtr 140 Class 100 Board 100 Del from £37.50 * **SERVICES:** Night porter **NOTES:** No dogs (ex guide dogs) Last d 9pm **CARDS:**

LEWIS, ISLE OF Western Isles — Map 13

STORNOWAY — Map 13 NB43

★★★ Cabarfeidh

HS1 2EU
Quality Percentage Score: 66%
☎ 01851 702604 🖹 01851 705572
Dir: *1m from town centre on main road to Tarbert, turn left at rdbt and take first turn on right*
Situated on the edge of town, this comfortable modern hotel is a popular venue for local functions and conferences. The attractive foyer lounge is a comfortable place to relax and there is a choice of bars as well as a smart restaurant. Bedrooms are mostly well proportioned with modern appointments and staff offer friendly, obliging service.
ROOMS: 46 en suite (bth/shr) (36 fmly) No smoking in 6 bedrooms s £69-£92; d £92-£98 (incl. bkfst) * LB Off peak **MEALS:** Lunch £6.25-£20 & alc Dinner £19.95-£30 & alc French Cuisine V meals Coffee am Tea pm **FACILITIES:** CTV in all bedrooms STV **CONF:** Thtr 350 Class 100 Board 35 Del from £65 * **SERVICES:** Lift Night porter Air conditioning 100P **NOTES:** No smoking in restaurant Last d 9pm **CARDS:**

LIVINGSTON West Lothian — Map 11 NT06

Travel Inn

Deer Park Av, Knightsridge EH54 8AD
☎ 01506 439202 🖹 01506 438912
Dir: *M8 junct 3*
This modern building offers accommodation in smart, spacious and well equipped bedrooms, all with en-suite bathrooms. Refreshments may be taken at the nearby family restaurant. For details about current prices consult the Contents Page under Hotel Groups for the Travel Inn phone number.
ROOMS: 40 en suite (bth/shr) d £39.95 *

LOCHCARRON Highland — Map 14 NG83

★★ Lochcarron

Main St IV54 8YS
Quality Percentage Score: 67%
☎ 01520 722226 🖹 01520 722612
Dir: *take A9 N from Inverness, then A835 at Tore rdbt for Ullapool, then A890 Kyle of Lochalsh, hotel is in E end of village on Lochcarron*
A friendly hotel, with a touch of Irish hospitality from the Graham family. Bedrooms, two with private sitting rooms, follow a modern decorative scheme. Meals and light snacks are available all day in the bar. In the dining room the emphasis is on fresh local seafood. Both bar and restaurant look out on the loch.

ROOMS: 10 rms (9 bth/shr) (2 fmly) No smoking in 2 bedrooms s £39-£41.50; d £78-£83 (incl. bkfst) * LB Off peak **MEALS:** Lunch £10-£25alc High tea £5-£16.50alc Dinner £25-£40 & alc Scottish & Continental Cuisine V meals Coffee am Tea pm **FACILITIES:** CTV in all bedrooms Pool table Hunting Shooting Fishing Xmas **SERVICES:** 40P **NOTES:** No smoking in restaurant Last d 9pm **CARDS:**

See advert on opposite page

LOCHEARNHEAD Stirling — Map 11 NN52

★ Lochearnhead

Lochside FK19 8PU
Quality Percentage Score: 67%
☎ 01567 830229 🖹 01567 830364
Dir: *A84 follow signs for Crianlarich/Callander. Lochearnhead is 30 miles away, once there turn right at T-junct, hotel is 500metres ahead*
This friendly hotel overlooks Loch Earn, a popular resort for visitors attracted by the extensive range of water pursuits. Lovely loch views can be enjoyed from all the public rooms. The varied menus offer a good range of home-cooked dishes in both bar and restaurant.
ROOMS: 12 rms (8 bth/shr) s £29-£38; d £48-£60 (incl. bkfst) * LB Off peak **MEALS:** Bar Lunch £1.20-£13.80 High tea £9 Dinner £17.50-£20 Scottish & French Cuisine V meals Coffee am Tea pm **FACILITIES:** CTV in all bedrooms STV Fishing Water skiing Windsurfing Sailing **SERVICES:** 82P **NOTES:** Last d 9pm Closed mid Nov-Mar **CARDS:**

LOCHGILPHEAD Argyll & Bute — Map 10 NR88

★★ ***The Stag***
Argyll St PA31 8NE
Quality Percentage Score: 65%
☎ 01546 602496 Fax 01546 603549
Dir: *from central Scotland A82 then A38, follow rd to Inveraray, turn right at mini rdbt into main st, hotel is large black/white turreted building*

This long established, family run hotel is situated in the town centre and offers good-value accommodation. Bedrooms, though not over large, have a wide range of amenities. At weekends, live music is a regular feature in the bar, and there is a quiet traditional lounge on the first floor adjacent to the smart dining room.

ROOMS: 17 en suite (bth/shr) **MEALS:** Scottish & Spanish Cuisine V meals Coffee am Tea pm **FACILITIES:** CTV in all bedrooms STV Pool table **CONF:** Thtr 50 Class 20 Board 30 **NOTES:** Last d 8.30pm **CARDS:**

LOCHINVER Highland — Map 14 NC02

★★★ **Inver Lodge**
IV27 4LU
Quality Percentage Score: 79%
☎ 01571 844496 Fax 01571 844395
Dir: *A835 to Lochinver continue through village and turn left after village hall, follow private road for 0.50m*

Inver Lodge is a smart, modern hotel with panoramic views across the river mouth and harbour. The public rooms are spacious and comfortable, good sized bedrooms are stylish and well equipped. The dining room capitalises on the view, formal service complements the cuisine, featuring local fish.

ROOMS: 20 en suite (bth) s £80-£130; d £120-£200 (incl. bkfst) * LB Off peak **MEALS:** Bar Lunch £6-£21alc Dinner £22-£28 Scottish & French Cuisine V meals Coffee am Tea pm **FACILITIES:** CTV in all bedrooms STV Fishing Snooker Sauna Solarium **CONF:** Thtr 70 Board 20 **SERVICES:** 30P **NOTES:** No coaches No smoking in restaurant Last d 9pm Closed Nov-Etr **CARDS:**

LOCHMADDY See North Uist, Isle of

LOCKERBIE Dumfries & Galloway — Map 11 NY18

★★★ ***Dryfesdale***
DG11 2SF
Quality Percentage Score: 66%
☎ 01576 202427 Fax 01576 204187
Dir: *from A74 take 'Lockerbie North' junct, 3rd left at 1st rdbt, 1st exit left at 2nd rdbt, hotel is 200yds on left hand side*

Set in wooded grounds outside the town, this family run hotel offers a peaceful retreat from the motorway, less than five minutes away. The restaurant overlooks the gardens and the bar stocks a fine collection of malt whiskies. The spacious ground-floor rooms are particularly attractive.

ROOMS: 15 rms (9 bth/shr) (1 fmly) **MEALS:** English & French Cuisine V meals Coffee am Tea pm **FACILITIES:** CTV in all bedrooms **CONF:** Thtr 80 Class 20 Board 20 **SERVICES:** 50P **NOTES:** No smoking in restaurant Last d 9pm **CARDS:**

LOCKERBIE Dumfries & Galloway — Map 11 NY18

★★ ***Somerton House***
35 Carlisle Rd DG11 2DR
Quality Percentage Score: 70%
☎ 01576 202583/202384 Fax 01576 204218
Dir: *off A74*

This fine Victorian mansion has been beautifully preserved and features magnificent woodwork, particularly in the restaurant. An attractive conservatory adds a new dimension to the inviting public areas and is an equally popular venue for bar meals.

ROOMS: 7 en suite (bth/shr) 4 annexe en suite (shr) (2 fmly) No smoking in 4 bedrooms **MEALS:** International Cuisine V meals Coffee am Tea pm **FACILITIES:** CTV in all bedrooms **CONF:** Thtr 25 Class 15 Board 15 **SERVICES:** 100P **NOTES:** No smoking in restaurant **CARDS:**

LOCKERBIE Dumfries & Galloway — Map 11 NY18

★★ **Kings Arms Hotel**
High St DG11 2JL
Quality Percentage Score: 66%
☎ 01576 202410 Fax 202410
Dir: *A74M, 0.5m into town centre, hotel is opposite Town Hall*

Reputedly one of the oldest in the town, this friendly hotel has hosted both Bonnie Prince Charlie and Sir Walter Scott in its time. Today it attracts custom to its inviting bars and restaurant, and its well equipped, comfortable bedrooms.

ROOMS: 13 rms (12 bth/shr) (3 fmly) s £30-£40; d £55-£75 (incl. bkfst) * LB Off peak **MEALS:** Bar Lunch £7-£15alc High tea £7-£15alc Dinner £8-£16alc International Cuisine V meals Coffee am Tea pm **FACILITIES:** CTV in all bedrooms Xmas **CONF:** Thtr 120 Class 60 Board 60 Del from £40 * **SERVICES:** Night porter 8P **NOTES:** No smoking in restaurant Last d 9pm **CARDS:**

Remember to return your Prize Draw card for a chance to win one of 30 relaxing leisure breaks with Corus and Regal hotels. See inside the front cover for the card and competition details.

LOCKERBIE Dumfries & Galloway **Map 11 NY18**

★ Ravenshill House

12 Dumfries Rd DG11 2EF
Quality Percentage Score: 64%
☎ 01576 202882 Fax 01576 202882
***Dir:** on A709 which is signed A74M Lockerbie junct, travel W of town centre. Hotel is 0.5m on right*

Cheerful and attentive service plus good value home cooked meals feature at this friendly family-run hotel, set in its own gardens on the edge of the town. It also boasts well equipped bedrooms, most of which are of a good size.

ROOMS: 8 rms (7 bth/shr) (1 fmly) s £35; d £50 (incl. bkfst) * LB Off peak **MEALS:** Sunday Lunch £9.75-£15alc Dinner fr £10.50 & alc Scottish, French, Italian & Indian Cuisine V meals **FACILITIES:** CTV in all bedrooms **CONF:** Class 20 Board 12 **SERVICES:** 35P **NOTES:** No smoking in restaurant Last d 9.30pm **CARDS:**

LOSSIEMOUTH Moray **Map 15 NJ27**

★★ Stotfield

Stotfield Rd IV31 6QS
Quality Percentage Score: 66%
☎ 01343 812011 Fax 01343 814820
***Dir:** A96 to Elgin then A941 to Lossiemouth, follow sign showing West Beach, Golf Club*

This substantial Victorian hotel is situated opposite the golf course and enjoys fine views over the Moray Firth. The spacious public areas include a comfortable foyer lounge, popular lounge bar and a large, attractive dining room where meals with an Italian influence are served. Bedrooms range from large superior rooms with sea views to more modest standard rooms.

ROOMS: 46 en suite (bth/shr) (4 fmly) No smoking in 11 bedrooms **MEALS:** Scottish, French & Italian Cuisine V meals Coffee am Tea pm **FACILITIES:** CTV in all bedrooms Sauna **CONF:** Thtr 120 Class 40 Board 25 **SERVICES:** 10P **NOTES:** No dogs (ex guide dogs) No smoking area in restaurant Last d 10pm **CARDS:**

L

LUNDIN LINKS Fife **Map 12 NO40**

★★★ Old Manor

Best Western

Leven Rd KY8 6AJ
Quality Percentage Score: 74%
☎ 01333 320368 Fax 01333 320911
***Dir:** 1m E of Leven on A915 Kirkaldy-St Andrews Rd*

Genuine hospitality together with high levels of guest care and award winning food, are all part of the appeal at this delightful tourist hotel. From its position beside the main road at the west end of the village, lovely views over the golf course to the Firth of Forth can be enjoyed. Bedrooms, with tasteful decoration and co-ordinated fabrics, are comfortably modern in appointment. Relaxing public areas include a small quiet lounge, and a well stocked bar. Adjacent, the Coachman's Grill and Ale House has recently been extended, and provides an interesting informal food option. The serious food is offered in the elegant surrounds of the Aithernie Restaurant where innovative treatment of local ingredients continues to provide the guest with a fine dining experience.

ROOMS: 24 en suite (bth/shr) (3 fmly) No smoking in 4 bedrooms s £70-£90; d £120-£170 (incl. bkfst) LB Off peak **MEALS:** Lunch £12.50-£15 High tea £7.50-£9.50 Dinner £25-£31 & alc Scottish & Continental Cuisine V meals Coffee am Tea pm **FACILITIES:** CTV in all bedrooms Complimentary membership of Lundin Sports Club Xmas **CONF:** Thtr 140 Class 70 Board 50 Del from £95 * **SERVICES:** 80P **NOTES:** No smoking in restaurant Last d 9.30pm **CARDS:**

See advert on opposite page

LUSS Argyll & Bute **Map 10 NS39**

★★★ *The Lodge on Loch Lomond*

G83 8PA
Quality Percentage Score: 71%
☎ 01436 860201 Fax 01436 860203
***Dir:** turn off A82 at Luss, hotel to N of main car park*

This modern hotel on the lochside enjoys panoramic views. Pine clad throughout, the hotel has executive rooms in a new wing which are larger than those in the original house. All but two rooms overlook the loch, each has its own sauna. There is a spacious open plan bar and restaurant overlooking the loch, and a small lounge in the foyer.

ROOMS: 29 en suite (bth/shr) (20 fmly) **MEALS:** V meals Coffee am Tea pm **FACILITIES:** CTV in all bedrooms STV Sauna fishing, boating **CONF:** Thtr 35 Class 18 Board 25 **SERVICES:** Night porter 82P **NOTES:** No coaches No smoking in restaurant Last d 9.45pm **CARDS:**

See advert on opposite page

MALLAIG Highland **Map 13 NM69**

★★ Marine

PH41 4PY
Quality Percentage Score: 67%
☎ 01687 462217 Fax 01687 462821
***Dir:** adjacent to railway terminal, first hotel on right off A830*

A friendly, family-run hotel, near the railway station, ferry terminal and harbour. Attractive public areas include a well stocked lounge bar with a small sitting area. The restaurant offers a good choice of dishes, fresh local seafood is a particular attraction.

ROOMS: 19 en suite (bth/shr) (2 fmly) s £35-£40; d £64-£70 (incl. bkfst) * LB Off peak **MEALS:** Bar Lunch fr £10.50alc Dinner fr £16alc Coffee am Tea pm **FACILITIES:** CTV in all bedrooms **SERVICES:** 6P **NOTES:** No smoking in restaurant Last d 9pm RS Nov-Mar **CARDS:**

MALLAIG Highland **Map 13 NM69**

★★ *West Highland*

PH41 4QZ
Quality Percentage Score: 63%
☎ 01687 462210 Fax 01687 462130
***Dir:** from Fort William turn right at rdbt then 1st right up hill, from ferry left at rdbt then 1st right uphill*

This family-run hotel enjoys fine views of the Isle of Skye and is a popular base for visiting tour groups. Bedrooms vary in size and style, some are attractively refurbished. The conservatory and open plan public areas are attractive and comfortable, a popular venue for the well prepared bar meals.

ROOMS: 34 en suite (bth) (6 fmly) No smoking in 6 bedrooms **MEALS:** V meals Coffee am Tea pm **FACILITIES:** CTV in all bedrooms Wkly live entertainment **CONF:** Thtr 100 Class 80 Board 100 **SERVICES:** 40P **NOTES:** No smoking in restaurant Last d 9pm Closed 15 Nov-15 Mar RS 15 Mar,1 Nov,15 Nov **CARDS:**

MARKINCH Fife **Map 11 NO20**

The Premier Collection

★★★★ Balbirnie House

Pride of Britain Member

Balbirnie Park KY7 6NE
☎ 01592 610066 Fax 01592 610529
***Dir:** turn off A92 onto B9130, entrance 0.5m on left.*
Half hour from Edinburgh & St Andrews

A luxury hotel with exemplary standards of hospitality in keeping with the Georgian mansion, centrepiece of a 416-

contd.

acre estate. The house has been lovingly restored and attracts a loyal clientele. Magnificent day rooms, warmed by open fires and furnished with antiques, include three sitting rooms, one with a bar. The elegant restaurant with views over the park serves the cuisine of Alan Gibb.

ROOMS: 30 en suite (bth/shr) (9 fmly) s fr £120; d fr £180 (incl. bkfst) * LB Off peak **MEALS:** Lunch £13.95-£17.50 Dinner fr £29.50 International Cuisine V meals Coffee am Tea pm **FACILITIES:** CTV in all bedrooms STV Golf 18 Pool table Croquet lawn Putting green Xmas **CONF:** Thtr 150 Class 70 Board 50 Del from £152 * **SERVICES:** Night porter 120P **NOTES:** No smoking in restaurant Last d 9.30pm **CARDS:**

MAYBOLE South Ayrshire — Map 10 NS20

The Premier Collection

★★ Ladyburn

KA19 7SG

☎ 01655 740585 01655 740580

Set in attractive gardens and bordered by fields and woodland, Ladyburn epitomises the perfect country house. Neither stuffy nor pretentious, guests here are welcomed as old friends. Jane Hepburn knows what looking after people is all about and this is what makes Ladyburn special. There are two lounges in which to relax and bedrooms are inviting. Jane's carefully prepared dinners are set three course affairs, and menus are discussed in the morning. Alternatives are offered and Jane will prepare special request dishes, if ingredients are available.

ROOMS: 8 rms (4 bth 3 shr) No smoking in 7 bedrooms s £100-£115; d £145-£165 (incl. bkfst) * LB Off peak **MEALS:** V meals **FACILITIES:** CTV in all bedrooms Croquet lawn Boules **SERVICES:** 12P **NOTES:** No dogs (ex guide dogs) No coaches No children 16yrs Last d 8pm RS Nov-Dec 2 weeks, Jan/Mar 4 weeks **CARDS:**

MELROSE Scottish Borders **Map 12 NT53**
★★★ Burt's
The Square TD6 9PN
Quality Percentage Score: 65%
☎ 01896 822285 01896 822870
Dir: *A6091, 2m from A68 3m S of Earlston*

Variable sized bedrooms are comfortably modern in style and offer the expected amenities. The well stocked bar, with its welcoming open fire, is a popular rendezvous and offers an informal food option. The elegant restaurant has earned praise for innovative use of fine Scottish ingredients.
ROOMS: 20 en suite (bth/shr) No smoking in all bedrooms s £50-£56; d £88-£90 (incl. bkfst) * LB Off peak **MEALS:** Lunch £13.50-£22 Dinner £20-£26.50 International Cuisine V meals Coffee am **FACILITIES:** CTV in all bedrooms Shooting Salmon Fishing **CONF:** Thtr 40 Class 40 Board 26 **SERVICES:** 40P **NOTES:** No coaches No smoking in restaurant Last d 9pm Closed 24-26 Dec **CARDS:**

M

MELROSE Scottish Borders **Map 12 NT53**
★★ Bon Accord
Market Square TD6 9PQ
Quality Percentage Score: 68%
☎ 01896 822645 01896 823474
Dir: *from A68 into Melrose, hotel in centre of square*
Colourful window boxes adorn the facade of this family run hotel beside the Market Square. Bedrooms, one with a four-poster, are brightly decorated, offer comfortable modern furnishings and a wide range of amenities. Attractive public areas include contrasting bars and a smart split-level dining room.
ROOMS: 10 en suite (bth/shr) (1 fmly) s fr £43; d £70-£72 (incl. bkfst) * LB Off peak **MEALS:** Bar Lunch £6-£12alc High tea fr £7.50 Dinner £8.50-£20alc V meals Coffee am Tea pm **FACILITIES:** CTV in all bedrooms STV Xmas **CONF:** Thtr 100 Class 60 Board 50 Del from £65 * **NOTES:** No dogs (ex guide dogs) No children 12yrs Last d 9pm Closed 25 Dec **CARDS:**

MELROSE Scottish Borders **Map 12 NT53**
★★ *George & Abbotsford*
High St TD6 9PD
Quality Percentage Score: 66%
☎ 01896 822308 01896 823363
Dir: *from A68 or A7 take A6091 to Melrose, hotel is in middle of High St*
Standing in the town centre, this substantial 18th-century former coaching inn enjoys a mixed trade from business persons, holiday makers and tours. It has a lounge bar which complements the dining room by serving a good range of bar meals.
ROOMS: 30 en suite (bth/shr) (3 fmly) **MEALS:** European Cuisine V meals Coffee am Tea pm **FACILITIES:** CTV in all bedrooms STV Fishing **CONF:** Thtr 130 Class 60 Board 30 Del from £65 * **SERVICES:** 102P **NOTES:** No smoking area in restaurant Last d 9.00pm **CARDS:**

MEY Highland **Map 15 ND27**
★★ Castle Arms
KW14 8XH
Quality Percentage Score: 65%
☎ 01847 851244 01847 851244
Dir: *on A836*
A modernised 19th-century coaching inn with uninterrupted views over the Pentland Firth to Orkney. Public areas include a well stocked lounge bar and adjoining dining room, offering a choice of light meals. There is an interesting photographic gallery of the Royal family. Most bedrooms are in a modern extension at the rear of the hotel, all are bright and airy.
ROOMS: 3 en suite (bth/shr) 5 annexe en suite (bth/shr) (1 fmly) s £33-£39; d £49-£58 (incl. bkfst) * Off peak **MEALS:** V meals Coffee am Tea pm **FACILITIES:** CTV in all bedrooms Fishing Pool table **SERVICES:** 30P **NOTES:** Last d 8pm RS Oct-Mar **CARDS:**

MILNGAVIE East Dunbartonshire **Map 11 NS57**
★★★ *The Black Bull*
Main St G62 6BH
Quality Percentage Score: 62%
☎ 0141 956 2291 0141 956 1896
Dir: *leave M8 junct 16 & head north on A879 for 6m, hotel on right hand side as you enter village*
Conveniently situated for access into Glasgow city centre or to the north, this former village inn displays much charm and character. Well equipped bedrooms vary in size, whilst there is a choice of bars, a comfortable cocktail bar and a public bar that proves popular with locals and visitors alike. A wide range of dishes is served in the traditional restaurant.
ROOMS: 27 en suite (bth/shr) (2 fmly) No smoking in 10 bedrooms **MEALS:** Scottish & Continental Cuisine V meals Coffee am Tea pm **FACILITIES:** CTV in all bedrooms STV **CONF:** Thtr 120 Class 30 Board 20 **SERVICES:** Night porter 30P **NOTES:** No smoking area in restaurant **CARDS:**

MOFFAT Dumfries & Galloway **Map 11 NT00**
see also **Beattock**
★★★ Auchen Castle
Beattock DG10 9SH
Quality Percentage Score: 70%
☎ 01683 300407 01683 300667
Dir: *1m N of Moffat village access sign posted from A74/M6*

Taking its name from the ruined castle, this is an imposing Victorian mansion in extensive grounds and terraced gardens 2 minutes from the motorway. Delightful public rooms retain a
contd.

gracious style, whilst bedrooms are being elegantly upgraded. Service is friendly and attentive.
ROOMS: 15 en suite (bth/shr) 10 annexe en suite (shr) (1 fmly) No smoking in 8 bedrooms s £45-£55; d £65-£95 (incl. bkfst) * LB Off peak **MEALS:** Sunday Lunch fr £9.65 Dinner fr £21.20 International Cuisine V meals Coffee am Tea pm **FACILITIES:** CTV in all bedrooms STV Fishing Clay pigeon shooting **CONF:** Thtr 70 Class 40 Board 28 Del from £75 * **SERVICES:** Night porter 37P **NOTES:** Last d 9.30pm Closed 3 wks Xmas-New Year **CARDS:**

MOFFAT Dumfries & Galloway — Map 11 NT00
★★★ Moffat House
High St DG10 9HL
Quality Percentage Score: 70%
☎ 01683 220039 Fax 01683 221288
***Dir:** from M74 at Beattock take the A701 in 1m hotel at end of High St*
This imposing Adam style mansion enjoys extensive gardens at the rear and is situated in the centre of the town. The public rooms include a number of relaxing lounges to suit all moods while the bedrooms, including some in the tastefully converted coaching house are attractively decorated and offer a stylish and comfortable environment.
ROOMS: 20 en suite (bth/shr) (2 fmly) No smoking in 6 bedrooms s fr £59; d fr £90 (incl. bkfst) * LB Off peak **MEALS:** Lunch £7.95-£12.50 High tea £6.75-£7.50 Dinner £17-£22 & alc Scottish & French Cuisine V meals Coffee am Tea pm **FACILITIES:** CTV in all bedrooms Xmas **CONF:** Thtr 70 Class 50 Board 40 Del from £65 * **SERVICES:** Night porter 61P **NOTES:** No smoking in restaurant Last d 9pm **CARDS:**

See advert on this page

MOFFAT Dumfries & Galloway — Map 11 NT00
★★ Beechwood Country House
Harthope Place DG10 9RS
Quality Percentage Score: 74%
☎ 01683 220210 Fax 01683 220889
***Dir:** at north end of town. Turn right at St Marys Church into Harthope Place and follow the 'Hotel' sign*

A delightful country house in attractive gardens, a short walk from the town. There are two comfortable lounges, one with a small bar. Bedrooms are named after local rivers. Carl Shaw continues to delight guests with imaginative cooking.
ROOMS: 7 en suite (bth/shr) (1 fmly) s £53; d £76 (incl. bkfst) LB Off peak **MEALS:** Lunch £14.50 Dinner £24.50 English & French Cuisine V meals Coffee am Tea pm **FACILITIES:** CTV in all bedrooms ch fac Xmas **SERVICES:** 15P **NOTES:** No coaches No smoking in restaurant Last d 8.45pm Closed 2 Jan-14 Feb **CARDS:**

See advert on this page

M

MOFFAT Dumfries & Galloway **Map 11 NT00**

★★ The Star

44 High St DG10 9EF
Quality Percentage Score: 66%
☎ 01683 220156 📠 01683 221524
Dir: *M74 Moffat, hotel is 2m from junct first hotel on right in High Street*

Smart, modern and well equipped bedrooms plus enjoyable food, served either in the bar or the restaurant, are just some of the virtues of this friendly hotel. Its claim to be the world's narrowest hotel is a novel conversation point.
ROOMS: 8 en suite (bth/shr) (1 fmly) s £40; d £56 (incl. bkfst) * LB Off peak **MEALS:** Lunch £4-£12 High tea £6.50 Dinner £5-£13 V meals Coffee am Tea pm **FACILITIES:** CTV in all bedrooms STV Pool table **NOTES:** No dogs (ex guide dogs) No smoking in restaurant Last d 8.45pm **CARDS:**

M

MOFFAT Dumfries & Galloway **Map 11 NT00**

The Premier Collection

★❀❀ Well View

Ballplay Rd DG10 9JU
☎ 01683 220184 📠 01683 220088
Dir: *on A708 from Moffat, pass fire station and first left.*

THE CIRCLE
Selected Individual Hotels
GREAT BRITAIN

This delightful Victorian house, dating back to 1864, is set on the edge of the spa town. Bedrooms, individually furnished, offer good comforts and include many useful extras. Good food is found on the six course menu, using fine ingredients that are locally sourced whenever possible.
ROOMS: 6 en suite (bth/shr) No smoking in all bedrooms s £60; d £90-£100 (incl. bkfst) * LB Off peak **MEALS:** Lunch fr £14 Dinner fr £28 Scottish & French Cuisine Coffee am Tea pm **FACILITIES:** CTV in all bedrooms Xmas **SERVICES:** 8P **NOTES:** No coaches No smoking in restaurant Last d 8.30pm Closed 2wk Jan & 1wk Nov **CARDS:**

MONTROSE Angus **Map 15 NO75**

★★★ Links Hotel

Mid Links DD10 8RL
Quality Percentage Score: 67%
☎ 01674 671000 📠 01674 672698
Dir: *turn off A90 at Brechin, take A935 to Montrose, 10m turn right at Lochside junct, left at swimming pool right by tennis courts hotel 200yds*

Good progress is being made with the refurbishment programme at this popular business and tourist hotel, a fine period house which has been extended. Bedrooms in the main house are individually decorated to a high standard, and those in the wing are smart and modern. There is a smart new coffee shop where all day food is now available. A night club adjoins the hotel and operates every Wednesday and Saturday.
ROOMS: 25 en suite (bth/shr) (12 fmly) No smoking in 11 bedrooms s fr £69; d fr £88 (incl. bkfst) * LB Off peak **MEALS:** Lunch £7.50-£15 Dinner £18.95 Scottish & French Cuisine V meals Coffee am Tea pm **FACILITIES:** CTV in all bedrooms STV Wkly live entertainment Xmas **CONF:** Thtr 169 Class 120 Board 70 Del from £95 * **SERVICES:** Night porter 30P **NOTES:** No smoking area in restaurant Last d 9.30pm RS 21-28 Dec & 3-9 Jan **CARDS:**

See advert on opposite page

MONTROSE Angus **Map 15 NO75**

★★★ *Park*

61 John St DD10 8RJ
Quality Percentage Score: 65%
☎ 01674 673415 📠 01674 677091
Dir: *from A935 follow signs for Montrose, turn right into High St then left into John St*

A warm welcome is assured at this popular business and tourist hotel convenient to central and recreational amenities. A major renovation plan includes the creation of more accommodation in the garden cottage annexe. Plans for the public areas include considerable alteration to the existing layout and improved conference facilities.
ROOMS: 59 rms (53 bth/shr) (4 fmly) No smoking in 6 bedrooms **MEALS:** International Cuisine V meals Coffee am Tea pm **FACILITIES:** CTV in all bedrooms **CONF:** Thtr 200 Class 80 Board 80 **SERVICES:** Night porter 50P **NOTES:** No smoking in restaurant Last d 9.30pm **CARDS:**

See advert on opposite page

MOODIESBURN North Lanarkshire **Map 11 NS67**

★★ Moodiesburn House

6 Cumbernauld Rd G69 0AA
Quality Percentage Score: 60%
☎ 01236 873172 & 872715
Dir: *on M80, N to Stirling. Easy access for all major motorways*

This successful hotel offers a range of bedrooms within different accommodation units. The reception and popular lounge/diner

contd.

are in the original house close to the function and leisure facilities.
ROOMS: 66 en suite (bth/shr) (16 fmly) No smoking in 15 bedrooms s £45-£55; d £55-£65 (incl. bkfst) LB Off peak **MEALS:** Lunch £6-£9 Dinner £7-£15 V meals Coffee am Tea pm **FACILITIES:** CTV in all bedrooms Indoor swimming pool (heated) Sauna Solarium Gym Jacuzzi/spa Wkly live entertainment Xmas **CONF:** Thtr 200 Class 50 Board 50 Del from £80 * **SERVICES:** 200P **NOTES:** No dogs (ex guide dogs) No smoking area in restaurant Last d 10pm
CARDS:

MORAR Highland — Map 13 NM69

★★ Morar

PH40 4PA
Quality Percentage Score: 63%
☎ 01687 462346 Fax 01687 462212
Dir: *in the village of Morar on the A830 "Road to the Isle". The hotel overlooks the silver sands of Morar*
A friendly family-run Highland hotel beside the scenic West Highland Railway, with views over the bay. The variable sized bedrooms are being upgraded, public areas include an open-plan foyer lounge and small bar. The spacious dining room overlooks the sea and offers good value home-cooking.
ROOMS: 27 en suite (bth) (3 fmly) s £30-£35; d £60-£70 (incl. bkfst) Off peak **MEALS:** Bar Lunch £2-£6 French Cuisine V meals Coffee am Tea pm **FACILITIES:** CTV in all bedrooms Fishing Wkly live entertainment **CONF:** Board 100 **SERVICES:** 50P **NOTES:** No smoking in restaurant Closed 22 Oct-Mar **CARDS:**

MOTHERWELL North Lanarkshire — Map 11 NS75

Travel Inn

Edinburgh Rd, Newhouse ML1 5SY
☎ 01698 860277 Fax 01698 861353
Dir: *leave M74 junct 6 onto A723 signposted Airdrie, Travel Inn on the A775 on the right*
This modern building offers accommodation in smart, spacious and well equipped bedrooms, all with en-suite bathrooms. Refreshments may be taken at the nearby family restaurant. For details about current prices consult the Contents Page under Hotel Groups for the Travel Inn phone number.
ROOMS: 40 en suite (bth/shr) d £39.95 *

MUIR OF ORD Highland — Map 14 NH55

★★ Ord House

IV6 7UH
Quality Percentage Score: 69%
☎ 01463 870492 Fax 01463 870492
Dir: *turn off A9 at Tore rdbt onto A832. Follow for 5m into Muir of Ord. Turn left outside Muir of Ord, to Ullapool still on A832. Hotel 0.5m on left*
A former Laird's house dating back to 1637, set in 60 acres of lawned and wooded grounds. It offers well proportioned accommodation in characterful, individually designed bedrooms. Public areas include inviting lounges with log fires and an informal timber-clad bar. The formal dining room provides enjoyable country cooking from a choice of menus.
ROOMS: 11 en suite (bth/shr) s £35-£54; d £78-£88 (incl. bkfst) * Off peak **MEALS:** Bar Lunch £4-£15alc Dinner fr £21 & alc Scottish & French Cuisine V meals Coffee am Tea pm **FACILITIES:** Croquet lawn Putting green Clay pigeon shooting ch fac **SERVICES:** 30P **NOTES:** No coaches No smoking area in restaurant Last d 9pm Closed Nov-Feb
CARDS:

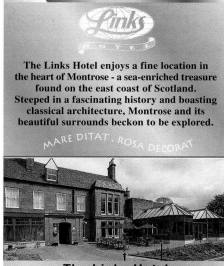

MUIR OF ORD Highland **Map 14 NH55**

The Premier Collection

★❀❀ The Dower House
Highfield IV6 7XN
☎ 01463 870090 🖷 01463 870090
Dir: *on Dingwall rd A862, 1m from town on left*
A charming hotel in four acres of secluded grounds. The welcoming sitting room features an open fire and much to read. The bedrooms offer quality and comfort, the house is full of thoughtful touches and fresh flowers. Set dinners and hearty breakfasts use fresh herbs and seasonal produce.
ROOMS: 5 en suite (bth/shr) 2 annexe en suite (bth) No smoking in all bedrooms s £55-£85; d £110-£120 (incl. bkfst) * LB Off peak **MEALS:** Lunch fr £17.50 Dinner fr £30 British & Mediterranean & Eastern Cuisine **FACILITIES:** CTV in all bedrooms Croquet lawn Xmas **SERVICES:** 20P **NOTES:** No dogs (ex guide dogs) No smoking in restaurant Last d 9.30pm Closed Xmas day & 1wk Mar **CARDS:**

M

MULL, ISLE OF Argyll & Bute **Map 10**

BUNESSAN **Map 10 NM32**

★★❀ Assapol House
PA67 6DW
Quality Percentage Score: 74%
☎ 01681 700258 🖷 01681 700445
Dir: *turn off A849 just after Bunessan School and follow signpost for 1m on minor road*
The Robertson family's small country house hotel sits on the shore of Loch Assapol. It offers cosy and inviting public areas as well as comfortable bedrooms. The dining room makes an attractive setting for the home-cooked meals that are a feature at Assapol. Served at 7.45pm, dinner is a 4-course affair with a choice for starters and puddings only.
ROOMS: 5 rms (4 bth/shr) No smoking in all bedrooms s £51-£56; d £66-£70 (incl. bkfst & dinner) LB Off peak **MEALS:** Dinner £25 **FACILITIES:** CTV in all bedrooms Fishing **SERVICES:** 8P **NOTES:** No dogs No coaches No children 10yrs No smoking in restaurant Last d 7.45pm Closed Nov-Mar **CARDS:**

DERVAIG **Map 13 NM45**

★★❀❀ Druimard Country House
PA75 6QW
Quality Percentage Score: 75%
☎ 01688 400345 & 400291 🖷 01688 400345
Dir: *from Craignure ferry terminal turn right towards Tobermory, go through Salen Village, after 1.5m turn left to Dervaig, hotel on right*
Wendy and Haydn Hubbard's cosy Victorian country house is set on the north-west side of the island. The prettily decorated bedrooms vary in size and are thoughtfully equipped. There are also a lounge and conservatory bar used for pre-dinner drinks. Wendy's five-course dinners are very much an attraction.
ROOMS: 5 en suite (bth/shr) 2 annexe en suite (shr) (2 fmly) s £71.50-£74; d £120-£147 (incl. bkfst & dinner) * Off peak **MEALS:** Dinner £28.50-£29.50 Scottish & French Cuisine V meals **FACILITIES:** CTV in all bedrooms **SERVICES:** 20P **NOTES:** No coaches No smoking in restaurant Last d 8.30pm Closed Nov-Mar **CARDS:**

KILLIECHRONAN **Map 10 NM54**

The Premier Collection

★★❀ *Killiechronan House*
Killiechronan Estate PA72 6JU
☎ 01680 300403 🖷 01680 300463
Dir: *leaving ferry turn right to Tobermory A849,in Salen (12m) turn left onto B8035, after 2m turn right to Ulva ferry B8073, hotel on right*
Set in the centre of the island, this delightful small country house hotel is close to the shore of Loch na Keal. Public areas include a choice of inviting sitting rooms and two elegant dining rooms where guests can enjoy five-course dinners. Bedrooms are very individual in style with pretty colour schemes and antique furnishings.
ROOMS: 6 en suite (bth) No smoking in all bedrooms
MEALS: Scottish, French & German Cuisine V meals **FACILITIES:** TV available Fishing Riding **SERVICES:** 10P **NOTES:** No coaches No children 12yrs No smoking in restaurant Last d 8.30pm Closed 1 Nov-28 Feb **CARDS:**

PENNYGHAEL **Map 10 NM52**

★★ Pennyghael
PA70 6HB
Quality Percentage Score: 69%
☎ 01681 704288
Standing by the road to Iona, this comfortable holiday hotel enjoys a spectacular outlook over Loch Scridain. Though limited in extent, public areas are nicely presented, and guests can enjoy excellent home cooking in the restaurant which overlooks the loch. Bedrooms are comfortably modern in style and offer a good range of amenities.
ROOMS: 6 en suite (bth) s £30-£46; d £60-£72 (incl. bkfst) * LB Off peak **MEALS:** Dinner £18.95 **FACILITIES:** CTV in all bedrooms **SERVICES:** 20P **NOTES:** No coaches No children 12yrs Last d 7pm Closed 24 Dec-Etr **CARDS:**

The AA Hotel Booking Service is a free benefit to AA members. See the advertisement on page 47

TOBERMORY **Map 13 NM55**

★★★ ***Western Isles***

PA75 6PR

Quality Percentage Score: 73%

☎ 01688 302012 📠 01688 302297

Dir: *Glasgow to Oban, ferry to Isle of Mull, after leaving ferry turn right to Tobermory*

Set high above the pier this Victorian hotel commands wonderful views over the bay to the Sound of Mull and the hills beyond. Its original character is combined with an Aladdin's cave of mementoes collected by the owners. The sitting room adjoins a conservatory bar where food is also served. One can also eat in the main dining room. Accommodation includes deluxe, master and standard rooms.

ROOMS: 26 en suite (bth/shr) (2 fmly) **MEALS:** French Cuisine V meals Coffee am Tea pm **FACILITIES:** CTV in all bedrooms **CONF:** Board 30 **SERVICES:** 20P **NOTES:** No smoking in restaurant Last d 8.30pm Closed 17-28 Dec **CARDS:**

TOBERMORY **Map 13 NM55**

★★ **Highland Cottage**

Breadalbane St PA75 6PD

Quality Percentage Score: 74%

☎ 01688 302030 📠 01688 302727

Dir: *A848 Craignure/Fishnish ferry terminal, pass Tobermory signs, ahead at mini rdbt across narrow bridge turn right. Hotel on right opp. Fire Station*

Situated in the upper part of Tobermory, this friendly and welcoming hotel is run by David and Josephine Currie. Bedrooms are individually furnished in period style, and have a host of extras. Public areas include a first floor lounge, a new conservatory and a restaurant.

ROOMS: 6 en suite (bth/shr) (1 fmly) No smoking in all bedrooms s £53; d £38-£41 (incl. bkfst) * LB Off peak **MEALS:** Bar Lunch fr £4.95alc Dinner fr £19.50 V meals Coffee am Tea pm **FACILITIES:** CTV in all bedrooms STV Xmas **SERVICES:** 4P **NOTES:** No coaches No smoking in restaurant Last d 9pm Closed 3wks Oct/Early Nov RS Oct-early Feb **CARDS:**

TOBERMORY **Map 13 NM55**

★★ **Ulva House**

PA75 6PR

Quality Percentage Score: 70%

☎ 01688 302044 📠 01688 302044

Dir: *on waterfront take only left hand turn. Within 100m sharp turn sharp right then hotel sign on left*

Standing on the hill above the town, this charming small hotel has the relaxed atmosphere of a country house. There is a lounge and a residents bar, while home-cooked meals are served in the dining room which enjoys views of the bay. Bedrooms are well maintained and attractively decorated. Wildlife tours of the island are also available.

ROOMS: 6 rms (1 bth 3 shr) No smoking in all bedrooms s £46.50-£52.50; d £93-£105 (incl. bkfst & dinner) * LB Off peak **MEALS:** Dinner £18.50 International Cuisine V meals **FACILITIES:** Landrover wildlife expeditions ch fac **SERVICES:** 8P **NOTES:** No smoking in restaurant Last d 8pm Closed Nov-Mar

NAIRN Highland **Map 14 NH85**

★★★★ **Golf View**

Seabank Rd IV12 4HD

Quality Percentage Score: 67%

☎ 01667 452301 📠 01667 455267

Dir: *off A96, next to Nairn Golf Course*

The leisure centre is a major attraction at this much improved business and tourist hotel. The conservatory provides an informal alternative to the more traditional restaurant. The bedroom enhancement program continues with many bedrooms offering very pleasant standards.

ROOMS: 48 en suite (bth/shr) (3 fmly) No smoking in 8 bedrooms s £80-£95; d £102-£133 (incl. bkfst) * LB Off peak **MEALS:** Lunch fr £11alc High tea £6-£7alc Dinner fr £24.75 & alc European Cuisine V meals Coffee am Tea pm **FACILITIES:** CTV in all bedrooms STV Indoor swimming pool (heated) Tennis (hard) Sauna Solarium Gym Putting green Jacuzzi/spa Cycle hire Xmas **CONF:** Thtr 120 Class 50 Board 40 Del from £120 * **SERVICES:** Lift Night porter 40P **NOTES:** No smoking in restaurant Last d 9.15pm **CARDS:**

NAIRN Highland **Map 14 NH85**

★★★★ **Newton**

Inverness Rd IV12 4RX

Quality Percentage Score: 67%

☎ 01667 453144 📠 01667 454026

Dir: *15m from Inverness on A96, turn left into tree lined driveway*

In 21 acres of mature grounds, this hotel has a combination of Georgian and Scottish Baronial architecture, also retained in public areas. Bedrooms and bathrooms in the main house are refurbished, and more spacious than those in the converted stable block (these are offered at a reduced rate and normally on sight). Guests may use leisure facilities at the nearby Golf View Hotel.

ROOMS: 57 en suite (bth/shr) (2 fmly) No smoking in 15 bedrooms s £75-£87; d £97-£128 (incl. bkfst) * LB Off peak **MEALS:** Sunday Lunch £10.25-£16.50alc High tea £6-£7alc Dinner £23-£25alc European Cuisine V meals Coffee am Tea pm **FACILITIES:** CTV in all bedrooms STV Tennis (hard) Fishing Use of leisure club at sister hotel "The Gulf View Hotel" Xmas **CONF:** Thtr 400 Class 250 Board 50 Del from £120 * **SERVICES:** Lift Night porter 80P **NOTES:** No smoking in restaurant Last d 9.15pm **CARDS:**

NAIRN Highland **Map 14 NH85**

★★★ **Boath House**

Auldearn IV12 5TE

Quality Percentage Score: 70%

☎ 01667 454896 📠 01667 455469

Dir: *2m past Nairn on A96 driving east towards Forres, signposted on main road*

A Georgian mansion set in 20 acres of lawned and wooded grounds. There are inviting lounges and an elegant dining room

contd.

N

overlooking the lake. Bedrooms, some generously proportioned, with lovely antique furnishings, are being upgraded.
ROOMS: 6 en suite (bth/shr) 1 annexe en suite (shr) (1 fmly) No smoking in all bedrooms s £80-£110; d £110-£175 (incl. bkfst) * LB Off peak **MEALS:** Lunch £15.50-£22 & alc Dinner £25-£32alc Scottish & Continental Cuisine V meals Coffee am Tea pm **FACILITIES:** CTV in all bedrooms STV Fishing Sauna Gym Croquet lawn Jacuzzi/spa Beauty & Hair salon Xmas **SERVICES:** Night porter 30P **NOTES:** No coaches No smoking in restaurant Last d 9pm **CARDS:**

NAIRN Highland **Map 14 NH85**
★★★ Claymore House
45 Seabank Rd IV12 4EY
Quality Percentage Score: 68%
☎ 01667 453731 & 453705 01667 455290
Dir: *turn into Seabank Rd from the A96 at the parish church. Hotel is halfway down on the right hand side*
Popular with all kinds of guests - from sporting enthusiasts to business people and holidaymakers. There are comfortable, modern bedrooms, four have direct access to the garden. Public areas include a lively bar serving a popular range of food, a conservatory lounge and adjoining restaurant. Golfing breaks can be arranged.
ROOMS: 16 en suite (bth/shr) (2 fmly) No smoking in 4 bedrooms s fr £42.50; d £75-£85 (incl. bkfst) * LB Off peak **MEALS:** Sunday Lunch £7-£13alc Dinner £10-£20alc International Cuisine V meals Coffee am Tea pm **FACILITIES:** CTV in all bedrooms Wkly live entertainment ch fac Xmas **CONF:** Thtr 50 Class 35 Board 35 Del from £67.50 * **SERVICES:** Night porter 30P **NOTES:** No smoking in restaurant Last d 9pm **CARDS:**

NAIRN Highland **Map 14 NH85**
★★ *Alton Burn*
Alton Burn Rd IV12 5ND
Quality Percentage Score: 65%
☎ 01667 452051 01667 456697
Dir: *follow signs from A96 via Sandown Farm Lane*
A traditional resort hotel, purpose built as a school at the turn of the century. Bedrooms are practically furnished and enhanced with colourful fabrics, the family rooms are particularly comfortable. Public areas include a spacious sun lounge and dining room, the supper menu offers a wide choice of dishes.
ROOMS: 19 rms (14 bth 3 shr) 7 annexe en suite (bth/shr) (6 fmly) **MEALS:** International Cuisine V meals Coffee am Tea pm **FACILITIES:** CTV in all bedrooms Outdoor swimming pool (heated) Tennis (hard) Putting green Games room ch fac **CONF:** Thtr 70 Class 30 Board 30 **SERVICES:** 30P **NOTES:** Last d 9pm RS Nov-Mar **CARDS:**

NEWBURGH Aberdeenshire **Map 15 NJ92**
★★❀ Udny Arms
Main St AB41 6BL
Quality Percentage Score: 70%
☎ 01358 789444 01358 789012
Dir: *turn off A92 at sign marked Newburgh, hotel 2m, in centre of village right hand side*
This comfortable hotel in the centre of the village enjoys views over the Ythan estuary. Bedrooms are well equipped and traditional in style, and day rooms consist of a choice of bars, a comfortable lounge and a split level bistro where seafood is a speciality.

ROOMS: 26 en suite (bth/shr) (1 fmly) No smoking in all bedrooms s £35-£66; d £50-£82 (incl. bkfst) LB Off peak **MEALS:** Lunch £16.95 & alc Dinner £16.95 & alc Scottish & French Cuisine V meals Coffee am Tea pm **FACILITIES:** CTV in all bedrooms Fishing Petanque **CONF:** Thtr 100 Class 30 Board 30 Del from £95 * **SERVICES:** 100P **NOTES:** No smoking in restaurant Last d 9.30pm **CARDS:**
See advert under ABERDEEN

NEWTON STEWART Dumfries & Galloway **Map 10 NX46**

The Premier Collection

★★★❀❀❀ Kirroughtree House
Minnigaff DG8 6AN
☎ 01671 402141 01671 402425
Dir: *from A75 take A712, New Galloway rd, for hotel on left*
Standing in landscaped gardens, this 17th-centry mansion offers comfort and elegance. Lounges have deep sofas and antique furniture. Spacious bedrooms are decorated with many personal touches and have all the expected facilities. Interesting dishes are served in the two stately dining rooms.
ROOMS: 17 en suite (bth/shr) s £75-£100; d £130-£170 (incl. bkfst) * LB Off peak **MEALS:** Sunday Lunch £13.50 & alc Dinner £30 Coffee am **FACILITIES:** CTV in all bedrooms STV Tennis (grass) Croquet lawn Pitch and putt Xmas **CONF:** Thtr 30 Class 20 Board 20 Del from £95 * **SERVICES:** 50P **NOTES:** No children 10yrs No smoking in restaurant Last d 9pm Closed 4 Jan-10 Feb
CARDS:

Symbols and Abbreviations are listed and explained on pages 4 and 5

NEWTON STEWART Dumfries & Galloway **Map 10 NX46**

★★★ Bruce

88 Queen St DG8 6JL

Quality Percentage Score: 61%

☎ 01671 402294 Fax 01671 402294

Dir: *leave A75 at Newton Stewart rdbt, hotel 600mtrs on right past filling station, at junction*

This hotel takes its name from Robert the Bruce. It offers good sized bedrooms which feature some ideal family units. The bar offers a selection of popular meals as an alternative to the restaurant and the first floor residents' lounge provides a quiet environment.

ROOMS: 18 en suite (bth/shr) (2 fmly) No smoking in 6 bedrooms s £35-£50; d £65-£80 (incl. bkfst) * LB Off peak **MEALS:** English & French Cuisine V meals Coffee am **FACILITIES:** CTV in all bedrooms Xmas **CONF:** Thtr 60 **SERVICES:** 20P **NOTES:** No smoking in restaurant **CARDS:**

NEWTON STEWART Dumfries & Galloway **Map 10 NX46**

★★ Creebridge House

DG8 6NP

Quality Percentage Score: 72%

☎ 01671 402121 Fax 01671 403258

Dir: *off A75*

This former shooting lodge lies secluded in attractive gardens. A comfortable drawing room and restaurant are supplemented by a traditional bar/bistro offering an interesting and wide selection of dishes. The smart bedrooms come in a variety of styles and include some family suites.

ROOMS: 19 en suite (bth/shr) (3 fmly) **MEALS:** Sunday Lunch £10.50-£12.50 Dinner £17.50-£25 & alc Scottish & French Cuisine V meals Coffee am Tea pm **FACILITIES:** CTV in all bedrooms STV Fishing Croquet lawn Putting green **CONF:** Thtr 70 Class 20 Board 30 **SERVICES:** 50P **NOTES:** No smoking in restaurant Last d 9pm RS Nov-Mar **CARDS:**

NORTH BALLACHULISH Highland **Map 14 NN06**

★★ Loch Leven

Onich PH33 6SA

Quality Percentage Score: 64%

☎ 01855 821236 Fax 01855 821550

Dir: *1st turning on right after crossing Ballachulish Bridge from S*

A welcoming Highland hostelry by the north shore of Loch Leven. A relaxed and friendly atmosphere prevails in the public areas which include a choice of bars. Delicious home-cooked fare, including seafood specialities, is served in the informal dining area adjacent to the bar.

ROOMS: 10 en suite (bth/shr) (7 fmly) s £25-£32; d £50-£64 (incl. bkfst) * LB Off peak **MEALS:** Bar Lunch £3.75-£10alc Dinner £5.25-£12.75alc Scottish, Continental & Oriental Cuisine V meals Coffee am Tea pm **FACILITIES:** CTV in all bedrooms Pool table Local fishing or shooting trips can be arranged **SERVICES:** 60P **NOTES:** No smoking area in restaurant Last d 9pm **CARDS:**

NORTH BERWICK East Lothian **Map 12 NT58**

★★★ The Marine

Cromwell Rd EH39 4LZ

Quality Percentage Score: 65%

☎ 01620 892406 Fax 01620 894480

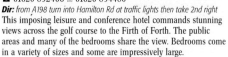

Dir: *from A198 turn into Hamilton Rd at traffic lights then take 2nd right*

This imposing leisure and conference hotel commands stunning views across the golf course to the Firth of Forth. The public areas and many of the bedrooms share the view. Bedrooms come in a variety of sizes and some are impressively large.

ROOMS: 83 en suite (bth/shr) No smoking in 20 bedrooms s fr £70; d £120-£200 * LB Off peak **MEALS:** Lunch £5.20-£8.95 High tea £5.50-£5.95 Dinner fr £15.95 & alc International Cuisine V meals Coffee am Tea pm **FACILITIES:** CTV in all bedrooms Outdoor swimming pool (heated) Tennis (hard) Snooker Sauna Solarium Putting green Childrens playground ch fac Xmas **CONF:** Thtr 300 Class 150 Board 100 Del from £95 * **SERVICES:** Lift Night porter 202P **NOTES:** No smoking in restaurant Last d 9.30pm **CARDS:**

NORTH BERWICK East Lothian **Map 12 NT58**

★ Nether Abbey

20 Dirleton Av EH39 4BQ

Quality Percentage Score: 59%

☎ 01620 892802 Fax 01620 895298

Dir: *at junct with A198, leave A1 and continue S to rdbt, take B6371 to N Berwick, hotel is second on left when entering town*

A popular hotel with golfers, the focus here is on its lively bar/bistro. A good range of tasty, home cooked dishes are on offer, representing excellent value for money. Bedrooms are a mixed bag some being more modestly furnished than others.

ROOMS: 16 rms (6 bth 5 shr) (4 fmly) s £47; d £74 (incl. bkfst) * LB Off peak **MEALS:** Bar Lunch £5.95 & alc High tea £7.95 Dinner £15-£20 & alc V meals Coffee am **FACILITIES:** CTV in all bedrooms Xmas **CONF:** Thtr 80 Class 50 Board 30 **SERVICES:** 40P **NOTES:** Last d 9.30pm **CARDS:**

N

NORTH UIST, ISLE OF Western Isles **Map 13**

LOCHMADDY **Map 13 NF96**

★★ Lochmaddy

HS6 5AA

Quality Percentage Score: 66%

☎ 01876 500331 Fax 01876 500210

Dir: *100yds from Lochmaddy ferry terminal*

A welcoming, long-established hotel, beside the ferry terminal, Lochmaddy is specially popular with anglers, but other country activities like deer stalking and wild fowling can be arranged. There is a choice of inviting lounges, some with peat fires, a popular bar and a formal dining room. Several of the bedrooms have fine sea views.

ROOMS: 15 en suite (bth/shr) (1 fmly) s fr £42; d fr £78 (incl. bkfst) * Off peak **MEALS:** Lunch £11-£16 & alc Dinner £16-£20 & alc V meals Coffee am Tea pm **FACILITIES:** CTV in all bedrooms Fishing Pool table **SERVICES:** 25P **NOTES:** No coaches No smoking in restaurant Last d 8.45pm **CARDS:**

OBAN Argyll & Bute **Map 10 NM83**

★★★ Columba

North Pier PA34 5QD

Quality Percentage Score: 62%

☎ 01631 562183 Fax 01631 564683

Dir: *A85 to Oban, first set of lights in town, turn right. The Columbia Hotel is facing you*

Attractively refurbished, this popular tourist hotel occupies an interesting position beside the North Pier and enjoys views over the bay to Kerrera and Mull beyond. Many of the comfortable

contd.

modern bedrooms overlook the bay. The public areas include a choice of contrasting bars and an attractive restaurant offering both carte and fixed price menus.

Columba, Oban

ROOMS: 48 en suite (bth/shr) (6 fmly) No smoking in 14 bedrooms s £35-£55; d £60-£90 (incl. bkfst) * LB Off peak **MEALS:** Bar Lunch £5-£9 Dinner £18-£24 Scottish & French Cuisine V meals Coffee am Tea pm **FACILITIES:** CTV in all bedrooms Wkly live entertainment Xmas **CONF:** Thtr 70 Class 30 Board 20 **SERVICES:** Lift Night porter 8P **NOTES:** No smoking in restaurant Last d 8pm
CARDS:

See advert on opposite page

OBAN Argyll & Bute **Map 10 NM83**
★★★ Alexandra
Corran Esplanade PA34 5AA
Quality Percentage Score: 61%
☎ 01631 562381 📠 01631 564497
Dir: *arrive Oban on A85, descend Hill, turn right at first rdbt, hotel 200yds further on seaside*

From its position on the esplanade, this privately owned, personally run hotel enjoys wonderful views over the bay to the islands of Kerrera and Mull. Bedrooms offer modern appointments and include two new ground-floor suites as well as some bedrooms with direct access from the car park. There is a comfortable lounge and well stocked bar. Extensive leisure facilities are also available.
ROOMS: 64 en suite (bth/shr) (6 fmly) s £35-£59; d £60-£95 (incl. bkfst) * LB Off peak **MEALS:** Bar Lunch £3-£5 Dinner £18-£24 Scottish Cuisine V meals Coffee am Tea pm **FACILITIES:** CTV in all bedrooms Indoor swimming pool (heated) Snooker Sauna Solarium Gym Steam room Games room Golf practice nets Wkly live entertainment Xmas **CONF:** Class 60 Board 60 **SERVICES:** Lift Night porter 80P **NOTES:** No smoking in restaurant Last d 8pm **CARDS:**

OBAN Argyll & Bute **Map 10 NM83**
★★ *Manor House*
Gallanach Rd PA34 4LS
Quality Percentage Score: 75%
☎ 01631 562087 📠 01631 563053
Dir: *Follow signs MacBrayne Ferries and pass ferry entrance for hotel on right*
The welcoming atmosphere, together with the high level of attention provided by the well motivated staff, and good food, are all part of the appeal of this charming small hotel, a former Georgian dower house. Wonderful views over Oban Bay and the nearby islands can be enjoyed. The public rooms are a delight to use, and Chef Neil O'Brien produces a daily-changing dinner menu, supported by a more adventurous carte, using only the best available produce. The non smoking bedrooms, with attractive colour schemes, have been thoughtfully equipped and are comfortably furnished.
ROOMS: 11 en suite (bth/shr) No smoking in all bedrooms **MEALS:** Scottish & French Cuisine V meals Coffee am Tea pm **FACILITIES:** CTV in all bedrooms **SERVICES:** 20P **NOTES:** No coaches No children 12yrs No smoking in restaurant Last d 9pm RS 1 Nov-28 Feb
CARDS:

OBAN Argyll & Bute **Map 10 NM83**
★★ Willowburn
PA34 4TJ
Quality Percentage Score: 72%
☎ 01852 300276 📠 300597
(For full entry see Clachan-Seil)

OBAN Argyll & Bute **Map 10 NM83**
★★ Foxholes
Cologin, Lerags PA34 4SE
Quality Percentage Score: 70%
☎ 01631 564982
Dir: *3m S of Oban*
George and Joan Waugh's charming small country hotel is set in a quiet glen just south of Oban. George looks after the front of house while Joan provides wholesome meals from the 5 course table d'hôte menu, which is supplemented by a short carte. The no-smoking bedrooms are decorated to a high standard, with some having patio doors to the garden. The relaxing lounge has a small dispense bar.
ROOMS: 7 en suite (bth/shr) s fr £37; d fr £56 (incl. bkfst) * Off peak **MEALS:** Dinner fr £18 **FACILITIES:** CTV in all bedrooms **SERVICES:** 8P **NOTES:** No dogs No coaches No smoking in restaurant Last d 8pm Closed 31 Oct-Mar **CARDS:**

OBAN Argyll & Bute **Map 10 NM83**
★★ Argyll
Corran Esplanade PA34 5PZ
Quality Percentage Score: 67%
☎ 01631 562353 📠 01631 565472
Dir: *A85 to town centre, Hotel 500yds from main rail, taxi and bus terminal*
Overlooking the bay, this relaxed, friendly hotel has an attractive lounge bar and a choice of eating options. Bedrooms, though variable in size, offer a good range of amenities.
ROOMS: 27 en suite (bth/shr) (5 fmly) No smoking in 9 bedrooms s £35-£45; d £57-£70 (incl. bkfst) * LB Off peak **MEALS:** European Cuisine V meals Coffee am Tea pm **FACILITIES:** CTV in all bedrooms STV Wkly live entertainment Xmas **CONF:** Thtr 600 Class 350 Board 200 **SERVICES:** Night porter 6P **NOTES:** No smoking in restaurant
CARDS:

OBAN Argyll & Bute **Map 10 NM83**

★★ Dungallan House Hotel

Gallanach Rd PA34 4PD

Quality Percentage Score: 66%

☎ 01631 563799 📠 566711

Dir: *at Argyll Square in town centre follow signs for Gallanch, hotel 0.5m from square*

From its elevated position set in attractive gardens, this friendly and relaxing hotel commands splendid views of Oban Bay. Public areas are comfortable and bedrooms well proportioned. Good home-cooked dinners and breakfasts are very enjoyable.

ROOMS: 13 rms (11 bth/shr) (2 fmly) s £37-£45; d £74-£90 (incl. bkfst) * LB Off peak **MEALS:** Lunch £10-£20alc High tea £10-£20alc Dinner £19.50-£25 V meals Coffee am Tea pm **FACILITIES:** CTV in all bedrooms Xmas **CONF:** Board 35 **SERVICES:** 20P **NOTES:** No coaches No smoking in restaurant Last d 8.15pm Closed Nov & Feb

CARDS:

OBAN Argyll & Bute **Map 10 NM83**

★★ Caledonian

Station Square PA34 5RT

Quality Percentage Score: 59%

☎ 01631 563133 📠 01631 562998

Dir: *opposite railway station at edge of Oban Bay*

A substantial hotel from the Victorian era which remains a popular base for visiting tour groups. Situated beside the railway station and ferry terminal, with lovely views over the bay. Bedrooms vary in size and style, there is a choice of restaurants.

ROOMS: 70 en suite (bth/shr) (10 fmly) s £59-£79; d £79-£109 (incl. bkfst) * LB Off peak **MEALS:** Bar Lunch £3-£15alc Dinner £12.50-£17.50 & alc European Cuisine V meals Coffee am Tea pm **FACILITIES:** CTV in all bedrooms Xmas **CONF:** Thtr 120 Class 60 Board 40 **SERVICES:** Lift Night porter 6P **NOTES:** No smoking in restaurant Last d 10.45pm

CARDS:

OBAN Argyll & Bute **Map 10 NM83**

★★ Lancaster

Corran Esplanade PA34 5AD

Quality Percentage Score: 59%

☎ 01631 562587 📠 01631 562587

Dir: *on seafront near St Columba's Cathedral*

From its position on the Esplanade this friendly, family run hotel, with its distinctive mock-Tudor frontage, enjoys wonderful views across the bay to the islands. There is a choice of bars and lounges, and the dining room has an especially impressive outlook. Bedrooms have been designed to make the best use of space.

ROOMS: 27 rms (3 bth 21 shr) (3 fmly) s fr £33; d fr £64 (incl. bkfst) * Off peak **MEALS:** V meals Coffee am Tea pm **FACILITIES:** CTV in all bedrooms STV Indoor swimming pool (heated) Sauna Solarium Pool table Jacuzzi/spa **CONF:** Thtr 30 Class 30 Board 20 **SERVICES:** 20P **NOTES:** No coaches Last d 8pm **CARDS:**

O

OLDMELDRUM Aberdeenshire **Map 15 NJ82**
★★ *Meldrum Arms*
The Square AB51 0DS
Quality Percentage Score: 62%
☎ 01651 872238 📠 01651 872238
Dir: *off the B947, in centre of village*
This long established hotel is situated in the centre of the village. Bedrooms make the best use of available space and offer all the expected amenities. Public areas have recently been upgraded. An extensive range of food is offered in both the bar and restaurant.
ROOMS: 7 en suite (shr) 4 annexe rms **MEALS:** V meals Coffee am Tea pm **FACILITIES:** CTV in all bedrooms Pool table **CONF:** Thtr 80 Board 40 **SERVICES:** 25P **NOTES:** No dogs (ex guide dogs) No smoking area in restaurant Last d 9.30pm **CARDS:**

OLD RAYNE Aberdeenshire **Map 15 NJ62**
★★ *Lodge*
AB52 6RY
Quality Percentage Score: 64%
☎ 01464 851205 📠 01464 851205
Dir: *just off A96*
A small hotel with a cosy bar-lounge and attractive restaurant. Bedrooms are split between the main building and a timber chalet on the other side of the car park.
ROOMS: 3 en suite (shr) 4 annexe en suite (bth/shr) (1 fmly) **MEALS:** Coffee am **FACILITIES:** CTV in all bedrooms **SERVICES:** 20P **NOTES:** Last high tea 6.30pm Closed 25-26 Dec & 1 Jan
CARDS:

ONICH Highland **Map 14 NN06**
★★★ Onich
PH33 6RY
Quality Percentage Score: 69%
☎ 01855 821214 📠 01855 821484
Dir: *beside A82, 2m N of Ballachulish Bridge*

With well-tended gardens sweeping down to the picturesque shore of Loch Linnhe, this friendly hotel is an ideal base for the touring holidaymaker. Public areas include a choice of comfortable bars and relaxing lounges, and the attractive restaurant offers interesting Scottish fare. Bedrooms, many with loch views, offer comfortable modern appointments together with the expected amenities.
ROOMS: 25 en suite (bth/shr) (6 fmly) s £53-£57; d £96-£104 (incl. bkfst) * LB Off peak **MEALS:** Bar Lunch £10.50-£21.25alc Dinner £22-£25 International Cuisine V meals Coffee am Tea pm **FACILITIES:** CTV in all bedrooms STV Solarium Pool table Jacuzzi/spa Games room Xmas **CONF:** Class 20 Board 20 Del from £67 * **SERVICES:** Night porter 50P **NOTES:** No smoking in restaurant Last d 9pm Closed 20-27 Dec **CARDS:**

See advert under FORT WILLIAM

ONICH Highland **Map 14 NN06**
★★★ Allt-nan-Ros
PH33 6RY
Quality Percentage Score: 68%
☎ 01855 821210 📠 01855 821462
Dir: *1.5m N of Ballachulish Bridge on A82*
Highland hospitality and good food are part of the appeal of this comfortable hotel, overlooking Loch Linnhe. Though variable in size, bedrooms are modern in style. Inviting public areas include a well-stocked bar and comfortable south-facing lounge. Superb loch views are enjoyed from the dining room.
ROOMS: 20 en suite (bth/shr) (2 fmly) s £67.50-£79; d £135-£158 (incl. bkfst & dinner) * LB Off peak **MEALS:** Lunch £5-£12.50 Dinner £28 Scottish & French Cuisine V meals Coffee am Tea pm **FACILITIES:** CTV in all bedrooms Xmas **SERVICES:** 30P **NOTES:** No coaches No smoking in restaurant Last d 8.30pm **CARDS:**

See advert under FORT WILLIAM

ONICH Highland **Map 14 NN06**
★★★ Lodge on the Loch
PH33 6RY
Quality Percentage Score: 67%
☎ 01855 821237 📠 01855 821238
Dir: *beside A82 - 5m N of Glencoe, 10m S of Fort William*
Palm trees grow in the attractive grounds of this comfortable holiday hotel, looking over Loch Linnhe to the mountains. Public areas include an inviting lounge, restaurant and snug canopy-draped bar. A smart new suite complements the range of accommodation available.
ROOMS: 20 rms (18 bth/shr) (2 fmly) s £68-£83; d £136-£166 (incl. bkfst & dinner) * LB Off peak **MEALS:** Dinner £29-£50 International & Scottish Cuisine V meals Coffee am Tea pm **FACILITIES:** CTV in all bedrooms Leisure facilities at sister hotel Wkly live entertainment Xmas **CONF:** Thtr 50 Class 30 Board 30 **SERVICES:** 25P **NOTES:** No coaches No children 12yrs No smoking in restaurant Last d 9pm Closed Jan-Mar **CARDS:**

See advert under FORT WILLIAM

ONICH Highland **Map 14 NN06**
★★ *Creag Mhor*
PH33 6RY
Quality Percentage Score: 66%
☎ 01855 821379 📠 01855 821579
Dir: *beside A82*
A comfortable hotel overlooking Loch Linnhe, with loch views from the spacious front-facing bedrooms. Rear rooms tend to be smaller and more practical though they are being enhanced. An ambitious improvement programme was being considered for the public areas at the time of our visit.
ROOMS: 14 en suite (bth/shr) (3 fmly) **MEALS:** V meals Coffee am Tea pm **FACILITIES:** CTV in all bedrooms **SERVICES:** 35P **NOTES:** No smoking in restaurant Last d 8.45pm Closed last 3 wks Nov & first 2 wks Dec RS Late Nov-17 Jan (open Xmas & New Year) **CARDS:**

See advert under FORT WILLIAM

ORKNEY **Map 16**

KIRKWALL **Map 16 HY41**
★★★ *Ayre*
Ayre Rd KW15 1QX
Quality Percentage Score: 66%
☎ 01856 873001 📠 01856 876289
Dir: *follow A9 north to Scrabster then P&O car ferry to Stromness, A965 to Kirkwall*
This friendly family-run hotel overlooking the harbour is an ideal base for both business and leisure visitors. Bedrooms vary

contd.

in size, are tastefully decorated and offer comfortable modern furnishings together with the expected amenities. Public areas include a combined bar/dining room where a range of dishes using local produce are available. There is also an attractive public bar and a good range of meeting/function rooms.

ROOMS: 33 en suite (bth/shr) (7 fmly) **MEALS:** Scottish & French Cuisine V meals Coffee am Tea pm **FACILITIES:** CTV in all bedrooms STV Pool table Wkly live entertainment **CONF:** Thtr 150 Class 50 Board 30 **SERVICES:** Night porter 20P **NOTES:** No coaches Last d 9pm **CARDS:**

See advert on this page

KIRKWALL

Map 16 HY41

★★ ***Albert***

Mounthoolie Ln KW15 1JZ

Quality Percentage Score: 64%

☎ 01856 876000 📠 01856 875397

Dir: *from Harbour turn onto Junction Road, turn 1st left into P&D car park, go around car park hotel adjacent to opticians*

Close to the harbour and the town centre, this comfortable tourist and commercial hotel is in the conservation area of old Kirkwall. Public areas include a choice of contrasting bars from the rustic Bothy to the modern Matchmakers, while the popular Stables Restaurant with its beamed walls and booth seating, offers a range of tempting island produce. Some bedrooms are furnished in pine while others offer solid fitted units.

ROOMS: 19 en suite (bth/shr) (2 fmly) **MEALS:** V meals Coffee am **FACILITIES:** CTV in 18 bedrooms Wkly live entertainment **CONF:** Thtr 90 Class 15 Board 20 **NOTES:** Last d 9.30pm **CARDS:**

PAISLEY Hotels are listed under Glasgow Airport.

PEAT INN Fife

Map 12 NO40

The Premier Collection

★★❀❀❀ **Peat Inn**

KY15 5LH

☎ 01334 840206 📠 01334 840530

Dir: *6m SW of St Andrews at junct B940/B941*

David and Patricia Wilson have built up an enviable reputation at this charming restaurant with rooms just six miles from St Andrews, the home of golf. Originally a coaching inn, it stands at the crossroads of the small village to which it has given its name. Chef David Wilson, is a legend in his own lifetime, producing dishes of consistently high quality, based mainly on local Scottish produce. The luxuriously furnished and appointed bedrooms offer a host of thoughtful extras, such as delicious home baking, books and board games, mineral water and fluffy bath robes. Hospitality is noteworthy.

ROOMS: 8 en suite (bth/shr) (2 fmly) s £95; d £145 (incl. cont bkfst) LB Off peak **MEALS:** Lunch £19.50 Dinner fr £28 & alc French Cuisine V meals **FACILITIES:** CTV in all bedrooms **SERVICES:** 24P **NOTES:** No coaches No smoking in restaurant Last d 9.30pm Closed Sun, Mon, Xmas day & New Years day **CARDS:**

PEEBLES Scottish Borders

Map 11 NT24

★★★❀ **Cringletie House**

EH45 8PL

Quality Percentage Score: 77%

☎ 01721 730233 📠 01721 730244

Dir: *2m N on A703*

This turreted baronial mansion is set in 28 acres of grounds and woodland and also features a superb walled garden, well worth

contd.

visiting in season. The house is immaculately maintained throughout, with delightful public rooms including a cocktail lounge with adjoining conservatory downstairs, and a small library, the main lounge and beautiful dining room are upstairs (there is a lift). Bedrooms are decorated individually and several boast fine original fireplaces and all enjoy the views. Resident manager Charles Cormack leads a small, dedicated team to provide an outstanding level of customer care.
ROOMS: 13 en suite (bth/shr) (2 fmly) s £65-£80; d £130-£160 (incl. bkfst) * LB Off peak **MEALS:** Lunch £7.95-£17.50 Dinner £29.50-£32.50 V meals Coffee am Tea pm **FACILITIES:** CTV in all bedrooms STV Tennis (hard) Fishing Croquet lawn Putting green Xmas **CONF:** Thtr 60 Class 30 Board 20 Del from £110 * **SERVICES:** Lift 30P **NOTES:** No coaches No smoking in restaurant Last d 9pm
CARDS:

See advert on opposite page

PEEBLES Scottish Borders **Map 11 NT24**
★★★ Peebles Hydro
EH45 8LX
Quality Percentage Score: 71%
☎ 01721 720602 📠 01721 722999
Dir: *on A702, one third mile out of town*
This well established family and conference hotel commands magnificent views across the valley from its hillside position on the eastern approach to the town. The welcome is friendly, and the long serving staff are attentive and caring in their approach. The well equipped bedrooms come in a variety of styles and sizes and include two-roomed family units. The range of leisure activities, both indoors and out, are second to none. Kids have their own dining room and there's also a lively brasserie open during the day.
ROOMS: 133 en suite (bth/shr) (24 fmly) s £83.25-£98.50; d £142.50-£195 (incl. bkfst & dinner) * LB Off peak **MEALS:** Lunch £15.50-£16 High tea fr £10 Dinner fr £23.50 Scottish & French Cuisine V meals Coffee am Tea pm **FACILITIES:** CTV in all bedrooms STV Indoor swimming pool (heated) Tennis (hard) Squash Riding Snooker Sauna Solarium Gym Pool table Croquet lawn Putting green Jacuzzi/spa Badminton Beautician Hairdressing Wkly live entertainment ch fac Xmas **CONF:** Thtr 450 Class 200 Board 74 Del from £111.50 * **SERVICES:** Lift Night porter 200P **NOTES:** No dogs (ex guide dogs) Last d 9pm
CARDS:

See advert on opposite page

PEEBLES Scottish Borders **Map 11 NT24**
★★★ Park
Innerleithen Rd EH45 8BA
Quality Percentage Score: 68%
☎ 01721 720451 📠 01721 723510
Dir: *in centre of Peebles opposite filling station*
The Park Hotel is little sister to the larger Hydro. Guests can use the Hydro's extensive leisure facilities. Public areas enjoy views of the gardens and include an attractive tartan-clad bar, a relaxing lounge and a well proportioned wood-panelled restaurant. Well equipped bedrooms vary in size, those in the original house are most spacious.
ROOMS: 24 en suite (bth/shr) s £64-£73.50; d £113-£131.50 (incl. bkfst & dinner) LB Off peak **MEALS:** Lunch £8.75-£16.90alc Dinner £20-£28.20 Scottish & French Cuisine V meals Coffee am Tea pm **FACILITIES:** CTV in all bedrooms Putting green Access to leisure facilities of Peebles Hotel Hydro Xmas **SERVICES:** Night porter 50P **NOTES:** Last d 9pm
CARDS:

PEEBLES Scottish Borders **Map 11 NT24**
★★ Castle Venlaw
Edinburgh Rd EH45 8QG
Quality Percentage Score: 73%
☎ 01721 720384 📠 01721 724066
Dir: *off A703 Peebles/Edinburgh road, 0.75m from peebles*
Castle Venlaw is a splendid turreted mansion which is peacefully set in four acres of wooded grounds overlooking the town. New owners John and Shirley Sloggie extend a personal welcome to guests old and new and are dedicated to carrying on the tradition of warm hospitality. Many of the bedrooms are spacious, with Stag furnishings, and most enjoy lovely views. Public areas include a cosy and well stocked library bar, a relaxing lounge, and a smart dining room.
ROOMS: 12 en suite (bth/shr) (3 fmly) s £50-£65; d £90-£110 (incl. bkfst) LB Off peak **MEALS:** Lunch £12-£20alc Dinner £21-£25alc V meals Coffee am Tea pm **FACILITIES:** CTV in all bedrooms STV Croquet lawn Xmas **CONF:** Thtr 40 Class 20 Board 24 Del from £85 **SERVICES:** 30P **NOTES:** No smoking in restaurant Last d 8.30pm
CARDS:

See advert on opposite page

PEEBLES Scottish Borders **Map 11 NT24**
★★ *Kingsmuir*
Springhill Rd EH45 9EP
Quality Percentage Score: 66%
☎ 01721 720151 📠 01721 721795
Dir: *cross Tweed Bridge from High St, then straight ahead up Springhill Rd, hotel is 300 yds on right hand side*
Friendly, attentive service continues to be a feature of this hotel which lies in a residential area on the south side of the River Tweed. There is a choice of lounges and a cosy bar, whilst good value home-cooked meals are available either there or in the dining room.
ROOMS: 10 en suite (bth/shr) (2 fmly) No smoking in 5 bedrooms **MEALS:** Traditional Scottish Cuisine V meals Coffee am Tea pm **FACILITIES:** CTV in all bedrooms **CONF:** Thtr 40 Class 20 Board 20 **SERVICES:** 35P **NOTES:** No coaches No smoking in restaurant Last d 9pm **CARDS:**

PENNYGHAEL See Mull, Isle of

PERTH Perth & Kinross **Map 11 NO12**
★★★❀❀ Kinfauns Castle
Kinfauns PH2 7JZ
Quality Percentage Score: 80%
☎ 01738 620777 📠 01738 620778
Dir: *2m beyond Perth on the A90 Perth/Dundee road*
A distinctive hotel, completely renovated in recent years but retaining many fine architectural features, such as ornate ceilings and marble fireplaces. These are set off by the owner's personal collection of Far Eastern artefacts, collected during many years in those parts. Good food prepared from quality produce is offered in the beautiful panelled restaurant. Bedrooms range from first class suites to master and standard rooms, all with antique or teak furnishings and luxurious bathrooms.
ROOMS: 16 en suite (bth/shr) s £120-£180; d £170-£280 (incl. bkfst) * Off peak **MEALS:** Lunch £18.50-£20.50 Dinner £32-£35 Scottish & French Cuisine V meals Coffee am Tea pm **FACILITIES:** CTV in all bedrooms STV Fishing Croquet lawn Putting green Xmas **CONF:** Thtr 60 Class 50 Board 24 Del from £150 * **SERVICES:** 40P **NOTES:** No coaches No children 8yrs No smoking in restaurant Last d 9pm
CARDS:

P

PERTH Perth & Kinross **Map 11 NO12**

★★★ Murrayshall Country House Hotel & Golf Course

New Scone PH2 7PH
Quality Percentage Score: 75%
☎ 01738 551171 Fax 01738 552595

Dir: *from Perth take A94 towards Coupar Angus, 1m from Perth turn right to Murrayshall just before New Scone*

The golf course is a major attraction at this converted mansion house set amid 300 acres of parkland. Bedrooms range from suites and executive rooms to the smaller standard rooms, all of which are tastefully appointed. Despite alteration and extension the Old Masters Restaurant has retained its refined ambience and is home to some fine cooking.

ROOMS: 27 en suite (bth/shr) (3 fmly) No smoking in 1 bedroom s £80; d £80-£120 (incl. bkfst) * LB Off peak **MEALS:** Lunch £14.95-£21 Dinner £21-£29 Scottish & French Cuisine V meals Coffee am Tea pm **FACILITIES:** CTV in all bedrooms STV Golf 18 Tennis (hard) Sauna Gym Croquet lawn Putting green Jacuzzi/spa Bowling green Driving range Xmas **CONF:** Thtr 180 Class 30 Board 30 Del from £95 * **SERVICES:** Night porter 50P **NOTES:** No smoking area in restaurant Last d 9.45pm **CARDS:**

PERTH Perth & Kinross **Map 11 NO12**

★★★ Huntingtower

Crieff Rd PH1 3JT
Quality Percentage Score: 73%
☎ 01738 583771 Fax 01738 583777

Dir: *3m W off A85*

Improvements are ongoing at this popular business and tourist hotel, a delightful Edwardian house set in attractive landscaped grounds. Bedrooms are comfortably modern, with a good range

contd.

of amenities. Inviting public areas include a lounge, well stocked bar, conservatory extension (offering a brasserie menu) and a restaurant where formal dining from an interesting menu takes place.
ROOMS: 31 en suite (bth/shr) 3 annexe en suite (bth/shr) (2 fmly) s £79.50-£99.50; d £99.50-£129.50 (incl. bkfst) * LB Off peak **MEALS:** Lunch £6.95-£25alc Dinner £6.95-£25alc Scottish & Continental Cuisine V meals Coffee am Tea pm **FACILITIES:** CTV in all bedrooms STV Wkly live entertainment Xmas **CONF:** Thtr 200 Class 140 Board 30 Del from £88 * **SERVICES:** Lift Night porter 100P **NOTES:** No smoking in restaurant Last d 9.30pm **CARDS:**

See advert on opposite page

PERTH Perth & Kinross **Map 11 NO12**
★★★ Queens Hotel
Leonard St PH2 8HB
Quality Percentage Score: 66%
☎ 01738 442222 Fax 01738 638496
Within a short walk of central amenities and close to the railway and bus stations, this popular business and tourist hotel has benefited from substantial refurbishment in recent years. Bedrooms, which range from superior to standard rooms, are tastefully decorated and comfortably modern in style. As well as good banqueting facilities, the hotel offers a well equipped leisure centre.
ROOMS: 51 en suite (bth/shr) (6 fmly) No smoking in 9 bedrooms s £75-£85.50; d £99-£109 (incl. bkfst) LB Off peak **MEALS:** Lunch £9.95-£11.95 High tea £6.50-£9 Dinner £16.50-£21.50 V meals Coffee am Tea pm **FACILITIES:** CTV in all bedrooms STV Indoor swimming pool (heated) Sauna Gym Pool table Jacuzzi/spa Steam room Xmas **CONF:** Thtr 270 Class 120 Board 70 Del from £82 * **SERVICES:** Lift Night porter 50P **NOTES:** No dogs (ex guide dogs) No smoking area in restaurant Last d 9.15pm **CARDS:**

See advert on opposite page

PERTH Perth & Kinross **Map 11 NO12**
★★★ Lovat
90 Glasgow Rd PH2 0LT
Quality Percentage Score: 61%
☎ 01738 636555 Fax 01738 643123
Dir: *from M90 follow signs for Stirling to rdbt, then turn right into Glasgow Rd, hotel situated 1.50m on right*
This popular business and tourist hotel stands beside the Glasgow Road on the south side of the city. Bedrooms, with pretty colour schemes, have been refurbished and offer a good range of amenities. Public areas include an inviting new conservatory lounge, a spacious bar where an extensive range of bistro/bar meals are offered, and a small restaurant with a more formal fixed-price menu and carte.
ROOMS: 31 en suite (bth/shr) (1 fmly) No smoking in 7 bedrooms s £74-£79; d £97-£102 (incl. bkfst) * LB Off peak **MEALS:** Lunch £10.25-£18.95 High tea fr £7.25 Dinner fr £18.95 V meals Coffee am Tea pm **FACILITIES:** CTV in all bedrooms STV Pool table Xmas **CONF:** Thtr 200 Class 50 Board 50 Del from £72.50 * **SERVICES:** Night porter 60P **NOTES:** No dogs (ex guide dogs) No smoking in restaurant Last d 9pm **CARDS:**

PERTH Perth & Kinross **Map 11 NO12**
★★★ Quality Hotel Perth
Leonard St PH2 8HE
Quality Percentage Score: 60%
☎ 01738 624141 Fax 01738 639912
Dir: *from A9 head for city centre & pass Perth Leisure Pool on right. Turn right & continue for 300yds*
High ceilings, wide corridors and large windows feature in this hotel, built at the height of the Victorian railway era. Spacious, airy public areas include bars and lounge areas. Bedrooms vary in size, Premier Plus rooms are rather larger and have mini bars and trouser presses.
ROOMS: 70 en suite (bth/shr) (4 fmly) No smoking in 25 bedrooms s £70-£81.50; d £81.50-£93.75 * LB Off peak **MEALS:** Lunch £2.95-£15.95alc Dinner fr £14.50 & alc English & Continental Cuisine V meals Coffee am Tea pm **FACILITIES:** CTV in all bedrooms STV Gym Mini-gym Golf simulator Xmas **CONF:** Thtr 300 Class 150 Board 30 **SERVICES:** Lift Night porter 100P **NOTES:** No smoking area in restaurant Last d 9pm **CARDS:**

PERTH Perth & Kinross **Map 11 NO12**
★ Woodlea
23 York Place PH2 8EP
Quality Percentage Score: 65%
☎ 01738 621744 Fax 01738 621744
Dir: *take A9 into Perth city centre, hotel is on left next to church & opposite library*
Genuine hospitality and good value are hallmarks of this small family run hotel. The well maintained bedrooms are carefully designed and offer the expected modern facilities. There is a small residents' lounge and, in the dining room, the high-tea menu is a popular feature.
ROOMS: 11 en suite (bth/shr) (1 fmly) s £29.50-£42; d £46-£50 (incl. bkfst) * LB Off peak **MEALS:** High tea £5.50-£10.25 Dinner £11 V meals Tea pm **FACILITIES:** CTV in all bedrooms **SERVICES:** Night porter 4P **NOTES:** No dogs (ex guide dogs) No smoking in restaurant Last d 7.30pm

PETERHEAD Aberdeenshire **Map 15 NK14**
★★★★ ***Waterside Inn***
Fraserburgh Rd AB42 1BN
Quality Percentage Score: 68%
☎ 01779 471121 Fax 01779 470670
Dir: *from Aberdeen A90, 1st rdbt turn left signed Fraserburgh, cross small rdbt, hotel at end of rd*

The warm welcome is a strength of this busy hotel beside the Fraserburgh Road. Its attractive lounge and bars are the ideal choice for afternoon tea or a relaxing drink, and there is also a restaurant. Well equipped bedrooms range from 'executive' rooms and suites to 'studio' rooms.
ROOMS: 69 en suite (bth/shr) 40 annexe en suite (bth/shr) (15 fmly) No smoking in 55 bedrooms **MEALS:** Scottish & French Cuisine V meals Coffee am Tea pm **FACILITIES:** CTV in all bedrooms STV Indoor swimming pool (heated) Snooker Sauna Solarium Gym Jacuzzi/spa Steam room, childrens play area ch fac **CONF:** Thtr 250 Class 100 Board 50 **SERVICES:** Night porter 250P **NOTES:** No smoking in restaurant Last d 9.45pm **CARDS:**

PETERHEAD Aberdeenshire **Map 15 NK14**

★★★ ***Palace***

Prince St AB42 1PL

Quality Percentage Score: 64%

☎ 01779 474821 📠 01779 476119

Dir: *from Aberdeen, take the A90 and follow signs to Peterhead, on entering Peterhead, turn into Prince Street, then right into main car park*

Situated in the centre of town, this comfortable business hotel offers good value and is also popular for local functions. Executive and standard rooms are available, all with modern appointments. The spacious lounge bar and popular café/diner are lively, and a more formal atmosphere can be found in the cocktail bar and smart split-level brasserie.

ROOMS: 66 en suite (bth/shr) (2 fmly) No smoking in 8 bedrooms **MEALS:** V meals Coffee am Tea pm **FACILITIES:** CTV in 69 bedrooms STV Snooker Pool table Wkly live entertainment **CONF:** Thtr 280 Class 100 Board 30 **SERVICES:** Lift Night porter 90P

CARDS:

PITLOCHRY Perth & Kinross **Map 14 NN95**

★★★ **Green Park**

Clunie Bridge Rd PH16 5JY

Quality Percentage Score: 70%

☎ 01796 473248 📠 01796 473520

Dir: *turn off A9 at Pitlochry, follow signs 0.25m through town, hotel on banks of Loch Faskally*

Under the care and direction of the McMenemie family, this delightful holiday hotel beside the picturesque shore of Loch Faskally, is going from strength to strength. Public areas include a choice of spacious lounges, together with a well stocked bar and a traditional dining room, where the fixed-price menu offers carefully prepared wholesome fare. Bedrooms continue to benefit

contd.

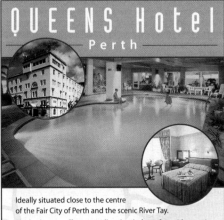

from enhancement and the majority of rooms enjoy views over the Loch.

Green Park Hotel, Pitlochry

ROOMS: 39 en suite (bth/shr) No smoking in all bedrooms s £40-£60; d £80-£120 (incl. bkfst & dinner) * LB Off peak **MEALS:** Dinner £23 British & French Cuisine V meals **FACILITIES:** CTV in all bedrooms Putting green Xmas **SERVICES:** 40P **NOTES:** No coaches No smoking in restaurant Last d 8.30pm **CARDS:**

See advert on page 865

PITLOCHRY Perth & Kinross **Map 14 NN95**
★★★ Pine Trees
Strathview Ter PH16 5QR
Quality Percentage Score: 69%
☎ 01796 472121 01796 472460
Dir: *along main street (Atholl Road), turn into Larchwood Road, follow signs for hotel*

A lovely mansion house, undergoing extensive refurbishment, in 14 acres of grounds. Public areas retain panelling, ornate plaster ceilings and a stained glass window. A marble staircase leads to the drawing room on the first floor. The Garden Restaurant provides tempting Scottish specialities on a daily fixed-price menu supported by a new carte. Bedrooms, currently varying in size and style, are due for complete refurbishment. A swimming pool is being considered.

ROOMS: 19 en suite (bth/shr) No smoking in all bedrooms s fr £54; d fr £96 (incl. bkfst) * LB Off peak **MEALS:** Sunday Lunch £9.75-£12.75 Dinner £20 & alc V meals Coffee am Tea pm **FACILITIES:** CTV in all bedrooms Putting green Wkly live entertainment Xmas **CONF:** Del from £65 * **SERVICES:** 20P **NOTES:** No coaches No smoking in restaurant Last d 9pm **CARDS:**

PITLOCHRY Perth & Kinross **Map 14 NN95**
★★★ Scotland's
40 Bonnethill Rd PH16 5BT
Quality Percentage Score: 67%
☎ 01796 472292 01796 473284

A major programme of refurbishment has transformed the bedrooms at this long established tourist hotel in the centre of town, the nicest of which are contained in the adjacent upgraded buildings. Extensive public areas include a choice of eating options and a good range of leisure facilities.

ROOMS: 75 en suite (bth/shr) (18 fmly) No smoking in 21 bedrooms s £67-£77; d £110-£120 (incl. bkfst) * LB Off peak **MEALS:** Bar Lunch £3-£7 High tea £5.95-£9.50 Dinner £18.95 British & French Cuisine V meals Coffee am Tea pm **FACILITIES:** CTV in all bedrooms Indoor swimming pool (heated) Sauna Solarium Gym Beauty room Xmas **CONF:** Thtr 200 Class 100 Board 30 **SERVICES:** Lift Night porter 87P **NOTES:** No dogs (ex guide dogs) No smoking in restaurant Last d 9pm **CARDS:**

PITLOCHRY Perth & Kinross **Map 14 NN95**
★★★ Dundarach
Perth Rd PH16 5DJ
Quality Percentage Score: 66%
☎ 01796 472862 01796 473024
Dir: *S of town centre on main route*

A warm welcome awaits at this extended mansion house, standing in several acres of grounds. Extensive public areas include a choice of lounges and a bar, and live entertainment features in the main season. Bedrooms in both the main house and the annexe offer a good level of comfort and facilities.

ROOMS: 20 en suite (bth/shr) 19 annexe en suite (bth/shr) (7 fmly) No smoking in 8 bedrooms s fr £56; d fr £80 (incl. bkfst) * LB Off peak **MEALS:** Dinner £19.50-£24.50 International Cuisine V meals Coffee am **FACILITIES:** CTV in all bedrooms STV Pool table Xmas **CONF:** Thtr 60 Class 40 Board 40 Del from £85 * **SERVICES:** 39P **NOTES:** No dogs (ex guide dogs) No smoking in restaurant Last d 6pm Closed Jan RS Dec-early Feb **CARDS:**

PITLOCHRY Perth & Kinross **Map 14 NN95**
★★★ Atholl Palace
Atholl Rd PH16 5LY
Quality Percentage Score: 61%
☎ 01796 472400 01796 473036
Dir: *South-Pitlochry rd off A9, hotel is just after railbridge on right into town. North-go straight through town and turn left just before railbridge*

Set in extensive grounds high above the town, this hotel benefits from fine views. Bedrooms are attractively furnished, day rooms are spacious and include a panelled bar where snacks are served, a comfortable lounge and a restaurant overlooking the river valley.

ROOMS: 76 en suite (bth/shr) (4 fmly) No smoking in 30 bedrooms s £32-£62; d £60-£104 (incl. bkfst) LB Off peak **MEALS:** Bar Lunch £3.50-£11.50 & alc Dinner £19.50-£19.95 & alc V meals Coffee am Tea pm **FACILITIES:** CTV in all bedrooms Outdoor swimming pool (heated) Tennis (hard) Snooker Sauna Solarium Pool table Putting green 9 Hole pitch & putt Games room Xmas **CONF:** Thtr 250 Class 120 Board 60 Del from £75 * **SERVICES:** Lift Night porter 120P **NOTES:** No smoking in restaurant Last d 9pm **CARDS:**

PITLOCHRY Perth & Kinross **Map 14 NN95**
★★ Knockendarroch House
Higher Oakfield PH16 5HT
Quality Percentage Score: 75%
☎ 01796 473473 01796 474068
Dir: *turn off A9 going N at Pitlochry sign. After railway bridge, take 1st right, then 2nd left*

Improvements continue at this delightful Victorian mansion, which stands in mature grounds with fine views over the Tummel Valley. There is no bar, but guests can enjoy a drink in the comfort of the inviting lounges while perusing the daily fixed-price menu. Bedrooms, which vary in size and in style, are comfortably modern and offer all the expected amenities. This is a no-smoking hotel.

ROOMS: 12 en suite (bth/shr) No smoking in all bedrooms s £59-£75; d £108-£114 (incl. bkfst & dinner) * LB Off peak **MEALS:** Dinner £18-£22 European Cuisine V meals **FACILITIES:** CTV in all bedrooms Leisure facilities at nearby hotel **SERVICES:** 30P **NOTES:** No dogs (ex guide dogs) No coaches No children 10yrs No smoking in restaurant Last d 8pm Closed Dec-Jan **CARDS:**

See advert on opposite page

PITLOCHRY Perth & Kinross **Map 14 NN95**

★★ Acarsaid

8 Atholl Rd PH16 5BX

Quality Percentage Score: 71%

☎ 01796 472389 🖷 01796 473952

Dir: *take main road from A9 Perth to Inverness to Pitlochry, hotel on right hand side as you enter town*

A warm welcome is assured at this hotel. Public areas include a choice of inviting lounges. The dining room provides an appropriate setting for the carefully prepared meals. The fresh and airy bedrooms come in various styles. A courtesy coach is available to convey guests to the Festival Theatre.

ROOMS: 19 en suite (bth/shr) (1 fmly) s £29-£36; d £58-£72 (incl. bkfst) * LB Off peak **MEALS:** Dinner £18.50 V meals Coffee am Tea pm **FACILITIES:** CTV in all bedrooms Xmas **SERVICES:** 20P **NOTES:** No dogs (ex guide dogs) No children 10yrs No smoking in restaurant Last d 8pm Closed 3 Jan-10 Mar **CARDS:**

PITLOCHRY Perth & Kinross **Map 14 NN95**

★★ Westlands of Pitlochry

160 Atholl Rd PH16 5AR

Quality Percentage Score: 71%

☎ 01796 472266 🖷 01796 473994

Dir: *turn off A9 into centre of Pitlochry, hotel situated at N end of town*

Standing in its own well maintained garden this family-run family hotel is just north of the town centre. The public areas include a well stocked bar, an inviting lounge, and an attractive Garden Restaurant which provides the setting for the enjoyable Taste of Scotland fare offered on both the carte and fixed price menus. Bedrooms are comfortably modern in style and offer a good range of amenities.

ROOMS: 15 en suite (bth/shr) (2 fmly) s £40-£50; d £80-£90 (incl. bkfst) * LB Off peak **MEALS:** Bar Lunch fr £10alc Dinner £18.50 & alc International Cuisine V meals Coffee am **FACILITIES:** CTV in all bedrooms Fishing Xmas **CONF:** Thtr 35 Class 24 Board 20 **SERVICES:** 28P **NOTES:** No smoking in restaurant Last d 9pm **CARDS:**

PITLOCHRY Perth & Kinross **Map 14 NN95**

★★ Balrobin

MINOTEL Great Britain

Higher Oakfield PH16 5HT

Quality Percentage Score: 70%

☎ 01796 472901 🖷 01796 474200

Dir: *leave A9 at Pitlochry junct, continue to town centre and follow brown tourists signs to hotel*

Views of the surrounding countryside can be enjoyed from this welcoming holiday hotel. Inviting public areas include a lounge, a well stocked bar and a restaurant offering a traditional four course menu. Bedrooms are comfortably modern in appointment.

ROOMS: 15 en suite (bth/shr) (2 fmly) s £25-£40; d £50-£74 (incl. bkfst) * LB Off peak **MEALS:** Dinner £15.50-£18.50 V meals Tea pm **FACILITIES:** CTV in all bedrooms **SERVICES:** 15P **NOTES:** No coaches No children 5yrs No smoking in restaurant Last d 8pm Closed Nov-Feb **CARDS:**

PITLOCHRY Perth & Kinross **Map 14 NN95**

★★ *Claymore*

162 Atholl Rd PH16 5AR

Quality Percentage Score: 69%

☎ 01796 472888 🖷 01796 474037

Dir: *turn off A9 into Pitlochry, hotel last on right hand side after passing through town centre - heading north*

A delightful holiday hotel standing in its carefully landscaped garden at the north end of town. Public areas offer inviting lounge and bar areas together with an attractive conservatory, popular for its good value bar meals. More formal dining is available in the restaurant. Bedrooms are decorated to a high standard and are comfortably furnished in the modern style.

ROOMS: 7 en suite (bth/shr) 4 annexe en suite (bth/shr) (1 fmly) No smoking in 7 bedrooms **MEALS:** European Cuisine V meals Coffee am Tea pm **FACILITIES:** CTV in all bedrooms **SERVICES:** 25P **NOTES:** No coaches Last d 9.00pm Closed 3 Jan-14 Feb **CARDS:**

AA Rosettes are awarded for quality of food,
see page 15 for an explanation of Rosette assessment.

PITLOCHRY Perth & Kinross **Map 14 NN95**

★★ Craigvrack

West Moulin Rd PH16 5EQ

Quality Percentage Score: 69%

☎ 01796 472399 Fax 01796 473990

Dir: *from the main street, turn into West Moulin Road, Craigvrack has three large flagpoles on the lawn and is illuminated at night*

Lovely views over the surrounding hills can be enjoyed from this welcoming holiday hotel which stands beside the Braemar Road. Bedrooms offer pretty colour schemes together with comfortable modern furnishings. Inviting public areas include a choice of lounges, a bar and restaurant which offers a wide range of food.

ROOMS: 16 en suite (bth/shr) (2 fmly) s £28-£46; d £56-£68 (incl. bkfst) * LB Off peak **MEALS:** Scottish & French Cuisine V meals Coffee am Tea pm **FACILITIES:** CTV in all bedrooms Xmas **CONF:** Thtr 30 Class 32 Board 16 Del from £59.95 * **SERVICES:** 20P **NOTES:** No smoking in restaurant Last d 9.00pm **CARDS:**

PITLOCHRY Perth & Kinross **Map 14 NN95**

★★ Moulin Hotel

11-13 Kirkmichael Rd, Moulin PH16 5EW

Quality Percentage Score: 68%

☎ 01796 472196 Fax 01796 474098

Dir: *turn off A9 into Pitlochry in centre of town take A924 signed Braemar. Moulin village 0.75m outside Pitlochry*

A delightful small hotel on the edge of town. The bar of the original Moulin Inn serves beers from the hotel's own brewery, and is popular for bar meals. The formal dining room has a daily changing menu, fresh seafood features strongly. Bedrooms vary in size and style with older rooms gradually being refurbished.

ROOMS: 15 en suite (bth/shr) (3 fmly) s £35-£65; d £40-£70 (incl. bkfst) * LB Off peak **MEALS:** Bar Lunch £9-£19alc High tea £6.45-£12.45alc Dinner £17.95 V meals Coffee am Tea pm **FACILITIES:** CTV in all bedrooms Pool table Wkly live entertainment **CONF:** Thtr 12 Class 8 Board 12 Del from £50 * **SERVICES:** 30P **NOTES:** No coaches Last d 9.30pm **CARDS:**

P

PITLOCHRY Perth & Kinross **Map 14 NN95**

★★ Birchwood

THE CIRCLE *Selected Individual Hotels* GREAT BRITAIN

2 East Moulin Rd PH16 5DW

Quality Percentage Score: 66%

☎ 01796 472477 Fax 01796 473951

Dir: *signposted from Atholl Rd on South side of town*

Enthusiastic new owners John and Viv Holmyard welcome guests old and new to their comfortable small hotel, which stands in four acres of mature grounds at the east end of the town. Inviting public areas include a relaxing lounge where refreshments are served from a dispense bar, and a smart dining room offering honest cooking. Bedrooms vary in size and style and are provided with extras such as fresh fruit.

ROOMS: 12 en suite (bth/shr) (4 fmly) No smoking in 6 bedrooms s £31-£39; d £62-£78 (incl. bkfst) * LB Off peak **MEALS:** Dinner £22 & alc V meals Coffee am Tea pm **FACILITIES:** CTV in all bedrooms Xmas **SERVICES:** 25P **NOTES:** No dogs (ex guide dogs) No smoking in restaurant Last d 8.15pm Closed Jan-mid Mar **CARDS:**

PITLOCHRY Perth & Kinross **Map 14 NN95**

★★ *Pitlochry Hydro*

Knockard Rd PH16 5JH

Quality Percentage Score: 63%

☎ 01796 472666 Fax 01796 472238

Dir: *turn off A9, proceed to town centre and turn right onto A924 Braemar Rd. Hotel is 0.5m on right*

This successful resort and conference hotel dominates the skyline of this delightful Perthshire town. The well equipped bedrooms are spacious and several have views across the Tummel Valley. The extensive public areas include a leisure complex, which has a good-sized swimming pool. The staff have a professional yet light-hearted approach.

ROOMS: 64 en suite (bth/shr) (6 fmly) **MEALS:** Scottish, English & French Cuisine V meals Coffee am Tea pm **FACILITIES:** CTV in all bedrooms STV Indoor swimming pool (heated) Snooker Sauna Solarium Gym Croquet lawn Putting green Jacuzzi/spa **CONF:** Thtr 120 Class 40 Board 40 **SERVICES:** Lift Night porter 100P **NOTES:** No smoking in restaurant Last d 8.45pm Closed Jan

CARDS:

PLOCKTON Highland **Map 14 NG83**

★★ Haven

Innes St IV52 8TW

Quality Percentage Score: 70%

☎ 01599 544334 & 544223 Fax 01599 544467

Dir: *turn off A87 just before Kyle of Lochalsh, after Balmacara there is a signpost to Plockton, hotel on main road just before lochside*

The picturesque village of Plockton is well known as the location for the TV series 'Hamish Macbeth'. This traditional hotel continues to attract much acclaim. Many of the smart bedrooms are refurbished and there are two new spacious suites. There are comfortable sitting rooms and a dispense bar.

ROOMS: 15 en suite (bth/shr) s £36-£38; d £72-£76 (incl. bkfst) * LB Off peak **MEALS:** Lunch £10-£18 Dinner £27 V meals Coffee am Tea pm **FACILITIES:** CTV in all bedrooms **SERVICES:** 7P **NOTES:** No coaches No children 7yrs No smoking in restaurant Last d 8.30pm Closed 20 Dec-1 Feb **CARDS:**

POLMONT Falkirk **Map 11 NS97**

★★★★ *Inchyra Grange*

MACDONALD hotels

Grange Rd FK2 0YB

Quality Percentage Score: 70%

☎ 01324 711911 Fax 01324 716134

Dir: *just beyond BP Social Club*

A former manor house, the building has been developed to include a well equipped leisure centre and extensive conference and banqueting suites. Spacious bedrooms are comfortably furnished, and there are two dining areas: the informal Peligrinos, overlooking the swimming pool, and the more formal Priory.

ROOMS: 109 en suite (bth/shr) (5 fmly) No smoking in 57 bedrooms **MEALS:** Scottish & French Cuisine V meals Coffee am Tea pm **FACILITIES:** CTV in all bedrooms STV Indoor swimming pool (heated) Tennis (hard) Sauna Solarium Gym Jacuzzi/spa Steam room Beauty therapy room Aerobics studio Aromatherapist ch fac **CONF:** Thtr 600 Class 250 Board 80 **SERVICES:** Lift Night porter 400P **NOTES:** No smoking in restaurant Last d 9.30pm **CARDS:**

POOLEWE Highland — Map 14 NG88

Pool House Hotel

IV22 2LD

☎ 01445 781272 Fax 01445 781403

***Dir:** 6m N of Gairloch on the A832. Located in the middle of Poolewe village, next to the bridge at the edge of the sea*

Pool House is an 18th century former clan Mackenzie hunting lodge standing on the shores of Loch Ewe and alongside the sub-tropical Inverewe Gardens. Majestic mountains and spectacular sunsets make a perfect backdrop. The restaurant features seafood landed daily, local lamb and venison.

ROOMS: 10 en suite (bth/shr) No smoking in all bedrooms s £65; d £130-£160 (incl. bkfst & dinner) * LB Off peak **MEALS:** Bar Lunch £12.95-£23.45alc Dinner £28 & alc Scottish & French Cuisine V meals Coffee am Tea pm **FACILITIES:** CTV in all bedrooms Xmas **SERVICES:** 20P **NOTES:** No dogs (ex guide dogs) No coaches No children 14yrs No smoking in restaurant Last d 8.45pm Closed Jan-Feb **CARDS:**

PORT APPIN Argyll & Bute — Map 14 NM94

The Premier Collection

★★★ Airds

PA38 4DF

☎ 01631 730236 Fax 01631 730535

RELAIS & CHATEAUX.

***Dir:** 16m S of Ballachulish Bridge turn off A828 and drive for 2m*

Overlooking Loch Linnhe, this is a welcoming hotel. Bedrooms are furnished with flair, and the lounges offer an environment in which to totally unwind. There is also an enclosed sun porch from which to take in the stunning views. In the kitchen, top quality ingredients are prepared with a light touch.

ROOMS: 12 en suite (bth/shr) d £166-£210 (incl. bkfst) * LB Off peak **MEALS:** Dinner fr £40 Coffee am Tea pm **FACILITIES:** CTV in all bedrooms Fishing Xmas **SERVICES:** 15P **NOTES:** No dogs (ex guide dogs) No coaches No smoking in restaurant Last d 8.30pm Closed Dec 23-Dec 27 **CARDS:**

PORT ASKAIG See Islay, Isle of

PORTMAHOMACK Highland — Map 14 NH98

★★ Caledonian

Main St IV20 1YS

Quality Percentage Score: 65%

☎ 01862 871345 Fax 01862 871757

***Dir:** from S A9 to Nigg rdbt then B9165 for 10m to village. From N travel through Tain, turn off for Portmahomack after 0.5m*

Situated in the centre of this pretty village, the Caledonian overlooks a sandy beach and the Dornoch Firth to the Sutherland hills. The hotel has been refurbished by the resident owners who provide friendly and attentive service. A popular range of food is available from the bar and dining room menus.

ROOMS: 16 en suite (bth/shr) (1 fmly) s £25-£30; d £45-£54 (incl. bkfst) * LB Off peak **MEALS:** V meals Coffee am Tea pm **FACILITIES:** CTV in all bedrooms Pool table **SERVICES:** 16P **NOTES:** No smoking in restaurant Last d 8.45pm **CARDS:**

PORT OF MENTEITH Stirling — Map 11 NN50

★★ *Lake of Menteith*

FK8 3RA

Quality Percentage Score: 72%

☎ 01877 385258 Fax 01877 385671

***Dir:** on B8034 to Arnproir*

A charming holiday hotel by the shore of the Lake of Menteith. The inviting sitting room and conservatory restaurant enjoy stunning views over the lake. Comfortable bedrooms range from spacious superior rooms to more cosy standard rooms. All are tastefully decorated and offer extras such as fresh flowers, fruit, and sweets.

ROOMS: 15 en suite (bth/shr) No smoking in all bedrooms **MEALS:** Scottish & French Cuisine V meals Coffee am Tea pm **FACILITIES:** CTV in all bedrooms **CONF:** Thtr 30 Board 20 **SERVICES:** 35P **NOTES:** No coaches No children 12yrs No smoking in restaurant Last d 8.30pm RS 1 Nov-28 Feb **CARDS:**

★

The Premier Collection, hotels with Red Star Awards are listed on pages 17-23

PORTPATRICK Dumfries & Galloway **Map 10 NX05**

★★★ Fernhill

DG9 8TD
Quality Percentage Score: 72%
☎ 01776 810220 🖷 01776 810596

Dir: *from Stranraer A77 to Portpatrick, 100yds past Portpatrick village sign, turn right before war memorial. Hotel is 1st on left*

This friendly hotel commands panoramic views over the harbour and the Irish Sea. It is ideally situated for access to the many activities in the area. Many of the bedrooms have magnificent views, as do the public rooms. The restaurant is renowned for the excellence of its cuisine.

ROOMS: 14 en suite (bth/shr) 6 annexe en suite (bth/shr) (1 fmly) s £63-£95; d £95-£120 (incl. bkfst) * LB Off peak **MEALS:** Lunch fr £10.75 Dinner fr £22.50 & alc Scottish & French Cuisine V meals Coffee am **FACILITIES:** CTV in all bedrooms Croquet lawn Xmas **SERVICES:** 32P **NOTES:** No coaches No smoking area in restaurant Last d 9.30pm **CARDS:**

See advert on page 869

PORTPATRICK Dumfries & Galloway **Map 10 NX05**

The Premier Collection

★★ Knockinaam Lodge

DG9 9AD
☎ 01776 810471 🖷 01776 810435

Dir: *from A77 or A75 follow signs to Portpatrick. 2m W of Lochans watch for hotel sign on the right, take next left and follow signs to hotel*

Bordered on three sides by cliffs, this hotel has lawns leading down to the beach. Public areas include a morning room which overlooks the sea, a drawing room and a bar, with a range of rare malt whiskies. Bedrooms vary in size, are brightly decorated and have many thoughtful touches.

ROOMS: 10 en suite (bth/shr) (6 fmly) s £100-£135; d £170-£320 (incl. bkfst & dinner) * LB Off peak **MEALS:** Lunch £28 High tea £5-£15 Dinner £38 International Cuisine Coffee am Tea pm **FACILITIES:** CTV in all bedrooms STV Croquet lawn ch fac Xmas **CONF:** Board 20 **SERVICES:** 20P **NOTES:** No coaches No smoking in restaurant Last d 9.30pm **CARDS:**

PORTREE See Skye, Isle of

AA Rosettes are awarded for quality of food, see page 15 for an explanation of Rosette assessment.

PORT WILLIAM Dumfries & Galloway **Map 10 NX34**

★★★ Corsemalzie House

DG8 9RL
Quality Percentage Score: 65%
☎ 01988 860254 🖷 01988 860213

Dir: *From A75 turn left at Newton Stewart rdbt onto A714, by passing Wigtown: turn right after crossing bridge at Bladnoch onto B7005 for Corsemalzie*

This 19th-century Scottish country mansion is set in 40 acres of woodland gardens and offers a comfortable retreat for those keen on outdoor pursuits. A good level of hospitality is provided by friendly and attentive staff.

ROOMS: 14 en suite (bth/shr) (1 fmly) No smoking in 3 bedrooms s £49-£61.50; d £98 (incl. bkfst) LB Off peak **MEALS:** Lunch £11.50-£13.50 & alc Dinner £22.50-£23.50 & alc Scottish & French Cuisine V meals Coffee am Tea pm **FACILITIES:** CTV in all bedrooms Fishing Croquet lawn Putting green Game shooting Xmas **SERVICES:** 31P **NOTES:** No coaches No smoking in restaurant Last d 9pm Closed 21 Jan-5 Mar & Xmas **CARDS:**

POWFOOT Dumfries & Galloway **Map 11 NY16**

★★ Golf

Links Av DG12 5PN
Quality Percentage Score: 66%
☎ 01461 700254 🖷 01461 700288

Dir: *turn off M74 at Gretna onto A75 round Annan bypass, hotel sign 2m on turn left onto B724 and follow sign to Powfoot village*

Popular with golfers and providing a retreat for business people, this hotel is next to the local golf course at the end of the village and enjoys panoramic views across the Solway Firth. You can dine well in both the bar and dining room. Bedrooms come in a variety of styles offering a good level of comfort.

ROOMS: 19 rms (18 bth/shr) (2 fmly) No smoking in 2 bedrooms s £42-55; d £58-£74 (incl. bkfst) * LB Off peak **MEALS:** Lunch £7-£16alc High tea £6.50-£10alc Dinner £17-£20alc V meals Coffee am Tea pm **FACILITIES:** CTV in all bedrooms Golf 18 Fishing Pool table Darts Bowls Xmas **CONF:** Thtr 150 Class 70 Board 70 Del from £65 **SERVICES:** Air conditioning 110P **NOTES:** No dogs (ex guide dogs) No smoking area in restaurant Last d 9pm **CARDS:**

POWMILL Perth & Kinross **Map 11 NT09**

★★★ Gartwhinzean Hotel

FK14 7NW
Quality Percentage Score: 66%
☎ 01577 840595 🖷 01577 840779

Dir: *from M90 junct 6 take A977 Kincardine Bridge Road, in approx 7m the village of Powmill, hotel at end of village*

A friendly and informal atmosphere prevails at this well known country inn. Most of the bedrooms are very well proportioned and contained in a modern wing. The comfortable lounge with panelled walls invites peaceful relaxation. The Bistro and restaurant have a more rustic feel.

ROOMS: 23 en suite (bth/shr) (6 fmly) No smoking in 6 bedrooms s fr £55; d fr £80 (incl. bkfst) * LB Off peak **MEALS:** Lunch £3.75-£21alc Dinner £7.50-£25alc Scottish & French Cuisine V meals Coffee am Tea pm **FACILITIES:** CTV in all bedrooms Pool table **CONF:** Thtr 250 Class 80 Board 30 Del from £75 * **SERVICES:** 150P **NOTES:** No dogs No smoking in restaurant Last d 9.30pm **CARDS:**

PRESTWICK South Ayrshire **Map 10 NS32**

★★★ Parkstone

Esplanade KA9 1QN
Quality Percentage Score: 65%
☎ 01292 477286 🖷 01292 477671

Dir: *from Prestwick Main St (A79) turn west to seafront - hotel 600yds*

Situated on the sea front in a quiet residential area, this family-

contd.

run hotel caters for business visitors as well as golfers. There is a wing of smart new bedrooms and the original rooms are also being refurbished to the same standard. In addition to restaurant meals, one can also eat in the lounge.

ROOMS: 22 en suite (bth/shr) (2 fmly) s £39.50-£44.50; d £59.50-£65.50 (incl. bkfst) * LB Off peak **MEALS:** V meals Coffee am **FACILITIES:** CTV in all bedrooms **CONF:** Thtr 100 **SERVICES:** Night porter 34P **NOTES:** No dogs No smoking in restaurant
CARDS:

RENFREW For hotels see **Glasgow Airport**

ROSEBANK South Lanarkshire **Map 11 NS84**

★★★ Popinjay

Lanark Rd ML8 5QB
Quality Percentage Score: 68%
☎ 01555 860441 🖷 01555 860204
Dir: *on A72 between Hamilton & Lanark*

An established hotel with Tudor style facade, grounds extend to the banks of the River Clyde. Public areas include a panelled bar with open fireplaces and a restaurant looking towards the river. Functions, especially weddings, are popular (the gardens provide a lovely backdrop). The well equipped bedrooms vary in size, some in a house across the road.

ROOMS: 40 en suite (bth/shr) 5 annexe en suite (bth/shr) (2 fmly) s £49-£59; d £65-£75 (incl. bkfst) * LB Off peak **MEALS:** Lunch fr £8.95 & alc Dinner fr £14.95 & alc International Cuisine V meals Coffee am Tea pm **FACILITIES:** CTV in all bedrooms STV Fishing Xmas **CONF:** Thtr 250 Class 120 Board 60 **SERVICES:** Night porter 300P **NOTES:** Last d 10pm **CARDS:**

See advert on this page

ROSLIN Midlothian **Map 11 NT26**

★★ Roslin Glen

2 Penicuik Rd EH25 9LH
Quality Percentage Score: 63%
☎ 0131 440 2029 🖷 0131 440 2229
Dir: *in the village of Roslin 1m from the A701 Edinburgh/Peebles Rd. 2m S of Edinburgh City bypass*

Handy for Rosslyn Chapel and The Institute, this family-run hotel provides a relaxed, welcoming atmosphere. The bright, cheery bedrooms come in a variety of sizes, a popular choice of dishes is available in the bar and cosy restaurant.

ROOMS: 7 en suite (bth/shr) (3 fmly) s fr £60; d fr £70 (incl. bkfst) * LB Off peak **MEALS:** Lunch £10-£23 & alc High tea fr £7 International Cuisine V meals Coffee am Tea pm **FACILITIES:** CTV in all bedrooms STV Pool table **CONF:** Class 50 Board 50 **SERVICES:** 6P
CARDS:

See advert under EDINBURGH

ROSYTH Fife **Map 11 NT18**

★★ Gladyer Inn

Heath Rd, Ridley Dr KY11 2BT
Quality Percentage Score: 63%
☎ 01383 419977 🖷 01383 411728
Dir: *from junct 1 of M90 travel along Admiralty Road, past roundabout then first road on the left*

Conveniently situated for the dockyard, naval base and with easy access to the M90 and Forth Bridge, this friendly hotel appeals to businessmen and is a popular venue for functions. Bedrooms, though compact, are comfortably modern and provide a good range of amenities. There is a choice of bars as well as a smart restaurant, which offers both carte and fixed-price menus.

ROOMS: 21 en suite (bth/shr) (3 fmly) s £39.50; d £55 (incl. bkfst) * LB Off peak **MEALS:** Lunch £5-£7.50 High tea £5.50-£7.50 Dinner £7.50-£15 V meals Coffee am Tea pm **FACILITIES:** CTV in all bedrooms STV Pool table Wkly live entertainment Xmas **CONF:** Thtr 100 Class 70 Board 80 Del from £37.50 * **SERVICES:** Night porter 81P **NOTES:** No dogs (ex guide dogs) Last d 9.30pm **CARDS:**

ROY BRIDGE Highland **Map 14 NN28**

★★★ **Glenspean Lodge Hotel**

PH31 4AW

Quality Percentage Score: 68%

☎ 01397 712223 🖷 01397 712660

Dir: *2m E of Roy Bridge, turn right off A82 at Spean Bridge onto A86*

A delightful country house in landscaped grounds with views of the glen and Nevis mountains. Public areas include a spacious bar and comfortable lounge. The restaurant carte offers interesting Scottish fare. Bedrooms, though variable in size, have attractive colour schemes and are furnished in pine.

ROOMS: 15 en suite (bth/shr) s £49-£60; d £80-£130 (incl. bkfst) * LB Off peak **MEALS:** Bar Lunch £6.15-£14.95alc High tea £11.75-£17.95alc V meals Coffee am Tea pm **FACILITIES:** CTV in all bedrooms Xmas **CONF:** Thtr 50 Class 25 Board 25 **SERVICES:** 50P **NOTES:** No smoking in restaurant Last high tea 4.30pm Closed Nov RS Dec-Mar

CARDS:

See advert under FORT WILLIAM

ROY BRIDGE Highland **Map 14 NN28**

★★ ***Stronlossit***

PH31 4AG

Quality Percentage Score: 62%

☎ 01397 712253

A friendly family run hotel at the east end of the village, with lovely mountain views. Public areas, mostly tastefully refurbished, include a comfortable small lounge. The restaurant carte offers competitively priced dishes, and a homely bar. Three smart new bedrooms are on the ground floor, the original accommodation remains mixed in size and style.

ROOMS: 9 en suite (bth/shr) (2 fmly) **MEALS:** V meals Coffee am Tea pm **FACILITIES:** CTV in all bedrooms **SERVICES:** 30P

NOTES: Last d 9.30pm Closed 10 Nov-10 Dec & Jan

CARDS:

ST ANDREWS Fife **Map 12 NO51**

see also **Leuchars**

★★★★★ **The Old Course Hotel**

KY16 9SP

Quality Percentage Score: 68%

☎ 01334 474371 🖷 01334 477668

Dir: *close to the A91 on the outskirts of the city*

Set beside the 17th hole of the famous championship course, this hotel attracts golfers from all over the world. The reception area leads to a choice of lounges and the conservatory, which provides an informal dining option. The cocktail bar has a stunning collection of single malts, and the Road Hole Grill offering innovative cooking. The new Sands brasserie serves from a menu influenced by the mediterranean and pacific rim. Bedrooms, including a range of stylish suites, are appointed to a high standard with inlaid furniture and marbled bathrooms.

ROOMS: 125 en suite (bth/shr) (6 fmly) s fr £245; d £270-£315 (incl. bkfst) * LB Off peak **MEALS:** Lunch fr £15.50 Dinner fr £38.50 & alc Scottish & French Cuisine V meals Coffee am Tea pm **FACILITIES:** CTV in all bedrooms STV Indoor swimming pool (heated) Golf 18 Sauna Solarium Gym Jacuzzi/spa Health spa Steam room Xmas **CONF:** Thtr 300 Class 150 Board 60 Del from £195 * **SERVICES:** Lift Night porter 150P **NOTES:** No smoking in restaurant Last d 10pm Closed 24-28 Dec

CARDS:

ST ANDREWS Fife **Map 12 NO51**

★★★★ **Rusacks**

Pilmour Links KY16 9JQ

Quality Percentage Score: 72%

☎ 01334 474321 🖷 01334 477896

Dir: *from W on A91 past golf courses, through an old viaduct, hotel 200m on left before rdbt*

Occupying an enviable position with fine views of the sea and part of the golf course, this imposing Victorian hotel offers well-appointed accommodation. The friendly staff provide an attentive level of service and guests in the restaurant and bar can enjoy the fine views which are said to be the best in town! Cuisine features freshly prepared dishes, using local produce where possible.

ROOMS: 48 en suite (bth/shr) **MEALS:** Lunch £9.95 Dinner £29 & alc V meals Coffee am Tea pm **FACILITIES:** CTV in all bedrooms STV Sauna Solarium Golf Mgr to organise golf **CONF:** Thtr 90 Class 40 Board 20 Del from £75 * **SERVICES:** Lift Night porter 21P **NOTES:** No smoking in restaurant Last d 10pm

CARDS:

ST ANDREWS Fife **Map 12 NO51**

★★★ **Rufflets Country House**

Strathkinness Low Rd KY16 9TX

Quality Percentage Score: 83%

☎ 01334 472594 🖷 01334 478703

Dir: *1.5m W on B939*

Rufflets, one of Scotland's oldest established country house hotels, is going from strength to strength. Situated just over a mile from St Andrews, the house is set amid 10 acres of beautiful award-winning gardens. Inviting public areas include a choice of relaxing lounges, filled with plump cushioned sofas and armchairs, and the well stocked Flints Bar. The Garden Restaurant provides a civilised setting for imaginative Scottish cuisine. Striking colour schemes do much to enhance the individually furnished bedrooms.

ROOMS: 21 en suite (bth/shr) 3 annexe en suite (bth/shr) (7 fmly) No smoking in 14 bedrooms s fr £95; d £170-£180 (incl. bkfst) * LB Off peak **MEALS:** Lunch £17 Dinner £30-£34.50 V meals Coffee am Tea pm **FACILITIES:** CTV in all bedrooms STV Putting green Golf driving net Xmas **CONF:** Thtr 50 Class 30 Board 25 Del from £110 * **SERVICES:** Night porter 52P **NOTES:** No dogs (ex guide dogs) No coaches No smoking in restaurant Last d 9pm

CARDS:

ST ANDREWS Fife **Map 12 NO51**

★★★ **St Andrews Golf**

40 The Scores KY16 9AS

Quality Percentage Score: 77%

☎ 01334 472611 🖷 01334 472188

Dir: *follow signs 'Golf Course' into Golf Place and in 200yds right into The Scores*

The Hughes family and their charming staff will assure you of a warm welcome and attentive service at their well-established hotel overlooking the bay. Rub shoulders with golfers from

contd.

around the world or simply relax in the inviting lounge with a magazine. The elegant restaurant offers cooking in the modern style but golfing appetites will be well satisfied. Bedrooms - several having sea views - come in a variety of sizes, and are stylishly decorated.

ROOMS: 22 en suite (bth/shr) (9 fmly) **MEALS:** Lunch £15 High tea fr £9 Dinner fr £28.50 Scottish & French Cuisine V meals Coffee am Tea pm **FACILITIES:** CTV in all bedrooms STV **CONF:** Thtr 200 Class 50 Board 20 **SERVICES:** Lift Night porter 6P **NOTES:** No smoking in restaurant Last d 9.30pm **CARDS:**

See advert on opposite page

ST ANDREWS Fife **Map 12 NO51**

★★★ Drumoig Golf Hotel

Drumoig KY16 OBE

Quality Percentage Score: 69%

☎ 01382 541800 01382 542211

(For full entry see Leuchars)

ST ANDREWS Fife **Map 12 NO51**

★★★ Scores

76 The Scores KY16 9BB

Quality Percentage Score: 64%

☎ 01334 472451 01334 473947

Dir: *on entering St Andrews follow signs to West Sands and Sea Life Centre, premises facing the sea diagonally opposite the Royal & Ancient Clubhouse*

Situated within a few yards of the Old Course and enjoying fine views over the bay, this welcoming hotel attracts an international clientele. Public areas include an all-day coffee-shop, and a choice of bars, one of which is full of golfing memorabilia. Fresh

contd.

Symbols and Abbreviations are listed and explained on pages 4 and 5

S

local seafood features strongly on the restaurant menu. Bedrooms come in a variety of sizes and styles.
ROOMS: 30 en suite (bth/shr) (1 fmly) s £85; d £142-£162 (incl. bkfst) * LB Off peak **MEALS:** Lunch £9-£11alc Dinner £9-£17alc Scottish & French Cuisine V meals Coffee am Tea pm **FACILITIES:** CTV in all bedrooms STV Xmas **CONF:** Thtr 150 Class 60 Board 40 **SERVICES:** Lift Night porter 10P **NOTES:** No dogs (ex guide dogs) No coaches No smoking in restaurant Last d 9pm
CARDS:

See advert on page 873

ST ANDREWS Fife — Map 12 NO51

★★ *Russell Hotel*

26 The Scores KY16 9AS
Quality Percentage Score: 69%
☎ 01334 473447 Fax 01334 478279
Dir: *A91-St Andrews turn right at 2nd rdbt into Golf Place, turn right again after 200yds into The Scores, hotel in 300yds on the left*
A warm welcome is assured at this comfortable family-run hotel, which enjoys lovely sea views. Though variable in size, the bedrooms are comfortable with attractive decor and modern furnishings. There is no lounge, but the lively Victorian bar is inviting and both here, and in the adjacent Supper Room, a wide range of dishes is offered.
ROOMS: 10 en suite (bth/shr) (3 fmly) **MEALS:** International Cuisine V meals Coffee am **FACILITIES:** CTV in all bedrooms STV **SERVICES:** Night porter **NOTES:** No dogs (ex guide dogs) No coaches No smoking in restaurant Last d 10pm **CARDS:**

ST ANDREWS Fife — Map 12 NO51

★★ *Ardgowan*

2 Playfair Ter KY16 9HX
Quality Percentage Score: 60%
☎ 01334 472970 Fax 01334 478380
Dir: *follow A91 straight into town, past first rdbt & then a mini rdbt, hotel 200 metres on left*
This family run hotel is situated near to the town centre, and is particularly popular for meals, which are taken in the lounge bar or in Playfair's Restaurant. Bedrooms have been cleverly furnished to make the best use of available space. The young staff are friendly and attentive.
ROOMS: 12 en suite (bth/shr) (2 fmly) **MEALS:** Scottish & French Cuisine V meals Tea pm **FACILITIES:** CTV in all bedrooms **NOTES:** Last d 10pm Closed 25-26 Dec 1-2 Jan **CARDS:**

S

ST ANDREWS Fife — Map 12 NO51

★★ Parklands Hotel & Restaurant

Kinburn Castle, Double Dykes Rd KY16 9DS
Quality Percentage Score: 60%
☎ 01334 473620 Fax 01334 473620
Dir: *opposite Kinburn Park and Museum*
Located opposite Kilburn Park this friendly family run hotel appeals to golfers, tourists, and visiting business guests. Bedrooms vary in size and style offering all the expected modern amenities. The attractive dining room is a focal point and chef/proprietor Brian McLellan's gourmet dinners continue to merit our rosette accolade.
ROOMS: 9 rms (7 bth/shr) (2 fmly) s fr £45; d fr £75 (incl. bkfst) * LB Off peak **MEALS:** Lunch £8.45-£12.50 High tea fr £6.95 Dinner fr £18.50 International Cuisine Coffee am **FACILITIES:** CTV in all bedrooms **SERVICES:** 9P **NOTES:** No dogs (ex guide dogs) No smoking in restaurant Last d 8.30pm Closed Xmas/New Year **CARDS:**

ST BOSWELLS Scottish Borders — Map 12 NT53

★★★ Dryburgh Abbey

TD6 0RQ
Quality Percentage Score: 76%
☎ 01835 822261 Fax 01835 823945
Dir: *at St Boswells turn onto B6404 & through village. Continue 2m, then turn left B6356 Scott's View. Through Clintmains village, hotel 1.8m*
An impressive red sandstone mansion, with stylish public areas, a choice of inviting lounges and a well stocked bar. In the restaurant a carefully selected wine list complements fresh local produce on the daily changing menu. Thoughtfully equipped bedrooms vary in size with suites and deluxe rooms available. There is smart accommodation in a new wing.
ROOMS: 37 en suite (bth/shr) 1 annexe en suite (bth/shr) (5 fmly) s £59-£110; d £59-£90 (incl. bkfst & dinner) * Off peak **MEALS:** Sunday Lunch £10.95-£16.95 High tea £8.50-£16.50alc Dinner £24 Scottish, English & French Cuisine V meals Coffee am Tea pm **FACILITIES:** CTV in all bedrooms Indoor swimming pool (heated) Fishing Putting green Xmas **CONF:** Thtr 120 Class 90 Board 70 Del from £120 * **SERVICES:** Lift Night porter 103P **NOTES:** No smoking in restaurant Last d 9.15pm **CARDS:**

ST BOSWELLS Scottish Borders — Map 12 NT53

★★ Buccleuch Arms

The Green TD6 0EW
Quality Percentage Score: 66%
☎ 01835 822243 Fax 01835 823965
Dir: *on A68, 8m N of Jedburgh*
Formerly a coaching inn, this charming hotel stands by the roadside opposite the village green and beside the local cricket pitch. It offers a good range of meals in both the recently refurbished bar and stylish restaurant. Morning coffees and afternoon teas are served in the attractive lounge which has an open fire in season. The well equipped bedrooms come in a variety of sizes.
ROOMS: 18 rms (17 bth/shr) (1 fmly) s fr £50; d fr £80 (incl. bkfst) * LB Off peak **MEALS:** Lunch £13.95-£16.95 High tea £7.25 Dinner £16.95-£19.95 International Cuisine V meals Coffee am Tea pm **FACILITIES:** CTV in all bedrooms Putting green Xmas **CONF:** Thtr 100 Class 40 Board 30 Del from £50 * **SERVICES:** 52P **NOTES:** No smoking in restaurant Last d 8.30pm Closed 25 Dec
CARDS:

ST FILLANS Perth & Kinross — Map 11 NN62

★★★ The Four Seasons Hotel

Loch Earn PH6 2NF
Quality Percentage Score: 64%
☎ 01764 685333 Fax 01764 685444
Dir: *on A85, towards W of village facing Loch*
This is a popular holiday hotel where most of the bedrooms enjoy a spectacular outlook over Loch Earn. Guests are sure to appreciate the relaxing atmosphere in the lounges. Informal dining can be had in the Tarken Room, or there is the main restaurant offering refreshingly uncomplicated cooking.
ROOMS: 12 en suite (bth/shr) 6 annexe en suite (bth/shr) s £36-£54; d £72-£88 (incl. bkfst) * LB Off peak **MEALS:** Bar Lunch £6.95-£26alc Dinner £23.95-£27.95 & alc V meals Coffee am Tea pm **FACILITIES:** CTV in all bedrooms Xmas **CONF:** Thtr 95 Class 45 Board 38 Del from £67 * **SERVICES:** 40P **NOTES:** No smoking in restaurant Last d 9pm Closed 3 Jan-Mar **CARDS:**

ST FILLANS Perth & Kinross — Map 11 NN62

★★ Achray House

Loch Earn PH6 2NF

Quality Percentage Score: 70%

☎ 01764 685231 Fax 01764 685320

Dir: *on A85 12 miles from Crieff*

This attractive small hotel enjoys a glorious outlook over Loch Earn. Bedrooms, with pretty colour schemes, are comfortably modern in appointment. As well as a lounge, public areas include a bar with conservatory extension, that provides an informal mealtime alternative to the dining room.

ROOMS: 9 rms (8 bth/shr) (1 fmly) s £37-£46.50; d £50-£69 (incl. bkfst) * LB Off peak **MEALS:** Sunday Lunch £10-£14alc Dinner £19.50 & alc V meals **FACILITIES:** CTV in all bedrooms Xmas **CONF:** Class 20 Board 20 Del from £60 * **SERVICES:** 30P **NOTES:** No dogs (ex guide dogs) No coaches No smoking in restaurant Last d 8.30pm Closed 4-22 Jan **CARDS:**

SANQUHAR Dumfries & Galloway — Map 11 NS70

★★ *Blackaddie House*

Blackaddie Rd DG4 6JJ

Quality Percentage Score: 65%

☎ 01659 50270 Fax 01659 50270

Dir: *turn off A76 just N of Sanquhar at Burnside Service Station. Private road to hotel 300mtrs on right*

Dating from 1540, Blackaddie House was originally a rectory, and stands in its own colourful gardens by the banks of the River Nith. Popular with tourists, business guests and sporting enthusiasts, the hotel has a friendly and relaxing atmosphere.

ROOMS: 9 en suite (bth/shr) (2 fmly) **MEALS:** Scottish & French Cuisine V meals Coffee am **FACILITIES:** CTV in all bedrooms Fishing Riding Game shooting Gold panning Bike hire ch fac **CONF:** Thtr 50 Class 20 Board 20 **SERVICES:** 20P **NOTES:** No dogs (ex guide dogs) No smoking in restaurant Last d 9pm **CARDS:**

SCALASAIG See Colonsay, Isle of

SCOURIE Highland — Map 14 NC14

★★ Eddrachilles

Badcall Bay IV27 4TH

Quality Percentage Score: 70%

☎ 01971 502080 Fax 01971 502477

Dir: *2m S on A894, 7m N of Kylesku Bridge*

An appealing holiday hotel in woodland beside the Badcall Bay, with sea views. There are inviting lounges and a popular conservatory overlooking the bay. The dining room, with its natural stone walls and flagstone floor, offers fixed-price and carte menus. The well equipped bedrooms are smartly refurbished.

ROOMS: 11 en suite (bth/shr) (1 fmly) s £46-£58; d £78-£84 (incl. bkfst) * LB Off peak **MEALS:** Bar Lunch fr £3.50alc Dinner fr £12.50 & alc V meals Coffee am **FACILITIES:** CTV in all bedrooms Fishing Boats for hire **SERVICES:** 25P **NOTES:** No dogs (ex guide dogs) No coaches No children 3yrs Last d 8pm Closed Nov-Feb **CARDS:**

SCOURIE Highland — Map 14 NC14

★★ Scourie

IV27 4SX

Quality Percentage Score: 64%

☎ 01971 502396 Fax 01971 502423

Dir: *situated on A894 in the village of Scourie*

An anglers paradise, with extensive fishing rights available on a 25,000-acre estate. Public areas include a choice of comfortable lounges, a cosy bar and a smart dining room offering wholesome fare. There is a relaxed and friendly atmosphere.

ROOMS: 18 rms (16 bth 1 shr) 2 annexe en suite (bth) (2 fmly) s £33-£43; d £55-£75 (incl. bkfst) * LB Off peak **MEALS:** Bar Lunch £10-£18alc Dinner fr £17 V meals Coffee am Tea pm **FACILITIES:** Fishing Pool table **SERVICES:** 30P **NOTES:** No smoking in restaurant Last d 8.30pm Closed mid Oct -end Mar **CARDS:**

SHETLAND — Map 16

BRAE — Map 16 HU36

★★★ Busta House

ZE2 9QN

Quality Percentage Score: 65%

THE CIRCLE
Selected Individual Hotels
GREAT BRITAIN

☎ 01806 522506 Fax 01806 522588

Dir: *after Brae follow road north, bearing left around Busta Voe, within 1m hotel signposted Muckle Roe*

This charming 16th-century former laird's home is set in grounds overlooking Busta Voe. Bedrooms are cleverly designed in pleasant country-house style to maximise available space, and day rooms include a choice of lounges, a first-floor library lounge, a bar popular for its meals, and an attractive dining room offering two fixed-price menus, one of which is vegetarian.

ROOMS: 20 en suite (bth/shr) (2 fmly) s fr £70; d fr £91 (incl. bkfst) * LB Off peak **MEALS:** Bar Lunch £9-£18alc Dinner £21-£23.50 International Cuisine V meals Coffee am Tea pm **FACILITIES:** CTV in all bedrooms Sea fishing Water sports **SERVICES:** 35P **NOTES:** No coaches No smoking in restaurant Last d 9pm Closed 23 Dec-2 Jan

CARDS:

LERWICK — Map 16 HU44

★★★ Shetland

Holmsgarth Rd ZE1 0PW

Quality Percentage Score: 69%

☎ 01595 695515 Fax 01595 695828

Dir: *opposite P&O ferry terminal, on main route north from town centre*

This modern hotel stands directly opposite the main ferry terminal. Public areas include a comfortable open plan bar-lounge and two choices for eating: Oasis Bistro and the more formal Ninian Restaurant. Bedrooms are well proportioned and comfortable.

ROOMS: 64 en suite (bth/shr) (4 fmly) No smoking in 14 bedrooms s £76.95; d £92.50 (incl. bkfst) * LB Off peak **MEALS:** Lunch £11.95 Dinner £23.50 & alc French Cuisine V meals Coffee am Tea pm **FACILITIES:** CTV in all bedrooms STV **CONF:** Thtr 320 Class 75 Board 50 **SERVICES:** Lift Night porter 150P **NOTES:** No dogs (ex guide dogs) No smoking in restaurant Last d 9.30pm **CARDS:**

S

LERWICK — Map 16 HU44

★★★ Lerwick

15 South Rd ZE1 0RB

Quality Percentage Score: 67%

☎ 01595 692166 Fax 01595 694419

Dir: *near town centre, on main road southwards to/from airport. 25m from main airport, located in central Lerwick*

This popular hotel has lovely views over Breiwick Bay to Bressay and Breiwick Islands. Bedrooms have modern facilities, there is an attractive foyer lounge, a pleasant Brasserie open for both lunch and dinner, and a more formal restaurant, with sea views, where a menu based on fine local produce is available at dinner.

ROOMS: 35 en suite (bth/shr) (3 fmly) s fr £72 (incl. bkfst) * LB Off peak **MEALS:** Lunch £10.85-£13.95alc Dinner £14.05-£24.40alc International Cuisine V meals Coffee am Tea pm **FACILITIES:** CTV in all bedrooms STV **CONF:** Thtr 60 Class 40 Board 20 **SERVICES:** Night porter 50P **NOTES:** No dogs (ex guide dogs) No smoking area in restaurant Last d 9.30pm **CARDS:**

UNST **Map 16 HP60**

★★ The Baltasound
ZE2 9DS
Quality Percentage Score: 60%
☎ 01957 711334 📠 01957 711358
This family-run hotel is the most northerly hotel in the British Isles. Apart from the separate breakfast room, public areas are open plan, with lounge, bar and dining room flowing through an L-shaped space. Some bedrooms are in the main building, but most are in pleasant log cabins dispersed round the grounds.
ROOMS: 8 rms (5 bth/shr) 17 annexe en suite (bth/shr) (17 fmly) s £39.50-£45; d £59 (incl. bkfst) * Off peak **MEALS:** Bar Lunch £8-£10.50alc Dinner £8.25-£16.25alc V meals Coffee am Tea pm **FACILITIES:** CTV in all bedrooms Fishing Pool table **CONF:** Class 20 **SERVICES:** 20P **NOTES:** No smoking in restaurant Last d 8.30pm **CARDS:**

SHIELDAIG Highland **Map 14 NG85**

★ Tigh an Eilean
IV54 8XN
Quality Percentage Score: 73%
☎ 01520 755251 📠 01520 755321
The 'house of the island' looks out on the bay and is surrounded by whitewashed crofts and fishermen's cottages, sheltered by pine trees. Bedrooms are well maintained, there is an 'honesty' bar and three comfortable lounges. The dinner menu features seafood and much local produce.
ROOMS: 11 en suite (bth/shr) (1 fmly) s £48.55; d £107.40 (incl. bkfst) * Off peak **MEALS:** Dinner fr £26.15 Scottish & French Cuisine Coffee am **SERVICES:** 15P **NOTES:** No coaches No smoking in restaurant Last d 8.30pm Closed Oct-Etr **CARDS:**

SKYE, ISLE OF Highland **Map 13**

DUNVEGAN **Map 13 NG24**

★★ Atholl House
IV55 8WA
Quality Percentage Score: 66%
☎ 01470 521219 📠 01470 521481
Dir: *over Skye bridge take A87 to Sligachan turn left onto A850 to Dunvegan, approach village hotel is 1m on right*
Personally run and warmly welcoming, this hotel is at the southern end of the village. The attractive public areas consist of the comfortable lounge where refreshments are willingly served, and the dining room which offers carefully prepared dishes from the carte menu at dinner; light lunches and high teas are also served. Bedrooms, of varying sizes, include two with four-posters, and are bright and airy with modern fitted furnishings.
ROOMS: 9 en suite (bth/shr) (1 fmly) s £45-£57; d £60-£84 (incl. bkfst) * LB Off peak **MEALS:** Lunch £2-£8alc High tea £2-£9alc Dinner £16-£18 & alc V meals Coffee am Tea pm **FACILITIES:** CTV in all bedrooms Xmas **CONF:** Thtr 30 Class 25 Board 25 **SERVICES:** 18P **NOTES:** No smoking in restaurant Last d 9pm Closed end Dec-end Feb
CARDS:

HARLOSH **Map 13 NG24**

The Premier Collection

★ Harlosh House
IV55 8ZG
☎ 01470 521367 📠 01470 521367
Dir: *A863 between Roag & Caroy, follow sign for Harlosh*
Magnificent views are to be had from this hotel, set on the shores of Loch Bracadale. The cottage style bedrooms are attractively furnished. Local seafood is put to good use in the set dinner menus. The main lounge is inviting and there is a further small lounge area.

ROOMS: 6 en suite (bth/shr) (2 fmly) No smoking in all bedrooms s £52.50-£105; d £85-£105 (incl. bkfst) * Off peak **MEALS:** Dinner £27.50 International Cuisine Coffee am Tea pm **FACILITIES:** TV available **SERVICES:** 10P **NOTES:** No dogs (ex guide dogs) No coaches No smoking in restaurant Last d 8.30pm Closed mid Oct-Etr
CARDS:

ISLE ORNSAY **Map 13 NG61**

★★ Kinloch Lodge
IV43 8QY
Quality Percentage Score: 75%
☎ 01471 833214 & 833333 📠 01471 833277
Dir: *6m S of Broadford on A851, 10m N of Armadale on A851*
At the end of a bumpy forest track, which replaces the former drive because of a damaged bridge, is the fine home of Lord and Lady Macdonald where guests are made to feel like friends by the owners and their charming staff. Some rooms have views over Loch Na Dal, and bedrooms are priced according to their size and location in the building. The two drawing rooms have log fires and comfortable settees; family portraits and photos are displayed throughout, and the elegant dining room complements Lady Claire's renowned cuisine. The latest development of a house in the grounds is now complete and contains five splendid new bedrooms, a homely lounge and Lady Claire's magnificent demonstration kitchen.
ROOMS: 10 rms (8 bth/shr) No smoking in all bedrooms s fr £45; d £90-£190 (incl. bkfst) * LB Off peak **MEALS:** Dinner £28-£37 Coffee am Tea pm **FACILITIES:** Fishing Deer Stalking Cooking demonstrations **SERVICES:** 18P **NOTES:** No coaches No smoking in restaurant Closed 22 Dec-31 Jan **CARDS:**

ISLE ORNSAY **Map 13 NG61**

★★ Hotel Eilean Iarmain
IV43 8QR
Quality Percentage Score: 69%
☎ 01471 833332 📠 01471 833275
Dir: *A851, A852, right to Isle Ornsay Harbour front*
Forming the nucleus of a restored fishing and crofting community, this 19th-century island inn provides traditional values of hospitality. Bedrooms, including those in the Garden House opposite the main building, are appropriately traditional in style and most have lovely views. There is a small cosy sitting room and the timber-clad pub often features impromptu ceilidhs, whilst the attractive candlelit dining room offers innovative

contd.

Scottish fare. The Gaelic-speaking staff under Effie Kennedy's fine management are friendly and willing to please.
ROOMS: 6 en suite (bth/shr) 6 annexe en suite (bth) (2 fmly) No smoking in 6 bedrooms s £85; d £130 (incl. bkfst) LB Off peak
MEALS: Lunch £16.50 Dinner £31 V meals Coffee am Tea pm
FACILITIES: CTV in 5 bedrooms Fishing Shooting Wkly live entertainment Xmas **CONF:** Thtr 50 Class 30 Board 25 Del from £100 *
SERVICES: 30P **NOTES:** No smoking in restaurant Last d 8.45pm
CARDS:

See advert on this page

PORTREE — Map 13 NG44
★★★ Cuillin Hills
IV51 9QU
Quality Percentage Score: 72%
☎ 01478 612003 Fax 01478 613092
Dir: *turn right 0.25m N of Portree off the A855 and follow signs for hotel*

Looking out across the bay to the Cuillin Hills beyond, this

contd.

smart hotel is a popular holiday destination. There are lounges and a separate bar. Bedrooms have attractive decor and the hotel has well advanced plans for a leisure centre. Additional de luxe bedrooms and an elegant restaurant are the result of upgrading.
ROOMS: 21 en suite (bth/shr) 9 annexe en suite (bth/shr) (2 fmly) No smoking in 7 bedrooms s £38-£56; d £76-£112 (incl. bkfst) * LB Off peak **MEALS:** Sunday Lunch fr £8.95 Dinner fr £26 & alc Scottish & French Cuisine V meals Coffee am Tea pm **FACILITIES:** CTV in all bedrooms STV Xmas **CONF:** Thtr 100 Class 60 Board 30 Del from £70 * **SERVICES:** 56P **NOTES:** No coaches No smoking in restaurant Last d 9pm **CARDS:**

See advert on page 877

PORTREE — Map 13 NG44
★★ Bosville
Bosville Ter IV51 9DG
Quality Percentage Score: 72%
☎ 01478 612846 Fax 01478 613434
This established family hotel, close to the town centre, provides attractively refurbished, well equipped accommodation. The public areas are limited to the restaurant, which offers two distinctive styles. The Chandlery offers interesting seafood dishes in the evening and the larger room serves a more popular style of food throughout the day.
ROOMS: 15 en suite (bth/shr) (2 fmly) No smoking in 10 bedrooms s £35-£60; d £58-£90 (incl. bkfst) * LB Off peak **MEALS:** Scottish & French Cuisine V meals Coffee am Tea pm **FACILITIES:** CTV in all bedrooms STV Xmas **SERVICES:** Night porter 14P **NOTES:** No dogs (ex guide dogs) No coaches **CARDS:**

See advert on opposite page

PORTREE — Map 13 NG44
★★ Rosedale
IV51 9DB
Quality Percentage Score: 72%
☎ 01478 613131 Fax 01478 612531
Dir: *follow the directions to the Village Centre and Harbour, hotel is on the waterfront of Portree Harbourside*

A holiday hotel converted from three 19th-century harbour-front buildings. It offers modern bedrooms in a range of shapes and sizes, decorated and furnished to a pleasant standard. Public areas on different levels include two lounges and a bar. The attractive upstairs restaurant overlooks the bay.
ROOMS: 20 en suite (bth/shr) 3 annexe en suite (bth/shr) (1 fmly) s £40-£46; d £68-£92 (incl. bkfst) * LB Off peak **MEALS:** Lunch £6.95-£13 Dinner £18-£25 Coffee am **FACILITIES:** CTV in all bedrooms **SERVICES:** 10P **NOTES:** No coaches No smoking in restaurant Last d 8.30pm **CARDS:**

PORTREE — Map 13 NG44
★★ Royal
IV51 9BU
Quality Percentage Score: 67%
☎ 01478 612525 Fax 01478 613198
Dir: *turn off A850 on to A855, hotel is on corner overlooking the harbour*
This established hotel overlooks the picturesque harbour and has a well-equipped leisure centre. The bistro, lounge and bars are attractively decorated. In the high season, live entertainment is provided in the Ceilidh Room. Bedrooms offer a good standard of comfort.
ROOMS: 21 en suite (bth/shr) No smoking in 6 bedrooms s £45-£52; d £60-£78 (incl. bkfst) LB Off peak **MEALS:** Lunch £8.50-£12 Dinner fr £17.50 & alc V meals Coffee am Tea pm **FACILITIES:** CTV in all bedrooms Sauna Solarium Gym Pool table Jacuzzi/spa Wkly live entertainment Xmas **CONF:** Thtr 130 Board 16 **SERVICES:** 14P **NOTES:** No coaches No smoking area in restaurant Last d 9.30pm **CARDS:**

UIG — Map 13 NG36
★★ *Uig*
IV51 9YE
Quality Percentage Score: 70%
☎ 01470 542205 Fax 01470 542308
An established hotel overlooking the bay and ferry terminal. The welcoming residents' bar offers fine views as well as a good range of tasty bar food, there is a simpler bar to the rear. The formal dining room provides some interesting and innovative dishes locally sourced. Bedrooms are spacious.
ROOMS: 10 en suite (bth/shr) 7 annexe en suite (bth/shr) (2 fmly) **MEALS:** V meals Coffee am Tea pm **FACILITIES:** CTV in all bedrooms Riding Sauna **SERVICES:** 20P **NOTES:** No coaches No smoking in restaurant Last d 9pm **CARDS:**

SOUTH QUEENSFERRY City of Edinburgh — Map 11 NT17
★★★ Forth Bridges
1 Ferrymuir Gait EH30 9SF
REGAL
Quality Percentage Score: 61%
☎ 0131 469 9955 Fax 0131 319 1733
Dir: *adjacent to Forth Road Bridge, follow signs - M90 then A8000, hotel on left*

The Firth of Forth with its famous bridges provides a breathtaking backdrop for this modern hotel situated only 20 minutes from both the centre of Edinburgh and the regional airport. The river-facing bedrooms are particularly spacious,

contd.

For Useful Information and Important Telephone Number Changes turn to page 25

while the upstairs restaurant also takes maximum advantage of the panoramic views.
ROOMS: 108 en suite (bth/shr) (19 fmly) No smoking in 43 bedrooms s £99-£115; d £120-£135 * LB Off peak **MEALS:** Lunch £7.50-£10.50 High tea fr £6.50 Dinner fr £14.50 International Cuisine V meals Coffee am Tea pm **FACILITIES:** CTV in all bedrooms Indoor swimming pool (heated) Squash Sauna Solarium Gym Jacuzzi/spa Dance studio Xmas **CONF:** Thtr 200 Class 90 Board 60 Del from £70 * **SERVICES:** Lift Night porter 200P **NOTES:** No smoking in restaurant Last d 9.45pm
CARDS:

SOUTH QUEENSFERRY City of Edinburgh **Map 11 NT17**

Travel Inn

Builyeon Rd EH30 3YJ
☎ 0131 311 5056 Fax 0131 331 4746
Dir: *leave M9 junct 1a take A8000 direction of Forth Road Bridge, at 3rd rdbt take 2nd exit into Builyeaon Road, do not go onto Forth Road Bridge*
This modern building offers accommodation in smart, spacious and well equipped bedrooms, all with en-suite bathrooms. Refreshments may be taken at the nearby family restaurant. For details about current prices consult the Contents Page under Hotel Groups for the Travel Inn phone number.
ROOMS: 47 en suite (bth/shr) d £39.95 *

STANLEY Perth & Kinross **Map 11 NO13**

★★ The Tayside

Mill St PH1 4NL
Quality Percentage Score: 65%
☎ 01738 828249 Fax 01738 827216
Dir: *from Perth Northbound on the A9 first exit B9099 to Stanley, signposted in villlage*
Under enthusiastic new ownership, this popular sporting, golfing, and tourist hotel is undergoing a programme of refurbishment. Public areas have a comfortable traditional feel and include a choice of contrasting bars, a cosy lounge, and a tartan and panelled dining room. Bedrooms are variable in size and offer both modern and traditional appointments.
ROOMS: 16 rms (4 bth 10 shr) (2 fmly) s £25-£60; d £40-£100 (incl. bkfst) * LB Off peak **MEALS:** Dinner £15-£17.50 & alc Scottish, English & French Cuisine V meals Coffee am Tea pm **FACILITIES:** CTV in all bedrooms Fishing Pool table Wkly live entertainment Xmas **CONF:** Thtr 100 Class 75 Board 75 Del from £45 * **SERVICES:** 42P **NOTES:** No smoking in restaurant Last d 9pm **CARDS:**

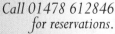

STIRLING Stirling **Map 11 NS79**

★★★★ Stirling Highland

SCOTTISH HIGHLAND HOTELS

Spittal St FK8 1DU
Quality Percentage Score: 67%
☎ 01786 272727 Fax 01786 272829
Dir: *take A84 into Stirling and follow signs to Stirling Castle until you reach the Albert Hall. Turn left and left again, following signs to Castle*
500 yards from the castle, this interesting hotel is the former high school. Meeting rooms are named after classrooms, drinks are served in the Headmasters Study and carefully prepared meals are taken in the Scholars restaurant! Rizzios is a more informal Italian restaurant, there is also a leisure club with a good size swimming pool.
ROOMS: 94 en suite (bth/shr) (4 fmly) No smoking in 56 bedrooms s £104-£116.50; d £140-£165 * LB Off peak **MEALS:** Lunch £5-£15 & alc High tea £7-£15 Dinner £19.95-£22.50 & alc Scottish & Italian Cuisine V meals Coffee am Tea pm **FACILITIES:** CTV in all bedrooms STV Indoor swimming pool (heated) Squash Snooker Sauna Solarium Gym Jacuzzi/spa Steam room Dance Studio Beauty therapist Xmas **CONF:** Thtr 120 Class 80 Board 45 Del from £130 * **SERVICES:** Lift Night porter 96P **NOTES:** No smoking in restaurant Last d 10pm
CARDS:

STIRLING Stirling **Map 11 NS79**

★★ Terraces

4 Melville Ter FK8 2ND

Quality Percentage Score: 67%

☎ 01786 472268 📠 01786 450314

Dir: *from A872 1st left at 2nd rdbt. At lights onto Melville Terrace (inside lane) parallel to main rd on left. Hotel at bottom*

Friendly attentive service is a feature of this hotel just off the town centre. Its bedrooms are well equipped and a good choice of dishes is available in the restaurant or as room service.

ROOMS: 18 en suite (bth/shr) (3 fmly) s £68-£69.50; d £80-£82.50 (incl. bkfst) * LB Off peak **MEALS:** Lunch £4.50-£11alc Dinner £12.75-£14 & alc International Cuisine V meals Coffee am Tea pm **FACILITIES:** CTV in all bedrooms STV Xmas **CONF:** Thtr 130 Class 60 Board 48 Del from £62.50 * **SERVICES:** Night porter 25P **NOTES:** No smoking in restaurant Last d 8.50pm **CARDS:**

STIRLING Stirling **Map 11 NS79**

⇧ Travel Inn

Whins of Milton, Glasgow Rd FK7 8EX

☎ 01786 811256 📠 01786 816415

Dir: *on A872, 0.25m from junct 9 of the M9/M80 intersection*

This modern building offers accommodation in smart, spacious and well equipped bedrooms, all with en-suite bathrooms. Refreshments may be taken at the nearby family restaurant. For details about current prices consult the Contents Page under Hotel Groups for the Travel Inn phone number.

ROOMS: 40 en suite (bth/shr) d £39.95 *

STIRLING Stirling **Map 11 NS79**

⇧ Travelodge

Pirnhall Roundabout, Snabhead FK7 8EU

☎ Central Res 8000 555300 📠 01525 878450

Dir: *junct M9/M80*

This modern building offers accommodation in smart, spacious and well equipped bedrooms, all with en-suite bathrooms. Refreshments may be taken at the nearby family restaurant. For details about current prices, consult the Contents Page under Hotel Groups for the Travelodge phone number.

ROOMS: 37 en suite (bth/shr) d £49.95 *

STONEHAVEN Aberdeenshire **Map 15 NO88**

★★ County Hotel & Leisure Club

Arduthie Rd AB39 2EH

Quality Percentage Score: 65%

☎ 01569 764386 📠 01569 762214

Dir: *off A90, opposite railway station*

A welcoming atmosphere prevails at this personally run hotel situated close to the railway station. Public areas include a choice of bars and an attractive dining room, which feature a collection of prints of celebrities. The bedrooms vary in size and style, and there are good leisure facilities.

ROOMS: 14 en suite (bth/shr) (1 fmly) s £40-£46; d £50-£60 (incl. bkfst) * LB Off peak **MEALS:** International Cuisine V meals Coffee am **FACILITIES:** CTV in all bedrooms Squash Sauna Gym Table tennis **CONF:** Thtr 150 Class 60 Board 32 **SERVICES:** 40P **NOTES:** No dogs (ex guide dogs) Last d 8.45pm **CARDS:**

STORNOWAY See Lewis, Isle of

STRACHUR Argyll & Bute **Map 10 NN00**

★★★ Creggans Inn

PA27 8BX

Quality Percentage Score: 67%

☎ 01369 860279 📠 01369 860637

Dir: *follow A82/A83 Loch Lomond road to Arrochar. Continue on A83 then take A815 Strachur*

A major transformation is taking place at this long established Highland Inn which stands beside the A815 enjoying spectacular views over Loch Fyne. On our recent visit, all the loch facing bedrooms had been tastefully refurbished with pretty co-ordinated colour schemes and individual furnishings. Rear facing rooms have been cosmetically enhanced with complete upgrade planned for the start of the 2000 season. Inviting public areas include a choice of inviting lounges and contrasting bars while the splendid lochview restaurant, with its candle lit tables, provides the appropriate setting for the innovative creations of the kitchen team which are based on the finest ingredients from Scotland's larder.

ROOMS: 17 en suite (bth/shr) s £57.50-£125; d £95-£150 (incl. bkfst) * LB Off peak **MEALS:** Bar Lunch £3.50-£30alc High tea £6.95-£12.95 Dinner £22.50-£25 V meals Coffee am Tea pm **FACILITIES:** CTV in all bedrooms Fishing Pool table Clay pigeon shooting Archery Off road driving Xmas **CONF:** Thtr 25 Class 25 Board 25 Del from £125 * **SERVICES:** Night porter 50P **NOTES:** No smoking in restaurant Last d 9.30pm **CARDS:**

STRANRAER Dumfries & Galloway **Map 10 NX06**

★★★★ North West Castle

DG9 8EH

Quality Percentage Score: 68%

☎ 01776 704413 📠 01776 702646

Dir: *on seafront, close to Stena ferry terminal*

This popular hotel overlooks the bay and ferry terminal. Public areas include an elegant dining room where a pianist plays at dinner and an adjoining lounge with large leather armchairs, and blazing fire in season. Bedrooms are well equipped and many are very spacious.

ROOMS: 70 en suite (bth/shr) 3 annexe en suite (bth/shr) (22 fmly) **MEALS:** Scottish & French Cuisine V meals Coffee am Tea pm **FACILITIES:** CTV in all bedrooms STV Indoor swimming pool (heated) Snooker Sauna Solarium Gym Pool table Jacuzzi/spa Curling (Oct-Apr) Games room **CONF:** Thtr 150 Class 60 Board 40 **SERVICES:** Lift Night porter 100P **NOTES:** No dogs (ex guide dogs) No coaches No smoking in restaurant Last d 9.00pm **CARDS:**

See advert on opposite page

STRATHAVEN South Lanarkshire **Map 11 NS74**

★★★ Strathaven

Hamilton Rd ML10 6SZ

Quality Percentage Score: 68%

☎ 01357 521778 📠 01357 520789

This Robert Adam designed mansion house on the outskirts of town is a popular venue for functions. A wing of smart new bedrooms have been added, all bedrooms are well equipped. Public areas include a comfortable lounge, dining room and attractive bar/lounge where meals are popular.

ROOMS: 22 en suite (bth/shr) No smoking in 12 bedrooms s fr £69; d fr £85 (incl. bkfst) * LB Off peak **MEALS:** Lunch fr £11.50 Dinner fr £18.50 Scottish & French Cuisine V meals Coffee am Tea pm **FACILITIES:** CTV in all bedrooms STV Xmas **CONF:** Thtr 180 Class 120 Board 30 Del from £92 * **SERVICES:** Night porter 80P **NOTES:** No dogs (ex guide dogs) No smoking in restaurant Last d 9.30pm **CARDS:**

STRATHBLANE Stirling — Map 11 NS57

★★★ Country Club Hotel

Milngavie Rd G63 9EH

Quality Percentage Score: 71%

☎ 01360 770491 Fax 01360 770345

Dir: *From Glasgow follow A81 through Strathblane. Turn left after leaving the village*

Under enthusiastic new ownership this country house set in 15 acres of grounds, has been totally transformed into a hotel of distinction. The mostly spacious bedrooms are attractively and comfortably furnished and public areas are much extended to include a choice of lounge areas and a popular brasserie as well. There is also a classically presented dining room, where a dedicated team of chefs produce food that attracts a discerning clientele.

ROOMS: 10 en suite (bth/shr) No smoking in all bedrooms
MEALS: V meals Coffee am Tea pm **FACILITIES:** CTV in all bedrooms
CONF: Thtr 120 Class 60 Board 40 **SERVICES:** Lift Night porter 100P
NOTES: No smoking in restaurant Last d 9.30pm
CARDS:

STRATHBLANE Stirling — Map 11 NS57

★★★ Kirkhouse Inn

G63 9AA

Quality Percentage Score: 63%

☎ 01360 770621 Fax 01360 770896

Dir: *A81 Aberfoyce Rd from Glasgow City Centre through Bearsden & Milnfarie.Strathblane on junct with A891*

This pleasant hotel which stands in the centre of the village, in the shadow of the Campsie Fells, is within easy reach of Glasgow. Bedrooms, including a suite and a room with a four-poster, are well equipped, and the best are those at the front. Good bar meals are a local attraction and there is also a separate restaurant and a foyer lounge.

ROOMS: 15 en suite (bth/shr) (2 fmly) **MEALS:** Scottish & International Cuisine V meals Coffee am Tea pm **FACILITIES:** CTV in all bedrooms STV Pool table Wkly live entertainment **CONF:** Thtr 40 Class 20 Board 20 **SERVICES:** Night porter 350P **NOTES:** Last d 9.30pm
CARDS:

STRATHPEFFER Highland — Map 14 NH45

★★ Brunstane Lodge

Golf Rd IV14 9AT

Quality Percentage Score: 72%

☎ 01997 421261 Fax 01997 421261

A Victorian house in landscaped gardens. The individually decorated bedrooms are well maintained and comfortable. There is a tartan-clad bar which is popular with locals as well as a quieter first-floor residents' lounge and a pretty dining room.

ROOMS: 7 rms (6 bth/shr) (2 fmly) **MEALS:** Lunch £9-£12 Dinner £16-£18 V meals **FACILITIES:** CTV in all bedrooms **SERVICES:** 20P
NOTES: No dogs No smoking in restaurant Last d 8.30pm Closed 1 & 2 Jan RS Oct-Mar **CARDS:**

New AA Guides for the Millennium are featured on page 24

Remember to return your Prize Draw card for a chance to win one of 30 relaxing leisure breaks with Corus and Regal hotels. See inside the front cover for the card and competition details.

STRATHYRE Stirling　　　　　　　Map 11 NN51

The Premier Collection

★ ⊛⊛ Creagan House
FK18 8ND
☎ 01877 384638 🖳 01877 384319
Dir: 0.25m N of Strathyre on A84

This old 17th-century farmhouse, in the heart of the Queen Elizabeth Forest Park, has been converted into a most charming, cosy hotel of some distinction. Carefully chosen antique pieces furnish the attractive bedrooms (including one with a hand-made four-poster bed) that are equipped with many extra little comforts and individual touches. The sitting room is comfortable and amply provided with books and magazines; refreshments are willingly served here before or after an enjoyable meal in the impressive baronial-style restaurant. Gordon Gunn cooks in a bold, innovative style, guests can choose from a short or more extensive menu.

ROOMS: 5 en suite (bth/shr) (1 fmly) No smoking in all bedrooms s £50; d £80 (incl. bkfst) LB Off peak **MEALS:** Dinner £18.50-£22.50 French & Scottish Cuisine Coffee am Tea pm **FACILITIES:** CTV in all bedrooms Xmas **CONF:** Thtr 35 Class 12 Board 35 **SERVICES:** 26P **NOTES:** No smoking in restaurant Last d 8.30pm Closed 2-28 Feb **CARDS:** 💳 ■ ■

STRONTIAN Highland　　　　　　Map 14 NM86
★★⊛⊛🢢 Kilcamb Lodge
PH36 4HY
Quality Percentage Score: 78%
☎ 01967 402257 🖳 01967 402041
Dir: off A861

A sympathetically modernised former hunting lodge with loch views. Open fires, deep cushioned sofas, flowers, books and magazines are found in the public rooms. The delightfully furnished bedrooms are thoughtfully equipped with items such as bathrobes. A short choice of well prepared dishes are supplemented by a carefully compiled wine list.

ROOMS: 11 en suite (bth/shr) (1 fmly) No smoking in all bedrooms s £75-£90; d £150-£200 (incl. bkfst & dinner) * LB Off peak **MEALS:** Bar Lunch £10-£15alc High tea £3-£7alc Dinner £29.50 Scottish & French Cuisine V meals Coffee am Tea pm **FACILITIES:** CTV in all bedrooms Fishing Mountain bike & Fishing rod hire Xmas **CONF:** Class 30 Board 20 **SERVICES:** 20P **NOTES:** No coaches No smoking in restaurant Last d 7.30pm Closed Dec-Feb (ex NY)
CARDS: 💳 ■ ■ ▩ ▨

TAIN Highland　　　　　　　　Map 14 NH78
★★★⊛⊛ Mansfield House
Scotsburn Rd IV19 1PR
Quality Percentage Score: 74%
☎ 01862 892052 🖳 01862 892260
Dir: A9 from S, ignore 1st exit signed Tain and take the 2nd exit signed police station

An impressive mansion house, in grounds opposite the Royal Academy. Inviting public areas include an attractive bar and formal dining rooms. Innovative dishes are found on the fixed-priced daily and carte menus. Bedrooms range from tastefully appointed de luxe rooms, furnished in period style, to pleasantly redecorated rooms in the wing.

ROOMS: 8 en suite (bth/shr) 10 annexe en suite (bth/shr) (6 fmly) No smoking in 4 bedrooms s £65-£85; d £100-£130 (incl. bkfst) * LB Off peak **MEALS:** Lunch £11.95 Dinner £25 & alc International Cuisine V meals Coffee am Tea pm **FACILITIES:** CTV in all bedrooms Croquet lawn Beauty salon Xmas **CONF:** Thtr 40 Class 20 Board 20 **SERVICES:** 100P **NOTES:** No smoking in restaurant Last d 9pm **CARDS:** 💳 ■ ■ ▩ ▨ ▨

TAIN Highland　　　　　　　　Map 14 NH78
★★★ Morangie House
Morangie Rd IV19 1PY
Quality Percentage Score: 70%
☎ 01862 892281 🖳 01862 892872
Dir: turn right off A9 northwards

A welcoming family-run hotel, with fine views of the Dornoch Firth. Attractive bedrooms in the new wing are comfortably modern, those in the main house are more traditional. All are well equipped with useful accessories. An extensive range of dishes is available in the formal dining room and smart Garden Restaurant.

ROOMS: 26 en suite (bth/shr) (1 fmly) No smoking in 4 bedrooms s £55; d £85-£90 (incl. bkfst) * LB Off peak **MEALS:** Lunch £6-£12 & alc High tea fr £6.80 Dinner fr £20 & alc Scottish & Continental Cuisine V meals Coffee am Tea pm **FACILITIES:** CTV in all bedrooms STV **CONF:** Thtr 40 Class 40 Board 24 **SERVICES:** Night porter 40P **NOTES:** Last d 9.30pm **CARDS:** 💳 ■ ■ ▩ ▨

TARBERT LOCH FYNE Argyll & Bute　　Map 10 NR86
★★★🢢 Stonefield Castle
PA29 6YJ
Quality Percentage Score: 68%
☎ 01880 820836 🖳 01880 820929
Dir: signed off A83, 2m N of Tarbert

An impressive Scottish baronial mansion, peacefully set in 60 acres of wooded gardens with rhododendrons and some exotic shrubs. Ornate ceilings, marble fireplaces and old family portraits add interest to the delightfully comfortable day rooms, which include a choice of lounges, a well stocked bar, and a spacious restaurant looking out over Loch Fyne. Most bedrooms are in a modern wing and are contemporary in style.

ROOMS: 33 en suite (bth/shr) (1 fmly) **MEALS:** European Cuisine V meals Coffee am Tea pm **FACILITIES:** CTV in all bedrooms Fishing Snooker Sauna Solarium **CONF:** Thtr 180 Class 100 Board 60 **SERVICES:** Lift 50P **NOTES:** No smoking in restaurant Last d 9pm **CARDS:** 💳 ■ ■ ▩ ▨ ▨

See advert on opposite page

For Useful Information and Important Telephone Number Changes turn to page 25

TAYNUILT Argyll & Bute — Map 10 NN03

★★ Polfearn
PA35 1JQ
Quality Percentage Score: 60%
☎ 01866 822251 Fax 01866 822251
Dir: *turn N off A85, continue 1.5m through village down to Loch Shore*

Ongoing improvements are continuing at this family owned hotel which stands one mile north of the village close to the shore of Loch Etive. It enjoys delightful all round views and offers friendly and informal service. A good range of food is available either in the bar or the dining room and the bedrooms provide several different styles.

ROOMS: 16 rms (3 bth 11 shr) (2 fmly) s £25-£33; d £20-£60 (incl. bkfst) * LB Off peak **MEALS:** Bar Lunch £6-£18 High tea £7-£17 Dinner £12-£22 V meals **FACILITIES:** CTV in all bedrooms Xmas **CONF:** Board 70 **SERVICES:** 21P **NOTES:** No smoking in restaurant Last d 8.45pm RS end of January **CARDS:**

THORNHILL Dumfries & Galloway — Map 11 NX89

★★ Trigony House
Closeburn DG3 5EZ
Quality Percentage Score: 73%
☎ 01848 331211 Fax 01848 331303
Dir: *1m S off A76*

Set in four acres of grounds, Trigony House was an Edwardian hunting lodge. Several bedrooms are particularly large. Day rooms include a lounge, a bar and a restaurant overlooking the garden. There is also a good range of bar meals.

ROOMS: 8 en suite (bth/shr) s £45-£50; d £75-£80 (incl. bkfst) LB Off peak **MEALS:** Lunch £7-£15alc Dinner £19.50-£23.50 V meals Coffee am **FACILITIES:** CTV in all bedrooms Fishing **SERVICES:** 30P **NOTES:** No dogs (ex guide dogs) No coaches No children 8yrs No smoking in restaurant Last d 8.45pm **CARDS:**

See advert on this page

THURSO Highland — Map 15 ND16

★★ Park Hotel
KW14 8RE
Quality Percentage Score: 69%
☎ 01847 893251 Fax 01847 893252
Dir: *situated on the right hand side of the A9, on approach to Thurso town centre*

A family run hotel is on the southern approach to the town. The conservatory extension has enhanced the convivial lounge bar where interesting bar meals are served, and the more formal dining room where an attractive carte menu is offered. Bedrooms are bright and well equipped, most are suitable for families.

ROOMS: 11 en suite (bth/shr) (8 fmly) s £30-£40; d £60-£70 (incl. bkfst) * LB Off peak **MEALS:** Lunch £7.45-£8.45alc High tea fr £7.25alc Dinner fr £13.25alc V meals Coffee am Tea pm **FACILITIES:** CTV in all bedrooms Pool table **CONF:** Thtr 100 Class 20 Board 40 Del from £40 * **SERVICES:** 40P **NOTES:** No smoking in restaurant Last d 9pm Closed 1-3 Jan RS 25 Dec **CARDS:**

contd.

TIGHNABRUAICH Argyll & Bute **Map 10 NR97**

Late entry ○ **Royal Hotel**

Shore Rd PA21 2BE

☎ 01700 811239 ▯ 01700 811300

Enthusiastic new owners Roger and Bea McKie have transformed this established hotel. All the refurbished non smoking bedrooms have pleasing colour schemes and are comfortably furnished in traditional style. Public areas include contrasting bars, one has a popular Brasserie providing informal food. Two other dining areas strongly feature seafood and game.

ROOMS: 11 en suite (bth/shr) (1 fmly) No smoking in all bedrooms d £74-£110 (incl. bkfst) * LB Off peak **MEALS:** Bar Lunch £9-£12 & alc Dinner £20-£30 V meals Coffee am Tea pm **FACILITIES:** CTV in all bedrooms Xmas **CONF:** Del from £80 * **SERVICES:** 20P **NOTES:** No coaches No smoking in restaurant Last d 9pm

CARDS:

TOBERMORY See Mull, Isle of

TOMINTOUL Moray **Map 15 NJ11**

★★ **The Gordon Hotel & Cromdales Restaurant**

The Square AB37 9ET

Quality Percentage Score: 70%

☎ 01807 580206 ▯ 01807 580488

Standing in the central square, the hotel has been delightfully refurbished. Its modern bedrooms, pleasantly furnished and equipped, range from de luxe to standard. A comfortable lounge and elegant restaurant are available. There is also a 'locals' bar to the rear where the hotel's own ales are served

ROOMS: 29 en suite (bth/shr) (2 fmly) s £25-£27; d £50-£54 (incl. bkfst) * Off peak **MEALS:** Lunch £12.50-£15 & alc Dinner £12.50-£15 & alc French Cuisine V meals Coffee am **FACILITIES:** CTV in all bedrooms Fishing Pool table Xmas **CONF:** Thtr 100 Class 120 Board 10 Del from £89 * **SERVICES:** Night porter 14P **NOTES:** No smoking in restaurant Last d 9pm **CARDS:**

TONGUE Highland **Map 14 NC55**

★★ **Ben Loyal**

Main St IV27 4XE

Quality Percentage Score: 70%

☎ 01847 611216 ▯ 01847 611212

Dir: *Tongue lies at the intersection of the A838/A836, hotel is in the centre of village*

This holiday and sporting hotel enjoys views of the Kyle of Tongue and Varrich Castle ruins. Bedrooms with attractive decor and pretty fabrics are comfortably furnished in pine. Public areas include a well stocked bar and a relaxing lounge. The attractive dining room features a short fixed-price menu offering a tempting range of Taste of Scotland specialities.

ROOMS: 11 en suite (bth/shr) s fr £35; d fr £70 (incl. bkfst & dinner) * LB Off peak **MEALS:** Bar Lunch £10-£20alc Dinner £25 V meals Coffee am Tea pm **FACILITIES:** CTV in all bedrooms Fishing Pool table Fly fishing tuition **SERVICES:** 20P **NOTES:** No coaches No smoking in restaurant Last d 8pm RS Nov-Mar **CARDS:**

TORRIDON Highland **Map 14 NG95**

★★★ **Loch Torridon Country House Hotel**

IV22 2EY

Quality Percentage Score: 79%

☎ 01445 791242 ▯ 01445 791296

Dir: *from A832 at Kinlochewe, take the A896 towards Torridon, do not turn into village carry on for 1m, hotel is on right*

This former shooting lodge is set in spectacular scenery overlooking Loch Torridon. The smartly decorated bedrooms vary in size and outlook, most have generous bathrooms. Day rooms include the reception lounge, panelled bar and an elegant lounge in peach and blue. The library is available as a meeting room. The spacious dining room in two sections is a formal setting for the daily five-course dinner menu. Winner of the AA Hotel of the Year Award for Scotland 1998/99.

ROOMS: 20 en suite (bth/shr) (1 fmly) No smoking in all bedrooms s £85-£235.50; d £110-£250 (incl. bkfst) * LB Off peak **MEALS:** Bar Lunch £6-£10alc Dinner fr £37.50alc V meals Coffee am Tea pm **FACILITIES:** CTV in all bedrooms STV Fishing Pool table Croquet lawn Xmas **SERVICES:** Lift 30P **NOTES:** No dogs (ex guide dogs) No coaches No smoking in restaurant Last d 8.30pm

CARDS:

TROON South Ayrshire **Map 10 NS33**

★★★★ **Marine Highland**

Crosbie Rd KA10 6HE

Quality Percentage Score: 67%

☎ 01292 314444 ▯ 01292 316922

Dir: *turn off A77 onto B749, hotel on left about 2m past municipal golf course*

What finer position could a hotel have than an outlook over the Royal Troon Golf Course and over the Firth of Clyde to Arran. Service is immaculate, and guests have a choice of restaurants, of which Fairways, open in the evening only, is the showcase. Bedrooms range from spacious suites to cosy standard rooms.

ROOMS: 74 en suite (bth/shr) (7 fmly) No smoking in 12 bedrooms s £94-£99; d £152-£160 * LB Off peak **MEALS:** Lunch £7.50-£16.95 Dinner £20-£27.50 International & Italian Cuisine V meals Coffee am Tea pm **FACILITIES:** CTV in all bedrooms STV Indoor swimming pool (heated) Tennis (hard) Squash Sauna Solarium Gym Putting green Jacuzzi/spa Aerobics Beautician Steam room Wkly live entertainment Xmas **CONF:** Thtr 220 Class 120 Board 60 Del from £129 * **SERVICES:** Lift Night porter 200P **NOTES:** Last d 10.00pm

CARDS:

TROON South Ayrshire **Map 10 NS33**

The Premier Collection

★★★ **Lochgreen House**

Monktonhill Rd, Southwood KA10 7EN

☎ 01292 313343 ▯ 01292 318661

Dir: *from A77 follow signs for Prestwick airport, 0.5m before airport take B749 to Troon. Hotel 1m on left*

Meticulous attention to detail remains the hallmark of this splendid house which, under the personal direction of Bill

contd.

and Catherine Costley, has developed into one of Scotland's finest country houses. Set in 30 acres of wooded and landscaped gardens, the house enjoys fine views over the golf course to the Firth of Clyde and Ailsa Craig. Inside, the house offers all the charm and elegance of a bygone era with ornate cornices, antique furnishings, and lovely oak and cherry panelling. There are two sumptuously furnished sitting rooms, one of which contains a dispense bar. Both areas are enhanced by lit fires in winter and beautiful paintings. One of the highlights of any visit to Lochgreen is the innovative cuisine offered in the classic setting of the dining room. Under the watchful eye of Bill Costley, the young kitchen team are producing some really excellent results. The menu changes weekly and reflects use of quality ingredients with seafood, game, and prime beef featuring strongly. This is supported by an extensive and carefully chosen list of fine wines from around the world. Bedrooms, including those in the recently converted stable block, are well proportioned and very individual in style with fine antiques, pretty fabrics, and luxurious bathrooms. Staff are friendly and willing to please.

ROOMS: 7 en suite (bth/shr) 8 annexe en suite (bth/shr) s £100-£115.95; d £140-£155 (incl. bkfst) * LB Off peak **MEALS:** Lunch £18.95-£22.50 Dinner £29.95-£35 European Cuisine V meals Coffee am Tea pm **FACILITIES:** CTV in all bedrooms Tennis (hard) Xmas **CONF:** Thtr 25 Board 16 Del from £150 * **SERVICES:** Night porter 50P **NOTES:** No dogs (ex guide dogs) No coaches No smoking in restaurant Last d 9pm **CARDS:**

TROON South Ayrshire **Map 10 NS33**
★★★ ***Highgrove House***
Old Loans Rd KA10 7HL
Quality Percentage Score: 74%
☎ 01292 312511 Fax 01292 318228

Standing on a hillside well above the town, this stylish hotel enjoys magnificent panoramic views over the Firth of Clyde. General manager Michael Poggi leads a friendly and efficient team and the hotel's popularity for good food is as strong as ever. The attractive split-level restaurant provides the ideal setting for impressively presented contemporary style cooking, whether from the good value lunch menu and evening Brasserie selection, or the more sophisticated dinner dishes. Booking is almost essential to ensure a seat in either the restaurant or the bar. Bedrooms come in a variety of sizes and are all well equipped and smartly presented.

ROOMS: 9 en suite (bth/shr) (2 fmly) **MEALS:** French Cuisine V meals Coffee am **FACILITIES:** CTV in all bedrooms **SERVICES:** Night porter 50P **NOTES:** No dogs (ex guide dogs) No coaches Last d 9.30pm **CARDS:**

TROON South Ayrshire **Map 10 NS33**
★★★ **Piersland House**
Craigend Rd KA10 6HD
Quality Percentage Score: 73%
☎ 01292 314747 Fax 01292 315613
Dir: *just off A77 on the B749 beside Royal Troon Golf Club*

Close to the championship golf course, this fine hotel has been much extended over the years and is a popular venue for business trade, tourists and locals. Public rooms feature delightful oak panelling and large open fires in season. The lounge bar offers an extensive menu, whilst fine dining is par for the course in the elegant restaurant, with its relaxing cocktail lounge adjoining. Residents can choose from three styles of bedroom, cottage suites situated in a row to the rear of the hotel, large superior rooms in the main house, or smaller standard rooms. Whatever the choice, all are very well equipped.

ROOMS: 15 en suite (bth/shr) 13 annexe en suite (bth/shr) (2 fmly) s £82.50; d £114-£140 (incl. bkfst) * LB Off peak **MEALS:** Lunch £12.95 High tea £7.95-£11.95 British & Continental Cuisine V meals Coffee am **FACILITIES:** CTV in all bedrooms STV Croquet lawn Xmas **CONF:** Thtr 100 Class 60 Board 30 Del £90 * **SERVICES:** Night porter 150P **NOTES:** No smoking in restaurant Last high tea 7pm **CARDS:**

See advert on this page

Indicates that the star classification has not been confirmed under the New Quality Standards, see page 7 for further information.

TURNBERRY South Ayrshire **Map 10 NS20**

The Premier Collection

★★★★★ Turnberry Hotel, Golf Courses & Spa
KA26 9LT
☎ 01655 331000 01655 331706
Dir: *from Glasgow take the A77/M77 S towards Stranraer, 2m past Kirkoswald, follow signs for A719 Turnberry Village, hotel 500m on right*

Superbly situated in over 800 acres of stunning countryside with spectacular views over the Firth of Clyde to Arran, the Mull of Kintyre and Ailsa Craig, this world-famous hotel offers a first class range of facilities. The golf courses have been host to the Open Championship on several occasions and the Ailsa is considered to be one of the best courses in the world. The Spa offers a wide range of health and beauty treatments, as well as a 20 metre pool. Bedrooms and suites are spacious and very thoughtfully equipped. The public rooms offer plenty of quiet corners for the less energetic. Apart from the Clubhouse, there are two restaurants; the Bay which specialises in lighter cuisine with a Mediterranean influence, and the main hotel restaurant which offers a more traditional atmosphere and classical cuisine.

ROOMS: 132 en suite (bth/shr) s £232-£270; d £270-£318 * LB Off peak **MEALS:** Lunch fr £24.50 High tea fr £13 Dinner fr £48 Scottish & French Cuisine V meals Coffee am Tea pm **FACILITIES:** CTV in all bedrooms STV Indoor swimming pool (heated) Golf 18 Tennis (hard) Squash Riding Snooker Sauna Solarium Gym Putting green Jacuzzi/spa Health spa Xmas **CONF:** Thtr 160 Class 115 Board 50 Del from £190 * **SERVICES:** Lift Night porter 200P **NOTES:** No coaches Last d 10pm **CARDS:**

TURNBERRY South Ayrshire **Map 10 NS20**

★★★ Malin Court
KA26 9PB
Quality Percentage Score: 77%
☎ 01655 331457 01655 331072
Dir: *On A74 take Ayr exit. From Ayr take the A719 to Turnberry and Maidens*

This comfortable hotel enjoys lovely views over the Firth of Clyde and Turnberry golf courses. Public areas include a choice of lounges, plus a cocktail lounge adjoining the restaurant. Standard and executive bedrooms are available, all equipped to a high standard.

ROOMS: 18 en suite (bth/shr) (9 fmly) s £72-£82; d £104-£124 (incl. bkfst) * LB Off peak **MEALS:** Lunch £9.50-£13.50alc High tea £5.45-£9.95alc Dinner £12.95-£22 V meals Coffee am Tea pm **FACILITIES:** CTV in all bedrooms STV Tennis (grass) Putting green Pitch & putt Childrens play area Xmas **CONF:** Thtr 200 Class 60 Board 30 Del from £65.50 * **SERVICES:** Lift Night porter 110P **NOTES:** Last d 9.00pm **CARDS:**

See advert on opposite page

UDDINGSTON South Lanarkshire **Map 11 NS66**

★★ Redstones
8-10 Glasgow Rd G71 7AS
Quality Percentage Score: 68%
☎ 01698 813774 & 814843 01698 815319
Dir: *1m along A721, opposite Uddingston railway station*

This friendly hotel, created by linking two sandstone Victorian villas, is enthusiastically run by Morris Inns. Public areas have all been attractively refurbished with the elegant restaurant offering an interesting menu. The Brooklands lounge and dining room is more informal. Bedrooms, two of which have four-posters, offer mixed modern appointments and a good range of amenities.

ROOMS: 14 en suite (bth/shr) (2 fmly) s £52-£75; d £65-£95 (incl. bkfst) * LB Off peak **MEALS:** Sunday Lunch fr £9.95 High tea fr £7.50 Dinner fr £18.95 & alc International Cuisine V meals Coffee am Tea pm **FACILITIES:** CTV in all bedrooms STV Xmas **CONF:** Board 20 Del from £90 * **SERVICES:** Night porter 27P **NOTES:** No smoking area in restaurant Last d 12pm **CARDS:**

UIG See Skye, Isle of

ULLAPOOL Highland **Map 14 NH19**

★★ Ceilidh Place
West Argyle St IV26 2TY
Quality Percentage Score: 64%
☎ 01854 612103 01854 612886
Dir: *come into Ullapool and go along Shore St, pass pier and take 1st right, hotel is straight ahead at top of hill*

Unique in style, The Ceilidh Place attracts a loyal following to diverse attractions such as music and drama festivals and art exhibitions. The coffee shop is very much the hub, while the more formal restaurant serves appropriate Scottish food. Residents have a comfortable first floor lounge with an honesty bar. Bedrooms vary in size, all are pleasantly functional. There is a well stocked bookshop.

ROOMS: 13 rms (10 bth) s £45-£60; d £90-£120 (incl. bkfst) * LB Off peak **MEALS:** Bar Lunch £6-£9 International Cuisine V meals Coffee am Tea pm **FACILITIES:** CTV in all bedrooms Xmas **CONF:** Thtr 60 Class 40 Board 24 **SERVICES:** 30P **NOTES:** No smoking in restaurant **CARDS:**

UNST See Shetland

UPHALL West Lothian Map 11 NT07

★★★★ ❀❀ ***Houstoun House***
EH52 6JS
Quality Percentage Score: 67%
☎ 01506 853831 🖷 01506 854220
Dir: *from M8 junct 3 follow signs for Broxburn, go straight over rdbt then at mini-rdbt turn right heading for Uphall, hotel is 1m on right*

An impressive house set in 20 acres of grounds, handy for Livingston and the airport. Tastefully extended, it has a smart new Country Club with stylish Italian bistro. In the original house, a stone staircase leads from the vaulted cocktail bar to three elegant dining areas. Bedrooms, particularly the 'executive' rooms, are inviting.
ROOMS: 25 en suite (bth/shr) 47 annexe en suite (bth/shr) (30 fmly) No smoking in 63 bedrooms **MEALS:** International Cuisine V meals Coffee am Tea pm **FACILITIES:** CTV in all bedrooms STV Indoor swimming pool (heated) Golf 18 Sauna Solarium Gym Croquet lawn Steam room Dance studio Beauty therapy room **CONF:** Thtr 350 Class 120 Board 70 Del from £155 * **SERVICES:** Night porter 200P **NOTES:** No dogs (ex guide dogs) No smoking in restaurant Last d 9.30pm **CARDS:**

WHITBURN West Lothian Map 11 NS96

★★★ **The Hilcroft**
East Main St EH47 0JU
Quality Percentage Score: 64%
☎ 01501 740818 🖷 01501 744013
Dir: *turn off M8 junct 4 follow signs for Whitburn, hotel 0.5m on left from junct*
This popular business hotel is in easy reach of the M8. Public areas have a bright contemporary style, with a split level bar and Bistro restaurant. Bedrooms are well equipped, the larger executive rooms are the best.
ROOMS: 31 en suite (bth/shr) (7 fmly) s £56-£59; d £68-£73 (incl. bkfst) * LB Off peak **MEALS:** Lunch £7-£11.95 & alc High tea fr £6.95 & alc Dinner fr £14.95 & alc French & Italian Cuisine V meals Coffee am Tea pm **FACILITIES:** CTV in all bedrooms STV Xmas **CONF:** Thtr 200 Class 50 Board 30 Del from £75 * **SERVICES:** Night porter 80P **NOTES:** No dogs (ex guide dogs) No smoking area in restaurant Last d 9.30pm **CARDS:**

Remember to return your Prize Draw card for a chance to win one of 30 relaxing leisure breaks with Corus and Regal hotels. See inside the front cover for the card and competition details.

WHITEBRIDGE Highland — Map 14 NH41

The Premier Collection

★★ Knockie Lodge

IV1 6UP

☎ 01456 486276 Fax 01456 486389

Dir: *signposted from B862*

Built as a shooting lodge by the chief of Clan Fraser, Knockie Lodge enjoys a dramatic setting overlooking Loch nan Lann. Afternoon tea is served in the comfortable lounge, there is also a conservatory and quieter lounge leading to the snooker room. The five-course set dinners are a grand occasion, preceded by canapés. Bedrooms come in a variety of sizes and styles, don't expect TV.

ROOMS: 10 en suite (bth/shr) **MEALS: FACILITIES:** Fishing Snooker Sailing **CONF:** Board 10 **SERVICES:** 10P **NOTES:** No coaches No children 10yrs No smoking in restaurant Last d 8.30pm Closed Nov-Apr **CARDS:**

WHITEBRIDGE Highland — Map 14 NH41

★★ Whitebridge

IV2 6UN

Quality Percentage Score: 66%

☎ 01456 486226 & 486272 Fax 01456 486413

Dir: *turn off A9 onto B851, follow signs to Fort Augustus*

A family-run hotel on the south eastern side of Loch Ness. Bedrooms are comfortable with modern and traditional appointments. Public areas include bars, a cosy sitting room, and an attractive dining room offering home-cooked fare.

ROOMS: 12 rms (10 bth/shr) (3 fmly) s £25-£30; d £44-£50 (incl. bkfst) * LB Off peak **MEALS:** Bar Lunch £6.50-£17alc Dinner £15 V meals Coffee am Tea pm **FACILITIES:** CTV in all bedrooms Fishing Pool table **CONF:** Class 30 Board 25 **SERVICES:** 32P **NOTES:** No coaches Last d 8.30pm Closed 21 Dec-Feb **CARDS:**

WICK Highland — Map 15 ND35

★★ Mackay's

Union St KW1 5ED

Quality Percentage Score: 67%

☎ 01955 602323 Fax 01955 605930

Dir: *opposite Caithness General Hospital*

The Lamont family have run this commercial hotel for over 40 years and are now nearing completion of an upgrading. The hotel stands on the south shore of the River Wick, close to the centre of the town, and provides a choice of bars and lounges as well as a formal dining room. Bedrooms are mostly refurbished and offer a good range of amenities.

ROOMS: 27 rms (19 bth/shr) (4 fmly) s fr £55; d fr £80 (incl. bkfst) * LB Off peak **MEALS:** Traditional Scottish Cuisine V meals Coffee am **FACILITIES:** CTV in all bedrooms STV Wkly live entertainment **CONF:** Thtr 100 Class 100 Board 60 **SERVICES:** Lift Night porter **NOTES:** No coaches No smoking in restaurant Closed 1-2 Jan **CARDS:**

Hotel of the Year Wales

St David's Hotel & Spa, Cardiff Bay, Cardiff

A

ABERCRAF Powys — Map 03 SN81

★★ *Maes-Y-Gwernen*
School Rd SA9 1XD
Quality Percentage Score: 75%
☎ 01639 730218 Fax 01639 730765

Situated on the edge of the Brecon Beacons this small hotel is surrounded by gardens and lawns that contain two annexe rooms and a building with gym equipment, sunbed and spa bath. Bedrooms are well appointed and an extensive menu is served in the spacious restaurant. An attractive conservatory and lounge offer pleasant areas in which to relax.
ROOMS: 10 en suite (bth/shr) No smoking in 1 bedroom
MEALS: European Cuisine V meals Coffee am Tea pm **FACILITIES:** CTV in all bedrooms STV Sauna Solarium Gym Jacuzzi/spa ch fac
SERVICES: 20P **NOTES:** No coaches No smoking in restaurant Last d 9pm **CARDS:**

ABERDYFI Gwynedd — Map 06 SN69

★★★ **Trefeddian**
LL35 0SB
Quality Percentage Score: 71%
☎ 01654 767213 Fax 01654 767777
Dir: *0.5m N off A493*

A holiday hotel overlooking the local golf course, surrounded by grounds and gardens. It provides sound modern accommodation, an indoor swimming pool and pitch-and-putt golf green. Children are welcome and recreation areas are provided. There are elegantly furnished lounges; bedrooms and bathrooms are well equipped and comfortable.
ROOMS: 46 en suite (bth/shr) (7 fmly) No smoking in all bedrooms s £55-£64; d £110-£128 (incl. bkfst & dinner) * LB Off peak
MEALS: Lunch £10.40-£11.40 Dinner £17.40 English & French Cuisine V meals Coffee am Tea pm **FACILITIES:** CTV in all bedrooms Indoor swimming pool (heated) Tennis (hard) Snooker Solarium Pool table Putting green Table tennis Play area Xmas **SERVICES:** Lift 68P
NOTES: No coaches No smoking in restaurant Last d 8.45pm Closed 4 Jan-5 Mar **CARDS:**

See advert on opposite page

ABERDYFI Gwynedd — Map 06 SN69

★★★ **Plas Penhelig Country House**
LL35 0NA
Quality Percentage Score: 66%
☎ 01654 767676 Fax 01654 767783
An impressive country house in 14 acres of beautiful grounds, and gardens which are open to the public. Guests may play croquet on the lawn. Bedrooms are bright and fresh, with modern facilities. The magnificent wood-panelled hall and adjacent lounge have log fires. Fish, game and other meats feature on the daily menu, which continues to merit our one-rosette award.

ROOMS: 11 en suite (bth/shr) s £48-£60; d £112-£120 (incl. bkfst & dinner) * LB Off peak **MEALS:** Lunch fr £13.50 Dinner fr £20 English & French Cuisine V meals Coffee am Tea pm **FACILITIES:** CTV in all bedrooms Croquet lawn Putting green **CONF:** Thtr 40 Class 20 Board 22 **SERVICES:** 40P **NOTES:** No coaches No children 10yrs No smoking in restaurant Last d 8.45pm Closed Jan & Feb **CARDS:**

See advert on opposite page

ABERDYFI Gwynedd — Map 06 SN69

★★ **Penhelig Arms Hotel & Restaurant**
LL35 0LT
Quality Percentage Score: 72%
☎ 01654 767215 Fax 01654 767690
Dir: *take A493 coastal road, hotel faces Penhelig harbour*
This delightful 18th-century hotel stands opposite the old harbour and there are views from many bedrooms and the dining room over the Dyfi Estuary to the mountains beyond. The bedrooms are well maintained, furnishings and fittings are of excellent quality, and rooms are well equipped. The public bar retains much of its original character and is much loved by locals who enjoy the bar food and real ale selections on offer. Robert and Sally Hughes and their staff offer a warm Welsh welcome to their guests.
ROOMS: 10 en suite (bth/shr) No smoking in all bedrooms s £39.50; d £69-£79 (incl. bkfst) * LB Off peak **MEALS:** Lunch £12.95 & alc Dinner fr £20 European Cuisine V meals Coffee am Tea pm
FACILITIES: CTV in all bedrooms **SERVICES:** 12P **NOTES:** No coaches No smoking in restaurant Last d 9.30pm Closed 25 & 26 Dec
CARDS:

ABERDYFI Gwynedd — Map 06 SN69

★★ **Harbour**
LL35 0EB
Quality Percentage Score: 70%
☎ 01654 767250 Fax 01654 767792
Dir: *on the A493 coastal road between Dolgellau & Machynlleth*
This delightful small hotel looks out over the beach towards the sand dunes of Ynyslas. Many of the tastefully decorated bedrooms enjoy the views and several family suites are provided. The elegant public areas are particularly attractive. There are

contd.

three restaurants, but their availability is seasonal. A wine bar opens every evening and provides an extensive range of meals, there is an all-day coffee shop and the hotel restaurant serves fixed-price menus. There is a first floor lounge bar and a residents' lounge.
ROOMS: 9 en suite (bth/shr) (3 fmly) No smoking in 3 bedrooms s £42.50-£64.50; d £59.50-£99 (incl. bkfst) * Off peak **MEALS:** Lunch £6-£20alc High tea £6-£10alc Dinner £9-£20alc International Cuisine V meals Coffee am Tea pm **FACILITIES:** CTV in all bedrooms **CONF:** Thtr 30 Class 12 Board 12 Del from £40 * **NOTES:** No smoking area in restaurant Last d 9pm RS 24-29 Dec **CARDS:**

ABERDYFI Gwynedd **Map 06 SN69**
★ **Maybank Hotel & Restaurant**
4 Penhelig Rd, Penhelig LL35 0PT
Quality Percentage Score: 68%
☎ 01654 767500 & 767622
Dir: *A493 from Machynlleth to Aberdovey. Hotel is 500yds on right past Aberdyfi village signpost*
This delightful small hotel enjoys a fine position overlooking the estuary and the sand dunes. Bedrooms are spacious, attractively furnished and some have views over the bay. There is a comfortable first floor residents' lounge. Downstairs, a cosy bar has blackboards showing the daily specials that supplement a varied menu. Car parking is available in a public car park 100

contd.

Some hotel groups have a central reservations telephone number, see pages 35, 37 and 38 for details.

A

yards away, where the hotel meets the cost for residents and assistance with luggage can be provided.
ROOMS: 5 en suite (bth/shr) (1 fmly) No smoking in all bedrooms s £26.95-£38.95; d £53.90-£61.90 (incl. bkfst) * LB Off peak **MEALS:** Dinner £19.95-£21.95 V meals Coffee am **FACILITIES:** CTV in all bedrooms Xmas **SERVICES:** Night porter **NOTES:** No coaches No smoking in restaurant Last d 9pm Closed 6 Nov-22 Dec & Jan-13 Feb, Xmas & N Y **CARDS:**

ABERGAVENNY Monmouthshire — Map 03 SO21
★★★ Llansantffraed Court
Llanvihangel Gobion NP7 9BA
Quality Percentage Score: 66%
☎ 01873 840678 01873 840674
Dir: *at A465/A40 Abergavenny intersection take B4598 signposted to Usk (do not join A40). Continue towards Raglan and hotel on left after 4.5m*
Set in extensive grounds, this imposing red brick country house enjoys views of the Brecon Beacons. The elegant ground floor public areas include an Italianate lobby and bar with a large lounge and spacious restaurant. Bedrooms are comfortably furnished with modern facilities.
ROOMS: 21 en suite (bth/shr) (3 fmly) No smoking in 7 bedrooms s £68-£80; d £85-£155 (incl. bkfst) LB Off peak **MEALS:** Lunch £10-£15.50 & alc Dinner £19.50-£25.50 & alc Welsh & French Cuisine V meals Coffee am Tea pm **FACILITIES:** CTV in all bedrooms STV Fishing Croquet lawn Putting green 20 Acres of walks and runs Ornamental troutlake Xmas **CONF:** Thtr 220 Class 120 Board 100 **SERVICES:** Lift Night porter 250P **NOTES:** No smoking in restaurant Last d 9.30pm **CARDS:**

ABERGAVENNY Monmouthshire — Map 03 SO21
★★★ Allt-yr-Ynys Country House Hotel
HR2 0DU
Quality Percentage Score: 65%
☎ 01873 890307 01873 890539
(For full entry see Walterstone (Herefordshire))

ABERGAVENNY Monmouthshire — Map 03 SO21
★★ Llanwenarth Arms
Brecon Rd NP8 1EP
Quality Percentage Score: 71%
☎ 01873 810550 01873 811880
Dir: *on A40 midway between Abergavenny and Crickhowell beside River Usk*
Sandwiched between the River Usk and the Sugar Loaf mountain, panoramic views of beautiful countryside are guaranteed at this hotel. The main building dates back to the 16th century, with a purpose-built annexe housing the attractively furnished and well equipped bedrooms. The traditional restaurant and bright conservatory lounge make the most of the riverside setting, and are complemented by a cosy bar. The restaurant menu makes extensive use of quality fresh produce and has a strong local flavour. Guests may also take advantage of the two stretches of trout and salmon fishing available to the hotel.
ROOMS: 18 en suite (bth/shr) (2 fmly) s £53-£63; d £63.01-£73 (incl. bkfst) * LB Off peak **MEALS:** Lunch £14-£25alc Dinner £14-£25alc International Cuisine V meals Coffee am **FACILITIES:** CTV in all bedrooms Fishing **SERVICES:** 60P **NOTES:** No dogs (ex guide dogs) No coaches Last d 9.30pm **CARDS:**

ABERGELE Conwy — Map 06 SH97
★★★ *Kinmel Manor*
St Georges Rd LL22 9AS
Quality Percentage Score: 65%
☎ 01745 832014 01745 832014
Dir: *at Abergele exit on A55*
Set in several acres of grounds, this 16th century manor house provides several function suites and a fully equipped leisure centre. Many original features have been retained, including superb fireplaces in the restaurant and the hall. Several family rooms are available and all bedrooms are equipped with modern amenities.
ROOMS: 51 en suite (bth/shr) (3 fmly) No smoking in 12 bedrooms **MEALS:** English & French Cuisine V meals Coffee am Tea pm **FACILITIES:** CTV in 42 bedrooms STV Indoor swimming pool (heated) Sauna Solarium Gym Jacuzzi/spa Steam room **CONF:** Thtr 250 Class 100 Board 70 **SERVICES:** 120P **NOTES:** Last d 9.30pm **CARDS:**

ABERPORTH Ceredigion — Map 02 SN25
★★★ *Hotel Penrallt*
SA43 2BS
Quality Percentage Score: 68%
☎ 01239 810227 01239 811375
Dir: *Take BA333 signed Aberporth Hotel 1 mile on the right*
An Edwardian mansion hotel in several acres of well maintained grounds, complete with tennis courts, a swimming pool and a children's play area. Inside, carved ceiling beams and a splendid stained glass window are among the attractions in the smart public areas that include an inviting restaurant and a popular bar. The bedrooms are generally spacious, with balcony, and family rooms both available.
ROOMS: 16 en suite (bth/shr) (2 fmly) **MEALS:** European & Oriental Cuisine Coffee am Tea pm **FACILITIES:** CTV in all bedrooms Outdoor swimming pool (heated) Tennis (hard) Sauna Solarium Gym Pool table Croquet lawn Putting green ch fac **CONF:** Class 60 Board 30 **SERVICES:** 100P **NOTES:** No coaches No smoking in restaurant Last d 9pm Closed 23-31 Dec **CARDS:**

ABERPORTH Ceredigion — Map 02 SN25
★★ Penbontbren Farm
Glynarthen SA44 6PE
Quality Percentage Score: 75%
☎ 01239 810248 01239 811129
Dir: *3.5m SE off A487*
A genuine farm-house with 90 acres of land, which has a truly Welsh flavour as the caring staff are native speakers and the bilingual menus are based mainly around Welsh cuisine. Courtyard style bedrooms are located in classical farm buildings, all of which are well equipped and decorated. Public areas include a pine-furnished restaurant and a spacious lounge; there is also a games room, a farm museum and a nature trail.
ROOMS: 10 annexe en suite (bth/shr) (6 fmly) s £46; d £80 (incl. bkfst) * LB Off peak **MEALS:** Dinner £15-£25alc European Cuisine V meals Coffee am Tea pm **FACILITIES:** CTV in all bedrooms Fishing Farm trail Xmas **CONF:** Thtr 50 Class 25 Board 30 Del £65.50 * **SERVICES:** 35P **NOTES:** No coaches No smoking in restaurant Last d 8.15pm Closed 24-28 Dec **CARDS:**

ABERPORTH Ceredigion — Map 02 SN25
★★ Highcliffe
SA43 2DA
Quality Percentage Score: 62%
☎ 01239 810534 01239 810534
Dir: *off B4333*
A coastal hotel enjoying an elevated position above Cardigan

contd.

Bay, with the sandy beaches close at hand. Hospitality is jovial and service is relaxed and informal. A wide range of meals is offered at good prices in the bar and restaurant. Bedrooms are comfortable and equipped with modern facilities.
ROOMS: 9 rms (6 bth 2 shr) 6 annexe en suite (bth) (4 fmly) s £36; d £53-£55 (incl. bkfst) * LB Off peak **MEALS:** Lunch £3.95-£12.50 Dinner £11-£14.50 & alc International Cuisine V meals Coffee am Tea pm **FACILITIES:** CTV in all bedrooms ch fac Xmas **SERVICES:** 18P **NOTES:** No smoking in restaurant Last d 9pm
CARDS:

ABERSOCH Gwynedd **Map 06 SH32**
★★★ Porth Tocyn
Bwlch Tocyn LL53 7BU
Quality Percentage Score: 73%
☎ 01758 713303 01758 713538
Dir: *2.5m S follow signs 'Porth Tocyn' and Blue Highway signs marked 'Gwesty/Hotel'*

Superbly located above Cardigan Bay, there are fine views over the area. Several elegantly furnished sitting rooms are provided, the hotel is surrounded by pretty gardens. Bedrooms are comfortably furnished. Children are especially welcome and have a play room. Fine food earns the restaurant a prestigious two-rosette award.
ROOMS: 17 en suite (bth/shr) (1 fmly) s £62.50; d £86-£116 (incl. cont bkfst) * LB Off peak **MEALS:** Sunday Lunch £9-£17.50 High tea £3-£6 Dinner £22.75-£30 V meals Coffee am Tea pm **FACILITIES:** CTV in all bedrooms Outdoor swimming pool (heated) Tennis (hard) ch fac **SERVICES:** 50P **NOTES:** No coaches No smoking in restaurant Last d 9.30pm Closed mid Nov-wk before Etr **CARDS:**

See advert on this page

ABERSOCH Gwynedd **Map 06 SH32**
★★★ White House
LL53 7AG
Quality Percentage Score: 68%
☎ 01758 713427 01758 713512
Dir: *on A499 from Pwllheli hotel is on the right just before entering Abersoch village*
A family-run hotel in an elevated position on the approach to Abersoch, with lovely views over Cardigan Bay from the attractive restaurant and many bedrooms. A log fire burns in the lounge during cold weather and the spacious bar has plenty of window seating. Bedrooms are smart, well equipped and decorated with co-ordinated fabrics.
ROOMS: 13 en suite (bth/shr) (1 fmly) No smoking in 6 bedrooms s £35-£45; d £70-£80 (incl. bkfst) * LB Off peak **MEALS:** Sunday Lunch fr £13.50 Dinner fr £20.50 & alc British & Welsh Cuisine V meals Coffee am **FACILITIES:** CTV in all bedrooms STV Xmas **CONF:** Thtr 100 Class 60 Board 40 **SERVICES:** 100P **NOTES:** No smoking in restaurant Last d 9pm **CARDS:**

A

ABERSOCH Gwynedd — Map 06 SH32

★★★ Riverside

LL53 7HW
Quality Percentage Score: 62%
☎ 01758 712419 📠 01758 712671

Dir: *situated overlooking the harbour just before entering the village of Abersoch*

This private hotel has been run by John & Wendy Bakewell for over 30 years. It is close to the village centre, harbour and beach. Bedrooms, including family and ground floor rooms, have modern facilities and equipment. Public areas include an attractive restaurant with spiral staircase, a lounge bar, lounges, pleasant riverside garden and small covered swimming pool.

ROOMS: 12 en suite (bth/shr) (4 fmly) **MEALS:** Bar Lunch £3.75-£10.50alc Dinner £18.95-£23.50 English & Continental Cuisine Coffee am Tea pm **FACILITIES:** CTV in all bedrooms Indoor swimming pool (heated) **SERVICES:** 25P **NOTES:** No dogs (ex guide dogs) No coaches No smoking in restaurant Last d 8.15pm Closed 16 Nov-Feb
CARDS:

ABERSOCH Gwynedd — Map 06 SH32

★★❀ Neigwl

Lon Sarn Bach LL53 7DY
Quality Percentage Score: 76%
☎ 01758 712363 📠 01758 712544

Dir: *on A499, drive through Abersoch, hotel on the left overlooking the sea*

The bar and restaurant at this delightful small hotel look out over Cardigan Bay, and there are lovely views from many bedrooms. These are attractively decorated and include two family suites. Meals are very enjoyable, and fresh local produce is used whenever possible.

ROOMS: 7 en suite (bth/shr) 2 annexe en suite (bth) (3 fmly) s £52; d £88 (incl. bkfst) LB Off peak **MEALS:** Dinner £20-£25 British Cuisine Coffee am Tea pm **FACILITIES:** CTV in all bedrooms Xmas **SERVICES:** 30P **NOTES:** No dogs (ex guide dogs) No coaches Last d 9pm **CARDS:**

ABERSOCH Gwynedd — Map 06 SH32

★★ Deucoch

LL53 7LD
Quality Percentage Score: 66%
☎ 01758 712680 📠 01758 712670

Dir: *through Abersoch village following signs for Sarn Bach. At cross roads in Sarn Bach (approx 1m from village centre) turn right, hotel on top of hill*

The White family, with local help, have welcomed guests for many years. The hotel enjoys lovely views over the area. There is a choice of bars and several food options. The regular carvery has attracted a large following, it provides excellent value for money and pre-booking is essential. Pretty bedrooms are equipped with modern amenities. The hotel specialises in golfing packages.

ROOMS: 10 en suite (bth/shr) (2 fmly) s fr £30; d fr £60 (incl. bkfst) * LB Off peak **MEALS:** Dinner fr £14.50 V meals **FACILITIES:** CTV in all bedrooms STV Xmas **SERVICES:** 30P **NOTES:** No coaches No smoking in restaurant Last d 8pm **CARDS:**

ABERYSTWYTH Ceredigion — Map 06 SN58

Courtesy & Care Award

★★★❀❀ Conrah

Ffosrhydygaled, Chancery SY23 4DF
Quality Percentage Score: 73%
☎ 01970 617941 📠 01970 624546

Dir: *on A487, 3.5m S*

This country house hotel stands in 22 acres of mature grounds, three miles south of Aberystwyth. The elegantly furnished public rooms include a choice of comfortable lounges with welcoming open fires. Conference and leisure facilities are available, while the cuisine which is French with modern influences, continues to achieve very high standards. Rooms are available in both the country house and a nearby annexe, and are well equipped and tastefully furnished. The team hold the AA Courtesy and Care Award for 1999-2000.

ROOMS: 11 en suite (bth/shr) 9 annexe en suite (bth/shr) (1 fmly) s £68-£78; d £90-£125 (incl. bkfst) * LB Off peak **MEALS:** Lunch £16.50-£16.75 Dinner £26 International Cuisine V meals Coffee am Tea pm **FACILITIES:** CTV in all bedrooms Indoor swimming pool (heated) Sauna Croquet lawn Table tennis **CONF:** Thtr 40 Class 20 Board 20 **SERVICES:** Lift 60P **NOTES:** No dogs No coaches No children 5yrs No smoking in restaurant Last d 9pm Closed 23 Dec-2 Jan **CARDS:**

ABERYSTWYTH Ceredigion — Map 06 SN58

★★★❀ *Belle Vue Royal*

Marine Ter SY23 2BA
Quality Percentage Score: 68%
☎ 01970 617558 📠 01970 612190

Dir: *near the Pier*

Dating back more than 170 years, this family owned hotel stands on the promenade, a short walk from the shops. Family and sea-view rooms are available, and all are well equipped. Public areas include extensive function rooms and a choice of bars. Food options include bar meals and more formal restaurant dining, where fresh local produce always satisfies the appetite of the guests.

ROOMS: 34 en suite (bth/shr) (6 fmly) No smoking in 10 bedrooms **MEALS:** International Cuisine V meals Coffee am Tea pm **FACILITIES:** CTV in all bedrooms STV **CONF:** Thtr 70 Class 20 Board 28 **SERVICES:** Night porter 15P **NOTES:** No dogs (ex guide dogs) No smoking area in restaurant Last d 9.15pm Closed 24-26 Dec
CARDS:

See advert on opposite page

ABERYSTWYTH Ceredigion **Map 06 SN58**

★★ Four Seasons

50-54 Portland St SY23 2DX
Quality Percentage Score: 68%
☎ 01970 612120 Fax 01970 627458
Dir: *in town centre, car park entrance in Bath Street*

Conveniently located between the town centre and the seafront, the Four Seasons is a well maintained and friendly hotel, which can also cater for small meetings. A cosy lounge is provided, plus a separate bar. A wide choice of food is available, and there is an enclosed rear car park. The bedrooms are attractive and well equipped.

ROOMS: 14 rms (13 bth/shr) (1 fmly) No smoking in 7 bedrooms **MEALS:** Sunday Lunch £12-£15 Dinner £18-£21 Welsh, English & Continental Cuisine V meals Coffee am **FACILITIES:** CTV in all bedrooms **CONF:** Thtr 25 Class 15 **SERVICES:** 10P **NOTES:** No dogs (ex guide dogs) No smoking in restaurant Last d 9pm Closed 25-31 Dec **CARDS:**

ABERYSTWYTH Ceredigion **Map 06 SN58**

★★ *Richmond*

44-45 Marine Ter SY23 2BX
Quality Percentage Score: 67%
☎ 01970 612201 Fax 01970 626706
Dir: *on entering town follow signs for Promenade*

This hotel lies in the centre of the promenade with good sea views from the public areas and from many of the bedrooms. The public areas and bedrooms are comfortably furnished and family rooms are available. An attractive dining room and comfortable lounge with a bar are provided. There is also a suite available for local functions.

ROOMS: 15 en suite (bth/shr) (6 fmly) **MEALS:** Welsh, British & International Cuisine V meals Coffee am Tea pm **FACILITIES:** CTV in all bedrooms STV **CONF:** Thtr 60 Class 22 Board 28 Del from £55 * **SERVICES:** 20P **NOTES:** No dogs (ex guide dogs) No coaches No smoking in restaurant Last d 8.30pm Closed 20 Dec-3 Jan **CARDS:**

ABERYSTWYTH Ceredigion **Map 06 SN58**

★★ *Groves*

MINOTEL Great Britain

44-46 North Pde SY23 2NF
Quality Percentage Score: 64%
☎ 01970 617623 Fax 01970 627068
Dir: *N on A487, in town centre*

Conveniently located just a few minutes walk from the shopping area and the sea front, the Groves Hotel is both a friendly and popular hotel. Functions and meetings of up to 50 people can be accommodated and the bar and cafe-style restaurant offer a good range of eating options. Bedrooms are well equipped with modern facilities.

ROOMS: 9 en suite (bth/shr) (1 fmly) No smoking in 2 bedrooms **MEALS:** International Cuisine V meals Coffee am **FACILITIES:** CTV in all bedrooms **CONF:** Thtr 50 **SERVICES:** 4P **NOTES:** No dogs (ex guide dogs) No smoking in restaurant **CARDS:**

AMLWCH See Anglesey, Isle of

AMMANFORD Carmarthenshire **Map 03 SN61**

★★ *Mill at Glynhir*

Glyn-Hir, Llandybie SA18 2TE
Quality Percentage Score: 68%
☎ 01269 850672 Fax 01269 850672
Dir: *turn off A483 Llandybie signposted Golf Course*

Nestling in beautiful countryside, this former water mill is situated adjacent to the local golf course. Popular with golfers and walkers, accommodation comprises restful and well equipped bedrooms around the mill. The bar/lounge and restaurant make up the public areas which also include a heated indoor swimming pool.

ROOMS: 11 en suite (bth/shr) **MEALS:** Welsh & French Cuisine V meals Coffee am **FACILITIES:** CTV in all bedrooms Indoor swimming pool (heated) Golf 18 Fishing **SERVICES:** 20P **NOTES:** No coaches No children 11yrs No smoking in restaurant Last d 8.15pm Closed Xmas RS 24-30 Dec **CARDS:**

ANGLESEY, ISLE OF Isle of Anglesey

AMLWCH **Map 06 SH49**

★★ Lastra Farm

Penrhyd LL68 9TF
Quality Percentage Score: 69%
☎ 01407 830906 Fax 01407 832522
Dir: *after 'Welcome to Amlwch' sign turn left across main road, left at T-junct on to Rhosgoch road*

This former 17th-century farmhouse offers pine-furnished, colourfully decorated bedrooms, as well as a comfortable lounge and a cosy bar area. A range of good-value food is available. Some way from the main building, a large suite with a conservatory has been built, popular for weddings and functions.

ROOMS: 5 en suite (bth/shr) 3 annexe en suite (bth/shr) (1 fmly) s £28-£30; d £48-£50 (incl. bkfst) * LB Off peak **MEALS:** Lunch £3.25-£8.75 High tea £7 Dinner £15 & alc Welsh & French Cuisine V meals Coffee am Tea pm **FACILITIES:** CTV in all bedrooms **CONF:** Thtr 100 Class 80 Board 30 **SERVICES:** Night porter 40P **NOTES:** No smoking in restaurant Last d 9.30pm **CARDS:**

A

AMLWCH Map 06 SH49

★★ Trecastell

Bull Bay LL68 9SA
Quality Percentage Score: 65%
☎ 01407 830651 01407 832114
Dir: *1m N on A5025, adjacent to Golf Club*
Near the local golf course, this traditional hotel overlooks Bull Bay. The popular bar serves a range of food, formal dining is found in the new brasserie. Refurbished bedrooms are well equipped, family and sea view rooms are available. There is a games room and cosy lounge.
ROOMS: 13 rms (11 bth/shr) (3 fmly) s £29.50-£35; d £45-£50 (incl. bkfst) * LB Off peak **MEALS:** Lunch £7.95-£12 & alc Dinner £7.95-£12 & alc V meals Coffee am Tea pm **FACILITIES:** CTV in all bedrooms Pool table Xmas **CONF:** Thtr 20 Class 10 Board 10 **SERVICES:** 60P **NOTES:** No smoking in restaurant Last d 9.30pm
CARDS:

BEAUMARIS Map 06 SH67

★★ Ye Olde Bulls Head Inn

Castle St LL58 8AP
Quality Percentage Score: 75%
☎ 01248 810329 01248 811294
Dir: *from Britannia road bridge follow A545*
Cromwell's General Mytton laid siege to the castle using the inn as his base. Charles Dickens and Samuel Johnson were regular visitors. Features include exposed beams, fireplaces and antique weaponry. Richly decorated bedrooms are well equipped. There is a spacious lounge, meetings and small functions are catered for. Food continues to attract praise and a new Brasserie has opened.
ROOMS: 14 en suite (bth/shr) 1 annexe en suite (bth/shr) No smoking in 4 bedrooms s £53-£56; d £83-£96 (incl. bkfst) LB Off peak **MEALS:** Dinner fr £27.50alc V meals Coffee am **FACILITIES:** CTV in all bedrooms **CONF:** Thtr 25 Board 16 **SERVICES:** 5P **NOTES:** No dogs (ex guide dogs) No coaches No smoking in restaurant Last d 9.30pm Closed 25-26 Dec & 1 Jan **CARDS:**

BEAUMARIS Map 06 SH67

★★ Bishopsgate House

54 Castle St LL58 8BB
Quality Percentage Score: 71%
☎ 01248 810302 01248 810166
Dir: *turn off in Menai Bridge onto A545. Follow the only road into Beaumans, hotel is on the left in the main street*
A delightful small hotel, immaculately maintained and dating back to 1760. Well equipped bedrooms are attractively decorated and include two with four-poster beds. The Chinese Chippendale staircase and fine examples of wood-panelling are impressive.
ROOMS: 9 en suite (bth/shr) s fr £40; d fr £62 (incl. bkfst) * LB Off peak **MEALS:** Lunch £8.95-£9.95 Dinner £14.95 & alc English & French Cuisine V meals Coffee am **FACILITIES:** CTV in all bedrooms **SERVICES:** 8P **NOTES:** No smoking in restaurant Last d 9pm Closed 28 Dec-31 Jan **CARDS:**

See advert on opposite page

BEAUMARIS Map 06 SH67

★★ *Bulkeley Arms*

Castle St LL58 8AW
Quality Percentage Score: 67%
☎ 01248 810415 01248 810146
Dir: *leave the A5 and follow signs for Menai Bridge. Take A545 from bridge to Beaumaris. Hotel in centre of town opposite pier overlooking waterfront*
A Grade I listed hotel built in 1831 to celebrate a visit by Princess Victoria, it has fine views from many rooms. Well equipped bedrooms are mostly spacious with pretty fabrics and wallpapers. There is a choice of bars, an all-day coffee lounge and health club. Regular jazz evenings, a resident pianist and friendly staff create a relaxed atmosphere.
ROOMS: 41 rms (40 bth/shr) (4 fmly) **MEALS:** V meals Coffee am Tea pm **FACILITIES:** CTV in all bedrooms Sauna Solarium Gym Climbing wall Wkly live entertainment **CONF:** Thtr 200 Class 180 Board 40 **SERVICES:** Lift Night porter 30P **NOTES:** No smoking in restaurant Last d 9.30pm **CARDS:**

HOLYHEAD Map 06 SH28

★★ *Bull*

London Rd, Valley LL65 3DP
Quality Percentage Score: 61%
☎ 01407 740351 01407 742328
Dir: *3.50 miles from ferry terminal, on A5 near junct with A5025*
A busy roadside hotel on the approach to Holyhead. Its popular bars offer good-value food and it acts as a base for local quizzes and other functions. Bedrooms are equipped with modern amenities, families can be accommodated, several rooms are in a nearby building.
ROOMS: 9 en suite (bth/shr) 5 annexe en suite (bth/shr) (4 fmly) **MEALS:** International Cuisine V meals Coffee am Tea pm **FACILITIES:** CTV in all bedrooms **SERVICES:** 130P **NOTES:** No dogs (ex guide dogs) Last d 9.30pm **CARDS:**

LLANFAIRPWLLGWYNGYLL Map 06 SH57

★★★ Carreg Bran Country Hotel

Church Ln LL61 5YH
Quality Percentage Score: 64%
☎ 01248 714224 01248 715983
Dir: *from Holyhead 1st junct for Llanfairpwll. Through village then 1st right before dual carriageway and bridge*
A family-run hotel close to the banks of the Menai Straits. Rooms are prettily decorated, spacious and well equipped. The restaurant is attractive and food has a local flavour. There is a choice of bars and a large function room, popular for weddings and business meetings.
ROOMS: 29 en suite (bth/shr) (3 fmly) No smoking in 7 bedrooms s £49-£55; d £69-£75 (incl. bkfst) * LB Off peak **MEALS:** Lunch £12-£14 Dinner £14-£17 V meals Coffee am Tea pm **FACILITIES:** CTV in all bedrooms Pool table Wkly live entertainment Xmas **CONF:** Thtr 130 Class 120 Board 100 Del from £80 * **SERVICES:** Night porter 100P **NOTES:** No smoking in restaurant Last d 9.45pm
CARDS:

MENAI BRIDGE Map 06 SH57

★★ *Anglesey Arms*

LL59 5EA
Quality Percentage Score: 64%
☎ 01248 712305 01248 712076
Dir: *on left after Menai Bridge*
This popular hotel next to the Menai Suspension bridge has pretty gardens, a popular background for wedding photographs. The hotel has been modernised and provides smart, well equipped accommodation. Bedrooms are attractively pine-furnished, equipped with trouser presses and other extras. There is a choice of bars and an excellent selection of meals.
ROOMS: 16 en suite (bth/shr) (2 fmly) **MEALS:** Welsh & English Cuisine V meals Coffee am Tea pm **FACILITIES:** CTV in all bedrooms **CONF:** Thtr 60 Class 40 Board 40 **NOTES:** No dogs (ex guide dogs) Last d 9.30pm **CARDS:**

MENAI BRIDGE — Map 06 SH57

★★ Gazelle

Glyn Garth LL59 5PD

Quality Percentage Score: 61%

☎ 01248 713364 Fax 01248 713167

***Dir:** 2m NE A545*

On the banks of the Menai Straits with views over Snowdonia, popular with local fishermen and yachtsmen. There is a large selection of bar food, substantial meals are served in the restaurant. Bedrooms are equipped with modern facilities.

ROOMS: 9 rms (4 bth 1 shr) s £25-£37.50; d £50-£65 (incl. bkfst) * Off peak **MEALS:** Lunch £11.50-£17.50 & alc Dinner £17.50-£25 & alc V meals Coffee am Tea pm **FACILITIES:** CTV in all bedrooms Sailing Sea fishing Watersports **CONF:** Thtr 20 Class 12 Board 12 Del from £50 * **SERVICES:** 40P **NOTES:** No dogs (ex guide dogs) Last d 9.30pm **CARDS:**

TREARDDUR BAY — Map 06 SH27

★★★ Trearddur Bay

LL65 2UN

Quality Percentage Score: 70%

☎ 01407 860301 Fax 01407 861181

***Dir:** from A5 turn left at lights in Valley toward Trearddur Bay, pass Power garage on right, turn left opposite garage, hotel on right*

A fine modern hotel with extensive function and conference facilities. Bedrooms are well equipped, many have sea views and several suites are available. An all-day bar with a conservatory serves a wide range of snacks and lighter meals, supplemented by a cocktail bar and the more formal hotel restaurant.

ROOMS: 37 en suite (bth/shr) (7 fmly) No smoking in 1 bedroom s £73-£105; d £108-£130 (incl. bkfst) * LB Off peak **MEALS:** V meals Coffee am Tea pm **FACILITIES:** CTV in all bedrooms STV Indoor swimming pool (heated) Croquet lawn Xmas **CONF:** Thtr 120 Class 60 Board 40 **SERVICES:** Night porter 300P **NOTES:** No smoking in restaurant **CARDS:**

TREARDDUR BAY — Map 06 SH27

★★★ Beach

Lon St Ffraid LL65 2YT

Quality Percentage Score: 62%

☎ 01407 860332 Fax 01407 861140

***Dir:** from mainland follow A5 to Valley Crossroads. Left at lights, hotel on right*

Improvements continue at this busy commercial hotel. The refurbished leisure centre provides excellent facilities, including a supervised play-centre for children. Light meals and snacks are available from the upgraded London Road bar, more formal dining is available in the main restaurant. Bedrooms are equipped with modern facilities.

ROOMS: 27 en suite (bth/shr) (3 fmly) s £35.50-£44.50; d £65-£70 (incl. bkfst) * LB Off peak **MEALS:** Sunday Lunch £8.95 Dinner £13.95 & alc V meals Coffee am Tea pm **FACILITIES:** CTV in all bedrooms Snooker Pool table Wkly live entertainment ch fac Xmas **CONF:** Thtr 70 Class 70 Board 40 Del from £42.50 * **SERVICES:** Night porter 100P **NOTES:** Last d 9.30pm **CARDS:**

BALA Gwynedd — Map 06 SH93

★★★ Pale Hall Country House

Llandderfel LL23 7PS

Quality Percentage Score: 75%

☎ 01678 530285 Fax 01678 530220

***Dir:** off the B4401 Corwen/Bala road 4m from Llandrillo*

This impressive Victorian mansion was once visited by Queen Victoria, and the room she occupied is now much in demand. The fine entrance hall, with vaulted ceiling and galleried oak staircase, is the centre of the house; leading off it are the library

contd.

bar, two elegant lounges and the smart dining room, where Wendy Phillips serves carefully cooked meals. Breakfast is taken in the old kitchen, complete with blackened range. The spacious bedrooms are furnished to the highest standards.
ROOMS: 17 en suite (bth/shr) (1 fmly) No smoking in 7 bedrooms
MEALS: English & French Cuisine V meals Coffee am Tea pm
FACILITIES: CTV in all bedrooms Fishing Clay pigeon & Game shooting
CONF: Board 22 **SERVICES:** 60P **NOTES:** No dogs No smoking in restaurant Last d 8.30pm **CARDS:**

See advert on page 897

BALA Gwynedd **Map 06 SH93**
★★ ***Plas Coch***
High St LL23 7AB
Quality Percentage Score: 65%
☎ 01678 520309 📠 01678 521135
Dir: *on A494*
A focal point for the bustling market town, this 18th-century coaching inn is popular with locals, tourists and business guests alike. The spacious public areas include a pleasant reception lounge, separate bistro-style restaurant, and the public and lounge bars. A very positive facelift will, by now, have fully refurbished the hotel.
ROOMS: 10 en suite (bth/shr) (4 fmly) **MEALS:** V meals Coffee am Tea pm **FACILITIES:** CTV in all bedrooms Windsurfing Canoeing Sailing **SERVICES:** 20P **NOTES:** No dogs (ex guide dogs) No coaches No smoking in restaurant Closed 25 Dec
CARDS:

BANGOR Gwynedd **Map 06 SH57**
⇧ **Travel Inn**
Menai Business Park
☎ 0870 242 8000
This modern building offers accommodation in smart, spacious and well equipped bedrooms, all with en-suite bathrooms. Refreshments may be taken at the nearby family restaurant. For details about current prices consult the Contents Page under Hotel Groups for the Travel Inn phone number.
ROOMS: 40 en suite (bth/shr) d £39.95 *

BANGOR Gwynedd **Map 06 SH57**
⇧ **Travelodge**
Llys-y-Gwynt LL57 4BG
☎ 01248 370345 📠 01248 370345
Dir: *junc A5/A55*
This modern building offers accommodation in smart, spacious and well equipped bedrooms, all with en-suite bathrooms. Refreshments may be taken at the nearby family restaurant. For details about current prices, consult the Contents Page under Hotel Groups for the Travelodge phone number.
ROOMS: 62 en suite (bth/shr) d £45.95 *

BARMOUTH Gwynedd **Map 06 SH61**
★★ ***Wavecrest Hotel***
8 Marine Pde LL42 1NA
Quality Percentage Score: 68%
☎ 01341 280330 📠 01341 280330
Dir: *Promenade Barmouth*
This delightful small hotel lies on the promenade and there are superb views from many rooms over Cardigan Bay towards the Cader Idris range of mountains. Bedrooms are decorated with pretty wallpapers and matching fabrics and several are suitable for families. The bar and restaurant are open plan and there is also a small seating area on the first-floor landing. Eric really pampers his guests and Shelagh, who is an accomplished chef, produces excellent food using only fresh local produce.
ROOMS: 10 rms (3 bth 4 shr) (4 fmly) No smoking in all bedrooms
MEALS: FACILITIES: CTV in all bedrooms **SERVICES:** 2P
NOTES: Last d 7.30pm Closed Nov-Feb **CARDS:**

BARMOUTH Gwynedd **Map 06 SH61**
★★ ***Ty'r Graig Castle Hotel***
Llanaber Rd LL42 1YN
Quality Percentage Score: 66%
☎ 01341 280470 📠 01341 281260
Dir: *0.75m from Barmouth on the Harlech road, Seaward side*
An unusual Gothic-style hotel featuring impressive stained glass windows and wood-panelled walls. There is a comfortable lounge and a modern conservatory bar with ocean views. Bedrooms are modern and well equipped, four are in rounded towers with views over Cardigan Bay. Food is of sound quality, staff and owners are friendly and welcoming.
ROOMS: 12 en suite (bth/shr) No smoking in 1 bedroom
MEALS: V meals Coffee am Tea pm **FACILITIES:** CTV in all bedrooms STV **CONF:** Thtr 50 Class 30 Board 20 **SERVICES:** 15P **NOTES:** No coaches No smoking in restaurant Last d 9pm Closed 25 Dec-5 Feb
CARDS:

BARMOUTH Gwynedd **Map 06 SH61**
★★ **Bryn Melyn**
Panorama Rd LL42 1DQ
Quality Percentage Score: 65%
☎ 01341 280556 📠 01341 280342
Dir: *off A496, 0.25m on left - Panorama Road - leaving Barmouth for Dolgellau*
This family-run hotel has superb views over the Mawddach Estuary to the Cader Idris mountains. Bedrooms are decorated with pretty wallpapers and fabrics and all are equipped with modern facilities. A comfortable lounge is provided and there is also an attractive cane-furnished conservatory. Good home cooking is on offer and vegetarians are well looked after.
ROOMS: 9 rms (8 shr) (1 fmly) s £28-£37.50; d £42-£64 (incl. bkfst) * LB Off peak **MEALS:** Lunch fr £14.95 Dinner fr £14.95 V meals Coffee am Tea pm **FACILITIES:** CTV in all bedrooms **SERVICES:** 10P
NOTES: No coaches No smoking in restaurant Last d 8.30pm
CARDS:

BARRY Vale of Glamorgan **Map 03 ST16**
★★★ **Egerton Grey Country House**
Porthkerry CF62 3BZ
Quality Percentage Score: 77%
☎ 01446 711666 📠 01446 711690
Dir: *from junct 33 of M4 follow signs for airport and turn left at rdbt for Porthkerry, after 500yds turn left down lane between thatched cottages*

An elegant country house that offers warm hospitality and attentive service. The charming public areas have a relaxed style,
contd.

period furnishings adorn the restaurant, lounge and library. Spacious bedrooms are similarly appointed, with some wonderful original bathroom furniture. Cuisine is taken seriously at both breakfast and dinner with a menu which includes exemplary Glamorgan sausages.

ROOMS: 10 en suite (bth/shr) (4 fmly) s £70-£105; d £95-£130 (incl. bkfst) * LB Off peak **MEALS:** Lunch £14.50-£14.95 & alc High tea £1.75-£6.50 Dinner fr £17.95 & alc V meals Coffee am Tea pm **FACILITIES:** CTV in all bedrooms STV Tennis Croquet lawn Croquet Xmas **CONF:** Thtr 30 Class 30 Board 22 Del from £120 * **SERVICES:** 41P **NOTES:** No coaches No smoking in restaurant Last d 9.30pm **CARDS:**

See advert under CARDIFF

BARRY Vale of Glamorgan — Map 03 ST16

★★★ Mount Sorrel

Porthkerry Rd CF62 7XY

Quality Percentage Score: 65%

☎ 01446 740069 📠 01446 746600

Dir: *from M4 junct 33 on A4232 signed Barry. Join A4050, pass Fire station, left at rdbt, over lights, 2nd left at rdbt, 1st left and left again*

Situated in an elevated position above the town centre this is an extended Victorian property offering comfortable accommodation for both the tourist and business trade. The public areas include a choice of conference rooms, restaurant and bar together with leisure facilities.

ROOMS: 43 en suite (bth/shr) (3 fmly) s £60-£72.50; d £80-£90 (incl. bkfst) LB Off peak **MEALS:** Lunch £10.50-£14.50 Dinner £12.75-£18.25alc English & Continental Cuisine V meals Coffee am Tea pm **FACILITIES:** CTV in all bedrooms STV Indoor swimming pool (heated) Sauna Gym Xmas **CONF:** Thtr 150 Class 100 Board 50 Del from £85 * **SERVICES:** Night porter 17P **NOTES:** No smoking in restaurant Last d 9.15pm **CARDS:**

BEAUMARIS See Anglesey, Isle of

BEDDGELERT Gwynedd — Map 06 SH54

★★★ *Royal Goat*

LL55 4YE

Quality Percentage Score: 66%

☎ 01766 890224 & 890343 📠 01766 890422

Dir: *off A498*

A privately owned hotel built over 200 years ago. Modern bedrooms are pretty and well equipped. Public areas include a choice of bars, a comfortable lounge, meeting and function rooms. Friendly staff are mostly Welsh speaking.

ROOMS: 32 en suite (bth/shr) (3 fmly) No smoking in 10 bedrooms **MEALS:** Welsh & French Cuisine V meals Coffee am Tea pm **FACILITIES:** CTV in all bedrooms STV Fishing Pool table **CONF:** Thtr 80 Class 70 Board 70 **SERVICES:** Lift Night porter 100P **NOTES:** No smoking in restaurant Last d 10pm **CARDS:**

BEDDGELERT Gwynedd — Map 06 SH54

★★ Tanronnen Inn

LL55 4YB

Quality Percentage Score: 71%

☎ 01766 890347 📠 01766 890606

This delightful small hotel lies in the centre of a lovely village which is itself surrounded by an area of outstanding beauty. Completely refurbished over recent years the hotel now offers comfortable and well appointed bedrooms and a range of attractive and relaxing public areas. The wide range of bar food on offer is popular with the many tourists to the area and more formal meals are served in the restaurant. Staff are friendly and helpful and there is a peaceful and relaxing atmosphere. Beddgelert has won the 'Britain in Bloom' competition for many years.

ROOMS: 7 en suite (bth/shr) (3 fmly) s £40; d £78 (incl. bkfst) * LB Off peak **MEALS:** Lunch £3.95-£9.95 & alc High tea fr £2.50 Dinner £6.95-£15.95 & alc English, French & Italian Cuisine V meals Coffee am **FACILITIES:** CTV in all bedrooms STV Xmas **SERVICES:** 15P **NOTES:** No dogs No smoking area in restaurant Last d 8.45pm **CARDS:**

BETWS-Y-COED Conwy — Map 06 SH75

see also **Llanrwst**

★★★ Royal Oak

Holyhead Rd LL24 0AY

Quality Percentage Score: 70%

☎ 01690 710219 📠 01690 710603

Dir: *on main A5 in centre of town, next to St Mary's church*

This fine hotel started life as a coaching inn, and now provides smart bedrooms and a wide range of public areas. Food is available in the bistro and in Stables Bar, a Grill Room for snacks, while more formal eating is available in the main dining room.

ROOMS: 26 en suite (bth/shr) No smoking in 6 bedrooms s £45-£52; d £70-£84 (incl. bkfst) * LB Off peak **MEALS:** Lunch £9.50-£12 High tea £6.99-£7.50alc Dinner £15.50-£19 & alc International Cuisine V meals Coffee am Tea pm **FACILITIES:** CTV in all bedrooms STV Pool table Golfing arranged Wkly live entertainment Xmas **CONF:** Board 20 **SERVICES:** Night porter 90P **NOTES:** No dogs (ex guide dogs) No smoking area in restaurant Last d 9pm Closed 25-26 Dec **CARDS:**

See advert on page 901

B

BETWS-Y-COED Conwy Map 06 SH75
★★★ Waterloo
LL24 0AR
Quality Percentage Score: 67%
☎ 01690 710411 📠 01690 710666
Dir: *close to A5, near Waterloo Bridge*

The Waterloo is a good base for touring Snowdonia and provides comfortable and well equipped accommodation. Most bedrooms are spacious, housed in modern buildings next to the main hotel, private suites are also available. Food options are wide ranging with formal dining in the fetching "Garden Restaurant", while a full choice of lighter meals is offered in the "Wellington Bar". The hotel also has an all day coffee shop at the fully equipped leisure centre.
ROOMS: 40 en suite (bth/shr) s £53-£63; d £86-£106 (incl. bkfst) * Off peak **MEALS:** Sunday Lunch £5.95-£12.95 High tea £4.95-£6.95 Dinner £14.75-£16.75 International Cuisine V meals Coffee am Tea pm **FACILITIES:** CTV in all bedrooms Indoor swimming pool (heated) Sauna Solarium Gym Pool table Jacuzzi/spa Steam room Xmas **CONF:** Thtr 75 Class 50 Board 25 Del from £65 * **SERVICES:** 200P
NOTES: Last d 9.30pm Closed 30 Dec-8 Jan
CARDS:

See advert on opposite page

BETWS-Y-COED Conwy Map 06 SH75
★★★ Craig-y-Dderwen Country House Hotel
LL24 0AS
Quality Percentage Score: 64%
☎ 01690 710293 📠 01690 710362
Dir: *A5 to town, cross Waterloo Bridge and take first left*
This Victorian country house hotel in well maintained grounds, lies alongside the River Conwy at the end of a tree-lined drive from the end of the famous Waterloo Bridge, making for very pleasing views which are enjoyed by many rooms. Comfortable lounges are provided, and two of the bedrooms have four-posters. The atmosphere is tranquil and relaxing.
ROOMS: 16 en suite (bth/shr) (5 fmly) d £55-£87.50 (incl. bkfst) * LB Off peak **MEALS:** Bar Lunch £2-£6.95alc Dinner fr £16.50 & alc V meals Coffee am Tea pm **FACILITIES:** CTV in all bedrooms Badminton,Golf driving range,Volleyball **CONF:** Thtr 50 Class 25 Board 12
SERVICES: 50P **NOTES:** No smoking in restaurant Last d 8.30pm Closed Nov-1 Mar **CARDS:**

BETWS-Y-COED Conwy Map 06 SH75
★★★ Glan Aber
Holyhead Rd LL24 0AB
Quality Percentage Score: 63%
☎ 01690 710325 📠 01690 710700
Dir: *turn off A5 onto the Waterloo Bridge and proceed a quarter mile. Hotel on left next to Midland Bank*
Glan Aber is located in the heart of the mountain resort and provides modern, well equipped bedrooms and comfortable public areas. A large menu is offered, supplemented by a good range of bar meals. There is a choice of bars, a separate pool room, and a secure car park. A first floor lounge is provided, and there is a spa bath and sun-bed.
ROOMS: 25 en suite (bth/shr) (3 fmly) s £24.50-£31.50; d £49-£63 (incl. bkfst) * LB Off peak **MEALS:** Sunday Lunch £9.95 & alc Dinner £10.95 Varied Cuisine V meals Coffee am Tea pm **FACILITIES:** CTV in all bedrooms STV Fishing Sauna Solarium Pool table Jacuzzi/spa
CONF: Thtr 30 Class 30 Board 20 **SERVICES:** Lift 21P
NOTES: Last d 8.45pm Closed 24-26 Dec **CARDS:**

See advert on opposite page

BETWS-Y-COED Conwy Map 06 SH75

The Premier Collection

★★ Tan-y-Foel Country House
Capel Garmon LL26 0RE
☎ 01690 710507 📠 01690 710681
Dir: *off A5 at Betws-y-Coed onto A470, travel 2m N sign marked Capel Garmon on right, take this turning towards Capel Garmon for 1.5m hotel sign on left*
With glorious views across the Conwy Valley towards the Snowdon mountain range, this immaculately maintained 16th-century manor house is run with enthusiasm and pride. Inside are two cosy lounges and both have cheerful log fires. The dining room has been extended into a conservatory area and is a fitting environment in which to enjoy the hotel cuisine, which uses fine local produce. Individually decorated and tastefully furnished bedrooms are all neatly presented, have many thoughtful extras and often enjoy delightful views.
ROOMS: 5 en suite (bth/shr) 2 annexe en suite (bth/shr) No smoking in all bedrooms s £70-£90; d £76-£150 (incl. bkfst) * LB Off peak **MEALS:** Lunch £16-£21alc Dinner £21-£29alc French Cuisine Coffee am Tea pm **FACILITIES:** CTV in all bedrooms
SERVICES: 9P **NOTES:** No dogs (ex guide dogs) No coaches No children 7yrs No smoking in restaurant Last d 7pm Closed mid Dec-1 Jan **CARDS:**

BETWS-Y-COED Conwy Map 06 SH75
★★ Park Hill
Llanrwst Rd LL24 0HD
Quality Percentage Score: 67%
☎ 01690 710540 📠 01690 710540
Dir: *north on A470*
This friendly hotel benefits from a peaceful location overlooking the village. Comfortable bedrooms come in a wide range of sizes

contd. on p. 902

THE EAGLE HOTELS GROUP

WATERLOO

Hotel & Leisure Centre

Betws - y Coed, Snowdonia • AA★★★

"The Hotel for all Seasons"

The leading hotel in Snowdonia, ideally situated for discovering the stunning mountain scenery and beautiful coastline with its many attractions for all ages. The hotel and modern cottage style rooms are located within attractive grounds, all en-suite with colour TV, telephone and tea/coffee tray and many with their own sitting room area.

Hotel facilities include indoor leisure complex with superb 14m swimming pool, jacuzzi, steam room, sauna, solarium, childrens splash pool and well equipped gymnasium.

Traditional Welsh restaurant with extended Table d'hote menu.

Wellington Bar with garden patio & cocktail bar.

WTB 5 DRAGONS RATING SELF CATERING COTTAGES are also available.

Best Western

Tel: 01690 710411

Fax: 01690 710666

Email: reservations@waterloohotel.co.uk www.waterloohotel.co.uk

Royal Oak Hotel

Holyhead Road
Betws y Coed, Gwynedd

Tel: 01690 710219 Fax: 01690 710603

AA ★ ★ ★

GWESTY ★★★ HOTEL

Picturesque former coaching inn overlooking River Llugwy with 27 luxury bedrooms, all en suite. NEW Stables Bistro Bar Open daily 10.30am to 10.30pm. Food served all day.

Our Grill is open daily 8am to 9pm offering varied menus, plus our excellent dining room specialising in fresh fish and meat delicacies. Our chef/manager is a member of the Chaine des Rotisseurs.

Central for coast, mountains, waterfalls, fishing, golf and riding.

Short breaks available - one day or more

Very competitive rates

PRINCES ARMS HOTEL

PRINCES ARMS COUNTRY HOTEL

Trefriw (nr Betws-y-Coed) - North Wales LL 27 0JP

Telephone 01492 640592 - Fax 01492 640559

Email: enquiries@princes-arms.co.uk

Website: http://princes-arms.co.uk

Quiet National Park location central to Snowdonia's mountains and coast. Superb en-suite bedrooms with bath and shower, satellite TV, telephone, tea/coffee, hairdryer, laundry. Spectacular views across the River Conwy. Our elegant AA rosette awarded restaurant has an enviable reputation for its cuisine, or alternatively dine in our less formal but stylish King's Brasserie. Whether you picnic by Lake Crafnant, stroll along forest tracks or browse around Bodnant Gardens the Princes Arms Hotel is really a rather nice place to find.

GLAN ABER HOTEL

BETWS-Y-COED

AA★★★ WALES TOURIST BOARD ★★★

A warm welcome awaits you at our hotel, renowned for its relaxing atmosphere and friendly staff. Situated in the centre of Betws-Y-Coed in the Snowdonia National Park, convenient for touring, walking, climbing, pony trekking, fishing and golf. Modernised to a high standard whilst retaining its old world charm with open fires. En-suite bedrooms with colour TV, radio, hospitality tray, hair dryer and trouser press. Facilities include first class restaurant, bar and lounge serving meals/snacks, games room, residents lounge, sauna/solarium, and drying room.

BETWS-Y-COED, CONWY LL24 0AB

TEL: 01690 710325 FAX: 01690 710700

and are well equipped. There is a choice of lounges and seating in the covered entrance porch.
ROOMS: 9 en suite (bth/shr) (2 fmly) **MEALS:** Bar Lunch fr £6.50 Dinner fr £14.50 Welsh, English & French Cuisine V meals **FACILITIES:** CTV in all bedrooms Indoor swimming pool (heated) Sauna Jacuzzi/spa **SERVICES:** 14P **NOTES:** No dogs (ex guide dogs) No coaches No children 6yrs No smoking in restaurant Last d 7.45pm
CARDS:

BETWS-Y-COED Conwy — Map 06 SH75
★ Fairy Glen
LL24 0SH
Quality Percentage Score: 68%
☎ 01690 710269 01690 710269
***Dir:** from A5 take A470 (Dolwyddelan road), hotel on left*
Dating back over 300 years, this former coaching inn is near the Fairy Glen beauty spot. It provides modern accommodation with good facilities and very friendly service. There is a cosy bar and separate lounge, good home cooking is served.
ROOMS: 8 rms (4 bth 2 shr) (2 fmly) s £21-£36; d £42-£48 (incl. bkfst) * LB Off peak **MEALS:** Dinner £13 V meals Coffee am Tea pm **FACILITIES:** CTV in all bedrooms **SERVICES:** Night porter 10P **NOTES:** No coaches No smoking in restaurant Last d 7pm Closed Nov-Jan **CARDS:**

BIRCHGROVE Swansea — Map 03 SS79
★★ Oak Tree Parc
Birchgrove Rd SA7 9JR
Quality Percentage Score: 62%
☎ 01792 817781 01792 814542
***Dir:** 300yds from M4 junc 44*
A large Victorian house, this family-run hotel standing in its own grounds provides a variety of accommodation including family-bedded rooms. The public areas comprise a lounge bar and a restaurant where an extensive range of varied dishes are served. At the time of publication, a wholesale refurbishment of the hotel was planned along with a significant extension.
ROOMS: 10 en suite (bth/shr) (2 fmly) s £39; d £55 (incl. bkfst) * Off peak **MEALS:** Lunch fr £9.95 & alc Dinner fr £12 & alc Welsh, English, French & Italian Cuisine V meals Coffee am Tea pm **FACILITIES:** CTV in all bedrooms **CONF:** Thtr 40 Class 25 Board 20 **SERVICES:** Night porter 40P **NOTES:** Last d 10pm Closed 25-31 Dec
CARDS:

BLACKWOOD Caerphilly — Map 03 ST19
★★★ *Maes Manor*
NP2 0AG
Quality Percentage Score: 68%
☎ 01495 224551 & 220011 01495 228217
Standing high above the town, this 19th-Century manor house is set in nine acres of its own gardens and woodland. Bedrooms are attractively decorated with co-ordinated furnishings and good in-room facilities. The restaurant is supplemented by a choice of bars with a lounge/lobby area and a large function room. The function room is the setting for regular live entertainment which is highly regarded in the local area.
ROOMS: 8 en suite (bth) 14 annexe en suite (bth) (2 fmly) **MEALS:** Welsh, English, French & Italian Cuisine V meals Coffee am Tea pm **FACILITIES:** CTV in all bedrooms ch fac **CONF:** Thtr 200 Class 200 Board 100 **SERVICES:** Night porter 100P **NOTES:** Last d 9.30pm
CARDS:

BLAENAU FFESTINIOG Gwynedd — Map 06 SH74
★★ *Queens Hotel*
1 High St LL41 3ES
Quality Percentage Score: 68%
☎ 01766 830055 01766 830046
***Dir:** on A470 adjacent to Ffestiniog railway, between Betws-Y-Coed & Dolgellau*
A flourishing hotel with an all-day bistro serving a full range of popular meals and snacks, and giving way to more formal dining in the evening. A large function room is available for weddings and other events, and business meetings can also be accommodated. Bedrooms are well equipped, attractively decorated and furnished, and some rooms are suitable for families. The hotel lies at the northern end of the famous Ffestiniog narrow gauge railway line.
ROOMS: 12 en suite (bth/shr) (4 fmly) **MEALS:** British & Italian Cuisine V meals Coffee am Tea pm **FACILITIES:** CTV in all bedrooms STV **CONF:** Thtr 100 Class 60 Board 40 **NOTES:** No dogs (ex guide dogs) No smoking in restaurant Last d 9.30pm Closed 25 Dec
CARDS:

BONTDDU Gwynedd — Map 06 SH61
★★★ Bontddu Hall
LL40 2UF
Quality Percentage Score: 71%
☎ 01341 430661 01341 430284
***Dir:** in Bontddu village halfway between Dolgellau and Barmouth on the A496*

Overlooking the beautiful Mawddach Estuary, this 19th-century house was once the country retreat of the Lord Mayor of Birmingham. Bedrooms are spacious and well equipped, three suites are available and several more are located in a nearby building. Elegant public areas include a choice of lounges and an attractive bar. In addition to the formal dinner menu, there is a lighter brasserie-style option.
ROOMS: 15 en suite (bth/shr) 5 annexe en suite (bth/shr) (6 fmly) s fr £62.50; d fr £100 (incl. bkfst) * LB Off peak **MEALS:** Lunch fr £13.95 & alc Dinner £23.50-£25 & alc British & French Cuisine V meals Coffee am Tea pm **FACILITIES:** CTV in all bedrooms 14 acres of gardens/woodland Xmas **SERVICES:** 50P **NOTES:** No coaches No children 3yrs No smoking in restaurant Last d 9.30pm Closed Jan & Feb
CARDS:
See advert under BARMOUTH

BRECHFA Carmarthenshire — Map 02 SN53
★★ *Ty Mawr Country Hotel*
SA32 7RA
Quality Percentage Score: 72%
☎ 01267 202332 01267 202437
***Dir:** off B4310 in centre of village*
Ty Mawr (the Big House), with the River Marlais flowing through its grounds, dates back some 450 years. The
contd.

accommodation is well maintained and public areas have charm and character. The hotel is establishing a reputation for friendly hospitality and good food.
ROOMS: 5 rms (4 bth/shr) (1 fmly) No smoking in all bedrooms **MEALS:** International Cuisine V meals Coffee am Tea pm **CONF:** **SERVICES:** 45P **NOTES:** No coaches No smoking in restaurant Closed Xmas week, last week Nov **CARDS:**

BRECON Powys **Map 03 SO02**
★★★ Nant Ddu Lodge
Cwm Taf, Nant Ddu CF48 2HY
Quality Percentage Score: 74%
☎ 01685 379111 Fax 01685 377088
(For full entry see Nant-Ddu)

BRECON Powys **Map 03 SO02**
★★ Castle of Brecon
Castle Square LD3 9DB
Quality Percentage Score: 70%
☎ 01874 624611 Fax 01874 623737
Dir: *follow signs to Town Centre. Turn opposite The Boars Head, towards Cradoc*
Standing next to the ruins of Brecon Castle, this early 19th century coaching inn has impressive views of the Usk Valley and the Brecon Beacons National Park. The public rooms include a choice of two bars and a separate lounge in addition to a large restaurant that is the venue for some imaginative cooking of quality produce. The bedrooms are modern and include a number of extra facilities. Conference and function rooms are also available.
ROOMS: 30 en suite (bth/shr) 12 annexe en suite (shr) (4 fmly) s £40-£49; d £54-£78 (incl. bkfst) * LB Off peak **MEALS:** Lunch fr £9.40 Dinner £20-£25 V meals Coffee am **FACILITIES:** CTV in all bedrooms STV **CONF:** Thtr 170 Class 150 Board 80 Del from £59 * **SERVICES:** 30P **NOTES:** No smoking in restaurant Last d 8.45pm Closed 23-25 Dec & 31 Dec-1 Jan **CARDS:**

BRECON Powys **Map 03 SO02**
★★ Lansdowne Hotel & Restaurant
The Watton LD3 7EG
Quality Percentage Score: 70%
☎ 01874 623321 Fax 01874 610438
Dir: *turn off A40/A470 onto the B4601, hotel in town centre*
A family-run hotel close to the town centre, it provides good value accommodation and friendly hospitality. The recently refurbished bedrooms are very well equipped. Family rooms and a ground floor room are available. Facilities include a traditionally furnished lounge, a split level dining room with original stone fireplace, and a bar.
ROOMS: 9 en suite (bth/shr) (2 fmly) s £27.50; d £47.50 (incl. bkfst) * LB Off peak **MEALS:** Dinner £13.75-£19.70alc English & French Cuisine V meals **FACILITIES:** CTV in all bedrooms Xmas **NOTES:** No dogs (ex guide dogs) No coaches No children 5yrs No smoking area in restaurant Last d 9.30pm **CARDS:**

BRIDGEND Bridgend **Map 03 SS97**
see also **Porthcawl**
★★★ The Great House Restaurant & Hotel
Laleston CF32 0HP
Quality Percentage Score: 75%
☎ 01656 657644 Fax 01656 668892
Dir: *at side of A473, 400yrds from its junction with A48*
A hotel housed in a Grade II listed building, dating back to 1550. Original features such as mullioned windows, flagstone floors, oak beams and inglenook fireplaces add character, especially the great stone arch over the fireplace in the bar. The restaurant offers a wide range of dishes. Bedrooms are located in the original building and a purpose built annexe, and decorated with rich colours and fabrics.
ROOMS: 8 en suite (bth/shr) 8 annexe en suite (bth/shr) No smoking in 4 bedrooms s £75-£80; d £110-£125 (incl. bkfst) * LB Off peak **MEALS:** Lunch fr £14.50 Dinner fr £21.50 & alc French Cuisine V meals Coffee am Tea pm **FACILITIES:** CTV in all bedrooms STV Sauna Gym Croquet lawn Jacuzzi/spa Health suite **CONF:** Thtr 40 Class 40 Board 20 Del from £99 * **SERVICES:** 40P **NOTES:** No dogs No smoking in restaurant Last d 9.30pm Closed 25 Dec-2 Jan
CARDS:

BRIDGEND Bridgend **Map 03 SS97**
★★★ Coed-y-Mwstwr
Coychurch CF35 6AF
Quality Percentage Score: 73%
☎ 01656 860621 Fax 01656 863122
Dir: *leave A473 at Coychurch and turn right at petrol station. Follow signs at top of hill*
Set in seventeen acres of grounds, just a few miles from the centre of Bridgend, this hotel retains many of its original features, including an impressive domed ceiling in the restaurant. The spacious bedrooms offer a good range of extra facilities.
ROOMS: 23 en suite (bth/shr) (2 fmly) No smoking in 10 bedrooms s £95; d £135 (incl. bkfst) * LB Off peak **MEALS:** Lunch £13.25 & alc High tea £4.75-£7.95 Dinner £24 & alc English & Mediterranean Influence Cuisine V meals Coffee am Tea pm **FACILITIES:** CTV in all bedrooms STV Outdoor swimming pool (heated) Golf 9 Tennis (hard) Croquet lawn Wkly live entertainment Xmas **CONF:** Thtr 225 Class 75 Board 60 Del from £140 * **SERVICES:** Lift Night porter 100P **NOTES:** No dogs (ex guide dogs) No smoking area in restaurant Last d 10.15pm
CARDS:

B

BRIDGEND Bridgend — Map 03 SS97
★★★ Heronston
Ewenny Rd CF35 5AW
Quality Percentage Score: 67%
☎ 01656 668811 📠 01656 767391
Dir: *exit M4 at junc 35, follow signs for Porthcawl, at fourth rdbt turn left towards Ogmore-by-Sea (B4265) hotel 200yds on left*
Well located for Bridgend town centre and for the major road network, this large modern hotel offers spacious well-equipped accommodation. Attractive public areas include an open plan lounge and bar together with a spacious restaurant. Leisure facilities include both indoor and outdoor pools. Conference rooms are available.
ROOMS: 69 en suite (bth/shr) 6 annexe en suite (bth/shr) (4 fmly) No smoking in 12 bedrooms s £85-£90; d £100-£110 (incl. bkfst) * LB Off peak **MEALS:** Lunch £15.95-£17.95 High tea £4.95 Dinner £17.95 & alc English & European Cuisine V meals Coffee am Tea pm **FACILITIES:** CTV in all bedrooms STV Indoor swimming pool (heated) Outdoor swimming pool (heated) Sauna Solarium Jacuzzi/spa Steamroom,Residential Aromatherapist and Masseur **CONF:** Thtr 200 Class 80 Board 60 Del from £135 * **SERVICES:** Lift Night porter 250P **NOTES:** No smoking area in restaurant Last d 9.30pm RS 25-26 Dec **CARDS:**

BRIDGEND Bridgend — Map 03 SS97
Travel Inn
Pantruthyn Farm, Pencoed CF35 5HY
☎ 01656 860133 📠 01656 864792
Dir: *situated immediately off the rdbt at junct 35 of the M4, between the service station and Sony factory*
This modern building offers accommodation in smart, spacious and well equipped bedrooms, all with en-suite bathrooms. Refreshments may be taken at the nearby family restaurant. For details about current prices consult the Contents Page under Hotel Groups for the Travel Inn phone number.
ROOMS: 40 en suite (bth/shr) d £39.95 *

BRIDGEND Bridgend — Map 03 SS97
Welcome Lodge
Welcome Break - Sarn Park, M4 CF32 9RW
☎ 01656 659218 📠 01656 768665
Dir: *M4 junct 36*
This modern building offers accommodation in smart, spacious and well equipped bedrooms, suitable for families and businessmen, and all with en-suite bathrooms. Refreshments may be taken at the nearby family restaurant. For details of current prices, consult the Contents Page under Hotel Groups for the Welcome Break phone number.
ROOMS: 40 en suite (bth/shr) d fr £40 *

BUILTH WELLS Powys — Map 03 SO05
★★★ *Caer Beris Manor*
LD2 3NP
Quality Percentage Score: 71%
☎ 01982 552601 📠 01982 552586
Dir: *SW on A483*
Some excellent fishing is available at this 19th-century country house, but you don't have to be an angler to appreciate the beautiful River Irfon that runs through the 30 acres of mature grounds. Recent years have seen many improvements taking place with both the public areas and many bedrooms benefiting from some elegant decoration. Meals can be taken in the oak-panelled dining room or in the less formal environs of the conservatory. There is plenty of space to relax including a lounge bar with log fire and a separate sitting room.
ROOMS: 22 en suite (bth/shr) (1 fmly) **MEALS:** International Cuisine V meals Coffee am Tea pm **FACILITIES:** CTV in 21 bedrooms STV Fishing Riding Sauna Gym Clay pigeon shooting **CONF:** Thtr 100 Class 75 Board 50 **SERVICES:** Night porter 32P **CARDS:**

BUILTH WELLS Powys — Map 03 SO05
★★ Pencerrig Gardens
Llandrindod Rd LD2 3TF
Quality Percentage Score: 66%
☎ 01982 553226 📠 01982 552347
Dir: *2m N on A483 towards Llandrindod Wells*
Enjoying a peaceful setting, with pretty gardens and grounds, the building dates partly from the 16th century. As well as the lobby lounge, bar and restaurant, there are several conference rooms. Bedrooms are well equipped and have modern facilities.
ROOMS: 20 en suite (bth/shr) (3 fmly) s £30-£55; d £60-£75 (incl. bkfst) * LB Off peak **MEALS:** Lunch £7.50-£9.95 Dinner £18.50 Welsh & French Cuisine V meals Coffee am Tea pm **FACILITIES:** CTV in all bedrooms Croquet lawn Xmas **CONF:** Thtr 75 Class 40 Board 30 Del from £62.50 * **SERVICES:** 40P **NOTES:** No smoking in restaurant **CARDS:**

CAERNARFON Gwynedd — Map 06 SH46
★★★ Seiont Manor
Llanrug LL55 2AQ
Quality Percentage Score: 78%
☎ 01286 673366 📠 01286 672840
Dir: *E on A4086, 2.5m from Caernarfon*
A high level of professional, yet friendly, service is provided at Seiont Manor. Created from the original barn buildings on this site, this splendid hotel is set amidst tranquil Welsh countryside, close to Snowdon. Bedrooms are well equipped, with lots of luxurious extra touches, and individually decorated with a sense of style. Public rooms are furnished in true country house fashion, cosy and comfortable. Capable cooking often features regional specialities, and there is the advantage of an attractive leisure centre for working off those extra calories.
ROOMS: 28 en suite (bth/shr) (7 fmly) No smoking in 8 bedrooms s £95-£115; d £140-£180 (incl. bkfst) * LB Off peak **MEALS:** Lunch fr £12.50 High tea fr £8.95 Dinner fr £23.50 & alc V meals Coffee am Tea pm **FACILITIES:** CTV in all bedrooms STV Indoor swimming pool (heated) Fishing Sauna Solarium Gym Jacuzzi/spa Xmas **CONF:** Thtr 100 Class 40 Board 40 Del from £130 * **SERVICES:** Night porter 150P **NOTES:** No dogs (ex guide dogs) No smoking in restaurant Last d 10pm **CARDS:**

CAERNARFON Gwynedd — Map 06 SH46
★★★ *Celtic Royal Hotel*
Bangor St LL55 1AY
Quality Percentage Score: 65%
☎ 01286 674477 📠 01286 674139
Recently re-opened after a major refurbishment, this well known hotel, close to the centre of the town, offers generally spacious and attractively furnished bedrooms. The lounge bar, serving snacks at lunchtime and in the evening, features local entertainment from time to time. The restaurant offers freshly prepared meals.
ROOMS: 110 en suite (bth/shr) **MEALS:** V meals Coffee am Tea pm **FACILITIES:** CTV in all bedrooms STV Indoor swimming pool (heated) Sauna Gym Jacuzzi/spa Aerobics **CONF:** Thtr 300 Class 170 Board 125 **SERVICES:** Lift Night porter 180P **NOTES:** No smoking area in restaurant Last d 9.30pm **CARDS:**

CAERNARFON Gwynedd — Map 06 SH46
★★ Ty'n Rhos Country Hotel & Restaurant
Llanddeiniolen LL55 3AE
Quality Percentage Score: 74%
☎ 01248 670489 Fax 01248 670079
Dir: *situated in the hamlet of Seion between B4366 and B4547*

Lynda and Nigel Kettle welcome visitors to their peaceful converted farmhouse, which is set in lovely countryside between Snowdon and the Menai Straits. The lounge, with its slate inglenook fireplace, is elegantly furnished and there is a small bar for pre-dinner drinks. Bedrooms are pine-furnished and include three new rooms in nearby buildings.

ROOMS: 11 en suite (bth/shr) 3 annexe en suite (bth/shr) No smoking in all bedrooms s £49-£75; d £70-£98 (incl. bkfst) * LB Off peak **MEALS:** Sunday Lunch fr £14.95 Dinner £19.50-£27 V meals Coffee am Tea pm **FACILITIES:** CTV in all bedrooms Croquet lawn **CONF:** Board 20 Del from £95 * **SERVICES:** 14P **NOTES:** No dogs (ex guide dogs) No coaches No children 6yrs No smoking in restaurant Last d 8.30pm Closed 24-30 Dec, Millenium & 1wk Aug RS Sun evening (rest closed to non-res) **CARDS:**

CAERNARFON Gwynedd — Map 06 SH46
★★ *Stables*
Llanwnda LL54 5SD
Quality Percentage Score: 64%
☎ 01286 830711 & 830935 Fax 01286 830413
Dir: *3m S of Caernarfon, on A499*

The restaurant and bar are found in a converted stable. Bedrooms, in a more modern block slightly away from the main house, are brightly decorated, several have four-poster beds. This building also has a breakfast room and reception area. The pleasant grounds have a swimming pool available in summer.

contd.

The popular bistro-style restaurant offers an extensive range of meals.
ROOMS: 15 annexe en suite (bth/shr) (3 fmly) **MEALS:** International Cuisine V meals **FACILITIES:** CTV in all bedrooms Outdoor swimming pool Guests may bring own horse to stables **CONF:** Thtr 50 Class 30 Board 30 **SERVICES:** 40P **NOTES:** No smoking area in restaurant Last d 8.30pm **CARDS:**

C

CAERNARFON Gwynedd — Map 06 SH46

★★ Menai Bank

North Rd LL55 1BD
Quality Percentage Score: 62%
☎ 01286 673297 01286 673297
Dir: *on A487 towards Bangor, on rdbt opposite Safeways foodmarket*
Built at the turn of the century as a private residence, it now provides bright, modern accommodation. It features original stained glass windows and tiled fireplaces. A comfortable lounge is provided for residents and there is a small bar and separate games room.
ROOMS: 16 en suite (bth/shr) (6 fmly) No smoking in 5 bedrooms s £30-£39; d £50-£58 (incl. bkfst) * LB Off peak **MEALS:** Dinner £15 English & French Cuisine V meals Coffee am **FACILITIES:** CTV in all bedrooms Pool table **SERVICES:** 10P **NOTES:** No smoking in restaurant Last d 9pm **CARDS:**

CAERPHILLY Caerphilly — Map 03 ST18

Travel Inn

Crossways Business Park, Pontypandy CF83 3NL
☎ 029 20888850 029 20863362
Dir: *A468 to Caerphilly, stay on ring road, until Crossways Business Park, adjacent to 4th rdbt. Travel Inn is on rdbt on right next to Great Mills*
This modern building offers accommodation in smart, spacious and well equipped bedrooms, all with en-suite bathrooms. Refreshments may be taken at the nearby family restaurant. For details about current prices consult the Contents Page under Hotel Groups for the Travel Inn phone number.
ROOMS: 40 en suite (bth/shr) d £39.95 *

CAPEL CURIG Conwy — Map 06 SH75

★★ Cobdens

THE CIRCLE
Selected Individual Hotels
GREAT BRITAIN

LL24 0EE
Quality Percentage Score: 64%
☎ 01690 720243 01690 720354
Dir: *on A5, 4m W of Betws-y-Coed*
For over 200 years this hotel at Moel Siabod in the heart of Snowdonia has been a centre for outdoor pursuits. The bedrooms are modern and well equipped, and many enjoy the lovely views. There are two bars, one with an impressive, exposed rock face. The hotel is run by a friendly team and offers a full range of good-value meals.
ROOMS: 16 en suite (bth/shr) (2 fmly) s £27.50-£29.50; d £55-£59 (incl. bkfst) * Off peak **MEALS:** Lunch £9.50-£10.50alc Dinner £10-£20alc International Cuisine V meals Coffee am Tea pm **FACILITIES:** CTV in all bedrooms Fishing Pool table Xmas **CONF:** Thtr 40 Class 30 Board 25 Del £55 * **SERVICES:** 60P **NOTES:** No coaches No smoking in restaurant Last d 9pm **CARDS:**

CARDIFF Cardiff — Map 03 ST17

see also **Barry**

Hotel of the Year

★★★★★ St David's Hotel & Spa

Havannah St, Cardiff Bay CF10 6SD
Quality Percentage Score: 72%
☎ 029 20454045 029 20487056
Chosen as Hotel of the Year for Wales, this striking modern hotel is at the heart of Cardiff's exciting waterfront development. Inside, an impressive seven-story atrium towers above the lobby, with a contemporary decor that extends throughout the hotel. The Spa and beauty facilities are extensive. Tides bar, with its unusual changing coloured light effect, leads on to the restaurant which looks out over the water. The bedrooms, with their own decks, enjoy views over Cardiff Bay.
ROOMS: 136 en suite (bth/shr) No smoking in 50 bedrooms d £110-£160 * LB Off peak **MEALS:** Lunch £14.50-£19.50 & alc Dinner £21.50-£35alc International Cuisine V meals Coffee am Tea pm **FACILITIES:** CTV in all bedrooms STV Indoor swimming pool (heated) Sauna Solarium Gym Jacuzzi/spa Wkly live entertainment Xmas **CONF:** Thtr 270 Class 110 Board 110 Del from £40 * **SERVICES:** Lift Night porter Air conditioning 80P **NOTES:** No dogs (ex guide dogs) No smoking in restaurant Last d 11pm **CARDS:**

CARDIFF Cardiff — Map 03 ST17

★★★★ Copthorne Cardiff-Caerdydd

MILLENNIUM
MILLENNIUM HOTELS
COPTHORNE HOTELS

Copthorne Way, Culverhouse Cross CF5 6DH
Quality Percentage Score: 71%
☎ 029 20599100 029 20599080
Dir: *exit at junct 33 of M4 and take A4232 for 2.5m in direction of Cardiff West and then A48*
Conveniently located for the city and airport, the Copthorne is a comfortable, popular, modern hotel with bright open-plan public areas. The well equipped bedrooms are smartly presented with rich colours and fabrics and comfortable seating. Guests can enjoy tasty meals in the restaurant overlooking a lake.
ROOMS: 135 en suite (bth/shr) (10 fmly) No smoking in 78 bedrooms s £115-£135; d £135-£155 * LB Off peak **MEALS:** Lunch £10-£15 High tea fr £4.95 Dinner £18.95 & alc International Cuisine V meals Coffee am Tea pm **FACILITIES:** CTV in all bedrooms STV Indoor swimming pool (heated) Snooker Sauna Solarium Gym Jacuzzi/spa Steam room Wkly live entertainment Xmas **CONF:** Thtr 300 Class 140 Board 80 Del £140 * **SERVICES:** Lift Night porter 225P **NOTES:** No smoking area in restaurant Last d 10pm **CARDS:**

CARDIFF Cardiff **Map 03 ST17**
★★★★ ***Thistle Cardiff***
Park Place CF1 3UD
Quality Percentage Score: 67%
☎ 029 20383471 Fax 029 20399309
This Victorian hotel, in the heart of the city, boasts a grand lobby, modern brasserie restaurant and new sports bar. Bedrooms vary in size but are smart and comfortable, with some offering that little extra in the way of luxury. The range of conference rooms is more extensive than is at first apparent.
ROOMS: 136 en suite (bth/shr) (7 fmly) No smoking in 30 bedrooms **MEALS:** English & French Cuisine V meals Coffee am Tea pm **FACILITIES:** CTV in all bedrooms STV **CONF:** Thtr 300 Class 170 Board 100 **SERVICES:** Lift Night porter 70P **NOTES:** No dogs (ex guide dogs) Last d 10.30pm **CARDS:**

CARDIFF Cardiff **Map 03 ST17**
★★★★ **Cardiff Marriott**
Mill Ln CF1 1EZ
Quality Percentage Score: 66%
☎ 029 20399944 Fax 029 20395578
Dir: *from M4 junct 29 follow signs City Centre. Turn left into High Street opposite Castle, then 2nd left, at bottom of High St into Mill Lane*
Located in the heart of the city, this large modern hotel boasts smart new public areas and a good range of services. Eating options include Chats café bar and the contemporary Mediterrano restaurant. The hotel also offers a first class gym with good pool facilities. The well equipped bedrooms are comfortable and furnished to a high standard, with the bonus of air-conditioning.
ROOMS: 182 en suite (bth/shr) (58 fmly) No smoking in 124 bedrooms d £99-£135 * LB Off peak **MEALS:** Lunch £15-£18 & alc High tea £6-£10alc Dinner £18 & alc Medditeranean Cuisine V meals Coffee am Tea pm **FACILITIES:** CTV in all bedrooms STV Indoor swimming pool (heated) Sauna Solarium Gym Jacuzzi/spa Steam room Wkly live entertainment Xmas **CONF:** Thtr 300 Class 200 Board 100 Del from £110 * **SERVICES:** Lift Night porter Air conditioning 110P **NOTES:** No dogs (ex guide dogs) No smoking area in restaurant Last d 10.30pm **CARDS:**

CARDIFF Cardiff **Map 03 ST17**
★★★★ **Jurys Cardiff**
Mary Ann St CF1 2EQ
Quality Percentage Score: 65%
☎ 029 20341441 Fax 029 20223742
Dir: *next to Ice Rink, opposite Cardiff International Arena*
A stylish city centre hotel located directly opposite the Cardiff International Arena. The comfortable, well-equipped bedrooms are situated around an impressive central atrium which gives access to the restaurant and Kavanagh's Irish theme bar. Extensive conference and function facilities are available in addition to a business centre and a fitness room.
ROOMS: 144 en suite (bth/shr) No smoking in 24 bedrooms d £105-£140 * LB Off peak **MEALS:** Lunch £11.95 Dinner £13.95 & alc International Cuisine V meals Coffee am Tea pm **FACILITIES:** CTV in all bedrooms STV Gym **CONF:** Thtr 200 Class 80 Board 50 Del £120 * **SERVICES:** Lift Night porter 55P **NOTES:** No dogs (ex guide dogs) No smoking area in restaurant Last d 9.30pm **CARDS:**

CARDIFF Cardiff **Map 03 ST17**
★★★★❀ **Cardiff Bay**
Schooner Way, Atlantic Wharf CF10 4RT
Quality Percentage Score: 64%
☎ 029 20475000 Fax 029 20481491
Dir: *leave M4 junct 33 follow signs to Cardiff Bay A4232, then to Atlantic Wharf & Cardiff Bay Hotel. Hotel at Schooner Way & Tyndall St junct*
Situated in the heart of Cardiff's exciting new Bay development area, this hotel has proved so popular that it recently doubled in size. The improvements have resulted in a smart new wing of bedrooms while the existing rooms have been upgraded. The public areas include leisure facilities and conference rooms, as well as extra lounge areas. Halyard's restaurant is the primary eating option, and lighter meals are available in two of the bars.
ROOMS: 156 en suite (bth/shr) (6 fmly) No smoking in 50 bedrooms s £105-£110; d fr £120 * LB Off peak **MEALS:** Lunch £7.50-£11.95 Dinner fr £18.50 & alc Continental Cuisine V meals Coffee am Tea pm **FACILITIES:** CTV in all bedrooms STV Indoor swimming pool (heated) Snooker Sauna Solarium Gym Pool table Jacuzzi/spa Wkly live entertainment Xmas **CONF:** Thtr 250 Class 90 Board 40 Del from £130 * **SERVICES:** Lift Night porter 150P **NOTES:** No smoking in restaurant Last d 10pm **CARDS:**

See advert on this page

CARDIFF Cardiff **Map 03 ST17**
★★★❀❀ **New House Country**
Thornhill CF4 5UA
Quality Percentage Score: 74%
☎ 029 20520280 Fax 029 20520324
Dir: *on A469*
Standing on the Cardiff side of Caerphilly mountain, the New House enjoys tranquil rural surroundings with panoramic views of the city centre. There is a country house feel to the public areas, which comprise a lounge and bar with deep cushioned seating and an elegant restaurant. The bedrooms are primarily

contd.

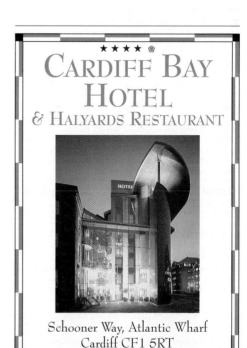

located in a nearby annexe and all are spacious, well appointed and imaginatively decorated.
ROOMS: 5 en suite (bth/shr) 28 annexe en suite (bth/shr) (3 fmly) No smoking in 3 bedrooms s fr £82.50; d fr £102.80 (incl. bkfst) * LB Off peak **MEALS:** Lunch £9.95-£13.95 Dinner fr £22.50 English & French Cuisine V meals Coffee am Tea pm **FACILITIES:** CTV in all bedrooms Xmas **CONF:** Thtr 200 Class 150 Board 200 **SERVICES:** Night porter 100P **NOTES:** No dogs (ex guide dogs) No smoking area in restaurant Last d 9.45pm **CARDS:** ⬤ ■ ⅃ ▣ ▨ ▞ ▢

≣ **CARDIFF** Cardiff   **Map 03 ST17**
★★★✿ **Manor Parc Country Hotel & Restaurant**
Thornhill Rd, Thornhill CF4 5UA
Quality Percentage Score: 73%
☎ 029 20693723 🖷 029 20614624
Dir: on A469
On the northern suburban edge of Cardiff, this hotel is located in pleasingly leafy grounds. There is a warm welcome and professional service delivered by smartly attired staff. The bedrooms are spacious and thoughtfully furnished and include a luxury suite. The public rooms offer a comfortable lounge and a restaurant with a magnificent lantern ceiling.
ROOMS: 12 en suite (bth/shr) (2 fmly) **MEALS:** International Cuisine V meals Coffee am Tea pm **FACILITIES:** CTV in all bedrooms STV Tennis (hard) **CONF:** Thtr 120 Class 80 Board 50 **SERVICES:** Night porter 70P **NOTES:** No dogs (ex guide dogs) No coaches Last d 10pm Closed 24-26 Dec & 1 Jan **CARDS:** ⬤ ■ ⅃ ▞ ▢

≣ **CARDIFF** Cardiff   **Map 03 ST17**
★★★ **Quality**
Merthyr Rd, Tongwynlais CF4 7LD
Quality Percentage Score: 72%
☎ 029 20529988 🖷 029 20529977
Dir: M4 junct 32, take exit for Tongwynlais off large rdbt
In a prime location on the major interchange between Cardiff and the M4 motorway, this modern hotel provides very well-equipped, comfortable bedrooms together with bright open-plan public areas and extensive leisure facilities. A good range of meeting rooms and extensive car parking make it a popular conference venue. Friendly service is dispensed by smartly attired staff.
ROOMS: 95 en suite (bth/shr) (6 fmly) No smoking in 47 bedrooms s £81.50-£107; d £105.50-£107 * LB Off peak **MEALS:** Dinner fr £14.50 English & Continental Cuisine V meals Coffee am Tea pm **FACILITIES:** CTV in all bedrooms STV Indoor swimming pool (heated) Sauna Solarium Gym Jacuzzi/spa Xmas **CONF:** Thtr 200 Class 80 Board 80 **SERVICES:** Lift Night porter 100P **NOTES:** No smoking area in restaurant Last d 9.45pm **CARDS:** ⬤ ■ ⅃ ▣ ▞ ▢

≣ **CARDIFF** Cardiff   **Map 03 ST17**
★★★ **St Mellons Hotel & Country Club**
Castleton CF3 8XR
Quality Percentage Score: 72%
☎ 01633 680355 🖷 01633 680399
Dir: from junct 28 of M4 follow signs into Castleton. Through village, then sharp left at brow of hill following hotel sign into driveway
In a quiet location on the Western edge of Cardiff, this country house style hotel offers quality accommodation with excellent leisure facilities. The bedrooms are located in nearby wings and

are spacious and well appointed. The main house offers relaxing lounges, a bar and an elegant restaurant.
ROOMS: 21 en suite (bth/shr) 20 annexe en suite (bth/shr) (9 fmly) s £80-£90; d £90-£100 (incl. bkfst) * LB Off peak **MEALS:** Lunch £12.95-£16.95 & alc Dinner fr £16.95 & alc International Cuisine V meals Coffee am Tea pm **FACILITIES:** CTV in all bedrooms Indoor.swimming pool (heated) Tennis (hard) Squash Sauna Solarium Gym Jacuzzi/spa Beauty salon Xmas **CONF:** Thtr 140 Class 70 Board 40 Del from £120 * **SERVICES:** Night porter 90P **NOTES:** Last d 9.45pm
CARDS: ⬤ ■ ⅃ ▣ ▨ ▞ ▢

≣ **CARDIFF** Cardiff   **Map 03 ST17**
★★★ *Cardiff Moat House*   ◆
Circle Way East, Llanederyn CF3 7XF   **MOAT**
Quality Percentage Score: 71%   HOUSE
☎ 029 20589988 🖷 029 20549092
Dir: off A48
This smartly decorated hotel is close to the city centre. The business client is well catered for with extensive conference facilities and a dedicated business centre. Comfortable, spacious bedrooms, good public areas and leisure facilities will suit a wide range of guests.
ROOMS: 132 en suite (bth/shr) (4 fmly) No smoking in 40 bedrooms **MEALS:** Welsh & Continental Cuisine V meals Coffee am Tea pm **FACILITIES:** CTV in all bedrooms STV Indoor swimming pool (heated) Sauna Solarium Gym Jacuzzi/spa Baby pool ,children's soft play area & climbing frame ch fac **CONF:** Thtr 290 Class 130 Board 65 **SERVICES:** Lift Night porter 305P **NOTES:** No dogs (ex guide dogs) No smoking area in restaurant Last d 10pm
CARDS: ⬤ ■ ⅃ ▣ ▨ ▞ ▢

≣ **CARDIFF** Cardiff   **Map 03 ST17**
★★★ **Posthouse Cardiff**
Pentwyn Rd, Pentwyn CF2 7XA   **Posthouse**
Quality Percentage Score: 70%
☎ 029 20731212 🖷 029 20549147
Dir: leave M4 Jct29, onto A48M, take 2nd exit (Pentwyn) 3rd exit off the rdbt. Hotel is located on the R.H.S, past the Mercedes garage
Suitable for both the business and leisure traveller, this bright hotel provides modern accommodation in well equipped bedrooms with en suite bathrooms.
ROOMS: 142 en suite (bth/shr) (50 fmly) No smoking in 55 bedrooms s £99; d £79-£119 * LB Off peak **MEALS:** International Cuisine V meals Coffee am Tea pm **FACILITIES:** CTV in all bedrooms Indoor swimming pool (heated) Sauna Solarium Gym Pool table Jacuzzi/spa Childrens play area ch fac **CONF:** Thtr 140 Class 70 Board 40 Del from £77.50 * **SERVICES:** Lift Night porter 300P **NOTES:** No smoking in restaurant Last d 10.30pm **CARDS:** ⬤ ■ ⅃ ▣ ▨ ▞ ▢

≣ **CARDIFF** Cardiff   **Map 03 ST17**
★★★ *Posthouse Cardiff City*
Castle St CF1 2XB   **Posthouse**
Quality Percentage Score: 66%
☎ 029 20388681 🖷 029 20371495
A large modern hotel with a wide range of services and amenities, designed particularly for the business traveller. Some bedrooms look out over the River Taff and the new National Stadium. Bedrooms are smart, comfortable and well equipped.
ROOMS: 155 en suite (bth/shr) No smoking in 102 bedrooms **MEALS:** International Cuisine V meals Coffee am Tea pm **FACILITIES:** CTV in all bedrooms STV Pool table **CONF:** Thtr 170 Class 65 Board 50 **SERVICES:** Lift Night porter 130P **NOTES:** Last d 10.30pm **CARDS:** ⬤ ■ ⅃ ▣ ▨ ▞ ▢

✛
Indicates that the star classification has not been confirmed under the New Quality Standards, see page 7 for further information.

CARDIFF Cardiff **Map 03 ST17**

★★ Sandringham

21 St Mary St CF10 1PL

Quality Percentage Score: 67%

☎ 029 20232161 🖷 029 20383998

Dir: *access via junct 29 on M4, follow 'City Centre' signs. Opposite the castle turn into High Street which leads to St Mary St*

Located in Cardiff city centre, the Sandringham offers convenient shopping and a friendly atmosphere. A smart restaurant and bar, 'Café Jazz' complements the hotel; as the name suggests live jazz is on offer several nights a week. The hotel also has a separate bar and a breakfast room. The bedrooms are well equipped with modern facilities and furnishings.

ROOMS: 28 en suite (bth/shr) (1 fmly) No smoking in 2 bedrooms s £32-£100; d £32-£130 * LB Off peak **MEALS:** Lunch £5.95-£7.95 & alc High tea £3-£5 Dinner £5.95-£7.95 & alc English, Welsh & French Cuisine V meals Coffee am Tea pm **FACILITIES:** CTV in all bedrooms Wkly live entertainment **CONF:** Thtr 100 Class 70 Board 60 Del from £65 * **SERVICES:** Night porter 6P **NOTES:** No dogs (ex guide dogs) No smoking area in restaurant Last d 10.30pm

CARDS:

See advert on this page

CARDIFF Cardiff **Map 03 ST17**

Campanile

Caxton Place, Pentwyn CF2 7HA

☎ 029 20549044 🖷 029 20549900

Dir: *take Pentwyn exit from A48 and follow signs for Pentwyn Industrial Estate*

This modern building offers accommodation in smart well equipped bedrooms, all with en-suite bathrooms. Refreshments may be taken at the informal Bistro. For details about current prices, consult the Contents Page under Hotel Groups for the Campanile phone number.

ROOMS: 50 annexe en suite (bth/shr) **CONF:** Thtr 35 Class 18 Board 20

CARDIFF Cardiff **Map 03 ST17**

Travel Inn Cardiff Bay

Keen Rd CF1 5JR

☎ 029 20489675 🖷 029 20489757

Dir: *follow signs to Cardiff Docks & Bay, after passing Docks & Heliport follow signs to city centre, Travel Inn on right, entrance at rear*

This modern building offers accommodation in smart, spacious and well equipped bedrooms, all with en-suite bathrooms. Refreshments may be taken at the nearby family restaurant. For details about current prices consult the Contents Page under Hotel Groups for the Travel Inn phone number.

ROOMS: 40 en suite (bth/shr) d £39.95 *

C

CARDIFF Cardiff **Map 03 ST17**

Travel Inn Cardiff (Roath)

David Lloyd Club, Ipswich Rd, Roath CF3 7AQ

☎ 029 20462481 029 20462482

Dir: *follow signs for docks, left at fork, then right at rdbt, at traffic lights (opposite Howells Motors) turn right and right again after Sainsbury's*

This modern building offers accommodation in smart, spacious and well equipped bedrooms, all with en-suite bathrooms. Refreshments may be taken at the nearby family restaurant. For details about current prices consult the Contents Page under Hotel Groups for the Travel Inn phone number.

ROOMS: 40 en suite (bth/shr) d £39.95 *

CARDIFF Cardiff **Map 03 ST17**

Travel Inn Cardiff West

The Walston Castle, Port Road, Nantisaf, Wenvoe CF5 6DD

☎ 029 20593896 029 20591436

Dir: *from junct33 on M4 head S on A4232, Travel Inn is 0.5m past Culver House Cross rdbt on A4050*

This modern building offers accommodation in smart, spacious and well equipped bedrooms, all with en-suite bathrooms. Refreshments may be taken at the nearby family restaurant. For details about current prices consult the Contents Page under Hotel Groups for the Travel Inn phone number.

ROOMS: 40 en suite (bth/shr) d £39.95 *

CARDIFF Cardiff **Map 03 ST17**

Travelodge

Granada Service Area M4, Pontyclun CF72 8SA

☎ 029 20891141 029 20892497

Dir: *M4, junct 33/A4232*

This modern building offers accommodation in smart, spacious and well equipped bedrooms, all with en-suite bathrooms. Refreshments may be taken at the nearby family restaurant. For details about current prices, consult the Contents Page under Hotel Groups for the Travelodge phone number.

ROOMS: 50 en suite (bth/shr) d £45.95 * **CONF:** Thtr 45 Board 34

CARDIFF Cardiff **Map 03 ST17**

Travelodge

Circle Way East, Llanedeyrn CF3 7ND

☎ 029 20549564 029 20549564

Dir: *M4 junc30, take A4232 to North Pentwyn Interchange. A48 & signs for Cardiff East & Docks. 3rd exit at Llanedeyrn Interchange, follow Circle Way East*

This modern building offers accommodation in smart, spacious and well equipped bedrooms, all with en-suite bathrooms. Refreshments may be taken at the nearby family restaurant. For details about current prices, consult the Contents Page under Hotel Groups for the Travelodge phone number.

ROOMS: 32 en suite (bth/shr)

CARDIGAN See **Gwbert-on-Sea**

CARMARTHEN Carmarthenshire **Map 02 SN42**

★★ **Falcon**

Lammas St SA31 3AP

Quality Percentage Score: 63%

☎ 01267 234959 & 237152 01267 221277

Dir: *in town centre opposite Monument*

Located in the centre of Carmarthen, this delightfully cosy hotel provides smart modern accommodation. There is a comfortable foyer, lounge and bar (which serves tea and coffee). The restaurant serves commendable meals using fresh local produce, and also caters for functions. Bedrooms are well equipped, some have four-poster beds.

ROOMS: 14 en suite (bth/shr) (1 fmly) s fr £52.50; d £59.50-£62.50 (incl. bkfst) * LB Off peak **MEALS:** Lunch £9.50-£10.95 Dinner fr £14.95 V meals Coffee am Tea pm **FACILITIES:** CTV in all bedrooms **CONF:** Thtr 100 Class 50 Board 40 **SERVICES:** 38P **NOTES:** No smoking area in restaurant Last d 9pm Closed 25-26 Dec RS Sun **CARDS:**

CASTLETON Newport **Map 03 ST28**

Travel Inn

Newport Rd CF3 8UQ

☎ 01633 680070 01633 681143

Dir: *leave M4 at junct 8, at rdbt take 2nd exit A48 Castleton and follow for 3m, Travel Inn on right*

This modern building offers accommodation in smart, spacious and well equipped bedrooms, all with en-suite bathrooms. Refreshments may be taken at the nearby family restaurant. For details about current prices consult the Contents Page under Hotel Groups for the Travel Inn phone number.

ROOMS: 47 en suite (bth/shr) d £39.95 *

CHEPSTOW Monmouthshire **Map 03 ST59**

★★★★ **Marriott St Pierre**

St Pierre Park NP16 6YA

Quality Percentage Score: 69%

☎ 01291 625261 01291 629975

Dir: *leave M48 junct 2. At rdbt on slip road take A466 Chepstow. At next rdbt take 1st exit Caerwent A48. Hotel approx 2m on left*

A popular hotel in a countryside setting, the Marriott St Pierre has elegant public rooms, a championship golf course, and extensive leisure and conference facilities. Bedrooms are situated in the main house, at the Lakeside, and in adjancent cottage

contd.

suites, and all are very well equipped. Meals can be taken in the formal Orangery or less formally in the Long Weekend Café.
ROOMS: 148 en suite (bth/shr) (4 fmly) No smoking in 53 bedrooms s £84-£114; d £94-£124 (incl. bkfst) * LB Off peak **MEALS:** V meals Coffee am Tea pm **FACILITIES:** CTV in all bedrooms STV Indoor swimming pool (heated) Golf 18 Tennis (hard) Sauna Solarium Gym Putting green Jacuzzi/spa Health spa ch fac Xmas **CONF:** Thtr 220 Class 160 Board 90 Del from £120 * **SERVICES:** Night porter 430P **NOTES:** No dogs (ex guide dogs) No smoking in restaurant **CARDS:**

CHEPSTOW Monmouthshire **Map 03 ST59**

★★★ The Old Course

Newport Rd NP16 5PR
Quality Percentage Score: 61%
☎ 01291 626261 01291 626263
Dir: *leave M48 junct 2, follow signs to Chepstow, A466 & A48 into town, hotel is on the left*

Convenient for both the M4 and the M48, this privately owned hotel lies just south of the town centre. The public areas include a spacious lounge bar, a comfortable lounge and an attractively appointed restaurant. There is a choice of conference rooms and a large ballroom.
ROOMS: 31 en suite (bth/shr) (4 fmly) s fr £39.50; d fr £42.50 * LB Off peak **MEALS:** Lunch £9.95-£14.50 Dinner fr £14.50 & alc Welsh & French Cuisine V meals Coffee am Tea pm **FACILITIES:** CTV in all bedrooms Xmas **CONF:** Thtr 240 Class 70 Board 70 Del from £77 * **SERVICES:** Lift Night porter 180P **NOTES:** No smoking in restaurant Last d 9.15pm **CARDS:**

CHEPSTOW Monmouthshire **Map 03 ST59**

★★ Castle View

16 Bridge St NP6 5EZ
Quality Percentage Score: 68%
☎ 01291 620349 01291 627397
Dir: *opposite the castle*

This 300-year-old building looks out onto the impressive Norman castle. The bedrooms, two of which are situated in a building at the end of the attractive garden, offer comfortable accommodation. The restaurant is supplemented by a bar and residents' lounge.
ROOMS: 9 en suite (bth/shr) 4 annexe en suite (bth) (7 fmly) s £40.95-£43.95; d £53.95-£58.95 * LB Off peak **MEALS:** Lunch £9.95-£10.95 Dinner £15.95-£18.95 V meals Coffee am **FACILITIES:** CTV in all bedrooms STV **NOTES:** No coaches No smoking in restaurant Last d 9pm **CARDS:**

See advert on this page

CHEPSTOW Monmouthshire **Map 03 ST59**

★★ Beaufort

Beaufort Square NP6 5EP
Quality Percentage Score: 67%
☎ 01291 622497 01291 627389
Dir: *off A48, at St Mary's church turn left and left again at end of public car park into Nelson St. Hotel car park 100yds on right*

Located in the town centre, this 16th Century coaching inn is a popular hotel. The bedrooms are furnished and equipped in a modern style, with ground floor and family rooms available. Public areas comprise a busy bar and a restaurant offering a wide choice of dishes including steaks and pasta.
ROOMS: 18 en suite (bth/shr) (2 fmly) s £35-£39.50; d £45-£49 * LB Off peak **MEALS:** Lunch £6-£13.95 & alc Dinner £13.95-£20 & alc English & French Cuisine V meals Coffee am **FACILITIES:** CTV in all bedrooms STV **CONF:** Thtr 40 Class 25 Board 20 Del from £59.50 * **SERVICES:** 14P **NOTES:** No smoking area in restaurant Last d 9.30pm **CARDS:**

contd.

C

CHEPSTOW Monmouthshire **Map 03 ST59**

★★ **George**

Moor St NP16 5DB

Quality Percentage Score: 67%

☎ 01291 625363 📠 01291 627418

Dir: *M48, junct 2, follow signs for town centre, hotel adjacent to 16th century town gate*

This former posting house retains a good deal of historic character. Located next to the 16th-century town gate, The George has a cosy, stylish bar and lounge, popular with locals and an informal, bistro-style restaurant. Well-equipped bedrooms are a good size and are smartly decorated in dark wood and traditional fabrics.

ROOMS: 14 en suite (bth/shr) No smoking in 7 bedrooms s £70; d £80 * LB Off peak **MEALS:** Sunday Lunch £2.50-£12 Dinner £2.50-£15 English & Continental Cuisine V meals Coffee am Tea pm **FACILITIES:** CTV in all bedrooms Xmas **CONF:** Thtr 40 Class 20 Board 26 Del £85 * **SERVICES:** 20P **NOTES:** No smoking in restaurant Last d 9.30pm **CARDS:**

See advert under Preliminary Section

CHIRK Wrexham **Map 07 SJ23**

★★★ ***Hand***

Church St LL14 5EY

Quality Percentage Score: 64%

☎ 01691 772479 📠 01691 773472

Dir: *in the centre of Chirk on the B5070*

Standing in the centre of Chirk, this Grade II listed property was once an important coaching house on the London to Holyhead route. Privately-owned, it provides modern accommodation, which includes a family bedroom and a room with a four-poster bed. Public areas include a number of lounges and bars, as well as a choice of eating options, one of which is the smartly appointed Regency restaurant. Other facilities include a beer garden with a play area for children.

ROOMS: 16 en suite (bth/shr) (1 fmly) **MEALS:** V meals Coffee am Tea pm **FACILITIES:** CTV in all bedrooms STV Sauna Solarium Gym Pool table **CONF:** Thtr 250 Class 225 Board 200 **SERVICES:** 50P **CARDS:**

COLWYN BAY Conwy **Map 06 SH87**

★★★ ***Norfolk House***

Princes Dr LL29 8PF

Quality Percentage Score: 67%

☎ 01492 531757 📠 01492 533781

Dir: *from A55 at Colwyn Bay exit into right lane of slip road right at traffic lights pass railway station continue hotel almost opposite filling station*

Norfolk House is a family-run hotel with a warm, friendly atmosphere, within easy walking distance of the seafront, town centre and railway station. The accommodation is well equipped, comfortable and relaxing. Bedrooms are prettily decorated with family suites offered. There are several lounges, a popular bar, and conference facilities available.

ROOMS: 22 en suite (bth/shr) (3 fmly) **MEALS:** English & French Cuisine V meals Coffee am Tea pm **FACILITIES:** CTV in all bedrooms **CONF:** Thtr 35 Class 15 Board 20 **SERVICES:** Lift Night porter 30P **NOTES:** Last d 8.30pm Closed 23 Dec-10 Jan **CARDS:**

See advert on opposite page

COLWYN BAY Conwy **Map 06 SH87**

★★★ **Hopeside**

Princes Dr, West End LL29 8PW

Quality Percentage Score: 66%

☎ 01492 533244 📠 01492 532850

Dir: *turn off A55 at Rhos-on-Sea exit, turn left at lights, hotel 50yds on right*

The promenade and town centre are within easy walking distance of this friendly hotel. The restaurant offers a good choice, and bar food and blackboard specials also feature. Bedrooms are mostly pine-furnished and all are attractively decorated. The hotel also holds a licence for civil marriage ceremonies.

ROOMS: 19 en suite (bth/shr) (1 fmly) No smoking in 4 bedrooms s fr £49; d fr £56 (incl. bkfst) * LB Off peak **MEALS:** Lunch £7.50-£16.50 & alc Dinner fr £16.50 & alc English & French Cuisine V meals Coffee am Tea pm **FACILITIES:** CTV in all bedrooms STV Solarium **CONF:** Thtr 50 Class 35 Board 26 Del from £65 * **SERVICES:** Night porter 25P **NOTES:** Last d 8.30pm **CARDS:**

See advert on opposite page

COLWYN BAY Conwy **Map 06 SH87**

★★ **Marine**

West Promenade LL28 4BP

Quality Percentage Score: 65%

☎ 01492 530295 📠 01492 530295

Dir: *turn off A55 at Old Colwyn to seafront. Turn left, and after pier turn left just before traffic lights, car park on corner*

This cheerful seaside hotel is close to the sea front and not far from town. Bedrooms are decorated attractively with modern facilities and many rooms enjoy good views. Tasty home cooking is available as well as the cosy bar and separate lounge.

ROOMS: 14 rms (12 shr) (4 fmly) No smoking in 4 bedrooms s £22-£26.50; d fr £44 (incl. bkfst) * LB Off peak **MEALS:** Bar Lunch £3-£6 Dinner fr £10 V meals Coffee am Tea pm **FACILITIES:** CTV in all bedrooms **SERVICES:** 11P **NOTES:** No coaches No smoking in restaurant Last d 7pm Closed mid Oct-Mar

CARDS:

COLWYN BAY Conwy **Map 06 SH87**

★★ ***Edelweiss***

Lawson Rd LL29 8HD

Quality Percentage Score: 61%

☎ 01492 532314 📠 01492 534707

Dir: *on the A55 take the Old Colwyn turning and then last exit at rdbt, follow to zebra crossing and turn right into Lawson Rd*

A 19th-century house lying in several acres of mature grounds with the bonus of being a short walk from the town centre and the seafront. Bedrooms, some on the ground floor, are equipped with modern facilities, and include family suites. A bar and a

contd.

games room are provided and a daily fixed-price menu with carte options is offered.
ROOMS: 26 en suite (bth/shr) (6 fmly) No smoking in 5 bedrooms **MEALS:** Welsh, English, French & Italian Cuisine V meals Coffee am Tea pm **FACILITIES:** CTV in all bedrooms STV Solarium Pool table Croquet lawn Children's play area Games room ch fac **CONF:** Thtr 70 Class 50 Board 30 **SERVICES:** Air conditioning 26P **NOTES:** No smoking in restaurant Last d 7.30pm **CARDS:**

COLWYN BAY Conwy **Map 06 SH87**
★★ ***Lyndale***
410 Abergele Rd, Old Colwyn LL29 9AB
Quality Percentage Score: 60%
☎ 01492 515429 Fax 01492 518805
Dir: *exit A55 Old Conwyn, turn left. At rdbt through village continue for 1m on A547*
Located at Old Colwyn this family-run hotel offers a range of comfortable accommodation including family suites and a four-poster room. There is a cosy bar and a comfortable foyer lounge. Weddings and other functions can be accommodated and there are facilities for business meetings.
ROOMS: 14 en suite (bth/shr) (3 fmly) **MEALS:** European Cuisine V meals Coffee am Tea pm **FACILITIES:** CTV in all bedrooms **CONF:** Thtr 40 Class 20 Board 20 Del from £30 * **SERVICES:** 20P **NOTES:** No smoking area in restaurant Last d 9pm **CARDS:**

CONWY Conwy **Map 06 SH77**
★★★ ***Groes Inn***
Tyn-y-Groes LL32 8TN
Quality Percentage Score: 71%
☎ 01492 650545 Fax 01492 650855
Dir: *leave A55 at Conwy turn off, cross Old Conwy Bridge, 1st left through Castle Walls on B5106 Trefriew road, follow road for approx 2m, hotel on right*

The original inn dates back at least to the 16th century and has charming features such as open beamed ceilings, log fires, and period furniture. There is a choice of bars and a restaurant with conservatory extension opening onto the garden. The comfortable, well equipped bedrooms are contained in a separate building, some with balconies or private terraces.
ROOMS: 14 en suite (bth/shr) (1 fmly) No smoking in 6 bedrooms **MEALS:** V meals Coffee am Tea pm **FACILITIES:** CTV in all bedrooms **SERVICES:** 100P **NOTES:** No dogs (ex guide dogs) No smoking area in restaurant Last d 9pm **CARDS:**

C

CONWY Conwy **Map 06 SH77**

★★★ The Castle

High St LL32 8DB

REGAL

Quality Percentage Score: 64%

☎ 01492 592324 Fax 01492 583351

Dir: *within town walls, on A55*

Centrally situated and convenient for the castle and quay this hotel dates back to 1500 and is one of Conway's distinguished historic buildings. Refurbishment of several bedrooms has considerably improved the accommodation, but guests will also enjoy the warm and hospitable atmosphere. Fine paintings by a local artist are featured in the public areas which are also enhanced by the presence of fresh flowers for most of the year.

ROOMS: 29 en suite (bth/shr) (2 fmly) No smoking in 16 bedrooms s £65-£85; d £75-£95 * LB Off peak **MEALS:** Sunday Lunch £7.50-£9.95 Dinner £12.50-£15.95 & alc V meals Coffee am Tea pm **FACILITIES:** CTV in all bedrooms Xmas **CONF:** Thtr 35 Class 20 Board 20 Del from £90 * **SERVICES:** Night porter 30P **NOTES:** No smoking in restaurant Last d 9.30pm **CARDS:**

CONWY Conwy **Map 06 SH77**

The Premier Collection

★★ The Old Rectory Country House

Llanrwst Rd, Llansanffraid Glan Conwy LL28 5LF

☎ 01492 580611 Fax 01492 584555

Dir: *0.5m S from A470/A55 junct on left hand side*

A charming hotel with delightful terraced gardens overlooking the Conwy Estuary and Snowdonia beyond. Inside, the intimate public rooms are complemented by classical interior design and antique pieces. Bedrooms are tastefully furnished in keeping with the building, and many thoughtful extra comforts are provided. Two bedrooms are located in the grounds and can be used as a family suite. The cuisine is excellent with well selected ingredients carefully put together in appealing yet reassuring combinations on the Anglo-French menu.

ROOMS: 4 en suite (bth/shr) 2 annexe en suite (bth/shr) No smoking in 4 bedrooms s £99-£129; d £119-£149 (incl. bkfst) LB Off peak **MEALS:** Dinner £29.90 British & French Cuisine Tea pm **FACILITIES:** CTV in all bedrooms **SERVICES:** 10P **NOTES:** No coaches No children 5yrs No smoking in restaurant Last d 8.15pm Closed Dec-Jan **CARDS:**

CONWY Conwy **Map 06 SH77**

★★ Castle Bank

Mount Pleasant LL32 8NY

Quality Percentage Score: 67%

☎ 01492 593888 Fax 01492 596466

Dir: *turn off A55 expressway at Conwy. Hotel is accessed through public car park on Mount Pleasant, adjacent to the Bangor Archway in town wall*

This friendly hotel near the old town walls is well located for touring the area. Bedrooms are bright, freshly decorated and well equipped. There is a spacious dining room with a bar attached and a comfortably furnished lounge.

ROOMS: 9 en suite (shr) (2 fmly) s fr £30; d fr £55 (incl. bkfst) * LB Off peak **MEALS:** Sunday Lunch £9.95 Dinner fr £14.95 V meals Coffee am Tea pm **FACILITIES:** CTV in all bedrooms Xmas **SERVICES:** 12P **NOTES:** No dogs (ex guide dogs) No coaches No smoking in restaurant Last d 7pm **CARDS:**

CONWY Conwy **Map 06 SH77**

★★ Tir-y-Coed Country House

Rowen LL32 8TP

Quality Percentage Score: 66%

☎ 01492 650219 Fax 01492 650219

Dir: *turn off B5106 into unclassified road signposted Rowen, hotel is on fringe of village about 60mtrs N of Post Office*

Located in the Conwy valley, this small and relaxing hotel resides at the edge of Conwy. Bedrooms are bright and freshly decorated with family rooms available. There is a small cocktail bar and a comfortable lounge. Freshly-cooked meals are served in the dining room.

ROOMS: 7 en suite (bth/shr) 1 annexe en suite (shr) (1 fmly) s £27.50-£31.50; d £51-£58.75 (incl. bkfst) LB Off peak **MEALS:** Bar Lunch £4-£9alc Dinner £13.50 Coffee am Tea pm **FACILITIES:** CTV in all bedrooms ch fac **SERVICES:** 8P **NOTES:** No coaches No smoking in restaurant Last d 7.30pm Closed Xmas & New Year RS Nov-Feb

CARDS:

CRICCIETH Gwynedd **Map 06 SH43**

★★★ **Bron Eifion Country House**

LL52 0SA

Quality Percentage Score: 68%

☎ 01766 522385 01766 522003

Dir: *0.5m outside Criccieth on A497 towards Pwllheli*

Improvements continue at this fine country house that lies in well maintained grounds just west of Criccieth. Bedrooms are nicely decorated and most are equipped with period and antique furniture. Several rooms have four-poster beds or attractive canopies. The central hall features a minstrel's gallery. Several comfortable lounges are provided and the restaurant overlooks the gardens.

ROOMS: 19 en suite (bth/shr) (2 fmly) s £63-£69; d £95-£125 (incl. bkfst) * LB Off peak **MEALS:** Lunch £12.75-£13.95 Dinner £21.50 & alc International Cuisine V meals Coffee am Tea pm **FACILITIES:** CTV in all bedrooms Croquet lawn Putting green Clock golf Xmas **CONF:** Thtr 30 Class 25 Board 25 Del from £75 * **SERVICES:** 80P **NOTES:** No smoking in restaurant Last d 8.30pm **CARDS:**

See advert on this page

CRICCIETH Gwynedd **Map 06 SH43**

★★ **Caerwylan**

LL52 0HW

Quality Percentage Score: 69%

☎ 01766 522547

Run by the friendly Davies family for over 30 years, this is a long established holiday hotel. It lies above the seafront, and many rooms have fine views of the castle and Cardigan Bay. A range of comfortably furnished lounges is available for residents and the five-course menu changes daily. Bedrooms are smart and modern and several have their own private sitting areas. The atmosphere is warm and dependable, and many guests return.

ROOMS: 25 en suite (bth/shr) s £18-£24; d £36-£48 (incl. bkfst) * LB Off peak **MEALS:** Sunday Lunch £9 Dinner £10.50 Coffee am Tea pm **FACILITIES:** CTV in all bedrooms **SERVICES:** Lift 16P **NOTES:** No smoking in restaurant Last d 7.35pm Closed Nov-Etr

CARDS:

CRICCIETH Gwynedd **Map 06 SH43**

★★ **Parciau Mawr**

High St LL52 0RP

Quality Percentage Score: 68%

☎ 01766 522368

Dir: *off the A497 in the village of Criccieth*

The original part of this hotel dates back more than 300 years and is set in several acres of attractive grounds. The restaurant is in a converted barn forming part of the main building. There is a choice of sitting rooms and bedrooms are bright and fresh, including several pine-furnished rooms in nearby outbuildings.

ROOMS: 6 en suite (bth/shr) 6 annexe en suite (shr) (1 fmly) s fr £31; d fr £59 (incl. bkfst) * LB Off peak **MEALS:** Dinner fr £13 English & French Cuisine Coffee am Tea pm **FACILITIES:** CTV in all bedrooms **SERVICES:** 30P **NOTES:** No coaches No children 5yrs No smoking in restaurant Last d 8pm Closed Nov-Mar **CARDS:**

CRICCIETH Gwynedd **Map 06 SH43**

★★ **Gwyndy**

Llanystumdwy LL52 0SP

Quality Percentage Score: 67%

☎ 01766 522720 01766 522720

Dir: *turn off A497 into village of Llanystumdwy follow road for 0.25m, hotel is next to church*

This popular hotel is made up of a 17th-century cottage and a nearby purpose-built bedroom complex. The original cottage contains the lounge, bar and restaurant, these are comfortably furnished. Exposed timbers feature and there are several stone fireplaces. Bedrooms are spacious and comfortably furnished.

ROOMS: 10 annexe en suite (bth/shr) (5 fmly) s £30-£32; d £50-£54 (incl. bkfst) * Off peak **MEALS:** British & French Cuisine Coffee am Tea pm **FACILITIES:** CTV in all bedrooms Fishing **SERVICES:** 20P **NOTES:** No coaches Closed Nov-Mar

CRICCIETH Gwynedd **Map 06 SH43**

★★ **Lion**

Y Maes LL52 0AA

Quality Percentage Score: 66%

☎ 01766 522460 01766 523075

Dir: *turn off A497 in the centre of Criccieth on to village green north, hotel located on green*

Long established, this hotel lies in the centre of a pretty seaside town, just a short walk from the castle and seafront; there are fine views from many rooms. The bars enjoy a good local following and staff are friendly and welcoming. Bedrooms are well decorated and furnished and a new block has recently been built from converted outbuildings. Regular live entertainment is held during the holiday season.

ROOMS: 34 en suite (bth/shr) 12 annexe en suite (bth/shr) (6 fmly) s fr £29; d fr £52 (incl. bkfst) * LB Off peak **MEALS:** Lunch £5.95-£7.95 Dinner £16.50-£19 Welsh & French Cuisine V meals Coffee am Tea pm **FACILITIES:** CTV in all bedrooms Pool table Wkly live entertainment ch fac Xmas **SERVICES:** Lift 30P **NOTES:** No smoking in restaurant Last d 8.30pm RS Nov-Mar **CARDS:**

New AA Guides for the Millennium are featured on page 24

C

CRICKHOWELL Powys — Map 03 SO21
★★★ Bear
NP8 1BW
Quality Percentage Score: 72%
☎ 01873 810408 📠 01873 811696
Dir: *on A40 between Abergaveny and Breen*

Offering impressive accommodation and cuisine, the character and friendliness of this 15th-century coaching inn are renowned. The bar and restaurant areas, divided into individual rooms, are furnished in keeping with the building. Denver Doddwell uses quality, local produce and provides both bar and restaurant food of real merit.
ROOMS: 13 en suite (bth/shr) 13 annexe en suite (bth) (6 fmly) s £47-£89; d £61-£115 (incl. bkfst) * Off peak **MEALS:** Lunch £12-£30alc Dinner £20-£30alc English & French Cuisine V meals Coffee am **FACILITIES:** CTV in all bedrooms **CONF:** Thtr 60 Class 30 Board 20 **SERVICES:** 38P **NOTES:** No smoking area in restaurant Last d 9.30pm
CARDS:

See advert on opposite page

CRICKHOWELL Powys — Map 03 SO21
★★★ *Manor*
Brecon Rd NP8 1SE
Quality Percentage Score: 70%
☎ 01873 810212 📠 01873 811938
Dir: *on A40, Crickhowell/Brecon, 0.5m from Crickhowell*
In a stunning location, perched on a hillside of the Usk Valley way above the town, this impressive manor house was the birthplace of Sir George Everest. The recently refurbished bedrooms and public areas retain an elegant yet relaxed atmosphere, and there are extensive leisure facilities. The restaurant has panoramic views and is the setting for some bold modern cooking. Guests also have the option of eating in the informal atmosphere of the nearby Nantyffin Cider Mill, the hotel's sister operation.
ROOMS: 17 en suite (bth/shr) (1 fmly) No smoking in 8 bedrooms **MEALS:** International Cuisine V meals Coffee am Tea pm **FACILITIES:** CTV in all bedrooms Indoor swimming pool (heated) Sauna Solarium Gym Jacuzzi/spa Fitness assessment, Sunbed **CONF:** Thtr 400 Class 300 Board 300 **SERVICES:** Night porter 200P **NOTES:** Last d 9.30pm **CARDS:**

See advert on opposite page

CRICKHOWELL Powys — Map 03 SO21
★★ Ty Croeso
THE CIRCLE
Selected Individual Hotels
GREAT BRITAIN
The Dardy, Llangattock NP8 1PU
Quality Percentage Score: 73%
☎ 01873 810573 📠 01873 810573
Dir: *at Shell garage on A40 take opposite road, down hill over river bridge. Turn right, after 0.5m turn left, up hill over canal, hotel signed*
Ty Croeso lives up to its name, meaning 'House of Welcome'. In the restaurant an interesting carte and a Taste of Wales fixed price menu are available. Glamorgan Sausages and laverbread are available at breakfast. Public areas are comfortable, with log fires. Bedrooms (one with a four-poster) are decorated with pretty fabrics and all have good facilities.
ROOMS: 8 en suite (bth/shr) (1 fmly) s £35-£50; d £55-£70 (incl. bkfst) * LB Off peak **MEALS:** Sunday Lunch £9.95-£15.95 & alc Dinner £15.95 & alc International Cuisine V meals Coffee am Tea pm **FACILITIES:** CTV in all bedrooms **SERVICES:** 20P **NOTES:** No coaches No smoking in restaurant Last d 9pm Closed 24-26 Dec
CARDS:

CRICKHOWELL Powys — Map 03 SO21
★★ Gliffaes Country House Hotel
NP8 1RH
Quality Percentage Score: 72%
☎ 01874 730371 & 0800 146719 (Freephone) 📠 01874 730463
Dir: *1m from A40 - 2.5m W of Crickhowell*
An 18th-century country house, the River Usk flows through the grounds. Bedrooms are furnished in sympathy with the building and provide good levels of equipment and comfort. The spacious restaurant serves quality meals. Lounges and a bar provide areas for relaxation.
ROOMS: 19 en suite (bth/shr) 3 annexe en suite (bth/shr) (3 fmly) s £52-£118.50; d £63-£129.50 (incl. bkfst) LB Off peak **MEALS:** Sunday Lunch fr £18.50 High tea fr £3.50 Dinner fr £24 European Cuisine V meals Coffee am Tea pm **FACILITIES:** CTV in all bedrooms Tennis (hard) Fishing Snooker Croquet lawn Putting green Golf practice net Cycling Birdwatching Walking ch fac **CONF:** Thtr 40 Class 16 Board 16 Del from £99 * **SERVICES:** 34P **NOTES:** No dogs (ex guide dogs) No smoking in restaurant Last d 9.15pm
CARDS:

CROSS HANDS Carmarthenshire — Map 02 SN51
Travelodge
Travelodge
SA14 6NW
☎ 01269 845700 📠 01269 845700
Dir: *on A48, westbound*
This modern building offers accommodation in smart, spacious and well equipped bedrooms, all with en-suite bathrooms. Refreshments may be taken at the nearby family restaurant. For details about current prices, consult the Contents Page under Hotel Groups for the Travelodge phone number.
ROOMS: 32 en suite (bth/shr) d £45.95 *

CRUGYBAR Carmarthenshire — Map 03 SN63
★★ Glanrannell Park
SA19 8SA
Quality Percentage Score: 72%
☎ 01558 685230 📠 01558 685784
Dir: *from A40 take A482 to Lampeter after 5.5m follow signs to hotel. From Llandeilo take B4302 for 10.5m , hotel is signposted*
This fine country house is surrounded by 23 acres of mature grounds, fronted by a lake where birds of prey are regular visitors. The hotel has a number of loyal guests who return year after year. Bedrooms are immaculately maintained and there is a bar and several comfortable sitting rooms. Good home cooking is offered from a fixed-price menu.
ROOMS: 8 en suite (bth) (2 fmly) s £41-£46; d £72-£80 (incl. bkfst) * LB Off peak **MEALS:** Bar Lunch £3-£7.50 Dinner £17-£19 International Cuisine Coffee am Tea pm **FACILITIES:** CTV in all bedrooms Fishing **SERVICES:** 33P **NOTES:** No coaches No smoking in restaurant Last d 8.30pm Closed Nov-Mar **CARDS:**

See advert on opposite page

C

C

CWMBRAN Torfaen — Map 03 ST29

★★★★ Parkway

Cwmbran Dr NP44 3UW

Quality Percentage Score: 62%

☎ 01633 871199 Fax 01633 869160

Dir: *from M4 head for Cwnbran until you see signs for Cwnbran-Llantarnam Park on the A4051. Turn right at rdabt then right for Hotel*

The Parkway is a purpose-built hotel complex that includes a spacious lounge/bar which doubles as a coffee shop during the day. Both carvery and carte menus are available for guests in Ravellos, and extensive leisure facilities are provided, which hotel residents use alongside the members. Several thoughtful extras are provided in the bedrooms.

ROOMS: 70 en suite (bth/shr) (4 fmly) No smoking in 24 bedrooms s £76.15-£94; d £88.20-£106 * LB Off peak **MEALS:** Lunch £7.90-£14.95 Dinner £8.50-£15.90 & alc V meals Coffee am Tea pm **FACILITIES:** CTV in all bedrooms STV Indoor swimming pool (heated) Sauna Solarium Gym Jacuzzi/spa Steam room Wkly live entertainment Xmas **CONF:** Thtr 500 Class 240 Board 144 Del from £98.70 * **SERVICES:** Night porter 300P **NOTES:** Last d 10pm Closed 24-31 Dec

CARDS:

See advert under NEWPORT

DEVIL'S BRIDGE Ceredigion — Map 06 SN77

★★ *Hafod Arms*

SY23 3JL

Quality Percentage Score: 67%

☎ 01970 890232

Built as a hunting lodge in the 18th century, this hotel provides a range of elegantly furnished public rooms and well equipped bedrooms. One room has a four-poster bed and family rooms are also available. The attractive restaurant serves from a daily fixed-price menu, and a separate Victorian-style tea room offers a full range of lighter meals.

ROOMS: 15 rms (11 bth/shr) (1 fmly) **MEALS:** International Cuisine V meals Coffee am Tea pm **FACILITIES:** CTV in all bedrooms **SERVICES:** 60P **NOTES:** No children 12yrs Last d 9pm Closed 2-31 Jan **CARDS:**

DOLGELLAU Gwynedd — Map 06 SH71

★★★ Penmaenuchaf Hall

Penmaenpool LL40 1YB

Quality Percentage Score: 72%

☎ 01341 422129 Fax 01341 422787

Dir: *off A470 onto A493 to Tywyn. Hotel entrance is approx. 1m on the left*

Built in 1860, this impressive hall stands in 20 acres of woodland and enjoys magnificent views. Careful restoration has created a comfortable and welcoming hotel which provides elegant public areas and attractive bedrooms. The wood-panelled restaurant serves fresh produce cooked in modern English style.

ROOMS: 14 en suite (bth/shr) (3 fmly) No smoking in 5 bedrooms s £70-£110; d £100-£160 (incl. bkfst) * LB Off peak **MEALS:** Lunch £14.25-£15.75 & alc High tea £7-£10alc Dinner fr £26.50 & alc V meals Coffee am Tea pm **FACILITIES:** CTV in all bedrooms Fishing Snooker Croquet lawn Xmas **CONF:** Thtr 50 Class 30 Board 22 Del from £100 * **SERVICES:** 30P **NOTES:** No coaches No children 6yrs No smoking in restaurant Last d 9.30pm **CARDS:**

DOLGELLAU Gwynedd — Map 06 SH71

★★★ Plas Dolmelynllyn

Ganllwyd LL40 2HP

Quality Percentage Score: 71%

☎ 01341 440273 Fax 01341 440640

Dir: *5m N of Dolgellau on A470*

Surrounded by three acres of terraced gardens with National Trust land beyond, this fine house dates back to the 16th century. Spacious bedrooms are attractively furnished and offer comfortable seating as well as many thoughtful extras. Dinner is served in the comfortable dining room, adjacent to the conservatory bar.

ROOMS: 10 en suite (bth/shr) No smoking in all bedrooms s £52.50-£60; d £95-£115 (incl. bkfst) * LB Off peak **MEALS:** Bar Lunch £3-£6alc V meals Coffee am Tea pm **FACILITIES:** CTV in all bedrooms STV Fishing Mountain walking Mountain Bike riding **CONF:** Thtr 20 Class 20 Board 20 **SERVICES:** 20P **NOTES:** No coaches No smoking in restaurant Closed Nov-Feb **CARDS:**

DOLGELLAU Gwynedd — Map 06 SH71

★★ Dolserau Hall

LL40 2AG

Quality Percentage Score: 72%

☎ 01341 422522 Fax 01341 422400

Dir: *1.5m outside town between A494 to Bala and A470 to Dinas Mawddwy*

The hospitality shown by owners and staff at this fine Victorian country house is one of the great strengths of the hotel and visitors return year after year. It lies in attractive grounds extending to the River Wnion and is surrounded by green fields. Several comfortable lounges are provided and wood burners and log fires cheer the air when needed. Huw Roberts leads the kitchen team and his efforts have earned our prestigious one-Rosette award. Bedrooms are smart and well equipped and all have comfortable armchairs or settees.

ROOMS: 15 en suite (bth/shr) (3 fmly) s £54-£69; d £85-£120 (incl. bkfst & dinner) * LB Off peak **MEALS:** Dinner £21.50 V meals **FACILITIES:** CTV in all bedrooms STV Xmas **SERVICES:** Lift 70P **NOTES:** No coaches No children 6yrs No smoking in restaurant Last d 8.30pm Closed mid Nov-early Feb (ex Xmas & New Year) **CARDS:**

DOLGELLAU Gwynedd — Map 06 SH71

★★ George III Hotel

Penmaenpool LL40 1YD

Quality Percentage Score: 70%

☎ 01341 422525 Fax 01341 423565

Dir: *turn left off A470 towards Tywyn, approx. 2miles, turn right for toll bridge then 1st left for hotel*

Idyllically located on the banks of the Mawddach Estuary, this delightful small hotel started life as an inn and a chandlers to the local boat yard. A nearby building, that now houses several bedrooms, was the local railway station. There is a choice of bars

contd.

providing a wide range of food with more formal dining available in the restaurant.
ROOMS: 6 en suite (bth/shr) 5 annexe en suite (bth/shr) s £40-£55; d £70-£94 (incl. bkfst) * LB Off peak **MEALS:** Sunday Lunch £12.95 & alc Dinner £17.70-£25.80alc Welsh, English & French Cuisine V meals Coffee am Tea pm **FACILITIES:** CTV in all bedrooms Fishing Free fishing permits Mountain bike hire **SERVICES:** 60P **NOTES:** No smoking in restaurant Last d 9pm **CARDS:**

DOLGELLAU Gwynedd — Map 06 SH71
★★ Fronoleu Farm
Tabor LL40 2PS
Quality Percentage Score: 67%
☎ 01341 422361 & 422197 Fax 01341 422361
Dir: *at junct of the A487 from Machynlleth with the A470. Take road signed Tabor opposite Cross Foxes and continue for 1.25m*
This 16th-century farmhouse lies under the shadow of Cader Idris. Carefully extended over recent years, it retains many original features. The bar and lounge are both located in the old building where there are exposed timbers and open fires. Most of the bedrooms are in a modern extension and these are spacious and well equipped. The wide range of food on offer attracts a large local following to the restaurant. There is also a recently opened cellar bar.
ROOMS: 11 rms (7 bth/shr) (3 fmly) No smoking in 6 bedrooms s £24.95-£35.95; d £43.50-£53.90 (incl. bkfst) * LB Off peak
MEALS: Lunch £5.95-£8.95alc Dinner £7.95-£16alc V meals Coffee am Tea pm **FACILITIES:** CTV in all bedrooms Fishing Pool table **CONF:** Thtr 150 Class 80 Board 80 **SERVICES:** 60P **NOTES:** Last d 10pm
CARDS:

DOLGELLAU Gwynedd — Map 06 SH71
★ Royal Ship
Queens Square LL40 1AR
Quality Percentage Score: 67%
☎ 01341 422209 Fax 01341 421027
The Royal Ship dates from 1813 when it was a coaching inn. There are three bars and several lounges, all most comfortably furnished and appointed. It is very much the centre of local activities and a wide range of food is available. Bedrooms are tastefully decorated and fitted with modern amenities.
ROOMS: 24 rms (18 bth/shr) (4 fmly) s £35; d £60 (incl. bkfst) * LB Off peak **MEALS:** Lunch £3.95-£9.95 & alc High tea fr £2.50 Dinner £6.95-£15.95 & alc English, French & Italian Cuisine V meals Coffee am Tea pm **FACILITIES:** CTV in 18 bedrooms STV Pool table Xmas
CONF: Thtr 80 Class 60 Board 60 **SERVICES:** 12P **NOTES:** No dogs (ex guide dogs) No smoking in restaurant Last d 9pm
CARDS:

See advert on this page

DOLWYDDELAN Conwy — Map 06 SH75
★★ Elen's Castle
LL25 0EJ
Quality Percentage Score: 64%
☎ 01690 750207 Fax 01690 750207
Dir: *on A470, 5m S of Betws-y-Coed*
This hotel operated as a tavern in the 18th century; the original bar, complete with a slab floor and pot-belly stove, remains and two cosy sitting rooms have open fires and exposed timbers. Two rooms have four-poster beds and families can be accommodated. A good range of bar and restaurant food is provided.
ROOMS: 9 rms (8 bth/shr) (2 fmly) No smoking in 2 bedrooms s £30-£40; d £34-£74 (incl. bkfst) * LB Off peak **MEALS:** Lunch fr £8.95alc Dinner £8.95-£25alc Welsh & Continental Cuisine V meals Coffee am Tea pm **FACILITIES:** CTV in all bedrooms STV Fishing Xmas **CONF:** Class 20 **SERVICES:** 40P **NOTES:** No dogs No smoking in restaurant Last d 9pm **CARDS:**

EGLWYSFACH Ceredigion — Map 06 SN69

The Premier Collection

★★★ Ynyshir Hall
SY20 8TA
☎ 01654 781209 Fax 01654 781366
Dir: *off A487, 5.5m S of Machynlleth, signposted from the main road*
A country house hotel set in 12 acres of scenic gardens. Individually designed bedrooms, varying in size, are delightfully furnished and equipped with a range of thoughtful extras. Both bar and drawing room are adorned with landlord Rob Reen's paintings of the local area while
contd.

the newly refurbished dining room continues to serve highly commendable cuisine.
ROOMS: 8 en suite (bth/shr) 2 annexe en suite (bth/shr) No smoking in all bedrooms s £110-£135; d £120-£195 (incl. bkfst) * LB Off peak **MEALS:** Lunch £21 Dinner £35 Welsh, English & French Cuisine V meals Coffee am Tea pm **FACILITIES:** CTV in all bedrooms Croquet lawn Xmas **CONF:** Thtr 25 Class 20 Board 18 Del from £150 * **SERVICES:** 20P **NOTES:** No coachesNo children 9yrs No smoking in restaurant Last d 8.45pm Closed 5-23Jan
CARDS:

E

EWLOE Flintshire — Map 07 SJ36
★★★★ St David's Park
St Davids Park CH5 3YB
Quality Percentage Score: 70%
01244 520800 01244 520930
Dir: *take A494 Queensferry to Mold for 4m,then take left slip road B5127 towards Buckley*
This is a fine modern hotel providing a full range of conference and function facilities. There is also a modern leisure club; a fully supervised children's play area has now been created. Further bedrooms have recently been added and these, like the existing rooms, are well equipped and comfortable. Suites are provided, many are suitable for families and disabled guests and others have four-poster beds. The restaurant offers a full range of eating options and the large team of staff are friendly and welcoming. Reduced green fees are offered for residents, on the nearby Northop Country Park championship course.
ROOMS: 145 en suite (bth/shr) (26 fmly) No smoking in 54 bedrooms d £109-£154 * LB Off peak **MEALS:** Lunch £13.95-£19.95 Dinner £19.50-£35 V meals Coffee am Tea pm **FACILITIES:** CTV in all bedrooms STV Indoor swimming pool (heated) Golf 18 Tennis (hard) Snooker Sauna Solarium Gym Pool table Jacuzzi/spa Steam bath, Beauty Therapist, Pool Room Wkly live entertainment ch fac Xmas **CONF:** Thtr 270 Class 150 Board 40 **SERVICES:** Lift Night porter 240P **NOTES:** No smoking in restaurant Last d 10pm
CARDS:

See advert under CHESTER

FISHGUARD Pembrokeshire — Map 02 SM93
★★ Tregynon Country Farmhouse Hotel
Gwaun Valley SA65 9TU
Quality Percentage Score: 71%
01239 820531 01239 820808
Dir: *at cross roads of B4313/B4329 take B4313 towards Fishguard, then first right and first right again proceed for 1.5m hotel drive on left*
This carefully converted 16th-century farmhouse, set in the picturesque Gwaun Valley, has a beamed sitting room dominated by an inglenook fireplace. There is also a cosy bar and a restaurant which serves very enjoyable dishes. The hotel has its own smoke house for gammon and bacon.
ROOMS: 1 en suite (bth/shr) 5 annexe en suite (bth/shr) (2 fmly) No smoking in all bedrooms d £65-£77 (incl. bkfst) * LB Off peak **MEALS:** Dinner fr £20.95 V meals Coffee am Tea pm **FACILITIES:** CTV in all bedrooms Xmas **SERVICES:** P **NOTES:** No dogs No coaches No children 6yrs No smoking in restaurant Last d 8.30pm Closed 2 wks in winter **CARDS:**

FISHGUARD Pembrokeshire — Map 02 SM93
★★ Cartref
15-19 High St SA65 9AW
Quality Percentage Score: 66%
01348 872430 01348 873664
Dir: *on A40 in town centre*
Conveniently placed for the nearby Irish Ferry port, this is a small and friendly hotel. It provides bright modern bedrooms and smart public areas. Some bedrooms are suitable for families, televisions and other modern facilities are provided. A large carte menu is on offer.
ROOMS: 10 en suite (bth/shr) (2 fmly) s fr £38; d fr £54 (incl. bkfst) * LB Off peak **MEALS:** Lunch £6-£7.95 Dinner fr £14 Welsh & Continental Cuisine V meals Coffee am Tea pm **FACILITIES:** CTV in all bedrooms **SERVICES:** Night porter 4P **NOTES:** No coaches No smoking in restaurant Last d 8.45pm **CARDS:**

See advert on opposite page

FISHGUARD Pembrokeshire — Map 02 SM93
★★ Abergwaun
The Market Square SA65 9HA
Quality Percentage Score: 63%
01348 872077 01348 875412
Dir: *on A40 in the centre of town*
Originally an 18th-century coaching inn, the Abergwaun stands on the main square of the town. It has been considerably modernised over recent years and now provides smart pine-furnished bedrooms. A comfortable bar serves a good range of bar food and the restaurant offers a selection of more substantial meals.
ROOMS: 11 rms (7 bth/shr) (2 fmly) s fr £39.50; d fr £54 (incl. bkfst) * LB Off peak **MEALS:** Lunch £8.95 Dinner £14.50 English, French & Italian Cuisine V meals Coffee am Tea pm **FACILITIES:** CTV in all bedrooms Pool table **CONF:** Thtr 50 Class 20 Board 24 Del from £50 * **SERVICES:** 3P **NOTES:** No smoking area in restaurant Last d 9pm
CARDS:

GLYN CEIRIOG Wrexham — Map 07 SJ23
★★★ Golden Pheasant
LL20 7BB
Quality Percentage Score: 64%
01691 718281 01691 718479
Dir: *take B4500 at Chirk, continue along this road for 5m, follow hotel signs*
This privately-owned 18th-century hostelry is on the edge of the village surrounded by hills and countryside. There is a choice of bars, as well as a lounge and a restaurant. To the rear is a courtyard with shrub and flower beds. One of its main features is an aviary containing exotic birds. Bedrooms include four-posters and family rooms.
ROOMS: 29 rms (19 bth/shr) (5 fmly) s £35-£45; d £59-£79 (incl. bkfst) * LB Off peak **MEALS:** Lunch £9.95-£12.95 Dinner £17.95-£19.95 English & French Cuisine V meals Coffee am Tea pm **FACILITIES:** CTV in all bedrooms Pool table Xmas **CONF:** Thtr 60 Board 10 **SERVICES:** 45P **NOTES:** No smoking area in restaurant Last d 8.45pm
CARDS:

GWBERT-ON-SEA Ceredigion — Map 02 SN15
★★★ *Cliff*
SA43 1PP
Quality Percentage Score: 66%
01239 613241 01239 615391
Occupying a headland location with views over Cardigan Bay, this privately owned hotel benefits from 30 acres of grounds including a nine-hole golf course. The spacious public areas make the most of the superb views. The restaurant has a huge picture window looking onto the sea. The accommodation is pleasant and there is a wide choice of bedroom sizes.
ROOMS: 70 en suite (bth/shr) (4 fmly) No smoking in 10 bedrooms **MEALS:** Welsh, English & French Cuisine V meals Coffee am Tea pm **FACILITIES:** CTV in all bedrooms Outdoor swimming pool (heated) Golf 9 Fishing Squash Snooker Sauna Solarium Gym Pool table Putting green Sea fishing **CONF:** Thtr 200 Class 100 Board 64 **SERVICES:** Lift Night porter 100P **NOTES:** No smoking area in restaurant Last d 8.45pm Closed 25-26 Dec **CARDS:**

See advert under CARDIGAN

HALKYN Flintshire — Map 07 SJ27

Travelodge

CH8 8RF
☎ 01352 780952 Fax 01352 780952
Dir: *on A55, westbound*

This modern building offers accommodation in smart, spacious and well equipped bedrooms, all with en-suite bathrooms. Refreshments may be taken at the nearby family restaurant. For details about current prices, consult the Contents Page under Hotel Groups for the Travelodge phone number.

ROOMS: 31 en suite (bth/shr) d £45.95 *

HARLECH See **Talsarnau**

HAVERFORDWEST Pembrokeshire — Map 02 SM91

★★ Hotel Mariners

Mariners Square SA61 2DU
Quality Percentage Score: 66%
☎ 01437 763353 Fax 01437 764258
Dir: *follow signs to town centre, over bridge, up High St, take 1st turning on the right Dark St hotel at the end*

Located just off the town centre, this friendly hotel dates back to 1625. The bedrooms are equipped with modern facilities and are well maintained. The popular bar is a focus for the town and offers a good range of food in addition to that available in the more formal restaurant. Conferences, meetings and functions are all catered for.

ROOMS: 28 en suite (bth/shr) (5 fmly) No smoking in 3 bedrooms s fr £51.50; d fr £71.50 (incl. bkfst) * LB Off peak **MEALS:** Bar Lunch £2.50-£15 Dinner £16-£23.50 English & French Cuisine V meals Coffee am Tea pm **FACILITIES:** CTV in all bedrooms Short mat bowls **CONF:** Thtr 50 Class 28 Board 28 **SERVICES:** Night porter 50P **NOTES:** Last d 9.30pm Closed 26-27 Dec & 1 Jan
CARDS:

HAVERFORDWEST Pembrokeshire — Map 02 SM91

★★ Wilton House

6 Quay St SA61 1BG
Quality Percentage Score: 66%
☎ 01437 760033 Fax 01437 760297

This friendly family-run hotel lies in a side-street off the bustling town centre, with the River Cleddau flowing behind it. Ground floor areas include several shops as well as a lounge bar cum bistro style restaurant where good value-for-money home made dishes are available. Spacious bedrooms are attractively decorated with pretty papers and good furnishings. Family rooms are available and one is located at ground-floor level. There is an out-door swimming pool for the warmer weather. On arrival, temporarily park outside and Mr and Mrs Bowie will guide you to the small carpark at the rear.

ROOMS: 10 en suite (bth/shr) (3 fmly) s £37.50; d £55 (incl. bkfst) * Off peak **MEALS:** Lunch £1.50-£4.95alc Dinner £7.50-£20alc V meals Coffee am **FACILITIES:** CTV in all bedrooms Outdoor swimming pool (heated) **SERVICES:** Night porter 6P **NOTES:** No dogs (ex guide dogs) No coaches No smoking in restaurant Last d 9pm
CARDS:

HAVERFORDWEST Pembrokeshire — Map 02 SM91

★★ Castle

Castle Square SA61 2AA
Quality Percentage Score: 59%
☎ 01437 769322 Fax 01437 769493
Dir: *from the main rdbt into Haverfordwest take the town centre turn off, follow the road for approx 200yds, hotel on right hand side*

This 19th-century inn lies in the town centre, overlooking the castle square. The spacious bar is popular with locals for its lively ambience and evening entertainment. The bedrooms are modern and comfortably furnished, and include one with a four-poster bed. Parking is on nearby streets, it is best to enquire about details on booking.

ROOMS: 9 en suite (bth/shr) (1 fmly) s £37.50-£40; d £50-£60 (incl. bkfst) * LB Off peak **MEALS:** Lunch £3.50-£9.95 Dinner £4.95-£11.75 V meals Coffee am **FACILITIES:** CTV in all bedrooms Wkly live entertainment **SERVICES:** Night porter **NOTES:** No dogs (ex guide dogs) No coaches No smoking area in restaurant Last d 9pm
CARDS:

HAY-ON-WYE Powys — Map 03 SO24

★★★ The Swan-at-Hay

Church St HR3 5DQ
Quality Percentage Score: 66%
☎ 01497 821188 Fax 01497 821424
Dir: *enter Hay-on-Wye on B4350 from Brecon, hotel on left. From any other route follow signs for Brecon & just before leaving town hotel on right*

Built as a coaching inn in 1821, it is close to the town centre. Well equipped accommodation includes rooms in former cottages across the courtyard car park. Facilities include a large function room, a room for smaller meetings, a choice of bars, a comfortable lounge and a bright and pleasant restaurant.

ROOMS: 16 en suite (bth/shr) 3 annexe en suite (bth/shr) (1 fmly) s £45-£50; d £65-£100 (incl. bkfst) * LB Off peak **MEALS:** Lunch £8.95-£10.95 Dinner £18.50-£22.50 European Cuisine V meals Coffee am Tea pm **FACILITIES:** CTV in all bedrooms Fishing Pool table Xmas **CONF:** Thtr 140 Class 60 Board 50 Del from £75 * **SERVICES:** 18P **NOTES:** No smoking in restaurant Last d 9.30pm
CARDS:

HAY-ON-WYE Powys **Map 03 SO24**

★★ Old Black Lion

26 Lion St HR3 5AD

Quality Percentage Score: 71%

☎ 01497 820841

With a history stretching back over several centuries, this fine old coaching inn was occupied by Oliver Cromwell during the siege of Hay Castle. Low ceilings and exposed beams abound, and bedrooms are cosy and well equipped, some being located in an adjacent building . A wide range of food is provided, with the restaurant attaining two AA Rosettes. Informal, friendly service is provided by John and Joan Collins and their willing team of loyal staff.

ROOMS: 6 rms (5 shr) 4 annexe en suite (bth/shr) (2 fmly) s £27-£30; d £55-£60 (incl. bkfst) * LB Off peak **MEALS:** Lunch £10 & alc Dinner £15-£22alc International Cuisine V meals Coffee am Tea pm **FACILITIES:** CTV in all bedrooms Fishing Xmas **SERVICES:** 20P **NOTES:** No coaches No children 5yrs No smoking in restaurant Last d 9.30pm **CARDS:**

H

HAY-ON-WYE Powys **Map 03 SO24**

★★ Kilverts

The Bull Ring HR3 5AG

Quality Percentage Score: 67%

☎ 01497 821042 & 820564 📠 01497 821580

Dir: *from Brecan on B4350, on entering Hay-on-Wye take 1st Right after Cinema Bookshop. Then take 1st Left and hotel is on your right after40yrds*

This privately owned and personally run town centre hotel is popular with both business and leisure visitors. The converted Victorian house provides well equipped bedrooms and has bustling public areas with both character and charm. Facilities include a spacious and attractive beer garden. Owner Colin Thomson is also the chef and his enjoyable and imaginative cooking uses good quality fresh produce which can be sampled in "Colin's Restaurant" or in the bar.

ROOMS: 11 en suite (bth/shr) (1 fmly) s £30-£44; d £60-£72 (incl. bkfst) * LB Off peak **MEALS:** Bar Lunch £10.50-£25alc Dinner £15.95-£25 & alc European Cuisine V meals Coffee am Tea pm **FACILITIES:** CTV in all bedrooms Croquet lawn **SERVICES:** 15P **NOTES:** No coaches Last d 9.30pm Closed 25 Dec **CARDS:**

HIRWAUN Rhondda Cynon Taff **Map 03 SN90**

Late entry ○ ***Ty Newydd Country Hotel***

Penderyn Rd CF44 9SX

☎ 01685 813433 📠 01685 813139

Dir: *off A4059, close to A465*

This country mansion set in 23 acres of woodland has been carefully restored and extended. The older bedrooms are antique furnished and most rooms are spacious, well equipped and comfortable. There is a small panelled bar and an attractive restaurant.

ROOMS: 27 en suite (bth/shr) (2 fmly) **MEALS:** International Cuisine V meals Coffee am Tea pm **FACILITIES:** CTV in all bedrooms STV Fishing ch fac **SERVICES:** Night porter 100P **NOTES:** Last d 9.30pm **CARDS:**

HOLYHEAD See Anglesey, Isle of

HOLYWELL Flintshire **Map 07 SJ17**

★★ *Stamford Gate*

Halkyn Rd CH8 7SJ

Quality Percentage Score: 64%

☎ 01352 712942 📠 01352 713309

Dir: *take Holywell turn off A55 on to A5026, hotel 1m on right*

This busy hotel provides well equipped bedrooms and spacious public areas. The bar and restaurant are both popular locally and there is a wide range of food options. Extensive function and conference facilities are provided and staff are friendly and welcoming. Breakfast room service is available and satellite television is also provided.

ROOMS: 12 en suite (bth/shr) **MEALS:** English & Italian Cuisine V meals Coffee am **FACILITIES:** CTV in all bedrooms STV Wkly live entertainment **CONF:** Thtr 60 Class 30 Board 30 **SERVICES:** 100P **NOTES:** No dogs (ex guide dogs) Last d 10pm **CARDS:**

ISLE OF

Placenames incorporating the words 'Isle' or 'Isle of' will be found under the actual name, eg Isle of Anglesey is under Anglesey, Isle of.

KNIGHTON Powys **Map 07 SO27**

★★★ The Knighton Hotel

MINOTEL Great Britain

Broad St LD7 1BL

Quality Percentage Score: 62%

☎ 01547 520530 📠 01547 520529

The impressive free-standing staircase at the centre of this market town hotel is reputedly the largest in Europe. The hotel is an amalgamation of a 16th-century coaching inn and a 19th-century manor house. The hotel changed hands in mid-1998 and the new owner has instituted an energetic programme of improvements. The public areas include a bar, lounge, steak bar and a spacious restaurant.

ROOMS: 15 en suite (bth/shr) s £45-£65; d £65-£90 (incl. bkfst) * LB Off peak **MEALS:** Lunch £13.50 Dinner £13.50 & alc European Cuisine V meals Coffee am Tea pm **FACILITIES:** CTV in all bedrooms Pool table **CONF:** Thtr 150 Class 75 Board 90 Del from £65 * **SERVICES:** Lift 15P **NOTES:** No dogs (ex guide dogs) No children 12yrs No smoking in restaurant Last d 9.15pm **CARDS:**

KNIGHTON Powys **Map 07 SO27**

★★ Milebrook House

Milebrook LD7 1LT

Quality Percentage Score: 77%

☎ 01547 528632 📠 01547 520509

Dir: *2m E, on A4113*

Set in the Teme Valley a mile or so to the east of the town, this charming house dates back to 1760. The Marsden family have established a very special small hotel here with impressive levels of customer care and a welcome emphasis on good food. The elegant bar (where a log fire burns) and restaurant are supplemented by a relaxing residents' lounge. The bedrooms are well-appointed and individually decorated. There is a ground floor bedroom particularly suitable for disabled guests.

ROOMS: 10 en suite (bth/shr) (2 fmly) No smoking in 5 bedrooms s £50.75; d £75 (incl. bkfst) * LB Off peak **MEALS:** Lunch fr £11.95alc Dinner £19.25-£23.25alc English & French Cuisine V meals Coffee am **FACILITIES:** CTV in all bedrooms Fishing Croquet lawn Badminton Xmas **CONF:** Class 30 **SERVICES:** 20P **NOTES:** No dogs No children 8yrs No smoking in restaurant Last d 8.30pm RS Mon **CARDS:**

LAMPETER Ceredigion **Map 02 SN54**

see also **Crugybar**

★★★ Falcondale Mansion

SA48 7RX

Best Western

Quality Percentage Score: 70%

☎ 01570 422910 📠 01570 423559

Dir: *800yds W of Lampeter High Street A475 or 1.5m NW of Lampeter A482*

This impressive mansion lies in 14 acres of attractive grounds. It provides a range of well equipped bedrooms which are generally very spacious. Good function facilities are provided and a licence

contd.

is now held to perform civil marriage ceremonies. Bars and lounge areas are particularly comfortably furnished.

ROOMS: 19 en suite (bth/shr) (8 fmly) s £55-£58; d £75-£85 (incl. bkfst) LB Off peak **MEALS:** Lunch fr £10.95 Dinner £18.95-£19.50 English, Welsh & French Cuisine V meals Coffee am **FACILITIES:** CTV in all bedrooms Tennis (hard) Fishing Putting green Xmas **CONF:** Thtr 60 Class 15 Board 30 **SERVICES:** Lift 80P **NOTES:** No dogs No smoking in restaurant Last d 9.30pm **CARDS:**

See advert on this page

LAMPETER Ceredigion — Map 02 SN54

★★ Black Lion Royal Hotel

High St SA48 7BG
Quality Percentage Score: 68%
☎ 01570 422172 Fax 01570 423630
Dir: *opposite Nat West bank*

Dating back to the early 18th century, the Black Lion started life as a coaching inn and remains at the heart of this busy university and market town. There is a choice of bars serving meals as well as a more formal restaurant. The pleasing bedrooms and public areas have all benefitted from recent improvements and investment.

ROOMS: 15 en suite (bth/shr) (4 fmly) s fr £39; d fr £62 (incl. bkfst) * Off peak **MEALS:** Lunch £2.50-£25alc V meals Coffee am Tea pm **FACILITIES:** CTV in all bedrooms STV Fishing Pool table Wkly live entertainment **CONF:** Thtr 100 Board 30 **SERVICES:** 31P **CARDS:**

See advert on this page

LAMPHEY See Pembroke

LANGLAND BAY Swansea — Map 02 SS68

★★★ Langland Court

Langland Court Rd SA3 4TD
Quality Percentage Score: 69%
☎ 01792 361545 Fax 01792 362302
Dir: *take B4593 towards Langland and turn left at St Peter's church*

A large, friendly, personally run Victorian property with lots of *contd.*

L

original character. Particularly impressive are the oak panelled public areas and the imposing stairway. Bedrooms are generally spacious, with some family rooms, and an annexe with ground floor access. There is a formal restaurant supplemented by the more relaxed surroundings of Polly's wine bar.
ROOMS: 14 en suite (bth/shr) 5 annexe en suite (bth/shr) (5 fmly) No smoking in 2 bedrooms s £62-£72; d £84-£91 (incl. bkfst) LB Off peak **MEALS:** Lunch £12.50-£15 Dinner £19.95-£21.25 Welsh, English & Continental Cuisine V meals Coffee am **FACILITIES:** CTV in all bedrooms STV **CONF:** Thtr 150 Class 60 Board 40 Del from £79 * **SERVICES:** 49P **NOTES:** No dogs (ex guide dogs) No smoking in restaurant Last d 9.30pm **CARDS:**

See advert under SWANSEA

LANGLAND BAY Swansea — Map 02 SS68

★★ Wittemberg

MINOTEL Great Britain

Rotherslade Rd SA3 4QN
Quality Percentage Score: 67%
☎ 01792 369696 Fax 01792 366995
Dir: *from Swansea follow bay to Mumbles. 1m from Mumbles turn right at White Rose Pub. Take 3rd left next to chapel then right into Rotherslade Rd*

Just a short walk from the beaches of Langland Bay, this friendly small hotel is also well located for the Mumbles, Swansea and the Gower peninsular. The public areas include a bar, lounge and a restaurant which is the venue for some good home cooking. Bedrooms are well maintained, comfortable and all have modern facilities.
ROOMS: 11 en suite (bth/shr) (2 fmly) s £40-£45; d £70-£75 (incl. bkfst) * LB Off peak **MEALS:** Lunch £9-£12 Dinner £13-£15 V meals **FACILITIES:** CTV in all bedrooms Jacuzzi/spa **SERVICES:** 12P **NOTES:** No coaches No smoking in restaurant Last d 8pm Closed Jan **CARDS:**

LLANARMON DYFFRYN CEIRIOG Wrexham — Map 07 SJ13

★★ West Arms

LL20 7LD
Quality Percentage Score: 72%
☎ 01691 600665 Fax 01691 600622
Dir: *turn off A483/A5 at Chirk, in Chirk take B4500 to Ceiriog Valley, Llanarmon is 11m at the end of B4500*

Set deep in the beautiful Ceiriog Valley, this fine hotel features an abundance of exposed beams. There is a particularly impressive entrance hall with a log fire and comfortable armchairs, a sitting room, and two bars where a wide range of meals is available; there is also a restaurant offering a short fixed-price menu of enjoyable, freshly cooked dishes. Bedrooms vary, having a mixture of modern and period furnishings, but all are attractively decorated.
ROOMS: 12 en suite (bth/shr) 3 annexe en suite (bth/shr) (3 fmly) s £42.50-£47.50; d £75-£85 (incl. bkfst) * LB Off peak **MEALS:** Lunch £12.50 Dinner £19.50 Welsh & French Cuisine V meals Coffee am Tea pm **FACILITIES:** CTV in all bedrooms Fishing Country pursuits programme available ch fac Xmas **CONF:** Thtr 75 Class 40 Board 30 Del from £80 * **SERVICES:** 35P **NOTES:** No smoking in restaurant Last d 9.30pm **CARDS:**

LLANBEDR Gwynedd — Map 06 SH52

★★ Cae Nest Hall Country House

LL45 2NL
Quality Percentage Score: 65%
☎ 01341 241349 Fax 01341 241349
Dir: *turn off A496 at Victoria Pub, turn left at the War Memorial (100yds from pub) then straight ahead to hotel approx 300yds*

A delightful small country house, the hotel dates back to the 15th century and lies in pleasant grounds extending to several acres. Many original features have been retained, with flagstoned floors in the bar and an old black stove in the dining room. Bedrooms have been modernised over the last few years and include many useful facilities.
ROOMS: 10 rms (9 bth/shr) (2 fmly) No smoking in all bedrooms s £33.50-£38.50; d £57-£67 (incl. bkfst) * LB Off peak **MEALS:** English, French, Japanese & Thai Cuisine **FACILITIES:** CTV in all bedrooms **SERVICES:** 10P **NOTES:** No dogs No smoking in restaurant

LLANBEDR Gwynedd — Map 06 SH52

★★ Ty Mawr

LL45 2NH
Quality Percentage Score: 63%
☎ 01341 241440
Dir: *travelling from Barmouth, turn right after the bridge in the village, hotel is 50yds on left*

Located in a picturesque village, this family-run hotel lies in pleasant grounds opposite the River Artro - known for its trout and salmon flows. The grounds are popular as a beer garden during better weather. The bar is attractively cane-furnished and a good choice of real ales is always available. There is a blackboard selection for bar food and a more formal offering in the restaurant. Bedrooms are smart and brightly decorated. Owners and staff are welcoming and friendly, there is a relaxed atmosphere throughout.
ROOMS: 10 en suite (bth/shr) (2 fmly) No smoking in 3 bedrooms s £35; d £58 (incl. bkfst) * LB Off peak **MEALS:** Lunch £7.50 & alc High tea £5-£7 Dinner £12-£18alc Welsh, English, French & Indian Cuisine V meals Coffee am Tea pm **FACILITIES:** CTV in all bedrooms STV Pool table **CONF:** Class 25 **SERVICES:** 30P **NOTES:** No smoking in restaurant Last d 8.45pm Closed 24-26 Dec **CARDS:**

LLANBERIS Gwynedd — Map 06 SH56

★★★ Royal Victoria

LL55 4TY

Quality Percentage Score: 66%

☎ 01286 870253 Fax 01286 870149

Dir: *on A4086 Caernarfon to Llanberis road, directly opposite Snowdon Mountain railway*

An established hotel near the foot of Snowdon, between the Peris and Padarn lakes. Pretty gardens and grounds are an attractive backdrop for the many weddings held there. Bedrooms have been refurbished and modernised in recent years and are well equipped. There are spacious lounges and bars, and a large dining room with a conservatory overlooking the lakes.

ROOMS: 111 en suite (bth/shr) (4 fmly) s £47.50-£50.50; d £95-£101 (incl. bkfst) * LB Off peak **MEALS:** Lunch £8-£12 & alc High tea £3.95-£8.75alc Dinner £11.85-£17.25 V meals Coffee am Tea pm **FACILITIES:** CTV in all bedrooms STV Pool table Mountaineering Abseiling Wkly live entertainment Xmas **CONF:** Thtr 130 Class 50 Board 40 Del from £56.50 * **SERVICES:** Lift Night porter 300P **NOTES:** No smoking in restaurant Last d 9pm **CARDS:**

See advert on this page

LLANBERIS Gwynedd — Map 06 SH56

★★ Lake View

Tan-y-Pant LL55 4EL

Quality Percentage Score: 66%

☎ 01286 870422 Fax 01286 872591

Dir: *1m from Llanberis on A4086 towards Caernarfon*

The lake which gives the hotel its name is impossible to miss, as the vast expanse of water is just over the road. Dramatic landscapes are all around, with Snowdon itself only a short distance away. Bar, restaurant and comfortable lounge have an appealing, country inn character. The bedrooms have modern facilities and are well maintained. The hotel is in easy reach of Caernarvon and Bangor.

ROOMS: 10 rms (9 shr) (3 fmly) s fr £31.95; d fr £45 (incl. bkfst) * Off peak **MEALS:** Lunch £10.95 V meals Coffee am Tea pm **FACILITIES:** CTV in all bedrooms **SERVICES:** 20P **CARDS:**

LLANDEGLA Denbighshire — Map 07 SJ25

★★★ ❀❀ *Bodidris Hall*

LL11 3AL

Quality Percentage Score: 71%

☎ 01978 790434 Fax 01978 790335

Dir: *in village take A5104 at Crown pub towards Corwen. Hotel 1m on left*

This impressive manor house, surrounded by ornamental gardens and mature woodlands, dates back many centuries and still retains original oak beams and inglenook fireplaces. Bedrooms are furnished with antique pieces and some have four poster beds. Dining at Bodidris is very enjoyable, the food is cooked with flair and stylishly presented. Provision can be made for weddings and business meetings.

ROOMS: 9 en suite (bth/shr) 2 annexe en suite (bth/shr) (2 fmly) No smoking in 4 bedrooms **MEALS:** British & French Cuisine V meals Coffee am Tea pm **FACILITIES:** CTV in all bedrooms Fishing Clay pigeon & Driven shooting Falconry **CONF:** Thtr 50 Class 25 Board 20 **SERVICES:** 80P **NOTES:** No smoking in restaurant Last d 9.30pm **CARDS:**

For Useful Information and Important Telephone Number Changes turn to page 25

LLANDEILO Carmarthenshire **Map 03 SN62**

★★★ ***The Plough Inn***

Rhosmaen SA19 6NP

Quality Percentage Score: 70%

☎ 01558 823431 📠 01558 823969

Dir: *1m N, on A40*

This pleasing inn, situated in gardens, provides well equipped modern accommodation including bedrooms on ground floor level and a room for disabled guests. Public areas comprise an attractively appointed restaurant and a cosy bar. Conference and leisure facilities are availiable.

ROOMS: 12 en suite (bth/shr) **MEALS:** Italian & Continental Cuisine V meals Coffee am Tea pm **FACILITIES:** CTV in all bedrooms STV Sauna Gym **CONF:** Thtr 45 Class 24 Board 24 **SERVICES:** 70P **NOTES:** No dogs Last d 9.30pm Closed 25 Dec RS Sun **CARDS:**

See advert on page 925

LLANDEILO Carmarthenshire **Map 03 SN62**

★★★ Cawdor Arms

Rhosmaen St SA19 6EN

Quality Percentage Score: 66%

☎ 01558 823500 📠 01558 822399

Dir: *centre of Llandeilo town, 20 mins from M4 junc 49. Follow signs to Llandeilo*

A warm welcome is offered to guests at this impressive Georgian hotel in the centre of Llandeilo. The hotel has elegantly furnished public rooms and bedrooms, some with four poster beds. An impressive menu is offered that is highly regarded locally.

ROOMS: 17 en suite (bth/shr) (2 fmly) s £45-£55; d £60-£75 (incl. bkfst) * LB Off peak **MEALS:** Lunch £11.50-£13.95alc V meals Coffee am Tea pm **FACILITIES:** CTV in all bedrooms Wkly live entertainment Xmas **CONF:** Thtr 60 Class 40 Board 26 **SERVICES:** 7P **NOTES:** No smoking in restaurant **CARDS:**

LLANDRILLO Denbighshire **Map 06 SJ03**

The Premier Collection

★★ Tyddyn Llan

Country Hotel & Restaurant

LL21 0ST

☎ 01490 440264 📠 01490 440414

Dir: *on B4401, Corwen-Bala road*

Set in landscaped gardens, this Georgian house provides an idyllic country retreat. Public rooms offer considerable comfort with a series of delightful lounges, and an elegantly appointed restaurant that offers an imaginative menu. Bedrooms are individually styled and tastefully furnished, and equipped with a range of useful facilities and thoughtful extras.

ROOMS: 10 en suite (bth/shr) (2 fmly) s £65-£82; d £100-£134 (incl. bkfst) * LB Off peak **MEALS:** Lunch £15.50 & alc Dinner £25-£27 V meals Coffee am Tea pm **FACILITIES:** CTV in all bedrooms Fishing Croquet lawn Xmas **CONF:** Thtr 30 Class 30 Board 20 Del from £115 * **SERVICES:** 30P **NOTES:** No smoking in restaurant Last d 9pm **CARDS:**

LLANDRINDOD WELLS Powys **Map 03 SO06**

see also **Penybont**

★★★ Hotel Metropole

Temple St LD1 5DY

Quality Percentage Score: 67%

☎ 01597 823700 📠 01597 824828

Dir: *on A483 in centre of town*

The centre of the famous spa town is dominated by this Victorian hotel. The lobby leads to a choice of bars, elegant lounge and an extensive restaurant. Bedrooms vary in style, all are quite spacious and well equipped. Additional facilities include a leisure centre, conference rooms and shop.

ROOMS: 121 en suite (bth/shr) (2 fmly) No smoking in 10 bedrooms s £55-£68; d £72-£90 (incl. bkfst) * LB Off peak **MEALS:** Lunch £6.50-£9.75 Dinner £17.95 Welsh, English & Continental Cuisine V meals Coffee am Tea pm **FACILITIES:** CTV in all bedrooms Indoor swimming pool (heated) Sauna Solarium Jacuzzi/spa Beauty salon Rowing & Cycling machines Wkly live entertainment ch fac Xmas **CONF:** Thtr 300 Class 200 Board 80 Del from £72 * **SERVICES:** Lift Night porter 150P **NOTES:** No smoking in restaurant Last d 9pm **CARDS:**

LLANDUDNO Conwy **Map 06 SH78**

The Premier Collection

★★★ Bodysgallen Hall

LL30 1RS

☎ 01492 584466 📠 01492 582519

Dir: *take A55 to intersection with A470, then follow A470 towards Llandudno. Hotel 1m on right*

Conwy Castle and Snowdonia provide the backdrop for this 17th-century country house set in 200 acres of parkland and superb formal gardens. The interior has a character to match the surroundings with wood panelled walls adorned with Old Masters, elegant furnishings, and open fires. The spacious bedrooms are thoughtfully appointed with extra comforts, some rooms are in converted cottages. The restaurant is the venue for some imaginative cooking using the finest local ingredients. A high level of service is

contd.

provided in all departments by a friendly and dedicated team.
ROOMS: 19 en suite (bth/shr) 16 annexe en suite (bth/shr) (3 fmly) No smoking in 3 bedrooms s £99-£105; d £150-£225 * LB Off peak **MEALS:** Lunch £14.50-£18.50 Dinner £32.50 V meals Coffee am Tea pm **FACILITIES:** CTV in all bedrooms Indoor swimming pool (heated) Tennis (hard) Sauna Solarium Gym Croquet lawn Jacuzzi/spa Spa with pool gym & beauty salons,sauna, steam room & club room Wkly live entertainment Xmas **CONF:** Thtr 50 Class 30 Board 24 **SERVICES:** Night porter 50P **NOTES:** No children 8yrs No smoking in restaurant Last d 9.30pm
CARDS:

LLANDUDNO Conwy — Map 06 SH78
★★★ Empire
Church Walks LL30 2HE
Quality Percentage Score: 76%
☎ 01492 860555 🖹 01492 860791
Dir: *A55 from Chester - Leave at intersection for Llandudno (A470). Follow signs for town centre - Hotel is at end & facing main street*

The Empire is considered to be one of the best hotels in North Wales. Bedrooms offer every modern facility and are luxuriously appointed. There is an indoor swimming pool, overlooked by an all-day restaurant, and a further outdoor pool and roof garden. The Watkins restaurant offers an excellent daily changing fixed-price menu.
ROOMS: 50 en suite (bth/shr) 8 annexe en suite (bth/shr) (3 fmly) s £55-£70; d £80-£120 (incl. bkfst) * LB Off peak **MEALS:** Sunday Lunch £14.50-£16.50 Dinner £24.50-£27.50 V meals Coffee am Tea pm **FACILITIES:** CTV in all bedrooms STV Indoor swimming pool (heated) Outdoor swimming pool (heated) Sauna Jacuzzi/spa Beauty treatments Wkly live entertainment **CONF:** Thtr 36 Class 20 Board 20 Del from £85 * **SERVICES:** Lift Night porter 40P **NOTES:** No dogs (ex guide dogs) No coaches No smoking area in restaurant Last d 9.30pm Closed 17-29 Dec **CARDS:**

See advert on this page

LLANDUDNO Conwy — Map 06 SH78
★★★ Imperial
The Promenade LL30 1AP
Quality Percentage Score: 67%
☎ 01492 877466 🖹 01492 878043
A large traditional seaside hotel. Many of the bedrooms have views over the bay and there are also several suites available. The elegant Chantrey restaurant offers a fixed-price menu which changes monthly and uses local produce. There is a fully

contd.

equipped leisure club and extensive conference and banqueting facilities.

Imperial, Llandudno

ROOMS: 100 en suite (bth/shr) (10 fmly) **MEALS:** Lunch £12-£14 Dinner £16.50-£24 V meals Coffee am Tea pm **FACILITIES:** CTV in all bedrooms STV Indoor swimming pool (heated) Sauna Solarium Gym Jacuzzi/spa Beauty therapist Hairdressing **CONF:** Thtr 150 Class 50 Board 50 **SERVICES:** Lift Night porter 40P **NOTES:** No smoking in restaurant Last d 9pm **CARDS:**

See advert on page 927

LLANDUDNO Conwy **Map 06 SH78**

★★★ St George's

The Promenade LL30 2LG

Quality Percentage Score: 65%

☎ 01492 877544 📠 01492 877788

Dir: *proceed along the promenade toward th*

This popular seafront hotel was the first to be built in the town and still retains many Victorian features including the splendidly ornate Wedgwood Room. The main lounges overlook the bay and incorporate a Coffee Shop serving hot and cold snacks. There is a wide variety of room sizes available and several have fine views over the sea and some also have balconies. Hotel staff are friendly and helpful.

ROOMS: 85 en suite (bth/shr) (4 fmly) No smoking in 12 bedrooms s £50-£60; d £90 (incl. bkfst) * LB Off peak **MEALS:** Sunday Lunch £7.95-£9.95 High tea fr £5.50 Dinner fr £15.95 English French & Welsh Cuisine V meals Coffee am Tea pm **FACILITIES:** CTV in all bedrooms STV Sauna Solarium Jacuzzi/spa Hairdressing Health & beauty salon Wkly live entertainment Xmas **CONF:** Thtr 250 Class 200 Board 45 Del from £75 * **SERVICES:** Lift Night porter 36P **NOTES:** No dogs (ex guide dogs) No smoking in restaurant Last d 9pm **CARDS:**

LLANDUDNO Conwy **Map 06 SH78**

★★★ Gogarth Abbey Hotel

West Shore LL30 2QY

Quality Percentage Score: 62%

☎ 01492 876211 📠 01492 875805

Dir: *A55 from Chester turn off rdbt signed Llandudno Junction continue to Llandudno turn left onto West Shore*

Whilst staying here as a guest of the Liddell family, Charles Dodgson (Lewis Carroll), was inspired to write "Alice in Wonderland" and "Alice through the Looking Glass". Public areas offer a choice of several lounges with no-smoking areas, an attractive restaurant and a lounge bar. A separate building contains the heated swimming pool and other leisure facilities.

ROOMS: 39 en suite (bth/shr) (4 fmly) **MEALS:** Lunch £5.95-£6.95 High tea £3.99 Dinner £18.95 English & French Cuisine V meals Coffee am Tea pm **FACILITIES:** CTV in all bedrooms STV Indoor swimming pool (heated) Sauna Solarium Gym Pool table Croquet lawn Putting green Table tennis Boules **CONF:** Thtr 40 Class 30 Board 30 Del £55 * **SERVICES:** Night porter 40P **NOTES:** No smoking in restaurant Last d 9pm **CARDS:**

LLANDUDNO Conwy **Map 06 SH78**

★★★ *Chatsworth House*

Central Promenade LL30 2XS

Quality Percentage Score: 59%

☎ 01492 860788 📠 01492 871417

This traditional family-run Victorian hotel enjoys a central position on the promenade and caters for many families and groups. Modern bedrooms are complemented by well maintained facilities and public areas, where varied entertainment is booked during the summer.

ROOMS: 72 en suite (bth/shr) (19 fmly) **MEALS:** British Cuisine V meals Coffee am Tea pm **FACILITIES:** CTV in all bedrooms Indoor swimming pool (heated) Sauna Jacuzzi/spa D **SERVICES:** Lift Night porter 9P **NOTES:** No smoking area in restaurant Last d 8.30pm

CARDS:

LLANDUDNO Conwy **Map 06 SH78**

★★★ Risboro

Clement Av LL30 2ED

Quality Percentage Score: 59%

☎ 01492 876343 📠 01492 879881

Dir: *A55 to Llandudno, follow A470 into town centre, at large roundabout turn left then take 3rd right*

Situated close to the base of the Great Orme, this popular family hotel provides agreeably furnished bedrooms. Amongst the extensive public areas are a comfortable lounge with a small terrace and a large restaurant overlooking the pool.

ROOMS: 65 en suite (bth/shr) (7 fmly) s £35-£40; d £70-£80 (incl. bkfst) * LB Off peak **MEALS:** Lunch £5-£7.50 Dinner £12.50-£15 English & French Cuisine V meals Coffee am Tea pm **FACILITIES:** CTV in all bedrooms STV Indoor swimming pool (heated) Squash Riding Sauna Solarium Gym Jacuzzi/spa Table tennis Wkly live entertainment Xmas **CONF:** Thtr 150 Class 100 Board 80 Del from £55 * **SERVICES:** Lift Night porter 40P **NOTES:** No smoking area in restaurant Last d 9.15pm

CARDS:

LLANDUDNO Conwy **Map 06 SH78**

The Premier Collection

★★ St Tudno

Promenade LL30 2LP

☎ 01492 874411 📠 01492 860407

Dir: *on reaching Promenade drive towards the pier, hotel is opposite pier entrance & gardens*

A high quality resort hotel which although not the place for buckets and spades, will receive toddlers as warmly as adults. Bedrooms, some with sea views, offer a wide choice of sizes and individual styles, so discuss exact requirements at the time of booking. Public rooms include a no-smoking lounge, a convivial bar-lounge, and a small indoor pool. The

contd.

air-conditioned Garden Room Restaurant is the focal point for enjoyable cuisine using good local produce.
ROOMS: 19 en suite (bth/shr) (2 fmly) No smoking in 3 bedrooms s £65-£75; d £95-£185 (incl. bkfst) LB Off peak **MEALS:** Lunch £15-£16.95 Dinner fr £27 V meals Coffee am Tea pm **FACILITIES:** CTV in all bedrooms STV Indoor swimming pool (heated) Wkly live entertainment Xmas **CONF:** Thtr 40 Class 25 Board 20 Del from £150 * **SERVICES:** Lift 12P **NOTES:** No coaches No smoking in restaurant Last d 9.30pm
CARDS:

LLANDUDNO Conwy **Map 06 SH78**
★★ Dunoon
Gloddaeth St LL30 2DW
Quality Percentage Score: 71%
☎ 01492 860787 01492 860031

THE CIRCLE
Selected Individual Hotels
GREAT BRITAIN

This comfortable and welcoming hotel is situated just a short walk from the promenade and shopping area of Llandudno. Attractively furnished bedrooms are well equipped, and generously priced meals are offered in the restaurant. There is a choice of lounges in which to relax, as well as a wood panelled bar.
ROOMS: 55 en suite (bth/shr) 3 annexe en suite (bth/shr) (10 fmly) s £39-£42; d £56-£84 (incl. bkfst) * LB Off peak **MEALS:** Lunch £9-£10.75 Dinner £14.50-£20.50 English & French Cuisine V meals Coffee am Tea pm **FACILITIES:** CTV in all bedrooms STV Solarium Pool table Jacuzzi/spa **SERVICES:** Lift 24P **NOTES:** No smoking area in restaurant Last d 8pm Closed mid Nov-mid Mar **CARDS:**

LLANDUDNO Conwy **Map 06 SH78**
★★ Epperstone
15 Abbey Rd LL30 2EE
Quality Percentage Score: 71%
☎ 01492 878746 01492 871223
Dir: *at junct of Abbey road and York road*
A delightful hotel with wonderful gardens located in a residential part of town, within easy walking distance of the seafront and shopping area. Bedrooms are attractively decorated and thoughtfully equipped. Two lounges are available, a comfortable no-smoking room and a Victorian-style conservatory. A daily changing menu is offered in the bright dining room.
ROOMS: 8 en suite (bth/shr) (5 fmly) No smoking in 6 bedrooms s £27-£30; d £54-£60 (incl. bkfst) * LB Off peak **MEALS:** Bar Lunch £4-£10 Dinner £16 V meals Coffee am Tea pm **FACILITIES:** CTV in all bedrooms STV Xmas **SERVICES:** 8P **NOTES:** No coaches No smoking in restaurant Last d 8pm **CARDS:**

LLANDUDNO Conwy **Map 06 SH78**
★★ Belle Vue
26 North Pde LL30 2LP
Quality Percentage Score: 70%
☎ 01492 879547 01492 870001
Dir: *follow the promenade towards the pier, as the road bends the Belle Vue Hotel is on the left*
This peaceful and relaxing hotel under the Great Orme is within easy distance of Llandudno town centre and boasts stunning views across the bay. The well equipped bedrooms are bright and fresh and include video recorders plus a large film library. A comfortable bar and separate lounge is provided for guests and the small daily menu offers good traditional cooking.
ROOMS: 15 en suite (bth/shr) (3 fmly) No smoking in all bedrooms s £37-£41; d £54-£62 (incl. bkfst) LB Off peak **MEALS:** Dinner £13 **FACILITIES:** CTV in all bedrooms **SERVICES:** Lift 12P **NOTES:** No coaches No smoking in restaurant Last d 7pm Closed Dec & Jan
CARDS:

LLANDUDNO Conwy **Map 06 SH78**
★★ Sandringham
West Pde LL30 2BD
Quality Percentage Score: 70%
☎ 01492 876513 & 876447 01492 872753
Dir: *enter Llandudno on A470 follow signs for West Shore, hotel is located in centre of West Shore Promenade*
This holiday hotel on the West Shore has superb views over the Conwy Estuary towards Snowdonia. There are two restaurants and a full range of bar food. Bedrooms are tastefully decorated with matching fabrics, some at ground floor level and others suitable for families.
ROOMS: 18 en suite (bth/shr) (3 fmly) s £26-£28.50; d £52-£57 (incl. bkfst) LB Off peak **MEALS:** Lunch £7.95-£11.95 & alc Dinner £13.95-£14.95 English & Continental Cuisine V meals Coffee am **FACILITIES:** CTV in all bedrooms STV Wkly live entertainment Xmas **CONF:** Thtr 70 Class 60 Board 30 Del from £35 * **SERVICES:** 6P **NOTES:** No dogs No smoking in restaurant Last d 8.30pm RS 25 & 26 Dec **CARDS:**

LLANDUDNO Conwy **Map 06 SH78**
★★ Tan-Lan
Great Orme's Rd, West Shore LL30 2AR
Quality Percentage Score: 70%
☎ 01492 860221 01492 870219
Dir: *turn off A55 onto A546 signposted Deganwy. Straight over 2 rdbts, approx 3m from A55, hotel on left just over mini rdbt*
Located under the Great Orme on the West Shore, a warm welcome is certain at this well presented small hotel. Bedrooms, many on the ground floor, are brightly decorated and well equipped. There is a cosy bar and a comfortable lounge, separated by the attractive restaurant, where freshly prepared meals are served in generous portions.
ROOMS: 17 en suite (bth/shr) (3 fmly) No smoking in 2 bedrooms s £25-£35; d £50-£54 (incl. bkfst) * LB Off peak **MEALS:** Dinner £15 V meals Coffee am Tea pm **FACILITIES:** CTV in all bedrooms Xmas **SERVICES:** 12P **NOTES:** No coaches No smoking in restaurant Last d 7.30pm **CARDS:**

LLANDUDNO Conwy **Map 06 SH78**
★★ Banham House
2 St Davids Rd LL30 2UL
Quality Percentage Score: 68%
☎ 01492 875680 01492 875680
Dir: *from Llandudno Station turn left, at traffic lights turn left into Trinity Avenue, take 3rd exit on right opposite school*
The front of the hotel is always adorned with lovely flower displays. Standards continue to be high with all areas fresh and impeccably maintained. Bedrooms are equipped with modern facilities and there is a relaxing lounge. An extensive range of food is available.
ROOMS: 6 en suite (bth/shr) No smoking in all bedrooms s £30; d £46-£50 (incl. bkfst) * Off peak **MEALS:** Lunch £9 Dinner £9 V meals Coffee am **FACILITIES:** CTV in all bedrooms A non-smoking hotel Xmas **SERVICES:** 5P **NOTES:** No dogs No coaches No children 16yrs No smoking in restaurant Last d 9.30pm Closed 31 Dec-2 Jan

LLANDUDNO Conwy **Map 06 SH78**
★★ *Sunnymede*
West Pde LL30 2BD
Quality Percentage Score: 68%
☎ 01492 877130
The Sunnymede Hotel lies on Llandudno's West Shore with views from many rooms over the Conwy Estuary and Snowdonia. Modern bedrooms are decorated with pretty

contd.

L

wallpapers. Lounge areas are particularly comfortable and attractive.
ROOMS: 18 rms (14 bth 3 shr) (3 fmly) **MEALS:** V meals Coffee am Tea pm **FACILITIES:** CTV in all bedrooms STV **SERVICES:** 18P **NOTES:** Closed mid Nov-Feb **CARDS:**

LLANDUDNO Conwy **Map 06 SH78**
★★ Tynedale
Central Promenade LL30 2XS
Quality Percentage Score: 68%
☎ 01492 877426 01492 871213
Dir: *on promenade opposite bandstand*
Tynedale is a holiday hotel on the promenade. Tour groups are well catered for and regular live entertainment is a feature. Public areas include good lounge facilities, and an attractive patio overlooking the bay. Bedrooms are fresh and well equipped, many have good views over the sea front and the Great Orme.
ROOMS: 56 en suite (bth/shr) (4 fmly) s £31-£41; d £50-£78 (incl. bkfst) * LB Off peak **MEALS:** Bar Lunch £2-£10alc Dinner £8-£12 English & Continental Cuisine V meals Coffee am Tea pm **FACILITIES:** CTV in all bedrooms Wkly live entertainment Xmas **SERVICES:** Lift Night porter 30P **NOTES:** No dogs (ex guide dogs) No smoking in restaurant Last d 8.30pm **CARDS:**

LLANDUDNO Conwy **Map 06 SH78**
★★ Wilton
South Pde LL30 2LN
Quality Percentage Score: 68%
☎ 01492 876086 & 878343 01492 876086
Dir: *from A470 head towards promenade, Pier & Great Orme. At Pier turn left before cenataph - Prince Edwards Sq. Hotel last on left before rdbt*
A well maintained hotel just off the promenade with the main shopping centre nearby. It has very pretty bedrooms, and most have four-poster beds; modern amenities are provided. There is a comfortable lounge bar for residents and good value meals are available.
ROOMS: 14 en suite (bth/shr) (7 fmly) No smoking in 4 bedrooms s £24-£26; d £48-£52 (incl. bkfst) * LB Off peak **MEALS:** Dinner £10-£12 V meals **FACILITIES:** CTV in all bedrooms STV ch fac **SERVICES:** 3P **NOTES:** No coaches No smoking in restaurant Last d 7.30pm Closed 28 Nov-6 Feb **CARDS:**

LLANDUDNO Conwy **Map 06 SH78**
★★ Bedford
Promenade LL30 1BN
Quality Percentage Score: 66%
☎ 01492 876647 01492 860185
Dir: *at intersection of A55/A470, take exit for Llandudno (A470) and continue until 4th rdbt. Take exit for Craig-Y-Don (B115) and turn right*
This hotel is located on the eastern approach to Llandudno at Craig-y-Don. Many of the well equipped bedrooms are suitable for families and enjoy fine views over the bay towards Great Orme. The hotel's Italian restaurant and pizzeria has a local following and supplements the traditional hotel restaurant. There is a comfortable lounge for residents.
ROOMS: 27 en suite (bth/shr) (2 fmly) No smoking in 3 bedrooms s £30; d £50 (incl. bkfst) LB Off peak **MEALS:** Dinner £12 & alc British, French & Italian Cuisine V meals Coffee am Tea pm **FACILITIES:** CTV in all bedrooms STV Xmas **CONF:** Thtr 30 Class 20 Board 20 **SERVICES:** Lift Night porter 21P **NOTES:** Last d 10.30pm **CARDS:**

LLANDUDNO Conwy **Map 06 SH78**
★★ *Leamore*
40 Lloyd St LL30 2YG
Quality Percentage Score: 66%
☎ 01492 875552
Comfortable and very well equipped bedrooms are provided at the Leamore Hotel. There is a comfortable lounge and a foyer bar, and satisfying local cooking is provided.
ROOMS: 12 rms (1 bth 6 shr) (4 fmly) **MEALS:** V meals **FACILITIES:** CTV in all bedrooms **SERVICES:** 4P **NOTES:** No dogs (ex guide dogs) No coaches Closed Dec

LLANDUDNO Conwy **Map 06 SH78**
★★ Somerset
St Georges Crescent, Promenade LL30 2LF
Quality Percentage Score: 66%
☎ 01492 876540 01492 863700
Dir: *on the Promenade*
With its sister hotel, The Wavecrest, this cheerful holiday hotel occupies an ideal location on the central promenade and there are superb views over the bay from many rooms. Regular entertainment is provided as well as a range of bar and lounge areas. Bedrooms are well decorated and modern facilities are provided.
ROOMS: 37 en suite (bth/shr) (4 fmly) s £30-£46 (incl. bkfst) * LB Off peak **MEALS:** Lunch £7.95 Dinner £15 V meals Coffee am **FACILITIES:** CTV in all bedrooms Pool table Games room Wkly live entertainment Xmas **SERVICES:** Lift Night porter 20P **NOTES:** No smoking in restaurant Last d 7.30pm Closed Nov-Feb
CARDS:

LLANDUDNO Conwy **Map 06 SH78**
★★ Stratford
8 Craig-y-Don Pde, Promenade LL30 1BG
Quality Percentage Score: 66%
☎ 01492 877962 01492 877962
Dir: *from A55 take A470 to Llandudno at 4th rdbt take Craig-y-don sign to Promenade*
A pleasant holiday hotel on the Craig-y-Don promenade. The Conference Centre and theatre are nearby, local shops a short walk away. The comfortable bedrooms have many beds with canopies. A daily changing menu provides generously priced home cooking. Guests have a comfortable lounge, separate bar and an inviting patio overlooking the sea.
ROOMS: 10 en suite (bth/shr) (4 fmly) s £21-£27; d £38-£50 (incl. bkfst) * LB Off peak **MEALS:** Dinner £10 V meals **FACILITIES:** CTV in all bedrooms STV ch fac **NOTES:** No coaches No smoking in restaurant Last d 5pm Closed Dec-Feb **CARDS:**

LLANDUDNO Conwy **Map 06 SH78**
★★ White Lodge
9 Neville Crescent, Central Promenade LL30 1AT
Quality Percentage Score: 66%
☎ 01492 877713
Dir: *A55 then A470, then onto the B5115*
This very friendly hotel is located on the promenade with all local amenities within easy walking distance. Many bedrooms enjoy good seafront views and have pretty canopies over the beds; family rooms are available. Good value food is on offer and guests have use of a comfortable lounge and a separate bar.
ROOMS: 12 en suite (bth/shr) (4 fmly) s £32-£36; d £52-£58 (incl. bkfst) * LB Off peak **MEALS:** Coffee am Tea pm **FACILITIES:** CTV in all bedrooms **SERVICES:** 12P **NOTES:** No dogs (ex guide dogs) No coaches No children 5yrs No smoking in restaurant Closed Nov-Mar
CARDS:

LLANDUDNO Conwy **Map 06 SH78**

★★ *Esplanade*

Glan-y-Mor Pde, Promenade LL30 2LL

Quality Percentage Score: 65%

☎ 0800 318688 (freephone) & 01492 860300 ▤ 01492 860418

Dir: *turn off A55 at Llandudno junct & proceed on A470*

One of the first hotels in Llandudno and popular for weekend and golfing breaks, the Esplanade Hotel is located in the centre of the promenade with the main shopping area nearby. Many bedrooms have superb views over the bay, and are all thoughtfully equipped. Live entertainment takes place regularly, and an all-day buttery serves snacks and refreshments.

ROOMS: 59 en suite (bth/shr) (20 fmly) **MEALS:** V meals Coffee am Tea pm **FACILITIES:** CTV in all bedrooms Wkly live entertainment **CONF:** Thtr 90 Class 40 Board 40 Del from £42.50 * **SERVICES:** Lift Night porter 30P **NOTES:** Last d 8.30pm **CARDS:**

LLANDUDNO Conwy **Map 06 SH78**

★★ Royal

Church Walks LL30 2HW

Quality Percentage Score: 64%

☎ 01492 876476 ▤ 01492 870210

Dir: *leave A55 for A470 to Llandudno. Follow through town to T-Jct - turn left into Church Walks. Hotel 200yds on left, almost opp. station*

A long established hotel lying under the Great Orme within easy reach of the promenade, town centre and other amenities. Bedrooms are furnished in a modern style, and many have views over the town and seafront. The hotel is popular with tour groups and is also a base for golf visitors. There is a bar and a spacious dining room, and seasonal live entertainment.

ROOMS: 38 rms (36 bth/shr) (7 fmly) s £30-£33; d £60-£70 (incl. bkfst) * LB Off peak **MEALS:** Lunch fr £3.95 Dinner fr £15 V meals Coffee am **FACILITIES:** CTV in all bedrooms Pool table Putting green Wkly live entertainment Xmas **CONF:** Class 50 Del from £40 * **SERVICES:** Lift Night porter 20P **NOTES:** No dogs (ex guide dogs) No smoking in restaurant Last d 8pm **CARDS:**

LLANDUDNO Conwy **Map 06 SH78**

★★ *Evans*

Charlton St LL30 2AA

Quality Percentage Score: 63%

☎ 01492 860784 ▤ 01492 860784

This friendly, privately owned hotel provides comfortable, well appointed bedrooms including family rooms. Spacious public areas include a well equipped games room and comfortable lounge bar, where regular live evening entertainment is held. Dinner is only served until 7 pm, but a non-cooked supper can be provided for later arrivals.

ROOMS: 50 en suite (bth/shr) (4 fmly) **MEALS:** V meals **FACILITIES:** CTV in all bedrooms STV Snooker Solarium Pool table Wkly live entertainment **SERVICES:** Lift **NOTES:** No dogs (ex guide dogs) No smoking in restaurant Closed Jan

LLANDUDNO Conwy **Map 06 SH78**

★★ Headlands

Hill Ter LL30 2LS

Quality Percentage Score: 63%

☎ 01492 877485

Lovely views over the town and seafront are enjoyed from the public areas and many bedrooms of this resort hotel, at the foot of the great Orme. Bedrooms with four-posters are available. There is a range of comfortable sitting areas and the hotel staff are friendly and welcoming.

ROOMS: 17 rms (15 bth/shr) (4 fmly) s £28-£38; d £56-£76 (incl. bkfst & dinner) * LB Off peak **MEALS:** Coffee am **FACILITIES:** CTV in all bedrooms Xmas **SERVICES:** 7P **NOTES:** No coaches No children 5yrs Last d 8.30pm Closed Jan-Feb **CARDS:**

LLANDUDNO Conwy **Map 06 SH78**

★★ Ormescliffe

East Pde LL30 1BE

Quality Percentage Score: 63%

☎ 01492 877191 ▤ 01492 860311

This family-run hotel lies at the eastern end of the promenade and is convenient for the theatre and conference centre. Bedrooms are modern and well equipped, several are suitable for families and most have superb views over the seafront and Great Orme. Comfortable bars and lounges are provided and there is a ballroom where live entertainment is regularly held. The atmosphere is warm and relaxing.

ROOMS: 61 en suite (bth/shr) (7 fmly) No smoking in 6 bedrooms s £35-£40; d £70-£80 (incl. bkfst) * LB Off peak **MEALS:** Bar Lunch £1.50-£3.50 Dinner £10.50-£12.50 V meals Coffee am Tea pm **FACILITIES:** CTV in all bedrooms Snooker Table tennis Xmas **CONF:** Thtr 120 Class 120 Board 80 **SERVICES:** Lift Night porter 15P **NOTES:** No smoking in restaurant Last d 7.45pm Closed 2 Jan-2 Feb **CARDS:**

LLANDUDNO Conwy **Map 06 SH78**

★★ Ravenhurst

West Pde LL30 2BB

Quality Percentage Score: 63%

☎ 01492 875525 ▤ 01248 681143

Dir: *on West Shore, opposite boating pool*

This comfortable hotel lies on Llandudno's West Shore with lovely views from many rooms over the Conwy Estuary towards Snowdonia. Smart accommodation includes several family suites. Two lounges and a small bar are provided, the dining room offers a daily fixed-price menu.

ROOMS: 25 en suite (bth/shr) (3 fmly) s fr £26; d fr £52 (incl. bkfst) * LB Off peak **MEALS:** Lunch £2.50-£8 High tea fr £2 Dinner £11-£13 V meals Coffee am Tea pm **FACILITIES:** CTV in all bedrooms Xmas **SERVICES:** 15P **NOTES:** No smoking in restaurant Last d 7pm Closed Dec-Feb **CARDS:**

LLANDUDNO Conwy **Map 06 SH78**

★★ Wavecrest

St Georges Crescent, Central Promenade LL30 2LF

Quality Percentage Score: 63%

☎ 01492 860615 ▤ 01492 863700

Dir: *on promenade behind Marks & Spencer*

The Wavecrest is the sister hotel of the adjoining Somerset, and public areas are shared. It lies on the central promenade and most bedrooms have lovely sea views. Lounge and bar areas are comfortably furnished and a games room is available. Staff are friendly and regular entertainment is staged.

ROOMS: 41 en suite (bth/shr) (7 fmly) s £30-£44; d £60-£88 (incl. bkfst & dinner) * LB Off peak **MEALS:** Lunch £6.25-£7.25 Dinner £15 V meals Coffee am Tea pm **FACILITIES:** CTV in all bedrooms Pool table Wkly live entertainment Xmas **CONF:** Class 70 **SERVICES:** Lift Night porter 12P **NOTES:** No smoking in restaurant Last d 7.30pm Closed Nov-Mar **CARDS:**

L

LLANDUDNO Conwy **Map 06 SH78**

★★ All Seasons Hotel

Hill Ter LL30 2LS

Quality Percentage Score: 62%

☎ 01492 876277 🖷 01492 876277

Dir: *at the top of the Promenade, & the base of the Great Orme*

Located on the slopes of the Great Orme, the All Seasons Hotel has far reaching views and provides good value breaks for tour parties and private guests. The attractive public areas include a bar and a choice of lounges.

ROOMS: 29 en suite (bth/shr) (3 fmly) No smoking in all bedrooms s £26-£28; d £52-£56 (incl. bkfst) * LB Off peak **MEALS:** V meals Coffee am Tea pm **FACILITIES:** CTV in all bedrooms Xmas **CONF:** Thtr 60 Class 40 Board 40 **SERVICES:** 4P **NOTES:** No children No smoking in restaurant Last d 6.30pm

LLANDUDNO Conwy **Map 06 SH78**

★★ *Branksome Hotel*

Lloyd St LL30 2YP

Quality Percentage Score: 62%

☎ 01492 875989 & 878808 🖷 01492 875989

This popular hotel lies between the town's two shores and is a short walk from the main shopping area. Family and ground floor rooms are available, with modern and well equipped accommodation across the board. Public rooms are spacious and comfortable, and regular live entertainment is provided.

ROOMS: 49 rms (44 bth/shr) (8 fmly) **MEALS:** V meals Coffee am Tea pm **FACILITIES:** CTV in all bedrooms **SERVICES:** Night porter 16P **NOTES:** Last d 7pm Closed Jan-Feb

L

LLANDUDNO Conwy **Map 06 SH78**

★ *Tan-y-Marian*

87 Abbey Rd, West Shore LL30 2AS

Quality Percentage Score: 68%

☎ 01492 877727

Situated at the foot of the Great Orme, near Llandudno's West Shore, this is a small and friendly hotel where guests receive a warm welcome. Everywhere is freshly decorated and a cosy bar and separate TV lounge are provided. Bedrooms are prettily decorated and food is home-cooked and wholesome.

ROOMS: 7 rms (1 bth 4 shr) (1 fmly) **SERVICES:** 5P **NOTES:** No dogs No coaches Closed Oct-Mar

LLANDUDNO Conwy **Map 06 SH78**

★ *Concord*

35 Abbey Rd LL30 2EH

Quality Percentage Score: 67%

☎ 01492 875504

This delightful hotel is located between Llandudno's two shores. Guests return year after year to this popular spot and are well cared for by the dedicated staff. Bedrooms are light and decorated with pretty wallpapers and fabrics. A comfortable lounge is provided and the home cooking is very popular.

ROOMS: 11 en suite (bth/shr) (7 fmly) **MEALS:** Coffee am **SERVICES:** 11P **NOTES:** No dogs (ex guide dogs) No coaches No children 5yrs No smoking in restaurant Last d 7pm Closed mid Oct-mid Mar

LLANDUDNO Conwy **Map 06 SH78**

★ Oak Alyn

2 Deganwy Av LL30 2YB

Quality Percentage Score: 65%

☎ 01492 860320

Dir: *situated in the centre of Llandudno, 200 yards from the Town Hall, opposite the Catholic Church*

This is a friendly resort hotel that lies in a residential part of Llandudno, near to the main shopping area and the seafront. Bedrooms are fresh and bright and all are equipped with modern facilities. There is a comfortable lounge for residents and a separate bar.

ROOMS: 12 en suite (bth/shr) (2 fmly) **MEALS:** Dinner £8.50-£10 V meals **FACILITIES:** CTV in all bedrooms **SERVICES:** 16P **NOTES:** No smoking in restaurant Closed 22-31 Dec **CARDS:**

LLANDUDNO Conwy **Map 06 SH78**

★ Min-y-Don

North Pde LL30 2LP

Quality Percentage Score: 63%

☎ 01492 876511 🖷 01492 878169

Dir: *leave A55 Expressway Llandudno junct taking A470. Through Martyn St, turn right at rdbt then left North Parade*

This is a cheerful family-run hotel located under the Great Orme and close to the pier. Bedrooms include several suitable for families and many have lovely views over the bay. Regular entertainment is held and there are comfortable lounge and bar areas.

ROOMS: 28 rms (2 bth 17 shr) (12 fmly) s £29; d £46-£50 (incl. bkfst) * LB Off peak **MEALS:** V meals Coffee am Tea pm **FACILITIES:** CTV in all bedrooms Xmas **SERVICES:** Air conditioning 7P **NOTES:** No dogs Closed Jan-Feb **CARDS:**

LLANDUDNO Conwy **Map 06 SH78**

★ *Quinton*

36 Church Walks LL30 2HN

Quality Percentage Score: 62%

☎ 01492 876879 & 875086 🖷 01492 876879

Dir: *150yds from St George's church*

Situated in a quiet side road and only a short walk from the town, this personally owned and run hotel offers well equipped bedrooms, a comfortable lounge and a basement bar with pool table.

ROOMS: 13 rms (4 bth 6 shr) (7 fmly) **MEALS:** Coffee am Tea pm **FACILITIES:** CTV in all bedrooms STV Pool table **SERVICES:** 10P **NOTES:** No smoking in restaurant

LLANDUDNO JUNCTION Conwy **Map 06 SH77**

⇧ Travel Inn

Afon Conway, Llandudno Junction LL28 5LB

☎ 01492 583320 🖷 01492 583514

Dir: *off the A55 at rdbt of A547 Conwy road and A470 to Betws-y-coed*

This modern building offers accommodation in smart, spacious and well equipped bedrooms, all with en-suite bathrooms. Refreshments may be taken at the nearby family restaurant. For details about current prices consult the Contents Page under Hotel Groups for the Travel Inn phone number.

ROOMS: 40 en suite (bth/shr) d £39.95 *

LLANELLI Carmarthenshire **Map 02 SN50**

★★★ Diplomat Hotel

Felinfoel SA15 3PJ

Quality Percentage Score: 66%

☎ 01554 756156 🖷 01554 751649

Dir: *from M4 exit junct 48 onto A4138 then B4303 hotel in 0.75m on the right*

A Victorian mansion in several acres of mature grounds. Public rooms include good lounge and bar areas, a large function suite

contd.

New AA Guides for the Millennium are featured on page 24

and fully equipped leisure centre. Bedrooms are well appointed and available in the mansion and the nearby coach house.
ROOMS: 23 en suite (bth/shr) 8 annexe en suite (bth/shr) (2 fmly) s £58.50-£65; d £78.50-£85 (incl. bkfst) * LB Off peak **MEALS:** Lunch £7.95-£10.95 & alc High tea £5.95 Dinner £8.95-£15.95 & alc V meals Coffee am Tea pm **FACILITIES:** CTV in all bedrooms Indoor swimming pool (heated) Sauna Solarium Gym Jacuzzi/spa Wkly live entertainment Xmas **CONF:** Thtr 250 Class 100 Board 100 Del £88 * **SERVICES:** Lift 250P **NOTES:** Last d 9.45pm **CARDS:**

LLANELLI Carmarthenshire — Map 02 SN50

★★ *Ashburnham*

Ashburnham Rd, Pembrey SA16 0TH
Quality Percentage Score: 66%
☎ 01554 834343 & 834455 Fax 01554 834483
Dir: *M4 junct 48, A4138 to Llanelli, A484 West to Pembrey, look out for road sign as entering village*

A friendly hotel in Pembrey with nineteenth century architecture, to the west of Llanelli. Amelia Earhart stayed here at the end of her historic Atlantic flight of 1928, and doubtless enjoyed her stay. Today, the bright bar and restaurant serve bar meals and a carte menu. Bedrooms have modern furnishings and facilities, family rooms are also available.
ROOMS: 12 en suite (bth/shr) (2 fmly) **MEALS:** V meals Coffee am Tea pm **FACILITIES:** CTV in all bedrooms STV Pool table **CONF:** Thtr 150 Class 150 Board 80 **SERVICES:** Night porter 100P **NOTES:** No smoking in restaurant Last d 9.30pm RS 25 Dec
CARDS:

LLANELLI Carmarthenshire — Map 02 SN50

★★ Miramar

158 Station Rd SA15 1YU
Quality Percentage Score: 65%
☎ 01554 754726 & 773607 Fax 01554 772454
Dir: *take junct 48 on M4. Follow road to Llanelli. In Llanelli follow railway station signs. Hotel is adjacent to the station*

A family-run hotel located opposite the railway station and conveniently near the town centre. Accommodation is well maintained and comfortable with modern facilities. There is a cheerful bar and two restaurants with an extensive choice of dishes, including a number of Portuguese specialities. Secure car-parking is an additional asset.
ROOMS: 10 rms (1 bth 7 shr) s £17-£24; d £30-£40 (incl. bkfst) * Off peak **MEALS:** Lunch £3-£12 & alc Dinner £3-£12 & alc International Cuisine V meals **FACILITIES:** CTV in all bedrooms **SERVICES:** 10P **NOTES:** No dogs (ex guide dogs) No smoking area in restaurant
CARDS:

LLANFAIRPWLLGWYNGYLL See Anglesey, Isle of

LLANFYLLIN Powys — Map 06 SJ11

★★ Cain Valley

High St SY22 5AQ
Quality Percentage Score: 67%
☎ 01691 648366 Fax 01691 648307
Dir: *at the end of A490 - Llanfillin, 12m from Welshpool. Hotel is situated in the centre of town on the square, car park at the rear*

A family run, grade II listed coaching inn with exposed beams and a Jacobean staircase. The comfortable accommodation includes family rooms. Quaint public areas include a choice of bars where a range of food is available. Alternatively, diners can choose from the extensive restaurant carte.
ROOMS: 13 en suite (bth/shr) (3 fmly) s £36-£39; d £59-£65 (incl. bkfst) LB Off peak **MEALS:** Lunch £6.95-£8.50 V meals Coffee am **FACILITIES:** CTV in all bedrooms **SERVICES:** 12P **NOTES:** No smoking in restaurant Closed 24-25 Dec **CARDS:**

LLANGAMMARCH WELLS Powys — Map 03 SN94

The Premier Collection

★★★ Lake Country House

PRIDE OF BRITAIN MEMBER

LD4 4BS
☎ 01591 620202 & 620474
Fax 01591 620457
Dir: *from Builth Wells head W on A483 to Garth (6m approx) turn left for Llangammarch Wells follow signs for hotel*

Perched on a hillside this country house hotel comes complete with golf course, lake and river. Lavish afternoon teas are served in the expansive lounge where a log fire burns on winter days. In addition to the high ceilinged restaurant there is a separate bar and also a billiard room. Bedrooms are individually decorated and with many extra comforts as standard. The kitchen upholds a good standard of cuisine.
ROOMS: 19 en suite (bth/shr) (1 fmly) No smoking in 6 bedrooms s £80-£100; d £120-£210 (incl. bkfst) * LB Off peak **MEALS:** Lunch £17.50 Dinner £30 English & French Cuisine Coffee am Tea pm **FACILITIES:** CTV in all bedrooms Golf 9 Tennis (hard) Fishing Snooker Croquet lawn Putting green Clay pigeon shooting Xmas **CONF:** Thtr 80 Class 30 Board 25 Del from £95 * **SERVICES:** Night porter 72P **NOTES:** No coaches No smoking in restaurant Last d 9pm **CARDS:**

LLANGOLLEN Denbighshire — Map 07 SJ24

see also **Glyn Ceiriog**

★★★ Bryn Howel

Best Western

LL20 7UW
Quality Percentage Score: 65%
☎ 01978 860331 Fax 01978 860119
Dir: *2m E of Llangollen on A539*

Built in 1896, this hotel is set in well tended gardens and enjoys magnificent views across the Vale of Llangollen. It provides attractive, modern, and thoughtfully equipped accommodation. The restaurant overlooks well tended gardens with a backdrop of mountains beyond, and there are comfortable lounges where guests can relax after dinner.
ROOMS: 36 en suite (bth/shr) s £71.50; d £90 * LB Off peak **MEALS:** Lunch £14.95 & alc High tea fr £5alc Dinner fr £21alc V meals Coffee am Tea pm **FACILITIES:** CTV in all bedrooms STV Fishing Sauna Solarium Pool table Croquet lawn Xmas **CONF:** Thtr 250 Class 60 Board 50 Del from £79 * **SERVICES:** Lift 200P **NOTES:** No dogs (ex guide dogs) No smoking in restaurant Last d 9pm
CARDS:

LLANGOLLEN Denbighshire — Map 07 SJ24

★★★ *The Wild Pheasant Hotel & Restaurant*

Berwyn Rd LL20 8AD
Quality Percentage Score: 64%
☎ 01978 860629 Fax 01978 861837

A professionally run hotel providing smart modern accommodation. Bedrooms are well equipped, several with four-poster beds. The reception area, modelled as an old village square, has comfortable seating areas. There is a choice of bars and a range of eating options including a formal restaurant. A self-contained function suite is available.

ROOMS: 34 en suite (bth/shr) (2 fmly) **MEALS:** Welsh & Continental Cuisine V meals Coffee am Tea pm **FACILITIES:** CTV in all bedrooms **CONF:** Thtr 200 Class 120 Board 50 **SERVICES:** 250P **NOTES:** No dogs (ex guide dogs) No smoking in restaurant Last d 9.30pm
CARDS:

LLANGOLLEN Denbighshire — Map 07 SJ24

★★★ Hand

Bridge St LL20 8PL
Quality Percentage Score: 61%
☎ 01978 860303 Fax 01978 861277

***Dir:** from A539, turn right over bridge, drive up Castle St, at lights turn left onto A5 towards Oswestry, hotel car park is 2nd turning on left hand side*

Situated close to the town centre and overlooking the River Dee, this 18th-century former coaching inn has gardens which lead down to the river, and to which the hotel has fishing rights. The majority of bedrooms have been refurbished, several to a very high standard although others are slightly more modest. A good standard of cuisine is provided in the restaurant, which has river views, or lighter meals and snacks are available in the hotel bar. Staff throughout are friendly and helpful.

ROOMS: 58 en suite (bth/shr) (3 fmly) No smoking in 11 bedrooms s £65; d £80 (incl. bkfst) * LB Off peak **MEALS:** Sunday Lunch £6.75-£8.50 Dinner £12.50-£14.95 English & Continental Cuisine V meals Coffee am Tea pm **FACILITIES:** CTV in all bedrooms Fishing Wkly live entertainment Xmas **CONF:** Thtr 100 Class 50 Board 50 Del from £55 * **SERVICES:** Night porter 40P **NOTES:** No smoking in restaurant Last d 8.30pm **CARDS:**

LLANGOLLEN Denbighshire — Map 07 SJ24

★★★ The Royal

Bridge St LL20 8PG
Quality Percentage Score: 61%
☎ 01978 860202 Fax 01978 861824

***Dir:** from A5 to Llangollen. Turn right into Castle St. Hotel is on junct with Bridge St. From Wrexham take A539 Llangollen, turn left across Bridge*

This traditional hotel, where Queen Victoria once stayed, is situated in the centre of the town overlooking the River Dee. The most recently refurbished bedrooms are comfortable and have been attractively decorated. All rooms have modern facilities and several have river views. The restaurant also overlooks the river as does the comfortable lounge. There are two bars, one in a modern theme, the other more in character with the age of the hotel. Staff are friendly and guests are assured of a warm welcome. The hotel has its own car park, opposite.

ROOMS: 33 en suite (bth/shr) (3 fmly) No smoking in 8 bedrooms s £55-£60; d £60-£80 * LB Off peak **MEALS:** Sunday Lunch £7.95-£9.95 Dinner fr £13.95 International & British Cuisine V meals Coffee am Tea pm **FACILITIES:** CTV in all bedrooms Fishing Pool table Xmas **CONF:** Thtr 70 Class 30 Board 20 Del from £95 * **SERVICES:** 20P **NOTES:** No smoking in restaurant Last d 9.30pm
CARDS:

LLANGYBI Monmouthshire — Map 03 ST39

★★★★ Cwrt Bleddyn Hotel & Country Club

NP5 1PG
Quality Percentage Score: 70%
☎ 01633 450521 Fax 01633 450220

***Dir:** from M4 junct 25 or 26, follow road through Caerleon. Hotel is 3m N on the road to Usk*

Cwrt Bleddyn is an attractive Victorian building set in parkland. Most of the bedrooms are smartly modernised; some have four-posters and carved oak furniture, and four are in a separate cottage, but all have many extras. There is a fine leisure complex, and Jesters restaurant is a colourful setting for a menu that makes the most of local produce.

ROOMS: 29 en suite (bth/shr) 4 annexe en suite (bth/shr) (4 fmly) No smoking in 9 bedrooms s fr £99; d fr £145 (incl. bkfst) * LB Off peak **MEALS:** Lunch £10.95-£13.95 Dinner £13.75-£24.50alc Welsh & European Cuisine V meals Coffee am Tea pm **FACILITIES:** CTV in all bedrooms STV Indoor swimming pool (heated) Tennis (hard) Squash Sauna Solarium Gym Jacuzzi/spa Boules Clay pigeon shooting Beauty salon Table tennis Xmas **CONF:** Thtr 200 Class 50 Board 40 **SERVICES:** Night porter 100P **NOTES:** No dogs (ex guide dogs) No coaches No smoking in restaurant Last d 10pm **CARDS:**

LLANIDLOES Powys — Map 06 SN98

★★ *Red Lion Hotel*

Long Bridge St SY18 6EE
Quality Percentage Score: 61%
☎ 01686 412270 & 413120

***Dir:** off A470*

The Red Lion is located in the centre of this peaceful Mid-Wales market town. Completely refurbished over recent years it provides modern pine-furnished bedrooms and these are equipped with telephones and remote-controlled televisions. The bars are spacious and welcoming and there is an attractive restaurant where a carte and fixed-price menu supplements the

contd.

less expensive bar food. Real ale is a speciality here and one of these, called 'Cobblers', is brewed on the premises.
ROOMS: 5 en suite (shr) 2 annexe en suite (shr) No smoking in all bedrooms **MEALS:** International Cuisine V meals Coffee am Tea pm **FACILITIES:** CTV in all bedrooms Pool table **SERVICES:** 12P
NOTES: Last d 9.30pm **CARDS:** 😊 ▬ ≖ ▦

☰ LLANRWST Conwy · Map 06 SH76
☰ see also **Betws-y-Coed**
★★★ *Maenan Abbey*
Maenan LL26 0UL
Quality Percentage Score: 62%
☎ 01492 660247 📠 01492 660734
Dir: 3m N on A470
Built as an abbey in 1850 on the site of a 13th-century monastery, now a popular venue for weddings. The grounds and magnificent galleried staircase make an ideal backdrop for photographs. Bedrooms are equipped with modern facilities, and a wide range of food is served in the hotel's two bars.
ROOMS: 12 en suite (bth/shr) (2 fmly) **MEALS:** Welsh, English & French Cuisine V meals Coffee am Tea pm **FACILITIES:** CTV in all bedrooms Fishing Clay pigeon shooting Wkly live entertainment **CONF:** Class 50 Board 50 **SERVICES:** 60P **NOTES:** Last d 8.45pm
CARDS: 😊 ▬ ≖ 💷

☰ LLANRWST Conwy · Map 06 SH76
★★ *Meadowsweet*
Station Rd LL26 0DS
Quality Percentage Score: 66%
☎ 01492 642111 📠 01492 642111
Dir: on the main A470 through Llanrwst
This small friendly hotel on the northern outskirts of the town is convenient for many local attractions such as Snowdonia National Park, Bodnant Gardens, Conwy and Llandudno. Rooms are spacious with modern facilities, there is a pleasant bar with an open fire. The attractive dining room offers both fixed-price and carte menus.
ROOMS: 10 en suite (shr) (3 fmly) **MEALS:** V meals **FACILITIES:** CTV in all bedrooms **SERVICES:** 9P **NOTES:** Last d 9.30pm
CARDS: 😊 ▬ ≖ ▦ ☒ 💷

☰ LLANTWIT MAJOR Vale of Glamorgan · Map 03 SS96
★★✧ **West House Country Hotel & Restaurant**
West St CF61 1SP
Quality Percentage Score: 70%
☎ 01446 792406 & 793726 📠 01446 796147
Dir: A48 for 10m at sign 'Llantwit Major', turn left onto B4268, at rdbt go straight over and under bridge, 1st right, follow road into West Street
Tucked away in a quiet street in the small town of Llantwit Major, this charming 16th-century building is a friendly, privately owned hotel. The bedrooms vary in size and style, and all are well equipped. The public areas are comfortably furnished and include a pleasant conservatory lounge which is licensed for marriage ceremonies.
ROOMS: 21 en suite (bth/shr) s £48-£55; d £62.50-£69.50 (incl. bkfst) * LB Off peak **MEALS:** Lunch £5-£12.50 High tea £3.50-£8.50 Dinner £7-£15.50 & alc English & French Cuisine V meals Coffee am Tea pm **FACILITIES:** CTV in all bedrooms STV **CONF:** Thtr 40 Class 70 Board 16 Del from £85 * **SERVICES:** Night porter 60P **NOTES:** No smoking in restaurant Last d 9.15pm **CARDS:** 😊 ▬ ≖ ▦ ☒ 💷

☰ LLANWDDYN Powys · Map 06 SJ01
★★★✸✸✸ ⚑ *Lake Vyrnwy*
Lake Vyrnwy SY10 0LY
Quality Percentage Score: 72%
☎ 01691 870692 📠 01691 870259
Dir: on A4393, 200yds past dam
Built at the end of the last century, this fine country house hotel lies in 26,000 acres of mature woodland above Lake Vyrnwy. It provides a wide range of bedrooms, most with superb views and many with four-poster beds and balconies. The extensive public rooms are elegantly furnished and include a choice of bars. The Tavern bar serves inexpensive meals and the main restaurant offers more formal dining. Fishing and shooting are available and the hotel holds a licence for performing civil marriages.
ROOMS: 35 en suite (bth/shr) (4 fmly) **MEALS:** V meals Coffee am Tea pm **FACILITIES:** CTV in all bedrooms Tennis (hard) Fishing Riding Game/Clay shooting Sailing Cycling Archery Quad trekking **CONF:** Thtr 120 Class 60 Board 40 **SERVICES:** 70P **NOTES:** No smoking in restaurant Last d 9.30pm **CARDS:** 😊 ▬ ≖ ▦ ☒ 💷

☰ LLANWRTYD WELLS Powys · Map 03 SN84
★★✸✸✸ **Carlton House**
Dolycoed Rd LD5 4RA
Quality Percentage Score: 73%
☎ 01591 610248 📠 01591 610242
Dir: centre of town
At the heart of this very individual small hotel is the cooking of Mary Ann Gilchrist, whose renown has spread far beyond the surrounding Mid-Wales countryside. Front of house is the province of husband Alan, who is an eloquent advocate for both his wife's cooking and his carefully compiled selection of wines. The bedrooms are striking in their decoration, each being appointed to an individual theme with high levels of comfort. The Edwardian origins of the house are reflected in the period furnishings of the lounge where a log fire burns during the colder weather.
ROOMS: 7 rms (5 bth/shr) (2 fmly) s £30-£40; d £60-£75 (incl. bkfst) * LB Off peak **MEALS:** Lunch £12-£15alc Dinner £16.50-£19.95 & alc V meals **FACILITIES:** CTV in all bedrooms Pony trekking Mountain biking **NOTES:** No coaches No smoking in restaurant Last d 8.30pm
CARDS: 😊 ≖ ▦ ☒ 💷

☰ LLANWRTYD WELLS Powys · Map 03 SN84
★★ **Lasswade Country House Hotel**
Station Rd LD5 4RW
Quality Percentage Score: 68%
☎ 01591 610515 📠 01591 610611
Dir: turn off A483 toward station Llangammarch Well, 200yds on right
An Edwardian country house set on the edge of town, Lasswade commands excellent countryside views. Bedrooms are comfortably furnished and feature thoughtful extra facilities. Dinner can be taken in the elegant dining room or in the bright conservatory. Guests can relax and take drinks in the lounge. Also on offer are rough shooting and trout fishing. The hotel is non-smoking throughout.
ROOMS: 8 en suite (bth/shr) No smoking in all bedrooms s £36.50; d £63.50 (incl. bkfst) * LB Off peak **MEALS:** V meals **FACILITIES:** CTV in all bedrooms STV Sauna **SERVICES:** 10P **NOTES:** No dogs No coaches No children 14yrs No smoking in restaurant
CARDS: 😊 ≖ ▦ ☒ 💷

L

≡ **LLYSWEN** Powys   **Map 03 SO13**

The Premier Collection

★★★★ ❀❀❀ ⚓ **Llangoed Hall**
LD3 0YP
☎ 01874 754525 🖷 01874 754545
Dir: follow A470 through village of Llyswen for 2m.
Hotel drive on right hand side
This imposing, largely Edwardian country house offers an exterior remodelled by Clough Williams-Ellis (of Portmeirion fame). Inside it is Sir Bernard Ashley's uncompromising touch that is responsible for a splendid balance between comfort, grandeur and interest. Wood-burning open fires and deep-cushioned sofas invite guests to admire the wealth of artwork, antiques, and eclectic artefacts that adorn dayrooms, corridors, and library. The bedrooms are appointed with a complementary mix of Laura Ashley designs and antiques together with smart bathrooms. Chef Ben Davies matches the opulent surroundings with some accomplished, imaginative cooking.
ROOMS: 23 en suite (bth) s £175-£385; d £205-£415 (incl. bkfst) * LB Off peak **MEALS:** Lunch £18-£21.50 & alc Dinner £35 & alc British & French Cuisine V meals Coffee am Tea pm
FACILITIES: CTV in all bedrooms STV Tennis (hard) Fishing Croquet lawn Mazes Clay pigeon shooting Xmas **CONF:** Thtr 60 Class 30 Board 28 Del from £155 * **SERVICES:** Night porter 85P
NOTES: No dogs (ex guide dogs) No coaches No children 8yrs No smoking in restaurant Last d 9.30pm
CARDS: 💳 ■ ■ ▣ ■ 💳 ⚏

≡ **LLYSWEN** Powys   **Map 03 SO13**
★★❀ **Griffin Inn**
LD3 0UR
Quality Percentage Score: 70%
☎ 01874 754241 🖷 01874 754592
Dir: on A470
A true country inn with log fires in the bar and a hearty menu of local game and other produce. Richard and Di Stockton offer a warm welcome and have attracted a loyal following. The bedrooms vary in size, all are prettily decorated and sympathetically furnished.
ROOMS: 8 rms (7 bth/shr) s fr £45; d £70-£80 (incl. bkfst) * LB Off peak **MEALS:** V meals Coffee am **FACILITIES:** CTV in all bedrooms Fishing **SERVICES:** 14P **NOTES:** No coaches No smoking in restaurant
CARDS: 💳 ■ ■ ▣ ■ 💳 ⚏

≡ **MACHYNLLETH** Powys   **Map 06 SH70**
≡ see also **Eglwysfach**
★★ **Wynnstay Arms**
Maengwyn St SY20 8AE
Quality Percentage Score: 64%
☎ 01654 702941 🖷 01654 703884
Dir: at junct of A487/A489
Long established, this hotel lies in the centre of the historic town. Bedrooms are equipped with modern facilities and upgrading is almost complete. Its bars are popular locally and a good range of food is available. The restaurant is home to more formal dining, guests choosing from a sizeable fixed price menu.
ROOMS: 23 en suite (bth/shr) (3 fmly) No smoking in 7 bedrooms s £45; d £70-£84 (incl. bkfst) * LB Off peak **MEALS:** Lunch £9 Dinner £9.95-£15.95alc English & Welsh Cuisine V meals Coffee am Tea pm
FACILITIES: CTV in all bedrooms **CONF:** Thtr 40 Class 20 Board 24
SERVICES: 30P **NOTES:** No smoking in restaurant Last d 9pm
CARDS: 💳 ■ ▣ ■ 💳 ⚏

≡ **MAGOR MOTORWAY SERVICE AREA**   **Map 03 ST48**
≡ Monmouthshire
⌂ **Comfort Inn**
Magor Service Area NP26 3YL
☎ 01633 881887 🖷 01633 881896
Dir: junct 23A M4
Operating as part of the Magor Services area, this modern lodge is located at Junction 23A of the M4 motorway. It provides a variety of well maintained accommodation, including family rooms and bedrooms suitable for travellers with disabilities. A meeting room is also available.
ROOMS: 43 en suite (bth/shr) d £44.95 * **CONF:** Thtr 24 Board 12

≡ **MALLWYD** Gwynedd   **Map 06 SH81**
★ **Brigand's Inn**
SY20 9HJ
Quality Percentage Score: 63%
☎ 01650 531208 🖷 01650 531460
Dir: junction of A470 and A458
This 15th-century coaching inn offers private fishing, country walks and shooting parties. Exposed timbers and uneven floors still feature, open fires burn during the colder months. Bedrooms include several suitable for families. There is a cosy bar and a comfortable character lounge.
ROOMS: 11 rms (5 bth 3 shr) (2 fmly) s £20-£28; d £40-£46 (incl. bkfst) * LB Off peak **MEALS:** Lunch £4.95-£7.95 High tea £2-£2.95 Dinner £17-£18.50 & alc V meals Coffee am Tea pm **FACILITIES:** Fishing Shooting Xmas **SERVICES:** 50P **NOTES:** No smoking area in restaurant Last d 9.15pm **CARDS:** 💳 ■ 💳 ⚏

≡ **MENAI BRIDGE** See Anglesey, Isle of

≡ **MERTHYR TYDFIL** Merthyr Tydfil   **Map 03 SO00**
≡ see also **Nant-Ddu**
★★★ **Tregenna**
Park Ter CF47 8RF
Quality Percentage Score: 138%
☎ 01685 723627 & 382055 🖷 01685 721951
Just to the north of the town centre, this family-run hotel provides well equipped, modern accommodation. The attractive ground floor public areas include a traditionally furnished restaurant which serves a good selection of wholesome dishes
contd.

with bar meals also available. Family and four-poster rooms are available.
ROOMS: 24 en suite (bth/shr) (9 fmly) No smoking in 2 bedrooms s £47-£57; d £57-£59 (incl. bkfst) * LB Off peak **MEALS:** Lunch £8.50-£15 & alc High tea £3.50-£6 Dinner £8.50-£15 & alc English, Indian, Italian & Philippino Cuisine V meals Coffee am Tea pm **FACILITIES:** CTV in all bedrooms STV Xmas **CONF:** Thtr 70 Class 70 Board 30 Del from £73 * **SERVICES:** Night porter 60P **NOTES:** No smoking area in restaurant Last d 10pm **CARDS:** ● ■ ■ ■ ■ ■

▤ MERTHYR TYDFIL Merthyr Tydfil   Map 03 SO00
⌂ **Travel Inn**
Pentrebach CF48 4BD
☎ 01443 693616 ▤ 01443 690188
Dir: from M4 junct 32 follow A470 to Merthyr Tydfil. At 2nd rdbt turn right to Pentrebach, follow signs to Ind Estate
This modern building offers accommodation in smart, spacious and well equipped bedrooms, all with en-suite bathrooms. Refreshments may be taken at the nearby family restaurant. For details about current prices consult the Contents Page under Hotel Groups for the Travel Inn phone number.
ROOMS: 40 en suite (bth/shr) d £39.95 *

▤ MILFORD HAVEN Pembrokeshire   Map 02 SM90
★★ *Lord Nelson*
Hamilton Ter SA73 3AW
Quality Percentage Score: 61%
☎ 01646 695341 ▤ 01646 694026
Dir: follow signs for railway station and docks
With fine views over the harbour and estuary from many bedrooms, this hotel (opened in 1795) was renamed after a stay here by Lord Nelson. Many types of bedroom are available, some are suitable for families and one has a four-poster bed. Public areas include the very popular Hamilton Bar, the Trafalgar Suite restaurant and a meeting room.
ROOMS: 32 en suite (bth/shr) (1 fmly) No smoking in 2 bedrooms **MEALS:** English & Italian Cuisine V meals Coffee am **FACILITIES:** CTV in all bedrooms Pool table Wkly live entertainment **CONF:** Class 40 **SERVICES:** Night porter 26P **NOTES:** No dogs (ex guide dogs) Last d 9.30pm Closed 25 Dec **CARDS:** ● ■ ■ ■ ■ ■

▤ MISKIN Rhondda Cynon Taff   Map 03 ST08
★★★★❀❀ **Miskin Manor**
Groes Faen, Pontyclun CF72 8ND
Quality Percentage Score: 71%
☎ 01443 224204 ▤ 01443 237606
Dir: leave M4 at junct 34 & follow hotel signs - 300yds on left
An imposing manor house in 20 acres of grounds and gardens. Many bedrooms are refurbished to a high standard, recent additions in former stables and cottages are very impressive. Public areas are attractive and elegant, the restaurant serves imaginative cooking. Frederick's health club has leisure facilities and a bar/bistro. Conference rooms are available.
ROOMS: 34 en suite (bth/shr) 8 annexe en suite (bth/shr) s £90-£110; d £120-£145 (incl. bkfst) * LB Off peak **MEALS:** Lunch £8.95-£25.95 & alc High tea £2.95-£10alc Dinner £25.95-£35 & alc V meals Coffee am Tea pm **FACILITIES:** CTV in all bedrooms STV Indoor swimming pool (heated) Squash Sauna Solarium Gym Croquet lawn Jacuzzi/spa Xmas **CONF:** Thtr 160 Class 60 Board 65 **SERVICES:** Night porter 200P **NOTES:** No dogs (ex guide dogs) No coaches No smoking in restaurant Last d 9.45pm **CARDS:** ● ■ ■ ■ ■

▤ MOLD Flintshire   Map 07 SJ26
▤ see also **Northop Hall**
★★★ **Beaufort Park Hotel**
Alltami Rd, New Brighton CH7 6RQ
Quality Percentage Score: 64%
☎ 01352 758646 ▤ 01352 757132
Dir: A55 - take Mold slip road, A494. Through Alltami traffic lights. Over mini rdbt by petrol station towards Mold, A5119. Hotel 100yds on right
With the North Wales Expressway just a short drive away, this large hotel attracts a business and holiday clientele. Accommodation is spacious and modern, and there are plenty of meeting and function rooms. Guests have the use of the hotel's squash courts and games room, and there is a wide range of eating options and several popular bars.
ROOMS: 106 en suite (bth/shr) (4 fmly) No smoking in 10 bedrooms s fr £70; d fr £85 (incl. bkfst) * LB Off peak **MEALS:** Lunch £6.50-£12.50 Dinner fr £19.50 International Cuisine V meals Coffee am Tea pm **FACILITIES:** CTV in all bedrooms Squash Pool table Darts, Games Room Wkly live entertainment Xmas **CONF:** Thtr 250 Class 120 Board 50 Del from £80 * **SERVICES:** Night porter 200P **NOTES:** No smoking area in restaurant Last d 9.30pm **CARDS:** ● ■ ■ ■ ■ ■

▤ MOLD Flintshire   Map 07 SJ26
★★ *Bryn Awel*
Denbigh Rd CH7 1BL
Quality Percentage Score: 64%
☎ 01352 758622 ▤ 01352 758625
Dir: NW edge of town, on A541
This small privately run hotel is in easy reach of the town centre. It provides well equipped modern accommodation. Some bedrooms are in a purpose built annexe. Public areas comprise a spacious lounge bar and attractive restaurant, a good choice is offered from the carte menu and an extensive selection of bar meals.
ROOMS: 8 rms (4 bth 3 shr) 10 annexe en suite (bth/shr) No smoking in 5 bedrooms **MEALS:** English & Continental Cuisine V meals Coffee am Tea pm **FACILITIES:** CTV in all bedrooms **CONF:** Thtr 35 Class 20 Board 20 **SERVICES:** 44P **NOTES:** Last d 9.30pm **CARDS:** ● ■ ■ ■ ■ ■

▤ MONMOUTH Monmouthshire   Map 03 SO51
▤ see also **Whitebrook**
★★ **Riverside**
Cinderhill St NP25 3EY
Quality Percentage Score: 70%
☎ 01600 715577 & 713236 ▤ 01600 712668
Dir: leave A40 signposted Rockfield & Monmouth hotel on left beyond garage & before rdbt
Close to the famous 13th-century bridge, this privately owned hotel offers comfortable accommodation and a relaxed atmosphere. The well equipped bedrooms include one ground floor room, with its own access. Facilities include a conservatory lounge, a pleasant bar and an attractive restaurant providing a fixed price menu and a short carte.
ROOMS: 17 en suite (bth/shr) (2 fmly) No smoking in 2 bedrooms s £39-£48; d £45-£71 (incl. bkfst) * LB Off peak **MEALS:** Sunday Lunch £7.95-£9.95 Dinner £12.95-£16.95 European Cuisine V meals Coffee am Tea pm **FACILITIES:** CTV in all bedrooms STV Pool table Xmas **CONF:** Thtr 200 Class 100 Board 80 **SERVICES:** 30P **NOTES:** No smoking in restaurant Last d 9.15pm **CARDS:** ● ■ ■ ■ ■

MONTGOMERY Powys — Map 07 SO29

★★ Dragon

MINOTEL Great Britain

SY15 6PA
Quality Percentage Score: 69%
☎ 01686 668359 ▯ 01686 668287
Dir: *behind the Town Hall*

This fine 17th-century coaching inn is located in the centre of the town. Beams and timbers from the nearby castle, which was destroyed by Cromwell, are visible in the lounge and bar. A wide choice of soundly prepared, wholesome food is available and there are also bar meals. Bedrooms are well equipped and include some suitable for families.

ROOMS: 20 en suite (bth/shr) (6 fmly) No smoking in 5 bedrooms s £44-£54; d £74 (incl. bkfst) * LB Off peak **MEALS:** Lunch £11.95-£17.95 & alc Dinner £17.95 & alc Welsh & French Cuisine V meals Coffee am Tea pm **FACILITIES:** CTV in all bedrooms Indoor swimming pool (heated) Wkly live entertainment Xmas **CONF:** Thtr 40 Class 30 Board 25 **SERVICES:** 21P **NOTES:** No smoking area in restaurant Last d 9pm **CARDS:**

MUMBLES (NEAR SWANSEA) Swansea — Map 02 SS68

★★ St Anne's

Western Ln SA3 4EY
Quality Percentage Score: 67%
☎ 01792 369147 ▯ 01792 360537
Dir: *follow A483/A4067 along coastal rd to Mumbles, on reaching village drive straight over mini rdbt and cont along rd, Western Lane is 3rd right*

Perched on the hillside above the town this privately-owned hotel enjoys some superb views over Swansea Bay. The accommodation is modern and bedrooms are well maintained with good facilities. Many offer an outlook over the sea as do the public areas that include a spacious lounge with a large picture window. The building was once a convent school and parts of the structure date back to 1823.

ROOMS: 33 en suite (bth/shr) (3 fmly) No smoking in 7 bedrooms s £45-£48; d £64.50 (incl. bkfst) * LB Off peak **MEALS:** Lunch £8.95-£13.95 Dinner £13.75 & alc International Cuisine V meals Coffee am Tea pm **FACILITIES:** CTV in all bedrooms **CONF:** Thtr 100 Class 50 Board 50 Del from £65 * **SERVICES:** 50P **NOTES:** No smoking in restaurant Last d 8.30pm **CARDS:**

NANT-DDU (NEAR MERTHYR TYDFIL) Powys — Map 03 SO01

★★★ Nant Ddu Lodge

Cwm Taf, Nant Ddu CF48 2HY
Quality Percentage Score: 74%
☎ 01685 379111 ▯ 01685 377088
Dir: *6m N of Merthyr Tydfil on main A470 between Merthyr and Brecon*

A fine Georgian House, the rivers Taff and Nant Ddu run through its extensive grounds. In recent years bedrooms and public areas have been transformed to a high standard. The charming bar and bistro areas are the focal point, serving good robust cooking. Meeting rooms are available and there is a comfortable lounge.

ROOMS: 12 en suite (bth/shr) 10 annexe en suite (bth/shr) (3 fmly) s £50-£65; d £69.50-£85 (incl. bkfst) * LB Off peak **MEALS:** Lunch £12.50-£22alc Dinner £12.50-£22alc International Cuisine V meals **FACILITIES:** CTV in all bedrooms **CONF:** Thtr 30 Class 15 Board 20 Del from £70 * **SERVICES:** 60P **NOTES:** No coaches No smoking in restaurant Last d 9.30pm RS 24-30 Dec **CARDS:**

See advert under BRECON

NEATH Neath Port Talbot — Map 03 SS79

★★ Castle Hotel

The Parade SA11 1RB
Quality Percentage Score: 65%
☎ 01639 641119 & 643581 ▯ 01639 641624
Dir: *M4 junct43, follow signs for Neath town centre, 500yds past railway station hotel is situated on right hand side*

Located in the heart of the town, this welcoming coaching inn was reputedly frequented by Lord Nelson; it is also where the Welsh Rugby Union was founded over a century ago. The bars and restaurant are popular local venues and there are function and conference rooms available. The bedrooms are well equipped and generally spacious and some have benefited from quite recent refurbishment.

ROOMS: 28 en suite (bth/shr) (3 fmly) No smoking in 4 bedrooms s £55; d £65 (incl. bkfst) * LB Off peak **MEALS:** Lunch £9.85-£17.05alc Dinner £9.85-£17.05alc English & Continental Cuisine V meals Coffee am Tea pm **FACILITIES:** CTV in all bedrooms STV **CONF:** Thtr 120 Class 75 Board 50 Del from £88 * **SERVICES:** Night porter 26P **NOTES:** No smoking area in restaurant Last d 10pm **CARDS:**

NEVERN Pembrokeshire — Map 02 SN03

★★ Trewern Arms

SA42 0NB
Quality Percentage Score: 64%
☎ 01239 820395 ▯ 01834 811 679
Dir: *off A487 coast road - midway between Cardigan and Fishguard*

Next to the river Nevern, this ivy clad 16th-century inn has a wealth of charm and character, which is enhanced by original features such as the stone flagged floors, exposed stone walls and beamed ceilings in the two bars and the attractively appointed restaurant. The modern bedrooms are spacious and comfortable, including family bedded rooms. A function area caters for up to 100 people.

ROOMS: 10 en suite (bth/shr) (4 fmly) s £35; d £50 (incl. bkfst) * Off peak **MEALS:** Sunday Lunch fr £8.50 Dinner £11-£18alc V meals Coffee am **FACILITIES:** CTV in all bedrooms Fishing Riding Pool table Xmas **SERVICES:** 100P **NOTES:** No dogs Last d 8.45pm **CARDS:**

NEWPORT Newport — Map 03 ST38

★★★★ The Celtic Manor

Coldra Woods NP18 2YA
Quality Percentage Score: 71%
☎ 01633 413000 ▯ 01633 412910
Dir: *leave M4 at junct 24, take A48 towards Newport town centre. Celtic Manor is 1st right turn past Newbridge Networks*

The beautifully restored 19th-century manor house remains the centrepiece of this impressive hotel and leisure complex, situated near Newport. An ambitious expansion of both accommodation and facilities was due to be completed around the time of publication, with significantly enhanced restaurant and leisure facilities, and a third championship standard golf course. Fine

contd.

dining currently takes place in Hedleys Restaurant, where the best of Welsh ingredients are employed to good effect.
ROOMS: 400 en suite (bth/shr) (30 fmly) No smoking in 136 bedrooms s fr £88; d fr £97 (incl. bkfst) * LB Off peak **MEALS:** Lunch £12-£15 High tea £9.50 Dinner £12-£25 Welsh, Continental & Mediterranean Cuisine V meals Tea pm **FACILITIES:** CTV in all bedrooms STV Indoor swimming pool (heated) Golf 54 Snooker Sauna Solarium Gym Pool table Putting green Jacuzzi/spa Golf Academy Wkly live entertainment ch fac Xmas **CONF:** Thtr 1500 Class 150 Board 50 Del from £128 * **SERVICES:** Lift Night porter Air conditioning 1300P **NOTES:** No dogs No smoking area in restaurant Last d 10.30pm
CARDS:

NEWPORT Newport — Map 03 ST38

★★★ Newport Lodge

Bryn Bevan, Brynglas Rd NP20 5QN
Quality Percentage Score: 67%
☎ 01633 821818 Fax 01633 856360

***Dir:** off M4 at junct 26 follow signs Newport Town centre. Turn left after 0.5m onto Malpal Road, up hill for 0.5m to hotel*

On the edge of the town centre, this friendly, personally run hotel has public areas that include a bistro-style restaurant that offers a wide range of freshly prepared dishes. The bedrooms are spacious, have modern facilities and are well presented.
ROOMS: 27 en suite (bth/shr) No smoking in 3 bedrooms s £60-£80; d £75-£95 (incl. bkfst) * LB Off peak **MEALS:** Dinner £15-£20alc British & French Cuisine V meals Coffee am **FACILITIES:** CTV in all bedrooms **CONF:** Thtr 25 Class 20 Board 20 **SERVICES:** Night porter 63P **NOTES:** No children 14yrs No smoking area in restaurant Last d 9.30pm
CARDS:

NEWPORT Newport **Map 03 ST38**
★★★ ***Kings***
High St NP9 1QU
Quality Percentage Score: 64%
☎ 01633 842020 ⎙ 01633 244667
Dir: *from town centre, take left hand road (not flyover) right hand lane to next rdbt, 3rd exit off across front of hotel then left for carpark*
Situated right in the town centre, this privately owned hotel offers comfortable bedroom accommodation and bright spacious public areas. The hotel's main dining room is supplemented by a separate, Chinese restaurant. There are also two bars, function rooms and a ballroom where live music features once a month.
ROOMS: 47 en suite (bth/shr) (15 fmly) No smoking in 10 bedrooms **MEALS:** V meals Coffee am Tea pm **FACILITIES:** CTV in all bedrooms STV **CONF:** Thtr 150 Class 70 Board 50 **SERVICES:** Lift Night porter 50P **NOTES:** No dogs (ex guide dogs) Last d 9.30pm Closed 26 Dec-4 Jan **CARDS:**

See advert on page 939

NEWPORT Newport **Map 03 ST38**
Travel Inn
Coldra Junction, Chepstow Rd NP6 2LX
☎ 01633 411390 ⎙ 01633 411376
Dir: *just N off junct 24 of M4*
This modern building offers accommodation in smart, spacious and well equipped bedrooms, all with en-suite bathrooms. Refreshments may be taken at the nearby family restaurant. For details about current prices consult the Contents Page under Hotel Groups for the Travel Inn phone number.
ROOMS: 63 en suite (bth/shr) d £39.95 *

N

NEWTOWN Powys **Map 06 SO19**
★★ **Elephant & Castle**
Broad St SY16 2BQ
Quality Percentage Score: 64%
☎ 01686 626271 ⎙ 01686 622123
Dir: *turn for Newtown town centre at traffic lights by St Davids Church, this rd meets main St, the hotel is opposite the junction next to the river*
Located beside the River Severn and near the town centre, this privately owned hotel is busy and popular. Bedrooms are well equipped and include several that are located in a separate building accessed from the car park. There is a choice of bars, a range of food options and extensive function facilities. A fitness centre is also provided.
ROOMS: 23 en suite (bth/shr) 11 annexe en suite (bth/shr) (2 fmly) s fr £39; d fr £58 (incl. bkfst) * LB Off peak **MEALS:** Lunch fr £9 Dinner fr £15 V meals Coffee am Tea pm **FACILITIES:** CTV in all bedrooms STV Solarium Gym **CONF:** Thtr 200 Class 100 Board 25 Del from £50 * **SERVICES:** Night porter 15P **NOTES:** No dogs (ex guide dogs) No smoking in restaurant Last d 9.15pm RS 24-26 Dec
CARDS:

NORTHOP Flintshire **Map 07 SJ26**
★★★ ***Soughton Hall***
CH7 6AB
Quality Percentage Score: 75%
☎ 01352 840811 ⎙ 01352 840382
Built as a Bishop's Palace in 1714, this is a truly elegant country house, lovingly restored by John and Rosemary Rodenhurst and surrounded by beautiful gardens. Bedrooms are individually decorated and furnished with fine antiques and rich fabrics. There are several spacious day rooms furnished in keeping with the style of the house. Michael Carney looks after the kitchens and offers an imaginative carte, supplemented by fish dishes in season.
ROOMS: 14 rms (11 bth/shr) (2 fmly) **MEALS:** V meals Coffee am Tea pm **FACILITIES:** CTV in all bedrooms Tennis (hard) Croquet lawn **CONF:** Thtr 60 Class 30 Board 20 Del from £128 * **SERVICES:** Night porter 100P **NOTES:** No dogs (ex guide dogs) No smoking area in restaurant Last d 10.30pm **CARDS:**

NORTHOP HALL Flintshire **Map 07 SJ26**
★★★ **Holiday Inn Garden Court**
Gateway Services, Westbound A55 CH7 6HB
Quality Percentage Score: 67%
☎ 01244 550011 ⎙ 01244 550763
Dir: *from M6 junct 20, follow M56 to Queensferry, follow signs for A55 Conwy. The Hotel is situated 500yrds past the A494 slip road*
This modern hotel is situated on the west bound carriageway of the A55 only a short distance from Chester and provides family accommodation, facilities for disabled persons, an executive suite and non smoking rooms. All are very well equipped and include satellite television, modem links and electronic bedroom locks. English and Continental Cuisine can be enjoyed in the attractive Conservatory Restaurant, which adjoins a comfortable lounge bar and there are also well appointed meeting and banqueting rooms and spacious car parking areas.
ROOMS: 55 en suite (bth/shr) (38 fmly) No smoking in 18 bedrooms d £44.50-£65 * LB Off peak **MEALS:** Lunch £7.95-£9.95 Dinner £12.95-£22.90alc English, French & Italian Cuisine V meals Coffee am Tea pm **FACILITIES:** CTV in all bedrooms STV Xmas **CONF:** Thtr 220 Class 90 Board 40 Del from £79 * **SERVICES:** Night porter 185P **NOTES:** No dogs (ex guide dogs) No smoking area in restaurant Last d 10pm Closed 24-27 December **CARDS:**

NORTHOP HALL Flintshire **Map 07 SJ26**
Travelodge
CH7 6HB
☎ 01244 816473 ⎙ 01244 816473
Dir: *on A55, eastbound*
This modern building offers accommodation in smart, spacious and well equipped bedrooms, all with en-suite bathrooms. Refreshments may be taken at the nearby family restaurant. For details about current prices, consult the Contents Page under Hotel Groups for the Travelodge phone number.
ROOMS: 40 en suite (bth/shr) d fr £39.95 *

PEMBROKE Pembrokeshire **Map 02 SM90**
★★★ **Court**
Lamphey SA71 5NT
Quality Percentage Score: 74%
☎ 01646 672273 ⎙ 01646 672480
Dir: *take A477 to Pembroke. Turn left at Village Milton. In Lamphey village hotel on right*

This fine Georgian mansion lies in several acres of mature

contd.

grounds and landscaped gardens. Bedrooms are well equipped and include several family suites, many located in a nearby converted coach house. Public areas include function and conference rooms and a modern conservatory.
ROOMS: 26 en suite (bth/shr) 11 annexe en suite (bth/shr) (15 fmly) s £69-£79; d £80-£130 (incl. bkfst) * LB Off peak **MEALS:** Sunday Lunch £7.95-£10.95 High tea fr £2.75 Dinner fr £18.95 & alc English & French Cuisine V meals Coffee am Tea pm **FACILITIES:** CTV in all bedrooms STV Indoor swimming pool (heated) Tennis (hard) Sauna Solarium Gym Jacuzzi/spa Yacht charter ch fac Xmas **CONF:** Thtr 80 Class 60 Board 40 Del from £99.50 * **SERVICES:** 50P **NOTES:** No smoking in restaurant Last d 9.30pm
CARDS:

See advert on this page

PEMBROKE Pembrokeshire **Map 02 SM90**
★★ Bethwaite's Lamphey Hall
Lamphey SA71 5NR
Quality Percentage Score: 72%
☎ 01646 672394 01646 672369
Dir: *on A4139 Pembroke/Tenby Road in centre of village, opposite parish church*
The pretty village of Lamphey is the setting for this welcoming family-run hotel. The two restaurants, one of which is an informal bistro, are at the hub of the operation and are popular with locals as well as visitors. Bedrooms are smart and modern and some are on ground floor level. Family bedded rooms are also available. A central lounge and a bar are available for residents.
ROOMS: 10 en suite (bth/shr) (2 fmly) s £35-£50; d £50-£80 (incl. bkfst) * LB Off peak **MEALS:** Lunch fr £8.95 Dinner fr £18.50 & alc English & French Cuisine V meals **FACILITIES:** CTV in all bedrooms ch fac **SERVICES:** 32P **NOTES:** No dogs No coaches No smoking area in restaurant Last d 9pm **CARDS:**

PEMBROKE Pembrokeshire **Map 02 SM90**
★★ *Old Kings Arms*
Main St SA71 4JS
Quality Percentage Score: 61%
☎ 01646 683611 01646 682335
Dir: *situated in Main Street Pembroke. Approach from Carmarthen, Tenby or Pembroke Dock*
A former coaching inn, now a bustling town centre hotel which is very much the heart of local activities. The bars are a popular drinking venue and the restaurant offers some good home-cooking. Surroundings are traditional with stone walls, flagged floors and roaring log fires all in evidence.
ROOMS: 21 en suite (bth/shr) **MEALS:** V meals Coffee am **FACILITIES:** CTV in all bedrooms **SERVICES:** 21P **NOTES:** Last d 10pm Closed 25-26 Dec & 1 Jan **CARDS:**

PEMBROKE DOCK Pembrokeshire **Map 02 SM90**
★★★ *Cleddau Bridge*
Essex Rd SA72 6UT
Quality Percentage Score: 64%
☎ 01646 685961 01646 685746
Dir: *M4 to Camarthen M40 to St Clears A477 to Pembroke Dock at rbut 2nd exit for Haverfordwest via the toll bridge take left before the toll bridge*
Close to the tolls at the end of the Cleddau Bridge, with some fine views over the river, this purpose built hotel provides modern and well equipped accommodation, all located on ground level and with several suites available. It is a very popular venue for weddings and other functions.
ROOMS: 24 en suite (bth/shr) (2 fmly) No smoking in 12 bedrooms **MEALS:** V meals Coffee am Tea pm **FACILITIES:** CTV in all bedrooms STV Outdoor swimming pool Wkly live entertainment **CONF:** Thtr 250 Class 150 Board 60 **SERVICES:** Night porter 120P **NOTES:** No smoking area in restaurant Last d 9.30pm **CARDS:**

PENARTH Vale of Glamorgan **Map 03 ST17**
★ Walton House
37 Victoria Rd CF64 3HY
Quality Percentage Score: 67%
☎ 029 20707782 029 20711012
Dir: *from M4 junct 33 into Penarth, 3rd left off rdbt at town center, through traffic lights, over railway bridge next left Victoria Rd, hotel 500yds*
Located in a quiet residential area, this attractive Victorian house is set in well tended gardens with a convenient car park to the rear. The hotel is family run and offers excellent hospitality. Bedrooms vary in size, and public rooms include a pleasant lounge/bar and traditionally furnished restaurant and breakfast room.
ROOMS: 13 rms (11 bth/shr) (7 fmly) s £27.50-£32.50; d £40-£47 (incl. bkfst) * LB Off peak **MEALS:** Sunday Lunch fr £9.95 High tea fr £3.95 Dinner fr £9.95 & alc English, French & Italian Cuisine V meals Coffee am Tea pm **FACILITIES:** CTV in all bedrooms **CONF:** Class 30 **SERVICES:** 13P **NOTES:** Last d 9pm **CARDS:**

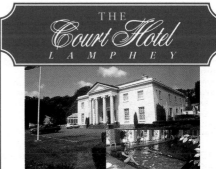

P

PENCOED Bridgend **Map 03 SS98**

★★★ St Mary's Hotel & Country Club

St Marys Golf Club CF35 5EA
Quality Percentage Score: 70%
☎ 01656 861100 & 860280 📠 01656 863400
Dir: *just off junct 35 of M4, on A473*

The stone buildings that comprise this modern hotel and golf course were formerly a 16th-century farmhouse. The two golf courses, 9 and 18 hole, surround the hotel buildings and form a pleasant backdrop to the public areas and bedrooms, many of which look out over the fairways. Inside, there is a choice of bars and Rafters Restaurant with its stone walls and exposed beams. The bedrooms are generous in size and benefit from good quality furnishings.

ROOMS: 24 en suite (bth/shr) (19 fmly) s £64-£89; d £78-£99 (incl. bkfst) * LB Off peak **MEALS:** Lunch £9.95-£15 & alc Dinner £15 & alc International Cuisine V meals Coffee am Tea pm **FACILITIES:** CTV in all bedrooms STV Golf 27 Tennis (hard) Putting green Jacuzzi/spa Floodlit driving range Xmas **CONF:** Thtr 120 Class 60 Board 40 Del £90 * **SERVICES:** Night porter 140P **NOTES:** No dogs (ex guide dogs) Last d 9.30pm **CARDS:**

See advert under BRIDGEND

PENCOED Bridgend **Map 03 SS98**

⌂ Travelodge

Old Mill, Felindre Rd CF3 5HU
☎ 01656 864404 📠 01656 864404
Dir: *on A473*

This modern building offers accommodation in smart, spacious and well equipped bedrooms, all with en-suite bathrooms. Refreshments may be taken at the nearby family restaurant. For details about current prices, consult the Contents Page under Hotel Groups for the Travelodge phone number.

ROOMS: 40 en suite (bth/shr) d £45.95 *

PENYBONT Powys **Map 03 SO16**

★★ Severn Arms

LD1 5UA
Quality Percentage Score: 67%
☎ 01597 851224 & 851344 📠 01597 851693
Dir: *5m from LLandrindod Wells on A44 at junct with A488*

An early 19th-century coaching inn, this friendly, family-run hotel lies in the centre of the village. There is a choice of character bars, a beamed restaurant and a first floor lounge for residents. Bedrooms are equipped with modern facilities and period furnishings add to the traditional character. Each room has a welcoming sherry decanter and even stamped postcards are provided. A full range of bar food is available and the restaurant offers fixed-price and carte menus.

ROOMS: 10 en suite (bth/shr) (6 fmly) s fr £28; d fr £50 (incl. bkfst) * LB Off peak **MEALS:** Sunday Lunch fr £7 Dinner fr £13.90 & alc V meals Coffee am **FACILITIES:** CTV in all bedrooms Fishing Pool table **SERVICES:** 62P **NOTES:** No smoking area in restaurant Last d 9.30pm **CARDS:**

PONTYPRIDD Rhondda Cynon Taff **Map 03 ST08**

★★★ Llechwen Hall

Llanfabon CF37 4HP
Quality Percentage Score: 69%
☎ 01443 742050 & 740305 📠 01443 742189
Dir: *A470 N towards Merthyr Tydfil, at rdbt turn R towards Nelson, at next rdbt turn R onto A4054, turn L next to factory and follow hotel signs*

Over the past nine years, this 17th-century hall has been transformed into an impressive country house hotel. Majestically located on a mountain top, in six acres of its own grounds, there are views of four valleys to be enjoyed. The bedrooms vary in size but are all thoughtfully and individually decorated, some having four-poster beds. The public areas include two eating options with the a la carte restaurant offering good cooking of fresh ingredients with some robust flavours.

ROOMS: 12 en suite (bth/shr) 8 annexe en suite (bth/shr) (4 fmly) No smoking in 8 bedrooms s £43.50-£95; d £53.50-£95 * LB Off peak **MEALS:** Lunch £9.95-£10.95 & alc Dinner £10.95-£18.95 & alc Welsh & French Cuisine V meals Coffee am Tea pm **FACILITIES:** CTV in all bedrooms STV Xmas **CONF:** Thtr 80 Class 30 Board 40 Del £75 * **SERVICES:** 100P **NOTES:** Last d 9.45pm **CARDS:**

PONTYPRIDD Rhondda Cynon Taff **Map 03 ST08**

★★★ Heritage Park

Coed Cae Rd, Trehafod CF37 2NP
Quality Percentage Score: 67%
☎ 01443 687057 📠 01443 687060
Dir: *off A4058, follow signs to the Rhondda Heritage Park*

Situated adjacent to the Rhondda Heritage Park and well located for the South Wales valleys, this modern hotel is equally suitable for the tourist and the business traveller. The spacious bedrooms include many on ground floor level, interconnecting rooms and a room for less able guests. Meals can be taken in the attractive, wood-beamed, Loft Restaurant where a wide range of popular dishes is available. Other facilities include a well equipped leisure suite together with extensive function rooms and conference areas.

ROOMS: 44 en suite (bth/shr) (4 fmly) No smoking in 19 bedrooms s £55-£70; d £69.50-£80 (incl. bkfst) * LB Off peak **MEALS:** Lunch £11 Dinner £15-£16.95 & alc V meals Coffee am Tea pm **FACILITIES:** CTV in all bedrooms STV Indoor swimming pool (heated) Sauna Solarium Gym Jacuzzi/spa Xmas **CONF:** Thtr 220 Class 60 Board 60 Del from £59.50 * **SERVICES:** Night porter 150P **NOTES:** No smoking in restaurant Last d 10pm **CARDS:**

PORT EINON Swansea — Map 02 SS48

★★ ***Culver House***

SA3 1NN

Quality Percentage Score: 64%

☎ 01792 390755

Dir: *in village continue past church turn right at post office, 50yds on turn left, hotel a further 100yds on left*

Just a few hundred yards from the shoreline, this friendly hotel is ideal for those visiting the Gower peninsular. The bedrooms are comfortably furnished and many of them have sea views. The restaurant serves generous homecooking and is supplemented by a bar and lounge.

ROOMS: 10 rms (8 shr) (3 fmly) No smoking in all bedrooms **MEALS:** V meals Coffee am Tea pm **FACILITIES:** CTV in all bedrooms **SERVICES:** 8P **NOTES:** No coaches No smoking in restaurant Last d 7.30pm Closed 1-30 Nov **CARDS:**

PORTHCAWL Bridgend — Map 03 SS87

★★★ **Atlantic**

West Dr CF36 3LT

Quality Percentage Score: 68%

☎ 01656 785011 📠 01656 771877

Dir: *leave M4 junct 35 or 37, follow signs for Porthcawl, on entering Porthcawl follow signs for Seafront/Promenade, hotel on seafront*

A friendly seafront hotel with a popular bar and restaurant. Located a short walk from the town centre, guests can enjoy seafront views from the sun terrace, bright conservatory and some of the bedrooms. The rooms are well kept and decorated, and feature good levels of equipment.

ROOMS: 18 en suite (bth/shr) (2 fmly) **MEALS:** Lunch £9.95-£13.50 & alc Dinner £13.50 & alc European Cuisine V meals Coffee am Tea pm **FACILITIES:** CTV in all bedrooms STV **CONF:** Thtr 50 Class 50 Board 25 Del from £85 * **SERVICES:** Lift 20P **NOTES:** No dogs (ex guide dogs) No coaches Last d 9pm **CARDS:**

PORTHCAWL Bridgend — Map 03 SS87

★★★ **Seabank**

The Promenade CF36 3LU

Quality Percentage Score: 63%

☎ 01656 782261 📠 01656 785363

Dir: *turn off junct 37 M4, follow A4229 to sea front, hotel is located after promenade on the right hand side*

This large privately owned hotel stands on the promenade and overlooks the sea. The well equipped accommodation includes many pleasant rooms with sea views. There is a spacious restaurant, a pleasant bar, and a choice of lounges in which to relax. Other facilities include two function rooms, and a mini gym.

ROOMS: 65 en suite (bth/shr) (2 fmly) No smoking in 15 bedrooms s £49.50-£59.50; d £75-£95 (incl. bkfst) * LB Off peak **MEALS:** Lunch £9.96 & alc Dinner £12.95-£14.95 & alc V meals Coffee am Tea pm **FACILITIES:** CTV in all bedrooms STV Sauna Gym Pool table Jacuzzi/spa Wkly live entertainment Xmas **CONF:** Thtr 250 Class 90 Board 70 Del from £85 * **SERVICES:** Lift Night porter 140P **NOTES:** No dogs (ex guide dogs) No smoking area in restaurant Last d 9.30pm **CARDS:**

See advert under BRIDGEND
See advert on this page

PORTHCAWL Bridgend — Map 03 SS87

★★ ***Glenaub***

50 Mary St CF36 3YA

Quality Percentage Score: 64%

☎ 01656 788242 788846 📠 01656 773649

Dir: *leave M4 junct 37 follow signs for Porthcawl town centre, turn left before Somerfield supermarket, 1st right into carpark*

Located just a short walk from both the town centre and the seafront, this personally run hotel offers comfortable accommodation and a warm welcome. The lounge bar has an attractive conservatory extension and there is a traditionally furnished dining room.

ROOMS: 18 en suite (bth/shr) **MEALS:** International Cuisine V meals Coffee am Tea pm **FACILITIES:** CTV in all bedrooms STV **SERVICES:** 12P **NOTES:** No dogs (ex guide dogs) No coaches Last d 10.30pm **CARDS:**

Symbols and Abbreviations are listed and explained on pages 4 and 5

PORTHCAWL Bridgend — Map 03 SS87
★★ *Rose & Crown*
Heol-y-Capel, Nottage CF36 3ST
Quality Percentage Score: 62%
☎ 01656 784850 Fax 01656 772345
Dir: *take A4229 towards Porthcawl and Nottage*
A popular and friendly traditional inn situated in the pretty village of Nottage on the outskirts of Porthcawl. The bedrooms are attractively decorated, with pine furnishings and modern facilities. The public areas include a choice of bars, a television lounge and a restaurant which also offers a carvery.
ROOMS: 8 en suite (bth) **MEALS:** V meals Coffee am Tea pm **FACILITIES:** CTV in all bedrooms **SERVICES:** 15P **NOTES:** No dogs (ex guide dogs) No smoking in restaurant Last d 9pm
CARDS:

PORTMEIRION Gwynedd — Map 06 SH53
★★★❀❀ The Hotel Portmeirion
LL48 6ET
Quality Percentage Score: 78%
☎ 01766 770000 Fax 01766 771331
Dir: *2m W, Portmeirion village is S off A487*

Nestling under the wooded slopes of the famous Italianate village, (The Village of 'The Prisoner' TV series fame) and looking out over the sandy estuary towards Snowdonia, this hotel must have one of the finest settings in Wales. Many rooms have balconies and private sitting rooms and most are located within the village and command spectacular views. Public areas are elegantly furnished and mostly Welsh-speaking staff offer warm hospitality.
ROOMS: 14 en suite (bth/shr) 25 annexe en suite (bth/shr) (4 fmly) s £85-£125; d £105-£160 * LB Off peak **MEALS:** Lunch £10.50-£15 Dinner £35 V meals **FACILITIES:** CTV in all bedrooms STV Outdoor swimming pool (heated) Tennis (hard) Xmas **CONF:** Thtr 100 **SERVICES:** Night porter 40P **NOTES:** No dogs No coaches
CARDS:

See advert on opposite page

PORT TALBOT Neath Port Talbot — Map 03 SS79
★★★❀ Aberavon Beach
SA12 6QP
Quality Percentage Score: 68%
☎ 01639 884949 Fax 01639 897885
Dir: *M4 junct 41 (A48) and follow signs for Aberavon Beach & Hollywood Park*
This large privately owned seafront hotel has benefited from a gradual programme of refurbishment of bedrooms and public areas. The latter are arranged on the ground floor and include a leisure suite comprising sauna, solarium and pool. The bedrooms are comfortable with modern furnishings and include family rooms. The restaurant is the setting for some bright imaginative cooking from a team led by new chef Wayne Williams.

ROOMS: 52 en suite (bth) (6 fmly) s fr £75; d fr £80 (incl. bkfst) * LB Off peak **MEALS:** Lunch £10-£12.50 Dinner fr £18.50 & alc Welsh, English & French Cuisine V meals Coffee am Tea pm **FACILITIES:** CTV in all bedrooms Indoor swimming pool (heated) Sauna Jacuzzi/spa All weather leisure centre Wkly live entertainment Xmas **CONF:** Thtr 300 Class 200 Board 50 Del from £89 * **SERVICES:** Lift Night porter 150P **NOTES:** No smoking in restaurant Last d 9.45pm
CARDS:

See advert under SWANSEA

PORT TALBOT Neath Port Talbot — Map 03 SS79
Travel Inn
Baglan Rd, Baglan SA12 8ES
☎ 01639 813017 Fax 01639 823096
Dir: *M4 junct 41 west or junct 42 east, follow A48 signed Briton Ferry*
This modern building offers accommodation in smart, spacious and well equipped bedrooms, all with en-suite bathrooms. Refreshments may be taken at the nearby family restaurant. For details about current prices consult the Contents Page under Hotel Groups for the Travel Inn phone number.
ROOMS: 40 en suite (bth/shr) d £39.95 *

PRESTEIGNE Powys — Map 03 SO36
Late entry ***Radnorshire Arms***
High St LD8 2BE
☎ 01544 267406 Fax 01544 260418
Dir: *A456 from Birmingham passing through Kidderminster, Bewdley and Tenbury Wells, through to Wooerton near Ludlow then change to the B4362 to Preseinge*
This delightful 17th-century timbered coaching inn features original panelling and real fires in the public rooms. Bedrooms are split between the main building and a new one across the pretty garden; most are spacious with good seating and a full range of facilities.
ROOMS: 8 en suite (bth/shr) 8 annexe en suite (bth/shr) (6 fmly) No smoking in 5 bedrooms **MEALS:** V meals Coffee am Tea pm **FACILITIES:** CTV in all bedrooms **CONF:** Thtr 30 Class 15 Board 18 **SERVICES:** 50P **NOTES:** No smoking in restaurant Last d 8.55pm
CARDS:

See advert under Preliminary Section

PWLLHELI Gwynedd — Map 06 SH33
★★❀❀❀ Plas Bodegroes
Nefyn Rd LL53 5TH
Quality Percentage Score: 79%
☎ 01758 612363 Fax 01758 701247
Dir: *on the A497, 1.5m W on Nefyn road*
Situated just to the west of Pwllheli, this beautiful Georgian Manor House has been stylishly refurbished to provide a

contd.

peaceful haven in which to relax and unwind. Privately owned, it is run by Gunna Chown, ably supported by her small team of dedicated staff. The bedrooms are individually styled with tasteful decoration and a combination of period furniture and contemporary equipment. Two of the bedrooms are located across a delightful courtyard, in a recently constructed building. Public rooms include the distinctive restaurant, where period-style furnishings have been sensitively combined with a restful colour scheme, Scandinavian track lighting and illuminated display cabinets. The result is a setting fit for the accomplished cuisine of chef Shaun Mitchell.

ROOMS: 9 en suite (bth/shr) 2 annexe en suite (bth/shr) No smoking in all bedrooms s fr £35; d £70-£120 (incl. bkfst) LB Off peak
MEALS: Sunday Lunch fr £12.50 Dinner £24.50-£29.50alc
FACILITIES: CTV in all bedrooms **SERVICES:** 15P **NOTES:** No coaches No smoking in restaurant Last d 9.30pm Closed Dec-Feb & Mon
CARDS:

RAGLAN Monmouthshire — Map 03 SO40

Travelodge

Travelodge

Granada Services A40, Nr Monmouth NP5 4BB
☎ 01600 740444
Dir: *on A40 near junct with A449*
This modern building offers accommodation in smart, spacious and well equipped bedrooms, all with en-suite bathrooms. Refreshments may be taken at the nearby family restaurant. For details about current prices, consult the Contents Page under Hotel Groups for the Travelodge phone number.
ROOMS: 42 en suite (bth/shr) d £39.95 *

REYNOLDSTON Swansea — Map 02 SS48

The Premier Collection

★★ Fairyhill

SA3 1BS
☎ 01792 390139 01792 391358
Dir: *just outside Reynoldston off the A4118 from Swansea in the middle of the Gower Peninsula*
Set in 24 acres of wooded grounds, this stone-built 18th-century mansion comes complete with stream and lake. Bedrooms are tastefully decorated and furnished in sympathy with the character of the house. The quality of accommodation is matched by the imaginative and accomplished cuisine, which features many local specialities like Penclawdd cockles, and superb Welsh beef and lamb.

ROOMS: 8 en suite (bth/shr) s £95-£145; d £110-£160 (incl. bkfst) * LB Off peak **MEALS:** Lunch £17.50-£19.50 Dinner £32 V meals Coffee am **FACILITIES:** CTV in all bedrooms Croquet lawn
CONF: Thtr 40 Class 20 Board 26 **SERVICES:** 50P **NOTES:** No dogs (ex guide dogs) No coaches No children 8yrs No smoking in restaurant Last d 9.15pm Closed 24 Dec-14 Jan
CARDS:

Indicates that the star classification has not been confirmed under the New Quality Standards, see page 7 for further information.

R

RHOSSILI Swansea **Map 02 SS48**

★★ **Worms Head**

SA3 1PP

Quality Percentage Score: 61%

☎ 01792 390512 📠 01792 391115

Dir: *from Swansea take A4118 to Scurlage. Turn right onto B4247 to Rhossili Drive, through village until car park on left, and hotel is opposite*

Occupying an unrivalled cliff-top position, many of the bedrooms at this privately run hotel have superb panoramic views. The bedrooms have modern facilities, some are family rooms, and a ground floor room has disabled access. There is a choice of bars and a restaurant.

ROOMS: 19 rms (17 bth/shr) (5 fmly) No smoking in 10 bedrooms s £42-£44; d £64-£68 (incl. bkfst) * LB Off peak **MEALS:** Sunday Lunch £9.95 High tea £5.95 Dinner £14.50 English & Continental Cuisine V meals Coffee am Tea pm **FACILITIES:** CTV in all bedrooms STV Pool table Xmas **SERVICES:** P **NOTES:** No smoking in restaurant Last d 9pm **CARDS:**

RHYL Denbighshire **Map 06 SJ08**

★★ ***Marina***

Marine Dr LL18 3AU

Quality Percentage Score: 60%

☎ 01745 342371 📠 01745 342371

Located on the seafront, the Hotel Marina is close to the town centre and Rhyl's many amenities. Several function suites are provided and there is a choice of bars. Live entertainment is regularly held. Bedrooms include several suitable for families and many have fine sea views.

ROOMS: 29 en suite (bth/shr) (6 fmly) **MEALS:** V meals Coffee am Tea pm **FACILITIES:** CTV in all bedrooms Pool table Wkly live entertainment **CONF:** Class 300 **SERVICES:** Lift Night porter 75P **NOTES:** No dogs (ex guide dogs) **CARDS:**

ROSSETT Wrexham **Map 07 SJ35**

★★★ ***Llyndir Hall***

LL12 0AY

Quality Percentage Score: 71%

☎ 01244 571648 📠 01244 571258

Dir: *5m S of Chester follow signs for Pulford on B5445. On entering Rossett hotel is set back off road*

Located on the English/Welsh border, this is a comfortable, modern hotel, that lies in several acres of mature grounds and is a popular conference venue. Bedrooms are spacious and the lounge is elegantly furnished. The hotel bar and the leisure centre serve snacks and light meals. Jeremy Stone leads the kitchen team and the food in the restaurant continues to be enjoyable and worthy of our one rosette award.

ROOMS: 38 en suite (bth/shr) (3 fmly) No smoking in 12 bedrooms **MEALS:** English & French Cuisine V meals Coffee am Tea pm **FACILITIES:** CTV in all bedrooms STV Indoor swimming pool (heated) Solarium Gym Croquet lawn Jacuzzi/spa Steam room **CONF:** Thtr 140 Class 60 Board 40 **SERVICES:** Night porter 80P **NOTES:** No dogs (ex guide dogs) No smoking in restaurant Last d 9.30pm **CARDS:**

See advert under CHESTER

ROSSETT Wrexham **Map 07 SJ35**

★★★ **Rossett Hall Hotel**

Chester Rd LL12 0DE

Quality Percentage Score: 69%

☎ 01244 571000 📠 01244 571505

Dir: *from the M56 take the M53 which becomes A55. Take Wrexham/Chester exit & head to Wrexham. Onto B5445 & Hotel entrance in Rossett village*

The original building, which dates back to 1750, has been carefully renovated and extended over recent years. It lies in several acres of mature lawns and gardens in the lovely Welsh border country. Extensive function and conference facilities are provided and weddings are especially popular. Pretty bedrooms are mostly spacious and all are well equipped and furnished. A comfortable foyer lounge is provided and Oscar's Bistro serves enjoyable food featuring some local produce.

ROOMS: 30 en suite (bth/shr) (2 fmly) No smoking in 10 bedrooms s £52.50-£70; d £67.50-£90 LB Off peak **MEALS:** Lunch £6.95-£16.10alc High tea £5.95-£7.95alc Dinner £8.50-£17.95alc International Cuisine V meals Coffee am Tea pm **FACILITIES:** CTV in all bedrooms STV Xmas **CONF:** Thtr 120 Class 50 Board 50 Del from £94 * **SERVICES:** Night porter 80P **NOTES:** No dogs (ex guide dogs) No smoking area in restaurant Last d 9.45pm **CARDS:**

See advert under CHESTER

RUTHIN Denbighshire **Map 06 SJ15**

★★★ **Ruthin Castle**

LL15 2NU

Quality Percentage Score: 62%

☎ 01824 702664 📠 01824 705978

In places, this impressive castle and its grounds date back many centuries. Original panelling and ornately carved ceilings are highlights, and the public areas, including a bar and restaurant, are elegantly appointed. There is a medieval banqueting hall, and a separate tea room. Many of the bedrooms are spacious and furnished with fine antiques.

ROOMS: 58 en suite (bth/shr) (6 fmly) s £75-£85; d £95-£128 (incl. bkfst) * LB Off peak **MEALS:** Lunch £6.95-£9.95 High tea £2.95-£3.95 Dinner £19.50-£19.95 International Cuisine V meals Coffee am Tea pm **FACILITIES:** CTV in all bedrooms Fishing Snooker Wkly live entertainment Xmas **CONF:** Thtr 150 Class 100 Board 30 Del from £85.95 * **SERVICES:** Lift Night porter 200P **NOTES:** No dogs (ex guide dogs) Last d 9.30pm **CARDS:**

The AA Hotel Booking Service is a free benefit to AA members. See the advertisement on page 47

RUTHIN Denbighshire **Map 06 SJ15**

★★ ***Ye Olde Anchor Inn***

Rhos St LL15 1DX

Quality Percentage Score: 68%

☎ 01824 702813 📠 01824 703050

Dir: *on the junction of the A494 and A525*

Originally an 18th-century drovers inn, this hotel retains much of its character. The accommodation is attractively furnished and inter-connecting rooms are available for families. The bar provides a happy mix of locals and visitors, as does the restaurant which offers a selection of freshly prepared and substantial meals.

ROOMS: 17 en suite (bth/shr) (1 fmly) **MEALS:** English Cuisine V meals Coffee am Tea pm **FACILITIES:** CTV in all bedrooms STV **CONF:** Board 50 Del from £50 * **SERVICES:** 20P **NOTES:** No smoking in restaurant Last d 9.30pm **CARDS:**

ST ASAPH Denbighshire **Map 06 SJ07**

★★★ **Oriel House**

Upper Denbigh Rd LL17 0LW

Quality Percentage Score: 63%

☎ 01745 582716 📠 01745 585208

Dir: *turn off A55 on to A525, left at cathedral 1m along A525 on right hand side*

Set in several acres of mature grounds south of St Asaph. Extensive function facilities are provided, catering for business meetings and weddings. Several bars are available and the Fountain Restaurant serves a wide choice of meals. Bedrooms are generally spacious and staff are friendly and hospitable.

ROOMS: 19 en suite (bth/shr) (1 fmly) **MEALS:** English & French Cuisine V meals Coffee am Tea pm **FACILITIES:** CTV in all bedrooms STV Fishing Snooker **CONF:** Thtr 250 Class 150 Board 50 **SERVICES:** 200P **NOTES:** Last d 9.30pm Closed 26 Dec

CARDS:

ST ASAPH Denbighshire **Map 06 SJ07**

★★ **Plas Elwy Hotel & Restaurant**

The Roe LL17 0LT

Quality Percentage Score: 65%

☎ 01745 582263 & 582089 📠 01745 583864

Dir: *turn left off A55 at junct A525 signposted Rhyl/St Asaph. On left opposite petrol station*

Parts of this hotel date back to 1850 and much original character has been preserved. Spacious bedrooms are provided in a purpose-built extension, one with a four-poster bed and another family suite of two rooms. Equally well equipped bedrooms are in the main building. Public rooms are smart and comfortably furnished, a range of food options is provided in the attractive restaurant.

ROOMS: 7 en suite (bth/shr) 6 annexe en suite (bth/shr) (2 fmly) s £40-£46; d £58-£68 (incl. bkfst) * LB Off peak **MEALS:** Sunday Lunch £8.50-£10.50alc Dinner £9-£30alc V meals Coffee am **FACILITIES:** CTV in all bedrooms **SERVICES:** 28P **NOTES:** No dogs (ex guide dogs) No coaches No smoking in restaurant Last d 10pm Closed 26-30 Dec

CARDS:

ST CLEARS Carmarthenshire **Map 02 SN21**

★★ **Forge**

SA33 4NA

Quality Percentage Score: 67%

☎ 01994 230300 📠 01994 231577

Dir: *1m E, beside A40*

This family owned business has developed over the last 45 years into a modern motel complex with adjoining leisure centre. The bedrooms are in modern buildings, which are spacious and furnished to high standards. Another building houses an all-day restaurant and bar, and also includes a function suite.

ROOMS: 18 annexe en suite (bth/shr) (8 fmly) s £42.50; d £60 (incl. bkfst) * Off peak **MEALS:** Lunch fr £6 & alc Dinner £10-£16alc British Cuisine V meals Coffee am Tea pm **FACILITIES:** CTV in all bedrooms Indoor swimming pool (heated) Sauna Gym **CONF:** Thtr 80 Class 80 Board 80 **SERVICES:** 80P **NOTES:** No coaches Last d 9.30pm Closed 25 & 26 Dec **CARDS:**

ST DAVID'S Pembrokeshire **Map 02 SM72**

★★★ **Warpool Court**

SA62 6BN

Quality Percentage Score: 77%

☎ 01437 720300 📠 01437 720676

Dir: *from Cross Square bear left beside Cartref Restaurant down Goat Street. Pass Farmers Arms on right, follow road to left and signposted at fork*

Sitting in the landscaped gardens, looking out to sea, it is easy to understand the inspiration this charming coastal scenery gave to many a famous artist. Though sympathetically extended, the main part of the Victorian building was originally the cathedral choir school. Rupert Duffin and his friendly team provide a warm welcome while chef John Daniels and his brigade produce gastronomic delights to complement the setting. Lounges are spacious with comfortable furnishings and log fires burning during colder weather. Bedrooms are well furnished and equipped with modern facilities.

ROOMS: 25 en suite (bth/shr) (4 fmly) s £83-£90; d £120-£180 (incl. bkfst) * LB Off peak **MEALS:** Lunch £15.50-£19.50 High tea fr £7.50 Dinner £25.50-£34.50 English & French Cuisine V meals Coffee am Tea pm **FACILITIES:** CTV in all bedrooms Indoor swimming pool (heated) Tennis (hard) Sauna Gym Pool table Croquet lawn Childrens play area ch fac Xmas **CONF:** Thtr 40 Class 25 Board 25 **SERVICES:** 100P **NOTES:** No smoking in restaurant Last d 9.15pm Closed Jan

CARDS:

ST DAVID'S Pembrokeshire **Map 02 SM72**

★★ **Old Cross**

Cross Square SA62 6SP

Quality Percentage Score: 70%

☎ 01437 720387 📠 01437 720394

Dir: *right in centre of St David's facing Cross Square*

Located in the centre of the historic city, parts of this friendly hotel date back to the 18th century. The entrance to the cathedral is just a short walk away from the pretty front gardens of the hotel. The bedrooms are generally spacious with good facilities and some are suitable for families. There is a choice of

contd.

S

comfortable lounges along with a bar and a restaurant serving an extensive range of dishes.
ROOMS: 16 en suite (bth/shr) (1 fmly) No smoking in 5 bedrooms s £37-£45; d £68-£78 (incl. bkfst) * LB Off peak **MEALS:** Bar Lunch fr £5 Dinner £17.50 & alc European & Oriental Cuisine V meals Coffee am **FACILITIES:** CTV in all bedrooms ch fac **SERVICES:** 18P **NOTES:** No coaches No smoking in restaurant Last d 9pm Closed Xmas-1 Mar
CARDS:

ST DAVID'S Pembrokeshire **Map 02 SM72**
★★ St Non's Hotel
Catherine St SA62 6RJ
Quality Percentage Score: 70%
☎ 01437 720239 01437 721839
Dir: *from Cross Square in St Davids bear left between Midland Bank and Restaurant, follow road for 700yds, hotel on the left*
At the gateway to Britain's only coastal National Park, St Non's lies in St Davids, which actually has city status, though is more like a gentle village with just 1600 inhabitants. Named after the mother of Wales' patron saint, the hotel is situated close to the cathedral and the 14th-century Bishops' Palace. Among the well equipped modern accommodation are ground floor and family rooms. The spacious restaurant offers a range of appealing dishes.
ROOMS: 21 en suite (bth/shr) (4 fmly) s £49-£51; d £74-£78 (incl. bkfst) * LB Off peak **MEALS:** Bar Lunch fr £3.50 High tea fr £5 Dinner £12.50-£18.50 English Cuisine V meals Coffee am Tea pm **FACILITIES:** CTV in all bedrooms **CONF:** Thtr 32 Class 32 Board 32 **SERVICES:** 40P **NOTES:** No smoking in restaurant Last d 9pm Closed Dec & Nov
CARDS:

ST DAVID'S Pembrokeshire **Map 02 SM72**
★★ Grove Hotel
High St SA62 6SB
Quality Percentage Score: 61%
☎ 01437 720341 01437 720770
Dir: *follow A487 from Haverfordwest to St Davids, hotel on right opposite new Tourist Information Centre, at top of High St*
This small, cosy, Regency property is personally managed and offers friendly service. With its attractive, enclosed grounds and gardens, it provides a peaceful holiday or an ideal touring base.
ROOMS: 10 rms (9 bth/shr) No smoking in all bedrooms s £35; d £70 (incl. bkfst) * LB Off peak **MEALS:** Bar Lunch £2.50-£6 Dinner £2.50-£6 & alc French Cuisine V meals Coffee am Tea pm **FACILITIES:** CTV in all bedrooms Pool table **SERVICES:** 30P **NOTES:** No smoking in restaurant Last d 8.30pm RS 25 Dec **CARDS:**

S

SAUNDERSFOOT Pembrokeshire **Map 02 SN10**
★★★ St Brides
St Brides Hill SA69 9NH
Quality Percentage Score: 67%
☎ 01834 812304 01834 813303
Dir: *on Tenby road, overlooking the harbour*
Perched high above the town, this hotel boasts superb views of the coastline. Bedrooms vary in size and style, some are suitable for families. Spacious public areas include a comfortable bar in addition to the restaurant. The hotel has well-tended gardens, and an outdoor heated swimming pool.

ROOMS: 43 en suite (bth/shr) (2 fmly) No smoking in 6 bedrooms s £65-£98; d £104-£160 (incl. bkfst) * LB Off peak **MEALS:** Lunch £11-£14.50 & alc Dinner £18.50-£21 & alc English & French Cuisine V meals Coffee am Tea pm **FACILITIES:** CTV in all bedrooms STV Outdoor swimming pool (heated) Wkly live entertainment Xmas **CONF:** Thtr 150 Class 80 Board 60 Del from £75 * **SERVICES:** Night porter 70P **NOTES:** Last d 9.15pm Closed 1-20 Jan
CARDS:

See advert on opposite page

SAUNDERSFOOT Pembrokeshire **Map 02 SN10**
★★ Jalna
Stammers Rd SA69 9HH
Quality Percentage Score: 65%
☎ 01834 812282 01834 812282
Dir: *turn off A478 at Pentlepoir onto B4316 into Saundersfoot, take 1st junction on the right leaving the village for Tenby, hotel is on the right*
This small hotel is run by the friendly King family and lies just 200 yards from the harbour. Bedrooms are well equipped, with modern amenities and some are suitable for families. A cosy lounge is available as well as a bar, and a daily fixed-price menu that offers good value. Guests also have use of a solarium.
ROOMS: 13 en suite (bth/shr) (7 fmly) No smoking in 6 bedrooms s £25-£35; d £50-£55 (incl. bkfst) * LB Off peak **MEALS:** V meals Coffee am **FACILITIES:** CTV in all bedrooms Solarium **SERVICES:** 14P **NOTES:** No smoking in restaurant Last d 6pm
CARDS:

SAUNDERSFOOT Pembrokeshire **Map 02 SN10**
★★ *Rhodewood House*
St Brides Hill SA69 9NU
Quality Percentage Score: 65%
☎ 01834 812200 01834 811863
Dir: *from St Clears, take A477 to Kilgetty, then A478 to Tenby, turn left onto B4316 signposted Saundersfoot*
In an elevated position above the harbour, this long established holiday hotel lies in pretty gardens that include a children's play area. Regular entertainment is provided for guests. Bedrooms are equipped with modern amenities and many extras such as satellite TV and hair dryers. A spacious bar and separate function room are available and there is also a snooker room.
ROOMS: 44 en suite (bth/shr) (6 fmly) No smoking in 6 bedrooms **MEALS:** V meals Coffee am **FACILITIES:** CTV in all bedrooms STV Snooker Wkly live entertainment **CONF:** Thtr 100 Board 100 **SERVICES:** Night porter 70P **NOTES:** No dogs (ex guide dogs) No smoking area in restaurant Last d 9.30pm Closed 4-29 Jan
CARDS:

SAUNDERSFOOT Pembrokeshire **Map 02 SN10**

★★ Merlewood

St Brides Hill SA69 9NP

Quality Percentage Score: 64%

☎ 01834 812421 & 813295 ▤ 01834 812421

Dir: *turn off A477 onto A4316, hotel on other side of village on St Brides Hill*

A purpose-built resort-style hotel, Merlewood has been family owned since 1972 and is popular with more mature guests, as it offers ground floor and family rooms among its modern equipped accommodation. Public areas include a bright dining room, a large lounge bar and a mini-launderette; outside is a lovely garden.

ROOMS: 30 en suite (bth/shr) (8 fmly) No smoking in all bedrooms s £40; d £74 (incl. bkfst & dinner) * LB Off peak **MEALS:** Dinner £10-£12 V meals **FACILITIES:** CTV in all bedrooms Outdoor swimming pool (heated) Pool table Putting green Children's swings & slide Wkly live entertainment Xmas **SERVICES:** 34P **NOTES:** No dogs (ex guide dogs) No smoking in restaurant Last d 8pm Closed Nov-Etr RS Etr-May & Oct **CARDS:**

SAUNDERSFOOT Pembrokeshire **Map 02 SN10**

★★ Cwmwennol Country House

Swallow Tree Woods SA69 9DE

Quality Percentage Score: 60%

☎ 01834 813430 ▤ 01834 813430

Set in several acres of mature woodland, this small family-run hotel lies a short walk from a sandy beach. Bedrooms include some suitable for families and several on the ground floor. A pretty lounge is provided and there is a large lounge bar with an adjoining suite for weddings and other functions.

ROOMS: 13 en suite (bth/shr) (2 fmly) No smoking in 3 bedrooms s £27-£28; d £44-£49 (incl. bkfst) * LB Off peak **MEALS:** Dinner £13 & alc English & French Cuisine V meals **FACILITIES:** CTV in all bedrooms Xmas **CONF:** Thtr 80 **SERVICES:** 35P **NOTES:** No smoking in restaurant Last d 8.30pm **CARDS:**

SWANSEA Swansea **Map 03 SS69**

see also **Port Talbot**

★★★★ Swansea Marriott

The Maritime Quarter SA1 3SS

Quality Percentage Score: 63%

☎ 01792 642020 ▤ 01792 650345

Dir: *M4 junct 42, follow A483 to the City Centre past Leisure Centre, then follow signs to Maritime Quarter*

This smart property is well situated on the marina, enjoying glorious views over the bay. Large and bustling, the hotel provides an ideal base for both business and leisure visitors. Abernethy's Restaurant offers comfortable relaxed surroundings in which to dine and, in addition, an extensive selection of dishes is available from room service. The well equipped bedrooms are spacious and benefit from large beds, in addition to such extra facilities as satellite TV and trouser press. The hotel has a number of meeting rooms, and a popular leisure club.

ROOMS: 117 en suite (bth/shr) (51 fmly) No smoking in 80 bedrooms d £87-£89 * LB Off peak **MEALS:** Lunch £12.70-£17.95 & alc Dinner fr £17.95 & alc Welsh & European Cuisine V meals Coffee am Tea pm **FACILITIES:** CTV in all bedrooms STV Indoor swimming pool (heated) Sauna Gym Jacuzzi/spa **CONF:** Thtr 250 Class 120 Board 30 Del from £85 * **SERVICES:** Lift Night porter Air conditioning 122P **NOTES:** No dogs (ex guide dogs) No smoking in restaurant Last d 10.30pm **CARDS:**

SWANSEA Swansea **Map 03 SS69**
★★★ ***Posthouse Swansea***
The Kingsway Circle SA1 5LS
Quality Percentage Score: 65%
☎ 01792 651074 01792 456044
Dir: *M4 junct 42, A483 Swansea exit. Signs for city centre W. At lights after Sainsbury's, turn R along Wind St then L at lights, hotel ahead at rdbt*

Posthouse

In the centre of town, this Posthouse offers comfortable accommodation and useful amenities, including a good Spa leisure club. Guests can eat in the lounge, The Junction restaurant or the new Mongolian Barbecue. Refurbishment of a number of bedrooms was imminent at the time of our last inspection.
ROOMS: 99 en suite (bth/shr) (12 fmly) No smoking in 66 bedrooms
MEALS: International Cuisine V meals Coffee am Tea pm
FACILITIES: CTV in all bedrooms Indoor swimming pool (heated) Sauna Solarium Gym **CONF:** Thtr 230 Class 120 Board 60 **SERVICES:** Lift Night porter 42P **NOTES:** No smoking area in restaurant Last d 10.30pm
CARDS:

SWANSEA Swansea **Map 03 SS69**
★★ **Fairyhill**
SA3 1BS
☎ 01792 390139 01792 391358
(For full entry see Reynoldston)

SWANSEA Swansea **Map 03 SS69**
★★ **Beaumont**
72-73 Walter Rd SA1 4QA
Quality Percentage Score: 74%
☎ 01792 643956 01792 643044
Dir: *M4 junct 42 - A483 to Swansea. Right on Oystermouth Rd to Kingsway R/A then left & 1st right to junct A4118 & turn left. Hotel 400yds on left*
The public areas at this family-run hotel are very attractive and, along with the bedrooms, have been furnished and decorated with quality and comfort in mind. The conservatory restaurant is the bright and airy venue for popular home-cooked dishes. Private secure parking is an asset.
ROOMS: 17 en suite (bth/shr) No smoking in 1 bedroom s £40-£49.50; d £59.50-£80 (incl. bkfst) * LB Off peak **MEALS:** Lunch £15.95 Dinner fr £10.95 & alc Welsh, French & Italian Cuisine V meals Coffee am Tea pm **FACILITIES:** CTV in all bedrooms **SERVICES:** 10P **NOTES:** No coaches Last d 9pm Closed 23 Dec-2 Jan
CARDS:

SWANSEA Swansea **Map 03 SS69**
★★ ***Windsor Lodge***
Mount Pleasant SA1 6EG
Quality Percentage Score: 73%
☎ 01792 642158 & 652744 01792 648996
Dir: *M4 exit 42 onto A483, turn right at lights past Sainsburys, turn left at station, turn right immediately after 2nd set of lights*
This elegant Georgian house is close to the town centre in a residential area. Bedrooms are attractively decorated and many have been enlarged and refurbished over recent years. There is a choice of comfortable lounge areas, and the popular restaurant has a small adjoining bar.

ROOMS: 18 en suite (bth/shr) (2 fmly) **MEALS:** English, French & Welsh Cuisine V meals Coffee am Tea pm **FACILITIES:** CTV in all bedrooms Sauna **CONF:** Thtr 30 Class 15 Board 24 **SERVICES:** 26P **NOTES:** No coaches No smoking in restaurant Last d 9.30pm Closed 25-26 Dec
CARDS:

AA Rosettes are awarded for quality of food,
see page 15 for an explanation of Rosette assessment.

SWANSEA Swansea **Map 03 SS69**
★★ **Oak Tree Parc**
Birchgrove Rd SA7 9JR
Quality Percentage Score: 62%
☎ 01792 817781 01792 814542
(For full entry see Birchgrove)

SWANSEA Swansea **Map 03 SS69**
★★ **Worms Head**
SA3 1PP
Quality Percentage Score: 61%
☎ 01792 390512 01792 391115
(For full entry see Rhossili)

SWANSEA Swansea **Map 03 SS69**
Travelodge
Penllergaer SA4 1GT
☎ 01792 896222 01792 898806
Dir: *M4 junct 47*

Travelodge

This modern building offers accommodation in smart, spacious and well equipped bedrooms, all with en-suite bathrooms. Refreshments may be taken at the nearby family restaurant. For details about current prices, consult the Contents Page under Hotel Groups for the Travelodge phone number.
ROOMS: 50 en suite (bth/shr) d £49.95 * **CONF:** Thtr 25 Class 32 Board 20

TALSARNAU Gwynedd **Map 06 SH63**

The Premier Collection

★★ ***Maes y Neuadd***
LL47 6YA
☎ 01766 780200 01766 780211
Dir: *3m NE of Harlech, signposted on an unclassed road off B4573*

PRIDE OF BRITAIN MEMBER

This Welsh granite house sits in its own grounds, overlooking the kitchen gardens and Snowdonia National Park. Parts of the house date back to the 14th century, with granite walls some five feet thick. Attractively furnished

contd.

bedrooms, four of which are in an adjacent coach house, boast many antique and period pieces.

ROOMS: 12 en suite (bth/shr) 4 annexe en suite (bth/shr) **MEALS:** V meals Coffee am Tea pm **FACILITIES:** CTV in all bedrooms Croquet lawn **CONF:** Thtr 20 Class 20 Board 16 Del from £135 * **SERVICES:** 50P **NOTES:** No coaches No smoking in restaurant Last d 9.15pm **CARDS:**

TALSARNAU Gwynedd **Map 06 SH63**
★★ **Estuary Motel**
LL47 6TA
Quality Percentage Score: 66%
☎ 01766 771155 01766 771697
Dir: *4m N of Harlech, on the A496*
At the edge of the village against wooded slopes, this family-run hotel has been refurbished in recent years to provide modern accommodation. Bedrooms are spacious and well equipped, there is a small lounge. The restaurant serves a carte menu of popular dishes and offers good value for money.
ROOMS: 10 en suite (bth/shr) (2 fmly) s £30; d £44.10-£49 (incl. bkfst) * LB Off peak **MEALS:** Sunday Lunch £7.25 Dinner £11.50 & alc British Cuisine V meals **FACILITIES:** CTV in all bedrooms **SERVICES:** Night porter 30P **NOTES:** No coaches No smoking in restaurant Last d 9pm **CARDS:**

TALSARNAU Gwynedd **Map 06 SH63**
★★ **Tregwylan**
LL47 6YG
Quality Percentage Score: 64%
☎ 01766 770424 01766 771317
Dir: *off A496, 0.5m N of Talsarnau and 4m N of Harlech*
Located above the bay and enjoying superb views, this family-run hotel offers genuine Welsh hospitality. The bedrooms are prettily decorated and there is an attractive restaurant and a cosy bar. Pretty grounds surround the hotel.
ROOMS: 10 en suite (bth/shr) (3 fmly) s fr £26; d fr £52 (incl. bkfst) * LB Off peak **MEALS:** Bar Lunch £3-£6 Dinner £12.50-£14.75 V meals Coffee am Tea pm **FACILITIES:** CTV in all bedrooms **SERVICES:** 20P **NOTES:** No dogs (ex guide dogs) No coaches No smoking in restaurant Last d 9pm Closed Jan-mid Feb **CARDS:**

TAL-Y-BONT (NEAR CONWY) Gwynedd **Map 06 SH76**
★★ **Lodge**
LL32 8YX
Quality Percentage Score: 68%
☎ 01492 660766 01492 660534
THE CIRCLE
Selected Individual Hotels
GREAT BRITAIN
Dir: *on B5106, hotel on right hand side of the road when entering village*
In a peaceful part of the Conwy valley, this garden hotel is so called because the bedrooms are in a separate building in the extensive gardens. Bedrooms are modern, individually furnished and decorated. A log fire burns in the bar lounge during winter months. There is a daily changing menu featuring produce from the hotel gardens, meals are served in generous portions.
ROOMS: 14 annexe en suite (bth/shr) s £35-£55; d £50-£80 (incl. bkfst) * LB Off peak **MEALS:** Lunch £6.25-£12.25 Dinner fr £16.95 & alc British & French Cuisine V meals Coffee am Tea pm **FACILITIES:** CTV in all bedrooms Xmas **SERVICES:** 50P **NOTES:** No smoking in restaurant Last d 8.45pm RS Winter **CARDS:**

TAL-Y-LLYN Gwynedd **Map 06 SH70**
★★ **Minffordd**
LL36 9AJ
Quality Percentage Score: 69%
☎ 01654 761665 01654 761517
Dir: *at junct of A487/B4405 midway between Dolgellau and Machynlleth*
Located in spectacular countryside below Cader Idris, this delightful hotel is a haven of peace and relaxation. It was once a drovers' inn and exposed timbers and thick stone walls remain in abundance. Smart modern bedrooms are now provided, however, and these are well equipped and comfortable. The lounge and bar are both elegantly furnished and there is a further sun lounge for residents' use. There is a character restaurant and local produce is used where possible. The hotel is non smoking throughout.
ROOMS: 6 en suite (bth/shr) No smoking in all bedrooms s £56-£65; d £102-£112 (incl. bkfst) * LB Off peak **MEALS:** V meals Tea pm **SERVICES:** 18P **NOTES:** No coaches No children 13yrs No smoking in restaurant Closed Nov-18 Mar **CARDS:**

T

TEN

TENBY Pembrokeshire Map 02 SN10
★★★ Penally Abbey Country House
Penally SA70 7PY
Quality Percentage Score: 77%
☎ 01834 843033 Fax 01834 844714
Dir: *1.5m from Tenby, off A4139, overlooking golf course, close to Penally village green*
Perched on the hillside above the pretty village of Penally, in superb gardens and with spendid views of the sea and Caldy Island. Owners Mr & Mrs Warren lead a friendly team who make every effort to ensure that guests feel relaxed and at home. All the bedrooms are spacious and comfortable with thoughtful decoration and superior furnishings. On the ground floor the drawing room, bar, restaurant and conservatory are all stylishly appointed.
ROOMS: 8 en suite (bth/shr) 4 annexe en suite (bth/shr) (3 fmly) s £114; d £148-£172 (incl. bkfst & dinner) * LB Off peak **MEALS:** Lunch £18 Dinner £26 Welsh & French Cuisine V meals Coffee am Tea pm **FACILITIES:** CTV in all bedrooms Indoor swimming pool (heated) Snooker Xmas **SERVICES:** Night porter 14P **NOTES:** No dogs (ex guide dogs) No coaches No smoking in restaurant Last d 9.30pm
CARDS:

TENBY Pembrokeshire Map 02 SN10
★★★ Atlantic
The Esplanade SA70 7DU
Quality Percentage Score: 73%
☎ 01834 842881 & 844176 Fax 01834 842881 ex 256
Dir: *take A478 into Tenby & follow signs to town centre, keep town walls on left then turn right at Esplanade, hotel half way along on right*
The Atlantic stands on the cliffs above Tenby's South Beach, overlooking the sea towards Caldy Island and beyond. The hotel is owned and personally run by the James family and there is much evidence of the personal care which they have lavished upon it. The well equipped accommodation includes a room with a four-poster bed, and rooms with sea views; there is also a fully equipped leisure centre. An elegant lounge and a formal dining room supplemented by a cellar bistro are available for guests' use. The hotel has a well deserved reputation for its very high level of customer care and friendliness.
ROOMS: 42 en suite (bth/shr) (11 fmly) No smoking in 2 bedrooms s £60-£63; d £84-£126 (incl. bkfst) Off peak **MEALS:** Welsh & French Cuisine V meals Coffee am Tea pm **FACILITIES:** CTV in all bedrooms STV Indoor swimming pool (heated) Solarium Jacuzzi/spa Steam room **SERVICES:** Lift Night porter 30P **NOTES:** No coaches No smoking area in restaurant Closed 17 Dec-21 Jan **CARDS:**

T

TENBY Pembrokeshire Map 02 SN10
★★★ Fourcroft
North Beach SA70 8AP
Quality Percentage Score: 66%
☎ 01834 842886 Fax 01834 842888
Dir: *from A478, after "Welcome to Tenby" sign bear left towards North Beach & walled town. On reaching sea front turn sharp left. Hotel on left*
A friendly, family-run hotel that offers a beachfront location together with a number of extra leisure facilities that make it particularly suitable for families with children. Guests have direct access to the beach through the hotel's own cliff-top gardens which also provide terraced gardens where refreshments can be taken. The bedrooms are all of a good size with modern facilities and are smartly decorated. Besides the bar, lounge and restaurant the public areas include an outdoor pool, jacuzzi, games room and play area.
ROOMS: 46 en suite (bth/shr) (9 fmly) No smoking in 30 bedrooms s £34-£46; d £68-£92 (incl. bkfst) * LB Off peak **MEALS:** Lunch £8-£19 High tea £5-£10 Dinner £12-£19 & alc International Cuisine V meals Coffee am Tea pm **FACILITIES:** CTV in all bedrooms Outdoor swimming pool (heated) Snooker Sauna Pool table Jacuzzi/spa Table tennis Indoor bowls Giant chess Human Gyroscope ch fac Xmas **CONF:** Thtr 80 Class 50 Board 40 Del from £75 * **SERVICES:** Lift Night porter 6P
NOTES: No smoking in restaurant Last d 8.30pm
CARDS:

TENBY Pembrokeshire Map 02 SN10
★★ Hammonds Park
Narberth Rd SA70 8HT
Quality Percentage Score: 69%
☎ 01834 842696 Fax 01834 844295
Dir: *take left turn off A478 into Narberth Rd leading to North Beach & Bus Park, look for white sign with hotel name in red*
Situated on a hill just north of the town, this small family-run hotel provides a friendly place to stay when visiting Tenby. The bedrooms vary in size but all benefit from modern facilities and the accommodation includes some family bedded rooms together with a bedroom on the ground floor. Many of the dining tables are situated in the bright conservatory which leads into a cosy bar. An additional room includes a spa bath and exercise equipment.
ROOMS: 14 en suite (bth/shr) (5 fmly) No smoking in all bedrooms s £41-£46; d £50-£54 (incl. bkfst) * LB Off peak **MEALS:** Lunch £8-£18alc Dinner £11 & alc Welsh & New Zealand Cuisine V meals Coffee am Tea pm **FACILITIES:** CTV in all bedrooms Gym Jacuzzi/spa Natural Therapy clinic ch fac **SERVICES:** 14P **NOTES:** No smoking in restaurant Last d 7.30pm **CARDS:**

TENBY Pembrokeshire Map 02 SN10
★★ Esplanade
The Esplanade SA70 7DU
Quality Percentage Score: 68%
☎ 01834 842760 & 843333 Fax 01834 842760
Dir: *in Tenby follow signs for South Beach, hotel on sea front next to Town Walls*
The Esplanade is just outside the old town walls and overlooks the sandy South Beach and Caldey Island. Some of the smart, modern bedrooms are suitable for families. The bright and well maintained public areas are open-plan.
ROOMS: 15 en suite (bth/shr) (3 fmly) s £40-£60; d £40-£80 (incl. bkfst) * Off peak **MEALS:** V meals Coffee am Tea pm
FACILITIES: CTV in all bedrooms **NOTES:** Closed Nov-Feb
CARDS:

TENBY Pembrokeshire Map 02 SN10
★★ Heywood Mount
Heywood Ln SA70 8DA
Quality Percentage Score: 68%
☎ 01834 842087 Fax 01834 842087
Dir: *follow signs for Wild Life Park when entering Tenby this will lead into Heywood Lane*
Situated in a peaceful location on the edge of the town but within easy reach of the beaches and town centre, this fine 18th-century house is surrounded by well tended lawns and gardens. The ground floor public areas include a lounge, bar and restaurant. Several bedrooms are on the ground floor. Owners Dennis and Jennifer Andrews lead a team of friendly staff.
ROOMS: 21 en suite (bth/shr) (4 fmly) No smoking in 11 bedrooms s £25-£30; d £50-£60 (incl. bkfst) * LB Off peak **MEALS:** Dinner fr £12 & alc British & Continental Cuisine V meals Tea pm **FACILITIES:** CTV in all bedrooms Xmas **CONF:** Class 50 Board 30 Del from £50 * **SERVICES:** 25P **NOTES:** No dogs (ex guide dogs) No smoking in restaurant Last d 9.30pm **CARDS:**

THREE COCKS Powys **Map 03 SO13**

★★ Three Cocks

LD3 0SL

Quality Percentage Score: 73%

☎ 01497 847215 🖷 01497 847215

Dir: *on A438, between Brecon & Hereford*

A unique 15th century inn surrounded by the rugged countryside of the Brecon Beacons National Park. Stone and timber abound in the public rooms which include the restaurant, bar and separate lounge. The impeccably kept bedrooms are simply decorated and do not have televisons. The owners' Belgian origins are much in evidence particularly in the cuisine.

ROOMS: 7 rms (5 bth 1 shr) (2 fmly) d £67 (incl. bkfst) * LB Off peak **MEALS:** Lunch fr £27 Dinner fr £27 Belgian Cuisine V meals Coffee am **SERVICES:** 40P **NOTES:** No dogs (ex guide dogs) No coaches Last d 9pm Closed Dec & Jan RS Sun lunch & Tue **CARDS:**

TINTERN Monmouthshire **Map 03 SO50**

★★ Parva Farmhouse Hotel & Restaurant

THE CIRCLE Selected Individual Hotels GREAT BRITAIN

NP6 6SQ

Quality Percentage Score: 72%

☎ 01291 689411 & 689511 🖷 01291 689557

Dir: *leave junct 2 M48, N of village on A466*

A 17th-century, stone-built farmhouse on the banks of the River Wye. Inside, the house retains many of its original features and a wealth of character and charm. Comfort is a priority and the lounge with its honesty bar, boasts leather chesterfields and a wood-burning stove. The tastefully furnished bedrooms include several with river views, a family room and a four-poster. The dining room features an inglenook fireplace and is the setting for wholesome and delicious home cooking.

ROOMS: 9 en suite (bth/shr) (3 fmly) s fr £48; d fr £72 (incl. bkfst) * LB Off peak **MEALS:** Dinner fr £17.50 European Cuisine V meals **FACILITIES:** CTV in all bedrooms Cycle hire **SERVICES:** 10P **NOTES:** No coaches No smoking in restaurant Last d 8.30pm **CARDS:**

TINTERN Monmouthshire **Map 03 SO50**

★★ Royal George

Best Western

NP16 6ST

Quality Percentage Score: 70%

☎ 01291 689205 🖷 01291 689448

Dir: *turn off M48 on to A466, 4m along this road into Tintern 2nd on left*

Privately owned and personally run, this delightful hotel provides well equipped and spacious accommodation, including bedrooms with balconies overlooking the pleasant garden. Family bedded rooms and rooms on ground floor level are available, as is a room recently converted for the convenience of disabled guests. The public areas include a choice of bars, and a large function room.

ROOMS: 2 en suite (bth/shr) 14 annexe en suite (bth/shr) (13 fmly) No smoking in 13 bedrooms s £62-£68; d £88-£98 (incl. bkfst) * LB Off peak **MEALS:** Bar Lunch £11 & alc High tea £6.75 Dinner £21 & alc English & French Cuisine V meals Coffee am Tea pm **FACILITIES:** CTV in 19 bedrooms Xmas **CONF:** Thtr 120 Class 40 Board 50 **SERVICES:** 50P **NOTES:** No smoking in restaurant Last d 9.30pm **CARDS:**

TREARDDUR BAY See Anglesey, Isle of

TREFRIW Conwy **Map 06 SH76**

★★ Princes Arms

LL27 0JP

Quality Percentage Score: 66%

☎ 01492 640592 🖷 01492 640559

Dir: *take A470 to Llanrwst left onto B5106 over bridge & follow to Trefriw, hotel just through village on left*

Located in the Conwy Valley, this hotel offers superb views from many bedrooms. Bedrooms are pleasingly decorated, and modern facilities are provided. The main restaurant is attractive and provides excellent food. There is also the newly opened Kings Brasserie which offers comfortable surroundings with log fires and a wide range of innovative dishes.

ROOMS: 14 en suite (bth/shr) (5 fmly) s £50-£52.50; d £99-£103 (incl. bkfst & dinner) LB Off peak **MEALS:** Lunch £8-£12.50 & alc High tea fr £6.50 & alc Dinner £16.50 & alc V meals Coffee am Tea pm **FACILITIES:** CTV in all bedrooms STV Xmas **CONF:** Class 60 Board 10 Del from £55 **SERVICES:** 40P **NOTES:** No dogs (ex guide dogs) No smoking in restaurant Last d 9.30pm **CARDS:**

See advert under BETWS-Y-COED

TYWYN Gwynedd **Map 06 SH50**

★ *Greenfield*

High St LL36 9AD

Quality Percentage Score: 62%

☎ 01654 710354 🖷 01654 710354

Dir: *on A493, opposite leisure centre*

In the middle of a small seaside town, this family-run hotel also operates a busy restaurant offering a good range of inexpensive meals. Bedrooms are plainly furnished but all are fresh and bright. Each has modern facilities and several are suitable for families.

ROOMS: 8 rms (6 bth/shr) (2 fmly) **MEALS:** V meals Coffee am **FACILITIES:** CTV in all bedrooms **NOTES:** No dogs (ex guide dogs) No coaches Last d 8.30pm Closed Jan RS Nov-Mar **CARDS:**

USK Monmouthshire **Map 03 SO30**

★★★ Three Salmons

Bridge St NP15 1RY

Quality Percentage Score: 74%

☎ 01291 672133 🖷 01291 673979

Dir: *turn off A449, 1m into Usk, hotel on the corner of Porthycarne St, B4598*

A former coaching inn dating back to the 17th century. Bedrooms are spacious, comfortably furnished and well maintained, with some rooms in a nearby annexe. Ostlers restaurant offers carefully prepared dishes. The bar serves an extensive range of meals and there is a pleasant rear garden.

ROOMS: 10 en suite (bth/shr) 14 annexe en suite (bth/shr) (1 fmly) s £66; d £90 (incl. bkfst) * LB Off peak **MEALS:** Dinner £16.50 & alc Continental Cuisine V meals Coffee am Tea pm **FACILITIES:** CTV in all bedrooms STV Xmas **CONF:** Thtr 100 Class 40 Board 50 Del £95 * **SERVICES:** Night porter 38P **NOTES:** No dogs (ex guide dogs) No coaches No smoking area in restaurant Last d 9.30pm **CARDS:**

See advert on page 955

U

USK Monmouthshire **Map 03 SO30**
★★★ ***Glen-yr-Afon House***
Pontypool Rd NP5 1SY
Quality Percentage Score: 69%
☎ 01291 672302 & 673202 Fax 01291 672597
Dir: *A472 through Usk High St, over river bridge following main rd around to the right hotel is 200yds on the left*
This large Victorian property provides well equipped accommodation, with no-smoking rooms, family rooms and a room equipped for disabled guests. Public areas comprise a comfortable lounge, a bar and a traditionally furnished restaurant with panelled walls. Other facilities include a function suite, a large ballroom and a smaller function room, which is licensed for marriage ceremonies.
ROOMS: 26 en suite (bth/shr) (1 fmly) No smoking in 13 bedrooms **MEALS:** V meals Coffee am Tea pm **FACILITIES:** CTV in all bedrooms STV Croquet lawn ch fac **CONF:** Thtr 100 Class 200 Board 30 Del from £93.85 * **SERVICES:** Lift Night porter 101P **NOTES:** No smoking in restaurant Last d 9pm **CARDS:**

WELSHPOOL Powys **Map 07 SJ20**
★★★ **Royal Oak**
SY21 7DG
Quality Percentage Score: 68%
☎ 01938 552217 Fax 01938 556652
Dir: *by traffic lights at junct of A483/A458*
A traditional market town hotel that dates back over 350 years, it provides well equipped bedrooms, a choice of bars and extensive function facilities. The 'cafe bar style' restaurant provides a good choice of popular dishes, food is available throughout the day and evening.
ROOMS: 24 en suite (bth/shr) (2 fmly) No smoking in 10 bedrooms s £35-£58.50; d £65-£85 (incl. bkfst) * LB Off peak **MEALS:** Dinner £9.50-£15.50alc Welsh, English, French & Italian Cuisine V meals Coffee am Tea pm **FACILITIES:** CTV in all bedrooms STV **CONF:** Thtr 120 Class 60 Board 80 Del from £65 * **SERVICES:** 40P **NOTES:** No smoking area in restaurant Last d 9.30pm
CARDS:

WELSHPOOL Powys **Map 07 SJ20**
★★ ***Golfa Hall***
Llanfair Rd SY21 9AF
Quality Percentage Score: 71%
☎ 01938 553399 Fax 01938 554777
Dir: *1.5m W of Welshpool on the A458 to Dolgellau*
Set on the Powys Castle estate, this fine modern hotel was originally a farmhouse. Bedrooms are well equipped and include family rooms. Public rooms are elegant and include a meeting room and a comfortable no smoking lounge. There is also a large, self-contained function suite. Service is friendly and the hotel has a well deserved reputation for its food.
ROOMS: 10 en suite (bth/shr) 4 annexe en suite (bth/shr) (3 fmly) **MEALS:** French, British & Welsh Cuisine V meals Coffee am Tea pm **FACILITIES:** CTV in all bedrooms **CONF:** Thtr 85 Class 50 Board 36 **SERVICES:** 100P **NOTES:** No smoking in restaurant Last d 9pm
CARDS:

W

WHITEBROOK Monmouthshire **Map 03 SO50**
★★ **Crown at Whitebrook**
NP25 4TX
Quality Percentage Score: 72%
☎ 01600 860254 Fax 01600 860607
Dir: *turn W off A466, 50yds S of Bigsweir Bridge*
Comfortable bedrooms, most enjoying views of the valley or the country garden, are attractively furnished, but it is at lunch or dinner that this hotel really comes into its own. There is an excellent fixed-price menu complemented by an award-winning wine list.
ROOMS: 10 en suite (bth/shr) s £66-£75; d £112-£130 (incl. bkfst & dinner) * LB Off peak **MEALS:** Lunch £15.95-£17.95 Dinner £27.95-£29.95 British & French Cuisine V meals **FACILITIES:** CTV in all bedrooms **CONF:** Thtr 18 Class 18 Board 18 Del from £100 * **SERVICES:** 40P **NOTES:** No coaches No children 12yrs No smoking in restaurant Last d 9pm Closed 2 wks Jan & 2 wks Aug
CARDS:

WOLF'S CASTLE Pembrokeshire **Map 02 SM92**
★★ **Wolfscastle Country Hotel**
SA62 5LZ
Quality Percentage Score: 73%
☎ 01437 741688 & 741225 Fax 01437 741383
Dir: *on the A40 in the village of Wolf's Castle, at top of the hill left hand side, 6m N of Haverfordwest*
This large, detached, stone-built house dates back to the mid-19th century. The well-maintained and well-equipped modern accommodation includes a room with a four-poster bed and a family room. There is a pleasant bar, plus an attractive restaurant, where a good range of soundly prepared dishes is available.
ROOMS: 20 en suite (bth/shr) 4 annexe en suite (bth/shr) (2 fmly) s £39-£47; d fr £73 (incl. bkfst) * LB Off peak **MEALS:** Lunch £10.50-£25alc Dinner £15-£25alc Welsh, English & French Cuisine V meals Coffee am **FACILITIES:** CTV in all bedrooms STV Squash **CONF:** Thtr 100 Class 100 Board 30 Del from £65 * **SERVICES:** 60P **NOTES:** No smoking in restaurant Last d 9pm Closed 24-26 Dec RS Sun nights
CARDS:

WREXHAM Wrexham **Map 07 SJ35**
★★★ **Llwyn Onn Hall**
Cefn Rd LL13 0NY
Quality Percentage Score: 66%
☎ 01978 261225 Fax 01978 363233
Dir: *between A525 Wrexham-Whitchurch road & A534 Wrexham-Nantwich road. Easy access Wrexham Ind Estate, 2m off main Wrexham-Chester A483*
Surrounded by open countryside this is a fine, ivy-clad, 17th-century manor house set in several acres of mature grounds. Exposed timbers remain, and the original oak staircase is still in use. Weddings and other functions are catered for. Bedrooms are equipped with modern facilities and one room has a four-poster bed which Bonnie Prince Charlie was once supposed to have slept in.
ROOMS: 13 en suite (bth/shr) (1 fmly) No smoking in 4 bedrooms s £62-£73; d £85-£95 (incl. bkfst) * LB Off peak **MEALS:** Lunch £7.95-£10.90 Dinner £16.95 & alc V meals Coffee am **FACILITIES:** CTV in all bedrooms **CONF:** Thtr 60 Class 40 Board 12 **SERVICES:** 40P **NOTES:** No dogs (ex guide dogs) No smoking in restaurant Last d 8.30pm **CARDS:**
See advert on opposite page

WREXHAM Wrexham **Map 07 SJ35**
★★★ ***Cross Lanes Hotel & Restaurant***
Cross Lanes, Bangor Rd, Marchwiel LL13 0TF
Quality Percentage Score: 64%
☎ 01978 780555 Fax 01978 780568
Dir: *3m SE of Wrexham, on A525*
Built as a private house in 1890 and standing in over six acres of beautiful grounds. Bedrooms are well equipped and meet the needs of today's traveller. The brasserie restaurant offers a fine
contd.

selection of well produced food and the hotel caters for conferences, weddings and functions.

ROOMS: 16 en suite (bth/shr) (1 fmly) **MEALS:** British & Continental Cuisine V meals Coffee am Tea pm **FACILITIES:** CTV in all bedrooms Indoor swimming pool (heated) Sauna Croquet lawn Putting green Fishing rights **CONF:** Thtr 120 Class 60 Board 40 Del from £88 * **SERVICES:** 80P **NOTES:** No smoking area in restaurant Last d 10pm Closed 25 Dec (night) & 26 Dec **CARDS:**

See advert under CHESTER

WREXHAM Wrexham **Map 07 SJ35**
★★★ Wynnstay Arms
Yorke St LL13 8LP
Quality Percentage Score: 61%
☎ 01978 291010 📠 01978 362138
Dir: *off A483 towards Wrexham. Right onto St Giles Rd at lights. Turn left at end of new road link, left again until pub and turn right,car park on left*
This large commercial hotel has a Georgian frontage. Extensive function and conference facilities are provided and there is a choice of bars. Bedrooms have been refurbished and are equipped with modern amenities. The restaurant offers a set menu and carte, bar snacks are served through the day.
ROOMS: 67 en suite (bth/shr) (7 fmly) No smoking in 4 bedrooms d £39.90 Off peak **MEALS:** Sunday Lunch £9.95 High tea £3.50 Dinner fr £12.95 & alc V meals Coffee am Tea pm **FACILITIES:** CTV in all bedrooms **CONF:** Thtr 50 Class 10 Board 20 **SERVICES:** Lift Night porter Air conditioning 70P **NOTES:** No dogs (ex guide dogs) No smoking in restaurant Last d 9.30pm
CARDS:

WREXHAM Wrexham **Map 07 SJ35**
⇧ Travel Inn
Chester Rd, Gresford LL12 8PW
☎ 01978 853214 📠 01978 856838
Dir: *on B5445 just off A483 dual carriageway near village of Gresford*
This modern building offers accommodation in smart, spacious and well equipped bedrooms. Refreshments may be taken at the nearby family restaurant. For details about current prices consult the Contents Page under Hotel Groups for the Travel Inn phone number.
ROOMS: 38 en suite (bth/shr) d £39.95 *

WREXHAM Wrexham **Map 07 SJ35**
⇧ Travelodge
Wrexham By Pass, Rhostyllen LL14 4EJ
☎ 01978 365705 📠 01978 365705
Dir: *2m S, A483/A5152 roundabout*
This modern building offers accommodation in smart, spacious and well equipped bedrooms. Refreshments may be taken at the nearby family restaurant. For details about current prices, consult the Contents Page under Hotel Groups for the Travelodge phone number.
ROOMS: 32 en suite (bth/shr) d £45.95 *

W

Hotel of the Year Ireland

The Lodge & Spa, Inchydoney Island

A

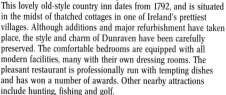

ADARE Co Limerick

Map 01 B3

★★★ Dunraven Arms

MANOR HOUSE HOTELS

Quality Percentage Score: 78%

☎ 061 396633 061 396541

Dir: *first building as you enter the village*

This lovely old-style country inn dates from 1792, and is situated in the midst of thatched cottages in one of Ireland's prettiest villages. Although additions and major refurbishment have taken place, the style and charm of Dunraven have been carefully preserved. The comfortable bedrooms are equipped with all modern facilities, many with their own dressing rooms. The pleasant restaurant is professionally run with tempting dishes and has won a number of awards. Other nearby attractions include hunting, fishing and golf.

ROOMS: 75 en suite (bth/shr) (1 fmly) **MEALS:** Irish & French Cuisine V meals Coffee am Tea pm **FACILITIES:** CTV in all bedrooms STV Indoor swimming pool (heated) Fishing Riding Sauna Gym Pool table Jacuzzi/spa Wkly live entertainment **CONF:** Thtr 300 Class 200 Board 50 **SERVICES:** Lift Night porter 90P **NOTES:** No smoking in restaurant Last d 9.30pm **CARDS:**

AGHADOWEY Co Londonderry

Map 01 C6

★★ Brown Trout Golf & Country Inn

209 Agivey Rd BT51 4AD

Quality Percentage Score: 67%

☎ 028 70868209 028 70868878

Dir: *on intersection of A54/B66 on main road to Coleraine*

Located by the banks of the Agivey River, this friendly inn caters particularly for golfers. A courtyard area houses cheerfully decorated and spacious bedrooms. The restaurant serves hearty home-cooked fare and food is also available in the bar lounge.

ROOMS: 17 en suite (bth/shr) (11 fmly) s £60; d £60-£85 (incl. bkfst) * LB Off peak **MEALS:** Lunch £10-£14 Dinner £14-£20alc V meals Coffee am Tea pm **FACILITIES:** CTV in all bedrooms Golf 9 Fishing Gym Putting green Game fishing river Wkly live entertainment Xmas **CONF:** Thtr 40 Class 24 Board 28 Del from £50 * **SERVICES:** 80P **NOTES:** No coaches No smoking in restaurant Last d 10pm **CARDS:**

AHERLOW Co Tipperary

Map 01 B3

★★★ Aherlow House

Quality Percentage Score: 62%

☎ 062 56153 062 56212

Dir: *8km from Tipperary, turn left at traffic lights coming from Limerick*

Located in coniferous forest with superb views of the Galtee Mountains, this Tudor-style house offers comfortable public rooms, including a relaxing drawing room, a spacious lounge bar, and restaurant, all of which have views of the forest. Accommodation is well equipped, and a new wing has recently been added. The attentive staff create a warm and friendly atmosphere, and golf, fishing, riding and climbing can be arranged.

ROOMS: 29 en suite (bth/shr) (23 fmly) **MEALS:** V meals Coffee am Tea pm **FACILITIES:** CTV in all bedrooms STV Wkly live entertainment **CONF:** Thtr 250 Class 150 Board 20 **SERVICES:** 200P **NOTES:** No dogs (ex guide dogs) No smoking area in restaurant Last d 9.30pm Closed 6 Jan-30 Mar **CARDS:**

ARDMORE Co Waterford

Map 01 C2

★ Round Tower

Quality Percentage Score: 62%

☎ 024 94494 & 94382 024 94254

Dir: *Ardmore is located off the main N25 Rosslare-Cork route. Turn off onto Route R673. Hotel is situated in centre of village*

This large country house is set in its own grounds in the picturesque fishing village which has a blue flag beach, lovely marked cliff walks, and much of early monastic interest. Owner-managed by Aidan Quirke, the atmosphere is friendly, and guests enjoy the relaxing ambience in the comfortable lounge, intimate panelled bar, and conservatory where bar food is served; an a la carte dinner menu is available in the restaurant, which always features 'catch of the day' seafood. Bedrooms are freshly decorated, there is a family room. Off-street parking.

ROOMS: 12 en suite (shr) (4 fmly) s IR£30-IR£22.50; d IR£50-IR£60 (incl. bkfst) * Off peak **MEALS:** V meals Coffee am Tea pm **FACILITIES:** CTV in all bedrooms **CONF:** Thtr 50 Class 25 Board 30 Del from IR£55 * **SERVICES:** Night porter Air conditioning 40P **NOTES:** No smoking area in restaurant Last d 9.15pm RS Oct-Apr

CARDS:

ARTHURSTOWN Co Wexford

Map 01 C2

★★★ Dunbrody Country House Hotel & Restaurant

Quality Percentage Score: 74%

☎ 051 389600 389601

Dir: *From N11 follow signs for Duncannon & Ballyhack (R733). Hotel is 20m on from turn off. Turn left at gate lodge on approaching Arthurstown*

Surrounded by peaceful parkland, this elegant Georgian manor house is situated near the coast. The priorities here are tranquility, generous hospitality and award-winning cuisine. The attractive bedrooms are all individually styled with new bathrooms. Nearby are beaches, walking, golf and horse riding.

ROOMS: 12 en suite (bth/shr) (1 fmly) No smoking in 2 bedrooms **MEALS:** International Cuisine V meals Coffee am Tea pm **FACILITIES:** CTV in all bedrooms Riding Croquet lawn clay pigeon shooting Wkly live entertainment ch fac **CONF:** Thtr 200 Class 100 Board 100 **SERVICES:** Night porter 40P **NOTES:** No dogs (ex guide dogs) No smoking area in restaurant Closed Jan

CARDS:

ASHFORD Co Wicklow

Map 01 D3

★★ The Chester Beatty Inn

Quality Percentage Score: 66%

☎ 0404 40682 0404 49003

Dir: *in centre of Ashford village route N11 Rosslare to Dublin*

Well situated for touring County Wicklow and convenient for the ferryport, guests are assured a warm welcome at this hotel. A restaurant and a lounge bar are available for guests' use. Bedrooms are attractive and simple.

ROOMS: 12 en suite (bth/shr) (10 fmly) No smoking in 8 bedrooms s IR£60-IR£70; d IR£90-IR£110 (incl. bkfst) * LB Off peak **MEALS:** Lunch IR£4.95-IR£6.95 & alc Dinner IR£20-IR£28 & alc International Cuisine V meals Coffee am **FACILITIES:** CTV in all bedrooms STV Snooker **SERVICES:** 52P **NOTES:** No dogs Last d 9.30pm Closed 25 Dec

CARDS:

★★ Cullenmore Hotel

Quality Percentage Score: 63%

☎ 0404 40187 0404 40471

Dir: *located N of Ashford on the N11 main Dublin/Wexford Rosslaire Road, 32km S of Dublin*

ROOMS: 17 en suite (bth/shr) (4 fmly) s IR£35-IR£45; d IR£56-IR£70 (incl. bkfst) * LB Off peak **MEALS:** Lunch IR£11.95-IR£15 Dinner IR£15.50-IR£25 Irish Cuisine V meals Coffee am Tea pm **FACILITIES:** CTV in all bedrooms STV **CONF:** Board 30 **SERVICES:** Night porter 100P **NOTES:** No dogs (ex guide dogs) No smoking area in restaurant Last d 10pm Closed 24-27 Dec

CARDS:

A

ATHLONE Co Westmeath **Map 01 C4**

★★★ Hodson Bay

Hodson Bay
Quality Percentage Score: 69%
☎ 0902 92444 0902 92688

Dir: *from N6 take N61 to Roscommon. Take right turn - hotel situated 1km on Lough Ree*

On the Co Roscommon side of the River Shannon and right on the shore of Lough Ree, this historic hotel has recently been reconstructed and extended to provide comfortable accommodation. With a golf course to the rear and a marina to the front, most of the rooms have excellent views.

ROOMS: 97 en suite (bth/shr) (23 fmly) s IR£78.50-IR£98; d IR£103-IR£122 * LB Off peak **MEALS:** Lunch fr IR£13 Dinner fr IR£25 & alc Irish & French Cuisine V meals Coffee am Tea pm **FACILITIES:** CTV in all bedrooms STV Indoor swimming pool (heated) Golf 18 Tennis (hard) Fishing Sauna Solarium Gym Steam room Wkly live entertainment Xmas **CONF:** Thtr 1000 Class 300 Board 300 Del from IR£84 * **SERVICES:** Lift Night porter 300P **NOTES:** No dogs (ex guide dogs) No smoking area in restaurant Last d 9.30pm **CARDS:**

See advert on opposite page

★★★ *Prince of Wales*

Quality Percentage Score: 64%
☎ 0902 72626 0902 75658

Dir: *in centre of town, opposite Bank of Ireland*

Situated in the centre of town, this modern hotel offers comfortable well equipped bedrooms. Its spacious restaurant and lounge bar have been extensively refurbished.

ROOMS: 73 en suite (bth/shr) (15 fmly) No smoking in 10 bedrooms **MEALS:** French Cuisine V meals Coffee am Tea pm **FACILITIES:** CTV in all bedrooms STV Wkly live entertainment **CONF:** Thtr 270 Class 140 Board 50 **SERVICES:** Night porter 35P **NOTES:** No dogs (ex guide dogs) No smoking area in restaurant Last d 9.30pm RS 24-25 Dec
CARDS:

★★ Royal Hoey Mardyke St

Quality Percentage Score: 68%
☎ 0902 72924 & 75395 0902 75194

Upholding a tradition of warm hospitality is the priority at this family-run hotel. Located in the centre of town, it has a comfortable foyer lounge bar and restaurant, and the coffee shop serves snacks all day. Bedrooms are carefully maintained.

ROOMS: 38 en suite (bth/shr) (8 fmly) No smoking in 10 bedrooms s IR£36-IR£45; d IR£70-IR£76 (incl. bkfst) * LB Off peak **MEALS:** Lunch IR£10 Dinner IR£18 & alc Irish, English & Italian Cuisine V meals Coffee am Tea pm **FACILITIES:** CTV in all bedrooms STV Wkly live entertainment **CONF:** Thtr 250 Class 130 Board 40 **SERVICES:** Lift Night porter Air conditioning 50P **NOTES:** No dogs (ex guide dogs) No smoking in restaurant Last d 8.30pm Closed 25-27 Dec
CARDS:

BALLINASLOE Co Galway **Map 01 B4**

★★★ Hayden's

Quality Percentage Score: 72%
☎ 0905 42347 0905 42347

Dir: *located on the main Dublin/Galway road N6*

Built around 1803, this fine hotel has been owned and run by successive generations of the O'Carroll family whose friendly staff offer an unfailingly good service. Meals are served throughout the day, either in the Gorbally Restaurant with its extensive à la carte menu or the award-winning coffee shop which serves full meals, snacks and home baking; both eating outlets overlook the garden.

ROOMS: 48 en suite (bth/shr) (7 fmly) s IR£33-IR£38; d IR£56-IR£60 * LB Off peak **MEALS:** Lunch IR£11.50-IR£12.50 High tea IR£14.50-IR£21alc Dinner IR£20-IR£22 International Cuisine V meals Coffee am Tea pm **FACILITIES:** CTV in all bedrooms STV Wkly live entertainment **CONF:** Thtr 300 Class 160 Board 50 Del from IR£63 * **SERVICES:** Lift Night porter 100P **NOTES:** No dogs (ex guide dogs) No smoking area in restaurant Last d 9.15pm Closed 24-26 Dec **CARDS:**

BALLON Co Carlow **Map 01 C3**

★★★ Ballykealey House

Quality Percentage Score: 63%
☎ 0503 59288 & 59212 0503 59297

Dir: *take N80 out of Carlow town, hotel approx. 12m on right hand side, 1m before Ballon village*

The house, set in seven acres of parkland, was built in the 1830s and features tudor chimney stacks, battlements, ornate plasterwork and fine oak reception room doors. Public areas include a pleasant lounge and lounge bar, banqueting suite and restaurant, serving good cuisine. Individually styled bedrooms are mostly spacious, two are restricted in size.

ROOMS: 12 en suite (bth/shr) (1 fmly) No smoking in 2 bedrooms s IR£60.50; d IR£99 (incl. bkfst) * LB Off peak **MEALS:** Lunch IR£15 High tea IR£8.50 Dinner IR£28.50 French Cuisine V meals Coffee am Tea pm **FACILITIES:** CTV in all bedrooms **CONF:** Thtr 200 Class 100 Board 100 Del IR£130 * **SERVICES:** 100P **NOTES:** No dogs No coaches No children 12yrs No smoking area in restaurant Last d 9.30pm Closed 24 Dec-28 Feb **CARDS:**

BALLYBOFEY Co Donegal **Map 01 C5**

★★★ Kee's Stranorlar

Quality Percentage Score: 70%
☎ 074 31018 074 31917

Dir: *2km NE on N15, in Stranorlar village*

This former coaching inn has been transformed into a very comfortable hotel. Bedrooms have been refurbished and new ones added. There is a Bistro as well as the conservatory lounge and popular Restaurant.

ROOMS: 53 en suite (bth/shr) (10 fmly) s IR£47-IR£57; d IR£85-IR£100 (incl. bkfst) LB Off peak **MEALS:** Sunday Lunch IR£13-IR£15 Dinner IR£23-IR£25 & alc V meals Coffee am Tea pm **FACILITIES:** CTV in all bedrooms STV Indoor swimming pool (heated) Sauna Solarium Gym Jacuzzi/spa Mountain bikes for hire Wkly live entertainment Xmas **CONF:** Thtr 250 Class 100 Board 30 Del IR£53 * **SERVICES:** Lift Night porter 90P **NOTES:** No smoking area in restaurant Last d 9.30pm **CARDS:**

BALLYCONNELL Co Cavan — Map 01 C4

★★★★ Slieve Russell Hotel Golf & Country Club

Quality Percentage Score: 67%

☎ 049 9526 444 Fax 049 9526 474

***Dir:** from Cavan head for Enniskillen, at Butlersbridge turn left towards Belturbet. Through village towards Ballyconnell, hotel is on left after 5 miles*

This imposing hotel stands in 300 acres. Public areas include a range of lounges, a restaurant and brasserie and a leisure centre. Bedrooms are tastefully furnished and equipped to a high standard.

ROOMS: 151 en suite (bth/shr) (74 fmly) s IR£95-IR£135; d IR£160-IR£220 (incl. bkfst) * LB Off peak **MEALS:** Irish & French Cuisine V meals Coffee am Tea pm **FACILITIES:** CTV in all bedrooms STV Indoor swimming pool (heated) Golf 18 Tennis (hard) Squash Snooker Sauna Solarium Gym Pool table Jacuzzi/spa Steam Room Hair & Beauty Salon Wkly live entertainment ch fac Xmas **CONF:** Thtr 800 Class 450 Board 40 Del from IR£76 * **SERVICES:** Lift Night porter 600P **NOTES:** No dogs (ex guide dogs) No smoking area in restaurant Last d 9.45pm **CARDS:**

BALLYCOTTON Co Cork — Map 01 C2

★★★ Bay View

Quality Percentage Score: 73%

☎ 021 646746 Fax 021 646075

***Dir:** turn off N25 at Castlemartyr and follow signs to Ballycotton*

The Bay View Hotel offers a mixture of past and present with its classic gabled exterior and modern interior, providing many comforts and facilities; inside the public areas are spacious. Bedrooms are comfortable, some with superb views over Ballycotton Bay. Staff are friendly and efficient.

ROOMS: 35 en suite (bth/shr) s fr IR£90; d fr IR£130 (incl. bkfst) * LB Off peak **MEALS:** Sunday Lunch fr IR£14.50 Dinner fr IR£28 V meals Coffee am Tea pm **FACILITIES:** CTV in all bedrooms STV Cruiser for hire Hillwalking Horse riding Fishing Golf Wkly live entertainment **CONF:** Thtr 60 Class 30 Board 24 Del from IR£95 * **SERVICES:** Lift Night porter Air conditioning 40P **NOTES:** No dogs (ex guide dogs) No smoking area in restaurant Last d 9pm Closed Nov-Apr **CARDS:**

See advert on this page

BALLYHEIGE Co Kerry — Map 01 A2

★★★ The White Sands

Quality Percentage Score: 64%

☎ 066 7133 102 Fax 066 7133 357

***Dir:** 18km from Tralee town on coast rd in North Kerry, the hotel is situated on left on main street*

This seaside hotel, in a village near Tralee, has warm attractive colour schemes, a good restaurant, two cosy bars and a pleasant staff. There is a car park to the rear with a sandy beach and a championship golf course nearby.

ROOMS: 81 en suite (bth/shr) s fr IR£45; d fr IR£81.50 (incl. bkfst) * LB Off peak **MEALS:** Lunch fr IR£10 Dinner fr IR£17 V meals Coffee am Tea pm **FACILITIES:** CTV in all bedrooms STV Wkly live entertainment **SERVICES:** Lift Night porter Air conditioning 40P **NOTES:** No smoking area in restaurant Last d 9.30pm Closed Nov-Feb **CARDS:**

BALLYLICKEY Co Cork — Map 01 B2

★★★ Sea View

Quality Percentage Score: 74%

☎ 027 50073 & 50462 Fax 027 51555

Dir: *5km from Bantry, 11km from Glengarriff on N71*

There is nowhere better to sample Irish hospitality than at this delightful country house overlooking Bantry Bay. Set in well tended gardens, it has cosy lounges with turf fires and comfortable, pleasantly decorated bedrooms. The hotel caters for the fishing and golfing enthusiast and is also a good touring base for West Cork and Kerry.

ROOMS: 17 en suite (bth/shr) (3 fmly) s IR£45-IR£55; d IR£90-IR£110 (incl. bkfst) * LB Off peak **MEALS:** Lunch fr IR£15 Dinner fr IR£25 V meals Coffee am Tea pm **FACILITIES:** CTV in all bedrooms STV **SERVICES:** 32P **NOTES:** No smoking in restaurant Last d 9.30pm Closed mid Nov-mid Mar **CARDS:**

BALLYMENA Co Antrim — Map 01 D5

★★★★ Galgorm Manor BT42 1EA

Quality Percentage Score: 68%

☎ 028 25881001 Fax 028 25880080

Dir: *1m outside Ballymena on A42, between Galgorm & Cullybackey*

This 19th-century mansion house by the River Maine has an 85-acre estate with equestrian centre and grand banqueting/conference hall. Public areas include a library lounge, cocktail bar, elegant restaurant and Gillies bar - a traditional Irish pub across a cobbled courtyard. Bedrooms are well proportioned and modern in style. Development plans include a leisure centre and 48 further bedrooms.

ROOMS: 24 en suite (bth/shr) (6 fmly) s £99; d £119 (incl. bkfst) * LB Off peak **MEALS:** Lunch £14.95 & alc Dinner £25.50 Irish & French Cuisine V meals Coffee am Tea pm **FACILITIES:** CTV in all bedrooms STV Fishing Riding Clay pigeon shooting Archery Wkly live entertainment Xmas **CONF:** Thtr 500 Class 200 Board 12 **SERVICES:** Night porter 170P **NOTES:** No dogs (ex guide dogs) No coaches Last d 9.30pm RS 25-26 Dec **CARDS:**

★★★ *Adair Arms* 1 Ballymoney Rd BT43 5BS

Quality Percentage Score: 65%

☎ 01266 653674

Public areas are spacious, well presented and enjoyable to use. Lounges are inviting, the bar well stocked, and the refurbished restaurant offers a good choice from the carte and fixed price menus. Lighter meals are available in the Lanyon Grill. All but a few of the well equipped bedrooms have been upgraded.

ROOMS: 40 en suite (bth/shr) (3 fmly) **MEALS:** English & French Cuisine V meals Coffee am Tea pm **FACILITIES:** CTV in all bedrooms STV Wkly live entertainment **CONF:** Thtr 250 Class 150 Board 60 **SERVICES:** Night porter Air conditioning 50P **NOTES:** No dogs (ex guide dogs) Last d 10pm Closed 25 Dec

CARDS:

See advert on opposite page

BALLYNAHINCH Co Galway — Map 01 A4

★★★★ Ballynahinch Castle

Quality Percentage Score: 73%

☎ 095 31006 & 31086 Fax 095 31085

Dir: *take Roundstone turn off from N59, 5km from turn off*

Situated at the foot of Ben Lettery, the hotel stands on the banks of the famous salmon river, in 350 acres of grounds with woodlands and scenic walks. Bedrooms are spacious, individually designed and comfortably equipped. In the popular Castle Bar, ghillie meets fishing enthusiast, and a marvellous atmosphere builds up. During the season there is often a fine salmon to display and game and fresh local produce inspire the menus offered in the charming restaurant. Understated elegance and informality are the keynotes here.

ROOMS: 40 en suite (bth/shr) No smoking in 4 bedrooms s IR£79.20-IR£126.50; d IR£123.20-IR£209 (incl. bkfst) * LB Off peak **MEALS:** Irish & French Cuisine V meals Coffee am Tea pm **FACILITIES:** CTV in all bedrooms STV Tennis (hard) Fishing Croquet lawn River & Lakeside walks Wkly live entertainment Xmas **CONF:** Thtr 30 Class 20 Board 20 **SERVICES:** Night porter 55P **NOTES:** No dogs (ex guide dogs) No coaches No smoking area in restaurant Closed Feb & 20-26 Dec **CARDS:**

BALLYVAUGHAN Co Clare — Map 01 B3

The Premier Collection

★★★ Gregans Castle

☎ 065 7077 005 Fax 065 7077 111

Dir: *3.5miles S of the village of Ballyvaughan on the road N67*

Standing at the foot of Corkscrew Hill with dramatic views over Galway Bay, the hotel is situated in an area which is rich in archaeological, geological and botanical interest. A high level of personal service and hospitality has earned the hotel special commendations in recent years, and the welcoming staff fulfill their reputation. The cuisine is also excellent with the emphasis placed on good food using fresh local produce.

ROOMS: 22 en suite (bth/shr) s IR£100; d IR£130 (incl. bkfst) * LB Off peak **MEALS:** Bar Lunch IR£10-IR£20alc Dinner IR£34 & alc V meals Coffee am Tea pm **FACILITIES:** Croquet lawn **SERVICES:** 25P **NOTES:** No dogs No coaches Last d 8.30pm Closed 18 Oct-31 Mar **CARDS:**

BALTIMORE Co Cork — Map 01 B1

★★★ Baltimore Harbour Resort Hotel & Leisure Ctr

Quality Percentage Score: 61%

☎ 028 20361 Fax 028 20466

Dir: *S from Cork city N71 to Skibbereen, continue on R595 13km to Baltimore*

Baltimore has much to offer visitors, and this smart new hotel adds to its attractions, set in a delightful position overlooking the harbour. The hotel has spacious, linked public areas; the restful lounge has deep sofas and a turf fire, and the bar and garden room open onto the patio and gardens. The staff are friendly, and enthusiastic, and fresh local ingredients are served in the dining room. Bedrooms are well appointed and all have sea views.

ROOMS: 64 en suite (bth/shr) (30 fmly) No smoking in 3 bedrooms s IR£59-IR£77; d IR£88-IR£104 (incl. bkfst) * LB Off peak **MEALS:** Sunday Lunch IR£12 & alc Dinner IR£20 & alc Irish & International Cuisine V meals Coffee am Tea pm **FACILITIES:** CTV in all bedrooms Indoor swimming pool (heated) Tennis (hard) Sauna Gym Pool table Croquet lawn Jacuzzi/spa Table Tennis, In-house video channel

contd.

Wkly live entertainment Xmas **CONF:** Thtr 120 Class 100 Board 30 Del from IR£60 * **SERVICES:** Night porter 80P **NOTES:** No dogs (ex guide dogs) No smoking in restaurant Last d 9pm Closed Jan-mid Feb
CARDS:

★★ Casey's of Baltimore

Quality Percentage Score: 66%
☎ 028 20197 🖹 028 20509
Dir: *follow R595 from Skibbereen*
Set in an elevated position overlooking the harbour, this warm and friendly hotel offers attractive, comfortable bedrooms. Both the lounge and the restaurant enjoy superb views. The restaurant features seafood dishes and there is a traditional pub. Ferry trips to nearby islands are popular.
ROOMS: 14 en suite (bth/shr) (1 fmly) s IR£51.50-IR£64; d IR£65-IR£90 (incl. bkfst) * LB Off peak **MEALS:** Lunch IR£10-IR£30 & alc Dinner IR£16-IR£30 & alc V meals Coffee am Tea pm **FACILITIES:** CTV in all bedrooms STV Wkly live entertainment **SERVICES:** 50P **NOTES:** No dogs No smoking area in restaurant Last d 9pm Closed 19-26 Feb,1-14 Nov & 21-27 Dec **CARDS:**

BANGOR Co Down — Map 01 D5

★★★ Clandeboye Lodge

10 Estate Rd, Clandeboye BT19 1UR
Quality Percentage Score: 68%
☎ 028 91852500 🖹 028 91852772
Dir: *from Belfast on A2 take Ballysallagh road. 500 yards turn left and take Crawfordsburn road. Hotel is on left.*
Situated three miles west of Bangor, Clandeboye Lodge sits in landscaped and wooded grounds, close to Blackwood Golf Course. A warm Irish welcome is assured and services and facilities are geared to cater for the needs of both the business and leisure guest. Good conference and banqueting facilities, together with a popular country-style pub, are housed in the older of two buildings. The newer Lodge offers comfortable, well-equipped accommodation with many thoughtful extra touches and some rooms offer special access for the less able. Public areas include a bright open-plan foyer bar and lounge, while the restaurant, with a feature gothic arch window, provides an attractive setting for the carefully prepared food.
ROOMS: 43 en suite (bth/shr) (2 fmly) No smoking in 13 bedrooms s fr £80; d fr £90 * LB Off peak **MEALS:** Sunday Lunch £5-£12.75 Dinner £16.50-£39.50 European Cuisine V meals Coffee am Tea pm **FACILITIES:** CTV in all bedrooms STV Petanque court **CONF:** Thtr 350 Class 110 Board 50 **SERVICES:** Lift Night porter 250P **NOTES:** No smoking area in restaurant Last d 9.45pm Closed 24-26 Dec
CARDS:

★★★ Marine Court The Marina BT20 5ED

Quality Percentage Score: 67%
☎ 028 91451100 🖹 028 91451200
Situated on the seafront, the Marine Court offers a good range of conference and leisure facilities. Public areas are extensive and include the first-floor restaurant and cocktail bar. The popular Lord Nelson's Bistro/Bar is more relaxed, and there is also a lively bar called Callico Jack's.
ROOMS: 52 en suite (bth/shr) (11 fmly) No smoking in 16 bedrooms
MEALS: Lunch £11.95 Dinner £14.95 & alc English, Irish & French Cuisine V meals Coffee am Tea pm **FACILITIES:** CTV in all bedrooms STV Indoor swimming pool (heated) Solarium Gym Jacuzzi/spa Steam room
CONF: Thtr 350 Class 100 Board 20 **SERVICES:** Lift Night porter 30P
NOTES: No dogs (ex guide dogs) No smoking area in restaurant Last d 10pm **CARDS:**

★★★ Royal Seafront BT20 5ED
Quality Percentage Score: 62%
☎ 028 91271866 028 91467810
Dir: *take A2 from Belfast. Proceed through Bangor town centre to seafront. Turn right-Hotel 300 yards overlooking Marina*
This substantial Victorian hotel overlooks the marina and offers bedrooms that are comfortably modern in style. Public areas are traditional and include a choice of contrasting bars and a popular brasserie. The serious eating is done in Quays restaurant at dinner.
ROOMS: 50 en suite (bth/shr) s £65-£75; d £80-£90 (incl. bkfst) * LB Off peak **MEALS:** Lunch £11.95-£13.95 & alc High tea £9.25-£15.65alc Dinner £17.50-£19.50 & alc European Cuisine V meals Coffee am **FACILITIES:** CTV in all bedrooms STV Pool table Wkly live entertainment **CONF:** Thtr 80 Class 60 Board 40 Del from £85 * **SERVICES:** Lift Night porter **NOTES:** No dogs (ex guide dogs) Last d 9.15pm Closed 25 Dec **CARDS:**

BANTRY Co Cork — Map 01 B2

★★★ Westlodge
Quality Percentage Score: 58%
☎ 027 50360 027 50438
This modern, busy hotel has a popular leisure centre and is set in grounds on the outskirts of the town, overlooking the bay.
ROOMS: 90 en suite (bth/shr) (20 fmly) **MEALS:** V meals Coffee am Tea pm **FACILITIES:** CTV in all bedrooms Indoor swimming pool (heated) Tennis (hard) Squash Snooker Sauna Solarium Gym Pool table Putting green Jacuzzi/spa Pitch & Putt Wkly live entertainment ch fac **CONF:** Thtr 400 Class 200 Board 24 **SERVICES:** Night porter Air conditioning 400P **NOTES:** No dogs (ex guide dogs) Closed 23-27 Dec **CARDS:**

BELFAST — Map 01 D5

★★★★ Culloden
Bangor Rd BT18 0EX
Quality Percentage Score: 75%
☎ 028 90425223 028 90426777
Dir: *on A2*
Culloden Hotel is an elegant baronial mansion with views across the estuary and to the city beyond. The day rooms include a bar and lounge areas. The restaurant is a suitable venue for some accomplished cooking. Recent improvements include some impressive new suites.
ROOMS: 79 en suite (bth/shr) (1 fmly) No smoking in 12 bedrooms s £135; d £160 * LB Off peak **MEALS:** Lunch £15-£25 & alc Dinner £24-£26 & alc Irish & Continental Cuisine V meals Coffee am Tea pm **FACILITIES:** CTV in all bedrooms STV Indoor swimming pool (heated) Tennis (hard) Squash Snooker Sauna Solarium Gym Pool table Croquet lawn Putting green Jacuzzi/spa Hair & Beauty Salon Aromatherapist Wkly live entertainment Xmas **CONF:** Thtr 500 Class 250 Board 88 Del from £133 * **SERVICES:** Lift Night porter 500P **NOTES:** No dogs (ex guide dogs) No smoking area in restaurant Last d 8.45pm Closed 24 & 25 Dec **CARDS:**

★★★★ Europa Hotel
Great Victoria St BT2 7AP
Quality Percentage Score: 69%
☎ 028 90327000 028 90327800
Dir: *leave Westlink at Grosvenor Rd rdbt, turn left into Grosvenor Rd. At traffic lights turn right, then 1st left into Glengall St*
Next to the Grand Opera House, the Europa is truly at the heart of the city with easy access to all facilities including the Waterfront complex. The rejuvenated facade gives way to impressive public areas that include a selection of bars, lounges and eating options. The latter include the informal Brasserie and the main Gallery restaurant on the first floor. Additional facilities include a beauty salon and a well equipped business centre. Bedrooms are modern and boast a good range of facilities.
ROOMS: 184 en suite (bth/shr) No smoking in 57 bedrooms s fr £105; d fr £150 * LB Off peak **MEALS:** Lunch £15.98 & alc Dinner £24.98 & alc International & French Cuisine V meals Coffee am Tea pm **FACILITIES:** CTV in all bedrooms STV Hairdressing & Beauty salon Wkly live entertainment Xmas **CONF:** Thtr 750 Class 250 Del £126 * **SERVICES:** Lift Night porter **NOTES:** No smoking area in restaurant Last d 11pm Closed 24-25 Dec **CARDS:**

★★★★ Stormont
587 Upper Newtownards Rd BT4 3LP
Quality Percentage Score: 67%
☎ 028 90658621 028 90480240
Dir: *4m E, off the A20*
Located opposite the impressive grounds of Stormont Castle, this popular, modern hotel is convenient for both the city centre and outlying areas. The public areas include open plan lounge and lobby areas that are smartly appointed, together with a bar and a choice of restaurants. The more formal McMasters offers some imaginative cooking on traditional lines whilst La Scala has a contemporary bistro feel to both the surroundings and the food. Business guests have the opportunity to make use of the well equipped Confex centre. The bedrooms are well kept and offer a number of extra in-room facilities.
ROOMS: 109 en suite (bth/shr) (3 fmly) No smoking in 25 bedrooms s £97-£102; d £130-£135 * LB Off peak **MEALS:** Lunch £12.50-£15.50 & alc High tea £9.50-£12.50 Dinner £20.50 & alc International Cuisine V meals Coffee am Tea pm **FACILITIES:** CTV in all bedrooms STV Wkly live entertainment Xmas **CONF:** Thtr 400 Class 120 Board 80 Del £127 * **SERVICES:** Lift Night porter 350P **NOTES:** No dogs (ex guide dogs) No smoking area in restaurant Last d 10pm Closed 25 Dec **CARDS:**

★★★★ The McCausland Hotel
34-38 Victoria St BT1 3GH
Quality Percentage Score: 61%
☎ 028 90220200 028 90220220
Dir: *Victoria St is one way, hotel next to First Trust building*

This exciting new hotel was created from the conversion of two warehouses built in 1850, with the original Italianate facade being retained. The bedrooms are well equipped. Refined dining is on offer in the restaurant, or there is a continental style cafe.
ROOMS: 60 en suite (bth/shr) (8 fmly) No smoking in 30 bedrooms s £130-£200; d £150-£200 (incl. bkfst) * LB Off peak **MEALS:** Lunch £14.50-£17.50 Dinner £25-£31.50alc International Cuisine V meals Coffee am Tea pm **FACILITIES:** CTV in all bedrooms STV Wkly live entertainment **CONF:** Thtr 60 Class 30 Board 30 Del from £145 * **SERVICES:** Lift Night porter 8P **NOTES:** No dogs (ex guide dogs) Last d 9.30pm Closed 25-27 Dec **CARDS:**

★★★ The Crescent Townhouse

13 Lower Crescent BT7 1NR
Quality Percentage Score: 66%
☎ 028 90323349 📠 028 90320646
Dir: *S towards Queens University, hotel is on Botanic Avenue opposite Botanic Train Station*

A fashionable Regency townhouse well located and adjacent to the botanic gardens. The popular Bar Twelve and Metro Brasserie are on the ground floor, and both reception and the stylishly furnished bedrooms are situated on the upper floors.

ROOMS: 11 en suite (bth/shr) No smoking in 2 bedrooms s £65-£110; d £90-£110 (incl. bkfst) * Off peak **MEALS:** Lunch £4.50-£8.50alc Dinner £5-£13alc Italian Cuisine V meals Coffee am Tea pm **FACILITIES:** CTV in all bedrooms **SERVICES:** Night porter **NOTES:** No dogs No coaches Last d 10pm Closed 25-27 Dec & 11-13 Jul
CARDS:

★★★ *Posthouse Belfast*

Posthouse

Kingsway, Dunmurry BT17 9ES
Quality Percentage Score: 66%
☎ 028 90612101 📠 028 90626546
Dir: *6 miles SW of Belfast City Centre on A1*

Situated just outside Dunmurry, this purpose built hotel is set in its own attractive landscaped grounds. Public areas are bright and comfortable with light meals being available all day, in addition to the more formal restaurant where both fixed-price and carte menus are offered. Bedrooms are comfortable, attractively decorated and furnished, and have good facilities.

ROOMS: 82 en suite (bth/shr) (6 fmly) No smoking in 55 bedrooms **MEALS:** International Cuisine V meals Coffee am Tea pm **FACILITIES:** CTV in all bedrooms **CONF:** Thtr 450 Class 230 Board 80 **SERVICES:** Lift Night porter 250P **NOTES:** No smoking area in restaurant Last d 10.30pm **CARDS:**

★★★ Lansdowne Court

657 Antrim Rd BT15 4EF
Quality Percentage Score: 64%
☎ 028 90773317 📠 028 90370125
Dir: *3m N of Belfast City Centre on the main Antrim road*

This bright modern hotel is situated north of the city centre beside the A6, and has particular appeal for the business guest. Bedrooms are tastefully decorated and offer smart furnishings together with a good range of amenities. Public areas include a spacious, lively bar and a themed restaurant.

ROOMS: 25 en suite (bth/shr) (3 fmly) s £38-£75; d £55-£95 (incl. bkfst) * LB Off peak **MEALS:** Sunday Lunch fr £10.50 & alc Dinner £15.50 & alc V meals Coffee am Tea pm **FACILITIES:** CTV in all bedrooms STV Wkly live entertainment **CONF:** Thtr 250 Class 60 Board 40 **SERVICES:** Night porter 50P **NOTES:** No dogs (ex guide dogs) No smoking area in restaurant Last d 9.15pm Closed 25 & 26 Dec
CARDS:

★★★ Malone Lodge

Best Western

60 Eglantine Av BT9 6DY
Quality Percentage Score: 62%
☎ 028 90382409 📠 028 90382706

Having particular appeal for the visiting businessman, this smart modern hotel is close to the university and within easy reach of central amenities. Smart public areas include an inviting foyer lounge, a tastefully appointed split-level restaurant, and a well stocked bar with a lively atmosphere. Bedrooms, though variable in size, are comfortably modern in appointment and offer a good range of amenities.

ROOMS: 50 en suite (bth/shr) (13 fmly) s £75; d £95 (incl. bkfst) * LB Off peak **MEALS:** European Cuisine V meals Coffee am Tea pm **FACILITIES:** CTV in all bedrooms STV Sauna Gym **CONF:** Thtr 150 **SERVICES:** Lift Night porter 45P **NOTES:** No dogs (ex guide dogs) No smoking area in restaurant Last d 10pm **CARDS:**

★★ *Balmoral*

Blacks Rd, Dunmurry BT10 0ND
Quality Percentage Score: 59%
☎ 028 90301234 📠 028 90601455
Dir: *take M1, 3m exit at Suffolk slip rd, turn right, hotel approx 300 yards*

This smart modern hotel is situated south of Belfast in the village of Drumurry and, with easy access to the M1 has particular appeal for business guests. Bedrooms vary in size and offer practical furnishings together with the expected amenities. Public areas include a choice of contrasting bars, one of which provides an informal food option to the main restaurant. Good banqueting facilities are available.

ROOMS: 44 en suite (bth/shr) **MEALS:** V meals Coffee am Tea pm **FACILITIES:** CTV in all bedrooms STV **CONF:** Thtr 150 Class 100 Board 80 Del from £65 * **SERVICES:** Night porter Air conditioning 300P **NOTES:** No smoking area in restaurant Last d 11pm Closed 25 Dec
CARDS:

See advert on this page

Indicates that the star classification has not been confirmed under the New Quality Standards, see page 7 for further information.

B

⌂ Holiday Inn Express Belfast
106a University St BT7 1HP
☎ 028 90311909 📠 028 90311910
Dir: *behind Queens University. Turn left at lights on Botanic Ave onto University St. Holiday Inn on left, 500yds down street*
This modern building offers accommodation in smart, spacious and well equipped bedrooms, all with en-suite bathrooms. Refreshments may be taken at the informal restaurant. For details about current prices, consult the Contents Page under Hotel Groups for the Holiday Inn Express phone number.
ROOMS: 114 en suite (bth/shr) (incl. bkfst) d £54.95-£64.95 **CONF:** Thtr 200 Class 100 Board 70 Del from £85 *

⌂ Travelodge
15 Brunswick St BT2 7GE
☎ 028 90333555 📠 028 90232999
Dir: *from M2 follow city centre signs to Oxford St turn right to May St, Brunswick St is 4th on left*
This modern building offers accommodation in smart, spacious and well equipped bedrooms, all with en-suite bathrooms. Refreshments may be taken at the nearby family restaurant. For details about current prices, consult the Contents Page under Hotel Groups for the Travelodge phone number.
ROOMS: 76 en suite (bth/shr) **CONF:** Thtr 65 Class 50 Board 34 Del from £104 *

Jurys Belfast Inn
Fisherwick Place, Great Victoria St BT2 7AP
☎ 028 90533500 📠 028 90533511
Dir: *at the intersection of Grosvenor Road and Great Victoria St, beside the Opera House*
In the heart of the city, this smart new hotel has particular appeal for business people. Public areas are contemporary in style and include a foyer lounge, well-stocked bar, and a smart restaurant. Bedrooms are spacious with pretty fabrics and offer a good range of amenities, including modem points.
ROOMS: 190 en suite (bth/shr) No smoking in 76 bedrooms d £63-£65 * Off peak **MEALS:** Bar Lunch £4.50-£6.95 International Cuisine V meals **FACILITIES:** CTV in all bedrooms STV Wkly live entertainment **CONF:** Thtr 35 Class 20 Board 20 **SERVICES:** Lift **NOTES:** No dogs (ex guide dogs) No smoking area in restaurant Closed 24-26 Dec
CARDS:

BETTYSTOWN Co Meath **Map 01 D4**

★★★★ Neptune Beach Hotel & Leisure Club
Quality Percentage Score: 63%
☎ 041 9827107 📠 041 9827412
Dir: *Bettystown is located just off the main Dublin/Belfast road N1*
This new hotel overlooks the sea and has access to a sandy beach. Public areas include an inviting lounge and an attractive Winter Garden. Many bedrooms enjoy sea views.
ROOMS: 38 en suite (bth/shr) No smoking in 14 bedrooms s IR£70-IR£100; d IR£90-IR£140 (incl. bkfst) * LB Off peak **MEALS:** Lunch IR£15 Dinner IR£27.50-IR£35 French & Mediterranean Cuisine Coffee am Tea pm **FACILITIES:** CTV in all bedrooms STV Indoor swimming pool (heated) Sauna Solarium Gym Jacuzzi/spa Steam room Kiddies pool Wkly live entertainment Xmas **CONF:** Thtr 250 Class 150 **SERVICES:** Lift Night porter 60P **NOTES:** No dogs (ex guide dogs) Last d 9.30pm
CARDS:

BIRR Co Offaly **Map 01 C3**

★★★ *Dooley's* Emmet Square
Quality Percentage Score: 61%
☎ 0509 20032 📠 0509 21332
This well known hotel dates back to the era of the horse-drawn Bianconi carriages, when it was used as a staging post. The hotel enjoys an excellent reputation for hospitality and cuisine. Dooly's is only a short stroll from Birr Castle Demesne with its great telescope.
ROOMS: 18 en suite (bth/shr) (4 fmly) **MEALS:** Irish & Continental Cuisine V meals Coffee am Tea pm **FACILITIES:** CTV in all bedrooms STV Wkly live entertainment **CONF:** Thtr 400 Class 200 Board 30 Del from IR£58 * **SERVICES:** Night porter **NOTES:** No dogs (ex guide dogs) No smoking area in restaurant Last d 9.30pm RS 25-26 Dec
CARDS:

★★★ *County Arms*
Quality Percentage Score: 60%
☎ 0509 20791 📠 0509 21234
Dir: *N7 from Dublin to Roscrea, N62 to Birr, hotel on right before church*
This fine Georgian house has comfortable bedrooms all furnished and decorated to a very high standard. These rooms overlook the meticulously kept Victorian walled gardens which supply the fruit, vegetables and herbs to the hotel kitchens. A new garden suite has been fully adapted for those with mobility problems. There is a choice of two restaurants, a bar and a comfortable lounge which has recently been refurbished.
ROOMS: 24 en suite (bth/shr) (4 fmly) No smoking in 2 bedrooms **MEALS:** Irish & French Cuisine V meals Coffee am Tea pm **FACILITIES:** CTV in all bedrooms STV Squash Wkly live entertainment **CONF:** Thtr 250 Class 250 Board 150 **SERVICES:** Night porter 150P **NOTES:** No dogs (ex guide dogs) Last d 9.30pm RS 25 Dec
CARDS:

BLARNEY Co Cork **Map 01 B2**

★★★ Blarney Park
Quality Percentage Score: 69%
☎ 021 385281 📠 021 381506
Dir: *located in the village of Blarney, just 10 minutes from Cork city on the N20 between Cork and Limerick*
Standing in 10 acres of gardens beneath the woods of Blarney Castle, the hotel offers comfortable lounges, a smart bistro, and a convivial bar. There is also an excellent leisure centre featuring a pool with a 40-metre slide and there are good facilities for children, with plenty of play space in the grounds.
ROOMS: 91 en suite (bth/shr) (20 fmly) No smoking in 2 bedrooms s IR£64-IR£74; d IR£98-IR£118 (incl. bkfst) * LB Off peak **MEALS:** Bar Lunch IR£3-IR£8 Irish / French Cuisine V meals Coffee am Tea pm **FACILITIES:** CTV in all bedrooms STV Indoor swimming pool (heated) Tennis (hard) Sauna Gym Steam room Childrens pool & playroom Wkly live entertainment ch fac Xmas **CONF:** Thtr 300 Class 130 Board 80 **SERVICES:** Lift Night porter 100P **NOTES:** No dogs (ex guide dogs) No smoking area in restaurant **CARDS:**

★★★ Christy's
Quality Percentage Score: 68%
☎ 021 385011 📠 021 385350
Dir: *N20, exit at the Blarney sign, at the R617 5km from Cork city*
Part of the famous Blarney Woollen Mills and skillfully converted into a hotel, Christy's stands within sight of the historic castle. Staff are pleasantly attentive and the Restaurant and Library have a relaxing atmosphere. Adjacent to the hotel is an interesting shopping complex which includes Christy's Pub and self-service restaurant.
ROOMS: 49 en suite (bth/shr) (2 fmly) No smoking in 10 bedrooms s IR£44.50-IR£61; d IR£69-IR£98 (incl. bkfst) * LB Off peak **MEALS:** Lunch IR£11 Dinner IR£17.50 V meals Coffee am Tea pm **FACILITIES:** CTV in all bedrooms Squash Sauna Solarium Gym Fitness classes **CONF:** Thtr 300 Class 100 Board 20 **SERVICES:** Lift Night porter 200P **NOTES:** No dogs (ex guide dogs) No smoking area in restaurant Last d 9.30pm Closed 24-26 Dec RS Good Friday
CARDS:

BLESSINGTON Co Wicklow — Map 01 D3

★★★ *Downshire House*
Quality Percentage Score: 61%
☎ 045 865199 📠 045 865335
Dir: *on N81*
This snug, family-run Georgian house is renowned for its friendly atmosphere, and is gradually being restored and extended. Bedrooms are comfortable though sizes vary, and the front lounge offers a perfect spot from which to observe village activities. Cooking is in good country house traditional style, and roasts come with all the trimmings and are followed by home-baked desserts.
ROOMS: 14 en suite (bth/shr) 11 annexe en suite (bth/shr) **MEALS:** V meals Coffee am Tea pm **FACILITIES:** CTV in all bedrooms Tennis (hard) Croquet lawn Table tennis **CONF:** Thtr 40 Class 20 Board 20 **SERVICES:** Night porter 30P **NOTES:** No dogs (ex guide dogs) No smoking area in restaurant Last d 9.30pm Closed 22 Dec-6 Jan
CARDS:

BOYLE Co Roscommon — Map 01 B4

★★ *Royal*
Quality Percentage Score: 64%
☎ 079 62016 📠 079 62016
Dir: *turn off N4 Dublin-Sligo road for Boyle, adjacent to bridge in town centre*
Set beside the river in the town centre, The Royal is a comfortable family-run hotel offering recently refurbished accommodation. Public areas are cosy and attractively furnished, and bedrooms are spacious and well maintained. Beautifully-prepared meals are served from a table d'hote menu, and food is also available from the bar and self-service buffet.
ROOMS: 16 en suite (bth/shr) (6 fmly) **MEALS:** Irish, French & Italian Cuisine V meals Coffee am Tea pm **FACILITIES:** CTV in all bedrooms STV ch fac **CONF:** Thtr 80 Class 35 Board 35 **SERVICES:** Night porter 120P **NOTES:** No smoking area in restaurant Closed 25-26 Dec
CARDS:

BRAY Co Wicklow — Map 01 D4

★★★ *Royal* Main St
Quality Percentage Score: 63%
☎ 01 2862935 📠 01 2867373
Dir: *from N11, First exit for Bray, 2nd exit from rdbt, through 2 sets traffic lights across bridge, hotel on the left side*
The Royal Hotel is situated on the main street near the seafront, just seven miles from the Dun Laoghaire ferryport. The hotel has a well equipped leisure centre, and free car parking is available.
ROOMS: 91 en suite (bth/shr) (3 fmly) **MEALS:** European Cuisine V meals Coffee am Tea pm **FACILITIES:** CTV in all bedrooms Indoor swimming pool (heated) Sauna Solarium Gym Jacuzzi/spa Children's pool Whirlpool spa Creche Massage and beauty clinic Wkly live entertainment **CONF:** Thtr 450 Class 300 Board 100 **SERVICES:** Lift Night porter 100P **NOTES:** No dogs (ex guide dogs) No smoking in restaurant Last d 11pm **CARDS:**

BUNBEG Co Donegal — Map 01 B6

★★★ Ostan Gweedore
Quality Percentage Score: 68%
☎ 075 31177 & 31188 📠 075 31726
Dir: *1km up coast from Bunbeg crossroads - first road left down to sea*
Day rooms here are designed to take full advantage of the ever-changing seascape and as such run the length of the hotel. Fresh seafood features daily on the carefully prepared menus. The bedrooms are spacious and provided with all the expected modern amenities.
ROOMS: 39 en suite (bth/shr) (6 fmly) s IR£50-IR£55; d IR£90-IR£95 (incl. bkfst) * LB Off peak **MEALS:** Dinner IR£25 V meals Coffee am Tea pm **FACILITIES:** CTV in all bedrooms STV Indoor swimming pool (heated) Sauna Solarium Gym Jacuzzi/spa Wkly live entertainment **CONF:** Thtr 250 Class 150 **SERVICES:** Night porter 80P **NOTES:** No dogs (ex guide dogs) No smoking area in restaurant Last d 8.50pm Closed Dec-Jan RS Oct, Nov, Dec, Feb & Mar **CARDS:**

BUNRATTY Co Clare — Map 01 B3

★★★ *Fitzpatrick Bunratty*
Quality Percentage Score: 61%
☎ 061 361177 📠 061 471252
Dir: *take Bunratty by-pass, exit off Limerick/Shannon dual carriageway*
Situated in the picturesque village of Bunratty, famous for its medieval castle, this modern ranch-style building is surrounded by lawns and flower beds. Bedrooms and public rooms are richly timbered, and there is a helipad in the grounds.
ROOMS: 115 en suite (bth/shr) (7 fmly) No smoking in 7 bedrooms **MEALS:** European Cuisine V meals Coffee am Tea pm **FACILITIES:** CTV in all bedrooms STV Indoor swimming pool (heated) Sauna Gym Jacuzzi/spa Steam room Wkly live entertainment **CONF:** Thtr 1000 Class 550 Board 100 **SERVICES:** Night porter 150P **NOTES:** No dogs (ex guide dogs) No smoking area in restaurant Last d 10pm RS 24-25 Dec
CARDS:

CAHERCIVEEN Co Kerry — Map 01 A2

★★ *Caherciveen Park Hotel* Valentia Rd
Quality Percentage Score: 60%
☎ 066 72548
Sitated in one of the villages on the Ring of Kerry, this pleasant hotel is near beaches and many places of interest. New ownership and a refurbishment programme have enhanced the hotel where there is also an inviting bar and restaurant. Caherciveen is well located for trips to the islands.

CAHERDANIEL Co Kerry — Map 01 A2

★★★ Derrynane
Quality Percentage Score: 63%
☎ 066 9475136 📠 066 9475160
Dir: *hotel is just off the main road. 2mins walk*
Strategically placed half-way around the famous Ring of Kerry, this modern hotel overlooking the sea offers a relaxed and friendly atmosphere. Manager Mary O'Connor and her team are attentive and helpful, and the gardens and some of the bedrooms take advantage of the spectacular sea views. The area is ideal for touring and enjoying the scenery, and there are plenty of beaches.
ROOMS: 74 en suite (bth) (30 fmly) s IR£50-IR£60; d IR£70-IR£90 (incl. bkfst) * LB Off peak **MEALS:** Dinner IR£22.50 International Cuisine V meals Coffee am Tea pm **FACILITIES:** CTV in all bedrooms STV Outdoor swimming pool (heated) Tennis (hard) Fishing Snooker Sauna Solarium Gym Pool table Wkly live entertainment **SERVICES:** Night porter 60P **NOTES:** No smoking in restaurant Last d 9pm Closed 4 Oct-15 Apr **CARDS:**

CAHIR Co Tipperary — Map 01 C3

★★★ *Cahir House* The Square
Quality Percentage Score: 70%
☎ 52 42727 📠 52 42727
Dir: *travelling S on N8 turn off at Cahir by-pass follow N24 to town, hotel on square in centre of town, car park at rear*
Cahir House, in the centre of the heritage town of Cahir, has been extending hospitality to travellers since the days of the famous Bianconi horse-drawn coaches. Much refurbished in recent years, to offer modern comforts in its well equipped and tastefully furnished rooms, Cahir House maintains traditional

contd.

standards of welcome and food. The hotel provides a veritable library of information on the surrounding area.
ROOMS: 31 en suite (bth/shr) (3 fmly) No smoking in 17 bedrooms **MEALS:** V meals Coffee am Tea pm **FACILITIES:** CTV in all bedrooms STV Wkly live entertainment **CONF:** Thtr 500 Class 300 Board 80 **SERVICES:** Night porter 80P **NOTES:** No dogs (ex guide dogs) No smoking area in restaurant Last d 9.30pm Closed 25 Dec RS 24-26 Dec & Good Fri **CARDS:**

C

CARLOW Co Carlow — Map 01 C3

★★★ Dolmen Kilkenny Rd
Quality Percentage Score: 72%
☎ 0503 42002 0503 42375
In 20 acres of landscaped grounds this hotel nestles in a peaceful, riverside location. Guests can relax in the grounds or take advantage of the free coarse fishing. Public areas include a spacious reception and foyer, a large bar and restaurant and a luxuriously appointed boardroom, which doubles as an additional lounge, overlooking the river. Bedrooms are all well equipped and comfortable.
ROOMS: 40 en suite (bth/shr) 12 annexe en suite (shr) (1 fmly) s IR£48.50-IR£65; d IR£79-IR£105 (incl. bkfst) * LB Off peak **MEALS:** Lunch IR£13.50 High tea fr IR£7.95 Dinner IR£17.50 French Cuisine V meals Coffee am Tea pm **FACILITIES:** CTV in 40 bedrooms STV Fishing Wkly live entertainment Xmas **CONF:** Thtr 1000 Class 300 Board 50 **SERVICES:** Night porter Air conditioning 300P **NOTES:** No dogs (ex guide dogs) No smoking area in restaurant Last d 9.15pm Closed 25 Dec **CARDS:**

See advert on opposite page

★★★ *Seven Oaks* Athy Rd
Quality Percentage Score: 65%
☎ 0503 31308 0503 32155
Near Carlow town centre, this hotel has a modern interior, while the majority of the rooms are contemporary in style and well equipped. Public areas are comfortable and there are separate function facilities that cater for a wide range of events.
ROOMS: 32 en suite (bth/shr) (3 fmly) **MEALS:** V meals Coffee am Tea pm **FACILITIES:** CTV in all bedrooms STV Fishing Wkly live entertainment **CONF:** Thtr 400 Class 150 Board 80 **SERVICES:** Lift Night porter Air conditioning 165P **NOTES:** No dogs (ex guide dogs) No smoking area in restaurant Last d 10pm Closed 25 Dec & Good Friday **CARDS:**

CARNLOUGH Co Antrim — Map 01 D6

★★★ *Londonderry Arms*
20 Harbour Rd BT44 0EU
Quality Percentage Score: 64%
☎ 028 28885255 028 28885263
Dir: *14m N from Larne on the coast road*
Genuine Irish hospitality is the hallmark of this comfortable ivy-clad coaching inn, close to the small harbour. For almost 50 years the O'Neill family have been welcoming guests old and new. Public areas include a choice of cosy lounges and well stocked bars, the restaurant offers a varied selection of wholesome Antrim fare.
ROOMS: 35 en suite (bth/shr) (5 fmly) **MEALS:** Irish & French Cuisine V meals Coffee am Tea pm **FACILITIES:** CTV in all bedrooms STV Fishing Cycles available **CONF:** Thtr 100 Class 50 Board 50 **SERVICES:** Lift Night porter 50P **NOTES:** No dogs No smoking area in restaurant Last d 9pm **CARDS:**

CARRICKFERGUS Co Antrim — Map 01 D5

★ Dobbins Inn 6-8 High St BT38 7AP
Quality Percentage Score: 68%
☎ 028 93351905 028 93351905
Dir: *from Belfast take M2, keep right at rdbt follow A2 to Carrickfergus, turn left opp castle*
Colourful flowering window boxes adorn the front of this popular inn, found near the ancient castle and other attractions. Public areas have undergone considerable alteration and improvement, care has been taken to preserve the original character. The bedrooms have also benefitted from refurbishment.
ROOMS: 15 en suite (bth/shr) (2 fmly) s £44-£46; d £64-£66 (incl. bkfst) * LB Off peak **MEALS:** Sunday Lunch £3-£12.95 High tea £13.95 Dinner £15 English & French Cuisine V meals Coffee am Tea pm **FACILITIES:** CTV in all bedrooms Wkly live entertainment **SERVICES:** Night porter **NOTES:** No smoking area in restaurant Last d 9pm Closed 25-26 Dec & 1 Jan RS Good Friday **CARDS:**

CARRICKMACROSS Co Monaghan — Map 01 C4

★★★★ Nuremore
Quality Percentage Score: 75%
☎ 042 61438 042 61853
Dir: *3km S of Carrickmacross, on main Dublin/Derry road*
Overlooking a lake and 18-hole golf course, the Nuremore is a quiet retreat with excellent facilities. This Victorian mansion has spacious public areas, and a wide variety of indoor and outdoor leisure and sporting facilities for the active and energetic. A very good restaurant serves imaginative dishes cooked with flair and confidence. A dedicated team ensures a pleasant visit to this friendly hotel with easy access to the N2 from the recently opened Northern section of the M50 Motorway in Dublin.
ROOMS: 72 en suite (bth/shr) s IR£100-IR£125; d IR£150-IR£190 (incl. bkfst) * LB Off peak **MEALS:** Lunch IR£14.50-IR£16.50 Dinner fr IR£26 European Cuisine V meals Coffee am Tea pm **FACILITIES:** CTV in all bedrooms STV Indoor swimming pool (heated) Golf 18 Tennis (grass) Fishing Squash Snooker Sauna Solarium Gym Putting green Jacuzzi/spa Xmas **CONF:** Thtr 250 Class 55 Board 30 **SERVICES:** Lift Air conditioning 200P **NOTES:** No dogs (ex guide dogs) No coaches Last d 9.30pm **CARDS:**

CASHEL Co Galway — Map 01 A4

The Premier Collection

★★★ Cashel House
☎ 095 31001 095 31077
Dir: *turn S off N59, hotel 1.5km W of Recess*
RELAIS & CHATEAUX.
Award winning gardens are the setting for this gracious country house hotel, which overlooks Cashel
contd.

Bay. Rich fabrics and antique furnishings contribute to the atmosphere of luxury and peaceful elegance created by the McEvilly family. The comfortable lounges have turf fires and antique furnishings, and the restaurant offers local produce such as Connemara lamb, skilfully prepared. Bedrooms are appealing, and luxury suites are available.
ROOMS: 32 en suite (bth/shr) (4 fmly) s IR£54-IR£80; d IR£108-IR£160 (incl. bkfst) * LB Off peak **MEALS:** Bar Lunch IR£8-IR£25alc Dinner IR£32-IR£34 Irish & French Cuisine V meals Coffee am Tea pm **FACILITIES:** CTV in all bedrooms STV Outdoor swimming pool Tennis (hard) Fishing Riding Xmas **SERVICES:** 40P **NOTES:** No coaches No children 5yrs No smoking area in restaurant Last d 8.45pm Closed 4 Jan-4 Feb **CARDS:**

★★★ Zetland Country House

MANOR HOUSE HOTELS

Cashel Bay
Quality Percentage Score: 77%
☎ 095 31111 Fax 095 31117
Dir: *N59 from Galway towards Clifden, turn right after recess onto R340, after approx 4m turn left onto R341, hotel is 1m ahead on right*
Set in very attractive gardens featuring an unusual mix of rock formation, flowers, shrubs and woodland, this peaceful and comfortable country house overlooking Cashel Bay is enhanced by attractive furnishings and decor. Public areas include a fine lounge and reading room as well as a smart cocktail bar; many of the bedrooms have sea or garden views - and the dining room has both. Warm hospitality is matched by good food and service, leisure facilities include shooting parties (snipe and woodcock). Riding is available close by.
ROOMS: 19 en suite (bth/shr) (10 fmly) s IR£82-IR£122; d IR£119-IR£159 (incl. bkfst) * LB Off peak **MEALS:** Bar Lunch IR£15-IR£20alc V meals Coffee am Tea pm **FACILITIES:** CTV in all bedrooms STV Tennis (hard) Fishing Snooker Croquet lawn **CONF:** Board 20 **SERVICES:** 32P **NOTES:** No smoking in restaurant Closed Nov-9 Apr
CARDS:

★★★ *Cashel Palace Hotel*

Quality Percentage Score: 70%
☎ 062 62707 Fax 062 61521
Dir: *in centre of town*
The Rock of Cashel, floodlit at night, forms a dramatic backdrop to this fascinating hotel which was originally built in the 18th century as a bishop's palace. It retains the integrity and character of its original building, although it has been totally restored and modernised. A lovely drawing room leads out to gardens whose focal point is two ancient mulberry trees and from which a private walk takes guests to the Rock of Cashel. For pre-dinner drinks there is a choice between the cosy library or the bar adjoining the Buttery Restaurant. All the bedrooms, whether designated 'superior' or 'standard', are comfortably well equipped and can be reached by elevator. The Cashel Palace is within easy reach of many historical sites and there are opportunities for fishing and horse riding.
ROOMS: 13 en suite (bth/shr) (4 fmly) No smoking in 5 bedrooms **MEALS:** V meals Coffee am Tea pm **FACILITIES:** CTV in all bedrooms STV ch fac **CONF:** Thtr 120 Class 45 Board 35 **SERVICES:** Lift Night porter 35P **NOTES:** No dogs (ex guide dogs) No smoking area in restaurant **CARDS:**

CASTLEBAR Co Mayo **Map 01 B4**

★★★ Breaffy House

Quality Percentage Score: 67%

☎ 094 22033 📠 094 22276

Dir: *on N60 in direction of Tuam and Galway*

This 19th-century manor house stands in 100 acres of leafy woodlands. Inside there is a new entrance and reception foyer, several new lounges and a wing of luxuriously appointed bedrooms which are an equal match for the attractively decorated rooms in the original house. Other facilities include a restaurant, a choice of bars, conference suites and a mini-gym.

ROOMS: 62 en suite (bth/shr) (3 fmly) s IR£60-IR£70; d IR£90-IR£110 (incl. bkfst) * LB Off peak **MEALS:** Lunch IR£9.75-IR£10.75 Dinner IR£20-IR£22 & alc Irish & International Cuisine V meals Coffee am Tea pm **FACILITIES:** CTV in all bedrooms STV Gym Croquet lawn Crazy golf Wkly live entertainment **CONF:** Thtr 250 Class 150 Board 50 Del from IR£75 * **SERVICES:** Lift Night porter 300P **NOTES:** No dogs (ex guide dogs) No smoking area in restaurant Last d 8.45pm Closed 23-26 Dec **CARDS:**

See advert on page 967

★★ Welcome Inn

Quality Percentage Score: 67%

☎ 094 22288 & 22054 📠 094 21766

Dir: *take N5 to Castlebar situated near the town centre via ring road & rdbts passed the Church of the Holy Rosary*

This town-centre hotel offers a range of modern facilities behind its Tudor frontage, including a new banqueting/conference centre. Bedrooms are well equipped and there is a night club with disco on some evenings as well as traditional music nights in the summer.

ROOMS: 40 en suite (bth/shr) (5 fmly) s IR£28-IR£39; d IR£55-IR£78 (incl. bkfst) * LB Off peak **MEALS:** Lunch IR£9.95-IR£13.95 Dinner IR£13.95-IR£19.95 & alc Irish & French Cuisine V meals Coffee am Tea pm **FACILITIES:** CTV in all bedrooms STV Wkly live entertainment **CONF:** Thtr 500 Class 350 **SERVICES:** Lift Night porter 100P **NOTES:** No dogs (ex guide dogs) No smoking area in restaurant Last d 9.15pm Closed 23-25 Dec **CARDS:**

CASTLECONNELL Co Limerick **Map 01 B3**

★★★ Castle Oaks House

Quality Percentage Score: 66%

☎ 061 377666 📠 061 377717

Dir: *turn off N7 8km outside Limerick City. Hotel is 3km on left*

A fine old Georgian house with grounds reaching down to the River Shannon, set in the tiny village of Castleconnell. The hotel has been extended and upgraded, and guests can enjoy first-class comfort in well-equipped modern bedrooms. Facilities include river walks, good fishing and free use of a leisure centre.

ROOMS: 20 en suite (bth/shr) (9 fmly) No smoking in 1 bedroom s IR£55-IR£71.50; d IR£76-IR£104.50 (incl. bkfst) * LB Off peak **MEALS:** Lunch IR£11 Dinner IR£22 & alc French Cuisine V meals Coffee am Tea pm **FACILITIES:** CTV in all bedrooms STV Indoor swimming pool (heated) Golf 9 Tennis (hard) Fishing Snooker Sauna Solarium Gym Jacuzzi/spa Angling centre Wkly live entertainment **CONF:** Thtr 350 Class 95 Board 40 **SERVICES:** Night porter 200P **NOTES:** No dogs (ex guide dogs) No smoking area in restaurant Last d 9pm Closed 24-26 Dec **CARDS:**

See advert on opposite page

CAVAN Co Cavan **Map 01 C4**

★★★ Kilmore Dublin Rd

Quality Percentage Score: 65%

☎ 049 32288 📠 049 32458

Dir: *approx 3km from Cavan on N3*

Set on a hillside on the outskirts of Cavan, this comfortable hotel features spacious public areas. Good food is served in the Annalee Restaurant, which is always appreciated by guests returning from a day's fishing, golf, windsurfing or boating (all available nearby).

ROOMS: 39 en suite (bth/shr) (17 fmly) s fr IR£48; d fr IR£76 (incl. bkfst) * LB Off peak **MEALS:** Lunch IR£4.50-IR£10 Dinner IR£19.50-IR£28 European Cuisine V meals Coffee am Tea pm **FACILITIES:** CTV in all bedrooms STV Wkly live entertainment Xmas **CONF:** Thtr 300 Class 200 Board 60 **SERVICES:** Night porter Air conditioning 450P **NOTES:** No dogs (ex guide dogs) No smoking area in restaurant Last d 9.30pm **CARDS:**

CLIFDEN Co Galway **Map 01 A4**

★★★ *Abbeyglen Castle* Sky Rd

Quality Percentage Score: 76%

☎ 095 21201 📠 095 21797

Dir: *take N59 from Galway to Clifden. Hotel is 1km from Clifden on the Sky Road*

Set in its own grounds with panoramic views over Clifden Bay, this friendly family-run hotel gives high priority to hospitality and good food. Musical evenings are a regular occurrence, creating a good atmosphere in the cosy bar with its turf fires. Extensive grounds include a helipad.

ROOMS: 36 en suite (bth/shr) No smoking in 10 bedrooms **MEALS:** International Cuisine V meals Coffee am Tea pm **FACILITIES:** CTV in all bedrooms STV Outdoor swimming pool (heated) Tennis (hard) Snooker Sauna Putting green Jacuzzi/spa Wkly live entertainment **CONF:** Thtr 100 Class 50 Board 40 Del from IR£121 * **SERVICES:** Lift 40P **NOTES:** No coaches No smoking area in restaurant Last d 9.30pm Closed 11 Jan-1 Feb **CARDS:**

★★★ *Rock Glen Country House Hotel*

Quality Percentage Score: 76%

☎ 095 21035 & 21393 📠 095 21737

Dir: *N6 from Dublin to Galway, N57 from Galway to Clifden*

John and Evangeline Roche run this converted 18th-century shooting lodge set in its own grounds. The emphasis is on traditional hospitality, with enjoyable cuisine under John's personal supervision. There are comfortable lounges with turf fires, and a cosy cocktail bar.

ROOMS: 29 en suite (bth/shr) (3 fmly) **MEALS:** Irish & French Cuisine V meals Coffee am Tea pm **FACILITIES:** CTV in all bedrooms STV Tennis (hard) Snooker Croquet lawn Putting green Wkly live entertainment **SERVICES:** 50P **NOTES:** No dogs (ex guide dogs) No smoking in restaurant Last d 9pm Closed 20 Nov-20 Dec & 7 Jan-7 Feb **CARDS:**

★★★ Ardagh Ballyconneely Rd

Quality Percentage Score: 69%

☎ 095 21384 📠 095 21314

Dir: *N59 Galway to Clifden, signposted for Ballyconneely*

A family-run hotel in a quiet location, just over a mile from Clifden. The restaurant overlooks the bay and serves award-winning food with good attention to detail, and fine lounges take full advantage of the views of Ardbear Bay.

ROOMS: 21 en suite (bth/shr) (2 fmly) s IR£57.50-IR£65; d IR£90-IR£105 (incl. bkfst) * LB Off peak **MEALS:** French/International Cuisine Coffee am Tea pm **FACILITIES:** CTV in all bedrooms Pool table **SERVICES:** 35P **NOTES:** No dogs No coaches No smoking area in restaurant Closed Nov-Mar **CARDS:**

★★★ Alcock & Brown Hotel

Quality Percentage Score: 60%

☎ 095 21206 21086 📠 095 21842

Dir: *Take N59 from Galway via Oughterard, hotel in centre of Clifden*

A comfortable, town-centre hotel, much of which has been refurbished. The bar and restaurant are inviting with particularly pleasant decor. The menu offers a good selection of fish dishes, but the food is consistently good throughout all courses. The friendly, attentive staff offer good service.

ROOMS: 20 en suite (bth/shr) s IR£45-IR£53; d IR£62-IR£78 (incl. bkfst) LB Off peak **MEALS:** Bar Lunch IR£5-IR£10 Dinner IR£12-IR£25alc European Cuisine V meals Coffee am Tea pm **FACILITIES:** CTV in all bedrooms Wkly live entertainment **NOTES:** No dogs (ex guide dogs) No smoking area in restaurant Last d 9.30pm Closed 23-25 Dec

CARDS:

CLONAKILTY Co Cork — Map 01 B2

Hotel of the Year

★★★★ The Lodge & Spa at Inchydoney Island

Quality Percentage Score: 75%

☎ 023 33143 📠 023 35229

Dir: *follow N71 West Cork road to Clonakilty, at entry rdbt in Clonakilty take 2nd exit and follow signs to Lodge and Spa*

Chosen as Hotel of the Year for Ireland, this luxurious hotel enjoys a stunning location on the coastline, with steps down to a sandy beach. The bedrooms are furnished in a warm, contemporary style and most rooms have sea views. The lounge is superb and there is a cocktail bar with a patio and a library. The restaurant serves an imaginative menu.

ROOMS: 67 en suite (bth/shr) (24 fmly) No smoking in 17 bedrooms s IR£120; d IR£160-IR£190 * LB Off peak **MEALS:** Lunch IR£16 Dinner IR£28 & alc Medditeranean Cuisine V meals Coffee am Tea pm **FACILITIES:** CTV in all bedrooms STV Indoor swimming pool (heated) Fishing Riding Snooker Sauna Gym Pool table Jacuzzi/spa Thalassotherapy spa Wkly live entertainment Xmas **CONF:** Thtr 300 Class 150 Board 100 Del from IR£120 * **SERVICES:** Lift Night porter 200P **NOTES:** No dogs No smoking area in restaurant Last d 10pm

CARDS:

CLONMEL Co Tipperary — Map 01 C2

★★★ Minella

Quality Percentage Score: 73%

☎ 052 22388 📠 052 24381

This mansion stands in nine acres of grounds on the banks of the River Suir. The public rooms are in the main building, while the east wing extension houses comfortable, well equipped bedrooms, some with jacuzzis. All rooms have good views. The hotel is owned and managed by the Nallen family.

ROOMS: 70 en suite (bth/shr) (8 fmly) No smoking in 16 bedrooms s IR£70-IR£90; d IR£100-IR£120 (incl. bkfst) * LB Off peak **MEALS:** Lunch IR£14-IR£20 High tea fr IR£15 Dinner IR£25-IR£35 & alc V meals Coffee am Tea pm **FACILITIES:** CTV in all bedrooms STV Indoor swimming pool (heated) Outdoor swimming pool (heated) Tennis (hard) Fishing Sauna Gym Croquet lawn Putting green Jacuzzi/spa Aerobics room **CONF:** Thtr 500 Class 300 Board 20 **SERVICES:** Night porter 100P **NOTES:** No dogs No smoking area in restaurant Last d 9.30pm Closed 24-26 Dec **CARDS:**

COBH Co Cork — Map 01 B2

○ Watersedge Yacht Club Quay

☎ 021 815566 📠 021 812011

Dir: *follow road signs for Cobh Heritage Centre*

ROOMS: 19 rms (18 bth/shr) (5 fmly) No smoking in 4 bedrooms **MEALS:** V meals Coffee am Tea pm **FACILITIES:** CTV in all bedrooms **SERVICES:** 27P **NOTES:** No dogs (ex guide dogs) **CARDS:**

COLLOONEY Co Sligo — Map 01 B5

★★★ Markree Castle

Quality Percentage Score: 62%

☎ 071 67800 📠 071 67840

Dir: *turn off N4 at Collooney Crossroads just north of junct with N17, 11km S of Sligo, hotel gates on right hand side after 1km*

This magnificent castle dates back to 1640 and is the ancestral home of Charles Cooper, the present owner, whose family tree is depicted in the stained glass window over the staircase. Considerable restoration work has taken place to transform this historic building into an hotel, and the imposing

contd.

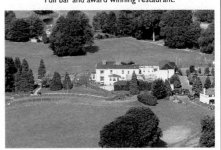

Knockmuldowney Restaurant gives a taste of the style, though service is informal.
ROOMS: 30 en suite (bth/shr) (2 fmly) s IR£66-IR£76; d fr IR£117 (incl. bkfst) LB Off peak **MEALS:** Sunday Lunch IR£13.50 Dinner IR£22-IR£26.90 Irish & French Cuisine Coffee am Tea pm **FACILITIES:** CTV in all bedrooms Riding Croquet lawn **CONF:** Thtr 50 Class 30 Board 20 **SERVICES:** Lift 60P **NOTES:** No smoking in restaurant Last d 9.30pm Closed 24-26 Dec **CARDS:**

C

CORK Co Cork — Map 01 B2

★★★★ Hayfield Manor
Perrott Av, College Rd
Quality Percentage Score: 78%
☎ 021 315600 021 316839
Dir: *1m W of Cork city centre-head for N22 to Killarney, turn left at University Gates off Western Rd. Turn right into College Rd, left into Perrott Ave*
Hayfield Manor offers privacy and seclusion within a mile of Cork city centre. This fine hotel is part of a grand two acre estate and gardens and inside has every modern comfort and maintains an atmosphere of tranquillity. The bedrooms are spacious and contain many thoughtful touches and extras. The rooms also have access to the exclusive health club. Throughout the public rooms, the elegant architecture has been carefully combined with fine furnishings and real fires to create an atmosphere of intimacy. In the Manor Room restaurant, dishes from the interesting carte provide the finishing touch to a fulfilling stay.
ROOMS: 56 en suite (bth/shr) No smoking in 15 bedrooms s IR£140-IR£180; d IR£180-IR£220 (incl. bkfst) * LB Off peak **MEALS:** Lunch IR£19.50 High tea IR£15 & alc Dinner IR£32.50 & alc International Cuisine V meals Coffee am Tea pm **FACILITIES:** CTV in all bedrooms STV Indoor swimming pool (heated) Gym Jacuzzi/spa Steam room Wkly live entertainment Xmas **CONF:** Thtr 100 Class 60 Board 40 Del IR£155 * **SERVICES:** Lift Night porter Air conditioning 80P **NOTES:** No dogs (ex guide dogs) No smoking area in restaurant Last d 9pm
CARDS:

See advert on opposite page

★★★★ The Kingsley Hotel Victoria Cross
Quality Percentage Score: 76%
☎ 021 800500 021 800527
Situated on the banks of the river Lee, the Kingsley is a luxurious new hotel with good facilities. Bedrooms are excellent and feature several extra touches. Guests have use of a comfortable lounge and library. Contemporary and informal trends are evident in the bar and restaurant.
ROOMS: 57 en suite (bth/shr) No smoking in 27 bedrooms
MEALS: Lunch fr IR£15 High tea IR£5-IR£12 Dinner IR£9.95-IR£15.95alc V meals Coffee am Tea pm **FACILITIES:** CTV in all bedrooms STV Indoor swimming pool (heated) Fishing Sauna Solarium Gym Jacuzzi/spa Wkly live entertainment **CONF:** Thtr 80 Class 50 Board 32 Del from IR£125 * **SERVICES:** Lift Night porter Air conditioning 250P **NOTES:** No smoking area in restaurant Last d 10pm Closed 25 Dec
CARDS:

★★★★ *Jurys* Western Rd
Quality Percentage Score: 69%
☎ 021 276622 021 274477
Dir: *close to city centre, on main Killarney road as you exit Cork*
Jurys enjoys a riverside setting near the University and within walking distance of the city centre. The public areas have a fresh outlook, with a comfortable library lounge, in addition to new leisure and conference facilities. Bedrooms are well equipped.
ROOMS: 185 en suite (bth/shr) (23 fmly) No smoking in 48 bedrooms
MEALS: International Cuisine V meals Coffee am Tea pm
FACILITIES: CTV in all bedrooms STV Indoor swimming pool (heated) Outdoor swimming pool (heated) Squash Sauna Gym Jacuzzi/spa Wkly live entertainment ch fac **CONF:** Thtr 700 Class 400 Board 150 **SERVICES:** Lift Night porter 231P **NOTES:** No dogs (ex guide dogs) No smoking area in restaurant Last d 11pm Closed 25-27 Dec
CARDS:

★★★★ *Fitzpatrick Silver Springs* Tivoli
Quality Percentage Score: 65%
☎ 021 507533 021 507641
Dir: *from N8 south-bound take Silver Springs exit. Turn right across overpass - hotel is on right*
Overlooking the River Lee, this hotel has excellent convention facilities and a fully equipped indoor leisure centre. The public areas have been refurbished and include a spacious lounge, two bars and a stylish restaurant. Many bedrooms have been refurbished and work is continuing on the remainder. There is also a helipad.
ROOMS: 109 en suite (bth/shr) (50 fmly) No smoking in 4 bedrooms **MEALS:** V meals Coffee am Tea pm **FACILITIES:** CTV in all bedrooms STV Indoor swimming pool (heated) Golf 9 Tennis (hard) Squash Snooker Sauna Gym Pool table Jacuzzi/spa Aerobics classes Wkly live entertainment **CONF:** Thtr 800 Class 500 Board 50 **SERVICES:** Lift Night porter 450P **NOTES:** No smoking area in restaurant Last d 10pm Closed 24-25 Dec **CARDS:**

★★★ *Arbutus Lodge*
Middle Glanmire Rd, Montenotte
Quality Percentage Score: 71%
☎ 021 501237 021 502893
A period town house in a residential suburb overlooking the city, with a friendly atmosphere. A variety of well equipped bedrooms are available, many with period furnishings. The elegant dining room has a good reputation for food and wine. Four suites of rooms with kitchens are housed in an elegant nearby building and are ideal for guests who want privacy allied to the convenience of having the hotel amenities.
ROOMS: 16 en suite (bth/shr) 4 annexe en suite (bth/shr) **MEALS:** Irish & French Cuisine V meals Coffee am **FACILITIES:** CTV in all bedrooms STV Tennis (hard) **CONF:** Thtr 100 Class 60 Board 30 **SERVICES:** Night porter 36P **NOTES:** No dogs (ex guide dogs) No coaches Last d 9.30pm Closed 24-28 Dec RS Sun **CARDS:**

★★★ *Imperial Hotel* South Mall
Quality Percentage Score: 69%
☎ 021 274040 021 275375
This fine hotel has a hospitable and welcoming atmosphere. The reception rooms are on a grand scale, particularly the foyer, with its beautiful crystal chandelier and paintings. Bedrooms are of a high standard and Clouds Restaurant is earning a reputation for good food.
ROOMS: 98 en suite (bth/shr) (12 fmly) **MEALS:** V meals Coffee am Tea pm **FACILITIES:** CTV in all bedrooms STV Wkly live entertainment **CONF:** Thtr 400 Class 200 Board 150 Del IR£89 * **SERVICES:** Lift Night porter 40P **NOTES:** No dogs (ex guide dogs) No smoking area in restaurant Last d 10pm Closed 24 Dec-2 Jan **CARDS:**

★★★ Ambassador Military Hill, St Lukes
Quality Percentage Score: 67%
☎ 021 551996 021 551997
Dir: *city centre, just off Wellington Road*
Many pleasing features distinguish this sandstone and granite building which dates from the 19th century. Today it is a fine hotel with views of the city and a feeling of space throughout.

contd.

Some bedrooms have balconies, but all are well equipped. Public areas include a cocktail lounge, bar and restaurant.
ROOMS: 60 en suite (bth/shr) (8 fmly) No smoking in 8 bedrooms s IR£60-IR£75; d IR£80-IR£95 (incl. bkfst) * LB Off peak **MEALS:** Lunch IR£6-IR£12.50 Dinner IR£24 & alc International Cuisine V meals Coffee am Tea pm **FACILITIES:** CTV in all bedrooms STV Wkly live entertainment **CONF:** Thtr 80 Class 40 Board 35 Del IR£74 * **SERVICES:** Lift Night porter 60P **NOTES:** No smoking area in restaurant Last d 9.45pm Closed 24-25 Dec **CARDS:**

★★★ Metropole MacCurtain St
Quality Percentage Score: 64%
☎ 021 508122 📠 021 506450
Dir: *hotel is in the city centre located on MacCurtain St - leading to N25 main Dublin Rd*
This city-centre hotel features secure free car parking in the rear garage. The Metropole has a new leisure centre which includes a supervised creche. The Waterside café overlooks the swimming pool and has been well designed with good use of natural light; bedrooms are pleasant. Conference rooms, and a bar and a choice of restaurants are also available.
ROOMS: 98 en suite (bth/shr) (3 fmly) No smoking in 6 bedrooms s fr IR£73; d fr IR£98 (incl. bkfst) * LB Off peak **MEALS:** Lunch IR£10 & alc Dinner IR£16 & alc Irish/International Cuisine V meals Coffee am Tea pm **FACILITIES:** CTV in all bedrooms STV Indoor swimming pool (heated) Snooker Sauna Solarium Gym Jacuzzi/spa Wkly live entertainment Xmas **CONF:** Thtr 500 Class 180 Board 60 Del IR£75 * **SERVICES:** Lift Night porter 254P **NOTES:** No dogs (ex guide dogs) No smoking area in restaurant Last d 9pm **CARDS:**

★★★ Jurys Inn Anderson's Quay
JURYS HOTEL GROUP
Quality Percentage Score: 58%
☎ 021 276444 📠 021 276144
Dir: *on E side of city, on the river Lee*
Attractively decorated in a modern style, this hotel overlooks the River Lee and is just a few minutes' walk from the main street. Accommodation prices are per room, and rooms can accommodate three adults or two adults and two children. The restaurant is informal in style and there is also a lively pub. A public car park adjoins the hotel.
ROOMS: 133 en suite (bth/shr) No smoking in 32 bedrooms **MEALS:** Bar Lunch IR£7.70-IR£8.20alc Dinner fr IR£15 & alc International Cuisine V meals Coffee am **FACILITIES:** CTV in all bedrooms STV Wkly live entertainment **CONF:** Thtr 35 Class 20 Board 20 **SERVICES:** Lift 22P **NOTES:** No dogs (ex guide dogs) No smoking area in restaurant Last d 9.30pm Closed 24-26 Dec **CARDS:**

★★ Vienna Woods Glanmire
Quality Percentage Score: 64%
☎ 021 821146 📠 021 821120
Dir: *from Dublin turn off for Glanmire at the 2nd rdbt you meet on the outskirts of Cork City*
This 18th-century house is situated in 20 acres of garden and woodlands overlooking Cork Harbour. Good meals and live entertainment are both available.
ROOMS: 20 en suite (bth/shr) (3 fmly) s IR£35-IR£40; d IR£55-IR£65 (incl. bkfst) * LB Off peak **MEALS:** Bar Lunch IR£6-IR£14alc Dinner IR£17.50 & alc V meals Coffee am Tea pm **FACILITIES:** CTV in all bedrooms STV Wkly live entertainment **CONF:** Thtr 400 Class 250 Board 50 Del from IR£44 * **SERVICES:** Night porter 150P **NOTES:** No dogs (ex guide dogs) Last d 9.45pm Closed 24-27 Dec
CARDS:

★★ *Hotel Ibis*
Lee Tunnel Roundabout, Dunkettle
Quality Percentage Score: 61%
☎ 021 354354 📠 021 354202
Dir: *situated off the N8 at Lee Tunnel rdbt, turn left in direction Waterford, at next rdbt turn left, hotel on left*
This new hotel is furnished to well established group standards that offer modern facilities at very affordable prices. While service is somewhat limited, a 24 hour snack service is a popular feature.
ROOMS: 100 en suite (shr) **MEALS:** International Cuisine V meals Coffee am Tea pm **FACILITIES:** CTV in all bedrooms STV **CONF:** Thtr 70 Class 40 Board 35 **SERVICES:** Lift Night porter 100P **NOTES:** No smoking area in restaurant **CARDS:**

Travelodge Blackash
Travelodge
☎ 01 21310722 📠 01 21310707
Dir: *at rdbt junc of South Ring Road/Kinsale Rd R600*
This modern building offers accommodation in smart, spacious and well equipped bedrooms, all with en-suite bathrooms. Refreshments may be taken at the nearby family restaurant. For details about current prices, consult the Contents Page under Hotel Groups for the Travelodge phone number.
ROOMS: 40 en suite (bth/shr) d IR£49.95 *

COURTMACSHERRY Co Cork **Map 01 B2**

★★ Courtmacsherry
Quality Percentage Score: 64%
☎ 023 46198 📠 023 46137
Dir: *take M71 to Bandon, R602 to Timoleague. From Timoleague head for Courtmacsherry, hotel is by the beach at the far end of the town*
This Georgian house is set in attractive grounds near the beach.
contd.

The hotel is family-run, it offers quality meals served in the kitchen and a riding school available to all ages.
ROOMS: 12 rms (9 bth 1 shr) (1 fmly) s IR£50-IR£58; d IR£64-IR£78 (incl. bkfst) * LB Off peak **MEALS:** Sunday Lunch fr IR£13 Dinner fr IR£20 International Cuisine V meals Coffee am Tea pm
FACILITIES: CTV in all bedrooms STV Tennis (hard & grass) Riding Shore fishing from hotel beach Wkly live entertainment **SERVICES:** 60P
NOTES: No smoking area in restaurant Last d 9pm Closed Oct-Mar
CARDS:

C

COURTOWN HARBOUR Co Wexford — Map 01 D3

★★ ***Courtown***
Quality Percentage Score: 68%
☎ 055 25210 & 25108 055 25304
Dir: *8km off N11*
Situated in a picturesque seaside resort, this long-established family-run hotel is noted for good food and the friendly atmosphere of its lounge bars. Summer entertainment takes the form of dinner theatre shows.
ROOMS: 21 en suite (bth/shr) (4 fmly) **MEALS:** Irish, English & French Cuisine V meals Coffee am Tea pm **FACILITIES:** CTV in all bedrooms Indoor swimming pool (heated) Golf 18 Tennis (hard & grass) Fishing Squash Riding Sauna Solarium Gym Jacuzzi/spa Steam room Massage Crazy golf Wkly live entertainment ch fac **SERVICES:** Night porter 10P
NOTES: No dogs (ex guide dogs) Last d 9.30pm Closed Nov-16 Mar
CARDS:

★★ ***Bay View***
Quality Percentage Score: 63%
☎ 055 25307 055 25576
Overlooking the beach and harbour, this family-run hotel complex offers a range of leisure facilities. Many of the bedrooms have sea views.
ROOMS: 17 en suite (bth/shr) (12 fmly) **MEALS:** Coffee am Tea pm
FACILITIES: CTV in all bedrooms Tennis (hard) Squash **SERVICES:** 30P
NOTES: No dogs (ex guide dogs) Closed Nov-14 Mar
CARDS:

CRAWFORDSBURN Co Down — Map 01 D5

★★★ ***Old Inn*** 15 Main St BT19 1JH
Quality Percentage Score: 68%
☎ 028 91853255 028 91852775
Dir: *A2, passing Belfast Airport and Holywood, 3m past Holywood sign for The Old Inn, 100yds turn L at lights, follow rd into village, hotel is on left*
Enjoying a quiet rural setting, but not far from Belfast, the Old Inn is reputed to date back to 1614. Much original character has been retained in the public areas which include bars, a bistro and a restaurant. Bedrooms vary in size and in style, and include a range of deluxe rooms.
ROOMS: 33 en suite (bth/shr) **MEALS:** V meals Coffee am Tea pm
FACILITIES: CTV in all bedrooms STV **CONF:** Thtr 120 Class 27 Board 40 Del from £90 * **SERVICES:** Night porter 65P **NOTES:** No dogs (ex guide dogs) Last high tea 7.30pm **CARDS:**

CROSSHAVEN Co Cork — Map 01 B2

★★ ***Whispering Pines Hotel***
Quality Percentage Score: 65%
☎ 021 831843 & 831448 021 831679
There is something inviting about this comfortable hotel with its sun lounge and bar overlooking the river. The hospitality is warming and the kitchen caters well for all its guests, particularly anglers, for whom fishing boats and equipment are available for hire. Transfers from Cork Airport can be arranged.
ROOMS: 15 en suite (bth/shr) (6 fmly) **MEALS:** Coffee am Tea pm
FACILITIES: CTV in all bedrooms STV Own angling boats fish daily
SERVICES: 40P **NOTES:** No dogs (ex guide dogs) No coaches
Last d 9.30pm **CARDS:**

DINGLE Co Kerry — Map 01 A2

★★★ ***Dingle Skellig Hotel***
Quality Percentage Score: 72%
☎ 066 51144 066 51501
On the outskirts of town overlooking the bay, this modern hotel has bright airy bedrooms and pleasant public areas, making it an excellent base for holidaymakers.
ROOMS: 115 en suite (bth/shr) **MEALS:** French Cuisine V meals Coffee am Tea pm **FACILITIES:** TV available STV Indoor swimming pool (heated) Tennis (hard) Solarium Gym Pool table Jacuzzi/spa Wkly live entertainment ch fac **CONF:** Thtr 250 Class 140 Board 80 Del from IR£105 * **SERVICES:** Lift Night porter **NOTES:** No dogs (ex guide dogs) No smoking area in restaurant Last d 9.30pm Closed Jan-mid Feb
CARDS:

DONEGAL Co Donegal — Map 01 B5

★★★ ***Harvey's Point Country***
Lough Eske
Quality Percentage Score: 74%
☎ 073 22208 073 22352
Dir: *from Donegal, take N56 then 1st right signposted Loch Eske/Harvey's Point. Hotel is approx 10 mins drive*
This modern hotel is in a superb lakeside location on Lough Eske, and was built with guests' peace and comfort in mind. There are spacious public rooms, excellent cuisine and a wide range of facilities.
ROOMS: 20 en suite (bth/shr) 12 annexe en suite (shr) **MEALS:** Irish, French & Swiss Cuisine V meals Coffee am Tea pm **FACILITIES:** CTV in all bedrooms STV Tennis (hard) Fishing Wkly live entertainment
CONF: Thtr 400 Class 400 Board 50 **SERVICES:** Night porter 200P
NOTES: No children 10yrs Last d 9.30pm Closed weekdays Nov-Mar
CARDS:

★★★ ***Abbey*** The Diamond
Quality Percentage Score: 63%
☎ 073 21014 073 21014
Dir: *located in centre of Donegal Down - N15 from Sligo*
This is a family run hotel overlooking the square in the town centre. The new Abbey Restaurant is an inviting place to eat lunch and dinner and hot food is also available all day in the lounge bar. The staff are friendly and helpful.
ROOMS: 49 en suite (bth/shr) (5 fmly) **MEALS:** International Cuisine V meals Coffee am Tea pm **FACILITIES:** CTV in all bedrooms STV
SERVICES: Lift Night porter Air conditioning 40P **NOTES:** No smoking area in restaurant Last d 9.30pm Closed 25-27 Dec
CARDS:

DOOLIN Co Clare — Map 01 B3

★★★ **Aran View House** Coast Rd
Quality Percentage Score: 64%
☎ 065 7074061 & 7074420 065 7074540
Situated in 100 acres of rolling farmland and commanding panoramic views of the Aran Islands, this hotel offers attractive and comfortably furnished accommodation. Staff are welcoming, the atmosphere is convivial, and there is traditional music and song in the bar three times a week.
ROOMS: 13 en suite (bth/shr) 6 annexe en suite (bth/shr) (1 fmly) s IR£45-IR£55; d IR£70-IR£80 (incl. bkfst) * LB Off peak **MEALS:** Dinner IR£18-IR£20alc V meals Coffee am Tea pm **FACILITIES:** CTV in all bedrooms **SERVICES:** 40P **NOTES:** No smoking area in restaurant Last d 9pm Closed 1 Nov-1 Apr **CARDS:**

See advert on opposite page

DROGHEDA Co Louth **Map 01 D4**

★★★ Boyne Valley Hotel & Country Club

Stameen, Dublin Rd

Quality Percentage Score: 61%

☎ 041 9837737 Fax 041 9839188

Dir: *N1 towards Belfast, north of Dublin Airport on right - up Avenue before town of Droghedah*

This historic mansion stands in 16 acres of gardens and woodlands on the outskirts of Drogheda. Much emphasis is placed here on good food and attentive service and all the accommodation is well furnished and provides high standards of comfort.

ROOMS: 35 en suite (bth/shr) (4 fmly) s IR£55; d IR£99 (incl. bkfst) * LB Off peak **MEALS:** Lunch IR£12 Dinner IR£22.50 & alc Irish & French Cuisine V meals Coffee am Tea pm **FACILITIES:** CTV in all bedrooms STV Indoor swimming pool (heated) Tennis (hard) Sauna Solarium Gym Putting green Jacuzzi/spa Pitch & putt Wkly live entertainment Xmas **CONF:** Thtr 150 Class 100 Board 25 **SERVICES:** Night porter 200P **NOTES:** No dogs (ex guide dogs) No smoking area in restaurant Last d 9.45pm **CARDS:**

DUBLIN Co Dublin **Map 01 D4**

see also **Portmarnock**

★★★★★ Radisson SAS St Helen's Hotel

Stillorgan Rd, Blackrock

Quality Percentage Score: 68%

☎ 01 2186000 Fax 01 2186010

Dir: *from city centre N11 due S, Hotel 4km on left of dual carriageway*

A fine 18th century mansion, with many period features, including a magnificent Italian marble fireplace in the lounge. The Orangerie is popular for drinks, and there are two restaurants. Many bedrooms have views of the lovely terraced gardens, and suites and penthouse suites are available, as well as standard rooms, and rooms for the disabled.

ROOMS: 151 en suite (bth/shr) No smoking in 39 bedrooms s IR£175; d IR£195 * Off peak **MEALS:** Lunch IR£19-IR£21 Dinner IR£29-IR£31 International Cuisine V meals Coffee am Tea pm **FACILITIES:** CTV in all bedrooms STV Snooker Gym Croquet lawn Beauty salon Wkly live entertainment Xmas **CONF:** Thtr 350 Class 210 Board 70 Del from IR£175 * **SERVICES:** Lift Night porter Air conditioning 230P **NOTES:** No dogs (ex guide dogs) No smoking area in restaurant Last d 11pm **CARDS:**

★★★★★ ❀❀❀ The Merrion Hotel Upper Merrion St

Quality Percentage Score: 78%

☎ 01 6030600 Fax 01 6030700

Dir: *situated at the top of Upper Merrion Street on the left hand side, beyond Government buildings which are on the right hand side*

The four Georgian town houses and modern Garden Wing offer the highest international standards. The main restaurant serves highly skilled cuisine, other dining options are available.

ROOMS: 145 en suite (bth/shr) No smoking in 65 bedrooms s IR£200-IR£240; d IR£220-IR£265 * LB Off peak **MEALS:** Lunch IR£13-IR£16 & alc Dinner IR£3-IR£19alc European Cuisine V meals Coffee am Tea pm **FACILITIES:** CTV in all bedrooms STV Indoor swimming pool (heated) Gym Steam room Xmas **CONF:** Thtr 60 Class 25 Board 25 Del IR£275 * **SERVICES:** Lift Night porter Air conditioning 60P **NOTES:** No dogs (ex guide dogs) No smoking area in restaurant Last d 10pm **CARDS:**

★

The Premier Collection, hotels with Red Star Awards are listed on pages 17-23

The Premier Collection

★★★★ ❀❀❀ The Clarence

6-8 Wellington Quay 2

☎ 01 6709000 Fax 01 6707800

Dir: *from O'Connell Bridge, drive west along quays, through 1st set of lights (at Ha'penny Bridge) hotel is 500mtrs*

Bedrooms are richly furnished, for sheer luxury, the two bedroom penthouse suite is outstanding. Public areas include a long gallery with luxurious sofas. The bar is smart and the restaurant serves well presented food.

ROOMS: 50 en suite (bth/shr) d IR£195-IR£210 * Off peak **MEALS:** Lunch IR£17-IR£32.75alc Dinner IR£26.50-IR£38alc European Cuisine V meals Coffee am Tea pm **FACILITIES:** CTV in all bedrooms STV **CONF:** Thtr 50 Class 24 Board 30 **SERVICES:** Lift Night porter P **NOTES:** No dogs (ex guide dogs) No coaches No smoking area in restaurant Last d 10.20pm **CARDS:**

★★★★ Conrad International
Earlsfort Ter
Quality Percentage Score: 75%
☎ 01 6765555 📠 01 6765424
***Dir:** just off St.Stephen's Green*
The National Concert Hall stands opposite this centrally located hotel. Facilities include two restaurants: the Alexandra and a less formal brasserie which offers good-value menus. Alfie Byrnes Dublin Pub and the lobby lounge are popular. Spacious bedrooms include some suites.
ROOMS: 191 en suite (bth/shr) No smoking in 60 bedrooms s IR£180-IR£195; d IR£200-IR£220 * LB Off peak **MEALS:** Lunch IR£15.50-IR£17.50 Dinner fr IR£18.50 Irish & Continental Cuisine V meals Coffee am Tea pm **FACILITIES:** CTV in all bedrooms STV Gym Wkly live entertainment Xmas **CONF:** Thtr 370 Class 150 Del from IR£250 * **SERVICES:** Lift Night porter Air conditioning 80P **NOTES:** No dogs (ex guide dogs) No smoking area in restaurant Last d 10.30pm
CARDS:

★★★★ The Herbert Park Hotel
Ballsbridge
Quality Percentage Score: 74%
☎ 01 6672200 📠 01 6672595
***Dir:** 2m from city centre Dublin*
Contemporary style bedrooms have extras such as air conditioning, mini-bars and safes. The marble tiled foyer leads to the Terrace Lounge, restaurant and bar. The Mezzanine lounge is for residents only, the Pavilion restaurant has views of the the park. Executive suites and rooms, conference facilities, a fitness suite and valet parking are available.
ROOMS: 153 en suite (bth/shr) (4 fmly) No smoking in 30 bedrooms s IR£150; d IR£185 * LB Off peak **MEALS:** Lunch IR£18.50 Dinner IR£26.65-IR£35.95alc European Cuisine V meals Coffee am Tea pm **FACILITIES:** CTV in all bedrooms STV Gym **CONF:** Thtr 100 Class 55 Board 50 **SERVICES:** Lift Night porter Air conditioning 80P **NOTES:** No dogs (ex guide dogs) No smoking area in restaurant Last d 9pm
CARDS:

★★★★ Jurys Hotel Dublin
Pembroke Rd, Ballsbridge
Quality Percentage Score: 70%
☎ 01 6605000 📠 01 6605540
***Dir:** from Dun Laighaire, follow signs for city to Merrion Rd, Ballsbridge & Pembroke Rd, hotel is at intersection of Pembroke Rd and Northumberland Rd*
This establishment has two identities: Jurys Hotel and The Towers at Jurys. The first is large and popular, boasting several restaurants and bars and good conference and leisure facilities. The Towers specialises in discreet luxury, with spacious bedrooms and private suites.
ROOMS: 294 en suite (bth/shr) (27 fmly) No smoking in 150 bedrooms s IR£155; d IR£195 * LB Off peak **MEALS:** Lunch IR£9.95-IR£17.95 & alc Dinner IR£25-IR£32 & alc International Cuisine V meals Coffee am Tea pm **FACILITIES:** CTV in all bedrooms Indoor swimming pool (heated) Outdoor swimming pool (heated) Sauna Gym Jacuzzi/spa Hairdresser Beauty Salon with Masseuse Xmas **CONF:** Thtr 850 Class 450 Board 100 Del IR£185 * **SERVICES:** Lift Night porter 280P **NOTES:** No dogs (ex guide dogs) No smoking area in restaurant Last d 10.15pm
CARDS:

★★★★ *Shelbourne Meridien Hotel*
St Stephen's Green
Quality Percentage Score: 70%
☎ 01 6766471 📠 01 6616006
***Dir:** in city centre*
A landmark since 1824, with strong literary and historical links, behind the elegant facade of this Georgian hotel are gracious reception rooms, a choice of restaurants, a leisure centre and popular bars. Bedrooms are smart and comfortable.

ROOMS: 164 en suite (bth/shr) (3 fmly) No smoking in 9 bedrooms **MEALS:** V meals Coffee am Tea pm **FACILITIES:** CTV in all bedrooms Beauty Salon **CONF:** Thtr 400 Class 180 Board 60 **SERVICES:** Lift Night porter **NOTES:** No smoking area in restaurant Last d 10.30pm
CARDS:

See advert on opposite page

★★★★ *Burlington* Upper Leeson St
Quality Percentage Score: 68%
☎ 01 6605222 📠 01 6603172
A few minutes from the city this comfortable hotel features well appointed bedrooms and some superior executive rooms. Public areas include the smart Diplomat restaurant and the residents' bar, which complement the popular Buck Mulligan's Dublin pub.
ROOMS: 526 en suite (bth/shr) (6 fmly) No smoking in 95 bedrooms **MEALS:** Irish & French Cuisine V meals Coffee am Tea pm **FACILITIES:** CTV in all bedrooms STV Use of facilities at fitness club **CONF:** Thtr 1500 Class 650 Board 40 **SERVICES:** Lift Night porter 400P **NOTES:** No dogs (ex guide dogs) No smoking area in restaurant Last d 11pm **CARDS:**

★★★★ Gresham O'Connel St
Quality Percentage Score: 67%
☎ 01 8746881 📠 01 8787175
***Dir:** on O'Connel St, just off M1 close to the GPO*

A commitment to traditional standards of hotel keeping is evident at the Gresham. Bedrooms are well equipped and there is a foyer lounge serving snacks and afternoon tea; a popular spot in which to relax. There is also the Aberdeen restaurant and 24-hour room service.

contd.

ROOMS: 288 en suite (bth/shr) (4 fmly) No smoking in 26 bedrooms d IR£200 * LB Off peak **MEALS:** Lunch fr IR£16alc Dinner fr IR£19alc International Cuisine V meals Coffee am Tea pm **FACILITIES:** CTV in all bedrooms STV Gym Xmas **CONF:** Thtr 300 Class 200 Board 100 Del from IR£130 * **SERVICES:** Lift Night porter Air conditioning **NOTES:** No dogs (ex guide dogs) No smoking area in restaurant Last d 10.15pm **CARDS:**

See advert on this page

★★★★ ***The Plaza Hotel*** Belgard Rd, Tallaght
Quality Percentage Score: 64%
☎ 01 4624200 📠 01 4624600
Dir: *6m from city centre, at S end of M50 motorway*
Contemporary in design, the Plaza is bright and spacious. The lounge and restaurant are located on the mezzanine and enjoy distant views of the Dublin mountains. Comfortable bedrooms are well equipped, facilities include modem points. There is a roof garden, conference rooms, a traditional Irish pub and carvery, and a sports-themed bar. Irish, French and mediterranean influences are found in the Olive Tree restaurant.
ROOMS: 122 en suite (bth/shr) (2 fmly) No smoking in 61 bedrooms **MEALS:** V meals Coffee am Tea pm **FACILITIES:** CTV in all bedrooms STV **CONF:** Thtr 200 Class 150 Board 50 **SERVICES:** Lift Night porter Air conditioning 520P **NOTES:** No dogs (ex guide dogs) No smoking area in restaurant Last d 10pm Closed 24-25 Dec
CARDS:

★★★★ **Red Cow Morans**
Red Cow Complex, Naas Rd
Quality Percentage Score: 64%
☎ 01 4593650 📠 4591588
Dir: *at junction of M50 & N7 Naas road on the city side of the motorway*
This smart hotel complex centres on the original Red Cow Inn, but has been attractively extended and now boasts excellent conference facilities. Bedrooms are spacious, smartly decorated and well equipped, and the lobby has an eye catching design.
ROOMS: 123 en suite (bth/shr) (5 fmly) No smoking in 44 bedrooms s IR£80-IR£105; d IR£115-IR£170 (incl. bkfst) * LB Off peak **MEALS:** Lunch IR£12-IR£14.50 Dinner IR£22.50 & alc Irish & Mediterranean Cuisine V meals Coffee am Tea pm **FACILITIES:** CTV in all bedrooms STV Wkly live entertainment **CONF:** Thtr 700 Class 520 Board 150 Del from IR£125 * **SERVICES:** Lift Night porter Air conditioning 700P **NOTES:** No dogs (ex guide dogs) No smoking area in restaurant Last d 10.30pm **CARDS:**

Courtesy & Care Award

★★★ **The Hibernian**
Eastmoreland Place, Ballsbridge
Quality Percentage Score: 77%
☎ 01 6687666 📠 01 6602655
Dir: *turn right from Mespil Rd onto Baggot St Upper, then take 1st left into Eastmorelad Place/St Mary's Rd, the hotel is at the end on the left*
This fine Victorian building, very close to the south city centre off Baggot Street features luxurious decor and well upholstered furniture. Manager David Butt and his

contd.

AA Rosettes are awarded for quality of food, see page 15 for an explanation of Rosette assessment.

professional staff create a friendly atmosphere, and the food is prepared by a confident, innovative chef.

ROOMS: 40 en suite (bth/shr) No smoking in 14 bedrooms s IR£120-IR£185; d IR£150-IR£185 (incl. bkfst) * LB Off peak **MEALS:** Lunch IR£14.95 Dinner IR£22-IR£29alc Irish & French Cuisine V meals Coffee am Tea pm **FACILITIES:** CTV in all bedrooms STV **CONF:** Board 20 **SERVICES:** Lift Night porter 25P **NOTES:** No dogs (ex guide dogs) No smoking area in restaurant Last d 10pm Closed 24-27 Dec
CARDS:

★★★ The Schoolhouse Hotel
2-8 Northumberland Rd
Quality Percentage Score: 70%
☎ 01 6675014 01 6675015
Dir: *from N11 turn right at Lesson St Bridge, Avis on right. Through 2 sets of lights, pass Mespil Hotel, & turn left. Hotel 100yds on right*
A period red brick building, dating from 1861, The Schoolhouse retains many original features. Satchels Restaurant and the Inkwell Bar continue the school theme. Bedrooms are inviting, and custom made oak furniture is very comfortable.
ROOMS: 31 en suite (bth/shr) No smoking in 10 bedrooms s fr IR£109; d IR£139-IR£190 (incl. bkfst) * LB Off peak **MEALS:** Lunch IR£11.95-IR£19 Dinner IR£25-IR£30 & alc Irish & French Cuisine V meals Coffee am Tea pm **FACILITIES:** CTV in all bedrooms STV **CONF:** Class 15 Board 20 **SERVICES:** Lift Night porter Air conditioning 21P **NOTES:** No dogs Last d 10.30pm Closed 24-28 Dec **CARDS:**

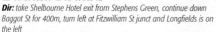

★★★ Longfield's Hotel
Fitzwilliam St
Quality Percentage Score: 69%
☎ 01 6761367 01 6761542
Dir: *take Shelbourne Hotel exit from Stephens Green, continue down Baggot St for 400m, turn left at Fitzwilliam St junct and Longfields is on the left*
This intimate town house hotel is situated close to the city centre. Particular emphasis is placed on personalised service, good food and a relaxed atmosphere.
ROOMS: 24 en suite (bth/shr) s fr IR£90; d fr IR£106 (incl. bkfst) * LB Off peak **MEALS:** Lunch IR£12.95-IR£14.95 & alc Dinner IR£25-IR£33 & alc French Cuisine V meals Coffee am Tea pm **FACILITIES:** CTV in all bedrooms STV **SERVICES:** Lift Night porter **NOTES:** No dogs (ex guide dogs) No coaches No smoking area in restaurant Last d 10.30pm RS 23 Dec-27 Jan **CARDS:**

★★★ Marine Sutton Cross
Quality Percentage Score: 69%
☎ 01 8390000 01 8390442
Dir: *take rd from M1 towards Dublin City Centre, take second exit for Coolocil, continue untilT-junct and turn left, after 1m hotel on right*
On the north shore of Dublin Bay with attractive gardens and seashore walks, the hotel features spacious public rooms. Bedrooms are attractively decorated and well equipped. It is close to the Howth rapid railway into the city centre, and the famous Portmarnock Golf Course.
ROOMS: 52 en suite (bth/shr) (7 fmly) No smoking in 7 bedrooms s IR£90-IR£110; d IR£140-IR£170 (incl. bkfst) * LB Off peak **MEALS:** Lunch IR£14.50-IR£14.95 Dinner IR£26-IR£28.50 & alc French Cuisine V meals Coffee am Tea pm **FACILITIES:** CTV in all bedrooms STV Indoor swimming pool (heated) Sauna **CONF:** Thtr 220 Class 140 Board 40 Del from IR£106.50 * **SERVICES:** Night porter 150P **NOTES:** No dogs (ex guide dogs) No coaches No smoking area in restaurant Last d 10.15pm Closed 25-27 Dec **CARDS:**

★★★ *Doyle Montrose* Stillorgan Rd
Quality Percentage Score: 68%
☎ 01 2693311 01 2691164
Smartly decorated, comfortable bedrooms are a feature of this hotel which overlooks the campus of University College. The public areas include good lounge space, a carvery bar and a more formal restaurant. The hotel is in a quiet suburb a short distance from the city.
ROOMS: 179 en suite (bth/shr) (6 fmly) No smoking in 12 bedrooms **MEALS:** V meals Coffee am Tea pm **FACILITIES:** CTV in all bedrooms STV Wkly live entertainment **CONF:** Thtr 80 Class 40 Board 40 **SERVICES:** Lift Night porter 150P **NOTES:** No dogs (ex guide dogs) Last d 10.30pm **CARDS:**

★★★ Clarion Stephen's Hall All-Suite Hotel
The Earlsfort Centre, Lower Leeson St
Quality Percentage Score: 67%
☎ 01 6381111 01 6381122
Dir: *from N11 into Dublin, hotel is on left after Hatch St junction, before St Stephens Green*
A famous landmark in central Dublin this hotel offers a wide range of all-suite accommodation. The choice includes penthouses, townhouses, double and single suites and four studios; each has a well equipped kitchen. A good range of food is served in the attractive bistro restaurant.
ROOMS: 37 en suite (bth/shr) (9 fmly) s IR£140; d IR£175 (incl. bkfst) * LB Off peak **MEALS:** Lunch IR£14.95 Dinner IR£24.50 & alc European & Modern Irish Cuisine V meals Coffee am **FACILITIES:** CTV in all bedrooms STV **CONF:** Thtr 30 Class 15 Board 20 **SERVICES:** Lift Night porter 40P **NOTES:** No dogs (ex guide dogs) No smoking area in restaurant Last d 9.45pm RS 24 Dec-4 Jan **CARDS:**
See advert on opposite page

★★★ *Doyle Green Isle* Naas Rd
Quality Percentage Score: 67%
☎ 01 4593406 01 4592178
Dir: *on N7, 10km SW of the city centre*
The Green Isle Hotel is situated on the outskirts of the city to the south. Bedrooms, both standard and executive, are generously proportioned and stylishly furnished. Public areas include the Tower Restaurant, a spacious lobby, and Rosie O'Gradys Bar.
ROOMS: 90 en suite (bth/shr) **MEALS:** Irish French & Italian Cuisine Coffee am Tea pm **FACILITIES:** CTV in all bedrooms **CONF:** Thtr 300 Class 100 Board 100 **SERVICES:** Lift Night porter 250P **NOTES:** No dogs (ex guide dogs) Last d 10pm **CARDS:**

★★★ *Doyle Skylon* Drumcondra Rd
Quality Percentage Score: 67%
☎ 01 8379121 01 8372778
In a convenient location with easy access to the city centre, this hotel offers very well appointed bedrooms. There is a spacious lobby lounge and a comfortable bar. Good value food is served in the restaurant.

contd.

ROOMS: 92 en suite (bth/shr) (10 fmly) **MEALS:** European Cuisine V meals Coffee am Tea pm **FACILITIES:** CTV in all bedrooms **CONF:** Thtr 35 Class 20 Board 20 **SERVICES:** Lift Night porter P **NOTES:** No dogs **CARDS:**

★★★ **Posthouse Dublin** Dublin Airport

Posthouse

Quality Percentage Score: 66%

☎ 01 8080500 📠 01 8446002

Dir: *the Hotel entrance is 1000yrds from main road entrance to Dublin airport, on the right hand side*

A large modern hotel with a wide range of services and amenities has been designed particularly for the business traveller. Bedrooms are smart, comfortable and well equipped.

ROOMS: 249 en suite (bth/shr) (3 fmly) No smoking in 100 bedrooms s IR£164; d IR£187 (incl. bkfst) * Off peak **MEALS:** Lunch IR£11.95-IR£15.95 Dinner IR£18.95-IR£20.95 & alc Irish,Chinese,European,Malaysian,Thai Cuisine V meals Coffee am Tea pm **FACILITIES:** CTV in all bedrooms STV Free use of nearby sports club-ALSAA Wkly live entertainment **CONF:** Thtr 130 Class 50 Board 40 Del from IR£120 * **SERVICES:** Night porter 250P **NOTES:** No dogs (ex guide dogs) No smoking area in restaurant Last d 11.30pm Closed 24-25 Dec RS 31 Dec **CARDS:**

★★★ **Temple Bar** Fleet St, Temple Bar

Quality Percentage Score: 66%

☎ 01 6773333 📠 01 6773088

Dir: *from Trinity College, head for O'Connell Bridge & take the 1st left onto Fleet St & the hotel is on the left hand side*

This stylish hotel lies in the heart of old Dublin and is ideally situated for sampling the cultural life of the city. Comfortable, well equipped bedrooms are moderately priced, and food is served throughout the day.

contd.

ROOMS: 129 en suite (bth/shr) (6 fmly) No smoking in 10 bedrooms s IR£99; d IR£130 (incl. bkfst) * LB Off peak **MEALS:** Lunch IR£9.50-IR£10.75 Dinner fr IR£17.50 & alc European Cuisine V meals Coffee am Tea pm **FACILITIES:** CTV in all bedrooms STV **CONF:** Thtr 40 Class 40 Board 80 **SERVICES:** Lift Night porter **NOTES:** No dogs (ex guide dogs) No smoking area in restaurant Last d 9.30pm Closed 24 & 25 Dec **CARDS:**

D

★★★ Buswells 23-27 Molesworth St

Quality Percentage Score: 65%
☎ 01 6146500 📠 01 6762090
Dir: *located on the corner of Molesworth St & Kildare St opposite Dail Eireann (Government Buildings)*
A popular rendezvous, Buswells is conveniently situated for the city's main shopping and cultural attractions. Bedrooms are well equipped and attractively decorated. The club-style bar is the focal point and there are two restaurants. Vouchers for overnight parking can be obtained from reception.
ROOMS: 69 en suite (bth/shr) (17 fmly) No smoking in 6 bedrooms s IR£99; d IR£156 (incl. bkfst) * LB Off peak **MEALS:** Lunch IR£15.95 Dinner IR£26.50 & alc International Cuisine V meals Coffee am Tea pm **FACILITIES:** CTV in all bedrooms Consession at nearby fitness club Complementary overnight parking Wkly live entertainment **CONF:** Thtr 84 Class 30 Board 24 Del IR£145 * **SERVICES:** Lift Night porter **NOTES:** No dogs (ex guide dogs) No smoking area in restaurant Closed 25 & 26 Dec RS 24 Dec **CARDS:**

★★★ *Doyle Tara Hotel* Merrion Rd

Quality Percentage Score: 65%
☎ 01 2694666 📠 01 2691027
The well equipped bedrooms of this hotel enjoy spectacular views of Dublin Bay and Howth Head. The attractively decorated public areas include a comfortable and relaxing foyer lounge, PJ Branagans Pub, and a split level conservatory restaurant.
ROOMS: 113 en suite (bth/shr) (2 fmly) **MEALS:** European Cuisine V meals Coffee am Tea pm **FACILITIES:** CTV in all bedrooms STV **CONF:** Thtr 300 Class 100 Board 40 **SERVICES:** Lift Night porter 140P **NOTES:** No dogs (ex guide dogs) No smoking area in restaurant Last d 9.30pm **CARDS:**

★★★ Abberley Court Belgard Rd, Tallaght

Quality Percentage Score: 64%
☎ 01 4596000 📠 01 4621000
Dir: *opposite The Square town Centre at the junction of The Belgard Rd and The Tallaglit by-pass (N81)*
Conveniently located beside a complex of shops, restaurants and a cinema, this hotel is very smartly furnished. Public areas include a lounge bar that serves food all day long and the first-floor Court Restaurant. There are sports facilities nearby.
ROOMS: 40 en suite (bth/shr) (34 fmly) s IR£50-IR£79; d IR£60-IR£98 (incl. bkfst) * LB Off peak **MEALS:** Bar Lunch IR£4.95-IR£7.20alc Dinner IR£12.95-IR£16.95alc Irish & Continental Cuisine V meals Coffee am Tea pm **FACILITIES:** CTV in all bedrooms **CONF:** Thtr 200 Class 70 Board 70 Del from IR£90 * **SERVICES:** Lift Night porter 450P **NOTES:** No dogs (ex guide dogs) No smoking area in restaurant Last d 10pm Closed 25 Dec **CARDS:**

★★★ Bewley's Hotel Newlands Cross

Newlands Cross, Naas Rd
Quality Percentage Score: 63%
☎ 01 464 0140 📠 01 464 0900
Dir: *from M50 junct 9 take N7 Naas road, hotel is short distance from junc of N7 with Belgard Rd at Newlands Cross*
This hotel on the outskirts of Dublin West has a bright, airy atmosphere. A spacious lobby and residents' lounge are provided, and there is a restaurant that serves snacks during the day, then more formal evening meals. Bedrooms are very good value and are furnished to a high standard.

ROOMS: 260 en suite (bth/shr) (260 fmly) No smoking in 165 bedrooms d IR£49-IR£55 * Off peak **MEALS:** Lunch IR£8-IR£12alc High tea IR£10-IR£15alc Dinner IR£15-IR£20alc International Cuisine V meals Coffee am Tea pm **FACILITIES:** CTV in all bedrooms STV **CONF:** Board 20 **SERVICES:** Lift Night porter 200P **NOTES:** No dogs (ex guide dogs) No smoking area in restaurant Last d 10pm Closed 24-26 Dec
CARDS:

See advert on opposite page

★★★ *The Mercer Hotel* Mercer St Lower

Quality Percentage Score: 62%
A young team of friendly staff create a pleasant atmosphere at this city centre hotel. Bedrooms are attractively appointed, and well equipped, with fridges and CD players as well as the usual amenities. Public areas include an inviting lounge with cocktail bar, and a restaurant. There is a public car park next door.

★★★ Mount Herbert Hotel

Herbert Rd, Lansdowne Rd
Quality Percentage Score: 62%
☎ 01 668 4321 📠 01 660 7077
Dir: *close Lansdowne Road Rugby Stadium, 220mtrs from Dart Rail Station*
ROOMS: 175 en suite (bth/shr) 10 annexe en suite (bth/shr) (15 fmly) s IR£54.50-IR£79.50; d IR£79-IR£99 (incl. bkfst) * Off peak **MEALS:** Bar Lunch IR£4-IR£8 & alc Dinner IR£16.50 & alc V meals Coffee am Tea pm **FACILITIES:** CTV in all bedrooms STV Sauna Solarium Childrens playground Badminton court **CONF:** Thtr 80 Class 60 Board 40 **SERVICES:** Lift Night porter 90P **NOTES:** No dogs (ex guide dogs) No smoking area in restaurant Last d 9.30pm **CARDS:**

★★★ Jurys Christchurch Inn

Christchurch Place
JURYS HOTEL GROUP
Quality Percentage Score: 59%
☎ 01 4540000 📠 01 4540012
Dir: *N7 onto Nass Rd, follow signs for city centre upto O'Connell St, cont past Trinity College turn R onto Dame St upto Lord Edward St Hotel is on left*
Centrally located opposite the 12th-century Cathedral, this hotel is close to the Temple Bar and all city amenities. The foyer lounge and pub are popular meeting places and there is an informal restaurant. The bedrooms are well appointed and each can accommodate families.
ROOMS: 182 en suite (bth/shr) No smoking in 37 bedrooms d fr IR£65 * Off peak **MEALS:** Lunch IR£4.10-IR£5.50 Dinner IR£16 & alc International Cuisine V meals Coffee am **FACILITIES:** CTV in all bedrooms Wkly live entertainment **SERVICES:** Lift Night porter **NOTES:** No dogs (ex guide dogs) No smoking area in restaurant Last d 9.30pm Closed 24-26 Dec **CARDS:**

★★★ *Jurys Custom House Inn*

Custom House Quay 1
Quality Percentage Score: 59%
☎ 01 607 5000 🖷 829 0400
Overlooking the River Liffey, this hotel is situated only seven minutes' walk away from the city's main shopping and tourist areas. Family rooms offer good value for money and facilities for business travellers are good.
ROOMS: 239 en suite (bth/shr) No smoking in 140 bedrooms
MEALS: International Cuisine V meals Coffee am Tea pm
FACILITIES: CTV in all bedrooms STV **CONF:** Thtr 90 Class 52 Board 40
SERVICES: Lift Night porter **NOTES:** No dogs (ex guide dogs) No smoking area in restaurant Last d 9.30pm Closed 25-26 Dec
CARDS:

★★★ The Parliament Hotel Lord Edward St

Quality Percentage Score: 56%
☎ 01 6708777 🖷 01 6708787
Dir: *adjacent to Dublin Castle in the Temple Bar area*
This attractive hotel near to the Temple Bar Area and Dublin Castle is part of the general revival of this area of the city. It offers well furnished bedrooms decorated in a modern style, and has a popular bar and separate restaurant.
ROOMS: 63 en suite (bth/shr) (8 fmly) No smoking in 22 bedrooms s IR£75-IR£110; d IR£100-IR£140 (incl. bkfst) * LB Off peak **MEALS:** Bar Lunch IR£5-IR£8 Dinner IR£15-IR£17 European Cuisine V meals Coffee am Tea pm **FACILITIES:** CTV in all bedrooms STV Wkly live entertainment **CONF:** Thtr 20 Board 10 **SERVICES:** Lift Night porter **NOTES:** No dogs (ex guide dogs) Last d 9.30pm
CARDS:

★★ *The Parnell West Hotel*

38/39 Parnell Square West
Quality Percentage Score: 66%
Friendly staff create a friendly atmosphere at this hotel, converted from interconnecting Georgian houses. There is a comfortable lounge bar, and a restaurant where enjoyable cuisine is served. There is a secure public car park a short walk away.

★★ Harding

Copper Alley, Fishamble St, Christchurch
Quality Percentage Score: 64%
☎ 01 6796500 🖷 01 679 6504
Dir: *located at the top of Dame St beside Christchurch cathedral, on the edge of Dublin's Temple Bar area*
At the heart of the fascinating Temple Bar area of the city this purpose-built hotel has a friendly atmosphere and offers good-value accomodation. Its Peruvian-style bar and Fitzers Restaurant are popular meeting places. There are plenty of shops, bars and restaurants nearby.
ROOMS: 53 en suite (shr) (14 fmly) s IR£45-IR£62.50; d IR£55-IR£125 * Off peak **MEALS:** European Cuisine V meals Coffee am Tea pm
FACILITIES: CTV in all bedrooms STV Wkly live entertainment
SERVICES: Lift **NOTES:** No dogs (ex guide dogs) Closed 23-26 Dec
CARDS:

★★ Hotel Ibis

Monastery Rd, Clondalkin 22
Quality Percentage Score: 60%
☎ 01 4641480 🖷 01 4641484
Dir: *off the M50, N7 turn off, in the direction of Naas, hotel is on the right, turn right into Monastery road, then next right again*
Close to Dublin airport and the M50, this hotel is contemporary in style. Its public rooms include a restaurant and lounge, where drinks may be taken. Bedrooms have modern appointments including large desks. Breakfast is self-service and a 24-hour snack service is available.
ROOMS: 150 en suite (shr) No smoking in 33 bedrooms d IR£50-IR£80 * Off peak **MEALS:** International Cuisine V meals Coffee am Tea pm
FACILITIES: CTV in all bedrooms STV **CONF:** Thtr 30 Class 18 Board 18
SERVICES: Lift 180P **NOTES:** No smoking area in restaurant Last d 10.30pm **CARDS:**

⇧ Travelodge Swords By Pass

☎ 01 8409233 🖷 01 8409257
Dir: *on N1 Dublin/Belfast road*
This modern building offers accommodation in smart, spacious and well equipped bedrooms, all with en-suite bathrooms. Refreshments may be taken at the nearby family restaurant. For details about current prices, consult the Contents Page under Hotel Groups for the Travelodge phone number.
ROOMS: 40 en suite (bth/shr) d IR£49.95 *

⇧ *Travelodge Castleknock*

Auburn Av Roundabout, Navan Rd
This modern building offers accommodation in smart, spacious and well equipped bedrooms, all with en-suite bathrooms. Refreshments may be taken at the nearby family restaurant. For details about current prices, consult the Contents Page under Hotel Groups for the Travelodge phone number.

> ✚ Indicates that the star classification has not been confirmed under the New Quality Standards, see page 7 for further information.

DUNDALK Co Louth — Map 01 D4

★★★ Ballymascanlon House

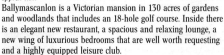

Quality Percentage Score: 69%
☎ 042 9371124 Fax 042 9371598
Dir: N of Dundalk take T62 to Carlingford. Hotel is approx 1km

Ballymascanlon is a Victorian mansion in 130 acres of gardens and woodlands that includes an 18-hole golf course. Inside there is an elegant new restaurant, a spacious and relaxing lounge, a new wing of luxurious bedrooms that are well worth requesting and a highly equipped leisure club.

ROOMS: 74 en suite (bth) (11 fmly) s IR£62-IR£74; d IR£85-IR£105 (incl. bkfst) LB Off peak **MEALS:** Lunch IR£14-IR£15 Dinner IR£24-IR£27 & alc Irish & French Cuisine V meals Coffee am Tea pm **FACILITIES:** CTV in all bedrooms STV Indoor swimming pool (heated) Golf 18 Tennis (hard) Sauna Gym Jacuzzi/spa Wkly live entertainment **CONF:** Thtr 300 Class 160 **SERVICES:** Lift Night porter 250P **NOTES:** Last d 9.30pm Closed 24-26 Dec **CARDS:**

★★★ Fairways Hotel & Leisure Centre

Dublin Rd
Quality Percentage Score: 61%
☎ 042 9321500 Fax 042 9321511
Dir: on N1 3km S of Dundalk

ROOMS: 48 en suite (bth/shr) (2 fmly) s IR£60-IR£65; d IR£90-IR£95 (incl. bkfst) * LB Off peak **MEALS:** Lunch fr IR£13.50 Dinner fr IR£19.50 European Cuisine V meals Coffee am Tea pm **FACILITIES:** CTV in all bedrooms STV Indoor swimming pool (heated) Tennis (hard) Squash Snooker Sauna Solarium Gym Jacuzzi/spa Badminton court Steam room Sports therapst Wkly live entertainment **CONF:** Thtr 350 Class 250 **SERVICES:** Night porter 300P **NOTES:** No smoking area in restaurant Last d 10pm Closed 25 Dec **CARDS:**

★★ Imperial Park St

Quality Percentage Score: 65%
☎ 042 9332241 Fax 042 9337909

A welcoming hotel in Dundalk town centre. The majority of the comfortable bedrooms are attractively decorated and have cherrywood furnishings and smart bathrooms. The coffee shop is open all day and there is a restaurant and a bar.

ROOMS: 47 en suite (bth) (47 fmly) s IR£50-IR£60; d IR£70-IR£80 (incl. bkfst) * LB Off peak **MEALS:** Lunch IR£11-IR£17 High tea IR£6-IR£10 Dinner IR£15-IR£20 English, Irish & Italian Cuisine V meals Coffee am Tea pm **FACILITIES:** CTV in all bedrooms STV **CONF:** Thtr 400 Class 125 Board 50 Del from IR£75 * **SERVICES:** Lift Night porter 25P **NOTES:** No smoking area in restaurant Last d 9.45pm Closed 25 Dec **CARDS:**

DUNFANAGHY Co Donegal — Map 01 C6

★★★ Arnold's

Quality Percentage Score: 65%
☎ 074 36208 Fax 074 36352
Dir: on N56 from Letterkenny hotel is on left entering the village

This hotel is situated on the coast, with miles of sandy beaches close at hand. Public areas offer comfortable seating, and facilities include two restaurants and two bars. There is a choice of bedrooms, from well equipped standard rooms to larger ones with sofas.

ROOMS: 30 en suite (bth/shr) (10 fmly) s IR£72; d IR£104 (incl. bkfst) * LB Off peak **MEALS:** V meals Coffee am Tea pm **FACILITIES:** CTV in all bedrooms STV Tennis (hard) Fishing Riding Croquet lawn Putting green Wkly live entertainment **SERVICES:** Night porter 60P **NOTES:** No dogs (ex guide dogs) Last d 9pm Closed Nov-mid Mar **CARDS:**

DUNGANNON Co Tyrone — Map 01 C5

Cohannon Inn

212 Ballynakilly Rd BT71 6HJ
☎ 028 87724488 Fax 028 87752217
Dir: 400yds from junct 14 on M1

The Cohannon Inn offers well maintained accommodation at competitive prices. Rooms are located behind the Inn complex in a separate block. The main food and beverage areas have been smartly upgraded and all day food is available.

ROOMS: 50 en suite (bth/shr) **CONF:** Thtr 150 Class 150 Board 100

DUNGARVAN Co Waterford — Map 01 C2

★★★ *Lawlors*

Quality Percentage Score: 56%
☎ 058 41122 & 41056 Fax 058 41000
Dir: off N25

An ideal touring centre, this family-run, streetside hotel caters for both leisure and business guests.

ROOMS: 89 en suite (bth/shr) (8 fmly) **MEALS:** V meals Coffee am Tea pm **FACILITIES:** CTV in all bedrooms Wkly live entertainment **CONF:** Thtr 420 Class 215 Board 420 **SERVICES:** Lift Night porter P **NOTES:** No smoking area in restaurant Last d 10pm Closed 25 Dec **CARDS:**

DUN LAOGHAIRE Co Dublin — Map 01 D4

★★★ Royal Marine Marine Rd

Quality Percentage Score: 65%
☎ 01 2801911 Fax 01 2801089
Dir: follow signs for 'Car Ferry'

Set in four acres overlooking Dun Laoghaire harbour, the Victorian Royal Marine has long been a local landmark. The hotel has a range of contemporary facilities including a restaurant, bars, the popular Bay Lounge, and attractive gardens. There is easy access to the city centre.

ROOMS: 103 en suite (bth/shr) No smoking in 10 bedrooms d IR£180 * LB Off peak **MEALS:** Lunch fr IR£14alc Dinner fr IR£18alc Irish & French Cuisine V meals Coffee am Tea pm **FACILITIES:** CTV in all bedrooms STV Gym Wkly live entertainment Xmas **CONF:** Thtr 500 Class 300 Del from IR£120 * **SERVICES:** Lift Night porter 300P **NOTES:** No dogs No smoking area in restaurant Last d 9.30pm **CARDS:**

★★ *Pierre*

Victoria Ter, Seafront
Quality Percentage Score: 71%
☎ 01 2800291 Fax 01 2843332

The atmosphere is relaxed in this Victorian townhouse hotel. Public areas include a conservatory lounge overlooking Dublin Bay, and the restaurant, which offers a good choice of dishes. The basement Pierre Cafe Bar hosts a popular Monday night jazz session. Bedrooms vary in size but all are well equipped.

contd.

ROOMS: 32 rms (30 bth/shr) (5 fmly) No smoking in 4 bedrooms **MEALS:** V meals Coffee am Tea pm **FACILITIES:** CTV in all bedrooms Wkly live entertainment **CONF:** Thtr 100 Class 40 Board 30 **SERVICES:** Night porter 20P **NOTES:** No dogs (ex guide dogs) No coaches Last d 10pm Closed 24-27 Dec **CARDS:**

ENNIS Co Clare **Map 01 B3**

★★★❀ *Temple Gate* The Square
Quality Percentage Score: 66%
☎ 065 6823300 🖷 065 6823322
Dir: *from Ennis follow signs for Temple Gate*

A smart new hotel in the centre of Ennis. Incorporating a 19th century gothic style building, public areas are carefully planned and include a comfortable lounge library, Preachers Pub and Le Bistro Restaurant. Bedrooms are well equipped and attractively decorated.

ROOMS: 74 rms (34 bth/shr) (3 fmly) No smoking in 11 bedrooms **MEALS:** Irish & French Cuisine V meals Coffee am Tea pm **FACILITIES:** CTV in all bedrooms STV Wkly live entertainment **CONF:** Board 35 **SERVICES:** Lift Night porter 52P **NOTES:** No dogs (ex guide dogs) Last d 9.45pm Closed 25 Dec **CARDS:**

★★★ West County Conference & Leisure Hotel Clare Rd
Quality Percentage Score: 66%
☎ 065 6823000 🖷 065 6823759
Dir: *10mins walk from Ennis Town, next to St Flannans College*

The comfortable lounge is an ideal spot in which to relax. The bedrooms are modern and include a wide range of facilities. The new conference centre has all the latest equipment for business needs.

ROOMS: 152 en suite (bth/shr) (56 fmly) No smoking in 4 bedrooms s IR£50-IR£90; d IR£70-IR£120 * LB Off peak **MEALS:** Lunch IR£10.95-IR£13 Dinner fr IR£20 International Cuisine V meals Coffee am Tea pm **FACILITIES:** CTV in all bedrooms STV Indoor swimming pool (heated) Sauna Solarium Gym Pool table Jacuzzi/spa Beauty treatments Kidsplus programme Wkly live entertainment ch fac Xmas **CONF:** Thtr 1650 Class 1120 Board 50 Del from IR£103 * **SERVICES:** Lift Night porter 370P **NOTES:** No dogs (ex guide dogs) No smoking area in restaurant Last d 9.30pm **CARDS:**

★★ Magowna House Inch, Kilmaley
Quality Percentage Score: 64%
☎ 065 6839009 🖷 065 6839258
Dir: *from R474 pass golf course, and after approx 5km, hotel is signposted off to right, 300mtrs from junction*

This small family-run hotel stands in 14 acres of grounds. The hotel provides a good standard of comfort and enjoyable meals. Good local fishing, boats for hire, and a golf practice area are among the amenities in the neighbourhood.

ROOMS: 10 en suite (bth/shr) (3 fmly) No smoking in 4 bedrooms s IR£35-IR£41; d IR£56-IR£64 (incl. bkfst) * LB Off peak **MEALS:** Lunch fr IR£10.95 Dinner IR£18.50-IR£21 V meals Coffee am Tea pm **FACILITIES:** CTV in all bedrooms 3 hole pitch & putt 3 Boats for hire **CONF:** Thtr 200 Class 200 Board 20 **SERVICES:** 60P **NOTES:** No smoking area in restaurant Last d 9.45pm Closed 24-26 Dec **CARDS:**

ENNISCORTHY Co Wexford **Map 01 D3**

★★★ *Riverside Park Hotel* The Promenade
Quality Percentage Score: 66%
☎ 054 37800 🖷 054 37900
Dir: *0.5km from New Bridge, centre of Enniscorthy town, N11 Dublin/Rosslare Road*

Situated in a picturesque position on the banks of the River Slaney, the hotel is easily distinguished by its terracotta and blue colourscheme. The foyer is equally dramatic and the public areas take advantage of the riverside views, including the Mill House pub. The spacious, attractively decorated bedrooms have every convenience.

ROOMS: 60 en suite (bth/shr) (50 fmly) No smoking in 6 bedrooms **MEALS:** European Cuisine V meals Coffee am Tea pm **FACILITIES:** CTV in all bedrooms STV Wkly live entertainment **CONF:** Thtr 800 Class 500 Board 100 **SERVICES:** Lift Night porter P **NOTES:** No dogs (ex guide dogs) No smoking area in restaurant Last d 9.30pm **CARDS:**

★ *Murphy-Flood's* Market Square
Quality Percentage Score: 60%
☎ 054 33413 🖷 054 33413
Dir: *follow signs to hotel in the town centre*

A family-run hotel in the centre of a lively market town, Murphy-Flood's has a comfortable bar where carvery lunches, grills and snacks are served throughout the day. The hotel is currently undergoing refurbishment.

ROOMS: 21 rms (5 bth 13 shr) (2 fmly) No smoking in 2 bedrooms **MEALS:** V meals Coffee am Tea pm **FACILITIES:** CTV in all bedrooms Wkly live entertainment **CONF:** Thtr 200 Class 100 Board 60 **SERVICES:** Night porter **NOTES:** No dogs (ex guide dogs) No smoking area in restaurant Last d 9.30pm Closed 25 Dec **CARDS:**

ENNISKERRY Co Wicklow **Map 01 D3**

★★❀ *Enniscree Lodge Hotel & Restaurant* Glencree Valley
Quality Percentage Score: 70%
☎ 01 2863542 🖷 01 2866037
Dir: *turn off N11 at Enniskerry Village exit, straight through village and up Kilcarron Hill, stay on road for approx 6km. Lodge is on the right hand side*

Enniscree is a comfortable lodge surrounded by the forests and parkland of the Glencree Valley. There are two inviting lounges and a cosy, intimate bar with a blazing turf fire. The en suite bedrooms, varying in size, have all the standard modern facilities. The restaurant has a good reputation. A warm and friendly service is provided by the owners Josephine and Raymond Power and their attentive team.

ROOMS: 10 en suite (bth/shr) (1 fmly) **MEALS:** Irish & French Cuisine V meals Coffee am Tea pm **FACILITIES:** CTV in all bedrooms **CONF:** Board 14 **SERVICES:** 20P **NOTES:** No dogs (ex guide dogs) No coaches No smoking area in restaurant Last d 9pm **CARDS:**

ENNISKILLEN Co Fermanagh **Map 01 C5**

★★★ Killyhevlin BT74 6RW
Quality Percentage Score: 69%
☎ 028 66323481 🖷 028 66324726
Dir: *2m S, off A4*

The Killyhevlin commands wonderful views over Lough Erne. The stylish public areas are comfortable and enjoyable to use. Attractive fabrics have been used to good effect in the smart bedrooms which are comfortably modern in style.

ROOMS: 43 en suite (bth/shr) (32 fmly) s £56.50-£67.50; d £80-£100 (incl. bkfst) * LB Off peak **MEALS:** Lunch £10.50-£13.50 High tea £6.75-£10.50 Dinner £19.50-£22.50 International Cuisine V meals Coffee am Tea pm **FACILITIES:** CTV in all bedrooms STV Fishing Wkly live entertainment **CONF:** Thtr 600 Class 350 Del from £85 * **SERVICES:** Night porter 500P **NOTES:** No dogs (ex guide dogs) No smoking area in restaurant Last d 9.30pm **CARDS:**

★ ***Railway*** BT74 6AJ
Quality Percentage Score: 66%
☎ 028 66322084 🖹 028 66327480
Since 1855 the Byrne family have been welcoming guests to their comfortable small hotel on the east edge of town. A railway theme features strongly throughout the tastefully decorated public areas, and a good level of local support is attracted by the competitively priced food options available throughout the day. Pretty fabrics have been used to good effect in the compact well equipped bedrooms.
ROOMS: 19 en suite (bth/shr) (4 fmly) **MEALS:** V meals Coffee am Tea pm **FACILITIES:** CTV in all bedrooms STV Wkly live entertainment **CONF:** Board 100 **SERVICES:** Night porter **NOTES:** No smoking area in restaurant Closed 25-26 Dec **CARDS:**

E

GALWAY Co Galway **Map 01 B4**

The Premier Collection

★★★★ ***Glenlo Abbey***
Bushypark
☎ 091 526666 🖹 091 527800
Dir: *4km from Galway City Centre on the N59*
Standing in a landscaped 134-acre estate, this restored 18th-century abbey overlooks the beautiful loch. The handsome original building now houses a boardroom, business centre, conference and banqueting facilities. The bedrooms are in a well designed modern wing with a library, restaurants, cocktail and cellar bars. Leisure facilities are situated in the grounds.
ROOMS: 45 en suite (bth/shr) No smoking in 10 bedrooms **MEALS:** Irish & Continental Cuisine V meals Coffee am Tea pm **FACILITIES:** CTV in all bedrooms STV Golf 18 Fishing Putting green Boating Clay pigeon shooting Wkly live entertainment **CONF:** Thtr 80 Class 60 Board 40 **SERVICES:** Lift Night porter 150P **NOTES:** No dogs (ex guide dogs) No smoking area in restaurant Last d 9.30pm **CARDS:**

★★★★ **Ardilaun Conference & Leisure Centre**
Taylor's Hill
Quality Percentage Score: 65%
☎ 091 521433 🖹 091 521546
Dir: *take 4th left after 4th rdbt leading from main Dublin road*
Formerly a country mansion this hotel has comfortable lounges and the dining room overlooks beautiful gardens. Bedrooms are spacious, well furnished and individually decorated. Guests can enjoy the extensive new leisure facilities.
ROOMS: 90 en suite (bth/shr) (16 fmly) No smoking in 6 bedrooms s IR£90-IR£110; d IR£156-IR£176 (incl. bkfst) LB Off peak **MEALS:** Lunch IR£15.50 Dinner IR£26 V meals Coffee am Tea pm **FACILITIES:** CTV in all bedrooms STV Indoor swimming pool (heated) Snooker Sauna Solarium Gym Jacuzzi/spa Treatment & Analysis Rooms Wkly live entertainment Xmas **CONF:** Thtr 450 Class 200 Board 16 **SERVICES:** Lift Night porter 220P **NOTES:** Last d 9.15pm Closed 22-28 Dec **CARDS:**

★★★★ **Galway Bay Hotel Conference & Leisure Centre**
The Promenade, Salthill
Quality Percentage Score: 65%
☎ 091 520520 🖹 091 520530
Dir: *on the promenade in Salthill on the coast road to Connemara. Follow signs to Salthill from all major routes*
A superbly situated hotel on the promenade, famous for its lovely views. The hotel entrance is at the back of the building to ensure that arrivals and departures do not interrupt the peace. The conservatory lounge and patio are the perfect setting in which to soak up the panorama. Dining options include the Lobster Pot restaurant, the Cafe Lido or a traditional Irish pub. Bedrooms are attractively furnished and comfortable.

ROOMS: 153 en suite (bth/shr) (6 fmly) No smoking in 30 bedrooms s IR£95-IR£105; d IR£135-IR£150 (incl. bkfst) * LB Off peak **MEALS:** Lunch IR£12.50-IR£15 Dinner IR£21-IR£23 Irish & French Cuisine V meals Coffee am Tea pm **FACILITIES:** CTV in all bedrooms STV Indoor swimming pool (heated) Sauna Gym Steam room Wkly live entertainment ch fac Xmas **CONF:** Thtr 1100 Class 325 Del IR£98 * **SERVICES:** Lift Night porter 300P **NOTES:** No dogs (ex guide dogs) No smoking area in restaurant Last d 9.30pm **CARDS:**
See advert on opposite page

★★★★ **Westwood House Hotel**
Dangan, Upper Newcastle
Quality Percentage Score: 65%
☎ 091 521442 🖹 091 521400
Dir: *from N6 enter Galway, continue on N6 following signs for Clifden (N59) once on Clifden Rd the Westwood House Hotel is on left*
Close to the university on the edge of the city, this new hotel is luxuriously appointed. The public rooms include a themed bar, a restaurant and lounges. Bedrooms are comfortable and equally well suited to both corporate and leisure guests.
ROOMS: 58 en suite (bth/shr) (10 fmly) s IR£99; d IR£149 (incl. bkfst) * LB Off peak **MEALS:** Lunch IR£12.50-IR£14 Dinner IR£10.95-IR£16.95alc International Cuisine V meals Coffee am Tea pm **FACILITIES:** CTV in all bedrooms STV ch fac **CONF:** Thtr 350 Class 275 Board 15 Del from IR£99.95 * **SERVICES:** Lift Night porter Air conditioning 130P **NOTES:** No dogs (ex guide dogs) No smoking area in restaurant Last d 10pm Closed 25-26 Dec **CARDS:**

★★★★ Park House Hotel & Eyre House Restaurants
Forster St, Eyre Square
Quality Percentage Score: 58%
☎ 091 564924 🖷 091 569219
Dir: *in city centre*
Easily accessible, this hotel is suited to the tourist and business client alike. Bedrooms vary in size, though all are well appointed. Public rooms include comfortable lounges, a spacious dining room and a carvery bar.
ROOMS: 57 en suite (bth/shr) s IR£55-IR£135; d IR£80-IR£135 (incl. bkfst) * Off peak **MEALS:** Sunday Lunch IR£14.25 High tea fr IR£15 & alc Dinner fr IR£22.95 & alc Irish & French Cuisine V meals Coffee am Tea pm **FACILITIES:** CTV in all bedrooms STV Wkly live entertainment **CONF:** Thtr 50 Class 30 Board 30 Del from IR£180 * **SERVICES:** Lift Night porter 26P **NOTES:** No dogs (ex guide dogs) No smoking area in restaurant Last d 10pm Closed 24-26 Dec **CARDS:**

★★★ *Galway Ryan* Dublin Rd
Quality Percentage Score: 67%
☎ 091 753181 🖷 091 753187
Dir: *follow signs to Galway West off N7*

This modern hotel has undergone major recent refurbishment to all public areas, which now include a spacious, well decorated lounge and a new leisure club.
ROOMS: 96 en suite (bth/shr) (96 fmly) No smoking in 6 bedrooms **MEALS:** French Cuisine V meals Coffee am Tea pm **FACILITIES:** CTV in all bedrooms STV Indoor swimming pool (heated) Tennis (hard) Sauna Gym Sports hall Steam rooms Wkly live entertainment **CONF:** Thtr 80 Class 110 Board 30 **SERVICES:** Lift Night porter 100P **NOTES:** No dogs Last d 9.45pm Closed 25 Dec **CARDS:**

★★★ Menlo Park Hotel Terryland
Quality Percentage Score: 61%
☎ 091 761122 🖷 091 761222
Dir: *located at Terryland rdbt off N6 and N84 (Castlebar Rd)*
ROOMS: 44 en suite (bth/shr) (6 fmly) No smoking in 10 bedrooms s IR£65-IR£95; d IR£75-IR£160 (incl. bkfst) LB Off peak **MEALS:** Lunch IR£12-IR£16 High tea IR£6.50-IR£9.50 Dinner IR£17-IR£21 Irish, American & Italian Cuisine V meals Coffee am Tea pm **FACILITIES:** CTV in all bedrooms STV Wkly live entertainment **CONF:** Thtr 200 Class 100 Board 40 Del from IR£45 * **SERVICES:** Lift Night porter Air conditioning 100P **NOTES:** No dogs (ex guide dogs) No smoking area in restaurant Last d 9.30pm Closed 24-25 Dec **CARDS:**

★★★ Jurys Galway Inn Quay St
Quality Percentage Score: 59%
☎ 091 566444 🖷 091 568415
Dir: *N6 follow signs for Docks. At Docks take Salthill Rd for 2-3 minutes*
This modern budget hotel stands at the heart of the city opposite the famous Spanish Arch. To the rear of the hotel are an attractive patio and a garden bounded by the river. The 'one price' room rate and comfortable bedrooms ensure its popularity.
ROOMS: 128 en suite (bth/shr) (6 fmly) No smoking in 39 bedrooms d IR£83.80-IR£125.70 * Off peak **MEALS:** Bar Lunch fr IR£4.50alc Dinner fr IR£15 International Cuisine V meals Coffee am **FACILITIES:** CTV in all bedrooms STV **CONF:** Thtr 40 Class 40 Board 40 **SERVICES:** Lift **NOTES:** No dogs (ex guide dogs) No smoking area in restaurant Last d 9pm Closed 24-26 Dec **CARDS:**

★★★ Lochlurgain
22 Monksfield, Upper Salthill
Quality Percentage Score: 59%
☎ 091 529595 🖷 091 522399
Dir: *off R336 behind Bank of Ireland*
This small family-run hotel stands in a quiet street, at Salthill, beside the Roman Catholic church. Service is personally supervised and the bedrooms offer a high standard of comfort, which includes electric blankets in season. Public rooms are attractively decorated.
ROOMS: 13 en suite (bth/shr) (3 fmly) s IR£35-IR£45; d IR£60-IR£70 (incl. bkfst) * LB Off peak **MEALS:** Lunch IR£15-IR£17 Dinner IR£16.50-IR£19.95 English & French Cuisine Coffee am Tea pm **FACILITIES:** CTV in all bedrooms STV **SERVICES:** 8P **NOTES:** No dogs (ex guide dogs) No coaches No smoking in restaurant Last d 8pm Closed 26 Oct-13 Mar **CARDS:**

★★★ Victoria Victoria Place, Eyre Square
Quality Percentage Score: 58%
☎ 091 567433 🖷 091 565880
Dir: *off Eyre Sq on Victoria Place, Beside the rail station*
This new city-centre hotel is conveniently located off Eyre Square, a few minutes' walk from a public car park. Bedrooms are well equipped, while other facilities include 24-hour room

contd.

service, a good bar and a pleasant restaurant. The atmosphere is relaxing and staff are friendly and attentive.
ROOMS: 57 en suite (bth/shr) (20 fmly) No smoking in 1 bedroom s IR£50-IR£70; d IR£70-IR£140 (incl. bkfst) * LB Off peak **MEALS:** Lunch IR£5.95-IR£20.95alc Dinner IR£10.95-IR£24.95alc Irish, French & Mediterraen Cuisine V meals Coffee am Tea pm **FACILITIES:** CTV in all bedrooms STV **CONF:** Thtr 50 Class 30 Board 25 **SERVICES:** Lift Night porter **NOTES:** No dogs (ex guide dogs) No smoking area in restaurant Last d 9.30pm Closed 25 Dec **CARDS:**

★★ Hotel Ibis Headford Rd

Quality Percentage Score: 58%
☎ 091 771166 📠 091 771646
Dir: *off rdbt at junct of N84 and N6*
Conveniently situated on the outskirts of the city on an open site off the Headford Road, this modern hotel offers good value accommodation in well equipped bedrooms. Open-plan public areas include a lounge and informal restaurant. Refreshments and a 24-hour light snack service are available, although there is no bar as such.
ROOMS: 100 en suite (shr) (50 fmly) No smoking in 23 bedrooms d IR£39.50-IR£49.50 * Off peak **MEALS:** Bar Lunch IR£1.95-IR£4.50alc Dinner IR£5.50-IR£12alc V meals Coffee am Tea pm **FACILITIES:** CTV in all bedrooms STV **CONF:** Thtr 65 Class 40 Board 40 Del from IR£68 * **SERVICES:** Lift Night porter 110P **NOTES:** No smoking area in restaurant Last d 10.30pm **CARDS:**

GARRYVOE Co Cork — Map 01 C2

★★ Garryvoe

Quality Percentage Score: 67%
☎ 021 646718 📠 021 646824
Dir: *turn off N25 onto L72 at Castlemartyr between Midleton and Youghal and continue for 6km*
A comfortable, family-run hotel with caring staff, the Garryvoe has recently been upgraded. It stands in a delightful position facing a sandy beach, and the first floor residents' lounge overlooks the sea. There is a hotel bar, and a public bar.
ROOMS: 19 en suite (bth/shr) (2 fmly) s IR£35; d IR£60 (incl. bkfst) * LB Off peak **MEALS:** Lunch IR£12-IR£22 Dinner IR£22 & alc V meals Coffee am Tea pm **FACILITIES:** CTV in all bedrooms Tennis (hard) Putting green **CONF:** Thtr 400 Class 250 **SERVICES:** 25P **NOTES:** No dogs (ex guide dogs) No smoking area in restaurant Last d 8.45pm Closed 25 Dec **CARDS:**

GLENDALOUGH Co Wicklow — Map 01 D3

★★★ *The Glendalough*

Quality Percentage Score: 64%
☎ 0404 45135 📠 0404 45142
Forest and mountains provide the setting for this long-established hotel run by the Casey family and situated beside the famous monastic site. The hotel has been refurbished, and additional new bedrooms, many with lovely views, are now available. The charming restaurant overlooks river and forest, and bar food is also served. The whole area is ideal for hill walking, golf and trout fishing.
ROOMS: 44 en suite (bth/shr) (3 fmly) **MEALS:** European Cuisine V meals Coffee am Tea pm **FACILITIES:** CTV in all bedrooms STV Fishing Pool table Wkly live entertainment **CONF:** Thtr 200 Class 150 Board 50 **SERVICES:** Lift 100P **NOTES:** No dogs (ex guide dogs) Last d 9pm Closed 1 Dec-Jan **CARDS:**

GOREY Co Wexford — Map 01 D3

The Premier Collection

★★★ Marlfield House

☎ 055 21124 📠 055 21572
Dir: *1.5km outside Gorey on the Courtown Harbour road*
RELAIS & CHATEAUX.
This distinctive Regency house was once the residence of the Earl of Courtown, and the hotel retains an atmosphere of elegance and luxury throughout its well proportioned day rooms, which include an entrance foyer, library, drawing room and dining room leading into a fine conservatory which looks out over the grounds and a wild-life preserve. Bedrooms are in keeping with the style of the downstairs rooms and there are some superb suites. Druids Glen and several other golf courses are within easy reach.
ROOMS: 19 en suite (bth/shr) (3 fmly) s IR£85-IR£95; d IR£156-IR£490 (incl. bkfst) * LB Off peak **MEALS:** Lunch IR£21-IR£22 Dinner IR£36-IR£41 V meals Coffee am Tea pm **FACILITIES:** CTV in all bedrooms STV Tennis (hard) Sauna Croquet lawn **CONF:** Thtr 60 Board 20 **SERVICES:** 50P **NOTES:** No coaches No smoking in restaurant Last d 9pm Closed 15 Dec-30 Jan
CARDS:

GOUGANE BARRA Co Cork — Map 01 B2

★★ *Gougane Barra*

Quality Percentage Score: 62%
☎ 026 47069 📠 026 47226
Dir: *off N22*
Right on the lake shore, the Gougane Barra Hotel is very popular with its guests. Recent refurbishments have further improved the restaurant, bedrooms and bathrooms, all of which have lovely views. Guests can be met from their train, boat or plane by prior arrangement.
ROOMS: 28 en suite (bth/shr) **MEALS:** Irish & French Cuisine V meals Coffee am Tea pm **FACILITIES:** CTV in all bedrooms STV Fishing **SERVICES:** 25P **NOTES:** No dogs (ex guide dogs) No coaches No children 6yrs Last d 8.15pm Closed 7 Oct-15 Apr
CARDS:

HILLSBOROUGH Co Down — Map 01 D5

★★★ *White Gables* 14 Dromore Rd BT26 6HS

Quality Percentage Score: 66%
☎ 028 92682755 📠 028 92689532
Dir: *join M2 (Belfast) then M1 west, join A1 at junct 7 to Dublin. Take Hillsborough turn, go through village, hotel is on right hand side*
A comfortable, well maintained, modern hotel appealing to visiting business people. Bedrooms range from executive rooms to smaller standard rooms; all comfortably modern in style, superior rooms have extra quality touches. Smart public areas
contd.

include a bright foyer lounge, attractive split-level restaurant and an all-day coffee shop.
ROOMS: 31 en suite (bth/shr) (2 fmly) **MEALS:** French Cuisine V meals Coffee am Tea pm **FACILITIES:** CTV in all bedrooms STV **CONF:** Thtr 120 Class 40 Board 25 **SERVICES:** Night porter **NOTES:** No dogs (ex guide dogs) No smoking area in restaurant Last d 9.15pm Closed 24-25 Dec RS Sun (residents only before 7pm) **CARDS:**

INISHANNON Co Cork — Map 01 B2

★★★ ***Inishannon House***
Quality Percentage Score: 68%
☎ 021 775121 021 775609
Dir: *off N71 at eastern end of village*
A charming hotel, the River Bandon flows by this eye-catching country house, complemented by attractive walks and gardens. Good food is prepared from the freshest ingredients, with seafood dishes a speciality.
ROOMS: 12 en suite (bth/shr) 1 annexe en suite (bth/shr) (4 fmly) **MEALS:** Irish & French Cuisine V meals Coffee am Tea pm **FACILITIES:** CTV in 14 bedrooms STV Fishing Wkly live entertainment **CONF:** Thtr 200 Class 80 Board 50 **SERVICES:** 100P **NOTES:** No smoking area in restaurant Last d 10pm Closed 15 Jan-15 Mar **CARDS:**

IRVINESTOWN Co Fermanagh — Map 01 C5

★★ **Mahons** Mill St BT74 1GS
Quality Percentage Score: 66%
☎ 028 686 21656 028 686 28344
Dir: *on A32 midway between Enniskillen and Omagh - beside town clock in centre of Irvinestown*
For over 100 years the Mahon family have been welcoming guests to their town centre hotel. Public areas, especially the bar, are filled with a collection of bric-a-brac. In the restaurant, the extensive carte offers a wide range of dishes. Bedrooms, though variable in size, have pretty decor.
ROOMS: 18 en suite (bth/shr) (4 fmly) s £30-£35; d £55-£65 (incl. bkfst) * LB Off peak **MEALS:** Lunch £10.50-£11.75 High tea £10-£12.50 V meals Coffee am Tea pm **FACILITIES:** CTV in all bedrooms STV Tennis (hard) Riding Solarium Pool table Wkly live entertainment **CONF:** Thtr 450 Class 200 **SERVICES:** Night porter 40P **NOTES:** No smoking area in restaurant Last high tea 9.30pm Closed 25 Dec **CARDS:**

KENMARE Co Kerry — Map 01 B2

The Premier Collection

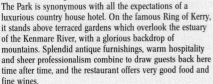

★★★★ **Park Hotel Kenmare**
☎ 064 41200 064 41402
Dir: *on R569 beside golf course*
The Park is synonymous with all the expectations of a luxurious country house hotel. On the famous Ring of Kerry, it stands above terraced gardens which overlook the estuary of the Kenmare River, with a glorious backdrop of mountains. Splendid antique furnishings, warm hospitality and sheer professionalism combine to draw guests back here time after time, and the restaurant offers very good food and fine wines.

ROOMS: 49 en suite (bth/shr) (2 fmly) No smoking in 5 bedrooms s IR£132-IR£152; d IR£244-IR£484 (incl. bkfst) * LB Off peak **MEALS:** Bar Lunch IR£5-IR£18 High tea IR£3.95-IR£6.95 Dinner IR£28.50-IR£39 & alc International Cuisine V meals Coffee am Tea pm **FACILITIES:** CTV in all bedrooms STV Golf 18 Tennis (hard) Snooker Gym Pool table Croquet lawn Putting green Wkly live entertainment Xmas **CONF:** Thtr 60 Class 40 Board 28 **SERVICES:** Lift Night porter 60P **NOTES:** No dogs (ex guide dogs) No smoking area in restaurant Last d 9pm Closed 3 Jan-13 Apr & 29 Oct-23 Dec **CARDS:**

New AA Guides for the Millennium are featured on page 24

The Premier Collection

★★★★ **Sheen Falls Lodge**
☎ 064 41600 064 41386
Dir: *from Kenmare take N71 to Glengarriff over the suspension bridge, take the first turn left*
This beautifully appointed hotel, beside the Sheen River, is surrounded by some of County Kerry's most stunning lake and mountain scenery. The cascading Sheen Falls are floodlit at night, creating a magical atmosphere which can be enjoyed from the the restaurant. A luxurious lounge, well stocked library, billiards room and cocktail bar complete the public rooms, and there are three grades of comfortable bedrooms.
ROOMS: 61 en suite (bth/shr) (14 fmly) No smoking in 10 bedrooms d IR£168-IR£258 * LB Off peak **MEALS:** High tea fr IR£9.50 Dinner fr IR£37.50 V meals Coffee am Tea pm **FACILITIES:** CTV in all bedrooms STV Indoor swimming pool (heated) Tennis (hard) Fishing Riding Snooker Sauna Solarium Gym Croquet lawn Jacuzzi/spa Table tennis Steam room Clay pigeon shooting Massage Seaweed therapy Cycling Wkly live entertainment Xmas **CONF:** Thtr 150 Class 65 Board 50 **SERVICES:** Lift Night porter 76P **NOTES:** No dogs (ex guide dogs) No smoking area in restaurant Last d 9.30pm Closed 30 Nov-21 Dec & 2 Jan-11 Feb **CARDS:**

★★★ Dromquinna Manor Blackwater Bridge
Quality Percentage Score: 68%
☎ 064 41657 🖹 064 41791
Dir: *take rd to Kenmare, take the N70 towards Sneem (ring of Kerry Rd). Hotel 3m down on the left*
Situated in the scenic Ring of Kerry in 42 acres of grounds sweeping down to the banks of the Kenmare River, this lovely hotel has at its heart the panelled Great Hall, and other pleasant sitting rooms, as well as the bar. Bedrooms vary in size, the largest being at the front, and there is a unique and much sought-after treehouse suite, perched 15ft above ground around the base of a huge tree. On the riverside are the bistro, a marina providing facilities for sailing, fishing and watersports, with a shallow pool, playground and small beach for children.
ROOMS: 28 en suite (bth/shr) 18 annexe en suite (bth/shr) (6 fmly) s IR£45-IR£90; d IR£90-IR£140 (incl. bkfst) * LB Off peak **MEALS:** Lunch IR£11.95 Dinner IR£18.50 International Cuisine V meals Coffee am Tea pm **FACILITIES:** CTV in 48 bedrooms Outdoor swimming pool Tennis (hard) Fishing Riding Croquet lawn Xmas **CONF:** Del from IR£65 * **SERVICES:** Night porter 80P **NOTES:** No dogs (ex guide dogs) No smoking area in restaurant Last d 9pm **CARDS:**

See advert on opposite page

★★★ *Riversdale House*
Quality Percentage Score: 63%
☎ 064 41299 🖹 064 41075
Nestling on the shores of Kenmare Bay in lovely woodland, but close to the town centre, the hotel has wonderful views. In the bedrooms, floor-length window alcoves take advantage of the clarity of light for which Kenmare is famous, and on the top floor are four mini-suites with balconies, well worth seeking out.
ROOMS: 64 en suite (bth/shr) **MEALS:** V meals Coffee am Tea pm **FACILITIES:** CTV in all bedrooms STV Wkly live entertainment **CONF:** Thtr 300 Class 250 Board 50 **SERVICES:** Lift Night porter 200P **NOTES:** No smoking area in restaurant Last d 10pm Closed Nov-Mar **CARDS:**

See advert on opposite page

KILKEE Co Clare — Map 01 B3

★★ *Halpin's* Erin St
Quality Percentage Score: 60%
☎ 065 56032 🖹 065 56317
The finest tradition of hotel service is offered at this family-run hotel which has a commanding view over the old Victorian town. The attractive bedrooms have recently been upgraded.
ROOMS: 12 en suite (bth/shr) (6 fmly) No smoking in 4 bedrooms **MEALS:** V meals Coffee am Tea pm **FACILITIES:** CTV in all bedrooms STV Tennis (hard) **CONF:** Thtr 60 Board 30 **SERVICES:** Night porter Air conditioning **NOTES:** No dogs Last d 9pm Closed 3 Jan-15 Mar **CARDS:**

AA Rosettes are awarded for quality of food, see page 15 for an explanation of Rosette assessment.

Remember to return your Prize Draw card for a chance to win one of 30 relaxing leisure breaks with Corus and Regal hotels. See inside the front cover for the card and competition details.

KILKENNY Co Kilkenny — Map 01 C3

★★★ Newpark
Quality Percentage Score: 71%
☎ 056 22122 🖹 056 61111
Recent refurbishment and extension of the public areas at this friendly hotel has provided an impressive new foyer lounge, a new bar/bistro, and conference suites. A new bedroom wing offers a choice of rooms, decorated and equipped to a high standard. Good car parking is available.
ROOMS: 111 en suite (bth/shr) (42 fmly) No smoking in 8 bedrooms s IR£56-IR£77; d IR£77-IR£99 * LB Off peak **MEALS:** Lunch IR£10.95-IR£13.95 High tea IR£5-IR£11 Dinner IR£18.95-IR£20.95 & alc International Cuisine V meals Coffee am Tea pm **FACILITIES:** CTV in all bedrooms STV Indoor swimming pool (heated) Sauna Solarium Gym Jacuzzi/spa Plunge pool Wkly live entertainment Xmas **CONF:** Thtr 600 Class 300 Board 50 Del from IR£80 * **SERVICES:** Night porter 350P **NOTES:** No dogs (ex guide dogs) No smoking area in restaurant Last d 9.45pm **CARDS:**

★★★ Hotel Kilkenny College Rd
Quality Percentage Score: 68%
☎ 056 62000 🖹 056 65984
Dir: *follow ring road to Callan/Clonmel rdbt hotel located on right*
Set in five acres of wooded grounds on the outskirts of Kilkenny, this hotel has facilities for both holidaymakers and business guests. There has recently been an extensive refurbishment, with new bedrooms and an attractive new restaurant which enjoys views of landscaped gardens. There is also a comfortable bar and a conservatory lounge.
ROOMS: 103 en suite (bth/shr) (15 fmly) s IR£62-IR£82; d IR£100-IR£125 (incl. bkfst) LB Off peak **MEALS:** Lunch fr IR£11 Dinner fr IR£22 French Cuisine V meals Coffee am Tea pm **FACILITIES:** CTV in all bedrooms STV Indoor swimming pool (heated) Sauna Solarium Gym Jacuzzi/spa Wkly live entertainment Xmas **CONF:** Thtr 400 Class 150 **SERVICES:** Night porter 250P **NOTES:** No dogs (ex guide dogs) No smoking area in restaurant Last d 10pm **CARDS:**

★★★ *Langton House* 69 John St
Quality Percentage Score: 63%
☎ 056 65133 🖹 056 63693
Dir: *take N9 & N10 from Dublin follow signs for city centre at outskirts of Kilkenny turn to left Langtons 500 metres on left after 1st set of lights*
Located on the main street, the exterior of this period town house hotel belies its internal size, which is large enough to include a ballroom. No expense has been spared in refurbishing the hotel, where lovely fabrics enhance the richness of specially designed mahogany furniture in the comfortable bedrooms, where marble tiled bathrooms also gleam. The well-known restaurant and pub are both very popular.
ROOMS: 10 en suite (bth/shr) 16 annexe en suite (bth/shr) No smoking in 4 bedrooms **MEALS:** European Cuisine V meals Coffee am Tea pm **FACILITIES:** CTV in all bedrooms STV Wkly live entertainment **SERVICES:** Night porter 60P **NOTES:** No dogs (ex guide dogs) No smoking area in restaurant Last d 10pm **CARDS:**

★★ Club House Patrick St
Quality Percentage Score: 59%
☎ 056 21994 🖹 056 71920
Dir: *city centre, nr Kilkenny castle*
This 200 year old hotel is located in the city centre and has its own car park to the rear of the building. The en suite bedrooms have all been refurbished, and ten more have recently been added. There is a lounge bar with an open fire, a Georgian

contd.

dining room, and a function suite. Personally supervised by the owner, this is a comfortable and friendly hotel.
ROOMS: 28 en suite (bth/shr) (2 fmly) s IR£35-IR£75; d IR£66-IR£125 (incl. bkfst) * LB Off peak **MEALS:** Lunch IR£10.95-IR£12.95 High tea IR£6.50-IR£12.50 Dinner IR£17.50-IR£19.50 Irish & French Cuisine V meals Coffee am Tea pm **FACILITIES:** CTV in all bedrooms STV Gym **CONF:** Thtr 100 Class 75 Board 35 **SERVICES:** Night porter 80P **NOTES:** No smoking area in restaurant Last d 9.30pm
CARDS:

KILL Co Kildare **Map 01 D4**

★★★ Ambassador

Quality Percentage Score: 62%
☎ 045 886700 📠 045 886777
Dir: *20/25 minutes from Dublin centre on the N7 to the South and South West*
Set beside the N7 - near Goffs Bloodstock Sales Complex, 16 miles from Dublin - the hotel offers comfortable, well appointed accommodation. The Ambassador Lounge carvery and the Diplomat Restaurant are the choices for meals, and there is also a bar. There are good parking facilities.
ROOMS: 36 en suite (bth/shr) (36 fmly) s fr IR£58; d fr IR£82 (incl. bkfst) * LB Off peak **MEALS:** Lunch fr IR£13 Dinner fr IR£20.50 European Cuisine V meals Coffee am Tea pm **FACILITIES:** CTV in all bedrooms STV Wkly live entertainment Xmas **CONF:** Thtr 260 Class 140 Board 60 Del from IR£78 * **SERVICES:** Night porter 150P **NOTES:** No dogs (ex guide dogs) No smoking area in restaurant Last d 10pm
CARDS:

KILLARNEY Co Kerry **Map 01 B2**

★★★★ Aghadoe Heights

Quality Percentage Score: 78%

☎ 064 31766 📠 064 31345

Dir: *16km S of Kerry Airport and 5km N of Killarney. Signposted off the N22 Tralee road*

In a superb setting, overlooking the Killarney Lakes, this hotel is a luxurious and hospitable haven concealed behind an austere façade. The award-winning restaurant continues to receive well deserved recognition and standards of service have also brought accolades.

ROOMS: 75 en suite (bth/shr) (5 fmly) s IR£105-IR£180; d IR£160-IR£245 (incl. bkfst) * LB Off peak **MEALS:** Lunch IR£23-IR£25 Dinner fr IR£37.50 Irish & French Cuisine V meals Coffee am Tea pm **FACILITIES:** CTV in all bedrooms STV Indoor swimming pool (heated) Tennis (hard) Fishing Sauna Solarium Gym Jacuzzi/spa Steam room Plunge pool Wkly live entertainment Xmas **SERVICES:** Night porter 120P **NOTES:** No dogs No smoking area in restaurant Last d 9.30pm Closed Nov-1 Apr **CARDS:**

★★★★ Killarney Park

Kenmare Place

Quality Percentage Score: 77%

☎ 064 35555 📠 064 35266

Dir: *N22 from Cork to Killarney. At 1st rdbt take 1st exit to Town Centre and at 2nd rdbt take 1st exit. Hotel is 2nd entrance on the left*

On the edge of town, this charming purpose-built hotel combines elegance with comfort. The entrance lobby with blazing fire gives the first hint of the warmth of atmosphere created by both the innovative decor, rich in colours and fabrics, and the friendly, efficient staff. Public rooms and bedrooms are very comfortable indeed.

ROOMS: 76 en suite (bth/shr) (4 fmly) No smoking in 28 bedrooms d IR£200-IR£320 (incl. bkfst) LB Off peak **MEALS:** Lunch IR£17.50 Dinner IR£28-IR£35 & alc Irish & European Cuisine V meals Coffee am Tea pm **FACILITIES:** CTV in all bedrooms STV Indoor swimming pool (heated) Snooker Sauna Gym Pool table Jacuzzi/spa Outdoor Canadian hot-tub Plunge pool Wkly live entertainment Xmas **CONF:** Thtr 150 Class 70 Board 35 **SERVICES:** Lift Night porter Air conditioning 70P **NOTES:** No dogs (ex guide dogs) No smoking area in restaurant Last d 9.15pm Closed 28 Nov-15 Dec 24-26 Dec **CARDS:**

See advert on opposite page

★★★★ *Muckross Park Hotel*

Muckross Village

Quality Percentage Score: 64%

☎ 064 31938 📠 064 31965

Dir: *from Killarney take road to Kenmare, hotel 4km on left*

Set in the heart of the Killarney National Park, this 18th-century hotel has been luxuriously refurbished to a high standard. Relaxing lounge areas feature comfortable furniture, warm colour schemes and chandeliers. Bedrooms are attractively decorated and well equipped. The adjacent thatched pub, Molly Darcys, offers an alternative to the formal Bluepool restaurant and has live entertainment.

ROOMS: 27 en suite (bth/shr) (2 fmly) No smoking in 2 bedrooms **MEALS:** European Cuisine V meals Coffee am Tea pm **FACILITIES:** CTV in all bedrooms STV **CONF:** Thtr 200 Class 80 Board 40 **SERVICES:** Night porter 250P **NOTES:** No dogs (ex guide dogs) No smoking in restaurant Last d 10pm Closed Dec-Feb **CARDS:**

See advert on opposite page

★★★ *Cahernane*

Muckross Rd

MANOR HOUSE HOTELS

Quality Percentage Score: 76%

☎ 064 31895 📠 064 34340

This fine old country mansion with a magnificent mountain backdrop enjoys panoramic views from its setting beside the lake. Elegant period furnishings, fresh flowers and the glow of silver combine to create a welcoming atmosphere. Service is attentive but unobtrusive, and cuisine is of a high standard.

ROOMS: 14 en suite (bth/shr) 33 annexe en suite (bth/shr) **MEALS:** Irish, French, German & Italian Cuisine V meals Coffee am Tea pm **FACILITIES:** Tennis (hard) Fishing Croquet lawn Wkly live entertainment **SERVICES:** Night porter 50P **NOTES:** No dogs (ex guide dogs) No smoking in restaurant Last d 9.30pm Closed 2 Nov-Mar **CARDS:**

★★★ *Castlerosse*

Quality Percentage Score: 67%

☎ 064 31144 📠 064 31031

Dir: *from Killarney town take R562 for Killorglin and The Ring of Kerry, hotel is 1.5km from town on the left hand side*

Set in 6,000 acres of lakeland overlooking Lough Leane, this beautifully situated hotel offers warm hospitality and good food as well as special facilities on the adjoining championship golf courses. Boating and fishing trips are available on the nearby lakes.

ROOMS: 110 en suite (bth/shr) (27 fmly) No smoking in 4 bedrooms **MEALS:** International Cuisine V meals Coffee am Tea pm **FACILITIES:** CTV in all bedrooms Indoor swimming pool (heated) Tennis (hard) Snooker Sauna Gym Jacuzzi/spa Golfing & riding arranged Wkly live entertainment **CONF:** Thtr 200 Class 100 **SERVICES:** Lift Night porter 100P **NOTES:** No dogs (ex guide dogs) No smoking area in restaurant Last d 9.30pm Closed Dec-Feb **CARDS:**

★★★ Gleneagle

Quality Percentage Score: 67%

☎ 064 31870 📠 064 32646

Dir: *1m outside Killarney town on the Kenmare Road - N71*

Set in 25 acres of parkland, this hotel has fine leisure facilities, and a hospitable atmosphere. Public rooms include spacious lounges, two bars, a coffee shop and a good restaurant. Bedrooms vary in size and style, with those in the modern wing

contd.

being more spacious. Entertainment is provided in the summer season.
ROOMS: 213 en suite (bth/shr) (35 fmly) No smoking in 20 bedrooms s IR£78; d IR£120 (incl. bkfst) * LB Off peak **MEALS:** Lunch fr IR£10.50 Dinner fr IR£19 V meals Coffee am Tea pm **FACILITIES:** CTV in 220 bedrooms STV Indoor swimming pool (heated) Tennis (hard) Fishing Squash Snooker Sauna Solarium Gym Pool table Jacuzzi/spa Pitch & Putt Table tennis Steam room Beauty therapist Wkly live entertainment Xmas **CONF:** Thtr 1000 Class 400 Board 70 **SERVICES:** Lift Night porter 500P **NOTES:** Last d 9.15pm **CARDS:**

★★★ Killarney Ryan
Cork Rd
Quality Percentage Score: 66%
☎ 064 31555 ▤ 064 32438
Dir: *on N22 route*

Conveniently situated on the outskirts of the town, this hotel offers good standards of comfort. Public rooms include a large lounge, a restaurant and lounge bar opening on to the gardens. Many of the bedrooms can accommodate families, and the Ryan Group offer an all-inclusive summer holiday rate which can be good value.
ROOMS: 168 en suite (bth/shr) (168 fmly) No smoking in 20 bedrooms **MEALS:** Bar Lunch IR£3-IR£8 & alc Dinner IR£18.90 & alc French Cuisine V meals Coffee am Tea pm **FACILITIES:** CTV in all bedrooms STV Indoor swimming pool (heated) Tennis (hard) Sauna Jacuzzi/spa Steam room Crazy golf Wkly live entertainment ch fac **SERVICES:** Lift Night porter 180P **NOTES:** No dogs No smoking area in restaurant Last d 10pm Closed Dec & Jan **CARDS:**

★★★ International
Kenmare Pl
Quality Percentage Score: 65%
☎ 064 31816 ▤ 064 31837
Dir: *town centre*
Refurbished to a high standard, this hotel offers quality bedrooms with modern comforts. Hannigan's Bar and the lounge are lively spots where bar snacks are available, while there is a more intimate dining room where soft candlelight glows against mahogany panelling. There is a library and a snooker room, and a keen interest is taken in golfing guests - tee times can be arranged at any of the numerous courses in the area.
ROOMS: 75 en suite (bth/shr) (6 fmly) s IR£35-IR£55; d IR£50-IR£90 (incl. bkfst) * LB Off peak **MEALS:** Lunch IR£12.50 High tea IR£5-IR£10 Dinner IR£12.50-IR£17.50 European Cuisine V meals Coffee am Tea pm **FACILITIES:** CTV in all bedrooms STV Pool table Wkly live entertainment **CONF:** Thtr 200 Class 100 Board 25 **SERVICES:** Lift Night porter **NOTES:** No smoking area in restaurant Last d 8.45pm Closed 23-27 Dec **CARDS:**

★★★ Lake
Muckross Rd
Quality Percentage Score: 64%
☎ 064 31035 📠 064 31902
Dir: *Kenmare road out of Killarney*
Approached down a wooded drive, this former mansion is stands in lovely countryside with lake and mountain views and woodland walks. Bedrooms are well equipped, and some have balconies and four-poster beds. Public rooms are spacious, and the lounge has kept an atmosphere of traditional comfort.
ROOMS: 65 en suite (bth/shr) (10 fmly) s fr IR£67; d IR£66-IR£160 (incl. bkfst) LB Off peak **MEALS:** Irish, French & Italian Cuisine V meals Coffee am Tea pm **FACILITIES:** CTV in all bedrooms STV Tennis (hard) Fishing Pool table Putting green Wkly live entertainment **CONF:** Thtr 80 Class 60 Board 40 **SERVICES:** Lift Night porter Air conditioning 143P **NOTES:** No dogs (ex guide dogs) Last d 8.45pm Closed 3 Dec-11 Feb **CARDS:**

★★★ *Killarney Court Hotel*
Tralee Rd
Quality Percentage Score: 63%
☎ 064 37070 📠 064 37060
Dir: *Travelling from Tralee on the main Tralee Rd, the 1st rdbt towards Killarney, hotel on left*
Purpose built to a high standard, this new stone-fronted hotel has spacious public areas, an inviting pub and a contemporary restaurant offering a mix of transatlantic influences and traditional cuisine. The large bedrooms are attractively furnished and very comfortable. Bar food is served all day, as well as a carvery lunch.
ROOMS: 96 en suite (bth/shr) (8 fmly) No smoking in 6 bedrooms **MEALS:** International Cuisine V meals Coffee am Tea pm **FACILITIES:** CTV in all bedrooms STV Sauna Gym Jacuzzi/spa Steam room **CONF:** Thtr 120 Class 70 Board 60 **SERVICES:** Lift Night porter 130P **NOTES:** No smoking area in restaurant Last d 10pm Closed 25 Dec **CARDS:**

★★★ *White Gates*
Muckross Rd
Quality Percentage Score: 61%
☎ 064 31164 📠 064 34850
Dir: *1km from Killarney town on Muckross road on left*
Distinctive blue and ochre paintwork draws the eye to this newly opened hotel. The same flair for colour combinations is evident throughout the interior, and bedrooms are particularly attractive. The natural harmony of wood and stone is a feature of the well designed lounge bar and the restaurant, with its conservatory front, is filled with light. There is also a very comfortable lounge.
ROOMS: 27 en suite (bth/shr) **MEALS:** V meals Coffee am Tea pm **FACILITIES:** CTV in all bedrooms STV Wkly live entertainment **CONF:** Class 50 **SERVICES:** Night porter 50P **NOTES:** No dogs (ex guide dogs) No smoking area in restaurant Closed 21-29 Dec **CARDS:**

★★★ *Scotts Garden Hotel*
College St
Quality Percentage Score: 59%
☎ 064 31060 📠 064 31582
Located in the town centre, this hotel now has a completely new building at the back of the old Scotts Hotel, with a new entrance, reception and bar, plus pleasant bedrooms and a patio garden. Special concessions are available at the sister Gleneagles Hotel's leisure facilities.
MEALS: Coffee am Tea pm **NOTES:** Last d 9pm **CARDS:**

★★❀ *Arbutus*
College St
Quality Percentage Score: 66%
☎ 064 31037 📠 064 34033
This attractive hotel has been completely renovated and its entrance now features a fine foyer lounge and a second lounge adjoining the bar. There is a good restaurant, serving freshly prepared dishes based on local Irish produce. Bedrooms are comfortable with modern facilities.
ROOMS: 39 en suite (bth/shr) (4 fmly) **MEALS:** V meals Coffee am **FACILITIES:** CTV in all bedrooms STV **SERVICES:** Night porter **NOTES:** No dogs (ex guide dogs) No smoking area in restaurant Last d 8.30pm Closed 19-30 Dec **CARDS:**

See advert on opposite page

★★ Darby O'Gills
Lissivigeen, Mallow Rd
Quality Percentage Score: 63%
☎ 064 34168 & 34919 📠 064 36794
A modern country house, offering smart, spacious and well-equipped bedrooms. Dinner is served in the restaurant, and bar food in the comfortable lounge bar. There is also a traditional Irish pub.
ROOMS: 13 en suite (bth/shr) (3 fmly) s IR£25-IR£35; d IR£40-IR£56 (incl. bkfst) * LB Off peak **MEALS:** Lunch fr IR£8.50 Dinner fr IR£15 Irish & French Cuisine V meals Coffee am Tea pm **FACILITIES:** CTV in all bedrooms STV Wkly live entertainment **CONF:** Thtr 250 Class 150 Board 60 Del from IR£45 * **SERVICES:** Air conditioning 150P **NOTES:** No dogs (ex guide dogs) No smoking area in restaurant Closed 25 Dec **CARDS:**

KILLINEY Co Dublin — Map 01 D4

★★★ *Fitzpatrick Castle*
Quality Percentage Score: 68%
☎ 01 2840700 📠 01 2850207
This converted castle with modern extensions is set in its own attractive gardens and grounds with views over Dublin Bay. There is a helipad, and a courtesy coach is available for transfers to and from the airport.
ROOMS: 113 en suite (bth/shr) (40 fmly) No smoking in 18 bedrooms **MEALS:** International Cuisine V meals Coffee am Tea pm **FACILITIES:** CTV in all bedrooms Indoor swimming pool (heated) Sauna Gym Beauty/hairdressing salon Steam room Wkly live entertainment **CONF:** Thtr 500 Class 240 Board 80 **SERVICES:** Lift Night porter 300P **NOTES:** No dogs (ex guide dogs) No smoking area in restaurant Last d 10.30pm **CARDS:**

★★★ Court
Quality Percentage Score: 65%
☎ 01 2851622 📠 01 2852085
Dir: *from Dublin-N11 via Donnybrook and Stillorgan, turn left off dual carriageway at traffic lights 1.6km after Cabinteely, right at next traffic lights*
In its own grounds overlooking the breathtaking Killiney Bay, this attractive Victorian mansion is in a convenient location, only 12 miles from Dublin and close to the fast commuter train service. The International Conference facilities include translating equipment.
ROOMS: 86 en suite (bth/shr) (29 fmly) No smoking in 8 bedrooms s IR£64.50-IR£99.50; d IR£89-IR£134 (incl. bkfst) * LB Off peak **MEALS:** Lunch IR£14.50-IR£15.50 & alc Dinner IR£23.95-IR£24.95 & alc International Cuisine V meals Coffee am Tea pm **FACILITIES:** CTV in all bedrooms Beach in front of hotel Wkly live entertainment Xmas **CONF:** Thtr 300 Class 180 Board 60 Del from IR£100 * **SERVICES:** Lift Night porter 200P **NOTES:** No dogs (ex guide dogs) Last d 11pm **CARDS:**

KINGSCOURT Co Cavan **Map 01 C4**

★★★ Cabra Castle

Quality Percentage Score: 65%

☎ 042 9667030 🖷 042 9667039

Rebuilt in 1808, the Castle stands in 100 acres of parkland and is part of a national park. The staff are friendly and welcoming and take a personal interest in guests' comfort. The courtyard bedrooms have car parking just outside the door and access to the hotel. The main reception rooms are elegant and invite relaxation, while the pleasant bar leads onto a patio garden. There is free golf to residents and fishing and archery nearby.

ROOMS: 20 en suite (bth/shr) 46 annexe en suite (bth/shr) (5 fmly) s IR£60-IR£120; d IR£80-IR£180 (incl. bkfst) * LB Off peak **MEALS:** Sunday Lunch IR£13.95 Dinner IR£24.95 English & French Cuisine V meals Coffee am Tea pm **FACILITIES:** CTV in all bedrooms Golf 9 Riding Wkly live entertainment **CONF:** Thtr 300 Class 100 Board 50 Del from IR£65 * **SERVICES:** Night porter 200P **NOTES:** No smoking area in restaurant Last d 9pm Closed 25-27 Dec **CARDS:**

KINSALE Co Cork **Map 01 B2**

★★★ Actons

Pier Rd

Quality Percentage Score: 73%

☎ 021 772135 🖷 021 772231

Dir: *hotel is located in the Town Centre area facing Kinsale Harbour, 500 yards from Yacht Club Marina*

The location of this hotel, set in gardens overlooking the waterfront and marina is a real bonus. The hotel has a bar and bistro, plus the Captain's Table restaurant which continues to offer enjoyable food. The luxurious lounge is comfortable and the bedrooms are all of good quality. Above all, it is the the friendly and attentive staff who contribute so much towards the enjoyment of a visit.

ROOMS: 76 en suite (bth/shr) (20 fmly) s IR£70-IR£95; d IR£90-IR£140 (incl. bkfst) LB Off peak **MEALS:** Sunday Lunch IR£14-IR£16 & alc Dinner IR£24-IR£26 & alc Irish & French Cuisine V meals Coffee am Tea pm **FACILITIES:** CTV in all bedrooms STV Indoor swimming pool (heated) Sauna Solarium Gym Wkly live entertainment Xmas **CONF:** Thtr 350 Class 200 Board 100 Del from IR£90 * **SERVICES:** Lift Night porter 70P **NOTES:** No dogs (ex guide dogs) No smoking area in restaurant Last d 9.45pm **CARDS:**

★★★ Trident

Worlds End

Quality Percentage Score: 68%

☎ 021 772301 🖷 021 774173

Dir: *take R600 from Cork city to Kinsale, drive along the Kinsale waterfront, the hotel is located just beyond the pier, on the waterfront*

Located at the harbour's edge, the Trident Hotel has its own marina with boats for hire. Many of the bedrooms have superb views and two have balconies. The restaurant and lounge both

contd.

overlook the harbour and pleasant staff provide hospitable service.
ROOMS: 58 en suite (bth/shr) (2 fmly) s IR£65-IR£85; d IR£90-IR£130 (incl. bkfst) * LB Off peak **MEALS:** Sunday Lunch IR£11 Dinner IR£20 & alc Irish & European Cuisine V meals Coffee am Tea pm **FACILITIES:** CTV in all bedrooms STV Sauna Gym Jacuzzi/spa Steam room Xmas **CONF:** Thtr 250 Class 170 Board 60 Del from IR£72.50 * **SERVICES:** Lift Night porter 60P **NOTES:** No dogs (ex guide dogs) No smoking area in restaurant Last d 9.30pm Closed 25-26 Dec
CARDS:

KNOCK Co Mayo — Map 01 B4

★★★❀ Belmont

Quality Percentage Score: 59%
☎ 094 88122 Fax 094 88532
Dir: *on the N17*
ROOMS: 64 en suite (bth/shr) (6 fmly) No smoking in 3 bedrooms **MEALS:** Sunday Lunch IR£11.50-IR£13.50 Dinner IR£20.50 & alc Irish & French Cuisine V meals Coffee am **FACILITIES:** CTV in all bedrooms STV Solarium Gym Jacuzzi/spa Steamroom Natural health therapies **CONF:** Thtr 500 Class 100 Board 20 **SERVICES:** Lift Night porter Air conditioning 110P **NOTES:** No dogs (ex guide dogs) No smoking area in restaurant Last d 9.30pm Closed 25 & 26 Dec **CARDS:**

LAHINCH Co Clare — Map 01 B3

★★★ *Aberdeen Arms*

Quality Percentage Score: 59%
☎ 065 81100 Fax 065 81228
Dir: *56km from Shannon airport, N18 to Ennis, N85 to Ennistymon, turn left, approx 3km to Lahinch, turn left at top of Main St*
A popular and recently modernised hotel offering very comfortable day rooms where guests can expect to mingle with the golfing fraternity playing the famous Lahinch Links Course. Bedrooms are furnished in a popular style and well equipped.
ROOMS: 55 en suite (bth/shr) **MEALS:** European Cuisine V meals Coffee am Tea pm **FACILITIES:** CTV in all bedrooms STV Snooker Sauna Pool table Jacuzzi/spa **CONF:** Thtr 200 Class 100 Board 50 **SERVICES:** Night porter 85P **NOTES:** No dogs (ex guide dogs) No smoking area in restaurant Last d 8.45pm **CARDS:**

LEIXLIP Co Kildare — Map 01 D4

★★★❀❀ *Leixlip House*

Captains Hill
Quality Percentage Score: 76%
☎ 01 6242268 Fax 01 6244177
This lovely old stone-built country house dates from the 18th century and retains many of the original features. Accommodation is of high quality, as is the service, and the restaurant serves enjoyable meals.
ROOMS: 15 en suite (bth/shr) (2 fmly) **MEALS:** V meals Coffee am Tea pm **FACILITIES:** CTV in all bedrooms STV **CONF:** Thtr 130 Class 60 Board 40 **SERVICES:** Night porter 64P **NOTES:** No smoking area in restaurant Last d 10pm **CARDS:**

LIMAVADY Co Londonderry — Map 01 C6

★★★★ Radisson Roe Park Hotel & Golf Resort

BT49 9LB
Quality Percentage Score: 67%
☎ 028 777 22222 Fax 028 777 22313
Dir: *on the A2 Londonderry/Limavady road, 16m from Londonderry, 1m from Limavady*
In a stunning location just outside the town, this country house offers a superb range of sporting, leisure and business facilities. The public lounges, restaurant and bar are grouped round cobbled courtyards and the Brasserie provides an interesting outlook on the golf course. Bedrooms are spacious and modern.
ROOMS: 64 en suite (bth/shr) (15 fmly) No smoking in 16 bedrooms s £90; d £130 (incl. bkfst) * LB Off peak **MEALS:** Lunch £11.95 French Cuisine V meals Coffee am Tea pm **FACILITIES:** CTV in all bedrooms STV Indoor swimming pool (heated) Golf 18 Fishing Sauna Solarium Gym Pool table Croquet lawn Putting green Jacuzzi/spa Floodlit driving range Practice area Xmas **CONF:** Thtr 450 Class 180 Board 100 Del £115 * **SERVICES:** Lift Night porter 300P **NOTES:** No dogs (ex guide dogs) No smoking area in restaurant **CARDS:**

LIMERICK Co Limerick — Map 01 B3

★★★★❀❀ Castletroy Park

Dublin Rd
Quality Percentage Score: 71%
☎ 061 335566 Fax 061 331117
Dir: *on N7, 5km from Limerick*
Encircled by gardens, this creatively designed hotel seems filled with light and combines modern comforts with attractive decor. Business guests will welcome the fax and computer points in the bedrooms. McLaughlin's Restaurant serves good food and is a popular meeting place. The hotel caters excellently for both business and leisure, and is near the University of Limerick, off the N7.
ROOMS: 107 en suite (bth/shr) (78 fmly) No smoking in 30 bedrooms s IR£112-IR£140; d IR£132-IR£160 (incl. bkfst) * LB Off peak **MEALS:** Bar Lunch fr IR£5.95 Dinner fr IR£26 International Cuisine V meals Coffee am Tea pm **FACILITIES:** CTV in all bedrooms STV Indoor swimming pool (heated) Sauna Gym Jacuzzi/spa Running track Steam room Wkly live entertainment **CONF:** Thtr 450 Class 270 Board 100 Del from IR£160 * **SERVICES:** Lift Night porter 160P **NOTES:** No dogs (ex guide dogs) No smoking area in restaurant Closed 24-26 Dec **CARDS:**

★★★❀❀ *Jurys*

Ennis Rd
Quality Percentage Score: 72%
☎ 061 327777 Fax 061 326400
Dir: *located at junction of Ennis Rd, O'Callaghan Strand and Sarsfield Bridge*
Standing in four acres of riverside grounds, with excellent corporate and leisure facilities, including executive rooms, conference rooms, indoor pool and leisure centre, the hotel offers two restaurants, the Copper Room for fine dining and the less formal Bridges.
ROOMS: 95 en suite (bth/shr) (22 fmly) No smoking in 16 bedrooms **MEALS:** International Cuisine V meals Coffee am Tea pm **FACILITIES:** CTV in all bedrooms STV Indoor swimming pool (heated) Tennis (hard) Sauna Gym Jacuzzi/spa Steam room Plunge pool Wkly live entertainment **CONF:** Thtr 200 Class 90 Board 45 **SERVICES:** Night porter 200P **NOTES:** No dogs (ex guide dogs) No smoking area in restaurant Last d 10.15pm Closed 24-27 Dec **CARDS:**

LIMERICK Co Limerick — Map 01 B3

★★★❀ Limerick Ryan

Ennis Rd
Quality Percentage Score: 72%
☎ 061 453922 Fax 061 326333
Dir: *on N18, Ennis road*
Conveniently situated close to the city, in its own grounds, the Limerick Ryan has smart public areas located in the original part of this refurbished period house. Spacious lounges and restaurants, and a cocktail bar with a fire, sofas and a pianist, are warm and relaxing. The well equipped bedrooms are located in the modern extension, and 24-hour room service is available.

contd.

Other facilities include conference suites, a business centre, patio gardens and a large car park.

ROOMS: 181 en suite (bth/shr) (181 fmly) No smoking in 19 bedrooms d IR£90-IR£125 * LB Off peak **MEALS:** Lunch fr IR£14alc Dinner fr IR£19alc French Cuisine V meals Coffee am Tea pm **FACILITIES:** CTV in all bedrooms STV Gym Gym nearby available free to guests Wkly live entertainment Xmas **CONF:** Thtr 130 Class 60 Board 40 Del from IR£110 * **SERVICES:** Lift Night porter 180P **NOTES:** No dogs No smoking area in restaurant Last d 9.30pm **CARDS:**

★★★ South Court Business & Leisure Hotel

South Court Roundabout, Raheen
Quality Percentage Score: 64%
☎ 065 6823000 065 6823759

A pleasant purpose-built hotel, set in a good location for both leisure and business guests. The latter will appreciate the well-equipped executive rooms, where fax machines, ISDN lines and laptop computers are available. All the rooms are very comfortable and there is a restaurant and a pub/bistro. Secretarial services are provided in the Business Centre.

ROOMS: 65 en suite (bth/shr) (65 fmly) No smoking in 6 bedrooms s IR£110; d IR£130 * LB Off peak **MEALS:** Lunch fr IR£12.50 Dinner IR£20-IR£27 & alc Irish & Continental Cuisine V meals Coffee am Tea pm **FACILITIES:** CTV in all bedrooms STV Sauna Solarium Gym Steam room (leisure centre due 2000) Wkly live entertainment Xmas **CONF:** Thtr 200 Class 120 Board 50 Del from IR£120 * **SERVICES:** Lift Night porter Air conditioning 250P **NOTES:** No dogs (ex guide dogs) No smoking area in restaurant Last d 10pm **CARDS:**

★★★ Greenhills

Caherdavin
Quality Percentage Score: 62%
☎ 061 453033 061 453307
Dir: *situated on the N18, approx 2m from City Centre*

Set in 3.5 acres of lovely landscaped gardens, this hotel has recently been refurbished and extended, adding some large, comfortable and well appointed bedrooms. It has superb conference and leisure facilities.

ROOMS: 58 en suite (bth/shr) (4 fmly) s IR£50-IR£63; d IR£70-IR£90 (incl. bkfst) * LB Off peak **MEALS:** Lunch IR£9.50-IR£12.50 Dinner IR£12.50-IR£19.50 International Cuisine V meals Coffee am Tea pm **FACILITIES:** CTV in all bedrooms STV Indoor swimming pool (heated) Tennis (hard) Sauna Solarium Gym Jacuzzi/spa Beauty parlour Massage Xmas **CONF:** Thtr 500 Class 200 Board 50 Del from IR£60 * **SERVICES:** Night porter 150P **NOTES:** No dogs No smoking area in restaurant Last d 9.30pm **CARDS:**

★★★ *Two Mile Inn*

Ennis Rd
Quality Percentage Score: 62%
☎ 061 326255 061 453783
Dir: *on N22, near Bunratty Castle & airport*

Situated on the outskirts of Limerick city near Bunratty Castle and Shannon Airport, the Two Mile Inn has a new pub and restaurant, as well as a spacious lounge and comfortable new bedrooms.

ROOMS: 123 en suite (bth/shr) (30 fmly) No smoking in 67 bedrooms **MEALS:** Irish & Continental Cuisine V meals Coffee am Tea pm **FACILITIES:** CTV in all bedrooms STV **CONF:** Thtr 350 Class 200 Board 40 **SERVICES:** Night porter 300P **NOTES:** No dogs (ex guide dogs) Last d 9.30pm **CARDS:**

★★★ Jurys Inn Limerick

Lower Mallow St
Quality Percentage Score: 60%
☎ 061 207000 061 400966
Dir: *from N7 follow signs for City Centre into O'Connell St, turn off at N18 (Shannon/Fanay), hotel is off O'Connell St*

A sizeable, smartly decorated new hotel, Jurys Inn is on the city side of the river, convenient for the shopping and business areas. Facilities include a spacious foyer, bar and restaurant, a board room for meetings and an elevator to all floors. Bedrooms are well equipped and offer good value, especially in the family rooms which can sleep either two adults and two children or three adults. The pleasant team of young staff, who go out of their way to be helpful and friendly, are a particular strength. There is a public car park at the rear of the hotel with pedestrian access into the hotel.

ROOMS: 151 en suite (bth/shr) (108 fmly) No smoking in 56 bedrooms d IR£51-IR£53 * Off peak **MEALS:** Bar Lunch IR£4.50-IR£5 Dinner IR£15-IR£15.95 & alc Irish & European Cuisine V meals Coffee am Tea pm **FACILITIES:** CTV in all bedrooms STV **CONF:** Thtr 50 Class 25 Board 18 **SERVICES:** Lift Night porter **NOTES:** No dogs (ex guide dogs) No smoking area in restaurant Last d 9.30pm Closed 24-26 Dec **CARDS:**

★★ Woodfield House

Ennis Rd
Quality Percentage Score: 63%
☎ 061 453022 061 326755
Dir: *on outskirts of city on main Shannon road*

This intimate little hotel stands on the N18 a short distance from the city centre. It offers well equipped en suite bedrooms, a restaurant, a lounge bar and good car parking.

ROOMS: 20 en suite (bth/shr) (3 fmly) s IR£40-IR£50; d IR£65-IR£85 (incl. bkfst) * LB Off peak **MEALS:** Lunch IR£11-IR£15alc High tea IR£10-IR£12alc Dinner IR£15-IR£20alc International Cuisine V meals Coffee am Tea pm **FACILITIES:** CTV in all bedrooms STV Tennis (hard) **CONF:** Thtr 130 Class 60 Board 60 **SERVICES:** Night porter Air conditioning 80P **NOTES:** No dogs (ex guide dogs) No smoking area in restaurant Last d 9.30pm Closed 24-25 Dec **CARDS:**

★★ *Royal George*

O'Connell St
Quality Percentage Score: 57%
☎ 061 414566 061 317171
Dir: *hotel is situated in the city centre on O'Connell Street*

The Royal George is a city centre hotel with car parking to the rear. Many of the bedrooms have been refurbished and are equipped with satellite TV, telephones, hairdryers and hospitality trays. A new addition, a traditional Irish bar is proving popular,

contd.

L

and has live music five nights a week. Other facilities include a lounge bar, self-service bistro grill, and a restaurant.
ROOMS: 54 en suite (bth/shr) (10 fmly) **MEALS:** European Cuisine V meals Coffee am Tea pm **FACILITIES:** CTV in all bedrooms STV Free access to fitness club Wkly live entertainment **CONF:** Thtr 70 Class 35 Board 30 **SERVICES:** Lift Night porter 30P **NOTES:** No smoking area in restaurant Last d 9.45pm Closed 25 Dec RS 24 Dec
CARDS:

LISDOONVARNA Co Clare **Map 01 B3**

★★❁❁ *Sheedy's Restaurant & Hotel*

Quality Percentage Score: 70%
☎ 065 74026 📠 065 74555
This well run family hotel provides warm hospitality, comfort, and good food from its award-winning restaurant. The hotel is situated beside a spa complex in well tended gardens in a fascinating region for tourists.
ROOMS: 11 en suite (bth/shr) **MEALS:** Irish, English & French Cuisine V meals Coffee am Tea pm **FACILITIES:** CTV in 2 bedrooms Tennis (hard) **SERVICES:** 42P **NOTES:** No dogs No coaches No smoking in restaurant Last d 9pm Closed Nov-1 Apr **CARDS:**

LISMORE Co Waterford **Map 01 C2**

★★ *Ballyrafter House*

Quality Percentage Score: 64%
☎ 058 54002 📠 058 53050
Dir: *1km from Lismore opposite Lismore Castle*
Noreen and Joe Willoughby have the gift of effortless hospitality which embraces all visitors to their country house, set in its own grounds opposite Lismore Castle. The Willoughbys are busy refurbishing this old house, and most of the bedrooms are now pleasant pine-furnished rooms with en-suite facilities. The bar and conservatory are where guests, anglers and locals meet to discuss the day's events. The hotel has its own salmon fishing on the River Blackwater.
ROOMS: 10 en suite (bth/shr) (1 fmly) **MEALS:** Irish & European Cuisine Coffee am Tea pm **FACILITIES:** CTV in 6 bedrooms Fishing Riding Putting green **SERVICES:** 20P **NOTES:** No dogs (ex guide dogs) No smoking area in restaurant Last d 8.30pm Closed Nov-Feb
CARDS:

LONDONDERRY Co Londonderry **Map 01 C5**

★★★★❁ Everglades

Prehen Rd BT47 2NH
Quality Percentage Score: 67%
☎ 028 71346722 📠 028 71349200
Dir: *1m from city centre*
An attractive, open-plan lobby, bar and lounge areas welcome the visitor to this stylish hotel. Situated to the south of the city, the hotel stands alongside the A5 with the River Foyle across the road. The bright and smart surroundings of the Satchmo restaurant serves modern cooking using plenty of local ingredients. There are four conference suites and a large banqueting facility. The bedrooms offer well-maintained modern accommodation and the staff offers consistently good levels of customer care.
ROOMS: 64 en suite (bth/shr) (2 fmly) s £48-£82; d £66-£98 (incl. bkfst) * LB Off peak **MEALS:** Lunch £11.25-£12.50 High tea fr £10.50 Dinner fr £13 & alc International Cuisine V meals Coffee am Tea pm **FACILITIES:** CTV in all bedrooms STV Wkly live entertainment ch fac Xmas **CONF:** Thtr 400 Class 150 Board 44 Del from £95 * **SERVICES:** Lift Night porter Air conditioning 200P **NOTES:** No dogs (ex guide dogs) No smoking area in restaurant Last d 9.45pm Closed 25 Dec
CARDS:

★★★❁ *Beech Hill Country House Hotel*

32 Ardmore Rd BT47 3QP
Quality Percentage Score: 71%
☎ 028 71349279 📠 028 71345366
Dir: *From A6 Londonderry-Belfast take Faughan Bridge turning and continue 1m to hotel opposite Ardmore Chapel*
Dating back to 1729, Beech Hill is an impressive mansion, standing in 32 acres of woodlands, waterfalls and gardens. Public areas are comfortable and attractive, and the splendid new bedroom wing provides spacious well equipped rooms in addition to those in the main house
ROOMS: 17 en suite (bth/shr) (4 fmly) **MEALS:** Irish & French Cuisine V meals Coffee am Tea pm **FACILITIES:** CTV in all bedrooms **CONF:** Thtr 100 Class 50 Board 30 Del from £75 * **SERVICES:** 75P **NOTES:** No dogs (ex guide dogs) No smoking in restaurant Last d 9.30pm Closed 24-25 Dec **CARDS:**

★★★ Trinity Hotel

22-24 Strand Rd BT48 7AB
Quality Percentage Score: 68%
☎ 028 71271271 📠 028 71271277
Dir: *to get to Derry City Centre cross River Foyle, follow signs for city centre, hotel is approx 0.5m from Guildhall adjacent to shopping centre/cinema*
The interior design at this modern hotel is modern and contemporary and has created a good deal of interest. Public areas include a continental-style café bar, while the former snug has been converted into a bar bistro. The panelled restaurant provides a more formal food option.
ROOMS: 40 en suite (bth/shr) (17 fmly) s fr £70; d fr £85 (incl. bkfst) * LB Off peak **MEALS:** Lunch fr £9.95 High tea fr £5.95 Dinner fr £14.95 & alc International Cuisine V meals Coffee am Tea pm **FACILITIES:** CTV in all bedrooms STV Conservatory & roof garden Wkly live entertainment Xmas **CONF:** Thtr 160 Class 80 Board 60 Del from £55 * **SERVICES:** Lift Night porter Air conditioning **NOTES:** No dogs (ex guide dogs) No smoking area in restaurant Last d 10pm
CARDS:

LUCAN Co Dublin **Map 01 D4**

★★★❁ Finnstown Country House Hotel & Golf Course

Newcastle Rd
Quality Percentage Score: 69%
☎ 01 6280644 📠 01 6281088
Dir: *turn off M50 at junct 7 for N4 heading West, after 3km turn off N4 for Newcastle, hotel is 1m along on the right hand side*
Set in 45 acres of wooded grounds, Finnstown is a calm and peaceful country house, popular both with business and leisure guests. Bedrooms vary in style, the newest being the garden suites. Reception rooms are inviting, furnished in period style.
ROOMS: 25 en suite (bth/shr) 26 annexe en suite (bth/shr) No smoking in 27 bedrooms s IR£75-IR£90; d IR£110-IR£150 (incl. bkfst) * LB Off peak **MEALS:** Lunch IR£16.50 High tea IR£5 Dinner IR£23-IR£31 International Cuisine V meals Coffee am Tea pm **FACILITIES:** CTV in all bedrooms STV Indoor swimming pool (heated) Golf 9 Tennis (hard & grass) Solarium Gym Pool table Croquet lawn Putting green Turkish bath Table tennis Massage Wkly live entertainment Xmas **CONF:** Thtr 100 Class 60 Board 30 Del from IR£125 * **SERVICES:** Night porter 90P **NOTES:** No smoking area in restaurant Last d 9.30pm
CARDS:

See advert under DUBLIN

★★★ Lucan Spa

Quality Percentage Score: 64%

☎ 01 6280495 & 6280497 Fax 01 6280841

***Dir:** hotel is located on N4, approx 11km from city centre, approx 20 mins from Dublin airport*

Set back from the road in its own grounds, the Lucan Spa is a fine Georgian house. Guests have complimentary use of Lucan Golf Course, which is adjacent to the hotel. A conference centre with facilities for 600 delegates is also available.

ROOMS: 71 rms (61 bth/shr) (15 fmly) No smoking in 21 bedrooms s fr IR£47.50; d fr IR£80 (incl. bkfst) * LB Off peak **MEALS:** Lunch IR£13-IR£13.50 Dinner fr IR£21.95 European Cuisine V meals Coffee am Tea pm **FACILITIES:** CTV in all bedrooms STV Golf 18 **CONF:** Thtr 600 Class 250 Board 80 **SERVICES:** Lift Night porter Air conditioning 90P **NOTES:** No dogs (ex guide dogs) No smoking area in restaurant Last d 10.30pm Closed 25 Dec **CARDS:**

See advert on this page

MACROOM Co Cork — Map 01 B2

★★ Castle

Main St

Quality Percentage Score: 72%

☎ 026 41074 Fax 026 41505

***Dir:** on N22*

The Castle Hotel contains a new leisure centre and some fine bedrooms. The hotel service is excellent and guests feel very much at home. There is a pleasant lounge and a function room, while the food in the restaurant and the bar is well cooked and imaginatively presented.

ROOMS: 42 en suite (bth/shr) (5 fmly) s IR£50-IR£59; d IR£64-IR£78 (incl. bkfst) * LB Off peak **MEALS:** Lunch IR£6.50-IR£10.50alc High tea IR£10-IR£15alc Dinner IR£17.50-IR£20alc V meals Coffee am Tea pm **FACILITIES:** CTV in all bedrooms STV Indoor swimming pool (heated) Sauna Gym Jacuzzi/spa **CONF:** Board 20 **SERVICES:** Night porter Air conditioning 30P **NOTES:** No dogs No smoking area in restaurant Last d 9pm Closed 25-27 Dec **CARDS:**

See advert on this page

MALLOW Co Cork — Map 01 B2

The Premier Collection

★★★ *Longueville House*

☎ 022 47156 & 47306 Fax 022 47459

***Dir:** 5km W of Mallow on N72 to Killarney*

RELAIS & CHATEAUX

Set in a wooded estate, this 18th-century Georgian mansion has many fine features. The comfortable bedrooms overlook the river valley and the courtyard maze. The two elegant sitting rooms have fine examples of Italian plasterwork and an Adams mantlepiece graces the Presidents Restaurant. Cuisine in the hotel restaurant is

contd.

exciting and inventive, and makes good use of excellent fresh produce.
ROOMS: 20 en suite (bth/shr) (5 fmly) No smoking in 5 bedrooms **MEALS:** French Cuisine V meals Coffee am Tea pm **FACILITIES:** CTV in all bedrooms STV Fishing Snooker Croquet lawn Billiards Table tennis **CONF:** Thtr 25 Class 16 Board 14 **SERVICES:** 50P **NOTES:** No dogs (ex guide dogs) No coaches No smoking in restaurant Last d 9pm Closed 20 Dec-mid Feb **CARDS:**

★★★ Springfort Hall Hotel
Quality Percentage Score: 63%
☎ 022 21278 ℻ 022 21557
Dir: *on Mallow/Limerick road N20, right turn off at 2 Pot House R581, hotel 500mtrs on right sign over gate*
ROOMS: 50 en suite (bth/shr) (4 fmly) s IR£47.50-IR£60; d IR£75-IR£100 (incl. bkfst) * LB Off peak **MEALS:** Lunch IR£15.50 High tea IR£2.50-IR£6 Dinner IR£23.50-IR£27 & alc Irish & European Cuisine V meals Coffee am Tea pm **FACILITIES:** CTV in all bedrooms STV **CONF:** Thtr 300 Class 200 Board 50 Del from IR£75 * **SERVICES:** 200P **NOTES:** No dogs (ex guide dogs) No smoking area in restaurant Last d 9.30pm Closed 23 Dec-2 Jan **CARDS:**

MAYNOOTH Co Kildare — Map 01 C4
★★★ *Moyglare Manor*
Moyglare
Quality Percentage Score: 74%
☎ 01 6286351 ℻ 01 6285405
Dir: *turn off N4 at Maynooth/Naas, then right to Maynooth town. Keep right at St Marys Church and continue 2m then left at X-roads*
Located just outside Maynooth in rich pasture land, this elegant 18th-century house is a haven of calm after the rush of the outside world. Guests arrive by way of an imposing tree-lined avenue and are greeted with genuine hospitality. Bedrooms are beautifully furnished in keeping with the Georgian style of the house, and there are several lounges offering peace and quiet or the conviviality of the bar lounge. Moyglare has earned a high reputation for its cuisine.
ROOMS: 17 en suite (bth/shr) (1 fmly) No smoking in 5 bedrooms **MEALS:** Irish & French Cuisine V meals Coffee am Tea pm **FACILITIES:** Tennis Wkly live entertainment **CONF:** Thtr 30 **SERVICES:** 120P **NOTES:** No dogs (ex guide dogs) No children 12yrs No smoking in restaurant Last d 9pm Closed 24-26 Dec **CARDS:**

MIDLETON Co Cork — Map 01 C2
★★★ *Midleton Park*
Quality Percentage Score: 66%
☎ 021 631767 ℻ 021 631605
Dir: *from Cork, turn off N25 hotel on right hand side. From Waterford, turn off N25, over bridge until T-junct, turn right, hotel on right*
This purpose-built hotel, situated in an area of great interest is just off the N25 Cork/Rosslare route ten miles from Cork. The hotel features fine, spacious and well appointed en suite bedrooms, while a comfortable restaurant offers good food and attentive service. Conference and banqueting facilities and on-site parking are all available.
ROOMS: 40 en suite (bth/shr) (12 fmly) No smoking in 6 bedrooms **MEALS:** Irish & French Cuisine V meals Coffee am Tea pm **FACILITIES:** CTV in all bedrooms STV **CONF:** Thtr 400 Class 200 Board 40 **SERVICES:** Night porter Air conditioning 500P **NOTES:** No dogs (ex guide dogs) Last d 9.30pm Closed 25 Dec **CARDS:**

MONAGHAN Co Monaghan — Map 01 C5
★★★★ Hillgrove
Old Armagh Rd
Quality Percentage Score: 62%
☎ 047 81288 ℻ 047 84951
Dir: *turn off N2 at Cathedral, continue for 400 metres, on left just beyond Cathedral*
ROOMS: 44 en suite (bth/shr) (2 fmly) s IR£47-IR£58; d IR£76-IR£96 (incl. bkfst) LB Off peak **MEALS:** Lunch fr IR£11.50 Dinner fr IR£19.50 & alc European Cuisine V meals Coffee am Tea pm **FACILITIES:** CTV in all bedrooms STV Jacuzzi/spa Wkly live entertainment Xmas **CONF:** Thtr 1200 Class 600 Board 200 **SERVICES:** Lift Night porter Air conditioning 430P **NOTES:** No dogs (ex guide dogs) No smoking area in restaurant Last d 9.30pm **CARDS:**

★★★ Four Seasons Hotel & Leisure Club
Coolshannagh
Quality Percentage Score: 65%
☎ 047 81888 ℻ 047 83131
Dir: *on N2, 1km from town centre*
This modern family run hotel is set back from the road in its own grounds. The public areas are attractively decorated and include a spacious foyer lounge, carvery bar, and bistro style restaurant. Bedrooms are well appointed and comfortable.
ROOMS: 44 en suite (bth/shr) (6 fmly) s IR£40-IR£60; d IR£80-IR£150 (incl. bkfst) * LB Off peak **MEALS:** Lunch IR£12-IR£20 Dinner IR£22-IR£35 European Cuisine V meals Coffee am Tea pm **FACILITIES:** CTV in all bedrooms STV Indoor swimming pool (heated) Fishing Riding Sauna Solarium Gym Jacuzzi/spa Steam room Wkly live entertainment **CONF:** Thtr 450 Class 250 Board 35 **SERVICES:** Night porter 200P **NOTES:** No dogs (ex guide dogs) No smoking area in restaurant Last d 9.30pm Closed 24-26 Dec **CARDS:**

NAVAN Co Meath — Map 01 C4
★★★ Ardboyne Hotel
Dublin Rd
Quality Percentage Score: 62%
☎ 046 23119 ℻ 046 22355
This welcoming hotel is situated on the edge of Navan. Bedrooms are comfortably furnished and freshly decorated, and overlook pretty gardens. Public areas are smartly furnished and include an inviting lounge warmed by an open fire, a well appointed dining room and a saloon style bar. Conference suites are available.
ROOMS: 27 en suite (bth/shr) (25 fmly) No smoking in 10 bedrooms s fr IR£56; d fr IR£80 (incl. bkfst) * LB Off peak **MEALS:** Lunch IR£18.95 & alc Dinner IR£18.95 & alc European Cuisine V meals Coffee am Tea pm **FACILITIES:** CTV in all bedrooms STV Wkly live entertainment **CONF:** Thtr 400 Class 200 Board 150 Del from IR£150 * **SERVICES:** Night porter 186P **NOTES:** No dogs No smoking area in restaurant Last d 9.45pm Closed 24-26 Dec **CARDS:**

NENAGH Co Tipperary — Map 01 B3
★★★ *Nenagh Abbey Court Hotel*
Dublin Rd
Quality Percentage Score: 68%
☎ 067 41111 ℻ 067 41022
Dir: *Hotel 2 mins from O'Connor's Shopping Centre on Dublin side of Nenagh*
ROOMS: 46 en suite (bth/shr) (3 fmly) No smoking in 10 bedrooms **MEALS:** French Cuisine V meals Coffee am Tea pm **FACILITIES:** CTV in all bedrooms STV **CONF:** Thtr 600 Class 150 Board 60 **SERVICES:** Lift Night porter Air conditioning 200P **NOTES:** No dogs (ex guide dogs) No smoking area in restaurant Closed 25 Dec **CARDS:**

M

NEWBRIDGE Co Kildare **Map 01 C3**

★★★ Keadeen

Quality Percentage Score: 71%

☎ 045 431666 045 434402

Dir: *M7 junct 10, (Newbridge, Curragh) at rdbt follow round to right and go in direction of Newbridge, hotel is on left 1km from rdbt*

This family-owned hotel is set in eight acres of landscaped gardens, and has good leisure facilities. Comfortable public areas include a spacious drawing room, reception foyer and two bars. The hotel is well placed for Dublin Airport and Goff's Blookstock Sales complex.

ROOMS: 55 en suite (bth/shr) (4 fmly) s IR£82.50-IR£200; d IR£121-IR£200 (incl. bkfst) * LB Off peak **MEALS:** Lunch IR£14.50-IR£18.50 Dinner IR£24.50-IR£27.50 French Cuisine V meals Coffee am Tea pm **FACILITIES:** CTV in all bedrooms STV Indoor swimming pool (heated) Sauna Solarium Gym Jacuzzi/spa Aerobics studio Treatment room Massage Wkly live entertainment Xmas **CONF:** Thtr 800 Class 300 Board 40 Del from IR£109 * **SERVICES:** Night porter 200P **NOTES:** No dogs (ex guide dogs) Last d 9.30pm Closed 24 Dec-3 Jan RS low season **CARDS:**

NEWCASTLE Co Down **Map 01 D5**

★★★★ Slieve Donard

Downs Rd BT33 0AH

HASTINGS hotels

Quality Percentage Score: 64%

☎ 028 43723681 028 43724830

Dir: *follow the A2 from Belfast into Newcastle. As you enter the town centre bear left onto Downs Road*

Idyllically situated, this impressive hotel has recently been refurbished. Bedrooms, many of them enjoying splendid views, are comfortable. Public areas include a choice of lounges. In addition to the wood panelled Oak Room restaurant, there is a grill and a bar for informal dining.

ROOMS: 130 en suite (bth/shr) No smoking in 12 bedrooms s fr £53; d fr £76 (incl. bkfst) * LB Off peak **MEALS:** Lunch £17-£21 High tea £10-£14 Dinner fr £21 European/Traditional Cuisine V meals Coffee am Tea pm **FACILITIES:** CTV in all bedrooms STV Indoor swimming pool (heated) Tennis (hard) Sauna Solarium Gym Putting green Jacuzzi/spa Steam room Wkly live entertainment Xmas **CONF:** Thtr 825 Class 250 Board 70 Del £105 * **SERVICES:** Lift Night porter 500P **NOTES:** No dogs (ex guide dogs) No smoking area in restaurant Last d 9.30pm **CARDS:**

★★ Enniskeen House

98 Bryansford Rd BT33 0LF

Quality Percentage Score: 64%

☎ 028 43722392 028 43724084

Dir: *from Newcastle town centre follow signs for Tollymore Forest Park, hotel 1m on left*

For 38 years now the Porter family have been welcoming guests to their peaceful hotel which enjoys a superb location in the shadow of the Mountains of Mourne. Public areas and bedrooms are all traditional in style. Wholesome fare is offered in the two dining areas.

ROOMS: 12 en suite (bth/shr) (1 fmly) No smoking in 3 bedrooms s £45-£55; d £70-£74 (incl. bkfst) * LB Off peak **MEALS:** Lunch £8.95-£11.25 High tea £10 Dinner £16 V meals Coffee am Tea pm **FACILITIES:** CTV in all bedrooms **CONF:** Thtr 60 Class 24 **SERVICES:** Lift 45P **NOTES:** No dogs No smoking in restaurant Last d 8.30pm Closed 12 Nov-14 Mar **CARDS:**

NEWMARKET-ON-FERGUS Co Clare **Map 01 B3**

★★★★★ *Dromoland Castle*

Quality Percentage Score: 71%

RELAIS & CHATEAUX. Relais Gourmands

☎ 061 368144 061 363355

Described as a "very large, early eighteenth century, gothic revival, castellated, irregular, multi-towered ashlar castle" Dromoland offers superbly appointed accommodation and facilities. The spacious, thoughtfully equipped and richly decorated bedrooms offer excellent levels of comfort. The magnificent public areas, warmed by log fires, are no less impressive. The hotel has two restaurants and the more formal Earl of Thomond Restaurant, earns our Two Rosette award. The hotel has immaculately maintained grounds with excellent leisure and meeting facilities.

ROOMS: 75 en suite (bth/shr) (20 fmly) **MEALS:** Irish & French Cuisine V meals Coffee am Tea pm **FACILITIES:** CTV in all bedrooms STV Golf 18 Tennis (hard) Fishing Snooker Sauna Solarium Gym Putting green Wkly live entertainment **CONF:** Thtr 450 Class 320 Board 80 **SERVICES:** Night porter 120P **NOTES:** No dogs No smoking in restaurant Last d 9.30pm **CARDS:**

★★★ Clare Inn Golf & Leisure Hotel

Quality Percentage Score: 61%

☎ 065 6823000 065 6823759

Dir: *on N18, 14km from Shannon International Airport*

The Clare Inn is set in open countryside next to an 18-hole golf course just 10 minutes from Shannon Airport. It is a comfortable hotel with excellent leisure facilities and friendly staff to ensure an enjoyable stay.

ROOMS: 182 en suite (bth/shr) (20 fmly) No smoking in 4 bedrooms s IR£70; d IR£110 * LB Off peak **MEALS:** Sunday Lunch IR£10-IR£12 & alc Dinner fr IR£20 & alc Irish & Continental Cuisine V meals Coffee am Tea pm **FACILITIES:** CTV in all bedrooms STV Indoor swimming pool (heated) Golf 18 Tennis (hard) Sauna Solarium Gym Pool table Croquet lawn Putting green Jacuzzi/spa Programme for children Crazy golf Horse riding Pitch and putt Wkly live entertainment ch fac Xmas **CONF:** Thtr 400 Class 250 Board 100 Del from IR£103 * **SERVICES:** Lift Night porter 300P **NOTES:** No dogs (ex guide dogs) No smoking area in restaurant Last d 9.30pm **CARDS:**

★★ *Carrygerry Country House*

Shannon

Quality Percentage Score: 61%

☎ 061 363739 061 363823

Dir: *N18 towards Shannon Airport then N19 at town rdbt turn right to Newmarket-on Fergus after 450mtrs at small rdbt turn left, opposite Shannon Aerospace*

Situated amidst acres of woodland, this 18th-century country house has recently been opened as a hotel. The two lounges are inviting and the attractive conservatory restaurant offers good food. The accommodation is of pleasing quality, while the coach house contains the bar and a private dining room. Local activities include golf, river and sea angling, and horse riding.

ROOMS: 6 en suite (bth/shr) 6 annexe en suite (bth/shr) (1 fmly) No smoking in all bedrooms **MEALS:** International Cuisine V meals Coffee am Tea pm **FACILITIES:** CTV in all bedrooms STV Snooker **CONF:** Class 60 Board 20 **SERVICES:** 25P **NOTES:** No coaches No smoking in restaurant Last d 9.30pm Closed 5 Jan-28 Feb **CARDS:**

NEW ROSS Co Wexford **Map 01 C3**

★★★ *Brandon House Hotel*

Wexford Rd

Quality Percentage Score: 59%

☎ 051 421703 051 421567

Dir: *1.5km outside New Ross on the N25*

Set in attractive grounds, this Victorian manor house has undergone a refurbishment programme under new owners. The fine big rooms of the period lend themselves particularly well to the reception foyer, lounge bar and the intimate dining room where good food is served. The bedrooms in the main house

contd.

tend to be larger than those in the extension wings. Numerous golf courses within driving distance.
CONF: Thtr 300 Class 200 Board 100

★★ The Old Rectory
Rosbercon
Quality Percentage Score: 59%
☎ 051 421719 📠 051 422974
Dir: *in New Ross cross the bridge, turn right and continue for 200mtrs up hill, hotel is on the right*
A small and cosy hotel set in two and a half acres of lovely gardens with mature trees. In an elevated position above New Ross and overlooking it from the River Barrow. Guests receive personal attention from the young proprietors, Claudia and Michael Whelan.
ROOMS: 12 en suite (bth/shr) s IR£50; d IR£75 (incl. bkfst) * LB Off peak **MEALS:** Lunch IR£10.95 Dinner IR£18.95 V meals Coffee am **FACILITIES:** CTV in all bedrooms STV **CONF:** Thtr 80 Class 48 Board 20 **SERVICES:** 37P **NOTES:** No dogs (ex guide dogs) No coaches No smoking in restaurant Last d 9.15pm Closed Nov-Jan
CARDS:

ORANMORE Co Galway — Map 01 B3
★★★ Galway Bay Golf & Country Club Hotel
Quality Percentage Score: 69%
☎ 091 790500 📠 091 790510
Dir: *follow signs from Oranmore for 3km entrance beside the Galway Bay Sailing Club*
A stylish and friendly hotel, overlooking the golf course on the Penville Peninsula. This championship course was designed by Christir O'Connor Jnr and there is a grandstand view of the first fairway from the smart lounge. The bedrooms, all well equipped, range from executive suites, with their own sitting rooms, to standard rooms. An accomplished chef cooks to a consistently high standard.
ROOMS: 90 en suite (bth/shr) **MEALS:** European Cuisine V meals Coffee am Tea pm **FACILITIES:** CTV in all bedrooms STV Golf 18 Putting green Golf practice range Parkland walks **CONF:** Thtr 160 Class 100 Board 30 **SERVICES:** Lift Night porter 200P **NOTES:** No dogs (ex guide dogs) No smoking area in restaurant Last d 9pm Closed 24-26 Dec
CARDS:

OUGHTERARD Co Galway — Map 01 B4
★★★ *Ross Lake House*
Rosscahill
Quality Percentage Score: 66%
☎ 091 550109 & 550154 📠 091 550184
Dir: *22km from Galway City on N59, Galway - Clifden road. Turn left after village of Rosscahill*
Set in a peaceful location in a woodland estate, this restored Georgian house is personally run and offers a warm welcome. Good food is a feature, and carefully chosen produce includes Connemara lamb and fresh fish. Golf, lake fishing and boating are all near by.
ROOMS: 13 en suite (bth/shr) **MEALS:** V meals Coffee am Tea pm **FACILITIES:** Tennis (hard) **SERVICES:** 150P **NOTES:** Closed Nov-mid Mar **CARDS:**

PARKNASILLA Co Kerry — Map 01 A2
★★★★ *Great Southern*
Quality Percentage Score: 79%
☎ 064 45122 📠 064 45323
Dir: *on Kenmare road 3km from Sneem village*
The Great Southern is superbly located on Kenmare Bay with fine sea views from many of its bedrooms. There are spacious, comfortable lounges, the excellent Pygmalion Retaurant and an impressive range of leisure facilities. Above all, it is the warmth of the welcome from the friendly and attentive staff that distinguishes this hotel.
ROOMS: 26 en suite (bth/shr) 59 annexe en suite (bth/shr) (6 fmly) No smoking in 11 bedrooms **MEALS:** International Cuisine V meals Coffee am Tea pm **FACILITIES:** CTV in all bedrooms STV Indoor swimming pool (heated) Golf 9 Tennis (hard) Fishing Riding Snooker Sauna Pool table Croquet lawn Jacuzzi/spa Bike hire Windsurfing Clay pigeon shooting Archery Wkly live entertainment **CONF:** Thtr 100 Class 80 Board 20 **SERVICES:** Lift Night porter 60P **NOTES:** No dogs (ex guide dogs) No smoking area in restaurant Last d 9pm
CARDS:

See advert on opposite page

PORTAFERRY Co Down — Map 01 D5
★★★ *Portaferry*
10 The Strand BT22 1PE
Quality Percentage Score: 65%
☎ 028 427 28231 📠 028 427 28999
Dir: *situated on Lough Shore opposite ferry terminal*
This charming hotel enjoys spectacular views over Strangford Lough. Public areas include a choice of inviting lounges, a well stocked bar, and the smart restaurant. Bedrooms, though varied in size, are comfortably modern in style and many enjoy lough views.
ROOMS: 14 en suite (bth/shr) **MEALS:** Irish & Continental Cuisine V meals Coffee am Tea pm **FACILITIES:** CTV in all bedrooms STV **SERVICES:** 6P **NOTES:** No dogs (ex guide dogs) Last d 9pm Closed 24-25 Dec **CARDS:**

PORTBALLINTRAE Co Antrim — Map 01 C6
★★ *Beach House*
The Sea Front BT57 8RT
Quality Percentage Score: 68%
☎ 02820 70331214 📠 02820 70331664
Since 1924 the MacLaine family have been welcoming guests to their substantially refurbished resort hotel, which enjoys spectacular sea views towards Donegal, Islay, and Kintyre. Public areas include a choice of lounges, a well stocked bar which has a nautical theme, and a spacious dining room. Bedrooms, which have recently benefited from a phased programme of refurbishment, offer modern comforts and amenities. Staff are friendly and willing to please.
ROOMS: 32 en suite (bth/shr) (17 fmly) **MEALS:** European Cuisine V meals Coffee am Tea pm **FACILITIES:** CTV in all bedrooms STV Pool table Table tennis **CONF:** Class 150 Board 35 **SERVICES:** Night porter 40P **NOTES:** No dogs (ex guide dogs) No smoking area in restaurant Last d 9pm **CARDS:**

PORTMARNOCK Co Dublin — Map 01 D4
★★★★ Portmarnock Hotel & Golf Links
Strand Rd
Quality Percentage Score: 77%
☎ 01 8460611 📠 01 8462442
Dir: *Dublin Airport-N1, rdbt 1st exit, 2nd rdbt 2nd exit, next rdbt 3rd exit, T-junct turn left, over crossrds and cont, hotel is left past the Strand*
Enjoying a superb location overlooking the sea and the PGA Championship Golf Links, this 19th century former home of the Jameson whiskey family is now a smart hotel. Guests may sample the creations of Chef Eric Faussurier in the Osborne restaurant.
ROOMS: 103 en suite (bth/shr) No smoking in 6 bedrooms s IR£135; d IR£195 (incl. bkfst) * LB Off peak **MEALS:** Lunch IR£12.05-IR£23.40alc Dinner IR£26.20-IR£38alc French Cuisine V meals Coffee am Tea pm **FACILITIES:** CTV in all bedrooms STV Golf 18 Putting green Xmas **CONF:** Thtr 300 Class 110 Board 80 Del from IR£127 * **SERVICES:** Lift Night porter 200P **NOTES:** No dogs (ex guide dogs) No smoking area in restaurant Last d 10.30pm **CARDS:**

See advert under DUBLIN

N

PORTRUSH Co Antrim — Map 01 C6

★★★ Causeway Coast

36 Ballyreagh Rd BT56 8LR
Quality Percentage Score: 62%
☎ 028 70822435 Fax 028 70824495
Dir: *on A2 between Portrush & Portstewart, opposite Ballyreagh Golf Course*

A purpose-built hotel and conference centre, on the western edge of town overlooking Ballyreagh golf course to the sea. Currently undergoing improvements, including the addition of 20 more bedrooms and the creation of a leisure centre. Further refurbishment will involve considerable alteration of public areas, and another wing of bedrooms.

ROOMS: 21 en suite (bth/shr) (2 fmly) s £55; d £85 (incl. bkfst) LB Off peak **MEALS:** V meals Coffee am Tea pm **FACILITIES:** CTV in all bedrooms Wkly live entertainment **CONF:** Thtr 500 Class 170 Del from £55 * **SERVICES:** Lift Night porter 172P **NOTES:** No dogs (ex guide dogs) Last d 9.30pm Closed 25 Dec **CARDS:**

RATHMULLAN Co Donegal — Map 01 C6

★★★ Fort Royal

Fort Royal
Quality Percentage Score: 71%
☎ 074 58100 Fax 074 58103
Dir: *take R245 from Letterkenny, through Rathmullan village, hotel is signposted*

MANOR HOUSE HOTELS

On the shores of Lough Swilly, this period house stands in 18 acres of grounds and has private access to a secluded beach. The sitting room is a restful place overlooking the sea. Enjoyable meals are served in the restaurant, and the bar is inviting. Bedrooms are attractively decorated.

ROOMS: 11 en suite (bth/shr) 4 annexe en suite (bth) (3 fmly) s IR£85; d IR£120 (incl. bkfst) * LB Off peak **MEALS:** Irish & French Cuisine V meals Coffee am **FACILITIES:** CTV in all bedrooms Golf 9 Tennis (hard) Squash **SERVICES:** 40P **NOTES:** No coaches No smoking in restaurant Closed Nov-Etr **CARDS:**

★ *Pier*

Quality Percentage Score: 59%
☎ 074 58178 & 58115 Fax 074 58115
Dir: *on sea front, near harbour*

This pleasant hotel stands directly opposite a sandy beach on the western shores of Lough Swilly. There is a comfortable lounge, a dining room and a bar. A good angling centre and golf course are available nearby.

ROOMS: 10 en suite (bth/shr) (2 fmly) **MEALS:** Coffee am Tea pm **FACILITIES:** Wkly live entertainment **NOTES:** No dogs (ex guide dogs) No smoking area in restaurant Last d 9.30pm Closed Nov-May RS Apr-May & Oct **CARDS:**

RATHNEW Co Wicklow — Map 01 D3

The Premier Collection

★★★ Tinakilly Country House & Restaurant

☎ 0404 69274 Fax 0404 67806
Dir: *follow the N11/M11 to Rathnew village, cont on R750 towards Wicklow. Entrance to hotel is approx 500mtrs from the village on left*

Built in 1870, it is an elegant house set in seven acres of 19th-century gardens with breathtaking views of the sea. The highest standards of accommodation and hospitality are offered and the bedrooms are tastefully decorated with period furnishings and some four-poster beds. Country house cuisine is served, including fresh fish, game and home-grown vegetables.

contd.

R

ROOMS: 53 en suite (bth/shr) (10 fmly) s IR£110-IR£117; d IR£130-IR£144 (incl. bkfst) * LB Off peak **MEALS:** Dinner IR£35 & alc Modern Irish Cuisine V meals Coffee am Tea pm **FACILITIES:** CTV in all bedrooms STV Tennis (hard) Croquet lawn Putting green 7 acres of gardens mapped for walking Fitness suite Wkly live entertainment Xmas **CONF:** Thtr 80 Class 60 Board 40 **SERVICES:** Lift Night porter 60P **NOTES:** No dogs (ex guide dogs) Last d 9pm RS 25-26 Dec & 31 Dec-2 Jan **CARDS:**

★★★ ***Hunter's***

Quality Percentage Score: 67%

☎ 0404 40106 📠 0404 40338

Dir: *1.5km from village off N11*

The hospitable Gelletlie family forms the fifth generation of Hunters who have been hosts at this delightful hotel which is one of Ireland's oldest coaching inns. Over the years they have made many improvements to introduce modern facilities, but none of this has detracted from the character of the original building. It is also noted for its prize-winning gardens bordering the River Vartry, where afternoon tea in summer is a special treat. The restaurant has a good reputation for carefully prepared dishes which make the best use of high quality local produce. An ideal centre for touring or for golf, Hunters caters equally well for the business traveller.

ROOMS: 16 en suite (bth/shr) (2 fmly) **MEALS:** Irish, English & French Cuisine Coffee am Tea pm **FACILITIES:** CTV in all bedrooms **CONF:** Class 40 Board 16 **SERVICES:** 50P **NOTES:** No dogs (ex guide dogs) No coaches Last d 9pm Closed 24-26 Dec

CARDS:

RECESS Co Galway — Map 01 A4

★★★ **Lough Inagh Lodge**

Inagh Valley

Quality Percentage Score: 75%

☎ 095 34706 & 34694 📠 095 34708

Dir: *after Recess take R344 towards Kylemore through Inagh valley, hotel is in middle of valley*

This 19th-century shooting lodge has been transformed into a luxurious hotel. Its setting, fronted by a good fishing lake, includes lovely mountain views. Large lounges and an oak-lined bar provide warmth and comfort, and the spacious bedrooms are beautifully furnished. The food is a highlight of a stay here.

ROOMS: 12 en suite (bth/shr) s IR£82.50-IR£106.70; d IR£110-IR£136.40 (incl. bkfst) * LB Off peak **MEALS:** Irish & French Cuisine V meals Coffee am Tea pm **FACILITIES:** CTV in all bedrooms Fishing **CONF:** Thtr 20 Class 20 Board 20 **SERVICES:** Air conditioning 16P **NOTES:** No coaches No smoking area in restaurant Last d 9pm Closed 15 Dec-15 Mar **CARDS:**

R

ROSCOMMON Co Roscommon — Map 01 B4

★★★ **Abbey**

Galway Rd

Quality Percentage Score: 64%

☎ 0903 26240 & 26505 📠 0903 26021

Dir: *on N63 opposite railway station*

Set in its own grounds at the edge of town, this fine manor house dates back over 100 years and has recently undergone major refurbishment. The bedrooms are well decorated, with a choice of period style rooms in the original part of the house, while those in the newer wing are more contemporary. The Grealy family and their friendly staff create a pleasant atmosphere.

ROOMS: 25 en suite (bth/shr) No smoking in 2 bedrooms s fr IR£65; d fr IR£95 (incl. bkfst) * LB Off peak **MEALS:** Lunch IR£12-IR£15 Dinner IR£21-IR£25 Irish & French Cuisine V meals Coffee am Tea pm **FACILITIES:** CTV in all bedrooms STV **CONF:** Thtr 300 Class 200 Board 25 **SERVICES:** Night porter 100P **NOTES:** No dogs No smoking area in restaurant Last d 9.30pm Closed 25-26 Dec **CARDS:**

ROSCREA Co Tipperary — Map 01 C3

★★★ **Grant's**

Castle St

Quality Percentage Score: 67%

☎ 0505 23300 📠 0505 23209

Dir: *off main N7 (Dublin/Limerick Road). Turn off for town centre and follow sign posts to hotel, opposite Roscrea Castle*

This attractive hotel stands opposite the 13th-century castle and Heritage Centre and is as inviting inside as out. Bedrooms are pleasantly furnished in warm-toned colours and there is an excellent, oak-panelled foyer lounge with deep leather armchairs and sofas. There is a choice of two restaurants, the Lemon Tree and the Bistro, as well as an informal pub with a cafe-bar area, Kitty's Tavern.

ROOMS: 25 en suite (bth/shr) (3 fmly) s IR£35-IR£45; d IR£60-IR£70 (incl. bkfst) * LB Off peak **MEALS:** Lunch IR£10.50-IR£11.50 High tea IR£5-IR£7 & alc Dinner IR£19-IR£21 & alc Irish & French Cuisine V meals Coffee am Tea pm **FACILITIES:** CTV in all bedrooms STV Wkly live entertainment **CONF:** Thtr 300 Class 150 Board 30 Del from IR£55 * **SERVICES:** Night porter 30P **NOTES:** No smoking area in restaurant Last d 9.30pm **CARDS:**

ROSSCARBERY Co Cork — Map 01 B2

★★★ **Celtic Ross**

Quality Percentage Score: 67%

☎ 023 48722 📠 023 48723

Dir: *on N71*

Overlooking a lagoon on the edge of a peaceful village this hotel is a striking landmark on the West Cork coastline. The spacious, light-filled public areas are luxuriously appointed with richly textured fabrics and highly polished Irish elm, yew bog oakwood and cherrywood. There is a cocktail bar, an Irish pub where a lunchtime carvery is on offer, conference and banqueting facilities and an indoor leisure centre. The restaurant specialises in seafood dishes. One bedroom is fully adapted for the disabled.

ROOMS: 67 en suite (bth/shr) (30 fmly) No smoking in 10 bedrooms s fr IR£85; d fr IR£140 (incl. bkfst) * LB Off peak **MEALS:** Lunch IR£12-IR£16 Dinner IR£22 & alc Irish & French Cuisine V meals Coffee am Tea pm **FACILITIES:** CTV in all bedrooms STV Indoor swimming pool (heated) Sauna Gym Jacuzzi/spa Steam room Wkly live entertainment Xmas **CONF:** Thtr 250 Class 80 Board 80 Del from IR£85 * **SERVICES:** Lift Night porter Air conditioning 200P **NOTES:** No dogs (ex guide dogs) Last d 9pm **CARDS:**

ROSSLARE Co Wexford — Map 01 D2

★★★★ ***Kelly's Resort***

Quality Percentage Score: 78%

☎ 053 32114 📠 053 32222

Since 1895 successive generations of the Kelly family have been running this popular seafront hotel. The range of facilities on offer is extensive, including a leisure centre, health treatments, indoor and outdoor tennis courts, a children's crèche and spacious gardens. La Marine Bistro is the setting for good modern cuisine, while the main restaurant continues to produce

contd.

award-winning food. Public rooms are adorned with contemporary Irish art.

ROOMS: 99 annexe en suite (bth/shr) (15 fmly) **MEALS:** English & French Cuisine Coffee am Tea pm **FACILITIES:** CTV in all bedrooms STV Indoor swimming pool (heated) Tennis (hard) Squash Snooker Sauna Solarium Gym Pool table Croquet lawn Jacuzzi/spa Bowls Plunge pool Badminton Crazy golf Wkly live entertainment ch fac **CONF:** Thtr 30 Class 30 Board 20 **SERVICES:** Lift Night porter 99P **NOTES:** No dogs No coaches No smoking area in restaurant Last d 9pm Closed mid Dec-late Feb **CARDS:**

ROSSLARE HARBOUR Co Wexford **Map 01 D2**

★★★ *Hotel Rosslare*

Quality Percentage Score: 57%

☎ 053 33110 📠 053 33386

Ideally situated for the car ferryport, this hotel overlooks the harbour and is a short distance from sandy `blue flag' beaches. A friendly atmosphere and good food are the priorities, and there is an interesting old bar full of seafaring lore and local history, with a pleasant beer garden outside.

ROOMS: 25 en suite (bth/shr) (6 fmly) **MEALS:** International Cuisine V meals Coffee am Tea pm **FACILITIES:** CTV in all bedrooms Squash Snooker Sauna Pool table Wkly live entertainment **CONF:** Thtr 120 Class 80 Board 50 **SERVICES:** Night porter P **NOTES:** No smoking area in restaurant Last d 9pm **CARDS:**

ROSSNOWLAGH Co Donegal **Map 01 B5**

★★★ Sand House

MANOR HOUSE HOTELS

Quality Percentage Score: 77%

☎ 072 51777 📠 072 52100

Dir: *on coast road from Ballyshannon in the centre of Donegal Bay*

Set in a crescent of golden sands five miles north of Ballyshannon, this owner-managed hotel is well known for its hospitality, good cuisine and personal service. Many rooms have sea views, and a conservatory lounge provides a relaxing retreat.

ROOMS: 46 en suite (bth/shr) (6 fmly) s IR£60-IR£70; d IR£90-IR£120 (incl. bkfst) * LB Off peak **MEALS:** Lunch IR£14-IR£16 Dinner IR£24-IR£25 Irish & French Cuisine V meals Coffee am Tea pm **FACILITIES:** CTV in all bedrooms STV Tennis (hard) Croquet lawn Putting green Mini-golf Surfing Canoeing Sailing Wkly live entertainment **CONF:** Thtr 60 Class 40 Board 30 Del from IR£75 * **SERVICES:** Night porter 42P **NOTES:** No smoking in restaurant Last d 9pm Closed mid Oct-Etr **CARDS:**

ROUNDSTONE Co Galway **Map 01 A4**

★★ *Eldons*

Quality Percentage Score: 70%

☎ 095 35933 & 35942 📠 095 35871

Dir: *off N59 through Toombedla then lt to village*

This distinctive building is situated on the main street of a picturesque fishing village. From Galway take the N59 to Clifden, near Recess turn left to Cashel and follow the coastline. The Conneely family are welcoming hosts and they maintain high standards throughout their hotel. The seafood restaurant, Bedla, serves a good choice of food.

ROOMS: 13 en suite (bth/shr) 6 annexe en suite (bth/shr) (2 fmly) **MEALS:** V meals Coffee am Tea pm **FACILITIES:** CTV in all bedrooms Wkly live entertainment **SERVICES:** Lift **NOTES:** No dogs No smoking area in restaurant Last d 9.30pm Closed 4 Nov-16 Mar **CARDS:**

SALTHILL See **Galway**

SLANE Co Meath **Map 01 D4**

★★★ *Conyngham Arms*

Quality Percentage Score: 63%

☎ 041 24155 📠 041 24205

Dir: *from N2 turn onto N51, hotel is 20mtrs on the left*

Situated in the picturesque village near the famous prehistoric tombs of New Grange, the hotel has very comfortable public rooms including the unique Estate Agent's Restaurant. There are attractive gardens to the rear, and this is an ideal location from which to explore the historic area which includes Tara and the Boyne Valley. Bedrooms are well appointed. Fishing, horse riding and tennis are available locally.

ROOMS: 16 rms (15 bth/shr) (4 fmly) **MEALS:** Irish & French Cuisine V meals Coffee am Tea pm **FACILITIES:** CTV in all bedrooms STV **CONF:** Thtr 150 Class 120 **SERVICES:** 12P **NOTES:** No dogs (ex guide dogs) Last d 9.45pm Closed Good Fri & Xmas **CARDS:**

SLIGO Co Sligo **Map 01 B5**

★★★ Sligo Park Pearse Rd

Quality Percentage Score: 71%

☎ 071 60291 📠 071 69556

Dir: *on N4*

Set in seven acres of parkland on the southern edge of Sligo, this recently refurbished hotel is an ideal touring centre for the many attractions of Yeats country and is also near Rosses Point Golf Club. Most of the bedrooms have recently been upgraded and offer all modern facilities, in particular the excellent 'executive' rooms. The restaurant is particularly attractive and inviting. A comprehensive leisure centre is an added attraction, and there are good beaches not far away.

ROOMS: 110 en suite (bth/shr) No smoking in 4 bedrooms s IR£50-IR£100; d IR£99-IR£200 * LB Off peak **MEALS:** Lunch IR£11-IR£12 Dinner fr IR£19 Irish & French Cuisine V meals Coffee am Tea pm **FACILITIES:** CTV in all bedrooms Indoor swimming pool (heated) Tennis (hard) Snooker Sauna Solarium Gym Jacuzzi/spa Steam room Plunge pool Wkly live entertainment Xmas **CONF:** Thtr 520 Class 350 Board 50 **SERVICES:** Night porter 200P **NOTES:** No dogs (ex guide dogs) No smoking area in restaurant Last d 9pm RS 24-26 & 31 Dec **CARDS:**

★★★ *Tower*

Quay St

Quality Percentage Score: 65%

☎ 071 44000 📠 071 46888

Dir: *in the centre of Sligo*

Pleasantly located beside the quay, this attractively furnished hotel is right in the town centre. There is a smart foyer lounge, a pleasant restaurant and bar; the bedrooms are comfortable and well equipped. Guests have access to the local leisure and fitness centre at reduced rates.

ROOMS: 58 en suite (bth/shr) No smoking in 12 bedrooms **MEALS:** V meals Coffee am **FACILITIES:** CTV in all bedrooms **CONF:** Thtr 200 Class 60 Board 50 **SERVICES:** Lift Night porter Air conditioning 20P **NOTES:** No dogs (ex guide dogs) No smoking in restaurant Last d 9.30pm Closed 21-30 Dec **CARDS:**

S

★★ Silver Swan

Quality Percentage Score: 61%

☎ 071 43231 🖷 071 42232

Dir: *situated on the banks of the Garavogue River in the town centre beside G.P.O. and on the junction of N4, N15, N16*

Family owned, this hotel is situated on the banks of the Garavogue River in the heart of Sligo and attracts both business guests and tourists. Recently redecorated bedrooms are well furnished and comfortable with good bathrooms, some with aero-spa baths. The Horseshoe Bar is a popular spot for snacks and drinks and there is a car park to the rear.

ROOMS: 29 en suite (bth/shr) s IR£48-IR£60; d IR£60-IR£75 (incl. bkfst) * Off peak **MEALS:** Lunch IR£10.50-IR£12.50 Dinner IR£19-IR£22 French Cuisine V meals Coffee am Tea pm **FACILITIES:** CTV in all bedrooms Wkly live entertainment **CONF:** Thtr 100 Class 60 Board 30 **SERVICES:** Night porter 40P **NOTES:** No dogs (ex guide dogs) No smoking in restaurant Last d 9.30pm Closed 25 & 26 Dec

CARDS:

STRAFFAN Co Kildare — Map 01 D4

The Premier Collection

★★★★★ The Kildare Hotel & Country Club

☎ 01 6017200 🖷 01 6017299

Dir: *from Dublin take N4, take exit for R406 hotel entrance is on right in Straffan*

A luxurious hotel set in 330 acres of park and woodland, with a golf course designed by Arnold Palmer - the venue for the 2005 Ryder Cup. Opulent reception rooms include the Chinese Drawing Room, overlooking the gardens and the River Liffey. Richly furnished bedrooms are most comfortable and extremely well equipped. Staff are very attentive, and there are extensive leisure and conference facilities.

ROOMS: 36 en suite (bth/shr) 9 annexe en suite (bth/shr) (10 fmly) * LB Off peak **MEALS:** Irish, French & Italian Cuisine V meals Coffee am Tea pm **FACILITIES:** CTV in all bedrooms STV Indoor swimming pool (heated) Golf 18 Tennis (hard) Fishing Squash Snooker Sauna Solarium Gym Pool table Croquet lawn Putting green Jacuzzi/spa Beauty salon Driving range Golf tuition Fishing tuition Wkly live entertainment Xmas **CONF:** Thtr 160 Class 60 Board 40 **SERVICES:** Lift Night porter 205P **NOTES:** No dogs No smoking area in restaurant **CARDS:**

★★★ Barberstown Castle

Quality Percentage Score: 76%

☎ 01 6288157 🖷 01 6277027

Embracing a heritage that dates from the 13th century, the castle has been elegantly refurbished and decorated in glowing colours to provide the highest standards of comfort. Inviting public rooms range from the original castle keep, now housing one of the two restaurants, to the soft warmth of the drawing room and cocktail bar. A new wing of high quality bedrooms has recently been added.

ROOMS: 22 en suite (bth/shr) s IR£85-IR£100; d IR£136-IR£156 (incl. bkfst) LB Off peak **MEALS:** Dinner IR£27.50 & alc Irish & French Cuisine V meals **FACILITIES:** CTV in all bedrooms STV Wkly live entertainment **CONF:** Thtr 50 Class 40 Board 30 Del from IR£130 * **SERVICES:** Night porter 200P **NOTES:** No dogs No children 12yrs No smoking in restaurant Last d 10pm Closed 24-26 Dec & 2-16 Jan

CARDS:

TEMPLEGLANTINE Co Limerick — Map 01 B2

★★★ The Devon Inn

Quality Percentage Score: 59%

☎ 069 84122 🖷 069 84255

Dir: *midway between Limerick City and Killarney on N21*

Major building and refurbishment work has resulted in a new look for this hotel, with its smart reception area, comfortable foyer lounge with big sofas and soft lighting, and all-day bar and restaurant. Twenty new bedrooms offer spacious accommodation with good quality wood finishes, and there are plans for further upgrading. Salmon and trout fishing and golf are available nearby.

ROOMS: 59 en suite (bth/shr) (20 fmly) s IR£35-IR£45; d IR£60-IR£80 (incl. bkfst) * LB Off peak **MEALS:** Lunch IR£9.50-IR£12 Dinner IR£15-IR£18 & alc French Cuisine V meals Coffee am Tea pm **FACILITIES:** CTV in all bedrooms STV Pool table **CONF:** Thtr 400 Class 200 Board 30 Del from IR£50 * **SERVICES:** Night porter 200P **NOTES:** No smoking area in restaurant Last d 9.15pm Closed 24-25 Dec

CARDS:

THOMASTOWN Co Kilkenny — Map 01 C3

The Premier Collection

★★★★ Mount Juliet

☎ 056 73000 🖷 056 73019

Dir: *take M7 from Dublin, M9 towards Waterford then to the Mount Juliet on the N9 via Carlow and Gowran*

Set in 1500 acres of parkland, including a Jack Nicklaus designed golf course where the Irish Opens were played in 1993 and 1994, this beautiful Palladian mansion is now a very special hotel. The elegant and spacious public rooms

contd.

S

retain much of the original architectural features, including ornate plasterwork and fine Adam fireplaces in the cocktail bar, restaurant and drawing room.
ROOMS: 32 en suite (bth/shr) 27 annexe en suite (bth/shr) s IR£120-IR£160; d IR£160-IR£260 * LB Off peak **MEALS:** Lunch fr IR£14.50 Dinner IR£35 & alc International Cuisine V meals Coffee am Tea pm **FACILITIES:** CTV in all bedrooms STV Indoor swimming pool (heated) Golf 18 Tennis (hard) Fishing Riding Snooker Sauna Gym Croquet lawn Putting green Beauty salon Archery Clay pigeon shooting Cycling Golf tuition Xmas **CONF:** Thtr 200 Class 80 Board 50 Del from IR£120 * **SERVICES:** Night porter 200P **NOTES:** No dogs (ex guide dogs) No smoking in restaurant Last d 9pm **CARDS:**

TIPPERARY Co Tipperary — Map 01 C3

★ Royal

Bridge St
Quality Percentage Score: 59%
☎ 062 33244 🖹 062 33596
ROOMS: 16 en suite (bth/shr) (3 fmly) s IR£35; d IR£70 (incl. bkfst) * LB Off peak **MEALS:** V meals Coffee am Tea pm **FACILITIES:** CTV in all bedrooms Wkly live entertainment **CONF:** Class 80 **SERVICES:** 200P **NOTES:** No dogs No smoking area in restaurant Last d 9pm
CARDS:

TRALEE Co Kerry — Map 01 A2

★★★ The Brandon

Quality Percentage Score: 67%
☎ 066 7123333 🖹 066 7125019
This modern hotel, completely refurbished, is situated in the town centre. It has excellent leisure facilities and is a golfer's paradise, within 30 minutes' of six superb courses.
ROOMS: 185 en suite (bth/shr) (4 fmly) **MEALS:** Sunday Lunch IR£15 French Cuisine V meals Coffee am Tea pm **FACILITIES:** CTV in all bedrooms STV Indoor swimming pool (heated) Sauna Solarium Gym Jacuzzi/spa Concessionary Green fees Wkly live entertainment
CONF: Thtr 1200 Class 600 Board 30 Del from IR£90 * **SERVICES:** Lift Night porter 300P **NOTES:** No dogs (ex guide dogs) No smoking area in restaurant Closed 23-28 Dec **CARDS:**

★★★ Abbey Gate

Maine St
Quality Percentage Score: 64%
☎ 066 7129888 🖹 066 7129821
Dir: *in town centre*
The Abbey Gate is a smartly appointed town centre hotel, with parking.The well equipped bedrooms include some suitable for those with mobility problems. Public areas include a spacious foyer and lounge area with attractive decor, a traditional pub, 'The Old Market Place' where carvery lunches are served, a cocktail bar, the Vineyard Restaurant, and banqueting and conference suites.
ROOMS: 100 en suite (bth/shr) (4 fmly) s IR£45-IR£95; d IR£70-IR£100 (incl. bkfst) * LB Off peak **MEALS:** Lunch IR£10.50-IR£15 High tea IR£8.50-IR£14alc Dinner IR£14.95-IR£20 & alc International Cuisine V meals Coffee am Tea pm **FACILITIES:** CTV in all bedrooms STV Wkly live entertainment Xmas **CONF:** Thtr 350 Class 250 Board 25
SERVICES: Lift Night porter 20P **NOTES:** No dogs (ex guide dogs) No smoking area in restaurant Last d 9.30pm Closed 25 Dec
CARDS:

★★★ *Tralee Court*

Castle St
Quality Percentage Score: 60%
☎ 066 21877

TRAMORE Co Waterford — Map 01 C2

★★★ *Majestic*

Quality Percentage Score: 63%
☎ 051 381761 🖹 051 381766
Dir: *turn off N25 through Waterford onto R675 to Tramore*
Set back from the sea front, a short distance from the beach, the Majestic is a white building with good sea views, situated close to the town centre. Entertainment is held in the lounge bar during the summer months, and there is an outdoor pool and attractive gardens. Bedrooms are comfortable with all modern facilities, and there is a lift to all floors.
ROOMS: 57 en suite (bth/shr) (4 fmly) No smoking in 5 bedrooms
MEALS: V meals Coffee am Tea pm **FACILITIES:** CTV in all bedrooms STV Outdoor swimming pool (heated) **SERVICES:** Lift Night porter 10P
NOTES: No dogs (ex guide dogs) No smoking area in restaurant Last d 9pm **CARDS:**

WATERFORD Co Waterford — Map 01 C2

★★★ Granville

The Quay
Quality Percentage Score: 71%
☎ 051 305555 🖹 051 305566
Dir: *take the N25 to the waterfront, city centre , opposite the Clock Tower*
Situated on the quayside, conveniently located opposite a public car park, this charming old hotel has been extensively refurbished to a high standard while retaining its character. The new bedrooms, with a choice of standard or executive rooms, and the restyled public areas and restaurant, are all very comfortable and appointed to a high standard.
ROOMS: 100 en suite (bth/shr) (5 fmly) No smoking in 20 bedrooms s IR£65-IR£150; d IR£100-IR£150 (incl. bkfst) * LB Off peak
MEALS: Lunch IR£11.95-IR£12.50 High tea IR£8.95-IR£10.95 Dinner IR£20-IR£25 International Cuisine V meals Coffee am Tea pm
FACILITIES: CTV in all bedrooms STV Wkly live entertainment
CONF: Thtr 200 Class 150 Board 30 Del from IR£65 * **SERVICES:** Lift Night porter 300P **NOTES:** No dogs (ex guide dogs) No smoking area in restaurant Last d 9.30pm Closed 25-26 Dec **CARDS:**

★★★ Dooley's

30 The Quay
Quality Percentage Score: 66%
☎ 051 873531 🖹 051 870262
Dir: *on N25*
Situated in the heart of Waterford overlooking the quayside, Dooley's is a family-run hotel recently completely refurbished to a high standard. The smart new public areas and bedrooms offer comfortable and stylish accommodation, and there is an elevator to all floors. The personalised attention of the owner and her team has not changed, and guests will experience their caring attitude and a friendly atmosphere.
ROOMS: 113 en suite (bth/shr) (3 fmly) No smoking in 17 bedrooms s IR£39-IR£50; d IR£95-IR£100 (incl. bkfst) * LB Off peak **MEALS:** Lunch IR£11.95 Dinner IR£11-IR£15.95 & alc International Cuisine V meals Coffee am Tea pm **FACILITIES:** CTV in all bedrooms STV Wkly live entertainment **CONF:** Thtr 260 Class 200 Board 100 **SERVICES:** Lift Night porter **NOTES:** No dogs (ex guide dogs) No smoking area in restaurant Last d 9.30pm Closed 25-27 Dec **CARDS:**

★★★ Tower
The Mall
Quality Percentage Score: 63%
☎ 051 875801 🖷 051 870129
Dir: *opposite Reginald's Tower in the centre of town*
Now completely upgraded, the hotel offers a full range of banqueting, conference and leisure facilities - the latter including a new swimming pool with air conditioned fitness centre - as well as an attractive restaurant and a pleasant bar overlooking the river. Helpful, friendly staff provide good service throughout.
ROOMS: 145 en suite (bth/shr) (10 fmly) **MEALS:** European Cuisine V meals Coffee am Tea pm **FACILITIES:** CTV in all bedrooms Indoor swimming pool (heated) Sauna Solarium Gym Jacuzzi/spa Wkly live entertainment **CONF:** Thtr 650 Class 300 Board 100 **SERVICES:** Lift Night porter 60P **NOTES:** No dogs (ex guide dogs) No smoking area in restaurant Last d 10pm Closed 25-26 Dec **CARDS:**

★★★ Waterford Marina Hotel
Canada St
Quality Percentage Score: 63%
☎ 051 856600 🖷 051 856605
Dir: *into Waterford across bridge turn left, continue to Quay, left at Tower hotel, in 0.5km left at Peoples Park, hotel on waterfront, carpark to rear*
Overlooking the River Suir, this smart new hotel features contemporary design and decor. The Marine Bar opens onto an outdoor seating area beside the river, while the colourful restaurant offers good value, carefully cooked modern cuisine. The comfortable bedrooms are all attractively decorated and equipped with many extras including ISDN lines. The young team of staff are all very pleasant.
ROOMS: 81 en suite (bth/shr) (4 fmly) No smoking in 15 bedrooms s IR£35-IR£55; d IR£70-IR£110 (incl. bkfst) * LB Off peak **MEALS:** Sunday Lunch IR£12.95-IR£16.95 Dinner IR£9.95-IR£16.95 & alc V meals Coffee am **FACILITIES:** CTV in all bedrooms STV Sauna Xmas **CONF:** Thtr 40 Class 20 Board 20 **SERVICES:** Lift Night porter Air conditioning 65P **NOTES:** No dogs (ex guide dogs) No smoking area in restaurant Last d 10pm **CARDS:**

★★★ *Jurys*
Ferrybank
Quality Percentage Score: 62%
☎ 051 832111 🖷 051 832863
Dir: *on N25 1km from City Centre*
Situated in parkland overlooking the city, this large modern hotel has spacious public rooms and caters for tourists and the commercial trade.
ROOMS: 98 en suite (bth/shr) (20 fmly) No smoking in 4 bedrooms **MEALS:** International Cuisine V meals Coffee am Tea pm **FACILITIES:** CTV in all bedrooms Indoor swimming pool (heated) Tennis (hard) Sauna Solarium Gym Jacuzzi/spa Steam room Plunge pool Jacuzzi Wkly live entertainment **CONF:** Thtr 700 Class 400 Board 100 **SERVICES:** Lift Night porter 300P **NOTES:** No dogs (ex guide dogs) No smoking area in restaurant Last d 9.15pm **CARDS:**

★★★ Bridge Hotel
1 The Quay
Quality Percentage Score: 61%
☎ 051 877222 🖷 051 877229
Dir: *the Hotel is located opposite the Waterford City Bridge when following the N25*
This busy hotel stands near the City Bridge, convenient for the shops and all local amenities. Extensive refurbishment has created really comfortable bedrooms and public areas include a country-style bistro, a restaurant, a traditional Irish pub and a relaxing lounge bar.
ROOMS: 100 en suite (bth/shr) (20 fmly) No smoking in 4 bedrooms s IR£45-IR£50; d IR£80-IR£90 (incl. bkfst) * LB Off peak **MEALS:** Lunch IR£9-IR£11.95 High tea IR£1.20-IR£3.25 Dinner IR£15-IR£18 & alc V meals Coffee am Tea pm **FACILITIES:** CTV in all bedrooms STV Wkly live entertainment **CONF:** Thtr 400 Class 300 Board 70 Del from IR£65 * **SERVICES:** Lift Night porter Air conditioning **NOTES:** No dogs No smoking area in restaurant Last d 9.30pm Closed 25 Dec
CARDS:

★★ Ivory's Hotel
Tramore Rd
Quality Percentage Score: 60%
☎ 051 358888 🖷 051 358899
Dir: *from Waterford city centre take the N25 to Cork. After 600yrds take exit to Trelore R675. Hotel is on Right hand side*
This distinctive modern hotel stands near the Waterford Glass factory, just south-west of the city. It offers good value accommodation, with family rooms as well as standard rooms, and all are furnished with writing desks as well as the usual amenities. The restaurant, with its 'Catch of the Day' selection of fresh seafood dishes from nearby Dunmore, is proving very popular. The hotel has a security-monitored car park and is close to no fewer than six golf courses where golfing packages can be arranged.
ROOMS: 40 en suite (bth/shr) (20 fmly) No smoking in 20 bedrooms s IR£45-IR£65; d IR£60-IR£90 (incl. bkfst) * LB Off peak **MEALS:** Lunch IR£7.50-IR£12.50 & alc High tea fr IR£5.95 Dinner IR£12.95-IR£16.95 & alc Irish & French Cuisine V meals Coffee am Tea pm **FACILITIES:** CTV in all bedrooms STV ch fac Xmas **SERVICES:** Night porter 40P **NOTES:** Last d 9pm **CARDS:**

⌂ Travelodge
Cork Rd
☎ 051 358885 🖷 051 358890
Dir: *On N25, 1km from Waterford Glass Visitors Centre*
This modern building offers accommodation in smart, spacious and well equipped bedrooms, all with en-suite bathrooms. Refreshments may be taken at the nearby family restaurant. For details about current prices, consult the Contents Page under Hotel Groups for the Travelodge phone number.
ROOMS: 32 en suite (bth/shr) d IR£45.95 *

WATERVILLE Co Kerry — Map 01 A2

★★★ *Butler Arms*
Quality Percentage Score: 72%
☎ 066 74144 🖷 066 74520
Dir: *centre of Waterville village on seafront. N70 Ring of Kerry*
Situated on the Ring of Kerry overlooking the ocean, the Butlers Arms has been owned by the same family for over three generations and offers high traditional standards of service. Most of the bedrooms have marble bathrooms and enjoy sea views, whilst public areas include spacious lounges and a billiards room. An 18-hole championship golf course is opposite.
ROOMS: 30 en suite (bth/shr) (1 fmly) **MEALS:** Irish & French Cuisine V meals Coffee am Tea pm **FACILITIES:** CTV in all bedrooms STV Tennis (hard) Fishing Snooker **SERVICES:** Night porter 30P **NOTES:** No dogs (ex guide dogs) No smoking area in restaurant Last d 9.15pm Closed Jan-Apr & Oct-Dec **CARDS:**

WESTPORT Co Mayo — Map 01 B4

★★★★ Knockranny House Hotel

Quality Percentage Score: 65%

☎ 098 28600 Fax 098 28611

Dir: *on the main Westport/Castlebar Road (N5) close to town of Westport*

Overlooking Westport with Clew Bay in the distance, the reception rooms of this family-run hotel take full advantage of the lovely views. The luxurious furnishings create an inviting and relaxing atmosphere throughout the lounge, bar and restaurant which are all located on the first floor. All types of rooms are well appointed. There is a helicopter landing area.

ROOMS: 54 en suite (bth/shr) (4 fmly) s IR£85; d IR£130 (incl. bkfst) * LB Off peak **MEALS:** Lunch IR£11.50-IR£15 High tea IR£7-IR£10 Dinner IR£23.50-IR£25 V meals Coffee am Tea pm **FACILITIES:** CTV in all bedrooms STV Tennis (hard) Jacuzzi/spa Full Leisure centre free to all guests, at associated hotel 3mins away Wkly live entertainment ch fac **CONF:** Thtr 700 Class 400 Board 40 Del from IR£95 * **SERVICES:** Lift Night porter 120P **NOTES:** No dogs (ex guide dogs) No smoking area in restaurant Last d 9.30pm Closed 24-26 Dec

CARDS:

★★★ *Hotel Westport*

The Demesne, Newport Rd

Quality Percentage Score: 67%

☎ 098 25122 Fax 098 26739

Dir: *N5 to Castlebar, N60 to Westport, at end of Castlebar St turn right, before bridge, right again, immediate left at hotel signpost follow rd to end*

Opposite the grounds of Westport House, this hotel offers welcoming accommodation including a new reception foyer, lounge, spacious restaurant and comfortable bedrooms including six suites. The hotel has much to offer the leisure and business guest, with a swimming pool, sauna and gym, and new conference and syndicate rooms.

ROOMS: 129 en suite (bth/shr) **MEALS:** Continental/Irish Cuisine V meals Coffee am **FACILITIES:** CTV in all bedrooms STV Indoor swimming pool (heated) Sauna Solarium Gym Jacuzzi/spa Steam room Lounger pool & childrens pool Jet stream Wkly live entertainment **CONF:** Thtr 500 Class 150 Board 60 **SERVICES:** Lift Night porter 220P **NOTES:** No dogs (ex guide dogs) No smoking area in restaurant Last d 9.30pm **CARDS:**

See advert on this page

★★ The Olde Railway

The Mall

Quality Percentage Score: 72%

☎ 098 25166 & 25605 Fax 098 25090

Dir: *overlooking the Carrowbeg River in the town centre*

Set on a tree-lined mall overlooking the river, this classic coaching inn offers a welcoming atmosphere with blazing turf fires. There is a variety of bedroom sizes, including some very spacious berths; all rooms are well equipped. Communal areas include an attractively furnished bar, a comfortable lounge and a new Conservatory Restaurant with access to the patio and barbecue area. Car parking is available.

ROOMS: 24 en suite (bth/shr) (2 fmly) s IR£45-IR£85; d IR£60-IR£90 (incl. bkfst) * LB Off peak **MEALS:** Lunch IR£11.95 Dinner IR£20-IR£25 & alc Irish/English Cuisine V meals Coffee am Tea pm **FACILITIES:** CTV in all bedrooms STV Fishing & Shooting arranged Wkly live entertainment **SERVICES:** Night porter 34P **NOTES:** No dogs (ex guide dogs) No smoking in restaurant Last d 10pm **CARDS:**

See advert on this page

WEXFORD Co Wexford — Map 01 D3

★★★ Ferrycarrig

Ferrycarrig
Quality Percentage Score: 73%
☎ 053 20999 Fax 053 20982
Dir: *on N11 by Slaney Estuary, beside Ferrycraig Castle*

Set in one of the most inspiring locations in Ireland, this lovely hotel has sweeping views across the estuary. The public rooms curve round the waterfront and include a fine leisure centre. The bedrooms have been refurbished to a high standard, while those in the new wing are worth their higher rate. Both restaurants are at the waters edge, the lively bistro offers a wide menu, while Tides, long time holder of AA Rosette awards, offers gourmet cuisine.

ROOMS: 90 en suite (bth/shr) (12 fmly) No smoking in 45 bedrooms s IR£65-IR£250; d IR£120-IR£450 (incl. bkfst) * LB Off peak **MEALS:** Lunch IR£8-IR£20 & alc Dinner IR£15-IR£27 & alc Irish & French Cuisine V meals Coffee am Tea pm **FACILITIES:** CTV in all bedrooms STV Indoor swimming pool (heated) Sauna Solarium Gym Jacuzzi/spa Aerobics Beauty treatments on request Wkly live entertainment Xmas **CONF:** Thtr 400 Class 250 Board 60 Del from IR£80 * **SERVICES:** Lift Night porter 235P **NOTES:** No dogs (ex guide dogs) No smoking area in restaurant Last d 9.15pm **CARDS:**

★★★ Talbot

Trinity St
Quality Percentage Score: 72%
☎ 053 22566 Fax 053 23377
Dir: *from Rosslare, take N11 & follow the signs for Wexford, hotel on the right hand side of the Quays - 12miles*

Centrally situated on the quayside, this hotel has been extensively refurbished, giving all the bedrooms custom-made oak furniture, attractive decor and new bathrooms. Day rooms include a spacious foyer, comfortable lounge, and a bar with an open fireplace. Cuisine is informal, in the country-kitchen style. There are good leisure facilities and an adjoining car park.

ROOMS: 100 en suite (bth/shr) (12 fmly) No smoking in 10 bedrooms s IR£65; d IR£105 (incl. bkfst) LB Off peak **MEALS:** Lunch IR£4.95-IR£8.95 & alc High tea IR£5-IR£6.50 & alc Dinner IR£21.50-IR£22.50 & alc International Cuisine V meals Coffee am Tea pm **FACILITIES:** CTV in all bedrooms STV Indoor swimming pool (heated) Sauna Solarium Gym Jacuzzi/spa Childrens room Beauty Salon Wkly live entertainment Xmas **CONF:** Thtr 600 Class 300 Board 110 Del from IR£79.50 * **SERVICES:** Lift Night porter 100P **NOTES:** No dogs (ex guide dogs) No smoking area in restaurant Last d 9.30pm **CARDS:**

See advert on this page

★★★ Whitford House

New Line Rd
Quality Percentage Score: 66%
☎ 053 43444 & 43845 Fax 053 46399
Dir: *located left off second rdbt on main Dublin to Rosslare rd, (N11)*

A family run hotel on the edge of Wexford with a choice of lounges, a spacious bar and a restaurant offering a good value table d'hote dinner menu that includes a variety of seafood dishes. The comfortable en suite bedrooms are equipped with all the modern facilities and there are de-luxe patio rooms available. Additional guest facilities include an indoor swimming pool, tennis courts, a children's playground and ample parking.

ROOMS: 23 en suite (bth/shr) (10 fmly) s IR£51.25; d IR£102.50 (incl. bkfst) * LB Off peak **MEALS:** Lunch fr IR£11.50 Dinner fr IR£23.50 & alc French Cuisine V meals Coffee am Tea pm **FACILITIES:** CTV in all bedrooms STV Indoor swimming pool (heated) Tennis (hard) Childrens playground Wkly live entertainment **CONF:** Board 50 **SERVICES:** Night porter 140P **NOTES:** No dogs Last d 9pm Closed 23 Dec-13 Jan RS 24 Dec-Jan **CARDS:**

★★★ River Bank House Hotel

Quality Percentage Score: 63%
☎ 053 23611 Fax 053 23342
Dir: *beside Wexford Bridge on R741*

This recently refurbished hotel is situated overlooking the river Slaney. Public areas include a very smart foyer, attractively decorated dining room and a victorian style bar where food is served all day. Bedrooms are comfortable and well equipped.

ROOMS: 24 en suite (bth/shr) s IR£60-IR£70; d IR£94-IR£114 (incl. bkfst) * LB Off peak **MEALS:** Lunch IR£12.95 Dinner IR£20 & alc French Cuisine V meals Coffee am Tea pm **FACILITIES:** CTV in all bedrooms STV Wkly live entertainment **SERVICES:** Night porter 40P **NOTES:** No dogs (ex guide dogs) No smoking area in restaurant Last d 10pm Closed 24-25 Dec **CARDS:**

★★★ White's Hotel

George St
Quality Percentage Score: 62%
☎ 053 22311 Fax 053 45000
Dir: *on entering Wexford Town from the N11 or N25 follow directional signs for Whites Hotel*

This historic former coaching inn has recently been refurbished, but retains much of its charm. The entrance is through a modern extension, and entertainment is provided in the converted saddlery and forge.

ROOMS: 76 en suite (bth/shr) 6 annexe en suite (bth/shr) (1 fmly) s IR£50-IR£91.50; d IR£70-IR£136 (incl. bkfst) * LB Off peak **MEALS:** Lunch IR£9.95-IR£12.50 & alc Dinner IR£16.95-IR£24 & alc International Cuisine V meals Coffee am Tea pm **FACILITIES:** CTV in all bedrooms STV Sauna Gym Jacuzzi/spa Nightclub Wkly live

contd.

W

entertainment Xmas **CONF:** Thtr 400 Class 250 Board 100 **SERVICES:** Lift Night porter 100P **NOTES:** No dogs (ex guide dogs) No smoking area in restaurant Last d 10pm
CARDS:

WICKLOW
Map 01 D3

See **Rathnew**

WOODENBRIDGE Co Wicklow
Map 01 D3

★★★ ❀ ***Woodenbridge***

Quality Percentage Score: 64%

☎ 0402 35146 🖷 0402 35573

Dir: *between Avoca & Arklow*

This comfortable hotel in the Vale of Avoca, about an hour's drive from the ferry ports of Dun Laoghaire and Rosslaire, and not far from the N11 Dublin to Wexford road, has been given a new lease of life by its new owners the O'Brien family who have recently extended it by creating 12 new bedrooms and a conference/banqueting suite. Hospitality and good food are the focus of their concerns. Golf and fishing are on the doorstep.
ROOMS: 23 en suite (bth/shr) (13 fmly) **MEALS:** V meals Coffee am Tea pm **FACILITIES:** CTV in all bedrooms STV Pool table **CONF:** Thtr 200 Class 200 Board 200 **SERVICES:** Night porter 100P **NOTES:** No dogs No smoking area in restaurant Last d 9pm **CARDS:**

YOUGHAL Co Cork
Map 01 C2

★★ ❀ ***Devonshire Arms***

Pearse Square

Quality Percentage Score: 64%

☎ 024 92827 & 92018 🖷 024 92900

This 19th-century hotel has been restored with considerable care and attention to detail. It offers good food in both the restaurant and the bar.
ROOMS: 10 en suite (bth/shr) (3 fmly) **MEALS:** Irish & French Cuisine V meals Coffee am Tea pm **FACILITIES:** CTV in all bedrooms **CONF:** Class 150 **SERVICES:** 20P **NOTES:** No dogs (ex guide dogs) Closed Xmas **CARDS:**

Y

KEY TO ATLAS

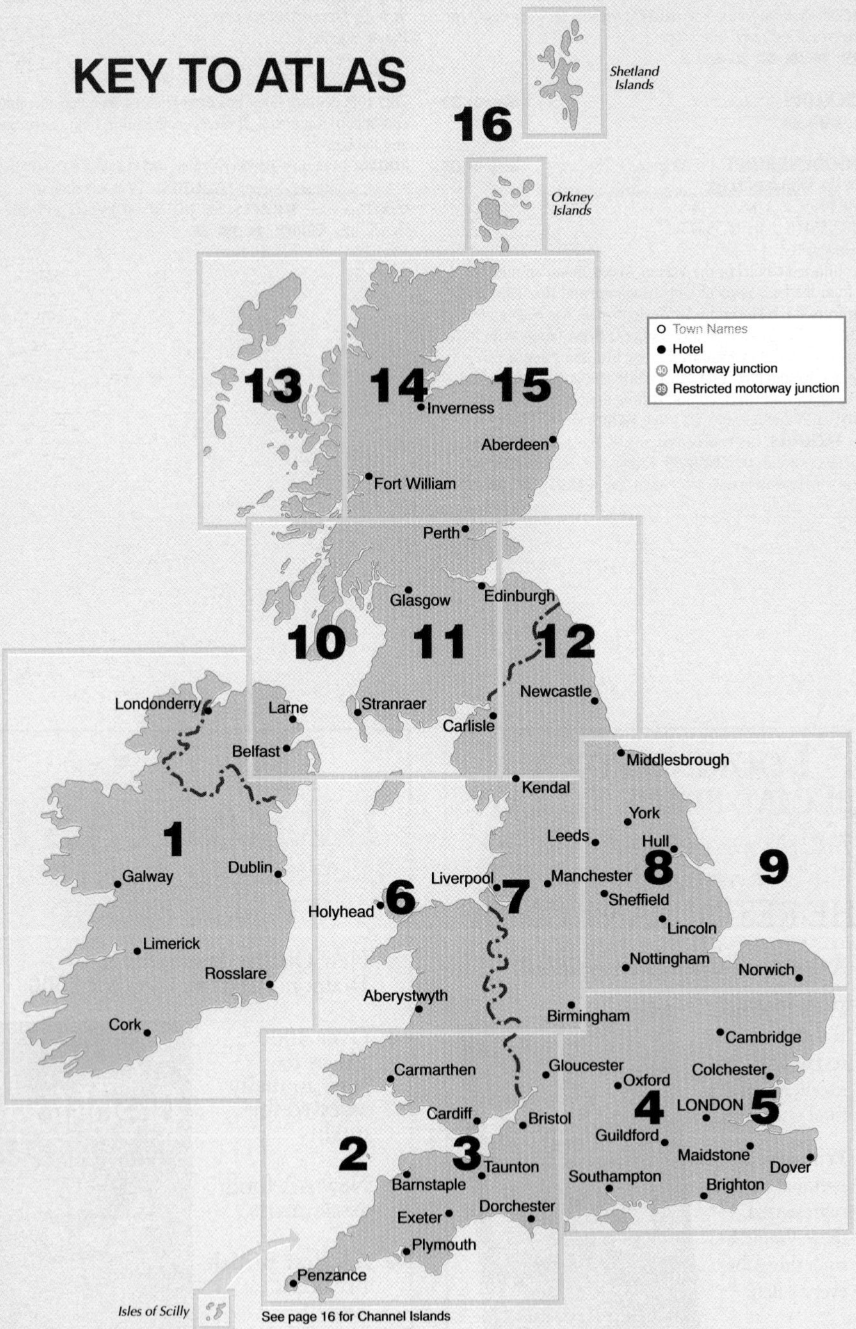

See page 16 for Channel Islands

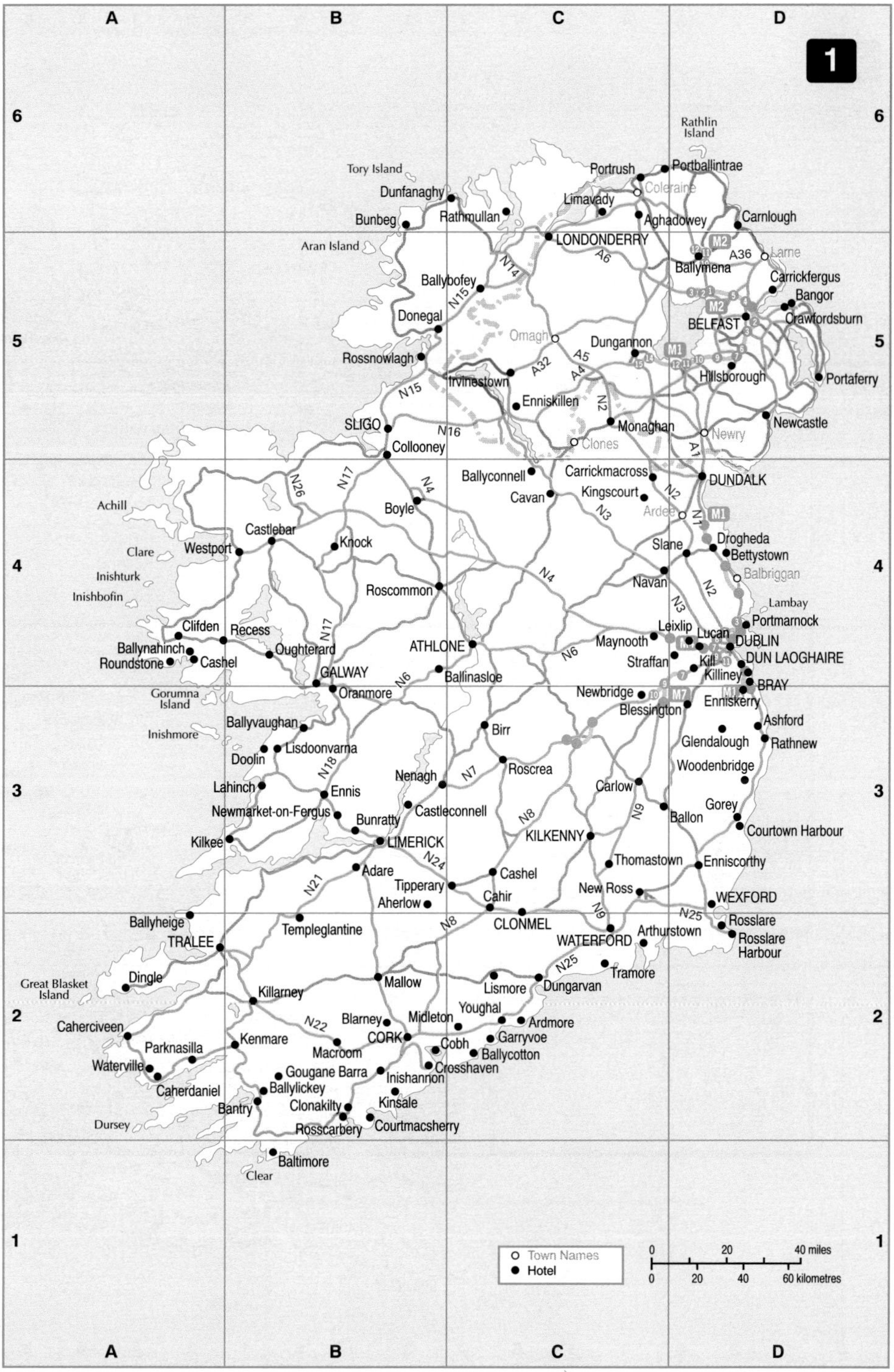

A
B
C
D
1
6
5
4
3
2
1
Rathlin Island
Tory Island
Portrush
Portballintrae
Coleraine
Dunfanaghy
Limavady
Aghadowey
Carnlough
Bunbeg
Rathmullan
LONDONDERRY
Aran Island
A6
M2
A36
Larne
Ballymena
N14
Carrickfergus
Ballybofey
N15
Bangor
M2
Donegal
Crawfordsburn
BELFAST
Omagh
Dungannon
M1
Rossnowlagh
A5
A32
Hillsborough
Portaferry
Irvinestown
A4
N15
N2
Enniskillen
Newcastle
Monaghan
SLIGO
N16
Newry
Clones
Collooney
A1
Ballyconnell
Carrickmacross
N26
N17
DUNDALK
N4
Cavan
Kingscourt
N2
Achill
Boyle
N3
Ardee
M1
N1
Castlebar
Drogheda
Knock
Slane
Clare
Westport
Bettystown
Inishturk
N4
Balbriggan
Navan
Roscommon
N2
Inishbofin
N3
Lambay
N17
Portmarnock
Clifden
Leixlip
Recess
Lucan
Ballynahinch
Maynooth
DUBLIN
Oughterard
ATHLONE
N6
Roundstone
Cashel
Kill
DUN LAOGHAIRE
Straffan
GALWAY
Killiney
N6
Ballinasloe
Oranmore
BRAY
Gorumna Island
Newbridge
M7
M11
Blessington
Enniskerry
Ballyvaughan
Ashford
Birr
Inishmore
Glendalough
Lisdoonvarna
Rathnew
Doolin
N18
Roscrea
Woodenbridge
Nenagh
N7
Lahinch
Carlow
Ennis
N9
Gorey
Castleconnell
Newmarket-on-Fergus
N8
Ballon
Bunratty
Courtown Harbour
KILKENNY
Kilkee
LIMERICK
N24
Thomastown
Enniscorthy
Adare
Cashel
N21
Tipperary
New Ross
WEXFORD
Cahir
Aherlow
N9
N25
Ballyheige
Rosslare
CLONMEL
N8
Templeglantine
Arthurstown
Rosslare Harbour
WATERFORD
TRALEE
N25
Tramore
Dingle
Mallow
Lismore
Dungarvan
Great Blasket Island
Killarney
Youghal
Caherciveen
N22
Blarney
Midleton
Ardmore
Kenmare
CORK
Garryvoe
Parknasilla
Macroom
Cobh
Ballycotton
Waterville
Gougane Barra
Crosshaven
Caherdaniel
Ballylickey
Inishannon
Bantry
Clonakilty
Kinsale
Dursey
Rosscarbery
Courtmacsherry
Baltimore
Clear
Town Names
Hotel
0
20
40 miles
0
20
40
60 kilometres

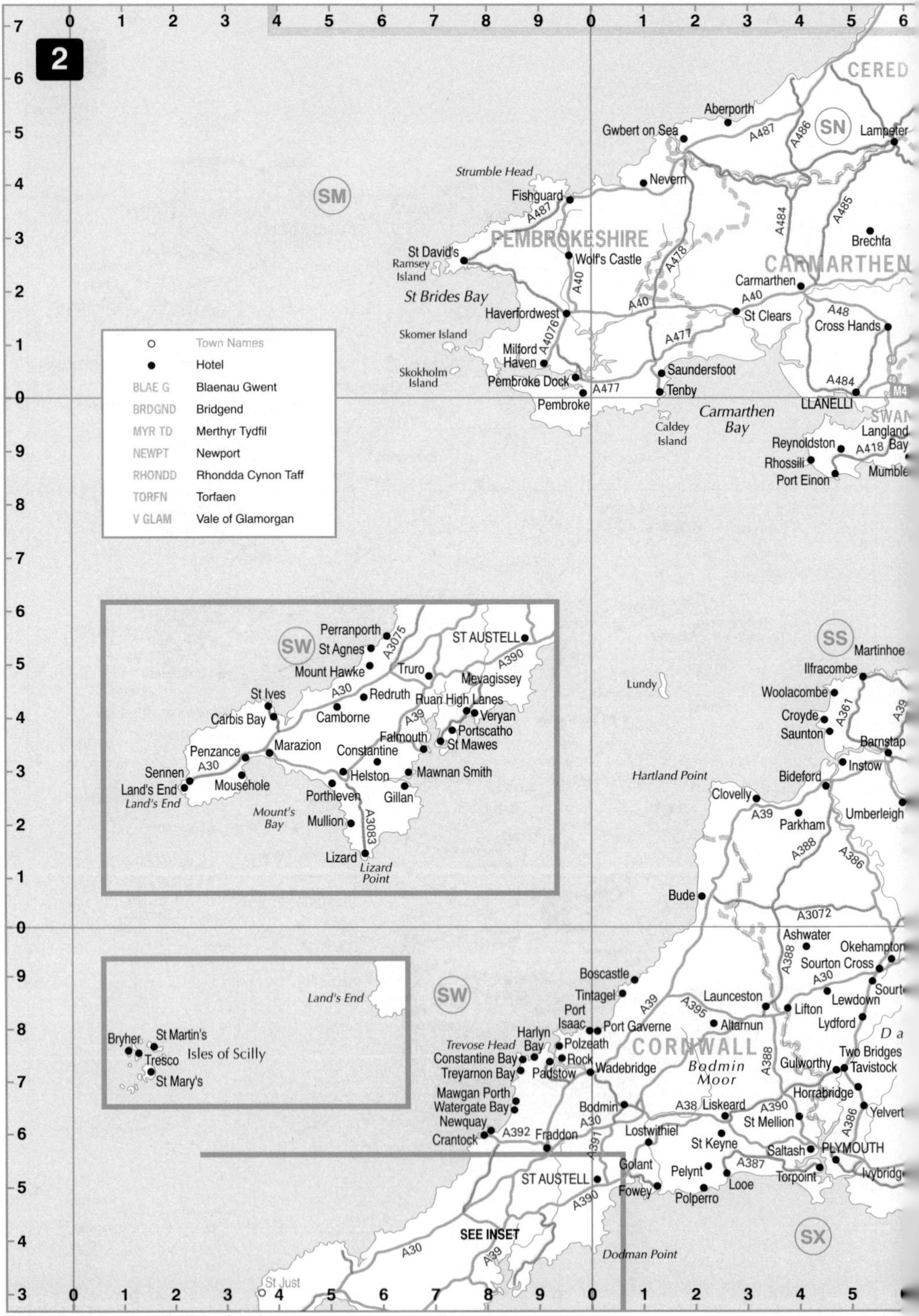

For continuation pages refer to numbered arrows

3
6
7
4
SO
ST
SY
POWYS
HEREFORDSHIRE
WORCESTERSHIRE
WARWICKSHIRE
GLOUCESTERSHIRE
WILTSHIRE
SOMERSET
DORSET
DEVON
Cotswolds
Brecon Beacons
Bristol Channel
Lyme Bay
Exmoor
Salisbury Plain
New Forest
Swansea Bay
Chesil Beach
Bill of Portland
Prawle Point
Severn
Penybont
Presteigne
Llandrindod Wells
Leominster
Droitwich
Kington
Weobley
Ullingswick
WORCESTER
Bransford
Builth Wells
Llanwrtyd Wells
Llangammarch Wells
Great Malvern
Severn Stoke
Fladbury
Stratford upon Avon
Hay-on-Wye
Upton upon Severn
Strensham SA
Crugybar
Llyswen
Three Cocks
HEREFORD
Ledbury
Tewkesbury
Fownhope
Brecon
Corse Lawn
Cleeve Hill
Walterstone
Much Birch
Llandeilo
Ross-on-Wye
CHELTENHAM
Crickhowell
Goodrich
GLOUCESTER
Abergavenny
East Symonds Yat
Nant-Ddu
Abercraf
Monmouth
Coleford
Painswick
Ammanford
MERTHYR TYDFIL
Raglan
Clearwell
Whitebrook
Stonehouse
Stroud
Cirencester
Birchgrove
Hirwaun
Usk
Tintern
Berkeley Road
Berkeley
NEATH & PORT TALBOT
Blackwood
Llangybi
Michael Wood SA
Nailsworth
Neath
Cwmbran
Chepstow
Falfield
Tetbury
SWANSEA
Magor SA
Severn View SA
Thornbury
Port Talbot
Pontypridd
Caerphilly
CAERPHILLY
Petty France
Malmesbury
BRIDGEND
Pencoed
NEWPORT
Alveston
Rangeworthy
SWINDON
Miskin
Castleton
Badminton
CARDIFF
Leigh Delamere SA
Porthcawl
Bridgend
Gordano SA
Tormarton
Castle Combe
Penarth
BRISTOL
Chippenham
Clevedon
Colerne
Calne
V GLAM
Llantwit Major
Barry
Keynsham
Weston-super-Mare
Churchill
Chelwood
Hunstrete
BATH
Melksham
Hinton Charterhouse
Bradford-on-Avon
Shipham
Midsomer Norton
Trowbridge
Lympsham
Axbridge
Woolverton
Woody Bay
Lynton
Lynmouth
Sedgemoor SA
Wookey Hole
Ston Easton
Beckington
Westbury
Porlock
Burnham-on-Sea
Brent Knoll
Highbridge
Minehead
Watchet
Holford
Frome
Dunster
Wells
Shepton Mallet
Nunney
Warminster
Exford
Williton
Nether Stowey
Wheddon Cross
Withypool
Winsford
Glastonbury
Bridgwater
Street
Hindon
Castle Cary
Dulverton
Wiveliscombe
Wincanton
Gillingham
SALISBURY
South Molton
TAUNTON
Podimore
Chittlehamholt
Bampton
Wellington
Shaftesbury
Taunton Deane SA
Martock
YEOVIL
Burrington
Sampford Peverell
Sherborne
Sturminster Newton
Tiverton
Ilminster
Chard
Yarcombe
Blandford Forum
Evershot
Crediton
Honiton
Axminster
Beaminster
South Zeal
Ottery St Mary
Colyford
Charmouth
Bridport
EXETER
Lyme Regis
Chideock
BOURNEMOUTH
Moretonhampstead
Sidmouth
Branscombe
West Bexington
Wareham
Bovey Tracey
Exmouth
Corfe Castle
WEYMOUTH
West Lulworth
Haytor
Ilsington
Dawlish
Portland
Teignmouth
Newton Abbot
Ipplepen
Staverton
TORQUAY
Totnes
Paignton
Brixham
Stoke Gabriel
Dartmouth
Bigbury-on-Sea
Kingsbridge
Thurlestone
Torcross
Hope Cove
Salcombe
M4
M5
M32
M48
M49
M50
M42
M40
A40
A44
A46
A49
A30
A31
A35
A36
A37
A38
A303
A350
A361
A338
A4
20 miles
30 kilometres

For continuation pages refer to numbered arrows

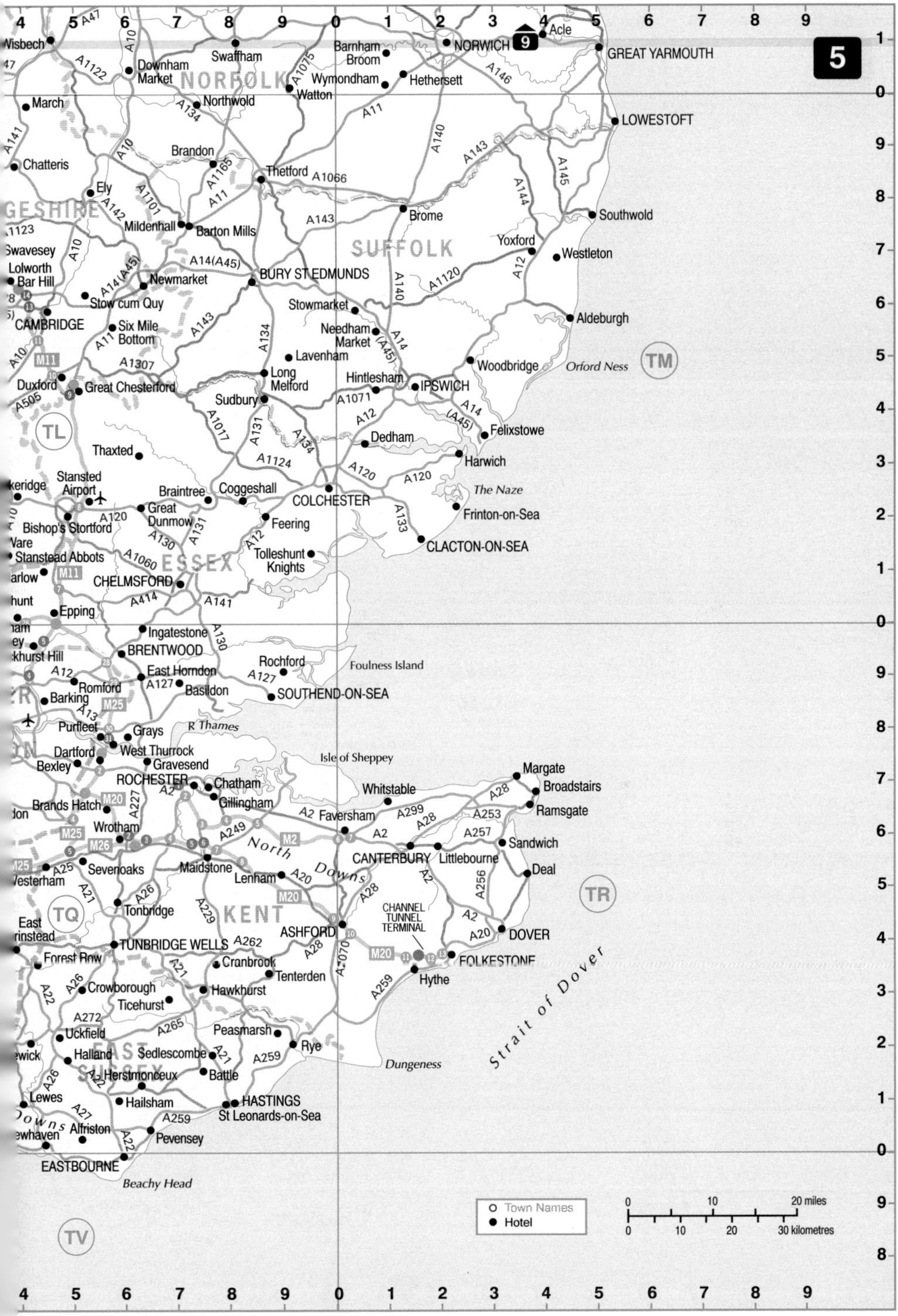
5
NORFOLK
SUFFOLK
ESSEX
KENT
EAST SUSSEX
Wisbech
Downham Market
Swaffham
Barnham Broom
Wymondham
Hethersett
NORWICH
Acle
GREAT YARMOUTH
Watton
March
Northwold
LOWESTOFT
Chatteris
Brandon
Thetford
Ely
Mildenhall
Barton Mills
Brome
Southwold
Swavesey
Lolworth
Bar Hill
Yoxford
Westleton
Newmarket
BURY ST EDMUNDS
Stow cum Quy
Stowmarket
CAMBRIDGE
Aldeburgh
Six Mile Bottom
Needham Market
Lavenham
Woodbridge
Orford Ness
TM
Duxford
Great Chesterford
Long Melford
Hintlesham
IPSWICH
Sudbury
Felixstowe
TL
Dedham
Thaxted
Harwich
Stansted Airport
Braintree
Coggeshall
The Naze
COLCHESTER
Great Dunmow
Frinton-on-Sea
Bishop's Stortford
Feering
CLACTON-ON-SEA
Stanstead Abbots
Tolleshunt Knights
CHELMSFORD
Epping
Ingatestone
BRENTWOOD
Rochford
Foulness Island
East Horndon
Romford
Basildon
SOUTHEND-ON-SEA
Barking
Purfleet
Grays
R Thames
West Thurrock
Dartford
Bexley
Gravesend
Isle of Sheppey
Margate
ROCHESTER
Chatham
Broadstairs
Whitstable
Brands Hatch
Gillingham
Ramsgate
Wrotham
Faversham
North Downs
Sandwich
CANTERBURY
Littlebourne
Westerham
Sevenoaks
Maidstone
Lenham
Deal
TR
TQ
Tonbridge
CHANNEL TUNNEL TERMINAL
East Grinstead
ASHFORD
DOVER
TUNBRIDGE WELLS
Forest Row
Cranbrook
FOLKESTONE
Tenterden
Hythe
Crowborough
Hawkhurst
Strait of Dover
Ticehurst
Uckfield
Peasmarsh
Halland
Sedlescombe
Rye
Battle
Herstmonceux
Dungeness
Lewes
Hailsham
HASTINGS
St Leonards-on-Sea
Alfriston
Pevensey
EASTBOURNE
Beachy Head
TV
Town Names
Hotel
20 miles
30 kilometres

For continuation pages refer to numbered arrows

7
12
8
4
3
North York Moors
NORTH YORKSHIRE
Yorkshire Dales
THE PENNINES
CUMBRIA
LANCASHIRE
WEST YORKSHIRE
SOUTH YORKSHIRE
GREATER MANCHESTER
MERSEYSIDE
CHESHIRE
DERBYSHIRE
NOTTINGHAMSHIRE
STAFFORDSHIRE
SHROPSHIRE
LEICESTERSHIRE
WEST MIDLANDS
WREXHAM
Peak District
SD
SE
SJ
SK
SO
SP
Elterwater
Ambleside
Troutbeck
Langdale
Coniston
Windermere
Hawkshead
Grizedale
Kendal
Newby Bridge
Crosthwaite
Witherslack
Heversham
Crooklands
Cartmel
Burton SA
Grange-over-Sands
BARROW-IN-FURNESS
Carnforth
MORECAMBE
LANCASTER
Hampson Green
Forton SA
Garstang
Chipping
Barton
BLACKPOOL
Lytham St Annes
PRESTON
Southport
Formby
Ormskirk
Killington Lake SA
Kirkby Lonsdale
Ravenstonedale
Austwick
Settle
Hawes
Askrigg
Carperby
Bainbridge
Buckden
Arncliffe
Malham
Skipton
Sawley
Clitheroe
Hurst Green
Langho
Blackburn
Accrington
Burnley
Darwen
Chorley
Adlington
Rochdale
Horwich
Bury
Heywood
Birch SA
Bolton
Parbold
Wigan
Upholland
Prestwich
Chadderton
Oldham
Haydock
Worsley
St Helens
Newton-le-Willows
Ashton-under-Lyne
MANCHESTER
Salford
LIVERPOOL
Burtonwood SA
Rainhill
Sale
Stockport
Widnes
Warrington
Altrincham
Cheadle
Marple
Bramhall
Manchester Airport
Wilmslow
BIRKENHEAD
Bebington
Bromborough
Runcorn
Childer Thornton
Ellesmere Port
Frodsham
Knutsford
Alderley Edge
Prestbury
Northwich
MACCLESFIELD
Sandiway
Holmes Chapel
Middlewich
CHESTER
Ewloe
Northop
Northop Hall
Halkyn
Puddington
Tarporley
Sandbach
Congleton
Rossett
Broxton
Burwardsley
CREWE
Alsager
Leek
Talke
WREXHAM
Nantwich
Newcastle-under-Lyme
STOKE-ON-TRENT
Onneley
Madeley
Llangollen
Chirk
Glyn Ceiriog
Oswestry
Hodnet
Market Drayton
Stafford SA
Stone
Uttoxeter
Sudbury
Nesscliffe
Newport
STAFFORD
Acton Trussell
Rugeley
Barton under Needwood
Penkridge
Cannock
Lichfield
SHREWSBURY
TELFORD
Shifnal
Hilton Park SA
Tamworth
Welshpool
Albrighton
WOLVERHAMPTON
Walsall
Sutton Coldfield
Wishaw
Montgomery
Much Wenlock
Church Stretton
Worfield
Pattingham
Bridgnorth
Himley
West Bromwich
Kingswinford
Oldbury
Alveley
Stourbridge
Dudley
BIRMINGHAM
Birmingham Airport
National Exhibition Centre
Hagley
Frankley SA
Kidderminster
Chaddesley Corbett
Solihull
Dorridge
Bewdley
Cleobury Mortimer
Stourport-on-Severn
Hartlebury
BROMSGROVE
Hockley Heath
Redditch
Abberley
Ludlow
Knighton
Tenbury Wells
Richmond
Leyburn
Middleham
West Witton
Northallerton
Ripon
Ramsgill
Pateley Bridge
Grassington
Burnsall
Bolton Abbey
HARROGATE
Ilkley
Keighley
Bingley
Haworth
Shipley
BRADFORD
LEEDS
Hebden Bridge
Halifax
Cleckheaton
Hartshead Moor SA
Brighouse
HUDDERSFIELD
Kirkburton
Glossop
SHEFFIELD
Buxton
Ashford-in-the-Water
Matlock
Thorpe
Ashbourne
DERBY
NOTTINGHAM
LOUGHBOROUGH
LEICESTER
COVENTRY
Malton
YORK
DONCASTER
M6
M55
M58
M61
M62
M65
M66
M56
M53
M54
M5
M42
M1
M18
M180
M181
M621
M69
M45
A1(M)
A1
A590
A593
A6
A65
A683
A685
A684
A6108
A167
A168
A172
A19
A170
A169
A61
A64
A59
A658
A58
A63
A163
A614
A638
A635
A628
A616
A631
A57
A620
A156
A159
A161
A619
A623
A621
A629
A640
A6068
A565
A56
A54
A53
A515
A523
A52
A50
A516
A518
A51
A38
A46
A6097
A617
A60
A564
A453
A606
A607
A5
A483
A41
A525
A495
A528
A49
A442
A458
A488
A489
A4117
A4113
A449
A34
A444
A4304
A427
A14
A508
A447
A42
A533
A628

For continuation pages refer to numbered arrows

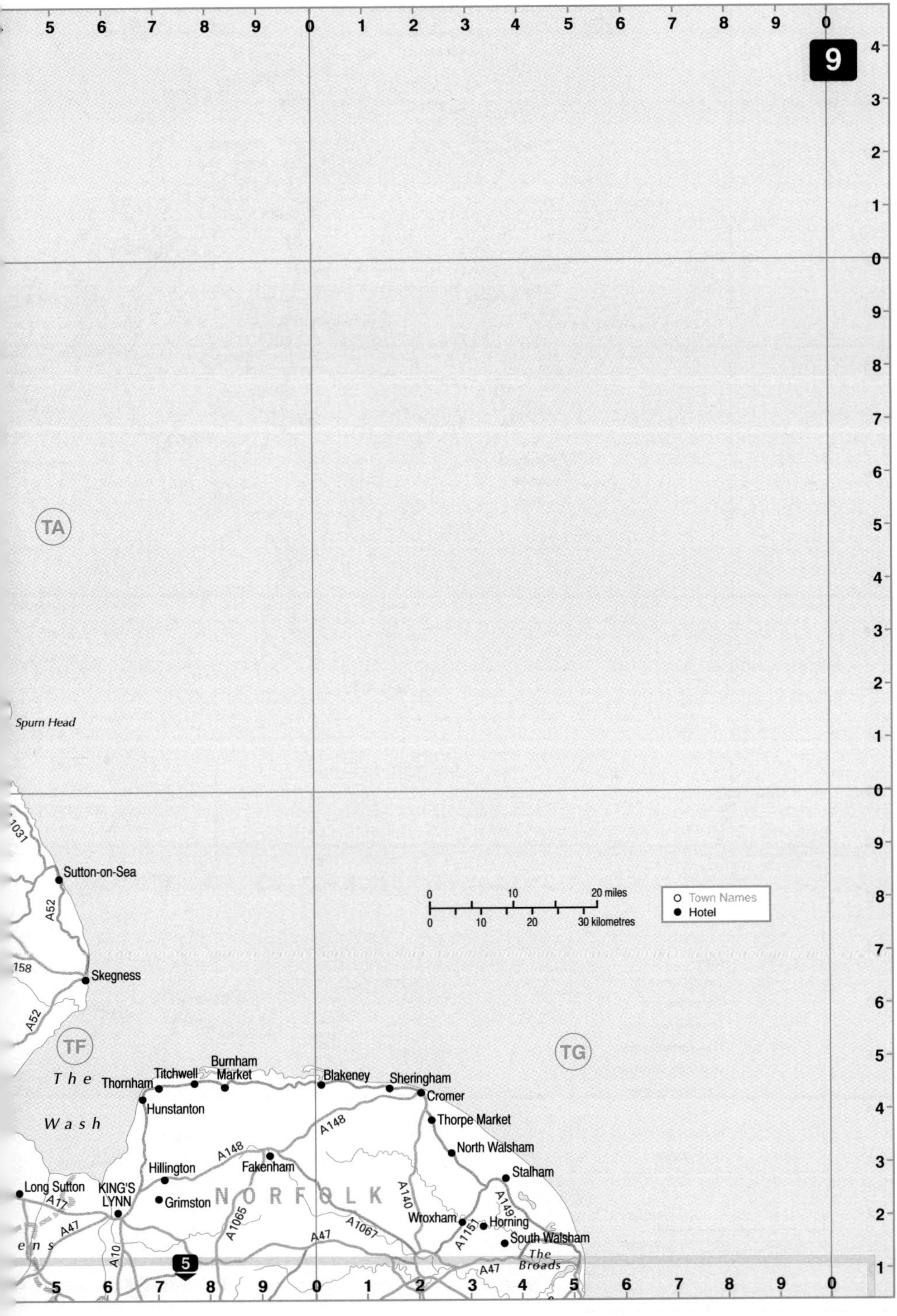

9
TA
Spurn Head
Sutton-on-Sea
A52
Skegness
A52
TF
The Wash
Thornham
Titchwell
Burnham Market
Blakeney
Sheringham
Cromer
Hunstanton
Thorpe Market
A148
North Walsham
A148
Hillington
Fakenham
Stalham
Long Sutton
KING'S LYNN
Grimston
NORFOLK
A140
A149
A17
Wroxham
Horning
A1151
South Walsham
A47
A1065
A1067
A47
A10
The Broads
A47
5
TG
0 10 20 miles
0 10 20 30 kilometres
Town Names
Hotel

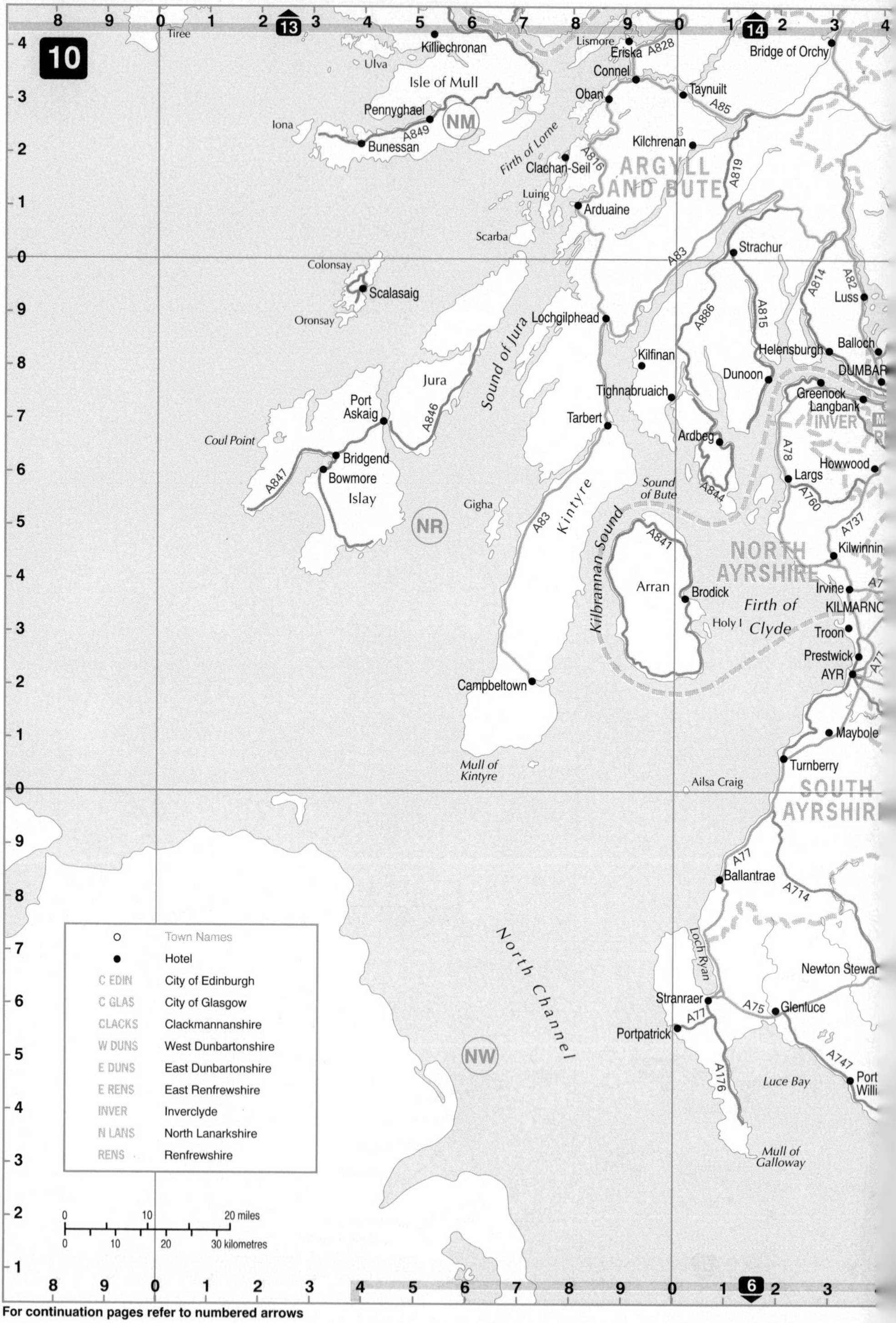

For continuation pages refer to numbered arrows

11
15
12
7
PERTH AND KINROSS
DUNDEE CITY
STIRLING
FIFE
FALKIRK
WEST LOTHIAN
EDINBURGH
MIDLOTHIAN
EAST LOTHIAN
SOUTH LANARKSHIRE
EAST AYRSHIRE
BORDERS (SCOTTISH)
DUMFRIES AND GALLOWAY
NORTHUMBERLAND
CUMBRIA
DURHAM
NORTH SEA
NN
NO
NS
NT
NX
NY
Dunkeld
Birnam
Kinclaven
Stanley
Coupar Angus
Auchterhouse
DUNDEE
Killin
St Fillans
Lochearnhead
Balquhidder
Comrie
Crieff
PERTH
Firth of Tay
Leuchars
St Andrews Bay
St Andrews
Strathyre
Auchterarder
Glenfarg
Cupar
Freuchie
Ladybank
Fife Ness
Callander
Kinnesswood
Markinch
Leven
Doune
Dunblane
Kinross
Glenrothes
Isle of May
Port of Menteith
Bridge of Allan
Powmill
STIRLING
KIRKCALDY
Dunfermline
Aberdour
Kincardine
Burntisland
Firth of Forth
Strathblane
Falkirk
Grangemouth
Inverkeithing
Rosyth
South Queensferry
Milngavie
Polmont
Cumbernauld
Uphall
Clydebank
Moodiesburn
Bathgate
Livingston
Dalkeith
Dunbar
St Abb's Head
Renfrew
Glasgow Airport
GLASGOW
Paisley
Bellshill
Whitburn
Roslin
Uddingston
Motherwell
Giffnock
Bothwell
Hamilton SA
East Kilbride
Hamilton
Lammermuir Hills
Berwick-upon-Tweed
Rosebank
Holy Island
Strathaven
Lanark
Peebles
Uplands
Galashiels
Biggar
Kelso
Abington
Jedburgh
The Cheviot Hills
Hawick
Sanquhar
Moffat
Beattock
Southern
Thornhill
Otterburn
Annandale Water SA
Lockerbie
DUMFRIES
Crocketford
Carrutherstown
Powfoot
Annan
Gretna
Castle Douglas
Hexham
Gatehouse of Fleet
Colvend
CARLISLE
Kirkcudbright
Auchencairn
Silloth
Wigtown Bay
Abbey Head
Solway Firth
Bassenthwaite
Mungrisdale
Penrith
WORKINGTON
Cockermouth
Keswick
Braithwaite
Whitehaven
Loweswater
Rosthwaite
Glenridding
Buttermere
Borrowdale
Patterdale
North Head
Cleator
Lake District
Gosforth
Grasmere
A827
A822
A826
A94
A92
A85
A90
A914
A91
A84
A9
A823
A915
A917
A81
A811
M9
M90
M80
M9
M73
M8
A8
A71
A70
A706
A702
A703
A7
A68
A198
A1
A1107
A6105
A697
A6112
A698
A73
A726
M74
A721
A72
A8089
A708
A701
A74(M)
A74
A6088
A702
A76
A709
A712
A713
A711
A75
A710
A696
A69
A695
A689
A686
A691
A596
A595
M6
A6
A66
A688
A84

For continuation pages refer to numbered arrows

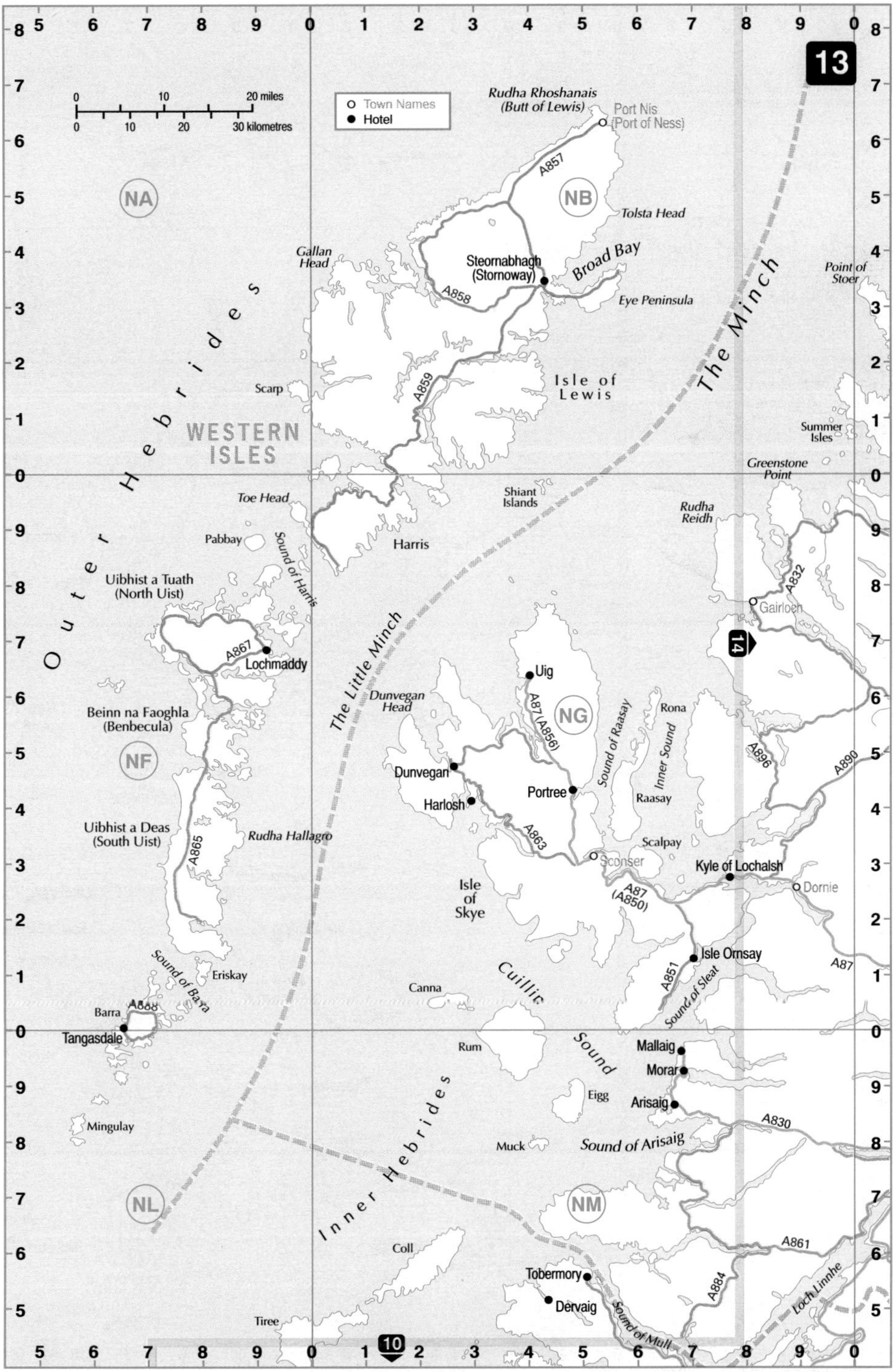
13
Town Names
Hotel
20 miles
30 kilometres
NA
NB
NF
NG
NL
NM
WESTERN ISLES
Outer Hebrides
Inner Hebrides
The Minch
The Little Minch
Rudha Rhoshanais (Butt of Lewis)
Port Nis (Port of Ness)
A857
Tolsta Head
Gallan Head
Steornabhagh (Stornoway)
Broad Bay
Eye Peninsula
A858
A859
Isle of Lewis
Scarp
Point of Stoer
Summer Isles
Greenstone Point
Toe Head
Shiant Islands
Rudha Reidh
Pabbay
Sound of Harris
Harris
Uibhist a Tuath (North Uist)
A832
Gairloch
A867
Lochmaddy
14
Uig
Dunvegan Head
Beinn na Faoghla (Benbecula)
A87 (A856)
Sound of Raasay
Rona
Inner Sound
A896
A890
Dunvegan
Harlosh
Portree
Raasay
Uibhist a Deas (South Uist)
A865
Rudha Hallagro
A863
Scalpay
Sconser
Kyle of Lochalsh
Dornie
Isle of Skye
A87 (A850)
Isle Ornsay
A87
A851
Sound of Sleat
Sound of Barra
Eriskay
Canna
Cuillin Sound
Barra
A888
Tangasdale
Rum
Mallaig
Morar
Eigg
Arisaig
A830
Mingulay
Muck
Sound of Arisaig
A861
Coll
Tobermory
Dervaig
A884
Loch Linnhe
Sound of Mull
Tiree
10

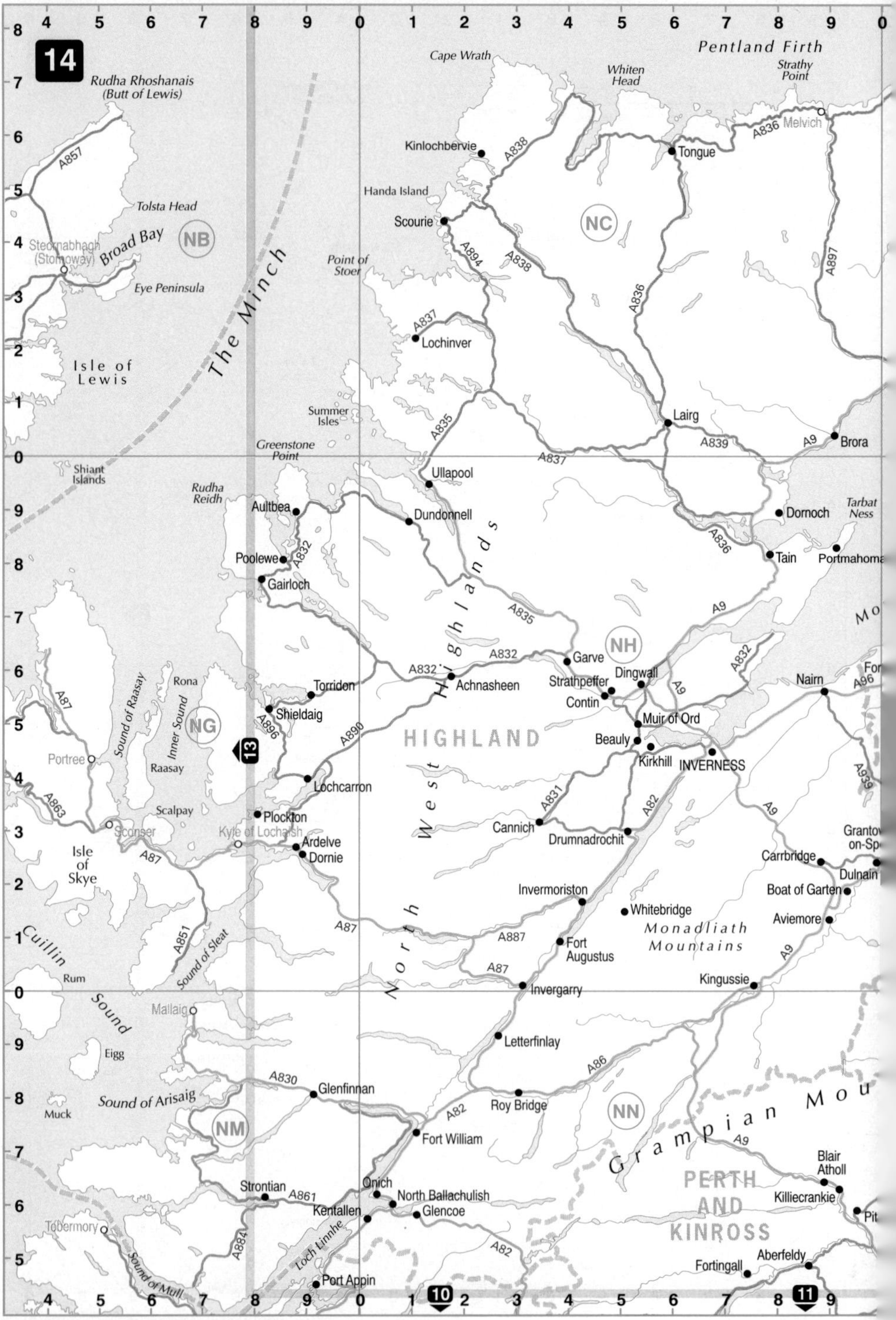

For continuation pages refer to numbered arrows

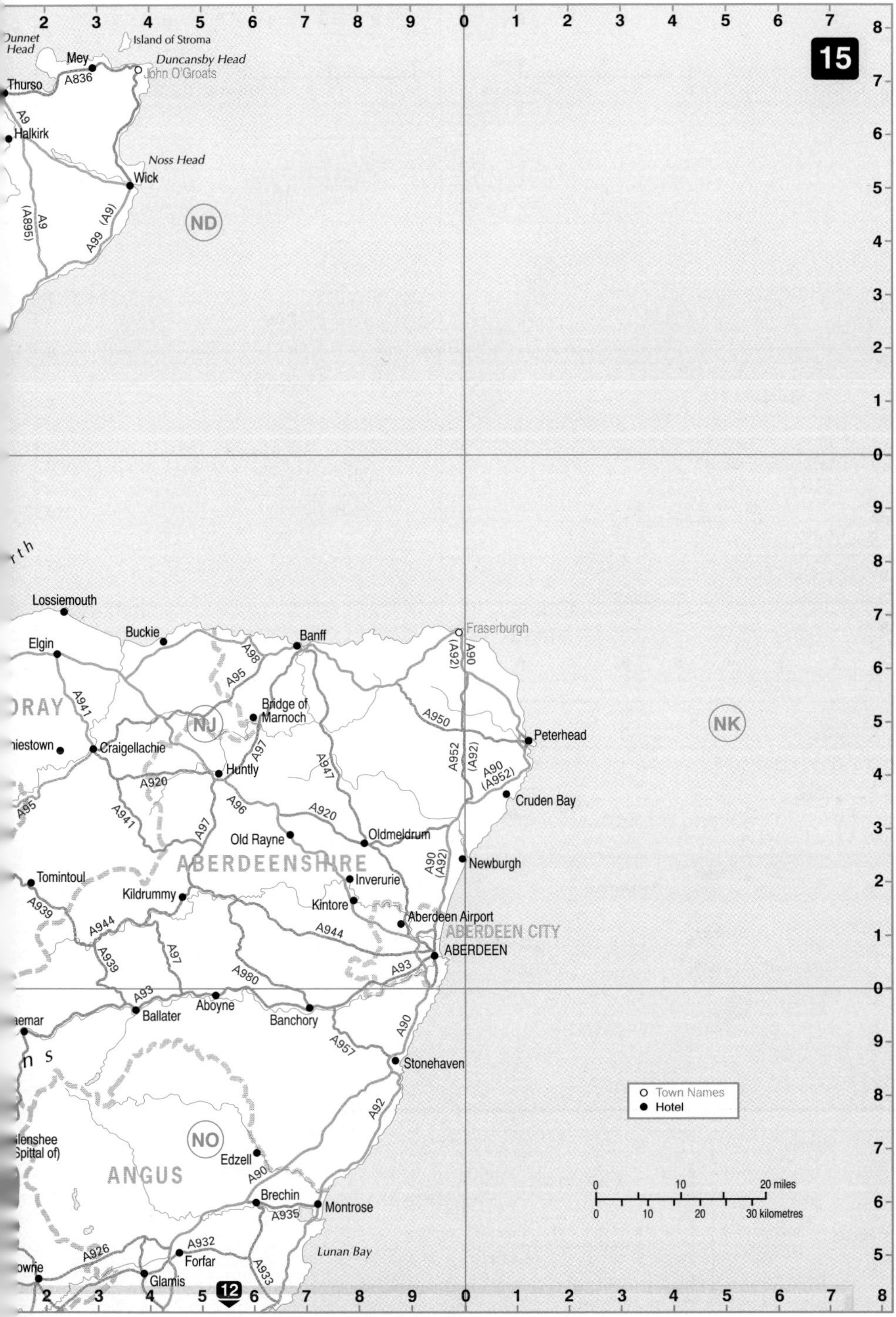

15
Dunnet Head
Mey
A836
Island of Stroma
Duncansby Head
John O'Groats
Thurso
A9
Halkirk
Noss Head
Wick
A9
(A895)
A99 (A9)
ND
rth
Lossiemouth
Elgin
Buckie
Banff
Fraserburgh
(A92)
A90
A98
A95
A941
ORAY
NJ
Bridge of Marnoch
A950
Peterhead
NK
iestown
Craigellachie
A97
A947
A952
(A92)
A90
(A952)
Huntly
A920
Cruden Bay
A95
A941
A96
A920
A97
Old Rayne
Oldmeldrum
A90
(A92)
Newburgh
ABERDEENSHIRE
Tomintoul
Inverurie
Kildrummy
Kintore
A939
Aberdeen Airport
A944
A944
ABERDEEN CITY
ABERDEEN
A939
A97
A980
A93
A93
Aboyne
Ballater
Banchory
emar
A90
A957
Stonehaven
Town Names
Hotel
A92
NO
lenshee
Spittal of)
Edzell
ANGUS
A90
Brechin
Montrose
A935
0
10
20 miles
0
10
20
30 kilometres
A932
A926
Forfar
Lunan Bay
owrie
Glamis
A933
12

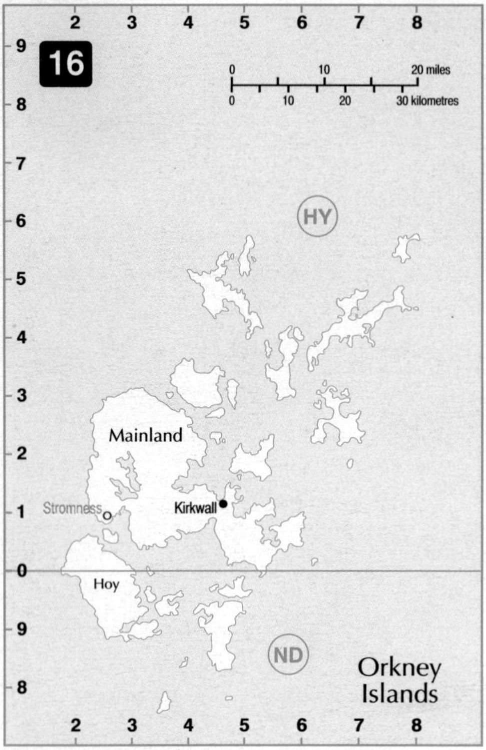
16
0 10 20 miles
0 10 20 30 kilometres
HY
ND
Mainland
Stromness
Kirkwall
Hoy
Orkney Islands
2 3 4 5 6 7 8
9 8 7 6 5 4 3 2 1 0 9 8

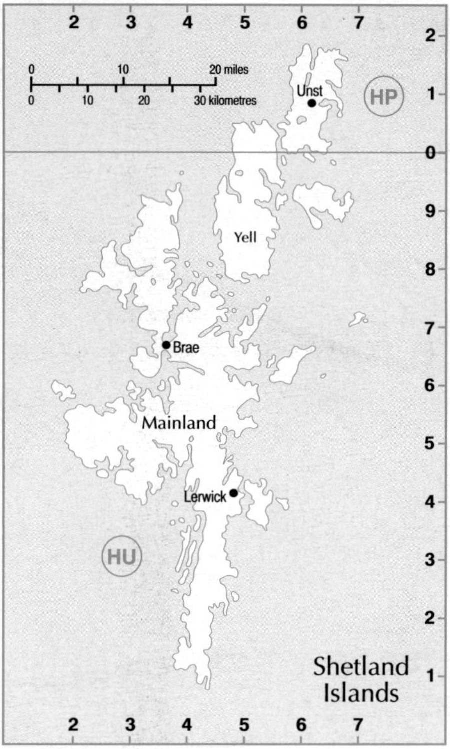
0 10 20 miles
0 10 20 30 kilometres
Unst
HP
Yell
Brae
Mainland
Lerwick
HU
Shetland Islands
2 3 4 5 6 7
2 1 0 9 8 7 6 5 4 3 2 1

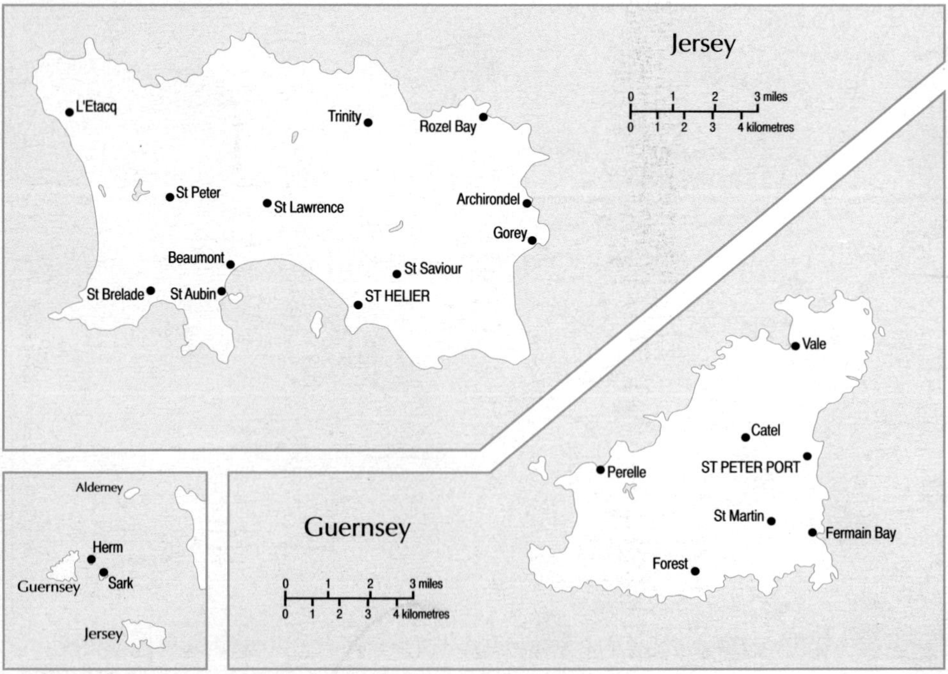
Jersey
0 1 2 3 miles
0 1 2 3 4 kilometres
L'Etacq
Trinity
Rozel Bay
St Peter
St Lawrence
Archirondel
Gorey
Beaumont
St Saviour
St Brelade
St Aubin
ST HELIER
Vale
Catel
Perelle
ST PETER PORT
St Martin
Fermain Bay
Forest
Guernsey
0 1 2 3 miles
0 1 2 3 4 kilometres
Alderney
Herm
Guernsey
Sark
Jersey